W. F. Poole

POOLE'S INDEX

TO

PERIODICAL LITERATURE

THIRD SUPPLEMENT

FROM JANUARY 1 1892 TO DECEMBER 31 1896

BY

WILLIAM I. FLETCHER, A.M.
LIBRARIAN OF AMHERST COLLEGE

AND

FRANKLIN O. POOLE, A.B.
ASSISTANT IN THE BOSTON ATHENÆUM LIBRARY

WITH THE COÖPERATION OF THE AMERICAN LIBRARY ASSOCIATION

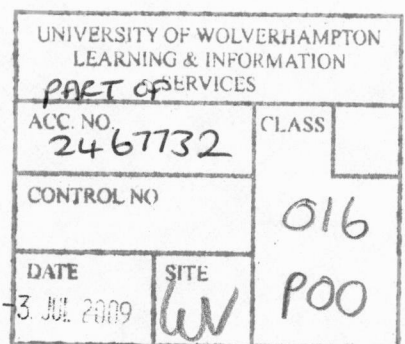

GLOUCESTER, MASS.
PETER SMITH
1963

REPRINTED 1938; 1958; 1963

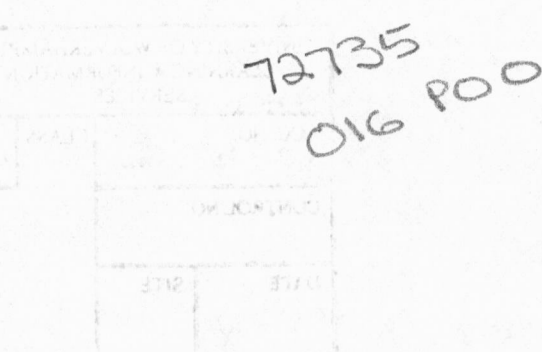

PRINTED IN THE UNITED STATES OF AMERICA

WILLIAM FREDERICK POOLE.

THE originator of this series of indexes, long known as the Nestor of American librarianship, was born in Salem, Massachusetts, December 14, 1821. His parents were Ward and Eliza (Wilder) Poole, and his American ancestry runs back to John Poole, who was settled in Cambridge in 1632, and in 1635 became the leading proprietor of Reading, which was named for the town in England from which he came.

William's decided bent for letters was not early developed, and it was not until he had spent several years of his later boyhood in outdoor work with his father on the farm or in the tanyard, and some months in learning the jewelry business, that he finally settled down to study and was fitted for college at Leicester Academy. Entering Yale College in 1842, he found it necessary, after the first year, to seek funds for the further prosecution of his studies. Three years were devoted to teaching for this purpose, and in 1846 he reëntered college as a sophomore, graduating with the class of 1849, of which President Dwight was a member.

During his sophomore year he became assistant librarian of his society, the Brothers in Unity, which had a library of about 10,000 volumes. The practical good sense which was always so characteristic of the man led him to observe the great value of the contents of the bound sets of periodicals with which the library was well furnished, and with characteristic industry he set to work to make a manuscript index by which these otherwise hidden treasures might be brought to light. No sooner was this index put into service than its great value became apparent and there arose a demand for its publication, which was effected in 1848, through Mr. George P. Putnam, of New York. The first edition was a small octavo of 154 pages. The book met with a warm reception, both in this country and in Europe, whence orders came for more than the entire edition, which was small. Thus encouraged, Mr. Poole commenced upon a larger work of similar character, which was published by C. B. Norton, in New York, in 1853, when Mr. Poole had become librarian of the Mercantile Library in Boston.

In a few years this edition was exhausted, but Mr. Poole was too busy to undertake the compilation of another; it was not until 1876 that he outlined to the conference of librarians held in Philadelphia, in connection with the Centennial Exposition, his scheme for the coöperative production of a new and greatly enlarged edition. His plan met ready acceptance and was successfully carried out, resulting in the large work published in 1882, to which this is the third "five-year" supplement.

Mr. Poole was successively librarian of the Mercantile Library of Boston, the Boston Athenæum, the public libraries of Cincinnati and Chicago, and the Newberry Library in the latter city. He was from the first a leader in the public library movement, which had its rise just as he came upon the stage, and to which he largely gave shape and direction. He was an active participant in the first convention of American librarians, held in New York in 1853, and was also one of the founders of the American Library Association in 1876, a constant attendant upon its meetings, and a frequent contributor to the Library Journal. With other American librarians, he attended the first International Conference of librarians in London in 1877, and was one of the vice-presidents of that meeting. He was always an intense believer in the underlying principles of the public library movement, had special sympathy with its freer and more popular aspects, and was an opponent of restrictive principles in library management. He did much to elucidate the subject of library architecture, especially to discredit the conventional and formal styles as applied to library buildings, and to introduce simplicity and adaptability as prime factors in their construction. In 1869 he was occupied for some months as a library expert, organizing libraries in several places in New England, as well as at the United States Naval Academy, Annapolis, Maryland; and during his residence in Chicago he rendered similar service for several of the larger towns in the West.

While thus active in library work, Mr. Poole found opportunity to pursue close and exhaustive studies in the field of American history, and published many papers on the witchcraft delusion, the history of slavery in America, the early settlements on the Maine coast, the Ordinance of 1787 and kindred subjects; his success in this kind of research gained for him the distinction of the presidency of the American Historical Association in 1887. In 1882 he received the degree of Doctor of Laws from the Northwestern University, Evanston, Illinois.

In 1893 Dr. Poole took an active part in the arrangements for the literary congresses connected with the Columbian Exposition, especially the World's Congress of Librarians. His arduous labors at that time, followed by others incurred in the removal of the Newberry Library to its new building the following winter, doubtless undermined his system, and he died on March 1, 1894, after a brief and apparently trifling illness.

Dr. Poole was a fine example of the *mens sana in sano corpore.* Enjoying perfect health all his life, his commanding presence and benign expression were truly representative of the strength and sweetness of his mental and moral character. To know him was to admire him for his gifts of person and of mind, and to be drawn to him by his large humanity and his earnest friendliness. In his life, as in his writings, he showed a native instinct for that which is honorable and of good report, and a corresponding dislike of all sham and pretence. No qualities were dearer to him than candor and sincerity, and it was the lack of these elements in the historical writings he reviewed that provoked his sharpest censure. In his own circle he came at the last to be spoken of as "the good Doctor." His immediate co-laborers and his associates in the American Library Association have joined to honor his memory by placing his bust in bronze in the magnificent new building of the Chicago Public Library. The institution itself is largely his monument, as it owes very much of what it is to him.

But his chief memorial must always be his Index to Periodical Literature. In its preparation he found delight and recreation; the tokens of its widespread acceptance and usefulness gave him the best satisfaction of his life. Through it he has achieved the truest fame, — great and abiding service to humanity.

W. I. F.

PREFACE.

USERS of the last Supplement to Poole's Index will remember that its preface commenced with a playful allusion to Dr. Poole's withdrawal from the collaboration, a withdrawal supposed to be temporary, and guarded by him with the proviso that he might resume the work when the pressure of other duties was somewhat lightened. But this was not to be. In a little more than a year after the date of that preface the life that had been so strong and so vigorous that one hardly associated age with it, even at seventy, was suddenly terminated in the midst of the activities of a busy and useful career. It has seemed fitting that this first issue of the Index after his death should bear his portrait and a slight biographical sketch.

The name of Poole, which must always be connected with this series of indexes, is now most pleasantly re-associated with it through the engagement, as co-editor of this Supplement, of Dr. Poole's nephew, Mr. Franklin O. Poole, A. B. (Harvard, '95,) Assistant in the Boston Athenæum Library. He has indexed over three hundred volumes for it, and has given much valuable assistance in the compilation of the material and the reading of the proofs.

It will be observed that this Supplement is one-third larger than either of the previous five-year volumes. The number of periodicals requiring inclusion in such an index is largely on the increase. Of the 187 sets covered by this volume, sixty are new, that is, have not been included in any previous issue, and of these, forty-two have had their origin since 1891. This increase is only partially offset by the dropping out of twenty-three sets which were represented in the list of five years ago, the net gain being thirty-seven. The number of volumes covered by this Supplement is 1,388 as against 1,068 in the previous one.

A comparison of the tables prefixed to Poole's Index and its supplements brings out some interesting facts as to the life of periodicals. In these tables a new entry is made for a periodical when it begins a new series with the name changed. On this basis the whole number of periodicals indexed in "Poole" from the beginning is 407, of which number 195, or 48 per cent., were continued beyond the year 1891.

The following tabular statement makes a striking exhibit of the rapid rise and fall of periodicals, although, if it took in all such publications instead of being confined to the comparatively substantial ones included in "Poole," the phenomena would be much more noteworthy.

Decade.	"Poole" sets originated.	Discontinued.	Net gain.
1801–10	6	0	6
1811–20	18	2	16
1821–30	22	15	7
1831–40	29	23	6
1841–50	47	21	26
1851–60	31	14	17
1861–70	57	29	28
1871–80	49	45	4
1881–90	91	37	54
1891–96 } 6 years }	55	23	32

Among the periodicals now first indexed are the Christian Union (now Outlook) and the Independent. The contents of these papers have not been thoroughly indexed, references being made only to "symposiums," or to unusually extended and important single articles. The Book Buyer, Book News, and Book Reviews are indexed only by references to their important articles, largely notices of authors with portraits. The entire set of the Magazine of Art (Cassell's) is here indexed, and its great store of valuable material on all art subjects thus becomes available.

Somewhat over two-thirds of the matter contained in this Supplement has appeared from year to year under the same editorship and collaboration, as one of the features of the Annual Literary Index, issued from the office of the Library Journal, in New York.

WILLIAM I. FLETCHER.

AMHERST COLLEGE LIBRARY,
October 1, 1897.

COLLABORATORS.

William I. Fletcher, Editor	Librarian Amherst College, Amherst, Mass.
Franklin O. Poole, "	Assistant, Boston Athenæum, Boston, Mass.

Prof. Herbert B. Adams	Johns Hopkins University, Baltimore, Md.
Willard Austin	Assistant Librarian Cornell University, Ithaca, N. Y.
James Bain, Jr.	Librarian Public Library, Toronto, Ont.
William Beer	Librarian Howard Memorial Library, New Orleans, La.
Silas H. Berry	Librarian Y. M. C. A., N. Y. City.
Walter S. Biscoe	Librarian [Catalog. Dept.] State Library, Albany, N. Y.
Caroline A. Blanchard	Librarian Tufts Library, Weymouth, Mass.
Geo. E. Bowerman	Reference Assistant, State Library, Albany, N. Y.
Isaac S. Bradley	Librarian State Historical Society, Madison, Wis.
Prof. Arthur N. Brown	U. S. Naval Academy, Annapolis, Md.
Nina E. Browne	Asst. Sec., A. L. A. Publishing Section, Boston, Mass.
Rev. Charles H. Burr	Librarian Williams College, Williamstown, Mass.
Edith E. Chase	Office Associated Charities, Boston, Mass.
Gratia Countryman	Assistant, Public Library, Minneapolis, Minn.
T. Franklin Currier	Harvard University Library, Cambridge, Mass.
John F. Davies	Librarian Public Library, Butte City, Mont.
Raymond C. Davis	Librarian University of Michigan, Ann Arbor, Mich.
Mabel A. Farr	Librarian Adelphi College, Brooklyn, N. Y.
Frederic W. Faxon	Boston Book Co., Boston, Mass.
William E. Foster	Librarian Public Library, Providence, R. I.
Geo. L. Fox	Rector Hopkins Grammar School, New Haven, Conn.
Samuel S. Green	Librarian Public Library, Worcester, Mass.
G. Wm. Harris	Librarian Cornell University, Ithaca, N. Y.
William C. Hawks	Assistant Librarian Hartford Theological Seminary, Hartford, Conn.
Caroline M. Hewins	Librarian Public Library, Hartford, Conn.
William J. James	Librarian Wesleyan University, Middletown, Conn.
William C. Lane	Librarian Boston Athenæum, Boston, Mass.
Josephus N. Larned	Superintendent Buffalo Library, Buffalo, N. Y.
Joseph D. Layman	Assistant Librarian University of California, Berkeley, Cal.
Geo. T. Little	Librarian Bowdoin College, Brunswick, Me.
Mary Medlicott	Assistant, City Library, Springfield, Mass.
A. Louise Morton	" " " " "
C. Alex. Nelson	Deputy Librarian, Columbia College Library, N. Y. City.
Mary O. Nutting	Librarian Mt. Holyoke College, South Hadley, Mass.
Helen P. Odell	Assistant, Y. M. C. A. Library, Brooklyn, N. Y.
Mary W. Plummer	Librarian Pratt Institute, Brooklyn, N. Y.
Josephine A. Rathbone	Assistant, Pratt Institute, Brooklyn, N. Y.
Abbie L. Sargent	Assistant, Public Library, Medford, Mass.
Mary E. Sargent	Librarian " " " "
Alice Shepard	Assistant, City Library, Springfield, Mass.
Adele Smith	Assistant, Public Library, Somerville, Mass.
Walter M. Smith	Librarian University of Wisconsin, Madison, Wis.
Willis K. Stetson	Librarian Public Library, New Haven, Conn.
William H. Tillinghast	Assistant Librarian, Harvard University Library, Cambridge, Mass.
Mary L. Titcomb	Librarian Free Library, Rutland, Vt.
Percy H. Tufts	Assistant, Harvard University Library, Cambridge, Mass.
Agnes Van Valkenburgh	Assistant, Public Library, Milwaukee, Wis.
Theresa H. West	Librarian Public Library, Milwaukee, Wis.
Carrie W. Whitney	Librarian Public Library, Kansas City, Mo.
Solon F. Whitney	Librarian Public Library, Watertown, Mass.
Eleanor B. Woodruff	Assistant, Pratt Institute, Brooklyn, N. Y.
Elizabeth A. Young	Assistant, Public Library, Chicago, Ill.

ABBREVIATIONS, TITLES, AND IMPRINTS.

Abbreviation.	Number in Chronological Conspectus.	Title.	Published.	Dates.	Number of Volumes.
Acad.	255	Academy	London	1892–96	10
Acad. (Syr.)	306	Academy. [Originally published at Syracuse]	Boston	1892	1
All the Year	133	All the Year Round	London	1892–95	7
Am. Antiq.	260	American Antiquarian	Chicago	1892–96	5
Am. Arch.	217	American Architect and Building News	Boston	1892–96	20
Am. Cath. Q.	218	American Catholic Quarterly	Philadelphia	1892–96	5
Am. Econ. Assoc. Pub.	304	American Economic Association Publications	New York	1892–96	5
Am. Hist. Reg.	401	American Historical Register	Philadelphia and Boston	1894–96	4
Am. Hist. R.	406	American Historical Review	New York	1896	1
Am. J. Archæol.	286	American Journal of Archæology	Princeton, N. J.	1892–96	4
Am. J. Philol.	246	American Journal of Philology	Baltimore	1892–96	5
Am. J. Pol.	366	American Journal of Politics	New York	1892–94	5
Am. J. Psychol.	314	American Journal of Psychology	Worcester	1892–96	5
Am. J. Sci.	17	American Journal of Science	New Haven	1892–96	10
Am. J. Soc. Sci.	188	[American] Journal of Social Science	Boston	1892–96	5
Am. J. Sociol.	405	American Journal of Sociology	Chicago	1896	1
Am. Law R.	171	American Law Review	St. Louis	1892–96	5
Am. M. Civics	395	American Magazine of Civics	New York	1895–96	4
Am. Natural.	172	American Naturalist	Philadelphia	1892–96	5
Am. Statis. Assoc.	313	American Statistical Association Publications	Boston	1892–96	3
And. R.	282	Andover Review	Boston	1892–93	3
Ann. Am. Acad. Pol. Sci.	323	Annals of the American Academy of Political Science	Philadelphia	1892–96	7
Anthrop. J.	202	Anthropological Institute, Journal of	London	1892–96	5
Antiq. n. s.	208	Antiquary [new series]	London	1892–96	8
Archit. Rec.	367	Architectural Record	New York	1892–96	5
Arena	324	Arena	Boston	1892–96	12
Argosy	165	Argosy	London	1892–96	10
Around World	394	Around the World	New York	1894	1
Art J.	112	Art Journal	London	1892–96	5
Asia. R.	292	Asiatic Quarterly Review [later, Imperial and Asiatic Quar. Rev.]	London	1890–96	14
Astron.	359	Astronomy and Astro-Physics	Northfield, Minn.	1892–94	3
Ath.	261	Athenæum	London	1892–96	10

Atlan.	131	Atlantic Monthly	Boston	1892–96	10
Bach. of Arts	397	Bachelor of Arts	New York	1895–96	3
Bank. M. (Lond.)	85	Bankers' Magazine	London	1892–96	10
Bank. M. (N. Y.)	104	Bankers' Magazine	New York	1892–96	8
Bapt. Q.	245	Baptist Quarterly Review	New York	1892	1
Belgra.	174	Belgravia	London	1892–96	15
Bib. World	373	Biblical World	Chicago	1893–96	8
Bibliographica	398	Bibliographica	London	1895–96	2
Bib. Sac.	86	Bibliotheca Sacra	Oberlin, O.	1892–96	5
Blackw.	13	Blackwood's Edinburgh Magazine	Edinburgh	1892–96	10
Bk.-Buyer	343	Book-Buyer	New York	1884–96	12
Bookman	396	Bookman	New York	1895–96	4
Bk. News	340	Book-News	Philadelphia	1883–96	14
Book R.	389	Book Reviews	New York	1893–96	3
Bookworm	347	Bookworm	London	1888–94	7
Bost.	390	Bostonian	Boston	1894–96	3
Canad. M.	376	Canadian Magazine	Toronto	1893–96	7
Cassier	358	Cassier's Magazine	London and New York	1891–96	10
Cath. World	160	Catholic World	New York	1892–96	10
Cent.	263	Century	New York	1892–96	10
Chamb. J.	89	Chambers's Journal	Edinburgh	1892–96	5
Char. R.	370	Charities Review	New York	1892–96	5
Chaut.	307	Chautauquan	Meadville, Pa.	1892–96	10
Chr. Lit.	386	Christian Literature	New York	1893–96	6
Chr. Un.	361	Christian Union	New York	1892–93	3
Church Q.	256	Church Quarterly Review	London	1892–96	10
Citizen	404	Citizen	Philadelphia	1896	2
Contemp.	166	Contemporary Review	London	1892–96	10
Cornh.	138	Cornhill Magazine	London	1892–96	10
Cosmopol.	300	Cosmopolitan Magazine	New York	1892–96	10
Critic	265	Critic	New York	1892–96	10
Crit. R.	354	Critical Review	Edinburgh	1891–96	6
Dial (Ch.)	230	Dial	Chicago	1892–96	10
Dub. R.	64	Dublin Review	London	1892–96	10
Ecl. M.	90	Eclectic Magazine	New York	1892–96	10
Econ. J.	329	Economic Journal	London	1892–96	5
Econ. R.	355	Economic Review	London	1892–96	6
Econ. Stud.	407	Economic Studies	Baltimore	1896	1
Ed. R.	1	Edinburgh Review	Edinburgh	1892–96	10

Abbreviation.	Number in Chronological Conspectus.	Title.	Published.	Dates.	Number of Volumes.
Educa.	232	Education	Boston	1892–96	5
Educa. R.	334	Educational Review	New York	1892–96	10
Engin. M.	330	Engineering Magazine	New York	1892–06	10
Eng. Hist. R.	290	English Historical Review	London	1892–96	5
Eng. Illust.	279	English Illustrated Magazine	London	1892–96	7
Eng. R.	335	English Review	London	1844–53	18
Eth. Rec.	348	Ethical Record	Philadelphia	1889–91	3
Folk-Lore	351	Folk-Lore	London	1890–96	7
Folk-Lore J.	342	Folk-Lore Journal	London	1883–89	7
Folk-Lore Rec.	336	Folk-Lore Record	London	1878–82	5
Fortn.	161	Fortnightly Review	London	1892–96	10
Forum	291	Forum	New York	1892–96	10
Garden & F.	362	Garden and Forest	New York	1892–96	5
Gent. M. n. s.	183	Gentleman's Magazine [new series]	London	1892–96	10
Geog. J.	374	Geographical Journal	London	1893–96	8
Good Govt.	372	Good Government	Washington	1893–96	4
Good Words	139	Good Words	London	1892–96	5
Green Bag	316	Green Bag	Boston	1892–96	5
Gunton's M.	400	Gunton's Magazine	New York	1896	2
Harper	116	Harper's Magazine	New York	1892–96	10
Harv. Grad. M.	378	Harvard Graduates' Magazine	Cambridge, Mass.	1893–96	4
Harv. Mo.	288	Harvard Monthly	Cambridge, Mass.	1892–94	6
Idler	363	Idler	London	1892–96	10
Illus. Archæol.	384	Illustrated Archæologist	London	1893–94	2
Indep.	360	Independent	New York	1892–96	5
Int. J. Ethics	326	International Journal of Ethics	Philadelphia	1892–96	5
Irish Mo.	209	Irish Monthly	Dublin	1892–96	5
Jew. Q.	349	Jewish Quarterly Review	London	1889–96	8
J. H. Univ. Studies	273	Johns Hopkins University Studies in History, etc.	Baltimore	1892–96	5
J. Am. Folk-Lore	341	Journal of American Folk-Lore	Boston	1888–96	9
J. Bib. Lit.	297	Journal of Biblical Literature	Boston	1892–96	5
J. Frankl. Inst.	33	Journal of the Franklin Institute	Philadelphia	1892–96	10
J. Hel. Stud.	296	Journal of Hellenic Studies	London	1892–96	6
J. Pol. Econ.	379	Journal of Political Economy	Chicago	1893–96	4
J. Soc. Arts	294	Journal of the Society of Arts	London	1892–96	5
J. Statis. Soc.	73	Journal of the Royal Statistical Society	London	1892–96	5

Jurid. R.	350	JURIDICAL REVIEW	Edinburgh	1889–96	8
Knowl.	268	KNOWLEDGE	London	1892–96	5
Law Q.	344	LAW QUARTERLY REVIEW	London	1885–96	12
Leis. Hour	236	LEISURE HOUR	London	1892–96	5
Lend a H.	301	LEND A HAND	Boston	1892–96	10
Lib. J.	226	LIBRARY JOURNAL	New York	1892–96	5
Lippinc.	184	LIPPINCOTT'S MAGAZINE	Philadelphia	1892–96	10
Lit. W. (Bost.)	257	LITERARY WORLD	Boston	1892–96	5
Liv. Age	91	LITTELL'S LIVING AGE	Boston	1892–96	20
Lond. Q.	120	LONDON QUARTERLY REVIEW	London	1892–96	10
Longm.	272	LONGMAN'S MAGAZINE	London	1892–96	10
Luth. Q.	200	LUTHERAN QUARTERLY	Gettysburg, Pa.	1892–96	5
McClure	387	MCCLURE'S MAGAZINE	New York	1893–96	7
Macmil.	140	MACMILLAN'S MAGAZINE	London	1892–96	10
M. Am. Hist.	221	MAGAZINE OF AMERICAN HISTORY	New York	1892–93	4
M. of Art	337	MAGAZINE OF ART (CASSELL'S)	London	1878–96	19
M. Chr. Lit.	317	MAGAZINE OF CHRISTIAN LITERATURE	New York	1891–92	3
Meth. R.	78	METHODIST REVIEW	New York	1892–96	5
Mid.-Cont.	402	MID-CONTINENT	Louisville, Ky.	1895	1
Mind	219	MIND	London	1892–96	5
Monist	331	MONIST	Chicago	1892–96	5
Month	157	MONTH	London	1892–96	15
Mo. Illust.	383	MONTHLY ILLUSTRATOR	New York	1895–96	5
Munsey	353	MUNSEY'S MAGAZINE	New York	1891–96	10
Music	356	MUSIC	Chicago	1891–96	10
Nation	163	NATION	New York	1892–96	10
Nat. Geog. M.	318	NATIONAL GEOGRAPHIC MAGAZINE	Washington	1892–96	5
Nat'l M. (Bost.)	403	NATIONAL MAGAZINE	Boston	1896	2
Nat'l M. (N. Y.)	352	NATIONAL MAGAZINE	New York	1891 94	5
National	276	NATIONAL REVIEW	London	1892–96	10
Nat. Sci.	364	NATURAL SCIENCE	London	1892–96	9
Nature	194	NATURE	London	1892–96	10
New Eng. M. n. s.	299	NEW ENGLAND MAGAZINE [NEW SERIES]	Boston	1892–96	10
N. E. Reg.	106	NEW ENGLAND HISTORICAL AND GENEALOGICAL REGISTER	Boston	1892–96	5
N. Eng.	82	NEW ENGLANDER	New Haven	1892	1
N. Church R.	391	NEW CHURCH REVIEW	Boston	1894–96	3
New R.	319	NEW REVIEW	London	1892–96	10
N. Sci. R.	399	NEW SCIENCE REVIEW	New York	1895–96	2
New World	369	NEW WORLD	Boston	1892–96	5

Abbreviation.	Number in Chronological Conspectus.	Title.	Published.	Dates.	Number of Volumes.
19th Cent.	222	Nineteenth Century	London	1892–96	10
No. Am.	12	North American Review	New York	1892–96	10
Open Court	345	Open Court	Chicago	1887–96	10
Our Day	315	Our Day	Boston	1892–96	8
Outing	305	Outing	New York	1892–96	10
Outl.	375	Outlook	New York.	1893–96	7
Overland, n. s.	186	Overland Monthly [new series]	San Francisco	1892–96	10
Pedagog. Sem.	332	Pedagogical Seminary	Worcester	1892–96	2
Pennsyl. M.	223	Pennsylvania Magazine of History	Philadelphia	1892–96	5
Philos. R.	368	Philosophical Review	Boston	1892–96	5
Poet-Lore	328	Poet-Lore	Boston	1892–96	5
Pol. Sci. Q.	289	Political Science Quarterly	New York	1892–96	5
Pop. Astron.	393	Popular Astronomy	Northfield, Minn.	1893–96	3
Pop. Sci. Mo.	206	Popular Science Monthly	New York	1892–96	10
Portfo.	197	Portfolio	London	1892–95	4
Presb. and Ref. R.	327	Presbyterian and Reformed Review	New York	1892–96	5
Psychic. R.	372	Psychical Review	Boston	1893–94	2
Psychol. R.	392	Psychological Review	New York	1894–96	3
Pub. Opin.	302	Public Opinion	New York	1892–96	10
Q. Illust.	381	Quarterly Illustrator	New York	1893–94	2
Q. J. Econ.	303	Quarterly Journal of Economics	Cambridge	1892–96	5
Quar.	6	Quarterly Review	London	1892–96	10
Ref. Q.	228	Reformed Quarterly Review	Philadelphia	1892–96	5
Reliquary	146	Reliquary	London	1892–96	5
R. of Rs. (N. Y.)	322	Review of Reviews	New York	1892–96	11
Sat. R.	252	Saturday Review	London	1892–96	10
School & Col.	371	School and College	Boston	1892	1
School R.	377	School Review	Ithaca and Chicago	1893–96	4
Science	277	Science	New York	1892–96	9
Sci. Prog.	388	Science Progress	London	1894–96	5
Scot. R.	274	Scottish Review	Paisley, Scot.	1892–96	10
Scrib. M.	309	Scribner's Magazine	New York	1892–96	10
Soc. Econ.	357	Social Economist	New York	1891–95	9
So. Hist. Pap.	220	Southern Historical Society Papers	Richmond	1892–96	5
So. M.	365	Southern Magazine	Louisville	1892–95	5
Spec.	253	Spectator	London	1892–96	10

Sund. M.	258	SUNDAY MAGAZINE	London	1892–96	5
Temp. Bar	148	TEMPLE BAR	London	1892–96	15
Theatre	240	THEATRE	London	1892–96	10
Theo. Mo.	321	THEOLOGICAL MONTHLY	London	1892–96	10
Thinker	385	THINKER	New York	1893	2
Time	338	TIME	London	1879–90	23
Un. Serv. (Phila.)	320	UNITED SERVICE	Philadelphia	1892–96	10
Un. Serv. M.	271	UNITED SERVICE MAGAZINE	London	1892–96	10
Univ. R.	346	UNIVERSAL REVIEW	London	1888–90	8
Univ. Q.	94	UNIVERSALIST QUARTERLY	Boston	1892–96	10
Walford's Antiq.	339	[WALFORD'S] ANTIQUARIAN AND BIBLIOGRAPHER	London	1882–87	12
Westm.	28	WESTMINSTER REVIEW	London	1892–96	10
Writer	310	WRITER	Boston	1893–96	4
Yale R.	380	YALE REVIEW	New Haven	1893–96	4

CHRONOLOGICAL CONSPECTUS.

SETS CONTINUED FROM PREVIOUS VOLUMES OF THE INDEX.

	1 Edinburgh Review.	6 Quarterly Review.	12 North American Review.	13 Blackwood's Magazine.	17 American Journal of Science.	28 Westminster Review.	33 Journal of the Franklin Institute.	64 Dublin Review.	73 Journal of the Royal Statistical Society.	78 Methodist Review.	82 New Englander.	85 Bankers' Magazine (London).	86 Bibliotheca Sacra.	89 Chambers's Journal.	90 Eclectic Magazine.	91 Littell's Living Age.	94 Universalist Quarterly.	104 Bankers' Magazine (New York).	106 N. E. Historical and Genealogical Register.
1892 . .	176	175	155	152	144	138	134	111	55	52	56	54	49	69	119	195	50	46	46
1893 . .	178	177	157	154	146	140	136	113	56	53	Continued as Yale Review. No. 377.	56	50	70	121	199	52	47	47
1894 . .	180	179	159	156	148	142	138	115	57	54		58	51	71	123	203	54	49	48
1895 . .	182	182	161	158	150	144	140	117	58	55		60	52	72	125	207	56	51	49
1896 . .	184	184	163	160	152	146	142	119	59	56		62	53	73	127	211	58	53	50

Chronological Conspectus. — *Continued.*

	112 Art Journal.	116 Harper's Magazine.	120 London Quarterly Review.	131 Atlantic Monthly.	133 All the Year Round.	138 Cornhill Magazine.	139 Good Words.	140 Macmillan's Magazine.	146 Reliquary.	148 Temple Bar.	157 Month.	160 Catholic World.	161 Fortnightly Review.	163 Nation.	165 Argosy.	166 Contemporary Review.	171 American Law Review.	172 American Naturalist.	174 Belgravia.
1892 . .	44	85	79	70	71	66	33	66	32	96	76	55	58	55	54	62	26	26	79
1893 . .	45	87	81	72	73	68	34	68	33	*99	79	57	60	57	56	64	27	27	82
1894 . .	46	89	83	74	75	70	35	70	34	103	82	59	62	59	58	66	28	28	85
1895 . .	47	91	85	76	76	72	36	72	35	106	85	61	64	61	60	68	29	29	88
1896 . .	48	93	87	78		74	37	74	36	109	88	63	66	63	62	70	30	30	91

* There is no volume 100.

CHRONOLOGICAL CONSPECTUS. — *Continued.*

	183 Gentleman's Magazine.	184 Lippincott's Magazine.	186 Overland Monthly.	188 [Amer.] Journal of Social Science.	194 Nature.	197 Portfolio.	200 Lutheran Quarterly.	202 Journal of the Anthropological Institute.	206 Popular Science Monthly.	208 Antiquary. New Series.	209 Irish Monthly.	217 American Architect.	218 American Catholic Quarterly.	219 Mind.	220 Southern Historical Society Papers.	221 Magazine of American History.	222 Nineteenth Century.	223 Pennsylvania Magazine of History and Biography.	226 Library Journal.
1892 . .	49	50	20	(NOS.) 30	46	23	22	21	41	26	20	38	17	17	20	28	32	15	17
1893 . .	51	52	22		48	24	23	22	43	28	21	42	18	18	21	30	34	16	18
1894 . .	53	54	24	31.32	50	(NOS.) 1-12	24	23	45	30	22	46	19	19	22		36	17	19
1895 . .	55	56	26	33	52	13-24	25	24	47	31	23	50	20	20	23		38	18	20
1896 . .	57	58	28	34	54	*	26	25	49	32	24	54	21	21	24		40	19	21

* Continued in such form that indexing seems undesirable.

CHRONOLOGICAL CONSPECTUS. — *Continued.*

	228 Reformed Quarterly.	230 Dial (Chicago).	232 Education.	236 Leisure Hour.	240 Theatre.	245 Baptist Review.	246 American Journal of Philology.	252 Saturday Review.	253 Spectator.	255 Academy.	256 Church Quarterly Review.	257 Literary World (Boston).	258 Sunday Magazine.	260 American Antiquarian.	261 Athenæum.	263 Century.	265 Critic.	268 Knowledge.	271 United Service Magazine.
1892 . .	39	13	12	41	29	14	13	74	69	42	34	23	21	14	1,2	22	21	15	5
1893 . .	40	15	13	42	31		14	76	71	44	36	24	22	15	1,2	24	23	16	7
1894 . .	41	17	14	43	33		15	78	73	46	38	25	23	16	1,2	26	25	17	9
1895 . .	42	19	15	44	35		16	80	75	48	40	26	24	17	1,2	28	27	18	11
1896 . .	43	21	16	45	37		17	82	77	50	42	27	25	18	1,2	30	29	19	13

Chronological Conspectus. — *Continued.*

	272 Longman's Magazine.	273 Johns Hopkins University Studies in Hist. and Polit. Science.	274 Scottish Review.	276 National Review.	277 Science.	279 English Illustrated Magazine.	282 Andover Review.	286 American Journal of Archæology.	288 Harvard Monthly.	289 Political Science Quarterly.	290 English Historical Review.	291 Forum.	292 Imperial and Asiatic Quar. Review.	294 Journal of the Society of Arts.	296 Journal of Hellenic Studies.	297 Journal of Biblical Literature.	299 New England Magazine.	300 Cosmopolitan.	301 Lend a Hand.
1892 . .	20	10	20	19	20	9	18		14	7	7	13	14	40	12	11	6	13	9
1893 . .	22	11	22	21	22	10	19	8	16	8	8	15	16	41	13	12	8	15	11
1894 . .	24	12	24	23	23 N. S.	11		9	18	9	9	17	18	42	14	13	10	17	13
1895 . .	26	13	26	25	1.2	13		10	*	10	10	19	20	43	15	14	12	19	15
1896 . .	28	14	28	27	4	15		11		11	11	21	22	44	16	15	14	21	17

* Continued, but not indexed.

Chronological Conspectus. — *Continued.*

	302 Public Opinion.	303 Quarterly Journal of Economics.	304 American Economic Assoc. Publications.	305 Outing.	306 Academy (Syracuse).	307 Chautauquan.	309 Scribner's Magazine.	310 Writer.	313 American Statistical Assoc. Proceedings.	314 American Journal of Psychology.	315 Our Day.	316 Green Bag.	317 Magazine of Christian Literature.	318 National Geographic Magazine.	319 New Review.	320 United Service (Phila.).	321 Theological Monthly.	322 Review of Reviews (New York).	323 Annals of the American Academy of Political and Social Science.	324 Arena.
1892 . .	13	6	7	20	7	15	12			4	10	4	5.6	3	7	8	8	5	2	6
1893 . .	15	7	8	22	Continued as School and College, No. 369.	17	14	6	3	5	12	5	7	4	9	10	10	8	3	8
1894 . .	17	8	9	24		19	16	7		6	13	6	Continued as Thinker, No. 382.	5	11	12	12	10	4	10
1895 . .	19	9	10	26		21	18	8	4	7	15	7		6	13	14	14	12	6	14
1896 . .	21	10		28		23	20	9	5	8	16	8		7	15	16	16	14	8	16

CHRONOLOGICAL CONSPECTUS. — *Continued.*

	326	327	328	329	330	331	332	334
	International Journal of Ethics.	Presbyterian and Reformed Review.	Poet-Lore.	Economic Journal.	Engineering Magazine.	Monist.	Pedagogical Seminary.	Educational Review.
1892 . .	2	3	4	2	3	2		4
1893 . .	3	4	5	3	5	3		6
1894 . .	4	5	6	4	7	4	2	8
1895 . .	5	6	7	5	9	5		10
1896 . .	6	7	8	6	11	6	3	12

CHRONOLOGICAL CONSPECTUS.

SETS NOW FIRST INDEXED.

	335	336	337	338	339	340	341	342	343	344	345	346	347	348	349	350	351	352	353	354
	English Review.	Folk-Lore Record.	Magazine of Art.	Time.	Walford's Antiquarian and Bibliographer.	Book News.	Journal of American Folk-Lore.	Folk-Lore Journal.	Book-Buyer.	Law Quarterly Review.	Open Court.	Universal Review.	Bookworm.	Ethical Record.	Jewish Quar. Review.	Juridical Review.	Folk-Lore.	National Magazine (N. Y.) [Contin. of Mag. West. Hist.]	Munsey's Magazine.	Critical Review.
	1844–53 Vols. 1–18	1878–82 Vols. 1–5	1878–91 Vols. 1–14	1879–90 Vols. 1–23	1882–87 Vols. 1–12	1883–91 Vols. 1–9	1888–91 Vols. 1–4	1883–89 Vols. 1–7	1884–91 Vols. 1–7	1885–91 Vols. 1–7	1887–91 Vols. 1–5	1888–90 Vols. 1–8	1888–90 Vols. 1–3	1889–91 Vols. 1–3	1889–91 Vols. 1–3	1889–91 Vols. 1–3	1890–91 Vols. 1–2	1891. Vol. 15	1891. Vol. 6. (Vols. 1–5 not indexed.)	1891. Vol. 1
1892			15			10	5		8	8	6		5		4	4	3	16	7	2
1893			16			11	6		9	9	7		6		5	5	4	18	9	3
1894			17			12	7		10	10	8		7		6	6	5	19	11	4
1895			18			13	8		11	11	9				7	7	6		13	5
1896			19			14	9		12	12	10				8	8	7		15	6

CHRONOLOGICAL CONSPECTUS. — *Continued.*

	355	356	357	358	359	360	361	362	363	364	365	366	367	368	369	370	371	372	373	374
	Economic Review.	Music.	Social Economist.	Cassier's Magazine.	Astronomy and Astro-Physics. [Contin. of Sid. Messenger.]	Independent.	Chris ian Union.	Garden and Forest. (Vols. 1–4 not indexed.)	Idler.	Natural Science.	Southern Magazine.	American Journal of Politics.	Architectural Record.	Philosophical Review.	New World.	Charities Review.	School and College. [Contin. of Academy (Syr.)]	Good Government.	Biblical World.	Geographical Journal.
1891	1		1	1																
1892	2	2	3	2	11	'92	45,46	5	2	1	1	1	1	1	1	1	1	*		
1893	3	4	5	4	12	'93	47	6	4	3	2	3	2	2	2	2		12	2	2
1894	4	6	7	6	13	'94		7	6	5	4	5	3	3	3	3		13	4	4
1895	5	8	9	8		'95		8	8	7	5		4	4	4	4		14	6	6
1896	6	10		10		'96		9	10	9			5	5	5	5		15	8	8
			Contin. as Gunton's Magazine, No. 400		Continued as Pop. Astronomy, No. 393		Continued as Outlook, No. 375.				Continued as Mid-Continent, No. 402	Contin. as Am. Mag. of Civics, No. 395					Continued as School Review, No. 377			

* Vols. 1-11 not indexed.

Chronological Conspectus. — *Continued.*

	375	376	377	378	379	380	381	382	383	384	385	386	387	388	389	390	391	392	393
	Outlook. [Contin. of Christian Union.]	Canadian Magazine.	School Review. [Contin. of School and College.]	Harvard Graduates' Magazine.	Journal of Political Economy.	Yale Review. [Contin. of New Englander.]	Quarterly Illustrator.	Psychical Review.	Monthly Illustrator. [Contin. of Quar. Illus.]	Illustrated Archæologist.	Thinker. [Contin. of Mag. Chr. Lit.]	Christian Literature. [Contin. of Thinker.]	McClure's Magazine.	Science Progress.	Book Reviews.	Bostonian.	New Church Review.	Psychological Review.	Popular Astronomy.
1892																			
1893	48	1	1	1	1	1	1	1		1	8.9		1						
1894	50	3	2	2	2	2	2	2		2		11	3	1.2	1	1	1	1	1
1895	52	5	3	3	3	3	Continued as Monthly Illustrator, No. 383		3.4.5		Continued as Christian Literature, No. 386	13	5	3	2	2	2	2	2
1896	54	7	4	4	4	4			*11.12			15	7	5	3	3	3	3	3
																Continued as National Magazine, No. 403			

* Absorbed Home and Country and took its vol. numbers.

Chronological Conspectus. — *Continued.*

	394	395	396	397	398	399	400	401	402	403	404	405	406	407
	Around the World.	Am. Magazine of Civics.	Bookman.	Bachelor of Arts.	Bibliographica.	New Science Review.	Gunton's Magazine.	American Historical Register.	Mid-Continent. [Contin. of Southern Mag.]	National Magazine (Bost.). [Contin. of Bostonian.]	Citizen.	American Journal of Sociology.	American Historical Review.	Economic Studies.
		Continued from Am. Jour. Politics.					Continued from Social Economist.							
1892 . .														
1893 . .														
1894 . .	1													
1895 . .		7	2	1	1	1		1.2	6					
1896 . .		9	4	3	2	2	10.11	4		4.5	1	1.2.	1	1

INDEX TO PERIODICAL LITERATURE.

THIRD SUPPLEMENT,

January 1, 1892 — January 1, 1897.

Aar, The Gorge of the, and its Teachings. (A. R. Wallace) Fortn. **66**: 175.
Aardvark. (R. Trimen) Longm. **27**: 266. Same art. Liv. Age, **208**: 379. — (R. Lydekker) Knowl. **15**: 221.
Aasen, Ivar. (E. Gosse) Ath. '96, **2**: 452.
Abalone or Haliotis Shells of the Californian Coast. (Mrs. M. B. Williamson) Am. Natural. **28**: 849.
Abandoned. (B. Lindsay) Atlan. **78**: 538.
Abandoned Farm, Hunting an, in Connecticut. (W. H. Bishop) Cent. **25**: 915.
Abandoned Farm; a poem. (J. Karl) Canad. M. **5**: 325.
Abarbanel, Don Isaac. (I. S. Meisels) Jew. Q. **2**: 37.
Abattoirs. (P. Hawes) National, **21**: 285.
— Cattle Ships and. (M. E. Haweis) Westm. **143**: 678.
Abattoir System, Progress in England. (H. F. Lester) J. Soc. Arts, **43**: 431.
Abbas Pasha, Khedive of Egypt. New R. **8**: 237. Same art. Liv. Age, **197**: 3.
Abbaye des Dunes, Flanders. Reliquary, **35**: 83.
Abbazia. (Louise Dodge) Garden & F. **7**: 202.
Abbey, Edwin A., with portrait. Bk. Buyer, **9**: 289. **13**: 513.
— Pastels of. (A. L. Baldry) M. of Art, **19**: 224. — (F. H. Smith) Scrib. M. **18**: 135. — (C. Monkhouse) Acad. **48**: 370.
Abbey, Henry Edwin. (O. Hackett) Munsey, **7**: 173.
Abbot, F. E., A Review of his "Scientific Theism." (L. Carrau) Open Court, **1**: 340.
Abbotsbury, England. (W. H. Hudson) Sat. R. **82**: 255.
Abbotsford. (E. K. Pearce) Gent. M. n. s. **48**: 167. — (M. M. Maxwell-Scott) Scot. R. **23**: 225.
— House-party at. (N. L. Smith) Cosmopol. **19**: 513.
Abbott, Chas. C., with portrait. Bk. News, **12**: 307.
Abbott, Lyman, New Progressive Orthodoxy of. (J. Cook) Our Day, **9**: 340.
Abbott, Saunders. (Maj. Broadfoot) Geog. J. **3**: 341.
Abbott, Sir James. (J. S. Cotton) Acad. **50**: 283.
Abbott, Sir John, with portrait. Green Bag, **5**: 537.
Abbott, Twyman W., with portrait. (C. W. Hobart) M. West. Hist. **13**: 421.
Abdul-Aziz and his Harem. (G. R. Watson) Mo. Illust. **11**: 215.
Abdul-Hamid, Sultan. Contemp. **67**: 43. Same art. Liv. Age, **204**: 361. Same art. Ecl. M. **124**: 303. — (E. F. Hay) Chaut. **23**: 79. — R. of Rs. (N. Y.) **13**: 33.
— Daily Life of. (D. Kelékian) Contemp. **70**: 784.
— A Few Facts concerning. Our Day, **16**: 42.
Abdûlla and his Money; a Persian Story. Nat'l M. (Bost.) **5**: 191.
Abdur Rahman Khan. (Sir L. Griffin) Fortn. **59**: 20. Same art. Liv. Age, **196**: 564.
— and Great Britain. (G. W. Leitner) Asia. R. **17**: 283.
— and the Press. Asia. R. **15**: 324.
— Wheeler's. (L. Griffin) Sat. R. **79**: 855.
Abelard and Early Universities, Compayré's. Sat. R. **79**: 259.
— and Héloise. (Anatole France) Cosmopol. **18**: 407.
— as a Theological Teacher, Church Q. **41**: 129.
— Life and Writings of. Eng. R. **5**: 318.
Aberdare, Lord, with portrait. (G. T. Goldie) Geog. J. **5**: 386.
Aberdeen, G. H. Gordon, Earl of. (J. A. Hamilton) Acad. **43**: 341. — With portrait. (P. A. A. Hind) Eng. Illust. **11**: 100.
— and Haddo House. Canad. M. **2**: 288.
— and Lady. With portraits, (W. T. Stead) R. of Rs. (N. Y.) **9**: 41. — McClure, **3**: 128. — (J. C. Hopkins) Canad. M. **2**: 170. — (Lyman Abbott) Outl. **48**: 545.
Aberdeen, Isabel, Countess of. (J. C. Hopkins) Chaut. **18**: 718.
Aberdeen and its Doctors. Blackw. **153**: 425.
Aberdeen University, History of, Bulloch's. Sat. R. **82**: 118.
Aberration, Problems of. (O. J. Lodge) Nature, **46**: 497.
— Stellar. Nature, **45**: 499.
Abingdon, W. L., with portrait. Theatre, **37**: 270.
Abinger, Lord, and the Bar. Temp. Bar, **101**: 519. Same art. Liv. Age, **201**: 423.
Ablaut, General Problems of. (C. D. Buck) Am. J. Philol. **17**: 267.
Abner. (L. R. Meekins) Cent. **30**: 691.
Abolition of Money, The; a story. (I. Zangwill) Idler, **6**: 593.
Abolition Journals, First. (S. C. Williams) New Eng. M. n. s. **10**: 633.
About, E., as a Journalist. Spec. **69**: 792.
"Above" and "Below," Disease of Language. (H. Hale) J. Am. Folk-Lore, **3**: 177.
Abraham at Bonn. (O. H. Gates) Bib. Sac. **53**: 75.
Abraham's Mother. (A. Flint) Lippinc. **51**: 484.
Abrahams, Woodward, with portrait. M. West. Hist. **10**: 174.
Abrantès, Laura, Duchess of. Temp. Bar, **103**: 317. Same art. Ecl. M. **124**: 29.
Absent Heart, The; a story. (G. G. Farquhar) Chamb. J. **70**: 700.
Absent-mindedness. Spec. **75**: 172.
Absentee Landlord, Irish, and his Tenants, 1768-92. (J. G. Alger) Eng. Hist. R. **10**: 663.
Absolute, The. (P. Carus) Open Court, **7**: 3594.

Absolute, The, and the Time-Process. (J. Watson) Philos. R. 4: 353, 486.
— Bradley's Theory of. (A. Seth) Contemp. 60: 694, 862.
Absorption, Physiological. (E. W. Reid) Sci. Prog. 2: 333.
Abstainers, Mistakes about. (F. W. Farrar) Contemp. 65: 545.
Abstraction. (P. Carus) Open Court, 7: 3569.
Abu'l Kásim, Persian Poet. (J. H. Parsons) Gent. M. n. s. 55: 419.
Abu-Simbel. Cornh. 70: 369.
Abyssinia. (J. J. O'Shea) Cath. World, 63: 227. — With map. (G. G. Hubbard) Nat. Geog. M. 7: 157.
— and the Abyssinians. (E. de Leon) Asia. R. 22: 395.
— and Italy. (F. H. Smith) Asia. R. 6: 327.
— Border and Antiquities of. Dub. R. 115: 171.
— Italian War in. (W. B. Harris) Sat. R. 81: 117. — (J. T. Bent) Fortn. 66: 363. — National, 27: 146.
— Marriage in. Time, 8: 148.
Abyssinians, The, and Negus Negusti. (F. Villiers) Cent. 22: 441.
Académie française. (A. Laugel) Nation, 61: 461. 62: 29. — (G. Holme) Munsey, 14: 607. — (H. Houssaye) Forum, 20: 682.
— Daudet on. Critic, 12: 307.
— Dictionary Session at. (E. Bergerat) Lippinc. 51: 118.
— Election of M. Hérédia to. Acad. 47: 484.
— Reception of Paul Bourget. (C. Nicholson) Acad. 47: 524.
— Reception of M. Challemel-Lacour. (C. Nicholson) Acad. 45: 102.
— Reception of Henry Houssaye. (C. Nicholson) Acad. 48: 545.
— Reception of M. Jules Lemaître. (C. Nicholson) Acad. 49: 77.
— Under the Valois, 1570–1585, Frémy on. (E. B. Hamilton) Eng. Hist. R. 3: 576.
Academies, American. (A. D. Mayo) Educa. 17: 203.
— in N. Y. State, State Aid for. School R. 3: 222.
Academy, The Christian. And. R. 17: 308.
— New England, Has it outlived its Usefulness? (G. M. Steele) Educa. 15: 513.
— of France, at Rome. Am. Arch. 47: 124.
— of the Visitation, Georgetown, D. C. (N. T. Taylor) Cosmopol. 13: 654.
— The Old Village. Atlan. 72: 853.
Academy, The; English Periodical. Acad. 50: 375.
Acadia and La Tour. (A. E. Allaben) Nat'l M. (N. Y. '91) 17: 422.
— Feudal Chiefs of. (F. Parkman) Atlan. 71: 25, 201.
— Vacation in. (F. H. Palmer) Educa. 14: 420.
Acadian Rambles. Outing, 26: 289.
Accad and the Early Semites. Open Court, 9: 4651.
Accepted with Pleasure. (V. Hall) New Eng. M. n. s. 13: 689.
Accessory after the Fact, An. (B. Woodbridge) Overland, n. s. 27: 258.
Accident in Invention and Discovery. (E. Mach) Monist, 6: 161.
Accidental Death; Is it Inevitable? (E. Watkin) Time, 1: 653.
Accidents, Incalculable. (W. A. Eddy) Pop. Sci. Mo. 41: 666.
Accipies Woodcut, The. (R. Proctor) Bibliographica, 1: 52.
Acclimatization. (W. Z. Ripley) Pop. Sci. Mo. 48: 662, 779.
Account Book of William Freke, 1619–1630. (G. W. Prothero) Eng. Hist. R. 7: 88.
Accountants, a Needed Profession. (J. L. Reid) No. Am. 159: 510.
Accused, The. (G. F. Tucker) Green Bag, 4: 55, 153.
— as a Witness. (F. Mead) 19th Cent. 31: 188.
Accused by the Dead; a tale. (E. McG. Lawson) Canad. M. 1: 503.
Ace of Hearts, The. (J. S. Fletcher) Chamb. J. 72: 620.
Acetylene. New Sci. R. 2: 348. — (J. M. Crafts) Science, n. s. 3: 377. — (W. J. Youmans) Pop. Sci. Mo. 49: 786.
— as Product of Electric Furnace. J. Frankl. Inst. 139: 72.
— Commercially Considered. (T. L. Willson and J. J. Suckert) J. Frankl. Inst. 139: 321.
— Practical Method of Producing. Dub. R. 116· 401.
Açheen, Sumatra. (A. T. Sibbald) Time, 8: 395.
Achill Island, Three Days in. (M. B. Pattison) Temp. Bar, 108: 213. Same art. Liv. Age, 210: 157.
Achilles, Story of, in Greek Art. (J. E. Harrison) Mag. of Art, 8: 33.
Achilli, G. G. Case against Cardinal Newman. Green Bag, 6: 11.
Achimenes IV. (W. E. Endicott) Garden & F. 8: 16.
Achthar; the Story of a Queen. (C. Sorabji) 19th Cent. 39: 1006. Same art. Ecl. M. 127: 279.
Acids, New Method of determining Relative Affinities of Certain. (M. C. Lea) Am. J. Sci. 147: 445.
Ackerman, Jessie A., An Interview with. (G. T. B. Davis) Our Day, 16: 607.
Acland, Sarah, Life of, ed. by Brunel. Sat. R. 77: 291.
Aconite Collectors on the Singalilas. Chamb. J. 72: 445.
Acorns as Food, Ancient Use of. (A. T. Sibbald) Time, 17: 600.
Acoustic Properties of Public Buildings. (H. C. Kent) Am. Arch. 39: 9.
Acoustics in Architecture. (J. L. Faxon) Am. Arch. 43: 107.
— in relation to Buildings. (H. W. Burrows) Am. Arch. 48: 65, 78.
— Researches in. (A. M. Mayer) Am. J. Sci. 147: 1. 151: 81.
Acquired Characters. (E. R. Lankester and others) Nature, 51: 8–126.
Acreage Returns, how obtained. Chamb. J. 69: 479.
Acrobats, Child-, Training of. (S. L. Bensusan) Eng. Illust. 16: 41.
Acropolis Museum, Archaic Statues of. (R. Lister) 19th Cent. 34: 560.
Across Dug Gap. (S. L. Bacon) Lippinc. 51: 94.
Across the Mesaba: a story. (J. Shephard) Outing, 27: 450.
Across the Moor. Good Words, 35: 520.
Across the Pond. All the Year, 73: 77.
Actæon; a poem. (E. Fawcett) Cosmopol. 15: 422.
Acting. (H. Irving) Fortn. 63: 369. — (W. Poel) Theatre, 30: 271.
— Amateur. (G. S. Lee) Critic, 29: 355.
— — of To-day. (W. G. Elliot) National, 24: 628.
— — Women and. (F. A. Mathews) No. Am. 159: 759.
— Art of. (M. Morris) Time, 7: 656.
— as an Art. (H. Irving) Fortn. 63: 369. Same art. Ecl. M. 124: 587.
— Can it be Taught? (H. Aïde) 19th Cent. 34: 452.
— Concerning. (R. Mansfield) No. Am. 159: 337.
— Criticism of. (W. Archer) New R. 12: 654.

Acting, An Epidemic of Slovenliness. (G. W. Dancy) Theatre, **38**: 97.
— "Gentleman" of Modern Drama. Theatre, **38**: 3.
— The Modern Cart of Thespis. (W. H. Crane) No. Am. **154**: 472.
— Is it a Healthy Profession? (A. J. Daniels) Theatre, **37**: 180.
— Momus; a Socratic Dialogue. (W. L. Courtney) National, **19**: 217.
— New. Critic, **27**: 283.
— Old and New. Sat. R. **80**: 799.
Actinism. (C. S. Wake) Science, **19**: 142.
Action, Unreasonable. (E. M. Sidgwick) Mind, **18**: 174.
"Active," Sloop, Case of. (H. L. Carson) Green Bag, **7**: 17. — (H. L. Carson) Pennsyl. M. **16**: 385.
Acton, Edward Hamilton. Nat. Sci. **6**: 351.
Action, J. E. E. D., Lord, as Professor of Modern History at Cambridge. Sat. R. **79**: 821.
Actor, The. (J. Drew) Scrib. M. **15**: 32.
— and his Tailor. Sat. R. **81**: 170.
— Legal Status of. (T. Marriott) Theatre, **32**: 260.
— Social Position of. (P. Fitzgerald and others) Theatre, **35**: 6.
— Manager, and the Public. (J. Malone) Forum, **20**: 235.
Actor-Manager, The. (H. Elliott) Theatre, **37**: 180.
Actors, American, in London. (A. Brereton) Theatre, **33**: 231.
— and Actresses in Westminster Abbey. Cornh. **67**: 373.
— — Stage Royalties. M. of Art, **7**: 384.
— and Audiences, French and English. (F. Febvre) New R. **7**: 365.
— and Puppets. Sat. R. **73**: 242.
— A Comparison. (F. Kerr) Theatre, **37**: 13.
— English; Her Majesty's Servants. (G. B. L. Woodburne) Gent. M. n. s. **51**: 60.
— Four "Leading Men," a Comparative Estimate. (W. A. L. Bettany) Theatre, **38**: 109.
— Goddard's Players of the Period. Spec. **68**: 273.
— Mummer Worship. (Geo. Moore) Univ. R. **2**: 105.
— of the New Generation. (W. D. Adams) Theatre, **31**: 247, 309.
— of the Past Generation. (W. D. Adams) Theatre, **30**: 316.
— On Some of the Old. (P. Fitzgerald) Gent. M. n. s. **52**: 82–170.
— Portraits of, in National Portrait Gallery. (P. Fitzgerald) Theatre, **37**: 204.
— Professional Amateur. (T. E. Pemberton) Theatre, **32**: 17.
— Puritans and. (W. Wheater) Gent. M. n. s. **50**: 178.
— Status of. (Dutton Cook) Time, **3**: 510.
— Strolling. Cornh. **72**: 87. Same art. Ecl. M. **125**: 374.
Actors' Association, The. (W. Lestocq) Theatre, **33**: 298.
Actress, Who is Greatest Living English? Idler, **8**: 393.
Actresses, Early English. (S. J. A. Fitzgerald) Theatre, **31**: 149.
— in Men's Parts. (L. H. Weeks) Lippinc. **57**: 88.
— Recollections of. (M. E. W. Sherwood) Lippinc. **53**: 92.
— The Stage and the Beauty Problem. (J. S. Metcalfe) Cosmopol. **22**: 13.
— Titled. (M. Bacheller) Munsey, **13**: 46.
— who have become Peeresses. (A. C. Wheeler) Cosmopol. **20**: 130.
Actualists, The; Impressions of Shilto Jessop, Artist. (M. Mempes) National, **23**: 544.
Adair, Gen. John. (Mrs. M. T. Daveiss) Am. Hist. Reg. **3**: 228.
Adam and Eve, Mohawk Legend of. (A. F. Chamberlain) J. Am. Folk-Lore, **2**: 228.
— Putting off the Old Man. (W. D. Gunning) Open Court, **1**: 67.
Adam, Mme. Juliette Lamber, Portraits of. McClure, **5**: 69.
Adam, Robert, Architecture by, in London. (P. Fitzgerald) J. Soc. Arts, **42**: 181.
Adam Brothers and Clodion, Thirion's. M. of Art, **8**: 212.
Adamawa, German Expedition to. (Dr. Passarge) Geog. J. **5**: 50.
Adams, Francis, Writings of. Sat. R. **78**: 75.
Adams, Hannah. (E. P. Gould) New Eng. M. n. s. **10**: 363.
Adams, John Clayton. (A. L. Baldry) M. of Art, **19**: 134.
Adams, John Couch. (Henriette Corkran) Temp. Bar, **105**: 519. — Acad. **41**: 109. — Ath. '**92**, **1**: 154. — Nature, **45**: 301. — With portrait. Pop. Sci. Mo. **41**: 545.
Adams, John Quincy, Death of, in the Capitol. (R. C. Winthrop) Scrib. M. **13**: 389.
Adams, W. Davenport. Apologia pro Vita Mea. Theatre, **32**: 70.
Adams, Rev. William, of New York, with his Adams and Bradford Descent. (Miss E. W. Leavitt) N. E. Reg. **48**: 190.
Adams, William T. (F. A. Munsey) Munsey, **8**: 58.
Adams Family, The. (J. A. Torrington) Munsey, **14**: 702.
Adams, Mt., Altitude of. (E. McClure) Nat. Geog. M. **7**: 151.
— Fourth of July on, 1891. (C. E. Rusk) Overland, n. s. **20**: 92.
Adaptation, Agglutination and. (E. W. Fay) Am. J. Philol. **16**: 1.
— Is it possible without Design? (J. Cooper) Bib. Sac. **51**: 117.
Adderley, J. Stephen Remarx. Spec. **70**: 779.
Adders or Vipers. (C. Parkinson) Gent. M. n. s, **50**: 272.
Addiscombe, Heroes and Men of, Vibart's. Sat. R. **78**: 357.
Addiscombe Military College. (W. Broadfoot) Blackw. **153**: 647. Same art. Liv. Age, **198**: 109. — (W. Broadfoot) Un. Serv. (Phila.) **10**: 40.
Addison, Joseph, as a Humorist. (M. O. W. Oliphant) Cent. **26**: 703.
— Essays, Green's ed. Spec. **69**: 193.
Adelaïda, Who was? (S. M. S. Pereira) Sund. M. **22**: 310. Same art. Liv. Age, **197**: 819.
Adelaide, South Australia, Art Gallery. Art. J. **46**: 344.
Adele Berthier; a Story of Old Quebec. (T. Swift) Canad. M. **6**: 43, 138.
"Adeste Fideles;" a story. (G. Rent) Bost. **3**: 213.
Adhesive Organs in Animals. (R. Lydekker) Knowl. **18**: 246.
Adirondack Idyl, An; a story. (C. C. Nott, jr.) Outing, **23**: 16.
Adirondack Park. (C. S. Sargent) Garden & F. **6**: 171.
Adirondack Reservation. (C. S. Sargent) Garden & F. **7**: 91.
— Plunder of. (C. S. Sargent) Garden & F. **9**: 101.
Adirondack Sketches. (W. Lecky) Cath. World, **58**: 554 — **59**: 492.
Adirondacks, Emerson, Agassiz and Lowell in. (W. J. Stillman) Cent. **24**: 598.

Adirondacks, Life in. (P. MacQueen and J. H. Smith) Munsey, **8**: 479.
— Map of. Around World, **1**: 151.
Adjustment of Accounts, An; a story. (W. McLennan) Harper, **88**: 360.
Adjutant's Swim, The. (M. Crommelin) Argosy, **61**: 251.
Adlamont Case. Green Bag, **6**: 69.
Adler, Nathan Marcus. (M. Friedländer) Jew. Q. **2**: 369.
Administrative Law, Goodnow on. (H. P. Judson) Dial (Ch.) **16**: 9.
Admirable Bandit, An; a story. (Mrs. J. G. Jebb) Blackw. **160**: 244. Same art. Liv. Age, **210**: 712.
Admiral's Yarn, The; a story. (C. S. Clarke) Eng. Illust. **12**: no. 6, 84.
Admiralty Surveys. Geog. J. **6**: 22.
Adolph, a Faithful Fool. (T. G. Randall) Outing, **27**: 476.
Adopted Child, An; a story. Argosy, **55**: 395. Same art. Liv. Age, **198**: 152.
Adowa, Battle of. Un. Serv. M. **13**: 214, 225.
Adriatic, Beyond the. (H. W. Preston) Cent. **27**: 737, 905. **28**: 118.
Adulterations in Groceries. Econ. R. **4**: 490.
— in Food. (H. W. Wiley) J. Frankl. Inst. **137**: 266.
— — Detection of. (I. M. Tarbell) McClure, **3**: 177.
— — in the U. S. (J. G. Speed) Chaut. **16**: 49.
Adventure in Philanthropy, An. (E. C. Martin) Scrib. M. **11**: 230.
Adventure of the Final Problem; a story. (A. C. Doyle) McClure, **2**: 99.
Adventure of a Lady of Quality. (M. J. Judah) Harper, **90**: 238.
Adventurer, The. (S. J. Weyman) Eng. Illust. **12**: no. 4, 3.
Adventures of Belzebub, The. (Emilia Dilke) Univ. R. **6**: 223.
Adventures of a Poet-Laureate. (M. F. Gibson) Gent. M. n. s. **54**: 473.
— of Walter Schnaffs. (G. de Maupassant) Idler, **2**: 252.
Adventuress, The. (Annie Edwardes) Temp. Bar, **102**: 289, 433. **103**: 1, 265.
Adventurous Week, An. (C. Edwardes) Chamb. J. **72**: 626–680.
Advertise; a story. (C. Lorinda) Belgra. **89**: 411.
Advertisement, Advance of. Cornh. **72**: 505.
— Self-. Theatre, n. s. **28**: 140.
Advertisements, Architecture and. (R. Evans) J. Soc. Arts, **42**: 35. — (R. Evans) Am. Arch. **43**: 18.
— Only the. (E. Stuart) Temp. Bar, **106**: 221. Same art. Ecl. M. **125**: 660.
Advertisement Nuisance. (W. E. H. Lecky and others) New R. **9**: 466.
Advertising, Artistic. (W. P. Frith and M. H. Spielmann) M. of Art, **12**: 421.
— as a Trespass on the Public. (R. Evans) 19th Cent. **37**: 968. Same art. Liv. Age, **206**: 131. Same art. Ecl. M. **125**: 314.
— Curiosities of. Chamb. J. **72**: 311.
— Economics of. (E. P. Harris) Soc. Econ. **4**: 171.
— Successful, Art of. (E. H. Heinrichs) Engin. M. **6**: 229.
Advertising Page, The. (W. H. McDougal) Overland, n. s. **22**: 569.
Advocate as a Verb. (F. Hall) Nation, **54**: 10.
Adye, Sir John, Military Recollections of. (W. O. Morris) Acad. **47**: 393.
Ægean Art and Writing, Beginnings of. (A. H. Sayce) Acad. **50**: 149.
Ægean Art, Pottery in Egypt. (W. F. Petrie; C. Torr) Acad. **41**: 476. **42**: 18–360.
Ægosthena. (E. F. Benson) J. Hel. Stud. **15**: 314.
Aerial Athletes and the Coming Race. (J. B. Walker) Cosmopol. **21**: 275.
Aerial Fleet, The; a poem. (L. S. Goodwin) Outing, **27**: 377.
Aerial Navigation. (H. Elsdale) Contemp. **65**: 362. — (C. B. Moore) Arena, **10**: 386. — (A. F. Zahm) J. Frankl. Inst. **138**: 265, 347. — (V. E. Johnson) Westm. **142**: 261. — All the Year, **75**: 318. — Cosmopol. **12**: 624. — (J. P. Holland) Cosmopol. **14**: 89. — Am. Cath. Q. **17**: 191. — (A. F. Zahm) Cath. World, **57**: 1. — (J. Fleury) Chaut. **17**: 682. — Dub. R. **112**: 167.
— Air Car, or Man-Lifting Kite. (B. B. Powell) National, **26**: 494.
— and Flying-Machines. (Gaston Tissandier) Cosmopol. **16**: 382.
— Development of. (H. S. Maxim) No. Am. **159**: 344.
— Empire of the Air. (A. Macivor) Gent. M. n. s. **56**: 520.
— Gliding Flight. (L. P. Mouillard) Cosmopol. **16**: 459.
— Maxim Airship. (H. J. W. Dam) McClure, **2**: 148.
— Present Status of. (O. Chanute) Engin. M. **11**: 47.
— Progress in. (H. S. Maxim) Fortn. **58**: 438. Same art. Ecl. M. **119**: 703.
— Prospects of. (H. S. Maxim) National, **24**: 42.
Aerial Vessels, Automatic Stability in. (T. Moy) Knowl. **18**: 29.
Aerial Warfare. (T. Moy) Knowl. **18**: 276.
Aeronautics, Experiments in. (H. S. Maxim) J. Soc. Arts, **43**: 21.
Aeroplane, The. (H. S. Maxim) Cosmopol. **13**: 202.
Æschylus. Agamemnon. Eng. R. **1**: 105.
— — at Bradfield College, 1892. (L. Dyer) Nation, **55**: 26.
— Choëphori, Verrall's. Sat. R. **76**: 19.
— Persians. (W. C. Lawton) Atlan. **70**: 228.
— Religious Teachings of. (M. T. Blauvelt) Poet-Lore, **4**: 415.
Æsop's Fables, Jacobs'. (T. F. Crane) J. Am. Folk-Lore, **3**: 245.
Æsthetic Principles, Marshall's. Sat. R. **80**: 480. — (E. E. Hale, jr.) Dial (Ch.) **19**: 141.
Æsthetics, Bosanquet on. (M. Mead) Dial (Ch.) **13**: 276.
— Hedonic. (H. R. Marshall) Mind, **18**: 15.
— Knight on. Spec. **70**: 607.
— of Simple Forms. (E. Pierce) Psychol. R. **3**: 270.
Affair at Islington, The; a novel. (M. White, jr.) Munsey, **12**: 150–620.
Affair of Dishonor, An. (W. C. Platts) Belgra. **84**: 43.
Affair of the Heart, An; a story. (G. King) Harper, **88**: 796.
Affectionate Son, An; a story. Cornh. **72**: 490. Same art. Ecl. M. **125**: 821. Same art. Liv. Age, **207**: 589.
Afghan Poetry of 17th Century. (C. E. Biddulph) Asia. R. **9**: 91.
Afghanistan, Alliance with. (E. K. Robinson) Fortn. **64**: 707.
— Amir of, Gray's. Sat. R. **80**: 805.
— Amir's Surgeon on. Dub. R. **116**: 188.
— Ethnography of. (H. W. Bellew) Asia. R. **12**: 261.
— Experiences at Court of. (J. A. Gray) J. Soc. Arts, **42**: 260.
— Frontier of, Rectification of. (J. Dacosta) Westm. **137**: 313.
— Hazaras of. Dub. R. **111**: 451.

Afghanistan in 1892, British Success and Danger in. Spec. 68: 632.
— Invasions of. Asia. R. 16: 35.
— Lord Salisbury's Policy. (T. P. Hughes) Arena, 6: 645.
— Our Relations with. Asia. R. 11: 28, 283.
— Political Relation of. Sat. R. 78: 427.
— Progress in. (J. A. Gray) Asia. R. 17: 305.
— Question of. (Archibald Forbes) Time, 1: 1.
— Ride into. (D. Ker) Chamb. J. 71: 321.
— Salter Pyne's Account of. Dub. R. 114: 434.
— Treaty with England. Asia. R. 16: 284.
— Tribes of. (H. G. Raverly) Asia. R. 17: 312.
Afghans, Peppered by. (A. Forbes) Cosmopol. 12: 434.
Africa, and the European Powers. Blackw. 151: 843. Same art. Ecl. M. 119: 105. Same art. Liv. Age, 194: 323.
— and India. (F. E. Younghusband) Asia. R. 22: 37.
— British Interest in, and European Action. (A. Silva White) Asia. R. 12: 63.
— Central, Belgium's Interest in. Sat. R. 74: 354.
— — British. Dub. R. 115: 175. — (H. H. Johnston) New R. 11: 14.
— — — and East, Commercial Prospects of. (G. S. Elliott) J. Soc. Arts, 44: 423.
— — — Cedar Forests in. Dub. R. 119: 167.
— — — Geography and Resources of. (A. Sharpe) Geog. J. 7: 366.
— — — Unexplored, A Journey to. (J. Thomson) Geog. J. 1: 97.
— — British Protectorate in. (H. H. Johnston) Geog. J. 5: 193.
— — Folk-Tales of. (E. Elmslie) Folk-Lore, 3: 92.
— — South, English in. (G. G. Hubbard) McClure, 7: 148.
— — Trade of, and the Nyassaland Water-Way. (A. Sharpe) Blackw. 151: 319.
— Chartered Government in. (A. S. White) 19th Cent. 35: 126.
— the Coming Continent, Vincent's. Sat. R. 80: 273.
— Congress on, at Chicago, 1893. (F. P. Noble) Our Day, 12: 279. — (F. P. Noble) Char. R. 2: 437.
— Degeneracy of Europeans in. (Max Nordau) Asia. R. 12: 68.
— East, American Trade Prospects in. (C. J. Zingg) Am. M. Civics, 6: 500.
— — and the Mombasa Railway. (G. S. Mackenzie) Fortn. 57: 566.
— — and West, in Parliament. (F. D. Lugard) Blackw. 155: 133.
— — Baumann's Journey Through. (E. Heawood) Geog. J. 4: 246.
— — British. Asia. R. 18: 58. 20: 65.
— — — Capabilities of. (F. Parry) Asia. R. 16: 106.
— — — Contributions to Physical Geography of. (J. W. Gregory) Geog. J. 4: 289, 408, 505.
— — — Crisis in. Asia. R. 13: 117.
— — — People, Places, and Prospects in. (C. W. Hobley) Geog. J. 4: 97.
— — British East Africa Co. (Marquis of Lorne) Asia. R. 16: 337. — (Gen. Sir A. B. Kemball) Fortn. 60: 707. — Spec. 70: 724.
— — British Empire in. Blackw. 154: 875.
— — British Interests in. Blackw. 155: 860.
— — British Trade with. Dub. R. 119: 430.
— — Equatorial, Anglo-German Boundary in. (C. S. Smith) Geog. J. 4: 424.
— — Höhnel's Discovery of Lakes Rudolf and Stefanie. (J. M. Hubbard) Nation, 59: 32.
— — Natives of, Customs among. (M. French-Sheldon) Anthrop. J. 21: 358.
— — Neumann's Journey in. Geog. J. 6: 274.
Africa, Physical Geography of, Gregory's. Dub. R. 119: 428.
— — Transport in. Dub. R. 114: 185. 115: 457.
— East Central, Customs in. (J. Macdonald) Anthrop. J. 22: 99. — (J. Macdonald) Pop. Sci. Mo. 42: 689. 43: 240.
— Englishmen in. All the Year, 74: 399.
— Equatorial, Count Götzen's Journey Across. Geog. J. 5: 354.
— — Parke's Experiences in. (D. F. Hannigan) Westm. 137: 28. — Nature, 45: 265.
— Ethnology of. (E. Heawood) Geog. J. 6: 465.
— Europe in. Lond. Q. 85: 205.
— European Influence in. (C. H. E. Carmichael) Asia. R. 14: 85.
— Evangelization of; Divine Program in the Dark Continent. (J. Cook) Our Day, 12: 193.
— Expedition to Ruwenzori and Tanganyika. (G. F. S. Elliot) Geog. J. 6: 301.
— Exploration in. Ed. R. 179: 267.
— — Ethics of. (R. N. Cust) Asia. R. 14: 348.
— Folk-Lore of, Chatelain on. (F. Starr) Dial (Ch.) 17: 261.
— Foreign Languages in, Function and Future of. (W. S. Scarborough) Meth. R. 54: 890.
— France and Germany in, 1894. Blackw. 156: 145.
— French Ambitions in. (G. T. Goldie) Asia. R. 17: 327.
— French Fighters in. (P. Bigelow) Harper, 90: 366.
— French Occupation of. (J. W. Lowther) National, 25: 306.
— German Policy in. (J. W. Gregory) 19th Cent. 39: 240.
— Glave in the Heart of. (E. J. Glave) Cent. 52: 918.
— Heart of. (E. C. Hore) Nat. Geog. M. 3: 238.
— How we Lost the United States of. (F. E. Garrett) National, 22: 681.
— Italian. Dub. R. 115: 170.
— Italy in. (J. W. Mario) Leis. Hour, 45: 467.
— Junker's Travels in, 1882–86. Dial (Ch.) 13: 208.
— Map of, by Treaty, Hertslet's. Sat. R. 79: 813.
— New British Markets in. (F. D. Lugard) 19th Cent. 38: 442.
— North; the New Winter-Land. (W. Sharp) 19th Cent. 35: 99.
— North of the Equator. (A. E. Pease) Contemp. 70: 37.
— Partition of. Pub. Opin. 15: 191. — (A. S. White) 19th Cent. 36: 23.
— — Keltie on. Sat. R. 80: 243. — (A. C. Coolidge) National, 57: 48.
— Past and Future of. (G. G. Hubbard) Nat. Geog. M. 1: 99.
— Portugal and England in. (G. de Vasconcellos Abreu) Asia. R. 11: 104, 319.
— Problem of. (E. W. Blyden) No. Am. 161: 327.
— Progress in, Causes of Retardation of. (H. Chatelain) J. Am. Folk-Lore, 8: 177.
— Races of, Problem of. (H. Elsdale) Asia. R. 21: 299.
— Railroad Development in. (C. C. Adams) Engin. M. 4: 693.
— Railways in. (L. Darwin) Geog. J. 8: 488.
— Recent Literature of. (E. G. Ravenstein) Geog. J. 3: 497.
— Reminiscences of. (T. H. Parke) Un. Serv. M. 6: 324–447.
— Re-partition of. (E. Bond) Un. Serv. M. 8: 136.
— Research in, Changes in Methods and Purposes of. C. C. (Adams) Chaut. 19: 701.
— Romans in. (A. Laugel) Nation, 63: 228.
— Rome in. (W. Sharp) Harper, 91: 95.

Africa, Routes in. (F. D. Lugard) National, 25: 765.
— Settlement of, by the Whites, Prospects of. (C. Peters) Forum, 16: 150.
— Since 1888. (G. G. Hubbard) Nat. Geog. M. 7: 157.
— South. (R. Colley) Month, 79: 311. — (A. G. C. Van Duyl) Asia. R. 20: 71. — Spec. 72: 621.
— — and Cecil Rhodes. (J. C. Hopkins) Canad. M. 3: 436.
— — and the Chartered Company. (C. Harrison) Contemp. 69: 339.
— — Anglo-Saxon Supremacy in, 1814–94. (F. I. Ricarde-Seaver) New Sci. R. 1: 11.
— — Animals in. Liv. Age, 208: 126.
— — Black and White in. (W. A. Wills) J. Soc. Arts, 42: 707.
— — British; 1200 miles in a Waggon. (Alice Balfour) National, 25: 183, 351. Same art. Ecl. M. 124: 751. 125: 22. Same art. Liv. Age, 205: 605.
— — British South African Company, Labouchere and. Spec. 71: 653.
— — Chartered Company; "Mr. Cecil Rhodes' Raid." (L. J. Maxse and others) National, 27: 719, 742.
— — Churchill on. Sat. R. 73: 607.
— — Climate of. (R. Roose) Fortn. 65: 104.
— — Developments in. (R. Ogden) Nation, 63: 44.
— — Empire-building in. (Albert Shaw) Cosmopol. 20: 472.
— — England's Duty in. (A. Michie) Blackw. 160: 265.
— — Expansion of, Wilmot's. Sat. R. 79: 448.
— — Fate of. (F. R. Harris) New R. 14: 331.
— — Future of the British Empire in. (D. Mills) Canad. M. 7: 62.
— — Germans in. (W. Greswell) Fortn. 65: 209.
— — Gold Era in. (W. B. Worsfold) Fortn. 65: 260. Same art. Ecl. M. 126: 334.
— — Gold Fields of. (G. F. Becker) Cosmopol. 22: 170. — (W. R. Lawson) National, 27: 412. Same art. Ecl. M. 127: 174.
— — High Commissionership of. (W. Greswell) Fortn. 65: 716.
— — Impressions of. (J. Bryce) Cent. 30: 48, 241, 442.
— — Languages of. Month, 75: 227.
— — Letters from. (C. W. Wood) Argosy, 57: 48–484. 58: 48–496.
— — The Liberals and. Quar. 178: 435.
— — Mining Industries of. (B. H. Brough) J. Soc. Arts, 41: 166.
— — Nature *vs.* The Chartered Company. (J. D. Montagu) 19th Cent. 40: 194.
— — New. Leis. Hour, 45: 326–581.
— — Problem of, and the Government. Asia. R. 22: 86.
— — Cecil Rhodes on. Spec. 69: 281.
— — Rhodesia, Crisis in. (E. M. Clerke) Dub. R. 119: 256.
— — Rhodesian Affairs. (H. L. W. Lawson) Fortn. 65: 704.
— — Rights and Duties of Great Britain in. Ed. R. 183: 273.
— — Lord Ripon and Mr. Rhodes. Spec. 71: 570.
— — Since 1888. (G. G. Hubbard) Nat. Geog. M. 7: 157.
— — Social and Political Problems of. (W. F. Bailey) National, 28: 543.
— — Social Questions in. (V. T. Kirby) Econ. R. 5: 125. 6: 90. — (W. F. Bailey) National, 28: 543.
— — Stray Thoughts on. (O. Schreiner) Fortn. 65: 510. 66: 1, 225.
— — Trouble in. (E. L. Godkin) Nation, 62: 25, 233.
— — Two Constitutions of. (J. Bryce) Forum, 21: 145.
Africa, White Man's: pt. 1. Jameson's Raid. (P. Bigelow) Harper, 93: 813.
— — — 2. President Kruger. (P. Bigelow) Harper, 94: 26.
— — Witwatersland and the Revolt of the Uitlanders. (G. F. Becker) Nat. Geog. M. 7: 349.
— — Work of the Chartered Company. (E. Dicey) Fortn. 65: 985.
— — Worsfold's. Sat. R. 81: 459.
— South of the Equator, by W. D. Cooley. Eng. R. 18: 340.
— Southeast, Anglo-Portuguese Delimitation Commission in. (J. J. Leverson) Geog. J. 2: 505.
— — Selous on. Ath. '93, 2: 513. — Spec. 71: 549. — (J. M. Hubbard) Nation, 57: 453.
— Southwest, English and German. (J. Count Pfeil) Geog. J. 2: 29.
— Transformation of. (J. M. Hubbard) Nation, 61: 306.
— Travel in, Paraphernalia of. (J. Johnston) Around World, 1: 89.
— Treaty-making in. (F. D. Lugard) Geog. J. 1: 53.
— Triangulation of. (E. F. Chapman) Geog. J. 5: 467.
— Tropical. (A. S. White) 19th Cent. 38: 455.
— Tropical, as Factor in Civilization. (C. C. Adams) Our Day, 13: 5.
— Two Women's Tramp in. (H. C. Black) Sund. M. 23: 261, 348.
— Ultimate: a poem. (J. E. Rankin) Our Day, 13: 495.
— Warning to Imperialists. (E. Lecky) 19th Cent. 40: 19.
— West, British in. Un. Serv. M. 11: 397.
— — British Administration in. (F. Buxton) Liv. Age, 192: 486. — Sat. R. 73: 360.
See also Mashonaland.
— — British Possessions in. (F. D. Lugard) Blackw. 157: 970.
— — Franco-German Delimitation Treaty in. Dub. R. 115: 174.
— — French in. (A. P. Crouch) Blackw. 153: 55.
— — Land of Palm Oil. Chamb. J. 72: 484.
— — Missionary Pioneers in; Women. (A. R. Buckland) Sund. M. 24: 841.
— — Railways for. Dub. R. 117: 455.
— — Service in. Un. Serv. M. 6: 72, 261.
— — Service in the Bights. Un. Serv. M. 5: 463.
— Why it can wait. (M. de Villiers) 19th Cent. 40: 338.
— Why it cannot wait. (E. Dicey) 19th Cent. 39: 721.
African Church, Schwartze on. (A. Macalister) Crit. R. 3: 410.
African Explorers: Martyrs to a New Crusade. (H. Ward) Eng. Illust. 11: 105.
African Legends. (H. M. Stanley) Fortn. 59: 797.
African Pioneers, French Society of. (S. P. Oliver) Asia. R. 21: 75.
African Races. (H. Chatelain) J. Am. Folk-Lore, 7: 289.
After Brer Rabbit in the Blue-grass. (J. Fox, jr.) Cent. 31: 97.
After Five Years; a story. (L. Butt) Belgra. 86: 65.
After Long Waiting; a poem. Argosy, 59: 66.
After Many Days; a story. Blackw. 158: 650.
After Many Days. (E. Nesbit) Longm. 23: 49.
After Much Suffering; a story. (L. Burrell) Belgra. 80: 268.
After —, the Deluge. (A. Eliot) Atlan. 72: 472.
After the Fact. (E. W. Hornung) Chamb. J. 73: 6–55.
After the Fire; a story. Overland, n. s. 23: 101–150.
After the Play; a story. (H. H. Fyfe) Theatre, 33: 242.

After Twenty Years; a story. (F. Friedland) Chaut. **18**: 596.
After Two Decades. (Lady Ramsay) Lond. Soc. **53**: 298.
Aftermath; a story. (W. J. Locke) New R. **13**: 103. Same art. Ecl. M. **125**: 399.
Afternoon Call, An; a story. Temp. Bar, **103**: 84. Same art. Liv. Age, **203**: 208.
Afterwards; a story. (I. Maclaren) McClure, **4**: 472.
Agassiz, Louis John Rudolph, at Penikese. (D. S. Jordan) Pop. Sci. Mo. **40**: 721.
— Marcou's Life of. Nation, **62**: 362. — Dial (Ch.) **20**: 304. — Sat. R. **81**: 510.
— Reminiscences of Penikese. (H. B. C. Beedy) Educa. **13**: 339.
Agava, An Arizona. Garden & F. **8**: 184.
Agave, New. (I. N. Rose) Garden & F. **6**: 5.
Age, Apology from, to Youth. Macmil. **67**: 126. Same art. Liv. Age, **196**: 167. — Spec. **69**: 846, 866.
— Old, and Youth. (F. L. Oswald) Open Court, **3**: 1683, 1741.
— — Endowment of. (J. F. Wilkinson) Contemp. **61**: 555. *See* Old Age; Pensions.
Age of Consent in U. S. (A. M. Powell and others) Arena, **11**: 192. **12**: 282. **13**: 88–353. **14**: 205, 401.
Agency and Trusteeship. (C. Sweet) Law Q. **8**: 220.
— Talmudical Law of. (L. M. Simmons) Jew. Q. **8**: 614
Agent and Servant essentially Identical. (C. C. Allen) Am. Law R. **28**: 25.
Agglutination and Adaptation. (E. W. Fay) Am. J. Philol. **16**: 1.
Aggregations, Names for. (B. Day) Writer, **7**: 52.
Agitator, An; a poem. (Lena Gyles) Temp. Bar, **108**: 406.
Agnostic, The, in Fiction. (W. L. Courtney) Univ. R. **2**: 71.
— Why I am not an. (F. M. Müller) 19th Cent. **36**: 890. Same art. Ecl. M. **124**: 99. Same art. Chr. Lit. **12**: 147.
Agnosticism. (M. D. Conway) Open Court, **2**: 1103.— (W. E. Hodgson) National, **20**: 327. — (J. G. Schurman) Philos. R. **4**: 241. — (W. Maccall) Monist, **4**: 31. — (A. Waters) Open Court, **6**: 3471.
— and Comte's Positivism. (P. Carus) Open Court, **3**: 1589.
— and Monism. (E. Montgomery) Open Court, **1**: 9, 37, 65.
— and the Theory of Life. (M. C. O'Byrne) Open Court, **3**: 1692.
— Balfour's Attack on. (T. Huxley) 19th Cent. **37**: 527.
— The Case of, Revised. (P. Carus) Open Court, **5**: 2993.
— Christianity and. (P. R. Shipman) Open Court, **3**: 1668.
— Common-sense View of. Westm. **144**: 278.
— Does it produce Better Results than Christianity? (W. L. Garrison, jr.) Open Court, **1**: 153.
— Evangelical. (D. H. Bauslin) Luth. Q. **26**: 217.
— Evolution and Bruce's Lectures on. (E. Buckley) Bib. World, **6**: 374.
— Field *vs.* Ingersoll on. Open Court, **2**: 1042, 1059.
— Free Thought, and Skepticism. (S. Dewey) Westm. **143**: 178.
— Huxley's Creed. Quar. **180**: 160.
— in "The Monist." (E. Thurtell) Open Court, **5**: 2950.
— in Theory and Practice. (J. Gerard) Month, **77**: 305.
Agnosticism, Monism, Dualism. (P. Carus) Open Court, **1**: 209.
— Passing of. (A. A. Berle) Bib. Sac. **52**: 505.
— Philosophical, and Monism. (L. G. James) Open Court, **5**: 2947.
— Questions of. Open Court, **4**: 2686.
— Rebound from; Balfour's Book. (J. G. Schurman) Forum, **19**: 364.
— Religion, Reason, and. (A. Bodington) Westm. **139**: 369. Same art. Ecl. M. **120**: 752.
— Roots of. (T. Seth) N. World, **3**: 458.
— Spencerian. (P. Carus) Open Court, **5**: 2951.
— Two Errors of. (P. Carus) Open Court, **3**: 1671.
— *versus* Gnosticism. (P. R. Shipman) Open Court, **4**: 2116–2189.
Agnostics; Are they in Good Faith? (C. Coupe) Dub. R. **110**: 71.
Agra, Blockade of, in 1857. Chamb. J. **71**: 715.
Agram Mummy. (M. L. McClure) 19th Cent. **33**: 796.
Agrapha: Sayings of our Lord not Recorded in the Gospels. (W. Locke) Chr. Lit. **10**: 111 a.
Agreements not to be Performed within a Year. (E. H. Bennett) Am. Law R. **29**: 481.
Agrell, Alfhild. Karin. Gent. M. n. s. **48**: 629.
Agricola, a British Pelagian. Church Q. **39**: 160.
Agricultural Banks, The Case for. (H. W. Wolff) Contemp. **69**: 584.
Agricultural Changes in New York. (L. H. Bailey) Garden & F. **7**: 203.
Agricultural Contracts in South Italy. (F. S. Nitti) Econ. R. **3**: 364.
Agricultural Depression. (C. S. Sargent) Garden & F. **9**: 391. — (W. D. Drysdale) Econ. R. **6**: 205. — (W. Hill) J. Pol. Econ. **4**: 505.
— and its Remedies. Quar. **176**: 521.
— and Light Railways. Sat. R. **80**: 793.
— in East Anglia. (R. Heath) Contemp. **64**: 443.
— Unmasked. (T. M. Hopkins) Westm. **145**: 552. Same art. Ecl. M. **127**: 74.
Agricultural Discontent in the United States, Analysis of. (C. F. Emerick) Pol. Sci. Q. **11**: 434–601.
Agricultural Experiment Centres, California. (C. H. Shinn) Garden & F. **7**: 442.
Agricultural Experiment Stations. (C. S. Sargent) Garden & F. **8**: 401. — (B. D. Halsted) Chaut. **16**: 284.
— Proper Work for. (C. S. Sargent) Garden & F. **9**: 321.
— Variety Tests in. (C. S. Sargent) Garden & F. **9**: 461.
Agricultural Experiments, Rothamsted. (C. Creyke) 19th Cent. **33**: 970.
Agricultural Laborer. (H. G. Pearce) Eng. Illust. **12**: no. 6, 43.
— Imperturbability of. Spec. **74**: 683.
— in England. Quar. **178**: 504. — Spec. **70**: 665.
— in Southeastern England. (R. Heath) Contemp. **64**: 852.
Agricultural Museums. (J. D. Crawford) Nat. Sci. **1**: 371.
Agricultural Population, An. (C. M. Weed) Pop. Sci. Mo. **42**: 638.
— of the United Kingdom. (W. E. Bear) Econ. J. **4**: 317, 707.
Agricultural Problem, The. (M. B. Morton) No. Am. **162**: 638.
Agricultural Rates Act, 1896, from an Historical Aspect. (R. M. Garnier) Econ. R. **6**: 456.
Agricultural Renaissance. (W. O. Atwater) Pub. Opin. **20**: 684.
Agricultural Science, Evolution of. (R. M. Garnier) Econ. R. **5**: 441.

Agricultural Syndicates and Coöperative Societies in France. (C. Gide) Econ. J. **5**: 195. — (H. W. Wolff) Q. J. Econ. **8**: 98. — (H. W. Wolff) Econ. J. **3**: 522.
Agricultural Unrest, Causes of. (J. L. Laughlin) Atlan. **78**: 577.
Agriculture, Advanced, Webb's. Sat. R. **79**: 70.
— and Economics. (C. A. Cripps) National, **20**: 782.
— — Roman and Anglo-Saxon Agrarian Conditions. (L. Hutchinson) Q. J. Econ. **7**: 205.
— Beginnings of. (L. Bourdeau) Pop. Sci. Mo. **46**: 678.
— Coöperation in. (H. W. Wolff) Contemp. **68**: 485.
— Declining. Chamb. J. **73**: 492.
— Electricity in. (Clarence D. Warner) Garden & F. **5**: 47.
— Energy as a Factor in. (M. Miles) Pop. Sci. Mo. **41**: 87.
— Experimental, Status of. (H. L. Bolley) Science, **19**: 270.
— Experimental Farms of Canada. Garden & F. **8**: 519.
— Experimental Work in the Improvement of Useful Plants. (C. S. Sargent) Garden & F. **6**: 261.
— Fallacies about Farm Prices. Soc. Econ. **6**: 321.
— Future Wheat Farming. (W. Aldrich) Soc. Econ. **6**: 224.
— in England. Agricultural Union. Dub. R. **112**: 445. — (Lord Winchelsea; G. B. Curtis) National, **20**: 587.
— — The British Farmer and the Deluge of Foreign Produce. (J. Long) Fortn. **60**: 184.
— — Climax of Disaster. (W. E. Bear) Fortn. **64**: 405.
— — Commission on. (L. L. Price) Econ. J. **6**: 389. — (P. A. Graham) New R. **14**: 549. — (J. Long) Fortn. **65**: 635.
— — Conference on, 1892. (L. L. Price) Econ. J. **3**: 128. — Spec. **69**: 640, 840. — Sat. R. **74**: 669.
— — Crisis in, 1892–93. Ed. R. **177**: 216.
— — Depression in. (E. Le Riche) Westm. **141**: 473.
— — — and its Effects on a Leading London Hospital. (J. C. Steele) J. Statis. Soc. **55**: 37.
— — — as shown in the Accounts of an Oxford College. (L. L. Price) J. Statis. Soc. **55**: 2.
— — — Cause of. (J. Collings) 19th Cent. **32**: 967.
— — — Coöperation and. (E. Mitchell) Westm. **142**: 241.
— — — New Evidence on. (W. E. Bear) National, **23**: 527.
— — How it is Affected by the Currency. (C. Wilson) National, **21**: 139.
— — A Plea for the Farmer. Westm. **140**: 440.
— — Problem of. (W. E. Bear) Econ. J. **3**: 391, 569.
— — Ruin of. (P. A. Graham) National, **20**: 177.
— in Europe; Distress on the Continent. Spec. **72**: 78.
— in France, Modern. (H. Blerzy) Chaut. **20**: 151.
— in Great Britain, Two Points on. Spec. **75**: 358.
— in Maine. (J. C. Rose) Nation, **55**: 159.
— in Public Schools. (C. S. Sargent) Garden & F. **6**: 37.
— in Russia, Crisis of. (I. A. Hourwich) Yale R. **1**: 411.
— in the South; Peons of the South. (G. K. Holmes) Ann. Am. Acad. Pol. Sci. **4**: 265.
— in the U. S. 100 Years Hence. (J. M. Rusk) No. Am. **156**: 255.
— Intensive Farming. Soc. Econ. **6**: 157.
— Mass. Society for Promoting. Garden & F. **5**: 371.
— on the Carolina Foot-Hills. (C. S. Sargent) Garden & F. **6**: 441, 518.
— Perish Agriculture! Quar. **180**: 406.
— Pessimist View of. Spec. **70**: 247.
— Pottering with. (P. A. Graham) New R. **13**: 443.
Agriculture, Preservation of Soil-Moisture by Shallow Tillage. (C. S. Sargent) Garden & F. **6**: 281.
— Relation to Science. Dub. R. **118**: 152.
— Science as a Factor in. (P. E. M. Berthelot) Pop. Sci. Mo. **42**: 481.
— Society for the Promotion of Agricultural Science. Garden & F. **7**: 339.
— Tillage of the Soil. (C. S. Sargent) Garden & F. **9**: 291.
— Wallace on. Garden F. & **9**: 19.
Agrostology in the Department of Agriculture. (F. L. Scribner) Science, n. s. **2**: 151.
Ahmed, the Cobbler; a Persian Story. Nat'l M. (Bost.) **5**: 286.
Ahmedabad. (S. H. Dunn) Month, **88**: 342. — All the Year, **74**: 440.
Aidan, St.; Was he an Anglican? Month, **74**: 188.
Aiken, Aunt Lizzie, Story of, with portrait. (Mrs. G. Anderson) Our Day, **15**: 125.
Aikman, Andrew. Bank M. (Lond.) **60**: 739.
Ailesbury, Thomas Bruce, 2d Earl of. (A. Lang) Blackw. **152**: 18. Same art. Liv. Age, **194**: 723.
Aino Folk-Lore. (J. Batchelor) J. Am. Folk-Lore, **7**: 15.
Ainos, Fresh Light on. Nature, **49**: 248.
— Hairy, Among the. Ed. R. **179**: 180.
— — Landor on. (D. MacRitchie) Acad. **44**: 570. — Sat. R. **77**: 15.
— of Japan, Bachelor's. Sat. R. **74**: 26.
— of Northern Japan. (H. T. Finck) Outing, **25**: 113.
— of Saghalien, and their Dogs. Dub. R. **114**: 427.
— — Howard on. (F. Starr) Dial (Ch.) **15**: 338.
— of Yezo. Dub. R. **114**: 429.
Ainslie, New, Memoir of. Sat. R. **74**: 398.
Ainsworth, Henry. Book of Psalms. (C. S. Nutter) New Eng. M. n. s. **10**: 201.
Ainsworth, W. F. Ath. '**96**, **2**: 799.
Air and Water, Relation of, to Temperature and Life. (G. G. Hubbard) Nat. Geog. M. **5**: 112.
— Atmospheric, Radiation of. (C. C. Hutchins) Am. J. Sci. **143**: 357.
— Bad, and Bad Health. (H. Wager and A. Herbert) Pop. Sci. Mo. **40**: 814. **41**: 97.
— Compressed. (W. L. Saunders) J. Frankl. Inst. **133**: 370. — (F. Richards) Cassier, **6**: 489.
— — Energy Transmitted by. (C. A. Hague) Cassier, **10**: 448.
— — for Street Railroads. (W. P. Pressinger) Cassier, **10**: 105. — (H. Haupt) Engin. M. **3**: 617.
— — for Workshops. (C. O. Heggem) Cassier, **8**: 440.
— — Practical Consideration of. (W. L. Saunders) Cassier, **2**: 128.
— — Widening Use of. (W. P. Pressinger) Engin. M. **6**: 145.
— — Work in. Chamb. J. **73**: 455.
— Electrification of, and other Gases. Nature, **51**: 495.
— — and Diselectrification of. Nature, **52**: 608.
— Expired, Composition of, and Effects on Life. Science, n. s. **1**: 481.
— Geography of the. (A. W. Greely) Nat. Geog. M. **2**: 49. **3**: 200. **4**: 85.
— Geological Work of. (S. Meunier) Pop. Sci. Mo. **48**: 355.
— Hot, and Steam, for Power. Cassier, **1**: 81.
— Liquefaction of. (J. Dewar) Nature, **53**: 329.
— Liquid. Pub. Opin. **14**: 475. — (J. J. Stewart) Knowl. **17**: 149.
— — and Oxygen. Dub. R. **112**: 162.
— Recent Researches on. (C. M. Aikman) Gent. M. n. s. **54**: 146.

Air and Water Supplied to Buildings, Purification of. (W. Key) J. Soc. Arts, **41**: 248.
— We Breathe. (S. A. Dunham) Chaut. **22**: 403–654. **23**: 143, 279.
Air-brush, Fountain. (C. L. Burdick) J. Soc. Arts, **42**: 344.
Air-car, The. (B. Baden Powell) National, **26**: 494. Same art. Liv. Age, **208**: 118.
Air-pump, Mercurial, Self-acting. (E. W. Morley) Am. J. Sci. **147**: 439.
Air-ship, Influence on War. (J. K. Cree) No. Am. **162**: 78. *See* Aerial.
Airy, Sir George B. Ath. '92, **1**: 55. — Nature, **45**: 232.
Alabama, Geology of, Miocene Group. (L. C. Johnson) Science, **21**: 90.
— Industrial Conditions of. (J. Ralph) Harper, **90**: 607.
— Pioneer Marriage in. (F. E. Herring) Canad. M. **5**: 375.
— Politics and the Race Question in. (J. C. Rose) Nation, **59**: 211.
— Post-Eocene Formations of the Coastal Plain of. (E. A. Smith) Am. J. Sci. **147**: 280.
"Alabama," The, Sinclair on. (C. H. Palmer) Dial (Ch.) **20**: 46. — (C. H. Stockton) Nation, **62**: 105.
Alabaster. (R. Benyon) Knowl. **18**: 245.
Alain of Halfdene; a story. (A. R. Brown) Lippinc. **55**: 435.
Alamo, Defence of the. (L. J. Hornibrook) Chamb. J. **73**: 401. — (R. H. Titherington) Munsey, **8**: 381.
— Heroine of. (Mena K. Ogan) Nat'l M. (N. Y. '91), **18**: 23.
Alaska. (J. G. Brady) Chaut. **23**: 729.
— Administrations in. (L. F. Bower) M. Am. Hist. **29**: 390.
— and its People. (C. W. Sarel) Westm. **139**: 616. **140**: 57.
— and Sheldon Jackson. (J. Eaton) R. of Rs. (N. Y.) **13**: 691.
— Boundary Line. (T. C. Mendenhall) Atlan. **77**: 517. (E. R. Scidmore) Cent. **30**: 143. — (R. E. Gosnell) Canad. M. **6**: 248. — (O. J. Klotz) Pop. Astron. **3**: 349, 395.
— Boundary Survey of. (Dr. Mendenhall) Nat. Geog. M. **4**: 177.
— Catholic Sisters in. (P. C. Yorke) Cath. World, **56**: 799.
— Chapter of. (C. E. Cabot) New Eng. M. n. s. **11**: 588. — (J. W. Bingham) Nation, **60**: 10, 28.
— Charles Bryant on. (C. E. Cabot) Nation, **60**: 72.
— Education in. Lend a H. **16**: 262.
— 1865–95. (W. H. Dall) Science, n. s. **3**: 37, 87.
— Ethnology of. (Franz Boas) J. Am. Folk-Lore, **1**: 215.
— Glaciers of. (H. G. Egerton) 19th Cent. **32**: 991. Same art. Liv. Age, **196**: 289.
— Gold Fields of. (R. Stein) R. of Rs. (N. Y.) **13**: 697.
— Landward Boundary of. (G. J. Varney) Green Bag, **8**: 152.
— Moravian Mission in. (J. T. Hamilton) M. Chr. Liter. **5**: 351.
— Pioneer Packhorses in. (E. J. Glave) Cent. **22**: 671, 869.
— Recent Explorations in. (E. R. Scidmore) Nat. Geog. M. **5**: 173.
— Revisited. (W. H. Dall) Nation, **61**: 6–220.
— Summer in. (Mabel H. Closson) Overland, n. s. **20**: 395.
— Summer Tour in. (L. M. Washburn) Cosmopol. **17**: 411.
Alaska, Thlinkets of. (A. M. Bugbee) Overland, n. s. **22**: 185.
— Under the Arctic Circle. (J. Keatley) Arena, **7**: 487.
— Undiscovered Island off the North Coast of. (M. Baker) Nat. Geog. M. **5**: 76.
— Voyage to. (F. De Laguna) Overland, n. s. **24**: 30.
— Work among Natives in. (R. S. Jackson) Lend a H. **14**: 179.
Alaskan Boats. (J. C. Cantwell) Outing, **23**: 388.
Alaskan Folk-Lore. (J. Deans) J. Am. Folk-Lore, **5**: 232. — (W. G. Chase) J. Am. Folk-Lore, **6**: 51.
Albany, Eng., and its Dukes. Time, **7**: 123.
Albany, N. Y., Colonial Buildings of. (M. T. Reynolds) Archit. Rec. **4**: 415.
Albatross, Sooty or Brown; with plate. Knowl. **19**: 196.
— White-breasted, on Laysan Island. Knowl. **18**: 79.
Albemarle, Earl of. (R. Noel) National, **19**: 526. Same art. Liv. Age, **194**: 387.
Albemarle, Va., in Revolutionary Days. (G. B. Goode) Nat. Geog. M. **7**: 271.
"Albemarle" in Albemarle Sound. (F. M. Bennett) Un. Serv. (Phila.) **11**: 438.
Albert, Prince, University Days of. (H. W. Wolff) Gent. M. n. s. **52**: 129.
Albert Edward, Prince of Wales, and his Set. Munsey, **13**: 164.
Albertina and National Gallery. (G. Ludwig) Art J. **48**: 359.
Albertinelli, Mariotto, and Fra Bartolommeo. (J. Cartwright) M. of Art, **6**: 426.
Albigenses, In the Country of. (E. H. Barker) Liv. Age, **192**: 295.
Albigensians and the Town of Albi. (R. Twigge) Dub. R. **114**: 309.
Alboni, Marietta. Sat. R. **77**: 686. — Ath. '94, **1**: 846.
Albrecht, Archduke. (S. Wilkinson) Spec. **74**: 261.
Albuquerque, Affonso d'. Sat. R. **74**: 419.
Albuquerque, Stephens's. (G. Smith) Nation, **56**: 202.
Alchemists of Egypt and Greece. Ed. R. **177**: 202.
Alchemy and Chemistry. (C. S. Peirce) Nation, **59**: 144.
— — Muir on. (H. McLeod) Nature, **50**: 50.
— in England. (R. Steele) Antiq. n. s. **24**: 99.
Alcohol and Happiness. (J. Gaule) Pop. Sci. Mo. **46**: 28.
— Discovery of, and Distillation. (P. E. M. Berthelot) Pop. Sci. Mo. **43**: 85.
— Expert Views of. Pub. Opin. **15**: 482.
— in its Relation to the Bible. (H. A. Hartt) Arena, **5**: 732.
— — Reply. (A. Gustafson) Arena, **6**: 461.
— — Rejoinder. (H. A. Hartt) Arena, **6**: 723.
— Question of. (R. Roose) New R. **7**: 66.
Alcoholism, Control of, by Baker-Rose Gold Cure. Bost. **1**: 542.
— Legal Preventives of. (J. Bergeron) Pop. Sci. Mo. **44**: 391.
Alcott, A. Bronson. Atlan. **73**: 549. — N. Church R. **1**: 305. — With portrait. Bk. Buyer, **10**: 250. — With portrait. Bk. News, **11**: 477.
— Conversations of. (E. D. Cheney) Open Court, **2**: 1131, 1142.
— Sanborn and Harris's Life of. Ath. '93, **2**: 548. — (T. W. Higginson) Nation, **57**: 103, 136. — Dial (Ch.) **14**: 356. — Critic, **22**: 348. — Monist, **4**: 144. — Sat. R. **76**: 184.
Alcott, Louisa May, with portrait. Bk. News, **5**: 227.
— Recollections of. (M. S. Porter) New Eng. M. n. s. **6**: 3.
Alcuin as an Educator. (F. Watson) Acad. **43**: 344.

Alden, Jonathan, of Marshfield, Letter of, 1722. (Mrs. C. L. Alden) N. E. Reg. **48**: 310.
Aldershot, Rise of. (T. A. L. Murray) Un. Serv. M. **8**: 321.
Aldines, Early Chronology of. (R. C. Christie) Bibliographica, **1**: 193.
Aldrich, Anne R., with portrait. Bk. News, **11**: 264. — With portrait. Bk. Buyer, **11**: 124.
Aldrich, Thos. B., with portrait. Bk. Buyer, **10**: 403.
Aldrich Public Buildings Bill. Am. Arch. **51**: 8.
Aldus, House of. Walford's Antiq. **11**: 308. **12**: 4.
Ale Drinking in Old Egypt and the Thrako-Germanic Race. (K. Blind) Scot. R. **25**: 23.
Aleutian Islands (W. R. Shoemaker) Un. Serv. (Phila.) **11**: 221.
Aleuts, Among the. Temp. Bar, **96**: 404.
Alexander VI., Pope. (T. B. Scannell) Dub. R. **118**: 309.
— Alleged Poisoning of. (R. Garnett) Eng. Hist. R. **9**: 355.
— and Cæsar Borgia; Were they Poisoned? (W. W. Story) Blackw. **154**: 843.
— Contemporary Oration on. (R. Garnett) Eng. Hist. R. **7**: 311.
— Demarcation Line of. (E. G. Bourne) Yale R. **1**: 35.
Alexander the Great, Legend of. (J. H. McDaniels) Nation, **63**: 406.
— Portraits of. M. of Art, **12**: 262.
— Tomb of. (Rev. H. Smith) Macmil. **67**: 208. Same art. Ecl. M. **120**: 349.
Alexander I. of Russia, and Napoleon. Quar. **177**: 416.
Alexander III. of Russia. (E. B. Lanin) Contemp. **63**: 1. Same art. Liv. Age, **196**: 387. Same art. Ecl. M. **120**: 259. — Spec. **70**: 5. — (W. T. Stead) R. of Rs. (N. Y.) **10**: 630. — (A. Laugel) Nation, **59**: 379. — Spec. **73**: 600. — (T. Schwartz) Munsey, **8**: 137.
— and his Advisers. (C. E. Smith) No. Am. **160**: 21.
— and Nicholas II. Pub. Opin. **17**: 765.
— and Russia of To-day. (W. T. Stead) R. of Rs. (N. Y.) **4**: 667.
— and What we may Expect of Him. (E. Borges) Harper, **9**: 129.
— Crowning of. (M. G. Thornton) Cent. **30**: 8.
— Death of, and the Peace of Europe. (T. A. Dodge) Forum, **18**: 396. — (S. Stepniak) No. Am. **159**: 735.
— Funeral of. Spec. **73**: 723.
— Lowe's. Sat. R. **79**: 100. — (I. F. Hapgood) Nation, **60**: 150.
— Personal Courage of. (A. Forbes) Contemp. **63**: 189.
Alexander I., Prince of Battenburg. (J. D. Bourchier) Fortn. **61**: 103. Same art. Liv. Age, **200**: 323.
Alexander, Mrs. C. F., Hymns of. (S. Gwynn) Sund. M. **25**: 55.
— Sunday Book of Poetry. Spec. **68**: 467.
Alexander, Francesca. (M. H. Spielmann) M. of Art, **18**: 295.
Alexander, George, Actor and Manager. (A. Bright) Theatre, **28**: 239.
— Four "Leading Men," a Comparative Estimate. (W. A. L. Bettany) Theatre, **29**: 109.
Alexander, Wm., Bp. (I. F. Mayo) Leis. Hour, **43**: 433.
Alexander Randall's Conversion. (M. C. Graham) Atlan. **71**: 231.
Alexandria. (M. MacColl) Sund. M. **22**: 807.
— Library of, Did Omar Destroy? (R. V. Rau) 19th Cent. **36**: 555.
— University of. (V. E. Johnson) Westm. **138**: 286.
Alexandria, A Walk in. (A. E. P. R. Dowling) 19th Cent. **33**: 813. Same art. Liv. Age, **198**: 177.
Alfred, King, in Somerset. (Mrs. C. G. Boger) Walford's Antiq. **7**: 14-118.
Alfonso XII. proclaimed King of Spain. (M. de Blowitz) Harper, **84**: 588.
Alfonso XIII., King of Spain. (A. Lynch) Eng. Illust. **15**: 499.
Algæ, Shell-boring. (T. Johnson) Nat. Sci. **5**: 17.
Algebra, Theoretical Knowledge and Practical Facility in. (J. M. Peirce) School & C. **1**: 535.
Algedonics, H. R. Marshall on. Nature, **50**: 3.
Alger, Horatio, jr. (F. A. Munsey) Munsey, **8**: 59.
— John Maynard, How I Came to Write. (H. Alger, jr.) Writer, **8**: 182.
Algeria. (S. J. Weyman) Leis. Hour, **41**: 14, 86
— New Pool of Bethesda. (G. O. Morgan) Gent. M. n. s. **52**: 15.
— Scenes in. (C. Edwardes) Liv. Age, **193**: 289.
— Situation in, 1892. Sat. R. **74**: 525.
— With two Canadians in. (A. Sullivan) Canad. M. **3**: 29.
Algerian Customs, Some. All the Year, **74**: 185.
Algiers. (J. A. Blaikie) M. of Art, **7**: 140, 177. — (C. Stewart) Idler, **6**: 771. — (W. H. Carpenter) Nation, **58**: 327. — (F. C. Sessions) M. West. Hist. **12**: 591.
— City of the White Dove. (A. J. H.-Antona) Outing, **29**: 128.
— Scenes in. (R. H. Titherington) Munsey, **7**: 165.
Algol and a New Stellar System. (A. Searle) Atlan. **69**: 814.
— Light Curve of, True Form of. (P. Plassmann) Astron. **11**: 419.
— Variable Star. (M. Ferrel) Astron. **12**: 429. — (J. E. Gore) Gent. M. n. s. **51**: 345.
Algonquin Indians, Migrations of. (C. S. Wake) Am. Antiq. **16**: 127.
Algonquin Legends. (T. C. Hamilton) J. Am. Folk-Lore, **7**: 201.
Algonquin Park, Canada. (E. B. Fraleck) Canad. M. **2**: 294. — (T. W. Gibson) Canad. M. **3**: 542.
Alhambra, Granada and the. (H. C. Chatfield-Taylor) Cosmopol. **21**: 451.
— Lights and Shadows of the. (E. R. Pennell) Cent. **30**: 198.
Ali Diâb's Tent. (G. A. Smith) Good Words, **37**: 238.
Aliens, Right of, to enter British Territory. (W. F. Craies) Law Q. **6**: 27.
Alimentation, Relation of, to some Diseases. (J. Wood) Science, **21**: 62.
Alison, Sir Archibald, Tory Economist. Soc. Econ. **9**: 256.
Alkali Carbonate Solution, Geologic Efficacy of. (E. W. Hilgard) Am. J. Sci. **152**: 100.
Alkali Lands, Steppes, and Deserts. (E. W. Hilgard) Pop. Sci. Mo. **48**: 602.
Alkali-making by Electricity. (C. F. Townsend) Knowl. **19**: 247.
Alkalies; Preliminary Note on a New Alkali Mineral. (W. M. Foote) Am. J. Sci. **150**: 480.
Alkali-metal Pentahalides. (H. L. Wells and H. L. Wheeler) Am. J. Sci. **144**: 42.
Alkaloids, Vegetable, Acidimetric Estimation of. (L. F. Kebler) J. Frankl. Inst. **141**: 141.
Alker, Henry. (G. W. Travers) M. West. Hist. **12**: 487.
All for Honour; a story. (Darcy Lever) Gent. M. n. s. **54**: 1.
All for a Life. (J. Heard, jr.) Outing, **22**: 173.
All I Could Never Be; a story. (M. Bradford-Whiting) Gent. M. n. s. **55**: 217.
All my Sad Captains. (S. O. Jewett) Cent. **28**: 737.

All Saints' Church, God's Hill. Am. Arch. 47: 59.
All the Way to the Mansion House. (G. M. Rogers) Canad. M. 7: 457.
Alladine and Palomides; a prose play. (M. Maeterlinck) Poet-Lore, 7: 281.
Allan, Robert, Sir H. Raeburn's Portrait of. M. of Art, 2: 268.
Allanite Crystals from Franklin Furnace, N. J. (A. S. Eakle) Am. J. Sci. 147: 436.
Allegheny, Pa. Carnegie Free Library. Lib. J. 18: 288.
Allen, Ethan. Oracles of Reason. (M. D. Conway) Open Court, 6: 3119.
Allen, Grant. British Barbarians. Sat. R. 80: 785.
— Hilltop Novels by. Spec. 75: 722.
— Millennium of. (J. Gardiner) Open Court, 4: 2659.
— My First Book. Idler, 2: 155.
— Poetry of. (E. Purcell) Acad. 45: 263.
— Woman Who Did. Sat. R. 79: 319. — (M. G. Fawcett) Contemp. 67: 625.
Allen, Hope, of Boston. (O. P. Allen) N. E. Reg. 47: 86.
Allen, Horatio. (A. Matthews) Cassier, 10: 471.
Allen, Jas. Lane, with portrait. Bk. News, 11: 380. — With portrait. (N. H. Banks) Bookman, 1: 303. — (H. L. Conard) M. West. Hist. 13: 487.
— and his Books. (E. A. Madden) Book R. 4: 151.
— Kentucky Cardinal. Sat. R. 82: 202.
Allen, Jeremiah Mervin. (P. H. Woodward) Cassier, 8: 616.
Allen, Jolley. (W. H. Winslow) Atlan. 70: 597.
Allen, Land-bill, Myth of. (W. Gladden) Cent. 25: 609.
Allen, Ralph. The Man of Bath. (A. Ballantyne) Longm. 28: 66. Same art. Liv. Age, 209: 616. — (R. C. Browne) Acad. 48: 309.
Allen, William V., with portrait. (A. Shaw) R. of Rs. (N. Y.) 10: 30.
Allerton Towers. (Mrs. P. Cudlip) Time, 6: 121–647. 7: 37–895.
Alliances, Talk of New. (F. Greenwood) New R. 12: 52.
Alligator Hunters of Louisiana, The. (A. Wilkinson) Cent. 21: 399.
Alligator-hunting in Mexico. (E. French) Outing, 27: 206.
— with Seminoles. (K. Munroe) Cosmopol. 13: 576.
Alligators and Crocodiles. Chamb. J. 70: 575.
— Indian. (C. T. Buckland) Longm. 23: 603. Same art. Liv. Age, 201: 299.
Allingham, Wm. Prose Works. (A. B. McMahan) Dial (Ch.) 17: 13. — Spec. 72: 471.
Allis, Edward P. (A. Hoppin) M. West. Hist. 7: 85.
Allison, William Boyd. (J. W. Kay) Mo. Illust. 11: 331.
— The Presidency and. Atlan. 77: 544.
Allon, Henry. (R. W. Dale) M. Chr. Liter. 6: 217. — (J. G. Rogers) Sund. M. 21: 387.
Allotments, Pages in the History of. (J. F. Wilkinson) Contemp. 65: 532.
Alloys. (N. C. Roberts-Austen) J. Soc. Arts, 41: 977–993.
— Chemical Nature of. (F. H. Neville) Sci. Prog. 4: 177.
— of Copper and Zinc. (T. K. Rose) Nature, 55: 130.
— of Tin and Iron, Study of Formation of. (W. P. Headden) Am. J. Sci. 144: 464.
— Recent Study of. (F. H. Neville) Sci. Prog. 4: 77.
Allport, Walter Webb; with portrait. (C. N. Johnson) Nat'l M. (N. Y. '91) 17: 376.
All's Fair in Love. Gent. M. 50: 541. Same art. Liv. Age, 198: 437.
All's Well; a story. All the Year, 75: 254.
Allston, Washington. (M. G. Van Rensselaer) M. of Art, 12: 145.
Allston as a Painter. (H. Greenough) Scrib. M. 11: 220.
— Flagg's Life of. (W. M. Conway) Acad. 43: 330. — (K. Cox) Nation, 56: 32. — Sat. R. 75: 354. — Atlan. 71: 698.
— Unpublished Correspondence of. Scrib. M. 11: 68.
Ally of Mr. Cross, An; a story. (J. J. à Becket) Scrib. M. 16: 122.
Allylene, New Method of Preparing. (E. H. Keiser; M. B. Breed) J. Frankl. Inst. 139: 304.
Allyn, Hon. Frank (Tacoma). (W. L. Visscher) M. West. Hist. 12: 81.
Alma-Tadema, Laurens. (E. Gosse) Cent. 25: 483. — With portrait. R. of Rs. (N. Y.) 9: 691. — (W. Maynell) M. of Art, 2: 193. — (M. H. Spielmann) M. of Art, 20: 42. — (R. R. Wilson) Mo. Illust. 12: 95. — (C. Monkhouse) Scrib. M. 18: 663.
— and his Work. (C. S. Johnson) Munsey, 8: 259.
— His Home and Pictures. (E. M. McKenna) McClure, 8: 32.
— House of, at Regent's Park. (W. Meynell) M. of Art, 5: 184.
— Seven Years Ago and Now. (W. Meynell) M. of Art, 4: 94.
Almanac of 16th Century. (G. White) Bookworm, 6: 32.
Almanacs. (R. W. McFarland) Pop. Astron. 2: 225, 358, 452. 3: 114, 303.
— Colonial. (A. M. Lathe) Chaut. 18: 722.
— Early American. (W. L. Andrews) Bookman, 2: 283.
— Literature of. (H. R. Plomer) Walford's Antiq. 11: 20, 332.
— Satirical. (H. R. Plomer) Walford's Antiq. 9: 27, 156.
Almeida-Garrett, João Baptista de. Brother Luiz de Sousa. (E. Prestage) Dub. R. 118: 79.
Almond Culture in California. (H. J. Philpott) Pop. Sci. Mo. 41: 328. — Garden & F. 5: 351.
Alms and the Man; a sketch. (E. C. Hamley) Belgra. 90: 313.
Alms of Monsieur l'Abbé. (J. J. à Becket) Cosmopol. 22: 148.
Almshouse Women; a Study. (Mary R. Smith) Am. Statis. Assoc. 4: 219.
Almshouses, Ancient English. Cornh. 71: 63.
— of Massachusetts. (C. E. Woodbury) Lend a H. 11: 524.
Alnoite. (F. D. Adams) Am. J. Sci. 143: 269.
— Containing an Uncommon Variety of Melilite. (C. H. Smyth) Am. J. Sci. 146: 104.
— Dikes of, at Manheim, N. Y. (C. H. Smyth, jr.) Am. J. Sci. 159: 290.
Alnwick Castle. Chamb. J. 69: 321. — (M. Creighton) Mag. of Art, 5: 140, 195.
Alone in China; a story. (J. Ralph) Harper, 91: 685.
Alone; a poem. (E. S. Robertson) M. of Art, 5: 282.
Along Shore. (S. O. Jewett) Liv. Age, 211: 761.
Along the Track; a Western Sketch. All the Year, 72: 84.
Along the Umpqua; a story. Overland, n. s. 19: 587.
Alpha Centauri and the Distance of the Stars. (J. E. Gore) Gent. M. n. s. 50: 407.
Alphabet, The, Evolution of. (G. Valbert) Pop. Sci. Mo. 42: 243.
— Early History of. (C. W. Super) Bib. Sac. 49: 496.
— of the Bureau of Ethnology. J. Am. Folk-Lore, 5: 236.
Alphabets, Asiatic, Lacouperie on. (I. Taylor) Acad. 46: 425.
— Handbook of Lettering, Strange's. Sat. R. 80: 584.

Alphabets of the Berbers. (D. G. Brinton) Science, 21: 104.
Alphege, Archbishop and Martyr. (C. A. Channer) Sund. M. 23: 559.
Alpine Climbing. (C. H. Parkhurst) Outl. 49: 1020.
Alpine Divorce, An; a story. (R. Barr) Eng. Illust. 11: 77.
Alpine Journal, An. (W. M. Conway) Contemp. 66: 210. Same art. Ecl. M. 123: 396.
Alpine Plants. (H. Correvon) Garden & F. 6: 152.
Alpine Root-Grubber. Cornh. 65: 611. Same art. Lit. Age, 194: 378.
Alpine Tit-Bits. (F. T. Wethered) Gent. M. n. s. 49: 390.
Alpinum in Botanic Garden of Tübingen. (D. T. MacDougal) Garden & F. 9: 372.
Alps and Caucasus, Mummery's Climbs in the. (C. W. Colby) Nation, 61: 65. — Sat. R. 80: 113.
— Ascents of, Famous. (A. Montefiore) Outing, 21: 257.
— Conway on. (Hiram M. Stanley) Dial (Ch.) 19: 178. — (C. W. Colby) Nation, 61: 351. — Sat. R. 80: 241.
— Day on the Rympfischhorn. Irish Mo. 16: 479.
— Death in. Liv. Age, 210: 458.
— Eastern, Lakes of. Geog. J. 1: 350.
— Gerschni. Macmil. 65: 365.
— Glacial Land-Forms of Margins of. (H. R. Mill) Geog. J. 5: 68. — Am. J. Sci. 149: 121.
— in 1880. Time, 4: 685.
— in Winter, Over the. (J. E. Muddock) Time, 3: 201.
— Mountain Climbing in. (W. S. Bridgeman) Munsey, 11: 646. — (C. E. Thomson) Outing, 23: 466.
— Plants of, and their Peculiarities. (H. Connevon) Garden & F. 9: 153.
— 1000 Miles through the. (W. M. Conway) Scrib. M. 20: 28.
— Western, Recent Contributions to Geology of. (J. W. Gregory) Sci. Prog. 3: 147.
Alsace and Lorraine. (S. J. Capper) Contemp. 66: (13). Same art. Liv. Age, 202: 387.
— Condition of, 1891. Un. Serv. M. 5: 264.
— How to Reconcile France and Germany. R. of Rs. (N. Y.) 10: 635.
Alsop Family, Pedigree of. N. E. Reg. 46: 366.
Alston Crucis; a story. (Helen Shipton) Good Words, 33: 48–793.
Altar of Mammon; a story. (Mrs. de Koven) Cosmopol. 18: 387.
Altar-Cloths. (B. C. Saward) Art J. 45: 349.
Altar-Stones, Marking. (J. Hirst and others) Antiq. n. s. 21: 75.
Altars, Christian, and their Accessories. (C. Coleman) Archit. Rec. 4: 251. 5: 245.
Alteration in Mr. Kershaw, The; a story. (W. P. Ridge) Idler, 10: 712.
Alternating Currents, Resonance Analysis of. (M. I. Pupin) Am. J. Sci. 148: 379, 473.
Alters, Micoñinovi Flute. (J. W. Fewkes) J. Am. Folk-Lore, 9: 241.
Altgeld, John P. (F. F. Browne) National, 28: 452.— With portrait. (R. P. Bishop) Nat'l M. (N. Y. '91) 16: 361.
— and the President. (E. P. Cook) Nation, 59: 22. — Pub. Opin. 17: 330.
Althorp Library. Bookworm, 5: 271, 313. — Gent. M. n. s. 49: 215.
— and its New Owner. Critic, 21: 111.
Altini, Francesco Fabj-. *See* Fabj-Altini.
Altitudes, High, and Climate. (H. R. Wray) New Sci. R. 2: 26.
Altitudes, Maximum and Ex-Meridian, Corrections of. (J. White) Nature, 51: 485.
Altruria. (E. B. Payne) Am. M. Civics, 6: 168.
— A Brief History of. (Sir Robert Harton) Cosmopol. 20: 218–545.
— Discovery of. (Sir Robert Harton) Cosmopol. 20: 85.
Altruism, Economic Value of. (L. G. James) Soc. Econ. 5: 11.
— Extravagance of. Spec. 68: 671. Same art. Ecl. M. 119: 97.
— in Economics. (W. H. Mallock) Forum, 21: 690.
Altruist in Corduroy. Gent. M. n. s. 49: 217. Same art. Liv. Age, 195: 394.
Altruistic Impulse in Man and Animals. (T. Gavanescul) Int. J. Ethics, 5: 197.
Alumina, Reduction, Considered from Thermo-chemical Standpoint. (J. W. Richards) J. Frankl. Inst. 139: 295.
Aluminum. (J. W. Richards) Cosmopol. 12: 277. — (H. Wurtz) Engin. M. 8: 482. — (J. Jamieson) Good Words, 37: 402.
— Coating, with other Metals. (Prof. Neesen) Am. J. Sci. 147: 133.
— Electro-Metallurgy of. (J. W. Richards) J. Frankl. Inst. 141: 357.
— Future of. Dub. R. 112: 161. — Spec. 71: 76.
— Manufacture and History of. (S. Rideal) Knowl. 19: 76, 148.
— Manufacture and Uses of. (A. E. Hunt) J. Frankl. Inst. 133: 241.
— Past and Future of. (J. Fleury) Pop. Sci. Mo. 44: 397.
— Production of. (E. P. Allen) Cassier, 1: 296, 418.
— Separation from Iron. (F. A. Gooch and F. S. Havens) Am. J. Sci. 152: 416.
— Specific Heat of. (J. W. Richards) J. Frankl. Inst. 133: 121.
— Substitute for Iron. (J. Fleury) Chaut. 17: 325.
— Uses and Applications of. (G. L. Addenbrooke) J. Soc. Arts, 40: 661. — (G. L. Addenbrooke) Am. Arch. 36: 150.
Aluminum Alloys, Resistance to Corrosion. (J. W. Richards) J. Frankl. Inst. 139: 69.
Aluminum Solders. (J. Richards) J. Frankl. Inst. 140: 351.
Alunite, from Red Mountain, Ouray County, Col. (E. B. Hurlburt) Am. J. Sci. 148: 130.
Alva, Fernando, Duke of. (A. M. Judd) Belgra. 85: 294.
Amalfi and its Inhabitants. (H. P. F. Marriott) Month, 75: 499.
— and Sorrento, Coasting by. (F. M. Crawford) Cent. 26: 325.
— From, to Ravello. (O. S. T. Drake) Time, 8: 328.
Amaryllis. Garden & F. 6: 177.
— Cultural Notes on. (E. O. Orpet) Garden & F. 9: 65.
Amateur Takes the Ribbons; a story. (W. S. Hutchinson) Overland, n. s. 20: 71.
Amateur Gamble, An. (Anna Fuller) Scrib. M. 14: 83.
Amateurs, Noble, in Art. (M. H. Spielmann) M. of Art, 16: 62.
— What about? (H. Maxwell) New R. 12: 641.
Amazing Marriage, The. (Geo. Meredith) Scrib. M. 17: 33–774. 18: 35–651.
Amazon River, Bates's Records of a Naturalist on. Spec. 68: 373.
— Tribes of. (C. R. Markham) Anthrop. J. 24: 236.
— Wild Night on. (M. S. Edmunds) Lippinc. 52: 117.
Amazonian Customs of the Caucasus. (J. Abercromby) Folk-Lore, 2: 171.

Amazon's Game, An; a story. (Mabel C. Pelletier) Bost. 2: 505.
Amazons, British. Chamb. J. 70: 298.
— Two West Indian. All the Year, 76: 59.
Ambassadors. (E. L. Godkin) Nation, 56: 246.
Amber. Chamb. J. 71: 209. — Cornh. 72: 278. Same art. Ecl. M. 125: 614. — Spec. 77: 853.
— English. (H. Conwentz) Nat. Sci. 9: 99, 161.
— Fossil Plants found in. (A. C. Seward) Nat. Sci. 1: 377.
Amber-producing Tree, American. (F. H. Knowlton) Science, n. s. 3: 582.
Amberite Powder. Chamb. J. 71: 191.
Ambition; a One-Act Play. (J. Staats) Lippinc. 51: 740.
Amboise, Chateau d'. Am. Arch. 49: 122.
Ambras Collection of Art Treasures, Vienna. (W. M. Conway) M. of Art, 5: 478.
Ambrosius, Johanna. (F. Sewall) Bookman, 4: 114. — Critic, 28: 87, 94.
— A Lyric Sudermann. (K. Francke) Nation, 63: 155.
Ambulances, Horse. (D. Leigh) 19th Cent. 40: 609.
Ambush against Ambush; a Franco-German War Story. (A. Forbes) Idler, 10: 320.
Ameer's Justice, The. Macmil. 72: 314.
Amen, Notes on its Use and Significance. (H. W. Hogg) Jew. Q. 9: 1.
America, Across, with "Junius Brutus Booth." (Eliz. Robins) Univ. R. 7: 375.
— Ancient Civilizations of. (J. S. Newberry) Pop. Sci. M. 41: 187.
— Ancient Inhabitants of. Around World, 1: 85.
— Asiatics in. (C. R. Conder) Scott. R. 28: 78.
— British Opinion of. (R. Whiteing) Scrib. M. 19: 371.
— Christian, Christianizing Christian Nations. (J. W. Mendenhall) Meth. R. 52: 93.
— Colonial History. Macmil. 75: 148.
— Discoverers of. (G. G. Hubbard) Nat. Geog. M. 4: 1.
— Discovery of. Quar. 177: 1. — Ed. R. 176: 147. Same art. Liv. Age, 194: 771.
— — and Naming of, Thacher on. (J. Winsor) Nation, 63: 143. — (B. A. Hinsdale) Dial (Ch.) 21: 111.
— — Bibliographies of. (C. W. Bump) J. H. Univ. Studies, 10: nos. 10–11, app.
— — by the Chinese. (F. J. Masters) Overland, n. s. 23: 576. — (R. S. Long) Ecl. M. 120: 201. — (A. K. Glover) M. Am. Hist. 27: 30. — (R. S. Long) Leis. Hour, 42: 91.
— — by Madoc, Stephens on. (R. B. Anderson) Dial (Ch.) 16: 138.
— — Causes which Led to. (J. B. Kieffer) Ref. Q. 40: 122.
— — Civil and Political Relations of. (C. S. Walker) Am. J. Pol. 1: 579.
— — Date of. (W. H. Thompson) Educa. 15: 88. — (W. Porter) Walford's Antiq. 1: 240. 2: 25.
— — Fiske's History of. Ath. '92, 2: 152. — (R. B. Anderson) Dial (Ch.) 13: 9. — (W. H. Tillinghast) Nation, 54: 449. — Sat. R. 74: 48.
— — Fourth Centennial. J. Frankl. Inst. 133: 69.
— — Harrisse on. (J. Winsor) Nation, 55: 244, 264.
— — Norse. (B. H. Du Bois) M. Am. Hist. 27: 369.
— — Portuguese Claim to. Dub. R. 116: 195.
— — Pre-Columbian. (H. Y. Oldham) Geog. J. 5: 221. — (J. P. McLean) Am. Antiq. 14: 33–316. — (E. Cantwell) M. West. Hist. 13: 139.
— — — Disclosures from Vatican Archives. (W. E. Curtis) Nat. Geog. M. 3: 197.
— — Providential Preparations for. (H. M. Scott) Our Day, 11: 1.
America, Discovery of, Religious Character of. (M. P. Villamil) Cath. World, 57: 244.
— — True. (J. W. Gambier) Fortn. 61: 49.
— — Value of. (E. E. Hale) Harv. Mo. 15: 131.
— — Voyages of the Cabots, Dawson's. Sat. R. 79: 659.
— — What was the Real? (L. Irving) Nat'l M. (N. Y. '91) 17: 39.
— — Winsor's Cartier to Frontenac. (E. G. Mason) Dial (Ch.) 16: 206.
— Equatorial, Travels in. Ed. R. 176: 33.
— for the Americans. (E. A. Bradford) Harper, 84: 599.
— Glimpse of. (Lord Brabazon) Time, 15: 148.
— History of, Chapters from Early. (T. B. Stephenson) Sund. M. 22: 125, 627.
— — Payne's. (W. Webster) Acad. 42: 277. — (W. H. Tillinghast) Nation, 55: 321. — Sat. R. 74: 253. — (F. J. Turner) Dial (Ch.) 13: 389.
— Impressions of, An Australian's. (C. H. Spence) Harper, 89: 244.
— Influence of, upon Old World. (J. Rein) Geog. J. 1: 539.
— Lyell's Travels in. Eng. R. 4: 72.
— Map of, La Cosa's. (L. C. de Lautreppe) Nation, 55: 410.
— Name of, must be called Columbia. (E. A. Oldham) M. Am. Hist. 27: 429.
— Northwest Coast, Early Voyages on. (G. Davidson) Nat. Geog. M. 3: 235.
— Notes from. (W. Besant) Cosmopol. 16: 64, 233.
— Peopling of; a New Theory. (A. H. Keane) Acad. 46: 173.
— Prefigured. (J. Winsor) Harv. Grad. M. 1: 236.
— Prehistoric. Spec. 70: 802.
— — Wilson on. (F. Starr) Dial (Ch.) 14: 178.
— Prehistoric Contact with Oceanic Peoples. (C. Thomas) Am. Antiq. 17: 101, 191.
— A Prophecy; a poem. (W. Blake) Poet-Lore, 5: 363.
— Republics in, Progress of. (W. E. Curtis) New Eng. M. n. s. 6: 311.
— Society in. The Point of View. (G. Hamilton) No. Am. 155: 171.
— Some Impressions of. (Walter Crane) New R. 10: 41, 150.
— Spanish Occupancy of; Bandelier's Gilded Man. (L. Carr) Nation, 57: 489.
— Tropical, Ford's. Ath. '93, 2: 618.
— — Stuart's. Sat. R. 73: 161.
"America," Hymn, How it was Written. Critic, 26: 69.
"America," Privateer. (J. G. Morse) New Eng. M. n. s. 11: 284.
American not a New Englishman, but a New Man. (H. G. Cutler) New Eng. M. n. s. 9: 24.
— out of doors. (G. Bradford, jr.) Atlan. 71: 452.
American Academy at Rome. (R. Cortissoz) Harper, 90: 626.
American Academy of Political and Social Science. Nation, 55: 46.
American Antiquities, Brinton's. (F. Boas) J. Am. Folk-Lore, 3: 168.
— Netting, Rope, and Wood Implements in a Mud Deposit in Western Florida. (C. D. Durnford) Am. Natural. 29: 1032.
— Study of. (W. W. Newell) J. Am. Folk-Lore, 3: 160.
American Archives at Upsal, Sweden. (C. J. Stillé) Pennsyl. M. 15: 481.
American Art and Artists. M. of Art, 2: 21–272.
American Artist, The. Pub. Opin. 15: 209.

American Artists' Association of Paris. (E. H. Wuerpel) Cosmopol. **20**: 402.
American Association for Advancement of Science. Science, n. s. **2**: 113. — (F. W. Putnam) Science, n. s. **2**: 171. — Nature, **50**: 484, 608.
— Early Years of. (W. H. Hale) Pop. Sci. Mo. **49**: 501.
— Springfield Meeting, 1895. (J. L. Howe and others) Science, n. s. **2**: 313, 349, 407.
American Authors, British Discourtesy to. Critic, **25**: 25, 191. — Reply. (A. J. Wyatt) Critic, **25**: 191.
— Society of. Critic, **20**: 294, 306.
American Bankers' Association and Law Reform. Bank. M. (N. Y.) **47**: 1.
American Board of Commissioners for Foreign Missions, Chicago Meeting of, 1892. And. R. **18**: 410.
— Decision of, in the Noyes Case. Pub. Opin. **16**: 79.
— Foreign Work of, Control of. And. R. **19**: 86.
— Latest Andover Attack on. (C. Hamlin) Our Day, **10**: 709.
— Dr. McKenzie's Letter Declining Election to the Prudential Committee. And. R. **18**: 519.
— Meeting at Worcester, 1893. And. R. **19**: 584, 715.
— Present Question in Regard to Applicants. And. R. **17**: 410.
— Prudential Committee, Proposed Enlargement of. And. R. **19**: 599.
— Dr. Storrs' Reply. And. R. **18**: 93.
— Dr. Storrs' Ultimatum. And. R. **17**: 613.
— "Supplementary Questions." And. R. **17**: 312.
American Character, Alien Degradation of. (S. G. Fisher) Forum, **14**: 608.
— in Politics. (A. B. Hart) Chaut. **22**: 142.
American Citizen, Public Relations of. Lend a H. **13**: 248.
American Citizenship, Distinctive. (A. Roeder) Am. M. Civics, **6**: 516.
American Civilization: Reply to Prof. Norton. (H. G. Chapman) Bach. of Arts, **2**: 755.
American Claimant, The. (Mark Twain) Idler, **1**: 1–697. **2**: 86–707.
American Colonies, British Convicts Shipped to. (J. D. Butler) Am. Hist. R. **2**: 12.
American Commercial and Financial Supremacy, Conditions for. (P. Leroy-Beaulieu) Forum, **20**: 385.
American Commercial Policy, Rabbeno on. (F. W. Taussig) Q. J. Econ. **10**: 102. — (W. Hill) J. Pol. Econ. **4**: 255.
American Dahlia Society, Meeting of. (L. H. Bailey) Garden & F. **8**: 418.
American Dead Sea Fruit. (A. M. Kerr) Overland, n. s. **25**: 189.
American Desert, Perils and Wonders of a True. (D. D. Gaillard) Cosmopol. **21**: 592.
American Dialect. (F. Hall) Acad. **43**: 265. **44**: 587.
American Diplomacy, Two Years of. (G. Gray) No. Am. **160**: 409.
American Diplomats in Europe. (H. C. Chatfield-Taylor) No. Am. **163**: 125.
American Economic Association. (L. P. Powell) Chaut. **15**: 601.
American English, Study of. (G. Hempl) Chaut. **22**: 436.
American Ethnology and Archæology. (J. F. Hewitt) Westm. **143**: 151.
American Exchange Bank Robbery. (C. Moffett) McClure, **5**: 179.
American Exhibition at Madrid, 1892; Exhibit of the United States at. (N. D. Davis) Nation, **55**: 349.
American Experiences, My. (E. Frey) No. Am. **158**: 129.
American Federation of Labor. Gunton's M. **10**: 134.
American Folk-Lore, Recent. (F. Starr) Dial (Ch.) **21**: 36.
American Folk-Lore Society, First Annual Meeting. J. Am. Folk-Lore, **3**: 1.
— 2d Annual Meeting of. J. Am. Folk-Lore, **4**: 1.
— 3d Annual Meeting of. J. Am. Folk-Lore, **5**: 1.
— 4th Annual Meeting of. J. Am. Folk-Lore, **6**: 1.
— 5th Annual Meeting of. J. Am. Folk-Lore, **6**: 291.
— 6th Annual Meeting of. J. Am. Folk-Lore, **8**: 1.
— 7th Annual Meeting of. J. Am. Folk-Lore, **9**: 67.
American Forestry Association, 10th Annual Meeting. Garden & F. **5**: 11.
American Gentleman. Atlan. **71**: 284.
American Girl, Origin of a Type of. (R. H. Davis) Mo. Illust. **3**: 3.
American Girls Early in the Century, Group of. (H. E. Smith) Cent. **31**: 163.
American Historical Review. (A. B. Hart) Nation, **60**: 274.
American History; How it is Written. Blackw. **159**: 107.
— How to Study. (A. B. Hart) Outl. **53**: 246.
— Isolation of. (W. MacDonald) Nation, **63**: 304.
— Proper Perspective of. (W. Wilson) Forum, **19**: 544.
American House Beautiful. All the Year, **74**: 153.
American Idea, The. (S. Dewey) Westm. **145**: 420.
American Ideal, The. (P. Carus) Open Court, **5**: 2807.
American Ideals, True. (T. Roosevelt) Forum, **18**: 743.
American Industries since Columbus. Pop. Sci. Mo. **42**: 433, 577.
American Influence over England, Growth of. (J. M. Ludlow, Atlan. **74**: 618.
American Institute of Architects; Amendments to the By-laws. Am. Arch. **49**: 125.
— 30th Annual Convention. Am. Arch. **54**: 35.
— 28th Annual Convention. Am. Arch. **46**: 19, 35.
— Ohio Chapter, Annual Convention. Am. Arch. **46**: 3.
American Institute of Civics. (H. R. Waite) Am. J. Pol. **5**: 56. — Pub. Opin. **17**: 333.
— Work and Needs of. (W. H. De Puy) Am. M. Civics, **8**: 431.
American Institutions and the Dutch Republic. (W. E. Griffis) Nat'l M. (N. Y. '91) **15**: 603.
— Are They of English Origin? (L. Irving) Nat'l M. (N. Y. '91) **17**: 129, 229.
American King, An; a poem. (H. C. Kirk) Educa. **16**: 111.
American Language. (T. B. Russell) Gent. M. n. s. **51**: 529.
American Library Association, Constitution, etc. Lib. J. **19**: 52.
— Exhibit at the World's Fair. (K. L. Sharp) Lib. J. **18**: 280.
— Meeting of, 1892. Critic, **20**: 306.
— — Proceedings. Lib. J. **17**: supp. 23.
— Meeting in Chicago, 1893. (C. A. Cutter) Nation, **57**: 150.
— — Proceedings. Lib. J. **18**: supp. 1.
— Meeting at Lake Placid, 1894. (W. I. Fletcher) Critic, **25**: 230. — (W. I. Fletcher) Lib. J. **19**: 344.
— — Proceedings. Lib. J. **19**: supp. 109.
— Denver Meeting, 1895. (C. A. Nelson) Lib. J. **20**: 311, supp.
— Cleveland Meeting, 1896. Lib. J. **21**: 410. — (W. I. Fletcher) Critic, **29**: 189.
— Post Conference, 1896. Historical Data. (R. G. Thwaites) Lib. J. **21**: 374.
American Library Association Index. (W. E. A. Axon) Acad. **43**: 457. — Nation, **56**: 259, 291.

American Life. (A. S. Northcote) 19th Cent. **34**: 476. Same art. Liv. Age, **199**: 226. Same art. Ecl. M. **121**: 471.
— Some Peculiarities of. (U. H. S. Aubrey) Univ. R. **7**: 565.
American Literature. (A. S. Cody) Critic, **20**: 92.
— Catholic Tendency in. (G. P. Lathrop) Am. Cath. Q. **18**: 372.
— Development of. (O. Thiergen) Pub. Opin. **13**: 340.
— Earliest Writer of. (C. F. Richardson) Bk. News, **8**: 307.
— Early. (T. J. Chapman) Nat'l M. (N. Y. '91) **15**: 27.
— English Criticism of. (W. Lewin) Acad. **42**: 307.
— Fifty Years of. (W. B. McCormick) Cath. World, **63**: 619.
— Has Immigration Dried Up? (S. G. Fisher) Forum, **16**: 560.
— Healthful Tone for. (R. Burton) Forum, **19**: 249.
— Is there an? (F. L. Pattee) Dial (Ch.) **21**: 243.
— Present State of. (W. R. Nicoll) Bookman, **4**: 344.
— Productive Conditions of. (H. Garland) Forum, **17**: 690.
— Study of, in Colleges. (N. W. Hall) And. R. **18**: 154.
— Symposium. Indep. Nov. 3, '92.
— Western, Garland on. Sat. R. **76**: 487.
American Love Story. (D. Prescott) New Eng. M. n. s. **15**: 309, 433.
American Magazines. (W. Besant) Critic, **25**: 126.
American Manufactures, Wider Markets for. (H. Hill) Engin. M. **7**: 145.
American Missionary Association. (C. J. Ryder) New Eng. M. n. s. **15**: 225.
American Mother, An. (M. L. Underwood) Scrib. M. **20**: 597.
American Museum of Natural History, New York. (W. Seton) Cath. World, **63**: 8. — Science, n. s. **4**: 849. — (W. Taylor) Munsey, **6**: 21.
American Money Abroad. (G. F. Duysters) Munsey, **11**: 101.
American Morals. (H. R. Chamberlain) Chaut. **14**: 673. **15**: 158.
American National Principles, Applications of. (A. Bierbower) Bapt. R. **14**: 411.
American Nationality, Growth of. (F. A. Walker) Forum, **19**: 385.
American Note, The. (H. Ward) No. Am. **161**: 507.
American Oriental Society. (A. V. W. Jackson) Acad. **43**: 373.
— Annual Meeting, 1896. (C. R. Lanman) Nation, **62**: 302.
American Patriotic Poems. (C. Porter) Poet-Lore, **5**: 342.
American People, Intellectual Life of. (C. F. Thwing) Chaut. **22**: 273.
— McMaster's History of. (F. W. Shepardson) Dial (Ch.) **18**: 319.
— Physical Condition of. (E. Hitchcock, jr.) Chaut. **23**: 151.
American Petty Tyrants. (M. O'Rell) No. Am. **161**: 321.
American Poetry, edited by Simonds. Sat. R. **79**: 48.
— Notable. Poet-Lore, **4**: 580.
— Recent, 1892. (W. Sharp) Acad. **41**: 82.
American Poets, Characteristics of. (T. Bradfield) Westm. **142**: 48.
American Political Philosophy. (W. A. Dunning) Yale R. **4**: 147.
American Protective Association. (A. Milne) Nation, **57**: 389. — Pub. Opin. **16**: 45. — (E. Hubbard) Arena, **10**: 76. — (W. Gladden) Cent. **25**: 789. — (J. L. Spalding) No. Am. **159**: 278.
American Protective Association, Aims and Methods of. (W. J. H. Traynor) No. Am. **159**: 67.
— Its Threatening Conflict with Romanism. (E. M. Winston) Forum, **17**: 425.
— Policy and Power of. (W. J. H. Traynor) No. Am. **162**: 658.
— Religious Intolerance in the Republic, Violence of. (F. R. Coudert and J. B. McMaster) Forum, **17**: 513.
— Revival of Know-Nothingism. (C. Robinson) Am. J. Pol. **5**: 504.
— Senator Hoar and. Pub. Opin. **19**: 232.
American Psychological Association. (J. M. Baldwin) Nation, **56**: 25.
American Race, Brinton's. Sat. R. **73**: 634.
American Republic, Some Reasons why it may Endure. (C. W. Eliot) Forum, **18**: 129.
American Revolution. (E. E. Hale) Bk. News, **8**: 239.
— and Commerce. (J. A. Stevens) M. Am. Hist. **29**: 243.
— James Barrett's Returns of Men Mustered into Service, 1777–78. (F. E. Blake) N. E. Reg. **50**: 468.
— Camp by Schuylkill Falls, Pa. (W. S. Baker) Pennsyl. M. **16**: 28.
— Causes of. (J. A Woodburn) J. H. Univ. Studies, **10**: no. 12.
— Diplomatic Correspondence of. (J. B. Moore) Pol. Sci. Q. **8**: 33.
— Finances of, Sumner on. (H. C. Adams) Dial (Ch.) **13**: 73. — (D. M. Means) Nation, **54**: 117.
— Fiske's. (J. A. Doyle) Eng. Hist. R. **8**: 164.
— French Aid in. Atlan. **74**: 128.
— King George's Personal Policy in England. (E. F. de Lancey) M. Am. Hist. **27**: 431.
— German Allies in. Atlan. **72**: 562.
— New York after. (H. P. Johnston) M. Am. Hist. **29**: 305.
— Officers under Washington, 1778, Roster of. Pennsyl. M. **18**: 64.
— Pay Rolls of, Miscellaneous. (F. E. Blake) N. E. Reg. **50**: 198.
— Portraiture of. (W. L. Andrews) Bookman, **3**: 271, 329.
— Prisoners of War, British and American, Returns of, 1778. Pennsyl. M. **17**: 159, 316.
— Proclamation of George III. against the Rebels, 1775. M. Am. Hist. **29**: 514.
— Songs and Ballads of. (L. B. Newcomb) New Eng. M. n. s. **13**: 501. — (H. Granville) Bach. of Arts, **3**: 207.
— Valuable Revolutionary Documents. M. Am. Hist. **29**: 163.
American School of Architecture at Rome. Am. Arch. **48**: 56.
American School of Classical Studies in Rome. (W. G. Hale) Harv. Grad. M. **4**: 569.
American Shipping and Farm Interests. (A. C. Houston) Am. J. Pol. **3**: 655.
— How to Rebuild. (T. Cox) Am. J. Pol. **1**: 377. — (T. Cox and E. Mead) Am. J. Pol. **1**: 587.
— A Present Chance for. (E. T. Chamberlain) No. Am. **158**: 277.
American Speech, Future of. Dial (Ch.) **14**: 233.
American Sportswoman. (E. C. Barney) Fortn. **62**: 263.
American Standard of Living. (J. R. Dodge) Chaut. **17**: 711.
American Stock in European Markets. (F. E. Clark) R. of Rs. (N. Y.) **11**: 293.
American Trade and England's Revenue. (A. D. Noyes) Nation, **62**: 338.
American Traits. (Martin Morris) New R. **13**: 296, 434. Same art. Ecl. M. **126**: 40.

American Tract Society. (G. L. Shearer) Cent. 22: 313.
American Type, Survival of the. (J. H. Denison) Atlan. 75: 16.
American Water Color Society. (W. Taylor) Munsey, 7 : 180.
American Wealth, True Source of. (B. F. Clayton) No. Am. 161: 612.
American Woman, Sentiments of an, during the Revolution. Pennsyl. M. 18: 361.
American Women. (C. de Thierry) Contemp. 70: 516.
— and American Literature. (H. H. Lusk) Forum, 22: 503.
Americanism, True. (H. C. Lodge) Harv. Grad. M. 3: 9.
— What it Means. (T. Roosevelt) Forum, 17: 196.
Americanisms. (I. W. Hartt) Educa. 13: 367. — Nation, 57: 484. — (A. Lang) Acad. 47: 193, (F. Hall) 278.
— English as used in America. Sat. R. 78: 321.
— English Speech, Wild Flowers of, in America. (E. Eggleston) Cent. 25: 848.
— Shakespeare's. (H. C. Lodge) Harper, 90: 252.
— Some so-called. All the Year, 76: 38. Same art. Liv. Age, 204: 438.
Americanists, A Carribbean among the. (N. D. Davis) Nation, 55: 333.
Americans, A Calendar of Great. (W. Wilson) Forum, 16: 715.
— Abroad. (F. B. Loomis) Lippinc. 53: 678.
— — Reflections of a Consul. (F. B. Loomis) Cosmopol. 18: 475.
— in Paris. (R. H. Davis) Harper, 91: 272.
America's Contributions to Civilization. (C. W. Eliot) Chaut. 24: 52.
America's Cup, The. Spec. 75: 332.
Americas, Three, Fundamental Geographic Relations of. (R. T. Hill) Nat. Geog. M. 7: 175.
Amerrique Indians of Nicaragua. (J. Crawford) Am. Antiq. 18: 269.
Ames, F. Lothrop. Garden & F. 6: 391. — (E. B. Willson) N. E. Reg. 49: 273.
Amesbury, Mass., Soldiers of. (F. E. Blake) N. E. Reg. 50: 338.
Amherst, Jeffery, Lord. (H. B. Adams) New Eng. M. n. s. 13: 749. — Un. Serv. M. 9: 528.
Amherst, Mass., Agricultural Experiment Station at. (A. W. Bailey) New Eng. M. n. s. 9: 65.
— Historical Landmarks near. (Fred. H. Law) Bach. of Arts, 2: 333.
Amherst College; Pres. Seelye's Administration. (J. Bigham) Educa. 13: 597.
— System of Government of. (J. Bigham) Educa. R. 3: 162.
— Tyler's History of. Nation, 60: 263.
Amiel, Henri Frédéric. (E. U. Clark) And. R. 18: 234.
— Journal of. Temp. Bar, 94: 47. — (Alex. H. Japp) Time, 14: 309.
Amiens, Notre-Dame d'. (W. Pater) 19th Cent. 35: 481.
Amma-San; a story. (A. A. Rogers) Cosmopol. 13: 551.
Ammonia, Liquid, Specific Heat of. (C. Ludeking and J. E. Starr) Am. J. Sci. 145: 200.
Ammonia Gas, Action on Molybdenyl Chloride. (E. F. Smith & V. Lenher) J. Frankl. Inst. 136: 149.
— Anhydrous, as a Motive Power. (T. W. Draper) Cassier, 4: 307.
Ammonia Gas Compressors, Oil, Use of. (H. von Strombeck) J. Frankl. Inst. 133: 297.
Ammonites, Sexes in. (S. S. Buckman and F. A. Bather) Nat. Sci. 4: 427.
Ammonium-Cuprous Double Halogen Salts. (H. L. Wells and E. B. Hurlburt) Am. J. Sci. 150: 390.
Ammonium-Lead Halides. (H. L. Wells and W. R. Johnston) Am. J. Sci. 146: 25.
Ammunition, Small Arm, Supply of. (D. J. Craigie) Un. Serv. (Phila.) 8: 211.
Amnesia, Case of. (C. L. Dana) Psychol. R. 1: 570.
Amœbæ, Artificial, Bütschli's. (J. B. Haycraft) Nature, 48: 594.
Amok! a Malayan Story. (R. Wildman) Overland, n. s. 23: 590.
Among the Wood-Goblins. (F. Whishaw) Longm. 25: 159.
Amongst Her Following; a story. (Mabel E. Wotton) Temp. Bar, 97: 417. Same art. Liv. Age, 197: 279.
Amongst the Missing; a story. Argosy, 56: 118.
Amour sublime, L'. (Villiers de l'Isle-Adam) Univ. R. 3: 483.
Amos. (C. H. Cornill) Open Court, 9: 4473.
Ampersand. (J. Hooper) Gent. M. n. s. 49: 488.
Amphibian Footprints from the Devonian. (O. E. Marsh) Am. J. Sci. 152: 374.
Amphioxus and the Ancestry of the Vertebrates, Willey on. (D. S. Jordan) Dial (Ch.) 19: 112.
Amphipoda, the, A Passage of Arms over. (T. R. R. Stebbing) Nat. Sci. 6: 257.
Amphiuma, Head of an Embryo. (J. S. Kingsley) Am. Natural. 26: 671.
— Tentacular Apparatus of. (A. Davison) Am. Natural. 30: 684.
Ampthill, Past and Present. (C. W. Williams) Westm. 143: 538.
Amputation, An Old-Time. (J. Albee) New Eng. M. n. s. 12: 309.
Amsterdam. (W. O. Tristram) Good Words, 33: 253.
— Jottings in. (R. D. Benn) Am. Arch. 49: 3.
Amsterdam Aquarium. Spec. 76: 701.
Amsterdam Zoo, Birds at. Spec. 76: 802.
Amulet, An; a story. Un. Serv. (Phila.) 8: 476.
Amulet Collection of Joseph Belucci. (T. Wilson) J. Am. Folk-Lore. 4: 144.
Amulets, Cranial, and Prehistoric Trepanning. (R. Munro) Fortn. 59: 208. Same art. Ecl. M. 120: 448.
— Gems used as. (G. F. Kunz). J. Am. Folk-Lore, 4: 29.
Amusements, Indolent. Spec. 70: 252.
— International. Spec. 73: 73.
— Law of the M. E. Church as to: Symposium. Meth. R. 56: 284.
— Methodist Legislation on. (G. P. Mains) Meth. R. 52: 375.
— A Year's. (F. A. Schwab) Cosmopol. 17: 18.
Amyl Alcohol, Action of, on Nitrates. (P. E. Browning) Am. J. Sci. 143: 386.
Anabaptism, Early: What We Owe to it. (R. Heath) Contemp. 67: 578.
Anabaptist Sect, An Oriental. (A. H. Newman) Chr. Lit. 15: 155.
Anabaptists, The. (W. E. Griffis) New World, 4: 647.
Anachronisms of Art. (J. Oldcastle) M. of Art. 3: 39.
Anæsthesia, Discovery of. (E. W. Morton) McClure, 7: 311.
— History of. (E. W. Emerson) Atlan. 78: 679. — (B. W. Richardson) Longm. 19: 489.
— Morton's Discovery of. (E. L. Snell) Cent. 26: 584.
Anaglyph. (A. F. Watch) J. Frankl. Inst. 140: 401.
Anagrams. (A. Inkersley) Lippinc. 58: 861. Belgra. 91: 236. Same art. Liv. Age, 211: 822.
"Anahuac" and "Nahuatl," On the Words. (D. G. Brinton) Am. Antiq. 15: 377.
Analogies and Homologies. (W. T. Freeman) Gent. M. n. s. 52: 37. Same art. Pop. Sci. Mo. 46: 91.

Analogies, Natural. (S. V. Clevenger) Am. Natural. 26: 195.
Ananias, Paul and, before the Sanhedrin at Jerusalem. (S. L. Bowman) Meth. R. 56: 570.
Anarchism. (V. Yarros) Arena, 7: 595.
— and the Napoleonic Revival. (K. Blind) No. Am. 158: 602.
— and Socialism. Open Court, 1: 754.
— Origin and Organization of. (C. B. Roylance-Kent) Gent. M. n. s. 54: 349.
— Rise and Progress of. (K. Blind) Contemp. 65: 140.
— Wave of, 1893. Spec. 71: 424.
Anarchist, Convicted, Reply of, to C. Lombroso. (M. Schwab) Monist, 1: 520.
— The Cry of. (E. V. Debs) Am. M. Civics, 6: 408.
Anarchist Law in France. Sat. R. 78: 36.
Anarchist Literature. Quar. 178: 1. — Spec. 73: 41.
Anarchist Meeting in Scotland. (D. Watson) Good Words, 35: 445. Same art. Ecl. M. 123: 371.
Anarchist Portraits, Some. (C. Malato) Fortn. 62: 315.
Anarchist Utopia. (G. Boglietti) Chaut. 19: 719. — Temp. Bar, 103: 521.
Anarchists, Among the. (Menzies Macdonald) Good Words, 35: 125.
— and Government in France. (A. Laugel) Nation, 59: 77.
— and their Theories in Europe. (P. Desjardins) Chaut. 18: 691.
— Antidote for. Sat. R. 73: 731.
— Asquith and. Spec. 71: 706.
— Chicago, of 1886, Crime and Trial of. (J. E. Gary) Cent. 23: 803.
— in Paris. (E. L. Godkin) Nation, 54: 335. — Sat. R. 73: 382, 497.
— Methods and Organization of. New R. 10: 1. — Reply. New. R. 10: 215.
— Physiognomy of. (C. Lombroso) Monist, 1: 336.
— Prescription for. (E. M. Winston) Am. Law R. 29: 681.
— Punishment of. (H. Holt) Forum, 17: 644.
— Socialistic, and the Salvation Army. (J. Cook) Our Day, 13: 532.
— Spanish. Spec. 68: 484.
— Vaillant on his Defence. Spec. 72: 36.
— What Shall be Done With? (R. L. Seymour) Chaut. 19: 732. — Pub. Opin. 17: 306. — (W. M. Salter) Open Court, 1: 530.
Anarchy and the Anarchists. Open Court, 1: 464.
— Culture and. Quar. 174: 317.
— Elements of, in Society. (W. Ferrero) Am. J. Pol. 5: 337.
— Evolution of. (J. F. Loba) Bib. Sac. 51: 604.
— Great Britain's Relation to. Spec. 72: 257.
— Ideals of. Quar. 184: 299. Same art. Liv. Age, 211: 616.
— In Defence of. (W. Donisthorpe) New R. 11: 283.
— Initial Anarchist. (G. H. Sandison) Soc. Econ. 3: 289.
— A Lance for. (V. de Cleyre) Open Court, 5: 2963.
Anatomy, Human and Comparative, at Oxford. (E. R. Lankester) Nature, 48: 616.
— Teaching of. (H. Allen) Science, 19: 85.
— Three-years' Course in; Best Order of Topics. Science, n. s. 1: 312.
Ancestor-Gods (Kalow-Vu) of the Fijians. (B. H. Thomson) Anthrop. J. 24: 340. Same art. Pop. Sci. Mo. 47: 671.
— in China. (S. R. Gundry) Fortn. 63: 225.
Ancestor-ridden: a Play in One Act. Blackw. 156: 205.
Ancestor Worship in China. Asia. R. 8: 141.
Ancestors, Collecting. Cornh. 71: 253.
Ancien Régime, L'. (St. G. Mivart) Am. Cath. Q. 19: 368.
Ancient, Fort. (W. K. Moorehead) Nat'l M. (N. Y. '91) 15: 147.
Ancient and Modern Civilizations. Soc. Econ. 1: 296, 371.
Ancient and Modern Life. (Barr Ferree) Soc. Econ. 1: 371.
Ancient Po-Who-Geh. (V. Z. Reed) Overland, n. s. 28: 644.
Ancients, The, Popular Superstitions of. (J. G. Frazer) Folk-Lore, 1: 145.
Ancona, March of. Am. Arch. 39: 123.
And One Unknown; a story. Temp. Bar, 102: 101. Same art. Ecl. M. 122: 834.
And so the Story Ends; a story. (J. De Boys) Eng. Illust. 13: 359.
Anderson, Isaac W. (Tacoma, Wash.). (W. L. Visscher) M. West. Hist. 12: 369.
Anger, Words for, in Certain Languages. (A. F. Chamberlain) Am. J. Psychol. 6: 585.
Angera Revolt. (Ion Perdicaris) Asia. R. 14: 330.
Angler's Dilemma, An; a story. (G. C. Audsley) Outing, 24: 107.
Angles and Position of Lines, Judgment of. (J. Jastrow) Am. J. Psychol. 5: 214.
Anglia and the Anglians. (R. J. Lloyd) Westm. 142: 196.
Anglican Catholic, Experiences of an. Contemp. 67: 395.
Anglican Orders. *See* Church of England.
Angling, Associations of. (W. T. Freeman) Gent. M. n. s. 57: 234.
— Bickerdyke's. Sat. R. 80: 176.
— New Departure in. Chamb. J. 72: 221.
— Poetry of. (J. Buchan) Gent. M. n. s. 54: 60. Same art. Ecl. M. 124: 270.
— Progress of. Ed. R. 179: 226.
— With Rod and Line. (A. Heron) Murray, 9: 653.
Angling Experiences in Lapland. (G. Lindesay) Blackw. 155: 416.
Angling Idyl, An. Chamb. J. 72: 398.
Angling Memories. (W. T. Freeman) Gent. M. n. s. 55: 634.
Angling Sketches, Lang's. Ath. '92, 1: 109.
Anglo-American Reunion, Possibilities of an. (A. T. Mahan; C. Beresford) No. Am. 159: 551.
Anglo-Catholic Theory. Eng. R. 17: 169.
Anglo-Egyptian Official. (J. Gorst) Time, 21: 561.
Anglo-Indian Marriage Customs. (G. Martell) Time, 1: 403.
Anglo-Indians, Retired, Australia for. (J. L. Parsons) Asia. R. 16: 344.
— — Australian Colonies as a Field for. Asia. R. 15: 354.
— — Hill Stations of India for. (R. A. Sterndale) Asia. R. 15: 168.
— — Twenty-five Years after India. (C. N. Cust) Asia. R. 21: 374.
Anglo-mania; Colonial Survival. (T. Roosevelt) Cosmopol. 14: 229.
Anglo-Saxon Conflict. (R. S. Norman) Am. M. Civ. 8: 267.
Anglo-Saxon Courts of Law, The. (F. Zinkeisen) Pol. Sci. Q. 10: 132.
Anglo-Saxon Language as a College Study. (C. F. Richardson) School & C. 1: 385.
Anglo-Saxon Race, Future of the. (W. Besant) No. Am. 163: 129.
— Are We Saxon or Roman? (Van Buren Denslow) Soc. Econ. 6: 289.

Anglo-Saxon Union. (G. Smith) No. Am. **157**: 170.
Angola, Folk-Tales of. (W. W. Newell) J. Am. Folk-Lore, **7**: 61, 311.
Angolan Customs. (H. Chatelain) J. Am. Folk-Lore, **9**: 13.
Angoulême, Duchess of. (F. T. Marzials) Acad. **43**: 100. — Blackw. **153**: 800.
Angoulême. (Miss Betham-Edwards) Time, **14**: 292.
— Churches of. (M. G. Van Rensselaer) Cent. **29**: 918.
Angra Pequena; the Parting of the Ways. Contemp. **69**: 190.
Anima Poetæ, Extracts. (S. T. Coleridge) New R. **13**: 353.
Animal and Man, Difference Between. (M. Müller) Open Court, **3**: 1980.
— as a Machine. (R. H. Thurston) No. Am. **163**: 607.
— — Thurston's. Nation, **59**: 52.
— as a Prime Mover. (R. H. Thurston) J. Frankl. Inst. **139**: 1, 100, 161. Same art. Science, n. s. **1**: 365.
— From, to Man. (J. LeConte) Monist, **6**: 356.
Animal Diet, Dainties of. Liv. Age, **210**: 696.
Animal Domestication. Spec. **76**: 200.
Animal Friends, Staples on. Sat. R. **73**: 664.
Animal Heat and Physiological Caliometry. (I. Rosenthal) Nature, **48**: 88. Same art. Liv. Age, **198**: 316.
Animal Helpers and Servers. (C. J. Cornish) Cornh. **74**: 56. Same art. Liv. Age, **210**: 375.
Animal Language. Spec. **77**: 550.
Animal Life, Abundance of. (A. Gaudry) Pop. Sci. Mo. **50**: 42.
— American Types of, Mivart on. (H. L. Osborn) Dial (Ch.) **14**: 362.
— and Intelligence, Lloyd-Morgan on. Spec. **68**: 683.
— Earliest Known Forms of, Homes and Migrations of. (H. Hicks) Nat. Sci. **5**: 417.
— Study of, by Kipling. Spec. **72**: 747.
— Thomson's. Sat. R. **74**: 397.
— War on, in America. Spec. **68**: 557.
Animal Materia Medica. Spec. **75**: 77.
Animal Mechanics. (M. Miles) Am. Natural. **28**: 555.
Animal Pets of Royalty. (G. B. Burgin) Idler, **3**: 243. — (E. M. Jessop) Idler, **4**: 3, 131.
Animal Symbolism in Ecclesiastical Architecture. (A. D. White) Pop. Sci. Mo. **50**: 187.
Animal Tempers. Cornh. **73**: 412. Same art. Liv. Age, **209**: 568.
Animal Warfare. Spec. **76**: 513.
Animal Worship in Mycenæan Age. (A. B. Cook) J. Hel. Stud. **14**: 81.
Animals, Æsthetic Sense and Religious Sentiment in. (E. P. Evans) Pop. Sci. Mo. **42**: 472.
— and Plants, Distinction between. (J. C. Arthur) Am. Natural. **29**: 961.
— Antipathies of. Spec. **77**: 480.
— as Machines, Relative Efficiency of. (M. Miles) Am. Natural. **30**: 784.
— Artist among. (F. S. Church) Scrib. M. **14**: 749.
— at the National Gallery. (Sophia S. Beale) Good Words, **36**: 454.
— Colors of. (M. J. Newbigin) Nat. Sci. **8**: 94.
— Comic. Spec. **77**: 13.
— Cornish's Life at the Zoo. Spec. **73**: 851.
— Crime among. (W. Ferrero) Forum, **20**: 492.
— Criminal. Spec. **69**: 349.
— Cruelty to. (L. de la Ramée) 19th Cent. **40**: 293.
— Cunning in. (W. L. Calderwood) Nat. Sci. **9**: 380.
— Distribution of. Sat. R. **79**: 215.
— — Affected by Temperature. (C. H. Merriam) Nat. Geog. M. **3**: 228.
Animals, Early Descriptions of. Sat. R. **73**: 179.
— Effect of Heat on. Spec. **76**: 868.
— Effect of Music on. Spec. **69**: 282.
— Evolution of, Bonavia's. Sat. R. **80**: 179.
— Extinct, Restoration of, Hutchinson on. Nat. Sci. **2**: 135.
— Extinction of. (R. Lydekker) Knowl. **16**: 21. — Sat. R. **73**: 595.
— Eye of, Expression in. Spec. **72**: 612.
— Feeding of, Science and. (V. Hallenbeck) Chaut. **14**: 425.
— Feeling of Beauty in. Chamb. J. **71**: 821.
— Feigning of Death by. (J. Weir) Lippinc. **57**: 838.
— Future State of. Spec. **72**: 295.
— Giant, Decay of. Spec. **74**: 849.
— Grateful. J. Am. Folk-Lore, **2**: 132.
— Grief in. Spec. **74**: 817.
— Have they Rights? Spec. **72**: 367.
— Humanity to, Ethical Basis for. (A. Leffingwell) Arena, **10**: 474.
— in Novels. Spec. **77**: 816.
— in Rain. Spec. **69**: 644.
— in Sickness, Conduct of. Spec. **69**: 123.
— Industries of. (F. Houssaye) Pop. Sci. Mo. **44**: 594.
— Industry in. Spec. **71**: 428. Same art. Liv. Age, **199**: 509.
— Intelligence of. (J. Weir, jr.) Am. Natural. **27**: 933. — (Edwin Arnold) Idler, **9**: 516.
— — Limits of. (C. L. Morgan) Fortn. **60**: 223. Same art. Liv. Age, **199**: 89.
— Land, Origin of, Simroth on. (W. J. Sollas) Nature, **46**: 271.
— Language of, New Observations on. (M. DeL. Duthiers) Pop. Sci. Mo. **40**: 528.
— Limit of Size in. Spec. **72**: 681.
— Little Children of Cybele. (E. M. Thomas) Atlan. **69**: 349.
— Luminous. (T. R. R. Stebbing) Blackw. **158**: 543.
— Mind in. Spec. **75**: 514.
— Nearness of, to Men. (E. P. Evans) Atlan. **69**: 171.
— Protective Resemblance in. (R. Lydekker) Knowl. **15**: 121.
— Rare. Sat. R. **78**: 232.
— Reasoning. (A. Pringle) Pop. Sci. Mo. **42**: 71.
— Rights of. (T. C. Laws) Open Court, **7**: 3791.
— — to Property. (E. P. Powell) Open Court, **9**: 4375.
— Sense of Humor in. Spec. **69**: 444.
— Senses and Intellect of: a Dream suggested by Sir John Lubbock. Ecl. M. **124**: 134.
— Sociability among. (A. de Neuville) Pub. Opin. **15**: 322.
— Some Interesting. (T. Wood) Sund. M. **22**: 318, 409.
— Speech of. (H. N. Lyon) Science, **22**: 324.
— Stories of. (L. Meadows) Argosy, **61**: 368–727. **62**: 91, 215.
— Stuffed, in Comic Groups. Idler, **6**: 559.
— Temper of. Ecl. M. **118**: 278.
— Temperature of. (M. S. Pembrey) Nat. Sci. **2**: 214.
— Training of. (J. E. LeRossignol) Am. J. Psychol. **5**: 205.
— — Torture in. (S. L. Bensusan) Eng. Illust. **15**: 25.
— Treatment of, Ethical Relations in. (E. P. Evans) Pop. Sci. Mo. **45**: 634.
— Variation in the Habits of. (G. C. Davenport) Pop. Sci. Mo. **47**: 619.
— Wanton Mutilation of. (G. Fleming) 19th Cent. **37**: 440.
— Wild, Management of. Spec. **76**: 269.
— — Popular Errors about. (T. B. Comstock) Science, **20**: 155.
— — Preservation of. Spec. **72**: 434.

Animals, Wild Traits in Tame; the Donkey. (L. Robinson) No. Am. **159**: 722.
— Will and Reason in. (W. R. Newbold) Am. Natural. **29**: 948.
— Winter Shifts of. Blackw. **151**: 446. Same art. Liv. Age, **193**: 426.
— Young. Spec. **77**: 641.
— — at the London "Zoo." Spec. **71**: 628.
Animism, Dr. Tylor on. (J. S. Stuart-Glennie) Folk-Lore, **3**: 289.
— and Teutonic Mythology. (P. D. Chautepie de la Saussaye) N. World, **3**: 443.
Anlagen. (P. C. Mitchell) Nat. Sci. **5**: 366.
Anna Pavlovna's Pilgrimage. (B. Russell) Sund. M. **24**: 773. Same art. Liv. Age, **207**: 689.
Annals of a Quiet Browning Club; a story. Poet-Lore, **7**: 436, 556.
Annandale, The Book of. (H. Maxwell) Blackw. **159**: 83. — (A. H. Millar) Scot. R. **28**: 203.
Annandale, House of. Ed. R. **182**: 307.
Annandale, N. Y., Reminiscences of. (J. N. Lewis) Am. Hist. Reg. **4**: 29–151.
Annapolis, Md., Colonial Architecture of. (T. H. Randall) Archit. Rec. **1**: 309.
Annapolis Valley, Canada, Fruit-growing in. (J. W. Longley) Canad. M. **1**: 621.
Anna's Engagement; a story. Argosy, **60**: 375.
Anne, Queen, and the Duchess of Marlborough. (M. O. W. Oliphant) Cent. **24**: 101.
Anne of Brittany, Château of, in the Valley of the Loire. (T. A. Cook) Scrib. M. **13**: 490.
Anne, Princess, of Denmark. (M. O. W. Oliphant) Cent. **23**: 904.
Anne des Deux Mondes, Ste. Macmil. **68**: 127.
Anne Marie and Jeanne Marie; a Balcony Story. (G. King) Cent. **24**: 372.
Annelids, Bifurcated. (E. A. Andrews) Am. Natural. **26**: 725.
Anntje; a story. Temp. Bar, **95**: 113.
Annexation, Philosophy of. Soc. Econ. **4**: 193.
— to the U. S. "Manifest Destiny." (C. Schurz) Harper, **87**: 737.
— Historic Policy of the U. S. as to. (S. E. Baldwin) Yale R. **2**: 131.
Annexed Territory, The Law of, as Declared by the Supreme Court of the United States. (J. Lowndes) Pol. Sci. Q. **11**: 672.
"Annie Laurie," True Story of. (F. P. Humphrey) McClure, **6**: 66.
Annie Tousey's Little Game; a story. (M. S. Briscoe) Harper, **91**: 179.
Annisquam, Mass. (E. M. Hallowell) New Eng. M. n. s. **12**: 706.
Anniversaire; a poem. (Paul Verlaine) New R. **10**: 571.
Anniversary, An. (A. H. Thorndike) New Eng. M. n. s. **12**: 595.
Annuals, Old. Atlan. **71**: 138.
Annuitants. Chamb. J. **69**: 97.
Annuities, Family. Bank. M. (Lond.) **55**: 337.
Annunciation, The, in Art. (J. Cartwright) M. of Art, **9**: 202.
Annunzio, Gabriele d'. (F. T. Cooper) Bookman, **3**: 18.
— With portrait. Bk. News, **15**: 45.
Anomalies, Significance of. (T. Dwight) Am. Natural. **29**: 130.
Anonymity. All the Year, **72**: 112.
— in Journalism. (J. MacIntyre) 19th Cent. **34**: 602. — (H. D. Traill) 19th Cent. **34**: 932.
Anonymous Letter, An; a story. (R. H. Davis) Harper, **88**: 445.
Anoplotherium, Phylogeny of. (C. Earle) Am. Natural. **30**: 665.
Another's Child. (K. G. Wells) New Eng. M. n. s. **10**: 669.
Anschauung, Meaning of. (P. Carus) Monist, **2**: 527.
Ansdell, Richard C. (W. W. Fenn.) M. of Art, **5**: 450.
Anselm, St., of Canterbury. (P. Schaff) Pres. and Ref. R. **5**: 25.
Answered Prayer, The; a poem. (G. Massey) Arena, **7**: 760.
Ant, South American, Fungus Gardens of. (J. C. Willis) Nature, **48**: 392.
— White, Sense-organs on Legs of. (A. C. Stokes) Science, **22**: 273.
— Wood or Fallow, of Southeastern Massachusetts. (J. B. Woodworth) Science, **22**: 132.
Antæus; a romance. (F. M. Bicknell) Outing, **23**: 24.
Antæus in Love. (R. B. Hale) New Eng. M. n. s. **9**: 783.
Antarctic's Challenge to the Explorer. (F. A. Cook) Forum, **17**: 505.
Antarctic Continent. Dub. R. **117**: 453.
— The "Antarctic's" Voyage. (C. E. Borchgrevink) Geog. J. **5**: 583. — Nature, **52**: 375.
— First Landing on. (C. E. Borchgrevink) Cent. **29**: 432.
— Murdoch's From Edinburgh to the. (W. H. Dall) Nation, **60**: 113.
Antarctic Expedition, A Proposed. (F. A. Cook) Around World, **1**: 55.
Antarctic Exploration. (C. C. Adams) Am. Natural. **28**: 693. — Dub. R. **118**: 176. — (W. S. Bruce) Knowl. **19**: 28. — (T. Southwell) Nat. Sci. **6**: 97. — Macmil. **72**: 250. Same art. Liv. Age, **206**: 614.
— Borchgrevink and. (A. W. Greely) Cent. **29**: 431.
— Bull's. Sat. R. **82**: 265.
— Need for. (C. R. Markham) 19th Cent. **38**: 706.
— Projects for. (H. R. Mill) Nature, **54**: 29.
— Renewal of. (J. Murray) Geog. J. **3**: 1. — Around World, **1**: 95.
Antarctic Regions, Physical Geography of. Am. J. Sci. **146**: 317. — Geog. J. **2**: 252.
— Voyage of the "Jason" to. (C. A. Larsen) Geog. J. **4**: 333.
Antarctic Seas, Cruise of the "Balaena" and the "Active" in. (W. S. Bruce) Geog. J. **7**: 502. — (C. W. Donald) Geog. J. **7**: 625.
— Voyage Toward, 1892–93. Geog. J. **2**: 429.
Antarctica; a Vanished Austral Land. (H. O. Forbes) Fortn. **61**: 194. — All the Year, **74**: 376. — (A. W. Greely) Cosmopol. **17**: 296.
Antediluvians, Long-lived. (W. R. Harper) Bib. World, **3**: 326.
Antelope, After, in Wyoming. (O. K. Davis) Outing, **26**: 401.
— Disappearing. Sat. R. **80**: 234.
Antelopes of Somali-land. (P. L. Sclater) Nat. Sci. **1**: 255.
Ante-mortem Condition of George Ramor. (G. B. McCutcheon) Nat'l M. (Bost.) **5**: 17.
Anterior Time, The; a story. (E. W. Pugh) New R. **13**: 175.
Anthemion, Greek, Lotiform Origin of. (W. H. Goodyear) Archit. Rec. **3**: 263.
Antholite from Ebsivir, Ontario. (A. P. Coleman) Am. J. Sci. **148**: 281.
Anthologia Palatina, Didot's Edition of Epigrams of. Third Volume. (R. Ellis) Am. J. Philol. **14**: 350.
Anthology, An Old. (F. I. Carpenter) Bookworm, **1**: 229.
Anthona, John de. (J. Brownbill) Antiq. n. s. **24**: 164.
Anthony, Elliott. (H. L. Conard) M. West. Hist. **13**: 126.

Anthracite Culm Heaps, Utilization of, in Production of Power. (N. W. Perry) J. Frankl. Inst. **142**: 26. — (E. H. Williams, jr.) Engin. M. **11**: 644.
Anthropological History of Europe. (J. Beddoe) Scot. R. **19**: 405. **20**: 146, 362.
Anthropological Work in America. (F. Starr) Pop. Sci. Mo. **41**: 289.
— in Europe. (F. Starr) Pop. Sci. Mo. **41**: 54.
Anthropology, Aims of. (D. G. Brinton) Science, n. s. **2**: 241. Same art. Pop. Sci. Mo. **48**: 59. — (D. G. Brinton) J. Am. Folk-Lore, **8**: 247.
— and Museums. (Sir H. Howorth) Nat. Sci. **9**: 182.
— and Sociology. (L. F. Ward) Am. J. Sociol. **1**: 426.
— at the University of Oxford. (F. Boas) Nation, **61**: 27.
— Christian, Thein's. (E. B. Brady) Cath. World, **55**: 541.
— Historical Sketch. (T. Hughes) Am. Cath. Q. **18**: 604.
— in Europe. (J. Beddoe) Scot. R. **21**: 162, 350. **22**: 84.
— in Universities and Colleges. (A. F. Chamberlain) Pedagog. Sem. **3**: 48.
— International Congress of, 1893, Memoirs of. Critic, **25**: 184. — J. Am. Folk-Lore, **7**: 259.
— Limitations of the Comparative Method of. (F. Boas) Science, n. s. **4**: 901.
— Prehistoric, Importance of the Study of. (T. Wilson) Am. Natural. **26**: 681, 809.
— Problems of (R. Virchow) Pop. Sci. Mo. **42**: 373.
— Relation of, to Study of History. (G. E. Fellows) Am. J. Sociol. **1**: 41.
— Spanish. (J. Beddoe) Sci. Prog. **3**: 99.
— True Basis of. (H. Hale) Am. Antiq. **15**: 15–212.
— What is? (F. Starr) Chaut. **19**: 25.
Anthropometric Identification of Criminals. (H. Vincent) Eng. Illust. **12**: no. 1, 73.
Anthropometric Statistics of Amherst College. (E. Hitchcock) Am. Statis. Assoc. **3**: 588.
Anthropometrical Measurements in Schools, Use of. (W. T. Porter) Educa. R. **11**: 126.
Anthropometry and Experimental Psychology. (E. B. Titchener) Philos. R. **2**: 187.
— in India. (J. Beddoe) Sci. Prog. **4**: 188.
— in the U. S. (E. M. Hartwell) Am. Statis. Assoc. **3**: 554.
— Legal. (E. R. Spearman) Green Bag, **7**: 33.
— Theory of. (F. Boas) Am. Statis. Assoc. **3**: 569.
Anthropomorphism. (S. D. Peet) Am. Antiq. **17**: 79.
Anthropophagy, A Chapter on. (R. Andree) Open Court, **4**: 2710. **5**: 2718.
Anthurioms, Notes on. (A. P. Meridith) Garden & F. **7**: 57.
Anti-Christ Saga, Armenian Form of the. Acad. **48**: 343.
Antidromy in Plants. (G. Macloskie) Am. Natural. **29**: 973.
"Anti-ism." Spec. **68**: 427.
Antimony, Double Halides of, with Rubidium. (H. L. Wheeler) Am. J. Sci. **146**: 269.
— Thermo-Electric Heights of Antimony and Bismuth Alloys. (C. C. Hutchins) Am. J. Sci. **148**: 226.
Antioch, the Birthplace of Christianity. (H. R. Reynolds) Thinker, **8**: 134.
— School of, Exegesis of. (H. S. Nash) J. Bib. Lit. **11**: 22.
Antipathy and Sympathy. (S. Bryant) Mind, **20**: 365.
Antiquarian Memories. (W. Brailsford) Antiq. n. s. **17**: 89.
Antiquarian Study, Scope and Charm of. Walford's Antiq. **1**: 3, 61, 121.
Antiquities, Forgery of. (Sir J. Evans) Longm. **23**: 142.
Antiquities, Greek and Roman, Smith's Dictionary of. Church Q. **33**: 477.
— in Benderloch. Chamb. J. **68**: 491.
Anti-Semitism, The Mask of. (F. L. Oswald) Open Court, **7**: 3907.
Anti-Slavery History and Biography. Atlan. **72**: 268.
Anti-Slavery Journals. *See* Abolition.
Antistes of Zurich. (J. I. Good) Presb. & Ref. R. **6**: 593.
Anti-toxin Cure for Diphtheria. R. of Rs. (N. Y.) **11**: 292. — (G. S. Woodhead) Nature, **51**: 402, 425. — (H. B. Donkin) New R. **12**: 191. Same art. Ecl. M. **124**: 453. — (W. H. Park) McClure, **4**: 365. — (L. E. Holt) Forum, **19**: 106. — Sat. R. **79**: 151. — (W. J. Fleming) Good Words, **36**: 115. — (S. T. Armstrong) Pop. Sci. Mo. **46**: 512. — (G. S. Woodhead) Nature, **51**: 402, 425. — (H. M. Biggs) McClure, **4**: 360. — (E. Klein) Sci. Prog. **3**: 1. — (G. A. Buckmaster) Sci. Prog. **3**: 193. — (L. Browne) Contemp. **70**: 119. — (W. P. Northrop) Forum, **22**: 53.
— from a Patient's Point of View. (D. C. Boulger) Contemp. **69**: 177.
— Ways and Means of. (N. Robinson) Pop. Sci. Mo. **48**: 826.
Antlers, Engraved. (W. A. Baillie-Grohman) Mag. of Art, **19**: 441.
Antoine, Andre, and the "Theatre Libre." Sat. R. **79**: 213.
Antoinette, Marie, La Rocheterie and Gaulot on. Ath. '94, **1**: 369.
Antokolsky, Mark. (I. Pavlovsky) Mag. of Art, **6**: 309.
Antonine, Wall of. (G. Neilson) Antiq. n. s. **23**: 250.
Antony and Cleopatra. (J. A. Froude) Cosmopol. **17**: 515.
Antraigues, Comte d'. Spec. **71**: 487.
Ants. (E. A. Butler) Knowl. **15**: 27–104.
— as Fertilisers. Dub. R. **110**: 458.
— as Mushroom Growers. (A. L. Smith) Good Words. **36**: 592. Same art. Ecl. M. **125**: 845. — (E. F. Smith) Am. Natural. **29**: 851.
— European and North American, Origin of. (C. Emery) Nature, **52**: 399.
— "Parasol," Classes among. (H. Spencer) Nature, **51**: 126.
Antwerp. (L. T. Meade) Sund. M. **23**: 814.
— Carillons of. (J. F. Rowbotham) Good Words, **36**: Xmas no. 44.
— How to see. (P. Fitzgerald) Gent. M. n. s. **50**: 335. Same art. Ecl. M. **120**: 706.
— International Exhibition, 1894. (E. Mitchell) Engin. M. **7**: 849. — (E. Sève) J. Soc. Arts, **42**: 283.
Anuradhapura; a pre-Christian City. (C. F. Gordon-Cumming) Ecl. M. **118**: 201. Same art. Liv. Age, **192**: 222.
— the Place of the Sacred Bo-tree. Cornh. **72**: 166.
Anvils, Portable, Found at Silchester. Illus. Archæol. **1**: 42.
Apache Dance, An. (N. Lupan) Outing, **22**: 189.
Apache Land, Building a State in. (C. D. Poston) Overland, n. s. **24**: 203–403.
Apache Mythology. (J. G. Bourke) J. Am. Folk-Lore, **3**: 209.
Apaches, Gentile System of the. (J. G. Bourke) J. Am. Folk-Lore, **3**: 111.
— Religion of. (J. G. Bourke) Folk-Lore, **2**: 419.
Apartment-houses, Parisian. (P. F. Marcou) Archit. Rec. **2**: 324. — (Maurice Saglio) Archit. Rec. **5**: 347.
— of New York and Paris. (Hubert, Pirsson, and Hoddick) Archit. Rec. **2**: 55.

Apartments, Furnished; a story. All the Year, **72**: 157.
Ape that Talked. (A. J. Kenealy) Outing, **24**: 292.
"Apergy:" Power without Cost. (C. Morris) New Sci. R. **2**: 174.
Apes, Anthropoid. (A. Keith) Nat. Sci. **9**: 250, 316, 372.
— Man-like. (R. Lydekker) Knowl. **17**: 151.
— Our Simian Cousins. Chamb. J. **72**: 750.
Aphasia. (A. Binet) Chaut. **15**: 50.
Aphides. (B. Kidd) Longm. **20**: 499.
— A Honey-dew Picnic. (W. H. Gibson) Harper, **85**: 24.
Apocalypse. *See* Bible; Revelation.
Apocalypse of Moses. (F. C. Conybeare) Jew. Q. **7**: 216.
Apocalypses, The Jewish. (G. H. Shodde) Bib. World, **6**: 97.
Apocrypha, The. (F. C. Porter) Bib. World, **8**: 272.
— Maccabees, Third Book of. (I. Abrahams) Jew. Q. **9**: 39.
— — Fourth Book of. (T. Tyler) Acad. **50**: 132.
— The New. (H. Lucas) Month, **77**: 1.
— Revised, Merits and Demerits of. (T. H. L. Leary) Gent. M. n. s. **56**: 126.
Apol, Lodewyk F. H. (A. C. Croiset van der Kop) Art J. **45**: 353.
Apollinarises of Laodicea. Church Q. **37**: 118.
Apollo and the Fates, Modern. (H. A. Clarke) Poet-Lore, **4**: 518.
— Delphic Hymn to. (A. C. Swinburne) 19th Cent. **36**: 315. — (J. H. McDaniels and F. P. Nash) Nation, **58**: 341. — (T. Ray) Temp. Bar, **103**: 396. — (A. W. Verrall) J. Hel. Stud. **14**: 1.
— — Another. (J. H. McDaniels and F. P. Nash) Nation, **61**: 112.
— in Picardy. (W. Pater) Harper, **87**: 949.
— A Palinode to. (H. W. Nevinson) Contemp. **70**: 529.
— Sanctuary of. (J. Gennadius) Forum, **22**: 327.
Apollo Flies; a story. Belgra. **84**: 64.
Apologetics. Church Q. **37**: 20.
Apologist, The. (N. Hapgood) Harv. Mo. **13**: 139.
Apostasy, Certificate of an, during the Persecution of Decian. (R. H. Beattie) Bib. World, **8**: 289.
— Danger of. (P. J. Glagg) M. Chr. Liter. **6**: 24.
Apostasy of Julian Fulke, The. (A. Adair) Macmil. **67**: 381, 467.
Apostasy of Paget, The. (C. D. Lanier) Southern M. **4**: 241.
Apostle of Port Royal; a story. (L. C. Cornford) Longm. **24**: 485. Same art. Liv. Age, **203**: 303.
Apostles' Creed, The. (Mrs. H. Ward and A. Harnack) 19th Cent. **34**: 152. Same art. Ecl. M. **121**: 241. — (J. C. Long) Bapt. R. **14**: 89.
— and the Monuments. (J. B. Fox) Luth. Q. **25**: 145.
— Communion of Saints. (J. W. Richard) Luth. Q. **24**: 24.
— Conflict in Germany over. (A. Zahn) Presb. & Ref. R. **4**: 267.
— Descent into Hell. (M. G. Boyer) Luth. Q. **24**: 223.
— Harnack on. (G. W. Fritsch) Luth. Q. **26**: 116. — Church Q. **35**: 472.
Apostolate, Limits of the. (E. Y. Hincks) J. Bib. Lit. **14**: 37.
Apostolic Delegation, The. (T. Bouquillon) Am. Cath. Q. **20**: 112.
Apostolic Fathers, Lightfoot's Edition. Quar. **182**: 369.
Apostolic Succession. (A. M. Mackay) Westm. **146**: 572.
Apostolic Testimony, Evidential Value of. (M. L. Young) Luth. Q. **24**: 173.
Apostolical Epistles, Perle's Annotations. Eng. R. **17**: 327.
Apothecaries' Lore, A Volume of. (W. Roberts) Bookworm, **4**: 111.
Appalachian Area, Hydrographic Examinations in. (C. C. Babb) Science, n. s. **4**: 103.
Appalachian Faulting, Conditions of. (B. Willis and C. W. Hayes) Am. J. Sci. **146**: 257.
Appalachians, Southern, Geo-morphology of. (C. W. Hays and M. R. Campbell) Nat. Geog. M. **3**: 63.
Appalachian Type of Folding in the White Mountain Range of Inyo County, California. (C. D. Walcott) Am. J. Sci. **149**: 169.
Apparition of Gran'ther Hill. (R. E. Robinson) Atlan. **76**: 680.
Apparitions, Podmore on. Sat. R. **78**: 435.
Appeal, Court of, in England. Green Bag, **7**: 377.
— in Criminal Cases. (Herbert Stephen) New R. **12**: 434.
Appeals to the Highest Court. (G. H. Westley) Green Bag, **7**: 501.
Appenines, Irish Saints in, Stokes on. Spec. **69**: 569.
Apperception. (M. K. Smith) School R. **3**: 548. — (J. Kodis) Psychol. R. **3**: 384.
— and the Study of the Classics. (H. C. Pearson) Educa. **17**: 27.
— Lange's. (F. Watson) Acad. **46**: 6.
Applause: Is It Necessary? (G. Gladden) Music, **8**: 431.
Apple, The; a story. (H. G. Wells) Idler, **10**: 288.
Apple Exhibits at the Columbian Exposition. (L. H. Bailey) Garden & F. **6**: 239.
Apple Orchards, Spraying. Garden & F. **7**: 25.
Apple Trees. (B. D. Halsted) Chaut. **23**: 415.
Applegate Courts, Review of the Facts by, in Actions at Law. (J. E. Reddick) Am. Law R. **26**: 329.
Apples, American Exports. Garden & F. **7**: 182.
— at the Midwinter Fair. (C. H. Shinn) Garden & F. **7**: 132.
— Birds Injuring. (F. W. Card) Garden & F. **7**: 414.
— Cultivation of, in Kansas. Garden & F. **6**: 404.
— Decay of, in Barrels. (B. D. Halsted) Pop. Sci. Mo. **43**: 76.
— Rare Varieties of. Garden & F. **5**: 11.
Apples of Gold; a story. (M. S. Briscoe) Scrib. M. **12**: 677.
Applied Art; a story. (W. T. Nichols) Lippinc. **56**: 273.
Appomattox, Surrender at. (C. Marshall) So. Hist. Pap. **21**: 353. — (H. H. Perry) So. Hist. Pap. **20**: 56.
Apprentice System in the Building Trades. (G. C. Sikes) J. Pol. Econ. **2**: 397.
Apprentices, Fair Number of, in a Trade. (C. P. Sanger) Econ. J. **5**: 616.
Après; a story. (G. de Maupassant) Cosmopol. **16**: 241.
April; a poem. (A. C. Swinburne) M. of Art, **16**: 207.
— Betwixt a Smile and Tear. (E. M. Thomas) Atlan. **71**: 536.
— Epic of. (G. Allen) Longm. **21**: 615.
— Once More; a poem. (E. Gosse) M. of Art, **8**: 253.
April Fool's Day, Origin of. Belgra. **83**: 358.
April Holiday, An. (P. Robinson) Eng. Illust. **15**: 21.
April's Passing; a poem. (E. P. Seabury) Outing, **26**: 28.
Apses. (G. Redon) Am. Arch. **41**: 163, 191.
Âpte, Mahâdeo Chimnâji. (G. A. Jacob) Acad. **46**: 403.
Apulia, Experiences in. (R. Church) Blackw. **155**: 622.
Aquarium, Sir Thomas Browne's. Liv. Age, **210**: 766.
Aquariums, Public, in Europe. (B. Dean) Pop. Sci. Mo. **50**: 13.
Aquatic Gardening. (J. H. Connelly) Cent. **28**: 726.
Aquatic Plants. Garden & F. **5**: 82.
— at Clinton, N. J. Garden & F. **5**: 310, 494.
— in California. (E. D. Sturtevant) Garden & F. **9**: 498.
— in Modern Gardening. (S. Henshaw) Garden & F. **6**: 197.
— in Southern N. J. (M. Treat) Garden & F. **5**: 363.
— Notes on. (W. Watson) Garden & F. **8**: 333.

Aquatic Plants; Water Garden. Garden & F. 5: 177, 477.
— Winter Flowering. (W. Tricker) Garden & F. 5: 44.
— Wintering. (W. Tricker) Garden & F. 8: 436.
Aquatic Sports in Australia. (G. E. Boxall) Outing, 25: 144.
Arab Dominion, Rise and Fall of. (H. A. Salmoné) Asia. R. 10: 434.
Arab Legend of a Buried Monastery. (H. C. Bolton) J. Am. Folk-Lore, 2: 227.
Arabi, Release of. (W. S. Blunt) 19th Cent. 32: 370.
Arabia; the Hadramut Valley. (J. T. Bent) 19th Cent. 36: 419.
— Historical Geography of. Eng. R. 3: 36.
— in the Middle Ages. Sat. R. 74: 314.
— Islam, and the Eastern Question. (W. H. Thomson) Harper, 91: 625.
— Land of Frankincense and Myrrh. (J. T. Bent) 19th Cent. 38: 595. Same art. Ecl. M. 125: 628.
— Southeast; Journal of an Excursion in Oman. (S. B. Miles) Geog. J. 7: 522.
— Southern; Exploration of the Frankincense Country. (J. T. Bent) Geog. J. 6: 109.
Arabian Art, Gayet's. Sat. R. 77: 176.
Arabian Day and Night. (P. Bigelow) Harper, 90: 3.
Arabian Nights, History as Told in. (J. F. Hewitt) Westm. 143: 253.
— Tr. by Burton, ed. by Smithers. Sat. R. 79: 322.
Arabian Poetry before the Days of Mohammed. (W. S. Blunt) New R. 14: 626.
Arabic Customs in the Rio Grande Valley. (J. G. Bourke) J. Am. Folk-Lore, 9: 81.
Arabic-English Vocabulary, Spiro's. (G. L'Estrange) Nation, 62: 475.
Arabic Inscriptions, Berchem's. Sat. R. 78: 127.
Arabic MSS. in the Convent on Mt. Sinai, Gibson's. Sat. R. 80: 768.
Arabic Schools. (G. W. Leitner) Asia. R. 18: 430.
Arachnids, Organs of. Nat. Sci. 5: 361.
— Stigmata of, as a Clue to their Ancestry. (H. M. Bernard) Nature, 49: 68.
Arachon and Oysters. (H. W. Lucy) Time, 20: 256.
Arago, Dominique-François, Statue of, by Mercié. M. of Art, 4: 96.
Araminta Passmore's Wrestle with Philosophy. (L. B. Chace Wyman) New Eng. M. n. s. 10: 731.
Aran Islands, Ethnography of. Nature, 49: 468.
— South. (L'A. Cole) Sund. M. 22: 839.
Ararat, Mt., Ascent of. (H. F. B. Lynch) Scrib. M. 19: 215.
Arb Dinner. (W. S. Blackstock) Canad. M. 4: 444.
Arber, Edward. English Garner. (C. H. Thurber) School R. 4: 549.
Arbes, Jakub. (J. G. Kràl) Poet-Lore, 4: 1.
Arbitration in Commercial Cases *vs.* Courts of Law. Sat. R. 77: 415.
— Industrial. (S. and B. Webb) 19th Cent. 40: 743. — (J. S. Lowell) Char. R. 2: 153. — Sat. R. 74: 556.
— — and the Wage Contract. (C. Reno) Am. Law R. 26: 834.
— — Bishop Potter as an Arbitrator. Gunton's M. 10: 399.
— — Compulsory. (Jerome Dowd) Gunton's M. 10: 138. — (N. T. Mason) Arena, 16: 622. — (L. Abbott) Arena, 7: 30. — (D. M. Frederiksen) Am. J. Pol. 5: 487. — (H. L. Wayland) Am. J. Soc. Sci. 31: lxiii. — (S. Schindler) Arena, 7: 396. — (C. A. Reed) Arena, 7: 587.
— — — an Impossible Remedy. (C. D. Wright) Forum, 15: 323.
— — in Belgian Coal Mines. (J. S. Lowell) Char. R. 2: 365.
Arbitration, Industrial, in the U. S. (E. C. Cummings) Q. J. Econ. 9: 353.
— — Industrial Conciliation and, in Europe and Australasia. (E. R. L. Gould) Yale R. 3: 376.
— — its Methods and Limitations. (S. N. D. North) Q. J. Econ. 10: 407.
— — Limits of. (D. MacG. Means) Nation, 59: 42.
— — State, in England. Spec. 70: 597.
— instead of Litigation. (J. M. M'Candlish) Jurid. R. 7: 53.
— International. (B. F. Trueblood) New Eng. M. n. s. 13: 21. — (E. P. Powell) Arena, 17: 97. — (H. White) Nation, 62: 133. — (J. B. Moore) New World, 5: 223. — (J. B. Walker) Cosmopol. 21: 103. — Westm. 146: 676. — (J. Westlake) Int. J. Ethics, 7: 1. — (F. R. Coudert) Harper, 87: 918. — (E. L. Lord) Ann. Am. Acad. Pol. Sci. 2: 471. — (W. S. Logan) Lend a H. 8: 19.
— — and International Law. (Lord Russell) Forum, 22: 192.
— — and our Relations with England. (E. J. Phelps) Atlan. 78: 26.
— — between England and America. Spec. 70: 845. — National, 27: 756. — Nation, 63: 63.
— — — Reasons for an Immediate Treaty. (C. W. Eliot) Forum, 21: 534.
— — — Symposium. Indep. My. 7, '96.
— — — Tribunal of. (J. R. Tucker) Lend a H. 16: 452. — (E. E. Hale) Lend a H. 17: 33. — (W. S. Logan; W. A. Butler) Lend a H. 17: 86.
— — — The United States and. (J. B. Moore) Am. Law R. 26: 66.
— — — Venezuela, Cuba, and the National Conference at Washington. (B. A. Lockwood) Am. M. Civics, 9: 12.
— — — Working of. (H. W. Wilson) Fortn. 66: 785.
— — Brotherhood and War. Sat. R. 81: 68.
— New Chambers of, London. (T. F. Utley) Am. Law R. 27: 175. — Sat. R. 78: 292.
— Successful. (W. L. Garrison) Am. Arch. 45: 45.
— Treaties of. (R. T. Paine) Lend a H. 15: 54.
Arbitration Treaty between Great Britain and the U. S. (G. H. Emmott) Arena, 13: 376.
Arbitrator, The; a story. (M. Roberts) Eng. Illust. 14: 89.
Arbitrary Lover, An; a story. Cornh. 72: 601. Same art. Liv. Age, 208: 94.
Arblay, F. B. d'. Diary and Letters, Ward's Edition. (A. B. McMahan) Dial (Ch.) 14: 143.
Arbona, Monastery of. (A. L. Frothingham, jr.) Am. J. Archæol. 7: 433.
Arbor in the Garden; a story. Cornh. 67: 509.
Arbor Day. Garden & F. 5: 169. — (C. S. Sargent) Garden & F. 6: 151. — (F. B. Harrison) Garden & F. 6: 329.
Arbuthnot, John, Life of, Aitken's. Ath. '92, 1: 333. — (W. P. Courtney) Acad. 41: 415. — (C. A. L. Richards) Dial (Ch.) 13: 97. — Sat. R. 73: 480. — Spec. 69: 162. — (G. A. Aitken) Ath. '92, 1: 792. — Ed. R. 177: 174. — Quar. 176: 317.
Arbutus, Origin of; a poem. (F. A. Tupper) M. Am. Hist. 27: 222.
— Trailing, Cultivation of. (J. G. Jack) Garden & F. 8: 15.
— — Guests of the Mayflower. (C. M. Weed) Pop. Sci. Mo. 45: 17.
Arcachon, France. Sat. R. 76: 490.
— A Sunday at. All the Year, 76: 184.
Arcades, Street, in North Italy. (H. E. Tidmarsh) M. of Art, 20: 19.
Arcady, Another. Liv. Age, 211: 718.

Archæan History, Subdivisions in. (J. D. Dana) Am. J. Sci. 143: 455. Same art. Nature, 46: 152.
Archæan Rocks of Central Piedmont, Virginia, Fossils in. (N. H. Darton) Am. J. Sci. 144: 50.
Archæological Recollections, Some. (W. F. Ainsworth) Antiq. n. s. 17: 1.
Archæology a Confirmation of Historic and Religious Truth. Walford's Antiq. 6: 218.
— and Biblical Criticism. (T. Tyler) Acad. 45: 281. — (A. Harper) Chr. Lit. 12: 89.
— and Old Testament Criticism. Meth. R. 56: 136.
— Errors and Fictions of. (J. C. Cox) Antiq. n. s. 30: 48.
— Greek, Relation to Folk-Lore. (C. Smith) Folk-Lore, 3: 529.
— in Greece. (E. A. Gardner) J. Hel. Stud. 14: 224.
— — 1889-90. (E. A. Gardner) J. Hel. Stud. 11: 210.
— — 1890-91. (E. A. Gardner) J. Hel. Stud. 12: 385.
— — 1892. (E. A. Gardner) J. Hel. Stud. 13: 139.
— — 1894-95. (E. A. Gardner) J. Hel. Stud. 15: 202.
— — Murray's. Sat. R. 74: 51.
— Notes on. Illus. Archæol. 1: 50, 113.
— Recent. (J. P. Mahaffy) 19th Cent. 35: 845. Same art. Liv. Age, 201: 674.
— Research in. (H. Howarth) Antiq. n. s. 30: 107.
Archæopteryx, Structure and Habits of. (C. H. Hurst) Nat. Sci. 6: 112, 180, 244.
— Wing of. (W. P. Pycraft) Nat. Sci. 5: 350, 437. 8: 261.
Archangel, Father, of Scotland. (T. G. Law) 19th Cent. 34: 782. — (R. B. C. Grahame) 19th Cent. 34: 384.
Archbishop's Unguarded Moment. (O. F. Adams) Cosmopol. 12: 612.
Archdale, John, and Descendants. (S. B. Weeks) M. Am. Hist. 29: 157.
Archelon Ischyros; a New Gigantic Testudinate. (G. R. Wieland) Am. J. Sci. 152: 399.
Archer, Fred. (A. Allison) Time, 15: 641.
Archer, James. (E. Hogan) Month, 74: 78.
Archer, Wm. (R. Buchanan) Univ. R. 3: 353.
— "The Drama in the Doldrum." (C. Scott) Theatre, 29: 147.
Archery. Sat. R. 74: 134. — Ed. R. 182: 27.
— Longman on. Sat. R. 78: 438.
Arches, Experiments on. Am. Arch. 51: 119.
— Three-Hinged, Maximum Stresses on. (E. A. Werner) J. Frankl. Inst. 134: 292, 366, 426. 135: 45, 129.
— Triumphal. (R. H. Titherington) Munsey, 11: 490.
Archimedes; an Old-World Mechanic. (G. Winterwood) Good Words, 34: 268.
Archimenes, Cultivation of. (W. E. Endicott) Garden & F. 7: 477, 506, 518.
Architect, The. (B. Champneys) Time, 19: 385
— and Client. (T. M. Clark) Am. Arch. 48: 13.
— and Engineer. (M. D. Burke) Am. Arch. 47: 125.
— — Relations Between. (G. Hill) Engin. M. 4: 808.
— and his Artists. (W. H. White) Am. Arch. 35: 12, 26.
— and his Materials. (G. P. Merrill) Am. Arch. 39: 133.
— as a Landscape Painter. Am. Arch. 44: 21.
— before the Law. Am. Arch. 35: 4. 42: 131.
— Education of an. (H. R. Marshall) Archit. Rec. 5: 82.
— How to Choose an. (B. McEvoy) Engin. M. 4: 529.
— Library for an. (T. R. Smith) Am. Arch. 42: 100.
— of Fashion. (L. Eidlitz) Archit. Rec. 3: 347.
— What He Does for His Money. (J. B. Robinson) Engin. M. 2: 729.
Architect's Office, U. S. Govt., Bill for Reorganization of. Am. Arch. 47: 9.
— — — Influences against. (J. M. Carrère) Am. Arch. 47: 84.
Architect's Vacation, An. (R. S. Peabody) Atlan. 76: 23-634.
Architects. (H. Spencer) Contemp. 69: 100. — (C. H. Blackall) Am. Arch. 46: 44.
Architects, British Institute of, and its Critics. Spec. 69: 739.
— Contemporary English, and their Work. (H. H. Statham) Eng. M. 10: 203.
— Duties and Responsibilities of. (W. J. Jennings) Am. Arch. 39: 91.
— German, Responsibility of. Am. Arch. 44: 123.
— Licensing. (J. B. Robinson) Engin. M. 9: 197.
— Office-helps for. (G. Hill) Am. Arch. 38: 20-44: 27.
— Responsibility of. (F. E. Kidder) Am. Arch. 45: 31.
Architects' Houses. (J. B. Robinson) Archit. Rec. 3: 188, 229, 354. 4: 45.
Architectural Chronicle, The English. Macmil. 73: 204.
Architectural Competition. (J. A. Fox; H. L. Warren) Am. Arch. 52: 11.
Architectural Competitions, Ethics of. (J. M. Carrère) Engin. M. 5: 144.
Architectural Construction. (Viollet-le-Duc) Am. Arch. v. 35-45.
Architectural Design, Authority in. (J. B. Robinson) Archit. Rec. 6: 71.
Architectural Designs, How Spoiled. (E. I. Bell) M. of Art, 4: 61.
Architectural Education for America. (A. Rotch) Engin. M. 7: 39-154.
Architectural Ethics. Am. Arch. 47: 78.
Architectural Garden at Indian Harbor, L. I. (C. S. Sargent) Garden & F. 19: 241.
Architectural Knockabout, An. (F. L. F. Hoppin) Am. Arch. 40: 120-41: 38.
Architectural League Exhibition, 9th. Am. Arch. 43: 17, 29.
— 10th. Am. Arch. 47: 99, 131. — (M. G. Van Rensselaer) Garden & F. 9: 88.
Architectural Sculpture in America. (R. Sturgis) Engin. M. 10: 883.
Architectural Shades and Shadows. (A. D. F. Hamlin) Am. Arch. 37: 196-40: 98.
Architectural Students' Work Abroad. (G. R. P. Spiers) Engin. M. 10: 33.
Architecture. (Barr Ferrée) Archit. Rec. 1: 199. — (H. W. Desmond) Archit. Rec. 1: 211. — (C. F. Osborne) Archit. Rec. 1: 281.
— Alphabet of. (H. W. Desmond) Archit. Rec. 3: 29, 175. 4: 477.
— American. (I. E. Dodd) So. M. 3: 117.
— — Problem of. (R. Kerr) Archit. Rec. 3: 121.
— — Schuyler on. (B. Lathrop) Dial (Ch.) 13: 136. — Archit. Rec. 2: 105.
— — through English Spectacles. (B. F. Fletcher) Engin. M. 7: 314.
— American Idea of. (B. Ferrée) Science, 17: 46.
— American Style of. Am. Arch. 41: 53. — (H. C. Butler) Critic, 23: 203. — (Barr Ferrée) Archit. Rec. 1: 39.
— — among the Poets. (H. Van Brunt) Atlan. 71: 524.
— and Landscape Work. (D. Vaux) Engin. M. 11: 1071.
— Art *versus* Archæology in. (E. I. Bell) M. of Art, 9: 50.
— Artistic Domestic, in America. (B. Ferrée) New Eng. M. n. s. 12: 451.
— as a Fine Art. (W. N. Black) Archit. Rec. 1: 295.
— Asiatic, in Polynesia. (R. A. Sterndale) Asia R. 10: 340.
— at the Royal Academy, 1894. (G. A. T. Middleton) Art. J. 46: 213.

Architecture, Bad, Causes of. (W. N. Black) Archit. Rec. 2: 149.
— Beginnings of. (H. C. Kirk) Engin. M. 3: 166.
— Bread and Butter Side of. (C. H. Blackall) Am. Arch. 49: 92.
— Burgundian School of. (A. de Baudot) Am. Arch. 42: 15, 31.
— Byzantine. (E. Corroyer) Am. Arch. 36: 79-95. — (George Aitchison) Archit. Rec. 1: 83-485. 2: 93-493.
— Champagne School of. (P. Planat) Am. Arch. 38: 143-191.
— Church, Roman Catholic Contemporary. (R. A. Cram) Cath. World, 58: 644.
— Colonial, History of. (M. Schuyler) Archit. Rec. 4: 312.
— — in Albany, N. Y. (M. T. Reynolds) Archit. Rec. 4: 415.
— — in Annapolis. (T. H. Randall) Archit. Rec. 1: 309.
— — in the Genesee Valley. (C. F. Bragdon) Am. Arch. 43: 141. 45: 26. 46: 11.
— — in Massachusetts. (G. C. Gardner) Am. Arch. 45: 99. 46: 89.
— — in New Jersey. (W. N. Black) Arch. Rec. 3: 245.
— — in Western Massachusetts. Am. Arch. 47: 39.
— — in the South. Arch. Rec. 3: 337.
— — So-called. (O. Z. Cewin) Am. Arch. 48: 63-130.
— Domestic. (R. Blomfield) M. of Art, 15: 79, 124.
— of Washington. (G. Brown) Engin. M. 11: 434.
— Early Christian, Romanesque and Gothic, Syllabus of. (M. Wergeland) Am. Arch. 49: 50-52: 14.
— Early Domestic, in Norfolk. Art. J. 46: 274.
— Eastern Asiatic. (C. T. Mathews) Archit. Rec. 5: 288.
— English House. (Banister Fletcher) Archit. Rec. 5: 321.
— English Secular, Pictorial Elements in. (E. I. Bell) M. of Art, 1: 158. 2: 65-225. 3: 251, 403.
— European. Am. Arch. 54: 101.
— — Influence of the Hanseatic League on. (J. T. Perry) Am. Arch. 45: 115. 46: 12, 45.
— Fads in. (G. Keister) Archit. Rec. 1: 49.
— Federal. (G. B. Post) Critic, 26: 205.
— First Principles in. (W. H. Goodyear) Engin. M. 8: 687.
— Floor-plan of a Building, Art in. (T. Hastings) Engin. M. 7: 492.
— French, Influence in United States. (E. Flagg) Archit. Rec. 4: 211.
— Gothic, Corroyer on. (P. G. Hamerton) Portfo. 24: 19.
— — and Saracen. (E. Johnson) Liv. Age, 192: 476.
— — French *vs.* English. (R. P. Spiers) M. of Art, 13: 358.
— — French View of. (R. Blomfield) M. of Art, 17: 33.
— — Introduction of, into Italy. (A. L. Frothingham, jr.) Am. J. Archæol. 7: 283, 433.
— — Philosophy of. Eng. R. 2: 397.
— — Plant Decorations in. (A. E. P. R. Dowling) Contemp. 63: 715.
— Great Classical Fallacy of the 18th Century. (G. Allen) M. of Art, 5: 282.
— Greek, in the U. S. (W. H. Goodyear) Chaut. 16: 5-259.
— High Office Buildings in N. Y. Soc. Econ. 5: 327.
— Historical, in Current Use. (W. H. Goodyear) Engin. M. 8: 391.
— Ile-de-France School of. (A. Saint-Paul) Am. Arch. 39: 35-84.
— in America. (J. Stewardson) Lippinc. 57: 132. Same art. Am. Arch. 51: 51.
— — City. (E. C. Gardner) Engin. M. 12: 30.
— — Official. (M. Schuyler) Engin. M. 6: 711.
Architecture in Campania, Remains of Early. (G. C. Gardner) Am. Arch. 38: 209.
— in Cities, Good. (B. Ferrée) Engin. M. 10: 671.
— in England and the U. S. (H. Townsend) Am. Arch. 38: 101.
— — Renaissance, Gotch and Brown on. Ath. '94, 2: 199.
— in France, Recent. (B. Ferrée) Engin. M. 8: 992. 9: 73.
— in Germany, of the Renaissance, Fritsch's. (J. S. Fiske) Nation, 54: 328.
— in Great Cities, Problems of. (B. Ferrée) Am. Arch. 38: 161.
— in Italy. (A. Melani) Am. Arch. 35: 3-67.
— in London. (P. Fitzgerald) M. of Art, 3: 18-443. — (B. Ferrée) Archit. Rec. 5: 1.
— in Paris. (P. G. Hamerton) Portfo. 24: 211, 238, 241.
— — Domestic. 19th Cent. 37: 593. Same art. Liv. Age, 205: 300.
— in Peru, and Engineering. (Mme. A. D. Le Plongeon) Engin. M. 7: 46.
— in Philadelphia. (W. P. Laird) Engin. M. 8: 75.
— in Rome. (W. Holmden) M. of Art, 9: 475.
— in Scotland, Castellated and Domestic. Sat. R. 74: 483.
— in the U. S. and England. (H. Townsend) Am. Arch. 38: 101.
— in Wood: a Protest. (G. B. Kimbrough) Engin. M. 4: 345.
— Japanese, Morse's Japanese Homes and their Surroundings. (W. Anderson) M. of Art, 9: 295.
— Lack of Originality in. (R. Sturgis) Engin. M. 6: 11.
— Landscape-gardening and. (C. S. Sargent) Garden & F. 6: 73.
— Languedocian School of. (A. Saint-Paul) Am. Arch. 39: 99-132.
— Lombard. (F. Dedartein) Am. Arch. 37: 159-175. 38: 3-51.
— Mediæval, Refinements in. (W. H. Goodyear) Archit. Rec. 6: 1.
— Mediæval Domestic. (B. Ferrée) Am. Arch. 47: 16.
— Modern. (B. Ferrée) New Eng. M. n. s. 7: 601. — (P. Planat) Am. Arch. 37: 3-111. — (H. W. Desmond) Archit. Rec. 1: 276. — (M. Schuyler) Archit. Rec. 4: 1.
— — Difficulties of. (A. D. F. Hamlin) Archit Rec. 1: 137.
— — Pessimism of. (J. H. Edelmann) Eng. M. 3: 44.
— Modern English. (W. M. Ellicott) Am. Arch. 43: 22.
— Mud, Persian and Eastern. (W. Simpson) Am. Arch. 37: 9, 25.
— Musical Ideals of. (H. T. Booraem) Archit. Rec. 4: 283, 379.
— National. (W. M. Aiken) Am. Arch. 54: 43.
— Natural Color in. Sat. R. 78: 502.
— New England. (A. G. Hyde) Macmil. 66: 454.
— New York. (A. G. Hyde) Gent. M. n. s. 48: 493.
— of Home-making. (C. E. Benton) Engin. M. 11: 696.
— of the Low Countries. (J. van Ysendyck) Am. Arch. 39: 147. 40: 51.
— of Modern Bank Buildings. (R. W. Gibson) Engin. M. 11: 74.
— of Municipal Buildings. (E. C. Gardner) Engin. M. 8: 609.
— Ornament in. (B. Ferrée) Am. Arch. 37: 99. — (L. H. Sullivan) Engin. M. 3: 633.
— Perry's Chronology of Mediæval and Renaissance. (J. S. Fiske) Nation, 58: 425.
— Picturesque in. (H. T. Booræm) Mo. Illust. 4: 240.
— Profession of, Reform of. (J. N. Porter) Time, 17: 163.

Architecture, a Profession or an Art? (Lord Grimthorpe) 19th Cent. 33: 65. — Reply. (T. G. Jackson) 19th Cent. 33: 405. — (Lord Grimthorpe) 19th Cent. 33: 631. — Sat. R. 75: 383. — (R. W. Gibson) Engin. M. 6: 322. — Sat. R. 79: 690. — (P. M. Horder) M. of Art, 15: 172.
— Professional Ethics of. (J. A. Fox) Am. Arch. 46: 68.
— Professional Institutions: Architect. (H. Spencer) Pop. Sci. Mo. 48: 412.
— Religious Aspect of. (R. A. Cram) Archit. Rec. 2: 351.
— Renaissance, in England. (B. F. Fletcher) Archit. Rec. 2: 31.
— Restraints upon the Practice of. (J. B. Robinson) Engin. M. 11: 307.
— Romanesque, in America. (M. Schuyler) Archit. Rec. 1: 151.
— — in New York. (M. Schuyler) Archit. Rec. 1: 7.
— Schools of Instruction in. (R. A. Cram) Am. Arch. 54: 107.
— Seaside. (H. C. Butler) Am. Arch. 49: 120.
— Self-helps in. (C. H. Blackall) Am. Arch. 53: 11.
— Shaw and Jackson on. Quar. 176: 40.
— Spanish. (C. A. Rich) Archit. Rec. 4: 14. 5: 47, 227.
— Study of, in America. Am. Arch. 49: 62.
— — in the Rural Districts of the West. (T. Holmes) Garden & F. 6: 132.
— Study of the History of. Am. Arch. 50: 100.
— Style in. Am. Arch. 49: 70. — (A. D. F. Hamlin) Archit. Rec. 1: 265, 405. — (L. Labrouste) Am. Arch. 44: 30–107.
— — Choice in. (E. A. Freeman) Archit. Rec. 1: 391.
— — Influence of Plate Glass and Steel Construction upon. (Dankmar Adler) Am. Arch. 54: 37. — (R. D. Andrews) Am. Arch. 54: 44. — (J. W. Yost) Am. Arch. 54: 45. — Discussion on the above Papers. Am. Arch. 54: 71.
— Styles, French. (E. Rivoalen) Am. Arch. 44: 131, 143. 45: 3.
— Tall Office Building Artistically Considered. (L. H. Sullivan) Lippinc. 57: 403. *See* Buildings, High.
— Town and Cloth Halls of Flanders. (A. Ansted) M. of Art, 17: 422.
— Van Brunt on. (E. E. Hale, jr.) Dial (Ch.) 16: 110.
— Vicissitudes of. (L. Eidlitz) Archit. Rec. 1: 471. 4: 147.
Archoplasm and Attraction Sphere. (J. E. S. Moore) Nature, 50: 478.
Arciszewski, Christopher. Acad. 44: 316.
Arctic and Antarctic Exploration; President's Address, Roy. Geog. Soc., 1894. (C. R. Markham) Geog. J. 4: 1.
Arctic Castaway, An. (R. G. Taber) Outing, 27: 272.
Arctic Expedition, American, in 1894. Dub. R. 116: 194.
— by F. Jackson. (A. C. Harmsworth) Eng. Illust. 14: 359.
— The Jackson-Harmsworth. (A. M. Brice) Geog. J. 8: 543. — Dub. R. 118: 177.
— Nansen's Proposed. Dub. R. 112: 180. — Geog. J. 2: 346.
— Nansen's Trip, 1894–96. Sat. R. 82: 179.
— of 1895. (R. D. Salisbury) Science, n. s. 2: 457.
— Peary's. (W. E. Hughes and B. Sharp) Lippinc. 50: 86.
— — and its Relief. (A. Heilprin) Engin. M. 2: 719.
— — Results of. Dub. R. 113: 666.
— Peary Auxiliary Expedition. (H. G. Bryant) Geog. J. 4: 531. — (A. Heilprin) Scrib. M. 13: 1.
Arctic Expedition, Proposed English, 1893. Dub. R. 112: 454.
— An; a poem. (E. Rhodes) Argosy, 58: 440.
Arctic Expeditions, 1894. Dub. R. 115: 458. — (H. R. Mill) Nature, 50: 57.
Arctic Exploration. (H. R. Mill) McClure, 1: 147.
— by R. E. Peary. (R. Brown) Acad. 45: 161.
— Glamour of. (A. C. Doyle) McClure, 2: 391.
— in 1896. (H. R. Mill) Nature, 54: 392. — (J. W. Gregory) Nat. Sci. 9: 233.
— The New Polar Quest. All the Year, 72: 15.
— North Pole Up To Date. (A. A. W. Drew) Eng. Ilust. 10: 735.
— Polar Probabilities of 1894. (A. W. Greely) No. Am. 157: 287.
— Recent Expeditions. (A. W. Greely) McClure, 3: 39.
— The Way to the North Pole. Cornh. 73: 297.
Arctic Explorations, Scope and Value of. (A. W. Greely) Nat. Geog. M. 7: 32.
Arctic Heroes. (F. L. Ford) Munsey, 14: 286.
Arctic Highlander, The. (B. Sharp) Scrib. M. 11: 241.
Arctic Highlanders, Curious Race of. (L. L. Dyche) Cosmopol. 21: 228.
Arctic Hurricane. (J. Diebitsch-Peary) Around World, 1: 197.
Arctic Life, The Problem of. Spec. 75: 365. — Liv. Age, 208: 703.
Arctic May-day. All the Year, 75: 84.
Arctic Regions; Beyond the Verge. Chamb. J. 70: 672.
— Collinson's Journey. (A. W. Greely) Nat. Geog. M. 4: 198.
— Color at. (F. W. Stokes) Cent. 26: 722.
— Heroes of. Cornh. 67: 405. Same art. Ecl. M. 120: 653. Same art. Liv. Age, 197: 625.
— in Arctic Seas. Belgra. 87: 189.
— Keely and Davis's. Dial (Ch.) 14: 10.
— Misconceptions regarding. (A. Heilprin) Around World, 1: 5.
— The North Polar Problem. (A. H. Markham) No. Am. 162: 486.
— The Race to the Pole. (Herbert Ward) New R. 11: 186.
— Trip to Arctic Ocean. All the Year, 73: 109.
Arctic Studio. (F. W. Stokes) Cent. 30: 408.
Arctic Temperatures and Exploration. (S. Jenkins) Pop. Sci. Mo. 45: 653.
Arden, Edward. (C. C. Stopes) Ath. '96, 1: 190.
Ardennes, Castle of the. All the Year, 72: 184.
Arditi, Signor, Reminiscences of. Theatre, 37: 262.
Area and Population, Statistics of. (E. Levasseur) J. Statis. Soc. 55: 298.
Areopagus, Did Paul Preach from? (J. I. Manatt) And. R. 18: 526.
Arequipa, Peru. (F. M. Edselas) Cath. World, 59: 595.
Aretino, P. (G. Norton) Nation, 63: 314.
Argenson, Marquis de, Saxe and. Ed. R. 176: 521.
Argentine Republic. (J. S. Attwell) New Eng. M. n. s. 6: 767. — (J. P. Wisser) Un. Serv. (Phila.) 11: 203.
— Agricultural Progress in. (W. E. Bear) Econ. J. 5: 516.
— Bibliography of. (R. Garnett) Bibliographica, 1: 262.
— Finances of. (W. R. Lawson) Bank. M. (Lond.) 55: 399.
— Hot Work in. (M. S. Edmunds) Lippinc. 53: 837.
— Housekeeping in. Chamb. J. 71: 182. Same art. Ecl. M. 122: 705.
— New Salt Industry in. Dub. R. 110: 456.

Argentine Republic, Social Life in. Chamb. J. **72**: 731.
— Quinta-life in. (J. B. James) Temp. Bar, **109**: 163. Same art. Ecl. M. **127**: 649.
— Turner on. Spec. **68**: 613.
— View of. Leis. Hour, **44**: 12, 90, 255.
Argon. J. Frankl. Inst. **139**: 390. — Liv. Age, **204**: 817. — Nature, **51**: 337. — (J. H. Gladstone) Nature, **51**: 389. — (Lord Rayleigh) Nature, **52**: 159. Same art. Science, n. s. **1**: 701. — (Lord Rayleigh) New Sci. R. **1**: 262. — (Lord Rayleigh and W. Ramsay) Nature, **51**: 347. Same art. Am. J. Sci. **149**: 275. (Lord Rayleigh and others) Nature, **51**: 337, 347. — (G. McGowan) Knowl. **18**: 49. — (J. T. Stoddard) Pop. Sci. Mo. **47**: 522. — (J. T. Stoddard) Nation, **60**: 160. — Dub. R. **116**: 396. — (A. H. Church) Acad. **47**: 130. — (Ira Remsen) Science, n. s. **1**: 309.
— and the Atmosphere. (C. M. Aikman) Scot. R. **26**: 244.
— and Helium. (G. McGowan) Knowl. **18**: 210. — Acad. **48**: 148. — Ed. R. **182**: 404. — (H. M. Stokes) Science, n. s. **2**: 533.
— — Additional Notes on. (E. A. Hill) Am. J. Sci. **150**: 359.
— — in Meteoric Iron. (W. Ramsay) Nature, **52**: 224.
— and the Kinetic Theory. (C. E. Basevi) Nature, **52**: 221.
— Discovery of. Sat. R. **79**: 183.
— Doubts Concerning. Sat. R. **79**: 576.
— Fluorescence of, and Combination with the Elements of Benzine. (P. E. Berthelot) Nature, **52**: 255.
— Liquefaction and Solidification of. Nature, **51**: 355.
— Mendeléeff on. Nature, **51**: 543.
— Prout's Hypothesis, and the Periodic Law. (E. A. Hill) Am. J. Sci. **149**: 405.
— Reasons for Predicting Existence of. (C. J. Reed) J. Frankl. Inst. **140**: 68.
Argos, Excavations at. (E. Robinson) Nation, **58**: 404. — (C. L. Brownson) Am. J. Archæol. **7**: 205.
— Heræum, Sculptures from. (C. Waldstein) Am. J. Archæol. **8**: 199.
— — Inscriptions from. (J. R. Wheeler) Am. J. Archæol. **9**: 351. — (R. B. Richardson) Am. J. Archæol. **11**: 42.
Arguments, A Critic of. (C. S. Pierce) Open Court, **6**: 3391, 3415.
Argus γ, Spectrum of. (L. A. Eddie) Pop. Astron. **3**: 123.
Argus, The; a Weekly Liverpool Review of 1876. (J. A. Noble) Idler, **7**: 248.
Argyll, G. D. C., Duke of. Philosophy of Belief. Ed. R. **184**: 430. — Quar. **184**: 215. — Church Q. **43**: 155.
Argyllshire. (W. C. Maughan) Scot. R. **24**: 125.
— Folk-Lore Objects of. (R. C. Maclagan) Folk-Lore, **6**: 144.
Argyrodite, Chemical Composition of. (S. L. Penfield) Am. J. Sci. **146**: 107.
Arid Regions of U. S. (F. H. Newell) Nat. Geog. M. **5**: 167.
— Conquest of. (W. E. Smythe) Cent. **28**: 85.
— Future of. (E. V. Smalley) Forum, **19**: 466. — (E. G. Ross) No. Am. **161**: 438.
— Reclamation of. (R. J. Hinton) Arena, **8**: 618.
— Our Sub-arid Belt. (E. V. Smalley) Forum, **21**: 486.
— Tenting in. (J. W. Hays) Outing, **28**: 436.
— Underground Waters of. (R. T. Hill) Engin. M. **3**: 653.
— Ways and Means in. (W. E. Smythe) Cent. **29**: 742.
Aridity, A Problem of. (C. M. Harger) No. Am. **163**: 711.
Ariosto, Ludovico. Temp. Bar, **97**: 37. Same art. Liv. Age, **196**: 498.
Aristides, Apology of. (J. H. Ropes) And. R. **19**: 120.
— Leptinean Orations ascribed to, Authorship of. (J. E. Harry) Am. J. Philol. **15**: 66.
Aristocracy, English; Hare's Story of Two Noble Lives. (W. O. Morris) Acad. **45**: 49.
— in America. Spec. **76**: 408.
— Influence of, upon the Stability of a Nation. (J. S. Hewitt) Westm. **146**: 216.
— Landed, Have We a? (G. M. Simonson) Munsey, **13**: 528.
Aristocratomania. (P. Carus) Open Court, **5**: 2846.
Aristophanes. The Frogs, at Oxford. (H. F. Wilson) Acad. **41**: 237. — Ath. '92, **1**: 318. — Sat. R. **73**: 244. — Temp. Bar, **95**: 238. — Theatre, **28**: 216.
— Poetry of, Philosophy of, According to Browning. (H. L. Reed) Poet-Lore, **5**: 237.
Aristotle and Christian Ethics. Church Q. **37**: 321.
— as an Historian. (G. W. Cox) Acad. **42**: 52–171.
— Constitution of Athens. Bookworm, **4**: 101. — (R. W. Macan) J. Hel. Stud. **12**: 17. — (P. Giles) Eng. Hist. R. **7**: 322.
— — Sanday's. Ath. '93, **1**: 568.
— His Conception of God. (J. Ten Broeke) Bapt. R. **14**: 1.
— Poetics of. Eng. R. **16**: 320. — (R. P. Hardie) Mind, **20**: 350.
— — Butcher's ed. Sat. R. **79**: 291.
— Politics, ed. by Susemihl. Sat. R. **79**: 417. — (W. W. Goodwin) Nation, **61**: 366.
— Theory of Reason. (F. Granger) Mind, **18**: 307.
— Tomb of, Finding of. (C. Waldstein) Cent. **22**: 414.
Aristotle's Doctrine of Barter. (W. J. Ashley) Q. J. Econ. **9**: 333.
Arithmetic and Elementary Science. (W. S. Jackman) Educa. R. **5**: 35.
— Essentials of. (A. G. Boyden) Educa. **14**: 390.
— — Southworth's. (D. E. Smith) School R. **4**: 180.
— Hindu. (F. Pincott) Knowl. **13**: 105.
— in the Report of the Committee of Fifteen. (F. L. Burk; J. A. McLellan) Educa. R. **11**: 74.
— Mental, Werner, Raub's. (D. E. Smith) School R. **4**: 239.
— Psychology of Number, McLellan and Dewey on. (D. E. Smith) School R. **4**: 102.
— Two Paths in. (W. D. Mackintosh) Educa. **16**: 481.
Arithmetical Books, Earliest, in European Vernaculars. Bookworm, **2**: 136.
Arithmetical Operations, Greek Method of Performing. (J. Tetlow) School & C. **1**: 22.
Arizona, Admission of, as a State. (J. N. Irwin) No. Am. **156**: 354.
— Building a State in Apache Land. (C. D. Poston) Overland, n. s. **24**: 87–403.
— Petrified Forest of. (S. A. Miller) Around World, **1**: 183.
— A Scrap of Frontier History. (C. Harkins) Overland, n. s. **21**: 265.
Arizona Speculation, An. (M. E. Stickney) Lippinc. **54**: 685.
Arkansas, Gypsy Camping in. (L. S. LaMance) Outing, **24**: 336.
— Paleozoic Sediments in. (J. C. Branner) Am. J. Sci. **152**: 229.
— Supreme Court of. (G. B. Rose) Green Bag, **4**: 417.
Arkansas Folk-Lore. (Alice French) J. Am. Folk-Lore, **5**: 121.
Arkansas Industrial University. (C. V. Kerr) Cassier, **5**: 405.
"Arkansas Traveler," On the Track of the. (H. C. Mercer) Cent. **29**: 707.

Arkins, John, with portrait. (A. N. Towne) M. West. Hist. **13**: 685.
Arklow, Barony of, in Ireland. (J. Wandesford-Butler) Walford's Antiq. **1**: 88.
Armadillo and its Oddities. (C. H. Coe) Pop. Sci. Mo. **47**: 354.
Armadillos. (R. Lydekker) Knowl. **15**: 221.
Armand's Mistake. Liv. Age, **195**: 77.
Armbruster, Violet, with portrait. Theatre, **28**: 91.
Armellini, Mariano, with portrait. (B. F. Broderick) Cath. World, **64**: 84.
Armenia. (G. McDermot) Cath. World, **64**: 295. — (E. J. Dillon) Contemp. **68**: 153. — (J. J. O'Shea) Cath. World, **60**: 553. — (F. S. Stevenson) Contemp. **67**: 201.
— and the Armenians. (A. von Schweizer-Lerchenfeld) Chaut. **22**: 697.
— and the Powers. Contemp. **69**: 628.
— and the Transvaal. (M. MacColl) Fortn. **65**: 313.
— An Appeal. (E. J. Dillon) Contemp. **69**: 1. Same art. Ecl. M. **126**: 194. Same art. Chr. Lit. **14**: 387.
— Atrocities in, Gladstone on. Sat. R. **79**: 3.
— Distribution of Relief in. (E. G. Porter) Lend a H. **16**: 188.
— English Failure in. (W. B. Harris) Sat. R. **81**: 141.
— Fiasco in. (E. J. Dillon) Fortn. **65**: 341.
— Immediate Future of. (W. K. Stride) Forum, **22**: 308.
— Impending Doom of: Our Duty. (M. M. Mangasarian) Forum, **21**: 449.
— Islam the Scourge of God. (H. H. Van Meter) Our Day, **16**: 325.
— La Turquie et son Souverain. (D. Kélékian) 19th Cent. **40**: 689.
— Moslem View of Abdul Hamid and the Powers. (R. Ahmad) 19th Cent. **38**: 156.
— Must have a European Governor. (R. Stein) Arena, **12**: 368.
— Past and Present. (H. Hyvernat) Cath. World, **62**: 312.
— A Poem. (L. Morris) Our Day, **16**: 56.
— Problem of Reform in Government of. Macmil. **71**: 340.
— Question of. (Hormuzd Rassam) Asia. R. **20**: 49. — (W. E. Gladstone) Chr. Lit. **14**: 337. — New R. **12**: 62. — (J. Bryce) Cent. **29**: 150. — (E. L. Godkin) Nation, **60**: 44.
— — England and. National, **28**: 141.
— — Europe or Russia? (H. F. B. Lynch) Contemp. **69**: 270.
— — in Russia. (H. F. B. Lynch) Contemp. **65**: 847. **66**: 91, 435.
— — Ottoman Lessons in Massacre. (J. Cook) Our Day, **14**: 121.
— — Possible Word for the Turk. (W. R. Claxton) Am. M. Civics, **9**: 321.
— — Turkey and. (R. Davey) Fortn. **63**: 197. — (T. Peterson) Cath. World, **61**: 665.
— — Turkish Atrocities. (C. Hamlin) Our Day, **14**: 9.
— — Unbiassed View of the. (W. B. Harris) Blackw. **158**: 483. Same art. Ecl. M. **125**: 641.
— Resolutions on, in Congress. (E. L. Godkin) Nation, **62**: 93.
— Roman Catholic Church in. (P. Terzian) Cath. World, **60**: 212.
— Russian, and British Trade. (A. V. Markoff) J. Soc. Arts, **43**: 225.
— — Queen Lukeria of Gorelovka. (H. F. B. Lynch) Harper, **93**: 36.
— Story of Woe in. (G. M. Manavian) Our Day, **16**: 20.
— Suffering. (B. F. Mills) Our Day, **16**: 581.
— Turks in. (F. de Pressensé) Chaut. **22**: 591.
Armenia; Van Industrial Bureau. (G. W. Kimball) Lend a H. **16**: 446.
— Winter Ride in. (E. Vizetelly) Eng. Illust. **15**: 135.
— Zeitun. (A. Vazarbek) Contemp. **69**: 513.
Armenian and Turk. (W. B. Harris) Sat. R. **80**: 614.
Armenian Church, History and Wrongs of. (F. S. Stevenson; G. B. M. Coore) New R. **9**: 201.
— — Reply. (Sadik Effendi) New R. **9**: 456.
— — Rejoinder. (F. S. Stevenson) New R. **9**: 648.
Armenian Exiles in Cyprus. (E. Cons) Contemp. **70**: 888.
Armenian Folk-Lore. (H. C. Bolton) J. Am. Folk-Lore, **9**: 293.
Armenian Melodies. (M. G. Reed) Music, **7**: 355.
Armenians, Massacres of. (J. G. Rogers; Earl Meath; J. Burns; H. A. Salmoné; W. E. Gladstone) 19th Cent. **40**: 654. Same art. Liv. Age, **211**: 393. — (W. M. Ramsay) Chr. Lit. **14**: 543. — National, **28**: 141. — (Cyrus Hamlin) Outl. **52**: 944.
— — in Constantinople. (W. M. Ramsay) Contemp. **70**: 435. Same art. Liv. Age, **211**: 352.
— — Review of Official Records. (H. H. Van Meter) Our Day, **16**: 559–641.
— Travels among. (J. T. Bent) Contemp. **70**: 695.
Armies, Can Europe Afford her? (C. W. Dilke) No. Am. **157**: 399.
— Private, Past and Present. (T. B. Preston) New Eng. M. n. s. **7**: 299.
— Standing, of Europe, Menace of. (F. Greenwood) Macmil. **68**: 414.
— — Some Advantages of. All the Year, **75**: 88.
Armitage, Edward. Ath. '**96**, **1**: 721.
Armitage, Thos. R., a Benefactor of the Blind. (A. Hirst) Sund. M. **25**: 736, 836.
Armor and Arms at the Tudor Exhibition. (Baron De Cosson) Antiq. n. s. **21**: 57. Same art. M. of Art, **13**: 317.
— Last Fight in. Temp. Bar, **102**: 501.
— of Old Japan. (M. S. Hunter) Cent. **27**: 386.
— A Retrospect. (Florence Peacock) Westm. **140**: 433.
Armor-plate, American, Development of. (F. L. Garrison) J. Frankl. Inst. **133**: 337–421. **134**: 20.
— Nickel-steel, Development of. (R. B. Dashiell) Engin. M. **5**: 763.
Armor-plate Question. (W. H. Jaques) Engin. M. **8**: 409.
Armor Protection for Heavy Guns in Battleships. (W. C. Foley) J. Frankl. Inst. **137**: 469.
Armorer of the Twentieth Legion. (H. D. Traill) Univ. R. **6**: 99.
Armorer's Bill, An, *temp.* Edward III. (H. Dillon) Antiq. n. s. **22**: 148.
Armories, Necessity for. (A. G. Marshall) Bost. **1**: 611. **2**: 49–617.
— Plutocracy's Bastiles. (B. O. Flower) Arena, **10**: 601.
Armour, Philip D., with portraits. (A. Warren) McClure, **2**: 260. — (C. H. Hepburn) Munsey, **9**: 56.
Armour Institute, Chicago. (W. J. Abbot) Outl. **48**: 993.
— — Department of Library Science. (K. L. Sharp) Lib. J. **19**: 162.
Arms and Armor. (C. King) Un. Serv. M. **9**: 45.
— — Art Ornamentation upon. (W. T. Nugent) M. of Art, **4**: 78.
— and the Men. (J. Latham) Time, **2**: 223.
— Ornamentation of Early Firearms. (W. O. Greener) M. of Art, **15**: 109.
Armstead, Henry Hugh. (M. P. Jackson) M. of Art, **3**: 420.
Armstrong, Gen. S. C. (H. Welsh) Educa. R. **6**: 105. — Lend a H. **11**: 3. — (L. C. Harvey) Chaut. **17**: 745. — (J. H. Denison) Atlan. **73**: 90. — (J. S. Emerson) Outl. **48**: 710.

Armstrong, Gen. S. C., and the Hampton Institute. (E. A. Start) New Eng. M. n. s. **6**: 442.
Armstrong, John D., with portrait. (H. D. Teetor) M. West. Hist. **13**: 57.
Armstrong, Sydney, Actress, and her Art. (A. Stoddart) Lippinc. **51**: 104.
Armstrong, W. G., Baron. Cassier, **9**: 488.
— Collection of Modern Pictures. (E. R. Dibdin) M. of Art, **14**: 158, 193.
Army. (E. Field) Un. Serv. (Phila.) **7**: 347.
— as a Career. (O. O. Howard) Forum, **21**: 34.
— Bogus Apotheosis of the. (A. Forbes) Contemp. **65**: 521.
— Competitive Examinations for, and Public Schools. (H. Knollys) Un. Serv. (Phila.) **14**: 160.
— Does it Pay to Enlist in? Un. Serv. M. **9**: 229.
— Education for. (H. F. Hardman) Un. Serv. M. **4**: 459, 551. **5**: 100, 209.
— Morale of an. (W. E. Montague) Un. Serv. M. (Phila.) **14**: 213.
— of Frederick the Great, and Army of Napoleon, Supplies of. Un. Serv. (Phila.) **13**: 201, 301, 450.
— of Northern Virginia, Allan's. (J. D. Cox) Nation, **56**: 85.
— or School? (G. W. Baird) Un. Serv. (Phila.) **10**: 303.
— Religious Service in. Blackw. **159**: 537.
Army of the Lord. (H. V. Brown) Lippinc. **54**: 132.
Army Bakery. Chamb. J. **70**: 314.
Army Legislation, Recent. (G. W. Baird) Un. Serv. (Phila.) **10**: 501.
Army Officer, British, The Ideal. Spec. **75**: 924.
— Italian, Life of. Chaut. **23**: 329.
Army Organization. Ed. R. **183**: 175.
Army Recruiting and Population. Un. Serv. M. **9**: 241.
Arnold, Edwin, with portrait. Bk. News, **9**: 283. — (L. C. Moulton) Arena, **6**: 46. — With portrait. Bk. Buyer, **7**: 491.
— Happy Hour with. (C. Scott) Eng. Illust. **12**: no. 3, 119.
— Light of Asia. (R. M. Ryan) Cath. World, **61**: 677, 809.
— Poetry of. (E. K. Chambers) Acad. **41**: 391.
— — Is it Consoling? Spec. **69**: 94. Same art. Ecl. M. **119**: 364.
Arnold, Isaac N., with portrait. (H. L. Conard) Nat'l M. (N. Y. '91) **15**: 62.
Arnold, Matthew. Dial (Ch.) **20**: 193. — (F. Harrison) 19th Cent. **39**: 433. Same art. Liv. Age, **209**: 362. — (A. B. Hyde) Meth. R. **53**: 867. — (L. Stephen) National, **22**: 458. Same art. Ecl. M. **122**: 300. Same art. Liv. Age, **200**: 90. — (J. H. Crocker) New Eng. M. n. s. **9**: 632. — (F. E. Coates) Cent. **25**: 931. — (J. Morley; W. E. Gladstone) 19th Cent. **38**: 1040. Same art. Liv. Age, **207**: 771. — (Geo. W. E. Russell) Time, **18**: 657.
— and the Celts. (M. E. Henry-Ruffin) Cath. World, **58**: 884.
— Bit of Art from. (L. A. Paton) Poet-Lore, **8**: 134.
— Blank Verse of His "Sohrab and Rustum." (H. E. Franklin) Poet-Lore, **7**: 497.
— Charm of. Spec. **75**: 814.
— Letters. (H. W. Mabie) Book R. **3**: 217. — (E. G. Johnson) Dial (Ch.) **19**: 376. — (H. Walker) Acad. **48**: 537. — (J. H. McDaniels) Nation, **61**: 451, 466. — (A. Austin) National, **26**: 471. Same art. Ecl. M. **126**: 223. Same art. Liv. Age, **208**: 46. — (E. Dowden) Sat. R. **80**: 757. — (D. F. Hannigan) Westm. **145**: 40. — (H. W. Paul) Forum, **20**: 616. — (M. Reed) New World, **5**: 262. — (C. A. L. Morse) Cath. World, **63**: 486.
— — Lesson in Style from. (J. W. Abernethy) Educa. **16**: 583.
Arnold, Matthew, Poems of, Note on. (Armine T. Kent) Time, **16**: 1.
— Poetic Characteristics of. (C. G. Barnard) Poet-Lore, **6**: 76.
— Poetry. Sat. R. **81**: 270. — Church Q. **39**: 106.
— — Ethical Tendency of. (T. Bradfield) Westm. **142**: 650. Same art. Ecl. M. **124**: 310.
— — from an Ethical Standpoint. (A. Flexner) Int. J. Ethics, **5**: 206.
— Popularity of. Spec. **70**: 382. **76**: 800.
— Some Aspects of. (G. LeG. Norgate) Temp. Bar, **109**: 540.
— Thyrsis. (C. Fisher) Temp. Bar, **108**: 388.
Arnold, Thomas, Educational Influence of. (G. Smith) Educa. R. **4**: 417.
— Semi-Centennial of Death of. Spec. **68**: 840.
Arnold Arboretum. (M. C. Robbins) Garden & F. **5**: 27. — (M. C. Robbins) Cent. **23**: 867.
Arnould-Plessy, Mme. Jeanne Sylvanie. (C. Hervey) Theatre, **18**: 194.
Aroostook County, Maine. (W. M. Thompson) New Eng. M. n. s. **13**: 65.
Arran, Isle of. (L. Higgin) M. of Art, **12**: 75-169.
Arranged Marriage. (D. Gerard) Longm. **25**: 1-551. **26**: 1.
Arrian as Legate of Cappadocia. (H. F. Pelham) Eng. Hist. R. **11**: 625.
Arrow-heads, Flint. (T. J. Chapman) M. West. Hist. **13**: 559.
Ars Amoris; a story. (B. Coll) Idler, **10**: 704.
Ars et Vita. (T. R. Sullivan) Scrib. M. **20**: 54.
Arsenic, Derivation of the Word. (F. Chance and others) Acad. **47**: 358, 381, 427. **48**: 53, 93.
— Detection and Separation of, Associated with Antimony and Tin. (F. A. Gooch and B. Hodge) Am. J. Sci. **147**: 382.
— Double-halides of, with Caesium and Rubidium, etc. (H. L. Wheeler) Am. J. Sci. **146**: 88.
— in Copper, Detection and Approximate Estimation of Minute Quantities of. (F. A. Gooch and H. P. Moseley) Am. J. Sci. **148**: 292.
— Manufacture of. Chamb. J. **70**: 149. Same art. Liv. Age, **198**: 189.
Arsenic Acid, Reduction of, by Hydrochloric Acid. (F. A. Gooch and I. K. Phelps) Am. J. Sci. **148**: 216.
Art, Advanced, Whistler as an Exponent of. (C. W. Dempsey) M. of Art, **5**: 358.
— Aims of. (G. F. Watts) M. of Art, **11**: 253.
— American, and Foreign Influence. (W. L. Fraser) Q. Illust. **2**: 3.
— — at the Paris Salon. (R. A. M. Stevenson) M. of Art, **8**: 512. — (P. Leroi) M. of Art, **9**: 485. — (C. Phillips) M. of Art, **10**: 421.
— — Types in, Some Imaginative. (R. Cortissoz) Harper, **91**: 165.
— American Taste in. M. of Art, **11**: 114.
— Ancient, in Ceylon. (J. Capper) M. of Art, **12**: 212.
— — Perrot on. (S. A. Hubbard) Dial (Ch.) **13**: 74. — Sat. R. **73**: 188.
— and Artists, American. M. of Art, **2**: 21-272.
— — of Burma. (H. L. Tilly) M. of Art, **15**: 367, 415.
— — of Scotland. Art J. **46**: 30.
— and the Common People. (D. Anderson) M. of Art, **11**: 102.
— and Ethics. (H. C. Alford) Dial (Ch.) **16**: 40.
— and Eyesight. (L. Howe) Pop. Sci. Mo. **47**: 458.
— and Handicraft. (L. F. Day) M. of Art, **11**: 410.
— and Industry. (W. E. Gladstone) Critic, **23**: 141.
— — in the 14th Century. (Wm. Morris) Time, **22**: 23.

Art and Life. (H. D. Croly) Archit. Rec. 1: 219.—(V. Paget) Contemp. 69: 658, 813. 70: 59. Same art. Ecl. M. 127: 1, 166, 378.
— — Once More. (J. Burroughs) Dial (Ch.) 15: 287.
— and Literature. (E. King) Mo. Illust. 4: 89.
— and Nature. (A. Trumble) Mo. Illust. 3: 75.
— and Religion, Reciprocity of. (F. M. Bristol) Meth. R. 54: 697.
— and Shoddy; a Reply to Criticisms. (F. Harrison) Forum, 15: 718.
— Applied, in East London. M. of Art, 19: 480.
— Artist and Artisan. (L. F. Day) M. of Art, 9: 294.
— as applied to Manufactures, National Policy in Relation to. (G. Wallis) M. of Art, 1: 173.
— as a Profession. (L. F. Day) M. of Art, 9: 122.
— Assyrian, 3,000 Years Ago. (H. Spencer) M. of Art, 19: 51.
— Byzantine. (H. Mayeux) Am. Arch. 36: 63.
— Canadian. (R. A. M. Stevenson) M. of Art, 9: 516.
— Christian. (H. Schmalz) Art J. 45: 72.
— — History of, Kraus's. Art J. 48: 223.
— — Lindsay's. Eng. R. 7: 104.
— Classical and Romantic. (P. Carus) Open Court, 2: 1095.
— Commonplace in. (W. Bayliss) M. of Art, 3: 329.
— Copyists in. (E. O. Kirk) Lippinc. 58: 506.
— Couture's Conversations on. (G. R. Halkett) M. of Art, 4: 41.
— Curiosities of. M. of Art, 3: 75.
— Current. M. of Art, 5: 388-472. 6: 170-448. 7: 347-441. 8: 346-464. 9: 345-441. 10: 109-376.—(M. H. Spielman) M. of Art, 11: 109-296. 12: 120-415.—(M. H. Spielmann and W. Armstrong) M. of Art, 13: 109-325.—(F. Wedmore and M. H. Spielmann) M. of Art, 14: 109-259.—(R. J. Slade and M. P. Jackson) M. of Art, 15: 117-289.—(C. Phillips and F. Wedmore) M. of Art, 16: 73, 109.—(M. P. Jackson and P. McNab) M. of Art, 17: 91.—(C. Phillips) M. of Art, 18: 121.—(R. J. Slade) M. of Art, 19: 92, 319, 337.
— Dawn of, Conway's. Sat. R. 73: 108.
— Decadents in, and Aubrey Beardsley. (M. Armour) M. of Art, 20: 9.
— Decline of Taste in. Sat. R. 79: 185.
— Development of Theories of. (J. E. Hodgson) M. of Art, 11: 262-361. 12: 32-279.
— Dualism in. (W. Bayliss) M. of Art, 2: 77-165.
— Early Irish. (J. R. Allen) M. of Art, 12: 118.
— Early Italian, at the New Gallery. (C. Phillips) M. of Art, 17: 145, 196.
— Education in, among the People. (G. Allen) M. of Art, 4: 145.
— Egotism in Contemporary. (R. Cortissoz) Atlan. 73: 644.
— Egyptian, of Khuenaten. (F. Petrie) M. of Art, 16: 235.
— English. (C. Adams) Mo. Illust. 3: 84.
— — Progress of, as shown at the Manchester Exhibition. (C. Phillips) M. of Art, 11: 42.
— — — as not shown at the Manchester Exhibition. (F. M. Brown) M. of Art, 11: 122.
— English Connoisseurship and Collecting. (J. C. Robinson) 19th Cent. 36: 523.
— English School in Peril. (E. Chesneau) M. of Art, 11: 25.
— — Reply. (G. Clausen) M. of Art, 11: 222.
— Eternal and Temporary. (H. Quilter) Eng. Illust. 10: 695.
— Evolution and Psychology in. (C. March) Mind, 21: 441.
— Festal Development of. (D. J. Hill) Pop. Sci. Mo. 42: 734.
Art for Art's Sake, Richard Burton on. (E. Fuller) Bookman, 1: 241.
— — Van Dyke's. (K. Cox) Nation, 56: 295.
— for Man's Sake. (G. Alexander) Poet-Lore, 6: 605.
— for the Villa. (G. Moore) M. of Art, 12: 296.
— Frauds in; the Artist's Ghost. M. of Art, 17: xlv.—(M. H. Spielmann) M. of Art, 17: 266, 311.
— French, at the Paris Exhibition, 1889. (C. Phillips). M. of Art, 13: 341-409.
— French Follies in. (P. G. Hamerton) Portfolio, 23: 144.
— Græco-Latin and Germanic. (A. Gehring) Philos. R. 5: 157.
— Græco-Roman Portraiture in Egypt. (J. F. Robertson) M. of Art, 12: 177.
— Greek, Myths in. (J. E. Harrison) M. of Art, 5: 502.
— Great Classical Fallacy of the 18th Century. (G. Allen) M. of Art, 5: 282.
— Higher Life in. (W. Bayliss) M. of Art, 1: 117.
— Historic. (F. Madox Brown) Univ. R. 2: 38.
— History of, Outline Studies in. (M. Burnside) Educa. 16: 425, 490, 549.
— — During the Renaissance in Italy, Müntz's. M. of Art, 12: 242.
— Humorists in, Exhibition of. (J. Grego) M. of Art, 12: 343.
— Illusions in. (T. J. Gullick) M. of Art, 17: 139.
— Immoral. (A. Comstock) Our Day, 13: 397.
— in America, Some Present Aspects. (C. Cook) Chaut. 23: 593.
— in Assyria. (W. Holmden) M. of Art, 9: 60, 112.
— in Australia. (W. J. Loftie) M. of Art, 9: 174.—(M. L. Manning) M. of Art, 18: 215.—(R. A. M. Stevenson) M. of Art, 9: 397.
— in South Australia and New South Wales. M. of Art, 10: 61.
— in Birmingham. (A. St. Johnston) M. of Art, 10: 159.
— in California, and What should be Done for it. (D. Tilden) Overland, n. s. 19: 509.
— in Early Education. (M. D. Hicks) Pedagog. Sem. 2: 463.
— in Education. (E. V. Eastman) Music, 5: 47.
— in Egypt. (W. Holmden) M. of Art, 9: 6.
— in England; the French Invasion. (E. R. Pennell) Nation, 57: 426.
— — French, in 18th Cent. 19th Cent. 31: 375. Same art. Liv. Age, 193: 280.
— — Future School of. (Duke of Marlborough) Fortn. 58: 595.
— — on the Queen's Accession. (J. Grego) M. of Art, 10: 366.
— in France. (W. C. Brownell) Scrib. M. 12: 329.
— — Administration of. (A. Barthélemy) Am. Arch. 52: 68.
— — Brownell's. (K. Cox) Nation, 55: 454.
— — Contemporary. (G. Mourey) Art J. 48: 215.
— — Impressionism in. (C. Waern) Atlan. 69: 535.
— in Germany, Leighton on. Art J. 46: 29.
— in Greece. (W. Holmden) M. of Art, 9: 338.
— — Mycenian, Perrot and Chipiez on. Sat. R. 79: 53.
— in Italy, Early. (L. F. Day) Art J. 46: 120.—(Penguin) Am. Arch. 43: 80.
— — How Italy retains her Hold on Art. Chaut. 15: 631.
— — in the Renaissance. (C. Phillips) Acad. 41: 19.
— — Problem of. (A. Rondani) Chaut. 17: 431.
— in its Relation to History. (W. Bayliss) M. of Art, 10: 410.
— in its Relation to Industry. (L. Alma-Tadema) M. of Art, 16: 8.
— in Japan, Treasures of. (J. H. Wigmore) Nation, 54: 319,

Art in London. (Penguin) Am. Arch. **44**: 88.
— in Metal. (J. H. Pollen) M. of Art, **1**: 51.
— in the Modern Church. (Barr Ferrée) Am. Arch. **51**: 139. **52**: 4.
— in Munich. (M. H. Spielmann) M. of Art, **18**: 73.
— in Munich: the Secessionists. (R. A. M. Stevenson) M. of Art, **17**: 415.
— in the Netherlands; the Gallery of Baron Steengracht at the Hague. M. of Art, **3**: 151, 460.
— in New York, Progress of. (G. P. Lathrop) Harper, **86**: 740.
— in New Zealand. (J. A. Blaikie) M. of Art, **10**: 32.
— in Persia. (W. Holmden) M. of Art, **9**: 166.
— in Phœnicia. (W. Holmden) M. of Art, **9**: 214.
— in Scotland, Recent. (J. L. Caw) Art J. **46**: 75.
— in Secondary Education. (J. S. Clark) Educa. R. **7**: 374.
— in the South. (W. Sartain) Southern M. **5**: 115.
— in the Streets of London. (P. Fitzgerald) M. of Art, **3**: 18-443.
— in Theory, Raymond on. (E. E. Hale, jr.) Dial (Ch.) **16**: 240.
— Indian, Notes on. (E. L. Weeks) Harper, **91**: 567.
— Individual Taste in. M. of Art, **1**: 90.
— Inspection of. (L. H. Stone) Psych. R. **1**: 126.
— Italian, and the New Art-Criticism. Quar. **184**: 454.
— Japanese. Anderson's Pictorial Arts of Japan. M. of Art, **9**: 63. — (C. Monkhouse) M. of Art, **9**: 391.
— — Note on. M. of Art, **5**: 174.
— — Personal View of. (M. Menpes) M. of Art, **11**: 192, 255.
— Life, and Literature, Quilter's Preferences in. (M. H. Spielmann) M. of Art, **16**: 139.
— Man in, Hamerton's. Spec. **70**: 362. — (W. Armstrong) Art J. **45**: 112.
— Manhood in. (W. O. Partridge) New Eng. M. n. s. **9**: 281.
— Modern and Public Taste. (W. P. Frith) Time, **20**: 122.
— — Antiquarianism in. (C. J. Shebbeare) National, **19**: 867.
— — in Belgium. M. of Art, **5**: 151.
— — in Florence. (L. Scott) M. of Art, **1**: 192. **2**: 234.
— — in Holland, and Anton Mauve. (E. Fles) M. of Art, **19**: 71.
— — Modern Life in. (F. Wedmore) M. of Art, **11**: 77.
— — of Austria-Hungary, Russia, Italy, and Spain, at the Paris Exhibition. (C. Phillips) M. of Art, **14**: 147.
— — of Belgium, at the Paris Exhibition. (C. Phillips) M. of Art, **14**: 15.
— — of Great Britain and the United States at the Paris Exhibition. (C. Phillips) M. of Art, **14**: 205.
— — of Holland, Germany, and Scandinavia at the Paris Exhibition. (C. Phillips) M. of Art, **14**: 52.
— — Thoughts on. (J. E. Millais) M. of Art, **11**: 289.
— Modern French, Feeling in. (B. Hamilton) M. of Art, **15**: 422.
— Modern Italian. (L. E. Baxter) M. of Art, **3**: 435.
— Municipal. (C. S. Sargent) Garden & F. **8**: 501.
— National Spirit in. (W. A. Sherwood) Canad. M. **3**: 498.
— Nationality in. (F. Cormon) M. of Art, **16**: 11. — Sat. R. **79**: 119.
— Nature and Evolution of. (A. Fouillée) Music, **11**: 134.
— The New Criticism. (M. Logan) Atlan. **76**: 263.
— New England, at the World's Fair. (W. H. Downes) New Eng. M. n. s. **8**: 352.
— New Phase of. (S. Dewey) Westm. **138**: 258.
— of Japan: Gonse's L'Art Japonais. M. of Art, **7**: 199.
— of Nuremberg. (W. M. Conway) M. of Art, **5**: 163.
Art of Periclean Athens. (L. R. Farnell) M. of Art, **8**: 239.
— of Savages. (A. Lang) M. of Art, **5**: 246, 303.
— of To-day, Thoughts on Our. (G. F. Watts) M. of Art, **12**: 90.
— Old Time Art and Artists. (F. Beard) Our Day, **16**: 85.
— Origin of. (L. Popoff) Pop. Sci. Mo. **44**: 827.
— Originality in. (H. Furniss) M. of Art, **16**: 20.
— Origins of, Grosse on. (A. C. Haddon) Nature, **51**: 241.
— Parisian. (A. T. Gibert) Mo. Illust. **3**: 17.
— Personality in. (G. H. Page) Westm. **139**: 646. — Same art. Ecl. M. **121**: 173.
— Philosophy of. (A. L. Frothingham, sr.) Am. J. Archæol. **9**: 165. — (A. E. Fletcher) Time, **14**: 271.
— Phœnician. (J. E. Harrison) M. of Art, **6**: 518.
— Pictorial, Accuracy in. (E. King) Mo. Illust. **3**: 153.
— Primitive, in Greece; Perrot and Chipiez on. (J. C. Van Dyke) Dial (Ch.) **18**: 142.
— Province of. M. of Art, **1**: 1.
— Purpose in. (H. Monroe) No. Am. **163**: 504.
— Realism *versus* Sloppiness in. (W. P. Frith) M. of Art, **12**: 6.
— Relation to Religion. (W. O. Partridge) Arena, **17**: 1.
— Revival of. (W. J. Stillman) Atlan. **70**: 248.
— Russian, Maskell's. (V. Stassoff) M. of Art, **9**: 249.
— Scottish, Special Exhibition of. (G. R. Halkett) M. of Art, **4**: 102.
— Seriousness in. (G. Gibbs) Mo. Illust. **13**: 67.
— Siena as a Cradle of. (R. Rodd) M. of Art, **10**: 391.
— Sporting Scenes in. (J. G. Millais, J. E. Harting, W. B. Tegetmeier, and W. A. Baillie-Grohman) M. of Art, **19**: 48-441.
— State-aided Instruction in. (A. J. Pitman) Westm. **141**: 533.
— Successful Efforts to teach, to the Masses. (H. Garland; A. C. Bernheim; J. Addams) Forum, **19**: 606.
— Talks about, W. M. Hunt's. (A. C. Meynell) M. of Art, **1**: 202.
— Teaching of. (Harry Quilter) Univ. R. **5**: 50.
— Theory of, Raymond's. Nation, **58**: 393.
— Thoughts on. (G. F. Watts) M. of Art, **12**: 253.
— Truth in. (G. F. Genung) N. World, **3**: 527.
— Utility in. (W. Tirebuck) M. of Art, **7**: 150.
— Venetian, at the New Gallery. Sat. R. **79**: 9.
— — at the New Gallery. (L. Cust) M. of Art, **18**: 208.
— Woman's Sphere in. (W. Ferrero) New R. **9**: 554.
— Works of, Spurious. (Sir C. Robinson) Ecl. M. **118**: 33.
Art Academies, Progress of, in Great Britain. (A. Beaver) M. of Art, **4**: 517.
Art Association in Western Towns, Work of. (H. Garland) Forum, **19**: 606.
Art Books of 1895. (F. Goldie) Dub. R. **119**: 271.
Art Collections, Illustrated Catalogues of. Sat. R. **73**: 738.
Art Commission, National. Am. Arch. **52**: 6.
Art Connoisseurship in England. (C. Robinson) 19th Cent. **38**: 838.
Art Crazes and Art Culture. (W. L. Courtney) Time, **3**: 213.
Art Criticism. (M. H. Spielmann) M. of Art, **13**: 116. — (A. L. Baldry) Art J. **46**: 327.
— Apologia pro Arte Meâ. (Harry Quilter) New R. **10**: 324.
— Diderot's Salons. (G. Saintsbury) M. of Art, **7**: 401.
— Foundations of. (P. G. Hamerton) Contemp. **64**: 405.
— Modern Affectations in. M. of Art, **2**: 213.
— The New and the Old. (M. W. Costello) 19th Cent. **35**: 828.

Art Education. (W. P. Frith) M. of Art, 12: 101. — (J. E. Hodgson) M. of Art, 12: 279.
— Elementary. (J. Ruskin) M. of Art, 11: 73.
— in American Life. (M. B. Martin) Am. J. Soc. Sci. 30: 12.
— for the People. (E. L. Jebb) M. of Art, 8: 294.
— National, Scheme for. (H. H. La Thanque) M. of Art, 10: 30.
— Plea for the Discouragement of. (E. R. Pennell) Nation, 55: 239.
— Posters as a Means of. M. of Art, 4: 298.
— Practical. (J. D. Linton) M. of Art, 10: 157.
Art Exhibitions in London in 1892, Autumn. (E. R. Pennell) Nation, 55: 447.
— in Whitechapel. (E. T. Cook) M. of Art, 7: 345.
— of 1893, in England. (W. Sharp) National, 21: 459.
Art Galleries, National, Common Sense in. (E. R. Pennell) Nation, 54: 49, 63.
Art Genius and Art Talent. (C. C. Billiani) Music, 5: 426.
Art Handiwork of 16th and 17th Centuries in Spitzer Collection. (A. Vallance) Art J. 45: 184.
Art Instruction at South Kensington. Art J. 46: 196.
Art Museums and Galleries in England, National. (J. C. Robinson) 19th Cent. 32: 1021.
Art Needlework. M. of Art, 3: 76-428.
— Royal School of. M. of Art, 5: 219.
Art Patrons. (F. M. Robinson) M. of Art, 10: 305, 373. 11: 158, 329. 12: 114, 307. 13: 157, 329.
Art Professorships. (W. M. Conway) M. of Art, 13: 25.
Art Sales, Curiosities of Early. Chamb. J. 73: 619. Same art. Liv. Age, 211: 660.
— of 1893. (A. C. R. Carter) Art J. 45: 270.
— Some Famous. All the Year, 72: 512.
Art School, An; What Should It Be? (B. C. Brown) Overland, n. s. 19: 30.
— Mass. Normal. (Katherine H. Parker) Bost. 1: 662.
Art Schools. (C. Cook) Mo. Illust. 4: 81.
— Artists and Art, Canadian. (J. A. Radford) Canad. M. 2: 462.
— of America. (W. S. Harwood) Cosmopol. 18: 27.
— of Paris. (L. H. Hooper) Cosmopol. 14: 59.
— of the Royal Academy. M. of Art, 2: 59.
— Slade Schools of the University of London. (C. J. Weeks) M. of Art, 6: 324.
Art Spirit. (O. A. Howland) Canad. M. 4: 493.
Art Students in Paris. (B. Day) M. of Art, 5: 510.
— — Girl. (A. Greene) M. of Art, 6: 286. — (S. H. Ward) Chaut. 15: 742. — (E. O. Somerville) M. of Art, 9: 152.
— Lady, in Munich. (C. J. Weeks) M. of Art, 4: 343.
Art Students' League of N. Y. (C. de Kay) Q. Illust. 1: 156.
Art Subjects, Experiences in Finding. (S. E. Waller) Art J. 48: 289.
— from Hinduism. (E. M. Bowden) Art J. 48: 241, 278.
Art Treasures, Destruction of. (A. Beaver) M. of Art, 10: 226.
— Found at Petrossa. M. of Art, 4: 148.
— Vicissitudes of. (R. H. Soden-Smith) M. of Art, 1: 19-77. 2: 109-168. 3: 363.
Art Unions and Art Lotteries. (J. Grego) M. of Art, 11: 245.
Art Work for Women. (L. E. Baxter) M. of Art, 7: 98.
Art of Living Together. (R. F. Horton) Sund. M. 25: 228, 411.
Artels: Co-operation in Russia. (Edith Sellers) Chamb. J. 72: 705.
Artemis and St. Nicholas. (E. Anichkoff) Folk-Lore, 5: 108.
Artesian Basin, South Dakota. (W. S. Hall) Science, 22: 29.
Artesian Boring at Galveston, Tex. (R. T. Hill) Am. J. Sci. 144: 406.
Artesian Waters in the Arid Region. (R. T. Hill) Pop. Sci. Mo. 42: 599.
Artesian Wells. (O. C. S. Carter) J. Frankl. Inst. 136: 230, 298.
— in Iowa. (E. E. Call) Science, 19: 310.
— Remarkable. Chamb. J. 71: 567.
Arthropoda, Classification of. (J. S. Kingsley) Am. Natural. 28: 118, 220.
Arthur, King, and Beowulf, as English Ideals. (S. J. McNary) Poet-Lore, 6: 529.
— Carr's. (A. B. McMahan) Dial (Ch.) 20: 160.
— Legend of. (M. Field) Munsey, 12: 64. — (C. Hanson) Theatre, 33: 291.
— — in Somerset. (Mrs. C. G. Boger) Walford's Antiq. 5: 225. 6: 12, 267.
— — Influence on Poetry and 19th Century Poets. Gent. M. n. s. 57: 105.
— Legends of. (F. Dixon) Temp. Bar, 109: 201.
— Morte d', Rhys's Malory's. (G. L. Kittredge) Nation, 58: 255.
Arthurian Legend, Rhys's. (C. F. Keary) Eng. Hist. R. 7: 130.
— on the Stage. (H. Elliott) Theatre, 33: 169.
— — at the Lyceum Theatre. Acad. 47: 65.
Arthur in Avalon; a poem. (J. A. Blaikie) M. of Art, 7: 433.
Arthur's Country, A Christmas Legend of. (Arthur Warren and J. L. Williams) Cosmopol. 20: 115.
Arthur, Prince, Appointment of, to the Aldershot Command, 1893. Spec. 71: 228.
Arthur, Chester A., Statue of. Garden & F. 6: 86.
Articular Infinitive with εἰς. (I. T. Beckwith) J. Bib. Lit. 15: 155.
Articulates, Some, Observations on the Derivation and Homologies of. (J. D. Dana) Am. J. Sci. 147: 325.
Artificial Limbs, Marks' Improvements on. J. Frankl. Inst. 136: 70.
Artillery and Cavalry. Sat. R. 77: 199.
— Distribution of, in an Army Corps. Un. Serv. M 10: 369.
— Field, of Future. (J. Gawne) Un. Serv. M. 5: 23.
— — Tactics. Un. Serv. M. 4: 432.
— for Coast Defense. (E. M. Weaver) Un. Serv. (Phila.) 7: 1.
— in 1870–71. (J. F. Maurice) Un. Serv. M. 7: 669.
— in Modern Warfare. Sat. R. 76: 153.
— Old. Antiq. n. s. 27: 144.
— Railway Batteries. (C. G. Boxall) Fortn. 64: 241.
— Russian Field, Regulations and Manœuvres. Un. Serv. (Phila.) 12: 16.
— Some Natural. (T. Wood) Sund. M. 25: 813.
Artillery Fire, Concentration of. (E. J. Granet) Un. Serv. M. 7: 1057.
— Concentration and Distribution of. (W. L. White) Un. Serv. M. 7: 923.
Artiodactyles, Miocene, from the Eastern Miohippus Beds. (O. C. Marsh) Am. J. Sci. 148: 175.
— Tertiary. (O. C. Marsh) Am. J. Sci. 148: 259.
Artist and Audience, Mutual Courtesy between. (E. B. Perry) Music, 2: 246.
— and his Model; a story. (P. Pollard) Cosmopol. 22: 175.
— Experiences of a War-. (Irving Montagu) New R. 11: 624.
— Holidays of an. (J. E. Hodgson) M. of Art, 12: 385.
— in Fiction. (K. de Mattos) M. of Art, 7: 157.
— of the Pavement; a story. Cornh. 65: 618.
— Random Reminiscences of a Special. (H. Furniss) M. of Art, 10: 316.

Artist, Trials of an; Humorous Sketch. (F. Miller) Idler, 3: 538.
Artist-life, Glimpses of. (M. H. Spielmann) M. of Art, 10: 80–228. 11: 55, 225. 12: 361. 13: 116. 17: 266. 18: 89.
Artistic Sense, Modern Life and the. (W. Crane) Cosmopol. 13: 152.
Artist's Ghost, The. (M. H. Spielmann) M. of Art, 17: 266, 311.
Artist's Romance, An. Argosy, 55: 77.
Artist's Vision, An; a story. (J. N. Robinson) Argosy, 55: 163.
Artists, Advice to Young, Leighton's. Art J. 45: 198.
Artists, Amateur, A Plea for. (Maria Theresa Earle) National, 27: 642.
— American. (W. H. Downes; F. T. Robinson) New Eng. M. n. s. 13: 289. 14: 131.
— — in Europe. M. of Art, 6: 1.
— — in Paris. (R. H. Sherard) M. of Art, 18: 224.
— as Historians. (C. Cook) Mo. Illust. 3: 97.
— Compensation of. (W. C. Lawton) Lippinc. 55: 429.
— Contemporary French, Claretie's, 2d Series. (R. A. M. Stevenson) M. of Art, 7: 461.
— Decorative, Women as. (L. E. Baxter) M. of Art, 6: 278.
— Four Australian. (R. J. Slade) M. of Art, 18: 389.
— Great Masters at Work. All the Year, 74: 373.
— Modern, and their Work. (C. S. Johnson) Munsey, 10: 337–563. 11: 3–561. 12: 3–557. 13: 3–565. 14: 3–641. 15: 48–515.
— Sketching Ground for. (K. de Mattos) M. of Art, 9: 508.
— Sketching Grounds of; Clovelly. (W. W. Fenn) M. of Art, 3: 87.
— — Ireland. (H. W. Sweny) M. of Art, 3: 165.
— — Lulworth Cove, Dorsetshire. (W. W. Fenn) M. of Art, 3: 212.
— — Oeschinnen See and Gemmi Pass. (S. Hodges) M. of Art, 3: 9.
— — Surrey Commons. M. of Art, 3: 52.
— Some Rising. (H. L. Postlethwaite) M. of Art, 17: 113.
Artists, The; a story. (V. M. Gaskins) Gent. M. n. s. 53: 1.
Artists' Haunts; Cornwall. (W. H. Tregellas) M. of Art, 1: 8, 141.
— Lynton and Lynmouth. (S. Hodges) M. of Art, 1: 225.
— Off the Track in Scotland. (S. Hodges) M. of Art, 1: 209.
— Porlock. M. of Art, 1: 169.
— Prague. (H. W. Sweny) M. of Art, 1: 37.
— Raglan Castle and the Wye. (S. Hodges) M. of Art, 1: 85.
— Sark. M. of Art, 1: 120.
Artists' Adventures Series: My First and Last Balloon Ascension. (R. V. V. Sewell) Cent. 25: 834.
— Celebrating the Fourth in Antwerp. (G. W. Edwards) Cent. 26: 457.
— Robbery on the French Coast. (A. Castaigne) Cent. 26: 926.
Artists' Association, American, of Paris. (E. H. Wuerpel) Cosmopol. 20: 402.
Artists' Orphans, Fund for. Art J. 48: 122.
Arts and Civilization, Evolution of. (G. LeBon) Pop. Sci. Mo. 42: 342.
— and Crafts, Fourth Exhibition. (L. F. Day) Art J. 45: 330. — (E. R. Pennell) Nation, 57: 284.
— — Fifth Exhibition, 1896. (L. F. Day) Art J. 48: 329. — M. of Art, 20: 32. — Sat. R. 82: 364.
Arts and Crafts Essays. Sat. R. 76: 448.
Artz, David A. C. (R. Walker) Good Words, 33: 550. Same art. Liv. Age, 194: 756.
Arun River, Along the. (C. Monkhouse) Art J. 45: 281–345.
Arundel, Philip, Earl of. (H. Thurston) Month, 86: 32.
Arundel, England, Past and Present. (A. M. Clarke) Cath. World, 64: 54.
Aryan Expulsion-and-Return Formula in Celtic Folk-Tales. Folk-Lore Rec. 4: 1.
Aryan Race. (G. D. Gurley) Ref. Q. 42: 331.
— Cradle of. (F. M. Müller) Open Court, 3: 2087.
Aryan Speech traced to the Stone Age. Knowl. 12: 77.
Aryanism, Revived, and the Modern Theistic Movement in India. (J. W. Brooks) Meth. R. 56: 559.
Aryans, Creed and Home of the Earliest. (W. F. Warren) Meth. R. 54: 76.
— Origin of. (J. S. Stuart-Glennie) Contemp. 62: 833.
Arzawa, Language of. (A. H. Sayce) Acad. 42: 154.
As Avon Flows. (H. S. Vince) Time, 10: 97–537. 11: 1–481.
As a Day in June. (M. D. Hatch) Lippinc. 55: 830.
As it Happened. (N. A. Cox) Cent. 26: 896.
As One Having Authority; a story. (H. C. Bunner) Scrib. M. 12: 201.
As the Sparks Fly Upwards; a story. (P. Bruce) Eng. Illust. 4: 465.
As Strangers. (Annie Trumbull) Scrib. M. 20: 189.
As Told to His Grace; stories. (W. McLennan) Harper, 88: 129–704.
As Told by Teresita. (A. Herrick) Overland, n. s. 27: 147.
Asaph; a story. (F. R. Stockton) Cosmopol. 13: 91.
Asbestos. (G. H. Guy) Am. Arch. 53: 47.
Ascending Magdalen; a poem. (M. C. Smith) Harper, 90: 559.
Ascetic Rake, The; a story. (A. J. Dawson) Idler, 10: 31.
Asceticism, Christian. (S. A. Alexander) Thinker, 8: 321, 509.
Asclepia. Stapelia Gigantea. (W. Watson) Garden & F. 8: 514.
Ascot Race-course. (R. H. Davis) Harper, 87: 251.
Asgill for Hayne. (Mrs. M. Richardson) Am. Hist. Reg. 1: 455.
Ash Tree. (G. Paxton) Knowl. 19: 234.
— White. (C. S. Sargent) Garden & F. 7: 402.
— Fraxinus Bungeana. (C. S. Sargent) Garden & F. 7: 5.
Ashantee; Celebration of the Yam Custom. Macmil. 73: 115.
— Troubles in. Sat. R. 80: 677, 679.
Ashbee, Henry Spencer. Bookworm, 2: 257.
Ashburnham MSS. Walford's Antiq. 3: 114.
Asheville, N. C., Round About. (Bailey Willis) Nat. Geog. M. 1: 291.
Ashmole, Elias. (E. Walford) Walford's Antiq. 9: 51, 99.
Ashton, James Martin, with portrait. (W. L. Visscher) M. West. Hist. 13: 187.
Ashton, John, Essays of. Spec. 72: 541.
Ashurbanipal; His Books and Buildings. (L. W. King) Illus. Archæol. 2: 65.
Ashwell, Lena, with portrait. Theatre, 36: 90.
Asia, Across, on a Bicycle. (T. G. Allen, jr., and W. L. Sachtleben) Cent. 26: 83–915.
— — — by Allen and Sachtleben. Sat. R. 79: 531.
— Central. (A. Vámbéry) 19th Cent. 32: 104. Same art. Ecl. M. 119: 238.
— — Across the Backbone of Asia. (H. Lansdell) Good Words, 35: 373.
— — Cartography of, Russian Contributions to. (R. Michell) Asia R. 12: 249. 13: 311. 14: 74.
— — China in. (M. Bell) Asia R. 9: 327.

Asia, Central, Chinese, Lansdell's. Church Q. 38: 327.
— — Development of, with English Capital. Asia R. 9: 241.
— — Expedition to, of Capt. Roborovsky and Lieut. Kozloff. Geog. J. 8: 161.
— — Grambcheffsky's Expedition. (W. B. Steveni) Asia. R. 13: 17.
— — Gray's Journey from Assam to Sources of the Irawadi. Geog. J. 3: 221.
— — Dr. Sven Hedin's Travels in. Geog. J. 5: 154.
— — Journey Across. (G. R. Littledale) Geog. J. 3: 447.
— — Journeyings in. (Earl of Dunmore) Geog. J. 2: 385.
— — Prjevalski's Last Journey. (C. Johnston) Asia. R. 18: 133.
— — Russia in. Liv. Age, 192: 323.
— — Russian Policy in. (J. M. Hubbard) Nation, 59: 400.
— — Younghusband's Travels in. Sat. R. 81: 485.
— Eastern, America's Interest in. (J. Barrett) No. Am. 162: 257.
— — Balance of Power in. Blackw. 154: 397.
— — Count Széchenyi's Travels in. (F. v. Richthofen) Geog. J. 3: 311.
— England and France in. (L. Griffin) 19th Cent. 34: 673.
— European Partners in. Contemp. 67: 609.
— Permanent European Dominion in. (A. C. Lyall) 19th Cent. 38: 381.
— Political and Commercial Affairs in, 1896. Ed. R. 183: 237.
— Railroad Invasion of. (C. Morris) Lippinc. 56: 83.
— Russia and England in, 1892. Sat. R. 74: 189–267.
— Western, Knight's Travels in. Sat. R. 75: 632.
Asia Minor and Syria, Early History of. (J. E. Gilmore) Eng. Hist. R. 10: 1.
— Glimpse of. Liv. Age, 192: 503.
— Historical Geography of, Ramsay's. Quar. 175: 211.
Asiatic Immigration to British Colonies. Chamb. J. 71: 406.
Asoka Edicts in Mysore. (J. Burgess) Acad. 43: 134.
Asoka Pillar in the Terai, The. (G. Bühler) Acad. 47: 360.
Asolan Country, In the. (E. Benson) New R. 15: 300. Same art. Liv. Age, 211: 115.
Asolo. (P. E. Pinkerton) M. of Art, 10: 173. — (C. DeKay) Critic, 20: 332.
Asparagus; a Vegetable with a Pedigree. Chamb. J. 71: 75.
— Cultivation of. (T. D. Hatfield) Garden & F. 9: 157.
— Culture of, for City and Village Lots. (W. W. Tracy) Garden & F. 9: 7.
— Decorative. (W. H. Taplin) Garden & F. 6: 79.
Asphalt and Bitumens. (S. P. Sadtler) Am. Arch. 49: 123. — (S. P. Sadtler) J. Frankl. Inst. 140: 198.
Asphaltic Pavement, Petroleum in its Relations to. (S. F. Peckham) Am. J. Sci. 147: 28.
Asphaltum, Analysis by Acetone. (S. F. Peckham) J. Frankl. Inst. 141: 219.
Aspinall, Clarke. (W. Tirebuck) Acad. 43: 387.
Aspinwall Family. (E. A. Bowen) N. E. Reg. 47: 342.
Aspirations; a story. (A. Hope) Idler, 7: 147.
Aspirations — Explanations; two dialogues. (A. Hope Hawkins) McClure, 8: 85.
Asquith, Herbert Henry. (W. T. Stead) R. of Rs. (N. Y.) 11: 553. — Sat. R. 80: 164. — New R. 10: 552.
Assam, Resources of. Dub. R. 110: 189.
Assassin in Private Life. (T. H. S. Escott) Time, 2: 513.
Assassins, Order of. (H. Porter) Bib. Sac. 52: 113.
Assaying at Mines and Works. (H. V. F. Furman) Engin. M. 10: 1093.
Asses, Wild and Tame. (M. Bell) Month, 76: 398.
Assessments, Political. (T. Roosevelt) Atlan. 70: 103.
Assignats, The. (E. Levasseur) J. Pol. Econ. 2: 179.
Assimilation and Association. (J. Ward) Mind, 18: 347. 19: 509.
Assisi and St. Francis. (M. S. Stillman) Nation, 55: 317.
Assisted Destiny, An. (F. Lynde) Scrib. M. 18: 92.
Associated Effort and its Influence on Human Progress. (M. L. Holbrook) Arena, 16: 462.
Association. (M. W. Calkins) Psychol. R. 3: 32, also supp. — (H. Münsterberg) Psychol. R. 1: 476.
— Cases of, Classification of. (M. W. Calkins) Philos. R. 1: 389.
— Mediate. (W. G. Smith) Mind, 19: 289. — (H. C. Howe) Am. J. Psychol. 6: 239.
Association of Colleges and Preparatory Schools of the Middle States and Maryland. (L. C. Hull) School R. 3: 87, 152.
Association Philosophy, The. (P. Carus) Open Court, 7: 3611.
Associations, Regulation of, in France, Bill for, 1892. Spec. 68: 256.
— Voluntary. (C. R. Henderson) Am. J. Sociol. 1: 327.
Assogue, The; a Peculiar British Mammal. (O. Thomas) Nat. Sci. 6: 377.
Assuân, Christmas Shopping at. (A. Repplier) Atlan. 75: 681.
Assyria, Discoveries in, History of. (Hormuzd Rassam) Asia. R. 18: 86.
— Excavations in. (R. F. Harper) Bib. World, 7: 23.
— First Contact with Israel. (R. W. Rogers) Meth. R. 55: 207.
— History of, Sketch of. (D. G. Lyon) Bib. World, 7: 425.
— Name, Continuance of. (D. A. Lincke) Asia. R. 17: 371.
Assyrian Arrowheads and Jewish Books. Talk at a Country House. (E. Strachey) Atlan. 73: 306.
Assyrian Dictionaries. (F. Brown) Nation, 60: 304.
Assyrian Monuments, Bible and the. (M. Jastrow, jr.) Cent. 25: 395.
Assyrian Stele, A New. (C. H. W. Johns) Acad. 48: 13.
Assyrians, Ethics of. (M. Jastrow) Eth. Rec. 3: 66.
Assyriology, Half-century of. (D. G. Lyon) Bib. World, 8: 125.
Asteck Opal, The; a story. (R. Ottolengui) Idler, 7: 359.
Asterisms, Early. (J. N. Lockyer) Nature, 48: 438, 518. 49: 199.
Asteroids Ceres, Pallas, Juno, and Vesta. (E. E. Barnard) Pop. Astron. 3: 143.
— Collision between, Effects of. (S. J. Corrigan) Astron. 12: 207, 304.
— Groups of. (D. Kirkwood) Astron. 11: 785.
— Relation of, to the Planetary System. (D. Kirkwood) Pop. Astron. 1: 19.
Astley, John Dugdale. Fifty Years of my Life. Sat. R. 77: 614.
Astor, J. J. and Wm.; with portraits. (F. Allaben) Nat'l M. (N. Y. '91) 18: 305.
Astor Family, The. (W. S. Bridgman) Munsey, 7: 527. — (H. Payne) Munsey, 11: 526.
Astor Library, N. Y. (F. Saunders) M. Am. Hist. 29: 150.
Astorga, Emmanuel de. (J. F. Rowbotham) Good Words, 37: 189.
Astounding Episode at No. 9. (E. Phillpotts) Idler, 6: 741.
Astragals. Reliquary, 35: 154.
Astrolabe, The. (Marg. L. Huggins) Pop. Astron. 2: 199, 261. 13: 793.
Astrologer at Large; an Interview with Old Moore. (L. F. Austin) Eng. Illust. 16: 396.
Astrology and Wm. Lilly. (E. Walford) Walford's Antiq. 10: 147.

Astrology: Forecast of Administration of Pres. Cleveland. (J. Erickson) Arena, 10: 536.
— at the Close of the 19th Century. (E. Lee) Arena, 6: 592.
— in London. (E. Lee) Arena, 7: 221.
— Man in his Relation to the Solar System. (J. H. Smith) Arena, 15: 755, 886.
— 17th Century. Pop. Sci. Mo. 45: 686.
— Survivals of. (M. B. Snyder) J. Am. Folk-Lore, 3: 127.
Astronomers, Catholic. (D. T. O'Sullivan) Am. Cath. Q. 17: 369.
— The Great. (Sir Robert Ball) Good Words, 35: 231-835.
— of 20th Century, Some Problems about to Confront. (J. K. Rees) Science, n. s. 3: 717.
Astronomical Instruments, Electric Controls and Governors for. (F. L. O. Wadsworth) Astron. 13: 265
Astronomical Photography. (R. A. Gregory) Good Words, 35: 190.
— Progress of. (H. C. Russell) Pop. Astron. 2: 101, 170.
Astronomical Symbols in America. (S. D. Peet) Am. Antiq. 18: 174.
Astronomy. (J. E. Gore) Gent. M. n. s. 49: 46, 331.
— America's Achievements in. (E. S. Holden) Forum, 15: 744.
— Ancient Egyptian. (J. N. Lockyer) Nature, 45: 296, 373.
— and Civilization. (A. W. Nitsch) Pop. Astron. 4: 206.
— and Geological Evolution. (R. G. M. Browne) Westm. 139: 430.
— and Geology, Union of. (Sir J. Cowell) New Sci. R. 1: 257.
— and Religion. (E. Arnold) No. Am. 159: 404.
— and Worship in Ancient Egypt. (J. N. Lockyer) 19th Cent. 32: 29.
— Babylonian. (A. L. Cortie) Month, 74: 528.
— Celestial Curiosities. (E. S. Dixon) Time, 6: 609.
— Celestial Mechanics, Progress of, since the Middle of the Century. (G. W. Hill) Science, n. s. 3: 333.
— Course of, for Engineering Students. (G. C. Comstock) Science, n. s. 2: 502.
— Dawn of, Lockyer's. Ed. R. 108: 418. — (C. S. Peirce) Nation, 58: 234.
— Descriptive, Teaching of. (H. A. Howe) Pop. Astron. 4: 225.
— Egyptian, and Exact Science. (W. M. Adams) Ath. '95, 2: 324.
— Fundamental, Neglected Field of. (J. R. Eastman) Astron. 12: 126, 315.
— Growth and Magnitude of Sidereal Heavens. (W. H. Lamaster) Pop. Astron. 3: 226.
— in High Schools. (E. Miller) Pop. Astron. 3: 161.
— Is the Universe Infinite? (Sir R. Ball) Fortn. 59: 620.
— Making it Popular. (Mary Proctor) Pop. Astron. 2: 418.
— Modern. (G. E. Latham) Munsey, 9: 95.
— The New. (Sir R. Ball) Fortn. 57: 10. Same art. Ecl. M. 118: 254. Same art. Liv. Age, 192: 515.
— — Ball on. Sat. R. 74: 57.
— Observations for Beginners. (W. W. Payne) Pop. Astron. 3: 14, 121.
— of the Incas. (J. Du Gourcq) Pop. Sci. Mo. 45: 823.
— The Old. (T. H. B. Graham) Gent. M. n. s. 49: 493. Same art. Ecl. M. 120: 44.
— Old and New, Proctor and Ranyard on. Ed. R. 177: 544. — Nature, 48: 361. — Pub. Opin. 15: 210.
— Phenomena for 1896. (H. C. Wilson) Pop. Astron. 3: 236.
— Photography in. (Camille Flammarion) Cosmopol. 21: 484.
Astronomy, Physical, Study of. (T. J. J. See) Pop. Astron. 2: 249, 289, 337.
— Pleasures of the Telescope. (G. P. Serviss) Pop. Sci. Mo. 47: 194.
— Program for 1895. (C. A. Young) Pop. Astron. 2: 308.
— Progress of, 1894. (J. K. Rees) Science, n. s. 2: 5.
— Recent Discoveries in. (G. M. Searle) Cath. World, 57: 164.
— Revelations of. (W. Mathews) Pub. Opin. 15: 277.
— Study of. (W. W. Payne) Pop. Astron. 4: 57, 116.
— What is? (G. P. Serviss) Chaut. 18: 541.
— Woman's Work in. (Mrs. M. Fleming) Astron. 12: 683.
— — at the Harvard Observatory. (H. L. Reed) New Eng. M. n. s. 6: 165.
— World's Debt to. (S. Newcomb) Chaut. 20: 286.
Asylum in Legations and Consulates and in Vessels. (J. B. Moore) Pol. Sci. Q. 7: 1-397.
Asylums, History of, Burdett's. Sat. R. 73: 252.
— Modern Private; Defence. (W. T. H. Haslett) Westm. 143: 307.
Asyma; a story. (A. D. Karkavitsas) Overland, n. s. 21: 181.
At the Academy; a poem. (C. Monkhouse) M. of Art, 13: 332.
At the Brewery; a story. (H. Garland) Cosmopol. 13: 34.
At the Bunch of Grapes Inn. (M. K. Champion) New Eng. M. n. s. 12: 313.
At a Conversazione; a story. (B. Durham) Eng. Illust. 13: 547.
At Cross Purposes; a story. All the Year, 73: 204.
At Duty's Bidding; a story. (G. W. Carryl) Munsey, 13: 42.
At the End of the World. All the Year, 75: 228.
At the Farm by the Sea. Liv. Age, 195: 113.
At the Grand Hotel du Paradis; a story. (T. A. Janvier) Harper, 91: 510.
At the Great Durbar; a story. (F. A. Steel) Cornh. 74: 503.
At the Green Dragon: an Episode. (B. Harraden) Blackw. 154: 159. Same art. Liv. Age, 198: 781.
At the Hands of Time; a story. (B. Vye) Belgra. 82: 179.
At the Hermitage; a story. (E. L. Brown) Harper, 87: 465.
At the Hop-pole Inn; a story. (E. E. Bigelow) Lippinc. 55: 503.
At the Hotel Grand St. Louis; a story. (G. Peel) Harper, 93: 780.
At the Ice-hills; a story. Cornh. 67: 34.
At the Keith Ranch. (A. Fuller) Cent. 23: 761.
At Last; a story. (Mrs. P. B. Pattisson) Un. Serv. M. 3 ('89): 547, 700. 4 ('89-'90): 53, 191.
At the Little Red House. (K. Jordan) Lippinc. 54: 522.
At Market Value. (G. Allen) Chamb. J. 71: 1-456.
At Marrini's. (R. H. Potts) Lippinc. 54: 113.
At the Meeting of the Circle. (J. M. Lippmann) New Eng. M. n. s. 8: 401.
At Point o' Bugles; a story. (G. Parker) Idler, 6: 603.
At a Private View; a story. (B. Matthews) Harper, 88: 491.
At the Rising of the Moon; a story. (F. Mathew) Idler, 2: 310.
At the Road-house; Verses in Memory of R. L. Stevenson. (B. Carman) Poet-Lore, 7: 397.
At the Rough-and-Tumble Landing. (C. G. D. Roberts) Lippinc. 54: 240.
At St. Margaret's; a story. (C. S. Ross) Outing, 21: 279.
At St. Mary's. (H. C. Hale) Scrib. M. 19: 770.
At Sea; a sketch. (M. Morris) 19th Cent. 40: 412.

At the Seigneurie; a story. (A. M. Trotter) Argosy, 58: 154.
At Set of Sun; a poem. (C. Burke) Temp. Bar, 103: 82.
At the Sign of the Eagle; a story. (G. Parker) National, 21: 518. Same art. Liv. Age, 198: 264.
At the Sign of the Pantuffel. Temp. Bar, 98: 83. Same art. Liv. Age, 198: 77.
At the Sign of the Red Cross. (G. H. Redding) Overland, n. s. 23: 612.
At the Spring; a poem. (N. M'Cormick) Argosy, 58: 26.
At the Stage Door. (R. N. Stephens) Lippinc. 50: 502.
At Sunrise; a story. (C. E. Huse) Un. Serv. (Phila.) 10: 430.
At the Turn of the Tide. (W. R. A. Wilson) New Eng. M. n. s. 13: 600.
At the Waterloo Banquet. Cornh. 72: 48. Same art. Liv. Age, 206: 536.
Atavism. (F. L. Oswald) Open Court, 7: 3705.
— and Evolution. (C. Lombroso) Contemp. 68: 42.
Atchison, Topeka, and Santa Fé Railroad. (C. S. Gleed) Cosmopol. 14: 465.
Athabasca River, Grand Rapids of the; a poem. (E. S. Colcleugh) Outing, 26: 31.
— Mount Brown and the Sources of the. (A. P. Coleman) Geog. J. 5: 53.
Athanasia in Search of a Creed. (H. E. M. Stutfield) Blackw. 153: 196.
Athanasian Creed, Date of. Eng. R. 11: 140.
Athanasianism. (L. L. Paine) N. World, 3: 634.
Athanasius, St., Select Works and Letters. Church Q. 36: 273.
Atheism and Philanthropy, Relations of. Spec. 69: 678. Same art. Ecl. M. 120: 54.
— Shelley's. (A. F. Sanborn) Open Court, 2: 1189.
— under Elizabeth and James I. (J. M. Stone) Month, 81: 174.
Athelwold; a play. (A. Rives) Harper, 84: 394.
Athena, Myth of. (P. Lafargue) Time, 23: 916.
Athénaïse. (K. Chopin) Atlan. 78: 232, 404.
Athens, Acropolis; Archaic Pediment Reliefs from, and Vase-painting. (C. L. Brownson) Am. J. Archæol. 8: 28.
— — Bronze Fragments of. (A. G. Bather) J. Hel. Stud. 13: 124.
— — Bronze Reliefs from. (P. Wolters) Am. J. Archæol. 11: 350.
— — Temple of, Burnt by the Persians. (H. N. Fowler) Am. J. Archæol. 8: 1.
— — Traces Connected with Original Entrance of. (F. C. Penrose) J. Hel. Stud. 15: 248.
— — Vase-fragments from. (G. C. Richards) J. Hel. Stud. 14: 186.
— American School at. (M. L. D'Ooge) Chaut. 16: 387, 515. — (J. R. Wheeler) Harv. Grad. M. 2: 18.
— and its Acropolis. Temp. Bar, 101: 568. Same art. Liv. Age, 201: 371.
— Archæological Schools in. Sat. R. 80: 406.
— British School at. Acad. 46: 71.
— Cycling in. (T. G. Allen, jr.) Outing, 28: 173, 310.
— Enneacrunus at. (J. W. White) Nation, 58: 120.
— Every-day. (N. W. Williams) Gent. M. n. s. 50: 368. Same art. Ecl. M. 120: 798.
— Fall of, Causes of. Macmil. 71: 311.
— — Church on. Spec. 73: 730.
— German Excavations at. (J. B. Bury) Ath. '96, 1: 257.
— Grave-monuments from. (T. W. Heermance) Am. J. Archæol. 10: 469.
— Heresy at, in the Time of Plato. (F. B. Tarbell) N. World, 2: 687.
Athens in 1895. Sat. R. 80: 573.
— Modern, In and About. (W. E. Waters) Chaut. 17: 131.
— Modern Maid of Athens and Her Brothers of To-Day. (W. E. Waters) Chaut. 17: 259.
— The New. Macmil. 69: 116.
— Religion of. (A. B. Hyde) Meth. R. 52: 576.
— Visit to. (W. C. Doane) Harper, 93: 3.
— Work and Wages in. (F. B. Jevons) J. Hel. Stud. 15: 239.
Athensville Crusade, The; a story. (W. L. Alden) Idler, 5: 312.
Atherton, G., Novels of. (W. S. Walsh) Lippinc. 50: 412.
Athlete, American, in England. (J. Corbin) Bach. of Arts, 1: 577.
— English, in America. (F. S. Horan) Bach. of Arts, 2: 145.
Athletes at the University of California. Overland, n. s. 20: 80.
— A Gallery of. (E. B. Osborn) New R. 12: 441.
— Training of. (M. W. Ford) Outing, 19: 421.
Athletic Clubs, Life at the. (D. Edwards) Scrib. M. 18: 4.
Athletic Extravagance. (W. Camp) Outing, 26: 81.
Athletic Life. (B. W. Richardson) Longm. 23: 251.
Athletic Prize Men in Greek Art. (W. Pater) Contemp. 65: 242.
Athletic Records, Past and Present. (S. Scoville, jr.) Outing, 22: 206.
Athletic Sports of Ancient Days. (T. J. de la Hunt) Lippinc. 56: 838.
— Question of. (F. L. Oswald) Open Court, 8: 4051.
Athletics. Spec. 77: 76.
— Amateur American, in 1896. (W. B. Curtis) Outing, 29: 161, 272.
— and Health. (E. L. Godkin) Nation, 59: 457.
— and Photography. Outing, 19: 404, 445.
— at Harvard. (W. D. Orcutt) Munsey, 11: 376.
— — Are the Harvard Teams Representative? (E. L. Conant) Harv. Grad. M. 3: 330.
— — Committee on. (J. W. White) Harv. Grad. M. 1: 209.
— — Report on. Lend a H. 14: 217.
— — Harvard's Policy. (A. B. Hart) Harv. Grad. M. 4: 209.
— at Oxford and Cambridge. (M. Shearman; R. W. Turner) Eng. Illust. 9: 441.
— College. (W. Camp) Cent. 24: 204. — (F. A. Walker) Harv. Grad. M. 2: 1.
— — and Higher Education. Spec. 76: 767.
— — Morality in. (O. S. Jones) No. Am. 160: 638.
— — Professionals in. Bach. of Arts, 1: 559.
— — Robt. J. Cook on. Bach. of Arts, 3: 145.
— Counter-Blast to. Spec. 69: 492.
— Craze for. (E. L. Godkin) Nation, 57: 422.
— Development of, in the United States. (C. W. Whitney) Fortn. 60: 412.
— Faculty Control of, at English Universities. (J. W. Laing) Outing, 27: 490.
— for City Girls. (M. T. Bissell) Pop. Sci. Mo. 46: 145.
— Glorification of. (R. Ogden) Nation, 55: 406.
— in Japan. (J. A. MacPhail) Outing, 21: 176.
— in Italy, Mosso's. Sat. R. 77: 49.
— International Contests of 1895. Outing, 26: 454. 27: 157.
— Intercollegiate, and Faculty Control. Outing, 26: 325.
— Limit of, for Brain Workers. (M. Thompson) Chaut. 19: 148.
— Outreachings of. Nation, 60: 235.
— Philosophy of the Bleachers. (G. Santayana) Harv. Mo. 18: 181.

Athletics, Place of. (B. W. Richardson) Sat. R. 80: 167.
— — in Popular Estimation. (R. R. Williams) Munsey, 8: 169.
— Professor's View of. (F. W. Taussig) Harv. Grad. M. 3: 305.
— Tournaments and Matches. Cornh. 68: 84. Same art. Ecl. M. 121: 721.
— Track, in California. (P. L. Weaver, jr.) Overland, n. s. 19: 609.
— — at Yale. (S. Scoville, jr.) Outing, 21: 450.
— — Starting and Starters. (J. Corbin) Outing, 22: 151.
— — Track and Field Records of English and American Universities. (S. Scoville, jr.) Bach. of Arts, 2: 647.
Atkins, Jearum, and his Inventions. (R. D. O. Smith) Cassier, 5: 109.
Atkinson, Canon, at Home. Sund. M. 23: 112.
Atkinson, Fort, on the Missouri. (W. H. Eller) Nat'l M. (N. Y. '91) 18: 29.
Atlanta, Georgia. (A. M. Young) Southern M. 4: 277.
— Capitol at. (A. H. Noll) Am. Arch. 39: 13.
— Cotton States and International Exposition. (C. Howell) R. of Rs. (N. Y.) 11: 159. — (W. A. Coffin) Nation, 61: 324. — (W. Y. Atkinson) No. Am. 161: 385. — (J. K. Ohl) Chaut. 21: 555.
Atlantic Cable, Possibilities of Communication by. (J. H. Heaton) No. Am. 160: 651.
Atlantic Cables, Two New. Chamb. J. 71: 303. Same art. Ecl. M. 123: 134.
Atlantic City. Cornh. 70: 474.
Atlantic Islands, Cycling in. (O. Howarth) Outing, 27: 288, 392.
Atlantic Ocean, Crossing the. Cornh. 69: 593. Same art. Liv. Age, 202: 30. Same art. Ecl. M. 123: 417.
— Geographical Knowledge in Time of Columbus. (A. Hautreux) Un. Serv. (Phila.) 10: 203.
— North, Currents of. (R. Beynon) Knowl. 15: 155.
— — Life in. (G. F. Wright) Nation, 59: 422.
— — Pilot Chart, U. S. Chamb. J. 72: 437.
— Race Across. Liv. Age, 193: 195.
Atlantic Record, A Run for the. (J. Milne) Gent. M. n. s. 52: 47. Same art. Ecl. M. 122: 562.
Atlantic Telegraph, Field on. Dial (Ch.) 14: 175.
Atlantis, Life from the Lost. (St. G. Mivart) Fortn. 65: 801. Same art. Liv. Age, 209: 810.
— Lost, Wilson on. (F. Starr) Dial (Ch.) 14: 178.
Atlas Mountains, Excursion in the. (W. B. Harris) Blackw. 160: 195. Same art. Liv. Age, 210: 739.
— Journey in, Harris's. Sat. R. 81: 176.
Atmosphere, and its Newly Discovered Properties. (A. E. Dolbear) Arena, 6: 1.
— General Circulation of. (J. M. Pernter) Nature, 45: 593.
— Hygiene of. (S. Lockwood) No. Am. 155: 446.
— in Art. (J. Hawthorne) Bk. News, 7: 1.
— New Element of the. (J. Dewar) New Sci. R. 1: 244.
— Physical Phenomena of the High Regions of. (A. Cornu) Nature, 53: 588.
— Pressure of. (H. Harries) Longm. 28: 373. Same art. Ecl. M. 127: 369.
— Secrets of. (H. A. Hazen) Science, 21: 202.
Atmospheres of the Moon, Planets, and Sun. (G. H. Bryan) Science, 22: 311.
Atmospheric Heat. (S. Charlesworth) Gent. M. n. s. 56: 49.
Atoll, A Growing. (H. R. Mill) Nature, 51: 203.
Atomic Theory; Atoms and Sunbeams. (Sir R. Ball) Fortn. 60: 464. Same art. Liv. Age, 199: 515. Same art. Ecl. M. 121: 721.
— Completed Chapter in History of. (E. W. Morley) Science, n. s. 4: 241.
Atomic Theory, Wilde on. (R. Meldola) Nature, 46: 568.
Atomic Weights, Notes on. (A. Scott) Sci. Prog. 5: 202.
— of the Elements, Numerical Relations Existing between. (M. C. Lea) Am. J. Sci. 151: 386.
Atoms and Molecules, The Individuality of. (H. H. Higgins) Open Court, 2: 1011, 1025.
— Color Relations of Molecules and. (M. C. Lea) Am. J. Sci. 149: 357.
— Ions and Molecules, Color Relations of. (M. C. Lea) Am. J. Sci. 151: 405.
— Space Relations of. (A. Eiloart) Sci. Prog. 3: 490. 4: 132, 448.
Atonement, The. (B. E. Howard) Arena, 5: 354.
— Anselmic Theory of. (A. J. Heller) Ref. Q. 41: 476.
— Conquering Cross of Christ. (J. Cook) Our Day, 13: 541.
— Development of Doctrine of, from the Time of Christ until 730 A. D. (C. E. Corwin) Ref. Q. 43: 375.
— — 730–1710 A. D. (C. E. Corwin) Ref. Q. 43: 497.
— the Divine Sacrifice. (E. M. Gaillard) Contemp. 67: 265.
— Incarnation and. (S. N. Callender) Ref. Q. 39: 201.
— Gladstone on. (J. K. Smyth) N. Church R. 2: 112.
— Methodist Doctrine of. (S. McChesney) Meth. R. 54: 268.
— New Testament Idea of. (A. G. Voigt) Luth. Q. 25: 310.
— Paul's Doctrine of. (C. C. Everett) New World, 5: 79.
Attempt and Intent, Recent Decisions Concerning. (S. Rogers) Law Q. 10: 164.
Attention, An Analysis of. (A. F. Shand) Mind, 19: 449.
— and Distraction. (Alice J. Hamlin) Am. J. Psychol. 8: 3.
— and Habit, Study in. (J. R. Angell and A. W. Moore) Psychol. R. 3: 245.
— and Visual Perception, Development of. (H. Griffing) Am. J. Psychol. 7: 227.
— and Will. (A. F. Shand) Mind, 68: 450.
— as Intensifying Sensation, Münsterberg on. (H. M. Stanley) Psychol. R. 2: 53.
— Disturbance of, During Simple Mental Processes. (E. J. Swift) Am. J. Psychol. 5: 1.
— Effective. (E. B. Titchener) Philos. R. 3: 429.
— Experimental and Critical. (F. Drew) Am. J. Psychol. 8: 533.
— Fluctuations of. (J. B. Hylan) Psychol. R. 3: 56.
— Intensifying Effect of. (H. Münsterberg) Psycholog. R. 1: 39.
— Is it Original or Derivative? (G. A. Cogswell) Philos. R. 3: 462.
— Memory After-Image and. (A. H. Daniels) Am. J. Psychol. 6: 558.
— Morbid States of. (T. Ribot) Open Court, 3: 1944.
— Phenomena of, Experimental Research upon. (J. R. Angell; A. H. Pierce) Am. J. Psychol. 4: 528.
— Physical Characteristics of. (R. MacDougall) Psychol. R. 3: 158.
— Psychology of. (T. Ribot) Open Court, 3: 1777–1868.
— Sensory Stimulation by. (J. G. Hibben) Psychol. R. 2: 369.
— Voluntary. (T. Ribot) Open Court, 3: 1873.
Attleboro, Mass. (G. Randall) New Eng. M. n. s. 11: 225.
Attorneys, "Sleeping." (J. D. Lindsay) Green Bag, 5: 11.
Attray's Wife. (H. F. Abell) Chamb. J. 73: 561–611.
Attucks, Crispus, and Boston Massacre. (F. J. Moses) Bost. 1: 641.

Atwater, Wm. O. R. of Rs. (N. Y.) **13**: 679.
Atwood, William. (C. P. Daly) Green Bag, **7**: 121, 188, 242.
Au Sucrérie; a sketch. (S. J. Robertson) Canad. M. **7**: 60.
Aubrey, John. Biographical Collections. (A. Clark) Eng. Hist. R. **11**: 328.
Auburn, A Scottish. (P. A. Graham) Chamb. J. **72**: 753.
Aucassin and Nicolette. (G. Petrie) Southern M. **5**: 87.
Auch; a Gascon City and its Church. (R. Twigge) Dub. R. **116**: 63.
Auchisaurus, Restoration of. (O. C. Marsh) Am. J. Sci. **145**: 169.
Auchmuty, Richard F. (E. E. Hale) Lend a H. **11**: 125.
Auckland Castle. (E. Venables) Good Words, **35**: 752.
Auction-room, Recollections of. (W. C. Hazlitt) Bookworm, **7**: 1, 33.
Auctions and Knock-outs. Chamb. J. **72**: 777.
Auditors. (A. H. Gibson) Bank. M. (Lond.) **58**: 481.
Audience, American. (K. Hackett) Music, **5**: 280.
Audiences. (E. E. Hale) Outl. **48**: 709.
— Are They too Patient? (A. Berlyn) Theatre, **28**: 140.
Audition, Colored, Problem of. (A. Binet) Pop. Sci. Mo. **43**: 812.
Auditoriums, How to find the Key-Note of. (E. Cutter) Am. J. Sci. **150**: 449.
Audley, Hugh. (G. Goodwin) Acad. **45**: 270.
Audubon, John James. (B. W. Duke) So. M. **3**: 3.
— Story of his Youth. Scrib. M. **13**: 267.
Augite and Plagioclase, Fibrous Intergrowth of. (W. S. Bayley) Am. J. Sci. **143**: 515.
Augsburg, The Angel of. (P. Carus) Open Court, **10**: 4901.
Augsburg Confession, Article 6. "The New Obedience." (C. S. Albert) Luth. Q. **22**: 385.
— Article 7, Holman Lecture on. (P. Bergstresser) Luth. Q. **23**: 301.
Augsburg Printers of 15th Century. Bookworm, **7**: 201.
August; a poem. (A. C. Swinburne) M. of Art, **11**: 335.
Augusta, Maine. (E. W. Hamlin) New Eng. M. n. s. **14**: 195.
Augustine, St., and the Donatists. (P. Burton) Dub. R. **112**: 397.
— and the Pelagian Controversy. (B. B. Warfield) Chr. Lit. **14**: 465, 577. **15**: 1–454. **16**: 1, 121.
Augustinianism, Pseudo-Athanasian. (L. L. Paine) N. World, **4**: 664.
Auk, Great, Gossip about. Chamb. J. **72**: 493.
Auk's Egg. (A. Newton; J. E. Harting) Nature, **49**: 412, 432.
Auld Curler's Prayer; a poem. (C. L. Clarke) Outing, **25**: 214.
Auld Lichte Causerie. National, **20**: 132.
Auld Robin Gray. (J. C. Hadden) Macmil. **66**: 291. Same art. Liv. Age, **195**: 121.
Aumale, Duc d'. A Pretender and his Family. (A. D. Vandam) Fortn. **62**: 582.
Aunt, The, the Nieces, and the Dog. (Sam. Butler) Univ. R. **4**: 126.
Aunt Angeline's Triumph. (W. A. Dromgoole) Arena, **11**: 391.
Aunt Anne. Temp. Bar, **94**: 140–**96**: 65. Same art. Liv. Age, **194**: 81–716.
Aunt Calista's Way; a story. (S. P. McManus) Our Day, **16**: 49.
Aunt Deborah. (Mrs. C. Carr) Good Words, **34**: 565.
Aunt Dorothy. (N. J. Welles) New Eng. M. n. s. **14**: 311.
Aunt Marthy's Secretary. (M. J. Garland) New Eng. M. n. s. **6**: 98.
Aurelio, the Conspirator. (W. Ruthven) New Eng. M. n. s. **14**: 726.
Auriga, New Star in. (E. E. Barnard) Pop. Astron. **2**: 307. — (H. C. Vogel) Astron. **13**: 48, 136, (H. Seeliger) 142, (W. H. Pickering) 201. — (E. C. Pickering) Astron. **11**: 228, (A. M. Clerke) 504, (W. Huggins and wife) 571, (R. Copeland) 593, (W. Sidgreaves) 604, (H. Seeliger) 904. — Nature, **45**: 344–498. — (W. Huggins) Fortn. **57**: 820. Same art. Ecl. M. **119**: 162. Same art. Liv. Age, **194**: 476. — (A. M. Clerke) Contemp. **61**: 546. Same art. Liv. Age, **193**: 630. — Ecl. M. **118**: 515. — Sat. R. **73**: 208. Same art. Liv. Age, **193**: 190. — (G. A. Hill) Science, **19**: 160. — Dub. R. **110**: 439. — (E. S. Holden) Forum, **16**: 211. — Pop. Sci. Mo. **42**: 542. — (A. L. Cortie) Astron. **12**: 521, (H. C. Vogel) 896.
— — Genesis of. (R. A. Gregory) Nature, **48**: 6.
— — Observations of. (C. A. Young and T. Reed) Astron. **11**: 289, (W. W. Campbell) 715, 820.
— — Spectrum of. (W. and Mrs. Huggins) Astron. **12**: 609, (W. W. Campbell) 722.
— — — in Feb. and March, 1892. (W. W. Campbell) Astron. **11**: 799.
— — — Photographic. (J. M. Boraston) Astron. **12**: 51.
Aurora Borealis. (W. A. Ashe) Science, **21**: 186, 276. — (A. E. Dolbear) Cosmopol. **18**: 759.
— of Nov. 23, 1894. (A. S. Herschell) Nature, **51**: 246.
— Oscillations of Lightning Discharges and of. (J. Trowbridge) Am. J. Sci. **146**: 195.
— Systematic Study of. (W. M. Payne) Astron. **12**: 602.
Austen, Jane. (W. Robertson) Time, **20**: 193. (H. W. Rolfe) Citizen, **2**: 196. — Liv. Age, **192**: 673.
— Adams' Life of. (A. French) Dial (Ch.) **13**: 342.
— and Miss Ferrier. (C. T. Copeland) Atlan. **71**: 836.
— A Girl's Opinion on. (Edith Edelmann) Temp. Bar, **94**: 343.
— In the Footsteps of. (O. F. Adams) New Eng. M. n. s. **8**: 594.
— Plagiarism of. (W. H. Pollock) National, **19**: 82.
— To; a poem. (A. Cochrane) Spec. **70**: 127. Same art. Ecl. M. **120**: 653.
Austin, Alfred, with portrait. Book News, **14**: 370. — (M. Nordau) Book R. **3**: 329. — With portrait. Bk. Buyer, **13**: 61. — Critic, **28**: 25. — (J. J. O'Shea) Cath. World, **62**: 822. — (W. E. Hodgson) Eng. Illust. **14**: 611. — (D. F. Hannigan) Westm. **145**: 251. — (J. Dennis) Leis. Hour, **45**: 292. — (H. W. Mabie) Outl. **53**: 148.
— as Poet-Laureate. Sat. R. **81**: 6. — Church Q. **42**: 124. — (C. D. Lanier) R. of Rs. (N. Y.) **13**: 199.
— Bibliography of. (E. D. North) Bk. Buyer, **13**: 126.
— England's Darling. (G. Cottrell) Acad. **49**: 298.
— The Garden That I Love. Sat. R. **77**: 617.
— Haunts of Ancient Peace. Spec. **73**: 301, 338, 370, 403.
Austin, Jane G., with portrait, Bk. Buyer, **11**: 194.
— List of books of. Lit. W. (Bost.) **25**: 111.
Austin, John. (J. Ross) Atlan. **69**: 763.
Austin, Sarah: a Modern Theodora. (S. R. Hershey) Cent. **29**: 952.
Austin, Stephen. Acad. **41**: 542.
Austin, Texas. The Great Dam. (F. E. Snyder) Engin. M. **8**: 245.
Austin Gang, Reminiscence of the. (E. A. Hamilton) Overland, n. s. **24**: 544.
Australasia and British Money. (N. Young) Contemp. **65**: 257.
— as a Field for Anglo-Indian Colonization. (E. N. Coventry Braddon) J. Soc. Arts, **41**: 493.
— Banks of, and British Deposits. Chamb. J. **69**: 625.
— Britisher's Impressions of. (Earl of Meath) 19th Cent. **33**: 493.
— Civil Service Problem in. (P. R. Meggy) R. of Rs (N. Y.) **12**: 447.

Australasia, Federation Movement in. (E. N. C. Braddon) 19th Cent. 40: 156.
— Finances of, in 1892. (R. M. Johnston) 19th Cent. 31: 606.
— Financial Position of. (G. C. Levey) Asia. R. 14: 102.
— Government Bonds of: Are they Safe? Bank. M. (Lond.) 53: 222, 577.
— History of, Laurie's. Sat. R. 81: 656.
— Resources and Prospects of. (E. Braddon) J. Soc. Arts, 40: 612.
— What Hinders Emigration to? Westm. 139: 402.
Australasian Colonies, History of, Jenks's. Sat. R. 80: 244.
Australasian Poets, Gallery of. (O. Smeaton) Westm. 144: 477.
Australia, Aborigines of. Chamb. J. 70: 735. — Anthrop. J. 24: 158.
— — of the Northwest. (P. W. Bassett-Smith) Anthrop. J. 23: 234.
— — Stone Cooking-Holes and Grooves for Stone-grinding used by. (R. H. Mathews) Anthrop. J. 25: 255.
— and the American Continent. (T. C. Hopkins) Am. J. Pol. 4: 587. — (G. L. Myers) Am. J. Pol. 5: 312.
— and the Empire, as to Defence. Un. Serv. M. 6: 145, 318.
— and Imperial Federation. (J. F. Hogan) Westm. 141: 1.
— and India, Financial Conditions and Mutual Relations of. Blackw. 154: 64.
— and New Zealand, Fauna and Flora of, Relation of. (C. Hedley) Nat. Sci. 3: 187.
— as a Strategic Base. (A. S. White) 19th Cent. 39: 457.
— Bank Crisis in. (G. Marsland) Bank. M. (N. Y.) 50: 336.
— Bank Failures in. Bank. M. (Lond.) 55: 712, 884.
— Bank Panic in. (Sir J. Vogel) Fortn. 59: 753.
— Banking in. (S. J. Murray) Bank. M. (Lond.) 60: 473.
— — Collapse of, Lessons of. (C. Gairdner) Econ. J. 4: 114.
— — Outlook in. Bank. M. (Lond.) 59: 195.
— Banks of. Bank. M. (Lond.) 55: 43. — (J. E. Bullard) Nation, 57: 42.
— Barrier Reef of. Ed. R. 178: 305. — Sat. R. 75: 519. — (A. Agassiz) Am. J. Sci. 152: 240. — (H. O. Forbes) Geog. J. 2: 540.
— — Kent on. Spec. 71: 519. — Nat. Sci. 2: 453. — Ath. '94, 1: 615.
— Centenary of. (H. Strong) Time, 19: 275.
— Coast Scenery of. (S. Thompson) M. of Art, 10: 321.
— Commonwealth of. (J. G. Bourniot) Scot. R. 26: 22.
— — Tregarthen's. Sat. R. 76: 601.
— Constitutional Evolution in. (W. K. Rose) Jurid. R. 4: 121, 233.
— Convicts and Bush-Rangers in. (T. W. Knox) Cosmopol. 21: 91, 173.
—Delusions about Tropical Cultivation. (G. W. Des Voeux) 19th Cent. 36: 38.
— Developments in. All the Year, 74: 414.
— Discovery of, Calvert's. Ath. '94, 1: 448.
— Ethnological Observations in. (R. Etheridge, jr.) Nature, 47: 594.
— Exploration of, Calvert on. Sat. R. 80: 274.
— Federation of. (E. Salmon) Fortn. 64: 67. — (O. Hall) Lippinc. 58: 237.
— — Outlook of. (E. Wilson) National, 25: 430.
— Financial Depression in. Canad. M. 1: 530. — (H. F. Hatton) National, 21: 436. — (R. Ogden) Nation, 56: 326. — (J. W. Fortescue) 19th Cent. 34: 22. — Sat. R. 75: 534. — Spec. 70: 663.
— — Effect of, upon Investors. Spec. 70: 445.
— Fossil Continent of. (W. Seton) Cath. World, 58: 180.
Australia, Geological Development of. (A. C. Gregory) Nature, 52: 20.
— Geology of. (R. Tate) Nature, 49: 277.
— Governors of, and their Ideals. (E. Lowe) Westm. 141: 553.
— Governorship in, A. National, 25: 641.
— Great West of. (M. Macfie) Westm. 137: 481.
— Growth of. (E. Reyer) Chaut. 20: 193.
— History of, Fifty Years of, Parkes's. Sat. R. 74: 658.
— in Rose-Color; Miss Shaw's Lecture. Spec. 72: 41, 684.
— Industrial Problem in. (E. Mitchell) Engin. M. 5: 1.
— Men of Mark in. (F. Adams) Fortn. 57: 194.
— Meteorological Work in. Nature, 51: 306.
— Money and Labor in. (J. E. Bullard) Nation, 56: 25.
— Naval Defence. Un. Serv. M. 4: 438.
— New Route to. (L. Goodrich) Time, 10: 619.
— Out-Door Sports in. (J. L. Lambert) Canad. M. 3: 269.
— Parkes on. (J. J. Halsey) Dial (Ch.) 15: 114.
— Plains of. (G. E. Boxall) Contemp. 69: 699. Same art. Liv. Age, 209: 764.
— Political Leaders in New South Wales. (J. T. Ryan) R. of Rs. (N. Y.) 12: 42.
— Politics of. (H. Parkes) R. of Rs. (N. Y.) 9: 434.
— Prospects of, in British Markets. (J. F. Dowling) J. Soc. of Arts, 44: 599.
— Revisited. (J. F. Hogan) Contemp. 67: 533.
— Lord Rintore's Journey across. Dub. R. 110: 184.
— Stage in. (E. Ballantyne) Theatre, 28: 186.
— Station Life in. (S. Dickinson) Scrib. M. 11: 135.
— Sundowners and Other Bush Types. Temp. Bar, 105: 117.
— Waterless. Sat. R. 74: 392.
— Western, Recent Explorations in, 1893. (A. F. Calvert) Eng. Illust. 10: 321.
— Westralian Mining Boom. (S. F. Van Oss) 19th Cent. 40: 711.
Australian Aboriginal, Skull of. (C. D. Cooper) Anthrop. J. 23: 153.
Australian Aboriginal Beliefs. J. Am. Folk-Lore, 9: 199.
Australian Aborigines, Paintings, Rock, and Carvings of. (R. H. Mathews) Anthrop. J. 25: 145.
Australian Alphabet. Sat. R. 75: 395.
Australian Bush Memories. (R. M. Dene) Outing, 25: 461.
Australian Colonies, Federation of. Asia. R. 17: 341.
Australian Crania, Aboriginal. (W. L. H. Duckworth) Anthrop. J. 23: 284.
Australian Literature. Bookworm, 1: 156.
Australian Natives, Influence of Geographical Position on the Development of. (E. Favenc) Geog. J. 2: 316.
Australian Rough-Riders. (R. Boldrewood) Macmil. 69: 430.
Australian Shields. (R. Etheridge) Anthrop. J. 26: 153.
Australian Watering Place and its Industries, An. (A. J. Rose-Soley) Westm. 142: 546.
Australian Writers. (C. M. Greene) Univ. R. 3: 465.
Austria. (E. Blum) Arena, 5: 657.
Austria and Bohemia. (L. Ordéga) Chaut. 19: 203.
Austria-Hungary, Army of. (Baron von Kuhn) Harper, 85: 50.
— Francis Joseph and his Realm. (A. Fournier) Forum, 21: 201.
— Military Strength of. (A. M. Murray) Un. Serv. M. 4: 32.
— Political Weakness of. Sat. R. 81: 519.
— Politics in, 1893. (E. B. Lanin) Contemp. 63: 279.
— Race Question in. (O. Wittelshöfer) Chaut. 20: 404.
— Resumption of Specie Payments in. (F. Wieser) J. Pol. Econ. 1: 380.

Austria-Hungary, Socialism and Social Politics in. (M. Kaufmann) Econ. R. 6: 334.
— Society, Politics, and Religion of. (S. I. de Z. de Nyevelt) Liv. Age, 192: 4.
— Suffrage in, Extension of. Spec. 71: 504, 572.
Austrian Museum of Art and Industry, Vienna. (W. M. Conway) M. of Art, 7: 369. 8: 382.
Auta, Doctrine of. (C. L. Morgan) Monist, 3: 161.
Author, Agent, and Publisher. (T. W. Laurie) 19th Cent. 38: 850.
— and Critic. (A. E. Barr) Bk. News, 7: 301.
Author's Dilemma; a story. (C. Burke) Argosy, 59: 360.
Authorcraft. (J. Dawson) Time, 22: 284.
Authority and Faith. (H. S. Holland) Sund. M. 21: 89.
— Anglicans on. (S. F. Smith) Month, 75: 457.
— Hatred of. Sat. R. 79: 377.
— in Christian Belief, Source of. (E. F. Bartholomew) Luth. Q. 23: 521.
— in Religion, Source of. (D. H. Bauslin) Luth. Q. 23: 477.
— in the Sphere of Conduct and Intellect. (H. Nettleship) Int. J. Ethics, 2: 217.
— Ultimate Ground of. (J. M. Sterrett) Philos. R. 1: 253.
Author's Choice of Company, On an. (W. Wilson) Cent. 29: 775.
Authors, Advice to. Lippinc. 58: 140.
— Allibone's Dictionary of, Kirk's Supplement to. (J. F. Kirk) Nation, 54: 147, 171.
— American, as Diplomatists. Critic, 23: 130.
— — Contemporary. (M. Thompson) Chaut. 23: 283.
— — Habits of, in Writing. (F. A. Burr) Lippinc. 51: 729.
— and Critics. (A. Birrell) New R. 6: 97.
— and Publishers. (W. R. Nicoll) Bookman, 1: 390.
— — Case of the American Author. (C. B. Todd) Forum, 13: 107.
— British Society of. (W. M. Conway) 19th Cent. 38: 975.
— — — Work of. (W. Besant) Forum, 13: 95.
— and their Public in Ancient Times, Putnam on. Critic, 25: 131.
— as Lecturers. (G. B. Burgin) Idler, 10: 337.
— Congress of, at Chicago, 1893. (S. S. Sprigge) Ath. '93, 2: 159, 192. — Dial (Ch.) 15: 27.
— Duties of. (Leslie Stephen) National, 23: 319. Same art. Ecl. M. 123: 1. — Dial (Ch.) 20: 325.
— England's New. (G. Holme) Munsey, 13: 336.
— Famous, Callow Flights of. Chamb. J. 69: 394.
— Favorite Books of. Pub. Opin. 13: 218.
— Five Indispensable: Homer, Dante, Cervantes, Goethe, Shakspere. (J. R. Lowell) Cent. 25: 223.
— I Have Known. (J. Murray) Good Words, 36: 87, 165.
— Inalienable Rights of. (R. McDonald Allen) Writer, 7: 19.
— Individual and Corporate. National, 19: 476.
— — Reply. (W. Besant) National, 19: 626.
— — Rejoinder. National, 19: 635. Same art. Ecl. M. 119: 194.
— Methods of. (H. Erichsen) Writer, 6: 89, 113, 131, 148. — Idler, 9: 344. — (G. B. Burgin) Idler, 10: 204.
— on Strike. Spec. 70: 44.
— Our Veteran. (G. Holme) Munsey, 13: 224.
— Publishers, and Reviewers. (F. Wicks) National, 20: 640. Same art. Ecl. M. 120: 342.
— Remuneration of. (A. Waugh) National, 21: 510.
— Some Notable Beginners in Chambers's Journal. Chamb. J. 72: 33.
— Unknown. (E. K. Cowing) Writer, 7: 81.
— *vs.* Publishers. Critic, 27: 446.
Authors, Why They Should not Marry. (E. Strong) Mid-Cont. 6: 87.
Authors' Club, Decennial Dinner of. Critic, 22: 134.
Authorship and Money, E. W. Bok on. (A. Schade van Westrum) Critic, 27: 316.
— Motives and Methods of. (G. Eyre-Todd) Chamb. J. 73: 97.
— Organization of. Dial (Ch.) 14: 201.
— Personality in. (W. A. Heidel) Meth. R. 52: 68.
Autobiographers, A Pair of. (C. Whibley) New R. 13: 674.
Autobiographies. Bookworm, 3: 119.
— Writing of. (G. A. Mendum) Bk. News, 8: 63.
Autobiography: A Bit of Editorial Experience. (R. T. Melcher) Writer, 6: 173.
— of a Criminal; a story. Our Day, 16: 93–385.
— of a President; a story. (T. C. Crawford) Cosmopol. 17: 583, 717.
— of a Professional Beauty. (E. P. Train) Lippinc. 53: 571.
Autograph-hunter, Confessions of. (C. Robinson) Cosmopol. 14: 305.
Autograph Letters and their Associations. Good Words, 37: 230.
Autographs. Bookworm, 4: 71.
— About a Book of. Blackw. 155: 372.
— Authors' Club. Critic, 22: 403.
— by a Collector. (L. Mendenhall) Munsey, 12: 589.
— in Books. (W. C. Hazlitt) Bookworm, 7: 145. — (Andrew Lang) Bibliographica, 1: 44.
— Talk Over. (G. B. Hill) Atlan. 75: 445, 669. 76: 46–605.
Automatic Maid-of-all-work; a tale. (M. L. Campbell) Canad. M. 1: 394.
Automatic Processes, Experimental Induction of. (W. R. Newbold) Psychol. R. 2: 348.
Automatic Writing. (E. T. Durgin) Psychic. R. 2: 267.
Automatism and Consciousness, Animal. (C. L. Morgan) Monist, 7: 1.
— and Spontaneity. (E. Montgomery) Monist, 4: 44.
— Are We Conscious Automata? (J. Seth) Philos. R. 3: 278.
— in Morality. (J. G. Hibben) Int. J. Ethics, 5: 462.
— Normal Motor. (L. M. Solomons and G. Stein) Psychol. R. 3: 492.
— Suggestibility, and Kindred Phenomena. (W. R. Newbold) Pop. Sci. Mo. 48: 193, 375, 520.
Automobile, The; a Forecast. (H. C. Marillier) New R. 13: 386. Same art. Ecl. M. 125: 774. *See* Carriages.
Autos-da-Fé. (F. L. Oswald) Open Court, 7: 3567.
Autumn. Atlan. 72: 449. — Spec. 69: 494. — (J. V. Cheney) Dial (Ch.) 17: 147.
— a Poem. (C. E. Meetkerke) Argosy, 58: 417. — (S. V. Ruby) Ref. Q. 41: 518. — (W. Cowan) Belgra. 60: 558.
— Thoreau's. (L. J. Block) Dial (Ch.) 13: 274.
Autumn Clouds. (E. Yolland) Belgra. 88: 169.
Autumn Dirge, An; a poem. (A. Austin) M. of Art, 17: 415.
Autumn Foliage and Unnatural Colors. (C. S. Sargent) Garden & F. 9: 471.
Autumn Gardens, Suggestions for. (C. S. Sargent) Garden & F. 8: 391.
Autumn Morning, An. All the Year, 75: 366.
Autumn Sessions in a Buchan Garden. National, 26: 180. Same art. Liv. Age, 207: 311.
Autumnal Changes in Leaves. (J. W. Folsom) Garden & F. 8: 383, 392.
Auvergne, Echoes from. Spec. 71: 45–192.
— in the 17th Century. (D. Sampson) Macmil. 66: 424. Same art. Liv. Age, 195: 745.

Auvergne, Les Grands Jours d'. (Lord Lamington) Time, 7: 668.
Avalanche at Gemmi, Sept. 11, 1895. (M. M. Ogilvie) Nature, 52: 573.
— Buried under an. (J. C. Werner) Canad. M. 4: 451.
— Great, in the Gemmi Pass. (H. V. Knox) Nat. Sci. 8: 17.
Avarice. Spec. 70: 188.
Ave Maria in Rome; a poem. (M. Blind) M. of Art, 17: 244.
Avenarius, Richard. (J. Kodis) Psychol. R. 3: 603.
Avenger of the Seven; a story. (J. J. à Becket) Cosmopol. 21: 394.
Aventurine Glass, Copper Crystals in. (H. S. Washington) Am. J. Sci. 148: 411.
Averages, Nature and Use of. (J. Venn) J. Statis. Soc. 54: 429.
Avery, S. P. Souvenirs of a Veteran Collector. (W. A. Coffin) Cent. 31: 231.
Avery Memorial Library. (J. A. Schweinfurth) Am. Arch. 51: 15.
Avesta, The. (S. A. Strong) Acad. 43: 525. — (A. V. W. Jackson) Bib. World, 1: 420.
— Date of. (F. Max Müller) Contemp. 64: 869.
Avianus and his Imitators. (R. Ellis) Acad. 45: 104, 128, 151.
Avignon; a story. All the Year, 75: 135, 161.
— The Great Schism of the West. (S. F. Smith) Month, 78: 77, 194.
Avon, River, Dockisation of the. Chamb. J. 72: 138.
Awaiting Judgment; a story. (W. G. Hewitt) Scrib. M. 16: 214.
Awakening; a poem. (M. Sangster) Harper, 90: 788.
Aweæ. (J. Six) J. Hel. Stud. 13: 131.
Awkward Fix, An. Chamb. J. 72: 733.
Awkward for Tabitha. (E. Godfrey) Belgra. 85: 262.
Axioms. Open Court, 7: 3752.
— the Basis of Mathematics. (E. Brooks) Open Court, 2: 1456.
Ayer, Benjamin F., with portrait. (H. L. Conard) Nat'l M. (N. Y. '91) 16: 613.
Ayesha, a Wife of the Prophet Mohammed. (W. B. Harris) Blackw. 155: 267. Same art. Liv. Age, 200: 734.
Aytoun, William Edmondstoune. (J. H. Millar) New R. 14: 103.
Azalea Indicum. Garden & F. 9: 394.
Azaleas, Indian. (T. D. Hatfield) Garden & F. 7: 486. 8: 177.
— at the Columbian Exposition. (L. H. Bailey) Garden & F. 6: 249.
— — Cultivation of. Garden & F. 8: 146.
— Hardy, at Knap Hill. Garden & F. 6: 262.
Azaleo-dendrons. Garden & F. 6: 264.
Azélie. (K. Chopin) Cent. 27: 282.
Azores as a Health Resort. (H. Canfield) Around World, 1: 161.
— Cycling in. (O. Howarth) Outing, 28: 35.
— Twilight Tales of the. (L. H. Weeks) Chaut. 21: 330.
Aztec Paintings, Humboldt's. (P. J. J. Valentini) Cosmopol. 18: 331.

B. A. *See* Bachelor of Arts.
Bäader. [Artists' Adventures Series.] (F. H. Smith) Cent. 25: 204.
Baalbek, Ruins of. (C. A. Rich) Am. Arch. 47: 3.
Bab, The, and Babism. (J. D. Rees) 19th Cent. 40: 56. Same art. Ecl. M. 127: 303. Same art. Liv. Age, 210: 451. — (H. Cottrell) Acad. 47: 220.
— Browne on. Spec. 68: 560. — Sat. R. 77: 44.
Baber, Zehir-ed-din Muhammed. (E. S. Holden) Cosmopol. 15: 204.
Babeuf, François. (M. D. Conway) Open Court, 9: 4367.
Babi Sect in Modern Persia. (C. Trotter) Scot. R. 19: 326.
Babies and Monkeys. (S. S. Buckman) Pop. Sci. Mo. 46: 371.
— in Art and Nature. (H. A. Kennedy) M. of Art, 13: 376.
— Some Comments on. (M. W. Shinn) Overland, n. s. 23: 2.
— The World's. (A. R. Buckland) Sund. M. 22: 671.
Babington, Charles Cardale. Ath. '95, 2: 133. — Nat. Sci. 7: 215.
Baboo's Good Tiger. (R. Wildman) Overland, n. s. 27: 628.
Baboo's Pirates. (R. Wildman) Overland, n. s. 25: 369.
Baby in the Siege, A. (J. C. Harris) Scrib. M. 19: 490.
Baby John. Chamb. J. 69: 634-695.
Baby Walter's Lapsus Linguæ. (F. Noble) Eng. Illust. 15: 121.
Baby-farming. (F. A. Burt) Lend a Hand, 10: 7.
Baby-talk, The World's. (C. Johnston) Fortn. 66: 494.
Baby's Christmas, The. (J. C. Harris) Cent. 25: 284.
Baby's Fortune, The. (J. C. Harris) Scrib. M. 20: 613.
Babylon, Modern. (S. A. Barnett) Time, 13: 129.
— Myth of. (T. G. Pinches) Knowl. 18: 52.
— True Story of. (T. G. Pinches) Knowl. 18: 169.
Babylonia, American Excavations in. (A. H. Sayce) Acad. 50: 83.
— Ancient Life in. (T. G. Pinches) Knowl. 19: 44.
— Discoveries in History of. (Hormuzd Rassam) Asia. R. 18: 94.
— Early History of. (H. H. Howorth) Acad. 42: 132.
— Education in Ancient. (C. G. Herbermann) Am. Cath. Q. 18: 449.
— Excavations in. (R. F. Harper) Bib. World, 8: 23.
— 4,000 Years Ago. (T. G. Pinches) Knowl. 19: 116.
— History of, The Earliest. Quar. 179: 338.
— Sketch of. (D. G. Lyon) Bib. World, 7: 425.
— under the Greeks and Parthians. (J. E. Gilmore) Eng. Hist. R. 7: 1.
Babylonian Myths in the Bible, Gunkel on. (J. D. Davis) Presb. & Ref. R. 6: 745.
Baylonians, Ethics of. (M. Jastrow) Eth. Rec. 3: 66.
Baccarat at Brighton. Sat. R. 74: 525.
— Derivation of. (F. Chance) Acad. 41: 207.
Bacchæ, the, Problem of. (A. G. Bather) J. Hel. Stud. 14: 244.
Bach, J. S., Festival, 1895. (H. H. Statham) Fortn. 63: 800. — (J. S. Shedlock) Acad. 47: 302, 322. — Sat R. 79: 475, 506.
— Matthew and John. Sat. R. 81: 346.
Bach-Schumann Violoncello Suites, Unpublished. (E. S. Kelley) Music, 3: 611.
Bacharach, Jair Chayim. (D. Kauffmann) Jew. Q. 3: 292-485.
Bache, Alexander Dallas, with portrait. Pop. Sci. Mo. 48: 112.
Bachelor Buttons; a story. (F. L. Guertin) Outing, 24: 280.
Bachelor Maid, A. (C. C. Harrison) Cent. 26: 427-876. 27: 73.
Bachelor of Arts Degree, Significance of. (J. M. Garnett) School & C. 1: 193.
— of Oxford, What does it Represent? (R. Jones) Educa. R. 4: 447.
Bachelor's Bridal. (Mrs. H. L. Cameron) Lippinc. 52: 259.
Bachelor's Christmas, The. (R. Grant) Scrib. M. 14: 663.
Bachelor's Counselings, A. (R. M. Johnston) Cent. 22: 775.

Bachiler, Rev. Stephen. (C. E. Batchelder) N. E. Reg. 46: 58–345.
Bacilli: Are They Causes of Disease? (G. W. Bulman) Westm. 139: 500. Same art. Ecl. M. 121: 163.
Bacillus of Love, The. Blackw. 152: 668.
Backboned Animals, Forerunners of. (A. S. Woodward) Nat. Sci. 1: 596.
Backgammon, Symbolism of. (W. W. Newell) J. Am. Folk-Lore, 3: 208.
Backsliding of Elder Pletus; a tale. (W. T. James) Canad. M. 1: 480.
Backwater of Life, The. (J. Payn) Cornh. 71: 517. Same art. Ecl. M. 124: 804. Same art. Liv. Age, 205: 569.
Bacon, Francis, How Shakespeare Illustrates. (H. M. Hugunin) Poet-Lore, 4: 200.
— Life of. Eng. R. 16: 276.
— Relations of, to Digby and Temple. (G. C. Robertson) Acad. 41: 110.
— *vs.* Professor Huxley. (Argyll) 19th Cent. 36: 959.
— *vs.* Shakespeare. (E. Reed) Arena, 6: 188–692. — (A. Nicholson) Arena, 7: 12.
— Worldly Wisdom of. Spec. 71: 661.
Bacon, N., Rebellion of, in Virginia. (A. G. Bradley) Macmil. 69: 22.
— Remembrance made by. (C. H. Townshend) N. E. Reg. 50: 64.
Bacon, Roger. (H. Maxwell) Blackw. 156: 610.
Bacteria. (G. C. Frankland) Longm. 22: 472.
— Action of Light on. (H. M. Ward) Am. Natural. 29: 671.
— and Carbonated Waters. (G. C. Frankland) Nature, 54: 375.
— and their Rôle in Nature. (J. J. Mackenzie) Canad. M. 1: 249.
— Color-producing. (C. A. Mitchell) Knowl. 18: 124.
— Fischer on. (E. F. Smith) Am. Natural. 29: 847.
— in our Dairy Products. (H. W. Conn) Pop. Sci. Mo. 40: 763.
— Nature and Function of. (E. Klein) Nature, 48: 82.
— Schenk on. Nature, 48: 562.
— Some Uses of. (H. W. Conn) Am. Natural. 26: 901, 987.
— which We Breathe, Eat, and Drink. (A. A. Kanthack) Nature, 55: 209.
Bacterial Diseases of Plants, Critical Review of Present Knowledge of. (E. F. Smith) Am. Natural. 30: 626, 716, 796, 912.
Bactericidal Action of Metals. (M. Bolton) Am. Natural. 29: 933.
Bacteriological Researches, Practical Results of. (G. M. Sternberg) Pop. Sci. Mo. 48: 735.
Bacteriology. Sat. R. 73: 93.
— in its General Relations. (H. L. Russell) Am. Natural. 27: 847, 1040.
— Modern, and Lady M. W. Montagu. (Mrs. H. M. Plunket) Pop. Sci. Mo. 45: 359.
— — Heim on. (G. C. Frankland) Nature, 51: 481.
— Recent Advances in, with Reference to Food. (M. V. Ball) J. Frankl. Inst. 140: 340.
Bad and Worthless; a story. (Mrs. A. Henniker) Eng. Illust. 11: 669.
Bad Lands of Nebraska and South Dakota. (F. C. Kenyon) Am. Natural. 29: 213.
Bad Men, Lives of Twelve, ed. by T. Seccombe. Dial (Ch.) 17: 223.
Bad Penny. Cornh. 68: 389. Same art. Liv. Age, 199: 571.
Badier, Florimond, Bookbindings of. (W. Y. Fletcher) Bibliographica, 1: 257.
Badollet, J., Sketch of, 1758–1837. (G. N. Lovejoy) M. Am. Hist. 27: 51.
Bag of Pop-Corn. (C. Ticknor) New Eng. M. n. s. 9: 489.
Bagehot, Walter. (W. E. Gladstone) 19th Cent. 38: 716. — (W. Wilson) Atlan. 76: 668.
— and the Catholic Church. Month, 86: 556.
Baginbun Stone, The. (R. A. S. Macalister and others) Acad. 46: 216–377.
Bagley Kidnapping, The. (M. A. Kimball) Overland, n. s. 22: 594.
Bagpipe, Highland. Chamb. J. 70: 827.
Bagpipe Music. (W. L. Calderwood) Scot. R. 27: 105.
Bagshot Park, Eng. (A. H. Beavan) Eng. Illust. 10: 727.
Bahama Folk-Lore. (C. L. Edwards) J. Am. Folk-Lore, 4: 247, 447.
Bahama Islands, Artist's Trip to. M. of Art, 2: 201.
— The Beautiful. (D. Macinnes) Canad. M. 3: 258.
— Songs and Stories of, Edwards's. (F. Starr) Dial (Ch.) 20: 15. — J. Am. Folk-Lore, 8: 243.
Bahar Planter, Reminiscences of a. (D. M. Reid) Gent. M. n. s. 56: 172.
Bahia, Struggle for, 1624–27. Eng. Hist. R. 11: 231.
Bahir and Zohar. (A. Neubauer) Jew. Q. 4: 357.
Bahrhoffer, Karl T., and his System of Naturalistic Monism. (E. Montgomery) Open Court, 2: 831–934.
Bail. (J. C. Macdonald) Jurid. R. 4: 341.
Bailey, James M., with portrait. (G. W. Hallock) Munsey, 11: 238.
Bailey, Nathaniel, Dictionary of. Bookworm, 2: 201.
Baillon, Henri Ernest. Nature, 52: 371. — Nat. Sci. 7: 288. — Ath. '95, 2: 134.
Baird, Abington; a Millionaire "Rough." Spec. 70: 383.
Baird, Henry M., with portrait. Bk. Buyer, 12: 429.
Baker, Lady Florence, in the Soudan. (H. Ward) Eng. Illust. 15: 443.
Baker, John Sherman, with portrait. (C. W. Hobart) M. West. Hist. 13: 416.
Baker, Sir S. W., and Exploration of Upper Nile. Around World, 1: 68. — Critic, 24: 6, 65.
— Murray's Life of. (E. G. Ravenstein) Geog. J. 6: 73. — (S. H. Peabody) Dial (Ch.) 19: 283. — (A. H. Keane) Acad. 47: 349. — Sat. R. 79: 513. — Blackw. 157: 949. Same art. Ecl. M. 125: 212. Same art. Liv. Age, 206: 150. — Ath. '94, 1: 20. — Nature, 49: 227. — With portrait. (E. G. Ravenstein) Geog. J. 3: 152. — Nat. Sci. 4: 228. — Pub. Opin. 16: 339.
Baker, W. Y., Collection of Pictures of. M. of Art, 16: 228, 336.
Baker of Beuly, The. (A. MacBain and W. A. Clouston) Folk-Lore, 3: 183.
Bakers, Operative, Industrial Conditions and Vital Statistics of. (S. N. Fox) Econ. J. 4: 106.
Bakeries, The Truth about the London. New R. 10: 607.
Bakhtiari Mts. and Upper Elam. (H. A. Sawyer) Geog. J. 4: 481.
Baku and its Oil Industry. (W. F. Hume) Nature, 54: 232.
— From, to Samarkand. (Frank Vincent) Cosmopol. 18: 394.
Balaam. (D. Merson) Thinker, 9: 215.
— and his Day. (A. B. Hyde) Meth. R. 53: 206.
— and Pedro; a story. (O. Wister) Harper, 88: 293.
— Prophecies of, Form and Import of. (W. W. Martin) Meth. R. 52: 699.
Balaclava, Charge at. (J. W. Wightman) 19th Cent. 31: 850. Same art. Ecl. M. 118: 801.
Balala's New Moon; a story. (H. Ward) Idler, 5: 17.
Balance of Power, The. (J. Hutton) Gent. M. n. s. 53: 487–595.

Balance of Power, European; Symposium. Indep. Dec. 3, '96.
Balance of Power; a story. (M. Thompson) Harper, 90: 796.
Balance of Trade. (Gen. Sir G. Chesney) Fortn. 60: 492.
Balconies, Street, in North Italy. (H. E. Tidmarsh) M. of Art, 16: 312.
Balcony at Lucerne, A; a story. Argosy, 54: 434.
Balcony Stories. (G. King) Cent 23: 279, 493. 24: 230-884.
Balder's Ball; a story. (P. von Schönthan) Idler, 3: 397.
Baldwin, J. Mark, on the Mind in Evolution. (H. Nichols) Am. Natural. 30: 697.
Balearic Islands. Cornh. 65: 423. Same art. Liv. Age, 193: 546.
— About the. (C. Edwards) Outing, 27: 404, 470.
— In the. (A. Solberg) Nation, 56: 290. 58: 119.
Balestier, Wolcott. (E. Gosse) Cent. 21: 923. — (H. James) Cosmopol. 13: 43.
Balfour, Arthur J. (H. W. Lucy) Eng. Illust. 9: 363. — (T. C. Hopkins) Canad. M. 1: 140.
— an Apostle of Naturalism. (G. Tyrrell) Month, 85: 215, 358.
— and Churchill, R. (E. L. Godkin) Nation, 56: 192.
— as Leader. Sat. R. 79: 436.
— as a Doubter. Sat. R. 79: 211.
— as a Theologian and as a Christian. (J. Denney) Chr. Lit. 12: 321.
— Attack on Agnosticism. (T. H. Huxley) Chr. Lit. 12: 325.
— Dialectics of. (H. Spencer) Fortn. 63: 861. Same art. Pop. Sci. Mo. 47: 327.
— Essays and Addresses. Sat. R. 75: 431.
— Foundations of Belief. (G. M. McCrie) Open Court, 9: 4495. — (W. Barry) Dub. R. 117: 128. — Ath. '95, 1: 241. — Blackw. 158: 33. — (W. T. Stead) R. of Rs. (N. Y.) 11: 429. — (A. M. Fairbairn; J. Martineau) Chr. Lit. 13: 9. — (A. M. Fairbairn) Contemp. 67: 457. — (F. W. Farrar) Eng. Illust. 13: 19. — (B. Kidd) National, 25: 35. Same art. Liv. Age, 204: 808. — (M. Todhunter) Westm. 143: 484. — (J. Martineau) 19th Cent. 37: 552. — (G. W. Steevens) New R. 12: 301. — (W. Wallace) Fortn. 63: 540. — (J. G. Schurman) Forum, 19: 364. — (Sir F. Pollock) Mind, 20: 376. — (R. Ogden) Nation, 60: 243. — (J. Seth) Philos. R. 4: 311. — Ed. R. 182: 192. — Quar. 180: 488. Same art. Liv. Age, 205: 657. — (A. W. Benn) Acad. 47: 207. — (S. D. F. Salmond) Crit. R. 5: 184. — (St. G. Mivart) Am. Cath. Q. 21: 53, 294, 541. — (A. Seth) Contemp. 70: 153. — (W. M. Daniels) Philos. R. 5: 59. — (J. DeWitt) Presb. & Ref. R. 7: 125.
— — and its Critics. (T. R. Slicer) New World, 5: 318.
— — Brahmanism and. (Vamadeo Shastri) Fortn. 64: 682.
— — "The Times" on. National, 27: 737.
— Philosophy of. Church Q. 41: 47.
— seen from a Distance. (N. Hapgood) Contemp. 68: 773.
— Work of, in the West of Ireland. (J. Verschoyle) Fortn. 58: 224. Same art. Liv. Age, 195: 167.
Balfour, Lady Blanche. (J. Robertson) Good Words, 37: 246, 302.
Balfour, Sir George. Geog. J. 3: 524.
Balfour, Jabez Spencer. (H. E. M. Stutfield) National, 26: 836.
Balkan Mountains, The. Time, 10: 16.
Balkan Peninsula. Lond. Q. 86: 35.
— Conflict of Peoples in. (C. de Stefani) Chaut. 21: 148.
— Russia and. (E. Dicey) Fortn. 62: 817.
Balkan Princess, The; a story. (E. M. Halliday) Munsey, 11: 496.
Balkan States and Greece. Chaut. 14: 573.
— In the. (H. Norman) Scrib. M. 19: 663.
Ball, Thomas. (W. O. Partridge) New Eng. M. n. s. 12: 291.
Ball, Valentine. Acad. 47: 527. — Ath. '95, 1: 808. — Nat. Sci. 7: 140.
Ball and Nozzle Phenomenon. (W. Hallock) Science, n. s. 2: 121.
Ball-Bearings, Anti-Friction. (G. F. Simonds) J. Frankl. Inst. 136: 289.
Ball Games, Evolution of. (H. G. Hutchinson) Blackw. 153: 751. Same art. Ecl. M. 120: 831.
Ball Nozzle. (A. Kitson) J. Frankl. Inst. 140: 123.
Ballard of the Elfin Knight, American Versions of the. J. Am. Folk-Lore, 7: 228.
Ballad of a Jester; a poem. (J. R. Williamson) Temp. Bar, 96: 227.
Ballad of a Shield, A; a poem. (C. Monkhouse) M. of Art, 15: 422.
Ballad of Books Unborn. Dial (Ch.) 13: 207.
Ballad of the Drum. (D. G. Adee) Lippinc. 54: 537.
Ballad of Love and Death. (E. Nesbit) Longm. 20: 394.
Ballad of the Thrush; a poem. (A. Dobson) M. of Art, 6: 108.
Ballad of the Tower; a poem. (Katrina Trask) Cosmopol. 21: 226.
Ballad of the White Lady. (E. Nesbit) Eng. Illust. 11: 308.
Ballade of a Choice of Ghosts; a poem. (A. Lang) M. of Art, 9: 73.
Ballade of Dead Actors; a poem. (W. E. Henley) M. of Art, 9: 33.
Ballade of the Yacht. (E. W. Barnard) Outing, 20: 440.
Ballade to a Bookman. (F. H. Williams) Dial (Ch.) 15: 289.
Ballads. Bookworm, 1: 103.
— of America. (Sarah L. Roys) Bach. of Arts, 1: 782.
— Gummere's Old English. (G. L. Kittredge) Nation, 59: 235.
— Two Ayrshire. (G. Eyre-Todd) Gent. M. n. s. 57: 269.
Ballantyne, Robert Michael. Acad. 45: 148.
— My First Book. Idler, 3: 527.
Ballast Fin, The. (A. J. Kenealy) Outing, 20: 228.
Ballet, The. (H. R. Haweis) Univ. R. 1: 248.
— Art in. (C. Wilhelm) M. of Art, 18: 12, 48.
— Corps de. (Dutton Cook) Time, 2: 699.
— History and Progress of. (Rosita Mauri) Cosmopol. 18: 449.
— Training of, at the Alhambra. (A. Mayhew) Idler, 2: 61.
Balley's Funeral. (S. J. Shields) Southern M. 4: 599.
Balliol College, Oxford, Reminiscences of. (A. Lang) Eng. Illust. 11: 122.
Balloon Ascension, My First and Last. (R. V. V. Sewell) Cent. 25: 834.
Ballooning. (A. H. Wall) Time, 6: 577, 666.
— Military. Cornh. 69: 72.
— Trip Heavenward. (B. B. Powell) Blackw. 158: 669. Same art. Liv. Age, 207: 660.
Balloons as a Means of Locomotion. (R. H. Sherard) McClure, 4: 493.
— in War. Macmil. 72: 337.
Ballot, The American. (H. H. Lusk) Forum, 22: 225.
— Australian, Advent of. (L. N. Dembitz) Nation, 54: 32, 87.
— — in Massachusetts. (R. H. Dana) Ann. Am. Acad. Pol. Sci. 2: 733.
— Different Forms of. (L. J. Vance) Chaut. 23: 713.
— Juggling with the. (J. W. Goff) No. Am. 158: 203.

Ballot: The Machine in Honest Hands. (H. B. Ames) Canad. M. 3: 101.
— Plural Voting. Spec. 74: 604.
— Secret, and the Election, 1892. (J. B. Bishop) Nation, 54: 442.
— — in Thirty-three States. (J. B. Bishop) Forum, 12: 589.
Ballots, Distinguishing Marks on. (H. T. Blake) N. Eng. 56: 170.
Ballot-Boxes, Patent, Defects of. (W. W. Tufts) Nation, 57: 155.
Ballot Law, Pennsylvania, of 1892. (C. C. Binney) Ann. Am. Acad. Pol. Sci. 2: 751.
Ballot Laws and Election Frauds. Nation, 58: 4.
Ballot Reform, A Campaign for. (E. B. Grubb) No. Am. 155: 684.
Balmaceda, Fall of. Blackw. 151: 129. Same art. Ecl. M. 118: 339. Same art. Liv. Age, 192: 556.
Balmoral; Queen Victoria's Highland Home. (J. R. Hunter) Harper, 91: 699.
Balmoral of Spain, The. Chamb. J. 73: 712.
Balochi Tales. (M. L. Dames) Folk-Lore, 3: 517. 4: 195–518.
Balochis, Northern, Customs and Folk-Lore of. (O. V. Yates) J. Soc. Arts, 43: 702.
Baltic, Eye of the. *See* Wisby.
— and North Sea Ship-Canal, The. Chamb. J. 72: 247. Same art. Liv. Age, 205: 442. — All the Year, 74: 607. — Liv. Age, 198: 127. — (W. H. Wheeler) Longm. 27: 485. Same art. Liv. Age, 209: 131.
Baltic Stream, The. (R. Beynon) Knowl. 18: 116.
Baltic, The; a London Exchange. Chamb. J. 73: 442.
Baltiperri, Laura. (L. E. Baxter) M. of Art, 14: 386.
Baltimore, City Government of. (T. P. Thomas) J. H. Univ. Stud. 14: 47.
— Daily Record Building. Archit. Rec. 2: 213, 360.
— Druid Hill Park. (M. C. Robbins) Garden & F. 7: 233.
— the Land of the Epicure. (C. D. Wilson) Cosmopol. 19: 661.
— The New. (S. Bonsal) Harper, 92: 331.
— Public Schools of. (J. M. Rice) Forum, 14: 145.
— Social Life in. (A. D. Wetmore) Southern M. 4: 631.
— Walters' Art Gallery. (M. Reizenstein) New Eng. M. n. s. 12: 545.
Baltimore National Bank. (J. T. Smith) Bank. M. (N. Y.) 52: 621.
Balzac, H. de. (G. Saintsbury) Book R. 3: 57.
— Human Comedy, Heroines of. (J. H. Browne) Lippinc. 53: 562.
— Influence of Swedenborg's Writings on. (T. F. Wright) N. Church R. 3: 481.
— La Musique dans. (L. de Fourcaud) Univ. R. 1: 111.
— Moral Influence of. (A. H. Tuttle) Meth. R. 55: 60.
— On Reading the Fiftieth Volume of. (W. P. Trent) Atlan. 78: 566.
— Realism of. (W. H. Gleadell) Gent. M. n. s. 52: 596.
— Wormeley's. Overland, n. s. 20: 103.
Balzani, Countess. Acad. 48: 31.
Balzi Rossi Caves, Prehistoric Interments of. (A. J. Evans) Anthrop. J. 22: 287.
Bamberg. (Sophia Beale) Good Words, 34: 176.
Bamboo, The. (J. F. Nott) Cosmopol. 18: 299.
— and its Uses. Chamb. J. 71: 694.
Bamboo Garden. Garden & F. 9: 239.
Bamboos in English Gardens. (W. Watson) Garden & F. 9: 206.
Banana, The. (R. Beynon) Knowl. 19: 9.
Banana Land Awheel. (E. M. Aaron) Outing, 27: 129.
Bananas. Chamb. J. 72: 517.
Bananas and Plantains. Garden & F. 5: 183.
— Cultivation of, in Jamaica. (A. Eric) Canad. M. 2: 71.
— Supply of, to N. Y. Garden & F. 6: 422.
— Where they Grow. (J. E. Humphrey) Pop. Sci. Mo. 44: 486.
Bancroft, Geo., with portrait. Bk. Buyer, 6: 133. — With portrait. Bk. News, 9: 220.
— Library of. Lib. J. 18: 149.
Bancroft, F. J., M. D. (H. D. Teetar) M. West. Hist. 11: 193.
Bancroft, Hubert Howe, with portrait. (S. D. Peet) Am. Antiq. 14: 230.
Bancroft Library, The; a Mine of Musty Manuscripts. (J. J. Peatfield) Overland, n. s. 25: 272.
Band Leaders, Famous American. (J. C. Harvey) Munsey, 12: 411.
Bandelier, A. F. (A. H. Noll) Dial (Ch.) 15: 389.
Bandinelli, Baccio, Statue of Hercules by. (L. E. Baxter) M. of Art, 3: 465.
Bandits, Corsican. Sat. R. 74: 46. — (C. Holland) Contemp. 64: 492. Same art. Liv. Age, 199: 622.
— of the Venetian Republic. (P. Fambri) Chaut. 23: 170.
Bandmaster of Claythorpe, The. (E. Mackay) Sund. M. 23: 748.
Bands, Military, of Europe. (S. P. Cadman) Chaut. 23: 57.
Bangkok. (P. C. Standing) Leis. Hour, 43: 364.
Bangs, J. K., with portrait. Book News, 14: 222.
Bangweolo, Lake, A Journey to. (J. Thompson) Geog. J. 1: 97.
Bank of England. (H. J. W. Dam) McClure, 4: 459. — (H. Townsend) Chaut. 23: 606.
— and Banks of France and Germany. Bank. M. (Lond.) 57: 369.
— Duty of. Bank. M. (Lond.) 57: 185.
— Facts about. Soc. Econ. 9: 91.
— Founders of. Macmil. 70: 184. Same art. Liv. Age, 202: 366.
— Discount at Two Per Cent. Chamb. J. 72: 321.
— — Rate of, Surprise Rise in. (R. Ewen) Westm. 146: 527.
— Recent Criticism on. Econ. J. 4: 348.
Bank of England Notes. Cornh. 70: 186. Same art. Liv. Age, 202: 630.
Bank of France, and Specie Reserve. Bank M. (Lond.) 56: 357.
— Renewal of Privileges of. Bank. M. (N. Y.) 46: 27–778.
Bank of Scotland, Bi-centenary of. Chamb. J. 72: 369.
Bank of Spain in 1892. (T. Lloyd) Econ. J. 2: 170.
Bank of the U. S., First. (Van Buren Denslow) Soc. Econ. 5: 84, 135.
— — Accounts of. Q. J. Econ. 6: 471.
Bank of Venice. (C. F. Dunbar) Q. J. Econ. 6: 308, 371. — (J. Davis) Arena, 9: 34, 633.
Bank Act, 1844–45, of Great Britain. Bank. M. (Lond.) 53: 541.
Bank Buildings, Architecture of Modern. (R. W. Gibson) Engin. M. 10: 1064.
Bank Circulation and Free Coinage. (J. J. Knox) Forum, 12: 772.
— Principles Underlying. Bank. M. (N. Y.) 47: 561.
— State and National. (A. B. Hepburn) Ann. Am. Acad. Pol. Sci. 3: 573.
Bank Clerks. Bank. M. (Lond.) 53: 70–909.
Bank Credits. (T. L. Greene) Nation, 56: 118.
Bank Currency in U. S. (T. Gilman) Bank. M. (N. Y.) 50: 347.
Bank Deposit Insurance, Colonial. Bank. M. (Lond.) 56: 849.

Bank Deposits, The Great Unclaimed. Blackw. **157**: 591.
— Insurance of. Bank. M. (Lond.) **59**: 773.
Bank Depositors, Protection of. (J. H. Eckels) No. Am. **163**: 564.
Bank Direction and Management. Bank. M. (Lond.) **56**: 795. **57**: 205. **58**: 158.
Bank Failures, Causes of. Bank. M. (N. Y.) **47**: 514.
Bank Forgers and their Methods. Bank. M. (N. Y.) **52**: 438.
Bank Inspection and Audit. Bank. M. (Lond.) **56**: 539, 676.
Bank Issues, Baltimore-Plan of. (J. L. Laughlin) J. Pol. Econ. **3**: 101.
Bank Notes. Chamb. J. **70**: 602.
— in Liverpool, 1793–95, Municipal. (E. C. K. Gonner) Econ. J. **6**: 484.
— Question of, and State Banks. (C. F. Dunbar) Q. J. Econ. **7**: 55.
Bank Panics and Runs. (J. Scot Henderson) Time, **2**: 626.
Bank Tax, Repeal of. Bank. M. (N. Y.) **48**: 801.
Banking. (J. R. Paget) Bank. M. (Lond.) **59**: 237–860. **61**: 244–696.
- Abuses and Uses of. (R. Ewen) Westm. **141**: 133.
— American, and the Money Supply of the Future. (M. D. Harter) Ann. Am. Acad. Pol. Sci. **3**: 559.
— and the Currency. (L. R. Harley) Am. M. Civ. **8**: 291.
— and Finance, Educational Papers on. Bank. M. (Lond.) **61**: 213–827.
— and Limited Liability. Bank. M. (Lond.) **53**: 891.
— Canadian and American. (T. L. Greene) Nation, **57**: 112.
— Canadian; Our Cash Reserves. (J. B. Peat) Canad. M. **5**: 461.
— Canadian System, 1817–90. (R. M. Breckenridge) Am. Econ. Assoc. **10**: 1.
— Competition and. (F. E. Steele) Econ. J. **3**: 637.
— Co-operative. (E. M. Lynch) Econ. R. **2**: 330. — (H. W. Wolff) Econ. R. **6**: 193. — (E. M. Leman) Econ. R. **6**: 371. — (H. W. Wolff) Econ. R. **6**: 382.
— — in Italy. (G. Fiamingo) Econ. J. **6**: 278.
— Co-operative-credit, in Germany. (H. W. Wolff) Econ. R. **2**: 460.
— First Principles in. (H. White) Engin. M. **10**: 391.
— Foreign and American. Gunton's M. **11**: 116.
— Fragment of History of. Soc. Econ. **9**: 38.
— Free Trade in. (R. Ewen) Westm. **146**: 527.
— Future of. Bank. M. (N. Y.) **47**: 481.
— Hill's. (G. W. Weippiert) Arena, **5**: 194.
— in Canada. (B. E. Walker) Econ. J. **4**: 227.
— — Free. Bank. M. (N. Y.) **49**: 286.
— in England; Abolition of the Bank Act. (R. Ewen) Westm. **138**: 190.
— in Great Britain, 1891. Bank. M. (Lond.) **53**: 9, 167.
— — 1892. Bank. M. (Lond.) **55**: 3, 179.
— — 1893. Bank. M. (Lond.) **57**: 1–529.
— — 1894. Bank. M. (Lond.) **59**: 15–529.
— — 1895. Bank. M. (Lond.) **61**: 1–534.
— in India and China. (J. W. Maclellan) Bank. M. (Lond.) **55**: 50–730.
— in Ireland. Chamb. J. **72**: 442.
— in London; "The Grasshopper" in Lombard Street, Martin's. Spec. **69**: 449.
— in Massachusetts in 18th Century. (A. McF. Davis) Q. J. Econ. **11**: 70.
— in Mexico, New Law of. Gunton's M. **11**: 351.
— in U. S. (J. Macbeth Forbes) Bank. M. (Lond.) **60**: 714.
— — 1846–96. Bank. M. (N. Y.) **52**: 21.
Banking in the U. S., 1893. (W. R. Lawson) Bank. M. (Lond.) **56**: 371.
— — Our Banking and Currency Plan. Soc. Econ. **8**: 1.
— Lincoln on a Government Bank. Soc. Econ. **9**: 1.
— Mortgage, in Germany. (D. M. Frederiksen) Bank. M. (N. Y.) **50**: 361.
— The New. Bank. M. (Lond.) **61**: 197.
— Old-fashioned. Chamb. J. **71**: 401.
— Path to Safe. Soc. Econ. **5**: 193.
— Proposal Concerning the Currency. Soc. Econ. **7**: 65.
— Reform in. (H. White) Nation, **63**: 416.
— Saxon Land Credit System. Gunton's M. **11**: 354.
— Scotch. (J. S. Nicholson) J. Pol. Econ. **1**: 487.
— Signs of Sound. Soc. Econ. **9**: 248.
— Some Points in Present Position of. Bank. M. (Lond.) **54**: 123.
— Springer on. (H. White) Nation, **57**: 386.
— State; Cleveland, G., and the Baltimore Plan. Pub. Opin. **17**: 807.
— The State as a Competitor in. Bank. M. (Lond.) **59**: 373. **60**: 697.
— State Banks of Issue. (F. L. McVey) Soc. Econ. **6**: 171.
— Suggestions on Currency and. (A. Ladenburg) Forum, **20**: 513.
— Sumner's History of American. (H. White) Nation, **63**: 32.
— Swiss Banks of Issue. Gunton's M. **11**: 207.
— Wildcat, in the 'teens. (J. B. McMaster) Atlan. **72**: 331.
— With and Without a Government Bank. (Van Buren Denslow) Soc. Econ. **5**: 209.
Banking Developments and Profits. (F. E. Steele) Bank. M. (Lond.) **54**: 497.
Banking Reform and Currency. (W. Knapp) Am. J. Pol. **3**: 140.
Banking System, Canadian. (D. R. Wilkie) Forum, **13**: 325.
— Old and New. (J. H. Walker) Ann. Am. Acad. Pol. Sci. **3**: 581.
Banking Systems. Bank. M. (N. Y.) **48**: 161.
Bankruptcy, After-acquired Property in. (E. C. Willis) Law Q. **10**: 240.
— Contingent Right in. (H. Goudy) Jurid. R. **5**: 212.
— In Difficulties. All the Year, **72**: 9.
— of Partners. (A. T. Murray) Law Q. **7**: 53.
— Preferential Payments in. (W. K. Morton) Jurid. R. **7**: 278.
— Uniform System of. (H. Teichmueller) Am. Law R. **26**: 231.
Bankruptcy Law Codification, International. (J. Jitta) Jurid. R. **7**: 305.
Bankruptcy Legislation. (E. S. Mack) Am. Law R. **28**: 1.
Banks, Agricultural. Char. R. **5**: 284. — (R. A. Yerburgh) J. Statis. Soc. **59**: 459.
— Amalgamation of. (F. E. Steele) Econ. J. **6**: 535. — Bank. M. (Lond.) **58**: 1.
— and Bank Reserves, New York. Soc. Econ. **8**: 150.
— and Bankers in England; Mr. Goschen's Mission. (A. E. Hake) National, **107**: 675.
— and Banking of California. (J. Finley) Overland, n. s. **26**: 657. **27**: 81.
— and the Panic. (A. D. Noyes) Pol. Sci. Q. **9**: 12.
— and Panics of 1893. Bank. M. (N. Y.) **48**: 721.
— and Sound Money. (G. Gunton) Gunton's M. **10**: 404.
— Bankers, and Banking in the North of England: M. Phillips. (R. Ewen) Westm. **143**: 278.
— Bogus. Bank. M. (N. Y.) **47**: 161.
— Coöperative. (H. W. Wolff) National, **24**: 253.
— Failure of, Causes of. Chamb. J. **70**: 417.

Banks for the People. (L. J. Vance) No. Am. 160: 382. — (L. J. Vance) Soc. Econ. 2: 305.
— in Italy, Popular. Bank. M. (N. Y.) 48: 131-369.
— — Scandal of. Pub. Opin. 14: 442.
— National. *See* National Banks.
— National and State. (H. White) Ann. Am. Acad. Pol. Sci. 3: 529.
— of Issue, History of, Conant's. Gunton's M. 10: 413. — (W. G. Sumner) Forum, 22: 182.
— of the North of England, Phillips on. Sat. R. 79: 228.
— Our Village Bank. (H. W. Wolff) Westm. 141: 503.
— People's. (T. Mackay) National, 22: 636.
— — for England. (H. W. Wolff) Econ. R. 3: 521.
— — Wolff on. Ath. '93, 2: 59.
— Remarks on. (R. Ewen) Westm. 146: 80.
— Runs on, 1866, 1892. Bank. M. (Lond.) 54: 633.
— Rural. (E. M. Lynch) Gent. M. n. s. 55: 160.
— Savings. *See* Savings Banks.
— Scotch, their Branches and Cash Credits. (A. S. Michie) Forum, 16: 86.
— Scotch System of Branch Banks. (J. S. Tait) Engin. M. 10: 1014.
— State. Pub. Opin. 15: 378, 568.
— — and Bank-Notes. (C. F. Dunbar) Q. J. Econ. 7: 55.
— — Congressman Harter on. (R. Ogden) Nation, 55: 253.
— — Currency and. (A. L. Ripley) Yale R. 3: 311.
— — Defeat of the Repeal Bill. Pub. Opin. 17: 237.
— — Do we need State-Bank Currency? (E. Atkinson) Engin. M. 4: 497.
— — Reëstablishment of. Pub. Opin. 14: 76.
See also State Banks.
— Taxation of. Bank. M. (N. Y.) 46: 535. 47: 112-916.
Banks, Fishing, Between Cape Cod and Newfoundland. (W. Upham) Am. J. Sci. 147: 123.
Bankside, The Stews of. (W. Rendle) Walford's Antiq. 2: 70.
Banneker, Benjamin, Letter of, to T. Jefferson. (F. Allaben) Nat'l M. (N. Y. '91) 17: 65.
Bannock Indians, A Brush with the. (N. A. Miles) No. Am. 161: 346.
— Home of. (A. Apache) Lend a Hand, 16: 247.
Bantu Customs and Legends. (J. Macdonald) Folk-Lore, 3: 337.
Bantu Languages, Torrend's Grammar of. Ath. '92, 2: 184.
Banville, Théodore de. Temp. Bar, 101: 595. Same art. Liv. Age, 201: 376.
Banziris of the Congo Basin. (F. J. Clozel) Pop. Sci. Mo. 49: 673.
Baptism. (P. Spener) Luth. Q. 23: 533.
— and Confirmation, Early History of. (J. R. Gasquet) Dub. R. 116: 136.
— Archæology of Mode of. (B. B. Warfield) Bib. Sac. 53: 601.
— Augsburg Confession, Art. IX. (R. W. Hufford) Luth. Q. 26: 453.
— Immersion not Essential to. (C. C. Starbuck) Ref. Q. 41: 401.
— in the English Church, Gorham Case. Eng. R. 13: 66, 374.
— Infant, Meaning and Efficacy of. (S. Schwarm) Luth. Q. 26: 540.
— — Order of Service for. (G. U. Wenner) Luth. Q. 25: 231.
— Spener on. (E. J. Metzler) Luth. Q. 23: 533.
— Word of God in. (J. Tomlinson) Luth. Q. 22: 259.
Baptismal Customs. (E. Howlett) Westm. 141: 265. Same art. Ecl. M. 122: 654.
Baptist, What makes a? (H. L. Wayland) Chaut. 18: 66.
Baptist Church in New York. (R. H. Titherington) Munsey, 7: 3.
— Journalism of, in U. S. (H. C. Vedder) Chaut. 21: 602.
Baptist Town, Religious Study of a. (W. B. Hale) Forum, 18: 694.
Baptists, Place of, in the Evolution of British Christianity. (J. Clifford) Time, 20: 625.
Bar, English and American. (A. O. Hall) Green Bag, 5: 237.
— — Contrasted. Green Bag, 5: 493.
— Pettifogging Law-Schools and an Untrained. (D. S. Jordan) Forum, 19: 350.
Bar Harbor. (F. M. Crawford) Scrib. M. 16: 268.
Barabins, Niccolò. (L. Villari) M. of Art, 15: 361.
Baraga, Frederick, Mission to the Chippewas. (R. R. Elliott) Am. Cath. Q. 21: 596.
Baram River, A Journey up. (C. Hose) Geog. J. 1: 193.
Barante, A. G. P. B. de. Memoirs. (A. Laugel) Nation, 54: 264. 56: 364. 58: 310. 60: 378, 420.
Barbadoes. All the Year, 70: 224, 256.
— as a Winter Resort. (T. H. Bindley) National, 20: 270.
— Pets and Pests in. (Maj. Battersby) Chamb. J. 73: 170.
— Visit to. (J. Reid; F. N. Clarke) Good Words, 35: 86.
Barbara; a story. All the Year, 70: 609.
Barbara of the Bell House; a story. (M. Pemberton) Eng. Illust. 14: 137.
Barbary, Peeps into. (J. E. B. Meakin) Harper, 93: 387.
Barbary; a story. (E. V. Wilson) McClure, 2: 282.
Barbary Corsairs. (F. H. Tyrrell) Asia. R. 10: 113, 388. 11: 438.
Barber, Amzi Lorenzo, with portrait. (F. Allaben) Nat'l M. (N. Y. '91) 15: 651.
Barber, Charles Burton. (H. Furniss) M. of Art, 19: 14.
Barberries, Hardy. (J. G. Jack) Garden & F. 6: 134.
— Study of Uses and Origin. (F. LeR. Sargent) Pop. Sci. Mo. 45: 594, 784.
Barber's Pound. (W. J. Lacey) Longm. 21: 95.
Barber-Surgeons. (J. F. Hewitt) Westm. 146: 23, 117.
Barbet de Jouy, Joseph Henry, Protector of the Louvre. Art J. 48: 260.
Barbizon School of Painters. Art J. 48: 119. — (W. Lawler) Idler, 8: 430. — (D. C. Thomson) M. of Art, 11: 181, 385. 12: 181-397.
Barbour, John, and Blind Harry as Literature. (W. A. Craigie) Scot. R. 22: 173.
Barcelona: a World's Wonder. (C. W. Wood) Argosy, 61: 683.
Barclay, Thomas, Selections from Correspondence of. (R. G. Thwaites) Dial (Ch.) 19: 43.
Bardienne, M., Bronze Founder. Acad. 41: 357.
Bare-Faced Deception, A; a story. (C. E. Brimblecom) Overland, n. s. 20: 257.
Barford, Povl Frederik. (R. N. Bain) Ath. '96, 2: 34.
Bargain of Faust, The; a poem. (A. W. Rollins) Cosmopol. 20: 626.
Barges and Bargemen. (A. Ansted) Good Words, 37: 412.
— on the Thames. (R. Spinner) M. of Art, 4: 520.
Bargis; a Story of Superstitions. (S. Maxwell) Gent. M. n. s. 49: 604.
Barham, Richard H. (G. Saintsbury) Macmil. 69: 105.
— in Kent. Temp. Bar, 106: 89. Same art. Liv. Age, 207: 244.
— Ingoldsby Legends. Eng. R. 7: 59. — Bookw. 6: 145.
Baring-Gould, S. *See* Gould, S. Baring.
Barium, Method for Determination of. (F. W. Mar) Am. J. Sci. 143: 521.
— Quantitative Separation of, from Strontium. (P. E. Browning) Am. J. Sci. 144: 459.

Barium, Separation from Calcium, by Amyl Alcohol. (P. E. Browning) Am. J. Sci. **143**: 314.
Barker, Wm. C., with portrait. (H. L. Conard) Nat'l M. (N. Y. '91) **15**: 557.
Barker; a story. All the Year, **72**: 541.
Barker's Second Honeymoon; a tale. (E. S. Atkinson) Canad. M. **7**: 470.
Barlaam and Josaphat Legend. (F. C. Conybeare) Folk-Lore, **7**: 101.
— Two Books about. (F. C. Conybeare) Acad. **49**: 223.
Barlow, Aaron, Book of Orders of. (C. B. Todd) Am. Hist. Reg. **3**: 662.
Barlow, Gen. F. C. (E. H. Abbot) Harv. Grad. M. **4**: 526.
Barlow, George. A Lost Mother. Spec. **69**: 856.
Barlow, Jane. (J. MacArthur) Critic, **24**: 325. — With portrait. Bk. News, **13**: 498.
Barnabas and Saul, Call and Ordination of, to Missionary Work. (A. Sutherland) Meth. R. **53**: 562.
Barnabas Rabbit's Rain-Cloud; a story. Cornh. **69**: 532.
Barnabee, Henry Clay. (F. A. Munsey) Munsey, **12**: 612.
Barnard, Edward Emerson. (S. W. Burnham) Harper, **87**: 530. — With portrait. (S. W. Burnham) Pop. Astron. **1**: 193, 341.
— Work of, at Lick Observatory. (S. W. Burnham) Pop. Astron. **1**: 441.
Barnard, Frederick. (G. Holme) Munsey, **10**: 37.
Barnard, George Grey. Critic, **29**: 348.
Barnard, Henry. (J. L. Hughes) New Eng. M. n. s. **14**: 560.
Barnardo, Dr. James, and his Work. (W. T. Stead) R. of Rs. (N. Y.) **14**: 181.
— Homes for Children. (F. W. Farrar) M. Chr. Lit. **7**: 17.
Barnby, Sir Joseph. Acad. **49**: 103. — Ath. '**96**, **1**: 157.
— A Last Reminiscence of. (Emily S. Judge) Westm. **116**: 267.
כר נשא; was this a Messianic Title? (N. Schmidt) J. Bib. Lit. **15**: 36.
Barnes, Catherine Weed. (M. A. Taft) Chaut. **15**: 730.
Barnes, James, with portrait. Bk. Buyer, **13**: 343.
Barnet and Barnet Field. (J. D. Symon) Eng. Illust. **14**: 259.
— Battle of. (J. H. Ramsay) Acad. **43**: 106–175.
Barnett, Henry Hyam Vincent, with portrait. Theatre, **29**: 24.
Barometers, Living. Chamb. J. **72**: 714.
Barometric Measurement of Heights. (J. E. Gore) Pop. Sci. Mo. **46**: 366. — (J. E. Gore) Gent. M. n. s. **51**: 139. Same art. Ecl. M. **121**: 352.
Barometric Pressure, Sub-Tropical Zones of High. (W. Ferrel) Science, **17**: 8.
Baron of Beaugard, The; a story. (G. Parker) Idler, **6**: 395.
Barr, Amelia E., with portrait. Bk. Buyer, **8**: 323. — With portrait. Bk. News, **7**: 238.
Barr, Robert, with portrait. Bk. News, **15**: 44. — With portrait. Bk. Buyer, **13**: 15. — (C. S. Allen) Canad. M. **4**: 545.
Barra, Island of. All the Year, **74**: 496.
Barras, P. F. J. N. Memoirs. Sat. R. **81**: 604. — (A. Laugel) Nation, **61**: 7, 44. **62**: 376, 393. — (J. H. M'Carthy) New R. **13**: 45. — (E. G. Johnson) Dial (Ch.) **18**: 338. — Sat. R. **79**: 832. — Ed. R. **182**: 374.
Barren Grounds, On Snow-Shoes to the. (C. W. Whitney) Harper, **92**: 10–717.
Barres, Maurice. Blessedness of Egoism. (R. P. Jacobus) Fortn. **65**: 40.
Barrett, Wilson. Pharaoh. Theatre, **29**: 202.
Barrett, Wilson, in "The Sign of the Cross," with portrait. Theatre, **36**: 129.
Barrie, James Matthew. Critic, **21**: 142. — With portrait. Bk. Buyer, **9**: 51. **11**: 473. **13**: 612. — With portrait. Bk. News, **11**: 261.
— and W. Robertson Nicoll, in New York. (J. B. Gilder) Critic, **29**: 301.
— Little Minister. Scot. R. **23**: 42.
— Sentimental Tommy. Sat. R. **82**: 526. — (A. T. Quiller-Couch) Contemp. **70**: 652. Same art. Liv. Age, **211**: 807. — Acad. **50**: 385.
— "Walker, London." Gent. M. n. s. **48**: 421. — Theatre, **28**: 202.
Barrington, George, the Convict Historian. Bookworm, **7**: 207.
Barrington, Mrs. Russell. Lena's Picture. Spec. **69**: 926. — (M. E. G. Duff) 19th Cent. **33**: 889.
Barrington's Marriage. All the Year, **75**: 323.
Barristers, A Chat about. Chamb. J. **73**: 468.
Barron, Commodore James. (J. H. Marr) Am. Hist. Reg. **2**: 755.
Barrow at Howe Hill, Yorkshire, Exploration of. (J. R. Mortimer; J. G. Garson) Anthrop. J. **22**: 3.
Bart, Jean; the Ex-Pirate of Dunkirk. Chamb. J. **71**: 733.
Barter, Aristotle's Doctrine of. (W. J. Ashley) Q. J. Econ. **9**: 333.
Barthélemy Saint-Hilaire, Jules. Lit. W. (Bost.) **27**: 73. — (T. Stanton) Nation, **61**: 406. — (J. B. Latham) Time, **13**: 548.
Bartholdi's Statue of Liberty, Lighting of. (D. P. Heap) Lippinc. **50**: 803.
Bartholomy's Story. (F. Brookfield) Eng. Illust. **11**: 791.
Bartlett, Ichabod, with portrait. (F. W. Hackett) Green Bag, **6**: 105.
Bartlett, John, with portrait. Bk. News, **13**: 75.
Bartlett, Thomas. (W. P. Stafford) Green Bag, **8**: 45.
Bartolommeo, Fra, and Mariotto Albertinelli. (J. Cartwright) M. of Art, **6**: 426.
Bartolozzi, F. Bk. Buyer, **2**: 148.
Barton, Benjamin Smith, with portrait. Pop. Sci. Mo. **48**: 834.
Barton, Bernard, Some Letters from. (M. Howitt) Good Words, **36**: 236.
Barton, Clara. (L. Whiting) Chaut. **22**: 725. — With portrait. (G. H. Pullman) Our Day, **16**: 16.
— and the Red Cross, with portrait. (S. W. R. Williams) R. of Rs. (N. Y.) **9**: 311.
Bartram, John. Purchase of his Farm for a Park by Philadelphia. (M. L. Dock) Garden & F. **9**: 121.
— and Wm., Sketch of. Pop. Sci. Mo. **40**: 827.
Barye, Antoine Louis, Work of, Balki's. M. of Art, **14**: 175.
Bas' Therese; a story. (J. P. Rudd) Outing, **25**: 273.
Basalts of Kula. (H. S. Washington) Am. J. Sci. **147**: 114.
Base-ball. (J. H. Mandigo) Chaut. **15**: 410. — Sat. R. **74**: 100. — (N. B. Young) Lippinc. **52**: 229.
Bashan, Across Southern. (G. R. Lees) Geog. J. **5**: 1.
— In. (J. Wells) Sund. M. **25**: 381. Same art. Liv. Age, **211**: 127.
— Travel in. (A. H. Sayce) Acad. **48**: 487.
Bashfulness in Children. (J. M. Baldwin) Educa. R. **8**: 434.
Bashkirtseff, Marie. (H. S. Wilson) Gent. M. n. s. **56**: 506.
Basilica of Montmartre, Paris. (J. M. Kiely) Cath. World, **63**: 398.
Basilides. Is He Quoted in the Philosophumena? (J. Drummond) J. Bib. Lit. **11**: 133.

Basingstoke. Guild of Holy Ghost. (F. C. Lefroy) Walford's Antiq. 3: 243.
Baskerville, Thomas; an Old English Topographer. Chamb. J. 72: 364.
Basket-plants. (W. H. Taplin) Garden & F. 5: 572.
Basque Books, Old and New. (W. V. Eys) Acad. 47: 152. — (E. S. Dodgson) Acad. 47: 318.
Basque Grammar, A. (L. Thomas) Acad. 45: 517.
Basque Music. (W. Webster) Acad. 41: 208.
Basques; their Country and their Origin. (T. L. Pipson) Gent. M. n. s. 56: 356.
— An Unconquered People. (E. T. Spring) Cosmopol. 17: 275.
Bass, Black, A Day with. (F. J. Lynde) Outing, 26: 369.
— — Fishing for. (F. J. Hagan) Outing, 22: 163.
— — — in Fox River. (F. J. Wells) Outing, 28: 130.
— — — in Maine. (A. Pierre) Outing, 22: 316.
— — — in New England. (C. F. Danforth) New Eng. M. n. s. 6: 661.
— Illinois, Sport with. (A. K. Stewart) Outing, 24: 257.
Bass Brooms. Chamb. J. 71: 447.
Bass Rock (Frith of Forth) and its Winged Inhabitants. (H. F. Witherby) Knowl. 18: 41.
Basse, William. Poems. Sat. R. 75: 245. — (E. K. Chambers) Acad. 44: 247.
Bassett, Allan Lee, with portrait. Nat'l M. (N. Y. '91) 19: 194.
Bassi, Ugo, A Portrait of. Good Words, 24: 560.
Bassompierre, François de, Marshal of France. (C. Whibley) New R. 15: 635.
Bastardy, Law of. (J. Kidd) Jurid. R. 8: 180.
Bastianini, Giovanni, Forgeries of. (N. Barstow) M. of Art, 9: 503.
Bastien-Lepage, Jules. (W. C. Brownell) M. of Art, 6: 265. — (C. Phillips) M. of Art, 15: 267. — (Julia Cartwright-Ady) Portfo. 1894: no. 4. — Spec. 69: 565.
— Personal Reminiscences of. (B. Karageorgevitch) M. of Art, 13: 83.
— Theuriet's. (K. Cox) Nation, 54: 343.
Bastile of Paris. (H. S. Howell) Canad. M. 2: 36.
— Last Governor of the. Liv. Age, 203: 318.
Bataks, Land of. (A. von Hügel) Geog. J. 7: 75, 175.
Batavians, Among the. (T. Edwin) Time, 5: 445.
Batchelder Family, Wills of. (C. E. Batchelder) N. E. Reg. 47: 356.
Bates, Arlo, with portrait. Bk. Buyer, 4: 252.
Bates, Henry Walter. Acad. 41: 186. — Ath. '92, 1: 248. — Nature, 45: 398. — With portrait. Pop. Sci. Mo. 42: 118. — (G. Allen) Fortn. 58: 798. — Liv. Age, 196: 679.
Bates College. (C. A. Chase) New Eng. M. n. s. 13: 513.
Bath, John Alexander Thynne, 4th Marquis of. (M. MacColl) Contemp. 69: 775. Same art. Liv. Age, 210: 44.
Bath, Maine. (E. C. Plummer) New Eng. M. n. s. 15: 353.
Bath Road, Old. All the Year, 73: 6.
Bath Stage, The. Gent. M. n. s. 49: 642.
Bath, German. (E. C. Cook) Gent. M. n. s. 49: 350. Same art. Liv. Age, 195: 627.
Bath Brick. Chamb. J. 73: 21.
Bathe, William. (E. Hogan) Month, 77: 532. 78: 244.
Bathing at the American Sea-shore Resorts. (J. H. Adams) Cosmopol. 19: 316.
— at the Continental Sea-shore Resorts. (J. H. Adams) Cosmopol. 19: 131.
— at the English Sea-shore Resorts. (J. H. Adams) Cosmopol. 19: 395.
— in Ancient Rome, and its Effects on Roman Character. (A. Inkersley) Educa. 16: 134.
Baths, Hot Sulphur, of Kusatsu. Chamb. J. 72: 118.
Baths, Hot-water Apparatus for. (W. P. Gerhard) Am. Arch. 44: 97.
— Public. (G. Brown) Char. R. 2: 143. — Citizen, 1: 249.
Bathurst, Benjamin; the Lost Ambassador. (M. Howitt) Good Words, 37: 40, 114. Same art. Liv. Age, 208: 563.
Batrachia and Reptilia of N. A. (E. D. Cope) Am. Natural. 30: 886, 1003.
Bats, Leathern Wings of. (F. Finn) Chamb. J. 70: 774.
Battacks, The, Notes on. (R. W. Shufeldt) Pop. Sci. Mo. 50: 34.
Battalion Organization. Un. Serv. M. 8: 247.
Battas, Folk-lore of. (E. B. Tylor) Acad. 47: 308.
Batteries. *See* Electrical Batteries.
— Storage. (P. G. Salom) J. Frankl. Inst. 5: 321.
— — Chloride. (H. Lloyd) J. Frankl. Inst. 136: 306.
Battery, Closed-circuit, Principles of Construction of. (E. F. Northrup) J. Frankl. Inst. 135: 223, 318, 396.
Battersea Polytechnic Institute. R. of Rs. (N. Y.) 9: 444. — (R. A. Gregory) Nature, 50: 114.
Battle; An Actual Experience under Fire. (J. B. Wilson) McClure, 2: 486.
— Human Animal in. (H. W. Wilson) Fortn. 66: 272.
— Losses in. Sat. R. 77: 93.
Battle in Crackerdom, A. (H. S. Edwards) Cent. 21: 457.
Battle of Salamanca. (B. P. Galdós) Lippinc. 55: 723
Battle of the Snow Plows; a Story of Railroading. (C. Warman) McClure, 8: 92.
Battle Hymn of Labor. (N. B. Simmons) Arena, 5: 401.
Battlefield up to Date, A; a story. (R. Marsh) Idler, 10: 46.
Battleship, The, as a Fighting Machine. (G. W. Melville) Engin. M. 7: 613.
— Evolution of a. (A. F. Matthews) Cent. 26: 347.
— in Action. (S. A. Staunton) Harper, 88: 653.
— Limits of. (W. Kent) Cassier, 1: 61.
Battleship Design, Absence of a Standard in. (R. Hunt) Engin. M. 12: 292.
Battles of English History, George's. Sat. R. 82: 45.
— Pictures of. (C. Williams) M. of Art, 19: 346.
Bauble Shop, a Play, Evolution of. (F. H. Morland) Theatre, 30: 181.
Baudelaire, Charles. (C. E. Meetkerke) Gent. M. n. s. 57: 592.
— and Poe, Edgar A. (E. Stuart) 19th Cent. 34: 65. Same art. Liv. Age, 198: 692.
Báudi, Miklós. (B. Elek) Longm. 29: 46.
Baudry, Paul. (C. Phillips) M. of Art, 9: 468.
Bauernfeld, Eduard, Austrian Dramatist. (E. Friend) Theatre, 28: 285.
Baur, F. C., and New Testament Criticism. (H. Holtzmann) New World, 3: 201.
Bavaria and its People. (W. C. Preston) Sund. M. 21: 669.
— Byways of. (J. E. Rogers) Outing, 26: 260.
Bayard, Thomas F., as a Diplomat. (L. R. Harley) Am. M. Civics, 7: 613.
Bayeux Tapestry, Evidence of its Probable Date. (F. H. B. Daniell) Eng. Hist. R. 7: 705.
— Reproduction in Facsimile of. (L. Higgin) M. of Art, 10: 345.
Baylor, Frances C., with portrait. Bk. Buyer, 4: 492.
Bayly, Ada Ellen, with portrait. Bk. News, 8: 64.
— Novels. Church Q. 35: 143.
Bayne, Peter. Acad. 49: 137.
Bayou, The American Word. (W. S. Wyman) Nation, 59: 361, 381.
Bayou Teche, Along the. (J. Ralph) Harper, 87: 870.
Bayreuth. (W. M. Payne) Music, 6: 594. 7: 58.
— Memories of. (E. H. Bell) Univ. R. 1: 560.

Bayreuth Revisited. (H. E. Krehbiel) Scrib. M. **11**: 98.
Bayreuth and Wagner, 1894. Spec. **73**: 207. — All the Year, **75**: 280. — Sat. R. **78**: 207. — (M. A. A. Galloway) 19th Cent. **36**: 507.
— Musical Festival, Criticism of. Sat. R. **82**: 132, 161.
— Hallucination of. (J. F. Runciman) New R. **15**: 331.
— Influence of. (J. A. Fuller-Maitland) 19th Cent. **40**: 360.
— Munich and. (C. Phillips) Fortn. **66**: 553.
— Wagner's Opera at. (L. A. Bourgault-Ducoudray) Chaut. **17**: 63.
Bazaine, Marshal. (Emily Crawford) Univ. R. **2**: 216.
— Alternative of. (A. Forbes) Un. Serv. M. **8**: 431.
Bazan, Emilia P. (S. Baxter) Cosmopol. **15**: 228. — With portrait. Bk. Buyer, **8**: 298.
Bdellostomids, Lepidosirenids and. (T. Gill) Am. Natural. **28**: 581.
Beaches, Sea. (N. S. Shaler) Scrib. M. **11**: 758.
Beachy Head, Battle of. Macmil. **72**: 222.
Beaconsfield, Benjamin Disraeli, Earl of. (G. Saintsbury) M. of Art, **9**: 221. — With portraits. (A. Badeau) Cosmopol. **14**: 501.
— as a Landscape Painter. (W. Sichel) Time, **18**: 533.
— as a Phrase-maker. (A. F. Robbins) Gent. M. n. s. **52**: 302. Same art. Ecl. M. **123**: 121.
— Characteristics of. (F. Greenwood) Cornh. **74**: 589.
— Death of, Political Effects of. Time, **2**: 428.
— Life of, Unexplored Passages in. Time, **1**: 129.
— Lyre of. (W. Meynell) Eng. Illust. **12**: no. 7, 28.
Beagles, Hunting with. (B. S. Turpin) Outing, **28**: 37.
Beams, Flexure of, Laws of, Apparatus for Experimenting with. (J. L. Greenleaf) J. Frankl. Inst. **140**: 27.
Beans, Jumping. (G. C. Nuttall) Chamb. J. **73**: 249.
Bear, The, and his Indian Wife; legend. (J. Deans) J. Am. Folk-Lore, **2**: 255.
— St. Elias. (W. H. Dall) Science, n. s. **2**: 87.
Bear-chasing in the Rocky Mountains. (F. Remington) Harper, **91**: 240.
Bear Flag, The. (J. Bidwell) Overland, n. s. **25**: 506.
— An Eye Witness's Story of the. (T. Lindsey) Overland, n. s. **27**: 218.
Bear Hunt, First. (F. Whishaw) Longm. **22**: 260. Same art. Liv. Age, **198**: 555.
Bear Hunt, Norwegian. Outing, **19**: 381.
Bear-hunting in British Columbia. (W. E. Coffin) Outing, **29**: 17.
— in Cashmere. (G. L. Morley) Un. Serv. M. **9**: 419.
— in Japan. Outing, **26**: 221.
— in Russia. Temp. Bar, **97**: 107. Same art. Liv. Age, **196**: 425.
Bear River Formation. (C. A. White) Am. J. Sci. **143**: 91.
— Stratigraphical Position of. (T. W. Stanton) Am. J. Sci. **143**: 98.
"Bear," U. S. Revenue Cutter, Arctic Cruise of. (S. Jackson) Nat. Geog. M. **7**: 27.
Beard, Daniel C. (A. N. Jervis) Q. Illust. **1**: 261. — With portrait. Bk. Buyer, **13**: 608.
Beard, William H. M. of Art, **5**: 14.
Beards. (R. E. Ingpen) Gent. M. n. s. **54**: 504. — Chamb. J. **68**: 671.
— and no Beards. (J. C. Haddon) Eng. Illust. **10**: 27.
Beardsley, Aubrey. Bookman, **1**: 159. — With portrait. Bk. Buyer, **12**: 26.
— and the Decadents. (M. Armour) M. of Art, **20**: 9.
Bearing-metal Alloys. (C. B. Dudley) J. Frankl. Inst. **132**: 81, 121.
Bearing-Reins. Time, **14**: 465.
Bearpaw Mountains of Montana. (W. H. Weed and L. V. Pirsson) Am. J. Sci. **151**: 283, 351. **152**: 136, 188.
Bear's-Head Brooch, The; a story. (E. Ingersoll) Outing, **19**: 251.
Bears; Bear and for Bear. (E. W. Sandys) Outing, **24**: 416.
— Himalayan, Amongst the. (C. Hastings) Argosy, **59**: 109. Same art. Liv. Age, **204**: 507.
— Polar, Shooting of. (F. Nansen) Longm. **24**: 253. Same art. Liv. Age, **202**: 283.
— Russian, Among the. (F. Whishaw) Outing, **27**: 463.
Beasts of Burden. (N. S. Shaler) Scrib. M. **16**: 82.
Beatification in the East. (L. M. Brunton) Contemp. **66**: 129. Same art. Liv. Age, **202**: 374.
Beatrix de Cusance. (H. W. Wolff) Gent. M. n. s. **48**: 550.
Beau of Modern Babylon. Eng. Illust. **16**: 300.
Beau's Stratagem; a story. All the Year, **75**: 110.
Beaufort, Joan. Belgravia, **79**: 132.
Beaulieu, Birds at. Spec. **76**: 919.
Beaumarchais, P. A. C. de. (Yetta B. de Bury) Time, **18**: 420.
Beaumont, Francis. Lecture on Grammar. (E. Scott) Ath. '94, **1**: 115.
— and Fletcher. (J. R. Lowell) Harper, **85**: 757.
— "Psyche." (C. F. S. Warren) Bookworm, **5**: 25, 43.
Beaumont, Sir George, and Wordsworth. (J. A. Noble) M. of Art, **7**: 206.
Beauport *Loup-garou*, The. (M. H. Catherwood) Atlan. **72**: 630.
Beaurepaire, Froment de. Thoughts of a Man of Thirteen Years. Church Q. **35**: 143.
Beautiful and the Sublime, Theories of. (J. L. Powell) Dub. R. **119**: 302.
— and the True, The. (M. Reid) Macmil. **65**: 266.
— Angel of the. (W. Boyd Carpenter) Sund. M. **21**: 155, 235.
— How to Become. (Agnes J. Burke) Time, **1**: 410.
Beautiful Delusion, A; a story. (Mrs. A. Phillips) Lond. Soc. **58**: 295.
Beauty. (M. E. W. Sherwood) Cosmopol. **17**: 259.
— Aids to. All the Year, **72**: 328.
— and Evolution. (St.G. Mivart) Univ. R. **3**: 101.
— and Sanity. (V. Paget) Fortn. **64**: 252.
— Character Note. Cornh. **70**: 174.
— Decay of. (F. Boyle) New R. **9**: 636.
— Ideals of, in Keats and Browning. (A. Groff) Poet-Lore, **5**: 247.
— Oriental Types of. (E. M. Bowden) Eng. Illust. **10**: 329.
— Strength of. (W. Hutchinson) Open Court, **10**: 4951, 4969.
Beauty for Ashes; a story. (L. C. Gibson) Our Day, **16**: 169.
Beauty of Voss, The. (C. Edwardes) Chamb. J. **71**: 574.
Beaver, American, Martin on. Spec. **70**: 131. — (R. Brown) Acad. **41**: 569.
Beaver Dam, Wis., Free Library. Lib. J. **21**: 182.
Beaver Eater, The. *See* Wolverine.
Beaver River, Inner Gorge Terraces of. (R. H. Hice) Am. J. Sci. **149**: 112.
Bechtel, John; his Contributions to Literature and his Descendants. (J. W. Jordan) Pennsyl. M. **19**: 137.
Bechuanaland, Among the Chiefs of. (J. T. Bent) Fortn. **57**: 642. Same art. Liv. Age, **194**: 37.
— British, Position of. Dub. R. **112**: 179.
Becke, Louis, with portrait. Bk. Buyer, **13**: 296.
— Ebbing of the Tide. Sat. R. **81**: 401.
Becket, Thomas à. *See* Thomas.
Beckford, Wm. (G. Barnett Smith) Time, **3**: **454**.

Beckford, Wm. Dreams, or Letters from Europe. (R. Garnett) Univ. R. 8: 112.
Beckington, Thomas, Bishop, and Henry VI. (G. G. Perry) Eng. Hist. R. 9: 264.
Beckwith, James Carroll. (C. W. Larned) Mo. Illust. 3: 131.
Beddoes, Thomas Lovell. (Mrs. Andrew Crosse) Temp. Bar, 101: 357. Same art. Liv. Age, 201: 157.
Bede, Venerable. Historical Works, Plummer's. Church Q. 43: 112.
Bedes, Bidding the. (J. Moyes) Dub. R. 115: 162.
Bedford, Mass., Governor John Winthrop's Farm in. (A. E. Brown) New Eng. M. n. s. 6: 325.
Bedouins of Palestine. Ali Diâb's Tent. (G. A. Smith) Good Words, 37: 238.
Beds and Bedrooms. (J. H. Pollen) M. of Art, 9: 81.
Bee, Honey, of the Future. Chamb. J. 70: 741.
— in Greek Mythology. (A. B. Cook) J. Hel. Stud. 15: 1.
— Leaf-cutting. (F. M. Duncan) Knowl. 19: 259.
Bee Hunting. (E. Cooper) Outing, 24: 475.
Bee Parasites. (E. A. Butler) Knowl. 15: 126–181.
Bee-ranching, Arcadian, in So. California. (N. Eames) Harper, 92: 509.
— in California. Chamb. J. 71: 789.
Bees. (J. K. Reeve) Lippinc. 58: 253.
— and Buckwheat. (C. C. Abbott) Lippinc. 53: 419.
— and Dead Carcasses. (W. F. Kirby) Nature, 49: 555.
— Employed in War. (W. Stokes) Acad. 50: 13.
— Honey. (C. G. Ridout) Munsey, 9: 340.
— Pleasant Occupation of Tending. (W. Z. Hutchinson) Cosmopol. 19: 29, 159.
Beech Tree. (G. Paxton) Knowl. 19: 282.
— Copper-Leaved, Origin of. Garden & F. 7: 2.
Beecher, Henry W. (A. H. Peters) Open Court, 1: 329.
— Anecdote of Boyhood. Bost. 2: 154.
— Recollections of. (H. C. King) Mo. Illust. 11: 581.
— Statue of, in Brooklyn, N. Y. (R. H. Titherington) Munsey, 6: 27.
Beecher, Lyman. (H. A. Glass) Sund. M. 24: 588, 682, 754.
Beef, Roast, of Old England. (H. Hall) Walford's Antiq. 2: 281.
Beefsteak, History of a. (J. Oldfield) Gent. M. n. s. 53: 533.
Beehive Huts. (S. Baring-Gould) Chamb. J. 70: 598.
Beer; Malt Liquors of the English. (T. H. B. Graham) Gent. M. n. s. 49: 52.
Beer-money, Work of, in England. (T. Rae) Contemp. 66: 508.
Beerbohm, Max. Works; with Bibliography by Lane. Sat. R. 82: 221.
Beere, Mrs. Bernard. Critic, 21: 300.
Beers, Jan Van. *See* Van Beers.
Beeswax, Examination of. (L. F. Kebler) J. Frankl. Inst. 137: 58.
Beet, Joseph Agar. Study in Scientific Theology and Study in Personal Religion. Church Q. 42: 432.
Beet Sugar Industry, American. (H. S. Adams) Cassier, 7: 504. — (H. W. Wiley) Engin. M. 7: 85.
— Effect of Bounties. (E. E. Williams) Sat. R. 82: 156, 208.
Beethoven, L. van. (Mrs. W. H. Wait) Chaut. 23: 335.
— at Home. Music, 2: 215.
— Heroic Symphony. Sat. R. 80: 797.
— Immortal Beloved. (M. Tenger) Music, 4: 1.
— Note Book of, of 1803. (G. Nottebohm) Music, 7: 371, 473. 8: 149.
— Piano Sonatas by. (W. S. B. Mathews) Music, 6: 200.
— — Impressions of. (F. H. Clark) Music, 1: 243–368.
— Symphonies of. Ed. R. 184: 455. — (J. F. Runciman) New R. 14: 669. 15: 34.
Beethoven Festival at Bonn. (J. S. Shedlock) Acad. 45: 403.
Beethoveniana. (P. Spitta) Open Court, 3: 1871, 1897.
Beetles, Bark-boring. (E. A. Butler) Knowl. 17: 4.
— Leaping. (E. A. Butler) Knowl. 18: 176.
Before and After. (H. Jones) Good Words, 34: 837.
Before the Break of Day. (B. Matthews) Harper, 89: 222.
Beggars and Philanthropy. Lend a Hand, 12: 170.
— How London deals with. (Lord Norton) No. Am. 161: 685.
— of Former Times. Sat. R. 77: 308.
— of Paris. (L. Paulian) Chaut. 19: 55.
— Some Peculiar. (R. Tangye) Chamb. J. 73: 801.
— Study of, and their Lodgings. (A. F. Sanborn) Forum, 19: 200.
Beggars, The; a poem. (William Young) Cosmopol. 16: 435.
Beggars of the Sea and Queen Elizabeth. (J. H. Round) Ath. '95, 2: 455.
Beggarstaff Bros. Idler, 8: 519.
Begging, Street, as a Fine Art. (K. K. Bentwick) No. Am. 158: 125.
Begging Letters and their Writers. Macmil. 70: 52. Same art. Ecl. M. 122: 851.
Beginner, The. (R. Broughton) Temp. Bar, 101: 1-489. 102: 1–145.
Beginner's Literary Experience, Another. (J. M. Loes) Writer, 7: 24.
Begonias. (J. N. Gerard) Garden & F. 5: 44, 76, 513.
— Cultivation of. (C. L. Allen) Garden & F. 5: 475. — (T. D. Hatfield) Garden & F. 7: 167.
— Notes on. (T. D. Hatfield) Garden & F. 5: 152. — (J. N. Gerard) Garden & F. 5: 452. 6: 356. — (R. Cameron) Garden & F. 8: 508. 9: 18, 527.
— Tuberous. (C. L. Allen) Garden & F. 6: 169.
— — as Bedding Plants. (W. N. Craig) Garden & F. 7: 157.
— Winter-Flowering. (J. N. Gerard) Garden & F. 6: 125. — (T. D. Hatfield) Garden & F. 9: 37.
Beguines and the Weaving Brothers. (A. M. F. Robinson) Time, 12: 177.
Behar, Disaffection in. (D. N. Reid) Fortn. 61: 808.
Behar Cadastral Survey, Spoliations in. (R. Lethbridge) Asia R. 16: 299.
Behar Planter, Reminiscences of a. Liv. Age, 208: 632.
Behind the Scenes. Atlan. 71: 856.
Behn, Mrs. Aphra, and Nell Gwyn. Ath. '94, 2: 396.
Behring, Cartography of First Voyage of. (A. W. Greely) Nat. Geog. M. 2: 205.
— First Expedition, Review of. (Wm. H. Dall) Nat. Geog. M. 2: 111.
Behring Sea, History of. (Hyde Clarke) Asia. R. 10: 273.
Behring Sea Controversy. (B. F. Butler; Marquis of Lorne) No. Am. 154: 562. — (T. B. Browning) Law Q. 7: 128, 315. — (E. Bond) Un. Serv. M. 7: 887. — (M. C. Seymour) 19th Cent. 33: 606. — (B. F. Tracy) No. Am. 156: 513. — (Q. A. Lash) Canad. M. 1: 289.
— Arbitration of. (A. S. Cameron) Nat'l M. (N. Y. '91) 19: 91. — (G. H. Knott) Am. Law R. 27: 684. — Spec. 71: 231.
— — The Award. (A. W. S. Hill) National, 22: 19. Same art. Ecl. M. 121: 503. — Sat. R. 76: 205. — (R. Ogden) Nation, 57: 113. — Pub. Opin. 15: 497, 522. — Blackw. 154: 745. — (G. H. Knott) Jurid. R. 6: 21.
— — — More Particulars of. (S. Webster) Nation, 57: 166.
— — Results of. (J. W. Foster) No. Am. 161: 693. — (E. L. Godkin) Nation, 61: 421.

Behring Sea Controversy, from an Economic Standpoint. (J. Stanley-Brown) Yale R. **2**: 195.
— A Naturalist's View. (P. L. Sclater) 19th Cent. **33**: 1038. Same art. Liv. Age, **198**: 251.
— Passing of the Fur-Seal. (H. L. Nelson) Harper, **92**: 462.
— Understanding with Russia. (C. D. Collet) Asia. R. **11**: 361.
Being, Philosophy of. (A. C. Stephens) Music, **2**: 448.
Beirut, Arabic Press of. (J. Orne) Bib. Sac. **51**: 281.
Belcher, Jonathan, a Royal Governor of Massachusetts. (G. E. Ellis) Atlan. **72**: 209.
Belding, Hiram H., with portrait. (H. L. Conard) Nat'l M. (N. Y. '91) **15**: 309.
Belfast, Bibliography of. (J. S. Crone) Bookworm, **3**: 289.
— Old, Young's. Sat. R. **81**: 562.
— Town Book of. Sat. R. **74**: 57.
Belfry, The. (S. Baring-Gould) Sund. **24**: 446.
Belgium, Constitution of the Kingdom of. Ann. Am. Acad. Pol. Sci. **7**: 295. — (H. H. Robbins) Gunton's M. **11**: 46.
— — Revision of, in 1893. (M. Vauthier) Pol. Sci. Q. **9**: 704. — (A. Le Ghait) No. Am. **157**: 550. — (J. M. Vincent) Nation, **54**: 186.
— Councils of Arbitration in. And. R. **17**: 609.
— The Danger in. Macmil. **72**: 1.
— Economics in. (E. Mahaim) Econ. J. **5**: 462.
— Elections under the New Law. Sat. R. **78**: 428.
— Electoral Experiment in. (W. C. Robinson) Dub. R. **116**: 109.
— Law Courts of. (J. B. Osborne) Green Bag, **8**: 158.
— Literary Movement in, New. (W. Sharp) 19th Cent. **34**: 416.
— Literature of, 1891-92. (P. Fredericq) Ath. '92, **2**: 5.
— — 1892-93. (P. Fredericq) Ath. '93, **2**: 7.
— — 1893-94. (P. Fredericq) Ath. '94, **2**: 7.
— — 1894-95. (P. Fredericq) Ath. '95, **2**: 7.
— — 1895-96. (P. Fredericq) Ath. '96, **2**: 7.
— Monetary Legislation in. (H. P. Willis) J. Pol. Econ. **3**: 222.
— Politics in, 1892. Result of the Elections. Spec. **68**: 837.
— Revolution in, 1893. Pub. Opin. **15**: 94.
— Situation in. (L. de Lorac) National, **24**: 334.
— Universal Suffrage for. Spec. **70**: 509.
Belgrade, Siege of, by Muhammad II., 1456. (R. N. Bain) Eng. Hist. R. **7**: 235.
Belief and Happiness. (C. P. Woolley) Open Court, **6**: 3160.
— Argument for. (H. M. Bompas) National, **21**: 632. Same art. Ecl. M. **121**: 289.
— Foundations of. *See* Balfour, A. J.
— Test of. (J. P. Gordy) Philos. R. **3**: 257.
— The Will in its Relation to. (W. James) New World, **5**: 327.
Beliefs of a Brother. (R. M. Smith) Bib. World, **3**: 30.
Belknap Genealogy. (A. A. Codman) N. E. Reg. **49**: 68.
Bell, Alexander Graham. Cassier, **8**: 55.
Bell, Charles H., Memoir of. (E. F. Slafter) N. E. Reg. **49**: 9.
Bell, Sir James, Picture Collection of. (R. Walker) M. of Art, **19**: 385.
Bell, John. Ath. '95, **1**: 449.
Bell, Lillian, with portrait. Bk. News, **12**: 70. — (E. D. Field) Writer, **9**: 84.
Bell and Everett Party. *See* Constitutional Union Party.
Bellamy, Edward, with portrait. Bk. Buyer, **5**: 275. — With portrait. Bk. News, **8**: 416.
Bellamy; a story. (J. Pain) Idler, **4**: 489.
Bellary, India, Rock-pictures at, Prehistoric. (F. Fawcett) Asia. R. **13**: 147.
Belle of St. Valerien; a story. (J. C. Harris) Atlan. **69**: 338.
Belle Isle, Prison Life at. (J. C. Helm) Cosmopol. **15**: 47.
Bellenger, Clément, Wood-Engraver. Scrib. M. **18**: 289.
Belle's Beaux; a story. (F. C. Baylor) Cosmopol. **21**: 487.
Belles of Caracas. (W. N. King) Cosmopol. **22**: 29.
Bellew, Henry Walter. (J. S. Cotton) Acad. **42**: 115. — Ath. '92, **2**: 198.
Bellew, Kyrle, in The Lights of Home. Theatre, **29**: 125.
Belligerency, Recognizing. (A. G. Sedgwick) Nation, **62**: 173.
Bellingham, John, Regina *vs.* Green Bag, **7**: 132.
Bellomont, Lady, at the Court of Hanover. (J. F. Chance) Eng. Hist. R. **11**: 527.
Bellomont, Richard, Earl of. (W. L. Stone) Nat'l M. (N. Y. '91) **17**: 1.
Bells and Bell Customs. (F. Peacock) Dub. R. **117**: 77.
— — in Lincolnshire. Reliquary, **33**: 137.
— and their Makers. (W. B. Paley) Gent. M. n. s. **50**: 250.
— California Mission. (C. H. Shinn) Overland, n. s. **19**: 1.
— Chat about. (H. R. Haweis) M. of Art, **5**: 94, 226.
— Christ Church. (R. A. Cram) New Eng. M. n. s. **11**: 640.
— Church. (S. S. Stanley) Am. Arch. **44**: 136.
— Folk-Lore of. (Mabel Peacock) Antiq. n. s. **30**: 156.
— Foreign, Dissertation on. (W. S. Sparrow) M. of Art, **17**: 353.
"Bells, The," First Production of. (F. Hawkins) Theatre, **37**: 305.
Bells of Linlaven, The; a story. (John Russell) Chamb. J. **69**: 425-487.
Bellwood, Bessie. Acad. **50**: 267.
Belmont, N. C. Mary Help Abbey. (J. S. Bassett) M. Am. Hist. **29**: 131.
Belodont Reptile, New (Stegomus), from the Connecticut River Sandstone. (O. C. Marsh) Am. J. Sci. **152**: 59.
Belostoma Americana; a Family of Water Kings. (C. M. Weed) Pop. Sci. Mo. **45**: 443.
Below the Salt; a story. (C. E. Raimond) New R. **15**: 1.
Below the Sea; a poem. (M. Kendall) M. of Art, **8**: 509.
Belton, Tex., Woman's Community at. (G. P. Garrison) Char. R. **3**: 28.
Belts, Conveying. (T. Robbins, jr.) Cassier, **10**: 285.
Belvoir Castle, Eng. (Duchess of Rutland) Eng. Illust. **10**: 804, 932.
— and its History. (F. Stephenson) M. of Art, **14**: 93.
Bemberg, the Composer. Elaine. Theatre, **29**: 90.
Bemersyde Tower. Sat. R. **73**: 413.
Bemis, Prof. E. W., and the University of Chicago. Pub. Opin. **19**: 296.
— Views on Social Problems. Bib. Sac. **53**: 145.
Ben. (A. M. Ewell) Atlan. **72**: 248.
Ben ma Chree; a poem. All the Year, **74**: 491.
Ben Nevis, Mt., Meteorological Observatory on. Nature, **48**: 428.
— On Top of. (E. Whymper) Leis. Hour, **43**: 694.
— Wintering on. (R. C. Mossman) Chamb. J. **71**: 353.
Benares, Festival at. All the Year, **74**: 228.
Bench-Ends, Cornwall. Reliquary, **36**: 162.
Bend Low and Hark; a poem. (L. C. Moulton) Cosmopol. **16**: 569.
Bend of the Road, The; a story. All the Year, **71**: 201.
Beneath the Mask. (H. Pyle) Scrib. M. **14**: 167.

Beneden, Pierre Joseph van. Nature, **49**: 293.
Benedetti, Count. Studies in Diplomacy. Am. Hist. R. **1**: 739.
Benedict, St., Tosti's Life of. Dub. R. **112**: 376.
Benediction of the Cattle in Switzerland. Atlan. **70**: 220.
Beneficence, Christian, and Property. (D. R. Breed) Pres. & Ref. R. **5**: 287.
— Negative and Positive, Spencer on. (J. G. Schurman) Philos. R. **2**: 720. — (P. Shorey) Dial (Ch.) **15**: 387.
Benefices Bill. National, **28**: 302.
Benefit of the Doubt; a drama. (V. Hunt) Eng. Illust. **12**: no. 2, 23.
Benefit Society Estate. (E. O. Fordham) Westm. **141**: 396.
Benefits Forgot; a story. (W. Balestier) Cent. **23**: 192–937. **24**: 51–939.
Benevolence, Cosmopolitan. Spec. **72**: 611.
Benevolences, Our. (H. N. Herrick) Meth. R. **56**: 205.
Benevolent Investment. Soc. Econ. **1**: 10.
Benevolent Rattlesnake, The. (P. Robinson) Eng. Illust. **12**: no. 3, 75.
Bengal, "Mafassal" Law Courts of. (A. D. Bolton) Gent. M. n. s. **53**: 75. Same art. Liv. Age, **203**: 182.
— Manuscript Records of. (H. M. Stephens) Acad. **46**: 23. — Sat. R. **78**: 387.
— Musulmans of. Asia. R. **18**: 21.
— Permanent Settlement of. (B. H. Baden-Powell) Eng. Hist. R. **10**: 276.
— Sanitary Struggles at Paukobil. (John Beames) Gent. M. n. s. **53**: 587.
— Zamindari Estates in. (B. H. Baden Powell) Q. J. Econ. **11**: 36.
Bengal Army, Caste Organization of. Un. Serv. M. **5**: 15, 125.
Bengáli, Place of, in Politics. (L. Griffin) Fortn. **57**: 811.
Bengali Philology and Ethnology. (C. Johnston) Asia. R. **14**: 110.
Benin Country, West Africa, Journeys in. (H. L. Gallwey) Geog. J. **1**: 122.
Benjamin-Constant, Jean Joseph. (J. M. Templeton) M. of Art, **14**: 181.
Bennett, Charles Henry. (M. H. Spielmann) M. of Art, **18**: 448.
Bennett, George. (J. Macaulay) Leis. Hour, **43**: 267.
Bennett, James Gordon. (J. R. Young) Lippinc. **51**: 185.
Bennett, Nelson, with portrait. (C. W. Hobart) M. West. Hist. **13**: 549.
Bennett's Partner. (J. K. Reeve) Lippinc. **56**: 844.
Bennettites, New Facts on. (A. C. Seward) Nature, **50**: 594.
Bensly, Robert Lubbock. Acad. **43**: 371. — Ath. '93, **1**: 537.
Benson, Arthur C. Spec. **72**: 302.
— Poetry of. (E. Gosse) Acad. **44**: 361. — (L. Johnson) Acad. **47**: 499.
Benson, E. F., with portrait. Bk. News, **12**: 281.
Benson, Edward White, Archbishop of Canterbury. (F. W. Farrar) Contemp. **70**: 623. Same art. Liv. Age, **211**: 560. Same art. Chr. Lit. **16**: 136. — (H. C. Shuttleworth) Sat. R. **82**: 411.
Bent, John, English Ancestors of. (E. C. Felton) N. E. Reg. **49**: 65.
Bent Family, The. (A. H. Bent) N. E. Reg. **48**: 288.
Bentham, Jeremy, Spanish Influence of. (C. Kenny) Law Q. **11**: 48.
Bentinck, George C., Lord, Kent's Reminiscences of. Ath. '92, **2**: 509. — Blackw. **152**: 627.
— Racing Life of. Sat. R. **74**: 479.
Bentinck, W., Lord, Boulger's. Sat. R. **74**: 19.
Bentley, George. Acad. **47**: 483. — Ath. '95, **1**: 739.
Bentley, George. In Memoriam; a poem. (J. J. Beresford) Temp. Bar, **105**: 289.
Bentley, Robert. Nat. Sci. **4**: 155.
Bentley's System; a story. (V. Roseboro') Cent. **21**: 438.
Benue River and Anglo-German Treaty, 1893. (E. G. Ravenstein) Geog. J. **3**: 42.
Benvenuti, Giambattista, called L'Ortolano, Altarpiece of. (G. Allen) Eng. Illust. **14**: 184.
Benzene Nucleus, Nature of. (A. E. Tutton) Nature, **49**: 614.
Benzon, Otto, and Edward Rose. The Plowdens; a Comedy. Theatre, **28**: 207.
Beowulf. (F. A. Comstock) Educa. **14**: 334.
— and Arthur as English Ideals. (S. J. McNary) Poet-Lore, **6**: 529.
— Earle's and Hall's. (J. M. Garnett) Nation, **57**: 295. — Ath. '92, **2**: 445. — Sat. R. **73**: 274.
— the English Homer. (L. E. Horning) Canad. M. **2**: 62.
— Oldest English Lyric. (R. Burton) Poet-Lore, **5**: 57.
Béranger, P. J. de. (C. Coquelin) Cent. **24**: 911.
Béraud, Jean. Chemin de la croix. (J. Bernac) Art J. **47**: 21.
Berbers of Morocco. (J. E. B. Meakin) Anthrop. J. **24**: 1.
Bere, Richard, Journal of. (M. A. S. Hume) Liv. Age, **192**: 106.
Berea College. (P. D. Dodge) Cent. **22**: 315.
Berengarian Controversy. (J. Rickaby) Month, **77**: 476. **78**: 24, 233.
Beresford, Lord Charles; a sketch. (R. Blathwayt) Idler, **4**: 275.
Berg, Gunnar. Acad. **45**: 19.
Bergamask, Baedeker and the. (J. S. Fiske) Nation, **59**: 358, 443.
Bergen, Biological Institution in. Nature, **50**: 271.
Bergen-op-Zoom, The Surprise of, 1814. Un. Serv. M. **13**: 386.
Bergerac, S. Cyrano de. *See* Cyrano.
Beri-beri, Altitude as a Cure of. (A. S. Ashmead) Science, **22**: 119.
— Etiology of. (A. S. Ashmead) Science, **20**: 281.
— Nature of. (A. S. Ashmead) Science, **22**: 48.
Beringer, Esmé, with portrait. Theatre, **36**: 283.
Berkeley, George, Huxley on. (G. G. Greenwood) Westm. **144**: 1.
— Positivism of. (P. Carus) Open Court, **8**: 4042.
Berkeley, Cal., Powder Explosion at, Aberration of Sound Illustrated by. (R. H. Chapman) Nat. Geog. M. **7**: 246.
Berkeley Castle. (P. Fitzgerald) M. of Art, **14**: 222. — (G. Winterwood) Sund. M. **21**: 94.
Berkshire Hills, Mass., Literary Associations of. (J. T. Cutler) New Eng. M. n. s. **9**: 3.
— Bryant and the. (A. Lawrence) Cent. **28**: 368.
— Reminiscences of. (H. D. Sedgwick) Cent. **28**: 552.
Berkshire Type, A. (Chas. B. Hubbell) Bach. of Arts, **2**: 501.
Berlin. (W. H. Hotchkiss) Munsey, **6**: 507. — (F. Spielhagen) Cosmopol. **14**: 515. — (S. B. Holabird) Un. Serv. (Phila.) **8**: 136.
— Art Museum at. M. of Art, **3**: 135.
— Cathedral of. Am. Arch. **51**: 30.
— Life in. Good Words, **37**: 612.
— People of. (F. Spielhagen) Cosmopol. **14**: 724.
— Police of. Nation, **59**: 140.
— Royal Polytechnikum. (A. F. M. Lange) Archit. Rec. **5**: 65.
— Socialistic Politics and Pleasure in. (J. K. Paulding) Nation, **57**: 117.
— Society in. (F. H. Geffcken) New R. **7**: 167.

Berlin, Triumphal Entry into, June 16, 1871. (A. Forbes) Scrib. M. **12**: 781.
— Unter den Linden. (P. Lindau) Scrib. M. **11**: 579.
— University; A Student Bierreise. (J. Matthewman) Bach. of Arts, **3**: 624.
Berlioz, Hector. (J. Trostler) Music, **10**: 353. — (C. Saint-Saens) Music, **5**: 94.
— Biographical Notes and Personal Reminiscences. (E. Reyer) Cent. **25**: 305.
— Works of. (Nora Teller) Music, **10**: 561.
Bermondsey, Old Houses of. (E. M. Boughton) Antiq. n. s. **27**: 100.
Bermuda or Somers Islands. (E. T. Mitchell) Time, **23**: 933. — Around World, **1**: 35.
— Bicycling in. (P. C. Stuart) Outing, **25**: 166.
— During the American Revolution. (I. J. Greenwood) N. E. Reg. **50**: 441.
— Early Church in. (W. R. Notman) Presb. & Ref. R. **7**: 630.
— Glimpses of. (F. Harwood) Canad. M. **1**: 219.
— in Blockade Times. (C. Hallock) New Eng. M. n. s. **6**: 337.
— Life in. Un. Serv. M. **10**: 506.
— Notes from. (A. Agassiz) Am. J. Sci. **147**: 411.
— Notes on. (A. Shaw) R. of Rs. (N. Y.) **9**: 563.
— Quaint Houses in. (M. F. Honeyman) Chaut. **23**: 749.
— Touring Awheel in. (T. B. Dowden) Outing, **27**: 236.
Bermuda Negroes, a Festal Rite of. (H. C. Bolton) J. Am. Folk-Lore, **3**: 222.
Bernard of Clairvaux. Lond. Q. **80**: 60.
— Life and Times, by Neander. Eng. R. **18**: 291.
— Storrs on. (C. A. L. Richards) Dial (Ch.) **14**: 140. — Church Q. **37**: 300.
Bernard of Cluny, Song of. (H. T. Henry) Am. Cath. Q. **18**: 793.
Bernardin de Saint-Pierre, J. H. (E. C. Price) Liv. Age, **192**: 479.
Berne-Bellecour, Etienne Prosper. Art J. **45**: 34.
Bernhardt and the Bear. (A. M. R. Gordon) Canad. M. **5**: 273.
Bernhardt, Sarah. (M. Bacheller) Munsey, **8**: 47. — (M. White, jr.) Munsey, **14**: 323.
— and Eleanora Duse. Sat. R. **79**: 787.
— as Cléopâtre. Sat. R. **73**: 654.
— in "La Femme de Claude." (A. Laugel) Nation, **59**: 283.
Bernheim, Abram C. Critic, **27**: 175.
Berosus, Ten Patriarchs of. (R. Brown, jr.) Acad. **43**: 485. **44**: 56.
Berries. Chaut. **23**: 602.
Berryer, Antoine Pierre. (T. B. Scannell) Month, **83**: 520. — (N. J. D. Kennedy) Jurid. R. **5**: 23.
Berthelot, P. E. M., and Renan. (A. D. Van Dam) Contemp. **68**: 862.
Bertie Martin's Blues; a story. Argosy, **58**: 342.
Bertolini, Antonio. (A. S. Macduff) Sund. M. **22**: 845.
Bertram, James G. Ath. '92, **1**: 342.
Berwick, Maine. (S. O. Jewett) New Eng. M. n. s. **10**: 585.
Besant, Annie. (W. E. Gladstone) 19th Cent. **36**: 317.
— Interview with Pusey. (C. Chapman) M. Chr. Lit. **5**: 385.
Besant, Walter, with portrait. Bk. News, **11**: 4. — With portrait. Bk. Buyer, **9**: 373. — With portraits. (J. Underhill) R. of Rs. (N. Y.) **8**: 428. — (F. Handley) Our Day, **14**: 63.
— and Advertising. National, **26**: 650.
— His First Book, with portrait. (W. Besant) Idler, **1**: 525.
— in America. Critic, **22**: 417.
— Knighted. Sat. R. **79**: 717.
Beset in Aravaipa Cañon. (W. Thomson) Lippinc. **55**: 845.
Bessemer, Sir Henry. (R. H. Thurston) Cassier, **10**: 323, 423.
Bessie; a story. (E. R. Esler) Chamb. J. **70**: 235.
Bessie of the Wolf's Ranche; a story. (M. S. Hancock) Gent. M. n. s. **49**: 109.
Best Man, The; a story. (J. E. V. Cooke) Chaut. **20**: 204.
Bête Humaine, La, and Criminal Anthropology. (C. Lombroso) Monist, **1**: 177.
Bethel and Shechem. (H. Vogelstein) Jew. Q. **4**: 513.
Bethlehem. (H. Schmalz) Art J. **45**: 337. — (S. S. McClure) McClure, **8**: 183.
— and Jerusalem. (G. W. Wood) Sund. M. **21**: 408.
Bethnal Green, Oxford House in. (W. R. Anson) Econ. R. **3**: 10.
Bethnal Green Museum, London, Dixon Bequest at. (W. S. Sparrow and R. J. Slade) M. of Art, **15**: 158-408.
Better Man, The; a story. Good Words, **35**: 481.
Betterment. (J. R. Adams) Law Q. **9**: 229.
Betterment and Local Taxation. Quar. **178**: 185.
— House of Lords and. (Lord Hobhouse) Contemp. **65**: 438. — Reply. (Duke of Argyle) 483. — Rejoinder. (Lord Hobhouse) 704.
— in its Legal Aspect. (P. V. Smith) Law Q. **10**: 117.
— Principles of. (H. H. L. Bellot) Westm. **141**: 405.
Betting and Betting Men. Chamb. J. **73**: 497.
Betting and Gambling. Westm. **143**: 140.
Betting on Horse Races; Our Sporting Zadkiels. (J. H. Horsley) New R. **9**: 515.
Betun, Roger de, Bishop of Hereford. (A. C. Benson) National, **28**: 522.
Between Mass and Vespers. (S. O. Jewett) Scrib. M. **13**: 661.
Between Night and Day; a story. (A. Gissing) Eng. Illust. **15**: 503.
Between Reliefs. (T. H. Wilson) Lippinc. **57**: 530.
Between the Seasons. All the Year, **73**: 414.
Between the Silences; a story. (C. Yorke) Belgra. **80**: 37.
Between Two Worlds. (C. K. Reifsnider) Arena, **15**: 304-1006. **16**: 147-993.
Beulah, with portrait. Bk. News, **10**: 505.
Beverages. (T. G. Allen) Chaut. **23**: 438.
Beveridge, Kühne. (G. Atherton) Lippinc. **51**: 643.
Beverley Minster, Norman Work in Nave of. (J. Bilson) Antiq. n. s. **27**: 18.
Beverly and Hull. (J. Leyland) Portfo. **23**: 83.
Bewick, Thomas, the Engraver. Bookworm, **2**: 65. — (A. Ritchie) Macmil. **67**: 236. Same art. Liv. Age, **196**: 442.
— Stray Notes on. (M. Howitt) Good Words, **37**: 730.
Bewitched; a story. All the Year, **75**: 236-379. Same art. Liv. Age, **203**: 94.
Beyle, Marie-Henri. (F. T. Cooper) Bookman, **3**: 216. — Acad. **41**: 613.
— and his Critics. (E. C. Price) Scot. R. **25**: 309.
— and his Sister. (A. Laugel) Nation, **54**: 464.
— as an Art Critic. (G. Smith) Portfo. **24**: 172, 183.
Beyond; a story. (K. Trask) Harper, **90**: 314.
Beyond the Frontier; a story. (B. Vye) Belgra. **90**: 414.
Beyond the Shadows; a story. (M. Holley) Arena, **12**: 277.
Beyrich, Heinrich Ernst. Nat. Sci. **9**: 209.
Bezoars. (E. Brightmen) Science, **21**: 50.
Bhils, The, Notes on. (R. W. Shufeldt) Pop. Sci. Mo. **50**: 34.
Bhogeraj Doosad, Private History of; a story. All the Year, **72**: 205. Same art. Liv. Age, **197**: 558.
Bhopal. All the Year, **75**: 471.

Bhopal, My Residence in. (H. C. E. Ward) National, **26**: 59. Same art. Liv. Age, **207**: 53.
Bhuridatta. (R. F. St. Andrew St. John) Folk-Lore, **2**: 90.
Bhut-baby, The. Macmil. **66**: 196.
B'hutt Gott; a story. Music, **3**: 288-636.
Biarritz, France. Sat. R. **75**: 454.
Bibi; a story. (H. Harland) Eng. Illust. **11**: 725.
Bible, The, and Christianity. (L. Staehlin) Luth. Q. **23**: 9.
— and the Church. (F. von Hügel) Dub. R. **115**: 313. **116**: 306. **117**: 275. — (J. K. Smyth) N. Church R. **3**: 104.
— and Free Thought. (P. Carus) Open Court, **2**: 953.
— and Higher Criticism. (E. L. Cutts) And. R. **19**: 137.
— and its Expositors. (L. A. Fox) Luth. Q. **25**: 541.
— and Jesus Christ; a New Era Dawning. (H. C. Hay) N. Church R. **1**: 405.
— and Modern Discoveries. (J. Cook) Our Day, **10**: 601.
— and Sacrament, Co-ordination of. (A. Stump) Luth. Q. **24**: 239.
— as Authority and Index. (A. A. Berle) Bib. Sac. **51**: 361.
— as Literature. (C. H. Toy) Harv. Mo. **18**: 137. — (R. Ogden) Nation, **61**: 76. — (R. G. Moulton, and others) Outl. **50**: 581-1128.
— — Study of. (W. H. Landon) Overland, n. s. **28**: 690.
— as a Strain of Music. Meth. R. **56**: 948.
— as a Text-book. (R. Ogden) Nation, **63**: 264.
— at Home and Abroad. Quar. **180**: 290.
— Authority of. (F. H. Foster) Bib. Sac. **52**: 69, 223.
— Between the Testaments. (T. R. Slicer) New World, **1**: 106.
— a Book of Spiritual Power. (J. K. Smyth) N. Church R. **2**: 423.
— Canonicity in, Apostolical Sanction the Test of. (W. M. McPheeters) Presb. & Ref. R. **6**: 26.
— Columnar Truths in. (J. Cook) Chaut. **18**: 78.
— Darwinism and. (W. M. Hughes) M. Chr. Lit. **6**: 401.
— Doctrinal Studies. N. Church R. **1**: 435, 585. **2**: 125-610. **3**: 121, 282, 421.
— Doctrine of, in Westminster Confession. (B. B. Warfield) Presb. & Ref. R. **4**: 582.
— Does it contain Scientific Errors? (C. W. Shields) Cent. **23**: 126.
— English, before the Reformation. (F. A. Gasquet) Dub. R. **115**: 122.
— — Early Printed Copies of. (J. R. Dore) Acad. **41**: 446.
— — in Theological Seminaries. (G. W. Gilmore) Bib. World, **4**: 287.
— — of 1539, Psalter of. Ath. '94, **1**: 338.
— — Place of in Modern Theological Education. (J. P. Taylor) And. R. **18**: 615.
— English Revised; How shall the Church utilize it? Meth. R. **56**: 131.
— — Wanted, an English Bible. (H. W. Horwill) Contemp. **69**: 705.
— Essentials and Circumstantials in. (J. Cook) Our Day, **10**: 902.
— First, Printed in America. (G. E. Sears) Bookworm, **1**: 187.
— Gladstone on. Spec. **76**: 543.
— Greek Mythology and. (J. Wedgwood) Contemp. **61**: 368.
— Hebrew, Lazarus de Viterbo on Integrity of. (D. Kaufmann) Jew. Q. **7**: 278.
— — Oldest MS. of. (W. S. Watson) Chr. Lit. **15**: 419. — (G. Margoliouth) Acad. **41**: 328.
— How it has come to us. (R. T. Talbot) Sund. M. **21**: 124-773.
Bible, The, Human Element in. (P. S. Moxom) New World, **3**: 23.
— Importance of Original Texts. (T. F. Wright) N. Church R. **1**: 605.
— in the British Museum. Quar. **178**: 157.
— in Chinese. Bishop Schereschewsky's Version. Lit. W. (Bost.) **26**: 265.
— in the College. (G. S. Burroughs) And. R. **18**: 253.
— in Luther's Time, Place of. (J. D. Pickles) Meth. R. **55**: 106.
— in Spain, Mayor on. (M. Todhunter) Westm. **146**: 36.
— in Young People's Societies. (L. A. Crandall) Bib. World, **8**: 49.
— Inerrancy of. (P. J. Cormican) Cath. World, **61**: 1. — (E. J. Wolf) Luth. Q. **23**: 229. — (T. S. Hamlin) Pub. Opin. **14**: 476.
— Inspiration of. (B. B. Warfield) Bib. Sac. **51**: 614. — (G. F. Wright) Bib. Sac. **52**: 1. — (F. H. Foster) Bib. Sac. **52**: 69, 232. — (W. Rupp) Ref. Q. **39**: 34. — (F. W. Chambers) Ref. Q. **39**: 435.
— — according to the Lutheran Symbols. (D. Nösgen, tr. F. H. Knubel) Luth. Q. **26**: 171.
— — and Authenticity of. (J. H. Fairchild) Bib. Sac. **49**: 1.
— — and Biblical Criticism. (H. I. D. Ryder) Cath. World, **56**: 742-**57**: 396.
— — and Heresy. (P. Cameron) Arena, **5**: 335.
— — and History. Church Q. **38**: 257.
— — Lutheran Church in Relation to. (J. J. Young) Luth. Q. **26**: 153.
— — Luther's Doctrine of. (F. Pieper) Presb. & Ref. R. **4**: 249.
— — Personal Factor in. (M. R. Vincent) New World, **2**: 103.
— — Real Problem of. (B. B. Warfield) Presb. & Ref. R. **4**: 177.
— — Roman Catholic View of. Spec. **72**: 679.
— — Sanday's Bampton Lectures on. Church Q. **38**: 359. — Sat. R. **77**: 318. — Spec. **72**: 850. — (S. Cheetham) Acad. **45**: 430. — And. R. **19**: 467.
— — Some Recent Views on. (J. A. Howlett) Dub. R. **113**: 532.
— Internal Sense of. N. Church R. **1**: 142.
— Interpretation of, Cheyne on. (G. H. Gwillim) M. Chr. Lit. **6**: 109.
— — Reply. (T. K. Cheyne) M. Chr. Lit. **6**: 114.
— its Mystery and Certainty, Divinity and Humanity. (J. K. Smyth) N. Church R. **1**: 579.
— its Relation to the World. (J. K. Smyth) N. Church R. **2**: 1.
— Light Thrown on, by Talmudic Usage. (M. Jastrow) J. Bib. Lit. **11**: 126.
— Literary Aspects of. Spec. **74**: 894.
— Mainz, 1455. (Russell Martineau) Bibliographica, **2**: 333.
— Manuscripts, The Lyon Pentateuch. (W. Sanday) Acad. **48**: 460.
— Metaphors of, Catalogue of. (C. G. Montefiore) Jew. Q. **3**: 623.
— Modern Discovery and; Symposium. Indep. My3, '94.
— The New. (F. B. Vrooman) Arena, **9**: 466.
— New Purple Codex. (A. L. Long) Ch. Lit. **15**: 143.
— Older than the Church. (J. Tomlinson) Luth. Q. **24**: 435.
— on the Stage. (H. A. Jones) New R. **8**: 183.
— Patriarchal Prophecy. New Church View of. (T. F. Wright) N. Church R. **1**: 321.
— Patriarchs' History, as Showing Stages of Regeneration. (L. P. Mercer) N. Church R. **2**: 511.
— Peerless, in the World's Parliament of Religions. (J. Cook) Our Day, **13**: 541.

Bible, The, Popular Use of. (K. Vaughan) Cath. World, **58**: 587.
— Printing and Distributing of. Chamb. J. **73**: 721.
— Religion of, Divine Origin of. (J. Monroe) Bib. Sac. **53**: 205, 409.
— Religious and Historical Uses of. (F. C. Porter) New World, **3**: 250.
— Religious Infallibility in, Sources of. (J. Cook) Our Day, **11**: 105.
— Russian. Church Q. **41**: 203.
— Scientific Methods in Relation to. (S. C. Wells) Luth. Q. **23**: 578.
— Septuagint Version. Quar. **183**: 473.
— — Are there Traces of Greek Philosophy in? (J. Freudenthal) Jew. Q. **2**: 205.
— — as related to New Testament Inspiration. (M. R. Vincent) M. Chr. Lit. **6**: 11.
— — Manuscripts of, in Italy. (H. A. Redpath) Acad. **42**: 362.
— — The Text of. (W. Sanday) Acad. **47**: 106.
— — *vs.* Hebrew Text. (H. H. Howorth) Acad. **44**: 233, 295, 549. **45**: 371, 478. **46**: 68–352. **47**: 215, (S. A. Cook) 279.
— — Study of, Distinctive Features of. (J. Poucher) Meth. R. **54**: 238.
— Spiritual or Internal Sense of. (G. F. Stearns) N. Church R. **1**: 546.
— Spiritual Supremacy of. (R. S. Storrs) Our Day, **9**: 326.
— Study of. (T. C. Hall; J. L. Withrow; O. P. Gifford; S. Burnham; W. H. P. Faunce) Bib. World, **3**: 28, 260, 417.
— — During the Middle Ages. (T. G. Law) Scot. R. **21**: 1.
— — Encyclical on. (Leo. XIII.) Am. Cath. Q. **19**: 177. — Translation. Am. Cath. Q. **19**: 388. — Commentary. (I. J. Conway) Am. Cath. Q. **19**: 412. — Contemp. **65**: 576. — (R. F. Clarke) Contemp. **66**: 42. — (T. F. Wright) N. Church R. **1**: 261.
— — — A Negative View of. (A. J. Maas) Am. Cath. Q. **20**: 162.
— — in College. Bib. World, **5**: 206, 287, 374.
— Teachings of, not Reducible to Set Terms. (T. B. Stork) Luth. Q. **22**: 272.
— Testimony of the Holy Spirit to. (J. De Witt) Presb. & Ref. R. **6**: 69.
— Translation of. (L. H. Tafel) N. Church R. **1**: 215.
— Trees of. (H. Macmillan) Sund. M. **22**: 263.
— Versions of. (C. W. Darling) M. West. Hist. **13**: 693.
— What is it? (T. G. Apple) Ref. Q. **39**: 5.
— The Wicked. (H. Stevens) Bookworm, **1**: 170.
— Woman's. (E. C. Stanton) Critic, **28**: 218.
— Word of God and the Sacraments, Objective Efficacy of. (J. A. Earnest) Luth. R. **25**: 289.
— Wycliffite, Authorship of. (F. D. Matthew) Eng. Hist. R. **10**: 91.
— Old Testament and Archæology. (S. R. Driver) Contemp. **65**: 408.
— — and Modern Criticism. Church Q. **37**: 276.
— — and the Monuments. (J. H. S. Moxly) National, **21**: 562.
— — Anomalies of Character in. (W. G. Blaikie) Thinker, **9**: 306.
— — Authority of, Teaching of Christ on. (C. J. Ellicott) M. Chr. Lit. **6**: 343–**7**: 228. — (C. J. Ellicott) Chr. Lit. **10**: 5 a–104 a.
— — British Criticism of. Ed. R. **176**: 453.
— — Canon of, Alleged Triple. (W. J. Beecher) J. Bib. Lit. **15**: 118.
— — Character of. (J. Wedgwood) Contemp. **64**: 531.
— — Christ's Treatment of. J. Bib. Lit. **15**: 87.
Bible, Old Testament; Christianity's Millstone. (Goldwin Smith) No. Am. **161**: 703.
— — — "Christianity's Millstone;" a Woman's View. (M. Nathan) No. Am. **162**: 252.
— — — Christianity's Foundation. (R. T. Ely) Our Day, **16**: 75.
— — — The Old Testament not a Millstone. (G. C. Workman) No. Am. **162**: 571.
— — Criticism of. Quar. **178**: 376. — Chr. Lit. **11**: 34 a, 57 a, 81 a.
— — — and Christianity. (W. Taylor Smith) Bib. World, **3**: 345.
— — — Archæology and. Meth. R. **56**: 136.
— — — Present State of. (E. L. Curtis) Cent. **23**: 727.
— — Driver's Introduction to. (A. W. Benn) Acad. **41**: 5. — Ath. '92, **1**: 77. — Church Q. **33**: 341. — (A. Blomfield) Contemp. **61**: 709, 865. Same art. M. Chr. Lit. **6**: 278, 333. — (W. E. Barton) Bib. Sac. **49**: 596. — (H. E. Ryle) Crit. R. **2**: 17.
— — German Criticism of. (T. K. Cheyne) Acad. **41**: 583.
— — Hebrew, Vulgate Chapters and Numbered Verses in. (G. F. Moore) J. Bib. Lit. **12**: 73.
— — Hebrew Text of. Meth. R. **56**: 473.
— — Higher Criticism of, Bishop Ellicott on. Church Q. **33**: 307.
— — in the Early Church. (J. Orr) Chr. Lit. **13**: 71.
— — in its Relation to Social Reform. (P. Vollmer) Ref. Q. **43**: 221.
— — Interpretation of, as affected by Modern Scholarship. (C. R. Brown) Bib. World, **5**: 88.
— — Israel's Deep Slumber. (E. Renan) New R. **8**: 397.
— — Message of Israel. (J. Wedgwood) Contemp. **62**: 579.
— — Monuments on, Verdict of the. Ed. R. **180**: 80.
— — Moral Difficulties of. (A. J. Heller) Ref. Q. **41**: 225.
— — The New. (N. Smyth) Cent. **28**: 299.
— — Notes on. (J. P. Peters) J. Bib. Lit. **15**: 106.
— — Notes on Difficult Passages in. (J. P. Peters) J. Bib. Lit. **11**: 38.
— — Pathos of. Spec. **71**: 236.
— — Poetry of, Are there Metres in? (E. C. Bissell) Presb. & Ref. R. **4**: 440.
— — Polychrome, and Paul Haupt. (C. H. Levy) R. of Rs. (N. Y.) **14**: 669. — Meth. R. **56**: 644.
— — Present Struggle Over. (Oettli) Luth. Q. **26**: 566.
— — Problems of. (Francis Brown) J. Bib. Lit. **15**: 63.
— — Recent Literature on. (A. W. Benn) Acad. **41**: 389.
— — Recent Books on. (T. K. Cheyne) Acad. **44**: 43.
— — Revised Version. (J. W. Chadwick) Arena, **7**: 298.
— — Service of, in educating the Race. (G. A. Smith) Bib. World, **8**: 91. Same art. Chr. Lit. **15**: 314, 363.
— — Goldwin Smith on. (R. Ogden) Nation, **61**: 423.
— — W. R. Smith on. (S. R. Driver) M. Chr. Lit. **7**: 59.
— — Sociological Value of. (O. H. Gates) Bib. Sac. **52**: 587.
— — Spirit of God in. (B. B. Warfield) Presb. & Ref. R. **6**: 665.
— — Theology of, Shultz on. Spec. **71**: 371.
— — Use of Mythic Elements in. (C. M. Cady) Bib. World, **6**: 115, 194.
— — Work in, in Theological Seminaries. (O. H. Gates) Bib. Sac. **50**: 119.
— Old Testament History, The Uniqueness of. (W. R. Harper) Bib. World, **5**: 81.
— Old Testament Literature, Chronology of. Bib. World, **5**: 290.
— Hexateuch, Authorship and Composition of. (C. van den Biesen) Dub. R. **111**: 246. **112**: 40.

Bible, Hexateuch, Biblical Criticism of, compared with other Books of the Old Testament. (C. R. Brown) And. R. 18: 205.
— — Principal Cave and the Composite Origin of. (S. R. Driver) Contemp. 61: 262.
— — Higher Criticism of. (L. W. Batten) Arena, 10: 59.
— — — Briggs on. (W. H. Green) Presb. & Ref. R. 4: 529.
— Pentateuch, Archæology of. (C. R. Conder) Scot. R. 26: 63.
— — Higher Criticism of. (W. H. Green) Pres. & Ref. R. 5: 369. — (W. S. Watson) Presb. & Ref. R. 6: 323.
— — Klostermann on. (W. H. Green) Pres. & Ref. R. 5: 261.
— — Mosaic Authorship of. (J. A. Howlett) Dub. R. 110: 264.
— — Prophetic Testimony to. (H. Hayman) Bib. Sac. 49: 109, 177.
— — Samaritan, Critical Copy of, Written in 1232. (W. S. Watson) Presb. & Ref. R. 4: 656.
— — Wellhausen on. (H. P. Laird) Ref. Q. 39: 326.
— Pentateuchal Codes. (H. Hayman) Bib. Sac. 53: 645.
— Genesis, Cosmogony of. (J. D. Dana) And. R. 9: 197. — (St. G. Mivart) Dub. R. 102: 180.
— — Documentary Theory in Regard to. Church Q. 36: 1.
— — Human and Divine Elements in Early Stories of. (W. R. Harper) Bib. World, 4: 266, 349, 467.
— — Lectures of W. R. Harper. (H. Osgood) Bib. Sac. 52: 323.
— — Naumann on. Crit. R. 2: 143.
— — not a Geological Treatise, but Spiritual States of Man. (P. B. Cabell) N. Church R. 2: 547.
— — Origin and Composition of. (E. C. Bissell) Presb. & Ref. R. 6: 1-614.
— — ch. i.-xi. (W. R. Harper) Bib. World 4: 184.
— — — and the Zendavesta. (A. Kohut) Jew. Q. 2: 223.
— — ch. i. in the Light of Modern Science. (H. P. Laird) Ref. Q. 43: 481.
— — ch. vi: 1-8. (W. H. Green) Pres. & Ref. R. 5: 654.
— — ch. xiv. (A. H. Sayce) M. Chr. Lit. 7: 156.
— Exodus, Septuagint Text of. (W. H. Hazard) Acad. 45: 309.
— Leviticus, Notes on, Driver's. (L. B. Paton) J. Bib. Lit. 14: 48.
— Deuteronomy. (C. H. Cornill) Open Court, 9: 4521.
— — Authorship of. (W. S. Watson, jr.) Bib. World, 6: 356.
— — Composition and Date of. (T. S. Potwin) Bib. Sac. 51: 1-231.
— — Driver's Commentary on. (G. C. M. Douglas) Presb. & Ref. R. 7: 137. — Church Q. 41: 334. — (G. A. Smith) Crit. R. 5: 339.
— — Final Chapters. (W. S. Watson) Bib. Sac. 53: 681.
— Judges, Moore's Commentary on. (W. M. McPheeters) Presb. & Ref. R. 7: 527. — Church Q. 42: 354. — Bib. Sac. 53: 266.
— — Origin and Structure of. (S. R. Driver) Jew. Q. 1: 258.
— — ch. v.; Deborah's Song. (R. G. Moulton) Bib. World, 6: 260.
— Ruth ii: 8. (M. Jastrow, jr.) J. Bib. Lit. 15: 59.
— I. and II. Samuel, Sources E and J in. (H. P. Smith) J. Bib. Lit. 15: 1.
— I. Sam. ix: 24. (M. M. Skinner) J. Bib. Lit. 19: 82.
— II. Kings v.; Drama of Naaman. (E. Duvall) Lippinc. 57: 571.
— Chronicles. (T. F. Wright) New Church R. 1: 455.
— Ezra, and the Ancient Monuments. (A. H. Sayce) Thinker, 8: 110.
Bible, Nehemiah ii: 12-15; Nehemiah's Night Ride. (T. F. Wright) J. Bib. Lit. 15: 129.
— Job. (B. Duhm) New World, 3: 328. — (J. F. Genung) Outl. 50: 930.
— — Hoffman on. (T. K. Cheyne) Crit. R. 1: 250.
— — Messianic Prophecy in. (E. L. Curtis) Bib. World, 1: 119.
— — Original Form of the Legend. (D. B. Macdonald) J. Bib. Lit. 14: 63.
— — Original Poem of. (E. T. Dillon) Contemp. 64: 108.
— — ch. xxvi: 12, 13, Text of. (D. G. Lyon) J. Bib. Lit. 14: 131.
— Psalms, Baethgen on. (T. K. Cheyne) Crit. R. 3: 20.
— — Cheyne's Origin, etc. of. (O. C. Whitehouse) Crit. R. 2: 8. — (S. C. Bartlett) Bib. Sac. 49: 292. — (W. W. Davies) Meth. R. 52: 884.
— — Date of. Church Q. 35: 162.
— — Development of the Psalter. (J. P. Peters) New World, 2: 285.
— — Mystic Passages in. (C. G. Montefiore) Jew. Q. 1: 143.
— — of the Pharisees. (F. C. Porter) Bib. World, 4: 167.
— — Poetry of. (H. Van Dyke) Outl. 50: 702.
— — Practical Use of. Spec. 72: 443.
— — Theology of. (T. W. Davison) Chr. Lit. 15: 227, 309.
— Psalm xxii: 25 and Nahum ii. 8. (T. K. Cheyne) J. Bib. Lit. 15: 198.
— Psalm cx. (G. Margoliouth) Acad. 41: 182. — (T. K. Cheyne and others) Acad. 41: 207-351. — (F. Chance and others) Acad. 41: 424, 447.
— Psalm cxxi. (G. A. Smith) Good Words, 33: 788.
— Proverbs, Date and Religious Value of. (C. G. Montefiore) Jew. Q. 2: 430.
— — Duties of Man as Taught in. (C. F. Kent) Bib. World, 3: 198.
— — Tests of Character in. (Countess of Cork) New R. 6: 542.
— Song of Solomon. (K. Budde) New World, 3: 56. — (W. W. Martin) Meth. R. 55: 775. — (R. Martineau) Am. J. Philol. 13: 307. — (T. A. Goodwin) Open Court, 9: 4671-4695. — (W. E. Griffis) Outl. 50: 1128.
— — Plot of. (M. Friedländer) Jew. Q. 6: 648.
— Ecclesiastes, and Buddhism. (E. T. Dillon) Contemp. 65: 153.
— — Course of Thought in. (F. B. Denio) Bib. World, 4: 326.
— — Design and Contents of. (M. Friedländer) Jew. Q. 1: 29, 359.
— Prophets. (C. W. Gallagher) Meth. R. 54: 597.
— — Alleged Socialism of. (A. W. Benn) New World, 2: 60.
— — Folk-Song of Israel in the Mouth of. (K. Budde) New World, 2: 28.
— — Kirkpatrick's Lectures on. (W. T. Davison) Crit. R. 3: 119.
— — Later. (C. H. Cornill) Open Court, 9: 4608.
— — Messianic Idea in. (T. W. Chambers) Presb. & Ref. R. 6: 224.
— Isaiah. (C. H. Cornill) Open Court, 9: 4577.
— — Cheyne's Introduction to. (A. W. Benn) Acad. 47: 457. — (G. C. M. Douglas) Presb. & Ref. R. 7: 704.
— — Child Prophecies of, ch. vii. 1-9. (G. W. Davis) Bib. World, 4: 259. — (W. R. Harper) Bib. World, 8: 417.
— — Critical Analysis of First Part of. (T. K. Cheyne) Jew. Q. 4: 562.
— — Critical Problems of Second Part of. (T. K. Cheyne) Jew. Q. 3: 588. 4: 102.

Bible, Isaiah, Duhm on. (A. B. Davidson) Crit. R. 3: 12.
— — Gleanings from. (G. H. Skipwith) Jew. Q. 7: 470.
— — Messianic Teaching of. (W. A. Shedd) Presb. & Ref. R. 5: 574.
— — Social Philosophy of. (C. F. Kent) Bib. World, 1: 248.
— — Virgin Oracle of. (T. G. Soares) Bib. World, 6: 58.
— — ch. xiii., Examination of. (W. H. Cobb) Bib. Sac. 49: 471.
— — ch. xiv., The Ode in. (W. H. Cobb) J. Bib. Lit. 15: 18.
— — ch. xxxviii: 8, Colophon at, in the Peshitta Version. (J. Binney) J. Bib. Lit. 14: 92.
— — ch. xl: 31, Practical Exegesis of. (A. W. Huizinga) Presb. & Ref. R. 5: 89.
— — ch. xl.-lxvi., Sufficient Reason for. (F. S. Potwin) Bib. World, 3: 435.
— — ch. lii: 13-53: Servant of Jehovah in. (S. I. Curtiss) Bib. World, 8: 354.
— Jeremiah, Provisional Analysis of. (G. H. Skipwith) Jew. Q. 6: 278.
— Lamentations. (J. Stalker) M. Chr. Lit. 5: 381.
— Ezekiel and the Holiness-code. (L. B. Paton) Presb. & Ref. R. 7: 98.
— — and the Priests' Code. (T. Whitelaw) Presb. & Ref. R. 5: 434.
— — Prophet of the Exile. (W. R. Betteridge) Bib. World, 5: 248.
— — Text- Critical Notes on. (C. H. Toy) J. Bib. Lit. 15: 54.
— Daniel. (J. E. H. Thomson) Thinker, 8: 116-487. 9: 7-486. — (W. H. Hinkley) N. Church R. 2: 570. — (J. A. Howlett) Dub. R. 117: 27.
— — Authenticity and Genuineness of. (J. J. Lampe) Presb. & Ref. R. 6: 440.
— — Daniel in the Critic's Den. (R. Anderson) Blackw. 157: 560.
— — D. A. Kamphausen on. (J. D. Prince) Bib. World, 1: 355.
— — Some Queries about the Book of. (I. M. Price) Bib. World, 6: 264.
— — ch. viii: 9-14. (G. F. Moore) J. Bib. Lit. 15: 193.
— Hosea. (K. Budde) New World, 4: 726.
— — in Light of Assyrian Research. (A. H. Sayce) Jew. Q. 1: 162.
— — Notes on Hosea's Marriage. (L. B. Paton) J. Bib. Lit. 15: 9.
— Amos ii: 7, vi: 10, viii. 3, ix: 8-10. (C. C. Torrey) J. Bib. Lit. 15: 151.
— Jonah. (J. Kennedy) Chr. Lit. 11: 8 a. — (H. J. Foster) Thinker, 9: 120. — (J. M. Whiton) Outl. 50: 847.
— — from New Church Standpoint. (T. F. Wright) N. Church R. 2: 481.
— — Haggai ii. 7. (M. S. Terry) Meth. R. 53: 268.
— Zechariah, Origin of Book of. (T. K. Cheyne) Jew. Q. 1: 76.
— — Quotations from, by St. Jude. (C. H. H. Wright) Thinker, 9: 126.
— Apocrypha; Book of Enoch. (J. Owen; R. H. Charles) Acad. 45: 93, 127.
— New Testament, Beyschlag's Theology of. (W. P. Dickson) Crit. R. 3: 142.
— — Canon of. (J. R. Gasquet) Dub. R. 112: 421.
— — — Beginning and Growth of. (D. Moore) Presb. & Ref. R. 7: 1.
— — Criticism of. Eng. R. 8: 277.
— — — and Religious Belief. (O. Cone) New World, 1: 445.
— — Demonology of. (F. C. Conybeare) Jew. Q. 8: 576.
— — Difficulty of Revision. (D. Brown) Presb. & Ref. R. 7: 228.
Bible, New Testament, Genesis of. (L. T. Townsend) Meth. R. 52: 26.
— — Earliest Quotation as Scripture. (D. Moore) Presb. & Ref. R. 6: 113.
— — Greek, Codex Bezae. (G. A. Simcox) Acad. 41: 544.
— — — Tischendorf's. Quar. 182: 181.
— — Historical Element in. (J. H. Thayer) J. Bib. Lit. 14: 1.
— — Inspiration of, Septuagint and. (M. R. Vincent) M. Chr. Lit. 6: 11.
— — Literature of, Anomalies of. (E. P. Gould) J. Bib. Lit. 11: 61.
— — of 1548. Ath. '93, 2: 227.
— — Origin or Formation of. (G. T. Purves) Presb. & Ref. R. 6: 239.
— — Study of, Sociology and. (W. R. Harper) Bib. World, 5: 1.
— — Textual Criticism of. Church Q. 39: 137.
— — Westcott and Hort Text of. (D. Brown) Thinker, 9: 413, 494.
— — Writers and Writings of, Testimony of 2d Century to. (B. O. True) Bapt. R. 14: 257.
— Gospels, Authenticity of. (A. F. Hewit) Cath. World, 57: 593.
— — Badham and Jolley on. (A. Wright) Crit. R. 3: 231.
— — Chronology of. Church Q. 33: 390.
— — The First-written Gospel. (L. Bradner, jr.) Bib. World, 1: 432.
— — Harmony of. (C. Leaman) Bib. Sac. 46: 73. — Eng. R. 16: 1.
— — — Robinson's. (C. Leaman) Bib. Sac. 46: 455.
— — Miraculous Element in. (J. Orr) Brit. and For. R. 36: 201.
— — Problem of, Ewald's. (J. T. Marshall) Crit. R. 2: 258.
— — Record of the Storm of Galilee. (W. W. Faris) Presb. & Ref. R. 7: 272.
— — Resch's Extra-canonical Parallel Texts. (J. T. Marshall) Crit. R. 3: 69.
— — Source of. Open Court, 2: 1079.
— — Synoptic Problem of. (S. C. Hodge) Presb. & Ref. R. 6: 703.
— — — Present Standing of, in Germany. (H. H. Wendt) New World, 4: 239.
— — Syriac, New. (J. R. Harris) Chr. Lit. 12: 78. — (R. H. Charles; A. S. Lewis; A. Rahlfs) Acad. 46: 556.
See Syriac.
— — Text of, Vindicated, Burgon's. Church Q. 43: 238.
— — Tissot's Illustr. of. (T. Stanton) Cent. 26: 244.
— — Tolstoi's Harmony of. Sat. R. 80: 271.
— — tr. from the Sinaitic Palimpsest, by Lewis. Sat. R. 79: 385.
— — Unity of. (W. R. Hartpence) Chris. Q. 8: 213, 385, 537.
— — Use of Four, by Justin Martyr. (H. M. Harman) Meth. R. 55: 81.
— Matthew, Fundamental Thought and Purpose of. (R. Kübel) Bib. World, 4: 194, 262.
— — Judaism of. (G. M. Harmon) J. Bib. Lit. 14: 114.
— — Syriac Version. (R. H. Charles and others) Acad. 47: 13-172.
— — ch. i., Priority of. (F. P. Badham) Acad. 48: 112.
— — ch. i: 1-8. (F. C. Conybeare, R. H. Charles, and others) Acad. 46: 447-556.
— — ch. xii: 39, 40. Interpretation of; a Symposium. (L. C. Barnes and others) Bib. World, 5: 417.
— — ch. xxvii: 9, 10, Old Testament Quotation in. (H. R. Hatch) Bib. World, 1: 345.
— Mark, Alternative Ending of. (J. R. Harris) J. Bib. Lit. 12: 96.

Bible, Mark. Indebtedness to Matthew. (F. P. Badham) R. 28: 310.
— — ch. xvi: 9–20, Genuineness of. (A. P. Peabody) And. R. 17: 631.
— Luke, Feine on. (J. H. Moulton) Crit. R. 2: 375.
— — Introduction to. (S. Mathews) Bib. World, 5: 336, 448.
— John. (A. B. Bruce) Bib. World, 7: 180.
— — After a Century of Criticism. (W. L. Ferguson) Bib. Sac. 53: 1.
— — as Correcting Luke. (E. A. Abbott) New World, 4: 459.
— — Critics and Characteristics. (W. W. Peyton) Ecl. M. 118: 58.
— — Discussions upon; Schürer and Sanday. (C. C. Starbuck) And. R. 17: 419.
— — Johannean Question, Present Position of. (W. Sanday) M. Chr. Lit. 5: 411–6: 203.
— — Köhler on. (A. Plummer) Crit. R. 3: 248.
— — Outline for Study of its Higher Criticism. (A. W. Anthony) Bib. World, 1: 190.
— — Peyton on. (W. Smith) Crit. R. 3: 29.
— — Place of, in New Testament Literature. (O. Cone) New World, 2: 1.
— — Prologue of. (J. R. Smith) Pres. & Ref. R. 5: 454.
— — Religious Value of. (C. G. Montefiore) Jew. Q. 7: 24.
— — Tatian and the Date of. (J. R. Harris) Contemp. 64: 800.
— — ch. vii: 53—viii: 11, Genuineness of. (A. P. Peabody) And. R. 17: 631.
— Acts, The Book of. (E. D. Burton) Bib. World, 6: 39.
— — Blass on. (G. T. Purves) Presb. & Ref. R. 7: 535.
— — Historical Method of Interpretation. (J. Brand) Bib. Sac. 52: 259.
— — On the Western Text of, as evidenced by Chrysostom. (F. C. Conybeare) Am. J. Philol. 17: 135.
— — Spitta on. (A. Menzies) Crit. R. 2: 168.
— — Textual Criticism of. (H. Lucas) Dub. R. 115: 30.
— — ch. xv: 21. (J. H. Ropes) J. Bib. Lit. 15: 75.
— Epistles, Pauline. (A. B. Bruce) Bib. World, 7: 6.
— — Classified according to External Evidence. (Mrs. C. T. Mead) Meth. R. 53: 735, 924.
— — General Conclusions from the Study of. (F. Godet) Ref. Q. 41: 379.
— — Godet's Introduction to. (J. H. Kerr) Presb. & Ref. R. 7: 713.
— — Lightfoot on. Sat. R. 80: 179.
— — Paul's Earliest Letters. (E. D. Burton) Bib. World, 6: 203.
— Romans. (E. D. Burton) Bib. World, 6: 367.
— — Paraphrase of. (G. B. Stevens) Bib. World, 8: 299, 390.
— — Sanday and Hort on. Church Q. 42: 321.
— — Sanday and Headlam on. (M. B. Riddle) Presb. & Ref. R. 7: 330.
— — ch. viii: 37, Sermon on. (M. Valentine) Luth. Q. 23: 247.
— Corinthians, Epistles to the. (E. D. Burton) Bib. World, 6: 278.
— I. Cor. xv: 42–44, Query respecting Translation of. (C. M. Mead) J. Bib. Lit. 14: 89.
— II. Cor. iii., Exegesis of. (S. T. Lowrie) Presb. & Ref. R. 7: 473.
— Galatians, Recent Critical Attack on. (C. W. Rishell) Meth. R. 54: 387.
— Philippians ii: 5–11. The Incarnation. (E. H. Gifford) Chr. Lit. 15: 472. — (W. Hull) Luth. Q. 26: 533.
— II. Thess. ii: 3–12. Man of Sin. (G. U. Wenner) Luth. Q. 25: 63.
Bible, I. Tim. iii: 16, ὤφθη ἀγγέλοις. (R. W. Micou) J. Bib. Lit. 11: 201.
— Hebrews. (A. B. Bruce) Bib. World, 7: 94. — (J. T. Marshall) Bib. World, 7: 359.
— — Authorship of. (W. M. Lewis) Thinker, 9: 199, 401.
— — on the Atonement. (W. F. Adeney) Thinker, 9: 534.
— — ch. i: 1–8, Exegesis of. (E. J. Wolf) Luth. Q. 25: 188.
— James, The Letter of. (E. D. Burton) Bib. World, 6: 121.
— — Faults of Early Christians as shown in. (E. P. Burtt) Bib. World, 4: 331.
— Epistles, Pastoral. (C. W. Votaw) Bib. World, 7: 130.
— Peter, Epistles of. (M. W. Jacobus) Bib. World, 7: 280.
— John, Epistles of. (E. D. Burton) Bib. World, 7: 359.
— I. John, Exposition of. (Prof. Rothe) M. Chr. Lit. 6: 469.
— — ch. iii: 9, Exposition of. (M. L. Culler) Luth. Q. 26: 244.
— Jude. (M. W. Jacobus) Bib. World, 7: 280.
— — Quotations from Zechariah in. (C. H. H. Wright) Thinker, 9: 126.
— Revelation. (M. S. Terry) Bib. World, 7: 207. — Church. Q. 37: 446.
— — and its Meaning. (E. Gould) N. Church R. 3: 572.
— — Originality of. (G. H. Gilbert) Bib. World, 5: 29, 114.
Bibles, Hieroglyphic. (W. A. Clouston) Bookworm, 7: 169.
— A Library of. Bookworm, 7: 217.
— of Coverdale and Cranmer. Bookworm, 2: 81.
Biblia Pauperum, A MS. of the. (E. M. Thompson) Bibliographica, 3: 385.
Biblical Archæology and the Higher Criticism. (A. H. Sayce) M. Chr. Lit. 5: 301.
Biblical Criticism. (H. Osgood) Bib. Sac. 50: 460. — (S. A. Alexander) Good Words, 34: 165.
— and the Authority of the Scriptures. (G. P. Fisher) M. Chr. Lit. 7: 235.
— and the Bible. (J. A. Howlett) Dub. R. 118: 282.
— and Philosophers. (H. Osgood) Presb. & Ref. R. 6: 688.
— and Science. (C. de Harlez) M. Chr. Lit. 6: 465.
— and Verdict of the Monuments. (W. D. Kerswell) Presb. & Ref. R. 6: 753.
— Archæological Stage of. (T. K. Cheyne) Contemp. 68: 89.
— Attitude of Catholics toward. (H. I. D. Ryder) Cath. World, 57: 396.
— Attitude of the Pope toward. Contemp. 63: 457.
— Conditions of Authoritative. (H. A. Buttz) Meth. R. 56: 191.
— Higher. (C. P. Grannan) Am. Cath. Q. 19: 562. — (S. F. Breckenridge) Luth. Q. 23: 349. — (W. Sanday) Arena, 9: 26. — (W. H. Green) M. Chr. Lit. 5: 475.
— — and Archæology. (J. A. Howlett) Dub. R. 115: 71. — (A. H. Sayce) Contemp. 68: 477.
— — and the Bible. (C. P. Grannan) Am. Cath. Q. 19: 562.
— — and the Supernatural. (A. W. Benn) New World, 4: 429.
— — Application to the Bible. (E. L. Curtis) And. R. 19: 137.
— — as Viewed by a Liberal Scholar. (J. H. Long) Arena, 12: 145.
— — Attitude of Christian toward. (L. W. Batten) Bib. World, 3: 275.

Biblical Criticism, Higher, Christological Implications of. (P. F. Jernegan) Bib. World, **3**: 420.
— — Common Sense and. Bapt. R. **14**: 234.
— — Conclusions of. (W. F. Scott) Thinker, **8**: 392.
— — Facts and Fancies of. (J. Cook) Our Day, **10**: 729.
— — History and Definition of. (H. Osgood) Bib. Sac. **49**: 529.
— — Questions of. (F. B. Denio) Bib. World, **6**: 95.
— — What it is not. (M. S. Terry) Bib. World, **6**: 22. — (A. C. Zenos) Bib. World, **6**: 189. — (W. J. Beecher) Bib. World, **6**: 351.
— in Some of its Theological and Philosophical Relations. (J. Ten Broeke) Bib. World, **2**: 330, 444.
— Modern. (H. Osgood) Bib. Sac. **51**: 674. — (A. A. Pfanstiehl) Ref. Q. **39**: 461. — Sat. R. **79**: 225.
— — Spirit of. (J. Cooper) Ref. Q. **41**: 388.
— Rights of, and Rights of the Church. (B. B. Warfield) M. Chr. Lit. **6**: 151.
— — Sayce on, and the Verdict of the Monuments. (S. R. Driver) Contemp. **65**: 408.
— True. Meth. R. **52**: 451.
Biblical Critics on the War-path. (A. H. Sayce) Contemp. **70**: 728. Same art. Chr. Lit. **16**: 165.
Biblical Facts and Science. (V. M. Olyphant) Bib. World, **2**: 92.
Biblical Geography, Recent Research in. (G. H. Schodde) Luth. Q. **23**: 1.
Biblical Sonnets, Three. (R. G. Moulton) Bib. World, **6**: 328.
Biblical Theology. (G. H. Gilbert) Bib. World, **6**: 6.
Biblical Truth, Self-evidencing Power of. Chr. Lit. **14**: 193.
Bibliographers, Some. Lib. J. **19**: 131.
Bibliographical Reverie; a poem. (F. S. Ellis) Bookworm, **7**: 91.
Bibliographical Society. (Falconer Madan) Bibliographica, **2**: 479.
Bibliographies, Recent. Bookworm, **7**: 185.
— Subject, International. (A. G. S. Josephson) Lib. J. **19**: 226.
Bibliography, American, General and Local. (G. W. Cole) Lib. J. **19**: 5.
— Battle of. (F. Campbell) Bookworm, **6**: 365.
— English Contemporary. (Edward Asher) Bibliographica, **3**: 173.
— of Folk-Lore. (G. L. Gomme) Folk-Lore Rec. **5**: 55.
Bibliolatry. (W. Lloyd) Westm. **137**: 113.
— Decline of. (T. H. Huxley) Pop. Sci. Mo. **41**: 594.
Bibliomania. (W. H. Tillinghast) Nation, **54**: 341.
Bibliophilism, Modern. (Octave Uzanne) Bibliographica, **1**: 63.
Bibliotaph, The. (L. H. Vincent) Atlan. **77**: 207.
Bicameral System in America, Rise and Development of. (T. F. Moran) J. H. Univ. Studies, **13**: 211.
Bicêtre. (T. Hopkins) Temp. Bar, **108**: 537. Same art. Ecl. M. **127**: 454. Same art. Liv. Age, **210**: 608.
Bickersteth, Rev. E., Memoirs of. Eng. R. **16**: 87.
Bicknell, E. M. (J. G. Speed) Q. Illust. **2**: 175.
Bicycle, Authors and the. Critic, **27**: 226.
— "Breaking a Bike." (F. H. Benson) Outing, **28**: 125.
— Cycling for Ladies. (W. H. Fenton) 19th Cent. **39**: 796.
— Economic Aspects of. (A. Shadwell) National, **28**: 345. Same art. Ecl. M. **127**: 811.
— Era of. (J. G. Speed) Lippinc. **56**: 230.
— Evolution and Perfection of. (R. Perkins) Engin. M. **9**: 281. — Sat. R. **80**: 343.
— in Europe, a Canadian. (C. R. Boulton) Canad. M. **6**: 530. **7**: 11.
— Invasion of Athens by. (T. G. Allen, jr.) Outing, **28**: 310.
Bicycle, its Pleasures and Perils. (R. L. Seymour) Chaut. **20**: 703.
— A Modern Centaur. (H. Ansot) Overland, n. s. **26**: 121.
— Social and Economic Influences of. (S. Baxter) Arena, **6**: 578. — (J. B. Bishop) Forum, **21**: 680.
— The Wheel of To-Day. (P. G. Hubert, jr.) Scrib. M. **17**: 692.
— Woman and the. (H. J. Garrigues) Forum, **20**: 578. — (Marguerite Merington) Scrib. M. **17**: 702.
Bicycle Disease. (A. Wilson) Pub. Opin. **15**: 390.
Bicycle Outlook. (I. B. Potter) Cent. **30**: 785.
Bicycle Riders. Blackw. **159**: 883.
Bicycle Tours — and a Moral. (E. H. Lacon-Watson) Westm. **142**: 166.
Bicycle Trip in the Tyrol. (S. Greer) Outing, **28**: 254.
Bicycles. (J. K. Starley) New R. **12**: 312.
— American, in England. (G. F. Parker) No. Am. **163**: 688.
— and Bicycle Riders. Pub. Opin. **19**: 342.
— and Dogs. Spec. **77**: 514.
— History of. Munsey, **15**: 131.
— Military, thro' the Dakotas. (De R. C. Cabell) Outing, **28**: 214.
— of the Day. (A. R. Savile) Un. Serv. M. **8**: 633.
— Social Effect of. Spec. **76**: 769.
Bicycling. (T. Stevens) Lippinc. **49**: 602.
— across Asia. (T. G. Allen, jr., and W. L. Sachtleben) Cent. **26**: 83-915.
— All Paris Awheel. (A. Alexandre) Scrib. M. **18**: 195.
— by Women. (Mrs. Humphry) Idler, **8**: 71.
— Doctor's View of. (J. W. Roosevelt) Scrib. M. **17**: 708.
— for Women. (Mrs. Reginald de Koven) Cosmopol. **19**: 386.
— in Bermuda. (P. C. Stuart) Outing, **25**: 166.
— in California. (M. Cerf) Overland, n. s. **22**: 391.
— My First Tour. (E. Ingersoll) Outing, **26**: 205, 273.
— Social Side of. (J. B. Townsend) Scrib. M. **17**: 704. *See* Cycling.
Bidding of the Bedes. (J. Moyes) Dub. R. **115**: 162. — (E. Bishop) Dub. R. **115**: 448.
Biddle, Charles, 1745-1831. (E. B. Bates) Lippinc. **51**: 83.
Biddle, Nicholas, and the Architecture of Girard College. Pennsyl. M. **18**: 354.
Bideford. (P. H. W. Almy) Temp. Bar, **109**: 367.
Bideford Bay, Natural History in. Macmil. **74**: 137.
Bierstadt, Albert. Visit to Colorado. (W. M. Byers) M. West. Hist. **11**: 237.
Big Claws and Little Klaus; a story. Sat. R. **74**: 615.
Big Game Shooting, C. Phillipps-Wolley on. Nature, **50**: 298. *See* Game.
Big Rodeo; Among the Cattle Ranges. (M. C. Johnson) Outing, **26**: 152.
Big Sandy, Battle of; a Forgotten Battle of the War of 1812. M. Am. Hist. **29**: 524.
Bigarré, Gen., Memoirs of. (A. Laugel) Nation, **57**: 171, 210.
Bighorn, After, in Kamschatka. (F. H. H. Guillemard) Blackw. **151**: 288.
Bijapur. All the Year, **76**: 102.
Billiards, Broadfoot on. Sat. R. **82**: 193.
Billings, Dr. John S., with portrait. Lib. J. **21**: 63.
Billington, Elizabeth W. (W. B. Squire) National, **26**: 512.
Billop Mystery; a story. (J. Hawthorne) Eng. Illust. **14**: 97.
Billroth, Christian Theodore, with portrait. R. of Rs. (N. Y.) **9**: 297.
— **Death of.** Pop. Sci. Mo. **45**: 350.

Bills of Exchange; Under Law of which State. Bank M. (N. Y.) 47: 609.
— of Sale. Ought they to be abolished? (J. B. Matthews) Law Q. 7: 74.
Billy Binks, Hero. (Guy Boothby) Chamb. J. 73: 145-198.
Biltmore Forest at Asheville, N. C. (C. S. Sargent) Garden & F. 7: 71. — (C. S. Sargent) Garden & F. 8: 481. — (F. C. W. Barbour) Chaut. 21: 320.
— Opening of. Gunton's M. 10: 33.
Biltmore House: 8 Plates. Archit. Rec. 5, following p. 96.
Biloxi Tales. (J. O. Dorsey) J. Am. Folk-Lore, 6: 48.
Bimetallic Arguments. (H. Schmidt) Bank. M. (Lond.) 59: 824.
Bimetallic Conference of 1894. (M. G. Mulhall) Contemp. 65: 866. — Pub. Opin. 17: 133.
Bimetallic League. F. A. Walker's Address. (J. H. Trilton) National, 28: 70.
Bimetallic Mystery, A; a story. Chamb. J. 71: 77.
Bimetallic Parity under a Gold Standard. (J. F. de Navarro) Forum, 15: 225.
Bimetallic Theory. (D. MacG. Means) Nation, 57: 22.
— in the Light of Recent History and Discussion. (H. W. Farnam) Yale R. 3: 203.
Bimetallism. (J. L. Greene) Am. J. Soc. Sci. 31: 9. — (A. J. Utley) Arena, 16: 85. — Canad. M. 7: 480. — (I. M. Scott) Overland, n. s. 28: 24. — (L. Courtney) National, 25: 337. — (H. A. Scomp) Am. M. Civics, 6: 21. — (J. B. Robertson) J. Statis. Soc. 58: 417. — Pub. Opin. 15: 386. — (A. de Rothschild) New R. 8: 40. — Reply. (W. H. Houldsworth) New R. 8: 206.
— American Bimetallic League, Chicago Convention, 1893. Pub. Opin. 15: 448.
— an Appeal. (G. K. Marischal) Westm. 145: 143.
— and Currency. (J. Douglass) Am. M. Civics, 7: 119, 253.
— and Legislation. (C. S. Thomas) Arena, 11: 378.
— and the Nature of Money. (W. H. Mallock) Fortn. 66: 207.
— as a Bubble. (H. D. MacLeod) 19th Cent. 37: 991.
— as a New Way to pay Old Debts. (J. W. Cross) 19th Cent. 37: 1001.
— Balfour on. Spec. 74: 458.
— Basis of Real. (J. H. Clark) Gunton's M. 11: 112.
— Bimetallist Committee of Boston and New England. (E. B. Andrews) Q. J. Econ. 8: 319.
— Committee for Promotion of International. Pub. Opin. 16: 569.
— Compensatory Theory of. (R. F. Hoxie) J. Pol. Econ. 1: 273.
— a Compromise. (D. Stange) Am. M. Civics, 8: 616.
— Conditions for American Commercial and Financial Supremacy. (P. Leroy-Beaulieu) Forum, 20: 385.
— Considered from Standpoint of National Interests. (A. J. Warner) Am. J. Pol. 4: 526.
— European Opinion on. Soc. Econ. 9: 58.
— H. S. Foxwell on. (E. Cannan) Econ. R. 3: 457.
— Germany and. (W. Lotz) Ann. Am. Acad. Pol. Sci. 4: 61.
— Giffen's Case against. (C. B. Spahr) Pol. Sci. Q. 8: 401. — (R. Hazard; C. B. Spahr) Pol. Sci. Q. 9: 224.
— Gospel of. (F. J. Scott) Am. J. Pol. 3: 408.
— How to Save. (Duc de Noailles) Ann. Am. Acad. Pol. Sci. 5: 557.
— in England. (H. White) Nation, 60: 177.
— in Europe and India. Bank. M. (N. Y.) 47: 849.
— in France, Operation of. (H. P. Willis) J. Pol. Econ. 3: 356.
Bimetallism, International. (R. Stein) Arena, 15: 212. — (H. W. Farnam) Yale R. 5: 182, 312. — (F. A. Walker) Yale R. 5: 303. — National, 27: 158. — (J. J. Valentine) Overland, n. s. 27: 422.
— — Prospects of. (G. K. Marischal) Westm. 146: 510.
— — Walker's. (L. L. Price) Econ. J. 6: 447.
— Is it a Delusion? (T. Tuck) 19th Cent. 37: 274.
— the Issue in '96. (A. J. Warner) Am. M. Civics, 6: 603.
— its Meaning and Aims. (H. S. Foxwell) Econ. R. 3: 297.
— Kernel of. (E. L. Godkin) Nation, 60: 316.
— Lexis on. Econ. J. 5: 276.
— MacLeod on. (T. E. Powell) National, 24: 795. — (H. P. Willis) J. Pol. Econ. 3: 486. — Sat. R. 79: 226.
— Mechanics of. (I. Fisher) Econ. J. 4: 527.
— Memphis Silver Convention. Pub. Opin. 18: 690.
— Monometallism or? Pub. Opin. 17: 159.
— Natural. (G. H. Lepper) No. Am. 163: 219.
— Objections to, Currency of India and. (L. L. Price) Econ. J. 3: 617.
— Once More. (L. Courtney) 19th Cent. 33: 619.
— Plea for. (J. F. McBlain) Un. Serv. (Phila.) 14: 1.
— Position of U. S. in Regard to. (F. J. Scott) Am. J. Pol. 4: 316.
— Practical, and Ideal Protection. (Frank Rosewater) Am. M. Civ. 8: 78.
— Protection and. Soc. Econ. 9: 26.
— The Ratio under. (G. J. F. Grant) Westm. 146: 95.
— Shaw's History of. (C. M. Walsh) Q. J. Econ. 10: 431.
— Ship Subsidies and. Soc. Econ. 8: 343.
— Six Centuries of. (H. White) Nation, 60: 356.
— Some Damaging Facts in its History. (F. I. Herriott) R. of Rs. (N. Y.) 13: 176.
— *vs.* the Single Standard. (L. B. Prince) Am. M. Civics, 6: 413, 483.
— Gen. Walker on. (H. White) Nation, 60: 250.
Bimetallist, A Pioneer: Charles C. Goodwin. (J. Dryden) Overland, n. s. 27: 657.
Bimetallist Agitation. Bank. M. (Lond.) 57: 836.
Bimetallists, Claims of. Soc. Econ. 8: 257.
Binding of the Lost; a sonnet. (E. Lee-Hamilton) M. of Art, 6: 374.
Bindon Hill. (W. W. Fowler) Macmil. 67: 17.
Bingham Genealogy. (T. A. Bingham) N. E. Reg. 49: 333.
Bingham's Idea. (E. L. Phillimore) Temp. Bar, 97: 91. Same art. Liv. Age, 196: 485.
Bink's Courtship; a story. All the Year, 72: 348.
Binney, Horace, with portrait. (H. L. Carson) Green Bag, 5: 441.
Biographical Myths. (J. Fenton) Folk-Lore Rec. 3: 26.
Biographies, Great. (G. Saintsbury) Macmil. 66: 97.
Biography. (L. Stephen) National, 22: 171. Same art. Liv. Age, 199: 451.
— and Biographies. Temp. Bar, 94: 578.
— L'Art de. (M. Schwob) New R. 14: 41.
— Candor in. (W. Ward) New R. 14: 445. Same art. Liv. Age, 209: 314.
— Commonplace. (T. M. Clark) New Eng. M. n. s. 6: 207.
— English, Stephen's Dictionary of. Ath. '92, 2: 182. — (L. Stephen) National, 27: 51. Same art. Liv. Age, 209: 25. — (S. Lee) Cornh. 73: 258.
— Parton's Rules for Writing. McClure, 1: 59.
— Suppression in. (E. S. Purcell) 19th Cent. 40: 533.
Biological Courses, Value of Experimental Physiology in. Science, 22: 21.
Biological Experiment Station of University of Illinois. Science, n. s. 2: 62.

Biological Work in Secondary Schools. (A. J. McClatchie) Pop. Sci. Mo. **46**: 634.
Biologist and Naturalist: a Comparison. (I. Muntz) Gent. M. n. s. **49**: 88.
Biology and Ethics. (Sir J. C. Browne) Pop. Sci. Mo. **44**: 671.
— Geographical. (J. W. Harshberger) Educa. **14**: 513.
— in Colleges. (C. H. Merriam) Science, **21**: 352.
— in Secondary Schools. (J. M. Coulter) School R. **1**: 141.
— in U. S. Nature, **51**: 81.
— Logical Method in. (F. Cramer) Pop. Sci. Mo. **44**: 372.
— Pseudo-. (F. A. Bather) Nat. Sci. **5**: 449.
— Psychology, and Sociology, Relations of. (H. Spencer) Pop. Sci. Mo. **50**: 163.
— Relation to Geological Investigation. (C. A. White) Nature, **52**: 258, 279.
— Relation to Sociology. (L. G. Janes) Pop. Sci. Mo. **41**: 206.
— Sanderson on. Sat. R. **76**: 324.
— Sociology rests indirectly upon. (L. F. Ward) Am. J. Sociol. **1**: 313.
— Teaching of. (C. Macmillan) Science, **21**: 184, 289. —(F. H. Herrick) Science, **21**: 220. —(H. F. Osborn) Science, **21**: 234. —(J. C. Bay) Science, **21**: 275. —(H. F. Nachtrieb) Science, **21**: 287.
— Weismann on. (D. S. Jordan) Dial (Ch.) **13**: 242.
— What is? (F. P. Mall) Chaut. **18**: 411.
— World's Debt to. (H. F. Osborn) Chaut. **23**: 564.
Birch, Chas. B. Ath. '93, **2**: 560. — M. of Art, **17**: 80.
Birch, R. B., with portrait. Bk. Buyer, **9**: 249.
Birch, Oil of. (H. Trimble) Garden & F. **8**: 303.
Birch Tree, The. (G. Paxton) Knowl. **19**: 90.
Birches, American White. (C. S. Sargent) Garden & F. **8**: 355.
— Hybrid. (J. G. Jack) Garden & F. **8**: 243.
Bird of Passage; a story. (B. Harraden) Blackw. **155**: 469. Same art. Liv. Age, **201**: 306. Same art. Ecl. M. **122**: 688.
Bird Foraging. Liv. Age, **201**: 46.
Bird Language: a speculation. (S. G. McClure) Chaut. **18**: 424.
Bird Life, Humors of. (R. B. Sharpe) Idler, **5**: 581.
— in Southern Scotland. Chamb. J. **72**: 77.
— in Spring. Spec. **74**: 531. Same art. Liv. Age, **205**: 446. —(J. B. Chandler) Eng. Illust. **10**: 508.
— in Summer. (J. B. Chandler) Eng. Illust. **10**: 685.
— Oddities in. (C. W. Swallow) Science, **21**: 121.
Bird Lyric, A. Argosy, **59**: 555. Same art. Liv. Age, **206**: 120.
Bird Notes in Southern California. (H. L. Graham) Overland, n. s. **28**: 156.
Bird Shooting in South Africa. Sat. R. **79**: 154.
Bird Songs in Spring. Spec. **74**: 645.
Bird Superstitions and Curiosities. All the Year, **71**: 87, 106.
Birds, Accidents to. Cornh. **72**: 384.
— Aftershaft in, Evolution and Use of. (H. L. Clark) Science, **21**: 160.
— Air-sacs and Hollow Bones of. (F. W. Headley) Nat. Sci. **3**: 346.
— Alaudarum Legio. (F. A. Fulcher) Fortn. **64**: 919.
— and the Atmosphere. (A. C. Baines) No. Am. **162**: 511.
— and "Birds." (E. M. Thomas) Atlan. **69**: 51.
— and Man. (W. H. Hudson) Longm. **29**: 143.
— and their Persecutors. (L. de La Ramée) 19th Cent. **37**: 45.
— as Dancers. (J. M. Murphy) Outing, **22**: 35.
— as Seed-Scatterers. (H. N. Ridley) Nat. Sci. **8**: 186.
— at the Amsterdam Zoo. Liv. Age, **210**: 126.
Birds at Dinner. (H. E. Richards) Pop. Sci. Mo. **49**: 337.
— at Dunluce. (F. A. Fulcher) Argosy, **58**: 200.
— at Yule-tide. (F. Bolles) Atlan. **72**: 757.
— August, in Cape Breton. (F. Bolles) Atlan. **74**: 158
— Autumn, in the Pine Barrens. (M. Treat) Garden & F. **9**: 452.
— Bills of Big. Cornh. **66**: 517. Same art. Ecl. M. **118**: 826.
— Brains of, Characteristics of. (C. H. Turner) Science, **19**: 16.
— British, and the Frosts of 1895. Sat. R. **79**: 375.
— — Destruction of. (Lord Lilford) National, **23**: 181.
— — Hudson's. (A. R. Wallace) Sat. R. **80**: 342.
— — Migration of, Dixon's. Sat. R. **80**: 83. —(M. G. Watkins) Acad. **47**: 546.
— British Game-, Dixon's. Sat. R. **75**: 302.
— Calendar of, by H. E. Parkhurst. Garden & F. **7**: 469.
— Care of, in Winter. (T. D. Hatfield) Garden & F. **7**: 48.
— Cliff-dwellers in the Cañon. (O. T. Miller) Atlan. **70**: 306.
— Colors of North American Land, Evolution of, Keeler on. Am. Natural. **27**: 547.
— Coöperation among. (C. Smiley) Chaut. **23**: 89.
— Courtship of. (J. Burroughs) Cosmopol. **14**: 119.
— Deserted Homes of. Blackw. **155**: 720.
— Distribution of. (R. B. Sharpe) Nat. Sci. **3**: 100.
— Dixon on. Sat. R. **77**: 98.
— Domestic, Law about. (R. V. Rogers) Green Bag, **7**: 182.
— Domesticated. (N. S. Shaler) Scrib. M. **18**: 501.
— Effects of Civilization on. (M. Gibbs) Science, **20**: 183.
— English Wood-Notes. (J. L. Allen) Cosmopol. **18**: 680.
— Feet of. (F. A. Lucas) Nat. Sci. **5**: 208.
— — Significance of. (F. Finn) Nat. Sci. **4**: 453.
— Flight of. (I. Lancaster) Am. Natural. **27**: 20. — (H. L. Ward) Science, **17**: 45.
— Foraging of. Cornh. **69**: 160.
— from Moidart. (J. E. Harting) Chamb. J. **73**: 81.
— Game, and Wild Food. Eng. R. **14**: 431.
— — Russian. (F. Whishaw) Longm. **20**: 60.
— Giant, of South America. (R. Lydekker) Knowl. **18**: 125.
— Gregarious; Birds of a Feather. (F. A. Fulcher) Sund. M. **22**: 335.
— Haunt of. (J. H. Crawford) Gent. M. n. s. **53**: 316.
— in Decoration. (A. Griffiths) M. of Art, **4**: 138.
— in Early September. N. Eng. **56**: 141.
— in Heligoland, Gaetke on. Sat. R. **80**: 582.
— in India. (C. T. Buckland) Liv. Age, **192**: 243.
— in Kensington Gardens. Sat. R. **79**: 184.
— in Kentucky. (L. S. Keyser) Southern M. **5**: 41.
— in New Zealand, Extinct, Remains of. (H. O. Forbes) Nature, **45**: 416. Same art. Science, **19**: 163.
— — Native. (Earl of Onslow) Nature, **46**: 502.
— in the New Forest. Cornh. **67**: 590.
— in a Pasture by the Great Salt Lake. (O. T. Miller) Atlan. **73**: 198.
— in Winter. Cornh. **71**: 133.
— Individuality in. (F. Bolles) Atlan. **71**: 619.
— Instinct and Education in. (H. C. Bumpus) Science, n. s. **4**: 213.
— Judgments of Men of. (M. Cunisset-Carnot) Pop. Sci. Mo. **44**: 110.
— Lament for. (S. F. Cooper) Harper, **87**: 472.
— Language of, Mimetic Origin and Development of. (C. A. Witchell) Am. Natural. **30**: 854.
— London. Sat. R. **75**: 593.

Birds, Migration of. (G. W. Bulman) Temp. Bar, 106: 517. Same art. Liv. Age, 208: 55. — (G. W. Bulman) Knowl. 16: 155. — (B. Torrey) Atlan. 70: 190. — (T. Wood) Liv. Age, 192: 376.
— — a Check on Production of Geographical Varieties. (T. H. Montgomery, jr.) Am. Natural. 30: 458.
— — Dixon on. Sat. R. 74: 315. — Spec. 69: 528. — Nature, 47: 169. — Nat. Sci. 1: 762.
— — in Great Britain and Ireland. Knowl. 19: 254.
— — Mystery of. Spec. 74: 681.
— — Wonders of. (C. Smiley) Chaut. 23: 466.
— Migratory. Liv. Age, 198: 57.
— Missing Fifth Wing-feather. Sat. R. 81: 619.
— Molting in, Study of. (W. Stone) Science, 21: 51.
— Music of. Chamb. J. 69: 81. Same art. Liv. Age, 193: 187.
— Nature's Training-school. Blackw. 157: 114.
— Nests and Eggs of, Resemblance of. (H. F. Witherby) Knowl. 19: 125.
— Nests of; Birds as Architects. Chamb. J. 71: 641.
— — Law of. (T. Champness) Sund. M. 21: 744.
— — Some Curious. (R. B. Sharpe) Good Words, 36: 528.
— Newton's Dictionary of. (J. A. Allen) Nation, 57: 415.
— Nocturnal Migration of. (F. M. Chapman) Pop. Sci. Mo. 45: 506.
— North American. (J. Worth) 19th Cent. 33: 586.
— of the Arnold Arboretum. (C. E. Faxon) Garden & F. 8: 292.
— of the Cliffs. (C. J. Cornish) Sund. M. 24: 302.
— of Devon and Cornwall. Quar. 183: 423.
— of England, and their Haunts. M. of Art, 4: 271-418.
— of the Florida Flat-Woods. (B. Torrey) Atlan. 72: 779.
— of the Grass Lands. (S. Trotter) Pop. Sci. Mo. 42: 453.
— of New Guinea. (G. S. Mead) Am. Natural. 29: 1-1056. 30: 710.
— of Northamptonshire, Lord Lilford's. Blackw. 160: 117.
— of Paradise from New Guinea. (G. S. Mead) Am. Natural. 28: 915.
— of Passage. (W. Haacke) Chaut. 20: 603.
— of a Sea-marsh. (F. A. Fulcher) Gent. M. n. s. 49: 618.
— Our Native, of Song and Beauty, by Henry Nehrling. Garden & F. 7: 159.
— Plumage of. (C. Whymper) M. of Art, 8: 276.
— — as used by Milliners. Spec. 72: 80.
— Precocious. (F. A. Fulcher) Sund. M. 21: 383.
— Protection of in England, Bill for, 1893. Ed. R. 178: 82. — Nature, 49: 54.
— Protective Resemblance in. (H. F. Witherby) Knowl. 19: 66.
— Rambles among. (H. G. Hutchinson) Longm. 26: 174. Same art. Ecl. M. 125: 102.
— Recent Books about. (S. A. Hubbard) Dial (Ch.) 19: 16.
— Respiration of. (T. Hornell) Nat. Sci. 3: 28.
— Roadside Singers and Covert Warblers. Blackw. 157: 879. Same art. Ecl. M. 125: 384.
— Sea. (J. H. Crawford) Belgra. 84: 189.
— — of the Cape. (Wm. Greswell) Good Words, 36: 311.
— Secret of the Wild Rose Path. (O. T. Miller) Atlan. 73: 487.
— Shore, Nests of, in Brading Harbor. Spec. 74: 576.
— Shore-shooting. (E. W. Sandys) Outing, 22: 219.
— — in New England. Outing, 20: 455.
— Silence of. (F. A. Fulcher) Argosy, 60: 283.
Birds, Soaring of, and Possibilities of Human Flight. Around World, 1: 79.
— Some Feathered Artists. (C. Smiley) Chaut. 21: 736.
— Some of the "Outliers" Among. (R. W. Shufeldt) Pop. Sci. Mo. 46: 760.
— Some Tennessee Bird-notes. (B. Torrey) Atlan. 77: 198.
— — in India. (W. T. Greene) Eng. Illust. 10: 269.
— Song of, in England. Spec. 73: 205.
— Songs of, Some. (R. C. Nightingale) Good Words, 37: 473.
— Spring. (N. C. Brown) Outing, 26: 69.
— Spring Migration of. (W. W. Brown) Lippinc. 55: 679.
— Study of, Out-of-doors. (F. M. Chapman) Pop. Sci. Mo. 47: 664.
— Testimony of, to the King. (B. Waugh) Sund. M. 24: 31.
— that we see. (E. E. Thompson) Scrib. M. 13: 759.
— Traits of. (F. Bolles) New Eng. M. n. s. 7: 93.
— Tramps with an Enthusiast. (O. T. Miller) Atlan. 75: 658.
— Wanderers. Macmil. 68: 25.
— Wet Day among the. All the Year, 72: 497.
— What shall we do with the? (F. W. Card) Garden & F. 8: 388.
— When Life stirs. National, 23: 232. Same art. Ecl. M. 122: 825.
— Whimsical Ways in Bird Land. (O. T. Miller) Atlan. 77: 670.
— Wild, Protection of. (H. Maxwell) Blackw. 156: 55.
— Wild Nature in London. M. of Art, 17: 246.
— Wingless. (F. V. Theobald) Chamb. J. 70: 718.
— Wings of. (W. H. Flower) Good Words, 35: 21.
— Winter. (H. G. Hutchinson) Longm. 26: 174.
— — of New England. (W. E. Cram) New Eng. M. n. s. 13: 547.
— Winter Faring of. (F. A. Fulcher) Chamb. J. 70: 81.
— Winter in the Pines. (Mary Treat) Garden & F. 6: 39.
— Young America in Feathers. (O. T. Miller) Atlan. 78: 112.
Birds' Eggs, Arrangement and Number of, in the Nest. (M. Gibbs) Science, 21: 148.
— Collecting. Atlan. 75: 288.
Birkinbine, John. (F. L. Bitler) Cassier, 4: 317.
Birmingham, Ala., Iron Industry. (W. Kent) Cassier, 1: 387.
Birmingham, Eng.; "Brummagem" Jewelry. (B. McEvoy) Canad. M. 2: 429.
— Grammar School. (A. M. Kersley) Educa. 13: 204.
— Municipal Finance, as Illustrated by. (E. O. Smith) J. Statis. Soc. 58: 327.
— Municipality at Work. (Frederick Dolman) New R. 11: 74.
— Musical Festival at. (J. S. Shedlock) Acad. 46: 262, 285.
— An Object Lesson in Municipal Government. (G. F. Parker) Cent. 31: 71.
— Progress of Art in. (A. St. Johnston) M. of Art, 10: 159.
— Ship Canal from, to Sea. (J. W. Robertson-Scott) Time 17: 16.
— United Nonconformist Action in. (L. F. Wiseman) Chr. Lit. 10: 339.
Birmingham Corporation Museum and Art Gallery. (A. St. Johnston) M. of Art, 10: 361.
Birney, W. Verplanck. (C. Childe) Q. Illust. 2: 145.
Birrell, Augustine, with portrait. Bk. Buyer, 4: 332.
— as a Critic. (J. A. Noble) Acad. 41: 605.
Birrens, Roman Station at. Acad. 50: 246.

Birth, The Mystery of. (G. Allen) Fortn. **64**: 113.
Birthday, A; a story. (N. Syrett) Longm. **19**: 512.
Birth-rate in the U. S., Diminishing. (J. S. Billings) Forum, **15**: 467.
— Significance of a Decreasing. (J. L. Brownell) Ann. Am. Acad. Pol. Sci. **5**: 48.
Births: Degree of Legitimate Natality. (J. Körösi) J. Statis. Soc. **57**: 690.
Biscuit Factories of Reading, Eng. (J. Hatton) Eng. Illust. **9**: 855.
Bisbee, Lewis H. (H. L. Conard) M. West. Hist. **12**: 679.
Biserta, Strategic Value of. (F. C. O. Johnson) Un. Serv. M. **7**: 1076.
Bishop, Mrs. Isabella Bird, Travels of. Dub. R. **119**: 435.
Bishop, Robert Hamilton. (E. D. Warfield) Nat'l. M. (N. Y. '91), **15**: 175.
Bishop, The, and the Football; a story. (B. Thomson) New R. **14**: 597.
Bishop in Partibus, A. Liv. Age, **209**: 798.
Bishop Hill Colony; a Religious Communistic Settlement in Henry County, Illinois. (M. A. Mikkelsen) J. H. Univ. Studies, **10**: no. 1.
Bishoprics, Right of Appointment to. Eng. R. **13**: 279.
Bishop's Nominee; a story. Cornh. **67**: 599.
Bishops, Inadvisability of Districting. Meth. R. **56**: 299.
— Office of, and their Visitations. Eng. R. **5**: 269.
— Proposal to have the Lutheran Bishops of Denmark Consecrate Bishops for the Episcopal Churches in America. (F. P. Manhart) Luth. **25**: 365.
Bishopsthorpe. (E. Venables) Sund. M. **23**: 447.
Bishopstone Church, Wilts, England. (S. Beale) Am. Arch. **54**: 6.
Biskra; an Algerian Winter-resort. (A. Griffiths) Fortn. **63**: 456. — (H. M. Field) Around World, **1**: 92.
— the Desert Queen. (R. W. W. Cryan) Westm. **145**: 50.
Bisley and the Nation Rifle Association. (W. Mackinnon) Un. Serv. M. **4**: 497.
Bismarck. (T. Schwartz) Munsey, **7**: 421. — (W. F. Day) Munsey, **11**: 366. — (P. Bigelow) Contemp. **61**: 609. Same art. Ecl. M. **118**: 835. — Eng. Illust. **13**: 289.
— American Friends of. (H. W. Fischer) Munsey, **13**: 481.
— and Caprivi. Pub. Opin. **14**: 201.
— and William II. Contemp. **62**: 153. Same art. Ecl. M. **119**: 420. — Spec. **69**: 7.
— and Prussian Monarchy. (W. H. Dawson) Fortn. **63**: 745.
— as a Ruler. Sat. R. **79**: 405.
— at Friedrichsruh. (E. Kinnikutt) Cent. **25**: 94.
— *Contra Coronam.* (M. Smith) Nation, **58**: 196, 217.
— followed up. Ecl. M. **118**: 368.
— Honored on his 80th Birthday. Sat. R. **79**: 468.
— Lowe's Life of. (M. Todhunter) Westm. **144**: 22.
— My Visit to. (S. Whitman) Chaut. **20**: 300.
— Outflanking Two Emperors. (Murat Halstead) Cosmopol. **17**: 424.
— Portraits of. McClure, **4**: 525.
— Reception of, in Vienna, 1892. Spec. **68**: 875.
— Reconciliation with William II. (Sidney Whitman) New R. **10**: 346.
— Secret Treaty of. Fortn. **66**: 904. — National, **28**: 446.
— Socialism of. (Sidney J. Law) Univ. R. **6**: 565.
— the Strongest Personality since Napoleon. (T. A. Dodge) Forum, **19**: 257.
— Table Talk. (C. H. Cooper) Dial (Ch.) **20**: 200. — Sat. R. **82**: 92.
— Thirty Years under Bismarck's Frown. (J. H. Wisby) Soc. Econ. **6**: 103.
Bismarck. The Three Chancellors. (Theodor Barth) New R. **11**: 557.
— A Visit to. (G. W. Smalley) Fortn. **60**: 1. Same art. Liv. Age, **198**: 643. Same art. Ecl. M. **121**: 200.
— A Wager with. (P. Andreæ) Eng. Illust. **14**: 317.
Bismarck Myth, The. Liv. Age, **211**: 878.
Bismuth. Thermo-electric Heights of Antimony and Bismuth Alloys. (C. C. Hutchins) Am. J. Sci. **148**: 226.
Bisnaga's Madeline. (W. LeC. Beard) Scrib. M. **17**: 165.
Bissell, E. C., Obituary of. (A. C. Zenos) Presb. & Ref. R. **5**: 684.
Bistolfi, Leonardo. (H. Zimmern) Art J. **48**: 335.
Bit of Blue Ribbon, A; a story. (S. B. Kennedy) Outing, **27**: 3, 145.
Bit of Blue Ribbon, A; a story. Temp. Bar, **101**: 233.
Bit of Forgotten Biography; a story. Overland, n. s. **19**: 65-377.
Bit of Land, A. (F. A. Steel) Macmil. **70**: 235.
Bit of Life; a story. (B. Carr) Munsey, **14**: 56.
Bittee; a story. (J. C. Bull) Munsey, **12**: 467.
Bitter Expiation, A. (A. M. Judd) Belgra. **88**: 149.
Bitter-sweet (Celastrus scandens). Garden & F. **5**: 568.
Bitter-sweet: an Adjustment; a story. (E. W. Abram) Idler, **10**: 541.
Bitumen in Paintings, Robinson on. Art. J. **46**: 326.
— Nitrogen Content of California Bitumen. (S. F. Peckham) Am. J. Sci. **148**: 250.
— of Park Co., Montana. (W. C. Day; A. P. Bryant) J. Frankl. Inst. **138**: 149.
— What is? (S. F. Peckham) J. Frankl. Inst. **140**: 370.
Bitumens and Asphalts. (S. P. Sadtler) J. Frankl. Inst. **140**: 198.
— Origin of. (S. F. Peckham) Am. J. Sci. **148**: 389.
Bjornson, Bjornstjerne. (S. Livingston) Canad. M. **1**: 93. — Critic, **21**: 196. — With portraits. (C. Collin) R. of Rs. (N. Y.) **6**: 411.
— Bibliography of. (W. H. Carpenter) Bookman, **2**: 65.
— and Ibsen. (Mrs. Alec. Tweedie) Temp. Bar, **98**: 536.
— Conversations with. (H. H. Boyesen) Cosmopol. **15**: 413.
— Pastor Sang. Sat. R. **77**: 205.
Black, Alexander. Miss Jerry, the First Picture Play. (Alex. Black) Scrib. M. **18**: 348.
Black, Jeremiah Sullivan. (J. P. Knott) So. M. **1**: 315.
Black, Wm., with portrait. Bk. Buyer, **5**: 269. — With portrait. Bk. News, **9**: 175.
Black, Wm. P., with portrait. (H. L. Conard) M. West. Hist. **13**: 476.
Black Affair, A. (W. W. Jacobs) Idler, **9**: 407.
Black and White Art, Herkomer's. Am. Arch. **51**: 101.
Black Art, Light on. (A. Herrmann) Cosmopol. **14**: 208.
Black Bat; a story. (F. M. Peard) Temp. Bar, **103**: 372.
Black Butterfly, The; a story. Temp. Bar, **95**: 495. Same art. Liv. Age, **196**: 23.
Black Country of England, Transformation of. Macmil. **71**: 377. Same art. Liv. Age, **205**: 245.
Black Death. All the Year, **75**: 11.
— Gasquet on. Ath. '**94**, **1**: 237.
Black Deuce. (W. Grant) New Eng. M. n. s. **7**: 392.
Black Dogs and the Thumbless Hand; a tale. (A. Lang) Cornh. **74**: 763.
Black Friars of England, Prelates of. (C. F. R. Palmer) Antiq. n. s. **26**: 213. **27**: 36, 111.
Black Forest, From the, to the Black Sea. (P. Bigelow) Harper, **84**: 329-85: 221.
Black Forest, Lorelei, A. (Constance A. M. Cotterell) Temp. Bar, **108**: 93. Same art. Liv. Age, **209**: 659.

Black Forest Wedding, A. Cornh. 72: 95. Same art. Liv. Age, 206: 334.
Black Friday of 1869. (H. White) Yale R. 3: 8.
Black Hawk, Home of. (I. B. Richman) New Eng. M. n. s. 7: 305.
Black Hills, Drive through. (A. Ogden) Atlan. 69: 449.
Black Knot upon Cherries and Plums. (E. G. Lodeman) Garden & F. 7: 508.
Black Lake of Surrey. Spec. 76: 445.
Black-letter Broadsheet, The. Chamb. J. 69: 698.
Black Mountains, Among the. All the Year, 73: 439.
Black Night, A; a poem. (W. Allingham) M. of Art, 9: 149.
Black Pointer, The; a story. (E. S. Drewry) Belgra. 79: 29. Christmas no.
Black River, Cleansing the. (F. M. Holmes) Gent. M. n. s. 50: 172.
Black Rod's Knock. (M. MacDonagh) Good Words, 37: 318.
Black Rudolph's Mass; a Christmas story. Argosy, 61: 48.
Black Sea, Physical Exploration of. (N. Andrusoff) Geog. J. 1: 49.
Black Sea Outing, A. (Charlotte D. Devon) Bach. of Arts, 1: 490.
Black Settlement, A; a story. (M. McCulloch-Williams) Harper, 93: 767.
Black Sheep, A; a story. Belgra. 88: 39.
Black Water, The; a story. (R. W. Chambers) Eng. Illust. 15: 546. — (A. F. Chamberlain) J. Am. Folk-Lore, 6: 77.
Blackberries, Cultivation of. Garden & F. 8: 439.
Blackfoot Indian Legends. (J. McLean) J. Am. Folk-Lore, 3: 296.
Blackfoot Lodge Tales, Grinnell's. (E. L. Huggins) Dial (Ch.) 14: 182.
Blackfoot Mythology. (J. Maclean) J. Am. Folk-Lore, 6: 165.
Blackfoot Sun and Moon Myth. (G. B. Grinnell) J. Am. Folk-Lore, 6: 44.
Blackie, John Stuart. Bk. News, 13: 338. — Leis. Hour, 44: 434. — Ed. R. 183: 465. — (A. H. Miller) Scot. R. 27: 12. Same art. Liv. Age, 208: 771. — Eng. Illust. 11: 1072. — Acad. 47: 465. — Ath. '95, 1: 312. — Blackw. 157: 662. 158: 715. — Liv. Age, 207: 612. — Critic, 26: 188. — (J. Douglas) Nation, 60: 256. — (Henriette Corkran) Temp. Bar, 105: 520.
— Biography of, Stoddard's. Sat. R. 80: 510.
— and his Doppel-gänger. (W. G. Blaikie) Good Words, 36: 297.
Blackmore, R. D. Lorna Doone, Descent of. (C. R. Ballard) Critic, 28: 259.
— — The Valley of the Doones. Atlan. 71: 573.
— Novels of. Blackw. 160: 409.
— Perlycross, Local History in. (R. D. Blackmore) Critic, 26: 66. — (G. Saintsbury) Acad. 46: 299. — (W. Corner) Critic, 25: 429.
Blackpool, Lancashire. All the Year, 74: 225.
Blackstone, Timothy B. M. West. Hist. 12: 298.
Blackwell, Alice Stone. Armenian Poems. Sat. R. 81: 561.
Blackwood, Sir Stevenson A. Sat. R. 82: 90.
Blades, William. Bookworm, 3: 221.
Blaine, J. G., with portraits. (H. P. Judson) R. of Rs. (N. Y.) 7: 159. — With portraits. (T. C. Crawford) Cosmopol. 14: 429. — (J. D. Long) Educa. 13: 455. — Pub. Opin. 14: 419. — Sat. R. 75: 116. — Spec. 70: 152.
— Commercial Policy of, with portraits. R. of Rs. (N. Y.) 5: 546.
— Declination of. Pub. Opin. 12: 471.
Blaine, J. G., Dodge's. (A. B. Hart) Am. Hist. R. 2: 181.
— His Defeat for the Presidency. (M. Halstead) McClure, 6: 159.
— Reminiscences of. (E. J. Edwards) Chaut. 17: 44.
Blair, Hugh. Scottish School of Rhetoric. (A. M. Williams) Educa. 13: 488.
Blair, James. *See* Bourchier.
Blake, William. Gent. M. n. s. 52: 429. — (E. A. Gowing) Belgra. 77: 357. Same art. Liv. Age, 193: 664. — (R. Garnett) Portf. 1895: no. 22. — (A. T. Story) Temp. Bar, 106: 525. Same art. Liv. Age, 208: 177. Same art. Ecl. M. 126: 319.
— and his Disciples. (A. T. Story) Art J. 45: 43.
— and his Wife. (J. Oldcastle) M. of Art, 4: 478.
— as an Impressionist. (L. Housman) Univ. R. 6: 209.
— Ellis and Yeats'. Sat. R. 75: 126.
— Romanticism of. (L. A. Paton) Poet-Lore, 5: 481.
— Story's. (K. Cox) Nation, 57: 376.
— Works. (L. Johnson) Acad. 44: 163.
Blanc, Mont, Ascent of, by Col. Beaufroy in 1787. (R. Edgcumbe) National, 22: 249.
— — The First. (R. Edgcumbe) National, 19: 772. Same art. Ecl. M. 119: 473. — (E. Whymper) Leis. Hour, 44: 615.
— in a Blizzard. (G. P. Serviss) McClure, 6: 560.
— Observatory at Top of. (I. M. Tarbell) McClure, 2: 289.
Blanchard, Joshua. (A. E. Brown) New Eng. M. n. s. 13: 390.
Bland, Mrs. Hubert, Poetry of. (C. Monkhouse) Acad. 41: 537.
Bland, Richard Parks, and a New Party. Arena, 13: 50.
Blanford, Henry F. Nature, 47: 322.
Blank Cartridges; a story. (E. Fawcett) Outing, 25: 24.
Blanket-making, Native American. (W. J. Hoffman) Mo. Illust. 4: 114.
Blasphemy Laws, Intellectual Liberty and the. (E. G. Taylor) Westm. 143: 117.
Blast Furnace. (J. Hartman) Cassier, 2: 331.
— Fuel of. (V. Cornish) Knowl. 15: 183.
— Blowing Engine. Cassier, 1: 326.
Blatchford, Lord Frederic. Acad. 50: 416.
Blatchford, Samuel, with portrait. (A. O. Hall) Green Bag, 5: 489.
Blavatsky, Helena Petrovna. (J. R. Bridge) Arena, 12: 177.
— and her Book "Isis Unveiled." (F. M. Müller) 19th Cent. 33: 769. — (A. P. Sinnett) 19th Cent. 33: 1015.
— and her Theosophy, Lillie's. Sat. R. 79: 533.
— and the Theosophical Society. (F. Podmore) Good Words, 33: 82.
— a Fraud. Sat. R. 79: 191.
— in India. (W. Q. Judge) Arena, 5: 472.
— Theosophy and. (K. B. Davis) Arena, 16: 292.
Bleaching by Electricity. (L. J. Matos) J. Frankl. Inst. 139: 177.
Bleckley, L. E. Autobiography, with portrait. Green Bag, 4: 49.
Blenner, Carle J. (A. Black) Q. Illust. 2: 37.
Blessing Disguised, A; a story. (F. W. Robinson) Idler, 3: 143.
Blessington, Countess of. (E. L. Didier) Chaut. 17: 605.
— Molloy's Life of. Sat. R. 81: 332.
Blight on Guestwick Hall; a story. Cornh. 68: 374.
Blighted Life, A; a story. Argosy, 55: 537.
Blighting of Mynheer Van Steen. (A. E. King) Cent. 28: 334.
Blind, Mathilde. (T. Watts-Dunton) Ath. '96, 2: 796. — Acad. 50: 497.
— Songs of the Orient and the Occident. Sat. R. 80: 241.

Blind, Chinese, Numeral-type for. (C. F. Gordon-Cumming) Sund. M. **23**: 754.
— Education of. (M. C. Jones) Scrib. M. **12**: 373.
— — How they are taught. (J. P. Ritter) Chaut. **15**: 65.
— Kindergarten for. Lend a Hand, **12**: 336. — (D. Sturgis) New Eng. M. n. s. **13**: 433.
— Kindergartens for. (J. Glenn) Char. R. **1**: 263.
— Magic Fingers. Chamb. J. **69**: 166–803.
— Printing for, Method of. Lend a Hand, **12**: 111.
— World of. (G. H. Pike) Sund. M. **23**: 130.
— Writing for, New System of. (J. A. Zahm) Cath. World, **61**: 32.
Blind Beggarman, A; a story. (F. Mathew) Idler, **3**: 82.
Blind Harry. *See* Henry the Minstrel.
Blind Larry; a story. All the Year, **75**: 452, 475.
Blind Victor Robair; a story. (C. E. Barnes) Music, **2**: 579.
Blindness, A Blind Man on. Spec. **71**: 552.
— and Musicianship. (J. S. Van Cleve) Music, **3**: 62. **5**: 21, 196.
— Voyage in the Dark. (R. E. Robinson) Atlan. **75**: 172.
Blister-beetles, Notes on. (J. B. Smith) Garden & F. **6**: 423.
Blizzard. *See* Storm of Mar. 11–14, 1888.
Blizzard, The; a story. (E. V. Wilson) McClure, **4**: 387.
Blizzard-bound; a sketch. All the Year, **76**: 53.
Block Island, Geology of. (O. C. Marsh) Am. J. Sci. **152**: 295, 375.
Blockade Runner, Watson's. Sat. R. **74**: 147.
Blockade Running. (J. N. Maffitt) Un. Serv. (Phila.) **7**: 147.
Blockades and Blockade Running. (S. H. Clarke) Un. Serv. M. **8**: 444.
Blodgett, Henry W., with portrait. (H. L. Conard) M. West. Hist. **12**: 413.
Blois, Château de. (W. T. Partridge) Am. Arch. **53**: 19, 67. **54**: 87.
Blomidon to Smoky, From. (F. Bolles) Atlan. **73**: 592.
Blondin, Chevalier. Eng. Illust. **11**: 547. — Chamb. J. **72**: 282.
Blood, Circulation of; Modern Developments of Harvey's Work. (T. L. Brunton) Nature, **50**: 625.
— Coagulation of. (W. D. Halliburton) Sci. Prog. **2**: 369. **3**: 127.
— Human, Legal Detection of. (E. Marshall) Green Bag, **7**: 61.
Blood Brotherhood. (T. L. Patterson) Nature, **53**: 604.
Blood Corpuscles, Separation of White from Red. (J. Daland) J. Frankl. Inst. **136**: 204.
Blood Royal. (G. Allen) Chamb. J. **69**: 561.
Blood-vessels, Shadows of, upon the Retina. (C. L. Franklin) Psychol. R. **2**: 392.
Blount, Edward: an Elizabethan Bookseller. (Sidney Lee) Bibliographica, **1**: 473.
Blousa-Bella; a story. (C. Young) Belgra. **84**: 390.
Blowing Engines. (J. Kennedy) Cassier, **5**: 34.
Blowing Machinery, American. (J. Birkinbine) Cassier, **11**: 109.
Blowitz, M. de. (W. T. Stead) R. of Rs. (N. Y.) **13**: 559. — With portraits. (W. M. Fullerton) McClure, **1**: 122, 166.
— Reminiscences. Contemp. **63**: 228.
Bloxsom, William Gibson, with portrait. Bank. M. (Lond.) **56**: 331.
Bluebeard, Case of. (P. Edwards) Green Bag, **5**: 543.
— Maréchal de Retz. Belgra. **80**: 58.
Blueberry, White Fruit. (E. J. Hill) Garden & F. **8**: 503.
Blue-bill Shooting. (E. W. Chubb) Outing, **24**: 73.
Blue Bonnet; a story. (C. Barnard) Chaut. **20**: 562, 682. **21**: 40.
Blue Dryad, The. Macmil. **69**: 44.
Blue-fish, A Bout with. (E. W. Sandys) Outing, **28**: 323.
— Fishing for, on Jersey Shoals. (H. P. Beach) Outing, **22**: 354.
Blue Grass Cycling Tour. (J. B. Carrington) Outing, **24**: 380.
Blue Hills of Milton, Massachusetts. (W. H. Downes and F. T. Robinson) New Eng. M. n. s. **14**: 707.
— Weather Studies at. (R. L. Bridgman) New Eng. M. n. s. **12**: 40.
Blue Jay; Little Boy Blue. (O. T. Miller) Atlan. **72**: 169.
Blue Laws. (F. M. Holland) Open Court, **1**: 92.
Blue Mt., Maryland, Geologist at. (C. D. Wolcott) Nat. Geog. M. **5**: 84.
Blue Mountain Forest Park. (T. J. Walker) New Eng. M. n. s. **12**: 355.
Blue Mountains, New South Wales, In the. (S. Thompson) M. of Art, **10**: 116.
Bluestone, North River. (H. B. Ingram) Pop. Sci. Mo. **45**: 352.
Blum, Robert F., with portrait. Bk. Buyer, **10**: 353.
— A Decorative Painting by. Scrib. M. **19**: 1.
Blunders. Spec. **71**: 42.
— Philosophy of. Blackw. **159**: 427. Same art. Ecl. M. **126**: 758. Same art. Liv. Age, **209**: 163.
Blunt, Wilfred S., with portrait. Bk. Buyer, **12**: 559.
— Poetry of. (P. Addleshaw) National, **26**: 202. — (P. Addleshaw) Acad. **41**: 503.
Blushing; Why We Blush. (C. Mélinard) Chaut. **18**: 448.
Boar, Hunting the. (R. S. Osborn) Munsey, **12**: 405. — Outing, **27**: 24.
Boar-hunt, Yaqui. (F. Crissy) Outing, **25**: 511.
Boars and Boar-hunting. (G. A. Stockwell) Outing, **23**: 21.
Board School Children and their Food. Lend a Hand, **14**: 262.
Boarder, Society. Spec. **69**: 187.
Boarding-out System for Children, Developments of. (H. Folks) Char. R. **2**: 254.
Boarding-schools, German. (J. E. Russell) Educa. R. **8**: 240.
Boase, Charles W. (F. C. Conybeare) Acad. **47**: 237. — Ath. '95, **1**: 345.
Boat of St. Avoye. Illus. Archæol. **2**: 106.
Boat-building. (H. R. Palmer) New Eng. M. n. s. **12**: 515.
Boat-race, After the. All the Year, **72**: 341.
— Oxford and Cambridge, 1893. Sat. R. **75**: 322.
— — — 1896. (W. H. Grenfell) Sat. R. **81**: 342.
— Harvard and Yale. (W. A. Brooks) Harper, **89**: 181.
Boat-races, Henley, 1896. (C. W. Dilke) Sat. R. **82**: 31. — (W. B. Curtis) Outing, **28**: 199.
Boat-racing, College, in England. (F. C. Drake) Idler, **3**: 221.
Boat-service Adventure, A; a story. Chamb. J. **70**: 462.
Boating Trip in Samoan Waters. (F. M. Turner) Outing, **25**: 199.
Boating Party of Two; a story. (L. Becke) Eng. Illust. **14**: 381.
Boats and Oars, American and English. (C. Mellen) Outing, **29**: 45.
— Combination Rowing and Sailing. (A. J. Kenealy) Outing, **24**: 145.
Bob. (M. L. Blanchard) New Eng. M. n. s. **11**: 91.
Bob, Story of. (D. S. Jordan) Pop. Sci. Mo. **44**: 145.
Bobbo. (T. Wharton) Harper, **91**: 346.
Boccaccio, Giovanni. (M. Hewlett) Acad. **46**: 469.
— Decameron. Ed. R. **178**: 500. — Atlan. **77**: 283.

Boccaccio, Giovanni, Country of, A Stroll in. (Janet Ross) National, **23**: 364. Same art. Liv. Age, **201**: 764.
— Genealogy of the Gods. (W. F. Melhuish) Bookworm, **3**: 125.
Bodenstedt, Friedrich von. (E. D. Keeling) Acad. **41**: 423. — Ath. '**92**, **1**: 535.
— Birthplace of. (H. C. Bierwith) Nation, **55**: 123.
Bodichon, B. L., Mme. (M. Betham-Edwards) Fortn. **57**: 213. Same art. Liv. Age, **193**: 40.
Bodkin Letter; a Christmas story. Argosy, **58**: 521.
Bodleian Dinnshenchas. (W. Stokes) Folk-Lore, **3**: 467.
Bodleian Library. Chamb. J. **69**: 232.
— in 1891. Acad. **41**: 494.
Body and Mind, or the Data of Moral Physiology. (F. L. Oswald) Open Court, **2**: 771-1476.
Body-snatching, Anatomy Laws *versus*. (T. Dwight) Forum, **22**: 493.
Böcklin, Arnold. (C. Phillips) M. of Art, **8**: 441.
Boehm, Sir Joseph Edgar. (M. H. Spielmann) M. of Art, **14**: 132. — (W. Meynell) M. of Art, **3**: 333.
Boehme, Jacob, compared with Swedenborg. (T. F. Wright) N. Church R. **2**: 214.
Boer, Africander, and Briton. (F. I. Ricardo-Seaver) Fortn. **64**: 197.
Boer Pastoral, A; a story. (H. A. Bryden) Blackw. **158**: 130. Same art. Liv. Age, **206**: 274.
Boers, In Praise of the. Liv. Age, **209**: 35.
— Manners and Customs of. (T. L. White) Forum, **21**: 118.
— Problem of. (T. A. Le Mesurier) Westm. **145**: 429.
— Question of. (H. H. Johnston) Fortn. **62**: 161.
— Who are the? (H. A. Bryden) Chamb. J. **73**: 385.
Boerhaave, Hermann, with portrait. (W. T. Lusk) Pop. Sci. Mo. **47**: 110.
Boethius, Stewart's. Sat. R. **73**: 48.
Bogdanovitch, M., Surveys by. (E. D. Morgan) Geog. J. **2**: 55.
Bogota, Golden Statuettes from. Reliquary, **35**: 151.
Bohemia and the Bohemians. (A. Heilprin) Nation, **60**: 305.
— Austria and. (L. Ordéga) Chaut. **19**: 203.
— An Evening in. Liv. Age, **210**. 119.
— in the Time of Zizka, 1415-24. Macmil. **72**: 346.
— Literature of, 1891-92. (V. Tille) Ath. '**92**, **2**: 6.
— — 1892-93. (V. Tille) Ath. '**93**, **2**: 8.
— — 1893-94. (V. Tille) Ath. '**94**, **2**: 8.
— — 1894-95. (J. Krejčí) Ath. '**95**, **2**: 8.
— — 1895-96. (V. Tille) Ath. '**96**, **2**: 8.
— Lützow's. Sat. R. **81**: 631.
— Peasant Life in. (F. P. Kopta) So. M. **5**: 394.
Bohemian Museum, Natural History Departments of. (M. I. Newbigin) Nat. Sci. **8**: 168.
Bohemian Music in 1894. (J. J. Kral) Music, **7**: 514.
Bohemian Popular Poetry. (J. J. Kral) Music, **3**: 485.
Bohemians, The Three. (J. J. Kral) Music, **5**: 103.
Bohn, H. G., and Bohn's Libraries. Book R. **1**: 125.
Bohun Wills, The. (M. M. Bigelow) Am. Hist. R. **1**: 414, 631.
Boiler Explosion, A Peculiar. (F. H. Daniels) Cassier, **3**: 123. — (J. M. Allen) Cassier, **1**: 191.
— Domestic. Am. Arch. **47**: 44.
Boiler Firing. (D. Ashworth) Cassier, **5**: 113.
Boiler Insurance. (W. H. Wakeman) Cassier, **6**: 175.
Boiler-making. (W. O. Webber) Cassier, **7**: 397.
Boilers at the World's Fair. (H. W. York) Cassier, **4**: 257, 390.
— Marine. Cassier, **1**: 243.
— — Maintenance and Repair of. (J. F. Walliker) Cassier, **10**: 452.
— — Modern. (A. B. Willits) Engin. M. **3**: 350.
— Steam. (A. A. Cary) Cassier, **10**: 197.
Boilers, Filtering Feed Water for. (W. H. Odell) Cassier, **10**: 365.
— Insurance and Inspection of. (W. A. Carlile) Cassier, **11**: 65.
— Selection of. (C. E. Emery) Engin. M. **11**: 1044.
Boiling-points. (E. M. Caillard) Good Words, **34**: 339.
Boise, James Robinson. (I. M. Price) Bib. World, **5**: 410.
Boker, G. H., with portrait. Bk. News, **6**: 94.
Bokhara Revisited. (H. Lansdell) Scrib. M. **11**: 50.
— Samarkand and. (F. Vincent) Cosmopol. **19**: 3.
Bol, Ferdinand, Old Dutch Master. (T. Cole) Cent. **27**: 933.
Bolaine, Elizabeth, a Kentish Miser. All the Year, **71**: 185.
Bold Deserter, A; a story. (J. C. Harris) Eng. Illust. **15**: 243.
Boldness, Wise. (A. H. Japp) Argosy, **56**: 288.
Bolero, The, in Seville. (G. W. Edwards) Cosmopol. **16**: 36.
Boleyn, Mary and Anne. (J. Gairdner) Eng. Hist. R. **8**: 53.
Bolivia. (J. P. Wisser) Un. Serv. (Phila.) **11**: 519.
— Capabilities of. Dub. R. **110**: 190.
— Southern Plateau of. (C. M. S. Pasley) Geog. J. **3**: 105.
Bolle, Berlin's Great Milkman. (H. Burwell) Chaut. **19**: 461.
Bologna, Gian, Desjardin's Life of. M. of Art, **6**: 303.
Bologna, About. (G. B. Stuart) Time, **19**: 303.
— Univ. of, and its Successors. (L. H. Weeks) Bach. of Arts, **2**: 294.
— — English Scholars at, during the Middle Ages. (A. Allaria) Dub. R. **112**: 66.
Bolomet Work, Recent Progress in, at Smithsonian Astro-Physical Observatory. (S. P. Langley) Astron. **13**: 41.
Bolometric Investigations in the Infra Red Spectrum of the Sun. (W. Hallock) Science, n. s. **2**: 174.
Bolton, Henry Carrington, with portrait. Pop. Sci. Mo. **43**: 688.
Bolton, Lavinia Fenton, Duchess of. Theatre, **29**: 168.
Bolton, Sarah Knowles, with portrait. Bk. News, **13**: 211.
Bolton Abbey. (A. Watson) M. of Art, **17**: 387.
— and the Bolton Woods. (T. R. Macquoid) M. of Art, **2**: 112.
— Sealed Altar Stone at. (C. R. Manning) Antiq. n. s. **25**: 163.
Bomareas. (W. Watson) Garden & F. **5**: 78.
Bombardier, The. (Gilbert Parker) Chamb. J. **72**: 481-519.
Bombardments; Battle of Mobile. (D. H. Maury) Southern M. **4**: 523.
Bombastes Furioso; a tale. (H. E. F. Potts) Canad. M. **7**: 143.
Bombay. All the Year, **74**: 350.
— Riots at, 1893. (Sir W. Wedderburn) New R. **9**: 285.
Bonamy Chadwick's Secret; a tale. (G. Fosbery) Argosy, **60**: 474.
Bonaparte, Elisa, Pauline, and Caroline, Sisters of Napoleon. (C. E. Shute) Munsey, **11**: 301.
Bonaparte, Joseph, in Bordentown. (F. M. Crawford) Cent. **24**: 81.
Bonaparte, Prince Lucien, Library of. (V. Collins) Critic, **29**: 299.
Bond, William Cranch, Sketch of, with portrait. Pop. Sci. Mo. **47**: 400.
Bond-holders, Slavery under. (J. Davis) Arena, **10**: 745.
Bond Syndicate and U. S. (B. Ives) Bank M. (N. Y.) **51**: 143.

Bond Syndicate, its Excellent Work. (A. B. Hepburn) Forum, **19**: 658.
— Government and the. (B. Ives) Yale R. **4**: 10.
Bondage, Last Days of, in England. (I. S. Leadam) Law Q. **9**: 348.
Bondage of George Berkley; a story. (Harriet W. Daly) Temp. Bar, **108**: 582. Same art. Liv. Age, **210**: 783.
Bondager, The; a story. (P. A. Graham) Longm. **27**: 497. Same art. Liv. Age, **209**: 335.
Bondager, The; a story. (Isabella Weddle) Gent. M. n. s. **57**: 433. Same art. Liv. Age, **211**: 714.
Bondei Country, Habits of Natives of. (G. Dale) Anthrop. J. **25**: 181.
Bonds, Free Coinage of Bonds. Soc. Econ. **8**: 133.
— U. S., New Issue of. Pub. Opin. **16**: 402. — (H. White) Nation, **58**: 60.
— — Sale of. (H. White) Nation, **60**: 158.
Bone-black, Iron in. (B. Terne) J. Frankl. Inst. **133**: 291.
Bone Skates. Reliquary, **36**: 33.
Bones and Shells, Why of Lime? Sat. R. **81**: 646.
— Folk-Lore of the. (D. G. Brinton) J. Am. Folk-Lore, **3**: 17.
Bonfires in London Streets. (G. L. Apperson) Gent. M. n. s. **55**: 355. Same art. Liv. Age, **207**: 380.
Bonghi, Raphael. Ath. '95, **2**: 571.
Bonheur, Rosa, with portrait. (G. Holme) Munsey, **11**: 58. — (J. Forbes-Robertson) M. of Art, **5**: 45.
Boniface VIII., Causes of Failure of Papal Assumptions of. (A. D. Campbell) Presb. & Ref. R. **4**: 429.
Bonifacio, Juan. (F. Watson) Acad. **47**: 421.
— Visit to. (J. N. Usher) Gent. M. n. s. **55**: 194. Same art. Liv. Age, **206**: 685.
Bonivard, François. (W. D. McCrackan) New Eng. M. n. s. **6**: 615.
Bonjean, Louis-Bernard. Month, **83**: 223.
Bonnat, Léon. (A. Meynell) M. of Art, **4**: 238.
— Atelier of. (B. Day) M. of Art, **5**: 138.
Bonnets. Chamb. J. **70**: 204.
Bonney, Anne, West Indian Amazon. All the Year, **76**: 59.
Bonsenyor, J. (M. Kayserling) Jew. Q. **8**: 632.
Bontebok Antelope Disappearing. Sat. R. **80**: 234.
Bonuses, Anticipated, in Insurance. Bank. M. (Lond.) **57**: 793.
— in Insurance. Bank. M. (Lond.) **61**: 497.
Bonvicino, Alessandro. (C. Phillips) Portfo. **23**: 153, 175.
Book, The. (W. Chapman) Bookworm, **1**: 191.
— of the Covenant, Original Form of. (L. B. Paton) J. Bib. Lit. **12**: 79.
— of the Dead. (Sara Y. Stevenson) New World, **4**: 321. — (J. Offord) Asia. R. **14**: 377.
— — and the Psalms. (J. H. Cooke) Contemp. **70**: 277.
— of the Rhymers' Club. Church Q. **35**: 201.
— Oldest. (J. H. Mitchiner) Knowl. **16**: 106. — (J. H. Mitchiner) Bookworm, **7**: 119.
Book-barrow man. (J. D. Symon) Eng. Illust. **12**: no. 1, 59.
Bookbinders, French, of To-day. (S. T. Prideaux) Scrib. M. **19**: 361.
— — Thoinan's. (S. T. Prideaux) Bibliographica, **1**: 82.
Bookbinding. Quar. **177**: 178. — Spec. **72**: 655. — (S. T. Prideaux) Antiq. n. s. **25**: 208. — (B. Quaritch) Walford's Antiq. **8**: 172.
— Art of. (J. V. Sears) Bk. News, **8**: 171.
— at Home. (Mrs. W. S. Hoyt) Bk. Buyer, **12**: 381.
— Commercial. (B. Matthews) Cent. **26**: 842.
— Design in. (S. T. Prideaux) Scrib. M. **19**: 199.
— Edge Decoration. (S. T. Prideaux) M. of Art, **15**: 94. — (Cyril Davenport) Bibliographica, **2**: 385.
— English. (W. Y. Fletcher) Portfo. **24**: 53, 79, 97.
Bookbinding for Libraries. (D. V. R. Johnston; R. B. Poole) Lib. J. **17**: supp. 13.
— for Library Use. (M. E. Sargent) Lib. J. **19**: 262.
— French. Bookworm, **2**: 8. — (W. Y. Fletcher) Portfo. 1894: no. 10.
— The Gentle Art of. (V. C. Tweedale) Chamb. J. **72**: 449.
— Historical and Artistic. (S. W. Kershaw) M. of Art, **5**: 146.
— History of, ed. by Brassington. Sat. R. **79**: 72.
— New Technique in. (D. S. MacColl) Art J. **48**: 147.
— Old and New. Bookman, **3**: 134.
— Use of Metal in Bound Books. (S. T. Prideau) M. of Art, **14**: 127, 316.
— its Processes and Ideal. (T. J. Cobden-Sanderson) Fortn. **62**: 214. Same art. Ecl. M. **123**: 475. Same art. Pop. Sci. Mo. **46**: 671.
Bookbindings. Acad. **50**: 605. — Bookworm, **2**: 369. — (A. Hayden) Bookworm, **7**: 137.
— Early London. Bookworm, **4**: 325.
— Historical, at the Grolier Club. Critic, **26**: 126. — Bookman, **1**: 55.
— in the British Museum. Bookworm, **1**: 297, 357.
— International Exhibition of. (W. H. Edmunds) M. of Art, **17**: 376.
— Little Gidding. (Cyril Davenport) Bibliographica, **2**: 129.
— of the Past. Bookworm, **7**: 245. — (B. Matthews) Cent. **26**: 60.
— of the Present. (B. Matthews) Cent. **26**: 277.
— of Roger Payne. (Cyril Davenport) Bibliographica, **3**: 371.
— Some Scottish. (S. T. Prideaux) M. of Art, **18**: 110.
See also Book Covers; Book Stamps.
Book-borrowers. Bookworm, **3**: 177, 208.
Book-buying. Bookworm, **2**: 281.
Book Catalogues, Some Old. Bookworm, **2**: 75.
Book Clubs, American. (E. D. North) Bibliographica, **2**: 369.
— Some. (G. L. Gomme) Bookworm, **1**: 65.
Book-collecting. Bookworm, **4**: 241.
— as a Fine Art. (J. Moore) Fortn. **64**: 699. Same art. Ecl. M. **125**: 805.
— in America. Bookworm, **6**: 71.
Book-collectors and Collections, English and Scotch. (W. C. Hazlitt) Bookworm, **7**: 65, 97, 151.
— Great, Elton on. (W. I. Way) Dial (Ch.) **15**: 296.
Book Cover Designs, a Competition. Bk. Buyer, **11**: 237–386.
— Embroidered. (S. T. Prideaux) M. of Art, **13**: 426. **14**: 61. — Bookworm, **1**: 297.
Book Friends, Some. (F. Cooper) Time, **9**: 556.
Book-hunter in England, Roberts's. Sat. R. **80**: 659.
— in Paris, Uzanne's. (W. I. Way) Dial (Ch.) **16**: 362.
Book-hunter's Spoils. Bookworm, **5**: 329.
Book-hunting, Romance of. Bookworm, **4**: 371.
Book-idolatry. Spec. **69**: 154.
Book Illustrations. (J. V. Sears) Bk. News, **7**: 33.
Book-lending. (O. Uzanne) Bookworm, **2**: 237.
— Gentle Art of. (G. S. Layard) 19th Cent. **37**: 1060.
Bookless House, The. (C. F. Richardson) Bk. News, **7**: 331.
Booklessness. Spec. **70**: 568.
Book Lotteries. Bookworm, **2**: 337.
Book-lovers' Societies, French. (W. Roberts) Bookworm, **2**: 253.
Book-plate Society. (J. R. Brown) Bookworm, **6**: 137.
Book-plates. Bookworm, **4**: 57. — (K. P. Garnett) Overland, n. s. **24**: 617. — Sat. R. **73**: 238. — Sat. R. **79**: 388. — (H. Gough) Scot. R. **21**: 315. — (F. J. Thirlwall) Walford's Antiq. **2**: 277. — Walford's Antiq. **3**: 2–274.

Book-plates, by J. Skinner of Bath. (W. J. Hardy) Bibliographica, 2: 422.
— American. Bk. Buyer, 11: 476. — (C. D. Allen) Book R. 2: 5. — (Laurence Hutton) Bk. Buyer, 3: 7–159.
— at the Grolier Club. Critic, 25: 263.
— Charm of Collecting. (F. E. Marshall) Bk. Buyer, 13: 79.
— Collections. Bk. Buyer, 12: 146–825.
— Dated. Bookworm, 7: 337.
— English. (W. J. Hardy) Walford's Antiq. 1: 173. 2: 53.
— — Castle on. Sat. R. 75: 77. — M. of Art, 17: 51.
— French and English. Bookworm, 6: 105.
— of English Authors. Critic, 22: 82.
— of Erasmus and Hector Pomer. (H. W. Pereira) Antiq. n. s. 25: 242.
Book-prices: Danze's Index Biblio-Iconographique. Bibliographica, 2: 494.
Book-reviewing. (G. Iles) Lib. J. 17: supp. 18.
Book-sales, English, 1676–86. (A. W. Pollard) Bibliographica, 1: 373. 2: 112.
— of 1891. (J. H. Slater) Ath. '92, 1: 87, 151.
Booksellers at the Sign of the Trinity. (E. G. Duff) Bibliographica, 1: 93, 175, 499.
— English: Long Shop in the Poultry. (H. R. Plomer) Bibliographica, 2: 61.
— of 17th Century. Bookworm, 5: 369.
— Picadilly. Chamb. J. 71: 529.
— Profits of. Sat. R. 78: 479.
Bookselling, Decay of. (D. Stott) 19th Cent. 36: 932.
— in England. Quar. 174: 158.
Bookstalling Reminiscences. Bookworm, 2: 1.
Book-stamps, English Armorial. (W. Y. Fletcher) Bibliographica, 3: 309.
Book-store Windows. Acad. 50: 437.
Book-trade, Early Italian. (R. Garnett) Bibliographica, 3: 29.
— English, Literature and. (L. de La Ramée) No. Am. 160: 157.
— — 1525, Literary References to. Bibliographica, 1: 252.
Bookworm, The. Bookworm, 1: 3.
— Natural History of. Bookworm, 1: 76.
— Ravages of. Lib. J. 19: 230.
Bookworms, Of. (W. Austin) Nation, 62: 305.
Books. (E. B. Titchener) Book R. 2: 331.
— about Books. (A. B. McMahan) Dial (Ch.) 20: 361.
— — Recent. Bookworm, 7: 185.
— Among the. National, 109: 123.
— and Culture. (H. W. Mabie) Bookman, 2: 409, 501.
— and Reading in Iceland. (W. E. Mead) Atlan. 71: 158.
— Arrangement of Matter in. Bookworm, 2: 265.
— as Necessaries of Life. (W. Gladden) Bk. News, 7: 179.
— Auction Prices of, in 17th and 19th Centuries. (J. Lawler) Bookworm, 1: 36.
— Bad Features of Good. (H. C. Bolton) Lib. J. 21: 265.
— Bits about. (W. Canton) Good Words, 36: 69–857.
— Chained. Reliquary, 32: 10. — (C. E. G. Dickinson) Sund. M. 23: 528.
— Choice of. (L. Stephen) National, 25: 165.
— Decoration of Backs of. Bookworm, 3: 241.
— Distribution of. (W. Chapman) Bookworm, 1: 286.
— Duty on. Dial (Ch.) 16: 67.
— Eastern; How they begin and end. (W. A. Clouston) Bookworm, 4: 121.
— First English Auction Sale of. (A. W. Pollard) Longm. 21: 634.
— for Boys. (R. E. Welsh) Sund. M. 25: 34. — (J. A. Cooper) Canad. M. 6: 282.
Books for Boys and Girls. Liv. Age, 209: 3.
— for Girls. (C. R. Coleridge) Sund. M. 25: 162. — (M. Merton) Canad. M. 6: 285.
— Friendship of. Bookworm, 6: 9.
— Gems at Auction in 1894–95. (F. M. Hopkins) Bookman, 1: 277.
— How to Choose. Acad. (Syr.) 7: 63.
— How to Treat. Bookworm, 4: 25.
— Illustrated, of 15th and 16th Centuries. (W. Roberts) Bookworm, 5: 97.
— Improper, in Libraries. Lib. J. 20: supp. 32.
— Increase of, 1880–90. Sat. R. 73: 36.
— In the Dozy Hours. (A. Repplier) Atlan. 74: 103.
— in Early Times. Bookworm, 2: 107.
— in Paper Covers. (B. Matthews) Cent. 28: 354.
— in Spain, Early History of. Bookworm, 2: 233.
— Libraries and Reading. (C. A. Ward) Bookworm, 3: 17.
— Little. (C. and M. Elton) Bibliographica, 3: 197, 485.
— Management of. Bookworm, 6: 297.
— Manufacturing of, Cheapness of. Lit. W. (Bost.) 27: 24.
— Names and Notes in. (Andrew Lang) Bibliographica, 1: 44.
— of Hours, French, Illustrations in. (A. W. Pollard) Bibliographica, 3: 430.
— — of Geoffroy Tory. (A. W. Pollard) Bibliographica, 1: 114.
— — Sforza. (T. C. Robinson) Bibliographica, 1: 428.
— of Trading Companies, Right of Inspection of. (J. M. Ludlow) Econ. J. 3: 704.
— Old, Duty on. (F. Solberg) Nation, 54: 351.
— — in America. Bookworm, 6: 273.
— — Third Shelf of. (Mrs. A. Fields) Scrib. M. 16: 338.
— Phonograph as Substitute for. (O. Uzanne) Scrib. M. 16: 221.
— Privately Printed. (W. G. Kingsland) Bookworm, 7: 289.
— Rare. Macmil. 68: 115.
— — and their Prices. (W. Roberts) 19th Cent. 33: 952. — Sat. R. 73: 617.
— Remarkable. Bookworm, 2: 285.
— Selling of. (J. Shaylor) 19th Cent. 40: 937.
— Some Friends of Mine in. (H. L. Cary) Educa. 16: 23.
— That have moulded Character. (S. C. Bartlett) M. Chr. Lit. 6: 56.
— Three Valuable Old. (S. E. M. Hardy) Am. Hist. Reg. 1: 349.
— Titles of. (A. Haultain) Blackw. 152: 392.
— Treatment of; Tattered Volumes. Chamb. J. 70: 715.
— Unfinished. Macmil. 73: 444. Same art. Liv. Age, 209: 536.
Boom at Los Almendros; a story. (G. De H. Browne) Munsey, 11: 207.
Boom Town Tragedy; a story. (A. Leland) Munsey, 14: 209.
Boom Towns, Causes of Failure in. (H. S. Fleming) Engin. M. 6: 276.
Boomellen, a Study from Life; a story. (Sarah Grand) Temp. Bar, 94: 351. Same art. Liv. Age, 193: 207.
Boomer's Baby, The. (P. C. R. Stone) Southern M. 4: 582.
Booth, Ballington. Our Day, 16: 213.
Booth, Mrs. Catharine. (S. K. Bolton) Chaut. 22: 467. — (Ruth Morse) Chaut. 17: 740. — (D. MacG. Means) Nation, 56: 257. — (W. T. Stead) Sund. M. 22: 58.
Booth, Miss Catherine, "La Maréchale." (F. E. Willard) Chr. Lit. 10: 286.

Booth, Edwin. (Adam Badeau) McClure, 1: 255. — (J. Jefferson) Critic, 25: 210. — (M. Bacheller) Munsey, 6: 434. — (M. M. Casseday) So. M. 2: 500. — Critic, 22: 384. — Pub. Opin. 15: 248. — (J. R. Towse) Nation, 56: 434. — (H. A. Clapp) Atlan. 72: 307.
— An Actor's Memory of. (J. Malone) Forum, 15: 594.
— and Julia Ward Howe. (F. M. Howe Hall) New Eng. M. n. s. 9: 315.
— as King Lear. Theatre, 29: 284.
— Grossman's Recollections of. (E. A. Barron) Dial (Ch.) 18: 17.
— Letters of. (E. B. Grossman) Cent. 26: 803.
— Memories and Letters of. (W. Bispham) Cent. 25: 132, 240.
— Players' Tribute to. Critic, 23: 327.
Booth, Newton. Speeches and Addresses; ed. by Crane. Sat. R. 82: 67.
Booth, Wilkes, Romance in Life of. (R. A. Mason) Theatre, 34: 162.
Booth, Wm., Social Scheme of. (F. W. Farrar) M. Chr. Lit. 6: 433. — (F. Peek) Contemp. 62: 59.
— — Investigation of, 1892. Spec. 69: 916.
— — Year of the Work of. (A. Shaw) Forum, 12: 762. — (Mrs. C. R. Lowell) Char. R. 1: 219.
Boots and Shoes, Manufacture of. (G. A. Rich) Pop. Sci. Mo. 41: 496.
Bora, Unvisited. (E. Pullen) Atlan. 75: 339.
Borax. (L. F. Kebler) J. Frankl. Inst. 138: 236.
Borchgrevink, Carsten Egeberg. Critic, 28: 113.
— and Antarctic Exploration. (A. W. Greely) Cent. 29: 431.
Bordeaux, Church of, During the Last Century of English Dominion. (E. Allain) Dub. R. 118: 63.
— the Land of Claret. Cornh. 73: 45. Same art. Ecl. M. 126: 746.
Borden Case, The. (J. H. Wigmore) Am. Law R. 27: 819.
Border Scenery. Chamb. J. 71: 272.
Borderland and its Dangers. Spec. 71: 106.
Boredom. Spec. 69: 251.
Borer, Bark, Destructive. Garden & F. 6: 76.
Bores. (H. Maxwell) 19th Cent. 35: 284. Same art. Ecl. M. 122: 362. Same art. Liv. Age, 200: 659. — Spec. 72: 157.
— A Chapter on. (C. Edwardes) Belgra. 85: 251.
— of Society. Sat. R. 77: 519.
Borgherini Palace, Florence. (L. E. Baxter) M. of Art, 9: 238.
Borghese, Gwendolin, Princess. Spec. 72: 540.
Borghese Library. (W. Roberts) Bookworm, 5: 217.
Borgia, Cæsar, and Pope Alexander VI.; Were they poisoned? (W. W. Story) Blackw. 154: 843.
Borgu, on the Niger, An Expedition to. (F. D. Lugard) Geog. J. 6: 205.
Borneo, Geology of. (F. H. Hatch) Nat. Sci. 1: 108.
— Highlands of, A Journey to. (C. Hose) Geog. J. 1: 193.
— Interior of. Dub. R. 118: 174.
— Natives of. (C. Hose) Anthrop. J. 23: 156. — (B. Low) Anthrop. J. 22: 22.
— Negritoes in. (H. L. Roth) Anthrop. J. 25: 262.
— Tiger-hunt in. (J. T. van Gestel) Lippinc. 58: 382.
Borneol and Isoborneol, Crystal Form of. (W. H. Hobbs) Am. J. Sci. 149: 449.
Borough, Origin of the. (F. W. Maitland) Eng. Hist. R. 11: 13.
Borrow, George. (J. Hooper) National, 26: 670. Same art. Liv. Age, 208: 298.
— Lavengro. Eng. R. 15: 362.
— Reminiscences of. (A. Jessopp) Ath. '93, 2: 65.
Borrowing and Borrowers. (W. G. Blaikie) Sund. M. 25: 117.
Boscombe. Temp. Bar, 97: 385.
Bosnia-Herzegovina. (W. B. Dawkins) Nature, 54: 78. — (E. B. Lanin) Contemp. 65: 735.
— and Dalmatia, Munro's Rambles and Studies in. (J. M. Hubbard) Nation, 63: 128. — Sat. R. 81: 411.
Bosnia, Baron de Kallay's Achievement in. Spec. 75: 428.
— A Trip to. (S. de Blowitz) 19th Cent. 36: 621. Same art. Ecl. M. 123: 636.
Boss of Lingfoo, The. (J. Ralph) Harper, 92: 620.
Bossuet as an Historian. (A. Laugel) Nation, 55: 219.
Boston, England, and Boston, Mass. All the Year, 73: 567.
Boston, Mass. (R. W. Emerson) Atlan. 69: 26.
— Ancient Burial Grounds of. (A. S. Cox) New Eng. M. 7: 607.
— Art and Artists in. Bost. 1: 215.
— Art Students' Association, Festival of. (M. C. Pelletier) Bost. 1: 354.
— Athenæum, The. (E. Winslow) Bost. 3: 227.
— Aurora Dramatic Club. (O. B. Stebbins) Bost. 2: 131.
— Back Bay. (W. B. Harte) Arena, 10: 1.
— Benedict Club. (J. H. Ward) New Eng. M. n. s. 14: 461.
— Charles River at. (C. S. Sargent) Garden & F. 7: 191.
— Charter of 1895. (E. J. Carpenter) Bost. 2: 531.
— Christ Church, Bells of. (R. A. Cram) New Eng. M. n. s. 11: 640.
— Churches of, Fifty Years Ago. Bost. 2: 346.
— — Old, of the North End. (J. H. Wiggin) Bost. 2: 165.
— the City of God. (C. G. Ames) New Eng. M. n. s. 10: 769.
— Common, in Winter. (L. Maynard) Bost. 1: 253. New Eng. M. n. s. 11: 425.
— — Mystery of: a story. (G. Braley) Bost. 2: 612.
— Early Drama. (C. H. Pattee) Bost. 2: 254.
— Exchange Club-house. Am. Arch. 47: 54.
— Fire Department. (R. G. Fitch) Bost. 3: 3.
— Floating Hospital. (R. B. Tobey) Lend a H. 16: 192.
— Freemasonry in. (W. B. Ellis) New Eng. M. n. s. 3: 3.
— Greater. (E. Atkinson) New Eng. M. n. s. 13: 377.
— Half a Century ago. (F. M. Edselas) Cath. World, 62: 733.
— Howells's. (S. Baxter) New Eng. M. n. s. 9: 129.
— In and about Old Bumstead Place. (K. G. Wells) New Eng. M. n. s. 9: 649.
— in 1827. Bost. 2: 72.
— Interesting Points near, for Half-holiday Excursions. (C. S. Sargent) Garden & F. 6: 187.
— King's Chapel and Christ Church. (Elizabeth G. Melcher) Bost. 1: 596.
— Latin School. (P. Brooks) New Eng. M. n. s. 8: 687.
— Literary, Thirty Years Ago. (W. D. Howells) Harper, 91: 865.
— Long Wharf. (J. W. Hammond) Bost. 3: 181.
— Marriages in. (Susan Channing) Open Court, 8: 3801.
— Massacre, 1770. (J. D. Lindsay) Nat'l M. (N. Y. '91) 17: 239.
— — and Crispus Attucks. (F. J. Moses) Bost. 1: 641.
— Metropolitan Park Movement. (S. Baxter) Garden & F. 5: 62.
— Metropolitan Reservations of. (C. Eliot) New Eng. M. n. s. 15: 117.
— Monuments and Statues in. (W. H. Downes) New Eng. M. n. s. 11: 353.

Boston, Museum, Wood's Early History of. (O. B. Stebbins) Bost. 1: 113.—(A. W. Brayley) Bost. 2: 125.
— Music in, in 1851 and 1852. (E. Swayne) Music, 7: 427.
— New Metropolitan Parks. (Sylvester Baxter) Garden & F. 7: 22.
— Newspapers of. (E. L. Godkin) Nation, 54: 206.
— Old Inns and Taverns. (B. F. Stevens) Bost. 2: 17.
— Old Milk Street. (H. A. Hill) New Eng. M. n. s. 12: 97.
— Old South Meeting-house, Builder of. (A. E. Brown) New Eng. M. n. s. 13: 390.
— Old State House. (F. N. Jones) Bost. 2: 77.
— Original Documents Relating to, 1713–55. N. E. Reg. 46: 121, 254.
— Parks of. (W. H. Downes) New Eng. M. n. s. 15: 193.
— — Proposed System. (C. S. Sargent) Garden & F. 6: 61.
— Poor in; North End Union. (Ellen M. Tower) Bost. 2: 393.
— Public Garden. Bost. 2: 379.
— — During Past 100 Years. (E. G. Heath) Bost. 2: 629.
— Public Institutions of. (J. Tunis) Lend a H. 10: 91.
— — Report for 1893. Lend a H. 12: 452.
— Public Library. (C. C. Soule) Lib. J. 17: 54–124.—Lib. J. 17: 425.
— — Characters in. (W. T. Niles) Bost. 2: 427.
— — New Building. (L. F. Gray) Lib. J. 19: 365.—Art J. 45: 126.—(T. R. Sullivan) Scrib. M. 19: 83.—(W. I. Fletcher) Critic, 28: 455.—Am. Arch. 48: 3, 70.—(C. H. Walker) New Eng. M. n. s. 12: 259.
— — — Abbey's Decorations for. Critic, 26: 190.—(E. R. Pennell) Nation, 60: 104.
— — — Handbook of. Critic, 28: 257.
— — — its Artistic Aspects. (M. G. Van Rensselaer) Cent. 28: 260.
— — — its Ideals and Working Conditions. (L. Swift) Cent. 28: 264.
— — — Macmonnies Bacchante Statue, The. Lit. W. (Boston) 27: 412.
— — — Sargent's Decorations in. (W. A. Coffin) Cent. 30: 163.
— — — Story of. (E. J. Carpenter) New Eng. M. n. s. 12: 737.
— — The Old and New. (A. W. Brayley) Bost. 1: 633.
— Pulpit in. (C. A. Bartol) New World, 2: 479.
— Railroads in, Early. (L. P. Loring) Bost. 1: 299.
— Real Estate Values in. (H. Whitmore) Am. Statis. Assoc. 5: 1.
— Revisited. (H. Harting) Temp. Bar, 109: 547.
— A Southern Woman's Study of. (F. A. Doughty) Forum, 18: 238.
— Schools and Teachers of. Arena, 13: 38.
— School Street. (H. F. Jenks) New Eng. M. n. s. 13: 259.
— State House. (T. A. Fox) Am. Arch. 48: 127. 49: 55.
— — Report on the Condition of. Am. Arch 48: 39.
— Subway in. (F. Foxcroft) New Eng. M. n. s. 13: 193.—(S. E. Turnbull) Bost. 2: 158.
— Suffolk Bank. (Edith Gerrier) Bost. 2: 603.
— Symphony Concerts. (H. A. Clarke) Music, 6: 3.
— Theatre, Early History of. (A. Corbett, jr.) Bost. 1: 3.
— Theatres of, 1895. (A. Brownell) Bost. 2: 655.
— Tremont House. (B. F. Stevens) Bost. 1: 329.
— Trinity Church. (P. Brooks) New Eng. M. n. s. 8: 139.—(H. H. Richardson) New Eng. M. n. s. 8: 158.
— Water-supply of. (F. Osgood) New Eng. M. n. s. 14: 389.
Boston, Words coined in. (C. W. Ernst) New Eng. M. n. s. 15: 337.
— Young Men's Christian Union. (G. Hutchinson) Lend a H. 16: 37.
— — Work of. Lend a H. 13: 296.
Boston Light and the Brewsters. (R. G. F. Candage) New Eng. M. n. s. 13: 131.
Boston Schoolgirl in 1771, A. (A. M. Earle) Atlan. 72: 218.
Boston Tea-party. (F. E. Abbot) New Eng. M. n. s. 8: 411.
Boston Terrier. (C. F. Leland) Outing, 23: 464.
Bostonians, The; Opera Company. (M. Bacheller) Munsey, 7: 560.—Music, 5: 241.
Boston's First "Marine;" a story. (W. H. Gardner) Bost. 2: 412.
Boswell, James, Proof-sheets of. Atlan. 74: 657.
— Johnson's. (Geo. S. Layard) Univ. R. 7: 535.
Botanic Gardens. (D. T. Macdougal) Pop. Sci. Mo. 50: 172.—(N. L. Britton) Garden & F. 9: 352, 362.—(N. L. Britton) Science, n. s. 4: 284.
— Cambridge. (W. Watson) Garden & F. 9: 443.
— Edinburgh. (W. Watson) Garden & F. 9: 483.
— Harvard, Notes from. (M. Barker) Garden & F. 5: 31–609.
— International, in the Alps of Switzerland. (G. H. Hicks) Garden & F. 7: 142.
— New York. (C. S. Sargent) Garden & F. 8: 261.—(C. S. Sargent) Garden & F. 7: 181.
— of Dublin. Garden & F. 5: 422.
— Tropical. Nature, 49: 453.
Botanical Freaks. Chamb. J. 70: 214.
Botanical Nomenclature. (J. Britton) Nat. Sci. 1: 612.—Garden & F. 5: 362.
Botanical Notes from Central Texas. (E. N. Plank) Garden & F. 5: 431, 579.
— from Texas. (E. N. Plank) Garden & F. 8: 72, 193.
Botanical Opportunity. (W. Trelease) Science, n. s. 4: 367.
Botany and Botanists in New England. (J. E. Humphrey) New Eng. M. n. s. 14: 27.
— at the German Universities. (G. J. Pierce) Educa. R. 9: 72.
— Beginnings in. (B. D. Halsted) Pop. Sci. Mo. 41: 515.
— Cañon near Ukiah, Cal. (Carl Purdy) Garden & F. 9: 482, 493.
— Elementary, in Schools and Colleges. (D. H. Campbell) School & C. 1: 211.
— Elements of, Bergen's. (R. H. Cornish) School R. 4: 554.
— Ethno-, Purposes of. (J. W. Harshberger) Am. Antiq. 18: 73.
— Everyday. (W. B. Hemsley) Knowl. 18: 217.
— Flora of the California Coast Range. (C. Purdy) Garden & F. 9: 192, 213, 233.
— Flora of the Sand-dunes of Indiana. (E. J. Hill) Garden & F. 9: 353–393.
— in Agricultural Colleges. Garden & F. 5: 493.
— Instruction in, Current Methods in. (C. Macmillan) Educa. 12: 460.
— June Flora of a Long Island Swamp. (Anna M. Vail) Garden & F. 8: 282.
— a Masquerade of Stamens. (W. H. Gibson) Cosmopol. 17: 570.
— Medical. (C. F. Millspaugh) Science, 20: 91.
— Modern. (C. R. Barnes) Science, 20: 62.
— Native Composites. (J. N. Gerard) Garden & F. 8: 376.
— New. (L. F. Ward) Science, 21: 43.
— Nomenclature in; the Vienna Propositions. (P. Ascherson; A. Engler) Am. Natural. 29: 1093.

Botany, Notes from a Botanic Garden. (W. J. Beal) Garden & F. 8: 304, 322.
— Notes from Harvard Botanic Garden. (R. Cameron) Garden & F. 8: 516.
— Physiological, L. H. Bailey's Survival of the Unlike. Garden & F. 9: 519.
— Practical Botany for Beginners, by F. O. Bower. Garden & F. 7: 359.
— Teaching, in High Schools. (C. R. Barnes) Science, 19: 91.
— Teratology in. (K. Groebel) Sci. Prog. n. s. 1: 84.
— of U. S.: Britton & Brown's Northern Flora. Garden & F. 9: 509.
Botany Bay. Chamb. J. 69: 801.
Botletli River, Sport and Natural History on. Liv. Age, 196: 113.
Botta, Vincenzo. Critic, 25: 248.
Botticelli, Sandro. (M. Hewlett) Acad. 46: 137.
— Coronation of the Virgin, by. (J. Cartwright) M. of Art, 6: 330.
— Pallas Athene. (H. Zimmern) Art J. 47: 188.
— — Discovery of. M. of Art, 18: 276.
— Spring. (G. Allen and others) Acad. 45: 109–214.
Botocudus, Lip and Ear Ornaments of. (J. C. Branner) Pop. Sci. Mo. 43: 753.
Boucher, François. (A. E. Hake) M. of Art, 5: 294.
Boucher de Perthes, J., Recollections of. Blackw. 157: 939. Same art. Liv. Age, 206: 232.
Boude Family of Pennsylvania. (E. St.C. Whitney) Am. Hist. Reg. 1: 367.
Boudinot, Elias, Boudinot's Life of. (W. C. Ford) Nation, 63: 255.
— Correspondence of. Pennsyl. M. 16: 439.
Bougainville. (C. W. Colby) Nation, 62: 347.
Bough, Sam. (R. Walker) M. of Art, 19: 425.
Boughton, George H. (A. Meynell) M. of Art, 5: 397. — (W. E. Griffis) New Eng. M. n. s. 15: 481. — (C. Cook) Q. Illus. 2: 107.
Bouguereau, W. A. (J. Bernac) Idler, 10: 511.
— and his Work. (C. S. Johnson) Munsey, 7: 535.
— Holy Women at the Tomb. Art. J. 47: 372.
Boulanger, Gen. G. (E. Crawford) Univ. R. 1: 83.
— An Object-lesson in French Politics. Blackw. 157: 297. Same art. Liv. Age, 204: 694.
— Will he succeed? Univ. R. 4: 157.
Boulanger, Gustave. (M. H. Spielmann) M. of Art, 12: 70.
Boulevard, Proposed, for N. Y. Garden & F. 6: 13. — (C. S. Sargent) Garden & F. 6: 431.
Boulogne. (Mrs. F. Pentrill) Irish Mo. 17: 543.
— Notre-Dame de. (R. S. Gundry) National, 20: 54. Same art. Liv. Age, 195: 407.
Bounties, Export, not the Remedy. Gunton's M. 10: 179.
Bounty, Protection by. (A. R. Smith) Soc. Econ. 9: 196.
Bourbons, Fall of the. Eng. R. 6: 1.
— Fortunes of the. (K. M. Rowland) Harper, 90: 171.
Bourchier, Arthur. Mr. Richards. Gent. M. n. s. 48: 424. — Theatre, 28: 208.
Bourget, Paul, with portrait. Bk. Buyer, 12: 136. — With portrait. Bk. News, 12: 67. — (G. Smith) Gent. M. n. s. 48: 370. — (E. Delille) Fortn. 57: 665. — (M. Todhunter) Westm. 144: 597.
— Andre Cornelis. (R. P. Jacobus) Fortn. 64: 179.
— as a Novelist. (J. Gray) Acad. 42: 188.
— in America. Critic, 23: 130.
— Novels. Ath. '93, 1: 78.
— Mark Twain and. (M. O'Rell) No. Am. 160: 302.
— on the U. S. (S. L. Clemens) No. Am. 160: 48.
Bourke, John Gregory. (W. Matthews) Science, n. s. 4: 820. — (F. W. Hodge) J. Am. Folk-Lore, 9: 139.
Bourne, Vincent. (A. C. Benson) Macmil. 71: 423.
Bournemouth and the New Forest. (Violet E. Mitchell) Mo. Illust. 13: 266.
Bova, or Initiation Ceremonies of the Kamilaroi Tribe. (R. H. Mathews) Anthrop. J. 24: 411.
Bovey Tracy, Surprise of. Macmil. 75: 28.
Bowditch, H. I., with portrait. (C. F. Folsom) Harv. Grad. M. 1: 38.
Bowditch, Nathaniel. Services to American Astronomy. (T. J. J. See) Pop. Astron. 2: 385.
Bowditch Family, Records of. (J. Williamson) N. E. Reg. 50: 436.
Bowell, Sir Mackenzie. (J. L. Payne) Canad. M. 6: 230.
Bowen, Charles, Lord. (H. Davey) Law Q. 10: 211. — Spec. 72: 497. — Sat. R. 77: 386.
Bowen, Griffith, of Boston. (E. A. Bowen) N. E. Reg. 47: 453.
Bower, Orie, with portrait. (G. R. Jones) Nat'l M. (N. Y. '91) 17: 183.
Bowery, The, and Bohemia. (H. C. Bunner) Scrib. M. 15: 452.
Bowl, Phœnician, in Metropolitan Museum, N. Y. (A. Marquand) Am. J. Archæol. 7: 19.
Bowlders, Drift, between the Mohawk and Susquehanna Rivers. (A. P. Brigham) Am. J. Sci. 149: 213.
— Remarkable. (D. A. Wells) Pop. Sci. Mo. 40: 340.
Bowles, William Lisle. (Mrs. Andrew Crosse) Temp. Bar, 103: 25.
Bowling Green, N. Y. City, Proposed Statue in. (C. S. Sargent) Garden & F. 8: 251.
Bowling Matches, Oxford and Cambridge. Sat. R. 72: 19.
Bowman, Sir William. (J. B. Sanderson) Nature, 45: 564.
Bowne Family of New Jersey. (A. H. Weatherby) Am. Hist. Reg. 3: 37.
Bows of the Ancient Assyrians and Egyptians. (C. J. Longman) Anthrop. J. 24: 49.
Box-elder and Russian Mulberry. (C. A. Keffer) Garden & F. 7: 493.
Boxing. (D. L. Dawson) Lippinc. 49: 96.
— Brutality of. Sat. R. 79: 86.
— in France with Hands and Feet. (R. Barr) Idler, 2: 115.
— under the Boston Athletic Association Rules. (R. C. Macdonald) Outing, 21: 23.
Boxley Abbey. (J. Cave-Browne) Antiq. n. s. 25: 75, 111.
Boy, The. (R. M. Stuart) Cent. 27: 624.
Boy and Dandelion, The. (C. Battersby) Sund. M. 25: 830.
Boy Choirs in America. (T. M. Prentice) Munsey, 9: 73.
Boy Orator of Zepata City, The; a story. (R. H. Davis) Harper, 85: 847.
Boyar of the Terrible. (F. Whishaw) Longm. 28: 185–535. 29: 1.
Boycotted Baby, A; a story. (P. L. McDermott) Chamb. J. 69: 215–281.
Boycotting, Peaceable. (C. A. Reed) Ann. Am. Acad. Pol. Sci. 5: 28.
Boyd, Benjamin, and the Solomon Islands. Chamb. J. 70: 593.
Boydell, John. (A. Beaver) M. of Art, 9: 110.
Boyer, Valentine A. M. West. Hist. 11: 659.
Boyesen, H. H., with portrait. Bk. Buyer, 3: 343. — With portrait. Bk. Buyer, 12: 557. — (G. M. Hyde) Dial (Ch.) 19: 323. — (J. D. Barry) Lit. W. (Bost.) 26: 351. — With portrait. Bk. News, 6: 537. — Critic, 27: 237.
— as Interviewer. Critic, 23: 131.
— — Reply. (H. H. Boyesen) Critic, 23: 142.

Boyesen, H. H., as a Teacher. (D. K. Dodge) Bach. of Arts, 2: 822.
— at Cornell University. (T. Stanton) Open Court, 10: 4812.
— Portraits of. McClure, 1: 22.
Boyhood of Great Men, Story of. (A. H. Yoder) Pedagog. Sem. 3: 134.
Boyle, Rev. G. D., Recollections of. Sat. R. 79: 258.
Boyle, Robert, with portrait. Pop. Sci. Mo. 42: 548.
Boylston, Nicholas. (B. Wendell) Harv. Grad. M. 4: 205.
Boys. Sund. M. 24: 632.
— and Boys' Schools. (D. C. Gilman) Cosmopol. 12: 461.
— Care of; Leading-strings. Spec. 70: 517.
— Poor City, in the Country. (A. F. Sanborn) No. Am. 160: 755.
— When we were. Macmil. 71: 442. 72: 43-414. Same art. Ecl. M. 124: 664. 125: 275, 848. Same art. Liv. Age, 205: 611, 627. 206: 312, 679. 207: 123, 425.
— Working. (Florence Kelley) Am. J. Soc. Sci. no. 34: 43. Same art. Am. J. Sociol. 2: 358.
Boys' Brigade, The. (H. Drummond) McClure, 2: 68.
— and Youthful Canada. (J. C. Hopkins) Canad. M. 4: 551.
Boys' Club, Story of a. (E. E. Hale) Cosmopol. 14: 549.
Boys' Clubs. (C. C. Lathrop) Lend a H. 15: 106.
Bozland. (P. Fitzgerald) Gent. M. n. s. 53: 447.
Bozon, Nicolas, Franciscan Monk. (Lucy Toulmin Smith) Eng. Hist. R. 7: 25.
Brabourne, E. H. Knatchbull-Hugessen, Lord. (W. K. R. Bedford) Blackw. 153: 474.
Brace, Charles L., with portrait. (H. B. Adams) Char. R. 1: 239.
Brace of Lions; a story. Temp. Bar, 104: 245.
Brachiopoda, Development of. (C. E. Beecher) Am. J. Sci. 144: 133.
— Palæozoic, Generic Evolution of. (A. Crane) Science, 21: 72.
Bracken, Thos. (O. Smeaton) Westm. 144: 500.
Brackenbury, Lieut.-Gen. H. (E. C. H. Price) Eng. Illust. 10: 251.
Bracton, Henry de, and the Roman Civil Law. (W. W. Edwards) Green Bag, 4: 196. 5: 348.
— Roman Law in. Law Q. 1: 425.
— Text of. (P. Vinogradoff) Law Q. 1: 189.
Braddock, Gen., Defeat of, Unpublished Contemporary Account of. Pennsyl. M. 20: 409.
— Route of. (R. G. Thwaites) New Eng. M. n. s. 15: 299.
Braddock Campaign, The. (G. Washington) Scrib. M. 13: 530.
Braddon, Edward, a Great Shikari. Blackw. 157: 949. Same art. Liv. Age, 206: 150. Same art. Ecl. M. 125: 212.
Braddon, Miss M. E. "My First Novel." Idler, 3: 19.
Bradford, Donald, with portrait. (C. P. Connolly) Nat'l M. (N. Y. '91) 15: 154.
Bradford, Wm., Bi-centenary of. Critic, 22: 236.
Bradford-on-Avon, Eng., Saxon Church at. Am. Arch. 39: 100.
Bradford, Mass., Soldiers of. (F. E. Blake) N. E. Reg. 50: 338.
Bradford Club's Publications. (E. D. North) Bibliographica, 2: 374.
Brading, Roman Villa at. (F. P. Cobbe) M. of Art, 4: 154.
Bradlaugh, Charles. Ath. '94, 2: 881. — (M. D. Conway) Open Court, 4: 2707. — (C. Waterer) Westm. 143: 511.
— Life and Work of. (H. B. Bonner) 19th Cent. 37: 349. — Sat. R. 79: 16. — (A. Webb) Nation, 60: 424.
Bradley, Justice Joseph P. (C. Parker) Am. Law R. 28: 481. With portrait. (F. W. Hackett) Green Bag, 4: 145. — Pub. Opin. 12: 427.
Bradley, Will H., with portrait. Bk. Buyer, 13: 233.
Bradshaw, Henry. Bookworm, 2: 221. — Walford's Antiq. 9: 125.
Bradstreet, Gov. Simon, Ancestry of. (I. J. Greenwood) N. E. Reg. 48: 168.
Bradwell, Myra. (M. M. Trumbull) Open Court, 8: 3999.
Brahan Castle. (Lady Jeune) Eng. Illust. 9: 392.
Brahe, Tycho. (Sir R. Ball) Good Words, 35: 231.
— and Uraniberg. (A. Hinrichs) Cath. World, 61: 589.
Brahmanism and Balfour's Foundations of Belief. (Vamadeo Shastri) Fortn. 64: 682.
— and Buddhism. Open Court, 10: 4851.
— and Hinduism, Monier-Williams on. (J. H. Crooker) Dial (Ch.) 12: 381.
— does not antedate the Mosaic Writings. (F. S. Chatard) Cath. World, 58: 729.
Brahmins, Secret Doctrine of. (H. Hensoldt) Arena, 9: 447.
Brahmo Somaj, Position and Principles of. (Protap Chunder Mozoomdar) New World, 1: 601.
Brahms, Johannes. Music, 7: 594.
Brain, Arrested Development of, and Responsibility. (T. S. Clouston) Jurid. R. 7: 38.
— The Blot on, Ireland's. (J. Jastrow) Dial (Ch.) 16: 46.
— Comparative Physiology of. (P. Carus) Open Court, 4: 2550.
— Growth of, Donaldson on. Sat. R. 81: 231.
— The Human. (P. Carus) Open Court, 4: 2239-2326.
— — Structural Plan of. (C. S. Minot) Pop. Sci. Mo. 43: 372.
— in the Light of Science. (S. M. Miller) New Sci. R. 2: 49.
— of Women. (L. Büchner) New R. 9: 166.
— Temperature of the. (A. Mosso) Nature, 46: 17.
Brain Activity, Localization of. (P. Carus) Open Court, 4: 2355-2379.
Brain Centres. (S. V. Clevenger) Am. Natural. 26: 734.
Brain Development as related to Evolution. (G. H. Scribner) Pop. Sci. Mo. 46: 525.
Brain Surgery. (W. A. Hammond) No. Am. 156: 390.
— in its Psychological Bearings. (S. M. Miller) Open Court, 9: 4431.
Brain-tapping. (A. A. Reade) Gent. M. n. s. 50: 362.
Brain Waves, A Theory of. (E. W. Wagstaff) National, 20: 140.
Brain Work, Measurement of. (J. M. Greenwood) Educa. 13: 583.
Brains and Sex. Open Court, 1: 379.
Bramante [Donato da Urbino]. (J. Klaczko) Pub. Opin. 15: 281. — (H. Mereu) Am. Arch. 47: 120.
Bramley, Frank. (P. G. Hamerton) Scrib. M. 15: 423.
Bramwell, Lord. (J. Macdonell) Temp. Bar, 108: 486. Same art. Liv. Age, 211: 31. — Bank. M. (Lond.) 53: 907. — (G. H. Knott) Jurid. R. 4: 347. — Sat. R. 73: 558. — Spec. 68: 668.
Branchiostomidæ, Genera of. (T. Gill) Am. Natural. 29: 457.
Brand of Discord; a story. (Mrs. A. Henniker) Eng. Illust. 16: 247.
Brandenburg, Ranke's Memoirs of the House of. Eng. R. 12: 395.
Brander's Wife; a Christmas story. (F. H. Loughead) Overland, n. s. 21: 61.
Brandes, Edward. The Visit. Gent. M. n. s. 48: 422. — Theatre, 28: 207.
Branding Cattle on the Plains. (A. MacGowan) McClure, 3: 100.

Branding, Conjugation of. (E. A. Andrews) Am. Natural. 29: 1021, 1121.
Brandon, Olga, in The Breadwinner. Theatre, 28: 252.
Brandram, Samuel. (W. K. R. Bedford) Blackw. 153: 256.
Brandt, Sebastian, Illustrated Books of. (G. R. Redgrave) Bibliographica, 2: 47.
Branford, Conn. Blackstone Library Building. Lib. J. 21: 326. — (Mrs. E. M. Gallaudet) New Eng. M. n. s. 15: 290.
Branginoco, a Burmese Bonaparte. (J. H. Ryley) Time, 15: 300.
Brangwyn, Frank, the Artist. (B. Boyle) Idler, 7: 263.
Brantôme, Pierre de Bourdeille, Seigneur de. (D. Hannay) New R. 15: 202. — Nation, 63: 452.
— Shakespeare's Compliment to. (C. H. Hunton) Poet-Lore, 4: 449.
Brasenose College, Oxford, and the High Street. (T. G. Jackson) M. of Art, 12: 332.
Brass Men, The Rising of the. Chamb. J. 72: 737. Same art. Liv. Age, 208: 123.
Brass Work, Birmingham. (J. M. O'Fallon) Art J. 46: 313.
— Some Oriental. (M. A. Wallace-Dunlop) M. of Art, 8: 56, 109.
"Brava Torera!" a story. (G. B. O'Halloran) Temp. Bar, 106: 68.
Brave Little Lass; a story. (M. Gaunt) Eng. Illust. 13: 459.
Bravest Deed of the War. (T. J. Mackey) McClure, 3: 272.
Brawley, F. W. S., with portrait. (H. L. Conard) M. West. Hist. 13: 230.
Bray, Rev. Thomas, and his American Libraries. (B. C. Steiner) Am. Hist. R. 2: 59.
Brazil, Constitution of, New. (J. W. Hawes) Overland, n. s. 19: 161.
— Crisis in, in 1891, and its Causes. (C. DeKalb) Forum, 12: 599.
— Dutch Power in. (G. Edmundson) Eng. Hist. R. 11: 231.
— Imperial and Republican. (J. G. Whiteley) Chaut. 18: 576.
— Italian Immigration into. Dub. R. 111: 446
— Politics and Finance in. Fortn. 59: 80.
— Rebellion in. Pub. Opin. 16: 449.
— — Latest Aspects of. (S. de Mendonça) No. Am. 158: 164.
— Republic of. (J. C. Redman) New Eng. M. n. s. 9: 701.
— Republicanism in. (R. Ogden) Nation, 57: 281. — (S. de Mendonça) No. Am. 158: 8.
— Treaty with, More Light on the. (R. Ogden) Nation, 54: 261.
— Von den Steinen's Natives of Central. (A. S. Gatschet) Nation, 58: 450.
— War in. (C. Eaglestone) Un. Serv. M. 8: 605.
Breach of Promise Cases. Spec. 71: 713.
Bread, Bleeding. (M. C. Cooke) Nature, 48: 578.
— Condiments and Fruits. (C. D. Wilson) Lippinc. 58: 704.
— Defects in. Soc. Econ. 3: 359.
— Excise on, in Boston, 1734. (J. Colburn) N. E. Reg. 48: 20.
— Price of, State Regulation of. (Stanley of Alderley) National, 20: 635.
Bread upon the Waters; a story. (R. Kipling) McClure, 8: 140.
Bread-and-Butter Miss, A; a story. All the Year, 72: 209-332.
Bread-and-Butter Question, The. (J. H. Browne) Harper, 88: 273.
Bread Laws and the Price of Bread. (J. Kirkland) Econ. J. 5: 413.
Breadtown Vixen, The; a story. All the Year, 72: 563.
Break of Day; a story. (J. A. Altsheler) Munsey, 13: 579.
Breakfast at Mme. Begue's; a story. (R. P. Skinner) Bost. 4: 298.
Breaking His Own Will: a story. (E. E. Seelye) Cent. 31: 253.
Breaking of the Drought; a story. Cornh. 68: 42.
Breaking-up of the Soho Anarchist League; a story. (R. Barr) McClure, 3: 228.
Breakwater, Building a. (H. Babson) New Eng. M. n. s. 11: 163.
Breakwaters, Sea-walls, and Jetties. (G. Y. Wisner) Engin. M. 7: 341.
Breath of Heaven, A. (E. M. Newton) Overland, n. s. 24: 131.
Breath-figures. (J. G. McPherson) Knowl. 18: 101.
— and Dust Photographs. Chamb. J. 71: 231.
Breathing, Art of. (A. W. Drayson) 19th Cent. 33: 611.
Breathing Movements as a Cure. (T. J. Mays) Cent. 24: 551.
Bréboeuf, Jean de. (T. B. Stephenson) Sund. M. 22: 627.
Breckinridge, John Cabell, Confederate Secretary of War, Escape of. (J. T. Wood) Cent. 25: 110.
— and Hannibal Hamlin. (H. L. Dawes) Cent. 28: 463.
Brecknock Beacons. All the Year, 73: 207.
Bremen, From Buffalo to. (J. H. Vincent) Chaut. 17: 643.
Bremer, Frederika, Reminiscences of. (A. Hope) Good Words, 34: 690.
Brendan, Saint, Fabulous Voyages of. (Marquess of Bute) Scot. R. 21: 371.
Brentwood, N. H., Quakers in. (B. A. Dean) N. E. Reg. 46: 252.
Brer Rabbit and Brer Fox; story. (Gerard Fowke) J. Am. Folk-Lore, 1: 148.
Breslau School and Judaism. (L. M. Simmons) Jew. Q. 4: 397.
Breton, Jules. (G. Smith) M. of Art, 11: 409.
— Autobiography. Ath. '92, 2: 520.
— Life of an Artist. (K. Cox) Nation, 52: 223.
Breton Fisherman's Song. (C. E. Meetkerke) Argosy, 57: 352.
Breton Homesteads. (M. C. Bradley) Time, 10: 560.
Brett, John, as Art Critic. Sat. R. 79: 439.
Breviary, The Roman. (J. Morris) Month, 78: 349.
Brewer, H. W., a Master-builder of Castles in the Air. (G. White) Argosy, 59: 151.
Brewster Tablet at Scrooby. Critic, 37: 200.
Briant, John, Descendants of. (P. Bryant) N. E. Reg. 48: 46.
Bribe Defeated, A. (C. B. Brown) Overland, n. s. 23: 35.
Bribery and the Law. (M. A. Hamm) Am. M. Civics, 9: 367.
— in England, Suppression of. (J. W. Jenks) Cent. 25: 781.
— in Small Transactions. (E. Fry) Sat. R. 82: 361.
Bric-à-brac, Fashions and Counterfeits of. (S. C. Hewett) Cosmopol. 13: 175.
Brick, Red, Artistic Use of in Architectural Design. (E. I. Bell) M. of Art, 4: 9.
Brickfield, A Kentish. (Beatrice A. Dan) Good Words, 36: 671.
Bricks, Enamelled. (G. B. Engle) Am. Arch. 43: 129.
Bricks, Manufacture of. (C. H. Schumann) Cassier, 4: 403.
Bricks without Straw; a story. (J. Hudspeth) Arena, 6: 481.
Bride Elect, A. Macmil. 73: 53-241.

Bride Roses: a scene. (W. D. Howells) Harper, 87: 424.
Bridge, City Avenue, over Schuylkill River, Philadelphia. (R. V. Merrick) J. Frankl. Inst. 139: 241.
— Great Metropolitan. Soc. Econ. 9: 329.
— Old, in Mass. Garden & F. 8: 42.
Bridge-building, Architecture of. (E. C. Gardner) Engin. M. 11: 844.
— in America. (T. K. Thomson) Engin. M. 4: 16.
Bridger, Fort. (E. S. Loud) Overland, n. s. 16: 251.
Bridges and Bridge Builders. (P. MacQueen) Cosmopol. 13: 395.
— Famous. (R. Jamison) Chaut. 20: 552.
— Sidewalks, Roads, and Pavements. (W. Howard) Engin. M. 8: 1014.
Bridges, Robert, with portrait. Bk. News, 13: 458.
— Eros and Psyche. Sat. R. 79: 41.
— Poems of. (J. C. Bailey) Temp. Bar, 99: 225. Same art. Liv. Age, 199: 556. Same art. Ecl. M. 124: 466. — Church Q. 35: 201. — (E. Dowden) Fortn. 62: 44. Same art. Liv. Age, 202: 451.
Bridgewater, Mass., East Parish of, Records of Marriages in, 1725–1803. N. E. Reg. 46: 55, 167.
Bridgnorth, England. (D. H. S. Cranage) Art. J. 48: 111.
Brierly, Oswald Walters. Acad. 46: 542.
Brigandage, Camorra, Maffia and. (S. Merlino) Pol. Sci. Q. 9: 466.
— in Egypt. Chamb. J. 69: 337.
— in Sicily. Spec. 69: 410. — Macmil. 74: 378.
Brigands, Apulian. (E. M. Church) Blackw. 152: 704. Same art. Ecl. M. 119: 821. Same art. Liv. Age, 196: 151.
— Three Famous Italian. Chamb. J. 70: 529.
Briggs, Chas. A., with portrait. Bk. Buyer, 8: 245. — With portrait. Bk. News, 11: 341.
— Acquittal of. Critic, 22: 7.
— and the Heretics' Sheol. (M. D. Conway) Open Court, 5: 3055.
— Case of. Pub. Opin. 15: 231, 254. — (C. A. Briggs) Pub. Opin. 15: 279. — And. R. 19: 99, 464.
— — Duty of Laymen in Regard to. (G. A. Strong) And. R. 19: 193.
— — Religious View of. Pub. Opin. 14: 357.
— — Secular View of. Pub. Opin. 14: 333.
— Heresy Trial of. (C. R. Gillett) N. World, 2: 141.
— — Effect of, upon Presbyterianism. And. R. 18: 90.
— — and Other Heresy Trials. (P. Schaff) Forum, 12: 621.
Brigham, Rachel, Burial Place of. (C. C. Stopes) Ath. '94, 1: 541.
Bright, John. (J. E. Thorold Rogers) Univ. R. 3: 431.
— on Woman Suffrage. (T. Stanton) Open Court, 9: 4348.
— Reminiscences of. (C. McLaren) No. Am. 155: 315.
Brightening of the Vane; a story. (C. J. K. Fenton) Argosy, 57: 527.
Brighthelmstone. (E. Walford) Walford's Antiq. 9: 1.
Brightlingsea and its Oysters. (A. H. Japp) Argosy, 62: 540.
Brighton, Old Roads to. All the Year, 73: 85.
— Wyndham in. Gent. M. n. s. 48: 104.
Brimmer, Martin. Critic, 28: 130.
Brimstone Pete; a story. All the Year, 73: 260, 283.
Brines, Specific Heat of. (H. von Strombeck) J. Frankl. Inst. 134: 154.
Bringing down the House. Cornh. 71: 141. Same art. Liv. Age, 204: 603.
Bringing of the Rose; a story. (H. L. Bradley) Harper, 92: 840.
Brinkerhoff, Gen. R., with portrait. (J. D. Byers) Char. R. 2: 429.
Brinton, D. G., with portrait. Bk. News, 11: 471.
Briscoe, Ralph, Newgate Clerk. (C. Whibley) New R. 14: 61.
Briseis; a novel. (W. Black) Harper, 92: 79–870.
Bristol, Eng., in the Time of Cabot. (J. B. Shipley) Harper, 86: 428.
Bristol Figure, A. (C. Monkhouse) M. of Art, 6: 417.
Bristow, George Frederic. (G. H. Curtis) Music, 3: 547.
Britain and her Rivals, 1713–89. Sat. R. 80: 624.
— Roman, Deities of. (T. H. B. Graham) Gent. M. n. s. 56: 195.
— — Trade Routes of. (T. H. B. Graham) Gent. M. n. s. 49: 189.
— Under the Cæsars in. (W. B. Paley) Gent. M. n. s. 53: 400.
Briticisms, Recent. (B. Matthews) Critic, 26: 245.
British America, Antiquities of. (J. Deans) Am. Antiq. 14: 41.
— Land of the Muskeg, Somerset's. Sat. R. 80: 317.
— New Route from. (D. Macarthur) Westm. 144: 178.
— On Snow-shoes to the Barren Grounds. (C. W. Whitney) Harper, 92: 10.
British Association for Advancement of Science, Meeting, 1892. Nature, 46: 316–555.
— 1894 Meeting. Nature, 50: 369. — Dub. R. 115: 437.
— — Echoes from. New Sci. R. 1: 232.
— — Geography at. Geog. J. 4: 355.
— — Notes from. Nat. Sci. 5: 214.
— — President's Address. (Marquis of Salisbury) Pop. Sci. Mo. 46: 33. Same art. Nature, 50: 338. Same art. Our Day, 13: 422.
— Meeting of 1896. Dub. R. 118: 146.
British Church, Early. Eng. R. 15: 1.
British Columbia. (J. Ralph) Harper, 84: 171, 491.
— Eldorado of. (E. M. Spragge) Canad. M. 2: 328.
— Elections in. (R. E. Gosnell) Canad. M. 3: 475.
— Garden of. (E. M. Spragge) Canad. M. 2: 422.
— Kwakiutl Indians of. (Franz Boas) J. Am. Folk-Lore, 1: 49.
— Life in. Chamb. J. 69: 219. — (T. L. Paton) Good Words, 36: 448.
— Mining Prospects in. Dub. R. 117: 457.
— Okanagan and Kootenay. (C. Lindsay) Canad. M. 5: 361.
— Rambles around Esquimault and Victoria. (A. Inkersley) Canad. M. 5: 514.
— Year in. (Chas. Edwardes) Time, 21: 654.
British Economic Association, Meetings of. Econ. J. 6: 177.
British Empire. *See* Great Britain, Empire of.
British Guiana, Four Months of Travel in. (G. G. Dixon) Geog. J. 5: 337.
— Rodway's History of. (N. D. Davis) Nation, 60: 111.
— Swamp Vegetation in. Dub. R. 117: 454.
British Investors and American Currency Regulations. (W. Wetherell) Forum, 16: 606.
British Isles, The. (Thomas H. B. Graham) Gent. M. n. s. 53: 474.
— Proposed Geographical Description of, Based on Ordnance Survey. (H. R. Mill) Geog. J. 7: 345.
British Librarian, The; the First Definite Work on English Bibliography and Book-lore. Bookworm, 1: 12.
British Museum. (A. C. Bickley) Bookworm, 1: 340, 366, 401. — (Sir E. M. Thompson) Leis. Hour, 45: 220–415.
— Archæological Departments. Walford's Antiq. 3: 17.
— Catalogue of. (R. Garnett) Univ. R. 2: 241.
— Facsimiles of Historic Letters in. Macmil. 73: 309.
— Library. (C. A. Cutter) Lib. J. 19: 289.
— Print Room and its Treasures. (A. Whitman) Good Words, 36: 680.
— Reading Room. (A. Grant) Time, 21: 449.

British Museum, Reference Library of. (R. S. Moffat) National, **20**: 856.
— Reminiscences of, by Dr. Garnett. Idler, **5**: 370.
— Sliding-press at. (R. Garnett) Lib. J. **17**: 422.
Brittany. (Y. King) M. of Art, **8**: 116.
— High. The Songs of Yesterday. Macmil. **74**: 359.
— of Cabbages and Kings. Ecl. M. **125**: 407.
— Quaint Artist Haunts in. (B. L. Harrison) Outing, **24**: 25.
— South, Costumes and Characteristics of. (T. R. Macquoid) M. of Art, **2**: 89.
— A Summer in. (A. Hoeber) Mo. Illust. **4**: 74.
— Twelve Days in. (C. B. Angier) Belgra. **84**: 54.
— Way-side Art in. (S. W. Kershaw) M. of Art, **3**: 66.
Broad Church Position Untenable. (A. F. Hewit) Cath. World, **59**: 94.
Broad Church Theology, Recent. (J. Owen) Acad. **41**: 272.
Broad Gauge, Birth and Growth of the. Gent. M. n. s. **55**: 489.
— Story of the. (G. A. Sekon) Gent. M. n. s. **49**: 59.
Broadmoor, Eng., Asylum for Insane. Green Bag, **5**: 165.
Broad-top Mountain, Pa. (M. L. Dock) Garden & F. **5**: 566, 603.
Broadus, John Albert. (W. C. Wilkinson) Bib. World, **5**: 327.
Broadwood, Henry Fowler. Music, **4**: 521.
Brocades, English. (C. P. Clarke) J. Soc. Arts, **40**: 576.
Brocklebank, Ralph, Collection of Pictures. (E. R. Dibdin) M. of Art, **14**: 86.
Brodhead, Eva W., with portrait. Bk. Buyer, **13**: 456.
Brodlique, Eve. (M. T. Bayard) Canad. M. **7**: 515.
Brodrick, Harold; a Modern Christ. Open Court, **7**: 3545.
Brohan Family, The. Dynasty of the Brohans. (A. Galdemar) Fortn. **60**: 71.
Broken Chord; a story. (A. H. Morrison) Canad. M. **2**: 476.
Broken Hill Silver Mine, A Visit to. (M. Frewen) Contemp. **68**: 358.
Broken Sword, A; a poem. (A. Dobson) M. of Art, **9**: 432.
Broken Tryst; a poem. All the Year, **75**: 419.
Broken Tryst, A; a story. (Mrs. C. Carr) Eng. Illust. **15**: 67.
Broker's Bay; a story. (W. C. Russell) Idler, **6**: 123.
Brome, R. (A. C. Swinburne) Fortn. **57**: 500.
Bromides, Two Ferroferric Double. (P. T. Walden) Am. J. Sci. **148**: 283.
Bromsgrove, England. Argosy, **60**: 663.
Bromvalerianic Acid. (J. G. Spenser) Am. J. Sci. **149**: 110.
Bron y Voel. (H. H. Lines) Antiq. n. s. **29**: 248.
Brontë, Charlotte. Acad. **50**: 520. — (A. W. Colton) Citizen, **1**: 253.
— and her Circle, Shorter on. (W. Reid) 19th Cent. **40**: 772.
— and Mrs. Gaskell. (C. K. Shorter) Bookman, **3**: 313.
— Place of, in Literature. (F. Harrison) Forum, **19**: 29.
— Unpublished Poem by. Critic, **22**: 100.
Brontë, Emily. (A. W. Colton) Citizen, **2**: 10. — (A. L. Salmon) Poet-Lore, **4**: 64. — (A. M. Williams) Temp. Bar, **98**: 431. Same art. Liv. Age, **199**: 59.
Brontës at Brussels. (F. Macdonald) Critic, **25**: 29.
— Haworth, the Home of the. (W. Davies) Temp. Bar, **107**: 132.
— in Ireland. (W. Wright) McClure, **1**: 177-335.
— — Wright's. (A. Webb) Nation, **57**: 468. — (J. D. Noble) Acad. **44**: 523. — Spec. **71**: 873.
— Relics of the. (H. E. Wroot) Good Words, **37**: 107. — (W. W. Yates) New R. **10**: 480.
Brontë Myths, A Crop of. (A. M. Mackay) Westm. **144**: 424.
Bronwen, Tomb of. (H. H. Lines) Antiq. n. s. **30**: 9.
Bronze Age in Bavaria, The. (A. J. Evans) Acad. **47**: 362.
Bronze Axe, The; a story. (A. Armitt) Gent. M. n. s. **53**: 325.
Bronze Box, The; a story. (J. C. Cowdrick) Munsey, **11**: 66.
Bronze Casting, Art of, in Europe. (G. Simonds) J. Soc. Arts, **44**: 654. — (G. Simonds) Am. Arch. **53**: 20, 30.
— in Japan. (W. Gowland) J. Soc. Arts, **43**: 523.
Bronze Flagon, 14th Century. Reliquary, **36**: 103.
Bronze Medallion, The; a story. Chamb. J. **70**: 763.
Bronze Statues of Grant and Lincoln. (C. Moffett) McClure, **5**: 419.
Bronze Weapons, Dartmoor. Reliquary, **35**: 104.
Bronzes, Japanese and Chinese. (G. Wallis) M. of Art, **5**: 401.
— — at Cernuschi's, Paris. (H. Wallis) Art J. **45**: 45.
— Russian. (J. F. Robertson) M. of Art, **10**: 239.
Brooch, Celtic, and how worn. (J. R. Allen) Illus. Archæol. **1**: 162.
Brook, George. Nature, **48**: 420.
Brook Farm, Boy's Recollections of. (A. Sumner) New Eng. M. n. s. **10**: 309.
— Codman on. (J. W. Chadwick) Nation, **60**: 207.
— Reminiscences of. (G. P. Bradford) Cent. **23**: 141.
— To-day. (A. A. McGinley) Cath. World, **61**: 14.
Brooke, Emma. Critic, **26**: 383.
Brooke, Fulke Greville, Lord, Selections from Works of. Sat. R. **79**: 588.
Brooke, James, Rajah of Sarawak. (H. Le Roux) Fortn. **62**: 410.
Brooke, Sir Victor, Life and Letters, ed. by Stephen. Sat. R. **78**: 509.
Brookes; a Story of the Civil Service. (J. Schayer) Cent. **26**: 817.
Brookline, Mass. (A. D. Chandler) New Eng. M. n. s. **8**: 777.
— Beaconsfield Terraces. (J. Waterman) New Eng. M. n. s. **5**: 625.
Brooklyn, Conn., Episcopal Church in. (W. H. Coleman) New Eng. M. n. s. **7**: 344.
Brooklyn, N. Y. (M. Halstead) Cosmopol. **15**: 131. — (J. Ralph) Harper, **86**: 651.
— and Kings County, Ostrander's History of. (J. W. Chadwick) Nation, **61**: 33.
— Government of, Idea of. (E. M. Shepard) Forum, **16**: 38.
— Prospect Park. (J. DeWolf) Engin. M. **3**: 16.
— Real Estate Exchange Building. Archit. Rec. **1**: 401.
Brooklyn Ethical Association, The. (L. G. Janes) Pop. Sci. Mo. **42**: 671.
Brooklyn Institute of Arts and Sciences. (F. W. Hooper) Lend a H. **15**: 193.
Brooks, Noah, with portrait. Bk. Buyer, **3**: 271.
Brooks, Phillips, with portrait. Bk. News, **10**: 233. — (J. H. Ward) And. R. **17**: 434. — (J. H. Ward) New Eng. M. n. s. **5**: 555. — (J. W. Bashford) Meth. R. **54**: 41. — (L. Parks) New Eng. M. n. s. **11**: 414. — (W. Lawrence) And. R. **19**: 183, 235. — (A. V. G. Allen) Atlan. **71**: 511. — (A. Brooks) Harper, **86**: 959. — With portrait. (C. C. Everett) Harv. Grad. M. **1**: 337. — (C. W. Eliot and others) Harv. Mo. **15**: 186. — Lend a H. **10**: 153. — Pub. Opin. **14**: 429. — (F. W. Farrar) R. of Rs. (N. Y.) **7**: 173. — Spec. **70**: 124. Same art. Ecl. M. **120**: 403. — (S. L. Bell) Sund. M. **22**: 454. — (C. A. Bartol) N. World, **2**: 479.

Brooks and Dean Stanley at Plymouth. (G. E. Ellis) New Eng. M. n. s. 8: 3.
— and Harvard University. (A. McKenzie) New Eng. M. n. s. 8: 275.
— as a Preacher. (C. F. Thwing) R. of Rs. (N. Y.) 7: 178.
— as a Theologian. (J. Fox) Presb. & Ref. R. 6: 393.
— as a Wrestler with Souls; with portrait. (J. Cook) Our Day, 11: 196.
— Letters from India. Cent. 24: 754.
— Letters to Children. Cent. 24: 503.
— Memorial Building to, at Harvard University. (E. H. Abbot) Harv. Grad. M. 2: 63.
— — English Coöperation in the. (L. Dyer) Nation, 57: 9.
— Preaching of. (H. G. Spaulding) New World, 4: 73.
— Statue of. Critic, 27: 44.
— Tributes to. Critic, 22: 69.
Brooks, William R. (F. W. Mack) Cent. 25: 838.
Brother Benedictus; a story. (J. C. Harvey) Munsey, 12: 255.
Brother Christian's Adventure. (P. W. Roose) Argosy, 59: 671.
Brotherhood; Address to Young Men. (L. Campbell) Time, 12: 169.
— Coming. (F. E. Willard) Arena, 6: 317.
— Greater, The. (F. Moscheles) Time, 22: 493.
— of Christian Unity. (T. F. Seward) Arena, 7: 721. — (T. T. Steward) Chr. Lit. 10: 102 a.
— of India. Arena, 10: 756. 13: 478.
— of Man. (W. A. Douglas) Canad. M. 6: 469.
— a Poem. (B. Arnold) Arena, 15: 463.
— Who are our Brethren? (W. D. Howells) Cent. 29: 932.
Brothers' Agency, The; a story. Idler, 3: 547.
Brother's Story. (J. C. Gwillim) Canad. M. 4: 307.
Brotherton, Alice W. (M. E. Cardwill) Writer, 7: 84.
Brotherton, Mistress Anne, Letters of. Temp. Bar, 108: 287.
Brough, Fanny, with portrait. Theatre, 28: 47.
Brougham, Henry, Lord, and Denman, Thomas, Lord. A Prophet and his Prophecy. (S. H. Boult) Gent. M. n. s. 51: 606.
Brower, Daniel R. S., M. D., with portrait. M. West. Hist. 11: 437.
Brown, Alice, with portrait. Bk. Buyer, 13: 634.
Brown, D. Russell, Ex-Gov. of R. I. Bost. 4: 313.
Brown, Ford Madox. Acad. 44: 325.— Ath. '93, 2: 526. — (F. G. Stephens) Portfo. 24: 62, 69. — Acad. 50: 395. — (L. M. Rossetti) M. of Art. 13: 289. — M. of Art, 17: 1.
— Note on the Cartoons of. M. of Art, 19: 29.
Brown, Fred, Teacher and Painter. (D. S. MacColl) M. of Art, 17: 403.
Brown, Ira, with portrait. (H. L. Conard) Nat'l M. (N. Y. '91) 15: 187.
Brown, James Henry (Denver). (H. D. Teetor) M. West. Hist. 12: 60.
Brown, John, Capt. (A. E. Allaben) Nat'l M. (N. Y. '91) 19: 23.
— and the Men of Harper's Ferry. (Col. R. J. Hinton) Time, 23: 728, 819.
— Farm of, in Adirondacks. (A. Shaw) R. of Rs. (N. Y.) 14: 311.
— — as a Public Park. (M. G. Van Rensselaer) Garden & F. 9: 47, 108.
— in Canada. (J. C. Hamilton) Canad. M. 4: 119.
— in Springfield. (H. A. Wright) New Eng. M. n. s. 10: 272.
— Raid of. (R. Shackelton, jr.) Nat'l M. (N. Y. '91) 17: 523.
Brown, John, Capt., What Support did he rely upon? (R. Shackleton) M. Am. Hist. 29: 348.
Brown, Dr. John. (J. M. Gray) Acad. 43: 454.
— Recollections of. Ecl. M. 122: 46. Same art. Liv. Age, 200: 57.
Brown, John, the Draughtsman. (J. M. Gray) M. of Art, 12: 310.
Brown, John G. (S. G. W. Benjamin) M. of Art, 5: 265.
Brown, Joseph E., with portrait. (H. L. Conard) M. West. Hist. 13: 255.
Brown, Nathaniel J. (H. L. Conard) Nat'l M. (N. Y. '91) 15: 667.
Brown, Robert. (J. S. Cotton) Acad. 48: 362. — Ath. '95, 2: 612. — Geog. J. 6: 577.
Brown, Vincent. Acad. 50: 424.
Brown, Wm. Hill. The real author of "Power of Sympathy." (A. W. Braley) Bost. 1: 224.
Brown-Séquard, Charles Edouard. Nat. Sci. 4: 393. — Nature, 49: 556.
— Alchemic Dream of. (G. M. Gould) Open Court, 3: 1859.
Browne, Chas. F. (G. J. H. Northcroft) Time, 18: 452.
— Relics of Artemus Ward. (D. C. Seitz) Cent. 24: 132.
Browne, Edward H., Kitchin on. Ath. '95, 1: 209.
Browne, George, with portrait. (P. A. O'Farrell) M. West. Hist. 13: 29.
Browne, Hablot Knight ("Phiz"), an Illustrator of Dickens. (A. Allchin) Cent. 23: 386.
Browne, Sir James. Blackw. 160: 149. Same art. Liv. Age, 210: 557.
Browne, Sir Thomas. (E. W. Adams) Gent. M. n. s. 54: 185. — (H. Allen) Pop. Sci. Mo. 50: 80.
Browne, Wm., of Tavistock. (G. Goodwin) Acad. 46: 134. — Spec. 72: 539.
Brownell, Henry Howard. (R. Burton) New Eng. M. n. s. 12: 601.
Brownell, Wm. Crary. (G. M. Hyde) Bookman, 4: 314.
Brownies on the Stage, Palmer Cox's. (B. Teal) McClure, 3: 404.
Browning, Origin of Surname. Am. Hist. Reg. 3: 650.
Browning, Elizabeth Barrett. (L. Whiting) Bookman, 3: 35. — (T. W. Hunt) Presb. & Ref. R. 7: 496. — Eng. R. 14: 307. — (W. B. Carpenter) Sund. M. 22: 767.
— Epilogues, Artistic Significance of. (D. G. Brinton) Poet-Lore, 4: 57.
— Ethical Impulse of her Poetry. (T. Bradfield) Westm. 146: 174. Same art. Ecl. M. 127: 447.
— A Little Girl's Recollections of. (H. Corkran) Ecl. M. 124: 345. Same art. Liv. Age, 204: 311.
— "A Musical Instrument." (H. Corson) Poet-Lore, 7: 259.
— on Tennyson. (W. G. Kingsland) Poet-Lore, 8: 23.
— Parentage of. (J. H. Ingram and others) Ath. '94, 1: 838. 2: 33-255.
— Poems. Eng. R. 4: 259.
— — Rare. (W. G. Kingsland) Poet-Lore, 4: 46.
— a Priestess of Liberty. (S. R. Tarr) Canad. M. 8: 176.
— Unpublished Letter from. Arena, 6: 296.
Browning, Robert. Acad. 50: 429. With portrait. Bk. News, 8: 173. — Time, 23: 1211. — (J. J. Chapman) Bach. of Arts, 3: 597, 731. — (G. Sarrazin) Univ. R. 3: 230.
— Alkestis. Does it interpret Euripides fairly? (P. S. Moxom) Poet-Lore, 8: 425.
— — and of Euripides. (C. A. Wurtzburg) Poet-Lore, 2: 344.
— and Elizabeth B. (Mrs. Andrew Crosse) Temp. Bar, 94: 29. Same art. Liv. Age, 192: 719. — (A. T. Ritchie) Harper, 84: 832.

Browning, Robert, Poe and. (J. L. Onderdonk) Dial (Ch.) 14: 353.
— and Tennyson, as Spiritual Forces. (C. C. Everett) N. World, 2: 240.
— — Love and Duty in. (E. F. R. Stilt) Poet-Lore, 4: 271.
— Andrea del Sarto. (H. Ford) Poet-Lore, 4: 144.
— Aprile, Democracy of. (C. G. Ames) Poet-Lore, 5: 27.
— as a Dramatic Poet. (H. Jones) Poet-Lore, 6: 13.
— as a Letter-writer. (W. G. Kingsland) Poet-Lore, 8: 78, 225.
— as a Musical Critic. (P. Jennings) Music, 5: 510.
— as Musician. (O. W. Pierce) Music, 8: 555.
— as a Religious Teacher. Jew. Q. 2: 230.
— as Theologian. Time, 22: 90.
— Bibliography of Writings of. (T. J. Wise) Ath. '94, 2: 193, 256, 422, 569.
— Caliban. (M. Wilkinson) Poet-Lore, 5: 562.
— Childe Roland, Danish Source of. (M. S. Brooks) Poet-Lore, 4: 425.
— Christianity of. (J. C. Collins) Sat. R. 81: 343.
— Classical Element in Work of. (W. C. Lawton) Am. J. Philol. 17: 197.
— Colombe's Birthday. Ath. '94, 2: 298, 363.
— — Study of. Poet-Lore, 4: 39.
— Criticism of Life by, Revell's. Spec. 69: 18.
— Definitive Edition of. Poet-Lore, 7: 102.
— Facettes of Love, from. (D. G. Brinton) Poet-Lore, 1: 1.
— Fifine at the Fair. (J. Morison) Acad. 42: 194.
— Form of. (F. H. Williams) Poet-Lore, 2: 300.
— His Mastery of Rhyme. (W. J. Rolfe) Poet-Lore, 5: 258.
— Impressions of, and his Art. (S. A. Brooke) Cent. 23: 238.
— Influence of Shelley on. (F. Converse) Poet-Lore, 7: 18.
— Interpretation of Romantic Love, compared with that of Plato, Dante, and Petrarch. (G. W. Cooke) Poet-Lore, 6: 225.
— Ixion. (G. D. Latimer) Poet-Lore, 4: 243. — (H. A. Clarke) Poet-Lore, 5: 626.
— Jones on. (T. B. Kilpatrick) Thinker, 9: 223.
— La Saisiaz. (A. T. Innes) Contemp. 70: 262. — (C. Malloy) Poet-Lore, 8: 256.
— — in 1895. Liv. Age, 210: 678.
— Letters, Excerpts from. (W. G. Kingsland) Poet-Lore, 4: 233.
— — New, and Mrs. Orr's Life. (W. G. Kingsland) Poet-Lore, 4: 522.
— Luria. (H. S. Pancoast) Poet-Lore, 1: 553. 2: 19. — (J. W. Chadwick) Poet-Lore, 6: 251.
— — compared with Othello. (L. A. Sherman) Poet-Lore, 6: 585.
— Mesmerism, from a Scientific Point of View. (F. E. White) Poet-Lore, 4: 261.
— Mildred. (J. J. Britton) Poet-Lore, 5: 266.
— Musical Symbolism in. (H. A. Clarke) Poet-Lore, 3: 260.
— on Philosophy of Music. (R. Hughes) Music, 3: 452.
— on Unconventional Relations. (D. G. Brinton) Poet-Lore, 4: 266.
— Optimism of, Source of. (M. M. Cohen) Poet-Lore, 4: 567.
— Paracelsus and the "Data of Ethics." (H. A. Clarke) Poet-Lore, 1: 117.
— — The Problem of. (J. Royce) New World, 3: 89.
— Philosophy of Art. (D. Dorchester) And. R. 19: 45.
— Pietro of Abano, Variants of. (C. Porter) Poet-Lore, 3: 577.
Browning, Robert. Pippa Passes. (I. F. Bellows) Poet-Lore, 6: 133.
— Poems. (M. Mackintosh) Educa. 13: 19, 228. — Eng. R. 11: 354.
— Poet of the People. (W. H. Anderson) Poet-Lore, 6: 244.
— Poetry of. (M. Mackintosh) Educa. 13: 270.
— Portraits of. (W. M. Rossetti) M. of Art, 13: 181–261.
— Rabbi Ben Ezra. (H. L. Wayland) Poet-Lore, 1: 57.
— Rarities on. (W. G. Kingsland) Poet-Lore, 6: 264.
— Relegation of Nature to Man in. (F. H. Williams) Poet-Lore, 4: 238.
— Religious Opinions of. (Mrs. S. Orr) Liv. Age, 192: 365.
— — Mrs. Orr on. Liv. Age, 192: 374.
— Reminiscences of. (W. G. Kingsland) Poet-Lore, 5: 229.
— Ring and the Book. (H. Corson) Poet-Lore, 6: 248.
— — Teachings of. (F. B. Hornbrooke) Poet-Lore, 1: 314.
— Science of. (E. Berdoe) Poet-Lore, 1: 353.
— Shorter Lyrics, Poetic Structure of. (E. Davis) Poet-Lore, 5: 436.
— Sludge the Medium. (F. B. Hornbrooke) Poet-Lore, 7: 240.
— Sordello. (A. T. Smith) Poet-Lore, 6: 238. — (C. C. Everett) Poet-Lore, 8: 243, 313.
— — Poetic Limitations of. (G. W. Cooke) Poet-Lore, 4: 612.
— Strafford, and Shakspere's Julius Cæsar. Poet-Lore, 4: 148.
— — Dramatic Motive in. (C. Porter) Poet-Lore, 5: 515.
— Theism of. (J. Royce) New World, 5: 401.
— Theology of. Our Day, 9: 93.
— True Greatness of. (A. Groff) Poet-Lore, 1: 470.
Browning, Robert, Father of the Poet, as Caricaturist. (F. G. Kitton) Art J. 48: 55.
Browning Club, Annals of a Quiet. Poet-Lore, 7: 225.
Browning Cyclopædia, Berdoe's. Ath. '92, 1: 107. — Spec. 68: 499.
Brownson, Orestes A. (G. P. Lathrop) Atlan. 77: 770.
Brozik, Vacslav. (R. H. Sherard) Art J. 47: 129.
Bruce, Alexander B. (A. Jenkinson) Thinker, 9: 25.
Bruce, Alexander Low. Geog. J. 3: 67.
Bruce, George, with portrait. (F. Allaben) Nat'l M. (N. Y. '91), 18: 176.
Bruce, Sir Geo. B. (J. R. Howatt) Chr. Lit. 10: 354.
Bruce, John Collingwood. Acad. 41: 357. — Ath. '92, 1: 475.
Brudenels, The; a story. (H. Aïde) National, 22: 409. Same art. Ecl. M. 121: 789.
Bruges, Belgium. (G. S. Morris) Am. Arch. 52: 91.
— Ship Canal. Dub. R. 118: 175.
Brugmann's Nasal Sonant Theory, Physiological Criticism of. (H. Schmidt-Wartenberg) Am. J. Philol. 17: 217.
Brugsch, Heinrich Karl. Ath. '94, 2: 361. Sat. R. 78: 291. — (W. M. Müller) Am. J. Archæol. 10: 47.
Bruighean Tales. (W. A. Craigie) Scot. R. 24: 270.
Brummell, Beau. (A. I. Shand) Cornh. 74: 769.
Bruncu Spina, Ascent of. All the Year, 73: 40.
Bruneau, G. Attaque du Moulin; an opera. Sat. R. 78: 11.
Brunelleschi, Filippo. (F. M. Robinson) M. of Art, 8: 318.
Brunetière, Ferdinand. Atlan. 73: 430. — (Y. Blaze de Bury) Fortn. 64: 497. — Liv. Age, 204: 572.

Brunetière, Ferdinand, Reception at the French Academy. (C. Nicholson) Acad. **45**: 169.
Brunn, Heinrich von. (P. Gardner) Acad. **46**: 122. — (A. Emerson) Am. J. Archæol. **9**: 366.
Brunner, John T. (F. Dolman) Eng. Illust. **14**: 277.
Bruno, Saint, Some Thoughts on. Macmil. **73**: 72. Same art. Liv. Age, **207**: 501.
Bruno, Giordano. (M. T. Kelly) Month, **75**: 527.
— Expulsion of the Beast Triumphant. (W. R. Thayer) N. World, **3**: 471.
— in England. (C. K. Paul) Month, **82**: 517.
Bruns, Karl Georg, German jurist. (M. Smith) Pol. Sci. Q. **10**: 664.
Brushwood Boy, The. (R. Kipling) Cent. **29**: 265.
Brussels, Exposition Nationale. M. of Art, **4**: 114.
— Treaty of, and Duty of the U. S. (L. Tree) Forum, **12**: 614.
Bryan, William Jennings. (W. J. Abbot) R. of Rs. (N. Y.) **14**: 161.
— and McKinley as Lawyers. (A. O. Hall) Green Bag, **8**: 393.
Bryanism, Meaning of, in American Politics. Gunton's M. **11**: 385.
Bryant, B. F., with portrait. (W. L. Osborne) M. West. Hist. **11**: 514.
Bryant, William Cullen. (T. Bradfield) Westm. **143**: 84. — (H. S. Nahmier) Arena, **15**: 28.
— and the Berkshire Hills. (A. Lawrence) Cent. **28**: 368.
— Centennial of. (W. R. Thayer) Nation, **59**: 136. — (A. Steadman) Dial (Ch.) **17**: 107. — (W. R. Thayer) R. of Rs. (N. Y.) **10**: 400. — Critic, **25**: 123.
— — a Poem. Lit. W. (Bost.) **25**: 264.
— Lesson on. (E. W. Barrett) Educa. **14**: 478.
— New England Home of. (H. S. Nahmer) New Eng. M. n. s. **6**: 65.
— Poet of Nature. (F. F. Emerson) New Eng. M. n. s. **11**: 148.
— Thanatopsis. Poet-Lore, **6**: 520.
— — Origin of. (T. W. Chadwick) Harper, **89**: 630.
Bryce, Prof. James, with portrait. Bk. News, **8**: 273.
— American Commonwealth. (E. J. James) Ann. Am. Acad. Pol. Sci. **7**: 377.
Brydges, James. *See* Chandos, Duke of.
Bryn Mawr College, Festivals in. (S. G. Walker) Cent. **25**: 429.
Bubbles from the Hooghly; a story. (E. C. Hamley) Gent. M. n. s. **57**: 1.
Buccaneers of America. Macmil. **69**: 149. — Spec. **73**: 345.
— Esquemeling's, edited by Powell. Ath. '**94**, **1**: 12.
— of the 17th Century. Leis. Hour, **41**: 171, 255.
— — A Floating Republic. Liv. Age, **192**: 600, 815.
— Jamaican. Sat. R. **73**: 383, 415.
Buchan. Quar. **179**: 387.
Buchan Garden, Autumn Sessions in a. (Mrs. R. Boyle) National, **26**: 180. Same art. Liv. Age, **207**: 311.
Buchanan, George. (A. Roberts) Crit. R. **1**: 127.
— and the Inquisition. (P. H. Brown) Scot. R. **21**: 296.
— a 16th Century Scholar. (G. Eyre-Todd) Gent. M. n. s. **49**: 35.
Buchanan, Sir George. Nature, **52**: 58.
Buchanan, James, W. M. Gwin and Judge Black on. (E. J. Coleman) Overland, n. s. **19**: 87.
Buchanan, Robert, and G. R. Sims. The Lights of Home. Theatre, **29**: 125.
— — The White Rose. Theatre, **28**: 307.
— Charlatan; a play. Sat. R. **77**: 94.
— Idyls and Legends of Inverburn. Idler, **3**: 385.
— Undertones. Idler, **3**: 385.
Buchanan, Robert. Wandering Jew. Spec. **70**: 128. — (J. S. Little) Acad. **43**: 191, (R. Buchanan) 243.
Bucket-shops. Chamb. J. **70**: 454.
Buckhounds, The. (Lord Ribblesdale) Eng. Illust. **10**: 452.
— Royal, History of, Hore's. Sat. R. **77**: 233.
Buckingham, George Villiers, First Duke of. (A. Buckler) Gent. M. n. s. **55**: 599.
Buckingham Palace. (W. J. Loftie) M. of Art, **9**: 89.
Buckland, William. (J. Macaulay) Leis. Hour, **44**: 148.
— Gordon's Life of. (S. A. Hubbard) Dial (Ch.) **18**: 172. — Sat. R. **79**: 451.
Buckley, James Matthias, with portrait. (C. W. Hobart) M. West. Hist. **13**: 183.
Buckley Lady, The; a story. (M. E. Wilkins) Harper, **88**: 499.
Bucks County, Pa. (H. C. Michener) M. Am. Hist. **27**: 225.
Bucrania. (J. Passepont) Am. Arch. **37**: 152. **38**: 24–194.
Bud-variation and Evolution. (G. Henslow) Nat. Sci. **7**: 103.
Bud Zunt's Mail; a Romance of the Simpkinsville Post-office. (R. McE. Stuart) Harper, **88**: 58.
Budapest, Popular Life in. (W. Singer) Harper, **84**: 215.
— Rise of a New Metropolis. (A. Shaw) Cent. **22**: 163.
Budapest Exhibition. (I. Zangwill) Critic, **29**: 99.
Budden, R. H. (E. M. Cesaresco) Acad. **48**: 567.
Buddha. (C. Galton) Month, **79**: 153.
— and Jesus as Literary Critics. (F. F. Kramer) Bib. World, **3**: 252.
— Christian Critics of. (P. Carus) Open Court, **9**: 4475–4483.
— The Great. (J. O'Neill) Good Words, **35**: 851.
Buddhism. (A. W. Benn) Acad. **43**: 145. — (W. Davies) Atlan. **74**: 334. — (T. F. Wright) N. Church R. **3**: 406. — (L. G. Cotton) Month, **88**: 75.
— and Brahmanism. Open Court, **10**: 4851.
— and Foreign Missions. (C. Pfoundes) Open Court, **9**: 4594.
— and Lamaism in Mongolia. (J. Sheepshanks) M. Chr. Lit. **5**: 329.
— Chinese; Our Lady of Pootoo. (R. S. Gundry) National, **22**: 491.
— Christianity and. (C. Schroder) Arena, **5**: 458. — (P. Carus) Open Court, **10**: 4783. — (J. H. Barrows) Our Day, **16**: 369. — (P. Carus) Monist, **5**: 65.
— Copleston's. (C. H. Toy) Nation, **56**: 182. — (M. Müller) New R. **8**: 107. — Spec. **70**: 612.
— Ecclesiastes and. (E. J. Dillon) Contemp. **65**: 153.
— Esoteric. (F. M. Müller) 19th Cent. **33**: 767. **34**: 296. Same art. Ecl. M. **121**: 58. — (A. P. Sinnett) 19th Cent. **33**: 1015. — (A. P. Sinnett) Time, **20**: 273.
— Essence of. (T. W. R. Davids) Chr. Lit. **12**: 350.
— Evangelical. (M. M. Snell) Bib. World, **7**: 182.
— Foundation of. (M. Bloomfield) New World, **1**: 246.
— in China. (R. S. Gundry) Ecl. M. **122**: 172.
— in Japan. (N. Kishimoto) Open Court, **8**: 4183–4211.
— Is Buddha's Teaching that of Christ? (D. Gilmore) Chr. Lit. **16**: 81.
— Japanese. (J. L. Atkinson) Bib. Sac. **49**: 313.
— Mahayana, in Japan. (A. E. Cheney) Arena, **16**: 439.
— Morality of. (C. Galton) Month, **78**: 4.
— of Tibet, Waddell's. Sat. R. **79**: 517.
— Original. (E. V. Gerhart) Ref. Q. **39**: 290.
— Plain Account of. (J. Beames) Asia. R. **22**: 145.
— Psychology of. (H. H. Williams) Open Court, **6**: 3407, 3418.
— Teachings of, Fundamental. (Zitsuzen Ashitzu) Monist, **4**: 163.

Buddhism, Theistic Evolution of. (J. E. Carpenter) New World, 1: 89.
— Through what Historical Channels did it influence Early Christianity? (J. G. R. Forlong) Open Court, 1: 382, 416, 439.
— Western. (H. G. McKerlie) Asia. R. 9: 192.
— What is? (Subhadra Bickshu) Arena, 5: 217.
Buddhist Confession. (E. M. Bowden) Eng. Illust. 11: 383.
Buddhist Doctrine and Ethics, Essentials of. (M. Bloomfield) Int. J. Ethics, 2: 313.
Buddhist Sanctuary of North China. (W. W. Rockhill) Atlan. 75: 758.
Buddhist Sects in Japan. (C. de Harlez) Dub. R. 116: 25.
Buddhist Temple at Buddha Gaya, Cunningham on. Sat. R. 74: 516.
Buddhists, Shall we become? (H. M. King) Chr. Lit. 14: 61.
Budenz, Joseph. Acad. 41: 402.
Bülow, Hans Guido v. Pub. Opin. 16: 482. — Acad. 45: 155. — Sat. R. 77: 170. — (S. V. Makower) New R. 11: 647. — (J. C. Hadden) Ecl. M. 126: 753. — (F. Regal) Music, 5: 681. — (Baron von Overbeck) Music, 8: 82.
— Letters. (H. T. Finck) Nation, 62: 141.
— Recollections and Anecdotes of. (B. Boekelman) Cent. 30: 461.
Buenos Ayres. Leis. Hour, 44: 166.
— British Expedition to, 1806–7. (J. W. Fortescue) Macmil. 71: 471.
Buffalo, N. Y. (W. H. Hotchkiss) Munsey, 7: 645. — — (F. J. Shepard) New Eng. M. n. s. 8: 237.
— and its Attractions. (A. Stocks) School R. 4: 494.
— Excise and Charity at. (F. Almy) Char. R. 4: 319.
— Grosvenor Library. Lib. J. 17: 202.
— Higher Life of. (W. B. Wright) Outl. 53: 1195.
— Public Schools of. (J. M. Rice) Forum, 14: 293.
Buffalo in Yellowstone Park. (C. S. Sargent) Garden & F. 7: 151.
— Last of the. (G. B. Grinnell) Scrib. M. 12: 267.
— Story of the. (H. Russell) Harper, 86: 795.
Buffalo Run at One Tree Creek, A. (L. R. Ord) Gent. M. n. s. 53: 297.
Buffum, Joseph H., M. D. (H. L. Conard) M. West. Hist. 12: 693.
Bufo of the Jewelled Head. (G. Winterwood) Good Words, 35: 684.
Building, Bogus. Econ. R. 5: 75.
— Combination of Iron, Brick and Stone in. (W. N. Black) Am. Arch. 39: 40.
— Construction of a Great. (F. H. Kimball) Engin. M. 8: 877.
— Mechanical Aids to. (G. Hill) Engin. M. 5: 500.
Building of a Bachelor. (A. E. Lawrence) New Eng. M. n. s. 15: 181.
Buildings, Careless Construction and Wilful Destruction of. (L. Windmüller) R. of Rs. (N. Y.) 12: 309.
— Cost per Cubic Foot. (F. E. Kidder) Am. Arch. 43: 76.
— Failure of. (Roger Smith) Am. Arch. 52: 36, 56.
— High. (A. L. A. Himmelwright) No. Am. 163: 580. — Am. Arch. 52: 86.
— — and Good Architecture. (T. Hastings) Am. Arch. 46: 67.
— — and their Art. (B. Ferree) Scrib. M. 15: 297.
— — Dangers of. (E. Flagg) Cosmopol. 21: 70.
— — Dangers from. (H. A. Goetz) Engin. M. 2: 792.
— — Fire-risks on. (E. Atkinson) Engin. M. 3: 149.
— — Foundations of. (W. B. Hutton) Am. Arch. 42: 88.
— — in England and America. (A. de Calonne) Chaut. 19: 427.
Buildings, High, Light in. (D. Adler) Engin. M. 4: 171.
— — Past and Future. (D. Adler) Engin. M. 3: 765.
— — The Sky-scraper. (F. C. Gordon) Am. Arch. 46: 101.
— Office, Modern. (B. Ferree) J. Frankl. Inst. 141: 47, 115.
— Steel. Pop. Sci. Mo. 47: 567.
Building and Loan Associations. Lend a H. 14: 450. — (J. M. Ludlow) Econ. R. 3: 64. — Spec. 70: 72.
— and the General Welfare of U. S. (S. Dexter) Am. J. Pol. 1: 622.
— and Savings Banks. Gunton's M. 10: 241.
Building Law in Boston, Failure of Joint Committee appointed to secure Certain Legislation in regard to. Am. Arch. 52: 103.
— of New York City. (W. J. Fryer, jr.) Archit. Rec. 1: 69.
Building Laws, Municipal, Comparison of. (H. A. Phillips) Am. Arch. vols. 35–40.
— Uniform, Need of. (W. J. Fryer) Engin. M. 5: 756.
Building-material Station, Switzerland. (E. Germain) Am. Arch. 49: 30.
Building-skeleton Construction. (W. J. Fryer, jr.) Archit. Rec. 1: 228.
Building Specifications. (T. R. Williamson) Am. Arch. 45: 79, 92.
Building Stone of U. S. (W. C. Day) J. Frankl. Inst. 141: 98.
Building Superstitions. Chamb. J. 69: 828.
Buitenzorg, Java, Botanical Garden of. (A. Tissandier) Pop. Sci. Mo. 48: 335.
Bulbous Plants, Autumn Flowering. (W. Watson) Garden & F. 9: 374.
— Desirable. (W. H. Taplin) Garden & F. 9: 487.
— Hardy. Garden & F. 5: 522.
— in Winter. (J. N. Gerard) Garden & F. 5: 126.
— New. (W. E. Endicott) Garden & F. 5: 79.
Bulbs, Cultivation of in North Carolina. (W. F. Massey) Garden & F. 6: 185.
— — — Progress of. (W. F. Massey) Garden & F. 7: 312.
— Some American. Garden & F. 6: 56.
— Spring, in '93. (W. E. Endicott) Garden & F. 6: 277.
Bulfinch, Charles. Am. Arch. 53: 101.
Bulgaria and her Ruler. Sat. R. 79: 180.
— in 1894, Dicey's. Sat. R. 78: 213.
— The New. (J. M. Hubbard) Nation, 60: 338.
— The Pomaks of Rhodope. (J. D. Bourchier) Fortn. 60: 509.
— Renaissance of. (M. S. Robinson) Meth. R. 54: 190.
— Russia and. (E. Dicey) Fortn. 65: 663.
— Youngest of the Nations. Chamb. J. 72: 385.
Bulgarian Dance and Song. (J. J. Kral) Music, 9: 159.
Bull, Capt. John; a Post-office Warrior. (A. H. Norway) Eng. Illust. 11: 799.
Bull Laudabiliter, The. (K. Norgate) Eng. Hist. R. 8: 18.
Bull-fight in Seville. (F. M. Wilcox) Lippinc. 52: 331.
— on the Border. (P. W. Avirett) Outing, 26: 27.
Bull-fighting. (E. F. Kimball) Munsey, 8: 400. — Spec. 73: 107.
— in France. (R. T. Mullin) Canad. M. 4: 110. — Gent. M. n. s. 53: 638.
— in Spain. (S. L. Bensusan) Eng. Illust. 14: 127.
Bull-fights, Francisco Goya y Luciente's Pictures of. (D. Hannay) M. of Art, 6: 501.
Bull Run, Battle of, 2d New Hampshire Regt. in. (F. S. Fiske) New Eng. M. n. s. 11: 153.
Bullant, Jean. (A. M. F. Robinson) M. of Art, 8: 298.
Bullen, George. Acad. 46: 303. — Ath. '94, 2: 494.
Bullet-proof Clothing, Dowe's. Spec. 70: 415.
Bullets, Flying. Nature, 55: 79.

Bullion, Fixed Value of, as a Standard. (A. Williams) Econ. J. 2: 280.
Bullock, Alex. H., Sketch of the Life of. (J. W. Dean) N. E. Reg. 50: 153.
Bullwinkle. (E. Gold) Lippinc. 58: 533.
Bully, The. (I. Turgenev) Liv. Age, 211: 387, 700.
Bulullicoo; a story. (C. E. Grimblecom) Overland, n. s. 23: 306–537.
Bulwer, Edward. *See* Lytton, E. L. B.
Bumpus, Edward. Acad. 50: 262.
Bunch of Wall Flowers; a story. (H. Landsberger) Chaut. 20: 76.
Buncle, John. (W. G. Waters) Gent. M. n. s. 54: 73.
Buncoed. Chamb. J. 68: 780.
Bundle Handkerchief. (E. M. Gosse) New Eng. M. n. s. 14: 62.
Bunhill Fields. Chamb. J. 70: 633.
Bunker Hill, Battle of. (C. F. Adams) Am. Hist. R. 1: 401.
— in 1829. (J. C. Johnson) Bost. 2: 283.
— Its First Monument. (J. T. Vose) Bost. 2: 227.
— Present Monument. (L. B. Titus) Bost. 2: 238.
Bunkum, Apology for. Spec. 70: 600.
Bunner, A. F. (G. P. Lathrop) Mo. Illust. 5: 150.
Bunner, Henry C., with portrait. Bk. Buyer, 13: 280. — (B. Matthews) Scrib. M. 20: 287. — (L. Hutton) Bookman, 3: 398. — Critic, 28: 352.
— as Editor and Story-writer. (H. G. Paine) Critic, 28: 363.
— as Poet. (F. D. Sherman) Critic, 28: 363.
— Fly-leaf and Friendly Verses of. (F. B. Paine) Bk. Buyer, 13: 345.
— Uncollected Poems of. Bookman, 3: 512.
Bunnoo, The Subjugation of, by Sir Herbert Edwardes. (F. Dixon) Un. Serv. M. 2 ('88–'89): 79.
Bunsen, Baron von, Birthplace of. (M. von Bunsen) Good Words, 33: 161.
Bunyan, John. (J. Royce) Psychol. R. 1: 22, 134, 230.
— Pilgrim's Progress. (K. M. Warren) Sund. M. 24: 669. — Bookworm, 1: 87, 201, 346.
— — and Anabaptism. (R. Heath) Contemp. 70: 541.
— — Bagster's Illustrated Edition of. (R. L. Stevenson) M. of Art, 5: 169.
Buoy, The Whistling. (L. Bell) Overland, n. s. 22: 605.
Burbank, E. A. (C. M. Skinner) Mo. Illust. 3: 246.
Burden of Isabel. (J. M. Cobban) Chamb. J. 70: 1–647.
Burdette, Robert J. (H. Parker) Munsey, 9: 608. — With portrait. Bk. News, 12: 4.
Burgess, Frederick. (W. Roberts) Bookworm, 4: 225.
Burgess, John Bagnold. M. of Art, 5: 133.
Burgh, Parish Register of. (A. Jessopp) Good Words, 35: 529.
Burghley, Lord. Memorial on Peace with Spain, 1588. (W. F. Tilton) Am. Hist. R. 1: 490.
Burghley, Sarah, Countess of. (J. Cartwright) M. of Art, 9: 281.
Burglar of Corn-Field Inn. (H. Babson) Outing, 27: 301.
Burglar Jim. Chamb. J. 71: 427–444.
Burglars and Safes. Chamb. J. 71: 101.
Burglars Three; a story. (J. H. Smith) McClure, 1: 268.
Burglary, Modern. Spec. 71: 941.
Burglary Season, The. All the Year, 71: 437.
Burgomaster Van Troon. (T. W. Speight) Chamb. J. 71: 73–104.
Burgon, John William. Lond. Q. 78: 121.
— Goulburn's. (G. A. Simcox) Acad. 41: 79. — Church Q. 34: 149. — Quar. 174: 453. — Macmil. 66: 145. — Sat. R. 73: 104.
Burgos, Casa del Cordon, Stories of. (R. Thirlmere) M. of Art, 19: 64.
Burgoyne, Gen., at Saratoga, With. Macmil. 75: 71.
— Letter of. Nat'l M. (N. Y. '91) 17: 159.
Burgoyne, Surrender of, 1777. Letter of Col. D. Colman. M. Am. Hist. 29: 279.
Burgoyne, Sir Roger. (M. M. Verney) Longm. 25: 72. Same art. Liv. Age, 203: 685.
Burgundio, John. Sat. R. 78: 429.
Burial, Art of. (L. C. Casartelli) Dub. R. 114: 1.
— in Borneo. (C. V. Creagh) Anthrop. J. 26: 33.
Burial of the Guns, The. (T. N. Page) Scrib. M. 15: 410.
Burial of the Sardine, The. (L. M. R. Walker) Belgra. 82: 416.
Burial Customs. (E. Howlett) Westm. 140: 166.
— Among the Sihanka. (J. Pearse) Sund. M. 23: 683.
— in Lincolnshire. (F. Peacock) Antiq. n. s. 31: 330.
— of Irish Peasantry. (Mrs. F. D. Bergen) J. Am. Folk-Lore, 8: 19.
— of New Britain. (B. Danks) Anthrop. J. 21: 348.
— of Northwest Indians. (J. Wickersham) Am. Antiq. 18: 204.
Burial Mound, in Florida. (C. B. Moore) Am. Natural. 26: 129.
Burial Place, Ancient, at Roseisle, Elgin. Reliquary, 35: 142.
Burial Service, Sermons on. Eng. R. 18: 38.
Buried Mother, The; a poem. (A. Meynell) M. of Art, 8: 317.
Buried Treasure; a Pirate Yarn. All the Year, 73: 443.
Burke, Edmund. (G. Smith) Cornh. 74: 17.
Burke, Father Thomas. Spec. 74: 22. — Sat. R. 79: 131.
Burke, Ulick Ralph. Acad. 48: 90. — Ath. '95, 2: 131.
Burke's Wife; a story. (B. Crocker) Overland, n. s. 20: 435.
Burlesque, Modern, Writers of, Plea for. (J. K. Angus) Belgra. 79: 196.
— Old and New. (W. D. Adams) Theatre, 36: 144.
— Past and Present. Time, 3: 127.
— Spirit of. (F. C. Burnand) Univ. R. 2: 163.
Burlesques, Old and New. (L. Wagner) Time, 15: 584.
Burlington, Vermont. (G. G. Benedict) New Eng. M. n. s. 11: 547. — (R. E. Lewis) New Eng. M. n. s. 15: 64.
Burlington House, Italian Pictures at. (J. P. Richter) Art J. 46: 62.
Burly, Derivation of. (W. W. Skeat) Acad. 45: 250.
Burma. Cornh. 73: 35.
— and the Burmese. Time, 8: 1.
— Cumming's Shadow of the Pagoda. Ath. '94, 1: 106.
— Education Department. (P. Hordern) Asia. R. 14: 29.
— Empire of, 1885. Blackw. 153: 658. Same art. Ecl. M. 121: 42. Same art. Liv. Age, 198: 18.
— Holidays in. Chamb. J. 72: 509.
— The Situation in, 1888. (P. Hordern) Univ. R. 2: 57.
— University for, at Rangoon. (Justice Jardine) Asia. R. 17: 71.
— Upper. (J. G. B. Stopford) Eng. Illust. 10: 383.
— — under British Rule. (H. T. White) J. Soc. Arts, 41: 150.
— Wa Tribe. (J. G. Scott) Asia. R. 21: 138.
— Women and Worship in. (V. Greville) 19th Cent. 31: 1001. Same art. Ecl. M. 119: 132.
— Women of. (H. Fielding) Blackw. 157: 776. Same art. Ecl. M. 125: 82. Same art. Liv. Age, 205: 801.
Burman Dacoity and Patriotism. (H. N. D. Prendergast) Asia. R. 15: 271.
Burmantofts Faïence. (C. Monkhouse) M. of Art, 8: 471.
Burmese Race, Extinction of. (G. H. Le Maistre) Asia. R. 16: 321.
— Nat-worship among the. (L. Vossion) J. Am. Folk-Lore, 4: 107.
— Notes on. (R. W. Shufeldt) Pop. Sci. Mo. 50: 34.

Burmese Traits. (H. C. Moore) Fortn. 58: 607. Same art. Liv. Age, 196: 42. Same art. Ecl. M. 120: 8.
Burnand, F. C. Some Old Friends. Spec. 69: 293.
Burne-Jones, Edward. *See* Jones, E. Burne.
Burnet, Wm., Governor of N. Y., 1720–28. (W. Nelson) Nat'l M. (N. Y. '91), 17: 399.
Burnett, Frances Hodgson, with portrait. Bk. Buyer, 3: 21. — With portrait. Bk. News, 8: 312.
— at Home. (Marie A. Belloc) Idler, 9: 645.
— Lady of Quality. Sat. R. 81: 627. — (M. C. Birchenough) 19th Cent. 40: 771.
— Novels of. (Clementina Black) Time, 12: 72.
— The Showman's Daughter. Gent. M. n. s. 48: 211. — Theatre, 28: 100.
Burnett, Henry L. Nat'l M. (N. Y. '91) 17: 272.
Burnett, J. P. "Jo," adapted from Dickens's Bleak House. Sat. R. 81: 523.
Burnham, Clara Louise. (L. A. Coonley) Writer, 8: 133.
Burnham, S. W. Address on Presentation of Gold Medal by Royal Astronomical Society. (W. DeW. Abney) Astron. 13: 283.
Burnham Beeches. (M. G. Fawcett) M. of Art, 8: 485.
Burning of the Sheas; a story. All the Year, 72: 189.
Burns, F. G., with portrait. M. West. Hist. 13: 52.
Burns, John. (R. J. Hinton) Arena, 12: 90.
— Blunders as a Socialist. Our Day, 14: 83.
— Sketch of his Life. (R. Blathwayt) Idler, 2: 669.
Burns, Robert. (C. A. Price) Belgra. 87: 248. Same art. Liv. Age, 206: 515. — (D. F. Hannigan) Westm. 142: 319. — (G. Holme) Munsey, 12: 196. — Blackw. 160: 184. — (H. Mann) Mo. Illust. 11: 645.
— Angellier's. Blackw. 154: 215.
— at Kirkoswald. (J. W. Oliver) Macmil. 67: 202.
— The Burns and Dunlop Correspondence. (L. M. Roberts) Fortn. 64: 662.
— Centenary of. Critic, 29: 121.
— Century of Biography of. (W. Wallace) Chamb. J. 72: 817.
— Completion of Statue of. Critic, 27: 157.
— Ethics of. (M. M. Trumbull) Open Court, 2: 1439.
— A French View of. (W. Wallace) Acad. 43: 301.
— Hogg's Life of. (T. Bayne) Ath. '93, 1: 764.
— Homes and Home Life of. (L. Stuart) Chaut. 16: 569.
— Nature of. (J. Campbell) Canad. M. 6: 395.
— Poetry; ed. by Henley and Henderson. Sat. R. 81: 353.
— a poem. (D. F. Hannigan) Westm. 145: 407.
— a poem. (A. C. Swinburne) 19th Cent. 39: 181.
— Poems. Sat. R. 73: 134.
— Portraits of, Authentic. (J. M. Gray) M. of Art, 17: 238.
— Religion of. (W. Walsh) Poet-Lore, 7: 57.
— Translations of, Jack's. (C. W. Colby) Nation, 62: 311.
Burns, Walter Hayes, with portrait. Bank. M. (Lond.) 53: 563.
Burnside, Gen. Ambrose E., in East Tennessee. (J. A. Joyce) Un. Serv. (Phila.) 10: 125.
Burnt Wood in Decoration. (J. W. Fosdick) Cent. 30: 495.
Burr, Aaron, Conspiracy and Trial of. (W. S. Drysdale) Harper, 84: 197.
Burr, Aaron, Dramatic Incident in Legal Experience of. (L. B. Proctor) Green Bag, 7: 223.
— Duel with Hamilton. (H. D. Teetor) M. West. Hist. 12: 232.
Burr, Pres. Aaron, Account Book of, 1755–58. (P. Van Dyke) M. Am. Hist. 28: 186.
Burr, Theodosia. The Wrecker's Story; a poem. (J. W. Palmer) Cent. 28: 860.
Burrawurra Brand, The; a story. (E. W. Hornung) Idler, 4: 349.
Burrell Libel Case, The; a story. (R. H. Sherard) Idler, 6: 465.
Burroughs, John, with portrait. Bk. Buyer, 6: 171. — With portrait. Bk. News, 6: 9.
Burroughs, Marie. (R. Edgarton) Lippinc. 51: 363.
Burton, Sir Frederick. M. of Art, 17: 310.
Burton, Lady Isabel. Acad. 49: 263.
— The Love of. (Margaret Lenox) Cosmopol. 22: 94.
Burton, John Hill. Bookworm, 2: 3[illegible]1.
Burton, Lord, and Burton-on-Trent. (F. Dolman) Eng. Illust. 12: no. 6, 60.
Burton, Sir Richard. (F. A. Gowing) Belgra. 84: 146. — (P. Addleshaw) Acad. 44: 333. — Ath. '93, 2: 149. — Ed. R. 178: 439. — (A. C. Coolidge) Nation, 57: 177. — Sat. R. 76: 101. — Spec. 71: 241. — (Mrs. Newton-Robinson) Westm. 140: 469. — (I. Burton) New R. 7: 562.
Burton, Richard, with portrait. Bk. Buyer, 12: 70.
Burton, Robert. (T. E. Brown) New R. 13: 257.
— and the Anatomy of Melancholy. (Edw. W. Adams) Gent. M. n. s. 57: 46. Same art. Ecl. M. 127: 264. — All the Year, 70: 199.
Burton, Stiles, with portrait. (H. L. Conard) M. West. Hist. 13: 704.
Burwell, Theodotus, with portrait. M. West. Hist. 8: 83.
Bury, Richard de. Bookworm, 2: 89.
Burying Alive. Spec. 75: 332.
Burying Ground of Honey Locust Hill. (E. C. Shipman) New Eng. M. n. s. 9: 501.
Burying of the Hatchet. (A. F. Brown) New Eng. M. n. s. 10: 644.
Busby, Richard. Cornh. 71: 416.
Bush, Rufus T. (V. B. Denslow) M. West. Hist. 13: 370.
Bushnell, Horace. (T. T. Munger) Chr. Lit. 15: 406, 467.
Bushrangers, The Ironclad. Chamb. J. 69: 12.
Bushwoman's Romance. (H. A. Bryden) Longm. 26: 261.
Business and Depression. Bank. M. (N. Y.) 50: 480.
— Improvement in, Indications of. Forum, 19: 380.
— Improving Condition of. Forum, 19: 508.
— May a Man conduct his, as he please? (C. D. Wright) Forum, 18: 425.
— Morality in. (J. Carter) Econ. R. 3: 318. 4: 221. — (S. B. Boulton) Econ. R. 4: 208.
— on Sentimental Principles. (D. M. Means) Nation, 55: 489.
- Private, is a Public Trust. (A. W. Small) Am. J. Sociol. 1: 276.
— Revival of, Evidences of. Gunton's M. 11: 414.
— Young Man in. (E. W. Bok) Cosmopol. 16: 332.
Business Arrangement, A; a story. (E. E. Kitton) Argosy, 59: 602.
Business Depression, Cause and Remedy for. (E. Atkinson) Engin. M. 11: 611.
— in 1847 and 1894. Bank. M. (Lond.) 58: 613.
Business Education, How to get. (M. J. Owens) Chaut. 22: 213.
Business Enterprise, Obstacles to. (F. H. Cooke) Am. J. Pol. 4: 425.
Business Idyll, A; a story. (E. Davies) Argosy, 58: 419.
Business Life, Social Science in. (J. Habberton) Chaut. 15: 682.
Business Men and Social Theorists. (C. R. Henderson) Am. J. Sociol. 1: 385.
Business Methods in Public Affairs, Obstacles to. (C. R. Woodruff) No. Am. 163: 758.

Business Outlook, The. (C. S. Smith; C. G. Wilson; J. O. Bloss; H. Hentz) No. Am. **157**: 385.
Business Revival, The. (E. Kemble; J. M. Glenn; A. K. Miller; W. G. Boyd) No. Am. **159**: 611.
— Evidences of. Engin. M. **8**: 1.
— Facts touching. Forum, **18**: 379.
— Outlook for. (J. E. Simmons) Engin. M. **7**: 1.
Business Situation in Review, 1895. (N. Sharp) Engin. M. **9**: 1005.
Business Success, Essentials to. (E. Gray) Chaut. **15**: 302.
Business Troubles of 1893. Bank. M. (N. Y.) **49**: 119.
Buss, Frances Mary, and her Work for Education. (J. E. Bulkley) School R. **4**: 635.
Bussaco in 1810. (J. de S. Silvestre) Gent. M. n. s. **52**: 281. Same art. Liv. Age, **199**: 292. Same art. Ecl. M. **121**: 530.
But also; a poem. (Hunter MacCulloch) Cosmopol. **16**: 331.
But an Envelope. (L. A. Dawson) Temp. Bar, **106**: 388.
But Men must work; a story. (R. N. Carey) Lippinc. **49**: 387.
Bute, Marquis of; the Man and the Town. (F. Dolman) Eng. Illust. **12**: no. 1, 8.
Butler, Arthur G. Poems. Spec. **68**: 303.
Butler, B. F. Pub. Opin. **14**: 370. — With portraits. (H. P. Judson) R. of Rs. (N. Y.) **7**: 169.
— Butler's Book. (J. D. Cox) Nation, **54**: 195.
— — Gen. W. F. Smith's Reply to. (J. D. Cox) Nation, **56**: 387.
Butler, Lady Eleanor. Gent. M. n. s. **55**: 401.
Butler, Mrs. Elizabeth Thompson. (J. Oldcastle) M. of Art, **2**: 257.
Butler, Joseph. (W. E. Gladstone) Good Words, **37**: 73–348. Same art. Chr. Lit. **14**: 234–475.
— Analogy of Religion to Nature. (T. F. Wright) N. Church R. **3**: 241.
— and his Censors. (W. E. Gladstone) 19th Cent. **38**: 715, 1056. Same art. Chr. Lit. **14**: 113.
— Gladstone and. (R. A. Armstrong) New World, **5**: 691.
— His Apologist. (L. Stephen) 19th Cent. **39**: 106. Same art. Chr. Lit. **14**: 502, 612.
— Works, edited by W. E. Gladstone. (J. Cooper) Bib. Sac. **53**: 494. — (C. A. L. Richards) Dial (Ch.) **20**: 232. — Church Q. **42**: 202. **43**: 1. — (J. Cooper) Ref. Q. **43**: 186, 441. — Book R. **3**: 308.
Butler, Marion. (C. Snyder) R. of Rs. (N. Y.) **14**: 429.
Buto, Megalithic Temple at. (A. W. Verrall) J. Hel. Stud. **16**: 158.
Butte County, Cal., and the Northern Citrus Belt. (S. G. Wilson) Overland, n. s. **27**: 419.
Butter-making, Danish. (Mrs. A. Tweedie) Fortn. **63**: 819.
Buttercups; a story. (E. Hatchett-Jackson) Gent. M. n. s. **54**: 325.
Butterflies at the London Zoo, 1893. Spec. **70**: 668.
— Among the. (W. Seton) Cath. World, **62**: 302.
— Bird-winged, of the East. (W. F. Kirby) Nature, **51**: 254.
— Colors of. (C. F. Marshall) Knowl. **18**: 128.
— Development of, under Artificial Conditions. Nature, **53**: 540.
— that come to Town. (M. E. Bamford) Overland, n. s. **22**: 639.
Butterflies; a Tale of Nature. (J. L. Allen) Cosmopol. **20**: 158–533.
Butterfly, The. (M. Dawson) Lippinc. **55**: 543.
— Training a. (Mrs. P. M. Goulèe) Cosmopol. **17**: 272.
Butterfly Episode; Moorland Idyll. (G. Allen) Eng. Illust. **12**: no. 6, 33.
Butterfly Years. (G. A. B. Dewar) Temp. Bar, **108**: 593.
Butters, William M., with portrait. Nat'l M. (N. Y. '91) **16**: 729.
Buttre, John Chester, with portrait. Nat'l M. (N. Y. '91) **19**: 203.
Buzelle, George B. Char. R. **2**: 432.
Buzzard's Bay, On the Shores of. (E. F. Kimball) New Eng. M. n. s. **7**: 3.
Bwlch yr Ddawfaen. (H. H. Lines) Antiq. n. s. **26**: 58, 100.
By Accident; a story. (H. F. Abell) Chamb. J. **70**: 135–184.
By Fair Woodcraft; a story. Temp. Bar, **101**: 579.
By Hook or Crook; a story. (R. Grant) Harper, **90**: 884.
By the Judgment of God; a tale. (R. F. Dixon) Canad. M. **5**: 263.
By Kibesillah. (V. Shanet) Overland, n. s. **26**: 540.
By Land and Sea. (H. Pyle) Harper, **92**: 3.
By the Light of a Camp-Fire; a story. Argosy, **58**: 248. Same art. Liv. Age, **203**: 286.
By the Light of the Lamp; a story. (H. Newman) Idler, **3**: 642.
By Right of Succession; a story. (E. Stuart) All the Year, **70**: 1–553.
By Right of Trove; a story. (Julie M. Lippmann) Overland, n. s. **20**: 11.
By Right of Womanhood; a story. Temp. Bar, **102**: 109.
By the Sea; a poem. (T. H. Rand) Canad. M. **3**: 94.
By Special Invitation. (F. Lynde) Scrib. M. **16**: 746.
By Telephone; a story. (F. E. Regal) Lippinc. **55**: 126.
By the Waters of Babylon. (J. B. Hopkins) Time, **6**: 694. **7**: 56–521.
Bynner, Edwin Lasseter. (E. E. Hale) New Eng. M. n. s. **9**: 568.
Byrne, Mrs. William Pitt. Ath. '**94**, **1**: 446.
Byrom, John. Temp. Bar, **104**: 563. **105**: 68. — (L. Stephen) National, **27**: 208.
— — and the Beginnings of Methodism. (J. Telford) Meth. R. **54**: 9.
Byron, Lord. (C. A. Price) Belgra. **80**: 137.
— and the Greek Patriots. (H. Hayman) Harper, **88**: 365.
— Chats with Jane Clermont concerning. (W. Graham) 19th Cent. **34**: 753.
— Glimpses of. (H. Hayman) Liv. Age, **192**: 41.
— In the Footsteps of. (E. L. Didier) Munsey, **14**: 422.
— Poems, ed. by Ward. Sat. R. **81**: 229.
— Some Portraits of. (F. G. Kitton) M. of Art, **17**: 253.
— Sonority of. (S. R. Elliot) Critic, **22**: 303.
— Unpublished Letters of. Bookworm, **6**: 45.
— Works of, edited by W. E. Henley. Acad. **50**: 551
Byron, Henry James. Fourteen Days; a comedy. Theatre, **28**: 153.
Byzantine Architecture. Ed. R. **181**: 460.
Byzantine Art and Culture in Italy. (A. L. Frothingham, jr.) Am. J. Archæol. **10**: 152.
Byzantine Artists in Italy, 6th–15th Cent. Am. J. Archæol. **9**: 32.

Cabane, La; a story. (W. McLennan) Harper, **84**: 702.
Cabanel, Alexandre. (A. Meynell) M. of Art, **9**: 271. — (C. S. Johnson) Munsey, **6**: 635.
Cabbages and Kings. Macmil. **72**: 134. Same art. Liv. Age, **206**: 240.
Cabinet, English, History of, Torrens's. Ed. R. **181**: 116.
Cabinet Council, In. (H. D. Traill) National, **22**: 400.
Cabinet Government in the U. S. (F. Snow) Ann. Am. Acad. Pol. Sci. **3**: 1.
Cabinet Minister, How I became a. Time, **3**: 233.

Cabinet Organ, The; a story. (O. Thanet) Harper, **93**: 238.
Cable, Geo. W., with portrait. Bk. Buyer, **2**: 246. — With portrait. Bk. News, **5**: 187.
— and Mrs. Dora Richards Miller. Critic, **22**: 63. — (Mrs. D. R. Miller) Critic, **22**: 167.
— Portraits of. McClure, **1**: 392.
Cable, the Bahama, How we saw. Chamb. J. **69**: 470.
— Electric, Improvements in. (E. Guillaume) Cassier, **4**: 463.
— Submarine, Laying a. (F. A. Hamilton) Canad. M. **4**: 469.
Cable-laying on the Amazon. (A. Siemens) Nature, **54**: 162.
Cable Railroad, Broadway, New York. (G. Iles) Engin. M. **4**: 351.
Cable Street-railway, The. (P. G. Hubert, jr.) Scrib. M. **15**: 371.
Cable-ways for Unloading Vessels. (W. Hewitt) Cassier, **8**: 448.
Cables, Submarine, of the World, with Chart. (G. Herrle) Nat. Geog. M. **7**: 102. — (M. P. Handy) New Sci. R. **1**: 347.
— Two New Atlantic. Chamb. J. **71**: 303.
— Value of all-British. (D. Osborn) Canad. M. **7**: 74.
Cabmen, London, and their Grievances. Spec. **71**: 364.
Cabot, John and Sebastian, Harrisse on. Am. Hist. R. **1**: 717. — Sat. R. **81**: 255.
Cabot, Sebastian. (E. H. McIntosh) Canad. M. **8**: 150.
Cabot Celebration, 1896. (J. Pope) Canad. M. **8**: 158.
Cabotiana. (J. Winsor) Nation, **57**: 433.
Cabots, The, and Columbus. (F. M. Holland) Open Court, **6**: 3474.
Cab's Father; a story. (Mrs. H. H. Penrose) Temp. Bar, **105**: 540. Same art. Liv. Age, **206**: 593.
Cabul, Campaign in, 1848. (F. Dixon) Temp. Bar, **99**: 27.
Cacao in the Sierra Nevada, Colombia. J. Soc. Arts, **42**: 726.
Cache-cache; a story. (W. McLennan) Harper, **88**: 528.
Cachuca Amorita; a story. (W. de Meza) Cosmopol. **14**: 481.
Cacti at the Columbian Exposition. (L. H. Bailey) Garden & F. **6**: 429.
Cactus, The. Around World, **1**: 83.
— Cereus Pecten-aboriginum. Garden & F. **7**: 334.
— Echinocactus Wislizeni. (J. W. Taumey) Garden & F. **8**: 154.
— Opuntias in Mexico. (J. W. Taumey) Garden & F. **9**: 2.
— Prickly Pear. (G. Allen) Longm. **19**: 377. Same art. Pop. Sci. Mo. **41**: 109.
Cactus Garden, Arizona. (J. W. Taumey) Garden & F. **9**: 432.
Cacus on a Black-figured Vase. (P. Gardner) J. Hel. Stud. **13**: 70.
Cad, The; a story. (M. Holland) Belgra. **87**: 370.
Cade, Jack, Rebellion of. (J. Greenstreet) Walford's Antiq. **3**: 165.
Cader Idris, On the Slopes of. (W. W. Hunt) Good Words, **34**: 816.
Cadiz and Seville. (F. C. Sessions) M. W. Hist. **12**: 270.
Cadmium as the Oxide, Estimation of. (P. E. Browning and L. C. Jones) Am. J. Sci. **152**: 269.
Caen, France. (Comtesse de Courson) Cath. World, **59**: 815.
— a City of Suffering. Cornh. **73**: 620. Same art. Liv. Age, **210**: 252.
Caer Llion and Caer Seion. (H. H. Lines) Antiq. n. s. **30**: 263.
Caerleon-upon-Usk. (E. Walford) Walford's Antiq. **7**: 166.
Cæsar, Julius, Dodge's. (J. D. Cox) Nation, **50**: 70.
Cæsar, Julius, Cicero's Case against. Quar. **184**: 395.
— Fowler's. Sat. R. **73**: 747. — Spec. **69**: 470.
Cæsars, Tragedy of, Gould's. Ed. R. **178**: 55. — Quar. **179**: 512. Same art. Liv. Age, **203**: 643.
Caesium and Cadmium, Double Chlorides, Bromides and Iodides of. (H. L. Wells and P. T. Walden) Am. J. Sci. **146**: 425.
— and Rubidium Chloraurates and Bromaurates. (H. L. Wells and H. L. Wheeler) Am. J. Sci. **144**: 157.
— — Crystallography of. (S. L. Penfield) Am. J. Sci. **144**: 160.
— and Zinc, Double Chlorides, Bromides, and Iodides of. (H. L. Wells and G. F. Campbell) Am. J. Sci. **146**: 431.
— and Zirconium, Double Fluorides of. (H. L. Wells and H. W. Foote) Am. J. Sci. **151**: 18.
— Quantitative Determination of, Method for the. (H. L. Wells) Am. J. Sci. **146**: 186.
— Rubidium, etc. (J. H. Pratt) Am. J. Sci. **149**: 397.
Cæsium Chloride, Double Salts of. (H. L. Wells and B. B. Boltwood) Am. J. Sci. **150**: 249.
Cæsium-cupric Bromides. (H. L. Wells and P. T. Walden) Am. J. Sci. **147**: 94.
Cæsium-cupric Chlorides. (H. L. Wells and L. C. Dupee) Am. J. Sci. **147**: 91.
Cæsium-lead Halides. (W. L. Wells) Am. J. Sci. **145**: 121.
Cæsium-mercuric Halides. (H. L. Wells) Am. J. Sci. **144**: 221.
— Crystallography of. (S. L. Penfield) Am. J. Sci. **144**: 311.
Cæsium Trihalides, On a Series of. (H. L. Wells) Am. J. Sci. **143**: 17.
Caffieri, Jean-Jacques. M. of Art, **7**: 171.
Caffyn, M., with portrait. Bk. Buyer, **11**: 193.
Cahenslyism *versus* Americanism. (J. Conway) R. of Rs. (N. Y.) **6**: 43.
Caillebotte, Gustave. Bequest of Paintings to the Luxembourg. (J. Bernac) Art J. **47**: 230.
Cain: the Cainite Civilization. (W. R. Harper) Bib. World, **3**: 264.
Caine, Hall. Critic, **27**: 116. — (W. A. Sherwood) Canad. M. **6**: 166. — (R. H. Sherard) McClure, **6**: 80. — With portrait. Our Day, **16**: 151. — With portrait. Bk. Buyer, **9**: 421. — With portrait. Bk. News, **10**: 350.
— Dinner to. Critic, **27**: 307.
— My First Book. Chr. Un. **46**: 408, 451. — Idler, **2**: 235.
— The Manxman. (H. Tattersall) Acad. **46**: 128. — Sat. R. **78**: 360.
— Novels of. (G. Saintsbury) Fortn. **63**: 180. Same art. Ecl. M. **124**: 818.
— Portraits of. McClure, **4**: 442.
Caird, Edward. (J. Iverach) Chr. Lit. **10**: 152 a.
— Essays. Ath. '92, **2**: 122.
Caird, Sir James. (P. G. Craigie) Econ. J. **2**: 196. — Sat. R. **73**: 173.
Caird, John. (A. Jenkinson) M. Chr. Lit. **7**: 161.
— in Glasgow University. (A. W. Stewart) Sund. M. **25**: 592.
Cairngorm in Winter. Chamb. J. **69**: 278.
Cairns, H. J., Earl, with portrait. Green Bag, **6**: 1. — (G. W. Hemming) Law Q. **1**: 365.
Cairns, John. (W. Wallace) Acad. **47**: 539. — M. Chr. Lit. **6**: 136.
— Life and Letters of. (A. Macewan) Presb. & Ref. R. **7**: 155.
Cairo, Egypt, Ancient Buildings at. Sat. R. **74**: 277.
— From Cape Town to. (H. W. Lucy) Fortn. **61**: 410.
— Old and New. (S. Lane-Poole) Sat. R. **80**: 863.
Cairo Scandal; a story. Temp. Bar, **104**: 427, 575.

Caithness, Summer in. (H. Maxwell) Blackw. 160: 16. Same art. Ecl. M. 127: 205.
Caithness Folk-Lore, Fragments of. (Frank Rinder) Scot. R. 26: 49.
Cajanello, Anne C. L., Duchess of. Ath. '92, 2: 630.
Cakes and Ale. (A. Repplier) Atlan. 78: 472.
Calabonna, Lake, South Australia, Recent Discovery of Fossil Remains at. (E. C. Stirling) Nature, 50: 184, 206.
Calabria, In. (G. W. Wood) Sund. M. 23: 168.
Calachortus, Cultivation of. (J. W. Gerard) Garden & F. 7: 255.
Caladiums. (E. O. Orpet) Garden & F. 9: 137.
— Cultivation of. (E. O. Orpet) Garden & F. 7: 177.
Calais, France. Sat. R. 75: 568.
— Journey to, in 1814. Argosy, 53: 16. Same art. Liv. Age, 192: 633.
Calais Gate, Hogarth's Picture of. (A. Dobson) M. of Art, 6: 508.
Calaverite from Cripple Creek, Colo. (W. F. Hillebrand) Am. J. Sci. 150: 128.
Calcium, Qualitative Separation of. (R. B. Riggs) Am. J. Sci. 143: 135. — (P. E. Browning) Am. J. Sci. 143: 386.
Calculating Machines. (H. S. Davis) Pop. Astron. 4: 20.
Calculus, Logical. (W. E. Johnson) Mind, 17: 3-140.
Calcutta and Madras. All the Year, 75: 569.
— Chinee Town in. Chamb. J. 72: 289.
— Royal Botanic Garden. Nature, 50: 308.
— Zoo in. (C. T. Buckland) Longm. 21: 468.
Caldecott, Randolph. (E. S. F. Dilke) Art J. 47: 138, 203. — (J. Grego) M. of Art, 10: 181.
Calder, River, in Yorkshire. Walford's Antiq. 6: 214, 263.
Calderon, Philip Hermogenes. (W. W. Fenn) M. of Art, 1: 197.
Caldonia of Red Cloud; a story. (L. H. Shuey) Overland, n. s. 19: 239.
Caldwell, Henry Clay. (J. B. Follett) Arena, 16: 177.
Calendar, The. (R. W. McFarland) Pop. Astron. 3: 441.
— Automatic, Prentiss. J. Frankl. Inst. 142: 98.
— Curiosities of the. (C. Flammarion) Cosmopol. 20: 560.
— Sacred, and Ancient Codices. (S. D. Peet) Am. Antiq. 17: 175.
— Sacrificial, from the Epakria. (R. B. Richardson) Am. J. Archæol. 10: 209.
Calendar of State Papers, Colonial. Macmil. 75: 148.
Calhoun, John C., Letter of, 1847. Am. Hist. R. 1: 314.
— Rhind's Statue of. McClure, 5: 550.
— Seward and Lincoln. (J. M. Ashley) M. West. Hist. 12: 599. 13: 1.
Calhoun, John C., 2d (b. 1843). (M. J. Verdery) Nat'l M. (N. Y. '91) 15: 546.
Calhoun, Simeon H. (C. W. Butterfield) M. West. Hist. 9: 405.
Calhoun Colored School. (P. Dillingham) Lend a H. 15: 206.
Calico Printing, Progress in. (L. F. Day) Art J. 47: 50.
California, Account of. (G. C. Perkins) Nat. Geog. M. 7: 317, 368.
— Along Coast of. (J. T. Connor) Munsey, 9: 52.
— Among the Old Missions of. (J. T. Connor) Chaut. 22: 185.
— Ancient Islanders of. (C. F. Holder) Pop. Sci. Mo. 48: 658.
— and the Railroad. (J. P. Irish) Overland, n. s. 25: 675.
— Artists of. (C. S. Greene; P. N. Boeringer) Overland, n. s. 27: 34-501.
— Bear Flag of. (J. Bidwell) Overland, n. s. 25: 506.
California, Breadstuffs in, Production and Trade. (H. Davis) J. Pol. Econ. 2: 517.
— By Northern Rivers of. (Ninetta Eames) Overland, n. s. 23: 225.
— Churches of, 1849. (A. Inkersley) Overland, n. s. 25: 533.
— Conquest of. (A. G. Brackett) Un. Serv. (Phila.) 7: 591.
— Constitution of, Genesis of First, 1846-1849. (R. D. Hunt) J. H. Univ. Studies, 13: 361.
— Deserts of. Chamb. J. 69: 171.
— Domestic Service in. Lippinc. 57: 268.
— Early Missions of. (C. P. Dorland) Nat'l M. (N. Y. '91) 16: 275.
— Eras of. (H. H. Bancroft) Lippinc. 50: 391.
— Exhibit of, at the Atlanta Exposition. (J. A. Fulcher) Overland, n. s. 27: 387.
— Farm Village in. (W. C. Fitzsimmons) Cosmopol. 13: 420.
— Forests of, Observations in. (C. H. Shinn) Garden & F. 8: 402.
— From New Orleans to San Francisco in 1849. (Mrs. T. F. Bingham) Overland, n. s. 20: 189.
— Fruit Exchange of. (M. A. Sudduth) Chaut. 23: 247.
— Fruit-farming Fiasco in. (J. L. Macdonald) National, 25: 804.
— Fruit Ranching in. (A. C. Twist) 19th Cent. 36: 807.
— Fruits of. Garden & F. 8: 512.
— Growth of La Fiesta. (Mabel Craft) Bost. 4: 280.
— Highlands of, Morning Ride in. (E. A. Yore) Outing, 21: 291.
— History of the United States in Paragraphs. (C. L. Norton) M. Am. Hist. 29: 61.
— Irrigation in. (Wm. H. Hall) Nat. Geog. M. 1: 277.
— Irrigation Surveying in. (C. E. Fowler) Engin. M. 9: 421.
— Journalism in. (M. H. de Young) Lippinc. 50: 366, 469.
— Labor in. (C. C. Plehn) Yale R. 4: 409.
— Legal Lore of 1849. (E. L. Keyes) Overland, n. s. 26: 201.
— Lower. (J. K. Reeve) Lippinc. 53: 71.
— Mountains of. (C. S. Sargent) Garden & F. 9: 81.
— — Muir on. (A. M. Earle) Dial (Ch.) 18: 75. — (H. T. Finck) Nation, 59: 366.
— of the Future. (S. H. Scudder) Overland, n. s. 19: 383.
— Our Great Pacific Commonwealth. (W. E. Smythe) Cent. 31: 300.
— Physical and Industrial Geography of. (E. W. Hilgard) Geog. J. 1: 536.
— Pioneering in; Story of Margaret M. Hecox. (M. Valhasky) Overland, n. s. 19: 535. 20: 98.
— Placers, Old, and their Possibilities. (C. D. Robinson) Overland, n. s. 23: 296.
— A Province of. (F. F. Victor) Overland, n. s. 22: 96.
— Railroad Commission of. (S. E. Moffett) Ann. Am. Acad. Pol. Sci. 6: 469.
— Ranch Life in. (B. Harraden) Bookman, 1: 326.
— Redwood Forest, Flora of, in April. (Carl Purdy) Garden & F. 9: 272.
— Republic of. (T. Lindsey) Overland, n. s. 27: 218.
— Schools in, Early. (S. S. Boynton) Overland, n. s. 26: 553.
— — under Spanish Rule. (C. H. Shinn) Educa. R. 6: 30.
— Situation in. (W. A. Linn) Nation, 59: 23.
— Southern, County Division in. (E. B. Clarke) Overland, n. s. 20: 430.
— — Camping with Fox Hounds in. (H. E. Bandini) Overland, n. s. 19: 148.
— — Italy of America. Chamb. J. 70: 351.

California, Southern, Life in Sage-brush Lands of. (G. H. Bailey) Gent. M. n. s. 52: 488. Same art. Ecl. M. 122: 844.
— — Revisited. (H. T. Finck) Nation, 57: 282.
— — the Summerland of America. (J. T. Connor) Munsey, 8: 271.
— To, in 1849. (H. O. Hooper) Overland, n. s. 22: 318.
— Topography of. (W. C. Morrow) Lippinc. 50: 407.
— University of. (M. W. Shinn) Overland, n. s. 20: 337–585.
— — and Practical Life. (C. T. Hopkins) Overland, n. s. 19: 421.
— — Athletes at. Overland, n. s. 20: 8.
— Upland Pastures. (Ninetta Eames) Cosmopol. 20: 518.
— Voyage to, by Way of Panama. (H. M. North) New Eng. M. n. s. 11: 602.
— What Indiana has done for. (J. A. Woodson) Overland, n. s. 26: 131.
California Fish Patrol, An Outing with the. (P. Weaver, jr.) Overland, n. s. 22: 23.
California Fruit Supply of New York. Garden & F. 6: 432.
California Lion, Hunting the, with Fox-hounds. (H. E. Bandini) Overland, n. s. 19: 392.
California Midwinter International Exposition. (P. Weaver, jr.) Overland, n. s. 22: 449.
California Peasants. (C. H. Shinn) So. M. 5: 452.
California Pioneers, Chronicles of. (H. L. Conard) Nat'l M. (N. Y. '91) 17: 313, 571.
Californian; a story. (G. Bonner) Harper, 90: 512.
Californians, Famous, of Other Days. (J. J. Peatfield) Overland, n. s. 24: 640. 25: 115.
Caligula, Quidde's. Sat. R. 78: 346.
— Ship of, Ancient Bronzes from. (W. Mercer) M. of Art, 19: 359.
Call, Wathen M. W., Life and Last Work of. (M. D. Conway) Monist, 2: 183.
Call, The. (D. Lowry) New Eng. M. n. s. 12: 369.
Call to Duty; a story. (J. Lychenheim) Our Day, 15: 31.
Calloway, Geo. Frederick, with portrait. (H. D. Teetor) M. West. Hist. 13: 167.
Callcott, Sir Augustus Wall. (G. D. Leslie and F. A. Eaton) Art J. 48: 334.
Callender, James Thomson, and Thos. Jefferson. (W. C. Ford) N. E. Reg. 50: 321, 445.
Calligraphy, English. (E. F. Strange) Bibliographica, 3: 256.
— in the Middle Ages. (E. M. Thompson) Bibliographica, 3: 257.
Calmette, A., and his Anti-venomous Serum. (P. C. Mitchell) Sat. R. 82: 104.
Calmour, Alfred C. The Breadwinner. Theatre, 28: 252.
Calvé, Emma. (Julia F. Opp) Munsey, 14: 524. — (F. E. Sawyer) Music, 5: 595.
Calumet, The, in the Champlain Valley. (G. H. Perkins) Pop. Sci. Mo. 44: 238.
Calvert, Edward, artist. Sat. R. 77: 21. — (S. Calvert) Ath. '94, 2: 261.
— Calvert's Memoir of. (M. H. Spielmann) M. of Art, 17: 49.
Calverley, Charles S. (R. R. Wilson) Mo. Illust. 12: 485.
Calvin, John, and Calvinism. Lond. Q. 80: 205.
— and Servetus. (P. Schaff) Ref. Q. 40: 5.
— Doctrine of Holy Scripture. (D. Moore) Presb. & Ref. R. 4: 49.
— in his Home Life. (P. Schaff) Ref. Q. 39: 163.
— Misapprehensions Concerning. (O. T. Lanphear) Bib. Sac. 53: 401.
Calvinism, Future of. (H. Bavinck) Presb. & Ref. R. 5: 1.
— in the Light of Reason and the Scripture. (P. Schaff) And. R. 17: 330.
— Misadventures of, in Scotland. National, 19: 419.
— the Origin and Safeguard of our Constitutional Liberties. (A. Kuyper) Bib. Sac. 52: 385, 646.
— Reformed Protestantism and Foreign Missions. (N. M. Steffens) Presb. & Ref. R. 5: 241.
Calypso. (M. G. Watkins) Gent. M. n. s. 50: 568.
Calypso Borealis. (E. I. Denny) Overland, n. s. 22: 113.
Cambodia, Life in, Incidents of. (A. Leclère) Pop. Sci. Mo. 44: 776.
Cambodian Primary School, A. (A. Leclère) Pop. Sci. Mo. 49: 688.
Cambray, League of, An Episode in the War of. Macmil. 74: 211.
Cambrian and Ozark Series. (G. C. Broadhead) Am. J. Sci. 146: 57.
— in Missouri, Notes on. (A. Winslow) Am. J. Sci. 145: 221.
Cambrian Rocks, Lower, in Eastern California. (C. D. Walcott) Am. J. Sci. 149: 141.
— of Pa., from Susquehanna to the Delaware. (C. D. Walcott) Am. J. Sci. 144: 469. 147: 37.
— of Virginia, etc., Notes on. (C. D. Walcott) Am. J. Sci. 144: 52.
Cambridge, Duke of, Transformation of Army by. (J. L. A. Simmons) 19th Cent. 38: 889.
Cambridge, Richard Owen. (A. Dobson) Temp. Bar, 108: 67.
Cambridge [Eng.], Apostles of, 1830. (R. Noel) New R. 8: 559. Same art. Ecl. M. 121: 12.
— in Winter. (A. G. Hyde) Atlan. 71: 185.
— Old Road to. All the Year, 74: 444.
Cambridge Antiquarian Society Publications. Eng. R. 4: 155.
Cambridge Teachers' College, Life at. (M. M. Hammond) Sund. M. 25: 470.
Cambridge University, Ethics in. (J. S. Mackenzie) Eth. Rec. 3: 35.
— Fitzwilliam Museum, Pictures at. (S. Colvin) M. of Art, 6: 122, 478.
— Hebrew MSS. in. (S. Schechter) Jew. Q. 4: 90, 245, 626. 5: 18–350. 6: 136.
— of To-day. Lit. W. (Bost.) 24: 256.
— Oxford *versus*. Temp. Bar, 101: 371.
— Post-graduate Study at. Nature, 52: 296.
— Science Scholarships at. Nature, 52: 271.
Cambridge, Mass., License and No-license in. (F. Foxcroft) New Eng. M. n. s. 13: 53.
Camel as a Freight-carrier in Australia. (E. Mitchell) Engin. M. 6: 70. — Chamb. J. 71: 767. — Dub. R. 116: 192.
— in the Army. Spec. 72: 785.
— Leonard on the. Sat. R. 78: 130.
— Transport by, Limits of. Spec. 74: 497.
Camel Corps. (C. Napier) Un. Serv. M. 11: 266.
Camelford, Thomas Pitt, Baron. (C. B. Angier) Argosy, 60: 25.
Camelot in Bond Street; a poem. (A. Lang) M. of Art, 7: 375.
— of Romance. (E. Capper) Good Words, 35: 37.
— Talk at a Country House. (E. Strachey) Atlan. 73: 46.
Cameo, A, and a Pastel. (B. Matthews) Harper, 86: 130.
Camera, and a Conscience, A; a story. (W. A. McClean) Nat'l M. (Bost.) 4: 425.
Camera-obscura, The; a story. (J. S. Fletcher) Chamb. J. 70: 589, 605.

Cameron, V. Lovett. Ath. '94, 1: 414. — Nature, 49: 537. — Nat. Sci. 4: 391.
Cameroons, The Peak of. (Mary H. Kingsley) National, 27: 357.
— — Throne of Thunder. Liv. Age, 209: 623.
Camorra, The American. (F. L. Oswald) Open Court, 5: 2723.
— Maffia, and Brigandage. (S. Merlino) Pol. Sci. Q. 9: 466. *See* Maffia.
Camp Chocorua; a Boy's Republic. (A. Balch) McClure, 1: 242.
Camp Cookery. (A. D. Gillette and W. S. McAndrew) Outing, 28: 120.
Camp Experience. (E. Stewart) Canad. M. 1: 475.
Campaign. *See* Political Campaign.
Campaniles, Italian. (E. M. Hurll) New Eng. M. n. s. 9: 322.
Campanini, Italo. Ath. '96, 2: 764.
Campbell, Colin. Letters from Camp during the Siege of Sebastopol. Macmil. 71: 393.
Campbell, Douglass, with portrait. Bk. Buyer, 10: 104.
Campbell, Mrs. Frederick, in "Magda." Sat. R. 81: 575.
Campbell, Fremont, with portrait. (W. L. Visscher) M. West. Hist. 13: 293.
Campbell, Sir George. Memoirs. Sat. R. 75: 547. — Spec. 68: 293.
Campbell, James Dykes. (T. Hutchinson) Acad. 50: 114. — (A. Symons) Acad. 47: 482. — (A. Ainger and W. Besant) Ath. '95, 1: 738. — (L. Stephen) Ath. '95, 1: 773.
Campbell, John McLeod. (A. M. Machar) And. R. 17: 549. 18: 591.
Campbell, Mrs. Patrick, as Juliet, with portrait. Theatre, 36: 5.
Campbell, Thomas. (Mary C. Agnew) Temp. Bar, 107: 116.
Campbell, William Wilfred. (C. A. Scott) Canad. M. 2: 270.
Campbell MSS. at Edinburgh. (A. Nutt) Folk-Lore, 1: 369.
Camphor. Nature, 54: 116.
Camping, Family. (E. H. Palmer) Outing, 26: 479.
— near Point Conception Light-house. (Bessie Taylor) Overland, n. s. 20: 39.
Camping Out for the Poor. (P. G. Hubert, jr.) Cent. 22: 632.
— Outfit for. (W. H. Hobbs) Outing, 26: 207.
Camptosaurus, Restoration of. (O. C. Marsh) Am. J. Sci. 147: 245.
Can it be? a poem. (W. W. Fries) Arena, 8: 392.
Canaan, History of, Sketch of, to 1000 B. C. (G. S. Goodspeed) Bib. World, 7: 459.
Canaanites, Alleged Cruelty of God to. (C. A. Hobbs) Bapt. R. 14: 455.
Canada, Dominion of. (J. G. Bourinot) Scot. R. 26: 22. — (W. H. Withrow) Chaut. 21: 565, 695.
— and the Canadian Pacific Railway. (J. C. Hopkins) Westm. 140: 154.
— and the Empire. (G. M. Grant) National, 27: 673. Same art. Canad. M. 8: 73. — Spec. 75: 329. — (G. F. Denison) Westm. 144: 248.
— and Imperial Federation. (J. F. Hogan) Westm. 141: 1.
— and Irish Home Rule Bill of 1893. (H. H. L. Bellot) Westm. 139: 469.
— and U. S. Tariff, 1893. (E. Wiman) Engin. M. 6: 125.
— and U. S., Political Reunion of. (L. Irwell) Am. J. Pol. 4: 430. — (F. W. Glen) Am. J. Pol. 3: 561.
— Annexation of. (W. S. Evans) Am. J. Pol. 4: 201. — (V. R. Andrew) Am. J. Pol. 4: 132. — Pub. Opin. 14: 349, 442.
Canada, Annexation of. Can she be coerced into the Union? (J. C. Murray) Open Court, 9: 4561.
— — Canadian Hostility to. (J. G. Hopkins) Forum, 16: 325.
— — Why Canadians do not favor. (J. G. Bourinot) Forum, 19: 276.
— as a Field for Mining Investment. (G. M. Dawson) National, 28: 242.
— as a Hostage. (E. W. Thomson) No. Am. 162: 119.
— Banking System of, Advantages of. (D. R. Wilkie) Forum, 13: 325.
— Britain, and the United States. Westm. 145: 28.
— Camping in, at the Sign of the Balsam Bough. (H. van Dyke) Harper, 91: 674.
— Canal System of. (A. R. Davis) Chaut. 17: 302.
— Change of Government of. (S. R. Tarr) Bach. of Arts, 3: 378.
— Church and State in. (G. R. Stetson) And. R. 17: 476.
— Civilization in, Contrasts of. Macmil. 67: 133.
— Colonial Conference, Ottawa. (J. L. Payne) Asia. R. 18: 353.
— A Colonial Court. (M. Mackenzie) Munsey, 12: 365.
— Confederation of, Twenty-nine Years of. (F. Yeigh) Canad. M. 7: 228.
— Conquest of, English. Eng. R. 12: 153. — (F. A. Roe) Am. Hist. Reg. 2: 1218.
— Constitution of. (E. Meek) Am. Law R. 29: 32. — (E. Meek) Canad. M. 3: 425. — (J. E. C. Munro) Law Q. 4: 184. — (J. G. Bourinot) Jurid. 2: 131, 209.
— — and the U. S. Constitution. (J. A. Cooper) Canad. M. 2: 415.
— Country Walk in. (A. Haultain) Blackw. 155: 143.
— Democracy and Socialism in. (J. A. Cooper) Canad. M. 3: 332.
— Destiny of. Pub. Opin. 14: 224.
— Did Lord Durham write his own Report on? (M. J. Griffin) Canad. M. 7: 521.
— Election in, Humors of an. (W. F. Stockley) Macmil. 68: 52. Same art. Liv. Age, 198: 380.
— Electoral Representation in. (S. Fleming) Am. J. Pol. 1: 262.
— English Settlement of. Macmil. 74: 177.
— Federal Government and the Distribution of Power in. (E. Meek) Am. Law R. 30: 203.
— Feeling of, for U. S. (D. C. Scott) Bookman, 3: 333.
— Finances of, and the Home Rule Bill. (H. H. L. Bellot) Westm. 140: 1.
— Fishing Trip in. (A. Haggard) Blackw. 153: 688.
— French, and the Empire. (J. C. Hopkins) Un. Serv. M. 10: 19.
— — Jean Baptiste and his Language. (H. A. Kennedy) Contemp. 69: 500. Same art. Liv. Age, 209: 387.
— — Restless. (G. Stewart) No. Am. 159: 379.
— Frontenac in. (G. Stewart) Cosmopol. 21: 427.
— Future of, as seen by Canadians. (H. Gregory-Flesher) Am. M. Civics, 6: 281.
— Geographical Work in, 1893. (G. M. Dawson) Geog. J. 3: 206.
— Governor-General, Functions of. (W. P. Reeves) National, 28: 554.
— The Great British Northwest Territory. (Lee Meriwether) Cosmopol. 18: 15.
— Great Plains of. (C. A. Kenaston) Cent. 22: 565.
— History of; First Annexation of, 1760. (J. G. Nicolay) Chaut. 14: 650.
— — Downfall of New France. (J. G. Nicolay) Chaut. 15: 269.
— — Fourth Century. (O. A. Howland) Canad. M. 4: 199.

Canada, History of; Jesuit Relations. (J. M. Parker) New Eng. M. n. s. **10**: 354.
— — Kingsford's. (G. W. Wrong) Am. Hist. R. **1**: 550. — Sat. R. **74**: 488. **77**: 103.
— Homes of. (J. Young) Canad. M. **3**: 512.
— in 1761. M. Am. Hist. **27**: 62.
— Institutions of, Character of. (J. G. Bourinot) Contemp. **62**: 590.
— Interest and Loyalty in. (E. Wiman) Contemp. **62**: 240.
— Lake Mestassini and James' Bay. (A. H. D. Ross) Canad. M. **3**: 573.
— Life in, by S. Moodie. Eng. R. **17**: 379.
— Literature in Western. (H. Scadding) Canad. M. **2**: 395.
— Local Self-government. (H. H. L. Bellot) Westm. **140**: 281.
— Loyalty of. Quar. **183**: 397.
— Military College, Kingston. Canad. M. **4**: 428.
— Militia of, Active. (J. H. Woodside) Outing, **19**: 323.
— Mission and Destiny of. (W. T. Stead) R. of Rs. (N. Y.) **9**: 61.
— Mortgage, Loan, and Building Companies of. (J. Hague) Bank. M. (N. Y.) **50**: 627.
— National Policy of, Anti-national Features of. (G. M. Grant) Canad. M. **1**: 9.
— National Song of. (J. A. Cooper) Canad. M. **6**: 176.
— National State. (C. A. Stuart) Canad. M. **1**: 85.
— Normal Schools of. (S. B. Sinclair) Pedagog. Sem. **3**: 461.
— Northern, Expedition through. (J. B. Tyrrell) Geog. J. **4**: 437.
— — Second Expedition through the Barren Lands of. (J. B. Tyrrell) Geog. J. **6**: 438.
— Northern Pikes. (W. B. Worsfold) Fortn. **58**: 539. Same art. Liv. Age, **195**: 549.
— Northwest. (M. Davitt) 19th Cent. **31**: 631. Same art. Ecl. M. **118**: 721. — (J. Nelson) Westm. **139**: 286.
— — American Emigration to. (S. A. Thompson) New Eng. M. n. s. **13**: 179.
— — Experiences in. (G. M. Standing) Canad. M. **5**: 309.
— — Her Majesty's Sporting Grounds. Outing, **20**: 81.
— — Mounted Policeman of. (H. C. Thomson) Canad. M. **8**: 10.
— — Rebellion, 1885. Un. Serv. M. **13**: 408, 524.
— — — Chapter from. (G. B. Brooks) Canad. M. **1**: 471.
— — — Suppression of. (F. Middleton) Un. Serv. M. **8**: 103-517.
— — Somerset's Travels in. Dub. R. **117**: 451.
— — Through the Sub-arctics. (J. W. Tyrrell) Canad. M. **7**: 411, 524. **8**: 35.
— Northwestern Forces of. (H. J. Woodside) Outing, **25**: 159.
— Paper Currencies of, 1685-1766. (R. M. Breckenridge) J. Pol. Econ. **1**: 406.
— Parliament, Dissolutions of. (M. J. Griffin) Canad. M. **7**: 3.
— — Member for the University. (T. Hodgins) Canad. M. **5**: 115.
— — Quintette of Veterans. (J. E. Atkinson) Canad. M. **6**: 427.
— a Poem. (G. W. Armstrong) Canad. M. **6**: 314.
— Policy, Want of a, in. (L. Irwell) Am. J. Pol. **1**: 628.
— Political Conditions of. (J. W. Longley) R. of Rs. (N. Y.) **10**: 160.
— Politics in, 1892, Cross Currents of. Westm. **137**: 641.
— — 1896. (J. W. Russell) R. of Rs. (N. Y.) **13**: 311.
— — Elections and their Result. (J. W. Russell) No. Am. **163**: 156. — (T. C. L. Ketchum) Am. M. Civics, **9**: 83.
Canada, Politics in, Significance of. (G. Stewart) Forum, **21**: 753.
— Position of. (J. C. Hopkins) Asia. R. **16**: 123.
— Present Position of. (L. Irwell) Asia. R. **14**: 365. — (L. Irwell) Westm. **138**: 294. **139**: 660. — (A. Haultain) Westm. **139**: 39.
— Progress of. Ed. R. **181**: 253. — Liv. Age, **205**: 451.
— Railway Development. (A. R. Davis) Chaut. **16**: 435.
— Religious Differences in. Sat. R. **79**: 469.
— Rise and Fall of New France. (F. J. Turner) Chaut. **24**: 31.
— Rod and Gun in. Outing, **20**: 241.
— Royal Military College. Canad. M. **4**: 376.
— Sacrament Week in the Lake Megantic Region. (M. Ross) Canad. M. **4**: 449.
— School Expenditures in. (R. G. Huling) Educa. **16**: 104.
— Sir John Schultz and the "Canada First" Party. (G. T. Dennison) Canad. M. **8**: 16.
— Science in. Science, n. s. **1**: 653.
— Scientific Investigation in. (G. M. Dawson) Nature, **51**: 236.
— Separate School Question in. (S. R. Tarr) Educa. R. **12**: 180.
— Singers of. (J. D. Miller) Munsey, **13**: 128.
— Goldwin Smith on. (C. G. D. Roberts) Dial (Ch.) **13**: 387.
— Society in. Spec. **68**: 852.
— — Past and Present. (Lady Jephson) New R. **9**: 85.
— Some Thoughts on. (Marquis of Lorne) No. Am. **160**: 712.
— Strong Men of. (E. M. Smith) Munsey, **15**: 344.
— Struggle for, Maryland's Attitude in. (J. W. Black) J. H. Univ. Studies, **10**: no. 7.
— Tariff of. Pub. Opin. **17**: 16.
— under British Rule. (H. L. Nelson) Harper, **87**: 100.
— Winter Pastimes in. (E. W. Sandys) Outing, **21**: 183.
— Winter Sports in. (R. S. Osborne) Munsey, **12**: 492.
— What then does Canada want? Macmil. **67**: 299.
— Wheat in, Production of. (S. C. D. Roper) Canad. M. **3**: 468.
— Winsor's Cartier to Frontenac. (J. D. Butler) Nation, **58**: 351.
Canada Company. (W. Clark) Canad. M. **8**: 181.
Canada National Park. (J. J. Bell) Canad. M. **2**: 265.
Canadian in New York. (E. Myers) Canad. M. **1**: 435.
Canadian Banking System, Breckenridge's. (F. E. Steele) Econ. J. **5**: 233.
Canadian Bank Stocks as Investments. (W. W. L. Chipman) Bank. M. (N. Y.) **50**: 899.
Canadian Club Movement. (W. S. Evans) Canad. M. **2**: 22.
Canadian Girl. (H. W. Charlesworth) Canad. M. **1**: 186.
Canadian Girl; a sketch. (R. Gourlay) Canad. M. **7**: 506.
Canadian Ghost Story; a tale. (H. H. Gowe) Canad. M. **1**: 682.
Canadian Historical Exhibition, 1897. (O. A. Howland) Canad. M. **7**: 165.
Canadian Immigrants. (A. Paterson) National, **25**: 399.
Canadian Literature. Dial (Ch.) **16**: 259.
Canadian Military College. Canad. M. **4**: 261.
Canadian Pacific Railway. (N. Gastin) Art. J. **44**: 169, 233. — (J. M. Oxley) Canad. M. **6**: 522. — (J. M. Oxley) Lippinc. **53**: 801. — (E. J. Devine) Month, **82**: 109, 345. **83**: 107. — (J. N. Porter) Time, **15**: 553.
— Canada and. (J. C. Hopkins) Westm. **140**: 154.
Canadian Pacific Steamships. (H. Fry) Canad. M. **3**: 173.
Canadian Poetry. (G. Waldron) Canad. M. **8**: 101.

Canadian Poets and Poetry, with portraits. (T. O'Hagan) Cath. World, 61: 783.
Canadian Short-story Writers. (A. D. Brodie) Canad. M. 4: 334.
Canadian Statute Book, An Old Provincial. (B. Russell) Canad. M. 1: 609.
Canadian Types; Artillery Bugler. (A. H. H. Heming) Canad. M. 6: 575.
Canadians, French. (H. J. Jephson) National, 21: 51. Same art. Liv. Age, 197: 435. Same art. Ecl. M. 120: 588.
— — in New England. (H. L. Nelson) Harper, 87: 180. — (P. Bender) New Eng. M. n. s. 6: 569.
— — Traditional Beliefs of. All the Year, 74: 484.
— — The U. S. for. (L. H. Frechette) Forum, 16: 336.
Canal, Ship, between New York and Philadelphia, Proposed. (L. M. Haupt) J. Frankl. Inst. 133: 172.
Canals, from Amsterdam to the Rhine. Dub. R. 111: 452.
— Great. (A. G. Menocal) Chaut. 20: 295.
— in Holland. Cornh. 65: 146. Same art. Liv. Age, 192: 810.
— of Commerce, The. (L. M. Haupt) New Sci. R. 1: 76.
— of the U. S. (J. A. Harman) Un. Serv. (Phila.) 14: 358.
— St. Lawrence Route. (A. R. Davis) Canad. M. 3: 148.
— Ship. (L. M. Haupt) J. Frankl. Inst. 134: 339.
— — Projects for. Pub. Opin. 19: 580. — (D. MacG. Means) Nation, 61: 180.
Canal-boat Propulsion, Electric. (J. Sachs) Cassier, 5: 500.
Canal System of Canada. (A. R. Davis) Chaut. 17: 302.
Canary, The. (P. White) New R. 12: 625.
Canary Culture. Spec. 73: 44.
Canary Islanders. (C. R. Conder) Scot. R. 19: 272.
Canary Islands. Eng. R. 15: 411.
— Ancient Inhabitants of. (J. W. Gambier) Antiq. n. s. 29: 15–94.
— Impressions of the. (H. Lynch) Good Words, 37: 736, 830.
Cancer, Electrical Cure of. (E. Faithful) Contemp. 61: 408. Same art. Ecl. M. 118: 591.
— Increase of. (H. P. Dunn) New R. 9: 393.
Cancerous Diseases, Parasitic Protozoa found in. (A. Bodington) Am. Natural. 28: 307.
Candid Friend, The. All the Year, 73: 465.
Candidate, The; a story. Liv. Age, 192: 361.
Candidate at Binnacle. (B. A. Goodridge) New Eng. M. n. s. 6: 796.
Candidate for West Drum; a story. (W. E. Hodgson) National, 19: 675. Same art. Ecl. M. 119: 375.
Candidates, Criticism of, Right of. (D. H. Pingrey) Am. Law R. 27: 14.
Candle-making. (J. Hatton) Eng. Illust. 9: 703.
Candolle, Alphonse de. (G. L. Goodale) Am. J. Sci. 146: 236. — Ath. '93, 1: 476. — Nat. Sci. 2: 396. — (W. T. Thiselton-Dyer) Nature, 48: 269.
Canfieldite, a New Germanium Mineral. (S. L. Penfield) Am. J. Sci. 146: 107.
Canine Pets; a poem. (W. C. Olmsted) Outing, 27: 356.
Canna Italia. Garden & F. 9: 134.
Cannabis Indica, Consciousness under the Influence of. (E. W. Scripture) Science, 22: 233.
Cannas. (T. D. Hatfield) Garden & F. 8: 367.
— at Bay Ridge, N. Y. (J. N. Gerard) Garden & F. 5: 478.
— at Tarrytown, N. Y. Garden & F. 7: 168.
— Cultivation of. (T. D. Hatfield) Garden & F. 7: 167, 336. 8: 116. — (W. Watson) Garden & F. 7: 176.
Cannas, Cultural Notes on. (T. D. Hatfield) Garden & F. 9: 166.
— New Hybrid. Garden & F. 9: 227.
Canned Foods, Poisonous. Pub. Opin. 15: 578. — Sat. R. 74: 650.
Cannes, Hotel Life at. Time, 3: 160.
Cannibal Islands, Among the. (L. G. Weld) Pop. Sci. Mo. 48: 229.
Cannibalism in America, Prehistoric. (A. N. Somers) Pop. Sci. Mo. 42: 203.
Cannibalistic Superstitions in China. (D. J. Macgowan) Pub. Opin. 13: 547.
Cannibals, African. Sat. R. 81: 544.
Canning, Charles J., Earl, Cunningham's. Ath. '92, 1: 173. — (H. G. Keene) Acad. 41: 58. — Spec. 68: 173.
Canning, Charlotte, Countess. Ed. R. 179: 382. Same art. Liv. Age, 201: 643.
— and Marchioness of Waterford, Hare on. (J. E. Roundell) Nation, 58: 256, 276. — Dial (Ch.) 16: 204. — Sat. R. 77: 151.
Canning, George. (Mary C. Agnew) Temp. Bar, 107: 111.
— and Denmark in 1807. (J. H. Rose) Eng. Hist. R. 11: 82.
— What he owed to an Irish Actor. (P. S. Cassidy) Cath. World, 61: 770.
Cannizzaro, Stanislao, Jubilee Celebration of. (A. Miolati) Nature, 55: 203.
Cannock Chase, On. All the Year, 74: 34.
Cannon, Charles Wesley, with portrait. (W. H. Maguire) Nat'l M. (N. Y. '91) 15: 657.
Cannon, Ancient Bombards of the Dardanelles. Chamb. J. 70: 108.
— High Velocity. Sat. R. 73: 177.
Canoe Found in Manchester Canal. Illus. Archæol. 2: 43.
Canoe Building, Modern, for Amateurs. (H. L. Strobridge) Outing, 23: 432. 24: 21.
Canoe Life. (W. P. Stephens) Lippinc. 50: 106.
Canoe Race, A Woman at. Outing, 24: 421.
Canoe Song. (M. Nicholson) Outing, 24: 24. — (C. R. Rogers) Outing, 28: 276.
— by Moonlight. (J. C. Bell) Canad. M. 5: 475.
Canoe Voyage on a French River. (E. H. Barker) Temp. Bar, 101: 531. Same art. Liv. Age, 201: 475.
Canoeing; Black Water and Shallows. (F. Remington) Harper, 87: 449.
— from Lake George to the Atlantic. (W. J. Warburton) Outing, 22: 464.
— in America. (L. J. Vance) Cosmopol. 15: 709.
— May-Day's. (F. E. Wilkes) Outing, 26: 101.
— the Mosquito Fleet. (W. G. Morrow) Overland, n. s. 20: 1.
— on the Concord and Merrimac Rivers. (J. N. Drake) Outing, 22: 16.
— on the Cuyumel. (E. W. Perry) Outing, 23: 234.
— on Pamedomcook. (W. A. Brooks) Outing, 28: 361.
— on the St. John. (W. C. Gaynor) Outing, 28: 109.
— on the Upper Delaware. (H. R. Wray) Outing, 20: 31.
— True. (R. B. Burchard) Outing, 26: 462.
— A Week in the "Wild Cat." (E. P. Johnson) Outing, 23: 45.
Canoes and Canoeists, American. (F. W. Crane) Munsey, 11: 509.
— Indian. (J. Rodway) Sat. R. 81: 144.
— Single-hand Cruiser, Modern. (C. C. Vaux) Outing, 22: 144.
Canon Law in England. (F. W. Maitland) Eng. Hist. R. 11: 446–641.
— Opening of a Judicial Instruction. (G. Péries) Am. Cath. Q. 20: 528.

Cañons of Southern France. (A. J. Jukes-Browne) Nat. Sci. **6**: 379.
Canova, Antonio. (L. E. Baxter) M. of Art, **9**: 150. — (C. S. Johnson) Munsey, **9**: 193.
Canrobert, François Certain, Marshal. Ed. R. **183**: 55. — (S. P. Oliver) Un. Serv. M. **10**: 541.
Cant. Spec. **77**: 891.
Cant Hooks and Peavey Stocks. (E. B. Ginty) New Eng. M. n. s. **12**: 83.
Cantaloupe, What is a? (F. F. Waugh) Garden & F. **8**: 183.
— Winter. (H. P. Harris) Garden & F. **8**: 457.
Cantata. (C. E. Meetkerke) Argosy, **55**: 233.
Canterbury, Eng. Chamb. J. **70**: 556.
— Archbishops of, and their Palace. (G. Leveson-Gowes) Walford's Antiq. **4**: 62, 122.
— Cathedral. (T. G. Bonney) M. of Art, **5**: 360, 416.
— St. Augustine's Abbey, Missal of. (H. Thurston) Month, **88**: 57.
Canticle of November; a poem. (G. T. Rider) Harper, **89**: 937.
Cantilever as applied to Building Construction. (J. B. Robinson) Engin. M. **12**: 220.
Cantillon, R., Place of, in Economics. (H. Higgs) Q. J. Econ. **6**: 436.
Canton, In the City of. (F. O'Driscoll) Cent. **26**: 59.
— the Paris of China. (A. J. H. Antona) Outing, **26**: 120.
— Province of, A Foreign Mission in. Liv. Age, **207**: 359.
— Scenes in; Punishment of Criminals, and the River Population. (F. O'Driscoll) Cent. **27**: 356.
Cantù, Cesare. (J. W. Mario) Nation, **60**: 254.
Canvassing, Tyranny of. (J. J. Davies) Westm. **138**: 43.
Caoutchouc, Concerning the Structure of. (H. F. Lueders) Am. J. Sci. **146**: 135.
Capay Valley, In the. (R. Wildman) Overland, n. s. **26**: 149.
Cape St. Vincent, Nelson at. (A. T. Mahan) Cent. **29**: 604.
Cape Town, Art Gallery at. Art J. **46**: 299.
— to Cairo, From. (H. W. Lucy) Fortn. **61**: 410.
Capello, Bianca. Belgra. **82**: 373. Same art. Liv. Age, **200**: 243.
— Story of. (H. Schultz Wilson) Liv. Age, **189**: 348.
Capern, Edward. Acad. **45**: 476.
— the Postman Poet. (P. H. W. Almy) Sund. M. **25**: 447.
Capital and Interest. (S. M. Macvane) Q. J. Econ. **6**: 129.
— and Labor. (W. G. Selleck) Am. J. Pol. **2**: 135.
— — Does Capital need High-priced Labor? (M. E. Partridge) Engin. M. **3**: 645.
— — No Natural Antagonism between. (N. F. Thompson) Pub. Opin. **20**: 557.
— — Our Industrial Image. (J. G. Clark) Arena, **8**: 286.
— — Relations of. (L. C. Warner) Bib. Sac. **52**: 411. — (C. S. Wake) Open Court, **5**: 2844.
— — Rights of Employers. (H. F. Henry) Soc. Econ. **3**: 193.
— Anti-capital Crusade. Gunton's M. **11**: 319.
— as Mental and Moral Energy. (H. A. Jones) National, **21**: 552. — (F. Wicks) National, **21**: 719.
— Boehm-Bawerk on. (H. White) Pol. Sci. Q. **7**: 133.
— Boehm-Bawerk's Definition of, and the Source of Wages. (T. B. Veblen) Q. J. Econ. **6**: 247.
— Boehm-Bawerk's Positive Theory of. (H. Bilgram) Q. J. Econ. **6**: 190.
— — Fundamental Error of. (F. B. Hawley) Q. J. Econ. **6**: 280.
— Combination of. (E. B. Andrews) Int. J. Ethics, **4**: 321.
Capital, Communism of. (J. Davis) Arena, **6**: 417.
— Economic Service of. Soc. Econ. **9**: 355.
— Ethics of. (W. Cunningham) Econ. R. **1**: 13.
— Genesis of. (J. B. Clark) Yale R. **2**: 302.
— — Clark on. (E. Boehm-Bawerk) Q. J. Econ. **9**: 113.
— Jannet on. (A. Tanzer) Nation, **55**: 129.
— Labor's Delusion Regarding. (A. H. Peters) Engin. M. **6**: 626.
— Marx on. (W. Lexis) Q. J. Econ. **10**: 1.
— Natural Law in the Economic World. (J. C. Kimball) Soc. Econ. **2**: 193.
— Positive Theory of. (J. B. Clark) Q. J. Econ. **9**: 257. **10**: 98.
— — and its Critics. (E. Boehm-Bawerk) Q. J. Econ. **9**: 235. **10**: 121.
— What is? (Irving Fisher) Econ. J. **6**: 509.
Capital Punishment. Pub. Opin. **13**: 33. — (H. Jones) Sund. M. **21**: 341, 417.
— Death Penalty. (J. Fergusson) Canad. M. **2**: 467.
— In Praise of Hanging. (W. S. Lilly) New R. **11**: 192.
— Ought it to be abolished? (G. R. Vicars) Westm. **143**: 561. — Gent. M. n. s. **55**: 308.
Capital of the U. S., 1789–1800, Life at. (H. L. Nelson) Harper, **89**: 862.
Capitalism, Evolution of, Hobson's. Sat. R. **78**: 183.
— What after it? (R. F. Bishop) Meth. R. **56**: 366.
Capitalist, A; a story. (G. Gissing) National, **23**: 273.
Capitalization, Fictitious Corporate, Vice of. (J. A. Logan) Am. J. Pol. **2**: 203.
Capitals (Architectural). (A. Joigny) Am. Arch. **35**: 131–195. **36**: 3–19.
— Sculptured Norman, Southwell Minster. (J. R. Allen) Illus. Archæol. **1**: 31.
Capitols, Southern. (A. H. Noll) Am. Arch. **38**: 69.
Capon, William. (W. J. Lawrence) M. of Art, **18**: 289.
Caprivi, Count. (T. Barth) New R. **11**: 557.
— and Bismarck. Pub. Opin. **14**: 201.
— and Count Kalnoky. Spec. **70**: 765.
— Dismissal of. Spec. **73**: 603.
Capsules, Suprarenal. (W. D. Halliburton) Sci. Prog. **4**: 461.
Captain and Passengers. Spec. **70**: 12.
Cap'n Ben. (A. Brown) New Eng. M. n. s. **11**: 692.
Captain Cleveland; a story. All the Year, **73**: 342.
Captain Close. (C. King) Lippinc. **54**: 3.
Captain Eli's Best Ear; a Christmas Story. (F. R. Stockton) Cent. **29**: 227.
Captain Francis Lawton; a story. Ecl. M. **127**: 67. Same art. Liv. Age, **210**: 14.
Captain Jerry. (H. S. Edwards) Cent. **25**: 478.
Captain John; a story. (J. Heard, jr.) Harper, **85**: 203.
Captain Jones of "The Rose;" a story. (W. C. Russell) McClure, **2**: 426.
Captain Kitty; a story. (L. Wassermann) Gent. M. n. s. **47**: 109.
Captain Ludwey's Jump; a story. Liv. Age, **192**: 145
Captain Molly. (M. A. Denison) Lippinc. **54**: 291.
Captain, my Captain! (W. Balestier) Cent. **22**: 65.
Captain Moratti's Last Affair. (S. L. Yeats) Chamb. J. **72**: 417–471.
Cap'n Patti. (E. W. Peattie) Lippinc. **53**: 523.
Captain Rooke; a story. (F. M. F. Skene) Argosy, **59**: 720.
Captain Scarlet at Fault; a story. (A. Stuart) Temp. Bar, **107**: 415. Same art. Liv. Age, **211**: 142.
Captain Scarlet's Coat; a story. (A. Stuart) Temp. Bar, **109**: 67.
Captain's Bet; a story. (T. S. Blackwell) Outing, **25**: 209.
Captain's Conviction, The; a story. All the Year, **75**: 301.

Captain's Dilemma, The; a story. (Sophie Hart) Idler, 10: 397.
Captain's Exploit, The. Chamb. J. 69: 460.
Captain's Story. (C. H. Rockwell) Un. Serv. (Phila.) 7: 494.
Captains Courageous; a novel. (R. Kipling) McClure, 8: 17, 165.
Captious Critic, A. Chamb. J. 72: 45.
Captor Captured; a tale. (D. Dare) Canad. M. 6: 60.
Captor of Old Pontomoc, The. (M. T. Earle) Scrib. M. 19: 749.
Capture of a Wolf. (M. P. Williams) Temp. Bar, 109: 254. Same art. Liv. Age, 211: 581.
Capturing a Highwayman. (S. S. Boynton) Overland, n. s. 22: 308.
Car-building Industry of the United States. (J. C. Wait) Engin. M. 9: 680.
Caracas; the Paris of America. (R. H. Davis) Harper, 92: 104.
Caraganas or Siberian Pea-trees. (J. G. Jack) Garden & F. 6: 265.
Caran d'Ache, at Passy. (M. A. Belloc) Eng. Illust. 14: 12.
Caraqueños, Los. (F. J. Stimson) Scrib. M. 13: 103.
Carausius, A Milestone of. (F. Haverfield) Acad. 47: 41.
Caravan, The. Sund. M. 22: 376.
— By, to Persia. (E. L. Weeks) Harper, 87: 651, 813.
Carbides and Acetylene commercially considered. (T. L. Willson and J. J. Suckert) J. Frankl. Inst. 139: 321.
Carbohydrates, Review of Recent Synthetic Work in. (H. A. Michael) J. Frankl. Inst. 142: 217.
Carbon, Energy of, Transformation of. (C. J. Reed) J. Frankl. Inst. 142: 1.
— Significance of, in the Universe. (R. Ball) Fortn. 61: 294. Same art. Liv. Age, 201: 3. Same art. Ecl. M. 122: 526.
Carbon Dioxide, Iodometric Method for the Determination of. (I. K. Phelps) Am. J. Sci. 152: 70.
— Lecture Experiment with Liquid. (C. Barus) Am. J. Sci. 152: 1.
— Precipitation and Gravimetric Determination of. (F. A. Gooch and I. K. Phelps) Am. J. Sci. 150: 101.
Carbonic Acid, New Industrial Uses of. Dub. R. 116: 436.
Carboniferous Flora, Southern. (W. T. Blanford) Nature, 52: 595.
— Williamson's Researches on. (D. H. Scott) Sci. Prog. 4: 253.
Carboniferous Fossils in the Norfolk County Basin, Mass. (J. B. Woodworth) Am. J. Sci. 148: 145.
Carboniferous Insects of Commentry, France. (S. H. Scudder) Am. J. Sci. 147: 90.
Carbonyls, Metallic. (L. Mond) Nature, 46: 230.
Carborundum. (F. A. J. Fitzgerald) Cassier, 9: 387.
— a New Abrasive Material. J. Frankl. Inst. 137: 401.
— Hardness of. (G. F. Kunz and O. W. Huntington) Am. J. Sci. 146: 470.
— History, Manufacture, and Uses of. (E. G. Acheson) J. Frankl. Inst. 136: 194, 279.
Cardinals, Some Noted. All the Year, 72: 151.
Cardinal Flower, The; a poem. (W. Packard) Outing, 27: 306.
Carducci, Giosuè. (M. Hargrave) Gent. M. n. s. 50: 163.
— and his Critics. (J. W. Mario) Nation, 57: 7.
— Professorship of, 35th Anniversary of. (J. W. Mario) Nation, 62: 175.
— Readings from Italian Renaissance. (J. W. Mario) Nation, 61: 361.
Career of Claudio. (Frances M. Peard) Temp. Bar, 109: 305, 449.
Caretaker, The; a story. Cornh. 68: 507. Same art. Liv. Age, 199: 758.
Carew, Bampfylde Moore. (Mrs. Andrew Crosse) Temp. Bar, 101: 121. Same art. Liv. Age, 200: 212. Same art. Ecl. M. 122: 189.
Carey, Henry C. and Greeley. Soc. Econ. 7: 134.
Carey, Patrick, Poems by, 1651. (G. White) Bookworm, 2: 187.
Carey, William, Founder of Modern Missions. (D. L. Leonard) Bib. Sac. 49: 615.
Caria and Lycia, Frontier of. (W. Arkwright) J. Hel. Stud. 15: 93.
Caribbees, Cruising among, Stoddard's. Sat. R. 81: 160.
Caribou, In Quest of. (S. R. Clarke) Outing, 23: 201.
— Hunting in Newfoundland. (W. Holberton) Outing, 19: 332.
— — in Quebec. (E. P. Rogers) Outing, 27: 217.
Caricature. (N. B. McCune) Lippinc. 56: 245.
— Aim and Tendencies of. (M. P. Jackson) M. of Art, 12: 276.
— Animals in. Spec. 75: 174.
— Early Political, in America. (J. B. Bishop) Cent. 22: 219.
— French, of To-day. (A. Alexandre) Scrib. M. 15: 477.
— History of. (G. W. Turner) M. of Art, 2: 136.
— Technical Tendencies of. (H. McBride) Mo. Illust. 4: 215.
Caricaturists and Cartoonists, American. (H. Payne) Munsey, 10: 538.
— and Humorists, Our Political. Spec. 75: 76.
Carl Hausen's Wife; a story. Music, 4: 180-382. 5: 63-665. 6: 106-301.
Carleton, George, Memoirs of. Who wrote them? (C. E. Doble) Acad. 43: 393, 438, 461, 482.
Carleton, Will, with portrait. Bk. News, 14: 73. — With portrait. Bk. Buyer, 5: 301.
Carleton Barker, First and Second. (J. K. Bangs) Scrib. M. 14: 465.
Carlisle, John G., Open Letter to. (G. W. Pepperell) Arena, 12: 77.
— Speech of, N. Y., Nov. 21, 1893. Am. J. Soc. Sci. 31: 40.
Carlos; a story. Temp. Bar, 107: 282. Same art. Liv. Age, 208: 653.
Carlos, Don, Son of Philip II. of Spain. (A. M. Judd) Belgra. 90: 258. Same art. Liv. Age, 210: 295.
— in History and Poetry. (G. Valbert) Chaut. 14: 700.
Carlsbad. (S. Boulter) Time, 17: 420.
Carlyle, Jane W. Letters to Amely Bölte. New R. 6: 608.
Carlyle, Thomas. (Mrs. I. F. Mayo) Leis. Hour, 45: 15, 93. — (G. S. Lee) Critic, 27: 359. — (L. Johnson) Acad. 42: 205.
— and Ecclefechan. Atlan. 71: 287.
— and Goethe. (H. S. Wilson) Gent. M. n. s. 51: 509. Same art. Ecl. M. 121: 775.
— and the "Rose-goddess." (G. Strachey) 19th Cent. 32: 470. Same art. Liv. Age, 195: 360.
— and Wordsworth; a parallel. Temp. Bar, 106: 262.
— Birthplace of. (H. C. Shelley) New Eng. M. n. s. 11: 194.
— Centenary of. Am. Arch. 51: 64. — Spec. 75: 810.
— Conversations with, Duffy's. Sat. R. 73: 722. — Contemp. 61: 120-576. Same art. Ecl. M. 118: 326-698. Same art. Liv. Age, 192: 531, 795. 193: 234, 596.
— Glimpses of. (L. Pelly) Fortn. 57: 723.
— History of Literature. Macmil. 65: 386. — Sat. R. 73: 162. — Spec. 68: 494, 531. — Spec. 69: 621.
— House in Chelsea. (E. R. Pennell) Nation, 62: 286.

Carlyle, T., House in Chelsea, Preservation of. (L. Stephen) Acad. 47: 12. — (R. Garnett) Nation, 60: 105.
— Influence of, on English Social Thought. (W. Clarke) New Eng. M. n. s. 9: 473.
— Interview with the Queen. Liv. Age, 204: 636.
— Latter-day Pamphlets. Eng. R. 16: 331.
— Letters and Conversations. Atlan. 73: 821.
— Letters from. (B. Atkinson) Good Words, 33: 459.
— Letters of, Unpublished. Scrib. M. 13: 416.
— Letters to Varnhagen von Ense. New R. 6: 408, 593. Same art. Liv. Age, 193: 744. 194: 480.
— Nichol's Life of. Sat. R. 74: 169. — Spec. 69: 226.
— Place of, in Literature. (F. Harrison) Forum, 17: 537.
— Recollections of. Blackw. 159: 31. Same art. Liv. Age, 208: 248. Same art. Ecl. M. 126: 213.
— Religion of. (M. D. Conway) Open Court, 3: 1719.
— Reminiscences of. (G. Strachey) New R. 9: 17.
— Sartor Resartus, "Blumine" of. (Eliz. A. Mercer) Westm. 142: 164.
— — Glimmerings of. (C. M. Sinclair) Canad. M. 1: 273.
— Some Portraits of. (D. Hannay) M. of Art, 7: 76.
— Varnhagen von Ense and. (W. S. Kennedy) Critic, 21: 21.
— Work and Influence of. (W. R. Thayer) Forum, 20: 465.
Carlyles, The, Mr. Zangwill on. Liv. Age, 208: 191.
Carmagnola, Francesco B.; the Story of a Free Lance. (C. Edwardes) Macmil. 67: 38. Same art. Liv. Age, 196: 52.
Carman, Bliss. Critic, 29: 164.
— Latest Poems. (H. W. Brown) Canad. M. 6: 477.
— Poetry of. (W. Sharp) Acad. 45: 7.
Carmelites in London. (M. Lambert) Eng. Illust. 11: 639.
Carmencita, Dancing of. Sat. R. 79: 441.
Carmichael, George S., with portrait. (H. L. Conard) Nat'l M. (N. Y. '91) 16: 617.
Carmichael, Jennings. (O. Smeaton) Westm. 144: 502.
Carmina Mariana. Spec. 70: 610.
Carn Brê Cornwall. Reliquary, 36: 108.
Carnarvon Peninsula, The. Cornh. 69: 482. Same art. Liv. Age, 201: 624.
Carnation Cuttings, Selection of. Garden & F. 8: 506.
Carnation Society, American. Garden & F. 8: 89, 99, 108.
Carnations. Garden & F. 5: 331. — (T. D. Hatfield) Garden & F. 5: 106. 7: 16. — (J. H. Connelly) Scrib. M. 19: 313.
— and Chrysanthemums. (T. D. Hatfield) Garden & F. 8: 427.
— Notes on. (W. N. Craig) Garden & F. 8: 26, 178, 277, 357, 476.
— and Pinks. (J. N. Gerard) Garden & F. 7: 286.
— Cultivation of. (E. D. Hatfield) Garden & F. 6: 166. — (W. N. Craig) Garden & F. 7: 237.
— Cultural Notes on. (W. N. Craig) Garden & F. 9: 55–466.
— for Market. Garden & F. 5: 608.
— How to grow Vigorous. (C. H. Allen) Garden & F. 6: 375.
— New and Old. (T. D. Hatfield) Garden & F. 9: 406.
— Notes on. (W. N. Craig) Garden & F. 7: 446.
— Rust on. Garden & F. 5: 18.
— Summer Flowering. (W. N. Craig) Garden & F. 7: 136.
— Summer Treatment of. (C. W. Ward) Garden & F. 6: 356.
Carnavalet House. Am. Arch. 46: 91.
Carnegie, Andrew. Blackw. 152: 556. — With portrait. Bk. Buyer, 5: 134. — (C. H. Hepburn) Munsey, 7: 672.
Carnegie, Andrew, Portraits of. McClure, 2: 438.
Carnegie Libraries, The. (W. B. Shaw) R. of Rs. (N. Y.) 12: 429.
Carnegie Library, Pittsburgh. Critic, 27: 353.
Carnielo, Rinaldo. (H. Zimmern) Art J. 45: 287.
Carnival at Rome. (P. M. Watkins) Gent. M. n. s. 51: 18.
— at St. Pierre, Martinique, West Indies. (E. Phillpotts) Idler, 2: 178.
— of Venice in the 18th Century. (V. Malamani) Chaut. 23: 394.
Carnival Ball; a poem for recitation. (W. Parke) Theatre, 28: 77.
Carnivorous Plants, Recent Studies of. (J. G. Smith) Am. Natural. 27: 413.
Carnot, Sadi. (R. H. Thurston) Cassier, 7: 410. — (Ernest Daudet) Cosmopol. 18: 541. — (R. C. Hawkins) No. Am. 159: 255. — (H. M. Minaud) Chaut. 19: 604. — (A. C. Swinburne) 19th Cent. 36: 1.
— Assassination of. Pub. Opin. 17: 288.
— — Moral of. (E. L. Godkin) Nation, 58: 480.
— — Paris after. (R. H. Davis) Harper, 90: 700.
Carob-bean Tree in New South Wales. (F. Turner) Nature, 46: 210.
Caroline Islands, Day's Sport in the. (S. H. Watts) Outing, 23: 391.
Carols of the Year; poems. (A. C. Swinburne) M. of Art, 16: 25–403.
Caron, Major Le. *See* Le Caron.
Carousal, The; Story of Thanet. (M. Pemberton) Eng. Illust. 13: 243.
Carp, the, History of. Cornh. 71: 284.
Carpaccio, Vittore. (F. M. Robinson) M. of Art, 7: 427. — (W. J. Stillman) Cent. 22: 244.
Carpenter, Matthew Hale, with portrait. (H. D. Ashley) Green Bag, 6: 441.
Carpenter, W. Boyd, Bishop, at Home. Sund. M. 23: 378.
Carpet Merchant of Damascus. (M. von Reichenbach) Chaut. 18: 471.
Carpet Weaving; an Ancient Craft. (H. Hendry) Good Words, 35: 744.
Carpets, Axminster, Making. (G. White) Art J. 47: 325. — (Harold Cox) Time, 23: 1067.
— Brussels and Tapestry, Making of. Art J. 47: 237.
— Design in Modern. (A. Millar) J. Soc. Arts, 42: 433.
— Designing of. (A. Millar) J. Soc. Arts, 43: 442.
— of Cork and Oil. Chamb. J. 73: 341.
— Oriental. (A. H. Church) Portfo. 23: 72.
Carpy; a Story of To-day. Blackw. 151: 378. Same art. Ecl. M. 119: 49. Same art. Liv. Age, 193: 265.
Carr, Joseph William Comyns. Forgiveness; a comedy. Theatre, 28: 97.
— King Arthur. Sat. R. 79: 93. — (R. W. Bond) Fortn. 63: 703.
Carr, Lyell. (M. Tracy) Q. Illust. 2: 268.
Carreno, Teresa. (W. S. B. Mathews) Music, 11: 142.
Carriages, American. (G. H. Thrupp) J. Soc. Arts, 42: 167.
— Art on Wheels. (R. Heath) M. of Art, 6: 49.
— Automobile. (H. H. Cunynghame) J. Soc. Arts, 44: 23, 55. — (W. W. Beaumont) J. Soc. Arts, 44: 87, 130, 150. — Blackw. 159: 276. — (P. G. Salom) J. Frankl. Inst. 141: 278. — Dub. R. 118: 427. — Spec. 77: 670. — (C. Moffett) McClure, 7: 153. — Ed. R. 183: 408. — Chamb. J. 73: 503. — Chamb. J. 72: 563. — Spec. 74: 812. — (W. Baxter) Engin. M. 11: 248.
— — Driven by Petroleum Motors. Sat. R. 80: 8.
— — Evolution of. (B. F. Spalding) Cassier, 9: 543.
— — Progress toward the Age of. (T. A. DeWeese) Cosmopol. 20: 417.
— — Race of, in France. Nature, 52: 300.

Carriages, Automobile, Trial of, N. Y. Cosmopol. 21: 544.
— Some English. (J. H. Pollen) M. of Art, 9: 276.
— Steam, on Common Roads, History of. (F. Bramwell) J. Soc. Arts, 42: 781.
Carrier by Water and his Responsibility. (J. B. C. Stephen) Law Q. 12: 116.
Carriere, Moritz. Acad. 47: 125.
Carriès, Jean, Sculptor and Potter. (E. Hovelaque) Cent. 27: 750.
Carrington, James Yates. Acad. 41: 453.
Carroll Family of Maryland. (E. L. Didier) Munsey, 16: 22.
Carroll's Cows. Lippinc. 56: 561.
Carrying-trade of the World. Chamb. J. 72: 533. — (M. G. Mulhall) Contemp. 66: 811.
Carson, Kit, On the War-path with. (W. Thomson) Lippinc. 57: 555.
Cartagena, Expedition against; a Recovered Chapter in American History. (W. Clark) Harper, 93: 753.
Carter, Robert, of Virginia. (Kate M. Rowland) M. Am. Hist. 30: 115.
— Recantation of. (M. D. Conway) Open Court, 3: 1837.
Carteret, Lady Elizabeth (1st). (A. H. Weatherby) Am. Hist. Reg. 2: 1445.
Carteret, Lady Elizabeth (2d). (A. H. Weatherby) Am. Hist. Reg. 2: 1446.
Carthage. Carthaginian Log. (Thos. H. B. Graham) Gent. M. n. s. 57: 304.
Carthusian. (A. Pigeon) Lippinc. 52: 374.
Carthusians, Books of the. (G. C. Williamson) Bibliographica, 3: 213.
— Somerset, History of the. Church Q. 42: 372. *See also* Charterhouse.
Cartier, Jacques. (K. W. Yeigh) Canad. M. 7: 103.
Cartier to Frontenac, Winsor's. (E. G. Mason) Dial (Ch.) 16: 206.
Cartis Folly. (F. Glover) Belgra. 91: 155.
Cartoons, Political, History of. (L. Sambourne) M. of Art, 15: 21, 42.
Cartouche, Louis-Dominique. (C. Whibley) New R. 12: 318.
Cartwright, Thomas, Capt., Muster Roll of his Company, 1777. (F. E. Blake) N. E. Reg. 50: 209.
Carus, Dr. Paul. (Prof. L. M. Billia) Open Court, 7: 3583.
Carved Door-posts in Brussels. (A. Elliot) Illus. Archæol. 1: 73.
Carved Newel Posts of the Pyrenees. (A. Elliot) Art. J. 45: 266.
Carving, Decorative, by Malagasy Tribes. (J. Sibree) Anthrop. J. 21: 230.
Carvings, Hindu. (L. H. Weeks) Chaut. 22: 59.
Casa Braccio. (F. M. Crawford) Cent. 27: 31-841. 28: 105-884.
Casado del Alisal Jose. (D. Hart) Art J. 48: 262.
Casanova, Jacopo. The Real Barry Lyndon. (W. E. G. Fisher) Eng. Illust. 14: 625.
Casario, Fra Lodovico da. (Comtesse de Courson) Cath. World, 62: 155.
Casaubon, Dorothy. (B. R. Belloc) Contemp. 65: 207. Same art. Liv. Age, 200: 728.
Cascade Mts., Triangulation in. (S. S. Gannett) Nat. Geog. M. 7: 150.
Casco Bay. (H. D. Waldron) New Eng. M. n. s. 14: 355.
— Romance of. New Eng. M. n. s. 6: 379-756. 7: 862.
Case, Jerome I., with portrait. (H. L. Conard) Nat'l M. (N. Y. '91) 15: 561.
Case, William Scoville. (W. L. Phelps) Writer, 8: 135.
Case for the Authors' Society, A. (E. N. L. Fry) Belgra. 89: 49.
Clase-aw, More. (J. Stanley) Time, 10: 578.
Case in Equity. (F. Lynde) Lippinc. 56: 291.
Case in Point, A; a story. (G. A. Hibbard) Scrib. M. 12: 323.
Case of Conscience, A; a story. (B. Witte) Scrib. M. 11: 496.
Case of Discipline, A. (C. Van Norden) Overland, n. s. 27: 282.
Case of the Guard-house Lawyer, The. (G. I. Putnam) Scrib. M. 18: 213.
Case of Heredity, A. (Ella B. Gittings) Overland, n. s. 23: 128.
Case of Hoodoo. (W. C. Elam) Lippinc. 54: 138.
Case of Lady Sannox, The. (A. C. Doyle) Idler, 4: 331.
Case of Mistaken Identity; a story. (J. D. Morrison) Canad. M. 3: 337.
Case of Sentiment, A. Liv. Age, 209: 815.
Casey, Thomas Lincoln. (S. Hayward) N. E. Reg. 50: 431.
Cash Capital of Sunset City. (H. Carruth) Cent. 23: 838.
Cashmere. *See* Kashmir.
Casimir-Périer, Position of. Spec. 74: 43.
— Resignation of. Spec. 74: 72.
Caspian Sea, New Islet in. Nature, 46: 212.
Cassatt, Miss Mary. (Wm. Walton) Scrib. M. 19: 353.
Cassie Quin's Atonement. Chamb. J. 72: 383.
Cassiterides, The. (J. Rhys) Acad. 48: 272. — (C. Torr and others) Acad. 48: 366-547. — (A. Hall) Antiq. n. s. 27: 207.
Cast of the Net; a story. (H. D. Ward) Harper, 87: 437.
Castagnola, C. di. (A. L. Frothingham, jr.) Am. J. Archæol. 7: 283.
Castaigne, André. Critic, 23: 57. — With portrait. Bk. Buyer, 12: 506.
Castanets, Australian. (R. Etheridge) Anthrop. J. 23: 320.
Caste. (E. C. Tait) Sund. M. 23: 762.
— Fiendishness of. (J. Cook) Our Day, 13: 320.
— in India. (J. A. Baines) J. Soc. Arts, 41: 457.
Caste; a story. (C. Adams) Belgra. 86: 163.
Castelar, E., and Republicanism. (R. Ogden) Nation, 58: 325.
Castellane, Marshal. (A. Laugel) Nation, 63: 45, 84, 119.
Castellion, Sebastien, Buisson's. Spec. 69: 264.
— and Religious Toleration. (T. Stanton) Monist, 4: 98.
Casterbridge, Eng., Ancient Earthworks at. (T. Hardy) Eng. Illust. 11: 281.
Castine, Me., Story of. (E. I. Stevenson) M. Am. Hist. 29: 21.
Casting Vote, The. (C. E. Craddock) Cent. 25: 47, 271.
"Castle" in certain Place Names. Reliquary, 33: 130.
Castle, Egerton. Light of Scarthey. Sat. R. 81: 357.
Castle Acre. (A. Jessopp) 19th Cent. 31: 263.
Castle Dangerous. Chamb. J. 72: 433.
Castle in the Air; a poem. (H. M. Burnside) Argosy, 59: 620.
Castle Kennedy. Sat. R. 74: 588.
Castle of Ice. (D. Prescott) New Eng. M. n. s. 10: 470-742. 11: 114-342.
Castle Roofs. Reliquary, 32: 101.
Castles, English. Quar. 179: 27.
— of the Channel Islands. (C. Rook) Art. J. 46: 238.
— German. (Countess v. Krockow) Am. Arch. 35: 102. 36: 83. 49: 131. 51: 58. 52: 27. 53: 51. 54: 59.
Castles; a poem. (S. B. Kennedy) Outing, 25: 209.
Castor, Orbit of. (S. W. Burnham) Pop. Astron. 4: 286.
Castro, Eugenio de. (E. Prestage) Acad. 48: 126.

Casuarina; New Group of Flowering Plants. (A. B. Rendle) Nat. Sci. 1: 132.
Casuistry, Limits of. (H. Rashdall) Int. J. Ethics, 4: 459.
Cat, The, in Catholic Ritual. Month, 87: 487.
— and the Rat, Early History of the. (H. A. Strong) Acad. 43: 81, (P. L. P. Renouf) 107.
— as a Wild Animal. Spec. 77: 333.
— in Law. (G. B. Rolfe) No. Am. 160: 251.
Cats. (A. Repplier) Atlan. 69: 753. — (T. Hopkins) Leis. Hour, 44: 107.
— and Dogs. Wild Traits in Tame Animals. (L. Robinson) No. Am. 163: 164.
— and their Affections. (C. B. Wister) Temp. Bar, 106: 557. 107: 84.
— as Pets. (A. Wellington) Bost. 3: 459.
— in Art. (M. H. Spielmann) M. of Art, 14: 21.
— A Kitten. (A. Repplier) Atlan. 72: 326.
— My Musical Critic. Atlan. 73: 139.
— Pictures of. (W. H. Pollock) M. of Art, 7: 89.
— Stray Thoughts on. Argosy, 57: 252.
— Uncared for. (C. H. Webb) Lippinc. 54: 246.
— Unprotected Vermin. (Mary Campbell Smith) Westm. 143: 204.
Cat and the Cherub, The. (C. B. Fernald) Cent. 28: 576.
Cat and the King, The; a story. (S. J. Weyman) McClure, 5: 438.
Catacombs of Paris, The. (N. W. Williams) Gent. M. n. s. 53: 97.
— Roman, The Church in the. (J. B. Fox) Luth. Q. 22: 572.
Catalepsy. (P. Carus) Open Court, 3: 1972.
Catalogue for the National Library of France. (C. A. Cutter) Nation, 58: 361.
— International, of Scientific Literature. Dub. R. 119: 405.
— Progressive Machine Index. (A. J. Rudolph) Nation, 55: 125.
Catalogues and Collecting of Books. (E. B. Titchener) Book R. 4: 97.
Catalogues, Library. (G. S. Ricci) Lib. J. 18: 423.
— — Card Volumes *vs.* Card Drawers. (H. E. Green) Lib. J. 17: 5.
— — Methods of Printing. (A. Growoll) Lib. J. 17: 157.
Cataloguing of Books. (J. T. Kay) 19th Cent. 34: 101. Same art. Lib. J. 19: 125. — (W. C. Lane) Lib. J. 18: 238.
— — in the Future. (E. I. Wade) Lib. J. 20: supp. 21.
— — Popular Errors in. (E. F. L. Gauss) Lib. J. 18: 5.
Catalpa Tree for Forest Planting. (R. Douglas) Garden & F. 7: 9.
— Hardy, in the West. (C. H. Keffer) Garden & F. 7: 512.
Catastrophe, The Final. (M. Proctor) Open Court, 7: 3552.
Catawba Indians. (W. B. Ardrey) Am. Antiq. 16: 266.
Catching a Runaway Engine; a story. (C. Warman) McClure, 6: 589.
Catechising, Hints in. Eng. R. 10: 390.
Catechism, Lutheran, Revised. Luth. Q. 23: 112.
Caterpillars. (E. A. Butler) Knowl. 15: 204, 226. 16: 4–104.
— Stinging. (B. Jones) Sund. M. 22: 680.
Cat-fish, the, History of. Cornh. 71: 291.
Cathedral, American, Significance of. (H. C. Potter) Forum, 13: 351.
— Modern. (R. W. Gibson) Archit. Rec. 1: 286, 435.
— Musings in an English. (D. M. Spence) Univ. R. 6: 372.
Cathedral Courtship; a story. (K. D. Wiggin) Atlan 69: 610.
Cathedral Establishments. Eng. R. 12: 88.
Cathedrals, Builders of. (M. S. Snow) New Eng. M. n. s. 7: 411.
— English. Church Q. 38: 50. — Atlan. 71: 270.
— — Curiosities in. Cornh. 65: 631. Same art. Liv. Age, 194: 367.
— — System of, Disastrous. (W. E. Dickson) 19th Cent. 34: 770.
— — A Word for. (A. Jessopp) 19th Cent. 35: 91.
— French. (A. S. Northcote) Blackw. 154: 249. — (B. Ferree) Cosmopol. 18: 287. — (B. Ferree) Archit. Rec. 2: 125, 303. 3: 87, 387. 5: 278, 363. 6: 21, 145.
— Use of. (R. Gregory) No. Am. 155: 84.
Catherine, St., of Siena. (Mrs. E. Garnett) Sund. M. 23: 554.
— in the National Gallery; that Great Painter Ignote. (G. Allen) Eng. Illust. 14: 237.
Catherine II. (W. K. Johnson) Fortn. 66: 655. Same art. Liv. Age, 211: 796. — Ed. R. 178: 168.
— A French Ambassador at the Court of. (Mrs. D'Arcy Collyer) Temp. Bar, 102: 169. Same art. Liv. Age, 202: 131.
— Girlhood of an Autocrat. (S. C. Woolsey) Atlan. 74: 166.
— Waliszewski's. (A. Laugel) Nation, 56: 120. 58: 481. — Sat. R. 79: 811. — Spec. 72: 269.
Catherine of Aragon, Divorce of, Froude's. Ed. R. 175: 201. — (A. Jessopp) Eng. Hist. R. 7: 360.
Catherine de' Medici, Death of. (H. F. Brown) Eng. Hist. R. 11: 478.
Catherine. (M. J. Jacques) Atlan. 70: 331.
Catherwood, Mary Hartwell, with portrait. Bk. News, 12: 277.
Cathetometer, A very Simple and Accurate. (F. L. O. Wadsworth) Am. J. Sci. 151: 41.
Cathode Rays. *See* Roentgen.
Catholicity. (H. A. Reed) Meth. R. 56: 377.
Catinat, Nicholas de. (E. M. Lloyd) Eng. Hist. R. 9: 493.
Catnip for Two. (E. Davis) New Eng. M. n. s. 7: 351.
Catopromancy, A Study in. (H. C. Bolton) J. Am. Folk-Lore, 6: 25.
Cats, Jacob. (A. Dobson) M. of Art, 5: 384.
"Catskill," Use of the Name. (J. J. Stevenson) Am. J. Sci. 146: 330.
Catskill Forests, New York State Commission on. Garden & F. 7: 41.
Catskill Mountains, Map of. Around World, 1: 129.
Catskin, the English and Irish *peau d'âne.* (H. C. Coote) Folk-Lore Rec. 3: 1.
Cattle, Beauty of. Spec. 69: 848.
— Domestic. Wild Traits in Tame Animals. (L. Robinson) No. Am. 162: 607.
Cattle Brands. (A. MacGowan) McClure, 3: 100.
Cattle Range Business, Harvard Graduates in the. (R. M. Allen) Harv. Grad. M. 2: 183.
Cattle Rearing in the Argentine. Dub. R. 117: 163.
Cattle Ships and Abattoirs. (M. E. Haweis) Westm. 143: 678.
Cattle Trade, English, Mr. Chaplin and the. (W. E. Bear) National, 19: 318.
Cattle Trails on the Prairies. (C. M. Harger) Scrib. M. 11: 732.
Catullus and his Models. (E. F. M. Benecke) Acad. 46: 377.
— Attis, translated by G. Allen. (R. Ellis) Acad. 43: 97. — Sat. R. 74: 685.
— Diminutives in. (S. B. Platner) Am. J. Philol. 16: 186.
— Merrill's. (W. C. Lawton) Dial (Ch.) 16: 142.

Catullus, Poems, ed. by Palmer. Sat. R. 81: 533.
Caucasus, Amazonian Customs of. (J. Abercromby) Folk-Lore, 2: 171.
— and Schamyl's Struggle against Russia. Macmil. 72: 213.
— Beyond the. (M. A. Morison) Sund. M. 21: 29, 175.
— Central. Geog. J. 8: 153.
— Exploration of, Freshfield's. (C. T. Dent) Art J. 48: 270. — Sat. R. 82: 91.
— Mountaineering in. (D. W. Freshfield) Sat. R. 82: 212.
— Prometheus and. (F. D. Allen) Am. J. Philol. 13: 51.
Caucus. (F. W. Dallinger) New Eng. M. n. s. 8: 754.
— Government by. (R. S. Moffat) Time, 7: 707.
— Reform of. Soc. Econ. 5: 112.
Caucus System, American Nomination Law. (J. B. Smith) Soc. Econ. 3: 170.
— a Problem of Democracy. Am. M. Civics, 9: 303.
Caught Napping. (P. W. Roose) Temp. Bar, 106: 248. Same art. Ecl. M. 125: 819. Same art. Liv. Age, 207: 509.
Caulfield's Crime; a story. (A. Perrin) Belgra. 79: 72. (Christmas no.) Same art. Liv. Age, 196: 598.
Cauliflower, Cultivation of. (E. O. Orpet) Garden & F. 6: 536.
— for Winter Forcing. Garden & F. 6: 435.
Causality, Idea of, Origin and Import of. (F. Jodl) Monist, 6: 516.
— Problem of. (P. Carus) Open Court, 2: 1200.
Causation, Humist Doctrine of. (W. W. Carlisle) Philos. R. 5: 113.
— its Alleged Universality. (W. W. Carlisle) Mind, 21: 90.
Cause of a Tragedy; a story. (C. H. New) Munsey, 13: 592.
Causses, The, of France; A New Holiday Ground. (M. B. Edwards) Eng. Illust. 11: 95.
Caustics, Demonstration of. (R. W. Wood) Am. J. Sci. 150: 301.
Cautious Youth, A; a story. (W. Pett Ridge) Idler, 10: 313.
Cavalier, Jean, An Almost Forgotten Man. (R. Greene) Gent. M. n. s. 55: 260.
Cavalier and Puritan; a story. (M. C. Lindsay) Argosy, 61: 754.
Cavaliers, Prince Rupert and the. Eng. R. 12: 1.
Cavalry, Achievements of. (E. Wood) Un. Serv. M. 6: 537, 559. 7: 724-1084.
— Dismounted. Sat. R. 75: 151.
— Long-distance Riding. (C. King) Cosmopol. 16: 295.
— Notes on. (S. B. Arnold) Un. Serv. (Phila.) 12: 61.
— Revolver or Sabre for? (W. P. Hall) No. Am. 161: 249.
— Russian. Sat. R. 74: 502.
— Tactical Power of. Un. Serv. M. 10: 431.
— Use of Firearms by. Sat. R. 75: 122.
Cavalry Arm of the British Service. Blackw. 156: 169.
Cavalry Problems. (C. Stein) Blackw. 155: 674.
Cavalry Stabling. Blackw. 160: 513.
Cavalry Troop, Beginnings of a. (K. Brown) Lippinc. 55: 276.
Cavazza, E. Bk. News, 11: 5.
Cave at the Higuerita Mine; a story. (J. Heard, jr.) Overland, n. s. 19: 625.
— Cheddar. Sat. R. 74: 414.
Cave-dwellers, American. (C. Lumholtz) Around World, 2: 8. — Scrib. M. 16: 31.
Cave-dwelling Animals. (E. A. Martel) Pop. Sci. Mo. 46: 815.
— Blind. (R. Lydekker) Knowl. 18: 208.
Cave-dwellings of Men. (W. H. Larrabee) Pop. Sci. Mo. 41: 27.
Cave Exploration in the United States. (H. C. Mercer) Am. Antiq. 18: 82.
Cave fauna of Kentucky, Origin of. (H. Garman) Science, 20: 240.
Cave-hunting in Derbyshire. Reliquary, 36: 209.
— in Pennsylvania. (H. C. Mercer) Around World, 1: 179.
Cave-men of Mentone. (A. V. Jennings) Nat. Sci. 1: 272.
Cave Paintings of Australia, Authorship and Significance of. (J. Mathew) Anthrop. J. 23: 42.
Cave Villages and Rock Sculpture in New Mexico. Dub. R. 114: 179.
Cavendish, Ada. (F. Wedmore) Acad. 48: 302.
Cavendish, House of, History of. (H. G. Skipton) Time, 13: 296.
Cavern of the Great Death. (S. Evans) Longm. 24: 503.
Caves, Martel on. Sat. R. 79: 260.
Cavils; a story. (A. T. Slosson) Harper, 94: 150.
Cavour as a Journalist. Atlan. 70: 557.
Cawdor Castle. Sat. R. 75: 147.
Cawein, Madison, with portrait. Bk. News, 11: 432.
Caxton, William, Importance of, in History of English Language. (H. H. Howorth) Ath. '94, 2: 715.
— Introduction of Printing into England by. (R. B. Whittemore) Educa. 12: 546, 616.
— Supposed Portrait of. Bookworm, 1: 60.
Caxton Club of Chicago, First Exhibit of. Bookman, 1: 91.
Caxton Press at Liverpool. (J. C. Morley) Bookworm, 4: 185, 232.
Caxton's Vision; a poem. (T. Bradfield) Westm. 144: 294.
Cayley, Arthur. Acad. 47: 107. — Ath. '95, 1: 151. — Nature, 51: 323.
Caymana Islands. (Maj. J. H. Lawrence-Archer) Time, 14: 576.
Cazin, Jean Charles, in America. Critic, 23: 288.
Cecca's Lover. (G. Allen) Longm. 23: 311.
Cecil, House of. (J. M. Bulloch) Eng. Illust. 14: 429.
Cecilia, St., Legend of. (M. Field) Munsey, 13: 345.
— Raphael's. (C. Duncan) M. of Art, 4: 6.
Cecils, In the Halls of the. (W. C. Sydney) Gent. M. n. s. 53: 570.
Cecrops, Three Daughters of. (J. E. Harrison) J. Hel. Stud. 12: 350.
Cedar of Algeria. Garden & F. 8: 332.
— of Lebanon. Garden & F. 5: 602.
— Planting Seeds of. Garden & F. 7: 457.
— Red. (C. S. Sargent) Garden & F. 8: 61.
Cedar Waxwing, Plumage of. (E. M. Hasbrouck) Science, 21: 144.
Cedars of Lebanon, The. Chamb. J. 70: 390.
Cegiha Language, Dorsey's. (A. F. Chamberlain) J. Am. Folk-Lore, 5: 255.
Ceilings, Decoration of. (G. T. Robinson) M. of Art, 15: 235, 351.
— Old English. (J. H. Pollen) M. of Art, 9: 228.
Celebrities, Glimpses of some Vanished. (F. M. F. Skene) Blackw. 158: 1.
Celery, Culture of. Garden & F. 7: 137.
— Greenhouse. (M. Barker) Garden & F. 8: 266.
Celestial Love, A; a story. (C. Flammarion) Arena, 17: 143.
Celibacy and the Struggle to get on. (H. E. M. Stutfield) Blackw. 156: 777. Same art. Ecl. M. 124: 359.
— and its Effects. (Mrs. S. Channing) Open Court, 3: 1911.
Cell, Recent Chemico-Physiological Discoveries Regarding. (R. H. Crittenden) Am. Natural. 28: 97.

Cell, Some Modern Views of the. (J. E. Humphrey) Pop. Sci. Mo. 49: 603.
Cell-theory, Present Position of. (G. C. Bourne) Sci. Prog. 5: 94, 227, 304.
Cells, Battle of the. (A. Wilson) Harper, 93: 136.
— Division of. (M. D. Hill) Nat. Sci. 4: 38, 416.
Cells and Hermitages. Reliquary, 33: 18.
Cellier, Alfred. Acad. 41: 22.
Cellini, Benvenuto. (T. A. Trollope) M. of Art, 5: 200. 6: 281.
— Autobiography. (P. Macnab) M. of Art, 11: 172.
Cellulose, Corn-pith, Marsden. (L. Nixon) J. Frankl. Inst. 141: 161. — (S. P. Sadtler) J. Frankl. Inst. 133: 393.
Cellulose Derivatives, New. (C. Beadle) J. Frankl. Inst. 138: 100.
Cellulose Thiocarbonates, Industrial Applications of. (A. D. Little) J. Frankl. Inst. 138: 111.
Celsus De Medicina, Grolier's Copy of. (W. Y. Fletcher) Bibliographica, 1: 1.
Celsus, the First Pagan Critic of Christianity, and his Anticipation of Modern Thought. (S. J. Barrows) Arena, 16: 1.
Celt, Revolt of the. (G. Allen; H. A. Smith) Univ. R. 1: 269, 407.
Celtic Element in French Romance. (A. Nutt) Ath. '95, 2: 162.
Celtic Language. (M. A. O'Byrne) Cath. World, 62: 764.
Celtic Law, Jubainville's. Sat. R. 79: 74.
Celtic Literature, Ancient. (T. J. Shahan) Am. Cath. Q. 19: 465.
Celtic Love Songs. (E. Rhys) Acad. 44: 314.
Celtic Monuments in Troubadour-land. (R. T. Mullin) Canad. M. 2: 253.
Celtic Myth and Saga. (A. Nutt) Folk-Lore, 1: 234. 3: 387. 4: 365.
Celtic Poetry, Anthology of; ed. by Sharp. Sat. R. 81: 245.
Celtic Tradition, Campbell's. Ath. '92, 1: 431.
Cement, Action of Heat on. (J. S. Dobie) Am. Arch. 53: 13.
— and Cement-testing. (S. B. Newberry) Engin. M. 7: 356.
— Slag. (R. W. Mahon) J. Frankl. Inst. 137: 184.
Cement Mortars, Adhesion of, to Brick Work. Am. Arch. 47: 35.
Cements, Natural and Artificial, in Canada. (H. P. Brumell) Science, 21: 177.
Cemeteries, Good Taste in. Garden & F. 5: 253.
— Management of. Garden and F. 5: 242.
— National, in the U. S. Pub. Opin. 15: 201.
— Public, and Churchyards. Eng. R. 2: 366.
— Quaker Burial-grounds. (M. C. Robbins) Garden & F. 5: 231.
— Restful Burial-grounds. Garden & F. 5: 301.
— Rural. (M. C. Robbins) Garden & F. 5: 290.
Cemetery of the Lilies, The; a Tale of the Jesuits. (M. H. Dziewicki) Blackw. 160: 165. Same art. Liv. Age, 210: 592. Same art. Ecl. M. 127: 534.
Cenci, Beatrice, Guido's Picture of. (T. A. Trollope) M. of Art, 4: 384.
Censorship, English. (W. Archer) New R. 6: 566.
Census, The U. S. (C. D. Wright) Forum, 20: 605.
— Misleading Statistics of. (H. L. Bliss) Am. J. Pol. 5: 417.
— 1890, Lessons from. (C. D. Wright) Pop. Sci. Mo. 40: 368-41: 756.
Census Bureau, A Permanent. (R. Mayo-Smith) Pol. Sci. Q. 11: 589.
Census Statistics, Use and Value of. (H. L. Bliss) J. Pol. Econ. 4: 86.
Census-taking in the British Dominions. (R. H. Hooker) J. Statis. Soc. 57: 298.
Centaur, The. (M. de Guérin) M. of Art, 15: 387.
Centenarians. Time, 15: 461.
— Some Lessons from. (J. M. French) Pop. Sci. Mo. 45: 756.
— Women as. (W. Kinnear) No. Am. 163: 755.
Centenaries. Spec. 71: 141.
Centennials, Literary. Dial (Ch.) 17: 371.
Central America, Ancient Civilization of. (A. P. Maudslay) Nature, 45: 617.
— and its Resources. (A. Gosling) No. Am. 163: 96.
— Polynesian Types in. (C. Thomas) Am. Antiq. 16: 99.
— Three Gringos in. (R. H. Davis) Harper, 91: 490, 730.
Central Pacific and Southern Pacific Railroads. (F. S. Stratton) Cosmopol. 15: 280.
Central Park, N. Y., Design of. (C. S. Sargent) Garden & F. 6: 331.
— Military Parades in. (C. S. Sargent) Garden & F. 6: 241.
Centralization, Corner Stone of Social Strife. (Theo. E. Cox) Soc. Econ. 4: 43.
— the Cure for Political Corruption. (L. P. Gratacap) Am. M. Civics, 9: 307.
Centre of the World. All the Yea , 76: 150.
Centrifugal Force and its Phenomena. (C. E. Emery) Cassier, 1: 355.
Centuries, Beginnings and Endings of. (Count de Mony) Chaut. 15: 450.
Century Cyclopedia of Names. (M. Anderson) Dial (Ch.) 18: 344.
Century Magazine. (H. Martyn) Q. Illust. 1: 93.
Cephalopod Beginnings. (F. A. Bather) Nat. Sci. 5: 422.
Ceramic Art of Japan, Audsley and Bowes on. M. of Art, 5: 522.
Ceramics. (M. L. Harman) So. M. 2: 480.
— Beauty in, Elements of. (C. F. Binns) J. Soc. Arts, 42: 409.
— Persian, Wallis on. Sat. R. 73: 396. 77: 371.
Ceramus and its Inscriptions. (E. L. Hicks) J. Hel. Stud. 11: 109.
Ceratops Beds of Converse County, Wyo. (J. B. Hatcher) Am. J. Sci. 145: 135.
Cercidiphyllum Japonicum. (C. S. Sargent) Garden & F. 7: 104.
Cerebral Discovery; a tale. (E. McG. Lawson) Canad. M. 1: 314.
Cerebral Radiation. (E. J. Houston) J. Frankl. Inst. 133: 488. — (E. J. Houston) Psych. R. 1: 150.
Cerebration, Unconscious. (J. H. Metcalf) Psych. R. 1: 230.
— — Statistics of. (C. M. Child) Am. J. Psychol. 5: 249.
Ceremonial Circuit among Village Indians. (J. W. Fewkes) J. Am. Folk-Lore, 5: 33.
Ceremonial Expenses of Our Forefathers. Walford's Antiq. 2: 301.
Cerillos Coal Fields. (J. J. Stevenson) Science, n. s. 3: 392.
Cernuschi, an Impenitent Italian Republican. (J. W. Mario) Nation, 62: 431.
Certitude. (W. Smith) Philos. R. 2: 665.
Certitudes and Illusions. (J. W. Powell) Science, n. s. 3: 426.
Cervantes, M. de. Don Quixote. (H. D. Sedgwick, jr.) Atlan. 77: 257.
— — and Hamlet. (I. Turgenief) Poet-Lore, 4: 169.
— — Sources of. (C. B. Leuffman; L. M. Lane) Temp. Bar, 106: 207. Same art. Liv. Age, 207: 277.
— — Watt's Translation. (A. R. Marsh) Nation, 61: 412.

Cervantes, M. de. Persiles. (J. Mew) National, **21**: 659.
— Zola, etc. (B. Matthews) Cosmopol. **14**: 609.
Cesnola, L. P. di, Richter on. Critic, **22**: 332.
Cestodes, Stiles' and Hassal's. (H. B. Ward) Am. Natural. **28**: 406.
Cetywayo. Un. Serv. M. **13**: 488.
— Visit to, at Cape Town. Time, **7**: 392.
Cevennes, Causses and Gorges of. (A. B. Hart) Nation, **59**: 6.
Ceylon. (A. W. Tocke) Asia. R. **22**: 109.
-- Big Game of. Outing, **23**: 227.
— British Rule in. (Thomas Berwick) Asia. R. **22**: 103.
— Coffee Planters in. Time, **3**: 556.
— A Dead City of. (O. Hall) Lippinc. **56**: 685.
— Gordon-Cumming on. Spec. **68**: 584.
— Hurst on. (H. A. Buttz) Meth. R. **52**: 362.
— January Days in. Cornh. **68**: 528, 600. Same art. Ecl. M. **121**: 823.
— Justice in. (L. B. Clarence) Law Q. **2**: 38.
— North, Folk-Lore from. (J. P. Lewis) Folk-Lore, **6**: 176.
— Wild Sport in. (F. F. R. Dixon) Outing, **21**: 163. **27**: 441.
Chacta. *See* Choctaw.
Chad, Saint, Ancient Offices of. (F. E. Gilliat-Smith) Dub. R. **114**: 22.
Chain, New Weldless. Chamb. J. **70**: 399.
Chain of Destiny; a story. (E. Robinson) Outing, **24**: 323, 455.
Chain-maker's Daughter, The. (H. Hill) Chamb. J. **71**: 156–173.
Chairman, Legal Position of the. (W. R. Herkless) Scot. R. **26**: 321.
Chairs, Chapter on. (J. H. Pollen) M. of Art, **9**: 36.
Chala Lake, First Circumnavigation of. (M. French-Sheldon) Arena, **6**: 133.
Chalcis, and What we saw therein. (D. W. Williams) Gent. M. n. s. **50**: 143.
Chaldea, American Expedition to. (W. St. C. Boscawen) Ath. '**93**, **2**: 297.
— Egypt and, in the Light of Recent Discoveries. (W. St. C. Boscawen) Harper, **88**: 190.
– Latest Discoveries in. (Marquis de Nadaillac) Science, **21**: 295.
— Sumiro-Accadians of, Legends of. (A. Bodington) Am. Natural. **27**: 14, 105.
Chaldeans, Oldest Civilized Men. (E. D. Cope) Am. Natural. **30**: 616.
Chalfont St. Giles, and Milton's Cottage. All the Year, **72**: 414.
Chalice and Paten at West Drayton. Reliquary, **32**: 1.
— from Isle of Man. Reliquary, **35**: 97.
Challemel-Lacour, Paul Armand. Critic, **29**: 269.
"Challenger" Voyage; Deep-sea Deposits. (J. W. Judd) Nature, **45**: 409.
— Murray's Report of. (A. Agassiz) Nation, **61**: 190, 208. — (H. R. Mill) Geog. J. **5**: 360.
— Reports of, Last of. (G. Murray) Nat. Sci. **6**: 317.
— Scientific Results of. (H. N. Dickson; J. W. Judd; G. R. M. Murray; C. B. Clarke; E. Haeckel; A. C. Haddon; A. R. Scott) Nat. Sci. **7**: 14, 107.
— The Voyage and its Achievements. (H. N. Dickson) Knowl. **18**: 235.
Chalmers, Thomas. (J. Macaulay) Leis. Hour, **42**: 523.
Chamberlain, Joseph. (B. C. Skottowe) National, **27**: 771. — R. of Rs. (N. Y.) **13**: 181. — New R. **12**: 393. — (J. C. Hopkins) Canad. M. **6**: 169. — (J. M'Carthy) Forum, **19**: 448.
— and Clémenceau, Eugene. Sat. R. **79**: 373.
— Colonial Schemes. (E. L. Godkin) Nation, **61**: 443.
— In Defence of. (F. A. Maxse) National, **22**: 104.
— Municipal Career of. (F. Dolman) Fortn. **63**: 904.
Chamberlain, Joseph, on Trade. Spec. **74**: 453.
— Portrait of. Bk. Buyer, **13**: 219.
Chambers, Charles. Nature, **53**: 561.
Chambers, C. Haddon. The Honorable Herbert; a play. Theatre, **28**: 95.
— and W. O. Tristram. Queen of Manoa. Theatre. **29**: 173.
Chambers, Robert W., with portrait. Bk. Buyer, **13**: 400.
Chambers, Talbot Wilson, with portrait. (J. P. Searle) Presb. & Ref. R. **7**: 577. — Chr. Lit. **14**: 651.
Chambers's Encyclopædia. Ath. '**93**, **1**: 401.
Chambord, Why he was not made King of France. (T. Stanton) Open Court, **10**: 5143.
Chambrier, Alice de. Temp. Bar, **95**: 227.
Chambrun, Jeanne, Comtesse de. Atlan. **73**: 834.
Chameleon, A; a story. (H. A. Vachell) Scrib. M. **19**: 378.
Chamois-driving. (W. A. Baillie-Grohman) Eng. Illust. **14**: 157.
Chamois Hunt, A. Outing, **22**: 141.
Chamois Hunter; a tale. (F. A. Fletcher) Canad. M. **1**: 318.
Chamois Hunting above the Snow-line. (H. E. M. Stutfield) Longm. **24**: 283. Same art. Liv. Age, **202**: 480.
— in the High Alps. (H. E. M. Stutfield) Blackw. **158**: 213.
Chamois-stalking. (W. A. Baillie-Grohman) Eng. Illust. **14**: 33.
Champ de Mars, Salon of, 1892. Ath. '**92**, **1**: 702, 736. **2**: 38.
— — 1893. Ath. '**93**, **1**: 644, 705, 803.
Champagne. (G. Harley) Contemp. **69**: 888. Same art. Ecl. M. **127**: 328.
— Gossip about. Chamb. J. **69**: 289.
— In the Land of. (C. Edwardes) Macmil. **65**: 212.
— Manufacture of. (F. B. Wilson) Lippinc. **50**: 775.
Champagne District, American. (L. J. Vance) Pop. Sci. Mo. **45**: 743.
Champerty and Maintenance, Law of. (A. H. Dennis) Law Q. **6**: 169.
Champlain Deposit of Diatomaceæ belonging to the Littoral Plain. (A. M. Edwards) Am. J. Sci. **145**: 835.
Champney, J. Wells. (C. Childe) Q. Illust. **2**: 290.
Champs Elysées, Salon of, 1892. Ath. '**92**, **1**: 639, 797.
— — 1893. Ath. '**93**, **1**: 578, 611, 803.
Chance, Comedy of. (P. Stapfer) Pub. Opin. **14**: 473.
Chance; a story. (J. F. Sullivan) Idler, **8**: 221.
Chance Meeting; a story. Argosy, **56**: 290.
Chancery, Common Law and Conscience in Ancient Court of. (L. O. Pike) Law Q. **1**: 443.
— Court of, English, Kerly on. Ath. '**92**, **1**: 174.
— Unclaimed Fortunes in. Chamb. J. **72**: 230.
Chancery Division of the English Judicature System. Green Bag, **7**: 416.
Chandler, John, Sketch of. (J. W. Dean) N. E. Reg. **49**: 141.
Chandler, William E. (H. C. Pearson) Munsey, **12**: 346.
Chandless, William. (G. E. Church) Geog. J. **8**: 77.
Chandos, James Brydges, Duke of, and the University of St. Andrews. (J. M. Anderson) Scot. R. **25**: 41.
Change, Measure of. (C. H. Cooley) Am. Statis. Assoc. **3**: 285.
Change for a Quarter. (M. A. P. Stansbury) New Eng. M. n. s. **11**: 418.
Change of Name, A; a story. Gent. M. n. s. **52**: 541.
Change-ringing. Walford's Antiq. **12**: 83.
Chanler, Wm. Astor, with portrait. Bk. News, **14**: 463.
— in Africa. (R. H. Davis) Harper, **86**: 632. — Geog. J. **2**: 534.

Channel Islands. (F. J. Austin) Belgra. 90: 359.—(Chas. Edwardes) Gent. M. n. s. 57: 150. Same art. Liv. Age, 210: 789.—(L. Barbé) Sund. M. 21: 262.
Channing, William Ellery. (C. A. Bartol) New World, 2: 479.
— Homes and Haunts of. (C. R. Thurston) New Eng. M. n. s. 15: 417.
Chansons de Geste. (M. Hayden) Dub. R. 114: 347.
Chant, Mrs. Laura Ormiston. An Interview, with portrait. Our Day, 16: 429.
— and the Empire Theatre. Lend a H. 14: 334.
Chanticleer; a poem. (K. Tynan) New R. 12: 503.
Chantilly Château and its Art Treasures. (D. A. Hart) M. of Art, 18: 351.
— Paintings at. (A. Laugel) Nation, 62: 116.
Chantrey, Sir Francis, Tomb of Lady Frederika Louisa Stanhope, by. M. of Art, 3: 155.
Chantries of Somerset. Reliquary, 32: 40.
Chap-books. Bookworm, 2: 311.
Chaparral Cock, The. Chamb. J. 71: 557.
Chapel of Ease; a story. (H. R. Davis) Lippinc. 55: 147.
Chaperonage. Spec. 71: 298.
Chaplains of the Navy. (E. K. Rawson) And. R. 18: 220.
Chaplin, Charles. (M. H. Dixon) M. of Art, 14: 408.
Chapman, Dr. John. Ath. '94, 2: 790.—(R. White) Ath. '94, 2: 828.—Westm. 143: 1.—(J. R. Lowell) Harper, 85: 561.
Character and Conduct. (S. Alexander) Int. J. Ethics, 3: 466.
— and the Emotions. (A. F. Shand) Mind, 21: 203.
— Building of. (W. P. Paterson) Good Words, 37: 754.
— Evolution of. (M. S. Gillihand) Open Court, 1: 63.
— Forces which determine. (H. H. Fairall) Meth. R. 56: 29.
— Higher Measurements of. (W. B. Chisholm) Am. M. Civics, 7: 455.
— Property in. Spec. 70: 478.
— Study of. Spec. 72: 682. Same art. Ecl. M. 123: 76.
— Sudden Changes in. Spec. 74: 527.
Character Notes. Ecl. M. 121: 40–756.
Character-writers, English. Chamb. J. 70: 33.
Characteristics, Lost. (A. Hyatt) Am. Natural. 30: 9.
Characteristics; a story. (S. W. Mitchell) Cent. 21: 423–859. 22: 35–338.
Characters in Biology. (G. Sandeman) Nat. Sci. 4: 267.
Characters in Fiction, Names of. (H. M. Hoke) Writer, 7: 177.
Charades. Atlan. 75: 569.
Charcoal Sketch, A. (L. B. Bridgman) Overland, n. s. 24: 311.
Charcot, Jean M. (Y. Blaze de Bury) New R. 9: 583. — With portrait. Pop. Sci. Mo. 44: 693.
— and his Work, with portrait. (W. Seton) Cath. World, 60: 798.
— Portraits of. McClure, 2: 137.
Charities, American, Warner's. (P. W. Ayres) Char. R. 4: 125.
— and Correction, Schools and Churches in Relation to. (R. T. Ely) Char. R. 4: 57.
— — Separation of. (R. Butler) Char. R. 2: 164.
— Nat'l Conference of. (E. E. Hale) Lend a H. 15: 3.
— — at Denver, 1892. Lend a H. 9: 308.
— Cyclopedia of. (F. B. Sanborn) Char. R. 5: 134.
— Endowed, Use and Abuse of. (L. R. Phelps) Econ. R. 2: 88.
— English. Lend a H. 9: 385.
— in the District of Columbia. (H. S. Everett) Lend a H. 8: 375. 9: 40, 324.
Charities, Instruction on, in University of Wisconsin. Lend a H. 14: 406.
— Medical, Confusion in. (C. S. Loch) 19th Cent. 32: 298.
— of the Netherlands. (S. R. Thayer) Lend a H. 15: 361.
— Organized; a Day's Work in New Haven. (S. O. Preston) Char. R. 3: 159.
— Superintendents of, Need of Training-schools for. (A. L. Dawes) Char. R. 3: 47.
— that have succeeded. (E. E. Hale) Lend a H. 15: 292, 354.
Charities of Dives; a story. (A. R. Carman) Arena, 8: 248.
Charity. All the Year, 73: 29.
— Administration of. (L. Twining) Econ. R. 5: 476.
— — its Abuses and their Remedy. (A. J. Bruen) Cosmopol. 21: 446.
— — Principles and Chief Dangers of. (B. Bosanquet) Int. J. Ethics, 3: 323.
— Almshouse at San Francisco. (Mrs. E. A. Weaver) Lend a H. 9: 28.
— and Pauperism. (J. C. Caldwell) Luth. Q. 24: 39.
Begins at Home. Spec. 70: 219.
— Business, Friendship, and. (L. G. McPherson) Pop. Sci. Mo. 47: 73.
— Criticism and Reform in. (M. E. Richmond) Char. R. 5: 169.
— Democracy and. (J. K. Paulding) Char. R. 4: 281.
— Disease of. (B. Hall) Am. J. Pol. 4: 225.
— Economic Bearing of. (Miss A. J. Mott) Lend a H. 16: 54.
— Emotional, and Archbishop Benson. Spec. 70: 41.
— Empire of. (R. T. Paine) Lend a H. 15: 298.
— Ethical Basis of. (W. A. Johnson) Open Court, 2: 927.
— Friendly Visitor, Opportunity of. (A. T. White) Char. R. 2: 323.
— Future Problem of. (J. G. Brooks) Ann. Am. Acad. Pol. Sci. 5: 1.
— Helping People to help themselves. (N. Straus) No. Am. 158: 543.
— in Japan. (C. Merriwether) Char. R. 1: 287.
— in New York City. (Mrs. C. R. Lowell) Lend a H. 15: 6. (J. P. Ritter) Soc. Econ. 7: 152.
— — Penny Provident Fund. (M. M. McBryde) Char. R. 1: 280.
— Individualism in. (A. N. Lincoln) Lend a H. 14: 411.
— Investigation in Cases for. (M. L. Birtwell) Char. R. 4: 129.
— its Basis, Sympathy. (J. Worcester) N. Church R. 2: 364.
— Legal Restraints on Gifts to. (L. S. Bristowe) Law Q. 7: 262.
— Movements in, in America. (J. H. Finley) Chaut. 18: 9.
— The New. (B. Hall) Arena, 16: 970.
— — and the Newest. (W. F. Crafts) Char. R. 5: 19.
— New-Church Doctrines Concerning. (J. Reed) N. Church R. 1: 258.
— New Hope for, in United Action. (J. G. Brooks) Lend a H. 12: 6.
— Old and New. (H. C. Vrooman) Arena, 11: 274.
— Organized. (A. G. Warner) Lend a H. 9: 403.
— — Economics of. (M. McG. Dana) Gunton's M. 11: 285.
— — Growth and Character of. (J. G. Schurman) Char. R. 1: 191.
See below, Charity Organization.
— Out-door Relief. (W. E. Welby-Gregory) National, 20: 849.—(A. M. White) National, 21: 283.
— — in Hartford, Conn. Lend a H. 8: 181.

Charity, Personal Problem of. (L. Abbott) Forum, 16: 663.
— Private Relief. (H. Spencer) Pop. Sci. Mo. 43: 307.
— Problem of. (F. G. Peabody) Char. R. 3: 1.
— Problems of. (R. T. Paine) Am. M. Civ. 8: 311. — (J. S. Lowell) Char. R. 5: 123.
— Public, and Private. (C. R. Henderson) Char. R. 3: 226.
— — Economic Study and. (J. Mavor) Ann. Am. Acad. Pol. Sci. 4: 34.
— Quasi-public, Incidentals of. (A. Johnson) Char. R. 1: 152.
— Reform in, Plain Path of. (W. Gladden) Char. R. 1: 251.
— Relief by Work in France. (M. Grossetete-Thierry) Char. R. 3: 17.
— Science of, School for. (J. G. Brooks) Eth. Rec. 3: 20.
— Scientific Basis of. (H. A. Wayland) Char. R. 3: 263.
— State Relief in Denmark. (C. H. Leppington) Econ. J. 3: 325.
— that Helps, and other Charity. (J. E. Robbins) Forum, 18: 502.
— Things to do. (A. B. Mason) Char. R. 1: 211.
Charity Chance. (W. Raymond) Good Words, 37: 433-793.
Charity Organization. (H. V. Toynbee) Longm. 21: 409. — (A. Johnson and others) Char. R. 2: 21.
— and Labor Bureaus. (J. H. Hyslop) Char. R. 4: 1.
— as an Educational Force. (C. D. Kellogg) Char. R. 2: 16.
— as Teacher of Ways to Self-help. (R. T. Paine) Lend a H. 14: 16.
— Conference on. Report, 1894. Lend a H. 13: 3.
— Development of. (J. M. Pullman) Lend a H. 11: 421.
— for Small Communities. Char. R. 3: 178.
— in America, Beginning of. (S. H. Gurteen) Lend a H. 13: 352.
— in Cities. (G. B. Buzelle) Char. R. 2: 3.
— in Southern Cities. (P. W. Ayres) Char. R. 4: 259.
— in Times Extraordinary. Char. R. 3: 275.
— a Necessity of Modern Conditions. (F. J. Kingsbury) Lend a H. 14: 3.
— Problem of. (F. Almy) Char. R. 4: 169.
— Remarks on. (C. J. Bonaparte) Char. R. 4: 337.
— Training of Volunteers in. Char. R. 4: 191.
— What is? (R. W. DeForest) Char. R. 1: 1.
— Winter Work in. (E. E. Hale) Lend a H. 15: 323.
Charity Organization Movement. (J. R. Brackett) Char. R. 4: 393. — (D. I. Green) Pub. Opin. 20: 238.
— Social Philosophy of. (J. A. Hobson) Contemp. 70: 710. Same art. Ecl. M. 127: 784.
Charity Organization Societies, The True Aim of. (J. S. Lowell) Forum, 21: 494.
Charity Organization Society. (C. F. Mallet) Time, 20: 236.
— and Christianity. (S. A. Barnett) Econ. R. 4: 189.
— Talk with Registrar of. (L. S. Cody) Chr. Lit. 12: 161.
— Work of. (C. J. Bonaparte) Char. R. 1: 201.
Charity Organization Work, Training-schools for. (A. L. Dawes) Lend a H. 11: 90.
Charity Organizations in Public Emergencies. (H. M. Todd) Lend a H. 14: 9.
Charity Schools. (H. W. Nevinson) 19th Cent. 39: 481. — (C. Scott) 19th Cent. 39: 871.
Charity Worker, Ideal of the. (W. F. Slocum) Char. R. 2: 10.
Charlatan, A. (M. Kendall) Longm. 27: 184. Same art. Ecl. M. 126: 108.
Charlemagne, Relation of, to the Church. (J. F. Hurst) Meth. R. 53: 345.
Charles I. of England; Attempt to annex Belgium. (A. M. Grange) Dub. R. 112: 360.
— Closing Years of. (R. C. Browne) Acad. 47: 118.
— Did he die for his Religion? (S. D. White) Westm. 146: 417.
— State Papers of. Ath. '92, 1: 181. — Sat. R. 73: 309.
— Unpublished Letters of, to St. John's College, Oxford. (W. H. Hutton) Eng. Hist. R. 7: 715.
Charles II., Court of, Jusserand on. Dial (Ch.) 13: 271.
— Draft of a Declaration to be issued by. (S. R. Gardiner) Eng. Hist. R. 8: 300.
— Eulogy of. (G. S. Street) New R. 12: 67.
— Voyage from Holland, 1650. Chamb. J. 72: 317.
— What became of? (C. T. W. Rouble) Gent. M. n. s. 50: 19.
Charles VII. of France, Beaucourt's. Ath. '92, 1: 661.
— and Agnes Sorel. (H. Bouchot) Cosmopol. 18: 35.
Charles IX. of France. (A. M. F. Robinson) M. of Art, 9: 290.
Charles X. An Unknown Exile; was he Charles X.? (H. C. Maine) M. Am. Hist. 29: 440.
Charles II. of Spain; Exorcism of Charles the Bewitched. (M. A. S. Hume) Gent. M. n. s. 51: 471.
Charles III. of Naples and Urban VI. Spec. 72: 618.
Charles IV. of Lorraine. *See* Beatrix de Cusance.
Charles XII. of Sweden. (Oscar Fredrik) 19th Cent. 33: 702.
— and the Campaign of 1712-13. (Oscar Fredrik) 19th Cent. 35: 158.
Charles of Orleans. (A. Walters) Temp. Bar, 95: 543.
Charles Edward Stuart, Prince. (Andrew Lang) Scrib. M. 17: 408.
— The White Rose on the Border. (Alison Buckler) Gent. M. n. s. 57: 25, 173.
Charles, Mme., and Lamartine. (A. Laugel) Nation, 55: 279.
Charles Pelham, Sportsman, his Holiday; a story. (G. L. Cook) Poet-Lore, 7: 49.
Charles River Basin. (W. H. Downes) New Eng. M. n. s. 15: 193.
Charles River Park at Boston. (C. S. Sargent) Garden & F. 7: 191.
Charleston and the Carolinas. (J. Ralph) Harper, 90: 204.
Charlestown, Mass., Ancient Line Feilde of (G. A. Gordon) N. E. Reg. 48: 57.
Charlie; a story. (R. Bergengren) Outing, 27: 197.
Charlie Miller. (R. B. Hale) New Eng. M. n. s. 10: 314.
Charlotte Elizabeth, "Madame." Liv. Age, 205: 504.
Charlton, John. (H. H. S. Pearse) Art J. 44: 33.
Charm, The; a farce. (Walter Besant and W. H. Pollock) Cosmopol. 20: 374.
Charm he never so wisely. (E. Stuart) Scrib. M. 20: 179.
Charmer of Men, A; a story. (T. C. Crawford) Cosmopol. 19: 91.
Charming Ghost, A. (M. Eastwood) Gent. M. n. s. 50: 109.
Charnock, Job. (Stephen Gray) Asia. R. 10: 163.
Charter of Liberties, An Unknown. (J. H. Round) Eng. Hist. R. 8: 288. — (H. Hall) Eng. Hist. R. 9: 326.
Charter Roll, History from. (F. W. Maitland) Eng. Hist. R. 8: 726.
Chartered Companies. (Marquis of Lorne) 19th Cent. 39: 375.
Charterhouse, London. (B. Champneys) M. of Art, 9: 309, 447.
Charterhouse School, Eng., Museum of. (O. H. Latter) Nat. Sci. 3: 40.

Charterhouse of Tyrol, The. (M. Howitt) Good Words, 33: 180.
Chartism, Character and Influence of. Gunton's M. 10: 117.
Chartist Movement, 1837–54, Gammage on. Sat. R. 80: 445.
Chartists and their Laureate. (E. Jones) Eng. R. 16: 55.
Chartreuse, La Grande, Monastery of. (Ch. Chaillé-Long) Cath. World, 60: 59.
— Six Months at. (A. Thorold) Dub. R. 110: 282.
Chase, Salmon P., Lincoln and Grant. (N. Brooks) Cent. 27: 607.
— Personal Recollections of. (E. L. Didier) Green Bag, 7: 313.
Chase, William M., Summer Vacation of. (J. G. Speed) Harper, 87: 3.
Chase, The, in Art and Morals. (R. St. J. Tyrwhitt) Univ. R. 3: 247.
Chase of an Heiress. (Christian Reid) Lippinc. 58: 723.
Chase of Saint-Castin. (M. H. Catherwood) Atlan. 72: 60.
Chastellain, George, and his Writings. (W. A. Smith) Bookworm, 7: 51.
Chastenay, Madame de. (A. Laugel) Nation, 62: 453, 489.
Château d'Azay-le-Rideau. Spec. 68: 299.
Château de Clères. Am. Arch. 43: 70.
Châteaux of the Loire. Liv. Age, 194: 707.
— of Touraine, Cook's. Spec. 69: 260. — Sat. R. 73: 334.
Château-hunting in France. (Mrs. C. Bodley) Blackw. 159: 95. Same art. Liv. Age, 208: 406. Same art. Am. Arch. 51: 43. Same art. Ecl. M. 126: 374.
Chateaubriand, Some Thoughts on. Macmil. 70: 390.
Chateaubriand's Tomb, St. Malo; a poem. (C. E. Meetkerke) Argosy, 60: 490.
Chatelaine of La Trinité, The. (H. B. Fuller) Cent. 22: 232–929.
Chatham, Eng., and its Dockyard. All the Year, 70: 533.
Chatham Hospital, Manchester. (W. T. Browne) Art J. 46: 147.
Chatham Islands and their Story. (H. O. Forbes) Fortn. 59: 669. Same art. Liv. Age, 198: 3.
Chats with a Chimpanzee. (M. D. Conway) Open Court, 1: 62–546.
Chatsworth House. (E. Bradbury) M. of Art, 3: 183, 218.
Chattanooga, Historic and Picturesque. (F. Lynde) So. M. 5: 517.
Chattels, Title to, by Possession. (J. F. Clerk) Law Q. 7: 224.
Chatterton, Thomas (Mrs. E. M. Davy) Belgra. 87: 18. — (A. L. Salmon) Poet-Lore, 4: 593.
Chatterton Family. Walford's Antiq. 4: 196.
Chatty Roof. (D. Upson) Am. Arch. 46: 88.
Chaucer, G. (W. W. Skeat and others) Ath. '94, 1: 742–837.
— and Italy. (Mary A. Scott) Nation, 63: 309, 365, 385.
— Canon of his Works. (W. W. Skeat) Acad. 46: 67.
— Canterbury Tales, ed. by Pollard. (H. Corson) Dial (Ch.) 17: 260.
— Date of his "Italian" Period. (A. W. Pollard) Acad. 42: 194.
— Did he meet Petrarch? (J. J. Jusseraud) 19th Cent. 39: 993.
— Folk-Lore from. Folk-Lore Rec. 2: 135.
— "Foo" and "Vitremyte" in. (F. S. Ellis) Ath. '92, 2: 322. — (W. W. Skeat; Jennett Humphreys) Ath. '92, 2: 353.
— Humor of. (J. B. Holmes) Harv. Mo. 17: 175.
— Is He Irreligious? (E. Baldwin) Poet-Lore, 4: 537.
Chaucer, G., Kelmscott edition of. (E. R. Pennell) Nation, 63: 173.
— Lounsbury's Studies in. (A. W. Pollard) Acad. 41: 173–230. — Atlan. 69: 554. — Ath. '92, 1: 462. — (O. F. Emerson) Dial (Ch.) 12: 351. — (G. L. Kittredge) Nation, 54: 214, 231. — Pub. Opin. 12: 415. — Sat. R. 73: 185.
— Manuscript Ballad of, in British Museum. Critic, 25: 29.
— Night-spell of. (W. J. Thoms) Folk-Lore Rec. 1: 145.
— Pardoner. (G. L. Kittredge) Atlan. 72: 829.
— Prioresses Tale, Sources of. (W. W. Skeat) Acad. 46: 153, 195.
— Troilus and Criseyde in Skeat's edition. (G. C. Macaulay) Acad. 47: 297, 338.
— Women of, A Study of. (Florence Maccunn) Good Words, 34: 775.
— Works, ed. by Skeat. Quar. 180: 521. — (E. Flügel) Dial (Ch.) 18: 116. — (G. L. Kittredge) Nation, 59: 309, 329. 60: 239. — Sat. R. 78: 353. — Ath. '94, 2: 313.
Chaunis Temoatan, Discovery of, 1586. (W. W. Tooker) Am. Antiq. 17: 3.
Chautauqua Movement, The. (H. H. Boyesen) Cosmopol. 19: 147. — (W. R. Harper) Outl. 54: 546. (E. E. Hale) Lend a H. 15: 163. — Lend a H. 13: 270.
— Aims and Influence of. (A. S. Cook) Forum, 19: 688.
— Literature of. (E. E. Hale) Bk. News, 7: 61.
Chavannes. *See* Puvis de Chavannes.
Cheam School. (A. Inkersley) Educa. 14: 137.
Cheapside, Down. All the Year, 76: 197.
— Ramblings in. (S. Butler) Univ. R. 8: 513.
Cheating at Letters. (H. C. Bunner) Cent. 27: 716.
Cheating the Gallows; a story. (I. Zangwill) Idler, 3: 3.
Chebyshev, P. L. *See* Tchebicheff.
Checa, Ulpiano. (P. G. Hamerton) Scrib. M. 16: 312.
Cheerful Godliness. (J. Vaughan) Sund. M. 25: 805.
Cheerfulness. (A. H. Japp) Argosy, 53: 255.
— Gains of. (J. Clifford) Sund. M. 22: 30.
Cheese, Cheshire. Chamb. J. 73: 743.
Cheever, Ezekiel. (L. P. Higgins) New Eng. M. n. s. 10: 481.
Chelsea, Eng., Beaver's. Spec. 69: 566.
— Hospital. Un. Serv. M. 9: 225.
Cheltenham College, Eng. (D. Sladen) Cosmopol. 13: 281.
Chemical Affinity. (J. Walker) Sci. Prog. 3: 419.
Chemical and Geographical Words, Changes in. (F. A. Fernald) Pop. Sci. Mo. 41: 690.
Chemical Elements, Classification of. (V. Cornish) Knowl. 15: 84.
Chemical Laboratories, Ira Remsen on. Nature, 49: 531.
Chemical Science, Immediate Work in. (A. B. Prescott) Science, 20: 127.
Chemical Technology, Recent Progress. (S. P. Sadtler) J. Frankl. Inst. 137: 1.
Chemical Terms, Spelling and Pronunciation of. (T. H. Norton) Science, 20: 272.
Chemistry, Agricultural. (H. W. Wiley) Science, n. s. 2: 442.
— Ancient and Mediæval. (P. E. Berthelot) Pop. Sci. Mo. 45: 109.
— Applied, Importance of. Sat. R. 82: 102.
— — Thorpe on. (H. E. Roscoe) Nature, 48: 145.
— Elementary, White on. (R. H. Cornish) School R. 4: 49.
— Elements of, Freer's. (J. J. Schobinger) School R. 4: 550.
— in relation to Pharmacotherapeutics and Materia Medica. Nature, 49: 587.

Chemistry; Laboratory Training, Aims of. (C. F. Maybery) Science, 19: 351.
— Mendeléeff's. Sat. R. 73: 163.
— Ostwald on. (J. W. Rodger) Nature, 48: 49.
— Physical. (H. C. Jones) Science, n. s. 4: 931.
— — Achievements of. (W. A. Noyes) Science, n. s. 4: 461.
— — The Major Premise in. (R. B. Warder) Science, n. s. 2: 651. Same art. Nature, 53: 139.
— — Recent Advances in. (W. Ostwald) Nature, 45: 590.
— Progress of, since 1851. (R. Meldola) Nature, 52: 477.
— Progress of, 1894. (J. W. Rodger) Sci. Prog. 3: 223, 290.
— Roscoe and Schorlemmer's. (M. M. P. Muir) Nature, 51: 193.
— The Spectroscope in Recent. (R. A. Gregory) Fortn. 64: 289. Same art. Ecl. M. 125: 473.
— Summer Courses of Instruction in. (J. Torrey, jr.) Educa. 14: 15.
— Symmetry in Compounds. Sat. R. 79: 344. Same art. Ecl. M. 124: 830.
— Synthetical, Rise and Development of. (T. E. Thorpe) Fortn. 59: 691.
— Teaching of. (C. F. Mabery) Science, 22: 129.
— Teaching of Beginners in. (P. C. Freer) Science, n. s. 4: 130.
— Theoretical; Nernst on. (M. M. P. Muir) Nature, 51: 530.
— Watt's Dictionary of. Sat. R. 74: 424.
— — Revised by Muir and Morley. Sat. R. 79: 293.
— What Engineering owes to. (A. L. Griswold) Engin. M. 4: 233.
— What is? (I. Remsen) Chaut. 18: 669.
— World's Debt to. (H. B. Cornwall) Chaut. 20: 417.
Chemists, American. (M. Benjamin) Chaut. 15: 453.
— as Leaders. (P. T. Austen) No. Am. 162: 381.
Cheney Family of Vermont, and Music. (E. Swayne) Music, 11: 117.
Cherbuliez, V. Le secret du précepteur. (L. de la Ramé) Fortn. 59: 829.
Chéret, Jules. (R. H. Sherard) M. of Art, 11: 368.
Chérie; a story. (C. N. Carvalho) Argosy, 62: 285.
Cherokee Claimant, A; a short story. (F. E. Newberry) Munsey, 12: 27.
Cherokee Indians and their Neighbors. (A. Downing) Am. Antiq. 17: 307.
— Myths of. (James Mooney) J. Am. Folk-Lore, 1: 97.
Cherokee Legends. (H. ten Kate) J. Am. Folk-Lore, 2: 53.
Cherokee Medicine. (J. Mooney) J. Am. Folk-Lore, 3: 44.
Cherokee Nation, Legal Episode in. (G. E. Foster) Green Bag, 4: 486.
Cherries, Russian. (T. H. Hoskins) Garden & F. 7: 16.
Cherry Picking on the Chilterns. (R. Pardepp) Temp. Bar, 108: 88.
Cherts of Missouri, Study of. (E. O. Hovey) Am. J. Sci. 148: 401.
Chesapeake Bay. (J. W. Palmer) Cent. 25: 252.
Cheshire Moor, Memories of a. All the Year, 75: 250.
Cheshire Salt Formation. Cornh. 66: 256.
Chesney, George. Acad. 47: 297.
Chess; Albin *vs.* Showalter. (I. Gunsberg) New R. 11: 555.
— by Electricity. (I. Gunsberg) New R. 10: 527.
— Champions and Champions. (I. Gunsberg) New R. 11: 111.
— Edgar Allan Poe on. (I. Gunsberg) New R. 10: 759.
— for the Parks. (I. Gunsberg) New R. 10: 383.
— International Tournament. (H. N. Pillsbury) Sat. R. 80: 264.
Chess; Ladies as Players. (I. Gunsberg) New R. 11: 667.
— Notes on. Sat. R. 77: 254, 307, 389, 441.
— Proposed Abolition of "Check." Sat. R. 76: 182.
— Some Strange Chess Games. (I. Gunsberg) New R. 10: 255.
— Dr. Tarrasch again Victorious. (I. Gunsberg) New R. 11: 443.
— The Two Rival Stars. (I. Gunsberg) New R. 11: 331.
— The Old Style and the New Method. (I. Gunsberg) New R. 11: 219.
— World's Championship. (I. Gunsberg) New R. 10: 647.
Chest of Kypselas. (H. S. Jones) J. Hel. Stud. 14: 30.
Chester, Earl of, and King Stephen. (J. H. Round) Eng. Hist. 10: 87.
Chester, Greville John. Acad. 41: 550.
Chester, England. (F. M. Robinson) M. of Art, 9: 115. — (V. E. Mitchell) Mo. Illust. 11: 485. — (B. O. Flower) Arena, 14: 175.
— City Companies. Reliquary, 32: 133. 33: 41.
— Grosvenor Museum. (G. W. Shrubsole) Illus. Archæol. 1: 20.
— Roman Remains at. (F. Haverfield) Ath. '92, 1: 509. 2: 71.
— Strolls Beyond the Walls of. (B. O. Flower) Arena, 14: 349.
Chesterfield, Lord. Letters, Bradshaw's Edition. Ath. '92, 1: 783. — Spec. 69: 392.
Chesterfield, England, Church with the Crooked Spire. (J. Pendleton) Eng. Illust. 16: 83.
Chestnut, Cultivation of, in the West. (C. A. Keffer) Garden & F. 8: 83.
Chestnut Tree at Llewellyn Park, N. J. Garden & F. 6: 13.
Chestnut Trees. (M. L. Dock) Garden & F. 9: 114.
Chestnut Weevil, Destroying. Garden & F. 8: 8.
Chestnuts with a History; a story. (M. B. Rudd) Outing, 26: 87.
Chetah, Hunting with the. (J. F. Nott) Cent. 25: 567.
Chevalier, Albert. Critic, 28: 259.
Chevalier de Resseguier. (T. B. Aldrich) Cent. 24: 73.
Chevedale, Up, and Down again. (C. S. Davison) Atlan. 74: 352.
Cheverny, Jean N. D., Comte de. Memoirs, Crevecœur's. (A. Laugel) Nation, 55: 491. 56: 9.
Cheviot, Round about the. (A. H. Drysdale) Good Words, 34: 24.
Chevrette, La, Cutting out of. Chamb. J. 68: 813.
Cheyne, Thomas Kelly. (A. S. Peake) Chr. Lit. 13: 249.
— and the Interpretation of the Bible. (G. H. Gwillim) M. Chr. Lit. 6: 109.
— — Reply. (T. K. Cheyne) M. Chr. Lit. 6: 114.
Chicago. (E. G. Mason) Atlan. 70: 33. — (J. Ralph) Harper, 84: 425. — Quar. 177: 297.
— Amateur Musical Club. (Mrs. T. Thomas) Music, 1: 204.
— Apollo Musical Club. Music, 2: 148.
— Architecture of. Am. Arch. 42: 75. — (B. Ferree) Lippinc. 52: 80.
— Art in. (L. B. Monroe) New Eng. M. n. s. 6: 411.
— Art Institute. Chr. Un. 47: 1015.
— Auditorium Building. (D. Adler) Archit. Rec. 1: 415.
— before the Fire, after, and to-day. (M. E. Stone) Scrib. M. 17: 663.
— Beginnings of. Nat'l M. (N. Y. '91) 16: 286.
— Bentzon on. Critic, 25: 109.
— Board of Trade Building. Archit. Rec. 3: 96.
— Books Published in, Who reads? (S. Waterloo) Dial (Ch.) 13: 206.

Chicago, Characteristics of. (N. Canby) Chaut. **15**: 610.
— Civic Federation of. (A. W. Small) Am. J. Sociol. **1**: 79.
— Civic Life of. (F. H. Stead) R. of. Rs. (N. Y.) **8**: 178.
— Democratic Convention at, 1892. (M. Halstead) Cosmopol. **13**: 585.
— Drainage-canal. (G. F. Wright) Nation, **60**: 320.
— Early Visitors to. (E. G. Mason) New Eng. M. n. s. **6**: 188.
— Educational Crisis in. (M. F. Washburne) Arena, **15**: 611.
— Endowments of Culture in. Dial (Ch.) **15**: 285.
— Fire in, 1871. (J. Kirkland) New Eng. M. n. s. **6**: 727.
— — and Chicago To-day. (E. Hoch) Nat'l M. (Bost.) **5**: 3.
— Heart of. (F. H. Head) New Eng. M. n. s. **6**: 551.
— Higher Evolution of. Dial (Ch.) **13**: 205.
— Higher Life of. (Melville E. Stone) Outl. **53**: 326.
— How to get to. (B. W. Ginsburg) Eng. Illust. **10**: 500.
— in its Infancy. All the Year, **75**: 198.
— in 1892. (N. Canby) Chaut. **15**: 323.
— Jackson Park. (M. C. Robbins) Garden & F. **6**: 293.
— — in June. (E. J. Hill) Garden & F. **9**: 288.
— — Geological Features of. (D. E. Willard) Science, **22**: 309.
— — A Memory of. (David Swing) Scrib. M. **11**: 691.
— — Revised Plan for. (C. S. Sargent) Garden & F. **9**: 201.
— Lincoln Park. (M. C. Robbins) Garden & F. **6**: 402.
— Literary. (W. M. Payne) New Eng. M. n. s. **7**: 683. — (M. P. Handy) Munsey, **12**: 77.
— Massacre at, in 1812. (J. Kirkland) M. Am. Hist. **28**: 111. — (J. Milne) Gent. M. n. s. **51**: 402.
— Medinah Temple. Archit. Rec. **4**: 82.
— Municipal Progress in. (J. Visher) Lend a H. **14**: 439.
— Music in. (G. P. Upton) New Eng. M. n. s. **7**: 477.
— Musical Centres of. (E. Swayne) Music, **5**: 439, 586. **6**: 73. **7**: 170.
— Newspapers of, and their Makers. (W. J. Abbot) R. of Rs. (N. Y.) **11**: 646.
— Orchestra, commercially considered. Music, **1**: 574.
— People's Institute. (Ray S. Baker) Outl. **52**: 630.
— Poor of. (J. Kirkland) Scrib. M. **12**: 3.
— Populist Campaign in. (W. J. Abbot) Arena, **11**: 330.
— Public Library, New. (L. Monroe) Critic, **27**: 185.
— Public Libraries in. (W. B. Wickersham) Lib. J. **20**: 274.
— Public Schools Crisis, 1896. Dial (Ch.) **20**: 157.
— Reliance Building. (C. E. Jenkins) Archit. Rec. **4**: 299.
— Riots of 1886. (H. M. Hyndman) Time, **14**: 687.
— Sanitary Condition of. (E. F. Ingals) Forum, **15**: 585.
— Society in. (J. Ralph) Harper, **87**: 286.
— Stock Yards of. (P. J. O'Keefe) New Eng. M. n. s. **6**: 358.
— "'T is Thirty Years Since" in. (J. D. Caton) Atlan. **71**: 588.
— The Two Babylons, London and Chicago. (W. T. Stead) New R. **10**: 560.
— University of. Dial (Ch.) **13**: 127. — (M. Smith) Nation, **55**: 216. — (J. L. Laughlin) Nation, **55**: 280. — Dial (Ch.) **19**: 201. **21**: 31. — (R. Herrick) Scrib. M. **18**: 399. — (H. P. Judson) Educa. **16**: 278. — (H. H. Boyesen) Cosmopol. **14**: 665.
— — and Music. (J. L. Mathews) Music, **6**: 550.
— — Architecture of. (C. E. Jenkins) Archit. Rec. **4**: 229.
— — Haskell Oriental Museum. (W. R. Harper; J. H. Barrows) Bib. World, **8**: 81, 85, (G. S. Goodspeed) 103, (E. G. Hirsch) 111.
— — Innovations at. (M. Smith) Nation, **55**: 255.
Chicago, University of, Library of. (Z. A. Dixson) Lib. J. **17**: 50.
— — — Departmental Libraries. (Z. A. Dixson) Lib. J. **20**: 375.
— — University Extension Work of. (W. A. Payne) Citizen, **2**: 260.
— — Yerkes Observatory. (G. E. Hale) Astron. **11**: 790.
— Women of. (Mrs. M. P. Handy) Munsey, **8**: 607.
— World's Columbian Exposition, 1893. (Marquis de Chasseloup-Laubat) Am. Arch. **39**: 58. — (J. Hermant) Am. Arch. **42**: 20. — (P. B. Wight) Am. Arch. **42**: 7-158. — (M. G. Van Rensselaer) Cent. **24**: 3. — (R. L. Fearn) Chaut. **16**: 521. — (T. Bentzon *et al.*) Critic, **23**: 331. — (B. Wendell) Harv. Mo. **17**: 1. — (J. Hawthorne) Lippinc. **51**: 496. **52**: 240. — Sat. R. **76**: 538. — Spec. **71**: 366. — (J. Dredge and others) J. Soc. Arts, **40**: 65, 225. **41**: 58. — (R. E. Webster) J. Soc. Arts, **42**: 7. — (N. Canby) Chaut. **15**: 460. — (M. H. DeYoung) Cosmopol. **12**: 599. — (J. Ralph) Harper, **84**: 205. — J. Frankl. Inst. **133**: 356. — (H. C. Bunner) Scrib. M. **12**: 399.
— — Africa at. (F. P. Noble) Our Day, **10**: 773.
— — and American Civilization. (H. Van Brunt) Atlan. **71**: 577.
— — and the Death-rate. (J. C. Bayles) Engin. M. **4**: 434.
— — and Industrial Art. (A. T. Goshorn) Engin. M. **4**: 645.
— — Anthropology at. (F. Starr) Pop. Sci. Mo. **43**: 610.
— — Architecture at. (B. Ferree) Engin. M. **5**: 651. — (H. Van Brunt) Cent. **22**: 81-897. — M. Schuyler) Archit. Rec. **3**: 291.
— — Art at. Art. J. **45**: supp. — (J. A. Radford) Canad. M. **2**: 128. — (E. Knaufft) R. of Rs. (N. Y.) **7**: 551.
— — Art of the White City. (Will H. Low) Scrib. M. **14**: 504.
— — Artist's View of. (F. Villiers) J. Soc. Arts, **42**: 49.
— — Balance-sheet of. (F. H. Head) Forum, **15**: 575.
— — Brahman's Impression of. (M. D. Vedant) Asia. R. **17**: 190. Same art. Liv. Age, **200**: 435.
— — British Section. (H. T. Wood) No. Am. **156**: 236.
— — — Report of Roy. Comm'n. J. Soc. Arts, **42**: 548.
— — Buildings of. (H. T. Wood) Eng. Illust. **10**: 222.
— — — Color on. Am. Arch. **38**: 201.
— — — through French Spectacles. (J. Hermant) Engin. M. **6**: 765.
— — Canada at. (G. Stewart) No. Am. **156**: 611.
— — Catholic Educational Exhibit. (J. Eaton) Am. Cath. Q. **20**: 66.
— — Ceramics at. Art J. **45**: 110, supp. 29.
— — Charges at. (G. R. Davis) No. Am. **156**: 385.
— — Charities and Correction, Bureau of, at. (N. S. Rosenau) Char. R. **2**: 91, 399.
— — Chemistry at. (M. Benjamin) Chaut. **18**: 320.
— — Chicago and. (J. P. Holland) Chaut. **17**: 136. — (H. T. Wood) 19th Cent. **31**: 553. Same art. Ecl. M. **118**: 660.
— — Chicago's Entertainment of Distinguished Visitors. (H. C. Chatfield-Taylor) Cosmopol. **15**: 606.
— — Chicago's Part in. (F. McVeagh) Scrib. M. **12**: 551.
— — Color in the Court of Honor at the Fair. (R. Cortissoz) Cent. **24**: 323.
— — Congresses at. (E. M. Henrotin) Cosmopol. **14**: 626. — Dial (Ch.) **15**: 59.
— — — of Authors. (W. Besant) Contemp. **65**: 123.
— — — of Catholics. (G. Koerner) Open Court, **7**: 3825.

Chicago, World's Columbian Exposition, Congresses at: Education. (F. H. Kasson) Educa. 14: 32.
— — — Literature. Dial (Ch.) 15: 5.
— — — Publications of, Bibliography of. (C. C. Bonney) Dial (Ch.) 20: 7.
See also names of different congresses, as Religion, *etc.*
— — Cost and Resources of. (J. Kirkland) Chaut. 16: 268.
— — Costa Rica at. (F. Starr) Science, 22: 239.
— — Decoration of. (F. D. Millet) Scrib. M. 12: 692. — (E. R. Pennell) Nation, 55: 84.
— — Decorative Painting at. (W. L. Fraser) Cent. 24: 14.
— — Dedication Ceremonies: Depew's Oration. Spec. 69: 585.
— — Designers of. (F. D. Millet) Harper, 85: 872.
— — A Dream City. (C. Wheeler) Harper, 86: 830.
— — Dress Reform at. R. of Rs. (N. Y.) 7: 312.
— — Eccentric Features of. (J. C. Eastman) Chaut. 17: 12.
— — Educational Exhibits at. (R. Waterman, jr.) Educa. R. 6: 268.
— — Electric and Power Plant at. (W. S. Monroe) Engin. M. 5: 661.
— — Electric Power at. (N. W. Perry) Engin. M. 6: 330.
— — Electricity at. (J. R. Cravath) R. of Rs. (N. Y.) 8: 35. — (M. Halstead) Cosmopol. 15: 577. — (W. Ingleheart) Chaut. 17: 264. — (C. M. Lungren) Pop. Sci. Mo. 43: 721. 44: 39.
— — Englishman's Impressions at. (F. H. Stead) R. of Rs. (N. Y.) 8: 30.
— — Ethnology at. (F. Boas) Cosmopol. 15: 607.
— — Europe at. (W. H. Edwards; J. M. Crawford) No. Am. 155: 623.
— — The Fair in Retrospect. (A. Carnegie, A. T. Goshorn, and others) Engin. M. 6: 417.
— — Farewell to the White City. (P. Bourget) Cosmopol. 16: 133.
— — Finances of. (L. J. Gage) Cosmopol. 16: 201.
— — Fine Arts at. (W. A. Coffin) Nation, 57: 79-303. — (E. Parsons) Open Court, 7: 3841.
— — First Impression of. (W. Besant) Cosmopol. 15: 528.
— — Flowers in Bloom. (L. H. Bailey) Garden & F. 6: 289.
— — Foreground and Vista at the Fair. (W. H. Gibson) Scrib. M. 14: 29.
— — Foreign Buildings. (P. Collier) Cosmopol. 15: 540.
— — Foreign Folk at. (J. Hawthorne) Cosmopol. 15: 567.
— — French Publishers at. (T. Stanton) Nation, 56: 289.
— — French Section. (T. Stanton) No. Am. 156: 236.
— — from a European Standpoint. (J. S. Jeans) Engin. M. 6: 265.
— — German Universities at. (P. Carus) Monist, 4: 106.
— — Glimpses of. (F. H. Kasson) Educa. 14: 104.
— — Gold, Diamonds, Silver, etc., at. (L. Macmillan) Chaut. 17: 422.
— — Government Building. Archit. Rec. 2: 333.
— — Great Britain at. (J. Dredge) Engin. M. 5: 276.
— — Grounds, Design of. Garden & F. 5: 278-302.
— — Harvard University Exhibits at. (H. P. Bowditch; E. Cummings) Harv. Grad. M. 1: 517. 2: 50.
— — Higher Aspects of. Dial (Ch.) 13: 263.
— — Household Arts at. (F. A. Fernald) Pop. Sci. Mo. 43: 803.
— — How shall it be opened? (B. A. Lockwood) Am. J. Pol. 1: 44.
Chicago, World's Columbian Exposition, Impressions of. (H. W. Mabie) Chr. Un. 47: 1200, 1248.
— — Ireland at. (Lady Aberdeen) No. Am. 157: 18.
— — Italy at. (A. O. Bourn) No. Am. 156: 43.
— — Japan at. (G. Tateno) No. Am. 156: 34.
— — Jesus, the Church, and. (B. O. Flower) Arena, 6: 250.
— — Lace at. (F. F. Miller) Art. J. 45: supp. 25.
— — Landscape Architecture of. (F. L. Olmsted) Am. Arch. 41: 151.
— — Landscape Gardening at. (C. S. Sargent) Garden & F. 6: 501.
— — — General Design. (C. S. Sargent) Garden & F. 6: 361.
— — Last Impressions of. (A. S. Hardy) Cosmopol. 16: 195.
— — Lesson from. (J. C. Adams) New Eng. M. n. s. 14: 3.
— — Lessons of. (C. E. Emery) Cassier, 5: 203. — (J. J. Ingalls) Cosmopol. 16: 141.
— — Letters of an Altrurian Traveller. (W. D. Howells) Cosmopol. 16: 218.
— — Liquor and Lawlessness at. (W. F. Crafts) Our Day, 10: 895.
— — Literary Tributes to. Dial (Ch.) 15: 176.
— — Machinery at. (A. Waters) Chaut. 18: 74.
— — Maine at. (C. P. Mattocks) New Eng. M. n. s. 10: 295.
— — Manufacturers' Building, Industrial Art in. (G. F. Kunz) Cosmopol. 15: 547.
— — Massachusetts at. (E. C. Hovey) New Eng. M. n. s. 9: 734.
— — Metal-work, Artistic, at the Chicago Exhibition. Art J. 45: supp. 21.
— — Midway Plaisance, Medley of the. (A. B. Ward) Outing, 23: 208.
— — A Midway Review. Dial (Ch.) 15: 105.
— — Mines and Metallurgy. (F. J. V. Skiff) Cosmopol. 15: 592.
— — Music at. (W. S. B. Matthews) Music, 3: 428. — Music, 1: 39-165. — Dial (Ch.) 14: 329. — Pub. Opin. 15: 433.
— — Musical Societies of the U. S. and their Representation at the World's Fair. (G. B. Upton) Scrib. M. 14: 68.
— — Nation of Discoverers. (H. C. Taylor) Cosmopol. 16: 187.
— — Natural Science at. (F. A. Bather) Nat. Sci. 3: 336.
— — New England Art at. (W. H. Downes) New Eng. M. n. s. 8: 352.
— — New Hampshire at. (E. M. Shaw) New Eng. M. n. s. 10: 135.
— — New World Fable. (H. H. Boyesen) Cosmopol. 16: 173.
— — No. 58; an Episode of. (C. K. Rathbone) Outing, 26: 13.
— — Opening of. Spec. 70: 594.
— — Ornamental Work at, Some British. (L. F. Day) Art J. 42: supp. 5.
— — Oration on 4th of July. (H. L. Carson) Pennsyl. M. 17: 491.
— — Painting at. (J. C. Van Dyke) Cent. 26: 439.
— — Peace Side of the Political Aspect of. (B. A. Lockwood) Am. J. Pol. 3: 107.
— — People who did not go. (R. Grant) Cosmopol. 16: 158.
— — Persia at. (C. Andrews) No. Am. 156: 611.
— — Photography at, Amateur. (H. H. Markley) Cosmopol. 16: 165.
— — Pictures at. Art J. 45: supp. 9.

Chicago, World's Columbian Exposition: The Picturesque Side. (F. H. Smith) Scrib. M. 14: 601.
— — Poachers' Exhibition. Spec. 70: 450.
— — Points of Interest. (B. Harrison) Cosmopol. 15: 610.
— — Police Protection at. (R. W. M'Claughry; J. Bonfield) No. Am. 156: 710.
— — Preliminary Glimpses of. (C. C. Buel) Cent. 23: 615.
— — Promises and Perils of. (J. Cook) Our Day, 12: 499.
— — Publicity Department. (W. Inglehart) Lippinc. 51: 478.
— — Publishers' Exhibit. (A. Growoll) Lib. J. 18: 262.
— — Results of, Some Lasting. (A. F. Palmer) Forum, 16: 517.
— — — to the City of Chicago. (F. H. Head) Forum, 16: 524.
— — Religious Congress at. R. of Rs. (N. Y.) 6: 318. — (J. H. Barrows) Our Day, 9: 252.
— — Religious Possibilities of. (J. H. Barrows) Our Day, 10: 560.
— — Rhode Island at. (J. C. Wyman) New Eng. M. n. s. 10: 427.
— — Roman Catholic Educational Exhibit at. (J. J. O'Shea) Cath. World, 58: 186.
— — Rumselling at. (J. Cook) Our Day, 10: 644.
— — Saturday Review on. Dial (Ch.) 15: 329.
— — Sculptors of. (J. H. Gest) Engin. M. 5: 427.
— — Sights at. (G. Kobbé) Cent. 24: 643.
— — South American Archæology at. (G. A. Dorsey) Am. Antiq. 15: 373.
— — Spain at. (Enrique Dupuy de Lŏme) No. Am. 156: 332.
— — Spanish Government Building. (R. Guastavino) Am. Arch. 41: 44.
— — State Buildings. (M. Schuyler) Archit. Rec. 3: 55.
— — State Exhibits. (W. Inglehart) Chaut. 17: 707.
— — Sunday Opening of. (O. P. Gifford) Arena, 7: 193. — Pub. Opin. 15: 279. — (W. F. Crafts) Our Day, 11: 139. — (J. L. Spaulding) Arena, 7: 45. — (H. C. Potter) Cent. 23: 138. — (J. Cook) Our Day, 9: 29. — (W. F. Crafts) Our Day, 10: 701. — (E. P. Clark) Nation, 55: 425. — (H. C. Potter) Forum, 14: 194. — (J. W. Chadwick) Forum, 14: 541. — (F. M. Holland) Open Court, 7: 3695.
— — — Field Work against. (W. F. Crafts) Our Day, 12: 19.
— — — Final Defeat of. (W. F. Crafts) Our Day, 12: 107.
— — — National Precedents for. (W. C. Wood) Our Day, 9: 1.
— — — Bishop Potter on. (E. P. Clark) Nation, 55: 235.
— — Transit Facilities at. (H. H. Windsor) R. of Rs. (N. Y.) 7: 548.
— — Transportation, Old and New. (J. B. Walker) Cosmopol. 15: 584.
— — Types and People at the Fair. (J. A. Mitchell) Scrib. M. 14: 186.
— — U. S. Government Exhibit. (F. T. Bickford) Cosmopol. 15: 603. — (C. Worthington) Chaut. 16: 393. — (C. King) Lippinc. 52: 349.
— — Vermont at. (H. H. McIntyre) New Eng. M. n. s. 10: 3.
— — Village Life at. (J. C. Eastman) Chaut. 17: 602.
— — What is it to celebrate? All the Year, 72: 175.
— — White Umbrella at. (F. H. Smith) Cosmopol. 16: 150.
— — Woman's Exhibit, Outsider's View of. (E. M. Henrotin) Cosmopol. 15: 560.
Chicago, World's Columbian Exposition: Woman's Part in. (Mrs. P. Palmer) Am. J. Pol. 1: 124. — (V. C. Meredith and others) R. of Rs. (N. Y.) 7: 417.
— — Women's Art at. (F. F. Miller) Art J. 45: supp. 13.
— — World's College of Democracy. (J. B. Walker) Cosmopol. 15: 517.
— — World's Religions at. (F. N. Riale) Arena, 6: 243.
Chicago Commons and its Summer School. (M. West) Our Day, 15: 167.
Chicago Platform, 1896. (H. White) Nation, 63: 42. — Gunton's M. 11: 81.
— Who is Responsible? Gunton's M. 11: 85.
"Chicago," U. S. S., Lesson from the. Fortn. 62: 30. Same art. Un. Serv. (Phila.) 12: 226.
Chichan-Kanab, Yucatan, Examination of Specimens from. (J. L. Howe and H. D. Campbell) Am. J. Sci. 152: 413.
Chichester, Henry Manners. Ath. '94, 1: 278.
Chichester, Eng.; Cissa's City. (W. C. Sydney) Gent. M. n. s. 57: 195.
Chickamauga. (B. Torrey) Atlan. 76: 310.
— Battle of. (E. T. Wells) Un. Serv. (Phila.) 16: 205.
Chickamauga and Chattanooga National Military Park. (H. V. Boynton) Cent. 28: 703. — (C. S. Sargent) Garden & F. 8: 371.
Chickasaws in Connecticut. (H. P. Robinson) Chaut. 18: 707.
Chief-making among the Passamaquoddy Indians. (Mrs. W. W. Brown) J. Am. Folk-Lore, 5: 57.
Chief Mountain Lakes. (G. B. Grinnell) Science, 20: 85.
Chiesanuova. (L. Villari) National, 21: 218.
Chilas. (M. A. S. Biddulph) Geog. J. 1: 342.
— Recent Events in. (G. W. Leitner) Asia. R. 15: 28.
Child, Francis James. (G. L. Kittredge) Atlan. 78: 738. — (A. G. Sedgwick) Nation, 63: 209. — Acad. 50: 262. — Critic, 29: 178. — (J. H. Morse) Critic, 29: 181.
— Obituary. (W. W. Newell) J. Am. Folk-Lore, 9: 219.
Child and his Fictions. (E. F. Seat) Lippinc. 57: 265.
— in Jewish Literature. (S. Schechter) Jew. Q. 2: 1.
— in Literature, The. (S. C. Hart) Harv. Mo. 14: 35.
— Mind of. (D. W. Fisher) Presb. & Ref. R. 6: 86.
— The New, and its Picture-books. Bookman, 4: 301.
— of the Covenant, A; a story. (E. W. McGlasson) Harper, 86: 897.
— of the Forest, The. Chamb. J. 73: 465.
— of the Jago, A; a story. (A. Morrison) New R. 15: 129-373.
— or Woman; a story. Argosy, 56: 81.
— The Primitive. (L. Robinson) No. Am. 159: 467.
— Spiritual Talents of. (T. F. Dornblaser) Luth. Q. 25: 16.
Child's Vocabulary, A. (A. Salisbury) Educa. R. 7: 289.
Child-growth, Phenomena of, in Education. (G. H. Hudson) Educa. 14: 466.
Child-labor. (C. D. Wright) Our Day, 16: 189.
— in the U. S. (W. F. Crafts) Pub. Opin. 20: 460.
Child-laborers and their Protection in Germany. (W. Stiedra) Chaut. 18: 88.
Child-life among the Omaha Indians. (A. C. Fletcher) J. Am. Folk-Lore, 1: 115.
— and the Kindergarten. (F. B. Vrooman) Arena, 13: 292.
— Fragments of. (E. H. Fowler) Longm. 24: 169. Same art. Liv. Age, 201: 811.
— in Bible Lands. (J. Wells) Sund. M. 24: 527.
— Social Responsibility toward. (A. G. Spencer) Lend a H. 11: 105.
Child-lore. (F. Starr) J. Am. Folk-Lore, 4: 55.
Child-marriage and Enforced Widowhood in India. Asia. R. 10: 421.

Child-nurture. (J. M. Gibson) Sund. M. 23: 373.
Child-problem, Legal Aspect of. (F. Wayland) Char. R. 2: 249.
Child-sacrifice in Hayti, Myth of. (W. W. Newell) J. Am. Folk-Lore, 1: 16.
Child-saving. (C. D. Randall) Lend a H. 11: 363.
— Michigan System of. (C. D. Randall) Am. J. Sociol. 1: 710.
Child-slavery in America. (A. P. Stevens; A. L. Woodbridge; T. E. Will) Arena, 10: 117.
Child-stealing Witch, Game of the. (W. W. Newell) J. Am. Folk-Lore, 3: 139.
Child-study. (M. V. O'Shea) Chaut. 23: 302. — (J. M. Greenwood) Educa. 16: 615. — (J. Sully) Pop. Sci. Mo. 45: 323, 577, 733. 46: 186-781. 47: 1-648. 48: 105, 166, 301.
— Aims and Status of. (E. W. Scripture) Educa. R. 8: 236.
— and Training of Teachers. (E. A. Kirkpatrick) R. of Rs. (N. Y.) 14: 687.
— the Basis of Exact Education. (G. S. Hall) Forum, 16: 429.
— A Bit of. Pedagog. Sem. 3: 314.
— in America, Sketch of History of. (S. E. Wiltse) Pedagog. Sem. 3: 189.
— in the Hospital: a Record of Six Hundred Cases. (H. D. Chapin) Forum, 17: 125.
— Methods and Difficulties of. (A. H. Barus) Forum, 20: 113.
— New Department of Education. (O. Chrisman) Forum, 16: 728.
— New Method of. (J. M. Baldwin) Science, 21: 213.
— New Study of Children. (J. Sully) Fortn. 64: 723. Same art. Liv. Age, 207: 579. Same art. Ecl. M. 126: 1.
— Preliminary Sketch of History of, 1896. (Sara E. Wiltse) Pedagog. Sem. 4: 111.
— Results of. (A. S. Whitney) Educa. 16: 466.
— Scheme of Classification for. (W. H. Burnham) Pedagog. Sem. 2: 185.
— Sully on. (A. B. Woodford) Dial (Ch.) 21: 116.
— Teacher's Record of her Pupils. (M. E. Laing) Forum, 17: 340.
Childe Rowland. (J. Jacobs) Folk-Lore, 2: 182.
Childers, H. C. E. Spec. 76: 159.
Childhood, American, from a Medical Standpoint. (H. L. Taylor) Am. J. Soc. Sci. 30: 44. 41: 721.
— and Education. (C. F. Carroll) Educa. 17: 79, 149.
— and Science. Chamb. J. 73: 486.
— Effect of Institution Life on. (W. Delafield) Char. R. 5: 403.
— Humorous Aspect of. (J. Sully) National, 27: 222. Same art. Liv. Age, 209: 293.
— in 1800. (A. L. Hill) New Eng. M. n. s. 15: 406.
— the Pleasantest or Most Miserable Time of Life? Idler, 3: 236.
— Volition in, Origin of. (J. M. Baldwin) Science, 20: 286.
Childish Errors, Tenacity of. Liv. Age, 202: 62.
Childocracy in Literature. (P. M. Cole) Writer, 7: 39.
Children. All the Year, 74: 584.
— and Dolls; a study. (A. C. Ellis and G. S. Hall) Pedagog. Sem. 4: 129.
— and Exercise. (W. P. Manton) Educa. 17: 138.
— and Friends. Chamb. J. 71: 113.
— and Modern Literature. (H. Sutton) Liv. Age, 192: 287.
— and Monkeys. (L. Robinson) Pub. Opin. 13: 36.
— and Parents. (R. F. Horton) Sund. M. 23: 596.
— as Gatherers of Food and Fuel. (A. R. Buckland) Sund. M. 23: 519.
— as Subjects in Painting. Sat. R. 79: 723.
Children as Teachers. (E. A. Kirkpatrick) Open Court, 5: 2789.
— Bashfulness in. (J. M. Baldwin) Educa. R. 8: 434.
— Beliefs and Customs of. (F. D. Bergen and W. W. Newell) J. Am. Folk-Lore, 2: 106.
— Books for. Atlan. 69: 854.
— by the Sea. Spec. 77: 205.
— Child Distress and State Socialism. (J. R. Diggle) National, 26: 519.
— Christianity and. (C. R. Henderson) Bib. World, 8: 473.
— Church and. (S. Z. Beam) Ref. Q. 43: 345.
— City, Curfew for. (Mrs. J. D. Townsend) No. Am. 163: 725.
— Cruelty to, Prevention of. (B. Waugh) Dub. R. 110: 140.
— — — National Society for. (F. W. Farrar) Chr. Lit. 10: 342.
— — — Society for, British. R. of Rs. (N. Y.) 4: 693.
— — — — New York. R. of Rs. (N. Y.) 4: 689.
— Dependent, Exclusive State System for the Care of. (G. A. Merrill) Lend a H. 13: 110.
— — in N. Y. City; Support in Private Institutions at Public Expense. Lend a H. 12: 421.
— — Minnesota System of Caring for. (H. W. Lewis) Char. R. 2: 261.
— — Reared in Families rather than in Institutions. (H. Folks) Char. R. 5: 140.
— Developing Interest of, in Good Literature. (W. E. Foster) Lib. J. 20: 377.
— Development of; Darwinism in the Nursery. (L. Robinson) Pop. Sci. Mo. 40: 674.
— — Normal, Statistics of. (F. Warner) Anthrop. J. 23: 205.
— Discipline of. (M. P. Bolton) Sund. M. 22: 762.
— Drawings of, in the Early Years. (H. T. Lukens) Pedagog. Sem. 4: 79.
— — A Study on. (E. Barnes) Pedagog. Sem. 2: 455.
— Ethical Training of. (W. DeW. Hyde) And. R. 17: 124.
— Exceptional, in School. Educa. R. 6: 431.
— Factory. Econ. R. 5: 370.
— French. (T. Bentzon) Cent. 27: 803.
— Growth of. (F. Boas) Science, 19: 256. 20: 351.
— — in St. Louis. (W. T. Porter) Am. Statis. Assoc. 4: 28. — (K. Pearson) Nature, 51: 145.
— Happiness of. Spec. 68: 331.
— Hearing of. (O. Chrisman) Pedagog. Sem. 2: 397.
— Home Environment of. (B. O. Flower) Arena, 10: 483.
— Home for, Miss Parker's. (M. P. Bolton) Sund. M. 23: 845.
— Imitation in. (E. M. Haskell) Pedagog. Sem. 3: 30.
— in Cities, Problem of. (J. H. Finley) R. of Rs. (N. Y.) 4: 683.
— in Fiction. (H. Sutton) National, 20: 67. Same art. Liv. Age, 195: 259.
— in Hospital, Three. Sund. M. 24: 413.
— in Painting and Sculpture. M. of Art, 4: 286.
— Industrial Schools for, in N. Y. City. (E. Hildane) Mo. Illust. 12: 52.
— Infirm, Glasgow Home for. (A. Lamont) Sund. M. 24: 263.
— Institution for, Construction, etc., of Ideal. (L. P. Alden) Lend a H. 13: 216.
— Institutions for Use of. (M. E. R. Cobb) Char. R. 2: 270.
— Labor of, in N. Y. (A. S. Daniel) Am. J. Soc. Sci. 30: 73.
— Language of, Psychology of. (J. Dewey) Psycholog. R. 1: 63.
— Letters of. Spec. 71: 397.

Children, Little, The Art of. (E. Barnes and others) Pedagog. Sem. 3: 302.
— Manners of. Spec. 77: 364.
— Mental and Physical Conditions. (F. Warner) J. Statis. Soc. 59: 125.
— Minds of, Ethical Contents of. (F. W. Osborn) Educa. R. 8: 143.
— Neglected and Friendless. (J. J. Kelso) Canad. M. 2: 213.
— — Boarding System for. (C. H. Pemberton) Lend a H. 13: 105.
— — Treatment of: Institutions or Families? (C. P. Worcester) Lend a H. 11: 487.
— New York City, Placing out of, in the West. (F. H. White) Char. R. 2: 215.
— of Charity. (A. S. Sherman) Am. M. Civics, 7: 177.
— of the Commune; a play. (W. Wemley) Eng. Illust. 11: 225.
— of the Poor. (J. A. Riis) Scrib. M. 11: 531.
— — Riis's. Ath. '93, 1: 429. — (J. B. Devins) Char. R. 2: 170.
— of the Regiment. Liv. Age, 207: 566.
— of the Road. (J. Flynt) Atlan. 77: 58.
— of the State of Massachusetts. (F. B. Sanborn) Char. R. 5: 89.
— Old-fashioned. (F. Adye) Macmil. 68: 286. Same art. Liv. Age, 198: 818.
— on the Stage. (A. Hornblow) Munsey, 12: 32.
— Our New Protectorate for. (B. Waugh) New R. 10: 458.
— Pauper, Education of. (E. Sellers) New R. 14: 429.
— — The Home or the Barrack for? (H. O. Barnett) Contemp. 66: 243.
— Peculiar and Exceptional, Study of. (E. W. Bohannon) Pedagog. Sem. 4: 3.
— Pictures of. (C. Monkhouse) M. of Art, 7: 133.
— Placing out in Country Homes of Homeless. Lend a H. 14: 34.
— Poor, Cottage Homes for. (Joanna M. Hill) Westm. 146: 660.
— — — Girl-life in Ilford Village. (J. Cassidy) Westm. 146: 194.
— — Duty of Government to. (R. Everett) Mo. Illust. 11: 596.
— Portraits of. (M. H. Dixon) M. of Art, 18: 330.
— Postures of. (M. L. Pratt) Educa. 14: 408.
— Punishment of. (M. M. Mangasarian) Int. J. Ethics, 4: 493.
— Questions by. Pop. Sci. Mo. 43: 238.
— Religious Consciousness of. (Mary W. Calkins) New World, 5: 705.
— Religious Ideas of, in California. (E. Barnes) Pedagog. Sem. 2: 442.
— Removal of, from Almshouses. (H. Folks) Lend a H. 13: 168.
— Rights of. (M. J. Savage) Arena, 6: 8. — (Kate D. Wiggin) Scrib. M. 12: 242.
— — as seen by themselves. (M. E. Schallenberger) Pedagog. Sem. 3: 87.
— Saturday's. (P. W. Roose) Argosy, 59: 629.
— School, Accuracy of Observation and Recollection in. (S. I. Franz and H. E. Houston) Psychol. R. 3: 531.
— — Application to Individual, of Anthropological Measurements from the Generalizing Method. (W. T. Porter) Am. Statis. Assoc. 3: 576.
— — Memory in. (J. C. Shaw) Pedagog. Sem. 4: 61.
— Scientific Method with. (H. L. Clapp) Pop. Sci. Mo. 44: 57.
— Secret Language of. (O. Chrisman) Science, 22: 303.
— Speech of. (A. Stevenson) Science, 21: 118.
Children, State Supervision of Agencies for Care of. (H. Folks) Lend a H. 16: 15.
— Study of, at the State Normal School, Worcester, Mass. (E. H. Russell) Pedagog. Sem. 2: 343.
— Suggestibility of. (M. H. Small) Pedagog. Sem. 4: 176.
— Support of, at Public Expense in Private Institutions in N. Y. City. Table of Statutes. Lend a H. 13: 339.
— Theology of. Cornh. 74: 188. Same art. Ecl. M. 127: 463.
— Thoughts and Reasonings of, Records of. (H. W. Brown) Pedagog. Sem. 2: 358.
— Unborn, and their Rights. (T. F. Utley) Am. Law R. 26: 50.
— Unbaptized, Condition of, after death. Month, 77: 160.
— Vexatious. (J. Watson) Sund. M. 25: 405.
— The Welcome Child. (Lady Henry Somerset) Arena, 12: 42.
— Too Many. (K. G. Wells) No. Am. 159: 254.
— What State and Society owe to. (A. G. Spencer) Lend a H. 14: 34.
— Yesterday and To-day. Quar. 183: 374. Same art. Liv. Age, 209: 707.
Children's Ability to Reason. (J. A. Hancock) Educa. R. 12: 261.
Children's Aid Society, New York, A Christmas Reminder of. (J. A. Riis) Forum, 16: 624.
— Farm at Kensico. (J. A. Riis) Cent. 29: 303.
Children's Book, An Old-fashioned. (F. Anstey) New R. 14: 392. Same art. Liv. Age, 209: 436.
Children's Bureau. Lend a H. 15: 212.
Children's Hour. (A. Jekyll) Longm. 22: 40.
Children's Questioning, Educative Value of. (H. L. Clapp) Pop. Sci. Mo. 49: 799.
Children's Rhymes and Incantations. (C. G. Leland) J. Am. Folk-Lore, 2: 113.
Children's Song in Berwickshire. (A. M. Bell) Antiq. n. s. 30: 12.
Childs, George W. (R. H. Titherington) Munsey, 7: 271. — With portrait. Our Day, 15: 171. — With portrait. (H. Parker) Munsey, 10: 576. — Ath. '94, 1: 179. — (E. J. Edwards) Chaut. 19: 34. — With portrait. (T. Williams) R. of Rs. (N. Y.) 9: 283. — Critic, 24: 100. — Pub. Opin. 16: 438.
— Manuscripts of. Ath. '94, 1: 348.
— Sketch of. Lit. W. (Bost.) 25: 46.
Chili. (M. Crommelin) Leis. Hour, 44: 516–804. — (C. H. Harlow) New Eng. M. n. s. 8: 96.
— Baltimore Affair. (R. Ogden) Nation, 55: 120. — Pub. Opin. 12: 419, 448. — Sat. R. 73: 118. — (F. Snow) Harv. Mo. 13: 176.
— — American Testimony from Chili. (J. Trumbull) Nation, 54: 50.
— — Democratic Congressmen and. (E. L. Godkin) Nation, 54: 24.
— Civil War in, 1891-92. Sat. R. 74: 563.
— Controversy about. (J. B. Moore) Pol. Sci. Q. 8: 467.
— Hancock's History of. (E. Wallace) Dial (Ch.) 16: 331. — Sat. R. 78: 355.
— Industrial Development of. (C. DeKalb) Engin. M. 8: 17.
— Nitrate Fields of. (C. M. Aikman) Blackw. 151: 437.
— War in. Un. Serv. M. 4: 506.
Chilkoot Pass, Over the, to the Yukon. (F. Fumston) Scrib. M. 20: 572.
Chillon, Prisoner of, The Real. (L. W. Bacon) Chr. Lit. 12: 313.
Chiltern Hundreds, The. (M. T. Pearman) Walford's Antiq. 3: 293. 4: 113.
— A Day among the. All the Year, 75: 534.

Chiltern Hundreds, On the. Liv. Age, **209**: 572.
— a Prehistoric Workshop. (J. E. Field) Gent. M. n. s. **56**: 265.
— Stewardship of. Quar. **178**: 215.
Chimney, Leaning, Straightening. (J. C. Platt) Cassier, **7**: 326.
Chimney-swallows; Up the Chimney. (F. Bolles) Pop. Sci. Mo. **45**: 24.
Chimney-tops, Italian. (H. E. Tidmarsh) M. of Art, **17**: 102.
Chimpanzee, The. (A. Keith) Nat. Sci. **9**: 250.
Chin and Kachin Tribes on Borderland of Burma. (Taw Sein Ko) Asia. R. **15**: 281.
Chin-Lushai Country, The. (E. O. Walker) Gent. M. n. s. **52**: 227.
China against the World. (G. Reid) Am. M. Civics, **7**: 617.
— and Russia. (E. H. Parker) Asia. R. **22**: 12.
— Alone in. (J. Ralph) Harper, **91**: 685.
— Americans in. (J. D. Butler) Nation, **54**: 392.
— and the Bible. (W. Wright) Sund. M. **24**: 327.
— and England. Quar. **178**: 460.
— and her Neighbors, Gundry's. Sat. R. **78**: 270.
— and its Government, Chirol on. Sat. R. **81**: 355.
— and Japan. (Viscount Wolseley) Cosmopol. **18**: 417. — (G. F. Seward) Cosmopol. **18**: 713. — (R. B. Brett) Contemp. **67**: 817. — New R. **11**: 222. — (W. H. Shock) Un. Serv. (Phila.) **13**: 101.
— — The New Situation in the Far East. (D. C. Boulger) Contemp. **68**: 815.
— and Russia. (R. S. Gundry) Fortn. **58**: 493.
— and the Western World. (L. Hearn) Atlan. **77**: 450.
— Army of. Pub. Opin. **15**: 295.
— — The Fighting Force of. (W. E. Gowan) New R. **11**: 522.
— Art and National Character in. (W. A. Cornaby) Contemp. **64**: 549.
— Awakening of. (M. R. Davies) Fortn. **64**: 454. Same art. Ecl. M. **125**: 597.
— British Interest in. (A. Michie) Asia. R. **21**: 41.
— British Ministers in, Six. Asia. R. **22**: 381.
— Caged in. (S. Lane-Poole) Eng. Illus. **12**: no. 2, 3.
— Civilization of, Vitality of. Sat. R. **78**: 10.
— Competitive Examinations in. (T. L. Bullock) 19th Cent. **36**: 87. Same art. Liv. Age, **202**: 501. — (J. T. Doyle) Good Govt. **14**: 39.
— Corea and Japan. (R. S. Gundry) Fortn. **62**: 618.
— Curio-hunting in. Temp. Bar, **104**: 284.
— Curzon's Problems of the Far East. (W. E. Griffis) Nation, **59**: 250. — Dial (Ch.) **17**: 189.
— Dungan Rebellion and Hankow. (Mark Bell) Asia. R. **21**: 55. **22**: 25.
— Early Civilization of, Lacouperie on. Sat. R. **78**: 328.
— Emperor of, to George III. (C. H. Parker) 19th Cent. **40**: 45. Same art. Liv. Age, **220**: 346.
— England and Russia. (R. S. Gundry) Fortn. **66**: 506.
— England's Interests in. (R. S. Gundry) Sat. R. **79**: 856. **80**: 464.
— Euphemism and Tabu in. (H. Friend) Folk-Lore Rec. **4**: 71.
— Every-day Scenes in. (J. Ralph) Harper, **91**: 358.
— A Far Eastern Question. (W. Robertson) Westm. **137**: 136. — Asia. R. **22**: 1.
— Folk-Lore of. (J. H. S. Lockhart) Folk-Lore, **1**: 359.
— Foot Distortion in. (G. A. Stockwell) Canad. M. **3**: 115.
— Foreign Missions in. (R. Ogden) Nation, **56**: 380.
— Foreign Trade of. Dub. R. **111**: 195.
— Foreigners Unsafe in. Sat. R. **73**: 354.
— Future of. Fortn. **66**: 159.
— Great Wall of. (J. A. Church) Engin. M. **4**: 654. — (R. Hitchcock) Cent. **23**: 327.
China, Great Wall of, Under. (A. Michie) Macmil. **67**: 172.
— — A Winter Ride to. (N. B. Dennys) Cent. **23**: 332.
— History of. (F. H. Balfour) Asia. R. **10**: 53.
— House-boating in. (J. Ralph) Harper, **91**: 3.
— in 1840–1843. Eng. R. **1**: 194.
— in 1895. Blackw. **157**: 501.
— In the Garden of. (J. Ralph) Harper, **91**: 188.
— In the Wild West of. (A. B. Little) 19th Cent. **39**: 58. Same art. Liv. Age, **208**: 221.
— Infanticide in. (A. M. Clarke) Cath. World, **60**: 769.
— Jesuit Missions in. Open Court, **10**: 5021.
— Jews in. (A. Newbauer) Jew. Q. **8**: 123.
— Journey to the Sacred Mountain in. (A. H. Savage-Landor) Fortn. **62**: 393.
— Journey through, Morrison's. Sat. R. **80**: 349.
— Labor Unions in. (W. N. Fong) Chaut. **23**: 320.
— Language of, Written. (J. C. Moffet) Educa. **16**: 31.
— Lenz's World Tour Awheel. Outing, **23**: 383. **24**: 284, 360, 432. **25**: 35, 152, 236.
— Mandarins and People of. (R. K. Douglas) Eng. Illust. **12**: no. 3, 171.
— Massacre in; a Word in Season. (E. L. Linton) New R. **13**: 267.
— Missionaries in. Macmil. **73**: 10.
— Murders in. Blackw. **154**: 592.
— Music of. (M. E. Simms) Music, **6**: 485.
— National and Religious Characteristics in. (J. C. Hopkins) Canad. M. **5**: 528.
— Navy. Blackw. **158**: 457, 609.
— Norman's People and Politics in the Far East. (W. E. Griffis) Nation, **60**: 308.
— North, Sledging Picnic in. (A. L. Craig) Outing, **25**: 399.
— Old Religion of. (A. B. Little) Sund. M. **25**: 766.
— Our Little War with, 1854. (P. Crosby) No. Am. **159**: 321.
— Our Trade with. (W. C. Ford) No. Am. **160**: 63.
— — and the Geary Act. (S. P. Read) Am. J. Pol. **3**: 234.
— Past and Present, Gundry's. Sat. R. **79**: 675.
— Peerage in. Cornh. **66**: 364. Same art. Ecl. M. **119**: 771.
— Problem of, and its Solution. (E. T. C. Werner) Fortn. **63**: 573.
— Problems of the Far East. Ed. R. **182**: 132. Same art. Liv. Age, **206**: 579.
— Public Work in. (W. Hornsby) Month, **88**: 350.
— Publication of Imperial Decrees in. Longm. **29**: 73.
— Railways in. (A. R. Colquhoun) Sat. R. **82**: 666.
— — Need of. Sat. R. **82**: 178.
— Religion of the Chinese People. (C. de Harlez) New World, **2**: 646.
— Riots in, 1891, Scene of. (W. B. Harris) Ecl. M. **118**: 145. Same art. Liv. Age, **192**: 406.
— Russia, Mongolia and. (E. Reclus) Contemp. **67**: 617. Same art. Liv. Age, **205**: 555.
— Secret Societies in. Blackw. **160**: 793.
— Social Organization and State Economy. Asia. R. **10**: 258.
— Some Peking Politicians. (R. K. Douglas) 19th Cent. **40**: 896.
— Southwest, Trade with. (R. S. Gundry) Sat. R. **81**: 369.
— Stage and Drama in. (L. Katscher) Time, **20**: 181.
— Tai-Ping Rebellion, Personal Recollections of. (E. Forester) Cosmopol. **22**: 34, 209.
— Through Oriental Doorways. (L. B. Starr) Cosmopol. **22**: 21.
— Treatment of, by the U. S., A Chinaman on. (Yung Kiung Yen) Forum, **14**: 85.

China *versus* Japan. (W. H. Shock) Un. Serv. (Phila.) **13**: 101.
— Western, as a British Market. (H. S. Hallett) 19th Cent. **38**: 236.
China Painting in America, Pioneer of. (E. A. Barber) New Eng. M. n. s. **13**: 33.
— Exhibition of, 1878. M. of Art, **1**: 176.
— Exhibition of, 1879. M. of Art, **2**: 269.
— Exhibition of, 1884. (C. Monkhouse) M. of Art, **7**: 245.
China-ware, Derby; Old and New. Time, **8**: 297, 445.
— Manufacture of, in Philadelphia, 1825–37. (E. A. Barber) Lippinc. **50**: 766.
China Wedding; a poem. (J. C. Bell) Canad. M. **6**: 151.
Chinaman Abroad, The. (E. Mitchell) 19th Cent. **36**: 612.
Chinamen from the Chinese Point of View. Sat. R. **77**: 559.
China's Extremity. Blackw. **157**: 501. Same art. Liv. Age, **205**: 287. **157**: 501.
Chinatown, San Francisco; Night Scenes in. (W. H. Gleadell) Gent. M. n. s. **54**: 576.
Chinese at Home. (A. M. Fielde) Around World, **1**: 217.
— Characteristics of, Smith's. Sat. R. **74**: 111. — Spec. **68**: 374.
— How they work and live. (F. O'Driscoll) Cent. **27**: 59.
— Illustrated Books of. (R. K. Douglas) Bibliographica, **2**: 452.
— Immorality of. (L. Lucas) National, **19**: 865.
— in America, Customs of. (S. Culin) J. Am. Folk-Lore, **3**: 191.
— — Divination and Fortune-telling among the. (S. Culin) Overland, n. s. **25**: 165.
— in Boston. (Mary Chapman) J. Am. Folk-Lore, **5**: 321.
— in California; Highbinders. (F. J. Masters) Chaut. **14**: 554.
— in New York City. (A. Forman) Arena, **17**: 620. — (H. F. Clark) Cent. **31**: 494.
— in San Franciso, New Light on. (H. B. McDowell) Harper, **86**: 3.
— in the U. S. (A. J. Hanson) Meth. R. **52**: 712.
— — Exclusion of. (R. G. Ingersoll; T. J. Geary) No. Am. **157**: 52. — (S. Dean) Am. J. Pol. **1**: 130.
— — — Geary Bill for. Pub. Opin. **13**: 28, 129. **15**: 171, 194, 162, 241. — (M. J. Farreley) Am. Law R. **28**: 734. — (R. Ogden) Nation, **57**: 23.
— — — — China's View of. (G. Reid) Forum, **15**: 407.
— — — — Decision on. (E. L. Godkin) Nation, **56**: 358.
— — — — in California. (C. H. Shinn) Nation, **56**: 365.
— — — Method of Restriction. (G. Reid) Am. J. Pol. **3**: 465.
— — Question of. (J. R. Young) No. Am. **154**: 596.
— Responsibility among the. (C. M. Cady) Cent. **29**: 341.
— Schools of the. (H. A. Giles) Time, **6**: 20.
— Scientific Knowledge of Ancient. Nature, **52**: 622.
— Social and Religious Ideas of, as Illustrated in Ideographic Characters of the Language. (R. K. Douglas) Anthrop. J. **22**: 159.
— Through an Official Window. (E. S. Bates) Overland, n. s. **22**: 138.
Chinese Beliefs about the North. (K. Minakata) Nature, **51**: 32.
Chinese Coinage, Recent. (W. Fisher) Q. J. Econ. **10**: 467.
Chinese Coins. Sat. R. **75**: 386.
Chinese Culture compared with European Standards. (Tcheng-Ki-Tong) Asia R. **11**: 380.
Chinese Curios. Am. Arch. **39**: 136, 152.
Chinese Dictionary, A New. Acad. **42**: 462.
Chinese Divination, Yih-king. (C. de Harlez) Asia. R. **20**: 107. **22**: 115.
Chinese Domestics. (H. A. A. Coate) Time, **13**: 78.
Chinese Drama, The. (G. Adams) 19th Cent. **37**: 497. — (F. J. Masters) Chaut. **21**: 434.
Chinese Education and the Book of the Three Words. (P. Carus) Open Court, **9**: 4567.
Chinese Encyclopædia, A. (H. A. Giles) Time, **7**: 753.
Chinese Festivals. (Helen G. Flesher) Munsey, **9**: 402. — (R. K. Douglas) Good Words, **36**: 23.
Chinese Folk-tales. (A. M. Fielde) J. Am. Folk-Lore, **8**: 185.
Chinese Funeral Ceremonies, in America. J. Am. Folk-Lore, **1**: 239.
Chinese Gentlemen and Virtuosos. Temp. Bar, **104**: 419. Same art. Liv. Age, **205**: 62.
Chinese Humbug. (E. H. Parker) Contemp. **70**: 876.
Chinese Labor, Plain Truth about. (J. Barrett) No. Am. **163**: 620.
Chinese Labor Unions in America. (W. N. Fong) Chaut. **23**: 399.
Chinese Letter-shops. (S. L. Gracy) Chaut. **21**: 309.
Chinese Literati at Peking University. (M. L. Taft) Meth. R. **56**: 921.
Chinese Literature. Ath. '**93**, **2**: 222.
Chinese London and its Opium Dens. (J. Platt) Gent. M. n. s. **55**: 272.
Chinese Lottery, A. (S. Culin) Overland, n. s. **24**: 249.
Chinese Menu, A. Chamb. J. **71**: 801.
Chinese Musical System, Psychological Aspects of. (B. I. Gilman) Philos. R. **1**: 54, 155.
Chinese Ornaments. Dub. R. **114**: 179.
Chinese Outrages, Origin of. (H. H. Van Meter) Our Day, **15**: 202.
Chinese Philosophy. (P. Carus) Monist, **6**: 188.
Chinese Pirates, An Adventure with. Liv. Age, **207**: 317.
Chinese Poetry, Allen's. Sat. R. **73**: 693. — Spec. **69**: 233.
— in English Verse. (H. A. Giles) 19th Cent. **35**: 115. Same art. Liv. Age, **200**: 351.
Chinese Question, Solution of. (K. von Staufen) Am. J. Pol. **3**: 294.
Chinese Sacred Books, transl. by Legge. Sat. R. **74**: 284.
Chinese Secret Societies in the U. S. (S. Culin) J. Am. Folk-Lore, **3**: 39.
Chinese "Six Companies," The. (W. N. Fong) Overland, n. s. **23**: 518.
Chinese Traits and Japanese Traits. (E. F. Fenollosa) Atlan. **69**: 769.
Chinese View of Missionaries. (J. C. Hayllar) 19th Cent. **38**: 769.
Chinese War of 1860, Recollections of the. (W. H. James) Macmil. **71**: 241. Same art. Ecl. M. **124**: 444. Same art. Liv. Age, **204**: 626.
Chino-Japanese War, 1894. Un. Serv. (Phila.) **14**: 331. — (John O'Neill) New R. **12**: 180. — (C. H. Stockton) Nation, **62**: 476. — (F. Maurice) Un. Serv. M. **9**: 540. **10**: 94–632. **12**: 105, 201. — (L. H. Foote) Overland, n. s. **24**: 524. — (G. Droppers) Nation, **59**: 320. — (D. C. Greene) Outl. **51**: 57.
— and After. (T. F. Wade) Contemp. **66**: 609. Same art. Ecl. M. **124**: 52.
— and the Eastern Problems. (J. T. Yokoi) Am. J. Pol. **5**: 561.
— and International Law. (T. E. Holland) Un. Serv. (Phila.) **14**: 108.
— Causes which led to. (K. Oishi) Arena, **10**: 721.
— Chinese Collapse at Sea. (S. Eardley-Wilmot) Fortn. **63**: 87.

Chino-Japanese War, 1894: China's Reputation Bubble. (H. Knollys) Blackw. 156: 714.
— Commercial Aspects of. (T. M. Uyeno) Engin. M. 7: 771.
— Influence of, upon the Future of the American People. (H. Weinstock) Our Day, 14: 238.
— International Law in. (T. E. Holland) Fortn. 63: 913.
— Military Lessons of. (H. A. Herbert) No. Am. 160: 685.
— a Military Study. (T. A. Dodge) Forum, 18: 314.
— Naval Aspects of. (E. R. Fremantle) Forum, 20: 531.
— The Naval War. (W. L. Clowes) Blackw. 157: 282. — Ed. R. 180: 497.
— Ping Yang and Yalu, Battles of. Pub. Opin. 17: 620.
— Significance of. (M. Hisa) Forum, 18: 216. — (S. Kurino) No. Am. 159: 529.
Chinook, The; a story. (L. Outram) Eng. Illust. 11: 394.
Chinook Indians, Doctrine of Souls among. (F. Boas) J. Am. Folk-Lore, 6: 39.
Chinook Songs. (F. Boas) J. Am. Folk-Lore, 1: 220.
Chinese Texts, Boas'. (W. W. Newell) J. Am. Folk-Lore, 8: 328.
Chione; a poem. (A. Lampman) Canad. M. 7: 496.
Chippendale Furniture. (C. Dempsey) M. of Art, 4: 494.
Chippewas, Father Baraga's Apostolate among the. (R. R. Elliott) Am. Cath. Q. 21: 596.
Chiswick Ferry. Leis. Hour, 42: 118.
Chitral. Geog. J. 1: 51. — (S. Wilkinson) National, 26: 246.
— and Frontier Policy. (L. Griffin) 19th Cent. 37: 981. — (A. Colvin) Sat. R. 80: 38.
— and the Hindu Kush. (F. E. Younghusband) J. Soc. Arts, 43: 487.
— as an Outpost of India. Un. Serv. M. 11: 327.
— Campaign of, Thomson on. Sat. R. 80: 469.
— — Uselessness of. Sat. R. 79: 684.
— Cost of Holding. (W. Wedderburn) Sat. R. 80: 233.
— Defence of. Fortn. 64: 1. Same art. Liv. Age, 206: 538.
— Description of. Dub. R. 116: 410.
— Drama of. Spec. 74: 520.
— Fables, Legends, and Songs of. (G. W. Leitner) Asia. R. 11: 145.
— From, to Gilgit. Cornh. 72: 368.
— Future of. (G. W. Leitner) Asia. R. 20: 29.
— Garrisoned. (H. B. Hanna) Sat. R. 80: 200.
— Hunza, and the Hindu Kush. (F. E. Younghusband) Geog. J. 5: 409.
— Moral Effect of Retaining. Sat. R. 80: 73.
— Recent Events in. (G. W. Leitner) Asia. R. 15: 28.
— Relief of. (H. B. Harington) Acad. 49: 7.
— Settlement of. Dub. R. 118: 434.
— Why we went to. Blackw. 158: 402.
— Younghusband on. Dub. R. 117: 165.
Chittagong, Hill-tribes of. (C. T. Buckland) Macmil. 60: 199. Same art. Liv. Age, 182: 460.
Chittenden, L. E. Legal Reminiscences. Green Bag, 6: 13, 67, 266, 515.
Chittenden, Simeon Baldwin. (N. Porter) N. Eng. 51: 45.
Chittenden, Wm. L., with portrait. Bk. News, 12: 125.
Chiuta, Lake, British Central Africa. (R. Codrington) Geog. J. 7: 183.
Chivalry and Matrimony. (W. Wheater) Gent. M. n. s. 49: 178.
— Concerning. All the Year, 68: 462.
— Tête de Chevalerie at Brussels, 1892. (J. B. Osborne) Cosmopol. 14: 187.
Chloe, Chloris, and Cytheria. (G. Hall) Scrib. M. 19: 586.
Chlorates and Nitrates, Estimation of. (Charlotte F. Roberts) Am. J. Sci. 146: 231.
Chlorine, Generation of, for Laboratory Purposes. (F. A. Gooch and D. A. Krieder) Am. J. Sci. 148: 166.
Chlorite Group and its Alternative, Tschermak's Theory of. (F. W. Clarke) Am. J. Sci. 143: 190.
Chloroform, Natural. (T. Wood) Sund. M. 21: 130, 189.
— Poisoning Cases. Green Bag, 6: 557.
— Sir James Simpson's Introduction of. (E. B. Simpson) Cent. 25: 412.
— *vs.* Ether, Reports on. Sat. R. 82: 319.
Chlorophyll. *See* Color in Plants.
Choate, Joseph H. (F. A. Munsey) Munsey, 15: 80.
Choate, Rufus. (W. Everett) New Eng. M. n. s. 15: 375.
Choctaw Indians. (J. A. Watkins) Am. Antiq. 16: 259.
— of Mississippi. (J. A. Watkins) Am. Antiq. 16: 69. — (H. L. Halbert) Am. Antiq. 15: 146.
Chocorua, Mt., at Night, Alone on. (F. Bolles) Atlan. 70: 758.
— Deed of. Green Bag, 5: 9.
— in Literature. Atlan. 71: 846.
Chodowiecki, Daniel. (A. Dobson) M. of Art, 8: 402. — (E. T. Heyn) Mo. Illust. 3: 193.
Choice of Cyril Harjohn, The. (J. K. Jerome) Idler, 10: 4.
Choice of Parents. (I. Zangwill) Cosmopol. 20: 209.
Choice Spirits; a story. (W. W. Jacobs) Idler, 10: 380.
Choir and Organ, Church. (C. A. Richmond) Chaut. 19: 704.
— — Position of. (H. W. Brewer) Am. Arch. 44: 108, 124.
Choir and the Pastor. (J. C. Griggs) Music, 5: 688. — (U. X. Buttles) Music, 6: 271.
Choirs, Mediæval. (D. Bearne) Month, 82: 503.
Choirs, Surpliced Boy, in America. (S. B. Whitney) New Eng. M. n. s. 6: 139.
Choisy, François Timoléon, Abbé de. (L. Latimer) National, 20: 368. Same art. Liv. Age, 196: 25.
Cholera. (H. Sheffield) Arena, 6: 707. — (F. H. Candy) Gent. M. n. s. 49: 584. — (E. Klein) Nature, 49: 492.
— and Articles of Diet. (G. C. Frankland) Nature, 48: 375.
— and Cleanliness in Russia. (E. B. Lanin) Fortn. 58: 304. Same art. Ecl. M. 119: 549.
— and Exchange. (Shastri) Asia. R. 14: 415.
— and Quarantine. (R. Ogden) Nation, 55: 178.
— and the Sultan. (E. Hart) 19th Cent. 36: 538.
— Arsenic as a Prophylactic against. (R. B. Leach) Arena, 8: 51.
— at Hamburg, 1892. Sat. R. 74: 272.
— Bhowani, the Cholera-goddess. (E. H. Hankin) 19th Cent. 40: 543.
— Coming, in 1893. (E. Hart) New R. 8: 290.
— Daremberg on. (A. A. Woodhull) Nation, 55: 228.
— How can it be stamped out? (E. Hart) No. Am. 157: 186.
— How can we guard against? (C. F. Shrady) Engin. M. 4: 64.
— How to prevent the coming of. (S. Wells) Forum, 14: 743.
— in 1892, Conference at Venice and. (J. Rochard) Chaut. 16: 306. — Spec. 69: 9, 310.
— — in New York Harbor, Dr. Jenkins and the other Doctors. (E. L. Godkin) Nation, 55: 214.
— in England, Are we prepared to resist an Epidemic of? (A. Smith) New R. 9: 353.
— in Germany in 1894. (G. C. Frankland) Nature, 53: 63.
— in the U. S., Prospect of, in 1893. (D. B. St. J. Roosa) Engin. M. 5: 135.
— Is it coming in '93? (P. H. Bryce) Canad. M. 1: 194.

Cholera, Macnamara on. Sat. R. **74**: 289.
— Memoranda of. (Sir W. Moore) Asia. R. **14**: 419.
— Origin and Diffusion of. (W. R. Cornish) New R. **7**: 158.
— Pilgrim Path of. (E. Hart) Pop. Sci. Mo. **43**: 634.
— Prevention of. (H. Hamilton) Science, **20**: 170.
— — and Vaccination. Nature, **46**: 466.
— — How to make a City Cholera Proof. (P. Bigelow) Cosmopol. **15**: 497.
— Propagation and Prevention of. (R. Roose) New R. **8**: 504. Same art. Ecl. M. **121**: 51.
— Protection against. (E. Hart) 19th Cent. **32**: 632. Same art. Ecl. M. **119**: 721.
— Protective Inoculation for. (S. T. Armstrong) Pop. Sci. Mo. **42**: 223.
— Safeguards against. (W. Wyman; C. G. Wilson; S. W. Abbott; C. Edson) No. Am. **155**: 483.
— Sanitary Science and the Coming. (C. R. Hammerton) Chaut. **17**: 152.
— Seed-ground of. Spec. **71**: 358.
— Treatment of, New Method of. Nature, **47**: 83.
— Vaccination against. R. of Rs. (N. Y.) **6**: 697. — (W. M. Haffkine) Fortn. **59**: 316.
— What it costs Commerce. (E. Wiman) No. Am. **155**: 545.
Cholera Camp; a poem. (R. Kipling) McClure, **7**: 414.
Cholera Considerations. (S. V. Clevenger) Open Court, **6**: 3395.
Cholmondeley, T., Thoreau and. (F. B. Sanborn) Atlan. **72**: 741.
Chongo, Chase of the. (C. F. Lummis) Cosmopol. **15**: 145.
Chopin, F., Willeby's. Sat. R. **74**: 538. — Spec. **69**: 820.
— and his Music. Temp. Bar, **109**: 261.
— A Visit to, and his Last Concert. Music, **7**: 262, 586.
Chopin, Kate, with portrait. Bk. News, **14**: 6. — (W. Schuyler) Writer, **7**: 115.
Choral Societies in England, Failure of. Sat. R. **79**: 578.
Chorus, Greek. Bookworm, **2**: 249.
— in Later Greek Drama. (E. Capps) Am. J. Archæol. **10**: 287.
— in Modern Drama. (W. V. Moody) Harv. Mo. **14**: 142.
Chose in Action, Is a Right of Action in Tort a? (T. C. Williams) Law Q. **10**: 143.
— What is a? (H. W. Elphinstone) Law Q. **9**: 311. — (C. Sweet) Law Q. **10**: 303.
Chosen Valley, The. (M. H. Foote) Cent. **22**: 106–823.
Christ. *See* Jesus Christ.
Christ Church, Philadelphia, Records of. (C. R. Hildeburn) Pennsyl. M. **15**: 486. **16**: 111.
Christ-life, How to interpret. (J. K. Smyth) N. Church R. **2**: 598.
Christendom, Civilization of, Bosanquet on. (J. S. Mackenzie) Int. J. Ethics, **4**: 389.
— Reunion of, Earle's. Sat. R. **79**: 419.
Christian Art, Early, Cutts on. Sat. R. **77**: 453.
— — The Scriptures in. (R. Seton) Am. Cath. Q. **19**: 620.
— Old Testament Subjects in Early. (R. Seton) Am. Cath. Q. **20**: 501.
Christian Brothers in Ireland. Am. Cath. Q. **18**: 42.
Christian Consciousness, Schleiermacher and. Bib. Sac. **53**: 668.
Christian Doctrine, Dale's Discourses on. Church Q. **39**: 442.
— Development of, by J. H. Newman. Eng. R. **4**: 386.
— Fisher's History of. (H. M. Scott) Presb. & Ref. R. **7**: 728.
Christian Doctrine, Restatement of. (A. S. Weber) Ref. Q. **42**: 291.
Christian Endeavor, Society of. (A. E. George) Bost. **2**: 387.
— — Boston Convention. (H. T. Emery) Bost. **2**: 323.
— — in Presbyterian Church. (D. R. Breed) Presb. & Ref. R. **7**: 648.
Christian Endeavor Era. (T. Chalmers) Lippinc. **53**: 125.
Christian Endeavor Movement. (F. E. Clark and others) New Eng. M. n. s. **6**: 513. — (F. E. Clark) M. Chr. Lit. **6**: 356. — (F. E. Clark) No. Am. **161**: 287. — Pub. Opin. **19**: 115.
— Leaders of. (J. L. Hill) New Eng. M. n. s. **12**: 586.
Christian Family Life, Peerlessness of. (J. Cook) Our Day, **13**: 335.
Christian Fellowship as affected by Race. (W. E. C. Wright) Bib. Sac. **51**: 421.
— Centrality of. (E. H. Delk) Luth. Q. **25**: 527.
Christian Law, The. (B. F. Dunelm) Econ. R. **6**: 1.
Christian Life, Questions of the. (A. W. Thorold) Good Words, **33**: 137, 209.
Christian Monuments, Early. Ed. R. **181**: 206.
Christian Motive, The. (B. Holland) National, **28**: 36.
Christian Nurture *vs.* Bad Heredity. (A. S. Cheeseborough) N. Eng. **56**: 230.
Christian Science. (K. Coolidge) Arena, **7**: 554. — (J. Ferguson) Canad. M. **6**: 183. — (S. V. Clevenger) Open Court, **1**: 320.
— New-Church View. (A. F. Frost) N. Church R. **3**: 10.
Christian Social Union, The. (B. F. Dunelm) Econ. R. **5**: 153.
— Church Quarterly Review on. (V. H. Stanton) Econ. R. **5**: 516.
— in the U. S. (F. W. Speirs) Lend a H. **8**: 164.
Christian Socialist Movement of the Middle of the Century. (J. M. Ludlow) Atlan. **77**: 109. — (J. M. Ludlow) Econ. R. **3**: 486. **4**: 24.
Christian Teachers of the 19th Century. (T. B. Kilpatrick) Chr. Lit. **13**: 211, 253.
Christian Unity. (H. F. Manning; A. B. Bruce; J. Martineau) M. Chr. Lit. **5**: 297. — Lond. Q. **87**: 205. — Pub. Opin. **17**: 751. — Pub. Opin. **19**: 591.
— Bishop Perowne's Scheme of. Spec. **69**: 375.
— Cardinal Gibbons and. Chr. Lit. **12**: 15.
— Church of England and. (G. O. Morgan) Westm. **145**: 260.
— Religious Coöperation, Local, National, and International. (J. Strong and others) R. of Rs. (N. Y.) **6**: 300.
— Symposium. Indep. Apr. 13, '94.
Christianity. (H. C. Beeching) Cornh. **74**: 723.
— Aggressive, in India. (G. F. Pentecost) Our Day, **10**: 801, 884.
— Amateur. (W. H. Mallock) Fortn. **57**: 678. Same art. Ecl. M. **119**: 80.
— and Agnosticism. (P. R. Shipman) Open Court, **3**: 1668.
— and Buddhism. (C. Schroder) Arena, **5**: 458.
— and Communism. (W. S. Lilly) New R. **11**: 340. Same art. Ecl. M. **123**: 721.
— and Culture. (E. J. Wolf) Bib. Sac. **51**: 185.
— and Empire. Spec. **71**: 138.
— and English Institutions. (D. H. Wheeler) Chaut. **20**: 395.
— and the Ethical Spirit in relation to Progress. (C. Ford) Westm. **146**: 404.
— and Evolution of Rational Life. (J. T. Gulick) Bib. Sac. **53**: 68.
— and the Experimental Method. (R. McC. Edgar) Presb. & Ref. R. **6**: 201.

Christianity and Mohammedanism. (Max Müller) 19th Cent. 35: 302. Same art. Ecl. M. 122: 468. — (B. F. Kidder) Meth. R. 56: 528.
— and Monism. (P. Carus) Open Court, 2: 1379.
— and the Moral Law. (C. Lanza) Open Court, 1: 203.
— and Orientalism. (J. K. Smyth) N. Church R. 1: 52.
— and Patriotism. (Leo Tolstoi) Open Court, 10: 4967-5007.—Spec. 73: 42.
— and Poverty. Spec. 69: 763.
— and Progress. (C. Patmore) Fortn. 58: 85. Same art. Ecl. M. 119: 329. Same art. Liv. Age, 194: 695.
— and Roman Paganism. (St. G. Mivart) 19th Cent. 34: 822. Same art. Liv. Age, 199: 790.
— and the Saxons. (J. Hart, sr.) Bapt. R. 14: 76.
— and Social Duty. (V. H. Stanton) Econ. R. 3: 87. — (W. Sanday) Econ. R. 3: 348.
— and the State. (E. H. Delk) Luth. Q. 23: 40.
— Apperceptive. (M. H. Richards) Luth. Q. 26: 40.
— Application of. (C. W. Clark) And. R. 19: 18.
— Argument for, from Tendency. (J. Cooper) Ref. Q. 40: 194.
— as it is preached. (B. A. Brooks) Arena, 10: 795.
— as seen in a Tour of the World. (F. E. Clark) Our Day, 12: 378.
— Aspects of. (W. R. Thayer) Open Court, 3: 1491, 1500, 1515.
— at the End of this Age, Condition of. (J. G. Noss) Ref. Q. 41: 211.
— Authority in. (G. C. Lorimer) Arena, 7: 543.
— Bruce's Apologetics. (C. Chapman) Crit. R. 3: 3. — (E. Buckley) Bib. World, 6: 289.
— Claims of, Lilly on. Spec. 73: 54. — (H. C. Lea) Nation, 59: 85.
— The Corner-stone of. Open Court, 5: 2986.
— Cosmopolitan, in 20th Cent. (J. B. Donaldson) Our Day, 13: 87.
— Crumbling Corner-stone of. (C. K. Whipple) Open Court, 5: 2983.
— Early, Aspects of. (C. W. Super) Meth. R. 53: 896.
— — Conybeare's Monuments. (V. Bartlett) Crit. R. 4: 268.
— — Cruttwell's Literary History of. Church Q. 38: 183. — (C. A. Scott) Crit. R. 3: 382.
— — Spitta on. (G. G. Findlay) Crit. R. 4: 276.
— Early British. (F. Haverfield) Eng. Hist. R. 11: 419. — (F. W. Farrar) Sund. M. 23: 21-234.
— Essence of. (A. Menzies) Contemp. 69: 554. — (O. Pfleiderer) New World, 1: 401.
— Ethical Aim of. (M. Valentine) Luth. Q. 22: 523.
— Ethnic Religions and. (T. M. Stuart) Meth. R. 53: 35.
— Eve of. (F. T. Richards) Sund. M. 24: 52-314.
— Evidences of. (W. B. Greene, jr.) Presb. & Ref. R. 6: 142. — (R. McC. Edgar) Presb. & Ref. R. 6: 201.
— — Some Recent Phases. (A. W. Huizinga) Presb. & Ref. R. 7: 34.
— Evolution of. (W. M. Lisle) Bib. Sac. 49: 431. — (L. Abbott) New World, 1: 1. — (E. M. Caillard) Contemp. 64: 434.
— — Abbott on. (O. Cone) Arena, 7: 654.
— Foregleams of. Church Q. 37: 179.
— Future of. (A. B. Bruce) Bib. World, 6: 248. — (W. M. Salter) New World, 1: 618.
— Genesis of, Prof. Pfleiderer on. (J. Sandison) Open Court, 8: 4007.
— Gerhart's Institutes. (T. G. Darling) Presb. & Ref. R. 7: 163.
— Godet's Lectures on. (W. B. Greene, jr.) Presb. & Ref. R. 7: 524.
— Higher Education and. (C. F. Thwing) Educa. 12: 257.
Christianity, Historical Preparation for. (S. Weir) Meth. R. 52: 926.
— Historical Study of. (A. C. McGiffert) Bib. Sac. 50: 150.
— How I came into. (Nobuta Kishimoto) New World, 1: 311.
— Ideal in, Office of. (C. Norton) Arena, 8: 294.
— Imperial Power in the Realm of Truth. (J. R. Buchanan) Arena, 16: 276.
— in America, Four Centuries of. (H. M. Scott) Our Day, 12: 1.
— in Contact with the Roman World. (H. R. Reynolds) Thinker, 8: 329.
— in the East. M. Chr. Lit. 6: 115.
— in our National Life. (B. W. Williams) Am. J. Pol. 5: 25.
— Incompatible with Outward Forms of Government. (L. Tolstoi) N. Church R. 2: 255.
— Is it an Evolution? Lond. Q. 79: 60.
— Is it losing Ground? (C. A. Briggs; F. Adler; P. Carus) Forum, 16: 366.
— Is its Power waning? — No. (H. K. Carroll) Forum, 21: 376.
— its Spirit and its Errors. (V. Solovieff) Open Court, 5: 2899, 2917.
— Judaistic, Hort's. Sat. R. 79: 658.
— Kaftan's Truth of. (B. L. Hobson) Presb. & Ref. R. 7: 116. — (J. Iverach) Crit. R. 4: 175.
— Letter and Spirit. Meth. R. 56: 777.
— a Life. (A. M. Schmidt) Ref. Q. 39: 407.
— Mallock on. Spec. 68: 635.
— Modern, Historical Christ and. (A. B. Bruce) Thinker, 8: 28.
— — Horton on. Spec. 70: 666.
— Modernizing. (M. G. Hansen) Ref. Q. 42: 351.
— Moral Influence of. (H. H. Fairall) Meth. R. 56: 29.
— National, Meaning of. (H. P. Hughes) R. of Rs. (N. Y.) 6: 315.
— Natural History of, Mackintosh's. (A. Cave) Crit. R. 4: 339. — (B. B. Warfield) Presb. & Ref. R. 6: 507.
— Naturalness of. (J. Stalker) Good Words, 35: 429.
— Next Step in. (S. D. McConnell) New World, 1: 281.
— St. Paul's Conception of, Bruce on. (G. Vos) Presb. & Ref. R. 6: 761.
— Practical; a Symposium. Arena, 17: 67.
— Preaching of Christ and Practice of his Churches. (L. Tolstoi) New R. 10: 55. — Reply. New R. 10: 186.
— Primitive. (J. Reed) N. Church R. 1: 522.
— Reason in, Function of. (W. B. Greene, jr.) Presb. & Ref. R. 6: 481.
— Relation to Judaism. (J. M. Stifler) Bib. Sac. 53: 691.
— Ripening Experience of Life. Meth. R. 56: 450.
— A Sermon for the Season. (J. Adderly) National, 25: 482.
— Sociality of. (G. D. Herron) Arena, 14: 385.
— Spiritual and Historical Sides of, Relation between. Spec. 68: 337.
— True and False. (F. W. Farrar) McClure, 2: 451.
— Truth of. (A. Menzies) New World, 4: 57.
— Vindicated by its Enemies. (D. Dorchester) Chaut. 24: 163.
— What the Working Classes owe to. (G. F. Greene) Bib. Sac. 53: 282.
— Why do Men remain Christians? (T. W. Fowle) Contemp. 63: 115.
Christiansen, Einar. (D. K. Dodge) Poet-Lore, 6: 301.
Christie, Chancellor R. Copley. Bookworm, 2: 129.
Christie's Auction House. (M. H. Spielmann) M. of Art, 11: 225.

Christie's Auction House, Reverie at. Longm. 20: 473.
Christina, Queen of Sweden. (S. L. Clayes) Educa. 13: 174. — (R. S. Mylne) Scot. R. 28: 122. — Bk. Buyer, 11: 190.
— and her Books. (C. I. Elton) Bibliographica, 1: 5.
Christmas among the Tules. (M. B. Gibson) Outing, 25: 337.
— Ananias of Shirak upon. (F. C. Conybeare) Chr. Lit. 16: 176.
— and After. (H. C. Potter) Forum, 12: 677.
— at Byland. Macmil. 75: 103. — Liv. Age, 211: 865.
— and Christmases. (P. Weaver, jr.) Overland, n. s. 21: 32.
— and New Year. (R. H. Story) Good Words, 37: 819.
— at the Ridge House, A; a story. Chamb. J. 70: 716. Same art. Liv. Age, 199: 660.
— Colonial, in the Red Hills of Georgia; a story. (E. F. Andrews) Chaut. 22: 299.
— Flora of. (A. E. P. R. Dowling) Contemp. 62: 817.
— The German. (A. Tille) Folk-Lore, 3: 166.
— in Art. (C. Cook) Chaut. 16: 321.
— in Calcutta. Sat. R. 77: 144.
— in Canton. Chamb. J. 68: 801.
— in England, as seen by G. Cruikshank. Bost. 1: 269.
— in the Olden Time. (A. W. Jarvis) Good Words, 37: 836.
— on the Nile. (W. W. Hunt) Gent. M. n. s. 56: 182. Same art. Liv. Age, 208: 760.
— a Poem. (Will Hill) Cosmopol. 20: 217.
— The Second, under Cromwell. Sat. R. 74: 737.
— The Third, under Cromwell, 1655. Sat. R. 76: 702.
— What the Christmas Spirit saith unto the Churches. (G. Hodges) New Eng. M. n. s. 15: 469.
— What the Spirit of Christmas saith to the Nations. (B. F. Trueblood) New Eng. M. n. s. 15: 401.
Christmas Angel, The. (H. L. Bradley) Atlan. 74: 777.
Christmas Bell, The. (J. Lemaitre) Bach. of Arts, 2: 1.
Christmas Betrothal; a story. (F. Coppée) Cosmopol. 18: 323.
Christmas Books. (R. A. Bowen) Book R. 4: 223.
Christmas Cards. M. of Art, 4: 74.
Christmas Carol, A. (W. Canton) McClure, 8: 110. — (A. Austin) National, 24: 717.
Christmas Carols and Customs, Early. (R. H. E. Starr) Bost. 3: 243.
Christmas Color. Acad. 50: 595.
Christmas Customs and Superstitions. (E. F. Seat) Lippinc. 55: 96.
— in Central France. (Mabel Peacock) Gent. M. n. s. 55: 551. Same art. Liv. Age, 207: 813. Same art. Ecl. M. 126: 189.
— in Newfoundland. J. Am. Folk-Lore, 6: 63.
Christmas Day; a story. Belgra. 79: 298.
Christmas Decorations, Art in. (M. A. Haweis) M. of Art, 11: 104.
Christmas Eve. Shepherds' Midnight Mass in Alassio. (J. Leete) Argosy, 61: 28.
— and Christmas Day at an English Country House. (Sir E. Strachey) Atlan. 74: 729.
— at the Corner Grocery; a story. (W. A. Dromgoole) Arena, 7: 111.
— in the Chapel of Villa Cristina. (E. Vere) Argosy, 56: 468.
Christmas Feel in the Air; a poem. (J. W. Riley) Cosmopol. 18: 211.
Christmas Fox-hunt in Old Virginia. (A. Hunter) Outing, 23: 274.
Christmas Greens, New York Traffic in. Garden & F. 9: 511.
— of America. (A. C. Sage) New Eng. M. n. s. 13: 461.
Christmas Guest; a monologue. (R. M. Stuart) Cent. 27: 198.
Christmas Kalends of Provence; a story. (T. A. Janvier) Cent. 31: 265.
Christmas Knock; a story. (E. E. Kitton) Argosy 57: 73.
Christmas Legend of King Arthur's Country. (Arthur Warren and J. L. Williams) Cosmopol. 20: 115.
Christmas Letters. (E. L. Hall) Bach. of Arts, 2: 53.
Christmas Maskings in Boston. (W. W. Newell) J. Am. Folk-Lore, 9: 178.
Christmas Memories; a story. (S. Fanny G. Wilder) Bost. 1: 240.
Christmas Mummers in Dorsetshire. Folk-Lore Rec. 3: 87.
Christmas Offices, Two Mediæval. (F. E. Gilliat-Smith) Dub. R. 116: 46.
Christmas Party, A; a story. (C. F. Woolson) Harper, 86: 40.
Christmas Picture, The; a story. (R. Barr) Idler, 6: 521.
Christmas Plays, Old. (A. W. Pollard) Univ. R. 5: 517.
Christmas Poultry. (P. A. Graham) Chamb. J. 73: 785.
Christmas Presents; a story. (J. Richepin) Idler, 2: 532.
Christmas Sermon. (P. Brooks) Cent. 25: 179.
Christmas Society, New York. (R. W. DeForest) Char. R. 1: 105.
Christmas Tragedy; a story. (A. H. Morrison) Canad. M. 2: 150.
Christmas Telegrams; a story. (L. Kip) Overland, n. s. 19: 18.
Christmas Tree, The German. (A. Tille) Folk-Lore, 3: 166.
Christmas Tree Vendor. (F. Smith) Eng. Illust. 14: 343.
Christmas Trees. Spec. 77: 932.
Christmas Vision, A. (E. M. Ayling) Theatre, 19: 300.
Christocentric Theology. (C. F. Dole) New World, 5: 422.
Christophe, Ernst Louis Aquilas. (E. F. S. Dilke) Art J. 46: 40.
Christopher, Saint. Irish Mo. 15: 216.
Christ's Hospital. (E. H. Pearce) New R. 12: 171.
Chromatophores of Animals. (W. Garstang) Sci. Prog. 4: 104.
Chromium, Qualitative Separation of, from Iron and Aluminum. (R. B. Riggs) Am. J. Sci. 148: 409.
Chronicles of Carter Barracks. Un. Serv. (Phila.) 13: 508.
Chronicles of Count Antonio, The. (A. Hope) Chamb. J. 72: 1–243.
Chronicles of Elvira House, The. (H. Keen) Idler, 9: 77–846.
Chronicles of San Lorenzo. (H. A. Vachell) Overland, n. s. 24: 298–504. 25: 69–483. 26: 91.
Chronicles of Westerly. Blackw. 151: 83, 216.
Chronograms. (J. Hilton) Antiq. n. s. 25: 167, 264. 26: 109, 216. 27: 255. 28: 163, 197.
Chronograph, Electric Clock Connections for operating. (G. W. Hough) Astron. 13: 184.
— New Pendulum. (E. C. Sandford) Am. J. Psychol. 5: 385.
— Pendulum, Simple. (C. Barus) Am. J. Sci. 148: 396.
— Tuning-fork. (W. L. Webb) J. Frankl. Inst. 134: 219.
Chronology, Misleading, of History. (S. W. Balch) Educa. 13: 291.
— Sacred. Eng. R. 6: 77.
— Some Points in. (R. W. McFarland) Science, 20: 213.
Chronoscope, Hipp, Pendulum as a Control Instrument for. (L. Witmer) Psycholog. R. 1: 506.

Chrysanthemum, "Golden-wedding." Garden & F. 5: 556.
— "Walter Hunnewell." (T. D. Hatfield) Garden & F. 5: 16.
Chrysanthemum Blight. (S. A. Beach) Garden & F. 5: 153.
Chrysanthemum Show, American Institute. Garden & F. 8: 469.
— Boston. Garden & F. 5: 550.
— Cincinnati. Garden & F. 5: 562.
— London. Garden & F. 5: 568.
— New York. Garden & F. 5: 539.
— Philadelphia. Garden & F. 5: 551.
Chrysanthemums. (J. N. Gerard) Garden & F. 5: 67, 381, 513. — (T. D. Hatfield) Garden & F. 8: 247, 377, 517.
— at Cornell University. (W. Miller) Garden & F. 8: 466.
— at Short Hills, N. J. Garden & F. 5: 526. 6: 469. 7: 449.
— Carnations and. (T. D. Hatfield) Garden & F. 8: 427.
— the Chicago Show. (F. C. Seavey) Garden & F. 6: 489.
— Cultivation of. (T. D. Hatfield) Garden & F. 6: 388, 517. 7: 97, 177, 255, 337, 408.
— — in the Open Air. Garden & F. 7: 447.
— Exhibitions of, Boston and Philadelphia. Garden & F. 9: 468.
— — in England. (W. Watson) Garden & F. 6: 503.
— for Exhibition. (J. N. Gerard) Garden & F. 6: 488.
— for Specimen Plants. (T. D. Hatfield) Garden & F. 8: 196.
— Frozen, at the Royal Aquarium. (L. Dodge) Garden & F. 5: 478.
— in Philadelphia and Boston. Garden & F. 7: 458.
— Late. Garden & F. 5: 595.
— Midsummer Care of. (T. D. Hatfield) Garden & F. 8: 287.
— Naturally Grown. (J. N. Gerard) Garden & F. 5: 573. — Garden & F. 7: 498. — (J. N. Gerard) Garden & F. 7: 519.
— Newer. (M. Barker) Garden & F. 8: 36.
— Notes on. (T. D. Hatfield) Garden & F. 9: 85, 476.
— Out-of-doors. (D. Dandridge) Garden & F. 9: 498.
— Popularity of. Garden & F. 6: 491.
— Propagation of. (T. D. Hatfield) Garden & F. 7: 76. 8: 46, 127.
— the Royal Flowers of Japan. (L. E. Purdy) Mo. Illust. 11: 307.
— Seedling. Garden & F. 5: 561.
— Show, of New York. Garden & F. 6: 478.
— Some Good. (F. D. Hatfield) Garden & F. 8: 436.
— Spring Cultivation of. Garden & F. 6: 126.
Chryselephantine Sculpture. M. of Art, 2: 116.
Chudleigh, John; an Elizabethan Adventurer. (R. W. Cotton) Macmil. 71: 190.
Chum, Etymology of. (W. W. Skeat and others) Acad. 49: 407, 429.
Chump's Sacrifice, The. (P. E. Quinn) Idler, 7: 110.
Church, Alfred J. Burning of Rome. Spec. 68: 20.
— Hymn of the Harvest. Dial (Ch.) 15: 199.
Church, Fred. S., with portrait. Bk. Buyer, 11: 196.
Church, Sir Richard. (R. Hughes) Acad. 48: 403.
— The End of the Story; from Unpublished Papers. (E. M. Church) Blackw. 156: 254.
Church, R. W., Dean. (W. Sanday) Crit. R. 1: 235. — Lond. Q. 84: 1. — (A. K. H. Boyd) Longm. 25: 604.
— Life and Letters of. Ath. '94, 2: 821. — Spec. 73: 842. — (G. A. Simcox) Acad. 47: 27. — (C. A. L. Richards) Dial (Ch.) 18: 176. — (J. W. Chadwick) Nation, 60: 348. — Church Q. 40: 85. — Sat. R. 79: 14.
Church, R. W. Village Sermons. Spec. 68: 372.
Church, Samuel H., with portrait. Bk. News, 13: 139.
Church, The. Meth. R. 52: 120.
— Aim and End of. (W. C. Schaeffer) Ref. Q. 40: 493.
— American, and the Primitive Church. (L. W. Bacon) Chr. Lit. 13: 177.
— and the Bible. (F. von Hügel) Dub. R. 116: 306, 313.
— and the Churches. (M. Loy) Luth. Q. 24: 412.
— and the Dispensations. (T. B. Hayward) N. Church R. 1: 557.
— and Economic Reforms. (C. H. Zimmerman) Arena, 10: 694.
— and the Empire, A. D. 250–312. (J. J. Shahan) Am. Cath. Q. 19: 57.
— and Ethical Societies. (G. von Gizycki) Eth. Rec. 2: 47.
— and the Kingdom of God. (J. M. Campbell) Bib. Sac. 51: 131.
— and Labor Problems. (W. How and others) M. Chr. Lit. 5: 463.
— and the Masses. (R. V. Hunter) Presb. & Ref. R. 4: 78.
— and Music. (W. R. Chamberlain) Music, 11: 10.
— and People, Alienation of. (C. A. Briggs) Forum, 16: 366.
— and Popular Skepticism. (S. A. Orb) Luth. Q. 26: 555.
— and the Press. (J. T. Bunce) National, 22: 387. Same art. Ecl. M. 121: 817. — (A. R. Buckland; P. W. Clayden; W. T. Stead) Chr. Lit. 11: 298.
— and Property. (R. Ogden) Nation, 60: 418.
— and Saloon as Political Antagonists. (J. G. Woolley) Our Day, 11: 12.
— and Social Reform. (D. Kinley) Bib. Sac. 50: 377. — (W. Gladden) Chr. Lit. 14: 68.
— and Social Work. (H. S. Holland) Econ. R. 5: 1.
— and State. (L. Johnston) Cath. World, 59: 731. — Eng. R. 5: 437. 9: 157. 10: 127. 11: 387. 18: 116.
— — in Canada. (G. R. Stetson) And. R. 17: 476.
— — in Early Maryland. (G. Petrie) J. H. Univ. Studies, 10: no. 4.
— — in New England. (P. E. Lauer) J. H. Univ. Studies, 10: nos. 2, 3.
— — — Effects upon American Congregationalism. (A. H. Ross) Bib. Sac. 49: 213.
— — in 12th and 19th Centuries. Eng. R. 14: 38.
— — Molinari on. (W. Lloyd) Westm. 137: 371.
— — Separation of. (A. Réville) Open Court, 1: 369, 396.
— — — Symposium: Indep. Jan. 14, '92.
— — Supremacy Question. Eng. R. 13: 173.
— — Union of. Eng. R. 11: 286.
— and the World. (P. Cameron) Arena, 6: 584. — (J. E. Learned) Meth. R. 52: 434.
— as a Missionary Field. (W. Vrooman) Arena, 9: 696.
— Attack on. National, 21: 230.
— Civic Function of. (L. S. Bean) Our Day, 13: 215.
— Civic, Stead's. (J. Cook) Our Day, 13: 440.
— The Coming Ideal. (A. A. Pfanstiehl) Ref. Q. 39: 234.
— Corruption of, through Wealth. (W. A. Evans) Arena, 14: 228.
— The Enlarged. (D. Swing) Forum, 14: 67.
— Fatal Mistake of. (W. A. Douglass) Canad. M. 6: 469.
— Five Theories of. (L. W. Bacon) Chr. Lit. 13: 241.
— Free, for America. (W. P. McKenzie) Arena, 8: 630.
— Function of. (E. M. Fairchild) Am. J. Sociol. 2: 220.
— Gore's Mission of. Church Q. 35: 507.

Church, Holy Catholic. (Canon McCormick) Chr. Lit. **10**: 30. — (R. E. Bartlett) Contemp. **63**: 398.
— Ideal of a. Eng. R. **2**: 179.
— in Apostolic Times, Unity of. (T. M. Lindsay) Contemp. **68**: 548.
— in the Middle Ages, Moeller's. Sat. R. **76**: 652.
— in the Roman Empire before 170, Ramsay on. Ath. '93, **2**: 123. — Church Q. **36**: 363. — (G. G. Findlay) Crit. R. **3**: 356.
— in the South. (A. E. P. Albert) Meth. R. **52**: 229.
— Institutional. (C. S. Mills) Bib. Sac. **49**: 453. — (G. W. Cooke) New Eng. M. n. s. **14**: 645. — (C. P. Woolley) Open Court, **9**: 4419.
— Is its Influence growing? (M. Fowler) Chr. Lit. **12**: 164.
— Its Position in Modern Reform Movements. (S. S. Seward) N. Church R. **1**: 481.
— Its Work becoming more Spiritual. (J. E. Mills) N. Church R. **2**: 408.
— Labor Problem and. (K. Hardie) Thinker, **8**: 105. — (J. M. Lang) Thinker, **8**: 295.
— Local, Expansion of. (A. E. Dunning) And. R. **17**: 12.
— Meaning of. (Archdeacon Sinclair) Chr. Lit. **12**: 285.
— Modern, Art in. (Barr Ferree) Am. Arch. **50**: 3-143.
— — Compared with the Ancient. (J. Reed) N. Church R. **3**: 529.
— Municipal Idea of. (W. Gladden) R. of Rs. (N. Y.) **6**: 305.
— New Jerusalem *vs.* Old Jerusalem. N. Church R. **1**: 623.
— not generally Attended by Young Men. N. Church R. **2**: 278.
— not Older than the Bible. (J. Tomlinson) Luth. Q. **24**: 435.
— of the Commonwealth, under Cromwell. (H. A. Glass) Contemp. **65**: 74.
— of England. Eng. R. **1**: 44. **2**: 55.
— — Absolution in. Eng. R. **12**: 196.
— — Alienation of Endowments of. (A. Jessopp) 19th Cent. **34**: 56.
— — and Christian Reunion. (Sir G. O. Morgan) Westm. **145**: 260.
— — and her Elementary Schools. (G. W. Gent) Econ. R. **4**: 353.
— — and Labor Combinations. (H. S. Holland) Econ. R. **2**: 441.
— — and the Parish Council Bill. Spec. **71**: 542.
— — and the Poor. Spec. **69**: 219.
— — and the Tithe Acts. (H. R. Farquharson) National, **26**: 379.
— — and the Unionist Party. National, **28**: 302.
— — Anglican Theory of the Church. (E. R. Hull) Month, **81**: 498. **82**: 129.
— — Anglican Theory of Continuity. (A. F. Marshall) Am. Cath. Q. **17**: 578.
— — Auricular Confession and. (T. T. Shore; T. T. Carter) Chr. Lit. **12**: 210, 280.
— — The Case for the Curates. (A. G. B. Atkinson) Contemp. **69**: 112.
— — Changes in. (R. Gregory) No. Am. **156**: 149.
— — Church Reform. (J. J. Lias) Contemp. **70**: 408.
— — Clerical Preferment under the Duke of Newcastle. (M. Bateson) Eng. Hist. R. **7**: 685.
— — Congress of, 1892. Spec. **69**: 441. Sat. R. **74**: 406.
— — — 1893. Spec. **71**: 457.
— — — 1895. (W. Lefroy) Sat. R. **80**: 467.
— — Convocation, Reform of. Spec. **70**: 186.
— — Constitutional History of, Makower's. Church Q. **42**: 82. — (C. L. Wells) Am. Hist. R. **1**: 709.
Church of England. Defence or Reform? (A. Jessopp) 19th Cent. **39**: 132, 356.
— — Disestablishment of. (H. M. Bompas) Fortn. **63**: 362. — (H. G. Morgan) National, **21**: 567. — (A. Birrell) New R. **10**: 37. — Quar. **175**: 258.
— — — After. (A. Berlyn) Westm. **139**: 386.
— — — and Disendowment, Moral Aspects of. (W. J. K. Little) Contemp. **67**: 29.
— — — and the State Bishops. (A. Graham-Barton) Westm. **139**: 257.
— — — Anti-. (A. Graham-Barton) Westm. **143**: 357.
— — — Aspects of. Sat. R. **78**: 157.
— — — in Scotland. Spec. **68**: 736.
— — — in Wales. (T. Darlington; C. H. Bromby) Contemp. **63**: 809. — (R. E. Webster; A. G. Boscawen) National, **23**: 449. Spec. **68**: 291.
— — — — Gladstone's Decision on. Spec. **71**: 393.
— — — — Canon Holland on. Spec. **70**: 697.
— — — in Wales and Ireland. (T. Darlington; A. Houston) Contemp. **65**: 649.
— — — Some Side Aspects of. National, **23**: 128.
— — — Unconsidered Contingencies. (W. R. Inge) National, **18**: 65.
— — Disestablishment Fictions. (A. G. Asaph) National, **25**: 705.
— — Ecclesiastical Law of, Phillimore's. Sat. R. **82**: 119.
— — Ecclesiastical Mediators. Spec. **68**: 771.
— — Education by. Eng. R. **1**: 390.
— — Endowment of. (J. G. Whiteley) Chaut. **22**: 337.
— — Gore on. Spec. **70**: 224.
— — High Church Party. (G. W. Child) Contemp. **62**: 736. Same art. M. Chr. Lit. **7**: 218.
— — High Church Position Untenable. (A. F. Hewit) Am. Cath. Q. **18**: 249.
— — Historic Protest of, and Reunion with Rome. (W. Sinclair) National, **27**: 614.
— — History of. Eng. R. **12**: 418.
— — in 19th Century, Overton's. Ath. '94, **1**: 205. — Sat. R. **77**: 156. — Church Q. **38**: 87. — (W. P. Courtney) Acad. **45**: 511.
— — The Kirk's Alarm. (Reuben Butler) New R. **13**: 75.
— — Lacking Order and Jurisdiction. (A. F. Marshall) Am. Cath. Q. **20**: 226.
— — Liberal Theology in. (T. C. Snow) Contemp. **61**: 106.
— — The New Clergy. (H. R. Haweis) Contemp. **68**: 591.
— — New Radicalism and. Spec. **69**: 344, 377.
— — Newspapers and. Spec. **69**: 120.
— — on the Continent. Eng. R. **2**: 453.
— — Opportunity of. (S. A. Barnett) Contemp. **68**: 348. Same art. Ecl. M. **125**: 577. Same art. Chr. Lit. **13**: 304.
— — Orders in: are they Valid? (C. J. Powers) Cath. World, **63**: 674, 812. — (W. Lloyd) Westm. **146**: 1. — Church Q. **41**: 281. **42**: 24. — (T. E. Bridgett) Dub. R. **118**: 1.
— — — Nature of. (A. M. Mackay) Westm. **146**: 388.
— — — Pope's Bull on. (Herbert Vaughan) Chr. Lit. **16**: 59.
— — Ordination in, Rome's Tribute to. Dub. R. **113**: 766.
— — Outlook for. Liv. Age, **211**: 585.
— — The Parish Priest before the Reformation. (A. Jessopp) 19th Cent. **36**: 468.
— — Patronage of, Bill for Regulation of, 1893. Spec. **70**: 318. — (R. C. Jenkins) Fortn. **59**: 543.
— — The Pope and the Anglicans. (T. A. Lacey; Catholicus) Contemp. **70**: 793.
— — Position of. (J. C. Hopkins) Canad. M. **4**: 30.

Church of England, Priest and Altar in. (F. Peek) Contemp. 64: 681.
— — Reform in. (A. G. Edwards) National, 26: 409. — Contemp. 68: 651. — (A. G. Boscawen) National, 28: 477.
— — Reformation and Reunion. (G. W. E. Russell) 19th Cent. 40: 34.
— — Sustentation Fund. (W. Lefray) National, 26: 685.
— — *Via-media* Position of. (G. J. Cowley-Brown) National, 22: 203. Same art. Ecl. M. 121: 677.
— — Vindication of. Eng. R. 7: 88.
— — What is Church Authority in? (T. T. Shore) 19th Cent. 37: 435.
— — What is the Law of the Church? (G. Serrell) Contemp. 70: 663.
— — C. Wordsworth on. Eng. R. 1: 180.
— of Scotland, Disruption of, Jubilee of. (J. Stalker) Sund. M. 22: 334.
— — Free, Semi-centennial of. (R. H. Howard) Meth. R. 53: 438.
— — General Assembly of, 1646-47, Records of. Spec. 69: 390.
— of the Upper Room, The. (J. Watson) Sund. M. 24: 517.
— Opportunity of. (G. D. Herron) Arena, 15: 42.
— Outer and Inner Growth of. (A. W. Lilly) Luth. Q. 22: 305.
— Position of, 1851. Eng. R. 13: 330. 16: 157.
— Primitive, and the See of Peter. Spec. 73: 176.
— Rational View of Sacraments and Rites of. (J. Copner) Westm. 144: 48.
— Relation of, to Labor. (A. E. Fletcher) R. of Rs. (N. Y.) 10: 407.
— Relations of, to Society. (C. Lathbury) Lend a H. 12: 413.
— Rest in. Eng. R. 9: 371.
— Rights of. (H. Rashdall) Econ. R. 6: 166.
— The Social Problem and. (M. I. Swift) Open Court, 1: 659.
— Social Questions and. (W. G. Blaikie) Thinker, 8: 8.
— The Stronghold of. (T. W. Higginson) Open Court, 1: 477.
— The Universal. (A. Taylor) Arena, 13: 185.
— Visible and Invisible. (J. C. F. Rupp) Luth. Q. 24: 64.
— Western, Early Chronicles of. Church Q. 35: 117.
— What is the? (W. Riddall) Thinker, 8: 423.
Church Authority; What is it? (T. T. Carter) 19th Cent. 37: 692. Same art. Chr. Lit. 13: 38.
Church Building; Symposium. Indep. Feb. 4, '92.
Church Chest, South Creake, Norfolk. Reliquary, 35: 102.
Church Council in relation to the Pastor. (S. J. Taylor) Luth. Q. 24: 164.
Church Dances at Seville. Spec. 68: 428. Same art. Liv. Age, 193: 575.
Church Discipline. Eng. R. 3: 79.
— Restoration of Corrective. Eng. R. 10: 77.
Church Emancipation. Eng. R. 14: 93.
Church Endowments. (F. Minton) Westm. 146: 477.
Church Entertainments, A Study of. (W. B. Hale) Forum, 20: 570. — (J. Reed) N. Church R. 3: 274.
Church Extension. Eng. R. 8: 141.
— and Reform. Eng. R. 11: 52.
Church Folk-Lore. (J. E. Vaux) M. Chr. Lit. 5: 483-7: 40.
— Vaux on. Sat. R. 77: 310.
Church-going, Alleged Decline of. Chr. Lit. 15: 517.
Church History, Literary Development of. (J. F. Hurst) Meth. R. 56: 681.
Church History, Studies in, Bright's. Church Q. 42: 342.
— Waymarks in, Bright's. Church Q. 39: 122.
Church Membership, Modern. (R. Ogden) Nation, 54: 83.
— Necessity of. (W. W. Lance) Meth. R. 56: 902.
Church Militant, The; a story. (Barry Pain) Idler, 9: 328.
Church Missionary Society and Proselytism. Church Q. 33: 492.
Church Missions, Irish. Eng. R. 16: 352.
Church Music. Eng. R. 5: 161. — (W. S. B. Mathews) Music, 5: 144.
— Ancient. (R. C. Hope) Walford's Antiq. 3: 24.
— Problem of. (E. Dickinson) Music, 6: 391.
— Some Available. (W. S. B. Mathews) Music, 10: 471.
Church Offices, Natural and Spiritual. (I. N. Carman) Bapt. R. 14: 65.
Church Parade. Liv. Age, 209: 425.
Church Pews, Free and Unappropriated. Spec. 76: 10.
Church Plate of Scotland. Reliquary, 32: 154.
— — Burns on. Sat. R. 74: 230.
Church Porch, The. (S. Baring-Gould) Sund. M. 24: 741.
Church Property, Taxation of. *See* Taxation.
Church Steeples, Old. (S. Wilson) Gent. M. n. s. 50: 85.
Church Union. (A. F. Marshall) Am. Cath. Q. 18: 815. — Eng. R. 10: 167. — (S. A. Ort) Luth. Q. 22: 208. — (A. M. Mackay) Westm. 146: 572.
— and the Episcopal Church. (J. W. Santee) Ref. Q. 41: 297.
— Encyclical on. (Leo XIII.) Am. Cath. Q. 19: 777.
— Grindelwald Conference, 1894. Chr. Lit. 11: 342.
— in Japan. (D. W. Learned) And. R. 17: 465.
— Is it Possible? (G. D. Boardman) Pub. Opin. 15: 86.
— Lambeth Conference and. (J. A. Faulkner) Meth. R. 53: 513, 615.
— Movement for, Ideals of. (H. S. Lunn) Chr. Lit. 11: 294.
— a Necessity; the Maine Experiment. (W. DeW. Hyde) Forum, 15: 154.
— Reunion of Christendom. (Lord Halifax) 19th Cent. 39: 850.
— True Bond of. (J. M. Cromer) Luth. Q. 22: 507.
Church Unity. (J. Fox) Presb. & Ref. R. 7: 371. — Pub. Opin. 18: 767. — (Viscount C. L. Halifax) National, 26: 415. — (W. Lloyd) Westm. 144: 552.
— Ideal in. (R. D. Mallary) Chr. Lit. 12: 1.
— in Apostolic Times. (T. M. Lindsay) Contemp. 68: 548. — Chr. Lit. 14: 82, 137.
— The One Flock of Christ. (C. A. Briggs) Ref. Q. 43: 302.
— Problem of the Divided Church. (G. Hodges) New World, 5: 438.
— Shields on. (H. M. Booth) Presb. & Ref. R. 7: 369.
— Spiritual or Ecclesiastical? (W. B. Carpenter) National, 27: 569.
— Symposium. Indep. Mar. 8, '94.
Church Work Changes and Church Workers. (H. Jones) Time, 19: 513.
Church Year. (G. U. Venner) Luth. Q. 24: 455.
Churches, Adaptation to Altered Condition of Life. (J. Strong) Chr. Lit. 11: 99.
— American, Foreigners and. (S. L. Loomis) Chaut. 17: 180.
— and Labor Unions. (J. P. Coyle) Forum, 13: 765.
— and the Masses. (T. C. Collings) Chr. Lit. 10: 87, 166, 224, 276.
— Anglican and Catholic, Is a Rapprochement between them Desirable? (E. Nelson; H. E. Fox; and Canon Bell) Chr. Lit. 11: 219.
— Clubs within. (R. Ogden) Nation, 59: 59.

Churches, Constitution of, in the Days of the Apostles. Church Q. **42**: 265.
— Coöperation between. (J. E. Bushnell) Luth. Q. **25**: 246.
— German, of Pennsylvania, Founding of. (J. H. Dubbs) Pennsyl. M. **17**: 241.
— Have we too many? (H. A. Bridgman) And. R. **17**: 488.
— in 1894; Symposium. Indep. Jan. 3, '95.
— in 1895; Symposium. Indep. Jan. 2, '96.
— in the U. S. in 1890. What the Census shows. (H. K. Carroll) Forum, **13**: 529.
Churches, English Country. (A. B. Bibb) Am. Arch. **49**: 11.
— French and English. (R. S. Peabody) Atlan. **76**: 174.
— in the Isle of Wight. (A. B. Bibb) Am. Arch. **50**: 5.
— of France, Some Great. 19th Cent. **35**: 481. Same art. Liv. Age, **200**: 792.
— of Périgueux and Angoulême. (M. G. Van Rensselaer) Cent. **29**: 918.
— of Provence. (M. G. Van Rensselaer) Cent. **27**: 117.
— Protestant, Design of. Am. Arch. **53**: 99.
— Restoration of. (J. T. Micklethwaite) Antiq. n. s. **26**: 162.
Churchill, Lord Randolph. (Sir H. Maxwell) National, **25**: 119. Same art. Liv. Age, **205**: 28. — New R. **12**: 245, 363. Same art. Ecl. M. **124**: 603. — (T. H. Escott) Fortn. **63**: 380. — R. of Rs. (N. Y.) **11**: 305. — Sat. R. **79**: 115, 686. — (A. West) 19th Cent. **40**: 567.
— and Modern Conservatism. Quar. **180**: 549.
— Resignation of. Time, **16**: 394.
Churchmen and their Politics. (C. L. Marson) Westm. **141**: 180.
Church Wardens, Old Accounts of. (E. Peacock) Dub. R. **110**: 152.
Churchyard by the Fen; a poem. (H. St. A. Denton) Argosy, **59**: 487.
Churchyards, English. Chamb. J. **70**: 357.
Cicero and his Case against Cæsar. Quar. **184**: 395.
— Commentariolum Petitiones, Authenticity of. (G. L. Hendrickson) Am. J. Philol. **13**: 200.
— De Oratore, Wilkins'. Sat. R. **74**: 227.
Cid, The, MS. of. (A. M. Huntington) Bookman, **4**: 31.
Cid Ruy, the Campeador; a poem. (J. Malone) Cent. **23**: 211.
— Legends of the; a poem. (A. De Vere) Cath. World, **55**: 741-**56**: 384.
Cider. (C. W. R. Cooke) J. Soc. Arts, **43**: 396.
Cider-making. (S. Baring-Gould) Good Words, **34**: 318.
Cigarette from Carcinto, A. (E. French) Outing, **20**: 13.
Cilatepetl, Mount. *See* Orizaba.
Cilicia, Eastern, Recent Discoveries in. (J. T. Bent) J. Hel. Stud. **11**: 231.
Cilicia Tracheia, Journey in. (J. T. Bent) J. Hel. Stud. **12**: 206.
Cima, Giovanni Battista. (B. Berenson) Acad. **46**: 284.
— Cost of his Altar-piece, "The Incredulity of Thomas." (F. Sacchi) Acad. **46**: 381.
Cimabue, Giovanni. Month, **80**: 197.
Cinch; a Christmas story. (W. A. Dromgoole) Arena, **11**: 100.
Cincinnati, O., Public Schools of. (J. M. Rice) Forum, **14**: 293.
Cincinnati Art Museum. M. of Art, **8**: 1, supp.
Cincinnati College of Music. Music, **2**: 75.
Cincinnati Ice Dam, The. (G. F. Wright) Pop. Sci. Mo. **45**: 184.
Cincinnati Southern R. R. (J. H. Hollander) J. H. Univ. Stud. **12**: 7.
Cincinnati, Society of the. (M. Benjamin) Chaut. **23**: 307. — (W. E. VerPlanck) New Eng. M. n. s. **14**: 676. — (J. Bunting) Lippinc. **51**: 609.
Cinderella. (R. H. Davis) Scrib. M. **19**: 460.
— and Britain. (A. Nutt and others) Folk-Lore, **4**: 133-413.
— Cox's. (W. W. Newell) J. Am. Folk-Lore, **6**: 159.
— Origin of. J. Am. Folk-Lore, **7**: 70.
— The Original. (G. Moore) Theatre, **28**: 26.
— a Spectacular Pageant, 1895. Bost. **1**: 579.
— up to Date. (E. Pullen) Cent. **30**: 132.
Cineraria, Origin of the Cultivated. (W. Bateson and others) Nature, **51**: 605. **52**: 3-128.
Cinerary Urn, Buckie, Banffshire. Reliquary, **35**: 229.
Cinerary Urns in Scotland. Reliquary, **36**: 178.
Cinque Port, Sunday at a. (W. V. Taylor) Sund. M. **25**: 254.
Cintla, Battle and Ruins of. (D. G. Brinton) Am. Antiq. **18**: 259.
Cipher-writing. (T. J. A. Freeman) Am. Cath. Q. **18**: 858.
Circassian Slave, The, in Turkish Harems. (E. B. Dietrick) Pop. Sci. Mo. **44**: 481.
Circle, Graduated, Determining Eccentricity of, with one Vernier. (F. L. O. Wadsworth) Am. J. Sci. **147**: 373.
— Squaring the. (H. Schubert) Monist, **1**: 197.
Circle in the Water, A. (W. D. Howells) Scrib. M. **17**: 292-428.
Circuit Notes; Court-room Sketches. Cornh. **71**: 357. Same art. Ecl. M. **124**: 671.
Circulating Libraries. All the Year, **74**: 488.
Circus, Advertising the. (C. T. Murray) McClure, **3**: 252.
— Behind the Scenes in the. (C. Moffett) McClure, **5**: 277.
— How it is put up and taken down. (C. Moffett) McClure, **5**: 49.
— A Week travelling with a. (G. Stewart) Eng. Illust. **16**: 63.
Cirques, Glacial. (I. C. Russell) Nature, **45**: 317.
Cisalpine Club. (W. Amherst) Dub. R. **112**: 107.
— Minute Book of. (W. Amherst) Dub. R. **112**: 321.
Cisco Fishing through the Ice. (E. W. Chubb) Outing, **19**: 305.
Cistercians, Settlement of, in England. (A. M. Cooke) Eng. Hist. R. **8**: 625.
Cities, American, Congested Districts in. (C. D. Wright) Our Day, **9**: 172.
— — Higher Life of. (Theodore Roosevelt) Outl. **52**: 1083.
— and Semi-public Corporations. (J. H. Gray) Am. J. Soc. Sci. no. **34**: 176.
— Charitable Work in. Lend a H. **14**: 251.
— Cleansing of, and Public Health. (G. E. Waring) Engin. M. **8**: 805.
— Congestion of: "Felix qui Causam Cognovit." (J. S. Lowell) Char. R. **2**: 420.
— Crowding of; The Flight from the Fields. (A. Gaye) Macmil. **65**: 293.
— Drift of Population to; Remedies. (H. J. Fletcher) Forum, **19**: 737.
— English, Municipal Insignia of. (R. S. Ferguson) Walford's Antiq. **6**: 66, 108.
— Enterprises of, Productivity of. (W. F. Willcox) Am. J. Sociol. **2**: 378.
— — Method of Determining Productivity of. (W. F. Willcox) Am. J. Soc. Sci. no. **34**: 162.
— Evolution of. (E. Reclus) Contemp. **67**: 246. Same art. Liv. Age, **204**: 707.
— Finance of. (F. R. Clow) Q. J. Econ. **10**: 455.

Cities, Finance of; Taxation and Expenditure as Illustrated by Birmingham. (E. O. Smith) J. Statis. Soc. 58: 327.
— German, The Government of. (A. Shaw) Cent. 26: 296.
— — What they do for their Citizens. (A. Shaw) Cent. 26: 380.
— Government of. (F. H. Cooke) Am. J. Pol. 3: 58. — (M. Storey) New Eng. M. n. s. 6: 432. — (A. Shaw) Our Day, 13: 472. — (Mrs. Cornelius Stevenson) Good Govt. 13: 123. — (C. E. Pickard) Am. J. Pol. 4: 378. — (J. R. Commons) Soc. Econ. 7: 28.
— — Brooklyn Idea in. (E. M. Shepard) Forum, 16: 38.
— — The Citizen and. (A. A. Bird) Citizen, 2: 100, 130.
— — Civil Service Reform in. (C. Schurz) Good Govt. 13: 93.
— — Cleveland Conference for Good City Government. (C. R. Woodruff) Am. M. Civics, 7: 167.
— — Democracy and. (E. A. Curley) Cosmopol. 14: 737.
— — Elections in, Separate from State. (J. B. Bishop) Nation, 58: 422.
— — First Nat'l Conference on Good City Government. Good Govt. 13: 84, 96.
— — Good. (C. R. Woodruff) Pub. Opin. 18: 536.
— — Good Govt. Clubs in N. Y. City. Good Govt. 13: 92, 112, 125. — (E. E. Hale) Cosmopol. 16: 735.
— — Home Rule for Cities. (W. H. Hotchkiss) R. of Rs. (N. Y.) 9: 682. — (F. J. Goodnow) Pol. Sci. Q. 10: 1. — (C. S. Palmer) Am. M. Civics, 9: 56.
— — in America, Failure of. (E. Porritt) National, 24: 245. Same art. Ecl. M. 123: 669.
— — in England. (E. Porritt) Chaut. 21: 168.
— — in Europe, Shaw on. (H. P. Judson) Dial (Ch.) 20: 43. — (C. E. Boyd) Am. Hist. R. 1: 535.
— — in Great Britain, Shaw's. (D. MacG. Means) Nation, 61: 120.
— — in the United States. (Seth Low) Outl. 53: 624.
— — The Mayor and the City. (H. N. Shepard) Atlan. 74: 85.
— — Movement for Good. (H. Welsh) Am. J. Pol. 5: 67.
— — Municipal Spirit in England. (R. P. Porter) No. Am. 161: 590.
— — Municipalities at Work, Birmingham. (F. Dolman) New R. 11: 74.
— — — Manchester. New R. 11: 499.
— — The New Municipal Movement. (W. F. McDowell) Meth. R. 56: 735.
— — of Baltimore. (T. P. Thomas) J. H. Univ. Stud. 14: 47.
— — of Birmingham. (G. F. Parker) Cent. 31: 71.
— — of St. Louis. (A. Shaw) Cent. 30: 253.
— — Official Complicity with Vice in. (W. H. Burke and others) Chr. Un. vols. 45, 46: — Chicago, 45: 1240; Louisville, 46: 18; Boston, 46: 65; San Francisco, 46: 115; Philadelphia, 46: 163; St. Louis, 46: 286.
— — Our Present Opportunity. (C. H. Parkhurst) No. Am. 158: 197.
— — Past, Present, and Future. (J. Chamberlain) New R. 10: 649.
— — Philadelphia Civic Club. Good Govt. 14: 5.
— — Problem of. (T. E. Will) Am. M. Civics, 7: 231. — (C. R. Woodruff) Am. M. Civics, 9: 382.
— — — Some Neglected Points in. (L. S. Rowe) Pub. Opin. 19: 810.
— — Problems of. (E. L. Godkin) Ann. Am. Acad. Pol. Sci. 4: 857.
— — Recent Books on. (H. P. Judson) Dial (Ch.) 18: 147.
Cities, Government of, Reform in. (T. E. Will) Arena, 10: 555. — (L. Williams) Arena, 9: 644. — (E. W. Bemis) Dial. (Ch.) 16: 175. — (R. L. Bridgman) New Eng. M. n. s. 11: 698.
— — — Progressive, of 1894–95. (C. R. Woodruff) Am. M. Civics, 7: 66.
— — — Why a Failure? (C. E. Burton) Am. M. Civics, 6: 611.
— — Reform of, by Proportional Representation. (M. N. Forney) Citizen, 1: 278.
— — — the Duty of the Hour. (H. S. Pingree) Our Day, 16: 521.
— — Requisites for Good. (W. A. Bancroft) Pub. Opin. 20: 77.
— — Responsibility in. (F. W. Kelley) Am. J. Pol. 4: 449.
— — Symposium on. Indep. Sept. 13, '94.
— — Tammany Points the Way. (H. C. Merwin) Atlan. 74: 680.
— — Town Meeting Idea in. (J. F. Thomas) Am. J. Pol. 2: 503.
— — Why a Failure. (S. Cooley) Am. J. Pol. 3: 178. *See* Municipal.
— Great, Comparative Rank of. Spec. 68: 841.
— — Growth of. (L. M. Haupt) Cosmopol. 14: 83. — (D. MacG. Means) Nation, 61: 92.
— Housing of the People in Great. Cath. World, 64: 110.
— Immigration to, Decline of. (E. Cannan) National, 22: 624.
— Improvement of; a Lesson from the White City. (J. C. Adams) New Eng. M. n. s. 14: 3.
— in Business for Profit. (S. M. Lindsay) Am. Soc. Sci. no. 34: 154.
— in the U. S., Growth of, 1880–90. (C. Boyd) Am. Statis. Assoc. 3: 416.
— Irish Conquest of our. (J. P. Bocock) Forum, 17: 186.
— Laying-out. (J. Steuben) Am. Arch. 42: 113.
— Movement toward. Pub. Opin. 15: 501.
— Municipal Methods, Needed Changes in. (J. H. Walker) Am. M. Civ. 8: 199.
— Municipal Ownership of Franchises. (F. M. Loomis) Engin. M. 11: 814.
— Municipal Problems in America. (L. G. Jones) Soc. Econ. 2: 395.
— Municipal Progress and the Living Wage. (D. M. Means) Forum, 20: 11.
— Municipal Reform. (W. H. Tolman) Arena, 16: 728.
— of the World, The. (A. W. Greely) Nat. Geog. M. 5: 89.
— Political Parties in, Need of. (St.C. McKelway) Good Govt. 15: 121.
— Population of, Distribution of. (M. B. Hammond) Am. Statis. Assoc. 4: 113.
— Power of, to regulate Telephone Charges, control Streets, and force Overhead Wires into Conduits. (H. C. McDougall) Am. Law R. 30: 381.
— Reform of, Modern. (St.C. M'Kelway) Am. J. Soc. Sci. no. 34: 126.
— — Programme for. (F. MacVeagh) Am. J. Sociol. 1: 551.
— Sanitary Condition of, and Fine Arts. (W. Bayliss) J. Soc. Arts, 41: 196.
— Slums of Great. (C. Osborn) Econ. J. 5: 474.
— Some Problems of. (E. W. Bemis) Forum, 21: 53.
— State Supervision for. (J. R. Commons) Ann. Am. Acad. Pol. Sci. 5: 865.
— Underground Topography of. (W. B. Parsons) Engin. M. 11: 1015.
— Unhealthfulness of. (F. Peek; E. T. Hall) Contemp. 61: 221.

Cities, Urban Populations. (R. C. Billing) Fortn. 59: 388.
Citizen, American, What True Patriotism demands of. (R. Sherman) Am. M. Civics, 6: 392.
— in Politics. (G. Urquhart) Am. J. Pol. 3: 162.
— The, a Sovereign. (W. H. Goodale) Am. M. Civics, 7: 23.
Citizen Schneider. (Erckmann-Chatrian) Temp. Bar, 99: 260. Same art. Ecl. M. 121: 846.
Citizens, Better, and Fewer Laws. (C. Nagel) Eth. Rec. 3: 106.
Citizenship. (W. J. Gaynor) Am. M. Civics, 9: 225.
— and the Republic. (W. B. Baldwin) Am. M. Civics, 8: 280.
— The Bad, of a Good Citizen. (G. W. Ochs) Pub. Opin. 20: 717.
— by Birth. (G. D. Collins) Am. Law R. 29: 385. — — (H. C. Ide) Am. Law R. 30: 241.
— Christian. (J. G. Woolley) Our Day, 16: 129.
— Civic and Ecclesiastic. (Adolph Roeder) Am. M. Civics, 8: 401.
— Coöperation in Work for Good. (L. Satterthwait) Pub. Opin. 19: 620.
— Education for. (W. S. Harley) Educa. 12: 16. — — (C. R. Skinner) Pub. Opin. 20: 653.
— Good. (T. H. Evans) Am. J. Pol. 5: 225.
— — Aids to. (R. Jones) Educa. R. 11: 233.
— — Decadence of. (S. H. Ransom) Am. M. Civics, 7: 411.
— — Elements of. (F. De Land) Am. M. Civics, 6: 181.
— Obligation of the Inactive. (K. Trask) Forum, 20: 489.
— Obligations of. (W. H. Goodale) Am. M. Civics, 9: 414. — (C. A. L. Richards) Am. M. Civics, 8: 1.
— of the United States under the 14th Amendment. (M. B. Woodworth) Am. Law R. 30: 535.
— Qualifications for. (M. B. C. True) Am. M. Civics, 8: 534.
— A Question of. (W. A. Linn) Nation, 59: 134.
— Religion carried into. (H. R. Waite) Am. J. Pol. 5: 645.
— Study of, in the Grammar Schools. (E. L. C. Morse) Nation, 63: 421.
— The True Citizen. (E. L. Briggs) Am. M. Civics, 8: 465.
— University Training and. (W. Wilson) Forum, 18: 107.
— What the Citizen owes the State. (L. W. Keplinger) Am. M. Civics, 6: 196.
Citric Acid. Chamb. J. 72: 405.
City, The American. (M. McG. Dana) Gunton's M. 11: 135.
— Church and the. (G. P. Mains) Meth. R. 54: 221.
— in Modern Life. Atlan. 75: 552.
— in the Valley, The; a story. Outing, 20: 371.
— Mediæval, Mutual Aid in. (Prince Kropotkin) 19th Cent. 36: 183, 397.
— Planning the Site for a. (L. M. Haupt) Engin. M. 8: 626.
City Councils, Work of. (A. A. Bird) Citizen, 1: 206.
City Engineering Bureau, Ideal. (F. Collingwood) Engin. M. 9: 445.
City Garden. (C. S. Sargent) Garden & F. 7: 161.
City Hall, The, in the U. S. (B. Ferrée) Engin. M. 4: 201.
City Life, Advantages of. (L. B. Halsted) Soc. Econ. 4: 219.
City Lots, Cultivation of Vacant. (M. A. Mikkelsen) Forum, 21: 313.
City Missions and Social Problems. (F. M. North) Meth. R. 53: 228.
City Missions. A Famous Night Mission in N. Y. (L. Hereward) Westm. 140: 272. Same art. Ecl. M. 121: 507.
City Noises, Plague of. (J. H. Girdner) No. Am. 163: 296.
City Square, Evolution of a. (S. Parsons, jr.) Scrib. M. 12: 107.
City Transit, Public Control of. (S. Baxter) Cosmopol. 18: 54.
City of Dreams; a poem. (A. S. Hardy) Cosmopol. 20: 233.
Civic Aphorisms. (A. Roeder) Am. M. Civics, 7: 422.
Civic Centre Movement in England. R. of Rs. (N. Y.) 6: 307.
Civic Church, The. (W. T. Stead) R. of Rs. (N. Y.) 8: 438.
Civic Duty. (J. B. Bishop) Nation, 57: 4.
— Teaching of. (J. Bryce) Forum, 15: 552. — (J. Bryce) Contemp. 64: 14. Same art. Ecl. M. 121: 217.
Civic Education. (J. H. Fleming) Chr. Lit. 10: 34.
— Popular, in France. (W. B. Scaife) Pub. Opin. 18: 504.
Civic Helps for Civic Life. (M. McG. Dana) Soc. Econ. 8: 226.
Civic Life, Conduct of the. (L. R. Harley) Am. M. Civics, 8: 644.
Civic Policy. (J. Schouler) Pub. Opin. 19: 703.
Civic Reform, Perils of. (Z. S. Holbrook) Pub. Opin. 20: 268.
Civic Religion. (W. Gladden) Am. M. Civics, 7: 624.
Civic Renaissance, Our. (A. Shaw) R. of Rs. (N. Y.) 11: 415.
Civics, American Institute of, Decennial of. (H. R. Waite) Am. M. Civics, 6: 632.
— and Politics at Philadelphia Summer Meeting. (S. Axson) Lend a H. 14: 445.
— as a School Study. (W. K. Wickes) Lend a H. 9: 172.
— — by the Parliamentary Method. (J. W. Macdonald) Acad. (Syr.) 7: 217.
— Course of Reading in. (E. T. Devine) Pub. Opin. 21: 45.
— in American Universities. (F. J. Warne) Am. M. Civics, 7: 74.
— in Public Schools. (T. J. Wool) Am. J. Pol. 5: 171.
— A Practical Example in. (T. W. Haskins) Am. J. Pol. 5: 617.
— Practical Instruction in. (J. Macy) Am. J. Soc. Sci. 32: 151.
— a Science for Citizens, and a Creed for Patriots. (H. R. Waite) Am. M. Civics, 6: 202.
— Temporary Enthusiasm or Permanent Results in. (E. E. Sparks) Pub. Opin. 20: 46.
Civil Government, Teaching of. (A. M. Mowry) New Eng. M. n. s. 7: 501.
Civil Service as a Career. (H. T. Newcomb) Forum, 20: 120.
— The Home. Chamb. J. 72: 504.
— How Chicago got her Law. (E. J. Phelps) Good Govt. 14: 137.
— Improvement of. (W. G. Rice) No. Am. 161: 602.
— in Great Britain, Discontent in the. National, 23: 236.
— in Illinois. (J. T. Doyle) Good Govt. 14: 193.
— in India, House of Commons and. (T. Beck) National, 23: 372. — Spec. 70: 795.
— in N. Y., Violations of State Law. Good Govt. 14: 21, 33.
— — How the Bill of 1895 was killed. (G. McAneny) Good Govt. 14: 207.

Civil Service in U. S.; Anti-spoils League. Good Govt. 13: 85. 14: 38.
— — Cleveland's Manifesto, Office-seekers and. (L. Windmüller) Forum, 15: 478.
— — Ex-office-holders and. Good Govt. 12: 117.
— — Fixed Terms for Fourth-class Postmasters. (F. M. Loomis) Good Govt. 13: 78.
— — History of Reform Movement. Good Govt. 13: 99. — (D. B. Eaton) 13: 107. — (H. Lambert) 13: 121, 135, 149.
— — Influence on Parties and People. (W. D. Foulke) Good Govt. 13: 17.
— — Investigation of. Pub. Opin. 16: 455.
— — Noah Webster's Letters on. Good Govt. 14: 48.
— — Old Employees in the Treasury. (E. I. Renick) Good Govt. 13: 79.
— — Patronage and the Constitution. (C. W. Watson) Good Govt. 13: 53.
— — Presidential Appointments. Are they for Sale? (W. D. Foulke) Forum, 16: 399.
— — Preventing Frauds in Identification. (R. L. Dickinson) Good Govt. 14: 7.
— — Reform of. Am. J. Pol. 2: 278. — (A. H. V. Colquhoun) Canad. M. 7: 569. — (T. Roosevelt) Chaut. 16: 543. — Pub. Opin. 14: 299. — Pub. Opin. 16: 524.
— — — and Democracy. (C. Schurz) Good Govt. 12: 131.
— — — and Labor. (H. Welsh) Good Govt. 14: 195.
— — — and President Cleveland. (A. J. Palm) Am. J. Pol. 2: 546.
— — — a Decade of the Merit System. (J. T. Doyle) Forum, 14: 216.
— — — George William Curtis and. (S. S. Rogers) Atlan. 71: 15.
— — — President Hayes and. (S. W. Burt) Good Govt. 12: 93, 121.
— — — in its Bearings upon the Interests of Working-men. (H. Welsh) Am. M. Civics, 8: 631.
— — — in the Indian Service. (H. Welsh) Good Govt. 13: 41.
— — — in Party Platforms. (W. D. Foulke) Good Govt. 12: 141.
— — — Necessity and Prospects of. (C. Schurz) Good Govt. 14: 75.
— — — Present Status of. (T. Roosevelt) Atlan. 75: 239.
— — — Progress of. (C. Schurz) Good Govt. 15: 165.
— — Reform law. Pub. Opin. 17: 205.
— — Relative Value of. (R. H. Dana) Good Govt. 14: 99.
— — Review of Two Administrations. (L. B. Swift) Forum, 14: 201.
— — Scheme for Re-classification of Departmental Officers. Good Govt. 13: 126.
— — Six Years of. (T. Roosevelt) Scrib. M. 18: 238.
— — Ten Years of. (C. Lyman) No. Am. 157: 571. — Good Govt. 12: 105.
— — Theory and Practice of. (W. D. Foulke) Good Govt. 14: 140.
— — Value of. (T. Roosevelt) Pub. Opin. 18: 343.
— Problem of. (J. A. Elliott) Time, 16: 76.
Civil Service Appointments by Nomination. Chamb. J. 73: 181.
Civil Service Commission, U. S., Treatment of, by Congress, from beginning. Good Govt. 14: 19.
Civil Service Principles in the Department of State. (E. T. Renick) Nation, 62: 357.
Civil War, A; a story. (J. McCrae) Canad. M. 8: 109.
Civility. (E. J. Hardy) Argosy, 56: 23.
Civilization. Spec. 75: 362.
— Ancient and Modern. Soc. Econ. 1: 296, 371.
Civilization and the Arts, Evolution of. (G. Le Bon) Pop. Sci. Mo. 42: 342.
— and Astronomy. (A. W. Nitsch) Pop. Astron. 4: 206.
— and Decay, Adams on Law of. (A. B. Kant) Bach. of Arts, 3: 223.
— and Money. (G. S. Kimball) Am. J. Pol. 2: 626.
— and the State. (A. A. Johnson) Am. M. Civics, 6: 456.
— Curse of. (F. Petrie) Critic, 27: 205.
— Does it enervate? Spec. 77: 202.
— President Eliot's Chautauqua Address. Bach. of Arts, 3: 584.
— Five American Contributions to. (C. W. Eliot) Atlan. 78: 433.
— Future of. (J. L. Davies) Contemp. 63: 879. Same art. Liv. Age, 198: 387. Same art. Ecl. M. 121: 145.
— Geographical Progress of. (G. G. Hubbard) Nat. Geog. M. 3: 1.
— in America, Some Aspects of. (C. E. Norton) Forum, 20: 641.
— Modern, Great War of. (P. Greenwood) Macmil. 68: 414.
— Origin of. (F. Legge) Scot. R. 24: 366.
— Silent Currents of. (B. O. Flower) Arena, 6: 765.
— a Transition in. (H. L. Biddle) Chaut. 23: 737.
— War and Progress. (L. G. Janes) Soc. Econ. 3: 331.
Civilized Man, Oldest. (E. D. Cope) Am. Natural. 30: 616.
Civitas Dei; a poem. (Lewis Morris) Cosmopol. 20: 660.
Claims, Private, against the State. (E. Freund) Pol. Sci. Q. 8: 625.
Clairmont, Mrs., "Geo. Egerton," with portrait. Bk. Buyer, 11: 243. — With portrait. Bk. News, 13: 266.
— Discords. Sat. R. 79: 416.
Clairvoyance, Long-distance, Experiments in. (M. M. Dawson) Psychic. R. 2: 294.
Claosaurus and Clevatosaurus, Restorations of. (O. C. Marsh) Am. J. Sci. 144: 343.
— Skull and Brain of. (O. C. Marsh) Am. J. Sci. 145: 83.
Clapp, David, Memoir of. (W. B. Trask) N. E. Reg. 48: 145.
Claque, The. (A. Escott) Theatre, 36: 259.
Clarence, Duke of. Blackw. 151: 326. — New R. 6: 129.
— Death of. Sat. R. 73: 57, 85.
— — A Poem. (A. Tennyson) 19th Cent. 31: 181.
— in India, Rees'. Spec. 68: 718.
Clarendon Press. Book R. 3: 155.
Claretie, Brichanteau, Comedien. (H. H. Fyfe) Theatre, 37: 198.
Clarissa Furiosa; a story. (W. E. Norris) Cornh. 73: 1–564. 74: 114–828.
Clark, F. E. (J. W. Baer) Outl. 54: 151.
Clark, George B., with portrait. (J. A. Brashear) Astron. 11: 367.
Clark, George Rogers. Intercepted Letters and Journal, 1778, 1779. Am. Hist. R. 1: 90.
Clark, Jas. G., with portrait. (B. O. Flower) Arena, 7: 607. 14: 52.
Clark, Major John. (E. W. Spangler) Pennsyl. M. 20: 77.
Clark, Robert. Ath. '94, 1: 380.
Clark, Rutherfurd, Lord. (A. W. Renton) Green Bag, 4: 543.
Clarke, George. Nat'l M. (N. Y. '91) 18: 1.
Clarke, George. (A. Croxton) Theatre, 31: 121.
Clarke, McDonald. (W. S. Hillyer) Mo. Illust. 12: 357.
Clarke, Marcus. (F. Adams) Fortn. 58: 352.
Clarke, Mary Cowden. My Long Life. Critic, 29: 344.

Clarke, Thomas B., Collection of Paintings. (C. de Kay) M. of Art, **10**: 37.
Clarke Papers. (J. H. Round) Ath. '94, **2**: 829.—(C. H. Firth) Ath. '94, **2**: 893.
Class and Labor Misrepresentations. Westm. **142**: 419.
Class Sympathies. (E. L. Linton) National, **26**: 400. Same art. Ecl. M. **125**: 839.
Class-day Madonna, The; a story. (J. Corbin) Outing, **23**: 40.
Class-room, My. (J. W. Abernethy) Educa. **14**: 26.
Classic-collecting. (W. Roberts) Bookworm, **7**: 25.
Classical Criticism in Oxford. Sat. R. **79**: 88–120.
Classical Education. (J. B. Walker) Cosmopol. **21**: 553.
Classical Languages, Place of, in Modern Schools. (O. Browning) Educa. R. **3**: 270.
Classical Poetry, Decline of the Writing of. Macmil. **69**: 470.
Classical Quotation, The Decay of. (H. Paul) 19th Cent. **39**: 636.
Classical Study, Defence of. (R. C. Jebb) New R. **9**: 494.
— How it may be made more Interesting. (W. D. Sheldon) School & C. **1**: 398.
Classical Studies in America. (B. L. Gildersleeve) Atlan. **78**: 728.
Classical Teachers, Conference of, Ann Arbor, 1896. (S. G. Ashmore) Book R. **3**: 1.
Classicism in Italian Ethics. (L. Ferri) Int. J. Ethics, **5**: 340.
Classics, Apperception and Study of. (H. C. Pearson) Educa. **17**: 27.
— Educational Value of. (W. W. Goodwin) Educa. R. **9**: 335.
— in the College Course. (F. May) Educa. **15**: 221.
— in Education. All the Year, **75**: 447.
— in Grade Work. (E. C. Thompson) Educa. **12**: 489.
— in the Middle Ages. (J. Leyland) Walford's Antiq. **8**: 159.
— Misuse of. (B. Winchester) Educa. **16**: 321.
— Study of. (E. B. Clapp) Overland, n. s. **28**: 93.
— Teacher of, Recollections of. (I. Flagg) School & C. **1**: 449.
— Translations of, in Secondary Schools. (A. J. George) Acad. (Syr.) **7**: 195.
Classification of Scientific Knowledge. (J. T. Kay) New Sci. R. **2**: 12.
Claude, a Sister-in-Law of Mary Queen of Scots. Blackw. **159**: 188. Same art. Liv. Age, **208**: 707.
Claude Gueux. (V. Hugo) Time, **3**: 389.
Claude Lorraine. (George Grahame) Portfo. no. 15.
Claudian. Old Man of Verona; with translation. (W. J. Courthope) National, **18**: 809.
Clausen, George. (W. Armstrong) M. of Art, **18**: 401.
Clavecin, Bruges. (G. W. Edwards) Cent. **22**: 277.
Clavichord, The. Music, **5**: 56.
Clavie Burning. Reliquary, **35**: 22.
Clavier, The. Music, **4**: 623.
Claw, The; a story. (R. Garnett) Eng. Illust. **11**: 90.
Clay, Henry, with portrait. (H. Coyle) Green Bag, **7**: 441.
— and Adams, J. Q. Were they Guilty of Bargain and Intrigue? (E. E. Hoss) Meth. R. **53**: 598.
— and his Friends. (John P. Peters) Nation, **63**: 101.
— and John Randolph of Roanoke. Lippinc. **52**: 443.
— as Speaker of the House. (M. P. Follett) New Eng. M. n. s. **6**: 344.
— Recollections of. (M. McDowell) Cent. **28**: 765.
— Controversy with John Randolph. (E. L. Gilliams) Nat'l M. (N. Y. '91) **15**: 505.
Clay, Burned, as Roofing Material. (J. R. Elder) Am. Arch. **39**: 75.
Clay, Mexican Art in. (E. P. Bancroft) Overland, n. s. **20**: 610.
Claypole, Mrs. Elizabeth. (R. W. Ramsey) Eng. Hist. R. **7**: 37.
Claypole, Osric. Time, **2**: 540.
Claypoole, John. (R. W. Ramsey) Gent. M. n. s. **49**: 457.
— Memorandum-Book of, 1781–82. (C. F. Jenkins) Pennsyl. M. **16**: 178.
Clayton-Adams, John. *See* Adams, John C.
Cleaning, Chemistry of. (V. Lewes) Nature, **50**: 256. Same art. Pop. Sci. Mo. **46**: 101.
Cleanthes. Hymn to Zeus. (R. T. Stevenson) Meth. R. **54**: 353.
Clearing House, New York. (W. A. Camp) No. Am. **154**: 684.
Clearing House System. (W. D. C. Street) Pub. Opin. **20**: 493.
Clearness, Importance of, and the Charm of Haziness. Open Court, **5**: 2923.
Cleavage and the Formation of Organs. Am. Natural. **28**: 272.
Cleavage-foliation, Plicated. (T. N. Dale) Am. J. Sci. **143**: 317.
Cleaveland, John and Ebenezer. M. Am. Hist. **28**: 391.
Cleg Kelly, Arab of the City; a story. (S. R. Crockett) Cornh. **72**: 1–561. **73**: 79–336.
Clematis and Ivy. (W. C. Kingsland) Poet-Lore, **6**: 1, 57, 182.
Clematis Paniculata. Garden & F. **9**: 72, 182.
Clémenceau, Eugene, and Chamberlain, Joseph. Sat. R. **79**: 373.
Clémenceau, G. B.; French Parnell. Spec. **70**: 842.
Clemens, Samuel L. [Mark Twain]. (J. H. Twichell) Harper, **92**: 817.—With portrait. Bk. Buyer, **7**: 149.
— A sketch. Illustrated. Idler. **9**: 901.
— and his Recent Works. (F. R. Stockton) Forum, **15**: 673.
— as an Historical Novelist. (W. P. Trent) Bookman, **3**: 207.
— Chance Recollections of. (M. M. Fairbanks) Chaut. **14**: 429.
— Interviews with. Idler, **1**: 79.
— on Paul Bourget. (M. O'Rell) No. Am. **160**: 302.
— on the Platform. Critic, **28**: 286.
— Poem on his 50th Birthday. (O. W. Holmes) Idler, **1**: 91.
— Portraits of. McClure, **7**: 73.—Bk. Buyer, **13**: 143.
— Tom Sawyer Abroad. Sat. R. **77**: 535.
Clement of Rome, Epistle of, and the Early Roman Church. Church Q. **39**: 174.
Clement, St., History of. (E. C. Richardson) Presb. & Ref. R. **6**: 108.
Clenardus [Nicolas Kleynartis]. Quar. **176**: 140.
— an Enterprising Scholar. (H. W. Preston and L. Dodge) Atlan. **74**: 386.
Cleopatra. Spec. **68**: 808.
— Antony and. (J. A. Froude) Cosmopol. **17**: 515.
— of Sardou and Sarah Bernhardt. Art J. **44**: 198.
Cleresby, Lord. (M. Carmichael) Month, **83**: 429.
Clergy and Social Morals. (J. H. Rylance) M. Chr. Lit. **6**: 97.
— Benefit of, and the "Neck Verse." (A. de G. Stevens) Time, **19**: 469.
— Dress of the. (D. Paton) Sund. M. **25**: 223.
— Effects of the Clerical Office on Character. (L. C. Stewardson) Int. J. Ethics, **4**: 430.
— Poverty of. Spec. **70**: 216, 633.
— — Convocation on. Spec. **70**: 350.
— Unpopularity of. Spec. **77**: 11.
Clergyman, Worldly, Passing of. (R. Drail) New Eng. M. n. s. **13**: 495.

Clergymen and Social Economics. (W. C. Gannett) Lend a H. **13**: 261.
— and the Rich. (R. Ogden) Nation, **54**: 184.
— Literary Culture of. And. R. **18**: 180.
— Pay of. (H. K. Carroll) Forum, **17**: 741.
— Scotch; Cromarty's Ministerial Miniatures. Spec. **69**: 450.
— Should they take to Trade? (C. N. Barham) National, **20**: 83.
— Some Talk about. (C. M. Gaskell) 19th Cent. **32**: 487.
See Ministers.
Clerical Duty. Cornh. **66**: 45. Same art. Liv. Age, **194**: 551.
Clerical Exterior. (L. B. Walford) Longm. **27**: 82.
Clerical Life, The. Chr. Lit. **12**: 152.
Clerk, Sir John, of Penicuik. (W. G. Scott-Moncrieff) Scot. R. **22**: 257.
Clerk of Fareleigh Minster; a story. (P. Dobson) Sund. M. **22**: 558.
Clerkenwell, Eng., Open Lending Library. (J. D. Brown) Lib. J. **20**: 51.
Clerks and Shop Assistants, German. (J. Bonar) Econ. J. **3**: 319.
Clermont, Jane, Chats with. (W. Graham) 19th Cent. **34**: 753. **35**: 76.
Clermont, Council of, and the First Crusade. (T. A. Archer) Scot. R. **26**: 274.
Clerodendrons. (W. H. Taplin) Garden & F. **9**: 257.
Cleveland, Grover, with portrait. (G. F. Parker) R. of Rs. (N. Y.) **6**: 28.
— Administration of. (D. Mowry) Am. J. Pol. **5**: 271. — (C. Snyder) Am. J. Pol. **4**: 505.
— — Astrological Forecast of. (J. Erickson) Arena, **10**: 536.
— — an Object Lesson. Soc. Econ. **5**: 1.
— — Failure (?) of. Forum, **17**: 139.
— Annual Message, 1893. Pub. Opin. **16**: 238, 261. — Sat. R. **76**: 641. — Soc. Econ. **5**: 129.
— Boyhood of. R. of Rs. (N. Y.) **7**: 299.
— Cabinet of, 1893. (W. Wilson) R. of Rs. (N. Y.) **7**: 286. — Pub. Opin. **14**: 491, 511.
— — Meaning of. (J. B. Bishop) Nation, **56**: 137.
— Inaugural Address, 1893. Pub. Opin. **14**: 536. — Spec. **70**: 313.
— Message of, to Extra Session of Congress, 1893. Pub. Opin. **15**: 469.
— Nomination of, 1892. (M. Halstead) Cosmopol. **13**: 585. — (J. B. Bishop) Nation, **54**: 480. — Pub. Opin. **13**: 295.
— — Letter of Acceptance. Pub. Opin. **13**: 613.
— Personal Force of. (E. J. Edwards) McClure, **1**: 493.
— Position respecting Silver. Pub. Opin. **16**: 17.
— Second Administration of. (G. W. Green) Forum, **21**: 540.
— Tasks and Opportunities of. (C. F. Adams) Forum, **15**: 298.
— Third Term for. Pub. Opinion, **19**: 455.
— What he stands for. (C. F. Adams) Forum, **13**: 662.
Cleveland, John, Life and Poetry of. (C. Scollard) Dial (Ch.) **14**: 268.
Cleveland, Eng., Hills and Dales. (J. Leyland) Portfo. **23**: 56.
Cleveland, Ohio. (H. E. Bourne) New Eng. M. n. s. **14**: 739.
— School of Art. (J. G. Speed) Q. Illust. **2**: 353.
— Street Railway Problem in. (W. R. Hopkins) Econ. Stud. **1**: 289.
Clever Chaperon, A; a story. Argosy, **59**: 488.
Clichés and Tags. Cornh. **70**: 301.
Cliff-climbers. Macmil. **70**: 60. Same art. Liv. Age, **201**: 755.
Cliff-dwellers, American. (C. R. Markham) Geog. J. **3**: 46.
— Among the. (C. L. Webster) Am. Natural. **27**: 435.
— and Cave-dwellers of Central Arizona. (J. W. Tourney) Science, **20**: 269.
— Land of the Living. (F. Schwatka) Cent. **22**: 27.
— of Périgord: Castles in the Air. Cornh. **69**: 631. Same art. Liv. Age, **203**: 107.
Cliff-dwellings and Cave-towns, Study of. (S. D. Peet) Am. Antiq. **18**: 285.
— of the Cañons of the Mesa Verde. (W. R. Birdsall) Am. Antiq. **14**: 123.
— Summer among. (T. M. Prudden) Harper, **93**: 545.
Clifford, Mrs. W. K. Aunt Anne. Spec. **69**: 195.
Cliff's End Farm; a story. (Florence Warden) Temp. Bar, **103**: 111.
Climate and Health. (C. F. Taylor) Pop. Sci. Mo. **47**: 313.
— and High Altitudes. (H. R. Wray) New Sci. R. **2**: 26.
— and Subsistence. (A. Woeikof) Pub. Opin. **15**: 276.
— Influence on Race. (J. W. Fortescue) 19th Cent. **33**: 862. Same art. Liv. Age, **198**: 48.
— Is it changing? (H. A. Hazen) Eng. M. **4**: 836.
— Variations in. (W. H. Larrabee) Pop. Sci. Mo. **40**: 804.
— Weather and. (R. H. Scott) Longm. **22**: 62.
Climatic Zones in Jurassic Times, Examination of the Arguments given by Neumayr for the Existence of. (A. E. Ortmann) Am. J. Sci. **151**: 257.
Climbing Plants, Summer Greenhouse. (M. Barker) Garden & F. **5**: 428.
Clinedinst, B. W., with portrait. Bk. Buyer, **12**: 562.
Clinton, DeWitt, Ingham Portrait of. (Mrs. W. J. Lamb) M. Am. Hist. **27**: 321.
Clinton, George, Governor of N. Y., 1743-53. (J. M. Gittermann) Nat'l M. (N. Y. '91) **18**: 209.
Clipper Ships. (H. Russell) Eng. Illust. **10**: 35.
— New England. (J. P. Bodfish) New Eng. M. n. s. **10**: 371.
Clippings, Filing, New System of. (W. H. Western) Writer, **7**: 145.
Clive, Robert, Lord, Death of. Spec. **71**: 629.
Cloak of Confession. (D. R. Goodale) New Eng. M. n. s. **13**: 629.
Clockmaker of Poissy. (S. J. Weyman) Eng. Illust. **12**: no. 1, 33.
Clodion, and the Adam Brothers, Thirion's. M. of Art, **8**: 212.
Cloisters, Cathedral, in England. Chamb. J. **69**: 657.
Cloister Life in the Days of Cœur de Lion. (H. Donald; M. Spence) Good Words, **33**: 514, 686. Same art. M. Chr. Lit. **7**: 28-207.
Cloncurry, Elizabeth, Lady. (M. O. W. Oliphant) New R. **14**: 241. Same art. Liv. Age, **209**: 59.
Closed Cabinet; a story. Blackw. **157**: 1. Same art. Liv. Age, **204**: 268, 332.
Closed Room, The; a poem. (Clinton Scollard) Cosmopol. **18**: 152.
Closson, William B. Scrib. M. **17**: 459.
Cloth Printing, A New Method of. Am. Arch. **52**: 127.
Clothes. (H. Maxwell) Blackw. **152**: 655. Same art. Liv. Age, **196**: 31.
Clothing as a Protection against Cold. (R. Roose) Fortn. **60**: 842.
— Historically Considered. (E. J. Lowell) Scrib. M. **14**: 288.
— Tailor-made, in Germany. (M. F. Billington) New R. **12**: 631.
— Where they make. Gunton's M. **11**: 26.
— Winter. Chamb. J. **72**: 55.

Cloud, Fog, and Haze. (J. G. McPherson) Gent. M. n. s. 53: 123.
Clouds and Cloudscapes. (A. Douglas) Eng. Illust. 11: 571.
— Artificial. Dub. R. 113: 654.
— Classification of. (D. Wilson-Barker) Science, 21: 89.
— Exhibition of the Royal Meteorological Society. Dub. R. 115: 153.
— Ley on. Nature, 51: 248.
— Luminous, Observations of. Nature, 46: 589.
— Night, Observation of. (W. Foerster; O. Jesse) Astron. 11: 859.
— Photography of. Nature, 49: 267.
Cloud Observations, International. (F. H. Bigelow) Science, n. s. 3: 653.
Clouet, Jean and François. (A. M. F. Robinson) M. of Art, 8: 477.
Clough, Anne. Acad. 41: 229. — Ath. '92, 1: 307. — (E. Skelding) Atlan. 72: 224.
Clough, Arthur Hugh. (M. Steede) Temp. Bar, 108: 35.
— and Emerson. (F. H. Williams) Poet-Lore, 6: 348.
Clough na Molla; a poem. (J. Kavanagh) Argosy, 57: 82.
Clovelly, England. (W. Harrison) Art. J. 48: 321.
— Description of. (W. W. Fenn) M. of Art, 3: 87.
Clovelly, A Romance of; a story. (K. D. Wiggin) Cosmopol. 19: 277.
Clovis, Baptism of. (A. Jessopp) 19th Cent. 40: 367. Same art. Chr. Lit. 15: 504. 16: 17.
Clown in Shakespeare's Twelfth Night. (W. Townsend) Canad. M. 4: 59.
Clowns and Fools of Shakespeare's Time. (H. E. Borradaile) Poet-Lore, 8: 206.
Club, Boys', The Drury Lane. (Frances H. Burnett) Scrib. M. 11: 676.
— Working-girls', A Model. (A. Shaw) Scrib. M. 11: 169.
Club Cup, The; a story. (W. E. Baldwin) Outing, 24: 141.
Club Ghost, The. (J. A. Simonds) Bach. of Arts, 1: 205.
Club-homes for Unmarried Working-men. (W. Moffatt) Blackw. 156: 701.
Club Life among Outcasts. (Josiah Flynt) Harper, 90: 712.
— *versus* Home Life. (G. S. Crawford) Arena, 16: 418.
Club Scandal: Thackeray and Edm. Yates. (E. Yates) Time, 2: 385.
Clubs. (G. H. Westley) Lippinc. 58: 559.
— Boys'. Lend a H. 8: 77.
— for Boys and Men in London. Sat. R. 78: 233.
— Household. (Countess of Aberdeen) 19th Cent. 31: 391.
— — in Small Households. (M. Hamilton) 19th Cent. 31: 807.
— Peoples'. (I. W. De Jonge) Soc. Econ. 3: 35.
— Political. Sat. R. 73: 650.
— Reading. (Louise Stockton) Bk. Buyer, 13: 63-626.
— Women's; a Symposium. (M. W. Sewall and others) Arena, 6: 362.
Clusia, Early Chronology of. (E. H. Parker) Acad. 50: 163.
Clyde Scenery. (P. G. Hamerton) Portf. 23: 186.
Clyde Sea Area, Physical Conditions of. (H. R. Mill) Geog. J. 4: 344.
Clymenia, Discovery of, in Western New York. (J. M. Clarke) Am. J. Sci. 143: 57.
Coaches of the London and Brighton Road. Sat. R. 77: 71.
Coaching, Road, up to Date. (T. S. Tailer) Cent. 23: 79.
Coaching Trip to Dorking. (G. Allen) M. of Art, 10: 283.
Coaching Trips out of London. (W. H. Rideing) Cosmopol. 17: 401.
Coaching and Cramming. (J. P. Owen) Ath. '92, 1: 502, 696. — (W. Wren) Ath. '92, 1: 600.
Coal, Anthracite. (O. C. S. Carter) J. Frankl. Inst. 138: 152.
— — Combinations. (G. O. Virtue) Q. J. Econ. 10: 296.
— — in Eastern England. Sat. R. 78: 532.
— — in the U. S. (H. M. Chance) Engin. M. 4: 544.
— — Markets for. Sat. R. 82: 249.
— Formation of. (H. Greene) New Sci. R. 2: 129.
— in England, Proposed Confiscation of. Spec. 68: 392.
— Influence of Combustion of, upon our Atmosphere. (Dr. C. Winkler) Open Court, 1: 197.
— of the World, The. Chamb. J. 72: 628.
— Relative Value of Different Coals. (H. M. Chance) Engin. M. 11: 40.
— Sampling and Testing Small Sizes of. (E. B. Coxe) Cassier, 5: 481.
— Spontaneous Ignition of. (V. B. Lewes) J. Soc. Arts, 40: 352.
— Storing. (T. W. Milnor) Cassier, 2: 213.
— Stratigraphy of the Kansas Coal Measures. (E. Haworth) Am. J. Sci. 150: 452.
— Structure and Formation of. (A. C. Seward) Sci. Prog. 2: 355, 431.
— Waste of, in Pennsylvania. (G. F. Wright) Nation, 55: 101.
— What is to be done when it is exhausted? (L. Sohncke) Open Court, 4: 2375, 2389.
Coal Calorimeter. (G. H. Barrus) Cassier, 4: 468.
Coal Combination, Great, and the Reading Leases. (C. L. Munson) Am. J. Soc. Sci. 30: 147.
Coal Conveyors, Modern. Cassier, 1: 490.
Coal-dust, Colliery Explosions and. (W. N. Atkinson) National, 23: 836. — Sat. R. 78: 221.
— — Stuart on. Nature, 51: 268.
Coal Industries of Great Britain. All the Year, 73: 590.
Coal Industry, The. (J. K. Reeve) Chaut. 16: 416.
— Anthracite, in the U. S. (H. M. Chance) Engin. M. 4: 544.
— in England. (J. S. Lloyd) Belgra. 79: 411.
Coal-mine, In the Depths of a. (S. Crane) McClure, 3: 195.
— Profits of. (G. P. Bidder) 19th Cent. 35: 807.
Coal Mines, Distribution of Power in. (L. B. Atkinson) Engin. M. 10: 236.
— Explosions in, Causes of. (D. A. Louis) Knowl. 18: 224.
— Nova Scotia. (T. W. Longley) Canad. M. 1: 111.
Coal Mining, Relation between Wages and Numbers employed in. (R. H. Hooker) J. Statis. Soc. 57: 627.
Coal-pit, A Scotch: Into the Jaws of Death. Macmil. 74: 93. Same art. Liv. Age, 210: 205.
Coal Question, The, and the Nationalization of Mines. (H. H. L. Bellot) Westm. 141: 117.
Coal-scuttles. (P. Fitzgerald) M. of Art, 5: 182.
Coal Strike Romance. (R. A. King) Belgra. 83: 148.
Coal Supply of the U. S., and its Distribution. (J. S. Harris) Forum, 13: 193.
— — and the Reading Leases. (A. A. McLeod) Forum, 13: 554.
Coal Trade, Rise of. (R. L. Galloway) Contemp. 62: 569. Same art. Liv. Age, 195: 498.
Coal War, The. (R. M. Grier and others) Econ. R. 4: 69.
Coal-working in Scotland in Former Days. Chamb. J. 71: 117.
Coalition, Reasons for a. National, 23: 17.
Coalitions, Political. Quar. 177: 525.
Coals of Fire. (L. Armstrong) Lippinc. 54: 544.

Coast and a Capture, A; a story. (V. N. Leeds) McClure, 7: 122. Same art. Eng. Illust. 16: 27.
Coast and Geodetic Survey, U. S. (H. G. Ogden) Nat. Geog. M. 1: 59. — (J. W. Powell) Chaut. 14: 422, 545.
Coast and Harbor Defence. Un. Serv. M. 4: 101.
Coast Defence of Germany and France. (C. A. Voigt) Un. Serv. M. 6: 357.
— A System of. (W. L. Clowes) Fortn. 63: 551.
— U. S. (J. A. Frye) Bost. 3: 513. 4: 441. — (J. B. Walker) Cosmopol. 21: 149.
Coast Defences. (G. E. Walsh) Lippinc. 58: 805.
— Electricity and. (C. L. Atwell) Cassier, 3: 323.
Cobbe, Frances Power. (J. W. Chadwick) New World, 4: 207. — (A. B. McMahan) Dial (Ch.) 19: 44. — With portrait. Bk. News, 13: 77.*
— Autobiography. (W. Lewin) Acad. 46: 321. — Sat. R. 78: 514. — Ath. '94, 2: 413. — (J. W. Chadwick) Nation, 59: 328. — Lit. W. (Bost.) 25: 326.
Cobbett, William. (G. Saintsbury) Liv. Age, 192: 301. — (L. Stephen) New R. 9: 362, 482. — Spec. 70: 284.
Cobden, Richard. (M. M. Trumbull) Am. J. Pol. 1: 1. — (T. Stanton) Open Court, 8: 4027.
— Decline of Cobdenism. (S. Low) 19th Cent. 40: 173.
— the Great Free Trader by his own Fireside. (J. M. Scovel) Overland, n. s. 22: 127.
— Jubilee of Corn Bill. Sat. R. 81: 641.
Cobdenism. Spec. 73: 168, 208, 241.
Cobden-Sanderson, T. J., with portrait. Bk. Buyer, 13: 442.
Cobra, The, and Other Serpents. (G. R. O'Reilly) Pop. Sci. Mo. 46: 67.
Coburg, Family of, and the English Court. (C. Lowe) Eng. Illust. 11: 11.
Coccidæ, Distribution of. (T. D. A. Cockerell) Am. Natural. 28: 1050.
Coccidology, Contributions to. (T. D. A. Cockerell) Am. Natural. 29: 725.
Cochineal Insect, Notes on. (T. D. A. Cockerell) Am. Natural. 27: 1041.
Cochití, The Wanderings of. (C. F. Lummis) Scrib. M. 13: 92.
Cock-fighting. Time, 2: 545.
— in Art. (W. B. Tegetmeier) M. of Art, 19: 408.
— in Wales. Reliquary, 36: 154.
Cock Lane Ghost, The. (H. Pyle) Harper, 87: 327.
Cockling at Morecambe. Sat. R. 77: 492.
Cockney Dialect. (R. P. Bolton) J. Am. Folk-Lore, 8: 222.
Cockneydom, Imperial. (Robert Buchanan) Univ. R. 4: 71.
Coco de Mer, The. All the Year, 71: 32.
Cocoa and its Manufacture. (J. Hatton) Eng. Illust. 9: 542.
— as a Substitute for Tobacco. Pub. Opin. 13: 112.
Cocoanut Palm. (A. Eric) Canad. M. 2: 354. — Garden & F. 7: 13.
Cocoons. (E. A. Butler) Knowl. 16: 214, 225.
— Jumping. Nature, 55: 65.
Cod, Cape. (M. G. Van Rensselaer) Garden & F. 5: 574.
— Early Autumn on. (E. S. Goss) Garden & F. 5: 465.
— Shore Towns of. (T. B. Harrison) Garden & F. 5: 9, 69, 93.
Codfish and Currency. (J. D. Butler) Nation, 63: 434.
— Historic, Removed to New State House, Boston. Bost. 2: 88.
Codification of U. S. Laws. (F. R. Coudert) No. Am. 156: 195.
Cod-liver Oil, Chemistry of, Möeller on. (J. Cameron) Nature, 51: 508.
Codman, Rev. John, D. D., Sketch of Life of. N. E. Reg. 48: 409.
Codrington College, Barbadoes. (T. H. Brindley) Macmil. 67: 99.
Codrus; a poem. (L. W. Smith) Overland, n. s. 21: 186.
Coe, George S., with portrait. Bank. M. (N. Y.) 50: 1.
Co-education. (F. Sarcey) Cosmopol. 19: 354. — (J. M. Cromer) Luth. Q. 23: 86.
— History of the Word. (F. N. Scott) Nation, 58: 48.
— in Colleges. (J. L. Pickard) Educa. 13: 259.
— in German Universities. (G. Pollak) Nation, 55: 42.
— Will the Co-educated Co-educate their Children? (M. F. Crow) Forum, 17: 582.
Cœlentera, Digestion in. (S. J. Hickson) Sci. Prog. 2: 447.
— Nervous System of. (S. J. Hickson) Sci. Prog. n. s. 1: 101.
Cœur, Jacques, a King's Treasurer. (H. C. Macdowall) Macmil. 67: 310. Same art. Liv. Age, 197: 32.
Cœur d'Alene. (M. H. Foote) Cent. 25: 502–895. 26: 102.
— Riots, 1892. (G. E. French) Overland, n. s. 26: 32.
Coffee-house as a Counteraction to the Saloon. (R. Graham) Char. R. 1: 215.
— as a Rival of the Saloon. (I. W. Howerth) Am. M. Civics, 6: 589.
Coffin, Charles Carleton. Critic, 28: 169. — (G. M. Adams) N. E. Reg. 50: 289. — With portrait. Bk. News, 9: 223.
Cognition, Knowledge, and Truth. Open Court, 2: 1458.
— Metaphysical x in. (P. Carus) Monist, 5: 510.
Cohesion, Laws and Nature of. (R. A. Fessenden) Science, 20: 48. 21: 113.
Coheleth, Dirge of. (C. Taylor) Jew. Q. 4: 533. 5: 5.
Coin, Circulation of, Evaluation of Amount of. (F. Y. Edgeworth) Econ. J. 2: 162.
Coin Clipping. Bank. M. (N. Y.) 49: 199.
Coin Collectors, Notes for. Walford's Antiq. 11: 172, 294.
Coinage, A Common, for all Nations. (C. W. Stone) No. Am. 163: 47.
— Decimal. (F. H. Perry Coste) Westm. 139: 22.
— — for Great Britain. (W. H. Broughton) Westm. 145: 668.
— English, New. (W. B. Robertson) Time, 16: 47. — (P. W. Steer) Art J. 45: 71.
— Free, and Prosperity. (J. B. Clark) Pol. Sci. Q. 11: 248.
— — Dangers of. (A. B. Dale) Am. M. Civics, 6: 42.
— — in Mexico. (C. N. Bennett) No. Am. 159: 630.
— — of Gold and Silver. Bank. M. (N. Y.) 47: 114. *See* Silver.
— Gold and Silver, Circulation of. (J. B. Delaney) Am. M. Civics, 9: 113.
— of Greeks. (G. F. Hill) Knowl. 18: 121.
— of Rome. (G. F. Hill) Knowl. 18: 241.
Coincidence, Delusions of. (F. L. Oswald) Open Court, 5: 2939.
— Tyranny of. Spec. 75: 43.
Coincidences. (F. Max Müller) Fortn. 66: 48.
— Contemporary. (A. W. Holmes-Forbes) Time, 23: 978.
Coins, Ancient, Educational Function of. (F. M. Bristol) Meth. R. 56: 874.
— Art in Miniature. (T. Sulman) Good Words, 37: 446.
— British. All the Year, 54: 101.
— Copper, of Queen Anne. Walford's Antiq. 2: 15.
— Discovery of a Hoard of Silver. Illus. Archæol. 2: 104.
— English. (G. F. Hill) Knowl. 19: 98, 172, 217. — (L. F. Day) M. of Art, 10: 416.
— — Designs for. (L. F. Day) M. of Art, 19: 275.
— Greek. (C. Oman) Acad. 42: 96.

Coins, Mysian. Sat. R. 74: 144.
— of Alexandria and the Nomes, Poole's Catalogue of. Sat. R. 74: 316.
— of Europe, Hazlitt on. Sat. R. 77: 424.
— of Ionia, Greece. Sat. R. 74: 343.
Coke, Mary, Lady, Foreign Tours of. Ed. R. 177: 519. Same art. Liv. Age, 198: 488.
— Letters and Journals. Temp. Bar, 95: 314. Same art. Liv. Age, 194: 608.
Coke, Manufacture of, in U. S. (W. G. Wilkins) Engin. M. 5: 469.
Coke-drawer, Mechanical. (R. A. Cook) Cassier, 10: 362.
Coke Industry, Development and Condition by Utilization of By-products. (B. Leistikow) J. Frankl. Inst. 135: 17.
— Vast Importance of the. (J. Fulton) Engin. M. 11: 208.
Colburn, Jeremiah, Memoir of. (J. W. Dean) N. E. Reg. 47: 425.
Cold. Cornh. 65: 30.
— and Heat, Extreme, Endurance of, by Man. (Marquis de Nadaillac) Science, 21: 49.
— Taking, How to avoid. (C. A. Hough) Cosmopol. 15: 683.
Cold Snap, A; a sketch. All the Year, 71: 418.
Cold Spring Harbor Biological Laboratory. (H. W. Conn) Am. Natural. 29: 228.
Cold Storage for Fruits and Vegetables. Garden & F. 7: 352.
Cole, George Vicat. Ath. '93, 1: 479. — (H. S. Wilson) M. of Art, 1: 149.
Cole, William J., with portrait. (L. A. Bond) Nat'l M. (N. Y. '91) 17: 484.
Cole Family. (J. R. Cole) Nat'l M. (N. Y. '91) 16: 226.
Coleman, William Tell. (A. S. Hallidie) Overland, n. s. 23: 71.
Coleoptera, Flight in, Nervous Centre of. (A. Binet) Monist, 4: 65.
Coleridge, Christabel Rose. Sund. M. 24: 764.
Coleridge, Henry James. Month, 78: 1, 153.
Coleridge, John D., Chief Justice, with portrait. (J. S. Cobb) Green Bag, 6: 305. — (G. H. Knott) Am. Law R. 28: 726. — Ath. '94, 1: 803.
— Reminiscences of. (Lord Russell) No. Am. 159: 257.
— Russell on. Sat. R. 78: 318.
Coleridge, S. T. Church Q. 37: 166. — (J. Wedgwood) Contemp. 67: 548. Same art. Liv. Age, 205: 387. — Atlan. 76: 397. — Lond. Q. 85: 58.
— and his Critics. (N. C. Smith) Fortn. 64: 340.
— and Nether Stowey. Ath. '93, 1: 765.
— and the Quantocks. (J. L. W. Page) Eng. Illust. 10: 344.
— and Wordsworth, Wordsworth on. Ath. '94, 2: 716, 829.
— Anima Poetæ. (W. E. G. Fisher) Acad. 48: 513. — (J. B. Bury) Sat. R. 80: 68.
— Christabel, and Keats's Lamia. Poet-Lore, 6: 32.
— Coleridgiana. (T. Hutchinson) Acad. 43: 481, 505.
— Confessions of an Enquiring Spirit. Eng. R. 12: 247.
— Introduction to the Lake District. (M. B. Benton) Atlan. 74: 95.
— Lectures by in 1818–19. (J. D. Campbell) Ath. '92, 1: 17.
— Letters of. (A. Lang) Contemp. 67: 876. Same art. Liv. Age, 206: 279. — (L. Stephen) National, 25: 318. Same art. Liv. Age, 205: 795. — (E. G. Johnson) Dial (Ch.) 18: 316. — Ed. R. 183: 99.
— Life, by Campbell. (E. Dowden) Sat. R. 82: 128. — (T. Hutchinson) Acad. 45: 141. — Sat. R. 77: 289.
— Note on. Ath. '94, 1: 114, 246.
Coleridge, S. T. Note-books, ed. by E. H. Coleridge. (T. F. Huntington) Dial (Ch.) 19: 244. — (C. Waterer) Westm. 145: 526.
— Osorio, and Remorse. (J. D. Campbell) Ath. '92, 1: 834.
— Poems, ed. by Campbell. Ath. '93, 1: 757. — Spec. 70: 804. — (G. Smith) Nation, 57: 196.
— Quotations by. Ath. '92, 2: 259.
— Ten Letters to Southey. Atlan. 73: 57.
— The Watchman, Prospectus of. Ath. '93, 2: 808.
Coles, Abraham. (A. H. Tuttle) Meth. R. 56: 580. — With portrait. (E. M. Hunt) Nat'l M. (N. Y. '91) 16: 228.
Colibri's Revenge, The. (A. Beresford) Argosy, 62: 297.
Colin; a story. (M. Mackenzie) Canad. M. 6: 338.
Coliseum, Fate of the. (R. Lanciani) Atlan. 78: 531.
Collaboration, Literary. (W. Besant) New R. 6: 200.
Collaboration; a story. (H. James) Eng. Illust. 9: 911.
Collacchione, Giovanni Battista. (W. Mercer) Acad. 48: 147.
Colladon, Jean D. (E. Sarasin) Nature, 48: 396.
Collar of S S, worn by English Judges. Green Bag, 7: 240.
Collating of Library Books. (W. I. Fletcher) Lib. J. 20: 80.
Collecting Fads. (W. Roberts) Temp. Bar, 108: 235.
Collecting Mania, The. (W. Hamilton) Bookworm, 7: 41.
Collection for the Saints, Pauline. (F. Rendall) Chr. Lit. 10: 43 a.
Collectivism, Limits of. (W. Clarke) Contemp. 63: 263.
Collectivist or Individualist, Which is most in Accord with Teaching of Christ? (F. Relton) Econ. R. 4: 499.
Collectivist Prospect in England. (W. Graham) 19th Cent. 37: 15.
Collector, Correspondence of a. (V. C. Prinsep) Art J. 44: 249.
Collector of Materials; a story. (B. McEvoy) Canad. M. 4: 13.
College, Admission to, by Certificate. (C. Northrop; M. E. Gates) Educa. R. 5: 187. — (J. H. Canfield; O. M. Fernald) Educa. R. 5: 291. — (M. Kellogg; J. Tetlow) Educa. R. 5: 384. — (C. K. Adams; E. W. Coy) Educa. R. 6: 69.
— — Different Methods of. (L. M. Salmon) Educa. R. 6: 223.
— American. Atlan. 75: 703.
— — First attempt to Found an. (W. A. Beardslee) M. Am. Hist. 29: 367. — (W. A. Beardslee) Nat'l M. (N. Y. '91) 18: 45.
— and the University. (N. Butler) Citizen, 2: 294, 328.
— — in the United States. (C. Gross) Educa. R. 7: 26.
— The Best Thing it does for a Man. (C. F. Thwing) Forum, 21: 44.
— Discipline in. (L. A. Selby-Bigge) 19th Cent. 36: 126.
— Entrance Requirements; Are they at Present too Great in Quantity? (J. C. Mackenzie) Educa. R. 12: 252.
— — Enlargement of Options in. (J. Tetlow) School R. 4: 745.
— — in English, Report of Conference on. Educa. R. 8: 176.
— — in Greek. (J. R. Bishop) School R. 4: 434.
— — in History. (A. B. Hart) Educa. R. 10: 417.
— — — Discussion of. (B. A. Hinsdale) School R. 4: 438.
— — — Unity in. (L. M. Salmon) Educa. R. 12: 151.
— — in Latin. (F. W. Kelsey) School R. 4: 443.
— — in Mathematics. (P. H. Hanus) School R. 4: 535.

College; Entrance Requirements in Modern Languages. (A. F. Nightingale) School R. 4: 424.
— — in Natural Sciences, Résumé and Critique of. (C. S. Palmer) School R. 4: 452.
— — in Science. (R. S. Tarr) Educa. R. 12: 57. — Science, n. s. 4: 929.
— — Papers of 5th Annual Meeting of the Harvard Teachers' Association. Educa. R. 11: 417.
— — Reform in. (W. Farrand) Educa. R. 10: 430.
— — Report on. (A. F. Nightingale) School R. 4: 415.
— — Systems of Admission. (B. A. Hinsdale; H. P. Judson; C. H. Moore) School R. 4: 301.
— — Tabular Statement of. (W. J. Chase and C. H. Thurber) School R. 4: 341.
— — Uniform. Conclusions reached by the Conferences held at Columbia College, Feb., 1896. Educa. R. 11: 494.
— Fitting for, in Public Schools. (J. J. H. Hamilton) Educa. 14: 329.
— — in English High Schools. (J. F. Casey) Pop. Sci. Mo. 46: 15.
— Future of. (E. D. Warfield) Educa. 15: 321.
— Government of, Student Coöperation in. (E. D. Warfield) Educa. R. 8: 442.
— Graduate Work in. (J. M. Taylor) Educa. R. 8: 62.
— Influence of, in American Life. (C. F. Thwing) No. Am. 163: 517.
— Instruction in, Cost of Undergraduate. (J. M. Coulter) Educa. R. 7: 417.
— Modern Side in. (T. B. Bronson) Educa. R. 8: 147.
— of France. *See* France, College of.
— Organization and Government of. (C. F. Thwing) Educa. R. 12: 16.
— Place of, in Higher Education. (H. T. Spangler) Ref. Q. 40: 96.
— Preparation for, Uniform Standards in. (W. H. Butts) Educa. R. 9: 148.
— The Private, and the State. (G. W. Knight) Educa. R. 10: 57.
— Qualifications for Admission to, Methods of Determining. (F. A. Waterhouse) School & C. 1: 519.
— Should your Boy go to? (C. M. Depew and others) Munsey, 13: 461.
— Studies in, Formal *versus* Concrete. (J. H. Gore) School R. 2: 21.
— What constitutes a, and what a Secondary School? (R. H. Jesse) School R. 4: 274.
— What should it do for a High School Graduate? (J. H. Baker) Educa. 16: 457.
— Where shall I send my Boy to? (E. L. Hall) Bach. of Arts, 1: 480.
College-bred Men in Business. (W. D. Sheldon) N. Eng. 56: 189.
— Influence of. (C. F. Smith) Nation, 60: 91, 124.
College Catalogues, Deficiencies of. (C. W. Gleason) School & C. 1: 343.
College Christmas, A. (Alice W. Rollins) Bach. of Arts, 2: 64.
College Commencements. Critic, 28: 379.
College Education, Cost of, Increasing. (C. F. Thwing) Forum, 18: 630.
— Drawbacks of a. (C. Thwing) Forum, 22: 483.
— in the U. S. Pub. Opin. 15: 485.
College Endowments, Well-meant but Futile: the Remedy. (C. F. Thwing) Forum, 20: 133.
College Finances: the Best Investment in the World. (C. F. Thwing) Forum, 19: 438.
College Girls, Self-help among. (E. L. Banks) 19th Cent. 39: 502.
College Government, Amherst College System of. (J. Bigham) Educa. R. 3: 162.
College Graduate and Public Life. (T. Roosevelt) Atlan. 74: 255.
— Civic Duties of. (J. B. Leavitt) Bach. of Arts, 1: 433.
College Graduates, Superabundance of. Sat. R. 76: 266.
College Libraries. (L. Ambrose) Lib. J. 18: 113.
College Life. (W. DeW. Hyde) Scrib. M. 19: 721.
— Drawbacks of. Spec. 76: 407.
— Girls', Stories of. (Abbe C. Goodloe) Scrib. M. 17: 356, 713. 18: 322.
— Ideal in. (C. E. Wagner) Ref. Q. 43: 519.
College Men First among Successful Citizens. (C. F. Thwing) Forum, 15: 494.
— in Journalism. (L. J. Vance) Bach. of Arts, 3: 161.
— in Politics. (J. La R. Burnett) Am. J. Pol. 1: 285. — (F. B. Debervill) Am. J. Pol. 1: 402.
College Oratory in the West. R. of Rs. (N. Y.) 11: 665.
College President, The. (C. F. Thwing) Educa. R. 3: 360.
College Presidents, American. (H. W. Mabie) Outl. 48: 338.
College Professor in Politics. (J. La R. Burnett) Am. J. Pol. 2: 317.
College Professors, American, The Pay of. (W. R. Harper) Forum, 16: 96.
— Some Aspects of. (M. L. Todd) Bach. of Arts, 2: 316.
College Progress, A. Macmil. 75: 22.
College Scouts; the Scout's Boy. Blackw. 157: 223.
College Settlements. *See* University Settlements.
College Sports, Camp's. (R. J. Cross) Nation, 57: 395.
College Students, Expenses of. Lend a H. 10: 349.
College Theatricals — as we have them. (E. I. Stevenson) No. Am. 158: 510.
College Women, A Generation of. (F. M. Abbott) Forum, 20: 377.
— Marriage Rate of. (M. W. Shinn) Cent. 28: 946.
— Why do they not marry? Bach. of Arts, 1: 711.
College Year, The Actual. (R. Ogden) Nation, 57: 444.
Colleges and the Country. Pub. Opin. 15: 394.
— and their Memories. Macmil. 72: 109.
— and Universities, Future of American. (D. C. Gilman) Atlan. 78: 175. — (A. D. White) School & C. 1: 65.
— Attendance at, Industrial Depression and. (W. Z. Ripley) Nation, 58: 47.
— Denominational. (J. B. Kieffer) Ref. Q. 42: 247.
— English System of, for America. (F. N. Smith) Bach. of Arts, 2: 596.
— Higher Life of. (J. E. Bradley) Educa. 17: 193.
— in the U. S., Attendance on, 1890–91. School & C. 1: 52.
— — Growth of. (A. M. Comey) Educa. R. 3: 120.
— — What they may demand of Preparatory Schools. (K. P. Harrington) School & C. 1: 257.
— Necessary Reforms in. (C. C. Ramsay) Educa. R. 9: 10.
— Personal Economics in. (F. B. Wilson) Lippinc. 49: 597.
— Preparatory Departments in. (C. W. Super) Educa. 13: 30.
— Relations and Duties of, to Preparatory Schools. (G. T. Ettinger) School & C. 1: 337.
— Smaller, Difficulties of. (E. P. Powell) Educa. 14: 504, 603.
— Southern, Entrance Examinations in. (J. H. Dillard) Nation, 57: 286. — (J. H. Kirkland) Nation, 57: 370.
— — Student Life in. (F. C. Woodward) Educa. R. 10: 461.
Collegian in Literature. (Winifred Johnes) Bach. of Arts, 2: 491.

Collet, Sophia Dobson. Ath. '94, 1: 445.
Collett, Jacobine Camilla. Ath. '95, 1: 345.
Collie, The, in Mendocino. (L. McNab) Overland, n. s. 23 481.
Collier, John. (W. H. Pollock) Art J. 46: 65.
Colliers and Colliery Explosions. Nature, 47: 481.
Collingwood, Cuthbert, Vice-Admiral Lord. Macmil. 72: 9.
Collins, E. B., with portrait. Bk. News, 14: 376.
Collins, Jennie, and her Boffin's Bower. (M. A. Allen) Char. R. 2: 105.
Collins, John Churton, as a Critic. (H. Walker) Acad. 48: 427.
— Essays and Studies. Sat. R. 79: 353.
Collins, Richard; Will and Inventory. Reliquary, 33: 104.
Collins, Wilkie, with portrait. Bk. Buyer, 6: 9.— With portrait. Bk. News, 7: 302.—Temp. Bar, 102: 320.
— Dickens' Opinion of. (F. T. Marzials) Acad. 42: 304.
— In Memoriam Amici. (H. Quilter) Univ. R. 5: 205.
— Reminiscences. Univ. R. 1: 182.
Collins, William, Poet. Temp. Bar, 102: 510. Same art. Liv. Age, 203: 60.
Collinson, Sir Richard, Arctic Journey of. (A. W. Greely) Nat. Geog. M. 4: 198.
Collinson, Samuel. Acad. 47: 401.
Collisions at Sea and International Law. (L. Franck) Law Q. 12: 260.
Colloid Solutions, On the Nature of. (C. E. Linebarger) Am. J. Sci. 143: 218.
Colman, Col. D., Letter of, 1777. M. Am. Hist. 29: 279.
Colman, Jeremiah J.; the Man and the Town (Norwich). (F. Dolman) Eng. Illust. 13: 196.
Colnbrook, An Ancient Inn of. (J. A. Owen) Blackw. 156: 843.
Colobognatha, New Character in the, with Drawings of Siphonotus. (O. F. Cook) Am. Natural. 30: 839.
Cologne Cathedral. (E. Bisland) Cosmopol. 12: 515. — (A. E. Hake) M. of Art, 4: 161.
Colombe's Birthday; a play, presented by the Marlowe-Taber Company. (O. L. Triggs) Poet-Lore, 7: 32.
Colombia, Business Opportunities in. (C. F. Z. Caracristi) Engin. M. 9: 883.
— Constitution of, with an Historical Introduction. (B. Moses) Ann. Am. Acad. Pol. Sci. vol. 3, supp.
— Lady's Life in. (B. C. Finch) Gent. M. n. s. 53: 63. Same art. Ecl. M. 123: 271. Same art. Liv. Age, 202: 429.
— Railroad Development of. (J. de la C. Posada) Engin. M. 5: 605.
Colonel, The; a story. (H. W. French) Lippinc. 53: 3.
Colonel and his Command. (J. Corbett) Am. Hist. R. 2: 1.
Colonel Burnaby's Parents; a story. (C. F. Little) Un. Serv. (Phila.) 7: 30.
Colonel Eva; a story. (C. Edwardes) Belgra. 78: 375.
Colonel Poparel; a story. (T. Hopkins) Eng. Illust. 13: 147.
Colonel's Christmas; a story. (H. P. Spofford) Harper, 90: 109.
Colonel's Last Campaign, The. (E. Wardman) Cent. 22: 508.
Colonel's "Nigger Dog," The. (J. C. Harris) Scrib. M. 18: 722.
Colonel's Plan, The. (R. Ramsay) Chamb. J. 73: 380–396.
Colonel's Romance, The; a story. Chamb. J. 70: 93.
Colonel's Story, The. Temp. Bar, 103: 75.
Colonel's System, The. (F. Gray) Southern M. 4: 491.
Colonel's Tea-party, The. (Bessie Chandler) Scrib. M. 18: 650.
Colonel's Wooing, The; a story. (K. Huddleston) Belgra. 82: 301.
Colonial and Indian Exhibition, 1886. (F. Banfield) Time, 14: 662.
Colonial Architecture. *See* Architecture, Colonial.
Colonial Clubs. (E. Heaton) Canad. M. 6: 259.
Colonial Conference at Ottawa. (C. Smith) Contemp. 67: 105.
Colonial Customs prior to 1730 in New England. (I. P. Fowle) Bost. 1: 258.
Colonial Dames, Our. (F. E. Myers) Overland, n. s. 27: 104.
Colonial Drinks. (Alice M. Earle) Nat'l M. (N. Y. '91) 16: 149.
Colonial Families, Some Stories of. (M. Newport) Am. Hist. Reg. 1: 44–558. 2: 650–1474. 3: 37–671.
Colonial Judge, The. (F. C. Williams) National, 18: 85.
Colonial Service, Recollections of. (Sir D. P. Chalmers) Jurid. R. 7: 24, 143.
Colonial Survival, A. (T. Roosevelt) Cosmopol. 14: 229.
Colonial Women, Some. (A. H. Wharton) Cosmopol. 16: 651.
Colonies. *See* Great Britain, Colonies.
Colonies, Tariffs, and Trade Treaties. Blackw. 153: 783.
Colonization, Ancient and Modern Earth Hunger. (A. R. MacMahon) Asia. R. 11: 323.
— as a Remedy for City Poverty. (F. G. Peabody) Forum, 17: 52.
— Compulsory. (E. Kelly) Char. R. 4: 78.
— Cultured. (M. Macfie) Westm. 143: 673.
— Experiments by. Hertzka's Freeland. (E. Salmon) Fortn. 63: 260.
— State. (Earl Meath) Time, 18: 543.
— A Tropical Colony. (F. Boyle) New R. 13: 272.
Colonizing, Two Ways of. New R. 13: 190.
Colonna, Prospero. Jacopo Palma's Portrait of a Poet. (W. F. Dickes) M. of Art, 16: 156, 202.
Colonna, Vittoria. (H. W. Preston and L. Dodge) Atlan. 71: 468.
Colony of Mercy, A. (D. MacG. Means) Nation, 58: 17.
Color. (J. G. McPherson) Longm. 23: 377. Same art. Liv. Age, 200: 742.—(J. E. Hodson) M. of Art, 12: 32.
— Analysis of Contrast-colors. (A. M. Mayer) Am. J. Sci. 151: 38.
— and Light, Sensations of, Lovibond's Measurement of. (W. de W. Abney) M. of Art, 17: 211.
— — Sensitiveness of the Eye to. (W. de W. Abney) Nature, 47: 538.
— Application of, to Architecture. (A. T. Sibbald) Am. Arch. 48: 11.
— Association of, with Words, Letters, and Sounds. (W. O. Krohn) Am. J. Psychol. 5: 20.
— Causes of. (J. J. Stewart) Knowl. 19: 197.
— Change of, in Animals. Animal Tinctumutants. (J. Weir, jr.) Pop. Sci. Mo. 46: 388.
Colors, Animal. Spec. 69: 592. 70: 731.
— — Beddard on. (E. B. Poulton) Nature, 46: 533.— (S. Garman) Nation, 56: 391.—Am. Natural. 27: 371.
— — Protective. (B. G. Johns) 19th Cent. 32: 454. Same art. Liv. Age, 195: 300.
— How to tell. (M. Benjamin) Chaut. 20: 325.
— in Animals, Science of. Chamb. J. 71: 299.
— in Drawing. (P. Souriau) Pub. Opin. 14: 585.
— in Flowering Plants. (A. Carter) Pop. Sci. Mo. 42: 75.
— in Insects, Changes of. (G. H. Carpenter) Nat. Sci. 2: 287.

Colors, in Painting. (M. P. Souriau) Pub. Opin. 14: 165.
— in Plants, Physiology of. (D. T. MacDougal) Pop. Sci. Mo. 49: 71.
— Influence of, on Estimation of Magnitude. (J. O. Quantz) Am. J. Psychol. 7: 26.
— Iridescent. (A. Hodgkinson) Nature, 47: 92.
— Nomenclature of. (H. Spencer) Nature, 52: 413.
— Organic. (F. T. Mott) Science, 21: 323.
— Photometric Method Independent of. (O. N. Rood) Am. J. Sci. 146: 173.
— Sensation of, Theory of. Art J. 46: 328.
— Simultaneous Contrast, Studies of the Phenomena of. (A. M. Mayer) Am. J. Sci. 146: 1.
— Standard Scheme of. (J. H. Pillsbury) Science, 21: 310.
— Tone Harmonies, and the Modern Scheme of. (C. W. Dempsey) M. of Art, 3: 257.
— Use of, in Architectural Design. (H. L. Warren) Am. Arch. 42: 45.
Color-blindness. Ed. R. 177: 129. — (W. de W. Abney) J. Soc. Arts, 40: 676.
— among North American Indians. (L. I. Blake; W. S. Franklin) Science, 21: 297.
— Pathology of, and Possible Remedy. (A. E. Wright) 19th Cent. 31: 648.
— Peril of. Pop. Sci. Mo. 47: 574.
Color Hearing, Problem of. (A. Binet) Chaut. 16: 447.
Color Music. (W. Schooling) 19th Cent. 38: 125. — Liv. Age, 206: 349.
Color Range, Indirect, Observations on. (G. W. A. Luckey) Am. J. Psychol. 6: 489.
Color Relations of Atoms, Ions, and Molecules. (M. C. Lea) Am. J. Sci. 151: 405.
Color Saturation. (L. M. Solomons) Psychol. R. 3: 50.
— and its Quantitative Relations. (A. Kirschmann) Am. J. Psychol. 7: 386.
Color-sense in Literature. (H. Ellis) Contemp. 69: 714.
— of Poets (A. St. Johnston) M. of Art, 8: 54.
Color-sergeant Rhodes; a story. Cornh. 69: 506.
Color-shadows. (A. E. Wright) 19th Cent. 37: 819. Same art. Liv. Age, 205: 560.
Color Standards, Scheme of. (J. H. Pillsbury) Nature, 52: 390.
Color System, On. (O. N. Rood) Am. J. Sci. 144: 263.
Color-teaching, System of. (E. W. Scripture) Educa. R. 6: 464.
Color Vision. (Prince Kropotkin) 19th Cent. 34: 253. Same art. Ecl. M. 121: 807. — Spec. 68: 848.
Colors of the Lawrence, The; a story. (C. Ross) McClure, 7: 208.
Colorado and its Capital. (J. Ralph) Harper, 86: 935.
— Bright Outlook of. (J. E. Leet) No. Am. 158: 247.
— History of the United States in Paragraphs. (C. L. Norton) M. Am. Hist. 29: 271.
— Situation in. (L. R. Ehrich) Yale R. 5: 51.
Colorado Health Plateau, The. (L. M. Iddings) Scrib. M. 19: 136.
Colorado River, Basin of, Physical Geology of. (A. Harker) Nat. Sci. 1: 205.
— Cañons of. (F. A. Nims) Overland, n. s. 19: 253. — (H. N. Hutchinson) Knowl. 15: 7, 29.
— Engineering in, with a Camera. (R. B. Stanton) Cosmopol. 15: 292.
— Grand Cañon of. (M. W. Fisher) Outing, 22: 261.
— Scenery on. (J. W. Powell) Am. Antiq. 17: 240.
Colorado Springs and Pike's Peak. (M. L. Todd) Nation, 57: 245.
— High School Building at. (G. B. Turnbull) School R. 1: 682.
— Water-works. (A. Lakes) Engin. M. 10: 273.
Colt, Officer and Gentleman; a story. (J. Lloyd) Munsey, 13: 137.
Coltart, William. Collection of paintings. (A. G. Temple) Art J. 48: 97.
Columba, St. (F. M. Robinson) M. of Art, 8: 105. — (E. H. Pearce) Sund. M. 21: 327.
— Orbit of. (A. Anscombe) Acad. 41: 542.
— — and Chronology of Early Kings of Alban. (A. Anscombe) Eng. Hist. R. 7: 570.
Columbia, America must be called. (E. A. Oldham) M. Am. Hist. 27: 429.
Columbia, Cruiser. (W. M. McFarland) Engin. M. 6: 686.
Columbia River, Up the, in 1857. (F. M. Stocking) Overland, n. s. 23: 186.
Columbia University, Dedication of New Site of. Science, n. s. 3: 681. — Critic, 28: 328.
— Library; New Building. Lib. J. 19: 379. Critic, 26: 368.
— Physical and Mental Measurements of Students of. (J. McK. Cattell and L. Farrand) Psychol. R. 3: 618.
— Work in Economic History. Soc. Econ. 6: 35.
Columbus, Christopher. (E. Castelar) Cent. 22: 123-921. — (S. Ruge) Harper, 85: 681. — With portrait. (J. L. Spalding) Cath. World, 56: 1. — (W. E. Curtis) Chaut. 15: 657. — (C. M. Depew) Our Day, 10: 851. — Gent. M. n. s. 49: 428. — (R. H. Clarke) Am. Cath. Q. 17: 47-733. — Lond. Q. 79: 306. — (A. Donovan) Reliquary, 32: 215.
— Ancestry and Education of. (L. A. Dutto) Cath. World, 54: 815.
— and the Cabots. (F. M. Holland) Open Court, 6: 34, 74.
— and Discovery of America. (Maria A. Brown) Time, 15: 429. — (H. B. Adams and H. Wood) J. H. Univ. Studies, 10: nos. 10-11.
— and his Friends. (I. B. Choate) New Eng. M. n. s. 7: 141.
— and La Rabida. (C. W. Currier) Cath. World, 55: 639.
— Apotheosis of, with portrait. (J. J. O'Shea) Cath. World, 57: 151.
— Autographs of. (E. P. Evans; J. Winsor) Nation, 55: 306.
— Birthplace of. (L. A. Dutto) Cath. World, 54: 478, 652.
— Book of Privileges. (J. Winsor) Nation, 59: 68.
— Boyhood and Youth of. (R. Davey) National, 20: 215. Same art. Ecl. M. 119: 733.
— Caravels of. (V. M. Concas) Nat. Geog. M. 5: 180.
— Celebration of, 1792. (E. F. de Lancey) M. Am. Hist. 29: 1.
— Character of. (D. Wise) Meth. R. 52: 745.
— The Columbian Fruition. Atlan. 78: 557.
— Columbus Day. (C. H. Townshend) N. E. Reg. 47: 164.
— Elton's. Sat. R. 74: 370.
— Enterprise of. (A. Harvey) M. Am. Hist. 27: 1, 98.
— Family and Descendants of. (W. E. Curtis) Chaut. 16: 315. — (Duke of Veragua) No. Am. 157: 113.
— Figure of. Atlan. 69: 409.
— First Landfall of. (J. W. Redway) Nat. Geog. M. 3: 179. — (H. A. Blake) 19th Cent. 32: 536. Same art. Un. Serv. (Phila.) 8: 527. Same art. Ecl. M. 119: 673.
— First Voyage, Las Casas' Narrative of. Cath. World, 56: 40.
— Forerunners of. (K. Blind) New R. 7: 346. Same art. Liv. Age, 195: 387.
— Fourth Centenary of. Addresses at Chicago, Oct. 21, 1892. M. Am. Hist. 28: 460.

Columbus, Fourth Centenary of: Celebration at Genoa. Sat. R. **74**: 326.
— — Celebration at Palos. Sat. R. **74**: 158.
— — New York's Great Object Lesson. (Mrs. M. J. Lamb) M. Am. Hist. **28**: 321.
— in Portugal. (L. A. Dutto) Cath. World, **55**: 44.
— in Romance. (A. Bierstadt) M. Am. Hist. **28**: 272.
— in Spain. (L. A. Dutto) Cath. World, **55**: 210.
— In the Wake of. (F. A. Ober) Nat. Geog. M. **3**: 187.
— Map by, Discovery of. (C. Peucker) Geog. J. **3**: 44.
— Markham's. (J. Winsor) Nation, **55**: 355.
— Memoirs of the Discovery of. (Otto, Count of Mosloy) M. Am. Hist. **28**: 358.
— Monuments. (W. E. Curtis) Chaut. **16**: 138.
— Mystery of. (E. Lawrence) Harper, **84**: 728.
— Old and the New in History; a poem. (W. I. Crandall) M. Am. Hist. **27**: 342.
— On the Track of. (H. J. Perry) New Eng. M. n. s. **6**: 290.
— Our Country and. (P. Freneau) M. Am. Hist. **28**: 351.
— a poem. (J. V. Cheney) Overland, n. s. **21**: 550.
— Portrait of, Lotto. (J. C. Van Dyke) Cent. **22**: 818.
— Portraits of. (W. E. Curtis) Cosmopol. **12**: 259, 409.
— Public Memorials to. (C. W. Bump) J. H. Univ. Studies, **10**: nos. 10–11, app.
— Recent Discoveries concerning. (C. K. Adams) M. Am. Hist. **27**: 161.
— Religion of. (F. M. Bird) Lippinc. **51**: 508.
— Second Wife of. (J. B. Healy) So. Am. **2**: 325.
— a sonnet. (A. J. Rupp) M. Am. Hist. **28**: 185.
— Spanish Memorials of. (J. G. Wilson) Nat'l M. (N. Y. '91) **17**: 137.
— Symposium on. Indep. June 2, '92.
— Third Centenary of, 1792. (C. T. Thompson) Chaut. **16**: 188.
— True Character of. (A. P. Dunlop) Arena, **6**: 603.
— Winsor's Life of. Ath. '92, **1**: 183. — (W. F. Poole) Dial (Ch.) **12**: 421. — (H. W. Haynes) Nation, **54**: 13. — Spec. **68**: 466. — (J. A. Mooney) Am. Cath. Q. **17**: 827.
Columbus in Love; a story. (G. A. Townsend) Lippinc. **51**: 387.
Columbus, Ohio; a brief history. Am. Arch. **49**: 53.
Columns, Cast-iron. Am. Arch. **45**: 46.
— — Safe Loads for. (F. E. Kidder) Am. Arch. **45**: 27.
Columns, Commemorative, and Ancestor Worship. (S. D. Peet) Am. Antiq. **15**: 261.
Colvin, John Russell, Life of. Sat. R. **79**: 792.
Comanche Series, Outlying Areas of, in Kansas, Oklahoma, and New Mexico. (R. T. Hill) Am. J. Sci. **150**: 205.
Combe, William. Dr. Syntax's Tours. (J. A. Blaikie) M. of Art, **6**: 394.
— Duke. (H. Lacey) Gent. M. n. s. **53**: 51.
Combination; the New Factor in Government. (J. A. Collins) Am. M. Civics, **7**: 268.
— Competition and. (G. Cohn) Econ. J. **5**: 550.
— of Capital. (E. B. Andrews) Int. J. Ethics, **4**: 21.
Combustion in Marine Boilers. (J. R. Fothergill) Cassier, **11**: 129.
Come Down; a story. (A. M. Ewell) Atlan. **75**: 230.
Come, Swallow, Come; a poem. (H. Boulton) M. of Art, **9**: 293.
Comédie Française, Acting of. (E. F. Spence) Theatre, **31**: 73.
— Art Treasures of. (T. Child) M. of Art, **15**: 151, 206.
— at Chicago. (F. Sarcey) Scrib. M. **13**: 677.
— at Orange. (T. A. Janvier) Cent. **28**: 165.
— Green-room. (F. Hawkins) Eng. Illust. **10**: 109.
— in London. (A. Galdemar) Fortn. **59**: 863.
— of To-day. (A. D. Vandam) New R. **9**: 314.
— Sculpture at the. (A. E. Hake) M. of Art, **7**: 171, 280.
Comedies of a Consulate, The. (Ben. H. Ridgeley) Scrib. M. **19**: 625.
Comedy, Bad. Sat. R. **81**: 473.
Comedy of Counterplots. (E. Fawcett) Outing, **21**: 243, 356.
Comedy of Courtship; a story. (D. S. Meldrum) National, **20**: 382. Same art. Liv. Age, **195**: 779.
Comedy of Errors; a story. (K. Wylde) Blackw. **154**: 518. Same art. Liv. Age, **199**: 524.
Comedy of War. (F. P. Humphrey) Cent. **30**: 454.
Comedy of the War, The; a story. (J. C. Harris) McClure, **1**: 69.
Comee-Comey Family. (A. H. Bent) N. E. Reg. **50**: 210.
Comenius, John Amos. (F. Watson) Acad. **43**: 149. — (W. S. Monroe) Educa. **13**: 212. — (J. G. Krall) Theatre, **28**: 195.
— Permanent Influence of. (P. H. Hanus) Educa. R. **3**: 226.
— Place of. (S. S. Laurie) Educa. R. **3**: 209.
— Text-books by. (C. W. Bardeen) Educa. R. **3**: 223.
— Was he called to the Presidency of Harvard? (W. S. Monroe) Educa. R. **12**: 378.
Comet, Barnard's, 1884, Probable Observations of. (L. Swift) Pop. Astron. **3**: 17.
— Brooks's, 1893, Nov. 10, Photograph of. (E. E. Barnard) Astron. **13**: 789.
— Brorsen's Short Period. (G. A. Hill) Astron. **11**: 7.
— A Captive. (C. L. Poor) Pop. Sci. Mo. **42**: 550.
— 1884 II., Barnard's Periodic. (H. C. Wilson) Pop. Astron. **2**: 321.
— 1889 V., Orbits of. (H. C. Wilson) Pop. Astron. **1**: 151.
— 1892 V., Photographic Discovery of. (E. E. Barnard) Pop. Astron. **3**: 13.
— *e*, 1894, and the Lost Comet of Vico, 1844 I. (H. C. Wilson) Pop. Astron. **2**: 241.
— Encke's, History of. (W. T. Lynn) Nature, **51**: 108.
— Holmes's. (W. W. Payne) Astron. **12**: 18.
— — Probable Origin of. (S. J. Corrigan) Astron. **12**: 24.
— Rordame. (W. J. Hussey) Pop. Astron. **2**: 353, 445.
— Swift's, Observations and Photographs of, March 6, 1892. (E. E. Barnard) Astron. **11**: 386.
— Tuttle's, and the August Meteors. (D. Kirkwood) Astron. **12**: 789.
Comets. (G. W. Coakley) Astron. **11**: 652. — (A. Elvins) Canad. M. **1**: 576.
— and Meteors, Notes on. (W. H. S. Monck) Astron. **11**: 274.
— Capture of, by Planets. (H. A. Newton) Astron. **11**: 12.
— — Theory of. Dub. R. **110**: 175.
— Determination of Positions of. (Mary W. Whitney) Pop. Astron. **4**: 177.
— Does the Sun repel? (G. W. Coakley) Astron. **11**: 97.
— Forms of, Tidal Theory of. (G. W. Coakley) Astron. **11**: 177.
— Forms of Tails of. (A. C. Ranyard) Knowl. **15**: 229.
— Magnitudes of. Nature, **53**: 93.
— of 1892. (H. C. Wilson) Astron. **12**: 121.
— of Short Period. (W. E. Plummer) Knowl. **19**: 40, 155.
— Periodical, due in 1895. (W. T. Lynn) Knowl. **18**: 13.
— Photography of. (W. J. Hussey) Pop. Astron. **2**: 353.
— Spectra of, Influence of Slit-width on Appearance of. (H. Kayser) Astron. **13**: 367.
Comfort Pease and her Gold Ring; a story. (M. E. Wilkins) Eng. Illust. **13**: 3.
Comic Papers. (J. F. Sullivan) M. of Art, **14**: 416.
— Rise of. (D. Anderson) M. of Art, **14**: 153.

Comines, Philippe de, and his Mémoires. (W. A. Smith) Bookworm, 7: 129.
Coming and Going. (G. T. Shettle) National, 20: 206. Same art. Liv. Age, 195: 691.
Coming and Going of Mr. Wicks; a story. (C. J. K. Fenton) Argosy, 62: 82.
Coming Home; a story. Argosy, 57: 553.
Coming of Love; a poem. (E. C. Cardoza) Cosmopol. 17: 450.
Cominges, Comte de, at the Court of Charles II., Jusserand's. Ath. '92, 2: 149. — Sat. R. 73: 752.
Commandments, Ten. *See* Decalogue.
Commencement, The College. (L. M. Salmon) Educa. R. 9: 427.
Commencement Season, The. Bach. of Arts, 1: 146.
Commerce, American and British. Liv. Age, 197: 126.
— Economic Aspect of Large Trading. Gunton's M. 10: 263.
— Ethics of. (A. R. Foote) Am. M. Civics, 8: 51.
— Evolution of. (G. G. Hubbard) Nat. Geog. M. 4: 1.
— (G. G. Hubbard) Science, 19: 216.
— Foreign, for 1894–95. Gunton's M. 10: 215.
— German and English, in Elizabeth's Time. (A. Tanzer) Nation, 62: 273.
— not an Accident. (C. E. Naylor) Overland, n. s. 28: 436.
— Ocean, driven from California by law. (C. E. Naylor) Overland, n. s. 28: 298.
— Western Nations and Eastern Markets. (H. S. Hallett) 19th Cent. 35: 379.
Commercial Alliances, New. (J. R. Elkins) Am. M. Civics, 8: 529.
Commercial Crises, Periodicity of, as exemplified in the U. S. (E. V. Grabil) Am. M. Civics, 8: 366.
Commercial Education, Higher. (T. W. Haddon) School & C. 1: 169.
Commercial Education in Belgium. (W. Layton) J. Soc. Arts, 43: 690.
Commercial Supremacy, America's Battle for. (J. R. Proctor) Forum, 16: 315.
Commercial Traveller, A; a story. (L. Dougall) Temp. Bar, 108: 349. Same art. Liv. Age, 210: 478.
Commerson, Philibert. The King's Naturalist. Ed. R. 177: 321. — Pop. Sci. Mo. 46: 112.
Commissions, Government by. (R. L. Bridgman; G. Bradford) New Eng. M. n. s. 10: 442.
— Illicit. Econ. R. 6: 217.
Committee of Ten. *See* Secondary Education in the U. S.
Common, Commonplace, and Romantic, The. (W. R. Alger) New World, 1: 51.
Common, Rights of, Origin of. (T. E. Scrutton) Law Q. 3: 373.
Common Consent. (R. A. Proctor) Open Court, 1: 386.
Common Sense, Philosophy of. (H. Sidgwick) Mind, 20: 145.
Commonest Possible Story, The. (B. Perry) Scrib. M. 11: 257.
Commonplace Books. (J. Buchan) Bookworm, 7: 83.
Commonplace Chapter, A; a story. (H. Crackanthorpe) New R. 10: 242, 365.
Commonplace Man. (K. Kenyon) Longm. 23: 614.
Commons, English, and Forests. Spec. 72: 303.
Commonwealth Hotel, Boston. Am. Arch. 48: 30.
Commonwealths, Ideal. (R. Wheatley) Meth. R. 53: 581.
Commune, Paris. Blackw. 155: 1. Same art. Liv. Age, 200: 466. Same art. Ecl. M. 122: 241.
— How it made the Republic. (P. Grousset) Time, 1: 106–750.
— What I saw f it. (A. Forbes) Cent. 22: 803. 23: 48.
Commune, Paris, What an American Girl saw of it. Cent. 23: 61.
Communion, Close, Reasons against. Bib. Sac. 52: 97.
— — Reasons for. (J. W. Willmarth) Bib. Sac. 52: 297.
Communion Tokens, Church. (A. M. Earle) Atlan. 74: 210.
Communism: Celibates of Economy. (M. T. Bayard) Canad. M. 7: 199.
— Christianity and. (W. S. Lilly) New R. 11: 340. Same art. Ecl. M. 123: 721.
— Colonial Experiment in. Soc. Econ. 8: 284.
— The Colony of New Australia, Paraguay. (A. J. Rose-Soley) Westm. 140: 523. Same art. Ecl. M. 121: 780.
Communistic Settlement in Africa, Proposed. Dub. R. 110: 460.
Communities. Seebohm's Tribal System in Wales. (C. M. Andrews) Am. Hist. R. 1: 120.
— Survival of. (F. W. Maitland) Law Q. 9: 36, 211.
Community, Woman's, at Belton, Tex. (G. P. Garrison) Char. R. 3: 28.
Companies, Conduct of Business by. Bank. M (Lond.) 60: 132.
Company. (C. C. Abbott) Lippinc. 58: 423.
Company Law, Proposed Changes in. (J. C. Lorimer) Jurid. R. 7: 352.
— Reform of. (E. Manson) Law Q. 11: 346.
Comparative Method, The. (A. H. Peters) Open Court, 6: 3111.
Compass, Deviation of the. (A. W. Reinold) J. Soc. Arts, 43: 558.
— Variation of, in British Isles. (P. L. Gray) Un. Serv. M. 5: 388.
Compassion, Evolution of. (Mona Caird) Westm. 145: 635.
Compatriot, A. (I. M. Tarbell) New Eng. M. n. s. 11: 83.
Compensation, Occult. (H. C. Lea) Int. J. Ethics, 4: 285.
Competition and Combination. (G. Cohn) Econ. J. 5: 550.
— Effect of, on Banking. (F. E. Steele) Econ. J. 3: 637.
— Recent Aspects of. Bank. M. (N. Y.) 47: 723, 819.
— Stress of, from Workman's Point of View. (R. Halstead) Econ. R. 4: 43.
Complaynt of Scotlande. (James Coville) Scot. R. 23: 90.
Complete Husband, The; a poem. New R. 12: 317.
Complete Lover, The; a poem. (Alex. Scott) New R. 12: 433.
Complete Recovery; a story. (B. Pain) Eng. Illust. 13: 191.
Composers, American. (R. Hughes) Munsey, 11: 157.
— Music, 2: 491.
— Great Living. (G. Holme) Munsey, 10: 227.
— Italian, Modern. (A. Veit) Music, 3: 353.
— To Young. (F. E. Sawyer) Music, 7: 488.
Composition, Literary, Scientific Basis of. (C. H. J. Douglas) Science, 22: 149.
Compositions, School, An Experiment in Correcting. (W. H. Maxwell) Educa. R. 7: 240.
— On Correcting. (H. G. Buehler) Educa. R. 7: 492.
Compostella and the Shrine of St. James. (B. O'Reilly) Am. Cath. Q. 17: 602.
Compromiser, The; a story. Overland, n. s. 20: 81.
Compurgation; Antiquities of Law of Evidence. (H. C. Black) Am. Law R. 27: 498.
Comrades; a story. (R. Penny) Temp. Bar, 107: 438.
Comrades in Arms; a story. (G. Gissing) Eng. Illust. 11: 1230.
Comrie, Alexander. (J. P. Lilley) Chr. Lit. 13: 151.
Comstock Mines, Consumption of Wood in. Garden & F. 8: 38.

Comte, Auguste, and his American Disciples. Atlan. 66: 136.
— and Turgot. (L. Belrose, jr.) Monist, 3: 118.
— Early Life of. (W. H. Schoff) Ann. Am. Acad. Pol. Sci. 8: 491.
— Gospel of Wealth. (L. Belrose, jr.) Open Court, 5: 2755.
— Mill and Spencer, Watson's. (C. S. Peirce) Nation, 60: 284.
— Positivism of, and Agnosticism. (P. Carus) Open Court, 3: 1589.
Comte's Atheism; Reply to F. Harrison. (H. Goodwin) 19th Cent. 21: 873.
Comte-calendar of Great Men, Harrison's. Macmil. 65: 388. — (C. S. Peirce) Nation, 54: 54. — (J. Morley) 19th Cent. 31: 312. Same art. Ecl. M. 118: 433.
Conanicut Island, R. I., Geology and Petrography of. (L. V. Pirsson) Am. J. Sci. 146: 363.
Conceit. Spec. 76: 79.
Concentration. (F. M. McMurray) Educa. R. 9: 27.
Concept, The, in Logical Doctrine. (J. H. Muirhead) Mind, 20: 508.
Conception as a Mental Act. (J. Ogden) Educa. 16: 227.
Conception, Psychology of. (J. Sully) Monist, 1: 481.
Concerts in London, Early. Chamb. J. 70: 794.
— Monday, Popular. (Michael Angelo) Time, 2: 443, 574.
— Popular, Musical Culture and. (H. Arthur Smith) Univ. R. 8: 542.
— Public, Early Days of. All the Year, 74: 592.
Conciergerie, The. Quar. 180: 354. Same art. Liv. Age, 205: 579.
Conciliator of Christendom; a story. (I. Zangwill) Eng. Illust. 16: 385.
Conclusions, Uncertainty of. (T. C. Mendenhall) Science, 20: 20.
Concord School of Philosophy. Open Court, 1: 355.
Concord, N. H. (F. M. Abbott) New Eng. M. n. s. 12: 476.
Concrete, Action of Heat on. (E. L. Ransome) Am. Arch. 53: 71.
— Use of, in Railway Structures. Am. Arch. 41: 69.
Concrete-iron Arches and Slabs. Am. Arch. 47: 86.
Condé, Prince of, and the Revocation of the Edict of Nantes. (A. Laugel) Nation, 62: 155.
— Princes of the House of, d'Aumale's. Ed. R. 176: 350. — Ed. R. 183: 207. — (W. O'C. Morris) Scot. R. 27: 226.
— Revolt of. (A. Laugel) Nation, 54: 376, 410.
Condensation, Cloudy, Colors of. (C. Barus) Am. J. Sci. 145: 150.
— in the Cylinder. (J. T. Hawkins) Cassier, 6: 484.
— in the Steam Jet, Rate of. (A. D. Palmer) Am. J. Sci. 152: 247.
Condensed Ghost, A; a story. (W. L. Alden) Idler, 4: 498.
Condenser, New Form of. Cassier, 3: 210.
— New Independent. Cassier, 2: 146.
Condensers for Steam Engines. (W. H. Weightman) Cassier, 10: 355.
Condensing Apparatus. (W. G. Starkweather) Cassier, 10: 16.
Condiments. (C. D. Wilson) Lippinc. 58: 704.
Conditional Sentences, Greek and Latin. (R. H. Smith; B. L. Gildersleeve) Nation, 60: 78.
Conduct and Manner. (W. Clark) Canad. M. 1: 22.
— A Test of. (F. M. Holland) Open Court, 4: 2676.
Conduit System for Electric Railways. (J. Sachs) Cassier, 6: 385.
Coney Island. (J. Ralph) Scrib. M. 20: 1.
Confederate States. (H. Watterson) Chaut. 15: 147.
— Army. Un. Serv. M. 11: 247.
— — Numerical Strength of. (A. B. Casselman) Cent. 21: 792.
— Fall of, Home Scenes at. (D. Dodge) Atlan. 69: 661.
— Finances of. (J. C. Schwab) Pol. Sci. Q. 7: 38.
— Foreign Loan of. (J. C. Schwab) Yale R. 1: 175.
— Navy. (V. Newton) So. Hist. Pap. 22: 87.
— Publications in. (L. J. Vance) Bach. of Arts, 2: 74.
Confederate Statistics once more. (D. H. Hill, jr.) Nation, 60: 71.
Conference Course of Study. (V. S. Collins) Meth. R. 55: 57.
Conferences, Economic. Open Court, 2: 950, 993, 1104.
Confession, A. (J. Achurch; C. Charrington) New R. 10: 488.
Confession and Absolution in English Church. Eng. R. 15: 249. — (T. T. Shore) 19th Cent. 37: 71. — (T. T. Carter) 19th Cent. 37: 281.
— Gresley on. Eng. R. 16: 281.
— Lea on. (E. Emerton) Am. Hist. R. 2: 113.
— Private, and Private Absolution in the Lutheran Church. (J. W. Richard) Luth. Q. 26: 336.
Confession, The; a story. (G. de Maupassant) Theatre, 32: 252.
Confession of Claude Leigh; a story. (G. Burgess) Eng. Illust. 11: 1179.
Confession of Colonel Sylvester. (C. Ross) Scrib. M. 20: 99.
Confession of Love, A; a story. Argosy, 53: 500.
Confession of Tibbie Law. Blackw. 156: 213. Same art. Liv. Age, 202: 719.
Confessional, The. (J. Morris) Month, 79: 341. 80: 69.
Confessions of a Suicide; a story. (C. Kernahan) Arena, 8: 240.
Confessions of a Village Tyrant. (E. Miller) 19th Cent. 34: 955.
Confessions of a Young Man. (Geo. Moore) Time, 17: 1-535.
Confirmation and Baptism, Early History of. (J. R. Gasquet) Dub. R. 116: 136.
— and its relation to Baptism. Church Q. 34: 1.
Conflict of Interests; a story. (W. P. Ridge) Eng. Illust. 15: 183.
Confucianism. (A. P. Happer) Pub. Opin. 14: 428.
Confucius, Ethics of, as seen in Japan. (J. H. De Forest) And. R. 19: 309.
— the Sage of China. (Mrs. Boyd Carpenter) Sund. M. 23: 239.
Congo, Cruelties in, overstated. (H. M. Stanley) Sat. R. 82: 307.
— Exploration of the. Dub. R. 113: 671.
— French. Dub. R. 114: 182.
— Tribes of, Ethnographical Notes on. (H. Ward) Anthrop. J. 24: 285.
Congo Basin, South-eastern, Explorations in. (E. G. Ravenstein) Geog. J. 1: 223.
Congo State, The. Un. Serv. M. 13: 314, 420.
— as a Factor in the Redemption of Africa. (J. A. Kasson) Our Day, 12: 301.
— International Beginnings of. (J. S. Reeves) J. H. Univ. Studies, 12: 527.
— Three Years' Travel in. (S. L. Hinde) Geog. J. 5: 426.
— Travel in. Sat. R. 78: 137.
Congregational Churches, Contribution of, to Modern Religious Life. (W. Calkins) And. R. 17: 453.
— New England. (E. E. Hale) New Eng. M. n. s. 10: 678.
— in the U. S., Walker's History of. (J. W. Chadwick) Nation, 59: 252.
Congregational Club. (A. H. Bradford) Cent. 22: 314.

Congregational Memorial Hall, London. (W. J. Woods) Sund. M. 24: 544.
Congregational National Council. Chr. Lit. 14: 78.
— of 1891, and Calvinism. (T. T. Munger) M. Chr. Lit. 5: 317.
Congregational Polity, The. (J. H. Crooker) New World, 2: 312.
Congregational Singing. (C. A. Richmond) Chaut. 14: 696.
Congregational Union, Tercentenary Literature of. Church Q. 36: 463.
Congregationalism, American, influenced by Union of Church and State in New England. (A. H. Ross) Bib. Sac. 49: 213.
— and the Historic Episcopate. (G. P. Fisher) Chr. Lit. 13: 322.
— and the Methodist Episcopacy. (C. A. Crane) Meth. R. 52: 429.
— in relation to Schools and Benevolent Societies. (C. B. Rice) Bib. Sac. 50: 429.
— Sociologically considered. (S. W. Dike) And. R. 18: 104.
— Southern. (A. H. Ross) Bib. Sac. 50: 561.
— What is? (A. J. F. Behrends) M. Chr. Lit. 7: 252.
Congregationalist, What makes a? (A. P. Foster) Chaut. 17: 438.
Congregations, How to win. Meth. R. 56: 133.
Congress and its Critics. (H. C. Hansbrough; N. Dingley; W. Elliott; G. B. M'Clellan; C. P. Taft) No. Am. 162: 355.
— at Work. (E. P. Lee) Am. J. Pol. 3: 368.
— Cabinet Officers in. (G. Bradford) Ann. Am. Acad. Pol. Sci. 4: 404.
— Cost of Legislation by. Pub. Opin. 17: 45.
— Extra Sessions of, Past. (C. M. Harvey) No. Am. 160: 379.
— How it votes Money. (C. F. Crisp) No. Am. 162: 14.
— How our Laws are made. (R. Ogden) Nation, 56: 191.
— How to purify. (M. V. Allen) No. Am. 159: 159.
— Important Problems confronting. (A. C. Fisk) Arena, 8: 338.
— Is it a Sovereign Legislature touching our External Relations? (St. G. T. Brooke) Am. Law R. 27: 33. — (G. G. Vest and J. N. Dolph) No. Am. 157: 234.
— Moral Tone of, in 1853 and 1893. (H. L. Dawes) Pub. Opin. 16: 66.
— Procedure in. How a Bill becomes a Law. (G. H. Walker) Chaut. 14: 569.
— Quorum in, Securing a. (C. C. Nott) Nation, 58: 148. — (R. Ogden) Nation, 58: 306.
— Reform of. (C. T. Hopkins) Overland, n. s. 20: 615.
— Rules of. (R. Ogden) Nation, 57: 60.
— Sound Economics in. Soc. Econ. 6: 129.
— Work of the Next. (M. W. Hazeltine; T. C. Catchings; J. P. Dolliver; G. N. Southwick; J. C. Bell) No. Am. 161: 641.
— 25th, Extra Session of. (R. Ogden) Nation, 57: 94.
— 51st and 52d, contrasted. (T. B. Reed) No. Am. 155: 227.
— 52d. Pub. Opin. 13: 441.
— — Work of. (D. MacG. Means) Nation, 55: 98.
— 53d, Extra Session. Pub. Opin. 15: 122, 355.
— — When shall its Work begin? Pub. Opin. 14: 271.
— — Work before. Pub. Opin. 14: 195.
— — Work of. R. of Rs. (N. Y.) 10: 269.
— 53d and 54th. Soc. Econ. 8: 193.
Congress Hall, Philadelphia, Restoration of. (G. C. Mason) Am. Hist. Reg. 4: 36.
Congressional Library. (E. A. Hempstead) Chaut. 23: 695. — (A. R. Spofford) Forum, 14: 369. — (A. R. Spofford) M. Am. Hist. 29: 492. — (A. Shaw) R. of Rs. (N. Y.) 9: 674.
Congressional Library, Building for. Critic, 23: 153. — (G. G. Bain) Am. Arch. 48: 95.
— — Authorship of the Designs for. (P. J. Pelz) Am. Arch. 48: 134.
— Reorganization of. (R. R. Bowker) Lib. J. 21: 357.
Congreve, William. Citizen, 1: 262.
Conifers. Cypresses of Monterey. (C. S. Sargent) Garden & F. 7: 241.
— Forms of European. (H. Christ) Garden & F. 9: 252, 273.
— How our Conifers have wintered. (M. C. Robbins) Garden & F. 7: 123.
— in Iowa. (L. M. Pammel) Garden & F. 8: 279.
— in the West. (C. A. Kepper) Garden & F. 8: 182.
— When to transplant. Garden & F. 7: 408.
Conjuring and Conjure-doctors in the South. J. Am. Folk-Lore, 9: 143, 224.
Conklin, J. M. D., with portrait. Bk. News, 14: 524.
Conkling, Roscoe, and Garfield, James Abram. (H. L. Dawes) Cent. 25: 341.
Connal, William, jr., Picture Collection of. (R. Walker) M. of Art, 17: 335, 361.
Connaught, Duke of. *See* Arthur, Prince.
Connecticut at the World's Fair. (J. H. Vaill) New Eng. M. n. s. 10: 555.
— Election of 1890; Decision of Supreme Court. (C. Deming) Nation, 54: 24.
— Election Sermons in, Statistics of. (B. C. Steiner) N. E. Reg. 46: 123.
— Hunting an Abandoned Farm in. (W. H. Bishop) Cent. 25: 915.
— Intestacy Law of. (C. M. Andrews) Yale R. 3: 261.
— Life in. J. Am. Folk-Lore, 9: 223.
— National Guard of. (W. H. C. Bowen) Outing, 19: 396, 456. 20: 60.
— Stone Age of. (J. Shepard) New Eng. M. n. s. 9: 327.
— Taxation in, History of, 1636–1776. (F. R. Jones) J. H. Univ. Studies, 14: 345.
— Trial Justices in. Green Bag, 6: 501.
Connecticut Public Library Committee. (C. M. Hewins) Lib. J. 21: 267.
Connecticut River, Flow of. (D. Porter) Science, n. s. 3: 579.
Connecticut Sandstone Group. (C. F. Hitchcock) Science, n. s. 1: 74.
Connemara, Coast Life in. (W. H. Bartlett) Art J. 46: 247.
Connemara Miracle, A; a story. (F. Mathew) Idler, 1: 666.
Conner, David, U. S. N., in Mexican War. (P. S. P. Conner) Un. Serv. (Phila.) 14: 32.
Conness, Mount, California, Occupation of. (G. Davidson) Overland, n. s. 19: 115.
Connoisseur, The; a story. (G. Fosbery) Argosy, 60: 544.
Conquered; a story. (Mrs. V. R. Cruger) Cosmopol. 14: 566.
Conquest, Morality of. Spec. 71: 711.
Conquest of Dona Jacoba. Ecl. M. 118: 754. — Same art. Liv. Age, 193: 523.
Conrad, Joseph. Outcast of the Islands. Sat. R. 81: 509.
Conrad, Timothy Abbott. (C. C. Abbott) Pop. Sci. Mo. 47: 257.
Conscience, The. (C. N. Starcke) Int. J. Ethics, 2: 342. — (H. Graham) Meth. R. 54: 345. — (H. Sturt) Mind, 21: 343. — (F. H. Smith) Our Day, 16: 43. — (W. Humphrey) Month, 77: 501.
— Cause and Function of. (S. E. Mezes) Philos. R. 5: 502.

Conscience, Definition of, Wanted. (H. A. Johnston) Presb. & Ref. 7: 622.
— Nature and Origin of. (W. W. Carlile) Int. J. Ethics, 6: 63.
Conscience Fund. (F. L. Chrisman) Lippinc. 54: 103.
Conscious Acts. (W. H. Hill) Am. Cath. Q. 17: 20.
Consciousness. (E. P. Powell) Open Court, 1: 125. — (T. Ribot) Open Court, 3: 1586.
— and Automatism, Animal. (C. L. Morgan) Monist, 7: 1.
— and Biological Evolution. (H. R. Marshall) Mind, 21: 367, 523.
— and Christian Faith. (F. C. Haddock) Meth. R. 55: 921.
— and Evolution. (G. T. Ladd and J. M. Baldwin) Psychol. R. 3: 296. — (J. M. Baldwin) Science, n. s. 2: 219.
— and Experience. (F. H. Bradley) Mind, 18: 211.
— and Time. (C. A. Strong) Psychol. R. 3: 149.
— Definitions and Problems of. (A. Bain) Mind, 19: 348.
— Double, in Hysterical Individuals. (A. Binet) Open Court, 3: 1739.
— — Suggestion in. (A. Binet) Open Court, 3: 2019.
— Doubling of, and the Graphic Method. (A. Binet) Open Court, 3: 1919.
— Evolution of. (C. L. Morgan) Nat. Sci. 1: 659.
— — and of the Cortex. (C. L. Herrick) Science, 21: 351.
— Imitation, The Natural History of. (J. M. Baldwin) Mind, 19: 26.
— Immediate and Mediate Testimony of. (T. E. Allen) Psych. R. 1: 246.
— Influence of Muscular States on. (E. B. Delabarre) Mind, 17: 379.
— Origin of, and Conservation of Spirit. (F. C. Russell) Monist, 2: 357.
— Primitive. (H. M. Stanley) Philos. R. 1: 433.
— Reflective. (S. H. Hodgson) Mind, 19: 208.
— Seat of. (P. Carus) Open Court, 4: 2523.
— Sub-. (A. Bodington) Open Court, 4: 2604, 2621.
— — Intensity of States of. (A. Binet) Open Court, 3: 1983.
— — or Mechanism. (A. Binet) Open Court, 3: 1886.
See also Personality.
Conscription. (L. de La Ramé) Fortn. 58: 211.
Consecration to Christ, Personal. (J. G. Noss) Ref. Q. 39: 93.
Conservatism and Radicalism in Theology. (C. Clever) Ref. Q. 40: 228.
— English, The New. Quar. 180: 549.
— in Scotland, Growth of. National, 18: 821.
— Mental Mummies. (F. L. Oswald) Monist, 3: 30.
Conservative Party in England, Fifty Years of, 1842-92. Blackw. 151: 1.
Conservatives, Ultra, Theological Restiveness of. And. R. 17: 75.
Conservatories, Bulbous Plants for. (W. H. Taplin) Garden & F. 6: 296.
— Plants for, in Summer. (W. H. Taplin) Garden & F. 6: 275.
— Small. Garden & F. 8: 437. — (J. Chamberlin) Garden & F. 5: 129.
Consols at 110. (S. F. Van Oss) 19th Cent. 39: 576.
Conspiracy, Law of. Spec. 68: 424.
Conspiracy of Daniel Dwarber; a story. (A. Cobham) Eng. Illust. 13: 111.
Conspiracy of Mrs. Bunker; a story. (Bret Harte) Idler, 1: 93, 206, 314.
Constable, Archibald, and Sir Walter Scott. Temp. Bar, 96: 473.
Constable, John. (J. Orrock) Art J. 47: 367. — (H. V. Barnett) M. of Art, 6: 334.
— Country of. (R. L. Everett) Eng. Illust. 10: 884. — (C. L. Burns) M. of Art, 14: 282.
Constable, Lord High. Spec. 74: 891.
— Office of. (H. B. Simpson) Eng. Hist. R. 10: 625.
Constabulary, Royal Irish. Chamb. J. 70: 551.
Constancy; a story. (C. H. Rockwell) Un. Serv. (Phila.) 9: 454.
Constant, Benjamin. (A. Laugel) Nation, 60: 47. — Sat. R. 80: 267. — Blackw. 158: 341.
Constant Crossbie. (W. E. Cule) Chamb. J. 73: 473.
Constantine and Christianity. (W. K. Marshall) Meth. R. 54: 82.
— Donation of, as applied by Roman Church. (F. Zinkeisen) Eng. Hist. R. 9: 625.
— Labarum of. (A. Harvey) Canad. M. 5: 164.
Constantinople. (J. P. Mahaffy) Chaut. 21: 442, 610, 722. — (F. M. Crawford) Scrib. M. 14: 714. 15: 3. — (W. C. Preston) Sund. M. 22: 519.
— after the Crimean War. Cath. World, 63: 581.
— American College for Girls in. (E. P. Gould) Educa. 13: 77.
— as an Historic City. (F. Harrison) Fortn. 61: 438. Same art. Liv. Age, 201: 322. Same art. Ecl. M. 122: 721.
— British Embassy at. (J. F. Fraser) Eng. Illust. 15: 97.
— Fall of, 1453. (A. Forbes) Cosmopol. 14: 69.
— Fortifications of. (R. von Bieberstein) Un. Serv. M. 4: 199, 301.
— Great Palace of, Paspati's. Ath. '94, 2: 228. — Scot. R. 23: 251.
— Grosvenor's. (T. Williams) Am. Hist. R. 1: 518. — (J. P. Peters) Nation, 62: 59. — Sat. R. 81: 202.
— Impressions of. (M. Prior) Eng. Illust. 16: 240.
— in 1893. (F. M. Müller) New R. 9: 595.
— Massacre at, 1895. (M. MacColl) Contemp. 68: 744.
— — 1896. Contemp. 70: 457. Same art. Chr. Lit. 16: 47. — (D. Kalopothakes) Nation, 63: 265. *See* Armenians.
— New Museum and the Sidon Sarcophagi. (F. M. Müller) New R. 10: 17.
— Ottoman Bank, Attack on the. National, 28: 141.
— A Personally Conducted Arrest in. (F. H. Smith) Cent. 29: 643.
— Problem of. (F. Harrison) Fortn. 61: 614. Same art. Liv. Age, 202: 87.
— Security from Attack. (S. Wilkinson) Sat. R. 82: 334.
— Value of. (S. Wilkinson) National, 28: 315. Same art. Liv. Age, 211: 694.
— Views about. (R. Davey) Art J. 47: 200.
— Walls of. (R. Davey) Art J. 48: 33.
— — Walls of Stamboul. M. of Art, 14: 44.
Constellation Figures, Phœnician Origin of. (R. Brown, jr.) Acad. 50: 351.
Constellations, Study of. (W. Upton) Pop. Astron. 1: 1-449.
Constitution, Written, Origin and Development of. (C. Borgeaud) Pol. Sci. Q. 7: 613.
Constitutions, Ancient, Two Books on. (L. Dyer) Nation, 57: 273.
— Revision of. (W. W. Phelps) Am. M. Civics, 6: 387.
Constitutional Amendment, Scheme of. (A. B. Farquhar) Am. J. Pol. 3: 10.
Constitutional Liberty, German Emperor and. (Poultney Bigelow) Cosmopol. 20: 17.
Constitutional Theories, English. (T. S. Jerome) Am. Law R. 26: 688.
Constitutional Union Party of 1860. (C. F. Richardson) Yale R. 3: 144.

"Constitution," Frigate, Escape of, 1812. M. Am. Hist. 29: 518.
— History of. (H. D. Smith) Un. Serv. (Phila.) 6: 41–577. 7: 15.
— Last Fight of. (J. J. Roche) Cent. 28: 749.
Construction, Cohesive. (R. Guastavino) Am. Arch. 41: 125.
— of English Houses. (B. T. Fletcher) Archit. Rec. 6: 114.
Construction, Legal, On the Limits of. (H. W. Elphinstone) Law Q. 1: 466.
— Literary. (V. Paget) Bookman, 2: 18, 112.
Constructive Faculty, Evolution of the. (J. M. Burnett) Engin. M. 3: 704.
Consuelo. (W. R. Perkins) Dial (Ch.) 15: 330.
Consular Invoices. Nation, 57: 8.
Consular Service and Spoils System. (J. B. Angell and others) Cent. 26: 306. — Nation, 56: 359.
— Attractions and Abuses of. (W. Slade) Forum, 15: 163.
— Faults in. (R. Adams) No. Am. 156: 461.
— Reform of. (O. S. Straus) Good Govt. 14: 97. — (W. A. Linn) Nation, 59: 398. — (E. L. Godkin) Nation, 61: 218. — (H. White) No. Am. 159: 711. — (W. F. Wharton) No. Am. 158: 412.
— Some Evils of. (A. H. Washburn) Atlan. 74: 241.
Consul's Wife, The; a story. Cornh. 73: 168.
Consumer, The. (I. L. Rice) Forum, 13: 594.
Consumer's Rent, J. S. Nicholson on. (F. Y. Edgeworth) Econ. J. 4: 151.
Consummation; a poem. (H. P. Kimball) Poet-Lore, 7: 453.
Consumption considered as a Contagious Disease. (A. L. Benedict) Pop. Sci. Mo. 48: 33.
— Facts about. (J. S. Billings) Pub. Opin. 14: 283.
— Hereditary, Mortality from. (H. Westergaard) Econ. J. 4: 139.
— a Hopeful Outlook. (J. Fergusson) Canad. M. 1: 628.
— in New England, Cause and Cure of. (W. P. Roberts) Lend a H. 10: 438.
— Robbing it of its Terrors. (H. M. Biggs) Forum, 16: 758.
Consumptives, Climate for. (J. W. Hayward) National, 20: 571.
— Marriage of. Inherited Wretchedness. (P. Paquin) Arena, 16: 605.
— Shall we have a National Sanitarium for? (W. T. Parker) Arena, 16: 196.
Contraband, How to abolish. (A. Wishart) Jurid. R. 2: 344.
Contraband of War; a story. (W. W. Jacobs) Idler, 9: 4.
Contemplation, Ode to the Spirit of. (Maud Walpole) National, 26: 57.
Contemporary, A; a story. (G. Fleming) New R. 14: 473. Same art. Ecl. M. 126: 814.
Contemporary Judgment, Value of. (H. A. Clarke) Poet-Lore, 5: 201.
Contempt of Court. Liv. Age, 203: 243.
Content and Function, Confusion of, in Mental Analysis. (D. S. Miller) Psychol. R. 2: 535.
— and Meaning. (A. Sidgwick) Mind, 20: 281.
Contestatio; a poem. (M. Maartens) Temp. Bar, 98: 45.
Continental Army at Totowa. (C. B. Todd) Am. Hist. Reg. 1: 254.
Continental Congress. (H. Friedenwald) Pennsyl. M. 19: 197.
— Diary of Richard Smith in. 1775–76. Am. Hist. R. 1: 288, 493.
— Draft of an Address of, to the People of the United States, 1776. (H. Friedenwald) Am. Hist. R. 1: 684.
Continental Trips. All the Year, 75: 585.
Continents, Growth of, and Geological Periods. (T. M. Reade) Nat. Sci. 4: 290, 337.
Continued Story, The. (M. W. Learoyd and M. L. Taylor) Am. J. Psychol. 7: 86.
Contract by Letter. (L. C. Innes) Law Q. 9: 316.
— History of. (J. W. Salmond) Law Q. 3: 166.
— of Employment, State Regulation of. (C. B. Labatt) Am. Law R. 27: 857.
— Religious Side of. Spec. 70: 319.
— Terminology in. (W. R. Anson) Law Q. 7: 337.
Contracting, Sub-, Code of Practice for. Am. Arch. 48: 28.
Contractors, Amateur. Am. Arch. 46: 39.
Contracts. (T. M. Clark) Am. Arch. 52: 11.
— Divisible, Rescission of. (V. Denslow) Am. Law R. 26: 20.
— Effect of War upon. (S. D. Thompson) Am. Law R. 30: 88.
— Independent Contractor Doctrine and its Limitations. (C. W. Pierson) Am. Law R. 29: 229.
— Lowest Bidder on, Rights of. (C. L. Allen; C. E. Hellier) Engin. M. 2: 476.
— Mercantile, Forms of. (H. D. Bateson) Law Q. 11: 266.
Contrary, The, and the Disparate. (F. H. Bradley) Mind, 21: 464.
Contrast, Some Effects of. (A. Kirschmann) Am. J. Psychol. 4: 542.
Contrast-colors, Note on the Analysis of. (A. M. Mayer) Am. J. Sci. 151: 38.
Contributors. National, 27: 793. Same art. Ecl. M. 127: 480. Same art. Liv. Age, 210: 755.
Convent, A Sojourn in a. Liv. Age, 210: 310.
Convention, In Praise of. (A. Clerk) New R. 12: 260. Same art. Ecl. M. 125: 363.
Convention, First National Nominating, 1831. (J. S. Murdock) Am. Hist. R. 1: 680.
Conventions, National, A Salutary Mandate to the. (W. Salomon) Forum, 21: 271.
— Party. (J. T. Morgan) No. Am. 155: 237.
Conversation. (J. P. Mahaffy) Chaut. 23: 586, 706. 24: 48. — (A. H. Japp) Argosy, 55: 282.
— Gift of. Spec. 72: 646.
— in France. (T. Bentzon) Cent. 26: 626.
— in Society. (Lady Jeune) Eng. Illust. 11: 1023.
— Polite, Swift on. Spec. 69: 448.
— True, Rarity of. Spec. 69: 591.
— Starting. Spec. 72: 192.
Converse, Allen, and Descendants. (W. R. Cutter) N. E. Reg. 50: 346.
Conversion of Trapper Lewis. (E. W. Sandys) Outing, 26: 64.
Conveyancing under the Ptolemies. (E. P. Fry) Law Q. 8: 56.
Convict who escaped. (J. P. Pollard) New Eng. M. n. s. 8: 233.
Convict Labor. Gunton's M. 11: 290. — (M. M. Trumbull) Open Court, 3: 1778.
— in Road-making. (A. Roberts) Engin. M. 3: 455.
Convicts, British, shipped to American Colonies. (J. D. Butler) Am. Hist. R. 2: 12.
— Discharged, in Europe. (S. J. Barrows) Lend a H. 16: 333.
— Education of. (J. A. Anderson) Green Bag, 4: 294.
— Question of. (J. Kellogg) Arena, 16: 445.
Convocation. Eng. R. 2: 36. 18: 166.
— of 1532. (S. F. Smith) Month, 84: 473.
— Revival of, Eng. R. 8: 289.
Conway, Wales. Sat. R. 73: 178.
Conyngham Foxe and the Charity Ball; a story. (A. H. Sydenham) Un. Serv. (Phila.) 11: 147.
Cook, Thomas, and Travelling. Sat. R. 74: 94.

Cook, Importance of the. Spec. 71: 43.
Cook Islands; Arcadia of the Southern Seas. All the Year, 74: 471.
Cooke, Josiah Parsons. Nature, 50: 551. — (C. L. Jackson) Harv. Grad. M. 3: 195.
Cooke, Rose Terry. Critic, 21: 47.
Cookeite from Paris and Hebron, Maine. (S. L. Penfield) Am. J. Sci. 145: 393.
Cookery. Aesthetics of the Dinner Table. (A. K. Herbert) National, 28: 205.
— and Heating by Electricity. (N. W. Perry) Cassier, 7: 418.
— Art of. (A. Kenney-Herbert) 19th Cent. 32: 763. — (A. K. Herbert) Ecl. M. 120: 77.
— as a Business. (M. Harrison) 19th Cent. 34: 110.
— Camp. (A. D. Gillette and W. and S. McAndrew) Outing, 28: 120.
— The Complete Dutch Kitchen-maid. (C. D. Chadwick) Scrib. M. 11: 250.
— Coöperation in. (G. S. Layard) 19th Cent. 33: 309.
— Elizabethan. (M. B. Wright) Chaut. 15: 622.
— English, Old. Quar. 178: 82.
— Literature of. (A. K. Herbert) Naticnal, 24: 676. 25: 776.
— New England, in the Olden Time. (F. E. Keay) Chaut. 17: 467.
— Principles which underlie. (T. G. Allen) Chaut. 23: 51.
— Schools of. Sat. R. 75: 566. — (M. A. Belloc) Idler, 8: 175.
— Scientific. (M. A. Boland) Pop. Sci. Mo. 43: 653.
Cooking-studies, Scientific, in the New England Kitchen. (E. H. Richards) Forum, 15: 355.
Cookman, Charles E. (Mary T. Earle) Mo. Illust. 13: 259.
Coolgardie. Chamb. J. 71: 581.
Coolie Passenger Traffic. Macmil. 71: 199.
Coolies. Liv. Age, 204: 403.
— Kanaka, Trade in. (J. G. Paton) Our Day, 11: 155.
— Melanesia and the Labor Traffic. (H. H. Montgomery) New R. 8: 549.
— Polynesian Labor Traffic. (R. Temple) National, 19: 639.
Coomans, Diana. (H. Bell) Mo. Illust. 4: 269.
Coomans, Héva. (H. Bell) Mo. Illust. 4: 155.
Coomans, Joseph, and his Work. (C. S. Johnson) Munsey, 7: 314.
Coombe Wood; a poem. (W. Pitt) National, 19: 297.
Coon-hunting in Maryland. (H. M. Howard) Outing, 24: 345.
Cooper, James Fenimore, and his novels. Macmil. 73: 281.
— Literary Offences of. (S. L. Clemens) No. Am. 161: 1.
Cooper, Thomas, Last of the Chartists. Spec. 69: 127. — (M. M. Trumbull) Open Court, 6: 3348.
Cooper, William White. (Mrs. Andrew Crosse) Temp. Bar, 102: 527. Same art. Liv. Age, 202: 668. Same art. Ecl. M. 123: 492.
Cooper Union Labor Bureau. (W. H. Tolman) Pub. Opin. 19: 739.
Coöperation. (N. O. Nelson) Outl. 51: 686.
— Agricultural. (Egerton of Tatton) 19th Cent. 39: 826. — (C. S. Sargent) Garden & F. 8: 451.
— — in Ireland. (T. A. Finlay) Econ. J. 6: 204.
— among California Farmers. (E. F. Adams) Forum, 20: 364.
— Ancient Experiments in. (H. G. Wells) Gent. M. n. s. 49: 418.
— and the Agricultural Depression. (E. Mitchell) Westm. 142: 241.
Coöperation and Profit-sharing. Lend a H. 9: 415. — (B. Jones) Econ. J. 2: 616.
— Brotherly Banking. (E. M. Lynch) Gent. M. n. s. 52: 372.
— Congress on, British, 1896. (A. Williams) Econ. J. 6: 455. — (H. Vivian) Econ. R. 6: 397.
— — International, 1895. (N. O. Nelson) Outl. 52: 580. — (A. Williams) Econ. J. 5: 456. — (H. W. Wolff) Econ. R. 5: 544. — (H. Vivian) Econ. R. 5: 398.
— Economic. (S. Cooley) Am. J. Pol. 4: 561. 5: 249. — (E. M. Burchard) Am. J. Pol. 5: 278. 6: 151.
— Educational Value of. (B. J. Westcott) Econ. R. 1: 5.
— in Building Trades. (H. H. Vivian) Econ. J. 6: 270.
— in 1892. Sat. R. 73: 676.
— Industrial. (D. D. Field) No. Am. 156: 61.
— Mutual Aid amongst Modern Men. (P. Kropotkin) 19th Cent. 39: 65, 914.
— or Compulsory Fraternalism? (M. A. Green) Our Day, 12: 144.
— Practical, at Harmelville, France. (J. G. Brooks) Forum, 13: 757.
— Science by. (T. Lindsay) Pop. Astron. 4: 84.
— *vs.* Competition. (N. S. Patton) Am. Arch. 50: 56. — (H. C. Hay) N. Church R. 2: 245.
— What is? (W. E. Snell) Econ. R. 6: 528.
Coöperative Alliance at Work. (H. W. Wolff) Econ. R. 6: 503.
Coöperative Banking. (E. M. Lynch) Econ. R. 2: 330.
Coöperative Competition. (E. Atkinson) New World, 4: 421.
Coöperative Courtship, A. (A. S. Winston) Scrib. M. 17: 767.
Coöperative Credit. (H. W. Wolff) Econ. R. 4: 366.
Coöperative Credit Banking in Germany. (H. W. Wolff) Econ. R. 2: 460.
Coöperative Ideal, The. (B. F. Dunelm) Econ. R. 4: 449.
Coöperative Industry. (E. E. Hale) Cosmopol. 14: 361.
Coöperative Labor Societies, Italian Report on. (D. F. Schloss) Econ. J. 6: 445.
Coöperative Movement, The. (W. H. Roberts) Univ. R. 1: 529.
Coöperative Production. (H. W. Wolff) Econ. R. 5: 19.
— Ethics of. (J. M. Ludlow) Atlan. 75: 383.
— in the British Isles. (J. M. Ludlow) Atlan. 75: 96.
— Jones'. Sat. R. 78: 238.
Coöperative Societies and Agricultural Syndicates in France. (C. Gide) Econ. J. 5: 195.
Coöperative Town, A Dutch. Am. Arch. 46: 91.
Coöperators and Profit-sharing. (W. E. Snell) Econ. R. 3: 201.
Coos Bay; a Province of California. (F. F. Victor) Overland, n. s. 22: 96.
Copais, Lake, Prehistoric Engineering at. (J. D. Champlin) Pop. Sci. Mo. 48: 209.
Cope, Charles W., Cope's Reminiscences of. Ath. '92, 2: 166. — Sat. R. 73: 430.
Cope-Montgomery Discussion, The. Open Court, 2: 776.
Copenhagen, Battle of, 1807. (W. S. Millard) Macmil. 72: 81.
— — Danish Account. (P. Toft) Un. Serv. (Phila.) 9: 15.
— Free Port of. (P. Vedal) Engin. M. 10: 899.
— Royal Danish Theatre. (W. Archer) Harper, 84: 443.
— Winter Life in. All the Year, 74: 60, 87.
Copernicus. (R. Ball) Good Words, 36: 252. Same art. Liv. Age, 205: 310.
— Was he a German? (J. J. Král) Nation, 57: 248.
Copleston, E., Bishop, Memoir of. Eng. R. 16: 243.
Copley, John Singleton. M. of Art, 2: 94.

Coppée, François, with portrait. Bk. Buyer, 10: 642. — With portrait. Bk. Buyer, 13: 355. — (M. Negreponte) Westm. 138: 236. — (T. Beaugeard) Theatre, 27: 277.
— For the Crown. (J. H. McCarthy) Gent. M. n. s. 56: 531.
Copper and Zinc, Alloys of. T. K. Rose) Nature, 55: 130.
— in Western Idaho. (R. L. Packard) Am. J. Sci. 150: 298.
— Refined American, Analysis of. (H. F. Keller) J. Frankl. Inst. 138: 54.
— Resources in, in the U. S. (J. Douglas) J. Soc. Arts, 41: 39.
— Separation of, from Cadmium by the Iodide Method. (P. E. Browning) Am. J. Sci. 146: 280.
Copper Mining in Nevada. (E. V. Clemens) Cassier, 4: 323.
— in U. S. (C. Kirchhoff) J. Frankl. Inst. 136: 338.
— Pre-Columbian, in North America. (R. L. Packard) Am. Antiq. 15: 67, 152.
Copper Region of Michigan. (F. B. Phelps) Engin. M. 4: 47.
Copperhead, The. (H. Frederic) Scrib. M. 14: 112-622.
Coptos, Egypt. Sat. R. 78: 209.
— Flinders Petrie at. Ath. '94, 1: 120, 153.
Copyholders, Security of, in 15th and 16th Centuries. (I. S. Leadam) Eng. Hist. R. 8: 684.
Copyright. (W. C. Maude) Month, 84: 431.
— American, French View of. Dial (Ch.) 15: 136.
— and Art. Art J. 47: 79.
— Architects'. (T. M. Reade) Am. Arch. 38: 45.
— Author's Control of a Copyrighted Book. Acad. 42: 131.
— Canadian. (Goldwin Smith) Sat. R. 81: 166. — Book R. 3: 125, 179. — Critic, 26: 353. 27: 89-373. — (D. A. Rose) Canad. M. 6: 81. — (Goldwin Smith) Canad. M. 5: 551. — (Hall Caine; W. E. H. Lecky; H. Rider Haggard; J. Murray; Macmillan & Co.) Contemp. 67: 477.
— — a Canadian Reply. (P. A. Hurd) Contemp. 67: 888.
— Hall Caine on. Critic, 27: 292.
— Covert Bill. Critic, 26: 170-246.
— Ethics of. (K. H. Claghorn) Yale R. 4: 426. — Critic, 28: 188, 298.
— in England, Registration of. (T. Solberg) Nation, 54: 66.
— in Works of Fine Art. (G. E. Samuel) M. of Art, 15: 375, 403.
— — Suggestions for a New Act. (M. H. Spielmann) M. of Art, 16: 127. — (G. E. Samuel) M. of Art, 18: 461.
— International. Critic, 20: 26. 27: 90.
— — Law of 1891. (C. Porter) Poet-Lore, 4: 155.
— — Protest against Hicks's Amendments. Critic, 25: 438.
— — Results of the Law. (G. H. Putnam) Forum, 16: 616.
— — Unsatisfactory Working of, in France. Critic, 20: 160.
— Is it a Chose in Action? (S. Brodhurst) Law Q. 11: 64.
— Literary Property, Ownership of. (G. H. Putnam) Chaut. 14: 690.
— Newspaper. (S. J. Low) National, 19: 648. — (H. Hardy) National, 19: 855. — (S. Brodhurst) National, 19: 859. — (D. M. Means) Nation, 54: 461.
— Property, Things in Action and. (T. C. Williams) Law Q. 11: 223.
— Shakespeare and. (H. Davis) Atlan. 71: 256.
Copyright Conference in Barcelona, 1894. (T. Solberg) Nation, 57: 324.
Copyright Congress in Antwerp, 1894. (T. Solberg) Nation, 59: 284.
— 1895. (T. Solberg) Nation, 61: 343.
Copyright Depositories, Need of Additional. (S. H. Ranck) Lib. J. 20: supp. 43.
Copyright Law, Curiosities of. (A. T. Carter) Law Q. 4: 172.
— of the U. S. of 1891. (C. J. Longman) Econ. R. 1: 203.
Copyright Legislation. Critic, 28: 375.
Coquelin, Benoît Constant. M. of Art, 8: 94.
Coques, Gonzales. Five Senses. (W. M. Conway) M. of Art, 6: 211.
Coquetdale; a Northumbrian Valley. (A. H. Japp) Gent. M. n. s. 52: 278.
"Cora," Slave-ship, Capture of. (W. Hall) Cent. 26: 115.
Coracle, From a. (A. G. Bradley) Macmil. 67: 458.
Coral Reef, Boringa. (W. W. Watts) Nature, 54: 201.
Coral Reef Controversy, The. (H. B. Guppy) Time, 19: 289.
Coral Sea, A Glimpse in the. (H. Milman) Good Words, 34: 328.
Corbett, Miles, and Malahide Castle. (Lord Talbot de Malahide) Walford's Antiq. 2: 225.
Corbin Park. Spec. 72: 434.
Corcoran Art Gallery, Washington, Architectural Plans for. Am. Arch. 43: 44.
Corday, Charlotte. (A. King) Argosy, 55: 464.
Cordelia's Night of Romance; a story. (J. Ralph) Harper, 90: 781.
Cordilleras, Crossing the. (M. Crommelin) Leis. Hour, 44: 457.
Cordite and its Manufacture. Chamb. J. 72: 495. Same art. Liv. Age, 206: 767.
Cordova. (D. Hannay) M. of Art, 6: 236.
— the City of Memories. (H. C. Chatfield-Taylor) Cosmopol. 21: 362.
— Observatory. (J. M. Thome) Astron. 13: 8. — (W. H. Pickering) Harv. Grad. M. 2: 350.
Corea. (A. Michie) Asia. R. 14: 317. — Scot. R. 24: 387. — (A. Kirchhoff) Around World, 1: 192.
— and the Coreans. (J. B. Bernadou) Nat. Geog. M. 2: 231.
— and its People, Notes on. (H. S. Saunderson) Anthrop. J. 24: 299.
— and the Sacred White Mountain, Cavendish's. Sat. R. 77: 700.
— and the Siberian Railway. Fortn. 64: 879. Liv. Age, 208: 131.
— China, and Japan. (R. S. Gundry) Fortn. 62: 618. (F. von Richthofen) Geog. J. 4: 556. — (W. E. Griffis) Chaut. 20: 70. — (W. E. Griffis) Lit. W. (Bost.) 25: 264. — (A. Heard; D. W. Stevens; H. Martin) No. Am. 159: 300.
See Chino-Japanese War.
— Conscience of. (E. H. Parker) Asia. R. 22: 291.
— The Corean Crux. (D. C. Boulger) 19th Cent. 36: 781.
— Curzon's Problems of. (W. E. Griffis) Nation, 59: 250. — (F. I. Maxse) National, 24: 263.
— Dolmens and Other Antiquities of. (W. Gowland) Anthrop. J. 24: 316.
— Execution in. Sat. R. 78: 531.
— from its Capital, Gilmore's. (W. E. Griffis) Nation, 56: 426.
— Holiday in. Spec. 73: 274.
— Japanese Invasion of, in 1592. (W. W. Ireland) Macmil. 71: 24. Same art. Liv. Age, 203: 611.

Corea, Mountains and Mountaineers of. (C. W. Campbell) Pop. Sci. Mo. **41**: 229.
— Mourning and Burial Rites of. (E. B. Landis) Anthrop. J. **25**: 340.
— Past, Present, and Future. (W. E. Griffis) Chaut. **22**: 461.
— People of. (R. K. Douglas) Good Words, **36**: 103.
— Problem of, Factors in. Spec. **73**: 164.
— Procession of the King. Sat. R. **78**: 502.
— Progressive Party in, Rise and Fall of. (G. Haddo) Chaut. **16**: 46.
— Question of. (N. Norman) Contemp. **66**: 305. — Liv. Age, **203**: 51.
— Royal Reception in. Chamb. J. **70**: 761.
— Russia and England in the Far East. Fortn. **65**: 865.
— Savage Landor's. Sat. R. **79**: 351.
— Unpleasant Reminiscences of. Chamb. J. **72**: 78.
— Village Scenes in. (A. L. Craig) Chaut. **16**: 332.
— Visit to. (A. H. Savage Landor) Fortn. **62**: 184. Same art. Ecl. M. **123**: 383. Same art. Liv. Age, **202**: 689.
Corean Customs and Notions. (T. Watters) Folk-Lore, **6**: 82.
Corean Games, Culin on. (F. Starr) Dial (Ch.) **20**: 302.
Corean Rebel, Story of. (H. Gordon) Lippinc. **55**: 662.
Corelli, Marie. Bk. News, **13**: 495.
— Barabbas; how written. (M. Corelli) Idler, **7**: 120.
— My First Book: Romance of Two Worlds. Idler, **4**: 239.
Corfu. (T. Ellis) M. of Art, **15**: 295. — (E. A. Richings) Belgra. **78**: 361. — (J. P. Mahaffy) Sund. M. **22**: 591.
Corinna's Fiammetta. (M. G. Van Rensselaer) Cent. **28**: 362.
Corinth, Gulf of. (Prof. Harrower) Good Words, **33**: 736, 814.
Corinth Canal. All the Year, **73**: 449.
— Progress of. Dub. R. **112**: 452.
Corinto, Out of the World at. (R. H. Davis) Harper, **91**: 933.
Cork, Cathedral of St. Fin Barre. (A. C. Robinson) M. of Art, **18**: 300.
— Southwest, and Kerry: a Congested District. Blackw. **157**: 208. Same art. Liv. Age, **204**: 750.
Cork Forests, Great. Chamb. J. **71**: 91. Same art. Liv. Age, **201**: 185.
Cork Oak, Cultivation of. (C. Mandin) Garden & F. **5**: 242.
— Fructification of. (C. E. Faxon) Garden and F. **8**: 52.
Corkey Minimus; a story. (E. Phillpotts) Idler, **9**: 778.
Corlear's Hook Park, N. Y. (C. S. Sargent) Garden & F. **7**: 422.
Cormorant, Etymology of. (F. Chance and others) Acad. **47**: 380, 404.
Cormorants. Spec. **75**: 928.
Corn, Indian, Fertile Crosses with. (J. W. Harshberger) Garden & F. **9**: 522.
— — Is it growing wild in America? (R. P. Harris) Garden & F. **9**: 422.
— — Silk and Tassel. (M. M. Williams) Cosmopol. **15**: 440.
— — Sugar from. (F. L. Stewart) Science, **22**: 143–171.
Cornbury, Lord, Governor of N. Y., 1702–8. (W. L. Stone) Nat'l M. (N. Y. '91) **17**: 95.
Cornelian, The Medici. (J. Cartwright) M. of Art, **8**: 70.
Cornelian Necklace, The; a story. (A. M. Trotter) Argosy, **60**: 210.
Cornelius, Peter von. (H. Zimmern) M. of Art, **7**: 74.
Cornell, John B., architect. Archit. Rec. **1**: 244.
Cornell Expedition to Greenland. (R. S. Tarr) Science, n. s. **4**: 520.
Cornell University, Ethics in. (J. S. Schurman) Eth. Rec. **2**: 143.
— Hazing at. Pub. Opin. **16**: 594.
— Horticulture at. (L. H. Bailey) Science, n. s. **2**: 831.
— Library. (W. Austin) Lib. J. **18**: 181.
— Quarter-centennial. (T. Stanton) Open Court, **7**: 3719.
— Sibley College. (R. C. Carpenter) Cassier, **1**: 104.
Cornflower; a Story of a Prairie Cornfield. (J. Blewitt) Canad. M. **6**: 315.
Cornhill Magazine, The First Number of. (Mrs. R. Ritchie) Cornh. **74**: 1.
Cornish Maid, A; a story. (B. Lake) Belgra. **81**: 92–**82**: 214.
Cornwall, William, Family of. (E. E. Cornwall) N. E. Reg. **49**: 39.
Cornwall, Bench-Ends in. (A. G. Langdon) Illus. Archæol. **1**: 246. — (R. J. Preston) Antiq. n. s. **25**: 61.
— Christmas in. Argosy, **58**: 484.
— Crosses in, Two. Walford's Antiq. **4**: 76.
— Early Christian Monuments of. (A. G. Langdon) Am. Arch. **46**: 69.
— Humours of the Duchy. Eng. Illust. **11**: 966.
— Land of a Lost Language. (W. C. Borlase) Eng. Illust. **12**: no. 3, 103.
— Prehistoric Remains in. (A. L. Lewis) Anthrop. J. **25**: 2.
— Scenery of. (W. H. Tregellas) M. of Art, **1**: 8, 141.
— Superstitions of. Macmil. **73**: 36.
Cornish Tin-mine. (L. Hind) Eng. Illust. **15**: 538.
Corona of the Nantahalas; a novel. (L. Pendleton) Munsey, **11**: 354, 465, 611. **12**: 22.
Coronal; a poem. (A. Fields) Harper, **90**: 50.
Coronation Oath, British. (T. E. Bridgett) Month, **86**: 305.
Coronations and Inaugurations. (F. S. Daniel) Cosmopol. **14**: 715.
Coroner, Early History of. (C. Gross) Pol. Sci. Q. **7**: 656.
Coroners' Rolls, Select Cases from, Gross's. (G. E. Howard) Am. Hist. R. **2**: 218.
Corot, Jean Baptiste Camille. (C. Thurwanger) New Eng. M. n. s. **5**: 692. — (R. A. M. Stevenson) New R. **14**: 408. Same art. Ecl. M. **126**: 625. — (D. C. Thomson) M. of Art, **11**: 181.
Corporal Punishment. (J. L. Payle) Canad. M. **7**: 476.
— Is it degrading? (A. J. Palm) Am. J. Pol. **1**: 187.
Corporate Authorship. (W. I. Fletcher) Lib. J. **21**: 493.
Corporate Organization, Foreign, to do Business at Home. (A. M. Alger) Am. Law R. **26**: 342.
Corporate Privileges, Abuses of. (S. D. Thompson) Am. Law R. **26**: 169.
Corporation, The, as a Form of Colonial Government. (H. L. Osgood) Pol. Sci. Q. **11**: 259, 502, 694.
— de facto, Liability of Members of a. (H. L. Woodward) Am. Law R. **27**: 209.
— Liability of, for Transferring Shares on Forged Powers of Attorney. (S. D. Thompson) Am. Law R. **26**: 809.
— Liability of Organizers of, for its Acts. (T. M. Avery) Am. Law R. **27**: 361.
— Must it go? (L. S. Richard) Am. J. Pol. **2**: 294.
Corporation Accounts, Examination of, by Auditors, (T. L. Greene) Engin. M. **12**: 449.
Corporation Plate and Insignia of Wiltshire. (E. H. Goddard) Illus. Archæol. **1**: 219.
Corporations and the Legislature. (C. C. White) Yale R. **3**: 35.
— and Public Morals. (W. Gladden) Bib. Sac. **52**: 607.
— and Trusts. (L. G. McPherson) Pop. Sci. Mo. **45**: 289.

Corporations, Company Law Reform. (H. E. M. Stutfield) National, **26**: 836.
— Consolidation of Competing. (J. C. Thomson) Am. Law R. **27**: 330.
— Control of Public Service. (A. R. Foote) Engin. M. **9**: 50.
— Foreign, Effect of War upon the Powers of their Agents. (S. D. Thompson) Am. Law R. **30**: 238.
— in Cities, Law of, A. R. Foote on. (I. A. Hourwich) J. Pol. Econ. **3**: 111.
— in Political Economy. (Wilbur Aldrich) Soc. Econ. **2**: 94, 218.
— Law of, Crying Need for Reforms in. (A. Emden) 19th Cent. **35**: 1033.
— — Philosophical View of. (C. T. Palmer) Open Court, **2**: 1331, 1346.
— Non-directing Directors. Soc. Econ. **2**: 211.
— Notice to, Mistakes on the Subject of. (S. D. Thompson) Am. Law R. **29**: 523.
— Priority as between Unrecorded Transfers of Shares and Attaching Creditors. (L. H. Hatfield) Am. Law R. **30**: 223.
— Private, Doctrine of *ultra vires* in relation to. (S. D. Thompson) Am. Law R. **28**: 376.
— Profits of. (W. F. Draper) Soc. Econ. **3**: 150.
— Public, and Private. (F. H. Cooke) Am. J. Pol. **3**: 239.
— — and the Right to Steal. (I. L. Rice) Forum, **16**: 204.
— — Municipal Ownership of. (M. J. Francisco) Engin. M. **9**: 41.
— Public Obstruction. (H. Powers) Soc. Econ. **1**: 348.
— Quasi-municipal, Validity of Contracts held by. (H. W. Williams) Am. Law R. **26**: 675.
— Ratio of Wages to Profit. (W. F. Draper) Soc. Econ. **4**: 84.
— Semi-public and the State. (A. W. Small) Am. J. Sociol. **1**: 398.
Corpus Christi, Feast of, in Seville. (C. E. White) Lippinc. **55**: 273.
Corpus Christi College, Oxford. (E. K. Chambers) Acad. **43**: 385.
Corpus Poetarum Latinarum, ed. by Postgate. Sat. R. **79**: 587.
Correggio. (W. J. Stillman) Cent. **22**: 916.
— 4th Centenary of. (B. Berenson) Nation, **59**: 156.
— Frescoes at Parma. M. of Art, **8**: 420.
— "Night" and "Day" of. (L. E. Baxter) M. of Art, **11**: 380.
— Ricci's Life of. Sat. R. **81**: 179. — (J. C. Van Dyke) Dial (Ch.) **20**: 41. — M. of Art, **19**: 449.
Correlation of Science and History. (N. S. Jackman) Educa. R. **9**: 464.
Correlation of Structure, Action, and Thought. (T. L. Brunton) Pop. Sci. Mo. **42**: 749.
Correspondence, An Impossible. (R. F. Murray) 19th Cent. **33**: 966.
Correspondent, Travelling. (W. J. C. Meighan) Lippinc. **49**: 573.
Corriveau, La. (L. Frechette) Arena, **8**: 747.
Corrodi, Hermann. (M. S. Taylor) M. of Art, **12**: 217.
Corrosion of Boilers and Steamships. (W. C. Ward) Cassier, **7**: 490.
— of Steam Drums. (J. McBride) Cassier, **6**: 399.
Corrupt Political Practices. (C. R. Woodruff) Am. M. Civics, **8**: 134.
— in Elections. (R. L. Bridgman) Chr. Un. **46**: 830.
Corrupt Practices Acts. (J. Hutchinson) Am. Law R. **27**: 345.
— British. (H. James) Forum, **15**: 129.
— Massachusetts. (J. Quincy) Forum, **15**: 142.
Corruption, Political, Centralization the Cure for. (L. P. Gratacap) Am. M. Civics, **9**: 307, 400.
— — The National Peril. (L. Satterthwaite) Am. M. Civics, **8**: 407.
— the Price of Peace. (J. B. Bishop) Cent. **26**: 667.
— Publicity as a Cure for. (H. Welsh) Forum, **14**: 26.
Corsica. (G. F. Bowen) Liv. Age, **192**: 439.
— and the Corsicans. (G. C. Rothery) Time, **23**: 833.
— Artist in. (E. T. Compton) M. of Art, **8**: 161, 200.
— Banditti of. (C. Holland) Contemp. **64**: 492. Same art. Liv. Age, **199**: 622. Same art. Ecl. M. **121**: 666.
— Boswell's Journal in. (E. S. Schuckburgh) Macmil. **66**: 432. Same art. Liv. Age, **195**: 605.
— Jaunt into. (C. H. Adams) Cent. **26**: 747.
— the Land of the Bandit. Cornh. **72**: 179.
— Life and Death in. (J. W. Keogh) Cath. World, **64**: 18.
— Society in. (B. Thomson) National, **19**: 349. Same art. Ecl. M. **119**: 73. Same art. Liv. Age, **194**: 111.
— Two Days in Cape Corse. Chamb. J. **70**: 377.
Corsican Affair, A; a story. All the Year, **74**: 381.
Cortex, Visual Area of, in Man. (H. H. Donaldson) Am. J. Psychol. **4**: 503.
Corti, Fibres of. (E. Mach) Open Court, **8**: 4087.
Cory, John. Acad. **41**: 613.
Coryate, Tom. Crudities. Walford's Antiq. **11**: 27. **12**: 202.
Coryphodon, Restoration of. (O. C. Marsh) Am. J. Sci. **146**: 321.
Cosby, William. Nat'l M. (N. Y. '91) **18**: 1.
Cosmic, The, and the Moral. (J. M. Baldwin) Int. J. Ethics, **6**: 93.
Cosmic Process, relation to the Ethical, Huxley on. (F. E. White) Int. J. Ethics, **5**: 478.
Cosmical Physics, J. Müller on. (W. J. Lockyer) Nature, **50**: 49.
Cosmogony, Hebrew. (C. B. Warring) Bib. Sac. **53**: 50, 522.
Cosmology and Sociology. (L. F. Ward) Am. J. Sociol. **1**: 132.
Cosmopolis City Club. (W. Gladden) Cent. **23**: 395, 566, 780.
Cosmopolitan [Magazine], Making of. Cosmopol. **14**: 259.
— New Home of. Cosmopol. **17**: 551.
Cosmos, Blight of. (B. D. Halsted) Garden & F. **7**: 464.
— Yellow-flowered. (J. N. Rose) Garden & F. **8**: 484.
Cosmotheism. (W. G. Todd) Open Court, **4**: 2154.
Cossa, Luigi. (A. Loria) Econ. J. **6**: 398. — J. Pol. Econ. **5**: 81.
Cossack as Cowboy, Soldier, and Citizen. (P. Bigelow) Harper, **89**: 921.
Cossacks in War. (R. G. Burton) Un. Serv. M. **13**: 602.
— Ural, and their Fisheries. (N. Borodine) Pop. Sci. Mo. **43**: 767.
Cost and Expense. (S. N. Patten) Ann. Am. Acad. Pol. Sci. **3**: 703.
— of Production as the Basis of Economic Movement. Soc. Econ. **1**: 287.
— Pain-cost and Opportunity-cost. (D. I. Green) Q. J. Econ. **8**: 218.
— and Utility. (S. N. Patten) Ann. Am. Acad. Pol. Sci. **3**: 409.
Costa, Giovanni. (J. Cartwright) M. of Art, **6**: 24.
— Exhibition of Pictures. M. of Art, **5**: 396.
Costa Rica, Day's Sport in. (A. H. Verrill) Outing, **29**: 265.
— Theralite in. (J. E. Wolff) Am. J. Sci. **151**: 271.
Costa Rica Packet Case, The. (J. F. Hogan) Westm. **141**: 362.
Coster-land, In. (D. Heath) Eng. Illust. **11**: 517.

Costume, English. (R. Heath) M. of Art, 11: 11-349.
— — Studies in. (R. Heath) M. of Art, 12: 235.
— Military; Buff Coats. (R. Hartshorne) M. of Art, 19: 54, 145.
— Modern. (W. D. McCrackan) Lippinc. 55: 425.
— of the Clans, Stuart's. Ath. '92, 2: 164.
— on the Stage. (P. Anderson) M. of Art, 17: 7.
Costume-designing for an Historical Play. (S. Lucas) M. of Art, 17: 276.
Costumes; Measures of Lawn. (Mrs. R. A. Pryor) Cosmopol. 16: 73.
Cotes, Merton Russell, Art Collection of. Art J. 47: 81-341.
Cotman, John Sell. (F. Wedmore) M. of Art, 11: 397.
Cotswold, In the Heart of. (C. Parkinson) Gent. M. n. s. 52: 529.
Cottage Homes. *See* Children, Homes for.
Cotteau, Gustave Honoré. Nat. Sci. 5: 390.
Cotterell, George, Poetry of. (W. Sharp) Acad. 46: 551.
Cotton Family, Needed Correction in the Pedigree of. (H. Williams) N. E. Reg. 49: 180.
Cotton as a Factor in Progress. (D. A. Tompkins) Engin. M. 5: 151.
— Culture and Preparation of, in the U. S. (H. S. Fleming) Cosmopol. 14: 539.
— Low Price of, Effect on the South of. (W. C. Estes) Nation, 61: 186.
— Romance of. Chamb. J. 71: 797. Same art. Liv. Age, 204: 188.
— Scarcity of, 1895. Bank. M. (N. Y.) 50: 175.
Cotton Cloth Manufacture, Crisis in. Gunton's M. 10: 347.
Cotton Industries, Future Location of. Soc. Econ. 1: 150.
Cotton Industry in Brazil. (J. C. Branner) Pop. Sci. Mo. 40: 666.
— in England, Alleged Decline of. (E. Helm) Econ. J. 3: 121.
— in Lancashire. Blackw. 152: 1, 284, 348.
— — Alleged Decline of. Econ. J. 2: 735.
Cotton Manufactures of New England. (E. Stanwood) Chaut. 17: 37.
Cotton Mill Operatives. (L. B. C. Wyman) Chaut. 18: 603.
— Indian *vs.* American. (J. W. Bennett) Am. M. Civics, 8: 69.
Cotton Mills in the South. (E. Porritt) New Eng. M. 12: 575.
Cotton Printing, Progress in. (L. F. Day) Art J. 47: 50.
Cotton-seed Oil. Chamb. J. 72: 612. — (F. G. Mather) Pop. Sci. Mo. 45: 104.
— Manufacture of. (E. W. Thompson) Engin. M. 3: 820.
Cottonwood Tree for Forest Planting on the Plains. (C. H. Keffer) Garden & F. 7: 502.
Cottons, Colored, of Peru. (A. F. Sears) Overland, n. s. 25: 359.
Couch, A. T. Quiller. First Book, Dead Man's Rock. Idler, 5: 47.
Couleur de Rose; a story. (G. E. Channing) Outing, 25: 96.
Coulomb, Charles Augustus. (E. J. Houston and J. B. J. Delambre) J. Frankl. Inst. 136: 455.
Counsel, Legal, License of Speech of. (I. Browne) Green Bag, 5: 467, 516, 539.
Counsel must hang too; a story. (F. H. Loughead) Overland, n. s. 23: 633.
Counsel of the Diplomatist, The; a story. Argosy, 54: 1.
Counsel of Myronides. (St.J. E. C. Hankin) Belgra. 82: 193.
Counterfeit Presentment, A; a story. (F. W. Broughton) Theatre, 28: 290.
Counterfeit Presentments; a story. (C. Milman) Temp. Bar, 95: 241.
Countess Radna, The; a story. (W. E. Norris) Cornh. 66: 80-632. 67: 82-635.
Counting the Ties; a story. All the Year, 71: 348.
Counting-out Rhymes. (H. C. Bolton) J. Am. Folk-Lore, 1: 31.
— Bolton on. (W. W. Newell) J. Am. Folk-Lore, 1: 240.
Country of the Pointed Firs. (S. O. Jewett) Atlan. 77: 5, 302. 78: 75, 352.
Country Boy *vs.* Town Boy. Soc. Econ. 3: 11, 98, 179.
Country Characters. All the Year, 74: 343.
Country Club, Evolution of the. (C. W. Whitney) Harper, 90: 16.
Country Clubs and Hunt Clubs in America. (E. S. Martin) Scrib. M. 18: 302.
Country Coquette, A. (G. H. Burgin) Chamb. J. 71: 636.
Country Gentlemen. (H. Maxwell) National, 20: 10.
— in England, Is there Hope for? Spec. 68: 112.
Country Homes. (W. T. Fryer, jr.) Archit. Rec. 2: 286.
— Transplanting to. (J. Visher) Lend a H. 16: 86.
Country House, Mediæval, The. (A. M. F. Robinson) Contemp. 63: 84. Same art. Liv. Age, 196: 530. Same art. Ecl. M. 120: 300.
Country-house Parties. (E. F. Benson) New R. 11: 355.
Country Life, Effect of, upon Women. (C. S. Sargent) Garden & F. 6: 1.
— in the Last Century. (T. W. Speight) Argosy, 61: 364. Same art. Liv. Age, 209: 125. Same art. Ecl. M. 126: 705.
— Is it lonely? (C. H. Crandall) No. Am. 159: 127.
— Kebbel on. Spec. 68: 240.
— Notes by an Artist. (E. F. Brewtnall) M. of Art, 11: 96.
— Privacy of. (C. S. Sargent) Garden & F. 9: 271, 309, 312.
— *versus* City Life. Macmil. 74: 279.
Country Printer, The. (W. D. Howells) Scrib. M. 13: 539.
Country-seat in California. (Carl Purdy) Garden & F. 6: 159.
Country-seats, Color and Form of. Garden & F. 5: 285.
— Color in Building. (M. G. Van Rensselaer) Garden & F. 5: 146.
— Names for. (M. C. Robbins) Garden & F. 5: 122.
— New England. Garden & F. 5: 321.
— Southern. (O. W. Blacknall) Garden & F. 5: 459.
— Wellesley Gardens. (M. Barker) Garden & F. 5: 298.
Country Town, Ideals of. (F. D. Huntington) Outl. 50: 1084.
— Social Problems of. (R. Stebbins) Lend a H. 10: 96.
Country Wedding, A. (S. M. Stevens) Bach. of Arts, 3: 819.
Country Week. (W. I. Cole) New. Eng. M. 14: 517.
County Council in Ontario. (J. M. McEvoy) Canad. M. 7: 148.
Coupons of Fortune, The; a story. (M. S. Cutting) Harper, 91: 670.
Courage. All the Year, 72: 536.
— in Battle, Crane on. Sat. R. 81: 44.
— of a Soldier. (S. R. Elliott) Atlan. 71: 236.
— What is it? (E. Belfort Bax) Time, 22: 461.
— Woman Question a Question of Courage. (H. Quilter) Fortn. 63: 979. Same art. Ecl. M. 125: 113.
Courci, John de, Conqueror of Ulster. (J. H. Round) Walford's Antiq. 3: 69-305. 4: 177, 288.

Courier, Paul Louis. (W. F. Rae) Temp. Bar, **96**: 209. Same art. Liv. Age, **195**: 537.
Course of Study, Attempted Improvements in. (P. H. Hanus) Educa. R. **12**: 435.
— Necessity of Five Coördinate Groups in. (W. T. Harris) Educa. **16**: 129.
Court, First, West of the Alleghanies. (S. C. Williams) Green Bag, **5**: 502.
— of Claims, Notable and Curious Cases in. (Kate Field) Green Bag, **7**: 12.
— Russian. (G. Knox) Green Bag, **7**: 297.
— Scenes in. (E. Manson) Green Bag, **6**: 452.
Court Presentations, English. Idler, **10**: 619.
Courtesy of Christian the Highwayman; a story. (A. Hope Hawkins) McClure, **5**: 313.
Courting of Jufrow van Loo. (A. E. King) Cent. **25**: 759.
Courtier, How to become a. Time, **3**: 349.
Courtney, W. L. Kit Marlowe. Theatre, **29**: 274.
Courts, Circuit, in England; an Autumn Circuit. Cornh. **65**: 295. Same art. Liv. Age, **193**: 351.
— Civil, and the Attendants. (J. W. Smith) Chaut. **15**: 685.
— Importance of the Lower. (J. W. Errant) Open Court, **2**: 773.
— Law, of England. Green Bag, **8**: 287-460.
— Martial. (V. Lushington) National, **21**: 870. — (W. H. Shock) Un. Serv. (Phila.) **12**: 147. — (A. Griffiths) Time, **2**: 1.
— of Conciliation in America. (N. Grevstad) Atlan. **72**: 671.
— Witty Encounters in. Green Bag, **7**: 449.
Courtship, Plantation. (F. D. Banks) J. Am. Folk-Lore, **7**: 147.
Courtship of Cale Sublett. (H. Robertson) Southern M. **4**: 38.
Courtship of Colonel Bill; a story. (J. J. Eakins) Harper, **92**: 306.
Courtship of Jack Curtis. (G. Gladdin) Outing, **28**: 420.
Cousin, Victor, and the United States. (T. Stanton) Nation, **60**: 27.
Cousin at the Vicarage, The; a story. (A. E. Courtenay) Sund. M. **21**: 319.
Cousin Charley; a story. Chamb. J. **72**: 265.
Cousin James. (J. Patterson) Southern M. **4**: 508.
Cousin Jane from South Africa. (B. Atkinson) Good Words, **37**: 67.
Cousinly Affection. Spec. **73**: 15.
Couture, Thomas. (G. P. A. Healy) Cent. **22**: 4.
Couvade, Derivation of. (J. A. H. Murray and others) Acad. **42**: 389-567.
— Signification of. (H. L. Roth) Anthrop. J. **22**: 204.
Covenanters, The. (D. Paton) Sund. M. **24**: 692, 779.
— Principles of. (J. M. Foster) Our Day, **13**: 102.
Covent Garden in the Early Morning. Spec. **75**: 202.
Covent Garden Theatre, The First. Theatre, **29**: 217.
Coventry Cross. (W. G. Fretton) Walford's Antiq. **1**: 117.
Coverley, Sir Roger de, and the Spectator. (J. S. Hugill) Bookworm, **3**: 321.
Cow, The; a poem. (R. L. Stevenson) M. of Art, **7**: 367.
Cowboy, Life of a. (T. Holmes) Chaut. **19**: 731. — Outing, **19**: 269, 357.
— on 'Change, A; a story. All the Year, **75**: 420.
Cowboy-land, In. (T. Roosevelt) Cent. **24**: 276.
Cowboys, Cracker, of Florida. (F. Remington) Harper, **91**: 338.
Cow-brute Tragedy; a sketch. All the Year, **54**: 368.
Cow-killing Riots in India. (G. W. Leitner) Asia. R. **16**: 329. **17**: 84.
Cow-mass, The. (E. Peacock) Folk-Lore, **4**: 303.
Cow-puncher, Evolution of the. (O. Wister) Harper, **91**: 602.
— Passing of. (W. T. Larned) Lippinc. **56**: 267.
Cowell, William. Boston Silversmith. (E. S. Holden) N. E. Reg. **50**: 297.
Cowen, F. Hymen. Harold. Sat. R. **79**: 786.
Cowley, Abraham, at the Restoration. (C. H. Firth) Acad. **44**: 296.
Cowpens, S. C., a Battle-field of the Revolution, Hannah's. (R. Shackleton, jr.) M. Am. Hist. **30**: 207.
Cowper, Wm. (C. A. Price) Belgra. **81**: 199. — (J. V. Cheney) Chaut. **15**: 402. — Lond. Q. **80**: 24.
— Some Beauties of. (Alice Law) Temp. Bar, **104**: 91. Same art. Liv. Age, **204**: 195.
— Some Unpublished MSS. of. (Adelaide Collyer) Univ. R. **7**: 271.
— Summer House of. Critic, **28**: 316.
— Wright's. Ath. '92, **2**: 769. — (W. P. Courtney) Acad. **41**: 581. — (G. Smith) Nation, **56**: 163. — (A. B. McMahan) Dial (Ch.) **14**: 82.
Cowslips; A Key-flower. (B. Lindsay) New R. **8**: 571.
Cox, David. (W. Bayliss) M. of Art, **1**: 62.
— and Peter de Wint, Redgrave's. (J. Orrock) M. of Art, **14**: 379.
— The Vale of Choyd. (J. Orrock) M. of Art, **15**: 385.
Cox, Kenyon, with portrait. Bk. Buyer, **8**: 415.
Cox, Palmer, with portrait. Bk. News, **12**: 382.
Coxe, Arthur Cleveland. (R. H. Newton) Critic, **29**: 67. — (F. P. Nash) Chr. Lit. **15**: 398.
Coxe, Brinton, with portrait. Pennsyl. M. **16**: supp.
Coxe, Eckley B. (W. Kent) Cassier, **3**: 129.
Coxe, Reginald Cleveland. (T. Purdy) Mo. Illust. **5**: 183.
Coxey, Jacob D., with portrait. R. of Rs. (N. Y.) **10**: 47.
Coxey Army. (H. Frank) Arena, **10**: 239. — (E. L. Godkin) Nation, **58**: 306, 358. — (T. B. Veblen) J. Pol. Econ. **2**: 456.
— and its Meaning. (W. N. Black) Engin. M. **7**: 307.
— Mission to. (J. V. Tracy) Cath. World, **59**: 666.
— Who is Responsible for? (E. L. Godkin) Nation, **58**: 322.
Coxeyism and the Interest Question. Soc. Econ. **6**: 345.
— Downfall of. (S. P. Austin) Chaut. **19**: 448.
— Menace of; Significance and Aims of the Movement. (O. O. Howard) No. Am. **158**: 687.
— — Character and Methods of the Men. (T. Byrnes) No. Am. **158**: 696.
— — Danger to the Public Health. (A. H. Doty) No. Am. **158**: 701.
Cox's Blunder; a Story of N. Y. Journalism. (A. Sperry) Idler, **4**: 302.
Coxwell, Henry. Morning Calls. (T. H. Lewis) Eng. Illust. **13**: 343.
Coyote, Hunting the, for Scalps. (C. B. Sedgwick) Overland, n. s. **19**: 192.
Coyote Hunting; a sketch. All the Year, **72**: 462.
Crabbing. (C. D. Wilson) Lippinc. **56**: 394.
Crabs. Chamb. J. **70**: 433.
— Land. (E. Step) Good Words, **35**: 541.
Cracks and Settlements in Buildings. Am. Arch. **45**: 101.
Cracow, Poland. (A. C. Coolidge) Am. Arch. **54**: 30. — (A. C. Coolidge) Nation, **63**: 137.
— and its Art-treasures. (H. Zimmern) M. of Art, **15**: 281.
Crackanthorpe, Hubert. Sentimental Studies. Sat. R. **80**: 117.
Cracksmen, Two. (Charles Whibley) New R. **13**: 422.
Craddock, C. E., with portrait. Bk. News, **6**: 224.
Cradle and Spade. (Wm. Sime) Time, **12**: 91-729. **13**: 83-592.

Cradle-songs of Negroes in N. Carolina. (E. M. Backus) J. Am. Folk-Lore, 7: 310.
Craftsman, The, and its Contributors. Bookworm, 2: 13.
Craftswomen in the Livre des métiers. (E. Dixon) Econ. J. 5: 209.
Craig, Thomas B. (P. King) Mo. Illust. 5: 229.
Craig Colony for Epileptics. (W. P. Letchworth) Lend a H. 16: 198.
Craigie, Mrs. T. O. H. "John Oliver Hobbes." With portrait. Bk. Buyer, 11: 127. — With portrait. Bk. News, 13: 415.
Crall, Leander H., with portrait. Nat'l M. (N. Y. '91) 17: 284.
Cramming and Coaching. (J. P. Owen) Ath. '92, 1: 502, 696. — (W. Wren) Ath. '92, 1: 600.
— Faculty of, Psychological Analysis and Practical Value of. (J. C. Murray) Educa. R. 5: 375.
— *versus* Education. (A. H. Morrison) Canad. M. 1: 167.
Cranberry Growing for Ornament. Garden & F. 8: 404.
Cranborne Chase, England. Cornh. 66: 373.
Cranbrook, James, and Religious Controversy in Scotland. (F. R. Statham) National, 28: 252.
Cranch, Christopher Pearse. Critic, 20: 74.
Crane, Bruce. (A. Trumble) Q. Illust. 1: 256.
Crane, Henry, and his Descendants. (Emily W. Leavitt) N. E. Reg. 46: 216. 47: 78, 325.
Crane, Stephen, with portrait. Bk. Buyer, 13: 140. — With portrait. Bookman, 1: 229. — With portrait. Bk. News, 15: 10. — Critic, 28: 163.
— College Days of. (C. L. Peaslee) Mo. Illust. 13: 27.
— Red Badge of Courage. (G. Wyndham) New R. 14: 30.
Crane, Walter. (L. F. Day) M. of Art, 10: 95.
Cranes, Electric Travelling. (A. E. Outerbridge, jr.) Cassier, 3: 419. — (A. Victorin) Cassier, 3: 184.
— Foundry. (A. E. Outerbridge, jr.) Cassier, 10: 211.
— Hoisting, American. (H. H. Suplee) Cassier, 1: 457. 2: 17.
— Locomotive. (W. L. Clements) Cassier, 7: 369.
— Travelling, Modern. (A. E. Outerbridge, jr.) J. Frankl. Inst. 135: 247.
Cranford Souvenirs. (Beatrix L. Tollemache) Temp. Bar, 105: 536. Same art. Liv. Age, 206: 575. Same art. Ecl. M. 126: 45.
Crania, Aboriginal Australian. (W. L. H. Duckworth) Anthrop. J. 23: 284.
Cranks. (E. R. Gregg and others) Am. J. Pol. 3: 659.
— and Crazes. (L. Linton) No. Am. 161: 667.
Cranmer, Thomas. (J. Stevenson) Month, 75: 65, 195.
— Legal View of his Execution. (A. Bailey) Eng. Hist. R. 7: 466.
Cranmer's Library and its Recovery. (E. Burbidge) Bookworm, 4: 209.
Crary, Benjamin Franklin. (F. D. Bovard) Meth. R. 56: 177.
Crauford, Isabella Valancy. (E. J. Hathaway) Canad. M. 5: 569.
Craven, Mrs. Augustus. Spec. 73: 778.
— Life and Letters of. Ed. R. 181: 315. Same art. Liv. Age, 205: 725. — Quar. 182: 454. — (E. M. Clerke) Dub. R. 116: 120. — (T. Hutchinson) Acad. 47: 141. — Quar. 182: 454.
Craven and the Dales of Yorkshire. (R. St.J. Tyrwhitt) M. of Art, 6: 409.
Crawfish, Day after. (F. Whishaw) Longm. 23: 496.
Crawford, F. M., with portrait. Bk. Buyer, 7: 5. — With portrait. Bk. News, 11: 216. — With portrait. (C. D. Lanier) R. of Rs. (N. Y.) 6: 712. — (J. N. Robinson) Westm. 137: 379. Same art. Ecl. M. 118: 770.
Crawford, F. M., Interview with. Critic, 21: 302. — (R. Bridges) McClure, 4: 316.
— Novels. (M. F. Egan) Am. Cath. Q. 17: 621.
— Taquisara. Acad. 50: 423.
— Views of. Critic, 22: 97.
Crayfish, Conjugation in an American. (E. A. Andrews) Am. Natural, 29: 867.
Crazy Wife's Ship; a sketch. (H. C. Bunner) Harper, 86: 115.
Cream, Thomas Neill, Crimes of. Spec. 69: 590.
Creation and the Deluge, Ancient Monumental Records of. (R. M. Ryan) Cath. World, 61: 223.
— Babylonian Account of. (W. Muss-Arnolt) Bib. World, 3: 6.
— by the Voice. (G. Maspero) Asia. R. 13: 365.
— Christian Doctrine of. (J. D. Robertson) Thinker, 8: 138.
— First Hebrew Story of. (W. R. Harper) Bib. World, 3: 1.
— Haeckel on. Sat. R. 75: 186.
— Hidery Story of. (J. Deans) Am. Antiq. 17: 61.
— Legend of, Negro. (A. F. Chamberlain) J. Am. Folk-Lore, 3: 302.
— Myth of the Tsimshians. (J. Deans) J. Am. Folk-Lore, 4: 34.
— Penobscot Indian Myth of. (A. L. Alger) Pop. Sci. Mo. 44: 195.
— Scientific. (J. Hawthorne) New Sci. R. 1: 50.
— Story of, among American Aborigines. (S. D. Peet) Am. Antiq. 17: 127.
— True Idea of. (J. H. Wythe) Meth. R. 52: 559.
Crécy, an Art Village. (G. Käsebier) Mo. Illust. 4: 9. — All the Year, 71: 557.
Credit and Instruments in Retail Trade. (D. Kinley) J. Pol. Econ. 3: 203.
— National, System of. (A. C. Houston) Am. M. Civics, 6: 172.
— Nature and Mechanism of. (S. Sherwood) Q. J. Econ. 8: 149.
Credit Associations in Germany. Gunton's M. 10: 323.
Credit Devices and the Quantity Theory. (H. P. Willis) J. Pol. Econ. 4: 281.
Credit Foncier and Pacific City. (A. K. Owen) Lend a H. 9: 344.
Creditors, Preferred, Power of Corporation as to. (S. D. Thompson) Am. Law R. 29: 846.
Credulity, National. Spec. 71: 13.
Creed, Apostles', Conflict in Germany over. (A. Zahn) Presb. & Ref. R. 4: 267.
Creed to be, The; a poem. (E. W. Wilcox) Arena, 7: 232.
Creede, Col. (J. A. Williams, jr.) Engin. M. 3: 325.
Creeds and Articles. Eng. R. 10: 26.
— Authority of. (W. H. Wynn) Luth. Q. 22: 409.
— Conformity to, Ethics of. (J. M. Sterrett) And. R. 18: 18.
— Ethics of. (A. Momerie) New World, 2: 676.
Creeping Shadow, The; a story. (R. Parpped) Belgra. 91: 144.
Creeps at the Theatre. (A. Fleming) Theatre, 30: 136.
Cremated Digger, The; a story. (A. Williams, jr.) Overland, n. s. 19: 289.
Cremation. (S. B. Gould) Chamb. J. 69: 428. — (J. W. Robertson-Scott) Time, 18: 596. — (A. S. Newman) Westm. 139: 654. Same art. Ecl. M. 121: 130.
— as an Incentive to Crime. (F. S. Horden) J. Soc. Arts, 41: 21.
— Desirability of, for Infected Bodies. (J. H. Smith) Arena, 15: 603.
— Oriental and Pseudo-Oriental. Asia. R. 14: 430.
— Progress of. (J. S. Cobb) Engin M. 3: 488.

Cremation, W. Robinson's "God's Acre Beautiful, the Cemeteries of the Future." M. of Art, 4: 21.
— Roman Catholic Decree on. Month, 75: 17.
Cremation of Colonel Calverly; a story. (J. Ayscough) Temp. Bar, 104: 305, 449.
Creole Folk-Lore from Jamaica. (W. C. Bates) J. Am. Folk-Lore, 9: 38, 121.
Creosote Stains. Am. Arch. 46: 106.
Crerar Library, Chicago. Dial (Ch.) 17: 323.
Cretaceous, at El Paso, Texas, Section of. (T. W. Stanton and T. W. Vaughan) Am. J. Sci. 151: 21.
— at Gay Head. (D. White) Science, 20: 332.
— of Northwestern Montana. (H. Wood) Am. J. Sci. 144: 401.
Cretaceous Formations of Mexico and their relations to North American Geographic Development. (R. T. Hill) Am. J. Sci. 145: 307.
Cretaceous Mammalia, Discovery of. (O. C. Marsh) Am. J. Sci. 143: 249.
Cretaceous Plant Population. (C. MacMillan) Am. Natural. 27: 336.
Crete, Archæological Researches in. (L. Mariani) Acad. 47: 198.
— Explorations in. (A. J. Evans) Acad. 49: 493, 512. 50: 17, 53.
— Inscriptions from. (J. L. Myres) J. Hel. Stud. 16: 178.
— Mycenæan Military Road in. (A. J. Evans; J. L. Myers) Acad. 47: 469.
— Question of. Fortn. 66: 451. — (J. Alden) Nation, 62: 136.
— Researches in. (F. Halbherr) Antiq. n. s. 25: 115-214. 27: 10, 195. 28: 12, 110.
— The Situation in. (Ypsiloritis) Contemp. 70: 316.
— Turks in. (F. H. Tyrrell) Asia. R. 9: 274.
Crew of the Flying Dutchman; a story. (H. A. Hering) Temp. Bar, 107: 49.
Crichton, William, Father. (T. G. Law) Eng. Hist. R. 8: 697.
Cricket. (W. K. R. Bedford) Eng. Illust. 10: 679, 758. — Macmil. 74: 203. — (F. Gale) Time, 7: 586. — (F. Gale) Univ. R. 1: 542.
— and Cricketers. Blackw. 151: 96.
— and Critics. (H. Hutchinson) Longm. 20: 278.
— at Haverford College. (A. C. Thomas) Outing, 28: 236.
— Australian. (T. R. Spofforth) New R. 10: 507, 626.
— Eton. (R. H. Lyttelton) National, 23: 424.
— — and Harrow Matches, 1858-64. (N. G. Lyttelton) National, 25: 690.
— W. G. Grace in. (R. H. Lyttleton) New R. 13: 129.
— Harrow. (S. W. Gore) National, 23: 670.
— in America. (T. Wharton) Outing, 20: 172.
— in England, 1892. (W. G. Grace) New R. 7: 404.
— in the United States. (G. S. Patterson) Lippinc. 50: 649.
— Leg before Wicket. (R. Stewart) Time, 18: 585.
— Old and New. (R. H. Lyttelton) Eng. Illust. 10: 871.
— Rustic. (G. Fiennes) New R. 8: 593.
Cricket Matches in Lord's Pavilion. Macmil. 74: 312.
Cricketers, Veteran. (P. Norman) Eng. Illust. 10: 184.
Crickets, American. (S. H. Scudder) Harper, 93: 691.
Crillon, Count Edward de. (H. Adams) Am. Hist. R. 1: 51.
Crim, Matt, with portrait. Bk. News, 11: 475.
Crime among Animals. (W. Ferrero) Forum, 20: 492.
— and Common Sense. (H. Laslett-Browne) Fortn. 64: 224.
— and Criminal Law in the U. S. Ed. R. 176: 1.
— and Criminals, The Study of. (A. MacDonald) Chaut. 18: 265.
Crime and Economics. (S. G. Smith) Lend a H. 17: 408.
— and Education in England, Growth of. Church Q. 35: 217.
— and the Enforcement of Law. (H. C. Vrooman) Arena, 12: 263.
— and Human Aggregation. (G. Tarde) Pop. Sci. Mo. 45: 447.
— and Immigration. (S. G. Fisher) Pop. Sci. Mo. 49: 625.
— and the Law. (F. Smyth) Scrib. M. 11: 26.
— and Natural Selection. (E. S. Morse) Pop. Sci. Mo. 41: 433.
— and its Punishment. (A. MacDonald) Lend a H. 10: 83. — (H. Hawkins; C. H. Hopwood; H. B. Poland) New R. 8: 617. — (H. B. Simpson) Contemp. 70: 91.
— Causes of, Economic Conditions and. (C. D. Wright) Ann. Am. Acad. Pol. Sci. 3: 764.
— Decrease of. (E. F. DuCane) 19th Cent. 33: 480.
— Detection of, by Photography. (T. C. Hepworth) Chamb. J. 69: 326. Same art. Green Bag, 4: 516.
— Development of Forms of. (L. Field) Open Court, 3: 1765.
— Disgrace and. Pub. Opin. 16: 97.
— Drink and. (F. W. Farrar) Fortn. 59: 783.
— Education and. Cath. World, 64: 322.
— Feeders of. (A. C. Applegarth) Green Bag, 5: 71.
— How to protect a City from. (T. Byrnes) No. Am. 159: 100.
— in Australia, White on. Sat. R. 79: 18.
— in England, Increase of. (W. D. Morrison) 19th Cent. 31: 950.
— in France, Problem of. (S. B. de Bury) Contemp. 62: 183.
— in India, Records of, Hervey's. Spec. 69: 451.
— in Large Cities; Ishmaelites of Civilization. (B. O. Flower) Arena, 6: 17.
— in Massachusetts: Has it increased? (W. F. Spalding) Forum, 12: 659.
— — Statistics of. (F. G. Pettigrove) Am. Statis. Assoc. 3: 1.
— in Paris, Phases of. (H. LeRoux) Ecl. M. 118: 221.
— Increased by Lax Enforcement of Law. (G. Huntington) Lend a H. 16: 327.
— Is it increasing? Pop. Sci. Mo. 43: 399.
— Modern Treatment of. (S. T. Dutton) Educa. 17: 12, 107.
— not Hereditary. (W. M. F. Round) Forum, 16: 48.
— Origins of. (W. B. Lewis) Fortn. 60: 329.
— Pauperism and. (J. B. Weber) Char. R. 3: 117.
— Philosophy of. (W. S. Lilly) Contemp. 65: 217. Same art. Ecl. M. 122: 500.
— Politics and. (A. G. Warner) Am. J. Sociol. 1: 290.
— Poor Abel! (L. de la Ramée) Fortn. 59: 535. Same art. Ecl. M. 120: 693.
— Poverty and. (H. Thomas) Westm. 145: 75.
— Prevention of. Westm. 146: 191.
— Preventive Legislation and. (C. H. Reeve) Ann. Am. Acad. Pol. Sci. 3: 223.
— Professional. (R. Anderson) Blackw. 159: 294.
— Psychology of. (H. Wood) Arena, 8: 529.
— Responsibility in, from a Medical Standpoint. (S. Brown) Pop. Sci. Mo. 46: 154.
— Science of. (A. MacDonald) Lend a H. 8: 83.
— Social Factor in. (J. K. Pershing) Am. Law R. 28: 358.
— Stamping out of. (N. Oppenheim) Pop. Sci. Mo. 48: 527.
— Study of. (W. D. Morrison) Mind, 17: 489.
Crime of Count Nicholas of Festenberg; a story. (A. Hope Hawkins) McClure, 5: 401.

Crimea, The Dead on the Battlefields of the. (W. Simpson) Eng. Illust. 16: 97.
— in 1854 and 1894. (E. Wood) Fortn. 62: 469, 593, 845. 63: 101, 285. Same art. Ecl. M. 123: 758. 124: 1–504. Same art. Liv. Age, 204: 169–668.
— — Wood's. Sat. R. 80: 210.
— Invasion of, Russell's. Sat. R. 79: 420.
Crimean War. (W. H. Russell) Un. Serv. (Phila.) 15: 432.
— Letters on. Ed. R. 182: 326.
— Lysons'. Sat. R. 80: 382.
Criminal, The. (St.J. E. C. Hankin) Westm. 140: 24. Same art. Ecl. M. 124: 478.
— and Prison Reform. (M. Davitt) 19th Cent. 36: 875.
— Can he be reclaimed? (H. S. Williams) No. Am. 163: 207.
— *vs.* Criminal Anthropologist. By an Ex-Convict. Chr. Un. 47: 910.
Criminal Anthropology applied to Pedagogy. (C. Lombroso) Monist, 6: 50.
— Developmental Aspects of. (T. S. Clouston) Anthrop. J. 23: 215.
— Fourth International Congress of. (J. M. Baldwin) Nation, 63: 247.
— Illustrative Studies in. (C. Lombroso) Monist, 1: 177, 336.
— its Origin and Application. (C. Lombroso) Forum, 20: 33.
Criminal Conspiracy, Law of. (K. E. Digby) Law Q. 6: 129, 363.
— — a Reply. (J. G. Butcher) Law Q. 6: 247.
Criminal Contagion. (A. MacDonald) National, 20: 422.
Criminal Festivals. (G. Ferrero) Pop. Sci. Mo. 43: 758.
Criminal Inquiries, Photography and. (Sir H. D. Littlejohn) Jurid. R. 8: 13.
Criminal Jurisprudence, Roman and Anglo-Saxon. (E. T. Felsenthal; M. Romero) No. Am. 163: 75, 383.
— English and Roman Systems of. (M. Romero) Green Bag, 8: 410.
Criminal Law, Contrasts in English. (H. L. Carson) Green Bag, 6: 505, 561.
Criminal Procedure and Appeal in Scotland and England. (J. C. Watt) Univ. R. 6: 88.
— in France. (M. McIlwraith) Law Q. 8: 193.
— Reform in. (C. Bissell) Green Bag, 8: 213.
Criminal Suggestion. (J. Delboeuf) Monist, 2: 363.
Criminals and Prisoners. (T. E. Will) Arena, 10: 409.
— and their Detection. (E. R. Spearman) New R. 9: 65.
— Capital. Should they be turned over to the Experimental Physiologist? (J. S. Pyle) Am. J. Pol. 3: 618.
— Confessions of. (Sir H. Stephen) New R. 15: 105.
— Dealing with. (H. S. Williams) Am. M. Civics, 6: 225.
— Executed, and Folk-medicine. (Mabel Peacock) Folk-Lore, 7: 268.
— Female. (A. Griffiths) No. Am. 161: 141.
— — Lombroso on. Sat. R. 79: 603.
— Habitual. (W. G. Scott-Moncrieff) Jurid. R. 8: 18. — Blackw. 157: 483.
— — Treatment of. Spec. 76: 834.
— — What to do with. (S. A. K. Strahan) Westm. 143: 660.
— Identification of. (I. M. Tarbell) McClure, 2: 355. — Chamb. J. 71: 325.
— — by Measurement. (H. Vincent) Eng. Illust. 12: no. 1, 73.
— Modern Methods with. (C. A. Collin) Am. J. Soc. Sci. 31: 93.
— Modern Penology. (G. Rayleigh Vicars) Gent. M. n. s. 53: 627.
Criminals, New Ways of Dealing with. (M. Crackanthorpe) 19th Cent. 34: 614.
— Our Penal System. (N. Nutt) Southern M. 4: 30.
— Punishment of. (C. S. Pierce) Open Court, 6: 3399.
— Reclamation of. Am. M. Civics, 9: 301.
— Responsibility of. (D. MacG. Means) Nation, 57: 167.
— Shall we look Backward or Forward in Dealing with? (H. S. Williams) Am. M. Civics, 6: 225.
— Treatment of. (G. R. Stetson) And. R. 19: 421.
Criminology. (W. R. Newbold) Am. Natural. 29: 1127. — (A. Macdonald) N. Eng. 56: 73.
— and Sociology. (C. Bell) Pub. Opin. 19: 587.
— Fundamental Principles of. (A. Macdonald) Lend a H. 11: 203.
— The Modern Frankenstein. (G. M. Gould) Open Court, 3: 1745, 1754.
— New School of. (W. W. Willoughby) Am. J. Pol. 2: 496. — (W. W. Willoughby) Pub. Opin. 15: 151.
— A Study. (W. S. Blackstone) Canad. M. 1: 523.
Crimson Poppies; a Legend of Life. (C. Vyvian) Belgra. 79: 46.
Crinoline, Defence of. (M. Jeune) New R. 8: 190.
— Folly of. (H. C. Ecob) Cosmopol. 15: 117.
Cripple Creek, Col., Calaverite from. (W. F. Hillebrand) Am. J. Sci. 150: 128.
— Gold Mines and the Stock Boom. (T. A. Rickard) Engin. M. 10: 605.
— in 1893. (E. Holloway) So. M. 3: 147.
— Story of. (C. Warman) R. of Rs. (N. Y.) 13: 161.
Crippled Hope; a Balcony Story. (G. King) Cent. 24: 374.
Cripples, Employment of. (A. M. Bowditch) Sund. M. 22: 686.
Crispi, Francesco. (W. J. Stillman) Cent. 27: 203. — With portrait. (W. F. Day) Munsey, 11: 366. — (G. M. James) R. of Rs. (N. Y.) 11: 297. — (W. S. Alden) 19th Cent. 37: 165.
— Administration of. (V. Riccio) Contemp. 68: 384.
— Dictatorship of. (L. de La Ramée) Contemp. 68: 241.
— The King, the Pope, and Crispi. (H. R. Haweis) Fortn. 62: 81.
— L' uomo fatale. Fortn. 61: 355.
Critic, The, and his Task. Dial (Ch.) 14: 97.
— The Music. (G. Alexander) Music, 8: 340.
Critic, The, 15th Anniversary of. Critic, 28: 46.
Critical Hour. (C. H. Chase) New Eng. M. n. s. 10: 413.
Critical Results, Wisdom in Teaching. (F. B. Denio) Bib. World, 3: 209.
Criticism. (H. A. Hicks) Canad. M. 1: 464. — (G. H. Page) Westm. 139: 646.
— and the Common Life. (A. A. Berle) Bib. Sac. 50: 52.
— and Culture. (J. R. Lowell) Cent. 25: 515.
— as Theft. (W. Knight) 19th Cent. 39: 257. Same art. Ecl. M. 126: 358. — Dial (Ch.) 20: 129.
— Bearing of, on Edification. (T. K. Cheyne) Bib. World, 3: 281.
— Biblical. *See* Biblical Criticism.
— Brief Defence of. (C. B. La Monte) Poet-Lore, 6: 332.
— Classical, in Oxford. Sat. R. 79: 88.
— a Critical Taboo. (A. Lang) National, 19: 603. Same art. Liv. Age, 194: 719.
— Dramatic, Difficulties of. (C. Howard) Theatre, 34: 218.
— — Modern. (R. Davey) Theatre, 35: 137.
— English, Position of, 1885. (Havelock Ellis) Time, 13: 669.
— English Literary, Vaughan's. (E. H. Lewis) School R. 4: 692. — Sat. R. 81: 581.

Criticism, Higher. *See* Biblical Criticism.
— Human Element in. (J. Buckham) Critic, **22**: 268.
— in Advance. (W. D. Adams) Theatre, **33**: 107. — (C. Scott) Theatre, **33**: 158.
— in the Provinces of England. (D. Ginaodh) Theatre, **37**: 143, 189, 246.
— Influence of. (A. Fitz-Gerald) Theatre, **33**: 238.
— Literary, American, and its Value. (H. H. Boyesen) Forum, **15**: 459.
— — Experimental Basis for. (C. Macmillan) Science, **21**: 296.
— — Realism and Idealism in. Sat. R. **82**: 184.
— — Views on, by Leading Novelists. Idler, **6**: 159.
— Modern. (A. Rickett) National, **21**: 717. — (Mary B. Whiting) Time, **23**: 699.
— Musical, On the Inherent Difficulties of. Music, **8**: 127.
— The New. (R. Ogden) Nation, **60**: 159.
— The Old. Cornh. **71**: 151.
— of Life. (E. Fuller) Bookman, **2**: 203.
— Relation of, to Art. (H. Quilter) National, **25**: 466.
— Stationariness of. (G. J. Holyoake) Open Court, **10**: 4903.
— Superficial. (G. Braden) So. M. **5**: 342.
— Touchstones of. Dial (Ch.) **18**: 335.
— Uncertainty of. Sat. R. **73**: 592.
Critics and Authors. (A. Birrell) New R. **6**: 97.
— Dramatic, Should they write Plays? (A. E. T. Watson) Theatre, **35**: 256, 317.
— Literary, Some Well-known. Idler, **5**: 500.
Croatans, The. (F. J. Melton) Mid-Cont. **6**: 195.
Crockett, David, Jackson and. (H. S. Turner) M. Am. Hist. **27**: 385.
Crockett, S. R., with portrait. Bk. Buyer, **11**: 200. — Critic, **24**: 425.
— at Home. (R. H. Sherard) Idler, **7**: 797.
— Cleg Kelly. Sat. R. **82**: 40.
— The Grey Man. Acad. **50**: 424.
— Men of the Moss-hags. (W. Wallace) Acad. **48**: 358.
— Novels of. (W. Wallace and others) Acad. **46**: 344, 376, 399, 423.
— A Talk with. Book R. **1**: 251.
Crocodile-birds. Sat. R. **75**: 483.
Crocodiles. Sat. R. **74**: 649.
— and Alligators. Chamb. J. **70**: 575.
Crocoite and Phoenicochroite, Synthesis of. (C. Ludeking) Am. J. Sci. **144**: 57.
— from Tasmania. (C. Palache) Am. J. Sci. **151**: 389.
Crofters of Island of Lewis. (W. C. Mackenzie) Westm. **145**: 301.
Croghan, George, Col., Letters of. Pennsyl. M. **15**: 429.
Croke, Archbishop. R. of Rs. (N. Y.) **12**: 313.
Croker, Richard. (E. J. Edwards) McClure, **5**: 542.
Croly, J. C., with portrait. Bk. News, **10**: 161.
Crome, John, the Elder. (E. Paget) M. of Art, **5**: 221.
Cromer, Lord, and the Khedive. (W. S. Blunt) 19th Cent. **33**: 571.
Cromwell, Oliver. (S. S. Smith) Munsey, **11**: 136. — Spec. **74**: 844.
— and the Expulsion of the Long Parliament in 1653. (C. H. Firth) Eng. Hist. R. **8**: 526.
— and the House of Lords. (C. H. Firth) Macmil. **71**: 151, 231.
— and Mazarin in 1652. (S. R. Gardiner) Eng. Hist. R. **11**: 479.
— and the "Saddle Letter" of Charles I. (E. B. Chancellor) Walford's Antiq. **11**: 148, 323.
— as a Soldier. (W. O'C. Morris) Temp. Bar, **96**: 343. Same art. Liv. Age, **196**: 643. — Liv. Age, **207**: 598. — (W. O'C. Morris) Un. Serv. (Phila.) **9**: 424.
Cromwell, Oliver, at Ripley Castle; painting. (R. G. Kingsley) Art J. **45**: 260.
— before Edinburgh, 1650. (W. S. Douglas) Scot. R. **26**: 258.
— Burial Place of. Walford's Antiq. **12**: 277.
— Emissary of, in France. (R. S. Long) Acad. **49**: 340.
— Hatred of. Sat. R. **79**: 819.
— his Daughter, Elizabeth Claypole. (R. W. Ramsey) Eng. Hist. R. **7**: 37.
— his Veterans in Flanders. (J. W. Fortescue) Macmil. **69**: 360. Same art. Liv. Age, **201**: 50.
— Major-Generals of. (D. W. Rannie) Eng. Hist. R. **10**: 471.
— Mask of. (F. Anderson) Eng. Illust. **14**: 115.
— The Surprise of Bovey Tracy. Macmil. **75**: 28.
— Tomb of. Chamb. J. **70**: 587.
— Views on Sport. (C. H. Firth) Macmil. **70**: 401. Same art. Liv. Age, **203**: 629.
Cromwell, Thomas. (E. C. Birney) Citizen, **2**: 202.
Cromwell Family, Waylen's. Sat. R. **73**: 521. — Spec. **68**: 169.
— Women of. (Sheila E. Braine) Good Words, **36**: 461.
Cromwellian Museum, A. Walford's Antiq. **4**: 16, 80.
Cromwells, The, of Putney. (J. Phillips) Walford's Antiq. **2**: 56, 178. **5**: 171.
Cronstadt and Peterhof, Around. (W. M. Inglis) Gent. M. n. s. **50**: 619. Same art. Ecl. M. **121**: 196.
Crook, Gen., Indian Campaigns of, Bourke on. Atlan. **69**: 270. — (C. King) Dial (Ch.) **12**: 383. — Sat. R. **73**: 51.
Crookes Tubes, Concerning. (C. C. Hutchins and F. C. Robinson) Am. J. Sci. **151**: 463.
Crops, Condition and Prospects of, 1895. (H. Farquhar) No. Am. **161**: 313.
— Rotation of. (A. Morgan) Pop. Sci. Mo. **42**: 377.
Crosland, Mrs. N. Chamb. J. **70**: 801.
Cross, John Woodrow, with portrait. Bank. M. (Lond.) **57**: 67.
Cross, Lonan, Isle of Man. Reliquary, **36**: 113.
— of Conbelin at Margam Abbey. Illus. Archæol. **2**: 45.
— Sign of, by extending the Arms. Church Q. **35**: 315.
— True, Early History of. (H. Thurston) Month, **75**: 88.
Crosses, English. (F. Peacock) Dub. R. **113**: 549.
— in Cornwall, Two. Walford's Antiq. **4**: 76.
— made of Straw. (W. H. Patterson) Illus. Archæol. **2**: 103.
— of Glamorganshire. (T. H. Thomas) Illus. Archæol. **1**: 207.
— Wayside, Yorkshire. (E. M. Cole) Antiq. n. s. **31**: 303.
Cross-country Running. (A. T. Sibbald) Bach. of Arts, **1**: 624.
Cross-examination. (Lord Bramwell) 19th Cent. **31**: 183.
— as an Art. (A. O. Hall) Green Bag, **5**: 423.
Cross-roads Ghost. (M. Crim) Lippinc. **52**: 341.
Crossbills in the Ohio Valley. (A. W. Butler) Am. Natural. **28**: 136.
Crosse, Mrs. A. Autobiographical Memories. Temp. Bar, **96**: 27. Same art. Ecl. M. **119**: 505. Same art. Liv. Age, **195**: 372. — Ath. '92, **2**: 809.
Crossin' the Bridge. (G. B. Burgin) Idler, **8**: 288.
Crossing of Plants. Garden & F. **5**: 2.
Crossley, James. (J. Pickford) Walford's Antiq. **4**: 198.
Crow, The Common. (W. H. Hudson) Fortn. **63**: 793. Same art. Liv. Age, **205**: 812.
Crow Indians, Sketching among. Outing, **24**: 83.
Crowe, Joseph Archer. Acad. **50**: 187. — Ath. '96, **2**: 361.

Crown Prince of Rexania. (E. S. Van Zile) Lippinc. 85: 343.
Crown's Right of Reply. (A. Cock) 19th Cent. 37: 304.
Crowns, Ancient and Modern. Chamb. J. 72: 539.
— Growth and Development of. (L. F. Day) M. of Art, 11: 277.
Croxden Abbey. (W. H. G. Flood) Month, 81: 264-569.
Croydon Palace. Walford's Antiq. 4: 190, 239.
Crucial, Derivation of. (C. B. Mount) Acad. 43: 130.
Crucifix, Origin, History, and Relation to Doctrine. (W. J. Reynolds) Bapt. R. 14: 322.
Crucifixion, Date of. (A. Wright) Bib. World, 2: 7-275.
Cruel — or Thoughtless? a story. Argosy, 56: 338.
Cruel Doubt, A; a novel. (Lady M. Majendie) Argosy, 60: 169-559.
Cruel Kindness; a story. All the Year, 74: 448.
Cruel Sports. (H. S. Salt) Westm. 140: 545.
Cruel Thousand Years. (C. B. Fernald) Cent. 30: 523.
Cruelty, Every-day. (L. Robinson) Fortn. 62: 104.
— in Europe and Asia. Spec. 70: 669.
— to Animals. (L. de la Ramé) 19th Cent. 40: 293.
— to Children, Causes of. Spec. 70: 637.
Cruger, Mrs. Van Rensselaer, with portrait. Bk. News, 9: 252.
Cruikshank, George. (F. G. Stephens) Portfo. 23: 233. — (A. Thompson) M. of Art, 3: 169, 244.
— Books illustrated by. Bookworm, 5: 167.
— a Defence. (G. S. Layard) Temp. Bar, 99: 560.
Cruikshank Outrage, A; a poem. (G. S. Layard) Gent. M. n. s. 54: 242.
Cruikshankiana. Bookworm, 6: 229.
Cruise of the Rover. (E. W. Gosse) M. of Art, 6: 45.
Cruise of the Snark. (G. A. Warder) Outing, 28: 259.
Cruise of the Two; a story. (C. G. Rogers) Outing, 26: 199, 276.
Cruiser, The Ocean. (H. W. Wilson) Un. Serv. M. 9: 465.
— and Battleship. (H. W. Wilson) Un. Serv. M. 11: 476.
— and Battleships, Launching. (Wm. J. Baxter) Scrib. M. 12: 488.
Crumbs; a story. (H. C. N. Wilson) Canad. M. 4: 228.
Crump, Arthur, with portrait. Bank. M. (Lond.) 56: 825.
Crusades, The. Quar. 183: 163. — (P. Schaff) Ref. Q. 40: 437.
— Archer and Kingsford's. Sat. R. 79: 52.
— Results of the. Ed. R. 179: 158.
Crusaders, Effigies of. Cornh. 72: 304.
Crustacea in Early Paleozoic Times, Life History of. (H. Woodward) Nature, 52: 114.
Crustaceans, Crafty. (T. R. R. Stebbing) Good Words, 35: 736.
Cryptography. Month, 81: 558.
See Cipher-writing.
Crystal, Atoms in, Arrangement of. (H. A. Miers) Sci. Prog. 3: 129.
Crystal Forms, Device for Simplifying the Drawing of. (A. J. Moses) Am. J. Sci. 151: 462.
Crystallography, Story-Maskelyne on. (H. A. Miers) Nature, 52: 145.
Crystals, Hemimorphic Wulfenite, from New Mexico. (C. A. Ingersoll) Am. J. Sci. 148: 193.
— Microscopic Investigation of, Improved Methods for, Klein on. (A. E. Tutton) Nature, 51: 608.
Csoma de Körös, Alexander. Time, 13: 699.
Cuba. (F. H. Osborne) Chaut. 23: 202.
— and Spain. (R. Ogden) Nation, 60: 319.
— and the Struggle for Liberty. (M. Halstead) R. of Rs. (N. Y.) 13: 419.
— and the United States. National, 27: 449.
— — and Spain. (R. Ogden) Chaut. 14: 565.
Cuba and the United States, Commercial Relations between. (E. S. Gould) Engin. M. 7: 500.
— Belligerency of, The Question of. (J. B. Moore) Forum, 21: 288.
— — Recognition of. (A. S. Hershey) Ann. Am. Acad. Pol. Sci. 7: 450.
— — — Grant's Precedent. Nation, 62: 137.
— Business Opportunities in. (E. J. Chibas) Engin. M. 4: 266.
— Catechism on. (A. G. Sedgwick) Nation, 62: 211.
— Causes of the Present War in. (H. L. De Zayas) Cath. World, 62: 807.
— Claims of, for Self-government. (R. Cabera) Gunton's M. 11: 423.
— Filibustering Expedition to, 1860. (R. F. Logan) Southern M. 4: 608.
— Fire and Sword in. (C. King) Forum, 22: 31.
— Five Weeks with the Insurgents. (H. Howard) Contemp. 69: 41. Same art. Liv. Age, 208: 259.
— Glimpse of. (J. K. Reeve) Lippinc. 55: 404.
— How it might have belonged to France. (G. Colmache) Fortn. 64: 747. Same art. Liv. Age, 207: 696.
— Industrial. (E. Vasquez) Gunton's M. 10: 447.
— Industrial Possibilities of. (R. Cabrera) Engin. M. 11: 875.
— Insurgents in, A Year with. (H. Howard) Un. Serv. (Phila.) 15: 127.
— Mr. Marcy, the Cuban Question, and the Ostend Manifesto. (S. Webster) Pol. Sci. Q. 8: 1.
— Negroes in, and the Revolution. Gunton's M. 11: 272.
— Ought we to annex? (F. R. Coudert and others) Am. M. Civics, 7: 37.
— Our Duty to. (H. C. Lodge) Forum, 21: 278.
— Problem of. Spec. 75: 359.
— Question of. (J. Fitzmaurice-Kelly) New R. 15: 144. Same art. Ecl. M. 127: 497.
— — Possible Complications of. (M. W. Hazeltine) No. Am. 162: 406.
— Revolt in. (W. S. Churchill) Sat. R. 81: 165, 244. 82: 213.
— — its Causes and Effects; by a Native Cuban. Engin. M. 10: 9.
— Shall it be Free? (C. King) Forum, 20: 50.
— Situation in. (S. Alvarez) No. Am. 161: 362.
— Struggle for Freedom. (J. F. Clark) Cosmopol. 19: 608. — (M. Garcia) Mo. Illust. 11: 227.
— Sympathy for. (R. Ogden) Nation, 61: 250.
— Symposium. Indep. Dec. 5, '95.
— Tertiary and Later History of. (R. T. Hill) Am. J. Sci. 148: 196.
— War in, and the Spanish Treasury. Gunton's M. 11: 122.
— What shall be done about? (M. W. Hazeltine) No. Am. 163: 731.
— Women of. (M. E. Springer) No. Am. 158: 255.
Cuckoo and the Myth of March. (G. W. Murdoch) Gent. M. n. s. 54: 233.
— Habits of. Nature, 53: 176.
— in the West of England. National, 21: 279.
— Popular History of. (J. Hardy) Folk-Lore Rec. 2: 47.
— Walling the. (H. Maxwell) 19th Cent. 32: 920.
Cuckoo Corner; a story. Blackw. 157: 865. Same art. Liv. Age, 206: 75. Same art. Ecl. M. 125: 179.
Cuckoos and Nightingales. Spec. 70: 635.
— and the Outwitted Cow-bird. (W. H. Gibson) Harper, 93: 934.
Cucumber Plants, Path of Water Current in. (E. F. Smith) Am. Natural. 30: 372, 451, 554.

Cuisine of Large Hotels. (I. H. Brainerd) Chaut. **19**: 421.
Culdees. (A. Allaria) Scot. R. **25**: 1.
Cullecoats, England. (R. J. Charleton) M. of Art, **9**: 456.
Cult in Literature. Dial (Ch.) **14**: 129.
Cultivation, Origin of. (G. Allen) Fortn. **61**: 578. Same art. Ecl. M. **122**: 788.
Culture and Anarchy. Quar. **174**: 317.
— and Books. (H. W. Mabie) Bookman, **2**: 409, 501.
— and Ethics. (F. Adler) Eth. Rec. **1**: 1.
— and Faith. Spec. **75**: 891.
— and Science. (C. E. Bessey) Science, n. s. **4**: 121.
— Criticism and. (J. R. Lowell) Cent. **25**: 515.
— Effect of, on Vitality. Spec. **70**: 479.
— General, Relation of, to Professional Success. (M. Mackenzie) New R. **7**: 323.
— The Gospel of. (N. C. Butler) Mid-Cont. **6**: 28.
— Home, for Americans. (N. Hapgood) New Eng. M. n. s. **13**: 721.
— Ideal of. (F. W. Gunsaulus) Chaut. **16**: 59.
— Meaning and Uses of. (J. A. Symonds) New R. **7**: 105. Same art. Liv. Age, **194**: 666.
— Mental, Zoölogy as a Factor in. (S. H. Gage) Science, n. s. **4**: 207.
— Politics and. (H. Seal) Westm. **144**: 650.
Culturkampf in the German Empire. (C. Clever) Ref. Q. **41**: 360.
Cumberland, Richard, Ethical System of. (E. Albee) Philos. R. **4**: 264, 371.
Cumberland, Eng., Coach Ride in. (D. N. Beach) Educa. **13**: 472.
— Statesmen of. Macmil. **67**: 194.
"Cumberland," Frigate, and the Merrimac. (T. O. Selfridge, jr.) Cosmopol. **15**: 176.
Cumberland Dialect. (T. H. B. Graham) Gent. M. n. s. **54**: 512.
Cumberland Etymology. (T. H. B. Graham) Gent. M. n. s. **56**: 402.
Cumberland Vendetta; a Tale of the Kentucky Mountains. (J. Fox, jr.) Cent. **26**: 163–497.
Cumberland Mountains, Home Arts in the. (A. M. Wakefield) Fortn. **66**: 596.
Cummings, Joseph. (J. M. King) Meth. R. **54**: 849, 942.
Cummington, Mass. (H. S. Nahmer) New Eng. M. n. s. **6**: 65.
Cundall, Joseph. Ath. '95, **1**: 91.
Cuneiform Inscriptions, Schrader's Collection of. (O. C. Whitehouse) Crit. R. **3**: 130.
Cuneiform Tablets from Egypt. Sat. R. **74**: 173.
Cunio Twins, Story of the. (H. V. Barnett) M. of Art, **8**: 454.
Cunliffe. (M. T. Wright) Scrib. M. **20**: 307.
Cunliffe-Owen, Sir Philip. *See* Owen.
Cunningham, Gen. Sir Alexander. (E. J. Rapson) Ath. '93, **2**: 777. — Acad. **44**: 513.
Cup of Ballafletcher. (E. S. Hartland) Illus. Archæol. **1**: 10.
Cup of Trembling, The. (H. M. Foote) Cent. **28**: 673.
Cup-and-ring Sculptures of Ilkley. Reliquary, **36**: 65.
Cupboard, An Old-world. (S. B. Gould) Sund. M. **25**: 108.
Cupboard Love; a story. Idler, **2**: 410.
Cupid the Fiddler. Macmil. **75**: 58. Same art. Ecl. **127**: 846.
Cupid in the Village. (J. Ramsay) Good Words, **36**: 615.
Cupid's Birth; a poem. (R. W. Bunny) Cosmopol. **20**. 189.
Curate of the Polton's; a story. (A. Hope) Eng. Illust. **11**: 1031.
Curate's Last Words; a story. (E. E. Kitton) Argosy, **62**: 253.
Curates, The Case for the. (A. G. B. Atkinson) Contemp. **69**: 112.
— Grievances of. Spec. **77**: 850.
— Supply of. Spec. **70**: 797.
Cure, Laws of. (M. W. Van Deaburg) Arena, **8**: 430.
Cures, Miraculous. (B. Taylor) Time, **23**: 1160.
— Old Scottish. (A. W. Stewart) Gent. M. n. s. **53**: 419.
Curfew, Origin and History of. (L. Cresswell) Gent. M. n. s. **54**: 599.
Curiosities of a Country Practice. Cornh. **70**: 515. Same art. Ecl. M. **123**: 793.
Curiosity, Nobler and Meaner. Spec. **68**: 602. Same art. Ecl. M. **118**: 832.
Curious Lottery, A; a story. Blackw. **157**: 188. Same art. Liv. Age, **204**: 651.
Curious Vehicle, The; a midnight story. (A. W. Drake) Cent. **25**: 217.
Curlew Lore. Chamb. J. **70**: 282.
Curling. (R. C. Whittet) Outing, **19**: 365.
— in the Northwest. (H. J. Woodside) Outing, **25**: 422, 497.
Curling Tongs, The; a poem. (J. M. Bulloch) Eng. Illust. **11**: 234.
Curran, Charles C., and his Work. (C. Cook) Mo. Illust. **11**: 289.
Currants, Greek, Over-production of. (V. Gabrielidis) Econ. J. **5**: 285.
Currency. (D. Ricardo) Econ. J. **6**: 64.
— and Banking, A Plea for a Sound System of. (A. R. Foote) Am. M. Civics, **7**: 133.
— — Suggestions on. (A. Ladenburg) Forum, **20**: 513.
— — Reform in. (W. Knapp) Am. J. Pol. **3**: 140.
— and Finance in the U. S. Bank. M. (Lond.) **56**: 529.
— and State Banks. (A. L. Ripley) Yale R. **3**: 311.
— and Taxation, Recent Literature on. (E. A. Ross) Dial (Ch.) **14**: 17.
— and Weight Standards, Metallic Origin of, Ridgeway on. (W. Ridgeway; I. Taylor) Acad. **42**: 218–341. — Ath. '92, **2**: 595.
— Appreciating, Evils of an. (E. B. Howell) R. of Rs. (N. Y.) **8**: 406.
— An Automatic, *vs.* a Fiat Currency. (E. L. Rector) Am. M. Civics, **7**: 382.
— Baltimore Plan. Soc. Econ. **7**: 327. — (H. White) Nation, **59**: 300. — (C. C. Homer and A. P. Hepburn) Engin. M. **8**: 377. — (A. P. Hepburn) Forum, **18**: 385.
— Banks and the Greenbacks. Gunton's M. **10**: 15.
— Best. (A. W. Tourgée) No. Am. **163**: 416.
— Creation of Money by Government. Soc. Econ. **8**: 36.
— Depreciation of, and Wages. Gunton's M. **11**: 332.
— Discussion of, in Massachusetts in 18th Cent. (A. McF. Davis) Q. J. Econ. **11**: 70.
— Double Standard: Is it desirable and is it possible to maintain it? (W. A. Richardson) Am. M. Civics, **9**: 31.
— An Elastic. Bank. M. (N. Y.) **48**: 910.
— — Do we want? (F. M. Taylor) Pol. Sci. Q. **11**: 133.
— English, under Edward I. (C. G. Crump and A. Hughes) Econ. J. **5**: 50.
— Expansion of, Object-lesson in. (A. D. Noyes) Nation, **55**: 41.
— Facts and Figures on. (A. P. Gardner) Bach. of Arts, **3**: 512.
— Fallacies that fool Fiatists. Soc. Econ. **8**: 83.
— The Financial Bronco. (T. S. Van Dyke) Forum, **21**: 651.
— Financing the U. S. Treasury. Soc. Econ. **9**: 81.
— Fixed, and Redeemable. Bank. M. (N. Y.) **48**: 244.

Currency, From a Silver to a Gold Standard in British Honduras. (A. Moloney) No. Am. **163**: 257.
— Greenback Issue returning. Soc. Econ. **9**: 184.
— Historical Aspects. (A. Del Mar) Soc. Econ. **9**: 34.
— History of, Shaw's. (C. Morrison) Econ. J. **5**: 230.
— Imperial National. (W. M. Gray) Canad. M. **5**: 547.
— in Austria, Gold Standard of. Q. J. Econ. **7**: 225.
— in the U. S., Democratic Party and. (R. P. Bland) No. Am. **156**: 485.
— — Our Variegated Currency. Pub. Opin. **16**: 158.
— — Problem of, through Fifty Years. (A. Brisbane) Arena, **8**: 467.
— Increase of Paper. Soc. Econ **2**: 80.
— Inflation of, Evidences of. (D. Kinley) Nation, **56**: 252.
— Legislation on, Early and Recent. (J. J. Lalor) Forum, **22**: 117.
— Money and. (J. H. Jones) Soc. Econ. **2**: 179.
— National, and Hard Times. (H. H. Trimble) Am. M. Civics, **8**: 449, 590.
— New York Banks and Reserves. Soc. Econ. **8**: 150.
— of Commerce, Real. (G. S. Coe) Engin. M. **6**: 1.
— of Great Britain. (J. P. Val d'Eremas) Asia. R. **18**: 76.
— — a Common-sense Currency. (R. Ewen) Westm. **138**: 416.
— — An Honest and Sufficient Currency. (C. Wilson) National, **20**: 427.
— Object Lessons. (W. Knapp) Am. J. Pol. **2**: 286.
— Old-time. (M. T. Sanders) Green Bag, **5**: 541.
— Paper, of Pennsylvania. (C. W. Macfarlane) Ann. Am. Acad. Pol. Sci. **8**: 50.
— Plan of President Cleveland. (W. J. Bryan) Arena, **11**: 321.
— Pleading for the Greenback. Soc. Econ. **9**: 263.
— Political Parties and the Public Peril. Soc. Econ. **9**: 161.
— Politics and. (E. L. Godkin) Nation, **55**: 405.
— Problem of. (J. B. Robertson) J. Soc. Arts, **41**: 210.
— — and its Solution. (A. Mills) Engin. M. **10**: 187.
— Proposal Concerning. Soc. Econ. **7**: 65.
— Proposed Clearing House. Gunton's M. **10**: 332.
— Question of. (H. C. Gibbs) National, **25**: 207. — Pub. Opin. **19**: 519. — (D. Barbour) National, **23**: 692. — (W. J. Bryan) Arena, **16**: 529. — (W. E. Chandler) National, **28**: 473.
— — Encouragements in the Present Crisis. (A. D. White) Forum, **22**: 16.
— — for Laymen. (B. Currie) National, **25**: 519. — (H. R. Beeton) National, **26**: 388.
— Reform in. (H. White) Nation, **63**: 358. — (J. C. Adams; A. K. Miller; H. Craig) No. Am. **163**: 743.
— — Greenback Controversy. Gunton's M. **11**: 408.
— Shall we degrade our Standards? (Lord Farrer) National, **24**: 165.
— Shrinkage in Volume of, Effects of. (I. E. Deen) Arena, **8**: 39.
— Small, Utility of. Chamb. J. **68**: 778.
— Sound, the Dominant Political Issue. (W. Salomon) Forum, **19**: 586.
— Systems of, 1892. J. Statis. Soc. **56**: 494.
— True Basis of. (M. M. Dawson) Arena, **6**: 84.
— U. S. Legal Tender Notes in California. (B. Moses) Q. J. Econ. **7**: 1.
— — A New. Bank. M. (N. Y.) **48**: 401.
— — Our Banking and Currency Plan. Soc. Econ. **8**: 1.
— — Our Government and. (A. B. and H. Farquhar) Am. J. Pol. **1**: 239.
— — Vacuum in our Currency System. Soc. Econ. **9**: 32.
— — Variegations of. (H. White) Nation, **55**: 23.
— — Volume of, 1892. (N. A. Dunning) Arena, **6**: 712.
Currency, U. S., Volume of, 1892, and Prosperity. (F. A. Walker) Econ. Stud. **1**: 25.
— — Way to equalize Gold and Silver. (J. H. Brown) Soc. Econ. **2**: 271.
— White on Money and Banking. Gunton's M. **10**: 90.
— Why Government Notes are Bad. Soc. Econ. **8**: 28.
See also Gold; Money; Silver; United States.
Currency Legislation, American, and British Investors. (W. Wetherell) Forum, **16**: 606.
Currency Reform. (W. Knapp) Am. J. Pol. **2**: 486.
— in Austria-Hungary. (J. Mandello) Am. Statis. Assoc. **3**: 477.
Currency Statistics, Imaginative. (J. B. Robertson) Fortn. **62**: 425.
Currency System, Rational. Bank. M. (N. Y.) **48**: 749.
Currency Systems of Different Nations. Bank. M. (N. Y.) **48**: 676.
Current Events, Teaching, in Schools. (E. O. Vaile) Pub. Opin. **14**: 17. — (O. F. Presbrey) Pub. Opin. **14**: 40.
Curriculum for Secondary Schools, Outlook for. (J. G. Schurman) School R. **1**: 67.
— School, Readjustment of. (R. S. Keyser) School R. **1**: 131.
Currie, Sir Philip, British Embassy at Constantinople. (J. F. Fraser) Eng. Illust. **15**: 97.
"Curry Favor," Derivation of. (H. Bradley) Acad. **45**: 228.
Curse of Conder; a story. (E. T. Fowler) Argosy, **55**: 435.
Cursed Bear. (F. Whishaw) Longm. **24**: 391. Same art. Liv. Age, **202**: 619.
Curtin, A. G., with portrait. Book News, **14**: 297.
Curtis, Edmund, the Boy Poet. Spec. **76**: 835. — Critic, **29**: 10.
Curtis, George William, with portrait. Bk. News, **4**: 373. — (W. Lewin) Acad. **41**: 441. **42**: 257. — Critic, **21**: 134–169. — (J. W. Chadwick) Critic, **21**: 183. — Dial (Ch.) **13**: 173. — Lit. W. (Bost.) **23**: 308. — (J. W. Chadwick) Nation, **55**: 180. — (W. Olney) Overland, n. s. **20**: 549. — (F. B. Sanborn) Am. J. Soc. Sci. **30**: xxx. — (E. B. Merrill) Am. J. Soc. Sci. **31**: ix. — (P. Godwin) Critic, **23**: 73. — (A. Cassot) Chaut. **17**: 165.
— and Civil Service Reform. (S. S. Rogers) Atlan. **71**: 15. — (W. G. Rice) Good Govt. **15**: 135.
— and Whittier. R. of Rs. (N. Y.) **6**: 280.
— as a Man of Letters. Atlan. **75**: 415.
— Autobiographical Sketch. Cosmopol. **17**: 703.
— Memorial Tablet. Critic, **29**: 178.
— Orations and Addresses. (C. F. McClumpha) Educa. R. **8**: 182.
— Recollections of. (J. W. Chadwick) Harper, **86**: 469.
Curtius, Ernst. Ath. '96, **2**: 97. — (R. P. Keep) Nation, **63**: 82.
— Festival at Olympia. (D. Kalopothakes) Nation, **60**: 378.
Curved Lines, About a Certain Class of, in a Space of *n* Manifoldness. (E. Lasker) Nature, **52**: 596.
Curzon, George. Travels in the Country Northwest of India. Dub. R. **116**: 406.
Cushing, Caleb, with portrait. (W. C. Todd) Green Bag, **4**: 1.
Cushing, Col. Job. (G. A. Gordon) N. E. Reg. **49**: 143.
Cushman, Charlotte Saunders, Life of, in Boston. (J. H. Wiggin) Bost. **1**: 87.
Cushman, Holbrook, Unpublished Papers by. Science, n. s. **2**: 757.
Cushman, Robert. (I. Cushman) Citizen, **2**: 89.
Custards. (F. R. Batchelder) New Eng. M. n. s. **15**: 476.

Custer, Gen. G. A., Last Battle of. (E. S. Godfrey) Cent. 21: 358.
Custine, Madame de, Bardoux on. (A. Laugel) Nation, 58: 135.
Custom in the Common Law. (F. A. Greer) Law Q. 9: 153.
Customs, Ancient, Mediæval, and Modern. (Lady Cook) Westm. 141: 19, 139, 271. Same art. Ecl. M. 122: 517, 735.
— Colonial, prior to 1730, in New England. (I. P. Fowle) Bost. 1: 258.
Cut, A, and a Kiss; a story. (A. Hope Hawkins) Eng. Illust. 12: no. 3, 35.
Cut-off and Compression, in Corliss Engines. (J. B. Stanwood) Cassier, 1: 217.
Cutting of Valley Falls Bridge; a story. (J. H. Schooling) Eng. Illust. 15: 155.
Cuyler, Theo. G., with portrait. Bk. News, 11: 224.
Cuyp, Aelbert. (T. Cole) Cent. 26: 58.
"Cyane," U. S. Steamer, Journal of, 1820. M. Am. Hist. 30: 92.
Cyanid Patents. (J. G. C. Wells) Engin. M. 11: 867.
Cyclamen, Cultivation of. (W. Scott) Garden & F. 7: 507.
— Double-flowered. (T. Holm) Garden & F. 5: 234.
— Hardy, of Asia Minor. (E. Whittall) Garden & F. 5: 465.
— Persian. (M. Barker) Garden & F. 6: 125, 146.
Cyclamens at the Columbian Exposition. (E. J. Hill) Garden & F. 6: 157.
— from Seed. (Beth Day) Garden & F. 9: 135.
Cycles. Sat. R. 78: 505.
— and Tires for 1893. (R. J. Mecredy) Fortn. 59: 237.
See also Bicycles.
Cycling. (R. J. Mecredy) Un. Serv. M. 6: 657. —(R. J. Mecredy) Sat. R. 81: 468.
— and Cycles. Fortn. 61: 669.
— Awheel in Jamaica. (E. M. Aaron) Outing, 27: 129.
— Blind Parisians awheel. (F. E. Thomas) Outing, 25: 364.
— A Century Ride. (G. E. Denison) Outing, 23: 56.
— Fast Ride of the Season. (G. E. Denison) Outing, 23: 217.
— for Health and Pleasure. Chamb. J. 72: 529.
— for Ladies, A Medical View of. (W. H. Fenton) 19th Cent. 39: 796. Same art. Ecl. M. 126: 798. Same art. Liv. Age, 209: 806.
— from Havre to Rouen. (J. W. Fosdick) Outing, 20: 83, 197.
— in Athens. (T. G. Allen, jr.) Outing, 28: 173.
— In Aztec Land awheel. (T. P. Terry) Outing, 23: 461.
— In Banana-land awheel. (E. M. Aaron) Outing, 25: 312.
— in the Desert. (D. G. Hogarth) National, 27: 701. Same art. Ecl. M. 127: 330. Same art. Liv. Age, 210: 361.
— in Germany. (F. B. Workman) Outing, 21: 110.
— in the Heart of England. (E. R. Holmes) Outing, 28: 20.
— in Jamaica. (E. M. Aaron) Outing, 27: 25.
— in the Jersey Pines. (H. M. Sayres) Outing, 26: 32.
— in Mid-Atlantic. (O. Howarth) Outing, 27: 288, 392. 28: 35.
— in Mid-Pacific. (C. E. Trevathan) Outing, 19: 347.
— in the White Mountains. (P. C. Stuart) Outing, 26: 372.
— Ladies on the Road. All the Year, 73: 105.
— Lenz's World Tour awheel. Outing, 24: 284, 360, 432. 25: 35, 152. 26: 224-467. 27: 51-467. 28: 47-456. 29: 57-267.
Cycling, Military. (T. DeB. Holmes) Un. Serv. M. 5: 415.— (A. R. Savile) Un. Serv. M. 7: 714.
— — French. Liv. Age, 207: 700.
— My Friends who cycle. Blackw. 159: 883. Same art. Liv. Age, 210: 184. Same art. Ecl. M. 127: 93.
— My Wheel and I. (J. P. Rudd) Outing, 26: 124.
— on Mt. Washington. (G. F. Smith) Outing, 22: 344.
— on Pablo Beach. (H. I. Greene) Outing, 21: 384.
— On the Palisades of the Hudson. (E. Ingersoll) Outing, 26: 442.
— Round the World with Wheel and Camera. (F. G. Lenz) Outing, 20: 339. 23: 241.
— Through Erin awheel. (G. E. Denison) Outing, 22: 28-445.
— thro' Virginia. (J. B. Carrington) Outing, 28: 204, 344.
— thro' Western England. (Mrs. A. L. Moqué) Outing, 28: 186, 232.
— Touring in Bermuda awheel. (T. B. Dowden) Outing, 27: 236.
— Trip in Trinidad. (H. Macbeth) Outing, 27: 433.
— What to avoid in. (B. W. Richardson) No. Am. 161: 170.
See Bicycling.
Cycling Tour, Bluegrass. (J. B. Carrington) Outing, 24: 272.
Cyclist's Vision, A; a poem. (K. Gerring) Outing, 27: 300.
Cyclomania. Chamb. J. 73: 458.
Cyclonic Indraught at the Top of an Anticyclone. (H. H. Clayton) Nature, 52: 243.
Cylinder Wall of Steam Engine, Temperature Cycle on. (E. T. Adams) Cassier, 7: 211.
Cylinders in the British Museum. Meth. R. 56: 799.
Cymatogaster, Sex Cells in, Origin and Differentiation of, and Idea of Continuity of Germ Plasm. (C. H. Eigenmann) Am. Natural. 30: 265.
Cynewulf. Christ, Gollancz's ed. Sat. R. 74: 746.
Cynthia's Love Affairs; a story. (B. Pain) Eng. Illust. 11: 323-763.
Cynthy's Joe; a story. (C. S. Ross) Outing, 20: 276.
Cyperaceæ, Studies upon. (T. Holm) Am. J. Sci. 151: 348. 152: 214.
Cypress, New, of Nyassaland. (W. T. T. Dyer) Nature, 51: 175.
— of the Sultana, The. (E. A. Kiching) Argosy, 60: 504.
Cypresses of Monterey. (C. S. Sargent) Garden & F. 7: 241.
Cyprian, St., Correspondence of. Church Q. 34: 381.
Cypriote Heads in Metropolitan Museum. (A. C. Merriam) Am. J. Archæol. 8: 184.
Cypripidium Bellatulum. (E. O. Orpet) Garden and F. 9: 528.
Cyprus. Temp. Bar, 95: 553.
— and England. (E. G. Browne) New R. 15: 510.
— Antiquities from, in the Fitzwilliam Museum. Acad. 41: 260.
— Christening in. (M. D. Conway) Open Court, 9: 4624.
— Convention concerning. (T. G. Bowles) Fortn. 66: 626.
— Excavations in. Acad. 50: 85.
— — 1889-90. (J. A. R. Munro; H. A. Tubbs) J. Hel. Stud. 11: 1. 12: 59, 298.
— A Glimpse of. Chamb. J. 69: 497.
— in 1893, Lewis's. Sat. R. 78: 187.
— Law of, and its Administration. (W. E. Grigsby) Law Q. 12: 67.
— Mediæval. Ed. R. 182: 440. Same art. Liv. Age, 207: 707.
— Ohnefalsch-Richter on. (C. R. Conder) Scot. R. 23: 126. — (C. H. Toy) Nation, 57: 174, 197.
Cyrano de Bergerac, Savinen. (F. J. Hudleston) Gent. M. n. s. 54: 585. — Time, 18: 590.

Cytology, Vegetable, Recent Advances in. (J. B. Farmer) Sci. Prog. 5: 22.
Czar and Emperor. (K. Blind) Fortn. 65: 767. Same art. Liv. Age, 209: 579.
— Coronation of. (Ian Malcolm) New R. 15: 242.
Czars, A Change of. Blackw. 157: 306. Liv. Age, 204: 579.
Czechs, Rival Leaders of the. (Edith Sellers) Temp. Bar, 107: 335. Same art. Liv. Age, 209: 236.

D'Abrichcourt Family. (J. Maskell) Walford's Antiq. 3: 285.
Dacquin, Mdlle. Jenny, and Prosper Mérimée. Macmil. 73: 211. Same art. Liv. Age, 208: 289.
Daddy Longlegs. (E. A. Butler) Knowl. 17: 245.
Daddy Longlegs and his Joanna; a story. Cornh. 71: 387.
Dæmme Vand, Glacier-Lake, Norway. (A. F. Mockler-Ferryman) Geog. J. 4: 524.
Daemonelix: is it a Burrow? Reply to Dr. Fuchs. (E. H. Barbour) Am. Natural. 29: 517.
Daffodils, English. Garden & F. 5: 198.
— in the Grass. (C. S. Sargent) Garden & F. 9: 231.
Daghestan, Lex Barbarorum of the. (M. Kovalevsky) Anthrop. J. 25: 112.
Dagnan-Bouveret, P. A. J. (W. A. Coffin) Cent. 26: 4. — (B. Karageorgevitch) M. of Art, 16: 121.
Dagonet, the Jester. Spec. 72: 557.
Daguerreotype in America. (D. T. Davis) McClure, 8: 3.
Dahabeah, Life on a. Spec. 69: 222.
Dahlias, Cactus and Show. (W. E. Endicott) Garden & F. 6: 487.
— Cultivation of. (J. N. Gerard) Garden & F. 6: 445.
— Single. (W. E. Endicott) Garden & F. 6: 415.
Dahn, Felix. Reminiscences. (J. T. Hatfield) Dial (Ch.) 14: 273.
Dahshur, Pyramids of, Recent Excavations at. (J. De Morgan) Harper, 92: 918. — Nature, 52: 131.
— Visit to. (Amy Strachey) National, 24: 809. Same art. Liv. Age, 204: 763.
"Daily Morning Chronicle." (A. Eliot) New Eng. M. n. s. 13: 307.
Daingerfield, Elliott. (D. R. Goodale) Mo. Illust. 3: 177.
Dainties, Local. Chamb. J. 72: 26.
Daira Sanieh of Egypt. Chamb. J. 70: 137.
Dairy Farming. (Lord Vernon) 19th Cent. 39: 267.
— English and Dutch. (H. H. Smith; E. C. Trepplin) 19th Cent. 40: 797.
Dairy Produce, England's Competitors in. Chamb. J. 72: 86.
Dairy Schools and Dairy Products. (F. W. Woll) Pop. Sci. Mo. 45: 234.
Daisies, Michaelmas, Cultivation of. (J. N. Gerard) Garden & F. 7: 396.
Daisy Venn; a story. (A. Gordon) Argosy, 59: 346.
Dakota, North and South. (J. Ralph) Harper, 84: 895.
— — Divorce Movement towards. (J. Realf, jr.) Arena, 5: 243.
— — Prairies and Coteaus of. (S. T. Clover) New Eng. M. n. s. 5: 735.
— Stubble and Slough in. (F. Remington) Harper, 89: 452.
Dakotas, Military Bicycling thro'. (De R. C. Cabell) Outing, 28: 214.
See North Dakota; South Dakota.
Dale, T. P., Life and Letters of. Ath. '94, 1: 272. — Sat. R. 77: 527.
Dale, R. W. (P. T. Forsyth) Sund. M. 24: 331. — (R. Thomas) Chr. Lit. 12: 348.
Dale, R. W., Recollections of. Westm. 144: 655.
Dalesman of Eyam. (C. Burke) Liv. Age, 196: 178.
Dalhousie, Lord, Unpublished Letters of. (G. W. Forrest) Ath. '96, 1: 218.
Dallas, George M. Diary. Sat. R. 74: 50.
Dalmatia. (W. B. Dawkins) Nature, 54: 78.
Dalmeny and Devonshire. (T. H. S. Escott) New R. 11: 256.
Dalmon, Charles William, Poetry of. (W. Sharp) Acad. 43: 124.
Dalou, Jules. (C. Phillips) Portfo. 24: 10.
Dalton, John, and the Atomic Theory. Nature, 52: 169.
Daly, Augustin, and Daniel Frohman Stock Companies contrasted. (A. Brownell) Bost. 3: 292.
— and the Modern Stage. Sat. R. 79: 860.
Daly, César. (M. Anderson) Am. Arch. 37: 64.
Daly, Charles P., with portrait. (A. O. Hall) Green Bag, 6: 489.
Damariscove. (W. Thompson) New Eng. M. n. s. 11: 34.
Damascus; a sketch. (A. M. Bell) Good Words, 35: 304.
Dame Periwinkle speaks. (E. B. Walling) New Eng. M. n. s. 7: 655.
Damma Island and its Natives. (P. W. Bassett-Smith) Anthrop. J. 23: 134.
Damme, Visit to. (J. Maskell) Walford's Antiq. 6: 60.
Damnosa Hæreditas; a story. (Eva Anstruther) New R. 10: 637.
Damrosch, Walter. (R. Stockton) Munsey, 7: 441.
Dams, and Cause of Bursting of the Dam at Bouzey, France. (W. C. Unwin) Cassier, 11: 9.
— Location and Construction of. (J. B. Johnson) Engin. M. 10: 654.
Dana, Charles A. (F. Morris) Chaut. 21: 325. — With portraits. (E. P. Mitchell) McClure, 3: 371.
— on Journalism. (H. T. Peck) Bookman, 2: 191.
Dana, James Dwight. Critic, 26: 295. — (E. S. Dana) Am. J. Sci. 149: 329. — Nature, 51: 611. — Nat. Sci. 6: 348. — (W. M. Davis) Geog. J. 5: 599. — Ath. '95, 1: 509. — (J. W. Powell) Science, n. s. 3: 181.
Dana, Richard H., and Herman Melville, Sea Stories of. (W. C. Russell) Critic, 20: 189.
Dana, Richard Henry, jr., and Thomas Starr King. (W. Everett) Overland, n. s. 28: 578.
Dana, Samuel Luther, with portrait. Pop. Sci. Mo. 49: 692.
Dana Family, The. Munsey, 16: 139.
Danbury, Eng.; A Corner of Essex. (J. Cartwright) National, 18: 626. Same art. Liv. Age, 192: 560.
Dance, A; a poem. (E. McGaffey) Cosmopol. 16: 360.
Dance No. Four; a story. (P. Crawford) Belgra. 77: 74.
Dance of Death. (J. M. Gray) Good Words, 34: 344.
Dancers, English Stage. (W. D. Adams) Theatre, 34: 76.
Dances, Country-house. Sat. R. 75: 68.
Dancing. Ed. R. 183: 336. — (A. W. Beckett) Westm. 143: 675.
— and Music. (H. Spencer) Pop. Sci. Mo. 47: 365.
— Bohemian, Zíbrt on. Sat. R. 79: 676.
— Emperor William on. Spec. 68: 51.
— Evolution of. (L. J. Vance) Pop. Sci. Mo. 41: 739.
— From Minuet to Skirt-dancing. All the Year, 73: 230.
— Greek. Art J. 46: 338.
— Grove on. Sat. R. 81: 52.
— History of. (Margaret Fleming) Munsey, 10: 287.
— in Churches. (J. Morris) Month, 76: 492.
— Origin of, Herbert Spencer on. Spec. 75: 12.

Dancing, Stage, Future of. (W. D. Adams) Theatre, 37: 252.
See Skirt-dancing.
Dancing Children of Harricombe; a story. All the Year, 72: 492. Same art. Liv. Age, 198: 401.
Dandy Jackson; a story. Gent. M. n. s. 55: 541. Same art. Liv. Age, 207: 781.
Danforth's Dilemma; a story. (F. M. Smith) Munsey, 13: 282.
Danger, Luxury of. Spec. 71: 544.
Dangerous Experiment; a story. Argosy, 55: 532.
Dangerous Experiment; a story. (M. Ogilvy) Canad. M. 6: 38.
Dangerous Side-path, A; a story. (J. S. Wood) Outing, 22: 209.
Daniel, Samuel. Macmil. 68: 433.
Daniels, William. M. of Art, 5: 341.
Danish Literature, 1891–92. (A. Ipsen) Ath. '92, 2: 9.
— 1892–93. (A. Ipsen) Ath. '93, 2: 9.
— 1893–94. (A. Ipsen) Ath. '94, 2: 9.
— 1894–95. (A. Ipsen) Ath. '95, 2: 9.
— 1895–96. (A. Ipsen) Ath. '96, 2: 9.
— Modern. (M. Wergeland) Dial (Ch.) 19: 135.
Danish Popular Tales. Folk-Lore Rec. 3: 201.
Dannat, William T. (J. F. Opp) Munsey, 13: 517.
Dannecker, Johann Heinrich. (E. S. Roscoe) M. of Art, 3: 13.
Dannel the Carter; a story. Chamb. J. 70: 685. Same art. Ecl. M. 121: 854.
Danovitch; a Russian Romance. Liv. Age, 192: 82.
Dante. Spec. 72: 657.
— and Sicily. (E. Moore) Univ. R. 4: 509.
— and Tennyson. (F. St.J. Thackeray) Temp. Bar, 102: 387. Same art. Liv. Age, 202: 259. Same art. Ecl. M. 123: 352.
— Beatrice and Other Allegorical Characters. (J. Conway) Am. Cath. Q. 17: 253.
— Biographical Notice of, in the 1494 Edition of "Speculum Historiale." (P. Toynbee) Eng. Hist. R. 10: 297.
— Botticelli's Illustrations to. (B. Berenson) Nation, 63: 363.
— R. W. Church on. Spec. 61: 757.
— Classical Studies of. Ed. R. 181: 284.
— Companion to, Scartazzini's. Sat. R. 77: 17.
— Did he study in Oxford? (W. E. Gladstone) 19th Cent. 31: 1032.
— Divina Commedia, Celtic Sources of. (M. Mulhall) Dub. R. 119: 343.
— — English Translations, Metre of. (A. Galton) Acad. 43: 258.
— — Historical Presuppositions and Foreshadowings of. (W. M. Bryant) And. R. 19: 525.
— — Manuscript of, at Lisbon. (L. Thomas) Acad. 49: 116.
— — Norton's Translation. (P. Toynbee) Acad. 41: 151. 42: 64. — (W. R. Thayer) Nation, 54: 134. 55: 110. — Sat. R. 74: 224.
— — Symbolism of. (E. F. Jourdain) Chr. Lit. 12: 102.
— — Use of the Divine Name in. (E. F. Jourdain) Chr. Lit. 13: 35.
— — Women of. (E. F. Jourdain) Chr. Lit. 13: 217.
— Francesca da Rimini, Russel's Translation. Eng. R. 1: 164.
— from a New-Church Standpoint. (S. W. Paine) N. Church R. 3: 542.
— Imperialism of. (A. R. Wall) Poet-Lore, 2: 501.
— Inferno; Butler's Translation. Sat. R. 73: 336.
— — Musgrave's Translation. (G. M. Harper) Dial (Ch.) 20: 136.
— — Vernon's Readings in. (W. R. Thayer) Nation, 59: 33. — Sat. R. 78: 295.
Dante, Letters of. (P. Toynbee) Acad. 41: 321.
— The "Oxford." (F. J. Snell) Acad. 46: 505.
— Paradise. (E. M. Mitchell) Poet-Lore, 7: 399.
— Power of. (M. O'Neill) Blackw. 155: 357. Same art. Liv. Age, 201: 166.
— "Quaestio de aqua et terra" of. (E. G. Gardiner) Nature, 47: 295.
— Recent Books on. (P. Toynbee) Acad. 47: 438.
— Religion of. (O. Browning) Time, 20: 134.
— Shadwell's Translation. (W. R. Thayer) Nation, 56: 128.
— — Translations of, by Boyd, Wright, and Shadwell. Church Q. 36: 182.
— Vita Nuova. (L. O. Kuhns) Meth. R. 54: 369. — Quar. 184: 24.
— Word-painting of. (A. F. Sadlier) Cath. World, 63: 746.
Dante Manuscripts, French. (G. R. Carpenter) Nation, 55: 339.
D'Antraigues, Pingaud's. (A. Laugel) Nation, 56: 176.
Danube, Canoes on the. (J. D. Butler) Nation, 55: 246.
— From the Black Forest to the Black Sea. (P. Bigelow) Harper, 84: 329–85: 261. Same art. Ecl. M. 120: 274.
— Iron Gates of, Destruction of. Chamb. J. 69: 769.
— Lower, Navigation of. Geog. J. 1: 243.
Danube Canal, Opening of. (A. Heilprin) Nation, 63: 286. — (K. Peucker) Geog. J. 8: 603. — (O. M. Norris) Sund. M. 25: 462. — (H. A. Gwynne) Longm. 27: 54.
Danubian States, Renaissance of. (M. S. Robinson) Meth. R. 54: 190.
Daphne. (Guy Boothby) Chamb. J. 72: 572.
Daphne Laurea; a poem. (J. P. Peabody) Atlan. 77: 640.
Daphne's Cruise on a Man-of-War. (A. L. Craig) Chaut. 19: 576.
Darbishire, Herbert Dukinfield. Acad. 44: 90.
Darboy, Georges, Archbishop. (E. W. Latimer) Cath. World, 56: 755.
D'Arcy, John, Lord, Monument of. Antiq. n. s. 27: 25.
Dardanelles, Through the. (C. Warman) McClure, 6: 103.
Dardistan, Legends, Songs, and Customs of. (G. W. Leitner) Asia. R. 13: 294. 14: 141, 442. 15: 143.
Darenth Valley, Kent, Roman Catholic Antiquities of. (A. M. Wilson) Dub. R. 118: 272.
D'Argenson, Marquis. Spec. 72: 373.
Dariel; a Romance of Surrey. (R. D. Blackmore) Blackw. 160: 443, 585, 725.
Darien, Isthmus of, and Sea Power, The. (A. T. Mahan) Atlan. 72: 459.
Darien Expedition, 1698. (B. Taylor) Scot. R. 19: 54.
Dark Design, A; a story. Argosy, 56: 527.
Dark Races, Future of. Spec. 70: 121.
Darkest before Dawn. (A. W. Holmes-Forbes) Time, 17: 683.
Darley, G. Sylvia. Sat. R. 74: 52.
Darlington, S. C., Bays of. (L. C. Glenn) Science, n. s. 2: 472.
Darmesteter, James. (Gaston Paris) Contemp. 67: 81. Same art. Liv. Age, 204: 387. — Atlan. 75: 571. — (J. S. Cotton) Acad. 46: 333, 380. — (A. V. W. Jackson) Critic, 25: 316. — Ath. '94, 2: 571.
— and his Studies in Zend Literature. (F. M. Müller) Jew. Q. 7: 173.
Darmstadt Polytechnic. (P. Magnus) Nature, 55: 34.
Dart River. (J. A. Blaikie) M. of Art, 8: 320–397. — (S. Hodges) M. of Art. 2: 50.
Dartmoor, Antiquities of. (C. Elton) Law Q. 6: 206.
Dartmoor Pony-drift. Spec. 77: 549.
Dartmoor Song-men. (S. B. Gould) Eng. Illust. 9: 468.

Dartmouth, England. (S. Baring-Gould) Sund. M. 23: 735.
Dartmouth College Case. (E. A. Otis) Am. Law R. 27: 525.
— Status and Tendencies of. (A. Russell) Am. Law R. 30: 321.
Darwaz and Karategin, Ethnological Sketch of. (C. Johnston) Asia. R. 13: 77.
Darwin, C., with portrait. (B. O. Flower) Arena, 7: 352. — With portrait. Bk. News, 9: 407.
— and after Darwin, Romanes on. (H. F. Osborn) Nation, 55: 266. — Sat. R. 74: 21. — (E. H. Griggs) Dial (Ch.) 20: 239.
— and Hegel, Ritchie's. (C. S. Peirce) Nation, 57: 393.
— and his Work. Open Court, 1: 40.
— F. Darwin's Reminiscences of. Critic, 22: 64.
— Home of. (O. J. Vignoles) Good Words, 34: 95.
Darwinian Theory, Marshall on. (D. S. Jordan) Dial (Ch.) 19: 140.
Darwinism and the Bible. (W. M. Hughes) M. Chr. Lit. 6: 401.
— and Christianity. (L. Noire) Open Court, 3: 1878.
— and Neo-Darwinism. (C. C. Coe) Univ. R. 5: 268.
— and Race Progress, Haycraft's. Sat. R. 79: 163. — (F. Starr) Dial (Ch.) 19: 89.
— and Socialism. (T. Kirkup) Econ. R. 1: 531.
— and Swimming; a theory. (D. Robinson) 19th Cent. 34: 721.
— The Deadlock in. (S. Butler) Univ. R. 6: 523. 7: 65, 238.
— Ethical Import of. (L. J. Vance) Open Court, 4: 2282–2310.
— The Newest. (St. George Mivart) Am. Cath. Q. 19: 673.
— of Darwin, and of the Post-Darwinian Schools. (G. J. Romanes) Monist, 6: 1.
— J. H. Stirling on. (A. R. Wallace) Nature, 49: 333. — (J. G. McKendrick) Crit. R. 4: 115.
— Wallace on. (J. C. F. Grumbine) Open Court, 5: 2813.
Dasent, Sir George Webbe. Ath. '96, 1: 811.
Dashur. *See* Dahshur.
Date Obolum Balisario; a poem. (A. Brodrick) Gent. M. n. s. 53: 426.
Date Palm. Garden & F. 7: 164.
Datolite from Loughboro', Ont. (L. V. Pirsson) Am. J. Sci. 145: 100.
Daubigny, Charles-François. (R. J. Wickenden) Cent. 22: 323. — (D. C. Thomson) M. of Art, 12: 300, 325.
Daubrée, Professor. Nature, 54: 132.
Daudet, Alphonse. (S. Henry) Bookman, 3: 118. — With portrait. Bk. Buyer, 9: 325. — (M. Thompson) Bk. News, 6: 53. — Book R. 4: 179. — (R. H. Sherard) McClure, 3: 137.
— at Home. (M. A. Belloc) Idler, 3: 595.
— Portraits of. McClure, 1: 24.
— Sherard's. Sat. R. 78: 576.
Daughter, Educating a. (E. Bisland) No. Am. 159: 627.
Daughter; a story. (I. Lamaison) Overland, n. s. 19: 516.
Daughter of the Church; a story. (C. Smith) Canad. M. 5: 378.
Daughter of Festus Hanks. (R. McDonald) Munsey, 10: 410–579. 11: 37, 146.
Daughter of Folly; a story. (A. E. Barr) Cosmopol. 21: 372.
Daughter of the King, A. (Beatrice Deakin) Chamb. J. 71: 487–536.
Daughter of the South; a story. (Mrs. B. Harrison) Cosmopol. 12: 296.
Daughter of the Sun: Tsimshian Legend. (J. Deans) J. Am. Folk-Lore, 4: 32.
Daughters and Mothers. (Mrs. F. Harrison) 19th Cent. 35: 313. Same art. Ecl. M. 122: 493.
— Evolution of the. (S. M. Amos) Contemp. 65: 515. Same art. Ecl. M. 122: 777.
— Reply from. (K. Cuffe) 19th Cent. 35: 437. — (A. W. P. Smith) 19th Cent. 35: 443. — (Gertrude Hemery) Westm. 141: 679.
— Revolt of the. (Lady Jeune) Fortn. 61: 267. Same art. Ecl. M. 122: 389. — (B. A. Crackanthorpe) 19th Cent. 35: 23, 424. — (M. E. Haweis) 19th Cent. 35: 430. Same art. Liv. Age, 200: 621.
Daughters of Job; a novel. (D. Dale) Belgra. 83: 80–418. 84: 82–424. 85: 89–423.
Daughters of Liberty. (Mrs. R. J. Barker) Am. Hist. Reg. 1: 29.
Dauncey, Sylvanus (pseud.). The Reckoning; a play. (C. Howard) Theatre, 28: 53. — Gent. M. n. s. 48: 104.
Dauphin's Birthday Ball. (J. Armstrong) New Eng. M. n. s. 14: 97.
Dauvray, Helen, in A Scrap of Paper. Theatre, 28: 203.
Dave; a story. (O. Rhoscomyl) Idler, 10: 609.
Davenport, Iowa. (M. Peck) Nat'l M. (N. Y. '91) 19: 56–276.
Daves Family of North Carolina. Am. Hist. Reg. 2: 779.
Davey, Henry. Cassier, 5: 349.
Davey, Sir Horace, with portrait. Green Bag, 6: 57.
David, The Historical. (B. W. Bacon) New World, 4: 540.
— in Hebrew Literature and Life, Place of. (W. R. Harper) Bib. World, 5: 241.
— "Son" and "Lord" of. (W. Milligan) Thinker, 8: 502.
— Statue of, by Michael Angelo. (L. E. Baxter) M. of Art, 3: 379, 417.
David, St. (Miss M. A. R. Tucker) Walford's Antiq. 9: 257.
David Copperfield's Childhood, Reminiscences of. (A. Ansted) Good Words, 35: 255, 333.
David Crowhurst's Ordeal; a story. All the Year, 75: 545–617.
David Deed. (G. Green) Overland, n. s. 24: 101.
Davidson, A. B., with portrait. (N. B. Bruce) Bib. World, 8: 255.
Davidson, John. (R. Le Gallienne) 19th Cent. 35: 952. — Spec. 73: 920. — (A. McC. Sholl) Bach. of Arts, 2: 618. — (H. D. Traill) Fortn. 63: 393. Same art. Ecl. M. 124: 616.
— Interview with. Bookman, 1: 85.
— Plays. Sat. R. 77: 342. — Spec. 72: 439.
— Poems of. Church Q. 39: 457.
— Poetry of. (L. Johnson) Acad. 47: 6. — Acad. 50: 421.
— Second Series of Fleet Street Eclogues. (G. Richards) Acad. 49: 112.
Davidson's Beat; a story. (G. G. Bain) Munsey, 13: 393.
Davie, Gen. W. R. (W. Clark) M. Am. Hist. 28: 415.
Davis, Henry William Banks. (M. P. Jackson) M. of Art, 4: 125.
Davis, Jefferson, Petition for Release of. (L. Young) M. Am. Hist. 27: 61.
— Reminiscences of, with portrait. (W. W. Scott) Southern M. 5: 178.
Davis, John, Forgotten Voyage of. (W. Foster) Geog. J. 2: 146.
Davis, Mrs. Mollie E. M., with portrait. Book News, 14: 335. — (A. Alain) Writer, 8: 152.
Davis, Richard Harding. Atlan. 75: 654. — With portrait. Bk. Buyer, 8: 197. — With portrait. Bk. News, 10: 469.

Davis, Richard Harding, Portraits of. McClure, **3**: 36.
Davis, Walter Renick. (W. A. Quayle) Meth. R. **55**: 618.
Davis's Discovery; a story. All the Year, **70**: 293.
Davos, Winter at. (C. W. Kennedy) Longm. **22**: 568.
Davy, Sir Humphry. Lond. Q. **87**: 311.
Davy-Faraday Laboratory. Dub. R. **119**: 406. — Nature, **55**: 208.
Dawn in San Diego; a poem. (C. H. Miller) Arena, **6**: 732.
Dawn of Spring, The; a story. (C. Campbell) Bost. **2**: 54.
Dawson, Daniel L., with portrait. Bk. News, **10**: 393.
Dawson, Rev. W. J., at Home. (C. Middleton) Sund. M. **25**: 246.
Day, Sir John, Collection of Paintings. (R. A. M. Stevenson) Art J. **45**: 261–309.
Day after, The; a story. (A. I. Harris) Temp. Bar, **105**: 392.
Day at Laguerre's, A. (S. M. Stevens) Bach. of Arts, **3**: 365.
Day in Asia; a story. (W. A. Dromgoole) Arena, **7**: 233.
Day in a Publisher's Life, A. (E. M. Green) Argosy, **58**: 172.
Day in Tophet, A. (M. M. Pope) Cent. **30**: 620.
Day of the Child; a story. (J. H. Barnabas) Overland, n. s. **19**: 93.
Day of Days; a poem. Argosy, **59**: 364.
Day of Encounters, A. (C. W. Wood) Argosy, **61**: 443.
Day of the Month. (L. C. Flint) New Sci. R. **2**: 326.
Day of the Recollection, a Russian. Chamb. J. **69**: 721.
Day of Silence, The; a story. (G. Gissing) National, **22**: 558. Same art. Liv. Age, **199**: 802.
Daybreak; a poem. (F. Courbière) Outing, **24**: 256.
Day Dreams and Realities. (H. Jones) 19th Cent. **34**: 94.
Day Dreams in the Dales. (R. F. Horton) Sund. M. **25**: 721.
Day-work or Piece-work. Cassier, **1**: 55.
Day's Drive in Three States. (B. Torrey) Atlan. **78**: 367.
Dayton, Charles Willoughby, with portrait. Nat'l M. (N. Y. '91) **19**: 310.
De Profundis; a story. (A. C. Doyle) Idler, **1**: 148. Same art. McClure, **3**: 513.
Deacon's Conversion; a story. (M. Purvis) Our Day, **16**: 409.
Deaconesses. (A. Cordes) Luth. Q. **22**: 172.
— Order of. How the Work is conducted. (G. T. B. Davis) Our Day, **16**: 393.
— Presbyterian. (G. W. Gilmore) M. Chr. Lit. **7**: 1.
Dead, Care of the. (Mrs. I. C. Barrows) Char. R. **5**: 198.
— Disposal of, by the Parsees: Towers of Silence. (W. Bourchier) Eng. Illust. **10**: 582.
— The Mighty. Gent. M. n. s. **49**: 323.
— Raising of, in the Gospels. (E. A. Abbott) New World, **5**: 473.
— Vicissitudes of the Remains of. (Eleanor Lewis) Cosmopol. **20**: 583.
Dead Dramatist, A; a dialogue. Theatre, **28**: 80.
Deadheads: Should they live? (H. C. Newton) Theatre, **37**: 147.
Dead-leaf Gully. (R. Horsley) Chamb. J. **71**: 108–119.
Dead Leaves; a poem. Argosy, **62**: 640.
Dead Leaves whisper; a poem. (P. B. Marston) Idler, **1**: 20.
Dead Man speaks, The. (G. Allen) Idler, **7**: 191.
Dead March, A; a poem. (C. Monkhouse) M. of Art, **8**: 88.
Deaf and Dumb, Education of. (H. A. Aikins) Educa. R. **12**: 236. — (M. E. Adams) Pop. Sci. Mo. **50**: 109. — (S. Fuller) Lend a H. **16**: 432. — (W. B. Peet) Scrib. M. **12**: 463.
— — Higher. (A. L. E. Crouter) Science, **19**: 199.
— — — Reply. (E. M. Gallaudet) Science, **19**: 231.
— — Values in. (E. M. Gallaudet) Educa. R. **4**: 16.
— — Facts about. (G. H. Pike) Sund. M. **23**: 561.
— Horace Mann School for, Sketch of. Lend a H. **13**: 346.
— Paris National Institution for. (F. Deltour) Chaut. **15**: 592.
— Speech for Deaf Children. (L. E. Warren) Pop. Sci. Mo. **44**: 363.
— Teaching to read Lips and Talk, Progress of, in the U. S. and Canada. (A. G. Bell) Science, **20**: 118.
Deaf, Dumb, and Blind, Treatment of. (S. M. Miller) Arena, **12**: 130.
Deaf Infants, Speech for. (E.V. Sutton) Educa. **15**: 464.
Deaf-mutism. (H. W. Hubbard) Leis. Hour, **43**: 576.
Deafness, and the Care of the Ears. (A. M. Fanning) Pop. Sci. Mo. **42**: 211.
Deal Boatmen. (T. S. Treanor) Leis. Hour, **41**: 337.
Deal on 'Change, A; a story. (R. Barr) Eng. Illust. **12**: no. 1, 77. Same art. McClure, **3**: 436.
Dealing in Futures; a Dramatic Sketch. (A. W. Rollins) Cosmopol. **16**: 90.
Dean of Bourges, The; a poem. (B. Wendell) Scrib. M. **11**: 117.
Deane, Silas. (C. J. Stillé) Pennsyl. M. **18**: 273.
— and the Coming of Lafayette. (G. A. Boutwell) New Eng. M. n. s. **8**: 167.
Dear Heart; a story. (A. Armitt) Belgra. **78**: 408.
Dear Lady Disdain. (J. Reid) Good Words, **35**: 207.
Dearest is Dearest; a story. (T. P. Battersby) Chamb. J. **68**: 775–808.
Death. (F. C. Mitchell) Nat. Sci. **1**: 434. — Sat. R. **79**: 376.
Death, Abolition of. (S. B. Goodnow) Bib. Sac. **49**: 650.
— and Burial Customs in Lincolnshire. (F. Peacock) Antiq. n. s. **31**: 330.
— and Life. (G. von Gizycki) Open Court, **2**: 1384.
— and the Player. Macmil. **67**: 284.
— and the Resurrection, Gerhard's. (J. M. Titzel) Ref. Q. **42**: 505.
— — Old-Testament Treatment of, Supposed Obscurity of. (L. W. Hayhurst) Bapt. R. **14**: 333.
— — Titzel's. (C. S. Gerhard) Ref. Q. **43**: 116.
— and Two Friends; a dialogue. (R. Le Gallienne) 19th Cent. **36**: 253.
— as represented on the Stage. (C. Edson) No. Am. **157**: 160.
— Beauty of. (W. Hutchinson) Open Court, **9**: 4639.
— in the Alps; a story. Blackw. **160**: 104.
— in Battle, Phenomena of. (G. L. Kilmer) Pop. Sci. Mo. **43**: 196.
— in Classical Antiquity. Ed. R. **180**: 131. Same art. Liv. Age, **202**: 643.
— In the Hour of. Macmil. **74**: 193. Same art. Liv. Age, **210**: 507.
— Is it a Finality? (P. Carus) Open Court, **4**: 2185.
— Old Age and. (C. A. Scott) Am. J. Psychol. **8**: 67.
— Omens of. (F. D. Bergen and W. W. Newell) J. Am. Folk-Lore, **2**: 12, 105.
— Origin of. (R. C. Schiedt) Ref. Q. **43**: 103.
— Prophesied in Dreams and by Voices. (S. K. Hart) Psychic. R. **2**: 262.
— Punishment of. (H. White) Nation, **59**: 456.
— Sudden. Spec. **77**: 510.
— Times to die. (Pauline W. Roose) Temp. Bar, **106**: 408.

Death, What is? Spec. 77: 933.
Death Chase, The; a poem. (D. T. Callahan) Overland, n. s. 25: 476.
Death Customs of South Carolina Negroes. J. Am. Folk-Lore, 7: 318.
— of the Sihanaka of Madagascar. (J. Pearse) Sund. M. 23: 539.
Death Dance, The; an Episode of the Hungarian Home Rule War. (E. Castle) Temp. Bar, 99: 353.
Death-dove in Folk-lore. (Mabel Peacock) Antiq. n. s. 31: 113.
Death Duties, New, in England. (Lord Winchilsea) No. Am. 160: 95.
Death-masks, Collection of. (L. Hutton) Harper, 85: 619–904.
Death-penalty, The. (A. M. Griffen) Open Court, 1: 572.
Death Rate in Great Britain. (A. J. H. Crespi) Scot. R. 21: 59.
— Low, in England. Pub. Opin. 14: 571.
Death Run, The; a railroad story. (C. Warman) McClure, 3: 248.
Death-signs, Superstitions concerning. (J. Am. Folk-Lore, 2: 72.
Death Valley, California, Flora of. (F. V. Coville) Science, 20: 342.
Death Valley Expedition, Report of. (E. D. Cope) Am. Natural, 27: 990.
Death Week in Russia. Spec. 68: 843. Same art. Liv. Age, 194: 766.
Debate and Composition: their Relation to Symmetrical Culture. (J. M. Buckley) Chaut. 13: 18.
— Preparation and Action in. (J. M. Buckley) Chaut. 18: 659.
— Principles and Practice of. (J. M. Buckley) Chaut. 18: 402.
— Public Oral. (J. M. Buckley) Chaut. 18: 532.
Debating, College. (C. Vrooman) Arena, 10: 677.
— in American Colleges. (M. M. Miller) Bach. of Arts, 2: 208.
Debs, E. V., Case of. (D. McG. Means) Nation, 59: 190.
Debs Insurrection and the American Republic. (Z. S. Holbrook) Bib. Sac. 52: 135, 209.
Debt, Imprisonment for, in U. S. (J. C. Thomson) Jurid. R. 1: 357.
Debt of Honor, A. Macmil. 67: 58. Same art. Ecl. M. 120: 17.
Debt of Honor, A; a story. (Lady H. Somerset) Sund. M. 24: 319.
Debts, Burden of Small. (H. Bosanquet) Econ. J. 6: 212.
Decadence of a Scholar. (W. P. Reeves) Dial (Ch.) 116: 71.
Decalogue: is it binding on the Gentiles? (W. A. Colcord) Arena, 5: 237.
— St. Paul's Seeming Abolition of the Law. (T. W. Chambers) Ref. Q. 42: 418.
— Recent Criticism upon. (C. G. Montefiore) Jew. Q. 3: 251.
Decay in Fruit, An Observation on. (B. D. Halsted) Garden & F. 6: 342.
Deccan, Agrarian Legislation for. (R. West) J. Soc. Arts, 41: 706.
— Ryots of. (J. W. Neil) Asia. R. 17: 396.
— Tour in. (J. D. Rees) Asia. R. 9: 402.
December; a poem. (A. C. Swinburne) M. of Art, 16: 55.
Deceptions, Psychological. (M. M. Trumbull) Open Court, 7: 3639.
Deck Hand, The. (C. King) Chamb. J. 69: 573.
Declaration of Independence and the Livingstons. (E. B. Livingston) Am. Hist. Reg. 1: 123.
Declaration of Independence by a Colonial Church [Edenton, N. C.]. (R. Dillard) M. Am. Hist. 28: 401.
— How it was received in the Old Thirteen. (C. D. Deshler) Harper, 85: 165.
— in the Light of Modern Criticism. (M. C. Tyler) No. Am. 163: 1.
— Story of the. (M. D. Conway) Open Court, 5: 2859.
Declaration of War: Is One Necessary? (D. C. Brench) Am. Law R. 28: 754.
Decoration, Animals in. (W. J. Nettleship) M. of Art, 9: 377. — (L. F. Day) M. of Art, 9: 494.
— External Color of Buildings. (H. Ricardo) M. of Art, 19: 311.
— Greek Textile. (A. Sacheverel-Coke) Univ. R. 3: 212.
— House. (G. Jekyll) National, 24: 519. Same art. Ecl. M. 124: 127.
— — Blanc's Grammaire des Arts Decoratifs. (C. Monkhouse) M. of Art, 5: 259.
— — How to beautify Home. (M. T. Bayard) Canad. M. 3: 168.
— Interior: an American Country House. M. of Art, 8: 45, 61, suppl.
— of the Home. (L. F. Day) M. of Art, 4: 98.
— — Woman's Part in. (L. F. Day) M. of Art, 4: 457.
— of a Room. (L. F. Day) M. of Art, 4: 182. — (C. Cook) Mo. Illust. 4: 323.
— — Place of Pictures in. (L. F. Day) M. of Art, 4: 319.
— Periodical Advice on. (L. F. Day) Art. J. 45: 85.
— Walls and Ceilings, Old English. (J. H. Pollen) M. of Art, 9: 228.
Decoration Day; a story. (S. O. Jewett) Harper, 85: 84.
Decorations, Domestic. (Gertrude E. Campbell) National, 18: 595.
— Kensington Interior. (L. F. Day) Art J. 45: 139.
Decorations, Foreign Orders and. (Edward Denloh) Cosmopol. 19: 294.
Decorative Art. (Candace Wheeler) Archit. Rec. 4: 409. — (L. F. Day) M. of Art, 3: 103–355.
— Crane on. (S. A. Hubbard) Dial (Ch.) 13: 212.
— and Elementary Education. (S. Image) J. Soc. Arts, 42: 679.
— English, from a Frenchman's Point of View. (V. Champier) M. of Art, 18: 31, 63.
— Evolution of. (H. Balfour) J. Soc. Arts, 42: 455.
— French, in London. (L. F. Day) Art J. 46: 5.
— in America, The Outlook for. (F. Fowler) Forum, 18: 686.
— in England, Revival of. (W. Crane) Fortn. 58: 810. Same art. (W. Crane) Ecl. M. 120: 164.
— Notes on. (L. F. Day) Art J. 48: 254.
— Plant Forms in, Lilley and Midgley's. Sat. R. 82: 9. — (G. McKenzie) M. of Art, 1: 74.
— Recent. (L. F. Day) Art J. 48: 92.
— seen in Shop Windows. (L. F. Day) Art J. 46: 52.
Decorative Design. Nature in Ornament. (L. F. Day) Garden & F. 5: 167.
Decorator in Rome, Impressions of a. (F. Crowninshield) Scrib. M. 13: 80–223.
Decree of Duke Deodonato; a story. (A. Hope) Eng. Illust. 12: no. 6, 49.
Dedham, Mass., Records, 1766–76. (D. G. Hill) Nat'l M. (N. Y., '91) 16: 160.
Dedicated to John Huntley; a story. New R. 10: 746.
Dedications, Curiosities of. Bookworm, 1: 150.
— to Englishmen by Foreign Authors. (W. D. Macray) Bibliographica, 1: 324, 455.
Deed of Daring, A. Spec. 68: 553. Same art. Ecl. M. 118: 790.

Deed with a Capital D. (C. M. Skinner) Lippinc. 52: 467.
Deeming, Conviction of. Spec. 68: 636.
Deep as First Love. (M. T. Wright) Scrib. M. 15: 218.
Deer and Deer-shooting. (E. W. Sandys) Outing, 25: 132.
— and Moose, Snap Shots at. (A. C. Shaw) Canad. M. 6: 412.
— and Other Animals for Parks. Sat. R. 78: 596.
— Hunting the Mule-deer. (R. Smith) Outing, 29: 229.
— Red, of New Zealand. Macmil. 74: 305.
Deer Forest, Life in a. (J. C. Lees) Good Words, 36: 822.
Deerhound, The Scotch. Good Words, 37: 770.
Deer Hunt in Uruguay. (G. A. Stockwell) Canad. M. 6: 114.
— in Old Virginia. Outing, 23: 61.
— with Akicitana, A. (J. O. Green) Outing, 27: 299.
Deer-hunting. (R. S. Osborne) Munsey, 13: 532. — (P. Pastnor) Outing, 27: 138.
— in Ceylon. (F. F. Dixon) Outing, 27: 441.
— on Exmoor. Macmil. 72: 241.
Deer-parks, English, Whitaker's List of. Sat. R. 74: 510.
Deer-stalking. (T. Speedy) Blackw. 158: 351. — Macmil. 69: 37.
— A Lucky Day in a Deer-forest. (G. W. Hartley) Blackw. 156: 272.
Deerfield, Mass. (M. E. Allen) New Eng. M. n. s. 7: 33.
— Negro Slavery in. (G. Sheldon) New Eng. M. n. s. 8: 49.
Defeat of Amos Wickliff; a story. (O. Thanet) Harper, 94: 86.
Defeated Transcendentalist, A; a story. (G. Dunn) Blackw. 153: 236. Same art. Liv. Age, 197: 76. Same art. Ecl. M. 120: 391.
Defeats of the Soul. (J. Watson) Sund. M. 25: 522.
De-facto Court, Can there be? (D. Fish) Am. Law R. 29: 833.
De-facto Principle in Law. (P. J. H. Grierson) Jurid. R. 2: 245.
Defalcations, Cause and Remedy of. (A. R. Barrett) Bank. M. (N. Y.) 52: 593.
Defective Classes. (A. O. Wright) Char. R. 5: 67.
— Legislation affecting, Recent. (W. B. Shaw) Char. R. 2: 128.
Defence, Imperial, What is? (P. H. Colomb) National, 24: 404.
— National, Chesney on. Eng. R. 17: 142.
Defendant Speaks, The; a story. (G. H. Rosenfeld) Lippinc. 55: 561.
Deficit, One Way to avoid. (J. E. Klock) Am. J. Pol. 2: 305.
Definitions wanted, Moral. (J. McCann) Theo. Mo. 3: 308. 4: 113.
Defoe, Daniel. (M. O. W. Oliphant) Cent. 24: 740. — (H. M. Stephens) Book R. 3: 303.
— Academy for Women. (E. Fairbairn) Time, 21: 508.
— and Malthus. Soc. Econ. 7: 203.
— Apparition of Mrs. Veal. (G. A. Aitkin) 19th Cent. 37: 95.
— Autograph Manuscript in British Museum. (K. D. Bülbring) Acad. 46: 280.
— Discourse on. Spec. 74: 21.
— in Trouble, 1703. (G. A. Aitken) Ath. '94, 2: 862.
— Life of, Wright's. Ath. '94, 2: 521. — Sat. R. 78: 485. — (J. R. Smith) Dial (Ch.) 19: 14.
— Political Career of. (H. Harrison) Univ. R. 8: 425.
— Robinson Crusoe, Illustrated Editions of. (G. S. Layard) Bibliographica, 2: 181.
— — New Illustrated Edition. (M. H. Spielmann) M. of Art, 15: 47.
Deformities and Monstrosities, Artificial Production of. (A. Stockwell) Canad. M. 3: 208.
Defregger, Franz. (H. Zimmern) M. of Art, 9: 183.
Degas, Hilaire G. E. (G. Moore) M. of Art, 13: 416. — (T. Duret) Art J. 46: 204.
Degeneracy, A Study in Youthful. (G. E. Dawson) Pedagog. Sem. 4: 221.
Degenerates, Literary. (J. E. Hogarth) Fortn. 63: 586.
— Society's Protection against the. (M. Nordau) Forum, 19: 532.
Degeneration: are we degenerating? (C. L. Dana) Forum, 19: 458. *See* Nordau, Max.
Degrees, Honorary, Conferred upon Artists. (M. H. Spielmann) M. of Art, 14: 334.
— in Pedagogy, Higher Academic. (S. G. Williams) Educa. R. 7: 180.
— University, Present System of. (F. S. Thomas) Educa. 13: 530, 611.
De Groot, Henry. (F. E. Birge) Overland, n. s. 22: 261.
De Haven, Frank. (E. M. Bacon) Q. Illust. 2: 143.
Deir el Bahari, Temple at. Am. Arch. 44: 51.
— Naville on. Sat. R. 79: 451.
Dejection, English. Spec. 71: 460.
De Kay, Charles, Dinner to. Critic, 25: 162.
Delacroix, Eugéne, et les peintres de l'école Anglaise. (C. Yriarte) 19th Cent. 38: 947.
Deland, M., with portrait. Bk. Buyer, 5: 387. — With portrait. Bk. News, 7: 180. — Critic, 25: 334.
Delaware Indian, The, as an Artist. (C. C. Abbott) Pop. Sci. Mo. 41: 586.
Delaware River and Harbor of Philadelphia, Improvement of. (J. Birkinbine) Engin. M. 9: 839.
— Along the. (M. White, jr.) Munsey, 9: 382.
Delaware River Channel, Improvement of. (W. Atlee) J. Frankl. Inst. 142: 401.
Delaware State Society of the Cincinnati. (H. H. Bellas) Am. Hist. Reg. 1: 203-301.
Deldir, Alina; Strange Story of an Indian Princess. Chamb. J. 71: 29.
Delepierre, Octave. (H. S. Ashbee) Bookworm, 4: 9.
Delhi, Days in. All the Year, 75: 6.
Deli, in Sumatra. (R. W. E. Eastwick) Fortn. 60: 634.
Delicacy, False. (P. W. Roose) Argosy, 61: 284.
— True and False. (W. Mathews) No. Am. 158: 507.
Delicate Affair. (G. King) Cent. 46: 884.
Delitzsch, Franz. (D. Kaufmann) Jew. Q. 2: 386.
Della Cruscanism in America. (J. L. Onderdonk) Am. Hist. Reg. 1: 446.
Delormais, Père. (C. W. Wood) Argosy, 61: 554.
Delorme, Philibert. (A. M. F. Robinson) M. of Art, 8: 506.
Delphi. (R. Lister) 19th Cent. 37: 241. Same art. Ecl. M. 124: 807.
— Excavations at. Am. Arch. 47: 45. 49: 15.
— Music from, Fragments of. Sat. R. 77: 549.
Delpit, Albert. (S. P. Oliver) Ath. '93, 1: 87.
Delsarte Theory, The. (Margaret Fleming) Munsey, 9: 32.
De Luce, Percival. (C. Cook) Mo. Illust. 3: 183.
Deluge, The. Spec. 75: 929.
— Ancient Monumental Records of. (R. M. Ryan) Cath. World, 61: 223.
— Chaldean Account of. (W. Muss-Arnolt) Bib. World, 3: 109.
— Hebrew Stories of. (W. R. Harper) Bib. World, 4: 20.
— in Other Literatures. (W. R. Harper) Bib. World, 4: 114.
— Prestwich on some Supposed New Evidence of. (G. F. Wright) Bib. Sac. 52: 724.
— Scientific Evidence of. (F. R. Wegg-Prosser) Dub. R. 117: 396.

Deluge, The, Geologies and. (W. T. Sollas) Nature, 50: 505. Same art. Pop. Sci. Mo. 46: 245.
Demagogues. (G. A. Townsend) Chaut. 17: 308.
Demagogy, Science of. (T. N. Carver) Am. J. Pol. 2: 271.
Demand and Supply. (J. R. Commons and Geo. Gunton) Soc. Econ. 4: 277.
Demavend, Mount, Ascent of. (E. G. Duff) Geog. J. 1: 149.
Demerara, Up a Creek in. Cornh. 66: 592. Same art. Ecl. M. 120: 186. Same art. Liv. Age, 196: 688.
Demeter in Art. (J. E. Harrison) M. of Art, 6: 145.
Democracies, Greek and American. (D. H. Wheeler) Chaut. 16: 18-276.
Democracy, American, Dominant Note of. (F. N. Thorpe) Harper, 93: 838.
— and Character. (E. H. Delk) Luth. Q. 24: 231.
— and Despotism. (A. Moses) Am. M. Civics, 9: 261.
— and Education. (N. M. Butler) Educa. R. 12: 120. — (W. H. Shaw) Citizen, 1: 35. — Dial (Ch.) 14: 351.
— and English Universities. (J. King) Contemp. 62: 692.
— and Leadership. Fortn. 66: 869.
— and Liberty, Lecky's. Ed. R. 183: 516. — Sat. R. 81: 400. — (C. R. Henderson) Dial (Ch.) 21: 143. — Church Q. 43: 132. — (J. A. Hamilton) Acad. 49: 357. — (W. G. P. Smith) Eng. Hist. R. 11: 531. — Liv. Age, 209: 643. — (A. L. Lowell) Am. Hist. R. 2: 153. — (A. G. Sedgwick) Nation, 62: 380. — (J. Morley) 19th Cent. 39: 697. Same art. Ecl. M. 127: 40.
— and Literature. (J. Burroughs) Outl. 51: 266.
— and the Poet. (N. P. Gilman) New World, 3: 311.
— and Progress. (Frank H. Hill) Univ. R. 6: 1.
— and Religion. (J. H. Crooker) New World, 4: 264.
— and Socialism. Bach. of Arts, 3: 454.
— and Subsidizing. (A. A. Baumann) Sat. R. 79: 784.
— at Home. (J. W. Breslin) Westm. 144: 62.
— Christian, An Object Lesson in. Liv. Age, 208: 490.
— Destinies of. (F. H. Giddings) Pol. Sci. Q. 11: 716.
— Disabilities of. (W. E. Hodgson) National, 20: 607.
— English, White's. Sat. R. 78: 22.
— Ethics of; Liberty. (F. J. Stimson) Scrib. M. 15: 648.
— False. (W. S. Lilly) 19th Cent. 33: 4.
— Godkin's Problems of. (W. R. Thayer) Nation, 63: 349.
— Guizot on. Eng. R. 13: 316.
— in America. (F. N. Thorpe) Atlan. 72: 814.
— — Checks on. (G. W. Smalley) 19th Cent. 35: 873. Same art. Ecl. M. 123: 162.
— Modern, Rise of. Spec. 73: 20.
— not Ideal. Sat. R. 79: 339.
— The Opportunity of. (W. H. Robinson) Westm. 144: 117. Same art. Ecl. M. 125: 467.
— Past and Present. (Theo. Cox) Soc. Econ. 3: 237.
— Possibilities of. (F. W. Grey) Westm. 137: 627. Same art. Ecl. M. 119: 191.
— Primitive, in British Trade Unionism. (S. & B. Webb) Pol. Sci. Q. 11: 307.
— Pure, Bed Rock of. (A. C. Houston) Arena, 6: 53.
— Pure, *vs.* Governmental Favoritism. (B. O. Flower) Arena, 8: 260.
— Real Problems of. (E. L. Godkin) Atlan. 78: 1.
Democratic Administration, Blunders of. (S. M. Cullom) Forum, 21: 713.
— A Year of. (W. E. Russell) Forum, 17: 257. — (S. M. Cullom) Forum, 17: 268.
Democratic Congress, Financial Danger from. (O. Ottendorfer) Forum, 15: 247.
Democratic Ideals. (W. Barry) 19th Cent. 35: 717. — (J. W. Kennedy) Westm. 144: 313.
Democratic Movement. Soc. Econ. 2: 263.
Democratic Opportunity, The Great. (S. Low) Forum, 15: 242.
Democratic Party, The Crisis of the; A Campaign for a Principle. (W. L. Wilson) Forum, 13: 158.
— Jefferson and his Party to-day. (W. E. Russell) Forum, 21: 513.
— Convention at Chicago, 1896. Pub. Opin. 21: 69.
— National, Convention of, at Indianapolis, 1896. Pub. Opin. 31: 325.
— — Rise of. (E. G. Dunnell) R. of Rs. (N. Y.) 14: 434.
— Platforms of, 1892. (J. S. Morrill) No. Am. 155: 268. — (R. Ogden) Nation, 54: 480.
— Promises of: have they been fulfilled? (F. W. Blackmar) Forum, 21: 425.
Democratic Theory and Practice. (W. L. Garrison, jr.) Open Court, 1: 316.
Democratization of England. (T. Davidson) Forum, 21: 460.
Democrats, Single Chamber. (R. Wallace) 19th Cent. 37: 177. Same art. Liv. Age, 204: 556.
Demon of Consumption: Cherokee Legend. (J. W. Terrell) J. Am. Folk-Lore, 5: 125.
Demon Leg, The. Blackw. 155: 686.
Demon-worship in Southern India. (Dr. Bulwer) J. Am. Folk-Lore, 7: 156.
Demon Possession and Mediumship. (W. R. Newbold) Pop. Sci. Mo. 50: 220.
— in Angola, Africa. J. Am. Folk-Lore, 6: 258.
— Modern Instances of. (E. P. Evans) Pop. Sci. Mo. 42: 159.
Demonology, Christian. (F. C. Conybeare) Jew. Q. 9: 59.
— — Influence of Ancient Greece upon. (P. Carus) Open Court, 10: 4867.
— — Northern Contributions to. (P. Carus) Open Court, 10: 4875.
— of New Testament. (F. C. Conybeare) Jew. Q. 8: 576.
Demont-Breton; a Painter of Motherhood. (L. Bacon) Cent. 31: 210.
Demorest, W. Jennings. A Character Sketch, with portrait. Our Day, 15: 9.
Demos's Maiden Aunt. (G. Allen) Univ. R. 6: 198.
Demurrer: Is it a Personal Affront? (C. Patteson) Green Bag, 7: 136.
Den of the Gray Wolf, The; a story. (C. G. D. Roberts) Cosmopol. 17: 360.
Denbigh, Rudolf, 8th Earl of. Month, 75: 1.
Denck, Hans. (R. Heath) Contemp. 62: 880. Same art. Liv. Age, 196: 615.
Dendrites. (S. Meunier) Pop. Sci. Mo. 41: 84.
Dendrolene as an Insecticide. (J. Troop) Garden & F. 9: 488.
Deneholes. (M. Christy) Reliquary, 35: 65. — (J. G. Waller) Reliquary, 36: 36.
Denison, Gen. Daniel. Autobiography. N. E. Reg. 46: 127.
Denison, Pedigree of. (J. L. Glascock) N. E. Reg. 46: 352.
Denman, Thomas, Lord. Appointment as Chief Justice. (S. H. Boult) Gent. M. n. s. 51: 606.
Denmark, Archæology in. (F. Starr) Pop. Sci. Mo. 47: 12.
— The Dane at Home. Cornh. 73: 154. Same art. Liv. Age, 208: 554.
— Kings of, Burial-place of. All the Year, 72: 588.
— An Old Page of History (12th century). Macmil. 74: 353.
— Peasant Wedding in. (M. H. Petersen) Chaut. 23: 753.
— Royal Family of. (T. Schwartz) Munsey, 9: 640.

Denmark under Bismarck's Frown. (J. H. Wisby) Soc. Econ. 6: 103.
Dennie, Joseph. (S. A. Bent) New Eng. M. n. s. 14: 666.
Dennis, John. Bookworm, 2: 145. 4: 289, 352.
Dennis, Robert, of Portsmouth, R. I., Descendants of. (O. M. Humphrey) N. E. Reg. 49: 441.
Denny, W. H., with portrait. Theatre, 28: 144.
Denominational School, Passing of the. (A. C. Hill) School R. 4: 158.
Denominational Schools in England. Can they obtain Help out of the Rates? Church Q. 37: 1.
Denominationalism and Sectarianism. (P. Schaff) Chr. Lit. 10: 144.
Denominations, Disturbed Feeling in. (W. H. Wynn) Luth. Q. 23: 551.
— Stability of the Great. (H. K. Carroll) Forum, 17: 62.
Dentistry, Mechanics of. (J. E. Sweet) Cassier, 3: 60.
— Shall it be taught as Medicine? (T. Fillebrown) Harv. Grad. M. 4: 214.
Denton, Dr. William, 1605–91. (M. M. Verney) Longm. 24: 364. Same art. Liv. Age, 202: 734.
Denudation, Catastrophic. (G. A. Lebour) Ath. '92, 2: 134.
Denver, Col. (T. Tonge) New Eng. M. n. s. 7: 251.
— and its Capitol. (J. Ralph) Harper, 86: 935.
Denza, F. Nature, 51: 179.
Department Store. Economic Aspect of Large Trading. Gunton's M. 10: 263.
Departure from Tradition. (R. Masson) Chamb. J. 72: 524–536. Same art. Liv. Age, 207: 15.
Departures in Life. (J. Watson) Sund. M. 25: 5.
Dependencies, Government of, Lewis on. Spec. 68: 174.
Depew, Chauncey Mitchell. (F. Morris) Chaut. 20: 694.
— Columbian Oration at Chicago, 1892. Spec. 69: 585.
— Home of. (M. Sheridan) Munsey, 6: 408.
DePeyster, Gen. J. Watts, portrait of. Bk. Buyer, 13: 519.
Deplorable Affair, A; a story. (W. E. Norris) Eng. Illust. 9: 520–784.
Deposits. Bank. M. (N. Y.) 49: 258.
— Ownership of. Bank. M. (N. Y.) 47: 682.
— Public, and the Banks. Bank. M. (N. Y.) 46: 1.
— Special. Bank. M. (N. Y.) 47: 619.
— Unclaimed. Bank. M. (Lond.) 59: 1.
Depravity, Total, and Soteriology. (N. M. Steffens) Presb. & Ref. R. 7: 303.
Depreciation, 18th Century Record of the Evils of. Q. J. Econ. 10: 240.
Depth, Relation of Accommodation and Convergence to our Sense of. (E. T. Dixon) Mind, 20: 195.
De Quincey, Thomas. How he wrote. Sat. R. 79: 246.
— in Glasgow. (Colin Rae-Brown) Univ. R. 5: 393.
— Thoughts on. Time, 17: 447.
Derby, Edw. G. S., 14th Earl of, Saintsbury's. Sat. R. 73: 604. — Spec. 69: 131.
Derby, Edward H. S., 15th Earl of. Spec. 70: 561. — Sat. R. 75: 447.
— Speeches and Addresses. Ed. R. 179: 201. — Sat. R. 77: 544. — (H. Tattersall) Acad. 46: 503.
Derby, George H. (Mrs. Launt Thompson) Un. Serv. (Phila.) 7: 239.
Derby, Eng., Museum and Art Gallery. (H. M. Cundall) Art J. 44: 123.
— Printers and Booksellers of, in the 18th Century. (J. P. Briscoe) Bookworm, 5: 89.
Derby Race-course. (R. H. Davis) Harper, 87: 251.
Derbyshire, England. In the Peak Country. All the Year, 71: 269.
Derelict; a story. (M. Pechell) Belgra. 90: 66.
Dereliction of the El Dorado; a story. (E. Carlton) Eng. Illust. 11: 1079.
Derenbourg, Joseph. (A. Neubauer) Jew. Q. 8: 189.
Derring do, Derring-do. (J. A. H. Murray) Nation, 61: 238.
Derringforth. (F. A. Munsey) Munsey, 10: 393–631. 11: 70–386.
Derry, Siege of, 1689, Dwyer's. Sat. R. 76: 17.
Derthick, Wilber M., and his Musical Clubs. (J. S. Van Cleve) Music, 6: 257.
Dervish Frontier, On the. 19th Cent. 40: 580. Same art. Liv. Age, 211: 523.
Derwentwater, James, Earl of. (Mrs. E. M. Davy) Belgra. 78: 173. Same art. Liv. Age, 194: 437.
Descartes, R., and his Works. (C. S. Peirce) Nation, 59: 476.
Descendant of the Doges; a story. (H. L. Bradley) Atlan. 69: 197.
Descent of Isaac Russ; a story. (F. M. Bicknell) Outing, 24: 243.
Deschamps, Louis. (P. G. Hamerton) Scrib. M. 16: 562.
Deschard of Oneaka; a story. (L. Becke) Eng. Illust. 14: 599.
Desclée, Aimée. Sat. R. 79: 472.
Desdemony; a story. (H. Musgrave) Liv. Age, 192: 331.
Desert, Californian, A Glimpse of. (W. W. Price) Overland, n. s. 19: 73.
— The Fringe of the. (D. G. Hogarth) Cornh. 74: 346.
— Great American. (W. F. G. Shanks) Lippinc. 49: 735.
— Great Persian, March through. (C. E. Biddulph) Liv. Age, 192: 57.
— Perils and Wonders of a True. (D. D. Gaillard) Cosmopol. 21: 592.
Desert Claim. (M. E. Stickney) Lippinc. 53: 291.
Deserts, North American. (Dr. J. Walther) Nat. Geog. M. 4: 163.
— Steppes, and Alkali Lands. (E. W. Hilgard) Pop. Sci. Mo. 48: 602.
Deserted Cottage. (M. B. Sanford) Eng. Illust. 11: 1051.
Deserted Kingdom; a story. (F. F. Brumback) Outing, 21: 282.
Desertion; its Causes and Prevention. Un. Serv. M. 5: 198. — (J. P. Finley) Un. Serv. (Phila.) 12: 330, 420.
Design. (W. Crane) M. of Art, 16: 79, 131.
— in its Dawn. Reliquary, 33: 171.
— Influence of Architectural Style upon. (W. Crane) M. of Art, 19: 129, 191.
Desire and Aversion, The Feeling-tone of. (H. Sedgwick) Mind, 17: 94, 400.
— Interest and Emotion. (S. F. M'Lennan) Psychol. R. 2: 462.
Desmond's Wake, The; a poem. (E. Lees) Temp. Bar, 103: 46.
De Soto, Camps of, in the Chickasaw Country, 1540–41. (T. H. Lewis) Nat'l M. (N. Y. '91) 15: 57[illegible]
Despard, Col. Marcus. (Rev. H. S. Fagan) Time, 21: 50.
Desuetude, as a Plea. (W. C. Smith) Jurid. R. 7: 173.
De Tabley, Geo. W., Lord. Acad. 48: 459. — (T. Watts) Ath. '95, 2: 754. — (M. E. Grant-Duff) Spec. 75: 818. — (E. Gosse) Contemp. 69: 84. Same art. Liv. Age, 208: 346.
— Poetry of. (C. Monkhouse) Acad. 47: 291. — (R. Le Gallienne) 19th Cent. 33: 899. — Ath. '93, 1: 497. — Sat. R. 75: 521. — Spec. 70: 776.
Détaille, Edouard, and his Work. (C. S. Johnson) Munsey, 8: 369.
Detective who failed. (J. Hudson) Belgra. 87: 64.
Detective Stories Gone Wrong; a story. (Luke Sharp) Idler, 1: 413.
Determined Young Person, A. (W. P. Ridge) Idler, 8: 33.

Determinism and Free Will. (P. Carus) Open Court, 2: 887. — Church Q. 35: 416.
— Ethical Implications of. (E. Ritchie) Philos. R. 2: 529. — (J. H. Gulliver and E. Ritchie) Philos. R. 3: 62.
— *vs.* Indeterminism. (G. von Gizycki) Open Court, 1: 729, 758.
Detroit, Mich., Early Social Life in. (R. R. Elliott) Cath. World, 59: 47.
— Gardening as a Means of Poor Relief in. (B. O. Flower) Arena, 15: 545. — (H. S. Pingree) Our Day, 14: 254.
— Hull's Surrender of, 1812. (S. C. Clarke) M. Am. Hist. 27: 343.
Detroit Art School. (H. E. Keep) Mo. Illust. 3: 243.
Deuce, Derivation of. (F. Chance) Acad. 41: 15. — (A. L. Mayhew) Acad. 41: 111, (F. Chance) 159, (D. S. Evans) 184.
Deuchar, David, with portrait. Bank. M. (Lond.) 53: 849.
Deutzias, Cultural Notes on. Garden & F. 9: 284.
Development, Deviation in, due to the Use of Unripe Seeds. (J. C. Arthur) Am. Natural. 29: 804, 904.
— Effect of External Conditions upon. (A. Weismann) Nature, 50: 31.
— Evolution and. (S. W. Dyde) Philos. R. 4: 1.
— Goethe and. (C. Thomas) Open Court, 2: 815, 847.
Development of Furlani, The; a story. (W. L. Alden) Idler, 9: 688.
De Vere, Aubrey. Cent. 26: 903.
— Mediæval Records and Sonnets. Spec. 72: 14.
— Recollections of. (A. de Vere) Cent. 26: 760, 904.
De Veres, Poetry of the. Quar. 183: 310. Same art. Liv. Age, 210: 67.
Deverell, Robert, a Mad Writer. (H. B. Wheatley) Bookworm, 1: 44.
Devil, The. (C. C. Everett) New World, 4: 1.
— De'il in Carglen. (A. Gordon) Gent. M. n. s. 51: 166.
— in Folk-Lore. (R. Bruce Boswell) Gent. M. n. s. 57: 472.
— the Prince of this World. (J. T. Gladhill) Luth. Q. 23: 402.
— Rôle of, in the Ancient Coptic Religion. (E. Amelineau) New World, 2: 518.
— Youthful Views of the. Ecl. M. 127: 742.
Devil inspires the Monk; a story. (L. T. Damon) Poet-Lore, 7: 301.
Devil-Bush of West Africa. J. Am. Folk-Lore, 9: 220.
Devil Conception in Protestant Countries. Open Court, 10: 4930.
Devil Contracts. Open Court, 10: 4961.
Devil Dance of Hemis. All the Year, 75: 510.
Devil-hunting in Elizabethan England. (T. G. Law) 19th Cent. 35: 397.
Devil-lore, Iroquois. (DeCost Smith) J. Am. Folk-Lore, 1: 184.
Devil Worship. (P. Carus) Am. Antiq. 18: 95.
Devil's Article, The; a story. (J. A. Lockwood) Overland, n. s. 28: 29.
Devil's Half Acre; a tale. (F. H. Holland) Canad. M. 1: 603.
Devil's One Good Deed. (E. R. Chesterman) Lippinc. 58: 275.
Devil's Own, The; a story. (L. C. Davidson) Temp. Bar, 98: 554. Same art. Liv. Age, 199: 271.
Devil's Tower, Wyoming, A Journey to. (T. Moran) Cent. 25: 450.
Devon, Clerical and Social Life in, in 1287. (Bishop of Clifton) Dub. R. 116: 1.
— North. (S. Wade) So. M. 1: 420.
— The Pleasant Land of. Quar. 178: 414.
— Red Cliffs of. Spec. 76: 49.
Devon, Shooting on the Yellow Clay Moors. Macmil. 73: 427.
Devonian Fossils in Strata of Carboniferous Age. (H. S. Williams) Am. J. Sci. 149: 94.
Devonian Rocks in California, Discovery of. (J. S. Diller and C. Schuchert) Am. J. Sci. 147: 416.
Devonian System of Eastern Pennsylvania. (C. S. Prosser) Am. J. Sci. 144: 210.
Devonshire, Duke of, Dalmeny and. (T. H. S. Escott) New R. 11: 256.
Devonshire, Dialect of, Hewett's. Sat. R. 74: 52.
— Pilgrim in. (A. Brown) Atlan. 72: 617.
— Rivers of. (J. L. W. Page) Portfo. 24: 4-73.
Devotee, A. (Mary Cholmondeley) Temp. Bar, 108: 465-109: 145.
Devotion of Enriquez. (B. Harte) Cent. 29: 37.
Dew, J. Harvie, with portrait. Nat'l M. (N. Y. '91) 16: 220.
Dew and Frost. (R. Russell) Nature, 47: 210.
Dewar, James, Chemical Researches of. (H. J. W. Dan) McClure, 1: 524.
Dewey Decimal Classification and International Catalogue of Science. (W. E. Hoyle) Nat. Sci. 9: 43. — (A. G. S. Josephson) Science, n. s. 4: 315.
— Difficulties in. (W. L. R. Gifford) Lib. J. 21: 494.
Dewing, Thos. Wilder, with portrait. (R. Cortissoz) Harper, 91: 167.
DeWint, Peter, and David Cox, Redgrave's. (J. Orrock) M. of Art, 14: 379.
Dextrine and Gum Arabic, Molecular Masses of. (C. E. Linebarger) Am. J. Sci. 143: 426.
Deyster, Louis and Anna. (L. E. Baxter) M. of Art, 10: 78.
Dhofar, the Land of Frankincense and Myrrh. (J. T. Bent) 19th Cent. 38: 595. Same art. Liv. Age, 207: 342.
Dhuleep Singh, Maharajah. Spec. 71: 575.
Diabolism in Spain. (H. C. Lea) J. Am. Folk-Lore, 3: 33.
Dial-Bearing Runes. Reliquary, 32: 65.
Dial, The, Score of Volumes of. Dial (Ch.) 20: 347.
Dialect in Literature. (J. W. Riley) Forum, 14: 465.
— Lingo in Literature. (W. C. Elam) Lippinc. 55: 286.
— Nuisance of. (W. B. Chisholm; M. A. Denison) Writer, 7: 49, 55.
— Plea for. (A. M. Jackson) Writer, 7: 27.
— Use and Abuse of. Dial (Ch.) 18: 67.
— Value of. (A. Wauchope) No. Am. 158: 640.
Dialect Dictionary, The. (E. H. Babbitt) Nation, 60: 201.
Diamond, Artificial Reproduction of. (L. Dex) Chaut. 18: 53.
— in the Cañon Diablo Meteoric Iron. (G. F. Kunz and O. W. Huntington) Am. J. Sci. 146: 470.
— Pitt or Regent. (V. Ball) Ath. '93, 1: 672.
— — Napoleon and. (C. S. Pratt) Lippinc. 56: 373.
Diamond Fields, South African, Story of. (J. Reid) Good Words, 34: 613.
Diamond Industry at Kimberley. (R. Churchill) Pop. Sci. Mo. 41: 455.
Diamond Mine, Puzzles from a. Chamb. J. 70: 310.
Diamond Necklace, The. Argosy, 53: 281.
Diamonds. (S. Brentworth) Chaut. 23: 629. — Chamb. J. 71: 369.
— and Gold; Anglo-Saxon Supremacy in South Africa, 1814–94. (F. I. Ricarde-Seaver) New Sci. R. 1: 11.
— Curiosities of. (H. J. Gibbons) Gent. M. n. s. 52: 243.
Diana: the History of a Great Mistake; a story. Blackw. 151: 180—152: 62.
Diana Tempest. (M. Cholmondeley) Temp. Bar, 97: 1—99: 449.

Diane de Poitiers. (A. M. F. Robinson) M. of Art, 9: 157.
Diaries and Diarists. All the Year, 72: 6.
Diary, Keeping a. Spec. 68: 525.
— Leaves from a. (P. Fitzgerald) Gent. M. n. s. 48: 35. 49: 473.
Diary of a Nervous Invalid. (E. L. Bynner) Atlan. 71: 33.
Diary of an Idle Doctor. Blackw. 153: 734. 154: 706. Same art. Ecl. M. 121: 821.
Diaspora in Egypt. (P. Hay-Hunter) Thinker, 9: 104.
Diatessaron, The; a reply. (J. R. Harris) Chr. Lit. 13: 268. *See* Tatian.
Diatoms, Classification of. (C. J. Elmore) Am. Natural. 30: 520.
— What are they? (E. L. Gregory) Pop. Sci. Mo. 41: 200.
Diaz, Narcisse Virgile, the Painter. (R. Cortissoz) Cent. 30: 3. — (D. C. Thomson) M. of Art, 12: 181, 231.
Diaz, Porfirio, with portraits. (H. W. Allen) R. of Rs. (N. Y.) 6: 677. — (G. Parker) Sat. R. 80: 168.
Dibbs, Sir George, with portrait. (J. T. Ryan) R. of Rs. (N. Y.) 10: 174.
Dice and Dolasses. Chamb. J. 72: 811.
Dick. (G. G. Bain) Lippinc. 53: 271.
Dick Stanesby's Hutkeeper; a story. (M. Gaunt) Eng. Illust. 10: 294, 363.
Dickens, C., with portraits. (A. D. Hurd) Munsey, 10: 647.
— and his Less Familiar Portraits. (F. G. Kifton) M. of Art, 11: 284, 321.
— and Thackeray. Eng. R. 10: 257.
— Barnaby Rudge, Reprint of First Edition. Spec. 69: 791.
— Boz-land. (P. Fitzgerald) Gent. M. n. s. 53: 447.
— Characters of. Bookworm, 3: 5.
— Christmas Books of. (C. Dickens, jr.) Good Words, 36: Xmas no., 52.
— Estimate of Wilkie Collins. (F. T. Marzials) Acad. 42: 304.
— First Editions of. (C. P. Johnson) Bookworm, 1: 81, 132.
— Following, with Camera. (H. H. Ragan) Outing, 23: 296.
— Further Travels in Boz-land. (P. Fitzgerald) Gent. M. n. s. 24: 116.
— A Girl's Recollections of. (E. W. Latimer) Lippinc. 52: 338.
— Glimpses of. (C. Dickens, jr.) No. Am. 160: 525, 677.
— How long will he hold his place? Spec. 69: 950.
— Illustrations to. Bookworm, 2: 345.
— in America. (F. M. Holland) Open Court, 9: 4580.
— In the Footsteps of. (H. H. Ragan) Cosmopol. 15: 3.
— in London. Bookworm, 2: 305.
— in Yorkshire. Ath. '94, 1: 83, 180.
— Pickwick Papers, First Edition of, Reprint of. Spec. 68: 677.
— — Topography of. (C. Dickens, jr.) Eng. Illust. 10: 186.
— Place of, in Literature. (F. Harrison) Forum, 18: 543.
— Pyrcroft House of "Oliver Twist." (P. Fitzgerald) M. of Art, 18: 432.
— Sam Weller and the Irony of the Streets. Spec. 71: 139.
— Thackeray, and Scott: Are they Obsolete? (W. H. Mallock) Forum, 14: 503.
— Tramp in Dickens Land, Hughes'. Spec. 68: 93.
— With, in Hertfordshire. (F. G. Kitton) Good Words, 37: 175.
Dickens, Charles, the Younger. Acad. 50: 66. — Ath. '96, 2: 130.
— Portrait of. Bk. Buyer, 13: 459.
Dickens Curios. (P. Fitzgerald) Gent. M. n. s. 52: 443.
Dickinson, Andrew Glassell. Nat'l M. (N. Y., '91) 16: 468.
Dickinson, Emily. Bk. Buyer, 9: 157. — With portrait. Bk. Buyer, 11: 485. — Bk. News, 13: 267.
— Letters. (M. L. Todd) Bach. of Arts, 1: 39. — (L. J. Block) Dial (Ch.) 18: 146. — Nation, 59: 446.
— Poems. Atlan. 69: 143.
Dickinson, John, and the Pennsylvania Constitution of 1776. (P. L. Ford) Nation, 57: 6.
Dick's Christmas Presents. (J. M. Fenners) Bach. of Arts, 2: 13.
Dicksee, Frank. (S. Hodges) M. of Art, 10: 217.
— Illustrations to Romeo and Juliet. M. of Art, 8: 82.
Dickson, Teamster. (M. Eyre) Longm. 21: 627. Same art. Liv. Age, 197: 571.
Dicky; a story. (L. Wyndham) Canad. M. 2: 89.
Dictator, The; a story. Ecl. M. 120: 133.
Dictionaries. Bookworm, 3: 49. — Gent. M. n. s. 49: 639.
— American. (T. Stanton) Westm. 139: 610.
Did he remember? a story. (J. L. Hornibrook) Temp. Bar, 109: 481.
Diderot, Denis. (J. Forster) Time, 15: 542.
Die, When to. (A. E. Ireland) Gent. M. n. s. 50: 627.
Dielman, Frederick. (A. Trumble) Mo. Illust. 5: 131.
Diet. (S. R. Elliott) New Eng. M. n. s. 8: 672.
— for Cold Weather, The Proper. (N. E. Yorke-Davies) Gent. M. n. s. 48: 140.
— for Hot Weather, Proper. (N. E. Yorke-Davies) Gent. M. n. s. 48: 517. Same art. Pop. Sci. Mo. 41: 365.
— Humanities of. (H. S. Salt) Fortn. 66: 426. Same art. Un. Serv. (Phila.) 16: 362.
Dietary for the Sick. (D. Duckworth) Pop. Sci. Mo. 43: 111.
Differentiation, The Logic of. (H. A. Clarke) Open Court, 5: 2837.
Difficult Choice, A; a story. Belgra. 77: 264.
Diffraction Gratings, Study of. (A. Cornu) Astron. 13: 207.
Diffusion, Problem of. (J. Jacobs and A. Nutt) Folk-Lore, 5: 129.
Digby, Sir Everard. Sat. R. 82: 399.
— Character of. (R. C. Browne) Acad. 49: 89.
Digestion. How Food is digested. (T. G. Allen) Chaut. 22: 708.
— in Plants. (J. Pentland-Smith) Knowl. 18: 171.
Digests of Cases. (J. D. White) Law Q. 12: 230.
Digger Indians. (Will. S. Green) Overland, n. s. 25: 282. — (M. L. Miller) Pop. Sci. Mo. 50: 201.
— Among the Diggers of Thirty Years Ago. (H. M. Carpenter) Overland, n. s. 21: 146, 389.
Dignity, Continental Sense of. Spec. 71: 832.
Dike, Newly Discovered, at DeWitt, near Syracuse, N. Y. (N. H. Darton and J. F. Kemp) Am. J. Sci. 149: 456.
Dikes, Complementary Rocks and Radial. (L. V. Pirsson) Am. J. Sci. 150: 116.
Dikkon's Dog; a story. (D. Lundt) McClure, 4: 31.
Dilettanteism in Literature. (P. Carus) Open Court, 3: 1708.
Dilîp Sinh. (F. Hall) Nation, 57: 390, 429.
Dilke, Sir Chas. Problems of Greater Britain. (Frank H. Hill) Univ. R. 6: 312.
Dillman, August. (T. W. Davies) Chr. Lit. 12: 262. 13: 76. — (G. L. Robinson) Bib. World, 4: 244. — (T. K. Cheyne) Acad. 46: 33.

Dillon, Chas., Reminiscence of. (H. Lowther) Time, 8: 213.
Dillon, John Forrest. (L. A. Bond) Nat'l M. (N. Y., '91) 15: 286.
Dime Social, A; a Western sketch. All the Year, 71: 110.
Dimensions, Physical, Electrostatic and Electromagnetic Systems of. (A. W. Rücker) Nature, 49: 387.
Diminishing Returns, Law of, Origin of, 1813–15. (E. Cannan) Econ. J. 2: 53.
Dinan and Brittany; Old Friends with New Faces. Good Words, 35: 117.
Dinichthyids, Relations of Certain Body-plates in. (C. R. Eastman) Am. J. Sci. 152: 46.
Dinictis, Two New Species of, from White River Beds. (G. I. Adams) Am. Natural. 29: 573.
Dining, Art of. (A. Kenney-Herbert) 19th Cent. 32: 203. Same art. Ecl. M. 119: 494.
Dining-room, A French. (Fernand Mazade) Archit. Rec. 5: 35.
Dinner, Derivation of. (F. Chance) Acad. 46: 50, 87.
— Ordering. Spec. 77: 142.
Dinner-hour, The. All the Year, 72: 473.
Dinner Parties, Large or Small? (G. von Beaulieu) Chaut. 23: 93.
Dinner Party, Ethics of a. (Lady Magnus) Good Words, 34: 341.
Dinner-table, Æsthetics of the. (A. K. Herbert) National, 28: 205. Same art. Ecl. M. 127: 683. Same art. Liv. Age, 211: 549.
Dinners and Diners. (Lady Jeune) No. Am. 158: 41.
— Free, for School Children. (J. L. Davies) Educa. R. 3: 61. — (H. C. Bourne) Macmil. 65: 186.
— Imperial. All the Year, 72: 295. 73: 151.
— Public, in London. (C. Dickens) No. Am. 159: 601.
— Stories of. All the Year, 71: 535.
Dinnshenchas, Bodleian. (W. Stokes) Folk-Lore, 3: 467.
— of Edinburgh. (W. Stokes) Folk-Lore, 4: 471.
Dinosaur Tracks, Three-toed, in the Newark Group at Avondale, N. J. (J. B. Woodworth) Am. J. Sci. 150: 481.
Dinosaurian Reptiles, Affinities and Classification of. (O. C. Marsh) Am. J. Sci. 150: 483.
— Horned, and Laramie Mammals, Where to find. (J. B. Hatcher) Am. Natural. 30: 112.
— Recent Restorations of. (R. Lydekker) Nature, 48: 302.
— Restoration of some European, with Suggestions as to their Place among the Reptilia. (O. C. Marsh) Am. J. Sci. 150: 407.
Dinuzulu, The Case for. (Harriet Colenso and H. R. Fox Bourne) Univ. R. 6: 541.
Diocletian, Edict of, Fragment of, Discovered at Plataia. (T. Mommsen) Am. J. Archæol. 7: 54.
— — New Portion of, from Megalopolis. (W. Loring) J. Hel. Stud. 11: 299.
— Persecution of Christians under. (W. M. Ramsay) Contemp. 70: 435.
Diocletian's Palace at Spalato. (P. Fitzgerald) Gent. M. n. s. 53: 266.
Dionysius, Homer's Hymn to. (A. Lang) M. of Art, 9: 368.
Dionysius of Halicarnassus, On a Legend of the Alban Lake told by. (K. F. Smith) Am. J. Philol. 16: 203.
Diphtheria in London. Spec. 71: 660.
— Inoculation against. Sat. R. 78: 529.
— New Treatment of, by Anti-toxin. (M. A. Ruffer) Nature, 51: 16. — Chamb. J. 71: 785.
— Recent Studies on. Nature, 52: 393.
Diphtheria, Recent Works on, and its Prevention. (J. C. Hoyle) Knowl. 18: 44.
— Spread of. (R. Roose) Fortn. 62: 873.
See Anti-toxin.
Diplacodon, New Species of. (J. B. Hatcher) Am. Natural. 29: 1084.
Diplograptus, Mode of Growth and Development of. (R. Ruedemann) Am. J. Sci. 149: 453.
Diplomacy. Time, 19: 1.
— American. (W. J. Stillman) Nation, 56: 251. 57: 407.
— and the Newspaper. (E. L. Godkin) No. Am. 160: 570.
— in the Time of Machiavelli. (E. Nys) Jurid. R. 5: 133.
— Palmerston Ideal in. (E. M. Chapman) Cent. 29: 541.
— Pleasures of. Spec. 68: 10.
Diplomatic Career, Plea for a. (S. P. Read) Am. J. Pol. 1: 561.
Diplomatic Salaries. (S. Webster) Nation, 57: 241.
Diplomatics, Giry's. (H. C. Lea) Nation, 58: 257.
Diplomats. Spec. 75: 512.
Diptera, Systematic Position of. (A. S. Packard) Science, 22: 199.
— S. W. Williston on. (J. M. Aldrich) Am. Natural. 30: 1053.
Directories in Public Reference Libraries. (R. G. Thwaites) Lib. J. 20: 341.
Dirge of Love; a poem. (M. A. Curtois) Gent. M. n. s. 54: 423.
Dirk, Etymology of. (W. W. Skeat) Acad. 47: 15.
Dirleton Castle. Sat. R. 74: 478.
Disappearance of George Driffell; a story. (J. Payn) Cornh. 73: 419–627.
Disappearance of Mr. Hiram Alldridge. (L. Springfield) Idler, 8: 531.
Disappearance of Mrs. Macquoid. (R. Ramsay) Chamb. J. 73: 769, 794.
Disappearance Syndicate, The; a story. (T. C. Crawford) Cosmopol. 16: 483, 589.
Disappearances of Men, Mysterious. (E. A. Osborne) Chaut. 19: 713.
Disarmament. (J. Simon) Contemp. 65: 609.
— of Civilized Nations. (J. M. Beck) Am. J. Pol. 3: 379.
Disbursement Sheet, The; a story. (W. W. Jacobs) Chamb. J. 73: 445.
Disciples, Church of: What makes a Disciple. (W. F. Black) Chaut. 19: 174.
Discipline. (R. Tellet) Longm. 22: 324. Same art. Liv. Age, 198: 634.
— Decay of. Temp. Bar, 102: 191. Same art. Liv. Age, 202: 49.
— Genesis of. Spec. 68: 491.
— Military. (J. F. Maurice) Un. Serv. M. 5: 59, 133.
— — Distaste for. Spec. 69: 553.
— Unconscious Element in. (H. S. Baker) Educa. 14: 264.
Discount at the Bank of England; Two per Cent. Chamb. J. 72: 321.
Discouragement; poem. (N. H. Dole) Poet-Lore, 4: 396.
Discursiveness. Spec. 73: 435. Same art. Ecl. M. 123: 673.
Disease-species. (C. Creighton) Time, 23: 1028.
Diseases, Infectious; Causation and Immunity. (G. M. Sternberg) Pop. Sci. Mo. 41: 616.
— — Immunity and Cure in. (V. U. Vaughan) Science, 22: 231.
— Strange, and Strange Remedies. Chamb. J. 68: 820.
Disfranchisement, Legal. Atlan. 69: 542.
Dishes, Ceremonial, of England. (Esther Singleton) Cosmopol. 19: 49.

Disinfectants and Disinfection. (D. Bevan) Science, 21: 298.
Disinfection, Maschek on. (G. C. Frankland) Nature, 46: 613.
Dismal Swamp, Great. (A. Hunter) Outing, 27: 70.
— Botany of. (C. L. Pollard) Garden & F. 9: 462.
Dismal Throng, The; a poem. (R. Buchanan) Idler, 3: 606.
Disorder, The Forces of. Macmil. 66: 187.
Dispensary Charity, Abuse of. (J. W. Roosevelt) Char. R. 3: 127.
Disraeli, Benjamin; Place in Literature. (F. Harrison) Forum, 18: 192. *See* Beaconsfield.
Distances, Far, of our Universe. (A. Giberne) Chamb. J. 73: 212. Same art. Liv. Age, 209: 377.
Distribution, Consumption of Wealth and. (W. Smart) Ann. Am. Acad. Pol. Sci. 3: 257.
— Ethical Basis of, and its Application to Taxation. (T. N. Carver) Ann. Am. Acad. Pol. Sci. 6: 79.
— Measures of. (G. K. Holmes) Am. Econ. Assoc. 3: 141.
— Subjective and Objective View of. (J. Hobson) Ann. Am. Acad. Pol. Sci. 4: 378.
— Walker's Theory of Shares in. (F. C. Hicks) J. Pol. Econ. 2: 77.
District Messenger System of London. Chamb. J. 73: 725.
District of Colorado, Surveys and Maps of. (M. Baker) Nat. Geog. M. 3: 149.
Disturber, A, in Carglen Kirk. (A. Gordon) Gent. M. n. s. 50: 297.
Disturbing Element, A; a story. (E. Fletcher) All the Year, 71: 356-404.
Ditas. Macmil. 70: 39.
Dithyrambic Poetry in Italy and Sicily. (P. Toynbee) Acad. 41: 32.
Dittmar, William. Nature, 45: 493.
Divers; Life under Water. (G. Kobbé) Scrib. M. 15: 426.
Diversions, Curious. All the Year, 70: 538.
Dives; a poem. (C. Monkhouse) M. of Art, 15: 98.
Dives Loquor; a story. Temp. Bar, 105: 355.
Dividend Day. All the Year, 73: 462.
Dividends, Right to, as between Life Tenant and Remainder-man. Am. Law R. 26: 1.
Dividing Fence: a Simpkinsville Episode. (R. McE. Stuart) Harper, 90: 81.
Divina Commedia, La; a poem. (F. R. Robinson) Cosmopol. 17: 58.
Divination by the Blade-bone. (W. J. Thoms) Folk-Lore Rec. 1: 176.
Divination-stone or Kali; a story. Blackw. 152: 372. Same art. Ecl. M. 119: 648.
Divine Response to Human Capacity. (E. M. Caillard) Contemp. 65: 554. Same art. Liv. Age, 201: 314.
Divining-rod. (L. J. Vance) J. Am. Folk-Lore, 4: 241.
Divinities, Anthropomorphic. (S. D. Peet) Am. Antiq. 17: 79.
Divinity that Hedges; a story. All the Year, 71: 513.
Divinity and Love. (E. J. Hardy) Gent. M. n. s. 57: 238.
Divis, Prokop, Inventor of the Lightning-rod. (J. J. Král) Pop. Sci. Mo. 42: 356.
Divorce. Church Q. 40: 1. — (C. W. Smith; H. L. Sibley; H. W. Rogers) Meth. R. 52: 212. — (H. L. Postlethwaite) Westm. 139: 394.
— Ancient Jewish Law on. (D. W. Abram) Green Bag, 4: 36, 493.
— and the Law of Domicile. (G. W. Burnett) Jurid. R. 7: 251.
— and Property. (W. C. Smith) Jurid. R. 6: 35.
— and Re-marriage. (J. A. Sewell) Westm. 145: 182.
Divorce and the Rights of Society. (H. G. Ager) Am. J. Pol. 3: 93.
— as a State Industry. (A. R. Kimball) Nation, 54: 334.
— The Bible and. (E. J. B. and W. W. Bolton) Overland, n. s. 25: 362.
— Census of. (C. D. Wright) Forum, 17: 484.
— Controversy on. Church Q. 41: 422.
— Ethics of. (F. Adler) Eth. Rec. 2: 200. 3: 1.
— from a French Point of View. (A. Naquet) No. Am. 155: 721.
— from a Layman's Point of View. (F. Chaffee) Green Bag, 7: 295.
— from a New-Church Standpoint. (W. H. Mayhew) N. Church R. 3: 518.
— in France. (J. Challamel) Jurid R. 2: 143.
— in the New Testament. (T. W. Chambers) Ref. Q. 42: 39.
— in North and South Dakota. (J. Realf, jr.) Arena, 5: 243.
— in South Dakota. (R. Ogden) Nation, 56: 60.
— Jewish Proceedings in. Green Bag, 6: 407.
— Law of, French, New. (E. Stocquart) Am. Law R. 27: 1, 876.
— Limits of. (C. G. Garrison) Contemp. 65: 285.
— made easy. (S. J. Brun) No. Am. 157: 11.
— Marriage after. (W. C. Maude) Month, 84: 213.
— Marriage and: Doctrine of the Church of England. (W. J. K. Little) Chr. Lit. 13: 259.
— — High-Church Doctrine of. (G. Serrell) Chr. Lit. 13: 186.
— — in Scotland. Westm. 146: 213.
— Reform in, in the U. S., National League for. Our Day, 11: 173.
— Statistics of, Need of. (S. W. Dike) Am. Statis. Assoc. 3: 513.
Divorce Act, New French. (T. Barclay) Law Q. 1: 355.
Divorce Law, A National. (S. W. Dike) Pub. Opin. 20: 397.
Divorce Laws, Chaos of. (J. H. Heaton) New R. 11: 157, 304.
Divorce Problem. (S. H. Wandell) Open Court, 4: 2560, 2579.
Divorced Persons, Marriage of Innocent. (Baron Grimthorpe) 19th Cent. 37: 325.
Divorces in English Law. (G. H. Knott) Jurid. R. 7: 219.
Dix, Dorothea L. (M. S. Robinson) Cent. 23: 468. — (E. A. Meredith) Am. J. Pol. 3: 252.
"Dixie," Music and Words of. So. Hist. Pap. 21: 212.
Dixon, A. S., Pictures owned by. M. of Art, 7: 238.
Dixon, Luther S. (H. L. Conard) Nat'l M. (N. Y. '91) 17: 562.
Dixon, Nathaniel. (I. Hooper) Liv. Age, 208: 78.
Do seek their Meat from God; a story. (C. G. D. Roberts) Harper, 86: 120.
Dobie, John. Acad. 46: 103.
Dobson, A., with portrait. Bk. Buyer, 4: 132.
— 18th Century Vignettes. (L. Johnson) Acad. 41: 531.
Dobson, William Charles Thomas. (J. Oldcastle) M. of Art, 1: 183.
Dock Life. All the Year, 74: 41.
Docks, India. All the Year, 71: 609.
Dr. Banks; a story. (Eliza W. Durbin) Bost. 3: 137, 237.
Dr. Carl; a story. Temp. Bar, 109: 510.
Doctor Gregory. Liv. Age, 193: 329.
Dr. Meredith's Assistant; a story. (M. Moule) All the Year, 74: 426-614. 75: 21, 42.
Doctor of the Old School, A; a story. (John Watson) McClure, 4: 266.

Doctor of Philosophy, Early History of the Degree of, in the U. S. (E. G. Bourne) Educa. R. **10**: 81.
Doctor of the Southern Cross; a story. (H. Lander) Idler, **6**: 76.
Dr. Pennington's Country Practice. (B. Munroe) Lippinc. **53**: 230.
Dr. Pike and his Wife; a story. (G. B. Stanton) Cosmopol. **21**: 203.
Dr. Smyle; a story. (J. F. Sullivan) Idler, **1**: 512.
Dr. Vyron; a story. (I. L. Cassilis) Belgra. **86**: 390.
Doctor's Relatives, The; a story. (K. Erickson) Scrib. M. **11**: 121.
Doctor's Romance. (Alex. Gordon) Good Words, **36**: Xmas no., 30.
Doctors and Doctors. (G. Everitt) Time, **16**: 193-693.
— Fees of, in England. (A. D. Vandam) Sat. R. **82**: 490.
— Medical, Etiquette of. Sat. R. **81**: 370.
Doctors of Holyland, The; a story. (A. C. Doyle) Idler, **5**: 227. Same art. McClure, **3**: 274.
Doctors, Our; Burlesques on Prominent Physicians. Time, **2**: 407-662. **3**: 331.
Doctors' Commons, History of. Sat. R. **78**: 347.
Doctrine, Fixed System of, Reasons for a. (W. F. Eyster) Luth. Q. **25**: 93.
— Importance of, in its Integrity. (A. J. Brown) Luth. Q. **22**: 237.
Documentary Discovery, Five Years of. Church Q. **36**: 35. Same art. Liv. Age, **198**: 323.
Dodd, Amzi, with portrait. Nat'l M. (N. Y. '91) **18**: 296.
Dodge, Mary Abigail. Critic, **29**: 123.
— Last Year of her Life. (M. B. Thrasher) Arena, **17**: 112.
Dodge, Mary Mapes, with portrait. Bk. Buyer, **5**: 575.
Dodge Family of Essex Co., Mass. (J. T. Dodge) N. E. Reg. **46**: 383.
Dods, Marcus, with portrait. (A. B. Bruce) Bib. World, **7**: 245.
Doellinger, J. J. I. von, on the Vatican Council. (A. Plummer) Crit. R. **1**: 21.
— as a Conversationalist. (J. Owen) Acad. **43**: 257.
— Conversations of, Koebel's. Ath. '92, **2**: 581.
— Life and Writings of. Ed. R. **175**: 48.
Doerpfeld, Wilhelm, Lectures of. (A. V. W. Jackson) Critic, **29**: 321.
Dog, The. (N. S. Shaler) Scrib. M. **15**: 692.
— Another. (F. H. Smith) Cosmopol. **19**: 86.
— in British Poetry. (R. M. Leonard) Gent. M. n. s. **53**: 84.
— in the Rig-veda. (E. W. Hopkins) Am. J. Philol. **15**: 154.
— Psychology of. (J. Monteith) Pop. Sci. Mo. **44**: 514.
Dog's Ghost, A; a story. Outing, **21**: 481.
Dog's Home, Battersea. (B. Tozer) Eng. Illust. **13**: 445.
Dogs. (Barbara C. Finch) Gent. M. n. s. **55**: 526. — (C. L. Hildreth) Munsey, **10**: 484.
— and Bicycles. Spec. **77**: 514.
— and Cats: Wild Traits in Tame Animals. (L. Robinson) No. Am. **163**: 164.
— and Dog Legislation. (A. Nicols) Time, **17**: 407.
— and the Law. (R. Pound) Green Bag, **8**: 172.
— as Beasts of Burden. (W. B. Noyes) Nat'l M. (Bost.) **5**: 284.
— Boston Terrier. (C. F. Leland) Outing, **23**: 464.
— Bull. (W. J. Rix) Eng. Illust. **10**: 372.
— A Four-footed Oddity. (W. W. Fowler) Macmil. **69**: 143.
— in British Poetry, Leonard on. Spec. **71**: 805.
— International Field Trials of 1891. Outing, **20**: 109.
— Laughter of. (Vicomte d'Aiglun) Pop. Sci. Mo. **50**: 89.
— Lee on. Sat. R. **77**: 423.
Dogs, Lloyd on. Sat. R. **76**: 105.
— Morals and Manners of. (L. Robinson) Contemp. **62**: 353. Same art. Liv. Age, **195**: 279. Same art. Pop. Sci. Mo. **42**: 171.
— Sad and otherwise. (Maj. W. Nelson) Time, **19**: 195.
— St. Bernard; Kennels of America. (E. H. Morris) Outing, **19**: 353, 441.
— Sporting. Sat. R. **77**: 333.
— — of Great Britain, Lee on. Sat. R. **75**: 435.
Dogs of War; a story. (E. B. Simpson) Art J. **44**: 362.
Dogbane and Milkweed. (E. M. Hardinge) Pop. Sci. Mo. **49**: 684.
Doggett's Last Migration. (H. Carruth) Cent. **22**: 884.
Dogma, Harnack's History of. (A. F. Hewit) Am. Cath. Q. **18**: 746. **19**: 1. — (J. S. Candlish) Crit. R. **1**: 273. — Sat. R. **79**: 485.
— Necessity of. (J. E. McTaggart) Int. J. Ethics, **5**: 147.
Dogmatic Thought, Recent, in Scandinavia. (C. E. Lindberg) Presb. & Ref. R. **4**: 562.
Dogmatics, Scope and Method of Christian. (M. S. Terry) Meth. R. **55**: 190.
Dolan, Philip A., with portrait. (W. R. McGarry) Nat'l M. (N. Y. '91) **16**: 727.
Dolbeares of Boston, The. (E. D. Harris) N. E. Reg. **47**: 24.
Dole, Charles F., with portrait. Bk. News, **13**: 265.
Dole, Charles S. (H. L. Conard) Nat'l M. (N. Y. '91) **18**: 311.
Dolet, Etienne. (E. A. Gowing) Belgra. **82**: 24.
Dolichos Japonicus. *See* Pueraria Thunbergiana.
Doll, A Historic. (C. A. Dugan) New Eng. M. n. s. **8**: 325.
Dollar, American, Evolution of. (T. Holmes) Educa. **13**: 496.
— Standard Gold, of U. S. Has it appreciated? (S. Newcomb) J. Pol. Econ. **1**: 503.
Dollar Bill, History of a. (H. W. George) Chaut. **14**: 679.
Dolls, A Study of. (A. C. Ellis and G. S. Hall) Pedagog. Sem. **4**: 129.
Dolly; a story. All the Year, **73**: 226.
Dolmen des Pierres Plattes. (F. S. Tremett) Illus. Archæol. **1**: 251.
Dolmens, France. Reliquary, **36**: 171.
Dolomites, Mountain-climbing in. Spec. **73**: 496.
— a Mountain Paradise. (A. B. Hart) Nation, **57**: 387.
Dolorous Stroke, The. (A. Tennyson) Ecl. M. **120**: 326.
Domesday Book. Walford's Antiq. **11**: 4, 269.
— and the Burton Cartulary. (F. Baring) Eng. Hist. R. **11**: 98.
— Brief Survey of. (Sir F. Pollock) Eng. Hist. R. **11**: 209.
Domestic Animals in India. (J. L. Kipling) Pop. Sci. Mo. **40**: 597.
— Shaler on. (E. Coues) Nation, **62**: 39.
— Wild Traits in. (L. Robinson) No. Am. vols. **158**–**163**.
Domestic Drama, A. Macmil. **73**: 372.
Domestic Industries, Survival of. (E. C. K. Gonner) Econ. J. **3**: 1.
Domestic Interior; a story. (G. King) Harper, **90**: 407.
Domestic Labor, a Belated Industry. (J. Addams) Am. J. Sociol. **1**: 536.
Domestic Science, Reformation of. (E. A. M. Lewis) 19th Cent. **33**: 127.
Domestic Servants, An Appeal in Behalf of. (C. Goodwin) Forum, **19**: 753.
— Our. (Mary Jeune) New R. **10**: 572. — Sat. R. **77**: 12, 120.
— Servant Girl of the Future. (K. G. Wells) No. Am. **157**: 716.

Domestic Servants, Sociology and. Yale R. 5: 3.
Domestic Service, The Dislike to. (C. Black) 19th Cent. 33: 454.
— Doom of the Domestic Cook. (G. S. Layard) 19th Cent. 33: 309.
— from the Standpoint of the Employee. (L. M. Salmon) Cosmopol. 15: 346.
— Historical Aspects of. (L. M. Salmon) New Eng. M. n. s. 8: 175.
— Problem of. (G. Vrooman) Arena, 14: 308.
— Statistical Inquiry concerning. (L. M. Salmon) Am. Statis. Assoc. 3: 89.
Domestic Tyrannies. (Mrs. E. L. Linton) National, 26: 170.
Domestication of Animals. (C. D. Wilson) New Sci. R. 2: 139.
Domett, Alfred. (O. Smeaton) Westm. 144: 484.
Domine, quo vadio? (W. Watson) Spec. 72: 615.
Dominic, St., History of, Drane's. Ath. '92, 1: 558.
Dominical Letter in Theory and Practice. (C. R. Ballard) Educa. 15: 209.
Dominican Order in England, Principal Priors of. (A. G. Little) Eng. Hist. R. 8: 519.
Dominican Sisters in the West. (I. Okey) Cath. World, 57: 609.
Dominoes, the National Game of China. (S. Culin) Overland, n. s. 26: 559.
Domninus. (S. Krauss) Jew. Q. 7: 270.
Don Juan. (James Fitzmaurice-Kelly) New R. 13: 504, 665.
Don Orsino. (F. M. Crawford) Macmil. 65: 161 — 67: 103. Same art. Atlan. 69: 1 — 70: 721.
Don Quixote, Hamlet and. (I. Tourgénieff) Fortn. 62: 191.
— on the Stage. (A. Escott) Theatre, 34: 267.
See Cervantes.
Donald, Colin Dunlap. Ath. '95, 1: 384.
Donald, James, Art Collection of. (R. A. M. Stevenson) Art J. 46: 257.
Donald Grey; a story. (A. B. Ward) Outing, 22: 399.
Donatists and St. Augustine. (P. Burton) Dub. R. 112: 397.
Doncaster and St. Leger. Eng. Illust. 9: 887.
Donegal. Blackw. 160: 467. Same art. Liv. Age, 211: 593.
— Cliff Scenery of. (C. Edwardes) Chamb. J. 71: 337.
— Sketches in. All the Year, 72: 447, 467.
— a Visit to Purgatory. Belgra. 86: 178.
Dongan, Thomas. (M. Benjamin) Nat'l M. (N. Y. '91) 16: 373.
Dongola Campaign. (F. Maurice) Un. Serv. M. 131: 113.
Donkey, The. Wild Traits in Tame Animals. (L. Robinson) No. Am. 159: 722.
Donkey-show, The Costers'. Spec. 75: 110.
Donkeys. Leis. Hour, 42: 16.
— and Horses. (B. C. Finch) Gent. M. n. s. 54: 409.
— Wild, in the Greek Archipelago. (W. R. Paton) Ath. '95, 2: 421.
"Donna" in 1891. Longm. 19: 259.
— in 1892. Longm. 21: 288.
— in 1893. Longm. 23: 280.
— in 1894. Longm. 25: 304.
— in 1895. Longm. 27: 270.
Donne, John, Life and Poetry of. (C. B. Furst) Citizen, 2: 229.
— Poetry of. (G. Bradford) And. R. 18: 350. — (E. Gosse) New R. 9: 236. Same art. Liv. Age, 199: 429.
Doom of London; a story. (R. Barr) Idler, 2: 391. — Same art. McClure, 3: 551.
Doomswoman, The; a story. (G. Atherton) Lippinc. 50: 263.
Doones, Country of the. (W. H. Rideing) New Eng. M. n. s. 10: 611.
Doors. Chamb. J. 69: 186.
Doorstep Neighbors [Insects]. (W. H. Gibson) Harper, 93: 420.
Doorways. (E. Rivoalen) Am. Arch. 41: 19, 35.
— of Old London. (P. Fitzgerald) M. of Art, 8: 420.
Doppler's Principle, Distance of the Stars by. (G. W. Colles) Am. J. Sci. 145: 259.
Dora, the Pretty Type-writer; a story. (W. Lutton) Canad. M. 5: 52.
Dora's Defiance. (Lady Lindsay) Lippinc. 54: 579.
Dorastus; a story. (G. Hall) Cosmopol. 14: 674.
Dorchester, Mass., Intentions of Marriage, 1744–47. (F. E. Blake) N. E. Reg. 50: 19.
— Some Dorchester Matters. (R. T. Swan) N. E. Reg. 49: 153.
— Warnings from the Town. (F. E. Blake) N. E. Reg. 50: 68.
Dorchester Deed, Abstract of, 1753. (E. S. Holden) N. E. Reg. 50: 168.
Dorchester House, London. (E. Balfour) M. of Art, 6: 397.
— Picture Gallery. (C. Phillips) M. of Art, 9: 422.
Dordrecht. *See* Dort.
Doré, Gustave. M. of Art, 6: 221. — (F. T. Marzials) Acad. 42: 75.
— and his Art. (F. Beard) Our Day, 16: 153.
— in London and Paris. (J. Hatton) Idler, 7: 481.
Dore, Cistercian Abbey of, in Herefordshire, Excavations at. Ath. '95, 2: 613.
Dore and Chinley Railway, Eng. Chamb. J. 69: 358.
Doris and I; a story. (J. Stafford) Chamb. J. 69: 333–345.
Dorner, A. Bk. Buyer, 1: 176.
Dorothy; a story. (H. L. Bradley) Atlan. 76: 788.
Dorothy; a story. (C. F. Woolson) Harper, 84: 551.
Dorothy; a story. (S. Alice Ranlett) Bost. 2: 637.
Dorothy Drew; a story. (M. Minor) Southern M. 5: 24.
Dorr, Julia C. R., with portrait. Bk. Buyer, 12: 144.
— With portrait. Bk. Buyer, 4: 15.
Dorset, A Holiday in. All the Year, 71: 5.
— Moule's Old. Ed. R. 180: 35.
Dorsey, J. O., Memorial of. (W. J. McGee) J. Am. Folk-Lore, 8: 79.
Dort, or Dordrecht. (W. Armstrong) M. of Art, 17: 259.
Dorval, Marie. (C. E. Meetkerke) Belgra. 89: 82.
Dosaris, Long Island. (G. M. Clapham) New Eng. M. n. s. 9: 201.
"Doss-house" Sketch, A. (A. Sherwell) Sund. M. 25: 685.
Dostoyevski, F. (A. L. Salmon) Poet-Lore, 6: 309.
— Poor Folk. (I. F. Hapgood) Nation, 59: 181.
Dot-and-go-one. (J. Bonner) Overland, n. s. 24: 16.
Doten, Elizabeth, Poems by. (G. B. Stebbins) Arena, 16: 228.
Double-bedded Room, The. Blackw. 156: 411. Same art. Liv. Age, 203: 267.
Double Blue, A; a story. Argosy, 53: 509.
Double Breach of Promise, A; a story. (F. Boyle) Idler, 8: 75.
Double-motion Mechanism, New Forms of. (F. L. O. Wadsworth) Astron. 13: 527.
Double Trap, A; a story. All the Year, 75: 427.
Doubles. Chamb. J. 72: 513.
Doubt, Value of, in the Study of History. (M. M. Trumbull) Open Court, 1: 715.
Doubt not; a poem. Argosy, 59: 191.
Doubter's Diary; a story. Temp. Bar, 104: 401. Same art. Ecl. M. 124: 704.
Doucette, Camille. Ath. '95, 1: 443.

Douglas, Amanda M., with portrait. Bk. News, 12: 7.
Douglas, Stephen A., Reminiscence of. (D. Roberts) Harper, 87: 957.
Douglas Book, The. Gent. M. n. s. 55: 27.
Douglass, Frederick. (J. Cook) Our Day, 15: 233. — Pub. Opin. 18: 191. — (F. M. Holland) Open Court, 9: 4415. — With portrait. Bk. News, 11: 307.
— as Orator and Reformer. (W. L. Garrison) Our Day, 14: 182.
— Character and Career of, with portrait. (J. E. Rankin) Our Day, 14: 171.
— in Paris. (T. Stanton) Open Court, 1: 151.
— Reminiscences of. (Jane M. Parker) Outl. 51: 552.
Douhault, Mme. de, Case of. (J. J. Brown) National, 25: 824.
Doune Castle. Sat. R. 77: 197.
Douw, Gerard. (T. Cole) Cent. 25: 656.
Dove, W., Trial of. Green Bag, 6: 371.
Dovecotes in Hereford. (A. Watkins) Eng. Illust. 10: 45. Same art. Am. Arch. 38: 117.
Dover, N. H., Documents, 1652, etc. (J. S. H. Fogg) N. E. Reg. 47: 468.
Dover Road, Old. All the Year, 73: 248.
Dow, Neal, and his Life Work. (A. A. Miner) New Eng. M. n. s. 10: 397.
— as Guest and Host. (Mrs. J. Cook) Our Day, 13: 315.
— Ninetieth Birthday of. (F. E. Willard) Our Day, 13: 1.
— Watchwords for the 20th Century. (J. Cook) Our Day, 14: 12.
Dowager's Companion, The; a story. (W. E. Norris) Harper, 93: 219.
Dowden, Edward, Lectures of. (H. C. Butler) Critic, 29: 321.
Dower, Common-law, Origin of. (F. G. Buckstaff) Ann. Am. Acad. Pol. Sci. 4: 233.
Dowie, Ménie Muriel. Gallia. Sat. R. 79: 383.
Down at the Salt Water; a story. All the Year, 75: 79.
Down in the World: the Flower-maker; a story. (E. D. Keeling) Ecl. M. 127: 268.
Down on the Desert; a story. (W. M. Wolfe) Outing, 25: 345.
Down the West Coast. (C. F. Lummis) Harper, 90: 391.
Down-draught Furnace. (W. H. Bryan) Cassier, 8: 572.
Downey, William. Eng. Illust. 14: 643.
Downfall of the House of Denayer. (B. C. Praed) Belgra. 83: 73.
Downing, A. J., Debt of America to. (C. S. Sargent) Garden & F. 8: 211.
Downman, John. (S. Colvin) M. of Art, 8: 126.
Downs, South, On the. Cornh. 71: 610.
Doyle, A. Conan, with portrait. Bk. Buyer, 11: 421. — (R. Barr) McClure, 3: 503.
— First Book. Idler, 2: 633. Same art. McClure, 3: 225.
— Interview with. Idler, 6: 341.
— Portraits of. McClure, 1: 488.
— Rodney Stone. (M. Beerbohm) Sat. R. 82: 665.
— Stark Munro Letters. Sat. R. 80: 417.
Doyle, Henry. Acad. 27: 213.
Doyle, James E. Ath. '92, 2: 921.
Draft, Artificial. (W. R. Roney) Cassier, 6: 222.
Dragomanov, Michael Petrovich. Acad. 48: 31.
Dragomiroff, Michael Iwanowitsh. Un. Serv. (Phila.) 12: 201.
Dragon, The, of Mythology, Legend, and Art. (J. Leyland) M. of Art, 14: 330, 369.
Dragons. (L. F. Day) M. of Art, 3: 375.
— Folk-Lore of. (L. J. Vance) Open Court, 6: 3439.
Drainage, House, Improved Methods of. (W. P. Gerhard) Am. Arch. 47: 6.
Drainage. Reclamation of Land in Low Countries. (C. S. Sargent) Garden & F. 6: 110, 202.
Drainage System of the Valley of Mexico. (M. Romero) Engin. M. 8: 597.
Drake, Sir Francis, Anchorage of. (E. L. Berthoud) Nat. Geog. M. 3: 208.
— on the Spanish Main, 1567–73. (G. Everitt) Time, 15: 559.
— Voyage round the World. Liv. Age, 199: 471.
Drake, Joseph Rodman. (R. H. Stoddard) Critic, 27: 83.
Drake, W. H., with portrait. Bk. Buyer, 12: 82.
Drake Sword. Illus. Archæol. 2: 113.
Drama, American, Beginnings of. (P. L. Ford) New Eng. M. n. s. 9: 673.
— as it is, The. (J. H. McCarthy) Gent. M. n. s. 49: 533.
— at the Universities. (W. L. Courtney) Time, 15: 576.
— Censorship of the. Sat. R. 79: 280.
— Decadent. (E. Fuller) Lippinc. 56: 423.
— A Dialogue on. (H. A. Kennedy) 19th Cent. 38: 322.
— Early English. (W. H. Withrow) Meth. R. 54: 534.
— Early, in Boston. (C. H. Pattee) Bost. 2: 254.
— English, before Shakespeare. Time, 10: 66, 373.
— — 1894–95. Sat. R. 80: 107.
— — Future of. (H. A. Jones) New R. 9: 177.
— — Lamb's Specimens. Ath. '94, 2: 265.
— French, of To-day. (W. M. Fullerton) Theatre, 34: 81.
— German, Modern. (E. Brain) Theatre, 34: 84.
— — — and its Authors. (F. Spielhagen) Cosmopol. 17: 177.
— — of the Hour. (Miss Braddon) Theatre, 34: 131.
— in America, Beginnings of. (R. Davey) National, 19: 802.
— in Australia. (L. Wingfield) New R. 7: 217.
— in the Doldrums. (W. Archer) Fortn. 58: 146.
— in relation to Truth. (H. A. Michael) Poet-Lore, 7: 149.
— in Semitic Literature. (D. B. Macdonald) Bib. World, 5: 16.
— in Tatters, A; a story. (W. B. Harte) Arena, 11: 251.
— H. Irving on. (E. A. Barron) Dial (Ch.) 15: 90.
— Literary. (H. A. Jones) New R. 6: 89.
— Literature and. (E. Fawcett) Dial (Ch.) 14: 38.
— Love-, of 10th Cent. (W. H. Hudson) Poet-Lore, 3: 489.
— Modern, Moral Purpose in a. (J. D. Hunting) Theatre, 28: 121.
— — Dr. Pearson on. (H. A. Jones) 19th Cent. 34: 543.
— Modern English. (Mrs. M. Craigie) Acad. 50: 428, 433, 468.
— The New. Quar. 182: 399.
— of the Middle Ages. (J. J. Jusserand) Chaut. 19: 65.
— of Modern England and H. A. Jones. (W. A. L. Bettany) Theatre, 31: 203.
— of the Past. (I. S. A. Herford) Walford's Antiq. 11: 379. 12: 95, 214.
— of Revolt, The. (H. H. Boyesen) Bookman, 1: 384.
— A Plain Talk on the. (R. Mansfield) No. Am. 155: 308.
— Plays and Acting of the Season, '93. (W. Archer) Fortn. 60: 255.
— Realism in the Modern. (H. D. Traill) 19th Cent. 36: 864.
— Recent Plays. (W. Archer) Fortn. 61: 600.
— Renascence of, H. A. Jones on. (C. Dickens) Theatre, 34: 322.
— Revival of. (F. Harrison) Forum, 16: 184.
— Serious, Difficulties of. (C. Dickens) Theatre, 36: 200.

Drama. Some Neglected Plays. (N. L. Parker) Belgra. **84**: 412.
— Some Plays of the Day. (A. B. Walkley) Fortn. **59**: 468.
— Technique of, Freytag on. (J. S. Nollen) Dial (Ch.) **18**: 77.
Dramatic Academies, Need of. Idler, **3**: 568.
Dramatic Art in the Far East. (R. W. E. Eastwick) Chamb. J. **72**: 521.
Dramatic Censorship. All the Year, **76**: 294. — (A. Goodrich) Theatre, **28**: 232.
Dramatic Criticism. (W. L. Courtney) Contemp. **64**: 691. Same art. Ecl. M. **123**: 63. — (J. H. McCarthy) Gent. M. n. s. **52**: 313. — (B. Stoker) No. Am. **158**: 325.
— and First-night Notices. (G. B. Burgin) Idler, **5**: 68.
— and the Renascent Drama. (W. A. C. Bettany) Theatre, **28**: 277.
— Archer and. Sat. R. **74**: 250.
— Ethics of. Gent. M. n. s. **49**: 528.
Dramatic Dangers of the Past. (A. J. Daniels) Theatre, **30**: 132.
Dramatic Difficulties. All the Year, **73**: 135.
Dramatic Essays, Forster and Lewes's. Sat. R. **81**: 622.
Dramatic Expression. (A. W. Rollins) Lippinc. **53**: 242.
Dramatic Funeral, A; a story. (F. Coppée) Theatre, **32**: 13.
Dramatic Point, A; a story. (R. Barr) McClure, **6**: 393.
Dramatic Realist to his Critics. (G. B. Shaw) New R. **11**: 56. Same art. Ecl. M. **123**: 326.
Dramatic Revolutions, Two. (C. Scott) No. Am. **157**: 476.
Dramatic Season, The. (E. Marshall) McClure, **4**: 179.
Dramatic Synchoregia at Athens. (E. Capps) Am. J. Philol. **17**: 319.
Dramatic Teaching at the Paris Conservatoire. (J. R. Solly) Univ. R. **1**: 386.
Dramatis Personæ. Macmil. **71**: 262.
Dramatist, The, and his Friends. All the Year, **71**: 509.
Dramatists, American. (A. Hornblow) Munsey, **12**: 159.
— French, Contemporary. (A. Hornblow) Cosmopol. **15**: 107.
— Old English, Lowell on. Spec. **70**: 524.
Draper, Prof. John W., with portrait. Bk. News, **5**: 263.
Draper, Lyman C., with portrait. Am. Antiq. **15**: 119.
Drapery, Expression in. (A. Williams) M. of Art, **12**: 61.
Draughts: a Popular Indoor Game. Chamb. J. **73**: 428.
Drawing and Nature-study. (M. V. O'Shea) Educa. **17**: 88.
— Children's. The Young Draughtsman. (J. Sully) Pop. Sci. Mo. **48**: 533.
— Error in, Compulsory Laws of. (A. L. Haddon) Nature, **48**: 402.
— in Elementary Schools. (H. V. Barnett) M. of Art, **8**: 326, 425.
— in General Education. (D. R. Augsburg) Educa. **14**: 268.
— in London Board Schools. (J. Runciman) M. of Art, **8**: 218.
— Language of Line. (W. Crane) M. of Art, **11**: 145, 415.
— Object, Psychology of. (W. A. Mason) Educa. **15**: 82.
— Proper Mode and Study of. (W. H. Hunt) M. of Art, **14**: 80, 116.
— a Study on Jam-pots. (R. St.J. Tyrwhitt) M. of Art, **4**: 377.
— Value of. (T. Woolner) M. of Art, **15**: 7.
Drawings, Artists', in the Louvre, Chennevières. (J. A. Blaikie) M. of Art, **6**: 474.
Drawings, at the British Museum. (W. Armstrong) M. of Art, **16**: 1.
— by Children in the Early Years. (H. T. Lukens) Pedagog. Sem. **4**: 79.
— in Black and White, at the Dudley Gallery. M. of Art, **4**: 410.
— made for and by an Architect, Ownership of. (J. W. Papworth) Am. Arch. **43**: 104.
— Malcolm, at the British Museum. (L. Cust) M. of Art, **17**: 188.
— Original, To prevent Loss of. (C. S. Wady) Writer, **8**: 82.
Drawing-room Entertainments. (Gertrude E. Campbell) National, **19**: 112.
Drawing-room Idyl. (A. C. Deane) Longm. **25**: 300. Same art. Liv. Age, **204**: 424.
Drayton, Michael, Introduction to, Elton's. Sat. R. **80**: 210.
— Polyolbion of. Bookworm, **2**: 209.
Dreadful Night; a hunter's tale. (E. L. Arnold) Belgra. **84**: 33.
Dream, Failure of Movement in. (F. H. Bradley) Mind, **19**: 373.
— of the Psychometer. (M. Kendall) Longm. **25**: 388.
Dream of a Wild White Doe; a story. (C. Glyn) Belgra. **80**: 164.
Dream Gown of the Japanese Ambassador; a story. (B. Matthews) Eng. Illust. **16**: 145.
Dream of our Birth, A; a poem. (A. L. Salmon) Blackw. **153**: 554.
Dreaming Bob. (C. C. Abbott) Lippinc. **57**: 540.
Dreaming of the Dead. (H. Ellis) Psychol. R. **2**: 458.
Dreams. (F. L. Oswald) Open Court, **3**: 1597, 1647. — — (W. D. Howells) Harper, **90**: 836. — Spec. **69**: 189.
— and Hallucinations. (W. Seton) Cath. World, **54**: 822. — (P. Carus) Open Court, **3**: 2014.
— and Perceptive Illusions. Chamb. J. **69**: 651.
— and their Mysteries. (E. Bisland) No. Am. **162**: 716.
— as Revelations. (J. Sully) Fortn. **59**: 354. Same art. Ecl. M. **120**: 607.
— Consciousness in, A Study of. (Florence M. Hallam; Emma D. Phinney) Am. J. Psychol. **7**: 405.
— go by Contraries; a story. (G. H. Jessop) McClure, **1**: 318.
— Greenwood on. Sat. R. **74**: 156. — Spec. **69**: 679.
— Imagination in. (F. Greenwood) Contemp. **62**: 165. Same art. Ecl. M. **119**: 446.
— Literature of. (L. W. Smith) Poet-Lore, **8**: 233.
— of Tasting. (E. B. Titchener) Am. J. Psychol. **6**: 505.
— Prophetic Faculty of Mind revealed in. (B. O. Flower) Arena, **12**: 123.
— Sleep, and Consciousness. (G. M. Gould) Open Court, **2**: 1433, 1444.
— Statistics of. (M. W. Calkins) Am. J. Psychol. **5**: 311.
— Study of. (F. Greenwood) New R. **7**: 591.
— What they are made of. (L. Robinson) No. Am. **157**: 687.
Dream-tracked in the Transvaal; a story. Blackw. **159**: 730. Same art. Liv. Age, **209**: 721.
Dredge, James, and his Work. (W. H. Wiley) Cassier, **1**: 284.
Dredging, Hydraulic. (A. W. Robinson) Cassier, **11**: 37.
— on the Pacific Coast. (J. J. Peatfield) Overland, n. s. **24**: 315.
— Pump, in Holland. (W. H. Booth) Cassier, **5**: 3.
Dresden. (S. B. Holabird) Un. Serv. (Phila.) **8**: 240. — All the Year, **70**: 272.
Dresel, Otto. (W. F. Apthorp) Atlan. **72**: 488, 638.
Dress. Cornh. **69**: 406. — M. of Art, **5**: 336.

Dress, Color in. (L. Hemingham) M. of Art, 5: 158.
— Development of. Quar. 175: 423.
— Dialogue on. (T. Chapman) 19th Cent. 36: 572.
— English, Hill's History of. Sat. R. 76: 654. — Spec. 71: 718.
— Extravagance in. (M. Jeune) National, 20: 794.
— Fashions in Waists. (R. Heath) M. of Art, 8: 185, 245.
— for Women, Freedom in. (F. E. Russell) Arena, 8: 70.
— Influence of, upon Development. (F. McDonald) Open Court, 1: 408.
— — Lady Jeune on. Spec. 70: 156.
— Male and Female, in various Nations and Ages. (E. B. Dietrick) Arena, 10: 353.
— Men's, Tubular System of. (H. Holiday) Eng. Illust. 10: 909.
— Modern, Artistic Aspect of. (A. C. Carr) M. of Art, 5: 242.
— Servility in. (H. Maxwell) Pop. Sci. Mo. 42: 530.
— a Symposium on. (M. W. Sewall and others) Arena, 6: 488, 621.
— Victims of Vanity. (Violet Greville) National, 21: 71.
— Women's, What Men think of. (C. H. Crandall) No. Am. 161: 251.
— — Parisian Folly *vs.* American Common Sense. (B. O. Flower) Arena, 8: 130.
Dress Reform at the Chicago Exposition. R. of Rs. (N. Y.) 7: 312.
— in the U. S. (F. E. Russell) Arena, 6: 325.
Drexel, Anthony. (H. C. Potter) Critic, 24: 65. — Bank. M. (N. Y.) 48: 128.
Drexel Institute, Philadelphia. (C. M. Depew) Engin. M. 2: 569. — (A. R. Burke) Chr. Un. 45: 252.
Drift-fruit of Jamaica. (D. Morris) Nature, 53: 64.
Drilling: Prospecting with the Diamond Drill. (J. P. Channing) Engin. M. 10: 1075.
Drink, Environment and. (J. F. Waldo; D. Walsh) No. Am. 161: 460.
— Question of, in Germany. (F. G. Peabody) Nation, 54: 167.
Drinking in England, Early. (C. Cooper) Gent. M. n. s. 48: 358.
— Intermittent: a Confession and a Theory. National, 20: 28.
— Moderate, the case for. (Dr. Farquharson) Blackw. 151: 788. Same art. Ecl. M. 119: 225.
— Perils of. (A. Gustafson) Our Day, 10: 494.
Drinking Habits, Old-time. (C. Northend) New Eng. M. n. s. 13: 49.
Drinking Vessels, Antique. (L. Jewitt) M. of Art, 7: 101.
Drinks. (J. K. Reeve) Lippinc. 57: 275.
— Aromatic. (J. Rochard) Chaut. 20: 579.
— Colonial. (Alice M. Earle) Nat'l M. (N. Y. '91) 16: 149.
— Curious. (G. C. Nuttall) Chamb. J. 73: 378.
Driven; a story of Strade Moor. Temp. Bar, 99: 237.
Driver with his Back to the Horses; a story. (R. Barr) Eng. Illust. 11: 1013.
Driving, Art of. (H. C. Merwin) Harper, 93: 513, 303.
— Form in. (C. D. English) Lippinc. 50: 664.
— Four-in-Hand. (C. D. English) Lippinc. 49: 487.
— Hints on, Knight's. Sat. R. 78: 79.
Dromana, Heiress of, 200 Years Ago. (J. F. Fuller) Walford's Antiq. 5: 66–217.
Dronne, Canoe Voyage on the. (E. H. Barker) Temp. Bar, 101: 531.
Dropmore Papers. Ed. R. 177: 145. 184: 386.
Droseras, Cultural Notes on. (G. W. Oliver) Garden & F. 9: 117.
Drought of 1893 in Great Britain. Nature, 48: 295.
Drought, Prolonged, Effect upon Animal Life. (C. C. Abbott) Pop. Sci. Mo. 48: 465.
Drought at San Anton, The. (W. H. Shelton) Scrib. M. 20: 760.
Drove Back; a story. (C. Russell) Idler, 6: 687.
Drover, The. Chamb. J. 73: 568.
Drowned; a poem. (C. G. Rogers) Canad. M. 3: 367.
Druidism. (T. H. B. Graham) Gent. M. n. s. 57: 599.
Druids, The Grave of the. (E. H. Barker) Temp. Bar, 105: 378. Same art. Liv. Age, 206: 287.
Drummer of Company E. (R. H. Fletcher) Cosmopol. 14: 13.
Drummond, Henry. (H. A. Bridgman) New Eng. M. n. s. 8: 725. — Critic, 25: 298. — (H. C. Shelley) Outl. 49: 1093.
— Ascent of Man. *See* Man, Ascent of.
— at Chautauqua. Critic, 23: 41.
— Natural Law in the Spiritual World. (J. Herbin) Open Court, 2: 1215.
— on the Struggle for the Life of Others. (E. L. Linton) Fortn. 62: 448.
— Portraits of. McClure, 1: 2. 2: 436.
— Religious Views of. (E. F. B. Horn) M. Chr. Lit. 7: 153.
Drummond, William, of Hawthornden. Poems, ed. by Ward. Sat. R. 79: 161.
Drummond, William. (S. B. Weeks) Nat'l (N. Y. '91) 15: 616.
"Drummond Castle," the Doomed Ship, My Voyage on. (C. Marquardt) Eng. Illust. 15: 379.
Drumsheugh's Love Story. (J. Watson) Bookman, 2: 27, 108.
Drumtochty, Visit to. (D. Davidson) Sund. M. 25: 524. — (F. C. Gordon) Bookman, 2: 288.
Drunkards, Habitual, Law Relating to. (J. B. Tuke) 19th Cent. 33: 1009.
Drunkenness and its Remedy. (L. E. Keeley) Am. J. Pol. 2: 657.
— A. Baer on. (A. MacDonald) And. R. 17: 259.
— a Curable Disease. (L. E. Keeley) Am. J. Pol. 1: 27.
— The Decline of. (A. Shadwell) National, 26: 558.
— in England. (J. B. Gough) Time, 1: 416.
— Law on, Massachusetts. (W. F. Spalding) Char. R. 1: 27.
— on the Stage. (A. Daudet) Theatre, 33: 48.
— Pathology and Treatment of. (L. E. Keeley) Am. J. Pol. 2: 143.
— Responsibility in. (T. S. Clouston) Jurid. R. 6: 147.
Drury Lane, Romance of. (John Coleman) Gent. M. n. s. 57: 365.
Drury Lane Court, In a. All the Year, 76: 279.
Drury Lane Theatre. Chamb. J. 69: 103.
— Discoveries at. (H. B. Baker) Theatre, 34: 91.
— Opening of; Real Rejected Addresses. (R. W. Lowe) Blackw. 153: 742. Same art. Ecl. M. 120: 817.
Druses in Hauran. (Abdullah Shámi) Asia. R. 22: 306.
— Life among the. Asia. R. 10: 358.
Dry Dock, New U. S., at Puget Sound. (W. M. Sheffield) Bost. 4: 343.
Dryburgh Abbey. *See* Abbotsford.
Dryden, John. Citizen, 1: 291.
— and Ben Jonson. (J. A. Evans) Temp. Bar, 95: 101.
— Works, ed. by Saintsbury. Sat. R. 76: 544.
"Drythe," used in Kent for "Drought." Acad. 44: 235.
Dual Organization of Mankind, Proposed. (W. G. Sumner) Pop. Sci. Mo. 49: 433.
Dualism, The Last Ditch of. (E. P. Powell) Open Court, 2: 977.
— Monism, and Agnosticism. (P. Carus) Open Court, 1: 209.

Dualistic Conception of Nature. (J. C. Murray) Monist, 6: 382.
Duality. (J. E. Walker) Bib. Sac. 49: 560.
— of Mind. (R. M. Bache) Monist, 1: 362.
— — T. J. Hudson's Theory of, disproved. (T. E. Allen) Arena, 13: 177.
Dublin, Ireland. (K. Tynan) Cath. World, 55: 93.
— Hall of Four Courts. (D. W. Douthwaite) Green Bag, 5: 457, 506.
— Museum of Science and Art. (H. M. Cundall) Art J. 44: 49.
— Museums of. (V. Ball) Nat. Sci. 5: 21.
— Old Huguenot, and its Weaving Industries. (R. S. Swirles) Good Words, 33: 801.
— Picturesque. (F. A. Gerard) Art J. 48: 265, 303.
Dublin National Gallery. (W. Armstrong) M. of Art, 13: 229, 281.
Dublin Review, Diamond Jubilee of. (L. C. Casartelli) Dub. R. 118: 245.
Dublin University, College Life at. (A. S. Cody) Bach. of Arts, 2: 309, 483.
— Tercentenary of. Ath. '92, 2: 96. — (J. P. Mahaffy) Chaut. 16: 56. — (H. T. Peck) Educa. R. 4: 287. — (J. C. Welling) Nation, 55: 43. — Sat. R. 74: 38.
Dubois, Paul. (P. Valery) Art J. 48: 134.
Dubourg, Comte de Castellane, Fate of. (C. S. Oakley) Cornh. 74: 339.
Dubs, Jacob, of Milford, Pa. (J. H. Dubbs) Pennsyl. M. 18: 367.
Ducal Butler, The; a story. (I. Clark) Munsey, 10: 626.
Ducali, Venetian. (J. W. Bradley) Bibliographica, 2: 257.
Du Camp, Maxime. (G. Koerner) Open Court, 9: 4551.
— Souvenirs. Ath. '94, 1: 214. — Spec. 72: 109.
Duccio di Buoninsegna; Story of an Old Picture. (C. Duncan) M. of Art, 4: 259.
Du Chaillu, P. B., with portrait. Bk. Buyer, 6: 355.
Duchartre, Pierre. Nature, 51: 344.
Duchâtelet, Gabrielle Emilie, Marquise. Temp. Bar, 95: 75. Same art. Liv. Age, 194: 51. — (H. W. Wolff) National, 19: 381.
Duck Shooting. Sat. R. 78: 94. — (J. D. Knap) Outing, 27: 97. — (E. A. Shepard) Outing, 27: 210.
— in Australia. (M. M. O'Leary) Cosmopol. 14: 245.
— in a City. (H. Rave) Outing, 23: 454.
— in a Crater. (H. D. Couzins) Outing, 26: 29.
— in the Ice. (J. D. Knap) Outing, 28: 67.
— in Maryland. (D. B. Fitzgerald) Cosmopol. 18: 61.
— in Southern California. (B. Douglas) Outing, 23: 129.
— on Savannah River. Outing, 27: 419.
Ducking Police, With. (D. B. Fitzgerald) Lippinc. 57: 117.
Ducklings. (C. L. Morgan) Science, 22: 63.
Ducks and Duck Shooting. (S. Jenkins) Canad. M. 5: 443.
— Decoy-shooting. (F. E. Kellogg) Outing, 29: 133.
— of Chesapeake Bay. (C. D. Wilson) Lippinc. 55: 80.
— Wild, and Tame Decoys. (H. Sears) Harper, 94: 95.
— Winter Day with. (J. R. Benton) Outing, 29: 249.
Duddon River. (H. Rix) Leis. Hour, 42: 532.
— The Valley of. Cornh. 72: 78. Same art. Liv. Age, 206: 419.
Du Deffand, Madame. Macmil. 70: 224. Same art. Liv. Age, 202: 323.
Dudevant, A. L. A. D. [Geo. Sand]. (T. Bentzon) Cent. 25: 457. — With portrait. Bk. Buyer, 10: 111.
— Convent Life of. Critic, 22: 148.
— Home of. (M. A. Taylor) Atlan. 77: 754.
— Recollections of. (Mme. J. Adam) No. Am. 156: 293.
Dudgeon, Patrick. Ath. '95, 1: 216.
Dudleian Lecture for 1891. (E. Emerton) And. R. 17: 238.
Dudley, Paul, 1675–1751. (E. Lord) New Eng. M. n. s. 7: 639. — (F. B. Hornbrooke) New Eng. M. n. s. 13: 634.
Dudley, Sir Robert. (Goldwin Smith) Nation, 60: 261.
Dudley, Thomas, Governor of Massachusetts. (M. S. Child) Bost. 2: 399.
Dudley Gallery, Exhibition of Pictures, 1877. M. of Art, 1: 11.
— — 1878. M. of Art, 2: 18.
Duel between Duke of Hamilton and Baron Oakhampton. Chamb. J. 72: 465. Same art. Liv. Age, 206: 637.
— The Last, in the Place Royale. Macmil. 72: 443.
Duel, A; a story. (H. Harland) Idler, 5: 184.
Duelling. (K. Blind) New R. 14: 660. — Spec. 68: 708. — Idler, 5: 212.
— at the Irish Bar. Green Bag, 6: 447.
— in France. Sat. R. 74: 38.
— in German Universities. (F. F. D. Albery) Bach. of Arts, 1: 603. — (W. T. Parker) Munsey, 6: 642.
— in Germany. Spec. 76: 592.
Duelling Grounds, Old London. Chamb. J. 72: 29.
Duels in France. (J. Pemberton-Grund) Cornh. 74: 780.
— Last, in America. (W. C. Elam) Lippinc. 57: 649.
— Some Curious. (J. C. Hadden) Gent. M. n. s. 57: 165. Same art. Liv. Age, 210: 761.
— Some Historic. (E. Castle) New R. 10: 177, 353.
Duerer, Albrecht. Bookworm, 2: 161. — With portrait. (M. A. Taggart) Cath. World, 59: 372.
— An Albrecht Duerer Town. (E. R. Pennell) Harper, 87: 537.
— and his Drawings, Ephrussi's. (S. Colvin) M. of Art, 5: 345.
— Conway's Literary Remains of. M. of Art, 13: 242.
— Engravings of. (L. Cust) Portfo. 1894: no. 11.
Dufferin, Helen, Lady. (T. Hutchinson) Acad. 46: 111.
— Poems and Verses. Quar. 179: 319. — Ed. R. 180: 433. — Spec. 73: 114. — Ath. '94, 2: 119. — Sat. R. 78: 73.
Dufferin, Marquis of. (C. Eaglestone) New R. 6: 332.
Duffy, Charles Gavan. (J. H. Heaton) Eng. Illust. 15: 395.
Dugdale, Sir William. (E. Walford) Walford's Antiq. 9: 153. 10: 3, 141.
Dukes and Duchesses, English. (R. H. Titherington) Munsey, 11: 15.
Dukinfield, North Carolina. (C. Hallock) New Eng. M. n. s. 9: 692.
Dulditch Angel; a story. (Mary E. Mann) Temp. Bar, 107: 549. Same art. Liv. Age, 209: 474.
Duluth. (S. A. Thompson) New Eng. M. n. s. 10: 327.
Dulwich Gallery. (H. Wallis) M. of Art, 4: 221. — (W. Armstrong) M. of Art, 15: 65, 100.
Dumas, Alexandre, *père*. (E. Crawford) Cent. 29: 726. — With portrait. Book News, 14: 224. — (T. Watts) 19th Cent. 35: 237.
— The Historical Novel. (G. Saintsbury) Macmil. 70: 321.
Dumas, Alex., *fils*. Critic, 27: 397. — (R. Davey) Theatre, 36: 12. — (A. Cohn) Bookman, 2: 382.
— and his Plays. (M. S. Van de Velde) Fortn. 65: 94.
— at Home. Lit. W. (Bost.) 24: 176.
— On Death of. (H. James) New R. 14: 288.
— Visit to. (A. Symons) Sat. R. 80: 724.
Dumas, Alexandre, *père* and *fils*. (C. E. Meetkerke) Argosy, 61: 156. Same art. Liv. Age, 208: 757.
Dumas Family. Atlan. 77: 141.

Du Maurier, George. (R. H. Sherard) McClure, 4: 391. — With portrait. Bk. Buyer, 11: 250. 13: 616. — With portrait. Bk. News, 13: 35. — Bk. News, 15: 77 — (W. D. Scull) M. of Art, 15: 229. — (F. Wedmore) Acad. 50: 290. — (E. Knaufft) R. of Rs. (N. Y.) 14: 565. — Ath. '96, 2: 491. — Critic, 29: 223.
— and William Morris. Art J. 48: 379.
— at Home. (A. Bright) Idler, 8: 415.
— in Bohemia with. (F. Moscheles) Cent. 30: 105.
— on Society. Spec. 67: 879.
— Peter Ibbetson. Spec. 68: 438.
— Trilby. (Mary G. Husband) Westm. 146: 446. — Sat. R. 78: 361. — Open Court, 9: 4465.
— — Causes of its Popularity. (F. Wedmore) Acad. 48: 392.
— — on the Stage. Critic, 27: 306. — (Justin H. McCarthy) Gent. M. n. s. 56: 207.
— — Trail of, in Paris. (A. D. Vandam) Forum, 20: 429.
— — Whistler's Protest against. Critic, 25: 331.
— Trilbyana. Critic, 26: 66. 27: 33.
— — in England. Critic, 27: 209.
Dumb Foxglove. (A. T. Slosson) Atlan. 75: 466.
Dummer Academy. (I. A. Herrick) Educa. 14: 571.
Dunbar, William. (F. R. Oliphant) Blackw. 154: 416.
Duncan, Francis. (J. G. C. Minchin) Acad. 42: 126.
Duncan, Sara Jeannette. (G. B. Burgin) Idler, 8: 113. — With portrait. Bk. Buyer, 8: 369. — With portrait. Bk. News, 10: 64.
Dundee Prior to the Reformation. (G. R. Merry) Acad. 43: 122.
Dunfermline Abbey. (F. T. Hodgson) Canad. M. 2: 335.
Dunkery Beacon. Chamb. J. 71: 433.
Dunlap Society's Publications. (E. D. North) Bibliographica, 2: 381.
Dunlop, Joseph R., Trial and Conviction of. Our Day, 16: 139.
Dunluce, Birds at. (F. A. Fulcher) Argosy, 58: 200.
Dunn, George W. (W. A. Wood) Green Bag, 4: 44.
Dunnottar Castle. Chamb. J. 72: 577.
Dunraven, Earl of, with portrait. (C. K. Cooke) McClure, 1: 429.
— and the Cup. (A. T. Quiller-Couch) Contemp. 68: 796.
— and the Physicians. National, 19: 280.
Dunsinane. (J. H. Crawford) Good Words, 34: 384.
Dunstable Land, Letter of Rev. Thomas Weld, 1684. (S. B. Doggett) N. E. Reg. 50: 305.
Dunstan, Saint, Ancient Offices of. (F. E. Gilliatt-Smith) Dub. R. 114: 22.
Dunstan's Ambassador; a romance. (G. B. Stuart) Argosy, 57: 415.
Dunster and its Castle. (G. Wallas) Eng. Illust. 9: 688.
Dunton, John, Bookseller. Gent. M. n. s. 53: 167.
Dunwich; a Lost English City. (H. M. Doughty) Blackw. 155: 515. Same art. Liv. Age, 201: 243.
Dunworth Crow, The; a story. (E. M. Weyer) Outing, 23: 102.
Duodecimal Enumeration, Plea for. (T. J. A. Freeman) Am. Cath. Q. 18: 202, 412.
Dupré, Giovanni. (L. E. Baxter) M. of Art, 6: 109.
Dupré, Jules. (E. Chesneau) M. of Art, 13: 45.
Dupuy, Fall of. Spec. 74: 73.
Duran, Carolus. (P. G. Hamerton) Scrib. M. 16: 232.
Duras, Madame la Duchesse de. (R. E. Prothero) 19th Cent. 33: 896.
Durham, In the Bishopric at. (J. W. Steel) Time, 1: 509.
Durham Cathedral. (T. E. Champion) Canad. M. 3: 350. — Reliquary, 35: 101.
Durham Cathedral and the Bishops Palatine. (W. C. Sydney) Gent. M. n. s. 55: 234. Same art. Liv. Age, 207: 205.
Durham Place, London: a Palace in the Strand. (M. A. S. Hume) Fortn. 60: 390.
Durrant Murder Case. (J. H. Wigmore) Am. Law R. 30: 29.
Duruy, Victor, Lavisse's Life of. (J. Bigelow) Am. Hist. R. 1: 142.
Durward, Charles P., with portrait. Cath. World, 59: 217.
Duse, Eleanora. (J. R. Towse) Cent. 29: 130. — (V. Blackburn) New R. 13: 39. — (W. Archer) Fortn. 64: 299. — Critic, 28: 128. — (M. C. Jones) Critic, 22: 67-117. — Sat. R. 75: 571.
— as Marguerite Gautier. (P. Houghton) Theatre, 32: 303.
— in Cavalleria Rusticana and La Locandiera. (P. Houghton) Theatre, 33: 27.
Du Seuil, Augustin. (S. T. Prideaux) Antiq. n. s. 25: 208.
Dusk; a poem. (W. W. Campbell) Cosmopol. 14: 500.
Dust and Fresh Air. (T. P. Teale) Pop. Sci. Mo. 41: 238.
— and Hygiene. All the Year, 76: 154.
— and Meteorological Phenomena. (J. Aitken) Nature, 49: 544.
— and Sand Storms in the West. (J. A. Udden) Pop. Sci. Mo. 49: 655.
— Atmospheric, and Meteorological Phenomena. (J. Aitken) Nature, 45: 299. — (A. Rankin) Nature, 45: 582.
— — Observations on, Friedlander's. Dub. R. 119: 402.
— Exclusion of. Dub. R. 110: 446.
— Explosive. Chamb. J. 71: 758.
See Coal-dust.
— Humanity as. (L. Hearn) Atlan. 78: 642.
— Protection from. (T. P. Teale) Am. Arch. 35: 157.
— Work of. (P. Lenard) Pop. Sci. Mo. 45: 647.
Dust Collectors in Workshops. (R. Kohfahl) Cassier, 4: 270.
Dutch, Influence of, in America. Atlan. 70: 698.
— — in New England. *See* Holland.
Dutch Etchers of the 17th Century. (Lawrence Binyon) Portfo. no. 21.
Dutch Kitty's White Slippers; a story. (J. Ralph) Harper, 90: 914.
Dutch Language, Study of. (W. H. Carpenter) Nation, 63: 209.
Dutch Literature, 1891-92. (T. H. de Beer) Ath. '92, 2: 18.
— 1892-93. (T. H. de Beer) Ath. '93, 2: 20.
— 1893-94. (T. H. de Beer) Ath. '94, 2: 18.
— 1894-95. (T. H. de Beer) Ath. '95, 2: 17.
— 1895-96. (H. S. M. van Wickevoort Crommelin) Ath. '96, 2: 18.
Dutch Raid on the Medway, 1667. Chamb. J. 70: 182.
Dutch West India Company. (D. Van Pelt) Nat'l M. (N. Y. '91) 15: 109.
Dutchmen, Down among the. (Henri Van Laun) Time, 2: 10.
Duties and Rights. (J. S. Mackenzie) Int. J. Ethics, 6: 425.
Duty; a poem. Argosy, 61: 111.
Duty the Aim of Life. (H. C. Shuttleworth) Sund. M. 24: 260.
Dutzia Discolor. Garden & F. 7: 284.
Duval and Du Vall Family of Maryland. (J. L. Raymond) Am. Hist. Reg. 2: 1474.
Duxbury, Mass., Old Ship-building Days at. (L. P. Higgins) New Eng. M. n. s. 8: 320.

Dvorák, Antonín. (H. E. Krehbiel) Cent. **22**: 657. — Critic, **21**: 236. — Sat. R. **81**: 323. — (J. J. Kral) Music, **4**: 561.
Dwarf Negroes of Andaman Islands. (W. C. Preston) Sund. M. **23**: 600. Same art. Liv. Age, **203**: 307.
Dwarfie Stone, Hoy, Orkney. Reliquary, **36**: 84.
Dwarfing Plants in Japan. (H. Izawa) Garden & F. **6**: 373.
Dwarfs and Dwarf Worship. (H. Crichton-Browne) Nature, **45**: 269.
— Forest, of the Congo. Chamb. J. **72**: 298.
Dwellers in Arcady. Liv. Age, **199**: 436.
Dwelling-house, Daylight in. (J. Brett) Am. Arch. **39**: 21.
Dwellings, Improved. (A. N. Lincoln) Char. R. **4**: 425.
— of the Poor. Lend a H. **15**: 135.
— Wanted, a House. (E. C. Tait) Good Words, **35**: 475.
Dwellings Company, Improved, of Brooklyn, N. Y. Lend a H. **16**: 128.
Dwight, John Sullivan. Music, **4**: 553. — (W. F. Apthorp) Music, **4**: 627.
Dwight Method of Legal Instruction. (G. C. Austin) Law Q. **9**: 171.
Dyce, William, Paintings by. Sat. R. **77**: 282.
Dyce and Forster Collection of Books. (F. G. Green) Bookworm, **3**: 273.
Dyck, Anthony Van, Michiel's and Guiffrey's Lives of. M. of Art, **5**: 422.
— Guiffrey's, tr. by Alison. Sat. R. **81**: 432.
Dyganwy. (H. H. Lines) Antiq. n. s. **30**: 263.
Dying, Art of. (I. A. Taylor) 19th Cent. **36**: 111. Same art. Ecl. M. **123**: 261. Same art. Liv. Age, **202**: 241.
— in Harness. Spec. **71**: 659.
Dynamic Economics, Theory of. (S. N. Patten) Q. J. Econ. **7**: 177.
Dynamics, Foundations of. (A. Gray) Nature, **49**: 389, (A. B. Bassett) 529. — (C. F. Fitzgerald) Nature, **51**: 283.
— Fundamental Axioms of. (O. Lodge) Nature, **48**: 62.
— Graphical, Subnormal in. (I. P. Church) J. Frankl. Inst. **133**: 23.
— Waterdale on. Nature, **47**: 601.
Dynamite. Chamb. J. **71**: 510.
— Ethics of. (A. Herbert) Contemp. **65**: 667.
Dynamite Conspirators, Extradition and the. National, **28**: 293.
Dynamite Explosion in French Chamber, Dec. 2, 1893. Nation, **57**: 442. — (W. J. Ashley) Nation, **57**: 482. — Sat. R. **76**: 669. — Spec. **71**: 860.
— in Paris, Nov. 8, 1892. Spec. **69**: 676.
Dynamite Explosion, A; a story. (R. Barr) Eng. Illust. **11**: 601.
Dynamite Outrages on the Continent, 1892. Spec. **68**: 395.
Dynamite Scare in Europe, 1892, and Anarchy. (S. Stepniak) New R. **6**: 529.
Dynamiters and Search Warrants. Sat. R. **77**: 196.
Dynamo, Constant-current, Closed-coil. (H. S. Carhart) J. Frankl. Inst. **137**: 140-209.
— and Motor Design. (G. S. Dunn) J. Frankl. Inst. **139**: 384.
Dynamo Construction, Urquhart on. Sat. R. **73**: 522.
Dynamos and Direct-connected Engines. (T. G. Smith, jr.) Cassier, **7**: 285.
— Calculation for. (C. H. Bedell) J. Frankl. Inst. **133**: 497.
— High-tension, Direct-current. (F. B. Crocker) Cassier, **5**: 341.
Dyonysus ἐν Δίμναις. (J. Pickard) Am. J. Archæol. **8**: 56.
Dyre, Major, William. (J. G. Leach) Am. Hist. Reg. **1**: 37.
Dysart in Fifeshire. (D. S. Meldrum) Eng. Illust. **9**: 337.

Eagle and the Child; a story. (T. Swift) Canad. M. **7**: 305.
— The Golden. Knowl. **18**: 269.
Eagre, The. (E. Peacock) Antiq. n. s. **26**: 26.
Eames, Emma. (O. Hackett) Munsey, **6**: 666.
Ear, Drum of, Pressure-sense of. (F. B. Dresslar) Am. J. Psychol. **5**: 344.
— Evolution of the Human. (H. Drummond) McClure, **1**: 52.
Earlier Manner, An; a story. (G. A. Hibbard) Cent. **28**: 878.
Earll, Robert Edward. (G. B. Goode) Science, n. s. **3**: 471.
Earlscourt; a Novel of Provincial Life. (A. Allardyce) Blackw. **153**: 1-839. **154**: 74-805. **155**: 67.
Early, Gen. J. A. (L. S. Marye) Southern M. **4**: 465. — (J. W. Daniel) So. Hist. Pap. **22**: 281.
Early-day Memory, An. (W. S. Hutchinson) Overland, n. s. **22**: 257.
Early Days in Elliot Bay. (R. Simmons) Overland, n. s. **23**: 181.
Earnestness, Breadth and. (C. P. Woolley) Open Court, **1**: 371.
Ears and Eyes in Spelling. (W. D. Parkinson) Educa. **16**: 106.
Earth, Age of the. (J. Perry and others) Nature, **51**: 224, 341, 439, 533, 582. — (Lord Kelvin) Nature, **51**: 438. — (W. J. McGee) Science, **21**: 309. — (C. King) Am. J. Sci. **145**: 1. — (W. Upham) Pop. Sci. Mo. **44**: 153.
— — Rigidity not to be relied upon in estimating. (O. Fisher) Am. J. Sci. **145**: 464.
— Axis of, Position of. (O. E. Harmon) Pop. Astron. **2**: 219.
— Bowels of. (A. C. Lane) Pop. Sci. Mo. **47**: 302.
— Crust of, Deformation of. (E. Reyer) Nature, **46**: 224.
— — Movements of. (J. Milne) Geog. J. **7**: 229.
— Density of. (J. H. Poynting) Pop. Astron. **3**: 232.
— Face of. (C. Lapworth) Nature, **49**: 614.
— Gigantic Model of. (A. R. Wallace) Contemp. **69**: 730. Same art. Liv. Age, **209**: 692.
— Idle. (R. Jefferies) Longm. **25**: 171.
— Interior of. (G. F. Becker) No. Am. **156**: 439.
— — Our Molten Globe. (A. R. Wallace) Fortn. **58**: 572. Same art. Ecl. M. **119**: 836. Same art. Liv. Age, **195**: 771.
— a Magnetic Shell. (F. H. Bigelow) Am. J. Sci. **150**: 81.
— Measurement of the. (J. H. Gore) J. Frankl. Inst. **134**: 358-415.
— Rotational Axis of, Displacements of. (W. Foerster) Nature, **50**: 488.
— Shape of, from a Pendulum. (J. H. Gore) Pop. Sci. Mo. **44**: 531.
— Story of Our Planet, Bonney's. Ed. R. **180**: 180.
— Surface of, Configuration of. (J. Lubbock) Geog. J. **6**: 545.
— the Theory of, Hutton on. (F. D. Adams) Nature, **52**: 569.
Earth Pressure, Theory of. (P. Vedel) J. Frankl. Inst. **138**: 139, 189.
Earthquake at Constantinople, July 10, 1894. (C. Davison) Nat. Sci. **8**: 27.
— at Port Royal, 1692. (A. B. Ellis) Pop. Sci. Mo. **40**: 774.
— at Zante, March and April, 1893. Pub. Opin. **15**: 253.

Earthquake at Strassburg in 1893. (E. v. Rebeur-Paschwitz) Nature, 51: 208.
— in Balúchistan, Dec. 20, 1892. Nature, 48: 348.
— in Greece, April, 1894. (C. Davison) Nature, 50: 607.
— in Japan, 1891. Dub. R. 110: 454. — (J. Milne) Liv. Age, 192: 443.
— — 1894. (B. Koto) Geog. J. 3: 213.
— of Dec., 1896. (C. Davison) Nature, 55: 179.
Earthquake-motion, A. Schmidt on. (C. Davison) Nature, 52: 631.
Earthquakes. Chamb. J. 69: 49.
— After-shocks of. (C. Davison) Nat. Sci. 6: 391.
— and how to measure them. (E. S. Holden) Cent. 25: 749.
— Building Construction against. Am. Arch. 54: 12.
— Cause of. (H. N. Hutchinson) Knowl. 15: 145. — (J. L. Lobley) Knowl. 18: 161.
— Explanation of. Pub. Opin. 14: 254.
— Falb's Theory of. (W. Stoss) Open Court, 2: 804.
— High Buildings and. (N. S. Shaler) No. Am. 156: 338.
— How to Observe. (C. Davison) Knowl. 19: 189.
— in Iceland. (J. Stefansson) Nature, 54: 574.
— Japanese on. Liv. Age, 192: 444.
— Phenomena of. Dub. R. 118: 150.
Earth-waves and Vibrations, Observations of. (J. Milne) Nature, 51: 548.
Earthworms. (C. F. Marshall) Knowl. 18: 259.
— and their Allies. (F. E. Beddard) Nat. Sci. 5: 45.
— Beddard on. (P. C. Mitchell) Sat. R. 80: 864.
— Luminous. (H. Friend) Nature, 47: 462.
— The Newest about. (F. E. Beddard) Blackw. 155: 412. Same art. Liv. Age, 201: 188.
Easements, Quasi-grant of, in English and Roman Law. (E. C. C. Firth) Law Q. 10: 323.
East, Alfred. (W. Armstrong) M. of Art, 18: 81.
East, The, Christianity in. (S. A. Barnett) Contemp. 61: 512.
— The Crisis in. (K. Blind) No. Am. 162: 84.
— Fate of. Contemp. 61: 842. Same art. Ecl. M. 119: 171.
— Far, Chirol on. (H. E. Bourne) Dial (Ch.) 20: 269.
— — Curzon on. (H. E. Bourne) Dial (Ch.) 20: 271. (W. E. Griffis) Nation, 59: 250.
— — Destinies of. (G. N. Curzon) National, 21: 315. — National, 22: 574.
— — Industrial Development of. Gunton's M. 11: 261.
— — Problems of. Ed. R. 182: 132.
— History of, Nöldeke's. Sat. R. 74: 595.
— Travel in. (A. Klein) Blackw. 151: 50-722. Same art. Liv. Age, 192: 612 — 193: 615.
— Travels in, Liddon's. Spec. 68: 403.
East (U. S.), Western Feeling towards the. (W. V. Allen) No. Am. 162: 588.
East and West. (E. Reclus) Contemp. 66: 475. Same art. Liv. Age, 203: 387.
East Boston Long Ago. (J. C. Johnson) Bost. 2: 409.
East India College of Haileybury. (A. Colvin) Blackw. 156: 107.
East Ruston Church. (J. L. André) Antiq. n. s. 31: 81.
East Winds in Hagar. (A. W. Colton) New Eng. M. n. s. 13: 371.
Easter. (T. M. Clark, A. G. Haygood, and others) M. Chr. Lit. 6: 142.
— in Russia. Chamb. J. 72: 145.
Easter; a poem. (J. Rand) Arena, 15: 827.
Easter in Florence; a poem. (Lord Houghton) M. of Art, 13: 276.
Easter Eggs. Walford's Antiq. 3: 233. 7: 172.
Easter Flowers. (C. S. Sargent) Garden & F. 7: 121.
Easter Hare, The. (C. J. Billson) Folk-Lore, 3: 441. — (G. J. Romanes) Open Court, 4: 2238.
Easter Homily, An. (L. J. Vance) Open Court, 4: 2180.
Easter Island. (W. J. Thomson) Nature, 46: 258.
Easter Observances. (T. E. Champion) Canad. M. 2: 458.
Easter Sepulchre, Ancient English Office of. (H. J. Feasey) 19th Cent. 37: 748.
Easter Story. (A. Theuriet) Temp. Bar, 94: 584.
Easter-tide in Greece. (Mrs. D. Boughton) M. Chr. Lit. 6: 139.
Easter-tide Recollections. All the Year, 70: 369.
Eastern Cadet, An. (L. B. Walford) Longm. 22: 334. Same art. Liv. Age, 199: 18.
Eastern Island and Evidences of a Lost Continent. (O. Smeaton) Westm. 144: 29.
Eastern Question. (S. Low) National, 26: 609. — (W. J. Stillman) Nation, 62: 27. — National, 28: 285. — Blackw. 160: 847.
— and Questions. (E. M. Bliss) Cent. 29: 473.
— Arabia, Islam, and the. (W. H. Thomson) Harper, 91: 625.
— The Greater. (R. K. Douglas) National, 26: 484.
— How the Sultan can save his Empire. (R. Ahmad) 19th Cent. 38: 1008.
— Immediate Future of Armenia. (W. K. Stride) Forum, 22: 308.
— Religious Basis of Russian Policy. (O. Novikoff) 19th Cent. 38: 1001.
— Russia and England. (A. J. French) Fortn. 63: 883.
— Shall the Frontier of Christendom be maintained? (J. W. Howe) Forum, 22: 321.
— Turkish Reforms and Armenia. (F. H. Geffcken) 19th Cent. 38: 991.
Eastern Questions, Far and Near. (R. C. Gundry; J. W. Gambier) Fortn. 66: 506.
— The Two. Fortn. 65: 193.
Easterton of Roseisle, Discoveries at. Reliquary, 36: 237.
Eastlake, Lady. Lond. Q. 86: 98.
Easton, Reginald. (W. P. Frith) M. of Art, 16: 150.
Easton Blues. (M. L. M. Howard) Am. Hist. Reg. 1: 533.
Eastport, Maine. (W. H. Kilby) New Eng. M. n. s. 14: 685.
Eastwick, Robert W. Life and Adventures. Spec. 68: 816.
Eating; Early English Fare. (C. Cooper) Gent. M. n. s. 48: 358.
Eaton, Daniel Cady. (W. H. Brewer) Am. J. Sci. 150: 184. — Nat. Sci. 7: 216. — (N. L. Britton) Science, n. s. 2: 57.
Eaton, William. (E. Shippen) Un. Serv. (Phila.) 13: 540.
Eaton, Wyatt. Critic, 28: 433.
Eb Hadley, Desert Teamster; a story. (J. R. Spears) Cosmopol. 17: 109.
Ebb and Flow; a poem. All the Year, 76: 13.
Ebb and Flow; a story. (E. Anstruther) Harper, 89: 219.
Ebb and Flow of the Tide; a poem. (J. Parr) Westm. 144: 273.
Ebb Tide, The; a story. (R. L. Stevenson and L. Osbourne) McClure, 2: 243 — 3: 89.
Ebers, George, with portrait. Bk. Buyer, 10: 308. — With portrait. Bk. News, 11: 520.
— Autobiography. Critic, 23: 58. — Dial (Ch.) 15: 87.
— How my Character was formed. Forum, 15: 738.
Ebner-Eschenbach, Marie von. Atlan. 74: 260.
Ebony Frame; a story. Ecl. M. 118: 414.
Ecclefechan, Scotland. Atlan. 71: 287. — (H. C. Shelley) New Eng. M. n. s. 11: 194.

Ecclesiastes, Book of. (A. N. Macnicoll) Time, 21: 157.
Ecclesiastical Impedimenta. (J. M. Sterrett) New World, 1: 431.
Ecclesiastical Persons. Duties of. Eng. R. 17: 391.
Echegaray, José. (W. Webster) Acad. 48: 358. — (H. Lynch) Contemp. 64: 576.
— Mariana; a play. Sat. R. 79: 547.
Echinoderms of N. E. America, Distribution of. (A. E. Verrill) Am. J. Sci. 149: 127, 199.
Echo from Willowwood; a poem. (C. G. Rossetti) M. of Art, 13: 385.
Echo in Egypt, An; a story. (R. Hichens) Temp. Bar, 109: 34.
Echo of Battle; a story. (A. M. Ewell) Atlan. 69: 218.
Eclipse of Iapetus, Nov. 1, 1889, Peculiarities of. (E. E. Barnard) Astron. 11: 119.
— of the Moon, Mar. 11, 1895. (L. A. Eddie) Pop. Astron. 2: 449.
— — Scientific Value of Total. (C. E. Furness) Pop. Astron. 3: 109.
— of the Sun, April 15-16, 1893. (H. S. Pritchett) Astron. 11: 454. — Astron. 11: 562. — (J. King) Astron. 11: 863. — (J. M. Schæberle) Astron. 12: 730. — (Sir R. S. Ball) Contemp. 63: 639. Same art. Ecl. M. 120: 805. Same art. Liv. Age, 197: 804. — (T. E. Thorpe) Fortn. 60: 55. Same art. Ecl. M. 121: 298. — (De la B. Pluvinel) Nature, 47: 304. — Nature, 48: 40. — Sat. R. 75: 652.
— — — Chili as a Field for Observation of. (J. King) Nature, 46: 561.
— — Aug. 9, 1896. (A. Fowler) Knowl. 19: 131. — (E. W. Maunder) Knowl. 19: 203. — Dub. R. 119: 411. — (A. Burton-Brown) Nature, 52: 633. — Nature, 54: 153, 197. — (J. M. Lockyer) Nature, 54: 395, 418, 441. — (A. L. Cortie) Month, 87: 476.
— — — Amherst Expedition to Japan. (M. L. Todd) Nation, 62: 468. 63: 84, 226, 267.
Eclipses. (J. Morrison) Pop. Astron. 4: 308.
— Graphic Construction of. (W. F. Rigge) Pop. Astron. 3: 247-454. 4: 67-184.
— of the Sun, Total, of 1889. (E. S. Holden) Cent. 21: 853.
Ecole des Beaux-Arts. (R. A. Cram) Am. Arch. 54: 108.
— Mathematics and Construction in. (J. M. White) Am. Arch. 49: 111.
— Prix de Rome at. (A. V. Parminter) M. of Art, 16: 26.
Economic and Statistical Studies at Chicago. (J. J. Halsey) Dial (Ch.) 15: 175.
Economic Doctrine. (W. Cunningham) Econ. J. 2: 1.
Economic Education, Problem of. (S. Newcomb) Q. J. Econ. 7: 375. — Soc. Econ. 7: 221.
Economic Experiences, Teaching of our Recent. (D. A. Wells) Forum, 16: 527.
Economic Fallacies, Argyll on. Ed. R. 177: 454.
Economic Freedom. (H. Teichmuller) Am. Law R. 29: 373.
Economic History, W. J. Ashley on. (W. A. S. Hewins) Econ. R. 3: 392.
Economic History, Perversion of. (W. Cunningham) Econ. J. 2: 491.
— Study of. (W. J. Ashley) Q. J. Econ. 7: 115.
Economic Ideas in France, Progress of. (M. Block) Ann. Am. Acad. Pol. Sci. 4: 1.
Economic Law, Moral Factor in. (W. Richmond) Econ. R. 1: 41.
Economic Laws, What are? (D. G. Ritchie) Econ. R. 2: 359.
Economic Legislation and Reports, English, Summary of. (E. Cannan) Econ. R. 5: 133, 263.
— of the States in 1894. (W. B. Shaw) Q. J. Econ. 9: 195.
Economic Legislation of the States in 1895. (W. B. Shaw) Q. J. Econ. 10: 218.
Economic Literature, Recent Tendencies in. (A. T. Hadley) Yale R. 3: 251.
Economic Man and the Clergy. (J. M. Sterrett) M. Chr. Lit. 6: 257.
Economic Progress, Theory of. (J. B. Clark) Econ. Stud. 1: 5. — Gunton's M. 11: 13.
Economic Reform short of Socialism. (E. B. Andrews) Int. J. Ethics, 2: 273.
Economic Revolution, The. (R. T. Ely) Chaut. 16: 398.
— in Europe. (E. P. Cheyney) Ann. Am. Acad. Pol. Sci. 2: 772.
Economic State. (L. M. Keasbey) Pol. Sci. Q. 8: 601.
Economic Study, Relation of, to Public and Private Charity. (J. Mavor) Ann. Am. Acad. Pol. Sci. 4: 34.
Economic Tendencies on the Continent. Soc. Econ. 1: 65.
Economic Terms, Misunderstandings about. (A. T. Hadley) Yale R. 4: 156.
Economic Theory concerning Value. (Van Buren Denslow) Soc. Econ. 6: 214.
— in America prior to 1776. (C. W. Macfarlane) Ann. Am. Acad. Pol. Sci. 6: 124.
Economic Variation, Universal Law of. (J. B. Clark) Q. J. Econ. 8: 261.
Economical Problem, Moral Aspect of. (E. Caird) Time, 18: 1.
Economics, Agriculture and. (C. A. Cripps) National, 20: 782.
— Altruism in. (W. H. Mallock) Forum, 21: 690.
— and Classics. Soc. Econ. 1: 278.
— and Ethics, Relation between. (J. S. Mackenzie) Int. J. Ethics, 3: 281. — (A. B. Woodford) Soc. Econ. 6: 297.
— at Berlin and Vienna. (H. R. Seager) J. Pol. Econ. 1: 236.
— Dishonest Newspaper. Soc. Econ. 9: 241.
— Dynamic, Patten on. (J. B. Clark) Ann. Am. Acad. Pol. Sci. 3: 30.
— Ethics of. (G. M. Gould) Open Court, 1: 689, 721, 747.
— Family. National, 23: 98.
— for the Young. (J. S. Kelsey) Soc. Econ. 4: 35.
— From a Woman's Point of View. (Amy Strachey) National, 23: 285, 403.
— Hadley's. (A. T. Hadley; G. G. Turrell) J. Pol. Econ. 5: 86. — Gunton's M. 11: 229.
— in the High School. (J. H. Clark) Soc. Econ. 9: 282.
— in Japan. (G. Droppers) Nation, 55: 286.
— Integrity of Economic Literature. Soc. Econ. 9: 11.
— Marshall on. (L. L. Price) Econ. J. 2: 17.
— Mathematical, Recent Contributions to. (C. P. Sanger) Econ. J. 5: 113.
— New. (W. W. Folwell) Am. Econ. Assoc. 8: 19.
— of Dynamic Society. Soc. Econ. 5: 335.
— Reality *vs.* Romance in. (T. E. Willson) Am. M. Civics, 8: 41.
— Recent Books on. (A. B. Woodford) Dial (Ch.) 14: 313.
— Relation of Engineering to. (W. Kent) Science, n. s. 2: 321.
— Relation of Sociology to. (A. W. Small) J. Pol. Econ. 3: 169.
— A School of. (C. D. Wright) Eth. Rec. 2: 209.
— Smart's Studies in. (L. L. Price) Econ. J. 6: 75.
— Teaching of. (J. L. Laughlin) Atlan. 77: 682.
— — in Secondary Schools. (H. W. Thurston) School R. 4: 604.
Economists and the Public. (S. M. Macvane) Q. J. Econ. 9: 132.

Economists as Mischief-makers. (W. Cunningham) Econ. R. 4: 1.
— Modern, Fallacies of. (A. Kitson) Pop. Sci. Mo. 42: 228.
Economy, Every-day. (Mrs. G. B. Jenks) Char. R. 1: 122.
Economy, Penn., Communistic Celibates at. (M. T. Bayard) Canad. M. 7: 199.
Ecstasy. (T. Ribot) Open Court, 3: 1970.
Ecuador. From the Sea to Quito. (W. P. Tisdel) Chaut. 18: 440, 584.
— its Cities and its People. (W. P. Tisdel) Chaut. 17: 321.
— Journey in. (M. B. Kerr) Nat. Geog. M. 7: 238.
— Western Lowland of. (T. Wolf) Geog. J. 1: 154.
— Wolf on. (C. De Kalb) Nation, 59: 272.
Edda, Derivation of. (E. Magnusson) Acad. 49: 15.
— Sources of the. (A. H. Gunlogsen) Open Court, 4: 2408.
Eddie. Overland, n. s. 23: 268.
Eddy, Clarence. Music, 7: 492.
Eden and the First Sin. (W. R. Harper) Bib. World, 3: 176.
Eden of the Gulf; a story. (A. J. H. Antona) Outing, 25: 514.
Eden River, England. (E. R. Dibdin) M. of Art, 18: 465.
Edentates, North American Origin of. (J. L. Wortman) Science, n. s. 4: 865.
Edenton, N. C., Declaration of Independence. (R. Dillard) M. Am. Hist. 28: 401.
— Historic Tea Party of, 1774. (R. Dillard) M. Am. Hist. 28: 81.
Edgehill, Battle of, and its Ghost Story. Argosy, 59: 381.
Edgeworth, Maria. (A. V. Dicey) Nation, 63: 162. — (J. Macaulay) Leis. Hour, 44: 296. — Lond. Q. 84: 15. — Temp. Bar, 105: 317. Same art. Ecl. M. 125: 191.
— and her Works. (Geo. Saintsbury) Macmil. 72: 161.
— Glimpse of. Argosy, 62: 283.
— Hare's Life and Letters of. (E. Purcell) Acad. 46: 525. — Spec. 73: 811. — (J. W. Chadwick) Nation, 60: 129. — Sat. R. 79: 288.
— Novels of. Quar. 182: 305.
Edict of Nantes, Revocation of. (R. Parsons) Am. Cath. Q. 19: 273.
Edinburgh. (J. J. O'Shea) Cath. World, 62: 195. — Leis. Hour, 41: 662.
— Ancient, Revels and Pageants of. (M. G. J. Kinloch) Month, 84: 370.
— House and its Owner, An. (D. Macleod) Good Words, 37: 742.
— in 1629. (J. B. Paul) Scot. R. 24: 1.
— International Exhibition, French and Dutch Pictures at. (R. A. M. Stevenson) M. of Art, 9: 482.
— — Old Edinburgh Street. (J. M. Gray) M. of Art, 9: 437.
— Museum of Science and Art, and its Director, Sir R. Murdock Smith. (H. M. Cundall) Art J. 44: 28.
— National Gallery. (W. Armstrong) M. of Art, 13: 1.
— Old Inns of. (A. W. Stewart) Gent. M. n. s. 52: 56. Same art. Ecl. M. 122: 264. Same art. Liv. Age, 200: 571.
— Queen's Park. (J. P. Croal) Art J. 46: 11.
— Royal Observatory at. Nature, 53: 605.
— St. Giles, Sunday Morning at. (A. W. Stewart) Sund. M. 25: 319.
— Schools of. (G. F. Adams) Educa. 14: 148.
— Sketches, Mason's. Sat. R. 73: 718.
— Society in, 1840–50. Longm. 21: 250. Same art. Liv. Age, 196: 606.
Edinburgh, University of. (Andrew Seth) Scot. R. 26: 159.
— — MacEwan Hall. (G. B. Brown) Art J. 46: 126.
— — — Decorations. (H. W. Bromhead) Art J. 48: 234.
— — Opening of. (Chas. A. Robinson) Bach. of Arts, 2: 326.
— — Story of Chair of Public Law in. (J. Lorimer) Law Q. 4: 139.
Edinburgh Dinnshenchas. (W. Stokes) Folk-Lore, 4: 471.
Edison, Thomas A., with portraits. (C. D. Lanier) R. of Rs. (N. Y.) 8: 41. — (C. Barnard) Chaut. 18: 677.
— Connection of the Family of, with Digby, N. S. (A. W. Savary) N. E. Reg. 48: 199.
— Home and Workshop of. (W. Taylor) Munsey, 6: 185.
— Life and Inventions of. (A. and W. K. L. Dickson) Cassier, 3: 3–445. 4: 56–445. 5: 16, 131.
— on Inventions. (R. R. Wilson) Mo. Illust. 11: 340.
— Portraits of. McClure, 1: 124.
— Telephone of. (J. Munro) Time, 3: 24.
— Unsolved Problems of. (C. Moffett) McClure, 1: 37.
— Visit to. Time, 1: 101.
Edited Story, An. (M. Roberts) Eng. Illust. 14: 541.
Editor, Diversions of a sub-. (J. Pendleton) Ecl. M. 126: 419.
Editor-in-Chief. (A. K. McClure) Lippinc. 49: 77.
— Literary. (M. Philips) Lippinc. 49: 457.
— Managing. (J. Chambers) Lippinc. 49: 195.
— of "The Cuadrilla," The. Macmil. 72: 57.
— Reminiscences of an. Forum, 20: 631.
— Sporting. (J. B. McCormick) Lippinc. 50: 633.
Editorial Talks with Contributors. (W. H. Ward and others) Writer, 8: 125–173.
Editor's Incubus. (I. Allen) Lippinc. 58: 285.
Editor's Story. (R. H. Davis) Harper, 89: 342.
Editor's Story, An. (C. N. Carvalho) Argosy, 61: 77.
Editors. National, 27: 505. Same art. Liv. Age, 210: 131. Same art. Ecl. M. 127: 77.
— and MSS.; are Editors to blame? (E. L. White) Writer, 7: 41.
— Chiefs of the American Press. (J. Creelman) Cosmopol. 18: 81.
— Evolution of. (L. Stephen) National, 26: 770. Same art. Liv. Age, 208: 643.
— Experiences with. (J. M. Oxley) Bookman, 2: 31, 122.
Educated Class, Irresponsible, Danger of, in a Republic. (H. H. Gardner) Arena, 6: 311.
Educated Men in a Democracy, Duty of. (E. L. Godkin) Forum, 17: 39.
— Mission of. (S. G. Valentine) Luth. Q. 23: 508.
— Need of. (D. S. Jordan) Pop. Sci. Mo. 46: 164.
— Public Duties of. Meth. R. 56: 782.
Education. (T. C. Laws) Open Court, 9: 4499, 4507.
— Academic Spirit in. (J. A. Hobson) Contemp. 63: 236. Same art. Ecl. M. 120: 467.
— Æsthetic Side of. (H. L. Clapp) Educa. 15: 449.
— Aim of Modern. (C. H. Henderson) Pop. Sci. Mo. 49: 485.
— Aims in, Efforts toward Clear. (G. S. Hall; T. Davidson; M. F. Crow) Forum, 19: 588.
— American, Need of a Distinctively. (E. P. Powell) Educa. 16: 202.
— among Roman Catholics, Outlook for. (W. S. Coward) Dub. R. 112: 150.
— and Childhood. (C. F. Carroll) Educa. 17: 79.
— and Crime in England, Growth of. Church. Q. 35: 217.
— and Evolution. (J. Le Conte) Educa. R. 10: 121.
— and Geologic Science. (N. S. Shaler) Science, n. s. 3: 609.
— and Instruction. (Lord Coleridge) Contemp. 64: 828.

Education and Literature. (Hiram M. Stanley) Dial (Ch.) 16: 296.
— and Maintenance. (T. K. Nuttall) Law Q. 10: 330.
— and Politics. (C. H. Reeve) Am. J. Pol. 1: 250.
— and Selection. (A. Fouillée) Pop. Sci. Mo. 43: 349.
— and the State. (J. G. Fitch) Contemp. 68: 134.
— and Vocation. (S. T. Dutton) Am. J. Soc. Sci. no. 34: 52.
— and Wealth. (H. G. Ager) Am. J. Pol. 3: 483.
— and the Will. (G. M. Steele) Educa. 16: 353.
— Art in. (E. V. Eastman) Music, 5: 47.
— Art in General. (J. S. Clark) Educa. R. 10: 331.
— as a Science. (E. W. Scripture) Pedagog. Sem. 2: 111.
— at the California Midwinter Fair. (T. R. Bacon) Overland, n. s. 23: 352.
— Basis of our Educational System. (J. J. Greenough) Atlan. 75: 528.
— A Bit of Psychology applied. (H. W. Crompton) Educa. R. 7: 343.
— Breadth in. (W. C. Lawton) Citizen, 1: 60.
— Catholics and Protestants in Coöperation. (S. J. Barrows) Lend a H. 14: 202.
— Cause and Effect in. (C. H. Henderson) Pop. Sci. Mo. 45: 51.
— Christian. (F. P. Manhart) Luth. Q. 24: 69.
— — Function and Scope of. (M. Rhodes) Luth. Q. 25: 393.
— — New Forms of. (M. A. Ward) New World, 1: 329.
— Classics and Modern Subjects. (H. S. Salt) Time, 7: 477.
— — and Science in. (E. Mach) Open Court, 8: 4295-4311.
— Compulsory. (C. De Graffenried) Lend a H. 16: 415.
— — in the U. S. (W. B. Shaw) Educa. R. 3: 444. 4: 47, 129.
— — Is it a Failure? (J. J. Davies) Westm. 137: 183.
— — Substitute for. (H. E. Monroe) Educa. 14: 352.
— Congresses of, Chicago, 1893. *See* Educational Congresses.
— Convent. (R. E. Scott) Month, 81: 217.
— Dangerous Tendencies in. (J. P. Monroe) Educa. R. 3: 145.
— Democracy and. Dial (Ch.) 14: 351. — (N. M. Butler) Educa. R. 12: 120.
— Direction of. (N. S. Shaler) Atlan. 75: 389.
— Duty of Young People to obtain Best Possible. (M. A. Whedon) Educa. 15: 354.
— Early, History of. (S. S. Laurie) School R. 1: 263, 668.
— Educator on Failure of. (E. P. North) Soc. Econ. 4: 157.
— Elementary. (W. T. Harris) No. Am. 160: 538. — (N. M. Butler) Nation, 60: 142. — (W. T. Harris) Nation, 60: 181.
— — An Experiment in. (M. A. Aber) Pop. Sci. Mo. 40: 377, 517.
— — and the Decay of Literature. (J. Ackland) 19th Cent. 35: 412.
— — Report on. Dial (Ch) 18: 167.
— — The Truth about. (A. Sonnenschein) Time, 12: 385, 565. 13: 419.
— Enliven it. (E. E. Hale) Lend a H. 17: 83.
— Evolutionary Psychology and. (Hiram M. Stanley) Educa. R. 12: 50.
— Exogenous and Indigenous. (C. A. Powell) Educa. 13: 45.
— An Experiment in. Soc. Econ. 1: 218.
— Experts in. (L. Dunton) Educa. 13: 327.
— Extension of the Public School. Soc. Econ. 3: 159.
— Few Words about. Dial (Ch.) 19: 105.
Education, Five L's in: Life, Liberty, Light, Law, Love. (S. Harris) And. R. 18: 437.
— for the People, Means of. Lend a H. 13: 163.
— Forces in. (C. F. Carroll) Educa. 15: 193.
— from a National Point of View. (F. Watson) Acad. 44: 314.
— Full-orbed. (J. R. Buchanan) Arena, 5: 417.
— Future of. (J. P. Mahaffy) 19th Cent. 34: 212. Same art. Ecl. M. 121: 367.
— Future of Economic. (C. De Garmo) Soc. Econ. 7: 221.
— Half-time System of, Results of, in England. (R. Waddington) Educa. R. 6: 65.
— High School, for Girls, Aims and Results of. (Mrs. H. Fawcett) Time, 18: 528.
— Higher, and Athletics. Spec. 76: 767.
— — and Christianity. (C. F. Thwing) Educa. 12: 257.
— — Duty of. (D. Quinn) Am. J. Soc. Sci. no. 34: 15.
— — Economics of. (D. J. Hill) Bapt. R. 14: 38.
— — for the Masses. (S. Channing) Open Court, 6: 3329.
— — in the U. S. (S. Low) Educa. R. 5: 1.
— — Outlook in. (G. S. Hall) Acad. (Syr.) 6: 543.
— — True Purpose of. (T. Dwight) Forum, 13: 311.
— History of Early; Aryan Races. (S. S. Laurie) School R. 2: 129, 214, 337, 419, 487.
— Home. (E. P. Powell) Educa. 14: 10.
— How shall the Child be taught? (J. M. Rice) Forum, 22: 385.
— Ideal, in Our Cities. (E. O. Buxton) Am. J. Pol. 1: 72.
— in Ancient Babylonia, Phœnicia, and Judea. (C. G. Hebermann) Am. Cath. Q. 18: 449.
— in Ancient Egypt. (C. G. Hebermann) Am. Cath. Q. 18: 176.
— in Ancient Greece. (C. G. Hebermann) Am. Cath. Q. 20: 766. — School R. 3: 16.
— in Argentine Republic. Lend a H. 12: 345.
— in Arkansas, Higher. (A. C. Millar) Educa. R. 4: 77.
— in China. Liv. Age, 196: 63.
— in Delaware, History of. Lend a H. 13: 43.
— in England. (E. Porritt) Nation, 59: 301. 62: 301. — Citizen, 2: 302.
— — Acland's New Code. (J. J. Davies) Westm. 144: 141.
— — Outlook for 1896. (J. R. Diggle) Fortn. 65: 72.
— — Bill of 1896. National, 28: 297. — Quar. 183: 58. — (E. G. Taylor) Westm. 145: 644. — (J. R. Diggle) National, 27: 435. — (J. Herlihy) Westm. 146: 367. — Church Q. 41: 489. 42: 196, 476. — (A. M. Fairbairn) Contemp. 69: 761. — (E. L. Stanley) Contemp. 69: 741. — (J. G. Rogers) 19th Cent. 39: 785. — (T. J. McNamara) 19th Cent. 39: 779. — (E. Porritt) New World, 5: 458.
— — — Flaws in. (J. G. Fitch) 19th Cent. 39: 881.
— — — From the Old Nonconformist Standpoint. (H. M. Bompas) Fortn. 66: 810.
— — — The Government's Opportunity. (J. R. Diggle) National, 28: 325.
— — — Policy of. (J. R. Diggle) Contemp. 70: 30.
— — — Reopening the Settlement of 1870. (E. L. Stanley) 19th Cent. 38: 915. — (J. R. Diggle; A. Riley) 19th Cent. 39: 44. — Reply. (E. L. Stanley) 19th Cent. 39: 328.
— — County Councils and Rural Education. (C. T. D. Acland) 19th Cent. 40: 596.
— — Crisis in. Church Q. 41: 1.
— — Day with a Diocese Inspector. (A. Thorold) Sund. M. 21: 747.
— — Denominational Schools and the Government. (J. F. Wilkinson) National, 28: 489.

Education in England. An Educational Interlude. Fortn. 65: 355. Same art. Liv. Age, 209: 179.
— — Elementary, and Voluntary Schools. Contemp. 62: 895.
— — Local Support of. (T. J. McNamara) 19th Cent. 40: 919.
— — Payment by Results, System of. (B. A. Hinsdale) Educa. R. 4: 105.
— — Prospects of. (J. E. Gorst) No. Am. 163: 427.
— — Public Schools in 1894. Ath. '94, 2: 65.
— — Recent Reform in. (J. R. Diggle) Sat. R. 81: 390.
— — Recent Tendencies of. (A. F. Palmer) School R. 4: 739.
— — Reopening the Settlement of 1870. (E. L. Stanley) 19th Cent. 38: 915.
— — The School Question, 1895. (E. Porritt) Nation, 61: 252.
— — Secondary. (F. Watson) Acad. 42: 280.
— — — Commission Report. (J. Massie) Contemp. 68: 783.
— — — Movement for. (H. E. Roscoe) Nature, 49: 203.
— — Upper Class, and its Amendment. (T. W. Fleming) Westm. 138: 428.
— — Voluntary Schools. (J. E. Gorst) 19th Cent. 40: 699. — (J. M. Wilson; F. W. Farrar; H. S. Holland; R. Eyton; W. Sinclair) Contemp. 68: 731.
— in France, Contemporary. (G. Compayré) Educa. R. 10: 313.
— — Recent Tendencies of. (A. F. Palmer) School R. 4: 739.
— — Secondary. (C. Schefer) Nation, 56: 100.
— in Germany, from the Standpoint of a German Teacher. (F. Reutter) Westm. 138: 156.
— in India. (J. A. Baines) J. Statis. Soc. 57: 254.
— in Ireland, Elementary. Church Q. 42: 174.
— — Intermediate. Chamb. J. 69: 794.
— — Question of. (T. W. Russell) Fortn. 57: 245.
— — Roman Catholic University for. Spec. 71: 264.
— in Italy. (A. Oldrini) Chaut. 18: 415.
— in Madras, System of. (G. F. Mackenzie) Dub. R. 119: 319.
— in Manitoba. (G. Bryce) Canad. M. 1: 512.
— in Paris, Free. (C. de Pratz) New R. 8: 675
— in Preparatory Schools. (C. F. Adams; W. W. Goodwin) Harv. Grad. M. 1: 177.
— in Prussia, Elementary, Bill for, in 1892. (N. M. Butler) Educa. R. 3: 355. — Pub. Opin. 12: 477. — Spec. 68: 111, 193.
— — Some Characteristics of Prussian Schools. (E. J. Goodwin) Educa. R. 12: 453.
— in Scotland. (J. Donaldson) Scot. R. 21: 183.
— — Edgar's History of Early. (J. Davidson) Educa. R. 8: 86.
— — Secondary. Scot. R. 19: 161.
— in the South, Advance of. (C. W. Dabney, jr.) Cosmopol. 13: 531.
— — for the Common People. (G. W. Cable) Cosmopol. 14: 63.
— — Problem of. (J. C. Hartsell) Meth. R. 52: 39.
— in the U. S. (W. T. Harris) Chaut. 15: 16.
— — Christian and Patriotic. (A. Young) Cath. World. 59: 444.
— — Nationalization of, and the Universities. (H. von Holst) Monist, 3: 493.
— — Organization of. (W. D. Hyde) Educa. R. 4: 209.
— — Roman Catholic Controversy about. (J. A. Mooney) Educa. R. 3: 237. — Reply. (T. Bouquillon) Educa. R. 3: 365. — Another reply. (T. O'Gorman) Educa. R. 3: 462.
— — Ten Years of. (W. Addis) School R. 1: 339.
— in the West. (C. F. Thwing) Harper, 85: 715.
Education, Initial Propositions in. (B. H. Holbrook) Educa. 15: 543.
— Innocence *vs.* Ignorance. (A. Rives) No. Am. 155: 287.
— Inspiration in. (J. E. Bradley) Educa. 15: 129.
— Isms in Schools. (J. S. Ewart) Canad. M. 1: 356.
— Is it Possible, without Freedom of the Will? (W. T. Harris) Educa. 16: 301.
— Is there a Science of? (R. H. Holbrook) Educa. 14: 272.
— Liberal. (G. W. Prothero) Scot. R. 28: 346.
— — Modern. (G. T. Ladd) Educa. R. 10: 218.
— — *vs.* Practical. (D. C. Gilman) Educa. R. 3: 105.
— — What is a? (F. M. Holland) Open Court, 7: 3631.
— London, *vs.* London Progressives. (J. R. Diggle) National, 24: 307.
— Lord Herschell on. Spec. 71: 625.
— Manitoba School Question. Soc. Econ. 9: 52.
— Modern Ideals of. (W. K. Hill) Contemp. 70: 568.
— National. Eng. R. 7: 401. — Time, 8: 38.
— — Disraeli on. (J. W. Hoste) Fortn. 65: 808.
— Natural or Scientific Method in. (W. Mills) Pop. Sci. Mo. 42: 10.
— Nervous System and its Relations to. (J. Ferguson) Pop. Sci. Mo. 47: 528.
— New. (N. M. Butler) Educa. R. 11: 58. — (C. B. Gilbert) Educa. 16: 37, 95, 151. — (J. R. Buchanan) Arena, 10: 590.
— — and Character-building. (J. R. Buchanan) Arena, 7: 268.
— — and its Practical Application. (J. R. Buchanan) Arena, 6: 653.
— — Another Phase of. (G. Buck) Forum, 22: 376.
— — a New-Church View of. (J. T. Prince) N. Church R. 3: 85.
— New Psychology as a Basis of. (G. S. Hall) Forum, 17: 710.
— Next Steps forward in. (E. B. Andrews) School & C. 1: 1.
— of an American Boy, Ideal. (T. Davidson) Forum, 17: 571.
— of Boys. (D. C. Gilman) Cosmopol. 12: 461.
— of the Foreign Element in Boston. (L. Wiener) Bost. 3: 34.
— of the Future. (C. King) Forum, 13: 20.
— of the Greek People, Davidson on. (W. M. Aber) School R. 4: 558.
— of Our Boys. Time, 23: 1083.
— of the Poor. Eng. R. 6: 127. — (Frances McNab) Temp. Bar, 109: 99.
— of a Prince. (E. E. Hale) Chaut. 20: 65.
— of the Whole of the Threefold Nature of Man. (H. C. Haithcox) Luth. Q. 25: 236.
— Oriental. (G. W. Leitner) Asia. R. 18: 421.
— Our Educational Finance. (J. D. White) Fortn. 65: 84.
— Over-. Sat. R. 474: 74. Same art. Ecl. M. 119: 818.
— Pauper, and Kneller Hall. Eng. R. 12: 107.
— Personal. (E. E. Hale) Lend a H. 8: 299.
— Philosophy and. (J. M. Baldwin) Presb. & Ref. R. 5: 36.
— Physical Element in. (E. L. Richards) Pop. Sci. Mo. 47: 471.
— Popular. Spec. 71: 514.
— — and Religious Liberty. (Cardinal Vaughan) New R. 15: 97.
— — at the University of Michigan. (H. C. Adams) Forum, 14: 123.
— — Wherein it has failed. (C. W. Eliot) Forum, 14: 411.

Education, Pre-Christian, Laurie on. (B. A. Hinsdale) Dial (Ch.) 19: 282.
— Present Sacrifice of. (C. Waterer) Westm. 145: 616.
— Principles of. (M. MacVicar) Educa. 12: 524–13: 165.
— Problem of. (J. S. Stahr) Ref. Q. 39: 421.
— Professional and Technical, Relation of, to General. (F. A. Walker) Educa. R. 8: 417.
— Public, Function of. (H. D. Chapin) No. Am. 162: 122.
— Public School Extension. Soc. Econ. 3: 27.
— A Public School Triumph. (D. Boyle) Canad. M. 3: 88.
— Purpose of. (T. E. Will) Open Court, 9: 4673.
— Reform in. (W. Mitchell) Int. J. Ethics, 6: 24.
— — Unity of. (C. W. Eliot) Educa. R. 8: 209.
— Relation to Vocation. (S. T. Dutton) Educa. R. 12: 335.
— Religious. (A. Henriques) Jew. Q. 3: 85. — (J. H. Jackson) Law Q. 12: 379.
— — Crisis in. (Bp. of Salford) National, 26: 448.
— — in Board Schools. (J. E. Graham) Jurid. R. 7: 13.
— — Jewish. (E. Harris and L. M. Simmons) Jew. Q. 6: 74.
— — of Children. Westm. 146: 61.
— Research in. (H. E. Armstrong) Nature, 51: 463. — (H. E. Armstrong) Sci. Prog. 4: 335.
— Roman. School R. 3: 143. — (S. S. Laurie) School R. 3: 211.
— Rousseau's Theory of. (A. E. Street) Macmil. 67: 50.
— School in an Air Castle. (W. Griffin) Canad. M. 5: 299.
— The Schoolhouse as a Centre. (H. E. Scudder) Atlan. 77: 103.
— Schools of the Olden Time. Canad. M. 2: 320.
— Science, Art, History, Studies in, Hinsdale on, (W. A. Mowry) School R. 4: 560.
— Science in, Place of. Nature, 53: 607.
— Secular. (T. A. Becker) Am. Cath. Q. 17: 176.
— Sham. (J. P. Mahaffy) 19th Cent. 33: 19. Same art. Ecl. M. 120: 289.
— Sociologic Basis of. (C. MacMillan) Educa. 16: 331.
— Some Political Principles applied to. (L. M. Salmon) Educa. R. 11: 220.
— Some Reasons for the School Board Rate. (C. A. Sim) Fortn. 65: 818.
— Spiritualization of, in America. (L. Whiting) Arena, 15: 286.
— State Aid in, Cost of. Spec. 74: 893.
— State and, in England and America. (I. Sharpless) Ann. Am. Acad. Pol. Sci. 3: 669.
— — and the "isms." (W. D. Le Sueur) Canad. M. 2: 3.
— — and Public. (L. G. Janes) Soc. Econ. 2: 152.
— — Limits of. (M. M. Trumbull) Am. J. Pol. 3: 225.
— — Purposes and Needs of. (W. M. Beardshear) Educa. 12: 293.
— — Secondary and Higher. (A. D. Mayo) 12: 252, 335.
— Study of, at Harvard University. (P. H. Hames) Educa. R. 72: 47.
— — at the Sorbonne. (H. Marion) Educa. R. 7: 122.
— — at Stanford University. (E. Barnes) Educa. R. 6: 360.
— — at the University of California. (E. E. Brown) Educa. R. 8: 169.
— — at the University of Edinburgh. (S. S. Laurie) Educa. R. 7: 55.
— — at the University of Michigan. (B. A. Hinsdale) Educa. R. 6: 443.
— Sympathy a Neglected Factor of. (W. Smith) Educa. 17: 211.
— Symposiums. Indep. Aug. 3, '93, Aug. 2, '94, Aug. 1, '95, Aug. 6, '96.
Education, Tendencies in, Current. (C. E. Lowrey) Educa. 14: 361.
— Thirteen Essays on. Sat. R. 73: 20.
— Tripartite Division of. (B. A. Hinsdale) School R. 4: 513.
— True Aim of. (A. S. Weber) Ref. Q. 41: 109. — (W. J. Greenstreet) Westm. 137: 394. — (E. E. White) Educa. 13: 65.
— Unappreciated Factors in. (— Austin) Educa. 15: 485.
— Utilitarian, Liberal and Jesuit. (T. Hughes) Cath. World, 57: 803.
— *versus* the Gold Fever. (E. V. Sutton) Educa. 14: 83.
Voluntary System applied to. Eng. R. 10: 306.
— Wholesale. (C. A. Powell) Lend a H. 9: 94.
Educational Aims and Educational Values. (P. H. Hanus) Educa. R. 9: 323.
Educational Congresses, International, at Chicago, 1893. (R. Waterman, jr.) Educa. R. 6: 158. — Dial (Ch.) 15: 81. — (G. Compayré) Educa. 14: 426, 489, 552. — (F. H. Kasson) Educa. 14: 32.
— — A Foreigner's Impressions of. (G. Compayré) Educa. R. 6: 257.
Educational Exhibits at the Columbian Exposition. (R. Waterman, jr.) Educa. R. 7: 129, 260.
— at World's Fairs since 1851. (R. Waterman, jr.) Educa. R. 5: 120, 219.
Educational Fads and Reforms. (E. L. Cowdrick) Educa. 17: 217.
— Psychology of. (J. W. Redway) Educa. R. 11: 179.
Educational Finance in England; Statistics of Girls' Schools. (S. Bryant) Econ. J. 4: 94.
Educational Institutions, Our, Coördination of. (E. H. Magill) Pop. Sci. Mo. 49: 176.
— in the Middle Ages. (P. Schaff) Ref. Q. 40: 205.
— in the West, The Church's Need of. (F. M. Porch) Luth. Q. 22: 562.
Educational Method. (H. K. Wolfe) Educa. R. 4: 27.
Educational Museums and Libraries of Europe. (W. S. Monroe) Educa. R. 11: 374.
Educational Organization, The County Unit in. (L. B. Evans) Educa. R. 11: 369.
Educational Problems in Europe, Some Phases of Present. (N. M. Butler) Educa. R. 7: 356.
— Symposium. Indep. Aug. 4, '92.
Educational Progress in America. (M. Louch) Educa. R. 7: 71.
Educational Statistics, Recent. (W. H. Norton) Meth. R. 53: 57.
Educational System in Fact, An American. (E. P. Powell) Forum, 19: 429.
Educational Thought in Germany, Contemporary. (E. von Sallwürk) Educa. R. 5: 313. — (W. Rein) Educa. R. 7: 460.
Educational Trend of the Northwest. (D. L. Kiehle) Atlan. 71: 832.
Educational Values. (J. H. Baker) Educa. R. 10: 209. — Dial (Ch.) 18: 229.
— Patten on. (J. W. Jenks) Educa. R. 31: 1.
Educational *versus* Logical Value. (F. W. Osborn) Educa. R. 11: 276.
Edward the Confessor, Saint. (E. C. Glyn) Cornh. 74: 739.
Edward III. Year Books, ed. by Pike. Sat. R. 73: 17.
Edward IV. Early Part of Reign of. Eng. R. 1: 415.
Edward VI. of England; Spoiler of Schools. (A. F. Leach) Contemp. 62: 368.
Edwards, Amelia Blandford. Acad. 41: 38. — (R. S. Poole; J. S. Cotton) Acad. 41: 397. — With portrait. (W. C. Winslow) Am. Antiq. 14: 305. — (M. B. Edwards) Ath. '92, 1: 534. — Critic, 20: 244. — Sat. R. 73: 473. Same art. Liv. Age, 194: 63. — With portrait. Bk. Buyer, 6: 363.

Edwards, Amelia Blandford, Childhood and Early Life of. (M. Betham-Edwards) New Eng. M. n. s. 7: 547.
Edwards, George Wharton. (P. Maxwell) Q. Illust. 1: 85.
Edwin, David, Catalogue of Engraved Works of. (C. R. Hildeburn) Pennsyl. M. 18: 97, 223.
Eel, Electric. Spec. 71: 110.
Eels. Leis. Hour, 43: 667. — (W. F. Nelson) Time, 16: 347. — (M. R. Davies) Gent. M. n. s. 50: 155.
— Gossip about. (T. Southwell) Longm. 21: 81.
Efferati Family, The; a story. (T. A. Janvier) Harper, 85: 763.
Effigies in Wood, English. (A. Hartshorne) Portfo. 24: 177, 202.
Egbert, Latin Penitential of, and Missing Work of Halitgar. (M. Bateson) Eng. Hist. R. 9: 320.
Egerton, Geo., *pseud.* *See* Clairmont, Mrs.
Egg Collector, Reminiscences of an. All the Year, 74: 301.
Eggs and their Foes. Sat. R. 77: 412.
Eggleston, Edward, with portrait. Bk. Buyer, 4: 96.
— With portrait. Bk. News, 6: 440.
Ego and Non-ego. (D. G. Watts) Psych. R. 1: 360.
— as Cause. (J. Dewey) Philos. R. 3: 337.
— Causality, and Freedom. (J. Hyslop) Philos. R. 3: 717.
— Blessedness of. (R. P. Jacobus) Fortn. 65: 40, 384.
— Duty of. Spec. 70: 513.
— et Rex Meus: a Study of Royalty. (L. de la Ramé) Forum, 21: 471.
Egotism. Spec. 70: 701.
Egotist's Whim, An. (East Owen) Temp. Bar, 109: 557.
Egremond, The Boy of. (J. Cartwright) M. of Art, 11: 62.
Egypt. (A. E. P. R. Dowling) Am. Cath. Q. 19: 754.
— Age of. (F. G. Fleay) Ath. '95, 2: 100.
— Agriculture in. (R. Wallace) J. Soc. Arts, 40: 596.
— Ancient. Chamb. J. 70: 785.
— — Astronomy and Worship in. (J. N. Lockyer) 19th Cent. 32: 29.
— — Conceptions of Death and Immortality in. (P. Carus) Open Court, 9: 4666.
— — Funeral Rites in. Ath. '94, 1: 283.
— — Mystery of. (W. M. Adams) New R. 9: 618. Same art. Liv. Age, 200: 182.
— — Poetry in. (F. C. H. Wendel) Chaut. 19: 589.
— — Prehistoric Times in. (J. W. Dawson) No. Am. 154: 672. 155: 68.
— and the Books of Moses. Eng. R. 3: 387.
— and Canaan. (F. A. Dewson) N. Church R. 2: 580.
— and Chaldea in the Light of Recent Discoveries. (W. St. C. Boscawen) Harper, 88: 190.
— and Great Britain; Coming Struggle on the Nile. (A. S. White) No. Am. 163: 326.
— and Israel. (W. M. F. Petrie) Contemp. 69: 617.
— and its Frontier. (A. Griffiths) Fortn. 65: 490.
— and Palestine, 1400 B. C. (M. Jastrow, jr.) J. Bib. Lit. 11: 95.
— Antiquities from, exhibited in London. Acad. 48: 16, 37.
— Archæological Explorations in. (W. M. F. Petrie and others) Acad. 41: 356, 379.
— Archæological Letters from. (A. H. Sayce; D. G. Hogarth) Acad. 41: 212-332. 43: 157-444. 45: 132-401. 47: 261, 385. 49: 225, 289, 310, 370.
— Archæological Researches in. (D. G. Hogarth and others) Acad. 47: 133-341.
— Army of, and Military Situation in. (O. G. Villard) Un. Serv. (Phila.) 14: 201.
— Art in, Primitive. (W. M. F. Petrie) J. Soc. Arts, 41: 673.
Egypt, British Explorations in. Time, 11: 89.
— British Occupation. (Abdullah Ash-Shámi) Asia. R. 20: 58. — Liv. Age, 192: 67.
— British Rights in. (M. J. Farelly) Macm. 70: 464.
— Contemporary. (F. C. Penfield) No. Am. 161: 13.
— *Coup d'Etat* in. (E. L. Godkin) Nation, 56: 61.
— Culture of, Origin of. (R. W. Rogers) Meth. R. 54: 51.
— Discoveries in, Recent. Am. Arch. 49: 112.
— Donkey-boys in. (E. H. and E. W. Bashfield) Scrib. M. 11: 32.
— — Egyptians and. Ecl. M. 118: 73.
— Eastern Desert of, Further Routes in. (E. A. Floyer) Geog. J. 1: 408.
— Georg Ebers'. (J. W. Mollet) M. of Arts, 4: 110.
— England in. Lond. Q. 80: 96. — (J. Adams; E. Dicey) New R. 6: 56. — (E. Dicey) New R. 8: 306. — Quar. 180: 255.
— — Milner on. R. of Rs. (N. Y.) 7: 185. — (G. R. Parkin) Nation, 56: 218.
— England's Work in. (Lord Farrer) National, 27: 166. 28: 443.
— — Difficulties of Withdrawal. (H. D. Traill) 19th Cent. 39: 544.
— — Our Promise to withdraw. (W. Reid) 19th Cent. 39: 557.
— English Failure in. Contemp. 67: 390.
— English Policy in. Sat. R. 79: 276.
— Evacuation of. (H. Norman) Contemp. 61: 487.
— Excavations in. (W. M. F. Petrie) Acad. 49: 309.
— Exploitations of, Sidelights on the. (F. C. Penfield) No. Am. 159: 479.
— Exploration in. Dub. R. 113: 674.
— 5000 Years Ago. Liv. Age, 201: 190.
— France and. (F. Deloncle) National, 27: 325.
— France and England in. (J. Adam) No. Am. 159: 34.
— Geology of. (P. Lake) Sci. Prog. 4: 395.
— Gods of. (Grant Allen) Univ. R. 8: 51.
— Hatesu. Cornh. 67: 186.
— History of; Date of Fourth Dynasty. (G. F. Hardy) Acad. 42: 391.
— — Mahaffy on. (J. H. Breasted) Dial (Ch.) 20: 359.
— — Petrie's. Sat. R. 79: 71. — (C. R. Gillett) Nation, 60: 188. — (A. Macalister) Crit. R. 5: 133.
— — Sketch of. (J. H. Breasted) Bib. World, 7: 438.
— How to save. (C. Whitehouse) Fortn. 60: 655.
— in 1882-1892. (W. T. Marriott) Fortn. 57: 782. Same art. Liv. Age, 194: 259.
— in 1896. Ed. R. 184: 237.
— In the Lotus Land. (C. W. Wood) Argosy, 53: 49-478. 54: 42-490. 55: 29-290.
— In the Mountains of. (E. N. Buxton) 19th Cent. 35: 495. Same art. Liv. Age, 200: 811. Same art. Ecl. M. 122: 534.
— Irrigation in. Dub. R. 119: 431. — (J. N. Lockyer) Nature, 50: 80.
— Justice in. (H. A. Perry) Law Q. 1: 342.
— Justice to. (Lord Farrer) National, 27: 483.
— Khedive and Lord Cromer. (W. S. Blunt) 19th Cent. 33: 571. 35: 177.
— Life in Modern. (C. B. R. Kent) Gent. M. n. s. 51: 351. Same art. Ecl. M. 121: 652. Same art. Liv. Age, 199: 498.
— Literary Discoveries in. Quar. 176: 344. Same art. Liv. Age, 197: 771.
— Mixed Courts of. (W. E. Grigsby) Law Q. 12: 252.
— Monuments of. Spec. 72: 194. Same art. Liv. Age, 200: 763. — (H. P. Laird) Ref. Q. 41: 504.
— — Israel and. Meth. R. 56: 976.
— Moses in. (W. R. Winston) Sund. M. 24: 375.
— Names in, Spelling of. (J. C. Dalton) Geog. J. 3: 504.
— Names of Towns in. Asia. R. 13: 328.

Egypt, Neutralization of. (Ar Rashîdî) Asia. R. 15: 345.
— New Crisis in, 1894. Spec. 72: 122.
— Newly-found Race in. (J. E. Quibell) Knowl. 18: 196. — (D. G. Brinton) Science, n. s. 2: 227. — Reliquary, 36: 115.
— Newspapers in. (W. F. Rae) 19th Cent. 32: 213.
— Nile Notes. Cornh. 68: 25.
— Oasis in, An unknown. (W. W. Hunt) Gent. M. n. s. 52: 421.
— Occult Sciences in the Temples of Ancient. (G. L. Leonard) Open Court, 1: 470, 496.
— of the Hebrews, Sayce's. (F. P. Nash) Nation, 63: 350. — Sat. R. 81: 458.
— Our Cleopatra. (H. D. Traill) National, 23: 118.
— Pharaoh Land. (C. C. Halkett) Belgra. 84: 369.
— Pharaohs, Fellahs, and Explorers, Edwards'. Spec. 68: 202. — Sat. R. 73: 247.
— Place of the Repose of Jesus Christ in. (A. R. Dowling) Am. Cath. Q. 19: 93.
— Present Position of Egyptology. (J. P. Mahaffy) 19th Cent. 36: 268.
— Progress of. Spec. 69: 406.
— Question of. (J. Simon) Contemp. 69: 609.
— Rae's. Blackw. 153: 152. — Spec. 69: 964.
— Real Estate Law of, in time of Joseph. (H. A. Lounsberry) Am. J. Pol. 4: 461.
— Recent Works on. Church Q. 39: 474.
— Regeneration of. (E. H. Woodruff) Nation, 54: 298.
— The situation in, 1894. (W. T. Marriott) Fortn. 63: 510.
— — 1893. Spec. 70: 150. 71: 933.
— Sketches in. (W. J. Loftie) M. of Art, 7: 15–57. — (S. J. Weyman) Leis. Hour, 41: 372–803.
— Strategic Importance of, for England. Sat. R. 76: 95.
— Strategic Value of. (O. Wachs) Contemp. 62: 442. Same art. Ecl. M. 119: 613.
— To Akasheh and after. (A. Griffiths) Fortn. 65: 791.
— To-day. (J. Lynch) Overland, n. s. 23: 453.
— Troubled, and the Late Khedive. (F. Scudamore) Blackw. 151: 263. Same art. Liv. Age, 192: 771.
— Tunis and. (J. St. Loe Strachey) National, 25: 21.
— under British Occupation. Spec. 69: 128.
— Upper, Cycling in. (D. G. Hogarth) National, 27: 701.
Egypt; a story. (E. S. Grew) Idler, 9: 672.
Egypt Exploration Fund. Acad. 41: 307. — (E. Naville) Acad. 43: 89. 44: 17. 47: 242. 48: 440. 49: 412. 50: 38. — (D. G. Hogarth) Acad. 45: 293, 421, 461. 46: 536. 47: 430.
Egyptian and Babylonian Triads. (Felix Robin) Asia. R. 17: 119.
Egyptian Ball, An. (Natalie de Kontski) Overland, n. s. 23: 645.
Egyptian Book of the Dead, ed. by Davis. Sat. R. 79: 20.
Egyptian Chronology. (S. Beswick) Am. J. Archæol. 8: 171.
Egyptian Fragment; a story. Cornh. 68: 514.
Egyptian Superstitions. (Hadji Raphael) Overland, n. s. 24: 215.
Egyptian Thief, The; a story. (Sir Edwin Arnold) Cosmopol. 19: 428.
Egyptian Tomb in Island of Elephantina. Reliquary, 35: 33.
Egyptian Wooden Toilet Spoon. Reliquary, 36: 102.
Egyptians, Ancient, Mythology and Psychology of. (J. Offord) Asia. R. 14: 377.
Egyptians, Wisdom of the. (J. N. Fradenburgh) Meth. R. 56: 229.
Eider Shooting in Cape Breton. (W. H. Mac) Outing, 21: 441.
Eidlitz, Cyrus, L. W. (M. Schuyler) Archit. Rec. 5: 411.
Eifel, The Volcanic. (K. S. Macquoid) Leis. Hour, 45: 640.
Eifel Hills, Prussia, Holiday Ramble in, Macquoid's. Sat. R. 82: 293.
Eiffel Tower, Experiments at, on Falling Bodies and Air-resistance. (E. Colardeau) Nature, 46: 262.
Eight-hour Agitation. (A. E. Outerbridge) Am. Arch. 53: 23. — Soc. Econ. 6: 262.
Eight-hours Bill for Miners. (W. T. Thomson) Westm. 141: 593. Same art. Ecl. M. 123: 312. — (D. A. Thomas) Fortn. 61: 593.
— The Aim behind. (W. Moffatt) Blackw. 155: 693.
— its Economic Effect. (E. Bainbridge) Contemp. 66: 457.
— Mather on. Sat. R. 77: 331.
Eight-hours Day and Foreign Competition. (J. Rae) Contemp. 65: 189.
— and the Unemployed. (J. Rae) Contemp. 63: 790.
— Effect of. (C. Beardsley, jr.) Q. J. Econ. 9: 450.
— in Australia. Soc. Econ. 1: 164.
— in England. Soc. Econ. 1: 48, 148, 267.
— Movement for, in the U. S. (R. Donald) Econ. J. 2: 549.
— Origin of, at the Antipodes. (H. H. Champion) Econ. J. 2: 100.
— Rae on. (J. A. Hamilton) Acad. 46: 187.
— Textile Operatives and. Spec. 69: 277.
Eight-hours Movement, Economic Aspects of. (J. E. Symes) Econ. R. 1: 51.
— in the U. S. (R. Donald) Econ. J. 2: 549.
— — London Times on. Soc. Econ. 6: 342.
Eight-hours Question. (J. T. Blanchard) Westm. 139: 526.
— Artisan's View of. (J. Naylor) Econ. R. 1: 370.
Eighteen Centuries Ago; a story. (H. A. Kennedy) Temp. Bar. 102: 365.
1891, Commercial History and Review of. J. Statis. Soc. 55: 88.
1892, The Year. Sat. R. 74: 764.
— Commercial History and Review of. J. Statis. Soc. 56: 101.
1893, The Year. Sat. R. 76: 732.
— Literary Year in Retrospect. Dial (Ch.) 16: 13.
1896, Political Events of. (W. A. Dunning) Pol. Sci. Q. 11: 764.
— Survey of Events. Westm. 146: 264, 616.
1899, The Year. (W. W. Crane) Overland, n. s. 21: 579.
Eighteenth Century, last Decade of. (J. W. Hales) Contemp. 62: 422. Same art. Ecl. M. 119: 537. Same art. Liv. Age, 195: 323.
Eily. (E. Chilton) Longm. 21: 595. Same art. Liv. Age, 197: 725.
Eisteddfod, The. (W. W. Davies) Chaut. 15: 568.
— Meaning of an. (E. Brower) Atlan. 75: 45.
Eisteddfods and Welsh Bards. Walford's Antiq. 4: 71.
El Azhar, the World's Oldest University. (F. E. Penfield) Idler, 10: 193.
El Behá Zoheir and his Poetry. (Prof. E. H. Palmer) Time, 8: 424.
Elam, 4,000 Years Ago. (T. G. Pinches) Knowl. 19: 116.
— Upper. (H. A. Sawyer) Geog. J. 4: 481.
Eland, The Vanishing. (H. A. Bryden) Chamb. J. 71: 673.
Elastic Lengthening, Law of. (J. O. Thompson) Am. J. Sci. 143: 32.
Elasticity, Mathematical, Love on. (A. G. Greenhill) Nature, 47: 529.
— Mathematical Theories of. (A. G. Greenhill) Nature, 50: 97.
Elbe Disaster, Lessons of the. (R. Gillham) Engin. M. 9: 92.

Elbe Disaster, Poem on. (J. J. Beresford) Argosy, 59: 607.
Elberfeld Farbenfabriken, Laboratory of. (H. E. Armstrong) Nature, 48: 29.
Elder Conklin. (F. Harris) Fortn, 57: 861.
Elderly Man at the Play, An; a poem. (R. Noel) M. of Art, 17: 214.
Eldorado. [Music for words by Poe.] (C. Hartog) Sund. M. 25: 732.
Eldridge, Barnabas. (H. L. Conard) Nat'l M. (N. Y. '91) 16: 95.
Eleanor, Queen of England, Monument to, in Lincoln Cathedral. (E. Edmunds) Art J. 44: 231.
Eleanor Keith's Strange Adventure. (E. F. Byrrne) Argosy, 59: 416.
Eleanore Cuyler; a story. (R. H. Davis) Harper, 84: 771.
Election and Foreordination. (C. Walker) Bib. Sac. 49: 276.
— Doctrine of, Homiletic Uses of. (H. W. Lathe) Bib. Sac. 50: 79.
— Paul's Doctrine of, in Rom. ix.-xi. (W. Rupp) Ref. Q. 43: 411.
Election, An, in England, North Country. (D. Bagot) 19th Cent. 32: 744.
— *vs.* Appointment of Officials. (J. G. Bourinot) Ann. Am. Acad. Pol. Sci. 5: 653.
Election Day in New York. (E. Ingersoll) Cent. 31: 3.
Election Experiences. Time, 14: 532.
Election Night in a Newspaper Office. (J. Ralph) Scrib. M. 16: 531.
Election Trials. (C. W. Dilke) No. Am. 163: 573.
Electioneering, Humors of. (C. W. Radcliffe-Cooke) Eng. Illust. 13: 389.
Elections and Corruption. Sat. R. 81: 140.
— Biennial. (R. L. Bridgman) New Eng. M. n. s. 8: 206.
— Contested. (H. Jephson) Time, 18: 678.
— — in Great Britain. (Lord Brabourne) Blackw. 151: 763.
— — The Costs of. (T. S. Ball) Westm. 143: 72.
— English. (H. C. Lodge) Harper, 93: 232.
— — Canvassing the Country. (Lucy B. Hill) Time, 21: 581.
— — Humors of Some. All the Year, 70: 582.
— — Old. (Lord Brabourne) Blackw. 152: 38-348.
— Fraudulent, in the U. S. (J. Cook) Our Day, 10: 814.
— in France, the French Electoral System. (A. Naquet; T. Stanton) No. Am. 155: 466.
— the Machine in Honest Hands. (H. B. Ames) Canad. M. 3: 101.
— Methods of, Swiss and French. (K. Blind) No. Am. 155: 575.
— Money in. (E. L. Godkin) Nation, 55: 274.
— Parliamentary, Should Canvassing be abolished at? (L. Emanuel) Westm. 146: 328.
— Purification of. (H. James; J. Quincy; J. B. Bishop) Forum, 15: 129.
— Rogers on. Sat. R. 73: 723.
Electives in Elementary Schools. (E. J. Goodwin) Educa. R. 10: 12.
— in the High School. (E. J. Goodwin) Educa. R. 5: 142. — (E. Giles) Educa. 14: 160.
— System of, at Indiana University, Results of. (R. G. Boone) Educa. R. 4: 53, 142.
Electoral Commission, Minority Report of, 1877. (J. G. Abbott) M. Am. Hist. 27: 81.
Electoral Reform. (R. L. Bridgman) New Eng. M. n. s. 11: 274.
Electoral Representation. (S. Fleming) Am. J. Pol. 1: 262.
Electoral Systems, American and English. (A. Shaw; E. Porritt) Chr. Un. 46: 280.
Electric and Cable Cars, Progress in England. Sat. R. 80: 721.
Electric Batteries, Secondary. (G. H. Robertson) J. Soc. Arts, 40: 44. — Science, 19: 324.
— Storage, and their Uses. (T. Wolcott) Engin. M. 7: 240.
— — Chloride. J. Frankl. Inst. 138: 241.
— — on Street Railways. (P. G. Salom) J. Frankl. Inst. 134: 145.
Electric Cables, High Pressure Concentric. (J. Hetherington) Cassier, 10: 382.
Electric Central Stations: Are they doomed? (M. Osterberg) Engin. M. 12: 456.
— Local Development of. (W. S. Barstow) Cassier, 10: 359.
Electric Conductivity in Rock Magmas, Change of, in passing from Liquid to Solid. (C. Barus and J. P. Iddings) Am. J. Sci. 144: 242.
Electric Conduit System for Street Railways. (A. Stetson) Cassier, 5: 503.
Electric Cooking. *See* Electric Heating.
Electric Currents, Measurement by Constant Shunt Method. (C. W. Pike) J. Frankl. Inst. 133: 476.
— Polyphased. (P. A. N. Winand) J. Frankl. Inst. 134: 312-388.
Electric Discharge through Gases. (J. J. Thompson) Nature, 51: 330.
Electric Elevator *vs.* Hydraulic. (W. Baxter, jr.) Engin. M. 11: 478.
Electric Fishes. (J. G. McKendric) Fortn. 60: 539. Same art. Liv. Age, 199: 489.
— Ewart's Investigation on. (G. Fritsch) Nature, 49: 222.
Electric Furnace in Chemistry. (H. Moissan) Pop. Sci. Mo. 48: 417.
— a Lecture-experiment. (W. C. Roberts-Austen) Nature, 52: 114.
Electric Heating and Cooking. Dub. R. 117: 154. — (R. E. Crompton) J. Soc. Arts, 43: 511. — Science, 22: 146. — (N. W. Perry) Cassier, 7: 418.
— Modern Science of. (W. S. Hadaway) Engin. M. 9: 302.
Electric Insulation, Fire Risks in. (A. C. Perrine) Eng. M. 5: 356.
Electric Inventions, Influence of. (T. D. Lockwood) Cassier, 5: 429.
Electric Lamps, Arc, Alternating. (T. Spencer) J. Frankl. Inst. 136: 389.
— Incandescent. (J. W. Howell) Engin. M. 7: 70.
— — Ram on. Nature, 50: 1.
Electric Light, Arc. (S. P. Thompson) J. Soc. Arts, 43: 943, 961, 980.
— — for Reading-rooms and Libraries. (B. A. Dobson) Am. J. Sci. 147: 76.
— — *vs.* Incandescent. (W. A. Anthony) Cassier, 6: 463.
— Reducing the Cost of. (N. W. Perry) Engin. M. 9: 57.
— St. Pancras (London) Installation. (H. Robinson) J. Soc. Arts, 42: 246.
Electric Light Fittings, Ornamentation of. (C. R. Ashbee) Art J. 47: 91.
Electric Light Fixtures, Art in. (R. Jope-Slade) M. of Art, 20: 13.
Electric Light Stations. (J. E. Talbot) Engin. M. 6: 655.
Electric Lighting. (F. Parsons) Arena, 13: 118, 381. 14: 86-439. 15: 95. — Chamb. J. 71: 463.
— and Town-refuse Disposal. (T. Tomlinson) Engin. M. 7: 522.

Electric Lighting, Arc, New System of Series. (T. Spencer) J. Frankl. Inst. 142: 303.
— Arc-lamp, Beginnings and Future of. (S. M. Hamill) Engin. M. 7: 700.
— Central Station. (P. G. Salom) J. Frankl. Inst. 137: 298.
— Engines for. (H. Lindley) Eng. M. 11: 232.
— Experiments in. (H. A. Howe) Astron. 12: 505.
— For Picture Galleries. (G. Wigan) M. of Art, 6: 358.
— for Residences. (A. Noll) Engin. M. 10: 1059.
— from Underground Mains. (E. J. Houston and A. E. Kennelly) Cassier, 9: 179.
— Gas-power for. Nature, 47: 284.
— Municipal, in Chicago. (W. J. Meyers) Pol. Sci. Q. 10: 87.
— of Office Buildings. (W. S. Monroe) Archit. Rec. 6: 105.
— of Streets. (F. L. Pope) Engin. M. 9: 261.
— Plants for. (N. W. Perry) Engin. M. 8: 272.
— Practical Exposition of. (W. A. Anthony) Engin. M. 11: 713.
— Public, Cost Statistics of. (V. Rosewater) Am. Statis. Assoc. 3: 293.
— Street, in American Cities. (R. J. Finley) R. of Rs. (N. Y.) 7: 68.
— — in Chicago. (M. A. Mikkelsen) Ann. Am. Acad. Pol. Sci. 2: 715.
— — Relative Cost of, and of Gas. (C. J. R. Humphreys) Engin. M. 4: 240.
— Viewed Financially. (E. Wiman) Cassier, 1: 463.
Electric Locomotive. (B. J. Arnold) Engin. M. 7: 539.
— of To-day. (G. L. Clark) Cassier, 5: 460.
Electric Locomotives on Steam Roads. (G. J. Varney) Lippinc. 55: 415.
Electric Machines, Direct-driven. (W. E. Hall) Cassier, 7: 314.
Electric Measure, Legal Units of. (T. C. Mendenhall) Science, n. s. 1: 9.
— U. S. Units of. Nature, 51: 518.
Electric Motor. (F. B. Crocker) J. Frankl. Inst. 137: 343. — (F. B. Crocker) Cassier, 7: 392.
— and the Farmer. (W. N. Black) Engin. M. 4: 260.
— Evolution of. (E. B. Rosa) Chaut. 22: 441.
— Will it supersede Steam? (J. Wetzler) Scrib. M. 17: 594.
Electric Nerves in the Torpedo, Gymnotus, etc. (G. Fritsch) Nature, 47: 271.
Electric Oscillations, Frequency of. (A. H. Patterson and C. H. Arnold) Am. J. Sci. 146: 359.
— of Low Frequency and their Resonance. (M. I. Pupin) Am. J. Sci. 145: 325, 420, 503.
— Poincaré on. (A. Gray) Nature, 51: 361.
Electric Power, Altruistic Effects of. (F. A. C. Perrine) Engin. M. 2: 509.
— Economics of. (H. L. Lufkin) Cassier, 5: 369.
— for Isolated Factories. (W. A. Anthony) Engin. M. 8: 869.
— from Central Stations. (W. C. Unwin) J. Soc. Arts, 41: 890, 965.
— in Canada. (J. S. Robertson) Cassier, 9: 301.
— in Mining. (I. Hale) Engin. M. 3: 774.
— in Small Units. (W. Elmer, jr.) Engin. M. 12: 233.
— in Southern Cotton Mills. (A. F. McKissick) Engin. M. 8: 1063.
— Transmission of. (F. J. Patten) New Sci. R. 1: 435.
— — Limits of. (A. D. Adams) Eng. M. 10: 269.
Electric Power Distribution. (H. C. Spaulding) Cassier, 1: 138.
Electric Power Station, A Small. (R. C. Carpenter) Cassier, 9: 339.
Electric Power Stations. (C. J. Field) Cassier, 9: 419.
— Equipment of. (R. C. Carpenter) Cassier, 7: 473.
Electric Railway at Budapest. (H. W. Bartol) J. Frankl. Inst. 133: 125.
— Brott. Lippinc. 56: 689.
— Probable Evolution of. (I. Hale) Engin. M. 8: 92.
— Storage Battery. (G. J. Varney) Lippinc. 53: 552.
— Triumph of. Spec. 68: 738.
— Trolley System. (O. M. Rau) Cassier, 6: 178.
— — the Successor of the Railway. (A. Morgan) Pop. Sci. Mo. 46: 750.
Electric Railways. Nature, 47: 570. — Spec. 70: 190.
— and Country Roads. (J. G. Speed) No. Am. 161: 382.
— Complete Metallic Circuit for. (J. H. Vail) Cassier, 6: 161.
— Conduit. (J. Sachs) Cassier, 6: 385.
— Development of. (F. J. Sprague) Cassier, 3: 15.
— in Competition with Steam Railroads. (C. Deming) Engin. M. 9: 823.
— Return Circuits of. (C. Hewitt) J. Frankl. Inst. 141: 51. — (T. J. McTighe) Cassier, 5: 331.
— Street, as Investments. (L. W. Serrell) Engin. M. 3: 216.
— Traction Apparatus in N. Y. (H. F. Parshall) J. Soc. Arts, 44: 395.
— Will Trunk Lines be operated by Electricity? (F. J. Sprague) Engin. M. 9: 642.
Electric Signalling without Wires. (W. H. Preece) J. Soc. Arts, 42: 274.
Electric Spark, Horse Power in. (J. Trowbridge) Chaut. 19: 42.
Electric Spark, An; a story. (G. M. Fenn) Chamb. J. 72: 273-756.
Electric Station Economics. (D. C. Jackson) Cassier, 5: 426.
Electric Storm on Mt. Elbert, Colorado. (P. A. Welker) Science, n. s. 2: 304.
Electric Strokes and their Treatment. Dub. R. 117: 446.
Electric Traction. (N. W. Perry) Engin. M. 6: 812. — (E. F. Bamber) Nature, 49: 567.
Electric Transmission of Intelligence. (T. D. Lockwood) Engin. M. 7: 61.
Electric Transmission of Power. (F. B. Crocker) Engin. M. 7: 389. — (F. B. Crocker) Cassier, 9: 231. — (E. Griffin) J. Frankl. Inst. 134: 169. — (Earl of Albemarle) 19th Cent. 31: 73. — (C. J. H. Woodbury) Cassier, 3: 274. 4: 175. — (L. Bell) Cassier, 4: 19.
— for 12 Miles. (T. H. Leggett) Cassier, 7: 355.
Electric Waves, Hertz on. (H. S. Carhart) Dial (Ch.) 18: 79.
— Velocity of. (J. Trowbridge and W. Duane) Am. J. Sci. 149: 297. 150: 104.
Electric Welding and Metal-working. (H. Lemp) Engin. M. 7: 680.
Electric Wires, Underground. (D. C. Jackson) Cassier, 5: 163.
Electric Wiring. (T. W. Flood) Am. Arch. 54: 88.
— and the Fire Hazard. (F. E. Cabot) Engin. M. 8: 1025.
— Conduits for. Am. Arch. 48: 133.
Electrical and Mechanical Engineering, Relations of. (E. E. Ries) Engin. M. 11: 425.
Electrical Business, Extravagance in. (B. E. Greene) Engin. M. 11: 837.
Electrical Congress at the Chicago Exhibition. Dub. R. 114: 167.
Electrical Discharge, Effects of Light on. Nature, 49: 226.
Electrical Discharges through Poor Vacua. (M. I. Pupin) Astron. 11: 483.

Electrical Discharges and Coronoidal Discharges. (M. I. Pupin) Am. J. Sci. **143**: 463.
Electrical Discovery, Latest. (J. E. H. Gordon) 19th Cent. **31**: 399. Same art. Liv. Age, **193**: 309.
Electrical Engineers, Technical Education of. (W. E. Ayrton) Nature, **45**: 326. — (D. C. Jackson) Science, **19**: 344.
Electrical Exhibition at the Crystal Palace. Dub. R. **110**: 448.
— at Frankfort. Dub. R. **110**: 437.
— N. Y., 1896. (R. Jamison) Chaut. **23**: 434.
Electrical Experiments, Nikola Tesla's. Dub. R. **111**: 175.
— Long-distance. (J. McGhie) Cassier, **9**: 359.
Electrical Metal Working. (J. Sachs) Cassier, **9**: 522.
Electrical Phenomena, Mechanical Conceptions of. (A. E. Dolbear) J. Frankl. Inst. **141**: 451. **142**: 59.
Electrical Range Finder of B. A. Fiske. J. Frankl. Inst. **134**: 249.
Electrical Research, Tendencies of. (M. I. Pupin) Science, n. s. **2**: 861.
Electrical Resistance Standards, Manufacture and Adjustment of. (E. G. Willyoung) J. Frankl. Inst. **133**: 309.
Electrical Science for Architects. (R. Robb) Am. Arch. **43**: 18–126. **44**: 16. **45**: 43. **46**: 5, 37. **47**: 91, 119. **48**: 48, 99. **49**: 12, 47, 75, 107.
Electrical Slip, An; a story. Eng. Illust. **11**: 711.
Electrical Study, An; a story. (V. Withington) Overland, n. s. **20**: 417.
Electrical Transmission in Factories. (R. E. B. Crompton) Cassier, **9**: 291.
Electrical Waves and Rays. (T. J. McCormack) Open Court, **3**: 1679–1705.
Electrician-in-charge. (H. L. Webb) Scrib. M. **16**: 316.
Electricians, Are we educating too many? (H. Floy) Engin. M. **10**: 648.
Electricity. (R. R. Bowker) Harper, **93**: 710. — Chamb. J. **69**: 177.
— Age of. (W. H. Preece) Time, **7**: 80–528.
— — Symposium. Indep. March 2, '93.
— Alternating Currents, Measurement of. (J. A. Fleming) J. Soc. Arts, **41**: 842 877.
— Alternating Current System. (A. J. Wurts) N. Eng. **56**: 210.
— Alternating Current Transformers. (J. A. Fleming) J. Soc. Arts, **44**: 699–735.
— and Electric Generators. (H. F. Parshall) Engin. M. **5**: 781.
— and High Rates of Speed on Railroads. (H. S. Maxim) Cassier, **1**: 250.
— and the Horseless-carriage Problem. (W. Baxter) Engin. M. **11**: 248.
— and Magnetism, Guillemin's. Sat. R. **74**: 539.
— and Plant-growing. (C. S. Sargent) Garden & F. **7**: 81.
— and Steam; a study in sociology. (A. A. Johnson) Am. M. Civics, **7**: 343.
— and Steam Power. (J. J. Wright) Cassier, **2**: 264.
— Applications of. (W. J. Hopkins) Citizen, **1**: 83.
— Applied to Farming. (G. E. Walsh) No. Am. **163**: 509.
— as a Nuisance. Juid. R. **5**: 159.
— Atmospheric. (A. Schuster) Nature, **53**: 207. — Dub. R. **119**: 407.
— — in the U. S., Observations of. (O. J. Lodge) Nature, **47**: 392.
— Benjamin on. (C. L. Peirce) Nation, **62**: 16.
— British School of. Sat. R. **79**: 7.
— Commercial Exploitation of. (B. E. Greene) Engin. M. **10**: 845.
— Cosmical. (E. Thomson) J. Frankl. Inst. **137**: 199.
Electricity, Current of, Value of the Force exerted by a. (S. T. Moreland) Am. J. Sci. **145**: 392.
— Development of, The Possible and the Impossible in. (W. Baxter, jr.) Engin. M. **12**: 113.
— Direct from Coal. (W. Ostwald) Engin. M. **7**: 673. — (B. H. Thwaite) 19th Cent. **36**: 919. — (W. W. Jacques) Harper, **94**: 144. — (G. H. Stockbridge) Engin. M. **11**: 658. — (A. H. Bucherer) J. Frankl. Inst. **139**: 378. — (L. Duncan) Cassier, **9**: 285.
— Distribution of. (G. Forbes) J. Soc. Arts, **40**: 862–897.
— Effect of, on Great Cities. Spec. **69**: 317.
— Fire-hazards of. (W. Brophy) Am. Arch. **40**: 57.
— for Marine Propulsion. (W. F. Durand) Cassier, **8**: 143.
— from Peat. (J. Munro) 19th Cent. **36**: 927.
— Future of. (E. Thomson) New Eng. M. n. s. **6**: 623.
— Generated by Windmills. (I. N. Lewis) Engin. M. **8**: 470.
— Human. (J. G. McKendrick) Fortn. **57**: 634. Same art. Ecl. M. **119**: 43.
— in Agriculture. (Clarence D. Warner) Science, **19**: 35. — (Clarence D. Warner) Garden & F. **5**: 47. — (A. F. McKissick) Engin. M. **4**: 708.
— in Country Houses. (Earl Russell; B. H. Thwaite) National, **20**: 764.
— in 1876 and in 1893. (E. Thomson) Engin. M. **6**: 442.
— in 1895. (T. C. Martin) Cassier, **9**: 312.
— in the Future. (J. Munro) Time, **23**: 758.
— in the Home and Office. (F. A. C. Perrine) Engin. M. **5**: 585.
— in the Iron and Steel Industries. (D. Selby-Bigge) Engin. M. **8**: 401.
— in Mining. (F. O. Blackwell) Cassier, **5**: 249.
— in the Modern City. (T. C. Martin) J. Frankl. Inst. **138**: 198–258.
— in Railroad Work, Future of. (L. Duncan) J. Frankl. Inst. **141**: 401.
— in relation to Science. (W. Crookes) Pop. Sci. Mo. **40**: 497.
— in Suburban Development. (E. Wiman) Engin. M. **6**: 679.
— in Textile Manufacturing. (L. Bell) Cassier, **7**: 275.
— Industrial Development of. All the Year, **75**: 328.
— Marvels of. (J. R. Buchanan) Arena, **14**: 33.
— Measurement of. (H. L. Webb) Engin. M. **4**: 72. — (N. W. Perry) Engin. M. **7**: 248. — (T. C. Mendenhall) Atlan. **73**: 605. — (A. E. Kennelly) Cassier, **6**: 77.
— — One-volt Standard Cell. (H. S. Carhart) Am. J. Sci. **146**: 60.
— — Future. (H. S. Carhart) Science, **21**: 86.
— Modern Theories as to. (H. A. Rowland) Engin. M. **8**: 589.
— Municipal Supply of, at Bradford, Eng. (J. N. Shoolbred) J. Soc. Arts, **40**: 630.
— Nationalization of. (S. Schindler) Arena, **10**: 84.
— Nature of. (A. E. Dolbear) Cosmopol. **18**: 123.
— of the Past. (F. A. Scheffler) Cassier, **6**: 479.
— on Steam Roads. (B. J. Dashiell, jr.) Cassier, **2**: 31.
— Operating Machine Tools by. (G. Richmond) Engin. M. **8**: 669.
— Portable. (J. Trowbridge) Chaut. **19**: 191.
— Possibilities of. (W. Crookes) Fortn. **57**: 173. Same art. Ecl. M. **118**: 391. Same art. Liv. Age, **193**: 93.
— Practical Phases of. (F. L. Pope) Chaut. **16**: 539.
— Practical Problems in. (S. P. Thompson) J. Soc. Arts, **41**: 620.
— Power, Light, and Heat in City Blocks. (J. E. Talbot) Engin. M. **9**: 457.
— Pre-scientific. (H. Hayden, jr.) New Sci. R. **1**: 358.

Electricity, Recent Developments in. (C. Hering) J. Frankl. Inst. 136: 447.
— Relations to Steam and Water Power. (C. E. Emery) J. Frankl. Inst. 142: 165.
— Remarkable Applications of. Chamb. J. 71: 22. Same art. Ecl. M. 122: 567.
— Resonance Analysis of Alternating Currents. (M. I. Pupin) Am. J. Sci. 148: 379, 473.
— Seeing and Hearing by. (A. G. Bell) McClure, 1: 39.
— Shifting Lines of Industrial Interest in. (G. H. Stockbridge) Engin. M. 11: 1062.
— Storage Battery of the Air. (A. McAdie) Harper, 89: 216.
— Storage of, Improvements in. (F. H. Bowman) Science, 22: 258.
— Supply of, Economic Points in. (G. Kapp) J. Soc. Arts, 41: 564.
— N. Tesla and. R. of Rs. (N. Y.) 12: 293. — (T. C. Martin) Cent. 27: 916.
— J. J. Thomson's Researches on. (A. Gray) Nature, 49: 357.
— Velocity of. (G. Le Clear) Pop. Sci. Mo. 48: 687.
— *vs.* Gas Direct from Coal. (D. M. Dunning) Engin. M. 11: 1008.
— — for Power Transmission. (N. W. Perry) Engin. M. 12: 49, 261.
— Wave Lengths of, on Iron Wires. (C. E. St. John) Am. J. Sci. 148: 311.
— What it is. New Sci. R. 1: 134. — (Mrs. B. Moore; C. J. Reed; H. Clay) New Sci. R. 1: 309.
— World's Debt to. (J. Trowbridge) Chaut. 20: 545.
Electrification and Light. (O. J. Lodge) Sci. Prog. 3: 175. 5: 417.
— of Air. Nature, 50: 280.
— — and other Gases. (Lord Kelvin; M. Maclean; A. Galt) Nature, 51: 495.
Electro-chemistry, Applied. (J. Swinburne) J. Soc. Arts, 44: 803–839.
— Recent Advances. (J. W. Richards) J. Frankl. Inst. 139: 351.
Electrodynamic Theories, Poincaré on. (A. Gray) Nature, 45: 367.
Electrolysis, Legal Aspects of. (H. C. Townsend) Cassier, 7: 457.
— Modern Theories of. (J. W. Richards) J. Frankl. Inst. 141: 192.
— of Buried Metal Pipes, How to prevent. (I. H. Farnham) Cassier, 8: 421.
— Theories of. (C. D. Whetham) Sci. Prog. 4: 293.
Electrolytic Phenomenon, Remarkable. (C. J. Reed) J. Frankl. Inst. 139: 283.
Electro-magnetic Machinery. (W. S. Aldrich) J. Frankl. Inst. 133: 130, 214.
Electro-magnetic Theory. (O. Heaviside) Nature, 51: 171.
— The Law of Electro-magnetic Flux. (M. I. Pupin) Am. J. Sci. 150: 326.
Electro-metallurgy. (A. E. Hunt) Engin. M. 7: 381. — (J. W. Swan) Nature, 46: 478.
Electrometer, Capillary, Method of Increasing Range of. (J. Whitmore) Am. J. Sci. 144: 64.
Electro-optics. (A. B. Basset) Nature, 48: 34.
Electropoise, The, and Nerve Force. (B. O. Kinnear) New Sci. R. 2: 298.
Electro-statics, Fundamental Concepts of. (E. Mach) Open Court, 8: 4247, 4254.
Elegie, The; a story. Ecl. M. 118: 11. Same art. Liv. Age, 192: 9.
Elegies, A Triad of. Liv. Age, 210: 410.
Elegy. (A. C. Swinburne) 19th Cent. 35: 523.
Elements, The. (W. Crookes) New Sci. R. 1: 385.
Elephant, African, Re-domestication of. Spec. 74: 161.
Elephant and the Lion, The Legend of the. (H. M. Stanley) McClure, 1: 351.
— White, Naming the. (B. H. Harrison) Outing, 23: 359.
Elephant-hunting. (P. F. Dixon) Outing, 27: 117.
— My First Elephant. Cornh. 67: 621.
— A Rogue Elephant. (F. F. R. Dixon) Outing, 21: 163.
Elephants. (R. Lydekker) Knowl. 15: 46, 64.
— Buried, in the Arctic Regions. (D. G. Whitley) Gent. M. n. s. 53: 275. Same art. Liv. Age, 203: 108.
— Wild, Capture of, in Mysore. (R. C. Woodville) Harper, 85: 290.
Eleusinia; a poem. (D. C. Bushby) 19th Cent. 35: 217.
Elevated Railway, Future of the. (E. Klapp) Engin. M. 11: 34.
Elevator, Electric. (J. Sachs) Cassier, 8: 388. — (G. E. Harding) Am. Arch. 46: 31.
— — *versus* Hydraulic. (W. Baxter, jr.) Engin. M. 11: 478.
— Passenger, American. (T. E. Brown, jr.) Engin. M. 5: 333.
Eleventh Juror, The; a tale. (Edith Wagner) Overland, n. s. 28: 146.
Elf-bolts. Chamb. J. 70: 153.
Eliduc, The Lay of. (A. Nutt) Folk-Lore, 3: 26.
Elijah. (C. H. Cornill) Open Court, 9: 4463.
Eliot, Charles W. (N. M. Butler) Educa. R. 8: 98.
— 25th Anniversary. (C. F. Thwing) Forum, 17: 355. — (C. F. Dunbar and others) Harv. Grad. M. 2: 450. — (E. L. Godkin) Nation, 58: 442.
Eliot, George and Dorothea Casaubon. (B. R. Belloc) Contemp. 65: 207. Same art. Liv. Age, 200: 728. Same art. Ecl. M. 122: 373.
— and Jane W. Carlyle. (A. I. Ireland) Gent. M. n. s. 40: 229.
— and her Neighborhood. (G. Morley) Liv. Age, 188: 42.
— as a Character Artist. (M. B. Whiting) Westm. 138: 406.
— Clematis and Ivy, a Record of Early Friendship. (W. G. Kingsland) Poet-Lore, 6: 1, 57, 182.
— Country and Country Characters of. (James Purves) Time, 21: 379.
— her Theory of Realism. (L. T. Damon) Harv. Mo. 15: 14.
— Humor of. Critic, 10: 69.
— Personality of. (M. H. Benton) So. M. 2: 131.
— Place of, in Literature. (F. Harrison) Forum, 20: 66.
— Portrait of, at thirty. Critic, 27: 46, 64.
— Revisited. (G. W. E. Russell) Contemp. 69: 357.
— Tito Melema; a study. (J. H. Gulliver) New World, 4: 687.
— Views of Religion of. (W. M. Salter) Eth. Rec. 2: 121.
— Was she a Hypocrite? (Mrs. Van R. Cruger) Cosmopol. 20: 312.
Eliot, John. (J. De Normandie) New Eng. M. n. s. 15: 259.
Eliot Bible at Jesus College, Cambridge, Eng. (J. G. Adami) Critic, 20: 330.
Elixir of Life, The. (L. E. Keeley) Am. J. Pol. 4: 146.
Elizabeth, Queen, Age of, Glance at. (G. G. Hepburn) M. Am. Hist. 29: 32.
— and the Beggars of the Sea. (J. H. Round) Ath. '95, 2: 455.
— and Elizabethan Fashions. Quar. 184: 423.
— and Ivan the Terrible. (W. B. Steveni) 19th Cent. 34: 944.
— and the Revolution in France. (J. M. Stone) Dub. R. 113: 599. 115: 358.

Elizabeth, Queen, and Amy Robsart. (J. Gairdner) Ath. '93, 1: 220-345. — (A. Lang) Ath. '93, 1: 311.
— Beesly's. Sat. R. 73: 254.
— Courtships of, Hume's. Sat. R. 81: 487.
— Death of, from Despatches of the Venetian Secretary. (G. le Strange) Temp. Bar, 107: 291.
— Ecclesiastical Policy of. (J. Stevenson) Month, 79: 24.
— Excommunication of. (M. Creighton) Eng. Hist. R. 7: 81.
— First 20 Years of the Reign of. Church Q. 40: 405.
— Hume's Calendar of State Papers, Spanish: Elizabeth, 1580-86. (W. F. Tilton) Am. Hist. R. 1: 529.
— Portraits of, O'Donoghue's Catalogue of. (J. M. Gray) Acad. 46: 197.
— Scandal about. (A. Lang) Blackw. 153: 209. Same art. Liv. Age, 197: 117.
— A Visit to. (J. H. Round) 19th Cent. 40: 619.
Elizabeth, Empress of Austria. Harper, 87: 30.
Elizabeth of France. Blackw. 153: 800.
Elizabeth; a story. (E. J. Gompf) New Eng. M. n. s. 10: 281.
Elizabeth Rivers; a Study in Crayons. (C. Burke) Argosy, 60: 287.
Elizabethan Literature, Revival of. (F. I. Carpenter) Dial (Ch.) 18: 297.
Elizabethan Period, English and French Literature during. (M. W. Easton) Poet-Lore, 1: 157.
Elizabethan Poets, Nature in. (G. Bradford, jr.) Poet-Lore, 7: 529.
Elizabethan Sea Kings. (J. Fiske) Atlan. 76: 91.
Elizabethan Sonnet Cycles, Crow on. (F. I. Carpenter) Dial (Ch.) 21: 186.
Elizabethan Stage. (W. Poel) Theatre, 31: 241.
Elk, After. (F. Prevost) Gent. M. n. s. 50: 42.
— Roping, in the Rockies. (H. S. Blanchard) Outing, 21: 375.
Elk-battue in Russia. (F. Whishaw) Outing, 25: 288.
Elk-hunt at Two-Ocean Pass. (T. Roosevelt) Cent. 22: 713.
Elk-hunting in Manitoba. Outing, 19: 268, 419.
— in Norway. A Handful of Lead. (Sir H. Pottinger) Fortn. 57: 24. Same art. Liv. Age, 192: 728.
— with Dogs. (E. D. White) Outing, 24: 342.
Elkin, W. L., Astronomical Work of. (S. C. Chandler) Pop. Astron. 3: 392.
Elkins, Stephen B. (F. A. Munsey) Munsey, 6: 520.
Elliott, Charlotte. (P. H. W. Almy) Sund. M. 23: 634.
Elliott, Stephen, and Elliottia Racemosa. (C. S. Sargent) Garden & F. 7: 201.
Elliott, Walter, Miscellaneous Notes. Asia. R. 11: 181.
Ellipsoid of Revolution, Homogeneous, Centre of Gravity for. (T. J. J. See) Astron. 13: 627.
Elliptic Functions, A. G. Greenhill on. (H. F. Baker) Nature, 49: 359.
Ellis, Arthur. Bank. M. (Lond.) 59: 258.
Ellis, Edwin J. Fate in Arcadia. (J. Todhunter) Acad. 42: 256.
Ellis, George Edward. (A. B. Ellis) New Eng. M. n. s. 14: 286.
— Retrospect of an Octogenarian. Atlan. 74: 452.
Ellsworth, Col. Ephraim Elmer. (J. Hay) McClure, 6: 354.
Elm-leaf Beetle. Garden & F. 9: 217.
Elm-tree, White, at Dauphin, Pa. (M. L. Dock) Garden & F. 9: 212.
Elmira Reformatory. (Z. R. Brockway) Fortn. 57: 729. — (J. W. Jenks) Char. R. 2: 126.
— Investigation of. Pub. Opin. 17: 44, 187, 910.
— System of. (C. D. Warner) Am. J. Soc. Sci. 32: 52.
Elms, Avenue of. Garden & F. 6: 172.
— of the St. Lawrence Valley. (T. H. Hoskins) Garden & F. 5: 86.
Elocution and Singing. (H. G. Hawn) Music, 7: 34.
Eloquence and Poetry. (J. Burroughs) Chaut. 15: 63.
Elotherium, Restoration of. (O. C. Marsh) Am. J. Sci. 147: 407.
Elphinstone, Mountstuart. (M. E. G. Duff) Acad. 41: 581. — Sat. R. 74: 87.
Elsbeth's Holiday. (D. Gerard) Longm. 22: 45.
Elsheimer, Adam. (S. Colvin) M. of Art, 6: 478.
Elsie; a story. (J. Stafford) Chamb. J. 70: 488-523.
Elsinore, A Day in. (C. Edwardes) Chamb. J. 70: 641.
Elswick Arsenal. (H. Hendry) Good Words, 33: 678.
Eltham Palace. All the Year, 71: 345.
Elton Pottery. (C. Monkhouse) M. of Art, 6: 228.
Elvira's Chance; a Kansas Idyl. (L. P. Bridgman) Overland, n. s. 25: 301.
Ely, R. T., Acquittal of. Econ. R. 5: 118.
— on Hard Times. (E. M. Burchard) Am. M. Civics, 7: 531.
— Sketch of, with portrait. Our Day, 16: 119.
— Trial of. (R. W. Conant) Dial (Ch.) 17: 109. — Pub. Opin. 17: 462.
Ely Cathedral. (T. E. Champion) Canad. M. 3: 356. — (W. E. Dickson) Good Words, 37: 520-607.
Ely Palace. (E. Venables) Good Words, 36: 554.
Elzevir Editions. (A. Lang) M. of Art, 7: 287.
Elzevirs, The. Bookworm, 2: 97. — (Althea Salvador) New Sci. R. 1: 333.
Emancipation of Mr. Samuel Banks. (C. S. Lanier) New Eng. M. n. s. 10: 424.
Embassy, An; a story. (A. Hope) Idler, 6: 551.
Embezzlement and Fraud; Causes and Remedies. (A. Barrett) Arena, 14: 196.
Emblems and their Significance. (H. S. Howell) Canad. M. 2: 501.
Embroideries and Laces, Verifying Ancient. (A. S. Cole) J. Soc. Arts, 43: 757, 769, 781.
Embroidery and Tapestry, Ancient. Chamb. J. 71: 629.
— Mediæval. (May Morris) J. Soc. Arts, 43: 384.
— on Book Covers. Bookworm, 6: 281.
Embryology, Experimental. (J. A. Thomson) Nat. Sci. 2: 294. — (E. A. Andrews) Am. Natural. 26: 367, 580.
— Preformation or New Formation, Hertwig on. (P. C. Mitchell) Nat. Sci. 5: 132, 184, 292.
— Wilson on. (D. S. Jordan) Dial (Ch.) 20: 13.
Emerald of Merida. (T. P. Terry) Outing, 25: 91.
Emerald Uthwart. (W. Pater) New R. 6: 708. 7: 42.
Emerald Beetle, The; a story. (R. Mace) Munsey, 11: 633.
Emergency Loans. (R. T. Paine) Lend a H. 11: 426.
Emerson, R. W. (J. V. Cheney) Chaut. 17: 687. — (C. A. Bartol) New World, 2: 479. — (C. A. Bartol) Critic, 24: 26. — (A. H. Peters) Open Court, 1: 329. — (J. W. Chadwick) Arena, 15: 12.
— and Clough. (F. H. Williams) Poet-Lore, 6: 348.
— and Alexander Ireland. (M. D. Conway) Nation, 60: 26, 44.
— and Walt Whitman, Friendship of. (W. S. Kennedy) Poet-Lore, 7: 71.
— as an Exponent of Beauty in Poetry. (H. A. Clarke) Poet-Lore, 5: 353.
— as a Philosopher. (F. C. Lockwood) Meth. R. 56: 702.
— Brahma, and Bhagavad Gita. (W. T. Harris) Poet-Lore, 1: 253.
— Correspondence with Thoreau. (F. B. Sanborn) Atlan. 69: 577, 736.
— Each and all. Poet-Lore, 6: 273.
— Fifty Years Ago. (F. M. Holland) Open Court, 5: 2787.

Emerson, R. W., E. E. Hale on. Critic, **22**: 364.
— in his Home. (F. B. Sanborn) Arena, **15**: 16.
— Letters of, to Carlyle. (M. D. Conway) Nation, **56**: 327.
— Limitations of, as a Poet. (C. P. Cranch) Critic, **20**: 129.
— Maeterlinck and. (H. Osgood) Arena, **15**: 563.
— Meeting with De Quincey. Blackw. **155**: 480. Same art. Ecl. M. **122**: 768. Same art. Liv. Age, **201**: 282.
— Natural History of Intellect. Poet-Lore, **6**: 93.
— Philosophy of. (W. L. Courtney) Time, **14**: 653.
— Portraits of. (F. B. Sanborn) New Eng. M. n. s. **15**: 449.
— Random Reminiscences of. (W. H. Furness) Atlan. **71**: 344.
— Religion of. (W. H. Savage) Arena, **10**: 736.
— Representative Men, Choice of. (I. McIlwraith) Canad. M. **1**: 689.
— Transcendentalist and Unitarian. (V. Paget) Contemp. **67**: 345.
— Wit and Humor of. (H. D. Lloyd) Forum, **22**: 346.
Emerson Mania, The. Eng. R. **12**: 139.
Emery, C. E. Cassier, **4**: 103.
Emery, Winifred. (W. A. L. Bettany) Theatre, **31**: 301.
Emery. (R. Beynon) Knowl. **19**: 210.
— and other Abrasives. (T. D. Paret) J. Frankl. Inst. **137**: 353–421.
Emery Wheels and some of their Uses. (J. W. Cole) Cassier, **5**: 239.
— and their Tests. (T. D. Paret) Cassier, **8**: 50.
Emigrant, An. (K. T. Hinkson) Good Words, **35**: 42.
Emigrants, Unhappy Predicament of. (H. H. Boyesen) Chaut. **15**: 607.
Emigration. (W. B. Paton) Time, **19**: 129.
— and Immigration in 1891, Statistics of. J. Statis. Soc. **55**: 311.
— in the Dark. Spec. **68**: 117.
— Pauper. Sat. R. **73**: 223.
— Upper-class. Chamb. J. **73**: 257.
See Immigration.
Emigration into the Laboring Class; a story. (Blanche Atkinson) Good Words, **35**: 698.
Em'ly; a story. (O. Wister) Harper, **87**: 941.
Emin Pasha, Death of. (R. D. Mohun) Cent. **27**: 591.
— Relief Expedition, New Light on. Asia. R. **11**: 337.
— Stuhlmann's. (J. M. Hubbard) Nation, **59**: 160.
Eminent Domain. (C. F. Randolph) Law Q. **3**: 314.
— Right of. (E. O. Brown) Arena, **9**: 442.
Emmanuel Hospital, Westminster. (W. J. Loftie) M. of Art, **17**: 228.
Emmet, Thomas Addis. (A. O. Hall) Green Bag, **8**: 273.
Emmitsburgh, Md., Roman Catholic Convent-school at. (H. M. Sweeney) Cath. World, **58**: 325.
Emmons, Ebenezer, with portrait. Pop. Sci. Mo. **48**: 406.
Emmons Ethnological Collection. (Franz Boas) J. Am. Folk-Lore, **1**: 215.
Emotion, Æsthetic. (B. Bosanquet) Mind, **19**: 154.
— and Pleasure-pain. (H. R. Marshall) Psychol. R. **2**: 57.
— Cosmic. (T. E. Fuller) Westm. **141**: 309.
— Descartes and Modern Theories of. (D. Irons) Philos. R. **4**: 291.
— Desire and Interest. (S. F. M'Lennan) Psychol. R. **2**: 462.
— Expression of, Origin of. (J. M. Baldwin) Psychol. R. **1**: 610.
— Morals and Music. (H. R. Haweis) Music, **4**: 595.
— Physical Basis of. (D. Irons) Mind, **20**: 92. — (W. James) Psychol. R. **1**: 516.
Emotion, Recent Developments in the Theory of. (D. Irons) Psychol. R. **2**: 279.
— Significance of. (J. Dewey) Psychol. R. **2**: 13.
— Theory of. (J. Dewey) Psychol. R. **1**: 553.
— — Professor James's. (D. Irons) Mind, **19**: 77.
Emotions and Infection. (C. Féré) Pop. Sci. Mo. **44**: 342.
— Natural History of the. Time, **11**: 185.
— *vs.* Pleasure-pain. (H. R. Marshall) Mind, **20**: 180.
Emotional Disorders. (T. Ribot) Open Court, **4**: 2651
Empire and Republic, Race between. Soc. Econ. **8**: 24.
Empiricism, Truth of. (J. Seth) Philos. R. **2**: 544.
Employees, Property Rights of. Char. R. **5**: 1.
Employer and Employee, Contract between, Statutory Limitations of. (F. C. Woodward) Am. Law R. **29**: 236.
— — under the Common Law. Am. Arch. **50**: 111. — (V. H. Olmstead and S. D. Fessenden) Lend a H. **16**: 111.
— and Workman, Relation of. (C. D. Wright) Am. Arch. **45**: 61.
— and the Young Man. (E. W. Bok) Cosmopol. **16**: 727.
— Place of, in Distribution. (F. W. Taussig) Q. J. Econ. **10**: 67.
Employers and Employed, Industrial Union of. (J. M. Ludlow) Econ. R. **5**: 549.
— — — Employer's View of. (T. W. Bushill) Econ. R. **4**: 195.
— — in France and Belgium, Joint Associations of. (A. M. Anderson) Econ. J. **5**: 641.
— Liability of. Spec. **72**: 125, 298. — (V. Nash) Fortn. **61**: 244. — (A. D. Provand) Contemp. **66**: 137. — (A. D. Provand) 19th Cent. **34**: 698.
— — in England. (H. D. Bateson) Law Q. **5**: 179.
— — Taking Stock of. (Lord Farrer) National, **26**: 356.
Employment, Fraudulent Advertisement of Lucrative. (P. G. Hubert, jr.) Lippinc. **54**: 657.
Employment Officers, Government. Lend a H. **12**: 133.
Empty Cage, The; a poem. (L. Morris) Cosmopol. **17**: 144.
En passant; a story. (M. V. Vernon) Belgra. **90**: 427.
Enamel, Simpson's Pictures in. (C. Monkhouse) M. of Art, **10**: 222.
Enamels. Chamb. J. **69**: 632.
— English. (J. S. Gardner) Portfo. **24**: 231, 249.
Enargite, Crystallization of. (L. V. Pirsson) Am. J. Sci. **147**: 212.
Enceladus; a poem. (C. J. O'Malley) Cent. **21**: 575.
Enchanted Mountains, The. (Kate P. Sieghold) Overland, n. s. **23**: 550.
Enclosures since 1760. (J. H. Green) Econ. R. **6**: 21.
Encore, The; a story. (V. Hunt) Eng. Illust. **13**: 89.
Encores. Sat. R. **77**: 253.
Encounter with Chinese Smugglers, An. (J. C. Nattrass) Overland, n. s. **23**: 206.
Encyclopædia, Chambers'. Sat. R. **74**: 116.
End of the Furrow, The. (T. L. Flood and Charles Barnard) Chaut. **17**: 524, 660.
End of the Game, The. (A. Brown) Cent. **27**: 551.
End of his Work, The; a story. (L. Walker) All the Year, **70**: 140–188.
End of it, The. Macmil. **72**: 454. Same art. Liv. Age, **207**: 337.
End of Phæacia, The. (A. Lang) Time, **14**: 45–280.
End of Tortoni's. (S. Dewey) Atlan. **73**: 751.
Endeavor after Well-being, The. (J. A. Thomson) Nat. Sci. **8**: 21.
Endemoniadas of Queretaro. (H. C. Lea) J. Am. Folk-Lore, **3**: 33.

Ending of Barstow's Novel, The; a story. (H. Campbell) Harper, **88**: 307.
Endothermic Decompositions obtained by Pressure. (M. C. Lea) Am. J. Sci. **146**: 413.
Endothermic Reactions effected by Mechanical Force, (M. C. Lea) Am. J. Sci. **146**: 241.
Endowment Insurance Policies. Sat. R. **77**: 147.
Endowment Order Craze in Mass. (F. P. Bennett) Am. J. Pol. **1**: 514.
Energy and Matter. (P. R. Shipman) Open Court, **8**: 4063.
— Conservation of, Principle of. (E. Mach) Monist, **5**: 22.
— Dissipation of. (Lord Kelvin) Fortn. **57**: 313. Same art. Ecl. M. **118**: 577. Same art. Liv. Age, **193**: 387.
— Mechanical. (W. C. Unwin) Cassier, **8**: 195.
— Natural Storage of. (L. F. Ward) Monist, **5**: 247.
— of the Universe, Heysinger on. Sat. R. **79**: 516.
— Physical and Spiritual; are they Identical? (Mrs. Mary Parmele) New Sci. R. **1**: 478.
— Radiant, Swedenborgian View of. (J. Whitehead) N. Church R. **3**: 366.
— Transformation of; Joule's Discovery. (V. E. Johnson) Westm. **138**: 645. Same art. Ecl. M. **120**: 234.
— Vital, Conservation of. Open Court, **3**: 2047.
— Wasted. (G. Hill) Cassier, **5**: 516.
Engadine; Some High Notes. Cornh. **67**: 608. Same art. Ecl. M. **121**: 123. Same art. Liv. Age, **198**: 366.
Engagement of Susan Chase; a story. (Mrs. H. Wood) Argosy, **55**: 1-272.
Engaño, Island of. (F. H. H. Guillemard) Geog. J. **4**: 153.
Engels, Friedrich. (J. Bonar) Q. J. Econ. **10**: 95.— Econ. J. **5**: 490.
Enghien, Duc d', Execution of. (W. H. Craig) Un. Serv. M. **10**: 266, 390.
Engine, Priestman. (C. Sellers) J. Frankl. Inst. **135**: 89.
Engines, English Traction. (W. Fletcher) Cassier, **10**: 135.
— Selection of. (C. H. Davis and J. S. Griggs, jr.) Engin. M. **12**: 15.
Engine Driver's Talk. (H. Macfarlane) Eng. Illust. **16**: 200.
Engine-room Interiors, Artistic. (E. T. Adams) Engin. M. **10**: 1046.
Engineer and Architect, Relations between. (G. Hill) Engin. M. **4**: 808.
— Growing Influence of. (J. F. Holloway) Engin. M. **7**: 96.
— in Naval Warfare. (G. W. Melville; W. S. Aldrich; I. N. Hollis; G. C. Sims; G. Uhler) No. Am. **162**: 513.—(J. G. Walker; A. T. Mahan; R. D. Evans; S. A. Stanton) No. Am. **163**: 641.
— of an Express Train, Life of an. (C. Moffett) McClure, **1**: 356.
— The Stationary. (L. A. Blake) Cassier, **1**: 173.
— Who is an? (O. Smith) Engin. M. **2**: 675.
Engineer's Life in the Tropics. (C. P. Yeatman) Engin. M. **10**: 632.
Engineers. Bearing of Shop Practice. (C. E. Emery) Engin. M. **10**: 423.
— Natural Science Training for. (N. S. Shaler) Engin. M. **9**: 1021.
— Present Status of. (H. F. J. Porter) Cassier, **3**: 477.
— Value of the Manual Training Schools. (A. E. Outerbridge, jr.) Engin. M. **10**: 428.
Engineering, Advances in. (J. W. Barry) Nature, **55**: 17.
Engineering and Abstract Science, Interdependence of. (W. Anderson) Nature, **48**: 65.
— Artistic Element in. (F. O. Marvin) Am. Arch. **54**: 21.—(F. O. Marvin) Science, n. s. **4**: 321.—(C. S. Sargent) Garden & F. **9**: 411.
— Correspondence Schools of. (E. P. Roberts) Cassier, **8**: 106.
— Domestic. (L. Allen) Engin. M. **6**: 86.
— Fallacies in. (H. Morton) Cassier, **7**: 200, 486. **8**: 428.
— Government, in the U. S., Worthless. (G. Y. Wisner) Engin. M. **2**: 427.—Reply. (W. R. King) Engin. M. **2**: 664.—Rejoinder. (G. Y. Wisner) Engin. M. **2**: 743.
— — Reform of. (G. Y. Wisner) Engin. M. **3**: 66.
— in Warships. (H. Williams) Un. Serv. M. **5**: 348, 482.
— Mechanical, Chalk Age of. (J. F. Holloway) Cassier, **6**: 23.
— Modern, Achievements of. All the Year, **75**: 540.
— on the Great Lakes. (J. Birkinbine) J. Frankl. Inst. **141**: 428. **142**: 42.
— Past and Future of. (G. B. Kimbrough) Engin. M. **5**: 103.
— Prehistoric, at Lake Copais. (J. D. Champlin) Pop. Sci. Mo. **48**: 209.
— Relation to Mathematics. (J. Hopkinson) Nature, **50**: 42.
— — to Economics. (W. Kent) Science, n. s. **2**: 321.
— — to Progress and Civilization. (F. R. Hutton) Cassier, **5**: 227.
— — to Science. (L. F. Vernon-Harcourt) Nature, **52**: 501.
— Relations of Electrical and Mechanical. (E. E. Ries) Engin. M. **11**: 425.
— Specialization and Education. (L. S. Randolph) Cassier, **8**: 533.
— 300 Years Ago. (W. F. Durfee) Cassier, **8**: 97.
— Various Kinds of. (R. Grimshaw) Cassier, **2**: 261.
— What Chemistry owes to. (J. Torrey) Engin. M. **6**: 345.
— What it owes to Chemistry. (A. L. Griswold) Engin. M. **4**: 233.
Engineering Colleges. (R. H. Thurston) Engin. M. **10**: 418.
Engineering Congress at Chicago Exposition, 1893. (J. K. Freitag) Engin. M. **5**: 485.
Engineering Education. (W. S. Aldrich) J. Frankl. Inst. **140**: 262.
— Foundations of. (G. Lanza) Nature, **52**: 405.
— Past and Present Tendencies in. (M. Merriman) Science, n. s. **4**: 255.
Engineering Magazine, An Early. (H. C. Kirk) Engin. M. **5**: 90.
Engineering Notes from China and Japan. (F. F. Prentiss) Cassier, **10**: 431.
Engineering Practice and Education. (G. Lanza) J. Frankl. Inst. **137**: 372-444. **138**: 31-459. **139**: 44, 122.
— Quackery in. (E. Kidwell) Engin. M. **11**: 200, (E. H. Williams, jr., and others) 514.
England, American hatred of. (E. L. Godkin) Nation, **62**: 46.—Liv. Age, **208**: 443. Same art. Ecl. M. **126**: 416.
— American Impressions and Comparisons. (E. L. Banks) 19th Cent. **37**: 634. Same art. Ecl. M. **125**: 172.
— and America, Causes of Distrust between. (Goldwin Smith) Sat. R. **81**: 190.
— — in 1863; a Chapter in the Life of Cyrus W. Field. Harper, **92**: 846.
— — in 1895-96; a poem. (G. E. Woodberry) Cent. **31**: 148.

England and America, What is the Relation? (E. L. Mason) Arena, 15: 930.
— and her Colonies. (D. MacG. Means) Nation, 54: 426.
— — as Represented at Ottawa. (J. C. R. Colomb) 19th Cent. 36: 939.
— — Social Conditions of. (A. Barry) Econ. R. 1: 185. *See* Great Britain, Colonies of.
— and Commercial Unity with the Colonies. (A. Loftus) 19th Cent. 33: 339.
— and the Coming Thunder Storm. (F. Boh) 19th Cent. 36: 678.
— and the Continental Alliances. (F. de Pressensé) 19th Cent. 40: 681. Same art. Liv. Age, 211: 880.
— and Denmark, Marriages between the Royal Families of. (J. D. Symon) Eng. Illust. 15: 303.
— and France; Anglo-French Problems. (J. W. Lowther) National, 25: 306. Same art. Liv. Age, 205: 707.
— — French Feeling towards England. (André Lebon) National, 23: 49.
— — Relations of. (F. de Pressensé) 19th Cent. 39: 189.
— and Germany, Commercial War between. (B. H. Thwaite) 19th Cent. 40: 925.
— and Ireland. (W. J. Corbett) Overland, n. s. 28: 520-664.
— and Rome, from the Conquest to 1688, Ingram on. (W. Hunt) Eng. Hist. R. 7: 763.
— and Russia. (A. Vambéry) No. Am. 160: 561.
— — in the Time of Queen Elizabeth. (W. B. Steveni) 19th Cent. 34: 944.
— and Scotland, Mackinnon's Union of. (C. W. Colby) Nation, 63: 55.
— and the U. S., War between. Dial (Ch.) 20: 5.
— and Wales, Atlas of, in 18th Century. (F. O. Whitaker) Gent. M. n. s. 57: 138.
— — Rateable Value of. (T. R. Luke) Westm. 144: 131.
— Art in. The Royal Academy and the New Gallery. (H. H. Statham) Fortn. 65: 958.
— as a Reservoir of Capacities. Spec. 75: 759.
— at the Time of Sir Thomas More. (B. O. Flower) Arena, 14: 278.
— Bad Times ahead for. Soc. Econ. 3: 39.
— Beauty of Rural. (A. McC. Hallock) Garden & F. 7: 198, 208.
— Commercial Treaty with Japan. Dub. R. 116: 190.
— Constitution of, Boutmy on. (J. O. Pierce) Dial (Ch.) 12: 321.
— Constructing a British Empire. Soc. Econ. 8: 328.
— Corn Stores for War Time. (R. B. Marston) 19th Cent. 39: 236.
— Counties of, Chats on. (J. Hutchinson) Time, 7: 635, 901.
— County Court System of. (M. D. Chalmers) Law Q. 3: 1.
— Crown of, as an Aid to Democracy. (J. Macy) Pol. Sci. Q. 7: 483.
— Cycling in. (E. R. Holmes) Outing, 28: 20.
— Defense of, Balfour on. Spec. 72: 121.
— — Coast Protection. (J. Tyndall) New R. 6: 430,
— Democratization of. (T. Davidson) Forum, 21: 460.
— Dislike of, abroad. (C. J. Darling) National, 27: 257. — (F. A. Maxse) National, 28: 180.
— Domestic Life in, 15th Century. (E. B. Stone) Lippinc. 57: 390.
— — 17th Century. (M. M. Verney) Longm. 27: 353.
— Eastern; Development of Certain English Rivers. (W. M. Davis) Geog. J. 5: 127.
— Economic History of, Ashley's. (C. Gross) Nation, 57: 468. — (W. Cunningham) Pol. Sci. Q. 8: 526.
— — Rogers on. Spec. 70: 548.
England, Election in, A General. (R. H. Davis) Harper, 87: 489.
— — Right and Wrong in Politics. (Sir E. Strachey) Atlan. 72: 50.
— Elections in Former Times. Leis. Hour, 41: 771.
— Ethical Movement in. (W. Clarke) Open Court, 1: 444.
— European Coalitions against. (T. E. Kebbel) 19th Cent. 39: 802.
— Financial Outlook in. (H. Withers) New R. 11: 268.
— Following Dickens with a Camera. (H. H. Ragan) Outing, 23: 296.
— Foreign Policy of. (W. O. Morris) Acad. 46: 41.
— Fortifications of. (E. Mitchell) Univ. R. 1: 210.
— Free Thought in. (H. B. Bonner) Open Court, 1: 147.
— A French Critic [A. De Staël] on. Macmil. 69: 435. Same art. Liv. Age, 201: 357.
— Future of, from a Biological Standpoint. Sat. R. 81: 118.
— German Account of, 1602. Ath. '92, 2: 65.
— History. Battle of the Sacred Standard, 1138. Sat. R. 76: 236.
— — Civil War, Gardiner's. (R. Dunlop) Acad. 41: 101, 150. — (M. W. Whelpton) Westm. 137: 305. — (H. Hayman) Dub. R. 111: 31. — (A. W. Ward) Eng. Hist. R. 7: 573. — (A. V. Dicey) Nation, 54: 360, 382. — Sat. R. 73: 488.
— — — Tracts on. Thomason Collection. (F. Madan) Bibliographica, 3: 291.
— — Commonwealth and Protectorate, Gardiner's. (W. O'C. Morris) Acad. 47: 5. — (A. V. Dicey) Nation, 60: 280. 61: 13. — (W. O'C. Morris) Scot. R. 25: 323. — Sat. R. 79: 293. — Ed. R. 181: 140.
— — Conversion of Wessex. (S. T. Holmes) Eng. Hist. R. 7: 437.
— — Flores Historiarum, Luard's Edition. (R. L. Poole) Eng. Hist. R. 7: 146.
— — for American Readers, Higginson's. Nation, 57: 214.
— — Irish Rebellion. Secret Service under Pitt, Fitzpatrick's. Spec. 68: 679.
— — Lancaster and York, Ramsay's. Ath. '92, 2: 117. — (G. Smith) Nation, 55: 71. — Sat. R. 73: 658. — Spec. 69: 354. — (T. F. Tout) Eng. Hist. R. 8: 557. — Ed. R. 177: 92.
— — Lindsay's, 1763. (R. Garnett) Eng. Hist. R. 7: 114.
— — New Light on. (E. Porritt) No. Am. 161: 119.
— — Oman's. Sat. R. 80: 177.
— — Revolution of 1688. (A. Shield) Dub. R. 119: 353.
— — — Naval Preparations of James II. (J. R. Tanner) Eng. Hist. R. 8: 272.
— — under Henry IV., Wylie's. Ath. '94, 1: 405.
— — Wace and his Authorities. (J. H. Round) Eng. Hist. R. 8: 677.
— Impending Revolution. (G. Smith) 19th Cent. 35: 353.
— in 1197; the Oxford Council. (J. H. Round) Eng. Hist. R. 7: 301.
— in 15th Century. (G. Winterwood) Good Words, 35: 627.
— in 1554; Visit of Philip II. (M. A. S. Hume) Eng. Hist. R. 7: 253.
— in 1644-45; Calendar of State Papers, etc. (C. H. Firth) Eng. Hist. R. 7: 369.
— in 1658; Letters Concerning the Dissolution of Cromwell's Last Parliament. (C. H. Firth) Eng. Hist. R. 7: 102.

England in 1678; Pepys and the Popish Plot. (J. R. Tanner) Eng. Hist. R. 7: 281.
— in 1689; a Diary. (S. Sewall) Walford's Antiq. 7: 110. 8: 129, 222.
— in the 18th Century. Church Q. 33: 467.
— in 1800. Sat. R. 75: 683.
— in 1892; "Merry England." (Duke of Marlborough) New R. 6: 31. Same art. Ecl. M. 118: 289.
— in the Orient. (A. Vambéry) No. Am. 156: 359.
— Individualism and Democracy in. (A. Waters) Open Court, 6: 3311.
— Industrial and Commercial History, Rogers's. Ath. '94, 1: 206. — (J. W. Jenks) Dial (Ch.) 13: 76. — (D. MacG. Means) Nation, 55: 226.
— Industrial Decline of Lancashire. Soc. Econ. 3: 257.
— Industrial History, Cunningham and McArthur's. Sat. R. 79: 606.
— Industry and Commerce of, Cunningham's. Ath. '92, 2: 911.
— Jews in, under the Angevin Kings. (J. Jacobs) Jew. Q. 4: 628. 5: 51.
— Journey to, in 1663. (J. J. Jusserand) 19th Cent. 32: 52. Same art. Ecl. M. 119: 335. Same art. Liv. Age, 194: 556.
— Labor and Politics in. (J. Mavor) Pol. Sci. Q. 10: 486.
— Labor Movement in. (Tom Mann) Soc. Econ. 3: 77.
— Labor Parliament of. (G. J. Harney) Open Court, 5: 2805.
— Lake Country of, Coach Ride in Cumberland. (D. N. Beach) Educa. 13: 472.
— Legislation in, Recent. (E. Porritt) Yale R. 5: 272.
— Liberty in, from the Reformation to William III. (M. Hennessey) Am. Cath. Q. 18: 295.
— Manners and Customs in; Picture of the Past. (E. L. Linton) 19th Cent. 32: 791.
— — 18th Century. (Mrs. E. L. Linton) Ecl. M. 120: 23.
— — Fifty Years Ago. (Mrs. E. L. Linton) Ecl. M. 120: 760.
— Miss Martineau's History. Eng. R. 13: 44.
— Morals and Religious Belief in the Reign of Edward VI. (N. Pocock) Eng. Hist. R. 10: 417.
— National Anthem of, Origin of. (F. K. Harford) Walford's Antiq. 1: 229, 285.
— Naval Supremacy of. (W. O. Morris) Acad. 43: 297.
— Navy of, under Charles I. (M. Oppenheim) Eng. Hist. R. 8: 467.
— Notes on. (P. Verlaine) Fortn. 62: 70. Same art. Liv. Age, 202: 345.
— Officialism in. (E. W. Huffcut) Pol. Sci. Q. 8: 58.
— Old, Castles of. (C. Turner) Mo. Illust. 4: 26.
— 100 Years Ago. Chamb. J. 71: 619.
— or Russia? (D. Mills) Canad. M. 4: 518.
— Our Invasions, Scares, and Panics. (R. V. Hamilton) 19th Cent. 39: 399.
— Outdoor Life in, Fisher on. Sat. R. 81: 403.
— Papal Letters Relating to, 1133–87. Eng. Hist. R. 9: 531.
— The Passing of. (Spenser Wilkinson) New R. 12: 236.
— Policy of, History of. (J. R. Seeley) Contemp. 66: 1. Same art. Liv. Age, 202: 473. Same art. Ecl. M. 123: 295.
— Political Evolution in. Blackw. 157: 651.
— Political Parties in, 1815. Eng. R. 4: 434.
— Population of, about 1164. (F. Lebermann) Eng. Hist. R. 11: 744.
— — 1259 to 1793. Time, 22: 250.
— Princesses of, Lives of Early. Eng. R. 15: 378.
— Progress of, Verney on. Spec. 68: 737.
— — Reply. (Sir H. Verney) Spec. 68: 744.
England, Prosperity of, Sources of. Spec. 70: 280.
— Provincial Courts, Reorganization of. (W. H. Owen) Law Q. 9: 321.
— Queens of, Miss Strickland's. Eng. R. 2: 339.
— Radicalism in, Old and New. Macmil. 74: 153.
— Religious Equality in, Movement for. (E. Porritt) New World, 3: 233.
— Religious Movements in. (F. Brown) New World, 5: 615.
— Rivers of the Lake District. (E. R. Dibdin) M. of Art, 19: 185.
— Roman Catholicism in; Devotion to Rome during a Thousand Years. (Bishop of Salford) Dub. R. 110: 243.
— Royal Palaces of. (W. Taylor) Munsey, 7: 699.
— Rural. An Architect's Vacation. (R. S. Peabody) Atlan. 76: 23.
— Rural Life in. Spec. 72: 748.
— Russia and France. (T. H. S. Escott) Fortn. 66: 648. Same art. Ecl. M. 127: 731.
— Seaman of the 16th Century, Froude's. Sat. R. 80: 144.
— Social, Traill's. (A. B. Woodford) Dial (Ch.) 18: 15. 19: 87. — (W. B. Weeden) Am. Hist. R. 1: 124.
— — Vol. 4. (A. B. Woodford) Dial (Ch.) 20: 203.
— Social Changes in. (E. S. Nadal) Critic, 27: 335.
— Social Disunion of. Spec. 69: 641.
— Social Life in, in 17th Century. (J. Ashton) Chaut. 20: 10.
— — in 18th Century. (J. Ashton) Chaut. 20: 138.
— — in 19th Century. (J. Ashton) Chaut. 20: 266.
— Social Theories in, and in America. Lend a H. 12: 83.
— Society in. (M. Jeune) Sat. R. 81: 571.
— South of, North *vs.* (F. Case) National, 23: 861.
— Sweden and Denmark in 1657–58. Correspondence of Thurloe and Meadowe. (E. Jenks) Eng. Hist. R. 7: 720.
— Telegraphic Isolation. (P. A. Hurd) Contemp. 69: 899.
— The Traveler's. Atlan. 73: 142.
— Two Tramps in. (J. Flynt) Cent. 28: 289.
— Under Henry IV., Wylie's. (C. L. Kingsford) Acad. 46: 4. — Sat. R. 81: 410.
— Vignettes from St. Pilgrim's Isle. (A. H. Morrison) Canad. M. 2: 224.
— Village Life and Politics in. (W. Tuckwell) Contemp. 61: 397. — (R. G. Thwaites) New Eng. M. n. s. 6: 275. — (S. H. Malmesbury) No. Am. 158: 304.
— Walks in the Country. (J. Penderel-Brodhurst) M. of Art, 7: 504.
— Western, Cycling thro'. (Mrs. A. L. Moqué) Outing, 28: 186. 29: 232.
Englefield, Sir Francis. (A. A. Harrison) Dub. R. 119: 34.
English and Americans in French Fiction. (A. de Ternant) Gent. M. n. s. 57: 287. Same art. Liv. Age, 211: 210.
English, The, in the United States. (J. R. Towse) Chaut. 15: 304.
English and American Manners. Soc. Econ. 9: 63.
English and German Literature of 18th Century. (O. Seidensticker) Poet-Lore, 2: 57, 169.
English and Scotch Fairy Tales. (A. Lang) Folk-Lore, 1: 289.
English Architecture, Secular, Pictorial Elements in. (E. I. Bell) M. of Art, 1: 158. 2: 65–225.
English Channel, Bridge over, Proposed. (Albert, Prince de Monaco) Fortn. 61: 832.
— Communication Across, Method of. (J. Fleury) Chaut. 16: 185.

English Channel, Geographical Evolution of. (A. J. Jukes-Browne) Contemp. **61**: 855.
— On Summer Seas. (Lady Arnold) Outing, **26**: 156.
— Proposed Tunnel. (E. J. Moeran) Time, **8**: 209.
— — Government and. Spec. **70**: 347.
— — Seizure of. Time, **7**: 91.
— The Short Sea Cross-Channel Routes. Blackw. **157**: 614.
— Strategical Condition of. (P. H. Colomb) Un. Serv. M. **5**: 225.
English Character, Influence of Historic Homes on. (Lord Brabourne) Forum, **15**: 232.
English Commons and Forests. (H. H. L. Bellot) Westm. **142**: 293.
English Composition at Harvard and elsewhere. (W. P. Garrison) Nation, **55**: 299.
— Conditions needed for Successful Teaching of. (S. Thurber) School R. **2**: 13.
— Effect of the Quarter System on Courses in. (R. W. Herrick) Educa. R. **8**: 382.
— Hart on. (M. W. Sampson) Dial (Ch.) **20**: 108. — (E. H. Lewis) School R. **4**: 105.
— in Colleges. (G. R. Carpenter) Educa. R. **4**: 438.
— in Preparatory Schools. Nation, **55**: 388.
— Limitations of Secondary Teaching of. (S. Thurber) Educa. **15**: 193.
— Sight Translations from the Classics as a Test of Proficiency in. (J. Tetlow) Educa. R. **12**: 75.
— Wendell on. Atlan. **69**: 129.
English Counties, Legends of. (C. G. Boger) Walford's Antiq. **1**: 125.
English Country-house Parties. (Lady Colin Campbell) Cosmopol. **18**: 687.
English Country Houses, Famous. (R. H. Titherington) Munsey, **9**: 397.
English Dictionary. *See* English Language; Dictionary.
English Drama, Fleay's Biographical Chronicle of. Spec. **68**: 749.
English Dramatists, Old. (J. R. Lowell) Harper, **85**: 75.
English Folk-Lore. (C. Burne) Folk-Lore, **1**: 313. *See* Folk-Lore.
English Friend, To an. (F. Eastman) Atlan. **74**: 790.
English Gentry; Disappearance of the Old Squires. Spec. **72**: 128.
English Grammar, Sweet's. Ath. '92, **2**: 120.
English House Architecture. (Banister Fletcher) Archit. Rec. **5**: 321.
English Immigrants in America. (M. B. Godsall) 19th Cent. **39**: 964.
English Imperialism, Lecky on. Spec. **71**: 741.
English Industry and Eastern Competition. (R. S. Gundry) Fortn. **64**: 609.
English Institutions, Christianity and. (D. H. Wheeler) Chaut. **20**: 395.
English Kings and Roman Pontiffs. (A. M. Marshall) Am. Cath. Q. **17**: 715.
English Language, The. Belgra. **90**: 319.
— Academic Treatment of. (H. E. Scudder) Atlan. **74**: 688.
— American, Study of. (G. Hempl) Chaut. **22**: 436.
— and English Grammar, Ramsey's. (G. L. Kittredge) Nation, **55**: 13.
— and the French. Spec. **69**: 156. Same art. Ecl. M. **119**: 399.
— and Literature, Study of, as a Part of a Liberal Education. (W. J. Courthope) National, **21**: 486. Same art. Ecl. M. **121**: 177. Same art. Liv. Age, **198**: 478.
— as Universal. (D. G. Porter) Am. J. Soc. Sci. **32**: 117.
— College. (E. L. Godkin) Nation, **61**: 219.
English Language, College Requirements in. (B. S. Hurlbut) Acad. **7**: 257. — (H. S. Pancoast) Educa. R. **3**: 132. — (J. E. Russell) Educa. R. **4**: 74.
— — at Yale. (H. A. Beers) Educa. R. **3**: 427.
— Conversational. (P. F. Bicknell) Dial (Ch.) **21**: 107.
— Corruption of. Gent. M. n. s. **48**: 429.
— Cracker. (E. F. Andrews) Chaut. **23**: 85.
— Democracy and. (J. C. Adams) Cosmopol. **14**: 459.
— Dictionaries of. Ath. '92, **1**: 78.
— Dictionary of, Century. Vol. 6. (M. B. Anderson) Dial (Ch.) **12**: 348.
— — Murray's. (W. P. Garrison) Nation, **54**: 91. **56**: 230. **57**: 67. **58**: 35. **60**: 167.
— — — Trials and Progress of. Sat. R. **81**: 393.
— — Philological Society's. *See above*, Murray's.
— — Sanford's, of Anglicised Words and Phrases. Sat. R. **74**: 655. — Gent. M. n. s. **49**: 639.
— — Standard. Atlan. **76**: 414. — (C. S. Peirce) Nation, **58**: 180.
— Educational Value of. (G. H. Browne) Educa. R. **9**: 377.
— Effective Use of, Teaching. (A. P. Marble) Educa. R. **3**: 22.
— English as she is spoke. Atlan. **76**: 717.
— Expressive Power of English Sounds. (A. H. Tolman) Atlan. **75**: 478.
— for Germans. Sat. R. **81**: 486.
— Future of. Chamb. J. **71**: 294.
— Grammar of, Historical, Primer of, Sweet's. (O. F. Emerson) School R. **4**: 236.
— — Teaching of, History of. (F. A. Barbour) Educa. R. **12**: 487.
— in College Curriculum. (S. V. Ruby) Ref. Q. **40**: 282.
— in India and the East. (Hyde Clarke) Asia. R. **10**: 149.
— in Newspapers. (R. I. Attwill) Bost. **3**: 543.
— Malay Words in. (R. C. Ford) Educa. **17**: 37.
— Mastery of. (J. Greene) School R. **1**: 546.
— on an Indian Reservation. (F. C. Sparhawk) Educa. **12**: 609.
— Orthography of, New. (J. I. D. Hinds) Science, **22**: 34.
— Practical Exercises in, Buehler's. (E. H. Lewis) School R. **4**: 242.
— Renascence in. (R. Burton) Forum, **20**: 181.
— Retrogression in. (P. F. Bicknell) Dial (Ch.) **19**: 204.
— School. (C. F. Adams) Nation, **61**: 309. — (W. W. Goodwin) Nation, **61**: 291.
— Spoken. (E. L. Godkin) Nation, **55**: 332.
— — Changes in. (A. B. Kingsbury) New Sci. R. **1**: 428.
— Study of. (J. Earle) Forum, **13**: 75.
— in American Colleges. (T. W. Hunt) Educa. R. **12**: 140.
— — Question of. (J. J. Greenough) Atlan. **71**: 656.
— — Reaction in. (S. B. Knowlton) School R. **4**: 682.
— Teaching of. Time, **16**: 564.
— — Emphasis in. (B. Groce) Acad. **61**: 529.
— — in Preparatory Schools. Nation, **63**: 364.
— Use of. (W. M. Thayer) Educa. **13**: 408.
— Writing. (J. A. Cooper) Canad. M. **8**: 80.
— — Bates on. (E. E. Hale, jr.) Dial (Ch.) **21**: 221.
English Law before Edward I. (R. W. Lee) Acad. **48**: 355.
English Liberty, The Church and. (M. Hennessy) Am. Cath. Q. **17**: 701.
English Literature. (T. Appel) Ref. Q. **42**: 487.
— and French; a contrast. Westm. **142**: 571.
— as a Study, Claims for. (T. W. White) Educa. **12**: 273.
— at Amherst College. (J. F. Genung) Dial (Ch.) **17**: 54

English Literature at Columbia College. (B. Matthews) Dial (Ch.) 16: 101.
— at Cornell University. (H. Corson) Dial (Ch.) 16: 201.
— at Harvard. (B. Wendell) Dial (Ch.) 16: 131.
— at Indiana University. (M. W. Sampson) Dial (Ch.) 17: 5.
— at Iowa State University. (E. E. Hale, jr.) Dial (Ch.) 16: 328.
— at Lafayette College. (F. A. March) Dial (Ch.) 16: 294.
— at Stanford University. (M. B. Anderson) Dial (Ch.) 16: 167.
— at University of California. (C. M. Gayley) Dial (Ch.) 17: 29.
— at University of Chicago. (A. H. Tolman) Dial (Ch.) 16: 356.
— at University of Illinois. (D. K. Dodge) Dial (Ch.) 16: 261.
— at University of Michigan. (F. N. Scott) Dial (Ch.) 17: 82.
— at University of Nebraska. (L. A. Sherman) Dial (Ch.) 17: 105.
— at University of Pennsylvania. (F. E. Schelling) Dial (Ch.) 17: 146.
— at University of Virginia. (C. W. Kent) Dial (Ch.) 16: 233.
— at University of Wisconsin. (D. B. Frankenburger) Dial (Ch.) 17: 187.
— at Wellesley College. (K. L. Bates) Dial (Ch.) 17: 219.
— at Yale University. (A. S. Cook) Dial (Ch.) 16: 69.
— at the Universities. Dial (Ch.) 16: 325. — (F. J. Carpenter) Dial, 19: 181.
— — in the South. (J. B. Henneman) Dial (Ch.) 17: 373.
— — A Summary. Dial (Ch.) 17: 249.
— at Oxford, New School of. Acad. 46: 511.
— Best Books of 1892. Lit. W. (Bost.) 24: 9.
— Brooke on. (C. H. Herford) Acad. 45: 222. — Spec. 69: 889. — Ath. '93, 1: 45.
— from the Standpoint of the Student. (C. W. Hodell) Dial (Ch.) 17: 148.
— Future of. (W. M. Colles) New R. 8: 571.
— Georgian Era of. (T. Hutchinson) Acad. 47: 49.
— High-school Course in. (G. J. Smith) Educa. R. 10: 445.
— History of, Jusserand's. Sat. R. 80: 550. — (W. M. Payne) Dial (Ch.) 18: 320.
— in Bohemia. Ath. '92, 1: 84.
— in the College. (L. A. Sherman) Educa. R. 10: 42.
— in Education of Girls. (S. Thurber) School R. 2: 321.
— in 1891. Ath. '92, 1: 19.
— in 1892. Ath. '93, 1: 19. — Lit. W. (Bost.) 24: 8.
— in a French University. Dial (Ch.) 17: 27.
— in the High School, First Year of. (J. G. Wight) School R. 1: 15.
— in New York State, Outlook for. (J. M. Hart) School R. 1: 195.
— — Regents' Diplomas in. (J. M. Hart) School R. 1: 24.
— — Regents' Work in. (J. R. Parsons, jr.) School R. 1: 226.
— in the Lower Schools. Dial (Ch.) 17: 3.
— in the Preparatory Schools. (C. F. Adams) Harv. Grad. M. 1: 177.
— in the Public Schools. (R. H. Alvey) Acad. 7: 19.
— — Parents' Point of View. (C. M. St. John) School R. 1: 491.
— in Secondary Schools. (F. B. Gummere) School & C. 1: 84. — (C. Davidson) School & C. 1: 577. — (B. Wendell) School R. 1: 168. — (S. Thurber) School R. 2: 468, 540.
— Laboratory Method in. (R. W. Herrick) Harv. Mo. 16: 133.
English Literature, of 19th Century, Saintsbury's. (T. Hutchinson) Acad. 49: 255. — Sat. R. 81: 423. — (M. Todhunter) Westm. 146: 378.
— of the Victorian Age. (F. Harrison) Forum, 16: 703.
— Outline of the Philosophy of, White on. (E. H. Lewis) School R. 4: 234.
— Outlook for. (J. M. Hart) School R. 2: 36.
— Renton on. Spec. 71: 665.
— Scherer on. Ath. '92, 1: 399.
— Seventeenth Century, America in. (I. B. Choate) New Eng. M. n. s. 6: 20.
— Study of. (E. Dowden) Liv. Age, 177: 3. — (W. H. Hudson) Overland, n. s. 27: 325.
— — Aim in. (G. E. Gardner) Educa. 15: 133, 221.
— — Collins on. Sat. R. 73: 24. — Spec. 68: 334.
— — in Public Schools. (A. P. Marble) School R. 1: 198.
— — in School and College. School R. 1: 462.
— Teacher's Equipment for. (S. Thurber) School R. 2: 65.
— Teaching. (B. Kellogg) School R. 1: 96, 152. — (B. Groce) Acad. 7: 202. — (L. W. Spring) Educa. 13: 83. — (R. Burton) Dial (Ch.) 19: 277.
— — Can it be taught? (B. Matthews) Educa. R. 3: 337.
— — Scientific Method in. (J. M. Hart) Acad. 7: 125.
— Tudor Translations. (W. Raleigh) Fortn. 64: 415.
— Uniform Entrance Examinations in. (B. L. Wheeler) School R. 2: 562.
— Victorian, Harrison on. Spec. 72: 263.
— — Mrs. Oliphant's. (L. E. Gates) Nation, 56: 351. — Sat. R. 74: 776. — Spec. 69: 958.
— Work in, in Secondary Schools. (B. Wendell) School R. 1: 638.
English Mercurie, The. Bookworm, 4: 169, 201.
English Nobility of Our Time. (H. Baumann) Chaut. 22: 83.
English Officer, The, as he was and is. (H. Knollys) Un. Serv. (Phila.) 14: 445.
English Officers and Soldiers — as they will be. (H. Knollys) Blackw. 159: 199.
English Opinion. What the English think of us. Gunton's M. 10: 172.
English People, Good Sense of the. (T. E. Kebbel) 19th Cent. 37: 382.
English Poetry, Courthorpe's History of. (G. L. Kittredge) Nation, 61: 152. — (W. M. Payne) Dial (Ch.) 19: 179. — Sat. R. 80: 85.
— Dixon on. Spec. 72: 138.
— Early History of. Church Q. 40: 461.
— Italian Influence on. Ed. R. 183: 28.
— Life of the Spirit in Modern. Atlan. 76: 130.
— Nature in Old. (R. Burton) Atlan. 73: 476.
English Prose, Craik's. (O. F. Emerson) Dial (Ch.) 15: 116.
— Growth of. Spec. 70: 641.
English Race: Is it degenerating? (H. P. Dunn) 19th Cent. 36: 300.
English Shakespeare, The; a story. (I. Zangwill) Idler, 1: 61.
English Shell, An; a poem. (A. C. Benson) National, 23: 786.
English Society; Disappearance of the Smaller Gentry, 1660–1800. Macmil. 72: 129.
— Revolution in. (H. A. Herbert) Cosmopol. 13: 475.
English Soldier, as he was and is. (H. Knollys) Un. Serv. (Phila.) 15: 22.
English-speaking Lands. (S. P. Cadman) Chaut. 21: 615, 727.
English-speaking People, Federation of. (J. Milne) Contemp. 66: 192.

English-speaking Peoples, Festival of, Proposed. (J. A. Cooper) 19th Cent. **32**: 380.
— Quarrel of. (H. Norman) Scrib. M. **19**: 513.
English Statesmen, Composite Portraits of. Idler, **1**: 39.
English Trees. (J. L. Allen) So. M. **5**: 419.
English Universities, Americans at the. (E. J. Smith) Nation, **58**: 208.
English Wife, A Plea for the. (E. M. Nicholl) No. Am. **161**: 759.
Englishman, The, in the Colonies. Chamb. J. **73**: 156.
Englishmen. How they Spend their Money. (P. Collier) Forum, **17**: 730.
Englishwomen abroad. (Mrs. Humphrey) Idler, **8**: 166.
— in India. (K. Lyttleton) New R. **6**: 682. Same art. Liv. Age, **194**: 237.
— of 17th and 19th Centuries. Eng. R. **6**: 235.
— Three Generations of, Ross's. Dial (Ch.) **14**: 207.
Engraving, Copper, Steel, and Bank-note. (C. W. Dickinson) Pop. Sci. Mo. **46**: 597.
— Neglect of, by Royal Academy. (R. S. Clouston) Art J. **48**: 217.
Enigma, An; a story. (W. Canton) Good Words, **34**: 332. Same art. Liv. Age, **198**: 246.
Enmities of Literature. Atlan. **73**: 717.
Ennis, Alfred, with portrait. (H. L. Conard) Nat'l M. (N. Y. '91) **17**: 380.
Ennis Abbey. (D. C. Parkinson) Antiq. n. s. **29**: 199.
Ennui. (A. Repplier) Atlan. **71**: 775. — Spec. **70**: 848.
Enoch, Book of. (J. Owen; R. H. Charles) Acad. **45**: 93, 127.
— — Ed. by Charles. Sat. R. **76**: 48.
— — Fragments of, New Greek. (G. H. Schodde) Bib. World, **1**: 359.
Enter the Earl of Tyne. (C. B. Fernald) Cent. **29**: 780.
Entertainer, The Public. Cornh. **65**: 285.
Entertainments which appeal to the Non-theatre-going Public, Educational Value of. (B. O. Flower) Arena, **15**: 726.
Enthusiasm and Intoxication. (E. D. Cope) Open Court, **5**: 3072.
Enthusiast, The. (E. H. Lacon Watson) Westm. **142**: 631.
Entirely Accidental; a story. (G. Allen) Eng. Illust. **16**: 47.
Entomology, Economic. (C. H. Fernald) Science n. s. **4**: 541.
— — Smith on. Garden & F. **9**: 498.
— Legal. (R. V. Rogers) Green Bag, **7**: 323.
— Speculative Method in. (R. Meldola) Nature, **53**: 352.
Envelopes, Civil-war. (J. H. Adams) New Eng. M. n. s. **12**: 121.
Environment, and Man in New England. (N. S. Shaler) No. Am. **162**: 726.
— Can Heredity be modified? (H. H. Gardiner) Arena, **10**: 145.
— Heredity and. (A. M. Holmes) Arena, **9**: 571.
— Society as. Poet-Lore, **6**: 40.
Envoy, The; a poem. (L. S. Porter) Cosmopol. **18**: 340.
Eocene Deposits of Maryland and Virginia, Geological Position of. (G. D. Harris) Am. J. Sci. **147**: 301.
— of New Jersey, Gigantic Bird from. (O. C. Marsh) Am. J. Sci. **148**: 344.
— Potomac River Section of Middle Atlantic Coast. (W. B. Clark) Am. J. Sci. **151**: 365.
— Upper Vicksburg, and Chattahoochee Miocene. (A. F. Foerste) Am. J. Sci. **148**: 41.
Eocene Mammals, Extinct, New Order of. (O. C. Marsh) Am. J. Sci. **143**: 445.
Eolian Action, Post-glacial, in Southern New England. (J. B. Woodworth) Am. J. Sci. **147**: 63.
Eon de Beaumont, Chevalier, as a Book Collector. (W. Roberts) Gent. M. n. s. **56**: 237. Same art. Liv. Age, **209**: 120.
— True Story of, Vizetelly's. Sat. R. **80**: 581.
Eos, Myths of, on Greek Vase-paintings. (J. E. Harrison) M. of Art, **17**: 59.
Eoves, The Vision of. (G. W. Wood) Sund. M. **21**: 814.
Eozoön and the Monte Somna Blocks. (H. J. Johnston-Lavis and J. W. Gregory) Nat. Sci. **6**: 398.
Ephemerides, Astronomical. (J. Morrison) Pop. Astron. **2**: 301.
Ephesus and the Temple of Diana. Temp. Bar, **104**: 355. Same art. Liv. Age, **205**: 153.
— Council of, and Anglican Writers. (S. Rivington) Dub. R. **110**: 296. **111**: 144.
— — Papal Supremacy at. (L. Rivington) Dub. R. **116**: 375.
— Memories of. (M. Harrison) Sund. M. **21**: 246.
Ephphatha; a poem. (C. Burke) Argosy, **60**: 472.
Epicureanism, Modern, A Phase of. (C. M. Williams) Int. J. Ethics, **4**: 80.
Epicurism. (R. Lewins) Open Court, **7**: 3544.
Epidemics and Providence. (E. D. Weigle) Luth. Q. **25**: 317.
— Early, in England, Creighton on. Spec. **68**: 580. — Sat. R. **73**: 661.
— Historic. All the Year, **70**: 228.
Epidote from Huntington, Mass., and its Optical Properties. (E. H. Forbes) Am. J. Sci. **151**: 26.
Epigenesis. (E. Haeckel) Open Court, **9**: 4514.
— Evolution or? (H. C. Hiller) Nature, **52**: 317.
— Haacke on. Nature, **50**: 242.
— Hertwig on. (G. C. Bourne) Nature, **51**: 265.
Epigœa. *See* Arbutus.
Epigrams, Some Ancient and Modern. (W. Cowan) Good Words, **34**: 827.
Epigraphy, Field. (J. Alden) Nation, **61**: 307.
— in Egyptian Research. (Flinders Petrie) Asia. R. **12**: 315.
Epileptics, Care of. (W. P. Letchworth) Lend a H. **17**: 280.
— Colony for. (E. Sellers) Contemp. **62**: 683. Same art. Pop. Sci. Mo. **42**: 663.
— Education of. (L. F. Bryson) Am. J. Soc. Sci. **31**: 100.
— Provision for. (W. P. Letchworth) Lend a H. **13**: 90.
— State Provision for. (W. F. Drewry) Char. R. **5**: 117.
Epiphany, Reflections on. (G. F. Mull) Ref. Q. **42**: 160.
Epiphytes. (P. Groom) Nat. Sci. **3**: 172.
Episcopacy in the First Two Centuries. (A. F. Hewit) Am. Cath. Q. **17**: 543.
Episcopal Claims, Bishop Coleman on. (C. Cort) Ref. Q. **41**: 263.
Episcopal Palaces of England, Venable's. Sat. R. **82**: 94.
Episcopal Scandal, An; a story. Cornh. **69**: 167. Same art. Ecl. M. **122**: 354.
Episcopalian, What makes an? (G. Hodges) Chaut. **18**: 452.
Episcopalian Polity, The. (W. Kirkus) New World, **3**: 260.
Episcopate, Historic. (J. C. Long) Bib. Sac. **51**: 444. — (R. J. Cooke) Meth. R. **55**: 371.
— — Congregationalism and. (G. P. Fisher) Chr. Lit. **13**: 322.
— — Development of. (V. Bartlett) Contemp. **65**: 795.
— — Symposium. Indep. April 12, '94.
— — in the Lutheran Church, Revival of. (E. H. Delk) Luth. Q. **24**: 555.
— — Shields on. (A. H. Bradford and others) Chr. Lit. **10**: 133 a, 165 a.
— Incomes of the. Eng. R. **7**: 426.

Episode in the Life of Robert the Simple. (H. E. Smith) Overland, n. s. 23: 197.
— in Mexico. (E. S. Sea) Cosmopol. 12: 546.
— in an Old Maid's Life, An; a story. (Blanche Atkinson) Good Words, 34: 414.
— in Two Lives; a story. Belgra. 86: 369.
— under the "Terror," An; a story. (H. de Balzac) Gent. M. n. s. 50: 1. Same art. Liv. Age, 196: 464.
Epistemology and Ontology. (A. Seth) Philos. R. 3: 568.
— Hartmann's. (W. Caldwell) Mind, 18: 188.
— in Locke and Kant. (A. Seth) Philos. R. 2: 167.
— of Neo-Kantianism. (A. Seth) Philos. R. 2: 293.
— of the Saints. Meth. R. 56: 120.
— Problem of. (A. Seth) Philos. R. 1: 504.
— Relation of Metaphysics to. (D. G. Ritchie) Philos. R. 3: 14.
— Some Epistemological Conclusions. (A. Seth) Philos. R. 3: 56.
Epitaph for a Husbandman; a poem. (C. G. D. Roberts) Cosmopol. 19: 146.
Epitaph Literature, Curiosities of. Chamb. J. 69: 254.
Epitaphs. (H. A. Lincoln) Good Words, 37: 526. — (J. D. P. Penhallow) J. Am. Folk-Lore, 5: 305.
— Curious. (T. E. Champion) Canad. M. 3: 502. — Canad. M. 4: 290.
— English. (I. A. Taylor) No. Am. 163: 595. — (Mrs. J. M. K. Fleming) Argosy, 60: 536.
— of the 17th Century, Three. (S. A. P. Andrews) J. Am. Folk-Lore, 7: 118.
'Επωύσως. (L. S. Potwin) J. Bib. Lit. 12: 15.
Epping Forest. (C. S. Sargent) Garden & F. 9: 301.
— Settlement of Question of. (R. Meldala) Nature, 50: 225.
Epsom and the Derby. Eng. Illust. 9: 656.
Epworth League. (J. F. Berry) M. Chr. Lit. 6: 359.
— Opportunities and Perils of. (E. A. Schell) Meth. R. 54: 412.
Equality. (D. G. Ritchie) Contemp. 62: 561.
— as the Basis of Good Society. (W. D. Howells) Cent. 29: 63.
Equatorial, Axis of, on Ball Bearings. (F. L. O. Wadsworth) Astron. 13: 723.
— Electric Control for. (G. W. Hough) Astron. 13: 524.
— Small, Adjustment of. (H. A. Howe) Pop. Astron. 3: 131, 193.
— 20-inch, of the Chamberlin Observatory. (H. A. Howe) Astron. 13: 826.
Equilibrium of Mrs. Tollmage, The; a story. (E. Castle) Temp. Bar, 103: 201.
Equity, Early English. (O. W. Holmes, jr.) Law Q. 1: 162.
— Thirteen Maxims of; a poem. (R. Palmer) Green Bag, 7: 27.
"er," Dialect Use of. Sat. R. 74: 328.
Eranthemums, Cultivation of. (N. J. Rose) Garden & F. 8: 516.
Erasmus, D. (F. St. J. Thackeray) Gent. M. n. s. 54: 91. — Quar. 180: 1. Same art. Liv. Age, 204: 771. — (J. M. Stone) Month, 87: 546.
— and the Pronunciation of Greek. (J. Gennadius) 19th Cent. 39: 87.
— and the Reformation. (J. C. Bailey) Temp. Bar, 104: 207. Same art. Liv. Age, 204: 643.
— and the Renaissance. (J. M. Stone) Month, 88: 98.
— in Italy. (E. H. R. Tatham) Eng. Hist. R. 10: 642.
— Life of, Froude's. Church Q. 40: 40. — (C. A. L. Richards) Dial (Ch.) 18: 73. — Ed. R. 181: 173. — (J. Gibb) Crit. R. 5: 71. — (K. Pearson) Acad. 46: 343. — Chr. Lit. 12: 35. — Sat. R. 78: 384. — Ath. '94, 2: 447. — Spec. 73: 524.
— Relation to the Reformation. (J. W. Santee) Ref. Q. 43: 81.
Erechtheum, North Doorway of. (R. W. Schultz; E. A. Gardner) J. Hel. Stud. 12: 1. — (S. H. Barnsley) J. Hel. Stud. 12: 381.
Eretria, Excavations by American School at, in 1891. (C. Waldstein; R. B. Richardson; A. Fossum; C. L. Brownson) Am. J. Archæol. 7: 233. — (J. Pickard) Am. J. Archæol. 7: 371.
— Gymnasium at. (R. B. Richardson and others) Am. J. Archæol. 11: 152.
— Temple in. (R. B. Richardson) Am. J. Archæol. 10: 326.
— Theatre in. (E. Capps) Am. J. Archæol. 10: 338.
— — Excavation of. (T. W. Heermance) Am. J. Archæol. 11: 317.
Ericas as Market Plants. (J. N. Gerard) Garden & F. 9: 138.
Erichsen, Sir John E. Acad. 50: 220. — Ath. '96, 2: 423. — (E. A. Schäfer) Nature, 54: 548.
Ericsson, John. (J. J. O'Shea) Cath. World, 61: 832. — With portrait. Pop. Sci. Mo. 44: 112. — (W. C. Church) Cassier, 7: 3-215.
— Church's Life of. Ed. R. 177: 31. Same art. Liv. Age, 196: 572.
— Recollections of. (G. H. Robinson) Un. Serv. (Phila.) 13: 10.
Erie Canal. How we towed our Way. (L. J. Sanderson) Outing, 22: 272.
— Ocean Traffic by. (E. P. North) Forum, 13: 371.
Erie, Lake, Correlation of New York Moraines with Raised Beaches of. (F. Leverett) Am. J. Sci. 150: 1.
— Deformation of Lundy Beach and Birth of. (J. W. Spencer) Am. J. Sci. 147: 207.
— Perry's Victory on. (J. C. Ridpath) Chaut. 15: 135.
Erkel, Francis. Acad. 43: 551.
Ernst II., Duke of Saxe-Coburg. (K. Blind) Contemp. 64: 478.
Eros and Psyche, Some Ancient Representations of. (E. Lecky) M. of Art, 13: 386.
— A Flying, from School of Praxiteles. (P. Bienkowski) J. Hel. Stud. 15: 211.
Erosion of the Soil, Economic Aspects of. (N. S. Shaler) Nat. Geog. M. 7: 328.
Erosion Epochs, Two. (W. J. McGee) Science, n. s. 3: 796.
Errand by Night, An; a story. (B. W. Chandler) Belgra. 89: 399.
Errant Wooing, An. (Mrs. B. Harrison) Cent. 27: 262-894. 28: 133.
Error in the Fourth Dimension; a story. (R. Kipling) Cosmopol. 18: 212.
Errors, The Consolation of. (P. Carus) Open Court, 7: 3891.
Erskine, Lord, American Correspondence of. (S. Erskine) No. Am. 157: 96.
— Letters of. Univ. R. 8: 597.
Erter, Isaac. (J. Chotzner) Jew. Q. 3: 106.
Erwin, Joseph, a Merchant of Philadelphia, 1768-91. (J. Erwin) Pennsyl. M. 19: 397.
Eschatology and Ethics. (M. C. O'Byrne) Open Court, 1: 190.
— Christian. (R. J. Cooke) Meth. R. 52: 849.
— Conditions of Life after Death. (A. Besant) 19th Cent. 40: 816.
— Jews and. (A. W. Goodnow) Bapt. R. 14: 443.
— Pauline. (O. Cone) New World, 4: 288.
— When this World is not. (H. W. Warren) Meth. R. 56: 849.
Escheat, Law of. (F. W. Hardman) Law Q. 4: 318.
Escomb Church. (C. C. Hodges) Illus. Archæol. 1: 225.
Escurial, The. (T. Child) Harper, 86: 531.

Esdras, First Book of. (H. H. Howorth) Acad. **43**: 13—**44**: 73.
— Character and Importance of. (H. H. Howorth) Thinker, **8**: 408.
Eskimo Customs. J. Am. Folk-Lore, **3**: 65.
Eskimo Maiden's Romance. (S. L. Clemens) Cosmopol. **16**: 53.
Eskimo Tales and Songs. (H. Rink and F. Boas) J. Am. Folk-Lore, **2**: 123. **7**: 45.
Eskimo Traditions. (H. I. Smith) J. Am. Folk-Lore, **7**: 209.
Eskimos; Arctic Highlanders. (L. L. Dyche) Cosmopol. **21**: 228.
— A Day's Hunting among. (F. Nansen) Pop. Sci. Mo. **46**: 446.
— Life of. Around World, **1**: 98.
— — Nansen on. (F. Starr) Dial (Ch.) **16**: 179.
— Northernmost, In the Land of the. (E. Astrup) Fortn. **65**: 466. Same art. Ecl. M. **126**: 593. Same art. Liv. Age, **209**: 102.
— of Alaska. (S. Jackson) Chaut. **18**: 193, 303. — (F. Boas) J. Am. Folk-Lore, **7**: 205.
— of Greenland. Dub. R. **113**: 667.
— Three Years among. (J. W. Tyrell) Canad. M. **3**: 119, 223.
Esmond, Miss Georgie, with portrait. Theatre, **29**: 112.
Esmond, Henry V., with portrait. Theatre, **28**: 198.
— and Wife, with portraits. Theatre, **36**: 36.
— Divided Way. Sat. R. **80**: 728.
Espartero, Death of. (R. Cortissoz) Harper, **93**: 596.
Espinasse, F. Reminiscences. Spec. **72**: 103.
Espionage as a Profession. Spec. **70**: 221.
Espronceda, José de, a Son of Spain. (O. F. Dabney) Poet-Lore, **7**: 546.
Essay, The, considered from an Artistic Point of View. (E. H. L. Watson) Westm. **141**: 559. Same art. Ecl. M. **123**: 50.
Essays, Contemporary. Atlan. **73**: 262.
Essen, Industrial Community at. (W. F. Willoughby) Lend a H. **17**: 371.
Essex, Katherine, Dowager Countess. Time, **7**: 187.
Essex, Across a Corner in. All the Year, **73**: 220.
— Barrett's. Sat. R. **74**: 261.
— Bibliography of. Walford's Antiq. **1**: 72.
— Farm Folk of. (A. T. Pask) Eng. Illust. **13**: 551.
Essex County, Mass. (F. T. Robinson) New Eng. M. n. s. **11**: 100.
Estate Duty and the Road round it. (A. H. Hastie) 19th Cent. **36**: 896.
— in England, Munro's. Sat. R. **79**: 534.
Estates Tail, Alienation of. (H. W. Elphinstone) Law Q. **6**: 280.
Esther. (R. B. Hale) New Eng. M. n. s. **12**: 561, 688.
Esthonia, Hero of, Kirby on. (W. R. Morfill) Acad. **46**: 550.
Estienne, Henry; an Old French Printer. (H. C. Macdowall) Macmil. **67**: 33.
Estrées, Gabrielle d'. Temp. Bar, **108**: 114. Same art. Ecl. M. **126**: 839.
Etching. (J. D. Smillie) Q. Illust. **2**: 265. — Chamb. J. **68**: 774.
— and Mezzotint by Herkomer. (P. G. Hamerton) Portfo. **23**: 97. — Sat. R. **73**: 222. — M. of Art, **15**: 204.
— The Art of Dry-point. (M. Menpes) M. of Art, **13**: 78.
— Bibliography of. Bookworm, **7**: 181.
— British. (F. Wedmore) M. of Art, **16**: 181-255.
— French Revival of. (F. Wedmore) M. of Art, **14**: 249.
— Seymour Haden on. M. of Art, **2**: 188-262.
— in England. M. of Art, **1**: 146, 217.
Etchings, The Printing of. (M. Menpes) M. of Art, **12**: 328.
Etelka Talmeyr, a Tale of Three Cities. (B. Matthews) Harper, **86**: 857.
Eternal Being, Ethics of. (T. Davidson) Int. J. Ethics, **3**: 336.
Eternal Past, The; a story. All the Year, **73**: 90-117.
Eternal Punishment; Aionian Punishment not Eternal. (W. E. Manley) Arena, **8**: 577.
— The Case against. Westm. **144**: 160.
Eternal Verities. (C. Anthony) Meth. R. **53**: 97.
Ethandune, Battle of. (W. Money) Antiq. n. s. **27**: 146.
Etheldreda, St., Retreat of. (J. A. Floyd) Cath. World, **62**: 441.
Etheostoma Caprodes, Color Variation of. (W. J. Monckhouse) Am. Natural. **28**: 641.
Ether, The, and its Functions. (G. F. Fitzgerald) New Sci. R. **1**: 414.
— as an Anæsthetic, Discovery by Dr. Jackson. Nat'l M. (Bost.) **5**: 46.
— Discovery of. (W. R. Hayden) Bost. **3**: 315.
— Dynamical Theory of. (J. Larmor) Nature, **49**: 260, 280.
— First Capital Operation under. (D. D. Slade) Scrib. M. **12**: 518.
— Interstellar. (O. Lodge) Fortn. **59**: 856. Same art. Liv. Age, **198**: 259.
— Luminiferous. (Sir G. G. Stokes) Nature, **48**: 306.
Ethical Culture, and Religion and Philosophy. (F. Adler) Int. J. Ethics, **4**: 335.
— Modern Skepticism and. (F. Adler) Forum, **16**: 379.
Ethical Education, Sociology in. (B. C. Mathews) Pop. Sci. Mo. **49**: 373.
Ethical Evolution. (E. D. Cope) Open Court, **3**: 1523.
Ethical Forces, Development of. (R. I. Munger) Lend a H. **15**: 33.
Ethical Meetings, Hymns and Music at. (A. W. Hutton) Eth. Rec. **2**: 98.
Ethical Movement, The Aim of the. (F. Adler) Open Court, **1**: 600.
— Defined. (S. Coit) Eth. Rec. **2**: 156. Same art. Time, **21**: 328.
— in America. (M. McCallum) Time, **19**: 171.
— Sheldon's Lectures. Meth. R. **56**: 1004.
Ethical Process, Relation to the Cosmic, Huxley on. (F. E. White) Int. J. Ethics, **5**: 478. **6**: 93.
Ethical Societies and the Church. (G. von Gizycki) Eth. Rec. **2**: 47.
— and the Labor Question. (W. Clarke) Eth. Rec. **3**: 91.
Ethical Society, Aim of. (F. Adler) Eth. Rec. **2**: 149.
— London, Work of. (H. Sidgwick) Int. J. Ethics, **4**: 1.
— What is an? (W. L. Sheldon) Eth. Rec. **2**: 165.
Ethical Training in the Public Schools. (C. DeGarmo) Ann. Am. Acad. Pol. Sci. **2**: 577.
See Moral.
Ethics, Abstract and Practical. (J. H. Muirhead) Am. J. Sociol. **2**: 341.
— Advancement of. (F. E. Abbot) Monist, **5**: 192.
— and Biology. (Sir J. C. Browne) Pop. Sci. Mo. **44**: 671. — (E. Montgomery) Int. J. Ethics, **5**: 44.
— and Cosmic Force, Huxley on. Spec. **70**: 698.
— and the Cosmic Order. (P. Carus) Monist, **4**: 403.
— and Culture. (F. Adler) Eth. Rec. **1**: 1.
— and Economics. (F. P. Powers) Lippinc. **56**: 531.
— — Relation between. (J. S. Mackenzie) Int. J. Ethics, **3**: 281.
— — Relations of. Soc. Econ. **6**: 297.
— and Eschatology. (M. C. O'Byrne) Open Court, **1**: 190.

Ethics and Formal Thought. (P. Carus) Open Court, 3: 1613.
— and Jurisprudence. (J. G. Hibben) Int. J. Ethics, 4: 133.
— and the Mosaic Law. (A. Maas) Am. Cath. Q. 17: 123.
— and Natural Science. (P. Carus) Open Court, 3: 1563.
— and Politics. (H. Macqueary) Am. M. Civics, 6: 86. — Quar. 175: 235.
— and Public Life. (W. M. Salter) Open Court, 2: 1071.
— and the Pulpit. (J. H. Clifford) Eth. Rec. 1: 48.
— and Psychology in the High School. (C. S. Buell) Educa. 14: 36, 92.
— and Religion, New Views of. (F. M. Holland) Open Court, 1: 519, 581.
— and the Struggle for Existence. (L. Stephen) Contemp. 64: 157. Same art. Ecl. M. 121: 379. Same art. Liv. Age, 198: 771. Same art. Pop. Sci. Mo. 44: 224.
— Animal, Spencer on. (H. Calderwood) Philos. R. 1: 241.
— Applied, and Philosophy, A School of. (F. Adler) Eth. Rec. 2: 1.
— — A Few Instances of. (A. Macdonald) Open Court, 5: 3008.
— as applied to Criminology. (A. Macdonald) Open Court, 5: 2861.
— as a Political Science. (A. T. Hadley) Yale R. 1: 301, 354.
— Basis of. (E. C. Hegeler and others) Open Court, 1: 18.
— Body and Mind, or the Data of Moral Physiology. (F. L. Oswald) Open Court, 2: 771-1476.
— Bonhöffer on. (W. Hammond) Philos. R. 3: 476.
— Bowne on. (J. Bascom) Dial (Ch.) 13: 308.
— Christian, Knight on. Spec. 72: 237.
— — Smyth on. (J. Bascom) Dial (Ch.) 13: 307. — (A. B. Bruce) Crit. R. 2: 341. — (D. S. Gregory) Presb. & Ref. R. 5: 350.
— — Strong's. Church Q. 43: 216.
— — Study of. (R. L. Ottley) Econ. R. 3: 229.
— Communal. (M. D. Conway) Open Court, 5: 2891.
— Criterion of, an Objective Reality. (P. Carus) Monist, 1: 552.
— D'Arcy's Short Study of. Sat. R. 82: 225.
— Darwinism in. (W. M. Salter) Open Court, 1: 77.
— Dewey on. (T. Davidson) Philos. R. 1: 95.
— Education in. (R. W. Conant) Open Court, 9: 4426.
— Eudæmonistic. (C. B. Brewster) And. R. 17: 293.
— Evolutionary. (T. C. Laws) Open Court, 6: 3369, 3377. — (R. Mathews) Pop. Sci. Mo. 44: 192.
— First Principles in. (W. M. Salter) Open Court, 6: 3191.
— from a Practical Standpoint. (Mrs. Bain) Mind, 21: 327.
— Gallwitz on the Problem of. (H. Jones) Crit. R. 2: 289.
— Hyslop's Elements of. (E. Albee) Philos. R. 4: 543.
— Idealist, Method of. (S. H. Mellone) Philos. R. 4: 47.
— Immoral. (A. Gilbertson) Westm. 144: 571.
— in Natural Law. (L. G. James) Pop. Sci. Mo. 46: 322.
— in Public Affairs. (M. M. Trumbull) Open Court, 1: 182.
— in our Public Schools. (P. Carus) Open Court, 5: 2816. — (W. E. Russell) Open Court, 5: 2926.
— International. (A. Pringle) Open Court, 3: 1892.
— Introspective Method in, Limitations of the. (F. C. Sharp) Philos. R. 5: 278.
Ethics, Italian, National Character and Classicism in. (L. Ferri) Int. J. Ethics, 5: 340.
— a Law of Nature. (P. Carus) Open Court, 4: 2440.
— Leading Principles in. (F. M. Holland) Open Court, 4: 2627.
— Metaphysical Method in. (J. Dewey) Psychol. R. 3: 181.
— Moral Science and Moral Life. (J. S. Mackenzie) Int. J. Ethics, 4: 160.
— Natural Law and Evolution. (J. Royce) Int. J. Ethics, 5: 489.
— The New Interest in. (W. Kawelin) Eth. Rec. 2: 227.
— of Literary Discussion. (P. Carus) Open Court, 2: 1230.
— of the Sexes, New. (S. Channing) Open Court, 5: 2798.
— of Struggle and Ethical Culture. (P. Carus) Open Court, 5: 3059.
— on a Scientific Basis. (J. T. Bixby) And. R. 19: 208.
— Physiological Conditions of. (M. I. Swift) Open Court, 5: 2736.
— Practical. (W. Knight) Int. J. Ethics, 4: 481.
— Practical Value of. (J. S. Mackenzie) Int. J. Ethics, 5: 98.
— Principles of, Seth on. (G. S. Patton) Presb. & Ref. R. 6: 578. — (J. G. Schurman) Philos. R. 4: 77.
— — Spencer's. (S. Alexander) Mind, 18: 102. — Ath. '93, 2: 309. — Church Q. 37: 84.
— The Problem of Right Living. (V. Paget) Contemp. 61: 653.
— Question of Authority in Early English. (N. Wilde) Philos. R. 4: 603.
— Revival of, and of Laughter. (W. E. Hodgson) National, 20: 41.
— School of, Plymouth, Mass. (R. G. Huling) School R. 2: 506.
— Science of, Georg von Gizycki and. (F. Jodl) Int. J. Ethics, 5: 500.
— Spencer's System. (Van Buren Denslow) Soc. Econ. 8: 96.
— Spinoza's. (E. Albee) Philos. R. 3: 350.
— Teaching, in the High School. (J. Dewey) Educa. R. 6: 313.
— Text-books of, New, in 1892. (J. H. Hyslop) Educa. R. 4: 372.
— Theoretical and Applied. (E. M. Bowden) Philos. R. 4: 616.
— Triple Standard in. (G. Batchelor) New World, 2: 267.
— Williams on. (W. H. Hudson) Dial (Ch.) 14: 249. — (E. Ritchie) Philos. R. 3: 221.
Ethiopia, Ancient Trade Route across. (J. T. Bent) Geog. J. 2: 140.
Ethiopian Cricket Match, An; a cricket story. (E. Phillpotts) Idler, 3: 512.
Ethnic Religions and Christianity. (T. M. Stuart) Meth. R. 53: 35.
Ethnography and the Sciences of Language. (G. W. Leitner) Time, 22: 579.
Ethnological Research, Aims of. (T. Achelis) Open Court, 4: 2323.
Ethnology and Music. (R. Wallaschek) Music, 9: 168.
— and Study of the Veda. (H. Oldenberg) Open Court, 10: 4889.
— Comparative. (T. Achelis) Open Court, 4: 2336.
— History and Development of. (T. Achelis) Open Court, 4: 2312.
— in Folk-lore, Gomme's. Sat. R. 73: 754.
— of Great Britain, Early. (H. Bradley) Acad. 41: 41.
— Ruling Races of Prehistoric Times. (D. F. Hannigan) Ecl. M. 126: 218.

Ethnology, Stratification and Displacement in. (C. C. Closson) Q. J. Econ. **11**: 92.
Etiquette, Absurdities of. (Mrs. Humphrey) Idler, **8**: 472.
— Animal. Liv. Age, **204**: 819.
— Marine. (A. O. Klaussmann) Chaut. **22**: 199.
— Snob's Guide. Spec. **70**: 417.
— Some Variations of. (W. G. Probert) Blackw. **155**: 634. Same art. Liv. Age, **201**: 604. Same art. Ecl. M. **123**: 212.
Etna, Mount. Cornh. **66**: 398. Same art. Ecl. M. **119**: 798.
— Ascent of. (A. F. Jaccaci) Scrib. M. **11**: 663.
— Eruption of, 1892. (G. Platano) Nature, **46**: 542.
— Up, in the Dog Days. All the Year, **73**: 55.
Eton Chapel. (E. M. Green) Sund. M. **25**: 750.
Eton College, Museum of. (W. L. Sclater) Nat. Sci. **4**: 201.
— Old Days at. (C. K. Paul) 19th Cent. **32**: 594.
— Old School-list of. (E. H. Knatchbull-Hugessen) Time, **1**: 527.
— Training of Boys at. (A. C. Benson) Forum, **13**: 464.
Eton Translations. (W. E. Gladstone) Contemp. **63**: 782.
Etoniana. (W. Durnford) National, **24**: 347.
Etruria, Ancient. (T. Wilson) Am. Antiq. **15**: 25.
— a Sleeping Beauty. (G. E. Channing) Cosmopol. **19**: 301.
Etruscan Book, Discovery of an. (A. H. Sayce) Fortn. **59**: 162. Same art. Ecl. M. **120**: 433. Same art. Liv. Age, **196**: 742. — (A. H. Sayce) Acad. **42**: 338.
Etruscan Discoveries at Vetulonia. Reliquary, **36**: 14.
Etruscan Gold-spinners, Divine Afflatus of the. (M. S. Lockwood) Arena, **16**: 813.
Etruscan Statues. Reliquary, **36**: 231.
Etshowe, Zululand. (H. R. Knight) Un. Serv. M. **8**: 582.
Etymological Diversions. (G. L. Apperson) Gent. M. n. s. **48**: 132.
Etymological Superstitions. Liv. Age, **210**: 701.
Etymology, Popular, in Greece and Rome. (J. R. S. Sterrett) Nation, **56**: 110.
Etz Chayim of Jacob b. Jehudah of London. (D. Kaufmann) Jew. Q. **5**: 353.
Eubœa, Summer Ride in. (N. W. Williams) Gent. M. n. s. **55**: 25. Same art. Liv. Age, **207**: 184.
Eucalyptus. Around World, **1**: 214.
— the Fever-tree. All the Year, **76**: 84.
Eucharis Amazonica, Cultivation of. (W. Scott) Garden & F. **7**: 86.
Eucharist of Earth; a poem. (C. W. Vernon) Canad. M. **7**: 59.
Eucharistic Congress at Jerusalem, 1893. Dub. R. **113**: 874.
Eudocia, Empress. (S. C. Upton) Overland, n. s. **21**: 402.
Eugene, Prince. (A. Laugel) Nation, **60**: 8.
— at Belgrade, 1716. (D. G. Adee) Un. Serv. (Phila.) **15**: 1.
Eugenia; a study from life. (S. Grand) Temp. Bar, **99**: 509.
Eugénie, Empress. (R. H. Titherington) Munsey, **7**: 675.
— and the Franco-Prussian War. (A. Forbes) 19th Cent. **32**: 285. Same art. Ecl. M. **119**: 457. Same art. Liv. Age, **195**: 37.
— — Reply. (J. L. A. Simmons) 19th Cent. **32**: 430.
Euphony. (M. Moszkowski) Music, **4**: 514.
Euphrates, Chesney's Survey. Eng. R. **14**: 13.
— Sources of. (W. F. Ainsworth) Geog. J. **6**: 173.
— Upper, Valley of. (V. W. Yorke) Geog. J. **8**: 317, 453.
Euripides, Alcestis, performed at Bradfield. (J. E. Sandys) Acad. **47**: 510.
Euripides, Andromache. (A. W. Verrall) Univ. R. **5**: 25.
— Iphigenia in Tauris, as performed at Cambridge, England. (H. F. Wilson) Acad. **46**: 477.
— the Rationalist, Verrall's. (C. Dodgson) Acad. **47**: 418. — (R. Y. Tyrrell) Sat. R. **80**: 40. — (B. L. Gildersleeve) Nation, **61**: 136. — (W. C. Lawton) Dial (Ch.) **20**: 16.
— Translations from, made while an Eton Schoolboy. (W. E. Gladstone) Contemp. **63**: 782.
Europe, An American at Home in. (W. H. Bishop) Atlan. **69**: 433. **70**: 314, 808.
— Armies of, in 1892. (T. A. Dodge) Forum, **13**: 561.
— Commercial Policy of. (W. Z. Ripley) Pol. Sci. Q. **7**: 633.
— Continent, Travelling on. (A. Webb) Nation, **55**: 428.
— Culture in, Asiatic Criticism of. (A. Vambery) New R. **9**: 428.
— Diplomatic, Debidour's History of. (J. W. Headlam) Eng. Hist. R. **7**: 599.
— Early Inhabitants of, Jubainville's. Sat. R. **78**: 132.
— Economic Revolution in. (E. P. Cheyney) Ann. Am. Acad. Pol. Sci. **2**: 772.
— Federation of. (C. D. Farquharson) Westm. **145**: 167.
— Finances of Continental. (M. G. Mulhall) No. Am. **158**: 751.
— from 1815 to 1871. (A. von Stern) 19th Cent. **37**: 341.
— "Going to." (E. L. Godkin) Nation, **58**: 307.
— Guide to, Moncrieff's. Around World, **1**: 132.
— Housekeeping in. (J. S. Fiske) Nation, **57**: 139.
— In the Days of the Grand Tour. All the Year, **75**: 585.
— in 1888, and England's Position. (C. W. Dilke) Univ. R. **1**: 5.
— in 1890–91. (S. B. Holabird) Un. Serv. (Phila.) **8**: 26–531. **9**: 230.
— in 1893: Armed Europe. (Gen. A. Alison) Blackw. **154**: 755.
— — European Outlook. (F. A. Maxse) National, **22**: 304.
— — An Oppressive Peace. Spec. **70**: 410.
— — The Situation Abroad and at Home. (F. Harrison) Fortn. **59**: 197.
— in 1894: Disquiet of the Continent. Spec. **72**: 39.
— — Outlook for War in. (A. Forbes) No. Am. **158**: 283.
— Northern, Plea for the Study of the History of. (A. C. Coolidge) Am. Hist. R. **2**: 34.
— Outskirts of. (J. D. Rees) National, **23**: 766. Same art. Liv. Age, **202**: 747.
— Peace of. (M. de Blowitz) McClure, **3**: 62.
— — in 1892, Kalnoky on. Spec. **69**: 486.
— Peace or War in. (M. de Blowitz) McClure, **1**: 63.
— Politics in. New Drift in Foreign Affairs. (F. Greenwood) Contemp. **66**: 327.
— — in 1892; Mediterranean Politics. Ed. R. **176**: 388.
— — — Bismarck's Alternative Plan. Spec. **69**: 637.
— — in 1896: the Quadruple Alliance. (E. J. Dillon) Contemp. **69**: 457.
— — Peace and the Quadruple Alliance. Contemp. **66**: 761.
— Russian Ascendency in. Fortn. **66**: 461.
— Situation in, 1896. (F. H. Geffsken) Forum, **21**: 100.
— Some Reminiscences of Eastern. (H. W. Preston) Atlan. **76**: 795.
— Summer Outings in. (J. Rochard) Chaut. **21**: 709.
— Touring in, on next to nothing. (J. P. Worden) Outing, **24**: 61–317.
— Travel in, Early Days of. Liv. Age, **209**: 757.
— — From the German Ocean to the Black Sea. (T. Stevens) Outing, **20**: 3–464.

Europe, Travel to, Our Annual. (F. Matthews) Chaut. 23: 569.
— The United States of. (E. E. Hale) Lend a H. 17: 17.
— Vegetation of, Influence of Discovery of America upon. Around World, 1: 26.
— War Expenses of. (H. Geffcken) 19th Cent. 36: 230.
— — must not increase. Contemp. 65: 761.
— Western, Strategic and Historic Geography of. (T. M. Maguire) Un. Serv. M. 7: 759.
European Literature, 1893–94. Critic, 25: 56.
Eusebius, Historical Works of. Church Q. 34: 95.
Euthanasia. (C. M. O'Leary) Cath. World, 62: 579.
Eutropius, Breviarium of. (J. W. Redway) Educa. R. 12: 508.
Evangel in Cyene. (H. Garland) Harper, 91: 375.
Evangelical Association of North America, Dissensions in. Meth. R. 53: 943.
Evangelical Movement in America. (C. F. Dole) New Eng. M. 12: 533.
Evangelicalism, Strength and Weakness of. (A. H. Craufurd) Thinker, 8: 201.
Evangeline, True Story of. (T. B. Stephenson) Sund. M. 22: 771, 834.
Evangelism, Hypo-. (J. P. Lilley) Presb. & Ref. R. 4: 222.
Evangelists, Four, Symbols of. (F. F. Irving) Theo. Mo. 3: 400.
Evangelists, Famous, of the U. S. (S. P. Cadman) Chaut. 20: 441.
— Need for. (W. F. Mallalieu) Meth. R. 55: 849.
— Place of, in Church Work. (A. R. Kremer) Ref. Q. 42: 178.
Evans, Amos A., Surgeon U. S. N. (A. W. Evans) Pennsyl. M. 19: 468.
— Journal kept by, on U. S. Frigate "Constitution," 1812. (A. W. Evans) Pennsyl. M. 19: 152.
Evans, Bernard. (A. J. Story) M. of Art, 15: 342.
Evans, George Essex. (O. Smeaton) Westm. 144: 501.
Evans, Henry H. (W. H. Maguire) Nat'l M. (N. Y. '91) 15: 97.
Evans, Principal Heber, at Home. (D. Paton) Sund. M. 25: 669.
Evaporation. (C. Abbe) Nature, 54: 283.
Evaporators, Marine. (D. B. Morison) Cassier, 11: 56.
Evarts, William M. (A. O. Hall) Green Bag, 8: 93.
Evelina's Garden; a story. (M. E. Wilkins) Harper, 93: 76.
Evelyn, John, Diary of. Quar. 183: 1.
Evelyn Moore's Poet. (G. Allen) Longm. 25: 487. Same art. Chaut. 20: 305, 434.
Even-light; a poem. (R. Rodd) M. of Art, 10: 115.
Evening; a poem. (C. E. Meetkerke) Argosy, 58: 47.
Evening; a story. (Lady Lindsay) Eng. Illust. 9: 713.
Evening with Hodge. (M. Hartier) Eng. Illust. 15: 253.
Evening Dress; a farce. (W. D. Howells) Cosmopol. 13: 116.
Evening Home and Library Association, Philadelphia. (O. Wister) Harper, 91: 268.
Evening Paper, The; a story. (L. Worthington) Munsey, 11: 326.
Evening Party; a story. (G. King) Harper, 89: 192.
Evening Schools among Roman Catholics. (W. M. Hunnybun) Dub. R. 112: 137.
— Continuation. (Lord Battersea) New R. 9: 134. — (J. J. Davies) Westm. 144: 670.
— in England. Sat. R. 76: 269.
Event at Milford, The; a story. Argosy, 53: 69.
Everest, Mt.: Can it be ascended? (C. T. Dent) 19th Cent. 32: 604.
Evergreens, Beauty of, in Snow. Garden & F. 5: 37.
— Broad-leaved. Garden & F. 5: 15.
— — Hardy. (W. F. Bassett) Garden & F. 5: 82.
Evergreens, Hardiness of. (J. Meshan) Garden & F. 5: 57.
— Hardy Hollies and Barberries. (J. G. Jack) Garden & F. 6: 196.
Everlastin' Buzzards' Sit, The. (C. McIlvaine) Lippinc. 54: 279.
Every Day Affair; a story. (O. Finch) Harper, 90: 590.
Every Day Egotist, An; a story. (E. Miller) Eng. Illust. 12: no. 5, 89.
Every Day Martyr, An. (A. M. Hays) Overland, n. s. 26: 332.
Everybody's Chance. (J. Habberton) Liv. Age, 208: 11.
Evesham Abbey. (D. M. Spence) Eng. Illust. 9: 595.
Evicted Tenants, The. (T. W. Russell) New R. 11: 113.
Evidence at the Common Law, Thayer on. Nation, 63: 126.
— Extrinsic, in Respect to Written Instruments. (C. A. Graves) Am. Law R. 28: 321.
— Hearsay, On the Rejection of. (L. Edmunds) Law Q. 5: 265.
— in Criminal Cases, Bill regulating. (G. Pitt-Lewis) 19th Cent. 39: 812.
— — — Argument against. (H. Stephen) 19th Cent. 39: 566.
— Law of, Antiquities of. (H. C. Black) Am. Law R. 26: 829.
— — on Examination as to Character. (E. Bowen-Rowlands) Law Q. 11: 20.
— Practical Tests in. (I. Browne) Green Bag, 4: 510, 555. 5: 13–268.
— Written, Superiority of. (J. W. Salmond) Law Q. 6: 75.
Evil, God not Responsible for. (J. T. Gladhill) Luth. Q. 24: 396.
— in the Natural World, Mystery of. (S. Z. Beam) Ref. Q. 49: 378.
— Popularization of. (R. Ogden) Nation, 58: 6.
Evil Eye, Superstition of the. (E. Clodd) Acad. 47: 459. — Quar. 182: 204.
Evil Eye; a story. All the Year, 74: 156, 180.
Evolution. (R. Whittingham) Cosmopol. 15: 473. — (J. Gerard) Month, 74: 14.
— Agnostic, Gaps in. (F. H. Hill) National, 26: 97. Same art. Ecl. M. 125: 766.
— and Christian Ethics. (T. G. Apple) Ref. Q. 40: 383.
— and Christianity. (H. Drummond) Chr. Lit. 11: 31 a, 54 a. — (St. G. Mivart) Cosmopol. 13: 146–613.
— and Classification. (C. E. Bessey) Nature, 48: 534.
— and Consciousness. (G. T. Ladd and J. M. Baldwin) Psychol. R. 3: 296. — (J. M. Baldwin) Science, n. s. 2: 219.
— and Cosmic Telepathy. (J. Cook) Our Day, 15: 171.
— and Darwinism. (G. M. Searle) Cath. World, 56: 223.
— and Development. (S. W. Dyde) Philos. R. 4: 1.
— and Doctrine of the Incarnation. (T. D. Bernard) Thinker, 9: 334.
— and Dogma, Jahm's. (F. David) Dub. R. 119: 245.
— and Education. (J. E. Le Conte) Educa. R. 10: 121.
— and Ethics. (L. M. B. Klein) Dub. R. 113: 589. — (R. Mathews) Pop. Sci. Mo. 44: 192. — (T. H. Huxley) Pop. Sci. Mo. 44: 18, 178. — (R. L. Gerhart) Ref. Q. 41: 318.
— — Huxley on. And. R. 19: 462. — (P. C. Mitchell) Nat. Sci. 3: 62. — National, 21: 713. — Sat. R. 75: 561.
— and Evangelical System of Doctrine. (F. H. Foster) Bib. Sac. 50: 408.
— and Evolution. (B. P. Bowne) Meth. R. 53: 681.
— and Human Progress. (J. Le Conte) Open Court, 5: 2779.
— and Idealism. (E. D. Cope) Open Court, 1: 655.
— and Immortality. (P. Carus) Open Court, 1: 726.

Evolution and the Incarnation. (J. K. Smyth) N. Church R. 3: 161.
— and Man's Place in Nature. Church Q. 40: 150.
— and Mind. Nat. Sci. 9: 297.
— and Palæobotany. (A. C. Seward) Sci. Prog. n. s. 1: 108.
— and Political Economy, Relation of. (C. S. Ashley) Pop. Sci. Mo. 44: 458.
— and Teleology. (F. H. P. Coste) New Sci. R. 2: 64.
— Ascent of Life. (S. Jarvis) Arena, 9: 1.
— Atavism and. (C. Lombroso) Contemp. 68: 42.
— Babies and Monkeys. (S. S. Buckman) 19th Cent. 36: 727. Same art. Pop. Sci. Mo. 46: 371.
— Bailey's Survival of the Unlike. Garden & F. 9: 519.
— Bonnet's Theory of. (C. O. Whitman) Monist, 5: 412.
— Bye-products in. Sat. R. 79: 155.
— Calderwood on. (P. Shorey) Dial (Ch.) 15: 66.
— Continuity of. (P. Carus) Monist, 2: 70.
— Cope's Theology of. (E. Montgomery) Open Court, 1: 160–300.
— Discontinuity in. (F. Galton) Mind, 19: 362.
— Divine. (H. Macmillan) Chr. Lit. 15: 130.
— Doctrine of, Constructive Power of. (E. P. Powell) New World, 4: 506.
— Drummond and Kidd on. (H. C. Minton) Presb. & Ref. R. 6: 136.
— Drummond on. (W. Gladden) McClure, 3: 235.—(E. Clodd) Acad. 46: 13.
See Man, Ascent of.
— Effects of, on Religious Ideas. (R. Crosbie) Ecl. M. 118: 177.
— Energy of. (E. D. Cope) Am. Natural. 28: 205.
— Ethics, and Natural Law. (J. Royce) Int. J. Ethics, 5: 489.
— Ethics of. (P. Carus) Open Court, 5: 3004.
— Experimental, amongst Plants. (L. H. Bailey) Am. Natural. 29: 318.
— — De Varigny on. (G. Baur) Dial (Ch.) 14: 278.
— Factors of. (J. Le Conte) Monist, 1: 321.
— Fast and Loose Theories of. (J. Cook) Our Day, 10: 500.
— the Fifth Gospel. (W. Hutchinson) Monist, 6: 99.
— For the Beauty of an Ideal. (A. Fogazzaro) Contemp. 67: 671. Same art. Ecl. M. 125: 1.
— Foundations of. (J. Gerard) Month, 74: 203.
— God's Will and Human Happiness. (St.G. Mivart) Cosmopol. 16: 344, 470, 609. 17: 102.
— Goethe on. (E. Haeckel) Open Court, 4: 2111.
— Hereditary Mechanism and the Search for the Unknown Factors of. (H. F. Osborn) Am. Natural. 29: 418.
— Heredity *vs.* (T. Gilman) Monist, 4: 80.
— How it evolves. (S. Jarvis) Arena, 14: 67.
— Human, and the Fall. (H. Wood) Arena, 12: 358.
— — an Artificial Process. (H. G. Wells) Fortn. 66: 590.—Reply. (G. A. Reid) Fortn. 66: 755.—(E. R. Lankester) Fortn. 66: 914.
— — Religion in. (F. Galton) National, 23: 755.
— — Work of, Ideas in. (G. Le Bon) Pop. Sci. Mo. 47: 451.
— Idea of. (J. Ming) Am. Cath. Q. 18: 762.
— Immorality of Evolutionary Ethics. (W. E. Hodgson) National, 22: 46.
— in Germany, 1892. (C. Sterne) Monist, 3: 97.
— in Professor Huxley. (St.G. Mivart) Pop. Sci. Mo. 44: 319.
— Life from the Lost Atlantis. (St.G. Mivart) Fortn. 65: 801.
— Limits on. (G. Howison) New World, 5: 237.
— Lord Salisbury on. (H. Spencer) Pop. Sci. Mo. 48: 564.
— Mechanics of. (J. Gerard) Month, 74: 491.
Evolution, Method of Organic. (A. R. Wallace) Fortn. 63: 211, 435.
— Missing Link in the Hypothesis. (D. Mills) Canad. M. 3: 207.
— Morality in Nature and. (J. T. Bixby) New World, 4: 444.
— "Nature's Method in." (A. R. Wallace) Nature, 50: 541.
— New Factor in. (J. M. Baldwin) Am. Natural. 30: 441, 536, 697.
— — J. M. Baldwin on. (H. Nichols) Am. Natural. 30: 697.
— of Evolution. (St.G. Mivart) Am. Cath. Q. 20: 673.
— of Man, Contemporary. (H. F. Osborn) Am. Natural. 26: 455.
— — Present, G. A. Reid on. (E. R. Lankester) Fortn. 66: 408.
— of the World, Unity in. (J. S. Stahr) Ref. Q. 41: 441.
— or Epigenesis? (H. C. Hiller) Nature, 52: 317.
— Organic, and Mental Elaboration. (H. M. Foston) Mind, 68: 472.
— Origin of Man and the Religious Sentiment. (A. Fogazzaro) Contemp. 68: 65. Same art. Ecl. M. 125: 289.
— H. B. Orr on. Nature, 50: 445.
— Osborne's From the Greeks to Darwin. (F. C. S. Schiller) Philos. R. 4: 85.
— Pantheistic, Latest Phases of. (J. J. Ming) Am. Cath. Q. 19: 492, 736.
— Popular Mistakes respecting. (B. P. Bowne) Meth. R. 53: 849.
— Present Problems of Organic. (E. D. Cope) Monist, 5: 563. Same art. Science, n. s. 2: 124.
— Present-day Conception of. (B. B. Warfield) Chr. Lit. 13: 277.
— Primer of, Clodd's. Sat. R. 79: 605.
— Recent Arguments for. (T. Hughes) Am. Cath. Q. 18: 19.
— A Restatement. (C. L. Morgan) N. World, 2: 223.
— Right of. (M. D. Conway) Monist, 1: 506.
— Salisbury on. (H. Spencer) 19th Cent. 38: 741.
— Social. (D. G. Ritchie) Int. J. Ethics, 6: 165.
— Spiritual. (W. T. Harris) Educa. 16: 413.
— Statistical Investigation of. Nature, 51: 510.
— Theory of. (W. Seton) Cath. World, 58: 787.
— — and Social Progress. (J. Le Conte) Monist, 5: 481.
— — Twenty-five Years of, 1869–94. (T. H. Huxley) Nature, 51: 1.
— Thoughts on. (J. Eddy) Open Court, 1: 463.
— Three Great Epochs of. (H. W. Conn) Meth. R. 56: 885.
— Variation and. (W. A. Gain) Science, 22: 7.
— Variation of Species, Bateson on. Sat. R. 78: 190.
— Weismann on. (D. Jordan) Dial (Ch.) 13: 242.
— What it teaches us. (L. Irwell) Westm. 142: 248. Same art. Ecl. M. 123: 607.
— What should be the Attitude of the Church towards, as a Working Theory of the Universe. (G. J. Burton) Chr. Lit. 13: 125.
— Wilson on. (D. S. Jordan) Dial (Ch.) 20: 13.
See Neo-Lamarckism; Neo-Darwinism.
Evolution of a Bishop. (O. F. Adams) New Eng. M. n. s. 11: 532.
Evolutionists, Extreme, Common-sense Criticism of. (C. J. Armistead) Am. Cath. Q. 18: 495.
Ewing, Juliana H. (E. A. Gowing) Belgra. 79: 244.
Ewing, Thomas, with portrait. (J. H. Kennedy) Nat'l M. (N. Y. '91) 15: 42.
Ex Libris. *See* Bookplates.
Exaggeration. All the Year, 74: 319.
— as an Æsthetic Factor. (F. Regnault) Pop. Sci. Mo. 49: 821.

Exaggeration, Tall Talk. All the Year, **70**: 465.
Examination Craze. (A. Sonnenschein) Time, **20**: 41.
Examination Curve. (C. L. Morgan) Nature, **51**: 617.
Examinations, Civil Service, in England. Sat. R. **80**: 572, 655, 688.
— College, and Student Honor. (W. L. Stevens) Forum, **18**: 732.
— Dangers of. (A. W. Drayson) New Sci. R. **1**: 267. — (W. B. Jacobs) School R. **4**: 675.
— Educational Value of. (J. Seth) Educa. R. **12**: 133.
— "for Revenue Only." Acad. **7**: 293.
— for Teachers' Certificates in England, Specimens of Papers. Macmil. **68**: 312.
— in Elementary and Secondary Schools. (A. Sonnenschein) Time, **19**: 455.
— Public School, Abolition of. Pub. Opin. **15**: 461.
— — Should they be abolished? (G. M. Steele) Educa. **14**: 542.
— True Lever of Education. (H. G. Wells) Educa. R. **4**: 380.
Examiner's Dream, An. Macmil. **74**: 367.
Examining, Science of. (P. T. Austen) Science, n. s. **2**: 223.
Exchange, Foreign. (E. Matheson) J. Soc. Arts, **40**: 495.
— Need of Better. (T. G. Shearman) Forum, **16**: 459.
Exchange is Robbery; a story. (R. Marsh) Idler, **4**: 526, 598.
Exchange-value, Monopoly and Rent, Geometrical Method of Treating. (H. Cunynghame) Econ. J. **2**: 35.
Exchanges, Foreign, and Movement of Gold, 1894–95. (W. C. Ford) Yale R. **4**: 128.
Exchequer, English, Antiquities of, Hall on. Spec. **68**: 60.
Excise Question, What shall we do with the? (W. Miller) No. Am. **162**: 287.
Excursions, Cheap. Spec. **69**: 593.
— Half-holiday, from Boston. (C. S. Sargent) Garden & F. **6**: 187.
Execution by Electricity. (J. Tunis) Lend a H. **10**: 389.
— in India, An. Macmil. **74**: 286.
Executor, Indemnity of, continuing Testator's Business. (A. T. Murray) Law Q. **9**: 331.
Exercise as a Remedy. (H. L. Taylor) Pop. Sci. Mo. **48**: 626.
Exeter, Bishops of, in the 13th and 14th Centuries. (A. Hamilton) Dub. R. **117**: 16.
— Case of Deanery of, 1839–40. (E. A. Freeman) Law Q. **3**: 280.
— Countess of, the Cottage Countess. Cornh. **72**: 375.
— St. Mary's Church, Visitation in 1301. (Monsignor Brownlow) Dub. R. **114**: 76.
Exeter Hall. (G. T. Brown) Sund. M. **25**: 311.
Exeter, N. H., and its Academy. (S. A. Ranlett) New Eng. M. n. s. **10**: 69.
Exhibitions, International, Advantages of. (T. Stanton) Lippinc. **58**: 405.
Exiles. Macmil. **72**: 274.
Exington Bank, The; a story. Temp. Bar, **106**: 35.
Exmoor. (J. Fortescue) M. of Art, **11**: 28.
Exmoor Forest, Rawle on. Sat. R. **77**: 129.
Exmouth, Edward Pellew, Admiral Lord. (A. T. Mahan) Atlan. **72**: 27.
Exoascaceæ. (G. F. Atkinson) Garden & F. **7**: 463.
Exodus, Place of, in the History of Egypt. (A. L. Lewis) Scrib. M. **15**: 109.
Expenditure, Middle-class, Some Statistics of. (E. Grubb) Econ. R. **6**: 359.
Experience. (P. Carus) Open Court, **7**: 3602.
Experiences; a poem. (I. F. Mayo) Argosy, **62**: 25.
Experiment, An; a story. (B. A. Clarke) Idler, **9**: 540.
Experiment Station, Amherst, Mass. (A. W. Bailey) New Eng. M. n. s. **9**: 65.
Experiment Stations, Among the. (C. H. Shinn) Overland, n. s. **24**: 164.
— Work of. (E. W. Hilgard) Garden & F. **6**: 462. — (C. S. Sargent) Garden & F. **6**: 381, 521.
Experts, Scientific, in Forensic Procedure. (C. F. Himes) J. Frankl. Inst. **135**: 407.
Expiation; a Story of the Chilian Revolt. (F. W. Evans) Chamb. J. **69**: 668.
Explanations; a story. (A. Hope) Idler, **7**: 333.
Exploration, Incentives to. Spec. **68**: 740.
— of the World. (J. L. Lobley) Knowl. **18**: 187.
— What is left to explore? (C. C. Adams) Chaut. **18**: 44. — (A. Heilprin) Forum, **15**: 680.
Explorations and Explorations. Spec. **69**: 443
— Early, Beazley on. Sat. R. **79**: 604.
Explosives. All the Year, **72**: 196. Same art. Liv. Age, **197**: 440. — All the Year, **76**: 298.
— High. (H. Maxim) J. Soc. Arts, **44**: 555.
— in War, Projectiles and. Ed. R. **180**: 447.
— Modern. (W. Lascelles-Scott) 19th Cent. **35**: 987.
— Modern Development of. (V. B. Lewes) J. Soc. Arts, **43**: 109–147.
Export Bounties. Are they Economic? Soc. Econ. **9**: 87.
— not the Remedy. Gunton's M. **10**: 179.
Export Trade, American, Growth of. (T. A. Eddy and C. Schurz) Engin. M. **9**: 413.
Exports. Foreign Commerce of the U. S., 1894-95. Gunton's M. **10**: 215.
— How to increase. (D. MacG. Means) Nation, **57**: 184.
Expression, Dramatic. (A. W. Rollins) Lippinc. **53**: 242.
— Facial, Acquired. (L. Robinson) Blackw. **155**: 536. Same art. Pop. Sci. Mo. **45**: 380.
— — Fate in the Face. (L. Robinson) Blackw. **159**: 680. Same art. Ecl. M. **127**: 16.
— — Pupil of the Eye as a Factor in. (S. Wilks) M. of Art, **15**: 265.
— — Trades and Faces. (L. Robinson) Pop. Sci. Mo. **47**: 627.
— Musical, Rules for. (R. Welton) Music, **3**: 227–594. **4**: 262. **8**: 383.
Extra-illustrating, Art of. (O. M. E. Rowe) Bookworm, **7**: 281.
— in New York. Bookworm, **6**: 177.
Extracts from MS. of Late Dr. Bernagius. (L. Biart) Time, **3**: 562–665. **4**: 203, 548. **5**: 574.
Extradition. Chamb. J. **70**: 129. Same art. Liv. Age, **197**: 508.
— and the Dynamite Conspirators. National, **28**: 293.
— in American Colonies. (J. D. Lindsay) Nat'l M. (N. Y. '91) **16**: 409–652.
— of Political Offenders. (E. L. DeHart) Law Q. **2**: 177.
— Right to Try an Extradited Fugitive for a Different Offense. (A. Stewart) Am. Law R. **28**: 568.
Extradition Treaty with Russia. (J. B. Moore) Forum, **15**: 629. — (E. L. Godkin) Nation, **56**: 450. — (I. A. Hourwich) Yale R. **3**: 68.
Extraordinary Events. Spec. **68**: 490.
Extraordinary Experience; a story. (T. H. Rand) Canad. M. **2**: 249.
Extra-territoriality of Orientals in England. Green Bag, **7**: 388.
Extravagance, Our National. (F. C. Baylor) Lippinc. **56**: 123.
Extreme Edge of Hazard, The; a story. (C. Ross) McClure, **7**: 379.
Eye, The, as an Optical Instrument. (A. Flint) Pop. Sci. Mo. **45**: 199.

Eye, Human, as affected by Civilization. (D. B. S. Roosa) Cosmopol. 13: 759.
— The Hysterical. (A. Binet) Open Court, 3: 1763.
— Sensitiveness of, to Light and Color. (W. de W. Abney) Nature, 47: 538.
Eye Hospital, Visit to. All the Year, 72: 251.
Eyes and Head, Relations between the Movements of the. (R. Boyle) Nature, 52: 184.
— The Bad-eye Factory. (E. W. Scripture) Outl. 53: 392.
— Bright Eyes and Dark Eyes. (Max Müller) New R. 7: 316.
— of the Dead, Images in. (E. Wallace) No. Am. 160: 248.
— Why has Man Two? (E. Mach) Open Court, 8: 4175.
Eyesight, Art and. (L. Howe) Pop. Sci. Mo. 47: 458.
— Defective, of School Children. Sat. R. 82: 57.
— in Middle Life and Old Age. (L. W. Fox) J. Frankl. Inst. 133: 454.
— of Railway Employees. (W. M. Beaumont) National, 19: 847.
Eylau Cemetery; a poem. (Victor Hugo, trans. by C. E. Meetkerke) Gent. M. n. s. 48: 609. Same art. Ecl. M. 119: 202.
Eymard, Père Julien, with portrait. (E. Lummis) Cath. World, 63: 184.
Eyoub, Turkey. (R. Davey) Art J. 47: 146. Same art. Ecl. M. 125: 604. Same art. McClure, 5: 361, 455.
Ezekiel. (C. H. Cornill) Open Court, 9: 4547.
— the Prophet of Individual Responsibility. (W. M. Sinclair) Good Words, 37: 711.
Ezra. (C. H. Cornill) Open Court, 9: 4599.
— Successors of. (G. S. Goodspeed) Bib. World, 2: 97.
Ezra Hardman, M. A. (S. Shelton) Scrib. M. 13: 383.

Fabert, Abraham, Life of, Hooper's. Ath. '92, 2: 447. — (W. O'C. Morris) Acad. 42: 303. — Spec. 69: 166.
Fabian Economics. (W. H. Mallock) Fortn. 61: 159, 393. Same art. Ecl. M. 122: 577. Same art. Liv. Age. 201: 131–214.
Fabian Society. (W. Clarke) New Eng. M. n. s. 10: 89.
Fabj-Altini, Francesco. M. of Art, 4: 510.
Fables, French, of the Middle Ages. (F. Brunetière) Chaut. 18: 333.
Face, Human, Evolution of. (A. H. Thompson) Am. Antiq. 14: 277.
— Fate in the. (L. Robinson) Blackw. 159: 680. Same art. Ecl. M. 127: 16.
Face of Death, The. (L. Dougall) Atlan. 76: 640.
Face of Mnemosyne, The. (E. B. Evans) Southern M. 4: 307.
Face on the Wall, The; a story. (M. Deland) Harper, 86: 510.
Face or Phantom; a story. (A. H. Morrison) Canad. M. 4: 47.
Faces in the Fire; a story. (J. Errol) Belgra. 79: 179.
Facial Expression; Trades and Faces. (L. Robinson) Blackw. 157: 689.
See Expression.
Fact and Fiction. Liv. Age, 205: 572.
Factions of Kitwyk. (A. E. King) Cent. 25: 27.
Factories, Accidents in. (K. P. Woods) Am. Statis. Assoc. 4: 303.
— and Workshops, New English Law for. (B. Shaw) Sat. R. 81: 192.
— Do they increase Immorality? (Carroll D. Wright) Forum, 13: 344.
Factory Act, The New English. Econ. J. 5: 471.
— — as it affects Women. (E. March-Phillips) Fortn. 61: 738.
Factory Acts, What brought. (W. F. Crafts) Soc. Econ. 9: 43.
Factory Inspection. (R. Watchorn) Am. J. Pol. 1: 546.
Factory Law, Illinois. (J. H. Wigmore) Nation, 60: 299.
Factory Legislation in Italy. (R. B. d'Ajano) J. Pol. Econ. 4: 309.
Factory Life, Old, in India. (J. T. Wheeler) Asia. R. 10: 412.
Factory System, Modern, Taylor on. (D. MacG. Means) Nation, 54: 92.
Facts and Mental Symbols. (E. Mach) Monist, 2: 198.
Faed, Thomas. M. of Art, 1: 92. — (M. H. Dixon) M. of Art, 16: 268.
Fags and Fagging. (H. G. Hutchinson) Cornh. 74: 237.
Failure, Individual, Social Value of. (G. D. Herron) Arena, 15: 633.
Failure? (M. Hawker) Good Words, 35: 349.
Fair Exchange. (A. M. Ewell) Atlan. 74: 194.
Fair Exchange; a story. (G. Allen) Eng. Illust. 15: 399.
Fair Trade and Authority. (M. S. Constable) National, 19: 293.
— Protection, and Free Trade. (Earl Grey) 19th Cent. 31: 38.
Fairbairn, A. M. (W. F. Adeney) Chr. Lit. 11: 87 a.
Fairchild, James H. Elements of Theology. (J. M. Williams) Bib. Sac. 51: 70.
Fairfax, H., Admiral, Court-martial of. Sat. R. 75: 32.
Fairfax, Thomas. Greenway Court, Va. (W. Y. Page) M. Am. Hist. 30: 137.
Fairfield, William Wells. (H. L. Conard) Nat'l M. (N. Y. '91) 15: 660.
Fairford, Gloucestershire, Stained Glass Window in the Church at. (E. S. Roscoe) M. of Art, 4: 437.
Fairies. All the Year, 74: 270.
— of the Balkan Peninsula. Chamb. J. 71: 779.
— Neo-Latin. (H. C. Coote) Folk-Lore Rec. 2: 1.
Fairs, The Great, of Russia. Chamb. J. 72: 550.
— Statute, in East Anglia; are they doomed? National, 18: 708.
Fairy Beliefs from County Leitrim. (L. L. Duncan) Folk-Lore, 7: 161.
Fairy Folk-Lore of Ireland. (M. Tyner) Walford's Antiq. 5: 140.
Fairy Gold; a story. (M. S. Cutting) McClure, 6: 573.
Fairy Gold; a story. (Netta Syrett) Temp. Bar, 109: 218.
Fairy Lore in "Midsummer Night's Dream." (E. G. Skeat) Poet-Lore, 3: 177.
— Latest. Spec. 68: 57.
Fairy Tales. All the Year, 73: 198.
— English and Scotch. (A. Lang) Folk-Lore, 1: 289.
— from Hebrew MSS. of the 9th and 12th Centuries. (M. Gaster) Folk-Lore, 7: 217.
— Irish, Yeats'. Sat. R. 73: 551.
— Science of, Hartland's. (W. W. Newell) J. Am. Folk-Lore, 4: 276.
Fairyland, Interregnum in. (J. Davidson) Good Words, 35: Xmas no., 28.
— Lapse of Time in. (W. W. Newell) J. Am. Folk-Lore, 9: 12.
Faith, Act of. (J. R. Downer) Bapt. R. 14: 349.
— and Authority. (H. S. Holland) Sund. M. 21: 89.
— and Creeds. (P. Carus) Open Court, 3: 1575.
— and Culture. Spec. 75: 891.
— and Reason. (J. Orr) Thinker, 9: 438.
— and Regeneration. (H. Ziegler) Luth. Q. 23: 372.
— and Science. (P. Topinard) Monist, 6: 28, 534.
— and Theology. (F. H. R. Frank) Luth. Q. 22: 52.
— and Works. (E. V. Gerhart) Ref. Q. 40: 460.
— Foresight of. (J. Watson) Chr. Lit. 12: 275.
— Fruitful, Identical in all Ages. (J. Cook) Our Day, 9: 109.

Faith, Light of. (F. David) Dub. R. **117**: 87.
— Obscurity of. (R. F. Clarke) Am. Cath. Q. **18**: 481.
— of Jesus Christ, The. (P. F. Jernegan) Bib. World, **8**: 198.
— Old, What can we give in Place of. (W. M. Salter) Eth. Rec. **1**: 35.
— Phases of. (G. M. Hammell) Meth. R. **56**: 437.
— Philosophical. (A. C. Fraser) Philos. R. **5**: 561.
— Preëminence of. (F. N. Upham) Meth. R. **54**: 404.
— Preliminaries of. (J. McCabe) Westm. **146**: 71. Same art. Ecl. M. **127**: 577.
— Return to. (A. C. Armstrong, jr.) Meth. R. **56**: 66.
— Tendencies to the Subversion of. Eng. R. **10**: 399.
— Universal. (T. B. Wakeman) Open Court, **2**: 1391. **3**: 1583.
Faith and Faithfulness; a story. (S. B. Elliott) Harper, **93**: 791.
Faith-cure. (J. M. Charcot) New R. **8**: 18.
Faith-healing. (J. Fergusson) Canad. M. **6**: 183. — (C. F. Nichols) Science, **19**: 43.
— Sixty Years Ago. (R. E. Bartlett) Time, **14**: 336.
Faithful Failure, A. (G. I. Putnam) Cent. **27**: 939.
Faithful Failure, A. (E. O. White) Atlan. **75**: 613.
Faithful Fortnight, The; a story. (B. Pain) Eng. Illust. **11**: 1159.
Faizullah. Macmil. **66**: 350.
Falaiseau, Marquise de, Broc's Memoirs of. Spec. **71**: 305.
— Exile of. (S. I. de Zuylen de Nyevelt) National, **21**: 500. Same art. Liv. Age, **198**: 350.
Falconer, Lanoe, *pseud.* *See* Hawker, M. E.
Falconry. (R. B. Lodge) Good Words, **36**: 686.
— Bibliography of, Harting's. Ath. '92, **1**: 536.
— Hood and Leash. (G. Lascelles) Time, **1**: 555.
— in Art. (J. E. Harting) M. of Art, **19**: 140, 180.
Faléro, Luis. (A. Trumble) Mo. Illust. **3**: 138.
Falkner's Genius; a story. (G. E. Montgomery) Lippinc. **49**: 472.
Fall of Man. (W. R. Harper) Bib. World, **3**: 176.
— and Human Evolution. (H. Wood) Arena, **12**: 358.
— Effect upon Nature. (W. A. Holliday) Presb. & Ref. R. **7**: 611.
— a poem. Westm. **145**: 23.
— a Scientific Fact. (A. J. Baker) Meth. R. **54**: 861.
Fall of Rhodes, The; a story. (H. N. Crellin) Gent. M. n. s. **55**: 109.
Fall River, Impotence of Churches in. (W. B. Hale) Forum, **18**: 288.
Fallen Elm, The; a poem. (A. Austin) National, **19**: 441. Same art. Ecl. M. **119**: 157.
Falling Leaves; a poem. (Maude Lyons) Cosmopol. **19**: 48.
Falloux, Alfred de. (C. de Mazade) Chaut. **17**: 449.
False Alarm, A; a story. Argosy, **54**: 233.
False Coin or True? (F. Montrésor) Good Words, **37**: 1–361.
False Fire. (J. Buckland) Blackw. **155**: 806. Same art. Liv. Age, **202**: 436.
Falstaff and the New Italian Opera. (J. A. F. Maitland) 19th Cent. **33**: 803.
— Verdi's. Critic, **26**: 109.
Fame. Penalties of a Well-known Name. (L. de La Ramé) No. Am. **154**: 733.
Fame's Little Day; a story. (S. O. Jewett) Harper, **90**: 560.
Families and Dwellings. (C. D. Wright) Pop. Sci. Mo. **41**: 474.
— Continued Care of. (F. A. Smith) Char. R. **4**: 418.
Familistère at Laeken, Life in a. Cornh. **73**: 278. Same art. Liv. Age, **209**: 187.
Family, Historical Development of the. (T. Achelis) Open Court, **2**: 806.
Family, The, in the United States. (S. W. Dike) Contemp. **64**: 724.
— Is it declining? (J. H. Muirhead) Int. J. Ethics, **7**: 33.
Family Budget, A. *See* Economics.
Family Council, The, in France. (M. Betham-Edwards) National, **26**: 351. **28**: 47. Same art. Liv. Age, **207**: 634. **211**: 160. Same art. Ecl. M. **127**: 613.
Family Life in America. (T. Bentzon) Forum, **21**: 1.
Family Names. Cornh. **71**: 405.
Family Rhymes and Proverbs. All the Year, **75**: 498.
Family Traits, Persistence of. Science, **19**: 155.
— — Rejoinder. Science, **19**: 157.
Family Tree. (M. L. Adams) New Eng. M. n. s. **6**: 257.
Famine in Russia, 1892, Cause of. (W. C. Edgar) Forum, **13**: 575.
See Russia.
Fanaticism of 18th Century. Sat. R. **73**: 300.
Fancher, Mollie, Clairvoyance of. (T. E. Allen) Arena, **12**: 329.
Fancy, Decline of. (B. Gilman) And. R. **18**: 30.
Fancy, my Falcon. (E. Fawcett) Cosmopol. **18**: 181.
Fan's Mammy; a story. (E. W. McGlasson) Harper, **86**: 76.
Fans of Japan, Salwey on. Art J. **46**: 181. — Spec. **72**: 377.
Fán T'án, Origin of. (S. Culin) Overland, n. s. **28**: 153.
Fanti-land, Social Life in. (R. M. Connolly) Anthrop. J. **26**: 128.
Faraday, M. Liv. Age, **192**: 637.
Farallone Islands, The. (C. S. Greene) Overland, n. s. **20**: 226.
Farewell; a poem. (D. H. Cornish) Argosy, **60**: 370.
Faribault, Minn., Schools of. (W. M. West) Chr. Un. **46**: 782.
Faris-el-Hakin, Bold American Diplomacy in Case of. (M. J. Wright) Southern M. **4**: 54.
Farm, Abandoned, Hunting an, in Connecticut. (W. H. Bishop) Cent. **25**: 915.
— — — in Upper New England. (W. H. Bishop) Cent. **26**: 30.
— Modern Massachusetts. Garden & F. **5**: 145.
Farms, Abandoned, and Wasted Forests. (C. S. Sargent) Garden & F. **6**: 201.
— — in New England. (C. Johnson) Cosmopol. **15**: 215.
— — in the United States. (J. G. Speed) Chaut. **16**: 310.
— — for Studio Purposes. (H. Bowdoin) Mo. Illust. **3**: 72.
— in England, Small. Sat. R. **73**: 622.
— — — Chaplin's Bill for, 1892. Spec. **68**: 289.
— Two Hampshire. (W. S. Seton-Karr) National, **18**: 699.
Farm Colony, Hadleigh. (C. S. Bremner) Nation, **59**: 154.
Farm-hand in Old England and in New. (F. W. Pelly) Cath. World, **63**: 242.
Farmhouses of England, Destruction of. (E. I. Bell) M. of Art, **3**: 353.
Farm Interests and American Shipping. (A. C. Houston) Am. J. Pol. **3**: 655.
Farm Life, English. Round about the Farm. (R. Spinner) M. of Art, **5**: 74.
Farm Machinery. Has it destroyed Farm Life? (E. V. Smalley) Forum, **17**: 241.
Farm-Mortgage Statistics, True Meaning of. (E. Atkinson) Forum, **17**: 310.
Farm Prices not made Abroad. Gunton's M. **10**: 339.
Farm Schools; Abbotsholme and Bedales. R. of Rs. (N. Y.) **8**: 680.
Farmer, American, and Railway Legislation. (H. C. Adams) Cent. **21**: 780.

Farmer, American, Condition and Prospects of. (C. E. Benton) Am. J. Pol. 5: 248.
— — Condition of. (T. L. Greene) Nation, 57: 460.
— — Discontent of. (E. W. Bemis) J. Pol. Econ. 1: 193.
— (J. R. Dodge) Cent. 21: 447.
— — Real Condition of. (G. E. Roberts) Engin. M. 5: 716.
— — Ruin of. (W. Maitland) 19th Cent. 32: 733.
— — Small, The Matter with. (R. M. Davis) Forum, 14: 381.
— — Some Hints to the. (A. Teisen) Overland, n. s. 22: 58.
— — What the Government is Doing for. (A. W. Harris) Cent. 22: 465.
— — What of? Pub. Opin. 19: 298.
— Education of. (S. J. Logan) Am. M. Civics, 6: 303.
— Fate of the. (F. P. Powers) Lippinc. 55: 261.
— How Science is helping. (C. S. Plumb) Pop. Sci. Mo. 43: 100.
— in American Politics. (J. Macy) Yale R. 3: 369.
— in the North. (Alice French) Scrib. M. 15: 323.
— in the South. (Alice French) Scrib. M. 15: 399.
— — Condition of. (F. W. Moore) Yale R. 3: 56.
— Politics and the. (B. F. Clayton) No. Am. 160: 166.
— Ruin of. (W. Maitland) Ecl. M. 120: 1.
— Western, Condition of, as illustrated by the Economic History of a Nebraska Township. (A. F. Bentley) J. H. Univ. Studies, 11: nos. 7-8.
— — Plight of. (D. MacG. Means) Nation, 63: 80.
— — Problems before. (L. D. Lewelling) No. Am. 160: 16.
— Why he does not get Rich. (N. Baldwin) Am. M. Civics, 8: 561.
Farmer Eli's Vacation. (A. Brown) Cent. 24: 557.
Farmer's Daughter; a sketch. (J. Blewett) Canad. M. 7: 535.
Farmers and Consumers. (H. Jones) National, 19: 135.
— and the State. (M. Brosius) Am. J. Pol. 2: 108.
— Coöperation among. (E. F. Adams) Forum, 20: 364.
— Depression among. Gunton's M. 11: 64.
— English, Jefferies on. Dial (Ch.) 14: 104.
— — Unrest of. (E. Porritt) Yale R. 2: 54.
— Fallacies, and Furrows. (J. S. Morton) Forum, 17: 385.
— Fox-hunters and. (Earl of Suffolk) National, 24: 546.
— in New England, Unrest of. (C. Deming) Yale R. 1: 291.
— Organization of. (A. P. Young) Am. J. Pol. 1: 320.
— Reform from their Point of View. (W. Aldrich) Am. M. Civics, 6: 399.
— What the Country is doing for. (W. S. Harwood) No. Am. 163: 527.
See Agriculture.
Farmers' Alliance. Soc. Econ. 1: 36.
— and Some of its Leaders. (A. L. Diggs) Arena, 5: 590.
— in Congress, 1892. (H. Garland) Arena, 5: 447.
— Women in. (A. L. Diggs) Arena, 6: 160.
Farmers' Movement. (C. S. Walker) Ann. Am. Acad. Pol. Sci. 4: 790.
— and the Sheffield Scientific School. Yale R. 2: 4.
Farming, American, Inside View of. Time, 3: 266.
— by Electricity, Practical. (A. F. McKissick) Engin. M. 4: 708.
— The Charm of. Spec. 74: 680.
— in England, Depression of. Sat. R. 80: 402.
— Isolation of Life on Prairie Farms. (E. V. Smalley) Atlan. 72: 378.
— on Vacant City Lots. (C. S. Sargent) Garden & F. 9: 91, 139.
— Profitable, and Employment of Labor. (J. B. Kinnear) Blackw. 153: 24.
Farming, Revival of. (H. E. Moore) Contemp. 65: 58.
— Self-reliance in. (L. H. Bailey) Garden & F. 9: 42.
— Small Farms. (E. March-Phillipps) Fortn. 59: 91.
— Teaching of, in Common Schools. (E. P. Powell) New Eng. M. n. s. 10: 55.
See Agriculture.
Farming the Taxes; a story. (S. J. Weyman) McClure, 5: 269.
Farnell, Geo. Stanley. Acad. 48: 410. — Ath. '95, 2: 682.
Farnese, Elizabeth, Armstrong's. Spec. 69: 597. — (W. O. Morris) Acad. 42: 185.
Farnham Castle. (E. Venables) Good Words, 63: 159, 258. — Spec. 75: 173.
Farnley Hall. (S. A. Byles) M. of Art, 10: 295.
Faroe Islands, The. (K. Grossmann) Geog. J. 7: 1.
— Wet Walk in. (C. Edwardes) Belgra. 79: 402.
Farquhar, G. (L. I. Guiney) Poet-Lore, 6: 406.
Farquharson, Joseph, and his Works. (M. P. Jackson) Art J. 45: 153.
Farr, Florence, with portrait. Bk. Buyer, 11: 383.
Farragut, D. G. (E. K. Rawson) Atlan. 69: 483.
— Mahan's Life of. Spec. 71: 522. — (H. L. Wait) Dial (Ch.) 14: 49. — (W. O. Morris) Acad. 44: 287.
— Reminiscences of. (C. V. Anthony) Meth. R. 54: 724.
Farrar, F. W. (F. G. Carpenter) Chaut. 23: 442.
— at Home. (A. Warren) McClure, 2: 3. Same art. Sund. M. 22: 38.
— Portraits of. McClure, 4: 51.
Farren, Nelly, the Actress, at Home. (W. Brook) Idler, 9: 67.
Fasci dei Lavoratori, The, and the Situation in Sicily. (E. Cavalieri) Chaut. 19: 13.
Fascination of the King. (G. Boothby) Chamb. J. 73: 481-788.
Fascine Training and Protection of River Banks. Nature, 55: 156.
Fashion. (C. A. Foley) Econ. J. 3: 458.
— and Intellect. (W. H. Mallock) No. Am. 158: 647.
— Economic Effects of Changes of. (J. L. Laughlin) Chaut. 19: 9.
— What is it? (A. H. Bigg) 19th Cent. 33: 235. Same art. Ecl. M. 120: 504.
Fashions. Sat. R. 73: 65.
— A Century of. (Henri Bouchot) Cosmopol. 19: 261.
— of the 19th Century. (A. M. Earle) Chaut. 21: 131, 260.
— of 1896. Bost. 4: 349.
— Origin of. Spec. 70: 135.
Fast and Thanksgiving Days of New England, Love on. (A. M. Earle) Dial (Ch.) 19: 41.
Fast Day in Massachusetts. Should it be continued? And. R. 17: 513.
Fasting of Cattle, Compulsory. (W. Stokes) Acad. 50: 115.
Fata Morgana. Pub. Opin. 14: 135.
Fatal Doubt, A. (C. D. Cowell) Overland, n. s. 22: 471.
Fatal Mistake, A; a story. (S. T. Heard) Corn. 74: 811.
Fatal Number, The. (M. Hargrave) Gent. M. n. s. 50: 581. Same art. Ecl. M. 121: 72.
Fatal Reservation, A; a story. (R. O. Prowse) Cornh. 70: 1-561. 71: 86-643.
Fate. Spec. 76: 917.
Fate of Clyde Moorfield, Yachtsman. (C. Ticknor) New Eng. M. n. s. 10: 636.
Fate of Fenella. Spec. 68: 751.
Fate of Guy Darrell; a story. (R. M. Strong) Eng. Illust. 10: 119.
Fate of Humphrey Snell; a story. (G. Gissing) Eng. Illust. 14: 1.
Fate of Three; a story. (J. D. Symon) Eng. Illust. 13: 285.

Father Jardine; a poem. (E. C. Stedman) Cosmopol. 18: 222.
Father Thames; a story. (R. Penn) Theatre, 28: 7.
Fathers, The. Early Patristic Literature. (E. C. Butler) Dub. R. 118: 94.
— Library of, Wace and Schaff's. Church Q. 36: 273.
Fatigue. (F. B. Dresslar) Pedagog. Sem. 2: 102.
Fats and Oils, Testing of. (E. Mailliau) J. Frankl. Inst. 136: 376, 433.
Faulkner, Charles J. (J. S. Cotton) Acad. 41: 205.
Faulting, Folds and. (W. F. Hume) Sci. Prog. 2: 399, 456.
Fauna, First, of the Earth. (J. F. James) Am. Natural. 29: 880, 970.
— Remarkable, at the Base of the Burlington Limestone, Mo. (C. R. Keyes) Am. J. Sci. 144: 447.
Faunas, Numerical Intensity of. (L. P. Gratacap) Am. Natural. 28: 752.
Faust, Legend of, Derivation of. (C. Merk) Acad. 46: 12.
— Salvation of. (F. M. Holland) Open Court, 7: 3831.
— Story of. (G. Holme) Munsey, 10: 401.
— a Story in Nine Letters. (I. Tourgénieff) Fortn. 62: 132.
— a Study in. (A. C. Roberts) Bach. of Arts, 3: 610.
Favor's Rebound, A; a story. (M. Giese) Chaut. 18: 729.
Favras, Thomas Mahi, Marquis de, Story of. (Mrs. E. M. Davy) Belgra. 81: 74. Same art. Liv. Age, 198: 241.
Fawcett, Henry, Statue of. Sat. R. 75: 622.
Fawcett, Joseph. Lippinc. 57: 725.
Fayal. (R. Dabney and H. Cunningham) New Eng. M. n. s. 7: 741.
Fayûm, The, and Lake Moeris. (J. C. Ross) Acad. 43: 375.
— Dead Cities of. Am. Arch. 53: 14.
Fear. (J. Sully) Pop. Sci. Mo. 47: 340.
— as Primitive Emotion. (Hiram M. Stanley) Psychol. R. 1: 241.
— Children's Sense of. (M. M. Harrison) Arena, 16: 960.
Fear of it, The; a story. (R. Barr) Idler, 3: 422.
Feast of the Marys. Play in Provence. (J. Pennell) Cent. 21: 884.
Feasts and Holidays, About. Liv. Age, 211: 422.
Feathers, Interlocking of, in Birds. (W. P. Pycraft) Nat. Sci. 3: 196.
February; a poem. (A. C. Swinburne) M. of Art, 16: 137.
Fechin, St., of Corca Bascinn. (E. Lawless) 19th Cent. 37: 421.
Fechner, Gustav Theodor, on Religion and Science. (P. Carus) Open Court, 6: 3225.
— Paradoxon. (T. R. Robinson) Am. J. Psychol. 7: 9.
Fechter, Charles, Recollections of. (A. W. á Beckett) Theatre, 31: 116.
Fecundation, New Studies in. (B. W. Barton) Am. Natural. 26: 424.
— Phenomena and Development of. (H. J. Webber) Am. Natural. 26: 103, 287.
Federal Government. (A. V. Dicey) Law Q. 1: 80.
Federal Jurisdiction in Case of Corporations. (S. D. Thompson) Am. Law R. 29: 864.
Federal Power in the U. S., Growth of. (H. L. Nelson) Harper, 85: 240.
Federal State, Nature of. (E. V. Robinson) Ann. Am. Acad. Pol. Sci. 3: 785.
Federal System, Failures of. Spec. 71: 423.
Federalism, American, Sources of. (W. C. Morey) Ann. Am. Acad. Pol. Sci. 6: 197.
— Creeping-on of. Spec. 70: 476.
Federalist, The, Authorship of. (P. L. Ford) Nation, 59: 440. — (R. Whitaker) Overland, n. s. 24: 64.
Federation. (C. D. Farquharson) Westm. 146: 237.
— and Pseudo-Federalism. (E. W. Burton) Law Q. 5: 170.
Feeble Atonement, A; a story. Chamb. J. 71: 474.
Feeble-minded. (G. H. Knight) Lend a H. 15: 18.
— Adult, Care of. (E. P. Bicknell) Char. R. 5: 76.
— Care of, in Denmark. (F. Starr) Char. R. 3: 79.
— Education of. (G. H. Knight) Lend a H. 11: 441.
— Manual Training for. (I. C. Barrows) Lend a H. 15: 222.
— Treatment of. (W. E. Fernald) Lend a H. 11: 255.
Feeble-minded Children, Bibliography of Literature on. (G. E. Johnson) Pedagog. Sem. 3: 299.
— Contribution to the Psychology and Pedagogy of. (G. E. Johnson) Pedagog. Sem. 3: 246.
Feehan, Patrick A., first Archbishop of Chicago, with portrait. Nat'l M. (N. Y. '91) 16: 484.
Feel in the Chris'mas Air; a poem. (J. W. Riley) Cosmopol. 18: 211.
Feeling and Motion. (P. Carus) Open Court, 4: 2424, 2435.
— as a Physiological Process. (P. Carus) Open Court, 4: 2506.
— Belief, and Judgment. (J. M. Baldwin) Mind, 17: 403.
— Evolutionary Psychology of, Stanley on. (J. Dewey) Philos. R. 5: 292.
— Monistic Definition of the Term. (P. Carus) Open Court, 5: 2909.
Feelings, The. (H. Nichols) Philos. R. 4: 506.
— and Elements of Feeling. (P. Carus) Monist, 1: 401.
Feena; a story. All the Year, 70: 204.
Feet-washing by Christ. (W. F. Gess) Thinker, 9: 312.
Felicity Brooke; a story. (B. M. Butt) Blackw. 156: 818. Same art. Liv. Age, 204: 11.
Felidæ, Extinct, of North America. (G. I. Adams) Am. J. Sci. 151: 419.
Feline Fate, A; a story. (A. R. Brown) Eng. Illust. 14: 251. Same art. McClure, 3: 496.
Fellow-feeling. (E. Brower) Lippinc. 57: 826.
Fellowship, Religious, Ethical Basis of. (W. M. Salter) Eth. Rec. 2: 51.
Fellowships, Scholarships, and the Training of Professors. (G. S. Hall) Forum, 17: 443.
Fellow-traveller, A; a story. (A. Prothero) Belgra. 79: 375.
Felméri, Lewis. Acad. 45: 456.
Felons on the Stage. (A. Escott) Theatre, 37: 150.
Feminine Phases. (T. S. Jarvis) Lippinc. 54: 235.
Fen Country, Before Breakfast in. Spec. 70: 157.
— Ely. Chamb. J. 70: 305.
Fencers, Bertrand on. Sat. R. 76: 596.
Fences. Garden & F. 6: 482, 502, 512.
Fencing. (E. Van Schaick) Lippinc. 51: 107. — Sat. R. 77: 442.
— and Fencers in Paris. (C. De Kay) Cosmopol. 12: 361.
— Castle's Schools and Masters of Fence. (D. Hannay) M. of Art, 8: 233.
— Italian. Sat. R. 73: 683.
— Metamorphosis of. (H. Ansot) Overland, n. s. 24: 566.
— Old and New. (H. A. C. Dunn) Outing, 25: 29.
Fénelon, F. de S. de la Mothe, Some Thoughts on. Macmil. 71: 462. Same art. Liv. Age, 205: 492.
— Janet's. (A. Laugel) Nation, 55: 45.
Fenian Spy, A. (C. Stein) Blackw. 157: 745. Same art. Liv. Age, 205: 715.
Fenn, Harry, House of. (R. Riordan) M. of Art, 9: 45.
Fenton, Lavinia. *See* Bolton, Lavinia Fenton, Duchess of.

Fenwick, George, Letters of, 1642–43. N. E. Reg. 46: 356.
Fenwick, John, in England. (C. W. Taylor) Am. Hist. Reg. 3: 668.
Fenwick Family of N. J. Am. Hist. Reg. 3: 221.
Ferdinand IV., King of Naples. Temp. Bar, 109: 332.
Ferguson, Sir Samuel. Blackw. 159: 613.
— in the Ireland of his Day. Sat. R. 81: 431.
Fergusson, Robert, Scottish Poet. (A. Gordon) Gent. M. n. s. 53: 375.
Fermanagh County, In. All the Year, 75: 557.
Fermentation, Modern Theories of. (F. Wyatt) J. Frankl. Inst. 142: 270, 336.
Fermentation Industries, Chemistry and Bacteriology of. (P. F. Frankland) J. Soc. Arts, 40: 911–947.
Fermentations of the Earth. (P. P. Dehérain) Chaut. 17: 585.
Fernald, Chester B., with portrait. Bk. Buyer, 13: 404.
Fernandez, James, with portrait. Theatre, 37: 154.
Fernandez-Guerra y Orbe, Aureliano. Ath. '94, 2: 35.
Fernando Noronha; a Brazilian Convict Island. Chamb. J. 70: 116.
Ferncliff-on-the-Hudson. (F. Allaben) Nat'l M. (N. Y. '91) 18: 305.
Ferns. Chamb. J. 70: 367. — (W. H. Taplin) Garden & F. 5: 308, 524. — Garden & F. 9: 417.
— and Mosses, Recent Work on. (F. O. Bower) Sci. Prog. 4: 358.
— Aposporous and Apogamous. (C. T. Druery) Sci. Prog. 5: 242.
— Aspidium. (G. E. Davenport) Garden & F. 9: 444, 484.
— Basket. (W. Scott) Garden & F. 7: 346.
— Coal-house. (W. H. Taplin) Garden & F. 5: 464.
— Filmy. (W. H. Taplin) Garden & F. 6: 237. — (W. Scott) Garden & F. 7: 368.
— — in Dwelling-houses. (G. W. Oliver) Garden & F. 9: 226.
— Gleichenias at Kew Gardens. (W. Watson) Garden & F. 9: 23.
— Hardy. (S. F. Goodrich) Garden & F. 5: 200.
— Hardy Ferneries. (E. O. Orpet) Garden & F. 6: 206.
— Notes on. (W. Scott) Garden & F. 8: 456.
— Potting. (W. H. Taplin) Garden & F. 5: 67.
— Raising, from Spores. (W. Scott) Garden & F. 7: 227.
— Rare. (S. F. Price) Garden & F. 6: 99.
— Suitable for House-culture. (W. H. Taplin) Garden & F. 6: 367.
— Todea Barbara of Australia. (D. P. Penhallow) Garden & F. 7: 394.
— Walking Fern and its Haunts. (L. S. La Mance) Garden & F. 7: 488.
Feroza. (F. A. Steel) Macmil. 67: 149. Same art. Liv. Age, 196: 268.
Ferrar, Nicholas. (A. Galton) Acad. 43: 318.
— and Little Gidding. Church Q. 35: 460.
Ferrara, Court of, in the 15th Century. (Conte Gaudini) Scot. R. 25: 70. Same art. Liv. Age, 204: 515.
Ferrari, Gaudenzio. (E. G. Gardner) Month, 81: 436.
Ferrel, William, with portrait. (W. M. Davis) Pop. Sci. Mo. 40: 686.
Ferrers, Earl, Trial of, 1760. (S. M. Hill) Belgra. 78: 141. Same art. Liv. Age, 194: 244.
Ferri, Enrico, on Homicide. (H. Zimmern) Pop. Sci. Mo. 49: 678, 828.
Ferrier, Susan E., Miss Austen and. (C. T. Copeland) Atlan. 71: 836.
Ferris, G. W. G., and the Ferris Wheel, with portrait. (C. Snyder) R. of Rs. (N. Y.) 8: 269.
Ferris Wheel and other Big Wheels. (F. G. Coggin) Cassier, 6: 214.
Ferry, Jules, Death of. Spec. 70: 376.
Ferry-boat of to-day. (E. A. Stevens) Cassier, 6: 275.
Fersen, Count Axel von. (F. T. Marzials) Acad. 45: 431. — (R. Gurnell) Gent. M. n. s. 48: 295. Same art. Liv. Age, 193: 368.
Fertilization, Cross, of Food-plants. (A. B. Rendle) Nat. Sci. 4: 272.
Fertilizer, Phosphate, for Fruit. (G. C. Caldwell) Garden & F. 6: 121.
Fertilizer Trade, Government Control of. J. Frankl. Inst. 134: 450.
Fertilizers and Flowers. (C. S. Sargent) Garden & F. 9: 361.
— for the Orchard. (J. Troop) Garden & F. 9: 517.
— for Small Fruits. (E. Williams) Garden & F. 6: 236.
Fête de Gayant. (A. Repplier) Atlan. 77: 51.
Fetish-Mountain in Krobo, The. (H. J. Bell) Macmil. 68: 210.
Fetishism, African. (H. Chatelain) J. Am. Folk-Lore, 7: 303.
"Feud, Deadly," Derivation of. (H. Bradley) Acad. 45: 229.
Feudal England, Round's. Sat. R. 80: 477.
Feudalism, Revolt against, in England. (E. Porritt) Pol. Sci. Q. 9: 64.
Feuillet, Octave, and Viaud. Sat. R. 73: 411.
Feuillet, Mme. Octave. Blackw. 156: 370. Same art. Liv. Age, 203: 37. Same art. Ecl. M. 123: 540.
Fever-tree, The. All the Year, 76: 84.
Fez, the Mecca of the Moors. (S. Bonsal) Cent. 24: 483.
— University of, to-day. (S. Bonsal) Fortn. 58: 470. Same art. Ecl. M. 119: 750. Same art. Liv. Age, 195: 489.
Fians, Tales of. (W. A. Craigie) Scot. R. 34: 270.
Fiatism, Natural History of. (F. P. Powers) Lippinc. 58: 377.
Fibres, Commercial. (D. Morris) J. Soc. Arts, 43: 891–921.
Fibulæ Worn in Pairs. Reliquary, 35: 157.
Ficoroni Cista, The. (J. E. Harrison) M. of Art, 7: 234.
Fiction, Advantage of. (M. G. Tuttiet) 19th Cent. 39: 123. Same art. Liv. Age, 208: 308.
— Analytic Spirit in. (P. Bourget) New R. 6: 48.
— and Ethics. (S. M. H. Gardner) Writer, 9: 62.
— Art of, A Claim for. (E. G. Wheelwright) Westm. 146: 205. Same art. Ecl. M. 127: 608.
— — Caine on. Sat. R. 78: 530.
— Art of Mystery in. (G. M. Fenn) No. Am. 156: 432.
— Art of the Novelist. (A. B. Edwards) Contemp. 66: 225.
— Bases of. (W. R. Thayer) Open Court, 4: 2393.
— British, Recent. (B. Matthews) Cosmopol. 13: 157.
— — Century of. All the Year, 75: 537.
— Craving for. (H. Maxwell) 19th Cent. 33: 1046. Same art. Ecl. M. 121: 76.
— Decadence of. Spec. 70: 481.
— Dominant Note of Some Recent. (T. Bradfield) Westm. 142: 537.
— Eroticism in. (J. S. Smith) So. M. 1: 1.
— Fact in. (F. M. Bird) Lippinc. 56: 140.
— Feminine. Sat. R. 78: 596.
— Fictions of. (H. H. Gardener) Open Court, 4: 2431, 2451.
— French, English Characters in. (A. F. Davidson) Macmil. 67: 420. Same art. Liv. Age, 197: 676.
— Future of. (H. Garland) Arena, 7: 513.
— Geographical. (G. Atherton) Lippinc. 50: 112.
— Good and Evil in. (C. H. Palmer) Open Court, 3: 1502.

Fiction, Great Characters in, Townsend on. Spec. 71: 11.
— Heredity of, from Author. (M. Sheffey-Peters) Writer, 7: 147.
— How to write. Sat. R. 80: 693.
— in Politics. Liv. Age, 189: 387.
— in Public Libraries. (E. H. Woodruff) Lib. J. 20: 342. — (G. W. Cole) Lib. J. 19: supp. 18. — (E. M. Coe) Lib. J. 18: 250.
— Living Writers of. Dial (Ch.) 16: 351.
— Magazine, and how not to write it. (F. M. Bird) Lippinc. 54: 650.
— Motion and Emotion in. (R. M. Daggett) Overland, n. s. 26: 614.
— The Novel with a Purpose. (L. Whiting) Chaut. 18: 82.
— of Our Day. Our Day, 16: 443.
— Old and New. Gent. M. n. s. 48: 322.
— A Prig in the Elysian Fields. (W. E. Hodgson) National, 19: 191.
— Reading, in the Country. (F. Bates) Dial (Ch.) 19: 11.
— Realism in. (E. I. Benson) 19th Cent. 34: 458.
— — Limits of. (P. Bourget) New R. 8: 201.
— Recent, A Dominant Note of Some. (T. Bradfield) Ecl. M. 124: 71.
— — in Britain. (G. N. Adam) Canad. M. 4: 218.
— Recent Text-books on. (B. Matthews) Educa. R. 9: 478.
— The Romantic Profession. Macmil. 68: 14.
— Scientific Method in. (W. R. Thayer) Open Court, 4: 2347.
— Sex in. (D. F. Hannigan) Westm. 143: 616.
— Social Morality and Hypocrisy in. (Y. E. Allison) So. M. 3: 45.
— Social Reformer in. (F. Dolman) Westm. 137: 528.
— Sound Logic in. (F. A. Doughty) Critic, 26: 431.
— Studies in Recent. (F. S. Townsend) Meth. R. 56: 911.
— Southern Grandee in. (A. T. Rotter) Critic, 22: 38.
— Tendencies in. (A. Lang) No. Am. 161: 153.
— Theology and Morality in. Church Q. 34: 82.
— Thrills in. Sat. R. 76: 440.
— Triumph of the Novelist. Dial (Ch.) 20: 225.
— Types in, The Two Eternal. (H. W. Mabie) Forum, 19: 41.
— Unchastity in. (J. W. Caldwell) So. M. 3: 51.
— Uses and Abuses of. Chamb. J. 71: 775.
— Why do Certain Works of, succeed? (M. Wilcox) New Sci. R. 1: 112.
— with a Purpose. All the Year, 76: 230.
— Women of. (H. S. Wilson) Gent. M. n. s. 53: 34.
— World of. (J. Hawthorne) Time, 1: 242.
Fiction Coach, The; a story. (F. Madoc) Argosy, 56: 29.
Fida; a Congo Story. Belgra. 78: 183.
Fiddle Figures, Fancy. (J. C. Hadden) Chamb. J. 73: 437.
Fiddle Mad; a story. (C. C. Halkett) Belgra. 81: Holiday no., 24.
Fiddle Told. (N. C. Franklin) Lippinc. 57: 720.
Fiddler of the Reels, The. (T. Hardy) Scrib. M. 13: 597.
Field, Cyrus W., with portrait. Bk. News, 11: 311. — With portrait. Bk. News, 14: 537.
— Chapter in the Life of. Harper, 92: 846.
Field, D. D., Reminiscences of, with portrait. Green Bag, 6: 209.
— Work of. (A. Abbott) R. of Rs. (N. Y.) 9: 545.
Field, Eugene, with portraits. (H. Garland) McClure, 1: 195, 314. — (C. Moffett) McClure, 6: 137. — With portrait. Bk. Buyer, 8: 101. — With portrait. Bk. News, 14: 145. — Critic, 27: 304–324. — Our Day, 15: 279. — Lit. W. (Bost.) 26: 390, (J. D. Barry) 420.
— and his Work. Atlan. 78: 265.
— Early Verse of. (J. N. Hilliard) Bk. Buyer, 13: 525.
— Home Life of. (J. Blewett) Canad. M. 6: 180.
— Verses to his Friends. (W. I. Way) Bk. Buyer, 12: 809.
— Works, Sabine edition. (L. J. Block) Dial (Ch.) 20: 333.
Field, Mrs. E. M. The Child and his Book. Church Q. 35: 143.
Field, Henry M., with portrait. Bk. Buyer, 13: 273.
Field, Kate. (J. L. Gilder) Critic, 28: 402. — (C. Wheeler) Critic, 29: 45. — (L. Whiting) Chaut. 24: 79. — (L. Whiting) Arena, 16: 919.
— Burial Place of. Critic, 29: 135.
Field, Matthew, of London: his Family and Arms. (O. Field) N. E. Reg. 48: 331.
Field, Michael. Underneath the Bough. (J. M. Gray) Acad. 44: 65.
Field, Stephen J. (R. H. Titherington) Munsey, 10: 146.
Field of Cloth of Gold, Story of. (G. Lambert) Walford's Antiq. 4: 259, 299. 5: 2.
Field of Isandhlwana; a story. (Lt.-Col. Mahony) Argosy, 56: 214.
Field Columbian Museum. Nature, 52: 137.
Field and Hedge Gleaners; by a Son of the Marshes. Eng. Illust. 14: 69.
Field-notes. (J. Burroughs) Cent. 26: 197.
Field Sports, Ethics of. (G. Greenwood) Westm. 138: 168.
— Future of. (G. W. Hartley) Macmil. 67: 365.
Fielding, H., and Smollett, Political World of. Liv. Age, 200: 297.
— as a Bookman. (Austin Dobson) Bibliographica, 1: 163.
— Morals of. Sat. R. 75: 421.
— Portrait, and the Taunton Bust of. (A. Dobson) M. of Art, 6: 371.
— Tom Jones, Verdict on Morality of. Critic, 24: 444.
Fields, Mrs. James T., and her Friends. (M. A. DeW. Howe) Bookman, 4: 308.
Fields, Beauty of the. (R. Jefferies) M. of Art, 5: 101.
Fife, Kingdom of. Ed. R. 184: 417.
Fifeshire. (J. H. Crawford) Scot. R. 21: 33.
Fifteen. (M. Richardson) Lippinc. 57: 272.
Fifth Avenue, New York City. (M. G. Van Rensselaer) Cent. 25: 5.
Fifth Picture, The. Macmil. 72: 112.
Fighting in 1600. Sat. R. 78: 234.
— Japanese Self-defence. (G. B. Burgin) Idler, 2: 281.
— with Four Fists. (R. Barr) McClure, 3: 294.
Figueur, Thérèse; the Real Madame Sans-Gêne. (A. D. Vandam) New R. 11: 24.
Figure-head of the White Prince; a story. (M. Roberts) Eng. Illust. 14: 243.
Figure-heads of Vessels, Historic. (R. G. Denig) Cosmopol. 14: 689.
Fiji and Imperial Federation. (J. F. Hogan) Westm. 141: 1.
— Leprosy Stones in. (B. G. Corney) Folk-Lore, 7: 5.
— Missions in. Dub. R. 112: 184.
— Path of the Shades in. (B. Thomson) New R. 14: 417.
Fijians, Ancestor-worship among. (B. H. Thomson) Pop. Sci. Mo. 47: 671.
Filbert Tree, A Serious Disease of. (B. D. Halsted) Garden & F. 6: 134.

Fildes, Luke, with portrait. R. of Rs. (N. Y.) **9**: 693. — (W. W. Fenn) M. of Art, **3**: 49.
Files, Facts about. (S. Nicholson) Cassier, **8**: 600.
Filian, St., Relics of. (Sir H. Maxwell) Good Words, **33**: 39.
Filibustering, Legislative. (J. B. McMaster) Forum, **16**: 470.
Filippi, Rosina, with portrait. Theatre, **36**: 219.
Filippo, Fra, the Man and Artist. (G. Tyrrell) Month, **88**: 465.
Film Holder, A New. Nature, **52**: 400.
Films, Liquid, Thin. (A. W. Reinold) Nature, **48**: 624.
Filters, Water, Organic Matter and. Knowl. **18**: 165.
Filtration of Water. Chamb. J. **73**: 39. — (S. Rideal) Knowl. **18**: 80, 270.
— Plea for. (S. C. Hooker) Citizen, **1**: 179.
— Sand, of Drinking Water. (G. W. Fuller) Engin. M. **6**: 663.
Fin de Cycle Incident, A. (E. C. Jackson) Outing, **28**: 192.
Fin de Siècle. (S. L. Fridenberg) New Eng. M. n. s. **8**: 757.
Fin de Siècle; a story. (R. C. V. Meyers) Harper, **84**: 437.
Finalmarina, Italy. Sat. R. **73**: 207.
Finance and its Influence upon Industrial Progress. (Arthur Kitson) Am. M. Civics, **8**: 420, 469.
— Back to Hamilton. Gunton's M. **11**: 126.
— President Cleveland's Plan. Gunton's M. **10**: 10.
— Is Sound Finance Possible under Popular Government? (J. B. McMaster) Forum, **19**: 159.
— Legislation suggested; Symposium. Soc. Econ. **5**: 75.
— The Middleman in. (F. E. Steele) Econ. J. **5**: 424.
— Modern, Dangers of. (S. Montagu) Fortn. **57**: 322. Same art. Liv. Age, **193**: 360.
— Our Cash Reserves. (J. B. Peat) Canad. M. **5**: 461.
— Patriotism and. (E. L. Godkin) Nation, **61**: 459.
— Public, Bastable on. (A. C. Miller) J. Pol. Econ. **1**: 133. — (S. Sherwood) Ann. Am. Acad. Pol. Sci. **3**: 243. — Ath. '92, **2**: 513. — (L. L. Price) Econ. J. **2**: 671. — (D. MacG. Means) Nation, **55**: 357. — (E. R. A. Seligman) Pol. Sci. Q. **7**: 708.
— Recent. National, **25**: 277. **26**: 267.
— Sherman and Cleveland on. Gunton's M. **10**: 110.
— Some Fictions in. (E. Mead) Am. J. Pol. **2**: 467.
Financial Boom of the Last Century. Liv. Age, **209**: 793.
Financial Crisis of 1890. (M. Wirth) J. Pol. Econ. **1**: 214.
— of 1893. (M. Marshall) Engin. M. **5**: 411. — (W. B. Cockran) No. Am. **156**: 739. — Pub. Opin. **15**: 32, 311, 400, 426. — (E. Wiman) Canad. M. **1**: 517.
— — and its Causes. (G. R. Gibson) Forum, **15**: 483.
— — in the U. S. (J. H. Eckels; S. Pennoyer) No. Am. **157**: 129.
— — Lesson of. (H. Lieb) Open Court, **7**: 3767.
— — Opinions of Men of Business. Fortn. **59**: 297.
— — Phenomenal Aspects of. (A. C. Stevens) Forum, **16**: 22.
— — Political Causes of. (W. E. Russell) No. Am. **157**: 641.
— — Repeal of Silver-purchase Law and. (F. W. Taussig) Econ. J. **3**: 733.
— — Southern View of. (G. C. Kelley) Arena, **9**: 118.
— — a Whirlwind of Disaster. (E. Wiman) Canad. M. **1**: 517. *See* Panics.
Financial Facilities. (R. Ewen) Westm. **142**: 601.
Financial Isolation, Industrial Effects of. (L. G. McPherson) Engin. M. **12**: 205.
Financial Outlook, 1891. (W. R. Lawson) Bank. M. (Lond.) **53**: 44.
Financial Panic, The Genesis of a. Nation, **57**: 192.
Financial Procedure in State Legislatures. (E. L. Bogart) Ann. Am. Acad. Pol. Sci. **8**: 236.
Financial Relief, Ready. (W. H. Van Ornum) Arena, **8**: 536.
Financial Situation, 1895. Bank. M. (Lond.) **60**: 22.
Financial System, An American. (I. E. Dean) Arena, **12**: 250.
— Conditions for a Sound. (E. W. Codington) Forum, **22**: 275.
Financial Trouble before Election of 1892. (A. D. Noyes) Nation, **61**: 402.
Financial Whimseys. (H. White) Nation, **57**: 61.
Finchampstead, England, Chronicles of, Lyon's. Sat. R. **80**: 353.
Finck, H. T., with portrait. Bk. Buyer, **10**: 307.
Finding of Fingall, The; a story. (G. Parker) McClure, **3**: 348.
Fine Art and Science. (E. Du Bois-Reymond) Pop. Sci. Mo. **40**: 751. **41**: 16.
Fine Arts, Boito on. Art J. **45**: 280.
— Education in, in Great Britain. (C. Lindsay) Time, **1**: 58.
— — French and English. (H. Quilter) Univ. R. **4**: 183.
— French School of, Influence of. (W. A. Sherwood) Canad. M. **1**: 638.
— History of, Educational Value of. (C. E. Norton) Educa. R. **9**: 343.
— How to study. (C. M. Fairbanks) Chaut. **18**: 275.
— in England. (Harry Quilter) Univ. R. **3**: 449. **4**: 27. **7**: 23, 163.
— in Phrygia, Lydia, etc., Perrot and Chipiez on. (J. R. S. Sterrett) Nation, **56**: 316.
— Modern, Decadence in. (F. Harrison) Forum, **15**: 428.
— New York Society of. (C. Kay) Cosmopol. **15**: 265.
— — Story-telling in. (H. Stannus) J. Soc. Arts, **41**: 262.
— Study of, in Universities. (C. H. Moore) Harv. Grad. M. **1**: 354.
Finger of Hankin, The. (C. J. C. Hyne) Chamb. J. **72**: 769–787.
Finger-Lake Region, N. Y., Glacial Erosion in. (D. F. Lincoln) Am. J. Sci. **147**: 105.
Finger-marks, Identification by. All the Year, **74**: 467. — (K. Minakata) Nature, **51**: 199.
— Galton on. Sat. R. **75**: 49.
Fingering, Systematic. (W. M. Cross) Music, **2**: 564.
Finland. Ed. R. **183**: 78. — (E. A. Freeman) Macmil. **65**: 321. Same art. Liv. Age, **193**: 259.
— and its Parliaments. (J. D. Shaw) Westm. **142**: 425.
— Fishing in. (F. Whishaw) Longm. **26**: 87. Same art. Outing, **27**: 56.
— A Fortnight in. (J. D. Rees) National, **22**: 215. Same art. Ecl. M. **121**: 696. Same art. Liv. Age, **199**: 546.
— in the 19th Century. Sat. R. **79**: 763.
— Science in. Pop. Sci. Mo. **47**: 566.
Finnegan's Absalom. (Alice MacGowan) Overland, n. s. **23**: 66.
Finns, Magic Songs of. (J. Abercromby) Folk-Lore, **1**: 17–331. **2**: 31. **3**: 49. **4**: 27.
— Myths of Origin of. (J. Abercromby) Folk-Lore, **3**: 308.
Finnish Folk-Lore, Collection of. J. Am. Folk-Lore, **5**: 48.
Fins, Evolution of. (A. S. Woodward) Nat. Sci. **1**: 28.
Finson, Vilhjálmr. Acad. **42**: 31.
Firdausi, Persian Poet. (J. H. Parsons) Gent. M. n. s. **55**: 419.
— Shah Námeh. (A. Grant) Time, **18**: 59.
Fire, Kindling of. (J. R. Allen) Illus. Archæol. **2**: 77.
— — Primitive. (E. Ingersoll) Mo. Illust. **4**: 251.

Fire, Losses by, and the Age of Clay. (H. B. Chess) Engin. M. 4: 561.
— — Methods of Reducing. (C. J. H. Woodbury) Cassier, 1: 27, 124.
— — Our Enormous Annual. (E. Atkinson) Engin. M. 7: 603.
— Origin of. (A. Macivor) Gent. M. n. s. 57: 508.
— Rite of Passing through. (A. Lang) Contemp. 70: 232.
Fire-alarm Telegraph System, Pneumatic. J. Frankl. Inst. 140: 81.
Fire-arms, Interchangeability in. (W. F. Durfee) Cassier, 5: 469.
Fire Boats. (H. deB. Parsons) Cassier, 10: 28.
Fire Congress at Amsterdam. Am. Arch. 50: 87, 98.
Fire-damp and other Gases, Detection of. (F. Clowes) J. Soc. Arts, 41: 307.
Fire-damp Indicator, Prof. Clowe's. Dub. R. 113: 652.
Fire Engines. (J. Sachs) Cassier, 7: 307.
— Turkish. (J. A. Grey) Cassier, 8: 581.
Fireplaces. (G. Aubry) Am. Arch. 36: 111–143. — M. of Art, 9: 187.
— Heating with. (W. W. Jackson) Am. Arch. 49: 79.
Fire-proof Buildings, Fire Losses in. (C. H. Bebb) Engin. M. 4: 731.
Fire-proof Construction and the Practice of American Architects. (P. B. Wight) Am. Arch. 41: 113.
— and Recent Tests. (A. L. A. Himmelwright) Engin. M. 12: 460.
— Interior. (J. M. Carrère) Engin. M. 4: 95.
— New. (H. B. Seely) Am. Arch. 46: 112. — (N. Poulson) Am. Arch. 39: 182.
— Test of the Roebling System of. Am. Arch. 54: 53.
Fire-proofing Tests. Am. Arch. 49: 99. — (S. A. Reed) J. Frankl. Inst. 142: 321.
— Report on. Am. Arch. 53: 59.
Fire-risk, External, or "Exposure." (S. A. Reed) Am. Arch. 40: 72.
Fire-seeker, The. (W. Packard) Overland, n. s. 28: 588.
Fire Ships of Antwerp. (A. A. C. Galloway) Un. Serv. M. 10: 294.
Fire-worship and Mythology in relation to Religion. (F. M. Müller) Open Court, 4: 2321.
Fires, Apparatus for Extinguishing. (J. G. Morse) Pop. Sci. Mo. 47: 477, 603.
— Causes of. (C. J. Hexamer) J. Frankl. Inst. 135: 288. 136: 53, 136.
— Drought. (F. L. Oswald) No. Am. 159: 506.
— Forest. (F. L. Oswald) Lippinc. 52: 355.
— Grass, in Africa, and their Effects. (G. F. S. Elliot) Sci. Prog. 5: 77.
— in London and Paris in 1891. J. Statis. Soc. 55: 137.
— in London in 1892. J. Statis. Soc. 56: 101.
— in Theatres, Statistics of. (W. P. Gerhard) Am. Arch. 46: 115.
— Protection against. (E. O. Sachs) J. Soc. Arts, 43: 42. — Bank. M. (Lond.) 59: 130.
— Steam Pumps for. (L. R. Alburger) Cassier, 1: 406.
— Some Famous. (J. Stephen) Eng. Illust. 16: 155.
Fireside, Evolution of. (M. J. Javage) Pub. Opin. 14: 305.
First and Last; a poem. (F. E. Coates) Cosmopol. 17: 372.
First Book, Their. (G. A. Mendum) Bk. News, 8: 207.
— Young Writer's. (M. K. Buck) Writer, 8: 165.
First-class Stowaway, A; a story. (H. C. Cox) Bost. 4: 339.
First Edition of Robinson Crusoe. Bookworm, 1: 173.
First Editions, Famous. Cornh. 69: 265.
— Mania for. (W. Roberts) Fortn. 61: 347. Same art. Ecl. M. 124: 77.
— of American Authors. Critic, 25: 382.
First Editions of Dickens. (C. P. Johnson) Bookworm, 1: 81, 132.
— of Shakespeare. Bookworm, 2: 314.
First Flight. (Mrs. V. R. Cruger) Lippinc. 51: 131.
First Foot. (M. Hunt) Longm. 28: 574. Same art Ecl. M. 127: 703.
— Superstition of, in the British Isles. (J. Rhys and T. W. E. Higgens) Folk-Lore, 3: 253.
— — in Aberdeenshire. (J. E. Crombie) Folk-Lore, 4: 315.
— — in Edinburgh. (G. Hastie) Folk-Lore, 4: 309.
First Impressions. (C. Edwardes) Belgra. 80: 187.
First Lodger, The; a story. (M. Douglas) Argosy, 54: 347.
First Mrs. Beckett, The. (C. J. Cutcliffe-Hyne) Eng. Illust. 11: 807.
First Night [of the Play], Impressions of a. Cornh. 73: 147. Same art. Ecl. M. 126: 370.
First Night; a story. Cornh. 67: 387.
First Night Criticism. (C. Scott) Theatre, 33: 100.
First Numbers. (F. B. Harrison) Time, 20: 66.
First Skylark of Spring; a poem. (W. Watson) Spec. 72: 437. Same art. Ecl. M. 122: 671.
First Stone, The. New R. 11: 662.
First Year, The; a story. (C. H. New) Munsey, 12: 355.
Fischer, Amand. Nature, 50: 272.
Fischer, Paul Henri. (E. Bordage) Nature, 49: 296. — Nat. Sci. 4: 74.
Fish, Hamilton. (J. C. B. Davis) Atlan. 73: 215.
— Old School and the New. (A. Badeau) Forum, 16: 289.
Fish, Acclimatization of, on the Pacific Coast. (H. M. Smith) Science, 22: 88.
— Distribution to Consumers, New Plan of. Westm. R. 140: 415.
— Immature, Destruction of. (E. W. L. Holt) Nature, 47: 160.
— Invisible Food of. Spec. 76: 372.
— Migrations of. Chamb. J. 72: 633.
— Non-edible, Economic Uses of. (R. F. Walsh) Pop. Sci. Mo. 45: 61.
— Preservation of our Game and. (G. Fay) Atlan. 77: 642.
— Practical Study of. Spec. 77: 893.
— Spearing, in Winter. (E. W. Sandys) Outing, 23: 295.
— Strange. (C. B. Hudson) Cosmopol. 19: 483.
Fish of M. Quissard, The; a story. (T. A. Janvier) Harper, 93: 823.
Fish Culture in the Highlands. (J. Bickerdyke) Blackw. 154: 835.
Fish Hatchery, New Sea-, at Dunbar. (L. N. Badenoch) Knowl. 18: 189.
Fish-hatching. (W. A. Smith) Scot. R. 26: 295.
Fish-shooting in the West Indies. (H. W. Lanier) Outing, 25: 455.
Fisher, Daniel, Diary of, 1755. Pennsyl. M. 17: 263.
Fisher, Geo. P., with portrait. Bk. Buyer, 3: 123.
Fisher, Fort, 1864–65. (W. Lamb) So. Hist. Pap. 21: 257.
— — Army of, True History. (H. C. Lockwood) Un. Serv. (Phila.) 10: 401.
— — Personal Reminiscences of Capture of. (E. Ketchum) Un. Serv. (Phila.) 16: 457.
Fisheries in American History. (G. A. Rich) Chaut. 17: 161.
— a Neglected Australian Industry. Chamb. J. 72: 645.
— New England. (G. A. Rich) New Eng. M. n. s. 10: 229.
— of California. (D. S. Jordan) Overland, n. s. 20: 460.
— on the Pacific Coast. (P. L. Weaver, jr.) Overland, n. s. 20: 149.
— of Scotland. (W. A. Smith) Scot. R. 21: 257.

Fisherman and the Stream; a poem. (Mrs. M. E. Gates) Outing, **24**: 284.
Fishermen, Among the. (F. M. Holmes) Gent. M. n. s. **53**: 289.
— New England. (W. M. Thompson) New Eng. M. n. s. **13**: 675.
Fishes, American Game. (L. M. Yale) Scrib. M. **15**: 754.
— Curious Bread-winners of the Deep. (C. B. Hudson) Cosmopol. **15**: 750.
— Evolution of; Latitude and Vertebræ. (D. S. Jordan) Pop. Sci. Mo. **45**: 346.
— Food, Distribution of. (H. N. Dickson) Nat. Sci. **6**: 30.
— Living and Fossil. (T. Gill) Science, n. s. **3**: 909.
— Teeth of. (W. G. Ridewood) Nat. Sci. **8**: 380.
— Young. (E. E. Prince) Longm. **19**: 300.
Fishing *à la Tourilli*. (N. B. Winston) Outing, **20**: 488.
— After the Herring. (A. Watson) M. of Art, **5**: 405, 454.
— Angling in Still Waters. (J. Buchan) Gent. M. n. s. **51**: 192.
— Bout with a King Fish. (E. W. Sandys) Outing, **20**: 97.
— Canoe-poling in the Cascapedia. (R. F. Hemenway) Outing, **22**: 201.
— A Day in a Catboat. (E. W. Sandys) Outing, **24**: 260.
— Drake's Bay. (J. H. Griffes) Overland, n. s. **24**: 453.
— Dry-fly. (Edward Grey) New R. **11**: 393.
— Fly, Fisher on. Sat. R. **74**: 25.
— Fly-books, Getting out the. (L. M. Yale) Scrib. M. **12**: 27.
— Game, in the Pacific. (C. F. Holder) Cosmopol. **20**: 138.
— in Art. Art J. **48**: 257.
— in England. Spec. **68**: 809.
— in Jamaica, A Day's. (A. J. Halliday) Outing, **23**: 205.
— in Scotland, Fontinalis. (C. Stein) Blackw. **154**: 256.
— in the Sea in Winter. (J. Bickerdyke) Sat. R. **81**: 165.
— in Wales; From a Coracle. (A. G. Bradley) Macmil. **67**: 458.
— The Last Fish. (T. I. Sherman) Outing, **24**: 301.
— Line-fishers *vs.* Beam-trawlers. (J. Quail) Blackw. **154**: 693.
— off Santa Barbara. (H. C. Booth) Outing, **26**: 355.
— Old-fashioned. (H. Van Dyke) Cent. **28**: 540.
— on Cherrystone Creek. (F. B. Jess) Outing, **20**: 52.
— on a Devonshire Trout Stream. Macmil. **72**: 94. Same art. Ecl. M. **125**: 500.
— on Lake Superior. (H. I. Woodside) Canad. M. **1**: 673.
— on Nashotah Lake. (E. W. Chubb) Outing, **26**: 264.
— on the Severn River. (W. Thomson) Outing, **24**: 452.
— Salmon, in the Columbia River. (M. W. Sheffield) Bost. **4**: 364.
— Sea, and the Territorial Waters. Blackw. **158**: 104.
— When Rustics went a-trouting. (E. French) Outing, **26**: 192.
— Winter. (E. W. Sandys) Outing, **27**: 282.
— with the Spear. (E. W. Sandys) Outing, **24**: 54.
Fishing Party; a story. (B. Thomson) New R. **14**: 229.
Fishing Tackle. (J. Cassidy) Gent. M. n. s. **55**: 390.
Fishwife of Le Conquet; a poem. (Isa J. Postgate) Gent. M. n. s. **57**: 427.
Fisk, Archie C., with portrait. Nat'l M. (N. Y. '91) **17**: 88.
Fiske, John, with portrait. Bk. Buyer, **7**: 241. — Critic, **26**: 310.
Fitch, Ashbel Parmelee, with portrait. Nat'l M. (N. Y. '91) **19**: 213.
Fitch, John. (C. F. Hammond) New Eng. M. n. s. **8**: 490.
Fitch, Joshua G. (F. Starr) Educa. R. **7**: 326.
Fitch, Ralph: First Englishman in Burmah. (J. Horton Ryley) Time, **15**: 589.
Fitch, Robert. Ath. '**95**, **1**: 478. — Nat. Sci. **6**: 352.
Fitch, Walter H. Nature, **45**: 302.
Fitchburg, Massachusetts. (J. G. Edgerly) New Eng, M. n. s. **12**: 321.
Fitton Portraits at Arbury. (C. G. O. Bridgeman) Acad. **41**: 40. — (T. Tyler) **41**: 66.
Fitz, Mary; Life-story of a Devonshire Ghost. (W. J. Hardy) Belgra. **83**: 25.
Fitzgerald, Edward. (M. Todhunter) Westm. **145**: 255. — Temp. Bar, **97**: 23. — Liv. Age, **192**: 99. — (E. Clodd) Eng. Illust. **11**: 529. — Lond. Q. **84**: 318. — (J. Dennis) Leis. H. **44**: 32.
— and Archdeacon Groome. Sat. R. **80**: 175.
— Letters of. Quar. **184**: 103. Same art. Liv. Age, **210**: 771. — Ed. R. **180**: 365. Same art. Liv. Age, **203**: 515.
— Letters to Fanny Kemble, 1871-83. Temp. Bar, **104**: 27-473. **105**: 33-486. — (W. P. Garrison) Nation, **61**: 297. — (W. G. Johnson) Dial (Ch.) **19**: 174. — (R. C. Browne) Acad. **48**: 451.
Fitzgerald, Percy, Memoirs of. Sat. R. **79**: 679.
Fitzherbert, Sir Anthony. "Boke Longyng to a Justice of the Peace." (E. A. McArthur) Eng. Hist. R. **9**: 305.
Fitzherbert, Mrs., George IV. and. (G. G. Bain) Munsey, **10**: 589.
Fitznoodle's Debut with the Ballyporeens. (T. S. Blackwell) Outing, **23**: 193.
Fitz-Walter, Maud. (L. Alldridge) Argosy, **61**: 119.
Five Dances and a Supper. (K. Cady) Overland, n. s. **24**: 94.
Five Grey Nuns, The; a story. All the Year, **71**: 300.
Five-pounder hooked Foul, A. (E. L. Kellogg) Outing, **28**: 252.
Five Voices from an Old Music-book; a story. Cornh. **65**: 544, 646. Same art. Liv. Age, **194**: 421, 495.
Five Years in a Convent. (E. C. Grenville-Murray) Time, **6**: 361-619.
Fizeau, Armand Hippolyte Louis. (A. Gray) Nature, **54**: 523.
Flag, U. S., First Salute to. (W. E. Griffis) New Eng. M. n. s. **8**: 576.
— Story of. (R. H. Titherington) Munsey, **13**: 401.
Flags, About. All the Year, **74**: 390.
Flagellants of the West of the U. S. Dub. R. **114**: 178.
Flagellante's Sin, The; a story. (T. M. Randall) Outing, **21**: 432.
Flame. (A. Smithells) Nature, **49**: 86.
Flameng, François. (P. G. Hamerton) Scrib. M. **16**: 63.
Flammarion, Camille. (R. H. Sherard) McClure, **2**: 569.
— Poet-astronomer. (F. Le C. de Lautreppe) Cosmopol. **17**: 146.
— Portraits of. McClure, **1**: 491.
Flanders. About the Flemings. All the Year, **73**: 376.
— Skating in. (C. J. K. Fenton) Argosy, **59**: 278.
Flanders Galleys, The. Chamb. J. **71**: 438.
Flannagan, William W., with portrait. Nat'l M. (N. Y. '91) **16**: 480.
Flash of Daring, A; a story. (E. V. Wilson) McClure, **5**: 144.
Flash-Lights. (L. Raynor) Cent. **26**: 145.
"Flaskisable," The Word. (Fitzedward Hall) Nation, **63**: 455.
Flat-fishes, Origin of Species among. (J. T. Cunningham) Nat. Sci. **6**: 169, 233.

Flatey Book; the Saga of Eric the Red. (H. H. Boyesen) Cosmopol. 16: 467.
Flats and Houses. Spec. 68: 462.
See Apartment Houses.
Flaubert, Gustav. (H. T. Peck) Bookman, 2: 130. — — (D. F. Hannigan) Westm. 144: 383. — (E. Newman) Fortn. 64: 813. — (H. James) Macmil. 67: 332.
— Letters of. (Garnet Smith) Gent. M. n. s. 50: 550.
— Tarver's Works and Correspondence of. (J. R. Smith) Dial (Ch.) 19: 208. — (W. Sharp) Acad. 48: 85. — Sat. R. 80: 443.
Flavia; a story. (A. Theuriet) Chaut. 23: 678. 24: 39, 168.
Flavorings. Chamb. J. 70: 490.
Flax, Culture of, in Scotland. Chamb. J. 70: 229.
Flaxman, John. (J. E. Hodgson and F. A. Eaton) Art J. 45: 326.
— Career and Works of. (E. S. Roscoe) M. of Art, 4: 368, 468.
Fleechy; a story. (L. Torre) Eng. Illust. 16: 226.
Flemish Art. (E. M. Vermorcken) Chaut. 18: 200.
Fletcher, Andrew. (J. R. MacDonald) Scot. R. 22: 61.
Fletcher, Benjamin. (C. B. Todd) Nat'l M. (N. Y. '91) 16: 627.
Fletcher, Giles, An Elizabethan Mystic. (G. Bradford) And. R. 19: 551.
Fletcher, P., Beaumont and. (J. R. Lowell) Harper, 85: 757.
Fleur-de-lis. (K. D. Wiggin) Cent. 25: 196.
Fleury, Tony Robert. (H. Bell) Mo. Illust. 4: 18.
Fliedner, Theodore, and Kaiserswerth. (E. Kinnicutt) Cent. 29: 84.
Fliegende Blätter. (W. D. Ellwanger and C. M. Robinson) Cent. 26: 448.
Flies as Conveyers of Infection. Dub. R. 117: 160.
— Courtship among. (J. M. Aldrich) Am. Natural. 28: 35.
— House, A Chapter on. Chamb. J. 73: 261.
Fly, House, Experiments on. (J. B. Smith) Science, 22: 205.
— Plague of, in South Africa. Chamb. J. 70: 806.
Flight, Human. (H. C. Kirk) Engin. M. 2: 650.
— — and the Soaring of Birds. Around World, 1: 79.
— Mechanical. (S. P. Langley) Cosmopol. 13: 55.
— Wind and. (F. W. Headley) Nat. Sci. 5: 344.
See also Flying.
Flight of Betsey Lane, The. (S. O. Jewett) Scrib. M. 14: 213.
Flight of Quails; Moorland Idyll. (G. Allen) Eng. Illust. 12: no. 5, 33.
Flinck, Govaert. (T. Cole) Cent. 27: 412.
Flinder, Matthew. (J. Macaulay) Leis. Hour, 41: 326.
Flint, Robert. History of the Philosophy of History. (R. M. Wenley) Scot. R. 24: 297.
Flint. (H. F. Wilson) M. of Art, 10: 404.
Flint Implements, Diminutive, from Hastings Kitchen Midden and Sevenoaks. (W. J. L. Abbott) Anthrop. J. 25: 137.
— from Berkshire, Eng. (O. A. Shrubsole) Anthrop. J. 24: 44.
— from Chalk. (A. M. Bell) Anthrop. J. 23: 266.
— — in Kent. (J. Prestwich) Anthrop. J. 21: 246.
Flint-knapping; the Oldest Trade in the World. Chamb. J. 73: 44. Same art. Liv. Age, 208: 440.
Flint-making; a Very Ancient Industry. (E. Lovett) Illus. Archæol. 1: 1.
Flint Saws and Sickles. (R. Munro) Illus. Archæol. 1: 176.
Flint Weapons, Caru Brê, Cornwall. Reliquary, 36: 45.
Flints, Gun, Making of. (P. A. Graham) Longm. 20: 580.
Flirtation as a Fine Art. (J. Wright) Lippinc. 58: 839.
— Ethics of. Spec. 72: 266.
Flirting Wives. (Mrs. A. E. Barr) No. Am. 156: 69.
Flittermouse, The; a story. (A. E. Abbott) Idler, 6: 62.
Floating Bethel, The. (L. S. Furman) Cent. 27: 297.
Flodden, Campaign of. (C. Stein) Un. Serv. M. 11: 295. Same art. Liv. Age, 206: 195.
— or Branxton? (W. S. Dalgleish) Good Words, 34: 669.
Flogging. Must we have the Cat-o'-nine Tails? (E. T. Gerry) No. Am. 160: 318.
Flood, Glacial Nightmare and, Howorth's. Ed. R. 178: 354.
Floods in the U. S., Recent. (J. W. Powell) No. Am. 155: 149.
— in Western Rivers. (C. B. Going) Engin. M. 8: 1038.
— — Effects of. (C. B. Going) Engin. M. 3: 795.
Floor-area, Advisability of Limiting. (E. Atkinson) Am. Arch. 43: 10.
Flora, Mountain, of Alabama. Garden & F. 5: 507.
— of Japan, Forest. (C. S. Sargent) Garden & F. 6: 26–532.
— of Smythe Co., Va. (H. M. Vail) Garden & F. 5: 364, 437.
— Sacra. (A. E. P. R. Dowling) Contemp. 62: 395.
— Vernal, Origin of. (J. Harshberger) Science, n. s. 1: 92.
— — Harshberger on. (C. Robertson) Science, n. s. 1: 371.
Flora Biology, Present Position of. (J. C. Willis) Sci. Prog. 4: 204.
Floras, Insular. (W. B. Hemsley) Sci. Prog. 2: 379. 3: 23, 447.
Florence, Description of. (O. Browning) M. of Art, 4: 45, 141.
— Duomo. (L. E. Baxter) M. of Art, 10: 233.
— History of. Eng. R. 11: 18.
— — Villari's. (H. C. Lea) Nation, 57: 252.
— in the 14th and 15th Centuries. (Guido Biagi) Blackw. 153: 327. Same art. Ecl. M. 120: 614. Same art. Liv. Age, 197: 259.
— in Spring. All the Year, 70: 448. Same art. Liv. Age, 194: 56.
— Laurenzian Library at. Leis. Hour, 43: 357.
— Literary Landmarks of. (L. Hutton) Harper, 93: 899.
— Men and Manners in. Cornh. 73: 597. Same art. Liv. Age, 210: 28. Same art. Ecl. M. 127: 60.
— Modern Art in. (L. Scott) M. of Art, 1: 192. 2: 234.
— National Library Building. (E. E. Clarke) Lib. J. 17: 483.
Florence, Mass., Sheffield's History of. (W. P. Garrison) Nation, 60: 264.
Florentine Artist, The. (E. H. and E. W. Blashfield) Scrib. M. 13: 165.
Florentine Episode, A; a story. (E. O. Kirk) Atlan. 70: 92, 173.
Florentine Fancies; poems. (Mary Negreponte) Westm. 139: 636. Same art. Ecl. M. 121: 278.
Florentine Villas. (Lee Bacon) Scrib. M. 19: 323.
Florian, Frédéric, Wood-engraver. Scrib. M. 18: 578.
Florian, Jean-Pierre Claris de. (A. Manston) Temp. Bar, 107: 235. Same art. Liv. Age, 208: 626.
Floriculture. (J. G. Jack) Garden & F. 5: 282.
— Civilizing Power of. (T. H. Haskins) Garden & F. 5: 410.
— Flora for Lake Shores and Water Fronts. (E. J. Hill) Garden F. & 6: 15, 51.
— for the Farmer. (C. S. Sargent) Garden & F. 7: 101.
— Fungous Troubles in Cutting-beds. (B. D. Halsted) Garden & F. 5: 91.

Floriculture. Society of Florists, American. Garden & F. 7: 349.
— — Annual Meeting, 1892. Garden & F. 5: 406.
— — — 1893. Garden & F. 6: 359.
Florida, Central, Midwinter Vegetation of. (A. N. Prentiss) Garden & F. 5: 52.
— Coast of, Pleasures and Perils of a Cruise on the. (W. Henn) Cent. 24: 163.
— First Landing in, 1512. (F. MacBennett) M. Am. Hist. 30: 32.
— Geography of. (J. N. MacGonigle) Nat. Geog. M. 7: 381.
— Geology of, Notes on. (L. C. Johnson) Am. J. Sci. 145: 497.
— In the Flat Woods. (B. Torrey) Atlan. 72: 779.
— in Winter. Cornh. 73: 370.
— Morning at the Old Sugar Mill. (B. Torrey) Atlan. 74: 373.
— On the Beach at Daytona. (B. Torrey) Atlan. 74: 66.
— Our own Riviera. (J. Ralph) Harper, 86: 489.
— Recollections of. (E. P. Scammon) Cath. World, 54: 691.
— South, West Indian Fauna in. (T. D. A. Cockerell) Nature, 46: 458.
— Story of a Recruit in. (D. Robinson) Un. Serv. (Phila.) 10: 153.
— Sub-tropical. (C. R. Dodge) Scrib. M. 15: 345.
— Traditions of. (H. P. Huse) Un. Serv. (Phila.) 7: 267.
— West. *See* West Florida.
— Winter Days in. (B. O. Flower) Arena, 13: 1.
Florida Blood Feud, A; a story. (F. Gribble) Idler, 2: 275.
Florida Gardens, Exotic Trees and Shrubs for. (H. Nehrling) Garden & F. 7: 33–132.
— Native Plants for. (H. Nehrling) Garden & F. 7: 13.
Florida Girl; a story. Cornh. 68: 162. Same art. Liv. Age, 199: 156.
Florida Pines. Garden & F. 5: 73.
Florida Sea Beans, So-called. (C. H. Coe) Garden & F. 7: 502.
Florissant, Stone Forest of. (A. Heilprin) Pop. Sci. Mo. 49: 479.
Flotsam. (H. S. Merriman) Longm. 27: 287–613. 28: 77–323. — (O. Hall) Lippinc. 57: 435.
Flotsam and Jetsam. (P. N. Boeringer) Overland, n. s. 24: 362.
Flour-milling in the Northwest. (T. L. Greene) Nation, 54: 424.
Flower, Charles E. (M. D. Conway) Nation, 54: 374. — Leis. Hour, 42: 473.
Flower, Natural History of the. (J. C. Willis) Nat. Sci. 4: 347.
— U. S. National, Maize as; a Symposium. Arena, 8: 92.
Flower and Fruit Mission, N. Y. Garden & F. 6: 232.
Flower of Death, The; a story. (F. S. Mines) Harper, 88: 442.
Flower of the Fields; a poem. (M. Cawein) Cosmopol. 20: 52.
Flower o' the World. (N. Stephenson) Scrib. M. 20: 737.
Flower Child, a Pastel. (W. E. Hunt) Canad. M. 7: 296.
Flower Day of the Midwinter Fair. (C. H. Shinn) Garden & F. 7: 232.
Flower Exhibition, St. Louis. Garden & F. 9: 479. *See* Flower Show.
Flower Festivals, Santa Barbara. (S. A. Higgins) Chaut. 21: 531.
Flower Garden. (E. O. Orpet) Garden & F. 5: 141, 150.
— at Wellesley. (T. D. Hatfield) Garden & F. 8: 358.
— Color in. (C. S. Sargent) Garden & F. 8: 321.
Flower Garden, Hardy. (J. N. Gerard) Garden & F. 7: 146. — (J. N. Gerard) Garden & F. 6: 218. — (E. O. Orpet) Garden & F. 6: 277.
— Island, in Jackson Park, Chicago. (F. C. Seavey) Garden & F. 7: 298.
— Notes on. (W. N. Craig) Garden & F. 8: 387.
— Work in. (E. O. Orpet) Garden & F. 7: 136.
Flower Gardens, Old Time. (A. M. Earle) Scrib. M. 20: 161.
Flower-lore. Atlan. 75: 858.
— of New England Children. (A. M. Earle) Atlan. 75: 459.
Flower Names, English. Sat. R. 77: 303.
Flower Pictures. (M. G. Van Rensselaer) Garden & F. 6: 83. — (C. S. Sargent) Garden & F. 6: 232.
Flower Seasons, Philosophy of. (H. L. Clarke) Am. Natural. 27: 769.
Flower Show at New York. Garden & F. 6: 209. 7: 459.
— at Philadelphia. Garden & F. 5: 166.
— at Temple Gardens. Spec. 74: 749. — (W. Watson) Garden & F. 7: 233.
— Autumn, in Chicago. Garden & F. 8: 468.
— in Boston. Garden & F. 8: 139. 9: 369, 379.
— English. Garden & F. 7: 258.
Flower Shows and their Uses. (C. S. Sargent) Garden & F. 6: 139.
— in California. (E. J. Mickson) Overland, n. s. 19: 472.
— in the U. S. (S. A. Wood) Chaut. 15: 180.
— Possibilities of. (M. C. Robbins) Garden & F. 7: 462.
Flowering Trees. (C. S. Sargent) Garden & F. 6: 231.
Flowers, according to Season, Mrs. W. S. Dana's. Garden & F. 7: 219.
— Affinities of. (F. Oswald) Knowl. 19: 212.
— and Flower Painters. (K. de Mattos) M. of Art, 6: 453.
— and Forests of the Far West. (A. R. Wallace) Liv. Age, 192: 467.
— and Insects. (F. W. Burbridge) Good Words, 33: 463. — (A. S. Wilson) Knowl. 17: 280.
— Annual, from Seed. (J. N. Gerard) Garden & F. 7: 67–108.
— Arranging. Spec. 68: 742.
— as Entertainers. Chamb. J. 70: 303.
— at N. Y. Farmers' Club. Garden & F. 7: 468.
— at Wellesley. Garden & F. 5: 586.
— Autumn Flowering Perennial Plants. (R. Cameron) Garden & F. 7: 406, 417.
— Changing Fashions in. Garden & F. 9: 413.
— Colors of, in relation to Season and Geographical Location. Around World, 1: 104.
— Cultivation of. (J. N. Gerard) Garden & F. 6: 245, 257.
— Cut, How to preserve. (M. C. Robbins) Garden & F. 6: 322.
— Doubling of. (G. H. Powell) Garden & F. 8: 448.
— Easter. (C. S. Sargent) Garden & F. 7: 121.
— — in Philadelphia. (W. H. Taplin) Garden & F. 5: 203.
— Favorite. (H. Christ) Garden & F. 6: 46.
— Fertilization of; Masquerade of Stamens. (W. H. Gibson) Cosmopol. 17: 570.
— Garden, and their Arrangement. (F. S. Mathews) Garden & F. 7: 252.
— Genesis of. (A. S. Wilson) Knowl. 17: 125.
— Hardy Perennials. Garden & F. 6: 156.
— Hardy Plants in Flower. (J. N. Gerard) Garden & F. 6: 237.
— in the Conservatory. Garden & F. 5: 585.
— in Town. (M. G. Van Rensselaer) Garden & F. 5: 195.
— in Winter. (W. A. Buckhout) Garden & F. 6: 81.

Flowers, Japanese Love of. Sat. R. 73: 547.
— Late-blooming Hardy Herbaceous Plants. (J. W. Manning) Garden & F. 8: 396, 406.
— Names for, Picturesque. (M. C. Robbins) Garden & F. 5: 614.
— Names of Garden. Garden & F. 6: 25.
— Names of, Latin. Sat. R. 76: 410.
— New York Cut Flower Co. Garden & F. 8: 452, 462.
— of Field and Forest. (B. D. Halsted) Chaut. 23: 138.
— of Japan. Art J. 44: 63.
— — and the Art of Floral Arrangement. Garden & F. 5: 22, 35.
— — Piggott on. Sat. R. 74: 369.
— of Spring. (C. S. Sargent) Garden & F. 6: 231.
— Origin of. (B. Kidd) Longm. 21: 392.
— Perforation of, by Insects. (J. G. Jack) Garden & F. 5: 29.
— Plants in Flower. (J. N. Gerard) Garden & F. 6: 315.
— Poets and. (P. Robinson) Contemp. 63: 825. Same art. Liv. Age, 198: 419.
— Popular Books about. (C. S. Sargent) Garden & F. 8: 201.
— Retail Prices of Cut. Garden & F. 9: 22.
— Rock-garden. (T. D. Hatfield) Garden & F. 6: 287.
— Some Unusual Androgynous Flower-clusters. (J. G. Jack) Garden & F. 8: 222.
— Southern. (P. Thum) Southern M. 4: 227.
— Spring, at Short Hills, N. J. Garden & F. 6: 247.
— — and Glaciers. (A. P. Coleman) Chaut. 17: 68.
— Spring Garden. (C. S. Sargent) Garden & F. 7: 141.
— Structure of. (A. S. Wilson) Knowl. 17: 163, 210.
— Town, Tyranny of. Argosy, 59: 47.
— Uses of. Garden & F. 5: 133.
— Vases for Cut. Garden & F. 7: 372.
— Welcomes of the. (W. H. Gibson) Harper, 88: 551.
— Wholesale Markets of, N. Y. City. Garden & F. 8: 232.
— Wild, British. Sat. R. 74: 40.
— — Early, in West Virginia. (Danske Dandridge) Garden & F. 7: 198.
— — Exhibition of, at Edinburgh, 1892. (W. R. Lazenby) Garden & F. 5: 382.
— — Hardinge's With the. Garden & F. 7: 279.
— — How to know. Garden & F. 6: 189.
— — in Cultivation. Garden & F. 5: 166.
— — of September. (D. E. Collins) Garden & F. 8: 409.
— — Plea for. (B. L. Putnam) Garden & F. 7: 118.
— Wind-fertilized. (A. S. Wilson) Knowl. 18: 199.
Flüggen, Joseph. M. of Art, 5: 188.
Fluffums; a story. (L. Merrick) Eng. Illust. 15: 417.
Fluids, Motion of, Discontinuity of. (W. Kelvin) Nature, 50: 549, 573, 597.
Flume, Log, Down a. (J. B. Kaye) Overland, n. s. 19: 45.
Fluorescence or Phosphorescence, and Photographic Action at Low Temperatures. (J. Dewar) New Sci. R. 1: 129.
Fluorine. Chamb. J. 69: 71.
— Presence of, as a Test for the Fossilization of Animal Bones. (T. Wilson) Am. Natural. 29: 301, 439, 719.
— Story of. (A. E. Tutton) Good Words, 34: 279.
Flute Altars, Oraibi. (J. W. Fewkes) J. Am. Folk-Lore, 8: 265.
— Micoñinovi. (J. W. Fewkes) J. Am. Folk-Lore, 9: 241.
Flute Celebration, Walpi. (J. W. Fewkes) J. Am. Folk-Lore, 7: 265.
Fly Country, The. Liv. Age, 200: 189.
Fly-fishing. (B. Field) Fortn. 61: 494.
Fly Larvæ, Silk-spinning. (H. Garman) Science, 22: 215.
Fly-Leaf Poem, A. (W. Watson) Acad. 50: 531.
Fly-wheels, Handling. (M. N. McLaren, jr.) Cassier, 7: 264.
Flygare, Carlén Emilie. Ath. '92, 1: 214.
Flying, Artificial, Langley on. Sat. R. 73: 51.
— Experiments on. (C. Runge) Nature, 49: 157.
— Lilienthal's Experiments in. Nature, 51: 177.
— Mechanical. (H. S. Maxim) Knowl. 18: 14.
— Problem of, New Lights on. (J. Le Conte) Pop. Sci. Mo. 44: 744.
See also Flight; Aerostation.
Flying through Flames; a story. (C. Warman) McClure, 3: 422.
Flying-fish Catching at Barbadoes. Chamb. J. 71: 44.
Flying Halcyon. (R. H. Savage) Lippinc. 53: 435.
Flying-machine; Aviator. (G. Trouvé) Pop. Sci. Mo. 40: 392.
— Birds in Flight and the. (H. S. Maxim) No. Am. 161: 405.
— The Maxim. (A. G. Greenhill) Nature, 52: 321.
— Maxim's Experiments. (H. S. Maxim) Cent. 27: 444.
— Wellner's Sail-wheel. (H. Bonfort) Pop. Sci. Mo. 46: 627.
Flying Machine Materials. (R. H. Thurston) Cassier, 6: 415.
Flying Machines. (J. P. Holland) Cassier, 3: 243. — (C. E. Duryea) Cassier, 6: 377. — Spec. 73: 204.
— Otto Lilienthal and. Nature, 53: 300.
— Progress of. (D. Archibald) Sat. R. 82: 181.
See Aeronautics.
Flying Man, The, and his Machine. McClure, 3: 323.
Flying March, A; a story. (W. L. Alden) Idler, 9: 829.
Foa, Edouard, in Africa. Sat. R. 79: 224.
Fog, Cloud, and Haze. (J. G. McPherson) Gent. M. n. s. 53: 123.
Fog on the Blumli's Alp; a story. (F. Gribble) Idler, 4: 146.
Fogs, Cyclonic. Dub. R. 115: 435.
— Effects of, upon Cultivated Plants. (F. W. Oliver) Nature, 48: 18.
— London. Spec. 68: 45.
— Scheme to abolish. (B. H. Thwaite) National, 20: 360. Same art. Ecl. M. 120: 72. — (O. C. D. Ross) Gent. M. n. s. 50: 228.
— Town; their Amelioration and Prevention. (E. S. Bruce) Dub. R. 114: 132.
Fog-idyl, A; a story. (D. Dale) Belgra. 80: 424.
Fogg Art Museum at Cambridge, Mass. (M. Brimmer; E. W. Hooper) Harv. Grad. M. 3: 301.
Fogy on Foot, A. (A. W. Quimby) Outing, 28: 364.
Foix, Gaston de, Tomb of. (J. Cartwright) M. of Art, 6: 381.
Folds and Faulting. (W. F. Hume) Sci. Prog. 2: 399, 456.
Foliage, Artificial, in Architecture. (H. Stannus) J. Soc. Arts, 42: 881–928.
Foliage Plants. (W. H. Taplin) Garden & F. 5: 537.
— for Bedding. (W. H. Taplin) Garden & F. 7: 207.
Folk, The. (J. Jacobs) Folk-Lore, 4: 233.
Folk-dancing. (L. J. Vance) Open Court, 8: 4068.
Folk-drama. (T. Fairman-Ordish) Folk-Lore, 2: 314. 4: 149.
Folk-foods of the Rio Grande Valley. (T. G. Bourke) J. Am. Folk-Lore, 8: 41.
Folkland. (P. Vinogradoff) Eng. Hist. R. 8: 1.
Folkestone, A Ramble Round. Blackw. 155: 660.
Folk-lore, African. (A. Werner) Contemp. 70: 377. Same art. Ecl. M. 127: 640. Same art. Liv. Age, 211: 172.
— African Legends. (H. M. Stanley) Fortn. 59: 797.

Folk-lore, American, Record of. (A. F. Chamberlain) J. Am. Folk-Lore, 8: 317.
— and Superstitions, Manx. (J. Rhys) Folk-Lore, 2: 284. 3: 74.
— An Old Mauma's. (John Hawkins) J. Am. Folk-Lore, 9: 129.
— Bahama. (C. L. Edwards) J. Am. Folk-Lore, 4: 47.
— Behar. Sat. R. 73: 365.
— Bibliography of. (G. L. Gomme) Folk-Lore Rec. 5: 55.
— Congress of, 1891. Sat. R. 75: 573.
— — Second International, 1892. J. Am. Folk-Lore, 4: 343.
— — Chicago, 1893. Folk-Lore, 4: 345.
— Corsican. Chamb. J. 69: 444.
— Cox's Introduction to. (A. Lang) Acad. 48: 559.
— English. (C. Burne) Folk-Lore, 1: 313.
— European, in the U. S. (J. Curtin) J. Am. Folk-Lore, 2: 56.
— Evolution in. (D. D. Wells) Pop. Sci. Mo. 41: 45.
— from Buffalo Valley, Pa. (J. G. Owens) J. Am. Folk-Lore, 4: 115.
— from Chaucer. Folk-Lore Rec. 2: 135.
— from Lesbos. (W. H. D. Rouse) Folk-Lore, 7: 142.
— German. Chamb. J. 70: 47.
— Handbook of, Gomme's. (W. W. Newell) J. Am. Folk-Lore, 4: 184.
— Horatian. All the Year, 72: 155.
— Huron. (Horatio Hale) J. Am. Folk-Lore, 1: 177.
— in First Series of Hardwicke's Science-Gossip, Index to. (J. Britten) Folk-Lore Rec. 1: 180.
— in Wills. (L. L. Duncan) Folk-Lore, 4: 513.
— Indian Origin of Popular Tales. (A. Lang) Acad. 41: 63.
— Interpretation of. (J. W. Powell) J. Am. Folk-Lore, 8: 97.
— Irish, Notes on. (G. H. Kinahan) Folk-Lore Rec. 4: 96.
— Iroquois. (W. M. Beauchamp) J. Am. Folk-Lore, 4: 39.
— Mohawk. (W. M. Beauchamp) J. Am. Folk-Lore, 8: 217.
— Natural History of. (O. T. Mason) J. Am. Folk-Lore, 4: 97.
— Necessity of Collection of. (W. W. Newell) J. Am. Folk-Lore, 3: 23.
— Norwegian. All the Year, 73: 474. — Chamb. J. 71: 203.
— of the Carolina Mountains. (J. Mooney) J. Am. Folk-Lore, 2: 95.
— of China. (J. H. S. Lockhart) Folk-Lore, 1: 359.
— of the Columbian Exposition. (S. Culin) J. Am. Folk-Lore, 7: 51.
— of Dragons. (L. J. Vance) Open Court, 6: 3439.
— of France. (A. Lang) Folk-Lore Rec. 1: 99.
— of India. (R. C. Temple) Folk-Lore Rec. 5: 33.
— of Ireland. (A. C. Haddon) Folk-Lore, 4: 349. — Quar. 179: 195.
— of Isle of Man. (A. W. Moore) Antiq. n. s. 31: 5-344.
— of Italy. (H. C. Coote) Folk-Lore Rec. 1: 187.
— of Leitrim County, Scotland. (L. L. Duncan) Folk-Lore, 4: 176.
— of Madagascar. (J. Sibree, jr.) Folk-Lore Rec. 2: 19, 336. — Folk-Lore Rec. 4: 45.
— of Melanesia. (R. H. Codrington) Folk-Lore, 4: 509.
— of the Mountain Whites of the Alleghanies. (J. H. Porter) J. Am. Folk-Lore, 7: 105.
— of New England. (J. M. Currier) J. Am. Folk-Lore, 2: 291.
— of the Sea. (W. Gregor) Folk-Lore, 2: 468.
Folk-lore of Old Wenlock. (Lady C. M. Gaskell) Ecl. M. 122: 407.
— of Western U. S. (C. M. Harger) Lit. W. (Bost.) 23: 244.
— Old Ballad. (J. Napier) Folk-Lore Rec. 2: 92.
— Oldest, of Iceland. (W. A. Craigie) Folk-Lore, 4: 219.
— Onondaga. (W. M. Beauchamp) J. Am. Folk-Lore, 8: 209.
— Oregonian. (A. S. Gatschet) J. Am. Folk-Lore, 4: 139.
— Pennsylvania German. (W. J. Hoffman) J. Am. Folk-Lore, 1: 125. 2: 23, 191. — (F. Starr) J. Am. Folk-Lore, 4: 321.
— Plantation. (L. J. Vance) Open Court, 2: 1029, 1074, 1092.
— Relation to Greek Archæology. (C. Smith) Folk-Lore, 3: 529.
— Research in 1892. (E. S. Hartland) Folk-Lore, 4: 80.
— Slavonic. (W. S. Lach-Szyrma) Folk-Lore Rec. 4: 52.
— Source of some of M. Galland's Tales. (H. C. Coote) Folk-Lore Rec. 3: 178.
— Study of. (T. F. Crane) Chaut. 16: 180. — (L. J. Vance) Forum, 22: 249.
— — in America. (L. J. Vance) Pop. Sci. Mo. 43: 586.
— Superstitions of the French Canadians. (B. L. Macdonell) Pop. Sci. Mo. 44: 520.
— Topics for Collection of. (F. D. Bergen and W. W. Newell) J. Am. Folk-Lore, 4: 151.
— Traditions of Historical Events in. (W. S. Lach-Szyrma) Folk-Lore Rec. 3: 157.
— West African. (A. B. Ellis) Pop. Sci. Mo. 45: 771.
— — Some Prototypes of the "Uncle Remus" Stories. (A. B. Ellis) Pop. Sci. Mo. 48: 93.
Folk-Lore Publication Fund. J. Am. Folk-Lore, 6: 12.
Folk-Lore Studies. (I. J. Vance) Open Court, 1: 612, 662.
Folk-Lore Study and Societies. (W. W. Newell) J. Am. Folk-Lore, 8: 231.
Folk-medicine and Executed Criminals. (Mabel Peacock) Folk-Lore, 7: 268.
Folk-music. (L. J. Vance) Open Court, 6: 3287.
— Harmony in. (J. C. Fillmore) Music, 5: 281.
Folk-prayers. (S. Baring-Gould) Sund. M. 23: 820. Same art. Chr. Lit. 12: 157.
Folk-psychology, Scope and Method of. (W. I. Thomas) Am. J. Sociol. 1: 434.
Folk Rhymes and Survivals. (E. B. Tylor) Acad. 43: 73.
Folk-Song and Popular Poetry, Williams'. (W. W. Newell) J. Am. Folk-Lore, 8: 94.
— Burgundy; tr. by E. F. Strange. Art J. 44: 350.
— German. (R. Lieber) Music, 8: 49.
Folk-Songs, Breton. (T. Bacon) Atlan. 70: 677.
— of Italy. (R. H. Busk) Folk-Lore, 1: 261.
— in the Finnish Kalevala. (C. J. Billson) Folk-Lore, 6: 317.
— Mexican, New. (C. F. Lummis) Cosmopol. 13: 720.
— Roumanian. Gent. M. n. s. 48: 212.
— Russian. (J. C. Fillmore) Music, 4: 123.
Folk-Speech. Spec. 74: 495.
— in America. (E. Eggleston) Cent. 26: 867.
Folk-Tale Research, 1890. (E. S. Hartland) Folk-Lore, 2: 99.
Folk-Tales, Diffusion of. (W. W. Newell) J. Am. Folk-Lore, 8: 7.
— English, in America. (W. W. Newell) J. Am. Folk-Lore, 1: 227. — (F. D. Bergen) J. Am. Folk-Lore, 2: 60, 213. 3: 291. 8: 143.
— Notes on. (W. R. S. Ralston) Folk-Lore Rec. 1: 71.
— of Angola, Chatelain's. (F. Starr) (Ch.) 17: 261.
— of Central Africa. (E. Elmslie) Folk-Lore, 3: 92.

Folk-Tales of India. (S. M. Taylor) Folk-Lore, 7: 83.
— Philosophy of. (L. J. Vance) Open Court, 5: 2935.
— Research on. (E. S. Hartland) Folk-Lore, 1: 108.
— — 1890-91. (E. S. Hartland) Folk-Lore, 3: 111.
— Sardinian. (E. S. Hartland) Ecl. M. 118: 166.
— Slavonic. (M. Dragomanov) Anthrop. J. 21: 456.
Folly of Mocking at the Moon. (Gaston Fray) Scrib. M. 16: 388.
Fonseca, Manual D. da, Rise and Fall of. (R. Adams, jr.) Cosmopol. 12: 453.
Fontainebleau. Ed. R. 177: 420. Same art. Liv. Age, 198: 131.
— Forest of. (M. Talmeyr, and J. P. Brodhurst) M. of Art, 11: 37-292.
— Painters at. (R. L. Stevenson) M. of Art, 7: 265, 340.
Fontenoy. (F. Dixon) Temp. Bar, 107: 187. Same art. Liv. Age, 208: 664.
Fonts at Alphington and Stoke Cannon. Illus. Archæol. 1: 252.
— Church. (C. F. Yonge) M. of Art, 18: 230.
Fonts, Norfolk. (J. L. André) Antiq. n. s. 27: 148.
Food and Genius. Sat. R. 78: 173.
— and Gladness. (W. G. Blaikie) Sund. M. 22: 818.
— Animal. (L. Tolstoi) New R. 7: 22. — Sat. R. 74: 195, 223.
— Composition of, and its Use in the Body. (T. G. Allen) Chaut. 22: 577.
— Familiar, Notes on. All the Year, 76: 7.
— Foreign. Blackw. 152: 175.
— Free, and Free Education. (A. G. Warner) Char. 1: 73.
— Nutritive Value and Digestibility of. (T. G. Allen) Chaut. 23: 174.
— of Mankind. (C. D. Wilson) Lippinc. 55: 716.
— The People's; a National Inquiry. R. of Rs. (N. Y.) 13: 679.
— — Question of. (A. W. Winthrop) Cath. World, 63: 768.
— Protection against Vermin. Reliquary, 36: 179.
— Science and. Spec. 72: 499.
— Unrecognized Dainties among. Spec. 72: 900.
— Waste of, in American Households. (W. O. Atwater) Forum, 16: 110.
— What the coming Man will eat. (W. O. Atwater) Forum, 13: 488.
Food Economy, Errors in. (W. O. Atwater) Char. R. 5: 146.
Food-nerves. (T. W. Nunn) New Sci. R. 1: 277.
Food Products, American, in Europe, Rusk's Crusade for. (J. Hawthorne) Lippinc. 49: 211.
Food Supply and Price of Wheat. (T. B. Veblen) J. Pol. Econ. 1: 365.
— in the Event of War, English. (W. E. Bear) National, 27: 133. — (R. B. Marston) National, 27: 302.
Foods in the Year 2000. (H. J. W. Dam) McClure, 3: 303.
Fool, The, in the Drama. (F. Helbig) Open Court, 1: 607, 657, 687.
Fool of the Four Corners. (G. B. Burgin) Good Words, 35: Xmas no., 67.
Fool to Fame, A; a story. (E. A. Alexander) Harper, 93: 301.
Fool's Gem; a poem. (E. King) Westm. 139: 50.
Fool's Wager, A. (John Mackie) Chamb. J. 73: 362.
Fools and Clowns of Shakespeare's Time. (H. E. Borradaile) Poet-Lore, 8: 206.
— of Shakespeare. (T. R. Slicer) New Eng. M. n. s. 12: 374.
Fools who Came to Scoff; a story. (R. B. Hale) New Eng. M. n. s. 7: 214.
Foot, Human, a Climbing Organ. (L. Robinson) 19th Cent. 31: 795.
Foot, Prehensile, of East Indians. (F. Regnault) Pop. Sci. Mo. 41: 489.
Football. Fortn. 61: 25.
— and its Abuses. Pub. Opin. 16: 220.
— and Manners. (E. L. Godkin) Nation, 59: 476.
— as Coachers see it. (J. L. Williams) Bach. of Arts, 3: 803.
— as a Moral Agent. (H. H. Almond) 19th Cent. 34: 899.
— Association, Plea for. (S. J. Watts) Outing, 24: 112.
— at Harvard College. (R. R. Dundee) Bost. 3: 115.
— Characteristics of Canadian. (A. C. Kingstone and C. A. S. Boddy) Outing, 27: 247.
— Church on University. (T. M. Osborne) Nation, 57: 395.
— Education of the Foot. (J. S. White) Cosmopol. 16: 508.
— How to reform. (L. F. Deland) Harv. Grad. M. 2: 316.
— in New Zealand. Chamb. J. 69: 783.
— in the South. (J. B. Robertson) Southern M. 3: 631. — (L. P. Miles) Outing, 25: 257.
— Intercollegiate. (E. A. Poe) Lippinc. 50: 235. — (J. W. White) No. Am. 158: 100.
— — on the Pacific Coast. (P. Weaver) Overland, n. s. 21: 117.
— Is it Educative or Brutalizing? (D. B. St. J. Roosa; J. G. Schurman; E. D. Warfield) Forum, 16: 634.
— The New. (E. L. Godkin) Nation, 59: 399.
— New Mania for. (C. Edwardes) 19th Cent. 32: 622.
— of 1891. (W. Camp) Outing, 21: 52, 102.
— of 1893. (W. Camp) Outing, 25: 56.
— of 1894. (W. Camp) Outing, 25: 169. 27: 81.
— of 1895. (W. Camp) Outing, 27: 169. 29: 62.
— of 1896. (W. Camp) Outing, 29: 176.
— on the Pacific Slope. (J. Craig) Outing, 22: 447.
— Professional. All the Year, 73: 558.
— Retrospective and Prospective. (W. Camp) Outing, 23: 119.
— Rugby. Sat. R. 74: 541. — Spec. 70: 134.
— The Situation in. (E. L. Richards) Pop. Sci. Mo. 45: 721.
— Training for. (J. G. Lathrop) Outing, 25: 84.
Foote, Henry S., Personal Recollections of. (G. Baber) Overland, n. s. 26: 162.
Foote, John J., with portrait. (H. L. Conard) Nat'l M. (N. Y. '91) 16: 103.
Foote, Mary Hallock, with portrait. Bk. Buyer, 11: 338.
Foote Collection of English Literature, Sale of. Critic, 26: 101, 164.
Foote's Catorium; a story. (W. L. Alden) Idler, 10: 262.
Footprints of Vertebrates in the Coal Measures of Kansas. (O. C. Marsh) Am. J. Sci. 148: 81.
Foot-racing. (J. Corbin) Outing, 23: 220.
Footstep from the Unseen. (J. Watson) Good Words, 36: Xmas no., 1. Same art. Liv. Age, 207: 817.
Footstep of Death; a story. Macmil. 65: 438.
Footsteps Overhead; a story. (R. Metcalfe) Sund. M. 23: 320, 418, 466.
For Angèle's Sake; a story. All the Year, 71: 571, 597, 620.
For a Birthday; a poem. (J. R. Lowell) Cosmopol. 13: 162.
For Bravery on the Field of Battle; a story. (T. B. Aldrich) Cent. 22: 880.
For their Brethren's Sake. (G. H. Peirce) Atlan. 74: 340.
For the Child's Sake; a story. Argosy, 61: 636.

For the Chiltern Hundreds; a story. (E. W. Abram) Temp. Bar, 106: 538.
For Conscience Sake; a story. (M. Hargrave) Gent. M. n. s. 52: 217.
For the Cross; a story. (Geo. L. Putnam) Scrib. M. 12: 751.
For the Dearest; a Valentine Story. (E. H. Miller) Chaut. 20: 593.
For Ever; a story. (G. Burgess) Eng. Illust. 15: 55.
For Ever; a story. (A. Hope) Idler, 7: 729.
For Falstaff he is Dead; a story. (G. M. Cooke) Atlan. 73: 210.
For Father's Sake; a story. (Lady Dunboyne) Argosy, 53: 247.
For God's Judgment; a story. (E. Gower) National, 22: 279.
For her Dear Sake. (A. L. Hannah) Bach. of Arts, 3: 528.
For her Ladyship's Sake. (L. Springfield) Idler, 7: 373.
For Humanity's Sake; a story. (W. L. Edmonds) Canad. M. 5: 411.
For Love of Marta; a story. (F. I. Currie) Munsey, 13: 256.
For the Love of the Stranger; a story. (A. Gordon) Good Words, 35: 767.
For Remembrance. (E. W. Bellamy) Lippinc. 53: 556.
For the Second Time; a story. (Q. Gordon) Belgra. 81: 273.
For Services Rendered; a story. (M. M. Helliwell) Canad. M. 7: 275.
For Ten Francs; a story. (George Fleming) New R. 13: 456. Same art. Ecl. M. 125: 695.
For Value Received; a story. (M. C. Graham) Cent. 31: 295.
Foraker, Joseph Benson. (F. B. Gessner) Munsey, 15: 59.
Foraminifera of the Chalk and of To-day. (H. W. Burrows and R. Holland) Nat. Sci. 8: 101.
Forbearance, Christian Ethics of. Spec. 72: 190.
Forbes, Archibald. Barracks, Bivouacs, and Battles. Spec. 69: 388.
— Memories of War and Peace. Sat. R. 80: 807.
Forbes, Stanhope A. (W. Meynell) Art J. 44: 65. — (M. H. Dixon) M. of Art, 15: 181. — (P. G. Hamerton) Scrib. M. 15: 688.
Forbes-Robertson, Johnston. Theatre, 30: 8.
Forbin, Claude de, More Adventures of. (E. P. Thompson) Gent. M. n. s. 55: 139.
Force. (J. B. Wood) Open Court, 3: 1503.
— as a Moral Influence. (E. L. Godkin) Nation, 61: 442.
Force Bill, Disastrous Effects of a. (H. Smith) Forum, 13: 686.
Forces, Inter-relation of. (A. H. Ivens) Westm. 140: 50. Same art. Ecl. M. 125: 369.
Ford, John, and Massinger. (J. R. Lowell) Harper, 85: 942.
Ford, Onslow. (M. H. Dixon) M. of Art, 15: 325.
Ford *vs.* De Pontes, 30 Beaven, 572; a story. (E. Myers) Canad. M. 3: 400.
Ford Castle. (A. Griffiths) M. of Art, 5: 108.
Fordham, Geo. (A. Allison) Time, 17: 513.
Foreglows and Afterglows. (J. G. McPherson) Gent. M. n. s. 52: 269.
Foreign Lands; a poem. (R. L. Stevenson) M. of Art, 7: 459.
Foreign Markets for the U. S., Outlook for. (A. D. Pentz) Engin. M. 4: 506.
Foreign Office, British. Chamb. J. 70: 705.
Foreign Office Romance; a story. (A. C. Doyle) McClure, 4: 70.
Foreign Trade, Railways and Ocean Steamers. Soc. Econ. 6: 283.
— The Search for New Markets. Soc. Econ. 6: 257.
Foreigner, Popular Prejudice against the. (C. D. Farquharson) Westm. 146: 237.
Foreigner, A; a story. (E. Gerard) Blackw. 156: 727. 157: 77–885. 158: 42–836.
Foreordination and Election. (C. Walker) Bib. Sac. 49: 276.
Fore-room Rug, The. (K. D. Wiggin) Atlan. 73: 316.
Foresight and Patience; a poem. (G. Meredith) National, 23: 164.
Forest, Battle of the. (B. E. Fernow) Nat. Geog. M. 3: 127.
Forest, German. (S. Whitman) Chaut. 21: 36.
Forest Air and Forest Soil, Hygienic Influence of. (B. E. Fernow) Garden & F. 6: 34.
Forest Conditions in the Sierras. (F. M. Gallaher) Garden & F. 9: 502.
Forest Fires. (C. S. Sargent) Garden & F. 7: 392. — (F. L. Oswald) Lippinc. 52: 355.
— American. Spec. 73: 298.
— Another Lesson from India. (C. S. Sargent) Garden and F. 9: 211.
— Are they a Necessary Evil? (B. E. Fernow) Garden & F. 8: 242.
— Causes and Effects of. (J. Gifford) Engin. M. 8: 187.
— How to stop them. Garden & F. 7: 172.
— in New Jersey. (J. Gifford) J. Frankl. Inst. 142: 102.
— Lesson of. (B. Hubbard) Pop. Sci. Mo. 46: 586.
— Minnesota, Sept. 1, 1894. (H. B. Ayres) Garden & F. 7: 362.
— New French Law for Prevention of. (W. R. Fisher) Nature, 49: 233.
Forest Growth. (W. W. Robertson) Garden & F. 7: 138.
Forest Interests in relation to the American Mind. (J. B. Harrison) New Eng. M. n. s. 9: 417.
Forest Land for Investment. (B. E. Fernow) Garden and F. 7: 88.
Forest Lands in Massachusetts. (C. S. Plumb) Garden & F. 9: 52.
Forest Life, Tragic Incidents in. (E. Stewart) Canad. M. 8: 68.
— With the Woodlanders. Blackw. 153: 556. Same art. Ecl. M. 120: 673.
Forest Management. (Gifford Pinchot) Garden & F. 8: 309, 319.
Forest Planting. (H. N. Jarchow) Garden & F. 6: 238.
Forest Preserves, Why not more? (R. U. Johnson) R. of Rs. (N. Y.) 10: 651.
Forest Reservations. Garden & F. 5: 589.
— Adirondack Reservation. (C. S. Sargent) Garden & F. 7: 91.
— California. (C. S. Sargent) Garden & F. 9: 131.
— — Cascade Range in Danger. (C. S. Sargent) Garden & F. 9: 111.
— in the U. S., Fifteen New. R. of Rs. (N. Y.) 8: 67. — (E. R. Scidmore) Forum, 46: 792.
— Management of. Garden & F. 5: 20.
— More. Garden & F. 5: 25.
— Our National. Garden & F. 5: 613.
Forest Tithes. Cornh. 67: 293.
Forest-trees in Spring. (C. S. Sargent) Garden & F. 8: 191.
Forestry. (T. H. Haskins) Garden & F. 5: 125. — (J. Michael) J. Soc. Arts, 43: 93. — Quar. 179: 177.
— Afforestation in British Isles. (W. R. Fisher) Nature, 49: 601.

Forestry. American Forestry Association, 10th Annual Meeting. Garden & F. 5: 11.
— and the Abandoned Farm. (C. S. Plumb) Garden & F. 8: 162.
— and the N. Y. Constitution. (C. S. Sargent) Garden & F. 9: 451.
— as a Business. (W. J. Beal) Engin. M. 5: 82.
— at Atlanta Exposition. Garden & F. 8: 449.
— Battle of the Forests. (B. E. Fernow) Nature, 51: 116, 139.
— Black-walnut in the West. (C. A. Keffer) Garden & F. 8: 12.
— British. Blackw. 156: 647.
— by Proclamation. (C. S. Sargent) Garden & F. 7: 491.
— California Experiment Station. (C. H. Shinn) Garden & F. 8: 62.
— Care of National Forests. (C. S. Sargent) Garden & F. 6: 351. 7: 201.
— Congress of, at Albany. (C. S. Sargent) Garden & F. 6: 251. — Garden & F. 7: 109.
— Conifers at Kansas Agricultural College. (F. C. Sears) Garden & F. 9: 453, 462.
— Desolation of Central Tunis. (C. S. Sargent) Garden & F. 6: 481.
— Devastation of our National Forest Reservations. (C. S. Sargent) Garden & F. 7: 312.
— Eastern Texas. Garden & F. 5: 399.
— An Experiment. (M. C. Robbins) Garden & F. 5: 434.
— Experiment Station at Santa Monica. (F. M. Gallaher) Garden & F. 5: 262.
— Farms and Forests on the Carolina Foot Hills. (C. S. Sargent) Garden & F. 6: 441, 518.
— for the Farmer. (G. Pinchot) Garden & F. 5: 104.
— for Farms. (C. S. Sargent) Garden & F. 8: 411.
— Forest as modified by Human Agency. Garden & F. 5: 356, 369.
— Forest Policy of European Nations. (B. E. Fernow) Garden & F. 9: 33.
— Forest Preservation a Protection to the Soil. (C. S. Sargent) Garden & F. 7: 101.
— Furst's Protection of Woodlands. Garden & F. 6: 439.
— German Forests. (W. Seliger) Garden & F. 5: 214.
— German View of the Value of. (C. S. Sargent) Garden & F. 9: 61.
— Hybrid Oaks in Western Missouri. (B. F. Bush) Garden & F. 8: 32.
— in the Constitution of the State of N. Y. (C. S. Sargent) Garden & F. 7: 361.
— in Eastern Nebraska. (E. J. Hill) Garden & F. 5: 201.
— in France; Statistical Account of French Forests. (W. R. Fisher) Nature, 51: 64.
— in the Land-Grant Colleges. (C. S. Sargent) Garden & F. 7: 301.
— in the Michigan Agricultural College. (W. F. Beal) Garden & F. 8: 148.
— in Natal. (W. R. Fisher) Nature, 51: 234.
— in Pennsylvania. (C. S. Sargent) Garden & F. 7: 511. — Garden & F. 9: 159. — (C. S. Sargent) Garden & F. 9: 521.
— in Prussia. Garden & F. 5: 393.
— in Russia. Garden & F. 5: 417.
— in the West. (R. Douglas) Garden & F. 6: 136.
— Legislation in Pennsylvania. (C. S. Sargent) Garden & F. 6: 271.
— Lesson in. (C. S. Sargent) Garden & F. 7: 471.
— Lower California. Garden & F. 5: 183.
— Lumbering and. (C. S. Sargent) Garden & F. 6: 451.
Forestry. Lumbering on State Lands. (C. S. Sargent) Garden & F. 7: 151.
— Lumberman and. (C. S. Sargent) Garden & F. 7: 111.
— Manual of, by Dr. W. Schlich. (G. Pinchot) Garden & F. 9: 87, 99, 118.
— Mathews' Familiar Trees and their Leaves. Garden & F. 9: 359.
— Meeting of the American and N. J. State Associations. Garden & F. 8: 229.
— Minnesota Forestry Assoc. Garden & F. 9: 39.
— Misconception as to Forest Growth. (T. H. Haskins) Garden & F. 7: 58.
— Mixed Oak and Beech Forests of the Spassart. (D. Brandis) Garden & F. 7: 218–329.
— Movement in the U. S. Garden & F. 5: 34.
— National Policy. Garden & F. 5: 397.
— National Reserve on Southern Appalachian Mountains. Garden & F. 5: 325.
— Need of Forest Schools in America. (G. Pinchot) Garden & F. 8: 298.
— Need of Protecting Young Trees. (C. S. Sargent) Garden & F. 6: 139.
— a Neglected Industry. (P. Thompson) Canad. M. 8: 24.
— N. H. Commission, Report of. (C. S. Sargent) Garden & F. 6: 109.
— New Jersey Legislatures Act for. (C. S. Sargent) Garden & F. 7: 121.
— Nisbet on. Sat. R. 78: 391. — (W. R. Fisher) Nature, 50: 193.
— Nomenclature. (G. B. Sudworth) Garden & F. 5: 98.
— Notes of Mexican Travel. (C. G. Pringle) Garden & F. 6: 172–263. 9: 102.
— Object Lessons in. (C. S. Sargent) Garden & F. 7: 291.
— of India. Garden & F. 5: 219.
— On Broad Top, Pennsylvania. (M. L. Dock) Garden & F. 6: 86.
— Our Land Office System. Garden & F. 5: 345.
— Pine. (G. L. Goodale) Nation, 63: 425.
— Pinetum at Wellesley, Mass. Garden & F. 5: 385.
— Plunder of the Adirondack Reservation. (C. S. Sargent) Garden & F. 9: 101.
— Practical. (J. D. Lyman) Garden & F. 5: 266.
— Practical Work for Associations. Garden & F. 7: 272.
— Preservation of Forests. Garden & F. 5: 229.
— Profitableness of Forest-culture. Garden & F. 5: 250.
— Public Forests and Public Parks. Garden & F. 5: 542.
— Public Indifference. Garden & F. 5: 157.
— Reforesting Waste Lands in Holland. (J. Gifford) Garden & F. 9: 423.
— Relation of, to the State. Garden & F. 7: 69.
— Seasonable Work among the Trees. (C. S. Sargent) Garden & F. 8: 461.
— Second Growth in California. (C. H. Shinn) Garden & F. 6: 228.
— Segregation of Trees. (R. Ridgway) Garden & F. 6: 148.
— Sierra Club of California. (C. H. Shinn) Garden & F. 6: 81.
— Silva of North America. (C. S. Sargent) Garden & F. 5: 83.
— Southern Forests. (L. Greenlee) Garden & F. 5: 164.
— Spring in Virginia. (M. G. Van Rensselaer) Garden & F. 6: 208.
— Spruces and Firs on the Maine Coast. Garden & F. 5: 97.
— Study in Lower Schools. (E. J. Houston) J. Frankl. Inst. 137: 22–107.

Forestry. Suggestions from the White Pine Forests of Minnesota. (H. B. Ayres) Garden & F. 6: 348.
— Summer in the Pines. (Mary Treat) Garden & F. 6: 314.
— Teak Forests of Burma. (C. S. Sargent) Garden & F. 9: 311.
— Timely Lessons from the Forests of India. (C. S. Sargent) Garden & F. 9: 191.
— Trees in Visalia, Cal. (C. H. Shinn) Garden & F. 9: 382.
— Trees of Minor Importance for Western Planting. (F. A. Waugh) Garden & F. 9: 23, 42.
— Western Larch. (C. S. Sargent) Garden & F. 9: 491.
— Western N. Y. Woodlands. (E. J. Hill) Garden & F. 8: 342, 382.
— What is? (C. S. Sargent) Garden & F. 9: 11.
— White Mountain. Garden & F. 5: 517.
— White Pines. Garden & F. 5: 1.
— Why we need Skilled Foresters. (C. S. Sargent) Garden & F. 8: 131.
— Wild Garden of the Sierra. (C. H. Shinn) Garden & F. 9: 343.
— Woods of Minnesota. Garden & F. 5: 297.
Forests and the Army. (J. D. W. French) Garden & F. 6: 95.
— and Commons of England and the Public, Lefevre on. Sat. R. 77: 236.
— and Floods. (C. S. Sargent) Garden & F. 9: 441.
— and Forestry in Europe and America. (H. Lambert) New Eng. M. n. s. 8: 664.
— and Rivers. Garden & F. 8: 371.
— Climatic and National Economic Influence of. (J. Nisbet) Nature, 49: 302.
— Climatic Influence of. (B. E. Fernow) Garden & F. 6: 147.
— Coniferous. (R. Douglas) Garden & F. 6: 252.
— Conservancy of, by the State. (J. B. Harrison) Cosmopol. 13: 300.
— English Commons and. Spec. 72: 303.
— in Danger. (E. T. Toker) Canad. M. 1: 339.
— Management and Protection of. (D. Brandis) Nature, 53: 510, 535.
— National, and the Government. (C. S. Sargent) Garden & F. 6: 511.
— of California. Garden & F. 5: 213, 237. — (C. Purdy) Garden & F. 5: 538.
— of Japan, Sargent's Studies of. (C. E. Bessey) Am. Natural. 29: 1049.
— of Minnesota. Garden & F. 7: 418.
— of the National Domain. (C. S. Sargent) Garden & F. 8: 1, 51.
— of Ne-Ha-Sa-Ne Park in Northern N. Y. Garden & F. 6: 168.
— of Pennsylvania. (J. F. Rothrock) J. Frankl. Inst. 140: 105.
— of Siberia. Garden & F. 7: 399.
— of the South. (H. L. Tolman) Garden & F. 6: 159.
— of the Wabash Valley. (C. S. Sargent) Garden & F. 8: 101.
— of Washington. (L. H. Wall) Garden & F. 5: 57.
— A Plan to save the. Cent. 27: 626.
— Preservation of, in California. (T. Magee) Overland, n. s. 19: 658.
— Reproductive Powers of. (L. C. Corbett) Garden & F. 9: 234.
— Tropical, Plant Life and Death in. (J. Rodway) Nat. Sci. 1: 528.
— Wasted. (C. S. Sargent) Garden & F. 6: 201.
— White Mountain. (J. B. Harrison) Garden & F. 6: 106.
— — in Danger. (J. H. Ward) Atlan. 71: 247.
Forests, White Mountain, Preservation of. (G. B. James) New Eng. M. n. s. 8: 712.
Forever and a Day; a story. (K. Jarboe) Munsey, 13: 624.
Forfarshire. (J. H. Crawford) Scot. R. 20: 276.
Forfeiture, Relief from. (W. C. Smith) Jurid. R. 5: 125.
Forged Madonna, The. (R. M. Strong) Chamb. J. 72: 774-809.
Forgeries, Edinburgh. Eng. Illust. 10: 466.
Forgers, Bank, and their Methods. Bank. M. (N. Y.) 52: 438.
Forgery as a Profession. (R. A. Pinkerton) No. Am. 158: 454.
— of Fictitious Names. (T. W. Brown) Am. Law R. 30: 500.
Forget not yet; a poem. (Sir T. Wyat) M. of Art, 18: 56.
Forgetting, Duty of. Spec. 71: 626.
Forging Press, The. (W. D. Allen) Cassier, 1: 292.
Forgotten Books. (A. M. Earle) Bach. of Arts, 3: 498.
Form and Formal Thought. (P. Carus) Open Court, 2: 1310, 1349, 1369.
— and Life. (G. Pouchet) Pop. Sci. Mo. 45: 521.
Formal, The. (P. Carus) Open Court, 7: 3679.
Formalin. (L. Stern) Am. Arch. 47: 21.
— as a Preservative Medium for Marine Animals. (J. Hornell) Nat. Sci. 6: 416. — (F. C. Kenyon) Am. Natural. 29: 82.
Formation of a Sphinx; a story. (W. Browne) Canad. M. 6: 268.
Formes, Karl. (A. Cox-Stephens) Music, 3: 625.
Formosa. (Alex. Man) Asia. R. 14: 56. — Geog. J. 2: 441. — (R. S. Gundry) Sat. R. 79: 574. — Liv. Age, 206: 440.
Forest, Gen. Nathan B. (G. Wolseley) Un. Serv. M. 5: 1, 113. Same art. So. Hist. Pap. 20: 325.
Forrester, Alfred Henry, as a Graphic Humorist. (G. S. Layard) M. of Art, 19: 393.
Fort Frederick. (H. Stockbridge) Am. Hist. Reg. 2: 748, 862.
Fort Griswold Massacre. New Eng. M. n. s. 12: 668.
Fort Independence, Boston. (M. C. Goodwin) Bost. 2: 644.
Fort Jenkins, Traditions of. (M. B. J. Richart) Am. Hist. Reg. 2: 1415. 3: 28-579.
Fort Mountain, Georgia. (R. Shackleton) Am. Antiq. 15: 295.
Fort Warren, Boston Harbor. (C. Campbell) Bost. 2: 259.
Fort Winthrop, Boston Harbor. (Mabel P. Cummins) Bost. 2: 491.
Forth River, The Inches of. (T. P. White) Scot. R. 26: 217.
Fortification. War's Use of the Engines of Peace. (J. L. Bent) Atlan. 73: 459.
Fortifications, Clarke on. Sat. R. 74: 423.
Fortitude. Spec. 71: 297.
Fortune, Byways to, by Sea. Blackw. 152: 839. Same art. Liv. Age, 196: 354.
Fortune-tellers. Spec. 70: 603.
Fortune-telling in America. (H. C. Bolton) J. Am. Folk-Lore, 8: 299.
Fortune's Wheel; a story. (G. B. Burgin) Good Words, 34: 632.
Fortunes, Large. Spec. 68: 775.
Fortuny, Mariano. M. of Art, 4: 77.
Fosca; a story. (A. Beresford) Argosy, 62: 614.
Foscolo-letters. (J. W. Mario) Nation, 54: 427.
Foss, S. W., with portrait. Bk. News, 11: 473.
Fossil Animals, Hutchinson on. Sat. R. 78: 305.

Fossil Botany, Solms-Laubach's. Sat. R. 74: 345.
Fossil Floras and Climate. (W. Dawson) Nature, 47: 556.
Fossil Men. (L. A. Fox) Luth. Q. 22: 11.
Fossil Plants of Canada. (J. W. Dawson) Nat. Sci. 4: 177.
— Report on. (Lester F. Ward) Nat. Geog. M. 2: 199.
Fossil Vertebrates from the Loup Fork Beds of Northwestern Nebraska. (J. B. Hatcher) Am. Natural. 28: 236.
— in U. S. National Museum. (R. Lydekker) Nature, 46: 295.
Fossil Wood. (A. S. Wilson) Knowl. 17: 43.
Fossils and Fossilization. (L. P. Gratacap) Am. Natural. 30: 902, 993.
— Chalk, Preparation and Mounting of. (A. W. Rowe) Nat. Sci. 9: 303.
— from Columbia Co., N. Y., Annotated List of. (J. M. Clarke) Am. J. Sci. 144: 411.
— Gigantic, New. (I. H. Barbour) Science, 19: 99.
— Living. (R. Lydekker) Knowl. 16: 55.
— Recent, near Boston. (W. Upham) Am. J. Sci. 143: 201.
Fossilization of Animal Bones, Presence of Fluorine as a Test for. (T. Wilson) Am. Natural. 29: 301.
Foster, James P., with portrait. (L. A. Bond) Nat'l M. (N. Y. '91) 16: 121.
Foster, John. (D. E. Snow) Bib. Sac. 51: 20.
Foster, Robert, of Kingston, Mass., Memoranda by. (C. E. Briggs) N. E. Reg. 48: 182.
Foster's Letter of Marque; a Tale of Old Sydney. (L. Becke and W. Jeffery) Eng. Illust. 16: 369.
Fotheringay, Tragedy of, Scott on. (Goldwin Smith) Nation, 61: 30.
"Foudroyant," The Ship. Sat. R. 74: 324.
Foudroyants, The Two. Macmil. 67: 66.
Fouilloux, Jacques de; a Master of Woodcraft. Macmil. 69: 462.
Foulis Art Academy, Glasgow, and James Tassie. (J. M. Gray) M. of Art, 17: 150.
Found Wanting; a novel. (A. F. Hector) Belgra. 80: 1—82: 337.
Found Wanting; a story. (F. M. F. Skene) Argosy, 58: 380.
Foundations, Bridge and Building. (G. E. Thomas) Am. Arch. 54: 70.
Founding a Society; a story. (B. A. Clarke) Idler, 10: 327.
Foundry, Economics in a. (C. O. Heggem) Cassier, 10: 51.
Fountain Air Brush, Burdick's. Dub. R. 115: 158.
Fountains. (L. Benouville) Am. Arch. 38: 67–127.
— Grotesque Heads for. M. of Art, 4: 187.
Fouquet, Jean. Nation, 63: 492.
Four as a Sacred Number. (A. W. Buckland) Anthrop. J. 25: 96.
Four Cameos; a symposium. (G. W. Steevens) New R. 12: 536.
Four-dimensional Space. (A. Bostwick) New Sci. R. 2: 146.
Four Dimensions. (C. S. Wake) Science, 19: 330.—(J. H. Hyslop) Philos. R. 5: 352.
— Mathematical and Spiritualistic. (H. Schubert) Monist, 3: 402.
Four Hundred, Myth of the. (Mrs. Burton Harrison) Cosmopol. 19: 329.
Four O'Clock in the Morning. (O. T. Miller) Atlan. 71: 729.
Four Students, The. (C. F. Keary) Macmil. 65: 226. Same art. Ecl. M. 118: 344.
Four Wise Virgins; a sketch. (S. J. A. Fitz-Gerald) Belgra. 86: 289.

Fourierism. (W. B. Shaw) New Eng. M. n. s. 8: 773.
Fournier, New Programme of, for French Navy. (C. R. R. Kent) Un. Serv. (Phila.) 16: 197.
Fourth-class Appointment, A; a story. (M. Deland) Harper, 84: 265.
Fourth Estate, The. Gent. M. n. s. 53: 40.
Fourth of July, First, Anecdotes of. (Elisabeth M. Williams) M. Am. Hist. 30: 91.
— How it should be celebrated. (J. W. Howe) Forum, 15: 567.
— in Antwerp, Celebrating the. (G. W. Edwards) Cent. 26: 457.
Fovea, Normal Defect of Vision in. (C. L. Franklin) Psychol. R. 2: 137.
Fowler, Edward Payson, with portrait. Nat'l M. (N. Y. '91) 19: 315.
Fowler, Frank. (R. Cortissoz) Q. Illust. 2: 51.
Fowler, Samuel P. (J. W. Dean) N. E. Reg. 46: 339.
Fowlers and Wild Fowling. Blackw. 151: 73.
Fowling on Longshore. Macmil. 68: 425.
Fowls of the Air. (H. Maxwell) Good Words, 36: 771.
Fox, George. Macmil. 68: 372. Same art. Liv. Age, 199: 259. Same art. Ecl. M. 122: 57.
Fox, John, jr., with portrait. Bk. Buyer, 13: 351.
Fox, Red, Mystery of the. (J. C. Harris) Scrib. M. 14: 418.
Fox Hunt, a Good Old. (E. W. Sandys) Outing, 28: 29.
— on the Little Obed. (M. W. Armstrong) Outing, 23: 145.
— A Rough-and-Ready. (H. Rave) Outing, 25: 74.
— Shepherd's. Temp. Bar, 107: 578.
Fox-hunters and Farmers. (Earl of Suffolk) National, 24: 546.
— — Lord Suffolk on: A Reply. (E. Heneage) National, 24: 764.
Fox-hunting. (R. H. Titherington) Munsey, 10: 571. —(E. L. Dorsey) Outing, 21: 13.—Outing, 27: 193.
— by Moonlight. (M. G. Humphreys) Outing, 26: 426.
— Cub-hunting. Sat. R. 74: 529.
— Decline of. Sat. R. 79: 343.
— in England. (C. W. Whitney) Harper, 89: 489.
— in the Genesee Valley. (E. S. Martin) Harper, 85: 511.
— in Great Britain. (R. M. Dene) Outing, 19: 292.
— in Kentucky. (J. Fox, jr.) Cent. 28: 620.
— in the United States. (C. W. Whitney) Harper, 90: 495.
— in Virginia. (D. B. Fitzgerald) Lippinc. 58: 824.
— Radcliffe on. Sat. R. 74: 745.
— Vyner on. Ath. '92, 1: 236.
Fox River, Black Bass Fishing in. (F. J. Wells) Outing, 28: 130.
Fox-hounds and Greyhounds. Spec. 70: 416.
— Puppies. Sat. R. 73: 681.
— Training of. (Y. Stewart) Eng. Illust. 16: 329.
Fox's Heart, The. (I. Abrahams) Jew. Q. 1: 216.
Fragmentary Correspondence, A. (Beatrix Duff) National, 23: 139.
Fragments. (J. R. Lowell) Cent. 26: 24.
France, Anatole. (Y. Blaze de Bury) Fortn. 66: 795.
— as a Critic. Sat. R. 80: 41.
— Chief Influences of his Career. Forum, 20: 344.
— Stories. Spec. 69: 794.
France Adorée; a story. (Ida M. Tarbell) Scrib. M. 11: 643.
France and Algeria. Sat. R. 74: 525.
— and Austria in 1781–1790; Correspondence of Count Mercy-Argenteau. (A. W. Ward) Eng. Hist. R. 7: 792.
— and Belgium, The Danger in. Macmil. 72: 1.
— and her Colonies. (L. Dutilh de la Tuque) Asia. R. 12: 78.

France and England. (J. Simon) Contemp. 67: 783.
— — and Russia. (T. H. S. Escott) Fortn. 66: 648. Same art. Ecl. M. 127: 731.
— — Attitude of France. (F. A. Maxse) National, 25: 851.
— — French Feeling. (André Lebon) National, 23: 49.
— — Misunderstandings of. Macmil. 75: 15.
— — Relations of. (F. de Pressensé) 19th Cent. 39: 189.
— — Les Sentiments de la France pour l'Angleterre. (E. Ollivier) New R. 12: 46.
— and Germany, Twenty-five Years of Peace. Sat. R. 80: 261.
— and her New Allies. (C. R. Roylance-Kent) Macmil. 70: 313.
— and Italy, Case against. (W. L. Alden) 19th Cent. 36: 175.
— — Question of. (E. Armstrong) Scot. R. 25: 141.
— and the Papacy. (C. B. R. Kent) Macmil. 67: 179.
— and Russia, Alliance between. (P. de Coubertin) R. of Rs. (N. Y.) 13: 700.
— — in 1893. Reception of Admiral Avellan. Spec. 71: 537.
— — Industrial Alliance of. (A. Laugel) Nation, 61: 114.
— — Instructions to French Ambassadors, 1648–1789, Rambaud on. (R. Lodge) Eng. Hist. R. 7: 373.
— — Pageantry in Politics. New R. 15: 545. Same art. Ecl. M. 127: 746.
— and Siam. (H. N. D. Prendergast) Asia. R. 21: 225.
— and Switzerland, Convention between. (C. Schefer) Nation, 56: 250.
— Army of. (F. N. Maude) Un. Serv. M. 4: 281.
— — Conscript's View of. (H. Belloc) Contemp. 63: 871. Same art. Un. Serv. (Phila.) 10: 160.
— — Discipline of Troops in Colonial Conquests. (J. D. Ross) Chamb. J. 72: 140.
— — Health Experiments in. (S. Dewey) Pop. Sci. Mo. 48: 204.
— Attractiveness of. Spec. 69: 342.
— The Bar in. (G. W. Wilton) Jurid. R. 3: 223, 331.
— Baring-Gould's Deserts in Southern. (A. B. Hart) Nation, 60: 53.
— By Wheel from Havre to Paris. (J. W. Fosdick) Outing, 20: 83, 197.
— Cabinet Crisis, 1892. Pub. Opin. 14: 300. — Sat. R. 74: 582, 729. — Spec. 69: 842, 913.
— — 1893. Spec. 71: 788, 824.
— Cabinet Government in. (G. Bradford) Nation, 58: 161, 181.
— Catholicism and Democracy in. (T. Stanton) Open Court, 1: 566.
— Celtic Monuments in. (R. J. Mullin) Canad. M. 2: 252.
— Centralization in. (A. Laugel) Nation, 61: 221.
— and Decentralization in. (T. Stanton) Open Court, 9: 4632.
— Chamber of Deputies, Membership of. Spec. 70: 725.
— — of 1889. (C. Schefer) Nation, 57: 62.
— Chambers. (J. W. Burgess) Chaut. 20: 272.
— Church in. Eng. R. 2: 295.
— — and State in. Am. Cath. Q. 17: 333.
— — The New Grievance of. Spec. 74: 714.
— Coast Defence of. (C. A. Voigt) Un. Serv. M. 6: 357.
— College of. (F. Carrel) Fortn. 59: 366. Same art. Liv. Age, 197: 387.
— Colonial Policy of. Ed. R. 177: 354. — (F. H. Geffcken) New R. 6: 723.
— Colonies in the East. (C. H. E. Carmichael) Asia. R. 8: 312.
— — Question of. (C. Schefer) Nation, 55: 161.
France, Commercial Policy of, Recent. (E. Levasseur) J. Pol. Econ. 1: 20. — Blackw. 154: 574.
— Constitution, Development of Present. (R. Saleilles) Ann. Am. Acad. Pol. Sci. 6: 1.
— Constitutional and Organic Laws of, 1875–89, with an Historical Introduction. (C. F. A. Currier) Ann. Am. Acad. Pol. Sci. 3: supp. 119.
— Constitutional Revolution in 1895. Sat. R. 81: 188.
— Criminal Law in. (Mme. J. Adam) No. Am. 156: 160.
— Criminal Procedure in. (M. McIlvraith) Law Q. 8: 193.
— Currency of. Bank. M. (Lond.) 60: 340.
— Depopulation of. (S. Dewey) Westm. 146: 597.
— Diary in, Wordsworth's. Eng. R. 4: 124.
— Divorce in. (J. Challamel) Jurid. R. 2: 143.
— Early Metallurgy of. (P. Mahler and B. H. Thwaite) Cassier, 5: 305.
— Elections in, 1893. Spec. 71: 261, 328. — Sat. R. 76: 231.
— Experimental Psychology in. (A. Binet) Open Court, 2: 1427.
— Finances of the Republic. (D. MacG. Means) Nation, 61: 443.
— Folk-Lore of. (A. Lang) Folk-Lore Rec. 1: 99.
— Foreign Companies in. (C. A. K. Hall) Jurid. R. 2: 234.
— "Fraternal," Maxse on. (C. C. P. Fitzgerald) National, 26: 258.
— Genius of. (H. Ellis) Atlan. 75: 72.
— Geographical Position of. (C. F. A. Currier) Chaut. 24: 26.
— Girlhood in. (L. de San Carlos) No. Am. 157: 81.
— Government of. (P. de Coubertin) R. of Rs. (N. Y.) 13: 307.
— — since 1870. Ed. R. 184: 185.
— Heroines of History of. (R. H. Titherington) Munsey, 10: 45.
— Historic Monuments of. (Russell Sturgis) Architec. Rec. 4: 308.
— History. Ancien Régime. (St. George Mivart) Am. Cath. Q. 18: 518.
— — — Fall of. Quar. 177: 212. Same art. Liv. Age, 199: 3.
— — 18th Century. Eng. R. 2: 88.
— — 1715–1815, Century of French History. Atlan. 71: 682.
— — Revolution. (Comte de Lally) New R. 7: 197. Same art. Liv. Age, 195: 220.
— — — Carlyle and Taine on. (H. S. Wilson) Gent. M. n. s. 53: 341.
— — — Carlyle's History of, Corrigenda in. (J. G. Alger) Westm. 145: 14.
— — — Directory, Memoirs of. (A. Laugel) Nation, 60: 144, 162, 182. — (H. M. Stephens) Am. Hist. R. 1: 473.
— — — Financial Causes of. (F. Rothschild) 19th Cent. 33: 375, 652. Same art. Liv. Age, 197: 195, 611. — Bank. M. (N. Y.) 47: 853.
— — — Grégoire and. (W. Gibson) 19th Cent. 34: 272. Same art. Liv. Age, 198: 759.
— — — Idyll during. Liv. Age, 200: 195.
— — — Lowell's Eve of. (A. V. Dicey) Nation, 57: 311.
— — — Miles' Correspondence on. (H. M. Stephens) Eng. Hist. R. 7: 184.
— — — Orators of. (E. Purcell) Acad. 42: 449. — (A. V. Dicey) Nation, 55: 377. — Spec. 69: 687.
— — — Paris in the Time of. M. of Art, 10: 48, 103.
— — — Sea Power and, Mahan on. Atlan. 71: 556. — (F. S. Bassett) Dial (Ch.) 14: 109. — Sat. R. 75: 72.

France. History. Revolution, 1792; Year 1. (D. G. Ritchie) Int. J. Ethics, **3**: 75.
— — — 1793–1893. (A. D. Vandam) Fortn. **60**: 377. Same art. Liv. Age, **199**: 284.
— — — Stephens' History of. Sat. R. **73**: 25.
— — — Symes on. Spec. **69**: 821.
— — — Von Holst's. Nation, **60**: 347. — (D. L. Shorey) Dial (Ch.) **18**: 10.
— — — Work of Committees of Legislation and Public Instruction in the Convention. (H. M. Stephens) Yale R. **4**: 305.
— — 1st Empire, Life under, Broc's. (A. Laugel) Nation, **60**: 297.
— — 2d Empire, Personal History of. (A. D. Vandam) No. Am. **160**: 1–726.
— — — Life in the Tuileries under. (A. L. Bicknell) Cent. **28**: 709.
— — — Side-lights on. (W. Graham) Fortn. **62**: 278, 498.
— — Franco-Prussian War. (M. Halstead) Cosmopol. **17**: 424, 603. — (R. C. Schiedt) Ref. Q. **43**: 149.
— — — Empress Eugénie and. (A. Forbes) 19th Cent. **32**: 285. Same art. Ecl. M. **119**: 457. Same art. Liv. Age, **195**: 37. — Reply (J. L. A. Simmons) 19th Cent. **32**: 430.
— — — Events leading up to. (E. Pinard) New R. **6**: 652. Same art. Liv. Age, **194**: 342.
— — — French Scare of 1870. (— de Blowitz) Harper, **86**: 948.
— — — Incidents of. (A. Forbes) Un. Serv. M. **8**: 431, 541.
— — — Origin of. (M. Smith) Nation, **62**: 122, 142.
— — Taine's Modern Régime. Ath. '94, **2**: 215. — (A. V. Dicey) Nation, **58**: 274.
— — Third Republic, Beginnings of. (A. D. Vandam) Fortn. **64**: 776, 902.
— in the East. (F. I. Scudamore) Time, **5**: 554, 686. **6**: 223, 560.
— in the 14th Century, Private Life in. (A. M. F. Robinson) Fortn. **57**: 369. Same art. Liv. Age, **193**: 213.
— Inland Navigation in, Census of, 1891. J. Statis. Soc. **55**: 482.
— Institute of. (H. de Varigny) Nature, **52**: 459.
— Jews of. (S. Debré) Jew. Q. **3**: 367.
— Law Schools of. (M. McIlwraith) Law Q. **6**: 42.
— Local Government in. (M. McIlwraith) Jurid. R. **1**: 163.
— Middle-class Life in. (L. de San Carlos) No. Am. **156**: 478.
— Modern, Revolution and Reaction in, Dickinson's. Ath. '92, **2**: 912.
— Moral Revival in. (A. Gorren) Atlan. **72**: 382.
— Naval Manœuvres, 1891. Un. Serv. M. **4**: 264, 321.
— — 1892. Un. Serv. M. **6**: 113.
— Navy, Early Years of. (G. Winterwood) Good Words, **35**: 110, 195.
— — 1639–1792. Sat. R. **74**: 203.
— — Loir's. (C. H. Stockton) Nation, **56**: 239.
— — New Programme of. (C. B. Roylance-Kent) Fortn. **66**: 302. Same art. Un. Serv. (Phila.) **16**: 197.
— Neo-Christian Movement in. (E. M. de Vogüé) Harper, **84**: 234.
— Newspapers in. (E. Delille) 19th Cent. **31**: 474.
— of To-day, Betham-Edwards'. Ath. '92, **2**: 85. — Spec. **69**: 322.
— Orleanism. New R. **13**: 19.
— Palaces of. (R. H. Titherington) Munsey, **9**: 621.
— People of. How they live. Leis. Hour, **42**. 394–549.
— Political Situation in. (G. Monod) Contemp. **67**: 592.
France, Political Situation in, 1893. (G. Monod) Contemp. **64**: 613. — (Y. Guyot) 19th Cent. **33**: 156.
— Political Stability and Economic Unrest in. (L. Lévy-Bruhl) Forum, **14**: 653.
— Politics in, in 1891. (G. Monod) Liv. Age, **192**: 259.
— — in 1892, Muddle in. Spec. **68**: 292.
— — — Party Government in France. Spec. **69**: 119.
— — — State of Parties. (C. Schefer) Nation, **54**: 482.
— — in 1893. Carnot's New Essay. Spec. **70**: 443.
— — — Election of Ferry. Spec. **70**: 281.
— — — French Lessons for English Politicians. (F. H. Hill) National, **20**: 732.
— — — The New Chamber of Deputies. (Emily Crawford) National, **22**: 189.
— — — Programme of the Premier. Spec. **71**: 740.
— — in 1896. (L. C. R. Duncombe-Jewell) Month, **88**: 217.
— Population of, Levasseur on. (R. Mayo-Smith) Pol. Sci. Q. **8**: 124.
— — Problem of. (Robt. Donald) Univ. R. **3**: 259.
— Presidents and Politics in. (A. Filon) Fortn. **63**: 337.
— "Pretenders" of. (W. F. Day) Munsey, **10**: 127.
— Protectionist Reaction in. (H. A. L. Fisher) Econ. J. **6**: 341.
— Protestantism in, Benevolences of. (L. S. Houghton) Char. R. **4**: 65.
— Protestantism, Liberal, in. (G. Bonet-Maury) Chr. Lit. **15**: 148.
— Recent Sociological Tendencies in. (J. H. Tufts) Am. J. Sociol. **1**: 446.
— Religious Outlook in, 1893. (T. Stanton) Monist, **3**: 450.
— Religious Question in, 1892. (C. Schefer) Nation, **55**: 408.
— Renaissance in. (G. A. T. Middleton) Archit. Rec. **6**: 126.
— a Republic. (Karl Blind) Time, **19**: 268.
— Republic of. (C. M. Andrews) Chaut. **24**: 10.
— — Third. (A. D. Vandam) Fortn. **60**: 377.
— Republicanism in. (F. V. Fisher) Westm. **139**: 229.
— Revival of, 1870–95. (A. Cohn) Atlan. **75**: 82.
— Revival of the Spiritual Ideal in. (Laura M. Lane) National, **21**: 424.
— Roads of. (M. H. Catherwood) Atlan. **77**: 355.
— Rural Dwellings in. (E. Castelot) Econ. J. **5**: 89.
— Senate of. (P. Robiquet) Jurid. R. **6**: 197.
— Social Prospect in. Spec. **71**: 901.
— Socialism and Militarism in. (A. Laugel) Nation, **58**: 8.
— Socialists in. (T. Stanton) Nation, **59**: 98.
— Society in during the Restoration. Eng. R. **4**: 100.
— Songs of, Popular. (E. C. Price) Contemp. **62**: 105.
— under the Regency, Perkins on. (G. Smith) Nation, **55**: 307.
— Universal Suffrage in. (J. Macé) No. Am. **156**: 27.
— Universities of, Admission of American Students to. (H. W. Cottell) Science, n. s. **3**: 341. — (S. Newcomb) Nation, **63**: 400.
— Village Life and Politics in. (W. Tuckwell) Contemp. **61**: 65.
— Village Life in. Contemp. **65**: 376. — (Marquis de Chambrun) Chaut. **18**: 643.
— Wealth of, and of other Countries. (A. de Foville) J. Statis. Soc. **56**: 597.
— Where Milk and Honey flow. (C. W. Wood) Argosy, **61**: 52.
Francesca di Rimini. (L. de La Ramé) Cosmopol. **18**: 259.
Franchise in England, Early Parliamentary. (T. Hodgins) Canad. M. **3**: 395.
Franchises, Inconsistent. (F. K. Henry) Lippinc. **54**: 416.

Francia, Il. Madonna and Child, with St. Anne. (G. Allen) Eng. Illust. **14**: 27.
Francis, St., of Assisi. (P. A. Sheehan) Irish. Mo. **18**: 468. — (Mme. Vincent) Liv. Age, **193**: 473. — (M. S. Stillman) Nation, **55**: 317.
— Sabatier's Life of. (C. A. Scott) Crit. R. **4**: 348. — (A. Laugel) Nation, **58**: 100. — (R. Steele) Acad. **46**: 96. — (C. A. L. Richards) Dial (Ch.) **17**: 150. — (B. B. Warfield) Presb. & Ref. R. **6**: 158. — Church Q. **40**: 436.
— Some Thoughts on. Macmil. **69**: 277. Same art. Liv. Age, **200**: 771.
Francis de Sales, St. (L. W. Bacon) Chr. Lit. **12**: 65. — Chr. Lit. **15**: 29, 112, 204. — Spec. **70**: 228.
Francis I., of France. (A. M. F. Robinson) M. of Art, **8**: 84.
— as an Art Patron. (F. M. Robinson) M. of Art, **13**: 329.
— Portraits of. (R. Heath) M. of Art, **5**: 366.
Francis Joseph, Emperor of Austria. (A. Fournier) Forum, **21**: 201.
Franciscans. English Popular Preaching in the 14th Century. (Lucy T. Smith) Eng. Hist. R. **7**: 25.
Franck, Richard. Bookworm, **6**: 112.
Franckenstein, George Arbogast von. (J. Alexander) Cath. World, **55**: 32.
Franco, Niccolò. The First Castilian Inquisitor. (H. C. Lea) Am. Hist. R. **1**: 46.
Franco-Russian Alliance. (A. Smith) Univ. R. **8**: 373.
Frangipani Ring, The. (L. Villari) Contemp. **69**: 879.
Frank and the Polish Frankists. (W. R. Morfill) Acad. **49**: 73.
Frankalmoign in 12th and 13th Centuries. (F. W. Maitland) Law Q. **7**: 354.
Frankford, Ky. So. M. **3**: 453.
Franklin, Benjamin, and Alexander Wedderburn. (T. J. Chapman) Nat'l M. (N. Y. '91) **17**: 35.
— as an Economist. (W. A. Wetzel) J. H. Univ. Stud. **13**: 419.
— Early Years of. (T. J. Chapman) Nat'l M. (N. Y. '91) **15**: 258.
— Explanatory Remarks. (P. L. Ford) Nation, **59**: 60, 76.
— Neglected Incident in Life of. (E. J. James) Nation, **60**: 296.
— 189th Birthday Celebration of. Critic, **26**: 69.
— Portrait of. M. Am. Hist. **27**: 472.
— — New. (P. L. Ford) Scrib. M. **15**: 617.
— Study of. (E. P. Powell) Arena, **8**: 477.
— Was he a Plagiarist? (Kate Stephens) Bookman, **4**: 24.
Franklin, Sir John. (Sir H. Elliott) 19th Cent. **32**: 118. Same art. Liv. Age, **194**: 579. Same art. Un. Serv. (Phila.) **8**: 228.
— Arctic Expedition, Fiftieth Anniversary of. Geog. J. **6**: 31.
— Work of. Leis. Hour, **44**: 493.
Franklin and Marshall College, Needs of, in 1894. (R. C. Schiedt) Ref. Q. **41**: 117.
Franks. Longm. **24**: 159.
— Conversion of the. (R. Parsons) Am. Cath. Q. **21**: 497.
— Salic, and their War-lord, Clovis. (J. J. O'Shea) Cath. World, **63**: 823.
Franz, Robert. (J. S. Shedlock) Acad. **42**: 394. — Ath. '92, **2**: 598. — (W. F. Apthorp) Atlan. **72**: 488, 638. — (P. Jennings) Music, **4**: 397.
— An Hour with. (H. T. Finck) Cent. **24**: 237.
Franz Josef Land. Leis. Hour, **45**: 430.
— English Expedition to. Dub. R. **115**: 178.
— Geography of. (A. Montefiore) Geog. J. **3**: 492.
Fraser, Jas., Second Bishop of Manchester. (C. D. Gordon) Time, **16**: 461.
Fraser, Patrick, Lord. (H. Goudy) Jurid. R. **1**: 178.
Fraser, Simon. (C. H. McIntosh) Canad. M. **8**: 150.
Fraternalism and Paternalism. (E. P. Powell) Educa. **13**: 468.
Frau Aja. *See* Goethe, J. W. von, Mother of.
Fraud and Embezzlement: Causes and Remedies. (A. R. Barrett) Arena, **14**: 196.
— Definition of. (M. M. Bigelow) Law Q. **3**: 419.
Frauds, Statute of, A Doubt on. (E. C. C. Firth) Law Q. **9**: 366.
Fraudulent Authoress, A; a story. (E. N. L. Fry) Belgra. **80**: 382.
Frazer, Persifor, Lieut.-Col., did not break his Parole. (P. Frazer) Pennsyl. M. **18**: 73.
Freak of Cupid, A. Temp. Bar, **109**: 183, 427. Same art. Liv. Age, **211**: 771–843.
Freaks. (C. Robinson) Lippinc. **53**: 277.
Freda; a story. (M. E. S. Penn) Argosy, **61**: 760.
Frederic, Harold, with portrait. Bk. Buyer, **8**: 151.
— Illumination. (F. Danby) Sat. R. **81**: 295. — (M. C. Birchenough) 19th Cent. **40**: 768.
Frederici; a Fatal First Night. (C. Warner) Theatre, **28**: 29.
Frederick the Great. Ed. R. **181**: 373.
— and the Lawyers. (O. F. Hershey) Green Bag, **8**: 58.
— Lavisse's Youth of. Spec. **69**: 619. — (C. H. Cooper) Dial (Ch.) **14**: 47.
— Menzel's Illustrations to Works of. (H. Zimmern) M. of Art, **7**: 476.
— A Mistaken Imperial Celebration. (K. Blind) 19th Cent. **40**: 1010.
Frederick the Wise and the Castle Church at Wittenberg. (J. Köstlin) Luth. Q. **23**: 211.
Free-board, Easy Method for Determining or Comparing. (A. Bod) J. Frankl. Inst. **138**: 367.
Free Boarder, The. (S. M. Stevens) Bach. of Arts, **3**: 655.
Free Burghs in the U. S. (J. H. Blodgett) Nat. Geog. M. **7**: 116.
Free Church Congress, 1894. (R. Westrope) Chr. Lit. **11**: 20.
Free List Vagaries. Theatre, **32**: 64.
Free Pardon. (M. Hunt) Longm. **22**: 135.
Free Thought, Crisis in. (S. Dewey) Westm. **143**: 547.
— its Truth and Errors. Open Court, **5**: 2902.
Free Trade. (H. Kingerly) Am. J. Pol. **1**: 496.
— and Protection. (J. Jarrett) Am. J. Pol. **1**: 529. — (T. B. Reed) Our Day, **13**: 156.
— — Viewed Morally. (A. Walkley) Am. J. Pol. **3**: 512.
— and Sugar Refining in England. (E. E. Williams) New R. **15**: 410.
— Edward Atkinson and his Economic Methods. Soc. Econ. **3**: 129. **3**: 227.
— Atkinson *vs.* Atkinson. (S. N. D. North) Soc. Econ. **3**: 341.
— British Wheat Production. Soc. Econ. **8**: 201.
— Case for Free Imports, A. (Marquis of Lorne) No. Am. **159**: 252.
— Decline of Cobdenism. (S. Low) 19th Cent. **40**: 173.
— Effect of an Import Duty. (J. Edgcome) National, **20**: 441.
— England's Policy of. Gunton's M. **11**: 202.
— Farreresqueries of. (F. Greenwood) National, **20**: 624.
— Federative Powers of. (A. Withy) Westm. **141**: 353.
— Foreign Market Delusion. Gunton's M. **11**: 249.
— From Cobden to Chamberlain. (E. Salmon) Fortn. **65**: 975.

Free Trade, Has England profited by? (Lord Masham, Forum, 14: 324.
— Imperative. (R. Ewen) Westm. 146: 296.
— in America. (J. B. Blake) Munsey, 7: 662.
— in Australia. (D. MacG. Means) Nation, 61: 74.
— in England, Results of. Sat. R. 82: 85.
— The New Party. (A. Reid) Fortn. 63: 874.
— No-profit Line in Wheat-raising. Soc. Econ. 8: 222.
— or Protection. (E. C. Hegeler) Open Court, 2: 1283.
— Our New Industrial Policy. Soc. Econ. 4: 1.
— Previous Experiences with. Soc. Econ. 6: 273.
— Prospects of, in the U. S. (C. M. Depew) 19th Cent. 35: 343.
— Protection, and the Empire. Soc. Econ. 5: 47.
— and Fair Trade. (Earl Grey) 19th Cent. 31: 38.
— Salisbury on. Pub. Opin. 13: 178.
— Thorough. (R. Ewen) Westm. R. 139: 304.
— a Variable Expedient. (F. Greenwood) National, 20: 310.
— *vs.* Protection for England. Sat. R. 82: 211.
— Views of Labor on. (J. K. Hardie; F. J. Whetstone) National, 20: 446.
— What Congress should do. Soc. Econ. 5: 65.
— Who profits by? (L. Courtney; Lord Masham) National, 20: 433.
Free Will and Determinism. Church Q. 35: 416.
— and Responsibility. (D. G. Ritchie) Int. J. Ethics, 5: 409.
— — Ritchie on. (J. H. Hyslop) Int. J. Ethics, 6: 101.
— Limits of. Spec. 68: 394.
— a Mechanical Possibility. (X. Clark) Open Court, 2: 975.
— Question of, Mathematical View of. (J. E. Oliver) Philos. R. 1: 292.
Freedom and the Proof of Determinism. (S. E. Mezes) Int. J. Ethics, 3: 366.
— and Psycho-genesis. (A. T. Ormond) Psychol. R. 1: 217.
- Anglo-Saxon, Hosmer's. Spec. 68: 680.
— Hegel's Conception of. (S. W. Dyde) Philos. R. 3: 655.
— Individual. (J. W. Appel) Ref. Q. 42: 397.
— the Germ of National Progress and Permanence. (T. F. Bayard) Am. Law R. 30: 1.
— a poem. (E. M. Thomas) Cosmopol. 20: 224.
— Responsibility, and Punishment. (J. H. Hyslop) Mind, 19: 167.
— Speculative Significance of. (B. P. Bowne) Meth. R. 55: 681.
— Spiritual, Evolution of. (T. W. Harris) N. Church R. 1: 187.
Freedom's Revéille; a poem. (J. G. Clark) Arena, 9: 96.
Freeland Colony Scheme. All the Year, 75: 65.
Freeland University. (W. L. Garver) Arena, 10: 777.
Freeman, Edward Augustus. (J. Fiske) Atlan. 71: 99. — (H. Taylor) Yale R. 2: 159. — (J. S. Cotton) Acad. 41: 301. — Ath. '92, 1: 374. — Critic, 20: 195, 239. — (J. Bryce) Eng. Hist. R. 7: 477. — (J. Bryce) Nation, 54: 336. — (W. Clarke) New Eng. M. n. s. 6: 606. — Quar. 175: 1. 182: 281. — Sat. R. 73: 324. — (C. K. Paul) Month, 84: 337.
— and the Quarterly Review. (T. A. Archer) Contemp. 63: 335.
— as an Historian. (J. Bryce) Nation, 54: 355.
— at Home. (D. L. Porter) Scrib. M. 14: 612.
— Historical Essays. Ath. '92, 1: 397. — (C. H. Haskins) Dial (Ch.) 13: 100. — Spec. 68: 437.
— — 4th Series. (G. W. Prothero) Eng. Hist. R. 8: 384.
— Recollections of. Temp. Bar, 109: 214. Same art. Liv. Age, 211: 442.
— Reminiscences of. (E. Venables) Fortn. 57: 739. Same art. Liv. Age, 193: 811.
Freeman, Edward Augustus, Review of Opinions of. (E. A. Freeman) Forum, 13: 145.
— the Scholar and Professor. (H. B. Adams) Yale R. 4: 231.
— Stephens's Life and Letters of. (H. B. Adams) Am. Hist. R. 1: 149. — (N. Pinder) Acad. 47: 517. — Sat. R. 79: 698. — Church Q. 41: 108. — (B. S. Terry) Dial (Ch.) 19: 37. — Nation, 61: 48.
Freeman, Thomas, with portrait. (H. L. Conard) Nat'l M. (N. Y. '91) 18: 70.
Freemasonry and the Roman Church. (C. Kegan Paul) Cornh. 74: 668.
— Dangerous Character of. Dub. R. 118: 192.
— Devil Worship and. (F. Legge) Contemp. 70: 466.
— in Boston. (W. B. Ellis) New Eng. M. n. s. 13: 3.
— in the Continental Army. (J. F. Sachse) Am. Hist. Reg. 2: 622.
— in the U. S. Bost. 2: 443.
— Knight Templar, in the U. S. Bost. 2: 477.
— Masonic Lodges of Boston. Bost. 2: 540.
— Royal Arch, in the U. S. Bost. 2: 469.
Freemasons, Roster of, of Tun Tavern, Philadelphia. (J. F. Sachse) Pennsyl. M. 20: 116.
Freesias, Cultivation of. (W. N. Craig) Garden & F. 9: 26.
Freight Rates, Railroad. (H. T. Newcomb) Cassier, 6: 114.
Fremont's Expedition, Story of. (J. W. Freeman) Cosmopol. 21: 400.
Fremund, St. Antiq. n. s. 27: 202, 247.
French, Alice. With portraits. Bk. Buyer, 6: 93. 12: 24. 13: 293.
French, Daniel Chester. (R. Cortissoz) Atlan. 75: 223. — (R. R. Wilson) Mo. Illust. 12: 283.
French, Frank, Wood Engraver. Scrib. M. 17: 689.
French, Thomas, of Guilford, Conn. (A. D. W. French) N. E. Reg. 47: 357.
French, Thomas Valpy, Bishop of Lahore. Church Q. 41: 372. Same art. Liv. Age, 208: 733. — Quar. 183: 86. Same art. Liv. Age, 208: 579. — (H. B. Harington) Acad. 48: 454.
French-Sheldon, Mrs. M. Sultan to Sultan. (D. Swing; Sir E. Arnold; T. W. Knox; C. McMichael) Arena, 7: 100.
Frenches of Ipswich, The. (A. D. W. French) N. E. Reg. 47: 362.
French, The; a Gray and Gay People. (S. Henry) Contemp. 64: 294.
— A Peep at. (G. Widdrington) Gent. M. n. s. 52: 459.
French for a Fortnight. (H. C. Bunner) Scrib. M. 16: 161.
French and Dutch Painters. (S. Beale) Am. Arch. 52: 35.
French and English. Macmil. 75: 15. Same art. Liv. Age, 211: 726.
French and Indian War, Frontier Forts of. (H. M. M. Richards) Am. Hist. Reg. 1: 519.
French Art, Romantic Movement in. Blackw. 159: 240.
French Canadian Race in America, Growth of. (J. Davidson) Ann. Am. Acad. Pol. Sci. 8: 213.
— in Maine. (W. MacDonald) Nation, 63: 285.
— Language of. (H. A. Kennedy) Contemp. 69: 500. Same art. Liv. Age, 209: 387.
— Superstitions of. (B. L. Macdonell) Pop. Sci. Mo. 44: 520.
French Children. (T. Bentzon) Cent. 30: 803.
French Colonization. (D. MacG. Means) Nation, 61: 145.
French Drama in Molière's Time. (F. M. Warren) Chaut. 24: 131.
French Element in American Population. (G. A. Rich) Soc. Econ. 6: 95.

French Fiction, English and Americans in. (A. de Ternant) Gent. M. n. s. 57: 287.
French Girls. (Mme. J. Adam) No. Am. 154: 447.
French Journalism. National, 26: 74. — (E. Davis) Canad. M. 3: 85.
French Language and the English Language. Spec. 69: 156. Same art. Ecl. M. 119: 399.
— and German in Public High Schools. (C. H. Grandgent) School & C. 1: 148.
— Do Americans need to speak? (A. Hennequin) Educa. 16: 170.
— Study of. Un. Serv. M. 6: 595.
French Legal Procedure, Peculiarities of. Green Bag, 7: 79.
French Literature, Contemporary; Apollo in the Latin Quarter. Macmil. 74: 411.
— contrasted with English. Westm. 142: 571.
— Decadence in. Quar. 174: 479. Same art. Liv. Age, 194: 67.
— 1891-92. (J. Reinach) Ath. '92, 2: 7.
— 1892-93. (J. Reinach) Ath. '93, 2: 10.
— 1893-94. (J. Reinach) Ath. '94, 2: 10.
— 1894-95. (J. Reinach) Ath. '95, 2: 10.
— 1895-96. (J. Reinach) Ath. '96, 2: 10.
— Essential Characteristic of. (F. Brunetière) Fortn. 58: 525. Same art. Ecl. M. 119: 683.
— Les Jeunes Revues. Atlan. 76: 141.
— Moral Drift in, New. (P. Bourget) Forum, 16: 282.
— Movement in. (E. Rod) Chaut. 24: 35.
— 19th Century. Blackw. 157: 171.
— Petit de Julleville's. (P. T. Lafleur) Nation, 63: 295.
— Recent. Atlan. 69: 123.
— Recent French Essays. Atlan. 69: 402.
— Souvenirs of Some Celebrated People of the Times. (J. Claretie) No. Am. 159: 165.
— Symbolism in. (T. S. Perry) Cosmopol. 13: 359. — Spec. 68: 579.
French Men and Manners, Vandam's. Sat. R. 80: 212.
French Peasant, The. (W. Webster and others) Acad. 42: 7-72.
French Peasantry. (L. de San Carlos) No. Am. 157: 209.
French Plays and English Audiences. (G. Barlow) Contemp. 64: 171.
— and English Money. (Wm. Archer) New R. 10: 86.
French Poetry. (A. Laugel) Nation, 56: 101.
— New School of. (E. Davis) Lit. W. (Bost.) 23: 356.
French Protestants, Theological Thought among, in 1892. (A. Grétillat) Presb. and Ref. R. 4: 390.
French Royalists, The. Macmil. 74: 457. Same art. Liv. Age, 211: 516.
French Soldiers. Chamb. J. 71: 287.
French Spoliation Period, Episodes of. (H. W. Hubbell) Am. Hist. Reg. 3: 660.
French Squire's Diary, A. Gent. M. 55: 442. Same art. Liv. Age, 207: 607.
French University Students. (T. Stanton) Open Court, 7: 3839.
French Wife, The. Liv. Age, 211: 819.
French Women, Group of Eminent. (E. L. Didier) Chaut. 24: 3.
Frenchman, The; Character Note. Cornh. 70: 251. Same art. Ecl. M. 123: 553.
Frenchy. (M. E. Seawell) Lippinc. 53: 79.
Freneau's National Gazette. (P. L. Ford) Nation, 60: 143.
Frere, Sir Bartle. (F. J. Goldsmid) Geog. J. 5: 462. — Ed. R. 182: 156.
— Martineau's. Blackw. 157: 351. Same art. Liv. Age, 205: 195. — Ath. '95, 1: 109. — Sat. R. 79: 320.
Frescoes, Maccari's Historic. (T. Tracey) Cosmopol. 22: 115.
Fresh Air Funds; the Poor Children's Holiday. (Lady Jeune) Fortn. 59: 846.
Fresh Air Work in New York City. (W. H. Tolman) Chaut. 21: 713.
Fressingfield, Eng., Families in, wishing to emigrate to America. N. E. Reg. 49: 337.
Frewen, Richard, Death of. Sat. R. 82: 208.
Freytag, Gustav, with portrait. (W. H. Carpenter) Bookman, 1: 315. — Dial (Ch.) 18: 287. — Open Court, 9: 4487. — (J. G. Robertson) Scot. R. 27: 71.
— and the Emperor Frederick. (Edm. Yates) Time, 21: 572.
Friant, Emile. (P. G. Hamerton) Scrib. M. 16: 675.
Friar Lawrence; a story. (E. Phillpotts) Idler, 1: 565.
Friars in Oxford. (G. B. Lancaster-Woodburne) Dub. R. 112: 84.
— of the Sack. (A. G. Little) Eng. Hist. R. 9: 121.
— of the West Indies. (J. I. Rodriguez) Am. Cath. Q. 17: 786.
Friction, Anti-, Materials. (K. Hedges) Cassier, 5: 423.
— of Lubricated Surfaces. (R. H. Thurston) Cassier, 2: 444.
Friend in Need, A. Sund. M. 25: 530.
Friend in Need, A; a story. (C. Shelley) Outing, 28: 163.
Friend of the Commune, A; a story. (G. Parker) Eng. Illust. 10: 61. Same art. Liv. Age, 195: 651.
Friend of the Family. (C. B. Davis) Cent. 22: 453.
Friend to the Devil. (M. Thompson) Lippinc. 56: 257.
Friendly Critic, A. Macmil. 74: 435.
Friendly Societies and their Congeners. (J. M. Ludlow) Econ. R. 6: 481.
— 1884-94. (E. W. Brabrook) J. Statis. Soc. 58: 286.
— Old-age Pensions and. (J. Chamberlain) National, 24: 592.
Friendly Society Finance. (J. F. Wilkinson) Econ. J. 2: 721.
— Illustrations of. (J. F. Wilkinson) J. Statis. Soc. 58: 303.
Friendly Society System. Quar. 182: 126.
Friendly Visiting. (L. O. Chant) Lend a H. 11: 431.
— Practical. (E. H. Bailey) Lend a H. 15: 60.
— the True Charity. (Mrs. A. K. Norton) Char. R. 3: 352.
Friendly Visitors. (Mrs. Q. D. Smith; Mrs. S. E. Tenney; B. Raeb) Char. R. 2: 48.
Friends, Dropping, Art of. All the Year, 70: 318.
Friends on the Astrakan Ranch; a poem. (S. F. Harrison) Canad. M. 4: 361.
Friends; a story. (E. B. Kaufman) Lippinc. 49: 609.
Friendship. All the Year, 72: 127. — (A. H. Japp) Argosy, 56: 202.
— Conduct of. (H. Maxwell) 19th Cent. 34: 399. Same art. Ecl. M. 121: 537.
— Ethics of. (E. Lynn Linton) Univ. R. 5: 332.
— Heaven Descended. Argosy, 58: 375.
— a Sermon. (R. W. Dale) Sund. M. 24: 418.
Friendships of J. Baldwin, The; a dialogue. (V. Paget) Contemp. 61: 653. Same art. Ecl. M. 118: 811.
— Terminable. Sat. R. 74: 708.
Frie's Rebellion. (L. R. Harley) Am. Hist. Reg. 4: 19.
Fringe-tree. Garden & F. 7: 325.
Fripp, Alfred D. Acad. 47: 262. — Ath. '95, 1: 383. — (G. F. Stephens) M. of Art, 18: 470.
Fripp, George Arthur. Ath. '96, 2: 569. — Acad. 50: 315.
Frisian Islands, North, Legends of the. (W. G. Black) Gent. M. n. s. 50: 508.
Frisian Summer Resort, A Winter Visit to a. (C. Edwardes) Chamb. J. 73: 382.
Frith, Walter. Her Advocate. Sat. R. 80: 438.
Frith, William Powell. (W. W. Fenn) M. of Art, 2: 80.

Frith Highland Gentleman. (G. Parker) Good Words, 34: 184.
Fritz, John, noted Captain of Industry. (J. F. Holloway) Cassier, 7: 339.
Froebel, Karl Friedrich. Ath. '94, 1: 681.
— and Herbart. (J. L. Hughes) Educa. R. 10: 239.
— from a Psychological Standpoint. (E. F. Buchner) Lend a H. 15: 105, 169.
— in Public Life. (E. P. Evans) Nation, 55: 305.
— Kindergarten of. (E. W. White) Cath. World, 56: 507.
— Reminiscences of. (E. P. Evans) Atlan. 71: 123.
Froeken Bergliot. (W. Sharp) Good Words, 34: 709.
Frog, The, for Pan and Pastime. (J. T. Wandle) Outing, 22: 301.
Frog that played the Trombone, The. (B. Matthews) Harper, 87: 911.
Frog Prince, Story of the. (W. A. Clouston) Folk-Lore, 1: 493.
Frogging in Northern Waters. Outing, 26: 196.
Frog's Eggs, Wrinkling of, during Segmentation. (C. B. Wilson) Am. Natural. 30: 761.
Frogs and their Uses. (R. W. Shufeldt) Pop. Sci. Mo. 49: 179.
— and Toads, Poisonous Secretion of. (G. A. Boulenger) Nat. Sci. 1: 185.
— Color Changes of. (C. M. Weed) Pop. Sci. Mo. 43: 490.
Froissart, Jean, the Historian. (G. C. Macaulay) Macmil. 71: 384.
— the Lover. (G. C. Macaulay) Macmil. 71: 223.
— Old Wine and New. (A. Repplier) Atlan. 77: 688.
From Clue to Climax. (W. N. Harven) Lippinc. 57: 739.
From the Dark Past. Macmil. 71: 207. Same art. Ecl. M. 124: 415.
From Dawn to Dusk; a poem. (A. L. Salmon) M. of Art, 17: 119.
From East to West; a tale. (G. Bartlett) Canad. M. 1: 153.
From the Error of his Way. (R. Ogden) Scrib. M. 20: 222.
From Generation to Generation. (E. E. Hale) New Eng. M. n. s. 13: 534.
From the Hebrid Isles; stories. (F. Macleod) Harper, 92: 45.
From Information received; a story. (A. Armstrong) Idler, 4: 533.
From the Jaws of Death. (R. F. Dixon) Canad. M. 5: 351.
From Leopold's Window; a story. (K. P. Woods) Harper, 85: 106.
From Macedonia; a story. (M. T. Wright) Scrib. M. 16: 510.
From the Memoirs of a Minister of France; stories. (S. J. Weyman) Eng. Illust. vols. 12, 13.
From the Note-Book of a Country Doctor. Macmil. 73: 36. Same art. Liv. Age, 207: 628. Same art. Ecl. M. 126: 92.
From out the Ruins; a story. (M. B. Goodwin) Outing, 28: 52.
From the Post-Bag; a story. (Mrs. H. Mansergh) Eng. Illust. 14: 459.
From a Suburban Window. (J. A. Ainscough) National, 20: 136.
From the Tower of Silence; a story. Chamb. J. 70: 269.
From the Valley of the Quenemo; a story. (J. Barnes) Cosmopol. 17: 61.
From the Valley o' the Shadder. (C. B. Morgan) Lippinc. 57: 680.
Fromentin, Eugène. (G. Smith) M. of Art, 18: 454.
Frontenac, Comte de, Lorin's. (G. M. Wrong) Am. Hist. R. 1: 545.
— in New France. (Geo. Stewart) Cosmopol. 21: 427.
Frontier Fight, A. (G. A. Forsyth) Harper, 91: 42.
Frontier Service in the '50s. (W. B. Lane) Un. Serv. (Phila.) 10: 522. 11: 46.
— On the. (G. W. Van Deusen) Outing, 27: 241.
Frost, A. B., with portrait. Bk. Buyer, 11: 57. — (H. C. Bunner) Harper, 85: 699.
Frost and Freedom. (F. L. Oswald) Open Court, 5: 2803.
— at Hong Kong, China, Jan. 1893. Nature, 47: 535.
— Dew and. (R. Russell) Nature, 47: 210.
— Protecting Plants from, by Water-evaporation. Garden & F. 9: 43.
Frost Forms on Roan Mountain. (H. R. Edson) Pop. Sci. Mo. 45: 30.
Frost Freaks. Chamb. 71: 805.
Frost Patterns, Arborescent. (G. J. Symons and others) Nature, 47: 162.
Frost Plants. (D. T. Macdougall) Science, 22: 351.
Frosty Flirtation, A. All the Year, 73: 614.
Frothingham, Octavius Brooks. (J. H. Morse) Critic, 27: 379. — (E. C. Stedman) Critic, 27: 430. — (J. W. Chadwick) Nation, 61: 405. — Ath. '95, 2: 872. — (T. W. Higginson) New World, 5: 1.
Froude, J. A., with portrait. Bk. Buyer, 10: 239. — (Mrs. Ireland) Contemp. 67: 17. Same art. Liv. Age, 204: 303. Same art. Ecl. M. 124: 262. Same art. Chr. Lit. 12: 203. — Quar. 182: 281. — Liv. Age, 204: 112. — (A. Birrell) Scrib. M. 17: 149. — Eng. Illust. 9: 723. — (E. L. Godkin) Nation, 54: 318. — (G. Smith) No. Am. 159: 677. — (A. Patchett Martin) National, 24: 488. — Sat. R. 78: 453. — Acad. 46: 329. — Pub. Opin. 17: 729. — Critic, 25: 274. — Ath. '94, 2: 568. — Dial (Ch.) 17: 251. — Spec. 73: 533. — (E. G. Bourne) Nation, 59: 302.
— and his Critics. (T. R. Holmes) Westm. 138: 174.
— as Historian. (T. H. S. Escott) Time, 1: 379.
— Pilgrimage of. (M. D. Conway) Open Court, 8: 4279–4300.
— Reminiscences of. (J. Skelton) Blackw. 157: 40.
— Some Letters of. (T. Stanton) Critic, 27: 400.
— Working with, on Fraser's Magazine. (M. D. Conway) Nation, 59: 378, 401.
Frugality and Content. Spec. 73: 401.
Fruit as a Food and Medicine. (H. Benjafield) Pop. Sci. Mo. 47: 677.
— Correlations of Quality. (L. H. Bailey) Garden & F. 5: 495.
— Display of, at the Columbian Exposition. (L. H. Bailey) Garden & F. 6: 409.
Fruit-barrow Man. (J. D. Symon) Eng. Illust. 12: no. 4, 59.
Fruit Culture, American Varieties. (L. H. Bailey) Garden & F. 5: 518.
— Bordeaux Mixture. (E. G. Lademan) Garden & F. 7: 456.
— — Does Mulching retard the Ripening of Fruits? Garden & F. 6: 495.
— in California. (W. Roberts) Fortn. 58: 621. — (H. Marshall) Eng. Illust. 9: 345.
— — Spirit of Growers. (C. H. Shinn) Garden & F. 5: 621.
— in Florida. Garden & F. 7: 189.
— in Scotland. Chamb. J. 71: 481.
— Insects injurious to. Garden & F. 5: 457, 490.
— New Types. Garden & F. 6: 206.
— Pacific Coast Seedling Fruits. (C. H. Shinn) Garden & F. 7: 243.
Fruit-drying, a Representative Rural Industry. (C. S. Sargent) Garden & F. 8: 441.

Fruit Exchange, California's. (M. A. Sudduth) Chaut. 23: 469.
Fruit-growing in Annapolis Valley, N. S. (J. W. Longley) Canad. M. 1: 621.
— in California, New Fields in. (W. H. Tisdale) Garden & F. 8: 258.
— New Factor in. (B. T. Galloway) Science, 22: 117.
— Spraying in. (T. H. Hoskins) Garden & F. 5: 370.
Fruit Industry in California. (C. H. Shinn) Pop. Sci. Mo. 44: 200.
Fruit of Sorrow; a poem. (F. S. Mines) Cosmopol. 14: 558.
Fruit Orchard. Are Varieties running Out? Garden & F. 6: 87, 131.
Fruit Raisers of California, Coöperation among. (E. F. Adams) Forum, 20: 364.
Fruit Trees, Girdling of, by Mice. (R. B. Hough) Garden & F. 6: 93.
— Forming the Heads of. (T. H. Hoskins) Garden & F. 7: 277.
— Methods of Setting Out. (T. H. Hoskins) Garden & F. 7: 156.
Fruits. (C. D. Wilson) Lippinc. 58: 704.
— and Seeds, Adaptations of. (J. W. Folsom) Pop. Sci. Mo. 43: 218.
— California. Garden & F. 8: 512.
— — at Home. (W. M. Tisdale) Garden & F. 9: 317.
— California Fruit Supply in New York. Garden & F. 6: 432.
— Citrous, at Columbian Exposition. (L. H. Bailey) Garden & F. 6: 309.
— Drying of Vegetables and. (E. W. Badger) J. Soc. Arts, 44: 540.
— Evolution of. (C. F. Marshall) Knowl. 18: 77.
— in the English Market. Spec. 71: 512.
— of Eastern Asia. (T. H. Hoskins) Garden & F. 5: 489.
— of the Year. (B. D. Halsted) Chaut. 24: 181.
— Ornamental, for the Conservatory. (W. H. Saplin) Garden & F. 7: 357.
— Preservation of, by Vapor of Alcohol. (F. A. Waugh) Garden & F. 9: 458.
— Slow Maturing of Trees and Shrubs. (J. G. Jack) Garden & F. 6: 494.
— Stone, at Columbian Exposition. (L. H. Bailey) Garden & F. 6: 398.
— Value of |Bud Varieties in. (G. H. Powell) Garden & F. 9: 513.
— Wild, in Southern California. (S. B. Parish) Garden & F. 6: 313.
— Wild, of New Jersey. (M. Treat) Garden & F. 5: 435.
Fry, C. B. "Fry of Wadham." (M. Beerbohm) Eng. Illust. 11: 1057.
Fryeburg, Me. (J. S. Barrows) New Eng. M. n. s. 9: 33.
Fuchs, Julius. Music, 5: 219.
Fuegia. (A. T. Sibbald) Overland, n. s. 19: 530.
Fuel, Choice of. (H. M. Chance) Engin. M. 12: 253.
— Compressed, Manufacture of, in U. S. (J. R. Wagner) Cassier, 11: 23.
— Liquid. Dub. R. 115: 432. — (G. Stockfleth) J. Soc. Arts, 42: 616.
— — for Steam-making. (F. R. Hutton) Eng. M. 4: 591.
— Newer Forms of. (H. Paul) Engin. M. 2: 521.
— Problems of. (J. D. Weeks) Cassier, 10: 298.
Fuels and their Use. (J. E. Reynolds) Nature, 46: 527.
Fujisan. (A. Parsons) Harper, 90: 269. — Nature, 47: 178.
— Ascent of. (M. L. and D. P. Todd) Cent. 22: 483.
Fulfilment of Failure; a story. (N. Ainsleigh) Temp. Bar, 95: 191.
Fulfilment; a story. (E. K. Carter) Lippinc. 55: 420.
Fulgurite from Waterville, Me. (W. S. Bayley) Am. J. Sci. 143: 327.
Fulham Palace. (W. S. Simpson) Sund. M. 24: 735, 845.
Fuller, George. Bk. Buyer, 3: 66. — (C. de Kay) M. of Art, 12: 349.
Fuller, Henry B., with portrait. Bk. Buyer, 12: 821.
— With portrait. (N. H. Banks) Bookman, 2: 15.
— Cliff-dwellers. (H. H. Boyesen) Cosmopol. 16: 373.
Fuller, Margaret, Critical Work of. (C. B. La Monte) Poet-Lore, 7: 477.
— Permanent Influence of. (K. West) Poet-Lore, 7: 377.
Fuller, Melville W., with portrait. (M. White, jr.) Munsey, 11: 80.
Fuller, Thomas. Sermons. Spec. 68: 681.
Fullwood, John. (A. T. Story) Art J. 48: 369.
Fulness of Life, The. (Edith Wharton) Scrib. M. 14: 699.
Fulton, Robert, and his Steamboats. (T. C. Purdy) Engin. M. 9: 868.
Fun as a Medicine. Spec. 77: 931.
Function and Content, Confusion of, in Mental Analysis. (D. S. Miller) Psychol. R. 2: 535.
Functions, Mathematical. (C. S. Peirce) Nation, 58: 196.
Fundy, Bay of, Tides and Marshes. (F. H. Eaton) Pop. Sci. Mo. 43: 250. — (G. Kobbé) Scrib. M. 14: 335.
Funera Nefunera; a story. (E. B. Osborn) New R. 13: 53.
Funeral, Moslem. Liv. Age, 196: 102.
Funeral Baked Meats. Antiq. n. s. 26: 11.
Funeral Customs, Omaha. (F. La Fiesche) J. Am. Folk-Lore, 2: 3.
— of the World. (J. H. Long) Pop. Sci. Mo. 45: 806.
Funeral Formalities. Spec. 74: 715.
Funeral Rite, Breaking of Vessels as a, in Modern Greece. (N. G. Politis) Anthrop. J. 23: 29.
Funeral Sacrifice in India. (J. D. Rees) 19th Cent. 31: 958. Same art. Liv. Age, 194: 375.
Funeral Wreaths, Collection of in Museum at Giseh. (Anna M. Vail) Garden & F. 8: 312.
Funerals, English. (H. C. Bolton) J. Am. Folk-Lore, 7: 233.
— New England. (P. M. Cole) J. Am. Folk-Lore, 7: 217.
Fungi, Comparative Morphology of. (J. E. Humphrey) Am. Natural. 25: 1055.
— Development of. (L. H. Pammel) Garden & F. 7: 248.
Fungi on Leaves, Parasitic. (A. S. Wilson) Knowl. 19: 242.
Funkias, Culture of. (R. Cameron) Garden & F. 9: 347.
Fur, Trade in, London. Chamb. J. 71: 625.
Fur Producers. (R. Lydekker) Knowl. 19: 10-271.
Furs in Russia. (I. J. Hapgood) Lippinc. 55: 413.
— Rare. Spec. 75: 721.
Furly, Benjamin. (J. F. Sachse) Pennsyl. M. 19: 277.
Furnace, High-temperature. (H. L. Gantt) J. Frankl. Inst. 142: 458.
Furnaces, Blast. (J. M. Hartman) J. Frankl. Inst. 134: 132.
Furnes, a Quaint Flemish Town. (J. Maskell) Walford's Antiq. 3: 7, 60.
Furness, H. H., with portrait. Bk. News, 11: 427.
Furness, William Henry. (J. W. Chadwick) Nation, 62: 114. — (C. G. Ames) Harv. Grad. M. 4: 545. — Ath. '96, 1: 183. — Critic, 28: 99.
Furness Abbey. All the Year, 76: 295.
— and its story. (W. C. Sydney) Gent. M. n. s. 56: 89. Same art. Liv. Age, 208: 500.

Furnished House, A. All the Year, 73: 113.
Furnishings, Household, from Antwerp Exhibition. (R. D. Benn) Art J. 46: 252.
Furniture. (R. Blomfield) M. of Art, 19: 488.
— Artistic Design in. (L. F. Day) Art J. 45: 302.
— Chests and Cabinets. (J. H. Pollen) M. of Art, 9: 144.
— Chippendale. (C. Dempsey) M. of Art, 4: 494.
— Colonial, of New England, Lyon's. (C. A. L. Richards) Dial (Ch.) 12: 387.
— French. (E. Balfour) M. of Art, 7: 522.
— — Havard's Dictionnaire de l'Ameublement. M. of Art, 11: 315.
— — in the 16th Century, Bonnaffé's. (C. Whibley) M. of Art, 10: 384.
— History of, Litchfield's. Spec. 69: 418.
— Old, Bits of. (S. Baring-Gould) Sund. M. 25: 558, 629.
— Sheraton's. (E. Balfour) M. of Art, 6: 190.
Furniture Draughting. (A. C. Nye) Am. Arch. 46: 56.
Furniture Exhibition at Bethnal Green Museum, 1878. M. of Art, 1: 245.
Furred and Feathered Youngsters; by a Son of the Marshes. Eng. Illust. 14: 629.
Further Adventures of a Guinea Pig. (C. J. Langston) Argosy, 57: 421.
Furze and Gorse. Cornh. 69: 286.
Fuseli, Henry, Milton Gallery of. (A. Beaver) M. of Art, 14: 166.
Futile Amendment, A; a story. (A. B. Lyon) Southern M. 4: 373.
Futteh por-Sikri, India. All the Year, 75: 102.
Future, In the. Chamb. J. 72: 209.
— Marvels of the; Predictions and Mottoes. McClure, 2: 199.
Future Life. (S. P. Wait) Arena, 7: 411.
— After Death — What? (C. F. Dole) No. Am. 156: 467.
— and the Condition of Man therein. (W. E. Gladstone) No. Am. 162: 1-740.
— Conception of, among Semitic Races. (E. Montet) Asia. R. 10: 319.
— Conceptions of a. (F. W. Farrar) No. Am. 156: 323.
— Doctrine of, in the Book of Job. (Samuel Plantz) Meth. R. 56: 45.
— Gladstone on. Spec. 76: 442.
— Glimmerings of a. (R. Hodgson) Forum, 21: 247.
— Hudson on. (J. Jastrow) Dial (Ch.) 20: 107.
— Ideas of, in the Pentateuch. (T. S. Potwin) Bib. Sac. 52: 423.
— Is Faith in it declining? (E. S. Phelps) Forum, 17: 380.
— Myers on. (W. M. Payne) Dial (Ch.) 15: 141.
— New-Church Belief in. N. Church R. 1: 460.
— Persian Doctrine of. (A. V. W. Jackson) Bib. World, 8: 149.
Future Punishment, Foster on Fallacies of. (G. R. Leavitt) Bib. Sac. 51: 37.
— Hell, Happiness in. (St. G. Mivart) 19th Cent. 32: 899.
— Hell no Part of Divine Revelation. (W. E. Manley) Arena, 14: 464.
— Mivart on. Spec. 69: 814.
Future Rights, Declaration of. (W. A. Bewes) Law Q. 8: 48.
Future State. "Eternal Hope" Delusion. (E. Shorthouse) Westm. 145: 206.
— Fancies concerning the. (P. W. Roose) Westm. 138: 382. Same art. Ecl. M. 119: 741.
Future Tense, Aryan. (E. W. Hopkins) Am. J. Philol. 13: 1.
Futures and Options. (W. D. Washburne) Am. J. Pol. 1: 449.
Futures, Legislation against. (H. C. Emery) Pol. Sci. Q. 10: 62.
Fyffe, Charles Alan. (J. S. Cotton) Acad. 41: 205.
Fyvie Castle; a Corner of the Kailyard. (R. S. Loveday) Eng. Illust. 16: 285.

Gabbro occurring in St. Lawrence County, N. Y., Metamorphism of. (C. H. Smyth, jr.) Am. J. Sci. 151: 271.
— in the Southwestern Adirondack Region. (C. H. Smyth, jr.) Am. J. Sci. 148: 54.
Gablentz, G. von der. Ath. '93, 2: 883.
Gabriel, and the Lost Millions of Perote; a story. (M. Kingsley) Harper, 87: 545.
Gaddis Case, The; Decision of Judge Bradley. Good Govt. 13: 137.
Gaelic Literature, Story of. (E. d'Esterre-Keeling) Dub. R. 119: 142.
Gailenruth Cave in 1894. (H. C. Mercer) Am. Natural. 28: 821.
Gainsborough, Thomas. M. of Art, 2: 2. — (H. V. Barnett) M. of Art, 8: 210. — (W. Armstrong) Portfo. 1894: no. 9.
Gainsburgh, 1642-48. (E. Peacock) Antiq. n. s. 28: 27, 48.
Galápagos Islands. (Dr. Wolf) Geog. J. 6: 560.
— Flora of. (W. B. Hemsley) Nature, 52: 623.
Galatian Churches, Location of. (C. W. Votaw) Bib. World, 3: 456.
Gale, Norman R. Critic, 22: 84.
— A Country Muse. (G. R. Tomson) Acad. 42: 186. — Spec. 68: 847. 69: 960.
Gale of Nov. 16-20, 1894. (C. Harding) Nature, 49: 294.
Galesburg, Ill., Social Structure of. (A. W. Dunn) Char. R. 5: 247, 303, 350, 415.
Galicia, Consular Town in. (L. M. R. Walker) Belgra. 82: 203.
Galilee. (J. S. Riggs) Bib. World, 4: 421.
Galilee, Sea of. (A. K. Parker) Bib. World, 7: 264.
Galileo. (Sir R. Ball) Good Words, 35: 592, 679.
— Case of, Retreat of Theology in. (A. D. White) Pop. Sci. Mo. 41: 145.
— Work of, on Saturn's Rings. (E. A. Partridge and H. C. Whitaker) Pop. Astron. 3: 408.
Galileo Celebration at Padua, 1892. (A. Favaro) Nature, 47: 180.
Gall-flies and their Work. Chamb. J. 70: 646.
Gall-making Insects of Australia. (W. W. Froggatt) Nat. Sci. 5: 109.
Galleys, Life on Board. (F. S. Bassett) Un. Serv. (Phila.) 9: 144.
Gallican Church, Origin of. Church Q. 38: 393.
Gallitzin, Prince Demetrius Augustine, with portrait. (K. Hart) Cath. World, 61: 94. — (H. D. Richardson) Lippinc. 49: 235.
Gallitzin, Princess Amelia. (C. Ford) Month, 83: 27.
Galloping Hoof-beats; a story. (R. Shackleton, jr.) Southern M. 4: 386.
Galloping Jess; a story. Temp. Bar, 103: 559.
Galloway and her Feudal Sheriffs. (J. Fergusson) Scot. R. 22: 104.
Galloway Fastnesses. Leis. Hour, 43: 567.
Galls and their Occupants. (E. A. Butler) Knowl. 16: 125-186.
— Vegetable. (G. B. Rothera) Nat. Sci. 3: 353.
Galt, John, Novels of. Blackw. 159: 871. Same art. Liv. Age, 210: 214. — (J. H. Millar) New R. 13: 207.
— Redivivus. (W. Wallace) Bookman, 2: 138.

Galton, Francis. (F. Starr) Dial (Ch.) 15: 12.
— on Inheritance. (W. K. Brooks) Pop. Sci. Mo. 48: 480, 617.
Galvani, Luigi, with portrait. Pop. Sci. Mo. 41: 408.
Galvanic Batteries, Maximum Efficiency of. (H. Morton) Cassier, 8: 131.
Galvanometer, Ballistic, and its Use in Magnetic Measurements. (T. Gray) Science, n. s. 1: 533.
— — New. (E. G. Willyoung) J. Frankl. Inst. 134: 474.
Galvanometers, d'Arsonval, Recent Improvements in. (N. H. Genung) J. Frankl. Inst. 135: 63.
— New Method for reading Deflections of. (C. B. Rice) Am. J. Sci. 152: 276.
Galvanotropism of Tadpoles. (A. D. Waller) Sci. Prog. 4: 96.
Galveston Deep Well, The. (E. T. Dumble and G. D. Harris) Am. J. Sci. 146: 38.
Galway, Glimpse of. (B. S. Knollys) Belgra. 78: 190. Same art. Liv. Age, 194: 349.
Galway Coast, Pictures of. (M. Moore) Cath. World, 60: 727.
Gambetta, L., in his New House. Time, 3: 689.
Gamblers, Female. (A. T. Sibbald) Green Bag, 8: 362.
Gambling and Betting. Westm. 143: 140.
— and Public Welfare. (J. W. Riddle) Am. J. Pol. 2: 121.
— and Speculation. (C. H. Hamlin) Arena, 11: 413.
— Ethics of. (J. Oliphant) Westm. 137: 518.
— Market. (W. E. Bear) Contemp. 65: 781. Same art. Ecl. M. 123: 153.
— Our Principles and Programme. (J. Hawke) New R. 10: 705.
— Suppression of. (N. Smyth) Forum, 19: 238.
— Symposium. Indep. May 5, '92.
— What is? (J. Bigelow) Harper, 90: 470.
Gambling System. Chamb. J. 74: 634.
Game and Fish, Preservation of. (G. Fay) Atlan. 77: 642.
— and Game Laws of Norway. Blackw. 160: 87.
— Big, Disappearing in the West. (T. Roosevelt) Forum, 15: 767.
— — Glance at. (E. W. Sandys) Outing, 21: 301.
— — of Ceylon. Outing, 23: 227.
— — of South Africa. Blackw. 159: 121.
— — — Extermination of. (H. A. Bryden) Fortn. 62: 538.
— in Ontario. (J. Dickson) Canad. M. 4: 3.
— New England, 250 Years Ago. (F. E. Keay) Chaut. 18: 187.
Game Animals, Measurements of, Ward's. Sat. R. 74: 487.
Game-book, Glimpses at a. (G. Manners) National, 19: 212.
— Leaves from a. (G. Manners) Blackw. 156: 543.
Game Farm in August. Spec. 77: 236.
Gamekeeper, Autobiography of a. Spec. 69: 263.
Gamekeepers. (T. E. Kebbel) National, 20: 229.
Gamekeeping. Sat. R. 73: 605.
Game Laws; how they work. (C. Roper) Westm. 140: 358.
— More Facts about the Working of. (W. Routh) Westm. 141: 373.
— Old. Sat. R. 74: 560.
Game-preserving, Some Aspects of. (C. W. Furse) Econ. R. 1: 375.
Game, An Ancient. (J. I. Minchin) Acad. 41: 440.
Game of Chess, A; a story. (H. N. Crellin) Idler, 5: 483.
Game of Goose. (H. C. Bolton) J. Am. Folk-Lore, 8: 145.
Game Postponed, A; a story. (G. Smith) McClure, 5: 564.
Game we might play, A. (Marquis of Lorne) Good Words, 36: 12.
Games. (H. Maxwell) Blackw. 152: 418.
— Ancient and Oriental, Falkener on. Sat. R. 73: 427. — Spec. 69: 452.
— Children's Song. (Joel Benton) Bach. of Arts, 1: 808.
— Churchyard, in Wales. Reliquary, 35: 136. 36: 154.
— Columbian Exposition Exhibit of. (S. Culin) J. Am. Folk-Lore, 6: 205.
— Education by. (G. E. Johnson) Pedagog. Sem. 3: 97.
— German Patience. Sat. R. 73: 46.
— Graeco-Roman, in California. (A. Inkersley) Outing, 24: 409.
— Korean. Sat. R. 82: 375.
— Street, of Boys. (S. Culin) J. Am. Folk-Lore, 4: 221.
— Traditional, Gomme's. Sat. R. 77: 561. — (W. W. Newell) J. Am. Folk-Lore, 7: 260.
Gamester's Inheritance; a story. Theatre, 33: 305.
Gamma Virginis, The Story of. (J. E. Gore) Gent. M. n. s. 54: 8.
Ganga's Wooing; a Legend from the Ramayana. (W. S. B. Mathews) Music, 3: 675.
Ganges, Expiring Sanctity of. Spec. 72: 820.
Garacontie, Iroquois Indian, 1600–1675. (J. M. Parker) Cath. World, 59: 69.
Garbage, Cremation of. (W. F. Morse) Am. Arch. 39: 155.
— Utilization of. (B. Terne) J. Frankl. Inst. 136: 221. — (B. Terne) Am. Arch. 41: 185.
Garda Lake, and Lake Iseo. (J. W. Mario) Nation, 59: 267.
Garden, Hugh R., with portrait. Nat'l M. (N. Y. '91) 16: 83.
Garden, A City. (C. S. Sargent) Garden & F. 7: 161.
— Grandmother's. (B. D. Halsted) Chaut. 23: 269.
— in Autumn. (C. S. Sargent) Garden & F. 7: 411. 9: 371.
— in relation to the House. (F. I. Thomas) Am. Arch. 51: 95. — (F. I. Thomas) J. Soc. Arts, 44: 241.
— in Stone, A. (A. E. P. R. Dowling) Ecl. M. 121: 587.
— in the Tropics, A. (J. Rodway) Gent. M. n. s. 50: 91.
— Japanese, 17th Century. (C. S. Sargent) Garden & F. 6: 49.
— of Dreams, A. Liv. Age, 206: 443.
— Rock. (M. Barker) Garden & F. 5: 272.
— Spring. (C. S. Sargent) Garden & F. 7: 171.
— that I love, The. (A. Austin) National, 22: 258–648. Same art. Liv. Age, 199: 663, 736. 200: 221, 485.
— Winter. (J. N. Gerard) Garden & F. 5: 116.
Garden Gossip. (M. C. Robbins) Garden & F. 6: 223.
Garden-plants, Uniform naming of. Garden & F. 7: 199.
Gardener, Helen H. An Unofficial Patriot. (J. C. Ridpath) Arena, 13: 74.
Gardener, The; a poem. (Katharine Tynan) New R. 12: 131.
Gardener-kings, The. (W. St. C. Boscawen) Chamb. J. 73: 405.
Gardener's Head; a story. (Percy White) New R. 13: 469.
Gardening. Quar. 184: 54.
— about State and Government Buildings, World's Fair. (L. H. Bailey) Garden & F. 6: 459.
— Accumulation without Disposition. (M. C. Robbins) Garden & F. 7: 472.
— Carpet Bedding. (H. A. Caparn) Garden & F. 7: 382.
— City. (J. N. Gerard) Garden & F. 6: 157.
— Delights of Rough. (D. H. R. Goodale) Garden & F. 9: 303.
— Experimental. Garden & F. 5: 33.
— — in England. Garden & F. 5: 269.

Gardening, Fertilizers and Flowers. (C. S. Sargent) Garden & F. 9: 361.
— Formal and Landscape. Ed. R. 176: 175.
— Hardy Plants. Garden & F. 5: 286.
— Historical Dissertation on. (R. M. Garnier) Econ. R. 6: 145.
— History of, in England. Garden & F. 9: 109.
— a Human Bond. Garden & F. 5: 481.
— in Brookline, Mass. (M. Barker) Garden & F. 5: 165.
— An Island Garden, by Celia Thaxter. Garden & F. 7: 199.
— Japanese. Garden & F. 5: 170.
— My. (R. K. Munkittrick) Bach. of Arts, 3: 38.
— an Outlet for American Vitality. (M. C. Robbins) Garden & F. 8: 42.
— Some Novelties in. (E. O. Orpet) Garden & F. 9: 327, 336.
— Use of Directions. Garden & F. 5: 587.
— Various Motives for. (C. S. Sargent) Garden & F. 9: 341.
Gardens. (H. Maxwell) Liv. Age, 192: 352. — (J. Cartwright) Portfo. 23: 211.
— and Garden Craft. Ed. R. 184: 161.
— and Garden Furniture. Spec. 71: 204.
— and their Associations. All the Year, 74: 127.
— Blomfield's Formal Garden in England. M. of Art, 16: 170.
— English, Unsuitable for America. (C. S. Sargent) Garden & F. 9: 281.
— Floating, of Mexico. (C. H. Coe) Garden & F. 8: 432.
— a Gossip on. Chamb. J. 73: 334. Same art. Liv. Age, 210: 54.
— Italian. (C. A. Platt) Harper, 87: 165, 393.
— of Christmastide. (E. M. Sexton) Overland, n. s. 22: 561.
— of Early New England. (D. D. Slade) Garden & F. 7: 282.
— Old-Fashioned. (C. S. Sargent) Garden & F. 8: 281.
— Old Italian. (V. Paget) Longm. 26: 311.
— Social Use of. (J. De Wolf) Garden & F. 8: 342.
Gardiner Lyceum. (J. H. Cooper) J. Frankl. Inst. 140: 275.
Gardner, Isaac, jr. (C. K. Boston) New Eng. M. n. s. 12: 107.
Garfield, James A. (M. Halstead) McClure, 6: 269.
— and Conkling, Roscoe. (H. L. Dawes) Cent. 25: 341.
— Portraits of. McClure, 3: 245.
— Ride at Chickamauga. (J. R. Gilmore) McClure, 5: 357.
Garfields, English, Notes on. (W. P. W. Phillimore) N. E. Reg. 49: 194–449.
Gargoyles in Mediæval Architecture. (G. R. Redgrave) M. of Art, 5: 462.
Garland, Hamlin. Atlan. 76: 840. — Lit. W. (Bost.) 27: 56.
— Crumbling Idols. (E. E. Hale, Jr.) Dial (Ch.) 17: 11.
— Gospel according to. (A. Inkersley) Educa. 15: 608.
— Portraits of. McClure, 2: 239.
Garnett, Richard, Poetry of. (W. Sharp) Acad. 45: 223. — Sat. R. 77: 504. — Spec. 72: 721.
Garonne, Along the. (S. J. Weyman) Eng. Illust. 11: 587.
Garrick, David, Knight's Life of. Ath. '94, 2: 329.
— Last Appearances of. (A. Dobson) Longm. 26: 590.
Garrick Club, Cambridge, Eng. Sat. R. 75: 480.
Garrison, William Lloyd. (L. W. Bacon) Chr. Lit. 13: 1, 65.
Garshine, Vsiévolode Michailovitch. Temp. Bar, 105: 523. — (Stepniak) Time, 22: 610.
Garter, Knights of, How degraded. (J. A. Porter) Walford's Antiq. 10: 167, 253.
Gary, Judge, and the Anarchists. (M. M. Trumbull) Arena, 8: 544.
Garza Raid and its Lessons. (M. Romero) No. Am. 155: 324.
Gas and Electricity, Relative Cost of. (C. J. R. Humphreys) Engin. M. 4: 240.
— as Fuel, System of American Gas Furnace Company. J. Frankl. Inst. 138: 321.
— as a Sanitarian. (L. C. D'Oyle) Gent. M. n. s. 52: 182.
— Coal, of London. Dub. R. 116: 179.
— — in London, and its Enrichment. (V. B. Lewes) J. Soc. Arts, 42: 419.
— Coal-gas and Water-gas. (C. J. R. Humphreys) Engin. M. 7: 227.
— Detection of, in the Air. (F. Clowes) J. Soc. Arts, 42: 793–827.
— Determination of the Simple or Compound Nature of, from its Spectrum. Dub. R. 118: 150.
— Enrichment of. (V. B. Lewes) Nature, 50: 175.
— Fuel. (K. M. Mitchell) Am. Arch. 37: 103.
— High Pressure, Geological Work of, Debrée on. Nature, 48: 226.
— Illuminating, for Heating Purposes. (F. Siemens) Engin. M. 9: 860.
— in Cleveite, Constituents of. (C. Runge and F. Paschen) Nature, 52: 520.
— in Living Plants. (J. C. Arthur) Am. Natural. 27: 1, 98. — (J. C. Arthur) Nature, 47: 427.
— Light from Coal. (V. B. Lewes) J. Soc. Arts, 41: 102–138.
— Liquefaction of, Dewar's Discoveries in. (R. O. Doremus) No. Am. 156: 543.
— Natural, and Oil Production. (S. D. Prentice) Cassier, 3: 405.
— — Drilling for, near Philadelphia. (O. C. S. Carter) J. Frankl. Inst. 138: 230.
— — Supply of, Limits of. (S. S. Gorby) Engin. M. 5: 419.
— Producer, for Steam-raising. (W. H. Blauvelt) Cassier, 7: 123.
— — Future of Producer-gas. (A. H. Sexton) Engin. M. 11: 905.
— *vs.* Electricity direct from Coal. (D. M. Dunning) Engin. M. 11: 1008.
— — for Power Transmission. (N. W. Perry) Engin. M. 12: 49, 261.
Gas Bills, How to reduce. Chamb. J. 73: 817,
Gas Companies and Consumers. (W. P. Gerhard) Cassier, 6: 229.
Gas Engines and Oil Engines. (A. Spies) Cassier, 3: 341–427. 4: 25–437. 8: 481.
— for Electric Light and Power. (N. W. Perry) Cassier, 9: 207.
— Limits and Possibilities of. (G. Richmond) Engin. M. 10: 853.
— Test of. (H. W. Spangler) J. Frankl. Inst. 135: 340.
Gas Fixtures. (W. P. Gerhard) J. Frankl. Inst. 137: 328–408. 138: 21.
Gas-lighting, Inventor of. (W. Fletcher) Engin. M. 6: 223.
Gas-making. (N. Tait) Good Words, 36: 479.
Gas Works, Municipal. (E. W. Bemis) Chaut. 16: 15.
— — in the U. S. (E. W. Bemis) R. of Rs. (N. Y.) 7: 61.
Gascon Tragedy, A. (Geo. H. Powell) Gent. M. n. s. 53: 17.
Gases, Constitution and Function of. (S. J. Corrigan) Pop. Astron. 4: 247.
— Constitution of. (J. J. Stewart) Knowl. 16: 53–195.
— Densities of. (Lord Rayleigh) Nature, 47: 567.
— Electrolysis of. (J. J. Thomson) Nature, 52: 451.

Gases, Kinetic Theory of. (G. H. Bryan) Nature, 51: 221, 319.
— Liquefaction of. Ed. R. 179: 361. Same art. Liv. Age, 201: 707. — (V. Cornish) Knowl. 15: 141. — (M. M. Pattison-Muir; J. Dewar) Nature, 51: 364, 413.
— — New Process for. Nature, 53: 515.
— Mineral, New. (J. N. Lockyer) Nature, 52: 547. — Nature, 53: 162.
— Ratio of Specific Heat of. (J. W. Capstick) Sci. Prog. 3: 272.
— Theory of. (L. Boltzmann) Nature, 51: 413.
— Waterston's Theory of. Nature, 46: 30.
Gaskell, Mrs. E. C. (M. Hompes) Gent. M. n. s. 55: 124. Same art. Liv. Age, 206: 623.
— and Charlotte Brontë. (C. K. Shorter) Bookman, 3: 313. — (J. L. Gilder) Critic, 28: 353.
— Knutsford in Fiction. Gent. M. n. s. 55: 507.
— Stray Notes from. (M. Howitt) Good Words, 36: 604.
Gasparin, Countess de. (Mrs. W. Cornish) Good Words, 37: 803.
Gasquet, Dom, as a Historian. (A. M. Grange) Am. Cath. Q. 19: 449.
Gass's Lewis and Clark, Two rare Editions of. (E. Coues) Nation, 58: 29.
Gasteropoda, Mechanical Cause of Folds in the Aperture of the Shell of. (W. H. Dall) Am. Natural. 28: 909.
— Tertiary and Triassic, of the Tyrol. Nature, 48: 567.
Gates, Adelia, with portrait. Bk. News, 2: 45.
Gates, City. (G. Redon) Am. Arch. 41: 95–123.
— Town, of Southern Germany. (L. von Krockow) Am. Arch. 39: 119.
Gates of the Reie; a story. Temp. Bar, 96: 396.
Gateways. All the Year, 73: 233.
Gattie, A. W., Honorable Member. Sat. R. 82: 61.
Gauchos at Home, The. Temp. Bar, 101: 289. Same art. Liv. Age, 200: 678.
Gauge, Automatic Micrometer, Haines, for Rolling-mill Work. (R. B. Haines, jr.) J. Frankl. Inst. 135: 42.
— Pressure-recording, Edson. J. Frankl. Inst. 137: 241.
— Recording. (C. A. Hague) Cassier, 8: 559.
— for Steam Pressure. (C. A. Hague) Cassier, 8: 500.
Gauger's Adventure, The. (A. Gordon) Good Words, 37: Xmas no., 55.
Gaul, Gilbert. (G. P. Lathrop) Q. Illust. 1: 235.
Gaul, Conquest of, Dramatic Incidents in. (J. R. Nelson) School R. 4: 617.
Gaun tae Glasgow; a story. (W. Robertson) Canad. M. 2: 398.
Gautier, Théophile. (F. T. Marzials) Acad. 44: 362. — (A. Laugel) Nation, 57: 326. — Temp. Bar. 99: 541.
Gay, John. (G. A. Aitken) Westm. 140: 386.
— Ladies' Petition. (G. A. Aitken) Acad. 47: 426.
— Polly. (G. A. Aitken) Ath. '93, 2: 202.
Gay Head. (P. R. Uhler) Science, 20: 176.
— Notes on the Miocene and Pliocene of. (W. H. Dall) Am. J. Sci. 148: 296.
Gay's Romance. (C. C. Harrison) Cent. 21: 728.
Gayarré, Charles E. A. Critic, 26: 128.
Gaynor, Jessie L. (Mrs. C. Adams) Music, 11: 154.
Gazetteer of the World, Longman's. (L. Heilprin) Nation, 62: 180.
Gear-wheels, Design of. (L. F. Rondinella) J. Frankl. Inst. 137: 288.
Geary Act, The. (S. P. Read) Am. J. Pol. 3: 234.
Gebirol, Solomon Ibn, Ethics of. (D. Rosin) Jew. Q. 3: 159.
Geer, Baron Louis de. (R. N. Bain) Ath. '96, 2: 450.
Geese, Canada, Sport with. (E. W. Sandys) Outing, 22: 52.
Geikie, Sir A. (A. de Lapparent) Nature, 47: 217. — With portrait. Pop. Sci. Mo. 43: 257.
Gelasian Sacramentary. Church Q. 38: 347.
Gellius, Aulus, Corrections and Additions to Lewis and Short's Lexicon. (C. Knapp) Am. J. Philol. 14: 216.
Gems and Precious Stones, Streeter on. Sat. R. 73: 577.
— A Handful of. (E. L. Cutts) Eng. Illust. 12: no. 2, 99.
Genealogical Dictionary, Savage's, Corrections and Additions in. (J. W. Porter) N. E. Reg. 46: 185.
Genealogical Gleanings in England. (H. F. Waters) N. E. Reg. 46: 44–417. 47: 104–497. 48: 105–481. 49: 105, 237, 369, 481. 50: 105, 249, 385, 504.
Genealogical Research in Public Libraries. (W. R. Cutter) Lib. J. 21: 222.
General, The. Macmil. 68: 70.
"General," The Locomotive, and the Andrews Raid. Am. Arch. 47: 85.
General Assembly, First, in the U. S. (A. Brown) Green Bag, 5: 216.
General Bain, of Sandy Beach; a story. (W. W. Campbell) Canad. M. 3: 527.
General Conference, Methodist, as a Working Body. (J. D. Walsh) Meth. R. 55: 712.
General Manager, The; a story. (C. H. New) Munsey, 11: 320.
General Theolcgical Seminary, N. Y., Glimpses of Life in. (C. A. Walworth) Cath. World, 59: 200 — 61: 60.
General's Bluff, The. (O. Wister) Harper, 89: 508.
General's Sword, The; a story. (R. C. V. Meyers) Harper, 87: 574.
Generation without Prospects, A. (M. I. Swift) Open Court, 2: 1410.
Genesee River. (B. Rogers) Science, 21: 121.
Genesis of a Docker; a story. (J. Kent) Gent. M. n. s. 54: 109.
Geneva and its Memories. (S. W. Kershaw) Sund. M. 24: 182.
— Concerning the use of Fagots at. (L. W. Bacon) Chr. Lit. 13: 121.
— National Exhibition at, 1896. (C. G. J. Reeve) Longm. 29: 172.
— Public Schools of. (W. B. Scaife) Educa. R. 10: 476.
Genial Editor, The. (John Reid) Good Words, 36: Christmas no., 12.
Genius. Spec. 71: 511.
— Ancestry of. (H. Ellis) Atlan. 71: 383.
— and Suicide. (C. W. Pilgrim) Pop. Sci. Mo. 42: 361.
— The Development of. (L. Arréat) Open Court, 2: 886.
— Lombroso on. Sat. R. 73: 78.
— the Model for Educational Methods. (W. G. Jordan) New Sci. R. 1: 397.
— New Criticism of. (A. Gorren) Atlan. 74: 794.
— Penalties of. (B. S. Lefroy) Canad. M. 5: 24.
— The Question of: Pathognomonic Law, Duality, and Retrospection. (S. McClelland) Arena, 16: 799.
— Something about. (F. B. Wilson) New Sci. R. 2: 228.
— Stimuli to. (J. J. Kral) Music, 8: 16.
— Transplanted. (S. R. Elliott) Dial (Ch.) 16: 71.
— Where it works. Chamb. J. 71: 586. Same art. Ecl. M. 123: 697.
Genius, The, and his Environment. (J. M. Baldwin) Pop. Sci. Mo. 49: 312, 522.
— at Home. (A. H. Wharton) Lippinc. 53: 708.
— Young; a sketch. (F. Greenwood) National, 22: 115.
Genlis, Madame de. (M. C. M. Simpson) Time, 21: 247, 369. — (A. King) Argosy, 56: 429. — (L. B. Lang) National, 19: 488. Same art. Liv. Age, 194: 488.

Genoa, Italy. (M. Halstead) Cosmopol. 12: 643. — (S. B. Holabird) Un. Serv. (Phila.) 9: 230.
— Campo Santo. (F. M. Edselas) Cath. World, 64: 181. — (M. Halstead) Cosmopol. 14: 591. — (W. Dallow) M. of Art, 4: 232.
— Easter at. (Lady V. Greville) Time, 3: 273.
Gent, Thomas. (A. Dobson) Longm. 27: 572.
Genth F. A. J. Frankl. Inst. 135: 448.
Gentility. Sat. R. 76: 622.
Gentle Craft. (H. Hutchinson) Longm. 22: 246.
Gentleman, A; a story. (A. Grey) Argosy, 58: 72.
Gentleman from Huron, The. (G. A. Hibbard) Scrib. M. 17: 743.
Gentleman in the Barrel. (C. B. Fernald) Cent. 28: 307.
Gentleman of France. (S. J. Weyman) Longm. 21: 221-549. 22: 1-487. 23: 1, 111.
Gentleman opposite. (E. Chilton) Longm. 21: 268.
Gentleman George; a story. (R. Horsley) Chamb. J. 70: 173.
Gentleman Jerry; or, how the kraal was saved. Chamb. J. 72: 460.
Gentleman Vagabond, A. (F. H. Smith) Cent. 26: 768.
Gentleman's Beauty, The. (E. F. Corby) Argosy, 62: 154.
Gentleman's Magazine, History of. (W. Roberts) Bookworm, 3: 97-353.
Gentlewoman in Society, Lady Greville's. Spec. 68: 375.
Gentry, the Smaller, Disappearance of, 1680-1800. Macmil. 72: 129. Same art. Liv. Age, 206: 106.
Geoffrey of Monmouth. Mons Badonicus. (E. W. B. Nicholson) Acad. 49: 222, 305.
Geoffroy, Jean. (P. G. Hamerton) Scrib. M. 15: 248.
Geographic Forms, Classification by Genesis. (W. J. McGee) Nat. Geog. M. 1: 27.
Geographic Names, Orthography of. (J. C. Dalton) Geog. J. 1: 431.
— U. S. Board on, Work of. (H. C. Gannett) Nat. Geog. M. 7: 221.
Geographic Nomenclature. (H. G. Ogden and others) Nat. Geog. M. 2: 261.
Geographical and Chemical Words, Changes in. (F. A. Fernald) Pop. Sci. Mo. 41: 690.
Geographical Bibliographies, Recent. (H. R. Mill) Geog. J. 7: 72.
Geographical Concentration in Agriculture. (J. Hyde) Am. Statis. Assoc. 3: 492.
Geographical Congress, German, The Eleventh. Geog. J. 5: 589.
— International, Sixth. (H. N. Dickson) Nat. Sci. 7: 241. — Geog. J. 5: 369. 6: 269.
Geographical Dispersal, A New Law of. (C. Dixon) Fortn. 63: 640.
Geographical Literature, Recent Russian. Geog. J. 6: 554.
Geography as a School Subject. (C. A. McMurray) Educa. R. 9: 448.
— as a Science in England. (H. R. Mill) Knowl. 19: 1.
— as a Sociological Study. (W. Z. Ripley) Pol. Sci. Q. 10: 636.
— at the British Association, Ipswich, 1895. Geog. J. 6: 460.
— at the Universities. (H. J. Mackinder and others) Geog. J. 6: 26.
— at World's Columbian Exposition. (C. T. Conger) Geog. J. 3: 130.
— Commercial. (H. R. Mill) Geog. J. 3: 124.
— Economic. (M. Loeb) Educa. R. 7: 286.
— Gigantic Model of the Earth. (A. R. Wallace) Contemp. 69: 730. Same art. Ecl. M. 126: 791.
— in European Universities. (H. R. Mill) Educa. R. 6: 417.
Geography in Public Schools. (W. B. Powell) Nat. Geog. M. 5: 137. — (W. M. Davis) School R. 1: 339.
— in the University. (R. S. Tarr) Book R. 4: 1.
— Modern, German and English. (H. J. Mackinder) Geog. J. 6: 367.
— Need of, in the University. (W. M. Davis) Educa. R. 10: 22.
— The New. (M. H. Paddock) Educa. 14: 482. — (A. P. Brigham) Pop. Sci. Mo. 48: 815.
— An Old. Chamb. J. 73: 123.
— Present Standpoint of. (C. R. Markham) Nature, 49: 69. — (C. R. Markham) Geog. J. 2: 481.
— Primary, Frye's. (F. W. Parker) Educa. R. 8: 395.
— Relation to History. (F. W. Parker) Nat. Geog. M. 5: 125.
— Teaching of. (W. M. Davis) Educa. R. 3: 417. 4: 6.
— — Improvement in. (W. M. Davis) Nat. Geog. M. 5: 68.
— — Status of. (J. W. Redway) Educa. R. 7: 33.
— Text-books of. (J. W. Redway) Educa. R. 5: 153.
Geological Atlas of the United States. (W. M. Davis) Nation, 56: 45. — Science, n. s. 2: 714, 787.
Geological Catastrophes, Geikie on. Sat. R. 74: 165.
Geological Congress, International. (W. Tapley) Nature, 50: 319.
Geological Evolution, Astronomy and. (R. G. M. Browne) Westm. 139: 430. Same art. Ecl. M. 121: 186.
Geological Investigation, Geographical Methods in. Nat. Geog. M. 1: 11.
Geological Laboratory, Notes on Apparatus for. (J. E. Wolff) Am. J. Sci. 147: 355.
Geological Myths. (B. K. Emerson) Science, n. s. 4: 328.
Geological Science and Education. (N. S. Shaler) Science, n. s. 3: 609.
— Value of, to Man. (N. S. Shaler) Chaut. 20: 170.
Geological Society of America, 5th Annual Meeting, 1892. Am. Natural. 27: 176.
Geological Study, Recent, Characteristics of. Pop. Sci. Mo. 47: 568.
Geological Survey of the United Kingdom. (A. Geikie) Nature, 49: 495, 518.
Geological Time, Estimates of. (W. Upham) Am. J. Sci. 145: 209.
— Ratios of. (W. Upham) Bib. Sac. 50: 131.
Geological Work of the Air. (S. Meunier) Pop. Sci. Mo. 48: 355.
Geologies and Deluges. (W. T. Sollas) Pop. Sci. Mo. 46: 245.
Geology and General Physics, Kelvin's. Sat. R. 78: 136.
— and Physical Geography, Limits between. Geog. J. 2: 518.
— at the British Association. (N. W. Watts) Science, n. s. 2: 493.
— Conquest of the under Earth. (N. S. Shaler) Chaut. 22: 280.
— Curiosities of. (G. W. Bulman) Gent. M. n. s. 51: 408.
— First Days of the World. (H. B. Bashore) Lippinc. 57: 261.
— Foreign Literature on the Older Rocks. (J. E. Marr) Sci. Prog. 3: 10.
— Geikie's Text-book of. (A. H. Green) Nature, 49: 287.
— History and Principles of, and its Aim. (J. C. Hartzell, jr.) Am. Natural. 30: 177, 271.
— in Schools and Colleges, Methods of Presenting. (M. E. Holmes) Science, 22: 175.
— Mathematical, W. Thomson on. (O. J. Lodge) Nature, 50: 289.

Geology, Neozoic, in Europe. (P. Lake) Sci. Prog. **2**: 476.
— of Natural Scenery. (F. J. H. Merrill) Pop. Sci. Mo. **46**: 240.
— Position of. (J. Prestwich) 19th Cent. **34**: 555. Same art. Pop. Sci. Mo. **44**: 537.
— Practical Use of. Chamb. J. **70**: 486.
— Relation to Physiography in Educational System. (T. C. Chamberlin) Nat. Geog. M. **5**: 154.
— Study of. (W. Seton) Cath. World, **56**: 761.
— Twenty-five Years' Progress of, in Britain. (A. Geikie) Nature, **51**: 367.
— What is? (N. S. Shaler) Chaut. **18**: 284.
— Why should we teach it? (A. S. Packard) Pop. Sci. Mo. **41**: 73.
Geometrical Researches, Lobatchewsky's. (C. S. Peirce) Nation, **54**: 116, 131.
Geometry, Abstract, Veronese on. Nature, **50**: 520.
— A Flaw in the Foundation of. (H. Grassman) Open Court, **2**: 1463.
— High School, Modern Methods in. (E. C. Goddard) School R. **4**: 70.
— Logic of. (B. A. W. Russell) Mind, **21**: 1.
— Non-Euclidian. Nature, **45**: 404. — (G. A. Miller) Science, **20**: 370.
— — and the Kantian *a priori*. (F. C. S. Schiller) Philos. R. **5**: 173.
— — Inevitable. (G. B. Halstead) Monist, **4**: 483.
— Old and New. (G. B. Halstead) Educa. R. **6**: 144.
— Old and New Methods in. (E. L. Richards) Educa. R. **3**: 31. — (G. C. Shutts) Educa. R. **3**: 264.
— Plane and Solid, Beman and Smith on. (A. S. Hathaway) School R. **4**: 334.
— — Elements of, Macnie on. (H. E. Slaught) School R. **4**: 183.
Geo-morphology, Walther, Rothpletz and Penck on. (J. W. Gregory) Nature, **51**: 313.
Geordie's Justice. (A. McF. Cleland) Chamb. J. **73**: 508–537.
George, St. (H. Thurston) Month, **74**: 457.
— and the Pope. Spec. **70**: 729.
George III. (Goldwin Smith) Cornh. **74**: 752. Same art. Liv. Age, **211**: 858.
— at Portsmouth in June, 1773. (G. Marsh) Un. Serv. M. '**87**, **1**: 517.
— Personal Policy of. (E. F. de Lancey) M. Am. Hist. **27**: 431.
George, Prince, of Wales. Eng. Illust. **9**: 579.
George, Henry, and the Encyclical of Leo XIII. (C. A. Ramm) Cath. World, **54**: 555.
— and Land Taxation. (M. M. Trumbull) Open Court, **2**: 1415.
— his "Perplexed Philosopher." (L. Belrose, jr.) Open Court, **7**: 3665.
— Tax Theory of, Criticism of. (A. Kitson) Am. J. Pol. **5**: 350.
George Dale's Ambition; a story. (L. Griswold) Outing, **20**: 89.
George Eliot. *See* Eliot, George.
George Fenton's Chance; a story. (D. J. Belgrave) Argosy, **59**: 30.
George Wentworth; a story. (J. S. King) Arena, **8**: 633.
Georgetown, S. C. (L. C. Harby) New Eng. M. n. s. **7**: 670.
— Episcopal Church and Soldiers' Monument. (F. A. Hagadorn) M. Am. Hist. **30**: 148.
Georgia and the Confederacy: Letters of 1865. Am. Hist. R. **1**: 97.
— Banking System of. Bank. M. (N. Y.) **48**: 357.
— Industrial Conditions of. (J. Ralph) Harper, **90**: 607.
Georgia, Middle, Rural Life in. (R. M. Johnston) Cent. **21**: 737.
Georgia Normal and Industrial College, Milledgeville. (M. A. Bacon) New Eng. M. n. s. **10**: 724.
— Superstitions in. (R. A. Moore) J. Am. Folk-Lore, **5**: 230. **7**: 305.
— Supreme Court of. (W. B. Hill) Green Bag, **4**: 18, 65.
Georgia and Russia. (W. R. Morfill) Acad. **41**: 536.
Georgian Literature. (W. R. Morfill) Acad. **47**: 479.
Georgian MSS. in Holy Cross Monastery at Jerusalem, Tsagarelli's Catalogue of. J. Bib. Lit. **12**: 168.
Georgians of the Caucasus. Sat. R. **74**: 11.
Gerard, St., of Gallinaro. Month, **85**: 72, 408.
Gerard, David. (W. H. J. Weale) Portf. '**95**: 24.
Gerbert. *See* Silvester II., Pope.
Germ Cells, Heredity and. (H. F. Osborn) Am. Natural. **26**: 642.
Germ Plasm, Continuity of, and Origin and Differentiation of Sex Cells in Cymatogaster. (C. H. Eigenmann) Am. Natural. **30**: 265.
— Weismann on. (H. L. Osborn) Dial (Ch.) **15**: 146.
Germain, Sophie, an Unknown Mathematician. (C. L. Franklin) Cent. **26**: 946.
German, The, and the German-American. (J. Flynt) Atlan. **78**: 655.
German-Americans and the Lord's Day. (W. C. Doane) Forum, **20**: 733.
German Bath, Notes at a. (E. C. Cook) Gent. M. n. s. **49**: 350. Same art. Liv. Age, **195**: 627.
German Character as reflected in the National Life and Literature. Int. J. Ethics, **3**: 202.
German Drama, The. (S. Whitman) Chaut. **21**: 163.
German Factory, Visit to. (S. Whitman) Chaut. **22**: 193.
German Folk-song. (R. Lieber) Music, **8**: 49.
German Forest, The. (S. Whitman) Chaut. **21**: 36.
German Grammar, Practical, Thomas's. (C. B. Wilson) School R. **4**: 237.
German Jurists and Poets. (A. Hermann) Green Bag, **6**: 3, 61.
German Language, Dictionary of, Flügel's Edition of 1892. Spec. **68**: 582.
— German Methods of Teaching. (R. D. Jones) Educa. **15**: 100.
— German Methods of Using. (R. D. Jones) Educa. **15**: 44.
— Teacher's Outfit in. (C. Thomas) School R. **2**: 401.
— Teaching of, in Higher Schools of Germany. (J. E. Russell) School R. **2**: 199.
German Literature and English Literature of 18th Cent. (O. Seidensticker) Poet-Lore, **2**: 57, 169.
— and Feeling. Eng. R. **10**: 357.
— and Imperialism. (M. G. Conrad) Pub. Opin. **15**: 209.
German Literature, Boyesen's. (G. E. Woodberry) Nation, **54**: 380.
— 1891–92. (R. Zimmermann) Ath. '**92**, **2**: 14.
— 1892–93. (R. Zimmermann) Ath. '**93**, **2**: 16.
— 1893–94. (R. Zimmermann) Ath. '**94**, **2**: 13.
— 1894–95. (R. Zimmermann) Ath. '**95**, **2**: 12.
— 1895–96. (R. Zimmermann) Ath. '**96**, **2**: 13.
— Paralysis of. (M. Delines) Bookman, **2**: 198.
Social Forces in, Francke on. (W. H. Carruth) Dial (Ch.) **21**: 224. — (C. H. Genung) Nation, **63**: 331.
German Music; das Lied. (S. Whitman) Chaut. **21**: 449.
— Realistic Trend of. (E. Blum) Arena, **8**: 211.
German Romanticism, A New Chapter in. (K. Francke) Nation, **63**: 248.
German Silver Commission, Declaration of Bimetallist Members of. (E. B. Andrews) R. of Rs. (N. Y.) **10**: 289.

German Student Life. (C. L. Crow) Southern M. 5: 136.
German Tenor; a story. (G. Fosbery) Argosy, 57: 537.
German Theology, A Century of. (J. Stalker) Chr. Lit. 12: 32.
German Unity, Krause on. Spec. 70: 261.
German Universities. (E. D. Perry) Educa. R. 7: 209. — (A. R. Crook) Chaut. 23: 560.— (E. F. Baldwin) Outl. 52: 256.
German Vote and the Republican Party. (F. W. Holls) Forum, 20: 588.
German Watering Place, Glimpse of a. (S. Whitman) Chaut. 20: 677.
Germanic Origins, Gummere on. Sat. R. 74: 55.
Germans, The. (S. Whitman) Chaut. 20: 43.
— as Emigrants and Colonists. (F. H. Geffcken) Forum, 13: 200.
— at Home. (V. Rendall) Gent. M. n. s. 54: 175. Same art. Ecl. M. 124: 422.
— French View of. Sat. R. 80: 374.
— in America, Plea for. (W. L. Sheldon) New Eng. M. n. s. 7: 106.
— National Traits of, as seen in their Religion. (O. Pfleiderer) Int. J. Ethics, 3: 1.
Germantown and Chestnut Hill, Pa., List of Inhabitants of, 1809. (T. H. Shoemaker) Pennsyl. M. 15: 449. 16: 42.
— Battle of, described by a Hessian Officer. Nat'l M. (N. Y. '91) 17: 456. — (F. E. von Münchausen) Pennsyl. M. 16: 197.
— Middle Ward Fire Company of. (T. H. Shoemaker) Pennsyl. M. 18: 429.
Germany and the Germans, Dawson's. Sat. R. 77: 207.
— Army. (J. J. O'Connell) Un. Serv. (Phila.) 16: 1, 155.
— — Commissions in. Cornh. 69: 606. Same art. Liv. Age, 202: 171.
— — Military Bill, 1892. Spec. 69: 437, 587.
— — Bill, 1892-93. Pub. Opin. 15: 143, 168.
— — — Defeat of. Spec. 70: 629. — Sat. R. 75: 506.
— — Manœuvres in the Rhineland, 1893. (F. Trench) Un. Serv. M. 8: 43.
— — of To-day. (Lt.-Col. Exner) Harper, 84: 869.
— — Side Lights on the German Soldier. (P. Bigelow) Harper, 87: 213.
— Banks of, and Specie Reserves. Bank. M. (Lond.) 56: 357.
— Church and the Social Question in. (J. G. Brooks) New World, 1: 673.
— Church of, Reformed, and Rationalism. (J. I. Good) Presb. & Ref. R. 5: 227.
— Cities in; What they do for their Citizens. (A. Shaw) Cent. 26: 380.
— Coast Defence of. (C. A. Voigt) Un. Serv. M. 6: 357.
— Code of. (E. Schuster) Law Q. 12: 17.
— — New. (F. Dahn) Jurid. R. 2: 15.
— Code of Criminal Procedure. (H. A. D. Phillips) Law Q. 10: 16.
— Competition of, in Trade. (G. Newcomen) Westm. 145: 276. — (E. E. Williams) New R. 14: 14-636.
— Constitutional Liberty in. (Poultney Bigelow) Cosmopol. 20: 17.
— Credit Associations in. Gunton's M. 10: 323.
— Crisis in, 1892, and the Emperor. New R. 6: 385. Same art. Liv. Age, 193: 707.
— Election, June, 1893. Pub. Opin. 15: 287, 332, 353. — Spec. 70: 844. 71: 8. — Sat. R. 76: 5.
— Empire of, Sybel's Founding of. (C. H. Cooper) Dial (Ch.) 12: 428. — (M. Smith) Nation, 55: 108, 130. — (Munroe Smith) Nation, 60: 204, 223.
Germany, Empire of, Twenty-fifth Anniversary of. Macmil. 73: 273. — (C. Thomas) Nation, 62: 134. — Sat. R. 81: 63. — (A. E. Evans) Contemp. 69: 167. Same art. Liv. Age, 208: 542.
— England's Relations with. Quar. 183: 545.
— Federal Council and the Emperor. (R. Hudson) Pol. Sci. Q. 10: 655.
— Foreign Policy of. (E. J. Dillon) Fortn. 66: 769.
— Government of; An Over-administered Nation. Macmil. 66: 39. Same art. Liv. Age, 194: 108.
— — Prussian Ministers and Imperial Rule. (E. W. Raynolds) Yale R. 1: 187.
— Greater, Idea of a. (H. H. Risley) Asia. R. 10: 233.
— History, German Struggle for Liberty. (P. Bigelow) Harper, 91: 202-822. 92: 66-901. 93: 122.
— Lamprecht's. (J. Tait) Eng. Hist. R. 7: 547.
— Home Colonies of. All the Year, 70: 591.
— Imperial. (F. C. Howe) Am. J. Pol. 2: 1.
— Industrial Decadence in. (J. C. Bayles) Engin. M. 4: 38.
— Industries of. New R. 14: 113-492.
— in the Middle Ages, Henderson's. Sat. R. 78: 240.
— in the 15th Century. (J. W. Wilstach) Cath. World, 63: 720.
— in 1826. Scot. R. 34: 106.
— in 1888. (J. P. Mahaffy) Univ. R. 2: 1.
— Judicial System of. (J. J. Cook) Jurid. R. 1: 70-298.
— Legislation of. (J. W. Burgess) Chaut. 20: 145.
— A Lesson in German. Fortn. 65: 177.
— Manufacturing in. New R. 14: 636.
— Militarism and Social Reform in. (F. Schumann) Chaut. 16: 577.
— Monetary Situation in, in 1893. (W. Lotz) Ann. Am. Acad. Pol. Sci. 4: 61.
— Music in. (M. D. Taylor) Music, 6: 516.
— New Storm and Stress in. (K. Francke) Atlan. 74: 408.
— of To-day. (S. Whitman) Chaut. 20: 167.
— Parliament of. (M. Smith) Nation, 57: 5.
— Partnership in. (J. Hirschfeld) Law Q. 9: 62.
— People of. Leis. Hour, 43: 173-384.
— Plant-geography of. (R. Pound) Am. Natural. 30: 465.
— Police in. (A. T. Sibbald) Green Bag, 8: 53.
— Political Parties in. (J. G. C. Minchin) Acad. 45: 284.
— Politics in, 1892. (G. W. Hinman) Chaut. 14: 561. — (C. H. Hull) Nation, 54: 375. — Sat. R. 73: 270.
— — 1893. Elections, Issue of. (J. H. Senner) No. Am. 157: 234.
— — 1894; the late German Crisis. Contemp. 66: 829.
— — 1896; Crisis in. (E. L. Godkin) Nation, 63: 208.
— Press and Government in. (A. Tanzer) Nation, 62: 49.
— Recent Home Politics in. Blackw. 159: 627.
— Royal Family. (G. H. Dryer) Chaut. 23: 668.
— Secret Treaty with Russia. National, 28: 446.
— Should we seek Alliance with? National, 27: 21.
— Situation in, 1893. Pub. Opin. 15: 214. — Spec. 70: 693.
— a Sketch. (M. Sutherland) 19th Cent. 38: 644.
— Sketches in. (K. Blyth) 19th Cent. 40: 383, 729. Same art. Ecl. M. 127: 768.
— Socialism and Literary Sterility in. (F. H. Geffcken) Forum, 14: 660.
— Socialistic Situation in. (K. Francke) Nation, 61: 132.
— Statesmen of. Liv. Age, 195: 242-741.

Germany, Village Life in. (A. F. Slack) Leis. Hour, 45: 34.
— We Girls awheel through. Outing, 20: 298.
Germinating Nuts and Acorns. (J. G. Jack) Garden & F. 8: 6.
Germs in the Air. (C. M. Aikman) Gent. M. n. s. 54: 146.
Gérôme, Jean Léon. M. of Art, 3: 453. — (R. R. Wilson) Mo. Illust. 12: 1.
— and his Work. (C. S. Johnson) Munsey, 7: 428.
Gerona. (C. W. Wood) Argosy, 61: 191–683.
Gerry, Elbridge, Letters of. (W. C. Ford) N. E. Reg. 49: 430. 50: 21.
Gerry, Elbridge, and the N. Y. Soc. for Prevention of Cruelty to Children, with portrait. R. of Rs. (N. Y.) 4: 689.
Gerrymander, The. (J. W. Dean) N. E. Reg. 46: 374.
— The Courts *versus*. (N. T. Mason) Am. J. Pol. 2: 150.
— A Cure for. (J. Haynes) Am. M. Civics, 7: 154.
— How to abolish. (J. R. Commons) R. of Rs. (N. Y.) 6: 541.
— Slaying of the. Atlan. 69: 678.
Gersoppa Falls, India. Chamb. J. 73: 253.
Gerund and Gerundive in Plautus and Terence. (S. B. Platner) Am. J. Philol. 14: 483.
— — Origin of. (L. Horton Smith) Am. J. Philol. 15: 194.
— The English. (J. W. Wilkinson) Educa. 15: 479.
Gervaise; a story. (M. E. Freeborn) Argosy, 61: 503.
Gesner, Conrad; an Old Naturalist. (W. K. Brooks) Pop. Sci. Mo. 47: 49.
Gessner, Solomon. Death of Abel. (J. A. Noble) Ecl. M. 114: 97.
Gesso-work. (W. Crane) Am. Arch. 41: 29.
Gesture, Written. (J. H. Schooling) 19th Cent. 37: 477.
Gethsemane Abbey. (L. G. Deppen) So. M. 2: 194.
Gettysburg, A Story of. (J. Ribchester) Un. Serv. (Phila.) 9: 9.
— Battle of. So. Hist. Pap. 23: 205.
— First Gun at. (J. L. Marye) Am. Hist. Reg. 2: 1225.
— Incident at the Battle of. (T. J. Mackey) McClure, 3: 68.
— Personal Recollections of Two Visits to. (A. H. Nickerson) Scrib. M. 14: 19.
— Thirty Years after. (H. White) Nation, 56: 326.
Gettysburg Week, The. (Philip Schaff) Scrib. M. 16: 21.
Gevers, Hélène. (P. G. Hubert, jr.) Mo. Illust. 3: 69.
Geyser, Artificial, Experiments with. (J. C. Graham) Am. J. Sci. 145: 54.
Geysers, At the. (R. Wildman) Overland, n. s. 26: 233.
Ghantur, Vapor Bath of. (A. Walker) Bib. World, 3: 53.
Gheel, Colony for Lunatics at. Cornh. 71: 577. Same art. Liv. Age, 206: 124.
Ghiberti, Lorenzo, Terracotta Sketch by. (A. Marquand) Am. J. Archæol. 9: 206.
Ghost of *nisi prius*; a story. (A. O. Hall) Green Bag, 7: 268, 343.
Ghost of Rhodes House. (W. T. Nichols) Lippinc. 55: 696.
Ghost of St. Elspeth; a story. (G. Fosbery) Argosy, 54: 516.
Ghost of the Sea, A; a story. (F. Prevost) Temp. Bar, 98: 411.
Ghost Dance at Pine Ridge, So. Dakota. J. Am. Folk-Lore, 4: 160.
— in Arizona. J. Am. Folk-Lore, 5: 65.
Ghost Raft, The; a yarn. Outing, 24: 440.
Ghost Stories. (L. J. Vance) Open Court, 2: 1248, 1259, 1273.
— and Beast Stories. (A. Lang) 19th Cent. 37: 258.
— Negro. (E. M. Backus) J. Am. Folk-Lore, 9: 228.
— Real, Stead's. (D. G. Ritchie) Westm. 137: 1.
— A Teton Dakota. (J. O. Dorsey) J. Am. Folk-Lore, 1: 68.
Ghost Train, A; a story. (W. L. Alden) Idler, 8: 556.
Ghost World, Dyer's. (T. F. Crane) Nation, 57: 253.
Ghost Worship and Tree Worship. (G. Allen) Pop. Sci. Mo. 42: 489, 648.
Ghostly Lights. (M. J. Walhouse) Folk-Lore, 5: 293.
Ghostly Premonitions. (L. C. Lillie) Harper, 90: 676.
Ghosts. (A. Repplier) Atlan. 74: 741. — Open Court, 5: 2811.
— and their Photos. (H. R. Haweis) Fortn. 59: 116. Same art. Ecl. M. 120: 250.
— and Things. (E. Worthington) Canad. M. 2: 507.
— before the Law. (A. Lang) Blackw. 155: 210.
— Doctrine of, among the Chinook Indians. (Franz Boas) J. Am. Folk-Lore, 6: 39.
— Duppies. (Alice Spinner) National, 25: 552. Same art. Ecl. M. 125: 124.
— The Lyttelton and Beresford. (C. B. Angier) Argosy, 61: 410.
— Modern View of. (A. Bodington) Open Court, 6: 3090, 3103.
— My Belief in. (J. C. Atkinson) Macmil. 67: 293.
— of the Living and of the Dead. (W. S. Blackstock) Canad. M. 3: 58.
— a Poem. (G. R. Tomson) Cosmopol. 16: 425.
— Some English. Chamb. J. 72: 721.
— Some Japanese Bogies. (A. Lang) M. of Art, 8: 15.
— up to Date. (A. Lang) Blackw. 155: 47.
— West African. (M. Kingsley) Cornh. 74: 79.
Ghosts' Ordinary. (W. B. Harte) New Eng. M. n. s. 9: 212.
Giannone, Pietro; a Forgotten Italian Worthy. (M. Macdonald) Good Words, 34: 611.
Giants and Giantism. (C. L. Dana) Scrib. M. 17: 179.
Gibbon, E., Art of. Ath. '94, 2: 633.
— as a Soldier. (R. Holden) Macmil. 71: 31. Same art. Liv. Age, 203: 669.
— Centenary of. (F. Harrison) 19th Cent. 36: 146. Same art. Ecl. M. 123: 220. Same art. Critic, 25: 280. — Am. Arch. 46: 127.
— Letters of, New. (R. E. Prothero) 19th Cent. 40: 143. Same art. Ecl. M. 127: 391. Same art. Liv. Age, 210: 416.
Gibbons, Abby H., with portrait. (S. S. Thayer) Char. R. 2: 379.
Gibbons, Grinling. (L. Cust) Eng. Illust. 11: 1115.
Gibbons, James, Cardinal, with portrait. (M. White, jr.) Munsey, 10: 398. — Portraits of. McClure, 3: 31.
Gibbs, Henry Hucks. (W. Roberts) Bookworm, 4: 193.
Gibbs, James. (J. R. Brown) Am. Arch. 48: 29.
Gibraltar. (E. Mitchell) Temp. Bar, 103: 398. Same art. Liv. Age, 203: 771.
— Cession of, Proposed. (J. W. Gambier) Fortn. 59: 722. — (W. F. Rae) Westm. 140: 126.
— for Twenty Centuries. Chamb. J. 68: 795.
— a Fortress of the Centuries. (M. T. Carpenter) Cosmopol. 19: 623.
— Grievance of. (C. Bill) National, 24: 816.
— Illustrated by Holst. Art J. 48: 238.
— Past and Future. (J. Adye) 19th Cent. 38: 814. Same art. Liv. Age, 207: 673.
— Reminiscences of. Canad. M. 7: 269.
— Uselessness of. (W. L. Clowes) Fortn. 59: 247.
Gibson, Charles Dana, with portrait. Bk. Buyer, 11: 487.

Gibson, Wm. Hamilton, with portrait. Bk. Buyer, 5: 18.—With portrait. Bk. Buyer, 13: 409.—Critic, 29: 63, 81.
Giddens, George, with portrait. Theatre, 37: 211.
Giddings, J. R., Julian's Life of. (J. W. Chadwick) Nation, 55: 206.—(S. Willard) Dial (Ch.) 13: 138.
— A Political Abolitionist. Atlan. 71: 701.
Gifford, William, and Keats. (D. Masson) 19th Cent. 31: 586. Same art. Liv. Age, 193: 719.
Gift of the Simple King, The. (G. Parker) Idler, 6: 255.
Gift, Title by. (W. C. Maude) Month, 88: 241.
Gifts. Atlan. 74: 142.
— Law of, Inconsistency of. (C. B. Labatt) Am. Law R. 29: 361.
— to Colleges. Critic, 28: 399, 450.
Gilbert, St. (J. A. Floyd) Cath. World, 63: 343.
Gilbert, Alfred. (W. C. Monkhouse) M. of Art, 12: 1, 37.
Gilbert, Sir John. (J. Macaulay) Leis. Hour, 42: 622. —(John Oldcastle) M. of Art, 1: 131.
— Pictures presented to London. Art J. 45: 199.
— Popular Art. (M. Jackson) Eng. Illust. 12: no. 2, 77.
Gilbert, John Gibbs, Actor. (J. H. Wiggin) Bost. 1: 530.
— and Wife. (J. H. Wiggin) Bost. 2: 62.
Gilbert, Sir Joseph Henry, with portrait. Pop. Sci. Mo. 45: 119.
Gilbert, Josiah. Acad. 42: 369.
Gilbert, W. S. The Mountebanks. Gent. M. n. s. 48: 206.—Theatre, 28: 112.
— Retirement of. (E. Kuhe) Theatre, 37: 127.
Gilbert Islands. (C. M. Woodford) Geog. J. 6: 325.
— Experiences of a Blackbirder at. (A. Inkersley and W. H. Brommage) Overland, n. s. 23: 565.
Gildas De Excidio Britanniae, Author and Date of. (A. Anscombe and others) Acad. 48: 206–411.—(W. H. Stevenson) Acad. 48: 522.
Gilder, R. W., with portrait. Bk. News, 8: 208.
Gilderoy. (C. Whibley) New R. 14: 215.
Gildersleeve, Richard. (C. M. Andrews) New Eng. M. n. s. 7: 702.
Gilead, Land of. (J. Wells) Sund. M. 25: 533.
Giles, Chauncey. (W. L. Worcester) N. Church R. 1: 1.
Giles; a story. All the Year, 74: 82.
Giles Corey, Yeoman; a play. (M. E. Wilkins) Harper, 86: 20.
Giles Dearlove; a story. (B. Lindsay) New R. 11: 98.
Giles's Resolution, Authorship of. (P. L. Ford) Nation, 61: 164.
Gilgit, From Chitral to. Cornh. 72: 368.
Gill Lineage. (J. D. Butler) N. E. Reg. 46: 212.
Gillet, Jonathan, Descendants of. (H. C. Alvord) N. E. Reg. 47: 168.
Gilliland, William. (H. Walworth) Am. Hist. Reg. 2: 1438.
Gillmore, Frank, with portrait. Theatre, 29: 129.
Gilly-f'ers. (M. E. Francis) Longm. 22: 233.
Gilpin, William. (J. A. Blaikie) M. of Art, 6: 322.
Gilsonite, Utah. (W. C. Day) J. Frankl. Inst. 140: 221.
Gindely, Anton. (A. W. Ward) Eng. Hist. R. 8: 500.
Ginger-beer Plant. Garden & F. 6: 50.
Ginseng. Chamb. J. 72: 359.
— Corean Export of. Dub. R. 117: 164.
— Cultivation of. (G. Stanton) Garden & F. 5: 223.
Gioberti, Vincenzo, Extracts from. (C. C. Starbuck) Ref. Q. 42: 82, 225, 315, 467.
Giolito, Gabriele. (H. F. Brown) Atlan. 69: 185.
Giorgione. (W. J. Stillman) Cent. 21: 715.
Giorgione. Madonna in the Hermitage. Is it by Giorgione? (C. Phillips) M. of Art, 18: 347.
Gipsies. *See* Gypsies.
Giraffe, The. (F. E. Beddard) Knowl. 19: 241.
— New. Sat. R. 78: 72.
Giraffe Hunting. Sat. R. 79: 123.
Giraffes. (R. Lydekker) Knowl. 16: 201.
— in the London Zoölogical Garden, Death of. 1892. Spec. 68: 524.
Girard, Stephen, and John Woolman. (G. M. Hammell) Meth. R. 55: 741.
Girard College. (W. H. Zeller) Chaut. 15: 717.
— Architecture of, N. Biddle and. Pennsyl. M. 18: 354.
Girdleton Gallery Mystery, The. Chamb. J. 73: 65–120.
Girl, The, and the Game; a drama. (G. E. Milton) Eng. Illust. 13: 428.
— and the Problem; a story. (V. Roseboro') Cent. 22: 254.
— from Madeira, The. (P. L. McDermott) Chamb. J. 71: 10–56.
— I left behind me, The. (W. W. Knollys) Time, 1: 611.
— Little, One Year with a. (O. Chrisman) Educa. R. 9: 52.
— The Modern. (S. Grand) No. Am. 158: 706.
— — A Defence of. Westm. 143: 54.
— of the Future. (G. Allen) Univ. R. 7: 49.
— of the Period, A; a story. (M. O. W. Oliphant) Eng. Illust. 9: 418.
— who believed in the Saints, The; a story. (L. Dougall) Temp. Bar, 104: 221. Same art. Liv. Age, 204: 720.
Girl Bachelors. (G. H. Hepworth) Chaut. 17: 735.
Girl-martyrs of Ku-Cheng. (A. R. Buckland) Good Words, 36: 676.
Girlhood, Squandered. (E. L. Gell) 19th Cent. 32: 930.
Girls during Adolescence, Effect of High School Work upon. (Helen P. Kennedy) Pedagog. Sem. 3: 469.
— in a Factory Valley. (L. B. C. Wyman) Atlan. 78: 391, 506.
— La Tour—Landry's Quaint Book of Advice to. (H. L. Reed) Chaut. 19: 219.
— Nervous, Education of. (L. F. Bryson) Critic, 21: 140.
— of Dangar. (L. R. Baker) New Eng. M. n. s. 7: 710.
— Tall. Liv. Age, 192: 188.
— What shall we do with our? (F. M. Edselas) Cath. World, 61: 538.
Girls' Schools in Past Times. (F. B. Cobbe) Time, 11: 222.
Girondins, Lamartine's History of. Eng. R. 11: 74.
Girton College, the Girls' College. Idler, 5: 532.
Gissing, George. Eve's Ransom. Sat. R. 79: 531.
— In the Year of Jubilee. Sat. R. 79: 99.
— Paying Guest. Sat. R. 81: 405.
Gist, Christopher. Journals. (J. D. Butler) Nation, 58: 108.
Giving. (A. H. Japp) Argosy, 55: 378.
— and Receiving, Carlyle on. Spec. 72: 228.
— Proportionate and Systematic. (J. K. Hilty) Luth. Q. 25: 358.
— Tribulations of a Cheerful Giver. (W. D. Howells) Cent. 28: 181, 417.
Gizeh Museum, Rearrangement of. Ath. '92, 2: 708.
Gizycki, Georg von, and the Science of Ethics. (F. Jodl) Int. J. Ethics, 5: 500.
Glacial Discoveries in England. [Map for Prof. Wright's Work.] Pop. Sci. Mo. 42: 169.
Glacial Drift, Diversity of, along its Boundary. (W. Upham) Am. J. Sci. 147: 358.

Glacial Gravels in the Lower Susquehanna Valley, Notes on. (H. B. Bashore) Am. J. Sci. 151: 281.
Glacial Ice Dam and a Limit to the Ice Sheet in Central Ohio. (W. G. Tight) Am. Natural. 28: 488.
Glacial Lake St. Lawrence of Professor W. Upham. (R. Chambers) Am. J. Sci. 149: 273.
Glacial Myth, An English. (G. F. Wright) Nation, 54: 318.
Glacial Nightmare and the Flood, Howorth's. Spec. 71: 114, 145.
Glacial Period. *See* Ice Age.
— in New England and the Upper Mississippi Basin. (J. D. Dana) Pop. Sci. Mo. 44: 816.
Glacial Phenomena between Lakes Champlain and George, and the Hudson River. (G. F. Wright) Science, n. s. 2: 673.
— Causes of, Howorth on. (T. McK. Hughes) Nature, 48: 242.
— of Newfoundland, Labrador, and Southern Greenland. (G. F. Wright) Am. J. Sci. 149: 86.
Glacial Pot-holes in California. (H. W. Turner) Am. J. Sci. 144: 453.
Glacial Studies in Greenland, Recent. (T. C. Chamberlin) Nature, 52: 139.
Glaciated Regions, Hint on Origin of Terraces in. (R. S. Tarr) Am. J. Sci. 144: 59.
Glaciation, Certain Astronomical Conditions favorable to. (G. F. Becker) Am. J. Sci. 148: 95.
— Epeirogenic Movements associated with. (W. Upham) Am. J. Sci. 146: 114.
— in the Finger-Lake Region of New York. (D. F. Lincoln) Am. J. Sci. 144: 290.
— in Western Montana. (H. R. Wood) Science, 20: 162.
Glacier on Montana Rockies. (L. W. Chaney, jr.) Science, n. s. 2: 792.
Glacier Bay, Alaska. (E. R. Scidmore) Nat. Geog. M. 7: 140.
— Discovery of. (J. Muir) Cent. 28: 234.
Glaciers, Cause of Movement of. (P. L. Addison) Knowl. 18: 65.
— Do they excavate? (T. G. Bonney) Contemp. 66: 108. — (T. G. Bonney) Geog. J. 1: 481.
— Motion of, Theories of. (H. N. Hutchinson) Knowl. 15: 66.
— Observations upon the Glacial Phenomena of Newfoundland, Labrador, and Southern Greenland. (G. F. Wright) Am. J. Sci. 149: 86.
— of Alaska. (H. G. Egerton) 19th Cent. 32: 991.
— of Greenland. (A. Heilprin) Pop. Sci. Mo. 46: 1.
— of Mt. St. Elias. (I. C. Russell) Am. J. Sci. 143: 169.
— Spring Flowers and. (A. P. Coleman) Chaut. 17: 68.
— Study of Existing. (Marshall-Hall) Nat. Sci. 6: 17.
— Work of. Around World, 1: 155.
Gladioli, Cultivation of. (J. N. Gerard) Garden & F. 7: 296.
— Origin of. (E. H. Krilage) Garden & F. 9: 446.
Gladstone, W. E. (G. H. Knott) Am. Law. R. 26: 64. — (H. W. Lucy) Eng. Illust. 9: 865. — With portraits. (W. T. Stead) R. of Rs. (N. Y.) 5: 437. 9: 417. — (W. Roberts) Bookworm, 3: 161. — With portrait. (J. MacVeagh) Cath. World, 58: 81. — (J. C. Hopkins) Chaut. 19: 198. — (R. H. Hutton) Contemp. 65: 616. — Liv. Age, 201: 579. — With portrait. (W. F. Day) Munsey, 7: 576. 11: 366. — (W. T. Stead) McClure, 7: 195.
— Age of, Unfitting him for the Premiership. National, 19: 119.
— and Mr. Chamberlain; a Chapter in Personal Politics. (T. H. S. Escott) Westm. 142: 15.
— and the Currency. (W. H. Grenfell) Fortn. 60: 297.
Gladstone, W. E., and his Portraits. (T. W. Reid) M. of Art, 12: 82.
— and Felix Gras, Correspondence of. Critic, 29: 392.
— and Ireland in 1892. (N. Carty) Chaut. 15: 702.
— and Lord Rosebery. (H. W. Massingham) Contemp. 65: 457. Same art. Ecl. M. 122: 635. Same art. Liv. Age, 201: 489.
— and Cardinal Manning. (S. F. Smith) 19th Cent. 39: 694.
— and Welsh Landlords. Spec. 69: 519.
— as a Book Collector. Acad. 50: 589.
— at Hawarden, with portraits. (W. H. Rideing) Cosmopol. 14: 45.
— Commemorative Album. M. of Art, 12: 428
— A Day with. (H. W. Massingham) McClure, 1: 44.
— The Gladstonian Secret. Fortn. 57: 757.
— Hopkins' Life of. (G. M. Grant) Canad. M. 6: 81.
— Letter to Pope Leo XIII. (W. Lloyd) Westm. 146: 1.
— Lucy's Life of. (M. Todhunter) Westm. 144: 22.
— Nonconformists and. (J. G. Rogers) Contemp. 61: 900.
— on Religious Liberty. Eng. R. 17: 337.
— Pamphlet on Irish Question. (W. Summers) Time, 15: 513.
— a Pamphleteer. (A. A. Baumann) Time, 15: 385.
— Phrases of. (A. J. Robbins) Gent. M. n. s. 56: 20.
— Portraits of. McClure, 4: 375.
— Qualities of, Defects of. Spec. 69: 53.
— Retirement of. National, 23: 175. — (A. Webb) Nation, 58: 191. — Soc. Econ. 6: 206.
— — The Nation's Loss. (R. S. Watson) Contemp. 65: 466.
— Return of, to Power. (E. L. Godkin) Nation, 55: 142.
— Return to Public Life. (H. D. Traill) National, 28: 27.
— Secret of. (E. L. Godkin) Nation, 56: 288.
— Speech of, at Liverpool, Dec., 1892. Spec. 69: 843.
Gladstone, Mrs. William Ewart. (M. G. Burnett) McClure, 1: 235.
Gladys Grey; a pastoral. (W. K. Honnywill) Belgra. 87: 307.
Glamour. (E. M. Thomas) Cent. 29: 308.
Glanville, Joseph, Writings of. Temp. Bar, 98: 250.
Glasgow. Chamb. J. 72: 49. — (W. E. Garrett Fisher) Fortn. 63: 607. Same art. Ecl. M. 124: 735.
— and Balliol. (P. A. W. Henderson) Blackw. 155: 342.
— and its Municipal Industries. (W. Smart) Q. J. Econ. 9: 188.
— Art Collections of. (H. M. Cundall) Art J. 45: 244.
— Art in. (E. R. Pennell) Harper, 90: 412.
— Home for Infirm Children. (A. Lamont) Sund. M. 24: 263.
— Municipal Work and Finance of. (W. Smart) Econ. J. 5: 35.
— Old. (R. Walker) Good Words, 37: 678.
— Old College at. Macmil. 69: 456.
— Social Condition of the Poor in. Scot. R. 20: 1.
— Water-supply of. (B. Taylor) Chamb. J. 73: 563.
Glasgow Corporation Gallery. (W. Armstrong) M. of Art, 13: 91, 138.
Glasgow Institute, The. Acad. 41: 164.
— and Royal Scottish Academy Exhibitions, 1879–81. (G. R. Halkett) M. of Art, 2: 184–265. 3: 341. 4: 212.
— — 1893–94. Acad. 43: 157. 45: 194.
Glasgow Technical College. (T. C. Fulton) Cassier, 4: 355.
Glass, Antique, Coleman Collection of. (R. Sturgis) Cent. 48: 554.

Glass, Austrian Sheet and Mirror. (J. Goldschmidt) Am. Arch. **37**: 120.
— Cameo, Modern. (A. St. Johnston) M. of Art, **10**: 187.
— Colored, American Art Supreme in. (L. C. Tiffany) Forum, **15**: 621.
— in Architecture. (Caryl Coleman) Archit. Rec. **2**: 265, 473.
— Modern Venetian. (M. A. W. Dunlop) M. of Art, **13**: 206.
— Painted. (N. H. J. Westlake) M. of Art, **1**: 162. — (L. F. Day) M. of Art, **8**: 377.
— — Cinque-cento Picture Windows. (L. F. Day) M. of Art, **8**: 341.
— — From Gothic to Renaissance. (L. F. Day) M. of Art, 8: 282.
— — Later Gothic, in England. (L. F. Day) M. of Art, **6**: 420.
— — of the 14th Century. (L. F. Day) M. of Art, **5**: 289.
— Some Modern Uses of. Chamb. J. **72**: 639. Same art. Liv. Age, **208**: 189.
— Stained; Earliest Cathedral Windows. (L. F. Day) M. of Art, **5**: 19.
— — What a Memorial Window should be. (J. P. Seddon) M. of Art, **13**: 67.
— Strengthened by Embedding Wire Netting, Shuman's Process. J. Frankl. Inst. **137**: 161.
— Venetian. (M. A. W. Dunlop) M. of Art, **7**: 20, 152.
— — Modern. (E. T. Blakely) M. of Art, **4**: 22.
— Wired-, Fire-retarding Qualities of. (C. A. Hexamer) J. Frankl. Inst. **142**: 81.
Glass Industry, The. (C. H. Henderson) Pop. Sci. Mo. **42**: 433, 577.
— in America. (R. M. Atwater) Engin. M. **4**: 883.
Glass-making, Domestic. (G. White) Art J. **48**: 21.
— English, in 16th and 17th Centuries. (E. W. Hulme) Antiq. n. s. **30**: 210, 259. **31**: 68.
Glass Painters. (F. Miller) Art J. **47**: 150.
Glasswork, Artistic. Chamb. J. **73**: 718.
Glasse, Mrs., Cookery Book, Early Editions of. (R. Hooper) Ath. '93, **2**: 628. — (J. Humphreys) Ath. **93**, **2**: 664.
Glasses. (H. James) Atlan. **77**: 145.
Glastonbury, Ancient Village at. Leis. Hour, **44**: 59.
— Reading, and Colchester, Abbots of, Document Relating to the Execution of. Dub. R. **118**: 154.
Glastonbury Abbey. (A. B. Bibb) Am. Arch. **45**: 73.
Glastonbury Lake-dwellers, The. (C. Edwardes) Chamb. J. **73**: 449.
Glave, Edward James, Career of, in Africa. (R. H. Russell) Cent. **28**: 865.
— Journey to the Livingstone Tree. (E. J. Glave) Cent. **30**: 765.
Gledstanes, Family of. (F. M. Gladstone) Scot. R. **27**: 324.
Glen Nevis, A Midsummer Day in. Good Words, **34**: 493.
Glenbaragh. Macmil. **70**: 276.
Glendower, Owen. Macmil. **74**: 254.
Glenfinnan, Ballad of, August, 1745. (H. C. Minchin) Temp. Bar, **102**: 385.
Glengarry, R. Macdonell, Chief of. Blackw. **154**: 323. Same art. Ecl. M. **121**: 459. Same art. Liv. Age, **199**: 323. — (L. C. R. Macdonnell) Blackw. **157**: 520.
Glenn, John. (D. C. Gilman) Char. R. **5**: 302.
Gliding Flight. (L. P. Mouillard) Cosmopol. **16**: 459.
Glimpse of an Artist. (Viola Roseboro') Scrib. M. **13**: 478.
Glimpse of Genteel Socialism; a story. Temp. Bar, **105**: 213.
Glimpses Back: a Hundred Years Ago. Temp. Bar, **99**: 104. Same art. Ecl. M. **121**: 445. Same art. Liv. Age, **199**: 371.
Glimpses of Garrison Life; a story. Un. Serv. (Phila.) **9**: 54.
Glimpses of Some Vanished Celebrities. Blackw. **158**: 1. Same art. Liv. Age, **206**: 337.
Globe; the Proposed Gigantic Model of the Earth. (A. R. Wallace) Contemp. **69**: 730.
Glommen, Falls of the. (C. Edwardes) Chamb. J. **71**: 214.
Glooscap, The Home of. (F. Bolles) Atlan. **74**: 47.
Glory of Woman. (F. A. Steel) Macmil. **69**: 474.
Gloucester, William, Duke of. Argosy, **53**: 194.
Gloucester, Eng. (H. D. M. Spence) Art J. **44**: 58.
— Musical Festival. (J. S. Shedlock) Acad. **42**: 221, 246.
Gloucester Cathedral. (T. E. Champion) Canad. M. **3**: 359.
Gloucester, Mass. (E. A. Start) New Eng. M. n. s. **6**: 687.
— Harbor of. (R. C. Coxe) Cent. **22**: 518.
— Marriages in, 1729. N. E. Reg. **48**: 420.
Gloucestershire Ship Canals. (W. J. Gordon) Leis. Hour, **42**: 232.
Glove, A; a prose play. (B. Björnson) Poet-Lore, **4**: 7–332.
Gloves, A Gossip on. (A. Isaacson) Good Words, **35**: 424.
Gloves, Historic. (S. W. Beck) M. of Art, **9**: 491. **10**: 24.
— Romance of. (S. W. Beck) Cosmopol. **13**: 450.
Glow-worm, The. Chamb. J. **69**: 543. — (E. A. Butler) Knowl. **17**: 268.
Gloxinias. (E. O. Orpet) Garden & F. **6**: 33. — Garden & F. **8**: 247.
Glück, Christoph, Newman on. Sat. R. **81**: 36.
Glück auf; a story. (J. P. Rudd) Outing, **28**: 3.
Glydon Ephscott's Bride; a tale. (A. M. Jolley) Canad. M. **7**: 81.
Glykas, Nikephoros, Bishop of Constantinople. (E. A. Grosvenor) New World, **5**: 527.
Gnarled Pine-tree; Moorland Idyll. (G. Allen) Eng. Illust. **13**: 33.
Gneist, Rudolf von. (C. Bornhak) Ann. Am. Acad. Pol. Sci. **7**: 253. — (M. Smith) Pol. Sci. Q. **10**: 664.
Gnosticism and Modern Pantheism. (G. J. Stokes) Mind, **20**: 320.
Go-backs. (J. H. Gore) J. Am. Folk-Lore, **5**: 107.
Goa, A Day in. (J. Lawson) Temp. Bar, **108**: 510. Same art. Liv. Age, **211**: 315.
Goal Reached, The; a story. (I. Kurz) Chaut. **19**: 87.
Goat-hunt, Rocky Mountain. (G. M. Dillard) Outing, **25**: 41.
Goats, White, Climbing for. (G. B. Grinnell) Scrib. M. **15**: 643.
— — Night with the. (M. T. Townsend) Outing, **28**: 391.
Goby, The Walking. (H. O. Forbes) Knowl. **19**: 97.
God and the World, Christian View as Centring in the Incarnation, Orr on. (T. G. Darling) Presb. & Ref. R. **6**: 359.
— as Lawgiver. (T. W. Chambers) Presb. & Ref. R. **5**: 503.
— Belief in. (F. M. Müller) Open Court, **5**: 2731.
— Character of, as Kind and Paternal. (J. Pitcher) Luth. Q. **22**: 109.
— Christian Conception of. (W. P. Odell) Meth. R. **56**: 728.
— Communion with, Herrmann on. (C. M. Mead) Presb. & Ref. R. **6**: 555.

God, Conception of, D'Alviella's Hibbert Lectures. (C. Chapman) Crit. R. 2: 249.
— Conceptions of. Open Court, 5: 2771.
— Derivation of Word. (C. Thomas) Open Court, 4: 2306.
— a Divine Man. N. Church R. 1: 139.
— The Divine Presence. (J. K. Smyth) N. Church R. 1: 123.
— Existence of. (H. B. Fry) Bib. Sac. 50: 668.
— — Ontological Proof of. (J. Cooper) Presb. & Ref. R. 5: 592.
— Fatherhood of, Homiletical Aspects of. (C. A. Salmond) Presb. & Ref. R. 4: 418.
— Fichte's Conception of. (J. A. Leighton) Philos. R. 4: 143.
— Goodness of. (A. F. Hewit) Cath. World, 58: 154.
— Government of, Vicarious Element in. (N. S. Burton) Bib. Sac. 50: 220.
— Hegel's Conception of. (J. A. Leighton) Philos. R. 5: 601.
— Help for Burdened Men. (J. Clifford) Good Words, 35: 786.
— His Benevolence in Harmony with His Justice. (E. H. Johnson) Bib. Sac. 51: 407.
— Immanence of, Doctrine of. (Henry Graham) Meth. R. 56: 35.
— Immanent, and the Incarnate Word. (W. H. Wynn) Luth. Q. 26: 66.
— in Evolution. (C. S. Wake) Open Court, 3: 1997.
— in Man, Worship of. (E. C. Stanton) Open Court, 7: 3850.
— Is He a Mind? Open Court, 5: 2978.
— Is Idea of, Tenable? (C. Royer) Open Court, 4: 2426.
— Love and Intelligence of. (J. C. Parsons) New World, 1: 535.
— Man's Conception of, from an Historical Standpoint. (J. W. Smith) Bib. World, 4: 349.
— Omnipresent Divinity. (H. Wood) Arena, 14: 77.
— "One Lord and His Name One." (S. R. Calthrop) New World, 3: 671.
— Real or Unreal? (W. H. Savage) Arena, 8: 320.
— Reasons for Belief in Him. (S. S. Seward) N. Church R. 2: 29.
— Righteousness of. (A. Robertson) Thinker, 9: 429.
— Spiritual Consciousness of. (M. H. Richards) Luth. Q. 22: 76.
— Talmudic Doctrine of, from Unitarian Point of View. (R. T. Herford) Jew. Q. 2: 454.
— Unity of, Anti-Nicene Doctrine of. (T. R. Slicer) New World, 3: 110.
— Unwritten Law of. (T. W. Chambers) Presb. & Ref. R. 6: 117.
— What is? (R. K. Carter) New Sci. R. 2: 278.
— Why we call Him "He." (M. M. Snell) Open Court, 7: 3764.
— Will of, and Human Happiness; Evolution. (St. G. Mivart) Cosmopol. 16: 344, 470, 609. 17: 102.
God-beloved. (M. B. Hardie) Longm. 27: 158. Same art. Liv. Age, 208: 139.
God of Lightning, The Aryan. (E. W. Fay) Am. J. Philol. 17: 1.
"God Save the Queen:" a Jacobite Hymn and Rebel Song. (S. Bateman) Gent. M. n. s. 51: 33.
Goddard, The, or Drinking-cup. (J. Goddard) Walford's Antiq. 2: 293.
Godefroi and Yolande, L. Irving's. (J. W. Thompson) Dial (Ch.) 20: 196.
Godfrey, G. W. Vanity Fair. Sat. R. 79: 579.
Godin, Jean B. A. (E. E. Hale) Lend a H. 9: 229.
Godiva, Lady. (E. S. Hartland) Folk-Lore, 1: 207.
Godiva of Hirst; a story. (A. W. Beckett) Idler, 8: 448.
Godkin, Edw. L., with portrait. Bk. Buyer, 13: 5.
— and his "Reflections and Comments." (H. T. Peck) Bookman, 2: 480.
Godliness. (D. B. Lady) Ref. Q. 40: 271.
Godmothers, The; a story. (H. P. Spofford) Cosmopol. 20: 461.
Godowsky, Leopold. Music, 10: 219.
God's Fool; a story. (M. Maartens) Temp. Bar, 94: 2—96: 279.
Gods and Men, Kinship of, among Early Semites. (G. A. Barton) J. Bib. Lit. 15: 168.
— The Maligned, of the Theatre. Theatre, 33: 8.
— of Greece; a poem. (F. Schiller) Blackw. 153: 383. Same art. Ecl. M. 120: 592.
— Personal, and Cultured Heroes of the Uncivilized Races. (S. D. Peet) Am. Antiq. 15: 348.
Godwin, William. (I. A. Taylor) Longm. 19: 412. Same art. Liv. Age, 193: 33.
— Political Justice. (H. S. Salt) Time, 22: 508.
Godwit, Southern. (J. Buckland) Eng. Illust. 16: 71.
Goethe and Carlyle. (H. S. Wilson) Gent. M. n. s. 51: 509. Same art. Ecl. M. 121: 775.
— and the Development Hypothesis. (C. Thomas) Open Court, 2: 815, 847.
— and Schiller, Xenions of. (P. Carus) Open Court, 1: 318. 8: 3939–3965.
— Arnold's Estimate of. (H. Preisinger) Acad. 41: 18.
— as a Minister of State. (H. W. Nevinson) Contemp. 62: 719. Same art. Liv. Age, 196: 67.
— a Buddhist. (P. Carus) Open Court, 10: 4832.
— Elpenor. (H. Wood) Am. J. Philol. 12: 458.
— Faust, on the German Stage, The Complete. (C. Thomas) Nation, 62: 340.
— — Translations of Angel Chorus. (R. McLintock) Acad. 48: 568.
— Iphigenia. (J. W. Sherer) Gent. M. n. s. 54: 388.
— Lighter Side of. (H. S. Wilson) Time, 22: 379.
— Maxims of. (Mrs. A. Crosse) Temp. Bar, 99: 417.
— Mother of. (J. Strauss) Liv. Age, 192: 340. — (H. S. Wilson) 19th Cent. 35: 649. Same art. Liv. Age, 201: 349.
— — The Original Frau Aja. (H. S. Wilson) Gent. M. n. s. 52: 297.
— New Points in Life of. (A. Zimmern) Bookman, 3: 408.
— on Evolution. (E. Haeckel) Open Court, 4: 2111.
— Rod against. (E. Dowden) Sat. R. 81: 618.
— Seeley on. Ath. '94, 1: 44.
— Two Days in Weimar. (E. Sigrid) Canad. M. 5: 250.
— Way of disposing of Old Manuscripts. (E. L. Hibberd) Writer, 8: 95.
Goethe and Schiller Archive House at Weimar. Sat. R. 73: 704. — (E. Schmidt) Forum, 19: 723.
Goethe-Schiller Cult in Germany. (T. Stanton) Nation, 56: 120.
Goff, Colonel, Etchings of. (F. Wedmore) M. of Art, 18: 102.
Goff, John W. (T. C. Quinn) Munsey, 12: 361.
Goffe, William, the Regicide. (J. Phillips) Eng. Hist. R. 7: 717.
Gogol, Nikolai V., Father of Russian Realism. (A. Tilly) National, 23: 650. Same art. Liv. Age, 202: 489.
Gohna, Landslip at, 1894. Geog. J. 4: 162.
Going Concern, A; a story. (A. E. Abbott) Idler, 5: 519.
Going of the White Swan, The. (G. Parker) Scrib. M. 17: 65.
Going out of Town. (M. T. Bayard) Canad. M. 3: 523.
Going Slow, On. All the Year, 73: 156.

Going without, Art of. (Eliz. Stuart Phelps) Outl. 48: 585.
Going Wrong; a story. All the Year, 71: 10.
Gold, Action of Ferric Chloride on Metallic. (P. C. McIlhiney) Am. J. Sci. 152: 293.
— and Silver. Cyanide Process of Extraction. (P. Argall) Engin. M. 7: 806.
— — Mining of, in South America. (A. L. Pearse) Engin. M. 7: 182.
— — Production of. Bank. M. (Lond.) 60: 581.
— — — World's, 1871–94. Bank. M. (N. Y.) 50: 503.
— Extraction Processes. (T. K. Rose) Sci. Prog. 5: 484.
— Free, in Granite, Occurrence of. (G. P. Merrill) Am. J. Sci. 151: 309.
— in Base Metals, Method of determining. (C. Whitehead) J. Frankl. Inst. 133: 470.
— in California, Discovery of, in 1841. (J. Murray) Overland, n. s. 19: 524.
— Increasing Difficulty of getting. (T. A. Rickard) Engin. M. 8: 313.
— Liquation of certain Alloys of. (E. Matthey) Nature, 54: 156.
— Nature's Method of Refining. (G. F. Baker) Cosmopol. 19: 362.
— Production of, Conditions of. (T. A. Rickard) No. Am. 160: 505.
— — 1893. Bank. M. (N. Y.) 49: 276.
— — in Colorado. (W. C. Wynkoop) Engin. M. 9: 97.
— — Increased. (E. Atkinson) No. Am. 162: 160.
— — is the Supply Sufficient? (J. E. Fraenkel) Forum, 16: 768.
— — These Golden Nineties. (D. H. Wheeler) Chaut. 21: 571.
— — The World's. (T. A. Rickard) Engin. M. 8: 251.
— Separated from Silver by Volatilization. (J. W. Richards) J. Frankl. Inst. 141: 447.
— South African Gold Boom. (A. Williams, jr.) Engin. M. 10: 399.
Gold Money. (Z. S. Holbrook) Bib. Sac. 53: 719.
— Accumulation of, in the Bank of England. Chamb. J. 71: 479.
— Alleged Appreciation of. (D. MacG. Means) Nation, 56: 22.
— and International Trade, Agio on. (W. Lexis) Econ. J. 5: 532.
— and the Prices of Farm Products. (L. G. Powers) Yale R. 5: 239.
— and Silver, Fallacies about. Gunton's M. 11: 175.
— Appreciation of. Bank. M. (N. Y.) 47: 801. — (R. Barclay) Fortn. 61: 645.
— — Index Numbers and. (N. G. Pierson) Econ. J. 5: 329.
— — or Depreciation of. (E. Atkinson) Bank. M. (N. Y.) 50: 905.
— as a Single Standard. (W. G. Sumner) Chaut. 24: 72.
— Basis fixed by Commerce itself. (E. Atkinson) Forum, 16: 737.
— Coming Flood of. Bank. M. (Lond.) 60: 481.
— English Industry and the Gold Standard. (J. T. Baylee) Westm. 146: 150.
— Exportations of, and Representative Money. (H. White) Engin. M. 10: 597.
— — Why Gold goes abroad. (A. C. Fisk) New Sci. R. 2: 290.
— Fallacy of; a Study of the Financial Situation. (J. C. Elliott) Am. M. Civics, 9: 207.
— Future of. (Alex Del Mar) Gunton's M. 11: 396. — (R. E. Preston) No. Am. 160: 38.
— Great Britain and the Gold Standard. (Lord Aldenham) National, 28: 165. — (D. MacG. Means) Nation, 63: 62.
Gold Money, has it risen? the Crux of the Money Controversy. (L. A. Garnett) Forum, 18: 573.
— The Impending Crisis. (W. H. Standish) Arena, 16: 974.
— in British Isles. (E. A. Smith) Knowl. 18: 33.
— in India; Demand for a Gold Currency. (C. Daniell) Blackw. 152: 597.
— — Past Action of the Government with regard to. (F. C. Harrison) Econ. J. 5: 52.
— in the U. S. Gold Reserve and Gold Payments. Pub. Opin. 15: 82.
— — Treasury. (T. L. Greene) Nation, 56: 96.
— Is it Sounder, as Money, than Silver? (G. C. Hill) Am. J. Pol. 3: 283.
— The Monometalist Creed. (H. D. MacLeod) 19th Cent. 36: 770.
— Movement of, and Foreign Exchanges, 1894–95. (W. C. Ford) Yale R. 4: 128.
— not Necessary for Foreign Trade. (W. M. Stewart) Overland, n. s. 26: 483.
— Past and Future of. (C. S. Ashley) Pop. Sci. Mo. 48: 39.
— A Plea for the Gold Standard. (W. R. Harper) Am. M. Civics, 7: 50.
— Present Value and Purchasing Power of. (H. M. Chance) Engin. M. 11: 193.
— Question of. Chamb. J. 71: 196. — (J. P. Heseltine) 19th Cent. 36: 438.
— — More about the. Chamb. J. 73: 147.
— A Scarcity of. (H. W. Stuart) J. Pol. Econ. 3: 362.
— — Pierson on. (F. Y. Edgeworth) Econ. J. 5: 109.
— Scramble for. (E. L. Godkin) Nation, 58: 463.
— — in India. (J. P. Heseltine) 19th Cent. 35: 58.
— Shipments of, Official Returns of. (G. O. Virtue) Q. J. Econ. 6: 465.
— Stored in the National Banks of Europe. Chamb. J. 72: 97.
— *vs.* Silver; Rule of the Gold Kings. (W. M. Stewart) No. Am. 154: 552.
— What shall the Ratio be? (W. M. Stewart; W. M. Springer; H. C. Hansbrough; R. P. Bland; J. Dalzell) No. Am. 155: 1.
— Why exported. (A. S. Heidelbach) Forum, 18: 647.
— without Gold. (N. C. Frederiksen) Bank. M. (Lond.) 54: 651.
See Gold Standard.
Gold and Silver Currency in the East. Bank. M. (Lond.) 54: 659.
Gold and Silver Hoarding in India. Bank. M. (N. Y.) 48: 210.
Gold-bearing Conglomerate, Jurassic, from the Sierra Nevada. (W. Lindgren) Am. J. Sci. 148: 275.
Gold-bearing Ores, Furnace for Roasting. (C. G. W. Lock) J. Soc. Arts, 43: 364.
Gold-bearing Veins of Meadow Lake, Cal. (W. Lindgren) Am. J. Sci. 146: 201.
Gold-camps in Colorado. (A. Lakes) Engin. M. 7: 623.
Gold Coast, Administration of Justice on. (H. Macleod) Jurid. R. 1: 272.
— Ellis' History of. Ath. '94, 1: 45.
Gold Deposit at Pine Hill, Cal. (W. Lindgren) Am. J. Sci. 144: 92.
Gold-digging in British Guiana. Liv. Age, 207: 446.
Gold-dredging in New Zealand. (T. A. Rickard) Engin. M. 7: 349.
Gold Export and its Dangers. Soc. Econ. 7: 1.
Gold-fields, African, A Woman in. (A. Russell) Cent. 24: 712.
— at Bendigo, Australia. (J. F. Markes) Engin. M. 4: 420.
— of Africa. (H. Smith) Bank. M. (N. Y.) 50: 646. — (S. F. Emmons) Nation, 61: 450.

Gold-Fields of Colorado, Less known. (T. Tonge) Engin. M. 11: 1029.
— of Ecuador. (R. F. Lord) Engin. M. 3: 244.
— of Guiana. (T. Dalgleish) Cent. 30: 716.
— of British Guiana. Chamb. J. 72: 79.
— of Dutch Guiana. (A. I. Mather) Engin. M. 5: 183.
— of South Africa. (G. F. Becker) Cosmopol. 22: 170. — (G. Hallé) Engin. M. 2: 582. 3: 523.
— — Zoutpansberg. (F. Jeppe) Geog. J. 2: 213.
— Scottish. Chamb. J. 72: 292.
Gold-mania, The. Chamb. J. 72: 790.
Gold-milling, Recent Improvements in. (H. M. Chance) Engin. M. 11: 461, 660.
Gold Mine of Kertch Bar; a story. (M. Roberts) Eng. Illust. 16: 278.
Gold-miners in the Past. Chamb. J. 72: 668.
Gold Mines of Queensland. Dub. R. 112: 456.
— Vanished. Chamb. J. 72: 782.
Gold Mining. (C. Snyder) R. of Rs. (N. Y.) 13: 167.
— Activity in Colorado. (T. A. Rickard) No. Am. 162: 473.
— Discovery of Large Nuggets. Chamb. J. 70: 511.
— in the Black Hills. (H. N. Hanson) Engin. M. 3: 683.
— in Montana. (W. D. Van Blascom, jr.) Nat'l M. (Bost.) 5: 33.
— in New Zealand. Chamb. J. 73: 756.
— in Rhodesia. (W. F. Wilkinson) J. Soc. Arts, 44: 687.
— in the Southern States. (H. B. C. Nitze) Engin. M. 10: 821.
Gold Ores, Concentration of. Nature, 53: 16.
— of California, Notes on. (H. W. Turner) Am. J. Sci. 147: 467. 149: 374.
Gold Ornaments and Gems in the British Museum. (A. W. Jarvis) Good Words, 37: 325.
Gold Power, Transformation of the Republic into a Plutocracy. (B. O. Flower) Arena, 16: 338.
Gold Reserve, The; its Function and its Maintenance. (F. Fetter) Pol. Sci. Q. 11: 237.
Gold Stamp-milling. (T. A. Rickard) Cassier, 5: 27.
Gold Standard. Bank. M. (N. Y.) 48: 827. — (B. Adams) Fortn. 62: 242. — Soc. Econ. vols. 1-9.
— and the Bond Sales. (F. W. Taussig) Forum, 22: 339.
— Desirability of. (R. T. Buerstatte) Am. J. Pol. 3: 534.
— in Austria. Q. J. Econ. 7: 225.
— in the Light of Recent Theory. (J. B. Clark) Pol. Sci. Q. 10: 389.
Gold Standard Party, Some Errors of. (O. Arendt) R. of Rs. (N. Y.) 13: 173.
Gold-supply, The World's. Spec. 75: 391.
Gold-work, Ancient. (C. H. Davenport) Harper, 85: 286.
Golden Ass, The. (J. F. Rowbotham) Gent. M. n. s. 51: 624.
Golden Ball, The; a fairy story. (C. Savile-Clarke) Eng. Illust. 11: 340.
Golden Bough, Frazer's. (W. W. Newell) J. Am. Folk-Lore, 3: 316.
Golden Bricks, The; a story. (C. Edwardes) Chamb. J. 70: 491.
Golden Calf at Dan, Was there a? (F. W. Farrar) Chr. Lit. 10: 8 a.
Golden Fleece, A. (L. T. Meade) Sund. M. 22: 413.
Golden Fleece; a story. (J. Hawthorne) Lippinc. 49: 515.
Golden House; a story. (C. D. Warner) Harper, 89: 165-893.
Golden-rod and Asters. (N. Boyce) Lippinc. 58: 257.
Golden-rod killing Horses. (J. L. Scott) Garden & F. 8: 477.
Golden Snail, The; a story. (A. Barczinsky) Gent. M. n. s. 48: 325.
Golden Wedding, The; a poem. (T. G. Hake) M. of Art, 9: 394.
Goldsbury Dilemma, The; a story. (V. Clement) Harper, 93: 888.
Goldsmith, Henry. Acad. 45: 148.
Goldsmith, Oliver. (C. A. Price) Belgra. 82: 138.
— Anecdotes of. Bookworm, 2: 59.
— Citizen of the World. Bookworm, 2: 217.
— Deserted Village. (H. C. Shelley) New Eng. M. n. s. 13: 323.
— Irving's Life of. (W. H. Browne) Chaut. 22: 545.
— Memoirs of a Protestant. Sat. R. 79: 627.
Goldsmiths and Silversmiths, Some Work of. (F. Miller) Art J. 48: 345.
Goldsmiths' Art at the Royal Academy. Art J. 47: 93.
Goldsmiths' Hall Marks in Sweden. Reliquary, 33: 224.
Goldsmiths' Halls in 1773. Reliquary, 33: 21.
Goldsmiths' Work, Exhibition of, at the Royal Academy. (C. Phillips) M. of Art, 18: 220.
— Past and Present. (Mrs. P. Newman) J. Soc. Arts, 42: 312.
Golf. Bach. of Arts, 3: 648. — (H. E. Howland) Scrib. M. 17: 531. — Time, 15: 466. — (J. G. Speed) Lippinc. 52: 609.
— and Golf Clubs in the U. S. (A. W. Tarbell) Nat'l M. (Bost.) 4: 481.
— and Golfing. (H. Hutchinson) Eng. Illust. 10: 54.
— Apotheosis of. (W. E. Norris) Cent. 22: 602.
— R. Clark on. (W. Rutherford) Nature, 49: 338.
— Evolution of. (E. Blake) Longm. 26: 200.
— Gossip on. (H. G. Hutchinson) Outing, 29: 156.
— in America to Date. (P. Collier) Outing, 29: 276.
— in 1892. Sat. R. 75: 36.
— in 1893. Sat. R. 76: 737.
— in England and Scotland. (P. Collier) Cosmopol. 20: 575.
— in the Old Country. (C. W. Whitney) Harper, 89: 760.
— Is it a First-Class Game? (A. Lyttelton) National, 22: 184.
— Long Driving at. Sat. R. 76: 207.
— Monstrous Regiment of the English. (T. Mackay) National, 22: 382.
— New Rules. Sat. R. 73: 11.
— The New Woman and. (Mrs. Reginald De Koven) Cosmopol. 21: 352.
— Old and New. (A. Lang) Harper, 91: 139.
— on the Continent. Sat. R. 75: 343.
— Park on. Sat. R. 82: 140.
— Physics of. (P. G. Tait) Nature, 48: 202.
— Pleasures of. All the Year, 74: 37.
— Should it be encouraged at Public Schools? Blackw. 157: 417.
— Simpson's. Sat. R. 73: 661.
— Something more than a First-class Game. (H. G. Hutchinson) National, 22: 568.
— The Year's, in England. Macmil. 71: 62.
Golf Club, The. (E. H. L. Watson) Gent. M. n. s. 49: 466.
Golf Links in France. Sat. R. 76: 462.
— Suburban. Sat. R. 75: 624.
Golfer, The, in Search of a Climate. (H. G. Hutchinson) Blackw. 156: 552.
Golgotha and the Holy Sepulchre, Site of. (M. MacColl) Contemp. 63: 167.
Goliath. (T. B. Aldrich) Cent. 23: 561.

Gombay, a Festival Rite of Bermudian Negroes. (H. C. Bolton) J. Am. Folk-Lore, **3**: 222.
Gompers, Samuel, A Talk with, with portrait. R. of Rs. (N. Y.) **10**: 27.
Goncourt, Edmond de, with portrait. Bk. Buyer, **13**: 445. — (Y. Blaze de Bury) Fortn. **66**: 333. — (A. Symons) Ath. '96, **2**: 129. — (R. H. Sherard) Bookman, **4**: 52. — Critic, **29**: 63. — Spec. **77**: 110. — (H. Frantz) Forum, **22**: 176.
— and his Friends. (A. Laugel) Nation, **54**: 300.
— and Jules de. (F. Wedmore) Acad. **46**: 504. — Atlan. **72**: 856.
— — Journal of. Critic, **29**: 195.
— — Last Volume. (A. Laugel) Nation, **63**: 27.
Gondola Days. (F. H. Smith) So. M. **3**: 228.
Gone to Coopertown. (C. W. Tyler) Southern M. **4**: 145, 253.
Goniometer, Use of, with Two Circles. (C. Palache) Am. J. Sci. **152**: 279.
Goniometry, Spiral, in its relation to the Measurement of Activity. (C. Barus) Am. J. Sci. **148**: 1.
Gontaut, Duchess de. (Y. Blaze de Bury) Blackw. **151**: 414. Same art. Liv. Age, **193**: 398. — Atlan. **71**: 390.
— Memoirs. Ed. R. **176**: 209. Same art. Liv. Age, **195**: 131.
Gontaut-Biron, Vicomte Elie de, Broglie's. Sat. R. **81**: 433.
Gooch, Sir Daniel. (J. A. Noble) Acad. **42**: 279. — Sat. R. **73**: 541. — Lond. Q. **79**: 263.
Good and Evil, Knowledge of. (E. M. Caillard) Contemp. **66**: 835. Same art. Ecl. M. **124**: 145. — (J. Royce) Int. J. Ethics, **4**: 48.
— — Problem of. (P. Carus) Monist, **6**: 580.
— Omnipotence of. (W. Hutchinson) Open Court, **9**: 4743.
Good Angel, The; a story. (Alice French) McClure, **3**: 21.
Good and Bad Children; a poem. (R. L. Stevenson) M. of Art, **7**: 459.
Good Government Clubs. (E. Kelley) Chr. Un. **47**: 1202. — (E. Kelley) Outl. **50**: 1125. — (P. Tucker) No. Am. **159**: 382.
Good Hope, Cape of, Observatory at. (H. Jacoby) Pop. Astron. **3**: 217.
— the Cape of Storms. Macmil. **70**: 143. Same art. Liv. Age, **202**: 53.
Good Hunting; a story. (R. Kipling) McClure, **5**: 195.
Good Morrow, Valentine! a story. All the Year, **70**: 156.
Good Nature. (E. E. Hale) Bk. News, **7**: 267.
Good-Natured Friend, A; a story. (R. K. Masterton) Temp. Bar, **109**: 527.
Good Will in Business. (J. R. Christie) Jurid. R. **8**: 71.
Goode, George Brown, with portrait. (T. Gill and S. P. Langley) Science, n. s. **4**: 365, 661. — Nat. Sci. **9**: 339.
Goodhart, H. C. Acad. **47**: 357.
Goodloe, A. C., with portrait. Bk. Buyer, **12**: 143.
Goodman, Arthur J., Artist. Idler, **9**: 803.
Goodness, Origin of. (M. J. Savage) New World, **3**: 78.
Goodwin, Alfred. Acad. **41**: 157.
Goodwin, Mrs. Almon, with portrait. Bk. Buyer, **13**: 215.
Goodwin, Charles C., a Pioneer Bimetallist. (J. Dryden) Overland, n. s. **27**: 657.
Goodwin, Harvey, Bishop of Carlisle. (W. B. Carpenter) M. Chr. Lit. **5**: 370. — Good Words, **33**: 305.
— Rawnsley's. Church Q. **43**: 51. — Sat. R. **81**: 282.
Goodwin Sands. Leis. Hour, **41**: 99.
Goodyear, Charles, *vs.* Horace H. Day, Case of. (A. Dutcher) Green Bag, **7**: 547.
Goose Shooting. (F. Gerald) Outing, **29**: 28.
— in Cape Breton. (W. H. Mac) Outing, **24**: 45.
— in the Dakotas. (F. B. Feetham) Outing, **25**: 141.
— in the South Platte Valley. (J. N. Hall) Outing, **21**: 172.
— on the Platte. (O. K. Davis) Outing, **20**: 16.
Gooseberry Culture, On. Chamb. J. **71**: 613.
Gopher, Tortoise, Florida Land. (H. G. Hubbard) Science, **22**: 57.
Gordon, Adam Lindsay. (F. Adams) Fortn. **58**: 352. — (O. Smeaton) Westm. **144**: 488.
Gordon, Adoniram Judson. Our Day, **14**: 144.
— as Preacher and Reformer. (J. Cook) Our Day, **14**: 225.
Gordon, Gen. C. G., Expedition for Relief of, Failure of. (A. Forbes) Contemp. **61**: 39.
— Home of. Chamb. J. **70**: 732.
— How he was really lost. (T. H. Parke) 19th Cent. **31**: 787. Same art. Ecl M. **119**: 23.
— Native Account of Death of. (C. H. Robinson) Geog. J. **2**: 451.
— Thornycroft's Statue of. M. of Art, **12**: 67.
— Why he perished. Sat. R. **81**: 607.
Gordon, George. Nat. Sci. **4**: 75.
Gordon, George Maxwell. (A. R. Buckland) Sund. M. **22**: 775.
Gordon, Julien. *See* Cruger, Mrs. Van Rensselaer.
Gordon Family of Scotland. Scot. R. **25**: 246.
Gordon Riots. (L. Johnson) Month, **78**: 60.
Gorges, Richard. Argosy, **62**: 120.
Gorges Society's Publications. (E. D. North) Bibliographica, **2**: 376.
Gorham Genealogy. Barnstable Gorhams. (F. W. Sprague) N. E. Reg. **50**: 32.
Gorilla, The. (A. Keith) Nat. Sci. **9**: 26.
— and his Cousins. (J. Weir) Southern M. **4**: 170.
Gorilla Brains, Collecting. (R. H. Nassau) Science, **19**: 240.
Gorillas, Among the. (R. L. Garner) McClure, **1**: 364.
Gorse, Furze and. Cornh. **69**: 286. Same art. Ecl. M. **122**: 556.
Gorst, Sir John. (J. J. Davies) Westm. **144**: 332.
Gorton, Samuel. (W. P. Sheffield) Nat'l M. (N. Y. '91) **19**: 34, 150.
Goschen, Geo. J., as a Conservative. Spec. **70**: 151.
Gospel, The, and the Gospels. (B. Weiss) Chr. Lit. **12**: 267.
— and Law. (E. V. Gerhart) Ref. Q. **41**: 5.
— The Primitive. (E. J. Dillon) Contemp. **63**: 857.
Gospels, Some Heretic. (F. Legge) Scot. R. **22**: 133.
Gosse, Edmund. (A. Waugh) Bookman, **4**: 205.
— Catalogue of his Library, reviewed. Bibliographica, **1**: 125.
— Critical Kit-kats. Sat. R. **81**: 377.
— Essays. Spec. **71**: 469.
Gosse, Philip. (Mrs. A. Crosse) Liv. Age, **192**: 235.
Gossip of the Century. Ath. '92, **2**: 311. — Spec. **69**: 421.
Gossip; a poem. (H. W. Boynton) Cosmopol. **71**: 426.
Gosson, Stephen. (A. C. Manston) Time, **8**: 525.
Got, M., Retirement of. (T. Barclay) Theatre, **34**: 20.
Gothenburg, Winter Scenes in. All the Year, **72**: 113.
Gothenburg System. (T. R. Willson) Leis. Hour, **45**: 181. — National, **24**: 726. — (D. N. Beach) New Eng. M. n. s. **11**: 785. — (E. S. Talbot) Good Words, **36**: 98. — (J. W. Leigh) Sat. R. **80**: 371.
— England and. (E. Goadby) Fortn. **63**: 165.
See Liquor Traffic.

Gothic Architecture in Italy, French Sources of. (C. H. Moore) Nation, 60: 285.
Gottschalk, Moreau. Music, 2: 117.
Goujon, Jean. (A. M. F. Robinson) M. of Art, 9: 86.
Gould, Benjamin Apthorp. (S. C. Chandler) Science, n. s. 4: 885. — Nature, 55: 132.
Gould, Edward. Bank. M. (N. Y.) 47: 770.
Gould, Jay, with portrait. (W. T. Stead) R. of Rs. (N. Y.) 7: 25.
— and Socialism. (A. T. Hadley) Forum, 14: 686.
— as Wrecker and Pirate. (W. O. McDowell) Our Day, 11: 83.
— Estate of, and the Inheritance Tax. (M. West) R. of Rs. (N. Y.) 7: 45.
— his Defence of Himself. Spec. 69: 847.
— Was he misjudged? (F. Allaben) Nat'l M. (N. Y. '91) 18: 79.
Gould, J. Nutcombe, with portrait. Theatre, 29: 22.
Gould, S. Baring. *See* Baring-Gould.
Gould Family, The. Munsey, 15: 448.
Goulding, Palmer, Petition of, 1741. N. E. Reg. 46: 215.
Gounod, Charles F. (J. S. Shedlock) Acad. 44: 349. — Ath. '93, 2: 561. — Critic, 23: 276. — (M. A. de Bovet and C. M. Widor) Fortn. 60: 824. Same art. Ecl. M. 122: 93. — (J. C. Hadden) Gent. M. n. s. 51: 580. Same art. Liv. Age, 200: 44. — With portrait. R. of Rs. (N. Y.) 8: 670. — Sat. R. 76: 458. — Spec. 71: 577. — With portrait. Book News, 14: 340. — (J. F. Rowbotham) Good Words, 35: 162. — (E. Cummings) Music, 5: 275. 8: 533.
— and Church Music. (H. T. Henry) Am. Cath. Q. 19: 320.
— as Author of Sacred Music. (G. Tebaldini) Music, 6: 224, 433.
— Autobiography of. (Baroness von Zedlitz) Theatre, 37: 136.
— Episode in the Life of. (A. D. Vandam) Temp. Bar, 95: 33
— Faust, Thematic and Other Significancies in. (E. I. Stevenson) Music, 9: 479, 592.
— in Italy and Germany. (C. F. Gounod) Cent. 21: 388.
— Redemption. Sat. R. 81: 371.
Goupil, Adolphe. (F. Masson) Art J. 45: 221.
Gourmets, Some Italian. All the Year, 73: 64.
Gournay, Marie Le J. de. *See* Le Jars de Gournay.
Gout, A New Theory of. (M. Granville) National, 26: 529.
Governess at Greenbush, The. (E. W. Hornung) Chamb. J. 72: 74-119.
Governing, Art of. (L. H. Berens) Westm. 142: 625.
Government by Injunction, So-called, and Labor Riots. (L. E. Curtis) Engin. M. 12: 381.
— Checks and Balances in. (L. R. Harley) Am. J. Pol. 4: 603.
— Essentials of Good. (J. Reed) N. Church R. 3: 321.
— Functions of. (A. E. Denslow) Am. J. Pol. 5: 257.
— — with relation to Natural Resources. (B. E. Fernow) Science, n. s. 2: 252.
— Functions of the State. (L. G. Janes) Soc. Econ. 2: 27.
— Interest of the Lieges. New R. 12: 605.
— Is the Hope of Our Century an Illusion? (A. Herbert) New R. 10: 164.
— Local, A Chapter on. (M. Parritt) Westm. 146: 459.
— — Failure of. (E. D. Cope) Open Court, 8: 4159.
— New Divine Right. (W. S. Lilly) New R. 12: 505.
— Origin and Nature of, Sir W. Temple on. (F. I. Herriott) Ann. Am. Acad. Pol. Sci. 3: 150.
— Popular, Development and Failure in Antiquity. (A. Moses) Am. J. Pol. 5: 381.
Government, Primary End of all. (W. H. Mallock) National, 21: 22.
— Province of. (H. Teichmueller) Am. Law R. 29: 21.
— State, Sovereign. A Triad of Political Conceptions. (C. M. Platt) Pol. Sci. Q. 10: 292.
— Study of. (W. MacDonald) Nation, 63: 418.
— Unrighteousness of. (C. C. Rudolf) Arena, 14: 476.
Government Administration of Industrial Enterprise. (A. T. Hadley) Yale R. 4: 398.
Government Buildings, Bill for the Employment of Architects for. Am. Arch. 44: 9. 45: 10, 53.
— Compared with Private Buildings. (G. Brown) Am. Arch. 44: 2, 24.
Government Competition with Private Enterprise. Bank. M. (Lond.) 57: 829.
Government Official, A; a story. (J. Maclaren Watson) McClure, 6: 241.
Government Paper, A Transaction in. (W. Forbes Mitchell) Chamb. J. 72: 589.
Governmental Waste. (R. Ogden) Nation, 60: 232.
Governor of Guèret; a story. (S. J. Weyman) Eng. Illust. 12: no. 6, 23. Same art. McClure, 5: 62.
Governor-general, Functions of a. (W. P. Reeves) National, 28: 554.
Governor's Prerogatives, The; a story. (M. T. Earle) McClure, 2: 562.
Governor's Reception; a story. (F. M. Abbott) New Eng. M. n. s. 6: 301.
Governors, New England, A Conference of. (F. T. Greenhalge) No. Am. 158: 366.
Gower, Lord Ronald. Eng. Illust. 13: 119.
— Speculum Meditantis. (G. C. Macaulay) Acad. 48: 71.
Goya y Lucientes, Francisco José de. (W. Rothenstein) Sat. R. 82: 252, 307.
Grace, W. G., and Cricket in 1895. (R. H. Lyttelton) New R. 13: 129.
Grace Cup of Thomas à Becket. Reliquary, 33: 114.
Gracian, Balthasar. (W. Webster) Acad. 43: 148.
Grade Crossings, Modern Problem of. (W. O. Webber) Engin. M. 9: 1034.
Grady, Henry W. (C. Howell) Chaut. 21: 703.
Græco-Egyptian Portraits. (M. A. Peck) Mo. Illust. 13: 219.
Graetz, Hirsch. (I. Abrahams) Jew. Q. 4: 165.
Graft, Symbiosis of Stock and. (E. F. Smith) Am. Natural. 29: 615.
Grafting. (A. W. Pearson) Garden & F. 5: 154-178. — Garden & F. 5: 315. — (T. H. Hoskins) Garden & F. 5: 558.
— Is it a Devitalizing Process? (L. H. Bailey) Garden & F. 5: 39, 50.
— on Grapes. (E. G. Lademan) Garden & F. 5: 498.
— Physiology of, Vöchting on. Nature, 47: 128.
Grafton Galleries. (R. Le Schonix) Antiq. n. s. 30: 54. — (A. L. Baldry) Art J. 45: 145. — (M. P. Jackson) M. of Art, 15: 348.
— Fair Women at. (C. Phillips) National, 23: 611. — Ath. '94, 1: 683. 2: 70.
Graham, George R. Critic, 25: 44.
Graham, Margaret Collier. (B. Harraden) Critic, 27: 127.
Graham, Peter. (W. W. Fenn) M. of Art, 2: 144.
Graham, William, Memorial Bronze, by Gilbert. (J. Graham) M. of Art, 13: 115.
Graham Family of Lawyers, with portraits. (A. O. Hall) Green Bag, 6: 353.
Graham's Bungalow; a story. (Sewall Read) Cosmopol. 16: 685.
Graham's Romance; a Corsican Love Story. Temp. Bar, 97: 130.

Graham's Voice; a story. (E. Macpherson) Harper, 89: 937.
Grahame, Kenneth, with portrait. Bk. Buyer, 13: 287.
Grail. *See* Holy Grail.
Grain Trade, Thirty Years in the. (E. R. Williams) No. Am. 161: 25.
Grammar, Bad, Our Inherited. (A. M. Spence) Poet-Lore, 7: 450.
— Parallel Study of. (E. A. Sonnenschein) Educa. R. 3: 450.
Grammar School, Curriculum of. (W. H. Maxwell) Educa. R. 3: 472.
— — Proposed Reform in. (D. C. Wells) And. R. 17: 47.
— — Shortening and Enriching the. (C. W. Eliot) School & C. 1: 153.
Grammar Schools, Departmental Teaching in. (F. W. Parker) Educa. R. 6: 342. — (F. A. Fitzpatrick) Educa. R. 7: 439.
— Reform in. (A. B. Hart) Educa. R. 4: 253.
— What can High Schools do to aid? (R. G. Huling) Educa. 14: 385.
Grammatical Stumbling Blocks. (E. F. Andrews) Chaut. 23: 339.
Grammont, Count Philibert de. Memoirs. (A. J. Gordon) Gent. M. n. s. 56: 380.
Gramophone. (E. Berliner) J. Frankl. Inst. 140: 419.
Granada. (D. Hannay) M. of Art, 8: 447.
— and the Alhambra. (H. C. Chatfield-Taylor) Cosmopol. 21: 451.
Granaries, National. (R. A. Yerburgh) National, 27: 197.
Granby, Lady, and her Pencil Drawings. (Mabel P. Haskell) Munsey, 16: 353.
Grand, Sarah, with portrait. Bk. News, 11: 515. — Critic, 23: 92. — Critic, 23: 361, 382.
— Ethics of. (T. B. Saunders) Open Court, 9: 4447.
— Heavenly Twins. (F. M. Bird) Lippinc. 52: 637.
Grand Army as a Pension Agency. (C. McK. Leoser) Forum, 15: 522.
— Decadence of. (A. W. Fiske) Nation, 60: 342.
— Decisive Breach in the. (A. R. Foote) Forum, 15: 452.
— Farnham Post Revolt, Complete History of. (J. J. Finn) Forum, 15: 532.
— on the Pacific Coast. (F. E. Myers) Overland), n. s. 27: 434.
Grand Cañon, From Flagstaff to. (H. T. Finck) Nation, 57: 169, 187.
Grand Cañon of the Yellowstone; a poem. (E. P. Gould) Educa. 15: 113.
Grand Prix and Other Prizes. (R. H. Davis) Harper, 91: 26.
Grand River, At the Mouth of. (T. L. M. Tipton) Canad. M. 1: 347.
Grand River, Labrador, Falls of. Around World, 1: 134. — Am. Natural. 28: 503.
Grande Demoiselle, La; a balcony story. (G. King) Cent. 23: 323.
Grandmother's Grandmother. (G. King) Cent. 24: 722.
Grandmother's Ways. (I. F. Mayo) Argosy, 55: 536.
Grandpapa's Clerk; a story. (M. C. Goodwin) Bost. 2: 293.
Grange and Coöperative Enterprises in New England. (F. J. Foster) Ann. Am. Acad. Pol. Sci. 4: 798.
— in Politics. (M. Whitehead) Am. J. Pol. 1: 113.
Grange Mystery, The; a story. Argosy, 61: 112.
Grangerism. (L. Hutton) Bookworm, 2: 361.
— and the Grangerites. (L. Hutton) Bk. Buyer, 4: 93-290.
Granite Industry in New England. (G. Rich) New Eng. M. n. s. 5: 742.
Granite Rock, Passage of, into Fertile Soil. (M. A. Ruffer) Nature, 46: 517.
Grant, Sir Francis. M. of Art, 1: 46.
Grant, Sir Hope. Leis. Hour, 42: 625. — With portrait. Un. Serv. M. 7: 777. 9: 398.
— Knolly's Life of. Ath. '94, 1: 533. — Sat. R. 77: 451.
Grant, James, with portrait. Nat'l M. (N. Y. '91) 19: 80.
Grant, Sir John Peter. Sat. R. 75: 70. — Spec. 70: 70.
Grant, Lewis Morrison. An Aberdeen Student of To-day. (I. F. Mayo) Ecl. M. 122: 234.
Grant, Robert, with portrait. Bk. Buyer, 9: 655. — Nature, 47: 36. Same art. Astron. 11: 878.
Grant, Thomas Rannie, with portrait. Bank. M. (Lond.) 55: 602.
Grant, Ulysses S., with portraits. (H. Porter and others) McClure, 2: 507.
— Abraham Lincoln and S. P. Chase. (N. Brooks) Cent. 27: 607.
— as a Colonel. (J. L. Crane) McClure, 7: 40.
— at Pilot Knob. (J. M. Thayer) McClure, 5: 433.
— Campaigning with. (H. Porter) Cent. 31: 16, 216.
— Early Life of. (H. Garland) McClure, 8: 125.
— his Life at the Outbreak of the Rebellion. (E. J. Edwards) McClure, 5: 38.
— Japanese Life of. Cent. 28: 435.
— The Mystery of. (A. Badeau) Cosmopol. 20: 483.
— Partridge's Statue of. (C. Moffett) McClure, 6: 590.
— under Fire. (T. R. Davis) Cosmopol. 14: 333.
Granther's Set-kittle. (K. Shelton) New Eng. M. n. s. 12: 500.
Grantley, Lady. Temp. Bar, 97: 237.
Grantley Manor; a story. (L. Meadows) Argosy, 62: 609.
Granville, Dr. Augustus Bozzi. Temp. Bar, 102: 455. Same art. Liv. Age, 202: 600.
Granville, Harriet, Countess, Letters of. Ed. R. 180: 211. Same art. Liv. Age, 202: 545. — (T. Hutchinson) Acad. 45: 341. — Sat. R. 77: 421. — (J. E. Roundell) Nation, 58: 411. — Spec. 72: 504, 535. — Ath. '94, 1: 305.
Grape Fruit and Shaddocks. (D. Morris) Garden & F. 9: 163.
Grapes, Cultivation of. (E. Williams) Garden & F. 5: 546.
— — Chautauqua Grape Belt. (L. J. Vance) Garden & F. 8: 438.
— European, Cultivation of. (A. W. Pearson) Garden & F. 5: 618.
— Fructification of. (A. W. Pearson) Garden & F. 5: 597.
— in January. (E. P. Powell) Garden & F. 7: 66.
— in Winter. (E. P. Powell) Garden & F. 6: 10.
— Keeping Grapes fresh all Winter. Garden & F. 8: 458, 499.
— Lake Keuka (N. Y.) Vineyards. (L. J. Vance) Garden & F. 8: 409.
— Neglected. (E. P. Powell) Garden & F. 5: 512.
— Notes from the Home-vineyard. (T. Greiner) Garden & F. 6: 447.
— Self-pollination of. Garden & F. 5: 451.
— Some California Raisin. (C. H. Shinn) Garden & F. 6: 265.
— under Glass. (P. Fisher) Garden & F. 6: 326. — (W. Tricker) Garden & F. 6: 475.
"Graphic, The," Making of. (W. L. Thomas) Univ. R. 2: 80.
— Some Artists of. (Harry Quilter) Univ. R. 2: 94.
Graphic Arts, Hamerton's. (S. Colvin) M. of Art, 6: 36.
Graptolites, The. (J. E. Marr) Sci. Prog. 5: 360.

Graptolites, Structure of. (C. Wiman) Nat. Sci. 9: 186, 240.
Grasmere August Festivals. Sat. R. 76: 235.
Grasp the Skirts of Happy Chance; a story. (M. Dyan) Belgra. 79: 277.
Grass and Flowers; a poem. (J. V. Cheney) Harper, 90: 836.
— Insects infesting. (J. B. Smith) Garden & F. 9: 463, 472.
Grasse. (M. Hunt) Longm. 25: 290. Same art. Liv. Age, 204: 480.
Grasses. (J. P. Smith) Knowl. 15: 185.
— Ornamental. (E. J. Canning) Garden & F. 9: 356. — (G. W. Oliver) Garden & F. 9: 457.
— — Native. (T. H. Kearney, jr.) Garden & F. 9: 152, 172.
— Some Promising. Garden & F. 5: 434.
— Troublesome, in Southern N. J. (Mary Treat) Garden & F. 8: 103.
Grasshopper and the Ant. (J. G. Vibert) Cent. 29: 261.
Grasshopper Vane in Boston. (D. W. Baker) N. E. Reg. 49: 24.
Grassington, Yorkshire, Prehistoric Remains at. (B. J. Harker) Antiq. n. s. 26: 147.
Grateful Joe; a story. (G. Allen) Eng. Illust. 11: 703.
Gratings, Rowland's Concave, Astigmatism of. (J. L. Sirks) Astron. 13: 763.
Graunt, John, or Petty? Authorship of Observations upon the Bills of Mortality. (C. H. Hull) Pol. Sci. Q. 11: 105.
Grave in Brent Hollow. (P. Wesley) New Eng. M. n. s. 10: 348.
Grave in St. Helena; a story. (C. F. Little) Un. Serv. (Phila.) 9: 301.
Grave-digger, The. (E. Verhaeren) Fortn. 66: 727.
Gravels, Story of. (H. B. Bashore) Lippinc. 55: 423.
Graves, A. P. "Father O'Flynn;" the story of a song. (M. A. Belloe) Eng. Illust. 11: 948.
Graves, Henry. Ath. '92, 2: 329.
Graves, Robert Perceval. Acad. 44: 319. — (J. P. Mahaffy) Ath. '93, 2: 552.
Graves, Decoration of, by Negroes. (H. C. Bolton) J. Am. Folk-Lore, 4: 214.
Gravière, Jurien de la, Admiral. Ath. '92, 1: 344.
Gravitation, Le Sage's Theory of. (W. Stoss) Open Court, 2: 804.
— Mystery of. (J. E. Gore) National, 18: 650. Same art. Liv. Age, 192: 690. — (Geo. Stearns) Open Court, 1: 557.
— Newtonian Constant of. Nature, 50: 330, 366, 417. — (C. V. Boys) Pop. Astron. 3: 128, 167. 4: 77, 120.
— Relation to Continental Elevation. (T. C. Mendenhall) Am. J. Sci. 149: 81.
Gravity Measurements, Use of Planes and Knife-edges in Pendulums for. (T. C. Mendenhall) Am. J. Sci. 145: 144.
Gray, Asa, as a Botanist. (F. Starr) Outl. 49: 310.
— Letters. Dial (Ch.) 15: 333. — (G. L. Goodale) Nation, 57: 377. — Garden & F. 6: 539. — Spec. 72: 88. — Ath. '94, 1: 413.
Gray, David. Spec. 76: 768.
Gray, Elisha, with portrait. (H. L. Conard) Nat'l M. (N. Y. '91) 18: 59.
Gray, John Edward. Acad. 50: 436.
Gray, John Miller. (G. Scharf) Ath. '94, 1: 781. — Acad. 45: 268.
Gray, Thomas, with portrait. Acad. 50: 532.
— and his Poetry. (Sir E. Brydges) Walford's Antiq. 5: 123.
— Elegy, Literary History of. (J. Maskell) Walford's Antiq. 4: 231, 281.
— New Portrait of. (G. Scharf) Ath. '94, 1: 251.
Gray, Thomas, Silhouette Portrait of. Ath. '94, 1: 483.
Gray Jacket, A. (T. N. Page) Cent. 22: 27.
Gray's Inn, London. (D. W. Douthwaite) Green Bag, 5: 65.
Great Belt, The, in Winter. (C. Edwardes) Chamb. J. 71: 65. Same art. Liv. Age, 200: 695.
Great Britain, Agricultural Policy of the New Ministry, 1892. Spec. 69: 248.
— Ancient Greek Trade-routes to. (W. Ridgeway) Folk-Lore, 1: 82.
— and the United States; their True Relations. (D. A. Wells) No. Am. 162: 385. — Reply. (M. W. Hazeltine) No. Am. 162: 594.
— Army. (Archibald Alison) Un. Serv. (Phila.) 7: 569. — (R. W. Hanbury) Fortn. 57: 846.
— — About Soldiers by a Soldier. Blackw. 151: 873.
— — Advancement in, 1895. (A. Griffiths) Un. Serv. (Phila.) 14: 547.
— — Aldershot Command, Appointment of the Duke of Connaught to, 1893. Spec. 71: 228.
— — Ammunition for. (S. Wilkinson) National, 25: 843.
— — and Civil War. Blackw. 153: 764.
— — An Army without Leaders. (L. Hale) 19th Cent. 39: 357.
— — Artillery Practice, June 29, 1893. Sat. R. 76: 40.
— — Autumn Manœuvres, for Civilians. (L. Hale) National, 24: 782.
— — Beginnings of. Infantry. Macmil. 70: 109.
— — — Artillery and Engineers. Macmil. 70: 265. Same art. Liv. Age, 202: 222, 302, 625.
— — — Cavalry. Macmil. 70: 195.
— — British Standing Army. All the Year, 75: 270.
— — Cavalry of. Macmil. 73: 1.
— — Cavalry Officers' Expenses. (Earl of Airlie) 19th Cent. 37: 467.
— — Civil Employment of Reserve. Time, 18: 689.
— — Competitive Examinations in. Sat. R. 77: 522.
— — Diet of. Blackw. 154: 865.
— — Discipline and. (G. W. Higginson) New R. 6: 187.
— — Division from West Indies. (C. Pearson) Un. Serv. M. 9: 150.
— — English Officer — as he was, and as he is. (H. Knollys) Blackw. 158: 527. Same art. Ecl. M. 125: 756.
— — English Officers and Soldiers — as they will be. (H. Knollys) Blackw. 159: 199. Same art. Ecl. M. 126: 655.
— — English Soldier, as he was and as he is. (H. Knollys) Blackw. 158: 850.
— — Estimates for 1896–97. (S. Wilkinson) Sat. R. 81: 321.
— — 44th Foot. (F. Dixon) Temp. Bar, 99: 27.
— — Has it grown with our Empire? (J. Adye) 19th Cent. 39: 1012.
— — Highland Regiments in. (W. E. Milliken) Time, 4: 577.
— — Horses for. Sat. R. 73: 510.
— — Improvement of. Sat. R. 73: 366.
— — Inefficiency of. (J. L. A. Simmons) 19th Cent. 31: 885. — (P. L. MacDougall) Blackw. 152: 267.
— — Infantry Drill, New. Sat. R. 76: 125.
— — Infantry Tactics, Proposed, 1892. Sat. R. 73: 387, 401.
— — Is our Military Administration Hopeless? (L. Darwin) National, 25: 538.
— — Medical Department. (F. Gillespie) Un. Serv. M. 8: 344. — Blackw. 160: 747.
— — Medical Organization. Un. Serv. M. 10: 278.
— — Medical Staff, Future of. (W. Hill-Climo) Un. Serv. M. 13: 83.

Great Britain. Army. Military Costume and Equipment. (W. Ash) Time, **8**: 717. **9**: 95–219.
— — Military Problem — for Civilian Readers. (F. I. Maxse) National, **26**: 545.
— — Mobilization Scheme, 1892. Spec. **69**: 378.
— — Mortality from Consumption in. (R. Lawson) J. Statis. Soc. **50**: 458.
— — of the "Forty-five." Chamb. J. **72**: 662.
— — Officers in, Selection of. (W. B. Scoones) 19th Cent. **34**: 807.
— — Origin of some Regiments. Chamb. J. **71**: 489.
— — Our Second Line of Defence. (A. Griffiths) Fortn. **65**: 304.
— — Our Young Soldiers in India. (T. A. P. Marsh) Westm. **146**: 156.
— — Our Military Problem. (F. I. Maxse) National, **26**: 657, 811.
— — Promotion. (Sir J. Adye) Un. Serv. M. **4**: 291.
— — Queen's Royal West Surrey Regiment, History of, Davis'. Sat. R. **79**: 795.
— — Recruiting of. (J. S. A. Herford) Un. Serv. M. **4**: 75, 170.
— — Recruiting for, in 1892, Official Report on. Spec. **68**: 359. — Sat. R. **73**: 145.
— — Recruiting Anglo-Indian Army. (W. Moore) Asia. R. **12**: 39.
— — Reform in. Spec. **68**: 519, 633.
— — Reorganization of. (C. W. Battine) National, **21**: 210.
— — Reserves, 1892. Sat. R. **73**: 644, 672.
— — Rise of the Buffs. Macmil. **74**: 392.
— — Route-marching. (P. C. Whalley) Temp. Bar, **94**: 105.
— — Short Service, Defence of. (Sir J. Adye) 19th Cent. **32**: 358.
— — Subaltern in India a Hundred Years Ago. Cornh. **68**: 474.
— — Transformation under Duke of Cambridge. (J. L. A. Simmons) 19th Cent. **38**: 889.
— — Volunteer Force. Un. Serv. M. **9**: 357. — (J. H. A. Macdonald) National, **27**: 80. — (Lord Raglan) National, **27**: 237. Sat. R. **74**: 710.
— — Volunteer Reform. Un. Serv. M. **4**: 488. **5**: 29–594.
— — Volunteers. (L. Brackenbury) Time, **1**: 698.
— — — Annual Manœuvres, 1893. Sat. R. **75**: 378.
— — War Office and. Quar. **183**: 188.
— — Wilkinson on. Sat. R. **81**: 379.
— — Wreath of Laurels. Cornh. **65**: 401.
— as a Naval Power, Position of, in 1893. Spec. **71**: 864.
— as an Absorbent. Pub. Opin. **14**: 473.
— Bank Act of 1844–45. Bank. M. (Lond.) **53**: 541.
— Cabinets, History of, Torrens'. Sat. R. **77**: 645.
— Civil Service in 1855. Good Govt. **15**: 107.
— Climate of. (R. H. Scott) Longm. **20**: 174.
— Colonial Empire. (M. G. Mulhall) Contemp. **67**: 632. — (H. Taylor) No. Am. **162**: 682.
— — and the Navy Question. (Sir C. Tupper) Canad. M. **6**: 307. — (A. H. Loring) Canad. M. **7**: 159.
— Colonial Office, History of. (A. W. Renton) Jurid. R. **1**: 287.
— Colonies, and the Empire. (C. E. Howard Vincent) National, **24**: 23.
— — and Free Trade; a Plea for Customs Union of the British Empire. (W. Peart-Robinson) Westm. **141**: 434.
— — and Maritime Defence. National, **23**: 593.
— — and Treaties. (C. M. Kennedy) J. Soc. Arts, **43**: 414.
— — Colonial Problems. (C. Bill) National, **24**: 816, (A. R. Whiteway) 822.
Great Britain. Colonies, Education for the. (A. Montefiore) Macmil. **66**: 212.
— — Exchange of. Asia. R. **9**: 374.
— — Extension of Trade of. (H. Vincent) J. Soc. Arts, **40**: 738.
— — Government of. Westm. **137**: 8.
— — Growth of. Sat. R. **74**: 83.
— — Home Rule in. (J. MacLachlan) Westm. **142**: 497.
— — John Bull and Company. (Max O'Rell) Cosmopol. **17**: 575.
— — Relationship to the Mother-land. (J. H. Long) Am. M. Civics, **6**: 379.
— — Self-government in. (D. Mills) Canad. M. **2**: 533.
— — Solution of Colonial Question. (R. Beadon) Asia. R. **15**: 83.
— — Study of, in Schools. (W. P. Greswell) Murray, **9**: 692.
— — Supplies of Dairy and Minor Food Products from. (C. R. Valentine) J. Soc. Arts, **44**: 469.
— — Women in. (Gilbert Parker) New R. **11**: 409.
— Commerce, Protection of, in War. (H. W. Wilson) Un. Serv. (Phila.) **15**: 321.
— Commercial Supremacy of. (A. W. Flux) Econ. J. **4**: 457, 595.
— Consols, The Coming Crisis in. (A. Chisholm) National, **28**: 126.
— Constitution of; Dicey's Leap in the Dark. Spec. **70**: 853.
— — Revision of. (Lord Salisbury) National, **20**: 289.
— — *vs.* Evolution. Westm. **144**: 393.
— Constructing a British Empire. Soc. Econ. **8**: 328.
— Currency of. Bank. M. (Lond.) **59**: 681.
— Current Educational Move in. Citizen, **1**: 163.
— Customs: Zollverein of British Dominions. (J. Vogel) 19th Cent. **32**: 498.
— Debt of. (Lawrence Irwell) Gunton's M. **11**: 133. — Chamb. J. **73**: 68.
— — Difficulties in Reducing. (D. Renton) Econ. J. **6**: 408.
— Defence of. (G. S. Clarke) Blackw. **157**: 665, 962. (A. H. Atteridge) Un. Serv. M. (Phila.) **13**: 1.
— — Advancement in the Army. (A. Griffiths) Fortn. **64**: 582.
— — Dungeness or Dover? (W. Verner) 19th Cent. **32**: 254.
— — Naval Warfare and. Quar. **174**: 534.
— — New Council of Defence. (H. O. Arnold-Forster) National, **26**: 50.
— — Our Military Unreadiness. Macmil. **65**: 275.
— Diplomacy of; Her Majesty's Service Abroad. Chamb. J. **72**: 708.
— Early Races of. (J. Garson) Nature, **51**: 67, 90.
— Elections in. Blackw. **153**: 312. — (J. B. Bishop) Nation, **55**: 446.
— — Old. (Lord Brabourne) Blackw. **152**: 38, 248.
— — Wanted; a New Corrupt Practices Act. (W. H. Mallock) National, **20**: 25.
— Electioneering Methods in England. (H. W. Lucy) No. Am. **155**: 338.
— Electoral Methods. (L. H. Courtney) National, **26**: 21.
— Electoral Reform in, A Scheme of. (W. Laird Clowes) Contemp. **68**: 363.
— Empire, and the Home Government. New R. **15**: 396.
— — Can it feed its People? (J. Long) 19th Cent. **39**: 16.
— — Commercial Federation of. (E. E. Williams) New R. **15**: 154. — (J. G. Colmer) National, **27**: 653. — (F. Young) 19th Cent. **40**: 27. — (J. G. Colmer) Econ. J. **6**: 563. — (R. Lethbridge) Asia. R. **22**: 272.

Great Britain. Empire, compared with Roman Empire. (J. B. Bury) Sat. R. 81: 645.
— — Federalizing the United Kingdom. Ed. R. 184: 341. — (J. Fergusson) Canad. M. 7: 455. — Fortn. 65: 738.
— — — Spalding on. Sat. R. 82: 195.
— — Federation and Consolidation of. Lond. Q. 79: 244.
— — Growth of. Blackw. 159: 364. Same art. Ecl. M. 126: 825.
— — Imperial Federation. Asia. R. 11: 111. — (A. S. White) Asia. R. 16: 356. — (J. Johnston) Un. Serv. M. 11: 320. — (A. H. F. Lefroy) Canad. M. 1: 176. (J. F. Hogan) Westm. 141: 1. — (J. Bonwick) Westm. 144: 622.
— — — Financial Incidents of War. (A. C. Galt) Canad. M. 5: 453.
— — — Fiscal Federation; is it Possible? (L. Irwell) Westm. 138: 621.
— — — for Naval Defence. (Lord Brassey) 19th Cent. 31: 90.
— — — from a Colonial Point of View. (W. B. Perceval) J. Soc. Arts, 41: 685.
— — — Herbey on. Spec. 68: 139.
— — — Home Rule and. (F. Pollock) National, 21: 841.
— — — How to federate. (C. Tupper) 19th Cent. 31: 525.
— — — Latest Aspects of. (Marquis of Lorne) No. Am. 157: 485.
— — — Parkin on. Sat. R. 74: 176.
— — — The Polity of the Future. (C. D. Farquharson) Westm. 139: 349.
— — Imperial Federation League. (J. P. Val d'Eremao) Asia. R. 17: 110.
— — Imperialism at the Intercolonial Congress. (J. Castell-Hopkins) Asia. R. 18: 364.
— — Is it Stable? (F. H. Geffcken) Forum, 18: 161.
— — Naval Defence of. (J. Vogel) Un. Serv. M. 9: 331.
— — Solidarity without Federation. (G. W. Wilton) Jurid. R. 4: 317. 5: 49, 248.
— External Trade of, Progress of. (S. Bourne) J. Statis. Soc. 56: 185.
— Fauna and Flora of, Effect of the Ice-age on. (G. W. Bulman) Nat. Sci. 3: 261.
— Finance, Democratic. Quar. 184: 76.
— Finances; Causes of the National Income. (W. H. Mallock) National, 21: 151-792. — (H. A. Jones) National, 21: 552. — (F. Wicks) National, 21: 719.
— — 1892; Cash Reserves and Gold, Insufficiency of. (G. H. Pownall) Econ. J. 2: 530.
— — — Goschen's Currency Proposals. (H. S. Foxwell; A. Crump) Econ. J. 2: 139.
— — John Bull's Purse Strings. (Henry C. Burdett) Univ. R. 3: 538.
— — Local. (G. H. Blunden) Pol. Sci. Q. 9: 78, 268.
— — — Budget of 1894. (John Lubbock) New R. 11: 1.
— Financial Relations of England and Ireland. (W. J. O'N. Daunt) Westm. 138: 483.
— Foreign and Indian Policy. (M. G. Duff) Un. Serv. M. 6: 1.
— Foreign Policy. (J. W. Gambier) Fortn. 64: 544. — (E. J. Dillon) Contemp. 68: 609. — (E. W. Beckett) Sat. R. 79: 470. — (H. M. Stephens) Nation, 62: 346.
— — British Guarantees and Engagements on the Continent. (C. E. Callwell) Westm. 139: 269.
— — in 1892. (H. Labouchere) No. Am. 155: 430.
— — — Conservative. (Sir C. W. Dilke) Fortn. 57: 1.
— — — Rosebery on. Spec. 68: 422.
— — Key Note of. (J. St. L. Strachey) National, 26: 741.
Great Britain. Foreign Policy, Our True. (H. O. Arnold-Forster) 19th Cent. 39: 204.
— — Seeley and Burrows on. (H. M. Stephens) Am. Hist. R. 1: 721.
— — Seeley's Growth of British Policy. (D. W. Rannie) Acad. 49: 109.
— — Spheres of Influence. (G. Taubman-Goldie) 19th Cent. 32: 984.
— Foreign Relations; England in Nicaragua and Venezuela. (G. H. D. Gossip) Fortn. 64: 829.
— — The Isolation of England. (E. Dicey) Fortn. 65: 330.
— — to European Powers. (C. H. O'Connell) Westm. 146: 55.
— — Turkey or Russia? (M. MacColl) Fortn. 64: 943.
— Geographical Description of the British Isles. Nat. Geog. M. 7: 208.
— Government; Law or Caprice? Westm. 146: 169.
— — Luck or Leadership for? Fortn. 66: 199.
— — The Schoolmaster at St. Stephen's. Fortn. 66: 436.
— — Socialist View of. (G. Lansbury) National, 25: 564.
— History, Early, Major's. Spec. 68: 536.
— Imperial Subventions in. (W. A. Hunter) Contemp. 64: 461.
— Imperial Veto. (G. Smith) Sat. R. 80: 499.
— in 1881-91; Lessons of a Decade. (T. W. Russell) 19th Cent. 32: 581.
— Industrial Supremacy of. "Made in Germany." (E. E. Williams) New R. 14: 14-636.
— Legislation in Modern. (F. E. Bradley) Law Q. 10: 32.
— Mammals of, Ancient. (R. Lydekker) Knowl. 17: 169-221.
— Mineral Wealth of. Bank. M. (Lond.) 61: 378.
— Ministerial Responsibility in. (S. Low) Fortn. 64: 210.
— Ministries, The Making of. National, 25: 750.
— Mint Operations. Bank. M. (Lond.) 58: 133.
— Mint Report, 1893. Bank. M. (Lond.) 56: 1.
— — 1895. Bank. M. (Lond.) 60: 1.
— Naval History, 1812-1815; the Post-office Packets. Macmil. 70: 282.
— Naval Supremacy. (E. Bond) Un. Serv. M. 9: 55.
— Navy. National, 27: 162. — (C. W. Dilke) New R. 12: 22. — Quar. 178: 289. — Sat. R. 77: 8. — (G. H. Jones) Westm. 141: 156.
— — Alarm about. (E. L. Godkin) Nation, 58: 4.
— — and the Colonies, The. (H. O. Arnold-Forster) New R. 13: 25.
See above, Great Britain. Colonial Empire.
— — Can England be invaded? (G. S. Clarke) National, 27: 338.
— — Carelessness of Officers. Sat. R. 74: 299.
— — Colonial Navies. Spec. 75: 328.
— — Colonies and Maritime Defence. National, 23: 593.
— — Children of Nelson. New R. 10: 129.
— — Command of the Sea and British Policy. (S. Wilkinson) National, 26: 758.
— — Compared with Foreign Navies. (H. W. Wilson) Sat. R. 81: 242.
— — Cost of. (Capt. C. Bridge) Time, 1: 385.
— — Cruisers in. Un. Serv. M. 7: 1045.
— — Engineering in. (R. C. Oldknow) New R. 13: 304.
— — Fighting Power of. (R. A. E. Scott) Murray, 9: 620.
— — Fleet in being. (David Hannay) New R. 13: 411.
— — Great Britain as a Sea-power. (T. A. Brassey) 19th Cent. 34: 121. Same art. Un. Serv. (Phila.) 10: 246.

Great Britain. Navy, Gun Muddle of. (H. C. Burdett) Univ. R. 3: 177.
— — Guns of. (H. O. Arnold-Forster) Sat. R. 80: 202.
— — How to join the. (C. Gleig) Chamb. J. 70: 501.
— — in 1805 and in 1896. (H. W. Wilson) Sat. R. 82: 436.
— — in 1893. (S. Eardley-Wilmot) Cosmopol. 14: 600.
— — in 1894. (W. L. Clowes) National, 24: 661.
— — Increase of. Chamb. J. 73: 326.
— — Is Our Sea-power to be maintained? (G. Hamilton) National, 22: 449.
— — Manning the. Blackw. 160: 678. — Spec. 76: 76. — (D. Hannay) New R. 12: 373, 490.
— — — in Time of War. (T. A. Brassey) 19th Cent. 40: 861.
— — Manœuvres in 1887. (D'A. G. Vincent) Un. Serv. M. '87, 2: 206.
— — — in 1889. Spec. 63: 234.
— — — in 1892. Spec. 69: 249. — (G. S. Clarke) Un. Serv. M. 6: 91.
— — — in 1893. (O. Churchill) Un. Serv. M. 8: 62. — Un. Serv. M. 9: 449.
— — — in 1894. (W. L. Clowes) 19th Cent. 36: 341. — Fortn. 62: 383. — (G. S. Clarke) Un. Serv. M. 10: 70.
— — — in 1895. (W. L. Clowes) Fortn. 64: 566. — (W. L. Clowes) Un. Serv. (Phila.) 14: 531.
— — — in 1896. (P. H. Colomb) Sat. R. 82: 127, 159.
— — The Marines. (D. Hannay) New R. 13: 655.
— — Men-of-war Names. (H. Mist) Un. Serv. M. 8: 227.
— — Merchant Ships as Auxiliaries to. Time, 16: 339.
— — Naval Estimates and Imperial Defence. (W. L. Clowes) Fortn. 65: 562.
— — Naval Grievances. Sat. R. 74: 679.
— — Navigating Officers. (W. Wilson) Un. Serv. M. 7: 912.
— — Navy Records Society. Macmil. 71: 416.
— — Needs of. (Sir T. Symonds) Fortn. 60: 282.
— — New Fleet at Chatham. Spec. 68: 294.
— — Notes on. Un. Serv. (Phila.) 15: 78.
— — of the Commonwealth, 1649-1660. (M. Oppenheim) Eng. Hist. R. 11: 20.
— — of the 18th Century, Rodney and. Ed. R. 175: 166.
— — Our Defenceless. Westm. 143: 543.
— — Our Naval Reserves. (A. G. Bagot) Fortn. 65: 422.
— — Protection of Our Commerce in War. (H. W. Wilson) 19th Cent. 39: 218.
— — Questions on. (H. O. Arnold-Forster) National, 23: 409.
— — Sea Power of England. (H. W. Wilson) Un. Serv. M. 10: 459.
— — Ships of. (W. L. Clowes) Engin. M. 6: 773.
— — Strength of. (H. O. A. Forster) Sat. R. 81: 65.
— — The Struggle before us. (H. W. Wilson) Fortn. 66: 731.
— — Tactics. Temp. Bar, 106: 318.
— — Teachings of the Crisis. (W. L. Clowes) 19th Cent. 39: 448.
— — 300 Years Ago. (H. Jones) Good Words, 35: 784.
— — under Queen Elizabeth. (M. Oppenheim) Eng. Hist. R. 9: 709.
— — under Charles I. (M. Oppenheim) Eng. Hist. R. 9: 92, 473.
— — under James I. (M. Oppenheim) Eng. Hist. R. 7: 471.
— — Unionist Policy in Naval Matters. Spec. 68: 839.
— — Weakness of. (B. Tillett) National, 27: 872.
— Ordnance Survey of. (J. Pierce, jr.) Nat. Geog. M. 2: 243. — Quar. 180: 36.
Great Britain. Parliament, Records of, 1305, ed. by Maitland. Sat. R. 78: 160.
— — 1892-95, Lucy's. Sat. R. 81: 532.
— Parties in, Future of. (R. Wallace) Fortn. 61: 705.
— Pensions, Civil List. (J. Jackson) Month, 81: 81.
— Political History, 1885-92, Clayden's. Sat. R. 73: 744.
— Political Organizations in the United States and England. (J. Bryce) No. Am. 156: 105.
— Politics and the Clergy. Spec. 75: 301.
— — Candidates, Society for Protection of. (J. A. Farrer) 19th Cent. 32: 975.
— — Conservatism and Democracy. Quar. 176: 254.
— — County Elections, Is Race a Factor in? Spec. 69: 86.
— — Democracy and Leadership. Fortn. 66: 869.
— — Extension of Trade in Political Principle. (F. Greenwood) Fortn. 52: 669.
— — The Future of. (H. Dyer) Westm. 145: 1. Same art. Ecl. M. 126: 311.
— — in 1832; Story of Eleven Days, May 7th-18th. (G. Wallas) Fortn. 58: 767.
— — in 1885; Franchise Bill. (W. R. Anson) Law Q. 1: 25.
— — in 1891. Sat. R. 73: 8.
— — in 1892. Spec. 68: 4.
— — — and in the U. S.; Impending Elections. (A. Carnegie) 19th Cent. 32: 141.
— — — An Appeal to the Country. National, 19: 585.
— — — Are Democracies Fickle? Spec. 69: 85.
— — — The Campaign. Pub. Opin. 13: 301, 325.
— — — — and after. (F. Greenwood) New R. 7: 641.
— — — Choice of England. (E. Dicey) 19th Cent. 32: 1.
— — — Coming Crisis. Ed. R. 175: 274.
— — — Coming Struggle. Blackw. 151: 904.
— — — Defence of the Union. (A. V. Dicey) Contemp. 61: 314.
— — — The Elections. And. R. 18: 182. — Blackw. 152: 138. — (J. C. Rose) Nation, 55: 25.
— — — — and after. (W. T. Stead) Contemp. 62: 288.
— — — — and Home Rule. (G. D. Campbell) No. Am. 155: 129.
— — — — Asquith on. Spec. 69: 759.
— — — — A Bird's Eye View. (A. A. Baumann) National, 19: 730.
— — — — Forecast of. (C. W. Dilke) New R. 6: 666.
— — — — Liberal Outlook. (T. W. Reid) 19th Cent. 31: 735. — (J. D. Holms) Westm. 137: 233.
— — — — The Real Radical Programme. (C. A. Whitmore) National, 19: 740.
— — — — Lessons Derived from. Westm. 138: 536.
— — — — Moral of. (S. Webb) Contemp. 62: 272.
— — — — The "Progressive" Victory. (C. A. Whitmore) National, 19: 252.
— — — — Results of. Blackw. 152: 293. — (E. Dicey) 19th Cent. 32: 333. Same art. Liv. Age, 144: 749.
— — — The Gladstone-Hartington Controversy. (F. Greenwood) Fortn. 57: 580.
— — — Gladstone's Majority; What will he do with it? Ed. R. 175: 559.
— — — Gladstone, Return of, to Power. (E. L. Godkin) Nation, 55: 142.
— — — — Tory Defiance of. Pub. Opin. 13: 399.
— — — Labouchere and the Government. Spec. 69: 373, 757.
— — — The New Government. Ed. R. 176: 557. — Spec. 69: 84. — (H. W. Massingham) New R. 7: 454. — Pub. Opin. 13: 470, 494. — Quar. 175: 538. — (W. T. Stead) R. of Rs. (N. Y.) 6: 287. — Sat. R. 74: 211. — Spec. 69: 244.

Great Britain. Politics in, 1892. The New Government, A Forecast of. (J. McCarthy) No. Am. 155: 293.
— — — — French View of. (J. Reinach) New R. 7: 257.
— — — New House of Commons. Pub. Opin. 13: 375.
— — — — and the Irish Question. (A. J. Balfour) No. Am. 155: 641.
— — — — Parties and Programmes in. (J. McCarthy; G. J. Shaw Lefevre; J. K. Hardie) New R. 7: 129.
— — — Nonconformists in. (J. G. Rogers) Contemp. 61: 498.
— — — Old and the New Ministry. National, 20: 1.
— — — Outlook for the New Year. Blackw. 151: 151.
— — — Parliamentary and Election Prospects. Quar. 174: 254.
— — — The Political Outlook. Fortn. 58: 243.
— — — Problem before Mr. Gladstone. Spec. 69: 116.
— — — Rosebery *vs.* Gladstone. (Lord Brabourne) Blackw. 151: 169.
— — — Tory Party, Future of. (F. R. Y. Radcliffe) National, 20: 145.
— — — Vote of Want of Confidence. Spec. 69: 180.
— — — Wanted — a New Party. (F. Greenwood) New R. 6: 555.
— — — Why I shall vote for the Unionists. (R. Gregory and others) 19th Cent. 32: 151.
— — — Why I voted for Gladstone. (Sir T. H. Farrer and others) 19th Cent. 32: 177.
— Politics, in 1893. Administration of Gladstone. Blackw. 153: 164.
— — — Autumn Session, Incidents of. National, 22: 664.
— — — A Cabinet Minister's Vade-mecum; a Satire. (A. Herbert) 19th Cent. 34: 504.
— — — English Political Leaders. (F. A. Maxse) National, 22: 115.
— — — Episodes of the Months. National, 22: 145–433.
— — — Future of the Labor Party. Spec. 70: 39.
— — — Government and the Country. Blackw. 153: 617.
— — — A Ground of Agreement for all Parties. (W. H. Mallock) National, 21: 22.
— — — Her Majesty's Opposition. (W. H. Robinson) Westm. 139: 489.
— — — Introduction of the Caucus into England. (M. Ostrogorski) Pol. Sci. Q. 8: 287.
— — — Liberal Party and the Claims of Wales. (S. T. Evans) New R. 9: 337.
— — — Liberals and the Labor Party. (J. L. Mahon) National, 21: 130.
— — — Liberalism and Social Reform. (L. A. Jones) New R. 9: 629.
— — — Making a Constitution. Ed. R. 178: 266.
— — — New Pocket-boroughs. Spec. 70: 793.
— — — Parliamentary Episodes. National, 21: 724.
— — — Party Manœuvres *vs.* Public Opinion. Ed. R. 178: 530.
— — — The Peers and the People. Blackw. 154: 597.
— — — The Political Situation. (F. S. Stevenson) Westm. 139: 1.
— — — The Radical Rush. (T. E. Kebbel) National, 21: 162.
— — — Registration Bill. Sat. R. 75: 233.
— — — The Session: I. Its Personal Aspects. II. Its Barren Labor. (Sir G. Baden-Powell) National, 22: 230.
— — — Unionist Campaign. Quar. 177: 265.
— — — Unionist Reaction. Quar. 176: 549.
— — — To your Tents, Oh Israel! Fortn. 60: 569.
Great Britain. Politics in, 1893. Tory Press and Tory Party. (F. Gardner; H. Cust; W. H. Pollock; W. E. Henley; S. J. Low) National, 21: 357.
— — — Waning of Liberalism. Spec. 71: 657.
— — — What Mr. Gladstone ought to do. (J. Fletcher-Moulton and others) Fortn. 59: 262.
— Politics in, 1894. Blackw. 156: 899.
— — — Alexander's Generals. Quar. 179: 553.
— — — Cabinet Counsels and Candid Friends. (T. H. S. Escott) Contemp. 66: 488.
— — — Chamberlain Coalition Programme. (E. Dicey) 19th Cent. 35: 367.
— — — Demagogues in British Politics. Quar. 178: 553.
— — — English Workmen and their Political Friends. (J. E. Gorst) No. Am. 159: 207.
— — — Labor Politics in a New Place. (E. Porritt) No. Am. 158: 378.
— — — Local Government Act, The. (H. H. L. Bellot) Westm. 141: 479.
— — — The Ministry of the Masses. Ed. R. 180: 235.
— — — The New Ministry. Ed. R. 179: 512.
— — — New Parties in Parliament. (J. McCarthy) No. Am. 158: 401.
— — — The Peril of Parliament. Quar. 178: 263.
— — — Political Bird's-eye View. (F. Greenwood) New R. 11: 366.
— — — Political Outlook in England. (E. Ashmead-Bartlett) No. Am. 158: 668.
— — — Position of Liberal Unionists. (T. W. Russell; H. O. Arnold-Forster; J. Parker-Smith; F. A. Maxse) National, 23: 219.
— — — Possibilities of Liberal Reunion. (T. H. S. Escott) Contemp. 66: 35.
— — — Problems and Perils of British Politics. (G. Smith) No. Am. 159: 11.
— — — Reasons for Coalition. National, 23: 17.
— — — Rosebery and the Liberal Crisis. (J. C. Hopkins) Forum, 17: 139.
— — — The Session. Ed. R. 179: 246. — Blackw. 156: 438.
— — — — Setting and the Rising Sun. New R. 10: 401.
— — — Some Features of. National, 24: 86.
— — — Why not dissolve? (H. W. Massingham) Contemp. 65: 903.
— Politics, in 1895. (W. Reid) 19th Cent. 37: 131.
— — — The Budget: a New Scheme. Contemp. 68: 697.
— — — The Conservatism of to-day. Quar. 180: 549.
— — — A Counterfeit Revolution. Ed. R. 181: 227.
— — — Economic Reforms of Late Liberal Administration. (E. Porritt) Yale R. 4: 269.
— — — The Failure of Government by Groups. (W. Rathbone) Fortn. 64: 843.
— — — Fall of the Government. (S. Wilkinson) National, 25: 843.
— — — A Foreign Affairs Committee. (S. Low) 19th Cent. 38: 506.
— — — General Election. (J. G. Rogers; E. Dicey) 19th Cent. 38: 177. — Pub. Opin. 19: 171.
— — — — and the Prospects of Social Legislation. (W. Cunningham) Econ. R. 5: 501.
— — — — Cause of the Collapse. (A. Withy) Westm. 144: 237. Another Cause. (S. Williams) Westm. 144: 567.
— — — — The Coalition. New R. 13: 117.
— — — — Crisis in English History. (H. Maxwell) Forum, 20: 144.
— — — — The Débacle and after. (H. W. Massingham) Contemp. 68: 299.

Great Britain. Politics in 1895: General Election. Defeat of the Liberal Party; why, whence and whither? (J. M'Carthy) Forum, 20: 170.
— — — General Election. I. General View. (C. S. Wortley). II. Lessons from Scotland. (Lady Frances Balfour) National, 26: 87.
— — — — Moral of. (H. H. L. Bellot) Westm. 144: 173.
— — — — Salisbury's Triumph. Fortn. 64: 355.
— — — — Significance of. (H. Maxwell; G. W. E. Russell; J. M'Carthy) Forum, 20: 160.
— — — — Triumph of Conservatism. Quar. 182: 538.
— — — The Great Democratic Joke. New R. 12: 161.
— — — Legislation, Parliamentary Inquiries, and Official Returns. (E. Cannan) Econ. R. 5: 133, 263, 406, 558.
— — — The Liberal Leadership. (James Annand) New R. 13: 367.
— — — The Liberal Party and its Candid Friends. Fortn. 63: 526.
— — — Liberal Programme, Wanted,—a New. (T. Scanlon) Westm. 144: 357.
— — — Need for a United Progressive Party. (R. Balmforth) Westm. 144: 624.
— — — The New Cabinet. Spec. 74: 889.—(C. W. Dilke) No. Am. 161: 196.—(T. E. Champion) Canad. M. 5: 345.
— — — The New Radicalism. Spec. 75: 103.
— — — Opening of Parliament. Green Bag, 7: 578.
— — — A Plague on both your Parties! (K. Wilkinson) Fortn. 63: 757.
— — — Political Retrospect. Ed. R. 182: 249.
— — — Political Situation. (D. Balsillie) Westm. 143: 603.
— — — Politics, Parties, and Imperial Defence. Ed. R. 182: 524.
— — — Predominant Partners and Unionist Discords. (T. H. S. Escott) Contemp. 67: 864.
— — — Reorganization of Liberalism. (James Annand) New R. 13: 494.
— — — Rival Leaders and Party Legacies. Quar. 182: 354.
— — — Rosebery and the Liberal Party. (W. L. Stobart) Fortn. 64: 234.
— — — The Rural Revolution. (R. Heath) Contemp. 67: 182.
— — — Timely Truths for the Outs and Ins. (K. Wilkinson) Fortn. 64: 170.
— — — Unionist Policy. (J. S. Stuart-Glennie) Fortn. 64: 849.
— — — Wilful Isolation. (F. Greenwood) Contemp. 67: 838.
— Politics, in 1896. The Country and the Ministry. Ed. R. 184: 514.
— — — Crisis in. Harper, 92: 954.
— — — Elections. (H. C. Lodge) Harper, 93: 232.—(L. Emanuel) Westm. 146: 328.
— — — The Election Petitions of 1895-96. (H. Chisholm) Fortn. 65: 759.
— — — The Happy Family; a Cabinet Meeting in 1895; a skit. Contemp. 70: 810.
— — — The Liberal New Year. (E. R. Russell) Contemp. 69: 137.
— — — Parliament, Session of. (J. M'Carthy) No. Am. 163: 304.—Nation, 63: 191.—(J. Herlihy) Westm. 146: 367.—National, 28: 297.
— — — Political Outlook. (F. Greenwood) National, 26: 703.
— — Jephson on. (W. Wilson) Dial (Ch.) 13: 213.
— — Legislation, Parliamentary Inquiries, and Official Returns. (E. Cannan) Econ. R. 6: 97-539.
Great Britain. Politics, in 1896. Liberalism of To-morrow. (W. T. Stead) Univ. R. 5: 1.
— — One Vote, one Value. (St. Loe Strachey) National, 18: 789.
— — Parliamentary Registration; Plea for Reform. (F. W. Palliser) National, 20: 567.
— — The Quadruple Alliance. (E. J. Dillon) Contemp. 69: 457.
— — — The Question of Alliances. Contemp. 69: 153.
— — The Queen in. (F. H. Hill) National, 19: 153.
— — Salisbury Administration. Spec. 69: 212.
— — A Septuagenarian's Retrospect. (J. G. Rogers) 19th Cent. 39: 158.
— — Tories, Neglected. (H. D. Traill) Fortn. 65: 919.
— — Why do Non-conformists follow Mr. Gladstone? (J. G. Rogers) Contemp. 61: 900.
— — Women in. (M. G. Fawcett) Forum, 14: 453.
— Prime Ministers. Quar. 183: 508.
— Private Bill Legislation. (R. V. Campbell) Jurid. R. 1: 26.
— Records, Public. (A. C. Ewald) Time, 2: 744.
— Royal Family, Income of. Spec. 70: 730.
— Service to Civilization. (A. S. Crowninshield) No. Am. 162: 634.
— Throne of, Order of Succession to. Spec. 68: 162.
— Treasury, its History and Associations. (C. E. D. Black) Westm. 143: 503.
— Union; a poem. (A. C. Swinburne) 19th Cent. 33: 725.
— War Office Reform. Contemp. 68: 326.
Great Good Heart of Corporal Dwight. (G. W. Carryl) Munsey, 14: 61.
Great Gulf, A; a story. Blackw. 157: 817. Same art. Liv. Age, 206: 12.
Great International Cricket Match; a story. (Basil Thomson) New R. 13: 398.
Great Island, N. H., Fort at. (F. W. Hackett) N. E. Reg. 50: 167.
Great K. & A. Train-robbery. (P. L. Ford) Lippinc. 58: 145.
Great Love; a poem. (L. C. Moulton) Cosmopol. 21: 512.
Great Men, Calendar of, Harrison's. Macmil. 65: 388.—(C. S. Pierce) Nation, 54: 54.—(J. Morley) 19th Cent. 31: 312. Same art. Ecl. M. 118: 433.
— How to grow. (E. A. Freeman) Univ. R. 1: 193.
— in Little Worlds; stories. (G. Gissing) Eng. Illust. 15: 127-487.
— The Twilight of. (R. Ogden) Nation, 61: 130.
Great Northern Railway, Eng., and its Locomotives. (A. J. Brickwell) Eng. Illust. 10: 423.
Great Plumstead Church. Reliquary, 32: 108.
Great Swamp Fight. (A. H. Clark) Am. Hist. Reg. 1: 530.
Great Talent, A; a story. Music, 4: 492, 604.
Great Water-cress Tragedy; a story. Blackw. 152: 105. Same art. Ecl. M. 119: 250. Same art. Liv. Age, 194: 621.
Great White Chief, The. (G. Parker) McClure, 2: 130.
Great Work; Magnum Opus. Ecl. M. 117: 592.
Greater Glory, The. (Maarten Maartens) Temp. Bar, 98: 283. 101: 423.
Greater Love; or, the Story of a Lone Woman. (Alex. Gordon) Good Words, 34: 781.
Greatest Man in the Country; a story. (H. D. Ward) Chaut. 22: 557.
Greatness of Man. (R. Le Gallienne) Cosmopol. 19: 617.
— Penalties of. All the Year, 71: 245.
Greaves, Lieut.-Gen. Sir G., with portrait. (E. C. H. Price) Eng. Illust. 10: 251.
Greece, Aerial Monasteries of. (C. Robinson) Lippinc. 57: 285.

Greece, Ancient, Murray's. Sat. R. 73: 340.
— and Modern Athens. (A. S. Peck) Around World, 1: 126.
— as revealed by Recent Excavations. Church Q. 35: 429.
— Battle of Chæroneia, B. C. 338. Sat. R. 79: 406.
— Christian: Bikelas and the Marquis of Bute. (J. S. Blackie) Blackw. 153: 126.
— Culture in, Environment of. (G. Perrott) Pop. Sci. Mo. 42: 193.
— Elections in, 1892. (J. H. McDaniels) Nation, 54: 462.
— English Policy in. Eng. R. 9: 388.
— Ethics of. (W. L. Sheldon) Open Court, 7: 3521.
— Excavations in. Am. Arch. 43: 56. — (C. Waldstein) New R. 6: 695.
— Financial Crisis in. (D. Kalopothakes) Nation, 58: 45.
— Five Weeks in. (J. C. Bailey) Temp. Bar, 99: 483.
— Higher Education in. (D. Quinn) Am. J. Soc. Sci. 32: 131.
— Highland, A Trip in. (A. W. Plant) Good Words, 36: 324.
— Historical Student in. (A. B. Hart) Nation, 58: 248.
— History of, Beloch's. (W. W. Fowler) Eng. Hist. R. 7: 119.
— — Egyptian Bases of. (W. M. F. Petrie) J. Hel. Stud. 11: 271.
— — Greek World under Roman Sway, Mahaffy's. (W. J. Arnold) Eng. Hist. R. 7: 124. — (J. H. McDaniels; B. L. Gildersleeve) Nation, 55: 89.
— — Holm on. Spec. 73: 732.
— — Myers's. (W. J. Chase) School R. 4: 696.
— — New Chapters in, Gardner's. Spec. 69: 709.
— — Problems in, Mahaffy on. Spec. 69: 422.
— Impressions of. (W. Miller) Westm. 142: 304.
— The Living Greek. (J. I. Manatt) R. of Rs. (N. Y.) 11: 398.
— Modern. (H. Lynch) Westm. 139: 155. Same art. Ecl. M. 120: 461.
— — Balkan States and. Chaut. 14: 573.
— — Customs and Lore of, Rodd's. Spec. 68: 170.
— Northern. (A. Phillippson) Geog. J. 3: 323.
— of To-day, Deschamps'. (M. S. Stillman) Nation, 55: 149.
— Politics in, in 1892: Result of the Elections. Spec. 68: 704.
— Recent Excavations in. (J. Gennadius) Forum, 21: 361, 735, 327.
— Religion in. (A. B. Hyde) Chaut. 17: 144.
— — Heresy at Athens at the time of Plato. (F. B. Tarbell) New World, 2: 687.
— Revisited. (E. Robinson) Nation, 58: 326, 362.
— Travels in. To the Brink of the Pirene. (M. Fullerton) National, 24: 58.
— Treatment of Criminals in. Blackw. 152: 54.
— A Wedding and a Christening in. (N. W. Williams) Gent. M. n. s. 49: 338.
Greek and Barbarian. (W. H. Norton) Educa. R. 7: 11.
Greek and Greek; a duologue. (N. Vynne) Theatre, 32: 145.
Greek and Latin in the Higher Schools in Germany. (J. E. Russell) School R. 4: 585, 664.
Greek Anthology and Teachings of Holy Scripture. (W. Cowan) Good Words, 34: 403. Same art. Liv. Age, 198: 445.
— Translating. Sat. R. 76: 330.
Greek Art, Characteristic Studies in. (M. Burnside) Educa. 16: 86.
— in the Age of Athletic Prizemen. (W. Pater) Contemp. 65: 242.
— Primitive, Perrot and Chipiez on. (J. C. Van Dyke) Dial (Ch.) 18: 142. — Art J. 47: 84.
Greek Church, The Divine Office in. (B. Zimmerman Month, 77: 72-369.
— Great Britain and America. (E. A. Grosvenor) New World, 5: 527.
— on the Pacific Coast. (A. Inkersley) Overland, n. s. 26: 469.
Greek Coins. (E. L. Cutts) Eng. Illust. 12: no. 5, 11.
Greek Comedians, Stories from, Church's. Spec. 69: 773.
Greek Courtship, A. (F. M. F. Skene) Argosy, 58: 117. Same art. Liv. Age, 202: 783.
Greek Drama, Chorus in Later. (E. Capps) Am. J. Archæol. 10: 287.
Greek Elements in Modern Religious Thought. (E. S. Carr) Bib. Sac. 53: 117.
Greek Epigrams. (J. H. McDaniels) Nation, 55: 304.
Greek Feast, A. (N. W. Williams) Gent. M. n. s. 52: 387.
Greek Fire. Chamb. J. 70: 319.
— Lightning from the East. Gent. M. n. s. 55: 450.
Greek Genius, Butcher on. Sat. R. 73: 77. — Spec. 69: 136.
Greek Head in Possession of T. H. Ward. (E. Sellers) J. Hel. Stud. 14: 198.
Greek Horizontal Curves in Maison Carrée, Nimes. (W. H. Goodyear) Archit. Rec. 4: 446.
Greek Idolatry, Hermai and Xoana. Reliquary, 36: 129.
Greek Language; Address of the Philological Association on the Study of, in the Schools. School R. 3: 434.
— and its Pronunciation, Modern. (J. P. Leotsakos) Nation, 59: 381.
— College Requirements in. (B. I. Wheeler) School R. 1: 73.
— Dictionary of, Prellwitz's. (E. R. Wharton) Acad. 41: 510.
— Elementary, as a College Study. (B. I. Wheeler) Educa. R. 4: 227.
— Imperfect and Aorist in. (C. W. E. Miller) Am. J. Philol. 16: 139.
— in the English of Modern Science. (F. A. March) Chaut. 17: 20.
— Instruction in, Elementary. (T. D. Seymour) School & C. 1: 88, 138.
— Is it Dead? (J. MacMullen) Educa. R. 4: 492. — (G. M. Whicher) Educa. R. 6: 379.
— Modern, Constantinides on. Sat. R. 74: 84.
— Modern, no Guide to the Ancient. (P. Shorey) Forum, 18: 602.
— Position of, in the Universities. (J. E. C. Welldon) Acad. (Syr.) 7: 1.
— Pronunciation of. (J. Gennadius) 19th Cent. 38: 681. — (R. J. Lloyd and others) Acad. 49: 39-511. — (A. Rose) Educa. 17: 65.
— Question of. (C. E. Fay) School & C. 1: 278.
— — at Cambridge University. (F. D. Moore) And. R. 17: 589.
— Spoken, Ancient and Modern. (A. N. Januaris) Contemp. 61: 566.
— Study of, in Germany. Educa. R. 3: 379.
— Teaching, as a Living Language. (J. Gennadius) Forum, 18: 228.
— — Experiment in. (M. W. Calkins) Educa. R. 7: 80.
Greek Lines, Van Brunt on. (E. E. Hale, jr.) Dial (Ch.) 16: 110.
Greek Literature, 1891-92. (S. P. Lambros) Ath. '92, 2: 17.
— in 1892-93. (S. P. Lambros) Ath. '93, 2: 20.
— in 1893-94. (S. P. Lambros) Ath. '94, 2: 17.
— in 1894-95. (S. P. Lambros) Ath. '95, 2: 16.
— in 1895-96. (S. P. Lambros) Ath. '96, 2: 17.

Greek Literature, Study of. (M. Thompson) Critic, 28: 249.
— Women in. (E. F. Wheeler) Chaut. 16: 531.
Greek Lyrics. (J. H. McDaniels) Nation, 54: 402.
Greek Music, Monro's. (F. P. Nash) Nation, 59: 364.
Greek Mythology. (F. B. Jevons) Folk-Lore, 2: 220.
— and the Bible. (J. Wedgwood) Contemp. 61: 368.
Greek Office-books. (S. G. Hatherly) Scot. R. 19: 113.
Greek Oracles. (T. D. Seymour) Chaut. 16: 163.
Greek Pay-bills, Some Ancient. (F. B. Jevons) Econ. J. 6: 470.
Greek Play at Bradfield College, 1892. (L. Dyer) Nation, 55: 26.
— at Iowa College; Electra of Sophocles. R. of Rs. (N. Y.) 2: 174.
— at Oxford, 1892. Sat. R. 73: 244.—Ath. '92, 1: 318.—Temp. Bar, 95: 238.
— Œdipus Tyrannus, at Cambridge. (C. Whibley) M. of Art, 11: 86.
— Jebb on. (P. Shorey) Dial (Ch.) 16: 107.—(J. H. McDaniels) Nation, 58: 159.
— Permanent Power of. (R. C. Jebb) Atlan. 72: 545.
Greek Portraits, Graf Collection of. (J. W. Fewkes) New Eng. n. s. 9: 612.
Greek Proper Names, Spelling and Pronunciation of. (C. M. Moss) Educa. R. 7: 495.
Greek Romances, Two Early. Westm. 137: 557.
Greek Social Life, Philosophy and. (A. W. Benn) New World, 3: 418.
Greek Spirit and Modern Life, Jebb on. Spec. 70: 351.
Greek Stage, Vitruvius on. (L. Dyer) J. Hel. Stud. 12: 356.
Greek Studies, Pater's. Sat. R. 79: 191.
Greek Subjects, English Poems on. (J. R. Joy) Chaut. 17: 271.
Greek Theatre of 5th Century B. C., Relative Position of Actors and Chorus in. (J. Pickard) Am. J. Philol. 14: 68-273.
Greek Trade-Routes to Britain. (W. Ridgeway) Folk-Lore, 1: 82.
Greek Tragedy, Smith's Specimens of. (J. H. McDaniels) Nation, 59: 179, 199.
Greek Tribal Society, Seebohm's. Sat. R. 82: 226.
Greek Worship of Stones. Reliquary, 36: 23.
Greeks in Contact with Romans. (E. J. Smith) Atlan. 72: 685.
— Mediæval. Use of the Term Helladikoi. (J. B. Bury) Eng. Hist. R. 7: 80.
Greeley, Horace. (J. R. Young) Lippinc. 51: 185.
— and Carey, H. C. Soc. Econ. 7: 134.
Green, Alexander Henry. Nat. Sci. 9: 276.—Acad. 50: 148.—Ath. '96, 2: 294.—Nature, 54: 421.
Green, Mrs. Everett. Ath. '95, 2: 645.
Green, Matthew; An Arm-chair Philosopher. Macmil. 74: 114.
Green, Sally Pratt McLean, with portrait. Bk. News, 12: 37.—With portrait. Bk. Buyer, 6: 142.
Green, Thomas Hill, and his Critics. (H. Haldar) Philos. R. 3: 168.
— Philosophy of, Theological Aspects of. (C. B. Upton) New World, 1: 139.
— — Recollections of. (C. P. Parker) Harv. Mo. 18: 1.
Green, Wm. Henry. (G. S. Duncan) Bib. World, 8: 46.
— Bibliography of. (J. H. Dulles) Presb. & Ref. R. 7: 509.
— Jubilee of. Presb. & Ref. R. 7: 507.
Green, Symbolism of. Chamb. J. 69: 367. Same art. Ecl. M. 122: 838.
Green Corn Festival of Seneca Indians. J. Am. Folk-Lore, 4: 71.
Green-Cub Mine. (R. Bain) Chamb. J. 73: 552.
Green Ferne Farm. Time, 1: 11-661. 2: 399, 529.
Green Flag, The; a story. (A. C. Doyle) McClure, 4: 155.
Green Gaffer, The. (L. Housman) Univ. R. 7: 313.
Green Lion Pavement. Longm. 20: 377.
Green Mountains, General Structure of Main Axis of. (C. L. Whittle) Am. J. Sci. 147: 347.
Green Room Club. (F. Hawkins) Theatre, 36: 17.
Green Rushes, O! a story. (S. Baring-Gould) Chamb. J. 72: 604.
Greenbacks, Banks and the. Gunton's M. 10: 15.
— must go. (H. White) Nation, 59: 438.
— Retire the. Gunton's M. 10: 24.
Greene, Anna Katharine, with portrait. Bk. News, 12: 8.
Greene, Robert; an Old Elizabethan. Spec. 73: 566.
Greenhill, William Alexander. Acad. 46: 232.—Ath. '94, 2: 421.
Greenhouse for Amateurs. (D. D. Slade) Garden & F. 5: 238.
— Insects in Soil of. (J. B. Smith) Garden & F. 5: 117.
— A Remodeled. Garden & F. 5: 6.
— Shading. (J. N. Gerard) Garden & F. 5: 200.
— Tropical. (T. D. Hatfield) Garden & F. 5: 383.
— under Trial. (J. N. Gerard) Garden & F. 5: 140.
Greenhouse Climbers. Garden & F. 7: 37.
Greenhouse Exhibits at the Columbian Exposition. (L. H. Bailey) Garden & F. 6: 448.
Greenhouse Plants, A Good Collection of. (T. D. Hatfield) Garden & F. 6: 179.
— Winter-flowering. (T. D. Hatfield) Garden & F. 6: 536.
Greenhouse Work. (E. O. Orpet) Garden & F. 6: 506.
Greenhouses, Economical Summer. (W. F. Massey) Garden & F. 6: 176.
— Small. (J. N. Gerard) Garden & F. 6: 92, 526.
Greenland, American Exploration of. Dub. R. 113: 665.
— East, Expedition, Lieut. Ryder's, 1891-92. Geog. J. 1: 43.
— Great White Journey across. (R. E. Peary) Around World, 1: 28.
— In the Land of the Northernmost Eskimo. (E. Astrup) Fortn. 65: 466.
— Von Drygalski's Expedition to. Geog. J. 3: 47.
Greenland Kayak, The. (G. F. Wright) Nation, 59: 213.
Greenstone God and the Stockbroker; a story. (F. Hume) Idler, 4: 563.
Greenway Court, Va. (W. Y. Page) M. Am. Hist. 30: 137.
Greenwich, Chronicles of. (E. Walford) Walford's Antiq. 8: 253.
Greenwich Observatory. Ath. '92, 1: 765.
— Annual Visitation of, 1893. (W. J. S. Lockyer) Nature, 48: 127.
Greenwood, Dr. J. G. Acad. 46: 254.
Gregariousness, a National Vice. (H. C. Merwin) Atlan. 71: 769.
Gregg, Josiah, Naturalist. Garden & F. 7: 12.
Gregoire, The Abbé, and the French Revolution. (W. Gibson) 19th Cent. 34: 272. Same art. Liv. Age, 198: 759.
Gregorovius, Ferd. (S. Münz) Eng. Hist. R. 7: 697.
— Euphorion. (J. E. Harrison) M. of Art, 8: 98.
— Roman Journal of. (E. Lecky) Longm. 24: 613. Same art. Liv. Age, 203: 617.
Gregory I., Pope, with portrait. (T. J. Shahan) Cath. World, 60: 507.
Gregory the Great and England. (M. Hennessy) Am. Cath. Q. 19: 40.

Gregory, Edward John. (F. Wedmore) M. of Art, 7: 353.
Gregory, William, Journal of, 1771. New Eng. M. n. s. 12: 343.
Gregory, Sir William H. (E. A. Gowing) Belgra. 88: 23.
— Autobiography of. Ath. '94, 2: 597. — (T. Hutchinson) Acad. 46: 391.
Gregory's Island. (G. W. Cable) Scrib. M. 20: 149.
Gregr, Edward. (Edith Sellers) Temp. Bar, 107: 335.
Greiffenhagen, Maurice. Art J. 46: 225.
Gresham, Law of, Formulation of. (W. M. Daniels) Ann. Am. Acad. Pol. Sci. 6: 280.
Gresham University Commission, Report of. Nature, 49: 405.
Gresollon, Daniel de. A Gentleman of the Royal Guard. (W. McLennan) Harper, 87: 609.
Gretchen's Wish. (M. T. Mott) Overland, n. s. 22: 170.
Greville, Eden E. Shakespeare. Theatre, 29: 79.
Grévy, Jules. (C. J. Wallis) Time, 14: 317.
Grey, Sir George, Rees'. Ath. '92, 2: 245. — (W. Wickham) Acad. 42: 255. — Sat. R. 74: 428. — Spec. 69: 564.
Grey, Henry, 3d Earl. Sat. R. 78: 399.
Grey and the Bay, The; a poem. (H. S. Wilson) Gent. M. n. s. 49: 97.
Grey Boy, The; a story. All the Year, 73: 500–642.
Grey Monk, The; a novel. (T. W. Speight) Argosy, 57: 1–353. 58: 1–441.
Grey Romance, A. (Lucy Clifford) National, 21: 682. Same art. Liv. Age, 198: 525.
Grey Sleeve, A; a story. (S. Crane) Eng. Illust. 14: 437.
Greyhounds and Foxhounds. Spec. 70: 416.
— How they hunt. (A. H. Powers, jr.) Outing, 26: 49.
Grez. (R. A. M. Stevenson) M. of Art, 17: 27.
Gridou's Pity. (G. H. Peirce) Atlan. 75: 325, 515.
Grief, Pleasures of. All the Year, 76: 88.
Grieg, Edvard Hagerup. (W. Mason) Cent. 25: 701.
Grier, R. M., with portrait. (F. Sherlock) Chr. Lit. 11: 339.
Griffin Family of Virginia. (S. N. Robins) Am. Hist. Reg. 2: 1233.
Griffith, Alfred. (J. A. McCauley) Meth. R. 52: 419.
Grimald, Nicholas. (J. M. Hart) Acad. 47: 126.
Grimm, Frédéric Melchior. Longm. 19: 603.
Grimsby, Eng.; Metropolis of Fishing Trade. (Geo. H. Robinson) Time, 8: 333.
Grindelwald Conference, 1892. Chr. Lit. 11: 342. — R. of Rs. (N. Y.) 6: 310.
Grindstone Island. (R. E. Burchard) Outing, 29: 138.
Griswold Mystery, The; a story. (W. Hinckley) Outing, 20: 441.
Grolier Club. (E. D. North) Bibliographica, 2: 377.
— Old English Books at. Critic, 22: 349.
Gröningen Land Lease System. (J. H. Gore) Gunton's M. 10: 440.
Groot, Gerhard, a Preacher of 14th Century. (M. T. Kelly) Month, 88: 259.
Groseilliers, Medard Chouart des, Radisson and. (H. C. Campbell) Am. Hist. R. 1: 226.
Grosley, Pierre Jean, 1718–85. (A. Dobson) Longm. 27: 244.
Gross, Samuel E., with portrait. (H. L. Conard) Nat'l M. (N. Y. '91) 17: 373.
Grossmith, George; a sketch of his Life. (R. Blathwayt) Idler, 3: 69.
Grossmith, Walter Weedon, with portrait. Theatre, 28: 91.
Grosvenor, Edwin A., with portrait. Book News, 14: 223. — Writer, 9: 9.
Grosvenor Gallery. M. of Art, 1: 50–110.
— Water-color Drawings at. M. of Art, 2: 30.
Grosvenor Gallery, Winter Exhibition of Pictures. (W. Meynell) M. of Art, 4: 177.
Grote, Hermann. Ath. '95, 1: 384.
Grotesque and Humorous in Mediæval Illuminations. (E. M. Thompson) Bibliographica, 2: 309.
— in Sacred Architecture. (F. Sewell) Am. Arch. 51: 87.
— Proper Limits and Functions of, in Art. (S. H. Statham) M. of Art, 4: 129.
Ground-rents, A Tax on: who would pay it? (R. Balmforth) Westm. 143: 297. Same art. Ecl. M. 124: 641.
— Taxation of. (I. P. Williams) 19th Cent. 33: 293. — (C. F. Bastable) Econ. J. 3: 255.
Ground-swells. (J. H. Walworth) Lippinc. 57: 147.
Grouse, by Macpherson and others. Sat. R. 78: 239.
— Pin-tailed, Shooting. (J. S. Crane) Outing, 24: 385.
— Still-hunting, on Snow. (J. R. Benton) Outing, 23: 215.
Grouse-moors. Sat. R. 74: 131.
— Scotch. Spec. 73: 337.
Grouse-shooting. Sat. R. 78: 320.
— Charm of. Sat. R. 80: 169.
— in Ireland. (H. A. Bryden) Sat. R. 82: 155. — (H. Jephson) Time, 19: 541.
— in Scotland. (C. Prescott) Outing, 20: 380.
Grove, Sir William Robert. (A. Gray) Nature, 54: 393. — Ath. '96, 2: 198.
Grover, Lewis C., with portrait. Nat'l M. (N. Y. '91) 18: 301.
Growse, Frederic Salmon. (J. S. Cotton) Acad. 43: 461.
Growth, Correlation of Factors in Organic. (E. Strasburger) Pop. Sci. Mo. 46: 397.
— of the Human Body. (G. M. West) Educa. R. 12: 284.
Grub, George. Ath. '92, 2: 451.
Grub Street and its Journal. (W. Roberts) Bookworm, 1: 20, 94.
Gruchy, the Birthplace of J. F. Millet. (G. Grahame) Portfo. 23: 106, 125.
Gruet, Jacques, Calvin's Ethical Victim. (M. D. Conway) Open Court, 10: 5068.
Grützner, Eduard. (C. S. Johnson) Munsey, 12: 397.
— Smiling Monks of. (C. de Kay) Mo. Illust. 3: 9.
Grundy, Sydney, and the Critics. (W. Watson) Theatre, 33: 161.
— A Fool's Paradise. Theatre, 28: 98.
— Slaves of the Ring. Sat. R. 79: 10.
Gruyère and its Castle. (W. D. McCrackan) New Eng. M. n. s. 9: 641.
Guanches, The, of the Canary Islands. (J. W. Gambier) Antiq. n. s. 29: 15–94.
— of Tenerife. (C. Edwardes) National, 19: 361. Same art. Liv. Age, 194: 165.
Guaramy, The. (J. Martiniano de Alencar) Overland, n. s. 21: 81 — 22: 529.
Guarantee Funds and Guarantors. (H. Moore) Music, 3: 187.
Guaranty. Bank. M. (N. Y.) 48: 656.
Guardian of Fort D'Albert; a story. (C. F. Little) Un. Serv. (Phila.) 8: 558.
Guardian of Stonehenge; a story. (A. Williamson) Eng. Illust. 14: 147.
Guarding the Pass; a poem. (E. M. Thomas) Cosmopol. 17: 75.
Guards, Brigade of, British. (H. A. Herbert; T. Donnelly) Cosmopol. 12: 551.
Guardsmen, Physical Training of. (W. T. Courtland) Un. Serv. (Phila.) 12: 101.
Guatemala; a Specimen Spanish-American Republic. Nation, 62: 153, 176.

Guérin, Maurice de. Centaur. (Mrs. J. T. Fields) Scrib. M. 12: 224.
Guests of Mrs. Timms. (S. O. Jewett) Cent. 25: 575.
Guests of the Wolfmaster; a story. (E. Castle) Temp. Bar, 108: 552.
Guiana and its Peoples. (H. Whates) Fortn. 65: 239.
— and Venezuela, Glimpses of. (W. N. King) Cent. 30: 358.
— British. Macmil. 73: 471. Same art. Ecl. M. 126: 731.
— — and its Resources. Dub. R. 118: 437.
— — Buck-pot, Swizzle-stick, and Cassirrie. (F. Banfield) Gent. M. n. s. 51: 247.
— — Gold Industry in. Dub. R. 111: 196.
— — Prospecting in. (J. E. Playfair) Gent. M. n. s. 51: 67.
— — Rodway's. (N. D. Davis) Nation, 54: 194.
— Caribs of. (N. D. Davis) Nation, 62: 193.
— Dutch Claims in. (H. Thurston) Month, 87: 396.
— Forest of, Day and Night in. Longm. 20: 603. Same art. Liv. Age, 195: 621.
— Evolution in. (J. Rodway) Nat. Sci. 2: 37.
— — — Rodway's. Sat. R. 79: 227.
— — Flowers in. (J. Rodway) Nat. Sci. 2: 412.
Guides; a Protest. (A. Repplier) Atlan. 76: 364.
Guido Reni, Picture of Beatrice Cenci. (T. A. Trollope) M. of Art, 4: 384.
Guildford, England. (W. J. Loftie) M. of Art, 9: 265.
Guildhall Library. Bookworm, 6: 361.
Guildhall Museum, Corner in. (F. G. Green) Bookworm, 3: 137.
— Loan Collection of Pictures. All the Year, 70: 444. — (A. G. Temple) Art J. 46: 133, 335.
Guilds and Guild-Laws. (G. Ravené) Green Bag, 4: 389.
— Art, Revival of. (W. S. Sparrow) Art J. 44: 365.
— Chinese and Mediæval. (F. W. Williams) Yale R. 1: 200, 275.
— Early. (G. Radford) Gent. M. n. s. 48: 187.
— English, Hibbert on. (Alice S. Green) Eng. Hist. R. 7: 758.
— — in Middle Ages. (W. D. Strappini) Month, 79: 478.
— History of. (C. Walford) Walford's Antiq. vols. 1-10.
— in Great Britain. Sat. R. 73: 372.
— Labor, Old Roman. (E. Eckstein) And. R. 18: 245.
— Lambert on. Ath. '92, 2: 55. — (C. Gross) Nation, 55: 14. — (A. S. Green) Eng. Hist. R. 8: 338.
— Neighborhood. (E. King) Char. R. 1: 77.
— of London. (E. Bisland) Cosmopol. 13: 259.
— Roman, and Charity. (J. P. Waltzing) Char. R. 4: 345.
— Turkish. (C. Sutcliffe) Fortn. 66: 820.
Guillotine, History of the. Sat. R. 73: 512.
Guilty or not Guilty; a story. (H. G. Sargent) Belgra. 89: 299.
Guilty Silence, A; a story re-told. Argosy, 53: 23-458. 54: 1-441.
Guimard, La. *See* Despréaux, Marie Madeline Guimard.
Guinea, The Story of the. Chamb. J. 73: 814.
Guineas and One-pound Notes. All the Year, 70: 41.
Guirlande de Julie. (J. W. Bradley) Bibliographica, 1: 291.
Guise, Familistère at. (C. Hancock) Fortn. 59: 418.
Guises, Assassination of, as described by the Venetian Ambassador. (H. Brown) Eng. Hist. R. 10: 304.
Gujarát, In Old. (E. W. Hopkins) Nation, 63: 471.
— Province of. (A. Rogers) Asia. R. 21: 380.
Guldin, Samuel. (J. H. Dubbs) Ref. Q. 39: 309.
Gulf & Inter-state Railway. (A. Griffin) Arena, 9: 777.
Gulf Coast, Summer on. (F. Lynde) Lippinc. 58: 208.
Gulf of Mexico, Cruising on. Outing, 27: 378.
Gulf Stream, and Labrador Current. (W. Libbey, jr.) Nat. Geog. M. 5: 161.
— Causes of. (R. M. Bache) Science, n. s. 2: 88.
— Density and Temperature of. (A. Lindenkohl) Science, n. s. 3: 271.
— Recent Discoveries concerning. (J. E. Pillsbury) Cent. 21: 533.
Gulls. (P. A. Graham) Longm. 27: 75.
Gully, Mr., as Speaker of the House of Commons. Spec. 74: 488.
Gulph Mill, Camp by the Old. (W. S. Baker) Pennsyl. M. 17: 414.
Gulstoniana. (C. F. S. Warren) Bookworm, 4: 281. 5: 241.
Gum, Quarter-sawed. Am. Arch. 51: 22.
Gun, First Days with. (H. Hutchinson) Longm. 29: 180.
Gunners and Gunsmiths; a true story. National, 19: 851.
Gunning, Prof. Wm. D. (F. M. Holland) Open Court, 2: 1271.
Gunpowder, Modern, and its Development. Chamb. J. 73: 165.
— Smokeless. (H. Maxim) J. Soc. Arts, 44: 555.
Gunpowder Plot. (R. G. Kingsley) Art J. 45: 286. — (F. Urquhart) Cornh. 74: 579. — (O. Abbott) Eng. Illust. 16: 138. — Blackw. 160: 775. — (J. Gerard) Month, 82: 487. 83: 1-478. 84: 33.
Guns and Shooting. (E. W. Sandys) Outing, 27: 63.
— in Battleships, Armor Protection for. (W. C. Foley) J. Frankl. Inst. 137: 469.
— Large, Certain Physical Difficulties in Construction of. (W. Le C. Stevens) Science, n. s. 4: 782.
— Testing, at Sandy Hook. (F. A. C. Perrine) Engin. M. 3: 357.
Gurnay, John de; a 14th Century Parson. (A. Jessopp) 19th Cent. 31: 964. Same art. Ecl. M. 119: 119. Same art. Liv. Age, 194: 355.
Gurney Family of Earlham, England. Lond. Q. 85: 232. — (A. E. Canton) Sund. M. 25: 173. — Church Q. 42: 138. Same art. Liv. Age, 208: 387.
— Hare on. Sat. R. 80: 478.
Gustavus III. and his Contemporaries, Bain's. Sat. R. 79: 67.
Gustavus Adolphus. (M. Lenz) Chaut. 20: 658. — (R. Parsons) Am. Cath. Q. 20: 510. — (S. Wilkinson) Cornh. 74: 193. Same art. Liv. Age, 210: 569.
— Death of. (J. McKay) Scot. R. 19: 400. Same art. Liv. Age, 194: 638.
— Dottge on. (J. D. Cox) Nation, 62: 672.
'Gustus Frederick; a story. (C. E. Raimond) New R. 12: 271.
Gutenberg, Johann, and Strasburg. (H. H. Howorth) Acad. 49: 12, 78.
— Parentage of. (H. H. Howorth) Acad. 48: 461.
Guthrie, F. A. Talk of the People. Spec. 69: 467.
Guthrie, Thomas. (N. Hall) Sund. M. 22: 488.
Guy of Warwick. (F. Conway) Walford's Antiq. 7: 160-279.
Guyau, Marie Jean, Faith of. (A. Fouille) Open Court, 3: 1611.
— on Irreligion of the Future. (E. Thurtell) Open Court, 9: 4705.
Guyot, Arnold H. Bk. Buyer, 1: 29.
Guyot, Yves. Three Years in the Ministry. Westm. 145: 149.
Guyot of Provins. (Edith Sellers) National, 25: 529. — Liv. Age, 206: 114.
Gwern Einion near Harlech. (H. H. Lines) Antiq. n. s. 28: 250.
Gwynn, Nell. (H. S. Edwardes) Time, 12: 428.
Gylden, Johan August Hugo. Nature, 55: 158.

Gymnasium, Girls'. (J. Pardee-Clark) Munsey, **15**: 737.
Gymnastics, Homely. (A. B. Tweedy) Pop. Sci. Mo. **40**: 524.
— Systems of. (H. Nissen) Educa. **13**: 150.
Gypsies in Hungary. (E. R. Pennell) Cent. **23**: 414.
— — Customs and Music of. (S. J. A. Fitz-Gerald) Belgra. **79**: 305.
— of Spain. (James Platt) Gent. M. n. s. **57**: 123.
— Scholar-. Macmil. **70**: 209. Same art. Liv. Age, **203**: 313.
— With the East-Anglian. (W. A. Dutt) Good Words, **37**: 120.
Gypsy Camping in Arkansas. (L. S. La Mance) Outing, **24**: 336.
Gypsy Lore Society. J. Am. Folk-Lore, **1**: 235.
Gypsy-moth and its Extermination. Garden & F. **5**: 81.
— — in Mass. (W. C. Wright) Garden & F. **8**: 108.
— Dendrolene as a Protection. Garden & F. **8**: 470.
Gypsy-moth Commission, Work of. (S. M. Weed) Am. Natural. **27**: 750.
Gypsy Music. (T. Moelling) Music, **3**: 371.
Gypsy Queen in America. J. Am. Folk-Lore, **2**: 156.
Gypsy Sorcery and Fortune-telling, Leland's. (W. W. Newell) J. Am. Folk-Lore, **4**: 187.
Gypsy-springs in Yorkshire. (H. Brierley) Nature, **53**: 177.
Gypsying by Water; a story. Temp. Bar, **108**: 436.

Haag, Carl. (F. Wedmore) M. of Art, **13**: 52.
Haakaland, A Ride in. (E. A. Irving) Blackw. **156**: 600. Same art. Liv. Age, **203**: 758.
Haanen, Cecil Van. *See* Van Haanen.
Habersham, Robert. (L. McK. Garrison) New Eng. M. n. s. **11**: 52.
Habit. (J. T. Prince) N. Church R. **1**: 224.
— and Attention, Study in. (J. R. Angell and A. W. Moore) Psychol. R. **3**: 245.
— and School Studies. (Mabel T. Wellman) Educa. **17**: 52.
— Deadening Power of, Bishop Temple on. Spec. **69**: 732.
— does not make the Monk, The; a poem. (E. F. Strange) M. of Art, **14**: 344.
Hachisch-eating. Cornh. **69**: 500. Same art. Ecl. M. **122**: 821.
Hack, William, and his Descendants. (C. A. Hack) N. E. Reg. **48**: 453.
Hackman, James, and Reay, Martha, Love Letters of. Sat. R. **80**: 115.
Hades, The Descent into. (P. Gardner) Contemp. **67**: 361.
Hading, Jane. (H. St. Maur) Munsey, **14**: 159. — (W. Alison) Theatre, **31**: 63.
Hadleigh Farm Colony. (C. S. Bremner) Lend a H. **13**: 285.
Hadley, Mass. (J. T. Bayne) New Eng. M. n. s. **7**: 329.
Hadramut, Expedition to. (J. T. Bent) Geog. J. **4**: 315.
— Journey in. (L. Hirsch) Geog. J. **3**: 196. — (J. T. Bent) 19th Cent. **36**: 419. Same art. Ecl. M. **123**: 527. Same art. Liv. Age, **203**: 81.
— Travels in. Dub. R. **115**: 176.
Hadrian, as an Art Patron. (F. M. Robinson) M. of Art, **11**: 329.
— Wall of. (F. Haverfield) Acad. **44**: 372.
Hadrian's Ode to his Soul. (W. Everett) Atlan. **74**: 669.
Haeckel, Ernst, with portrait. Nat. Sci. **5**: 161.
— Celebration of 60th Birthday. Nat. Sci. **5**: 237.
— Religion of. Spec. **73**: 883.
Haendel, G. F. (E. MacMahon) Belgra. **84**: 264. — (F. J. Crowest) Blackw. **155**: 825. Same art. Liv. Age, **202**: 195.
— and his Portraits. (R. A. M. Stevenson) M. of Art, **8**: 309.
— English Experience and Influence of. (F. J. Crowest) Good Words, **37**: 620.
— in the 19th Century. (D. E. Hervey) Music, **5**: 653.
Háfiz, Persian Poet. (J. H. Parsons) Gent. M. n. s. **55**: 419. — Quar. **174**: 33.
— From the Persian of; a poem. Temp. Bar, **108**: 233.
Hafiz of Shiraz; a poem. (E. Arnold) Cosmopol. **16**: 406.
Hagar; a Poem. (E. P. Nicholson) Cosmopol. **16**: 10.
Hagenbeck, Carl, the Moltke of Menagerie Owners. (C. J. Cornish) Eng. Illust. **14**: 82.
Haggada, Pre-Talmudic. (K. Kohler) Jew. Q. **5**: 399. **7**: 581.
Haggard, Henry Rider, with portrait. Bk. Buyer, **4**: 156. — With portrait. Bk. News, **8**: 344.
— and the New School of Romance. (A. M. Moore) Time, **16**: 513.
— as a Politician. Sat. R. **79**: 372.
— Joan Haste. Sat. R. **80**: 386.
— My First Book; Dawn. Idler, **3**: 279.
— Nada the Lily. Sat. R. **73**: 629.
— Portraits of. McClure, **2**: 134.
Hague, George, with portrait. Bank. M. (Lond.) **55**: 237.
Hague, The, Exhibition of Old Masters at. (W. M. Conway) M. of Art, **4**: 337.
Haida Indian Legend. (J. Deans) J. Am. Folk-Lore, **5**: 43.
Haidar Ali, Bowring's. Sat. R. **77**: 202.
Haidas, Family Life of. (C. Harrison) Anthrop. J. **21**: 470.
Haidas Legend. (J. Deans) J. Am. Folk-Lore, **2**: 255.
Haig, Axel H. (C. L. Hind) Art J. **44**: 1.
Hail, Damage by, in Austria. J. Statis. Soc. **55**: 668.
Hail Stones, Remarkable, at Cleveland, O., May 17, 1894. (F. H. Herrick) Nature, **50**: 173.
Hail Storms, Remarkable. Chamb. J. **71**: 741.
Hail Storms. (H. C. Russell) Nature, **47**: 573.
Hailes, Lord, The Humor of. (F. P. Walton) Jurid. R. **6**: 223.
Haileybury College, Old. Quar. **179**: 224.
Hain's Repertorium, Coppinger's Supplement to. Bibliographica, **2**: 489.
Hair, Fashions in. (W. F. Nelson) Time, **21**: 531.
— Will the Coming Woman lose her? (E. F. Andrews) Pop. Sci. Mo. **42**: 370.
Hair-growths. All the Year, **76**: 227.
Hairs of Plants, Functions of. (J. Pentland-Smith) Knowl. **18**: 138.
Haité, George C., Artist. (H. W. Bromhead) Idler, **10**: 85.
Haiti. *See* Hayti.
Hake, Thomas Gordon. Acad. **47**: 57. — (T. Watts) Ath. '95, **1**: 84, 118.
— Memoirs. Ath. '92, **2**: 733.
— Poems of. Ath. '94, **1**: 435. — Sat. R. **79**: 122.
Haldeman, Donald Carmichael, with portrait. Bank. M. (Lond.) **58**: 597.
Hale, Edward, an Eton Master. Blackw. **156**: 693. — Geog. J. **4**: 373.
Hale, Edward Everett, with portrait. Bk. Buyer, **4**: 188. — With portrait. Bk. News, **6**: 262. — With portrait. (W. H. McElroy) Char. R. **1**: 335. — With portraits. (H. D. Ward) McClure, **1**: 120, 291. — (S. F. Coles) Munsey, **8**: 52.
— Autobiography, A Chapter of. (E. E. Hale) Outl. **52**: 1064.

Hale, Edward Everett. My College Days. Atlan. 71: 355, 458.
Hale, John P., a Presidential Candidate of 1852. (G. W. Julian) Cent. 30: 870.
Hale, Nathan, Monument to. Critic, 23: 366.
Hale, Robert Beverly. New Eng. M. n. s. 13: 481.
Haleakala, Mt., a Dead Volcano. (M. H. Closson) Overland, n. s. 21: 236.
Hales Abbey, Gloucestershire. (J. Hooper) Gent. M. n. s. 56: 422.
Half-brothers; a story. (H. Stretton) Sund. M. 21: 1-793.
Half-burnt Letter, The; a story. (C. N. Carvalho) Argosy, 60: 121.
Half Way between the Stiles. (M. L. Molesworth) Longm. 25: 374.
Half Way Covenant in New England. (W. Walker) N. Eng. 56: 93.
Halford, Sir Henry. (C. J. Robinson) Acad. 48: 481. — Quar. 183: 212.
Haliburton, Hugh. New Poems. Spec. 68: 338.
Haliburton, T. C. (F. B. Crofton) Atlan. 69: 355. — With portrait. (J. A. Chisholm) Green Bag, 7: 489.
Halicarnassus, Mausoleum of. (T. Sulman) Sund. M. 24: 832.
Halifax, Heroes of. (W. B. Wallace) Canad. M. 5: 235.
— A Yankee in. (Allan Eric) Canad. M. 4: 401.
Haliotis Shells. *See* Abalone.
Hall, Asaph, with portrait. Pop. Sci. Mo. 45: 833.
Hall, Chas. F., and Jones Sound. Nat. Geog. M. 7: 308.
Hall, Fitzedward. Acad. 47: 299. — (W. P. Garrison) Nation, 60: 221.
Hall, John, of Gray's Inn, 1627-56. (F. Watson) Gent. M. n. s. 52: 476.
Hall, Joseph, Bishop: Mundus Alter et Idem. (E. A. Petherick) Gent. M. n. s. 57: 66.
Hall, Newman, at Home. Sund. M. 22: 470.
— Jubilee Remembrances of Persons I have met. (N. Hall) Sund. M. 22: 162-707.
Hall, William Edward. (T. E. Holland) Law Q. 11: 113.
Hall-mark, The; a story. (Katrina Trask) Cosmopol. 18: 235.
Hallam, Arthur Henry, on the Tennysons. (W. G. Kingsland) Poet-Lore, 8: 23.
Hallamshire, Early Condition of, Addy's. Sat. R. 78: 78.
Hallé, Sir Charles. Ath. '95, 2: 615. — Acad. 48: 371.
Halle, University of, Bicentenary of. (A. V. W. Jackson) Educa. R. 8: 265. — Ath. '94, 2: 193.
Halley, Edmund. (Robert Ball) Good Words, 36: 750.
Halliwell-Phillips, James Orchard. (J. P. Norris) Poet-Lore, 1: 64.
Hallowe'en Reformation, A. (H. Butterworth) Cent. 27: 48.
Hallucinations. (T. B. Snow) Dub. R. 117: 245.
— and Alienations of Personality. (T. Ribot) Open Court, 4: 2691.
— and Dreams. (P. Carus) Open Court, 3: 2024. — (W. Seton) Cath. World, 54: 822.
See Illusions.
Halogens in Mixed Silver Salts, Estimation of. (F. A. Gooch and C. Fairbanks) Am. J. Sci. 150: 27.
Hals, Frans. (T. Cole) Cent. 25: 323.
Halstead, Murat. (A. Shaw) R. of Rs. (N. Y.) 13: 439.
— Early Editorial Experiences of. Lippinc. 49: 710.
Halswelle, Keeley. (W. W. Fenn) M. of Art, 4: 406.
Halt! Universal Deficit of Europe. Contemp. 65: 761. Same art. Liv. Age, 202: 228.
"Ham," The Suffix. (J. H. Pring) Walford's Antiq. 6: 276.
Hambrough, Lieut. W. D. C., Alleged Murder of. Sat. R. 76: 727. — Spec. 71: 940.
Hamburg. Around World, 1: 174. — (M. Halstead) Cosmopol. 14: 35.
— Harbor Life at. (Louis Barbe) Good Words, 34: 363.
— Killed by the Baltic Canal. Liv. Age, 206: 254.
— New Sanitary Impulse. (A. Shaw) Atlan. 73: 787.
— Reminiscences of a Pleasure-trip. (R. Ganthony) Eng. Illust. 13: 561.
Hameln, Rat-catcher of. *See* Rat-catcher of Hameln.
Hamerton, Philip Gilbert. (F. Wedmore) Acad. 46: 381. — Critic, 25: 316. — Ath. '94, 2: 648. — M. of Art, 18: 119.
— Autobiography. (K. Cox) Nation, 63: 439. — (J. L. Gilder) Critic, 29: 407.
— Chief Influences on his Career. Forum, 18: 415.
Hamilton, Alexander. (H. F. Barnes) Am. J. Pol. 4: 250. — Macmil. 72: 461. Same art. Ecl. M. 125: 830. Same art. Liv. Age, 207: 259.
— and Adam Smith. (E. G. Bourne) Q. J. Econ. 8: 328.
— and J. P. Zenger. (B. C. Steiner) Pennsyl. M. 20: 405.
— as a Guide in Modern Finance. Gunton's M. 11: 126.
— as a Political Economist. (E. C. Lunt) J. Pol. Econ. 3: 289.
— as a Lawyer. (A. O. Hall) Green Bag, 7: 537.
— Company of Artillery commanded by, 1776. (W. C. Ford) N. E. Reg. 47: 472.
— in our Education. (E. P. Powell) New Eng. M. n. s. 14: 699.
Hamilton, Capt. Alexander; a 17th Century Scot in the Far East. Chamb. J. 72: 568.
Hamilton, Andrew, with portrait. (J. F. Fisher) Pennsyl. M. 16: 1.
Hamilton, Emma, Lady. Ed. R. 183: 380. — (M. Todhunter) Westm. 144: 367. — (Mrs. R. P. Porter) Cosmopol. 18: 643.
— Life of, Gamlin's. Ath. '92, 1: 46.
— Some Portraits of. (E. B. Nash) M. of Art, 8: 492.
Hamilton, Eugene Lee, Sonnets of. (J. A. Noble) Acad. 46: 145.
Hamilton, James, 4th Duke of; an Historic Duel. Chamb. J. 72: 465. Same art. Liv. Age, 206: 637.
Hamilton, John McLure. (H. S. Morris) Art J. 48: 341.
Hamilton, William; Jacobite Laureate. Macmil. 67: 374.
Hamilton, William D. Ath. '94, 2: 290.
Hamilton Family. (A. B. Hamilton) Pennsyl. M. 17: 175.
Hamilton-Burr Duel. (D. Van Pelt) Nat'l M. (N. Y. '91) 16: 549.
Hamilton Palace Library and Works of Art. Walford's Antiq. 2: 83, 141. 3: 35, 80. — Bk. Buyer, 1: 90.
— Sale of. Walford's Antiq. 4: 90. M. of Art, 5: 440.
Hamlet. (D. Dorchester, jr.) Meth. R. 52: 390.
— and Ajax. (W. B. L. Howell) Canad. M. 6: 205.
— and Don Quixote. (I. Tourgenieff) Fortn. 62: 191.
— Insanity of. (R. C. MacDonald) Acad. (Syr.) 7: 29. — (H. B. Lathrop) Acad. (Syr.) 7: 89.
Hamley, Sir Edward B. Blackw. 154: 446. — (A. C. Gleig) Gent. M. n. s. 55: 515. — Quar. 184: 1. Same art. Liv. Age, 210: 515.
— and the Egyptian Campaign. (W. F. Butler) Contemp. 68: 212.
— and Lord Wolseley. (F. Maurice) Un. Serv. M. 11: 414, 439.
— Shand's Life of. Blackw. 158: 583. — Sat. R. 79: 761.
Hamley, William G. Blackw. 153: 879.
Hamlin, Cyrus. (C. M. Nichols) Our Day, 14: 117.
Hamlin, Hannibal, and John C. Breckenridge. (H. L. Dawes) Cent. 28: 463.

Hammam, Sid. Spec. 69: 440.
Hammer-throwing. (M. W. Ford) Outing, 20: 448.
Hammock's Complaint, The; a poem. (E. W. Wilcox) Outing, 23: 259.
Hammond Family of Maryland. Am. Hist. Reg. 2: 874.
Hampden, John, Sword of. Walford's Antiq. 4: 227.
Hampshire, Christ Church. (T. G. Bonney) M. of Art, 4: 415, 445.
— Roman Roads of. (T. W. Shore) Antiq. n. s. 26: 263.
Hampshire Monasteries, Dissolution of. (F. A. Gasquet) New R. 14: 192.
Hampshire Moors. (R. G. Kingsley) Eng. Illust. 9: 511.
Hampstead Heath. (P. Robinson) Contemp. 66: 119. Same art. Ecl. M. 123: 358. Same art. Liv. Age, 202: 314.
Hampstead Heath Treasure-trove. Chamb. J. 70: 71.
Hampton, New Hampshire. (N. M. Hall) New Eng. M. n. s. 14: 611.
"Hampton," The Place-name. (J. H. Pring) Walford's Antiq. 3: 127.
Hampton Court. Macmil. 65: 446. Same art. Liv. Age, 193: 554.
Hampton Institute, Va. (E. A. Start) New Eng. M. n. s. 6: 442.
— and its Founder. (L. C. Harvey) Chaut. 17: 745.
— Education of our Colored Citizens. (M. W. Goodwin) Pop. Sci. Mo. 42: 789.
Hanbury, Lily, with portrait. Theatre, 27: 253.
Hancock, John, Three Letters from, to Dorothy Quincy. (H. C. Walsh) New Eng. M. n. s. 6: 531.
Hancock, Gen. W. S., Walker's. (J. D. Cox) Nation, 60: 188.
Hand of Time; a story. (E. B. Kaufman) Lippinc. 50: 378.
Handel, G. F. *See* Haendel, G. F.
Hands, History of. Cornh. 71: 182.
— of Men and Children, Relation of Strength to Flexibility in. (J. A. Hancock) Pedagog. Sem. 3: 308.
Handsome Humes; a novel. (W. Black) Harper, 87: 40–835.
Handwriting and Character. (W. Preyer) Chaut. 19: 594. — Spec. 69: 680. — (Lady M. Boynton) Longm. 22: 69. — (L. Brough) Munsey, 9: 144.
— — Lombroso on. Sat. R. 79: 629.
— Experts in. Chamb. J. 70: 767.
— Illustrious. Chamb. J. 70: 671. Same art. Ecl. M. 122: 134.
— Present-day. (J. Jackson) Educa. R. 4: 290.
— Proof by Comparison of, History of. (J. H. Wigmore) Am. Law R. 30: 481.
— Vertical, Argument for. (J. V. Witherbee) Pop. Sci. Mo. 44: 86.
Hane, Joachim. Journal; ed. by Firth. Sat. R. 81: 256.
Hanging in Chains. (R. Blair and C. Cox) Antiq. n. s. 22: 213.
— In Praise of. (W. S. Lilly) New R. 11: 190.
Hangman's Daughter, The. (Emilia F. S. Dilke) Univ. R. 8: 499.
Hanna, Marcus A. (M. Halstead) R. of Rs. (N. Y.) 14: 421.
Hanna, my Abyssinian Servant. (F. Scudamore) Blackw. 156: 663.
Hannah; a story. Temp. Bar, 102: 483. Same art. Ecl. M. 123: 558. Same art. Liv. Age, 202: 811.
Hannale; a poem. (G. Hauptmann) New R. 10: 280, 430.
Hannen, Sir James, with portrait. Green Bag, 4: 505.
Hannibal, Dodge's. Ath. '92, 2: 57.
Hannington, James. (E. A. Gowing) Belgra. 81: 138.
Hanover. (S. B. Holabird) Un. Serv. (Phila.) 8: 26.
— Schools of. (G. A. Fisher) Educa. 16: 344.
Hans Guteman's Winnings. (M. G. Jenkins) New Eng. M. n. s. 6: 703.
Hansaland. (C. H. Robinson) Geog. J. 8: 201.
— and the Central Sudan. Dub. R. 119: 162.
Hansard, Septimus. (J. M. Ludlow) Econ. R. 6: 297. — Chamb. J. 73: 433.
Hansoms and their Drivers. (W. H. Wilkins) 19th Cent. 33: 470.
Hanssen, Georg. (G. Cohn) Econ. J. 5: 141.
Hant er Buzzard's Nes', De. (V. F. Boyle) Cent. 21: 581.
Hanway, Jonas, Travels. (A. Dobson) Longm. 20: 257.
Happenings in Old Calaveras; a story. (W. S. Hutchinson) Overland, n. s. 19: 405.
Happiest Heart; a poem. (J. V. Cheney) Harper, 89: 673.
Happiest Man in London. Cornh. 70: 164.
Happiness. (A. Lampman) Harper, 93: 309. — Spec. 69: 186.
— and Belief. (C. P. Wooley) Open Court, 6: 3160.
— and Ethics. (E. C. Hegeler) Open Court, 2: 1169.
— and the Gospel of Work. (V. Yarros) Open Court, 7: 3807.
— Hunt for. (F. Adams) Fortn. 60: 807.
— — Adams on. Spec. 71: 831.
— Pursuit of. (E. C. Cardozo) Cosmopol. 19: 595.
— a story. (G. de Maupassant) Theatre, 33: 13.
— Tolstoi on. Our Day, 14: 133.
Happy-go-lucky Beach. (C. Rice) Outing, 26: 405.
Happy Land, The. All the Year, 75: 614.
Happy Pairs at Dunmow. Cornh. 68: 405.
Happy Returns. Gent. M. n. s. 48: 425.
Happy Valley, Wales. Belgra. 83: 138.
Haps and Mishaps of a Florida Maroon. Outing, 25: 224.
Hapsburgers, The Unhappy. (H. W. Fischer) Munsey, 12: 167.
Har Dalam Cavern. Nature, 49: 514.
Harada, Toyokitsi. Nat. Sci. 6: 350.
Harbor Defenses: Should they be controlled by the Navy? (Clarence Deems) Un. Serv. (Phila.) 7: 58.
Harcourt, Sir William Vernon. (H. D. Traill) Contemp. 70: 737. — (J. St. Loe Strachey) National, 26: 140. — Spec. 74: 40, 890. — (W. T. Stead) R. of Rs. (N. Y.) 9: 429. — With portrait. (L. Irwell) Green Bag, 6: 257.
— His Budget. (Lord Farrer) Contemp. 66: 153.
Hard, Unnoticed Sense of the Word. (F. Hall) Nation, 58: 388.
Hard Answer. (A. MacGowan) Lippinc. 58: 400.
Hard-hearted Woman, A. (F. Axtens) Good Words, 37: Xmas no., 37.
Hard Little Cuss, A; a story. (Mrs. H. H. Penrose) Temp. Bar, 99: 63, 205. Same art. Liv. Age, 199: 204, 450.
Hard Man's Charity, A; a story. (L. Jackson) Argosy, 54: 77.
Hard Times, Benefits of. (E. Atkinson) Forum, 20: 79.
— Cause of. Sat. R. 80: 368.
— Causes and Remedies. I. Free Trade and Protection. (I. M. Scott) Overland, n. s. 27: 57. II. The Scarcity of Money. Overland, n. s. 27: 153, 561.
Hard Times in the Colonies; a story. Overland, n. s. 19: 490.
Hard Times Review. (I. M. Scott) Overland, n. s. 28: 417–557.
Hard Trigger, The. (H. S. Edwards) Cent. 27: 780.
Hardenburgh, F. von. (G. M. Hammell) Meth. R. 53: 721.
Hardinge, Charles Stewart, Viscount. Acad. 46: 90.
Hardwick, Philip C. Ath. '92, 1: 188.
Hardwick Hall. (E. Bradbury) M. of Art, 10: 247.

Hardy, Arthur S., with portrait. Bk. Buyer, 7: 323.
Hardy, Sir Charles. (J. G. Wilson) Nat'l M. (N. Y. '91) 19: 1.
Hardy, Dudley, Artist. Idler, 9: 371.
Hardy, Rev. E. J. Bk. Buyer, 9: 15. — Critic, 21: 22.
Hardy, Thomas, with portrait. Bk. Buyer, 9: 151. — (M. Thompson) Bk. News, 6: 223. — With portrait. Bk. News, 12: 274. — (H. W. Preston) Cent. 24: 353. — (J. Newton-Robinson) Westm. 137: 153.
— and his Novels. (W. Sharp) Forum, 13: 583.
— Art of, Johnson on. (A. M. Logan) Nation, 60: 225.
— as a Decadent. (A. J. Butler) National, 27: 384.
— as a Novelist. (W. P. Trent) Citizen, 1: 284.
— Country of. (J. W. White) Nation, 55: 184, 200.
— In the Country of. Temp. Bar, 108: 150. Same art. Ecl. M. 126: 774.
— Jude the Obscure. (R. Y. Tyrrell) Fortn. 65: 857. — (D. F. Hannigan) Westm. 145: 136. — Our Day, 16: 101. — (R. le Gallienne) Idler, 9: 114.
— Tess of the D'Urbervilles. (W. Watson) Acad. 41: 125. — Gent. M. n. s. 49: 321. — Spec. 68: 121. — (D. F. Hannigan) Westm. 138: 655.
— Trumpet Major. Critic, 29: 8.
Hardy-plant Garden. (T. D. Hatfield) Garden & F. 6: 246.
Hare, Augustus J. C. Story of my Life. Sat. R. 82: 447. — Nation, 63: 459.
Hare, Robert, with portrait. Pop. Sci. Mo. 42: 695.
Harel, Christian. (N. Moore) Ath. '94, 2: 36.
Hares and Hare-hunting. (E. W. Sandys) Outing, 29: 236.
Hargrove's Madonna; a story. (M. E. Francis) Art J. 44: 338.
Harington, Sir John. (W. Raleigh) New R. 15: 277.
Harlakenden Family. (C. C. Baldwin) N. E. Reg. 46: 368.
Harland, Henry. Bookman, 1: 87.
Harlech, Remains near. (H. H. Lines) Antiq. n. s. 29: 76, 111.
Harlem River Speedway. (C. S. Sargent) Garden & F. 7: 311.
Harley Family Papers. Ath. '94, 2: 387.
Harmel, Léon. An Object Lesson in Christian Democracy. (V. M. Crawford) Fortn. 65: 58.
Harmelville, France. An Example of Organized Thrift. (J. G. Brooks) Forum, 13: 757.
Harmony, Causes of. (E. Mach) Open Court, 8: 4136.
— in Folk-Music. (J. C. Fillmore) Music, 5: 281.
— Modern, and Acquired Sense Perception. (W. S. B. Mathews) Music, 5: 257.
— of the Spheres, The. (P. Carus) Open Court, 1: 33.
Harmsworth, Alfred C., at Elmwood. Eng. Illust. 16: 203.
Harnack, Adolf, with portrait. (J. H. Ropes) Bib. World, 7: 22. — (D. Macfadyen) Chr. Lit. 14: 17.
Harold Cameron's Love-story. All the Year, 71: 548.
Harold Hardrada; Battle of Stamford Bridge. (D. Lever) Gent. M. n. s. 55: 80.
Harp, Magic, of Suomi. (A. C. Stephens) Music, 6: 499.
Harpenden, England. (F. G. Kitton) Art J. 46: 107.
Harper, Edward B., with portrait. Nat'l M. (N. Y. '91) 17: 186.
Harper's Book of Facts, Wiley's. (C. W. Colby) Nation, 61: 206.
Harper's Magazine. (J. H. Chapman) Q. Illust. 1: 56.
Harpies in Greek Art. (Cecil Smith) J. Hel. Stud. 13: 103.
Harraden, Beatrice, with portrait. Bk. Buyer, 11: 241. — With portrait. Bk. News, 12: 399. — (J. L. Gilder) Critic, 24: 327, 343.
Harraden, Beatrice. Ships that pass in the Night. (B. Harraden) McClure, 4: 144.
— — How it was written. Critic, 26: 441.
Harrar, A Recent Visit to. (W. B. Harris) Blackw. 156: 350. Same art. Liv. Age, 203: 215. — Dub. R. 115: 460.
Harrington, Christopher. Monumental Brass and Will. Reliquary, 32: 211.
Harris, Sir Augustus. Theatre, 37: 5. — Ath. '96, 1: 851. — (J. S. Shedlock) Acad. 49: 535.
— as Opera Manager. Sat. R. 82: 12, 34.
— at Home. (Marie A. Belloc) Idler, 8: 439.
Harris, Gen. George, Lord. Life in America, etc. Eng. R. 5: 1.
Harris, David Bullock. So. Hist. Pap. 20: 395.
Harris, Frank. Elder Conklin, and other Stories. (C. Patmore) New R. 11: 655. — (P. Addleshaw) Acad. 46: 488.
Harris, Joel Chandler, with portrait. Bk. Buyer, 3: 540. — With portrait. Bk. Buyer, 13: 65. — With portrait. Bk. News, 10: 429. — (W. M. Baskerville) Chaut. 24: 62.
— On the Plantation. (A. C. McClurg) Dial (Ch.) 13: 46.
Harris, John Henry. (E. S. Cronise) Cassier, 6: 84.
Harris, M. C., with portrait. Bk. News, 12: 39.
Harris, Thomas L. Works. (W. Lewin) Acad. 41: 127.
Harris, Townsend. (W. E. Griffis) Atlan. 70: 161.
Harrisburg, Pa. Harrisburg Terraces. (H. B. Bashore) Am. J. Sci. 147: 98.
Harrison, Benjamin, with portraits. (T. J. Morgan) R. of Rs. (N. Y.) 5: 669.
— Administration of. (J. R. Hawley) Forum, 13: 650. — (H. L. Dawes; J. N. Dolph; A. H. Colquitt) No. Am. 154: 641. — Pub. Opin. 14: 539.
— Foreign Policy of. (R. Ogden) Nation, 55: 140.
— Fourth Annual Message. Pub. Opin. 14: 219.
— Renomination of, 1892. Pub. Opin. 13: 247.
— — Letter of Acceptance. Pub. Opin. 13: 537.
Harrison, Mrs. Burton, with portrait. Bk. Buyer, 7: 647. — Bk. News, 13: 261. — (C. W. Martin) Southern M. 5: 67.
Harrison, Carter H., with portraits. R. of Rs. (N. Y.) 8: 663.
— Assassination of, Lesson of. Pub. Opin. 16: 140.
Harrison, Frederic. Religion of Humanity. (W. H. Mallock) 19th Cent. 38: 661.
Harrison, George Tucker, with portrait. Nat'l M. (N. Y. '91) 16: 216.
Harrison, William Anthony. Acad. 41: 181.
Harrison, Gen. W. H., Bravery of. Am. Hist. Reg. 1: 59.
— New Statue of. (F. B. Gessner) McClure, 6: 172.
Harrison Family, The. (E. J. Edwards) Munsey, 14: 395.
Harrison, Fort, in History. (A. C. Duddleston) M. Am. Hist. 28: 20.
Harrodsburg, Ky. (H. C. Wood) New Eng. M. n. s. 7: 750.
Harry Lossing; a story. (A. French) Scrib. M. 13: 208.
Harry's Career at Yale. (J. S. Wood) Outing, 19: 300 — 21: 477.
Harshaw Bride, The. (M. H. Foote) Cent. 30: 90, 228.
Harte, F. Bret, with portrait. Bk. Buyer, 7: 49. — With portrait. Bk. News, 5: 295. — With portraits. (H. J. W. Dam) McClure, 4: 38.
— A California "Colonel Newcome." Gent. M. n. s. 49: 107.
— Early Recollections of. (C. W. Stoddard) Atlan. 78: 673.
— First Book. Idler, 4: 553.

Harte, F. Bret, Two Interviews with. (Luke Sharp, G. B. Burgin) Idler, 1: 301.
Harte, Walter B., with portrait. Bk. News, 14: 289.
— Meditations in Motley. Poet-Lore, 7: 34.
Hartebeest. Am. Natural. 30: 755.
Hartford, Conn., a New England Literary Colony. (E. S. Echols) Munsey, 13: 647.
— Public Library and the Public Schools. (C. M. Hewins) Lib. J. 19: 292.
— Wadsworth Athenæum. Lib. J. 18: 12.
Hartley, Jonathan Scott. (R. Hughes) Munsey, 11: 515. — (R. R. Wilson) Mo. Illust. 12: 485.
Hartmann the Anarchist; a story. (E. D. Fawcett) Eng. Illust. 10: 637-891.
Hartnup, John. Acad. 41: 427.
Hartwick Seminary. (W. Hull) Luth. Q. 23: 206.
— and a North East College for Lutherans. (W. E. Hull) Luth. Q. 24: 269.
Hartz District and its Towns. (C. A. Channer) Good Words, 35: 164.
Hartz Mts., Afoot in the. (W. H. Hotchkiss) Outing, 24: 117.
Harvard, John, Parish Church of. (J. A. Locke) Cath. World, 63: 98.
Harvard College. (W. Besant) Critic, 23: 251.
— An Administrative Problem. (F. Bolles) Harv. Grad. M. 3: 1.
— Admission to, Requirements for, in 1892. (J. J. Greenough) Atlan. 69: 671.
— and the Church. (C. C. Everett) Harv. Mo. 13: 133.
— and Yale in the West. (C. F. Thwing) Harv. Grad. M. 1: 194.
— Another Year of, 1892. (W. P. Garrison) Nation, 54: 105.
— Archives of. (W. G. Brown) N. E. Reg. 49: 35.
— Are the Athletic Teams Representative? (E. L. Conant) Harv. Grad. M. 3: 330.
— Athletics at. (W. D. Orcutt) Munsey, 11: 376.
— Clubs and Club-life at. (W. D. Orcutt) New Eng. M. n. s. 6: 81.
— Composition and Rhetoric at. Critic, 27: 244.
— Dudleian Lecture for 1891. (E. Emerton) And. R. 17: 238.
— Engineering at. (I. N. Hollis) Harv. Grad. M. 4: 187.
— Ethics in. (J. Royce) Eth. Rec. 2: 138.
— Exhibitions of, Prior to 1800. (A. McF. Davis) N. E. Reg. 46: 233.
— Founding of. (S. B. Kenyon) Gunton's M. 10: 421.
— Grounds and Buildings. (R. S. Peabody) Harv. Grad. M. 4: 521.
— Hill on. (B. A. Hinsdale) Dial (Ch.) 18: 295. — (W. R. Thayer) Nation, 60: 14.
— in Early Days. (A. McF. Davis) Harv. Grad. M. 1: 363.
— in 1820-24. (A. B. Muzzey) Harv. Mo. 13: 185.
— in 1840-45. (H. J. Perry) New Eng. M. n. s. 9: 208.
— in 1887-92. (W. C. Lane) Harv. Grad. M. 1: 43.
— Initiation Ceremonies and Intemperance at. Our Day, 9: 98.
— Latin Play, 1894. (M. H. Morgan) Harv. Grad. M. 2: 345, (H. W. Haynes) 515. — (J. B. Greenough) New Eng. M. n. s. 10: 491.
— Library of. (C. K. Bolton) New Eng. M. n. s. 9: 433.
— New-comer at, how received. (F. C. de Sumichrast) Harv. Grad. M. 3: 162.
— President Eliot's Administration. (C. F. Dunbar and others) Harv. Grad. M. 2: 450.
— Presidents of, and the Election of Messrs. Quincy and Eliot. (W. A. Richardson) N. E. Reg. 49: 59.
— — Some. (E. E. Hale) Harv. Grad. M. 4: 562.
Harvard College, Recollections of, 1825-29. (S. F. Smith) Harv. Grad. M. 2: 162.
— School Examination Board of. (P. H. Hanus) School R. 2: 257.
— Spirit and Ideals of. (G. Santayana) Educa. R. 7: 313.
— Statistics of. Harv. Mo. 15: 126.
— Student Diet at. (R. W. Greenleaf) Harv. Grad. M. 2: 171.
— "'Tis Sixty Years Since" at. (E. E. Hale) Atlan. 78: 496.
— Three Youngest Graduates of. (E. Lord) New Eng. M. n. s. 7: 639.
— Undergraduate Life at, 1830-34. (T. Cushing) Harv. Grad. M. 1: 547.
— University Club at, Shall we have? (W. R. Thayer) Harv. Grad. M. 3: 468.
— Voluntary Prayers at. (F. G. Peabody) Harv. Mo. 15: 1.
— Volunteer Charity Work at. (R. Calkins) Harv. Grad. M. 3: 323.
— Was Comenius called to the Presidency of? (W. S. Monroe) Educa. R. 12: 378.
— What Phillips Brooks did for. (C. W. Eliot) Harv. Mo. 15: 186.
— Where the Students come from. (J. H. Beale) Harv. Grad. M. 3: 464.
Harvard and Yale Boat-race. (W. A. Brooks) Harper, 89: 181.
Harvard Botanic Garden, Notes from. (M. Barker) Garden & F. 6: 68-468.
Harvard College Observatory, Stations of. (W. H. Pickering) Astron. 11: 353.
Harvard Divinity School. (C. C. Everett) Nation, 56: 213. — (J. W. Chadwick) New Eng. M. n. s. 11: 740.
— Non-sectarian Character of. (G. E. Ellis) Harv. Grad. M. 2: 192.
Harvard House, N. Y. City. Critic, 25: 31. — (L. McK. Garrison) Harv. Grad. M. 3: 23.
Harvard Law Review and the New York Law School. (G. Chase) Am. Law R. 26: 155.
Harvard Medical School, Bacteriological Laboratory at. (H. C. Ernst) Harv. Grad. M. 3: 336.
Harvard Teachers' Association, Fifth Annual Meeting of. Educa. R. 11: 417.
Harvest. Macmil. 65: 204.
— in England, 1893. Spec. 71: 234.
— in Great Britain, 1892. Spec. 69: 314.
Harvest; a poem. (N. Gale) M. of Art, 17: 347.
Harvest Song. (N. Boyce) Outing, 24: 480.
Harvest Songs, English. (L. A. Smith) Gent. M. n. s. 53: 153.
Harvey, William, Work of, Modern Developments of. (T. L. Brunton) Nature, 50: 625.
Harvey, William Hope, with portrait. Bookman, 1: 306.
Harvy, John de; a Bedfordshire Squire of the 14th Century. (A. Hervey) Good Words, 37: 171.
Harwood, Elizabeth Franklin, "Mrs. Jarley." Critic, 20: 257.
Hasemann, Wilhelm, Home of, in the Black Forest. (M. E. Bowles) M. of Art, 16: 239.
Hasheesh. *See* Hachisch.
Haskins Massacre, The. (L. C. Embree) Nat'l M. (Bost.) 4: 494.
Haslemere, Old. (H. Candy) Gent. M. n. s. 52: 206.
Hassan the Barber; a story. (H. N. Crellin) Idler, 5: 413.
Hastings, Francis Rawdon, Marquis of. (H. G. Keene) Acad. 43: 279.

Hastings, Warren, and the Rohilla War, Strachey's. (S. J. Owen) Eng. Hist. R. 8: 373. — (G. Smith) Nation, 55: 168. — Sat. R. 73: 451. — Spec. 68: 468.
— Malleson's. Sat. R. 79: 69.
Hastings, Battle of. (K. Norgate; J. A. Archer) Eng. Hist. R. 9: 1, 602. — Quar. 177: 73.
— — Freeman on. (T. A. Archer) Contemp. 63: 335. — (J. H. Round) Eng. Hist. R. 9: 209.
— Kitchen Middens at. (W. J. L. Abbott) Anthrop. J. 25: 122.
— Old and New. Art J. 47: 225.
Hasty Pudding Club at Harvard. (L. McK. Garrison) Bach. of Arts, 2: 200.
Hat, The Tall, and its Ancestors. (R. S. Loveday) Eng. Illust. 15: 276.
Hatesu. Cornh. 67: 186. Same art. Liv. Age, 197: 108.
Hatfield House. (W. C. Sydney) Gent. M. n. s. 53: 570. — (J. Penderel-Brodhurst) M. of Art, 8: 24, 72.
— Historic Pictures at. (T. Sulman) Good Words, 36: 760, 815.
Hathaway, Anne, Cottage of. All the Year, 70: 415.
Hathaway, Benj., with portrait. (H. E. Starrett) Arena, 10: 24.
Hatton, Joseph, Personal Recollections by. Idler, 9: 532, 679, 837. 10: 173, 371, 519.
Hats and Caps. (G. Winterwood) Good Words, 34: 388.
— Chimney Pot. (J. Cassidy) Gent. M. n. s. 56: 32.
— Concerning. All the Year, 70: 65.
— Women's, and the Height of Absurdity. (R. S. Loveday) Eng. Illust. 15: 409.
Hatteras, Cape, Engineering off. (J. W. Walters) Engin. M. 3: 512.
Haunted; a story. Belgra. 80: 85.
Haunted by a Bard; a story. (H. F. Lester) Argosy, 59: 352.
Haunted Ashchurch. Argosy, 56: 509.
Haunted Farm House, The; a story. (Mrs. N. Fiennes) Belgra. 90: 382.
Haunted Hand, The. (H. S. Merriman) Idler, 5: 575.
Haunted Hearts. (J. P. Simpson) Time, 7: 1003. 8: 96–305.
Haunted Station; a story. (H. Nisbet) Belgra. 79: Christmas no., 1.
Haunted Valley, A. Chamb. J. 71: 314.
Haunting Memories; a story. All the Year, 76: 174.
Haunts of Ancient Peace. (Alfred Austin) Spec. 73: 301–403. Same art. Ecl. M. 124: 82. Same art. Liv. Age, 203: 249–700.
Haupt, Paul, and the Polychrome Bible. (C. H. Levy) R. of Rs. (N. Y.) 14: 669.
Hauptmann, Gerhard. (J. D. Barry) Lit. W. (Bost.) 27: 120.
— Works. Spec. 71: 436.
Hauptmann, Moritz. Letters. Sat. R. 73: 749.
Hausa Pilgrimages from Western Soudan. (C. H. Robinson) Geog. J. 2: 451.
Hauser, Kaspar, Evans's. (C. Thomas) Nation, 56: 34.
Hauteville House, Guernsey, Home of Victor Hugo. (H. Rix) Good Words, 33: 823.
Havana. Cornh. 72: 526. Same art. Liv. Age, 207: 560. Same art. Ecl. M. 126: 20.
— Flying Visit to. (A. J. H. Antona) Outing, 27: 220.
— People of, Habits and Conditions of. (J. K. Reeve) Chaut. 15: 674.
— Water-supply of. (R. Cabrera) Eng. M. 12: 101.
Haverford College Cricket. (A. C. Thomas) Outing, 28: 236.
Hawaghy wa'l Bint; an Egyptian Idyl. Blackw. 160: 328.
Hawaii. (L. N. Badenoch) Asia. R. 13: 409. — (A. A. Black) Chaut. 17: 52. — (E. L. Godkin) Nation, 60: 121. — Pub. Opin. 16: 330–545. 17: 263.
— and our Future Sea-power. (A. T. Mahan) Forum, 15: 1.
— and its Missionaries. (B. J. Clinche) Am. Cath. Q. 19: 139.
— and Samoa, Importance of. (W. F. Draper) Soc. Econ. 6: 352.
— and Vancouver. (H. H. Gowen) Canad. M. 2: 451.
— Annexation of. (F. H. Palmer) Educa. 13: 413. — (T. G. Gribble) Engin. M. 4: 898. — (F. Snow) Harv. Mo. 16: 45. — (L. A. Thurston; G. T. Curtis) No. Am. 156: 265. — (J. Cook) Our Day, 12: 393. 13: 124. — Pub. Opin. 15: 217.
— — Grave Obstacles to. (T. M. Cooley) Forum, 15: 389.
— — Missionary Argument for. (R. Ogden) Nation, 58: 380.
— — Practical and Legal Aspects of. (C. J. Swift) Overland, n. s. 25: 586.
— — Report of Republicans of House on. Pub. Opin. 16: 359.
— — Will it pay the United States? (P. C. Jones) Overland, n. s. 25: 580.
— Bibliography of Articles on, in the Overland. Overland, n. s. 25: 685.
— Birds of. (A. Newton) Nature, 45: 465.
— Cable to. (Hugh Craig) Overland, n. s. 25: 653.
— Cleveland's Policy with. (R. Ogden) Nation, 58: 96.
— Climate of. (C. J. Lyons) Overland, n. s. 25: 602.
— Coffee-planting in. (C. D. Miller) Overland, n. s. 25: 669.
— Commercial Development of. (T. G. Thrum) Overland, n. s. 25: 613.
— Commercial Relations of U. S. with. (F. R. Clow) J. Pol. Econ. 1: 280.
— Constitutional History of. (H. E. Chambers) J. H. Univ. Stud. 14: 7.
— Controversy on, in Light of History. (C. Robinson) Am. J. Pol. 4: 477.
— — Review of. (J. Schouler) Forum, 16: 670.
— Disturbances in the Direction of the Plumb-line in. (E. D. Preston) Am. J. Sci. 149: 271.
— The Facts and the Law. (J. E. Bacon) Southern M. 4: 64.
— for Tourists. (J. D. Spreckels) Overland, n. s. 25: 660.
— Glimpse of. (A. W. Gulick) R. of Rs. (N. Y.) 9: 572.
— Gravity Determinations at. (E. D. Preston) Am. J. Sci. 145: 256.
— How has it become Americanized? (S. E. Bishop) Overland, n. s. 25: 507.
— In the Wilds of. (E. Wilson) Overland, n. s. 21: 225.
— Japan in. (W. B. Oleson) Pub. Opin. 15: 169.
— Land Tenures in, Evolution of. (S. B. Dole) Overland, n. s. 25: 565.
— Law and Policy for. (T. S. Woolsey) Yale R. 2: 347.
— Monarchy in, Rise and Decline of. (H. H. Gowen) Cosmopol. 15: 159.
— Physical Characteristics of. Around World, 1: 45.
— Picturesque and Beautiful in. (J. R. Musick) Mo. Illust. 13: 204.
— Political Importance of. (J. A. Harman) No. Am. 160: 374.

Hawaii, Revolution in, 1893. (A. Hoffnung) Asia. R. 15: 406. — (T. H. Davies) 19th Cent. 33: 830. — (E. T. Chamberlain; J. L. Stevens; W. M. Springer) No. Am. 157: 731. — Spec. 70: 153. — (E. L. Godkin) Nation, 56: 96. — (W. P. Garrison) Nation, 56: 190. — (R. Ogden) Nation, 56: 154. 57: 362. — (T. H. Davies) No. Am. 156: 605.
— — and British Interests. (G. R. Parkin) Nation, 56: 362.
— — Cleveland's Message. Pub. Opin. 16: 287, 306. — (E. L. Godkin) Nation, 57: 460.
— — Pres. Harrison on. (E. L. Godkin) Nation, 57: 384.
— — Stevens's Defence. (R. Ogden) Nation, 57: 422.
— — United States and. Pub. Opin. 15: 145, 242.
— — — Our Flag Hauled Down. (R. Ogden) Nation, 56: 286. — Pub. Opin. 15: 69.
— Schools in. (W. R. Castle) Overland, n. s. 26: 399.
— Something about. (H. S. Howell) Canad. M. 1: 426.
— Sugar Industry in. (H. P. Baldwin) Overland, n. s. 25: 663.
— Traditions of. (A. Fornander) Lippinc. 53: 531.
— United States and. (J. A. Donaldson) Am. J. Pol. 4: 161.
— United States in. (S. Bishop) R. of Rs. (N. Y.) 7: 180.
— — Our Policy; Symposium. Indep. Feb. 8, '94.
— Volcanoes of. Chamb. J. 71: 472. Same art. Liv. Age, 203: 506.
— What to do with. (E. L. Godkin) Nation, 58: 42.
— Wild Flowers of. (G. C. K. Thompson) Overland, n. s. 25: 157.
Hawaiian Oddities, Some. Nation, 58: 60.
Hawaiian Pastimes. (H. C. Bolton) J. Folk-Lore, 4: 21.
Hawaiian Treaty, The, and the Monroe Doctrine. (G. Koerner) Open Court, 7: 3623.
Hawk, A, descends on a Japanese War-ship. Liv. Age, 204: 443.
Hawk and the Dove; a story. (E. A. Richings) Belgra. 87: 283.
Hawke, Admiral Lord; Father of the British Navy. Macmil. 73: 420.
Hawker, Mary E., with portrait. (T. G. L. Hawker) Writer, 6: 25.
Hawker, Sir P. Diary. Ath. '93, 2: 617. — Sat. R. 76: 495. — Spec. 73: 529.
Hawker, R. S. Essays. Spec. 70: 777.
Hawking. Chamb. J. 71: 577.
Hawkins, Anthony Hope, with portrait. Bk. Buyer, 12: 489. — With portrait. Bk. News, 13: 8. — (R. H. Sherard) Idler, 8: 24.
— Prisoner of Zenda, on the Stage. (J. H. McCarthy) Gent. M. n. s. 56: 315. — Idler, 9: 359.
— Works of. Sat. R. 8: 145.
Hawkins, Sir Henry, with portrait. Green Bag, 5: 57.
Hawkins, Sir John. (J. A. Froude) Longm. 22: 422.
Hawk's Een; a story. (A. E. Abbott) Idler, 6: 617.
Hawks as Fruit-watchers. Chamb. J. 72: 431.
Hawkshaw, Benjamin. Eng. R. 3: 151.
Hawkwood, Sir John. Macmil. 73: 232. Same art. Liv. Age, 208: 226.
Haworth, Joseph. Bost. 1: 545.
Haworth Thirty-seven Years Ago. (Wm. Davies) Liv. Age, 208: 314.
Hawtayne, Mrs. Margaret Washington, Will of, 1616. (G. H. Hawtayne) N. E. Reg. 47: 303.
Hawthorne, Julian, with portrait. Bk. Buyer, 13: 121.
Hawthorne, Nathaniel, with portrait. Bk. News, 3: 257. — (M. Thompson) Bk. News, 6: 261.
Hawthorne, Nathaniel and Mrs., in Lenox; Told in Letters. (R. H. Lathrop) Cent. 27: 86.
— as an Interpreter of New England. (K. Hillard) New Eng. M. n. s. 12: 732.
— at North Adams. (B. Perry) Atlan. 71: 675.
— Homes and Haunts of. (W. S. Nevins) New Eng. M. n. s. 9: 289.
— Lessons on. (E. W. Barrett) Educa. 14: 417.
— Marble Faun. (J. K. Curtis) And. R. 18: 139.
— — An Interpretation. (M. T. Gale) N. Eng. 56: 26.
— Personal Recollections of. (H. Bridge) Harper, 84: 257-510.
— Romances of. (T. Bradfield) Westm. 142: 203.
— Some Memories of. (R. H. Lathrop) Atlan. 77: 173-649.
Hawthorns, American. Garden & F. 5: 217.
Hawtrey, Edward Craven, Memoir of, Thackeray's. Sat. R. 82: 323.
Hawtry, Charles, Mr. Martin. (G. B. Shaw) Sat. R. 82: 416.
Hay, Spontaneous Combustion of. Dub. R. 117: 449.
Hay Fever as an Idiosyncrasy. (J. M. Cooper) Chaut. 15: 407.
Haydon, Benjamin Robert. (J. Oldcastle) M. of Art, 4: 250, 501. — Temp. Bar, 94: 202-541. Same art. Liv. Age, 193: 152, 536.
Hayes, R. B. Pub. Opin. 14: 369. — With portrait. (W. M. F. Round) Char. R. 2: 197. — With portraits. (H. P. Judson) R. of Rs. (N. Y.) 7: 167.
— Administration of. (J. D. Cox) Atlan. 71: 818.
— and Civil Service Reform. (S. W. Burt) Good Govt. 13: 93, 121.
— Personal Recollections of. (W. McKinley, jr.) Chaut. 17: 42.
Haygood, Bishop, as a Philosopher and Reformer. (H. M. Du Bose) Meth. R. 56: 587.
Haymaking. Spec. 68: 879.
Hayne, Paul H. (W. H. Hayne) Lippinc. 50: 793.
Haynes, Walter, of Sudbury, Mass., Descendants of. (F. H. Newell) N. E. Reg. 47: 71.
Haynes-Williams, J., Work of. (F. Wedmore) Art J. 46: 289.
Haynes Family, Material Relating to the Essex, Eng., Family of Haynes. (A. M. Haines) N. E. Reg. 49: 304.
Hays, Reuben, Sioux Indian. (G. T. Kercheval) Lend a H. 9: 82.
Hayti and its Future. Asia. R. 11: 357.
— Geography of. Geog. J. 3: 49.
Hayward, Abraham. Bk. Buyer, 1: 60.
Haze. (J. G. McPherson) Longm. 20: 270.
— Cloud, and Fog. (J. G. McPherson) Gent. M. n. s. 53: 123.
Hazels; Carylus Rostrata. (J. G. Jack) Garden & F. 8: 345.
Hazlitt, William. (L. I. Guiney) Cath. World, 58: 489.
— and James Northcote. (J. A. Noble) M. of Art, 7: 34.
— Unpublished Correspondence. (W. C. Hazlitt) Atlan. 71: 443.
Hazlitt, William Carew. Bookworm, 2: 353.
He and She. (L. Parr) Longm. 25: 89. Same art. Liv. Age, 203: 750.
He Cometh Not; a story. Temp. Bar, 107: 245. Same art. Liv. Age, 208: 782.
He served the King. (D. Lowry) New Eng. M. n. s. 13: 84.
He whistled as he went; a poem. (D. Fuguet) Cosmopol. 27: 371.
He would a-wooing go. (F. P. Humphrey) Cent. 2: 599.

Head, Form of, influenced by Growth. (W. Z. Ripley) Science, n. s. **3**: 888.
הֶעָלֶיהָ, I. Sam. ix. 24. (M. M. Skinner) J. Bib. Lit. **15**: 82.
Headaches. (A. S. Eccles) National, **25**: 328.
Head-gear; Child's Wimples and Crisping-Pins. Spec. **73**: 925.
— Female. (R. Heath) M. of Art, **8**: 333-480. **9**: 427.
— in the 15th Century. (R. Heath) M. of Art, **7**: 467, 499.
Head-lines. (W. T. Larned) Lippinc. **54**: 410.
Head Rights in Virginia, Certificates of. (J. H. Lea) (N. E. Reg.) **47**: 60-350.
Healers in an Age of Science. (R. Ogden) Nation, **61**: 383.
Healey, John P. (J. W. Dean) N. E. Reg. **46**: 207.
Healing, Divine, or Works. (E. Hatch) Arena, **15**: 989.
Healing of Mrs. Chichester. (Z. Cocke) New Eng. M. n. s. **15**: 19.
Health. All the Year, **76**: 250.
— and Condition. (N. E. Yorke-Davies) Gent. M. n. s. **49**: 260. Same art. Ecl. M. **119**: 558.
— and Horticulture. (W. R. Lazenby) Science, n. s. **4**: 548.
— A National Bureau of. (G. M. Sternberg) No. Am. **158**: 529.
— — Nationalization of. (H. Ellis) Time, **23**: 690.
— — Ellis on. Spec. **71**: 307.
— of Boston and Philadelphia. (J. S. Billings) Forum, **17**: 595.
— Our National. (F. L. Oswald) Chaut. **17**: 281.
— Public and Private; Symposium. Indep. Dec. 7, '93.
— — Duty of the Nation in guarding it. (T. M. Prudden) Cent. **24**: 245.
— — the National Defence. (F. B. Vrooman) Arena, **13**: 425.
— U. S. National Department of. (W. W. Willoughby) Ann. Am. Acad. Pol. Sci. **4**: 292.
— Weak, Literary Advantages of. Spec. **73**: 520. Same art. Liv. Age, **203**: 509.
Health Insurance. (G. W. Steeves) 19th Cent. **35**: 32.
Health Resort; Leysin-sur-Aigle. (H. D. Rawnsley) Blackw. **158**: 680.
— Meteorology of. Dub. R. **112**: 163.
Healy, Father. Spec. **76**: 202.
Heard, John, jr., with portrait. Bk. Buyer, **12**: 438. — Critic, **21**: 142.
Hearing, Sense of, in Animals. Chamb. J. **69**: 822.
Hearing my Requiem; a story. (G. A. Townsend) Lippinc. **50**: 494.
Hearn, Lafcadio, with portrait. Bk. Buyer, **13**: 209. — With portrait. Bk. News, **13**: 378.
Hearne, Thomas, an Antiquary of Last Century. Bookworm, **6**: 88, 119.
Hearse, The Word; its Changes of Meaning. (E. Peacock) Am. Cath. Q. **18**: 852.
Heart of the Fire Spirit. (A. H. Sydenham) Lippinc. **55**: 686.
Heart of Life. (W. H. Mallock) Fortn. **62**: 730, 895. **63**: 133-996. **64**: 132.
Heart of Oak. (W. Clark) Good Words, **36**: 58-845.
Heart of the Princess Osra; a story. (A. H. Hawkins) McClure, **5**: 219.
Heart-leaf from Stony Creek Bottom. (M. E. M. Davis) Atlan. **71**: 57.
Hearts Insurgent; a novel. (T. Hardy) Harper, **90**: 188-940. **91**: 117-894.
Hearts Unfortified; a story. (A. Eliot) McClure, **7**: 281.
Heartsease. (A. Brown) Atlan. **74**: 505.
Heat and Cold, Extreme, Endurance of, by Man. (Marquis de Nadaillac) Science, **21**: 49.
— Animal. (V. Cornish) Knowl. **17**: 65.
— Atmospheric Radiation of. (C. Abbe) Am. J. Sci. **143**: 364.
— Conductivity of, Change of. (C. Barus) Am. J. Sci. **144**: 1.
— Mechanical Equivalent of. (A. Perot) J. Frankl. Inst. **133**: 55, 93.
— Radiant, Note on Absorption of, by Alum. (C. C. Hutchins) Am. J. Sci. **143**: 526.
— Radiation of, Experimental Comparison of Formulæ for Total. (W. Le C. Stevens) Am. J. Sci. **144**: 431.
— Waste, under Steam Boilers. (D. Ashworth) Cassier, **4**: 107.
— Wastes of. (W. Kent) Cassier, **1**: 203.
Heat Engines, Experimental Study of. (W. C. Unwin) Nature, **52**: 89.
Heat Insulation. Am. Arch. **50**: 90.
Heat Waves. *See* Hot Waves.
Heath, Dwellers on the. All the Year, **76**: 77.
Heath; Erica Hyemalis. (W. Watson) Garden & F. **5**: 136.
Heating and Ventilating, Blower System of. (W. B. Snow) Cassier, **4**: 97.
— — Plants in the Suffolk County Court House, and the Massachusetts State House. (P. N. Kenway) Am. Arch. **50**: 121.
— — Tall Buildings. (L. Allen) Engin. M. **9**: 476.
Heating, Combination. (G. D. Hoffman) Ann. Arch. **41**: 71.
— of Buildings. (George Hill) Arch. Rec. **5**: 204.
— of Houses. (L. Allen) Engin. M. **3**: 394-832.
— — Problem of. Am. Arch. **39**: 154.
— of Large Buildings. (A. R. Wolff) J. Frankl. Inst. **138**: 45, 116.
See Warming.
Heaths, Mosses, and Meres. Blackw. **158**: 293.
Heaven and Hell, Rational Views of. (G. St. Clair) Arena, **5**: 572.
— — Recent Romancings on. (G. B. Rolfe) No. Am. **158**: 119.
— Episcopal View of. (R. H. Howe) No. Am. **157**: 456.
— The Gates Ajar — Twenty-five Years After. (E. S. Phelps) No. Am. **156**: 567.
— Religious Reserve on Subject of. (P. Whitefoord) Chr. Lit. **12**: 17.
— What Sort of a Place is? Overland, n. s. **24**: 327.
Heavenly Law in the Universe. (Lydia F. Dickinson) N. Church R. **2**: 56.
Heavenly Wind, The. (H. Macmillan) Sund. M. **25**: 372.
Heavens, Photographic Chart of. Astron. **13**: 20.
— Sidereal, Growth and Magnitude of. (W. H. Lamaster) Pop. Astron. **3**: 226.
Heber, Reginald. Church Q. **42**: 159.
Hébert, E. Bk. Buyer, **1**: 269.
Hebrew, Mnemonic Formulæ for Radical and Servile Letters in. (D. Rosin) Jew. Q. **6**: 475.
— Use of, in New Testament Study. (J. Poucher) Bib. World, **6**: 88.
Hebrew Archæology, Benzinger's. (O. C. Whitehouse) Crit. R. **4**: 127.
Hebrew Bible and English Translation, Humor of. (Dr. Chotzner) Asia. R. **13**: 124.
Hebrew Collection, The Lewis-Gibson. (S. Schechter) Jew. Q. **9**: 115.
Hebrew Historiography. (T. G. Soares) Bib. World, **2**: 178.
Hebrew Legislation, Humane Spirit in. (J. Poncher) Meth. R. **55**: 39.

Hebrew Poetry. (F. A. Gast) Ref. Q. 43: 5.
Hebrew Weight, Inscription upon a. (W. R. Smith) Acad. 44: 443.
Hebrideans as Patriots and Naval Reservists. (D. N. Reid) Gent. M. n. s. 54: 41.
Hebrides, The. (W. M. Gilbert) M. of Art, 19: 280, 327.
— Antiquities of. Reliquary, 35: 200.
— Barra in the Minch. Chamb. J. 70: 778.
— From the. (F. Macleod) Harper, 92: 45.
— Legendary Lore of. (Frank Rinder) Scot. R. 27: 54.
Hebron, Harem at, Interior of. Good Words, 35: 264.
Hecatompedon, Ancient, on the Site of the Parthenon. (F. C. Penrose) J. Hel. Stud. 12: 275. 13: 32.
Hecker, Rev. Isaac T., with portrait. (M. E. Jordan) Cath. World, 60: 489.
Hecker, Isaac. (W. Barry) Dub. R. 111: 63.
Hecox, Margaret M., The Story of. (Marie Valhasky) Overland, n. s. 19: 535 — 20: 98.
Hecucka Society, Songs of. (J. O. Dorsey) J. Am. Folk-Lore, 1: 65.
Hedera, Κισσός and. (L. Horton-Smith) Am. J. Philol. 16: 38.
Hedgehogs; a Thorny Subject. (W. A. Smith) Good Words, 34: 464.
Hedgeley-Haskins Lawsuit, The. (A. M. Belding) Chamb. J. 73: 705-759.
Hedgerows. (M. G. Watkins) Longm. 20: 46.
Hedges for Cold Climates. Garden & F. 7: 158.
Hedonism, The New. (G. Allen) Fortn. 61: 377. — (F. Greenwood) Contemp. 65: 635.
— Rational. (E. E. C. Jones) Int. J. Ethics, 5: 79. — (M. S. Gilliland and others) Int. J. Ethics, 5: 376.
Hedonistic Theories, Watson's. Sat. R. 81: 232.
Heere, Lucas de. (L. Cust) M. of Art, 14: 354.
Hegel. (R. B. Haldane) Contemp. 67: 232.
— Dialectic of, Changes of Method in. (J. E. McTaggart) Mind, 17: 56, 206.
— — Time and the. (J. E. McTaggart) Mind, 18: 490. 19: 190.
— Ethics of. (J. M. Sterrett) Int. J. Ethics, 2: 176.
— Logic of. (J. E. Creighton) Philos. R. 4: 187.
— Monism and Christianity of. (E. Digby) Monist, 7: 114.
— on the State. (L. F. Ward) Soc. Econ. 7: 32.
— Problem of. (J. Watson) Philos. R. 3: 546.
— Some Aspects of his Philosophy. (H. Haldar) Philos. R. 5: 263.
— Theory of Punishment. (J. E. McTaggart) Int. J. Ethics, 6: 479.
Hegelianism and its Critics. (A. Seth) Mind, 19: 1.
— Psychological Basis of. (A. Fraser) Am. J. Psychol. 5: 472.
Hegemony of Science and Philosophy. (A. Fouillée) Int. J. Ethics, 6: 137.
Hegesias, the Cyreniac. (J. C. Murray) Philos. R. 2: 24.
Hegira of Gabe Freer. (R. G. Taber) Bach. of Arts, 2: 216.
Heidelberg University, Quincentenary of. (E. C. Thomas) Time, 141.
— Student Life at. (E. A. U. Valentine) Bach. of Arts, 2: 507.
Heilprin, A., with portrait. Bk. News, 11: 511.
Heimskringla; Olaf, King and Saint. (W. Morris and S. Magnusson) Sat. R. 78: 239.
— Morris's Translation. (W. H. Carpenter) Nation, 58: 471.
Heimweh; a story. (E. S. Nordhoff) Harper, 89: 422.
Heine, Heinrich. (Marion M. Miller) Bach. of Arts, 2: 778.
— as an Art Critic. (G. Smith) M. of Art, 10: 402.
Heine, Heinrich, Book of Ideas. (Alice G. Royston) Univ. R. 7: 437.
— Family Life of. Sat. R. 75: 46.
— Letters of, Unpublished. New R. 8: 139. Same art. Liv. Age, 196: 814. — Critic, 22: 46.
— Recent Heine Literature. (R. M'Lintock) Acad. 43: 364.
— Some Passages in the Life of. (Mrs. E. M. Davy) Belgra. 83: 291.
— Works, translated by Leland. Sat. R. 73: 749. Spec. 68: 92. 76: 497.
Heine Fountain Controversy. (W. Steinway) Forum, 20: 739.
Heinrich Hoffman's History; a poem. (J. R. Mallett) Temp. Bar, 103: 95-529. 104: 87-422. 105: 80-352.
Heinzen, Karl. (K. Peter) Open Court, 1: 451.
Heir, Power of, over an Executory Devise, and over a Condition Subsequent. (F. Goodwin) Am. Law R. 30: 69.
Heir of the McHulishes. (F. B. Harte) Cent. 24: 763, 921.
Heiress of Golden Falls, The. (H. Hill) Chamb. J. 71: 615.
Heirs of Kellie; a story. Blackw. 159: 325. Same art. Liv. Age, 209: 78-138.
Held in Ambush. (Edwin Whelpton) Good Words, 35: Xmas no., 22.
Held up; a story. (R. Barr) McClure, 2: 308.
Held up; a story. (M. B. Gibson) Outing, 21: 402.
Helen of Troy, in Art. (J. E. Harrison) M. of Art, 6: 55.
Helen Challoner; a story. Argosy, 57: 212.
Helgorn, The, a Welsh Mystery; a story. (E. Laws) Temp. Bar, 98: 379. Same art. Liv. Age, 198: 661.
Heligoland, Bird-catching in. (J. Cordeaux) Chamb. J. 73: 193.
— Ceded to Germany in 1890. (W. F. B. Laurie) Asia. R. 10: 36.
— Gätke's Bird-Lore at. (E. Coues) Nation, 61: 99.
Heliochromoscope. (F. E. Ives) J. Frankl. Inst. 135: 35.
Heliochromy, Composite. (F. E. Ives) J. Soc. Arts, 40: 687.
Heliographic Longitudes and Solar Prime Meridian. (F. H. Bigelow) Astron. 12: 821.
Helium. Dub. R. 117: 153. — (J. N. Lockyer) Sci. Prog. 5: 249.
— and Argon. (H. N. Stokes) Science, n. s. 2: 533. — Ed. R. 182: 404. — (G. McGowan) Knowl. 18: 210.
— and Parhelium. (E. W. Maunder) Knowl. 19: 284.
— a Constituent of Certain Minerals. Nature, 52: 306, 331.
— Identification and Properties of. (C. A. Young) Pop. Sci. Mo. 48: 339.
— is it Terrestrial? (W. W. Payne) Pop. Astron. 3: 16.
— Liquefaction of. Nature, 54: 377.
— Spectrum of. (E. W. Maunder) Knowl. 19: 86. — (W. Crookes) Nature, 52: 428. — (W. Crookes) Am. J. Sci. 150: 302.
— The Story of. (J. N. Lockyer) Nature, 53: 319, 342.
— Terrestrial. (S. E. Tillman) Cosmopol. 20: 450. — (J. N. Lockyer) Nature, 51: 586. — (W. Ramsay and others) Nature, 52: 7, 55.
— Wave Length of the D_3 Helium Line. (A. De F. Palmer, jr.) Am. J. Sci. 150: 357.
Hell. (J. P. Newman) Meth. R. 52: 345.

Hell, Happiness in. (St. G. Mivart) 19th Cent. 33: 320—34: 979. Same art. Ecl. M. 120: 172. — (R. F. Clarke) 19th Cent. 33: 83. — (J. H. Newman) 19th Cent. 33: 635.
— — Roman Catholic Church on. (R. F. Clarke) 19th Cent. 34: 489.
— St. George Mivart on. Church Q. 38: 152.
— Moslem. (J. Mew) 19th Cent. 31: 433.
— No Part of Divine Revelation. (W. E. Manley) Arena, 14: 464.
— Recent Romancings on. (G. B. Rolfe) No. Am. 158: 119.
Hell Fire: Is it Material? Month, 78: 208.
Hellas, History of Name. (J. B. Bury) J. Hel. Stud. 15: 217.
Hellebores, Cultivation of. Garden & F. 5: 8.
Helleu, M., Drypoints and Pastels of. (F. Wedmore) Acad. 47: 177. — (F. Wedmore) M. of Art, 18: 252.
Hellriegel, Hermann. Nature, 53: 11.
Helmholtz, H. L. F. Bk. News, 13: 207. — (A. W. Rücker) Fortn. 62: 651. — Nature, 50: 479. — (J. S. Shedlock) Acad. 46: 199. — Critic, 25: 175. — (T. C. Mendenhall) Science, n. s. 3: 189. — (C. R. Mann) Scrib. M. 18: 568. — (T. C. Martin) Cent. 27: 687. — Dub. R. 116: 181.
— and the New Psychology. (C. Stumpf) Psychol. R. 2: 1.
— Physical Work of. Nature, 51: 472, 493.
Helmick, Howard. (C. Cook) Q. Illust. 2: 357.
Helvellyn, A Night on. All the Year, 76: 125.
Hemenway, Mrs. Mary. Leis. Hour, 43: 708. — (C. G. Ames) Lend a H. 13: 31. — (E. E. Hale) Lend a H. 12: 243.
Hemlock for Tanneries. Garden & F. 9: 222.
Hemy, C. Napier, and his Boat Studio. (M. W. Freeman) Art J. 45: 201.
Hénault, President. (A. Laugel) Nation, 56: 437, 470.
Henbury Parish 1000 Years Ago. (T. Kerslake) Walford's Antiq. 3: 279.
Henderland Hill Fort, Peebles-shire. Reliquary, 35: 99.
Henderson, Alexander, Collection of Pictures. (W. S. Sparrow) M. of Art, 15: 12.
Hendriks, Augustus, with portrait. Bank. M. (Lond.) 58: 103.
Henism, Monism and. (P. Carus) Monist, 4: 228.
Henley, W. E. (H. B. M. Watson) Bookman, 2: 186. — Gent. M. n. s. 49: 213.
— and Stevenson, R. L. Macaire. Sat. R. 79: 756.
— New Poetry and. (G. Parker) Lippinc. 52: 109.
— Plays of. Gent. M. n. s. 49: 529.
— Poetry of. (A. Symons) Fortn. 58: 182.
— Song of the Sword, and Other Poems. Gent. M. n. s. 49: 213. — Spec. 68: 716.
Henley, England. (R. H. Davis) Harper, 87: 251.
— An American, Proposed. (S. Scoville, jr.) Bach. of Arts, 3: 305.
Henley Idyll, A; a story. (E. Markwick) Temp. Bar, 106: 231.
Henlopen, Cape. (A. Pyle) Harper, 85: 586.
Hennell, S. S. (W. E. Gladstone) 19th Cent. 38: 721.
Henner, Jean-Jacques. (F. Wedmore) M. of Art, 11: 217.
— and his Work. (C. S. Johnson) Munsey, 8: 142.
Henri Christophe I., King of Hayti. (L. G. Billings) Cosmopol. 13: 28.
Henri-deux Ware. (T. T. Greg) Art J. 44: 253.
Henrietta, Daughter of Charles I. of England. Church Q. 38: 138.
Henry II. of England and the Criminous Clerks. (F. W. Maitland) Eng. Hist. R. 7: 224.
Henry IV. of England, Wylie's. Sat. R. 77: 373.
Henry V. and David Rothesay. Belgra. 85: 417.
Henry VI. of England, Proposed Canonization of. (E. Peacock) Antiq. n. s. 29: 18.
Henry VIII., Divorce of. (J. Gairdner) Eng. Hist. R. 11: 673.
— First Divorce of, Hope's. Sat. R. 78: 163.
— Reign of. Ath. '92, 1: 239.
Henry IV., of France. Blair's Life of. (W. H. Carruth) Dial (Ch.) 18: 144. — Sat. R. 79: 102.
— Letters of. (A. Tilley) Macmil. 68: 344. Same art. Ecl. M. 121: 611. Same art. Liv. Age, 199: 218.
Henry of Orleans, Prince, Journey of, in 1895. Dub. R. 119: 168.
Henry, Prince, the Navigator. (Mrs. M. J. Lamb) M. Am. Hist. 27: 37. — (E. G. Bourne) Yale R. 3: 187. — Geog. J. 3: 388.
— Beazley on. Sat. R. 79: 604.
— 500th Anniv. of. Nature, 49: 443.
Henry, Patrick. (A. G. Bradley) Macmil. 65: 346.
— and John Adams, Correspondence of, 1776. M. Am. Hist. 27: 54.
— Letter of, 1776. (J. S. H. Fogg) N. E. Reg. 50: 19.
— Life of, Henry's. (H. C. Vedder) Bapt. R. 14: 251. — (W. F. Poole) Dial (Ch.) 13: 41. — (J. C. Welling) Nation, 54: 306, 327.
— New Study of. (M. C. Tyler) Yale R. 1: 345.
Henry, The Minstrel, and Barbour, as Literature. (W. A. Cragie) Scot. R. 22: 173.
Henry. (E. D'Esterre-Keeling) Gent. M. n. s. 56: 623.
Henry. (M. S. Cutting) Lippinc. 57: 395.
Henslow on Natural Selection. (A. R. Wallace) Nat. Sci. 5: 177.
Henson, Medora. (E. S. Wayne) Music, 11: 47.
Henty, G. A., with portrait. Bk. Buyer, 5: 237.
Hepburn Line. (M. J. Holmes) Lippinc. 52: 387.
Her Boy; a story. (R. Stewart) Harper, 92: 460.
Her Brother-in-law; a story. (M. Hargrave) Cornh. 74: 531. Same art. Liv. Age, 211: 514.
Her Dying Words. (T. B. Aldrich) Scrib. M. 14: 204.
Her First Smile. (J. Payn) Idler, 1: 32.
Her Garden; a poem. (K. Carter) M. of Art, 10: 390.
Her Mother's Success. (V. Roseboro') Cent. 26: 461.
Her Passport into Heaven; a story. (I. J. Armstrong) Eng. Illust. 14: 207.
Her Prerogative; a story. (E. A. Alexander) Harper, 93: 430.
Her Prussian Lover; a story. (M. Breck) Outing, 24: 428.
Her Son's Wife; a story. (C. S. Clarke) Eng. Illust. 11: 1087.
Her Tam O'Shanter; a poem. (J. W. Parker) Outing, 26: 364.
Herakles and Eurytos on a Cylix at Palermo. (P. Hartwig) J. Hel. Stud. 12: 334.
Heraldry, Abuses of. (A. S. van Westrum) Lippinc. 58: 677.
— British and Foreign. (H. Gough) Scot. R. 19: 245.
— Exhibition of. Sat. R. 77: 612.
— Hulme's. Sat. R. 73: 23.
— Humors of. Cornh. 70: 375. Same art. Liv. Age, 203: 443.
— in America. (E. Zieber) Lippinc. 58: 264.
— Modern Misuse of Coats of Arms. Sat. R. 82: 488-580.
— Notes on. Reliquary, 33: 156. — Sat. R. 77: 388.
— A Plea for its Resurrection. (E. Green) 19th Cent. 39: 1025.
— Scottish. (J. M. Gray) Acad. 42: 268. — (J. B. Paul) Scot. R. 20: 233.
— Woodward and Burnett on. Ath. '92, 1: 281, 312.
Herbaceous Plants, Hardy. Garden & F. 6: 391.

Herbage, William, with portrait. Bank. M. (Lond.) 54: 703.
Herbal, Stearns's American. (S. P. Boyle) Canad. M. 5: 178.
Herbals, Old German and Italian. (J. F. Payne) M. of Art, 8: 362.
Herbarium; Another Pest. (J. G. Jack) Garden & F. 8: 323.
— in relation to Botany. (J. P. Lotsy) Pop. Sci. Mo. 47: 360.
Herbart, J. F., and Froebel. (J. L. Hughes) Educa. R. 10: 239.
— and Pestalozzi compared. (W. T. Harris) Educa. R. 5: 417. — (W. Rein) Forum, 21: 346.
— Attitude of Scientific Thought in Germany toward Doctrines of. (C. Ufer) Educa. R. 12: 209.
— De Garmo on. Sat. R. 79: 194.
— Science of Education. (F. Watson) Acad. 43: 8.
— Significance of, for Secondary and Higher Education. (C. De Garmo) Educa. R. 11: 40.
— Unmoral Education. (W. T. Harris) Educa. 16: 178.
— Views of, on Mathematics and Natural Science. (C. H. Douglas) Educa. R. 3: 490.
Herbartian Literature in English. (J. J. Findlay) School & C. 1: 478, 541.
Herbartian Teachers, Some Suggestions to. (C. B. Gilbert) Educa. 14: 75.
Herbartism, Every-Day Uses of. (J. T. Prince) Educa. 15: 328.
Herbert, Auberon. Windfall and Waterdrift. (L. de la Ramé) 19th Cent. 40: 760.
Herbert, Edward, of Cherbury, Lord, Philosophy of. (W. R. Sorley) Mind, 19: 491.
Herbert, George. Spec. 72: 199. — Temp. Bar, 96: 116.
Hercules, Statue of, by Baccio Bandinelli. (L. E. Baxter) M. of Art, 3: 465.
Herculis ζ, Motion of, in Line of Sight. (A. Belopolsky) Astron. 13: 130.
Herder, J. G. von. Life, Kuehenmann's. Sat. R. 81: 657.
Herderite, Crystallization of. (S. L. Penfield) Am. J. Sci. 147: 329.
— from Hebron, Me. (H. L. Wells and S. L. Penfield) Am. J. Sci. 144: 114.
Here it is; a poem. M. of Art, 8: 15.
Hérédia, José-Maria de. Critic, 24: 443. — (E. Grosse) Contemp. 65: 471.
Hereditary Legislators. Sat. R. 80: 375.
Hereditary Transmission of Micro-organisms. (G. A. Buckmaster) Sci. Prog. 5: 324.
Heredity. (H. H. Gardiner) Arena, 9: 769. — (St. G. Mivart) Harper, 90: 631.
— and Environment. (A. M. Holmes) Arena, 9: 571.
— and the Germ Cells. (H. F. Osborn) Am. Natural. 26: 642.
— and Instinct. (J. M. Baldwin) Science, n. s. 3: 438, 558.
— and Pre-natal Influence, Effect of, on a Child. (B. O. Flower) Arena, 13: 243.
— and Rejuvenation. (C. S. Minot) Am. Natural. 30: 1.
— Are individually acquired Characters Inherited? (A. R. Wallace) Fortn. 59: 490, 655.
— Bad, Christian Nurture *versus*. (A. S. Cheeseborough) N. Eng. 56: 230.
— Cellular Genesis explains. (T. B. Wakeman) Open Court, 7: 3871.
— Criminals not the Victims of. (W. M. F. Round) Forum, 16: 48.
— Essays on, Weismann's. Sat. R. 79: 160.
— Evolution of. (C. H. Hurst) Nat. Sci. 1: 578.
— Galton on. (F. Starr) Dial (Ch.) 15: 12.
Heredity in Art. (D. E. Colnaghi) Art J. 48: 86.
— in Plants, Weismann's Theory of. (G. Henslow) Nat. Sci. 1: 171.
— in relation to Education. (W. Mills) Pop. Sci. Mo. 44: 472.
— in U. S. Political History. (H. King) Chaut. 21: 387.
— Lessons of. (H. S. Williams) No. Am. 157: 341.
— Mimicry of. (G. Batchelor) New World, 3: 735.
— Modification and Variation in. (C. L. Morgan) Science, n. s. 4: 733.
— Morbid. (C. Féré) Pop. Sci. Mo. 47: 388.
— Mystery of Birth. (G. Allen) Fortn. 64: 113.
— Nature of. (C. H. Hurst) Nat. Sci. 1: 502.
— of Acquired Characters. (M. Miles) Am. Natural. 26: 887. — (C. C. Nutting) Am. Natural. 26: 1009.
— once more. (A. Weismann) Contemp. 68: 420. — (H. Spencer) Contemp. 68: 608.
— Progressive, Problem of. (E. Haeckel) Open Court. 8: 3975.
— Spencer-Weismann Controversy on. (P. C. Mitchell) Nature, 49: 373.
— Theory of, Difficulties in. (H. F. Osborn) Am. Natural. 26: 537.
— Triple Standard in Ethics. (G. Batchelor) New World, 2: 279.
— *vs.* Evolution. (T. Gilman) Monist, 4: 80.
— *vs.* Individual Variation. Sat. R. 79: 89.
— Weismann on. (H. Spencer) Contemp. 64: 893. — (H. L. Osborn) Dial (Ch.) 15: 143. — (C. L. Morgan) Monist, 4: 20. — (D. S. Jordan) Dial (Ch.) 13: 242.
— Weismann's Concessions. (L. F. Ward) Pop. Sci. Mo. 45: 175.
— Weismann's Theory of. (St. George Mivart) Am. Cath. Q. 19: 673.
— What is Inheritance? (A. Wilson) Harper, 83: 355.
Herefordshire, Country Life in. Longm. 29: 60.
— Nooks and Corners of. (C. J. Robinson) Acad. 43: 148.
Heresy and Schism, Place of, in the Modern Church. (W. E. Gladstone) 19th Cent. 36: 157, 664. Same art. Chr. Lit. 11: 105 a, 129 a. Same art. Liv. Age, 202: 579.
— — Gladstone on. Church Q. 39: 76. — (R. Ogden) Nation, 59: 136.
— Dishonesty of. (J. Cooper) Ref. Q. 40: 319.
— from another Point of View. (G. V. Smith) 19th Cent. 36: 332.
Heretics, The. (W. F. Adeney) New World, 5: 654.
— Salvability of. (C. C. Starbuck) Meth. R. 55: 720.
Herford, Oliver, with portrait. Bk. Buyer, 12: 280.
Herkomer, Hubert, with portrait. (G. Campbell) Cosmopol. 14: 273. — (W. Meynell) M. of Art, 3: 259. — With portrait. R. of Rs. (N. Y.) 9: 698.
— and his Pupils. (M. P. Jackson) M. of Art, 19: 31.
— House of, at Bushey. (A. Meynell) M. of Art, 6: 96.
— School of. Art J. 44: 289.
Herkomer Pictorial Music-play. (H. Herkomer) M. of Art, 12: 316.
Hermann, Father. (T. L. L. Teeling) Am. Cath. Q. 17: 276.
Hermaphroditism, Successive Protandric and Proterogynic, in Animal. (T. H. Montgomery, jr.) Am. Natural. 29: 528.
Hermas, Witness of, to the Gospels, Taylor on. (J. Massie) Crit. R. 2: 377.
Hermippus Redivivus. (W. Sydney) Bookworm, 1: 361.
Hermit, The; a story. (C. J. Cutliffe Hyne) Chamb. J. 73: 27.
Hermitage Wharf; a story. Argosy, 60: 736.

Hermits, Ancient and Modern. All the Year, **54**: 282.
Herndon, N. H., with portrait. Bk. News, **11**: 219.
Herne, James A. Autobiography, with portrait. Arena, **6**: 401.
— in "Shore Acres." (B. O. Flower) Arena, **8**: 304.
Hero, Coming. (A. A. Johnson) Meth. R. **53**: 915.
Hero, A; a story. (P. Groussac) Cosmopol. **18**: 107.
Hero, A; a short story. (A. S. Duane) Munsey, **11**: 393.
Hero; a tale. (T. G. Randall) Outing, **27**: 30.
Herodas. *See* Herondas.
Herodotus, Humor of. (E. Manson) Westm. **141**: 52. Same art. Ecl. M. **122**: 346.
— Macan's. (J. H. McDaniels) Nation, **63**: 13.
Heroes, Certain accepted. (H. C. Lodge) Cosmopol. **13**: 713.
— Culture and Deified Kings. (S. D. Peet) Am. Antiq. **16**: 143.
— How they are made. Time, **1**: 694.
Heroic Couplet, The. (St. Loe Strachey) National, **23**: 815. Same art. Ecl. M. **123**: 448.
Heroine, Evolution of. (H. H. Boyesen) Lippinc. **54**: 425.
— Past and Present. (N. R. Allen) Lippinc. **58**: 429.
Heroism in the Mission-field. (A. R. Buckland) Sund. M. **22**: 231-822.
— in Music. (C. Bellargue) Chaut. **16**: 581.
— The true. (G. Dobbs) Our Day, **15**: 4.
Heroism of Lauders, The. (A. S. Pier) Scrib. M. **18**: 780.
Heron Court, Eng. (Lady S. Malmesbury) Eng. Illust. **10**: 378.
Herondas. Mimes. Acad. **42**: 93-195. — (R. Ellis) Acad. **42**: 413. — (C. Whibley) Liv. Age, **192**: 49.
— Notes on. (T. G. Tucker and others) Acad. **41**: 64, 88. — (W. Headlam and others) Acad. **41**: 112, 134. **42**: 72, 195.
— Translations of. (R. Ellis) Acad. **45**: 230.
Heronry at Richmond Park, Eng. Spec. **70**: 801.
— The Virginia Water. Liv. Age, **209**: 822.
Herons, The. Macmil. **71**: 1-401. **72**: 20, 143.
— in England. Spec. **72**: 498.
Heronscourt; a story. Argosy, **60**: 668.
Herr Dolle's Diamonds; a story. (H. Keen) McClure, **8**: 57.
Herreshoff, J. B. and N. G., and their Boats. (H. R. Palmer) New Eng. M. n. s. **12**: 515.
Herrick, Robert. (H. M. Sanders) Gent. M. n. s. **56**: 590. — (P. Edgar) Citizen, **2**: 332.
— and his Friends. (A. W. Pollard) Macmil. **67**: 142. Same art. Liv. Age, **196**: 220.
— A dream of; a poem. (T. B. Dilks) Temp. Bar, **107**: 123.
— Poems, Pollard's Edition. Ath. '**92**, **2**: 124.
Herring and Herring Fishery. (W. F. Nelson) Time, **17**: 567.
— Feeding-ground of. (A. Turbyne) Nature, **52**: 617.
— Mysterious Migration of. (A. H. Gouraud) New Sci. R. **2**: 162.
— The Persecuted. Chamb. J. **73**: 177.
Herron, George D. (C. Beardsley) Arena, **15**: 784. — With portrait. Bk. News, **12**: 385.
— and his Work in California. (A. Knapp and others) Arena, **14**: 110.
— as a Leader. (F. H. Foster) Presb. & Ref. R. **5**: 561.
— The Kingdom of God; Résumé of the Teachings of, with portrait. (H. P. Douglass) Our Day, **14**: 274.
Herschel, Sir John. (Sir R. Ball) Good Words, **35**: 835. Same art. Ecl. M. **124**: 205.
Herschel, William. (Sir R. Ball) Good Words, **35**: 463.
Hertfordshire, Rambles in. (A. Grant) Temp. Bar, **107**: 382. Same art. Liv. Age, **209**: 114.
Hertz, Heinrich. Nature, **49**: 265. — With portrait. (H. Bonfort) Pop. Sci. Mo. **45**: 401. — Dub. R. **114**: 425.
— Helmholtz's Tribute to. Pop. Sci. Mo. **46**: 182.
— Miscellaneous Papers of. Nature, **55**: 6.
— Work of. (O. Lodge) Nature, **50**: 133.
Hertzka, Dr. Theodor. Freeland. Gent. M. n. s. **48**: 108. — (E. Salmon) Fortn. **63**: 260.
Hervey, Arthur C., Bishop. Ath. '**94**, **1**: 773.
Hervey de Saint Denys, Marie Jean Léon, Marquis d'. Acad. **42**: 487.
Hervey, Mary Lepel, Lady. (A. Dobson) Longm. **28**: 452. Same art. Liv. Age, **211**: 89.
Hervieu, Paul. Armature. Sat. R. **79**: 836. — (H. Lynch) Fortn. **66**: 472.
Herz, Dr. Cornelius, Imprisonment of. Green Bag, **7**: 496.
Herzegovina and Bosnia. (E. B. Lanin) Contemp. **65**: 735.
— Baron de Kallay's Achievement in. Spec. **75**: 428.
Hesiod. Works and Days. (J. B. Bury) Scot. R. **23**: 31.
Hesperornis, New Cretaceous Bird allied to. (O. C. Marsh) Am. J. Sci. **145**: 81.
Hessian Fly. (E. A. Butler) Knowl. **18**: 30.
Hester; a story. Chamb. J. **72**: 93.
Hexapod, brain of, Mushroom Bodies of. (F. C. Kenyon) Am. Natural. **30**: 643.
— — Meaning and Structure of. (F. C. Kenyon) Am. Natural. **30**: 643.
Hey, Tutti, Taitie; the story of an old song. Chamb. J. **69**: 659.
Hey Willow Waly, O. (M. Eyre) Longm. **21**: 176.
Heyse, Paul. Atlan. **71**: 410. — With portrait. Bk. News, **10**: 391.
Heywood, Thomas, Plays of. (A. C. Swinburne) 19th Cent. **37**: 646. **38**: 397.
Hezekiah, Sargon, and Sennacherib. (J. Horner) Meth. R. **53**: 74.
Hiawatha. (W. M. Beauchamp) J. Am. Folk-Lore, **4**: 295.
Hiawatha; a poem. (C. A. Goodwin) Outing, **26**: 104.
Hibbard, Geo. A., with portrait. Bk. Buyer, **12**: 377.
Hibbert Lectures and the Gaulish Pantheon. (S. A. Strong) Open Court, **2**: 1297.
Hichborn, Philip. (R. G. Skerrett) Cassier, **8**: 140.
Hick, Thomas. Nat. Sci. **9**: 209.
Hickathrift, Thomas; the Norfolk Giant-killer. (J. Hooper) Gent. M. n. s. **56**: 39.
Hickories; why certain ones died. (J. B. Smith) Garden & F. **8**: 352.
Hickory Nuts, Abnormal. (F. H. Herrick) Am. J. Sci. **152**: 258.
Hicks, Seymour. This World of Ours. Theatre, **29**: 126.
Hidden Lives. (A. Macleod) Sund. M. **23**: 314.
Hieroglyphics and Pictographs, California. (T. H. Hittel) Science, **21**: 146.
— How Egyptian Monuments were read. Cornh. **65**: 259. Same art. Liv. Age, **193**: 414.
— in Crete. Acad. **46**: 136.
— Maya, Interpretation of. (H. T. Cresson) Science, **22**: 325.
— — Minor Phonetic Elements of. (H. T. Sisson) Science, **21**: 325.
— of Central America. (M. H. Saville) J. Am. Folk-Lore, **7**: 237.
Hieropolis, in Phrygia. (W. M. Ramsay) Contemp. **64**: 563.
Higgie, Thomas. (J. Coleman) Theatre, **31**: 17.

Higgins, Van Hollis, with portrait. (H. L. Conard) Nat'l M. (N. Y. '91) 16: 619.
Higginson, Nesta, "Moira O'Neill," with portrait. Bk. Buyer, 11: 371.
Higginson, Thos. W., with portrait. Bk. News, 6: 344.
— Cheerful Yesterdays; Autobiography. Atlan. 78: 586, 758.
Higginson Family, English Ancestry of. (T. W. Higginson) N. E. Reg. 46: 117.
High Oaks, The; a poem. (A. C. Swinburne) 19th Cent. 40: 341.
High Sand, The. Liv. Age, 208: 574.
High School, Admission to, Mode of. Overland, n. s. 27: 556.
— American. Dial (Ch.) 19: 373.
— — Future of. (J. R. Bishop) School R. 3: 287.
— and its Enemies. (T. Vickers) School R. 1: 83.
— Argument for. (R. S. Keyser) Acad. (Syr.) 7: 265.
— Courses of Study in, Unification and Consolidation of. (C. W. Groves) Acad. (Syr.) 7: 106.
— Differentiation of, the Coming Movement in Education. (H. Miller) School R. 1: 418.
— Election of Studies in. Overland, n. s. 27: 553.
— Elective Study in. (E. Giles) Educa. 14: 160. — (E. J. Goodwin) Educa. R. 5: 142.
— English, Preparation for College by. (J. F. Casey) Pop. Sci. Mo. 46: 15.
— Future of the. (F. W. Kelsey) Educa. R. 11: 157.
— Influence upon Educational Methods. (J. Dewey) School R. 4: 1.
— of the Future. (M. H. Paddock) Educa. 17: 103.
— Place of, in an Ideal Scheme. (S. Low) School R. 2: 379.
— Preparatory and Non-preparatory Pupils in. (W. R. Butler) Educa. R. 12: 473.
— Small, Curriculum of. (E. J. Goodwin) School R. 3: 268.
— Status of, in New England. (C. H. Douglas) Educa. R. 5: 27.
— Teacher of, Equipment in French. (A. H. Edgren) School R. 3: 257.
— What can it do to aid the Grammar School? (R. G. Huling) Educa. 14: 385.
— Work of the. (F. L. Soldan) Educa. R. 11: 335.
— Zoölogy in. (C. M. Weed) Am. Natural. 28: 1003.
High School Classical Library, Most Essential Books for. (C. L. Meader) School R. 4: 149.
High School Discipline. (C. L. Biedenbach) School R. 4: 228.
High School Period. (J. H. Baker) Educa. R. 9: 472.
High School System. (L. R. Harley) Ann. Am. Acad. Pol. Sci. 8: 332.
High School Work, Effect of, upon Girls during Adolescence. (Helen P. Kennedy) Pedagog. Sem. 3: 469.
Higher Aim; sonnet. (W. M. Payne) Dial (Ch.) 19: 105.
Higher Hand, A; a Detective Story. (P. Andreæ) Eng. Illust. 12: no. 3, 13.
Higher Law, A; a story. Temp. Bar, 104: 288.
Highland Folk-tale and its Foundation in Usage. (G. L. Gomme) Folk-Lore, 1: 197.
Highland Lochs, Sailing in, for Ladies. (C. Creyke) 19th Cent. 40: 478.
Highland Regiments and their Origin. (C. E. Macdonald) Canad. M. 7: 259.
Highland Seers. Good Words, 34: 196.
Highlands, Scottish, Development of. (J. H. Fullarton) Scot. R. 25: 291.
— My Stay in. (C. M. Gaskell) 19th Cent. 34: 230. Same art. Liv. Age, 199: 169.
— Summer Tour in the. (T. L. James) Cosmopol. 21: 571.
Highlands, West, New Route to. Chamb. J. 71: 129.
Highway, World's Future. (T. G. Gribble) Engin. M. 3: 1-306.
Highwaymen; Knights of the Road in Berkshire. (P. H. Ditchfield) Gent. M. n. s. 57: 60.
Highways, Care of Existing. (W. E. McClintock) Engin. M. 5: 233.
— The People's. (F. Parsons) Arena, 12: 218, 393.
Higinbotham, George, Morris' Life of. (J. G. C. Minchin) Acad. 47: 440.
Hilda Strafford; a California Story. (B. Harraden) Blackw. 159: 483, 652. Same art. Cosmopol. 20: 627. 21: 30, 191.
Hilda's Race; a story. Outing, 24: 16.
Hildebrand, Adolf. (H. Zimmern) M. of Art, 17: 53.
Hildesheim, Germany, and its Churches. (J. K. Paulding) Archit. Rec. 2: 9.
— Ecclesiastical Art Work at. (H. Cole) M. of Art, 4: 36.
— an Old World City. (Sophia Beale) Univ. R. 5: 413.
Hill, Daniel Harvey. (A. C. Avery) So. Hist. Pap. 21: 110.
Hill, David B., with portrait. (H. Parker) Munsey, 12: 16. — With portraits. (C. A. Collin) R. of Rs. (N. Y.) 5: 19.
— Another View of. R. of Rs. (N. Y.) 5: 26.
— Political Career and Character of. Forum, 18: 257. — Pub. Opin. 17: 759.
Hill, Captain, Collection of Pictures at Brighton. (A. Meynell) M. of Art, 5: 1-116.
Hill, Frederick, Autobiography of. Sat. R. 77: 395. — Ath. '94, 1: 105. — Spec. 72: 200. — (W. P. Garrison) Nation, 58: 140.
Hill, L. Raven. (M. H. Spielmann) M. of Art, 19: 493.
Hill, Nathaniel Peter. (B. W. Steele) Nat'l M. (N. Y. '91) 15: 428.
Hill, Nicholas. (M. Hale) Green Bag, 8: 185.
Hill, Rowland, and Penny Postage. (A. G. Bowie) Time, 22: 185.
Hill of Seven Trees; a story. (R. Horsley) Chamb. J. 70: 347.
Hillegas, John Frederic. (M. R. Minnich) Pennsyl. M. 18: 85.
Hillegas Family, Some Data of. (M. R. Minnich) Am. Hist. Reg. 1: 23.
Hiller, Ferdinand. Temp. Bar, 106: 240.
Hills, Rose Dunster. (W. S. Hills) N. E. Reg. 49: 146.
Hillsborough River, Along the. (B. Torrey) Atlan. 72: 597.
Hillside Farm; a story. (J. B. Rowell) Un. Serv. (Phila.) 12: 433.
Hilton, Ensign William, of York, Me. (J. T. Hassam) N. E. Reg. 50: 206.
Hiltons' Holiday, The. (S. O. Jewett) Cent. 24: 772.
Hiltzheimer, Jacob, Diary of, 1768-98. Pennsyl. M. 16: 93, 160, 412.
Himalayas. (E. A. Richings) Belgra. 90: 83.
— Ascents of. (E. Whymper) Leis. Hour, 42: 193, 228.
— Central, Dr. Diener's Expedition to. Geog. J. 2: 258.
— — Geology of, Griesbach on. (H. B. Woodward) Nat. Sci. 1: 442.
— Exploration in. Chamb. J. 71: 545.
— — Conway's. Sat. R. 79: 49.
— Geology of. Nature, 45: 308.
— Karakoram, Conway's Climbing in. Around World, 1: 220. — (L. Stephen) National, 23: 460. — (J. Ritchie, jr.) Nation, 59: 123. — Ath. '94, 1: 671. — Nature, 50: 199.
— Mountaineering in. (W. M. Conway) All the Year, 74: 559.

Hind, Captain James; Master Thief of England. Macmil. **73**: 345.
Hind, John Russell. (W. E. Plummer) Nature, **53**: 201.
Hind, W. M. Nat. Sci. **5**: 313.
Hinderer, Anna. (A. R. Buckland) Sund. M. **24**: 194.
Hindolvestone Church, Norfolk. Reliquary, **33**: 28.
Hindostan, Awakening of. (A. Webb) Nation, **58**: 268.
Hindu and Moslem. (E. L. Weeks) Harper, **91**: 651.
Hindu Carvings. (L. H. Weeks) Chaut. **22**: 59.
Hindu Civilization under British Rule. (J. F. Hewitt) Westm. **145**: 510. — Sat. R. **81**: 409.
Hindu Family Life. Asia. R. **11**: 398.
Hindu Grammar, Recent Studies in. (W. D. Whitney) Am. J. Philol. **14**: 139.
Hindu Historical Mythology. (J. F. Hewitt) Westm. **145**: 357.
Hindu Kush, Chitral, Hunza and. (F. E. Younghusband) Geog. J. **5**: 409.
— Eastern. (A. Durand) Contemp. **66**: 685. Same art. Liv. Age, **203**: 788.
— Exploration in. Dub. R. **112**: 181.
— Races and Language. (G. W. Leitner) Asia. R. **12**: 139.
Hindu Logic, Inference in. (S. N. Gupta) Mind, **20**: 159.
Hinduism, Art Subjects from. (E. M. Bowden) Art J. **48**: 241, 278.
— Evangelical. (M. M. Snell) Bib. World, **6**: 270.
— Moral Evils of. (A. Besant and H. S. Lunn) Chr. Lit. **11**: 149.
— Points of Contact with Christianity. (M. M. Snell) Bib. World, **3**: 189, 349. **4**: 98.
Hindus, Political Training of. (J. T. Wheeler) Asia. R. **9**: 61.
— Religion of. Eng. R. **5**: 300.
— Sea-voyages by. (S. E. Gopalacharlu) Asia. R. **14**: 49, 300.
Hine, Henry George. Ath. '95, **1**: 384. — Acad. **47**: 283. — (F. Wedmore) M. of Art, **16**: 87.
Hingham, Mass., Old Meeting-house in. (P. Collier) New Eng. M. n. s. **8**: 477.
Hinkson, Katharine T., with portrait. Bk. Buyer, **13**: 447.
Hint o' Hairst, The; a story. (M. M. Dowie) Chamb. J. **70**: 73–119. Same art. Liv. Age, **197**: 529, 592.
Hippolyte Foncé Tract, The; a story. Outing, **19**: 280.
Hippolytus and his Age, Bunsen's. Eng. R. **18**: 239.
Hippopotami, Ancient and Modern. (R. Lydekker) Knowl. **17**: 106.
Hird, Ben, a South Sea Trader. Macmil. **75**: 66.
Hired Man, The. Atlan. **73**: 283.
Hirn, Gustav Adolph. (B. Donkin) Cassier, **4**: 232.
Hirsch, Baron Maurice de. (O. S. Straus) Forum, **21**: 558. — (A. White) Eng. Illust. **15**: 191. — Spec. **76**: 590.
Hirsch, Samson Raphael. (S. A. Hirsch) Jew. Q. **2**: 109.
Hirsch Fund. (M. S. Isaacs) Char. R. **1**: 30.
Hirschberg, Silesia, Churchyard of. (L. von Crockow) Am. Arch. **50**: 131.
Hirst, Father J. Ath. '95, **2**: 540.
Hirst, Thomas A. Nature, **45**: 399.
His Advocate. (G. G. Farquhar) Chamb. J. **72**: 779.
His Bad Angel; a story. (R. H. Davis) Harper, **87**: 381.
His Balance at the Bank; a story. (E. Everett-Green) Sund. M. **22**: 607.
His Duty; a story. (O. Thanet) Harper, **93**: 612.
His Enemy; a story. (E. E. Kitton) Belgra. **90**: 399.
His Father's Memoirs; a story. (A. E. Lawrence) Nat'l M. (Bost.) **4**: 589.
His Football Father. (Chas. R. Elston) Bach. of Arts, **3**: 782.
His Ghostly Wife. Argosy, **59**: 67.
His Grace. (W. E. Norris) Longm. **20**: 1–613.
His Great Disappointment; a story. Argosy, **62**: 211.
His Highness Prince Kwakoo, an African Story. (H. Bell) Idler, **10**: 685.
His Highness's Playthings. (Headon Hill) Chamb. J. **72**: 689–710.
His Honor. (E. Mackubin) Atlan. **74**: 463.
His Letter; a story. (H. Newman) Argosy, **56**: 374.
His Magnificence; a story. (S. F. Bullock) Eng. Illust. **12**: no. 5, 53.
His Nameless Enemy. (C. T. C. James) Gent. M. n. s. **51**: 433–541.
His Own Counsel; a story. (A. F. King) Belgra. **81**: 257.
His Passport into Hell; a story. (I. J. Armstrong) Eng. Illust. **16**: 175.
His Passport into Peace; a story. (I. J. Armstrong) Eng. Illust. **15**: 221.
His Sister; Comedietta. (H. A. Spurr) Eng. Illust. **13**: 319.
His Special Providence; a story. All the Year, **74**: 13.
His Trenchant Pen; a story. (M. E. Cardwill) Nat'l M. (Bost.) **5**: 134.
His Vanished Star. (M. N. Murfree) Atlan. **72**: 1–789. **73**: 99–384.
Hispar Pass, Crossing the. (W. M. Conway) Geog. J. **1**: 131.
Hiss, Natural History of the. (L. Robinson) No. Am. **157**: 104.
Hissing in Theatres. (W. H. Pollock) Theatre, **34**: 147.
Histology, Physiological, A Plea for. (S. H. Gage) Science, n. s. **2**: 209.
Historians, English, Young. (M. Reid) Macmil. **67**: 91. Same art. Liv. Age, **196**: 694.
— Modern. (H. A. L. Fisher) Fortn. **62**: 803.
Historic Homes, Influence on English Character. (Lord Brabourne) Forum, **15**: 232.
Historical Argument, Importance and Limitations of. (A. T. Swing) Bib. Sac. **52**: 48.
Historical Enquiry, New Methods of. Quar. **184**: 122.
Historical Industries. (J. Schouler) Yale R. **3**: 24.
Historical MSS. Commissioners, References to Books in the Reports of. (H. R. Plomer) Bibliographica, **3**: 142.
Historical Novel, The. (W. H. Carruth) Dial (Ch.) **19**: 8. — (G. Saintsbury) Macmil. **70**: 321, 410.
Historical Perspective. Meth. R. **56**: 115.
Historical Research. (J. Schouler) Nat'l M. (N. Y. '91) **15**: 250.
Historical Spirit. Atlan. **73**: 409.
History, American, Teaching of. (G. White) School & C. **1**: 286, 326.
— and Democracy. (W. M. Sloane) Am. Hist. R. **1**: 1.
— and Fable. Quar. **178**: 31.
— and Mystery. Month, **88**: 457.
— as the Teacher. Spec. **68**: 260.
— Beginnings of. (S. D. Peet) Am. Antiq. **17**: 273.
— College Entrance, Unity in. (L. M. Salmon) Educa. R. **12**: 151.
— — Report of the Conference on. School R. **3**: 469.
— Definition of, and a Forecast. (M. S. Barnes) Ann. Am. Acad. Pol. Sci. **6**: 128.
— Educational Value of. (A. B. Thompson) Educa. R. **9**: 359.
— Five Books of. (J. W. Powell) Science, n. s. **1**: 157.
— for Ready Reference, Larned's. (A. H. Noll) Dial (Ch.) **17**: 152, **19**: 90.

History, Hinsdale's How to study and teach. (W. H. Tillinghast) Nation, 59: 201.
— How to study. (A. B. Hart) Chaut. 18: 17.
— in the Common Schools. (E. J. Rice) Educa. R. 12: 169. — (S. S. Laurie) School R. 4: 649.
— in Secondary Education. (R. G. Huling) Educa. R. 7: 448. 8: 43.
— Instruction in. (C. H. Levermore) School & C. 1: 218.
— Local, Study of. New Eng. M. n. s. 8: 28.
— — Teaching of. (M. S. Barnes) Educa. R. 10: 481.
— Logic of. (R. M. Wenley) Scot. R. 24: 297.
— The Most Valuable. (H. C. Kirk) Educa. 16: 15.
— The New Spirit in. (W. S. Lilly) 19th Cent. 38: 619. Same art. Ecl. M. 125: 721. Same art. Liv. Age, 207: 737.
— of Clare Tollison; a story. (B. Pain) Eng. Illust. 16: 233.
— of a Failure; a story. (E. Chilton) Liv. Age, 192: 457.
— of the Fairchild Family, an Old-fashioned Child's Book. (F. Anstey) New R. 14: 392.
— On the Writing of. (W. Wilson) Cent. 28: 787.
— Philosophy of. (J. B. Rust) Ref. Q. 39: 64.
— — Flint's History of the. (D. Irons) Philos. R. 3: 726. — Ed. R. 180: 392. — Sat. R. 77: 393. — Spec. 72: 437, 472. — (G. B. Adams) Nation, 58: 454.
— Prophecy and the Monuments, McCurdy's. (A. B. Davidson) Crit. R. 5: 3.
— Ranke and the Beginning of the Seminary Method in Teaching. (E. G. Bourne) Educa. R. 12: 359.
— The Real Historian. Macmil. 66: 221. Same art. Ecl. M. 119: 359.
— Royal Road to. (F. Harrison) Fortn. 60: 478.
— Should it be taught backwards? (R. K. Wilson) Contemp. 70: 391. Same art. Liv. Age, 211: 259.
— Study of. (T. R. Bacon) Overland, n. s. 27: 427.
— — at Oxford. Nation, 60: 274.
— — Lecky on. Spec. 69: 524.
— — Methods of. (L. R. Harley) Educa. 15: 332.
— Teaching. (J. W. MacDonald) Acad. (Syr.) 7: 36. — (E. D. Warfield) School R. 3: 33.
— — in Elementary Schools. (E. D. Warfield) Educa. 14: 1.
— Truth of. (W. H. Mills) Un. Serv. (Phila.) 10: 17.
— Universal, from Socialist Standpoint. (E. B. Bax) Time, 1: 712.
— Use of. Sat. R. 74: 438.
— Why learn? (G. W. Prothero) National, 24: 460. Same art. Ecl. M. 124: 349.
— Writing of. (A. J. Gossip) Gent. M. n. s. 56: 484.
— — Art of. (W. E. H. Lecky) Forum, 14: 715.
Hitchcock, Pres. Edward, with portrait. Pop. Sci. Mo. 47: 689.
Hittite Inscription, The New Bilingual. (A. H. Sayce) Acad. 41: 43. — (T. Tyler) Acad. 41: 91.
Hittite Inscriptions. (P. Jenson) Acad. 46: 450.
— Decipherment of. (A. H. Sayce) Acad. 41: 494. — (C. R. Conder) Acad. 41: 566.
— Jensen on. (A. H. Sayce) Acad. 46: 259.
Hittite Seals. (W. H. Ward) Am. J. Archæol. 9: 361.
Hittites and Pelasgians, The. (A. H. Sayce) Acad. 47: 446.
— Semitism of. (T. Tyler and others) Acad. 43: 329-464.
Hjaltland. (T. B. White) Scot. R. 28: 1. Same art. Liv. Age, 210: 643.
Ho! for the Pines; a ballade. (E. A. Raleigh) Outing, 24: 335.
Hoadly, George, with portrait. (J. H. Kennedy) Nat'l M. (N. Y. '91) 15: 52.
Hoagland, Cornelius N., with portrait. (F. Allaben) Nat'l M. (N. Y. '91) 15: 649.
Hoar, Ebenezer Rockwood. (D. E. Ware) Atlan. 76: 162.
— How he ceased to be Attorney-General. (J. D. Cox) Atlan. 76: 162.
Hoar, Senator George F., and the A. P. A. Pub. Opin. 19: 232.
Hoard of the Vazir Khanji. (H. Hill) Chamb. J. 69: 747. Same art. Liv. Age, 196: 302.
Hobart, Garret A. (T. Roosevelt) R. of Rs. (N. Y.) 14: 289.
Hobart, Tasmania, Exhibition of 1894. (G. C. Levey) J. Soc. Arts, 42: 481.
Hobbema, Meyndert. (T. Cole) Cent. 25: 832.
Hobbes, John Oliver. *See* Craigie, Mrs.
Hobbes, Thomas. (F. Pollock) National, 24: 29. Same art. Liv. Age, 203: 131.
Hobby, Value of a. Spec. 74: 896.
Hochelaga, Fall of. (H. Hale) J. Am. Folk-Lore, 7: 1.
Hockey, Ice. (B. Bogert) Outing, 21: 252.
— in the Canadian Northwest. (H. J. Woodside) Canad. M. 6: 242.
Hockey Match, Championship, in Canada. (C. G. Rogers) Outing, 23: 408.
Hocking, Silas K., at Home. Sund. M. 22: 112.
Hodge in the Saddle; a poem. Spec. 74: 464.
Hodgson, Brian Houghton. (J. S. Cotton) Acad. 45: 459. — Nat. Sci. 5: 151. — Ath. '94, 1: 710.
— Hunter's Life of. Acad. 50: 579.
Hodgson, John Evan. Ath. '95, 1: 844. — Acad. 47: 549.
Hodson, of Hodson's Horse, The Charges against, substantiated. (T. R. E. Holmes) Eng. Hist. R. 7: 48.
Hoefer, Andreas. (R. Heath) Leis. Hour, 43: 225. — (W. D. McCrackan) New Eng. M. n. s. 14: 548.
Hoehnel, Lieut. von. Geog. J. 2: 534.
Hoffman, Francis. (E. Solly) Walford's Antiq. 9: 6.
Hoffman, Heinrich. Struwelpeter. Spec. 73: 398, 406.
Hoffman, Heinrich, Painter, Studio of. (M. C. Crowley) Cath. World, 60: 653.
Hoffman, Ogden. (A. O. Hall) Green Bag, 5: 297.
Hofmann, August W. von. Ath. '92, 1: 635.
Hoffmann, Ernst T. W. Serapion Brethren. Sat. R. 74: 400.
Hofman's Object Lesson; a story. (J. J. à Becket) Cosmopol. 21: 618.
Hog, Wild, of Louisiana. (G. Reno) Outing, 21: 364.
Hogarth, William. (W. Roberts) Bookworm, 5: 129. — (A. Dobson) M. of Art, 5: 441. — (J. Grego) M. of Art, 18: 375, 412. — (C. Cook) Mo. Illust. 11: 453.
— Dobson's Life of. (F. Wedmore) Acad. 41: 93. — Ath. '92, 2: 391, 423. — (E. G. Johnson) Dial (Ch.) 12: 345. — (C. Phillips) Portfo. 23: 10.
— House and Tomb of. (A. Dobson) M. of Art, 6: 70.
— Some Portraits by. (A. Dobson) M. of Art, 8: 40.
— Was he a Plagiarist? M. of Art, 19: 228.
Hogg, James. (J. C. Hadden) Gent. M. n. s. 49: 283.
Hoghton Tower. (M. Creighton) M. of Art, 10: 19, 68.
Hogue, La, Battle of. Quar. 176: 461.
Hogun, Gen. James, Career of. (W. Clark) M. Am. Hist. 28: 284.
Hohenlohe-Langenburg, Victor, Prince of. Fortn. 58: 366.
Hohenlohe-Schillingsfürst, Prince. (T. Barth) New R. 11: 557.
Hohenzollerns, The White Lady of. (Emma H. Nason) Munsey, 9: 178.

Hokusaï. (S. Bing) M. of Art, **14**: 242, 307.
Holbein, Hans. (W. Armstrong) Portfo. **23**: 131.
— The Ambassadors. M. of Art, **19**: 155.
— — Mystery of. (W. F. Dickes) M. of Art, **15**: 1-275.
— in London. (F. M. Robinson) M. of Art, **9**: 350.
Holbein, Hans, the Younger. (F. M. Robinson) M. of Art, **9**: 194. — (A. F. Ferry) New Eng. M. n. s. **10**: 101. — With portrait. (M. A. Taggart) Cath. World, **59**: 744.
Holbein-Rippel, L'Affaire. Univ. R. **5**: 377.
Holberg, Ludwig, influenced by Addison. Sat. R. **80**: 413.
Holborn. All the Year, **75**: 438.
Holcroft, Thomas, author of the Road to Ruin. (H. G. Hibbert) Theatre, **28**: 132.
Holdheim, Samuel. (I. H. Ritter) Jew. Q. **1**: 202.
Hole, Samuel Reynolds. Critic, **25**: 275.
— Memories. Dial (Ch.) **14**: 42. — All the Year, **71**: 614, 624. — Sat. R. **74**: 657. — Spec. **69**: 738.
— More Memories. Critic, **26**: 1.
— on America. Critic, **26**: 171.
Holford, R. S., Art Collection of. Sat. R. **76**: 103.
Holgate, Robert, Archbishop, Papers of. (N. Pocock) Eng. Hist. R. **9**: 542.
Holiday, The Autumn. (H. D. Traill) National, **25**: 755.
Holiday in the Hills. (C. G. Rogers) Canad. M. **3**: 368.
Holiday Bush Adventure. (G. A. Stockwell) Canad. M. **6**: 344.
Holiday Moods. All the Year, **75**: 293.
Holidays: Distraction and Diversion. Spec. **71**: 203.
— An Experiment in. (H. Preston-Thomas) Blackw. **152**: 364.
Holiness, Growth in; a Friendly Word with my Critics. (James Mudge) Meth. R. **56**: 125.
Holinshed, Judith. (J. Hawthorne) Critic, **28**: 83.
Holkham Lake, Wild Fowl of. Spec. **76**: 81.
Holl, Frank. (W. Meynell) M. of Art, **3**: 187. — (M. H. Spielmann) M. of Art, **11**: 412.
Holland, Josiah Gilbert, with portrait. Bk. News, **4**: 337.
— Arthur Bonnicastle, "Mr. Bird" in, Source of. Educa. **12**: 545.
Holland, Surveyor-General. (H. Scadding) Canad. M. **5**: 521.
Holland. Blackw. **160**: 626.
— and Friesland, A Ladies' Skating Tour in. Liv. Age, **208**: 233. Same art. Ecl. M. **126**: 350.
— Blok's Geschiednis van. (W. E. Griffis) Am. Hist. R. **2**: 122.
— Defensive Position of. (S. R. Van Campen) Time, **23**: 804.
— Electoral Reform in. (A. L. Pincoffs) Nation, **56**: 416.
— Elizabeth Stuart and her Family in. (S. I. de Zuylen de Nyevelt) National, **19**: 52.
— Fiscal Reform in. (H. B. Greven) Econ. J. **3**: 534.
— Home Colonies of. All the Year, **70**: 591.
— Houses and Housekeeping in. (M. L. F. Mohr) Around World, **1**: 211.
— how it was made. (F. Crowell) Engin. M. **9**: 204.
— In Dutch Water-meadows. (T. D. Pigott) Contemp. **62**: 210.
— Influence of, in New England. (W. E. Griffis) Harper, **88**: 213. — (F. W. Shepardson) Dial (Ch.) **17**: 61.
— Land wrested from the Sea. (M. Beck) Chaut. **21**: 597.
— Literary. (W. E. Griffis) Critic, **21**: 181.
— Literature in. (W. E. Griffis) Lit. W. (Bost.) **26**: 248.
— — 1891-92. (T. H. de Beer) Ath. '**92**, **2**: 18.
See Dutch Literature.
Holland. On the Shores of the Zuyder Zee. (G. A. T. Middleton) M. of Art, **16**: 64.
— Peasantry in. (S. I. de Zuylen de Nyevelt) National, **19**: 467. Same art. Liv. Age, **194**: 315.
— Poor Colonies of. (J. H. Gore) Lend a H. **16**: 203.
— Printers and Wood-cutters of. (W. M. Conway) M. of Art, **4**: 190, 505.
— Skating Trip in. Leis. Hour, **41**: 183. Same art. Liv. Age, **192**: 697.
— Social, Artistic, and Literary. (W. E. Griffis) Chaut. **18**: 433.
— Some Dutch Characteristics. (C. Edwardes) Chamb. J. **69**: 665.
— Sport among the Dykes. (B. Webber) Time, **7**: 685.
— Universities in. (S. Nusbaum) Educa. **17**: 18.
— Winter in. All the Year, **73**: 536.
Holland House. Am. Arch. **48**: 42. — (E. L. Didier) Chaut. **17**: 387.
— and its Associations. (W. C. Sydney) Gent. M. n. s. **50**: 188.
— Library of. Bookworm, **3**: 153.
Hollingshead, John. (J. Knight) Theatre, **35**: 26.
— Life of. Sat. R. **79**: 763.
Hollis, Thomas. (A. McF. Davis) Harv. Grad. M. **3**: 342.
Hollow Ruby, The; a story. (J. Hawthorne) Eng. Illust. **12**: no. 6, 3.
Holloway College Picture Gallery. (W. S. Sparrow) M. of Art, **14**: 234, 269.
Holly, European Eryngiums. (H. Correvon) Garden & F. **6**: 496.
— Hardy Evergreen, and Barberries. (J. G. Jack) Garden & F. **6**: 196.
Holly Berries. (R. K. Munkittrick) Bach. of Arts, **2**: 34.
Holme, Thomas, Surveyor-General of Pennsylvania and Provincial Councillor. (O. Hough) Pennsyl. M. **19**: 413. **20**: 128, 248.
Holmes, Oliver Wendell. Blackw. **152**: 174. — With portrait. Bk. Buyer, **5**: 174. — With portrait. Bk. News, **4**: 266. — With portrait. Bk. News, **13**: 70. — With portrait. Bk. News, **14**: 477. — (Maria S. Porter) Bost. **2**: 243. — (J. A. Noble) Leis. Hour, **44**: 82. — Lond. Q. **87**: 77. — (H. V. Clarke) Munsey, **7**: 400. — (H. C. Lodge) No. Am. **159**: 669. — (J. W. Chadwick) Forum, **18**: 279. — (H. E. Scudder) Atlan. **74**: 831. — (E. Gosse) Critic, **25**: 382. — With portrait. (E. E. Hale) R. of Rs. (N. Y.) **10**: 495. — With portraits. (E. E. Hale) McClure, **1**: 99, 214. — Critic, **25**: 242. — Ath. '**94**, **2**: 492. — (G. E. Woodberry) Nation, **59**: 264. — Dial (Ch.) **17**: 215. — Pub. Opin. **17**: 707. — (W. Lewin) Acad. **46**: 279. — Sat. R. **78**: 407. — Lit. W. (Bost.) **25**: 350. — Spec. **73**: 485. Same art. Liv. Age, **203**: 503. — Lippinc. **55**: 107. — (T. T. Munger) New World, **4**: 33. — Quar. **180**: 189. Same art. Ecl. M. **124**: 433. Same art. Liv. Age, **204**: 537. — (L. Stephen) National, **27**: 626. Same art. Ecl. M. **127**: 359. Same art. Liv. Age, **210**: 259. — (W. D. Howells) Harper, **94**: 120. — (A. K. H. Boyd) Longm. **28**: 344.
— the Anatomist. (D. W. Cheever) Harv. Grad. M. **3**: 154.
— and Tennyson; a parallel, with portraits. Cath. World, **60**: 521.
— as Professor of Anatomy. (Thos. Dwight) Scrib. M. **17**: 121.
— Chambered Nautilus. Poet-Lore, **6**: 570.
— Health Code. (F. L. Oswald) Chaut. **20**: 321.
— An Hour with. (J. L. Hughes) Canad. M. **2**: 134.
— in his Library. (G. Le Baron) Nat'l M. (Bost.) **5**: 231.

Holmes, O. W., Morse's Life of. (J. W. Chadwick) Nation, 62: 456. — (L. C. Moulton) Bookman, 3: 417. — (E. G. Johnson) Dial (Ch.) 20: 299. — Atlan. 77: 830. — (J. L. Gilder) Critic, 28: 325.
— on Immortality. Spec. 76: 699.
— Personal Recollections and Unpublished Letters. (A. Fields) Cent. 27: 505.
— Personal Tributes to. Writer, 7: 161, 183.
— a Poem. (C. G. D. Roberts) Dial (Ch.) 19: 169.
— Recollections of. (E. E. Hale) Arena, 15: 21.
— Religion of his Poems. (M. J. Savage) Arena, 11: 41.
— Reminiscences of. (E. S. Phelps) McClure, 7: 114.
— Sic Sedebat. Atlan. 77: 830.
— To, on 83d Birthday, a poem. (J. G. Whittier) Atlan. 70: 401.
— With the Autocrat. Lippinc. 55: 107.
— with his Classmates. (S. May) Harv. Grad. M. 3: 154, 159.
— Works. Spec. 69: 387.
Holmes, Judge O. W., Sentimental Jingoism of. (W. P. Garrison) Nation, 61: 440.
Hololepta Fossularis, Larva and Pupa of. (H. F. Wickham) Am. Natural. 28: 816.
Holst, Hans P. (R. N. Bain) Ath. '93, 1: 734.
Holst, Hermann von. Awakening. (V. Yarros) Am. J. Pol. 5: 496.
Holst, L. Art J. 48: 238.
Holt, Joseph, Irish Rebel Leader. (C. J. Hamilton) Time, 20: 304.
Holtzendorff, Franz von. (E. Grueber) Law Q. 5: 190.
Holtzendorff's Encyclopädie. (E. Grueber) Law Q. 1: 62.
Holy Alliance, The, Doctrine of. (T. F. Wright) N. Church R. 1: 201.
Holy Coat, Blood Stains on the. (E. Gautier) New Sci. R. 1: 157.
Holy Days. (P. Marshall) Open Court, 7: 3554.
Holy Grail, Legend of. (M. Gaster) Folk-Lore, 2: 50, 198. — (A. Nutt) Folk-Lore, 2: 211.
Holy Island Pilgrimage. (E. Skelding) Atlan. 77: 325.
Holy Land. *See* Palestine.
Holy Mountain, The. (E. W. Hopkins) Nation, 63: 491.
Holy Sepulchre at Jerusalem, Sunday Morning at Church of. (T. Conant) Canad. M. 4: 531.
— Life at the. (G. Schilling) No. Am. 159: 77.
Holy Spirit and His Office. (H. H. W. Hibshman) Ref. Q. 40: 259.
— as the Administrator of the Church. (J. Cook) Our Day, 15: 288.
— as known to Science. (J. Cook) Our Day, 15: 77.
— Doctrine of the. (S. M. Merrill) Meth. R. 56: 513.
— The Female of the Godhead. (F. Jay) Open Court, 10: 4770.
— in Natural Law. (J. Cook) Our Day, 15: 181.
— in Scripture, Science, and Life. (J. Cook) Our Day 14: 176.
— New Church Belief concerning. (P. B. Cabell) N. Church R. 2: 74. — (E. D. Daniels) N. Church R. 2: 369.
— Offices of. (E. H. Johnson) Bib. Sac. 49: 361.
— Scriptural Teaching respecting. (F. B. Denio) J. Bib. Lit. 15: 135.
Holyoake, G. J. Autobiography. Ath. '92, 2: 909. — Sat. R. 74: 688.
Holywell, Wales, in 1894. (M. Maher) Month, 83: 153.
Holywood, Christopher. (E. Hogan) Month, 78: 398, 554. 79: 104, 243.
Homans, Smith, with portrait. (S. Homans) Bank. M. (N. Y.) 52: 23.
Homburg and its Waters. (N. E. Yorke-Davies) Gent. M. n. s. 57: 88.
Home, D. D., Case of Mrs. Lyon against. Green Bag, 6: 222.
Home, American. Shall it be saved? (W. S. Beard) Am. M. Civics, 8: 113.
— Four Pillars of. (R. F. Horton) Good Words, 33: 281.
— Hope of a. (E. Wiman) No. Am. 156: 228.
— Study at, for School-children. Lend a H. 14: 131.
Home again. (J. W. Riley) Cent. 26: 551.
Home again; a story. (E. E. Hale) Lend a H. 8: 10.
Home again, 40 to 1; a sketch. (S. J. Robertson) Canad M. 8: 87.
Home Arts and Industries. Spec. 73: 14.
— Association for. (E. L. Jebb) M. of Art, 8: 294.
Home at Last; a poem. (C. Scott) Theatre, 28: 12.
Home-beauty; a poem. (A. Dobson) M. of Art, 6: 277.
Home-coming. Cornh. 68: 186.
Home Culture. (G. W. Cable) Outl. 51: 952.
Home Life. (P. Browne) Ecl. M. 124: 767.
— English and American. (P. Collier) Forum, 17: 345.
Home-making, Architecture of. (C. E. Benton) Engin. M. 11: 696.
Home Missions; the Minute-Man on the Frontier. Chaut. 19: 598.
Home-ownership, Decadence of, in the United States. (J. A. Collins) Am. M. Civics, 6: 56. — Reply. (G. L. Eberhart) Am. M. Civics, 6: 291. — (H. L. Bliss) Am. M. Civics, 7: 361.
Home Rule. (J. D. Miller) Am. J. Pol. 4: 25.
— and British Industry. Spec. 68: 806.
— and Federation, American View of. (A. Shaw) Contemp. 62: 305.
— — Reply. (T. Raleigh) Contemp. 62: 525.
— and the Irish Party. (T. P. O'Connor) Contemp. 70: 179.
— Campaign for. (J. Chamberlain) National, 23: 305.
— English Elections, 1892, and. (Argyll) No. Am. 155: 129.
— Forms of. (R. T. Reid) Contemp. 61: 472.
— — Reply. (G. Pitts-Lewis) Contemp. 61: 779.
— How to drive Home Rule Home. (F. Harrison) Fortn. 58: 273.
— in Canada. Sat. R. 74: 162.
— in the Colonies. (J. MacLachlan) Westm. 142: 497.
— in Croatia. (D. Crawford) Contemp. 63: 316.
— in Guernsey and Jersey. (H. G. Keene) Westm. 140: 138.
— in Ireland. *See* Ireland.
— in the Isle of Man. (A. N. Laughton) Westm. 142: 361.
— in Norway. Sat. R. 78: 476.
— Lord Knutsford and Colonial Opinion on. (E. J. C. Morton) Contemp. 61: 214.
— Mr. Bright's Compromise. Contemp. 70: 1.
— The New House of Commons and the Irish Question. (A. J. Balfour) No. Am. 155: 641.
— New Political Departure. (M. MacColl) Univ. R. 1: 457.
— Nonconformists and. (H. M. Bompas) Fortn. 58: 6.
— Provincial. (Marquis of Lorne) Contemp. 62: 258.
— Rally for. (A. Webb) Nation, 63: 211.
— Scotland's Revolt against. (R. Wallace) New R. 8: 1.
— *Sine qua non* of. (W. T. Stead) Contemp. 62: 753.
— The Taxpayer under. Blackw. 154: 587.
— Ulster and. Contemp. 62: 16.
— United States and. Spec. 71: 170.
— Vindication of. (W. E. Gladstone) No. Am. 155: 385.

Home Rule, What has become of? (J. E. Redmond) 19th Cent. **36**: 665.
See Ireland.
Home Secretary, The; a story. (Carmen Sylva) Sund. M. **21**: 49, 102.
Homesickness; a poem. Cornh. **66**: 71.
Home-winning Problems. (J. L. Payne) Canad. M. **2**: 18.
Home Work, The Cry against. (A. Heather-Bigg) 19th Cent. **36**: 970.
Homeless at Night. (L. Noble) Eng. Illust. **9**: 572.
Homer. (A. Lang) Scrib. M. **12**: 500.
— and the Epic, Lang's. Church Q. **37**: 472. — (J. H. McDaniels) Nation, **58**: 314. — (P. Shorey) Dial (Ch.) **15**: 15. — Sat. R. **75**: 325. — Spec. **70**: 423.
— and the Higher Criticism. (A. Lang) National, **18**: 758.
— and Recent Discoveries. Quar. **175**: 372.
— Chapman's Translation. Spec. **70**: 515.
— Clerke's. Sat. R. **73**: 520.
— Comic Ballads of. (T. Hodgins) Canad. M. **3**: 1.
— Figures of. (J. H. Caverno) And. R. **17**: 146.
— Humor of, Butler on. Spec. **68**: 555.
— Iliad, Companion to, Leaf's. Sat. R. **74**: 106.
— — Song of Roland and. (A. Lang) National, **20**: 195.
— — Womanhood in. (W. C. Lawton) Atlan. **71**: 784.
— Landscapes of. (W. W. Lloyd) Portfo. **23**: 37, 51.
— Local Cults in. (A. Fairbanks) New World, **4**: 716.
— Odyssey, in Art. (E. Parsons) Chaut. **17**: 3.
— — Plot of. (W. C. Lawton) Atlan. **76**: 319.
— — Topography of. (S. Butler) Ath. '92, **1**: 149, 245.
— — Trans. by Palmer. Sat. R. **73**: 220.
— Odyssey VI., Bain on. (F. M. Bronson) School R. **4**: 111.
— Picturesque in. (W. W. Lloyd) Portfo. **24**: 193, 208.
— To-day. (A. B. Hyde) Meth. R. **55**: 894.
— Translating. (R. Garnett) Univ. R. **5**: 226.
— Writing in. (W. Ridgeway and others) Acad. **48**: 54–147.
Homeric Hymns, Text of. (T. W. Allen) J. Hel. Stud. **15**: 136, 251.
Homeric Warfare. (J. B. Bury) National, **28**: 334.
Homes, Rev. William, of Chilmark, Martha's Vineyard, Diary of. (C. E. Banks) N. E. Reg. **48**: 446. **49**: 413. **50**: 155.
Homes, American; Are they Decreasing? (G. L. Eberhart) Am. M. Civics, **6**: 291.
— — Development of. (M. G. Van Rensselaer) Forum, **12**: 667.
— — Workingman's Plea for. (J. B. Hammond) Am. M. Civics, **8**: 56.
— Broken. (J. Watson) Sund. M. **25**: 85.
— for Girls, Miss Steer's. (M. P. Bolton) Sund. M. **23**: 678.
— for Wage-earners, Need of Better. (C. de Graffenried) Forum, **21**: 301.
— for the Working Classes. Soc. Econ. **1**: 10. — Lend a H. **12**: 99. — Chamb. J. **73**: 601.
See Housing.
— Owned and Rented. (J. C. Rose) Nation, **57**: 114.
Homestead, Pa., and its Perilous Trades. (H. Garland) McClure, **3**: 3.
— as seen by One of its Workmen. McClure, **3**: 163.
— Labor Troubles at. (F. W. Taussig) Econ. J. **3**: 307. — Pub. Opin. **13**: 345. **14**: 203. — (J. D. Weeks) M. Chr. Lit. **6**: 372. — (G. T. Curtis) No. Am. **155**: 364. — (W. C. Oates) No. Am. **155**: 355. — (T. V. Powderly) No. Am. **155**: 370. — (E. C. Hegeler) Open Court, **6**: 3351. — (W. M. Jones) Am. J. Pol. **1**: 275.
Homestead, Pa., Labor Troubles at, The Lesson of; a Remedy for Labor Troubles. (C. F. Black) Forum, **14**: 14.
— — Merits of. (D. MacG. Means) Nation, **55**: 22.
— — Congressman Oates' Report on. (H. White) Nation, **55**: 99.
— — Object Lesson of. (J. B. Walker) Cosmopol. **13**: 572.
— — Reflections on. (J. Hawthorne) Engin. M. **3**: 759.
— — Warring Protectionists. (D. MacG. Means) Nation, **55**: 40.
Homicide, Enrich Ferri on. (H. Zimmern) Pop. Sci. Mo. **49**: 828.
— How to arrest the Increase of, in America. (T. C. Parker) No. Am. **162**: 667.
— in the U. S. (E. Wakefield) Liv. Age, **192**: 27.
— — in 1890, Census Report on. J. Statis. Soc. **55**: 474.
— When is it Justifiable? (C. K. Whipple) Open Court, **2**: 1236.
Homicides, American and Southern. (Van Buren Denslow) Soc. Econ. **8**: 163.
Homilies, A Discourse on the. Macmil. **69**: 139.
Homing of Animals. (J. Weir, jr.) Lippinc. **58**: 687.
Homologies and Analogies. (W. T. Freeman) Gent. M. n. s. **52**: 37.
Honduras, British. Leis. Hour, **43**: 783. — Macmil. **75**: 41.
— Paddling a Pipanti in. (E. W. Perry) Outing, **27**: 396.
Honest Heathen; a story. (E. S. Cummins) Lippinc. **50**: 783.
Honest People; a story. (Paul Heyse) Cosmopol. **20**: 649.
Honey and Honey Bees. (C. G. Ridout) Munsey, **9**: 340.
— and Honey Plants. (G. G. Groff) Pop. Sci. Mo. **43**: 545.
— Out of the Lion. (F. M. Abbott) New Eng. M. n. s. **10**: 619.
Honeymoon, The; a story. (G. Gissing) Eng. Illust. **11**: 895.
Honeymoon on Wheels, A. (H. Follett) Outing, **29**: 3.
Honeysuckle; Lonicera Karolkomii. (O. Stapf) Garden & F. **7**: 34.
Honeysuckles. Garden & F. **9**: 344.
— Climbing. (J. G. Jack) Garden & F. **6**: 314.
Hong-Kong. Asia. R. **22**: 338.
— and the Straits Settlements. (R. S. Gundry) Fortn. **63**: 965.
— English Colony in, Jubilee of, 1891. Cornh. **65**: 188.
— Plague in. Un. Serv. M. **11**: 60.
Honnie; a Study of Irish Peasant Life. Temp. Bar, **104**: 367. Same art. Liv. Age, **204**: 793.
Honor, Court of; is it Possible? (J. M'Crea) Time, **2**: 641.
— Unpublished Essay on, by Aaron Burr. (W. E. Curtis) Cosmopol. **21**: 557.
Honor among Thieves; a story. (S. Gibney) Belgrav. **78**: Holiday no., 33.
Honorable Actions, Inspiring Pupils to. (J. M. Richardson) Educa. **12**: 283.
Honorable Jane, The; a novel. (Mrs. P. Cudlip) Belgra. vols. 77–79.
Honorable Patrick Kilfinane Winch; a story. (M. Carmichael) Temp. Bar, **106**: 253.
Honorat, St.: Iona of the South. (H. MacMillan) Thinker, **9**: 295, 392.
Honoré, Henry H., with portrait. (H. L. Conard) Nat'l M. (N. Y. '91) **16**: 718.
Honorius and Liberius, Pontiffs. (A. F. Marshall) Am. Cath. Q. **19**: 82.
Honoweable Intentions; a story. All the Year, **73**: 187.
Hooch, Pieter de. (T. Cole) Cent. **27**: 700.

Hood, Sir Samuel. Letters, 1781-83; ed. by Hannay. Sat. R. **82**: 222.
Hood, Thomas. (C. A. Price) Belgra. **83**: 178. — (M. M. Trumbull) Open Court, **1**: 461. — (W. J. Rolfe) Poet-Lore, **8**: 535. — With portrait. Acad. **50**: 498.
Hood, Mt., Ascent of. (E. M. Wilbur) Outing, **24**: 348.
Hooft, Pieter Corneliszoon. (G. Edmundson) Eng. Hist. R. **9**: 77.
Hooghly, Bubbles from the. Liv. Age, **210**: 395.
Hook, James Clarke. (W. W. Fenn) M. of Art, **2**: 10. — With portrait. R. of Rs. (N. Y.) **9**: 695.
Hook, Theodore. (W. S. Walsh) Lippinc. **51**: 759. — (G. Saintsbury) Macmil. **69**: 105.
— Satirist and Novelist. Temp. Bar, **103**: 465. Same art. Liv. Age, **204**: 3.
— Unpublished Letters of. (F. G. Waugh) Gent. M. n. s. **56**: 338.
Hooker, Rev. Thomas, Origin and Ancestry of. (E. Hooker) N. E. Reg. **47**: 189.
Hooks, Ancient Bronze, Double. Reliquary, **35**: 38.
Hop, Hornbeam, Ostrya Knowltoni, a New Species of. (F. V. Coville) Garden & F. **7**: 114.
Hop-picker, Day as a. All the Year, **73**: 180.
Hop-picking in California. (N. Eames) Cosmopol. **16**: 27.
— in a Washington Hopfield. (L. H. Wall) Atlan. **74**: 379.
Hope, Anthony. *See* Hawkins, A. Hope.
Hope, Duty of. (B. J. Snell) Sund. M. **23**: 229.
Hope; a story. (E. E. Green) Sund. M. **22**: 129-273.
Hope Deferred. (L. A. North) Lippinc. **51**: 348.
Hope of the Universe, The. (G. Macdonald) Sund. M. **21**: 659, 770.
Hopkin's Safe; a story. (W. L. Alden) Idler, **6**: 43.
Hopkins, Mark. (F. H. Kasson) Educa. **14**: 164. — With portrait. Bk. Buyer, **4**: 220.
— Carter's Life of. (E. P. Anderson) Dial (Ch.) **13**: 17.
Hoppe-Seylier, Ernest Felix Immanuel. (A. Gamgee) Nature, **52**: 575, 623.
Hopper's Old Man. (R. C. V. Meyers) Scrib. M. **19**: 247.
Hopper's Wife, A; a story. (F. A. McKenzie) Eng. Illust. **12**: no. 6, 71.
Hoppner, John. (R. Walker) Good Words, **33**: 94.
Hops and Hop-pickers. (C. E. Edwardes) National, **22**: 59. Same art. Ecl. M. **121**: 516. Same art. Liv. Age, **199**: 249.
— Eelworm Disease of. (J. Percival) Nat. Sci. **6**: 187.
Hopscotch, Game of, as Played in Denmark. (H. F. Feilberg) Folk-Lore, **6**: 359.
Horace. (W. Everett) Atlan. **76**: 18. — Macmil. **65**: 423. Same art. Ecl. M. **118**: 742. Same art. Liv. Age, **193**: 731. — Quar. **174**: 127.
— and the Elegiac Poets, Sellar's. (A. S. Wilkins) Acad. **41**: 81.
— and his Translators. Quar. **180**: 111.
— Carmen Seculare; a poem. (S. E. De Vere) Temp. Bar, **103**: 492.
— Criticism of. Eng. R. **18**: 147.
— Hexametrical. Atlan. **71**: 426.
— in English. (Chas. Cooper) Gent. M. n. s. **57**: 455. Same art. Liv. Age, **211**: 611.
— Love Odes. (W. E. Gladstone) 19th Cent. **35**: 701.
— Ode 11, Bk. 3, Translated. (S. E. De Vere) Ecl. M. **120**: 71.
— Odes, Gladstone's Edition. (E. A. Meredith) Canad. M. **5**: 102. — (H. T. Henry) Am. Cath. Q. **20**: 327. — (E. D. A. Morshead) Acad. **46**: 487. — Blackw. **156**: 793. — Sat. R. **78**: 537.
— Sabine Farm of. (J. A. Lawson) Walford's Antiq. **3**: 288.
Horace, trans. by Milman. Eng. R. **11**: 260.
Horace Chase; a novel. (C. F. Woolson) Harper, **86**: 198-882. **87**: 140-755.
Horatio as a Friend. (H. P. Goddard) Poet-Lore, **7**: 203.
Horden, Bishop. (A. R. Buckland) Sund. M. **22**: 526.
Horn and Horn-books. Walford's Antiq. **2**: 165.
— Impressed, English Work in. (C. H. Read) Portfo. **24**: 23.
Horn-book, History of the, Tuer's. Bibliographica, **3**: 353. — (P. L. Ford) Nation, **63**: 129.
Horn, Cape, Adventure off. All the Year, **75**: 423.
Hornaday, W. T., with portrait. Bk. News, **14**: 421.
Hornbills, Remarkable Nests of. (J. Buckland) Eng. Illust. **15**: 363.
Hornblower Family of N. J. Nat'l M. (N. Y. '91) **18**: 189.
Hornby, Sir Geoffrey T. P. (W. L. Clowes) National, **25**: 226. — Sat. R. **79**: 309. — (W. E. G. Fisher) Acad. **50**: 254.
Horne, Herbert P. Diversi Colores. (L. Johnson) Acad. **42**: 355.
Horner, Fred. Happy Returns; a Farcical Comedy. Theatre, **28**: 205.
Hornets; a Familiar Guest. (W. H. Gibson) Harper, **91**: 76.
Horoscope of Pharaoh, The; a story. (A. Upward) Idler, **10**: 624.
Horoscope of Two Portraits; a story. (C. Wheeler) Harper, **91**: 303.
Horrid Suspicion, A; a story. (H. C. Marillier) Idler, **5**: 647.
Horse, The. (N. S. Shaler) Scrib. M. **16**: 566.
— and his Competitors. (R. L. Seymour) Chaut. **22**: 196.
— Arabian. (H. C. Merwin) Atlan. **70**: 58.
— — Mistakes about. Sat. R. **77**: 63.
— — Origin of. (W. S. Blunt) New R. **15**: 46.
— — Tweedie on. Blackw. **157**: 424. — Ed. R. **180**: 198. — Sat. R. **77**: 506. — Un. Serv. (Phila.) **13**: 328.
— from an Artistic Point of View. (H. Hayes) J. Soc. Arts, **42**: 21.
— Future of the. Sat. R. **82**: 579.
— The Greek. (J. H. McDaniels) Nation, **57**: 432.
— Hackney. (L. N. Megargee) Lippinc. **49**: 203.
— How to teach to jump. (T. A. Dodge) Idler, **9**: 697.
— in America. (C. T. Dodge) No. Am. **155**: 667.
— — Fiction and Truth on the. (E. L. Trouessart) Science, **20**: 188.
— London, at Home. Liv. Age, **200**: 510.
— of Apollo. Am. Arch. **46**: 128.
— of Modern Fiction. Spec. **70**: 43.
— of Society. (E. B. Abercrombie) Outing, **27**: 320.
— on Ancient Monuments. (J. H. S. Moxly) National, **21**: 562.
— or Motor. (O. McKee) Lippinc. **57**: 379.
— Owning a, Experience in. (E. J. Hardy) Gent. M. n. s. **51**: 489.
— Paces of the, in Art. (W. G. Simpson) M. of Art, **6**: 198.
— Teeth of. (W. G. Ridewood) Nat. Sci. **6**: 249.
— Trotting, Development of. Pub. Opin. **13**: 523.
— — Evolution of the. (H. Busberg) Scrib. M. **19**: 564, 699.
— Wild Traits in Tame Animals. (L. Robinson) No. Am. **158**: 477.
— Worship of the. Spec. **68**: 637.

Horse Chestnut, Dwarf. (J. G. Jack) Garden & F. 7: 444.
Horse-market, The. (H. C. Merwin) Cent. 27: 691.
Horse Progress on the Pacific Coast. Overland, n. s. 26: 622.
Horse-racing, Curzon on. Sat. R. 73: 608.
— Derby Anecdotes. (H. B. Bromhead) Eng. Illust. 10: 663.
— Fascinations of. (T. Longueville) New R. 6: 740.
— in America, The Spirit of. (J. G. Speed) Forum, 21: 109.
— in Australia. (S. Dickinson) Scrib. M. 12: 577.
— in England. Spec. 69: 953.
— La revanche de Vaterloo. Temp. Bar, 98: 592.
— Tendencies of. (C. H. Crandall) No. Am. 159: 373.
See also Turf, The.
Horse Show, Coming, at San Francisco. Overland, n. s. 24: 409.
— at New York, 1892, Lessons of. Outing, 19: 384.
Horse-training. (W. J. Gordon) Leis. Hour, 44: 524.
Horseback-riding, Cesaresco on. Sat. R. 77: 341.
— The Inheritance of the Centaur. Atlan. 72: 575.
Horseback Sketches. (J. F. O'Donnell) Outing, 19: 307 — 21: 11.
Horseless Age, The. (H. W. Fischer) Munsey, 13: 143.
Horseless Carriages in France. Soc. Econ. 9: 278.
— Progress and Future of. Idler, 9: 577.
— Some Speculations regarding Rapid Transit. (J. B. Walker) Cosmopol. 20: 26.
See Automobile.
Horseman, Professional. (H. C. Merwin) Atlan. 74: 201.
Horsemanship. Un. Serv. (Phila.) 15: 211. — (F. A. Munsey) Munsey, 6: 56.
— and Polo. (F. Keene) Lippinc. 49: 336.
— Art of. Quar. 183: 139.
— Riders, Algerian. (T. A. Dodge) Harper, 87: 256.
— — of Egypt. (T. A. Dodge) Harper, 87: 626.
— — of Syria. (T. A. Dodge) Harper, 87: 771.
— — of Tunis. (T. A. Dodge) Harper, 87: 406.
— — of Turkey. (T. A. Dodge) Harper, 87: 933.
— — of Many Lands, Dodge's. (C. C. Nott) Nation, 57: 450.
See also Riding.
Horses and Donkeys. (B. C. Finch) Gent. M. n. s. 54: 407.
— and Horse Market in London. (W. J. Gordon) Leis. H. 41: 27-531.
— Army, Shoeing of. (G. Fleming) Un. Serv. M. 5: 240.
— Breeding, for Profit. Overland, n. s. 28: 573.
— — in Austria. (F. Wrench) 19th Cent. 31: 661.
— — in India. Sat. R. 78: 206.
— City, Rough Usage of. Sat. R. 73: 40.
— Emperor William's Stud-farm and Hunting-forest. (P. Bigelow) Harper, 88: 742.
— for Draught. Sat. R. 73: 273.
— Glanders and Farcy in. (C. Colvile) National, 20: 478.
— Historic: Two Famous Charges of Napoleon and Wellington. (M. P. Jackson) M. of Art, 16: 306.
— in relation to Art. M. of Art, 1: 124-206.
— Loss of, in War. (F. Smith) Un. Serv. M. 7: 1130.
— of the Pampas. (R. B. Cunninghame-Graham) Time, 22: 370.
— Pedigrees of British and American. (J. I. Lupton) 19th Cent. 35: 922.
— Polydactyle, Recent. (O. C. Marsh) Am. J. Sci. 143: 339.
Horses, Prominent, of the Season. (E. B. Abercrombie) Outing, 29: 109.
— Ranches and Racing beyond the Rockies. (A. Bennett) Southern M. 3: 570.
— Saddle-, Training of. (J. G. Speed) Lippinc. 53: 390.
— Substitutes for, as Beasts of Burden. Spec. 71: 461.
— Trotting and Pacing Champions of 1894. Outing, 26: 181.
— — of To-day. (E. B. Abercrombie) Outing, 28: 245.
— Trotting: Kings and Queens of the Turf. Outing, 22: 97, 192, 265.
— Wild, of the Pampas. (A. Livingstone) Outing, 28: 127.
Horses; a story. (S. Crane) New R. 14: 140.
Horseshoe, Folk-lore of the. (R. M. Lawrence) J. Am. Folk-Lore, 9: 288.
Horseshoe Superstition, The. Cornh. 66: 526.
Hort, Fenton John Anthony. (A. W. Benn) Acad. 50: 321. — Sat. R. 82: 348.
— and the Cambridge School. Lond. Q. 87: 53.
— Judaistic Christianity. Church Q. 4: 187.
Hospital, In the. (J. W. Roosevelt) Scrib. M. 16: 472.
Hospital Romance, A. (A. M. Cameron) Sund. M. 23: 626.
Horticultural Congress at Chicago. Garden & F. 6: 359.
Horticultural Education. Garden & F. 5: 553. — (C. S. Sargent) Garden & F. 9: 31.
Horticultural Exhibition, London, 1892. Spec. 68: 810.
— Philadelphia. Garden & F. 8: 458.
Horticultural Novelties. (C. S. Sargent) Garden & F. 7: 61.
Horticultural Society, Iowa, Meeting of. Garden & F. 9: 8.
— Nebraska. Garden & F. 7: 39. 8: 47, 57, 67. 9: 48, 58.
— of N. J., Meeting of. Garden & F. 9: 29.
— of Pennsylvania. Garden & F. 9: 69.
— — Meeting of. Garden & F. 9: 38.
— — Spring Show of. Garden & F. 6: 137.
— of Vermont, Meeting of. Garden & F. 9: 508.
— Western N. Y., 37th-41st Annual Meetings. Garden & F. 5: 58, 70. 6: 57, 70. 7: 48, 58. 8: 58, 68, 79. 9: 49-78.
Horticultural "Sports." (C. T. Druery) Nat. Sci. 5: 265.
Horticulture. (W. H. Taplin) Garden & F. 7: 6.
— American. (C. S. Sargent) Garden & F. 7: 481.
— and Health. (C. S. Sargent) Garden & F. 9: 431.
— at the World's Fair. (C. S. Sargent) Garden & F. 6: 341.
— — Front Esplanade of Horticultural Building. (L. H. Bailey) Garden & F. 6: 379.
— — Japanese. (L. H. Bailey) Garden & F. 6: 369.
— — Plant Effects in Horticultural Building. (L. H. Bailey) Garden & F. 6: 349.
— California Experiment Centres. (C. H. Shinn) Garden & F. 7: 442.
— Chino Valley (Cal.) Experiment Station. (C. H. Shinn) Garden & F. 8: 212.
— Cold Winter, in North Carolina. (W. F. Massey) Garden & F. 6: 74.
— Education in, in France. Garden & F. 6: 284.
— Evolution of, in New England. Garden & F. 9: 168.
— Garden Herbariums. (F. W. Card) Garden & F. 8: 242.
— Improvement of Cultivated Plants. Garden & F. 7: 31.
— in Belgium. (G. Nicholson) Garden & F. 6: 353.
— in England. (W. Watson) Garden & F. 6: 204-533.
— — and America. (C. S. Sargent) Garden & F. 7: 271.
— in France. Garden & F. 6: 214.

Horticulture, in Kern Valley, California. (C. H. Shinn) Garden & F. 7: 403.
— in Mexico, Notes on. (C. G. Pringle) Garden & F. 6: 172-263.
— Institute held at Fredonia, N. Y. Garden & F. 7: 409.
— Kansas State Soc'y, 26th Annual Meeting. Garden & F. 5: 622.
— Notes on a Summer Journey in Europe. (J. G. Jack) Garden & F. 6: 4-140.
— A Novel School of. (C. S. Sargent) Garden & F. 8: 21.
— Schools of. (C. S. Sargent) Garden & F. 8: 471. — (L. Bevier) Garden & F. 8: 508.
— Selecting Shrubs for Planting. (C. S. Sargent) Garden & F. 6: 321.
— Specialized. Garden & F. 5: 565.
— Study of Principles as a Help in. Garden & F. 8: 511.
— Why do some New Varieties Fail? (L. H. Bailey) Garden & F. 6: 2.
— World's Debt to. (D. B. Alsted) Chaut. 23: 709.
Horton, Robert Forman. (O. A. Curtis) Meth. R. 54: 252.
— at Home. Sund. M. 22: 735.
Horton, Samuel Dana. (F. A. Walker) Econ. J. 5: 304. — (F. W. Holls) R. of Rs. (N. Y.) 11: 412.
Hosanna of Ka-Bob; a story. (F. Crissey) Arena, 8: 379.
Hosea. (C. H. Cornill) Open Court, 9: 4479.
Hosken, James Dryden. Dramas. (E. D. A. Morshead) Acad. 42: 125. — Spec. 69: 230.
Hospital Construction. (C. E. Owen-Smith) Am. Arch. 42: 147.
Hospital Management in London. (J. C. Collins) Sat. R. 81: 594.
Hospital Nurse, Experiences of a. (K. M. Warren) Sund. M. 25: 433.
Hospital Stories. (G. B. Burgin) Chamb. J. 70: 206, 780.
Hospitalfield Mansion. (A. H. Millar) Art J. 48: 246.
Hospitals and Asylums of the World, Burdett's. (J. S. Billings) Nation, 56: 240.
— and Public Health. (J. S. Billings) Lend a H. 11: 168.
— Architecture of Modern. (E. C. Gardner) Engin. M. 9: 1086.
— Financial Support of. Lend a H. 14: 45.
— Floating. (R. B. Tobey) Lend a H. 11: 356.
— Hard Labor in. (Gertrude Dix) Westm. 140: 627.
— in London, Metropolitan. (H. C. Bourne) Macmil. 66: 362. — (Chas. Marvin) Time, 15: 1.
— Modern. Quar. 177: 464.
— — European. (Alphonse de Calonne) Archit. Rec. 6: 29.
— Needs of our. (Walter Pye) Time, 14: 427.
— Planning of. (A. Hutton) Am. Arch. 45: 64.
— Ventilation of. (M. Wyman) Am. Arch. 48: 47, 102.
Hostess by Proxy; a story. (Mrs. Armstrong) Belgra. 79: 190.
Hot Trail, A; a story. (P. Clarke) Cosmopol. 17: 706.
Hot Wave in England, Aug., 1893. Nature, 48: 395.
— in Europe, 1892. (Sir R. S. Ball) Contemp. 62: 478. Same art. Ecl. M. 119: 782.
Hotchkiss, Chauncey C., with portrait. Bookman, 2: 274.
Hotel, American, of To-day. (R. C. Hawkins; W. J. Fanning) No. Am. 157: 197.
Hotel du Cheval Blanc; a story. Argosy, 54: 412.
Hotel Life, Ethics of. (E. L. Linton) Chamb. J. 70: 721.
Hotels, Cuisine of Large. (I. H. Brainerd) Chaut. 19: 421.
— Past and Present of. Atlan. 70: 424.
Hotman, François. Franco-Gallia. (H. M. Baird) Am. Hist. R. 1: 609.
Houdon, Jean-Antoine. (C. Phillips) Art J. 45: 78. — (A. E. Hake) M. of Art, 7: 280.
— Three Newly Discovered Busts by. (P. Valéry) Art J. 48: 228.
Hough, Richard. (O. Hough) Pennsyl. M. 18: 20.
Houghton, Arthur Boyd, a forgotten Book-illustrator. (L. Housman) Bibliographica, 1: 275.
Houghton, Henry O., with portrait. Bk. Buyer, 12: 501. — (J. H. Ward) New Eng. M. n. s. 13: 159. — Lit. W. (Bost.) 26: 280. — Critic, 27: 136.
— a Representative Publisher. (Margaret Deland) Outl. 52: 700.
Hounds and Hunting, Irish. (T. S. Blackwell) Outing, 25: 393.
Hour and the Man; a story. (R. Barr) Eng. Illust. 11: 1139. Same art. McClure, 5: 45.
Hour is near, The; a poem. (W. J. Armstrong) Arena, 9: 134.
Hour of her Life, The; a story. (Mabel E. Wotten) Temp. Bar, 105: 107.
House of Commons. (J. W. Longley) Canad. M. 6: 27. — (M. J. Wright) Arena, 13: 31. — (S. Low) 19th Cent. 36: 146. — (A. Birrell) Scrib. M. 14: 593.
— and the House of Representatives. (H. A. Herbert) No. Am. 158: 255. — (H. Taylor) No. Am. 159: 225. — (R. F. D. Palgrave) No. Am. 161: 740.
— at Work. (M. MacDonagh) Temp. Bar, 109: 413. Same art. Liv. Age, 211: 704.
— Business of. (Chas. Bradlaugh) Univ. R. 2: 145.
— Can it be Saved? (H. Spender) New R. 9: 409.
— Chamberlain on. Spec. 68: 421.
— Decline of. (S. Low) 19th Cent. 37: 567. Same art. Liv. Age, 205: 411.
— Enlargement of. (C. Barry) 19th Cent. 33: 541.
— "Gag" in. (T. W. Russell; J. E. Redmond; Viscount Cranborne) New R. 9: 113.
— Humors of. Chamb. J. 72: 183. Same art. Ecl. M. 124: 700.
— If it were Abolished? Liv. Age, 204: 88.
— Ladies' Gallery. Chamb. J. 69: 113.
— Lobby of. Chamb. J. 69: 209.
— Management of. Macmil. 65: 477.
— Members of, Payment of. Spec. 70: 380.
— The New, 1892. (J. C. Rose) Nation, 54: 462.
— A Night in the Reporters' Gallery. (M. MacDonagh) 19th Cent. 37: 516. Same art. Liv. Age, 205: 50.
— Obstruction in: what is it? (L. Courtney and others) New R. 8: 385.
— Peers and. (St. L. Strachey) Contemp. 61: 725.
— A Plea for Action. (J. F. Moulton) Contemp. 67: 305.
— Relation of the House of Lords to. (G. W. Prothero) National, 25: 259.
— Romance of. (Chas. Bradlaugh) Univ. R. 3: 317. 4: 92.
— The Speaker in. (A. Webb) Nation, 57: 116.
— — Powers of. Spec. 68: 389.
— Speakership of. (D. Crawford) Nation, 60: 253.
— The Stranger in. Macmil. 65: 394. 66: 395.
— Structure, Rules and Habits of. (T. P. O'Connor) Harper, 88: 34.
— Unpopularity of. (T. Mackay) National, 27: 802. — Spec. 71: 388.
— Voting Supplies in. (M. MacDonagh) Chamb. J. 73: 529.

House of the Dragons, The; a story. (I. M. van Etten) Cosmopol. **14**: 615.
House of Lords. Ed. R. **178**: 404. — (R. W. McL. Fullarton) Jurid. R. **6**: 257. — (Sir H. S. Northcote) National, **24**: 685. — Green Bag, **7**: 329. — (Lord Ribblesdale) 19th Cent. **38**: 199. — (B. D. Mackenzie) Westm. **141**: 68. — (D. Crawford) Nation, **59**: 402. — (G. W. Smalley) Harper, **88**: 686.
— Abolish its Veto. (T. W. Reid) 19th Cent. **35**: 553.
— and the Home Rule Bill. (Earl of Donoughmore) No. Am. **157**: 298.
— and Ireland. (J. J. O'Shea) Cath. World, **60**: 51.
— An Appeal. (St. Loe Strachey) National, **22**: 738. Same art. Ecl. M. **122**: 449.
— as a Constitutional Force: a Symposium. New R. **10**: 257.
— as a Court of Appeal, The. (M. MacDonagh) Good Words, **37**: 808.
— Besant on. Critic, **25**: 220.
— A Dangerous Anachronism. (T. Burt) 19th Cent. **35**: 547.
— Edinburgh Review and. Spec. **71**: 571.
— History of, Pike's. Sat. R. **78**: 458.
— How to mend the. (Earl of Meath) 19th Cent. **37**: 195.
— How to preserve. (A. R. Wallace) Contemp. **65**: 114.
— Lord Rosebery's Enterprise against. (L. A. A. Jones) 19th Cent. **36**: 837. — (Lord Salisbury) National, **24**: 450. — Spec. **73**: 601.
— Lord Salisbury and the. (R. B. Haldane) National, **24**: 705.
— — Mr. Haldane's Policy. (A. Lyttleton) National, **24**: 863.
— Lords and Commons; a dialogue. (H. D. Traill) National, **23**: 742.
— Macpherson on. Spec. **70**: 487. — Sat. R. **75**: 298.
— Peculiarities of the Upper House. Chamb. J. **71**: 769.
— Plea for Deliberation. (J. F. Moulton) Contemp. **67**: 153.
— Position of. Westm. **142**: 22. — (Lord Hobhouse) Contemp. **66**: 774. Same art. Liv. Age, **204**: 32.
— Reform of the. (F. S. Pulling) Time, **18**: 401. — (Pembroke) Univ. R. **1**: 100.
— A Reformed. (T. A. Le Mesurier) Westm. **143**: 413.
— Shall Indian Princes sit in? (Earl Meath) 19th Cent. **35**: 710.
— Sham Crusade. National, **24**: 355.
— Short Way with. (J. G. Swift McNeill) Fortn. **63**: 1.
— since the Reform Act. (C. B. Roylance-Kent) Fortn. **63**: 14.
— Single-chamber Democrats. (R. Wallace) 19th Cent. **37**: 177.
— Stability of. (J. C. Hopkins) Forum, **17**: 329.
— A Strong Second Chamber. (E. S. Beesly) Fortn. **54**: 161.
— a Suggestion. (E. S. Robertson) National, **20**: 574.
— An Unfair Penalty on Peers. (G. Smith) 19th Cent. **35**: 525.
— Unionists and the. (A. V. Dicey) National, **24**: 690.
— The Useless. (J. McCarthy) No. Am. **157**: 215.
— *vs.* Commons. (E. L. Godkin) Nation, **57**: 207.
House of Representatives, and the House of Commons. (H. A. Herbert) No. Am. **158**: 257. — (H. Taylor) No. Am. **159**: 225. — (R. F. D. Palgrave) No. Am. **161**: 740.
— Leaders of. (E. J. Edwards) Chaut. **20**: 186.
— Limitation of Number of Members. (M. Brosius) Arena, **6**: 569.
House of Representatives, Rules of. (R. Ogden) Nation, **54**: 102.
House Divided, The; a story. (J. D. Whiting) McClure, **6**: 370.
House of the Wicked Baker, The. Macmil. **68**: 368.
House on the Hill-top, The. (G. E. Channing) Scrib. M. **14**: 135.
House on the Lone Tree Meadow; a story. (H. P. Beach) Outing, **23**: 313.
House over the Way, The; a story. (C. E. Caryll) Scrib. M. **12**: 96.
House that Jack built. (H. P. Brewster) J. Am. Folk-Lore, **2**: 209.
House that Jack built. (P. A. Tucker) Lippinc. **53**: 281.
House they took, The; a story. (J. W. Tompkins) Munsey, **14**: 155.
House with the Broken Shutter; a story. (G. Parker) Eng. Illust. **12**: no. 1, 1.
House with the Paint wore off; a story. (M. Richardson) Lippinc. **55**: 525.
House with the Tall Porch; a story. (G. Parker) McClure, **1**: 533.
House-boat, A Painter's. (W. H. Boot) M. of Art, **11**: 309.
— Plea for. (C. L. Norton) Outing, **20**: 243.
House-hunting. All the World, **71**: 156.
House-painting; The Outer Coloring of Houses. (A. C. Meynell) M. of Art, **3**: 366.
House-plants. (J. N. Gerard) Garden & F. **6**: 416.
Household Decoration. (A. Vallance) Art J. **44**: 23-372.
Household Furnishings. (Helen Campbell) Archit. Rec. **6**: 97.
Household Management, Art of. (A. Kenney-Herbert) 19th Cent. **34**: 304.
Household Pests. Spec. **70**: 768.
Householders, The; a story. (A. Q. Couch) McClure, **6**: 421.
Housekeeping, British: is it a Success? (Ellen W. Darwin) National, **26**: 619. Same art. Ecl. M. **126**: 248.
— Coöperative. (H. C. Walsh) Lippinc. **53**: 549.
— Education in. (L. M. Salmon) New Eng. M. n. s. **10**: 185.
— Penalties of Ignorance of Scientific Methods. (E. Priestley) 19th Cent. **37**: 579.
— Schools of. (E. Priestley) 19th Cent. **32**: 652.
Housekeeping Problem, How to solve the. (F. M. Abbott) Forum, **14**: 778.
Housemaids, Boy. Spec. **77**: 204.
Housetops, The City on the. Atlan. **74**: 28.
Houses, Architects'. (J. B. Robinson) Archit. Rec. **3**: 188, 229, 354.
— Country, Modern American. (J. B. Robinson) Engin. M. **5**: 365.
— Habitable. Spec. **69**: 558.
— Old, in Praise of. (V. Paget) Longm. **20**: 287.
— Old Dutch, on the Hudson. (W. E. Ver Planck) New Eng. M. n. s. **12**: 71.
Housing, Economics of Improved. (E. R. L. Gould) Yale R. **5**: 8.
— Half a Century of Improved. (W. H. Tolman) Yale R. **5**: 288.
— of the Poor. (Robert Donald) Outl. **53**: 204.
— — in American Cities. (M. T. Reynolds) Am. Econ. Assoc. **8**: 139.
See Homes.
Housman, Lawrence. House of Joy. Sat. R. **80**: 879.
Houssaye, Arsène. Critic, **28**: 169. — (R. Davey) Theatre, **36**: 271.
Houston, Edwin J. Cassier, **6**: 184.
Houston, Sam, with portrait. Bk. News, **12**: 76.

Houston, Sam, Williams' Life of. Dial (Ch.) **15**: 257. — (J. C. Welling) Nation, **58**: 90.
Hovey, Richard. (H. Aïdé) 19th Cent. **35**: 240.
How, George M., with portrait. (H. L. Conard) Nat'l M. (N. Y. '91) **15**: 314.
How the Battle was lost. (L. Osbourne) Scrib. M. **13**: 255.
How Mrs. Binnywig checked the King; a story. Overland, n. s. **20**: 513.
How the Captain made Christmas. (T. N. Page) Scrib. M. **14**: 779.
How Cassie saved the Spoons; a story. (A. H. Fréchette) McClure, **1**: 301.
How Dr. Davidson kept his Last Christmas at Drumtochty. (J. Watson) McClure, **8**: 114.
How Florence rings her Bells; a poem. (A. Austin) National, **21**: 289.
How Hawkins was regulated. (H. A. Parker) Lippinc. **58**: 413.
How he came out at the Other Side. (W. Canton) Good Words, **35**: Xmas no., 14.
How he left the Hotel. Argosy, **58**: 349.
How I became a Bashi-bazouk. (E. Vizetelly) Eng. Illust. **12**: no. 6, 76.
How I broke our A. D. C.; a poem. (C. Bingham) Theatre, **29**: 158.
How I found the Baron. (E. Wakefield) Lippinc. **54**: 397.
How I found Maria; a story. Overland, n. s. **19**: 481.
How I gained an Income. Lippinc. **53**: 669.
How I sent my Aunt to Baltimore. (C. S. Davison) Scrib. M. **12**: 249.
How I went Duck Hunting; a story. (C. G. Rogers) Canad. M. **4**: 164.
How Joseph won Asenath; a Story of Egypt. (S. R. Allen) Canad. M. **6**: 503.
How Keturah left the Conqueror. (F. H. Sweet) Bost. **3**: 479.
How "The Kid" won his Medal. (T. H. Wilson) Cent. **39**: 547.
How King Shaillu was punished. Macmil. **74**: 419.
How the Kroomen took the Gunboat. Chamb. J. **73**: 734.
How the La Rue Stakes were lost. (C. N. Hood) Lippinc. **56**: 384.
How the Law got into the Chaparral. (F. Remington) Harper, **94**: 60.
How the Light came. (J. A. Knox) Lippinc. **52**: 625.
How Lin McLean went East; a story. (O. Wister) Harper, **86**: 135.
How the Major learned to fish; a story. (J. E. Gunckel) Outing, **22**: 85.
How the Man-eater was killed. Chamb. J. **72**: 490.
How Martha did n't Marry a Sumpman. (F. Risom) Longm. **21**: 375. Same art. Liv. Age, **196**: 728.
How Matt lost his Nerve. (W. L. Alden) Idler, **5**: 607.
How the Minister went to Jerusalem. (Mary Bell) Overland, n. s. **28**: 671.
How the Other Half lives; Stories. (E. L. Banks and others) Eng. Illust. **11**: 845, 1063. **12**: no. 4, 59, no. 6, 43. **13**: 73-539. **14**: 51. **15**: 51, 341.
How Peg's Runners rusted. (C. F. McClure) Outing, **29**: 280.
How Phœbe came Home. (K. Wylde) Macmil. **66**: 369. Same art. Ecl. M. **119**: 621. Same art. Liv. Age, **195**: 336.
How she got out of it; a story. Cornh. **65**: 180. Same art. Liv. Age, **193**: 148.
How Sir Roger Darrell broke his Word. (E. Halsted) Sund. M. **22**: 695.
How they boomed the Elgin St. Church. (A. R. Carman) Arena, **10**: 245.
How Timmy saved the Piece. (L. B. Morse) Lippinc. **58**: 854.
How to live on Nothing a Year; a story. (Mrs. E. T. Cook) Gent. M. n. s. **54**: 433.
How Tomkins enjoyed it; a story. (E. F. Turner) Eng. Illust. **10**: 473.
How the Town was saved. Chamb. J. **72**: 541.
How Uncle Nottoway "Squashed" the Indictment. (W. A. Dromgoole) Arena, **5**: 611.
How we Apples swim; a story. (C. E. Morland) Belgra. **77**: 281.
How we played Robinson Crusoe in the Straits of Malacca. (R. Wildman) Overland, n. s. **28**: 35.
How we went Blundering; a story. (J. P. Rudd) Outing, **20**: 436.
How Whalebone caused a Wedding. (J. C. Harris) Scrib. M. **16**: 606.
Howard, Mr. George, Pictures owned by. (S. Colvin) M. of Art, **7**: 83.
Howard, H. R. (M. H. Spielmann) Ath. '95, **2**: 362.
Howard, John, Relics of. (H. Edwards) M. Am. Hist. **28**: 288.
Howard, Gen. Oliver Otis. (H. Johnson) Chaut. **20**: 198.
Howe, E. W. Bk. Buyer, **2**: 46. — With portrait. Book News, **10**: 97.
Howe, George E., with portrait. (M. D. Leggett) Nat'l M. (N. Y. '91) **16**: 353.
Howe, Henry; the Quaker Actor. Acad. **49**: 247.
— Reminiscences of. (J. Coleman and G. W. Baynham) Theatre, **36**: 263.
Howe, Joseph, and his Times. (J. W. Longley) Canad. M. **2**: 207. **3**: 531. **4**: 77. — (J. A. Cooper) Canad. M. **7**: 562.
Howe, Julia Ward, and Edwin Booth. (F. M. Howe Hall) New Eng. M. n. s. **9**: 315.
— and Her Daughters. (M. Field) Munsey, **12**: 527.
Howe, Lyman, of Sudbury, Mass. (Mrs. C. Van D. Chenoweth) New Eng. M. n. s. **10**: 265.
Howe, Maud, with portrait. Bk. Buyer, **6**: 205.
Howe, Richard, Admiral. (A. T. Mahan) Atlan. **73**: 20.
Howe, S. G., with portrait. (S. M. Jackson) Char. R. **1**: 174.
Howe, Wm., Lord, his Commission to pacify the Colonies. (P. L. Ford) Atlan. **77**: 758.
Howel the Good, Quaint Laws of. (G. H. Westley) Green Bag, **8**: 167. — All the Year, **70**: 325, 348.
Howell, James. Letters. Spec. **69**: 620.
— Prose Style of. (E. K. Chambers) Acad. **42**: 327.
Howell Family of Penn. and N. J. (M. R. J. Bellas) Am. Hist. Reg. **3**: 578. — (S. S. Robeson) Am. Hist. Reg. **4**: 59.
Howells, William Dean, with portrait. Bk. News, **5**: 41. — (M. Thompson) Bk. News, **6**: 93. — With portraits. (H. H. Boyesen) McClure, **1**: 3. — (C. P. Woolley) New Eng. M. n. s. **9**: 408.
— and his Work. (H. H. Boyesen) Cosmopol. **12**: 502.
— as a Country Printer. Scrib. M. **13**: 539.
— Boston of. (S. Baxter) New Eng. M. n. s. **9**: 129.
— English Criticism of. Critic, **25**: 193.
— Literary Methods of. (T. C. Crawford) Critic, **21**: 36.
Howland, A. C. (M. Tracy) Mo. Illust. **3**: 230.
Hoxton, Eng., Haunted. Chamb. J. **70**: 753.
Hoyt, Charles H., the Playwright. Bost. **3**: 386.
Hoyt, Colgate, with portrait. (J. H. Kennedy) Nat'l M. (N. Y. '91) **15**: 418.
Hroswitha. (G. de Dubor) Fortn. **65**: 443.
— Love-drama of. (W. H. Hudson) Poet-Lore, **4**: 489.

Hryniewicki, Charles, Bishop of Vilna, Sketch of. (M. E. Herbert) Dub. R. **117**: 265.
Hubbard, Thomas, Obituary of. N. E. Reg. **47**: 480.
Huckleberries, White. (W. G. Farlow) Garden & F. **6**: 363.
Huddleston, John W., Baron. Green Bag, **5**: 165.
Hudson, Henry, the Navigator. (Mary L. D. Ferris) M. Am. Hist. **30**: 214.
— Voyage of, and its Results. (J. G. Wilson) Nat'l M. (N. Y. '91) **15**: 221.
Hudson Family, Record of. (H. W. Lloyd) Pennsyl. M. **16**: 108.
Hudson River, Bridge Across, at N. Y. (G. Lindenthal) Engin. M. **6**: 213.
— Will it pay? (G. Lindenthal) Engin. M. **10**: 261.
— Old Dutch Houses on. (W. E. Ver Planck) New Eng. M. n. s. **12**: 71.
— Palisades of, and Orange Mountain of New Jersey. Around World, **1**: 103.
— Steamboats of. (S. W. Stanton) Engin. M. **8**: 849.
— Through Inland Waters. (H. Pyle) Harper, **92**: 828. **93**: 63.
Hudson River Fiord. (A. M. Edwards) Am. J. Sci. **143**: 182.
Hudson's Bay. (W. W. Fox) Canad. M. **1**: 31. — (G. H. Bradbury) Canad. M. **4**: 141.
— and Fort Nelson. (D. B. Read) Canad. M. **1**: 233.
— Fort Prince of Wales. (J. Schultz) Canad. M. **2**: 562.
— Is the Land around, at Present Rising? (J. B. Tyrrell) Am. J. Sci. **152**: 200.
— — Proofs of it. (R. Bell) Am. J. Sci. **151**: 219.
Hudson's Bay Company. (J. Ralph) Harper, **84**: 373.
Hudson's Bay Railway, Nature's Outlet. (H. Sutherland) Canad. M. **3**: 519.
Hudson's Bay Route. (H. Sutherland) Canad. M. **3**: 347. — (D. Macarthur) Westm. **144**: 178.
Huggate Dikes. (E. M. Cole) Antiq. n. s. **30**: 7.
Huggins, William, with portrait. Pop. Sci. Mo. **41**: 260.
Hugh Holroyd; a sketch. (W. K. Honnywell) Belgra. **83**: 800.
Hugh Wynne, Free Quaker. (S. W. Mitchell) Cent. **31**: 54, 194.
Hughes, John R., Letters of, 1743-49. Eng. Hist. R. **8**: 307.
Hughes, Thomas. Acad. **49**: 263. — (J. M. Ludlow) Econ. R. **6**: 297. — Ath. '96, **1**: 414. — Macmil. **74**: 78. Same art. Liv. Age, **209**: 819. — Spec. **76**: 443. Same art. Liv. Age, **209**: 382. — Lit. W. (Bost.) **27**: 104. — Critic, **28**: 220, 227. — With portrait. Bk. News, **12**: 241.
— and "Tom Brown." (C. D. Lanier) R. of Rs. (N. Y.) **13**: 567.
— Letter from. Critic, **28**: 258.
— Notes on. Sat. R. **81**: 320.
Hughey; a story. (R. Macknight) Scrib. M. **17**: 316.
Hugo, Victor, and Sainte-Beuve. Liv. Age, **211**: 465.
— At the Tomb of. (F. Coppée) Nat'l M. (Bost.) **4**: 497.
— Conversations and Opinions of. (O. Uzanne) Scrib. M. **12**: 558.
— Dieu. (A. C. Swinburne) Fortn. **57**: 109. Same art. Liv. Age, **192**: 569.
— Esme Stuart. Scot. R. **28**: 223.
— Hauteville House, Guernsey, Home of. (H. Rix) Good Words, **33**: 823.
— Journeys in France and Belgium. (A. Laugel) Nation, **55**: 85.
Hugo, Victor. Legend of the Centuries. (C. E. Meetkerke) Argosy, **57**: 114.
— Letters. Acad. **50**: 415. — Sat. R. **82**: 499. — (E. G. Johnson) Dial (Ch.) **21**: 247. — (P. T. Lafleur) Nation, **63**: 389.
— L'homme qui rit. Sat. R. **75**: 374.
— Mabilleau's Life of. Spec. **71**: 580. — (A. Laugel) Nation, **57**: 285.
— A Meeting with. (H. Latchford) Time, **2**: 292.
— Notes of Travel. (A. C. Swinburne) Fortn. **58**: 485.
— Recovered Papers of. Gent. M. n. s. **49**: 105.
— Social Ideals of. (B. O. Flower) Arena, **10**: 104.
— Toute la lyre. (A. C. Swinburne) 19th Cent. **34**: 733.
— Two Busts of. M. of Art, **7**: 127.
Huguenots, The. Atlan. **77**: 413. — (W. Loughman) Month, **76**: 70, 234.
— and the Edict of Nantes, Baird's. (A. C. Zenos) Presb. & Ref. R. **7**: 344. — (W. Walker) Nation, **62**: 15. — (H. E. Bourne) Dial (Ch.) **19**: 285.
— History of. Eng. R. **10**: 1.
— in New England. (H. Graves) New Eng. M. n. s. **11**: 497.
Huie, D. R. W., with portrait. Bank. M. (Lond.) **57**: 401.
Huldah, the Prophetess; a story. (K. D. Wiggin) Harper, **92**: 115.
Hulero, Home of the. (E. W. Perry) Outing, **23**: 353.
Hulke, John Whitaker. Nat. Sci. **6**: 277.
Hull, Isaac, Commodore, Birthplace of. (J. De F. Shelton) Harper, **85**: 30.
Hull, Gen. William. (S. C. Clarke) N. E. Reg. **47**: 141, 305.
— Surrender of Detroit, 1812. (S. C. Clarke) M. Am. Hist. **27**: 343.
Hull, England, Strike at. (W. H. Abraham) Econ. R. **3**: 357.
— Taking of J. Hallam at. (T. T. Wildridge) Antiq. n. s. **25**: 16.
Hull House, Chicago. (A. Miller) Char. R. **1**: 167. — (J. Addams) Forum, **14**: 226. — (H. B. Learned) Lend a H. **10**: 318. — (Emily Herndon) Chr. Un. **45**: 351.
— and its Civic Aspects. (Mrs. J. Humpal-Zeman) Pub. Opin. **20**: 364.
— Art-work done by. (J. Addams) Forum, **19**: 614.
— Maps and Papers of. (M. West) Dial (Ch.) **18**: 239.
— Settlers in the City Wilderness. Atlan. **77**: 118.
— A Social Settlement. (A. L. Muzzey) Arena, **16**: 432.
Human Automaton, Thoughts of a. (H. Blanchamp) Fortn. **27**: 390. Same art. Ecl. M. **118**: 599.
Human Body, Changes in Proportions of, During Period of Growth. (W. S. Hall) Anthrop. J. **25**: 21.
Human Cost and Utility. (J. A. Hobson) Econ. R. **6**: 10.
Human Development, Phases of. (Mona Caird) Westm. **141**: 37, 162.
Human Document, A. (W. H. Mallock) Fortn. **57**: 127-590.
Human Documents: Portraits of Distinguished People at Different Periods of their Lives. (S. O. Jewett) McClure, **1**: 16 — **3**: 345.
Human Figure, Brüke on the. Sat. R. **73**: 158.
— Proportions of the. (C. Roberts) M. of Art, **4**: 466.
Human Habitation, A; a poem. (H. Garland) Arena, **9**: 130.
Human Judgment, Reversal of. (G. Matheson) Good Words, **35**: 140.

Human Life, the Greatest Drama. (T. W. Longley) Canad. M. 1: 341.
— Quantity of. (J. L. Williams) Am. Natural. 27: 193.
Human Nature. (M. A. M. Marks) Argosy, 61: 540.
— Relation of Hume's Treatise to the Inquiry. (W. B. Elkin) Philos. R. 3: 672.
Human Problem, The, according to Law. (A. M. Diaz) Arena, 15: 619.
Human Progress, Past and Future. Arena, 5: 145.
Human Race: is it Degenerating. (H. P. Dunn) 19th Cent. 36: 301. Same art. Ecl. M. 123: 483.
Humane Ideas and Feelings, Cultivation of. (W. Mills) Pop. Sci. Mo. 43: 46.
Humane Progress in History. (H. F. Hegner) Lend a H. 15: 103.
Humanities, The. (J. W. Powell) Science, n. s. 1: 15.
Humanity, The New. (R. E. Neighbor) Bapt. R. 14: 45.
— New Movement in. (W. J. Tucker) Harv. Grad. M. 1: 17.
— on the Ocean. Spec. 69: 12.
— Religion of. (W. C. Coupland) Open Court, 1: 577.
Humbert, King of Italy. (E. Panzacchi; F. Lampertico) Chaut. 17: 593.
Humble, William Pickering, with portrait. (J. P. Bishop) Nat'l M. (N. Y. '91) 16: 724.
Humble Advocate; a story. (W. A. Dromgoole) Arena, 14: 322.
Humboldt, A., Monument to, in Berlin. (C. Balle) Garden & F. 7: 42.
Humboldt, Wilhelm von. Eng. R. 9: 1.
Humboldt, California, and its Redwoods. (M. M. Vaughan) Overland, n. s. 28: 328.
Humboldt Bay and its Jetty System. (W. E. Dennison) Overland, n. s. 28: 381.
Hum-drum Girl, A. (J. Wren) Belgra. 88: 179.
Hume, David, Huxley on. (G. G. Greenwood) Westm. 144: 1.
Hume, Fergus. Island of Fantasy. Spec. 69: 291.
Humming-bird, Ruby. (E. Phillpotts) Eng. Illust. 11: 217.
Humming-birds. (O. T. Miller) Atlan. 77: 737. — (S. Goodhue) Cosmopol. 16: 570.
— of Chocorua. (F. Bolles) Pop. Sci. Mo. 45: 588.
Humor, American, Fugitive. Time, 8: 42.
— Concerning. (J. L. Ford) Bach. of Arts, 2: 174.
— English and American. (A. Repplier) Cosmopol. 16: 361.
— Future of. (H. D. Traill) New R. 10: 27.
— — Traill on. Spec. 71: 939.
— in Dickens and Eliot. (R. Y. Tyrrell) Sat. R. 81: 521.
— Irish. (P. Glenelg) National, 18: 712.
— New, and Non-humorists. (J. L. Toole) National, 21: 449.
— On the Make-up of. (D. H. Hill, jr.) So. M. 5: 558.
— Peculiarities and Illustrations of. (T. V. Hutchinson) Canad. M. 2: 77.
— The Penalty of. (B. Matthews) Harper, 92: 897.
— Wit, Fun, and Satire. (J. R. Lowell) Cent. 25: 124.
Humor; a story. Temp. Bar, 94: 276.
Humorist, The Analytical. (H. D. Traill) Fortn. 66: 137.
— The Unconscious. Macmil. 70: 271. Same art. Liv. Age, 203: 231.
Humorists, American. (L. A. Sherman) Chaut. 22: 160.
— of the 19th Century, Four English, Lilly's. Sat. R. 80: 766.
— Three: Hook, Barham, Maginn. (G. Saintsbury) Macmil. 69: 105.
Humors of Bench and Bar. (W. H. Blake) Canad. M. 2: 166.
Humpbacking in the Friendly Islands. (F. T. Bullen) Good Words, 36: 627.
Humperdinck, Engelbert. "Hansel und Gretel." (B. Stavenhagen) Cent. 29: 257.
Humphrey, Frank P. New England Cactus. Spec. 69: 102.
Humphrey, Maud. (W. McK. Bangs) Q. Illust. 2: 31.
Humphry, Sir George Murray. Acad. 50: 240. — Ath. '96, 2: 454.
Humpty Dumpty. Cosmopol. 12: 324.
Hunchback to his Linnet, A; a poem. (G. K. Menzies) Temp. Bar, 104: 505.
Hundred, Problem of the. (E. Jenks) Eng. Hist. R. 11: 510.
Hundred, The; a story. (G. Hall) Harper, 94: 70.
Hundredth Regiment, Reminiscences of. Canad. M. 7: 269.
Hungarian Confession, The. (S. F. Smith) Month, 87: 333, 511.
Hungarian Literature, 1891-92. (L. Katscher) Ath. '92, 2: 19.
— 1892-93. (L. Katscher) Ath. '93, 2: 21.
— 1893-94. (L. Katscher) Ath. '94, 2: 19.
— 1894-95. (L. Katscher) Ath. '95, 2: 19.
— 1895-96. (L. Katscher) Ath. '96, 2: 20.
Hungarians, Origin and Early Homes of. (J. B. Bury Scot. R. 20: 1.
Hungary. (T. Lindsay) Canad. M. 7: 464.
— and the Hungarians. Eng. R. 14: 1.
— and the Vatican. (B. Molden) Fortn. 64: 33.
— at the Close of her First Millennium. (E. Reich) 19th Cent. 39: 837.
— Home Rule War in, An Episode of. (E. Castle) Temp. Bar, 99: 353.
— Millennial of. (E. I. Stevenson) Outl. 54: 504.
— — Exhibition. Sat. R. 81: 469, 496, 645.
— Nationality in, Kossuth and. (F. Amouretti) Chaut. 20: 24.
— New Marriage Law of. (F. P. Walton) Jurid. R. 8: 189.
— Sabbatarians of. (W. Bacher) Jew. Q. 2: 465.
— Sacred Crown of. (J. Horowitz) Eng. Illust. 15: 405.
— to Gipsyland. (E. R. Pennell) Cent. 23: 109, 258.
— Wandering Minstrels of. (O. Hensel) Music, 2: 425.
Hunger. Atlan. 71: 429.
Hungerford, M. H., "The Duchess," with portrait. Bk. News, 13: 5.
Hunnewell, H. S. Notes from Gardens at Natick, Mass. (T. D. Hatfield) Garden & F. 9: 278.
Hunnis, William. (Mrs. C. C. Stopes) Acad. 41: 331.
Hunnish Cemetery at Cziko. Reliquary, 35: 7.
Huns in Pennsylvania. (W. F. Gibbons) Am. M. Civics, 7: 315.
Hunt, Alfred William. Ath. '96, 1: 625. — (F. Wedmore) M. of Art, 14: 104.
Hunt, Leigh. Cornh. 65: 480. Same art. Ecl. M. 119: 28. Same art. Liv. Age, 194: 131. — (F. W. Cornish) Temp. Bar, 108: 186. Same art. Ecl. M. 127: 30. Same art. Liv. Age, 210: 3.
— and his Books. (W. I. Way) Bookworm, 7: 115.
— Dramatic Essays. Ath. '94, 2: 463.
— Monkhouse's Life of. Ath. '93, 1: 725. — (J. A. Noble) Acad. 43: 409. — Sat. R. 75: 575. — Spec. 71: 433.
Hunt, Richard Morris. (H. Van Brunt) Am. Arch. 50: 53. — Critic, 27: 89. — Am. Arch. 49: 70.
— Works of. (M. Schuyler) Archit. Rec. 5: 97.
Hunt, Thomas Sterry. Acad. 41: 187. — Ath. '92, 1: 249. — Am. J. Sci. 143: 246. — (W. Topley) Nature, 45: 400.

Hunt, Thornton, and G. H. Lewes. (Mrs. Lynn Linton) Bookman, 3: 520.
Hunt, William Holman. (J. Orrock) Art J. 47: 12. — (W. W. Fenn) M. of Art, 3: 384.
Hunt, William Morris. (H. M. Knowlton) New Eng. M. n. s. 10: 685.
Hunt, The. (R. S. Osborne) Munsey, 12: 131.
Hunter, Agnes, and Neil Livingston. (H. C. Shelley) Sund. M. 22: 109.
Hunter, Dr. John. (A. H. Millar) Acad. 45: 419.
— at Home. Sund. M. 23: 254.
Hunter, Robert, Governor of N. Y., 1710-19. (C. B. Todd) Nat'l M. (N. Y. '91) 17: 287.
Hunter, William. (A. H. Millar) Acad. 45: 419.
— and John. (G. E. Mather) Nature, 50: 169.
Hunters, Irish, Improvement of. (F. Wrench) 19th Cent. 35: 470.
Hunting and Snakes. (W. B. Lane) Un. Serv. (Phila.) 11: 317.
— as represented in Art. (J. G. Millais) M. of Art, 19: 48-348.
— Big Game, Phillipps-Wolley on. Sat. R. 77: 447.
— the Buck in Warwickshire. Eng. Illust. 16: 185.
— Christmas among the Tules. (M. B. Gibson) Outing, 25: 337.
— Craft of. Macmil. 73: 131, 291.
— A Day on the Uplands. (E. W. Sandys) Outing, 29: 72.
— in India. (E. Braddon) Blackw. 156: 387.
— — Thirty Years of. (E. Braddon) Blackw. 155: 276.
— in the Midlands. (Mary E. Kennard) Univ. R. 3: 67.
— in Modern France. (T. R. R. Stebbins) Blackw. 153: 262.
— Large Game. (N. A. Miles) No. Am. 161: 484.
— A Mixed Bag. (E. W. Sandys) Outing, 23: 65.
— Stray Shots. (O. W. Howarth) Outing, 24: 52.
— Summer. (G. Lascelles) New R. 7: 177.
— with Beagles. (B. S. Turpin) Outing, 28: 37.
— With the Hounds in France. (H. Sears) Harper, 90: 257.
Hunting of Rothiemuir; a poem. (G. R. Tomson) Art J. 44: 119.
Hunting Parties, Famous, of the Plains. (W. F. Cody) Cosmopol. 17: 131.
Hunting Recollections, Some. Macmil. 73: 192.
Huntington, Agnes. Lippinc. 49: 113.
Huntington, Collis P. (F. A. Munsey) Munsey, 9: 421.
Huntsman, Benjamin, Inventor of Crucible Steel. (R. A. Hadfield) Cassier, 7: 78.
Hunza, Nagyr, and Pamir. (G. W. Leitner) Asia. R. 13: 53.
— Language and Customs of. (G. W. Leitner) Time, 22: 579.
Huon of Bordeaux, retold by Steele. Sat. R. 81: 652.
Hurd, Harvey B., with portrait. (H. L. Conard) Nat'l M. (N. Y. '91) 17: 84.
Huron Folk-Lore. (H. Hale) J. Am. Folk-Lore, 1: 177. 2: 248. 4: 289.
Huronian, Structural Relations of. (R. Pumpelly and C. R. Van Hise) Am. J. Sci. 143: 224.
Hurricanes, West Indian, and Solar Magnetic Influence. (H. A. Halen) Astron. 13: 105, 441.
Hurst, Hal, the Artist. (R. Compton) Idler, 9: 657.
Hurst of Hurstcote; a story. Temp. Bar, 98: 263.
Husband, The, Authority of. (E. Manson) Law Q. 7: 244.
— Does the Ideal Husband exist? (M. A. Livermore) No. Am. 162: 210.
Husband-seducer, The. Am. Law R. 26: 36.
Husbands, A Study in. (M. Harland; B. Harrison; E. Bisland) No. Am. 162: 103.
Huss, John. (G. F. Behringer) Luth. Q. 22: 223.
Huss, John, Letters to his Church in Prague. (M. J. Crumer) Chr. Lit. 13: 179.
Hutchinson, Francis. Relation to Utilitarianism. (E. Albee) Philos. R. 5: 24.
Hutchinson, Thomas, Hosmer's. (A. C. Goodell, jr.) Am. Hist. R. 2: 163.
Hutchinson, W. R. Acad. 48: 70.
Hutchinson Family, Story of. (G. J. Clarke) Dial (Ch.) 21: 222.
Huth, A. H. (W. Roberts) Bookworm, 3: 225.
Hutten, Ulrich von, in the light of Recent Investigation. (F. P. Goodrich) Yale R. 3: 45.
Hutton, Catherine. Letters. Spec. 69: 231.
— Reminiscences of. (A. Galton) Acad. 42: 330.
Hutton, James. Ath. '93, 1: 442.
Hutton, Laurence, with portrait. Bk. Buyer, 6: 267. — Bookworm, 3: 105.
Hutton, R. H. (H. Walker) Bookman, 2: 498.
— Works. (W. Wallace) Scot. R. 24: 157.
Huxley, Thos. H., with portrait. Bk. News, 13: 494. — (J. M. Macfarlane) Citizen, 1: 155. — (R. H. Hutton) Forum, 20: 23. — (O. C. Marsh) Am. J. Sci. 150: 177. — Science, n. s. 2: 85. — Lit. W. (Bost.) 26: 222. — Nature, 52: 226. — (M. Foster) Nature, 52: 318. — Pop. Sci. Mo. 47: 557. — Dial (Ch.) 19: 35. — Ath. '95, 2: 33. — (G. W. Smalley) Scrib. M. 18: 514. — Sat. R. 80: 6. — Acad. 48: 10. — Critic, 27: 1. — (P. C. Mitchell) New R. 13: 147. Same art. Liv. Age, 206: 666. — With portrait. (E. R. Lancaster and others) Nat. Sci. 7: 119. — (J. W. Chadwick) New World, 5: 25. — (W. Ward) 19th Cent. 40: 274. Same art. Ecl. M. 127: 627. Same art. Liv. Age, 210: 579. — (M. D. Conway) Open Court, 9: 4711.
— and the Deluge. (J. L. Clarke) Good Words, 33: 411.
— and his Work. (T. Gill) Science, n. s. 3: 253.
— and Karl Vogt. (E. Haeckel) Fortn. 64: 464.
— and the "New Reformation." Church Q. 41: 151.
— and Religion. Pub. Opin. 19: 83.
— as Anthropologist. (E. B. Tylor) Fortn. 64: 311.
— as Biologist. Fortn. 64: 313.
— as Evolutionist. (W. F. Reid) Westm. 144: 558.
— as Philosopher. (W. L. Courtney) Fortn. 64: 317.
— as a Theologian. (W. Sanday) Contemp. 62: 336. Same art. M. Chr. Lit. 7: 6.
— the British Diagoras. (F. L. Oswald) Open Court, 9: 4559.
— Creed of. Quar. 180: 160.
— Essays. (W. K. Brooks) Forum, 20: 284. — Ath. '95, 1: 571.
— — Vol. I. (C. S. Peirce) Nation, 58: 36. — Sat. R. 76: 470. — Church Q. 36: 57.
— Essays on Controverted Questions. (W. Barry) Cath. World, 60: 181, 333. — (F. Harrison) Fortn. 58: 417. — Sat. R. 74: 23. — Spec. 69: 352.
— Evolution in. (St. G. Mivart) 19th Cent. 34: 198. Same art. Pop. Sci. Mo. 44: 319.
— Forty-seven Years Ago. (C. Hedley) R. of Rs. (N. Y.) 12: 552.
— From the Point of View of a Disciple. (T. J. Parker) Nat. Sci. 8: 161.
— Funeral of. Nature, 52: 248.
— the Great Agnostic. Spec. 75: 10.
— Greatest Service of. (D. MacG. Means) Nation, 61: 5.
— Memorial to. Science, n. s. 2: 796.
— Memorial Tribute to. (H. F. Osborn) Science, n. s. 3: 147.
— on Hume and Berkeley. (G. G. Greenwood) Westm. 144: 1.
— on Sunday Observance. (Jane A. H. Simpson) Westm. 144: 266. Same art. Ecl. M. 125: 584.

Huxley, Thos. H., Reminiscences of. (W. H. Flower) No. Am. 161: 279.
— Scientific Work of. Dub. R. 117: 443.
— Some Personal Characteristics of. (G. C. Brodrick) Fortn. 64: 308.
— Student's Recollections of. (A. Heilprin) Pop. Sci. Mo. 48: 326.
— *versus* Genesis I. (C. B. Warring) Bib. Sac. 49: 638.
— *versus* Lord Bacon. (Argyll) 19th Cent. 36: 959.
— Witch of Endor and. (A. Lang) Contemp. 66: 165.
Huygens, Christian. Correspondence. (A. M. Clerke) Nature, 45: 434.
Huysmans, J. K. (A. Symons) Fortn. 57: 402.
— as Mystic. Sat. R. 79: 312.
— En Route; tr. by Kegan Paul. Sat. R. 82: 139.
Hyacinthe, Père. His Testament. Contemp. 64: 41.
Hyacinths, Good Varieties of. Garden & F. 7: 217.
H'yakusho's Summer Pleasures. (Sen Katayama) Harper, 90: 403.
Hybridism exemplified in the Genus Colaptes. (S. N. Rhoades) Science, 20: 325.
Hybridization. Early Experiments in Crossing Plants. (E. J. Hill) Garden & F. 9: 32.
Hybrids, Crosses and Crossing of Plants. Garden & F. 5: 2.
Hyde Park. *See* London.
Hyde Park Garden Tragedy, The; a story. (L. Springfield) Idler, 5: 422.
Hydraulic Machine Tools. (R. H. Tweddell) Cassier, 7: 55.
Hydraulic Works and System of Hydraulic Power-supply at Geneva, Switzerland. (W. C. Union) Am. Arch. 42: 37.
Hydrazine, Free, Isolation of. (A. E. Tutton) Nature, 51: 544.
Hydrocarbon, Illuminating, Commercial Synthesis of. (V. B. Lewes) J. Soc. Arts, 43: 156.
Hydrocarbons, Origin of. (M. E. Jones) Science, 22: 358.
Hydrogen and Oxygen, Relative Densities of. (Lord Rayleigh) Nature, 46: 101.
— Liquefaction of. New Sci. R. 1: 240.
Hydrographic Research to the North of Scotland. Geog. J. 5: 581.
Hydrography and Navigation. Scientific Results of the "Challenger" Expedition. (T. H. Tizard) Nat. Sci. 7: 10.
— in the U. S. (F. H. Newell) Nat. Geog. M. 7: 146.
Hydroids, Reproduction of Plumularian. (C. C. Nutting) Am. Natural. 29: 966.
Hydroxylamine, Free. (A. E. Tutton) Nature, 49: 105.
Hyères, France. (E. B. Ricketts) Eng. Illust. 9: 435. — (R. Barr) Idler, 1: 329.
Hygiene, Congress of, 8th International, 1894. Am. Statis. Assoc. 4: 69.
— Defects in our Bread. (L. Irwell) Soc. Econ. 3: 359.
— Modern, in Practice. (A. Schofield) Ecl. M. 126: 681. 127: 242.
— Science of Change of Air. (L. Robinson) National, 27: 663.
— Social. (K. Georgi) Pub. Opin. 14: 283.
Hygienic Education, Higher. (G. W. Linn) Educa. 17: 30.
Hygienic Influence of Forest Air and Forest Soil. (B. E. Fernow) Garden & F. 6: 34.
Hygrometer, Hair. (C. C. Trowbridge) Science, n. s. 4: 62.
Hylozoism. (W. A. Hammond) Philos. R. 4: 394.
Hymeneal Fiasco, A; a story. Cornh. 72: 390. Same art. Liv. Age, 207: 406.
Hymettus, Behind. (J. I. Manatt) Atlan. 73: 636, 763.
Hymn, What constitutes a Good? (W. W. How) Sund. M. 25: 361.
— to Canada; a poem. (K. Livingston) Canad. M. 7: 534.
Hymnody, Early English Catholic. (O. Shipley) Month, 84: 385. 85: 95.
— of Foreign Missions. (J. H. Ross) Bib. Sac. 51: 269.
Hymnology. (G. A. Simcox) Acad. 43: 51.
— Dictionary of, Julian's. Ath. '92, 1: 303. — Atlan. 69: 843. — Church Q. 34: 433. — (F. M. Bird) Nation, 54: 432. — Quar. 175: 38. — Spec. 68: 47. Same art. Ecl. M. 118: 380. — Sat. R. 73: 484. — Ed. R. 179: 300.
— English. (O. Shipley) Month, 80: 201, 341.
— of the Christian Church. (J. Telford) Scot. R. 19: 377.
Hymns and Hymn-writers of the 18th Century. (E. W. Howson) Sund. M. 23: 461, 550.
— Latin, and English Versions. (H. T. Henry) Am. Cath. Q. 18: 272.
— Most Popular. (W. C. Preston) Sund. M. 25: 81.
— Negro Camp-meeting. (H. C. Wood) New Eng. M. n. s. 6: 60.
— Songs of the Church. (J. Strong) Meth. R. 53: 258.
Hyperides and the New Papyri. Quar. 178: 531.
Hypnotic States, Nature and Induction of. (A. Howton) Open Court, 6: 3137.
— Trance, and Ecstasy. (W. R. Newbold) Pop. Sci. Mo. 48: 804.
Hypnotism. All the Year, 71: 136. — (G. M. Aylsworth) Canad. M. 5: 279. — (J. Daland) Lippinc. 52: 366. — (Annie Besant) Univ. R. 6: 145. — (C. N. Barham) Univ. R. 8: 66.
— and Clairvoyance. (J. M. Soames) Contemp. 61: 809.
— and Humbug. (E. Hart) 19th Cent. 31: 24.
— and its relation to Psychical Research. (B. O. Flower) Arena, 5: 316.
— and Justice. (H. M. Steele) No. Am. 160: 505.
— and the Law. Green Bag, 6: 143.
— and Mental Suggestion. (B. O. Flower) Arena, 6: 208.
— and Modern Psychology. (J. Luys) Open Court, 3: 1835.
— and Moral Responsibility. (J. A. Hayes) N. Church R. 2: 563.
— and Suggestion. (F. W. H. Myers) Mind, 18: 95.
— Applications of. (C. L. Tuckey) Ecl. M. 118: 1.
— Benedikt on. Sat. R. 77: 335.
— Common Sense of. (L. Storr-Best) New R. 8: 363. Same art. Ecl. M. 120: 734.
— Educational uses of. (R. O. Mason) No. Am. 163: 448.
— The Eternal Gullible, with Confessions of a Professional Hypnotist. (E. Hart) Cent. 26: 833.
— Ethics of. (G. M. Gould) Open Court, 4: 2172.
— Hart on. (J. Jastrow) Dial (Ch.) 15: 113.
— Legal Aspects of. (J. W. Brodie-Innes) Jurid. R. 3: 51.
— Dr. Luys' Experiments. (R. H. Sherard) McClure, 1: 547.
— Mesmer, Animal Magnetism and. (J. Jastrow) Cosmopol. 20: 360.
— Posthypnotic and Criminal Suggestion. (W. R. Newbold) Pop. Sci. Mo. 49: 230.
— Practical Application of, to Modern Medicine. (J. R. Cocke) Arena, 9: 73.
— Psychology of. (J. Weir, jr.) Am. Natural. 28: 921.
— Recent Work in. (W. R. Newbold) Am. Natural. 29: 1027.
— Revival of Witchcraft. (E. Hart) 19th Cent. 33: 347. Same art. Pop. Sci. Mo. 43: 206. Same art. Ecl. M. 120: 406. — (C. L. Tuckey) Contemp. 63: 416.

Hypnotism, Significance of. (P. Carus) Open Court, 4: 2129.
— Suggestion and Fiction. (J. Jastrow) Nation, 55: 227.
— Tuckey on. Spec. 68: 55.
— Value of, as Means of Surgical Anæsthesia. (J. R. Cocke) Arena, 10: 289.
— What is? (P. Carus) Open Court, 3: 1958.
— With Dr. Bernheim at Nancy. (J. M. Baldwin) Nation, 55: 101.
Hypnotist, The; a story. (O. Thanet) Harper, 93: 678.
Hypnotized Ghost, The; a story. (J. E. V. Cooke) Overland, n. s. 21: 464.
Hypocritical Romance, A; a story. (C. Ticknor) Cosmopol. 19: 203.
Hypotheses, Origin of. (G. K. Gilbert) Science, n. s. 3: 1.
Hyrtl, Carl Joseph. Nat. Sci. 5: 153.
Hysteria, Epidemics of. (W. Hirsch) Pop. Sci. Mo. 49: 544.

I do not Love; a poem. (J. Kavanagh) Argosy, 57: 154.
I Dreamed; a poem. (D. Fuguet) Cosmopol. 21: 617.
Iago, Conscience of. (A. M. Spence) Poet-Lore, 5: 194.
Iberian Peninsula, Geography and Social Conditions of. (T. Fischer) Geog. J. 1: 347.
Iberville and the Mississippi. (G. King) Harper, 89: 722.
Ibn Ezra in England. (M. Friedländer) Jew. Q. 8: 140.
Ibraim Pasha, Marriage of. (H. F. Brown) Atlan. 70: 617.
Ibsen, H., with portrait. Bk. Buyer, 6: 317. — (C. H. Herford) Acad. 41: 247. — With portrait. Bk. News, 8: 242. — (C. E. Maurice) Econ. R. 1: 348. — (A. N. Meyer) Lippinc. 53: 375. — (E. O. Achorn) New Eng. M. n. s. 13: 737. — (A. Symons) Univ. R. 3: 567.
— and B. Björnson. (Ethel B. Tweedie) Temp. Bar, 98: 536.
— and the Morbid Taint. Belgra. 83: 59.
— as an Artist. (L. Simons) Westm. 140: 506.
— as he is translated. (Wm. Archer) Time, 22: 37.
— at Christiania. (E. J. Goodman) Theatre, 35: 146.
— Bibliography of. (W. H. Carpenter) Bookman, 1: 275.
— Books about. (R. B. Johnson) Acad. 45: 285.
— Boyesen on. Spec. 72: 652. — Sat. R. 78: 359.
— Brand. (W. M. Payne) Dial (Ch.) 16: 236.
— Bygmester Solness. (W. M. Payne) Dial (Ch.) 14: 68.
— Comedy of Love. (H. H. Boyesen) Dial (Ch.) 14: 132.
— Doll-house. (H. H. Boyesen) Cosmopol. 16: 84.
— Dramatic Poem by. (E. D. Cheney) Open Court, 4: 2557.
— Earlier Work of. (C. H. Herford) Lippinc. 49: 351.
— Ghosts, Art and Moral of. Poet-Lore, 6: 356.
— in London. (H. Waring) Theatre, 33: 164.
— Interpretations of. (M. Wergeland) Dial (Ch.) 16: 262.
— John Gabriel, Bookman. Sat. R. 82: 654.
— Little Eyolf. Acad. 50: 465. — (G. B. Shaw) Sat. R. 82: 563, 623. — Poet-Lore, 7: 99. — (W. M. Payne) Dial (Ch.) 18: 5.
— — Note on. (W. L. Courtney) Fortn. 63: 277.
— Master Builder. Sat. R. 75: 241. — Spec. 70: 285.
— Mausoleum of. (W. Archer) Fortn. 60: 77.
— The New. (G. W. Steevens) New R. 12: 39. Same art. Liv. Age, 205: 239.
— Nora, and Shakespeare's Katharine. (E. Crowell) Poet-Lore, 8: 192.
Ibsen, H. Peer Gynt. (H. H. Boyesen) Chaut. 17: 293. — Gent. M. n. s. 49: 533. — Sat. R. 74: 417. — (G. B. Shaw) Sat. R. 82: 542.
— Poems, Philosophical. (E. Tissot) Chaut. 16: 53.
— — With portrait. (H. H. Boyesen) Cosmopol. 15: 91.
— Sarcey on. (W. D. Adams) Theatre, 37: 19.
— Beerbohm Tree on. Gent. M. n. s. 48: 103.
— Wild Duck. (H. H. Boyesen) Dial (Ch.) 15: 137.
— Women of. (D. K. Dodge) N. Eng. 56: 118.
Ibsen Legend. Dial (Ch.) 18: 259.
Ibsenism. Lond. Q. 78: 227.
Icarian Community. (E. F. Robinson) Open Court, 4: 2474, 2503.
Ice, Ground, Notes on. (R. D. Oldham) Nat. Sci. 4: 450.
— Growth and Sustaining Power of. (P. Vedel) J. Frankl. Inst. 140: 355, 437.
— Manufacture of. (L. Allen) Engin. M. 2: 762.
— Wall of, at Hull, Mass., Jan. 1893. (J. B. Woodworth) Science, 21: 71.
Ice Age about New York, Some Records of. (T. M. Prudden) Harper, 89: 593.
— Altitude as the Cause of. (W. Upham) Science, 22: 75.
— and the Antiquity of Man. Church Q. 38: 123.
— and Post-glacial Flood. (D. G. Whitley) Scot. R. 22: 381.
— and its Work. (A. R. Wallace) Fortn. 60: 616, 750. Same art. Pop. Sci. Mo. 44: 681, 781. 45: 40, 244.
— Astronomical Explanation of. (R. Ball) Knowl. 15: 1. — (E. P. Culverwell) Nature, 51: 33.
— — Ball on. (G. H. Darwin) Nature, 45: 289. — Sat. R. 73: 81. — (H. H. Howorth) Nature, 52: 594.
— Causes, Stages, and Time of. (W. Upham) Pop. Sci. Mo. 49: 354.
— Central Michigan and the Post-glacial Submergence. (E. H. Mudge) Am. J. Sci. 150: 442.
— Climate of Europe during. (C. Reid) Nat. Sci. 1: 427.
— Continuity of. (G. F. Wright) Am. J. Sci. 147: 161.
— Diversity of. (T. C. Chamberlin) Am. J. Sci. 145: 171.
— Epochs and Stages of. (W. Upham) Am. J. Sci. 149: 305.
— Geikie on. (R. D. Salisbury) Dial (Ch.) 19: 246.
— Glacial Theory. (Argyll) 19th Cent. 35: 337.
— Great. Lond. Q. 85: 20.
— Howorth's Glacial Nightmare. (D. G. Whitley) Thinker, 9: 33.
— in Australia, Ancient Epoch of. (E. Dunn) Nature, 47: 55.
— in North America. Ed. R. 175: 297.
— is it Periodic? Chamb. J. 70: 782.
— Man and the, Wright on. (R. D. Salisbury) Nation, 55: 496.
— Man in, in Ohio, Evidences of. (G. F. Wright) Pop. Sci. Mo. 43: 29.
— — Are there Evidences of him? (J. W. Powell) Pop. Sci. Mo. 43: 316.
— — Wright on. (E. D. Cope) Am. Natural. 27: 550.
— Minor Time-divisions of. (W. Upham) Am. Natural. 29: 235.
— Mystery of, and its Solution. (A. W. Drayson) New Sci. R. 1: 1.
— Necessary Consequence of the Earth's Movements. (J. C. Cowell) Science, 22: 341.
— of Great Britain and Ireland, Lewis's. Sat. R. 78: 21.
— Recent Glacial Theory. (Argyll) 19th Cent. 35: 337.

Ice Age, Some Theories of. Quar. 178: 105.
— Theory of Interglacial Submergence in England. (G. F. Wright) Am. J. Sci. 143: 1.
— Unity of. (G. F. Wright) Am. J. Sci. 144: 351.
— View of, as Two Epochs, the Glacial and Champlain. (W. Upham) Science, n. s. 2: 529.
— Wright on. (T. C. Chamberlain) Dial (Ch.) 13: 303. — (G. F. Wright; W. J. McGee) Science, 20: 275, 317, 360.
Ice Caves and Ice-gorges. Around World, 1: 194.
Ice Cliffs on the Kowak River. (J. C. Cantwell) Nat. Geog. M. 7: 345.
Ice Crystals, Hollow Pyramidal. (K. Grossmann and J. Lomas) Nature, 50: 600.
Ice Fishing in Winter; a poem. (J. H. Keene) Outing, 23: 463.
Ice Floe, Life on an. (T. Wood) Sund. M. 21: 685.
Ice Hills, At the. Ecl. M. 120: 243.
Ice Yachting. (C. L. Norton) Outing, 21: 411.
— in the Gulf of Finland. (G. Anderson) Outing, 21: 297.
Icebergs. (M. E. Jennings) Cosmopol. 15: 405. — (N. S. Shaler) Scrib. M. 12: 181.
Iced Bar Base Apparatus of the United States Coast and Geodetic Survey, Preliminary Account of. (R. S. Woodward) Am. J. Sci. 145: 33.
Iceland. Chamb. J. 70: 278. — (T. Anderson) J. Soc. Arts, 40: 397. — (T. G. Paterson) M. of Art, 11: 349.
— Across. (K. Grossmann) Geog. J. 3: 261.
— and its People. (R. Shaffner) Chaut. 22: 259.
— Books and Reading in. (W. E. Mead) Atlan. 71: 158.
— Commonwealth of. (A. H. Gunlogsen) Open Court, 4: 2328.
— Fortnight on a Farm in. (W. E. Mead) Meth. R. 55: 513.
— Oldest Folk-Lore of. (W. A. Craigie) Folk-Lore, 4: 219.
— School for Women in. Lend a H. 14: 272.
— Dr. Thoroddsen's Explorations in. Geog. J. 2: 154.
— To-day. Quar. 179: 58. Same art. Liv. Age, 202: 515.
— Women of. (R. Shaffner) Chaut. 22: 469.
Icelandic Sagas, tr. by Dasent. Sat. R. 79: 21.
Ichabod. (C. E. Laughlin) New Eng. M. n. s. 15: 220.
Iconoclastic Episode, An. (Emma M. Newton) Overland, n. s. 26: 366.
Iconography, Mediæval, from the Psalms. (C. Dodgson) Acad. 48: 570.
Ida, Mount. *See* Bob, Mount.
Idaho, Recent Botanical Explorations in. (D. T. MacDougal) Science, 20: 311.
— Snake Plains of, Zoölogy of. (C. H. Merriam) Am. Natural. 26: 218.
Iddesleigh, Lord. (O. A. Fermor) Time, 16: 129. — (H. W. Lucy) Liv. Age, 188: 111.
Ideal in College Life, Place of. (C. E. Wagner) Ref. Q. 43: 519.
— the Need of the People. (J. P. Fruit) Southern M. 4: 520.
— Plea for the. (W. T. Field) Dial (Ch.) 14: 206.
Ideal Shoeblack, An; a story. (R. Allen) Good Words, 34: 425.
Idealism. (F. Vanderem) Pub. Opin. 12: 505.
— and Epistemology. (H. Jones) Mind, 18: 289, 457.
— and Physical Science. (W. M. Salter) Open Court, 1: 552.
— Balfour on. (W. M. Daniels) Philos. R. 5: 59. — (R. B. Johnson) Philos. R. 5: 401.
— Ethical and Religious Import of. (May Sinclair) New World, 2: 694.
Idealism, Evolution and. (E. D. Cope) Open Court, 1: 655.
— In the Club Smoking-Room. (H. Knight-Horsfield) National, 20: 415.
— A Misconception of. (W. M. Salter) Open Court, 1: 478.
— of Spinoza. (J. C. Murray) Philos. R. 5: 473.
— Panlogist Phase of. (E. D. Fawcett) Monist, 7: 41.
— Positive. (G. M. M'Crie) Open Court, 4: 2531.
— Realism and Monism. Open Court, 2: 919.
— Refutations of, in the Löse Blätter. (J. H. Tufts) Philos. R. 5: 51.
Idealist, The American. (G. Bradford) Atlan. 70: 85.
Idealist, An; a story. (M. Hawker) New R. 9: 502.
Idealistic Theories, Criticising of Current. (A. J. Balfour) Mind, 18: 425.
Ideas, Community and Association of. (J. Jastrow) Psycholog. R. 1: 152.
— Community of, of Men and Women, Jastrow on. (C. C. Nevers) Psychol. R. 2: 363.
— Motor Power of. (H. Nichols) Philos. R. 4: 174. — (H. Münsterberg) Psycholog. R. 1: 441.
— their Origin and Destiny. (P. Carus) Open Court, 7: 3529.
— Thrust of. (M. H. Richards) Luth. Q. 24: 49.
Identification by Finger-marks. *See* Finger-marks.
— of Criminals. (E. R. Spearman) 19th Cent. 36: 356. — (A. F. B. Crofton) Cosmopol. 20: 34.
Idiocy and Responsibility. (T. S. Clouston) Jurid. R. 7: 38.
— Feeble-minded Children. (D. Galton) 19th Cent. 35: 276.
— Prevention of. (H. S. Williams) Am. J. Pol. 3: 516.
Idiot's Wife, An; a story. (E. P. Allen) Southern M. 5: 46.
Idiots savants. (F. Peterson) Pop. Sci. Mo. 50: 232.
Idle Days, the Lake, and a Little Music; a social sketch. (B. McEvoy) Canad. M. 5: 369.
Idle Summer, An; a story. (W. E. Saxon) Argosy, 62: 29.
Idleness and Immorality. (E. L. Godkin) Forum, 13: 334.
— In Praise of. (H. J. Jennings) Gent. M. n. s. 49: 383.
— Sin of. (H. S. Holland) Sund. M. 22: 258.
Idlers Both; a story. All the Year, 75: 132.
Idol and the Iconoclasts, The; a story. Temp. Bar, 97: 391. Same art. Ecl. M. 120: 550.
Idol of High Price, An; a story. (F. B. Millard) Overland, n. s. 19: 465.
Idolatry. (P. Carus) Open Court, 7: 3619.
Idols and Images. (S. D. Peet) Am. Antiq. 14: 197.
Idy. (M. C. Graham) Cent. 23: 879.
Idyll, An. (Mrs. P. Pattison) Eng. Illust. 14: 555.
Idyll of the 40's; a story. (C. Bissell) Lippinc. 55: 280.
Idyll of the Ice. (G. Allen) Eng. Illust. 11: 776.
Idyll of an Idol. (C. E. Morland and A. d'Elmard) Belgra. 80: 69.
Idyll of London, An; a story. (B. Harradeen) Eng. Illust. 11: 289.
Idyll of Swiftwater Ferry, The; a story. (C. T. C. James) Gent. M. n. s. 49: 433. Same art. Liv. Age, 196: 11.
Idyllic Art, French and English. (H. Quilter) Univ. R. 4: 309.
Ie-sound in Accented Syllables in English. (E. W. Bowen) Am. J. Philol. 15: 51.
If, Chateau d'. (W. H. Pollock) Eng. Illust. 13: 221.
If; a story. (H. P. Lewis) Argosy, 58: 27. Same art. Liv. Age, 202: 402.

If it could be! a story. (A. French) Scrib. M. **11**: 178.
If Jesus came to Boston. (E. E. Hale) New Eng. M. n. s. **11**: 402.
Ightham Moat House. (B. Champneys) M. of Art, **6**: 184.
Ignatius, St., Syriac Epistles of. Eng. R. **4**: 309.
Ignatius, Father, of Llanthony Abbey. (R. Blathwayt) Idler, **4**: 401.
Ignatius Loyola, St. *See* Loyola.
Igneous Rock Fusion, Relation of Melting Point to Pressure in. (C. Barus) Am. J. Sci. **143**: 56.
Igneous Rocks, Classification and Naming of. (W. S. Bailey) Science, **21**: 87.
— of the Sweet Grass Hills, Montana. (W. H. Weed and L. V. Pirsson) Am. J. Sci. **150**: 309.
— of Yogo Peak, Montana. (W. H. Weed and L. V. Pirsson) Am. J. Sci. **150**: 467.
Ignis Æternus. (A. F. Hewit) Cath. World, **57**: 14.
Ilford Village Homes. (J. Cassidy) Westm. **146**: 194.
Ilkley Wells, Yorkshire, Fairies at. Folk-Lore Rec. **1**: 229.
Illegitimate Children, Care of, in England. Sat. R. **82**: 6.
Illinois, Map of, in 1680. (H. W. Beckwith) Am. Antiq. **17**: 213.
— National Guard of. (W. R. Hamilton) Outing, **26**: 75, 160, 240.
— Naval Reserve. (W. H. Burke) Outing, **24**: 465.
— State Historical Library. Lib. J. **17**: 244.
— Taxation in. A Remarkable Statistical Report. (J. Malcolm) Arena, **16**: 585.
Illinois Town, Spirit of an. (M. H. Catherwood) Atlan. **78**: 168, 338, 480.
Illiteracy in the United States. (J. H. Blodgett) Educa. R. **8**: 227.
— of American Boys, Growing. (E. L. Godkin) Nation, **63**: 284.
Illuminated Certificate, The; a story. (M. Davies) Overland, n. s. **20**: 642.
Illuminated MSS., English, 700–1066. (E. M. Thompson) Bibliographica, **1**: 129.
— — 12th–15th Centuries. (E. M. Thompson) Bibliographica, **1**: 385. **2**: 1.
— Middleton on. Sat. R. **74**: 115.
— of the Middle Ages, Grotesque and Humorous in the. (E. M. Thompson) Bibliographica, **2**: 309.
Illuminating, Art of. (J. V. Sears) Bk. News, **7**: 207.
Illumination of Books, of the Middle Ages, Notes on. (W. Morris) M. of Art, **17**: 83.
— of Manuscripts, as originally practiced. (A. Warren) M. of Art, **3**: 359–450.
Illumination, Artificial. (W. P. Gerhard) Am. Arch. **42**: 109.
— of Buildings, Internal. Am. Arch. **36**: 168.
— New Methods of. Chamb. J. **72**: 582.
Illusions and Certitudes. (J. W. Powell) Science, n. s. **3**: 263, 426.
— and Hallucinations. (W. R. Newbold) Pop. Sci. Mo. **49**: 630.
Illustrated Journalism. (H. Townsend) J. Soc. Arts, **42**: 233.
Illustration, American, of To-day. (W. A. Coffin) Scrib. M. **11**: 106–333.
— Bicknell's New Process. (H. V. Barnett) M. of Art, **6**: 22.
— Book. (J. Pennell) Art J. **47**: 136–361. — (G. Du Maurier) M. of Art, **13**: 349, 371.
— — and Newspaper. (H. Blackburn) Am. Arch. **43**: 78. — (H. Blackburn) J. Soc. Arts, **42**: 93, 105, 121.
Illustration, Book, Byways of. M. of Art, **5**: 169, 384. — (R. L. Stevenson) M. of Art, **6**: 8.
— — English. (J. Pennell) J. Soc. Arts, **44**: 455.
— — for Children. M. of Art, **6**: 127.
— — from the Author's Point of View. (W. Black) M. of Art, **14**: 28.
— — from the Humorous Artist's Point of View. (H. Furniss) M. of Art, **14**: 99.
— — Italian. (A. W. Pollard) Portfo. **25**: no. 12.
— — One Way of. (A. G. Coburn) Bk. News, **8**: 343.
— Decorative Idea in. (A. Black) Mo. Illust. **5**: 193.
— Inconsistencies in. (H. C. Cox; E. B. Warman) Writer, **7**: 98, 146.
— Modern, Pennell on. Sat. R. **82**: 43.
— of Newspapers in England. (C. N. Williamson) M. of Art, **12**: 104, 173. **13**: 297–391.
— Pictorial Imagination *vs.* Spec. **74**: 683.
— The Special Artist. (H. V. Barnett) M. of Art, **6**: 163.
Illustrative Art, Past and Present. (H. Nisbet) Gent. M. n. s. **48**: 258.
Illustrator, Recollections of a Veteran. (J. R. Chapin) Mo. Illust. **3**: 104.
Illustrators, American Women. (H. Payne) Munsey, **11**: 47.
— and Illustrating. (P. R. Paulding) Munsey, **13**: 151.
— Book. Bk. Buyer, **11**: 12–487. **12**: 81–562. **13**: 17–636.
— Concerning some "Punch" Artists. (W. S. Hunt) M. of Art, **14**: 296.
— French, Glimpses of the. (F. N. Doubleday) Scrib. M. **14**: 446, 579.
— Some San Francisco. (P. N. Boeringer) Overland, n. s. **26**: 70.
Ilmington Hills. (Sigma Smith) Time, **11**: 75–238.
Image, Selwyn. Poems and Carols. Sat. R. **79**: 8. — (L. Johnson) Acad. **47**: 271.
Image, The; a story. (Vernon Lee) Cornh. **73**: 516.
Imagery of American Students. (A. C. Armstrong) Psychol. R. **1**: 496.
Imaginary Companions, Study of. (C. Vostrovsky) Educa. **15**: 393.
Imagination, The. (J. R. Lowell) Cent. **25**: 716. — (A. Lovell) New Sci. R. **2**: 311.
— and Faith. Spec. **71**: 794.
— Goschen on. Sat. R. **75**: 563.
— in Children. (J. Sully) Pop. Sci. Mo. **45**: 323.
— — Individual Differences in. (W. H. Burnham) Pedagog. Sem. **2**: 204.
— Measure of. (G. Galton) Nature, **47**: 319.
— Types of. (R. H. Stetson) Pyschol. R. **3**: 398.
Imagination; a story. (A. Hope) Idler, **6**: 411.
Imagination; a story. (E. Fawcett) Outing, **23**: 83.
Imaginationalism, Immoral. (A. Comstock) Our Day, **16**: 191.
Imaginations. (M. Eyre) Longm. **21**: 405.
Imbecility, Relation of, to Pauperism and Crime. (M. L. Clark) Arena, **10**: 788.
Imbert de Saint-Amand, with portrait. Bk. Buyer, **7**: 287.
Imbrications as Architectural Ornaments. (L. Passepont) Am. Arch. **36**: 65–193.
Imerina, In. (Pasfield Oliver) New R. **13**: 554.
Imitation. (J. Royce) Psychol. R. **2**: 217.
— among Atoms and Organisms. (E. Noble) Pop. Sci. Mo. **48**: 492.
— Natural History of Consciousness. (J. M. Baldwin) Mind, **19**: 26.
Imitative Functions and their Place in Human Nature. (J. Royce) Cent. **26**: 137.
Immaculate Conception and Modern Thought. (J. Orr) Thinker, **9**: 136.

Immanuel, Isaiah's Suggestion Regarding. (F. C. Porter) J. Bib. Lit. 14: 19.
Immanuel di Romi, as 13th Century Hebrew Poet. (J. Chotzner) Jew. Q. 4: 64.
Immigrants; Day in the New Castle Garden. (F. Balgarnie) Eng. Illust. 13: 155.
— Handling of, in New York. (H. M. Sweeney) Cath. World, 63: 497.
— What they contribute to Industry. (G. F. Parker) Forum, 14: 600.
— Where do they go? (C. C. Adams) Chaut. 23: 551.
Immigration. (N. Canby) Chaut. 16: 197. — (J. Cook) Our Day, 11: 42.
— Alien. (G. Drage) J. Statis. Soc. 58: 1. — (A. White) Fortn. 63: 501. — (G. Drage) Fortn. 63: 37.
— Alien Degradation of American Character. (S. G. Fisher) Forum, 14: 608.
— and the Census. (H. C. Lodge) Cent. 24: 737.
— and Crime. (H. H. Hart) Am. J. Sociol. 2: 369. — (S. G. Fisher) Pop. Sci. Mo. 49: 625.
— and the Foreign-born Population in the U. S. (R. Mayo-Smith) Am. Statis. Assoc. 3: 304.
— and Inter-state Migration. Lend a H. 9: 155.
— and the Labor Problem. (T. N. Carver) Am. J. Pol. 3: 78.
— and the Land Question. (C. J. Buell) Arena, 10: 807.
— and Naturalization. (H. S. Everett) Atlan. 75: 345.
— and the Sweating System. (G. E. Walsh) Chaut. 18: 174.
— Economic Aspects of. (J. A. Roebling) Am. M. Civics, 9: 235.
— European Peasants as Immigrants. (N. S. Shaler) Atlan. 71: 646.
— Evils of. (R. Gale) Lippinc. 58: 231.
— — Practical Remedy for. (G. H. Schwab) Forum, 14: 805.
— from Italy. (J. H. Senner) No. Am. 162: 649.
— Harm of. (E. L. Godkin) Nation, 56: 42.
— Has it increased Population? (S. G. Fisher) Pop. Sci. Mo. 48: 244.
— History of. (C. S. Hoyt) Lend a H. 11: 276.
— How to deal with. (E. E. Hale) Soc. Econ. 4: 75.
— How we restrict. (J. H. Senner) No. Am. 158: 494.
— in England, Alien. (C. E. H. Vincent) New R. 7: 606.
— — Pauper. (Earl of Dunraven) 19th Cent. 31: 985.
— in the U. S. Pub. Opin. 14: 221-296. — (F. A. Walker) Yale R. 1: 125.
— Incalculable Room for. (E. Atkinson) Forum, 13: 360.
— Indiscriminate, Burden of. (J. H. Twells) Am. J. Pol. 5: 608.
— into Great Britain: Strangers within Our Gates. Chamb. J. 72: 344.
— Is it a Menace to the Nation? (W. G. Puddefoot) Am. M. Civics, 9: 1.
— Is it practicable to regulate? (J. Chetwood, jr.) Overland, n. s. 23: 166.
— Italian. (P. F. Hall) No. Am. 163: 252.
— Laws concerning, Needed Changes in. (F. W. Hamilton; W. E. Weyl; L. H. Knox) Pub. Opin. 14: 583.
— Our Attitude toward Foreigners. (B. W. Williams) Am. M. Civics, 8: 64.
— Our National Dumping-ground. (J. B. Weber; C. S. Smith) No. Am. 154: 424.
— Philosophy of. Soc. Econ. 4: 193.
— Problem of. (W. H. Jeffrey) Am. J. Pol. 2: 132. — Public Opin. 16: 122. — (S. E. Turner) Soc. Econ. 2: 359. — Westm. 138: 65. — (E. P. Clark) Nation, 54: 4. — (R. DeC. Ward) Char. R. 3: 390.
Immigration, Problem of, Present State of. (J. H. Noble) Pol. Sci. Q. 7: 231.
— Question of. (R. H. Sylvester) Am. J. Pol. 2: 567. — (W. H. Jeffrey) Am. J. Pol. 4: 320.
— Regulation of. (E. E. Hale) Lend a H. 10: 1.
— Restriction of. (A. Cassot) Am. J. Pol. 3: 244. — (F. A. Walker) Atlan. 77: 822. — (E. W. Bemis) Bib. Sac. 53: 560. — (H. C. Lodge) Our Day, 16: 281. — (Arnold White) Char. R. 3: 70. — (E. B. Dietrick) Soc. Econ. 5: 21.
— — Methods of. (W. E. Chandler) Forum, 13: 128.
— Shall it be suspended? (W. E. Chandler) No. Am. 156: 1.
— Statistics of. Gunton's M. 11: 431.
— Symposium on. Indep. Nov. 2, '93.
— Unrestricted, Danger of. Pub. Opin. 15: 173, 221.
— — Dangerous to American Institutions. (W. R. Wood) Am. J. Pol. 2: 512.
— Why it should not be suspended. (H. C. Hansbrough) No. Am. 156: 220.
— Workingman and. (J. W. Knight) Char. R. 4: 363.
Immorality, French *versus* Anglo-Saxon. (M. O'Rell) No. Am. 159: 545.
— Idleness and. (E. L. Godkin) Forum, 13: 334.
— Laws Favoring. (B. O. Flower) Arena, 11: 167.
— Present-day, Well-springs of. (B. O. Flower) Arena, 8: 394.
— Social Conditions as Feeders of. (B. O. Flower) Arena, 11: 399.
— Wellsprings and Feeders of. (B. O. Flower) Arena, 11: 56. 12: 337.
Immortal Monkey, An; a story. (F. Whishaw) Idler, 6: 327.
Immortal Three; a poem. (R. B. Wilson) Cosmopol. 21: 115.
Immortality. (G. M. Gould) Monist, 1: 372. — (T. B. Wakeman) Open Court, 6: 3487. — (G. M. McCrie) Open Court, 10: 4904. — (W. Knight) Time, 19: 30.
— Ancient Beliefs in. (T. K. Cheyne) M. Chr. Lit. 5: 287.
— and the Buddhist Soul-conception. (P. Carus) Open Court, 8: 4259.
— and Nothingness. (P. Bayne) Good Words, 37: 243.
— and Resurrection. (G. Allen) Fortn. 60: 317.
— and Science. Open Court, 5: 3023.
— The Conception of, in Spinoza's Ethics. (A. E. Taylor) Mind, 21: 145.
— Doctrine of, in the Old Testament. (S. Holmes) Westm. 145: 92.
— Ethical Consequences of Doctrine of. (W. Lutoslawski) Int. J. Ethics, 5: 309.
— Evolution and. (P. Carus) Open Court, 1: 726.
— Hebrew Doctrine of. (M. S. Terry) Bib. World, 2: 87.
— in the Old Testament, Modern Religion and. (A. B. Davidson) Chr. Lit. 13: 82.
— Is there Another Life? (Goldwin Smith) Forum, 21: 607.
— Natural History of, Reynolds'. Spec. 68: 647.
— Personal. (G. G. Thompson) Open Court, 1: 172.
— Salmond on. (E. D. Morris) Presb. & Ref. R. 7: 558.
— a Scientific Truth. (P. Carus) Open Court, 8: 4155.
— Seal of the Hope of. (W. Sinclair) Sund. M. 23: 35.
— that is now. (G. J. Romanes) Monist, 4: 481. Same art. Pub. Opin. 18: 381.
— that Science teaches, The. (L. F. Ward) Open Court, 1: 199.
— Voysey on. Spec. 72: 715.
Immortals to the Sleepers, The; a poem. (B. Pares) Gent. M. n. s. 55: 618.

Imogen, Fair, upon the Stage. (C. E. L. Wingate) Cosmopol. 12: 525.
Impending Sword. (H. A. Vachell) Lippinc. 57: 595.
Imperial Federation, Canada's Call to the Empire. (H. Vincent) Canad. M. 6: 264.
— Financial Incidents of War. (A. C. Galt) Canad. M. 5: 453.
See Great Britain, Empire.
Imperial Federation League; why it was dissolved. (R. Beadon) National, 22: 814.
Imperial Institute, German. (P. Magnus) Nature, 53: 32.
Imperial Institute, London. (Sir S. Vine) Eng. Illust. 10: 539. — (Sir G. Baden-Powell) Fortn. 59: 890.
— — Opening of. All the Year, 72: 488. — Spec. 70: 631.
Important Man, An; a story. (W. Simpson) Eng. Illust. 11: 425.
Impostor, Extraordinary, of Stuart Era. (J. F. Fuller) Walford's Antiq. 1: 290. 2: 124.
Impostors? a story. (E. Yolland) Belgra. 83: 393.
Impressing Others, Love of. Spec. 68: 706.
Impressionism and Pre-Raphaelitism. (W. P. Frith) M. of Art, 11: 187.
— in Art. (P. Gsell) Pub. Opin. 13: 119.
— in France. Art J. 45: 28. — (C. Waern) Atlan. 69: 535.
— in Painting. (W. H. Downes) New Eng. M. n. s. 6: 600.
— Remarks on. Art J. 45: 103.
Impressionists; a story. (J. F. Raffaëli) Scrib. M. 17: 630.
Imprisonment for Debt. (B. F. Washer) Green Bag, 7: 410.
— Terms of. (F. Galton) Nature, 52: 174.
Improbable Story, An. (H. W. Kespa) Belgra. 77: 172.
In Acadie; a tale. (G. Bartlett) Canad. M. 5: 536.
In Ambush at the Lake-side. (F. Whishaw) Longm. 23: 633.
In Another World than Ours. (G. E. Channing) Outing, 23: 397.
In Arcady. (G. S. Street) New R. 13: 157.
In Arcady; a poem. (C. Monkhouse) M. of Art, 8: 108.
In Arcady; a story. (K. Grahame) New R. 12: 225.
In the Bear Latitudes. All the Year, 76: 207.
In the Best of all Possible Worlds; a story. (F. M. Wilson) Belgra. 81: 42.
In Birling Deep; a story. Temp. Bar, 109: 396.
In the Bitter Root Mountains. (E. Higginson) Lippinc. 54: 700.
In the Bonnie North Countree; a story. (M. L. Cameron) Eng. Illust. 16: 362.
In the Box Tunnel; a tale. All the Year, 74: 417.
In Breton Land; a poem. (E. Leith) Argosy, 60: 90.
In the Burst of the Southwest Monsoon. (R. Wildman) Overland, n. s. 24: 509.
In the Camp of Philistia. (V. W. Cloud) Lippinc. 52: 755.
In the Camp of the Shadow of Death. (E. E. Luthell) Belgra. 87: 140.
In a Caravan. Cornh. 67: 285. Same art. Liv. Age, 197: 418.
In Case of Discovery. (Mrs. W. K. Clifford) Fortn. 64: 470.
In a Cathedral; a story. (G. H. Page) Argosy, 54: 532.
In Collusion with Fate. (H. H. Boyesen) Scrib. M. 20: 73.
In the Convent Garden; a poem. (T. A. Janvier) Cosmopol. 16: 578.
In a Corner of Paris; a story. (J. Canning) Eng. Illust. 11: 523.
In a Country Omnibus; a story. Cornh. 69: 34.
In the Cypress View Neighborhood; a story. (O. Reid) Cosmopol. 15: 235.
In a Dahabieh; a poem. (F. Peterson) Cosmopol. 15: 60.
In the Darkroom. (F. R. Batchelder) New Eng. M. n. s. 14: 245.
In the Days of the Cagots; a tale. (E. Yolland) Belgra. 91: 245.
In the Dozy Hours. (A. Repplier) Atlan. 74: 103.
In 1812; a story. (S. Livingston) Canad. M. 5: 385.
In the Evening of Life. Chamb. J. 69: 430.
In Fableland; a poem. (W. Toynbee) Gent. M. n. s. 52: 54.
In a Field of Buckwheat; a story. (J. P. Rudd) Outing, 26: 331.
In the Fifth Flat; a story. (A. Leach) Munsey, 10: 507.
In the First Christmastide; a poem. (H. P. Spofford) McClure, 8: 121.
In Fly Time; a story. (R. Grant) Harper, 89: 296.
In a Fool's Paradise; a story. (O. Crawfurd) New R. 10: 517.
In Foro Conscientiæ; a story. (W. Mills) Arena, 14: 495.
In Granada; a song of exile. (A. Gordon) Cent. 24: 370.
In the Hands of Jefferson; a story of the West Indies. (E. Phillpotts) Idler, 3: 612.
In Hazy Days; a poem. (L. Williams) Outing, 23: 118.
In the Heart of the Country. Belgra. 85: 78.
In Honor Bound; a story. (G. Gissing) Eng. Illust. 13: 79. Same art. Liv. Age, 205: 470.
In Hour of Need; a sketch. Argosy, 55: 257.
In Jackson's Administration. (L. L. Pleasants) Atlan. 74: 755.
In King Arthur's Land; a story. (E. H. Brodlique) Cosmopol. 18: 91.
In the Land of Shadows; a story. Canad. M. 4: 210.
In the Little Church down the Street. (B. Matthews) Harper, 88: 462.
In a Little Old Trunk. (J. S. Barrows) New Eng. M. n. s. 6: 213.
In Louisa County. (C. P. Lamar) Lippinc. 58: 218.
In Lurid Light; a story. (E. Stuart) Blackw. 152: 510. Same art. Liv. Age, 195: 590.
In Memory's Mirror; a poem. (C. Burke) Argosy, 62: 768.
In the Midst of Alarms. (R. Barr) Lippinc. 52: 131.
In de Miz; a story. (L. C. Pickett) Arena, 8: 642.
In the Name of the Czar; a tale. (W. M. Graydon) Munsey, 10: 421-611.
In the Name of the Law; a story. (S. J. Weyman) McClure, 1: 110.
In the Name of the Most High; a story. (R. W. Chambers) Eng. Illust. 16: 305.
In Narrow Ways; a story. (Mary Hartier) Temp. Bar, 109: 353.
In the Never, Never Country; a story. (R. Monckton-Dene) Un. Serv. (Phila.) 8: 48-368.
In the Next Room; a story. (A. Perrin) Belgra. 81: Holiday no., 13.
In Northern Waters. (T. C. Evans) Scrib. M. 17: 479.
In Oakham Pastures; a story. Blackw. 151: 114.
In an Old Porch; a story. (W. Raymond) Temp. Bar, 101: 386.
In Passion's Wake. (L. Jackson) Belgra. 85: 41.
In the Permanent Way; a story. (Mrs. Steel) Eng. Illust. 11: 331.
In the Pine Lands of Georgia; a story. (E. F. Andrews) Chaut. 21: 413, 579.
In the Piney Woods; a story. (Mrs. B. F. Mayhew) Harper, 89: 713.
In the Portrait Class. (M. M. Piggot) Southern M. 4: 180.

In the Preacher's Heart; a story. (L. Jackson) Belgra. 90: 53.
In the Redwoods; a story. (J. C. Bull) Munsey, 13: 286.
In Rented Rooms. (G. I. Putnam) Scrib. M. 13: 463.
In the River Pei-ho; a poem. (W. L. Clowes) Blackw. 155: 856.
In the Rukh; a story. (R. Kipling) McClure, 7: 23.
In the St. Peter's Set; a story. (T. A. Janvier) Cosmopol. 13: 131.
In a Scotch Loch; a story. (D. Lerron) Eng. Illust. 9: 756.
In Search of the Picturesque. (S. M. Stevens) Bach. of Arts, 3: 534.
In the Season; a play. (L. E. Mitchell) Theatre, 30: 260.
In the Shadow of the Church; a poem. (D. McCaig) Canad. M. 3: 506.
In the Shadow of Nineveh; a story. (W. Hinckley) Outing, 22: 1.
In the Shadow of the Guillotine; a story. (E. Lambre) Chaut. 23: 408, 545.
In Shake Rag Alley. (V. Starnes) Southern M. 4: 302.
In Sight of the Goddess. (H. R. Davis) Lippinc. 56: 579.
In a Silent Sea. Chamb. J. 69: 507.
In the South; a poem. (A. M. F. Robinson) M. of Art, 9: 332.
In Summer; a poem. (M. A. Mason) Outing, 26: 289.
In Summer Heat. Cornh. 68: 499.
In Sunny June; a story. (L. G. Ackroyd) Argosy, 59: 738.
In Tenebras; a parable. (H. Pyle) Harper, 88: 392.
In Three Weeks; a story. (W. Besant) Idler, 5: 115.
In the Time of our Sickness (A. D. 1348); a story. Temp. Bar, 104: 537.
In the Time of the Sweetbrier; a story. (H. P. Spofford) McClure, 7: 305.
In the Track of the Wandering Jew; a story. Cornh. 71: 164.
In Trust. (M. H. Goodrich) Overland, n. s. 22: 349.
In the Vale of the White Horse; a story. (R. M. Kettle) Argosy, 57: 341.
In the Valley; a poem. (M. A. M. Marks) Argosy, 62: 28.
In Viger again. (D. C. Scott) Scrib. M. 14: 457.
In the Wine-cellar. (H. C. Bunner) Scrib. M. 20: 475.
In a Woman's Doss-house. (T. Sparrow) New R. 11: 176.
In the Year Ten Thousand; a story. (W. N. Harden) Arena, 6: 743.
Ina, King, of Wessex. (Mrs. C. G. Boger) Walford's Antiq. 8: 256. 9: 21.
Inactive, Obligation of the. (K. Trask) Forum, 20: 489.
Inadequacy; a poem. (E. M. Thomas) Dial (Ch.) 17: 217.
Inaudi, Jacques; the Latest Arithmetical Prodigy. (A. Binet) Pop. Sci. Mo. 42: 60. — (A. Binet) Chaut. 15: 670. — (A. Binet) Pub. Opin. 13: 574.
Inaugurations and Coronations. (F. S. Daniel) Cosmopol. 14: 715.
Incandescent Arc Light. (L. B. Marks) Cassier, 5: 23.
Incandescent Lamps, Age-coating in. (E. L. Nichols) Am. J. Sci. 144: 277.
— of To-day. (J. H. Cuntz) Cassier, 7: 329.
Incandescent *versus* Arc Lighting. (W. A. Anthony) Cassier, 6: 463. *See* Electric Light.
Incantations, Children's. (C. G. Leland) J. Am. Folk-Lore, 2: 113.
Incarnation, The. (E. H. Gifford) Chr. Lit. 15: 472.
— and Atonement. (S. N. Callender) Ref. Q. 39: 20.
— and Common Life. Church Q. 38: 70.
— and the Eucharist. Church Q. 41: 303.
Incarnation, The, Dissertations on Subjects connected with, Gore's. (W. Gildea) Dub. R. 118: 347.
— Doctrine of, Otley's. Church Q. 43: 28.
— — Philosophical Aspects of. (F. C. Conybeare) Jew. Q. 7: 607.
— Does the Church believe in? (C. C. Starbuck) N. Eng. 56: 152.
— Gore's Bampton Lectures on. Church Q. 33: 273. — (R. Rainy) Crit. R. 2: 115.
— in Modern Theology. Lond. Q. 80: 41.
— in the Religions of the World. (W. W. Peyton) Contemp. 60: 825. Same art. Ecl. M. 127: 289.
Incas, The Ancient. Chamb. J. 72: 758.
Incas Eyes. (W. S. Miller) Science, 21: 74.
Inchbald, Elizabeth. Temp. Bar, 99: 317. Same art. Liv. Age. 199: 643. — (I. A. Taylor) Longm. 19: 412. — Ecl. M. 122: 30.
Incident from Borderland, An; a story. Cornh. 72: 514.
Incident in the Career of the Rev. Luke Tremain; a story. (A. Jessopp) 19th Cent. 34: 314. Same art. Liv. Age, 198: 725.
Incident of the Wild West, An. (B. Mitford) Idler, 6: 429.
Inclined Railway Systems. (T. C. Ives) Engin. M. 7: 163.
Incognito. (W. S. Walsh) Lippinc. 54: 668.
Incognito; a story. (C. Shelley) Outing, 27: 425.
Income, Management of the. (P. Browne) Ecl. M. 124: 497.
Income Tax. Bank. M. (N. Y.) 48: 428. — (A. Abbott) Bank. M. (N. Y.) 50: 185. — (E. J. James) Citizen, 1: 81. — (G. H. Blunden) Econ. J. 2: 637. — (F. J. Lippitt) Nation, 60: 217. — (G. Bradford) Nation, 60: 298. — (C. J. Swift) Overland, n. s. 25: 184. — (Austin Abbott) Outl. 50: 500. — (E. R. A. Seligman) Pol. Sci. Q. 9: 610. — Pub. Opin. 16: 353, 476, 543. — (W. T. Dutton) Am. J. Pol. 4: 496. — (E. R. A. Seligman) Econ. J. 4: 639. — (C. F. Dunbar) Q. J. Econ. 9: 26.
— and Economic Science. (N. C. Frederiksen) Bank. M. (Lond.) 55: 979.
— and Federal Revenues. (F. C. Howe) Ann. Am. Acad. Pol. Sci. 4: 65.
— Beauties of the Law. (R. Ogden) Nation, 58: 133.
— Civil War, History of. (J. A. Hill) Q. J. Econ. 8: 416, 491.
— I. Decision of the Supreme Court. (G. S. Boutwell) No. Am. 160: 589. — II. Spirit of the Tax. No. Am. 160: 601.
— The Decision on. (E. L. Godkin) Nation, 60: 272, 394. — J. Pol. Econ. 3: 509. — Pub. Opin. 18: 400. — (L. Allen) Am. Law R. 29: 847. — Reply. (S. Pennoyer) 29: 856. — (J. K. Beach) Yale R. 5: 58.
— — and Constitutional Construction. (C. G. Tiedeman) Ann. Am. Acad. Pol. Sci. 6: 268.
— — and the Power of the Supreme Court to nullify Acts of Congress. (S. Pennoyer) Am. Law R. 29: 550.
— — Political Dangers of. (E. B. Whitney) Forum, 19: 521.
— — Salutary Results of. (G. F. Edmunds) Forum, 19: 513.
— France and the. (T. Stanton) No. Am. 158: 373.
— Graduated. (J. J. O'Neill) Am. J. Pol. 3: 650. — (J. Burns) Westm. 146: 555.
— Graver Evils of. (R. Ogden) Nation, 58: 24.
— in the American Colonies and States. (E. R. A. Seligman) Pol. Sci. Q. 10: 221.
— in England. (J. Lubbock) No. Am. 158: 150. — (E. Porritt) Outl. 49: 312.
— — Schemes for. Spec. 70: 595.

Income Tax, in France; Bill of 1895. (H. P. Willis) J. Pol. Econ. 4: 409.
— in Prussia. (J. A. Hill) Q. J. Econ. 6: 207.
— in the U. S. Sat. R. 79: 500.
— Is it Constitutional? (N. Trickett) Am. Law R. 29: 73.
— Is it Constitutional and Just? (E. R. A. Seligman) Forum, 19: 48.
— Is it Desirable? (D. A. Wells) Forum, 17: 1.
— Is it Socialistic? (W. H. Mallock) Forum, 19: 707.
— Is it Unconstitutional? (R. Sewell) Am. Law R. 28: 808. — (D. A. Wells) Forum, 18: 537.
— Legislative History of the Second Law. (G. Turrell) J. Pol. Econ. 3: 311.
— National Finance and the. (A. C. Miller) J. Pol. Econ. 3: 255.
— of 1894 [Text of the Bill]. Q. J. Econ. 9: 223.
— on Corporations. (W. L. Wilson) No. Am. 158: 1.
— Phantom Quality in Incomes. Soc. Econ. 7: 7.
— A Progressive. (G. H. Blunden) Econ. J. 5: 527.
— Proposed. Pub. Opin. 15: 169, 193, 218, 242, 264. — (H. White) Nation, 57: 404.
— Reasons in its Favor. (U. S. Hall) Forum, 17: 14.
Income Taxation in France. (H. P. Willis) J. Pol. Econ. 4: 37.
Income Taxes in 1787. (S. Webster) Nation, 60: 215.
Incomplete Highwayman, The; a story. (C. J. C. Hyne) Eng. Illust. 12: no. 3, 111.
Incongruence, Spiritual. (J. H. Phillips) Educa. R. 10: 384.
Inconvenient Keepsake, An. (W. Pain) Idler, 8: 467.
Incorporator's Case, The Bona-fide. (C. Sweet) Jurid. R. 7: 314.
Incorrigible Poet, An. (B. Perry) Scrib. M. 15: 22.
Incredulity. All the Year, 75: 606.
— Credulous. Spec. 77: 639.
Incubation among Egyptians. (J. T. Baylee) Nature, 52: 414.
Incurable; a story. (I. Zangwill) McClure, 1: 478.
Indefinite Article, An; a story. All the Year, 71: 492.
Indenture for Military Service, 1421. Antiq. n. s. 25: 58.
Independence in Politics. (W. D. Foulke) Good Govt. 15: 23.
— — a Protest. (L. Satterthwaite) N. Eng. 56: 180.
Independent Vote in the U. S., Power of. (J. B. Bishop) Nation, 54: 164.
Independents, The American, of 1896, A National Platform for the. (W. P. St. John) Arena, 16: 67.
Index, Roman. Cornh. 69: 256.
Index Expurgatorius and my Articles on Hell. (St. G. Mivart) 19th Cent. 34: 979.
Indexing. (J. B. Nichols) Lib. J. 17: 406.
— Geographical. (J. B. Nichols) Lib. J. 19: 330.
India. Outing, 27: 232.
— Akbar in the 16th Century, by Abul-Fazl. Sat. R. 79: 867.
— Administration of, Hunter on. Sat. R. 74: 200.
— Agricultural Credit in, Reorganization of. (W. Wedderburn) J. Soc. Arts, 40: 646.
— Agricultural Folk-lore Notes. (R. C. Temple) Folk-Lore Rec. 5: 33.
— Agricultural Needs of. (J. A. Voelcker) J. Soc. Arts, 40: 554.
— Agriculture and Canals of. (D. N. Reid) Gent. M. n. s. 57: 373.
— and Afghanistan. Our Last War with the Mahsuds. (S. S. Thorburn) Blackw. 158: 76.
— and Africa. (F. E. Younghusband) Asia. R. 22: 37.
— and Australia, Financial Conditions and Mutual Relations of. Blackw. 154: 64.
India and Ceylon, Carpenter's. (J. D. Butler) Nation, 56: 219.
— and China, Alliance of. (A. Michie) Asia. R. 16: 274.
— — Relations of. (A. Michie) Asia. R. 13: 1.
— and Lancashire, Cotton Trade of. (R. Garth) Asia. R. 21: 1.
— and the Viceroyalty. (E. K. Robinson) Fortn. 64: 439.
— Anglo-Indian Life, Two Aspects of. (P. Hordern) Univ. R. 6: 68.
— Anthropology in, Progress of. (H. H. Risley) Asia. R. 17: 432.
— Archæological Survey of. (J. S. Cotton) Acad. 45: 521. — Acad. 48: 96.
— Army in. (H. N. D. Prendergast) Asia. R. 22: 254. — Un. Serv. M. 10: 410.
— — Imperial Service Troops. Blackw. 160: 5.
— — Native. (D. C. Macdonald) Lippinc. 58: 501.
— — Officering of. Asia. R. 9: 124. — (M. I. Gibbs) Un. Serv. M. 5: 587.
— — Proposed Changes in. (F. H. Tyrrell) Asia. R. 16: 15.
— — Sickness and Mortality in. (T. A. P. Marsh) Westm. 146: 156.
— — Sikh Auxiliaries. (N. G. Lyttleton) New R. 7: 430.
— — Silladar Cavalry. (E. A. W. Stotherd) Un. Serv. M. 6: 484.
— Art of, Notes on. (E. L. Weeks) Harper, 91: 567.
— Aryanism in, and the Modern Theistic Movement. (J. W. Brooks) Meth. R. 56: 559.
— as affected by Russia and France. (G. N. Curzon) 19th Cent. 34: 177.
— Australian View of. (C. W. Dilke) Fortn. 58: 704.
— Beast and Man in, Kipling's. Spec. 68: 123. — (J. D. Butler) Nation, 54: 90. — Sat. R. 73: 52.
— Beasts and Reptiles of. Ed. R. 175: 469.
— British, Constitutional Union for. Asia. R. 18: 36.
— British Government in, compared with Roman System. (W. Lee-Warner) J. Soc. Arts, 43: 61.
— — Home Charges. (W. M. Wood) Asia. R. 16: 75.
— British Possessions in. (G. B. Wolseley) Blackw. 157: 537.
— British Rulers in. (W. S. Seton-Karr) National, 26: 226.
— Cantonments of, Sanitary Condition of. (W. Hill-Climo) Un. Serv. M. 11: 557.
— Carpenter on. Dial (Ch.) 15: 110.
— Carrier-bards of. Dub. R. 111: 445.
— Cavalry Soldier of. (R. H. Morrison) Un. Serv. M. 13: 511.
— Census of, 1891. Dub. R. 111: 443. — (J. Beames) Asia. R. 17: 76. — (E. O. Walker) Gent. M. n. s. 53: 133. — (J. A. Baines) Geog. J. 3: 216.
— — Administration of. (J. A. Baines) J. Soc. Arts, 40: 717.
— Central Province of, Civil Litigation in. (J. W. Macdougall) Jurid. R. 6: 242.
— Chance of Change in. Spec. 74: 716.
— Child-marriages and Widows in. (P. R. Telang) Forum, 18: 95. — (F. M. Müller) Our Day, 13: 563.
— Christian Church in, Earlier. Meth. R. 55: 441.
— Christianity in. (G. F. Pentecost) Our Day, 10: 801, 884.
— Civil Service in. (G. W. Leitner) Asia. R. 16: 90. — (P. C. Roy) Westm. 140: 495.
— — and the Universities. (F. J. Lys) Fortn. 59: 525.
— Closing of the Mints. (Brassey) 19th Cent. 38: 649.

India, Colonial Policy for. (R. A. Sterndale) Asia. R. 12: 49.
— Commercial Travelling in. Chamb. J. 72: 5.
— Cotton Duties in. (Uma Sankar Misra) Asia. R. 18: 50.
— — and Imperial Commercial Federation. (R. Lethbridge) Asia. R. 22: 272.
— The Cow Agitation. (O. P. Singh) 19th Cent. 35: 667.
— Cow-killing Riots in. Spec. 71: 359.
— Creditor and Debtor in. (E. J. Kitts) Law Q. 12: 41.
— Currency of. Bank. M. (Lond.) 54: 504. — (W. R. Lawson) Blackw. 155: 440. — (G. L. Molesworth) Ann. Am. Acad. Pol. Sci. 4: 1. — (J. B. Robertson) J. Soc. Arts, 42: 353. — J. Statis. Soc. 56: 482.
— — Bimetallism and. (L. L. Price) Econ. J. 3: 617.
— — Commission for. Blackw. 154: 293.
— — Currency Committee's Report. Econ. J. 3: 511. — (W. Fowler) Econ. J. 3: 628.
— — Question of. (F. C. Harrison) Econ. J. 4: 262. — (D. Barbour) National, 25: 219.
— — Recent Legislation on. (T. Beauclerk) Econ. J. 4: 119.
— — Rupee Difficulty. (E. Hubbard) National, 22: 68.
— — Suspended Rupee and the Policy of Contraction. (D. Horton) Econ. J. 3: 475.
— — Variorum Notes on. Econ. J. 3: 517.
— Dak to Peshawur. (A. H. Morrison) Canad. M. 1: 280.
— Defence of. (Lord Chelmsford) Asia. R. 16: 1, 265.
— Difficulties of District Officers in. (H. C. E. Ward) Asia. R. 21: 275.
— Discontent in. Westm. 142: 481.
— Discontent of Officers in. Sat. R. 74: 221.
— Domestic Animals in. (J. L. Kipling) Pop. Sci. Mo. 40: 597.
— Drama; Bharata Nâtya Sâstra. (H. H. Dhruva) Asia. R. 22: 349.
— Duties on Cotton Goods in. (E. Helm) Econ. J. 6: 110.
— Economic Products of, Watt on. Nature, 51: 4.
— Education of. (Uma Sankar Misra) Asia. R. 9: 365.
— Lord Elgin as Viceroy. (R. Lethbridge) Asia. R. 17: 59.
— England and. Pub. Opin. 19: 491.
— England's Frontier in. Quar. 184: 161.
— England's Honor toward. (Dadabhai Naoroji) Asia. R. 14: 311.
— English in. (W. Bonnar) Contemp. 68: 564.
— Englishmen who won Fame in. (S. P. Codman) Chaut. 19: 692.
— European Military Adventurers in, Compton's. Spec. 70: 826.
— Famine of 1896. (L. Griffin) Sat. R. 82: 489. Same art. Liv. Age, 211: 886. — (T. M. Kirkwood) Fortn. 66: 856.
— Farther, MacMahon's. (S. Wheeler) Acad. 41: 535.
— Finance Troubles. (H. S. Cunningham) Asia. R. 17: 251.
— Finances of. Sat. R. 80: 336.
— — Silver and. (S. Montagu) Fortn. 58: 545.
— Financial Condition of. (A. K. Connell) Asia. R. 21: 261.
— Folk-Tales of. (S. M. Taylor) Folk-Lore, 7: 83.
— Forecasting Famines in. (D. Archibald) Knowl. 19: 265.
— Forward Policy. Asia. R. 17: 15.
— French and English View of. Atlan. 78: 552.
— French in. (L. B. Bowring) Fortn. 61: 83.
— Frontier of, English Expeditions to. (J. Dacosta) Westm. 137: 36.
India. Frontiers and Finance. (A. Colvin) 19th Cent. 38: 870.
— Prince Galitzin's Travels in. Dub. R. 110: 451.
— Geography of, Evolution of. (R. D. Oldham) Geog. J. 3: 169.
— Gods of. (F. M. Crawford) Cent. 25: 925.
— Gold Currency for. (C. Daniell) Blackw. 152: 597.
— Gold Standard in, Plans to establish. Bank. M. (Lond.) 54: 157.
— Government of. (C. A. Elliott) Asia. R. 22: 233.
— — Parliament and. Macmil. 68: 449.
— — Reflections on the Way Home. (H. E. M. James) National, 22: 335.
— — Twelve Years of. Ed. R. 181: 1.
— Growth of State Expenditure. (A. Colvin) 19th Cent. 36: 645.
— Half-Breeds in; Eurasians. (G. Sandberg) Contemp. 61: 880. — (S. J. Duncan) Pop. Sci. Mo. 42: 1.
— Hospitals in, Origin and Progress of. (W. J. Moore) Asia. R. 14: 286.
— How it has suffered in the Race of Wealth. (D. N. Reid) Gent. M. n. s. 56: 612.
— Hunter's. Sat. R. 75: 328.
— Hurst on. (H. A. Buttz) Meth. R. 52: 362.
— Imperial, Prinsep's. M. of Art, 2: 120.
— Import Duties on Cotton Goods and Yarns. (E. Helm) Econ. J. 5: 269.
— Impressions of. (C. F. Keary) New R. 12: 29-395. Same art. Ecl. M. 124: 370-772.
— Improving our Position in. (R. Carstairs) Asia. R. 20: 268. 21: 19.
— in the Days of John Company. (Col. Herbert) Macmil. 67: 119. Same art. Liv. Age, 196: 296.
— in 18th Century. Sat. R. 73: 281.
— in 1882-92. (C. E. D. Black) Geog. J. 3: 506.
— in 1892, Mutterings from. National, 19: 582.
— In the Jungles of. (E. O. Walker) Gent. M. n. s. 54: 13.
— in Parliament in 1894-95. (R. Temple) Asia. R. 20: 1.
— In the 7th Century, I-tsing's Record of. Acad. 47: 62.
— Is it Safe from Russia? (L. H. Griffin) Asia. R. 16: 26.
— Judiciary of, Necessity of Independence of. (Manomohan Ghose) Asia. R. 21: 31.
— A Khud in the Punjab. (E. Carrington) Ecl. M. 125: 780.
— Land Question. (R. Lethbridge) Asia. R. 18: 325.
— — Is the State Owner? (H. H. Baden-Powell) Asia. R. 18: 1.
— Land Legislation in. (J. W. MacDougall) Jurid. R. 8: 167.
— Land Revenue Settlements. (A. Rogers) Asia. R. 22: 61.
— Land Survey of, Proposed. Sat. R. 76: 352.
— Land Systems of, B. H. B. Powell on. (A. C. Powell) Law Q. 9: 23.
— Land Tenure in. (J. W. Macdougall) Jurid. R. 5: 218.
— Landed Aristocracy in, Decay of. (O. P. Singh) 19th Cent. 31: 830.
— Lord Lansdowne as Viceroy. Asia. R. 17: 53. — Sat. R. 78: 212.
— Latent Religion of. (G. M. Cobban) Contemp. 67: 853. Same art. Liv. Age, 206: 50.
— Law of, Codification of. (C. P. Ilbert) Law Q. 5: 347.
— Legislative Council in, Powers of. (C. D. Field) Law Q. 11: 278.
— Lenz's World Tour Awheel. Outing, 26: 224-467. 27: 51-226, 313.

India, Life in Anglo-, Recent Impressions of. (E. L. Weeks) Harper, **91**: 903.
— Little Wars on the Indian Frontier. Blackw. **157**: 930.
— Local Self-government in. (Umá S. Misra) Univ. R. **4**: 589.
— Looting of Lucknow, 1857. (W. H. Russell) Idler, **9**: 36.
— MacGeorge's Ways and Works in. (G. S. Morison) Nation, **60**: 130.
— Mammals of, Blanford's. (R. Lyddeker) Nat. Sci. **1**: 60.
— Manufactures in. (J. Danvers) J. Soc. Arts, **41**: 602.
— Medical Needs of. (K. N. Bahadurji) Asia. R. **22**: 298, 406.
— Meteorology of. Nature, **45**: 217.
— Military Resources of. (E. Lawrence) Time, **18**: 339.
— Military Weakness of England in. (C. B. Norman) Un. Serv. M. **4**: 153-354.
— Mints of. Chamb. J. **71**: 561.
— — Closing of. (W. H. Houldsworth) National, **21**: 805.
— Missionary Work in. (P. C. Mozoomdar) Outl. **49**: 862.
— Missions; a Forgotten Oxford Movement, 1681. (Sir W. W. Hunter) Fortn. **65**: 689.
— Monetary History of. (J. L. Laughlin) J. Pol. Econ. **1**: 593.
— Monetary Problem of. (L. C. Probyn) Asia. R. **17**: 271. **20**: 241.
— Mountain March in. (A. H. Morrison) Canad. M. **1**: 497.
— Mutiny of 1857-58. Sat. R. **76**: 157.
— — Lieut. Mackenzie's Ride. (T. R. Holmes) National, **21**: 58.
— — Maude on. Ath. '94, **1**: 339. — Sat. R. **77**: 345.
— — Missing Link in the Chain of. (Deputy Surgeon-Gen. Paske) Eng. Illust. **11**: 1205.
— — Mitchell's Reminiscences of. Ath. '94, **1**: 203. — Sat. R. **77**: 498.
— — My First Battle in the. (S. D. White) Westm. **145**: 78.
— — Recollections of. (J. R. Oliver) Un. Serv. M. **13**: 55-255.
— — Romantic Tales of. (W. F. Mitchell) Chamb. J. **71**: 654-669.
— National Congress of, Origin and Aims. (A. Mundy) Asia. R. **21**: 388.
— Naval Requirements for. Un. Serv. M. **6**: 150.
— Native, and England. (T. Beck) National, **24**: 375.
— Native Chivalry in, True Story of. Spec. **73**: 266.
— Native Press of. Liv. Age, **207**: 164.
— Native Princes of. (Lepel Griffin) Asia. R. **9**: 1.
— Native States of. Quar. **176**: 198.
— New Danger and Fresh Wrongs. (G. W. Leitner) Asia. R. **20**: 288.
— A Night in. (S. C. Logan) 19th Cent. **36**: 71. Same art. Liv. Age, **202**: 296. Same art. Ecl. M. **123**: 346.
— Night-Traveling in. (S. C. Logan) 19th Cent. **37**: 101. Same art. Liv. Age, **204**: 426.
— North-East, Nágá and Other Tribes of. (Gertrude M. Godden) Anthrop. J. **26**: 161.
— Northwest Frontier of. (H. Beauchamp) Fortn. **63**: 721. — (J. D. Poynder) National, **28**: 103.
— Occupation and Caste in. (J. A. Baines) J. Soc. Arts, **41**: 457.
— Opium Legislation of. (J. W. Macdougall) Jurid. R. **6**: 14.
— Original Inhabitants, Oppert on. Sat. R. **77**: 263.
— Outings in. (A. Hudson) Art J. **44**: 52-205.
— Paper Currency of. Bank. M. (Lond.) **55**: 345.
India, Past and Present. (J. D. Rees) Asia. R. **20**: 253.
— Police of. (A. Ollivant) Un. Serv. M. **6**: 610.
— Political Outlook. (G. Chesney) 19th Cent. **35**: 890.
— Polity in, Chesney on. Sat. R. **79**: 447.
— Popular Religion in. Spec. **73**: 115.
— Population of. Geog. J. **1**: 242.
— — Distribution and Movement of. (J. A. Baines) J. Statis. Soc. **56**: 1.
— — Rapid Growth of. (R. Temple) Fortn. **57**: 426.
— Press of. Asia R. **20**: 16.
— Princes of, Relation to the Empire. (R. Lethbridge) Asia. R. **20**: 312. **21**: 11.
— — Jurisdiction of, and of the Paramount Power. Asia. R. **22**: 263.
— — Protected (R. Lethbridge) Asia. R. **18**: 36.
— — — Warner's. Sat. R. **77**: 672.
— Progress of, under the Crown. (W. W. Hunter) J. Soc. Arts, **41**: 329.
— Public Opinion in. Quar. **182**: 429.
— Pundits, Priests, and Missions in. Eng. R. **11**: 404.
— Ragozin's Story of Vedic India. (M. Bloomfield) Am. Hist. R. **1**: 103.
— Railroad to. (C. E. D. Black) Contemp. **67**: 569. — (F. R. Maunsell) Un. Serv. M. **5**: 525.
— Railroads in. (Jos. Walton) J. Soc. Arts, **42**: 393.
— — Coming. (J. W. Parry) J. Soc. Arts, **43**: 569.
— Recent Run to the East. (Lord Brassey) 19th Cent. **35**: 971.
— Religions of, Recent Books on. (G. S. Goodspeed) Dial (Ch.) **19**: 289.
— Religious Movements in. (B. Khuda) Spec. **75**: 47. Same art. Liv. Age, **206**: 572.
— Reminiscence of Travel in. (C. J. Gillis) Around World, **1**: 144.
— Representative Government in. (D. MacG. Means) Nation, **61**: 23.
— Revenue in. (W. H. Grimley) Univ. R. **3**: 285.
— Rulers of. (M. E. G. Duff) Un. Serv. M. **7**: 705-1231.
— Rupee, and Silver. (F. C. Harrison) Econ. J. **5**: 272.
— — How to save. (H. Cox) National, **24**: 69.
— Rupee Circulation, Composition and Amount of. (F. C. Harrison) Econ. J. **6**: 122.
— Russian Approach to. (K. Blind) Lippinc. **51**: 214. — (G. J. Younghusband) 19th Cent. **33**: 727.
— Russianized, Officialism in. (Sir W. Wedderburn) Asia. R. **15**: 1.
— Sanitation in, and International Congress of Hygiene. (Sir W. Moore) J. Soc. Arts, **40**: 372.
— Scramble for Gold in. (J. P. Heseltine) 19th Cent. **35**: 58.
— Scientific Frontier of, Hanna on. Sat. R. **80**: 315.
— Silk Manufacture. (L. N. Badenoch) Asia. R. **16**: 455.
— Silver Crisis of. Pub. Opin. **16**: 423. — Spec. **72**: 124.
— — Effects of Depreciation. (J. S. Nicholson) Econ. J. **4**: 59.
— Silver, Wheat and Cotton. (S. Leavitt) Arena, **10**: 192.
— Situation in, in 1893. (Sir L. H. Griffin) Pub. Opin. **15**: 446.
— Sketches of. (S. H. Dunn) Month, **88**: 342, 536.
— Society in, Variety of. Spec. **70**: 352.
— Some Further Reflections on. (H. E. M. James) National, **22**: 772.
— South, Early Races of. (F. Fawcett) Folk-Lore, **5**: 18.
— — Murder Trials in. (E. Sewell) Folk-Lore, **5**: 14.

India, Station in, A. Liv. Age, **207**: 755. Same art. Ecl. M. **125**: 810.
— Statistics of, 1894–95. Dub. R. **119**: 430.
— Subaltern in, a Hundred Years Ago. Cornh. **68**: 474. Same art. Liv. Age, **199**: 683. Same art. Ecl. M. **122**: 52.
— Survey of. Chamb. J. **72**: 151.
— — 1891–92. Geog. J. **2**: 152.
— — 1892–93. (C. E. D. Black) Geog. J. **4**: 31.
— — 1893–94. (C. E. D. Black) Geog. J. **6**: 27.
— Tariffs of. New R. **14**: 67.
— Things Missed in. (P. Hordern) Univ. R. **4**: 284.
— Thirty Years of Shikar, Braddon's. Sat. R. **79**: 657.
— Three Moral Cancers of. Our Day, **11**: 348.
— Tiger Hunting in. (J. H. Porter) Outing, **28**: 140.
— to Kâbul, Journey from. (R. C. Drummond) Belgra. **85**: 379.
— Trade with Far East, and the New Rupee. (F. B. Forbes) Econ. J. **4**: 127.
— Trans-frontier Expeditions. (J. Dacosta) Asia. R. **15**: 15.
— Travel and Sport in, Gardner's. Sat. R. **80**: 84.
— Travels in, Twining's. Sat. R. **77**: 20. — Ath. '**94**, **1**: 271.
— Trigonometrical Survey. Liv. Age, **205**: 58.
— Vernacular Literature of. Acad. **46**: 89. — (A. Pedler) Acad. **50**: 164.
— Viceroys of. (E. Arnold) Eng. Illust. **11**: 406.
— The Village in. (W. J. Ashley) Pol. Sci. Q. **9**: 119. — (Anne C. Wilson) Good Words, **35**: 690. Same art. Ecl. M. **123**: 676.
— Village Communities in Southern. (C. K. Menon) J. Soc. Arts, **43**: 310.
— Village Money-lenders in. Chamb. J. **70**: 300.
— A Vision of. Macmil. **70**: 100.
— Voices of the Night in. Sund. M. **24**: 405, 606, 751.
— Water Supply and Sanitation in N. W. (A. Colvin) J. Soc. Arts, **42**: 515.
— The Wife in. (R. V. Rogers) Green Bag, **8**: 7.
— Women of. (S. E. J. Clarke) J. Soc. Arts, **43**: 262.
— Would India gain by the Extinction of European Government? (R. N. Cust) Asia. R. **9**: 257.
— Yellow Men of. (C. Johnston) Asia. R. **15**: 102.
— Zhob Field Force in 1890, McFall on. Sat. R. **80**: 24[illegible].
India Exhibition, London. (S. Beale) Am. Arch. **49**: 102.
India-rubber. (G. Allen) Longm. **24**: 492.
Indian, American, as a Citizen. (J. Wickersham) Am. Antiq. **17**: 329.
— — What and Whence. (J. Campbell) Canad. M. **2**: 305.
Indian Agents. (H. Welsh) Lend a H. **17**: 430.
Indian Association, Connecticut, Report for 1893. (C. E. Swartwout) Lend a H. **12**: 37.
— Maine. Report, 1893. (A. Blanchard) Lend a H. **12**: 107.
— Massachusetts. Report, 1893. (M. E. Dewey) Lend a H. **12**: 17.
— Woman's National. Lend a H. **10**: 30.
Indian Bibliographies. (R. R. Elliott) Am. Cath. Q. **18**: 698.
Indian Bureau; its Transfer to the War Department. Am. Cath. Q. **19**: 244.
Indian Corn, Fertile Crosses with. (J. W. Harshberger) Garden & F. **9**: 522.
— in Italy. (H. C. Mercer) Am. Natural. **28**: 971.
— An Indian on. (T. H. Hoskins) Garden & F. **8**: 23.
— Use of, in Europe, as a Human Food. (G. W. Hill) Chaut. **16**: 293.
Indian Emeralds, The; a story. (S. Crewe) Argosy, 58: 559.
Indian Fair, An, in the Mexican Hot Country. (S. Baxter) Harper, **84**: 757.
— in South New Jersey. (J. Gifford) Science, **22**: 113.
Indian Lover, An; a story. (J. G. Menard) Canad. M. **5**: 242.
Indian Maiden's Grave; a story. (C. Traill) Canad. M. **4**: 280.
Indian Names, North and South American. (M. V. Moore) Pop. Sci. Mo. **44**: 81.
Indian Ocean in Antiquity. (H. Schlichter) Asia. R. **12**: 305.
Indian Princess, An [American]. (Mary F. Kalor) Bost. **3**: 64.
Indian Princess, Strange Story of an. Chamb. J. **71**: 29.
— Visit to. (Mrs. W. Dixon) Sund. M. **22**: 692.
Indian Rajah at Home. (J. P. Val d'Eremao) Asia. R. **14**: 181.
Indian Relics in New York State, Nature and Distribution of. (W. M. Beauchamp) Science, **22**: 159.
Indian Reservation, English Language on an. (F. C. Sparhawk) Educa. **12**: 609.
Indian River, A Glimpse of. (R. A. Moore) So. M. **2**: 3.
Indian River Country, Florida. Chamb. J. **71**: 424.
Indian Songs. (J. G. Fillmore) J. Am. Folk-Lore, **8**: 138.
— Personal Studies of Indian Life. (A. C. Fletcher) Cent. **25**: 421.
Indian Summer. (F. N. Jones) Bost. **3**: 170.
Indian Summer; a poem. (A. Watters) Temp. Bar, **103**: 407.
Indian Territory. (A. Hendricks) Lippinc. **58**: 670.
— Failure of Government in. (W. M. Fishback) Am. M. Civics, **6**: 96.
— Problems in. (O. H. Platt) No. Am. **160**: 195.
— Survey and Subdivision of. (H. Gannett) Nat. Geog. M. **7**: 112.
Indian Treaties in Ontario and Manitoba. (J. C. Hamilton) Canad. M. **3**: 556.
Indian War Clubs. (J. Wickersham) Am. Antiq. **17**: 72.
Indian Warfare on the Frontier. Atlan. **69**: 270.
Indian Wars and Warriors. (E. Goodale-Eastman) Cosmopol. **16**: 409.
Indian Words, Transliteration of. (M. J. King-Harman) Asia. R. **13**: 91.
Indiana, State Bank of. (W. F. Harding) J. Pol. Econ. **4**: 1, 109.
— Supreme Court of. (W. W. Thornton) Green Bag, **4**: 207, 249.
Indiana Campaign; a story. (S. Crane) Eng. Illust. **16**: 320.
Indiana Charivari, An. (L. Armstrong) Southern M. **4**: 355.
Indiana University, Elective Studies at. (R. G. Boone) Educa. R. **4**: 53, 142.
Indianapolis. (T. Hughes) Month, **74**: 559.
— Public Schools of. (J. M. Rice) Forum, **14**: 429.
Indian's Hand; a story. (L. Stoddard) Lippinc. **50**: 227.
Indian's Grave; a poem. (H. A. Cody) Canad. M. **7**: 147.
Indians of America. (W. E. Dougherty) Overland, n. s. **19**: 225–337. — (T. B. Stephenson) Sund. M. **22**: 242.
— Administration of Indian Service, Change in. (P. C. Garrett) Lend a H. **11**: 328.
— Allotment of Land to, Experiences in. (E. J. Gay) Lend a H. **9**: 241.
— and the U. S. (J. E. Greene) Lend a H. 17: 128.

Indians. Are they becoming Extinct? (J. W. Powell) Forum, 15: 343.
— Artists' Adventures with; the Rush to Death. (W. Shirlaw) Cent. 25: 41.
— Beauty from an Indian's Point of View. (R. W. Shufeldt) Cosmopol. 18: 591.
— Bows and Quivers of. (E. Ingersoll) Mo. Illust. 5: 119.
— Canadian, Treatment of. (W. Trant) Westm. 144: 506.
— Civil Service and Indian Service. (H. Welsh) Good Govt. 13: 41.
— Civilizing the. (R. Shaffner) Chaut. 23: 259.
— Condition of, in 1892. (M. E. Dewey) Lend a H. 8: 225. — (G. T. Kercheval) Lend a H. 9: 18.
— — 1895. (W. T. Larned) Lippinc. 55: 647.
— Dakota, Emblematic Use of the Tree by. (Alice C. Fletcher) Science, n. s. 4: 475.
— Depredations of, Claims for. (L. W. Colby) Lend a H. 11: 337.
— Disappearance of the Race a Popular Fallacy. (J. W. Pope) Arena, 16: 945.
— Education of. (F. W. Blackmar) Ann. Am. Acad. Pol. Sci. 2: 813. — (R. H. Pratt) Pub. Opin. 18: 730.
— — Fruits of. (D. O. Lewis) Canad. M. 5: 425.
— — Government Schools and Contract Schools. (D. Dorchester) Lend a H. 10: 118.
— — How educated? (J. H. Kyle) No. Am. 159: 434.
— — Symposium. Indep. April 7, '92.
— Educational Work for. (W. N. Hailman) Lend a H. 13: 367.
— English Institutions and. (J. A. James) J. H. Univ. Stud. 12: 467.
— Famous; Portraits of Some Indian Chiefs. (C. E. S. Wood) Cent. 24: 436.
— Food of. (L. Carr) Lend a H. 15: 347.
— Government Policy toward, Crisis in. (H. L. Dawes) Lend a H. 11: 346.
— Half-blood. (F. Boas) Pop. Sci. Mo. 45: 761.
— Hidatsu, Folk-tale of. Folk-Lore Rec. 1: 136.
— Homes of, Comparative Study of. (R. W. Shufeldt) Pop. Sci. Mo. 41: 798.
— in Maine, 1724. Letters of Col. T. Westbrook and others. N. E. Reg. 46: 22-359.
— in New York State, Location of Tribes of. (W. M. Beauchamp) Science, 19: 76.
— Incoming Administration and, Feb., 1893. (H. Welsh) Lend a H. 10: 112.
— Is the Race Exceptional? (W. W. Wotherspoon) Lend a H. 8: 318.
— Languages of, Bibliographies of. (R. R. Elliott) Am. Cath. Q. 19: 545. 20: 238, 721.
— — Characteristics of. (D. G. Brinton) Am. Antiq. 16: 33.
— — Morphologic Traits of. (D. G. Brinton) Am. Antiq. 16: 336.
— Law for. (E. E. Hale) Lend a H. 8: 1.
— Legends and Fables of. Folk-Lore Rec. 5: 93.
— Letter of Guy Johnson, 1775. M. Am. Hist. 28: 372.
— Life of, Personal Studies of; Politics and Pipe-dancing. (A. C. Fletcher) Cent. 23: 441. 28: 691.
— Magic among. (H. Kellar) No. Am. 157: 591.
— Music of. (A. C. Fletcher) Music, 6: 188.
— — and its Investigators. (A. C. Fletcher) Music, 4: 452.
— — Study of. (J. C. Fillmore) Cent. 25: 616.
— Myths of. (S. D. Peet) Am. Antiq. 16: 275.
— Mythologies of, Growth of. (F. Boas) J. Am. Folk-Lore, 9: 1.
Indians. Nations of the Great Lakes. (W. M. Beauchamp) Am. Antiq. 17: 321.
— Need of. (M. E. Dewey) Lend a H. 9: 77.
— Northwestern, Characteristics of. Pop. Sci. Mo. 43: 823.
— Nova Scotian, Folk Tales of, Rand on. (F. Starr) Dial (Ch.) 17: 14.
— of the Atlantic Slope, Prehistoric Migrations of. (C. Thomas) Am. Antiq. 18: 346.
— of British Columbia, Potlach Dance. (D. O. Lewis) Canad. M. 5: 337.
— of Minnesota. (H. B. Whipple) Lend a H. 14: 97.
— of New Mexico. Dub. R. 114: 176.
— of the North Pacific, Decorative Art of. (F. Boas) Science, n. s. 4: 101.
— of the Southwest, Bandelier's. (L. Carr) Nation, 56: 54.
— One Good Indian. (D. A. Goodsell) Chaut. 23: 179.
— Origin of. (C. Thomas) Am. Antiq. 16: 3. — (J. Wickersham) Am. Antiq. 16: 325. — (C. Thomas) Am. Antiq. 17: 44.
— — Indian Traditions of. (Wm. E. Read) Overland, n. s. 20: 577.
— Peonage in Mexico. (W. L. Logan) Soc. Econ. 5: 98.
— Poetry of American Aboriginal Speech. (A. F. Chamberlain) J. Am. Folk-Lore, 9: 43. — (D. G. Brinton) Poet-Lore, 4: 329.
— Pottery of. (W. J. Hoffman) Mo. Illust. 4: 209, 377. 5: 87, 216, 361. — (W. J. Hoffman) Mo. Illust. 11: 237, 530, 663. 12: 79.
— Preparation of, for Citizenship. (A. C. Fletcher) Lend a H. 9: 190.
— Problem of, and how we are solving it. R. of Rs. (N. Y.) 5: 551.
— — by an Indian. (S. Po-ka-gon) R. of Rs. (N. Y.) 12: 694.
— Proper Training and Future of. (J. W. Powell) Forum, 18: 622.
— Question of. (C. A. Huntington) Overland, n. s. 22: 516.
— — Some Phases of. (H. Welsh) Pub. Opin. 18: 408.
— Roman Catholic Church and. (D. Manley) Cath. World, 55: 473.
— School System for, The Evolution of. (H. D. Sheldon) Educa. 16: 7.
— Schools for, Supt. Hailman on. Lend a H. 14: 361.
— — in the U. S., in 1892. (M. E. Dewey) Lend a H. 10: 229.
— — Industrial Training in. (R. H. Pratt) Educa. R. 10: 325.
— Scotch Highlanders and. (M. E. Strieby) Lend a H. 15: 376.
— Spoils System and Indian Service. (F. E. Leupp) Pub. Opin. 18: 570.
— Through Camps of, in a Government Ambulance. (E. Grinnell) Southern M. 4: 405.
— Tour of Observation among, Meserve on. Lend a H. 14: 133.
— Trading-Houses or Factory System. (J. A. James) Nat'l M. (N. Y. '91) 16: 32.
— Training of. (M. E. Dewey) Lend a H. 11: 163. — Lend a H. 17: 436.
— Types of. (G. Holme) Munsey, 9: 152.
— U. S. Indian Service. (H. Smith) Lend a H. 14: 170.
— Virginia, Government and Religion of. (S. R. Hendren) J. H. Univ. Stud. 13: 539.
— With Gun and Palette among. Outing, 25: 355.
Indictments. (H. L. Stephen) Law Q. 12: 167.
Indifference of the Miller of Hofbau; a story. (A. Hope Hawkins) McClure, 5: 533.

Indifferentism. (C. Coupe) Am. Cath. Q. **20**: 266.
Indigo; an Old Industry. (M. H. Leonard) Pop. Sci. Mo. **46**: 649.
Individual, The, and the Community. (W. Wundt) Open Court, **6**: 3183–3217.
— and the State. (W. E. Hart) Soc. Econ. **4**: 29.
— Rights of the. (H. Rashdall) Econ. R. **6**: 317.
— Value of. (W. N. Ashman) Ref. Q. **40**: 396.
Individual Determinism and Social Science. (G. Fiamingo) Ann. Am. Acad. Pol. Sci. **7**: 270.
Individual Mind and Nature. (K. Lasswitz) Monist, **6**: 396.
Individualism. (T. Hedge) Luth. Q. **25**: 506. — Soc. Econ. **1**: 75. — (W. Schooling) Westm. **138**: 521.
— and Monism. (W. Lutoslawski) Monist, **6**: 351.
— and Political Economy. (V. Yarros) Open Court, **7**: 3591.
— and Societism. (Z. S. Holbrook) Bib. Sac. **53**: 540.
— as a Sociological Principle. (E. B. Andrews) Yale R. **2**: 13.
— Progressive. (J. R. Commons) Am. M. Civics, **6**: 561.
— Pseudo-; the Present Slavery. (A. Withy) Westm. **142**: 485.
— True. (W. E. Brokaw) Am. M. Civics, **8**: 537.
— *versus* Collectivism. (L. Courtney) Pop. Sci. Mo. **50**: 215.
Individualist or Collectivist, Which is most in Accord with Teaching of Christ? (F. Relton) Econ. R. **4**: 499.
Individualists and Socialists, An Eirenikon to. (J. E. Symes) Westm. **142**: 644.
Individuality, Cultivation of. (H. S. Brodie) Belgra. **78**: 423.
— Moral, in Catholic Christianity, The Principle of. (G. Frommel) New World, **5**: 634.
— A Plea for. (F. A. Comstock) Educa. **16**: 46.
Individuals, Importance of. (W. James) Open Court, **4**: 2437.
Indo-China, Crisis in. (D. C. Boulger) 19th Cent. **34**: 187.
— England and France in. (H. N. D. Prendergast) Asia. R. **17**: 1.
— France in. Dub. R. **117**: 161.
— French, Journeys in. (G. N. Curzon) Geog. J. **2**: 97, 193.
— A Journey from Tonkin. (Henri d'Orleans) Geog. J. **8**: 566.
— Partition of. Fortn. **65**: 370.
— Recent Travels in. (Lord Lamington) J. Soc. Arts, **40**: 278.
— Traveling in. (G. N. Curzon) Around World, **1**: 16.
Induction Coils, Large, Improved Form of Interrupter for. (F. L. O. Wadsworth) Am. J. Sci. **148**: 496.
Inductive Inquiry, Methods of. (H. Laurie) Mind, **18**: 319.
Indulgences, Historical Argument for. (J. Hirst) Month, **75**: 347.
— Lea's History of. (W. Webster) Acad. **50**: 324. — (E. Emerton) Am. Hist. R. **2**: 113.
— Luther's Theses on. (J. C. Long) Bapt. R. **14**: 385.
Indus-delta Country, M. R. Haig's. (F. J. Goldsmid) Geog. J. **6**: 260.
Industrial America. By C. B. Spahr. Outl. **48**: 66–627.
Industrial and Social Situation. (W. Gladden) Bib. Sac. **49**: 383.
Industrial Art at the Paris Salons, 1896. (H. Frantz) M. of Art, **19**: 457.
— Russian. (E. D. Morgan) Am. Arch. **41**: 11.
Industrial Arts, Teaching of, in Italy. (A. Melani) Am. Arch. **42**: 125.
Industrial Competition. (T. Scanlon) Westm. **145**: 286.
Industrial Conditions and the Money Markets. (M. L. Muhleman) Engin. M. **11**: 1.
Industrial Crisis. Gunton's M. **10**: 347.
Industrial Decline of Lancashire. Soc. Econ. **3**: 257.
Industrial Depression, The Present. (R. H. I. Palgrave) National, **25**: 105.
Industrial Depressions; Cause and Cure. (F. H. Cooke) Am. J. Pol. **3**: 597.
Industrial Disputes, Settlement of, by Law. (W. L. Stobart) Westm. **137**: 667.
Industrial Education in Old and New England. (S. N. D. North) Am. J. Soc. Sci. no. **34**: 29.
— Why push it in the South? (B. T. Washington) Pub. Opin. **20**: 750.
See Manual Training.
Industrial Features in Boston Public Schools. (H. M. Winslow) New Eng. M. **9**: 369.
Industrial History, English, Cunningham and McArthur's. Sat. R. **79**: 606.
Industrial Independence, American. (A. R. Foote) Am. J. Pol. **1**: 593.
Industrial Life, Philosophy and. (J. C. Murray) Monist, **4**: 533.
Industrial Order, The Coming. (J. G. Clark) Arena, **11**: 238.
Industrial Organization, The. (D. H. Wheeler) Meth. R. **55**: 595.
Industrial Outlook and our National Policy. (C. Mills) Engin. M. **12**: 1.
Industrial Peace, Growth of. (J. Rae) Contemp. **62**: 319. Same art. Ecl. M. **119**: 594.
— Methods of. (W. J. Ashley) Econ. R. **2**: 297.
— State Promotion of. (D. F. Schloss) Econ. J. **3**: 218.
Industrial Problem, Woman's View of. (A. L. Woodbridge) Am. M. Civics, **9**: 71.
Industrial Problems, Present, in the Light of History. (E. Atkinson) Forum, **18**: 42.
Industrial Question, The Impending. And. R. **18**: 272.
Industrial Reform. (J. G. Stevenson) Arena, **14**: 317.
Industrial Residuum. (H. Dendy) Econ. J. **3**: 500.
Industrial Schools and Juvenile Crime. (A. A. W. Drew) Contemp. **63**: 732.
— of the Netherlands. (M. A. Dooly) Arena, **7**: 714.
Industrial Slavery. (F. H. Hurd) Am. J. Pol. **1**: 471.
Industrial Success, Relations of Finance to. (H. Clews) Engin. M. **11**: 809.
Industrial Training in Public Schools, Limitations and Possibilities of. (C. J. Ryder) Educa. **12**: 581.
See Manual Training.
Industrialism, Ethics of. (R. R. Marett) Econ. R. **2**: 342.
— Relation to Morality. (M. C. Remick) Arena, **17**: 32.
Industries, Great American. X. A Bar of Iron. (R. R. Bowker) Harper, **88**: 408.
— — XI. A Steel Tool. (R. R. Bowker) Harper, **88**: 587.
— — XII. Electricity. (R. R. Bowker) Harper, **93**: 710.
— Location of. (E. A. Ross) Q. J. Econ. **10**: 247.
— Public Regulation of. (W. D. Dabney) Ann. Am. Acad. Pol. Sci. **2**: 433.
— Relations of, to Advancement of Chemical Science. (W. McMurtie) Science, n. s. **2**: 283.
Industriously, Use of the Word. (F. Hall) Nation, **61**: 149.
Industry, American: why it languishes. (H. A. Herbert) No. Am. **163**: 488.
— Evolution of, Dyer's. Sat. R. **80**: 442.
— Place of, in the Social Organism. (W. Smart) Int. J. Ethics, **3**: 437.
— Protectionist Idea of. (D. A. Wells) Am. J. Pol. **1**: 225.

Industry, Threefold Contention of. (J. B. Weaver) Arena, 5: 427.
— Victims of. (C. Rolleston) Westm. 141: 417.
Inebriation in Plants and Animals. (C. Sterne) Open Court, 4: 2419, 2459.
Inebriety and Insanity. (L. E. Keeley) Arena, 8: 328.
— as a Disease. (Norman Kerr) Cosmopol. 21: 547.
— Bichloride of Gold Cure for. (H. Wood) Arena, 7: 145. — (L. Keeley) Arena, 7: 450. — (J. R. Barlow) Chaut. 15: 61.
— — Historical Notes on. (H. C. Bolton) Pop. Sci. Mo. 41: 469.
— Keeley Cure. (A. B. O'Neill) Cath. World, 57: 320.
— Specifics for the Cure of. (T. D. Crothers) Pop. Sci. Mo. 41: 732.
Inefficiency, Adler on. (S. Schindler) Educa. 15: 200.
Inevitable Thing, The; a story. (E. Pugh) Eng. Illust. 14: 411.
Infancy, The Scientific Investigation of. Liv. Age, 208: 60.
Infant, Legal Deed of an. (T. R. Harris) Am. Law R. 26: 502.
Infant Life, Perils and Protection of. (H. R. Jones) J. Statis. Soc. 57: 1.
Infant Phenomenon, The; a farce. (W. Pett Ridge) Idler, 9: 582.
Infant Prodigies, Literary. Spec. 68: 741.
Infanticide in China. (A. M. Clarke) Cath. World, 60: 769. — (C. de Harlez) Dub. R. 111: 117.
— in India. Chamb. J. 69: 517.
Infants, Distance- and Color-perception by. (J. M. Baldwin) Science, 21: 231.
— Movements of. (J. M. Baldwin) Science, 19: 15.
— Nursing and Care of: Maggie's Baby. Lend a H. 11: 18.
Infantry, Drill Regulations of New System. (W. H. Powell) Un. Serv. (Phila.) 9: 403.
— Action of, and our New Drill Regulations. (C. Reichman) Un. Serv. (Phila.) 8: 105-218.
— Drill Regulations and our Next War. (J. S. Pettit) Un. Serv. Phila. 10: 1.
— Mounted. (Sir F. Middleton) Un. Serv. M. 5: 178. 6: 163. — (E. T. H. Hutton) Un. Serv. M. 7: 748.
— Offensive Tactics of. (G. F. R. Henderson) Un. Serv. M. 7: 945.
— Organization of. (C. Pearson) Un. Serv. M. 9: 313.
— Swiss. Macmil. 73: 106.
— Training and Organization of. (A. Hardinge) Un. Serv. M. 8: 173.
Infantry Attack. (F. N. Maude) Un. Serv. M. 6: 602. — (A. W. A. Pollock) Un. Serv. M. 10: 523.
Infection and Emotions. (C. Féré) Pop. Sci. Mo. 44: 342.
Infectious Diseases. (H. Engel) Science, 20: 225.
— Explanation of Acquired Immunity from. (G. M. Sternberg) Science, n. s. 1: 346.
Infelix; a poem. (M. E. Sangster) Cosmopol. 21: 393.
Inference, Theory of. (W. W. Carlile) Philos. R. 4: 407.
Infidelity. (R. B. Westbrook) Open Court, 3: 1709.
Infinite and Infinitesimal. (J. M. Gibson) Sund. M. 21: 36.
— Is the, a Religious Idea? (P. Carus) Open Court, 5: 2732.
Infinitive, Cleft. (F. Hall) Nation, 56: 274, 312.
Infinitude and Eternity. (P. Carus) Open Court, 2: 870.
Inflammation, Pathology of, Metschnikoff on. (E. R. Lankester) Nature, 45: 505.
Influenza. (J. Althaus) Contemp. 62: 225. — (R. Sisley) Univ. R. 6: 20.
— Bacillus in, Alleged Discovery of. Nature, 45: 250.
Influenza, Epidemic of, in England, 1889-90. (R. Russell) Nature, 49: 210.
— — 1891-92. Spec. 68: 81.
— — Moral Effect of. Spec. 68: 115.
— — in France, in the 16th Century. Macmil. 68: 441.
— Nervous and Mental Phenomena of. (C. K. Mills) Pub. Opin. 12: 507.
— Propagation of. Dub. R. 111: 183.
— Salicin in Treatment of. (T. J. Maclagan) 19th Cent. 31: 329. — Reply. (Earl of Dunraven) National, 19: 32.
Information, Undesirable. (E. F. Benson) Contemp. 68: 125. Same art. Liv. Age, 206: 490. Same art. Ecl. M. 125: 222.
— — Benson on. Sat. R. 80: 37.
Informer's Family, An. Liv. Age, 206: 380.
Informers, Jewish, in the Middle Ages. (D. Kaufmann) Jew. Q. 8: 217.
Infusoria, Immortality of. (A. Binet) Monist, 1: 21.
Ingalls, J. J., and Political Economy. (W. J. Armstrong) Arena, 8: 592.
— Portraits of. McClure, 1: 216.
Ingalls, Mount, Cal., Lavas of. (H. W. Turner) Am. J. Sci. 144: 455.
Ingelow, Jean, with portrait. Bk. News, 11: 70.
Ingenue of the Sierras, The; a story. (Bret Harte) Idler, 3: 361. Same art. McClure, 3: 150.
Ingersoll, Robert G. (E. V. Debs) Am. J. Pol. 2: 198.
— and Facts. (W. M. Boucher) Open Court, 3: 1621.
Inglefield, Sir Edward. Geog. J. 4: 464.
Inglis, John. (A. W. Renton) Green Bag, 4: 132. — (J. McLaren) Jurid. R. 4: 14.
— Watt's Life of. Spec. 70: 455.
Ingoldsby, Thomas, With, in Kent. (H. M. Stephens) Temp. Bar, 106: 89. Same art. Ecl. M. 125: 541. *See* Barham, R. H.
Ingonish, by Land and Sea. (F. Bolles) Atlan. 73: 781.
Inheritance and Wills, Laws regarding. (Lady Cook) Westm. 143: 187.
— Dynamical Hypothesis of. (J. A. Ryder) Science, n. s. 1: 597, 617.
— Study of. (W. K. Brooks) Pop. Sci. Mo. 48: 480, 617.
Inheritance Laws. An Inheritance for the Waifs. (C. F. Taylor) Arena, 17: 59.
Inhibition and the Freedom of the Will. (J. H. Hyslop) Philos. R. 1: 369.
Initial Blocks of some Italian Printers. (A. J. Butler) Bibliographica, 1: 418.
Initials, Pictorial and Heraldic. (A. W. Pollard) Bibliographica, 3: 232.
Initiative and Referendum System of Law-making, The. (C. W. Bowne) Arena, 16: 553.
— — How to introduce. (W. D. McCrackan) Arena, 7: 696.
— — in Switzerland. (W. D. McCrackan) Arena, 7: 548.
— — Relation of, to Labor. (A. L. Lowell) Int. J. Ethics, 6: 51.
See Referendum.
Injector, The. (R. C. Carpenter) Cassier, 1: 211-378.
Injunction, as against Organized Labor. (C. C. Allen) Am. Law R. 28: 828.
— Government by, and the Wage-earners. Gunton's M. 11: 243.
— Labor and. Gunton's M. 11: 44.
Injunctions and Strikes. (W. H. Upson) Bib. Sac. 52: 549.
— Modern Use of. (F. J. Stimson) Pol. Sci. Q. 10: 189.
Injuries to Free Passengers. (J. Schouler) Am. Law R. 26: 212.
Ink and Paper, Best. (R. T. Swan) Lib. J. 20: 163.

Inks for Library Use. Lib. J. 19: 84, 124.
Inkberrow Parish, Account Books of. (W. Bradbrook) Gent. M. n. s. 56: 367.
Inmate of the Dungeon. (W. C. Morrow) Lippinc. 53: 380.
Inn, An Ancient. (J. A. Owen) Blackw. 156: 843.
Inn of San Jacinto. (Z. D. Underhill) Harper, 89: 463.
Inness, George. (E. Daingerfield) Mo. Illust. 3: 258. — Pub. Opin. 18: 207.
— Characteristics of. (G. W. Sheldon) Cent. 27: 530.
— Exhibition of Paintings of. Critic, 26: 17.
— The Man and his Work. (M. Schuyler) Forum, 18: 301.
Innocence at the Price of Ignorance. (S. Schindler) Arena, 8: 185.
Innocent Impostor, An; a story. (F. E. Regal) Music, 1: 432.
Innocent Offender, An. (A. Turner) Cent. 27: 949.
Innocent Thief, An. (M. E. S. Penn) Argosy, 57: 256.
Inns and Taverns, English. (P. Fitzgerald) M. of Art, 7: 485.
— Notable, around London. (N. L. Beal) Chaut. 21: 659.
— of Chancery. (W. J. Loftie) M. of Art, 7: 413.
— of Court, London. (W. J. Loftie) M. of Art, 7: 166. — (W. J. Loftie) Portfo. 23: 1-241.
— — as Schools of Law. (M. Crackanthorpe) 19th Cent. 32: 773.
— — Student life at. Green Bag, 4: 371.
— of Salt Hill, The Old. (J. W. Sherer) Gent. M. n. s. 49: 169.
— The Old Life of the. (S. E. Braine) Good Words, 37: 462. Same art. Ecl. M. 127: 560.
— Old, of Boston. (B. F. Stevens) Bost. 2: 17.
Innsbruck Home, An. (M. Howitt) Sund. M. 22: 392.
Inquisition, Achilli's Dealings with. Eng. R. 15: 322.
— George Buchanan and the. (P. H. Brown) Scot. R. 21: 296.
— as an Alienist. (H. C. Lea) Pop. Sci. Mo. 43: 289.
— Lea's History of. (W. W. Newell) J. Am. Folk-Lore, 1: 172.
— Spanish. (S. F. Smith) Month, 74: 375.
Insane, Asylums for, Modern. (G. H. Bibby; E. A. E. Woodrow) Am. Arch. 40: 147 — 44: 49.
— — Ought Private, to be abolished? (J. F. G. Pietersen) Westm. 142: 688.
— Care of. (S. G. Smith) Char. R. 4: 138.
— — and Cure of. (Richard Greene) Univ. R. 4: 493.
— County Care of, under State Supervision. (J. E. Heg) Lend a H. 17: 175.
— Criminal Responsibility of. (E. F. Willoughby) Jurid. R. 2: 220.
— Duty of the State to. (A. Macfarlane) Pop. Sci. Mo. 43: 741.
— Hospitals for Care of. (E. Gorton) Am. J. Pol. 5: 140.
— in Montenegro. (C. Mÿatovich) Good Words, 33: 351.
— Politics and. (H. S. Williams) No. Am. 161: 394.
— Public, Examination and Commitment of. (M. D. Field) Am. J. Soc. Sci. 30: 19.
— Social Relations of. (H. S. Williams) No. Am. 157: 611.
Insane Colony at Gheel. (S. G. Smith) Lend a H. 16: 356.
Insane Hospitals; A Girl's Visit to a Swiss Madhouse. (A. Kennedy) Belgra. 91: 91.
Insanity and Crime. Green Bag, 6: 503.
— and Criminal Law. (C. Scott) Jurid. R. 1: 237, 333. 2: 64.
— and Genius. (A. McDonald) Arena, 8: 1.
— as Portrayed by Shakespeare. (F. Winslow) Arena, 15: 414.
Insanity, Communicated. (C. W. Pilgrim) Pop. Sci. Mo. 46: 828.
— How it is propagated. (W. J. Corbett) Westm. 142: 153.
— in Royal Families. (A. Bodington) Am. Natural. 29: 118.
— Increase of. (W. J. Corbet) Fortn. 59: 7. 65: 431.
— is it increasing? (T. Drapes) Fortn. 66: 483.
— Modern Form of. (H. S. Williams) No. Am. 154: 719.
— Moral, as a Defense to Crimes. (F. B. Livingstone) Green Bag, 7: 368.
— Popular. (A. Moses) Am. M. Civics, 7: 599.
— Premonitions of. (F. Winslow) Harper, 92: 471.
Inscription, Gortynian, Procedure of. (J. W. Headlam) J. Hel. Stud. 13: 48.
— Sepulchral, from Athens. (W. C. Poland) Am. J. Archæol. 8: 191.
Inscriptions at Santa Cruz, Cal. (B. F. Leeds) N. E. Reg. 50: 438.
— from Ceramus. (E. L. Hicks) J. Hel. Stud. 11: 109.
— from Cilicia. (E. L. Hicks) J. Hel. Stud. 11: 236. 12: 225.
— from the Hauran and Gilead. (G. A. Smith) Crit. R. 2: 55.
— Greek and Latin, Story of the. Macmil. 69: 286. Same art. Ecl. M. 122: 475.
— of Cos, Paton and Hicks on. Ath. '92, 1: 349.
— on Gravestones, Great Valley, Pa. (H. W. Lloyd) Pennsyl. M. 15: 440.
Insect Immigrants in Ohio. (F. M. Webster) Science, 21: 57.
Insect Pests; Kerosene Attachment for Spraying-pumps. (E. S. Goff) Garden & F. 8: 143.
— Legislation against. (C. S. Sargent) Garden & F. 8: 41.
Insect Pests, Some New Indian. Chamb. J. 69: 599.
Insect Secretions. (E. A. Butler) Knowl. 17: 103-223.
Insect Wax. Chamb. J. 69: 661.
Insecticides in Glass Houses. Garden & F. 9: 167.
Insectivorous Plants. *See* Dogbane; Milkweed.
Insects and the Fertilization of Flowers. Sat. R. 79: 440.
— and Flowers. (A. S. Wilson) Knowl. 17: 280. — (F. W. Burbridge) Good Words, 33: 463.
— as Gods. Cornh. 69: 45. Same art. Ecl. M. 122: 214.
— Cannibalism among. (C. Berg) Nat. Sci. 2: 444.
— Colors of. (F. H. P. Coste) Nature, 45: 513, 541.
— Development of. (G. H. Carpenter) Nat. Sci. 1: 279.
— Doorstep Neighbors. (W. H. Gibson) Harper, 93: 420.
— Embryology of, W. M. Wheeler's Contribution to. Am. Natural. 27: 745.
— Habits of. (G. H. Carpenter) Nat. Sci. 4: 365.
— Injuries and Benefits of. (B. G. Johns) Sund. M. 23: 759.
— Injurious; Increasing Number of Plant Pests. (C. S. Sargent) Garden & F. 7: 51.
— — Legislation against. (C. S. Sargent) Garden & F. 6: 401.
— — Quarantine against. (C. S. Sargent) Garden & F. 7: 441.
— Injurious to Agriculture. Garden & F. 5: 457, 601.
— Instinct of, Evolution of. (C. Perton) Pop. Sci. Mo. 50: 105.
— Intelligence of, in Relation to Flowers. (A. S. Wilson) Knowl. 18: 60.
— Literature on, Some Recent. (G. H. Carpenter) Nat. Sci. 7: 179.
— Nervous Ganglia of. (A. Binet) Monist, 3: 35.

Insects, Nest-building. Chamb. J. 71: 414.
— Neuter, and Darwinism. (J. T. Cunningham) Nat. Sci. 4: 281.
— — and Lamarckism. (W. P. Ball) Nat. Sci. 4: 91.
— Parasitic and Predaceous. (C. V. Riley) Pop. Sci. Mo. 45: 678.
— Prevalence of, in England in the Summer of 1893. (E. A. Ormerod) Nature, 48: 394.
— Remarkable. (W. J. Fox) Pop. Sci. Mo. 43: 527.
— Senses of, Riley on. Nature, 52: 209.
— Social. (L. N. Badenoch) Pop. Sci. Mo. 49: 641.
— — Certain Habits and Instincts of. (M. Hartog) Science, n. s. 1: 98.
— — Homes of. (L. N. Badenoch) Pop. Sci. Mo. 45: 338.
— Stinging. (E. A. Butler) Knowl. 17: 40–77.
— Tracheæ of, Structure of. (A. C. Stokes) Science, 21: 44.
— Transformations of. (L. C. Miall) Nature, 53: 152.
— Walking of. (H. H. Dixon) Nature, 47: 56.
— Wings of. (L. Wright) Leis. Hour, 43: 354.
— Winter Life of. (E. A. Butler) Knowl. 18: 83, 113.
Insects' Eggs. (V. Brandicourt) Pop. Sci. Mo. 48: 256.
Insignia of Mayoralty. (L. F. Day) M. of Art, 12: 27.
— of Office of Towns of England and Wales, Jewitt and Hope's. (F. G. Stephens) M. of Art, 19: 324.
Inskip Pride, The; a story. (G. M. Martin) Munsey, 12: 325.
Insley, Albert. (D. R. Goodale) Mo. Illust. 5: 155.
Insolvency, Ethics of. (L. G. Rosenblatt) Eth. Rec. 1: 88, 124.
Insomnia and Recent Hypnotics. (W. A. Hammond) No. Am. 156: 18.
— Pillow-Problems, Dodgson on. Spec. 71: 238.
— A Struggle with. (F. B. Millard) Overland, n. s. 20: 33.
Inspection, An; a Story of American Army Life. (D. Lundt) Poet-Lore, 5: 305.
Inspiration and Truth. (W. Lloyd) Westm. 137: 16.
— Limits of. (I. Zangwill) Critic, 28: 175.
— of the Bible. (S. R. Driver) M. Chr. Lit. 5: 282. — (W. Rupp) Ref. Q. 39: 34. — (T. W. Chambers) Ref. Q. 39: 435.
— Plenary, and the Investigations of Biblical Criticism. (M. G. Hansen) Ref. Q. 41: 171.
— Sanday on. (G. T. Purves) Presb. & Ref. R. 6: 175.
— Smith on. (B. B. Warfield) Presb. & Ref. R. 5: 600.
— Theories of. (M. A. Wilcox) Bib. World, 5: 169. — (C. S. Albert) Luth. Q. 22: 87.
Inspiration, An; a story. (G. Gissing) Eng. Illust. 14: 268.
Inspirational Writings. (T. E. Allen) Psychic. R. 2: 312.
Instinct. Chamb. J. 69: 86.
— and Heredity. (J. M. Baldwin) Science, n. s. 3: 438, 558.
— and Intelligence in Chicks and Ducklings. (C. L. Morgan) Open Court, 8: 4058.
— Definitions of. (C. L. Morgan) Nature, 52: 389. — (C. L. Morgan) Open Court, 9: 4635.
— Holiness of. (W. Hutchinson) Monist, 6: 481.
— in Chicks. (C. L. Morgan) Nat. Sci. 4: 207.
— Limits of Animal Intelligence. (L. Morgan) Fortn. 60: 223.
— Our Social Instincts. (E. P. Powell) Soc. Econ. 5: 220.
— Problem of. Am. Natural. 29: 773.
— Reflex Action, Instinct and Reason. (G. A. Reid) Fortn. 65: 269.
— Some Definitions of. (C. L. Morgan) Nat. Sci. 6: 321.
— What Men call. Cornh. 68: 396.
Instincts, Moral. (F. L. Oswald) Open Court, 6: 3089.
Institute of Chartered Accountants, London, Decoration of. (R. Blomfield) M. of Art, 18: 185.
Institute of France, Centenary of. (E. Lecky) Longm. 27: 174.
Institute of Painters in Oil Colours, London, Exhibition, 1884. M. of Art, 7: 160.
— — 1886. M. of Art, 9: 139.
Institution of Mechanical Engineers. Nature, 51: 377.
Institutional Church League, The. (H. R. Waite) Am. J. Pol. 5: 645.
Institutional Study, Recent Aspects of. (C. M. Andrews) Yale R. 1: 381.
Institutions, Research on. (G. L. Gomme) Folk-Lore, 2: 485.
Instruction and Study, Methods of. (H. C. Kirk) Educa. 16: 230.
Insurance. Chamb. J. 70: 561.
— Accident. Bank. M. (Lond.) 61: 125. — (H. W. Wolff) Contemp. 67: 68. — (H. W. Wolff) Econ. R. 5: 297.
— — Claims in. Bank. M. (Lond.) 61: 889.
— — Milan Congress on. (H. W. Wolff) Econ. R. 5: 121.
— amongst Banks. Bank. M. (Lond.) 55: 703.
— and Annuity. Bank. M. (Lond.) 57: 342.
— and Business Profits. (J. B. Clark) Q. J. Econ. 7: 40.
— Anticipated Bonuses in. Bank. M. (Lond.) 57: 793.
— as a Profession. Bank. M. (Lond.) 55: 803.
— Assessment. Sat. R. 76: 463.
— Compulsory State; its Effect in Germany. (J. G. Brooks) Forum, 16: 122.
— Effects of Free Surrender and Loan Privileges in. (M. M. Dawson) Am. Statis. Assoc. 4: 84.
— Endowment. Bank. M. (Lond.) 61: 629.
— Fire. Sat. R. 76: 409.
— — Barnacles of. (L. Windmüller) Forum, 18: 751.
— — British. Bank. M. (Lond.) 58: 429.
— — Does it cost too much? (G. U. Crocker) No. Am. 160: 470.
— — Municipal. (R. Donald) Contemp. 68: 839.
— Government. (S. Schindler) Arena, 10: 379.
— Imperial. (F. N. Maude) National, 22: 601.
— Life. (A. Hewat) Bank. M. (Lond.) 53: 501, 633. — (J. Burns) Jurid. R. 8: 129.
— — American Methods. (M. M. Dawson) Ann. Am. Acad. Pol. Sci. 4: 753.
— — as an Investment. Sat. R. 79: 154–861. 80: 109–652.
— — Best Form of. (G. A. Litchfield; E. B. Harper) No. Am. 156: 594.
— — for Army and Navy Officers. (H. Brackenbury) Un. Serv. M. 4: 377. — (W. G. Kirby) Un. Serv. M. 8: 456.
— — Government; how not to do it. (J. Vogel) Fortn. 62: 225.
— — Hints on. (Thos. Welton) Univ. R. 4: 61.
— — in 1889. (Walter M. Gattie) Univ. R. 3: 495.
— — Industrial. (F. J. Brown) Westm. 138: 397.
— — Infantile, in Europe. (C. W. Chancellor) Char. R. 5: 128.
— — Novelties in. Sat. R. 76: 565.
— — of Seamen. Lend a H. 12: 299.
— — Policies, Negotiability of. (E. N. Adler) Bank. M. (Lond.) 53: 331.
— — Rise and Growth of. (D. N. Holway) Arena, 6: 64.
— Methods in. (J. Ferguson) Canad. M. 4: 322.
— Modern, and its Possibilities. (R. A. McCurdy; J. L. Greene; S. Homans; C. H. Kelsey) No. Am. 156: 303.

Insurance, Naval, in England, Proposed. (C. Gleig) Chamb. J. 70: 757.
— of Bank Deposits. Bank. M. (Lond.) 54: 89. 59: 773.
— of Colonial Bank Deposits. Bank. M. (Lond.) 56: 849.
— of Engines. (H. B. Spence) Cassier, 8: 554.
— of Limited Interests. (W. Harvey) Law Q. 10: 48.
— Old Age. Lend a H. 12: 286. — (J. H. Richardson) Westm. 139: 362.
— Risks in Sale in relation to. (W. Harvey) Jurid. R. 4: 248.
— Sanitary. Bank. M. (Lond.) 57: 936.
— Workingmen's. (R. Mayo-Smith) Char. R. 1: 49. — (H. W. Wolff) Econ. J. 5: 612.
— — and the Chicago Exposition. (J. G. Brooks) Econ. J. 3: 138.
Insurance Bonuses. Bank. M. (Lond.) 61: 497.
Insurance Companies and Ground Rent. Bank. M. (Lond.) 54: 279.
Insurance Laws, German. (J. E. Hogarth) Econ. J. 6: 283.
Insurance Mortality Tables. (W. S. B. Woolhouse) Bank. M. (Lond.) 53: 137.
Insurance Organizations, Bogus. Bank. M. (N. Y.) 47: 161.
Insurance Policies, Valued. (J. Trayner) Jurid. R. 6: 1.
Insurance Policy Values. (T. J. Searle) Bank. M. (Lond.) 53: 985.
Insurance Surrender Values. Bank. M. (Lond.) 60: 289.
Intellect; Brains and Inches. (P. Kent) Gent. M. n. s. 48: 580.
Intellecta; a story. Cornh. 68: 312.
Intellectual Ability and Physical Development in Children. (G. M. West) Science, n. s. 4: 156.
Intellectual Detachment. (H. Maxwell) 19th Cent. 38: 41. Same art. Liv. Age, 206: 387.
— Sir Herbert Maxwell on. Spec. 75: 11.
Intelligence, Human, Fraser's Account of. (J. E. Creighton) Philos. R. 4: 167.
Intemperance and Crime. (F. W. Farrar) Fortn. 59: 783.
— Beatty-Kingston on. Sat. R. 73: 518.
— Cure of. Lend a H. 12: 403.
— The Evil and the Remedy. (J. M. Cleary) Cath. World, 58: 11.
— in England. (F. W. Farrar) Contemp. 65: 545.
— — How combated. (Duchess of Rutland) New R. 6: 76, 460.
— Newspaper Responsibility for. (W. W. Ramsay) Meth. R. 55: 568.
— Old-time, in New England. (C. Northend) New Eng. M. n. s. 13: 49.
— Past and Present. (A. Shadwell) National, 26: 189.
Intent and Attempt, Recent Decisions concerning. (S. Rogers) Law Q. 10: 164.
Inter-American Commerce. (K. v. Staufen) Am. J. Pol. 4: 649.
Intercepted Heiress. (F. M. Bird) Lippinc. 49: 581.
Interchangeability of Mechanism. (W. F. Durfee) Cassier, 4: 418.
Intercolonial Railway. (P. F. Cronin) Canad. M. 4: 458.
Interdenominational Fellowship. (Francis E. Clark) Chr. Un. 45: 152.
Interest, as related to Will, Prof. John Dewey's Doctrine of. (W. T. Harris) Educa. R. 11: 486.
— Desire, and Emotion. (S. F. M'Lennan) Psychol. R. 2: 462.
— The Doctrine of. (W. E. Wilson) Educa. R. 11: 254.
— Herbart's Doctrine of. (W. T. Harris) Educa. R. 10: 71.
Interest of Pupils and the Transcendental Will. (A. F. Ames) Educa. R. 11: 392.
— Some Objections to it. (F. M. McMurry) Educa. R. 11: 146.
Interest. (J. R. Christie) Jurid. R. 6: 362. 7: 119.
— and Profits. (A. T. Hadley) Ann. Am. Acad. Pol. Sci. 4: 337.
— Basis of. (B. F. Hughes) Ann. Am. Acad. Pol. Sci. 3: 65.
— — Natural. (F. W. Sanders) J. Pol. Econ. 4: 494.
— Boehm-Bawerk's Theory of. (F. A. Walker) Q. J. Econ. 6: 399.
— Henry George's Theory of. (D. M. Lowrey) Ann. Am. Acad. Pol. Sci. 2: 629.
— Influence of Monetary Appreciation and Depreciation on Rate of. (I. Fisher) Am. Econ. Assoc. 11: 331.
— Origin of. (J. B. Clark) Q. J. Econ. 9: 257. — (E. Boehm-Bawerk) Q. J. Econ. 9: 380.
— Real Issues concerning. (J. B. Clark) Q. J. Econ. 10: 98.
— Teaching of, in School. (J. V. Collins) Educa. 16: 554.
— Theory of, Place of Abstinence in. (T. N. Carver) Q. J. Econ. 8: 40.
Interestingness of Things. Ecl. M. 126: 696.
Interference, Wrongful, by Third Parties. (W. L. Hodge) Am. Law R. 28: 47.
Interior; a drama for Marionettes. (M. Mæterlinck) New R. 11: 543.
Interloper, An. (Frances M. Peard) Temp. Bar, 101: 135-605. 102: 115-551.
Interlude, An; a story. (G. King) Harper, 89: 918.
Intermediary, The. Macmil. 69: 129.
Intermediate State. (W. F. Ulery) Luth. Q. 22: 537.
Internal Improvements in U. S. (B. Moses) Chaut. 22: 664.
Internal Revenue System of the U. S. (W. W. Carruth) Chaut. 16: 288.
International Affairs, Real Interests of the Public in. (C. D. Farquharson) Westm. 145: 167. Same art. Ecl. M. 126: 383.
International Congresses. (R. Ogden) Nation, 57: 263.
International Delusions, Some. (F. E. Clark) No. Am. 163: 28.
International Geographical Conference, Chicago, 1893. Nat. Geog. M. 5: 97.
International Institutions. (C. Barnard) Chaut. 16: 11.
International Jealousy. (J. P. Mahaffy) 19th Cent. 39: 529. Same art. Ecl. M. 126: 721.
International Justice. (D. J. Hill) Am. J. Soc. Sci. no. 34: 98.
International Law. (Lord Russell) Law Q. 12: 311.
— and Acts of Parliament. (T. E. Holland) Law Q. 9: 136.
— Duty of Neutral Nations. (John Gibbons) Am. M. Civics, 9: 88.
— in the War between Japan and China. Fortn. 63: 913. Same art. Liv. Age, 206: 67.
— Is it a Science? (W. L. Scruggs) Science, 21: 275.
— Private. (A. V. Dicey) Law Q. 6: 1. 7: 113.
— — Basis of. (M. J. Farrelly) Law Q. 9: 242.
— — New Italian School of. (M. J. Farrelly) Jurid. R. 5: 105, 197.
International Prejudice. Liv. Age, 211: 490.
International Prison Congress, 5th, 1895. (S. J. Barrows) Pop. Sci. Mo. 48: 395.
International Psychological Congress, Third, Education at. (S. I. Franz) Educa. R. 12: 280.
International Quarrels and their Settlement. (L. H West) Int. J. Ethics, 3: 64.

International Questions, Settlement of. (P. Fiore) Int. J. Ethics, 7: 20.
International Relations, "Intention" in. (R. Ogden) Nation, 62: 301.
International Statesman, The. (W. B. Chisholm) Am. M. Civics, 8: 501.
International Statistical Institute. (R. P. Falkener) Am. Statis. Assoc. 4: 358.
Internationalism, Growth of. (B. F. Trueblood) Lend a H. 15: 98.
Interoceanic Canal from the Standpoint of Self-interest. (T. S. Woolsey) Yale R. 4: 357.
— in the Light of Precedent. (T. S. Woolsey) Yale R. 4: 246.
Interoceanic Canals. (G. E. Walsh) Chaut. 23: 723. — (E. L. Godkin) Nation, 61: 382.
— Diplomacy and Law of. (S. Webster) Harper, 87: 602.
— Suez and Panama. (W. H. Wheeler) Longm. 25: 394.
Interrupted Current. (H. M. Yost) Lippinc. 58: 579.
Interrupted Story, An. (W. McLennan) Harper, 88: 704.
Interrupted Wooing, An. (W. A. Dromgoole) Southern M. 5: 148.
Interstate Commerce, Federal Power to regulate, and Police Power of the States. (H. B. Shoemaker) Am. Law R. 29: 59.
Interstate Commerce Commission. (A. Morgan) Pop. Sci. Mo. 41: 212.
— and the Courts. (T. L. Greene) Nation, 54: 46.
— Statistical Division of. (H. C. Adams) Citizen, 1: 203.
Interstate Commerce Law. (J. A. Logan) Am. J. Pol. 2: 401.
— Has it been Beneficial? (A. F. Walker) Forum, 17: 207.
Interstate Law at the West. (T. L. Greene) Nation, 54: 205.
Interstate Migration, Decrease of. (W. F. Willcox) Pol. Sci. Q. 10: 603.
Interval, Least Observable, between Stimuli addressed to Disparate Senses and to Different Organs of the Same Sense. (A. J. Hamlin) Am. J. Psychol. 6: 564.
Interval, An; a story. (E. S. Grew) Idler, 6: 293.
Intervention, An; a story. Chamb. J. 71: 301.
Interview, An, with Miss Marlenspuyk; a story. (B. Matthews) Harper, 92: 61.
Interviewed by a Comudi; a story. (A. Ferguson) Temp. Bar, 107: 124. Same art. Ecl. M. 126: 254.
Interviewers and Interviewing. All the Year, 71: 422.
Interviewing. (F. Banfield) National, 26: 367. Same art. Ecl. M. 126: 32.
— Canadian Newspaper. (P. S. Barydardt) Canad. M. 5: 46.
— Difficulties and Delights of. (H. Friederichs) Eng. Illust. 10: 338.
Intestacy Law, Connecticut. (C. M. Andrews) Yale R. 3: 261.
Into the Jaws of Death; a mining story. Macmil. 74: 93.
Intonation, Perfect. Is it Practicable? (J. P. White) Music, 7: 441, 606. 8: 65, 262.
Intoxicated Ghost, The. (A. Bates) Cent. 24: 393.
Intuition and Reason. (C. L. Franklin) Monist, 3: 211.
Intuitionism, Relation of, to the Ethical Doctrine of Self-realization. (H. Calderwood) Philos. R. 5: 337.
Invalid Aid Society, The Service of an. (C. F. Nichols) R. of Rs. (N. Y.) 11: 290.
Invalids, Migration of. (S. A. Eliot) Nature, 9: 423.
Invention and Design, Relation of, to Mechanical Progress. (C. L. Redfield) Engin. M. 12: 286.
Invention, Dependence of the New Civilization on. (W. T. Harris) Monist, 2: 178.
— Ethical Influence of. (C. D. Wright) Soc. Econ. 1: 268, 338.
— How it is made. (A. D. Pentz) Engin. M. 3: 96.
— Law of. (H. Pettit) J. Frankl. Inst. 138: 433. 139: 20.
— March of. (N. S. Shaler) Chaut. 22: 151. — Gunton's M. 11: 266.
— Opposition to. (W. C. Dodge) Engin. M. 10: 907.
— Relation of, to the Conditions of Life. (G. H. Knight) Cosmopol. 12: 441.
— — to Labor. (C. D. Wright) Soc. Econ. 1: 193.
— Some Peculiarities of. (G. R. Fleming) Good Words, 37: 547.
Inventive Faculty. Is it a Myth? (W. H. Smyth) Engin. M. 9: 851.
Inventor, The American. Am. Arch. 40: 121.
— The Professional Mechanical. (H. H. Suplee) Engin. M. 8: 842.
Inventors and Official Science. (E. Turpin) Cosmopol. 18: 252.
— Early Life of Great. (L. Allen) Engin. M. 7: 639.
— Our Debt to. Shall we discourage them? (R. H. Thurston) Forum, 19: 356.
— Precautionary Hints for. (F. Richards) Engin. M. 6: 853.
Invertebrates, Physiology of, Griffith on. Sat. R. 74: 262.
Investigation, Units of, in the Social Sciences. (A. F. Bentley) Ann. Am. Acad. Pol. Sci. 5: 915.
Investments, Casuistry and Ethics of. (P. Gardner) Econ. R. 3: 501.
— Diminishing Returns from. (U. H. Crocker) Soc. Econ. 4: 213.
— for British Investors. Contemp. 70: 144, 292, 599.
— in the United States, English View of. (R. H. I. Palgrave) Forum, 15: 191.
Investors and their Money. (H. E. M. Stutfield) National, 26: 501.
Invisible Chains; a story. (L. D. Mitchell) Outing, 23: 339.
Invitations, English Forms of. (A. Badeau) Cosmopol. 16: 39.
Iodates, Alkaline. (H. L. Wheeler) Am. J. Sci. 144: 123.
Iodic Acid, Action of Reducing Agents on. (C. F. Roberts) Am. J. Sci. 148: 151.
Iodide, Blue, of Starch. (C. F. Roberts) Am. J. Sci. 147: 422.
Iodine, Compounds containing Lead and Extra. (H. L. Wells) Am. J. Sci. 150: 21.
— Determination of, in Haloid Salts by the Action of Arsenic Acid. (F. A. Gooch and P. E. Browning) Am. J. Sci. 145: 334.
— in the Animal Organism. (W. D. Halliburton) Sci. Prog. 5: 454.
Iolite, Chemical Composition of. (O. C. Farrington) Am. J. Sci. 143: 13.
Iona, Two Days at. (G. B. Smith) Time, 6: 69.
— A Visit to. (J. Oldbuck) National, 19: 576.
Ionic Capital, Lotiform Origin of. (W. H. Goodyear) Archit. Rec. 3: 137.
Ionides, Constantine, Collection of Pictures. (C. Monkhouse) M. of Art, 7: 36–208.
Ions, Migration of. (G. F. Stradling) J. Frankl. Inst. 135: 387.
I. O. U., An. (M. S. Briscoe) Scrib. M. 14: 308.
Iovanovich, Zmai Iovan, the Chief Servian Poet. (N. Tesla) Cent. 26: 130.
Iowa, Agricultural College. (G. W. Bissell) Cassier, 5: 59.

Iowa, Association of Colleges in. (I. Loos) Educa. R. 11: 271.
— Politics, 1892. Is it a Doubtful State? (J. N. Irwin) Forum, 13: 257.
— University of. (J. J. McConnell) Educa. 16: 400.
Iowa Legends. (G. W. Weippiert) J. Am. Folk-Lore, 2: 287.
Ipomœas Tree of Mexico. (J. N. Rose) Garden & F. 7: 366.
Ipswich, England, and its Neighborhood, Geology of. (C. Reid) Nat. Sci. 7: 173.
Ireland, Mrs. Annie Elizabeth. Acad. 44: 320.
Ireland, J., Archbishop. (Albert Shaw) Chr. Un. 45: 977.
— Educational Policy of. (T. O'Gorman) Educa. R. 3: 462.
Ireland. (Wm. Mackay) Time, 15: 155.
— Agricultural Coöperation in. (T. A. Finlay) Econ. J. 6: 204.
— and the Government. (J. McCarthy) New R. 11: 333.
— and Great Britain, Financial Relations of. Sat. R. 82: 276.
— Arbitration for, The Question of. (W. O'Brien) 19th Cent. 39: 746.
— as a Field for Tourists. (J. A. Steuart) Fortn. 66: 416.
— Census of, 1891. J. Statis. Soc. 55: 601.
— The Church in. Eng. R. 4: 24. 15: 282. 18: 309.
— — Prospects of, under Home Rule. Church Q. 36: 202.
— Condition of. (J. J. O'Shea) Cath. World, 63: 371.
— Congested District in. Blackw. 157: 208.
— Congested Districts Board; a Great Experiment. (T. W. Russell) Fortn. 62: 61.
— Constabulary of. Sat. R. 76: 208. — Westm. 143: 379.
— Constitution for, Haldane on the Evolution of. Spec. 68: 802.
— Convent National Schools in. (W. J. Walsh) Contemp. 61: 350.
— — Reply. (T. W. Russell) Contemp. 61: 630.
— Coöperation and Farming in. (E. Mitchell) Westm. 142: 241.
— County Government in. (J. T. C. Humphreys) Jurid. R. 1: 369.
— Disaffection in. Eng. R. 9: 128.
— Early Religious Buildings of. (G. H. Orpen) Leis. Hour, 44: 643, 732.
— Education in. (Lord Powerscourt) 19th Cent. 39: 286.
— — Catholic and Protestant. (H. A. Hinkson) Westm. 144: 80.
— — Intermediate. Chamb. J. 69: 794.
— England's Opportunity in. Quar. 183: 255. — (J. McGrath) Fortn. 66: 602.
— England's Policy towards. Eng. R. 3: 408.
— Evicted Tenants' Bill. (Lord Monteagle) 19th Cent. 35: 1026. — (T. W. Russell) Fortn. 61: 421. — (M. Davitt) 19th Cent. 35: 560.
— Evictions in: Are the Evicted Tenants Knaves? (W. O'Brien) New R. 7: 385.
— — Government and the Evicted Tenants. Spec. 69: 343.
— Farmer in, Evolution of. (G. H. Bassett) No. Am. 160: 509.
— Field-club Work in. (G. A. J. Cole) Nat. Sci. 6: 313.
— Financial Grievance of. (J. J. Clancy) 19th Cent. 40: 982.
— Folk-Lore of. (A. C. Haddon) Folk-Lore, 4: 349. — (G. H. Kinahan) Folk-Lore Rec. 4: 96. — (E. P. Thompson) J. Am. Folk-Lore, 6: 259.
Ireland. From Bantry to Killarney. (F. B. Sawvel) Educa. 15: 32.
— From the Democratic Standpoint. (Wm. Wallace) Time, 14: 129.
— Futile Legislation for. (M. O'Brien) Nation, 59: 265.
— Geology and Scenery in. (G. A. J. Cole) Nature, 50: 323.
— The Glens and their Speech. (M. O'Neill) Blackw. 154: 367.
— History, Early Treatises on. (G. C. Brodrick) National, 20: 495.
— — French Invasion of 1798. Chamb. J. 69: 798.
— — Joyce's. (W. O'C. Morris) Acad. 44: 579.
— Home Rule for. Blackw. 153: 458, 903. 154: 462. — (J. McCarthy) 19th Cent. 33: 369. — (G. McDermot) Cath. World, 55: 225, 785. — (St. Loe Strachey) National, 24: 216.
— — American Sidelights on. (T. W. Russell) Fortn. 59: 341.
— — and the Irish Party. (T. P. O'Connor) Contemp. 70: 179.
— — and the Land Question. (A. Withy) Westm. 142: 58.
— — Aspects of. (W. E. H. Lecky) Contemp. 63: 626.
— — in 1888. (F. H. Hill; T. P. O'Connor) Univ. R. 1: 161, 309.
— — in 1892, Gladstone and. Pub. Opin. 13: 519.
— — Is it near? (B. J. Clinch) Am. Cath. Q. 17: 853.
— — Bill for, 1893. (J. J. O'Shea) Cath. World, 56: 622 — 57: 407. — (G. McDermot) Cath. World, 56: 845. — (F. Harrison; J. E. Redmond; D. Crawfurd) Contemp. 63: 305. — Ed. R. 177: 565. — (E. L. Godkin) Nation, 56: 80. — (A. Webb) Nation, 56: 156. 57: 209. — (F. Greenwood) National, 21: 739. — (H. D. Traill) National, 22: 36. — (Lord Ashbourne) National, 22: 161. — (O'C. Don) National, 22: 531. — Pub. Opin. 15: 94, 166, 352, 516,
— — — and the Army. (Lord Ashbourne) National, 21: 145.
— — — and the Canadian Constitution. (H. H. L. Bellot) Westm. 139: 469.
— — — Canadian Finance and. (H. H. L. Bellot) Westm. 140: 1.
— — — A Bill of Wrongs. National, 21: 1.
— — — A Bill for Weakening Great Britain. (J. Chamberlain) 19th Cent. 33: 545.
— — — Danger of Delay. (J. E. Redmond) 19th Cent. 34: 688.
— — — The Dishonored Bill. Quar. 177: 552.
— — — Exclusion or Retention of Irish Members. (H. Jephson) 19th Cent. 33: 189.
— — — Financial Aspect of. (J. J. Clancy) Contemp. 63: 25.
— — — Financial Clauses of. Fortn. 59: 574. — (J. J. Clancy) Fortn. 59: 610.
— — — Financial Scheme of. Contemp. 63: 609.
— — — Fresh Puzzle of. (F. Pollock) National, 21: 841.
— — — Gladstone's Battle for. (A. A. Black) Chaut. 18: 336.
— — — House of Lords and. (Earl of Donoughmore) No. Am. 157: 298. — Sat. R. 76: 288, 319.
— — — Ireland's Decay and Ulster's Defiance. (S. J. Low) National, 21: 292.
— — — Ireland's Reply. (J. E. Redmond) New R. 8: 12.
— — — Irish Constabulary and. Fortn. 59: 901.
— — — Irish Opinion on. (E. Dowden) Fortn. 59: 593.
— — — Is it needed? (W. J. O'N. Daunt) Westm. 139: 589.
— — — Ministerial Tactics. (E. Dicey) 19th Cent. 34: 1.

Ireland, Home Rule for, Bill for, 1893. The 9th Clause. (R. Wallace) 19th Cent. 34: 10.
— — — Police Clauses of. National, 21: 553.
— — — Tactics of the Opposition. (T. M. Healy) New R. 9: 94.
— — Cavour on the Repeal of the Union. (M. Wood) 19th Cent. 33: 874.
— — Earl of Mar's Bill. (S. Erskine) Dub. R. 115: 382.
— — Killing with Kindness. (J. E. Redmond) 19th Cent. 38: 905.
— — Prospects of. (M. Dalton) Westm. 144: 456.
— — Readjustment of the Union, Nationalist Plan for. (J. E. Redmond) 19th Cent. 32: 509.
— — Mr. Redmond and South Meath. (H. W. Forster) Fortn. 59: 290.
— — Reply to Lord Salisbury. (T. B. Grant) Am. J. Pol. 5: 30.
— — Second Thoughts on. (J. E. Redmond) 19th Cent. 33: 559.
— — Some Objections. (T. P. O'Connor) Time, 14: 641.
— — The South Meath Election. (J. E. Redmond) Fortn. 59: 1.
— — Ulster and. (J. G. Colclough) Contemp. 63: 761.
— House of Lords and. (J. J. O'Shea) Cath. World, 60: 51.
— Illiterate Voters in. Spec. 75: 230.
— in 1659 and 1893; a Historical Parallel. Macmil. 68: 136.
— in 1882, State and Prospects of. (R. S. Moffat) Time, 7: 401.
— in 1892. Balfour's Failure. (E. L. Godkin) Nation, 54: 185.
— — Gladstone and. (N. Cantry) Chaut. 15: 702.
— — Morley's Task in. (W. O'Brien) Fortn. 58: 585.
— — New Departure in. (T. W. Russell) New R. 7: 533.
— in 1895; an Irish Compromise? (Lord Stanmore; L. A. A. Jones; R. W. Hanbury; Sir J. Leng) National, 24: 737.
— — by a Disenchanted Nationalist. Fortn. 64: 512.
— — Mr. Morley and the Irish Land Bill. (T. W. Russell) Fortn. 63: 347.
— in 1896: Mr. Lecky and Irish Affairs. (J. G. Swift MacNeill) Fortn. 65: 18.
— — The New Movement. (S. O'Grady) New R. 15: 666.
— Influence on Thought and Literature of. (J. M'Carthy) Time, 22: 405.
— The Irish Fiasco. (H. Jephson) 19th Cent. 38: 17.
— Justice to England. (E. Dicey) 19th Cent. 36: 824.
— Land Acts. (H. O. Arnold-Forster) National, 25: 410.
— Land in: Bill of Lord Salisbury's Government. (O. Morris) Fortn. 65: 879. — National, 28: 3. — (T. M. Healy) Sat. R. 82: 154.
— — Compulsory Purchase of. (A. Traill) Contemp. 64: 847.
— — Dual Ownership of, a Myth. (G. McDermot) Cath. World, 60: 251.
— — Legislation on, since 1845. (W. A. Dunning) Pol. Sci. Q. 7: 57, 500.
— Land Laws, Select Committee on, 1894. (M. O'Brien) Nation, 58: 117.
— — Latest Land Bill. (Lord Monteagle) 19th Cent. 37: 629.
— Land Purchase in. (G. Fottrell) 19th Cent. 40: 829.
— — Compulsory. Spec. 68: 454.
— Land Question in. (M. O'Brien) Nation, 60: 340. — (W. Glenny-Crory) Time, 16: 535.
Ireland, Land Question in, Settling the. (H. de F. Montgomery) National, 25: 142.
— — To-day. (Monteagle) 19th Cent. 39: 756.
— Land Registry in. (J. W. Craig) Jurid. R. 2: 325.
— Land System of. (W. O'C. Morris) Law Q. 3: 133. 4: 1. — (O. Morris) Fortn. 65: 249.
— Land Tenure in, The Muddle of. (W. E. Bear) Fortn. 66: 70.
— — 25 Land Acts in 26 Years. (H. O. Arnold-Forster) 19th Cent. 40: 345.
— Landlord in, Budget of. National, 23: 626. 24: 142. — (T. W. Russell) National, 23: 781.
— Local Government in. (G. McDermot) Cath. World, 54: 833.
— — Bill for, 1892. (J. E. Redmond) Fortn. 57: 621.
— — From the Landlord's Point of View. (L. A. Ellis) National, 18: 705.
— Morris's, 1494–1868. (A. Webb) Nation, 63: 293.
— Myths and Folk-Lore of, Curtin's. (W. W. Newell) J. Am. Folk-Lore, 3: 250.
— of To-day. Fortn. 60: 686. Same art. Liv. Age, 199: 771.
— of To-day, and Ireland To-morrow. (H. Plunkett) Fortn. 61: 277.
— of To-morrow. Fortn. 61: 1. Same art. Liv. Age, 200: 387.
— Official Life in, Experiences of. (A. E. Turner) National, 21: 134.
— Ordnance Survey of. (E. Mitchell) Gent. M. n. s. 56: 373.
— Our Parish in. (E. Blake) New R. 6: 617.
— Outlook for. (B. J. Clinche) Am. Cath. Q. 20: 859. — (Earl of Crewe) No. Am. 161: 366.
— Pagan, W. G. Wood-Martin on. Nature, 53: 82.
— Parliament of, The Old. Westm. 138: 16.
— Parties in, and the Ministry. (T. M. Healy) New R. 10: 468.
— Party Struggle in. Westm. 146: 604.
— Peasant Life and Industries in. (A. C. Haddon) J. Soc. Arts, 44: 387.
— Sir R. Peel's Government of. Eng. R. 4: 173.
— Phœnix Park Tragedy, '82, and Rebellion of 1798. Time, 7: 341.
— Place of, in the Financial System of the United Kingdom. (C. F. Bastable) Econ. J. 6: 185.
— A Plea for. (E. Dowsley) Canad. M. 2: 233, 566.
— Pre-Christian Antiquities, Wood-Martin's. Sat. R. 80: 511.
— Priest-ridden. Blackw. 154: 264.
— Priestly Intimidation in. Spec. 69: 808.
— Progress in. Sat. R. 82: 210.
— Protestanism, Protest of. (A. V. Dicey) Contemp. 62: 1.
— Public Works in. Ed. R. 183: 358.
— Question of, An American View of. (R. H. Dana) Forum, 13: 709.
— — How to whittle away at. Spec. 69: 638.
— — Round Table Conference. (St. Loe Strachey) Time, 16: 257.
— Questions about, Three. Time, 15: 24.
— The Rebel South. Westm. 140: 241. Same art. Ecl. M. 121: 521.
— Recent Politics. Sat. R. 80: 132.
— Religion in. Eng. R. 8: 257.
— Remedies for Evils of. Time, 4: 355.
— Repeopling of. (G. H. Bassett) No. Am. 163: 753.
— Resources of Industry in. (W. Glenny-Crory) Time, 15: 184.
— revisited. (A. Austin) Blackw. 158: 634. — Liv. Age, 207: 532.

Ireland, Rhetoricians of. Fortn. 60: 713. — Liv. Age, 200: 67.
— Round Towers of. (G. E. Orpen) Leis. Hour, 45: 626, 724.
— — and Irish Art. (F. T. Hodgson) Canad. M. 4: 38.
— A Royal Residence in. (J. St. L. Strachey) National, 25: 746.
— Sketching Grounds of. (H. W. Sweny) M. of Art, 3: 165.
— A Snipe-bog in. (A. G. Bradley) Macmil. 66: 473.
— State Papers, 1592-96; ed. by H. C. Hamilton. (R. Dunlop) Eng. Hist. R. 7: 168.
— Surnames in. Spec. 72: 435, 468.
— Varieties of. (Wm. M'Grath) Time, 23: 988.
— Taxes in, and in England. Sat. R. 82: 5.
— That Damnable Country. (A. Austin) Blackw. 156: 309. Same art. Ecl. M. 123: 615. Same art. Liv. Age, 203: 290.
— To; a poem. (A. Austin) National, 26: 165.
— Travels in. (H. G. Fagan) Time, 15: 317.
— Trip in, 1634. (Jas. Bowker) Time, 17: 659.
— Under Grattan's Parliament. (W. J. O'N. Daunt) Westm. 138: 109.
— under the Land League, Lloyd's. Sat. R. 73: 549. — Spec. 69: 423.
— under the Tudors, Bagwell on. (E. G. Atkinson) Eng. Hist. R. 7: 365.
— Unionism in, Strength and Prospects of. Fortn. 58: 125.
— A Unionist Policy for. (X; Lord Monteagle; V. B. Dillon; Lord Castletown; W. O'Brien; H. de F. Montgomery) National, 26: 306.
— Unsolved Problem of. (O'C. Don) National, 22: 531.
— Unvisited. (Lord Houghton) National, 25: 598. Same art. Liv. Age, 206: 496.
— Village Life in. (J. P. Mahaffy) Chaut. 18: 259.
— Week in. (J. Shaylor) Gent. M. n. s. 57: 465.
— The West of. Blackw. 159: 708.
— — Fairy Folk-Lore of. (M. Tyner) Walford's Antiq. 5: 140.
— West Coast of, Poverty on. Sat. R. 73: 418.
— Arthur Young in. (A. Webb) Nation, 56: 401.
Irene; a poem. (W. C. Cooper) Arena, 15: 841.
Iris, Cultivation of. (J. N. Gerard) Garden & F. 5: 606, 619.
— Earliest. (J. N. Gerard) Garden & F. 7: 126.
— Kempfer's. (E. O. Orpet) Garden & F. 5: 452.
Iris Caroliniana. Garden & F. 6: 334.
Iris Hexagona. (Laura S. La Mance) Garden & F. 8: 329.
Iris Lorteti. (M. Foster) Garden & F. 5: 429.
Irises. Garden & F. 5: 573. — (J. N. Gerard) Garden & F. 8: 246.
— American. (J. N. Gerard) Garden & F. 8: 286.
— and their Cultivation. (J. N. Gerard) Garden & F. 6: 9-55.
— Bulbous. (M. Foster) Garden & F. 5: 258.
— Cultural Notes on. (J. N. Gerard) Garden & F. 9: 437.
— Current Notes on. (J. N. Gerard) Garden & F. 7: 195, 208.
— Garden of. Garden & F. 7: 122.
— Oncocyclus. (T. B. Ellis) Garden & F. 7: 386.
Irish, Annie, with portrait. Theatre, 28: 247.
Irish at Nantes. (P. Hurley) Dub. R. 110: 351.
— — and a Bishop of Cork. (P. Hurley) Dub. R. 110: 38.
— Conquest of our Cities by. (J. P. Bocock) Forum, 17: 186.
— How they pass the Winter. Cornh. 71: 279.
— in America. (W. Lecky) Cath. World, 63: 355.
Irish in American Life. (H. C. Merwin) Atlan. 77: 289.
Irish Americans: do they hate England? (T. B. Grant) Am. M. Civics, 7: 516.
Irish and Norse Literature. (W. Larminie) Contemp. 68: 575, 665.
Irish Burial and Holiday Customs. (Mrs. F. D. Bergen) J. Am. Folk-Lore, 8: 19.
Irish Cathedral Churches. Reliquary, 32: 17-78.
Irish Channel, Artificial Isthmus across. (E. A. Le Sueur) Pop. Sci. Mo. 45: 472.
Irish Gentleman a Hundred Years Ago; a poem. (P. Lawdeshayne) Canad. M. 5: 553.
Irish Idylls. Atlan. 72: 699.
Irish Judicial Joker. All the Year, 73: 164.
Irish Landlord; a Visit to his Property. Macmil. 70: 215.
Irish Literature. (G. Sigerson) Contemp. 62: 505.
— Ireland's Position in Literature. Westm. 141: 289.
— Sir Charles G. Duffy on. Spec. 69: 712.
Irish Loyalists, Who are the? (T. Scanlon) Westm. 138: 1.
Irish Mirabilia in Norse "Speculum Regale." (K. Meyer) Folk-Lore, 5: 299.
Irish Nationalism, Argyll's. Sat. R. 75: 488.
Irish Parliament, Old. All the Year, 72: 247.
Irish Peasant-woman, An. (K. T. Hinkson) New R. 14: 53. Same art. Liv. Age, 210: 238.
Irish Poetry, National. (M. MacDonagh) Time, 22: 603.
Irish Police, Localizing of the. Blackw. 157: 798.
Irish Politics, Future of. Fortn. 63: 685.
Irish Priesthood, The. (M. MacDonagh) Contemp. 69: 529. Same art. Liv. Age, 209: 481.
Irish Question, — National Poverty. Sat. R. 79: 779.
Irish Race, Convention of. Cath. World, 65: 573.
Irish Rajah of Hariána, The. Chamb. J. 72: 635. Same art. Liv. Age, 208: 162.
Irish Recklessness. Sat. R. 73: 329.
Irish Saints in Italy. (R. Hughes) Acad. 42: 231. — (E. M. Clerke) Am. Cath. Q. 19: 288.
— Wanderings of, on the Continent, in Early Times. (E. M. Clerke) Dub. R. 118: 364.
Irish Songs. (J. E. T. Dow) Cent. 25: 586.
Irish Spies and Informers. Ed. R. 176: 81. Same art. Liv. Age, 195: 88.
Irish Superstitions. (A. Gregory) Spec. 74: 533.
Irish Surnames. (W. H. Whitmore) Nation, 58: 383.
Irish Types and Traits. (K. Tynan) M. of Art, 11: 19, 127. 15: 210.
Irishmen in the British Cabinet. Spec. 70: 214.
Irmas Lions. Chamb. J. 68: 669.
Irnerius. (J. D. Wilson) Jurid. R. 6: 304.
Iron and Steel, Mechanical Testing of, Our Present Knowledge of. (H. Beare) Sci. Prog. 4: 216.
— — Production of, in Germany. New R. 14: 113.
— — Rustless Coating for. Am. Arch. 45: 94.
— — Tests for. Am. Arch. 48: 6.
— — Works of the United States. Am. Arch. 53: 69.
— A Bar of. (R. R. Bowker) Harper, 88: 408.
— Bog Iron Ore: Traces of a Vanished Industry of South Jersey. (J. Gifford) Pop. Sci. Mo. 42: 827.
— Boom in. (J. H. Ryley) Time, 23: 1042.
— Carbides of. (F. L. Garrison) J. Frankl. Inst. 140: 464.
— Carburization of. (J. Parry) Nature, 46: 283.
— Clinton Iron Ore. (C. H. Smyth, jr.) Am. J. Sci 143: 487.
— Cost of, as related to Industrial Enterprises. (G. H. Hull) Engin. M. 12: 420.
— Desulphurization of. (J. Parry) Nature, 48: 427.

Iron, Ferrous Determination of, in Silicates. (J. H. Pratt) Am. J. Sci. **148**: 149.
— Future of the American Iron Trade. (J. M. Swank) Engin. M. **10**: 613.
— How made. (J. Birkinbine) Cassier, **7**: 23–249.
— in Homer. (F. B. Jevons) J. Hel. Stud. **13**: 25.
— Manganese, and Calcium, Separation of, by the Acetate and Bromine Methods. (R. B. Riggs) Am. J. Sci. **143**: 135.
— Manufacture of. (H. Garland) McClure, **3**: 3.
— — in America, Bell on. (J. Parry) Nature, **47**: 195.
— Mining of. (J. Birkinbine) J. Frankl. Inst. **135**: 259, 375.
— Pig-, Locations for Production of. (J. Birkinbine) Engin. M. **4**: 858.
— Pig-iron Industry, Changes in. (W. Kent) Cassier, **2**: 105.
— Place of, in Nature. (J. T. Kemp) Knowl. **18**: 100.
— Product of, in Mexico. (R. T. Hill) Engin. M. **4**: 744.
— Sussex. (W. C. Symons) Illus. Archæol. **2**: 89.
— Wrought. (H. Nodet) Am. Arch. **45**: 51, 59.
— — Conditions Causing it to be Fibrous. (W. F. Durfee) J. Frankl. Inst. **142**: 110.
— — Decorations in. (J. M. O'Fallon) Art J. **47**: 269.
Iron Alloys. Nature, **47**: 58.
Iron and Steel Institute, 1894 Meeting. Nature, **50**: 37.
Iron and Steel Workers, Amalgamated Association of. (C. D. Wright) Q. J. Econ. **7**: 400.
Iron Casting, First done in America. (A. Spies) Cassier, **7**: 65.
Iron-clad, First. (R. H. Thurston) Cassier, **6**: 312.
Ironclads, 1855–95, Wilson on. (E. G. Johnson) Dial (Ch.) **20**: 90.
— in Action, Wilson on. Sat. R. **81**: 76.
Iron Construction in New York. (L. D. Berg) Archit. Rec. **1**: 448.
Iron Crane, Overton, Flintshire. Reliquary, **35**: 37.
Iron-founding, Art of, Evolution of. (S. Bolland) Engin. M. **5**: 298.
Iron Industry, American. Gunton's M. **11**: 344.
— of England. (W. T. Jeans) Chamb. J. **73**: 708.
Iron Mask, Man of the. (A. Hartshorne) Antiq. n. s. **30**: 198.
Iron-mill, Working in an. McClure, **3**: 163.
Iron Mine, Determining the Value of an. (N. P. Hulst) Engin. M. **11**: 91.
Iron Mines of Minnesota, Monopoly and the. (C. J. Buell) Arena, **16**: 124.
Iron Ore in Mexico, Hematite and Martite. (R. T. Hill) Am. J. Sci. **145**: 111.
— Magnetic Separation of. (C. M. Ball) Engin. M. **9**: 908.
— Mining and Smelting of. (J. Birkinbine) Cassier, **4**: 163–425. **5**: 43.
— of Marquette District. (C. R. Van Hise) Am. J. Sci. **143**: 116.
Iron-ore Industry, Lake Transportation and the. (G. G. Turrell) J. Pol. Econ. **5**: 23, 110.
Iron-ore Region of Lake Superior. (R. A. Parker) Engin. M. **6**: 152, 285.
Iron Situation in U. S. (A. I. Findley) Bank. M. (N. Y.) **50**: 633.
Iron Smelting, Modern. (J. Birkinbine) Engin. M. **9**: 483.
Iron Trade, The. (T. L. Greene) Nation, **56**: 269.
Ironwork, Art. Chamb. J. **69**: 118. — (G. Wallis) M. of Art, **3**: 112, 139.
— at South Kensington. (J. S. Gardner) M. of Art, **19**: 402.
— Constructive, Protection of. (T. B. Grierson) Am. Arch. **43**: 8.
Ironwork, Decorative. (G. Wallis) M. of Art, **4**: 295. **5**: 61.
— Gardner on. (A. H. Church) Portfo. **23**: 256.
— Plant Forms for Art Decoration in. (G. McKenzie) M. of Art, **3**: 62.
Irony; is it a Form of the Ludicrous? Spec. **76**: 627.
Irony of Fate; a story. (T. E. Souther) Chamb. J. **69**: 777–835.
Irony of Progress; a story. (W. B. Harte) Poet-Lore, **8**: 113.
Iroquois Indians, Early Religion of. (W. M. Beauchamp) Am. Antiq. **14**: 344.
— Origin of. (W. M. Beauchamp) Am. Antiq. **16**: 61.
— The Pagan. (A. H. H. Heming) Canad. M. **3**: 463.
— Wampum Records of. (H. M. Converse) Mo. Illust. **4**: 342.
Iroquois Condolence. (W. M. Beauchamp) J. Am. Folk-Lore, **8**: 313.
Iroquois Country, Roman Catholic Influence in. (R. R. Elliott) Am. Cath. Q. **18**: 78.
Iroquois Folk-lore. (W. M. Beauchamp) J. Am. Folk-Lore, **4**: 39. **5**: 223.
Iroquois Games. (W. M. Beauchamp) J. Am. Folk-Lore, **9**: 269.
Iroquois Witchcraft and Demonism. (De Cost Smith) J. Am. Folk-Lore, **1**: 184.
Irrawaddy, A Thousand Miles Up the. (W. R. Winston) Sund. M. **23**: 687.
Irrepressibles. (Mrs. Lynn Linton) Chamb. J. **72**: 593.
Irrigation. (A. B. Wyckoff) J. Frankl. Inst. **140**: 241. — Lend a H. **14**: 243.
— The Conquest of Arid America. (W. E. Smythe) Cent. **28**: 85.
— for Kansas Farms and Orchards. Garden & F. **8**: 518.
— in the Arid Regions of America. (H. S. Inglis) Canad. M. **3**: 449. — (C. H. Shinn) Pop. Sci. Mo. **43**: 145.
— in the Australian Colonies. All the Year, **70**: 172.
— in California. (W. S. Green) Overland, n. s. **26**: 407.
— in Egypt. Dub. R. **119**: 431. — Engin. M. **8**: 821.
— — Perennial. Nature, **50**: 80. Same art. Liv. Age, **201**: 820.
— — Regulation of. Sat. R. **74**: 359.
— in the Punjab. (J. Broadwood) J. Soc. Arts, **44**: 286.
— in the San Joaquin. (C. S. Greene) Overland, n. s. **26**: 320.
— in the U. S., A Great Domain by. (J. N. Irwin) Forum, **12**: 740.
— — Idea of, and the Los Angeles Congress. (W. E. Smythe) R. of Rs. (N. Y.) **8**: 394.
— in the West. (C. Warman) McClure, **3**: 355.
— — Problem of. (H. M. Wilson) Engin. M. **4**: 386.
— — Progress of. (W. E. Smythe) R. of Rs. (N. Y.) **10**: 396.
— Modern, and the Law of Water. (R. J. Hinton) Engin. M. **10**: 699.
— Pump, on the Great Plains. (H. V. Hinckley) Engin. M. **11**: 16.
— Pumping Water for. (W. G. Starkweather) Cassier, **11**: 49.
— Shall we irrigate Orchards in N. Y. State? (L. H. Bailey) Garden & F. **8**: 236.
— Sub-. Garden & F. **6**: 516.
— — in Greenhouse and Garden. (T. Greiner) Garden & F. **7**: 146.
— Symposium. Indep. May 4, '93.
Irrigation States of North America. Spec. **76**: 337.
Irritability, Scientific. (E. J. Hardy) New Sci. R. **1**: 493.
Irvine; Memories of an Old Scottish Burgh. Chamb. J. **72**: 497.

Irvine Family of Georgia. (J. G. Bullock) Am. Hist. Reg. 3: 308.
Irving, Sir Henry. (F. Hawkins) Acad. 44: 197. — With portrait. Theatre, 34: 129. 35: 1.
— Address at Harvard College. Critic, 24: 204.
— and the Dignity of the Stage. Sat. R. 79: 182.
— and English Drama. (G. Barlow) New R. 7: 655.
— as Becket. (H. D. Traill) National, 21: 14.
— as Cardinal Wolsey. Theatre, 28: 101.
— as Henry VIII. (F. H. Hill) Contemp. 61: 73. — Gent. M. n. s. 48: 209.
— as King Lear. (H. J. Jennings) Gent. M. n. s. 49: 624, 634. — Sat. R. 74: 676. — Theatre, 29: 278. — (E. J. Russell) 19th Cent. 33: 44.
— as Shylock. (A. B. McMahan) Dial (Ch.) 15: 215.
— Boyhood of. (J. Hatton) Idler, 6: 669.
— Claims of. (W. Wallace) National, 28: 75.
— Criticism of. Theatre, 37: 175.
— Early Work of. (W. S. Hunt) Theatre, 32: 198.
— Four Favorite Parts of. (H. Irving) Eng. Illust. 10: 925. — Forum, 16: 33.
— How he rose to Fame. (H. Saint Maur) Munsey, 14: 652.
— in Cymbeline. Theatre, 37: 268.
— in King Arthur. (J. W. Cunliffe) Canad. M. 6: 75. — Bost. 3: 87.
— in the Ridiculous. Sat. R. 79: 619.
— in "A Story of Waterloo." (A. Brereton) Theatre, 33: 179.
— Influence of, on the American Stage. (W. T. W. Ball) New Eng. M. n. s. 10: 173.
— — in America. (S. Fiske) Theatre, 36: 75.
— Knighted. Sat. R. 79: 718.
— on the Art of Acting. (L. de la Ramé) 19th Cent. 37: 786.
— a review. (Rev. T. Parker) Idler, 3: 91.
Irving, Washington. (W. W. Gist) Chaut. 18: 48. — (C. D. Warner) Critic, 22: 220. — Temp. Bar, 96: 321. Same art. Liv. Age, 195: 791.
— Knickerbocker's History of New York. Sat. R. 77: 70.
— Outline of Lesson on. (E. W. Barrett) Educa. 15: 167.
— Reminiscences of, with portrait. (J. Morris) Cath. World, 62: 627.
— Study of. (G. F. Adams) School R. 2: 29.
Irvingism. Eng. R. 9: 13.
I 's Niver Feared for my Ould Man. (J. E. T. Dowe) Cent. 23: 934.
Is he Living or is he Dead? (S. L. Clemens) Cosmopol. 15: 629.
Is it Well? a poem. (A. Price) Belgra. 78: 373.
Is it worth while to Live? a poem. (F. Blanchard) Overland, n. s. 21: 438.
Isabel Dysart. (M. O. W. Oliphant) Chamb. J. 70: 7-56.
Isabella I., Queen of Castile. (R. M. Johnston) Cath. World, 54: 541.
— at Segovia. (H. Pierson) Cosmopol. 13: 336.
Isabella, ex-Queen of Spain. (C. R. Montgomery) Munsey, 8: 44.
Isaiah. (C. H. Cornill) Open Court, 9: 4488.
Isam and the Major. (H. S. Edwards) Cent. 25: 692.
Isandhlwana, Zululand, 1894. Liv. Age, 206: 248.
Isaurians, Emperor Zeno and. (E. W. Brooks) Eng. Hist. R. 8: 209.
Isham Books. (R. E. Graves) Bibliographica, 3: 418.
Ishmael. (R. M. Johnston) Lippinc. 52: 359.
Ishmael; a story. (W. P. Brown) Southern M. 4: 49.
Islam and its Critics. (Ameer Ali) 19th Cent. 38: 361.
Islam and its Critics; a Reply. (Ameer Ali) 19th Cent. 38: 778. — (M. MacColl) 19th Cent. 38: 1075. — (J. Knowles) 19th Cent. 38: 1075.
— and Soofeeism. (Mohammed Barakatullah) Westm. 144: 674.
— Apology for. Quar. 174: 345.
— Future of. (Ibn Ishak) Arena, 6: 389.
— — Reply. (T. P. Hughes) Arena, 6: 532.
— Future of. Open Court, 8: 4339.
— Holy Places of. (C. D. Warner) Harper, 85: 813.
— The New. (E. Sell) Contemp. 64: 282.
— Past and Present. (F. W. Sanders) Arena, 8: 115.
— Propagation of. Dub. R. 113: 741.
— Spirit of. (H. Hirschfeld) Jew. Q. 5: 212.
See also Mohammedanism.
Island of Penance. Liv. Age, 196: 755.
Island of Philadelphia; a story. (Dr. Garnett) Eng. Illust. 12: no. 2, 69.
Island Floras. (W. B. Hemsley) Sci. Prog. 5: 286, 374.
Island Hostelry, An. (A. Walters) Gent. M. n. s. 49: 578.
Island Plant, An. (M. C. Lee) Atlan. 71: 597, 751.
Islay, Carved Stones of, Graham on. Sat. R. 79: 834.
— Prunus Ilicifolia. Garden & F. 5: 469.
Isle of Man. *See* Man, Isle of.
Isle of Wight. *See* Wight, Isle of.
Ismail Pasha. Liv. Age, 192: 771.
Isocrats. New Party; ed. by Reid. Sat. R. 77: 692.
Isoperimetrical Problems. (Lord Kelvin) Nature, 49: 515.
Ispahan to Kurrachee, From. (E. L. Weeks) Harper, 88: 231.
Israel. *See* Jews.
Israëls, Josef. Leis. Hour, 45: 648. — (D. C. Thomson) M. of Art, 13: 397.
Isostacy, Gulf of Mexico as a Measure of. (W. J. McGee) Am. J. Sci. 144: 177.
Israphel; a poem. (F. E. Coates) Cosmopol. 17: 602.
Issa, Life of, Carus on. Monist, 5: 116.
Issik Kul. *See* Kirghese.
Istia. (F. C. Sparhawk) New Eng. M. n. s. 11: 243.
It is the Season; a poem. (R. L. Stevenson) M. of Art, 8: 53.
It is a Voice; a poem. (H. N. Crellin) Gent. M. n. s. 57: 212.
It might have been; a poem. (H. St. A. Denton) Argosy, 61: 256.
It might have been Mrs. General Rayburn. (W. W. Woodson) Southern M. 4: 167.
It was a Lordling's Daughter; a poem. (W. Shakespeare?) M. of Art, 19: 97.
It was too Good to be True; a story. (A. F. King) Belgra. 79: 362.
Italian Art of the New Gallery. (C. Whibley) 19th Cent. 35: 330.
Italian Fiction, Recent, Politics in. Blackw. 160: 647. Same art. Liv. Age, 211: 778.
Italian Garden; a poem. (E. Nesbit) Argosy, 59: 175.
Italian Gardens, Old. (V. Paget) Longm. 26: 311. Same art. Liv. Age, 206: 546. Same art. Ecl. M. 125: 388.
Italian Immigrants and their Enslavement. (S. Merino) Forum, 15: 183.
— Protection of. (L. Bodio) Chaut. 23: 42.
Italian Literature. (R. Bonghi) Ath. '94, 2: 20.
— and Art. (E. Panzacchi) Chaut. 18: 142.
— 1891-92. (R. Bonghi; G. Zannoni) Ath. '92, 2: 20.
— 1892-93. (R. Bonghi; G. Zannoni) Ath. '93, 2: 22.
— 1894-95. (R. Bonghi) Ath. '95, 2: 20.
— 1895-96. (A. Manzi) Ath. '96, 2: 21.
— Popular Modern. Ed. R. 179: 103.

Italian Masters, Cole's Old. (K. Cox) Nation, 55: 379. — (J. A. Symonds) New R. 8: 497.
Italian Merrymaking, A bit of. (M. Scott-Uda) Cent. 28: 532.
Italian Novelists of the Present Day. (M. Hargrave) Gent. M. n. s. 49: 519.
Italian Officer, Life of an. Chaut. 23: 329.
Italian Opera in London. (F. Hawkins) Theatre, 34: 272.
Italian Operas. Sat. R. 81: 499.
Italian Poetry, Contemporary. (W. Sharp) Acad. 44: 433.
— in 1892. (J. S. Fiske) Nation, 55: 469.
Italian Poets of To-day. (H. Zimmern) Blackw. 151: 350. Same art. Liv. Age, 193: 451.
Italian Villas. Am. Arch. 46: 38.
Italian Women of 15th Century. No. Am. 160: 126.
— of the 16th Century. (E. P. Jacobsen) Westm. 140: 17.
Italians: Are they a Dangerous Class? (I. W. Howerth) Char. R. 4: 17.
— Immigration into U. S. (V. Grossi) Chaut. 21: 270.
— in Boston; the Padrone Question. (E. E. Hale) Lend a H. 12: 449.
Italy and the Pope. Spec. 68: 80.
— and the Ruin of Political Liberty. (T. Hughes) Am. Cath. Q. 21: 449.
— and the Triple Alliance. (D. MacG. Means) Nation, 54: 482. — (W. J. Stillman) Nation, 58: 26.
— Archæological Notes from. (F. Halbherr) Ath. '92, 1: 575. '93, 2: 198.
— Archæological Research in. (F. von Duhn) J. Hel. Stud. 16: 120.
— Army and Navy of. (G. Goiran) Chaut. 18: 13.
— Art-centre of the World. (J. Flaxman) M. of Art, 12: 73.
— Artistic Problem in. (A. Rondani) Chaut. 17: 431.
— Awakening of. (L. de La Ramé) Fortn. 65: 541.
— Bank Scandals in. (N. Colajanni) Fortn. 61: 510. — (J. W. Mario) Nation, 56: 98, 175. — (R. Dalla Volta) J. Pol. Econ. 2: 1.
— Blind Guides of. (L. de La Ramé) Fortn. 57: 65.
— Bourget's Sensations d'Italie. Spec. 68: 610.
— Cabinet Crisis in, 1893. Spec. 71: 866.
— Canadian Bicycle in. (C. B. Boulton) Canad. M. 7: 113, 216.
— Capitalists and Land Owners in. (G. Fiamingo) Econ. J. 5: 128.
— Church and State in. (W. J. D. Croke) Cath. World, 60: 579.
— Cities of, and their Development. (A. Oldrini) Chaut. 18: 672.
— — Recent Progress in. (A. Shaw) R. of Rs. (N. Y.) 12: 553.
— Colonies in Africa. (R. Bonghi) Asia. R. 11: 79.
— Constitution of, Amendments to. (G. A. Rutz) Ann. Am. Acad. Pol. Sci. 6: 227.
— Crime and Politics in. (J. W. Mario) Nation, 55: 350.
— Crisis in, Some Causes of. (W. R. Thayer) Atlan. 73: 537.
— Crispi in Power again. (J. W. Mario) Nation, 58: 9.
— Disunion in. (J. Crooklands) Fortn. 63: 940. Same art. Liv. Age, 206: 25.
— A Doomsday Book Doomed. (J. W. Mario) Nation, 62: 8.
— Drive in. All the Year, 73: 125, 159.
— During the Renaissance. (B. O. Flower) Arena, 12: 185.
— Economics in. (U. Rabbeno) Pol. Sci. Q. 6: 439.
Italy, Every-Day. (C. F. Bragdon) Am. Arch. 51: 71-127. 52: 3.
— Financial Crisis, 1893. (P. Villari) Chaut. 18: 527. — (M. G. Mulhall) Contemp. 65: 496.
— Finances of, 1893. Spec. 71: 540. — (M. Ferrario) Chaut. 18: 270. — (W. J. Stillman) Nation, 57: 81. — (F. S. Nitti) Econ. J. 3: 156.
— — 1894. Spec. 72: 261.
— Folk-Lore of. (H. C. Coote) Folk-Lore Rec. 1: 187.
— Folk-Songs of. (R. H. Busk) Folk-Lore, 1: 261.
— Foreign Companies in. (M. McIlwraith) Law Q. 10: 176.
— Foreign Policy of. (E. de Laveleye) Contemp. 61: 153.
— — Effects of. (F. M. Warren) Chaut. 19: 162.
— Friendship with England. Fortn. 65: 451.
— Future of, Sursum Corda, or. (R. Bonghi) Chaut. 19: 144.
— Glimpses of. (E. C. Foster) Cath. World, 61: 254.
— Government of, Practical Questions in. (V. Pareto) Chaut. 14: 448.
— Her Needs *vs.* her Art Treasures. (C. A. Dougherty) Am. Arch. 45: 83.
— History, 1409–1530, Browning's. Sat. R. 82: 224.
— — 1820–48. (A. Oldrini) Chaut. 18: 30, 159.
— Hodgkin's Italy and her Invaders. Am. Hist. R. 1: 108.
— How it is governed. Nation, 62: 413.
— How Law is taught in. (J. Kirkpatrick) Jurid. R. 1: 137.
— How People of, live. Leis. Hour, 42: 11-185.
— Humiliation and Prowess in Africa. (J. W. Mario) Nation, 62: 284.
— Ideas and Tendencies of Modern. (A. Oldrini) Chaut. 19: 29.
— In. (J. H. Vincent) Chaut. 18: 387.
— in Africa. (J. W. Mario) Leis. Hour, 45: 467. — (J. W. Mario) Nation, 60: 179.
— in 1892. (W. F. Lord) 19th Cent. 31: 363.
— in 1894. (J. W. Mario) Nation, 58: 287.
— Independence of, Thayer's Dawn of. Atlan. 71: 551. — (F. P. Nash) Nation, 56: 181.
— King, The, the Pope and Crispi. (H. R. Haweis) Fortn. 62: 81. Same art. Ecl. M. 123: 303.
— Kingdom of, Twenty-five Years of. (F. Z. Rooker) Chr. Lit. 13: 329.
— Liberation of. (Countess Evelyn Martinengo Cesaresco) 19th Cent. 37: 337.
— Marriage of the Crown Prince of. (J. W. Mario) Nation, 63: 324.
— Monumental Sculpture of. (S. Thompson) M. of Art, 3: 95.
— Navy. (S. Eardley-Wilmot) Un. Serv. M. 7: 692. — (J. Leyland) Un. Serv. M. 8: 357.
— New Criminal Code of. (T. B. Bruce) Law Q. 5: 287.
— The New Reformation of. (A. Robertson) Chr. Lit. 12: 342.
— North, Notes on a Tour in. (Emily Crawford) National, 22: 612. Same art. Liv. Age, 200: 342.
— of the Renaissance. (B. O. Flower) Arena, 11: 310. 12: 50.
— of To-day. Fortn. 61: 295. Same art. Liv. Age, 200: 683.
— Parliament of, Convicts in. (E. S. Morgan) Time, 16: 81.
— Parliamentary Régime in. (V. Pareto) Pol. Sci. Q. 8: 677.
— Philosophy of, National Character and Classicism in. (L. Ferri) Int. J. Ethics, 5: 63.
— The Pities of. (George Widdrington) Gent. M. n. s. 53: 613.

Italy, Political Situation in. (Deviti De Marco) 19th Cent. **38**: 548. Same art. Ecl. M. **125**: 677. — (C. B. Roylance-Kent) Macmil. **71**: 431.
— Politics in, 1892. Result of the Elections. (J. W. Mario) Nation, **55**: 427.
— Poor Relief in. (F. S. Nitti) Econ. R. **2**: 1.
— Preservation of Ancient Buildings in. Am. Arch. **46**: 62.
— Protectionism and Socialism in. (J. W. Mario) Nation, **58**: 384.
— Reconciliation with the Holy See. (W. C. Robinson) Am. Cath. Q. **20**: 389.
— Religious Prospects of. (E. D. Cheney) Open Court, **5**: 2885.
— Religious Sentiment and Moral Problem in. (G. Barzellotti) Int. J. Ethics, **4**: 445.
— Religious Tableaux in Churches of. (W. H. D. Rouse) Folk-Lore, **5**: 4.
— Roba d'Italia. (C. S. Strong) Gent. M. n. s. **53**: 504. Same art. Liv. Age, **211**: 235.
— the Roman's Villeggiatura. (Countess M. Cesaresco) Contemp. **68**: 509. Same art. Liv. Age, **207**: 417. Same art. Ecl. M. **126**: 47.
— Rome and. (R. de Cesare) Chaut. **22**: 686.
— Royal Pageant in. (M. S. Stillman) Nation, **63**: 381.
— Scientific Societies of. (W. C. Cahall) Pop. Sci. Mo. **42**: 107.
— Senate of. (F. Nobili-Vitelleschi) 19th Cent. **34**: 922. Same art. Liv. Age, **200**: 131.
— Silver Jubilee of. (W. Poland) Am. Cath. Q. **20**: 571.
— Situation in, 1892. (F. Crispi) No. Am. **155**: 106.
— Social Regeneration in. (J. W. Mario) Nation, **62**: 358.
— Society in, in 18th Century, Mrs. Piozzi on. Spec. **69**: 101.
— Some Cities of. (O. Browning) Time, **2**: 249, 315.
— South, Agricultural Contracts in. (F. S. Nitti) Econ. R. **3**: 364.
— — Early Settlement of Jews in. (A. Neubauer) Jew. Q. **4**: 606.
— — Notes of a Journey in. (J. A. Symonds) Fortn. **60**: 551.
— State Expenditures as compared with National Wealth. (V. Pareto) Econ. J. **2**: 561.
— under the Lombards. (J. B. Bury) Scot. R. **27**: 33.
— Unification of, O'Clery's. Sat. R. **73**: 482.
— United, and Modern Rome, 1860–90. Agriculture, Emigration, Industry, and Commerce. (A. Oldrini) Chaut. **18**: 287.
— Universities of. (F. Martini) Chaut. **19**: 452.
— Votive Offerings in. (W. H. D. Rouse) Folk-Lore, **5**: 11.
— What the United States owes to. (G. Morosini) Lippinc. **52**: 103.
— Why it is not Rich. (W. J. Stillman) Nation, **62**: 488.
— Woman Novelists in, at the Present Day. (M. Hargrave) Gent. M. n. s. **53**: 145.
Ivan IV., the Terrible. (J. Errol) Belgra. **88**: 262. — (R. Green) Gent. M. n. s. **52**: 569.
Ivan Aksentieff's Petition. (O. M. Norris) Sund. M. **24**: 564.
Ivan of the Mask; a story. (E. L. Dorsey) Outing, **23**: 262.
Iviza, Sketches in. All the Year, **72**: 31. Same art. Liv. Age, **196**: 634.
Ivories. Sat. R. **75**: 404.
— Carved. Chamb. J. **70**: 725.
Ivory. Chamb. J. **72**: 726.
Ivory Gate, The; a story. (Walter Besant) Chamb. J. **69**: 1–483.
Ivory Leg and the Twenty-four Diamonds, The. (F. Hume) Idler, **5**: 155.
Ivy, Poison. (W. H. Harrison) Garden & F. **8**: 268.
— — When most Active. (H. Havard) Garden & F. **8**: 203, 239.
— Structure and Growth of. (A. S. Wilson) Knowl. **18**: 17.
Iyemitsu, Temple of. (C. T. Mathews) Am. Arch. **52**: 83.

Jack, Derivation of. (E. W. B. Nicholson) Acad. **41**: 90, 183. — (F. Chance) Acad. **41**: 278. — (E. W. B. Nicholson and others) Acad. **41**: 470, 593. **42**: 33, 53.
Jack Hilton's Love-affair; a story. (T. H. Farnham) Un. Serv. (Phila.) **10**: 224.
Jack-in-the-box; a story. (T. R. Sullivan) Scrib. M. **12**: 211.
Jack Moore's Temptation; a story. (D. Vane) Chamb. J. **69**: 360–392.
Jack Smith, Boy; a story. (M. Pemberton) Eng. Illust. **12**: no. 4, 85.
Jack's Friends. Liv. Age, **210**: 637.
Jackson, Andrew, and David Crockett. (H. S. Turner) M. Am. Hist. **27**: 385.
— and the Land Banks. (F. Rivers) So. M. **3**: 80.
— at the Battle of New Orleans, 1815. (H. King) M. Am. Hist. **29**: 19.
— The "Hermitage," the Home of. (W. J. Lisle) So. M. **1**: 531.
— Unpublished Letters of. Overland, n. s. **19**: 138.
Jackson, Helen Hunt. Bk. Buyer, **2**: 195.
Jackson, Gen. Henry. (J. W. Dean) N. E. Reg. **46**: 111.
Jackson, Howell E., with portrait. (H. M. Doak) Green Bag, **5**: 209.
— Nomination of. Pub. Opin. **14**: 443.
Jackson, Sheldon. (J. Eaton) R. of Rs. (N. Y.) **13**: 691.
Jackson, Thomas J., "Stonewall," and Lee, Robert E., Gentler Side of. (G. W. Cable) Cent. **25**: 292.
— Boyhood of. So. Hist. Pap. **22**: 157.
— The Real. (D. H. Hill) Cent. **22**: 623.
— Reminiscences of, with portrait. (W. W. Scott) Southern M. **5**: 37.
Jackson-Harmsworth Polar Expedition. (F. G. Jackson) Geog. J. **4**: 141. — (A. Montefiore) Geog. J. **6**: 497. — (A. M. Brice) Geog. J. **8**: 543.
— Fitting out the. (A. C. Harmsworth) Eng. Illust. **14**: 359.
Jacksonville, Florida; Panama Park. (B. G. Sargent) Nat'l M. (Bost.) **4**: 473.
Jacob; a story. (K. S. Macquoid) Ecl. M. **125**: 442.
Jacobinism, Revival of. (G. H. Powell) National, **19**: 290.
Jacobite Tracts, Late. (Andrew Lang) Bibliographica, **3**: 407.
Jacobite's Farewell, 1715; a poem. (A. C. Swinburne) M. of Art, **12**: 81.
Jacobites, Spain and the. (Benjamin Taylor) Scot. R. **27**: 253.
Jacobitism, Revival of. (S. D. White) Westm. **146**: 417.
Jaffa, Railway from, to Jerusalem. Liv. Age, **200**: 441. — (S. Merrill) Scrib. M. **13**: 289.
Jagannath. (C. W. Leadbeater) Gent. M. n. s. **48**: 387. Same art. Ecl. M. **118**: 751.
Jails. An American Lock-up. Cornh. **62**: 290.
— and Jubilees. (E. E. Stanton) Open Court, **1**: 175.
— County, as Reformatory Institutions. (E. B. Merrill) Am. J. Soc. Sci. **30**: 29.

Jainism and its Founder. (J. T. Bixby) New World, 5: 541.
Jake Peterkin's Surprise Party. (C. Gilbert) Southern M. 4: 295.
Jake Stanwood's Gal. (A. Fuller) Cent. 26: 673.
Jakobowski, Edward. Mynheer Jan; comic opera. Theatre, 18: 163.
Jalalabad, Defence of. (W. Broadfoot) Eng. Hist. R. 8: 93.
Jamaica. (H. M. Sweeney) Cath. World, 59: 402. — (G. Gaul) Cent. 23: 682.
— and Mauritius. (J. W. Fortescue) Liv. Age, 192: 491.
— as a Field for Investment. (H. A. Blake) No. Am. 162: 341.
— Blue Mountains of. All the Year, 70: 562.
— and the Blue Hills. Around World, 1: 66.
— An Evening Chat in. Cornh. 72: 636. Same art. Liv. Age, 208: 109. Same art. Ecl. M. 126: 678.
— Folk-Lore of. (W. C. Bates) J. Am. Folk-Lore, 9: 38, 121.
— for Cyclists. (A. Eric) Outing, 23: 379.
— In Banana-land awheel. (E. M.-Aaron) Outing, 25: 312. 27: 25, 129.
— in the Past and Present. (F. Cundall) J. Soc. Arts, 44: 104.
— Museum Work in. (J. E. Duerden) Nat. Sci. 8: 318.
— Negro Customs and Folk-stories of. (A. W. Trowbridge) J. Am. Folk-Lore, 9: 279.
— New England Farmer in. (D. Buffum) New Eng. M. n. s. 11: 469.
— Old Churches in. All the Year, 73: 487.
— Opportunities for Young Men in. (H. A. Blake) No. Am. 155: 661.
— Rebellion of the Maroons, 1795-1800. (J. W. Fortescue) Macmil. 71: 72.
— Recently discovered Remains of the Aboriginal Inhabitants of. (W. H. Flower) Nature, 52: 607.
— resurgens. (Duke of St. Albans) 19th Cent. 32: 97.
James I. and VI. (O. Smeaton) Westm. 146: 635.
— Coronation of. (Guy le Strange) Scot. R. 28: 293.
— Court and Times of. Eng. R. 5: 120.
— Kingis Quair, Doubtful Authorship of, Brown on. Sat. R. 82: 55.
— Library of. (G. F. Warner) Ath. '93, 1: 17.
— Parliaments of, and Plantation of America. (A. Brown) Green Bag, 6: 36.
— Wedding Tour of. (A. H. Millar) Scot. R. 21: 142. Same art. Liv. Age, 197: 161.
James II. at Saint-Germains. (Herbert Vivian) New R. 13: 525. Same art. Liv. Age, 207: 682.
James I. of Aragon, Life and Times of, Swift's. Sat. R. 77: 289.
James, the Old Pretender. (A. Shield) Month, 88: 16.
James, Bartholomew, 1752-1828. Journal. Sat. R. 82: 116.
James, Henry, Jr. (N. Hapgood) Bach. of Arts, 3: 477. — (Annie Macdonell) Bookman, 4: 20. — (A. M. Logan) Nation, 57: 416. — (R. Buchanan) Univ. R. 3: 353.
— at Play-writing. Sat. R. 78: 662.
— English Criticism of. Critic, 22: 52.
— Guy Domville. Sat. R. 79: 43.
James, Sir Henry, with portrait. Green Bag, 4: 193.
James, Kate, with portrait. Theatre, 28: 197.
James, Wm., with portrait. Bk. Buyer, 12: 61.
Jameson, Mrs. Anna M. Bk. Buyer, 12: 653. — (A. Oldcastle) M. of Art, 2: 123.
Jameson, Dr. Leander S., Rhodes and. (J. Verschoyle) Fortn. 65: 483.
— Raid of. Sat. R. 81: 266.
— — and Sir Jacobus de Wet. Sat. R. 81: 507.
Jameson, Dr. Leander S., Raid of, and the Trial at Bar. (E. Dicey) Fortn. 66: 319.
— — Comments on. (R. B. C. Graham) Sat. R. 81: 340.
— — Maps and Notes. Sat. R. 81: 553.
— — True Motive of. (G. S. Fort) 19th Cent. 39: 873.
— — Trial of, in its Legal Aspects. Green Bag, 8: 397.
— — — Result of. Sat. R. 82: 100. — Nation, 63: 6, 118.
Jamestown Romance. (S. B. Kennedy) Outing, 25: 179-484.
Jamie; a story. (H. V. Brown) Gent. M. n. s. 54: 541.
Jamie; a story. (Ian Maclaren) Harper, 91: 559.
Jamie the Kid; a story. (J. Flynt) Harper, 91: 776.
Jamieson's Dictionary. Scot. R. 12: 270.
Jamison, Celia V., with portrait. Bk. News, 12: 462.
Jamrach's. Spec. 72: 265.
Jan Pengelly. (J. Patey) Chamb. J. 73: 417-470.
Janauschek, Fanny, Portraits of. McClure, 3: 346.
Jane Field; a novel. (M. E. Wilkins) Harper, 84: 815 — 85: 828.
Jane Hubbs's Salvation; a story. (H. Huntington) Harper, 92: 598.
Jane's Holiday. (V. H. Berry) Lippinc. 52: 235.
Janet; a story. All the Year, 76: 108, 131.
Janissaries, The. (H. Macmillan) Good Words, 37: 564. Same art. Liv. Age, 210: 807.
Jannet, Claudio. Econ. J. 4: 745.
Jansenists and their Schools. (H. C. Bowen) Educa. R. 6: 485. 7: 64.
Janssen, Johannes. (J. Alexander) Cath. World, 55: 572. — (C. Galton) Month, 77: 385.
January; a poem. (A. C. Swinburne) M. of Art, 16: 95.
Japan. (H. H. Gardener) Arena, 11: 176. — (D. W. Stevens) Nat. Geog. M. 3: 193.
— After the War. (L. Hearn) Atlan. 76: 599.
— Ainu of. (A. H. Keane) Acad. 42: 207.
— Alps of. Dub. R. 118: 432. — Acad. 50: 552.
— — Exploration of, 1891-94. (W. Weston) Geog. J. 7: 125.
— and China. (Viscount Wolseley) Cosmopol. 18: 417. — (G. F. Seward) Cosmopol. 18: 713.
— — Engineering Notes from. (F. F. Prentiss) Cassier, 10: 431.
— — a Symposium. New R. 11: 221.
— — Treaty Questions. Sat. R. 79: 571.
— — War between. *See* Chino-Japanese War.
— and her Constitution. (F. T. Piggott) Asia. R. 14: 1. 15: 50.
— and England. (A. G. Boscawen) National, 27: 424.
— and the European Powers. Sat. R. 79: 540. — (E. A. Cheney) Arena, 8: 455.
— and her Outlook. Pub. Opin. 20: 427.
— and the United States. (E. W. Clement) M. Am. Hist. 28: 129.
— — Relations between. (W. E. Griffis) M. Am. Hist. 27: 449. — (W. E. Griffis) New Eng. M. n. s. 11: 257.
— — Treaty Relations of. (J. L. Atkinson) Our Day, 9: 273.
— Architecture of. (C. T. Mathews) Archit. Rec. 5: 383.
— Arnold on. Sat. R. 73: 75.
— Art in, Contemporary. (E. F. Fenollosa) Cent. 24: 577.
— — Stray Notes on. (F. T. Piggott) Fortn. 59: 184. Same art. Ecl. M. 120: 632.
— Art Industries in. (E. Hart) J. Soc. Arts, 43: 869, 881.
— An Artist in. (R. Blum) Scrib. M. 13: 399-729.
— as an Industrial Power. (W. E. Griffis) Chaut. 24: 201.

Japan. At Hakata. (L. Hearn) Atlan. 74: 510.
— Autumn in. (A. Parsons) Harper, 90: 767.
— Bric-à-brac; An Artist's Letters from Japan. (J. La Farge) Cent. 24: 419.
— Bronze Casting in. (W. Gowland) J. Soc. Arts, 43: 523.
— Buddhism in. (N. Kishimoto) Open Court, 8: 4183–4211.
— Burning Questions of. (A. H. Savage-Landor) Fortn. 62: 636. Same art. Liv. Age, 203: 812. Same art. Ecl. M. 124: 114.
— Cabinet Changes in. (G. Droppers) Nation, 63: 399.
— Case of, in Late War. (T. Okamura) Un. Serv. M. 10: 209.
— Causes Célèbres in. Green Bag, 4: 563.
— Chinese Philosophy in. (J. H. Wigmore) Nation, 54: 411.
— Christianity in Old. (T. R. Beck) Ref. Q. 41: 409.
— Color-prints of. (E. F. Strange) New R. 14: 680.
— Commercial Morality in. (R. Young) 19th Cent. 40: 721. — (G. C. Perkins) Overland, n. s. 28: 393. — (A. R. Foote) Engin. M. 11: 705. — Gunton's M. 10: 206. — (J. P. Young) Overland, n. s. 28: 82.
— — Influence of, upon the Industries of America. (W. H. Mills) Overland, n. s. 27: 587.
— — Is it a Myth? (R. P. Porter) No. Am. 163: 144.
— Commercial Treaty with Great Britain. Dub. R. 116: 190.
— Constitution of, The New. (C. B. Roylance-Kent) Macmil. 70: 420. — Liv. Age, 203: 418.
— Constitutional Crisis and the War. Contemp. 68: 457. Same art. Liv. Age, 207: 323.
— Corea, China and. (R. S. Gundry) Fortn. 62: 618. — (M. A. Hamm) Overland, n. s. 25: 130.
— Currency and Finances of. (J. Soyeda) Econ. J. 5: 662.
— Curzon on. Dial (Ch.) 17: 189. — (W. E. Griffis) Nation, 59: 250. — Sat. R. 78: 211. 81: 404.
— Description of Customs and Sights. (N. Roofs) Idler, 8: 540.
— Early Summer in. (A. Parsons) Harper, 89: 522.
— Earthquake in, 1891. (Mrs. E. Hart) Leis. Hour, 41: 418.
— Failure as a Colonizer. Sat. R. 82: 358.
— Feast of Flags. (C. M. Salwey) Asia. R. 22: 388.
— Festival of the Cherry Blossom. (C. M. Salwey) Asia. R. 22: 139.
— Folk-tales of. (C. Pfoundes) Folk-Lore Rec. 1: 118.
— Foreign Jurisdiction in. (J. H. Wigmore) Nation, 56: 26.
— Foreign Policy of. (E. W. Clement) Am. J. Pol. 5: 408.
— Forests of, Sargent's. (C. E. Bessey) Am. Natural. 29: 1049.
— From my Japanese Diary. (L. Hearn) Atlan. 74: 609.
— Future of. (S. Kurino) No. Am. 160: 621. — Spec. 73: 915.
— Genius of Japanese Civilization. (L. Hearn) Atlan. 76: 449.
— Girls in. (C. Scott) Eng. Illust. 11: 135.
— Hearn on. (E. W. Clement) Dial (Ch.) 17: 258. — (E. Buckley) Dial (Ch.) 18: 241.
— Home Life in. (W. D. Eastlake) Pop. Sci. Mo. 43: 1.
— Imperial Family of. Liv. Age, 205: 822.
— In the Mountains of. (L. B. Starr) Outing, 26: 7.
— Introduction of Buddhism into. (P. Carus) Open Court, 8: 4321.
— Japanese View of. (K. T. Takahashi) Canad. M. 3: 110.
Japan, Josses in: In the Twilight of the Gods. (L. Hearn) Atlan. 75: 791.
— Justice for. (B. O. Flower) Arena, 10: 225.
— Labor Problem in. (F. Takano) Gunton's M. 11: 106.
— Land of the Mikado. (J. C. Hopkins) Engin. M. 8: 195.
— Land Taxation in. (S. Sugiyama) Gunton's M. 11: 6.
— Language and Literature in. (E. W. Clement) Dial (Ch.) 19: 137.
— Lenz's Tour awheel. Outing, 23: 324.
— Love and Marriage in. (Sir E. Arnold) Cosmopol. 12: 387.
— Maps of, Early. (G. Collingridge) Geog. J. 3: 403.
— Married Life in. (L. Hearn) Atlan. 72: 761.
— Military. (E. G. Barrow) Un. Serv. M. 7: 1271.
— Modern Development of. Sat. R. 78: 344.
— Moral Life in. (W. D. Eastlake) Pop. Sci. Mo. 43: 327.
— Murray's. (E. W. Clement) Dial (Ch.) 16: 181.
— Music of. (L. A. Smith) 19th Cent. 36: 900. — (E. C. Bell) Music, 2: 533.
— National Debt of. (J. Soyeda) Econ. J. 5: 289.
— Natural Science in. (F. A. Bather) Nat. Sci. 4: 19, 98, 183.
— New. (F. T. Piggott) Fortn. 58: 335. Same art. Ecl. M. 119: 577. Same art. Liv. Age, 195: 352.
— — and England. (H. W. Wilson) Un. Serv. M. 11: 109.
— — Signs of the Times in. (M. Ichihara) Our Day, 9: 237.
— New British Treaty with. (M. J. Farrelly) Macmil. 71: 69. — (G. Droppers) Nation, 59: 404.
— Norman's. Sat. R. 73: 100.
— Notes from a Traveling Diary. (L. Hearn) Atlan. 76: 815.
— Occult, Lowell on. (E. W. Clement) Dial (Ch.) 18: 45.
— Of the Eternal Feminine. (L. Hearn) Atlan. 72: 761.
— Old, Legal System of. (J. H. Wigmore) Green Bag, 4: 403, 478.
— — Spirit of. (Arthur Diósy) Asia. R. 16: 179.
— Open Furrows in the Orient. (J. Cook) Our Day, 15: 13.
— Parliament. Session of 1894. (G. Droppers) Nation, 59: 78.
— Parliamentary Affairs in. (J. H. Wigmore) Nation, 54: 85.
— Parsons's Pictures of. (M. G. Van Rensselaer) Garden & F. 6: 127.
— Party Government in. (G. Droppers) Nation, 56: 416, 436.
— Party Politics in. (G. Droppers) Nation, 62: 375.
— Political Crisis in. (C. M. Huntington) Soc. Econ. 6: 166.
— Political Development in. (G. Droppers) Nation, 62: 94.
— Politics of. (C. T. Long) Canad. M. 4: 407. — (C. Meriwether) R. of Rs. (N. Y.) 10: 277. — (G. Droppers) Nation, 58: 325, 343.
— Position of, in 1894. Blackw. 156: 878.
— Pottery of, Art. (E. Hart) J. Soc. Arts, 40: 315.
— Prehistoric Peoples of. (R. Hitchcock) Am. Antiq. 16: 209.
— Present and Future of. (M. Komatz) Arena, 12: 1.
— Problems of the Far East. Ed. R. 182: 132. Same art. Liv. Age, 206: 579.
— Rambles in. (H. B. Tristram) Leis. Hour, 44: 155–781.
— Recent Books on. Atlan. 75: 830.
— Recent Growth of. Sat. R. 79: 500.

Japan, Recent Works on, 1892. Ath. '92, 1: 205.
— Religion in. (C. Pfoundes) Open Court, 9: 4372, 4377.
— Religions of, Griffis on. (E. Buckley) Nation, 60: 260.
— Religious Situation in, as altered by the War. (J. T. Yokoi) Chr. Lit. 12: 265.
— Religious Thought in. (K. M. Hirai) Arena, 7: 257.
— Report of the Work of the A. B. C. F. M. for 1891-92. And. R. 18: 185.
— Revenue Measures in. (G. Droppers) Nation, 62: 414.
— revisited. (Sir E. Arnold) Cosmopol. 14: 3, 132, 285.
— Shintoism in. (N. Kishimoto) Pop. Sci. Mo. 46: 206.
— Silver Wedding of the Emperor. (C. T. Long) Canad. M. 3: 382.
— Some Wanderings in. (A. Parsons) Harper, 90: 900.
— Soshi-ism in. (G. Droppers) Nation, 60: 321.
— Sword of, and its Ornaments. Mo. Illust. 4: 245.
— Symbolism in. (Mrs. C. M. Salwey) Asia. R. 18: 439.
— Tea Ceremony of. (J. K. Matumoto) Lippinc. 56: 115.
— Theology of, Crudity of. (J. L. Atkinson) Our Day, 13: 113.
— Tidal Wave in, 1896. Dub. R. 119: 433. — (J. Milne) Geog. J. 8: 157. — (E. R. Scidmore) Nat. Geog. M. 7: 285.
— Time of the Lotus in. (A. Parsons) Harper, 90: 51.
— Tracy's. Sat. R. 74: 341.
— Transformation of. (Countess of Jersey) 19th Cent. 34: 369, 570. Same art. Ecl. M. 121: 491, 624. Same art. Un. Serv. (Phila.) 10: 437, 508.
— A Trip to. (Alfred East) Univ. R. 6: 331, 508.
— Triumph of. (R. K. Douglas) 19th Cent. 37: 156. — (E. Arnold) Chaut. 20: 449.
— *versus* Europe. Sat. R. 73: 248.
— Victorious. (G. Droppers) Nation, 60: 377.
— War and Labor in. (F. Takona) Soc. Econ. 9: 30.
— What to do in. (H. J. Baird-Huey) Around World, 1: 109.
— Women of. (A. B. de Guerville) Munsey, 14: 341. — (A. M. Hart) Sat. R. 80: 500.
Japanese, American Naturalization of. (J. H. Wigmore) Am. Law R. 28: 818.
— and the War. (G. Droppers) Nation, 60: 122.
— Ethical Ideas of. Spec. 76: 48.
— Ethical Life and Conceptions of. (T. Yokoi) Int. J. Ethics, 6: 182.
— Future of. Our Day, 14: 185.
— Humor of. M. of Art, 4: 16.
— Mental Characteristics of. (G. T. Ladd) Scrib. M. 17: 79.
Japanese Anomatopes and the Origin of Language. (W. G. Aston) Anthrop. J. 23: 332.
Japanese Art, Faces in. (L. Hearn) Atlan. 78: 219.
— on Puget Sound. (J. Wickersham) Am. Antiq. 16: 47, 78.
Japanese Art Work, Lawrence's Collection. Sat. R. 80: 213.
Japanese Book Illustration. (R. K. Douglas) Bibliographica, 3: 1. — (H. Shugio) Bk. Buyer, 5: 12.
Japanese Bride, Tamura's. (W. E. Griffis) Nation, 56: 299.
Japanese Characteristics. Spec. 77: 815.
Japanese Curiosities, Collection of. (E. Hart) Art. J. 47: 7-336.
Japanese Customs. (F. T. Piggott) Fortn. 57: 508. Same art. Liv. Age, 193: 797.
— compared with English. (D. Goh) Idler, 5: 239.
Japanese Fighting; the Art of Self-defence. (G. B. Burgin) Idler, 2: 281.
Japanese Firemen, A Night with. Temp. Bar, 94: 419. Same art. Liv. Age, 193: 698.
Japanese Folk-songs. Out of the Street. (L. Hearn) Atlan. 78: 347.
Japanese Garden, In a. (L. Hearn) Atlan. 70: 14.
Japanese Imbroglio. 1895. Blackw. 158: 309.
Japanese Interior, Bacon on. (F. W. Gookin) Dial (Ch.) 16: 17.
Japanese Language, Importance to Western Nations. (Daigoro Goh) Asia. R. 15: 461.
Japanese Lanterns. (L. B. Starr) Cosmopol. 17: 737.
Japanese Lyric Drama. (F. B. Harris) Chaut. 15: 574.
Japanese Match-box Labels. Eng. Illust. 15: 361.
Japanese Mountaineers. Dub. R. 118: 432.
Japanese Play, A. Belgra. 86: 359.
Japanese Religious Practices, Minor. (B. H. Chamberlain) Anthrop. J. 22: 355.
Japanese Smile. (L. Hearn) Atlan. 71: 634.
Japanese Theatre. (E. B. Rogers) Outing, 25: 191.
Japanese Traits and Chinese Traits. (E. F. Fenollosa) Atlan. 69: 769.
Japanese Vase-handles. (A. H. Church) Portfo. 23: 140.
Japanese Vegetation in California. (C. H. Shinn) Garden & F. 8: 302.
Japanese War Caricatures. (F. Lucas) Mo. Illust. 11: 445.
Japanese Ways, Chamberlain on. Sat. R. 73: 453.
Japonica. (H. Oertel) J. Am. Folk-Lore, 2: 149.
Jareb, Pul, Tiglath-Pilezer. (J. Horner) Meth. R. 54: 928.
Jarley, Mrs. *See* Harwood, Elizabeth Franklin.
Jarras, Gen. Ath. '92, 2: 314.
Jarrow Church, Northumberland. Reliquary, 33: 148.
Jarry, Alfred. Ubu roi. (A. Symons) Sat. R. 82: 645.
Jarvis Island: Under the Southern Cross. (M. H. Closson) Overland, n. s. 21: 205.
Jasmin, J., the Gascon Poet. Temp. Bar, 95: 39. — (J. G. C. Minchin) Acad. 41: 249. — All the Year, 71: 441-491.
Jasper Mines, Prehistoric, in the Lehigh Hills. (H. C. Mercer) Pop. Sci. Mo. 43: 662.
Jàtaka, The. (J. F. Hewitt) Westm. 145: 622.
Java, Dutch Society in. (W. B. Worsfold) Fortn. 59: 330. Same art. Liv. Age, 197: 243.
— Opera in. (A. H. Grant) Time, 7: 1055.
— Pilgrimage to the Temples of. (R. Rivington) Westm. 145: 321.
— Six Weeks in. (H. Collett) Blackw. 156: 78. Same art. Liv. Age, 202: 561.
Jay, John. (E. Jones) Nat'l M. (N. Y. '91) 17: 310.
Jay, William, Tuckerman's. (W. P. Garrison) Nation, 58: 16.
Jay's Treaty. (H. White) Nation, 61: 460.
JE in Middle Books of the Pentateuch. (B. W. Bacon) J. Bib. Lit. 11: 177. 12: 23.
Jeaffreson, J. Cordy, Recollections of. (A. H. Japp) Gent. M. n. s. 52: 70. — Sat. R. 76: 522.
Jealousy. Sat. R. 77: 275.
"Jeannette" Relics, So-called. (W. H. Dall) Nat. Geog. M. 7: 93.
Jeans, J. Stephen. (G. Cawley) Cassier, 6: 243.
Jebb, John Gladwyn. (J. S. Little) Acad. 46: 488. — Sat. R. 78: 636.
Jebus, Expedition against. (F. J. Davies) Un. Serv. M. 5: 629.

Jecks, Clara, with portrait. Theatre, 29: 286. — With portrait. Theatre, 37: 126.
Jefferies, Richard. (M. A. Nicholas) Chr. Un. 45: 1197. — (A. T. Q. Couch) Critic, 23: 262. — (E. Garnet) Univ. R. 2: 357.
— About the Home of. (P. A. Graham) Art J. 45: 16.
— as a Descriptive Writer. (I. Muntz) Gent. M. n. s. 53: 514. Same art. Liv. Age, 203: 794. Same art. Ecl. M. 123: 843.
— Essays. Spec. 69: 888.
— Naturalist. (B. G. Johns) Sund. M. 23: 334.
— Poetical Tribute to. (Mary Geoghegan) Temp. Bar, 94: 28.
— A Study of. (C. Fisher) Temp. Bar, 109: 502.
— Toilers of the Field. (E. Purcell) Acad. 42: 599.
Jefferson, Joseph. (M. Bacheller) Munsey, 12: 497.
— and his Art. (R. W. Gilder) Chr. Un. 47: 410.
— as a Painter. (G. MacDonough) Mo. Illust. 5: 267.
— at the Normal College. Critic, 27: 284.
— Winter's Life of. Dial (Ch.) 17: 256.
Jefferson, Thomas, and Callender, James Thomson. (W. C. Ford) N. E. Reg. 50: 445.
— and the French Revolution. Nation, 61: 61.
— and his Party To-day. (W. E. Russell) Forum, 21: 513.
— and Religion. (E. P. Powell) Open Court, 10: 4943.
— and the Social Compact Theory. (G. P. Fisher) Yale R. 2: 403.
— as an Architect. (J. K. Peebles) Am. Arch. 47: 29.
— as a Geographer. (A. W. Greely) Nat. Geog. M. 7: 269.
— in our Education. (E. P. Powell) New Eng. M. n. s. 14: 699.
— in Undress. (P. L. Ford) Scrib. M. 12: 509.
— Manuscripts of. (E. E. Hale) Bk. News, 14: 65.
— Notes on Virginia. (P. L. Ford) Nation, 58: 80, 98.
— Writings of. Ford's ed. (W. H. Smith) Dial (Ch.) 14: 110.
Jeffersonian Heresy, The Mayflower Compact and the. (H. B. Sprague) Our Day, 15: 145.
Jeffrey; an Editor's Letters. Liv. Age, 204: 252.
Jeffreys, George, Lord Chancellor. (F. Watt) New R. 15: 193.
Jeffries, Maud, with portrait. Theatre, 28: 49.
— in the Sign of the Cross. Theatre, 36: 129.
Jeffrys, Ellis, with portrait. Theatre, 37: 303.
Jehudah Halevi, Poems by, English Version of. (Mrs. H. Lucas) Jew. Q. 5: 652.
Jekyl Island, Georgia. (F. H. Head) New Eng. M. n. s. 8: 393.
Jekyll, Joseph, Correspondence of. (T. Hutchinson) Acad. 45: 221. — Sat. R. 77: 316. — Ath. '94, 1: 171. — Spec. 72: 240.
Jelly-fishes. (A. Wilson) Eng. Illust. 14: 493.
Jem, Prince, Thouasne's. Ath. '92, 2: 546.
Jem's Trouble; a story. (F. B. Spencer) Belgra. 84: 295.
Jena, Summer School at, 1893. (J. J. Findlay) Educa. R. 6: 364.
Jennings, Louis. Ath. '93, 1: 221.
Jenny Wren; a story. (A. M. Trotter) Argosy, 54: 64.
Jenolan Caves, Through the. (F. C. T. Mann) Westm. 143: 426. Same art. Ecl. M. 124: 789.
Jenoure, Aida, with portrait. Theatre, 29: 22.
— in The Mountebanks. Gent. M. n. s. 48: 206.
Jensen, Adolf. (A. von Ende) Music, 9: 257.
Jephtha's Daughter at Honolulu. (M. D. Conway) Open Court, 1: 86.
Jeremiah. (C. H. Cornill) Open Court, 9: 4527.
Jeremiah's Roll, The Burning of. (E. B. Pollard) Bib. World, 6: 15.
Jermyn's Portrait; a story. (C. Lanza) Lippinc. 49: 221.
Jeroboam and the Disruption. (C. F. Kent) Bib. World, 4: 38.
Jerome of Prague. (P. Felts) Luth. Q. 26: 380.
Jerome, Jerome K., with portrait. Bk. News, 9: 496.
— Childhood Recollections by. Idler, 1: 47.
— my First Book; "On the Stage and Off." Idler, 4: 440.
— Rise of Dick Halward. Sat. R. 80: 543.
Jerrold, Douglas. (E. Copping) New R. 7: 358.
Jerry; a Personality. (E. Cadazza) Atlan. 73: 498.
Jersey, Isle of. (E. Bradbury) M. of Art, 4: 513. — (M. Hasbrouck) Cosmopol. 13: 515.
— and Mulberry. (H. C. Bunner) Scrib. M. 13: 641.
— Ethnology of. (A. Dunlop) Anthrop. J. 22: 335.
Jersey City, Free Public Library of, Educational Work of. (E. E. Burdick) Lib. J. 21: 359.
— New City Hall. Archit. Rec. 5: 77.
Jersey Villas; a story. (H. James) Cosmopol. 13: 314, 433.
Jerusalem. (J. S. Riggs) Bib. World, 4: 177. — (C. R. Conder) Scot. R. 24: 337. — (R. M. Ryan) Cath. World, 62: 667. — Eng. R. 12: 171.
— and Bethlehem. (G. W. Wood) Sund. M. 21: 408.
— and thereabouts. (A. K. Parker) Bib. World, 7: 342.
— Archæological Explorations at. Am. Arch. 49: 123.
— The Church of the Resurrection, or of the Holy Sepulchre. (J. R. Macpherson) Eng. Hist. R. 7: 417, 669.
— Cotton Grotto in. (C. Adler) Jew. Q. 8: 384.
— in the 7th Century, An Armenian Visitor to. (E. W. Brooks) Eng. Hist. R. 11: 93.
— Literary Landmarks of. (L. Hutton) Harper, 90: 546.
— Modern Improvements in. Spec. 69: 347.
— Oliphant's. Sat. R. 73: 455. — Spec. 68: 89.
— Painter's Pilgrimage to. (H. Schmalz) Art J. 45: 96.
— The Poor of. (G. R. Lees) Sund. M. 24: 469.
— Recent Visit to. (C. A. Dana) McClure, 2: 86.
Jerusalem Chamber. (E. D. Morris) Presb. & Ref. R. 7: 595.
Jervis, John. *See* St. Vincent, Earl of.
Jessekiah Brown's Courtship; a story. (R. McE. Stuart) Harper, 84: 933.
Jessel, Sir George, with portrait. (J. Willard) Green Bag, 5: 1.
Jessie French's Experiment; a story. (E. R. Esler) Eng. Illust. 15: 43.
Jests, Asiatic, in Europe. (W. A. Clouston) Asia. R. 10: 372.
Jesuit and the Mexican Coin, The; a story. (F. Hume) Idler, 5: 378.
Jesuit Doctrine of Obedience. (J. A. Symonds) Fortn. 59: 745.
Jesuit Martyrs, Land of the. (T. O'Hagan) Cath. World, 63: 71.
Jesuit Relations. (J. M. Parker) New Eng. M. n. s. 10: 354.
Jesuitism, Modern. (C. C. Starbuck) New World, 3: 720.
Jesuits and Pope Ganganelli [Clement XIV.]. Eng. R. 8: 1.
— Educational System of. (T. Hughes) Cath. World, 56: 80.
— — Hughes on. Sat. R. 74: 174.

Jesuits, General Chapter of. (R. Beauclerk) National, 20: 351.
— in Canada. (S. C. Richards) Month, 84: 261.
— in China, Jenkins on. Sat. R. 79: 99.
— in the 18th Century. Eng. R. 9: 391.
— In the Tarumensian Woods. (R. B. C. Graham) 19th Cent. 36: 244.
— Mornings among the. Eng. R. 12: 30.
— New Chief of, 1892. Spec. 69: 487.
— Order of, Constitutions and Principles. Eng. R. 5: 15.
— Reusch's History of. (A. Plummer) Crit. R. 4: 241.
— Training of. (R. F. Clarke) 19th Cent. 40: 211. Same art. Liv. Age, 210: 546. Same art. Chr. Lit. 15: 369.
Jesus Christ, The Adoration of. (S. Coit) Eth. Rec. 1: 13.
— in Apostolic Age. (I. Zahn) Bib. Sac. 51: 314, 389.
— Alleged Sojourn in India. (M. Müller) Chr. Lit. 12: 4.
— Anæmic Birth of. (F. P. Badham) Acad. 49: 446.
— and the Apostles. (J. R. Buchanan) Arena, 16: 897.
— and Buddha as Literary Critics. (F. F. Kramer) Bib. World, 3: 252.
— and the Christians. (P. Carus) Open Court, 7: 3696.
— and the Creation. (J. C. Adams) And. R. 17: 225.
— and his Time, a Biography. (D. L. Sharp) Nat'l M. (Bost.) 5: 115, 211.
— and the Repentant Thief. (W. E. Barton) Bib. Sac. 53: 100.
— and Science. (W. W. Kinsley) Bib. Sac. 50: 93-656.
— as a Poet. (C. S. Nutter) Meth. R. 52: 774.
— as a Preacher. (W. C. Wilkinson) Bib. World 6: 476.
— as shown in Myths. (E. D. Daniels) N. Church R. 3: 204.
— Ascension of. (J. Brubaker) Luth. Q. 24: 155.
— — and Heavenly Priesthood of, Milligan's. Church Q. 34: 128.
— Authority of, as a Lawgiver. (G. F. Genung) And. R. 19: 155.
— Birth of. (F. C. Conybeare and others) Acad. 46: 400, 424.
— — and Infancy of. (A. Réville) New World, 1: 695.
— — and Childhood of. (A. C. Zenos) Bib. World, 6: 433.
— — Story of. (G. T. Purves) Bib. World, 8: 423.
— — The Virgin-birth, Expectation and Publication of. (W. F. Steele) Meth. R. 52: 9.
— Bloody Sweat of. (W. W. Keen) Bapt. Q. 14: 169.
— Burial of, Place of. (J. C. Jackson) Meth. R. 54: 177.
— Character of, a Basis of Confidence in the Gospel Record. (N. S. Burton) Bib. World, 8: 30.
— the Chief Corner Stone. (A. J. Heller) Ref. Q. 40: 110.
— Childhood of. (H. van Dyke) Harper, 87: 723. — (F. W. Farrar) McClure, 4: 75. — (W. G. Wilkinson) Bib. World, 8: 458.
— Coming Kingdom of. (A. F. Hewit) Am. Cath. Q. 19: 225.
— Consciousness of. (W. J. Tucker) And. R. 17: 186.
— Crucifixion of, Day of. (C. W. Heisler) Luth. Q. 25: 209.
— — in Celtic Art. (J. R. Allen) M. of Art, 14: 189.
— — Real Meaning of. (L. G. Holck) N. Church R. 3: 504.
— Death of, and Religious Fanaticism. (J. J. Young) Luth. Q. 25: 516.
— — New Testament Doctrine of. (W. H. Ward) Bib. Sac. 51: 246.
Jesus Christ, the Demagogue. (W. Walsh) Contemp. 69: 427.
— Departure of, Expediency of. (G. Matheson) Thinker, 8: 21.
— Descent into Hell. (M. G. Boyer) Luth. Q. 24: 223.
— Divine-human Person of. (T. G. Apple) Ref. Q. 39: 277.
— Divinity of. And. R. 17: 510 — 18: 633. — (S. H. Giesy) Ref. Q. 39: 522. — And R. 19: 78.
— — and the Divine in Men. (A. Bjorck) N. Church R. 1: 176.
— — Attacks on. And. R. 17: 402.
— Exterior of. (J. V. Tracy) Cath. World, 57: 538.
— Fairbairn's Place of, in Modern Theology. (J. S. Candlish) Crit. R. 3: 369.
— The Faith of. (T. C. Hall) Bib. World, 3: 247.
— Feet-washing by. (W. F. Gess) Thinker, 9: 312.
— Foreshadowings of, in the Old Testament. (W. R. Harper) Bib. World, 6: 401. — (G. S. Goodspeed) Bib. World, 8: 376, 485.
— Gracious Truth of. (W. H. Ryder) Ref. Q. 43: 32.
— The Greatest Reformer. (A. S. Weber) Ref. Q. 39: 389.
— Hall of, at Chautauqua. (J. H. Vincent) Bib. World, 6: 530.
— Harnack's Theories of Christology. (F. H. Foster) Bib. Sac. 49: 240.
— Headship and Sonship of. (S. H. Giesy) Ref. Q. 39: 364.
— Herrmann's Verkehr des, mit Gott. (J. Orr) Crit. R. 3: 401.
— Hindrances to the Acceptance of. (M. Dods) Chr. Lit. 14: 518.
— The Historic and the Ideal Christ. (C. C. Everett) New World, 1: 14.
— Historical, and Modern Christianity. (A. B. Bruce) Thinker, 8: 28.
— — and the Christs of Faith. (D. Connor) Contemp. 70: 365. Same art. Chr. Lit. 15: 488.
— Human Soul of. (A. F. Hewit) Cath. World, 57: 297.
— Humanity and Mediation of. (W. Rupp) Ref. Q. 40: 71.
— in Art. (R. Phees) Bib. World, 6: 490.
— in Creation. (A. H. Strong) M. Chr. Lit. 7: 166.
— in Gethsemane. (J. W. Schwartz) Luth. Q. 22: 267.
— in History. (A. M. Fairbairn) Bib. World, 6: 518.
— in Modern Art. (R. R. Wilson) Mo. Illust. 11: 469.
— in Modern Theology. (A. B. Bruce) Contemp. 63: 682. — Church Q. 37: 50. — (J. Rickaby) Month, 79: 167-535. 80: 222, 406. 81: 57.
— in Nazareth; the New-Church Interpretation. (J. K. Smyth) N. Church R. 1: 272.
— in Poetry. (F. W. Gunsaulus) Bib. World, 6: 504.
— in Theology. (W. H. Dunbar) Luth. Q. 25: 490.
— Incarnation of. (E. H. Gifford) Chr. Lit. 16: 25, 153. — (P. E. Pratt) Thinker, 9: 20.
— — Evolution and. (Prof. Bernard) Thinker, 9: 334.
— — Gore's. Sat. R. 80: 692.
— — not Incompatible with Evolution. N. Church R. 3: 161.
See Incarnation.
— Infancy of, Legendary. (F. W. Farrar) Sund. M. 25: 18.
— Infinite Humanity of. (T. F. Wright) N. Church R. 3: 589.
— Influence of, on Character: Short Sunday Readings. (W. B. Carpenter) Good Words, 34: 67-855.
— Josephus and. (S. L. Bowman) Meth. R. 55: 272.
— Language spoken by. (Agnes S. Lewis) Cent. 31: 307. — (J. E. Warren) N. Church R. 3: 398.
— Last Refuge and Journey of. (M. Harrison) Sund. M. 21: 463.

Jesus Christ, Life of, Helps to the Study of. (S. Mathews) Bib. World, 6: 524.
— — in Art. Church Q. 39: 396.
— — — Farrar's. M. of Art, 18: 191.
— — Lacunæ in. (W. H. Wynn) Luth. Q. 25: 25.
— — Prior to his Public Ministry. (F. Godet) Chr. Lit. 13: 92.
— — Renan's. (E. H. Hall) New World, 5: 493.
— — Sources of. (E. D. Burton) Bib. World, 6: 424.
— Light of Man. (P. J. Gloag) Thinker, 9: 520.
— the Light and Life of Men. (J. Clifford) Good Words, 33: 854.
— Likeness of, History of. (Bayliss) Eng. Illust. 10: 435.
— Love of. (A. W. Thorold) Sund. M. 21: 306-803.
— — in the Life to come. (A. W. Thorold) Good Words, 35: 281.
— Manliness of, Hughes'. Sat. R. 79: 291.
— Mind of the Master, Watson's. (S. T. Lowrie) Presb. & Ref. R. 7: 749.
— Ministry of. (W. A. Stevens) Bib. World, 6: 444.
— Miracles of, in relation to his Personality. (E. V. Gerhart) Ref. Q. 39: 147.
— Miraculous Conception and Virgin Birth of. (C. J. H. Ropes) And. R. 19: 695.
— The Modern Conception of. (J. K. Smyth) N. Church R. 3: 50.
— Modern Jewish View of. (J. Voorsanger) Overland, n. s. 23: 29.
— A Modern View of. (J. B. Crozier) Fortn. 66: 373.
— Nativity of, Drama of. (A. Bierbower) Luth. Q. 22: 34.
— — Illustrated. (H. Mann) Mo. Illust. 11: 423.
— — in Art. (J. Cartwright) M. of Art, 6: 74.
— — in the National Gallery. (J. E. Hodgson) M. of Art, 13: 37.
— Natural and the Supernatural in. (A. M. Fairbairn) Bib. World, 6: 168.
— or Cæsar, as Guide. (B. O. Flower) Arena, 9: 522.
— Passion of, at the National Gallery. (J. E. Hodgson) M. of Art, 13: 212.
— Pauline Teaching of the Person of. (O. Cone) New World, 3: 274.
— Perfecting of. (C. H. Dickinson) And. R. 17: 339.
— Person of. (T. G. Apple) Ref. Q. 40: 179.
— Place of, in Modern Theology. (R. Watts) Presb. & Ref. R. 5: 532.
— — in Modern Thought. (C. A. Beckwith) And. R. 19: 385.
— Prayer of, in Gethsemane, Meaning of. (T. West) Chr. Lit. 14: 285.
— Prophesied in Isaiah, ch. liii. (W. W. Martin) Bib. Sac. 51: 143.
— Recent Books on. (J. Bascom) Dial (Ch.) 20: 17.
— Religion of, in its relations to Christianity and Reforms. (G. D. Coleman) Arena, 16: 721.
— Renan on. (J. D. McPherson) Arena, 12: 289. — (M. N. Oliver) Bib. Sac. 50: 309.
— Repose in Egypt, Place of the. (A. R. Dowling) Am. Cath. Q. 19: 93.
— Resurrection of. (A. Réville) New World, 3: 498. — (L. A. Gotwald) Luth. Q. 24: 546.
— — Credibility of. (W. N. Rice) Meth. R. 55: 177.
— Resurrection Body of, Nature of. (S. Hutchings) Bib. Sac. 52: 708.
— Righteousness of. (B. W. Bacon) Bib. World, 6: 334.
— Scenes from Life of. (R. H. Titherington) Munsey, 13: 18.
— Self-consciousness of. (T. H. Root) Bib. World, 2: 265, 353, 412.
Jesus Christ, Self-designation of, in the Synoptics. (O. Cone) New World, 2: 492.
— Social Ethics of. (J. S. Sewall) Bib. Sac. 52: 271.
— Son of the Carpenter. (L. Abbott) Cosmopol. 16: 515.
— Student's Life of, Gilbert's. Meth. R. 56: 1001.
— Studies in Christology. (F. H. Foster) Bib. Sac. 52: 531. 53: 250, 444.
— Suffering of. Was it in his Divine Nature? (C. R. Lane) Ref. Q. 39: 173.
— the Supreme God, proved by Scripture. N. Church R. 3: 561.
— Teaching of. (G. B. Stevens) Bib. World, 5: 7-431. — (A. B. Bruce) Bib. World, 6: 455. — (M. Dods) Bib. World, 6: 467.
— — as related to that of the Apostles. And. R. 17: 70.
— — Wendt on. (J. Stalker) Chr. Lit. 15: 232, 293.— Crit. R. 1: 359.
— Temptation of. (J. Wedgwood) Sund. M. 23: 126, 194.
— Times of. (H. M. Scott) Bib. World, 6: 413.
— Tissot's Life of. (E. Coues) Cent. 29: 289.— (R. H. Sherard) M. of Art, 18: 1.
— Trial and Condemnation of, as a Legal Question. (E. W. Hatch) Green Bag, 5: 398, 449.
— Unknown Life of, Notovitch's. (E. E. Hale) No. Am. 158: 594.
— — The Chief Lama of Himis on. (J. A. Douglas and F. M. Müller) 19th Cent. 39: 667. Same art. Chr. Lit. 15: 55.
— Walk to Emmaus. (H. Allon) Good Words, 33: 570.
— The Word Incarnate. (T. F. Wright) N. Church R. 1: 535.
Jetty at Mouth of Columbia River; Longest in the World. (A. H. Sydenham) Overland, n. s. 22: 362.
Jew, The, and Modern Thought. (I. H. Isaacs) Westm. 140: 261.
— from a Gentile Standpoint. (K. M. Nesfield) Overland, n. s. 25: 410.
— Glorification of the. (A. S. Isaacs) No. Am. 158: 94.
— The Modern. Quar. 183: 29.
— What makes a? (A. S. Isaacs) Chaut. 18: 168.
Jew and the Jewel, The; a story. Temp. Bar, 104: 1.
Jewel, Bishop, Works of. Eng. R. 14: 334.
Jewel Bright in a Setting Rude, A; a tale. (E. Dowsley) Canad. M. 5: 429.
Jewel Caskets, Artistic Treatment of. (J. W. Tonks) J. Soc. Arts, 40: 338.
Jewel Mysteries. (M. Pemberton) Eng. Illust. 11: 207-1165.
Jewelry as an Art. (A. Mullins) M. of Art, 19: 236.
— as an Artistic Production. (C. R. Ashbee) Art J. 45: 247.
— Cinque-cento. (C. R. Ashbee) Art J. 46: 152.
— Hints for Buyers of. (A. Vallance) Art J. 45: 357.
— Kabyle. (M. A. Wallace-Dunlop) M. of Art, 6: 316.
— of Birmingham. (J. M. O'Fallon) Art J. 46: 112.
Jewels, Famous. All the Year, 75: 126.
Jewett, Benjamin, Diary of, 1758. Nat'l M. (N. Y. '91) 17: 60.
Jewett, Sarah Orne, with portrait. Bk. Buyer, 11: 329. — With portrait. Bk. News, 7: 361.
Jewish Dietary Laws, Dr. Wiener on. (C. G. Montefiore) Jew. Q. 8: 392. — (Frances A. Joseph) Jew. Q. 8: 643.
Jewish Doctors. Chamb. J. 69: 761.
Jewish Folk-life in America. (F. S. Krauss) J. Am. Folk-Lore, 7: 72.
Jewish Ideals. (J. Jacobs) Jew. Q. 2: 494.
Jewish Informers in Middle Ages. (D. Kaufmann) Jew. Q. 8: 217.

Jewish Law, Ancient, Chapters from. (D. W. Amram) Green Bag, **6**: 407.
— Growth of. (D. W. Amram) Green Bag, **8**: 253, 298.
Jewish Liturgies, Arabic. (H. Hirschfeld) Jew. Q. **6**: 119. **7**: 418.
Jewish New Year and its Liturgy. (M. Friedmann) Jew. Q. **1**: 62.
Jewish Philosophy, Optimism and Pessimism. (J. Owen) Jew. Q. **3**: 182.
Jewish Prayer-book in England before 1290. (D. Kaufmann) Jew. Q. **4**: 20.
Jewish Religion, Effect of Biblical Criticism upon. (C. G. Montefiore) Jew. Q. **4**: 293.
See also Judaism.
Jewish Religious Education. (Mrs. H. Lucas) Jew. Q. **2**: 270.
Jewish Sibylline Oracles. (S. A. Hirsch) Jew. Q. **2**: 406.
Jewish Tax-gatherers at Thebes in Age of Ptolemies. (A. H. Sayce) Jew. Q. **2**: 400.
Jews, The. (Ednah D. Silver) N. Church R. **3**: 414.
— among the Nations, Leroy-Beaulieu on. (R. Gottheil) R. of Rs. (N. Y.) **13**: 52.
— and the Egyptian Monuments. Meth. R. **56**: 976.
— and Eschatology. (A. W. Goodnow) Bapt. R. **14**: 443.
— and Emperor Julian. (M. Adler) Jew. Q. **5**: 591.
— and Puritans. (J. G. Dow) Jew. Q. **3**: 52.
— Anti-Semitism, Classical. (M. H. Morgan) Nation, **61**: 50.
— — in America. (A. H. Tuttle) Meth. R. **54**: 90.
— Are they a Nation To-day? (M. H. Harris) Jew. Q. **2**: 166.
— Babylonian Exile of. (J. Wellhausen) New World, **2**: 601. — (C. H. Cornill) Open Court, **9**: 4537.
— Beliefs, Rites, Customs of, with Respect to Death, Burial, and Mourning. (A. P. Bender) Jew. Q. **6**: 317, 664. **7**: 101, 259.
— Captivity, Return from. (C. H. Cornill) Open Court, **9**: 4587.
— Colony of, in London. (Mrs. Brewer) Sund. M. **21**: 16, 119.
— Early Religion of, Robertson on. (W. J. Davison) Crit. R. **2**: 153.
— Early Settlement of, in Southern Italy. (A. Neubauer) Jew. Q. **4**: 606.
— Emancipation from the. National, **27**: 576.
— Ethics of. (C. Zeublin) Int. J. Ethics, **2**: 462.
— Exile, Literary Achievements of. (C. H. Cornill) Open Court, **9**: 4573.
— Expulsion of, from England, 1229. (B. L. Abrahams) Jew. Q. **7**: 75-428.
— Health of, influenced by the Bible. (M. N. Adler) Asia. R. **13**: 136.
— Hebrew Monarchy, Economic Conditions of. (W. H. Bennett) Thinker, **8**: 126, 299. **9**: 16.
— History of, Earliest Ages of. (C. R. Conder) Scot. R. **22**: 274.
— — Edersheim's. Sat. R. **82**: 118.
— — Graetz's. Church Q. **35**: 68. — Spec. **71**: 309.
— — Renan's. Ath. '93, **2**: 377. — (E. G. Hirsch) Dial (Ch.) **20**: 105.
— — to 1000 B. C. (I. M. Price) Bib. World, **7**: 472.
— — to Establishment of the Kingdom. (E. T. Harper) Bib. World, **7**: 483.
— — Wellhausen's. Ed. R. **176**: 58.
— in China. (A. Neubauer) Jew. Q. **8**: 123.
— in England, Early History of. (H. Bradley) Acad. **44**: 8.
— — under Angevin Kings. (J. Jacobs) Jew. Q. **4**: 628. **5**: 51.
— in Europe, The. (E. L. Gookin) Nation, **56**: 24.
— in France. (S. Debré) Jew. Q. **3**: 367.
Jews in France. Private Life in France in the 14th Century. (A. M. F. Robinson) Fortn. **57**: 369.
— in Morocco. (J. E. B. Meakin) Jew. Q. **4**: 369.
— in New York. (R. Wheatley) Cent. **21**: 323, 512. — (J. A. Riis) R. of Rs. (N. Y.) **13**: 58. — Meth. R. **53**: 290.
— in Palestine. Chamb. J. **70**: 97.
— in Political, Business, and Social Life. (A. E. Bloom) Am. J. Pol. **2**: 525.
— in Russia, Persecution of. Asia. R. **11**: 63.
— — — Official Defence of. (J. Jacobs) Cent. **24**: 359.
— — the Russian and his Jew. (P. Bigelow) Harper, **88**: 603.
— — Truth about. (A. White) Contemp. **61**: 695. Same art. M. Chr. Lit. **6**: 227.
— in San Francisco. (G. A. Danziger; Mrs. D. M. Nesfield) Overland, n. s. **25**: 381.
— in Spain during the Middle Ages. (M. P. Villamil) Cath. World, **55**: 649.
— — Expulsion of, in the 15th Century. (M. P. Villamil) Cath. World, **55**: 851.
— — MS. Sources of History of. (J. Jacobs) Jew. Q. **6**: 597.
— — Truth about. (M. P. Villamil) Cath. World, **58**: 49.
— in the Works of Church Fathers. (S. Krauss) Jew. Q. **5**: 122. **6**: 82, 225.
— Israel. Quar. **176**: 106. Same art. Liv. Age, **197**: 451.
— Israel among the Nations. (W. E. H. Lecky) Forum, **16**: 442.
— — Leroy-Beaulieu's. (J. W. Chadwick) Nation, **63**: 53.
— Israel and the Gospel. (G. H. Shodde) Bib. Sac. **51**: 468.
— Israel in Egypt. (C. H. Toy) New World, **2**: 121.
— Jew-baiting on the Continent. (E. Reich) 19th Cent. **40**: 422.
— Leroy-Beaulieu on. (E. G. Johnson) Dial (Ch.) **20**: 64.
— Literary Productions of, before the Division of the Kingdom. (J. D. Davis; H. F. Mallory) Bib. World, **7**: 497, 510.
— Marriage and Kinship among Ancient. (A. B. Ellis) Pop. Sci. Mo. **42**: 325.
— Message of, Wedgwood's. (A. B. Bruce) Contemp. **66**: 77.
— Mission of the. Harper, **88**: 259.
— The Modern Jew and the New Judaism. (H. Cohen) Fortn. **65**: 457, 624.
— Mosach's Contes Juifs. (S. M. Samuel) M. of Art, **12**: 358.
— Movement against. (S. Whitman) Contemp. **63**: 699.
— Music of. (N. H. Imber) Music, **6**: 496.
— Non-Hebrew Languages used by. (A. Neubauer) Jew. Q. **4**: 9.
— Objections to Christianity. Meth. R. **54**: 280.
— Political Life of, Early. (C. F. Kent) Bib. World, **7**: 520.
— Pre-prophetic Religion of Israel. (C. H. Toy) New World, **5**: 123.
— Prejudices against. (A. Moses) Am. J. Pol. **4**: 71.
— Primitive, Polytheism among. (A. H. Sayce) Jew. Q. **2**: 25.
— Propaganda in the time of Christ. (B. Pick) Luth. Q. **23**: 149. **24**: 115.
— Prophets of, the, Reaction against. (C. H. Cornill) Open Court, **9**: 4503.
— Question of. (Josephus) Cent. **21**: 395. — (M. Jastrow, jr.) Int. J. Ethics, **6**: 457.

Jews. Rabbinic Theology. (S. Schechter) Jew. Q. 6: 405, 633. 7: 195. 8: 1, 363.
— Religion and History of. (F. Meinhold) New World, 4: 98.
— Rise of. (C. H. Cornill) Open Court, 3: 1619, 1633, 1643.
— Russian, as Desirable Immigrants. (I. M. Van Etten) Forum, 15: 172.
— — Immigration of, to the U. S. (A. Slutzski) Lend a H. 11: 293.
— Tunisian. (Mrs. Reichardt) Good Words, 34: 45.
— Wellhausen on One God, One Sanctuary. (W. L. Baxter) Thinker, 9: 419, 499.
— Why they are not Farmers. (M. Kaufman) So. M. 1: 363.
— Wit and Humor of. (H. Adler) 19th Cent. 33: 457. Same art. Ecl. M. 120: 530. Same art. Liv. Age, 197: 361.
Jezebel. (Julian Corbett) Univ. R. 4: 555.
Jezreelites, The: their Prophet and Prophetess. (J. H. Ryley) Time, 19: 163.
Jhering, Rudolf von, with portrait. (A. Rivier) Jurid. R. 5: 1. — (M. Smith) Pol. Sci. Q. 10: 664. 11: 278.
Jiltings, Certain Royal. (E. F. Corby) Argosy, 60: 116.
Jim, the Bond. (R. Metcalfe) Sund. M. 22: 328.
Jim Bowers's Hoss. (S. Reid) Lippinc. 58: 511.
Jim Curley, Bad Man; a story. (H. White) Munsey, 13: 488.
Jim Lancy's Waterloo; a story. (E. W. Peattie) Cosmopol. 17: 211.
Jimtown's Bride. (E. A. Robinson) Overland, n. s. 27: 375.
Jimty; a story. (M. S. Briscoe) Harper, 91: 439.
Jingoes and Silverites. (E. Atkinson) No. Am. 161: 554.
Jingoism in America. (W. T. Stead) Contemp. 68: 334. Same art. Ecl. M. 125: 588.
— War upon Domestic Industry. (E. Atkinson) Engin. M. 10: 801.
Joan, First Princess of Wales. (C. Leigh) Belgra. 88: 134.
Joan and Mrs. Carr; a novel. (Mrs. E. M. J. von Booth) Belgra. 89: 1, 113, 225. 90: 1–337. 91: 1, 113.
Joan of Arc. (T. O'Gorman) Cath. World, 55: 629, 803. 56: 193. — (E. M. Clerke) Dub. R. 115: 295. — Eng. R. 6: 227. — (C. W. Colby) Nation, 63: 51. — (A. Lang) Eng. Illust. 16: 315. — Quar. 180: 461. — (C. S. Hill) 19th Cent. 37: 848.
— and the New Womanhood. (I. M. O'Reilly) Am. Cath. Q. 19: 582.
— Ayrolles'. Sat. R. 77: 448. Same art. Liv. Age, 200: 699.
— Beatification of. (J. J. O'Shea) Cath. World, 59: 251. — Sat. R. 77: 117.
— The False Pucelle. (A. Lang) 19th Cent. 37: 859.
— Gower on. (A. French) Dial (Ch.) 15: 67. — Spec. 71: 118.
— Home of. (W. D. McCrackan) Cosmopol. 17: 161.
— in History. (J. G. Colclough) Month, 83: 252.
— Last Fight of. (A. Lang) Macmil. 70: 69. Same art. Liv. Age, 201: 801.
— Lowell on. (R. W. Moore) School R. 4: 471. — (B. S. Terry) Am. Hist. R. 2: 131.
— Miracle of the Maid of Orleans. R. of Rs. (N. Y.) 8: 303.
— National Hero of France. (B. de Monvel) Cent. 21: 119.
— Personal Recollections of. (S. L. Clemens) Harper, 90: 485, 680. 91: 227–879. 92: 135–655.
Joan of Arc, Recent Books on. (J. W. Thompson) Dial (Ch.) 20: 351.
Joanna I. of Naples, Baddeley's. Sat. R. 75: 129.
Joanna; a story. (K. T. Hinkson) Good Words, 35: 314.
Joanna's Bracelet. Cornh. 61: 211.
Job, Certain Lessons from. (R. F. Horton) Good Words, 35: 855.
Jocky's Ladder. (E. H. Bell) Sund. M. 24: 823.
Jocularities, Inane. Spec. 70: 75.
Jocularity, Plague of. (H. H. Boyesen) No. Am. 161: 528.
Jocund Feud; a story. (Maurice Thompson) Cosmopol. 20: 259.
Joel, the Prophet. (W. Boyd Carpenter) Good Words, 33: 475–604.
Joel Garside; a story. (Mrs. Woods) Temp. Bar, 97: 221. Same art. Liv. Age, 197: 99.
Joey Mason, a sketch. (C. M'Leod) Canad. M. 6: 272.
Jogues, Père. (T. B. Stephenson) Sund. M. 22: 322.
Johannes, Count. (I. Browne) Green Bag, 8: 435.
Johannesburg the Golden. Temp. Bar, 107: 227. Same art. Liv. Age, 208: 567. Same art. Ecl. M. 126: 612.
— Story of an Amateur Revolution. Liv. Age, 209: 303.
— To-day in. Chamb. J. 73: 4.
John the Baptist, Message of, to Jesus. (M. Dods) Chr. Lit. 12: 344.
John, St. (J. Stalker) Good Words, 36: 41–834.
— and Paul, House of, at Rome. (Padre Germanus) Am. J. Archæol. 7: 25.
— in Asia Minor. Church Q. 37: 446.
— Theology of, and of Paul. (G. B. Stevens) Bib. World, 3: 161.
— — Peculiarities of. (G. B. Stevens) New World, 2: 612.
John, King, and the Abbot of Bury. (T. Arnold) Contemp. 63: 843.
John Anderson, My Jo; a Love Story. Canad. M. 8: 116.
John Ballantyne, American. (H. Campbell) New Eng. M. n. s. 7: 568, 764. 8: 122–705. 9: 81–534.
John Bentley's Mistake; a story. (T. A. Freeland) Canad. M. 2: 144.
John Bull asks Advice. (Julius Vogel) Time, 1: 19.
John Gavin's Accident; a story. Cornh. 71: 296.
John Gray; a story. (J. L. Allen) Lippinc. 49: 643.
John Henderson, Artist; a Psychological Study from Life. (G. Kennan) Cent. 25: 57.
John Malala, Historian; his date. (E. W. Brooks) Eng. Hist. R. 7: 291.
John March, Southerner. (G. W. Cable) Scrib. M. 15: 53 — 16: 769.
John Mitchell's Indictment. (F. H. Loughead) Overland, n. s. 22: 16.
John Nelson's Luck; a story. (C. Leigh) Belgra. 80: 153.
John O'Conner Goes a'-fishing. (C. S. Davison) Bach. of Arts, 1: 16.
John Parmenter's Protégé. (W. B. Harte) New Eng. M. n. s. 5: 792.
John Peter Macnab, Commission Agent, and Practical Golfer. Blackw. 158: 391.
John Sanders, Laborer; a story. (F. H. Smith) Harper, 90: 344.
John Upcraft's Crime; a story. (J. St. E. Hake) Chamb. J. 70: 409–473.
John-a-combe, the Moving Wood; a Forgotten Estimate of Bacon. (C. C. Stopes) Poet-Lore, 7: 185.

Johnnie Rawson and Chunky Peters; a story. (W. McLennan) Harper, 84: 539.
Johnny Boy; a story. (Bret Harte) Idler, 5: 563.
Johns Hopkins Marine Laboratory, Jamaica, Notes from. (W. S. Windle) Pop. Sci. Mo. 44: 449.
Johnson, Andrew, Impeachment of. (E. G. Ross) Forum, 19: 595.—(E. G. Ross) Scrib. M. 11: 519.
Johnson, Digby, with portrait. Bank. M. (Lond.) 59: 363.
Johnson, E. Pauline. (H. Hale) Critic, 28: 7.
— Poems. (H. Charlesworth) Canad. M. 5: 478.
Johnson, Eastman. (S. G. W. Benjamin) M. of Art, 5: 485.—(E. King) Mo. Illust. 4: 265.
Johnson, Edward. (C. E. Banks) N. E. Reg. 47: 153.
Johnson, Lionel, as a Critic. (E. K. Chambers) Acad. 46: 297.
— Poems. Sat. R. 79: 553.—(E. D. A. Morshead) Acad. 47: 394.
Johnson, Samuel, at Oxford. (E. B. Parry) Leis. Hour, 45: 651, 713.
— in Lichfield. Critic, 27: 353.
— The Johnson Club. (G. B. Hill) Atlan. 77: 18.—Lit. W. (Bost.) 27: 8.—Critic, 26: 170.
— Letters, Hill's Edition. Ath. '92, 1: 657.—Church Q. 34: 295.—Gent. M. n. s. 48: 635.—Liv. Age, 195: 67.—Macmil. 66: 151.—(T. R. Lounsbury) Nation, 54: 415.—Quar. 175: 394.—Sat. R. 73: 606.—Spec. 69: 468.
— on Book-collecting. Bookworm, 7: 363.
— painted by Reynolds. Walford's Antiq. 4: 1.
— Rambles in Johnson-land. (P. Fitzgerald) Gent. M. n. s. 51: 145. Same art. Ecl. M. 121: 356.
— Round the Town with. (G. Whale) Gent. M. n. s. 50: 120.
— Tavern Resorts and Conversations. (C. A. Ward) Bookworm, 1: 225–383.
Johnson, Samuel Wm., with portrait. Pop. Sci. Mo. 43: 117.
Johnson, Thomas Loftin, with portrait. (H. Parker) Munsey, 11: 574.
Johnson, Wm. M., with portrait. Bk. Buyer, 13: 17.
Johnston, Charles. Chrysal. Macmil. 72: 122.
Johnston, Richard Malcolm, with portrait. Bk. News, 11: 35.
— School Experiences of. Lippinc. 54: 703.
Johnstone, Henry Campbell. (J. T. Walker) Geog. J. 7: 209.
Johnstone Family of N. J. (M. Newport) Am. Hist. Reg. 1: 44–145.
Johore. (H. Lake) Geog. J. 3: 281.
— In the Court of. (R. Wildman) Overland, n. s. 27: 137.
Johore Tea. Chamb. J. 70: 629.
Joinery, Hardwood. (H. W. Barnes) Am. Arch. 43: 6.
Joint Owners in Spain; a story. (A. Brown) Atlan. 75: 30.
Joint-stock Companies, Legal Position of Auditors of. (R. S. Brown) Jurid. R. 8: 254.
Joints, Formation of, among the Invertebrata. (B. Sharp) Am. Natural. 27: 89.
Jókai, Mór, Hungarian Novelist. Sat. R. 77: 37.
— Literary Recollections. Forum, 19: 667.
Jokes, Old, in New Form. All the Year, 73: 544.
Jollie, Thomas, Diary of, 1670–93. (G. Neilson) Ath. '92, 1: 244.
Jonah. (C. H. Cornill) Open Court, 9: 4616.
— and Christ. (P. H. Hunter) Good Words, 37: 210.
— in Nineveh. (H. C. Trumbull) J. Bib. Lit. 11: 53. Same art. Bib. Sac. 49: 669.
Jonas Biddlecome's Christmas Gift; a story. (T. Thompson) Nat'l M. (Bost.) 5: 240.
Jonathan; a story. (F. H. Smith) Cosmopol. 19: 654.
Jonathan Holt's "Third;" a story. (J. Gardner) Harper, 89: 953.
Jones, Edward Burne. (C. M. Fairbanks) Chaut. 15: 429.—(C. Phillips) M. of Art, 8: 286.—With portrait. R. of Rs. (N. Y.) 9: 689.—(C. Monkhouse) Scrib. M. 15: 135.—(L. T. Meade) Sund. M. 23: 392, 471.
— and his Art. (H. Brooke) Eng. Illust. 10: 230.
— and the Royal Academy. M. of Art, 16: xxi, xxiii.
— Art and Influence of. (M. R. L. Bryce) Blackw. 153: 861.
— Bell on. (J. Cartwright) Art J. 45: 82.—Ath. '93, 2: 392.—Sat. R. 75: 103.—M. of Art, 16: 102.
— Drawings of. (A. L. Baldry) M. of Art, 19: 343.
— Exhibition of the Work of. (E. R. Pennell) Nation, 56: 46.—Ath. '93, 1: 58, 127.—Spec. 70: 46.
— Merlin and Nimuë. Art J. 48: 221.
— Mosaics by, at Rome. M. of Art, 18: 256.
— Recent Paintings. Sat. R. 81: 544.
— Sidonia. (Mrs. J. M. Ady) Art J. 48: 353.
— Work of. (K. Cox) Nation, 55: 395.
— Works of. (J. Cartwright) Art J. 45: 1.—Sat. R. 75: 41.
Jones, Ernest, Chartist Laureate. Eng. R. 16: 55.
Jones, Henry Arthur. (R. Blathwayt) Idler, 4: 67.—With portrait. (J. A. Hamilton) Munsey, 11: 174.—(H. C. Newton) Theatre, 36: 150.
— and Modern English Drama. (W. A. L. Bettany) Theatre, 31: 203.
— Dancing Girl, Moral Purpose in. (J. D. Hunting) Theatre, 28: 121.
— Judah. Theatre, 28: 152.
— The Noble Vagabond, a drama. Theatre, 18: 44, 107.
— Rogue's Comedy. Sat. R. 81: 426.
— Saints and Sinners; a play. Theatre, 28: 151.
— Triumph of the Philistines. Sat. R. 79: 650.
Jones, Inigo, Latter Days of. Am. Arch. 50: 146.
Jones, James K. (W. J. Abbot) R. of Rs. (N. Y.) 14: 427.
Jones, Joseph. So. Hist. Pap. 23: 382.
Jones, Paul. (M. E. Seawell) Cent. 27: 873.
— and the Capture of the "Serapis." (J. C. Ridpath) Chaut. 14: 643.
— Letter of, 1777. N. E. Reg. 48: 461.
Jones, William, Deputy Governor, Saybrook Branch of the Family of. (E. A. Hill) N. E. Reg. 49: 310.
Jones, Winslow. (W. P. Courtney) Acad. 48: 146.
Jones Family, Records of. (N. J. Herrick) N. E. Reg. 47: 470.
Jones Sound, C. F. Hall and. Nat. Geog. M. 7: 308.
Joneses' Telephone, The: a story. (A. H. Fréchette) McClure, 1: 394.
Joniaux, Madame, Case of. Green Bag, 7: 239.
Jonson, Ben. (T. E. Brown) New R. 14: 514.
— and his Lyrics, with portrait. Acad. 50: 390, 432.
— Best Plays of. Spec. 71: 716.
— Dryden and. (J. A. Evans) Temp. Bar, 95: 101.
— in Edinburgh. (D. Masson) Blackw. 154: 790.
— Epicoene, Revival of, at Harvard College. (G. P. Baker) Harv. Grad. M. 3: 493.
— Shakespeare burlesqued by. (H. Wood) Am. J. Philol. 16: 273.
Joplin Zinc-mining District. (H. S. Wicks) Eng. M. 6: 699.

Jopling, Louise.. (W. Meynell) M. of Art, 3: 304.
Jordan, David Starr, with portrait. (M. B. Anderson) Pop. Sci. Mo. 44: 546.
Jordan, Dorothy. (J. F. Molloy) Eng. Illust. 9: 567.
Jordan, The Painter's. (G. Allen) Eng. Illust. 15: 371.
Jordan Valley and the Perea. (J. S. Riggs) Bib. World, 5: 36.
Jordan Art Gallery, Boston. (Mabel C. Pelletier) Bost. 1: 457.
Jorgensen, Jorgen, The Convict King. All the Year, 69: 486.
Josaphat and Barlaam Legend. (F. C. Conybeare) Folk-Lore, 7: 101.
José: a Tale of Old Socono. (W. R. Leighton) Cosmopol. 15: 624.
José and Téo; a story. (F. B. Millard) Overland, n. s. 21: 475.
Josef Helmuth's Goetz. (F. R. Burton) Lippinc. 54: 382.
Joseph, St., Eastern Devotion to. (W. H. Kent) Dub. R. 116: 245.
Joseph and Shakespeare. (L. R. Meekins) New Eng. M. n. s. 13: 571.
Joseph, the Dreamer; a story. (I. Zangwill) Cosmopol. 20: 63.
Josephine, Empress. (L. E. Tiddeman) Belgra. 89: 260.
— In the Land of. (W. L. Beasley) Outing, 23: 318, 373.
— 90th Anniversary of Crowning of. (E. Duff) Lippinc. 55: 104.
Josephinite, a New Nickel-iron. (W. H. Melville) Am. J. Sci. 143: 509.
Josephus, Flavius, and Jesus. (S. L. Bowman) Meth. R. 55: 272.
— and the New Testament. Church Q. 36: 92.
Joshee, Anandabia, Dr. Open Court, 1: 156.
Josiah's Alarm. (M. Holley) Lippinc. 51: 198.
Josselin; a Kitwyk Story. (A. E. King) Cent. 27: 101.
Jotchie; a story. (F. F. Robertson) Eng. Illust. 14: 41.
Jouett, James Edward. Un. Serv. (Phila.) 16: 523.
Joule, James Prescott. (Lord Kelvin) Cassier, 6: 405.
Journal of a Solitary. (A. Daudet) Canad. M. 2: 367.
Journalism. (C. A. Dana) McClure, 4: 555.
— as a Career. (J. W. Kellar) Forum, 15: 691.
— as a Profession. (M. de Blowitz) Contemp. 63: 37. — (F. Wilson) Westm. 146: 427. — (W. L. Stansfield) Westm. 146: 686. — (M. Y. Beach) Writer, 9: 80.
— Blowitz on. (E. L. Godkin) Nation, 56: 62.
— Borderland of Literature. Spec. 71: 513.
— Bucolic, of the West. (M. E. Stickney) Lippinc. 55: 516.
— Chapters in. (G. W. Smalley) Harper, 89: 426.
— College Training for. (C. F. Thwing) Educa. R. 6: 17.
— Complete Leader-writer. Macmil. 70: 359.
— Contemporary, Some Phases of. (J. A. Cockerill) Cosmopol. 13: 695.
— C. A. Dana on. (H. T. Peck) Bookman, 2: 191.
— Early, in San Francisco. (J. M. Scanland) Overland, n. s. 24: 260.
— Ethics of. (C. M. Huntington) Soc. Econ. 5: 163.
— Foreign Correspondent. (T. Stanton) Lippinc. 51: 746.
— French, before the 2d Empire. (Y. Blaze de Bury) Time, 19: 44.
Journalism, French, from 1852 to 1888. (Y. Blaze de Bury) Time, 19: 402.
— from the Interior. Scot. R. 28: 354.
— in New York. (F. A. Munsey) Munsey, 6: 379. — (R. Ogden) Nation, 57: 78.
— in the U. S. Time, 16: 22, 152.
— Institute of. Gent. M. n. s. 53: 40.
— Leaders of Public Thought. (Jas. M'Crea) Time, 3: 289.
— London Pen and Gown in the Sixties and Since. (T. H. S. Escott) Fortn. 63: 238.
— A Menace to Literature. (M. Deland) No. Am. 158: 157.
— Modern, Ethics of. (A. Gorren) Scrib. M. 19: 507.
— The New. (E. M. Phillips) New R. 13: 182.
— Power of the British Press. (H. W. Lucy) No. Am. 163: 168.
— Practical. Can it be taught in College? (A. F. Matthews) Chaut. 17: 48.
— that pays. (Le R. Armstrong) Lippinc. 58: 681.
— Varieties of. (M. Halstead) Cosmopol. 14: 202.
— Vicious. Open Court, 1: 129.
— Women in. (E. G. Jordan) Lippinc. 51: 340.
— Work of, in India. Sat. R. 76: 704.
Journalist in Fiction. Church Q. 36: 73.
— Musical. (G. B. Armstrong) Music, 4: 377.
Journalistic Remuneration. Chamb. J. 73: 753.
Journalists and Journalism. (Wm. Maxwell) Time, 20: 577.
— in France. (A. Hornblow) Cosmopol. 14: 153.
— Education of. (C. H. Dana) Our Day, 14: 188.
— Institute of. National, 20: 274.
— Pay and Rank of. (H. King) Forum, 18: 587.
Journey in a Chaise. (J. Boylston) New Eng. M. n. s. 12: 440.
Journeymen Smugglers; a story. (C. J. C. Hyne) Temp. Bar, 107: 581.
Jowett, Benjamin. (J. S. Cotton) Acad. 44: 293, (F. T. Palgrave) 321. — Ath. '93, 2: 491. — Dial (Ch.) 15: 213, 253. — (W. J. Ashley) Nation, 57: 266. — (F. W. Farrar) R. of Rs. (N. Y.) 8: 667. — Sat. R. 76: 401. — Spec. 71: 458. — Temp. Bar, 99: 473. — (F. W. Farrar) Chr. Lit. 10: 87. — (W. M. Hardinge) Temp. Bar, 103: 173. — Liv. Age, 200: 37. — Ecl. M. 122: 166. — Liv. Age, 203: 554. — Critic, 24: 82. — Church Q. 41: 440. — (I. A. Taylor) Longm. 26: 78. — Spec. 75: 603.
— and Manchester College. (L. Dyer) Nation, 57: 367.
— College Sermons. Sat. R. 80: 527.
— In Memoriam; a poem. (M. Sinclair) Ecl. M. 122: 128.
— Memories of. Cornh. 68: 586. Same art. Liv. Age, 199: 816.
— Recollections of. (A. C. Swinburne) 19th Cent. 34: 912.
— Some more Recollections of. Macmil. 73: 266. Same art. Liv. Age, 208: 686.
Joy, Charles A., with portrait. Pop. Sci. Mo. 43: 405.
Joy, Edmund L., with portrait. Nat'l M. (N. Y. '91) 19: 197.
Juarez, Benito, President of Mexico, Burke's. Sat. R. 77: 259.
Jub River, An Expedition up. (F. G. Dundas) Geog. J. 1: 209.
— Italian Explorations in. (E. G. Ravenstein) Geog. J. 3: 134.
Judæo-German Element in the German Language. (L. Wiener) Am. J. Philol. 15: 329.
— spoken by the Russian Jews. (L. Wiener) Am. J. Philol. 14: 41, 456.

Judaism and the Breslau School. (L. M. Simmons) Jew. Q. 4: 397.
— and Christianity. (J. M. Stifler) Bib. Sac. 53: 691.
— — Misconceptions of, by Each Other. (C. G. Montefiore) Jew. Q. 8: 193.
— — Spirit and Letter in. (M. Güdemann) Jew. Q. 4: 345.
— and Faith. (O. J. Simon) Jew. Q. 2: 53.
— and Unitarianism. (M. H. Harris) No. Am. 160: 632.
— Authority and Dogma in. (O. J. Simon) Jew. Q. 5: 231. — Reply. (M. Hyamson) Jew. Q. 5: 469.
— Dogmas of. (S. Schechter) Jew. Q. 1: 48, 115.
— English. (I. Zangwill) Jew. Q. 1: 376.
— Expansion of. (O. J. Thatcher) Bib. World, 1: 99.
— in Literature. Church Q. 37: 364.
— Mission of. (O. J. Simon) Fortn. 66: 577.
— Missionary. (O. J. Simon) Jew. Q. 5: 664. — Spec. 72: 10.
— Modern Teaching of. (G. W. Tooley) Chr. Lit. 10: 210.
— National Idea in. (Lady Magnus) Jew. Q. 1: 353.
— New Testament, Development of. (G. H. Schodde) Bib. Sac. 50: 193.
— Position of. (I. Zangwill) No. Am. 160: 425.
— Reformed. (O. J. Simon) Jew. Q. 6: 262.
— Significance of. (H. Graetz) Jew. Q. 1: 4. 2: 257.
— Tendencies of Thought in Modern. (D. Philipson) New World, 4: 601.
— Zangwill on. Sat. R. 79: 504
Jude the Obscure. (T. Hardy) *See* Hearts Insurgent.
Judea, Education in Ancient. (C. G. Herbermann) Am. Cath. Q. 18: 449.
Judge, Mark H., Testimonial to. (S. A. Barnett) Westm. 146: 19.
Judge Ashcraft's Experiment. (R. Y. Toombs) Southern M. 3: 646.
Judge's Daughter, The; a story. (J. W. Sherer) Gent. M. n. s. 52: 1.
Judge's Guinea; a tale. (C. P. Dwight) Canad. M. 6: 460.
Judges and Juries. (H. Hodges) Westm. 145: 441.
— Are they above the Law? (H. H. L. Bellot) Westm. 145: 388.
— of the English Bench, Some. Temp. Bar, 107: 269. Same art. Liv. Age, 208: 804.
— Superannuation of. Sat. R. 80: 496. 82: 360.
Judgment, Final. (E. B. Fairfield) Bib. Sac. 49: 62. 50: 487.
Judgment, Value of Good, in Business. (H. L. Biddle) Chaut. 22: 74.
Judgment Hill; a story. All the Year, 71: 275.
Judgments, Some Peculiar. (G. H. Westley) Green Bag, 8: 243.
Judicial Anthology, A; American Specimens. (H. A. Chaney) Green Bag, 5: 34.
— British Specimens. (H. A. Chaney) Green Bag, 4: 592.
Judicial Error. (M. M. Pope) Lippinc. 58: 1.
Judicial Ignorance of the Law. Soc. Econ. 8: 94.
Judicial Power. (W. M. Little) Nation, 57: 269, 287. — (H. H. L. Bellot) Westm. 145: 237.
— Coxe on. (C. C. Nott) Nation, 58: 350.
Judicial Procedure in England, Improvement of. Sat. R. 74: 187.
Judith, Book of; a Hebrew political romance. (J. A. Duncan) Bib. World, 3: 429.
Judith and Holofernes, Passages from. (T. B. Aldrich) Atlan. 78: 262.
Jug and the Bottle, The; a story. (H. B. M. Watson) New R. 13: 325.
Juggler, The. (C. E. Craddock) Atlan. 78: 597, 804.
Juggling. All the Year, 73: 534.
— Hindoo. (A. E. Rood) Nat'l M. (Bost.) 5: 161.
Julia; a story. (C. Macnaughton) Eng. Illust. 14: 151.
Julian, Emperor, and the Jews. (M. Adler) Jew. Q. 5: 591.
— Gardner's. Sat. R. 80: 414.
Julie's Dowry, and How it was won; a tale. Canad. M. 1: 595.
Julius Cæsar, Dodge's Life of. (S. Willard) Dial (Ch.) 16: 47.
July, 4th of. The Birthday of Liberty. (C. M. Depew) Munsey, 13: 350.
July; a poem. (A. C. Swinburne) M. of Art, 16: 301.
Jumper Adams; a story. Chamb. J. 70: 316.
Jumpers; New England Religious Sect. (E. C. Cord) New Eng. M. 12: 272.
Jumping. (M. W. Ford) Outing, 20: 235.
— The Standing Jump. (M. W. Ford) Outing, 19: 450.
Jumping Frog Story, Private History of the. (S. L. Clemens) No. Am. 158: 446.
Junction Jack; a story. (E. Moore) Argosy, 58: 82.
June. (F. Viggars) Longm. 22: 155.
June; a poem. (A. Lampman) Cosmopol. 15: 173.
June; a poem. (A. C. Swinburne) M. of Art. 16: 279.
June, 1993; a story. (J. Hawthorne) Cosmopol. 14: 450.
June of Long Ago. (C. L. Field) New Eng. M. n. s. 9: 225.
Jungle Circus, A; a story. (B. Vye) Idler, 5: 270.
Junior Promenade; a story. (W. Camp) Outing, 25: 396.
Juniper Tree. (N. J. Rose) Garden & F. 9: 114.
Junius; did he commit Suicide? (A. Lang) Blackw. 157: 406.
— on Priestcraft. (W. F. Rae) Ath. '95, 1: 476.
— Revealed, Francis's. (W. Everett) Nation, 59: 253. — Ath. '94, 1: 337, 371, 412.
— Who was? (W. F. Rae) Ath. '95, 1: 568. — (A. Hayden) Bookworm, 7: 161.
Juno of Argos. (C. Waldstein) Cent. 24: 218.
Jupiter, The Planet. (W. F. Denning) Nature, 51: 227. 53: 33. — (G. W. Hough) Pop. Astron. 2: 145.
— and his Period of Rotation. Nature, 53: 558.
— and its Satellites. (W. H. Pickering) Astron. 12: 193. — Dub. R. 110: 172.
— and its System. (J. E. Gore) Gent. M. n. s. 52: 337.
— at Opposition. (E. A. Bowen) Pop. Astron. 1: 133.
— Comet Family of. (W. W. Payne) Pop. Astron. 1: 25, 62.
— Observations of, at Goodell Observatory, 1891-92. (H. C. Wilson) Astron. 11: 189.
— Opposition of 1895-96. (G. W. Hough) Pop. Astron. 3: 519.
— Orbit of. (H. A. Newton) Am. J. Sci. 149: 420.
— Physical Constitution of. (G. W. Hough) Astron. 13: 89.
— Red Spot on. (W. F. Denning) Nature, 49: 104. — (E. W. Maunder) Knowl. 19: 4. — Dub. R. 118: 421.
— — and its Changes. (E. E. Barnard) Astron. 11: 686.
— — and other Markings on. (E. E. Barnard) Astron. 13: 736. — (E. E. Barnard) Pop. Astron. 2: 129.
— Satellite of, Fifth. (E. E. Barnard) Pop. Astron. 1: 76. — (R. S. Ball) Liv. Age, 196: 259.
— Satellites of. (W. H. Pickering) Astron. 12: 390.

Jupiter, Satellites of, Discs of. (W. J. S. Lockyer) Nature, **50**: 320.
— — Forms of. (E. E. Barnard) Astron. **13**: 272, (W. H. Pickering) 423, 438.
— — New. (R. S. Ball) Fortn. **58**: 733. — Sat. R. **74**: 356. Same art. Ecl. M. **119**: 664.
— — Outer, Rotation of. (W. H. Pickering) Astron. **12**: 481.
— — Pseudo-, in 17th Century. (C. W. L. Johnson) Nature, **51**: 285.
— — Recent Observations of. (W. H. Pickering) Pop. Astron. **2**: 121. — (W. H. Pickering) Astron. **13**: 728.
— Spots and Markings of. (G. W. Hough) Astron. **11**: 193.
Jura-Trias Trap of New Haven Region, Additional Observations on. (J. D. Dana) Am. J. Sci. **144**: 165.
Jurassic Formation on the Atlantic Coast. (O. C. Marsh) Am. J. Sci. **152**: 433.
Juries. Are they to judge the Law, in any Case. (P. Edwards) Green Bag, **6**: 466.
Jurisdiction, Criteria of. (A. V. Dicey) Law Q. **8**: 21.
— Summary. (W. J. Stewart) Law Q. **9**: 129.
Jurisprudence, Abstract, Difficulties of. (W. W. Buckland) Law Q. **6**: 436.
— American and Grecian compared. (S. M. Davis) Chaut. **17**: 33.
— — Progress in. (D. D. Field) Am. Law R. **27**: 641.
— Analytic, Historical, and Philosophical Schools of. (A. J. G. Mackay) Jurid. R. **7**: 209.
— and Legal Education. (E. C. Clark) Law Q. **1**: 201.
— Conception of Morality in. (T. W. Taylor) Philos. R. **5**: 36.
— English, New Departure in. (G. H. Smith) Am. Law R. **28**: 867.
— English and French Systems of. (L. E. Chittenden) Green Bag, **7**: 56.
— Ethnological. (A. H. Post) Monist, **2**: 30.
— Historical and Philosophical Methods in. (A. Thomson) Jurid. R. **7**: 66.
— in American Universities. (E. W. Huffcut) Ann. Am. Acad. Pol. Sci. **2**: 488.
— Pollock's First Book of. (A. V. Dicey) Nation, **63**: 234.
See also Law.
Jury, Trial by, Decay of. Spec. **72**: 8.
— in Bengal. (C. D. Field) Asia. R. **15**: 309.
— — Abolition of. Spec. **70**: 9.
— in Civil Cases. (M. D. Chalmers) Law Q. **7**: 15.
— in India. Sat. R. **75**: 3.
— Indian Official Opinions. (J. Jardine) Asia. R. **15**: 293.
— Layman's View of. Green Bag, **6**: 239.
— Medical Study of. (T. D. Crothers) Pop. Sci. Mo. **47**: 375.
— Origin and Growth of. (J. E. R. Stephens) Westm. **144**: 70. Same art. Ecl. M. **125**: 323.
— the Palladium of Liberty. (V. Yarros) Arena, **12**: 209.
— Reform in. (H. F. Cutter) Am. M. Civics, **6**: 621.
— System of. (A. C. Applegarth) Green Bag, **4**: 110.
— The Wrongs of the Juryman. (H. M. Shepard) Atlan. **76**: 258.
Jury System, Threatened Annihilation of. (W. K. Townsend) Forum, **22**: 107.
Jusqu'au Revoir. (C. W. Wood) Argosy, **56**: 478.
Just a Freak; a story. Cornh. **73**: 610. Same art. Liv. Age, **210**: 138.
Just a Sub. (M. Crichton) Belgra. **87**: 47.
Just in Time; a story. (W. R. Walkes) Theatre, **31**: 151.
Justice. All the Year, **73**: 582. — (W. M. Salter) Open Court, **6**: 3381. — (P. Carus) Open Court, **7**: 3535.
— Administration of. (G. W. Wakefield) Am. J. Pol. **3**: 422.
— and Charity. (S. King) Lend a H. **15**: 274.
— and Labor. (V. Yarros) Open Court, **7**: 3647.
— Art of. (A. Clerk) New R. **12**: 527. Same art. Ecl. M. **125**: 17. Same art. Liv. Age, **205**: 643.
— Distributive, Criterion of. (F. C. Sharp) Am. J. Sociol. **2**: 264.
— Eternal. (R. Barr) Good Words, **34**: 542.
— Free Administration of. (V. Yarros) Am. J. Pol. **4**: 138.
— Ideas of, in Plato's Republic. (P. Shorey) Eth. Rec. **2**: 185.
— Herbert Spencer on. Church Q. **34**: 313. — (J. G. Schurman) Philos. R. **1**: 79. — (H. Sedgwick) Mind, **17**: 107. — Soc. Econ. **2**: 105.
— Theory of. (T. Whittaker) Mind, **20**: 99.
— *versus* Egoism and Altruism. (W. M. Salter) Open Court, **6**: 3409.
— What is? (H. Rashdall) Econ. R. **1**: 466. **2**: 161.
Jute in Transit. Chamb. J. **69**: 5.
Jutes, Traces of, in Hampshire and Isle of Wight. (T. W. Shore) Antiq. n. s. **29**: 100.
Juvenile Crime and Industrial Schools. (A. A. W. Drew) Contemp. **63**: 732.
Juvenile Delinquents. Eng. R. **17**: 241. — (M. McG. Dana) Lend a H. **15**: 87.
Juvenile Offenders, and the Conditions which produce them. (W. D. Morrison) Int. J. Ethics, **5**: 162.
— Treatment of; Symposium. Indep. Mar. 3, '92.
Juvenile Literature, Modern. Are the Characters Real? (E. G. Alcom) Writer, **6**: 153.

Kaala, the Flower of Lanai. (E. E. Carey) Overland, n. s. **24**: 117.
Kaa's Hunting; a story. (R. Kipling) McClure, **3**: 45.
Kabul, British Mission to, Journey of. Dub. R. **114**: 181.
— 1879–80. (G. T. Pretyman) Un. Serv. M. **13**: 347–628.
— Slavery in. (Jamshâd) Asia. R. **21**: 153.
Kabyle Language, Notes on. (R. S. Charnock) Asia. R. **13**: 346.
Kabylia, In the Mountains of. (W. H. Carpenter) Nation, **58**: 467.
Kaddour; a story. (W. E. Norris) Eng. Illust. **11**: 235.
Kaemmerer, Frederic Henri. (J. Bernac) Art J. **46**: 161.
Kaffir, Humor of the. (W. Mackay) Time, **22**: 400.
Kaffir Finance. (W. R. Lawson) National, **27**: 412.
Kaffirs, The, in British South Africa. Chamb. J. **72**: 574.
— of the Hindu Kush, Origin of. (T. H. Holdich) Geog. J. **7**: 42.
Kaffiristan. Asia. R. **22**: 278. — (G. S. Robertson) Geog. J. **4**: 193.
— and the Kaffirs, England's Relation to. (N. Chamberlain) Sat. R. **81**: 494.
— and the Khalîfa Question. (G. W. Leitner) Asia. R. **21**: 284.
— Explorations in. Dub. R. **115**: 458.
Kaiana and the Shark-God. (Mabel H. Closson) Overland, n. s. **23**: 90.
Kaikai; a story. Cornh. **72**: 624. Same art. Ecl. M. **126**: 113.
Kaiserswerth and its Deaconesses. (W. H. Withrow) Chaut. **18**: 219.
— and its Founder. (E. Kinnicutt) Cent. **29**: 84.

Kakemono, The, and its Usage. Mo. Illust. **4**: 65.
Kalahari, Notes on a Portion of. (E. Wilkinson) Geog. J. **1**: 324.
Kalakaua, Queen, Trip around the World. (W. N. Armstrong) Overland, n. s. **25**: 644.
Kaler, James Otis, with portrait. Bk. News, **13**: 377.
Kalevala, The. (A. C. Stephens) Music, **2**: 133.—Sat. R. **74**: 482.
— A Story from the. (N. F. Milburn) Chaut. **17**: 91.
Kalligas, Paul. (S. P. Lambros) Ath. '96, **2**: 484.
Kalmias, Collecting. (J. G. Jack) Garden & F. **7**: 314.
Kalnoky, Count, and Caprivi. Spec. **70**: 765.
Kamehameha the Great. (Joaquin Miller) Overland, n. s. **25**: 629.
Kameké, Von. (M. Rose) Un. Serv. M. **8**: 256.
Kamelot. *See* Camelot.
Kames, Henry Home, Lord. Scottish School of Rhetoric. (A. M. Williams) Educa. **13**: 281–488.
Kamilaroi Tribe, Bora or Initiation Ceremonies of. (R. H. Mathews) Anthrop. J. **25**: 318.
Kanahee; a story. (T. W. Hall) Munsey, **12**: 19.
Kanaka, The, in Queensland. (A. Forbes) New R. **6**: 641.
Kanaka Traffic in the Pacific, Paton on. Our Day, **13**: 65.
Kandahar in 1880. (S. P. Oliver) Un. Serv. M. **7**: 898.
Kandyans, Ceremonies observed by, in Paddy Cultivation. (T. B. P. Kehelpannala) Anthrop. J. **25**: 104.
Kangaroo, The Conversational. (P. Robinson) Eng. Illust. **12**: no. 2, 45.
— Hunting the. (E. Wakefield) Outing, **22**: 168.—(R. M. Dene) Outing, **26**: 97.
— in America. (R. C. Auld) Overland, n. s. **20**: 164.
Kanjut Valley and its Inhabitants. Dub. R. **116**: 406.
— Campaign in, 1891. Ed. R. **178**: 199.
Kano, Commercial Importance of. Dub. R. **119**: 163.
Kansas, 1541–1891. (J. J. Ingalls) Harper, **86**: 696.
— Is New York more civilized than? (J. W. Gleed) Forum, **17**: 217.
— Railroad Commission of. (A. R. Greene) Cosmopol. **12**: 337.
— Situation in. (E. P. Clark) Nation, **56**: 43.
— State Horticultural Society, 26th Annual Meeting. Garden & F. **5**: 622.
— Struggle for Freedom in. (T. Ewing) Cosmopol. **17**: 76.
— — Robinson's. (J. W. Chadwick) Nation, **54**: 490.
— Supreme Court of. (H. Inman) Green Bag, **4**: 321.
Kansas Coal Measures, Stratigraphy of. (C. R. Keyes) Am. J. Sci. **150**: 239.
Kansas River. (A. P. Davis) Nat. Geog. M. **7**: 181.
Kant, I., Antimony of, Third. (W. T. Harris) Philos. R. **3**: 1.
— Bibliography of: German. (E. Adickes) Philos. R. vols. 2–4.
— Critical Problem of. (J. G. Schurman) Philos. R. **2**: 129.
— Doctrine of the Schemata. (H. H. Williams) Monist, **4**: 375.
— Epistemology in. (A. Seth) Philos. R. **2**: 167.
— Epistemology of Neo-Kantianism. (A. Seth) Philos. R. **2**: 293.
— Ethics of, Spencer on. (P. Carus) Monist, **2**: 512, app. 1.
— Relation to Utilitarianism. (N. Wilde) Philos. R. **3**: 289.
Kant, I., Herbert Spencer on. (P. Carus) Open Court, **4**: 2492.
— Theory of Religion, Some Aspects of. (J. Orr) Chr. Lit. **13**: 318.
Kantian Theism. (C. W. Hodge) Presb. & Ref. R. **5**: 478.
Karagheuz and the Stage in Turkey. (R. Davey) Theatre, **37**: 257.
Karen; a Novelette. (A. Kielland) Poet-Lore, **4**: 385.
Karens of Burmah. Dub. R. **114**: 183.
Karen Sites and Inscriptions. (W. R. Paton; J. L. Myres) J. Hel. Stud. **16**: 188.
Karin. Gent. M. n. s. **48**: 629.
Karl; a story. (B. Kennedy) Idler, **8**: 383.
Karl Ludwig, Archduke of Austria. (Edith Sellers) Temp. Bar, **106**: 23. Same art. Liv. Age, **207**: 23.
Karma à la Mode; a story. (Mrs. A. G. Rose) Cosmopol. **17**: 229.
— and Nirvâna. (P. Carus) Monist, **4**: 417.
Karroo, My Pupils in. Macmil. **67**: 444. Same art. Liv. Age, **197**: 633.
Karroo Love Story, A. (L. Butt) Belgra. **90**: 296.
Kashmir. (W. R. Lawrence) Asia. R. **21**: 127.—(L. Griffin) 19th Cent. **38**: 931. Same art. Liv. Age, **208**: 67.—(W. M. Conway) Nation, **57**: 227.
— Bear-shooting in. (G. L. Morley) Un. Serv. M. **9**: 419.
— Camp Life in. Cornh. **68**: 413. Same art. Ecl. M. **121**: 635.
— Knight on. Dial (Ch.) **15**: 9.
— People and Products of. (W. R. Lawrence) J. Soc. Arts, **44**: 491.
— Travels in. Dub. R. **116**: 406.
— Vale of, Agriculture in. Dub. R. **113**: 673.
Kashmir Politics. Sat. R. **73**: 121.
Kashmir Railway. Asia. R. **11**: 275.
Kashmir Valley, Lawrence's. (L. Griffin) Sat. R. **80**: 539.
Kaslo, British Columbia. Chamb. J. **72**: 602.
Katangaland, Stairs Expedition to. (J. A. Moloney) Geog. J. **2**: 238.
Katchins, In Camp with the. (H. E. Colville) Scrib. M. **14**: 531.
Kate Carnegie; a story. (J. Watson) Bookman, **2**: 387–489. **3**: 138–500. Same art. Canad. M. **6**: 509.
Kate Negley's Leadings. (L. S. Furman) Cent. **27**: 548.
Kathleen: Maid of all Work. (G. H. Page) Good Words, **35**: 779.
Katie. Chamb. J. **72**: 333.
Katie; a story. (K. T. Hinkson) Good Words, **35**: 676.
Kattie's Wedding. All the Year, **75**: 14.
Katzenjammer. (W. D. Gunning) Open Court, **1**: 4.
Kauffmann, Angelica. (A. Ritchie) Macmil. **68**: 353.—Spec. **69**: 562.
— and her Engravers. (E. B. Nash) M. of Art, **10**: 259.
— Gerard's. Sat. R. **74**: 421.
— Love Affairs of. (J. Oldcastle) M. of Art, **5**: 32.
— Note on. Art J. **45**: 26.
Kauffman, Hugo, Street Sketches of. M. of Art, **2**: 240.
Kaulbach, Wilhelm and Fritz August von. (Margaret Field) Munsey, **9**: 367.
Kauri Gum. Chamb. J. **73**: 223.
Kaweah, Colony of. Spec. **68**: 194.
— a Modern Utopia. All the Year, **70**: 462.
Kay, John, and his Portraits. (J. M. Gray) M. of Art, **13**: 312.

Kea, the Sheep-eating Parrot of New Zealand, Habits of. (W. Garstang) Nature, **52**: 629. Same art. Liv. Age, **207**: 575. — (J. Buckland) Eng. Illust. **14**: 203.
Kearny, Philip; a Personal Tribute. (Philippe, Comte de Paris) Cent. **25**: 747.
Keary, C. F. A Wanderer. (Mrs. W. K. Clifford) Bookman, **2**: 189.
Keasbey, Anthony Q., with portrait. Nat'l M. (N. Y. '91) **18**: 299.
Keats, John. (E. A. Price) Belgra. **87**: 404. — (J. G. Speed) McClure, **5**: 458. — (K. West) Chaut. **22**: 691. — With portrait. Acad. **50**: 429. — (P. B. Goetz) Harv. Mo. **15**: 60. — (T. C. Carrington) Mid-Cont. **6**: 174. — (Kenyon West) Outl. **52**: 683.
— American Monument to. Critic, **24**: 388.
— and Severn. (W. Graham) New R. **10**: 593. — Spec. **68**: 496.
— — Graves of. (J. L. Hurst) Critic, **27**: 269.
— Centenary of. Am. Arch. **51**: 19. — (M. Schuyler) Forum, **20**: 356.
— Character and Works of. (J. B. Kenyon) Meth. R. **56**: 353.
— Gifford and. (D. Masson) 19th Cent. **31**: 586. Same art. Liv. Age, **193**: 719.
— in Hampstead. (K. West) Cent. **28**: 898.
— Influence of. (H. van Dyke) Cent. **28**: 910.
— Lamia, and Coleridge's Christobel. Poet-Lore, **6**: 32.
— Manuscript of. (T. W. Higginson) Forum, **21**: 420.
— Memorial Monument to. Sat. R. **78**: 66.
— — Address of Edmund Gosse. Critic, **25**: 78.
— Memorial to. Critic, **21**: 364.
— MS. (F. G. Kitton) Ath. '94, **2**: 894.
— Poem in Memory of. (R. Thirlmere) Westm. **142**: 621.
— Poetical Works, Palgrave's ed. Spec. **68**: 779.
— Reading in the Letters of. (L. H. Vincent) Atlan. **74**: 399.
— Some Unedited Letters of. (A. F. Sieveking) Fortn. **60**: 728.
— Stray Thoughts about. (E. J. H.) Critic, **27**: 259.
Keble, John. (G. A. Simcox) Acad. **43**: 234. — Church R. **36**: 416. — Spec. **70**: 358.
— Christian Year. Church Q. **42**: 417.
— Poetry of. (A. C. Benson) Contemp. **67**: 825. Same art. Liv. Age, **206**: 97.
Keeley Cure for Inebriety. (W. G. Haskell) Arena, **16**: 222.
Keeley League and its Purpose. (J. J. Flinn) Am. J. Pol. **1**: 654.
Keeleys, The. (W. D. Adams) Theatre, **35**: 328.
Keely, John E. W., and his Discoveries. (W. Lascelles-Scott) New Sci. R. **1**: 200.
— Air-ship, Propeller of. (Mrs. Bloomfield Moore) New Sci. R. **1**: 33.
— Physical Discoveries of. (C. J. Moore) Lippinc. **50**: 797.
— The Veil withdrawn. (Mrs. Bloomfield Moore) New Sci. R. **1**: 465.
Keely Motor and the Dogmatism of Science. (Mrs. Bloomfield Moore) New Sci. R. **2**: 75.
— Some Truths about. (Mrs. B. Moore) New Sci. R. **2**: 321.
Keen, Herbert, and James Leader. The Broken Melody. Theatre, **29**: 123.
Keene, Robinson & Co., London. Belgra. **83**: 66.
Keene, Charles. All the Year, **71**: 176, 204. — (G. S. Layard) Scrib. M. **11**: 499. — (M. H. Spielmann) M. of Art, **14**: 145.
Keene, Charles, Layard's Life of. (M. H. Spielmann) M. of Art, **15**: 331. — Spec. **69**: 21. — Sat. R. **73**: 686.
Kehoeite, a New Phosphate. (W. P. Headden) Am. J. Sci. **146**: 22.
Keij, Willem. *See* Key.
Keiller Collection of Paintings. (R. A. M. Stevenson) Art J. **46**: 54.
Kekulé, August. Nature, **54**: 297.
Kelám-i-pîr and Esoteric Muhammadanism. (G. W. Leitner) Asia. R. **16**: 159.
Keller, Helen. (J. T. McFarland) Chaut. **23**: 672. — (E. V. Sutton) Educa. **14**: 341. — Lend a H. **10**: 357.
— at Radcliffe College. Critic, **29**: 303.
— Psychological Notes on. (J. Gastrow) Psychol. R. **1**: 356.
Keller Institute, Copenhagen. (F. Starr) Char. R. **3**: 79.
Kellogg Families of Colchester, Conn. (J. H. Perrin) N. E. Reg. **48**: 59.
Kelly, Edgar Stillman. (R. Hughes) Music, **10**: 279.
— Puritania Music. Music, **3**: 323.
Kelly, Frances Maria. (A. H. Wall) Time, **8**: 201.
Kelly, James E. (A. Leach) Munsey, **14**: 446. — (A. Trumble) Cath. World, **58**: 65.
Kelmscott Press, The. (E. R. Pennell) Nation, **56**: 196.
— End of. Acad. **50**: 530, 572.
— Publications of, Bibliography of. Bk. Buyer, **12**: 550.
Kelp-making in Shetland. Chamb. J. **73**: 749.
Kelpers, Among the. (D. J. Robertson) Longm. **27**: 33.
Kelpius, John, Pietist. (F. H. Williams) New World, **3**: 218.
Kelvin, Lord. Leis. Hour, **43**: 56. — With portraits. (J. Munro) R. of Rs. (N. Y.) **8**: 53. — (A. Gray) Nature, **54**: 151.
— Jubilee of. (S. P. Thompson) Sat. R. **81**: 617. — (D. Macleod) Good Words, **37**: 378.
Kelvingrove Art Galleries and Museum, Glasgow. (O. Fleming) M. of Art, **16**: 92.
Kemble, E. W., with portrait. Bk. Buyer, **11**: 293.
Kemble, Frances Anne. (H. Lee) Atlan. **71**: 662. — (E. MacMahon) Belgra. **80**: 373. Same art. Liv. Age, **197**: 692. — (Mrs. Ritchie) Macmil. **68**: 190. — Sat. R. **75**: 67. — (H. James) Temp. Bar, **97**: 503. — Temp. Bar, **102**: 326. — (J. Coleman) Theatre, **30**: 139.
— at Lenox. (C. B. Todd) Lippinc. **52**: 66.
— Death of. Critic, **22**: 37.
— Fitzgerald's Letters to. *See* Fitzgerald, Edw.
— in America. (A. J. Upson) Critic, **22**: 152.
— a Poem. Temp. Bar, **97**: 572.
Kemeys, Edward. (H. Garland) McClure, **5**: 120.
Kemp, David Robert, with portrait. Bank. M. (Lond.) **57**: 573.
Kemp, George Mickle. (J. M. Gray) Acad. **42**: 116.
Kemp, Will, and his Dance from London to Norwich. Walford's Antiq. **10**: 243.
Kempis, Thomas à, Birthplace of. (L. A. Wheatley) Bookworm, **1**: 53.
Kendal, Henry. (O. Smeaton) Westm. **144**: 495.
Kendal, Mrs., and the American Public. (R. H. Davis) Theatre, **32**: 91.
Kendal, Eng., Singing Contest at, 1893. Sat. R. **75**: 428.
Kennebec River, Lower. (W. Thompson) New Eng. M. n. s. **11**: 675.
Kennedy, H. H. The New Wing; farcical comedy. Theatre, **28**: 106.
Kennedy, J. P. Horseshoe Robinson, Summary of. (E. Spencer) M. Am. Hist. **28**: 131-465. **29**: 42.
Kennedy, John S., with portrait. (A. F. Schauffler) Char. R. **1**: 228.

Kenneth; a Golfing story. Cornh. 72: 266.
Kennion, G. Wyndham, Bp., with portrait. Chr. Lit. 11: 288.
Kennst du? poem. (E. C. Stedman) Cent. 29: 656.
Kenrick, F. P., Archbp., and P. R. (J. Gibbons) Am. Cath. Q. 17: 382.
Kenrick, Peter Richard, Archbishop. (L. W. Bacon) Chr. Lit. 14: 653.
Kensington Fifty Years Ago. (W. J. Loftie) M. of Art, 11: 420.
Kensington Minor. (G. H. Page) Argosy, 55: 345.
Kent, Constance, Trial of, for Murder. Green Bag, 6: 526.
Kent, James, Chancellor, with portrait. (C. S. Martin) Green Bag, 7: 153.
Kent, Drowsy. (C. de Kay) Cent. 25: 676.
— Prehistoric Metropolis in. (H. Stopes) Ath. '95, 2: 325.
Kentish Arcadia, A. (Linda Gardiner) Temp. Bar, 109: 520.
Kentish Proverbs. (J. A. Sparvel-Bayly) Walford's Antiq. 11: 17, 145.
Kentucky; Blue-Grass Cycling Tour. (J. B. Carrington) Outing, 24: 272.
— History of a Municipal Charter in. (E. J. McDermott) Ann. Am. Acad. Pol. Sci. 7: 63.
— Homesteads of the Blue-grass. (J. L. Allen) Cent. 22: 51.
— How it became a State. (G. W. Ranck) Harper, 85: 46.
— Humors of Political Campaigning in. (E. J. McDermott) Cent. 28: 826.
— Settlement and Early Social Condition of. J. Am. Folk-Lore, 7: 150.
— Making of a State. (Mrs. M. J. Lamb) M. Am. Hist. 28: 50.
— Watering-places in, Old. (S. E. M. Hardy) Am. Hist. Reg. 2: 1385.
Kentucky Cardinal, The; a story. (J. L. Allen) Harper, 88: 926. 89: 20.
Kentucky Resolutions of 1798, Jefferson's Draft of. (P. L. Ford) Nation, 62: 156.
Kenya, Mount, Expedition to. (J. W. Gregory) Fortn. 61: 327. Same art. Liv. Age, 201: 177.
Kenyon Family Papers. Ath. '94, 2: 752.
Kenyon's Innings; a story. (E. W. Hornung) Longm. 19: 614. Same art. Liv. Age, 193: 584.
Kepler, J. (Sir R. Ball) Good Words, 35: 402.
Kepler's Problem, Method of Solving. (F. R. Moulton) Pop. Astron. 3: 136.
Kepplestone Collection of Pictures. (J. Dow) M. of Art, 11: 378, 425.
— Portrait Gallery. (J. Dow) M. of Art, 12: 206.
Kerbela, A Pilgrimage to. Blackw. 159: 287. Same art. Liv. Age, 208: 659.
Kermoozer's Club, The. (M. H. Spielmann) M. of Art, 12: 361.
Kerry, November in. (H. S. Fagan) Time, 16: 29.
Kertch, Recent Excavations at. (W. R. Morfill) Acad. 50: 102.
Kestrel Hawk. (H. F. Witherby) Knowl. 18: 218.
Kettell, John; was he killed by the Indians? (G. F. Clark) N. E. Reg. 50: 483.
Kew Gardens, Aquatic Life in. Spec. 75: 140.
— Botanical Library at. (E. W. Crofts) Bookworm, 5: 7.
— Flowers at. Spec. 76: 410.
— in May. Spec. 74: 682.
— Jubilee Year of. Garden & F. 5: 26.
— Landscape Effects at. (W. Watson) Garden & F. 9: 523.
— Notes from. (G. Nicholson) Garden & F. 6: 424.
Kew Gardens, Observatory for Measurement of Temperature, Apparatus of. (E. H. Griffiths) Nature, 53: 39.
— Queen's Cottage at. (W. Watson) Garden & F. 6: 463.
Key, Willem. (A. R. Evans) M. of Art, 10: 113.
Key to Sixty-Six; a story. (E. M. Halliday) Munsey, 11: 97.
Key West, Railroad to. (J. B. Browne) Nat. Geog. M. 7: 203.
Keys found in Lochleven. (E. E. Guthrie) Liv. Age, 199: 190.
— Old. (T. W. Greene) M. of Art, 2: 75. 3: 15, 174.
Khama. (J. S. Little) Acad. 48: 265.
Khartum, Siege and Fall of. (F. R. Wingate) Un. Serv. M. 4: 406, 537. 5: 69-393.
Khayyam, Omar, Rubaiyat, Dole's Edition. Bk. Buyer, 13: 295.
Khnopff, Fernand. (W. S. Sparrow) M. of Art, 14: 37.
Khu-en-aten, Abandoned Archives of. (J. N. Fradenburgh) Meth. R. 52: 570.
Khurasan, Trade of. Asia. R. 20: 148.
Khyber Pass, A Drive to the. (E. C. Tait) Sund M. 23: 547.
— Through the. (S. Wilkinson) 19th Cent. 34: 533. Same art. Liv. Age, 199: 482.
Kiama. (A. J. Rose-Soley) Westm. 142: 546.
Kicking, Scientific. (R. Barr) McClure, 3: 294.
Kidd, Benj., with portrait. Bk. News, 12: 424. — Lit. W. (Bost.) 25: 238.
— Larger Issues of his Position. (L. P. Jacks) New World, 4: 528.
— Social Evolution. (B. A. Kant) Bach. of Arts, 1: 26. — (F. M. Crawford) Book R. 1: 247.
— — Some Fallacies of. (J. M. Whiton) New World, 4: 87.
Kidnapped Bride. (M. H. Catherwood) Atlan. 74: 326.
Kidnapping of the "Squaller," The. (Mary L. Pendered) Idler, 7: 527.
Kieff, Russian Holy City. (I. F. Hapgood) Atlan. 74: 489.
Kieft, William. (J. W. Gerard) Nat'l M. (N. Y. '91) 15: 447.
Kiel, Celebration at. Spec. 74: 743.
Kielland, Alexander. (W. H. Carpenter) Bookman, 4: 229.
Kilauea, Mt. (M. L. Cheney) Overland, n. s. 19: 561.
— Gases in. (W. Libby) Am. J. Sci. 147: 371.
— in April, 1892. (S. E. Bishop) Am. J. Sci. 144: 207.
— in August, 1892. (F. S. Dodge) Am. J. Sci. 145: 241.
— Recent Eruption in the Crater of. (L. A. Thurston) Am. J. Sci. 148: 338.
— A View of. Nature, 53: 490.
Kilby Brooke; a story. (I. J. Roberts) Munsey, 13: 90.
Kilima-njaro, Mammals of. (P. L. Sclater) Nat. Sci. 2: 257.
Killarney, Lakes of. (C. Turner) Mo. Illust. 3: 364.
— — and Dells of. Idler, 6: 20.
Killing of the Captain; a story. (J. Heard, jr.) Cosmopol. 17: 440.
Kilt, The, in Danger. (E. L. Godkin) Nation, 56: 229.
Kilwa Island, in Lake Mweru. (A. Blair-Watson) Geog. J. 6: 458.
Kimball, Grace, and her Relief Work in Armenia. (R. of Rs. (N. Y.) 13: 444.
Kimberley, Exposition at, Proposed. (L. Atkinson) J. Soc. Arts, 40: 305.
— From, thro' Transvaal to Delagoa Bay. (Geo. Kilgour) Univ. R. 3: 515.
Kina Balu, Mount, in Borneo, Exploration of. Dub. R. 118: 173.

Kindergarten and the Elementary School. (C. C. Van Liew) Educa. R. 9: 172.
— Child-life and. (F. B. Vrooman) Arena, 13: 292.
— for the Blind. (D. Sturgis) New Eng. M. n. s. 13: 433.
— Froebel's. (E. W. White) Cath. World, 56: 507.
— from the College Standpoint. (F. B. Gould) Educa. R. 12: 384.
— in Elementary Schools. (Sarah Corbett) Time, 22: 503.
— In His Name. (H. E. Monroe) Educa. 12: 430.
— in Japan. (L. W. Mason) Lend a H. 15: 442.
— Kate Douglas Wiggin's. (F. C. W. Barbour) Chaut. 16: 462.
— a Natural System of Education. (J. L. Hughes) Pop. Sci. Mo. 45: 207.
— of the Church. (M. C. Foster) Chaut. 23: 91.
— Miss Peabody and the. (L. Wheelock) Educa. 15: 27.
— The Second Gift. (H. L. Jerome) Educa. 14: 80.
Kindergarten Age, The. (H. Butterworth) R. of Rs. (N. Y.) 14: 681.
Kindergarten Christmas, A. (N. A. Smith) Overland, n. s. 21: 5.
Kindergarten Movement. (T. Williams) Cent. 23: 369.
Kindergartens and Manual Training. (Mrs. H. M. Plunkett) Pop. Sci. Mo. 41: 375.
Kindly Crocodile ; a story. (J. Lawson) Gent. M. n. s. 57: 54.
Kindness of the Celestial. (B. Pain) Idler, 1: 552.
Kineto-phonograph, Edison's Invention of. (A. and W. K. L. Dickson) Cent. 26: 206. — (A. and W. K. L. Dickson) Cassier, 7: 145.
Kinetoscope of Time, The. (B. Matthews) Scrib. M. 18: 733.
King, Alice, the Blind Authoress. Argosy, 58: 469.
King, Capt. Chas., with portrait. Bk. Buyer, 6: 553. — With portrait. Bk. News, 13: 375.
— Portraits of. McClure, 3: 134.
King, Edward, Bishop of London, Judgment in the Case of. And. R. 18: 278.
— — Protest against. Spec. 70: 282.
— — Lord Grimthorpe and. Spec. 69: 312.
King, E. Joseph Zalmonah. Westm. 140: 312.
King, Francis S. ; engraver. Scrib. M. 17: 291.
King, Grace, with portrait. Bk. Buyer, 13: 139. — With portrait. Bk. News, 12: 312.
King, Capt. John, Muster-roll of Company of, 1775. (E. B. Hill) N. E. Reg. 49: 206.
King, K. Douglas. Scripture Reader of St. Mark's. (M. C. Birchenough) 19th Cent. 40: 770.
King, Thomas Starr, and R. H. Dana, jr. (W. Everett) Overland, n. s. 28: 578.
King Family of Suffield, Conn. (E. J. Cleveland) N. E. Reg. 46: 370.
King of Currumpaw ; a wolf story. (E. E. Thompson) Scrib. M. 16: 618.
King of Foula, The ; a story. (C. J. C. Hyne) Temp. Bar, 105: 506. Same art. Liv. Age, 206: 725.
King of Schnorrers, The ; a story. (I. Zangwill) Idler, 4: 24-610.
Kingdom of God, The. (D. Macleod) Good Words, 33: 497.
— Enthusiasm of. (I. Maclaren) Chr. Lit. 13: 325.
— Jesus' Idea of. (A. C. Zenos) Bib. World, 3: 35.
Kingdom of Heaven in Matthew. (T. J. Ramsdell) Bib. World, 4: 124.
— Keys of. (G. U. Wenner) Luth. Q. 23: 364.
Kinglake, A. W. "Eothen" and the Athenæum Club. (A. Gregory) Blackw. 158: 797. Same art. Liv. Age, 207: 748.
— Reminiscences of. New R. 10: 726.
King's Daughter, A ; a story. Ecl. M. 127: 124.
King's Mountain, Battlefield of. (R. Shackleton) M. Am. Hist. 30: 38.
King's Norton Parish Library. Bookworm, 7: 315.
King's Peace, The. (Sir F. Pollock) Law Q. 1: 37.
King's Treasure, The ; a story. (H. B. M. Watson) New R. 13: 1.
King's Well ; a story. (F. A. Steel) Eng. Illust. 12: no. 3, 65.
Kings, Deified, Culture Heroes and. (S. D. Peet) Am. Antiq. 16: 143.
Kings of Owascoag. (Mrs. J. K. Van Rensselaer) Am. Hist. Reg. 1: 461.
Kingsburg, John H. A. Macdonald, Lord. (A. W. Renton) Green Bag, 4: 567.
Kingsley, Charles, as a Christian Teacher. (F. H. Woods) Chr. Lit. 12: 144, 200.
— as an Economist. Dub. R. 113: 662.
— as Novelist. (F. Tupper, jr.) Citizen, 2: 47.
— Place of, in Literature. (F. Harrison) Forum, 19: 560.
— Saint's Tragedy. Eng. R. 12: 378.
— Sermons. Eng. R. 18: 267.
— Water Babies. (W. Clark) Canad. M. 1: 373.
— Westward Ho ! (R. G. Moulton) Chaut. 20: 548.
Kingsley, Elbridge. Bk. Buyer, 2: 248. — Scrib. M. 18: 32.
Kingsley, George H. Ath. '92, 1: 214.
Kingsley, Henry, with portrait. Bk. Buyer, 11: 723.
Kingsley, Mary, with portrait. Theatre, 28: 297.
Kingsley-land, Literary History of. (P. H. W. Almy) Temp. Bar, 109: 367.
Kingston, Can., Military College. Canad. M. 4: 428.
Kingston, N. Y. (M. I. Forsyth) New Eng. M. n. s. 9: 345.
Kiowas, Brush with. (W. Thomson) Lippinc. 56: 711.
Kipling, Rudyard, with portrait. Bk. Buyer, 7: 377. — With portraits. Bk. Buyer, 13: 589. — (F. Adams) Ecl. M. 118: 47.
— and W. Balestier. The Naulahka. Spec. 69: 196. — Sat. R. 74: 226.
— as Journalist. Acad. 50: 458.
— as a poet. (M. Schuyler) Forum, 22: 406.
— at Home in Vermont. Critic, 22: 34.
— Ballads. Sat. R. 73: 580. — Spec. 68: 644.
— Bibliography of First Editions. (E. D. North) Bk. Buyer, 13: 595.
— First Book of. (R. Kipling) McClure, 3: 563. Same art. Idler, 2: 477.
— in England. (E. K. Robinson) McClure, 7: 99.
— Jungle Books. Idler, 9: 115.
— Poetry of. (L. Johnson) Acad. 41: 509.
— Seven Seas. Acad. 50: 377. — Sat. R. 82: 549. Same art. Liv. Age, 211: 827.
— Some Tales of. (S. R. Crockett) Bookman, 1: 23.
— Stories. (G. Cope) Gent. M. n. s. 49: 136.
— Tales. Quar. 175: 132.
— Verse. (F. Adams) Fortn. 60: 590.
— Work of, so far. (W. H. Bishop) Forum, 19: 476.
Kirby's Canadian Idylls ; a review. (S. A. Curzon) Canad. M. 6: 568.
Kirckhoff, Gustav R. (R. von Helmholtz) Open Court, 2: 783.
Kirghese, the Kara, Issik Kul and. (H. Lansdell) Gent. M. n. s. 48: 346. Same art. Liv. Age, 193: 689.
Kirk, Ellen Olney, with portrait. Bk. Buyer, 6: 140.
Kirke, John. A Curious and Rare Old Play. (S. J. A. Fitzgerald) Theatre, 28: 3.
Kirke & Company's Wife. (F. M. Bicknell) Southern M. 3: 616.

Kirkham, Garvin, Open-air Evangelist. (G. H. Pike) Sund. M. 23: 741.
Kirkland, Joseph, with portrait. Bk. Buyer, 6: 65. — Critic, 24: 301.
Kirkpatrick, A. J., Picture Collection of. (R. Walker) M. of Art, 18: 41.
Kirkpatrick, J. A., Romantic Marriage of. (E. Strachey) Blackw. 154: 18. Same art. Liv. Age, 198: 540.
Kirschner, Lula. [Ossip Schubin] (J. Hoops) Acad. 41: 255.
— Novels of. Westm. 140: 653.
Kirtland or Kirkland Family. (V. C. Sanborn) N. E. Reg. 48: 66.
Kiss for a Blow, A. (G. B. Burgin) Good Words, 35: 564.
Kiss of Gold; a story. (K. Jordan) Lippinc. 50: 423.
Kisses, Royal. All the Year, 73: 52.
Kissing on the Stage. (E. Rose) Theatre, 34: 149.
Kissingen; a German Watering Place. (S. Whitman) Chaut. 20: 677.
Κισσός and Hedera. (L. Horton-Smith) Am. J. Philol. 16: 38.
Kistler, Cyrill. Kunihild. (W. A. Ellis) Ath. '93, 1: 289.
Kistvaens, Dartmoor. Reliquary, 35: 161.
Kitchen Affair; a story. (V. Berryman) Canad M. 7: 155.
Kitchen-range Boilers, Explosion of. Chamb. J. 70: 171.
Kite, The, as a Life-saver at Sea. (J. W. Davis) Engin. M. 7: 213.
Kite-flying, Scientific. (C. Moffett) McClure, 6: 379.
Kittery, Me., Document, 1755. (J. S. H. Fogg) N. E. Reg. 47: 469.
Kites and Meteorological Observations. (H. H. Clayton) Nature, 55: 150.
Kitty Alone; a Story of Three Fires. (S. Baring-Gould) Good Words, 35: 1-793.
Kizil Irmak River. (Lieut. Marcker) Geog. J. 3. 327.
Klamath Indians. (H. Hale) Science, 19: 6-29.
— Gatschet's. (A. F. Chamberlain) J. Am. Folk-Lore, 5: 252.
Klapka, George, and Kossuth. (K. Blind) Scot. R. 20: 379.
Klein, Bruno Oscar, "Kenilworth" by. Music, 8: 36.
Kleynartis, Nicolas. *See* Clenardus.
Knaus, Ludwig. (H. Zimmern) M. of Art, 8: 327.
— Morning after the Fête. Art J. 47: 53.
Knee-jerk in a Case of Terminal Dementia. (W. Noyes) Am. J. Psychol. 4: 343.
Kneipp, Sebastian. Month, 74: 28.
— Visit to Wörishofen. (A. Quarry) Argosy, 59: 745.
Kneipp Spa, at a. (H. W. Wolff) Gent. M. n. s. 50: 589.
Kneller, Godfrey. Ath. '94, 2: 611.
Kneller Hall and Military Bands. All the Year, 71: 465.
Knickerbocker, Joshua C., with portrait. Nat'l M. (N. Y. '91) 16: 488.
Knickerbockers of New York. (E. B. Pennell) Art J. 45: 343.
Knight, Joseph. Bookworm, 3: 1.
Knight, Madam Sarah, and her Journal. (F. Allaben) Nat'l M. (N. Y. '91) 15: 158.
Knight, Thos. A., Botanist. (L. H. Bailey) Garden & F. 8: 512.
Knight, William, as Editor of Wordsworth. (T. Hutchinson) Acad. 50: 5, 233.
Knight and the Lady, The; a story. Blackw. 158: 16.
Knight of the Legion of Honor; a story. (F. H. Smith) Cent. 23: 223.
Knight of Pentecost; a poem. (H. P. Spofford) Cent. 24: 31.
Knight Service, Introduction of, into England. (J. H. Round) Eng. Hist. R. 7: 11.
Knighthood, American, An Order of. (W. H. Smith) Am. J. Pol. 4: 337.
Knightlow Wroth Silver. (G. L. Gomme) Antiq. n. s. 29: 1.
Knights, Military, of Windsor. All the Year, 75: 484.
— of St. John of Jerusalem. (J. Wortabit) Good Words, 34: 378.
— of the Temple. (A. Grange) Dub. R. 117: 329.
Knights Templars; Boston Conclave. Bost. 2: 486.
Knightsbridge Road, On the Old. Macmil. 67: 216.
Knives, Spoons, and Forks. (A. Vallance) Art J. 44: 266.
Knockers. All the Year, 72: 521. — (P. Fitzgerald) M. of Art, 5: 23.
— Mediæval. Antiq. n. s. 31: 202.
— Some Venetian. (H. F. Brown) M. of Art, 8: 197.
Knole. (F. G. Stephens) M. of Art, 14: 423.
Knowledge. (W. Smith) Mind, 68: 489. — (P. Carus) Open Court, 7: 3588.
— and Feeling in Spirituality, Crowder's. (J. W. Webb) Meth. R. 56: 963.
— Maleficent Aspects of. Spec. 72: 262.
— on Sight. (R. Ogden) Nation, 57: 41.
— Physical Basis of. (J. Ferguson) Canad. M. 3: 317.
— Superficial, Lord Justice Bowen and Prof. Mahaffy on. Spec. 70: 74.
— Tree of. New R. 10: 675.
— What Knowledge is of Most Worth? (N. M. Butler) Educa. R. 10: 105.
Know-nothingism in Kentucky. (T. J. Jenkins) Cath. World, 57: 511.
— Local History of. (G. H. Haynes) New Eng. M. n. s. 15: 82.
— Riotous Career of. (J. B. McMaster) Forum, 17: 524.
Knox, Alexander, and his Friends. (Mrs. A. Crosse) Temp. Bar, 94: 495.
Knox, John. (J. S. Blackie) Contemp. 62: 263. Same art. M. Chr. Lit. 6: 412. — Pub. Opin. 12: 512.
— and St. Giles. (I. Harris) Sund. M. 23: 405.
— Hume Brown on. (A. F. Mitchell) Presb. & Ref. R. 7: 546.
Knox, Major John, Journal of the French and Indian War, 1757-60. Macmil. 72: 62.
Knox, John Jay. Bank. M. (Lond.) 53: 584. — Bank. M. (N. Y.) 47: 267.
Knox, Thomas W., with portrait. Bk. News, 10: 281. — Critic, 25: 29.
Knox College, Galesburg, Ill. (Madame Blanc) McClure, 4: 541.
Knutsford, Cheshire. Latter-day Cranford. (A. Brown) Atlan. 77: 526.
— in Fiction. (Geo. A. Payne) Gent. M. n. s. 55: 507.
Knyphausen, Wilhelm, Baron. Pennsyl. M. 16: 239.
Koch, Robert, Discovery of. (H. Bernheim) Open Court, 4: 2636.
Koerner, Gustav. Open Court, 10: 4879.
Kōhēn, Use of Word, in the Old Testament. (L. B. Paton) J. Bib. Lit. 12: 1.
Kolgueff Island. (A. Trevor-Battye) Geog. J. 5: 97.
— Trevor-Battye on. Sat. R. 80: 147. — (Hiram M. Stanley) Dial (Ch.) 19: 253.
Kolokotronês, Theodore Gennaios. (E. M. Edmonds) Acad. 45: 437.

Konde Country. (Rev. Dr. Merensky) Geog. J. 2: 321.
Königsmark, Aurora. (H. S. Wilson) Gent. M. n. s. 49: 369.
Koniscope, The. (J. G. McPherson) Knowl. 17: 258.
Kootenay Indians. (A. F. Chamberlain) Am. Antiq. 15: 292. 16: 271. 17: 68.
Kootenay Legend. (A. F. Chamberlain) J. Am. Folk-Lore, 7: 195.
Kophetua the 13th. (Julian Corbett) Time, 18: 476-730. 19: 94-599. 20: 87, 203.
Kopp, Hermann F. M. (T. E. Thorpe) Nature, 45: 441.
Koptos, Sculptures from. (S. Y. Stevenson) Am. J. Archæol. 10: 347.
Koran, Introduction to the. (G. Weil) Bib. World, 5: 181, 438. 6: 26, 105.
Koran Schools. (G. W. Leitner) Asia. R. 18: 421.
Korea. *See* Corea.
Kosh-she-she-bog-a-mog. (E. Wiman) Canad. M. 4: 95.
Kossuth, Louis. (Madam Adam) Cosmopol. 17: 329. — With portraits. R. of Rs. (N. Y.) 9: 551. — Sat. R. 77: 301. — (J. Nichol) Macmil. 70: 153. — (S. K. Schonberg) Munsey, 7: 542. — (M. M. Trumbull) Open Court, 8: 4023. — (J. B. Moore) Pol. Sci. Q. 10: 95, 257.
— and George Klapka. (K. Blind) Scot. R. 20: 379.
— and Hungarian Nationality. (F. Amouretti) Chaut. 20: 27.
— and the War of Liberation. (S. J. Low) National, 23: 350. Same art. Ecl. M. 123: 54. Same art. Liv. Age, 201: 515.
— Career of. Our Day, 13: 263.
— in New England. (G. S. Boutwell) New Eng. M. n. s. 10: 525.
— On a Mission for. (W. J. Stillman) Cent. 26: 270.
— Predictions of. (F. L. Oswald) No. Am. 158: 635.
Kovalevsky, Sonya, with portrait. Bk. Buyer, 12: 395. — With portrait. Bk. News, 13: 499. — (I. F. Hapgood) Cent. 28: 536. — Sat. R. 80: 51. — (E. W. Carter) Fortn. 63: 767. Same art. Ecl. M. 125: 50. Same art. Liv. Age, 205: 679. — (C. C. Burnham) Astron. 11: 281. — Critic, 25: 213.
— The Cost of Glory. (A. Barine) Chaut. 19: 571.
Kowak River, Ice-cliffs on. (J. C. Cantwell) Nat. Geog. M. 7: 345.
Krakatoa Eruption, The. (J. T. Van Gestel) Cosmopol. 18: 719. — (E. R. Hodges) Knowl. 18: 265. Same art. Liv. Age, 207: 823.
Krasinska, Françoise, Countess. Ed. R. 184: 113. Same art. Liv. Age, 211: 221.
Kraut-cutter of Montafun. (S. Baring-Gould) Chamb. J. 71: 305.
Kray, Wilhelm. (C. S. Johnson) Munsey, 7: 668.
Krelage, J. H., Horticultural Library of. Bookworm, 5: 353.
Kropotkine, Prince. (E. Sellers) Contemp. 66: 537. Same art. Ecl. M. 123: 653.
— Conquête du Pain. Temp. Bar, 103: 521.
Krüdener, Madam de. (S. M. S. Pereira) Good Words, 35: 410.
— Ford's Life and Letters of. (I. F. Hapgood) Nation, 56: 441. — Spec. 71: 691. — Dial (Ch.) 14: 333.
Krüger, Dr. Adalbert. Nature, 54: 14.
Krüger, Paul, President. (P. Bigelow) Harper, 94: 26. — Sat. R. 80: 197. 81: 421, 446.
Kruell, Gustav; engraver. Scrib. M. 17: 186.
Krupp Foundries, Social Work at. (S. M. Lindsay) Ann. Am. Acad. Pol. Sci. 3: 330.
Krystallês, Konstantine. (E. M. Edmonds) Acad. 45: 475.
Ku-Cheng, Massacre of Missionaries at. Sat. R. 80: 164. — (J. Lawson) Gent. M. n. s. 54: 244. Same art. Ecl. M. 124: 659.
Kuenen, Abraham. (P. H. Wicksteed) Jew. Q. 4: 571. — (C. H. Toy) M. Chr. Lit. 5: 494. — (C. H. Toy) New World, 1: 64. — And. R. 17: 201.
Kumys Cure, Russian. (I. F. Hapgood) Atlan. 71: 47.
Kundt, August. (H. Du Bois) Nature, 50: 152.
Kunjer Doctor, The. (B. Winston) Southern M. 4: 360.
Kurdistan. (F. R. Maunsell) Geog. J. 3: 81.
— Persian, Journey in, with map. (W. B. Harris) Geog. J. 6: 453.
— — Wanderings in. Blackw. 158: 735. Same art. Liv. Age, 207: 476.
— Travels in, Bishop's. Ath. '92, 1: 75.
Kurds. (W. B. Harris) Sat. R. 80: 724.
Kürschner, Lola. *See* Kirschner, L.
Kutho-daw, The. (F. M. Muller) 19th Cent. 38: 494. — Acad. 47: 505.
Kuyper's, Abraham, Theological Encyclopædia. (A. H. Huizinga) Presb. & Ref. R. 6: 502.
Kwapa Folk-lore. (J. O. Dorsey) J. Am. Folk-Lore, 8: 130.
Kwakiutl, The, Songs and Dances of. (Franz Boas) J. Am. Folk-Lore, 1: 49.
— A Woman's Song of the. (J. C. Fillmore) J. Am. Folk-Lore, 6: 285.
Kyōto, Trip to. (L. Hearn) Atlan. 77: 613.
Kyrle Society, The. M. of Art, 3: 210.

La Baraonda, Rovetta's. (A. Gorren) Dial (Ch.) 19: 169.
La Bastie, A. D'Arces de. Blackw. 154: 132.
La Bourboule, France. (E. C. Vansittart) Belgra. 88: 197.
La Charité, France; a Fossil Town. Sat. R. 74: 334.
La Chasse-galerie. (H. Beaugrand) Cent. 22: 497.
La Haute Ecole; a story. Un. Serv. (Phila.) 7: 174.
La Revanche; a story. (F. Gribble) Idler, 10: 249.
Labarum: Was Constantine's Sign a Sun-dog? (A. Harvey) Canad. M. 5: 164.
Labīd, Poetry of. (C. J. Lyall) Acad. 41: 280.
Labor and Capital. (W. G. Selleck) Am. J. Pol. 2: 135. — (W. Barry) Dub. R. 112: 341.
— — the Coming Struggle. (F. E. Tasker) Am. M. Civics, 9: 277.
— — Judicial Opinions affecting, 1893. Pub. Opin. 14: 619.
— — No Natural Antagonism between. (N. F. Thompson) Pub. Opin. 20: 557.
— — Psychology of. (R. Wallace) Fortn. 60: 676. Same art. Ecl. M. 122: 17.
— — Relative Strength of. (J. S. Nicholson) Econ. J. 2: 478.
— — Rights of Employers. (H. F. Henry) Soc. Econ. 3: 193.
— — Strife between; Symposium. Indep. Feb. 7, '95.
— — Two New Social Departures. (L. M. Ludlow) Atlan. 77: 360.
— and Hours of Labor. (W. Mather) Contemp. 62: 609.
— and the Injunction. (E. Woollen) Yale R. 5: 39.
— and Labor Unions; Symposium. Indep. May 2, '95.
— and Laborers. (H. Jones) Sund. M. 24: 88.
— and the Popular Welfare, Mallock's. Sat. R. 76: 631.

Labor and Tariff, Problems of, in New South Wales. (J. E. Bullard) Nation, 54: 84.
— Autonomy of. (H. W. Wolff) Contemp. 70: 191. Same art. Ecl. M. 127: 470.
— Cabinet Secretary of. (M. L. Swift) Am. M. Civics, 8: 489.
— Casual; a Winter's Experiment. (H. V. Toynbee) Macmil. 69: 54.
— Cheap, and Cost of Production. Spec. 69: 948.
— — Dearness of. (D. F. Schloss) Fortn. 59: 54. Same art. Engin. M. 5: 41.
— Civil Service Reform and. (H. Welsh) Good Govt. 14: 195.
— Claims and Methods of. (V. Yarros) Open Court, 8: 4305.
— Claims of. Eng. R. 2: 257.
— — on Organized Christianity. Soc. Econ. 4: 359. 5: 365.
— Condition of, Leo XIII. on. (H. S. Holland) Econ. R. 1: 455.
— Co-partnership of. (H. Vivian and A. Williams) Econ. R. 4: 297.
— Current Sophisms about. (H. Gourlay) National, 20: 749.
— Delusion of, regarding Capital. (A. H. Peters) Engin. M. 6: 626.
— Dignity of, as taught in the Talmud. (Hermann Gollancz) Asia. R. 12: 129.
— Emancipation of, by Machinery. (A. E. Outerbridge) Engin. M. 9: 1012.
— English, in and out of Parliament in 1893. (E. Porritt) Yale R. 2: 418.
— Ethics of. (F. W. Howard) Cath. World, 59: 847.
— Friends of, Genuine. (J. B. Bishop) Nation, 54: 279.
— Future of. (R. C. Adams) Open Court, 1: 575.
— Hobhouse on. (S. Ball) Int. J. Ethics, 4: 520.
— Hours of. (H. Jones) Macmil. 65: 367.
— — in Europe. (L. Irwell) Soc. Econ. 7: 160.
— — Ten Hour Movement. Soc. Econ. 4: 330.
See Eight Hours.
— in America, Macaulay on. Gunton's M. 11: 195.
— in England, Chamberlain's Programme. (T. Burt and others) 19th Cent. 32: 864.
— — Commission on. National, 23: 201.
— — Department of. Q. J. Econ. 7: 359.
— — — Reorganization of. (D. F. Schloss) J. Statis. Soc. 56: 44.
— — Failure of. (B. Webb) 19th Cent. 36: 2.
— — The Government and. (H. W. Massingham) Contemp. 64: 765.
— — Home Office and the Deadly Trades. (V. Nash) Fortn. 59: 169.
— — in 1892, Platform of, New Style. (T. Mann; B. Tillett) New R. 6: 166.
— — — Reply. (G. Howell) New R. 6: 472.
— — Land and. (Lord Thring; W. E. Bear; Mrs. S. Batson) 19th Cent. 31: 150. — (J. Shortrede) New R. 6: 362.
— — Lords and Laborers. (J. Arch) New R. 8: 129.
— — National Free Labor Association. (J. M. Ludlow) Econ. R. 5: 110.
— — New Unionism. (T. Mann) New R. 8: 272.
— — Pressing Reforms. (C. W. Dilke) New R. 8: 257.
— — Quest of. (J. Chamberlain) 19th Cent. 32: 677.
— — Report on. Ed. R. 180: 333. — (L. L. Price) Econ. J. 4: 444.
— — Royal Commission of. (J. Ral) Econ. J. 3: 164, 339.
— — — Teachings of. (C. H. d'E. Leppington) Contemp. 64: 388.
Labor in England. Social Remedies of the Labor Party. (W. H. Mallock) Fortn. 59: 505. Same art. Ecl. M. 120: 721.
— — Unemployed. (J. Burns) 19th Cent. 32: 845.
— — Mrs. Sidney Webb's Attack on. (G. Drage) 19th Cent. 36: 452.
— in Europe, Ancient and Modern. Soc. Econ. 6: 30.
— in France. (H. K. Landis) Gunton's M. 11: 37.
— in Great Britain, New Government and. Spec. 75: 8.
— in Japan. (F. Takano) Gunton's M. 11: 106.
— in London, Waterside. (H. L. Smith) Econ. J. 2: 593.
— in New Zealand, Adult Male. (E. Reeves) Westm. 144: 631.
— in U. S. (P. Vedel) Am. M. Civics, 6: 32.
— Income of, Future. (W. H. Mallock) National, 21: 620.
— Industrial Agreements and Conciliation. (C. C. Kingston) R. of Rs. (N. Y.) 10: 647.
— Infringing a Political Patent. (St. Loe Strachey) 19th Cent. 37: 206.
— Leaders of. (W. L. Sheldon) Am. J. Pol. 5: 152.
— Legislation on, in the U. S. (H. G. Wadlin) Chaut. 23: 288.
— Liquor, and Land. Fortn. 64: 12.
— Man's Birthright. (J. K. Smyth) N. Church R. 2: 233.
— Organization of. (T. V. Powderly) Chaut. 17: 15.
— — as affected by Law. (Mrs. C. R. Lowell) Char. R. 1: 6.
— Organized. (N. O. Nelson) New Eng. M. n. s. 13: 338.
— — and the Law. (N. T. Mason) Am. J. Pol. 3: 188. — (E. Ardon) Chaut. 17: 140.
— — in the U. S. in the Campaign of 1892. (S. Gompers) No. Am. 155: 91.
— — Injunction and. (C. C. Allen) Am. Law R. 28: 828.
— — Relation to Trade Instruction. (E. W. Bemis) Ann. Am. Acad. Pol. Sci. 5: 209.
— Political Future of. (T. R. Threlfall) 19th Cent. 35: 203.
— Policy of. (C. Edwards) Contemp. 66: 269.
— Premium Plan for Paying for. (F. A. Halsey) Econ. Stud. 1: 75.
— Problem of. (Nelson Baldwin) Am. M. Civics, 8: 138, 234. — (F. E. Russell) Arena, 15: 960. — (M. H. Richards) Luth. Q. 23: 55.
— — and of Immigration. (T. N. Carver) Am. J. Pol. 3: 78.
— — Aspects of. (N. A. Flood) Am. J. Pol. 4: 14.
— — Church and. (W. Howard and others) M. Chr. Lit. 5: 463. — (K. Hardie) Thinker, 8: 105. — (J. M. Lang) Thinker, 8: 295.
— — in the U. S. (A. Bierbower) Overland, n. s. 21: 217.
— — What Attitude should the Pulpit take toward? (W. L. Sheldon) Int. J. Ethics, 2: 439.
— Question of. (G. Drage) J. Soc. Arts, 43: 234.
— — Church and the. (H. H. Barber) Am. M. Civics, 6: 65.
— — Historical Sketch of. (A. Mills) National, 19: 145.
— — in America. (E. Aveling) Time, 16: 298–705.
— — in South Africa. (A. Cartwright) Westm. 140: 46.
— — Manufacturers' View of. (Joseph H. Walker) Soc. Econ. 1: 378.
— — Moral Forces in Dealing with. (W. M. Salter) Int. J. Ethics, 5: 296.
— — Once More. (Joel Benton) Soc. Econ. 3: 23.

Labor, Question of. Our National Ideal. Soc. Econ. 2: 141.
— — Recent Books on. (E. W. Bemis) Dial (Ch.) 18: 342.
— — Women on. (J. A. Kellogg and others) Arena, 14: 268.
— Recent Movement of; Hours and Wages. (J. S. Jeans) J. Statis. Soc. 55: 620.
— Relation of Invention to. (C. D. Wright) Soc. Econ. 1: 193.
— Relation of the Referendum and Initiative to. (A. L. Lowell) Int. J. Ethics, 6: 51.
— Representation of. (F. Hammill) Fortn. 61: 546. — (E. Salmon) Time, 19: 87.
— Right of, to Free Speech. (Kemper Bocock) Soc. Econ. 3: 136.
— The Right to. (F. J. Stimson) Nation, 60: 251.
— Rights of, Judge Grosscup on. Pub. Opin. 17: 359.
— Rulings on, by Federal Courts. (A. F. Walker) Forum, 15: 311.
— Social Condition of. (E. R. L. Gould) Contemp. 63: 125. — (E. R. L. Gould) Chaut. 17: 267. — (E. R. L. Gould) J. H. Univ. Studies, 11: no. 1.
— Social Improvement of European. (E. R. L. Gould) Engin. M. 8: 384.
— Specialization of Labor Functions. Soc. Econ. 5: 235.
— Spiritual and Material Benefits of. (J. T. Prince) N. Church R. 2: 384.
— State Tribunals of, Necessity of. (N. T. Mason) Am. M. Civics, 7: 160.
— Statistics of, European Bureaus of. (E. R. L. Gould) Yale R. 2: 386.
— Surplus Gains of. (J. B. Clark) Ann. Am. Acad. Pol. Sci. 3: 607.
— Unemployed. (H. C. Bourne) Macmil. 67: 81.
— U. S. National Department of. (C. D. Wright) Cosmopol. 13: 229.
— Unrest of. Spec. 69: 121.
— Unskilled; What ails it in America? (P. Vedel) Am. M. Civics, 6: 32.
— Waterside, in London. (C. Booth) J. Statis. Soc. 55: 521.
— Wealth of, Palmer on. Lend a H. 14: 91.
— What it wants. (R. Grieve) Arena, 14: 259.
— White-slave Trade. (J. J. O'Shea) Cath. World, 59: 418.
— with a Capital L. (Joel Benton) Soc. Econ. 2: 281.
Labor Bureau, Free, of New York. Lend a H. 16: 253.
Labor Bureaus. All the Year, 73: 605.
— Charity Organization and. (J. H. Hyslop) Char. R. 4: 1.
— A Conversation with C. D. Wright. (H. Johnston) Chaut. 21: 62.
Labor Church, A. (R. Ogden) Nation, 54: 27. — Spec. 72: 530, 533, 582.
— Religion of the Labor Movement. (J. Trevor) Forum, 18: 597.
Labor Colonies. Time, 18: 432.
— German. (A. G. Warner) Q. J. Econ. 6: 462.
— — and the Unemployed. (J. Mavor) J. Pol. Econ. 2: 26.
— in Europe. (D. M. Stevenson) New R. 7: 493.
— in South Australia. (J. Berry) Contemp. 67: 665.
Labor Commission, English. (Tom Mann) Soc. Econ. 2: 296.
Labor Congress at Belfast, 1893. Sat. R. 76: 290.
Labor Congresses, International, London, 1896–97. (R. D. Melville) Westm. 146: 543.
Labor Day. Am. Arch. 45: 109. — (P. Carus) Open Court, 8: 4207.
— Significance of. (E. V. Debs) Arena, 14: 303.
Labor Disputes, A Legislative Remedy for. (H. A. Drake) Am. M. Civics, 8: 337.
Labor Exchange, The. (F. W. Cotton) Arena, 14: 141.
Labor Federations. (C. Edwards) Econ. J. 3: 205, 408.
Labor Functions, Specialization of. Soc. Econ. 5: 235.
Labor Homes of the Church Army in England. (E. Clifford) Eng. Illust. 10: 574.
Labor Insurance in Germany. Gunton's M. 11: 437.
Labor Leader. (C. E. Robie) Lippinc. 57: 415.
— Conversation with. (H. Johnston) Chaut. 18: 569.
Labor Legislation. Soc. Econ. 9: 176.
— in England. (R. S. Viktorov) Engin. M. 5: 640.
— in the United States. (G. K. Holmes) Engin. M. 9: 1027.
Labor Market. (E. E. Hale) Lend a H. 15: 403.
Labor Misrepresentations, Class and. Westm. 142: 419. Same art. Ecl. M. 123: 744.
Labor Movement and International Peace. (R. T. Ely) Our Day, 16: 194.
— and the New Labor Party. (H. W. B. Mackay) Am. M. Civics, 7: 608.
— in England. (Tom Mann) Soc. Econ. 3: 77.
— — Four Leaders in. (F. E. Willard) Our Day, 11: 241.
Labor Organizations, Confederation of. (E. V. Debs) Am. J. Pol. 1: 63.
— in Law. (O. B. Taft) No. Am. 156: 65.
— Influence of. (G. Gunton) Soc. Econ. 2: 10.
Labor Outlook. Soc. Econ. 5: 171. — (Edw. Thimme) Soc. Econ 5: 242.
Labor Party in England. (J. L. Garvin) Fortn. 64: 325. — (J. Keir Hardie) 19th Cent. 37: 1. — Spec. 73: 879.
— — and the General Election. (J. L. Mahon) National, 23: 637.
— — Case for. (J. K. Hardie) New R. 10: 718.
— — What it may achieve. (N. Young) National, 19: 706.
— in Queensland. (A. Bertram) Contemp. 69: 399.
Labor Power of Nations, Food and. (F. S. Nitti) Econ. J. 6: 30.
Labor Reform. (G. W. Weippiert) Am. J. Pol. 1: 427.
Labor Riots and so-called Government by Injunction. (L. E. Curtis) Engin. M. 12: 381.
Labor Settlement, Week on a. (J. Law) Fortn. 62: 206.
Labor Statistics, English, 1895. (A. L. Bowley) Econ. J. 6: 465.
— of Russian Factories. (H. Schoenfeld) Cath. World, 64: 397.
— Value of. (C. D. Wright) Engin. M. 6: 134.
Labor-tests, Concerning. (A. Wilcox) Char. R. 4: 119.
— Municipal, Economy of. (F. Almy) Char. R. 4: 440.
Labor Troubles. (W. P. Reeves) R. of Rs. (N. Y.) 10: 178.
— and the Tariff. (C. J. Harrah) Engin. M. 4: 411.
— Causes and Proposed Remedies. (J. H. Hyslop) Int. J. Ethics, 5: 444.
— in the United States between 1834 and 1837. (E. Woollen) Yale R. 1: 87.
— Settlement of. (D. MacG. Means) Nation, 59: 23.
— Significance of, in America. (C. D. Wright) Int. J. Ethics, 5: 137.
— Stock-sharing as a Preventive of. (L. R. Ehrich) Forum, 18: 433.
— True Cause of. (J. G. Gray) Engin. M. 4: 569.
Labor Trust, A. (E. M. Burchard) Am. J. Pol. 5: 634.
Labor Unions and the Churches. (J. P. Coyle) Forum, 13: 765.
— Chinese, in America. (W. N. Fong) Chaut. 23: 399.
— in China. (W. N. Fong) Chaut. 23: 320.

Labor Unions, Profit-sharing, of Antwerp. (J. H. Gore) Forum, **18**: 177.
See Trade Unions.
Labor War. (H. Thomas) Westm. **144**: 438.
— American, Bitterness in. Spec. **73**: 70.
Laboratories, Research, for Women. (A. W. Rücker) Nature, **48**: 590.
Laboratory, The, in the School. (L. F. Griffin) School & C. **1**: 469.
Laboratory Apparatus, Notes on Convenient Forms of. (F. A. Gooch) Am. J. Sci. **144**: 239. — (D. A. Kreider) Am. J. Sci. **150**: 133.
Laborer and his Hire. (E. Chilton) Longm. **25**: 57.
Laborer, The; Character Note. Cornh. **70**: 593. Same art. Ecl. M. **124**: 124.
Laborer, The; a poem. (G. Meredith) Ecl. M. **120**: 516.
Laborers, Italian. (B. Landreth) Un. Serv. (Phila.) **12**: 240.
Laboring Classes. (Chas. Barnard) Soc. Econ. **5**: 146.
— Central Bureau for Promotion of Welfare of, Conference of, 1892. (L. S. Rowe) Ann. Am. Acad. Pol. Sci. **3**: 73.
— Church and the. (C. Clever) Ref. Q. **43**: 318.
— Condition of, and its Remedies. (J. S. Vaughan) Dub. R. **114**: 41.
— Discontent of, as Illustrated in Cartoons. (B. O. Flower) Arena, **16**: 298.
— In the Country of Dollars. Soc. Econ. **9**: 217.
— in England. In the Wake of the Red Van. (G. Blake) National, **19**: 401.
— in Japan. (F. Takona) Soc. Econ. **9**: 30.
— Industrial Equity. Soc. Econ. **1**: 110.
— Literature and Life. Soc. Econ. **2**: 203.
— Natural Limits of a Day. Soc. Econ. **7**: 231.
— The Plough and the Platform. (T. E. Kebbel) National, **19**: 175.
— Problem of the Unemployed. Soc. Econ. **6**: 11.
— Railroad Labor. (W. E. Hart) Soc. Econ. **1**: 99.
— Shorter Working Year for. (Mathew Middleton) Soc. Econ. **5**: 103.
— Standard of Living of, English. (Tom Mann) Soc. Econ. **4**: 95.
— Tobacco and Clothing Workers. Soc. Econ. **5**: 353.
— Unemployed. (C. D. Wright) Soc. Econ. **2**: 71.
— University and. (Seth Low) Soc. Econ. **1**: 7.
— Wages in England. Soc. Econ. **9**: 253.
Labrador. Liv. Age, **206**: 451. — Lond. Q. **84**: 284.
— Expedition to, 1894. (C. E. Hite) Am. Natural. **29**: 143.
— Explorations through the Interior of, 1893–94. (A. P. Low) Geog. J. **5**: 513.
— Grand Falls of. (H. G. Bryant) Cent. **22**: 643.
— In Rugged. (R. G. Taber) Outing, **27**: 16, 91, 329, 388.
— Outing in. (R. G. Taber) Outing, **27**: 213.
Labouchere, H., with portrait. (H. Parker) Munsey, **11**: 350.
Laboulbeniaceæ, Thaxter's Studies of. (R. Pound) Am. Natural. **28**: 605.
Labrunie, Gérard. (C. E. Meetkerke) Argosy, **59**: 752.
Labussière, Charles Hippolyte. Temp. Bar, **94**: 381. Same art. Liv. Age, **193**: 445.
Lace. (Mrs. B. Palliser) M. of Art, **1**: 179. — (A. S. Cole) M. of Art, **2**: 249.
— at the South Kensington Museum. (A. Cole) M. of Art, **18**: 419.
— Dreams in Woven Thread. (M. S. Lockwood) Cosmopol. **20**: 177.
— English, in 1896. (E. B. Clarke) Art J. **48**: 297.
— Honiton, Recent. (A. S. Cole) M. of Art, **15**: 30.
— Irish. M. of Art, **6**: 438.
Lace, Irish, Some Recent. (A. S. Cole) M. of Art, **14**: 211.
— Irish Papal Jubilee. (M. P. Lalor) M. of Art, **11**: 200.
— Nottingham, and Fashion. (J. D. Firth) Econ. J. **3**: 709.
— Old Venetian Point. M. of Art, **7**: 66.
Lace-making in Ireland, Outlook of. (A. S. Cole) M. of Art, **11**: 202.
Lace School at Burano. (F. M. Robinson) M. of Art, **7**: 257.
Laces of Queen Margherita of Italy. (E. B. Clarke) Art J. **47**: 296.
— Verifying Ancient. (A. S. Cole) J. Soc. Arts, **43**: 757, 769, 781.
Lacedæmon. (W. Pater) Contemp. **61**: 791. Same art. Ecl. M. **119**: 145. Same art. Liv. Age, **194**: 284.
Lachine, Derivation of. Nation, **56**: 384.
Lachish, Recovery of. (T. Harrison) Chr. Lit. **10**: 12 a. — (J. Wells) Sund. M. **25**: 111.
Lackington, James, and his Memoirs. (A. L. Humphreys) Bookworm, **1**: 197, 242.
Lacouperie, Albert Terrien de. (J. S. Cotton) Acad. **46**: 308. — Ath. '**94**, **2**: 531.
Lacquer Collection of Sir T. Lawrence. (M. B. Huish) Art J. **45**: 211.
Lacrosse. (F. Weir) Lippinc. **49**: 743. — (R. MacKenzie) Outing, **21**: 76.
Lad with a Barley Loaf. (Mrs. W. Palmer) Sund. M. **23**: 28–246.
Ladd, G. T. Philosophy of the Mind. (A. L. Hodder) Nation, **60**: 226.
Ladder of Grief, The; a story. (A. French) McClure, **7**: 214.
Ladies as Domestic Servants. Spec. **69**: 92. — (E. M. Phillipps) Fortn. **58**: 193.
— Employments for. Spec. **71**: 635.
— Great. Spec. **70**: 636.
Lady, A Perfect. Spec. **68**: 164.
— a Plea for the Word. Atlan. **76**: 431.
Lady and the Trumps. (W. L. Taylor) New Eng. M. n. s. **11**: 756.
Lady Banksia, The; a story. (W. M. Tisdale) Overland, **21**: 289.
Lady Bountiful; a poem. (A. Dobson) M. of Art, **7**: 14.
— up to Date. (C. R. Coleridge) Sund. M. **25**: 584.
Lady Cecilia's Emeralds; a story. (J. Leete) Argosy, **59**: 608, 685. **60**: 52, 230.
Lady Etheldreda's "at Home;" a story. (C. Milman) Temp. Bar, **94**: 437.
Lady Featherflight: an English Folk-tale. (W. W. Newell) J. Am. Folk-Lore, **6**: 54.
Lady Hazleton's Confession. (Mrs. I. K. Spender) Time, **22**: 3–561. **23**: 673–1233.
Lady Jane's Jam-pot. (E. St. Leger) Belgra. **85**: 53.
Lady Jean's Vagaries; a story. Temp. Bar, **103**: 289, 441. **104**: 132, 161.
Lady Joan; a story. (E. Chilton) Argosy, **59**: 283. Same art. Liv. Age, **205**: 14.
Lady John's Suitors. (M. C. Whitwick) Argosy, **58**: 68.
Lady Journalist, A; a story. (G. Paston) Eng. Illust. **12**: no. 4, 65.
Lady Kilpatrick; a story. (R. Buchanan) Eng. Illust. **10**: 491–914.
Lady Maud's Walk; a Legend. (E. d'Argent) Belgra. **81**: 190.
Lady of Las Cruces. (C. Reid) Lippinc. **55**: 579.

Lady of the Line, A. (G. I. Putnam) Scrib. M. **15**: 255.
Lady of the Lock. (M. E. Francis) Longm. **28**: 357. Same art. Liv. Age, **210**: 660.
Lady of Lucerne. (F. H. Smith) Cent. **28**: 284.
Lady of New York, A. (R. Stewart) Cent. **27**: 393.
Lady of the Pool. (A. Hope) Longm. **25**: 181, 264.
Lady of the Studio. (W. W. Fenn) Argosy, **58**: 205.
Lady Rosalind. (E. Marshall) Sund. M. **25**: 43-818.
Lady Travellers. Blackw. **160**: 49. Same art. Liv. Age, **210**: 279.
Lady's Chamber, The; a story. (H. B. M. Watson) New R. **12**: 473.
La Farge, John, Art of. (C. Waern) Atlan. **75**: 690. — R. of Rs. (N. Y.) **11**: 535.
Lafayette, Marquis de, as a Free-Mason. (A. Jordan) Am. Hist. Reg. **4**: 147.
— Bardoux's. (A. Laugel) Nation, **55**: 123, 164.
— in the American Revolution, Tower on. (C. J. Stillé) Pennsyl. M. **19**: 1. — (P. L. Ford) Nation, **60**: 222. — (D. L. Shorey) Dial (Ch.) **18**: 208.
— Silas Deane and the Coming of. (G. A. Boutwell) New Eng. M. n. s. **8**: 167.
— Visit of, to U. S. Am. Hist. Reg. **2**: 1151-1363. **3**: 1-621. **4**: 1-133.
Lafayette Formation, Age and Origin of. (E. W. Hilgard) Am. J. Sci. **143**: 389.
La Fontaine, Jean de. (J. C. Bailey) Temp. Bar, **98**: 337. Same art. Liv. Age, **199**: 67.
— Lafenestre's. (A. Laugel) Nation, **62**: 74.
Lagarde, Paul Anton de. Acad. **41**: 63. — And. R. **17**: 201. — (A. Neubauer) Ath. '92, **1**: 53. — (W. Muss-Arnolt) M. Chr. Lit. **6**: 62.
Laggard in Love, A. (M. McC. Williams) Scrib. M. **14**: 640.
Lagoa Santa. (E. F. Smith) Science, n. s. **1**: 510.
La Hogue, Battle of, 1692, Contemporary Account. (W. C. Boulter) Eng. Hist. R. **7**: 111.
Lahore and the Punjaub. (E. L. Weeks) Harper, **89**: 651.
Lailler, Jean. (S. G. Ayres) Meth. R. **54**: 776.
Laird's Daughter, The; or, a Day in the Heather. (A. Gordon) Good Words, **35**: Xmas. no., 53.
Laissez Faire, Individual and the State. (W. E. Hart) Soc. Econ. **4**: 29.
Lake of the Great Slave, The; a story. (G. Parker) Idler, **6**: 143.
Lake Basins, Origin of. (Duke of Argyll) Nature, **47**: 483. — (A. R. Wallace; H. H. Howorth) Nature, **49**: 220. — (J. Aitken; R. S. Tarr) Nature, **49**: 315. — (A. M. Hansen; T. D. La Touche) Nature, **49**: 364.
Lake Country, English. (D. N. Beach) Educa. **13**: 472, 544, 601.
— Churches in. (C. Edwardes) Temp. Bar, **109**: 267.
— Fauna of, Macpherson on. Nature, **47**: 457.
— Off Beaten Tracks in the. All the Year, **75**: 54.
— Rawnsley's Literary Associations of. Ath. '94, **2**: 182.
— Waterways of. (J. E. Marr) Geog. J. **7**: 602.
Lake Dwellers of Switzerland. (W. D. McCrackan) Arena, **6**: 40. — (A. E. Wilson) Gent. M. n. s. **48**: 570. Same art. Ecl. M. **119**: 185.
Lake Poets, Cradle of the. (W. C. Sydney) Gent. M. n. s. **51**: 590. Same art. Liv. Age, **200**: 154. Same art. Ecl. M. **122**: 119.
— in 1823. Bookworm, **3**: 41.
Lake Region of America, Ancient. (J. Richardson) Harper, **84**: 681.
Lake St. John Country. (H. Van Dyke) Scrib. M. **18**: 291.
Lake Simcoe Lore. (H. Scadding) Canad. M. **6**: 537.
Lake Yacht Racing Association. (P. S. Peer) Outing, **26**: 315.
Lakeland, Three Days in. All the Year, **73**: 346.
Lakeland Once More; a poem. (W. Watson) Spec. **72**: 132.
Lakes, Disappearance of in Minnesota and Dakota. Garden & F. **8**: 482.
— English, Bathymetrical Survey of. With Maps. (H. R. Mill) Geog. J. **6**: 46, 135.
— — Survey of. (H. R. Mill) Geog. J. **4**: 237.
— Great, of U. S. (C. Reid) Nat. Sci. **1**: 117.
— — Birth of. Science, **22**: 295.
— — Commerce of, and Ways to the Sea. (C. K. Davis) Forum, **12**: 729.
— — — Growth of. (H. C. Pearson) Eng. M. **5**: 793.
— — Cruise on Inland Seas. (E. A. Richings) Belgra. **85**: 27.
— — Currents of, Harrington on. Nature, **49**: 592.
— — From, to the Sea. (E. V. Smalley) R. of Rs. (N. Y.) **12**: 305.
— — How they were built. (J. W. Spencer) Pop. Sci. Mo. **49**: 157.
— — Transportation on. (G. Turrell) J. Pol. Econ. **4**: 243, 332, 413.
— — — and the Iron-ore Industry. (G. G. Turrell) J. Pol. Econ. **5**: 23, 110.
— Outlets to. (G. F. Wright) Nation, **55**: 217.
— of Minnesota, Formation and Deformation of. (C. W. Hall) Science, **21**: 314.
Lakin Family, The. (S. A. Green) N. E. Reg. **48**: 444.
Lally, T. A., Count, Visit of, to England, in 1745. (F. Dixon) Eng. Hist. R. **8**: 284.
Lalo, Edouard. Acad. **41**: 454.
La Luzerne, Chevalier de. Letter to Jefferson, 1781. M. Am. Hist. **29**: 381.
Lamaism and its Sects. (L. A. Waddell) Asia. R. **17**: 137.
— Eucharist of. (L. A. Waddell) Asia. R. **17**: 379.
Lamar, L. Q. C., with portrait. (W. B. Hill) Green Bag, **5**: 153. — Pub. Opin. **14**: 421. — (H. P. Judson) R. of Rs. (N. Y.) **7**: 165.
Lamarck, Chevalier de, with portrait. (W. Seton) Cath. World, **64**: 98.
Lamarckians and Charles Lyell. (W. K. Brooks) Nat. Sci. **8**: 89.
Lamartine, A., and Madame Charles. (A. Laugel) Nation, **55**: 279.
Lamb, Charles, and Mary, Unpublished Letters of. Cornh. **66**: 610. Same art. Liv. Age, **196**: 310.
— Elia, in Secondary Schools. (G. L. Deering) School & C. **1**: 229.
— Library of. (E. D. North) Chr. Un. **45**: 588, 641.
— Lines to Sara and her Samuel. Ath. '94, **2**: 318.
— Two Views of. (E. M. de Vogüé) Chaut. **15**: 199.
— Webster, and Swinburne. (W. Archer) New R. **8**: 96.
Lamb, Mrs. Martha J. (D. Van Pelt) M. Am. Hist. **29**: 126.
Lamb that hath been slain. (J. L. Fonda) Bib. World, **4**: 94.
Lambert, Johann H. (H. Griffing) Philos. R. **2**: 54.
Lambert, Thomas Ricker, Memoir of. (J. W. Dean) N. E. Reg. **47**: 293.
Lambeth Faience. (W. H. Edwards) M. of Art, **2**: 39.
Lambeth Palace. (J. G. Paget) Am. Arch. **42**: 124. — (J. Cave-Browne) Good Words, **36**: 696, 765. — (S. W. Kershaw) M. of Art, **3**: 34, 43.
— Library of. (W. Roberts) Bookworm, **1**: 69.

Lambeth Poisoning Case. Green Bag, **5**: 75.
Lambing-time. Spec. **74**: 646.
Lambs, Motherless. (W. Botham) Sund. M. **24**: 536.
Lamennais, H. F. R. de. (G. J. Harney) Open Court, **5**: 2959. — (W. K. Firminger) Econ. R. **6**: 29.
Lament, A; a poem. (J. R. Robinson) Westm. **143**: 435.
Lamont, Daniel Scott. (C. Robinson) Un. Serv. (Phila.) **11**: 328.
Lamoureux, Charles, and his Orchestra in London. Sat. R. **81**: 395.
Lamp, Story of the. All the Year, **76**: 107.
Lamp of Psyche, The. (Edith Wharton) Scrib. M. **18**: 418.
Lampman, Glance at. (A. J. Stringer) Canad. M. **2**: 545.
Lampreys of the Severn and the Teme. (C. Parkinson) Longm. **19**: 638.
Lamps, American. (R. Riordan) M. of Art, **8**: 73, suppl.
— in Old Times. (H. M. Beal) Bost. **3**: 447.
Lancashire and the Cotton Duties. (W. Tattersall) Fortn. **65**: 291.
— and Yorkshire, Nomenclature in. Walford's Antiq. **4**: 69.
— Hand Loom Weavers, The Last. (E. W. Abram) Leis. Hour, **42**: 737.
— History of, Fishwick's. Sat. R. **79**: 76.
— in 1892. (J. C. Fielden) Blackw. **152**: 284.
— Prospective Decline of. (W. A. Abram) Blackw **152**: 1.
— — The Remedy for. (H. S. Hallett) Blackw. **152**: 348.
Lancaster, Edmund, Earl of. (W. E. Rhodes) Eng. Hist. R. **10**: 1, 209.
Land and the Land Question, Bibliography of Literature dealing with. (T. E. Will) Arena, **16**: 380.
— English Commons and Forests. Spec. **72**: 303.
— Farmer and the. (W. D. McCrackan) Arena, **9**: 625.
— Folk-. (P. Vinogradoff) Eng. Hist. R. **8**: 1.
— Held out of Use. (J. W. Bengough) No. Am. **158**: 512.
— How to attract Capital to. (Lord Vernon) 19th Cent. **33**: 1028.
— in England; Considerations for Small Holders. (Earl Percy) National, **25**: 647.
— — Laborer and. (J. Shortrede) New R. **6**: 362. — (Lord Thring; W. E. Bear; Mrs. S. Batson) 19th Cent. **31**: 150.
— — Pottering with Agriculture. (P. A. Graham) New R. **13**: 443.
— — Settlement of Landed Property. (Lord Vernon) 19th Cent. **31**: 352.
— — The Squirearchy and the Statute Book. Quar. **180**: 231.
— — Tenure of: Organization of Real Credit. (H. de F. Montgomery) National, **20**: 241.
— — — The Words *solinum* and *solanda*. (J. H. Round) Eng. Hist. R. **7**: 708.
— in France and Belgium, Tenure of, Early, Brutails and Errera on. (F. W. Maitland) Eng. Hist. R. **7**: 748.
— in Great Britain, New Valuation Act. (S. B. Armour) Jurid. R. **8**: 55.
— — Reform in. (R. M. Ferguson) Contemp. **64**: 509.
— in the Highlands. Should Government legislate? (W. C. MacKenzie) Westm. **145**: 301.
— in Wales. Sat. R. **78**: 317.
— — Question of. Spec. **71**: 539.
Land in Wales, Royal Commission on. (Lord Stanley of Alderley) National, **21**: 827.
— Law of. (W. A. McClean) Green Bag, **6**: 288, 449.
— Liquor and Labor. Fortn. **64**: 12.
— Making of. (W. H. Wheeler) Longm. **26**: 422.
— Monopoly in, Evils of. (B. W. Williams) Arena, **16**: 538.
— Nationalization of. (C. M. Bailhache) Westm. **137**: 513.
— Ownership of, Attractiveness of. Spec. **69**: 708.
— — Principles of. (H. H. L. Bellot) Westm. **141**: 10.
— Private Property in. (M. M. Trumbull) Open Court, **3**: 1758.
— Property in. Are we becoming a Homeless Nation? (J. O. Yeiser) Arena, **16**: 286.
— — Origin and Evolution of. (H. H. L. Bellot) Westm. **140**: 644. Same art. Ecl. M. **122**: 151.
— Public. *See* Public Land.
— Question of. (E. B. Brokaw and others) Arena, **10**: 622.
— — and the Single Tax. (S. B. Riggen) Arena, **10**: 332.
— — Daylight on. (E. Withy) Westm. **145**: 123.
— — First Principles of. (L. F. Post) Arena, **9**: 758.
— — George and Spencer on. (J. Armsden) Westm. **144**: 317.
— — Immigration and. (C. J. Buell) Arena, **10**: 807.
— — Policy of Thorough. (W. T. Thomson) Westm. **142**: 381.
— — Pseudo Individualism. (A. Withy) Westm. **142**: 485.
— Re-peopling the. (H. W. Wolff) Contemp. **67**: 653.
— Taxation of, in Japan. (S. Sugiyama) Gunton's M. **11**: 6.
— Tenure of, among the Negroes. (P. Dillingham) Yale R. **5**: 190.
— — Curiosities of. (R. A. Bennett) Time, **14**: 302.
— — How to multiply Small Holdings. (H. E. Moore) 19th Cent. **36**: 947.
— — in England and Scotland. (R. Campbell) Law Q. **1**: 175, 400. **2**: 166.
— — in Tuscany. (J. Ross) Macmil. **71**: 195. Same art. Liv. Age, **204**: 380.
— — Legal Execution and. (E. Jenks) Eng. Hist. R. **8**: 417.
— Transfer of. (H. W. Elphinstone) Law Q. **2**: 12.
— — Reform in. (C. F. Libby) Am. Law R. **28**: 196.
— Underground Waste of. (H. B. Woodward) Nat. Sci. **2**: 124.
— Value of, How to find. (W. C. Albro) Open Court, **3**: 1781.
— Waste and Gain of the Dry Land. Pop. Sci. Mo. **41**: 403.
Land and Sea; ballade. (E. Leith) Argosy, **58**: 88.
Land of Counterpane; a poem. (R. L. Stevenson) M. of Art, **7**: 367.
Land of Lost Delights. (D. J. Robertson) Longm. **22**: 151.
Land of Promise; a poem. (F. E. Coates) Cosmopol. **18**: 406.
Land of the Sun. (F. C. Tiernan) Cath. World, **56**: 531 — **57**: 832.
Land Bank (Massachusetts) of 1740, Alphabetical List of the Partners in. (A. M. Davis) N. E. Reg. **50**: 187, 308.
Land Deeds, Registration of. (T. Key) Law Q. **2**: 324. — (J. Erskine) Jurid. R. **7**: 162. — (E. K. Blyth) Law Q. **12**: 354.
Land Law of Scotland. (E. Jenks) Law Q. **12**: 155.
Land Lease System, Groningen. (J. H. Gore) Gunton's M. **10**: 440.
— in India. (J. W. MacDougall) Jurid. R. **8**: 167.

Land Owners, London's Great. Chamb. J. **73**: 285. Same art. Liv. Age, **210**: 61.
Land System of India, Baden-Powell on. Ath. '92, **2**: 770.—Sat. R. **74**: 256.
— of Russia: Cause of the Famine. (W. C. Edgar) Forum, **13**: 575.
Land Systems of Australasia. (A. Duckworth) Econ. J. **5**: 76.
— — Epps on. (D. MacG. Means) Nation, **60**: 186.
Land Tax. Blackw. **156**: 118.—Sat. R. **78**: 297.
Land Titles in Australia, Registry of. (E. Atkinson) Cent. **21**: 586.
— in England, Registration or Simplification of. (H. Greenwood) Law Q. **6**: 144.
Landais, Pierre de. (H. D. Smith) Un. Serv. (Phila.) **8**: 32.
Landed Gentry, Burke's, New Edition of. Ath. '94, **1**: 735.
Landed Proprietor, A; a poem. (C. Burke) Argosy, **58**: 288.
Landelle, Charles. (A. Trumble) Mo. Illust. **4**: 94.
Landes, A Day in the. (C. Edwardes) Chamb. J. **72**: 257.
Landladies of Fiction. Chamb. J. **73**: 586. Same art. Liv. Age, **211**: 406.
Landlords, New. (E. O. Fordham) Westm. **141**: 396.
Landmarks. (C. C. Abbott) Lippinc. **57**: 128.
Landor, Walter Savage. (G. Saintsbury) Macmil. **67**: 267. Same Art. Liv. Age, **196**: 746.—(A. C. Benson) National, **28**: 524.—(J. Fyvie) Temp. Bar, **105**: 253. Same art. Liv. Age, **206**: 3.
— Imaginary Conversations, Crump's ed. (M. B. Anderson) Dial (Ch.) **13**: 71.—Sat. R. **74**: 279.
Landscape at the National Gallery. (J. Brett) Fortn. **63**: 623.
— Hamerton on. (R. A. M. Stevenson) M. of Art, **8**: 259.
— in Art. (W. Bayliss) M. of Art, **5**: 8.
— in Fiction. (W. W. Fenn) M. of Art, **3**: 318.
— New Facts in. (R. Jefferies) M. of Art, **5**: 470.
— Out of Doors with the Artists. (C. M. Fairbanks) Chaut. **19**: 523.
— Painter's Weather. (W. W. Fenn) M. of Art, **12**: 355.
— Self-painted Pictures. (F. M. Brown) M. of Art, **12**: 184.
— Some Thoughts on. (N. W. Williams) Westm. **144**: 409. Same art. Ecl. M. **125**: 742.
See below, Landscape Painting.
Landscape Art in the Military Parks. (C. S. Sargent) Garden & F. **8**: 381.
Landscape by Constable; a story. (F. M. Wilson) Harper, **87**: 455.
Landscape Gardening. Garden & F. **5**: 205-433.—(W. Robinson) Garden & F. **5**: 467.—(M. G. Van Rensselaer) Garden & F. **6**: 229.—(C. S. Sargent) Garden & F. **8**: 361.—(C. Eliot) Garden & F. **9**: 132.—(B. Day) M. of Art, **5**: 464. **6**: 251. **7**: 191.
— Æsthetic Value of Roads and Walks. (H. H. Caparn) Garden & F. **7**: 272.
— and Architecture. (C. S. Sargent) Garden & F. **6**: 73.
— and the Harlem Speedway. (C. S. Sargent) Garden & F. **7**: 401.
— Art and Nature in. (C. S. Sargent) Garden & F. **7**: 261, 341.
— at Indian Harbor, L. I. (C. S. Sargent) Garden & F. **9**: 241.
— at Natick, Mass. (T. D. Hatfield) Garden & F. **9**: 278.
— at Newport. Garden & F. **7**: 452.
Landscape Gardening at Wellesley, Mass. (M. C. Robbins) Garden & F. **5**: 338.
— Blomfield and Thomas on. Sat. R. **73**: 191.
— Competitive Examination for. (C. S. Sargent) Garden & F. **9**: 231.
— Composition in. (H. H. Caparn) Garden & F. **6**: 522.
— Debt of America to A. J. Downing. (C. S. Sargent) Garden & F. **8**: 211.
— Doing too much. (C. S. Sargent) Garden & F. **8**: 291, 311.
— for Small Places. (S. W. Parsons, jr.) Chr. Un. **45**: 881, 1147.
— for Women. Garden & F. **5**: 482.
— Formal. Does it conflict with Natural Style? (C. S. Sargent) Garden & F. **6**: 119.
— — Some Uses of. (C. S. Sargent) Garden & F. **6**: 161.
— — Where it can be used to Advantage. (C. S. Sargent) Garden & F. **6**: 129.
— Imagination in. (M. C. Robbins) Garden & F. **7**: 492.
— in America, German View of. Garden & F. **7**: 41.
— in Japan, Conder on. Garden & F. **6**: 418. **7**: 179.
— in Public Parks. (C. S. Sargent) Garden & F. **6**: 191.
— in Small Grounds. (C. S. Sargent) Garden & F. **9**: 341.
— Japanese, at the World's Fair. (M. C. Robbins) Garden & F. **6**: 302.
— Key-note in. (C. S. Sargent) Garden & F. **6**: 531.
— Nature and the Rich. (C. S. Sargent) Garden & F. **7**: 251.
— Necessity of Planning. (C. Eliot) Garden & F. **9**: 342.
— Plans for. Garden & F. **5**: 13.
— — for Home Grounds. (C. S. Sargent) Garden & F. **8**: 241.
— Privacy in Suburban Life. (C. S. Sargent) Garden & F. **9**: 271, 309, 312.
— School-grounds. (C. S. Sargent) Garden & F. **8**: 491.
— Sculpture in. (C. S. Sargent) Garden & F. **8**: 111.
— Simplicity in. Garden & F. **5**: 313.
— Small Seashore Places. (C. S. Sargent) Garden & F. **8**: 341.
— Utility and Landscape. (Sylvester Baxter) Garden & F. **8**: 2.
— Vegetable Sculpture in China. (A. B. Westland) Garden & F. **7**: 92.
— What shall we plant? (C. S. Sargent) Garden & F. **6**: 471.
— Where it should begin. (H. A. Capen) Garden & F. **7**: 62.
Landscape Painters, English, Country-sides of. (F. Wedmore) Time, **1**: 479.
Landscape Painting, Choice of Subjects in. M. of Arts, **4**: 481.
— Fact in. (W. W. Fenn) M. of Art, **4**: 393.
— in the Pictures of the Old Masters. M. of Art, **3**: 344.
— in the Studio. (A. Mackworth) M. of Art, **9**: 255.
— Modern. (L. J. Block) Open Court, **6**: 3167.
— Pleasures of. (W. W. Fenn) M. of Art, **4**: 118.
— Poetry in. (J. E. Hodgson) M. of Art, **18**: 9.
Landscape Work and Architecture. (D. Vaux) Engin. M. **11**: 1071.
Landscapes with Figures. (J. K. Paulding) Atlan. **78**: 752.
Landseer, Sir Edwin. (J. G. Waring) Munsey, **11**: 166.
— Lions in Trafalgar Square. (R. Jefferies) Longm. **19**: 528.

Landslide at Gohna, 1894. Geog. J. 4: 162. — Nature, 50: 231.
— at Sandgate, Eng., 1893. (J. F. Blake) Nature, 47: 467. — (A. Irving) Nature, 47: 581.
Landslips. All the Year, 72: 324. Same art. Liv. Age, 197: 697.
Lane, Richard James. M. of Art, 4: 431.
Lane, William, Founder of New Australia. (A. J. Rose-Soley) Westm. 140: 523.
Lang, Andrew, with portrait. Bk. Buyer, 7: 369. — With portrait. Bk. News, 8: 33. — (A. Macdonell) Bookman, 3: 114. — (B. Matthews) Cent. 25: 375.
— and Criticism. Sat. R. 82: 32.
— and the Ethics of Reprinting. Critic, 29: 30, 123.
— as a Poet. (W. Canton) Bookman, 2: 24.
— Cockneydom. (Rob't Buchanan) Univ. R. 4: 71.
— Literary Recollections by. Idler, 1: 21.
— Poetry of. (G. R. Tomson) Acad. 45: 451.
— Portraits of. McClure, 2: 341.
— Yellow Fairy Book. Sat. R. 78: 413.
Lang, B. J. (W. F. Apthorp) Music, 4: 347.
Lang, Dr. Marshall, at Home. Sund. M. 24: 167.
Langbridge, Frederic. Scales of Heaven. Acad. 50: 456.
Langdale, Charles. (W. J. Amherst) Dub. R. 111: 395. 113: 515, 836.
Lange, Julius Henrik. (E. Gosse) Ath. '96, 2: 362.
Langham Sketching Club. Art J. 47: 1, 54.
Langland, W., what he saw. (Kate M. Warren) Good Words, 36: 306.
Langsyne. (A. H. M. Macleod) Good Words, 36: Xmas no., 58.
Language. (E. P. Powell) Open Court, 1: 684, 750.
— Analysis of. (F. M. Müller) Open Court, 3: 2016.
— and Brain Disease. (H. T. Pershing) Pop. Sci. Mo. 41: 775.
— and Ethnology, Sciences of. (G. W. Leitner) Asia. R. 9: 348.
— and Literature, their Connection in Education. (T. R. Price) Educa. R. 11: 12.
— and Man. (H. Hale) Am. Antiq. 15: 15–212.
— and Thought. (C. N. Barham) Westm. 143: 437. Same art. Ecl. M. 124: 721. — (F. M. Müller) Monist, 1: 572.
— — Identity of. (F. M. Müller) Open Court, 1: 281, 309.
— — F. M. Müller on. (G. J. Romanes) Monist, 2: 56.
— as a Fine Art. (F. B. Cowgill) Meth. R. 56: 940.
— as a Test of Mental Capacity. (H. Hale) Anthrop. J. 21: 413.
— Clark on. (D. K. Dodge) Dial (Ch.) 16: 178.
— Cosmopolitan, Prospects and Practicability of. (M. Q. Holyoake) Cosmopol. 14: 19.
— Development of. (J. E. Werren) N. Church R. 2: 198.
— Diversity of, and National Unity. (V. Wilker) Meth. R. 53: 576.
— Effect of Nomad Life on Growth of. (Joseph Edkins) Asia. R. 12: 288.
— Evolution of. (M. L. Johnson) Westm. 145: 557. Same art. Ecl. M. 127: 8.
— Festal Origin of. (J. Donovan) Mind, 17: 325.
— How to learn a. (J. S. Blackie) R. of Rs. (N. Y.) 6: 51.
— — in Six Months. (W. T. Stead) R. of Rs. (N. Y.) 5: 701.
— in Elementary Schools. (J. Ogden) Educa. 15: 363.
— Learning of, Preliminary Report on. (H. T. Lukens) Pedagog. Sem. 3: 424.
— Lesson taught by Science of. (F. M. Müller) Open Court, 3: 2030.
Language, Music of, as Illustrated in Shakespeare's Venus and Adonis. (S. E. Bengough) Poet-Lore, 4: 562.
— No Mystery in. (F. M. Müller) Open Court, 3: 1991.
— of Childhood. (F. Tracy) Am. J. Psychol. 6: 107.
— or Languages. (E. P. Powell) Educa. 16: 65.
— Origin of. (L. Noire) Open Court, 4: 2221–2266.
— Progress in, with Special Reference to English, Jespersen's. (O. F. Emerson) School R. 4: 633.
— Simplicity of. (F. M. Müller) Open Court, 1: 225, 253.
— Study of Foreign, in Grammar Schools. (J. Tetlow) Educa. R. 7: 111.
— Thought without Words. (F. Galton and others) Open Court, 1: 441, 472, 498.
— A Universal. (J. P. Mahaffy) 19th Cent. 40: 782. Same art. Liv. Age, 211: 675.
— The Universal. Macmil. 65: 372.
— *versus* Literature at Oxford. (J. C. Collins) 19th Cent. 37: 290.
— Volapük, The Universal. Open Court, 1: 523.
Language Studies, Limitation of, to Secondary Schools. (D. W. Abercrombie) School R. 1: 455.
Languages, Learning of. (P. G. Hamerton) Forum, 13: 219. — Chamb. J. 72: 236.
— Method of Teaching. (J. S. Blackie) Contemp. 67: 278. Same art. Liv. Age, 205: 232.
— Modern, as a Mental Discipline. (O. Heller) Educa. 13: 102.
— — Instruction in, Reform in. (J. J. Findlay) Educa. R. 5: 334.
— — Mass. Teachers' Association on. (C. H. Grandgent; A. N. Van Daell; C. E. Fay) Acad. 6: 562.
— — Teaching of, New Method of. Educa. R. 4: 80. — (W. Victor) Educa. R. 6: 351.
— Teaching of, Gouin's System of. (W. T. Stead) R. of Rs. (N. Y.) 7: 193.
Langue d'Oc, Intellectual Awakening of. (T. Stanton) Monist, 2: 95.
Languedoc, Lagoons of. (M. B. Edwards) Time, 23: 1048.
Lanier, Sidney. (C. Lanier) Chaut. 21: 403. — (A. Allen) Mid-Cont. 6: 81. — (H. Wilson) So. M. 2: 11.
— Letters of. (W. R. Thayer) Atlan. 74: 14, 181.
— Poems. Ed. by Calloway. (W. M. Baskervill) Dial (Ch.) 18: 299.
Lansdowne House. (E. L. Didier) Chaut. 18: 62.
Lantara, Simon Mathurin. (A. E. Hake) M. of Art, 8: 274.
Lantern, Magic, in the School. (W. F. C. Morsell) Educa. 13: 558. *See* Magic Lantern.
Lanty Riordan's Red Light; a story. (R. M. Craig) Temp. Bar, 107: 570. Same art. Ecl. M. 126: 691.
Laos States, Upper Siam. (E. Satow) J. Soc. Arts, 40: 182.
Lao-Tsze, a Chinese Mystic. (J. T. Bixby) Arena, 7: 75. — Temp. Bar, 95: 48.
— Tao-teh-king of. Open Court, 10: 5146.
Lapham, Increase A., with portrait. Am. Antiq. 15: 119.
Laplace, P. S., Eulogy, on, with portrait. (Baron Fourier) Pop. Astron. 3: 1.
Lapland. (Wm. C. Preston) Good Words, 33: 523. — (W. V. Taylor) Sund. M. 22: 447.
— Angling Experiences. (G. Lindesay) Blackw. 155: 416. Same art. Liv. Age, 201: 117.
— Nomads of the North. (C. J. C. Hyne) Outing, 23: 289.
— Two Visits to. (H. H. Boyesen) Cosmopol. 13: 15.
La Plata, British Expedition to 1806-7. (J. W. Fortescue) Macmil. 71: 471. Same art. Liv. Age, 205: 429.

La Plata, Hudson's Naturalist in. (R. Lydekker) Nat. Sci. 1: 144. — (A. R. Wallace) Nature, 45: 553.
La Plata Museum. (R. Lydekker) Nat. Sci. 4: 27, 116.
Lapwing's Artifice, The. Chamb. J. 71: 225.
La Ramée, Louisa de. Gent. M. n. s. 57: 322.
— Toxin; a sketch. Sat. R. 80: 661.
Laramie Formation, Notice of New Reptiles from. (O. C. Marsh) Am. J. Sci. 143: 449.
Laramie Mammals and Horned Dinosaurs, Where to find. (J. B. Hatcher) Am. Natural. 30: 112.
Larceny Law, A Moot Point in. (T. W. Marshall) Jurid. R. 8: 65.
Larch, Western. (C. S. Sargent) Garden & F. 9: 491.
Larchmont, N. Y. (R. Stockton) Munsey, 7: 517.
Larcom, Lucy, with portrait. Bk. News, 5: 399. — Critic, 22: 258. — (J. L. Onderdonk) Dial (Ch.) 14: 267.
— Addison's Life of. (J. W. Chadwick) Nation, 60: 289.
Lark, Song of. (I. G. Tompkins) Music, 10: 340, 451.
La Rochefoucauld. (A. Laugel) Nation, 61: 147.
La Rochejaquelein, Madame de. (Mrs. A. Crosse) Temp. Bar, 105: 17. Same art. Ecl. M. 124: 795. Same art. Liv. Age, 205: 751.
Larrabee, William, Will of, 1691-92. (W. B. Trask) N. E. Reg. 50: 40.
Larry. Overland, n. s. 22: 431.
Larunda; a poem. (K. Carter) M. of Art, 10: 427.
La Salette, Our Quinzaine at. (A. P. McIlvaine) Atlan. 74: 527.
La Salle, R. C., Girouard on. (E. G. Mason) Dial (Ch.) 16: 52.
Las Casas, Bartholomew, and Democracy. (C. C. Starbuck) New World, 5: 305.
Las' Furrer, Th'; a story. (E. Higginson) Overland, n. s. 19: 432.
Lassalle, Ferdinand, Episode in Life of. (M. Waters) Univ. R. 7: 521.
— Socialism of. (G. B. Dibblee) Econ. R. 1: 497.
Last Drink, The; a story. (A. E. Abbott) Idler, 5: 61.
Last Drive, The. (L. Q. Couch) Eng. Illust. 13: 497.
Last Hours, Stories of. (Maj. W. G. Nelson) Time, 21: 89.
Last Joke of Muley Hassan. (W. A. Curtis) Overland, n. s. 24: 387.
Last Mass; a reminiscence. (Maurus Jokai) Cosmopol. 20: 505.
Last of the First. (A. M. Ewell) Atlan. 78: 782.
Last of the Peplows. (G. B. Burgin) Chamb. J. 70: 140. Same art. Liv. Age, 197: 685.
Last of the Thrustons, The; a story. (Mrs. Macquoid) Temp. Bar, 102: 55.
Last of the Vampires; a story. (P. Robinson) Contemp. 63: 410. Same art. Ecl. M. 120: 558. Same art. Liv. Age, 197: 296.
Last Parade; a poem. (J. L. Molloy) Temp. Bar, 105: 191.
Last Resort, A. (Ada E. Ferris) Overland, n. s. 23: 76.
Last Ride together, The. (R. H. Davis) Scrib. M. 20: 705.
Last Saturday in August, The; a story. Argosy, 60: 362.
Last Scene, A; a story. (A. Agrell) New R. 9: 268.
Last Sonnet, The, of Prinzivalle di Cembino; a story. (T. Wharton) Harper, 92: 126.
Last Straw, The; a story. (Mrs. Andrew Dean) Temp. Bar, 107: 370.
Last that was First, The. (Julia M. Lippmann) Overland, n. s. 23: 317.
Latas, Dionysios. (E. M. Edmonds) Acad. 46: 151.
Late in Life; a novel. (A. Perrin) Belgra. 86: 91-421. 87: 92-430. 88: 94-323.
Late Miss Crofton, The. (Mrs. Newman) Time, 2: 649.
Late Mr. Lympet; a story. All the Year, 74: 108.
Late Mr. Watkins of Georgia. (J. C. Harris) Lippinc. 53: 422.
Late Mrs. Vernon, The; a story. (A. Moberly) All the Year, 71: 67-331.
Late Returning, The; a story. (Gertrude Hall) Cosmopol. 18: 663.
Late War in Europe, The; a story. (H. P. Robinson) Scrib. M. 18: 542.
La Thangue, Henry Herbert. (J. S. Little) Art J. 45: 169.
Latin Inscriptions, Introduction to the Study of, Egbert's. (F. E. Rockwood) School R. 4: 555.
Latin Language, and Greek in the Higher Schools of Germany. (J. E. Russell) School R. 4: 664.
— Course in, Difficulties and Discouragements in the Early Stages of the. (E. J. Goodwin) School R. 4: 80.
— Elementary, Old and New Methods of Teaching. (B. L. D'Ooge) Educa. R. 12: 368.
— — Reading at Sight in Teaching. (C. E. Bennett) Educa. R. 12: 269.
— in the Secondary School. (C. E. Bennett) School R. 1: 269.
— Preparatory Work in. (E. T. Merrill) School R. 1: 408.
— Reading Matter in, for Beginners. (C. W. Super) School & C. 1: 321.
— Six Years' Course. (A. F. West) School R. 3: 321. — (A. F. Nightingale) School R. 3: 335. — (W. G. Hale) School R. 3: 334.
— Study of, Elementary, Hints for Teachers in. (J. C. Rolfe) Acad. (Syr.) 7: 96.
— — in High School. (J. H. Harris) School R. 2: 356. — (F. W. Kelsey) Educa. R. 8: 25. — Reply. (H. S. Vaile) Educa. R. 8: 294.
— — Report of the Committee of Twelve of the American Philological Association on. School R. 4: 472.
— Subjunctive in, Comparative Clause in. (W. G. Hale) Am. J. Philol. 13: 62.
— Syllabus of Instruction in. (W. C. Collar) School R. 2: 1.
— Teaching of. (W. C. Collar) School & C. 1: 74-588.
— What shall we teach in and how shall we teach? (W. C. Collar) School R. 3: 1.
Latin Lessons for Beginners, Coy's. (J. C. Grant) School R. 4: 467.
Latin Lexicography, Contribution to. (C. Knapp) Am. J. Philol. 16: 52.
Latin Literature, History of, Mackail's. Sat. R. 80: 552.
Latin Play. Phormio at Harvard. (F. G. Ireland) Educa. R. 8: 54.
Latin Poetry, Early. (R. Y. Tyrrell) Atlan. 73: 505.
— of the Cæsarean Epoch. Quar. 178: 129.
— of the Decline. Quar. 179: 117.
— Tyrrell's. Sat. R. 80: 509. — (W. H. Johnson) Dial (Ch.) 18: 267. — (W. Everett) Nation, 60: 388.
Latin Prose and Verse, Peck's Roman Life in. (M. H. Morgan) Nation, 60: 283.
Latin Versification, Modern. Eng. R. 17: 33.
Latini, Brunetto; the Teacher of Dante. (N. H. Dole) Bach. of Arts, 1: 721.
Latitude and Longitude, Determination of, by Photography. (C. Runge) Nature, 50: 102.
— by Elongation. (O. J. Klotz) Pop. Astron. 3: 199.
— Variation of. (J. K. Rees) Science, n. s. 1: 561. — (E. Doolittle) Pop. Astron. 3: 105.

Latitude, Variation of, Laplace on. (A. B. Hancock) Pop. Astron. **2**: 349.
— Variations of. (C. L. Doolittle) Nature, **48**: 451.
Latitude Work, German Variation of. (H. Jacoby) Astron. **11**: 471.
La Tour, C., and Acadia in the Suffolk Deeds. (A. E. Allaben) M. Am. Hist. **29**: 108.
La Tour, Fort, Site of. (W. F. Ganong) Nat'l M. (N. Y. '91) **18**: 242.
La Tour D'Auvergne, Princess de, at Jerusalem. (O. R. Seward) Cath. World, **62**: 351.
La Tour-Landry, Sir Geoffrey de, Book of. (A. B. Stone) Lippinc. **56**: 100.
— Quaint Book of Advice to Girls. (H. L. Reed) Chaut. **19**: 219.
La Toussaint; a story. (S. J. Weyman) McClure, **4**: 353.
La Trappe, Monastery at. (C. Smith) Canad. M. **3**: 453.
Laud, William, Simpkinson's Life of. (R. C. Browne) Acad. **47**: 417. — Spec. **74**: 395. — Church Q. **40**: 80. — Sat. R. **79**: 355. — Church Q. **40**: 63.— (Goldwin Smith) Nation, **60**: 346. — Sat. R. **77**: 338. — Ath. '**94**, **1**: 829.
— Unpublished Letter of. (W. H. Hutton) Eng. Hist. R. **7**: 715.
Lauder, Sir Thomas D., and the Royal Scottish Academy. Art J. **46**: 271.
Lauder, Wm. Masenius, and Milton. (J. C. H. Flood) Walford's Antiq. **3**: 221, 300.
Laughter, Chat about. All the Year, **75**: 397.
— of Dogs. (Vicomte d'Aiglun) Pop. Sci. Mo. **50**: 89.
— Philosophy of. (C. Whibley) M. of Art, **13**: 28.
— Why we Laugh. (C. Mélinand) Chaut. **21**: 195.
Laun, Henri van. Ath. '**96**, **1**: 120.
Launay, Count de. Cornh. **69**: 538.
Laureateship, The. Critic, **21**: 255–281.
See Poet Laureate.
Laurel; Kalmia-cuneata. (C. S. Sargent) Garden & F. **8**: 434.
Laurels. Garden & F. **5**: 349.
— Islay. Garden & F. **5**: 469.
Laurens, Jean Paul. (E. F. S. Pattison) M. of Art, **7**: 51.
Laurens, Fort. (R. Shackelton, jr.) Nat'l M. (N. Y. '91) **16**: 398.
Laurentian and Huronian, Relations of, on the North Side of Lake Huron. (A. E. Barlow) Am. J. Sci. **144**: 236.
— Further Contribution to our Knowledge of. (F. D. Adams) Am. J. Sci. **150**: 58.
Laurie, Annie. *See* Annie Laurie.
Laurie, S. S. (F. Watson) Educa. R. **9**: 1. — With portrait. School R. **2**: 465.
Laurier, Wilfrid. (J. A. Barron) Canad. M. **6**: 237.— With portrait. (W. B. Wallace) R. of Rs. (N. Y.) **10**: 158.
Lausanne; a Sunny Corner of Europe. All the Year, **75**: 174.
Lauth; a story. (F. Norris) Overland, n. s. **21**: 241.
Lauzun, A. L., Duc de, and the Private Court of Louis XV. (Y. Blaze de Bury) Fortn. **63**: 949.
Lava Beds at Meriden, Conn., Quarries in. (W. M. Davis) Am. J. Sci. **151**: 1.
— In the. (J. H. Hamilton) Overland, n. s. **24**: 97.
Lavalette, Count Marie Chamans. Memoirs. Sat. R. **82**: 20.
Lavas of Mount Ingalls, Cal. (H. W. Turner) Am. J. Sci. **144**: 455.
Lavater, Study of. (A. O. Commelin) Open Court, **4**: 2364.
Lavatories, Medieval. Reliquary, **32**: 193.
Laveleye, Emile de. (E. Mahaim) Econ. J. **2**: 193. — (P. Fredericq) Ath. '**92**, **1**: 115.
Lavender, Sweet. Chamb. J. **71**: 511.
La Verna Monastery, A Visit to. (E. Bale) M. of Art, **18**: 24.
Lavigerie, Charles M. A., Cardinal. And. R. **18**: 646.
— With portrait. (J. R. Slattery) Cath. World, **56**: 593.
— Work in North Africa. (W. Sharp) Atlan. **74**: 214.
Lavisse, Ernest, as a Historian. (H. M. Stephens) Acad. **46**: 250, (S. Reinach) 282.
— The Students' Academician. Atlan. **72**: 573.
Lavoisier, Antoine-Laurent. (T. E. Thorpe) Liv. Age, **188**: 3.
Law, William. Sat. R. **75**: 301. — Church Q. **37**: 193.
Law, The, and the Boy. (I. E. Crouch) Educa. **13**: 98.
— and Gospel. (E. V. Gerhart) Ref. Q. **41**: 5.
— and Laughter. (E. J. Hardy) Argosy, **57**: 375.
— and the Lawyers. (W. M. Thompson) Time, **22**: 159.
— — Disgusted Layman's Views of. Green Bag, **6**: 403.
— — My Impressions of. (R. D. Doyle) Southern M. **4**: 245.
— and Legislation. (J. W. Greene) Am. J. Soc. Sci. no. **34**: 117. — (John F. Dillon) Am. Law R. **26**: 658.
— and Morality. (H. Teich Teichmuller) Am. Law R. **28**: 510.
— and Order Leagues, Work of. Lend a H. **12**: 295.
— and Order Movement and the Citizen. (A. P. Wilder) Lend a H. **12**: 437.
— and Public Opinion as Factors in Social Control. (E. A. Ross) Am. J. Sociol. **1**: 753.
— Anglo-Saxon. (F. Pollock) Eng. Hist. R. **8**: 239.
— Are Judges above the? (H. H. L. Bellot) Westm. **145**: 237.
— as a Profession. National, **24**: 49.
— Bench and Bar of Chicago. (H. L. Conard) M. West. Hist. **12**: 563, 672. **13**: 114-615.
— Cases as the Original Sources of the. (D. A. Jones) Green Bag, **6**: 421.
— Classification of. (R. H. Curtis) Ann. Am. Acad. Pol. Sci. **4**: 738.
— — for Lawyers. (E. McClain) Am. Law R. **26**: 223.
— Codification in the U. S. (D. D. Field) Jurid. R. **1**: 18.
— — Progress of. (J. D. Wilson) Jurid. R. **3**: 97.
— Commercial, Proposed Imperial Code of. (J. D. Wilson) Jurid. R. **8**: 329.
— Common, and Civil Law. (L. E. Chittenden) Green Bag, **7**: 56.
— — Custom in. (F. A. Greer) Law Q. **9**: 153.
— — Early. (W. G. Hammond) Green Bag, **4**: 283.
— — Vocation of. (Sir F. Pollock) Law. Q. **11**: 323.
— Concept of, in Ethics. (F. C. French) Philos. R. **2**: 35.
— Constitutional, Thayer's Cases on. (S. E. Baldwin) Am. Hist. R. **1**: 163.
— Curiosities of the. (J. M. Lely) Time, **16**: 323.
— Development of, Illustrative Chapter on. (W. W. Dillson) Pop. Sci. Mo. **44**: 802.
— Early. (P. J. H. Grierson) Jurid. R. **7**: 97.
— — Study of. (G. Neilson) Jurid. R. **3**: 12.
— Economical Administration of. (S. L. Holland) Econ. R. **2**: 192.
— Education in. *See* Legal Education.
— Enforcement of, Crime and. (H. C. Vrooman) Arena, **12**: 263.

Law, Enforcement of, Voluntary Organizations for. (C. Greeley) Lend a H. 13: 138.
— English, Early History of. Ed. R. 183: 428.
— — History of. (T. C. Williams) Jurid. R. 7: 260.
— — Pollock and Maitland's History of. (M. M. Bigelow) Am. Hist. R. 1: 112. — (H. Brunner) Pol. Sci. Q. 11: 534. — (J. J. Halsey) Dial (Ch.) 20: 44.
— Ethics of. (J. T. Holmes) Green Bag, 7: 428. — (W. E. Glanville) Green Bag, 8: 209.
— Foreign, Proof of. (J. Hirschfeld) Law Q. 11: 241.
— History of, Uses of. (M. Crackanthorpe) Law Q. 12: 337.
— in England, Civil and Canon. (J. E. R. Stephens) Gent. M. n. s. 55: 585.
— Jewish, Growth of. (D. W. Amram) Green Bag, 8: 253, 298.
— Judicial Ignorance of. Soc. Econ. 8: 94.
— Language of. (W. W. Marshall) Walford's Antiq. 11: 244.
— Literature of. (E. W. Huffcut) Green Bag, 4: 52.
— Lorimer's Theory of. (A. Thomson) Jurid. R. 8: 242.
— Modern, Archaism in. (Sir F. Pollock) Law Q. 9: 271.
— Nature and Meaning of. (Sir F. Pollock) Law Q. 10: 228.
— Necessity of Allegiance to. (A. Mason) N. Church R. 2: 341.
— of the Land. (W. A. McClean) Green Bag, 4: 59–490.
— of Life; a story. (Ida Lemon) Argosy, 57: 34.
— of Nature. (J. W. Salmond) Law Q. 11: 120.
— Penological, Reforms in. (P. Edwards) Green Bag, 4: 386.
— Positive, and other Laws; a Comparison and Contrast. (C. M. Platt) Pol. Sci. Q. 9: 53.
— Preparation for the Study and Practice of. (C. F. Thwing) Educa. 14: 321, 400.
— Profession of. Has it been commercialized? (W. B. Hornblower) Forum, 18: 679.
— — Influence of. (C. M. Depew) Am. M. Civics, 9: 392.
— — Position and Prospects of. (E. S. Roscoe) Law Q. 1: 314.
— Professional Ideal in, True. (J. F. Dillon) Am. Law R. 28: 671.
— Reign of. (F. J. Kingsbury) Am. J. Soc. Sci. 32: ix.
— Reminiscences of Bench and Bar in Canada. (C. A. Durand) Canad. M. 5: 314.
— Romance of. (R. T. Barton) Green Bag, 4: 125.
— Specialism in. (Sir F. H. Jeune) Law Q. 11: 11.
— State of the Law. (S. A. T. Rowlatt) National, 28: 262.
— Treatises on, Modern. (F. H. Bacon) Am. Law R. 29: 688.
— Uncertainty of the. Open Court, 2: 1238.
— Universality of. (H. Wood) Arena, 5: 199.
— Unjust Expense of. Sat. R. 73: 144.
— What is? (T. D. Marshall) Am. Law R. 27: 540.
— Where to find the. (P. Edwards) Green Bag, 5: 355.
See also Jurisprudence.
Law and Prophets, Reading of, in Triennial Cycle. (A. Büchler) Jew. Q. 5: 420. 6: 1.
Law Codes, Anglo-Indian. (W. Graham) Jurid. R. 7: 330.
Law Dictionaries. (W. C. Anderson) Am. Law R. 28: 531.
Law French. (W. W. Marshall) Walford's Antiq. 12: 224.
Law Latin Love Story. A. (F. J. Stimson) Scrib. M. 20: 725.
Law Proceedings, The Place of Truth in. (E. Manson) Jurid. R. 7: 367.
Law Reform, Congress of. (B. A. Lockwood) Am. J. Pol. 3: 321.
Law Reporting, Present System of. (J. Mews) Law Q. 9: 179.
Law Reports, English, Daniel's History of. (N. Lindley) Law Q. 1: 137.
Law Schools, American, Proper Course of Study for. (W. G. Hammond) Am. Law R. 26: 705.
Law Students, Advice to, in 1668. (E. A. Frost) Green Bag, 4: 446.
Law Teaching, Dwight Method of. (G. C. Austin) Law Q. 9: 171.
— Some Aspects of. (E. Fry) Law Q. 9: 115.
Lawes, Henry. Temp. Bar, 109: 24.
Lawford Hall, Essex, History of. Sat. R. 74: 514.
Lawless, Emily. Grania. Spec. 68: 431. — (Mrs. H. Ward) New R. 6: 399.
Lawlessness and the Reason of Law. (Austin Abbott) Outl. 48: 758.
— The New. (R. Ogden) Nation, 58: 340.
Lawn, Color for, in November. Garden & F. 5: 555.
— Essentials of a Good. (J. Troop) Garden & F. 9: 106.
Lawn Tennis. (F. A. Kellogg) Bach. of Arts, 1: 316.
— Champions at. (C. Hobart) Outing, 24: 296.
Lawns, Formation and Care of. Garden & F. 5: 618.
— Notes on. (W. Tricker) Garden & F. 6: 427.
Lawrence, Eugene. Critic, 25: 127.
Lawrence, George, Descendants of. (E. W. Leavitt) N. E. Reg. 46: 149.
Lawrence, Lord H. M., Aitchison's. Sat. R. 74: 780.
Lawrence, Capt. Thomas. Billeting Roll of his Company. (F. E. Blake) N. E. Reg. 50: 352.
Lawrence, Sir Thomas. M. of Art, 2: 129–230.
— Mr. and Mrs. Angerstein. (H. Ward) Art J. 48: 154.
Lawrence Family of Long Island. (L. B. Thomas) Am. Hist. Reg. 3: 671.
Lawrence, Mass., History of Banking in. Bank. M. (N. Y.) 47: 210.
— Public Library Building. Lib. J. 17: 199.
Lawrence Scientific School, at Harvard College. (I. N. Hollis) Harv. Grad. M. 4: 187.
Law's Delay. (J. S. Rubenstein) Fortn. 65: 122.
Laws, Conflict of, Dicey on. (A. G. Sedgwick) Nation, 63: 292.
— English and American, Dillon on. (M. Starr) Dial (Ch.) 17: 115.
— Normal, Formulation of, and Theory of Utility. (S. N. Patten) Ann. Am. Acad. Pol. Sci. 7: 426.
— State, Uniform, Necessity for. (J. F. Colby) Forum, 13: 541.
— Too many. (C. Nagel) Eth. Rec. 3: 106.
— Uniformity of, through National and Inter-state Codification. (L. A. Jones) Am. Law R. 28. 547.
Lawson, Cecil Gordon. (H. Owen) M. of Art, 17: 1, 64.
Lawson, Sir E. Eng. Illust. 11: 733.
Lawyer as a Teacher and Leader. (T. M. Cooley) Am. Law R. 28: 641.
— Country, in English Life. (E. Porritt) Green Bag, 8: 365.
— from a Moral Standpoint. (J. F. Dennis) Am. J. Pol. 5: 76.
— Obligations of, to the Public. (T. M. Cooley) Am. M. Civics, 7: 511.
— Position of, in Society. (G. C. Lee) Green Bag, 8: 246.
— Relation of, to his Fellows. (J. F. Dennis) Am. J. Pol. 4: 260.

Lawyer, The Young. (J. W. Peddie) Green Bag, **7**: 165.
Lawyers, American. (W. D. J. Foulkes) Time, **1**: 562.
— as Biographers. (T. W. Dwight) Green Bag, **4**: 100.
— English, Ease of. Sat. R. **82**: 153.
— A Lawyer on. (A. C. Applegarth) Green Bag, **4**: 316.
— Legal Luminaries of England. (S. P. Cadman) Chaut. **23**: 313.
Lawyers' Bills: Who should pay them? (Sir R. K. Wilson) Law Q. **12**: 368.
Lawyer's Secret, The. (J. K. Leys) Chamb. J. **71**: 417–819.
Lay of Earl Harold; a poem. (C. Kingsley) Eng. Illust. **10**: 447.
Lay Work and how to secure it. (C. Clever) Ref. Q. **40**: 350.
Layard, Sir Austen Henry. Acad. **46**: 34. — Ath. '94, **2**: 66. — Sat. R. **78**: 10. — Geog. J. **4**: 370. — (J. F. Boyes) Art J. **44**: 103.
— Picture Collection of. (H. Brown) M. of Art, **19**: 217.
Layer Marney Tower and Church in Essex. (T. M. Mundle) Art J. **47**: 17.
Laymen, Religious Movement of. (T. F. Seward and others) R. of Rs. (N. Y.) **5**: 45.
Laywoman, Rule of the. (Mrs. S. Batson) Liv. Age, **208**: 373.
Lazarette of the "Huntress," The; a story. (C. Russell) Idler, **5**: 339.
Lazarus, Emma. (M. M. Cohen) Poet-Lore, **5**: 320.
Lazarus and Dives. (C. Matheson) Good Words, **33**: 107.
Lea, Marion, as Deborah. Theatre, **28**: 202.
Lead and Extra Iodine, Compounds containing. (H. L. Wells) Am. J. Sci. **150**: 21.
— Double Halides of. (H. L. Wells) Am. J. Sci. **146**: 34.
— White, Manufacture of. (J. Barrett-Leonard) Fortn. **59**: 591.
— — Process for making. (S. E. Tillman) Cosmopol. **22**: 112. — (W. Tatham) J. Frankl. Inst. **142**: 309.
— — Production of non-Poisonous. (P. F. Nursey) J. Soc. Arts, **41**: 445.
— — Substitutes for. (A. P. Laurie) J. Soc. Arts, **42**: 133.
Leadhillite in Missouri, Occurrence of, and its Chemical Composition. (L. V. Pirsson and H. L. Wells) Am. J. Sci. **148**: 219.
Leadhillite Pseudomorphs at Grandby, Mo. (W. M. Foote) Am. J. Sci. **150**: 99.
Leadville, Colo., in 1893. (A. F. Wuensch) Engin. M. **5**: 567.
Leaf from Life; a story. (J. E. Bennett) Munsey, **13**: 360.
League of American Wheelmen in Politics. (F. H. Kerrigan) Overland, n. s. **28**: 285.
Leah; a poem. (L. P. Nicholson) Cosmopol. **17**: 546.
Leap in the Dark, A; a story. (J. T. McKay) McClure, **6**: 519.
Leap-years and their occasional omission. (W. T. Lynn) Nature, **54**: 126.
Learning, Revival of; the Century of Sir Thomas More. (B. O. Flower) Arena, **10**: 838.
— Transmission of. (H. L. Clapp) Educa. **15**: 1.
Leased Premises, Appropriation of, for Public Purposes. Does it abate the Payment of Rent? (J. H. Taulane) Am. Law R. **29**: 351.
Leathart, James, Collection of pre-Raphaelite Paintings. (W. M. Rossetti) Art J. **48**: 129.
Leather in the Ornamental Arts. Reliquary, **32**: 3.
Leather-making. (G. A. Rich) Pop. Sci. Mo. **41**: 339.
Leather Pocket-book; a story. (L. Street) Argosy. **60**: 112.
Leather Work. (L. F. Day) M. of Art, **19**: 88.
Leaves, Falling of. (A. B. Rendle) Nat. Sci. **1**: 680.
— Forms of, Rainfall and. (A. L. Smith) Nat. Sci. **3**: 95.
— Groove in the Petiole of. (A. Nelson) Science, **21**: 115.
— of Land Plants. Do they absorb Water? (E. A. Burt) Science, **22**: 51.
— Radiation and Absorption of Heat by. (A. G. Mayer) Am. J. Sci. **145**: 340.
— Significance of. (F. S. Mathews) Pop. Sci. Mo. **49**: 793.
Leaves from Fra Giovanni's Diary. Temp. Bar, **103**: 233. Same art. Liv. Age, **203**: 532.
Leaves from Pocket-book of a State Prisoner. (P. Grousset) Time, **2**: 237–695. **3**: 31.
Le Bon, Gustave, in India. (W. M. Conway) Geog. J. **1**: 444.
Le Bon Sauveur Convent Lunatic Asylum at Caen. Cornh. **73**: 620. Same art. Liv. Age, **210**: 253.
Le Brun, Charles; Genevay's Le Style Louis Quatorze. M. of Art, **9**: 127.
Le Brun, Madame Vigée. (I. F. Mayo) Argosy, **62**: 668.
Le Caron, Major H., Credibility of. Spec. **69**: 556.
— Critics of, and their Methods. (H. Le Caron) New R. **7**: 683.
Leclercq, Carlotta. (J. Coleman) Theatre, **31**: 166.
Leconte de Lisle, C. M. R. (F. Brunetière) Contemp. **66**: 890. — Atlan. **74**: 712. — (A. Symons and others) Ath. '94, **2**: 99, 130, 223. — (E. Stuart) Fortn. **64**: 121. Same art. Liv. Age, **206**: 432. — (P. T. Lafleur) Atlan. **75**: 694.
— and his Fellow Poets. Sat. R. **79**: 689.
— Memorial Ode. (A. C. Swinburne) Sat. R. **78**: 595.
Lecouvreur, Adrienne. (C. E. Meetkerke) Argosy, **55**: 106.
Lectern, On the. Chamb. J. **72**: 767. Same art. Liv. Age, **208**: 62.
Lecture Platform, Mission of. (M. B. Thrasher) New Eng. M. n. s. **15**: 212.
— Twenty-five Years on. (M. A. Livermore) Arena, **6**: 261.
Lecture System, Want of Economy in. (J. Trowbridge) Atlan. **75**: 102.
Lecturers, A Gentle Warning to. (A. Repplier) Forum, **17**: 235.
Lectures, Free. (H. M. Leipziger) Critic, **28**: 329. *See* Lyceum.
Lecythus from Eretria. (E. A. Gardner) J. Hel. Stud. **14**: 170.
Led to Gold; a story. (C. B. Sedgwick) Overland, n. s. **20**: 58.
Lee, Sir Harry, The Real. Antiq. n. s. **28**: 241.
Lee, Homer; with portrait. (J. H. Kennedy) Nat'l M. (N. Y. '91) **15**: 208.
Lee, Jane. Acad. **48**: 410.
Lee, Mary Catherine. (H. P. Robinson) Writer, **8**: 183.
Lee, Robert E., and Jackson, Thomas J., Gentler Side of. (G. W. Cable) Cent. **25**: 292.
— During the Campaign of the Seven Days. (E. G. Scott) Atlan. **73**: 446.
— Friendship with Scott. (J. W. Jones) Southern M. **4**: 514.
— Reminiscences of, with portrait. (W. W. Scott) Southern M. **4**: 628.
Lee Family, The. (V. Cousins) Munsey, **15**: 217.
— of Virginia. (J. H. Lea) N. E. Reg. **46**: 64, 161. — (W. B. Lee) N. E. Reg. **47**: 21.
Lee-Metford Rifle. Un. Serv. M. **5**: 614.

Leech, John. (W. P. Frith) All the Year, **70**: 84. — (F. G. Kitton) Temp. Bar, **95**: 207. Same art. Liv. Age, **194**: 429.
— Art Life of. (H. Silver) M. of Art, **16**: 115.
— as Sketcher of Hunting Horses. (F. G. Kitton) Art J. **48**: 293.
— Home Life of. (H. Silver) M. of Art, **16**: 162.
— Life of, Frith's. Ath. '92, **1**: 409. — Spec. **68**: 407.
Leeds Castle. (Maj. Ricketts) Eng. Illust. **11**: 1199.
Leeds Musical Festival. (J. S. Shedlock) Acad. **42**: 318, 341. — Sat. R. **74**: 446.
Le Fanu, W. R. Seventy Years of Irish Life. Spec. **71**: 771.
Lefebvre, Jules. (M. Tracy) Mo. Illust. **3**: 305.
Lefevre, Raoul, and "Le Recueil des Histoires de Troye." (H. O. Sommer) Bibliographica, **1**: 31, 502.
Lefroy, Edward C. (J. A. Symonds) New R. **6**: 341. Same art. Liv. Age, **193**: 250.
Left no Address. (M. Hunt) Longm. **24**: 376.
Left-handed Folk. Chamb. J. **70**: 43.
Left-handedness. (R. A. Lundie) Chamb. J. **73**: 9.
Legacies, Abatement of, where an Estate shows a Deficiency of Assets. (P. L. Edwards) Am. Law R. **27**: 243.
Legal Business, Causes of Decrease in Volume of. (L. E. Chittenden) Green Bag, **7**: 364.
Legal Education at the Universities. (E. C. Clark) Law Q. **12**: 386.
— Existing Question on. (A. Abbott) Am. Law R. **27**: 801.
— in Modern Japan. (J. H. Wigmore) Green Bag, **5**: 17, 78, 129.
— in U. S. (L. R. Meekins) R. of Rs. (N. Y.) **10**: 502.
— Inductive Method in. (W. A. Keener) Am. Law R. **28**: 709.
Legal Information, Free, Bureaus of. (W. B. Scaife) Pub. Opin. **18**: 698.
Legal Medicine, Hamilton's System of. (A. A. Woodhull) Nation, **59**: 163.
Legal Procedure, English, Reform in. (D. MacG. Means) Nation, **55**: 160.
— French, Some Peculiarities of. Green Bag, **7**: 79.
Legal Professions, A Plea for Amalgamation. Westm. **142**: 524.
Legal Reform, Imperativeness of. (W. M. Thompson) Time, **22**: 389.
Legal Reminiscences. (L. E. Chittenden) Green Bag, **5**: 307, 378. **7**: 544. **8**: 48, 101.
Legal Suicide, A, 1996. (P. Weaver, jr.) Overland, n. s. **28**: 680.
Legal Technicalities, Resort to. Am. M. Civics, **9**: 305.
Legal Tender, Ethics of. (M. M. Trumbull) Open Court, **7**: 3760.
Legal Vulgar Errors. Green Bag, **6**: 168.
Le Gallienne, Richard. Critic, **26**: 295.
— as a Critic. Sat. R. **81**: 511. — (T. Hutchinson) Acad. **50**: 155.
— Poetry of. (P. Addleshaw) Acad. **47**: 519.
— Prose Fancies. Sat. R. **82**: 113.
— Robert Louis Stevenson and Other Poems. Sat. R. **79**: 699.
Legato, Mental Basis of. (C. B. Cady) Music, **1**: 264.
Legend, A. (H. Fielding) Blackw. **155**: 567.
Legend of Holland Cove. (F. Gerald) Canad. M. **7**: 499.
Legend of Invershield. (M. A. Marks) Argosy, **60**: 415.
Legend of Lapwater Hall. (A. Morrison) Macmil. **66**: 108.
Legend of Prince Maurice, A. (H. A. Bryden) Chamb. J. **72**: 7-23.
Legend of Rodeo Cañon. (H. E. Bandini) Overland, n. s. **20**: 170.
Legend of Wonalansett. (C. H. Glidden) New Eng. M. n. s. **8**: 797.
Legends of the Crucifixion. (F. W. Farrar) Sund. M. **25**: 217.
Legerdemain, Psychology of. (M. Dessoir) Open Court, **7**: 3599-3633.
Legion of Honor, The. (D. MacG. Means) Nation, **61**: 111.
— by a Knight of the Order. Eng. Illust. **14**: 293.
Legislation and Law. (J. W. Greene) Am. J. Soc. Sci. no. **34**: 117.
— Direct. (Eltweed Pomeroy) Outl. **51**: 267. *See* Referendum.
— Energy of. (E. P. Powell) Am. M. Civics, **6**: 274.
— Field of. Pub. Opin. **15**: 566.
— How a Law is made. (J. L. Mitchell) No. Am. **159**: 537.
— of Fear. (L. de la Ramé) Fortn. **62**: 552.
— Political Betterments through improved. (W. F. Crafts) Am. M. Civics, **8**: 73.
— Society of Comparative. (C. P. Ilbert) 19th Cent. **38**: 142.
— Unconstitutional, Coxe on. (H. P. Judson) Dial (Ch.) **17**: 62.
Legislature, American. (M. Story) Am. Law R. **28**: 683.
— Authority of, Trumbull on. Pub. Opin. **17**: 687.
— Biennial Sessions of. (R. L. Bridgman) New Eng. M. n. s. **8**: 206.
Legislatures; a Defence and a Criticism. (R. L. Bridgman) Am. J. Pol. **5**: 598.
Legouvé, E. Recollections. Spec. **71**: 402.
Legros, Alphonse. (C. Monkhouse) M. of Art, **5**: 327.
Legs of Sister Ursula, The; a story. (R. Kipling) McClure, **2**: 347. Same art. Idler, **3**: 485.
Leguat, François, Adventures of. Ed. R. **175**: 342. — Sat. R. **73**: 610.
Leguminosæ, Root Tubercles of. (E. F. Smith) Am. Natural. **29**: 898.
Lehman, Rudolph. Cromwell at Ripley Castle; painting. (R. G. Kingsley) Art J. **45**: 260.
Leibnitz, Godfrey William, and Protestant Theology. (J. Watson) New World, **5**: 102.
— Monadology of, Dillmann on. (J. Watson) Philos. R. **2**: 710.
Leibnitz Day of the Berlin Academy of Sciences. (K. Francke) Nation, **61**: 60.
Leicester Corporation Art Gallery. (S. J. Viccars) M. of Art, **16**: 12, 44.
Leicester Square. All the Year, **70**: 88.
Leifchild, Henry Stormouth. (J. Sparkes) M. of Art, **14**: 322.
Leigh, Henry S. (B. Webber) Time, **10**: 157.
Leighton, Miss Dorothy. Thyrza Fleming. Sat. R. **79**: 126.
Leighton, Frederick, Lord. Acad. **50**: 568. — (F. Wedmore) Acad. **49**: 101. — Art J. **48**: 90. — Ath. '96, **1**: 154. — Critic, **28**: 82. — (C. Monkhouse) Scrib. M. **19**: 399. — Sat. R. **81**: 120. — Spec. **76**: 163. — (G. Campbell) Cosmopol. **14**: 273. — (V. Butler) Lippinc. **52**: 463. — With portrait. R. of Rs. (N. Y.) **7**: 565. — (H. S. Wilson) M. of Art, **1**: 57. **2**: 1. — (M. H. Spielmann) M. of Art, **19**: 197.
— and his South Kensington Frescoes. M. of Art, **19**: 373.
— and his Art. (W. B. Richmond) 19th Cent. **39**: 465.
— Drawings. (S. P. Cockerell) 19th Cent. **40**: 809. Same art. Liv. Age, **211**: 814. — National, **28**: 505. — Sat. R. **82**: 647.

Leighton, Frederick, Lord. Garden of the Hesperides. (E. Radford) Art J. **47**: 11.
— House of, in Holland Park Road. (W. Meynell) M. of Art, **4**: 169.
— Many Moods of. (W. Meynell) M. of Art, **4**: 51.
— Minor Memories of. (W. Meynell) Eng. Illust. **14**: 583.
— Pictures at the Royal Academy. M. of Art, **12**: 224.
— Ray's. (R. Sturgis) Archit. Rec. **5**: 310.
— A Sketch. (M. Dean) Belgra. **89**: 374.
— Studio of. Ath. '**96**, **1**: 256.
Leighton Buzzard, Ancient Preaching Cross. Reliquary, **35**: 42.
Leipzig, Book Trade of. (L. Katscher) Bookworm, **5**: 151.
— New Psychological Laboratory at. (G. M. Stratton) Science, n. s. **4**: 867.
Leisler Troubles in N. Y., 1688–92. (A. G. Vermilye) Nat'l M. (N. Y. '91) **16**: 505.
Leisure. (Vernon Lee) Contemp. **70**: 853. — (A. Repplier) Scrib. M. **14**: 63.
— Distaste for. Spec. **69**: 643.
Leitrim County, Fairy Beliefs from. (L. L. Duncan) Folk-Lore, **7**: 161.
— Folk-Lore Gleanings from. (L. L. Duncan) Folk-Lore, **4**: 176.
Le Jars de Gournay, Marie, Adopted Daughter of Montaigne. (F. J. Hudleston) Belgra. **87**: 126. Same art. Liv. Age, **206**: 169.
Lejeune, General, Souvenirs of. (A. Laugel) Nation, **61**: 344, 386.
Le Keux, John Henry. Ath. '**96**, **1**: 224.
Lekythoi, Attic. (R. C. Bosanquet) J. Hel. Stud. **16**: 164.
— — from Eretria. (E. Sellers) J. Hel. Stud. **13**: 1.
— Two Sepulchral. (P. Gardner) J. Hel. Stud. **15**: 325.
Lekythos, Protokorinthian, in the British Museum. (C. Smith) J. Hel. Stud. **11**: 167.
Leland, Charles Godfrey. (W. Lewin) Acad. **45**: 75. — With portrait. Bk. Buyer, **11**: 7. — With portrait. Bk. News, **12**: 196.
— Memoirs. Critic, **23**: 428. — (C. S. Peirce) Nation, **57**: 414. — Sat. R. **76**: 444. — Dial (Ch.) **16**: 9.
Leland Stanford, jr., University, Educational Policy of. (D. S. Jordan) Educa. R. **4**: 1.
Leloir, Louis, Illustrations to Molière. M. of Art, **8**: 38.
Lemaire, Madeleine, with portrait. Bk. Buyer, **12**: 227.
Lemaitre, Jules. (Y. Blaze de Bury) Fortn. **65**: 547. — Sat. R. **79**: 857.
Lemons and Oranges, California. (C. H. Shinn) Garden & F. **5**: 561.
— at Massa-Lubrense. Chamb. J. **72**: 188.
— Cultivation of, in Southern California. (W. M. Tisdale) Garden & F. **8**: 168.
— Growing, in California. (W. M. Tisdale) Garden & F. **9**: 477.
Le Moyne, William J. (M. White, jr.) Munsey, **13**: 31.
Lemurs. (R. Lydekker) Knowl. **16**: 14.
— Ghosts of the Tropical Forest. Spec. **70**: 321.
Lenapé Conversations. (D. G. Brinton) J. Am. Folk-Lore, **1**: 37.
Lenau, Nicolaus. (E. Poesche) Open Court, **6**: 3288, 3298.
Lenbach, F. von. Autobiographical Notes. Cosmopol. **16**: 3. — (C. Phillips) M. of Art, **9**: 51.
L'Enfant, Pierre Charles. (C. B. Todd) Am. Arch. **53**: 53.
Lennette. (E. Davis) New Eng. M. n. s. **6**: 231, 372.
Lenox, Charlotte. (A. Dobson) National, **19**: 312.
Lenox, Mass. (G. A. Hibbard) Scrib. M. **16**: 420.
Lens, Crystalline. (C. H. Hurst) Nat. Sci. **7**: 113.
— Dioptric, for Lighthouse Illumination, Progress of. (C. A. Stevenson) Nature, **46**: 514.
Lenses; Assisted Sight. (Sir H. Maxwell) Good Words, **35**: 270.
— Measurement of. (S. P. Thompson) J. Soc. Arts, **40**: 22.
Lent. (H. Thurston) Month, **83**: 553.
— among the Mahometans. (F. G. Carpenter) Cosmopol. **14**: 646.
Lenten Customs at St. Malo. Macmil. **73**: 454. Same art. Liv. Age, **209**: 493. Same art. Ecl. M. **127**: 23.
Lenten Observances. (T. E. Champion) Canad. M. **2**: 458.
Lentils, About. Chamb. J. **72**: 102.
Leo X., Pope, as an Art Patron. (F. M. Robinson) M. of Art, **13**: 157.
Leo XIII., Pope, with portrait. Bk. News, **15**: 55.
— and the Future of the Papacy. (F. H. Geffcken) Forum, **12**: 577.
— and the Higher Criticism. Contemp. **63**: 457.
— and his Household. (F. M. Crawford) Cent. **29**: 590.
— and Historical Research. (E. Soutif) Am. Cath. Q. **20**: 750.
— and the Poor, The. (E. L. Godkin) Nation, **54**: 7.
— and the Social Question. (J. A. Zahm) No. Am. **161**: 200.
— Encyclical of. (A. F. Hewit) Cath. World, **60**: 721. — Pub. Opin. **18**: 136.
— — on the School Question. Pub. Opin. **15**: 301. — (P. Carus) Open Court, **5**: 2877.
— — on Labor, Canon Holland on. Dub. R. **110**: 180.
— — — Ethical Aspects of. (Brother Azarias) Int. J. Ethics, **2**: 137.
— Encyclicals of. Atlan. **73**: 692.
— Jubilee of, 1893. (J. Moyes) Dub. R. **112**: 245. — Spec. **70**: 249.
— Letter concerning Anglican Ordinations. Dub. R. **119**: 392.
— Letter to the English People. (F. W. Farrar) Contemp. **67**: 788. Same art. Chr. Lit. **13**: 140.
— A Morning with. (W. H. W. Campbell) Munsey, **6**: 689.
— Policy of, 1892. Contemp. **62**: 457. Same art. M. Chr. Lit. **7**: 125. — (S. M. Brandi) Contemp. **63**: 663. — Reply. Contemp. **63**: 899.
— Reactionary Phases in Pontificate of. (H. C. Sheldon) Meth. R. **55**: 877.
— Triumphs of. (J. W. Mario) Nation, **63**: 7.
Leoncavallo, R. Pagliacci. Sat. R. **73**: 708.
Leoni, Leone, and Pompeo, Plon's. M. of Art, **10**: 206.
Leonids, Importance of Accurately Observing, this Year, 1896. (G. J. Stoney) Pop. Astron. **4**: 134.
— of November 15, 1896. (A. S. Herschel) Nature, **55**: 176.
Leonile, Australian Aboriginal Weapon. (R. Etheridge) Anthrop. J. **23**: 317.
Leopard, The. Around World, **1**: 39.
— Man-eating. Chamb. J. **69**: 813.
— Marauding. (E. F. R. Dixon) Outing, **19**: 427.
— Night with a. (M. Challinor) Cosmopol. **12**: 581.
Leopard Hunt in Ceylon. (F. F. Dixon) Outing, **23**: 449.
Leopardi, Giacomo. (G. Bradford, jr.) Poet-Lore, **5**: 385.
— Loves of. (Chas. Edwardes) Time, **12**: 272.
Leopards. (C. T. Buckland) Longm. **22**: 333. Same art. Liv. Age, **199**: 116.
Lepel, Mary. *See* Hervey, Mary Lepel, Lady.

Leper of the Cumberlands, The; a story. (W. A. Dromgoole) Arena, 7: 497.
Leper Village, Chinese, Visit to a. (E. T. C. Werner) Gent. M. n. s. 51: 463.
Lepère, A., Wood-engraver. Scrib. M. 18: 718. Same art. Ecl. M. 125: 702.
Lepers, Home for, at Mandelay. (W. R. Winston) Sund. M. 22: 632.
— in Siberia. Dub. R. 112: 182. — (K. Marsden) Eng. Illust. 10: 75.
— — Miss Kate Marsden among. R. of Rs. (N. Y.) 6: 178. — (I. F. Hapgood) Nation, 56: 258.
— — Outcast. All the Year, 72: 132.
— on Darcey Island, British Columbia. (C. H. Gibbons) Nat'l M. (Bost.) 4: 515.
Lepidoptera, Classification of. (V. L. Kellogg) Am. Natural. 29: 278.
— — on Larval Characters. (H. G. Dyar) Am. Natural. 29: 1066.
— Habits and Tastes of. (C. J. Mansford) Chamb. J. 72: 325.
— Mouth Parts of. (V. L. Kellogg) Am. Natural. 29: 546.
— New Classification of. (A. S. Packard) Am. Natural. 29: 636, 788.
— Wing of, Affinities of. (V. L. Kellogg) Am. Natural. 29: 709.
Lepidosiren; a Fish with a History. Chamb. J. 71: 572.
Lepidosirenids and Bdellostomids. (T. Gill) Am. Natural. 28: 581.
Leprosy, Immunity from, in the Fifth Generation. (A. S. Ashmead) Science, 20: 309.
— in Brittany. Macmil. 74: 193.
— in India. (George Birdwood) Asia. R. 9: 438. — Sat. R. 76: 217.
— Tebb on. (A. A. Woodhull) Nation, 57: 275.
Leprosy Commission in India, Report of. (G. Thin) Fortn. 61: 93.
Le Puy, France, Churches of. (M. P. Thompson) Am. Arch. 53: 9.
Lerida, Spain. (C. W. Wood) Argosy, 62: 191, 299.
Lerwick, Pictish Burgh near. (E. M. Cole) Antiq. n. s. 31: 83.
Le Sage. Gil Blas, Smollett's Translation of. (F. Hall) Nation, 55: 411.
Lesbos, Folk-Lore from. (W. H. D. Rouse) Folk-Lore, 7: 142.
Lescot, Pierre. (A. M. F. Robinson) M. of Art, 8: 394.
Lescure, Victorine de. *See* La Rochejaquelein.
Lesdiguières, Constable. (E. Armstrong) Eng. Hist. R. 10: 445.
Leslie, C. E., and his Work. Music, 2: 223.
Leslie, Charles Robert. M. of Art, 2: 152. — (R. C. Leslie) Temp. Bar, 107: 353.
Leslie, Frank, with portrait. Bk. News, 11: 342.
Leslie, George. *See* Archangel.
Leslie, George Dunlop. (W. Meynell) M. of Art, 3: 232.
Leslie, Henry. Ath. '96, 1: 225.
Lespedeza Bicolor. (J. G. Jack) Garden & F. 5: 112.
Less than Kin; a story. (Mrs. W. C. Hawksley) Chamb. J. 70: 759-825.
Lesseps, Ferdinand de. (T. Schwartz) Munsey, 12: 617. — Am. Arch. 47: 31. — Atlan. 76: 285. — Pub. Opin. 17: 920. — (R. R. Sherard) McClure, 1: 83.
— and the Panama Canal Scandal. (G. W. Hinman) Chaut. 16: 587.
— and the Suez and Panama Canals. (W. H. Wheeler) Longm. 25: 394.
Lessi, Tito. (P. G. Hamerton) Scrib. M. 15: 319.
Lessing, G. E. Dramaturgie. (J. W. Thomas) Poet-Lore, 5: 593.
— Grucker's. (A. Laugel) Nation, 62: 194.
— Nathan the Wise. (W. W. Davies) Meth. R. 54: 746.
— Place in German Literature. (T. W. Rolleston) Contemp. 64: 237.
— Story of the Three Rings. (T. Bradfield) Westm. 144: 666.
Lesson in the Art, A; a story. (A. Hope) Idler, 6: 115.
Lesson in Thrift, A; a story. (E. Chilton) Macmil. 66: 228.
Lesson of Content, A; a poem. (J. H. May) Educa. 16: 77.
Lesson of the Master. (H. James) Univ. R. 1: 342, 494.
Le Sueur, Charles A., with portrait. (D. S. Jordan) Pop. Sci. Mo. 46: 547.
Let the Best Man win; a drama. (M. H. Dixon) Eng. Illust. 12: no. 5, 47.
Let no Man put Asunder; a story. (A. J. Halliday) Outing, 24: 3.
Lethargy. (P. Carus) Open Court, 3: 1972.
Letter from the Pacific, A; a poem. (T. Watts) M. of Art, 15: 61.
Letter of Credit, The; a story. (C. C. Nott, jr.) Outing, 22: 115.
Letter of Farewell, A. (B. Matthews) Scrib. M. 19: 644.
Letter of Introduction; a farce. (W. D. Howells) Harper, 84: 243.
Letter to Town, A. (H. C. Bunner) Scrib. M. 19: 760.
Letter-writer, The Complete. (S. E. Braine) Good Words, 37: 330. Same art. Ecl. M. 126: 771. Same art. Liv. Age, 210: 58.
Letter-writers. Gent. M. n. s. 48: 635.
Letter-writing, English, in the 19th Century. Ed. R. 183: 306. — Liv. Age, 209: 598.
Letters. (M. E. G. Duff) Cornh. 74: 464.
— Biographical Value of. Macmil. 73: 309.
— Fictitious. Bookworm, 3: 185.
— from a French Atelier. Temp. Bar, 104: 105. Same art. Liv. Age, 204: 369.
— of an Altrurian Traveller. (W. D. Howells) Cosmopol. 16: 110-697. 17: 46-610.
— of a Man of Leisure. Temp. Bar, 97: 23.
— Old, A Packet of. (Mrs. A. Crosse) Temp. Bar, 97: 199. Same art. Ecl. M. 120: 595. Same art. Liv. Age, 197: 42.
— An Old Maid's. (S. Baring-Gould) Good Words, 37: 478-594.
— Private, of King James's Reign. (W. Scott) Scrib. M. 14: 733.
— A Sheaf of. Temp. Bar, 102: 217. Same art. Liv. Age, 262: 109.
— to Clarinda. (J. K. Jerome) Idler, 9: 56-874. 10: 128-554.
Letting in the Jungle; a story. (R. Kipling) McClure, 4: 128.
Lettres de Cachet, Issue of, in Blank. (H. M. Baird) Nation, 61: 446.
Leuciscus Balteatus (Richardson). (C. H. Eigenmann) Am. Natural. 29: 10.
Leucite, Basic Dike near Hamburg, N. J., thought to contain. (J. F. Kemp) Am. J. Sci. 145: 298.
Leucocytes, Action of, toward Foreign Substances. (E. J. Claypole) Am. Natural. 28: 316.
— Function of. (A. Wilson) Harper, 93: 136.
— Varieties of. (C. S. Sherrington) Sci. Prog. 2: 415.

Levees, Mississippi River. Engin. M. **3**: 387. — (C. N. Dutton; H. S. L. Coppée) Engin. M. **3**: 623. — (W. Starling) Engin. M. **4**: 247.
— — Louisiana and. (L. A. Sheldon) Arena, **5**: 187.
Léveillé, A., Wood-engraver. Scrib. M. **18**: 167
Levens Hall, England. Sat. R. **73**: 303.
Lever, Charles. Writings. Sat. R. **73**: 180, 210
Leverett, Gov. John, Three Letters in Cipher. (W. P. Upham and G. Sheldon) N. E. Reg. **48**: 316.
Levin, Rahel, and her Times. Macmil. **74**: 264. Same art. Liv. Age, **210**: 538.
Levitical System, Evidence of Psalter to. (H. Hayman) Bib. Sac. **50**: 238.
Lewes, George Henry, and the Stage. (W. Archer) Fortn. **65**: 216.
— and Thornton Hunt. (Mrs. Lynn Linton) Bookman, **3**: 520.
— as Dramatic Critic. (W. D. Adams) Theatre, **27**: 337.
Lewes, Battle of. (J. P. Gilson) Eng. Hist. R. **11**: 520.
Lewes, Song of, Kingsford's Edition. (G. W. Prothero) Eng. Hist. R. **7**: 144.
Lewins, Robert. (G. M. McCrie) Open Court, **9**: 4607.
Lewis, Charles B. (H. Parker) Munsey, **9**: 608.
Lewis, Henry Francis; with portrait. (J. P. Bishop) Nat'l M. (N. Y. '91) **16**: 242.
Lewis, James. (J. L. Gilder) Critic, **29**: 177.
Lewis, John Frederick. (C. Phillips) Portfo. **23**: 89.
Lewis, Meriwether, and Clark, as American Explorers. Around World, **1**: 32.
— — Expedition of, Coues's Edition. (F. T. Turner) Dial (Ch.) **16**: 80. — (J. D. Butler) Nation, **57**: 312, 331.
— Death of. (V. S. Pease) Southern M. **4**: 17.
Lewis, William. (W. Primrose) Pennsyl. M. **20**: 30.
Lewis, The, Traditions, Customs, Superstitions of. (M. MacPhail) Folk-Lore, **6**: 162.
Lewiston, Me. (C. A. Chase) New Eng. M. n. s. **13**: 513.
Lexow Committee; Putrid Police. Soc. Econ. **7**: 9.
Leyden and its Archives. (W. E. Griffis) Nation, **55**: 143.
— Ethnological Museum at. (H. Ten Kate) Nature, **49**: 165.
Leyland, Frederic. (V. Prinsep) Art J. **44**: 129.
Leyland Collection, The. (L. Robinson) Art J. **44**: 134.
Leysin-sur-Aigle. (H. D. Rawnsley) Blackw. **158**: 680.
Leystone, Three Abbeys of. (H. M. Doughty) Gent. M. n. s. **57**: 439.
Lézeau, Marie de. Macmil. **66**: 46. Same art. Liv. Age, **194**: 176.
L'Homme propose, Dieu dispose; a story. (I. Mar) Gent. M. n. s. **49**: 1.
Li Hung Chang. (S. J. E. C. Hankin) Acad. **48**: 179. — (D. C. Boulger) Contemp. **70**: 18. Same art. Ecl. M. **127**: 197. Same art. Liv. Age, **210**: 387. — (C. Holcombe) Eng. Illust. **15**: 285. Same art. McClure, **7**: 427. — (J. W. Foster) Cent. **30**: 560. — (A. Michie) 19th Cent. **40**: 226. — (A. R. Colquhoun) Sat. R. **82**: 80. — (G. T. Ferris) Cosmopol. **17**: 643. — With portrait. R. of Rs. (N. Y.) **10**: 386. — (A. W. Tarbell) Nat'l M. (Bost.) **4**: 507. — (A. Michie) Un. Serv. (Phila.) **16**: 348.
— and General Grant. (Frederick D. Grant) Outl. **54**: 367.
— at Home again. (R. S. Gundry) Sat. R. **82**: 675.
— Diplomacy of. (E. H. Parker) New R. **15**: 167.
— Douglas's. Sat. R. **80**: 81.
— Transit of. Cornh. **74**: 452.
Li Hung Chang. Visit to England. Blackw. **160**: 526.
Liability, Limited. (B. D. Mackenzie) Gent. M. n. s. **51**: 46.
Liar, On the Elench of the. (Hiram M. Stanley) Philos. R. **4**: 185.
Liars, Americans a Nation of. (I. T. Headland) Chaut. **19**: 565.
Lib and the Others. All the Year, **76**: 276.
Libanius; why he could not become a Christian. (F. W. Farrar) Good Words, **37**: 418.
Libel, Law of. (Wm. Mackay) Time, **16**: 268.
— — History of. (J. R. Fisher) Law Q. **10**: 158.
Libel Law, The New New York. (E. L. Godkin) Nation, **58**: 207.
Liberal Churches and Skepticism. (M. D. Shutter) Arena, **8**: 18.
— Tendencies of Thought in. (S. M. Crothers) New World, **5**: 669.
Liberal Party in England, The. (D. Crawford) Nation, **60**: 46.
— Causes of its Defeat. (G. W. E. Russell) Forum, **20**: 160.
— Fabian Society's Attacks on. (M. Davitt) 19th Cent. **34**: 849.
— Future of. Macmil. **72**: 383.
— Leadership of. (James Annand) New R. **13**: 367.
— Position of. (J. G. Rogers) 19th Cent. **35**: 189.
— Unification of the. (H. H. L. Bellot) Westm. **143**: 477.
Liberal Reunion. Time, **16**: 385.
Liberal Theology, New England. (F. T. Curnick) Meth. R. **56**: 599.
Liberal Unionism, Evolution of. (G. O. Morgan) Contemp. **64**: 299.
Liberalism and Roman Catholicism. (B. Herford) Chr. Lit. **14**: 157.
— Demoralization of. (James Annand) New R. **13**: 248.
— Modern. (H. Genone) Open Court, **9**: 4471.
— Re-organization of. (James Annand) New R. **13**: 494.
— Resurrection of. (W. H. Robinson) Westm. **145**: 497.
— True and False. (H. D. Atchison) Meth. R. **55**: 552.
— *versus* Socialism. (E. B. Bax) Time, **23**: 1184.
Liberia, Bishop Potter on. (J. Cook) Our Day, **13**: 333.
— Negro Emigration to. (J. E. Rankin) Our Day, **13**: 224.
Liberius and Honorius, Pontiffs. (A. F. Marshall) Am. Cath. Q. **19**: 82.
Liberty. (M. D. Conway) Open Court, **7**: 3887, 3905, 3919.
— The Actualities of. (J. C. Macdonald) Westm. **143**: 182.
— and License. All the Year, **75**: 465.
— Civil, and the Reformation. (D. H. Bauslin) Luth. Q. **22**: 547.
— — A Doctrine of. (H. L. Sibley) Meth. R. **55**: 528.
— Effects of. (E. B. Dietrick) Soc. Econ. **5**: 301.
— in England from the Reformation to William III. (M. Hennessey) Am. Cath. Q. **18**: 295.
— Individual, Limits of, and of State Authority. (J. M. Smith) Am. M. Civics, **9**: 288.
— Intellectual. Contemp. **66**: 280.
— Nature of. (W. D. Howells) Forum, **20**: 401.
— of a Christian Man. (A. G. Voigt) Luth. Q. **22**: 584.
— Personal. All the Year, **71**: 81. — (E. Atkinson and E. T. Cabot) Pop. Sci. Mo. **40**: 433.
— — in Scots Law. (J. Harvey) Jurid. R. **8**: 28, 142.

Librarian as Administrator. (F. M. Crunden) Lib. J. **19**: 44.
— Assistants, and the Public. (L. E. Stearns) Lib. J. **21**: 489.
— Duty of, as a Citizen. (C. K. Bolton) Lib. J. **21**: 219.
— How should he read? (G. E. Wire) Lib. J. **20**: supp. 16.
— Training of. (A. L. Hayward) Lib. J. **17**: 478.
Librarians and Teachers, Coöperation of. (G. W. Cole) Lib. J. **20**: 115.
— Training of. (A. R. Hasse) Lib. J. **20**: 202, 239, 272, 303.
— — at Armour Institute, Chicago. (K. L. Sharp) Lib. J. **19**: 162.
— — Schools for, in the United States. Lib. J. **19**: 296.
— Women. (M. S. R. James) Lib. J. **18**: 146.
Libraries, American, Rev. Thos. Bray and. (B. C. Steiner) Am. Hist. R. **2**: 59.
— Astor and Lenox. Bk. Buyer, **12**: 128.
— at Lisbon. (L. Thomas) Acad. **49**: 96.
— Bibliothèque Nationale. (C. A. Cutter) Lib. J. **19**: 193, 289.
— Books and Reading. (C. A. Ward) Bookworm, **3**: 17.
— College, Public Use of. (S. H. Ranck) Lib. J. **20**: 235.
— — Relations to the People. (J. C. Rowell) Lib. J. **19**: 50.
— Free, in London, Day at. All the Year, **70**: 305.
— Free Public. (H. H. Barber) Lend a H. **14**: 366. **15**: 246.
— — Establishment of. (W. I. Fletcher) Citizen, **1**: 9.
— — Failure of. (W. Roberts) New R. **13**: 316.
— Free Public Library Commission of Massachusetts. (H. S. Nourse) Lib. J. **21**: 10.
— Great, of the U. S. (W. I. Fletcher) Bk. Buyer, **11**: 343. — (H. Putnam) Forum, **19**: 484.
— Home. (C. W. Birtwell) Lib. J. **19**: supp. 9. — (M. S. Cutler) Lib. J. **21**: 60.
— — of Children's Aid Society, Boston. (C. W. Birtwell) Lend a H. **13**: 35.
— Impressiveness of. Spec. **68**: 877. Same art. Ecl. M. **119**: 236.
— in Secondary Schools. (K. L. Sharp) Lib. J. **20**: supp. 5.
Large Gifts to. Critic, **29**: 127.
— of Lisbon. Lit. W. (Bost.) **27**: 72.
— of New York. Critic, **21**: 84.
— of Science in New York City, Plea for. (H. C. Bolton) Lib. J. **19**: 12.
— Public, Access to the Shelves in. (W. H. Brett) Lib. J. **17**: 445. — (B. C. Steiner and S. H. Ranck) Lib. J. **19**: supp. 87. — (J. D. Brown) Lib. J. **20**: 9.
— — Accession Department of. (G. M. Jones) Lib. J. **18**: 234.
— — Adaptation of, to Local Needs. (A. L. Peck) Lib. J. **20**: 45.
— — Aids and Guides in, Report on, 1893–94. (W. H. Austin) Lib. J. **19**: supp. 77.
— — and Proprietary. (C. A. Cutter) Lib. J. **18**: 247.
— — and the Public School. (C. C. Young) Lib. J. **21**: 140. — (G. W. Peckham) Educa. R. **8**: 358.
— — and Teachers. (J. C. Dana) Lib. J. **21**: 133.
— — and University Extension. (T. L. Montgomery) Lib. J. **19**: supp. 64.
— — Architecture of. (T. H. West) Lib. J. **19**: supp. 96.
— — as Bureaus of Information. (S. S. Green) Lib. J. **21**: 324.
— — as an Educational Factor. (M. E. Comstock) Lib. J. **21**: 147.
Libraries, Public, at the World's Columbian Exposition. (C. H. Garland) Lib. J. **18**: 284.
— — Books and Readers in. (C. B. Tillinghast) Forum, **16**: 60.
— — Books in, Line of Exclusion of. (W. Learned) Lib. J. **21**: 320.
— — Branches and Deliveries. (G. W. Cole) Lib. J. **18**: 220.
— — Bulletins, Publishing of Periodical. Lib. J. **19**: supp. 50.
— — Cards for the "Two-book" System. (G. M. Jones) Lib. J. **20**: 168.
— — Charging Systems and Statistics. (C. K. Bolton) Lib. J. **19**: 225.
— — the Child and the School. (L. A. Eastman) Lib. J. **21**: 134.
— — Children's Departments in. (M. E. Dousman) Lib. J. **21**: 406.
— — Circulation Statements. (A. E. Bostwick) Lib. J. **21**: 96.
— — Classification and Catalogues, Report on, 1893–94. (C. A. Nelson) Lib. J. **19**: supp. 69.
— — Classification in. (H. Kephart) Lib. J. **18**: 240.
— — Combined Receipt and Cash Register. (H. Kephart) Lib. J. **19**: 86.
— — Connection of, with Schools and Museums. (W. Orr, jr.) New Eng. M. n. s. **15**: 245.
— — Delivery Stations. (G. W. Cole) Lib. J. **17**: 480.
— — Development of. (J. Winsor) Lib. J. **19**: 370.
— — Economical Features of. (T. L. Kelso) Arena, **7**: 709. Same art. Lib. J. **15**: 473.
— — Employees in, Training of. (A. R. Hasse) Lib. J. **20**: 202, 239, 272.
— — Executive Department of. (F. M. Crunden) Lib. J. **18**: 232.
— — Fixtures, Furniture and Fittings. (H. J. Carr) Lib. J. **18**: 225.
— — Floors and Floor-Coverings of. (W. Beer) Lib. J. **19**: supp. 100.
— — Free. (F. M. Crunden) Lend a H. **10**: 399.
— — — How to popularize. (P. Cowell) New R. **9**: 440. Same art. Lib. J. **18**: 461.
— — from the Readers' Point of View. Lib. J. **18**: 179, 216.
— — Future of Local. (J. Winsor) Atlan. **71**: 815.
— — Gifts and Bequests to, 1893–94. (H. Kephart) Lib. J. **19**: supp. 61.
— — Government, Constitution, and Trustees. (H. M. Utley) Lib. J. **18**: 225.
— — Helping Inquirers in. (G. E. Little) Lib. J. **20**: supp. 19.
— — Improper Books in. Lib. J. **20**: supp. 32.
— — in England, Growth of. (W. E. Gladstone) Lib. J. **17**: 200.
— — in Europe, Facilities for Study in. (J. H. Gore) Educa. R. **6**: 58.
— — in Germany. (L. Ambrose) Lib. J. **21**: 53.
— — in Russia. (A. V. Babine) Lib. J. **18**: 75.
— — in relation to Schools. (H. P. James) Lib. J. **18**: 213.
— — in United States, Progress of, 1893–94. (F. P. Hill) Lib. J. **19**: supp. 56.
— — Information Desk. (W. E. Foster) Lib. J. **19**: 368.
— — International Mutual Relations of. (K. Dziatzko) Lib. J. **18**: 465.
— — Lectures, Museums, Art Galleries, etc., in Connection with. (J. Bain, jr.) Lib. J. **18**: 214.
— — Loan Systems. (M. W. Plummer) Lib. J. **18**: 242.
— — Maintaining by Endowment. (M. E. Hazeltine) Lib. J. **21**: 93.

Libraries, Public, Movement for, in the U. S. (J. L. Harrison) New Eng. M. n. s. 10: 709. — (W. I. Fletcher) Cosmopol. 18: 99.
— — Moving of. (C. R. Gillett) Lib. J. 20: 48.
— — Newspapers, Current, in. Lib. J. 19: supp. 42.
— — of the U. S. Dial (Ch.) 15: 327.
— — Present Problem of. (W. H. Brett) Lib. J. 19: supp. 5.
— — Printed Lists for. (K. M. Henneberry) Lib. J. 19: 9.
— — Problem of Small. (W. P. Garrison) Nation, 56: 210.
— — Progress of Government Aids to. (A. R. Spofford) Lib. J. 18: 248.
— — Reading for the Young in. (L. E. Stearns) Lib. J. 19: supp. 81. — (C. M. Hewins) Lib. J. 18: 251.
— — Recent Improvements in. (E. C. Hovey) No. Am. 158: 376.
— — Recent Progress of. (W. I. Fletcher) Citizen, 1: 56.
— — Reference Books in. (E. C. Richardson) Lib. J. 18: 254.
— — Reference Work among School Children in. (A. L. Sargeant) Lib. J. 20: 121.
— — Regulations for Readers. (W. H. Brett) Lib. J. 18: 230.
— — Relation of, to Public Schools. (E. M. Coe) Lib. J. 17: 193.
— — Replacing Books in. (B. C. Steiner; S. H. Ranck) Lib. J. 21: 397.
— — Scrap-books, Clippings, etc., in. (W. A. Bardwell) Lib. J. 18: 258.
— — Selection of Books for. Lib. J. 19: supp. 30. — (J. N. Larned) Lib. J. 20: 270. — (M. S. Cutler) Lib. J. 20: 339.
— — Service in. (F. P. Hill) Lib. J. 18: 228.
— — Shelf-notation in. (H. H. Langton) Lib. J. 21: 441.
— — Technical Collections in. (C. W. Andrews) Lib. J. 20: 6.
— School. (H. E. Scudder) Atlan. 72: 678. — (M. W. Shinn) Overland, n. s. 27: 644.
— — and College. (G. T. Little) Lib. J. 18: 431.
— Some Continental. (M. W. Plummer) Nation, 59: 305, 338, 441. 60: 7, 180, 358.
— Travelling, Free. (W. R. Eastman) Forum, 18: 616. — Critic, 27: 138.
— — in Farming Communities. (F. A. Hutchins) Lib. J. 21: 171.
— University and Higher Education. (C. E. Lowrey) Lib. J. 19: 264.
— — and the University Curriculum. (W. F. Poole) Lib. J. 18: 470.
— — Functions of. (H. L. Koopman) Lib. J. 19: supp. 24.
Library, District, Evolution of a. (A. R. Phelps) Lib. J. 21: 362.
— A Mediæval. Bookworm, 5: 57.
— National, for Ireland. Eng. R. 7: 314.
— A New National. Gent. M. n. s. 49: 216, 319.
— of Congress. Lib. J. 19: 309.
— Public, Changing a Subscription Library to. (C. W. McClintock) Lib. J. 20: supp. 46.
— — The Free. (H. H. Barber) Am. M. Civics, 6: 469.
— The Writer's. (W. H. Hills) Writer, 8: 158.
Library Association of the United Kingdom, Meeting at Paris, 1892. Ath. '92, 2: 416.
— 1894 Meeting. Ath. '94, 2: 353.
Library Associations, State, Work accomplished by. (E. L. Adams) Lib. J. 20: 380.
Library Building, Ideal Free Public. (E. C. Hovey) No. Am. 160: 118.
Library Buildings. (J. L. Smithmeyer) Am. Arch. 41: 192.
— Construction of, and the Card Catalogue. (E. E. Clarke) Lib. J. 17: 229.
Library Conference at Atlanta. Lib. J. 21: 15.
Library Economies. (W. I. Fletcher) Lib. J. 17: supp. 1.
Library Economy, Handbook of. (A. H. Hopkins) Lib. J. 20: supp. 41.
Library Examinations in Schools. (C. K. Bolton) Lib. J. 20: 122.
Library Exhibit, German, at the World's Fair. (L. Ambrose) Lib. J. 18: 499.
Library Journal and Library Organization. (R. R. Bowker) Lib. J. 21: 5.
Library Laws, Iowa. (G. W. Wakefield) Lib. J. 19: 331.
— of the State of New York. Lib. J. 17: 448.
Library Legislation in New Hampshire. (W. I. Fletcher) Critic, 26: 367.
— in Ohio. (W. H. Johnson) Critic, 26: 426.
Library Notes, Keeping of. (N. E. Browne) Lib. J. 20: 306.
Library Papers. Lib. J. 17: 48.
Library School, New York State, Life at. (M. E. Robbins) Lib. J. 21: 13.
Library Thieves. Lib. J. 17: 243.
Library Window, The; a story of the Seen and the Unseen. Blackw. 159: 1. Same art. Ecl. M. 126: 393. Same art. Liv. Age, 208: 266.
Library Work, State University. (C. Bennett) Educa. 14: 298.
Libyans; Newly-found Race in Egypt. (J. E. Quibell) Knowl. 18: 196.
License and No-license in Cambridge, Mass. (F. Foxcroft) New Eng. M. n. s. 13: 53.
License Question. (J. J. Cockshott) Econ. R. 4: 463.
License System, Substitute for. (L. Satterthwait) Am. J. Pol. 2: 476.
Lichenology, American. (W. W. Calkins) Science, 20: 205.
Lichens, Notes on Mexican. (T. A. Williams) Am. Natural. 29: 480.
— Symbiosis and Mutualism in. Pound) Am. Natural. 27: 509.
Lichtenberg, Castle of. How it became a Ruin; tr. by Mrs. Childers. Good Words, 35: 556, 638, 693.
Lick Observatory. Chr. Un. 45: 784. — (A. Fowler) Nature, 51: 201. — (M. W. Shinn) Overland, n. s. 20: 479. — (E. S. Holden) Univ. R. 3: 165.
— Astronomy on Top of a Mountain. (I. H. Fikel) Chaut. 17: 313.
Liddon, H. P., Canon. (J. Gibb) Crit. R. 1: 63.
Lide; a story. (R. C. V. Mayers) Harper, 86: 359.
Lie, Jonas, with portrait. Bookman, 2: 200.
— One of Life's Slaves; tr. by J. Muir. Sat. R. 79: 675.
Liebermann, Max. (F. H. Meissner) Art J. 45: 225.
Liebig, Justus von. Autobiographical Sketch. Pop. Sci. Mo. 40: 655.
Liebknecht, William. (E. Sellers) Fortn. 65: 997.
Liebling, Emil. Music, 5: 90.
Liechtenstein; the Smallest Principality in Europe. Chamb. J. 73: 550.
Liederbuch des Königs Denis von Portugal, Lang's. (A. R. Marsh) Nation, 61: 373.
Liège, Fortifications near. (E. M. Lloyd) Un. Serv. M. 6: 24.
— Old Towers of. (A. Elliot) Illust. Archæol. 1: 150.

Lien, Maritime. (J. Mansfield) Law Q. 4: 379.
Lieutenant, The; a story. Un. Serv. (Phila.) 10: 341.
Life, Active. All the Year, 71: 321.
— and its Environment. (E. Mancini) Chaut. 21: 550.
— and Labor. (E. Zola) New R. 9: 56. Same art. Ecl. M. 121: 318.
— Animal and Vegetable, Retrogression in. (A. Weismann) Open Court, 3: 1801–1855.
— Ascent of. (S. Jarvis) Arena, 9: 482, 601, 723.
— Aspects of. (Sir E. Arnold) Longm. 23: 31.
— at Low Pressures. Chamb. J. 69: 343.
— Backwater of. (J. Payn) Cornh. 71: 517.
— before Fossils. (C. Morris) Am. Natural. 30: 188, 279.
— Conditions of. (W. Preyer) Open Court, 2: 863–1407.
— Continuity of. (J. Watson) New Sci. R. 1: 487. Same art. Chr. Lit. 13: 130.
— Duration of. Sat. R. 79: 248.
— Eternal. (W. Hutchinson) Open Court, 10: 4855.
— Final Aim of. (S. B. Weston) Eth. Rec. 1: 73.
— Guesses at the Riddle of. (G. Smith) No. Am. 161: 230.
— How long can the Earth sustain? (Sir R. Ball) Fortn. 57: 478. Same art. Ecl. M. 118: 682. Same art. Liv. Age, 193: 656.
— How to make the most of. (Sir B. W. Richardson) Longm. 25: 39. — Spec. 73: 206.
— How to prolong. (W. Kinnear) No. Am. 163: 249.
— Inequalities of. (R. Thomas) Chr. Lit. 12: 218.
— Infinitely and Divinely worth living. (F. Sewall) N. Church. R. 3: 89.
— Is Human Life overvalued? (F. M. Bird) Soc. Econ. 4: 339.
— Is it Universal? (E. J. Chappel) New Sci. R. 2: 41.
— Is it worth living? (W. James) Int. J. Ethics, 6: 1. — (T. Davidson) Int. J. Ethics, 6: 231.
— Material View of, and its Relation to the Spiritual. (G. Lusk) Pop. Sci. Mo. 43: 533.
— Nature of, the Foundation of Medical Science. (L. S. Beale) Science, n. s. 2: 644.
— Pelagic Origin of. (W. K. Brooks) Am. Natural. 28: 585.
— Physical. (M. J. Greenman) Chaut. 14: 418.
— Plant and Animal, Mutual Relations of. (B. D. Halsted) Chaut. 19: 194.
— Problem of, in Terms of Chess. Ecl. M. 118: 172.
— Prolonging. (W. Kinnear) No. Am. 159: 635.
— Simple Forms of. Sat. R. 79: 10.
— Simpler, Plea for. Chamb. J. 73: 17.
— The Struggle for. (J. Reed) N. Church R. 2: 321.
— Suspended. Spec. 68: 196.
— Synthesis of Living Beings. (A. Sabatier) Pop. Sci. Mo. 42: 49.
— Tasting. Spec. 73: 202.
— to come, The. (J. M. Gibson) Sund. M. 21: 588.
— Varied, in Other Worlds. (R. A. Proctor) Open Court, 1: 595.
— What is it? (E. Montgomery) Monist, 5: 166.
Life of a Brown Rabbit. All the Year, 73: 630.
Life of Nancy. (S. O. Jewett) Atlan. 75: 175.
Life of the Party, The; a story. All the Year, 75: 276.
Life-guards, The. Chamb. J. 71: 220.
Life-saving Service, British. Chamb. J. 69: 145. — (C. W. Macara) New R. 10: 232.
— — Is our Lifeboat System effectual? (E. H. Bayley) New R. 10: 71.
— U. S. (T. J. A. Freeman) Am. Cath. Q. 18: 650. — (H. L. Piper) J. Frankl. Inst. 133: 1.
Life's Episodes; a story. (R. M. Burnand) Belgra. 81: holiday no., 90.
Life's Possibilities; a story. (M. S. Hancock) Belgra. 90: 198.
Lifeboat Rescue, A. (T. S. Treanor) Sund. M. 25: 517.
Light. (N. Tesla) J. Frankl. Inst. 136: 1-401.
— Aberration and Atmospheric Refraction of. (G. C. Comstock) Astron. 13: 329.
— Action of, on Animal Life. (G. C. Frankland) Nature, 52: 86.
— and Color, Sensitiveness of the Eye to. (W. de W. Abney) Nature, 47: 538.
— and Electrification. (O. J. Lodge) Sci. Prog. 3: 175. 5: 417.
— and Other High Frequency Phenomena. (N. Tesla) Nature, 48: 136.
— Artificial, Standards of. (W. J. Dibdin) J. Soc. Arts, 44: 223.
— Cold. (A. E. Dolbear) Cosmopol. 18: 255.
— Influence of, upon the Discharge of Electrified Bodies. (E. Merritt) Science, n. s. 4: 853, 890.
— of the Future. (D. McF. Moore) Cassier, 6: 236.
— Perception of. (G. G. Stokes) Nature, 53: 66.
— Poincaré on Maxwell and Hertz. Nature, 50: 8.
— Sensation of, New Theory of. (C. L. Franklin) Science, 22: 18.
— — Intensity and Duration of Stimulation in. (J. E. Lough) Psychol. R. 3: 484.
— — Theories of. (C. L. Franklin) Mind, 18: 473.
— Velocity of. (E. Mach) Open Court, 8: 4167.
— Waves of, and their Application to Meteorology. (A. A. Michelson) Nature, 49: 56. Same art. Astron. 13: 92.
Light and Shadow; a novel. (E. Garnett) Univ. R. 4: 244, 417, 571. 5: 138.
Light in the East. (B. O. Flower) Arena, 10: 342.
Light o' Carglen, A. (A. Gordon) Macmil. 66: 126.
Light of the World, The. (W. M. Sinclair) Sund. M. 22: 307.
Light Brigade, Balaclava. (J. W. Wightman) Un. Serv. (Phila.) 8: 90.
Lightfoot, J. B., Bishop. Quar. 176: 73.
— and Cardinal Newman. Ed. R. 178: 248.
— and the Early Roman See. (D. C. Butler) Dub. R. 113: 497.
Lighthouse Apparatus. (J. Kenward) Science, 21: 216.
Lighthouse Illuminants. Chamb. J. 62: 563. — (W. P. Anderson) Science, 21: 260.
Lighthouse Keeper's Story. (B. Chandler) New Eng. M. n. s. 12: 723.
Lighthouse Service. (E. P. Adams) Cassier, 6: 297–355.
Lighthouses; a Cruise of the "Ameria," Supply-ship. (K. Munroe) Scrib. M. 20: 460.
— in Foreign Countries. Am. Cath. Q. 17: 413.
— in the United States. Am. Cath. Q. 17: 644, 873.
— Oil for. (E. Price Edwards) J. Soc. Arts, 40: 260.
— Recent Improvements in. Nature, 53: 56.
— Silent Sentinels of the Cornish Coast. (J. M. Price) Eng. Illust. 11: 1222.
Lighting, Artificial, for Workshops. (B. A. Dobson) Cassier, 5: 417.
— Corporations for, State and. (W. S. Allen) Ann. Am. Acad. Pol. Sci. 2: 707.
Lightning. (M. Henshaw) Science, 19: 249.
— and Lightning-conductors. (O. J. Lodge) Engin. M. 8: 68.
Lightning, Effect of, on Trees. Knowl. 18: 162.
— Effects of, in Ben Nevis Observatory. (W. S. Bruce) Nature, 52: 244.

Lightning, Injury from. (G. M. Minchin) Nature, **53**: 5.
— Note on Globular. (O. C. Marsh) Am. J. Sci. **151**: 13.
— Protection of Buildings from. (N. D. C. Hodges) Science, **19**: 197.
— Protection from. (A. McAdie) Am. Arch. **50**: 77. — (A. McAdie) Pop. Sci. Mo. **43**: 453. — (A. J. Wurts) Cassier, **9**: 435.
— Sheet, in India. Dub. R. **118**: 151.
Lightning Arresters and why they sometimes fail. (A. J. Wurts) J. Frankl. Inst. **139**: 439.
— of Alex. Jay Wurts. J. Frankl. Inst. **138**: 247.
Lightning Conductors, Reynold's Instructions for Erecting and Testing. Am. Arch. **39**: 188.
— Inventor of. (J. J. Kral) Pop. Sci. Mo. **42**: 356.
Lightning Discharges, Oscillations of, and of the Aurora Borealis. (J. Trowbridge) Am. J. Sci. **146**: 195.
Lightning Figures. (C. Tomlinson) Chamb. J. **69**: 847.
Lights in Mediæval Churches. (F. W. Weaver) Antiq. n. s. **25**: 23.
Lightship, A Bishop's Visit to a. (T. S. Treanor) Sund. M. **25**: 664.
Like Father, Like Son; a story. Argosy, **54**: summer no., 53. Same art. Liv. Age, **194**: 678.
Like the Good God. (M. Wilcox) Harper, **90**: 590.
Like a Mountain Path; a story. (M. L. Radford) Canad. M. **4**: 480.
Like Other Folks. (G. Morton) New Eng. M. **12**: 434.
Lilac Thief, The. (C. Battersby) Sund. M. **24**: 696.
Lilacs. Garden & F. **8**: 224.
— The Best. Garden & F. **6**: 457.
— Best Varieties of. Garden & F. **7**: 168.
Lilburne, John, as a Pamphleteer. (H. H. Sparling) Bookworm, **6**: 315.
Lilienthal, Otto, the Flying Man. McClure, **3**: 323.
Lilies as Articles of Food and Commerce. (I. Nitaba) Garden & F. **9**: 12.
— at Kew Gardens. (G. Nicholson) Garden & F. **6**: 413.
— Autumn Flowering. (G. Reuthe) Garden & F. **6**: 45, 55.
— Beauty of. (C. C. Abbott) Mo. Illust. **3**: 209.
— Cultivation of. (E. O. Orpet) Garden & F. **8**: 115, 426. — (F. H. Horsford) Garden & F. **9**: 44.
— Culture of, in Pots. (J. Douglas) Garden & F. **6**: 114.
— Hardy. (E. O. Orpet) Garden & F. **5**: 462.
— in Autumn. (C. L. Allen) Garden & F. **5**: 501.
— Lilium Giganteum. (J. Brydon) Garden & F. **6**: 373.
— Luther Burbank's Hybrid. (Carl Purdy) Garden & F. **8**: 328.
— Notes on. (F. H. Horsford) Garden & F. **8**: 7, 17, 276.
— Timely Hints on. (E. O. Orpet) Garden & F. **6**: 394.
Lilies of France. (H. M. Ingersoll) Mo. Illust. **4**: 49.
Lilies of Nola, The. (M. Scott-Uda) Cent. **28**: 532.
Liliuokalani, Queen. (C. F. Nichols) Overland, n. s. **27**: 526.
Lille, France, Roman Catholic University. Cath. World, **59**: 780.
Lilly, William. (E. Walford) Walford's Antiq. **10**: 147.
— a 17th Century Zadkiel. (C. Lord) Bookworm, **7**: 265, 296.
Lilly, W. S. Great Enigma. Spec. **70**: 104.
Lily Flower in Art. (L. B. Thompson) Art J. **47**: 363.
Lily-of-the-Valley, Cultivation of. Garden & F. **5**: 249.
— for Out-door Planting. (E. O. Orpet) Garden & F. **7**: 475.
Lily of the Valley; a poem. (A. H. Japp) Argosy, **62**: 153.
Lima, Peru, Housekeeping in. (S. R. Bogue) Overland, n. s. **22**: 520.
Limbo. (Vernon Lee) Longm. **27**: 388. Same art. Ecl. M. **126**: 739. Same art. Liv. Age, **208**: 812.
Limerick Cathedral. Reliquary, **32**: 25.
Limestone, Bethany, of the Western Interior Coal Field. (C. R. Keyes) Am. J. Sci. **152**: 221.
— Flexibility of, Illustration of. (A. Winslow) Am. J. Sci. **143**: 133.
Limestone Formations, Mount Bob, N. Y. (T. W. Harris) Am. J. Sci. **143**: 236.
Limestone Regions, Dr. Cvijić on Phenomena of. Geog. J. **3**: 320.
Limitation as a Social Remedy. (J. C. Ridpath) Arena, **15**: 741.
— Statutes of, and Property. (W. C. Maude) Month, **87**: 388.
Limitations. (E. F. Benson) Temp. Bar, **107**: 305, 449. **108**: 1-598. **109**: 118, 282.
Limited Liability Act, A National. Am. J. Pol. **2**: 233.
Limoges. (Miss Betham-Edwards) Time, **14**: 292.
Limpets, Habits of. (J. R. A. Davis) Nature, **51**: 511.
Lin McLean's Honeymoon; a story. (O. Wister) Harper, **90**: 283.
Linarias, Cultivation of. (E. Mische) Garden & F. **7**: 438.
Lincoln, Derivation of the Name. (H. Bradley and others) Acad. **44**: 344, 369, 416, 439.
Lincoln, Abraham, Ancestry of. (J. H. Barrett) N. E. Reg. **48**: 327.
— Appeals to Clemency of. (L. J. Perry) Cent. **29**: 251.
— as Commander-in-chief. (A. K. McClure) McClure, **4**: 253.
— as a Strategist. (A. Forbes) No. Am. **155**: 53, 160.
— Assassination of. (H. King) New Eng. M. n. s. **9**: 425.
— — Recollections of. (S. Munroe) No. Am. **162**: 424.
— — Thwarting of the First Plot. (C. Moffett) McClure, **3**: 519.
— Brooks on. (E. G. Johnson) Dial (Ch.) **19**: 241.
— S. P. Chase and Grant. (N. Brooks) Cent. **27**: 607.
— The Close of his Career. (N. Brooks) Cent. **28**: 18.
— Complete Works, ed. by Nicolay and Hay. (B. A. Hinsdale) Dial (Ch.) **17**: 33.
— Conspiracies against, Four. (V. L. Mason) Cent. **29**: 889.
— Gettysburgh Address. (J. G. Nicolay) Cent. **25**: 596.
— Glimpses of, in War Time. (N. Brooks) Cent. **27**: 457.
— His Journey to Washington in 1861. (A. K. McClure) McClure, **5**: 91.
— in his Relations to Women. (Mrs. Van R. Cruger) Cosmopol. **18**: 205.
— Life of, with Illustrations. (I. M. Tarbell) McClure, **5**: 481. **6**: 2-526. **7**: 79-401. **8**: 43.
— Literary Experiments of. (J. G. Nicolay) Cent. **25**: 823.
— Morse's Life of. (W. Lewin) Acad. **44**: 245. — (J. J. Halsey) Dial (Ch.) **15**: 263. — (H. White) Nation, **56**: 407.
— Nomination of. (I. H. Bromley) Scrib. M. **14**: 645.
— — to Congress, 1846. Am. Hist. R. **1**: 313.
— on a Government Bank. Soc. Econ. **9**: 1.

Lincoln, Abraham, Personal Recollections of. (Marq. de Chambrun) Scrib. M. **13**: 26.
— Place of, in History. (J. C. Adams) Cent. **25**: 590.
— Recollections of. (J. M. Scovel) Lippinc. **51**: 237.
— Reëlection of. (N. Brooks) Cent. **27**: 865.
— Religion of. Chr. Lit. **14**: 641.
— Some Memories of. (J. F. Wilson) No. Am. **163**: 667.
— Symposium. Indep. April 4, '95.
— What was his Creed? (G. M. McCrie) Open Court, **5**: 3031.
— Whitney's. (J. W. Chadwick) Nation, **56**: 127.
Lincoln Cathedral, Restoration of. Antiq. n. s. **25**: 194.
— Statutes of. Church Q. **35**: 97. — Spec. **69**: 601.
— Walk Round. (E. Venables) Sund. M. **22**: 552, 600.
— Yuletide in. (C. Logsdail) New Eng. M. n. s. **9**: 383.
Lincoln Co., Me., Intentions of Marriage in. (B. N. Goodale) N. E. Reg. **46**: 11.
Lincoln Palace. (A. R. Maddison) Sund. M. **25**: 725, 807.
Lincoln's Inn. All the Year, **74**: 535.
Lincoln's Inn Fields. (R. Hunter) Eng. Illust. **11**: 991.
— Round. All the Year, **74**: 317.
Lincolnshire Cars, Legends of. (M. C. Balfour) Folk-Lore, **2**: 251, 401.
Lincolnshire Churches. (A. G. Hill) Walford's Antiq. **2**: 62.
Lincolnshire Water-lore. (M. Peacock) Antiq. n. s. **31**: 366.
Lind, Jenny. (R. J. McNeill) Cent. **23**: 207.
— and the Old Songs. (G. F. Root) Music, **2**: 15.
— First Concert in America. (I. G. Tompkins) Music, **10**: 145.
— in Northampton, Mass. (E. Le B. Marsh) New Eng. M. n. s. **6**: 393.
Linden Trees. (G. Paxton) Knowl. **19**: 171.
Linderhof. Liv. Age, **211**: 670.
Lindisfarne. *See* Holy Island.
Line upon Line; a poem. Argosy, **59**: 452.
Line-man's Wedding. (J. Ralph) Harper, **89**: 828.
Lineage, Ancient. (Edward Harlow) Cosmopol. **20**: 317.
Lineff's Russian Choir. Music, **4**: 590.
Lines Written on returning a Lady's Violin; a poem. (Will Hill) Cosmopol. **19**: 300.
Lingg, Hermann, with portrait. Bk. News, **12**: 347.
Linguist, The; a story. (E. Nesbit) Liv. Age, **192**: 167.
Linked! not United; a story. (Mrs. P. Cudlip) Belgra. **78**: holiday no., 10.
Links and Chains; a story. (B. Oulet) Argosy, **55**: 470. Same art. Liv. Age, **198**: 465.
Linlithgow. (D. Macleod) Good Words, **33**: 828.
Linn, Dr. Lewis F. (C. Aldrich) M. Am. Hist. **28**: 54.
Linnell, John. (A. T. Story) M. of Art, **15**: 130.
— Country of. (A. T. Story) Art J. **44**: 301.
— Story's. (F. Wedmore) Acad. **41**: 512. — Ath. '**92**, **2**: 860. — Sat. R. **74**: 627. — Spec. **69**: 927.
Linoleum. (G. McGowan) Knowl. **19**: 195.
Linotype, The. (E. Aveling) Time, **22**: 412.
Linotyping of Library Catalogues. Lib. J. **19**: 257.
Linton, Eliza Lynn. (Mrs. Alec Tweedie) Temp. Bar, **102**: 355.
Linton, Sir J. D. (F. G. Stephens) Portfo. **24**: 224.
Linton, Wm. James. (G. J. Harney) Open Court, **5**: 2969.
— Recollections. (E. G. Johnson) Dial (Ch.) **18**: 43.
— Studio and Library of, by Himself. Lippinc. **55**: 711.
Lion-hunt in North-Western Colorado. (C. A. Hardy) Outing, **27**: 317.
Lion-Hunt, South American. (C. Bullman) Outing, **21**: 48.
Lion-hunting. (L. D. Rees) Outing, **27**: 370.
— Beyond the Haud. (H. C. Lowther) 19th Cent. **38**: 474. Same art. Liv. Age, **207**: 108. Same art. Ecl. M. **126**: 54.
— in Somaliland, Melliss's. Sat. R. **79**: 793.
Lion-tiger and Tiger-lion Hybrids. (V. Ball) Nature, **47**: 390.
Lions, African, Adventure with. (T. Genone) Outing, **29**: 144.
at the London Zoo, 1893. Spec. **70**: 220.
— in Trafalgar Square. Liv. Age, **196**: 446.
— My First; Hunting Fierce Game in Eastern Africa. (H. W. Seton-Karr) Cent. **25**: 22.
Lions [Society], in the Twenties. Liv. Age, **208**: 416.
Lippi, Fra Filippo. (J. A. Crowe) 19th Cent. **40**: 643.
— Browning's. (F. Wilson) M. of Art, **12**: 163.
Lipsius, Richard Adelbert. Acad. **42**: 193.
Liquids, Forms of. (E. Mach) Open Court, **8**: 3935.
— Surface Tension and Chemical Constitution. (C. E. Linebarger) Am. J. Sci. **144**: 83.
— — of Mixtures of. (C. E. Linebarger) Am. J. Sci. **152**: 226.
— — Apparatus for the Rapid Determination of. (C. E. Linebarger) Am. J. Sci. **152**: 108.
— under High Pressures, Behavior of. (J. W. Rodger) Nature, **49**: 506.
Liquor, Actual Effects of Restricting Sale of. (G. H. Bolland) Econ. R. **3**: 418.
— and Law. (W. C. Doane) No. Am. **162**: 292.
— and Politics. (K. Bocock) Soc. Econ. **4**: 164.
— and Tobacco. Why should they be taxed? (M. Malagrowther) National, **19**: 148.
— Drink Evil, The; Symposium. Indep. Oct. 4, '94.
— Drink Problem. (Axel Gustafson) Chr. Un. **45**: 203–590.
— Government by Brewery Interests. (G. A. Gates) Arena, **15**: 797.
— Immoral Use and Sale of. (A. F. Hewit) Cath. World, **50**: 1.
— Land and Labor. Fortn. **64**: 12.
— Local Option. (J. Halpin) Month, **74**: 233.
See Saloons.
Liquor Laws in England, Five Centuries of. (E. Porritt) Pol. Sci. Q. **10**: 615.
Liquor Legislation. (D. MacG. Means) Nation, **57**: 423.
Liquor Licenses; Excise Law and the Saloon. (W. C. Doane) No. Am. **155**: 395.
— in England; Bishop of Chester on Public Houses. Spec. **69**: 279, 346.
— — Lord Randolph Churchill and. Spec. **71**: 573.
Liquor Problem, Some Aspects of. (H. O. Ward) Am. M. Civics, **6**: 426.
Liquor Question. (J. P. St. John) Am. J. Pol. **1**: 407.
Liquor Traffic. (J. S. Hopkins) National, **25**: 72.
— Abolition of Laws on. Pub. Opin. **16**: 593.
— Chamberlain on Reform in Licensing. Lend a H. **13**: 184.
— Christ and the Liquor-seller. (H. M. Gougar) Arena, **7**: 461. — (G. G. Brown) Arena, **8**: 201.
— Gothenburg System. Cath. World, **58**: 431. — J. Statis. Soc. **56**: 316. — R. of Rs. (N. Y.) **8**: 548. — (J. G. Brooks) Forum, **14**: 514. — Spec. **69**: 918. — (T. F. Moran) Char. R. **3**: 282. — Spec. **73**: 40. — (J. G. Brooks) Econ. J. **4**: 209. — (P. Carlson) Cath. World, **59**: 224. — (E. O. Achorn) Bost. **2**: 120.
— — and Kindred Systems. Lend a H. **10**: 244.

Liquor Traffic. Gothenburg System and our Liquor Traffic. (E. R. L. Gould) Forum, 17: 103.
— — in America. (E. R. L. Gould) Atlan. 72: 538.
— — in England, Sir W. Harcourt's Bill for. Spec. 70: 277.
— — — The Veto Bill. (C. Walker) Fortn. 59: 734.
— — in Norway, and its Application to England. (T. M. Wilson) Contemp. 65: 836.
— — not a Failure. (J. Koren) Cath. World, 59: 553.
— Government Control of. (R. B. Rockham) Econ. R. 5: 285.
— How to deal with. (A. A. Miner and others) Arena, 9: 827.
— in New York and Pennsylvania. (R. Wheatley) Chaut. 19: 178.
— in Norway. Sat. R. 75: 628–680.
— in the South Seas. (J. G. Paton) Our Day, 11: 155.
— in Switzerland, Question of. (W. Milliet) Ann. Am. Acad. Pol. Sci. 3: 429.
— Is Liquor Selling a Sin? (H. M. Gougar) Arena, 8: 710.
— Is Prohibition of, Practicable? (M. F. Brown) Am. J. Pol. 1: 570.
— Political Parties and. National, 20: 859.
— Popular Control. (F. S. M. Bennett) Econ. R. 5: 338.
— Possible Reformation of. (W. S. Rainsford) No. Am. 156: 586, 728.
— Regulation of. (F. Gottsberger) No. Am. 161: 635. — (J. Mann, jr.) Scot. R. 21: 419.
— Roman Catholic Church and. (F. A. Satolli) Our Day, 13: 434.
— Mgr. Satolli and. Pub. Opin. 17: 438.
— Shall we nationalize it? (A. L. Cornwall) Am. M. Civics, 6: 317.
— South Carolina Law. (B. R. Tillman) No. Am. 158: 140.
— — A Last Word on. (B. R. Tillman; W. F. Dargan) No. Am. 159: 46.
— — Lesson of Outbreak against. Spec. 72: 459.
— — Our Whiskey Rebellion. (B. R. Tillman) No. Am. 158: 513.
— State Control of, in South Carolina. Pub. Opin. 15: 271, 355, 376.
— State Monopoly of. (D. MacG. Means) Nation, 61: 74.
— Successful Public-house Reform. (F. J. Jayne) No. Am. 158: 520.
— Three Methods of Dealing with. Pub. Opin. 17: 142.
— without Private Profits. (J. Koren) Arena, 9: 561.
Liquor-tax Law, Raines. (J. Raines) No. Am. 162: 481.
Lirica and Xerica, James F. F. Stuart, Duke of, Diary of. Quar. 174: 192. Same art. Liv. Age, 193: 105.
Lisbon, Voyage to, Fielding's. Sat. R. 73: 660.
Lishoy, Ireland. (H. C. Shelley) New Eng. M. n. s. 13: 323.
Lismore Cathedral. Reliquary, 32: 28.
Lister, Sir Jos. (H. Tillmanns) Nature, 54: 1.
Liszt, Franz, with portrait. Bk. Buyer, 11: 254. — (C. Saint-Saëns) Cent. 23: 517. — (W. S. B. Mathews) Music, 4: 52. — (H. K. Moore) Time, 15: 286.
— and Paderewski. (H. T. Finck) Nation, 56: 308.
— Dante Symphony. (E. V. Eastmann) Music, 3: 304.
— Letters, tr. by Bache. Sat. R. 77: 477. — (H. T. Finck) Nation, 58: 158. — Dial (Ch.) 17: 8.
Literary Activities, Directions and Volume of. (A. R. Spofford) Forum, 16: 598.
Literary Activity, Extensions of. Dial (Ch.) 21: 176.
Literary Advice and Patronage. (R. Ogden) Nation, 61: 323.
Literary Agent, The. (W. R. Nicoll) Bookman, 1: 249. — Reply. (W. Besant) 19th Cent. 38: 979. — National, 26: 650.
Literary Amenity. Dial (Ch.) 16: 5.
Literary Anachronisms. Bookworm, 2: 140.
Literary Art, Resemblances in. (W. H. Olding) Time, 14: 552.
Literary Conferences. (W. Besant) Contemp. 65: 123.
Literary Coincidences. (J. Dennis) Liv. Age, 192: 822.
Literary Construction. (V. Paget) Contemp. 68: 404. Same art. Ecl. M. 125: 530.
Literary Dilettanteism. (W. G. Kingsland) Poet-Lore, 6: 512.
Literary Forms, Origin of. (C. Letourneau) Pop. Sci. Mo. 43: 673.
Literary Frauds in England in 1892. Spec. 69: 438.
Literary Hack and his Critics. Forum, 20: 508.
— Confessions of a. Forum, 19: 629.
Literary Independence of the U. S. (B. Matthews) Cosmopol. 13: 343.
Literary Judgment, Finality in. (W. M. Dixon) Westm. 143: 401.
Literary Man, The, as a Man of Business. (W. D. Howells) Scrib. M. 14: 429.
Literary Masquerader, A. (G. F. Lynch) Bach. of Arts, 3: 742.
Literary Men, Letters and Recollections of. Cornh. 65: 368. Same art. Liv. Age, 193: 673.
Literary Model, A. (M. B. Sheldon) Atlan. 78: 256.
Literary Necrology for 1891. Lit. W. (Bost.) 23: 29.
— for 1894. Lit. W. (Bost.) 26: 13.
Literary Personality. All the Year, 72: 225.
Literary Production, Present Conditions of. (P. Shorey) Atlan. 78: 156.
Literary Property. (E. Zola) Bookman, 3: 412.
— A Good. (Helen E. Starrett) Educa. 17: 158.
Literary Spirit in the Colleges. (F. H. Stoddard) Educa. R. 6: 126.
Literary Students' League. (F. W. Coburn) Writer, 8: 77.
Literary Studies, Tendencies in. (A. R. Marsh) Harv. Mo. 14: 177.
Literary Study, Aims of. (H. Corson) Poet-Lore, 6: 473.
— — Corson on. (E. E. Hale, jr.) Dial (Ch.) 18: 109.
Literary Taste, Decay of. (E. Gosse) No. Am. 161: 109.
— Developing, in Students. (E. T. MacLaughlin) Educa. R. 5: 17.
— of the Public, On Pleasing the. (B. Matthews) Forum, 21: 219.
Literary Theory and Practice. (S. Axson) Citizen, 2: 169.
Literary Wife, A; a story. (E. C. Cook) Gent. M. n. s. 48: 541.
Literary Woman at the Picnic. (E. W. Wilcox) Lippinc. 56: 400.
Literature, Ancient, Romance of. (W. F. Petrie) Leis. Hour, 41: 12–260.
— and the Drama. (E. Fawcett) Dial (Ch.) 14: 38.
— and Language, their Connection in Education. (T. R. Price) Educa. R. 11: 12.
— and Life. Soc. Econ. 2: 203.
— and the Ministry. (L. W. Spring) Atlan. 69: 546.
— and Philology. (G. M. Whicher) Educa. R. 11: 279.
— — Relations of. (O. F. Emerson) Educa. R. 5: 130.
— and the Religious Feeling. (A. A. Berle) Bib. Sac. 50: 261.

Literature and the Scientific Spirit. (O. L. Triggs) Poet-Lore, 6: 113. — (L. A. Sherman) Poet-Lore, 6: 323.
— The Approach to. Dial (Ch.) 16: 199.
— Art of. (E. V. Ingram) Westm. 142: 392.
— as a Career. (W. Besant) Forum, 13: 693.
— as a Means of Moral Training in the Schools. (C. F. Brusie) Educa. 14: 129.
— as a Resource. (H. W. Mabie) Chaut. 22: 65.
— Best Books, 1892. Lit. W. (Bost.) 23: 8.
— — 1893. Lit. W. (Bost.) 25: 8.
— — 1894. Lit. W. (Bost.) 26: 8.
— Comforts of. (T. W. Higginson) Chr. Un. 45: 300.
— Common and Human in. (W. B. Harte) New Eng. M. n. s. 8: 641.
— Contemporary, Mediocrity of. Lit. W. (Bost.) 26: 350.
— Decadent. (H. E. M. Stutfield) Blackw. 157: 833. Same art. Ecl. M. 125: 162.
— Decadent Movement in. (A. Symons) Harper, 87: 858.
— Decay of Spirituality in. (L. Hunt) Critic, 27: 297.
— Democratic and Aristocratic in. (R. Burton) Poet-Lore, 8: 57, 129.
— Democratic Ideal in. (C. Porter) Open Court, 7: 3560.
— European, Continental, 1892. Dial (Ch.) 15: 55.
— — — 1893. Dial (Ch.) 17: 51, 79.
— Evaluation of. (G. Iles) Lib. J. 17: supp. 18.
— for Art's Sake. (H. M. Hoke) Writer, 7: 23.
— Greek Influence in. (J. Burroughs) Critic, 24: 177. — Reply. (M. Thompson) Critic, 24: 212.
— Hill's Lectures on Spec. 68: 241.
— How to make a Living by. (W. D. Adams) Bookman, 2: 124.
— How to study. (M. Thompson) Chaut. 18: 147.
— Immoral: Corrupt Classics. (A. Comstock) Our Day, 13: 397.
— — Suppression of. (R. Ogden) Nation, 57: 323.
— Immorality in Recent. (H. Quilter) Contemp. 67: 761.
— in America. (M. D. Conway) Open Court, 10: 4971.
— in 1891. Lit. W. (Bost.) 23: 24.
— Instruction in, Aims and Methods in. (M. Hill) Acad. (Syr.) 7: 84.
— Last Fifteen Years in. (F. E. Lester) Critic, 28: 35.
— Localism in. (J. L. Onderdonk) Mid-Cont. 6: 228.
— Mechanism of. (C. P. Nettleton) Writer, 9: 111.
— Mere. (W. Wilson) Atlan. 72: 820.
— Money the Modern King of. (E. W. Bok) Forum, 20: 334.
— Moral and Immoral. (H. MacQueary) Arena, 8: 447.
— New Era in Letters. (A. Waugh) National, 21: 510. Same art. Ecl. M. 121: 168.
— New Studies in, Dowden's. Sat. R. 80: 49.
— of the Century. (E. Gosse) Bookworm, 6: 357.
— of the Future. (J. Viaud) Forum, 14: 178.
— of the Kailyard. (J. H. Millar) New R. 12: 384.
— on the Stage. Dial (Ch.) 13: 336.
— Place of, in Reform. (R. M. Alden) Pub. Opin. 18: 376.
— Present State of. (A. J. Balfour) Critic, 22: 402.
— — Balfour on. Spec. 70: 566.
— Sex in Modern. (B. A. Crackanthorpe) 19th Cent. 37: 607.
— Spoken. (C. Barnard) Chaut. 16: 439.
— The Stage and. (W. Archer) Fortn. 57: 219.
— Study of. (N. Butler) Educa. 16: 589.
Literature, Study of, Aims and Methods in. (S. Thurber) Educa. 16: 449. — (N. Butler) Educa. 16: 529.
— — at the Universities. Dial (Ch.) 14: 134.
— Success in. (H. Caine) Critic, 26: 384.
— Teaching of. Dial (Ch.) 14: 65. — (F. I. Carpenter; L. A. Sherman; K. L. Bates; H. Carson; O. L. Triggs) Poet-Lore, 6: 377. — (H. Carson; E. M. Hurll) Poet-Lore, 6: 536.
See English.
— — Emerson's Ideas of. (E. Mims) Dial (Ch.) 20: 98.
— — New Ideas in; a Symposium. Poet-Lore, 8: 432.
— Teaching the Spirit of. (W. P. Trent) Atlan. 78: 414.
— Temporizing, and Superficial Criticism. (G. Barden) So. M. 5: 342.
— Victorian Age of, and its Critics. (D. F. Hannigan) Westm. 145: 519. Same art. Ecl. M. 126: 809.
— Vocal Interpretation of. (T. O'Hagan) Canad. M. 5: 439.
Literature Congresses at Chicago, 1893. Dial (Ch.) 15: 5.
Litho-carbon. Am. Arch. 37: 12.
Lithography, A Century of. (E. R. Pennell) Nation, 61: 289.
— Renaissance of. (M. H. Spielmann) Scrib. M. 20: 545.
— Revival of. (F. Wedmore) Art J. 48: 11, 41.
— Transfer. (W. Sickert) Sat. R. 82: 667.
Litigants, Some Famous. (B. F. Burnham) Green Bag, 6: 399.
Litigation in England and Wales. (J. Macdonell) J. Statis. Soc. 57: 452.
Litre, Where is the? (S. H. Emmens) Science, 21: 141. — (T. G. Mendenhall) Science, 21: 219.
Litt'la-iza; a story. Cornh. 67: 46.
Little Amber Monkey, The. Chamb. J. 71: 365.
Little Aymery; a poem. (Victor Hugo) Gent. M. n. s. 52: 629.
Little Bell of Honor. (G. Parker) Cent. 29: 881.
Little Betty's Kitten tells her Story. (F. H. Burnett) Eng. Illust. 12: no. 3, 3.
Little Child shall lead them. (D. Macleod) Good Words, 34: 813.
Little Chorister, The. Macmil. 70: 365. Same art. Liv. Age, 203: 74.
Little Clay God, The. Macmil. 70: 435.
Little Convent Girl; balcony story. (G. King) Cent. 24: 547.
Little Coquette, A; a story. All the Year, 74: 260, 285, 305.
Little Darby. (T. N. Page) Scrib. M. 16: 285, 457.
Little Disappointment. (L. B. Walford) Longm. 21: 487. Same art. Liv. Age, 197: 205.
Little Domestic, A. (M. H. Catherwood) Atlan. 77: 217.
Little Fairy's Constancy; a story. (J. Ralph) Harper, 92: 856.
Little Fiddler, The; a story. (L. B. Tisdale) Eng. Illust. 12: no. 6, 37.
Little Fool, A. (A. B. Poor) Cent. 30: 825.
Little General, The. (R. Stephens) Chamb. J. 73: 603. Same art. Liv. Age, 211: 336.
Little Green Door; a story. (M. E. Wilkins) Eng. Illust. 15: 293.
Little Lady Lee. (Mrs. H. L. Cameron) Lippinc. 56: 147.
Little Leaven. (A. E. P. Searing) New Eng. M. n. s. 15: 279.

Little Legacy. (L. B. Walford) Longm. **28**: 47. Same art. Liv. Age, **209**: 783.
Little Maid at the Door. (M. E. Wilkins) Harper, **84**: 349.
Little Maid Marion; a story. (A. D. Brodie) Canad. M. **3**: 136.
Little Manual; a true ghost story. (C. M. Tilden-Brown) Overland, n. s. **24**: 25.
Little Misunderstanding, A. (A. Upward) Idler, **2**: 641.
Littl' Modder, De; a story. (W. McLennan) Harper, **84**: 167.
Little Napoleon of Caribou, The. Cornh. **66**: 56. Same art. Ecl. M. **119**: 312. Same art. Liv. Age, **194**: 785.
Little Number Three; a story. (F. J. Fraser) Belgra. **91**: 356.
Little Old Ladies of the Creek; a story. (C. Burke) Argosy, **59**: 543. Same art. Liv. Age, **205**: 597.
Little Out of the Way, A; a story. (A. Thomas) Belgra. **81**: holiday no., 1.
Little Pharisees in Fiction. (Agnes Repplier) Scrib. M. **20**: 718.
Little Regiment, The; a story. (S. Crane) McClure, **7**: 12.
Little Snow White Märchen. (A. Nutt) Folk-Lore, **3**: 26.
Little Tailor of the Ritten. (J. P. Rudd) Outing, **26**: 167.
Little White-Cap; a story. (B. Dempster) All the Year, **70**: 20–114.
Little Wizard; a story. (S. J. Weyman) Leis. Hour, **42**: 21–170.
Little Woolly Dog, A. (B. Jones) Good Words, **34**: 772.
Littré, Emil, Defence of. (L. Belrose, jr.) Monist, **2**: 403.
— Positivism of; a reply. (P. Carus) Monist, **2**: 410.
Liturgical Culture, Thoughts on. (A. R. Kremer) Ref. Q. **41**: 154.
Liturgical Developments of New Testament Times. (J. L. Reeder) Meth. R. **56**: 926.
Liturgical Question. (J. A. Seiss) Luth. Q. **26**: 305.
— in Germany. Eng. R. **3**: 192.
Liturgies, Greek, Missa Catechumenorum of. (H. Lucas) Dub. R. **112**: 268.
— Modern German. Eng. R. **3**: 297.
— The Tropes and the Gradual. Church Q. **40**: 132.
Liturgy, Gallican, Early. (H. Lucas) Dub. R. **113**: 564. **114**: 112.
Live Ghost. (E. Mackubin) Lippinc. **54**: 839.
Live-loads (in Architecture). Am. Arch. **43**: 21, 118.
Live Oak, Florida. (R. H. Lamborn) Garden & F. **5**: 483.
Liver, Story of the. (Dr. A. Wilson) Harper, **90**: 957.
Livermore, Mary A. (E. L. Didier) Chaut. **23**: 392.
— Autobiography. Arena, **6**: 261.
Liverpool, First Library and its Founders. (J. C. Morley) Bookworm, **4**: 133.
— To-day. (R. Machray) Canad. M. **5**: 397.
— Walker Art Gallery. (H. M. Cundall) Art J. **47**: 247.
Liverpool Congress of 1890. (Eleanor Marx-Aveling) Time, **23**: 1088.
Liverpool Corporation Collection of Pictures. (E. R. Dibden) M. of Art, **12**: 14, 50.
Liverworts, Adaptation in. (J. Reeves) Nat. Sci. **4**: 194.
Living, Art of. (R. Grant) Scrib. M. **17**: 3–752. **18**: 48–581.
Living, Cheaper, and the Rise of Wages. (C. D. Wright) Forum, **16**: 221.
— Cost of. (V. Rosewater) Char. R. **1**: 268. — Sat. R. **80**: 13.
— — The Bread-and-butter Question. (J. H. Browne) Harper, **88**: 273.
— — Compared, in the U. S. and Great Britain. (A. Carnegie) Contemp. **66**: 318. Same art. Engin. M. **8**: 9.
— Standard of. (J. R. Dodge) Chaut. **17**: 711.
Living Christ, The; a poem. (J. G. Clark) Arena, **15**: 724.
Living God, A. (L. Hearn) Atlan. **78**: 833.
Living of East Wispers, The. Macmil. **74**: 54. Same art. Liv. Age, **209**: 591.
Living Pictures in the Louvre. (A. F. Sanborn) Lippinc. **54**: 823.
— in Public. Sat. R. **79**: 443.
— a Symposium. New R. **11**: 461.
Living together, Art of. (R. F. Horton) Sund. M. **25**: 145.
Livingston, Neil, and Agnes Hunter. (H. C. Shelley) Sund. M. **22**: 109.
Livingston Family and Declaration of Independence. (E. B. Livingston) Am. Hist. Reg. **1**: 123.
— of N. Y. (E. B. Livingston) Am. Hist. Reg. **2**: 650.
Livingstone, David, The Heart of. Cent. **28**: 100.
Livingstone, Robert R., with portrait. (I. Browne) Green Bag, **6**: 393.
Livingstone Family, The. (W. F. Livingstone) Munsey, **15**: 585.
Liz; a story. All the Year, **74**: 515.
Liza's Lout; a story. Cornh. **71**: 266.
Lizard, The Frilled. (W. Saville-Kent) Nature, **53**: 395.
Lizards at the London Zoo, 1893. Spec. **70**: 516.
— From Southern California, Two New Species. (S. P. Gage) Am. Natural. **30**: 833.
— Hypnotized. (W. T. Van Dyck) Nature, **52**: 148.
— Psychology of. (J. Delboeuf) Pop. Sci. Mo. **43**: 682.
— The Tuatara. (J. Buckland) Eng. Illust. **16**: 381.
Llan Dâv, Book of. Sat. R. **78**: 48.
Llanfairfechan, Celtic Remains at. (H. H. Lines) Antiq. n. s. **27**: 58.
Llangollen, Ladies of. Gent. M. n. s. **55**: 401. Same art. Liv. Age, **207**: 285.
Llano Estacado; a story. (J. P. Duncan) Outing, **28**: 92.
Llanover, Lady. Ath. '96, **1**: 118.
Llanthony Abbey and Two of its Priors. (A. C. Benson) National, **28**: 519.
Llewellyn Park. Garden & F. **5**: 578.
Lloyd, Henry D., as a Social Reformer, with portrait. (H. Latchford) Arena, **10**: 577.
Lloyd, W. Watkiss. Ath. '93: **2**: 916.
Lloyd's, Past and Present of. (R. Derechef) Eng. Illust. **11**: 143.
Loan of Half-orphans. (T. A. Janvier) Cent. **26**: 44, 218.
Loan Associations, Benevolent, in France. (A. P. McIlvaine) Char. R. **2**: 315.
— Rural in Germany. (H. F. Merritt) Char. R. **5**: 259.
Loan-offices in Europe, Public. (C. H. Hull) Nation, **58**: 171.
Loan Societies, Provident. (E. W. Peet) Chr. R. **4**: 181.
Loans, Popular and Syndicate. (A. D. Noyes) Nation, **62**: 48.
Lobanoff, Prince, Diplomacy of. Sat. R. **82**: 248.

Lobbying, Evils of, and Proposed Remedy. (S. Maxwell) Am. Law R. **30**: 398.
— in the House of Commons. Macmil. **72**: 195.
— Suppression of, Necessity for. (S. Maxwell) Am. Law R. **28**: 211.
Lobengula, King of the Matabele, with portrait. R. of Rs. (N. Y.) **8**: 555.
Lobster at Home. (G. Allen) Longm. **28**: 270.
— in Commerce and Science. (T. R. R. Stebbing) Nat. Sci. **9**: 38.
— Notes on Biology of. (F. H. Herrick) Science, n. s. **1**: 263.
Lobster-spearing in Nova Scotia. Outing, **22**: 348.
Local Government in the Canadian Village. (H. H. L. Bellot) Westm. **140**: 281.
— in England in 1892, Bill for. Spec. **68**: 257.
— — Act of 1894. (H. H. L. Bellot) Westm. **141**: 479. — National, **22**: 664. — Sat. R. **77**: 641.
— in Japan. (E. W. Clement) Pol. Sci. Q. **7**: 294.
— in the South and the Southwest. (E. W. Bemis and others) J. H. Univ. Studies, **11**: nos. 11-12.
— of Country Communities in Prussia. (C. Bornhak) Ann. Am. Acad. Pol. Sci. **3**: 393.
Local History, Collections of, in Public Libraries. (H. J. Carr) Lib. J. **19**: supp. 67.
— Study of. (W. Boughton) Educa. **13**: 400.
— Value of, in Public Libraries. (M. A. Sanders) Lib. J. **20**: supp. 40.
Local View, A. (P. L. M'Dermott) Chamb. J. **73**: 353-505.
Locality and Industries. (E. A. Ross) Q. J. Econ. **10**: 247.
Loch Brora, a June Midnight by. (H. Miller) Blackw. **152**: 101.
Loch Etive, Pastoral Life on, during the Last Century. (W. Jolly) Good Words, **33**: 588, 666.
Loch Fyne. Sat. R. **74**: 647.
Loch Katrine in Glasgow. (B. Taylor) Chamb. J. **73**: 563.
Loch Lomond, A Day's Skating on. (C. M. Aikman) Westm. **145**: 337.
Loch Torridon; a poem. (A. C. Swinburne) M. of Art, **13**: 73.
Lochman, Augustus H. (A. Stump) Luth. Q. **22**: 180.
Locke, John, Epistemology in. (A. Seth) Philos. R. **2**: 167.
— Essay on the Understanding, edited by Fraser. Sat. R. **78**: 272.
— Pocket Book of. (G. Williamson) New R. **10**: 223.
— Theory of Mathematical Knowledge, and of a Possible Science of Ethics. (J. Gibson) Mind, **21**: 38.
Locker-Lampson, Frederick. (T. Hutchinson) Acad. **49**: 337. — Critic, **28**: 293. — (A. Birrell) Scrib. M. **19**: 39. — With portrait, Bk. Buyer, **13**: 223. — (W. Roberts) Bookworm, **3**: 65. — (C. Kernahan) 19th Cent. **38**: 634. Same art. Liv. Age, **207**: 306. — Critic, **26**: 423. — Ath. '95, **1**: 740.
— My Confidences: Autobiographical. Sat. R. **81**: 435. — (E. G. Johnson) Dial (Ch.) **20**: 328. — Liv. Age, **211**: 362.
Lockhart, John Gibson, Lang's Life of. (T. Hutchinson) Acad. **50**: 341. — (W. Everett) Nation, **63**: 425. — Chamb. J. **73**: 737. — Blackw. **160**: 607. Same art. Ecl. M. **127**: 796. — Sat. R. **82**: 525.
— Notes on. Temp. Bar, **105**: 175. Same art. Liv. Age, **206**: 177.
Lockhart, William. Acad. **41**: 517. — Ath. '92, **1**: 665.
Lockouts and Strikes, Ethics of. (C. H. Reeve) Am. J. Pol. **2**: 75.
Lock-up, American. Cornh. **68**: 290.
Locks and Safes, Construction of. (H. W. Chubb) J. Soc. Arts, **41**: 510.
— Bibliography of. J. Soc. Arts, **41**: 525.
Lockwood, Crosby. Ath. '95, **1**: 316.
Lockwood, Frank; a Sketch of his Life. (R. Blathwayt) Idler, **4**: 477.
Locoed Cattle. Chamb. J. **69**: 815.
Locomotion, Animal, Chromo-photographic Study of. (E. J. Marey) Nature, **49**: 41.
Locomotive, Compound. (A. von Borries) Cassier, **6**: 146.
— — of Rhode Island Locomotive Works. J. Frankl. Inst. **133**: supp.
— Modern, Construction of, Hughes on. (N. J. Lockyer) Nature, **51**: 97.
— Present and Future. (D. L. Barnes) Engin. M. **7**: 396.
— Raub Gravity. (W. R. Covert) Am. J. Pol. **3**: 207.
— Thousand Mile Ride on. (C. Warman) McClure, **2**: 164.
Locomotive that lost herself; a story. (C. Warman) McClure, **7**: 89. Same art. Eng. Illust. **15**: 433.
Locomotive Works at Crewe. (C. J. B. Cooke) Eng. Illust. **9**: 377.
— at Derby. (C. H. Jones) Eng. Illust. **9**: 673.
— at Strafford. (A. P. Parker) Eng. Illust. **9**: 761.
— at Swindon. (A. H. Malan) Eng. Illust. **9**: 559.
Locomotives, American and Foreign. (D. L. Barnes) Cassier, **5**: 494.
— English and French. (C. Warman) McClure, **5**: 156.
— of the Great Northern Railway, Eng. (A. J. Brickwell) Eng. Illust. **10**: 423.
— of the Great Western Railway. (A. H. Malan) Eng. Illust. **10**: 199.
— of the Northeastern Railway. (W. Worsdell) Eng. Illust. **9**: 816.
— Some Unusual Forms of. (G. L. Clark) Cassier, **10**: 243.
Locust, Grouse, Unusual Flights of, in N. E. Illinois. (J. L. Hancock) Am. Natural. **28**: 483.
Locust Trees. Garden & F. **5**: 349.
Locusts. The Plague of Africa. (H. Michel) Chaut. **15**: 196.
Lodge, Robert John; with portrait. Bank. M. (Lond.) **56**: 99.
Lodge, Thomas. (J. Buckham) Poet-Lore, **3**: 601.
— Poet, Author, Physician. (W. H. Long) Walford's Antiq. **3**: 189.
Lodger in Maze Pond; a story. (G. Gissing) National, **24**: 847.
Lodging-house, a Dock. (E. M. Phillipps) Fortn. **57**: 668.
Lodging-houses, Boys', in New York. (W. P. Johnson) Lend a H. **8**: 304.
— Common London. (A. Mearns) Sund. M. **22**: 16, 102.
— in a Woman's Doss-house. (T. Sparrow) New R. **11**: 176.
— Municipal. (A. Shaw) Char. R. **1**: 20.
— — and other. All the Year, **72**: 276.
Lodgings in Thule; a story. Cornh. **69**: 381.
Loeb, Isidore. (A. Neubauer) Jew. Q. **5**: 1.
Loeningg, Allart van, Guild of the Skippers of Middleburg. (R. Temple-Barre) M. of Art, **19**: 113.
Loewe, Carl. (J. S. Shedlock) Acad. **50**: 55.
Loftus, Augustus, Lord. Diplomatic Reminiscences. Ath. '92, **2**: 409. '94, **1**: 569. — Dial (Ch.) **13**: 300. — Sat. R. **74**: 365. — Spec. **69**: 417.
Loganberry, of California. (C. H. Shinn) Garden & F. **7**: 465.

Logarithms. (N. Hill) J. Frankl. Inst. **140**: 130.
— Chart of, Scale-lines in. Nature, **52**: 272.
— in Musical Science. (J. P. White) Music, **3**: 399, 565.
Logging Camp, Life in a. (A. Hill) Scrib. M. **13**: 695.
Logging Camps; Under the Far-west Greenwood Tree. (L. H. Wall) Atlan. **71**: 194.
Logic and Metaphysics, Outlines of, Erdmann's. Sat. R. **82**: 141.
— and Psychology. (G. H. Howison) Psychol. R. **3**: 652. — (G. M. Stratton) Psychol. R. **3**: 313.
— Anomalies in. (J. H. Hyslop) Philos. R. **3**: 129.
— as Relation Lore. (F. C. Russell) Monist, **3**: 272.
— Content and Meaning. (A. Sidgwick) Mind, **20**: 283.
— Is it a Dualistic Science? (J. Dewey) Open Court, **3**: 2040.
— Literary Lack of. Atlan. **71**: 853.
— Psychological Interpretation of Certain Doctrines of. (A. H. Lloyd) Psychol. R. **3**: 422.
— Reform in. (A. Sidgwick) Mind, **18**: 145.
— Regenerated. (C. S. Peirce) Monist, **7**: 19.
— Relation to Psychology. (D. G. Ritchie) Philos. R. **5**: 585.
Logical Judgment, Nature of. (E. E. C. Jones) Mind, **18**: 441.
Logical Theory, Future Position of. (E. T. Dixon) Monist, **2**: 606.
Logos, Doctrine of, Origin of. (R. D. Hahn) Bapt. R. **14**: 176, 300.
Logsdail, William, and Lincoln, Eng. Art J. **44**: 321.
Loire Campaign, 1870. (A. Bothmer) Un. Serv. M. **7**: 1032. **8**: 487.
Lollards. (A. Snow) Dub. R. **118**: 40.
Lollardism. Spec. **69**: 884. Same art. Liv. Age, **196**: 316.
Lolling, H. G. (R. B. Richardson) Am. J. Archæol. **9**: 371.
Lolos, The, a Horned People. All the Year, **71**: 197.
Lombards, The; Fair Rosamund, the First. (W. W. Hunt) Gent. M. n. s. **54**: 458.
Lombardy, Community of, Williams on. Spec. **69**: 469.
Lombroso, C., Reply of Convicted Anarchist to. (M. Schwab) Monist, **1**: 520.
London after the Great Fire. (C. Creighton) Blackw. **152**: 736.
— Amalgamation of. (F. Harrison) Contemp. **66**: 737. — Sat. R. **78**: 375-400.
— Amusements in Reign of George III. Walford's Antiq. **10**: 204.
— and the Kingdom, Sharpe's. Sat. R. **80**: 274.
— and the Water Companies. (J. Lubbock) 19th Cent. **37**: 657.
— Arcades and Bazaars of. (G. Clinch) Eng. Illust. **14**: 562.
— Architecture in. (Barr Ferree) Archit. Rec. **5**: 1.
— as the Capital of the Empire. (L. Gomme) Contemp. **69**: 692.
— Awakening of. Cornh. **73**: 75.
— Beautiful. (G. Allen) Fortn. **60**: 42.
— Beautifying. (C. A. Whitmore) National, **27**: 92.
— Besant's. (F. Ryland) Acad. **41**: 582. — (G. Smith) Nation, **55**: 338. — Sat. R. **74**: 363.
— Brill, The Lost. (J. MacL. Coblan) Time, **4**: 44.
— Chamber of Arbitration. (E. Manson) Law Q. **9**: 86.
— Charities of. Lend a H. **10**: 107.
— — Kodak Views of. Lend a H. **10**: 199.
— Charm of. Spec. **69**: 414. **77**: 851.
— Children's Shelter. (Baroness Burdett-Coutts) Sund. M. **21**: 42, 164.
London, Churches of 17th and 18th Centuries, Birch's. Sat. R. **82**: 144.
— — St. Bartholomew the Great. (W. Dampier) Walford's Antiq. **10**: 51.
— City of, Queer Customs. (J. C. Thornley) Chaut. **21**: 173.
— City Temple, Sunday Morning at. (G. T. Brown Sund. M. **25**: 103.
— Coaching Trips out of. (W. H. Rideing) Cosmopol. **17**: 401.
— Corporation Art Gallery. (A. G. Temple) Art J. **46**: 302.
— County Council. (T. G. Fardell; C. Harrison) New R. **6**: 257. — (J. Burns; R. E. Prothero) 19th Cent. **31**: 496. — (A. A. Baumann) Univ. R. **7**: 493.
— — and its Assailants. (Lord Hobhouse) Contemp. **61**: 332.
— — and its Work. (G. L. Fox) Yale R. **4**: 80. — (S. Webb) Contemp. **67**: 130.
— — Conservatives and the. (C. A. Whitmore) National, **21**: 175.
— — Election, 1892. Sat. R. **73**: 296.
— — Elections of. (C. A. Whitmore) National, **25**: 239.
— — Proposed Building for. Spec. **70**: 796.
— — Work and policy of. (R. M. Beachcroft; H. P. Harris) National, **24**: 828.
— Crosses in. (G. Clinch) Eng. Illust. **14**: 305.
— Crystal Palace; East African Show. (C. J. Cornish) Eng. Illust. **14**: 82.
— Debt of, Repayment of. (A. Hoare) 19th Cent. **31**: 403.
— Disappearing Dickensland. (C. Dickens) No. Am. **156**: 670.
— Diseases of, Mortal. (H. P. Dun) 19th Cent. **34**: 875.
— Docks of. All the Year, **70**: 253. — (W. Senior) Good Words, **33**: 326.
— Drawings of, by Caneletto. (R. R. Holmes) Art J. **46**: 129.
— Early Concerts in. (G. P. Gordon) Gent. M. n. s. **56**: 495.
— Early Italian Opera in. (F. Hawkins) Theatre, **34**: 272.
— East End. (A. Streeter) Month, **83**: 202.
— — and Crime. (A. O. Jay) New R. **11**: 401. Same art. Ecl. M. **123**: 627.
— — Aspects of Social Life in. (S. Moody) Chaut. **20**: 399.
— — Booth's Life and Labor of the People. Spec. **70**: 389.
— — Charles Booth and his Work. (M. McG. Dana) Gunton's M. **10**: 189.
— — General Readers in. (G. H. Pike) Good Words, **37**: 668.
— — Marriage in. (H. Dendy) Contemp. **65**: 427.
— — People's Palace. (J. Tunis) Lend a H. **8**: 151. — (Mrs. S. S. Blanchard) Lend a H. **9**: 340.
— Electric Supply of. Chamb. J. **73**: 225.
— Exhibition of 1851, Early History of. J. Soc. Arts, **44**: 899.
— Fire Brigade, Condition of. Sat. R. **76**: 645.
— Free Shelters of. Leis. Hour, **42**: 256.
— from West to East. (E. A. Eardley-Wilmot) Good Words, **37**: 617.
— German Colony in. (A. Shadwell) National, **26**: 798.
— Government of. (Sir J. Lubbock) Fortn. **57**: 157. — (A. Shaw) R. of Rs. (N. Y.) **5**: 282. — (Sir J. Lubbock and others) National, **24**: 530.
— — Future. (G. L. Gomme) Contemp. **66**: 746.
— — in 1893: New London Programme. Spec. **71**: 168.

London, Government of. Let London live. (J. Burns) 19th Cent. 31: 673.
— — Municipal Administration. Ed. R. 175: 500.
— Government Offices, Proposed New. (H. H. Statham) Fortn. 66: 879.
— Gower Street and its Reminiscences. Temp. Bar, 97: 46.
— Guildhall, Loan Collection of Pictures at. All the Year, 70: 444.
— Health of. Nature, 52: 298.
— Heights of. (C. N. Barham) Gent. M. n. s. 54: 138.
— History of, Besant's. (H. Bradley) Acad. 44: 506.
— Hospitals in, Voluntary, Hake on. (E. S. L. Buckland) Westm. 139: 125.
— House of Shelter. (H. Boulton) Fortn. 61: 215.
— Houses in, Historic. (P. Norman) Eng. Illust. 12: no. 4, 41.
— How the Other Half lives. The Pitman. (G. E. Mitton) Eng. Illust. 14: 547.
— Hyde Park. (F. Watt) Art J. 48: 225.
— Hydraulic Power in. (E. B. Ellington) Cassier, 11: 95.
— Imperial Institute. (S. Vine) M. of Art, 13: 169.
— Improvements in. (F. Harrison) New R. 7: 414.
— In, and Out of it. All the Year, 72: 558, 584.
— in the Past. Quar. 174: 393.
— in the Poets. All the Year, 74: 293. — Liv. Age, 203: 123.
— in the Season. (R. H. Davis) Harper, 87: 898.
— in the Small Hours. Eng. Illust. 10: 705.
— Influence of, upon Literature. Spec. 68: 163.
— Inns of Court. (W. J. Loftie) Portfo. 23: 1-241.
— — as Schools of Law. (M. Crackanthorpe) 19th Cent. 32: 773.
— Jewish Colony in. (Mrs. Brewer) Sund. M. 21: 16, 119.
— Law Courts and Proposed Changes. (G. H. Knott) Jurid. R. 7: 130.
— Life and Labor in, Booth's. Sat. R. 78: 386. — (C. Booth) J. Statis. Soc. 56: 557.
— Life of the Working Classes in. (W. Clarke) New Eng. M. n. s. 10: 572.
— Literary. (Katharine Hinkson) Lit. W. (Bost.) 24: 240.
— Livery Companies of. (F. Hawkins) Acad. 42: 353. — (E. Bisland) Cosmopol. 13: 259.
— — Hazlitt on. Spec. 69: 568.
— Map of, in 1677. (P. Norman) Acad. 47: 425.
— Markets of, Two Old. (A. Dobson) M. of Art, 6: 216.
— Milk Trade, Three Months in. Econ. R. 4: 177.
— Modern, Ancient Rome and. (E. J. Gibbs) National, 19: 516. Same art. Ecl. M. 119: 179. Same art. Liv. Age, 194: 451.
— The Monument. Chamb. J. 69: 55.
— Mortality in, Old Bills of. (W. Ogle) J. Statis. Soc. 55: 437.
— Municipal Problems of. (G. R. Tyler) No. Am. 159: 448.
— Music Halls and the County Council. Theatre, 33: 277.
— Names in, Some more Old. Chamb. J. 70: 22.
— National Gallery of British Art, and Mr. Tate's Collection. (M. H. Spielmann) M. of Art, 16: 145-263.
— National Portrait Gallery, Medallion Portraits on. M. of Art, 18: 429.
— — Should there be a British Artist's Room in the? (M. H. Spielmann) M. of Art, 13: 98, 404.
— of Charles II. (W. Besant) Harper, 84: 292.
— of the Future. Spec. 68: 874.

London of George II. (W. Besant) Harper, 84: 619.
— of Old Catholic Times and Ecclesiastical Establishments. (H. W. Brewer) Month, 81: 371, 511.
— of To-day. Quar. 182: 59.
— of Whittington's Time. (John F. Rolph) Time, 15: 665.
— Old Inns of. (W. E. Milliken) Time, 7: 353, 578.
— Older Churches of. (W. J. Loftie) M. of Art, 8: 177, 353.
— Omnibus in, Romance of. (F. T. Jane) Eng. Illust. 11: 691.
— Open Spaces in, County Council and. (Earl of Meath) New R. 7: 701.
— Near, Out-of-the-way Tramping. (F. Abell) Time, 7: 536.
— Parks of. Garden & F. 5: 366.
— Past and Present. Church Q. 34: 20.
— People's Palace Library. (M. S. R. James) Lib. J. 18: 427.
— Picturesque in. (H. F. McDermott) Time, 19: 205.
— Plague and Fire, Book on. (T. A. Cooper) Bookworm, 3: 25.
— Playhouse, The Globe. (W. Rendle) Walford's Antiq. 8: 209.
— Playhouses at Bankside in Time of Shakespeare. (W. Rendle) Walford's Antiq. 7: 207, 274. 8: 55.
— Polytechnic, Regent Street. (F. W. Farrar) M. Chr. Lit. 7: 97.
— Poor of. (W. A. Gibbs) Time, 11: 42.
— — Homes of. (D. F. Schloss) Time, 13: 18.
— Poor Relief in. (C. S. Loch) Lend a H. 16: 436.
— Poverty in. (E. Reeves) Westm. 138: 244.
— Present London School Board and the Coming Election. (E. L. Stanley) New R. 11: 445.
— Railway Stations of. Eng. Illust. 10: 658.
— Rebuilding of. (J. Parker) Eng. Illust. 13: 174.
— Regent's Park Zoölogical Gardens. (C. J. Cornish) Cornh. 74: 369.
— Relics of the Past in. (A. Webb) Nation, 60: 357.
— Revisited. (W. O'Brien) Contemp. 69: 805. Same art. Liv. Age, 210: 228.
— Royal Courts of Justice. (W. Armstrong) M. of Art, 5: 37.
— Royalty Theatre, Reminiscences of. (F. C. Burnand) Theatre, 27: 6, 70.
— St. Dunstan's-in-the-East. Antiq. n. s. 31: 15.
— St. James Parish, Ratcliffe. (W. Besant) Scrib. M. 12: 149.
— St. James' Park, Water-fowl in. Macmil. 70: 354.
— St. James's Square, Dasent's. Sat. R. 80: 601.
— — Memories of. (W. C. Sydney) Gent. M. n. s. 57: 558.
— St. Katharine Cree Church. (W. J. Loftie) Antiq. n. s. 31: 363.
— St. Mary Berking Church, Chantry or Royal Free Chapel of. (J. Maskell) Walford's Antiq. 2: 109, 288.
— St. Olave, Hart Street, Church Annals, Povah's. Sat. R. 79: 132.
— St. Paul's Cathedral. (M. G. Van Rensselaer) Cent. 21: 643.
— — and Old City Life, Simpson's. Sat. R. 78: 388.
— School Board. (F. Miller) Time, 2: 183.
— — Controversy as to. (C. W. A. Brooke) Westm. 142: 637. — Spec. 73: 685. — Church Q. 39: 204.
— — Elections for. Church Q. 39: 501.
— — Progressives *vs.* London Education. (J. R. Diggle) National, 24: 307.
— — Religion and. (E. L. Stanley) 19th Cent. 34: 739.
— — — Reply. (J. R. Diggle) 19th Cent. 34: 998.
— — Theologians of. Spec. 71: 826.

London School Board, Work of. (T. J. Macnamara) Educa. R. 12: 1.
— School Board Rate. (G. L. Bruce) Contemp. 69: 597.
— Six Days' Tour in. (P. Fitzgerald) Gent. M. n. s. 54: 361.
— Slums of County Council and. (L. S. Rowe) Citizen, 2.
— — Stamping out the. (E. Marshall) Cent. 29: 700.
— Social Awakening in. (R. A. Woods) Scrib. M. 11: 401.
— Society in. (Lady Jeune) No. Am. 154: 603.
— — Reply. (W. H. Mallock) No. Am. 155: 25.
— — Rejoinder. (Lady Jeune) No. Am. 155: 456.
— — A Last Word on. (Lady F. Balfour) No. Am. 155: 217.
— — Lady Jeune on. (G. O. Morgan) Contemp. 62: 85. Same art. Ecl. M. 119: 355.
— — Past and Present. When Plancus was Consul. (E. L. Linton) New R. 8: 451.
— Soho and its Associations, Rimbault's. Sat. R. 81: 656.
— Some Historic Landmarks of. (J. Gennings) Chaut. 20: 387.
— Stock Exchange under Fire. Bank. M. (Lond.) 56: 15.
— Strand, Palace in. Fortn. 60: 390. Same art. Liv. Age, 199: 300.
— The Strand Improvements. (H. P. Horne) Fortn. 58: 319.
— Street Cries in. (G. A. Sala) Eng. Illust. 10: 125.
— Street Improvements in, Cawston on. Spec. 71: 173.
— Street Life of. (M. I. Wooding) Chaut. 22: 473, 729. — (A. R. Buckland) Good Words, 33: 86–742.
— Street Traffic. (W. W. Fenn) Time, 1: 426.
— Streets and Building Act. (E. A. E. Woodrow) Am. Arch. 46: 99.
— Streets of. (M. Roberts) Liv. Age, 188: 159.
— Suburbs of, Fitzgerald's. (T. Runciman) Art J. 45: 175.
— Summer's Night about. All the Year, 71: 250.
— Taxation in. Bitter Cry of the Taxed. (B. F. C. Costelloe) Contemp. 65: 293.
— — Demand for Changes in. (C. A. Whitmore) National, 21: 375.
— Technical Instruction in, Scheme for. (H. L. Smith) Contemp. 61: 741.
— Thackeray's. Chamb. J. 69: 641. — Temp. Bar, 105: 422.
— to Beauvais: a Lightning Tour. (P. Fitzgerald) Gent. M. n. s. 56: 470. Same art. Liv. Age, 210: 35.
— The Theatre in. (G. S. Street) New R. 12: 558.
— Theatres in and Circuses, Vanished. Sat. R. 76: 66.
— — Early. (H. B. Baker) Theatre, 33: 294.
— — County Council and. Theatre, 33: 105. — (C. Dickens) Theatre, 34: 140.
— — of the Past. Theatre, 30: 91, 207.
— Tower of. Time, 9: 264. 10: 174.
— — Armor in. Antiq. n. s. 29: 25, 193.
— — Ceremony of the "Keys." (C. F. Winter) Canad. M. 1: 555.
— — Money-making at. Gent. M. n. s. 54: 304.
— Tower Bridge. Am. Arch. 39: 139. — Leis. Hour, 43: 498.
— Toynbee Hall. (T. H. Nunn) Econ. R. 2: 478.
— Trees of. Spec. 71: 365.
— The Two Babylons, London and Chicago. (W. T. Stead) New R. 10: 560.
— under England's Old Laws. (W. S. Hardy) Sund. M. 24: 124.
London, Underground. Chamb. J. 72: 673.
— Underground Railway in. (A. E. Daniell) Chaut. 20: 654.
— — Round the, on an Engine. Eng. Illust. 10: 787.
— Underground Railways of. (E. R. Pennell) Harper, 92: 278.
— — Projects for. Sat. R. 73: 597.
— Unification of. Am. Arch. 46: 68. — Lond. Q. 83: 322. — (C. A. Whitmore) National, 21: 375.
— — City Metropolitan Law Courts. (G. H. Knott) Am. Law R. 29: 395.
— — Commission on. (C. Harrison) Fortn. 59: 836.
— — A True. (M. Crackanthorpe) Fortn. 62: 828.
— University for, A Great. (L. Playfair) 19th Cent. 38: 699.
— — Making a Great. (S. P. Thompson) J. Soc. Arts, 44: 180.
— — Proposed Teaching. (C. H. Herford and others) Acad. 41: 14–89. — (G. Young) Acad. 41: 112, 134. — (H. P. W. Bunting) Contemp. 61: 754. — (K. Pearson) Acad. 41: 589. 45: 189. — (W. T. Thiselton-Dyer) Nature, 45: 392. — Nature, 46: 121, 169. 47: 1. — (J. C. Collins) 19th Cent. 31: 243. — Quar. 174: 222. — (T. W. Haddon) School & C. 1: 112. — Spec. 68: 262. — (J. S. Hill) Westm. 137: 165, 497. — (J. G. Fitch) Educa. R. 5: 209. — (W. P. Wynne) Nature, 51: 297.
— University of. (W. P. Wynne) Nature, 50: 269. — Nature, 53: 103.
— — Slade Schools. (C. J. Weeks) M. of Art, 6: 324.
— *versus* the Water Companies. (B. F. C. Costelloe) Contemp. 67: 801.
— Vices of. Time, 13: 410.
— Water for, from the Sea. (F. W. Grierson) J. Soc. Arts, 44: 210. — (F. W. Grierson) Am. Arch. 51: 74.
— Water-supply of. Chamb. J. 72: 502. — (E. Frankland) Nature, 53: 619. — (E. Frankland) Sci. Prog. 5: 163. — (Sir J. Lubbock) 19th Cent. 31: 224. — Quar. 174: 63. — Sat. R. 73: 356.
— — Companies for. (A. E. Dobbs) Contemp. 61: 26.
— Waterside Labor in. (H. L. Smith) Econ. J. 2: 593. — (C. Booth) J. Statis. Soc. 55: 521.
— Waterworks for. Antiq. n. s. 31: 243, 361.
— West and East Ends of. (R. H. Davis) Harper, 88: 279.
— Will's Coffee-house. Temp. Bar, 96: 547.
— Zoo in Winter. Spec. 71: 871.
— — Revisited. (P. Robinson) Eng. Illust. 11: 297–1147. Same art. Liv. Age, 206: 412.
London Bridge. Am. Arch. 47: 76.
— Bookselling on. (W. Roberts) Walford's Antiq. 12: 21.
London Hospital, Receiving Room of. (F. H. Low) Eng. Illust. 15: 175.
London Monument, Man on the. (G. E. Mitton) Eng. Illust. 16: 15.
London Post, The. (E. Walford) Walford's Antiq. 9: 147.
London Progressives, The. (J. Stuart) Contemp. 61: 521.
London Rivers, Old. Chamb. J. 71: 686.
London Rose, A. (E. Rhys) Macmil. 65: 225.
London School of Economics and Political Science. (W. A. S. Hewins) Ann. Am. Acad. Pol. Sci. 6: 283.
London Seasons, My. Temp. Bar, 106: 335.
London Society of Arts. (A. Beaver) M. of Art, 10: 123.
London Sparrow; a poem. (T. Russell) Temp. Bar, 108: 80.

London Times, The. (J. Creelman) McClure, 5: 387. — (E. Vincent) Eng. Illust. 9: 922. — (Harry Quilter) Univ. R. 4: 1.
— in 1861. (C. K. Tuckerman) M. Am. Hist. 27: 290.
Londonderry, Siege of, Walker on. Spec. 71: 181.
Lonely Man, The. (J. W. Roosevelt) Scrib. M. 20: 746.
Lonely Soul, A; a story. (M. Milton) McClure, 4: 175.
Long, Armistead Lindsay. (C. D. Maclean) So. M. 3: 353.
Long and the Short of it, The; a story. (F. Madoc) Belgra. 82: 281.
Long Arm of Coincidence, The; a story. Chamb. J. 73: 103.
Long Chase, A. (Owen Hall) Scrib. M. 19: 206.
Long Good-bye, A; a poem. (M. Kendall) M. of Art, 9: 465.
Long Innings, A. Sund. M. 23: 530.
Long Island, Battle of, 1776. (C. F. Adams) Am. Hist. R. 1: 650.
Long Lost Friend, A; duologue. (Mrs. Hugh Bell) Temp. Bar, 105: 402.
Long Run, the, Law of. (T. C. Mendenhall) Science, n. s. 2: 825.
Long Shop in the Poultry. (H. R. Plomer) Bibliographica, 2: 61.
Long Vacation Romance; a story. All the Year, 73: 253.
Long Valley Moor. Cornh. 66: 32.
Longevity and Death. (G. J. Romanes) Monist, 5: 161.
— of Great Men. Critic, 25: 30.
— of the Patriarchs. (W. R. Harper) Bib. World, 3: 326.
— Where People live the Longest. (S. S. McClure) Pub. Opin. 12: 406.
Longfellow, Henry Wadsworth. (R. H. Stoddard) Lippinc. 57: 95. — (G. Holme) Munsey, 12: 243. — (J. F. McLaughlin) Cath. World, 58: 528.
— A Glimpse of. (M. J. Savage) Arena, 15: 183.
— Golden Legend, and its Analogues. Poet-Lore, 4: 91.
— Homestead of. (H. S. Howard) Canad. M. 3: 389.
— Lesson on. (E. W. Barrett) Educa. 14: 539.
— Places and People of. (R. H. Titherington) Munsey, 9: 259.
— Portraits and Reminiscences of. (E. S. Phelps) McClure, 7: 110.
— Religion of. (W. H. Savage) Arena, 11: 145.
— Ship of State. (W. Everett) Atlan. 76: 18.
— Song of Hiawatha. (F. B. Sawvel) Educa. 16: 290.
— Spanish Student. Poet-Lore, 6: 161.
— Tales of a Wayside Inn. (A. S. Cook) Chaut. 22: 412.
— Wayside Inn. (M. J. Nesbet) Canad. M. 2: 275.
— — Landlord of the. (Mrs. C. Van D. Chenoweth) New Eng. M. n. s. 10: 265.
— The White. (W. D. Howells) Harper, 93: 327.
Longfellow, Samuel. Bk. News, 12: 426. — (O. F. Adams) New Eng. M. n. s. 11: 205.
Longipennes, Classification of. (R. W. Shufeldt) Am. Natural. 27: 233.
Longitude, Telegraphic Determination of, by U. S. Bureau of Navigation. (Lieut. Norris) Nat. Geog. M. 2: 1.
Longleat. (P. Fitzgerald) M. of Art, 14: 325.
Longmeadow, Mass., Inscriptions at. (O. B. Stebbins) N. E. Reg. 49: 335.
Lonsdale, Earl of. Manuscripts. (J. B. Paul) Scot. R. 24: 1. — Ed. R. 180: 317.
Loochow Islands and their Inhabitants. (B. H. Chamberlain) Geog. J. 5: 289, 446, 534.
Loofs, Friedrich. (W. F. Slater) Chr. Lit. 14: 513.
Looker-on, The. Blackw. 157: 902.
Lookout Mountain. (B. Torrey) Atlan. 76: 545.
Loomis, Elias, with portrait. Pop. Sci. Mo. 40: 405.
Loomis, John Mason, with portrait. Nat'l M. (N. Y. '91) 16: 493.
Loop, Etymology of. (W. W. Skeat) Acad. 49: 448, (S. O. Aldy) 470.
Loosened Cord, The; a Midnight Story. (A. Drake) Cent. 26: 203.
Looting of the Second National. (W. Brooks) Overland, n. s. 25: 151.
"Loover" of a Hall, Etymology of. (A. L. Mayhew and others) Acad. 46: 424, 536.
Lope de Vega. Quar. 179: 486.
— Grillparzer on. (W. Webster) Acad. 48: 266.
Lopez, Ruy, Conspiracy of. (A. Dimock) Eng. Hist. R. 9: 440.
Lord, Richard Halkett. (J. Hawthorne) Critic, 21: 331.
Lord of Chateau Noir, The; a story. (A. C. Doyle) McClure, 4: 310.
Lord Bateman; a Ballad, with Thackeray's Illustrations. (Comment by A. T. Ritchie) Harper, 86: 124.
Lord Beauprey. (H. James) Macmil. 65: 465 — 66: 133.
Lord Macao's Watch; a story. (J. W. Sherer) Gent. M. n. s. 53: 433.
Lord Mayor's Day Pageants, Poets of. (A. de Ternant) Gent. M. n. s. 56: 282.
— Artistic Aspect of. (J. Grego) M. of Art, 13: 8.
Lord Ornington; a story. (Barry Pain) Idler, 10: 146.
Lords, House of. *See* House of Lords.
Lord's Prayer. Debts or Trespasses? (M. Valentine) Luth. Q. 22: 379.
— English Version of. (A. N. Jannaris) Contemp. 66: 580.
— The Kingdom of Darkness. (J. B. Rust) Ref. Q. 42: 47.
Lord's Supper. Character of Christ's Last Meal. (N. Schmidt) J. Bib. Lit. 11: 1.
— Jewish View of. (K. Kohler) Pub. Opin. 13: 238.
— Judas and, as affecting Baptist Practice. (J. E. Gregory) Bapt. R. 14: 431.
— Lutheran Doctrine of. (W. S. Sigmund) Luth. Q. 26: 248.
Loreto. (J. Dolan) Month, 81: 545.
— the New Nazareth, Garratt's. Sat. R. 82: 66.
Loria, Achille, Landed System of Social Economy of. (U. Rabbeno) Pol. Sci. Q. 7: 258.
Lorimer, J. H. (R. A. M. Stevenson) Art J. 47: 321.
Lorimer, James, with portrait. (R. Flint) Jurid. R. 2: 113.
Lorraine, Claude, Duchess of. (Mrs. M. Scott) Blackw. 159: 188.
Lorraine, Plateau of. Geog. J. 2: 52.
— Rural Wedding in. Folk-Lore Rec. 3: 258.
Los Amigos Fiasco, The; a story. (A. C. Doyle) Idler, 2: 548.
Los Angeles Public Library, Charging System of. (A. R. Hasse) Lib. J. 19: 195.
Loss of Time; a poem. (D. Fuguet) Cosmopol. 22: 169.
Loss of the "Vanity;" a story. (M. Gaunt) Eng. Illust. 9: 843.
Lossing, Benson J., with portrait. Bk. News, 9: 449.

Lost; a Story of the Australian Bush. (M. Gaunt) Eng. Illust. **9**: 456.
Lost Address, A. (F. H. Sweet) Nat'l M. (Bost.) **5**: 26.
Lost Ambassador, The. (M. Howitt) Good Words, **37**: 40, 114. Same art. Liv. Age, **208**: 238.
Lost Arrow, The; a Legend of the Yosemite. (K. E. Robinson) Overland, n. s. **28**: 187.
Lost Battle, A; a True Story. Sund. M. **24**: 805.
Lost Chance, A; a story. (C. M. Norris) Belgra. **79**: 28.
Lost Child, The. (H. C. Bunner) Scrib. M. **19**: 342.
Lost Cipher, The; a story. (S. J. Weyman) Eng. Illust. **12**: no. 5, 37. Same art. McClure, **5**: 349.
Lost Duchess, The; a story. Cornh. **71**: 40. Same art. Ecl. M. **124**: 394.
Lost Engine, The. (W. L. Alden) Idler, **6**: 447.
Lost Friend, The; a Turkish Story. (R. Lindau) Chaut. **20**: 341.
Lost Ideal, A. (A. S. Swan) Sund. M. **23**: 1-793.
Lost Ideal; a story. Argosy, **55**: 84.
Lost in Wooing; a story. (P. Andreae) Eng. Illust. **14**: 57.
Lost Island, The; a story. (E. J. Austen; L. V. Sheldon) Cosmopol. **14**: 365.
Lost Letter, The; a story. (H. Herman) Eng. Illust. **10**: 239.
Lost or Stolen; a story. (E. F. Jenkinson) Gent. M. n. s. 48: 109.
Lost Park, Camping out in. All the Year, **71**: 587.
Lost Pine Mine; a story. (A. H. Sydenham) Un. Serv. (Phila.) **10**: 53.
Lost Property Office. Time, **20**: 356.
Lost Pueblo. (V. L. Reed) New Eng. M. n. s. **8**: 71.
Lost Singer. (V. Woods) New Eng. M. n. s. **15**: 412.
Lost Will, The; a story. (I. P. Whitfield) Argosy, **62**: 761.
Lost Years, The; a story. (L. H. Neff) McClure, **1**: 182.
Lot, Divination by. Chamb. J. **69**: 331.
Lot No. 249; a story. (A. C. Doyle) Harper, **85**: 525.
Lotbiniere Family. (I. J. Greenwood) N. E. Reg. **50**: 53.
Lothrop, Daniel. (E. E. Hale) Lend a H. **9**: 253.
Loti, Pierre, *pseud.* *See* Viaud, Julien.
Lo-To-Kah and The Golden Woman. (V. Z. Reed) Overland, n. s. **25**: 426.
— and the Witch. (V. Z. Reed) Overland, n. s. **24**: 585.
Lotteries, Art, and Art Unions. (J. Grego) M. of Art, **11**: 245.
— Book. Bookworm, **2**: 337.
— English, History of, Ashton's. Sat. R. **77**: 643.
— Federal Taxation of. (T. M. Cooley) Atlan. **69**: 523.
— New and Old. All the Year, **70**: 152.
— Suppression of, by Taxation. (H. White) Forum, **12**: 807.
Lottery, Louisiana. Pub. Opin. **12**: 319, 474. — Spec. **68**: 49.
— — Charitable Career of; or, the Degradation of a State. (C. C. Buel) Cent. **21**: 618.
— — History of. (E. H. Farrar) Chr. R. **1**: 143. — (J. C. Wickliffe) Forum, **12**: 569.
— — Shall its Charter be renewed? (F. McGloin) Forum, **12**: 555. Same art. Our Day, **9**: 181.
— — Suppression of. (N. Smyth) Forum, **19**: 238.
— — — Campaign for. Chr. Un. **45**: 60, 101, 149.
Lottery Duel, A; a story. (C. J. C. Hyne) Cornh. **74**: 66.
Lotto, Lorenzo. (W. J. Stillman) Cent. **21**: 842.
— Berenson's. (K. Cox) Nation, **60**: 76. — (J. Cartwright) Art J. **47**: 233.
Lotus, Grammar of the. (W. H. Goodyear) Archit. Rec. **2**: 165, 391.
— — Goodyear's. (W. P. P. Longfellow) Nation, **54**: 287.
Lotus Eater, Page from the Diary of a. (E. F. Benson) Fortn. **66**: 844.
Lotus-eating and Opium-eating. (J. G. Alexander) Contemp. **66**: 337.
Lotus Symbolism in Homer, etc. (A. R. Brown) Poet-Lore, **2**: 625.
Lotze, R. H. Antithesis between Thought and Things. (A. Eastwood) Mind, **17**: 305, 470.
— Doctrine of Thought. (H. Jones) New World, **3**: 1.
— Influence on Theology. (G. T. Ladd) New World, **4**: 401.
— Jones's Critical Account of the Doctrine of. (F. C. S. Schiller) Philos. R. **4**: 435.
— Monism. (F. C. S. Schiller) Philos. R. **5**: 225.
Lou and Liz; a story. (G. Gissing) Eng. Illust. **10**: 793.
Lough Derg, the Island of Penance. All the Year, **71**: 544.
Lough Swilly, Co. Donegal. Belgra. **89**: 38.
Loughborough, Lord, and Benjamin Franklin. (T. J. Chapman) Nat'l M. (N. Y. '91) **17**: 35.
Louis XIV., An English Princess at the Court of. Liv. Age, **201**: 631.
— Hassall's. Sat. R. **82**: 224.
Louis XVII., and Eleazer Williams, Evans's. Ath. '94, **1**: 141. — (J. D. Butler) Nation, **58**: 417. — Spec. **71**: 876.
Louis Philippe and his Brothers. (M. Lansing) Educa. **14**: 20.
— Fall of. (Emile Ollivier) Cosmopol. **18**: 424.
— in a Cherokee Wigwam. Atlan. **69**: 286.
Louisbourg, N. S. (J. G. Bourinot) M. Am. Hist. **27**: 177.
— Capture of, Anniversary of. Critic, **26**: 484.
— — Sir W. Pepperrell and. (V. Reed) New Eng. M. n. s. **12**: 415.
— Past and Present. (H. Pell) Am. Hist. Reg. **1**: 354.
— Siege of, and the Louisburg Cross. (D. D. Slade) Bost. **3**: 551. — Am. Hist. Reg. **2**: 939.
Louisbourg Monument. Am. Hist. Reg. **2**: 1242.
Louise, Queen. (T. Schwartz) Munsey, **11**: 532.
Louise, Lake, in the Canadian Rocky Mts. (W. D. Wilcox) Geog. J. **7**: 49.
Louise of Savoy and Francis I., De Maulde's. (A. Laugel) Nation, **60**: 199.
Louisiana and the Levees. (L. A. Sheldon) Arena, **5**: 187.
— Customs and Superstitions of. (Alcée Fortier) J. Am. Folk-Lore, **1**: 136.
— Discovery and Settlement of. (J. Doniphan) M. Am. Hist. **28**: 346.
— Folk-tales of, Fortier's. J. Am. Folk-Lore, **7**: 317.
— History, Heroes of. (L. F. Hinsdale) Am. Hist. Reg. **1**: 154.
— Nursery Tales of. (Alcée Fortier) J. Am. Folk-Lore, **1**: 140.
— Purchase of. (S. M. Davis) Chaut. **14**: 658.
— Studies in, Fortier's. (W. W. Newell) J. Am. Folk-Lore, **7**: 171.
Louisville, Ky. (G. H. Yenowine) Cosmopol. **14**: 179.
— Romance of the Origin of. (R. T. Durrett) Southern M. **4**: 445.

Loup Rivers, Nebraska, Evolution of. (L. E. Hicks) Science, **19**: 59. — (W. M. Davis) Science, **19**: 107.
Lourdes, Cures at. (J. R. Gasquet) Dub. R. **115**: 342.
— — Medical Estimate of. Month, **75**: 371, 476.
— Miracles at. Cath. World, **54**: 897. — (E. Berdoe) 19th Cent. **38**: 614. Same art. Ecl. M. **125**: 802.
— Pilgrimage to. (S. Bonsal) Cent. **25**: 659.
Louth Grammar School. (J. W. Hales) Gent. M. n. s. **49**: 562.
Loutherbourg, Phillipe Jacques de. (W. J. Lawrence) M. of Art, **18**: 172.
Lovat, Simon Fraser, Lord. (W. Donaldson) Scot. R. **21**: 81. Same art. Liv. Age, **196**: 771.
Love. (H. Maxwell) 19th Cent. **35**: 999.
— among the Saints; a poem. (A. M. F. Robinson) M. of Art, **7**: 114.
— and Art. (E. O. Kirk) Atlan. **74**: 227.
— and Bread; a story. (A. Strindberg) Poet-Lore, **6**: 501.
— and Death; a poem. (L. A. Tadema) Harper, **90**: 151.
— and Death; a poem. (E. F. Strange) M. of Art, **11**: 35.
— and Law. (A. W. Verrall) Univ. R. **5**: 466.
— and Marriage. (Sir E. Strachey) Atlan. **72**: 358. — Westm. **140**: 349.
— — in Japan. (Sir E. Arnold) Cosmopol. **12**: 387.
— and Spring; a poem. (A. A. Sewall) Cosmopol. **16**: 746.
— and Thought; a poem. (J. R. Lowell) Cosmopol. **13**: 299.
— at the Ship; a story. Chamb. J. **69**: 22.
— Evolutionary. (C. S. Peirce) Monist, **3**: 176.
— Expectant; a poem. (W. St. Leger) M. of Art, **17**: 18.
— for God. (C. Vander Veen) And. R. **17**: 57.
— Free, and Monogamy. Open Court, **4**: 2699.
— the Gift; a story. (M. Brooke) Argosy, **60**: 156.
— in the Afternoon. (C. E. Laughlin) Lippinc. **57**: 704.
— in the Big Barracks; a story. (J. Ralph) Harper, **90**: 421.
— in a Cottage, Sudermann's. (C. Thomas) Nation, **62**: 28.
— in Idleness; a Fortnight at Bar Harbor. (F. M. Crawford) Cent. **26**: 401, 594, 777.
— in a Mist. (W. Sharp) Good Words, **34**: 845.
— Little Easy on. (J. Wright) Lippinc. **57**: 422.
— of the Natural; a story. (V. de l'I. Adam) Poet-Lore, **7**: 388.
— of the Prince of Glottenberg, The; a story. (A. Hope Hawkins) McClure, **6**: 23.
— on the Road; a story. (Margaret Hunt) Temp. Bar, **108**: 50. Same art. Liv. Age, **209**: 526.
— or Money? a story. (J. Leete) Argosy, **62**: 547.
— a poem. (R. McE. Stuart and A. B. Paine) Cosmopol. **21**: 503.
— Reality or Fiction? Idler, **3**: 108.
— Stronger than Death. (A. W. Thorold) Good Words, **35**: 67.
— the Supreme Law of the Moral World. (J. M. Williams) Bib. Sac. **50**: 640.
Love Birds and Pigmy Parrots. (W. T. Greene) Eng. Illust. **9**: 836.
Love Letters of a Poet; a story. (E. Turner) Cornh. **74**: 663. Same art. Liv. Age, **211**: 668.
— of Superfine Gold; a story. (J. Ralph) Harper, **93**: 276.
— Literary. (R. W. Herrick) Atlan. **74**: 814.
Love Passage, A. (W. W. Jacobs) Idler, **10**: 103.
Love-philtres. Chamb. J. **70**: 76.
Love-poems, Anthology of, Watson's. Spec. **69**: 737.
Love song; a poem. (L. G. Ackroyd) Argosy, **59**: 554.
Love-songs, Caine's. Spec. **69**: 532.
Love-tokens; a poem. (I. J. Postgate) Gent. M. n. s. **54**: 318.
Love 's a Tyrant. (Mrs. Pender Cudlip) Time, **15**: 724. **16**: 95–731. **17**: 94–729. **18**: 90, 224.
Love's Court; a poem. (E. C. Cardozo) Cosmopol. **20**: 129.
Love's Farewell; a poem. (A. Mackay) Argosy, **62**: 46.
Love's Handicap. (J. J. à Becket) Scrib. M. **20**: 363.
Love's Ironies; a story. (W. H. Gleadell) Belgra. **91**: 59.
Love's Limitation. (Mabel Boyd) Cosmopol. **22**: 174.
Love's Looking-glass; poems by H. C. Beeching and others. Church Q. **35**: 201.
Love's Madness; a story. All the Year, **71**: 181.
Love's Rubicon; a poem. (K. Carter) M. of Art, **13**: 403.
Love's Tragedy at Scratch's Point; a story. (W. W. Campbell) Canad. M. **3**: 324.
Lovelace, Francis. (A. G. Vermilye) Nat'l M. (N. Y. '91) **16**: 129.
Lovelace, Lord, and Second Canadian Campaign, 1708–10. (J. G. Wilson) Nat'l M. (N. Y. '91) **17**: 189.
Loven, Sven Ludvig. (F. A. Bather) Nat. Sci. **7**: 283. — Ath. '95, **2**: 359.
Lover, Samuel, as a Graphic Humourist. (G. S. Layard) M. of Art, **19**: 393.
Lover, The, despairing to attain; a sonnet. (Sir T. Wyat) M. of Art, **15**: 386.
Lover's Lexicon, Greenwood's. Spec. **71**: 949.
Low, James E. (H. L. Conard) Nat'l M. (N. Y. '91) **18**: 316.
Low, Will H., with portraits. Bk. Buyer, **12**: 5. — (C. Moffett) McClure, **5**: 291.
Lowe, Robert, as a Journalist. (A. P. Martin) National, **22**: 352. Same art. Liv. Age, **200**: 145.
Lowe, Mount, and Santa Monica. (R. Wildman) Overland, n. s. **26**: 353.
Lowell, J. R. (H. James) Atlan. **69**: 35. — (R. H. Stoddard) Lippinc. **50**: 534. — Temp. Bar, **96**: 88. Same art. Liv. Age, **195**: 416. — With portrait. Bk. News, **5**: 82. — (C. E. Norton) Harper, **86**: 846. — (E. S. Nadal) Critic, **22**: 105. — (W. C. Lawton) Lippinc. **56**: 717.
— and Whitman. (H. L. Traubel) Poet-Lore, **4**: 22.
— as a Prose Writer. (T. W. Hunt) Presb. & Ref. R. **4**: 275.
— Biglow Papers. (J. H. Gilmore) Chaut. **23**: 19.
— Celebration of 73d Birthday of. Critic, **20**: 147.
— The Dead Poet; a poem. (W. W. Campbell) Lit. W. (Bost.) **23**: 24.
— Essays. Sat. R. **73**: 255.
— — and Addresses. Ath. '92, **1**: 235.
— in England. (G. W. Smalley) Harper, **92**: 788.
— Letters. Acad. **44**: 505. — (C. E. Norton) Harper, **87**: 553. — Ath. '93, **2**: 580. — Dial (Ch.) **15**: 291. — (T. W. Higginson) Nation, **57**: 488. — Sat. R. **76**: 546. — Spec. **71**: 748. — (W. J. Stillman) Atlan. **70**: 744. — Church Q. **38**: 97. — (J. W. Chadwick) Forum, **17**: 114. — Ecl. M. **122**: 335.
— Letters to Poe. Scrib. M. **16**: 170.
— Memorial in Westminster Abbey. Critic, **23**: 365.
— Memorial Park. Critic, **28**: 395.
— A Morning with. (M. J. Savage) Arena, **15**: 1.
— on Art Principles. (F. Lockwood) Scrib. M. **15**: 186.
— Poem to, on his Fortieth Birthday. (R. W. Emerson) Cent. **25**: 3.
— Religion of Poems of. (M. J. Savage) Arena, **9**: 705.

Lowell, J. R. Sir Launfal. Poet-Lore, 6: 47.
— Socialism of. (E. Grubb) New Eng. M. n. s. 6: 676.
— Study of. (F. M. Drew) Acad. (Syr.) 7: 271.
— Three Letters from. (M. A. Clarke) Cent. 29: 545.
— Underwood's Life of. Critic, 22: 274.
— Visit to. (Clara M. Parker) Chr. Un. 45: 1146.
— Writings of. (J. V. Cheney) Chaut. 16: 554.
— Yorkshire Haunts of. (E. Skelding) Atlan. 76: 181.
Lowell, Orson, with portrait. Bk. Buyer, 13: 289.
Lowell Institute. (H. K. Smith) New Eng. M. n. s. 11: 713.
Lowell Observatory and its Work. (A. E. Douglass) Pop. Astron. 2: 395.
— New 24-inch Refracting Telescope at. (T. J. J. See) Pop. Astron. 4: 297.
Lowlands *versus* Highlands. (E. R. Vicars) Gent. M. n. s. 53: 202.
Lowndes, Lloyd, with portrait. Bank. M. (N. Y.) 52: 305.
Loyal Heart, A; a story. Argosy, 54: 25, 112.
Loyal Lover, A; a story. (J. Edgeworth) Chaut. 23: 65, 185.
Loyal Traitor. (C. W. Shipman) New Eng. M. n. s. 14: 411.
Loyalists in the American Revolution. (M. C. Tyler) Am. Hist. R. 1: 24. — (C. G. D. Roberts) Canad. M. 6: 127.
— Plea for New Patriotic Society for Descendants of. (J. M. Parker) Am. Hist. Reg. 2: 632.
Loyalty to our Country. (M. Dix) M. Am. Hist. 27: 265.
Loyola, Ignatius, St., Rose's. Sat. R. 73: 548.
— and his Educational System. (F. Watson) Acad. 42: 407.
— as a Basque. (W. Webster) Acad. 50: 235.
— Writings of, Genuineness of. (C. C. Starbuck) And. R. 18: 283.
Luapula, Upper, A Journey to. (A. Sharpe) Geog. J. 1: 524.
Lubbock, Sir John, with portrait. Bk. News, 11: 382.
— and the Teaching University for London. Nature, 52: 295.
Lubricants, from a Maker's Standpoint. (C. M. Everest) Cassier, 7: 228.
Lucas, Seymour. (E. Gosse) M. of Art, 11: 1.
Lucas, Winifred. Units. Acad. 50: 383.
Luce, Siméon. Acad. 43: 12. — Ath. '92, 2: 891.
Luchuan Language. (B. H. Chamberlain) Anthrop. J. 26: 47.
Lucian. Dialogues, tr. by Irwin. Sat. R. 78: 186.
Luciani, S. (C. Phillips) Portfo. 24: 131.
Lucifera; a story. (A. Hope) Idler, 6: 275.
Lucille: a Tale of the Franco-German War. (A. W. Arnold) Blackw. 160: 386. Same art. Liv. Age, 211: 271.
Lucinda. (L. E. Mitchell) Cent. 28: 63.
Luck. All the Year, 73: 228. — Sat. R. 75: 565.
Luck; a story. (E. A. Thurston) Overland, n. s. 19: 78.
Luck of the Atkinses; a story. (M. B. Yeates) Lippinc. 55: 409.
Luck of Neri Boldwig, The. Macmil. 72: 203. Same art. Liv. Age, 206: 460.
Lucknow, The Looting of, 1857. (W. H. Russell) Idler, 9: 36.
— Siege of, Lady Inglis's. Sat. R. 73: 515.
Lucky Catch, A; a story. Chamb. J. 69: 795.
Lucky Man, The; a story. (J. Achurch) Eng. Illust. 14: 345.
Lucky Sixpence, A; a story. New R. 10: 105.
Lucretius. (R. Y. Tyrrell) Atlan. 74: 56.
— and his Science. (E. W. Adams) Gent. M. n. s. 53: 188. Same art. Liv. Age, 202: 726.
Lucy, Sir Thomas. (C. C. Stopes) Ath. '95, 2: 67.
Ludicrous, Theory of the. (W. S. Lilly) Fortn. 65: 724. Same art. Liv. Age, 209: 737. Same art. Ecl. M. 126: 781.
Ludington, Nelson, with portrait. (H. L. Conard) Nat'l M. (N. Y. '91) 17: 480.
Ludlow, Gen. Edmund. (R. Dunlop) Acad. 46: 79. — (Goldwin Smith) Nation, 59: 84. — Spec. 72: 904. — Sat. R. 78: 106. — Ath. '94, 2: 247.
Ludlow, Thomas W. Critic, 24: 289.
Ludwig II. of Bavaria. (L. Mead) Munsey, 9: 526.
— Palaces of. (B. Wirth) M. of Art, 10: 85.
Ludwig, Carl. (W. Stirling) Sci. Prog. 4: 155. — (L. Asher) Sci. Prog. 4: 323.
— and Modern Physiology. (J. B. Sanderson) Sci. Prog. 5: 1.
Luini, Bernardino. (W. J. Stillman) Cent. 22: 47. — (F. W. Farrar) Univ. R. 7: 393.
— Lugano Frescoes of. (C. Duncan) M. of Art, 6: 294.
Lukari's Story. (G. Atherton) Cosmopol. 14: 29.
Luke Meadow's Warning. Chamb. J. 71: 764.
Lukeria, Queen, of Gorelovka. (H. F. B. Lynch) Harper, 93: 36.
Lukis, Rev. W. C. (W. Gregson) Science, 22: 63.
Lullabies. (Laura A. Smith) Gent. M. n. s. 50: 604. Same art. Liv. Age, 198: 374.
Lullaby; a poem. (A. S. Hardy) Cosmopol. 14: 494.
Lullaby; a poem. (N. F. MacLean) Cosmopol. 17: 143.
Lullaby; a poem. (H. E. Boulton) M. of Art, 10: 157.
Lulworth Cove, Dorsetshire, England. (W. W. Fenn) M. of Art, 3: 212.
Lumber, Dimensions of. Minnesota Pine. Garden & F. 7: 148.
— Northern White Pine. (R. A. Parker) Engin. M. 7: 193.
— Pine Industry in the South. (G. L. Fowler) Engin. M. 7: 368.
Lumber Camp, Life in a. (G. A. Woodward) Munsey, 11: 604.
Lumber Industry, Canadian. (J. S. Robertson) Engin. M. 10: 17.
Lumber Supply, White Pine, in America. Garden & F. 7: 21.
Lumbering and Forestry. (C. S. Sargent) Garden & F. 6: 451.
— Humboldt. (M. H. Closson) Overland, n. s. 22: 155.
— in Muskoka. (A. Sullivan) Canad. M. 2: 556.
— in the Northwest. (J. E. Jones) Cosmopol. 15: 63.
— in Washington. (F. I. Vassault) Overland, n. s. 20: 23.
— on the St. Lawrence. (E. C. Grant) Canad. M. 2: 549.
— on State Lands. (C. S. Sargent) Garden & F. 7: 151.
Lumbermen and Forestry. (C. S. Sargent) Garden & F. 7: 111.
— Canadian. (L. J. Vance) Eng. Illust. 9: 879
Lumby, Joseph Rawson. Acad. 48: 459.
Luminous Animals. (T. R. R. Stebbing) Blackw. 158: 543. Same art. Ecl. M. 125: 685. Same art. Liv. Age, 207: 430.
Lumley Castle, England. (A. Griffiths) M. of Art, 4: 1.

Lunacy Laws in England. (T. Raleigh) Law Q. **1**: 150.
Lunatic Asylums, Private. Ought they to be abolished? (W. J. Corbet) Westm. **142**: 369.
Lunatics at Large. Time, **16**: 204.
Lundy Beach, Deformation of, and Birth of Lake Erie. (J. W. Spencer) Am. J. Sci. **147**: 207.
Lundy's Land, In. (W. P. Garrison) Pennsyl. M. **19**: 340.
Lundy's Lane, Battle of. (E. S. Brooks) Chaut. **15**: 263.
Lung-Tests, Two. (F. L. Oswald) Pop. Sci. Mo. **46**: 343.
Lungs, Origin of; a Chapter in Evolution. (C. Morris) Am. Natural. **25**: 975.
Lunt, Orrington, with portrait. (H. L. Conard) Nat'l M. (N. Y. '91) **15**: 500.
Lupton's Guest; a story. (L. Becke) New R. **13**: 515.
Lupus, Hugh, Mr. Watt's Equestrian Statue of. M. of Art, **3**: 150.
Lushais, The, and their Country. (J. Shakespear) J. Soc. Arts, **43**: 167.
Lushington, Edmund Law. Acad. **44**: 72.
Lustigs, The. (M. G. Van Rensselaer) Cent. **23**: 605.
Lustre Ware. (W. De Morgan) J. Soc. Arts, **40**: 756.
Luther, Martin. (G. Freytag) Open Court, **10**: 5063–5159.
— at Worms. (F. A. M. Mignet) Luth. Q. **26**: 394.
— Carlyle's Lecture on. Acad. **41**: 158.
— Hymns of. (E. Dickinson) Bib. Sac. **52**: 676.
— Income and Possessions of. (G. F. Behringer) Luth. Q. **26**: 236.
— Language of, Sources of. (F. R. Hochdoerfer) Luth. Q. **25**: 260.
— Luther League of America. (C. Eckhardt) Chr. Lit. **15**: 449.
— Mental and Moral Characteristics of. (W. N. McElroy) Luth. Q. **24**: 565.
— Portraits of. (R. Heath) M. of Art, **7**: 28.
— Translation of the Bible. (C. H. Merk and K. Pearson) Acad. **47**: 127, 150.
Lutheran, What is a? (S. Stall) Our Day, **16**: 619. — (C. S. Albert) Chaut. **18**: 324.
Lutheran Church and the Masses. (J. F. Scherer) Luth. Q. **26**: 374.
— and Science. (E. C. Hegeler) Open Court, **3**: 1811.
— Confessional History of the General Synod. (J. W. Richard) Luth. Q. **25**: 458.
— Doctrines of, in the 19th Century. (J. Wagner) Luth. Q. **23**: 194.
— General Synod, German Theological Seminary of. (J. D. Severinghaus) Luth. Q. **22**: 453.
— in U. S., Augustana Synod, Educational Work of the Kansas Conference of. (C. A. Swensson) Luth. Q. **25**: 253.
— — Union of, Problem of. (H. E. Jacobs) M. Chr. Lit. **6**: 177.
— Manual of, Remensnyder's. (M. Valentine) Luth. Q. **24**: 183. — (J. B. Remensnyder) Luth. Q. **24**: 311.
— — and Prof. Pieper. (J. B. Remensnyder) Luth. Q. **24**: 283.
— a Missionary Church. (L. A. Gotwald) Luth. Q. **22**: 488.
— Private Confession and Private Absolution in. (J. W. Richard) Luth. Q. **26**: 336.
— Revival of the Historic Episcopate in. (E. H. Delk) Luth. Q. **24**: 555.
— Separation from Reformed in 16th Century. (E. Boehl) Presb. & Ref. R. **5**: 415.
Lutheran Church, Synod of Southwest Virginia. Luth. Q. **22**: 98.
Lutheran Churches, Suggestions for Building. (Dr. von Lechler) Am. Arch. **43**: 148.
Lutheran Dissension in the U. S., Grounds of. (J. W. Richard) M. Chr. Lit. **6**: 1.
Lutheranism and Christian Liberty. (T. F. Dornblaser) Luth. Q. **22**: 317.
— and the Real Presence. (J. W. Santee) Ref. Q. **42**: 195.
— Central Principle of. (J. W. Richard) Luth. Q. **25**: 162.
— in American Liberty vindicated. (L. M. Heilman) Luth. Q. **24**: 81.
— in the General Synod. (E. J. Wolf) Luth. Q. **22**: 592.
Lutherburg, Philippe Jacques. (J. Penderel-Brodhurst) M. of Art, **9**: 101.
Luttrell, Lord Amelius. (J. W. Sherer) Time, **3**: 279.
Luttrell, Henry. (Mrs. A. Crosse) Temp. Bar, **104**: 47. Same art. Liv. Age, **204**: 487. Same art. Ecl. M. **124**: 236.
Lutyens, Charles. (A. E. Torrens) M. of Art, **6**: 133.
Lux Mundi. (A. De Vere) Dub. R. **111**: 337.
Luxembourg Gallery, Caillebotte Bequest to. (J. Bernac) Art J. **47**: 308, 358.
Luxury. (Leslie Stephen) National, **23**: 29. Same art. Ecl. M. **122**: 588. Same art. Liv. Age, **201**: 67. — (H. Sidgwick) Int. J. Ethics, **5**: 1.
— Culpable. Spec. **77**: 511. Same art. Liv. Age, **211**: 591.
— Economics of. (Ellis Merriam) Soc. Econ. **1**: 233.
— Office of. (P. L. Beaulieu) Pop. Sci. Mo. **47**: 25.
— Sidgwick on. Spec. **72**: 79. Same art. Ecl. M. **122**: 351.
— a Social Study. (P. Leroy-Beaulieu) Chaut. **20**: 456.
Lyall, Edna. *See* Bayly, A. E.
Lycée, French, Life in. (G. Jamin) Educa. R. **5**: 266.
Lycett, Edward. (E. A. Barber) New Eng. M. n. s. **13**: 33.
Lyceum, The. (J. B. Pond) Cosmopol. **20**: 595.
— Great Orators and the. (J. B. Pond) Cosmopol. **21**: 247.
— New England, Rise and Decline of. (E. P. Powell) New Eng. M. n. s. **11**: 730.
Lyceum Theatre, London, Rehearsals at the. (G. B. Burgin) Idler, **3**: 123.
Lycia and Caria, Frontier of. (W. Arkwright) J. Hel. Stud. **15**: 93.
— and Pisidia, Inscriptions from. (G. F. Hill) J. Hel. Stud. **15**: 116.
— Greek Inscriptions from. (G. Davies) J. Hel. Stud. **15**: 100.
Lycopods, Paleozoic, Development of Exogenous Structure in. (D. White) Science, n. s. **3**: 754.
Lydia Gibson. (L. Parr) Longm. **26**: 295.
Lyell, Charles, and the Lamarckians. (W. K. Brooks) Nat. Sci. **8**: 89.
Lying. (W. P. Roberts) Good Words, **35**: 645.
— Truth and the White Lie. (E. M. Thomas) Atlan. **76**: 836.
— Why Children lie. (N. Oppenheim) Pop. Sci. Mo. **47**: 382.
Lyly, John. Quar. **183**: 110.
— and his Euphues. (H. Lacey) Gent. M. n. s. **54**: 292. Same art. Liv. Age, **205**: 225.
— Endymion. (E. K. Chambers) Acad. **48**: 332.
— Plot of his Sapho and Phao. (F. J. Teggart) Poet-Lore, **8**: 29.

Lyly, John, Shakspeare and. (H. Davis) Poet-Lore, 5: 177.
Lymph, Formation of. (W. D. Halliburton) Sci. Prog. 3: 409.
Lynch Law. (N. J. D. Kennedy) Jurid. R. 3: 213. 4: 44. — (I. B. Wells) Our Day, 11: 333.
— Case of Henry Smith. Pub. Opin. 14: 448.
— in America. Spec. 72: 743.
— in the South. (F. Douglass) No. Am. 155: 17.
— in the U. S. (W. Roberts) Fortn. 57: 91.
— Trial by. (R. B. Townshend) 19th Cent. 32: 243. Same art. Ecl. M. 119: 413.
Lynching and the Law's Delays. (W. Le C. Stevens) Nation, 61: 426.
— as a Fine Art. (L. H. Blair) Our Day, 13: 307.
— Educative Effect of. (E. L. Godkin) Nation, 57: 222.
— Horrors of. (C. F. Aked) Chr. Lit. 11: 96.
— Last Hold of the Southern Bully. (W. H. Page) Forum, 16: 303.
— Mobs and. (G. C. Holt) Am. J. Soc. Sci. 32: 67.
— Negro Outrage no Excuse for. (L. E. Bleckley) Forum, 16: 300.
— of Black People because they are Black. (F. Douglass) Our Day, 13: 298.
— of Negroes in the South. (C. F. Aked) Contemp. 65: 818.
— Southern. (E. L. Godkin) Nation, 57: 322. — Pub. Opin. 15: 618. — (F. M. Noa) Nation, 61: 407.
— — Cause of. Nation, 61: 463.
— Symposium. Indep. Feb. 1, '94.
— True Remedy for. (W. Clark) Am. Law R. 28: 801.
Lynn, England. (O. F. Adams) New Eng. M. n. s. 10: 204.
Lynton, England, Scenery of. (S. Hodges) M. of Art, 1: 225.
Lyon, George W. Music, 5: 474.
Lyon, Matthew, Col., a Vigorous Politician of the Olden Time. (J. G. Speed) Harper, 88: 698.
Lyon in Mourning, The; or, Reminiscences of the 45. Chamb. J. 72: 785.
Lyonnesse, Souvenirs of. (F. Banfield) Gent. M. n. s. 50: 396.
Lyra Sacra, ed. by H. C. Beeching. Sat. R. 79: 625.
Lyræ β, Spectrum of. (H. C. Vogel) Astron. 13: 358, 561, (J. N. Lockyer) 575.
Lyric, What is a? Spec. 76: 735.
Lyric Drama and Libretti. (S. J. A. Fitzgerald) Theatre, 29: 161.
Lyric Poetry, World-anthology of. (F. L. Thompson) Dial (Ch.) 21: 214.
Lyrics of 17th Century, Saintsbury's. Sat. R. 74: 366. — Spec. 68: 817.
Lysikrates, Choragic Monument of, at Athens, Frieze of. (H. F. De Cou) Am. J. Archæol. 8: 42.
Lyttelton, Thomas, Edward, and Timothy, Legal Portraits of. (G. Scharf) Ath. '93, 1: 125.
Lyttelton, Thomas, Lord. Did Junius Commit Suicide? (A. Lang) Blackw. 157: 406.
Lytton, E. L. Bulwer, Lord. (J. W. Sherer) Gent. M. n. s. 55: 299.
— and the Caxtons. Eng. R. 12: 303.
— The Poetry of. (G. Saintsbury) Forum, 22: 467.
— Some Unpublished Letters. (G. Stewart) Canad. M. 4: 297.
Lytton, E. R., Lord. (L. C. Moulton) Arena, 6: 46.
— King Poppy. (G. Cotterell) Acad. 43: 299. — Sat. R. 74: 714.
— Marah. National, 19: 200.
— Morris, and Arnold. (L. C. Moulton) Arena, 6: 46.
Lytton, E. R., Lord, Poetry and. (W. H. Mallock) Fortn. 57: 795.
— Poetry of. (R. B. Johnson) Acad. 41: 415.
— Rank of, in Literature. (W. S. Blunt) 19th Cent. 31: 566. Same art. Liv. Age, 193: 805.
Ma P'tite Philomène. (T. G. Randall) Outing, 25: 381.
Maartens, M., with portrait. Bk. Buyer, 9: 667. — With portrait. Bk. Buyer, 11: 233.
— Question of Taste. Spec. 68: 719.
Mabie, Hamilton W., with portrait. (J. McArthur) Bookman, 2: 298.
Mabinogion Studies. (A. Nutt) Folk-Lore Rec. 5: 1.
Mabuse, Jan van. (W. M. Conway) M. of Art, 8: 462.
Macaire; a farce. (W. E. Henley and R. L. Stevenson) New R. 12: 685.
Macallester, Oliver; study of a spy. (A. Lang) Eng. Illust. 13: 214.
Macaronic Poetry. Walford's Antiq. 10: 153.
Macaronics. Sat. R. 78: 70.
Macaulay, T. B., and the Reformers. Eng. R. 14: 307.
— and Water. (W. J. Ashley) Nation, 56: 16.
— Enduring Characteristics of. (T. Bradfield) Westm. 145: 152.
— Essays, Proof Sheets of. Good Words, 35: 26.
— His Place in Literature. (F. Harrison) Forum, 18: 80.
— on American Institutions. Gunton's M. 11: 195.
Maccall, William. (A. Waters) Open Court, 7: 3779.
Maccari's Historic Frescoes. (T. Tracey) Cosmopol. 22: 115.
McCarthy, Justin. Autobiography, An. Outl. 54: 1081.
McCarthy, Justin Huntly. By the Midland Sea. Theatre, 29: 77.
— Ring of Polycrates. Theatre, 29: 78.
McClellan, G. B. (E. G. Scott) Atlan. 70: 1.
— and his Mission. (J. B. Fry) Cent. 26: 931.
— Peninsular Campaign, First Six Weeks of. (J. F. Rhodes) Am. Hist. R. 1: 464.
— Recollections of. (W. F. Biddle) Un. Serv. (Phila.) 11: 460.
McClure's Magazine. (McClure) 4: 487.
McCord, George H. (C. M. Skinner) Q. Illust. 2: 164.
McCormick, Cyrus H., with portrait. (H. L. Conard) Nat'l M. (N. Y. '91) 16: 594.
McCosh, James, with portrait. Bk. Buyer, 3: 207. — Critic, 25: 354. — Pub. Opin. 17: 820. — (F. L. Patton) Presb. & Ref. R. 6: 643.
— as a Teacher of Philosophy. (A. T. Ormond and S. M. Hamilton) Educa. R. 9: 122.
— Sloane's Life of. (J. W. Chadwick) Nation, 63: 276. — (G. J. Clarke) Dial (Ch.) 21: 114.
McCrea, Samuel Harkness, with portrait. (H. L. Conard) Nat'l M. (N. Y. '91) 15: 324.
McCulloch, George. Collection of Paintings. Art J. 48: 137, 355.
McCulloch, Oscar C. Lend a H. 8: 38. — With portrait. (A. Johnson) Char. R. 1: 97. — (I. C. Barrows) Lend a H. 9: 113.
McCullough, John Griffith, with portrait. (H. L. Conard) Nat'l M. (N. Y. '91) 16: 100.
McCunn, Hamish. Queen Hynde of Caledon. Theatre, 28: 218.
Macdonald, Alexander. Collection of Pictures. (J. Dow) M. of Art, 11: 378, 425.
McDonald, Flora. (C. McD. Smith) Munsey, 13: 398.
MacDonald, George, with portrait. Bk. News, 11: 303.
— at Bordighera. Critic, 25: 209.

MacDonald, George, Poetry of. (J. A. Noble) Acad. 44: 146. — Spec. 71: 243.
Macdonald, Sir John A. (W. F. Maclean) Canad. M. 4: 253. — (G. M. Adams) Nation, 60: 94. — Ath. '95, 1: 41. — Sat. R. 73: 490. — Spec. 73: 848.
Macdonald, Marshal. Recollections. Ed. R. 176: 114.— Ath. '92, 1: 365. — (H. M. Stephens) Acad. 41: 269. — (J. D. Cox) Nation, 54: 434. — Sat. R. 73: 306. — (W. O'C. Morris) Scot. R. 20: 67. Same art. Liv. Age, 195: 3. — Spec. 68: 561.
Macdonald's Return; a story. Cornh. 68: 71.
Macdonell, George Paul. Acad. 47: 504.
McDonogh, John, with portrait. (C. D. Lanier) Char. R. 1: 315.
McDonogh Farm School, Maryland. (C. D. Lanier) R. of Rs. (N. Y.) 5: 429.
McDougall, Archibald, Letter of. (J. S. H. Fogg) N. E. Reg. 50: 12.
MacDowell, Edward A. (E. Brower) Atlan. 77: 394. — (J. L. Mathews) Music, 10: 31.
Macedonia and the Macedonians. Contemp. 68: 305. Same art. Liv. Age, 207: 131.
— Question of. (J. M. Hubbard) Nation, 63: 64.
Maceo and his Race. Spec. 77: 892.
McEwan, Tom, Sketch of. Art J. 48: 15.
McGaffey's Poems; a review. (J. Blewitt) Canad. M. 6: 571.
McGill University, Montreal. (A. H. U. Colquhoun) Canad. M. 6: 418.
— Physics and Engineering at. Nature, 50: 558.
— Physics Building. (F. Thomason) Canad. M. 7: 425.
M'Graw. (F. Lynde) Cent. 27: 136.
Macgregor, John. (J. Macaulay) Leis. Hour, 44: 43.
— Hodder's. Ath. '94, 2: 559. — (G. H. Pike) Sund. M. 23: 741.
Mach, E. Scientific Lectures, Popular. (A. E. Dolbear) Dial (Ch.) 18: 176.
Machako's to Kitwyi, A Journey from. (J. Ainsworth) Geog. J. 7: 406.
Machias, Me. (M. E. C. Smith) New Eng. M. n. s. 12: 672.
Machiavelli, Niccolo. Lond. Q. 79: 20. Same art. Liv. Age, 196: 131.
— and the English Reformation. (W. A. Phillips) 19th Cent. 40: 907.
— Mandragola. (J. Mew) Fortn. 57: 530.
— The Prince. (W. R. Thayer) Int. J. Ethics, 2: 476.
— — Burd's Ed. (M. Creighton) Eng. Hist. R. 7: 354.
Machina ex-Cœlo; a story. Temp. Bar, 107: 205. Same art. Liv. Age, 208: 528.
Machine-building in America. (E. François) Cassier, 11: 141.
Machine Designing, Racial Traits in. (A. Williams, jr.) Engin. M. 10: 92.
Machine Production and Oriental Lands. Gunton's M. 11: 261.
— Evolution of Modern Capitalism. Soc. Econ. 9: 81.
Machine-shop Construction. (J. E. Sweet) Cassier, 3: 223.
Machine-shop Economics. (H. L. Arnold) Engin. M. 11: 59-1089. — (O. Smith) Cassier, 8: 127.
Machine-shop Instruction in Technical Schools. (J. Torrey) Engin. M. 6: 17.
Machine-shop Management. (J. Brady) Engin. M. 8: 433.
Machine-tools, Modern American. (O. Smith) Engin. M. 8: 54.
Machinery. Soc. Econ. 2: 86.
— and Culture. Soc. Econ. 1: 129.
— and Morals. Soc. Econ. 1: 210.
Machinery and Progress. Decline of Rome. Soc. Econ. 2: 385. 3: 46.
— as a Factor in Social and Industrial Evolution. (J. M. H. Frederick) Am. M. Civics, 9: 136.
— The Democratic Movement. Soc. Econ. 2: 263.
— Economic Theory of, Graziani's. (S. Wood) Ann. Am. Acad. Pol. Sci. 2: 522.
— — Reply. (A. Graziani) Ann. Am. Acad. Pol. Sci. 2: 838.
— Educational Influence of. (A. E. Outerbridge) Engin. M. 9: 225.
— Emancipation of Labor by. (A. E. Outerbridge) Engin. M. 9: 1012.
— False Ideas of Beauty in. (W. Fletcher) Cassier, 5: 147.
— Influence of, upon Employment. (J. A. Hobson) Pol. Sci. Q. 8: 97. — (J. Todd) Meth. R. 53: 393.
— Manufacturing it — or Building it? (O. Smith) Cassier, 7: 157.
— Miniature. Chamb. J. 73: 807.
Machines, Designing of, Intuition in. (J. T. Hawkins, Engin. M. 3: 480.
Machinist, The. (F. J. Miller) Scrib. M. 14: 314.
Machyn, Henry, Diary of. (A. Hayden) Bookworm, 7: 17.
McIlwraith, the Canadian Ornithologist. (J. M. Le Moine) Canad. M. 3: 91.
Macintyre's Baranta; a story. (L. W. Montagnon) Gent. M. n. s. 56: 433.
Mackay, Charles, Writings of, in relation to the present Uprising of the People. (B. O. Flower) Arena, 16: 865.
Mäckay, Eric, at Home. (B. Boyle) Idler, 6: 471.
— Nero and Actéa. Ath. '92, 2: 298.
Mackay, John W. (J. R. Young) Munsey, 6: 267.
McKean, Thomas, Letter to Gen. Washington, 1789. Am. Hist. R. 2: 98.
Mackenzie, Alexander. (C. H. McIntosh) Canad. M. 8: 150.
Mackenzie, Dr. Alex. C. Bethlehem. Sat. R. 77: 414.
Mackenzie, Sir Morell, with portrait. (W. T. Stead) R. of Rs. (N. Y.) 5: 189.
MacKenzie Delta, A Woman in. (E. Taylor) Outing, 25: 44, 120, 229, 304.
MacKenzie River. In Northwest Wilds. (W. Ogilvie) Canad. M. 2: 516. 3: 67, 160, 272.
Mackerel, A School of. (E. Step) Good Words, 37: 14.
— Supply of, Conservation of. (R. F. Walsh) Pop. Sci. Mo. 42: 821.
Mackey, Charles William, with portrait. (L. A. Bond) Nat'l M. (N. Y. '91) 17: 550.
Mackinac, the Gate of Lake Michigan. (J. A. Currie) Canad. M. 3: 416.
Mackinac Island, Highest Old Shore Line on. (F. B. Taylor) Am. J. Sci. 143: 210.
— Scenes at. (M. N. Wishard) Chaut. 16: 89.
McKinley, William, with portraits. (F. B. Gessner and E. J. Edwards) McClure, 2: 22, 80. — (M. Halstead) Outl. 54: 132. — (E. V. Smalley) R. of Rs. (N. Y.) 14: 33.
— and Bryan as Lawyers. (A. O. Hall) Green Bag, 8: 393.
— and the Presidency. (N. R. Flood) Am. M. Civics, 8: 385.
— Nominated for President. Sat. R. 81: 614.
Mackintoshite, etc. (W. E. Hidden) Am. J. Sci. 146: 98.
Macklin, Thomas, Gallery of. (A. Beaver) M. of Art, 9: 462.
Mackonochie, Rev. Alex. H., and Ritualistic Movement. Time, 18: 137.

McLachlan, Thomas Hope. (S. Image) M. of Art, **18**: 57.
Maclagan, Gen. Robert. Geog. J. **4**: 179. — (W. Broadfoot) Blackw. **156**: 247.
Maclaren, Ian. *See* Watson, John.
Maclean, A. Petruccio; a prize opera. Sat. R. **80**: 9.
Maclean, John. Acad. **47**: 237.
McLean, Sally Pratt. *See* Green, Sally P. McL.
MacLean, Thomas Nelson. (J. A. Blaikie) M. of Art, **9**: 233.
Macleod, Dr. Donald, at Home. (A. W. Stewart) Sund. M. **24**: 382.
Macleod, Fiona. The Mountain Lovers. (G. Cotterell) Acad. **48**: 125.
— The Washer of the Ford. (G. Cotterell) Acad. **50**: 25.
Macleod, Fort, in 1885. (B. W. Antrobus) Canad. M. **8**: 3.
MacMahon, M. P. de, Marshal. (A. D. Vandam) New R. **9**: 449. — (W. O'C. Morris) Scot. R. **23**: 59. — (M. Rose) Un. Serv. M. **8**: 256.
— and his Forbears. (E. Crawford) Contemp. **64**: 788. Same art. Liv. Age, **200**: 21.
— The Soldier and the Man. (J. Hogan) Am. Cath. Q. **19**: 348.
McMaster, John B., with portrait. Bk. News, **7**: 62.
McMaster University. (E. P. Wells) Canad. M. **3**: 309.
McMichael, James, Lieut., Diary of. (W. P. McMichael) Pennsyl. M. **16**: 129.
Macmillan, Alexander. Critic, **28**: 80, 127. — Acad. **49**: 95. — Ath. '**96**, **1**: 150. — (H. W. Mabie) Outl. **53**: 1200.
— A Personal Reminiscence. Macmil. **73**: 397.
Macmillan & Co., Publishers. Book R. **1**: 103.
Macmonnies, Frederick. (Will H. Low) Scrib. M. **18**: 617.
McNeill's Zareba as a Surprise. (W. Huyshe) Sat. R. **79**: 511, 551.
Macpherson, James, Saunders's Life of. (T. Hutchinson) Acad. **46**: 205. — Sat. R. **77**: 669.
Macpherson, Wm. Ath. '**93**, **1**: 536.
Macquoid, Katherine. (J. MacArthur) Critic, **25**: 450.
McTaggart, William. (J. L. Caw) Art J. **46**: 243.
Mad Medlicott; a story. (G. Allen) Eng. Illust. **10**: 619.
Mad Sentinel, The; a story. (W. H. Woods) Southern M. **5**: 155.
Madagascar. (Vazaha) Fortn. **62**: 574. — Fortn. **63**: 77. — (F. Taylor) No. Am. **163**: 479.
— and its People, Glimpse of. (A. H. Grant) Time, **8**: 329.
— and Mauritius. (F. C. Williams) National, **20**: 377.
— Customs connected with Royalty among Tribes of. (J. Sibree) Anthrop. J. **21**: 215.
— Deadlock in. (Vazaha) Fortn. **59**: 896.
— England's Futile Scheme to colonize. (Julian Corbett) Macmil. **71**: 358.
— Expedition to, and Neutrals. (M. J. Farrelly) Am. Law R. **29**: 539.
— Exposition de, at the Jardin des Plantes. (P. L. Sclater) Nat. Sci. **7**: 251.
— Fictitious French Claim to. (K. Blind) Contemp. **66**: 883.
— Folk-lore of. (J. Sibree, jr.) Folk-Lore Rec. **2**: 19. — Folk-Lore Rec. **4**: 45.
— — Birds in. (J. Sibree, jr.) Folk-Lore, **2**: 336.
— Forest of. Cornh. **69**: 181. Same art. Liv. Age, **200**: 552.
— French in. Ed. R. **182**: 499. — (P. Oliver) New R. **12**: 547. — (F. C. Maude) Sat. R. **80**: 105. — Quar. **184**: 245. — (S. P. Oliver) Un. Serv. M. **10**: 155–484. **11**: 100–642.
— — Inefficiency of. Sat. R. **82**: 137.
Madagascar, French in, Routier on. Sat. R. **79**: 552.
— French Design against. Spec. **72**: 76.
— History, An Unpublished Page in. (Alice Zimmern) Temp. Bar, **104**: 262. Same art. Liv. Age, **204**: 609.
— In Imerina. (P. Oliver) New R. **13**: 554.
— in War-time, Knight's. Sat. R. **81**: 534.
— Invasion of. Spec. **75**: 294.
— Journeying in. (F. Vincent) Pop. Sci. Mo. **47**: 239.
— Languages spoken in. (J. T. Last) Anthrop. J. **25**: 46.
— Military Situation in. (Vazaha) Fortn. **57**: 437.
— Music in. (F. A. Van Stantford) Music, **8**: 399.
— New Animals from. (R. Lydekker) Knowl. **18**: 68.
— Question of. (M. Ordinaire) Chaut. **20**: 279.
— Roman Catholic Missions in. (B. J. Clinch) Am. Cath. Q. **18**: 392.
— Sacred City of Ambohimanga. (F. C. Maude) Sat. R. **80**: 233.
— The Sancho Panza of. (J. Corbett) Macmil. **71**: 358. Same art. Liv. Age, **205**: 147.
— The Situation in. Meth. R. **56**: 143.
— War Literature of. (S. P. Oliver) Ath. '**95**, **2**: 416.
— Western, and the Antinosi Country, Notes on. (J. T. Last) Geog. J. **6**: 227.
Madam Celeste. (R. C. Falls) Southern M. **4**: 25.
Madame; a story. (E. T. Fowler) Argosy, **58**: 326.
Madame Annalena. (B. Perry) Scrib. M. **19**: 97.
Madame la Comtesse; a story. Argosy, **59**: 115.
Madame's Bass; a story. (A. C. Hurlburt) Outing, **26**: 375.
Madam's Chicken Shoot, The; a story. (E. W. Sandys) Outing, **22**: 365.
Maddocks, Councillor J., Collection of Pictures. (B. Wood) M. of Art, **14**: 298, 337.
Madeira. Idler, **2**: 437.
— English Chaplaincy in. Eng. R. **9**: 298.
— Levada-walking in. (E. H. Robertson) Good Words, **37**: 309.
Mademoiselle Clémence. (E. Pouvillion) Chaut. **21**: 290.
Mademoiselle de Maupin; a story. (H. de V. Stacpoole) Temp. Bar, **106**: 86.
Madhouses. *See* Insane Hospitals.
Madison, James, at Princeton. (J. L. McLeish) Bach. of Arts, **1**: 634.
— Letters by. (W. C. Ford) Nation, **59**: 46.
— — The Revelation contained in. (C. C. Nott) Nation, **60**: 380, 398.
— Retreat of. (J. D. Warfield) Am. Hist. Reg. **2**: 857.
Madison Square Garden, New York. (M. G. Van Rensselaer) Cent. **25**: 732.
Madness of Gabrielle Rousillon; a story. (C. Holland) Belgra. **80**: 310.
Madonna and Child; a poem. (A. A. Sewall) Harper, **90**: 14.
— — in Art. (W. H. Low) McClure, **6**: 33.
Madonna of a Day, The. (L. Dougall) Temp. Bar, **106**: 145, 289, 433. **107**: 1, 161.
Madras and Calcutta. All the Year, **75**: 569.
— Determination of the Longitude of. (A. Houtum-Schindler) Acad. **49**: 449.
— Land Taxation in. (R. Lethbridge) Asia. R. **20**: 8.
Madrazo, Raimundo de. (D. Hannay) M. of Art, **7**: 10.
Madre; a story. (D. E. Beaty-Pownall) Temp. Bar, **99**: 113. Same art. Ecl. M. **121**: 562.
Madre de Dios River in Bolivia and Peru, Recent Discoveries in Basin of. (C. R. Markham) Geog. J. **7**: 187.
Madrid. (H. C. Chatfield-Taylor) Cosmopol. **21**: 121.

Madrid, Expoçicion Historico-Americano, 1892. Am. Natural. 37: 840, 907.
— Royal Palace in. (D. M. Hart) Art J. 45: 236.
— Saunterings in. (S. Culin) Overland, n. s. 24: 8.
Madura, India. All the Year, 76: 31.
Maes, Nicholaas. (T. Cole) Cent. 25: 563.
Maeterlinck, Maurice. (W. Sharp) Acad. 41: 270. — (J. Heard, jr.) Critic, 20: 354. — (R. Burton) Atlan. 74: 672. — (R. Hovey) 19th Cent. 37: 491. — (I. Zangwill) Critic, 26: 451. — With portrait. (J. T. Stoddart) Bookman, 1: 246. — Poet-Lore, 5: 151.
— and Emerson. (H. Osgood) Arena, 15: 563.
— at Home. (M. Pidoux) Bookman, 2: 104.
— Impressions of, and the Theatre de l'Œuvre. (R. Hovey) Poet-Lore, 7: 446.
— Plays. Spec. 69: 455.
— Princess Maleine and the Intruder. Ath. '92, 1: 525.
Mafassal Law Courts of Bengal. (A. D. Bolton) Gent. M. n. s. 53: 75.
Mafia, The. Chamb. J. 69: 385. Same art. Liv. Age, 194: 572.
— Camorra, and Brigandage. (S. Merlino) Pol. Sci. Q. 9: 466.
Magallon, Paul Peter Raphael de. (E. Schreiber) Month, 82: 15.
Magazine, 18th Century. (W. T. Brewster) Harv. Mo. 14: 105.
— Illustrated, Making of an. Cosmopol. 14: 259.
Magazine Articles, Evils of Signing. Sat. R. 74: 133.
Magazine Fiction, and how not to write it. (F. M. Bird) Lippinc. 54: 650.
Magazine-writers, Relations of Editors to. (F. M. Bird) Lippinc. 56: 859.
Magazines, Cheap. McClure, 5: 287.
— Christmas, 1892, and Literary Decay. Poet-Lore, 5: 39.
— Old-time. (F. H. T. Bellew) Cosmopol. 12: 343.
— Writing for. (F. M. Bird) Lippinc. 58: 713.
Magdalen, the, Types and Legends of. (M. Field) Munsey, 13: 258.
Magdalens of Society. (J. W. Sproull) Am. J. Pol. 2: 179.
Magdalen Islands. Chamb. J. 70: 193.
Magdalene; a story. (C. Warner) Theatre, 30: 17.
Magee, W. C., Archbishop. (F. W. Farrar) Contemp. 62: 534. — (F. W. Farrar) Contemp. 70: 623. — Same art. Liv. Age, 211: 560. Same art. Chr. Lit. 16: 136.
— Sermons. Spec. 68: 436.
— Speeches and Addresses. Sat. R. 74: 337.
Magellan Straits and Smyth's Channel. (A. P. Crouch) Un. Serv. M. 5: 568.
Magic. (C. Morritt) Theatre, 30: 23.
— among the Red Men. (H. Kellar) No. Am. 157: 591.
— and Prodigy in the East. (M. Jastrow, jr.) Poet-Lore, 4: 118.
— Characteristics of, in Eastern and Western Literature. (T. Williams) Poet-Lore, 4: 126.
— High Caste Indian. (H. Kellar) No. Am. 156: 75.
— Hindoo. (H. Hensoldt) Arena, 9: 46.
— Indian. Spec. 72: 432, 467.
— Midsummer. (V. Paget) Macmil. 66: 206. Same art. Ecl. M. 119: 350.
— Modern. Ed. R. 181: 82.
— Natural History of. (L. J. Vance) Open Court, 5: 2763, 2773, 2783.
Magic Circle; a poem. (Isa J. Postgate) Gent. M. n. s. 57: 627.
Magic Egg, The. (F. R. Stockton) Cent. 26: 290.
Magic Ink; a story. (W. Black) Good Words, 33: 73.
Magic Pot, The. (L. Kip) Overland, n. s. 23: 54.
Magic Ring, The. (K. Grahame) Scrib. M. 20: 693.
Magic Square. (H. Schubert) Monist, 2: 487.
Maginn, William. (G. Saintsbury) Macmil. 69: 105.
Magistrates, County, in England, Appointment of. Spec. 70: 412, 565.
Magnesia, Asia Minor, Excavations at. Sat. R. 77: 660.
Magnesium, Action of, upon Vapors of the Alcohols. (E. H. Keiser and M. B. Breed) J. Frankl. Inst. 139: 304.
— as a Source of Light. (F. J. Rogers) Am. J. Sci. 143: 301.
Magnesium Chloride, Separation of, from Chlorides of Sodium and Potassium. (R. B. Riggs) Am. J. Sci. 144: 103.
Magnetic Elements at Principal Magnetic Observatories of the World, Value of. (C. Chree) Sci. Prog. 3: 390.
Magnetic Field, Graphic Representation of. (E. J. Houston) J. Frankl. Inst. 134: 75.
— Photographic Method of Mapping. (C. B. Thwing) Am. J. Sci. 144: 374.
— Robert Boyle's Conception. (E. J. Houston) J. Frankl. Inst. 133: 208.
Magnetic Fields, Phenomena of Alternating. (E. Thomson) Engin. M. 7: 530.
Magnetic Induction. (J. A. Ewing) Nature, 46: 552.
Magnetic Needle. (V. Cornish) Knowl. 18: 93.
— Secular Motion of a Free. (L. A. Bauer) Science, 20: 218.
Magnetic Observations, General Bearings of. (E. W. Creak) Sci. Prog. 5: 81.
Magnetic Pole, Expedition to the North. (W. H. Gilder) McClure, 1: 159.
Magnetical Science, Early. (C. S. Peirce) Nation, 58: 124, 141.
Magnetism, Animal, Mesmer and Hypnotism. (Joseph Jastrow) Cosmopol. 20: 360.
— Feats of, Explained. (N. W. Perry) Cassier, 7: 236.
— Terrestrial, Distribution and Secular Variation of. (L. A. Bauer) Am. J. Sci. 150: 109, 189, 314. — (L. A. Bauer) Science, n. s. 1: 673.
— — in England; Whiston's Discoveries. (L. A. Bauer) Nature, 51: 295.
— — Secular Variation of, Wilde on. (L. A. Bauer) Nature, 51: 103.
— Wilde's Explication. (L. A. Bauer) Am. J. Sci. 143: 496.
Magnetization, Electro-chemical Effects due to. (G. O. Squier) Am. J. Sci. 145: 443.
Magnets. Damping of Bell-magnets and Ring-magnets by Surrounding Copper. (A. Kendrick) Am. J. Sci. 147: 454.
— Hard Steel, Induction Coefficients of. (B. O. Peirce) Am. J. Sci. 152: 347.
— Large Guns as. (W. R. King) Cassier, 7: 464.
Magnificence. Spec. 75: 635.
Magnolia Glauca. (T. C. Porter) Garden & F. 7: 398.
Magnolia Stellata. Garden & F. 9: 194.
Magnolias as Garden Plants. (C. S. Sargent) Garden & F. 8: 161.
— Early Flowering. (J. G. Jack) Garden & F. 7: 144.
Magnus, St., of the Isles. (W. M. Metcalfe) Good Words, 34: 626.
Magothy Formation of Northeastern Maryland. (N. H. Darton) Am. J. Sci. 145: 407.
Magrath, Miler. (P. G. Smyth) Cath. World, 61: 44.
Magruder, Julia, with portrait. Bk. News, 12: 71.

Mahalapsi Diamond, The. (H. A. Bryden) Chamb. J. **73**: 209–263.
Mahan, A. T., Honors to, from English Universities. Critic, **25**: 43.
Maharaja Duleep Singh. (L. Griffin) Asia. R. **17**: 21.
Mahatman, A Real. (F. M. Müller) 19th Cent. **40**: 306.
Mahdi, Epistles of the. (A. E. Turner) National, **20**: 767.
Mahomet. *See* Mohammed.
Mahon, Lord, as a Historian. Eng. R. **3**: 1.
Mahon's Guest; a story. (M. E. Francis) Temp. Bar, **101**: 412.
Mahsuds, Our Last War with the. Blackw. **158**: 76. Same art. Liv. Age, **206**: 468.
Maid of Doon, The. (A. Deir) Gent. M. n. s. **50**: 433.
Maiden Dreams; a poem. (W. H. Pollock) M. of Art, **6**: 23.
Maiden of Dreams, A; a poem. (A. L. Salmon) M. of Art, **13**: 27.
Maid's Progress, The. (A. Goode) Scrib. M. **20**: 234.
Maidstone. (G. Payne) Good Words, **37**: 95.
— Battle of, 1648. (H. E. Malden) Eng. Hist. R. **7**: 533. — Sat. R. **74**: 249.
Maignan, Albert. Whither? Art J. **48**: 118.
Mail Carrier's Daughter; a story. (J. F. O'Donnell) Outing, **24**: 96.
Mail Delivery, Free, in Rural Districts. (J. M. Stahl) No. Am. **161**: 511.
Mail Service of U. S., New. (W. B. Robertson) Time, **16**: 44.
— Overland, Development of. (T. L. James) Cosmopol. **20**: 603.
Maillat, François Clément. Nat. Sci. **5**: 313.
Mails, Exclusion from; a Blow at the Freedom of the Press. (H. Taylor) No. Am. **155**: 694.
Maimon, Solomon; Autobiography. (J. Fyvie) Time, **21**: 193.
Maimonides, Discovery of an Unknown Work of. (M. Gaster) Acad. **46**: 195.
Maine, Sir Henry. (A. C. Lyall) Law Q. **4**: 129. — Quar. **176**: 287. — Spec. **70**: 17.
— as a Jurist. Ed. R. **178**: 100.
Maine at the World's Fair. (C. P. Mattocks) New Eng. M. n. s. **10**: 295.
— Conquest of. (G. J. Varney) Green Bag, **8**: 443.
— Early History of. (E. P. Scammon) Cath. World, **56**: 181, 365.
— Election in, 1896: as Maine goes, so goes the Union. (T. B. Reed) Forum, **22**: 257.
— — 1894. Pub. Opin. **17**: 587.
— Farming in. (J. C. Rose) Nation, **55**: 159.
— Folk-Lore. (G. Decrow) J. Am. Folk-Lore, **5**: 318.
— National Guard. (C. B. Hall) Outing, **29**: 77, 181, 285.
— Simanca's Map of, 1610. (B. F. De Costa) N. E. Reg. **46**: 84–401.
— Supreme Court of. (C. Hamlin) Green Bag, **7**: 457, 504, 553. **8**: 14, 61, 111.
— Trade Depression in. (C. Osborn) Econ. J. **5**: 476.
Mainotes, The. (R. Rodd) Macmil. **66**: 54.
Maintenance and Champerty, Law of. (A. H. Dennis) Law Q. **6**: 169.
— and Education. (T. K. Nuttall) Law Q. **10**: 330.
Maintenon, Madame de. (E. L. Didier) Chaut. **24**: 5.
Mainz Psalter of 1457. (Russell Martineau) Bibliographica, **1**: 308.
Maisaja, G., Cardinal. (E. M. Clerke) Dub. R. **112**: 293.
Maistre, Casimir, Journey of, from Congo to Shari and Benue. Geog. J. **2**: 323.
Maistre, Joseph de. (T. L. L. Teeling) Am. Cath. Q. **20**: 807.
Maitland, S. R. Essays in England 9th to 12th Centuries. Eng. R. **1**: 362.
Maiwand Pass. (S. P. Oliver) Un. Serv. M. **7**: 1018.
Maize, Nativity of. (J. Wickersham) Am. Antiq. **16**: 201.
— Value of, as Human Food. (I. I. Murphy) Chaut. **18**: 69.
Majendie's Heroism; a story. (T. Garvey) Argosy, **59**: 731.
Majolica, Roman Maker of. (T. A. Trollope) M. of Art, **4**: 243.
Major, John, Scottish Scholastic, 1470–1550. (T. G. Law) Scot. R. **19**: 345.
Major, The; an Election Sketch. (L. C. Doyle) Gent. M. n. s. **51**: 1.
Major Kinfaun's Marriage; a story. Cornh. **69**: 271.
Major Randall's Warning; a story. (Jessie Macleod) Chamb. J. **69**: 298–329.
Major's Astral Body; a story. (G. B. Stuart) Argosy, **55**: 419.
Major's Diplomacy, The; a story. (A. Marryat) Belgra. **91**: 438.
Major's Mistake; a story. Argosy, **57**: 347.
Major's Silhouette; a story. (W. A. Curtis) Munsey, **11**: 553.
Majorca. (C. Edwards) Outing, **27**: 404, 470.
— In the Mountains of. All the Year, **71**: 126.
Majorities, Political, Nature and Conduct of. (F. H. Giddings) Pop. Sci. Q. **7**: 116.
Majority's Hearth; a story. (G. Livingston) Chaut. **15**: 707.
Makart, Hans, and his Work. (C. S. Johnson) Munsey, **7**: 22.
Maker of Moons; a story. (R. W. Chambers) Eng. Illust. **15**: 315.
Making a Living. (E. E. Hale) Cosmopol. **13**: 374.
Making of a Pessimist; a story. (E. A. Alexander) Harper, **93**: 925.
Making a Point of it; a story. (C. J. K. Fenton) Argosy, **59**: 747.
Making up, The Art of. (Sara Bernhardt) Cosmopol. **20**: 530.
Makowsky, Constantine Egorovitch. (S. F. Coles) Munsey, **9**: 332.
Makran, Ancient and Mediæval. (T. H. Holdich) Geog. J. **7**: 387.
Malabar, Marriage Law in. Law Q. **8**: 314.
Malacca Straits Settlement. (W. A. Pickering) Asia. R. **21**: 90, 329.
Malachi; a story. (G. Parker) Eng. Illust. **12**: no. 2, 9.
Malacology, Recent Advances in. (W. H. Dall) Science, n. s. **4**: 770.
Malagasy, Divination among the. (J. Sibree, jr.) Folk-Lore, **3**: 193.
Malagasy Ghost Story, A. Chamb. J. **70**: 571.
Malagrida, Gabriel, Trial of. Green Bag, **7**: 299.
Malahide, The Talbots of. Walford's Antiq. **4**: 251.
Malan, Solomon Cæsar. Acad. **46**: 451.
Malaria, What is? (C. Edson) No. Am. **162**: 120.
Malarial Fevers, Parasites of. (J. W. Gregory) Nat. Sci. **5**: 195.
Malatesta, Gismondo. (M. Creighton) M. of Art, **5**: 270.
Malatesta, Paolo de, and Francesca di Rimini. (L. de La Ramé) Cosmopol. **18**: 259.
Malay Festival, A. (B. A. Cody) Month, **83**: 542.
Malay Peninsula, The. (A. Keyser) 19th Cent. **34**: 437.
— Life in. (J. Fairlie) Cent. **23**: 577.

Malay Peninsula, Mekong Treaty and. (W. A. Pickering) Asia. R. 21: 241.
Malay Sketches, Swettenham's. Sat. R. 80: 513.
Malayan Christmas, A. (R. Wildman) Overland, n. s. 26: 618.
Malaysia, British. Sat. R. 81: 389.
— British Rule in. Dub. R. 119: 166.
— Child-life in. (R. Wildman) Overland, n. s. 27: 270.
Malbrouk, Song of, (D. G. Adee) Harper, 91: 505.
Malet, Claude François de, Conspiracy of. All the Year, 73: 632.
Malibran, Madame, The Battle of. (A. de Pontmartin) Overland, n. s. 20: 214.
Maliseet Legends. (Edward Jack) J. Am. Folk-Lore, 8: 193.
Mallard, Ernest. Nature, 50: 428.
Mallard Shooting. Outing, 25: 78.
— on Goose Lake. (E. W. Chubb) Outing, 25: 221.
Mallarmé, Stéphane. (E. Gosse) Acad. 43: 5. — (F. Carrel) Fortn. 63: 446. — (A. Manston) Temp. Bar, 109: 242.
Mallein, Diagnostic and Therapeutic Use of. (G. A. Buckmaster) Sci. Prog. 4: 437.
Mallery, Garrick. Acad. 46: 426.
Mallet, David, and "William and Margaret." (W. L. Phelps) Harvard Mo. 13: 191.
Mallet, John L. Autobiography. Ed. R. 175: 369.
Mallett, Peter, with portrait. (C. S. Sotheran) Nat'l M. (N. Y. '91) 15: 541.
Mallock, Wm. H. (A. W. Benn) Acad. 48: 83.
— as a Defender of Natural Religion. (E. R. Hull) Am. Cath. Q. 21: 618.
— Heart of Life. Sat. R. 80: 147.
— Human Document. Sat. R. 74: 86. — Spec. 69: 17.
— Poetry of. (J. S. Little) Acad. 43: 387.
— Proposed Trumpet Performance of. (G. B. Shaw) Fortn. 61: 470.
— Studies of Contemporary Superstition. (F. Harrison) 19th Cent. 38: 214.
Mallorca, Try. (Alan Walters) Chamb. J. 72: 428.
Malmaison, La. Chamb. J. 69: 29.
Malouin; a story. (W. McLennan) Harper, 84: 910.
Malt Liquors of the Ancients. (T. H. B. Graham) Gent. M. n. s. 48: 415.
— of the English. (T. H. B. Graham) Gent. M. n. s. 49: 52.
Malta, Church of St. John at. (W. K. Riland-Bedford) Walford's Antiq. 9: 243.
— Knights of. (W. K. R. Bedford) Portfo. 1894: no. 2.
— Recollections of. (E. J. Hardy) Sund. M. 21: 599.
— Springtide Journey to. (J. Rodenberg) Chaut. 17: 345.
— A Trip to, and back. Liv. Age, 210: 813.
Maltese Cat, The; a story. (Rudyard Kipling) Cosmopol. 19: 303.
Malthus, T. R., Doctrine of, and Modern Society. (L. R. Harley) Am. M. Civics, 6: 13.
— Recent Critics of. (T. N. Carver) Am. J. Pol. 5: 535.
— The Reversal of. (A. W. Tourgee) Am. J. Sociol. 2: 13.
Malthusian Anti-Socialist Argument. (E. Cannan) Econ. R. 2: 71.
Malthusianism. Soc. Econ. 2: 35.
— and Working-Women. (F. H. Giddings) Eth. Rec. 3: 84.
Maltworme's Madrigal; a poem. (A. Dobson) M. of Art, 8: 209.
Malwood Eclogues; Pollio. (C. L. Graves) Cornh. 74: 109.
Mamelukes of Egypt, Muir's. Sat. R. 81: 279.
Mammalia, American, Some Proposed Changes in the Nomenclature of. (S. N. Rhoads) Am. Natural. 28: 523.
— Ancient, and their Descendants. (W. Seton) Cath. World, 60: 401.
— Geography of. (W. L. Sclater) Geog. J. 3: 95. 4: 35. 5: 471. 7: 282. 8: 378.
— in North America. (H. F. Osborn) Am. J. Sci. 146: 379, 448.
— — Rise of. (H. F. Osborn) Nature, 49: 235, 257.
— of the Malay Peninsula. (H. N. Ridley) Nat. Sci. 6: 23, 89, 161.
— Oldest. (R. Lydekker) Knowl. 15: 212.
— Study of, in 1891. (R. Lyddeker) Nat. Sci. 1: 36, 103.
Mammoth Bones under London. Sat. R. 73: 626.
Mammoth Cave in March. (H. C. Hovey) Science, 21: 189.
Mammoths, Destruction of. Lond. Q. 85: 20.
Ma'moiselle. (F. L. Guertin) Munsey, 12: 144.
Man above Nature. (L. Curtis) And. R. 18: 113.
— and Animal, Difference between. (M. Müller) Open Court, 3: 1980.
— and Domestic Animals. (E. E. Hale) Lend a H. 17: 108.
— and the Glacial Period, Wright on. (T. C. Chamberlain) Dial (Ch.) 13: 303. — (R. D. Salisbury) Nation, 55: 496.
See Ice Age.
— and Language. (H. Hale) Am. Antiq. 15: 15-212.
— and the Lower Animals. (E. Noble) Open Court, 7: 3575.
— and Men in Nature. Atlan. 74: 541.
— and Nature, The Oneness of. (P. Carus) Open Court, 2: 1107.
— and the Town. (F. Dolman) Eng. Illust. v. 12-14.
— Animal View of. Spec. 68: 298. Same art. Liv. Age, 194: 254. Same art. Pop. Sci. Mo. 41: 260.
— An Answer to Some Critics. (C. H. Pearson) Fortn. 60: 149.
— Antiquity of. (J. A. Zahm) Am. Cath. Q. 18: 225-719. 19: 260.
— — and the Glacial Period. Church Q. 38: 123.
— — The Greater. (J. Prestwich) 19th Cent. 37: 617. Same art. Ecl. M. 125: 74.
— — in N. America. (E. D. Cope) Am. Natural. 29: 593.
— — Primigenial Skeletons, the Flood, and the Glacial Period. (H. P. F. Marritt) Pop. Sci. Mo. 48: 14.
— as a Microcosm. (C. Sterne) Open Court, 3: 1847, 1865.
— Ascent of, Drummond's. Our Day, 13: 351. — (T. E. Mayne) Westm. 142: 431. Same art. Ecl. M. 123: 679. — (W. Gladden) McClure, 3: 235. — (J. G. McKendrick) Crit. R. 4: 227. — (H. C. Minton) Presb. & Ref. R. 6: 136.
— Beginning and Antiquity of. (D. G. Brinton) Forum, 16: 452.
— Dr. Brinton on. (E. D. Cope) Am. Natural. 28: 902.
— Creation of, African Legends of. (H. M. Stanley) Fortn. 59: 797.
— Debrutalisation of. (B. Leppington) Contemp. 67: 725. Same art. Ecl. M. 125: 145.
— Destiny of. (W. E. Manley) Arena, 13: 454.
— Earliest Abodes of. (S. D. Peet) Am. Antiq. 15: 1.
— East and West. (S. A. Barnett) 19th Cent. 31: 123. Same art. Ecl. M. 118: 263.
— Effeminisation of. (E. D. Cope) Open Court, 7: 3847.
— Evolution of the Human Race. (W. J. Sollas) Nature, 53: 150. — (F. Harrison) Fortn, 60: 28.

Man, The First, Parsic and Jewish Literature of. (A. Kohut) Jew. Q. **3**: 231.
— Fossil. (J. G. Rothermel) Pop. Sci. Mo. **44**: 616. — (A. Keith) Sci. Prog. **3**: 348.
— From Animal to. (J. Le Conte) Monist, **6**: 356.
— Genealogy of. (E. D. Cope) Am. Natural. **27**: 321.
— Glacial, Fresh Relics of. (G. F. Wright) Am. Natural. **30**: 781.
— — in Ohio, New Evidence of. (G. F. Wright) Pop. Sci. Mo. **48**: 157.
— Glassy Essence of. (C. S. Peirce) Monist, **3**: 1.
— Higher Evolution of. (H. Wood) Arena, **10**: 214.
— in Art, Hamerton's. Lit. W. (Bost.) **23**: 469.
— in the Light of Evolution. (E. M. Caillard) Contemp. **64**: 873.
— in Nature. (P. Topinard) Pop. Sci. Mo. **42**: 445.
— — Topinard's. Nature, **45**: 457.
— Is the Race Deteriorating? (M. G. Mulhall) No. Am. **162**: 174.
— Miocene, in India. (T. R. Jones) Nat. Sci. **5**: 345.
— Natural History of. Eng. R. **1**: 271.
— The New. (E. B. Sherman) Critic, **28**: 364.
— of Genius, Lombroso's. (C. S. Peirce) Nation, **54**: 151.
— of the Moment, The. (S. Grand) No. Am. **158**: 620.
— of Peace; a Highland Tradition. (J. S. Campbell) New R. **7**: 719.
— Origin of Mankind. (L. Büchner) Fortn. **61**: 74. Same art. Ecl. M. **122**: 228.
— — and the Religious Sentiment. (A. Fogazzaro) Contemp. **68**: 65.
— — and State of Innocence. (W. R. Harper) Bib. World, **3**: 97.
— Palæolithic, in Europe, W. B. Dawkins on. (H. C. Mercer) Am. Natural. **28**: 448.
— — in No. America. (C. C. Abbott) Science, **20**: 270, 344.
— Petrified, Observations on a So-called. (J. M. Stedman) Am. Natural. **29**: 326.
— Pithecoid. (E. P. Evans) Pop. Sci. Mo. **46**: 183.
— Place of, in the Cosmos, Huxley on. (A. Seth) Blackw. **154**: 823.
— — in Nature, and his Antiquity in America. Around World, **1**: 112.
— Plateau, in Kent. (W. J. L. Abbott) Nat. Sci. **4**: 257.
— Prehistoric, in the Eastern Mediterranean. (J. L. Myres) Sci. Prog. **5**: 335.
— Present Evolution of, Reid's. Sat. R. **82**: 372.
— Primeval. (S. B. Goodenow) Bib. Sac. **51**: 158.
— — Day with. (H. D. Traill) Univ. R. **3**: 303.
— the Primeval Savage, W. C. Smith on. (W. B. Dawkins) Nature, **51**: 194.
— Solidarity of the Race. (H. Wood) Arena, **5**: 307.
— Study of. (W. M. F. Petrie) National, **28**: 119. — (A. Macalister) Pop. Sci. Mo. **42**: 303.
— Three-fold Nature of. (P. J. Gloag) Thinker, **9**: 204.
— Varieties of the Human Species. (G. Sergi) Nature, **51**: 595.
Man, A, and his Model; a story. (A. Hope) Eng. Illust. **12**: no. 4, 51.
Man at Amnat, The. (W. B. Harris) Blackw. **160**: 764.
Man Beyant, The. (A. G. Cowan) Overland, n. s. **22**: 463.
Man from Aidone, The. (E. Cavazza) Atlan. **72**: 433–721.
Man from the Four Corners, The; a story. (G. B. Burgin) Good Words, **34**: 114.
Man from Grimsby, The. (G. G. Farquhar) Chamb. J. **71**: 460.
Man from Staleybridge, The. Macmil. **75**: 35.
Man in the Green Turban; a story. Cornh. **68**: 269. Same art. Liv. Age, **199**: 336.
Man in the Iron Mask, The. Acad. **44**: 343.
Man in Red, The. (T. R. Sullivan) Scrib. M. **13**: 329.
Man of Feeling, A. (H. Spender) Eng. Illust. **16**: 81.
Man of Millions; a story. (C. Stewart) Eng. Illust. **13**: 57.
Man of Monceaux, The; a story. (S. J. Weyman) McClure, **5**: 113.
Man of Promise; a story. (R. Hichens) Temp. Bar, **105**: 129, 227. Same art. Liv. Age, **206**: 140, 208. Same art. Ecl. M. **125**: 257, 353.
Man of Silence; a story. (E. Pugh) New R. **13**: 688. Same art. Ecl. M. **126**: 232.
Man of Sin. [2 Thess. ii. 3–12.] (G. U. Wenner) Luth. Q. **25**: 63.
Man-that-draws-the-handcart, The. (E. Eggleston) Harper, **88**: 466.
Man who came to Town. (C. D. Rhodes) Lippinc. **57**: 125.
Man who died at Amdheran. (V. W. Cloud) Lippinc. **54**: 664.
Man who feared the Dark; a story. (H. Bates) Arena, **8**: 496.
Man who lived a Plot. (E. J. Appleton) New Eng. M. n. s. **8**: 586.
Man who was Brave, The; a story. (Mrs. J. E. Holloway) Eng. Illust. **9**: 735.
Man with the Cough. (L. Molesworth) Longm. **23**: 506.
Man with the Iron Mask. (F. Funck-Brentano) Chaut. **20**: 531.
Man with the Ivory Pass, The. (T. W. Speight) Argosy, **60**: 759.
Man with no Grit, The; a story. (L. C. D'Oyle) Gent. M. n. s. **48**: 433.
Man with no Voice; a story. Cornh. **68**: 655. Same art. Liv. Age, **200**: 51.
Man without a Memory, A. (W. H. Shelton) Scrib. M. **16**: 68.
Man, Isle of. Lond. Q. **83**: 304. — (E. Bradbury) M. of Art, **4**: 54. — (E. R. Dibdin) M. of Art, **18**: 178.
— Folk-Lore of. (A. W. Moore) Antiq. n. s. **31**: 5–344.
— — and Superstitions of. (J. Rhys) Folk-Lore, **2**: 284. **3**: 74.
— Home Rule in. Sat. R. **75**: 153.
— Manx Life and Manxland. (T. E. Brown) Contemp. **66**: 642.
— Peculiarities of Laws of. (G. H. Westley) Green Bag, **8**: 55.
— Superstitions of. J. Am. Folk-Lore, **6**: 65.
— Walpole's. Ed. R. **178**: 32. — (W. J. Ashley) Nation, **56**: 300.
Man-eater, The; a story. Argosy, **62**: 418.
Man-eater, The; a story. (M. Roberts) Idler, **4**: 295.
Man-eaters, Adventures with. Time, **8**: 420.
Man-hater's Romance, A; a story. (L. Hensel) Chaut. **19**: 743.
Man-making and Verse-making. (W. E. Gladstone) New R. **15**: 116.
Man-of-war, English, Life on. Chamb. J. **69**: 843.
Man-of-war Pets. Chamb. J. **72**: 698.
Man's Heart, A; a story. (A. Goddard) Theatre, **32**: 26.
Manager's Safe, The; a story. (G. Fosery) Argosy, **54**: 326. Same art. Liv. Age, **195**: 733.

Mañana. Chamb. J. 73: 571.
Manassas Industrial School. (Mrs. B. Whitman) Lend a H. 14: 297.
Manatee, Florida, Present Standing of, in Indian River Waters. (O. Bangs) Am. Natural. 29: 783.
— Young, at the London Zoo. Chamb. J. 70: 799.
Manchester, England, Art Gallery. (H. M. Cundall) Art J. 46: 35.
— City Hall, Mural Paintings. (T. H. Caine) M. of Art, 5: 114.
— Municipal Technical School. (H. E. Roscoe) Nature, 47: 201.
Manchester School, The. (G. Smith) Contemp. 67: 377. Same art. Ecl. M. 124: 594.
Manchester Ship Canal. Chamb. J. 70: 817. — Dub. R. 111: 452. — (D. Paton) Good Words, 33: 100. — (E. Porritt) Yale R. 3: 295. — (H. Y. Oldham) Geog. J. 3: 485. — All the Year, 54: 132, 161, 173. — (Egerton of Tatton) 19th Cent. 35: 12. — Liv. Age, 200: 374. — (L. M. Haupt) J. Frankl. Inst. 137: 176. — Sat. R. 77: 13. — Spec. 72: 9.
Manchuria, Central, Journey through. (J. A. Wylie) Geog. J. 2: 443.
— Chinese, English Commercial Relations with. (A. R. Agassiz) Geog. J. 4: 534.
— Chinese Colonization in. Dub. R. 119: 167.
— Russian Acquisition of. Blackw. 153: 631. 154: 199.
Manchus, Marriage Ceremonies among. (J. H. S. Lockhart) Folk-Lore, 1: 481.
— Religion of the. (C. de Harlez) New World, 5: 43.
Mancini, Pasquale Stanislao, with portrait. (D. Lioy) Jurid. R. 1: 113.
Mandalay, "Bloody Hand" at. (R. C. Temple) Acad. 48: 363.
Mandamus Cases, Interest in. (F. J. Goodnow) Pol. Sci. Q. 8: 48.
Mandarin, Making of. Liv. Age, 192: 550.
Mandeville, Geoffrey de, Round's. Ath. '92, 2: 54. — — (F. Liebermann) Eng. Hist. R. 8: 544.
Mandombe's Sacrifice. (F. B. Troup) Sund. M. 25: 567.
Mandy. (Ednah Robinson) Overland, n. s. 26: 602.
Mandy's Baby. (A. E. P. Searing) New Eng. M. n. s. 14: 15.
Manet, Edouard. (C. Mauclair) Art J. 47: 274. — (P. G. Hamerton) Scrib. M. 15: 48.
Manette Andrey; or, Life during the Reign of Terror. (Paul Perret) Liv. Age, 200: 11. 201: 268.
Mangan, Jas. C. Poetry from a Dublin Garret. (C. J. Hamilton) Time, 18: 713.
Manganese, Manufacture of, on Commercial Scale. (W. H. Greene and W. H. Wahl) J. Frankl. Inst. 135: 218.
— Separation of. (R. B. Riggs) Am. J. Sci. 143: 135.
Manganese Beds of the Batesville Region of Arkansas, Age of. (H. S. Williams) Am. J. Sci. 148: 325.
Manganese Mines of St. Marcel, Piedmont, Italy, Minerals from. (S. L. Penfield) Am. J. Sci. 146: 288.
Manganese Mining in Colombia. (E. J. Chibas) Engin. M. 12: 426.
Manganine, Thermo-electric Properties of. (B. O. Peirce) Am. J. Sci. 148: 302.
Mangano-Columbite, Occurrence of, at Rumford, Me. (H. W. Foote) Am. J. Sci. 151: 457.
Mangle, Wooden Hand. Reliquary, 36: 227.
Mangrove Tree. (C. S. Sargent) Garden & F. 6: 97.
Manhattan, a Proposed New State. (A. H. Peters) Am. J. Pol. 2: 266.
Manifest Destiny. (C. Schurz) Harper, 87: 737.
Manikin Lion, The. (P. Robinson) Eng. Illust. 12: no. 6, 90.
Manipur, England's Relations with. Asia. R. 12: 6.
Manitoba. (C. M. Miall) Belgra. 89: 148.
— Mail-carrying in. Chamb. J. 70: 730.
— Our Western Heritage. (G. H. Ham) Canad. M. 5: 560.
— Public School Law. (D'Alton McCarthy) Canad. M. 1: 1.
— Red and White Races in. (J. Maclean) J. Soc. Arts, 40: 548.
— Revista. (B. Cumberland) Canad. M. 4: 313.
— School Question. (C. Bryce) Canad. M. 1: 512. — (J. S. Ewart) Canad. M. 2: 107. — (E. Meek) Canad. M. 5: 90. — (H. H. L. Bellot) Westm. 144: 11. — (C. Sifton) R. of Rs. (N. Y.) 12: 452. — (J. S. Ewart) Am. Cath. Q. 20: 839. — (J. G. Colclough) Month, 87: 230. — (C. H. Tupper) National, 27: 375. — (G. Smith) Forum, 21: 65. — (T. C. Down) 19th Cent. 40: 117.
— Study of Civil Government in. (E. V. Smalley) R. of Rs. (N. Y.) 11: 167.
— With the Prairie Chicken. (R. S. Masson) Canad. M. 3: 446.
Manitou Islands of Lake Nipissing, Geology of. (J. M. Goodwillie) Science, 22: 101.
Mankind, Hittell's Mental Growth of. (M. H. Morgan and G. L. Kittredge) Nation, 59: 105, 124.
Mann, Horace. (F. W. Parker) Educa. R. 12: 65. — (W. T. Harris) Educa. R. 12: 105.
— and the Revival of Education in Massachusetts. (G. H. Martin) Educa. R. 5: 434.
Mann, Tom, with portrait. (J. C. Carlile) Chr. Lit. 10: 91. — (J. C. Carlile) R. of Rs. (N. Y.) 8: 660.
Manner and Manners. Chamb. J. 69: 785.
Mannerism in Art. (G. Smith) Portfo. 24: 127.
Manners. Are they degenerating? Spec. 77: 13.
— Are they disappearing from Great Britain? 19th Cent. 40: 137. Same art. Liv. Age, 210: 315.
— Changes of. Sat. R. 73: 327. Same art. Ecl. M. 118: 636.
— Cultivation of, in Schools. Spec. 68: 878.
— 18th Century, Bath as Mirror of. Spec. 72: 297.
— English and American. Soc. Econ. 9: 63.
— English and French. (F. Carrel) Fortn. 61: 680. Same art. Ecl. M. 123: 31.
Manning, Frederick and Maria, Case of. Green Bag, 7: 15.
Manning, H. E., Cardinal. (A. Galton) Acad. 41: 534. — (A. F. Marshall) Am. Cath. Q. 17: 356. — With portrait. (J. G. Kenyon) Cath. World, 54: 633. — (O. Shipley) Cath. World, 54: 712, 841. — (H. C. Kent) Cath. World, 54: 793. — (K. Tynan) Cath. World, 55: 180. — Church Q. 34: 198. — (W. Meynell; S. M. S. Amos; B. Waugh) Contemp. 61: 172. Same art. Ecl. M. 118: 399. Same art. Liv. Age, 193: 3. Same art. M. Chr. Lit. 5: 449. — (J. Bryce) Nation, 54: 105. — Quar. 175: 188. — With portrait. (W. T. Stead) R. of Rs. (N. Y.) 5: 182. — Sat. R. 73: 61. — Spec. 68: 78. — (L. Johnson) Acad. 44: 223. — (E. A. Gowing) Belgra. 83: 253. — Ed. R. 184: 1. — Scot. R. 27: 304. — (S. Buxton) Fortn. 65: 576. — (St. G. Mivart) New World, 5: 201. — Lond. Q. 86: 137. — (J. Morris) Month, 74: 153. — (S. F. Smith) Month, 86: 153, 395.
— and the Catholic Revival. (A. M. Fairbairn) Contemp. 69: 306. Same art. Chr. Lit. 14: 625. 15: 14. Same art. Liv. Age, 209: 195.
— Anglican and Roman. (C. C. Tiffany) Forum, 21: 577.

Manning, H. E., Cardinal, as a Man of Letters. (W. Meynell) Ath. '92, 1: 116.
— Conversion of. (B. Holland) National, 27: 111.
— Exposure of. Chr. Lit. 14: 527.
— Fresh Lights. (R. G. Wilberforce) 19th Cent. 39: 896.
— Hutton's. Sat. R. 73: 662. — Spec. 68: 752.
— in his Anglican Days. (E. S. Purcell) Dub. R. 110: 381. — (R. G. Wilberforce) 19th Cent. 31: 280.
— Letter from Gladstone. 19th Cent. 40: 541.
— Personal Reminiscences of. (A. De Vere) Contemp. 69: 327.
— Portraits of. (W. Meynell) M. of Art, 11: 361.
— Purcell's Life of. (H. Vaughan; W. Meynell) 19th Cent. 39: 249. — (G. A. Simcox) Acad. 49: 149, 169. — Blackw. 159: 809. — (A. F. Hewit) Cath. World, 62: 836. — Church Q. 42: 1. — (T. F. Huntington) Dial (Ch.) 20: 169. — (W. H. Kent) Dub. R. 118: 388. — (J. W. Chadwick) Nation, 62: 161. — (J. T. Smith) Forum, 22: 93. — Lit. W. (Bost.) 27: 104. — Sat. R. 81: 255. — Our Day, 16: 277.
— — Ethics of Suppression in Biography. (E. S. Purcell) 19th Cent. 40: 533. Same art. Chr. Lit. 16: 35.
— The Real. New R. 14: 269.
— Reminiscences of. (W. Lockhart) Dub. R. 110: 372.
— Sermons. Eng. R. 2: 359.
— Successor of. Spec. 68: 228.
Manning of the Fleet. (D. Hannay) New R. 12: 373.
Mannington House and the Walpoles, Nevill on. Sat. R. 78: 189.
Manns, August. Acad. 47: 387.
— as Orchestra Leader. Sat. R. 79: 546.
Manoa Company, The. (H. White) Nation, 62: 5.
Manocryometer, On the. (De Visser) Am. J. Sci. 147: 130.
Manor, Mediæval. (E. P. Cheyney) Ann. Am. Acad. Pol. Sci. 4: 275.
— Old English, Andrews's. (P. Vinogradoff) Eng. Hist. R. 8: 540.
— Manorial Jurisdiction. (G. H. Blakesley) Law Q. 5: 113.
Manresa, Spain. (C. W. Wood) Argosy, 62: 175.
Manrique, Jorge, Coplas de [in the Original]. Overland, n. s. 20: 555.
Mansfeld, Schloss. Chamb. J. 72: 284.
Mansfield, Mt., To the Crest of. (W. C. Gaynor) Outing, 20: 385.
Mansfield Summer School of Theology. (N. H. Smith) Chr. Lit. 11: 282.
Mantegazza, Paolo, with portrait. (F. Starr) Pop. Sci. Mo. 43: 549.
Mantegna's Sepia Drawing of Judith, On; a poem. (E. L. Hamilton) M. of Art, 7: 315.
Mantle of Osiris, The. (W. L. Palmer) Scrib. M. 16: 718.
Mantz, Paul. Acad. 47: 110.
Manual Training. (C. H. Henderson) Pop. Sci. Mo. 46: 48, 799. — (R. Scotter) Westm. 138: 377. — (I. C. Barrows) Char. R. 1: 60.
— and Kindergartens. (Mrs. H. M. Plunkett) Pop. Sci. Mo. 41: 375.
— for Women. (G. Vrooman) Arena, 14: 308.
— in Boston. Lend a H. 10: 193.
— in relation to Health. (Sir P. Magnus) Educa. R. 3: 78.
— Influence of, on Character. (F. Adler) Eth. Rec. 1: 113.
— Moral and Educational Value of. (B. F. McDaniel) Lend a H. 10: 165.
Manual Training, Relation to Public Schools. (Z. Richards) Educa. 13: 623.
— Schools for. (C. M. Woodward) Cassier, 5: 478.
— *versus* the Old Method of Education. (A. H. Heinemann) Arena, 9: 427.
Manufacturing Industries in Massachusetts, Net Profits of. (F. B. Hawley) Am. Statis. Assoc. 3: 38. — (W. F. Draper) Am. Statis. Assoc. 3: 192.
Manuscript of Axel Hermelin; a story. Argosy, 59: 756.
— An Oriental. (W. A. Clouston) Bookworm, 4: 37.
Manuscript Age. (R. B. Poole) Lib. J. 18: 71, 109.
Manuscripts, Author's, On compelling Careless Editors to pay for. (H. P. Arms) Writer, 8: 111.
— British, in Cottonian Library. Blackw. 157: 846.
— Illuminated. (W. Roberts) Bookworn, 5: 289, 336.
— in European Archives relating to America, Stevens's Facsimiles of. (L. Swift) Nation, 58: 88, 370. 59: 87. 60: 112, 307. 63: 110.
— Interchange of, between Libraries. (O. Hartwig) Lib. J. 18: 503.
— Prize Offers for. (E. L. Martin) Writer, 8: 45.
— Relating to America in the British Museum. (N. Darnell Davis) Nation, 61: 146, 270, 291.
— Three, Experience of. (M. E. Ireland) Writer, 8: 126.
— Venetian Ducali. (T. W. Bradley) Bibliographica, 2: 257.
Manutius, Aldus. Bk. Buyer, 12: 442. — (M. A. Taggart) Cath. World, 59: 85.
Manx Folk-Lore. *See* Man, Isle of.
Manx Mystery; a Cycling Experience. (T. D. Dickson) Outing, 25: 472.
Maori of To-day. Spec. 69: 190.
Maori Chief, Thoughts of a. Spec. 70: 187. Same art. Liv. Age, 197: 56.
Maori Meeting, A. (Earl of Meath) 19th Cent. 31: 778.
Maori Tangi; a tale. (H. S. Brodie) Belgrav. 78: 63.
Maori Traits, Some. All the Year, 70: 232.
Maoris, The. (A. Webb) Nation, 62: 250. — (W. Colenso) Nature, 47: 41. — (E. Tregear) Pop. Sci. Mo. 42: 781. — (F. J. Moss) Fortn. 60: 775.
— Industries of. (J. W. Davis) Nat. Sci. 2: 110.
— Political and Social Life of the Native New Zealander. (L. Becke and others) R. of Rs. (N. Y.) 12: 440.
Map, Walter. (A. W. Colton) Poet-Lore, 5: 537.
Map of the World, Colossal. Chamb. J. 70: 257.
Mapes, James Jay. Critic, 28: 281.
Maple, Carstorphine Sycamore. (C. S. Sargent) Garden & F. 6: 202.
Maple, Sugar-, Fastigiate. Garden & F. 7: 65.
Maple Leaf Forever; a song. (A. Muir) Canad. M. 6: 177.
Maple Sugar. Garden & F. 6: 198.
— Flavor of. (T. H. Hoskins) Garden & F. 7: 128.
— Modern Process. (C. S. Plumb) Garden & F. 7: 98.
— Old-time Sugar-making. (R. E. Robinson) Atlan. 77: 466.
— Old Way and the New. (T. Wheeler) Garden & F. 6: 120, 141, 173.
Maple Syrup, Flavor of. (C. S. Plumb) Garden & F. 7: 188.
Maples, Bishop Chauncy. (H. Waller) Geog. J. 6: 481. — Eng. Illust. 14: 170.
Maples, Sugar, in Ohio. (F. L. Right) Garden & F. 5: 375.
Mapping, Topographic, Art and Development of. (A. Winslow) Engin. M. 6: 24.

Maps. (H. C. Badger) Lib. J. 17: 375.
— American, Study of Early. (S. D. Peet) Am. Antiq. 17: 219.
— and Map Makers. (C. C. Adams) Chaut. 15: 294.
— Care of, in Public Libraries. (F. H. Parsons) Lib. J. 20: 199.
— Early American, Paris Exhibition of. (Le C. de Lautreppe) Nation, 55: 278.
— Governmental, in Schools. (W. M. Davis) Educa. R. 7: 232.
— MS. Charts in the English Public Records Office. (N. D. Davis) Nation, 55: 471.
— Topographic, of the U. S. Geological Survey. (W. M. Davis) Science, 21: 225.
— used by Herodotus, Attempt to reconstruct. (J. L. Myres) Geog. J. 8: 605.
Mar, J. Erskine, Earl of. (S. Erskine) Ath. '93, 2: 523.
Mar, The Braes o'. (P. MacQueen) Mo. Illust. 13: 137.
— Earldom of. Walford's Antiq. 1: 178.
— Later Earldom of. (J. H. Round) Walford's Antiq. 2: 114, 231.
Mara; a story. All the Year, 71: 451–524.
Marat, J. P., in England. (W. Roberts) Bookworm, 6: 193.
Marble, Temperature Variation of Thermal Conductivity of. (B. O. Peirce and R. W. Willson) Am. J. Sci. 150: 435.
Marblehead, Mass. (J. W. Chadwick) New Eng. M. n. s. 12: 611.
Marble-workers of Carrara. (H. Zimmern) Eng. Illust. 11: 719.
Marbles, Ancient, at Leeds. (E. L. Hicks) J. Hel. Stud. 11: 255.
Marbot, Gen. Memoirs. (Sir G. Chesney) Blackw. 151: 200. Same art. Ecl. M. 118: 523. — Ed. R. 175: 114, 435. — (A. Hassall) Eng. Hist. R. 7: 593. — (G. Shaw-Lefevre) Liv. Age, 192: 195. — Liv. Age, 193: 55. — Quar. 174: 95. — Spec. 68: 812. — Lond. Q. 78: 297. — (Sir G. Chesney) Un. Serv. (Phila.) 7: 380. — (E. E. Hatch) Un. Serv. (Phila.) 9: 521.
Marbury *vs.* Madison, Case of. (S. Pennoyer) Am. Law R. 30: 188.
Marceau-Desgraviers, Francois-Severin. (E. P. Thompson) Gent. M. n. s. 49: 147. — (A. Laugel) Nation, 55: 258.
Marcel Garant; a story. (Elinor Halsted) Good Words, 34: 838.
Marcelline; a story. All the Year, 54: 403.
March, Francis A. (J. C. Mackenzie) Educa. R. 11: 264.
March; the Crocus Month. (F. W. Burbidge) Good Words, 34: 194.
— Cuckoo and the Myth of. (G. W. Murdoch) Gent. M. n. s. 54: 233.
March; a poem. (A. C. Swinburne) M. of Art, 16: 169.
March; a poem. (E. Stoddard) Cosmopol. 14: 625.
Marching, Methods of. (H. R. Brinkerhoff) Un. Serv. (Phila.) 8: 315.
Marcken, Island of. (E. Verhaeren) M. of Art, 19: 413.
Maremma, Tuscan, Pastoral Life in. (E. Cecconi) Good Words, 37: 391.
Marengo, Battle of. (J. Petit) McClure, 4: 164.
Margaret, Queen of Italy. (E. Panzacchi and F. Lampertico) Chaut. 17: 593. — (Fannie C. W. Barbour) Munsey, 10: 238. — (F. B. Clark) Cosmopol. 18: 153.
— as a Mountaineer. (E. T. Cook) Eng. Illust. 11: 447.
Margaret of Anjou. Belgra. 78: 301.
Margaret Tudor, Lady. Macmil. 74: 449.
Margaret; a sketch in black and white. National, 23: 847. Same art. Liv. Age, 202: 592.
Margaret, To; a poem. (G. Halford) Temp. Bar, 100: 242.
Margaret Ward, Spinster. Macmil. 72: 426. Same art. Liv. Age, 207: 459.
Margaritana, Validity of the Genus. (C. T. Simpson) Am. Natural. 29: 336.
Marginal Utility and Value. (S. M. Macvane) Q. J. Econ. 7: 255.
Margot; a story. (H. E. V. Stannard) Eng. Illust. 11: 301.
Marguerita's Pack; a story. (G. T. Kercheval) Lend a H. 8: 96.
Marguerite de Bourbon. Blackw. 153: 800. Same art. Liv. Age, 198: 407. Same art. Ecl. M. 121: 308.
Marguerite of Navarre. Gent. M. n. s. 52: 214.
— Memoirs of. Gent. M. n. s. 48: 538.
— Last Poems of. (J. Manson) Acad. 49: 483. — (G. Norton) Nation, 62: 382.
Marguerites; a poem. (A. H. Japp) Argosy, 61: 670.
Maria Caroline, Queen of Naples. Temp. Bar, 109: 332.
Maria Clementina, Escape of. (A. Lang) Macmil. 71: 302. Same art. Liv. Age, 205: 131.
Marie Antoinette. Chamb. J. 70: 822.
— and the Stage. (F. Hawkins) Theatre, 37: 80.
— in Petit Trianon. (G. Bapst) Cosmopol. 17: 387.
— La Rocheterie's Life of. Spec. 71: 715. — Sat. R. 78: 296.
— On some Portraits of. (R. Gower) M. of Art, 15: 338.
— Prison-life of, Bishop's. Spec. 70: 705.
Marie-Therese Charlotte, Princesse. Blackw. 153: 800. Same art. Liv. Age, 198: 407. Same art. Ecl. M. 121: 308.
Mārie; a story. (W. McLennan) Harper, 84: 345.
Marié-Davy, G. H. Nature, 48: 351.
Mariemont, Belgium, Miners of. (J. H. Gore) Cath. World, 63: 456.
Marienbad-Elegy, The New. (F. Wedmore) New R. 11: 209.
Marietta, Ohio, Journey to, in 1794. (I. Putnam) New Eng. M. n. s. 13: 642.
Marine Animals, Distribution of. (O. Maas) Nat. Sci. 2: 92.
— and Temperature. (O. Maas) Nat. Sci. 5: 276.
— Preservation of. (W. A. Redenbaugh) Am. Natural. 29: 399.
Marine Biological Laboratory, Woods Holl, Mass. (J. S. Kingsley) Pop. Sci. Mo. 41: 604.
Marine Biological Observatory, A. (C. O. Whitman) Pop. Sci. Mo. 42: 459.
— the Prime Need of American Biology. (C. O. Whitman) Atlan. 71: 808.
Marine Biology, European Laboratories of. Nature, 48: 404.
— Problem of. (G. W. Field) Am. Natural. 26: 799. Same art. Nature, 46: 623.
Marine Etiquette. (A. O. Klaussmann) Chaut. 22: 199.
Marine Floras, Distribution of. (G. Murray) Nature, 48: 257.
Marine Laboratories in the U. S. (J. P. Campbell) Nature, 47: 66.
— of Europe. (B. Dean) Am. Natural. 27: 625, 697.
Marine Laboratory, St. Andrews, New Buildings for. Nature, 50: 301.
Marine Machinery, Corrosion of. (H. Maccoll) Cassier, 10: 468.

Marine Organisms, Chemical Action of. (J. W. Judd) Fortn. 61: 65. Same art. Ecl. M. 122: 313. Same art. Liv. Age, 200: 564.
Marine Underwriters, Frauds on. (C. T. Hopkins) Overland, n. s. 21: 602.
Marine Zoölogical Station, Swedish. (F. A. Bather) Nat. Sci. 6: 407.
Marines, The. (David Hannay) New R. 13: 655.
— Evolution of the Blue-jacket. (P. H. Colomb) No. Am. 161: 268.
Marion, Gen. Francis. (F. A. Hagadorn) M. Am. Hist. 30: 148.
— Grave of. (S. C. Hughson) M. Am. Hist. 27: 145.
Marionette Theatre in Brooklyn. (S. Culin) J. Am. Folk-Lore, 3: 155.
Marionettes. At the Opra di li Pupi. (E. Cavazza) Atlan. 73: 797.
Marital Authority. (E. Manson) Law Q. 7: 244.
Marital Liability. (E. P. Train) Lippinc. 58: 289.
Marked Half-sovereign, The. (J. S. Fletcher) Chamb. J. 73: 589.
Marken, Quaint. (C. S. Pelham-Clinton) Eng. Illust. 15: 367.
Market-day in an Italian Country Town. Chamb. J. 71: 133. Same art. Liv. Age, 201: 57.
Market Gambling. (W. E. Bear) Contemp. 65: 781.
Market-place, Romance of the. Chamb. J. 70: 218.
Markets, Influence of Opinion on. (A. Ellis) Econ. J. 2: 109.
Markham, John, Admiral. All the Year, 74: 55.
Mark's Monument. (E. C. Plummer) New Eng. M. n. s. 14: 601.
Marks, Gilbert, Silver Plate by. (F. S. Robinson) M. of Art, 19: 437.
Marks, Henry Stacy. (W. W. Fenn) M. of Art, 2: 97.
— Decorations by. (A. Griffiths) M. of Art, 4: 138.
— Pen and Pencil Sketches. Sat. R. 78: 461.
Marlborough, Duchess of, and Anne of England. (M. O. W. Oliphant) Cent. 24: 101.
Marlborough, Duke of. (S. J. Low) New Sci. R. 1: 96.
— Alison's Life of. Eng. R. 17: 1.
— and James FitzJames, Duke of Berwick, Legrelle's Secret Negotiations of. Ed. R. 180: 158.
— Dispatches. Eng. R. 3: 257.
— Letters at The Hague. (W. Bliss) Eng. Hist. R. 11: 117.
— Wolseley's Life of. (A. Alison) Blackw. 155: 847. Same art. Liv. Age, 202: 3. — Same art. Un. Serv. (Phila.) 12: 117. — Ed. R. 180: 259. — (Goldwin Smith) Nation, 58: 430 — (A. Lang) Contemp. 65: 828. Same art. Liv. Age, 202: 117. — (W. O'C. Morris) Scot. R. 24: 252. — National, 23: 391. — Belgra. 84: 22. — Quar. 179: 439. — Dub. R. 115: 402. — Sat. R. 77: 444. — Dial (Ch.) 16: 358. — Ath. '94, 1: 605. — Spec. 72: 584. — Un. Serv. (Phila.) 12: 521.
Marlborough, Dukes of. (R. H. Titherington) Munsey, 14: 414.
Marlborough House, Mural Paintings at. (M. Q. Holyoake) Art J. 44: 349.
Marlowe, Christopher. (J. R. Lowell) Harper, 85: 194. — (John H. Ingram) Univ. R. 4: 381.
— Death of. (W. L. Courtney) Univ. R. 6: 356.
— Faustus. Temp. Bar, 98: 515.
— — arranged by Poel. Sat. R. 82: 36.
— New Facts about. (S. Lee; H. P. Stokes) Ath. '94, 2: 235, 299.
Marlowe, Julia. (M. Aldrich) Arena, 6: 148. — (W. T. Strong) Bost. 1: 385.
Marm Lisa. (K. D. Wiggin) Atlan. 78: 297, 452, 619.
Marmion, Land of. (W. S. Dalgleish) Good Words, 34: 669.
Marmontel, J. F. Moral Tales, ed. by Saintsbury. Sat. R. 80: 354.
Marne, Farm in. (M. H. Catherwood) Atlan. 77: 31.
Maroma, Killing a. Gent. M. n. s. 57: 500.
Marriage. All the Year, 71: 221.
— among Early Slavs. (P. Kowalewsky) Folk-Lore, 1: 463.
— and Divorce. (J. A. Sewell) Westm. 145: 182.
— — Census of. (C. D. Wright) Forum, 17: 484.
— — Doctrine of the Church of England. (W. J. K. Little) Chr. Lit. 13: 259.
— — High Church Doctrine of. (G. Serrell) Contemp. 68: 21. Same art. Chr. Lit. 13: 186. — (W. J. Knox Little) Contemp. 68: 256.
— — in Scotland. Westm. 146: 213.
— — Statistics of, Condition and Needs of. (S. W. Dike) Am. Statis. Assoc. 3: 513.
— and Immovables. (H. Nelson) Law Q. 6: 307.
— and Kinship among the Ancient Israelites. (A. B. Ellis) Pop. Sci. Mo. 42: 325.
— Anti-marriage League. (Mrs. Oliphant) Blackw. 159: 135.
— Apparent Decline of. Sat. R. 79: 721.
— Bigamy under the Canadian Code. (R. J. Wicksteed) Canad. M. 5: 304.
— Breach of Promise of. (J. D. White) Law Q. 10: 135.
— by Purchase. (E. S. Hartland) Pub. Opin. 15: 31.
— Conditions in Restraint of. (T. C. Williams) Law Q. 12: 36.
— Divine Laws of, Watkins'. Sat. R. 80: 211.
— Early, Evils of. (C. Edson) No. Am. 158: 230.
— English Law of, Notes on. (H. W. Elphinstone) Law Q. 5: 44.
— Future of. (W. Donisthorpe) Fortn. 57: 258.
— — A Reply. (Countess of Malmesbury) Fortn. 57: 272.
— How we marry. (Laura B. Cameron) Westm. 145: 690.
— in China. (H. L. Beek) Chaut. 15: 471.
— in East London. (H. Dendy) Contemp. 65: 427. Same art. Ecl. M. 122: 708.
— in England, Valid. (I. Browne) Green Bag, 4: 308.
— in France. (S. Dewey) Westm. 146: 597.
— in Turkey, viewed from a Harem. (Adalet) 19th Cent. 32: 118. Same art. Ecl. M. 119: 276.
— Infant. Gent. M. n. s. 53: 322-427.
— — and Widows; Home Life in India. (P. R. Telang) Forum, 18: 95.
— Intentions of, Lincoln County, Me. (B. N. Goodale) N. E. Reg. 46: 11.
— Love and. (Sir E. Strachey) Atlan. 72: 358. — Westm. 140: 349.
— Luckock's History of. Cath. World, 60: 682.
— A Man's Thoughts on. (E. B. Fox) Gent. M. n. s. 50: 63.
— The Matrimonial Puzzle. (H. H. Boyesen) No. Am. 160: 203.
— Men and. Westm. 142: 146.
— Mistakes of. (F. Marryat) Belgra. 78: holiday no., 1.
— Morality, Christianity, and. (L. Tolstoi) Univ. R. 7: 154.
— The New Wedlock. (V. Greville) National, 19: 328.
— of Children in England in the 16th Century. (F. J. Furnivall) Acad. 44: 275. — (W. E. A. Axon) Acad. 44: 465.
— Philosophy of. (E. Lynn Linton) Univ. R. 2: 21.
— a Poem. (E. Nesbit) Argosy, 58: 341.
— Prospects of, for Women. (C. E. Collet) 19th Cent. 31: 537.

Marriage, Remarkable Side of. All the Year, **71**: 629.
— Roman Catholic Doctrine and Law of. (C. C. Starbuck) Meth. R. **53**: 878.
— Romance after. (C. P. Selden) New Eng. M. n. s. **13**: 593.
— The Sacred. (G. M. Godden) Folk-Lore, **6**: 225.
— Short History of. (Lady Cook, *née* Tennessee Claflin) Westm. **141**: 380.
— Some Disused Roads to. (F. Watt) New R. **14**: 162.
— Some Modern Ideas about. Westm. **143**: 520.
— A Study in Vital Statistics. (W. F. Willcox) Pol. Sci. Q. **8**: 69.
— Theory of. (S. W. Dike) And. R. **19**: 672.
— Westermarck on. (C. N. Starcke) Int. J. Ethics, **3**: 452. — Reply (E. Westermarck) Int. J. Ethics, **4**: 94. — Spec. **68**: 243.
— Why Men don't marry. (A. Pollard) Longm. **23**: 156. — Spec. **69**: 348.
— with Deceased Wife's Sister, Law of. Eng. R. **3**: 129. **11**: 159. **13**: 197.
Marriage Ceremonies. Chamb. J. **71**: 604.
— among Aborigines of Bengal. (E. S. Hartland) Asia. R. **15**: 183.
— among the Manchus. (J. H. S. Lockhart) Folk-Lore, **1**: 481.
Marriage Contracts, Successional Provisions in. (J. D. Wilson) Jurid. R. **6**: 118.
Marriage Customs. (E. Howlett) Westm. **140**: 602.
— Early. (F. Shelley) Lippinc. **53**: 134.
— Early New England. (A. M. Earle) J. Am. Folk-Lore, **6**: 97.
— in Scotland. Chamb. J. **69**: 537.
— of the Mordvins. (J. Abercromby) Folk-Lore, **1**: 417.
Marriage Eve; a poem. (N. McCormick) Argosy, **61**: 606.
Marriage Law of Hungary. (F. P. Watton) Jurid. R. **8**: 189.
Marriage Laws, Chaos of. (J. H. Heaton) New R. **11**: 157, 304.
— Should they be revised? (W. A. Jaycox) Am. M. Civics, **8**: 164.
Marriage Market at Babylon. (J. F. Rowbotham) Argosy, **59**: 662.
— French and English. (M. A. de Bovet) New R. **7**: 80.
Marriage Problem, The. (E. D. Cope) Open Court, **2**: 1308, 1320.
— and Artificial Selection. (Hiram M. Stanley) Monist, **2**: 51.
Marriage Rate in Massachusetts. (F. S. Crum) Am. Statis. Assoc. **4**: 322.
— in Michigan. (W. F. Wilcox) Am. Statis. Assoc. **4**: 1.
Marriage Tie, Sanctity and Abuse of. (E. L. Lynton) New R. **6**: 218.
Marriages are made in Heaven. (I. Abrahams) Jew. Q. **2**: 172.
— Asiatic Mixed. (M. L. Agarwala) Law Q. **11**: 373.
— Decisive, in English History. (S. Walpole) New R. **9**: 384. Same art. Liv. Age, **199**: 579.
— Foreign. Why our Women marry abroad. (E. S. Martin) No. Am. **159**: 755.
— in Army "Without Leave." (S. P. H. Statham) Un. Serv. M. **6**: 295.
— Irregular, and Illegitimacy in Scotland. (G. Bizet) Westm. **146**: 437.
— Performed by Daniel Wetherell in New London Co., Ct. (F. F. Starr) N. E. Reg. **50**: 485.
Marriages. Should they be Indissoluble? (T. S. Potwin) N. Eng. **56**: 43.
Married to Order; a Romance. (E. Stuart) All the Year, **74**: 1-601. **75**: 2-211.
Marrying in the Valley; a poem. (A. Austin) National, **20**: 725. Same art. Ecl. M. **120**: 457.
Mars. (W. H. Pickering) Astron. **11**: 668, 849. — (Sir R. Ball) Fortn. **58**: 288. Same art. Ecl. M. **119**: 527. Same art. Liv. Age, **195**: 195. — Sat. R. **74**: 302. — (P. Lowell) Atlan. **75**: 594, 749. **76**: 103, 223. — (P. Lowell) Astron. **13**: 538, 814. — (P. Lowell) Pop. Astron. **2**: 1, 56, 91, 154. **4**: 113, 202. — (G. Schiaparelli) Astron. **13**: 714. — (W. W. Payne) Pop. Astron. **3**: 385. — (E. M. Clerke) Month, **76**: 185.
— and its Inhabitants. (C. Flammarion) No. Am. **162**: 546. — Sat. R. **81**: 345.
— and Jupiter. (F. L. Blake) Canad. M. **4**: 224.
— as a Habitable World. Month, **79**: 1.
— as he now appears. (W. J. S. Lockyer) Nature, **50**: 476.
— as seen at the Opposition in 1894. (W. J. S. Lockyer) Nature, **54**: 625.
— as a World. (G. Winterwood) Good Words, **34**: 677. Same art. Ecl. M. **121**: 619.
— Canals of. (J. R. Holt) Astron. **13**: 347. — (S. E. Peal) Canad. M. **1**: 202. — (S. E. Peal) Science, **21**: 242. — (E. W. Maunder) Knowl. **17**: 249. — (P. Lowell) Pop. Astron. **2**: 255.
— Circulation of Water in Atmosphere of. (C. Flammarion) Knowl. **18**: 73.
— Climate of. (E. W. Maunder) Knowl. **15**: 167. — (M. Manson) Pop. Astron. **2**: 371.
— Colors exhibited by. (W. H. Pickering) Astron. **11**: 449, 545.
— Communication with. (C. Flammarion) New R. **6**: 106. Same art. Ecl. M. **118**: 315.
— — Do we need Wider Horizons? Spec. **69**: 253.
— Do People live on? (W. J. Baker) Chaut. **17**: 443.
— Eye of. (E. W. Maunder) Knowl. **18**: 55.
— Flagstaff Photographs of. (P. Lowell) New Eng. M. n. s. **12**: 643.
— Flammarion on. (W. J. S. Lockyer) Nature, **47**: 553.
— Latest News of. (E. S. Holden) No. Am. **160**: 636.
— Lines on, Gemmination of. (C. B. Warring) Science, **20**: 177.
— — Interpretation of. (Hiram M. Stanley) Science, **20**: 235.
— — Origin of. (H. W. Parker) Science, **20**: 282.
— Lowell on. (T. J. J. See) Dial (Ch.) **21**: 42.
— Markings in the Syrtis Major of. (P. Lowell) Pop. Astron. **4**: 289.
— Micrometric Measures of Diameters of. (P. Lowell) Pop. Astron. **3**: 287.
— New Views about. Ed. R. **184**: 368. — Liv. Age, **211**: 533.
— — Edinburgh Review on. Liv. Age, **211**: 732.
— Non-glaciation of. (J. R. Holt) Pop. Astron. **2**: 78.
— Oases of. (P. Lowell) Pop. Astron. **2**: 343.
— Observations of. Nature, **51**: 40.
— — at Goodsell Observatory. (H. C. Wilson) Astron. **11**: 684.
— — at Halsted Observatory. (C. A. Young) Astron. **11**: 675.
— — at Lick Observatory. (E. S. Holden) Astron. **11**: 663. — (E. E. Barnard) Astron. **11**: 680.
— — at Nice Observatory. (M. Perrotin) Nature, **46**: 482.
— — at the Washburn Observatory. (G. C. Comstock) Astron. **11**: 679.

Mars, Opposition of, 1892. (J. N. Lockyer) Nature, **46**: 443.
— Polar Cap of. (A. E. Douglass) Astron. **13**: 738.
— Projections on. (W. J. S. Lockyer) Nature, **50**: 499.
— The Ruddy Planet. (D. P. Todd) Nation, **59**: 282.
— Schiaparelli on. Nature, **51**: 87. — (W. H. Pickering) Astron. **13**: 632.
— Seas of. (W. H. Pickering) Astron. **13**: 553. — Pop. Astron. **4**: 300.
— Seasonal Changes on. (P. Lowell) Nature, **51**: 259.
— South Polar Cap of, Micrometrical Measures of. (E. E. Barnard) Pop. Astron. **2**: 433.
— Spectrum of. (W. W. Campbell) Astron. **13**: 752.
— Telegraphing to. Spec. **69**: 218.
— Twilight Arc upon. (P. Lowell) Nature, **52**: 401.
— What we really know about it. (E. S. Holden) Forum, **14**: 359.
Mars Hill, Cleanthes and Paul on. (R. T. Stevenson) Meth. R. **54**: 353.
— Did Paul preach on? (R. Parsons) Meth. R. **56**: 546.
Marseillaise, The. (J. Koren) Music, **3**: 161.
Marseilles. (W. H. Pollock) Longm. **26**: 384. Same art. Liv. Age, **207**: 572.
— Old and New. (W. H. Pollock) Eng. Illust. **13**: 315.
Marsh-lands, Value of. Garden & F. **6**: 98.
Marshall, Arthur Milnes. Nature, **49**: 250. — With portrait. Nat. Sci. **4**: 150.
Marshall, Benjamin, Extracts from Letter-book of, 1763–66. (T. Stewardson) Pennsyl. M. **20**: 204.
Marshall, Christopher, Correspondence of Children of. Pennsyl. M. **17**: 336.
Marshall, Humphrey. (C. S. Sargent) Garden & F. **6**: 461.
Marshall, John, Chief Justice. (Sallie E. M. Hardy) Green Bag, **8**: 479.
Will of. (S. E. M. Hardy) Green Bag, **8**: 4.
Marshes in England: Alders and Reeds. Blackw. **152**: 828.
Marshland Churches. (J. C. Cox) Antiq. n. s. **26**: 154.
Marsick, M., violinist. (M. E. Wales) Music, **2**: 599.
Marston, John, Shakespeare burlesqued by. (H. Wood) Am. J. Philol. **16**: 273.
— Shakespearianisms of. (L. M. Griffiths) Poet-Lore, **2**: 289, 360.
Marston, Philip Bourke. (W. Sharp) Acad. **41**: 6. — (C. Kernahan) Fortn. **57**: 81. Same art. Ecl. M. **118**: 319. — (Henriette Corkran) Temp. Bar, **108**: 278.
— Last Poems of. Gent. M. n. s. **48**: 90.
Marston, Westland. Donna Diana. (G. B. Shaw) Sat. R. **82**: 492.
Marsupial, New Australian. Sat. R. **74**: 443.
Marteilhe, Jean. Memoirs, tr. by Goldsmith. Sat. R. **79**: 627.
Martha's Head-stone. (E. Brower) Lippinc. **55**: 669.
Martha's Vineyard, or Martin's? (C. E. Banks) N. E. Reg. **48**: 201, 468.
Martial: a Roman of Greater Rome. (A. W. Verrall) Univ. R. **1**: 123.
Martial Law, What is the Justification of? (G. N. Lieber) No. Am. **163**: 549.
Martial Music. All the Year, **72**: 181.
Martian, The; a novel. (G. Du Maurier) Harper, **93**: 659, 869. **94**: 39.
Martin, St., of Tours. (A. Jessopp) 19th Cent. **37**: 112. Same art. Liv. Age, **204**: 239.
Martin, Edward S., with portrait. Bk. Buyer, **11**: 185.
Martin, Henry Newell. (M. Foster) Nature, **55**: 56.
Martin Brothers, Pottery. (C. Monkhouse) M. of Art, **5**: 433.
Martin the Shepherd. (L. Wassermann) Gent. M. n. s. **50**: 325.
Martineau, Harriet, in New England. (E. P. Powell) Gent. M. n. s. **15**: 282.
Martineau, James. (M. D. Conway) Open Court, **9**: 4519. — Spec. **74**: 574. — (A. W. Jackson) Chr. Lit. **13**: 41.
— at Ninety. Critic, **26**: 417.
Martinetti, Giacomo. After the Crucifixion. (I. M. Anderton) Art J. **48**: 253.
Martinez, Ferrand, and the Massacres of 1391. (H. C. Lea) Am. Hist. R. **1**: 209.
Martinique; In the Land of Josephine. (W. L. Beasley) Outing, **23**: 318, 373.
— to Trinidad. (J. Symington) Southern M. **5**: 3.
Martlet Seal; a story. (J. H. Walworth) Lippinc. **50**: 131.
Martyn, Henry. Lond. Q. **79**: 205.
— Smith's. Spec. **69**: 391.
Martyrdom of John the Baptist, The; a story. (W. Le C. Beard) Scrib. M. **17**: 633.
Martyrdom of the Mouse; a story. (E. Pugh) New R. **14**: 318.
Martyrs, English, Unpublished Acts, by J. H. Pollen. (T. G. Law) Eng. Hist. R. **7**: 165.
— of Africa, 208 A. D. (H. Hayman) Cath. World, **61**: 481.
— of Industry. (E. D. McCreary) Am. M. Civics, **8**: 351.
— Woman's. (F. M. Holland) Open Court, **5**: 2999.
Marvell, Andrew. Macmil. **65**: 194.
— Correspondence of. (David Lindsay) Gent. M. n. s. **57**: 570.
— Poetry of. (E. K. Chambers) Acad. **42**: 230.
Marvellous Madonna, The; a poem. (W. Archer) M. of Art, **8**: 114.
Marvellous Prayer of Aubrey Saul. (W. J. Lacey) Longm. **26**: 192.
Marwedel, Emma, and the Kindergarten. (W. S. Monroe) Educa. **14**: 338.
Mary, Virgin, Anthology of, Shipley's. Sat. R. **77**: 205.
— Types of. (T. Child) Harper, **86**: 57.
Mary Tudor, Queen of England. (J. D. Breen) Dub. R. **117**: 102.
Mary, Queen, Accession of, Guaras on. Sat. R. **74**: 25.
Mary, Queen of Scots, at Saint Germain. Macmil. **74**: 42. — Liv. Age, **209**: 747.
— Death of, Bourgoing on. Sat. R. **79**: 515.
— Execution of. (R. C. Brown) Acad. **48**: 43.
— First Wooing of. (A. Buckler) Gent. M. n. s. **54**: 556.
— Scottish Castles and Residences of. (J. C. Hadden) Eng. Illust. **10**: 348.
— Skelton's Life of. Ath. '93, **2**: 653. — Spec. **71**: 633.
Mary of Modena, Queen. (E. Fawcett) Cosmopol. **15**: 718.
Mary Hitchcock Memorial Hospital, Hanover, N. H. (E. Cowles) Am. Arch. **49**: 59.
Mary; a story. Cornh. **67**: 149.
Mary; a story. (Mrs. S. Van Rensselaer) Scrib. M. **20**: 776.
Marya Smirnova's Mission. (M. A. Morrison) Good Words, **34**: 324.
Maryland and Virginia, Early Relations between. (J. H. Latané) J. H. Univ. Studies, **13**: 129.
— Attitude of, in the Struggle for Canada. (J. W. Black) J. H. Univ. Studies, **10**: no. 7.
— Court of Appeals. (E. L. Didier) Green Bag, **6**: 225, 274.
— Eastern Shore of, Customs of. (Mrs. F. D. Bergen) J. Am. Folk-Lore, **2**: 295.

Maryland, Farming in. (J. D. Frederiksen) Nation, 59: 324.
— Genealogical Information in, Sources of. (B. F. Cummings, jr.) N. E. Reg. 46: 403.
— Homes and Ways in, Old. (J. W. Palmer) Cent. 27: 244.
— National Guard. (H. Hiss) Outing, 20: 149, 217.
— Old, Certain Worthies and Dames of. (J. W. Palmer) Cent. 29: 483.
— or Rhode Island, which established Religious Liberty First? (R. H. Clarke) Am. Cath. Q. 20: 289.
— Political Corruption in. (C. J. Bonaparte) Forum, 13: 1.
— Provisional Government of, 1774–77. (J. A. Silver) J. H. Univ. Studies, 13: 477.
— Revolution of 1689, Causes of the. (F. E. Sparks) J. H. Univ. Studies, 14: 477.
— Wheat Farmers in. (C. Meriwether) Nation, 59: 116.
Maryville, Mo., Roman Catholic Convent-school at. Cath. World, 56: 673.
Mas' Craffud's Freedom. (H. S. Edwards) Cent. 30: 82.
Masai Arts. Sat. R. 73: 64.
Masailand, Exploration in. Dub. R. 112: 459.
Mascagni, Pietro. (A. Veit) Music, 3: 353. — (A. R. Willard) New Eng. M. n. s. 8: 334.
— Irantzau. Sat. R. 74: 589.
Masenius, Lauder and Milton. (J. C. H. Flood) Walford's Antiq. 3: 221, 300.
Mashonaland. Lond. Q. 81: 287. — (W. Greswell) National, 22: 394. — All the Year, 72: 389. 73: 390, 424. — Ed. R. 177: 283. — (F. Mandy) Scrib. M. 11: 455.
— and its Inhabitants. (J. T. Bent) New R. 6: 580. Same art. Liv. Age, 194: 44.
— and its Neighbors. (E. M. Clerke) Dub. R. 114: 145.
— and its People. (J. T. Bent) Contemp. 64: 642. Same art. Liv. Age, 199: 749.
— Another View of. All the Year, 73: 519.
— Bent's Ruined Cities of. (J. M. Hubbard) Nation, 56: 130. — Dial (Ch.) 14: 137. — (A. H. Keane) Acad. 41: 582. — Spec. 69: 770.
— Eastern, Notes in. (W. A. Eckersley) Geog. J. 5: 27.
— England's Latest Conquest in Africa. (C. A. Orr) Cosmopol. 17: 35.
— King Rhodes and King Lobengula. Spec. 71: 299.
— Matabele Deadlock. Spec. 71: 390.
— Memories of, Bruce's. Sat. R. 80: 765.
— Natives of. Dub. R. 112: 448.
— Progress in. Dub. R. 112: 177.
— Recent Views on. Dub. R. 110: 457.
— Rhodes on. Spec. 69: 809. — R. of Rs. (N. Y.) 5: 309.
— Road from. (J. T. Bent) Fortn. 57: 182. Same art. Liv. Age, 193: 160.
— Ruined Temples in. (R. M. W. Swan) Anthrop. J. 26: 2.
— Ruins in. Geog. J. 2: 438.
— — Origin of. (J. T. Bent) 19th Cent. 34: 991.
— Tableland of. Dub. R. 110: 458.
Mashonaland Mice at Eavesdropping. New Eng. M. n. s. 5: 581.
Mask, The; a story. (R. Marsh) Gent. M. n. s. 49: 541.
Maskelyne, J. N., the Great Wizard of the West. (T. H. Lewis) Eng. Illust. 12: no. 4, 74.
Mason, A. E. W. Courtship of Morrice Buckler. Sat. R. 82: 21.
Mason, George, Rowland's Life of. (A. C. McLaughlin) Dial (Ch.) 13: 181. — (J. C. Welling) Nation, 54: 468, 487. — (J. A. Doyle) Eng. Hist. R. 8: 589.
Mason, Lowell. (J. H. Ross) Educa. 14: 411. — Music, 4: 527. — (F. H. Jenks) New Eng. M. n. s. 11: 651.
— and Music in America. (W. M. Derthick) Music, 9: 378, 575.
— Centennial of. Music, 1: 400.
— Recollections of. (S. F. Smith) New Eng. M. n. s. 11: 648.
— Reminiscences of. (W. A. Mowry) Educa. 15: 335.
Mason, Luther W., and School Music. Music, 2: 474.
Masonry, Effects of Frost on. Am. Arch. 46: 47.
Masquerade of Stamens, A. (W. H. Gibson) Cosmopol. 17: 570.
Masquerade Ball, The; a story. (A. M. Trotter) Argosy, 53: 166.
Masquerades and Tea-gardens 100 Years Ago. All the Year, 74: 277.
Masrium. (A. E. Tutton) Nature, 46: 79. Same art. Science, 19: 329.
Mass, The. (B. F. C. Costelloe) Time, 21: 345.
— Doctrine of, at Council of Trent. (C. Walker) Bib. Sac. 52: 629.
— for the Dead, The; a story. (E. Nesbit) Argosy, 53: 345.
Mass-books, Roman; Gelasian Sacramentary. (E. Bishop) Dub. R. 115: 245.
Massachusetts, Acts and Resolves of. (J. A. Saxe) Green Bag, 6: 327.
— Alleged Religious Persecution in. (A. D. Barber) New Eng. 56: 255.
— Ancient Punishments in. Nat'l M. (N. Y. '91) 15: 67.
— at the World's Fair. (E. C. Hovey) New Eng. M. n. s. 9: 734.
— Chancery in. (E. H. Woodruff) Law Q. 5: 370.
— Coast of, a Bicycle Trip along the. (J. C. Abbott) Bost. 2: 211.
— — Land of the Pilgrims. (A. Eric) Canad. M. 4: 26.
— Constitution of. Why did not Massachusetts have a Saybrook Platform? (W. Walker) Yale R. 1: 68.
— Crime, Lunacy, and Charity in. (G. E. Littlefield) Lend a H. 10: 189.
— Early Court Records of. (G. H. Brennan) New Eng. M. n. s. 11: 301.
— Historians of, Adams's. (W. Walker) Nation, 58: 33. — (W. F. Poole) Dial (Ch.) 16: 74.
— History, Adams's Three Episodes of. (G. Batchelor) Dial (Ch.) 14: 15. — Lit. W. (Bost.) 23: 383. — (J. C. Welling) Nation, 55: 394.
— — Hale's. Nation, 54: 173.
— in the Civil War. (T. S. Townsend) New Eng. M. n. s. 12: 3.
— Legislature of, Anarchy in. (G. Bradford) Nation, 56: 177.
— — Nativity and Occupation of Members of. (H. F. Howland) Am. Statis. Assoc. 4: 15.
— Manufacturing Industries in, Net Profits of. (F. B. Hawley) Am. Statis. Assoc. 3: 38. — (W. F. Draper) Am. Statis. Assoc. 3: 192.
— Militia of. (T. F. Edmands) New Eng. M. n. s. 11: 770.
— — First Corps Cadets Mass. Vol. Militia. (A. L. Spring) Outing, 23: 464.
— Representation and Suffrage in, 1620-91. (G. H. Haynes) J. H. Univ. Studies, 12: 377.
— School Legislation in, Early. (G. H. Martin) New Eng. M. n. s. 8: 526.
— Schools of, before the Revolution. (G. H. Martin) New Eng. M. n. s. 9: 356.

Massachusetts, Survey and Map of. (H. Gannett) Nat. Geog. M. **1**: 78.
Massachusetts Charitable Fire Society. Lend a H. **12**: 69.
Massachusetts Charitable Mechanics Association. (M. A. McBride) Bost. **2**: 25.
Massachusetts Institute of Technology. Nature, **49**: 20.
Massachusetts Library Commission. (H. S. Nourse) Citizen, **1**: 14.
Massachusetts Railroad Commission. (W. A. Crafts) Engin. M. **10**: 286.
Massachusetts State Library. Lib. J. **20**: 85.
Massage, Action of, upon the Muscles. (D. Graham) Pop. Sci. Mo. **44**: 677.
— in Sprains, Bruises, and Dislocations. (D. Graham) Pop. Sci. Mo. **49**: 381.
Massena, Marshal, An Aide-de-Camp of. Temp. Bar, **94**: 191.
— Estimate by Marbot. (E. Shippen) Un. Serv. (Phila.) **7**: 537.
Massenet, Jules. (R. N. Sherard) Music, **8**: 393
— Autobiographical Notes. Cent. **23**: 122.
— Thais. (A. Ernst) Music, **7**: 156.
— Werther; an opera. Sat. R. **77**: 635.
Masses, Alleged Estrangement of the. (R. F. Bishop) Meth. R. **54**: 64.
— The Contented. (A. French) Forum, **18**: 204.
Massey, Gerald. (B. O. Flower) Arena, **8**: 767. **9**: 136. — (M. M. Trumbull) Open Court, **1**: 745. — Open Court, **10**: 4789.
Massinger and Ford. (J. R. Lowell) Harper, **85**: 942.
Massorah, Rise and Development of. (I. Harris) Jew. Q. **1**: 128, 223.
Massoretic Studies. (L. Blau) Jew. Q. **9**: 122.
Massys, Quintin. *See* Matsys.
Master Craftsman, The. (W. Besant) Chamb. J. **73**: 1–407.
Master John Horsleigh, Knight; a story. (T. Hardy) McClure, **1**: 136.
Master Masons, Scotland. Scot. R. **24**: 31.
Master of Arts. (J. A. Nicklin) Gent. M. n. s. **57**: 586.
Master of Brookfield, The; a story. (S. B. Kennedy) Outing, **29**: 32.
Master of the "Chrysolite." (G. B. O'Halloran) Gent. M. n. s. **50**: 217. Same art. Liv. Age, **197**: 334.
Master of Deceit, A; a story. (I. Maclaren) Blackw. **158**: 333. Same art. Liv. Age, **207**: 84. Same art. McClure, **5**: 470.
Master of the Situation. (S. W. Reigart) Ref. Q. **41**: 458.
Masterpiece, The; a story. (H. F. Huntington) Nat'l M. (Bost.) **5**: 246.
Masterpiece of Diplomacy, A; a farce. (W. D. Howells) Harper, **88**: 371.
Masters, Old and New. (E. B. Perry) Music, **1**: 106.
Masters; a poem. (M. Hayden) Arena, **7**: 602.
Mastic. Garden & F. **6**: 272.
Mastodon Americanus, Restoration of. (O. C. Marsh) Am. J. Sci. **144**: 350.
— and the Mound-builders. (S. D. Peet) Am. Antiq. **14**: 59.
Masuirs. (G. H. Blakesley) Law Q. **8**: 323.
Matabele, The. (R. N. Cust) Asia. R. **22**: 330.
— and their War Dance. (W. Siltwell) Un. Serv. M. **8**: 213.
— Sidelights on. (Bertram Mitford) Asia. R. **17**: 96.
Matabeleland, The Alarm in. (Sir J. Willoughby) New R. **14**: 703.
— and how we got it, Newman's. Sat. R. **80**: 385.
— and its People. (H. T. Cousins) Sund. M. **23**: 51.
Matabeleland, Campaigning in. National, **23**: 662. Same art. Liv. Age, **202**: 443.
— The Chartered Company in. (F. G. Shaw) National, **26**: 786. (F. R. Statham) **27**: 33.
— Life in. Leis. Hour, **43**: 114.
— Rebellion in, by an Eye-witness. Argosy, **62**: 411.
— Religion of. (J. M. Orpen) 19th Cent. **40**: 187.
— under the British South Africa Company. (F. Frankland) R. of Rs. (N. Y.) **12**: 436.
— War in. Sat. R. **76**: 508, 561. — (A. Webb) Nation, **57**: 408. — Spec. **72**: 72.
— — Cause and Effect of. (F. C. Selous) National, **23**: 250.
Match-box Making at Home. (C. Black) Eng. Illust. **9**: 625.
Match Factory at Bow, Eng. (W. C. Preston) Sund. M. **21**: 447.
Matchmaker, The. (L. B. Walford) Longm. **23**: 74–551. **24**: 1–551.
Matchmaking. (C. O. Tiswolde) Longm. **28**: 157.
Match-making Customs in Munster. (K. Tynan) Eng. Illust. **12**: no. 1, 45.
Matches: Only a Match. (C. Falkenhorst) Pop. Sci. Mo. **47**: 683.
Mater Triumphans; a poem. (R. L. Stevenson) New R. **12**: 21.
Materialism, Controversial. (E. Noble) Open Court, **5**: 3033.
— Error of. (P. Carus) Open Court, **5**: 2823.
— Psycho-physical. (S. S. Laurie) Mind, **19**: 56.
— Reaction against. (P. Carus) Open Court, **4**: 2169.
— Scientific. (I. Remsen) Science, n. s. **3**: 225.
— — Emancipation from. (W. Ostwald) Sci. Prog. **4**: 419.
— — Failure of. (W. Ostwald) Pop. Sci. Mo. **48**: 589.
— Transcendentalism and. (E. M. Caillard) Contemp. **70**: 78.
— Untenable. (A. E. Dolbear) Monist, **5**: 501.
Materialization of Charles and Mivanway. (J. K. Jerome) Idler, **10**: 572.
Mathematical Consciousness, A Study of the. (M. W. Calkins) Educa. R. **8**: 269.
Mathematical Curiosities of the 16th Century. (V. Brandicourt) Pop. Sci. Mo. **44**: 106.
Mathematical Knowledge, Nature of. (H. Schubert) Monist, **6**: 294.
Mathematical Master's Love Story. (B. Harraden) Blackw. **151**: 651. Same art. Liv. Age, **194**: 14.
Mathematical Thought, Modern. (S. Newcomb) Nature, **49**: 325.
Mathematics and Engineering. (J. Hopkinson) Nature, **50**: 42.
— and Love. Open Court, **2**: 1251.
— Applied, as an Educational Factor. (F. R. Hutton) Cassier, **4**: 459.
— Committee of Ten's Report on. (J. M. Greenwood) Educa. **15**: 65, (H. H. Seerley) 239.
— Cajori's History of. Nation, **58**: 316.
— Educational Value of. (F. A. Hill) Educa. R. **9**: 349.
— in Liberal Culture. (J. J. Hardy) School & C. **1**: 459.
— in Secondary Schools of Germany. (J. E. Russell) School R. **2**: 479, 549.
— Laws of. (E. T. Dixon) Monist, **3**: 127.
— — Reply. (P. Carus) Monist, **3**: 133.
— The Old and the New. (P. Carus) Open Court, **2**: 1468.
— Preparation in, for College. (L. H. Safford) Acad. (Syr.) **7**: 210.
— Present State of. (F. Klein) Monist, **4**: 1.

Mathematics, Pure, Principles of, Veronese on. Nature, **50**: 493.
— Teacher's Outfit in. (J. M. Taylor) School R. **4**: 215.
— Teaching of. (S. Newcomb) Educa. R. **4**: 277. — (W. H. H. Hudson) Educa. R. **5**: 482. — (S. Newcomb) Educa. R. **6**: 332. — (L. L. Conant) School R. **1**: 210.
— — Use of History in. (G. Heppel) Nature, **48**: 16.
Mather, Cotton. (A. E. Moore) Bost. **2**: 146. — (L. Swift) Nation, **55**: 414. — (E. Lord) New Eng. M. n. s. **7**: 639.
— Was he a Fellow of the Royal Society? (N. D. Davis) Nation, **54**: 127. — (N. D. Davis) N. E. Reg. **46**: 114.
Mather, Increase. (A. E. Moore) Bost. **2**: 146.
Mather, William Williams, with portrait. Pop. Sci. Mo. **49**: 550.
Mather Family, Abstracts of Wills of. (J. P. Rylands) N. E. Reg. **47**: 38–330.
— of Lancashire, Some Deeds of. (J. P. Rylands) N. E. Reg. **49**: 29.
Matheson, George. (A. Jenkinson) M. Chr. Lit. **7**: 244.
Mathilde, Queen of Denmark. (F. St. J. Brenon) Time, **11**: 32.
Mathurâ, Epigraphic Discoveries at. (G. Bühler) Acad. **49**: 367.
Matineian Reliefs. (C. Waldstein) Am. J. Archæol. **7**: 1.
Matlock Will Case. Green Bag, **5**: 547.
Mato Tepee. (I. C. Russell) Around World, **1**: 106.
Matriarchal Family System. (E. B. Tylor) 19th Cent. **40**: 81.
Matriarchy, Origins of, S. Glennie on. (A. Nutt and J. Jacobs) Folk-Lore, **2**: 367.
— What was? (E. D. Cope) Open Court, **3**: 1518.
Matrimonial Agency, The; a story. (L. Springfield) Idler, **6**: 173.
Matrimonial Market. (E. Cary) Forum, **21**: 747.
Matrimonial Tontine Benefit Association. (R. Grant) Scrib. M. **16**: 679.
Matrimony and Chivalry. (W. Wheater) Gent. M. n. s. **49**: 178.
Matrons, Some Seventeenth Century, and their Housekeeping. Longm. **27**: 353. Same art. Liv. Age, **208**: 434.
Matsys, Quinten. (T. Cole) Cent. **26**: 593. — (A. E. Evans) M. of Art, **9**: 414.
Matt Decker, a Sketch from the Life; a story. (A. Gordon) Gent. M. n. s. **49**: 271. Same art. Liv. Age, **195**: 481.
Matt Digby's Meddling. (W. N. Harben) Lippinc. **56**: 108.
Mattawa River, Sharp Time on the. Outing, **24**: 92.
Matter. (E. M. Caillard) Good Words, **35**: 379. Same art. Ecl. M. **123**: 278.
— and Energy. (P. R. Shipman) Open Court, **8**: 4063.
— and Force, Modern View of. Sat. R. **80**: 370.
— Fourth State of. (E. M. Caillard) Good Words, **35**: 92. Same art. Ecl. M. **122**: 420.
— Fundamental Properties of. (J. G. Vogt) Open Court, **2**: 820, 852, 897.
— a Property of Energy, Hiller's. Sat. R. **79**: 516.
— Relation of Mind to. (E. D. Cope) Open Court, **1**: 527.
— Unity of. New Sci. R. **1**: 502.
Matter o' Coin, A. (A. E. Abbott) Idler, **7**: 41.
Matter of Course, A; a story. Temp. Bar, **97**: 123.
Matter of Taste, A. (S. Dawson) Belgra. **86**: 35.
Matterhorn, Ascent of. (G. P. Serviss) McClure, **5**: 339.
Matterhorn, Woman's Ascent of. (A. S. Peck) Eng. Illust. **16**: 53. Same art. McClure, **7**: 127.
Matthew; a Story of Ennui. (W. M. Hardinge) Temp. Bar, **94**: Same art. Liv. Age, **192**: 653.
Matthew Austin; a story. (W. E. Norris) Cornh. **69**: 1–585. **70**: 81–633.
Matthews, Brander, with portrait. Bk. Buyer, **3**: 166. — (H. C. Bunner) Bookman, **3**: 40.
Matthews, C. P., Collection of Pictures. (A. Griffiths) M. of Art, **4**: 265, 333.
Matthews, Ethel, with portrait. Theatre, **28**: 144.
Matthews, Kate. So. M. **5**: 504.
Matthews, William. Critic, **28**: 299.
Matty Island, Ethnography of. (J. Edge-Partington) Anthrop. J. **25**: 288.
Maturin, Rev. Charles Robert. Gent. M. n. s. **48**: 535.
Maulbronn, Cistercian Abbey of. (H. Barber) Antiq. n. s. **25**: 250.
Mauley, The Barons de. (C. L. Kingsford) Eng. Hist. R. **11**: 515.
Mauna Loa, Eruption of, Jan., 1887. (N. E. Fuller) Overland, n. s. **21**: 231.
Maundeville, Sir John. (H. G. Keene) Westm. **146**: 39.
Maunsell, John, Gen. (M. Van Rensselaer) M. Am. Hist. **27**: 419.
Maupassant, G. de. (L. N. Tolstoi) Arena, **11**: 15. — (W. E. Garrett Fisher) Temp. Bar, **103**: 495. — (A. Symons) Ath. '93, **2**: 97. — Critic, **23**: 40. — (F. C. de Sumichrast) Nation, **57**: 25. — (G. Saintsbury) National, **21**: 817. — Spec. **71**: 77. — With portrait. Bk. Buyer, **7**: 197. — (E. Delille) Fortn. **58**: 50.
— Insanity of. Critic, **20**: 43.
— Souvenirs of. (Eugene Davis) Lit. W. (Bost.) **24**: 448.
— Tolstoi on. (A. Laugel) Nation, **59**: 44.
Maurice, Edmund, and wife, with portraits. Theatre, **36**: 69.
Maurice, Frederick Denison. (H. R. Haweis) Contemp. **65**: 873.
— as Christian Socialist. (T. Hughes) Econ. R. **1**: 209.
— Lincoln's Inn Sermons. Spec. **69**: 261.
Maurice the Teetotaler; a play. (N. Vynne) Theatre, **33**: 54.
Mauritius; an Answer to F. C. Williams. (V. Naz) National, **21**: 422.
— and Jamaica. (J. W. Fortescue) Liv. Age, **192**: 491.
— before the Cyclone. Blackw. **152**: 208.
— Cyclone in, April 29, 1892. (H. E. H. Jerningham) Blackw. **152**: 342. — Dub. R. **111**: 192.
— the Gem of the Ocean. All the Year, **75**: 205.
— Madagascar and. (F. C. Williams) National, **20**: 377.
Maury, Matthew F., Reminiscences of, with portrait. (W. W. Scott) Southern M. **5**: 179.
Mauvais Quart d'Heure, Un; a summer sketch. (G. S. Reinhart) Harper, **89**: 236.
Mauve, Anton. (A. C. Loffelt) Art J. **46**: 101.
— and the Modern Dutch School. (E. Fles) M. of Art, **19**: 71.
— Incidents in Early Life of. Art J. **47**: 348.
Maverick. (M. H. Foote) Cent. **26**: 544.
Maverick Family, The. (I. J. Greenwood) N. E. Reg. **48**: 207.
Mavourez, Everard. (M. Carmichael) Month, **84**: 128.
Mavourez, Humphrey. (M. Carmichael) Month, **83**: 573.
Mavourez, Ludovic. (M. Carmichael) Month, **83**: 278.
Max, Gabriel. M. of Art, **3**: 224.
— and his Work. (C. S. Johnson) Munsey, **7**: 140.

Maxim, Hiram S. (J. B. Smith) Cassier, **7**: 436.
— Experiments in Aërial Navigation by. Cent. **27**: 444.
Maxim Gun, The Latest. (S. E. Tillman) Cosmopol. **19**: 584.
Maximilian I. and Mexico. (J. Heard, jr.) Scrib. M. **15**: 663.
— as an Art Patron. (F. M. Robinson) M. of Art, **12**: 307.
Maximilianus Transylvanius. (C. H. Coote) Ath. '92, **2**: 101.
Maxwell, Andrew, Picture Collection of. (R. Walker) M. of Art, **17**: 221.
May, Dorothy, and her Relations. (C. H. Townshend) N. E. Reg. **50**: 462.
May, Phil. (M. H. Spielmann) M. of Art, **17**: 348. — (A. H. Lawrence) Idler, **10**: 633.
May; a poem. (A. C. Swinburne) M. of Art, **16**: 226.
May and December; a poem. (P. B. Strong) Outing, **27**: 179.
May Day. All the Year, **72**: 401.
— at Cheltenham. (W. H. D. Rouse) Folk-Lore, **4**: 50.
— Games on. Walford's Antiq. **9**: 195. — (G. Clinch) Eng. Illust. **11**: 781.
May Meetings. (Jas. M'Crea) Time, **3**: 170.
May Queen Festival, A; with Letters from Mr. Ruskin. (J. P. Faunthorpe) 19th Cent. **37**: 734.
Maytime in West England. Sat. R. **79**: 825.
Maya Codices. (C. Thomas) Am. Antiq. **14**: 328.
Maya Hieroglyphic Writing. Is it Phonetic? (C. Thomas) Science, **20**: 197.
— Brinton on. (F. Starr) Dial (Ch.) **19**: 46.
Mayas, Customs and Superstitions of. (Mrs. A. D. Le Plongeon) Pop. Sci. Mo. **44**: 661.
— Language of. (W. W. Skeat) Ath. '95, **2**: 453.
— Time-periods of. (C. Thomas) Science, **21**: 128.
Maybrick, Mrs., Imprisonment of. R. of Rs. (N. Y.) **6**: 416.
— An Open Letter to the Queen. (M. A. Dodge) No. Am. **155**: 257.
Maybrick Case, Medico-legal View of. (H. D. Littlejohn) Jurid. R. **1**: 352.
Mayence Cathedral, Doorways of. (A. B. Bibb) Am. Arch. **51**: 83.
Mayfair and the Muses. (A. Haultain) Blackw. **155**: 814. Same art. Ecl. M. **123**: 184.
Mayfairs, The; a story. (R. A. Garland) Overland, n. s. **21**: 348.
May-flies in March. Spec. **70**: 385.
Mayflower. *See* Arbutus.
Mayflower Compact and the Jeffersonian Heresy. (H. B. Sprague) Our Day, **15**: 145.
Mayhew, Rev. J., Letter of, to R. Clarke, 1765. N. E. Reg. **46**: 15.
Maynard, Isaac H., Case of. Pub. Opin. **16**: 44.
— Reappointment of. (E. L. Godkin) Nation, **55**: 488.
Maynooth College. Eng. R. **3**: 328.
— Centenary of. (J. F. Hogan) Am. Cath. Q. **20**: 37. — (G. McDermot) Cath. World, **61**: 205.
— Centenary History, Healy's. (P. Lynch) Dub. R. **118**: 129.
Mayor, English, Municipal Insignia of. (R. S. Ferguson) Walford's Antiq. **6**: 66, 108.
Mayor of Sawmill Flat. (W. Atkinson) Chamb. J. **69**: 503–519.
Mayor's Lamps, The; a story. (J. K. Bangs) Harper, **93**: 455.
Mayor's Secret, The. Cornh. **70**: 606. Same art. Liv. Age, **204**: 202.
Mazarin, Cardinal, and Cromwell, in 1652. (S. R. Gardiner) Eng. Hist. R. **11**: 479.
Mazel, Lady, Murder of. (A. J. Gordon) Belgra. **90**: 141.
Mazer Bowl at Clynnog Fawr. (H. Hughes) Illus. Archæol. **2**: 107.
Mazzini, G., Love Episode in Life of. (D. Melegari) 19th Cent. **37**: 765. — (J. W. Mario) Nation, **61**: 75.
— Political Philosophy of. (A. Chandler) Econ. R. **2**: 63.
Meacham, Capt. William, at Bunker Hill. (E. S. Willcox) N. E. Reg. **49**: 203.
Mead, Richard, Library of. (Austin Dobson) Bibliographica, **1**: 404.
Meade, Mrs. L. T., at Home. Sund. M. **23**: 615.
Meade County, Kan., and Adjoining Territory, Local Deformation of Strata in. (E. Haworth) Am. J. Sci. **152**: 368.
Meadowcroft, Robert, with portrait. (H. L. Conard) Nat'l M. (N. Y. '91) **18**: 69.
Meadows, Kenny. (M. H. Spielmann) M. of Art, **19**: 301.
Meaning and Metaphor. (Lady V. Welby) Monist, **3**: 510.
Meaningless, Cult of the. (F. Morgan) Writer, **7**: 99.
Meanness, Pet. (F. C. Baylor) Lippinc. **56**: 708.
Mearne, Samuel, Bookbindings of. (Cyril Davenport) Bibliographica, **3**: 129.
— Roger Payne's Indebtedness to. (Cyril Davenport) Bibliographica, **3**: 371.
Mears, Nathan, with portrait. Nat'l M. (N. Y. '91) **16**: 238.
Measles, Murder by. (F. J. Waldo; D. Walsh) 19th Cent. **39**: 957.
Measure for Measure; a story. (E. Gower) Eng. Illust. **11**: 853.
Measurement as applied to the Mental Sciences. (J. McK. Cattell) Philos. R. **2**: 316.
Measurements of Precision. (T. C. Mendenhall) Nature, **50**: 584.
Measures, as derived from Light-waves. (A. A. Michelson) Astron. **13**: 92.
Meat, Live, Importation of, in England. Chamb. J. **70**: 412.
Meat Supply of Great Britain. (E. M. Nelson) J. Soc. Arts, **43**: 420.
Meat-trade, Australian. Chamb. J. **71**: 245.
Meats. (C. D. Wilson) Lippinc. **56**: 855.
Meayll Stone Circle, Isle of Man. (P. M. C. Kermode) Illus. Archæol. **2**: 1.
Mecca. (C. D. Warner) Harper, **85**: 813.
— Pilgrimage to. Chamb. J. **72**: 691.
— and the Propagation of Disease. (A. Proust) Chaut. **21**: 574.
Mechanic and Employer, Hints for. (E. Woodward) Engin. M. **9**: 493.
Mechanical Art, Style in. (F. Baumann) Am. Arch. **38**: 81.
Mechanical Conception of the World. (W. Harrison) Meth R. **55**: 932.
Mechanical Drawing-room. (C. W. MacCord) Engin. M. **7**: 855.
Mechanical Energy, Transformation into Chemical Energy. (M. C. Lea) Am. J. Sci. **147**: 377.
Mechanical Powers, Birth of. Chamb. J. **70**: 583. Same art. Liv. Age, **199**: 444.
Mechanical Testing, Kirkaldy's System of. Ath. '92, **1**: 729.
Mechanical Triumphs, An Era of. (R. H. Thurston) Engin. M. **6**: 456.
Mechanics, American. Are they Boasters? (T. F. Hagerty) Engin. M. **4**: 443.
— Skilled, Prevailing Scarcity of. (A. E. Outerbridge, jr.) Engin. M. **10**: 227.

Mechanics, Applied, Supremacy of U. S. in. (C. Sellers) Engin. M. 2: 443-771.
— Science of, An Historical Survey of. (R. S. Woodward) Science, n. s. 1: 141.
— — Mach's History of. (C. S. Peirce) Nation, 57: 251. — (A. G. Greenhill) Nature, 51: 49.
Mechanism; Interchangeable Construction, History of. (W. F. Durfee) J. Frankl. Inst. 136: 413. 137: 44-118.
— Modern, Benjamin on. Nature, 47: 241.
Mechmet, the Wrestler, a Brigand of Turkey. (C. J. Cornish) Blackw. 155: 518.
Mechoopdas, or Rancho Chico Indians. (A. K. Bidwell) Overland, n. s. 27: 204.
Mecklenburg Declaration of Independence. (D. B. Hill) So. Hist. Pap. 20: 335.
Medal of Honor Legion. (F. S. Frisbie) Am. Hist. Reg. 1: 67.
Medallions, Some Modern. M. of Art, 8: 384.
— Syracusan, Evans on. Ath. '92, 2: 358.
Medallists of the Renaissance, Heiss's. (C. Phillips) M. of Art, 8: 519.
Medals, American Indian. (W. M. Beauchamp) M. Am. Hist. 29: 65.
— and Medal Collecting. Chamb. J. 69: 124.
— Italian. (G. F. Hill) Knowl. 19: 17.
— Military and other. All the Year, 75: 246.
— of British Army and Navy, Grey on. Sat. R. 74: 234.
— Some Rare Napoleonic. (J. H. Adams) Cosmopol. 17: 286.
Mediæval Lore, Steele's. Sat. R. 75: 238.
Mediæval Schoolgirl, A. (S. Beale) Univ. R. 5: 551.
Median, the, Practical Computation of. (E. W. Scripture) Psychol. R. 2: 376.
Medical Books for Small Public Libraries. (G. E. Wire) Lib. J. 20: supp. 37.
Medical Climatology. Climate of South Africa. (R. Roose) Fortn. 65: 104.
Medical Congress, Eleventh International, at Rome. (C. A. Siegfried) Nation, 58: 361. — Nature, 49: 563, (P. Giacosa) 578.
Medical Crisis of the 18th Century. (C. W. Cram) Arena, 16: 908.
Medical Education. (A. L. Benedict) Lippinc. 56: 673.
— in America. (J. Madden) New Sci. R. 2: 152.
— in the U. S., Recent Advances in. (W. D. Harnaker) Chaut. 24: 177.
Medical Etiquette. Time, 20: 321.
— Quacks and Secret Remedies. (F. Hart) Forum, 16: 195.
Medical Jurisprudence in the U. S. (Sir H. D. Littlejohn) Jurid. R. 8: 346.
Medical Mission, Deptford. (W. C. Preston) Good Words, 34: 821.
Medical Missionaries at Home. Another Use for our Churches. (J. A. Bevington) Lend a H. 12: 191.
— in Palestine. (J. Wells) Sund. M. 25: 741.
Medical Press, The. (E. Berdoe) Univ. R. 1: 241.
Medical Recipes from Topsell. Sat. R. 74: 332.
Medical Schools, Scotland. Scot. R. 23: 1.
Medical Science. (C. R. Hammerton) Chaut. 16: 159.
— and the State. National, 19: 278.
Medical Service, Free and Paid. (N. Oppenheim) Soc. Econ. 7: 352.
Medical Student, Life of. (A. L. Benedict) Lippinc. 58: 389.
Medici, Alessandro de, a Florentine Despot. Macmil. 74: 128. Same art. Liv. Age, 210: 176.
Medici, Lorenzo de', Wedding of. (J. Cartwright) M. of Art, 9: 365.
Medici, a Grand-ducal Family. (E. Lewis) Cosmopol. 13: 186.
Medicine, Advancement of, by Research. (H. P. Bowditch) Science, n. s. 4: 85.
— and Recent Advances in Science. (M. Foster) Nature, 54: 580, 600.
— and Society. (J. B. Yeo) 19th Cent. 38: 1025.
— as a Career. (J. S. Billings) Forum, 14: 725. — (Sir W. B. Dalby) Longm. 22: 556. 23: 56.
— as a Profession. (A. L. Benedict) Lippinc. 54: 811.
— Fads of Medical Men. (C. Edson) No. Am. 156: 287.
— *Fin de siècle.* (A. S. Eccles) National, 21: 785. Same art. Ecl. M. 121: 440. Same art. Liv. Age, 199: 122.
— in Scotland, in the Days of Queen Mary. (T. G. Stewart) Blackw. 153: 885. Same art. Liv. Age, 198: 451.
— Mediæval. (E. A. King) 19th Cent. 34: 145. Same art. Liv. Age, 199: 40.
— Modern, Drift of. (G. M. Carfrae) New R. 15: 182. Same art. Pub. Opin. 21: 656. Same art. Ecl. M. 127: 621.
— New Outlooks in the Science and Art of. (T. M. Prudden) Pop. Sci. Mo. 48: 359.
— Practice of, Legislative Restriction, on. (H. Wood) Arena, 8: 680.
— Preventive, the New Science. (A. Ruffer) Ecl. M. 118: 183.
— Progress in. Sat. R. 82: 338.
— Psychologic Development of. (J. H. McCormick) Am. Antiq. 18: 211.
— Study of, Preparation for. (E. L. H. Rusk) Science, 19: 282.
— Treatment of, in Fiction. (C. W. Latimer) New Sci. R. 2: 253.
— Twenty-five Years of. (Mrs. H. M. Plunkett) Pop. Sci. Mo. 46: 302.
— World's Debt to. (J. S. Billings) Chaut. 20: 668.
Medicine Arrows of Oregon Indians. (A. S. Gatschet) J. Am. Folk-Lore, 6: 111.
Medicine Men, Indian. (L. G. Yates) Overland, n. s. 28: 171.
— Omaha. (F. La Flesche) J. Am. Folk-Lore, 3: 215.
Medicine Woman, French. (M. Negreponte) Argosy, 55: 532.
Medicines, Quack. Sat. R. 73: 277.
Medina. (C. D. Warner) Harper, 85: 813.
Mediocrity, Revenges of. (T. W. Higginson) Pub. Opin. 15: 362.
Mediterranean, the, Braggadocio about. (W. L. Clowes) 19th Cent. 37: 875.
— Eastern, Hydrography of. Geog. J. 3: 138.
— England and. (G. S. Clarke) 19th Cent. 37: 541. — (P. H. Colomb) No. Am. 158: 583. — Un. Serv. M. 10: 56.
— The Millstone round the Neck of England. (Wm. L. Clowes) 19th Cent. 37: 369.
— Should England hold it in War? (H. Elsdale) 19th Cent. 37: 215.
Medium, Confessions of a. Sat. R. 74: 142.
Medley of the Midway Plaisance, A. (A. W. Bailey) Outing, 23: 208.
Médoc, The, and its Wines. Chamb. J. 72: 609.
— Chateaux in. (Henry W. Lucy) Univ. R. 4: 341.
— Vintage of. All the Year, 71: 159.
Medusæ, Living. (E. Ingersoll) Mo. Illust. 5: 299.
Medway, Mass., Births in, 1714-44. (E. O. Jameson) N. E. Reg. 49: 280, 444.
Medway River. (D. Hannay) M. of Art, 9: 20, 66.
— Voyage up. All the Year, 73: 322.
Meehan Nurseries, Germantown, Pa. Garden & F. 6: 377.

Meeting-house Feud. (D. E. Nelson) New Eng. M. n. s. 12: 90.
Meeting-houses, Some Early. Cornh. 68: 152.
Megalopolis, Excavations at. Sat. R. 76: 339.
— Theatre at. (W. Loring) Ath. '93, 2: 200. — (E. A. Gardner and others) J. Hel. Stud. 11: 294.
Megascops, Evolution and Dichromatism in the Genus. (E. M. Hasbrouck) Am. Natural. 27: 521, 638.
Mehan, John Dennis. (E. Swayne) Music, 9: 422.
Meigs, Gen. Montgomery C. Pub. Opin. 12: 321.
Meigs, Return J. (M. J. Wright) M. Am. Hist. 28: 125.
Meiron, Burning of; Jewish Ceremony. Macmil. 74: 428.
Meissonier, Jean Louis Ernest. (A. Meynell) M. of Art, 4: 133. 8: 31. — (W. Armstrong) M. of Art, 14: 199. — (P. G. Hamerton) Portfo. 24: 90.
— Exhibition of Paintings by. (C. Phillips) M. of Art, 16: 280.
— his Life and his Art, Gréard's. Nation, 63: 476.
— in London. (S. Beale) Am. Arch. 40: 116.
— Paintings of. (G. Berne-Bellecour) Art J. 45: 135.
Mekong, Shans and Hill Tribes on the. (R. G. Woodthorpe) Anthrop. J. 26: 13.
Melancholy in Literature. (E. Verhaeren) Univ. R. 5: 104.
Melancholy Man. Macmil. 70: 47. Same art. Liv. Age, 202: 186.
Melanesia and the Labor Traffic. (H. H. Montgomery) New R. 8: 549.
— Folk-Lore of. (R. H. Codrington) Folk-Lore, 4: 509.
Melanesians, Codrington's. (W. M. Ferriss) Nation, 55: 91.
Melba at Home. (F. E. Thomas) Munsey, 12: 393.
Melbourne, Lord. Queen Victoria and her First Prime Minister. (R. B. Brett) Ecl. M. 122: 181.
Melbourne, University of. (E. Jenks) Ath. '92, 1: 308, 824. — (T. G. Tucker) Ath. '92, 1: 762.
Melchizedek, Order of. (J. N. Fradenbergh) Meth. R. 53: 426.
Melford, Mark. The Maelstrom. Theatre, 28: 254.
Melia Azedarach; Pride of China Tree. Garden & F. 7: 92.
Melilla and the Moors. (José P. Val d'Eremao) Asia. R. 17: 103.
— Spaniards at. (O. G. Villard) Nation, 58: 27.
Mellen, William Solon, with portrait. Nat'l M. (N. Y. '91) 15: 290.
Mellingford Bank Failure; a story. Belgra. 91: 174.
Meloban, The, and the Pentheroy. (J. Creelman) Cosmopol. 16: 426.
Melons; Benton Harbor, Mich., Melon Industry. (L. H. Bailey) Garden & F. 6: 412.
Melun, Viscount Armand de, with portrait. (F. X. McGowan) Cath. World, 63: 754.
Melville, Sir Andrew. (J. G. Alger) Scot. R. 26: 1.
Melville, Herman. (H. S. Salt) Gent. M. n. s. 48: 248. Same art. Ecl. M. 118: 517. — Spec. 70: 859.
— Romances. Lit. W. (Bost.) 23: 352.
Melville Bay, A Journey round. (E. Astrup) Geog. J. 5: 345.
Memling, Hans, Wauter's Studies of. M. of Art, 17: 282.
Memminger, C. G. (J. C. Schwab) Yale R. 2: 288.
Memoirs of a Minister of France. (S. J. Weyman) Eng. Illust. 12: no. 1, 33.
Memorial Day at the Corners. (H. Copeland) New Eng. M. n. s. 14: 472.
Memories of Bluemeadow. (C. Lyon) New Eng. M. n. s. 13: 694. 14: 86-345.
Memories of Books, Authors, and Events. (J. Bertram) Chamb. J. 72: 17.
Memorizing. (P. T. Austen) Educa. 16: 18.
Memory. (H. Münsterberg) Psychol. R. 1: 34, 453.
— Affective. (E. B. Tichener) Philos. R. 4: 65.
— and Organized Substance. (P. Carus) Open Court, 3: 1900.
— and Personality. (T. Ribot) Open Court, 4: 2709.
— as a General Function of Organized Matter. (E. Hering) Open Court, 1: 141, 169.
— Experimental Study of. (E. A. Kirkpatrick) Psychol. R. 1: 602.
— for Square Size. (J. M. Baldwin and W. J. Shaw) Psychol. R. 2: 236.
— Freaks and Fancies of. (J. C. Hadden) Gent. M. n. s. 52: 588. Same art. Ecl. M. 123: 192.
— Growth of, in School Children. (T. L. Bolton) Am. J. Psychol. 4: 362.
— Illusions of. (W. H. Burnham) Scrib. M. 11: 185.
— in Animals. Chamb. J. 69: 43.
— in Education. (G. T. W. Patrick) Educa. R. 4: 463.
— in School Children. (J. C. Shaw) Pedagog. Sem. 4: 61.
— Lapses of. Spec. 77: 814.
— Muscular. (Theodate L. Smith) Am. J. Psychol. 7: 453.
— Physiological, Experiments upon. (J. A. Bergström) Am. J. Psychol. 5: 356.
— Repetition in. (W. G. Smith) Psychol. R. 3: 21.
— Relation of Attention to. (W. G. Smith) Mind, 20: 47.
— Romance of. (S. R. Elliott) Atlan. 70: 346.
— Short, Advantages of a. (P. W. Roose) Argosy, 58: 286.
— Training in the Public Schools. (W. Vaughan) Educa. 12: 468.
— Wilful. (A. K. H. Boyd) Longm. 21: 517.
Memory; a poem. (C. Brontë) Cornh. 67: 185. Same art. Ecl. M. 120: 405.
Memory, A; a poem. (W. E. Henley) M. of Art, 9: 385.
Memory, A; a story. (Harold MacFarlane) Cosmopol. 22: 60.
Memory After-image and Attention. (A. H. Daniels) Am. J. Psychol. 6: 558.
Memory Clearing House; a story. (I. Zangwill) Idler, 1: 572.
Memory Processes, Visual and Aural. (L. G. Whitehead) Psychol. R. 3: 258.
Memory Training, Use of Correlations in. (C. Moffett) Educa. 16: 541.
Memphis and Sakkarah, Egypt. (C. W. Wood) Argosy, 56: 381.
Memphis, Tenn., Development of Club Idea in. (A. R. Watson) Mid-Cont. 6: 144.
Men and Women as Social Beings. (I. A. Safford) Open Court, 7: 3615.
— — Mutual Relations of. (A. Clerk) New R. 13: 375.
— — Relative Sensitivity of, at Nape of the Neck. (F. Galton) Nature, 50: 40.
— Oldest Civilized. (E. D. Cope) Am. Natural. 30: 616.
Men and Women and Horses; a story. (B. Matthews) Harper, 91: 813.
Men call it Conscience; a tale. (M. Marstyn) Canad. M. 7: 449.
Men in Stone, The; a story. (C. J. C. Hyne) Chamb. J. 72: 157.
Men in the Storm, The; a story. (S. Crane) Arena, 10: 662.
Men of the Hills, The. Liv. Age, 207: 30.
Men of Letters and the State. (W. E. Hodgson) National, 18: 618.

Men of the Moss-Hags, The. (S. R. Crockett) Good Words, 36: 1-793.
Men who might have been Presidents. (J. M. Rogers) No. Am. 162: 558.
Menage Scientific Expedition. (W. S. Harwood) Chaut. 17: 723.
Menagerie, Management of a. (C. Moffett) McClure, 2: 544. 3: 71.
Ménagiana, An Old French Jestbook. (M. E. Grant Duff) Cornh. 74: 41. Same art. Ecl. M. 127: 221.
Menagier de Paris. (E. B. Stone) Lippinc. 56: 100.
Mendelssohn, Elijah. Sat. R. 81: 522.
Mendelssohn, Felix. (H. H. Statham) Fortn. 64: 926.
— in Scotland. Chamb. J. 70: 361.
Mendelssohn, Moses, 1729-86. (J. Strauss) Gent. M. n. s. 51: 361.
Mendelssohn Club of Philadelphia. (J. Bunting) Music, 3: 646.
Mendenhall, James W. (W. F. Whitlock) Meth. R. 52: 681.
— Four Years Ago; a remembrance. Meth. R. 56: 620.
Mender of Hearts. (S. Myrick) New Eng. M. n. s. 14: 152.
Mendip Hills, Eng. Chamb. J. 70: 481.
Mendocino, Camping in. (C. S. Greene) Overland, n. s. 22: 337.
Mendon, Mass., Story of Parish in. New Eng. M. n. s. 7: 789.
Menelik, King, and his Court. Dub. R. 112: 183.
Ménèval, Baron, Memoirs. (J. J. O'Shea) Cath. World, 60: 698. — (C. H. Levermore) Nation, 60: 151 182. — (W. O'C. Morris) Acad. 46: 143. — Dial (Ch.) 17: 111. — Ath. '94, 1: 827. 2: 85.
Menhir Autel at Kernuz. (F. S. Tremlett) Illus. Archæol. 2: 16.
Menhirs reërected on Dartmoor. Reliquary, 35: 35.
Mental Activity, Conditions of. (J. A. Bergström) Am. J. Psychol. 6: 247.
Mental Capacity, Measure of. (E. Kraepelin) Pop. Sci. Mo. 49: 756.
Mental Congruence, Laws of, in Education. (B. A. Hinsdale) Educa. R. 10: 152.
Mental Defect and Disorder from the Teacher's Point of View. (J. Royce) Educa. R. 6: 209-449.
Mental Development in the Child and the Race, Baldwin on. Am. Natural. 29: 687.
Mental Dulness and Other Defects, Causes of. (F. Warner) J. Statis. Soc. 59: 125.
Mental Dyspepsia, What is? (B. F. Herrick) Writer, 7: 114.
Mental Education, Some Principles of. (E. W. Scripture) School R. 3: 533.
Mental Effort, Motor Phenomena of. (E. H. Lindley) Am. J. Psychol. 7: 491.
Mental Epidemics, A Study of. (B. Sidis) Cent. 30: 849.
Mental Evolution. (C. L. Morgan) Monist, 2: 161.
Mental Forms, Statistical Study of. (M. W. Calkins) Am. J. Psychol. 5: 439.
Mental Growth of Mankind in Ancient Times, Hittell on. (F. Starr) Dial (Ch.) 17: 117.
Mental Imagery. (A. Binet) Fortn. 58: 95. Same art. Ecl. M. 119: 344. Same art. Liv. Age, 194: 545.
Mental Images. (E. A. Kirkpatrick) Science, 22: 227.
Mental Philosophy, What is? (G. T. Ladd) Chaut. 19: 157.
Mental Suggestion, Ochorowicz on. Sat. R. 73: 101.
Mental Telegraphy. (C. S. Coles) New Sci. R. 2: 73.
— again. (Mark Twain) Harper, 91: 521.
— Logic of. (J. Jastrow) Scrib. M. 18: 571.
Mental Training; a Remedy for Education. (W. G. Jordan) New Sci. R. 1: 140.
Mentation, Arrested. (C. Ferrero) Monist, 6: 60.
— Science of. (E. Gates) Monist, 5: 574.
Mentone, Notes from. (Mrs. H. Chetwynd) Belgra. 86: 24.
— Stories from. (J. B. Andrews) Folk-Lore Rec. 3: 40.
Mentone Caves, Man of. (A. J. Evans) Nature, 49: 42.
Menzel, Adolf. (H. Zimmern) M. of Art, 7: 291.
— and Frederick the Great. (H. Zimmern) M. of Art, 7: 476.
— Greatest Painter of Modern Germany. (C. Waldstein) Harper, 93: 42. — R. of Rs. (N. Y.) 13: 63.
Mephisto; a story. (Mrs. O. Booth-Daphne) Temp. Bar, 95: 529.
Meran, Hofer Play at, 1893. (H. M. Poynter) Spec. 71: 431.
Mercenary Spirit in Public Life. Meth. R. 55: 116.
Merchandise Marks, Legislation on. (C. Stuart-Wortley) National, 20: 469.
Merchant of Venice, Two Legends of. (G. Chiarini) Chaut. 17: 702.
Merchantmen, The; a ballad. (R. Kipling) McClure, 1: 163.
Merchants, English, and German Traders. (C. Marvin) Time, 16: 136.
— of New York, Old Shipping. (G. W. Sheldon) Harper, 84: 457.
Merciful Mandarin, The. (E. York) Good Words, 34: 706.
Mercur, A. H., with portrait. Bk. News, 12: 245.
Mercurial Columns. (A. B. Calkins) Cassier, 1: 398.
Mercy-Argenteau, Count de, Secret Correspondence of. (A. W. Ward) Eng. Hist. R. 7: 792.
Mère Angèle. (M. S. Hancock) Belgra. 86: 297.
Mère Loubet; a story. (Mary Negreponte) Westm. 138: 424.
Meredith, Geo., with portrait. Bk. Buyer, 5: 580. — With portrait. Bk. Buyer, 12: 121. — (J. A. Newton-Robinson) Ecl. M. 118: 124. — Temp. Bar, 97: 589.
— The Amazing Marriage. (W. E. G. Fisher) Acad. 49: 27. — Idler, 9: 119.
— and his Country Home. (A. W. Lothrop) Idler, 4: 343.
— and his Critics. (R. Le Gallienne) Time, 22: 307.
— as a Journalist. (F. Dolman) New R. 8: 342.
— in his Poems. (E. Dowden) Fortn. 57: 337. Same art. Ecl. M. 118: 650. Same art. Liv. Age, 193: 495.
— Lord Ormont and his Aminta. (L. Johnson) Acad. 46: 3.
— Maiden Speech of. (W. R. Nicoll) Bookman, 2: 34.
— Nature Poetry of; Earth and Man. (W. F. Revell) Westm. 142: 506.
— New Edition of his Works. Acad. 50: 389.
— Novels. (E. F. Wheeler) Chaut. 19: 561. — Ed. R. 181: 33. — Sat. R. 74: 719. — (F. Mary Wilson Parsons) Temp. Bar, 108: 262.
— Ordeal of Richard Feverel. Acad. 50: 498.
— A Summer with: in particular, Richard Feverel. (E. L. Menefee) Poet-Lore, 7: 505.
— Women of. (G. Smith) Fortn. 65: 775.
Meredith, William Ralph, at Home. (T. E. Champion) Canad. M. 3: 184.
Merely an Incident; a story. (W. Western) Munsey, 13: 550.
Merenptah: Pharaoh of the Hard Heart. (W. M. F. Petrie) Cent. 30: 500.
Meriden, Conn., Quarries in the Lava Beds at. (W. M. Davis) Am. J. Sci. 151: 1.
Mérimée, Prosper. Macmil. 73: 18. Same art. Liv. Age, 207: 515.

Mérimée, Prosper, and M'lle Dacquin. Macmil. 73: 211.
— Carmen, Dramatized. Sat. R. 81: 597.
Merit System in Government Appointments. (T. Roosevelt) Cosmopol. 13: 66.
Merivale's Masterpiece; a story. All the Year, 71: 469.
Merlin, the Prophet of the Celts. Walford's Antiq. 12: 9, 135.
Merlin Myth, its Scottish Origin. (A. Grant) Scot. R. 20: 321.
Mermaid's Pool; a tale. (L. Wyndham) Canad. M. 7: 336.
Merriam, Augustus Chapman. (C. H. Young) Am. J. Archæol. 10: 227—(R. B. Richardson) Ath. '95, 1: 156.
— Death of. Critic, 26: 69.
Merriam, Lucius S., Memorial of, with portrait. J. H. Univ. Studies, 12: 97.
Merrick, Frederick. (W. G. Williams) Meth. R. 55: 345.
Merrimac, The, of the C. S. Navy. So. Hist. Pap. 20: 1.
— and the Cumberland. (T. O. Selfridge, jr.) Cosmopol. 15: 176.
Merriman, Henry Seton. Sat. R. 82: 191.
Merrington-Manning Affair; a story. (F. L. Guertin) Munsey, 12: 652.
Merry Andrew, The First. (E. Walford) Walford's Antiq. 9: 249. 10: 111.
Merry Maid of Arcady; a story. (Mrs. B. Harrison) Harper, 90: 378.
Merry Thanksgiving of the Burglar and Plumber, The; a story. (A. French) McClure, 5: 515.
Méry, Joseph. (J. W. Sherer) Macmil. 71: 104.
Mesdag, Hendrik Willem. (L. Hind) Art J. 45: 49.—(E. D'Esterre-Keeling) Leis. Hour, 44: 447.
Mesmer, Animal Magnetism and Hypnotism. (Joseph Jastrow) Cosmopol. 20: 360.
Mesmerism, New, Real Wonder of. Spec. 70: 42.
Mesodactyla. (O. C. Marsh) Am. J. Sci. 143: 445.
Mesopotamian Kings. Ath. '94, 1: 50.
Mesozoic Flora of Portugal compared with that of U. S. (L. F. Ward) Science, n. s. 1: 337.
Mesozoic Plants from near Oroville, Cal. (W. M. Fontaine) Am. J. Sci. 152: 273.
Mesozoic Vertebrate Fossils. (O. C. Marsh) Am. J. Sci. 144: 171.
Mess of Pottage. (L. Stockton) Lippinc. 54: 124, 264.
Message from the Desert; a story. (E. Favenc) Chamb. J. 70: 695-743.
Message from the Flood; a story. Chamb. J. 69: 301.
Message of the Cherokee Rose; a story. (M. W. Emerson) Lend a H. 10: 279.
Messe de l'aurore, La; a story. (B. G. Moore) Canad. M. 2: 83.
Messengers and Modes of Communication, Strange. Chamb. J. 70: 234.
Messiah, The Indian. (A. C. Fletcher) J. Am. Folk-Lore, 4: 57.—(W. W. Newell) J. Am. Folk-Lore, 4: 106.—J. Am. Folk-Lore, 4: 162.
— Cheyenne Account of the. J. Am. Folk-Lore, 4: 61.
— Jack Wilson. (A. S. Gatschet) J. Am. Folk-Lore, 6: 108.
Messiah of the New Testament, Briggs on. (G. Vos) Presb. and Ref. R. 7: 718.
— Teachings of Jesus and the Jews respecting. (H. M. Scott) Bib. World, 1: 408.
Messianic Belief, References to "King" in Psalter in their Bearing on. (C. B. Gray) Jew. Q. 7: 658.

Metal, Art in. (J. H. Pollen) M. of Art, 1: 51.
Metal-work, Art in. (L. F. Day) M. of Art, 9: 241.
Metal-work, Celtic. (J. R. Allen) M. of Art, 8: 456. 9: 285.
— Ecclesiastical, at Hildesheim. (H. Cole) M. of Art, 4: 36.
— Indian, at the Imperial Institute. (Sir G. Birdwood) M. of Art, 16: 172.
— of India. (J. R. Royle) M. of Art, 3: 236-469.
— Saracenic, in Venice. (S. Lane-Poole) M. of Art, 9: 450.
— Singer's. (A. H. Church) Portfo. 23: 121.
Metallic Oxides, Reduction of. (W. H. Greene and W. H. Wahl) J. Frankl. Inst. 135: 453.
Metallic Reducing Agents, Recent Progress in. (H. F. Keller) J. Frankl. Inst. 138: 306.
Metallurgists, Practical Laboratory Training for. (R. H. Richards) Engin. M. 8: 657.
Metallurgy, Early, of France. (P. Mahler and B. H. Thwaite) Cassier, 5: 305.
— Electro-, as applied to Silver Refining. (G. Faunce) J. Frankl. Inst. 140: 287.
— Recent American Methods. (J. Douglas) J. Soc. Arts, 43: 809-845.
Metals and Alloys, Composition and Characteristics of. (G. Hill) Am. Arch. 38: 207.
— at High Temperatures. (W. C. Roberts-Austen) Nature, 45: 534.
— Diffusion of. (W. C. Roberts-Austen) Nature, 54: 55. Same art. Science, n. s. 3: 827.
— Fuse, Defects experimentally considered. (W. E. Harrington) J. Frankl. Inst. 141: 464.
— Nitro-. (A. E. Tutton) Nature, 48: 524.
— Rarer, their Alloys. (W. C. Roberts-Austen) Nature, 52: 14, 39.
— Specific Heat of, (J. W. Richards) J. Frankl. Inst. 136: 37, 116, 178.
— used in Building, Chemistry of. (J. M. Thomson) J. Soc. Arts, 44: 861, 885.
Metamorphosis, the Meaning of. (A. Hyatt and J. M. Arms) Nat. Sci. 8: 395.
Metamorphoses of Johnson, The. (R. Barr) Idler, 5: 40.
Metaphor of Every-day Life. Atlan. 72: 287.
— Slang and. (E. F. Andrews) Chaut. 23: 462.
Metaphysic and Psychology. (J. Watson) Philos. R. 2: 513.
Metaphysicism. (P. Carus) Open Court, 3: 1995.
Metaphysics, Bradley on. (J. Royce) Philos. R. 3: 212.
— Relation of, to Epistemology. (D. G. Ritchie) Philos. R. 3: 14.
— Sectarian Criticism. (K. Pearson) Fortn. 64: 674.
— Use and Meaning of the Word. Open Court, 2: 1313.
Metaplastid Cell and Protoplastid Body. (J. E. S. Moore) Sci. Prog. 3: 323.
Metasomatic Changes in Limestones. (A. Harker) Sci. Prog. 4: 50.
Metcalf, W. L., with portrait. Bk. Buyer, 11: 121. —(H. M. Steele) Mo. Illust. 3: 93.
Meteor and Meteor-streak of Aug. 26, 1894. (W. F. Denning) Nature, 50: 537.
— of Jan. 25, 1894. (H. C. Russell) Nature, 49: 324.
Meteoric Irons, Two. (G. F. Kunz and E. Weinschenk) Am. J. Sci. 143: 424.
Meteorite, Beaver Creek. (E. E. Howell) Am. J. Sci. 147: 430.
— Cañon Diablo, Constituents of. (O. A. Derby) Am. J. Sci. 149: 101.
— from Cross Roads, N. C. (E. E. Howell) Am. J. Sci. 146: 67.

Meteorite, from Farmington, Kans. (G. F. Kunz and E. Weinschenk) Am. J. Sci. **143**: 65. — (H. L. Preston) Am. J. Sci. **143**: 65. **144**: 400.
— from Forsyth Co., N. C. (E. A. de Schweinitz) Am. J. Sci. **151**: 208.
— from Garratt Co., Md. (A. E. Foote) Am. J. Sci. **143**: 64.
— from Hamblen Co., Tenn. (G. P. Merrill) Am. J. Sci. **152**: 149.
— from Jafferabad, India. (J. W. Judd) Nature, **49**: 32.
— from Kenton Co., Ky. (H. L. Preston) Am. J. Sci. **144**: 163.
— from Pennsylvania. (W. G. Owens) Am. J. Sci. **143**: 423.
— from Mt. Joy, Pa. (E. E. Howell) Am. J. Sci. **144**: 415.
— from Western Australia. (J. R. Gregory) Nature, **47**: 90.
— Is the Santa Catherina Iron a? (O. A. Derby) Science, **20**: 254.
— Lines of Structure in the Winnebago County. (H. A. Newton) Am. J. Sci. **145**: 152.
— New, from Hamblen, Tenn. (L. G. Eakins) Am. J. Sci. **146**: 283.
— from Japan. (H. A. Ward) Am. J. Sci. **145**: 153.
— of Jan. 13, 1893. (H. A. Newton) Am. J. Sci. **146**: 161.
— Photography of, Instrument for. (W. L. Elkin) Astron. **13**: 626.
— Plymouth, Ind. (H. A. Ward) Am. J. Sci. **149**: 53.
— Seen to fall at Bath, S. D. (A. E. Foote) Am. J. Sci. **145**: 64.
Meteorites, Probable Origin of. (G. W. Coakley) Astron. **11**: 753.
— Two New. (E. E. Howell) Am. J. Sci. **150**: 252.
Meteorological Conference. Dub. R. **110**: 438.
Meteorological Discovery, A Chapter in. (J. C. Adams) Pop. Sci. Mo. **41**: 787.
Meteorological Stations, High-level. (A. L. Rotch) Nature, **52**: 236.
— on Mount Wellington. Nature, **52**: 599.
Meteorological Work in Australia. (C. Todd) Nature, **51**: 306.
Meteorology. Climatic Influence of Forests. (B. E. Fernow) Garden & F. **6**: 147.
— Elementary, Davis'. Sat. R. **77**: 646.
— in Schools. (W. M. Davis) School R. **2**: 529.
— in the Universities. (T. Stanton) Open Court, **7**: 3923. — (C. Abbe) Science, n. s. **2**: 709.
— Progress of. (F. Waldo) No. Am. **160**: 580.
— Recent Contributions to. Nature, **49**: 217.
— Waldo's. Sat. R. **75**: 406.
Meteors and Comets. (W. H. S. Monck) Astron. **11**: 274.
— Andromed, of Nov. 23 and 27, 1892. (H. A. Newton) Am. J. Sci. **145**: 61.
— April. (W. F. Denning) Nature, **48**: 5. **52**: 33.
— August, Heights of. (A. S. Herschel) Nature, **52**: 437.
— — and December, Photographs of. (Dr. Elkin) Am. J. Sci. **147**: 154.
— Biela. *See* Andromedes.
— Leonids, or Meteors of Nov. 13. (D. Kirkwood) Astron. **12**: 385.
— Perseids, or August Meteors. (D. Kirkwood) Astron. **12**: 789.
— Shooting Stars. (W. F. Denning) Pop. Astron. **1**: 34–147.
Method, New Manual of, Garlick's. (C. C. Van Liew) **School R. 4: 631.**
Method of Britta, the Dane; a story. (H. Campbell) New Eng. M. n. s. **11**: 311.
Methodism and the Andover Theology. (J. A. Faulkner) And. R. **18**: 487.
— and the General Conference. (F. C. Inglehart) No. Am. **162**: 635.
— The Tasks of. Meth. R. **56**: 625.
— World-wide, Glimpses of. (J. Mudge) Meth. R. **55**: 538.
Methodist, An Old-fashioned. Sund. M. **22**: 682.
— What makes a? (J. M. Buckley) Chaut. **17**: 589.
Methodist Book Concern. (W. C. Robinson) Cath. World, **55**: 159.
Methodist Episcopacy in Transition. (J. M. Thoburn) Meth. R. **55**: 764.
— Life Tenure of. Meth. R. **52**: 105.
Methodist Episcopal Church, Book of Discipline, Opening Sentences. (W. F. Warren) Meth. R. **52**: 61.
— Constitution of. (John Pearson) Meth. R. **56**: 260.
— Fragmentary Nature of. (J. H. Potts) Meth. R. **52**: 719.
— Constitutional Problem in. (B. F. Rawlins) Meth. R. **54**: 548.
— Episcopacy of, Congregationalism and. (C. A. Crane) Meth. R. **52**: 429.
— General Conference of. Our Day, **16**: 315.
— — as a Working Body. (J. D. Walsh) Meth. R. **55**: 712.
— — Powers and Procedure of. (H. L. Sibley) Meth. R. **54**: 591.
— History of the Third Restrictive Rule. (T. H. Pearne) Meth. R. **56**: 430.
— in the South. (Daniel Stevenson) Meth. R. **56**: 384.
— in the United States. (T. B. Neely) Meth. R. **56**: 213.
— — Bishops of, Terms of Service of. (T. H. Pearne) M. Chr. Lit. **6**: 64.
— Itinerants' Club of. (J. H. Vincent) Meth. R. **53**: 190.
— Journalism in. (T. L. Flood) Chaut. **20**: 313.
— Men and Women in. (W. F. Warren) Meth. R. **54**: 735, 900.
— Ministry in; Removal of the Time-limit. (E. W. Caswell) Meth. R. **54**: 433.
— New England Conference, and what it has done for Education in the South and West. (W. F. Warren) New Eng. M. n. s. **14**: 351.
— Polity of, in Foreign Fields. Meth. R. **56**: 141.
— — Methods and Principles of. (D. G. Downey) Meth. R. **56**: 420.
— Power of Appointment. Meth. R. **56**: 294.
— Wesley's Sunday-service Book for. (T. B. Neely) Meth. R. **53**: 215.
Methodist Laymen. (T. A. Goodwin) Meth. R. **52**: 241.
Methodist Review, Seventy-five Years of. (J. Mudge) Meth. R. **54**: 513.
Metres, English, Development of. (W. Larminie) Contemp. **66**: 717.
Metric System. (J. V. Collins) Educa. **15**: 229. — Nature, **53**: 84. — (H. Spencer) Pop. Sci. Mo. **49**: 186. — (T. C. Mendenhall) Pop. Sci. Mo. **49**: 721. — (W. Le C. Stevens) Science, n. s. **3**: 793. — (F. M. Lyte) Westm. **146**: 397.
— in England. Science, n. s. **2**: 119.
— in the U. S. (E. E. Slosson) Science, n. s. **4**: 59.
— Proposed Legislation in regard to. Science, n. s. **3**: 457.
Metropolitan College of Music. Music, **6**: 381.
Metropolitan Museum of Art. (C. S. Johnson) Munsey, **6**: 145.

Metropolitan Museum of Art. Handbooks. Critic, **28**: 305.
— New Wing of. Critic, **25**: 317.
Metsu, Gabriel. (T. Cole) Cent. **26**: 744.
Metsys, Quentin. *See* Matsys, Quinten.
Metz. All the Year, **71**: 389.
— Siege of. (C. Edwardes) Gent. M. n. s. **52**: 407.
Meuer, A. Josef, with portrait. (A. N. Towne) Nat'l M. (N. Y. '91) **15**: 295.
Meuse, Fortifications on. (E. M. Lloyd) Un. Serv. M. **6**: 24.
Mews, Royal English. (J. Forrest) Eng. Illust. **9**: 479.
Mexican Dancing Girl; a poem. (J. L. R. Burnett) Outing, **23**: 378.
Mexican Heraldry. (Agnes Crane) Science, **20**: 174.
Mexican Village, Feast-day in. (E. W. Deming) Mo. Illust. **4**: 147.
Mexican War, Home Squadron during. (P. S. P. Conner) Un. Serv. (Phila.) **16**: 419, 470.
— Mexican Battle-flags presented to the Historical Society of Pennsylvania. Pennsyl. M. **17**: 185.
— U. S. Cavalry in. (W. B. Lane) Un. Serv. (Phila.) **15**: 482.
— Veterans of, in California. (K. M. Nesfield) Overland, n. s. **26**: 258.
Mexico and its People. (P. H. Bryce) Canad. M. **2**: 435.
— Annexation of. (H. W. Allen) Arena, **9**: 476.
— Archæological Studies in. (A. P. Maudslay) Nature, **54**: 274. — (W. H. Holmes) Am. Antiq. **18**: 137.
— as an Iron-producing Country. (R. T. Hill) Engin. M. **4**: 744.
— as the Cradle of Man's Primitive Traditions. R. of Rs. (N. Y.) **12**: 49.
— Banking Law of, New. Gunton's M. **11**: 351.
— Busy Days of an Idler in. (E. M. Slayden) Cosmopol. **16**: 14.
— Census of. Nat. Geog. M. **7**: 211.
— Drainage Canal, in Plain of. (F. H. Cheesewright) J. Soc. Arts, **44**: 251.
— Early Political Organization of. (B. Moses) Yale R. **4**: 256, 383.
— Education in, What Catholics have done for. (K. Vaughan) Cath. World, **59**: 120.
— Ferry in. (A. D. Stewart) Overland, n. s. **20**: 628.
— Floating Gardens of. (C. H. Coe) Garden & F. **8**: 432.
— Folk-lore of Ancient. (Zelia Nuttall) J. Am. Folk-Lore, **8**: 117.
— Folk-usages of. (J. G. Bourke) J. Am. Folk-Lore, **9**: 81.
— The Free Zone in. (M. Romero) No. Am. **154**: 459.
— The French in, and the Monroe Doctrine. (F. Bancroft) Pol. Sci. Q. **11**: 30.
— Glimpses of. (W. Gilman) Cath. World, **59**: 475.
— Hospitality in. (A. Paterson) Temp. Bar, **105**: 476. Same art. Liv. Age, **206**: 816.
— In Aztec Land awheel. (T. P. Terry) Outing, **23**: 461.
— Industrial Conditions in. (J. Birkinbine) Engin. M. **6**: 633.
— Land of the Noonday Sun. (W. Clark) Arena, **15**: 349-912. **16**: 44.
— Land of the Sun. (F. C. Tiernan) Cath. World, **56**: 531 — **57**: 832.
— Lawsuit in. (W. S. Logan) Am. J. Soc. Sci. **33**: 134.
— Life in, Glimpses of. (H. S. G. Macdonald) Canad. M. **4**: 66.
— Men and Things in. (A. Leigh) Canad. M. **2**: 359.
— Midwinter Travels in. (A. Schachner) Mid-Cont. **6**: 99, 267.
Mexico, Notes of Travel in. (C. G. Pringle) Garden & F. **7**: 152, 162, 172. **8**: 272. **9**: 102.
— of To-day, President Diaz and. (H. W. Allen) R. of Rs. (N. Y.) **6**: 677.
— An Outpost of Civilization. (F. Remington) Harper, **88**: 71.
— Popular Rhymes of. (A. S. Gatschet) J. Am. Folk-Lore, **2**: 48.
— Popular Celebrations in. (Frederick Starr) J. Am. Folk-Lore, **9**: 161.
— Present and Past. (E. J. Howell) J. Soc. Arts, **41**: 181.
— Prospects of. (W. M. O'Dwyer) No. Am. **159**: 120.
— Recent Economic Progress in. (M. Macfie) Westm. **142**: 33.
— Republic of. (A. Inkersley) Chaut. **22**: 3, 131. — (C. Romero) New Eng. M. n. s. **6**: 579.
— Revolutions in, Philosophy of. (M. Romero) No. Am. **162**: 33.
— Supreme Court of. (W. Clark) Green Bag, **8**: 203.
— under President Diaz. (A. de Iturbide) No. Am. **158**: 715. — Pub. Opin. **17**: 217.
— Valley of. Drainage System. (M. Romero) Engin. M. **8**: 597.
— Village Life in. (T. J. Hughes) Chaut. **19**: 3.
— Winter Regatta in. (A. Inkersley) Outing, **23**: 302.
— Women of. (Jeannie A. Marshall) Munsey, **15**: 713.
Mexico, City of, Holy Week in. Lippinc. **57**: 522.
— Strolls about. (S. Baxter) Am. Arch. **35**: 41. **37**: 54-146.
— Topographical and Architectural History of. (A. H. Noll) Am. Arch. **40**: 69 — **43**: 42.
Mexico, Gulf of. Around World, **1**: 33. — All the Year, **75**: 487.
— as a Measure of Isostacy. (W. J. McGee) Am. J. Sci. **144**: 177.
— Density and Temperature of Waters of. (A. Lindenkohl) Science, n. s. **3**: 271.
Meyer, Lothar. (M. M. P. Muir) Nature, **52**: 81.
Meyer, Mrs. Lucy Rider, Interview with. (G. T. B. Davis) Our Day, **16**: 393.
Meynell, Alice. (E. K. Chambers) Bookman, **3**: 516. — (C. Patmore) Fortn. **58**: 761.
— Essays. (E. E. Hale, jr.) Dial (Ch.) **21**: 255. — (C. Patmore) Sat. R. **81**: 593.
— — Two Books of. (G. Meredith) National, **27**: 762. Same art. Liv. Age, **210**: 707.
Meyerheim, Paul. (F. H. Meissner) Art J. **47**: 301.
Meza, Wilson de. (F. Fowler) Q. Illust. **1**: 169.
Mica, and Mica Mines. (C. H. Henderson) Pop. Sci. Mo. **41**: 652.
Mica-peridotite from Kentucky. (J. S. Diller) Am. J. Sci. **144**: 286.
Micas and Chlorites, Experiments on Constitution of. (F. W. Clarke and E. A. Schneider) Am. J. Sci. **143**: 378.
Micawberism, Political. (J. J. Davies) Westm. **143**: 206.
Mice as a Field Pest. Sat. R. **73**: 529.
— — in Southern Scotland. Chamb. J. **69**: 406. — Sat. R. **74**: 164. — Spec. **68**: 766. Same art. Liv. Age, **194**: 250. — Spec. **70**: 449. — (F. A. Fulcher) Westm. **138**: 639.
— of Town and Country. Spec. **77**: 725.
— Waltzing. (E. R. Waite) Nat. Sci. **7**: 101.
Michael and his Lost Angel, Jones's. (E. E. Hale, jr.) Dial (Ch.) **21**: 149.
Michael Angelo. (J. Ross) 19th Cent. **32**: 818. — (H. P. Horne) Fortn. **59**: 54. — Liv. Age, **196**: 94. — Church Q. **35**: 366.
— The "David" of. (L. E. Baxter) M. of Art, **3**: 379, 417.

Michael Angelo, The Lost "Cupid" of. (J. Cartwright) M. of Art, 9: 74.
— Ollivier's. (E. Müntz) Ath. '92, 2: 230.
— Plagiarisms of. (C. Phillips) M. of Art, 12: 257.
— a Sketch. (C. Duncan) M. of Art, 3: 266-296.
— Sonnets. (J. J. Chapman) Bach. of Arts, 1: 175.
— Symonds' Life of. (M. Hewlett) Acad. 42: 415.— Lit. W. (Bost.) 23: 440.—(K. Cox) Nation, 55: 434. —Spec. 69: 961.—(W. Armstrong) Art J. 45: 96. —Portfo. 24: 84.—Ath. '93, 1: 446.—Atlan. 71: 406.—(C. Whibley) M. of Art, 16: 419.
— Three Books on. (M. Hewlett) Acad. 42: 136, 156.
Michael Darcy's Heiress. Chamb. J. 73: 425.
Michel, Claude. *See* Clodion.
Michel, George, the Painter of Montmartre. (V. Vaughan) Cent. 25: 71.
Michel, Louise, with portraits. (W. T. Stead) R. of Rs. (N. Y.) 6: 155.
Michell, John. (J. R. Sutton) Knowl. 15: 188.
Michigan, Archæology of. (H. I. Smith) Am. Antiq. 18: 144.
— Banking Law of. Bank. M. (N. Y.) 46: 45.
— Central, and the Post-glacial Submergence. (E. H. Mudge) Am. J. Sci. 150: 442.
— National Guard. (C. B. Hall) Outing, 24: 75, 156, 310.
— New England in. (E. P. Powell) New Eng. M. n. s. 13: 419.
— Public Schools in, Course of Study, Revision of. (S. MacKibbin) Educa. 12: 538, 606.
— Relations of the Lower Menominee and Lower Marquette Series in Michigan. (H. L. Smyth) Am. J. Sci. 147: 216.
— Schoolmasters' Club, Report of 22d Meeting of, 1894. School R. 2: 373.
— — Report of 25th Meeting of, 1895. (F. W. Kelsey) Educa. R. 11: 81.
— University of, Ethics in. (J. Dewey) Eth. Rec. 2: 145.
— — Popular Education at. (H. C. Adams) Forum, 14: 123.
— The Spirit and Ideals of. (B. A. Hinsdale) Educa. R. 11: 356, 476.
Michigan, Lake, Ancient Outlet of. (W. M. Davis) Pop. Sci. Mo. 46: 217.
Mickiewicz, Adam. (W. R. Morfill) Acad. 48: 334.
Micmacs, Magic and Medicine of. (Stansbury Hogar) J. Am. Folk-Lore, 9: 170.
— Rand's, Legends of. (A. F. Chamberlain) J. Am. Folk-Lore, 7: 163.—(F. Starr) Dial (Ch.) 17: 14.— Sat. R. 77: 101.
Microbe, The, as a Social Leveller. (C. Edson) No. Am. 161: 421.
Microbes as Factors in Society. (L. Capitan) Pop. Sci. Mo. 47: 103.
— Half an Hour with. (Mrs. P. Frankland) Good Words, 35: 266.
— in the Air. (C. M. Aikman) Gent. M. n. s. 54: 146.
— Influence of Heat and Cold upon. (L. Irwell) New Sci. R. 1: 193.
— Sunshine and. (P. Frankland) 19th Cent. 35: 838. Same art. Ecl. M. 123: 72.
Microcephalic Hindu, Skull of. (R. W. Reid) Anthrop. J. 24: 105.
Micrographic Analysis. (W. C. Roberts-Austen) Nature, 52: 367.
Microlite at Rumford, Me., Occurrence of Pollucite, Mangano-Columbite and. (H. W. Foote) Am. J. Sci. 151: 457.
Micronesia. (Isaiah Bray) Overland, n. s. 23: 40.
Micro-organisms and Chemical Change. (P. F. Frankland) Nature, 46: 135.
Micro-organisms of the Soil. (A. Springer) Nature, 46: 576.
— Physiological Function of the Nucleus in. (A. Binet) Open Court, 2: 1343.
— Psychic Life of. (A. Binet) Open Court, 2: 1127-1235.—(G. J. Romanes) Open Court, 3: 1715.
Microscope, Carpenter on, ed. by Dallinger. (E. R. Lankester) Nature, 45: 313.—(H. L. Osborn) Dial (Ch.) 13: 11.
— Contributions of, to the Physical History of the Earth. (T. G. Bonney) Nature, 46: 180.
— Gage on. (W. H. Dallinger) Nature, 46: 440.
— Modern Optics and. (W. H. Dallinger) Nature, 47: 409.
Microscopes, Evolution of. (A. B. Steele) Knowl. 19: 199.
— Unnecessarily Expensive. (H. G. Wells) Sat. R. 82: 277.
Microscopical Study of Living Matter. (C. S. Minot) No. Am. 162: 612.
Microscopy, Forensic. (L. A. Harding) Science, 20: 242.
— Useful Methods in. (E. A. Minchin) Nat. Sci. 3: 112.
'Mid Eternal Snow; a poem. (C. C. Bass) Outing, 29: 231.
Middendorff, Alexander T. von. Nat. Sci. 4: 229.
Middle-aged Woman. (R. B. Hale) New Eng. M. n. s. 13: 471.
Middle Ages, Art in, Spirit of. (B. M. Ranking) Time, 10: 183, 251.
— Art of War in. Macmil. 72: 171.
— Classics of. (J. Leyland) Walford's Antiq. 3: 283.
— Glamour of, and its Antidotes. (D. MacRitchie) Am. Antiq. 18: 87.
— Habits and Customs of. (Lady Cook) Westm. 141: 139. Same art. Ecl. M. 122: 601.
— Mediæval Life in England. (A. F. Sanborn) Lippinc. 56: 793.
— Political Theory of the Early. (A. J. Carlyle) Econ. R. 5: 319, 464.
Middle Classes in England. Sat. R. 74: 651.
Middle Hall; a Sequel to The Dividing Fence. (R. M. Stuart) Harper, 90: 306.
Middle Years, The. (H. James) Scrib. M. 13: 609.
Middleboro, Mass., Religious Analysis of. (W. B. Hale) Forum, 17: 71.
Middlebury College. (C. E. Blake) New Eng. M. n. s. 11: 129.
Middlemen and Parasites. (H. A. Jones) New R. 8: 645. Same art. Ecl. M. 121: 158.
Middleton, Conyers. Westm. 142: 68.
Middleton, Henry, of South Carolina. Missed a Crown. (McD. Furman) Educa. 16: 115.
Middleton, John Henry. (J. S. Cotton) Acad. 49: 514. Ath. '96, 1: 816.
Middleton, Stanley. (C. Adams) Q. Illust. 2: 170.
Middy Hero, A; a story. (A. L. Knight) Eng. Illust. 9: 551.
Midges, Larvæ of Marine and Fresh-water. (G. Swainson) Science. 22: 107.
Midland Counties Art Museum, Nottingham. (E. Bradbury) M. of Art, 5: 65.
— Exhibition of Pictures. (W. G. Beardmore) M. of Art, 2: 55.
— Industrial Art at. M. of Art, 1: 154, 237.
Midnight: New Year's Eve; a poem. Argosy, 59: 46.
Midnight Attack, A. Chamb. J. 73: 349.
Midnight Tryst, A; a story. (C. B. Morgan) Overland, n. s. 19: 196.
Midroï, Subterranean River, Ardèche, France. (P. Raymond) Pop. Sci. Mo. 49: 253.
Midshipmite. (A. E. P. Searing) New Eng. M. n. s. 13: 428.

Midsummer Day; a poem. (J. Davidson) Sat. R. **79**: 697.
Midsummer Madness. (G. Gissing) Eng. Illust. **12**: no. 3, 55.
Midsummer Memory; a poem. (H. M. Burnside) Argosy, **57**: 536.
Midsummer Midnight, A. (B. Matthews) Harper, **88**: 221.
Midsummer Night, A. (B. Kidd) Cent. **29**: 222.
Midsummer Night's Marriage; a story. (J. M. Falkner) National, **27**: 851. Same art. Liv. Age, **211**: 16.
Midwinter Fair. *See* San Francisco.
Migrations of the Nations. (J. B. Bury) Scot. R. **21**: 329.
— of Races of Men. (J. Bryce) Contemp. **62**: 128. Same art. Ecl. M. **119**: 289. Same art. Liv. Age, **194**: 515.
Milan, The Castle at. (J. S. Fiske) Nation, **59**: 117.
— Manners and Customs, early in the 18th Century. Macmil. **72**: 291.
— Student Life in. Sat. R. **74**: 218, 303.
— Working-class Settlements in Mulhouse and. (C. Hancock) Fortn. **62**: 94.
Mildew in Drawing Paper. (W. J. Russell) M. of Art, **19**: 98.
Mildmay, H. Bingham, Sale of Picture Collection of. M. of Art, **11**: 375.
Miles, Gen. Nelson A. (G. E. Pond) McClure, **5**: 562. — (E. Hildane) Mo. Illust. **11**: 183.
— Portraits of. McClure, **5**: 398.
Militarism as a Social Force. (T. H. S. Escott) Time, **2**: 25.
— European, and an Alternative. (C. Roberts) Econ. R. **4**: 87.
— in Education. Fostering the Savage in the Young. (B. O. Flower) Arena, **10**: 422.
— in the Republic. (B. O. Flower) Arena, **10**: 601.
— Socialism and. (R. S. Long) Westm. **146**: 681.
— Spirit of. (A. B. Ronne) Pop. Sci. Mo. **47**: 234.
Military and the Magistrates. (G. Irving) Fortn. **60**: 358.
Military Bands and Kneller Hall. All the Year, **71**: 465.
Military College, Kingston. Canad. M. **4**: 261, 377.
Military Discipline. (J. F. Maurice) Un. Serv. M. **5**: 59, 133.
Military Drill, Ancient. Sat. R. **76**: 379.
— for Boys' Clubs. Char. R. **4**: 235.
— in Schools. Dial (Ch.) **20**: 293. — (W. Graham) Munsey, **15**: 459. — (C. W. Fowler) Educa. R. **11**: 183.
— — For and against. Pub. Opin. **17**: 266.
— in Schools, Colleges, and Churches. (A. H. Love) Am. J. Pol. **5**: 205.
Military Education. Sat. R. **74**: 192.
— in 1893. Sat. R. **76**: 181.
— in Colleges. (J. K. Cree) Educa. **15**: 398, 473.
Military Engineering, Recent Progress in. (J. Mercur) Chaut. **21**: 156.
Military Etiquette, Official and Social. (W. R. Hamilton) Un. Serv. (Phila.) **11**: 407.
Military Lore in an Old College Library. (L. S. A. Herford) Gent. M. n. s. **55**: 283.
Military Manœuvre, A. (K. L. Ashley) Lippinc. **54**: 252.
Military Punishments. (J. Mew) Un. Serv. M. **6**: 196.
Military Schools of the United States. (W. R. Hamilton) Outing, **20**: 330–473.
Military Studies, Modern. Sat. R. **78**: 348.
Military Systems of Europe and America. (W. Ludlow) No. Am. **160**: 72.
Military Training and Discipline, Value of, in Schools. (T. B. Bronson) School R. **2**: 281.
— in Italy. (A. Mosso) Chaut. **18**: 398.
— in the U. S. Is it adequate? (C. W. Larned) Forum, **12**: 783.
Militia, Canadian. (Lt. Col. O'Brien) Canad. M. **2**: 101.
— — Active. (J. H. Woodside) Outing, **19**: 323. **22**: 227, 288.
— — Northwestern Forces. (H. J. Woodside) Outing, **25**: 159.
— — Re-armament of. (C. F. Winter) Canad. M. **5**: 107.
— Connecticut. (W. H. C. Bowen) Outing, **19**: 396, 456. **20**: 60.
— Illinois. (W. R. Hamilton) Outing, **26**: 75, 160, 240.
— Iowa. (A. C. Sharpe) Un. Serv. (Phila.) **9**: 1.
— Maine. (C. B. Hall) Outing, **29**: 77–285.
— Maryland. (H. Hiss) Outing, **20**: 149, 217.
— Massachusetts. (T. F. Edmands) New Eng. M. n. s. **11**: 770.
— — First Corps Cadets, Mass. Vol. Militia. (A. L. Spring) Outing, **23**: 464.
— Michigan. (C. B. Hall) Outing, **24**: 75, 156, 310.
— — National Guard, The New. (F. V. Greene) Cent. **21**: 483.
— Nebraska. (W. R. Hamilton) Outing, **28**: 157.
— Nevada. (W. R. Hamilton) Outing, **27**: 493. **28**: 78.
— New Hampshire. (G. H. Moses) Outing, **27**: 77, 165, 252, 332, 413.
— New Jersey. (W. H. C. Bowen) Outing, **21**: 60–237.
— New York State. (E. E. Hardin) Outing, **25**: 251.
— Ohio. (W. H. C. Bowen) Outing, **21**: 406, 470.
— Pennsylvania, and its Antecedents. (C. A. Booth) Outing, **23**: 73–412.
— South Dakota. (P. Leary, jr.) Outing, **22**: 77, 156.
— U. S. Army and. (J. H. James) Un. Serv. (Phila.) **12**: 365. — (H. R. Brinkerhoff) Un. Serv. (Phila.) **13**: 501.
— Vermont. (W. L. Greenleaf) Un. Serv. (Phila.) **9**: 215.
See also Naval Reserve.
Milk. (C. M. Aikman) Good Words, **37**: 763.
— Absence of Cow's, from Japan. (A. S. Ashmead) Science, **20**: 211.
— and Cream, imported into England. (R. H. Wallace) Chamb. J. **72**: 657.
— and Milk Products in Great Britain, Statistics of. (R. H. Rew) J. Statis. Soc. **55**: 244.
— Boiling. (G. C. Frankland) 19th Cent. **40**: 454.
— Constancy of Bacterial Species in. (H. L. Bolley) Am. Natural. **30**: 184.
— Human, Artificial. (E. Frankland) Nature, **52**: 546.
— Pasteurization of. Sat. R. **82**: 197.
— Pasteurized, for Babes. (L. E. Hogan) Pop. Sci. Mo. **45**: 491.
— Quantity and Quality of. (W. W. Cooke) Science, **22**: 38.
— Sterilized, and the New York Death-rate. (N. Straus) Forum, **18**: 361.
— Sterilizing of. (L. E. Hogan) Lippinc. **49**: 503.
Milk-trees. Chamb. J. **70**: 566.
Milkweed and Dogbane. (E. M. Hardinge) Pop. Sci. Mo. **49**: 684.
Milky Way, The. (J. E. Gore) Gent. M. n. s. **48**: 307. Same art. Liv. Age, **193**: 316. — (Sir R. Ball) Leis. Hour, **44**: 28.
— Dark Lanes of. (E. W. Maunder) Knowl. **18**: 36.
— Distance of Stars in. (C. Easton) Knowl. **18**: 179.

Milky Way, Photographic Nebulosities and Star Clusters of. (E. E. Barnard) Astron. 13: 177.
— Southern, with the Sydney Star Camera. (E. W. Maunder) Knowl. 18: 87.
Milky Way, The; a poem. (W. Bruce) Harper, 87: 265.
Mill, John Stuart. (F. Harrison) 19th Cent. 40: 487.
— and the London and Westminster Review. (C. M. D. Towers) Atlan. 69: 57.
— Ethical Views of. (P. Carus) Open Court, 6: 3186–3210.
Mill of Minnony; a story. All the Year, 75: 60. Same art. Liv. Age, 203: 168.
Mill-girls. (E. Morris) Lippinc. 54: 119.
Millais, Sir John E. Acad. 50: 134. — Art J. 48: 318. — (J. and E. R. Pennell) Fortn. 66: 443. Same art. Ecl. M. 127: 592. — (D. Macleod) Good Words, 37: 693. — (E. R. Pennell) Nation, 63: 156. — (C. Monkhouse) Scrib. M. 20: 659. — Spec. 77: 241. — (S. Beale) Am. Arch. 51: 134. 53: 84. — Ath. '96, 2: 232. — Critic, 29: 123. — (R. R. Wilson) Mo. Illust. 12: 189. — Sat. R. 82: 160, 183, 214. — (M. Dean) Belgra. 90: 33. — With portrait. (G. Campbell) Cosmopol. 14: 273. — (H. S. Wilson) M. of Art, 2: 33. — (M. H. Spielmann) M. of Art, 19: supp. i. — (C. S. Johnson) Munsey, 6: 537. — R. of Rs. (N. Y.) 11: 543.
— and "Once a Week." (G. S. Layard) Good Words, 34: 552.
— Clarissa. Art J. 47: 87.
— House of, at Palace Gate. (J. Oldcastle) M. of Art, 4: 290.
— Isabella Supper, The. (H. Quilter) Univ. R. 3: 145.
Millar, Harold R. (W. Lawler) Idler, 8: 228.
Millard, Evelyn, with portrait. Theatre, 36: 317.
Millard, James Elwin. Acad. 46: 232.
Millbank Prison, Rise and Fall of. (G. R. Vicars) Gent. M. n. s. 50: 492.
Millenialism. (J. F. Pollock) Luth. Q. 26: 11.
Millenniums, Machine-made. (W. J. Lhamon) Our Day, 13: 17.
Miller, Charles Henry. (S. G. W. Benjamin) M. of Art, 7: 94. — (L. H. French) Q. Illust. 2: 54.
Miller, Hugh (the younger). Acad. 49: 40.
Miller, Joaquin. (H. E. Gregory-Flesher) Arena, 12: 86. — (E. B. Sherman) Critic, 29: 20. — (C. W. Stoddard) Overland, n. s. 27: 664. — (H. V. Clarke) Munsey, 9: 308.
— The Building of the City Beautiful. (B. O. Flower) Arena, 9: 553.
— An Hour with. (C. S. Brown) Southern M. 5: 194.
Miller, Olive Thorne, with portrait. Bk. News, 12: 346.
Miller, Samuel F. (W. A. Maury) Jurid. R. 3: 21.
Miller, William, Wood Engraver. Scrib. M. 18: 525.
Miller of Hascombe, The; a story. (W. E. Alexander) Gent. M. n. s. 56: 217.
Miller's Hand; a story. (G. A. Scott) Longm. 20: 54.
Miller's River, Mass. (J. Lee) Outing, 22: 285.
Millet, Jean François. (I. F. Mayo) Leis. Hour, 43: 15. Same art. Ecl. M. 121: 765. — (W. H. Low) McClure, 6: 499. — (D. C. Thomson) M. of Art, 12: 375, 397.
— as an Art Critic. M. of Art, 6: 89.
— Life at Barbizon. (P. Millet) Cent. 25: 908.
— Story of his Early Life. (P. Millet) Cent. 23: 380.
— Work of. Sat. R. 79: 98.
Millet, Madame J. F. (J. Cartwright) Art J. 47: 72.
Milling. (W. C. Edgar) Chaut. 16: 169.
Milling Machine, Economic Possibilities of the. (H. L. Arnold) Engin. M. 9: 65.
Milling Machines. (H. B. Binesse) Cassier, 10: 338.
Million Pound Bank-note. (S. L. Clemens) Cent. 23: 338.
Millionaire, The. (J. R. Vernon) Argosy, 59: 621.
Millionaires, American. Cornh. 74: 159.
— — Public Gifts of. R. of Rs. (N. Y.) 7: 48.
— Foreign. (W. F. Day) Munsey, 8: 661.
— Malady of. Sat. R. 74: 678.
— Socialism for. (G. B. Shaw) Contemp. 69: 204. Same art. Ecl. M. 126: 340. Same art. Liv. Age, 208: 676.
— The Unspeakable. (D. MacG. Means) Nation, 61: 22.
Millom, Cumberland. (S. Barber) Walford's Antiq. 12: 27.
Mills and Factories, Men in. (W. H. Wakeman) Engin. M. 8: 48.
— and Millers. (M. G. Watkins) Gent. M. n. s. 50: 24.
Mills of God, The; a story. (E. Castle) Temp. Bar, 102: 199.
Millward, Jessie, with portrait. Theatre, 37: 241.
Milsand, Joseph, a French Friend of Browning. (Th. Bentzon) Scrib. M. 20: 108.
Milton, John, and Randolph. (F. C. B. Terry and others) Ath. '94, 2: 194, 225, 254.
— as an Educator. (P. Brooks) New Eng. M. n. s. 8: 385.
— Astronomical Science of. (M. Mitchell) Poet-Lore, 6: 313.
— Concordance to, Bradshaw's. Sat. R. 78: 577.
— Descendants of. (J. Bradshaw) Ath. '92, 2: 741.
— His Indebtedness to Vondel. (G. Duflou) Acad. 47: 379.
— in Westminster. Bookworm, 2: 173.
— Local Memories of. (D. Masson) Good Words, 34: 39, 130, 170, 232.
— Lycidas. (C. Fisher) Temp. Bar, 108: 388.
— Macbeth considered by, as the Subject of a Drama. (J. W. Hales) Ecl. M. 118: 230. Same art. Liv. Age, 192: 431.
— Masenius and Lauder. (J. C. H. Flood) Walford's Antiq. 3: 221, 300.
— Prosody of. (R. Bridges) Ath. '94, 1: 372.
— — Bridges on. (E. H. Lewis) School R. 4: 553.
— Theology of. (F. McElresh) Meth. R. 53: 69.
— To Chalfont and Milton's Cottage. All the Year, 72: 414.
— Unknown Portrait of. Walford's Antiq. 2: 1.
Milton's Daughters; a story. (V. de L'Isle Adam) Poet-Lore, 7: 601.
Milwaukee. (C. King) New Eng. M. n. s. 6: 110.
— Public Library and Museum Building. (T. West) Lib. J. 21: 177.
Mimicry. (A. Playfair) Theatre, 30: 15.
— Recent Observations on. (F. E. Beddard) Nat. Sci. 1: 10.
Mimi's Marriage. (G. King) Cent. 23: 493.
Mind and Body. (P. Shorey) Psychol. R. 2: 43.
— — Auto-suggestion and Concentration. (H. Wood) Arena, 12: 136.
— — Münsterberg's Theory of. (C. A. Strong) Philos. R. 1: 179.
— and Evolution. Nat. Sci. 9: 297.
— Are we Products of? (E. Montgomery) Open Court, 1: 423–617.
— Building of a. (S. M. Miller) New Sci. R. 2: 335.
— Duality of. (R. M. Bache) Monist, 1: 362.
— Dynamics of. (H. Wood) Arena, 11: 302.
— Hegel's Philosophy of. (E. B. Tichener) Philos. R. 4: 196.
— Individual, Totality of. (B. F. Underwood) Psych. R. 1: 111.
— Influence of Stomach upon. (W. Nathan) Westm. 146: 185.
— Integration of. (E. Montgomery) Mind, 20: 307.

Mind, Ladd's Philosophy of. (J. E. Creighton) Philos. R. **4**: 427.
— Law of. (C. S. Peirce) Monist, **2**: 533.
— Nature of. (P. Carus) Open Court, **2**: 999.
— Origin of. (P. Carus) Monist, **1**: 69.
— Pace of. Spec. **68**: 230.
— Powers of, Correlation of Physical Powers and. (J. Venn) Monist, **4**: 5.
— Prospective Reference of. (W. M. Urban) Psychol. R. **3**: 73.
— Relation to Body, H. Höffding on. (W. M. Salter) Monist, **1**: 118.
— Sully on. (G. F. Stout) Mind, **17**: 409. — (W. James) Nation, **55**: 285.
— Variety in, Biologic Origin of. (H. Nichols) Am. Natural. **30**: 964.
— What it is. (E. D. Cope) Open Court, **2**: 992.
Mind-building by Sense Development. (S. M. Miller) Educa. **16**: 218.
Mind Cure. (J. L. Hasbrouck) Arena, **8**: 346. — (J. R. Cocke) Arena, **9**: 746. — (J. Fergusson) Canad. M. **6**: 183.
— Has it any Scientific Basis? (H. Wood) New Sci. R. **2**: 85.
— in its Relation to Modern Thought. (H. W. Dresser) Arena, **16**: 131.
Mind-reading. (M. J. Savage) Open Court, **1**: 149.
Mind-study, Laboratory Methods of. (E. W. Scripture) Forum, **17**: 721.
Mindoro, Island of. (J. B. Steere) Am. Natural. **25**: 1041.
Mine Explosion, After a. Chamb. J. **73**: 582.
Mine Laborers in Pennsylvania. (H. Rood) Forum, **14**: 110.
Mine Own Familiar Friend; a story. (C. Burke) Argosy, **62**: 624.
Mine Surveying. (B. H. Brough) J. Soc. Arts, **40**: 798, 809, 822.
Miner, The Law and the. (T. L. Ford) Overland, n. s. **28**: 310.
Mineral Industry, Rothwell's. (J. Douglas) Nation, **63**: 275.
Mineral Kingdom, Individuality in. (H. A. Miers) Nature, **54**: 208.
Mineral Lands in the U. S., Public Ownership of. (G. O. Virtue) J. Pol. Econ. **3**: 185.
Mineral Products, Minor, of the United States. (D. T. Day) Engin. M. **11**: 299, 504.
Mineral Species, Views on. (H. A. Miers) Sci. Prog. **3**: 429.
Mineral Transformations. (H. A. Miers) Sci. Prog. **4**: 273.
Mineralogy, Contributions to. (F. A. Genth) Am. J. Sci. **143**: 184.
— The New. (G. P. Grimsley) Pop. Sci. Mo. **45**: 663.
Minerals, Law of. (M. G. Davidson) Jurid. R. **7**: 341.
— New. Am. Natural. **28**: 59.
— of High Specific Gravity, Devices for the Separation of. (S. L. Penfield) Am. J. Sci. **150**: 446.
Miners, Coal, in Pennsylvania. Adopted Home of the Huns. (W. F. Gibbons) Am. M. Civics, **7**: 315.
— Congress of, 1892. Sat. R. **73**: 675.
— in the German Harz, Life of. (J. G. Brooks) Q. J. Econ. **6**: 474.
— Pits and. (J. Pendleton) Time, **19**: 257.
— Tennessee, Revolt of, 1892. Pub. Opin. **13**: 489.
Miners' Vengeance, The. (S. S. Boynton) Overland, n. s. **22**: 303.
Minerva Press, The Old. Bookworm, **1**: 388.
Minerva's Mother; a story. (Annie G. Gale) Overland, n. s. **20**: 377.
Mines, American, English Money in. Westm. **142**: 268.
Mines and Miners, English. (S. P. Cadman) Chaut. **19**: 606.
— Eight Hours for. (W. T. Thomson) Westm. **141**: 593.
— English Practice in Transmitting Power in. Engin. M. **12**: 470.
— Explosions in. Nature, **51**: 211.
— Lost. (A. Williams, jr.) Chaut. **17**: 692.
— Management and Superintendence of. (C. Johnson) Engin. M. **8**: 1032.
— Nationalization of. (H. H. L. Bellot) Westm. **141**: 117.
Reports on, and Mine Salting. (W. McDermott) Engin. M. **9**: 311.
Miniature, The; a story. (A. Leach) Munsey, **12**: 349.
Miniature Painting, English School of. (J. L. Propert) M. of Art, **14**: 7-345.
— in England. (J. J. Foster) Art J. **48**: 101-365.
— Modern. (J. C. Harvey) Munsey, **12**: 295.
— Painters in Little. (N. H. Banks) Cosmopol. **19**: 598.
Mining, American, in 1891. (A. Williams, jr.) Engin. M. **2**: 608.
— Electricity in. (F. O. Blackwell) Cassier, **5**: 249.
— Perils of. (A. Williams, jr.) Chaut. **18**: 429, 556.
— Placer, in South America. (O. F. Pfordte) Cassier, **10**: 62.
— Profits of, and the Cost of Silver. (J. D. Hague) Forum, **15**: 60.
— The Prospector. (B. R. Atkins) Canad. M. **5**: 66.
— Scientific Phases of. (A. Williams, jr.) Chaut. **17**: 29.
Mining Industry at the World's Fair. (R. W. Raymond) Engin. M. **6**: 489.
Mining Law, American. (W. C. Wynkoop) Engin. M. **8**: 62.
Mining Life in So. Africa. (G. Halle) So. M. **3**: 267.
Mining School, Practical Work at. (E. S. Cranson) Engin. M. **3**: 379.
Minister, Christian, and Sociology. (J. R. Commons) Lend a H. **8**: 117. — (J. H. Vincent) M. Chr. Lit. **6**: 67.
— How to become a Better. (G. C. Henry) Luth. Q. **25**: 385.
— Mediating Function of. (P. S. Moxom) And. R. **77**: 1.
— Place of, in Politics. (Canon Barker and others) M. Chr. Lit. **5**: 360.
— Training of. (T. F. Wright) N. Church R. **3**: 427.
Ministerial Blues. (J. Love, jr.) Bapt. R. **14**: 150.
Ministerial Retreats. Meth. R. **56**: 312.
Ministerialists and Unionists. Blackw. **157**: 807.
Minister's Business Day, A Queen's. Cosmopol. **22**: 87.
Minister's Children: Character Sketches. Our Day, **16**: 459.
Minister's Dog, The. (Maarten Maartens) Good Words, **35**: Xmas no., 1.
Minister's Money. (W. J. Lacey) Longm. **21**: 314.
Ministers, Her Majesty's. (M. MacDonagh) Chamb. J. **73**: 372.
— Prime, of Queen Victoria. (R. B. Brett) 19th Cent. **37**: 32.
Ministry, Christian. Its Present Claim and Attraction. (F. C. Pease) And. R. **19**: 649.
— and Current Social Problems. (E. D. Weigle) Luth. Q. **24**: 467.
— Compensations of the. (W. Hull) Luth. Q. **24**: 538.
— Educated, Plea for. (W. M. B. Glauding) Luth. Q. **23**: 258.
— Gregory's Christ's Trumpet Call to the. (G. T. B. Davis) Our Day, **16**: 487.
— in New England. (E. E. Hale) Lend a H. **9**: 412.
— Literature and. (L. W. Spring) Atlan. **69**: 546.

Ministry, Primary Qualifications for. (D. N. Beach) And. R. 19: 288.
Minneapolis. (J. Ralph) Harper, 84: 576.
— Republican Convention at, 1892. (M. Halstead) Cosmopol. 13: 507.
Minnehaha. (E. W. McGlasson) Scrib. M. 16: 763.
Minnesota, Northern. Through Darkest America. (T. White) Outing, 21: 3-461.
— Sketch in. All the Year, 73: 610.
— Supreme Court of. (C. B. Elliott) Green Bag, 4: 110, 161.
Minnie-Wah-Wah. (W. A. Jones) Overland, n. s. 23: 195.
Minor, John Barbee, with portrait. (T. J. Michie) Green Bag, 7: 400.
Minor Chord, Acoustic Relations of. (J. C. Fillmore) Music, 1: 119.
— Art, not Nature, Responsible for. (H. A. Clarke) Music, 1: 395.
Minor Mode, Value and Application of the. (E. von Adelung) Music, 4: 372.
Minorca. Chamb. J. 70: 401. Same art. Liv. Age, 198: 572.
— English Occupations of. Temp. Bar, 106: 465.
Minorcans; Philosophers Afloat. (H. H. Gardener) Arena, 19: 480.
Minority, Filibustering, How to deal with a. (J. B. McMaster) Forum, 16: 470.
Minot's Ledge; Life in a Lighthouse. (G. Kobbé) Cent. 25: 364.
— Lighthouse, Building of. (C. A. Lawrence) New Eng. M. n. s. 15: 131.
Minstrels, Irish, and Minstrelsy. (D. Spillane) Cath. World, 55: 496.
— Wandering. (J. F. Rowbotham) Good Words, 35: 30.
Mint at London Tower. Gent. M. n. s. 54: 304.
Minto, William. (J. S. Cotton) Acad. 43: 221.
Miocene, Chattahoochee, and Vicksburg Eocene. (A. F. Foerste) Am. J. Sci. 148: 41.
— in S. W. Georgia, Apparent Time-break between the Eocene and Chattahooche. (R. Pumpelly) Am. J. Sci. 146: 445.
Miocene Mammal, New. (O. C. Marsh) Am. J. Sci. 147: 409.
Miocene Mammalia, Description of. (O. C. Marsh) Am. J. Sci. 146: 407.
Miocene Man, Alleged, in Burma. (R. D. Oldham) Nat. Sci. 7: 201.
Miohippus Beds, Eastern Division of, with Notes on some of the Characteristic Fossils. (O. C. Marsh) Am. J. Sci. 148: 91.
Minxes, French and English. (L. B. Lang) Longm. 29: 131. Same art. Liv. Age, 211: 871.
Mira, Variable Star. (J. A. Parkhurst) Pop. Astron. 3: 165.
Mirabeau. Temp. Bar, 94: 84. Same art. Liv. Age, 192: 579.
— Life of, Mézières. Spec. 68: 236, 271.
— Recent French Works on. (H. M. Stephens) Eng. Hist. R. 7: 587.
Miracle. (C. K. Paul) Month, 76: 217.
Miracle, A; a story. (M. E. M. Davis) Harper, 91: 38.
Miracle Chapel, The. (G. King) Cent. 23: 497.
Miracle Play of the Rio Grande. (J. G. Bourke) J. Am. Folk-Lore, 6: 89.
— Persian. (M. Pechell) Belgra. 91: 209. Same art. Liv. Age, 211: 370.
Miracles and Christian Faith. (J. E. Russell) New World, 5: 9.
— Biblical. (A. H. Huizinga) Bib. Sac. 49: 129.
— Evidential Value of. (M. L. Young) Luth. Q. 22: 429.
Miracles in French Canada. (E. Farrer) Pop. Sci. Mo. 48: 234.
— in Religion. (C. P. Wooley) Open Court, 8: 4024.
— in the Synoptic Gospels. (A. Réville) New World, 4: 626.
— Indicative of Superhuman Power. (C. H. Drew) New Church R. 1: 245.
— Mediæval. All the Year, 70: 180.
— Modern. (E. P. Evans) Pop. Sci. Mo. 43: 192.
Miraculous Explorer, The; a story. (G. Allen) Eng. Illust. 12: no. 3, 99.
Mirage in Western Canada. (T. Flesher) Canad. M. 2: 34.
Miramar, Castle of. All the Year, 70: 497. Same art. Liv. Age, 194: 509.
Mirror-gazing Superstition, Scientific Analysis of. (M. Dessoir) Monist, 1: 87.
Mirror-reading. All the Year, 70: 79.
Mirrors, Ancient and Modern. Chamb. J. 72: 122.
— Glass, Silvering. (A. A. Common) Astron. 11: 859.
— Magic, Japanese. Dub. R. 113: 655.
— Note on. Atlan. 73: 572.
Mirth, A School for. Macmil. 66: 357.
Mis' Pettigrew's Silver Tea-set. (J. Spencer) Lippinc. 57: 384.
Misadventures of an American Princess; a story. (C. L. Strong) Temp. Bar, 108: 124.
Misdemeanor of Pamela Rosevear. (L. Quiller Couch) Idler, 7: 81.
Miser Morgan. (W. E. Norris) Longm. 27: 371. Same art. Liv. Age, 208: 467.
Misericordia of Florence. (M. Zucchi) Dub. R. 114: 333.
Miserly Spendthrift. (M. B. O'Reilly) New Eng. M. n. s. 14: 375.
Miserrimus-stone, The; a poem. (C. Burke) Argosy, 61: 127.
Miser's Doom; a Modern Greek Morality. (J. L. Myers) Anthrop. J. 25: 102.
Miser's Secret, The; a story. (E. Yolland) Belgra. 79: 383. Same art. Liv. Age, 196: 365.
Misers, About. Chamb. J. 69: 604.
Misoneism. (C. Lombroso) Monist, 1: 344.
Miss Agatha. Chamb. J. 71: 252.
Miss Anne; a sketch. (K. Carr) Argosy, 56: 242.
Miss Carruthers's Partner; a story. (A. J. Halliday) Outing, 22: 60.
Miss Dangerlie's Roses. (T. N. Page) Scrib. M. 12: 650.
Miss de Maupassant; a story. (C. E. Raimond) New R. 13: 233. Same art. Ecl. M. 125: 547.
Miss Delamar's Understudy. (R. H. Davis) Scrib. M. 18: 183.
Miss Falkines; a story. (L. Butt) Belgra. 86: 405.
Miss Featherly's Cup of Tea; a story. (H. F. Kimball) Lend a H. 9: 328.
Miss Garth; a story. All the Year, 74: 117-211.
Miss Gwynne's Burglar; a story. (V. E. Mitchell) Outing, 23: 13.
Miss Helen; a story. (Vivian Brooke) Chamb. J. 70: 414.
Miss Latimer of Bryans; a story. (E. C. Price) All the Year, 70: 577, 601. 71: 1-625. 72: 19-162.
Miss Latymer; a story. (G. A. Hibbard) Scrib. M. 12: 731.
Miss Liz'beth; a story. (Z. A. Norris) Bost. 4: 394.
Miss Maloney's Public House; a story. (B. Atkinson) Good Words, 33: 172.
Miss Maria's Revival; a story. (S. B. Elliott) Harper, 93: 461.

Miss Methuen's Masterpiece; a story. All the Year, **70**: 439, 469.
Miss Miffin's Crime. (Mary L. Pendered) Idler, **7**: 33.
Miss or Mrs.? Westm. **145**: 454.
Miss Peekskill's Spirometer; a story. (J. Hawthorne) Eng. Illust. **16**: 344.
Miss Penrose; a story. (M. Holland) Argosy, **61**: 671.
Miss Polly Lopp; a story. (O. Read) Eng. Illust. **12**: no. 5, 69.
Miss Royston's Gloves; a story. (R. H. Savage) Cosmopol. **16**: 352.
Miss Stuart's Legacy. (F. A. Steel) Macmil. **67**: 241 — **68**: 458.
Miss Thankful's Love Affair. (K. W. Patch) Nat'l M. (Bost.) **4**: 522.
Miss Theodora. (H. L. Reed) New Eng. M. n. s. **12**: 656. **13**: 21–273.
Miss Tom and Peepsie. (A. M. Elwell) Atlan. **71**: 489.
Missals, Venetian. (H. P. Horne) Fortn. **62**: 711.
Missed and Won; a story. (S. Dawson) Belgra. **82**: 154.
Missing Evidence in "The People *vs.* Dangering." (W. H. Sullivan) Scrib. M. **16**: 199.
Missing Interpreter; a story. (H. D. Ward) Atlan. **69**: 87.
Missing Link, The. (W. Hart) New Sci. R. **2**: 99. — (Thos. Tyler) Time, **8**: 476.
— Eugene Dubois on. Nature, **53**: 115.
Missing the Prize of Life. (J. Watson) Sund. M. **25**: 317.
Missing Word Competitions. Spec. **69**: 818, 881.
Mission, Catholic, in Canton. (E. A. Irving) Blackw. **158**: 555.
— German Inner, Rise of. (C. R. Henderson) Am. J. Sociol. **1**: 583, 676. **2**: 58.
— Scotch, at Blantyre. Dub. R. **110**: 191.
Mission in Life, A; a story. (Mrs. E. Cartwright) Belgra. **88**: 277.
Mission Enterprise, A Century of. (G. Smith) Sund. M. **21**: 693.
Mission Indians, Decline of the. (J. M. Scanland) Overland, n. s. **24**: 634. — (E. P. Clark) Overland, n. s. **25**: 89.
Mission Legend; a story. (J. C. Bull) Munsey, **13**: 424.
Mission Music and Musicians. (J. J. Peatfield) Overland, n. s. **25**: 348.
Missionaries, Christian, in India. Are they Frauds? (J. H. Mueller) Arena, **16**: 806.
— Early Spirit of. (S. B. Hedges) Cath. World, **58**: 794.
— French, and the French Government. Spec. **70**: 664.
— Heroism of. (A. R. Buckland) Sund. M. **22**: 231, 775, 822.
— in Algeria. Sat. R. **74**: 39.
— in China. (R. S. Gundry) Fortn. **60**: 240. — Macmil. **73**: 10. Same art. Ecl. M. **126**: 26.
— in India, Decennial Conference of. (J. Aberly) Luth. Q. **23**: 235.
— Misleaders of. (G. F. Pentecost) Our Day, **12**: 69.
Missionary, Modern, in China. (F. H. Balfour) Asia. R. **9**: 12.
— Qualifications of a. (H. K. Fenner) Luth. Q. **25**: 82.
Missionary Farm in Borneo, A Model. (E. M. Clerke) Dub. R. **114**: 294.
Missionary Methods, Cust on. Sat. R. **79**: 161.
Missionary Ridge, An Idler on. (B. Torrey) Atlan. **76**: 807.
Missionary Sheriff, The: a story. (O. Thanet) Harper, **92**: 773.
Missionary Spirit in the Home Churches. (D. H. Bauslin) Luth. Q. **25**: 1.
Missionary Temptations. (R. Ogden) Nation, **61**: 360.
Missionary's Story, The. (J. G. Vibert) Cent. **29**: 82.
Missions. Eng. R. **2**: 137. **7**: 42.
— and Civilization. (C. C. Starbuck) And. R. **17**: 496. **18**: 58. **19**: 167.
— and Colonies. (C. C. Starbuck) And. R. **19**: 428, 681.
— and Diplomacy. (S. G. W. Benjamin) M. Chr. Lit. **7**: 193.
— and Missionaries, Misrepresentations of. (H. K. Carroll) Meth. R. **56**: 273.
— and Political Science. (H. W. Hulbert) Presb. & Ref. R. **5**: 254.
— and Reformed Protestantism. (N. M. Steffens) Presb. & Ref. R. **5**: 241.
— Around the World for Christ. (G. T. B. Davis) Our Day, **16**: 607.
— as seen at the Parliament of Religions. (H. R. Bender) Meth. R. **55**: 907.
— as seen by a Brahman. (P. R. Telang) Forum, **18**: 481.
— as seen by a Missionary. (J. M. Thoburn) Forum, **18**: 490.
— Christian. Monist, **5**: 264.
— Church, Progress and Prospects of. Quar. **178**: 52.
— Comparative Religion and. (A. Menzies) Chr. Lit. **12**: 335.
— Debate on. (J. M. Thoburn; V. R. Gandhi; P. Carus) Monist, **5**: 264.
— English, Birthday of. (W. G. Blakie) Sund. M. **21**: 373.
— English Protestant Missionaries and West Africa. (Mary H. Kingsley) National, **27**: 66.
— Failures of, Non-Christian View of. Asia. R. **10**: 300.
— The Heroic in. (A. R. Buckland) Sund. M. **21**: 778, 831.
— Hindrances in, and their Remedies. (F. F. Ellinwood) Presb. & Ref. R. **7**: 193.
— Home Relation to. (P. S. Moxom) M. Chr. Lit. **6**: 452.
— Hymns of. (J. H. Ross) Our Day, **12**: 210.
— in Central Africa: Hore's Tanganyika. Spec. **69**: 454.
— in India. (D. L. Leonard) Bib. Sac. **51**: 298. — (V. R. Gandhi) Arena, **11**: 157.
— — Effect of Parliament of Religions on. (H. H. Jessup) Our Day, **14**: 98.
— — Hunter on. Sat. R. **80**: 444.
— — Portuguese. (G. T. Mackenzie) Dub. R. **112**: 27.
— — Success of. (F. P. Powers) Forum, **17**: 475.
— — Why they have failed. (V. R. Gandhi) Forum, **17**: 160.
— in the Light of Fact. (Judson Smith) No. Am. **162**: 21.
— in the Turkish Empire, Problems of. (C. C. Starbuck) And. R. **17**: 23.
— incentives to Activity in. (P. C. Croll) Luth. Q. **24**: 260.
— Modern, Genesis of. (J. A. Singmaster) Luth. Q. **22**: 117.
— Native Agents in, and their Training. (J. S. Dennis) M. Chr. Lit. **7**: 137.
— New Style. (R. Ogden) Nation, **61**: 235.
— Peerlessness of. (J. Cook) Our Day, **13**: 448.
— Protestant, before 1792. (C. C. Starbuck) And. R. **18**: 478.
— Question of. Pub. Opin. **19**: 274.
— Roman Catholic. (E. D. Weage) Bib. Sac. **51**: 45.
— — in Africa. (J. T. Murphy) Am. Cath. Q. **21**: 576.

Missions, Roman Catholic, in Canada. (E. S. Colcleugh) Cath. World, 61: 108.
— Study of, in Theological Seminaries. Meth. R. 56: 318.
— Within and Without Christendom. (C. C. Starbuck) And. R. 17: 277.
Mississagua Indians. (A. F. Chamberlain) J. Am. Folk-Lore, 1: 150.
— Legend of Nānībōjū. (A. F. Chamberlain) J. Am. Folk-Lore, 5: 291.
— Tales of. (A. F. Chamberlain) J. Am. Folk-Lore, 2: 141. 3: 149.
Mississippi, In Sunny. (J. Ralph) Harper, 90: 819.
Mississippi Basin, Upper, in the Glacial Period. (J. D. Dana) Pop. Sci. Mo. 44: 816.
— Winsor's. (E. Coues) Nation, 61: 67. — (B. A. Hinsdale) Dial (Ch.) 19: 110.
Mississippi River, Bank Revetment on the. (H. St. L. Coppée) Engin. M. 11: 486.
— Hydrology of. (J. L. Greenleaf) Am. J. Sci. 152: 29.
— Levees and Fascine Training. Nature, 55: 156.
— Old Way to Dixie. (J. Ralph) Harper, 86: 165.
— Problem of. Engin. M. 3: 387. — (C. N. Dutton; H. S. L. Coppée) Engin. M. 3: 623. — (W. Starling) Engin. M. 4: 247.
— — Geology and. Engin. M. 4: 536.
— Territory West of. (W. A. Wood) M. Am. Hist. 27: 298.
— Upper, Basin of, New England and, in the Glacial Period. (J. D. Dana) Am. J. Sci. 146: 327.
Mississippi Roustabout. (S. Cooley) New Eng. M. n. s. 11: 290.
Missouri, Lawyers of, Group of Giant. (J. Doniphan) M. Am. Hist. 27: 213.
— North, Devonian of. (G. C. Broadhead) Am. J. Sci. 152: 237.
— Yarns of. (W. A. Wood) Green Bag, 4: 84, 174.
Missourite, a New Leucite Rock from the Highwood Mountains of Montana. (W. H. Weed and L. V. Pirsson) Am. J. Sci. 152: 315.
Missus and I; a poem. (A. Broderick) Gent. M. n. s. 53: 95.
Mistaken Souls. (F. Hall) Nation, 56: 122.
Mistassini, Lake, and James's Bay. (A. H. D. Ross) Canad. M. 3: 573.
Mistletoe. Ecl. M. 118: 116. Same art. Liv. Age, 192: 421.
— and Mistle Thrush. (G. W. Murdoch) Knowl. 18: 284.
— in Medicine. Bookworm, 7: 358.
Mistral, Frédéric. (M. L. Elmendorf) Poet-Lore, 2: 401, 449.
Mistress Marion; a Story of the Revolution. (F. S. Williams) Outing, 23: 179.
Mistress of Brae Farm; a novel. (R. N. Cary) Argosy, 61: 1-641. 62: 1-641.
Mistress of the Foundry; a story. (E. Joslyn) McClure, 3: 261.
Mistress of Pascesla Post Office, The. (S. A. Ranlett) Bost. 3: 437.
Mistress Sarah's Romance. All the Year, 73: 540.
Mistress Sherwood's Victory. (E. L. Ogden) New Eng. M. n. s. 12: 338.
Misunderstanding, A; a poem. (C. Burke) Argosy, 58: 568.
Misunderstanding, A; a story. (C. Edwardes) Chamb. J. 70: 284.
Misunderstandings. Cornh. 71: 158.
Mitchell, D. G., with portrait. Bk. Buyer, 3: 303. — With portrait. Bk. News, 11: 380.
Mitchell, John A., with portrait. Bk. Buyer, 13: 134.
Mitchell, John T. W. (A. Williams) Econ. J. 5: 306.
Mitchell, Langdon Elwyn. Deborah; a play. Theatre, 28: 202.
Mitchell, Maria, with portrait. Bk. News, 14: 536.
— Kendall's Life. (C. L. Franklin) Nation, 63: 235.
Mitchell, S. Weir, with portrait. Bk. News, 6: 54.
Mitchells, The; a Brunette Darby and Joan. (Helen M. Carpenter) Overland, n. s. 26: 292.
Mitford, Mary Russell, Extracts from Letters of. Longm. 24: 159.
— In the Country of. Eng. Illust. 14: 515.
— Our Village. (S. M. S. Pereira) Good Words, 35: 455.
— Some Letters from. (Margaret Howitt) Good Words, 36: 377.
Mithraism. (J. M. Robertson) Time, 20: 405.
Mithras, Unconquered. (T. H. B. Graham) Gent. M. n. s. 55: 58. Same art. Liv. Age, 206: 306.
Mitla, Ruins of. (E. Steger) Southern M. 4: 590.
Mitylene, In, with the Late Sir Charles Newton. Blackw. 157: 596. Same art. Liv. Age, 205: 477.
Mivart, St. George, Action of the Holy Office in the Case of. (W. R. Sullivan) Westm. 140: 489.
— Essays. (M. Mead) Dial (Ch.) 13: 143.
— on the Ethical Motive. (H. Spencer) 19th Cent. 38: 536.
— Sectarian Criticism. (K. Pearson) Fortn. 64: 674.
Miyajima: an Island without Death. (E. R. Scidmore) Cent. 30: 483.
Mizon, Lieut., and the Royal Niger Company. Spec. 69: 152.
Moas of New Zealand. (H. O. Forbes) Nat. Sci. 2: 374.
— History of. (R. Lyddeker) Nat. Sci. 1: 588.
Mob, Study of the. (B. Sidis) Atlan. 75: 188.
Mob Law. (Duane Mowry) Am. M. Civics, 8: 62.
Mobs. Blackw. 153: 109. Same art. Liv. Age, 196: 451.
— and Lynching. (G. C. Holt) Am. J. Soc. Sci. 32: 67.
— Human Aggregation and Crime. (G. Tarde) Pop. Sci. Mo. 45: 447.
— Mental and Moral Character of. (C. H. d'E. Leppington) National, 20: 578.
— A Study of. (C. Lombroso) Chaut. 15: 314.
Mobile, Battle of. (D. H. Maury) Southern M. 4: 523. — (D. B. Conrad) Un. Serv. (Phila.) 8: 261.
Mocking-bird, The. (M. Thompson) Cosmopol. 14: 193. — (Z. Cocke) New Eng. M. n. s. 8: 572.
— Southern. (J. W. Blake) Pop. Sci. Mo. 49: 258.
— Why it left New Jersey; a Geological Reason. (S. Lockwood) Am. Natural. 26: 635.
Model Crime, A; a story. (W. P. Ridge) McClure, 7: 478.
Models, Artist's. (G. Holme) Munsey, 10: 527.
— — Girls trained for. (A. D. Vandam) Sat. R. 80: 649.
— Beautiful, of Paris. (F. T. Sisson) Cosmopol. 18: 529.
— in Photographic Art. (A. Van B. Berg) Cosmopol. 21: 22.
— Men and Women as. (Dutton Cook) Time, 2: 119.
— Some Types of Artists'. (Katharine Pyle) Cosmopol. 21: 14.
Moderation. (A. H. Japp) Argosy, 56: 168. — (E. M. Thomas) Atlan. 75: 217.
Modern Cinderella. (M. Hunt) Longm. 22: 438.
Modern Day Saint, A; a story. Belgra. 85: 279.
Modern Fairy Tale; a story. (T. C. Crawford) Cosmopol. 21: 606. 22: 39, 151.

Modern Genie; a story. (B. Gwynfe) Argosy, **57**: 507.
Modern Hero, A. Temp. Bar, **103**: 145, 409.
Modern Knight, A; a story. (G. Thow) Idler, **9**: 350.
Modern Language Association Meeting, 1896. Critic, **28**: 64.
— Pedagogical Section of. (E. H. Babbitt) Educa. R. **7**: 188.
Modern Languages, Educational Value of. (H. K. Schilling) Educa. R. **9**: 385.
— Teaching of. Dial (Ch.) **16**: 129.
— — in Secondary Schools. (W. M. Payne) School R. **2**: 74.
Modern Latchkey, A; a story. Argosy, **60**: 491.
Modern Lear, A. (E. Wetherald) New Eng. M. n. s. **6**: 603.
Modern Life and the Artistic Sense. (W. Crane) Cosmopol. **13**: 152.
— and Sedatives. (T. Robinson) National, **19**: 723.
— from the Spanish. (R. Navarette) Liv. Age, **211**: 604.
Modern Magician, A; a story. (H. Pyle) Cosmopol. **17**: 461.
Modern Odyssey; or, Ulysses up to date. Spec. **68**: 305.
Modern Samson, A; a story. (R. Barr) Eng. Illust. **11**: 191.
Modern Sindbad, A. Macmil. **74**: 187.
Modern Vengeance. (D. Prescott) New Eng. M. n. s. **9**: 601.
Modoc Songs. Pop. Sci. Mo. **47**: 569.
Modoc War, 1872–73. (James Jackson) Un. Serv. (Phila.) **8**: 1.
Modjeska, Helena, as Lady Macbeth. Poet-Lore, **4**: 42.
— Farewell Performances. (A. Brownell) Bost. **3**: 472.
Moeller, Louis. (F. W. Ruckstuhl) Q. Illust. **2**: 347.
Moeran's Moose; a hunting story. (E. W. Sandys) Outing, **20**: 419.
Mogul, Great, Legend of the. (E. A. Richings) Belgra. **80**: 180.
Mogul Empire, Travels in. Quar. **176**: 490.
Mohammed and the Koran. (J. T. Bixby) Arena, **12**: 17.
— Life and Teaching of. Quar. **182**: 220.
— Passing of. (E. Arnold) Cent. **27**: 584.
Mohammed Play in England. Asia. R. **11**: 195.
Mohammedan Fanaticism. Spec. **76**: 836.
Mohammedan Literature of the Day. Bookworm, **3**: 257.
Mohammedan Marriage and Life. (A. N. Jannaris) Arena, **51**: 60.
Mohammedan Peoples, Future of. Spec. **77**: 508.
Mohammedan States, England in Relation to. (R. Ahmad) National, **21**: 187.
Mohammedanism. (G. W. Leitner) Time, **21**: 101.
— Christianity and. (G. Washburn) Contemp. **64**: 654. Same art. Ecl. M. **121**: 746. — (F. M. Müller) 19th Cent. **35**: 302. Same art. Ecl. M. **122**: 468. — (B. F. Kidder) Meth. R. **56**: 528.
— Future of. (T. Davidson) Forum, **22**: 152.
— in Bengal. Spec. **71**: 541.
— in Defence of Islâm. (Rafiuddin Ahmad) Fortn. **65**: 165.
— Islam and its Critics. (A Quarterly Reviewer) Fortn. **64**: 621.
— A Mohammedan on. (D. F. Hannigan) Westm. **138**: 8.
— Outlook for. (D. L. Leonard) Bib. Sac. **51**: 660.
— Pool's Studies in. Spec. **69**: 167.
Mohammedanism, Sketch of, with Bibliography. (T. W. Davies) Bib. World, **8**: 337.
— Some Fallacies about Islam. (M. MacColl) Fortn. **65**: 613.
— The Sultan and his Priests. (R. Davey) Fortn. **65**: 1.
See also Islâm.
Mohammedans, can they be Friendly with Non-Mohammedans? (Mushtak Hussain) Asia. R. **10**: 136.
— of the East. (J. F. Hewitt) Westm. **143**: 253.
Moharrem Festival in Natal. (J. Meldrum) Good Words, **36**: 232.
Mohawk Indians, Church of. Sund. M. **21**: 546.
— Folk-Lore of. (W. M. Beauchamp) J. Am. Folk-Lore, **8**: 217.
Mohegans, The; an Historical Sketch of the Tribe. (H. A. Baker) Bost. **1**: 369, 503, 671.
Mohican's Derby; a story. (L. Springfield) Idler, **5**: 540.
Mohl, Mary, Madame. Blackw. **154**: 41. Same art. Liv. Age, **199**: 45.
Mohonk Conferences. (F. C. Sparhawk) Am. M. Civics, **6**: 206.
— Indian Conference, 1893. Lend a H. **11**: 323.
— — 1895. Lit. W. (Bost.) **26**: 350.
Mohonk Platform, The. Lend a H. **13**: 372.
Moisture in the Soil, Conservation of. (C. S. Sargent) Garden & F. **9**: 401.
Mojave Desert, Miners' Homes in the. (J. R. Spears) Chaut. **18**: 713.
Mojave Indians, Cosmogony and Theogony of. (J. G. Bourke) J. Am. Folk-Lore, **2**: 169.
Molding, by Machinery. (H. Tabor) Cassier, **2**: 197.
Molecular Physics, Recent Work on. (R. A. Fessenden) J. Frankl. Inst. **142**: 187.
Molecular Vibrations, New Law connecting. (A. Schuster) Nature, **55**: 200.
Molecules, Color Relations of Atoms, Ions, and. (M. C. Lea) Am. J. Sci. **149**: 327. **151**: 405.
Moles. (R. Lydekker) Knowl. **16**: 81.
— Australian Marsupial. (E. Trouessart) Pop. Sci. Mo. **40**: 650.
— the First Engineers. Cornh. **68**: 259.
Moleschott, Jacob, with portrait. (E. P. Evans) Pop. Sci. Mo. **49**: 399.
Molière, J. B. P. de. (E. Duvall) Lippinc. **56**: 391.
— as Dramatist. (H. D. Lawhead) Poet-Lore, **8**: 197.
— Last Appearance of; a poem. (Nellie K. Blissett) Temp. Bar, **104**: 185.
— L'Avare. (J. C. Bracq) Chaut. **24**: 158.
— Les Femmes Savantes. (A. Fortier) Chaut. **24**: 145.
— Le Tartuffe. (H. M. Trollope) Blackw. **154**: 641.
— Life of. (J. A. Harrison) Chaut. **24**: 154.
— on the Stage. (A. De Ternant) Gent. M. n. s. **54**: 252.
— Six Phases of Life of. (J. Coleman) Theatre, **31**: 98–315.
— Survival of Plays of. (F. Fyles) Chaut. **24**: 139.
— Women Characters of. (M. Merington) Chaut. **24**: 150.
Moll Cutpurse, the Queen of Thieves. Macmil. **72**: 407.
Mollie Ahearne; a story. All the Year, **76**: 62.
Mollien, Count. Memoirs. Temp. Bar, **101**: 76. Same art. Liv. Age, **200**: 411.
Mollusca, Archetype of. (A. E. Verrill) Am. J. Sci. **152**: 91.
— Collecting of. (W. H. Dall) Nature, **47**: 140.
— from Northwestern Louisiana, and Harrison County, Texas. (T. W. Vaughan) Am. Natural. **27**: 944.
— from Pampean Formation. (H. v. Ihering) Science, n. s. **1**: 421.

Mollusca, Geographical Distribution of. (F. C. Baker) Science, n. s. 2: 179.
Molluscs, Morphology of. (W. Garstang) Sci. Prog. 5: 38.
— Shell-bearing, of Portage County, O. (G. W. Dean) Am. Natural. 26: 11.
— Shells and. Ed. R. 182: 351.
— Sleep of. (C. T. Simpson) Pop. Sci. Mo. 45: 99.
Molly Maguires, The. Macmil. 75: 110.
— Overthrow of. (C. Moffett) McClure, 4: 90.
Moltke, Helmuth Karl Bernhard, Graf von. (W. O'C. Morris) Scot. R. 24: 74. Same art. Liv. Age, 203: 323. — Ath. '94, 2: 311. — (S. Whitman) Fortn. 63: 47. Same art. Liv. Age, 204: 323. Same art. Ecl. M. 124: 294. Same art. Chaut. 20: 413, 557. (G. Wolseley) Un. Serv. M. 4: 1. — (D. F. Hannigan) Westm. 139: 32. Same art. Un. Serv. (Phila.) 9: 223. — Dial (Ch.) 14: 74.
— and his Generalship. (J. von Verdy du Vernois) Forum, 21: 628.
— as a Writer. (M. Smith) Nation, 58: 15.
— Campaign in Bohemia. Ed. R. 179: 412.
— Essays, Speeches, and Memoirs. Sat. R. 76: 474.
— in War. (A. Forbes) McClure, 5: 209.
— Outflanking Two Emperors. (M. Halstead) Cosmopol. 17: 424.
— Tactical Problems, 1858–82, tr. by Donat. Sat. R. 77: 588.
Moluccas, Martin on. (H. R. Mill) Nature, 52: 217.
Molybdic Acid, Iodometric Estimation of. (F. A. Gooch and C. Fairbanks) Am. J. Sci. 152: 156.
Mom Cely's Wonderful Luck. (E. W. Bellamy) Atlan. 71: 316.
Momentary Indiscretion; a story. (Sarah Grand) Cosmopol. 20: 169.
Moment's Passion, A; a story. All the Year, 71: 317.
Mommsen, Theodor, the Great Historian. (F. G. Carpenter) Chaut. 17: 319.
Mona, Anglesea. (H. H. Lines) Antiq. n. s. 30: 71. 31: 87, 249.
Monads, Leibnitz's Theory of, Dillmann's Restatement of. (W. Wallace) Mind, 18: 224.
Monadnock, Mount. (E. W. Emerson) New Eng. M. n. s. 15: 33.
— and Ben Nevis. (W. M. Davis) Nation, 59: 99, 118.
Monasteries, Aerial, of Greece. (C. Robinson) Lippinc. 57: 285.
— Buddhist and Tao-ist, on the Lo Fau San. (E. A. Irving) Blackw. 157: 453. Same art. Liv. Age, 205: 37.
— English, Character of, on the Eve of their Suppression. (F. A. Gasquet) Dub. R. 114: 245.
— — Dissolution of. Quar. 182: 83. Same art. Liv. Age, 207: 67.
— of Crete, Visit to. (R. Rodd) New R. 9: 328. Same art. Liv. Age, 199: 243.
— of the Levant. (G. N. Curzon) Liv. Age, 192: 387.
Monastery, A North Carolina. (J. S. Bassett) M. Am. Hist. 29: 131.
Monasticism and Mysticism, Thorold on. Sat. R. 81: 513.
— Christian, Smith's. Spec. 68: 717. — Westm. 138: 35.
— Ideals and History of. (A. Harnack) Chr. Lit. 12: 9, 71, 136.
— in Scotland. (E. Austin) Cath. World, 61: 740.
— Revival of. Eng. R. 2: 424.
— Rules for Monks and Secular Canons after Revival under King Edgar. (M. Bateson) Eng. Hist. R. 9: 690.
— Woman under, Eckenstein's. (J. M. Vincent) Am. Hist. R. 2: 120.
Monazite and its uses. Chamb. J. 73: 54.
Monboddo, James Burnett, Lord. (F. P. Walton) Jurid. R. 8: 360.
Monckton, Lady. Theatre, 37: 179.
Moncrieff, H. J., Baron. (A. W. Renton) Green Bag, 4: 238.
Monda; a story. (G. P. Lathrop) Mo. Illust. 3: 45–369.
Monderisch; a Turkish story. (L. von Sacher-Masoch) Chaut. 21: 216.
Monet, Claude. (T. Robinson) Cent. 22: 696. — (J. D. Barry) Lit. W. (Bost.) 27: 108.
Monetary Agreement, Need of an International. (F. H. Head) Forum, 17: 455.
Monetary Conference at Brussels, 1892. (E. B. Andrews) Cosmopol. 15: 242. — (E. B. Andrews) Pol. Sci. Q. 8: 197. — (C. Foster) No. Am. 156: 493. — (H. White) Nation, 55: 424. — (H. S. Foxwell) Contemp. 62: 797. — Pub. Opin. 14: 235. — Spec. 69: 812. — (G. K. Marischal) Westm. 146: 511.
— — End of. (H. White) Nation, 55: 466.
— — French View of. (E. L. Godkin) Nation, 55: 424.
— International, 1893. (F. W. Hackett) Am. J. Pol. 2: 159.
Monetary Programme of the U. S. (J. L. Laughlin) Forum, 20: 652.
Monetary Reform and Tariff Reform. (E. B. Andrews) No. Am. 158: 464.
— in Russia. (A. N. Miklashevsky) Econ. J. 6: 632.
— in Santo Domingo. (J. L. Laughlin) Atlan. 74: 107.
— a Monetary Panacea. (A. S. Browne) Am. J. Pol. 4: 178.
— Thoughts on. (F. Y. Edgeworth) Econ. J. 5: 434.
Monetary Sectionalism, Remedy for. Gunton's M. 10: 433.
Monetary Situation, The Present. (W. Lexis) Econ. Stud. 1: 215.
Monetary Standard, The. (Wm. H. Hale) Bach. of Arts, 3: 315.
— The Multiple. (J. A. Smith) Ann. Am. Acad. Pol. Sci. 7: 173.
Monetary Standards. (J. Cummings) J. Pol. Econ. 2: 349. — (J. F. Orton) J. Pol. Econ. 3: 338.
— Fancy. (R. Giffen) Econ. J. 2: 463.
Monetary Treaty, Vienna, of 1857. (H. P. Willis) J. Pol. Econ. 4: 187, 270.
Money. (T. J. E. Freeman) Am. Cath. Q. 19: 198, 637. — (J. A. Quarles) Am. M. Civics, 6: 113, 237.
— American Sound Money Problem and its Solution. (A. Higgins; M. Frewen) National, 26: 422.
— and Bank Credits in U. S. (H. W. Williams) Ann. Am. Acad. Pol. Sci. 6: 531.
— and Banking. (H. White) Engin. M. 10: 391.
— — White's. (F. Franklin) Nation, 62: 57.
— and Civilization. (G. S. Kimball) Am. J. Pol. 2: 626.
— and Credit Paper in the Modern Market. (W. Fisher) J. Pol. Econ. 3: 391.
— and its Functions. (L. J. Gage) Open Court, 5: 2715.
— — A Debate on. (M. M. Trumbull) Open Court, 5: 2734.
— and Investments. Contemp. 70: 449, 750.
— and Monetary Problems, Nicholson's. (L. L. Price) Econ. J. 5: 563.
— and Prices. (S. McL. Hardy) Bank. M. (N. Y.) 50: 790.
— — Popular Superstitions on. Gunton's M. 11: 309.
— and Social Problems, Harper's. Sat. R. 82: 201.

Money as an International Question. (E. B. Andrews) Atlan. 71: 543.
— Bank Monopoly — Specie Contraction — Bond Inflation. (A. Roberts) Arena, 15: 998.
— Battle of the Standards, and the Fall of Prices. (E. Atkinson) Forum, 19: 143.
— — in America. (W. L. Alden; W. Dillon) 19th Cent. 40: 199. Same art. Ecl. M. 127: 433.
— The Business World *vs.* the Politicians. (J. H. Eckels) Forum, 19: 1.
— Coin's Financial School and its Censors. (W. H. Harvey) No. Am. 161: 71.
— — and its Critics. (W. Fisher) Q. J. Econ. 10: 187. — Reply. (J. L. Laughlin) Q. J. Econ. 10: 337.
— — Food for the Gullible. (J. L. Laughlin) Forum, 19: 573.
— — Various Replies to. (H. White) Nation, 60: 374.
— Concerning. (G. H. Smith) Am. J. Pol. 3: 337.
— Demand for More. (E. W. Bemis) Bib. Sac. 53: 306.
— Economic Effect of an Appreciating. Gunton's M. 11: 233.
— Evolution of. (J. D. Hancock) Am. M. Civics, 9: 191, 246.
— Famine of, How to prevent a. (J. H. Eckels) No. Am. 158: 50.
— Lord Farrer on the Standard. (H. S. Foxwell) National, 24: 637.
— Fiat. (C. Q. De France) Am. M. Civics, 9: 324. — Pub. Opin. 19: 262.
— Functions of. (E. L. Rector) Am. J. Pol. 5: 470.
— Gold and Silver and the Money of the World. (L. C. Probyn) J. Statis. Soc. 58: 559.
— Historical Aspect of the Question. (A. Del Mas) Fortn. 63: 565.
— History of, in England, Shaw's. (H. S. Foxwell) Econ. J. 6: 226.
— Hoarding, Effect of. (D. MacG. Means) Nation, 57: 77.
— — Folly of. Pub. Opin. 15: 467.
— Honest. (F. U. Laycock) J. Pol. Econ. 3: 472.
— — and Dishonest. (J. Davis) Arena, 10: 91.
— — Fonda on. Sat. R. 80: 530.
— in Circulation in U. S. Bank. M. (N. Y.) 46: 301.
— in Legislation of U. S. (S. Sherwood) Chaut. 22: 407.
— in Politics. (J. Davis) Arena, 10: 317.
— in the U. S., Problem of. Pub. Opin. 19: 70.
— — Supply of, American Banking and. (M. D. Harter) Ann. Am. Acad. Pol. Sci. 3: 559.
— — What should Congress do about? R. of Rs. (N. Y.) 8: 151.
— Is it a Mere Commodity? (W. Smart) Fortn. 60: 646. Same art. Ecl. M. 121: 759.
— Laws of. (M. M. Trumbull) Open Court, 3: 1657.
— Legal Tender for England. (R. Ewen) Westm. 146: 296.
— Measurement of Utility by. (F. Y. Edgeworth) Econ. J. 4: 342.
— More, as a Relief to Financial Distresses. (G. W. Pepperell) Arena, 12: 233.
— Natural Law of. (J. J. Valentine) Overland, n. s. 28: 121.
— Need, not of More, but of Better Exchange. (T. G. Shearman) Forum, 16: 459.
— New Basis for. (A. I. Fonda) Am. J. Pol. 3: 99.
— of the Far East. (G. Peel) National, 27: 546. Same art. Ecl. M. 127: 101.
— of the U. S., Character and Volume of. (M. L. Muhleman) Am. Statis. Assoc. 3: 463.
— Origin of. (K. Menger) Econ. J. 2: 239.
Money, Outline of a New Philosophy of. (A. J. Webb) Arena, 13: 199.
— Payment in Promises to pay. Open Court, 3: 1703.
— A Perfect Coinage System. (M. D. Harter) Forum, 17: 603.
— Philosophy of. (E. Atkinson) Monist, 6: 337.
— Problem of. (M. Green) Pub. Opin. 15: 203.
— — Development of. (L. G. McPherson) Pop. Sci. Mo. 49: 20, 202.
— Quantity of, and Prices, 1860–91. (S. M. Hardy) J. Pol. Econ. 3: 145.
— Quantity-theory of. (F. A. Walker) Q. J. Econ. 9: 372. — (W. E. Mitchell) J. Pol. Econ. 4: 139.
— — and Credit Devices. (H. P. Willis) J. Pol. Econ. 4: 281.
— — History and Present Application. (H. P. Willis) J. Pol. Econ. 4: 417.
— Question of. (J. Davis) Arena, 5: 547.
— — and Constructive Enterprise. (J. R. Dunlap) Engin. M. 10: 1005.
— — and the Unemployed. (G. G. Merrick) Am. J. Pol. 4: 622.
— — The Crux of: has Gold risen? (L. A. Garnett) Forum, 18: 573.
— — Engineer's View of. (A. F. Nagle) Cassier, 5: 105.
— — Is it a Class Question? (L. H. Transom) Overland, n. s. 28: 478.
— — Marine Solution of. (W. W. Bates) Soc. Econ. 4: 205.
— Recent American Books on. (W. Fisher) Q. J. Econ. 10: 324.
— Reign of. (A. Leroy-Beaulieu) Chaut. 21: 69.
— Representative, and Gold Exportations. (H. White) Engin. M. 10: 597.
— Right Use of: Symposium. Indep. Sept. 7, '93.
— Scientific Analysis of. (E. Schalk) Engin. M. 5: 710.
— Should the Government retire from Banking? (W. C. Cornwell) Forum, 18: 641.
— Silver, Coinage. Soc. Econ. 2: 328.
— Sound. Are we a Nation of Rascals? (J. Oker) Am. M. Civics, 8: 506.
— — Banks and. (G. Gunton) Gunton's M. 10: 404.
— — Question of. Pub. Opin. 18: 592.
— — the Safeguard of Labor. (R. B. Mahany) No. Am. 163: 98.
— Value of. (F. A. Walker) Q. J. Econ. 8: 62.
— What is? (J. R. Musick) Am. J. Pol. 3: 449. — Bank. M. (N. Y.) 48: 665.
See Currency; Gold; Silver.
Money-borrowers. (J. H. Browne) Harper, 92: 636.
Money-lending in Australia. (Sir R. G. C. Hamilton) 19th Cent. 32: 194.
— in the East. Spec. 76: 234. Same art. Liv. Age, 208: 765.
Money-market and the Industrial Conditions. (M. L. Muhleman) Engin. M. 11: 1.
Money Matters. (R. Ewen) Westm. 145: 43.
Money Power in Government. (C. H. Monroe) Arena, 12: 106.
— in the U. S., Slavery Power and. (C. W. Cram) Arena, 8: 690.
Money-spider, The; a story. (P. Roberson) Gent. M. n. s. 53: 109. Same art. Liv. Age, 202: 659.
Money-spinner; a story. Cornh. 67: 28.
Money Unit of the U. S. (E. O. Leech) Bank. M. (N. Y.) 51: 15.
Mongolia and Tibet, Journey in. (W. W. Rockhill) Geog. J. 3: 357.
— The Insurrection in. Blackw. 151: 894. Same art. Liv. Age, 194: 414.

Mongolia, Northern, Notes of a Journey in, 1893. (A. A. Borradaile) Geog. J. 5: 562.
— — Review of above. (N. Elias) Geog. J. 5: 572.
— Obrucheff's Explorations in. Geog. J. 5: 260.
Monism. Bapt. R. 14: 202. — (E. Haeckel) Monist, 2: 481. — (D. F. Strauss and others) Open Court, 1: 384.
— and Agnosticism. (E. Montgomery) Open Court, 1: 9, 37, 65. — (A. Waters) Open Court, 6: 3471.
— and Henism. (P. Carus) Monist, 4: 228.
— and Individualism. (W. Lutoslawski) Monist, 6: 351.
— and Materialism. (P. R. Shipman) Open Court, 6: 3151.
— and Monistic Thinkers. Open Court, 1: 376.
— and Philology. Open Court, 2: 884.
— and Religion. (P. Carus) Open Court, 1: 694. — (D. Theophilus and others) Open Court, 2: 834, 911, 1179, 1192.
— as the Formal Principle of Cognition. Open Court, 2: 1478.
— Dualism and Agnosticism. (P. Carus) Open Court, 1: 209.
— Ethical. (A. J. F. Behrends) Meth. R. 55: 357.
— Hindu. (R. Garbe) Monist, 3: 51.
— in Arithmetic. (H. Schubert) Monist, 4: 561.
— Lotze's. (F. C. S. Schiller) Philos. R. 5: 225.
— Message of, to the World. (P. Carus) Monist, 4: 545.
— of India. (C. Johnston) Open Court, 10: 4847.
— of "The Open Court." (E. Montgomery) Open Court, 4: 2461, 2476.
— Psychical. (E. Montgomery) Monist, 2: 338.
— Religious Character of. (P. Carus) Open Court, 2: 1381.
— Three Aspects of. (C. L. Morgan) Monist, 4: 321.
— Unity of Thought and Thing. (R. Lewins) Monist, 4: 208.
"Monist, The;" a Review of its Work. Open Court, 5: 3073.
Monistic Mental Science. (S. V. Clevenger) Open Court, 1: 400, 429-553.
Monistic Method, The. (W. S. Ross) Open Court, 7: 3551.
Monistic Theory of Mind. (L. F. Ward) Monist, 4: 194.
"Monitor" and the "Merrimac," Fight between. (S. D. Greene) Un. Serv. (Phila.) 10: 350.
Monkey, Apology for. Spec. 72: 532.
— Fossil, from Madagascar. (R. Lydekker) Nature, 55: 89.
— Story of a. (M. J. Dybowski) Pop. Sci. Mo. 48: 637.
Monkey House at the Zoo. (F. Miller) Eng. Illust. 13: 327.
Monkeys. (T. Wood) Sund. M. 21: 334.
— and Children. (L. Robinson) Pub. Opin. 13: 36.
— and Men, from a Simian Point of View. (H. K. Horsfield) Liv. Age, 192: 53.
— Speech and Thought of. (R. L. Garner) Cosmopol. 13: 72.
— Speech of. (R. L. Garner) Forum, 13: 246. — (R. L. Garner) New R. 6: 181. Same art. Liv. Age, 193: 121.
— — Garner on. (J. Jastrow) Dial (Ch.) 13: 215. — Spec. 69: 227.
— — Jim the Orang and his Cousins. (R. L. Garner) New R. 7: 439.
— — Monkey's Academy in Africa. (R. L. Garner) New R. 7: 282.
— — What I expect to do in Africa. (R. L. Garner) No. Am. 154: 713.
— Story of Bob. (D. S. Jordan) Pop. Sci. Mo. 44: 145.
— Strangers yet. (J. Kent) Gent. M. n. s. 51: 158.
— Two Rare. (L. Heck) Pop. Sci. Mo. 41: 389.
Monk's Life as depicted in Paintings. (A. T. Winslow) Nat'l M. (Bost.) 5: 271.
Monkshood; a poem. (C. E. Meetkerke) Argosy, 60: 111.
Monkwearmouth Church. Reliquary, 33: 141.
Monmartre, The Capital of Paris. Macmil. 75: 97.
Monmouth, Battle of. (J. G. Nicolay) Chaut. 14: 515.
— Drummer Boy of. (C. J. Denton) Am. Hist. Reg. 1: 515.
Monogamy and Free Love. Open Court, 4: 2699.
Monometallism and Protection. (C. S. Thomas) Arena, 10: 169.
Monometallist Arguments. (H. Withers) Bank. M. (Lond.) 59: 831.
Monometallist Creed, The. (H. D. MacLeod) 19th Cent. 36: 770. Same art. Bank. M. (N. Y.) 50: 41.
Monopolies and Patents. Cornh. 72: 256.
— and Revenue. Spec. 74: 843.
— Capitalistic, and their Relation to the State. (J. W. Jenks) Pol. Sci. Q. 9: 486.
— Legislation against, in the U. S. (J. D. Forrest) Am. J. Social. 1: 411.
— Natural, and Protection. (J. R. Commons) Q. J. Econ. 6: 479.
— — and the Workingman. A Programme of Social Reform. (R. T. Ely) No. Am. 158: 294. — Pub. Opin. 16: 575.
Monopolies, Old; story of. All the Year, 71: 392.
Monopoly. Is it always Victorious? (G. L. Eberhart) Am. Civics, 6: 584.
Monotony, Plea for. Spec. 68: 775.
Monotype Machine, Lanston's. J. Frankl. Inst. 142: 161.
Monotypes, The making of. (H. W. Faulkener) Mo. Illust. 13: 50.
Monroe Doctrine, The. (Thos. E. Jevons) Bach. of Arts, 2: 437. — New R. 14: 47. — (M. Frewen) National, 26: 595. 27: 156. — (H. S. Henriques) Westm. 145: 271. Same art. Ecl. M. 126: 590. — (J. B. Moore) Pol. Sci. Q. 11: 1. — Spec. 75: 478. — (M. B. Dunnell) Am. Law R. 29: 839. — (G. Smith) Sat. R. 80: 794.
— and its History. (W. F. Burrough) Am. M. Civics, 8: 47.
— and Nicaragua. Sat. R. 79: 541.
— and Nicaragua Canal. (L. M. Keasbey) Ann. Am. Acad. Pol. Sci. 7: 1.
— and Some of its Applications. (J. A. Woodburn) Chaut. 22: 549.
— and the Venezuela Dispute. (T. M. Etting) Citizen, 2: 6.
— Defence, not Defiance. (A. C. Cassat) Forum, 20: 456.
— Definition and Interpretation of. Gunton's M. 10: 81.
— Development of. (E. L. Godkin) Nation, 62: 4, 90.
— England, Venezuela, and. (H. C. Lodge) No. Am. 160: 651.
— English View of. Gunton's M. 10: 84.
— French in Mexico and. (F. Bancroft) Pol. Sci. Q. 11: 30.
— A German View of. (L. vom B. Göttingen) Am. M. Civics, 8: 574.
— D. C. Gilman on. (G. Koerner) Open Court, 10: 4801.
— Growth of. Sat. R. 81: 4.
— in 1895. (E. D. Cope) Open Court, 10: 4777.
— More about. (E. L. Godkin) Nation, 61: 304.
— of President Cleveland. (T. S. Woolsey) Forum, 20: 705.
— — and Olney. (D. Mills) Canad. M. 6: 365.
— Philosophy of. Gunton's M. 10: 1.

Monroe Doctrine. Proposed Dual Organization of Mankind. (W. G. Sumner) Pop. Sci. Mo. **49**: 433.
— Recent Pseudo-Monroeism. (J. W. Burgess) Pol. Sci. Q. **11**: 44.
— Lord Salisbury and. (O. S. Strauss) Forum, **20**: 713.
— Some Myths of. (R. Ogden) Nation, **60**: 356.
Monselet, Chas. (C. H. Palmer) Time, **21**: 414.
Monseigneur; a sketch. (E. Keith) Argosy, **57**: 168.
Monsieur Alcibiade. (C. C. Harrison) Cent. **21**: 601.
Monsieur le Comte; a story. Blackw. **157**: 764. Same art. Liv. Age, **205**: 648.
Monsieur le Comte; a story. (W. McLennan) Harper, **88**: 255.
Monsieur Paul; a story. (F. F. Robertson) Eng. Illust. **16**: 289.
Monsoons, Big and Little, of Ceylon. (E. D. Archibald) Nature, **48**: 175.
Monsters, Human. Spec. **68**: 426.
Mont Doré, Auvergne. Time, **4**: 35.
Mont St. Michel. (J. H. Adams) Cosmopol. **18**: 515. — (R. Barr) Idler, **4**: 201.
Montagu, Mrs. Elizabeth. (E. L. Didier) Chaut. **23**: 210. — Temp. Bar, **101**: 31. Same art. Liv. Age, **200**: 277.
Montagu, Lady Mary Wortley. All the Year, **74**: 114. — (E. L. Didier) Chaut. **23**: 209. — Temp. Bar, **98**: 187. Same art. Ecl. M. **121**: 95. Same art. Liv. Age, **198**: 290.
— and Modern Bacteriology. (Mrs. H. M. Plunkett) Pop. Sci. Mo. **45**: 359.
— Letters; Ropes's ed. Spec. **68**: 465.
Montaigne, Michel de. (A. Tilley) Macmil. **66**: 177. — Spec. **70**: 226. — (L. E. Tiddeman) Temp. Bar, **106**: 48. Same art. Liv. Age, **207**: 195.
— Florio's. (G. Norton) Nation, **57**: 69.
— A Holiday with. (H. D. Sedgwick, jr.) Atlan. **78**: 187.
— On the Track of. (E. H. Barker) Temp. Bar, **99**: 381.
— a Practical Philosopher. (Mrs. Lynn Linton) Chamb. J. **71**: 289.
— The Satirist. (H. H. Chamberlin) Bach. of Arts, **2**: 804.
Montaigne's Adopted Daughter. Belgra. **87**: 126. Same Art. Liv. Age, **206**: 169.
Montalba, Henrietta. (M. Hepworth-Dixon) Art J. **46**: 215.
Montana, Irrigation Problem in. (H. M. Wilson) Nat. Geog. M. **2**: 213.
— Sporting Vacation in. (G. M. Dillard) Outing, **27**: 41.
— the Treasure State. (J. Ralph) Harper, **85**: 90.
Montana Divorce Suit, A. (W. L. Alden) Idler, **6**: 703.
Montanism. (P. J. Gloag) Presb. & Ref. R. **5**: 398.
Montcalm, Marquis de, and Levis, Casgrain's. Atlan. **69**: 560.
Monte Carlo. (C. H. Farnham) Cosmopol. **14**: 387.
— Idling at. All the Year, **74**: 297. Same art. Liv. Age, **201**: 250.
— Science and. (K. Pearson) Fortn. **61**: 183.
Monte de Piedad, at Madrid. (M. Belmas) Am. Arch. **49**: 30.
Monte Rosa, Climbing. (F. Parsons) Bach. of Arts, **3**: 80.
Montenegro and its Borderlands. (W. H. Cozens-Hardy) Geog. J. **4**: 385.
— Excavations in. (J. A. R. Munro) Ath. '93, **2**: 459-632.
— Journeys in. (K. Hassert) Geog. J. **3**: 508.
Montenegro, Mountaineering in; an Interview with Prince Nicholas. (M. Miller) Westm. **142**: 403.
— 200th Anniversary of. (W. Miller) Gent. M. n. s. **57**: 391.
Montenero, Eighth of September at. (E. Cecconi) Good Words, **36**: 598.
Monterey, Del Monte and. (R. Wildman) Overland, n. s. **26**: 581.
Monterey County Pastoral, A. (K. P. Siegbold) Overland, n. s. **25**: 643.
Montesquieu, C. de S. de, with portrait. (A. H. di Farini) Green Bag, **4**: 305.
Montezuma Emerald, The. (R. Ottolengui) Idler, **7**: 13.
Montferrat, Marquis de. (A. C. Lyall) 19th Cent. **35**: 946.
Montfort, Simon de, A Song on the Death of. (Ed. by F. W. Maitland) Eng. Hist. R. **11**: 314.
Montgomerie, John, Governor of N. Y., 1728-32. (D. Van Pelt) Nat'l M. (N. Y. '91) **17**: 493.
Montgomery, Dr. Edmund. Open Court, **1**: 103.
— on the Theology of Evolution. (E. D. Cope) Open Court, **1**: 285, 358.
Month of Mary; a poem. All the Year, **74**: 444.
Months, Assyro-Babylonian, and their Regents. (W. Muss-Arnolt) J. Bib. Lit. **11**: 72, 160.
Monticelli, Adolphe. (M. Drage) Fortn. **65**: 412. — (M. H. Dixon) Art J. **47**: 211.
Monticellite, Optical Properties of. (S. L. Penfield and E. H. Forbes) Am. J. Sci. **151**: 129.
Montmarte, Church of the Sacred Heart. (H. Rauline) Archit. Rec. **3**: 3.
Montmorency Falls, Electric Power from. (E. C. Chesney) Cassier, **10**: 1.
Montpelier, a French Provincial City. (A. B. Hart) Nation, **58**: 465.
Montreal and Quebec, March to, 1775. (C. B. Todd) Am. Hist. Reg. **2**: 641.
— Attempt to destroy the Nelson Monument. Spec. **71**: 739.
— Mt. Royal Park. (M. C. Robbins) Garden & F. **6**: 523.
Montrigone, Shrine of St. Anne at. (Samuel Butler) Univ. R. **2**: 317.
Montrond, M. de. (A. Laugel) Nation, **60**: 234.
Montrose, James, Marquis of. (J. Pryce) Acad. **44**: 265.
— Last Campaign of. Ed. R. **179**: 122.
— Morris's. Sat. R. **73**: 130.
— Wishart's Memoirs of. Spec. **71**: 148.
Montserrat, Spain. (C. W. Wood) Argosy, **62**: 47. — Chamb. J. **69**: 431.
Monument to Corder, The; a story. (E. W. McGlasson) Harper, **88**: 693.
Monumental Effigy at Llanarmon-in-Yale. Reliquary, **35**: 1.
Monuments. Open Court, **1**: 521.
— Ancient, Fresh Light from. (J. Cook) Our Day, **9**: 428.
— Commemorative. (L. C. Boileau *fils*) Am. Arch. **40**: 111 — **41**: 3.
— Equestrian. Am. Arch. **35**: 87-181. **36**: 40-97.
— Funeral Orations in Stone and Word. (C. Waldstein) Harper, **85**: 3.
— in City Streets and Parks. (C. S. Sargent) Garden & F. **9**: 21.
— Inscriptions on Public. (M. G. Van Rensselaer) Garden & F. **8**: 87.
— Lessons from the. Liv. Age, **207**: 643.
— National. (Frank Sewall) Am. Arch. **51**: 114.
— of London. (F. Ford) M. of Art, **10**: 168.
— Some New American. M. of Art, **8**: supp. 27.

Monvel, Jacques Boutet de. Temp. Bar, **94**: 335.
Monvel, Maurice Boutet de. (W. H. Low) Cent. **26**: 253.
Moods and Fancies. All the Year, **70**: 268.
— of a Man, Two. (M. M. Singleton) 19th Cent. **31**: 208. Same art. Ecl. M. **118**: 490.
Moody, Dwight Lyman. (H. Drummond) McClure, **4**: 188. — (H. W. Webb-Peploe) Outl. **54**: 379. — With portraits. (H. Drummond) McClure, **4**: 53.
— Schools at Northfield and Chicago. (G. F. Magoun) Our Day, **10**: 790.
Moody, Francis Wollaston, as an Art Teacher. (O. Gibbons) M. of Art, **11**: 404.
Moon, The. (R. S. Ball) Good Words, **33**: 121–260. — (W. W. Payne) Pop. Astron. **1**: 289. **2**: 67. **3**: 176. **4**: 143, 242.
— Atmosphere of, and the Recent Occultation of Jupiter. (W. H. Pickering) Astron. **11**: 778.
— Craters on. (W. M. Davis) Nation, **56**: 342.
— — Tycho. (A. C. Ranyard) Knowl. **16**: 149.
— Eclipse of, Bering's Alleged Observations. (M. Baker) Nat. Geog. M. **2**: 167.
— Ephemeris of. (J. Morrison) Pop. Astron. **3**: 362, 467.
— Influence on Rainfall. (M. Merriman; H. A. Hazen) Science, **20**: 310.
— Myths of. All the Year, **75**: 276.
— Observations of, First. (M. E. Byrd) Pop. Astron. **1**: 216.
— Photographs of. (E. S. Holden) Overland, n. s. **19**: 58.
— — Taken at the Paris Observatory. Nature, **52**: 439.
— Pictures of. Dub. R. **110**: 442.
— Progress of; Selenography. (A. Mee) Knowl. **18**: 133.
— Surface of, Advances in our Knowledge of. (E. S. Holden) McClure, **3**: 443.
— — New Theory of Markings of. (E. Miller) Pop. Astron. **3**: 273.
— — Possible Cause of Change on. (C. Davison) Knowl. **19**: 278.
— Visibility of Change in. (H. G. Wells) Knowl. **18**: 230.
— Walled Plain of Clavius on. (E. W. Maunder) Knowl. **19**: 227.
Moon, Mountains of. (W. Meyer) Pub. Opin. **13**: 136.
— — and the Nile. Dub. R. **112**: 451.
Moonlight. Ecl. M. **125**: 92.
— Perpetual, Laplace's Plan for. (D. Kirkwood) Pop. Sci. Mo. **44**: 36.
Moonlight; a poem. (M. I. McNeal) Outing, **27**: 271.
Moonlight; a story. (G. de Maupassant) Theatre, **32**: 3.
Moon-maiden; a poem. (C. A. Fraser) Canad. M. **1**: 444.
Moon Man or Moon Maid. (W. Canton) Good Words, **35**: 312.
Moon-set; a poem. (E. P. Johnson) Outing, **25**: 43.
Moonshee, Portrait of a. (J. W. Sherer) Macmil. **69**: 270. Same art. Liv. Age, **200**: 689.
Moonshiner of Fact. (F. Lynde) Lippinc. **57**: 66.
Moon-stricken, The; a story. (B. E. J. Capes) Cornh. **74**: 795.
Moore, Albert. Acad. **44**: 278. — Ath. '93, **2**: 459. — Art J. **46**: 88. — (C. Monkhouse) M. of Art, **8**: 191.
— and the Royal Academy. M. of Art, **17**: i.
— Celibates. (F. Danby) Sat. R. **80**: 105.
— Life of, Baldry's. Art J. **47**: 48. — (R. Sturgis) Nation, **60**: 110.
— Painting of. Art J. **45**: 334.
— Picture by. Sat. R. **77**: 89.
Moore, Albert, Pictures by, owned by W. Connal. (R. Walker) M. of Art, **17**: 361.
— Rise of, with portrait. (H. T. Peck) Bookman, **1**: 322.
Moore, Charles L. (S. W. Mitchell) Forum, **13**: 430.
Moore, F. Frankfort. The Mayflower; a comedy. Theatre, **28**: 106. — Gent. M. n. s. **48**: 211.
Moore, George. Bk. News, **13**: 10. — (R. Buchanan) Univ. R. **3**: 353.
— and the Mummers. (L. F. Austin) Time, **19**: 524.
Moore, Henry. Ath. **95**, **1**: 843. — Acad. **47**: 548. — (M. H. Spielmann) M. of Art, **18**: 378.
— Death of. Art J. **47**: 280.
Moore, John. Cross at Sibstone. Reliquary, **33**: 193.
Moore, Thomas, Glimpses of. (J. P. O'Byrne) Westm. **138**: 146.
Mooredge Dwellers and their Doings. (B. Atkinson) Sund. M. **22**: 53.
Moorish Café, An Evening in a. (J. E. B. Meakin) Gent. M. n. s. **54**: 418. Same art. Ecl. M. **124**: 852.
Moorland Idylls. (G. Allen) Eng. Illust. vols. **12**, **13**.
Moorland Parish, Atkinson's. Church Q. **34**: 453.
— Jottings from a. Temp. Bar, **96**: 497. Same art. Liv. Age, **196**: 242.
Moors, Among the, Montbard's. Sat. R. **77**: 621.
— in Spain, Among the. Chamb. J. **72**: 132.
Moors, English, and what lives and grows there. (B. Atkinson) Sund. M. **22**: 458.
Moose and Deer. (A. C. Shaw) Canad. M. **6**: 412.
— How I killed my First. (C. H. Gooderham) Canad. M. **4**: 269.
— The Vanishing, and their Extermination in the Adirondacks. (M. Grant) Cent. **25**: 345.
Moose Call, The. (F. H. Risteen) Outing, **28**: 450.
Moose Hunt on the Yukon. (V. Wilson) Outing, **27**: 279.
Moose Hunting. (S. R. Clarke) Outing, **21**: 192.
— in British America. (A. Haggard) Blackw. **155**: 787.
Moquis, Legend of the Snake Order of. (A. M. Stephen) J. Am. Folk-Lore, **1**: 109.
Moraine of Central Massachusetts. (R. S. Tarr) Am. J. Sci. **143**: 141.
Moraine-fringe, Extra, in Eastern Pennsylvania, Age of. (E. H. Williams, jr.) Am. J. Sci. **147**: 34.
Moraines, Correlation of, with Raised Beaches of Lake Erie. (F. Leverett) Am. J. Sci. **143**: 281.
Moral, The, and the Cosmic. (J. M. Baldwin) Int. J. Ethics, **6**: 93.
— Non-survival of. (H. C. B. Cowell) Am. J. Pol. **4**: 630.
Moral Conduct. Can it be taught in Schools? (G. H. Palmer) Forum, **14**: 673.
— Motives to. (A. Döring) Int. J. Ethics, **5**: 361.
Moral Crisis, A. (E. T. Corbett) Munsey, **13**: 51.
Moral Culture and Nature Study. (D. S. Jordan) Science, n. s. **4**: 149.
Moral Deficiencies as determining Intellectual Functions. (G. Simmel) Int. J. Ethics, **3**: 490.
Moral Educability. (E. P. Jackson) Pop. Sci. Mo. **40**: 647.
Moral Education. (L. V. Price) Educa. **16**: 1.
— and Will-training. (G. S. Hall) Pedagog. Sem. **2**: 72.
— in Schools. (S. E. Warren) Educa. **15**: 297.
— Spencer on. (S. S. Laurie) Educa. R. **4**: 485.
Moral Evolution, Harris on. (J. H. Crooker) Dial (Ch.) **20**: 357. — (J. W. Chadwick) Nation, **63**: 127, 140.
Moral Forces, Correlation of. (W. Knight) National, **20**: 600. Same art. Ecl. M. **120**: 361.
Moral Law, Authority of. (P. Carus) Open Court, **4**: 2606.

Moral Life, A Help to. (W. M. Salter) Eth. Rec. 3: 31.
Moral Motive, Green's Theory of. (J. Dewey) Philos. R. 1: 593.
Moral Obligation, Consciousness of. (J. G. Schurman) Philos. R. 3: 641. — (W. W. Carlile) Philos. R. 4: 303.
Moral Obliquity, A. (F. Lynde) Scrib. M. 17: 189.
Moral Progress, Economic Causes of. (S. N. Patten) Ann. Am. Acad. Pol. Sci. 3: 129.
Moral Slovenliness. (W. Page-Roberts) Good Words, 37: 451.
Moral Standard, The. (W. H. Hudson) Pop. Sci. Mo. 50: 1.
Moral Standards. Are they shifting? (A. B. Hart) Forum, 18: 513.
Moral Training, The Chaos in. (J. Dewey) Pop. Sci. Mo. 45: 433.
— Pyschological Aspects of. (J. Royce) Int. J. Ethics, 3: 413.
Moral Unity. (W. J. Potter) Open Court, 1: 88.
Morality and Virtue. (P. Carus) Open Court, 5: 3011.
— and Work. (W. Ferrero) Forum, 22: 358.
— as Freedom. (H. Jones) Time, 18: 314.
— Basis of. (C. S. Wake) Open Court, 3: 1862. 6: 3355, 3363.
— Commercial. (J. Carter) Econ. R. 3: 318. 4: 221. — (S. B. Boulton) Econ. R. 4: 208.
— in Business and Professional Life. (D. Swing) Am. J. Pol. 2: 337.
— in Nature and Evolution. (J. T. Bixby) New World, 4: 444.
— Independent of Theology. (G. J. Holyoake) Open Court, 10: 4984.
— Inductive. (F. Nobili-Vitelleschi) 19th Cent. 40: 439.
— the Last of Dogmas. (A. Llano) Philos. R. 5: 371.
— of Art. Spec. 75: 722.
— Religion and. (A. H. Bradford) And. R. 17: 537. — (L. Tolstoi) Contemp. 65: 326.
— — Kidd on. (W. B. Greene, jr.) Presb. & Ref. R. 7: 697.
— — Pfleiderer on. (E. Ritchie) Philos. R. 5: 619.
— — Relations of. (W. Bender) New World, 2: 453.
— Religious Belief as a Basis of. (E. P. Evans) Pop. Sci. Mo. 45: 83.
— Sanctions of. Westm. 138: 506. — (L. Ramsey) Westm. 139: 169.
— that is. (A. Hodder) Int. J. Ethics, 6: 338.
— that ought to be. (A. L. Hodder) Philos. R. 3: 412.
— Wealth and. (W. E. Hart) Soc. Econ. 3: 96.
— Windelband's Principles of. (C. W. Hodge) Philos. R. 5: 623.
— without Religion. Is it Possible and Desirable? (O. Pfleiderer) Philos. R. 5: 449.
Morals and Politics. (J. Gibbons) Am. M. Civics, 8: 359.
— Are they Improving or Deteriorating? (D. G. Thompson) Forum, 16: 588.
— Economics, and Statistics, Relations between. (Lord Farrer) J. Statis. Soc. 57: 595.
— Emotion and Music. (H. R. Haweis) Music, 4: 595.
— English, and Christianity. (D. H. Wheeler) Chaut. 20: 522.
— Evolution of. (F. E. White) Open Court, 3: 1775, 1788.
— Little. (E. J. Hardy) Good Words, 35: 160.
— Natural Selection in. (S. Alexander) Int. J. Ethics, 2: 409.
— Progress in. (J. R. Sutherland) Am. J. Pol. 1: 466.
— Public and Private. And. R. 19: 95.
— School Statistics and. (W. T. Harris) School R. 1: 218.
Moran, Thomas. (S. G. W. Benjamin) M. of Art, 5: 89.
Morant Bay, Underhill's Tragedy of. (Goldwin Smith) Nation, 61: 97.
Moravian Anabaptism; Living in Community. (R. Heath) Contemp. 70: 247.
Moravian Mission in Alaska. (J. T. Hamilton) M. Chr. Lit. 5: 351.
Moray Firth and Vicinity. Sat. R. 78: 263.
Mordvins, Marriage Customs of. (J. Abercromby) Folk-Lore, 1: 417.
More, Alexander Goodman. Nat. Sci. 6: 351.
More, Hannah: an Old-world Girlhood. All the Year, 75: 513.
— A Word for. Temp. Bar, 101: 224. Same art. Ecl. M. 122: 385. Same art. Liv. Age, 200: 707.
More, Sir Thomas. (B. O. Flower) Arena, 15: 112. — Church Q. 34: 55. — Quar. 184: 329.
— and Bishop Fisher, Letter of 1535 concerning. (J. Gairdner) Eng. Hist. R. 7: 712.
— Bridgett's Life of. (W. H. Hutton) Eng. Hist. R. 7: 159.
— Century of. (B. O. Flower) Arena, 10: 838.
— Utopia. (B. O. Flower) Arena, 15: 296, 391.
More Adventures of M. de Forbin. (E. P. Thompson) Gent. M. n. s. 55: 139.
More than Coronets. (F. M. White) Chamb. J. 71: 136-200.
More than Kin. (M. V. Terhune) Lippinc. 50: 551.
Moreau, Gustave. (C. Phillips) M. of Art, 8: 228.
— Illustrations to La Fontaine. (C. Phillips) M. of Art, 10: 101.
Morehouse, George T. (H. L. Conard) Nat'l M. (N. Y. '91) 17: 570.
Morel-Ladeuil, Work of. (L. F. Day) M. of Art, 13: 271.
Morelli, Giovanni. M. of Art, 16: 154.
Morgan, Mrs. Mary J., Collection of Pictures. (C. de Kay) M. of Art, 9: 245.
Morgan, Sydney Owenson, Lady. Temp. Bar, 97: 341. Same art. Liv. Age, 197: 131.
— the Queen of Irish Society. All the Year, 74: 420.
Morgue, Derivation of. (F. Chance) Acad. 43: 131, 199.
Morlaix, Finistère; an Old Breton Town. (S. Thompson) M. of Art, 3: 288.
Morley, Henry. Bk. Buyer, 11: 237. — Critic, 24: 349. — (H. F. Heath and T. G. Foster) Acad. 45: 417. — Ath. '94, 1: 645. — Pub. Opin. 17: 173.
— List of Works of. Lit. W. (Bost.) 25: 174.
Morley, John. New R. 8: 430.
— with Portrait. (H. W. Lucy) Eng. Illust. 10: 291.
Mormonism. Eng. R. 13: 399. — (J. Cook) Our Day, 11: 39.
— Spiritual Gifts and Spiritual Delusions. Eng. R. 14: 122, 263.
Mormons, The. Am. Cath. Q. 20: 486. — (H. R. Haweis) Contemp. 65: 94, 345.
— Amnesty to. Pub. Opin. 14: 347.
— Problem of. (F. S. Beggs) Meth. R. 56: 754.
Mormon Church. Has it re-entered Politics? (G. Miller) Forum, 20: 499.
Morning of the Year, The; a poem. (H. M. Burnside) Argosy, 61: 47.
Morning on a Trout Stream; a poem. (J. H. Keene) Outing, 26: 267.
Morning Calls. Eng. Illust. 13: 47-343. 14: 12-643. 15: 210. 16: 15, 208.
Morning Glory, Double. Garden & F. 5: 592.
Morning Mists. (J. Gordon) Lippinc. 56: 404.
Morning Song; a poem. (Sir Lewis Morris) Cosmopol. 19: 370.

Morning Star, The; a story. Temp. Bar, **105**: 268. Same art. Ecl. M. **125**: 242.
Morocco. (R. N. Cust) Asia. R. **10**: 87. — Nature, **47**: 298.
— Agitation in, 1892. Spec. **69**: 86, 214.
— and England, Strained Relations. (Ali ben Abd-Es-Salam) Asia. R. **15**: 339.
— and European Powers. Sat. R. **74**: 99.
— and its Races. (C. Rolleston) J. Soc. Arts, **42**: 157.
— Bonsal's. Ath. '**92**, **2**: 735. — Nation, **56**: 159.
— British Subjects in. (W. B. Harris) Asia. R. **14**: 340.
— Camp Life and Pigsticking in. (H. G. Egerton) 19th Cent. **31**: 623. Same art. Liv. Age, **193**: 740.
— Coming Crisis in. (H. R. Haweis) Fortn. **57**: 491.
— Condition of. (Ion Perdicaris) Asia. R. **14**: 330. **22**: 315.
— English Mission to, 1893. Spec. **70**: 40.
— From Spanish Light to Moorish Shadow. (A. J. Weston) Scrib. M. **13**: 193.
— Future of. Spec. **69**: 150.
— Jews of. (J. E. B. Meakin) Jew. Q. **4**: 369.
— A Land of Incredible Barbarity. (Earl Meath) 19th Cent. **36**: 136.
— Moorish Politics, 1891-93. (W. B. Harris) Blackw. **153**: 446.
— My Escape from Mulai Bushta. (W. B. Harris) Blackw. **157**: 98.
— New Sultan of. (W. B. Harris) Blackw. **156**: 467. Same art. Liv. Age, **203**: 451.
— On Muleback in. (S. J. Weyman) Eng. Illust. **9**: 614.
— Past and Present. Lond. Q. **83**: 57.
— Ras Doura Village. (R. B. C. Graham) Sat. R. **80**: 646.
— Recent Changes in. (W. B. Harris) Sat. R. **81**: 219.
— Situation in. (Ion Perdicaris) Asia. R. **18**: 340. — Spec. **69**: 55.
— Spaniards in. Spec. **71**: 624.
— Truth about. Asia. R. **12**: 83.
Morong, The, as a Relic of Pre-marriage Communism. (S. E. Peal) Anthrop. J. **22**: 244.
Morphology at the National Museum. (W. G. Ridewood) Nat. Sci. **7**: 258.
— General Physiology and. (C. O. Whitman) Am. Natural. **27**: 802.
Morrey, Humphrey, first Mayor of Philadelphia, 1691-92. (J. G. Leach) Pennsyl. M. **18**: 419.
Morris, Clara, in Repertoire. (A. Brownell) Bost. **3**: 470.
Morris, Francis Orpen. Leis. Hour, **42**: 487.
— the Naturalist of Nunburnholme. (E. W. Abram) Good Words, **34**: 621.
Morris, John. Month, **79**: 305, 457.
Morris, Dr. John G. (J. G. Morris) Pennsyl. M. **17**: 200.
Morris, Lewis. Eng. Illust. **11**: 861.
— Knighted. Sat. R. **79**: 718.
— Songs without Notes. Spec. **73**: 113.
Morris, Richard. (J. S. Cotton) Acad. **45**: 417.
— List of Works of. Lit. W. (Bost.) **25**: 174.
Morris, Wm., with portrait. Bk. Buyer, **12**: 545. **13**: 619. — With portrait. Bk. News, **13**: 303. **15**: 113. — Eng. Illust. **13**: 47. — (M. Bell) Fortn. **66**: 693. Same art. Ecl. M. **127**: 777. — (R. Steele) Acad. **50**: 261. — (A. Lang) Longm. **28**: 560. Same art. Liv. Age, **211**: 323. — (T. Watts-Dunton) Ath. '**96**, **2**: 487. — Critic, **29**: 207, 247. — Liv. Age, **211**: 380. — (E. R. Pennell) Nation, **63**: 306. — Spec. **77**: 478. — With Bibliography. Dial (Ch.) **21**: 209.
Morris, Wm., and Du Maurier, George. Art J. **48**: 379.
— and the Meaning of Life. (F. W. H. Myers) 19th Cent. **33**: 93.
— and some of his Later Works. (B. O. Flower) Arena, **17**: 42.
— as a Dramatist. (G. B. Shaw) Sat. R. **82**: 385.
— as Poet. (A. Symons) Sat. R. **82**: 387.
— as Printer. (H. P. Horne) Sat. R. **82**: 438.
— at the Kelmscott Press. Eng. Illust. **12**: no. 7, 47.
— Funeral of. (R. B. Cunninghame-Graham) Sat. R. **82**: 389.
— Home of. Critic, **27**: 119.
— Lord Lytton, and Sir E. Arnold. (L. C. Moulton) Arena, **6**: 46.
— The Man and his Work. (W. Sharp) Atlan. **78**: 768.
— Poems. Ath. '**92**, **1**: 336.
— Poems by the Way. (O. Elton) Acad. **41**: 197.
— Poetry of. (G. Saintsbury) Critic, **25**: 101.
— Socialistic Thread in Life and Writings of. (O. L. Triggs) Poet-Lore, **5**: 113, 210.
— Unpublished Letters on Socialism. (W. G. Kingsland) Poet-Lore, **7**: 473, 543.
— A Visit to his Factory. (R. F. Zueblin) Outl. **54**: 770.
— The Well at the World's End. (A. C. Swinburne) 19th Cent. **40**: 759. — (H. G. Wells) Sat. R. **82**: 413.
— Workshop of. Liv. Age, **211**: 461.
Morris, William O'Connor. (H. Tattersall) Acad. **47**: 371.
Morris-dancing. Walford's Antiq. **9**: 195.
Morris's Friend; a story. All the Year, **70**: 55.
Morrison, Alfred, House of. M. of Art, **2**: 140-206.
Morrison, Arthur, with portrait. Bk. Buyer, **12**: 333.
— Realism of. Acad. **50**: 531.
Morrison, Daniel, of Newbury, Mass., Descendants of. (L. A. Morrison) N. E. Reg. **48**: 413.
Morrison-Grant, Lewis. (J. Anderson) Good Words, **35**: 202.
Mors et Vita; a story. (C. A. Price) Belgra. **89**: 386.
Morse, Alpheus C. Am. Arch. **42**: 126.
Mortality in 23 Cities of Mass. (C. E. Burnap) Am. Statis. Assoc. **5**: 78.
— in Various Occupations. Bank. M. (Lond.) **54**: 903.
— in the U. S. (J. S. Billings) Chaut. **16**: 146.
Mortality Standard, International. (J. Körösi) Am. Statis. Assoc. **3**: 450.
Mortar and Cement, Tests of. (A. S. Cooper) J. Frankl. Inst. **140**: 321.
Mortars, Coast Defense, American. (A. A. Fuller) Cassier, **8**: 57.
Mortgage-banking in America. (D. M. Frederiksen) J. Pol. Econ. **2**: 203.
— in Germany. (D. M. Frederiksen) Bank. M. (N. Y.) **50**: 361. — (D. M. Frederiksen) Q. J. Econ. **9**: 47.
— in Russia. (D. M. Frederiksen) Ann. Am. Acad. Pol. Sci. **5**: 242.
Mortgagees and Trustees. (A. J. P. Menzies) Jurid. R. **5**: 241.
Mortgages. Bank. M. (Lond.) **59**: 621.
— and Farm and Home Proprietorship in the U. S. (G. K. Holmes) J. Statis. Soc. **56**: 443.
— Decade of, 1880-90. (G. K. Holmes) Ann. Am. Acad. Pol. Sci. **4**: 904.
— Freedom of Contract in. (E. C. C. Firth) Law Q. **11**: 144.
Mortmain, Codification of Law of. (R. E. Mitcheson) Law Q. **5**: 387.
Morton, Henry. (C. Sellers) Cassier, **6**: 337.
Morton, Julius Sterling. Atlan. **77**: 388.
Morton, Levi P., with portrait. (J. Ford) Munsey, **12**: 273.

Morton, Levi P., as a Presidential Candidate. (T. C. Platt; C. M. Depew; W. Miller; E. Lauterbach; C. W. Hackett) No. Am. **162**: 497.
Morton, Gov. Oliver P., and the Sons of Liberty. (W. D. Foulke) Atlan. **72**: 73.
Morton, T. New English Canaan. (B. F. De Costa) N. E. Reg. **48**: 329.
Morton, W. T. G., Discoverer of Anæsthesia. (E. L. Snell) Cent. **26**: 584.
Morton Family. The old Morton and Taylor Estates, Dorchester, Mass. (D. Clapp) N. E. Reg. **46**: 78.
Mortuary Chest, The; a story. (A. Brown) Harper, **93**: 562.
Morwenstow and Hawker. Chamb. J. **71**: 449. Same art. Liv. Age, **203**: 364.
Mosaic. (C. H. Townsend) J. Soc. Arts, **41**: 748, 772, 782.
— Art of. Chamb. J. **71**: 709.
— as an Independent Art. (Isabella De Barbieri) Archit. Rec. **2**: 291.
— Indian Pietra-dura Work. (H. G. Keene) M. of Art, **4**: 58.
— Making. Leis. Hour, **42**: 697.
— Modern. (A. C. Nye) Am. Arch. **39**: 23.
Mosaic Decoration. M. of Art, **3**: 338.
Mosaic Factory, A. Liv. Age, **199**: 182.
Mosaic Pavements, Bolton on. Ath. '**92**, **1**: 796.
— at St. Paul's Cathedral. (H. J. Powell) Contemp. **69**: 418. — Macmil. **74**: 16.
— in St. Paul's, Richmond's. Ath. '**92**, **2**: 37.
— Modern. (Isabella De Barbieri) Archit. Rec. **3**: 314. **4**: 277.
— Modern English. (L. F. Day) Archit. Rec. **2**: 79.
Mosaics by Burne-Jones, at Rome. M. of Art, **18**: 256.
Mosaic Law, The, in the Light of Ethics. (A. Maas) Am. Cath. Q. **17**: 123.
Moscow, Disaster at, 1896. (T. G. Allen, jr.) Bach. of Arts, **3**: 490.
— in 1893. Westm. **143**: 66.
Moser, James H. (T. Jenks) Mo. Illust. **4**: 102.
Moses, Age and Work of. (N. Schmidt) Bib. World, **7**: 30, 105.
— as a Political Economist. (T. N. Carver) Meth. R. **52**: 598.
— in Hebrew History, Place of. (W. R. Harper) Bib. World, **5**: 161.
— Law of. (A. B. Bruce) Chr. Lit. **12**: 20.
— — and the Higher Criticism. (A. F. Hewit) Cath. World, **61**: 728. — Church Q. **40**: 282.
— Recent Criticism upon. (C. G. Montefiore) Jew. Q. **3**: 251.
— Religion of. (C. H. Cornill) Open Court, **9**: 4455.
— Theology of. (P. H. Steenstra) J. Bib. Lit. **14**: 72.
— Veil of. (P. J. Gloag) Thinker, **8**: 308.
Moses, Stainton, Lillie's. Sat. R. **77**: 75.
Moslem, Hindoo and. (E. L. Weeks) Harper, **91**: 651.
Moslem Sacred History. Sat. R. **73**: 395.
Moslems, Modern. (C. R. Conder) Scot. R. **23**: 344.
Mosler, Henry. (A. Trumble) Mo. Illust. **4**: 259.
Mosque of Hassan. (C. W. Wood) Argosy, **55**: 298.
Mosques of Cairo. (C. W. Wood) Argosy, **55**: 490.
Mosquito, Great: Iroquois Legend. (W. M. Beauchamp) J. Am. Folk-Lore, **2**: 284.
— Mission of the. (E. A. Jepson) Gent. M. n. s. **50**: 616.
Mosquito Coast, The, and Nicaragua. (R. N. Keely, jr.) Pop. Sci. Mo. **45**: 160.
Mosquitoes and their Enemies. (L. Irwell) Westm. **146**: 332.
Moss, Gilbert, Collection of Paintings owned by. (A. T. Story) M. of Art, **17**: 120.
Mosses and Ferns, Recent Work on. (F. O. Bower) Sci. Prog. **4**: 358.
— British. Knowl. **15**: 4-61.
— in Literature. Chamb. J. **70**: 427. Same art. Ecl. M. **122**: 275.
— of the Southern States. (L. M. Underwood) Garden & F. **9**: 263.
Most Unfortunate Affair, A. All the Year, **74**: 542.
Moszkowski and his Compositions. (E. Liebling) Music, **9**: 117.
Mote, A; a story. (W. Ramal) Cornh. **74**: 209.
Mother and Son; a story. (W. B. Hale) Munsey, **13**: 465.
Mother, The, as a Power for Woman's Advancement. (Mrs. B. Smith) Pop. Sci. Mo. **46**: 622.
— Rule of. (C. P. Selden) No. Am. **161**: 637.
Mother in Israel, A; a story. (H. H. Boyesen) Harper, **92**: 377.
Mother of Felipe, The; a story. (M. Austin) Overland, n. s. **20**: 534.
Mother of John, The; a story. (E. Pugh) New R. **14**: 559.
Mother Goose. Spec. **69**: 133.
Mother Song, The; a story. (J. Ralph) Harper, **90**: 102.
Motherhood and Citizenship; Woman's Wisest Policy. (K. Trask) Forum, **18**: 609.
— and the New Woman. Sat. R. **79**: 752.
Mother's Hands; a story. (B. Björnson) New R. **8**: 281-517.
Mothers and Daughters. (E. B. Harrison) 19th Cent. **35**: 313. Same art. Liv. Age, **200**: 627. Same art. Ecl. M. **122**: 493.
— and Infants, How to deal with. (Annette J. Shaw) Char. R. **5**: 408.
— and Sons of Gods. (M. D. Conway) Open Court, **7**: 3671, 3687, 3703.
— Good and Bad. (Mrs. A. E. Barr) No. Am. **156**: 408.
— not Politicians, wanted. (H. Lieb) Open Court, **7**: 3816.
— of Great Men. (J. H. Myers) Chaut. **17**: 85.
— Tyranny of the. Belgra. **86**: 415.
Moths, Day-flying. (L. N. Badenoch) Knowl. **19**: 244.
— of North America. (W. F. Kirby) Nature, **50**: 619.
Motion. (E. M. Caillard) Good Words, **35**: 761. Same art. Ecl. M. **123**: 788.
— and Feeling. (P. Carus) Open Court, **4**: 2424, 2435.
— and Heat. (D. S. Troy) Science, **19**: 132, 147.
— Nature of. (J. W. Powell) Monist, **5**: 55.
— Without Apparent Contact. Spec. **73**: 917.
Motions, Reflex. (G. H. Schneider) Open Court, **1**: 696.
Motive Power, Selection of. (C. E. Emery) Engin. M. **8**: 638, 797.
— Ethical Significance of. (D. G. Ritchie) Int. J. Ethics, **4**: 89.
Motley, John Lothrop. (L. Irving) Nat'l M. (N. Y. '91) **16**: 59.
Motor, Induction. (L. Bell) Cassier, **9**: 241.
— Synchronous, Single-phase. (F. Bedel and H. J. Ryan) J. Frankl. Inst. **139**: 197.
— without Fuel. (H. Mehner) J. Frankl. Inst. **134**: 89.
Motor Ability. (J. A. Hancock) Pedagog. Sem. **3**: 9.
— Voluntary, Development of. (W. L. Bryan) Am. J. Psychol. **5**: 125.
Motor Carriages and Cycles. (G. R. Fleming) Good Words, **37**: 842.
See Carriages, Automobile.

Motteux, Pierre Antoine. (H. S. Ashbee) Bookworm, **4**: 261.
Mottl, —, as Opera Leader. Sat. R. **80**: 649.
Motto changed, The; a Christmas Story. (Jean Ingelow) Good Words, **34**: Xmas no.
Motto Mongering. (W. C. Bitting) Bapt. R. **14**: 242.
Mottoes, Texts and. Cornh. **68**: 52.
Mouchez, Admiral. Ath. '92, **2**: 36. — Nature, **46**: 253.
Moulton, Louise Chandler, with portrait. Bk. News, **6**: 393.
— Poems. (B. C. Flower) Arena, **6**: 288. — (C. Kernahan) Fortn. **59**: 499.
— Portraits of. McClure, **3**: 243.
Moulton, R. G., with portrait. Bk. News, **9**: 321.
Mound-builders. (W. H. Withrow) Chaut. **19**: 735.
— Age of. (T. L. Gaertner) Am. Antiq. **15**: 195.
— and the Mastodon. (S. D. Peet) Am. Antiq. **14**: 59.
— Cultus of, and Village Life. (S. D. Peet) Am. Antiq. **14**: 247.
— Effigy, and the Modern Indians. (S. D. Peet) Am. Antiq. **17**: 19.
— of Ohio. (Harriet P. Eaton) M. Am. Hist. **29**: 70.
— Symbolic Carvings of. (F. W. Putnam) Am. Antiq. **18**: 55.
— Water Cult among. (S. D. Peet) Am. Antiq. **14**: 3.
Mounds, Ancient, in Northern Minnesota. (T. H. Lewis) Am. Antiq. **17**: 316.
— and Relics of Manitoba. (C. N. Bell) Am. Antiq. **15**: 207.
— and Stone Cists at St. Paul, Minn. (T. H. Lewis) Am. Antiq. **18**: 314.
— Effigy, of Wisconsin. (T. H. Lewis) Am. Antiq. **15**: 164.
— — Tribal Record in. (S. D. Peet) Am. Antiq. **15**: 90.
— The Hopewell Find. (W. K. Moorehead) Am. Antiq. **18**: 58.
— in the Mississippi Valley. (L. Carr) Nation, **61**: 306.
— in Tennessee. (G. P. Thurston) Am. Antiq. **14**: 95.
— Sand, of the St. John's River, Florida. (H. C. Mercer) Am. Natural. **29**: 76.
— Serpent Effigy. (S. D. Peet) Am. Antiq. **16**: 15.
Mounet-Sully, as Œdipe Roi and Le Cid. Critic, **24**: 242.
Mount Auburn. (F. Foxcroft) New Eng. M. n. s. **14**: 419.
Mount de Chantal, W. Va., Roman Catholic Convent-school at. (E. S. Houston) Cath. World, **56**: 822.
Mount Desert. (C. Waern) Garden & F. **5**: 530.
Mount Holyoke College, Festivals in. (H. E. Hooker) Cent. **27**: 431.
Mount Loretto, N. Y., Roman Catholic Schools at. (J. J. O'Shea) Cath. World, **58**: 19.
Mount Lowe Railroad, near Pasadena, Cal. (F. Van Vleck) Cassier, **5**: 449.
Mount Royal, Florida. (C. B. Moore) Around World, **1**: 191.
Mount Royal; a poem. Canad. M. **4**: 409.
Mt. Vernon Association. (Mrs. R. A. Pryor) Am. Hist. Reg. **1**: 407.
Mountain Art. (H. L. A. Culmer) Overland, n. s. **24**: 341.
Mountain Ascent, Highest, and Effects of Rarefied Air. (E. S. Balch) Pop. Sci. Mo. **46**: 668.
Mountain Ash, Sweet, as a Fruit Tree. (C. V. Hartman) Garden & F. **8**: 162.
Mountain Climbing. (W. M. Conway) Fortn. **60**: 345.
— Falls in. (W. M. Conway) Contemp. **66**: 821. Same art. Liv. Age, **204**: 121.
Mountain Climbing, Physiological Effects of. (C. Dent) Geog. J. **1**: 46.
— A Slip on the Ortler. (C. S. Davison) Atlan. **72**: 319.
Mountain Europa, A. (J. Fox, jr.) Cent. **22**: 760, 846.
Mountain Exploration, Development of. (W. M. Conway) New R. **10**: 736.
Mountain-lover, Protest of the. (A. B. Hart) Nation, **62**: 430.
Mountain Maid. (J. Albee) New Eng. M. n. s. **8**: 461.
Mountain Plants. (H. Carrevon) Garden & F. **6**: 152.
Mountain Railways, Great. (J. H. Means and J. C. Branner) Chaut. **21**: 426.
Mountain Ranges, Genesis of. (T. M. Reade) Nat. Sci. **3**: 371.
— Origin of. (J. Le Conte) Nature, **48**: 551.
Mountain Sickness. (C. S. Roy) Sci. Prog. **3**: 85.
Mountain Vegetation. (H. Carrevon) Garden & F. **9**: 153.
Mountain Vigil, A; a story. (A. P. Stone) Outing, **26**: 448.
Mountain Whites of the Alleghanies, Folk-lore of. (J. H. Porter) J. Am. Folk-Lore, **7**: 105.
Mountaineering, Adventure in. (F. Gribble) McClure, **1**: 417.
— A Chat with Sir W. M. Conway on. (J. F. Fraser) Eng. Illust. **15**: 481.
— Dent on. Ath. '92, **2**: 213. — Sat. R. **74**: 260.
— Episodes of. (E. L. Weeks) Scrib. M. **15**: 531.
Mountaineering Memories. (H. Preston - Thomas) Blackw. **158**: 92. Same art. Liv. Age, **206**: 296.
Mountaineers and Mountaineering. (E. Whymper) Leis. Hour, **45**: 150.
Mountains. (D. W. Freshfield) Geog. J. **3**: 228. — (A. H. Green) Good Words, **33**: 43.
— Ascents of, Highest Possible. Around World, **1**: 12.
— Coasting down some Great. (H. L. Wells) Cosmopol. **20**: 240.
— Formation of. Chamb. J. **69**: 295.
— Forms of. (J. E. Marr) Nat. Sci. **6**: 240.
— of California. (C. S. Sargent) Garden & F. **9**: 81.
Mounted Police of N. W. Canada. (J. G. A. Creighton) Scrib. M. **14**: 399.
Mourie, Sanctuary of. (G. M. Godden) Folk-Lore, **4**: 498.
Mourning, Royal and Other. (M. A. Belloc) Idler, **8**: 275.
Mourning Customs. Gent. M. n. s. **49**: 108.
Mousall, John, of Woburn. (W. R. Cutter) N. E. Reg. **47**: 462.
Mouse-Tower on the Tyne; a story. (M. G. Hancock) Belgra. **81**: 384.
Mouthe Cave, The. Nature, **55**: 55.
Movements, Involuntary. (J. Jastrow) Pop. Sci. Mo. **40**: 743. **41**: 636.
— Voluntary, Causes affecting Rapidity of. (F. B. Dressler) Am. J. Psychol. **4**: 514.
Moving of Heavy Masses by the Ancients. (W. F. Durfee) Engin. M. **6**: 611–793.
Moving House; a sketch. (B. McEvoy) Canad. M. **1**: 669.
Mowat, John Lancaster Gough. Acad. **46**: 102.
Mowat, Sir Oliver. (F. Yeigh) Canad. M. **2**: 582.
Mowgli leaves the Jungle forever; a story. (Rudyard Kipling) Cosmopol. **19**: 670.
Mowlson, Ann, Lady. (A. McF. Davis) New Eng. M. n. s. **9**: 773.
Moxley's Chum; a story. (V. Berry) Outing, **19**: 481.
Mozarabic Offices, Pseudo-. Church Q. **40**: 169.
Mozart, Wolfgang Amadeus. Don Giovanni. Sat. R. **79**: 858.

Mozart, Wolfgang Amadeus, Estimate of. (F. J. Crowest) Blackw. 151: 37. Same art. Ecl. M. 118: 462. Same art. Liv. Age, 192: 747.
Mozley, Anne, Essays of. Church Q. 34: 410.— Liv. Age, 195: 46.—Spec. 68: 406.
Mozley, Thos. (W. Mercer) Ath. '93, 1: 798.
Mr. Anthony Jones of New York; a story. (H. Vedder) Eng. Illust. 12: no. 1, 17.
Mr. Benjamin Franklin Gish's Ball; a story. (M. E. M. Davis) Harper, 85: 949.
Mr. Brown. (H. P. Stephens) Time, 15: 679. 16: 14, 142.
Mr. Burbitt's Bible Class. (M. Edwards) New Eng. M. n. s. 8: 90.
Mr. Carter's Client; a story. (E. F. Byrrne) Argosy, 57: 295.
Mr. Castonel; a novel. (Mrs. Henry Wood) Argosy, 59: 49-561.
Mr. Cummin's Relinquishment. (R. M. Johnston) Cent. 25: 140.
Mr. Duddel's Temptation; a story. All the Year, 76: 13.
Mr. Ebenezer Bull's Investments; a Story of Philemon Perch. (R. M. Johnston) Cent. 25: 558.
Mr. Gadsbury's Brother. (M. F. S. Williams) Cent. 24: 124.
Mr. Jones's Experiment. (J. S. Norton) Cent. 24: 590.
Mr. Keegan's Elopement. (W. Churchill) Cent. 30: 215.
Mr. Menelaws, a Long Vacation Study: a story. Temp. Bar, 96: 96.
Mr. Mortimer; a story. All the Year, 75: 492.
Mr. Pate's Only Infirmity. (R. M. Johnston) Cent. 26: 134.
Mr. Pattin's Penchant. (C. J. K. Fenton) Longm. 27: 259.
Mr. Presterton; a story. (I. T. Sullivan) Idler, 1: 170.
Mr. Robert Bullock's Method; a story. All the Year, 70: 420.
Mr. Snagg of London; a story. (H. Vedder) Eng. Illust. 13: 451.
Mr. Somerby's Plot. (J. K. Leys) Chamb. J. 73: 237.
Mr. Stein's Grandmother; a story. Argosy, 53: 342.
Mr. Surtrees. (D. S. Meldrum) Good Words, 36: Xmas no., 15.
Mr. Taswell Langdon of Seville; a story. (M. Wilcox) Cosmopol. 13: 704.
Mr. Tewksbury's New Year; a story. (Louise Lyndon) Bost. 3: 335.
Mr. Warrenne, Medical Practitioner; a story. (M. E. Edwards) Argosy, 55: 54—56: 441.
Mr. Wrong; a story. (Lise Boehm) Temp. Bar, 108: 447. Same art. Liv. Age, 210: 335.
M'randy Ann's Romance. (H. M. Winslow) New Eng. M. n. s. 9: 751.
Mrs. Bligh; a story. (Rhoda Broughton) Temp. Bar, 96: 124-553.
Mrs. Chimp; a story. (W. E. Tirebuck) Idler, 9: 650.
Mrs. Cliff's Yacht; a story. (F. R. Stockton) Cosmopol. 20: 612. 21: 45-304.
Mrs. Crichton's Creditor. (A. F. Hector) Lippinc. 57: 3.
Mrs. Cronarty's Maid; a tale. (F. H. Holland) Canad. M. 7: 348.
Mrs. Curgenven of Curgenven; a story. (S. B. Gould) Cornh. 66: 1-561. 67: 1-561.
Mrs. Délire's Euchre Party. (E. Lynne) Southern M. 4: 188.
Mrs. Driffield; a story. Macmil. 65: 434. Same art. Liv. Age, 193: 696.
Mrs. Hallam's Companion. (M. J. Holmes) Lippinc. 54: 723.
Mrs. Janz's Jar; a story. Argosy, 55: 194.
Mrs. Jeff; a story. Temp. Bar, 103: 507.
Mrs. Juliet. (Mrs. A. W. Hunt) Longm. 19: 312—21: 111.
Mrs. Lofter's Ride. (J. A. Mitchell) Scrib. M. 20: 217.
Mrs. Lofty's Diary, Extracts from. (B. Lindsay) Overland, n. s. 23: 600. 24: 425. 25: 237, 470. 26: 64, 502. 27: 611.
Mrs. McGlory's Niece. (M. Hunt) Longm. 23: 387.
Mrs. Martin's Company; a story. (Jane Barlow) National, 23: 708. Same art. Liv. Age, 202: 359. Same art. Ecl. M. 123: 373.
Mrs. Melrose's Companion; a story. (R. Warfield) Chamb. J. 70: 667.
Mrs. Naseby's Denial. (E. F. Benson) Longm. 23: 271.
Mrs. O'Donnell's Report; a story. (E. Lawless) Eng. Illust. 10: 717.
Mrs. Pettibone's Dinner-horn. (C. B. Loomis) Cent. 24: 304.
Mrs. Pickering's Vanity; a story. (I. Garvey) Argosy, 54: 249.
Mrs. Ponsonby's Poodle; a story. (L. H. Armstrong) Belgra. 79: Christmas no., 50.
Mrs. Rex's Brahmin. (K. G. Wells) New Eng. M. n. s. 7: 85.
Mrs. Riddle's Daughter; a story. All the Year, 74: 253.
Mrs. Risley's Christmas Dinner; a story. (E. Higginson) Lippinc. 55: 102.
Mrs. Romney. (R. N. Carey) Lippinc. 51: 515.
Mrs. Santa Claus; a story. (M. Richardson) Lippinc. 55: 87.
Mrs. Teddy's Skating Party; a story. (Constance Milman) Temp. Bar, 97: 549.
Mrs. Tonkin at Home. Liv. Age, 205: 204.
Mrs. White-Smith's Afternoon Party. (H. W. Lucy) Idler, 4: 418.
Much Ado about Nothing; a poem. Gent. M. n. s. 54: 491.
Mud as a Material in Architecture. (W. Simpson) J. Soc. Arts, 40: 697. Same art. Pop. Sci. Mo. 41: 762.
— Value of. Ecl. M. 118: 103.
Mud-Daubing, Facts from Bihar about. (W. Egerton) 19th Cent. 36: 279.
Mud-line, Murray's. (J. Chumley) Nat. Sci. 6: 395.
Mudie's Library. (Wm. C. Preston) Good Words, 35: 668.
Muehlig, Hugo. (J. J. Raulston) Mo. Illust. 3: 191.
Mueller, August. Ath. '92, 2: 417.
Müller, Carl. Acad. 44: 158.
Mueller, Ferdinand von. Nat. Sci. 9: 340.—Ath. '96, 2: 530.
Mueller, Max, and the Science of Thought. (J. Chappellsmith) Open Court, 2: 943.
— Denounced for Heresy. Open Court, 5: 2829.
Mueller, Peter Paul. (C. de Kay) Q. Illust. 2: 255.
Mueller, Wilhelm, Poetry of. (J. T. Hatfield) Meth. R. 55: 581.
Mueller, William, Painter. (J. Orrock) Art J. 47: 154.
Muenier, Jules Alexis. (P. G. Hamerton) Scrib. M. 15: 587.
Muensterberg and his Critics. (E. B. Titchener) Mind, 17: 251, 397.
Muff, Reign of the. (S. E. Braine) Good Words, 36: 832.
Mugwumps, Ancient and Modern. Atlan. 75: 284.
Muhlenberg, Gotthilf Heinrich Ernst, with portrait. Pop. Sci. Mo. 45: 689.
Muir, John. (J. Swett) Cent. 24: 120.

Muir Glacier, Alaska, Studies of. (H. F. Reid) Nat. Geog. M. **4**: 19.
Muirhead, James, with portrait. (G. Carle) Jurid. R. **2**: 27.
Mulai Bushta, My Escape from. (W. B. Harris) Blackw. **157**: 98. Same art. Ecl. M. **124**: 250. Same art. Liv. Age, **204**: 457.
Mulai Hassan, Sultan of Morocco. (C. F. Goss) 19th Cent. **32**: 311.
— Last Journey of. Dub. R. **118**: 436.
Mulais, Religion of. Asia. R. **15**: 417.
Mulberry Bend; Clearing of a New York Slum. (J. A. Riis) R. of Rs. (N. Y.) **12**: 172.
Mulberry Tree, Red. Garden & F. **7**: 23.
— Russian. (C. A. Keffer) Garden & F. **7**: 493.
Mule-skinner's Coincidence, A. (W. B. Cameron) Overland, n. s. **28**: 463.
Mules: my Forthcoming Book. (W. B. Tegetmeier) Eng. Illust. **11**: 880.
Mulhouse, Working-class Settlements in, and in Milan. (C. Hancock) Fortn. **62**: 94.
Mull, Naturalist's Notes off. (N. Lochaber) Good Words, **34**: 850.
Mullany, P. F. [Brother Azarias], with portrait. (G. E. Hardy) Educa. R. **6**: 475.
— Phases of Thought and Criticism. Atlan. **71**: 126.
Mulready, W. (E. F. S. Dilke) Fortn. **58**: 346. Same art. Liv. Age, **195**: 434.
Mulso, John. (L. B. Lang) Longm. **26**: 492. Same art. Liv. Age, **207**: 177.
Multiple Standard, The. (H. Winn) Am. M. Civics, **7**: 567.
Mummies, Egyptian, in Cambridge Anatomical Museum. (A. Macalister) Anthrop. J. **23**: 101.
Mummy, the, Budge on. Ath. **'94**, **1**: 283.
Mummy-wheat. Spec. **73**: 437, 524, 559.
Mun, Count de, with portrait. (E. Davis) Cath. World, **60**: 345.
Munby, Arthur J. Faithful Servants. Gent. M. n. s. **48**: 106.
Munchausen's Travels. Bookworm, **2**: 273.
Mungo Mah Lobeh, Ascent of. (Mary H. Kingsley) National, **27**: 357.
Munich and Bayreuth. (C. Phillips) Fortn. **66**: 553.
— as an Art Centre. (C. De Kay) Cosmopol. **13**: 643.
— Court Theatre of. (J. G. Robertson) National, **25**: 247.
— International Art Exhibition. (J. Forbes-Robinson) M. of Art, **3**: 29-69.
— Music in, 1893. Ath. **'93**, **1**: 742.
— Salon of. (A. B. Bibb) Am. Arch. **50**: 133.
— Schäfflertanz and Metzgersprung in. Cath. World, **64**: 306.
— Suburbs of. (H. H. Lusk) Mo. Illust. **5**: 306.
Municipal Art. (C. S. Sargent) Garden & F. **8**: 501.
Municipal Buildings, Architecture of. (E. C. Gardner) Engin. M. **8**: 608.
Municipal Corruption, Science of. Forum, **15**: 43.
Municipal Government. (M. McG. Dana) Soc. Econ. **8**: 226.
— Civil Service in. (S. Low) Good Govt. **13**: 29. — (C. Richardson) Good Govt. **13**: 65.
— a Corporate, not a Political Problem. (F. Morison) Forum, **13**: 788.
— Evils of. (W. N. Black) Engin. M. **3**: 73.
— Good, A Case of. (F. G. Peabody) Forum, **13**: 53.
— in England. Soc. Econ. **8**: 212.
— in Quincy, Mass., Lessons from. (C. F. Adams) Forum, **14**: 282.— (W. P. Garrison) Nation, **55**: 197.
Municipal Government in the U. S., Failures in. (G. Bradford) Ann. Am. Acad. Pol. Sci. **3**: 691.
— — Home Rule for American Cities. (E. P. Oberholtzer) Ann. Am. Acad. Pol. Sci. **3**: 736.
— Modes of, in the West. (J. Ralph) Harper, **84**: 709.
— Science of, Study of. (F. P. Prichard) Ann. Am. Acad. Pol. Sci. **2**: 450.
See Cities.
Municipal Institutions in America and England. (J. Chamberlain) Forum, **14**: 267.
Municipal League of Boston. (S. B. Capen) Am. J. Pol. **5**: 1.
— of Philadelphia. (C. R. Woodruff) Am. J. Pol. **5**: 287. — (A. B. Woodford) Soc. Econ. **2**: 366.
Municipal Monopolies. (R. Ogden) Nation, **58**: 285.
Municipal Ownership, Fallacy of. (M. J. Francisco) Engin. M. **5**: 725.
— of Public Corporations. (M. J. Francisco) Engin. M. **9**: 41.
Municipal Problems in England, Literary and. (F. Harrison) Forum, **14**: 644.
— of New York and London. (A. Shaw) R. of Rs. (N. Y.) **5**: 282.
— Other Side of. (R. Ogden) Nation, **56**: 449.
Municipal Reform, A Definite Step toward. (H. Welsh) Forum, **17**: 179.
Municipal Terms, Certain. (C. W. Ernst) Green Bag, **6**: 219.
Municipalities at Work: Birmingham. (Frederick Dolman) New R. **11**: 74.
— Manchester. New R. **11**: 499.
Municipality, Christian Citizen and the. (W. D. Maxon) Am. M. Civics, **7**: 543.
— Modern, Political Organization of. (W. D. Lewis) Ann. Am. Acad. Pol. Sci. **2**: 458.
Munkacsy, Michael. (J. B. Atkinson) M. of Art, **4**: 441.
Munro, Sir Thomas, and the Madras Presidency, Bradshaw's. Sat. R. **78**: 268.
Munster, Faction-fighting in. (J. F. MacNamara) Westm. **144**: 417.
— Match-making Customs in. (K. Tynan) Eng. Illust. **12**: no. 1, 45.
— Pope Alexander VI.'s Bull and the Treaty of. (N. D. Davis) Nation, **62**: 213.
Murad V., Sultan of Turkey. Sat. R. **80**: 8, 39.
Mural Decoration. (F. Crowninshield) Am. Arch. **49**: 55.
— in America. (R. Cortissoz) Cent. **29**: 110.
Mural Painting with Soluble Silicates. (Mrs. L. Merritt and Prof. Roberts-Austen) J. Soc. Arts, **44**: 39.
Mural Paintings. (L. Merritt and Prof. Roberts-Austen) Am. Arch. **51**: 3.
— in Berkshire. Reliquary, **32**: 137.
— in the Panthéon and Hôtel de Ville of Paris. (W. H. Low) Scrib. M. **12**: 661.
Murat, Prince and Princess Achille, in Florida. (M. L. McConnell) Cent. **24**: 513.
Murderous Mixture, A; a story. (Geo. M. Fenn) Chamb. J. **70**: 13.
Murders in China. Blackw. **154**: 592.
— in Massachusetts. (W. M. Cook) Am. Statis. Assoc. **3**: 357.
Murphy, Lady Blanche. (D. D. Slade) New Eng. M. n. s. **9**: 757.
Murray, Sir Charles. Ath. **'95**, **1**: 738.
Murray, David. (M. H. Dixon) Art J. **44**: 144.
Murray, David Christie, with portrait. Bk. News, **13**: 137. — (W. Armstrong) M. of Art, **14**: 397.
— my First Book, Grace Forbeach. Idler, **4**: 155.

Murray, George. Verses and Versions. (A. G. Doughty) Canad. M. 5: 476.
Murray, John. (J. S. Cotton) Acad. 49: 350. — Ath. '92, 1: 469. — (A. Repplier) Lippinc. 50: 115. — Sat. R. 73: 412.
Murrieta, Joaquin, a Californian Fra Diavolo. (J. M. Scanland) Overland, n. s. 26: 530.
Murty Mulligan's Revenge; a story. All the Year, 74: 234.
Musaccio. Novellino; tr. by Waters. Sat. R. 81: 106.
Muscat. (J. T. Bent) Contemp. 68: 871. Same art. Liv. Age, 208: 169.
Muscatine, Iowa. Mascoutin. (I. B. Richman) M. Am. Hist. 28: 89.
Muscle-building. (E. Checkley) Lippinc. 50: 522.
Muscles and Morals. (M. E. Blake) Lippinc. 54: 286.
Muscoe Plate, The; a story. (M. F. S. Williams) Overland, n. s. 19: 176.
Muscular Contraction, On the Nature of. (T. W. Engelmann) Nature, 51: 519.
Muscular Reaction, Sensorial and. (A. R. Hill and R. Watanbe) Am. J. Psychol. 6: 242.
Muscular Sense and its Location in the Brain Cortex. (M. A. Starr) Psychol. R. 2: 33.
Muse of the Halls, The; a story. (G. Gissing) Eng. Illust. 11: 313.
Musette. (W. Boosey) Temp. Bar, 103: 241.
Museum of Natural History, Plans for a. (P. André) Am. Arch. 42: 143, 155.
Museum Methods. (F. A. Lucas) Science, n. s. 3: 573.
Museums, Architecture of. (E. Rümler) Am. Arch. 42: 95, 107.
— as Aids to Technical Art Instruction. (E. F. Strange) M. of Art, 13: 278.
— Casual Thoughts on. (H. H. Howorth) Nat. Sci. 7: 97, 319. 8: 114, 377.
— Classifications of. (G. B. Goode) Science, n. s. 3: 154.
— in Educational Work. (F. Starr) Educa. R. 3: 254.
— Local. (G. Payne) Antiq. n. s. 27: 241.
— New Museum and the Sidon Sarcophagi. (T. M. Muller) New R. 10: 17.
— Notes on. Illus. Archæol. 1: 59. 2: 30.
— of Paris, Municipal. (F. Harrison) Fortn. 62: 458.
— Place of, in Education. (T. Greenwood) Science, 22: 246.
— Public, If we have Public Libraries, why not have? (E. S. Morse) Atlan. 72: 112.
— Relationships and Responsibilities of. (G. B. Goode) Science, n. s. 2: 197.
— Some Casual Thoughts on. (H. Howorth) Nat. Sci. 7: 319.
Mushrooms and Toadstools. Time, 17: 282.
— — A few Edible. (W. H. Gibson) Harper, 89: 390.
— Cultivation of. (E. O. Orpet) Garden & F. 6: 436. 9: 456. — (W. Downs) Garden & F. 8: 27.
— Notes for Eaters of. (W. G. Farlow) Garden & F. 7: 32-82.
— Our Edible Toadstools and. (W. H. Gibson) Garden & F. 8: 488.
Music. (B. J. Lang) Atlan. 73: 207.
— Ability to listen to. (A. R. Schlesinger) Music, 8: 345.
— Accessorial, in Plays. (W. Beatty-Kingston) Theatre, 34: 143. — (J. A. F. Maitland) Theatre, 34: 200.
— American. How can it be developed? (H. Moore) Music, 1: 321.
— Americanism in. (A. Weld) Music, 5: 633. — (H. J. Krum) Music, 6: 544.
— and the American Poets. (H. A. Clarke) Music, 6: 63-282.
— and Ethnology. (R. Wallaschek) Music, 9: 168.
Music and the Individual. (C. B. Cady) Music, 1: 54.
— and the Inner Life of Man. (W. S. B. Mathews) Music, 7: 403.
— and the Intellect. (R. P. Rider) Music, 2: 32, 178.
— and Life. (Mrs. J. V. Cheney) Music, 11: 1.
— and Musicians in England, Poor. Sat. R. 82: 60.
— — Statham on. Sat. R. 73: 18.
— and Nutrition. (E. B. Perry) Music, 6: 559.
— and Poetry. (W. M. Derthick) Music, 10: 24.
— and the Poets. (H. Arthur Smith) Univ. R. 8: 275.
— and its Processes. (R. R. Manners) Music, 4: 365.
— and Western Papers. (R. J. Jessup) Music, 5: 153.
— the Art of the 19th Century. (F. A. Gevaert) Music, 9: 284, 351.
— Art of, Parry on. Spec. 72: 856.
— as Discipline and Culture. (W. S. B. Mathews) Music, 6: 349.
— as an Educator. (P. C. Hayden) Music, 11: 41.
— as a Medicine. Chamb. J. 71: 145. — (J. C. Hadden) Music, 9: 359.
— as a University Study. (W. S. Pratt) Music, 6: 413.
— Bohemian, in 1894. (J. J. Kral) Music, 7: 514.
— Chamber, Educational Value of. (J. S. Van Cleve) Music, 5: 641.
— Chinese. (M. E. Simms) Music, 6: 485.
— Church, and Congregational Singing. (E. P. Thesiger) Eng. Illust. 9: 695.
— — Recent Decrees on. (H. T. Henry) Am. Cath. Q. 20: 82.
— Conception of. (K. J. Belling) Music, 2: 540.
— Conservatory of, Uses of. (E. Dickinson) Music, 8: 366.
— Descriptive. Macmil. 68: 109. 69: 122. Same art. Liv. Age, 198: 357.
— Development of, in America. (A. Seidl) Forum, 13: 386.
— Difference of Time and Rhythm in. (R. Wallaschek) Mind, 20: 28. — (E. T. Dixon) Mind, 20: 236.
— Dignity of. (J. S. Van Cleve) Music, 1: 7.
— Emotion, and Morals. (H. R. Haweis) Music, 4: 595.
— English. Sat. R. 78: 535.
— — History of. (J. C. Hadden) Scot. R. 28: 264.
— Essence of. (J. P. White) Music, 8: 466.
— for the Masses. (Mrs. J. Marshall) 19th Cent. 32: 67.
— for the People. (K. Hackett) Music, 10: 125.
— Form and Spirit in. (B. M. Whiteley) Music, 2: 544.
— French Masters of, Hervey's. Sat. R. 77: 262.
— from the Standpoint of Sociology. (C. Ballaigne) Chaut. 23: 455.
— Grace Notes and Ornaments in. (C. Sternberg) Music, 8: 61.
— hath Charms. Macmil. 73: 217.
— Heavenly Maid. (T. T. Munger) Cent. 29: 282.
— Histories of. (J. S. Shedlock) Acad. 41: 22.
— History of, Impelling Forces in. (J. C. Fillmore) Music, 9: 19.
— — Matthews'. Sat. R. 74: 258.
— — Weber's. Sat. R. 74: 453.
— How we think of Tones and. (R. Wallaschek) Contemp. 66: 258.
— in America. (A. Dvořák) Harper, 90: 428.
— in the Courts. (J. J. Kral) Music, 7: 315.
— in Emergency. (F. J. Crowest) Gent. M. n. s. 51: 79.
— in England. Sat. R. 80: 542. — (F. J. Crowest) Blackw. 158: 819.
— in Germany. (M. D. Taylor) Music, 6: 516.
— in the Language of the People. (K. Hackett) Music, 9: 519.
— in Madagascar. (F. A. Van Stantford) Music, 8: 399.
— in the Making. Belgra. 84: 75.

Music in Mysticism. (N. H. Imber) Music, 7: 573.
— in North America. (J. C. Fillmore) Music, 8: 171–599.
— in Norway. (A. von Ende) Music, 6: 475.
— *in profundis*. (J. A. F. Maitland) Time, 21: 19.
— in Public Schools. (J. C. Johnson) Bost. 1: 622.
— Influence of, upon Life and Health. (E. A. Smith) Music, 8: 361.
— Instrumental, Early, in Boston. (G. Brayley) Bost. 1: 189.
— Is the Musical Idea Masculine? (E. Brower) Atlan. 73: 332.
— Isolation of. (W. S. Pratt) Forum, 21: 501.
— Italian, of 18th Century. "Il bel canto" of Svengali. (G. A. Dennen) Music, 8: 551.
— Italian Church, Golden Age of. (E. Dickinson) Bib. Sac. 51: 88.
— Italian Masters, Streatfeild's. Sat. R. 80: 708.
— its Laws and Tendencies. (Eleanor P. Sherwood) Music, 10: 376.
— Japanese, Pigott on. Sat. R. 76: 302.
— Licensing, in London. Sat. R. 78: 501, 534.
— Masters of. (G. Holme) Munsey, 13: 468.
— Military, Kappey on. Sat. R. 77: 451.
— The Minor Triad and the Chord of the Diminished Seventh. (J. P. White) Music, 10: 16, 116.
— Modern Romantic School of. Music, 4: 549.
— Money and. (J. C. Hadden) Chamb. J. 73: 90.
— Morals in. (H. Arthur Smith) Univ. R. 7: 428.
— Mother-tone of, and Tonalonomatopy. (C. C. Converse) Monist, 5: 375.
— National, Origin and Growth of. (J. Moos) Music, 1: 531.
— Nature and Object of. (C. Saint-Saens) Music, 5: 557.
— — and Women. (H. A. Clarke) Music, 7: 453.
— of the Jews. (N. H. Imber) Music, 6: 496.
— of the Spheres, The. (Mary Proctor) New Sci. R. 2: 305.
— Old English, Popular, Chappell on. Sat. R. 77: 479.
— Omaha Indian, Fletcher's. (F. Boas) J. Am. Folk-Lore, 7: 169.
— Pedagogical Needs in. (T. Tapper) Music, 1: 68.
— Permanent Element in. (W. S. B. Mathews) Music, 11: 28.
— Pianoforte Sonata, Shedlock on. Sat. R. 80: 472.
— Plato on. (K. J. Belling) Music, 1: 197–317.
— Primitive, Wallascheck's. (J. C. Fillmore) J. Am. Folk-Lore, 7: 165.
— Printing, Early. (W. B. Squire) Bibliographica, 3: 99, 483.
— Private Teacher of, versus Conservatory. (W. S. B. Mathews) Music, 8: 487.
— Public Schools. (S. W. Cole) New Eng. M. n. s. 13: 328.
— Pure. (E. B. Perry) Music, 8: 113.
— Revealed through Clairaudience. — (H. M. Poole) Psych. R. 1: 207. (E. W. Marchant) Psych. R. 1: 353.
— Ruskin on. Ed. by Wakefield. Sat. R. 78: 299.
— Russian. (C. Lichtenberger) Music, 6: 506.
— Scales of Alypius. Sat. R. 78: 152.
— Significance of. (P. Carus) Monist, 5: 401.
— Sight-reading, Need of Instruction in. (W. H. Pontius) Music, 6: 289.
— Street, Regulation of. (J. C. Hadden) 19th Cent. 39: 950.
— String Quartets. (H. Knapp) Music, 10: 41.
— Studies in, Hadow's. Sat. R. 79: 701.
— Study of, for Children. (C. W. Landon) Music, 3: 542.
— Teaching of. (F. W. Wodell) Music, 11: 159.
Music, Teaching of, in Elementary Schools. (W. G. McNaught) J. Soc. Arts, 41: 411.
— Tone and Color in. (C. S. Wake) Music, 11: 171.
— Unemotional, Some Uses of. (E. P. Reese) Int. J. Ethics, 5: 471.
— University Work in. (H. G. Hanchett) Music, 10: 360.
— — Women and Men in. (C. Selden) Music, 7: 322.
— Writing Words for. (F. R. Burton) Writer, 9: 93.
Music Books of 17th Century. Bookworm, 3: 233.
Music Extension, Plan for. (F. W. Root) Music, 9: 131.
Music Hall, At the. (D. Wallis) Longm. 22: 163.
— History of the. Sat. R. 77: 91.
— Pedigree of the. (E. R. Pennell) Contemp. 63: 575. Same art. Ecl. M. 120: 792.
Music Halls, Costers and. (A. Chevalier) Eng. Illust. 10: 479.
— London. (J. K. Jerome) Idler, 1: 121. — (J. Hatton) Idler, 1: 239. — (F. Wedmore) 19th Cent. 40: 128.
— London County Council and. (W. Archer) Contemp. 67: 317.
Music Lessons. (M. Moszkowski) Music, 4: 73.
Music Teacher, the Pupils and the Parents. (C. W. Landon) Music, 2: 504.
Music Teachers, Necessity of a Standard for. (E. Van Valkenburg) Music, 10: 370.
Musical, Who is? (W. Malmene) Music, 9: 70, 412.
Musical Art, French. (C. Willeby) Eng. Illust. 11: 419.
— National Element in. (J. Moos) Music, 3: 35.
Musical Books, List of. Music, 6: 536.
Musical Celebrities of Vienna. (W. von Sachs) Harper, 93: 622.
Musical Clefs, Abolition of. (E. Glode Ellis) Univ. R. 4: 223.
Musical Composition and Psychology. (F. Paulham) Music, 5: 28.
Musical Compositions, American. (F. W. Root) Music, 2: 1.
Musical Conception, Development of. (B. C. Henry) Music, 10: 442.
Musical Conductors of the Day. (J. Bennett) Eng. Illust. 10: 3.
Musical Criticism. Sat. R. 78: 155.
— and the Critics. (J. F. Runciman) Fortn. 62: 170. — (J. Bradford) Westm. 142: 530.
— Former. Sat. R. 73: 332.
— Gentle Art of. (J. F. Runciman) New R. 12: 612.
— in England, Some Aspects of. (C. V. Stanford) Fortn. 61: 826.
— Recent. Ed. R. 182: 468.
Musical Curiosity, A. (S. Baring-Gould) Chamb. J. 72: 81.
Musical Expressiveness, Experimental Test of. (B. I. Gilman) Am. J. Psychol. 4: 558. 5: 42.
Musical Festival at Gloucester. Sat. R. 80: 376–407.
— of the Lower Rhine. (J. S. Shedlock) Acad. 47: 490.
Musical Instrument, Primitive. Reliquary, 36: 221.
Musical Instrument Factory. Music, 8: 351.
Musical Instruments as Works of Art. (J. Leyland) M. of Art, 6: 298.
— at the Vienna Exhibition, 1892. Ath. '92, 2: 457, 525.
— Day on. Sat. R. 73: 99.
— of the World. (I. H. Hall) Cosmopol. 18: 165.
— Orchestral. (D. Spillane) Pop. Sci. Mo. 40: 793.
Musical Journalism and Journalists. (W. S. B. Mathews) Music, 2: 231, 331.
Musical Journalist, The. (G. B. Armstrong) Music, 4: 377.

Musical Library, A. (T. Tapper) Music, 5: 693.
— Books for a. (J. G. Adams) Music, 3: 407.
Musical Life, What is a? (W. L. Tomlins) Music, 1: 161.
Musical-literary Clubs, Reading for. (W. S. B. Mathews) Music, 3: 316.
Musical Literature, Curiosities of. (A. Veit) Cosmopol. 13: 493.
Musical Memory, Cultivation of. (F. E. Regal) Music, 7: 218.
Musical Neighbors. Spec. 69: 883.
Musical Notations. Music, 3: 666.
Musical Performers of the Day. (J. Bennett) Eng. Illust. 9: 643.
Musical Pitch. *See* Pitch, Musical.
Musical Prime Numbers. (J. P. White) Music, 2: 553.
Musical Progress and the American People. (W. L. Tomlins) Music, 7: 541.
Musical Scales, Harmonic Nature of. (J. Moss) Music, 6: 13–293. 7: 19, 138.
Musical Science and Musical Performance. (J. Moss) Music, 1: 347.
— Logarithms in. (J. P. White) Music, 3: 399, 565.
Musical Sensibility, Emotional Basis of. (A. E. Brand) Music, 5: 300.
Musical Snapshots. (H. R. Haweis) Contemp. 70: 286.
Musical Societies of New York. (J. M. Prentice) Munsey, 10: 458.
Musical Taste, Catholicity in. (O. Wister) Atlan. 72: 650.
Musical Temperament, The, and its Manifestations, (W. W. Hutchins) Blackw. 160: 29. Same art. Liv. Age, 210: 367.
Musical Terms, Persian, Old. (C. E. Wilson) Ath. '92, 2: 863.
Musical Transmigration. (Nimmo Christie) Gent. M. n. s. 57: 325.
Musical World, Over-production in the. (J. A. Fuller Maitland) National, 24: 557.
Musicians, Street. (P. Gsell) Music, 8: 374.
Musk-ox, The. (J. Parry) Nature, 47: 560.—(H. T. Martin) Pop. Sci. Mo. 40: 364.
— Hunting, with the Dog Ribs. (Frank Russell) Scrib. M. 19: 235.
Muskallonge Fishing. (E. W. Sandys) Outing, 27: 134.
Musketry Training. Un. Serv. M. 5: 253.
Muskogee Nation, and the U. S. Lend a H. 12: 445.
Muskoka Days and Doings. (C. Bluefield) Canad. M. 5: 488.
Muskoka Marvel-lands. (E. W. Sandys) Outing, 20: 163.
Musset, Alfred de. (L. Katscher) 19th Cent. 33: 525.
— Illustrations to. M. of Art, 7: 274.
Mussulman Secret Societies. (N. Ney) Cosmopol. 17: 556.
Mussulmans of India and the Armenian Question. (Ghulamus-Saqlan) 19th Cent. 37: 926.
Mustagh-Ata, Attempts to ascend. (S. Hedin) Geog. J. 6: 350.
— Exploration in. (W. M. Conway) Geog. J. 2: 289.
Mustard Manufacture. (J. Hatton) Eng. Illust. 10: 99.
Muster, Militia, in New Hampshire, Old. (H. T. Perry) New Eng. M. n. s. 7: 97.
Muswell Hill Murder. Green Bag, 8: 399.
Mutilations, Transmission of, Cases of Apparent. (O. vom Rath) Am. Natural. 28: 1.
Mutiny on board the "Caswell," 1875. (J. Amos) Idler, 6: 35.
Mutiny on the "Jinny Aiken." (H. Phelps Whitmarsh) Cent. 29: 912.
Mutton-bird of the Furneaux Islands. Chamb. J. 70: 165.
Mutual Aid among Barbarians. (Prince Kropotkin) 19th Cent. 31: 101.
— among Modern Men. (Prince Kropotkin) 19th Cent. 39: 65, 914. Same art. Ecl. M. 126: 289.
Mutual Benefit Societies in Conn. (S. M. Hotchkiss) Am. J. Soc. Sci. 31: 54.
Mutual Societies, New Belgian Law on. Lend a H. 13: 326.
Mutualism, Philosophy of. (F. Parsons) Arena, 9: 783.
Muzzioli, Giovanni, Note on. Art J. 48: 110.
Mweru, Lake, A Journey to. (A. Sharpe) Geog. J. 1: 524.
My Adventure with a Lion. (H. Rave) Outing, 24: 14.
My Best Fare; a story. Chamb. J. 71: 141.
My Boarder; a true story. Overland, n. s. 21: 468.
My Brother Aaron. (E. Searchfield) Sund. M. 23: 694, 771, 826.
My Canada; a poem. (J. Blewett) Canad. M. 6: 465.
My Christmas Dinner; a story. (Mrs. E. Kennard) Belgra. 79: Christmas no., 21.
My Cousin Colas. All the Year, 74: 68, 92.
My Cousin Fanny; a story. (T. N. Page) Cent. 23: 178.
My Dead Self; a story. (R. F. Dickson) Canad. M. 4: 233.
My First Big Trout. (S. A. George) Longm. 24: 154.
My First Kill; a story. Temp. Bar, 106: 336.
My First Night; a story. (A. Daudet) Theatre, 32: 299.
My Friend Arcanieva. Macmil. 73: 139.
My Friend Beppino. Macmil. 71: 372.
My Friend Jimmy. (B. Atkinson) Sund. M. 22: 758.
My Friend Will; a story. (C. F. Lummis) McClure, 3: 531.
My Friendly Jap; a story. All the Year, 71: 37, 62.
My Friend's Contributor; a story. All the Year, 73: 61.
My Ghosts. (L. H. Harris) Southern M. 4: 136.
My Goddaughter; a story. (Gustav Kobbé) Cosmopol. 19: 37.
My Grandmamma; a story. (J. Reid) Good Words, 34: 272.
My Great-aunt Martha; a story. Temp. Bar, 99: 568. Same art. Liv. Age, 200: 104.
My Guests; a poem. (E. Arnold) Cosmopol. 18: 133.
My Indian Plunder. (Julian Ralph) Scrib. M. 20: 637.
My Kaffir. (J. A. Barry) Chamb. J. 73: 804–819.
My Lady passes; a song. (Marguerite Merington) Cosmopol. 20: 544.
My Lady's Chair; a story. (J. F. Fraser) Eng. Illust. 12: no. 6, 57.
My Lady's Garden. (F. Madoc) Argosy, 53: 464.
My Last Proposal; a story. Cornh. 65: 439. Same art. Liv. Age, 193: 714.
My Lord; a sketch. Cornh. 71: 399. Same art. Ecl. M. 124: 710.
My Lord; a story. Argosy, 61: 34.
My Lord the Elephant. (R. Kipling) Macmil. 67: 161.
My Lord Mayor; a story. (Evelyn Sharp) Temp. Bar, 108: 249.
My Maid of Honor. (H. Fielding) Blackw. 158: 261. Same art. Liv. Age, 207: 36. Same art. Ecl. M. 126: 83.
My Match with Eileen. (L. O. Robbins) Outing, 28: 277.
My Matinee; a story. Cornh. 65: 507.
My Maverick; a story. (R. B. Townshend) 19th Cent. 33: 789.
My Mysterious Client. Chamb. J. 72: 189.

My Mysterious Model; a story. All the Year, 70: 248, 277.
My Next-door Neighbour. Argosy, 53: 465.
My Nurse; a poem. (C. Burke) Argosy, 58: 425.
My Nursery revisited. Cornh. 68: 299. Same art. Liv. Age, 199: 364.
My own Murderer; a story. (E. J. Goodman) Idler, 3: 557.
My own Petard; a story. All the Year, 72: 421.
My Peasant Host of the Dordogne. Blackw. 160: 423. Same art. Liv. Age, 211: 115.
My Pool; Scenes and Seasons at an Inland Reservoir. Cornh. 66: 147.
My Preëmption; a Western sketch. All the Year, 71: 487.
My Professor of History. Liv. Age, 188: 120.
My Queer Friend; a story. Chamb. J. 72: 223.
My Rival's Revenge. Chamb. J. 71: 396.
My Rural Experiences. (H. H. Boyesen) Lippinc. 58: 121.
My Second Marriage. (J. Theodore Bent) Liv. Age, 188: 49.
My Servant Andreas; a story. (A. Forbes) Idler, 3: 48.
My Servant John; a story. (A. Forbes) Idler, 3: 448.
My Sister Kate. (Mary S. Hancock) Gent. M. n. s. 51: 109. Same art. Liv. Age, 199: 78.
My Son Absalom; a story. (J. Laird) Cosmopol. 14: 237.
My Stepmother; a story. (J. Mortimer) Eng. Illust. 11: 491.
My Strange Patient. (W. T. Nichols) Lippinc. 56: 435.
My Sunday at Home. (R. Kipling) Idler, 7: 388. Same art. McClure, 5: 18.
My Tenants at the Dower House; a story. All the Year, 70: 373, 397.
My Troublesome Sonar. (A. Keatinge) Lend a H. 8: 107.
My Tutorship. Liv. Age, 188: 139.
My Uncle's Pictures; a story. Cornh. 73: 491.
My Uncle's Warning. Macmil. 71: 450.
My Unwilling Neighbor; a story. (F. R. Stockton) McClure, 8: 154. Same art. Eng. Illust. 16: 402.
Mycenæ, Antiquities of. (W. M. F. Petrie) J. Hel. Stud. 12: 199.
— Latest Discoveries at. Antiq. n. s. 25: 35.
Mycenæan, What People produced Objects called? (W. Ridgeway) J. Hel. Stud. 16: 77.
Mycenæan Art. Acad. 48: 32, 58.
— Perrot and Chipiez on. Sat. R. 79: 53.
Mycenæan System of Writing in Crete. Ath. '94, 1: 813.
Myers, Philip. (H. L. Conard) Nat'l M. (N. Y. '91) 15: 663.
Myology, Value of, as an Aid in the Classification of Animals. (F. G. Parsons) Nat. Sci. 7: 336.
Mysie; a story. Liv. Age, 196: 78.
Mysie, the Tale of a Bonnet. (L. B. Walford) Longm. 21: 55.
Mysore and the Late Maharajah. (Sir G. Wolseley) Leis. Hour, 44: 237.
— Glimpse of an East Indian State. (J. N. Ghose) Arena, 15: 981.
— Ten Days in. (J. D. Rees) Asia. R. 9: 75.
Mysteries, The Ancient. Church Q. 42: 405.
— Early English. (C. S. Palmer) Writer, 7: 51. — Spec. 72: 167.
— Greek, Use of, in New Testament. (A. S. Carman) Bib. Sac. 50: 613.
Mysterious Spotley; a story. (B. McEvoy) Canad. M. 4: 505.
Mystery and History. Month, 88: 457.
— Pleasures of. All the Year, 75: 18.
— Value of. Spec. 76: 198.
— Word, in the New Testament. (H. J. Foster) Thinker, 8: 408.
Mystery, A; a poem. (F. B. Cabell) Cosmopol. 16: 696.
Mystery of the Balkans; a story. (P. Andreae) Eng. Illust. 16: 350.
Mystery of Black Rock Creek, The. (J. K. Jerome) Idler, 6: 303.
Mystery of Dave Gurney. (L. G. Wilson) New Eng. M. n. s. 14: 119.
Mystery of the Dover Express, The; a story. (M. F. Baly) Belgra. 90: 277.
Mystery of the Golden Llama, The. (E. J. R. Surrage) Chamb. J. 72: 561-614.
Mystery of Miss Carew; a story. (M. E. S. Penn) Argosy, 60: 349.
Mystery of Modern Florence; a story. Argosy, 59: 100. Same art. Liv. Age, 204: 163.
Mystery of Pilgrim Gray, The. (T. St. E. Hake) Chamb. J. 72: 218-259.
Mystery of the Sea, A. (W. J. Henderson) Scrib. M. 19: 620.
Mystery of Witch-Face Mountain. (M. N. Murfree) Atlan. 76: 331, 525, 651.
Mystery Play, A, in the Black Country. Chamb. J. 72: 401. Same art. Liv. Age, 206: 251.
— A Modern. (M. C. O'Byrne) Open Court, 1: 290.
Mystics among the New England Hills. (D. Calvert) New Eng. M. n. s. 12: 571.
— English. (W. Webster) Acad. 43: 367.
— of the Middle Ages, Catholic. Ed. R. 184: 298.
Mysticism. (F. M. Crawford) Book R. 2: 49-231.
Myth of the Mountain Chant, Navajo, and Old World Myths and Customs. (A. W. Buckland) Anthrop. J. 22: 346.
— Place of, in Modern Education. (E. L. Guptill) Educa. 14: 461, 546.
Mythologic Religions. (C. D. B. Mills) Open Court, 1: 201.
Mythology and the Bible. Contemp. 61: 368. Same art. Ecl M. 118: 546.
— Christian, The Decadence of. (W. S. Kennedy) Open Court, 1: 71.
— Comparative. (H. Oldenberg) Open Court, 10: 4881.
— Frazer's Golden Bough. (A. Macalister) Crit. R. 1: 144.
— Greek. (F. B. Jevons) Folk-Lore, 2: 220.
— Teutonic. (F. Y. Powell) Folk-Lore, 1: 118.
— — Animism and. (P. D. Chautepie de la Saussaye) New World, 3: 443.
— Vedic. Quar. 177: 443.
Myths, Australian. Belgra. 79: 86.
— of America. (S. D. Peet) Am. Antiq. 14: 336.
— Scandinavian. All the Year, 76: 130.
— Scottish, from Ontario. (C. A. Fraser) J. Am. Folk-Lore, 6: 185.
— Transformation. (S. D. Peet) Am. Antiq. 16: 275.

Nachmanides. (S. Schechter) Jew. Q. 5: 78.
Nadaud, Martin. Childhood and Youth of a French Maçon. (J. M. Ludlow) Atlan. 76: 68.
— Political and Professional Life of a French Maçon. (J. M. Ludlow) Atlan. 76: 187.
Naden, Constance C. W., Poems of. Temp. Bar, 103: 187. Same art. Liv. Age, 203: 487.
— "World-scheme" of. (G. M. M'Crie) Open Court, 6: 3335-3360.

Nagualism, Brinton's. (W. W. Newell) J. Am. Folk-Lore, 7: 172.
Nails and Chains, In the Land of. All the Year, 76: 179.
Nakai, Yoshigusu, with portrait. Bank. M. (Lond.) 61: 69.
Nameless Hero, A. Macmil. 67: 187. Same art. Liv. Age, 196: 546.
Nameless Man, The. (R. Ottolengui) Idler, 6: 711.
Names. (P. Carus) Open Court, 9: 4379.
— Archaic Place-. Reliquary, 32: 70.
— Art of giving. Spec. 73: 74.
— Art of Nomenclature. Cornh. 73: 524.
— Century Cyclopædia of. Nation, 59: 447.
— ending in "Man," Origin of. (A. A. Codman) N. E. Reg. 47: 202.
— English. (G. Allen) Longm. 21: 360.
— Fundamentals of Nomenclature. (E. L. Greene) Science, n. s. 3: 13.
— Indian, North and South American. (M. V. Moore) Pop. Sci. Mo. 44: 81.
— Jewels Five Words Long. Chamb. J. 72: 447.
— of Places, On the Poetry of. (B. Matthews) Scrib. M. 20: 22.
— Our Children's. (W. C. Preston) Sund. M. 25: 649.
— Personal. Blackw. 151: 504. Same art. Ecl. M. 118: 732.
— Scottish Local, Significance of. (J. S. Blackie) Good Words, 34: 738.
— "Taft" and "Craft" in. Cornh. 69: 521.
See Towns, Names of.
Namur, Fortifications near. (E. M. Lloyd) Un. Serv. M. 6: 24.
Nanibozhu among the Algonquins. (A. F. Chamberlain) J. Am. Folk-Lore, 4: 193.
Nanking, Woman's Life in. (H. L. Beebe) Chaut. 15: 619.
Nan's Deerhunt. (G. Roberts) Outing, 26: 365.
Nansen, Fridtjof. (C. C. Adams) McClure, 8: 99. — (Ethel B. Tweedie) Temp. Bar, 97: 187. 98: 31. Same art. Ecl. M. 120: 420. Same art. Liv. Age, 198: 118.
— and the Polar Basin. Dub. R. 119: 435.
— at Home. (H. Ward) Eng. Illust. 16: 123.
— North Polar Expedition of. Geog. J. 2: 346. — With portrait. (A. W. Greely) Nat. Geog. M. 7: 98. — (E. A. Man) Nat. Geog. M. 7: 339. — (H. Mohn) Geog. J. 8: 389. — (H. Ward) Eng. Illust. 15: 15. — Nature, 54: 374.
— Reception of, at Christiania. Knowl. 19: 228.
— Return of. Geog. J. 8: 279. — Nat. Geog. M. 7: 290.
— "Throwing Stick." (J. Murdoch) Pop. Sci. Mo. 49: 173.
Napa, Cal., Insane Asylum. (C. W. Coyle) Overland, n. s. 21: 161.
Napa Soda Springs. (R. Wildman) Overland, n. s. 28: 321.
Napier, Gen. Sir Chas. Time, 14: 414.
Napier, Charles James. Temp. Bar, 94: 131. Same art. Liv. Age, 192: 755.
Naples. (S. B. Holabird) Un. Serv. (Phila.) 9: 121.
— and the Neapolitans. All the Year, 72: 220, 256.
— Bay of, Extinct Crater of. (H. P. F. Marriott) Month, 81: 352. 82: 101, 428. 83: 511.
— Biological Station. Sat. R. 75: 119.
— Canadian Bicycle in. (C. R. Boulton) Canad. M. 7: 111.
— Collette's History of. Eng. R. 4: 354.
— The End of the Story. (E. M. Church) Blackw. 156: 254. Same art. Ecl. M. 123: 461.
Naples, Froebel Institution in. (Adele von Portugal) Time, 18: 513.
— Reminiscence of. (F. Mayne) Belgra. 77: 413.
— St. Joseph's Day in. (J. W. Mario) Nation, 54: 281.
— Society in. (C. Edwardes) National, 18: 771. Same art. Liv. Age, 193: 173.
— Under the Shadow of Vesuvius. (E. Fawcett) Cosmopol. 22: 3.
— Water Works of. Am. Arch. 46: 49.
— Women of. (C. Eaglestone) Ecl. M. 118: 195. Same art. Liv. Age, 192: 426.
Napo River. (C. D. Tyler) Geog. J. 3: 476.
Napoleon I. (J. Davis) Arena, 13: 271, 438. 14: 129, 290. 15: 124. — With portraits. (I. M. Tarbell) McClure, 3: 471. 4: 1–409. — (J. Davis) Arena, 15: 448, 765. — Gent. M. n. s. 53: 228. — Temp. Bar, 103: 317.
— and Alexander I. (A. Laugel) Nation, 62: 214, 252. — Quar. 177: 416.
— and the American War of 1812. (R. S. Guernsey) Nat'l M. (N. Y. '91) 19: 164.
— and English Commerce. (J. H. Rose) Eng. Hist. R. 8: 704.
— and the Fair Sex, Masson on. (W. O'C. Morris) Acad. 46: 548.
— and the Stage. All the Year, 70: 559.
— Arraignment of. (R. H. Titherington) Munsey, 8: 621.
— as Captain, at Toulon. (G. Bapst) Harper, 88: 207.
— as a Dramatic Critic. (Dutton Cook) Time, 7: 843.
— at St. Helena. Gent. M. n. s. 54: 638. Same art. Liv. Age, 206: 61. — (A. L. Royce) Un. Serv. (Phila.) 15: 475.
— Bibliographical Notes on. (T. Stanton) Critic, 28: 394.
— Chaptal's Recollections of. (A. Laugel) Nation, 56: 402.
— Conversation with, at Elba. Macmil. 71: 81. Same art. Liv. Age, 204: 101.
— Daniel Webster against. (A. B. Bates) Cent. 28: 468.
— Decline and Fall of, Wolseley's. Sat. R. 79: 552. — Spec. 71: 948.
— Deportation of, to Elba. (T. Ussher) Cent. 23: 664.
— — to St. Helena. (J. R. Glover) Cent. 24: 826. 25: 81.
— English Idea of. (J. H. Adams) Cosmopol. 17: 451.
— Grande Armée of. (H. M. Stephens) Acad. 41: 485.
— House where he was born. (C. Holland) Eng. Illust. 12: no. 2, 29.
— in Egypt. (A. H. Wall) Time, 7: 807.
— in Time, Levy's. (A. Laugel) Nation, 56: 212.
— Last Charges of. (R. Holden) Un. Serv. M. 6: 476.
— Life of. (W. M. Sloane) Cent. v. 27–30.
— Marriage with Marie-Louise. (B. Morgan) Cath. World, 61: 145.
— Méneval's Memoirs of. *See* Méneval.
— Mother of. Chamb. J. 69: 677.
— on Board H. M. S. "Bellerophon." Un. Serv. M. 11: 282. Same art. Liv. Age, 206: 184.
— on the Island of Elba. (H. Houssaye) Chaut. 21: 14.
— Pasquier's Memoirs. (A. Laugel) Nation, 57: 25–427. — Atlan. 72: 834. *See* Pasquier.
— Pitt's Prophecy on. (A. V. Dicey) Contemp. 70: 305, (Reply) 582.
— Portraits of. (R. Heath) M. of Art, 11: 81–176.
— Private Life of, Levy's. (W. O'C. Morris) Acad. 45: 409. — Dial (Ch.) 16: 172. — Spec. 72: 588.
— Quadrilles at the Court of. (F. Masson) Cosmopol. 16: 529.

Napoleon I., Relations with the United States. (I. M. Tarbell) McClure, 5: 24.
— Revival of Worship of. (J. W. Russell) Canad. M. 5: 226.
— Second Funeral of. (I. M. Tarbell) McClure, 4: 504.
— Sisters of. (C. E. Shute) Munsey, 11: 301.
— Some Unpublished Reminiscences of. (N. G. Lyttelton) New R. 11: 276. Same art. Liv. Age, 203: 282.
— Story by, from an Unpublished Manuscript. Cosmopol. 16: 645.
— Views of. (T. R. Bacon) Yale R. 4: 23.
— Voyage to St. Helena. Blackw. 160: 540. Same art. Liv. Age, 211: 372. — Un. Serv. (Phila.) 16: 397.
— Wax Cast of the Face of. (Baron de St. Pôl) McClure, 4: 231.
— Wolseley's. (J. D. Cox) Nation, 59: 291.
Napoleon II., King of Rome. (E. S. Perkins) Lippinc. 56: 548.
Napoleon III. Ed. R. 184: 269.
— at Sedan. (A. Forbes) 19th Cent. 31: 419. Same art. Liv. Age, 193: 226. Same art. Un. Serv. (Phila.) 7: 452.
— Life of. (A. Forbes) Idler, 10: 55, 213, 296, 439, 665.
— A Little Girl's Recollections of. (H. Corkran) Ecl. M. 124: 345. Same art. Liv. Age, 204: 311.
Napoleon, Eugene, Prince Imperial, Death of. (A. Forbes) Cent. 24: 179.
Napoleon, Prince Louis; Two Lost Kingdoms. (E. B. Biggar) Canad. M. 2: 256.
Napoleonic Medals, Some Rare. (J. H. Adams) Cosmopol. 17: 286.
Napoleonic Revival, Anarchism and the. (K. Blind) No. Am. 158: 602.
Narcisse's Friend; a story. (C. Smith) Canad. M. 3: 51.
Narcissus. (J. N. Gerard) Garden & F. 5: 209.
— Hardy. Garden & F. 5: 270, 283. — (E. O. Orpet) Garden & F. 5: 382.
— Notes on. (E. O. Orpet) Garden & F. 8: 207.
— Poeticus. Garden & F. 5: 308. — (G. H. Engleheart) Garden & F. 7: 386.
Narcissus Season. (J. N. Gerard) Garden & F. 6: 207.
Narcotics used by the Nicobar Islanders. (E. H. Man) Anthrop. J. 23: 232.
Narragansett Indians, Hartford Treaty with, 1638. (C. H. Townshend) N. E. Reg. 46: 354.
Narrative of Golden Row. (G. B. Stuart) Argosy, 58: 167.
Narrow Escape. (G. Montbard) Lippinc. 58: 243.
Narrowseas Church, In Search of. Chamb. J. 71: 106. Same art. Liv. Age, 203: 378.
Naruta Whirlpool, Through the. Chamb. J. 70: 49.
Naser-ed Din, Shah of Persia. Good Words, 34: 532. — (Mirza Husain Kuli Khan) Asia. R. 22: 77.
— Assassination of. (E. L. Browne) New R. 14: 651. Same art. Liv. Age, 210: 93.
Nassau, Spring Days at. (W. H. Downes) New Eng. M. n. s. 10: 37.
Nassi, Don Joseph. (D. Kaufmann) Jew. Q. 2: 291.
Nast, Thomas, with portraits. McClure, 4: 153.
Nat-worship among the Burmese. (L. Vossion) J. Am. Folk-Lore, 4: 107.
Natal, Black and White in. (H. E. Colenso; A. Werner) Contemp. 61: 205.
— by one who knows it. Chamb. J. 71: 599.
— Forestry in. (W. R. Fisher) Nature, 51: 234.
— The Highlands of. (E. M'Master) Contemp. 69: 846. Same art. Liv. Age, 210: 195.
Natality, Degree of Legitimate. (J. Körösi) J. Statis. Soc. 57: 690.
Natchez under the Old Régime. (A. G. Haydon) Mid-Cont. 6: 35.
Nathaniel Dixon, Naturalist; a story. (I. Hooper) Temp. Bar, 106: 489.
Nation, Duty of, to her Citizens. (V. R. Andrew) Am. J. Pol. 3: 426.
— What is a? (J. P. Mahaffy) New R. 8: 349. Same art. Ecl. M. 120: 698.
National Academy of Design of N. Y. (J. G. Speed) Q. Illust. 1: 241.
National Airs, Some, and their Associations. Chamb. J. 72: 700.
National and Albertina Galleries. (G. Ludwig) Art J. 48: 359.
National Anthem, English; a Jacobite Hymn and Rebel Song. (S. Bateman) Gent. M. n. s. 51: 33.
National Bank Act of 1863, Debate on. (J. W. Million) J. Pol. Econ. 2: 251.
— Judicial Meaning of. Bank. M. (N. Y.) 47: 19-178.
National Bank Receiver. Bank. M. (N. Y.) 48: 34.
National Banking System. Bank. M. (N. Y.) 43: 895. — (L. G. McPherson) Pop. Sci. Mo. 49: 327.
— Can it be perpetuated? (W. H. Ainey) Bank. M. (N. Y.) 49: 203, 269.
— Completion of. Bank. M. (N. Y.) 48: 174.
— Is it a Monopoly? (L. J. Gage) Open Court, 2: 978.
National Banks. (J. L. Laughlin) Chaut. 16: 32.
— and the Clearing House. (A. B. Hepburn) No. Am. 156: 365.
— and Panic of 1893. Bank. M. (Lond.) 58: 337.
— Basis of Security for. (H. Bacon) Ann. Am. Acad. Pol. Sci. 3: 597.
— Charters of, Forfeiture of. Bank. M. (N. Y.) 44: 202.
— Fluctuations in Secured Circulation of. (C. A. Conant) Am. Statis. Assoc. 3: 471.
— Liquidation of. Bank. M. (N. Y.) 43: 682.
— Notes of, New Guarantees for. (A. Tanzer) Nation, 55: 372.
— Popular Character of. Bank. M. (N. Y.) 50: 165.
— Taxation of. Bank. M. (N. Y.) 47: 195.
— *versus* State Banks. Bank. M. (N. Y.) 47: 588.
National Character, Race Mixture and. (L. R. Harley) Pop. Sci. Mo. 47: 86.
National Debt, Funding the; a Business Man's Plan. (W. A. Amberg) Am. M. Civics, 7: 655.
National Educational Association. (A. Gove) Educa. R. 12: 466.
— at Denver. (C. H. Thurber) School R. 3: 422.
National Emblems and Colors. All the Year, 73: 490.
National Free Labor Association. (J. M. Ludlow) Econ. R. 5: 110.
National Gallery, London. (F. M. Brown) M. of Art, 13: 133.
— British Art in. (S. J. Viccars) New R. 9: 536.
— Difficulty of, 1892. (M. H. Spielmann) New R. 6: 229.
— Exhibition, 1891-92. Ath. '92, 1: 29.
— New Administration. Art J. 46: 348.
— Notes on. (C. Phillips) National, 24: 475.
— £100,000 Worth of Art. (Thos. Sulman) Good Words, 36: 318.
— Romance of. (Emily C. Cook) National, 98: 332. Same art. Liv. Age, 198: 232.
— Site for. Ath. '92, 1: 251.
— Treasures of. (C. Monkhouse) M. of Art, 10: 142-213.
— Veronese Paintings in. (J. P. Richter) Art J. 47: 37.

National Gallery of Ireland. (W. Armstrong) Art J. 45: 54.
National Geographic Society, Work of. Nat. Geog. M. 7: 253.
— — Eighth Annual Meeting. Nat. Geog. M. 7: 259.
National Greatness. Soc. Econ. 3: 1.
National Guard. *See* Militia.
National Life and Character, Pearson's. Ath. '93, 1: 273.—Church Q. 36: 349.—Ed. R. 178: 277.—(F. Greenwood) Macmil. 67: 391.—(A. C. Lyall) 19th Cent. 33: 892.—Quar. 177: 105.—Spec. 70: 71.
— — An Answer to Some Critics. (C. H. Pearson) Fortn. 60: 149.
— Evolution of Our Race. (F. Harrison) Fortn. 60: 28.
National Portrait Gallery, The. (C. Monkhouse) Scrib. 20: 317.
— History and. Ed. R. 184: 218.
— A Walk around. (P. Fitzgerald) Gent. M. n. s. 57: 520.
National Safe Deposit, London. Am. Arch. 43: 92.
National Sculpture Society. Am. Arch. 54: 39.
National Sentiment, Growth of. (C. B. R. Kent) Macmil. 69: 340. Same art. Ecl. M. 122: 641.
National Struggle for Existence. (A. B. Woodford) Soc. Econ. 9: 125.
National University, Why we need a. (S. Newcomb) No. Am. 160: 210.
Nationalism. (S. Schindler) New Eng. M. n. s. 7: 53.
— as an Economic Factor. (N. A. Flood) Am. J. Pol. 1: 148.
— Comtean. Soc. Econ. 2: 43.
— Experience of Italy with. (D. MacG. Means) Nation, 54: 409.
— First Steps to. (S. Schindler) Arena, 13: 26.
— Machine-made Millenniums. (W. J. Lhamon) Our Day, 13: 17.
— Progress of, in the United States. (E. Bellamy) No. Am. 154: 742.
— Proportions of. (E. Arden) Chaut. 14: 437.
Nationalists, Programme of the. (E. Bellamy) Forum, 17: 81.
Nationalities; a story. (H. A. Winthrop) Bach. of Arts, 1: 67.
Nationality, Double, Some Cases of. (C. Maugham) Jurid. R. 4: 135.
— Economic Aspects of. (S. C. Parmiter) Econ. R. 6: 49.
— of Children of a Naturalized British Subject born abroad after the Naturalization. (T. Barclay) Law Q. 12: 279.
Nationality Movement of the 19th Century. (J. Downie) Westm. 141: 620. Same art. Ecl. M. 123: 145.
Nationalization. Enthusiasm or Hysteria? (T. Mackay) National, 23: 468. Same art. Ecl. M. 123: 317.
Nations, Food and Labor-power of. (F. S. Nitti) Econ. J. 6: 30.
— Unity of. (C. Richet) Pub. Opin. 12: 322.
Nation's Lament: a poem. (J. Cook) Our Day, 13: 319.
Nativity, The, in Art. (J. Cartwright) M. of Art, 6: 74.
— A Middle-English. (J. Corbin) Harper, 94: 4.
Natura Naturans. (W. W. Carlile) Philos. R. 4: 624.
Natural Bridge in Virginia. (C. D. Walcott) Nat. Geog. M. 5: 59.
Natural History, Applied. (W. L. Calderwood) Nature, 47: 492.
— Forest Tithes. Cornh. 67: 293.
Natural History from Christchurch Bay. Cornh. 67: 365.
— From a London Window. Cornh. 65: 528.
— in the Primary Schools of France. (F. Bignon) Pop. Sci. Mo. 50: 250.
— In Summer Heat. Cornh. 68: 499.
Natural Law, Ethics, and Evolution. (J. Royce) Int. J. Ethics, 5: 489.
Natural Philosophy in the Village; a story. (A. Stuart) Idler, 7: 550.
Natural Religion. Does it reveal only One God? (J. W. Schwartz) Luth. Q. 25: 382.
Natural Requital. (N. Pearson) 19th Cent. 39: 937. Same art. Ecl. M. 127: 181.
Natural Science and Art. (E. du Bois-Reymond) Nature, 45: 224.
— and the Philosophy of Nature. (B. C. Burt) Philos. R. 1: 284.
— Educational Value of. (J. F. Woodhull) Educa. R. 9: 368.
— in the High School Course. (E. E. Call) Science, 20: 1.
Natural Sciences, Books of Reference in. (C. D. Sherborn) Nat. Sci. 5: 115.
— Formulation of. (E. D. Cope) Am. Natural. 30: 101.—(E. D. Cope) Science, n. s. 3: 299.
Natural Selection. (St. G. Mivart) Cosmopol. 13: 329.—(W. T. Freeman) Gent. M. n. s. 49: 196.
— and Crime. (E. S. Morse) Pop. Sci. Mo. 41: 433.
— Socialism and. (K. Pearson) Fortn. 62: 1.
See also Selection, Natural.
Natural Selection, A; a story. Belgra. 89: 88.
Natural Theology, The New. (J. W. Buckham) And. R. 18: 563.
— and Evolution, Barry's Bampton Lectures on. Church Q. 37: 257.
— Stokes's Gifford Lectures. (A. Macalister) Crit. R. 2: 40.
Naturalism. (C. L. Morgan) Monist, 6: 76.—(D. W. Fisher) Presb. & Ref. R. 7: 56.
— and Ethics. (A. J. Balfour) Int. J. Ethics, 4: 415.
— New Gospel of. (E. Magevney) Cath. World, 59: 233.
— The Term, in Recent Discussion. (A. Seth) Philos. R. 5: 576.
Naturalist and Biologist: a Comparison. (I. Muntz) Gent. M. n. s. 49: 88.
— Education of a. (J. C. Branner) School R. 3: 134.
— in the Jungle. Sund. M. 23: 842.
— in La Plata, Hudson's. (S. Garman) Nation, 55: 501.
— Work of, in the World. (C. S. Minot) Pop. Sci. Mo. 47: 60.
Naturalists, A Group of. (Mrs. A. Crosse) Temp. Bar, 98: 356. Same art. Liv. Age, 198: 681.
— in La Plata. (G. J. Romanes) 19th Cent. 33: 886.
— Old and New. (C. L. Morgan) Nature, 53: 9.
— Rustic. Spec. 68: 459.
— Travelling in America. Quar. 175: 445.
Naturalization in the U. S. Continued Residence of Applicant. (F. Van Dyne) Am. Law R. 29: 52.
— Immigration and. (H. S. Everett) Atlan. 75: 345.
— Needed Reform in. (J. B. Moore) Forum, 13: 475.
Naturals, Village. Chamb. J. 71: 139.
Nature. (J. Weir, jr.) Outing, 26: 305.
— Adaptations of, to Highest Wants of Man. (G. F. Wright) Bib. Sac. 51: 206.
— — to Intellectual Wants of Man. (G. F. Wright) Bib. Sac. 51: 560.
— American Literature and. (C. S. Sargent) Garden and F. 8: 181.
— and Eternal Youth. (G. von Gizycki) Open Court, 2: 1403.

Nature and Eternity. (R. Jefferies) Longm. **26:** 38. Same art. Liv. Age, **205:** 760. Same art. Ecl. M. **125:** 254.
— and the Individual Mind. (K. Lasswitz) Monist, **6:** 396.
— and the Rich. (C. S. Sargent) Garden & F. **7:** 251.
— as Drama and Enginery. (G. Iles) Pop. Sci. Mo. **45:** 496.
— Aspects of, in England and in America. Atlan. **70:** 573.
— Behind the Scenes of. (A. P. Sinnett) 19th Cent. **36:** 211.
— From, to Art; a poem. (Edgar Fawcett) Cosmopol. **19:** 90.
— Gospel in. (H. H. Moore) Meth. R. **53:** 23.
— in the Earlier Roman Poets. (Countess M. Cesaresco) Contemp. **69:** 576. Same art. Liv. Age, **209:** 372.
— Love of. Garden & F. **5:** 193–529.
— — as Root of Teaching and Learning the Sciences. (W. A. Hoyt) Pedagog. Sem. **3:** 61.
— Morning at the Old Sugar Mill. Atlan. **74:** 373.
— Observation of, Impulse to. Spec. **69:** 381.
— Philosophical Tour in Seen and Unseen Regions. (R. G. Mackley Browne) Westm. **141:** 78. Same art. Ecl. M. **122:** 326.
— Revelation through. (H. Wood) Arena, **5:** 436.
— Self-consciousness, Social Consciousness and. (J. Royce) Philos. R. **4:** 465, 577.
— Sympathy with. (E. K. Robinson) Time, **11:** 93.
— Sympathy with Human Suffering. (S. Urban) Gent. M. n. s. **55:** 319.
Nature Essays. From Winter Solstice to Vernal Equinox. (E. M. Thomas) Atlan. **73:** 67.
Nature Studies. (W. M. Thayer) Educa. **15:** 407. — Cornh. **67:** 141. Same art. Liv. Age, **196:** 820.
Nature Study and Intellectual Culture. (J. M. Coulter) Science, n. s. **4:** 740.
— and Moral Culture. (D. S. Jordan) Science, n. s. **4:** 149.
— in Our Schools. (B. B. Russell) Educa. **12:** 345.
— Nature and Purpose of. (H. L. Clapp) Educa. **15:** 597.
— Representative Expression in. (W. S. Jackman) Educa. R. **10:** 248.
Nature's Planting Plans. (J. Dawson) Garden & F. **7:** 353.
Nature's Training-school. Blackw. **157:** 114. Same art. Liv. Age, **204:** 502.
Nature's Triumph. (J. Rodway) Pop. Sci. Mo. **46:** 456.
Naulahka, The; a story. (R. Kipling and W. Balestier) Cent. **21:** 343–890. **22:** 135–375.
Nausikaa. (M. G. Watkins) Gent. M. n. s. **52:** 633.
Nautilus, the, In the Home of. (A. Willey) Nat. Sci. **6:** 405.
Nautilus, The; a poem. (E. Gosse) Cosmopol. **16:** 705.
Navajo, The; a poem. (E. McGaffey) Cosmopol. **16:** 541.
Navajo Indians, Gentile System of the. (W. Matthews) J. Am. Folk-Lore, **3:** 89.
— A Fight with. Chamb. J. **71:** 238.
— A Legend of. (W. C. Duxbury) Cosmopol. **22:** 73.
— Legendary Evolution of. (T. S. Van Vleet) Am. Natural. **27:** 69.
— Songs of Sequence of. (W. Matthews) J. Am. Folk-Lore, **7:** 185.
Navajo Legends. (W. W. Newell) J. Am. Folk-Lore, **9:** 211.
Navajo Myth: Noqðilpi, the Gambler. (W. Matthews) J. Am. Folk-Lore, **2:** 89.
Naval Academy, United States, The. *See* U. S. Naval Academy.
Naval Annual, 1894, ed. by Brassey. Sat. R. **77:** 532.
Naval Architects, Institution of. Nature, **51:** 568.
— — 1894 Meeting. Nature, **49:** 490. **50:** 328.
Naval Architecture. The Battle-ship of the Future. (W. T. Sampson) No. Am. **157:** 653.
— The Fight off the Yalu River. (H. A. Herbert) No. Am. **159:** 513.
Naval Armaments. Ed. R. **179:** 447.
— Possible Developments in. (J. Eastwick) Contemp. **66:** 374.
Naval Aspects of the Japan-China War. (E. R. Fremantle) Forum, **20:** 531.
Naval Battle, A Modern. Spec. **75:** 75.
— of To-morrow. (H. W. Wilson) Un. Serv. M. **9:** 387.
Naval Education. (C. F. Goodrich) Am. J. Soc. Sci. **33:** 29.
Naval Experts. (C. N. Robinson) New R. **13:** 161.
Naval Forces of Europe. (A. Alison) Blackw. **155:** 313.
Naval Gun Factory, United States. (T. F. Jewell) Harper, **89:** 251.
Naval History, The Teaching of. (David Hannay) New R. **12:** 132.
Naval Manœuvre Cruise with a British Light Squadron. (F. T. Jane) Good Words, **37:** 162.
Naval Militia, The. (W. H. Stayton) Outing, **28:** 394.
Naval Misadventures. All the Year, **72:** 439.
Naval Needs of the Pacific. (I. M. Scott) Overland, n. s. **24:** 367.
Naval Progress, 1895. Un. Serv. (Phila.) **15:** 167, 252.
Naval Reserve, Illinois. (W. H. Burke) Outing, **24:** 465.
— U. S. (E. B. Mero) Outing, **22:** 334, 436.
Naval Review at New York, 1893, Lesson of. (H. A. Herbert) No. Am. **156:** 641. — (C. H. Rockwell) Un. Serv. (Phila.) **10:** 14.
Naval Stores, Gathering. (L. J. Vance) Pop. Sci. Mo. **48:** 469.
Naval Tactics. (M. Hamilton) Un. Serv. M. **8:** 498, 624.
Naval Titles and Sea Phraseology. Chamb. J. **71:** 236.
Naval Utopia, A. Blackw. **159:** 795.
Naval War in the East. Ed. R. **180:** 497.
Naval War College in Rhode Island. (R. S. Osborne) Munsey, **12:** 638.
Naval Warfare, The Engineer in. (G. W. Melville; W. S. Aldrich; I. N. Hollis; G. C. Sims; G. Uhler) No. Am. **162:** 513.
— Future of. (W. Mitchell) Atlan. **76:** 644. — (H. Geffcken) Contemp. **65:** 29.
— in 1896. (O. Hall) Lippinc. **57:** 817.
— The Meloban and the Pantheroy. (J. Creelman) Cosmopol. **16:** 426.
— On Board the Aquidaban. (M. R. Watt) Canad. M. **2:** 345.
— under Modern Conditions. (S. B. Luce) No. Am. **162:** 70.
— Wilson on. (E. G. Johnson) Dial (Ch.) **20:** 99.
Navalism. (E. L. Godkin) Nation, **54:** 44.
Navies, Development of, Eardley-Wilmot's. (C. H. Stockton) Nation, **54:** 307. — Sat. R. **73:** 248. — Spec. **69:** 135.
— The New. (W. L. Clowes) Eng. Illust. **11:** 534.
— Official Estimate of Rival. New R. **10:** 385.
Navigation in Spain, History of. (J. de Perott) Science, n. s. **2:** 63.
— Problems in, Graphical Solution of. Nature, **47:** 547.
Navigation Laws, Our. (C. H. Cramp) No. Am. **158:** 433.
Navy as a Career. (A. T. Mahan) Forum, **20:** 277.
— A Modern. (W. H. White) Un. Serv. M. **9:** 9.

Navy, War Training of. Un. Serv. M. 9: 129.
Navy Yard Regeneration. (J. B. Bishop) Nation, 61: 41.
Nazareth. (G. A. Smith) Bib. World, 8: 435.
— Reminiscence of. (A. K. Parker) Bib. World, 7: 189.
Nazareth, Ky., Roman Catholic Convent-school at. Cath. World, 56: 464.
Neal, David. (J. R. Tait) M. of Art, 9: 95.
Neale, Edward Vansittart, as Christian Socialist. (T. Hughes) Econ. R. 3: 38, 174.
Neapolitan in Love. (F. M. Crawford) Liv. Age, 211: 757.
Near-sightedness among Schoolboys. (E. Hart) Atlan. 72: 681.
Neb; a story. (E. A. Atkinson) Canad. M. 2: 282.
Nebraska, National Guard of. (W. R. Hamilton) Outing, 28: 157.
— — in the Sioux War. (W. R. Hamilton) Outing, 28: 317.
— Volcanic Ash in. (R. D. Salisbury) Science, n. s. 4: 816.
— University of, Accredited School System of. (J. H. Canfield) Educa. R. 7: 184.
Nebula and Clusters. (L. Swift) Pop. Astron. 1: 369.
— in Orion. (W. W. Campbell) Astron. 13: 384, (J. E. Keeler) 476. — (H. C. Wilson) Pop. Astron. 1: 433. — (E. E. Barnard) Pop. Astron. 2: 151. — (E. S. Holden) Overland, n. s. 19: 401.
— — Photographic. (E. E. Barnard) Astron. 13: 811.
— Trifid, Photograph of. (E. E. Barnard) Astron. 13: 791.
— What is a? (E. W. Maunder) Knowl. 18: 253.
Nebulæ, Photographs of Elliptical and Spiral. (I. Roberts) Knowl. 18: 207.
Nebular Hypothesis. (J. E. Keeler) Astron. 11: 567-768.
Necessitarians, Reply to. (C. S. Peirce) Monist, 3: 526.
— Reply. (P. Carus) Monist, 3: 571.
Necessity, Doctrine of. (C. S. Peirce) Monist, 2: 321.
— — Reply. (P. Carus) Monist, 2: 560.
— Idea of, Basis and Scope of. (P. Carus) Monist, 3: 68.
— Superstition of. (J. Dewey) Monist, 3: 362.
Necromancer, Some Adventures of a. (C. Herrmann) No. Am. 155: 418.
Nectanebo, Pharaoh and Magician. (D. G. Hogarth) Eng. Hist. R. 11: 1.
Ned Clark, Poacher; a story. (J. Edgar) Gent. M. n. s. 55: 179.
Need-fire. (J. R. Allen) Illus. Archæol. 2: 77.
Needle-craft. Cornh. 67: 497.
Needles in Tunnelling, Use of. Am. Arch. 43: 33. 44: 127.
— Wandering, in the Human Body. Chamb. J. 73: 197.
Needlework, Art. M. of Art, 3: 76-428.
— — Royal School of. M. of Art, 5: 219.
— as Art, Alford's. (K. de Mattos) M. of Art, 9: 304.
— Decorative. (M. A. L. Wright) Canad. M. 4: 282.
— — English. (L. Higgin) M. of Art, 10: 43, 151.
Neef, Joseph; a Pestalozzian Pioneer. (A. Carman) Pop. Sci. Mo. 45: 373.
— and Pestalozzianism in America. (W. S. Monroe) Educa. 14: 449.
Negotiable Instruments. Bank. M. (N. Y.) 48: 206-779.
— Early History of. (E. Jenks) Law Q. 9: 70.
Negotiable Paper, Law of. (W. A. McClean) Green Bag, 5: 86.
Negreponte, Mme., Poetry of. (R. Thirlmere) Westm. 140: 62.
Negro, The, in America. (H. Watterson) Chaut. 15: 20.
— in America. (E. Parham) Mid-Cont. 6: 255.
— — Developmental Status of. Pub. Opin. 18: 171.
— — Race Traits and Tendencies of. (F. L. Hoffman) Am. Econ. Assoc. 11: 1.
— as a Mechanic, The. (R. Lowry) No. Am. 156: 472.
— as a Soldier. (T. G. Steward) Un. Serv. Phila. 11: 323.
— Awakening of the. (B. T. Washington) Atlan. 78: 322.
— Future of, in Fiction. (L. H. Egan) Dial (Ch.) 18: 70.
— Mortality of. (T. G. Steward) Soc. Econ. 9: 204.
— New England, The; a Remnant. (J. De F. Shelton) Harper, 88: 533.
— Southern Social Problem. (K. Bocock) Soc. Econ. 4: 22.
— — — Unaided Solution of. (A. S. Van de Graaff) Forum, 21: 330.
Negro Citizens. Shall they be banished? (F. M. Holland) Open Court, 3: 2079.
Negro Folk-Lore and Witchcraft in the South. (L. Pendleton) J. Am. Folk-Lore, 3: 201.
— Christensen's. (W. W. Newell) J. Am. Folk-Lore, 5: 258.
Negro Lore, Baltimore. (C. Lee) J. Am. Folk-Lore, 5: 110.
Negro Music. (J. Tonsor) Music, 3: 119.
Negro Myths from the Georgia Coast, Jones's. (W. W. Newell) J. Am. Folk-Lore, 1: 169.
Negro Plot in N. Y. in 1741. Nat'l M. (N. Y. '91) 18: 128.
Negro Problem, Solution of. (W. A. Curtis) Am. J. Pol. 3: 352.
Negro Question. (C. S. Wake) Open Court, 4: 2353. — (T. B. Wakeman) Open Court, 4: 2433.
— in U. S. (E. D. Cope) Open Court, 3: 2052.
Negro Stories from Jamaica. (P. C. Smith) J. Am. Folk-Lore, 9: 278.
Negro Suffrage a Failure. Shall we abolish it? (J. C. Wickliffe) Forum, 14: 797.
Negro Superstitions. Atlan. 75: 136.
Negro Tales. (Mrs. W. P. Johnston) J. Am. Folk-Lore, 9: 194.
Negro Vote in South Carolina. (R. I. Manning) Nation, 60: 299.
Negro Woman, The New. (B. T. Washington) Lend a H. 15: 254.
Negro Women, Southern. (O. R. Jefferson) Chaut. 18: 91.
Negroes. Æsthetic Capacity of the Afro-American. (J. E. Rankin) Our Day, 13: 289.
— and the Baptists. (J. R. Slattery) Cath. World, 63: 265.
— Black Shadow in the South. (A. G. Haygood) Forum, 16: 167.
— Burning of, in the South. (B. O. Flower) Arena, 7: 630.
— Calhoun School for. (P. Dillingham) Lend a H. 15: 369.
— Capacity of. Spec. 75: 927.
— Christian Industrial Education of. (B. T. Washington) Our Day, 16: 343.
— Colored Children in the District of Columbia. (H. W. Lewis) Char. R. 5: 94.
— Education of. (A. A. Gundy) Am. J. Pol. 1: 295. — (J. L. M. Curry) Am. M. Civics, 8: 168.

Negroes, Education of, Calhoun School, Report of. (C. R. Thorn and M. W. Dillingham) Lend a H. 13: 52.
— — Symposium. Indep. April 7, '92.
— Emigration and Deportation of. Pub. Opin. 18: 370.
— Free, of Louisiana. (P. F. de Gournay) Lippinc. 53: 511.
— Future of. (M. H. Kingsley) Spec. 75: 930.
— Higher Education of. (H. L. Wayland) Am. J. So. Sci. no. 34: 68.
— in the District of Columbia. (E. Ingle) J. H. Univ. Studies, 11: nos. 3-4.
— in the South, M. E. Church and. (W. W. W. Wilson) Meth. R. 54: 713.
— in the U. S., Condition of, Present and Future. (J. Slattery) Cath. World, 58: 219.
— — Conference of, at Tuskegee, Ala., 1892. (R. C. Bedford) Lend a H. 8: 251.
— — Constitutional Rights of. (F. A. Noble) Our Day, 12: 459.
— — Education of. (W. T. Harris) Atlan. 69: 721. — (J. R. Slattery) Cath. World, 56: 28.
— — — Expense of. Does the Negro pay it? (G. W. Cable) Forum, 13: 640.
— — Have they too much Liberty? (C. H. Smith) Forum, 16: 176.
— — An Open Letter. (O. P. Fitzgerald) 19th Cent. 34: 291.
— — Outrages by, no Excuse for Lynching. (L. E. Bleckley) Forum, 16: 300.
See Lynching.
— — Problem of. (J. Bryce) Our Day, 9: 51.
— — Question of. (T. E. Watson) Arena, 6: 540.
— — — Mississippi and. (A. C. McLaughlin) Atlan. 70: 828.
— — — New Aspects of. (S. M. Davis) Our Day, 10: 469.
— — — Scientific Aspects of. (N. S. Shaler) Pub. Opin. 18: 147.
— — — A Southerner on. (T. N. Page) No. Am. 154: 401.
— — Religious Progress of. (H. K. Carroll) Forum, 14: 75.
— — Unsolved Race Problems. (J. Cook) Our Day, 12: 35.
— — Vital Statistics of. (F. L. Hoffman) Arena, 5: 529.
— in the West Indies. (F. L. Hoffman) Am. Statis. Assoc. 4: 181.
— Industrial Education of. (B. T. Washington) Our Day, 16: 79.
— Lingo of, in Literature. Lippinc. 55: 286.
— Redemptive Work for. (G. W. Moore) Lend a H. 17: 355.
— Suffrage of, History of. (S. B. Weeks) Pol. Sci. Q. 9: 671.
— — Problem of, in America. (C. F. Aked) Contemp. 65: 818.
— Under Northern Conditions. (G. L. Lee) Gunton's M. 10: 52.
— The White Problem. (R. T. Greener) Lend a H. 12: 354.
— Whites and. Spec. 75: 427.
Negro's Place in History, The. (W. Boughton) Arena, 16: 612.
Negus Negusti and the Abyssinians. (F. Villiers) Cent. 22: 441.
Nehemiah. (C. H. Cornill) Open Court, 9: 4599.
— Night Ride of. (T. F. Wright) J. Bib. Lit. 15: 129.
Neighbor, Understanding One's. (X. Clark) Open Court, 2: 780.
Neighbor King; a story. (C. Shackelford) McClure, 6: 96.
Neighborhood Rooster; a story. (Maurice Thompson) Cosmopol. 21: 504.
Neighbor's Landmark; a Winter Story with a Christmas Ending. (S. O. Jewett) Cent. 27: 235.
Nell Latore; a Tale, in Verse, of the Canadian Rebellion of 1885. (G. Parker) Good Words, 34: 64. Same art. Ecl. M. 120: 213.
Nelson, Horatio, Lord. (C. Russell) Eng. Illust. 16: 115, 257. — New R. 13: 485. — Sat. R. 80: 243.
— and Naval Warfare. Church Q. 41: 451.
— and the "Victory," with portrait. (F. A. Walker) Southern M. 4: 59.
— at Cape St. Vincent. (A. T. Mahan) Cent. 29: 604.
Nema; a story. (H. Peek) Eng. Illust. 12: no. 2, 85.
Nematinæ, American, C. L. Marlatt on. Am. Natural. 30: 1056.
Nemesis of Perkins, The. (J. K. Bangs) Harper, 93: 918.
Nemi, The Mysterious Wreck of. (R. Lanciani) No. Am. 162: 225.
Nennius, Zimmer on. (A. Nutt) Acad. 44: 132, 151.
Neo-Buddhist Movement. Time, 22: 597.
Neo-Christian Movement in France. (E. M. de Vogüé) Harper, 84: 234.
— Effects of. (J. H. Leuba) Am. J. Psychol. 5: 496.
Neo-Darwinism and Neo-Lamarckism. (L. H. Bailey) Am. Natural. 28: 661.
Neo-Stundism, Skoortsoff on. (E. J. Dillon) R. of Rs. (N. Y.) 7: 317.
Neocene: Correlation Papers of U. S. Geological Survey. Am. J. Sci. 145: 351. — Am. Natural. 27: 246.
Neot, St., Legend of. (Mrs. C. G. Boger) Walford's Antiq. 7: 14-118.
Nepigon Indians to Canada; a poem. (K. F. M. Sullivan) Canad. M. 7: 510.
Nepotism, Plea for. (C. Robinson) Am. J. Pol. 3: 203.
Neptune, Ammannati's Statue of, Florence. (L. E. Baxter) M. of Art, 8: 373.
Nerval, Gérard de. *See* Labrunie, Gérard.
Nerve, Observations on Isolated. Nature, 54: 18.
Nerve-action in relation to Modern Nerve-Cell, Two Fundamental Laws of. (A. D. Waller) Sci. Prog. 3: 186.
Nerve Centres, Minute Structure of. (Prof. Ramon y Cajal) Nature, 49: 464.
Nerves and Nervousness. Spec. 72: 11. Same art. Ecl. M. 122: 278.
— Visceral and Allied. (T. G. Brodie) Sci. Prog. 1: 34.
Nervous Diseases and Modern Life. (T. C. Allbutt) Contemp. 67: 210. Same art. Ecl. M. 124: 645.
— Are they increasing? (P. C. Knapp) Cent. 30: 146.
Nervous Impulse, Velocity of. (C. S. Dolley; J. M. Cattell) Psychol. R. 1: 159.
Nervous System and its Relation to Education. (J. Ferguson) Pop. Sci. Mo. 47: 528.
— Education of. (H. H. Donaldson) Educa. R. 9: 105.
— Specific Energies of. (E. Hering) Open Court, 1: 609, 664.
Nervousness, Modern, and its Cure. (Dr. Bilsinger) Pop. Sci. Mo. 42: 90. Same art. Pub. Opin. 14: 110.
— the National Disease of America. (E. Wakefield) McClure, 2: 302.
Nesbitt. (A. M. Peck) New Eng. M. n. s. 7: 736.
Nest-building, Extraordinary. Chamb. J. 70: 255.
Nestlings [Bird]. (T. Wood) Sund. M. 24: 267.
Nestorian Church, Liturgy of. (F. E. Brightman) Acad. 41: 610.

Nests I have known. (L'Aigle Cole) Sund. M. 25: 333.
Netherlandish Masters at the Burlington Fine Arts Club. (C. Phillips) Acad. 41: 619.
Netherlandish Pictures at the Burlington Club. (W. Armstrong) Portfo. 23: 188.
Nethersole, Olga, the Actress. Idler, 3: 383.
— as Camille. Critic, 25: 300.
— in "The Transgressor." Critic, 25: 259.
Netje. (M. F. Upton) Overland, n. s. 22: 579.
Netsukés, their Makers, Use, and Meaning. (H. S. Trower) M. of Art, 12: 153.
Nettleship, Henry. (J. S. Cotton) Acad. 44: 51.
Nettleship, J. T. Artist, Chat with. (R. Compton) Idler, 10: 361.
Nettleship, Richard Lewis. Acad. 42: 193. — (H. D. Rawnsley) Good Words, 34: 55.
Neumann, F. Nature, 52: 176.
Neumann, John N., Bishop, with portrait. (J. Wüst) Cath. World, 56: 322.
Neuropathic Wanderers; the Wandering Jew at the Salpêtrière. (H. Coupin) Pop. Sci. Mo. 44: 525.
Neustadt, Joanna Mitchels, Memorial to. Critic, 27: 136.
Neuville, Alphonse de. M. of Art, 8: 525.— (A. Meynell) M. of Art, 4: 353.
— and his Work. (C. S. Johnson) Munsey, 8: 3.
Neuville, G. H., Baron de. Blackw. 154: 90.
Nevada, National Guard of. (W. R. Hamilton) Outing, 27: 493. 28: 78.
Nevada Silver. (C. H. Shinn) Pop. Sci. Mo. 49: 734.
Nevers, and its Pottery. Sat. R. 73: 471.
Neville, Henry, as Jack Holt. (C. Howard) Theatre, 28: 155.
New and the Old, The. (E. L. Linton) Univ. R. 6: 270.
New Amsterdam. *See* New York.
New Australia, Paraguay, Communistic Work at. (A. J. Rose-Soley) Westm. 140: 523. Same art. Ecl. M. 121: 780.
New Boy at Stanhope's; a story. Argosy, 58: 538.
New Bedford, Massachusetts. (G. F. Tucker) New Eng. M. n. s. 15: 97.
New Brunswick; Memories of Bathurst. (E. B. Biggar) Canad. M. 3: 18.
New Caledonia. Chamb. J. 72: 543. — (Countess of Jersey) 19th Cent. 32: 524. Same art. Liv. Age, 195: 672.
New Capitalist, A; a story. (F. Adams) Ecl. M. 118: 242.
New Cashier; a story. (E. Eggleston) Cent. 23: 189.
New Castle, N. H., Records of. (E. S. Stearns) N. E. Reg. 50: 458.
New Centurion. (J. Eastwick) Longm. 26: 504-603.
New Church. *See* Swedenborgian.
New Child, The. (Mrs. E. T. Cook) Good Words, 36: 522.
New Contribution, A. (Mrs. H. Mansergh) Eng. Illust. 15: 525.
New Corn from Old Fields. (W. Canton) Good Words, 33: 378, 545.
New Crusade, The; a poem. (B. Hathaway) Arena, 8: 273.
New England and the Formation of America. (P. O'Callaghan) Cath. World, 64: 344.
— and the Upper Mississippi Basin in the Glacial Period. (J. D. Dana) Am. J. Sci. 146: 327.
— Appreciation of Nature in. Spec. 69: 681.
— Baxter's Pioneers of New France. (C. C. Smith) Am. Hist. R. 1: 542.
— Country Life in, Sixty Years Ago. (L. E. A. Kebler) New Eng. M. n. s. 5: 797. 6: 48.
— Customs of. (E. N. Blair) Chaut. 22: 294.
New England, Dutch Influence in. (W. E. Griffis) Harper, 88: 213.
— Early Religious History of. (J. A. Faulkner) Ref. Q. 40: 510.
— Folk-lore of. (J. M. Currier) J. Am. Folk-Lore, 4: 253.
— Glimpses of Life in, Two Centuries Ago. (W. B. Weeden) New Eng. M. n. s. 14: 277.
— in the Glacial Period. (J. D. Dana) Pop. Sci. Mo. 44: 816.
— In the Gray Cabins of. (R. H. Davis) Cent. 27: 620.
— Influence of Physical Features on. (E. K. Alden) New Eng. M. n. s. 8: 653.
— Journey of William Gregory in, 1771. (M. G. Powell) New Eng. M. n. s. 12: 343.
— My First Visit to. (W. D. Howells) Harper, 89: 40, 228, 441.
— Names of Places in. (E. F. Hayward) New Eng. M. n. s. 13: 345.
— Old. (E. Porritt) Leis. Hour, 45: 83, 185. — Ecl. M. 123: 20. Liv. Age, 201: 387.
— — Earle on. Dial (Ch.) 15: 219. — Spec. 71: 837.
— Religious Situation in. (D. Dorchester) Meth. R. 54: 875.
— Revolt of. (W. L. Sawyer) Bach. of Arts, 1: 654.
— Transformation of. Is it Decay or Development? (W. D. Hyde; E. Atkinson) Forum, 15: 107.
— What it owes to the United States. (L. G. James) New Eng. M. n. s. 10: 510.
New England Association of Colleges, 1893 Meeting. (R. G. Huling) School R. 1: 587.
— — 1894 Meeting. School R. 2: 593.
— Report of. (R. G. Huling) School R. 4: 713.
New England Boyhood. (E. E. Hale) Atlan. 70: 148-765.
— Hale's. (C. S. Peirce) Nation, 57: 123.
New England Children in the 17th Century. (L. A. Phillips) Bost. 3: 329.
New England Conscience. (A. E. Brand) New Eng. M. n. s. 13: 759.
New England Farm, A. (F. French) Scrib. M. 13: 426.
New England Historic Genealogical Society, Necrology of. (H. A. Hill) N. E. Reg. 46: 95-406.
New England Kitchen, Scientific Cooking-studies in. (E. H. Richards) Forum, 15: 355.
New England Lawyers, Old. (H. C. Merwin) Am. Law R. 30: 365.
New England Pirate, A; a story. (D. Buffum) New Eng. M. n. s. 11: 373.
New England Primer, The. (P. L. Ford) Bookman, 4: 122. — (R. Colles) Bookworm, 5: 123.
— A fresh Note on. (B. F. De Costa) N. E. Reg. 48: 64.
New England Prophet; a story. (M. E. Wilkins) Harper, 89: 601.
New England Senates, Colonial Origins of. (F. L. Riley) J. H. Univ. Studies, 14: 101.
New England Woodpile. (R. E. Robinson) Atlan. 76: 736.
New English Art Club Exhibition. Art J. 48: 60. — Sat. R. 81: 394.
New Examiner, The; a story. (E. H. L. Watson) Gent. M. n. s. 52: 147.
New Forest, The. (M. G. Fawcett) M. of Art, 8: 1, 45. — (C. J. Cornish) Portfo. 1894: no. 8. — Spec. 73: 344.
— and Bournemouth. (Violet E. Mitchell) Mo. Illust. 13: 266.
— and the War Office. (J. King) Westm. 137: 261.
— In the. Cornh. 67: 590. Same art. Liv. Age, 198: 504.
— under Fire. (F. H. Candy) Gent. M. n. s. 48: 290.

New France, Decade of the History of. (T. P. Bedard) Canad. M. 4: 84.
— Study of Exploration in. Atlan. 76: 559.
New Galatea; a story. (L. H. Armstrong) Belgra. 78: 386.
New Gallery. (M. P. Jackson) M. of Art, 17: 306. 18: 285. — Ath. '94, 1: 55, 118, 416, 619, 810.
— Exhibition, Summer, 1892. (C. Phillips) Art J. 44: 187-241. — Ath. '92, 1: 574, 700. — Spec. 69: 647.
— — Autumn, 1892. Ath. '92, 2: 490.
— — Summer, 1893. Ath. '93, 1: 576, 677. — Sat. R. 75: 510. — Spec. 70: 606.
— — 1895. Sat. R. 79: 577. — Ath. '95, 1: 24, 154, 413.
— Italian Pictures at. (J. P. Richter) Art J. 46: 62.
— Spanish Pictures at. (R. A. M. Stevenson) M. of Art, 19: 152.
New Guinea. (J. P. Bocock) Lippinc. 56: 555. — Time, 8: 385.
— Birds of. (G. S. Mead) Am. Natural. 30: 195, 285, 710.
— British, as a Colony. (H. O. Forbes) Blackw. 152: 82.
— — Languages of. (S. H. Ray) Anthrop. J. 24: 15.
— — Recent Exploration in. Nature, 50: 609.
— — Thomson on. (H. O. Forbes) Nat. Sci. 1: 766. Same art. Nature, 47: 345.
— Ornithology of. (J. S. Mead) Am. Natural. 28: 389.
— Sir Wm. MacGregor's Journey across. (J. P. Thomson) Nature, 55: 157.
New Hampshire at the World's Fair. (E. M. Shaw) New Eng. M. n. s. 10: 135.
— National Guard of. (G. H. Moses) Outing, 27: 77-413.
— Royal Pines of. (W. H. Stone) New Eng. M. n. s. 15: 26.
— Third Regiment in the Revolution. (C. B. Dahlgren) Am. Hist. Reg. 2: 997.
New Hebrides; Ambrym Island, Eruption of. (H. E. Purey-Cust) Geog. J. 8: 585.
— Islands of. (B. T. Somerville) Anthrop. J. 23: 2.
— Notes on. (B. T. Somerville) Anthrop. J. 23: 363.
"New Ironsides" off Charleston, 1863. (G. E. Belknap) Un. Serv. (Phila.) 15: 147.
New Jersey National Guard. (W. H. C. Bowen) Outing, 21: 60-237.
— Northern, Rivers of. (W. M. Davis) Nat. Geog. M. 2: 81.
— Slavery in, A Study of. (H. S. Cooley) J. H. Univ. Studies, 14: 419.
— West, Council of Proprietors of, organized 1687. (J. Clement) Pennsyl. M. 18: 496.
New Jersey Highlands. (C. S. Sargent) Garden & F. 6: 491.
New Jerusalem, Descent of. (W. E. Barton) Bib. Sac. 52: 29.
New Jerusalem Church. *See* Swedenborgian.
New Jerusalem Magazine (Lond.), History of. New Church R. 1: 432.
New London, Conn. (H. R. Palmer) New Eng. M. n. s. 14: 291.
— Fort Griswold Massacre. New Eng. M. n. s. 12: 668.
— Public Library. Lib. J. 18: 153.
New Mecklenburgh, Count Pfeil on. Dub. R. 115: 460.
New Member of the Club; a story. (B. Matthews) Cent. 23: 101.
New Mexico, Admission of, as a State. (L. B. Prince) No. Am. 156: 346.
— Botanical Journey through. (E. N. Plank) Garden & F. 9: 322.
— Cities that were forgotten. (C. F. Lummis) Scrib. M. 13: 466.
New Mexico, Lummis's. (L. Carr) Nation, 58: 127.
— Rural Industry in. Dub. R. 114: 177.
— A Traveller's Views. (J. R. Spears) Chaut. 23: 540.
— Twenty-two Years Ago. (E. P. Clark) Nation, 62: 337.
New Orleans. (J. Ralph) Harper, 86: 364.
— Battle of. (H. King) M. Am. Hist. 29: 19.
— — who won? Scrib. M. 17: 507.
— Butler in; a Diary. So. Hist. Pap. 23: 182.
— Convents in. (E. A. Starr) Cath. World, 64: 357.
— Higher Life of. (Grace King) Outl. 53: 754.
— Streets of the Vieux Carré in. (L. O. Harris) So. M. 5: 381.
— The Tragedy at. (M. M. Trumbull) Open Court, 5: 2776.
New Paltz, N. Y., Huguenot Refugees of. (E. Eltinge) M. Am. Hist. 30: 142.
New Patriotism, The; a poem. (M. M. Dawson) Arena, 16: 512.
New Pool of Bethesda, A. (G. O. Morgan) Gent. M. n. s. 52: 15.
New Resident at Slocombe; a story. (C. A. Price) Belgra. 81: Holiday no., 98.
New River. Cornh. 68: 249.
— Source of, Travels to. (Percy Fitzgerald) Gent. M. n. s. 55: 559. Same art. Ecl. M. 126: 327.
New Song of Spring Gardens; a poem. (A. Dobson) M. of Art, 8: 352.
New South Wales, Bush Fires in. Liv. Age, 208: 638.
— Industries, etc., of. (J. Inglis) J. Soc. Arts, 42: 666.
— Labor Party in. (H. Parkes) Contemp. 61: 197.
— National Gallery of. Art J. 44: 77.
— Physical Geography and Climate of. (H. C. Russell) Nature, 47: 258.
— Protectionists of. (H. Parkes) Contemp. 61: 621.
New Tenants of Linden Lodge; a story. (T. W. Speight) Argosy, 62: 745.
New Tenor, The. (C. V. Chippendale) Eng. Illust. 13: 335.
New Time, The, and how its Advent may be hastened. (B. O. Flower) Arena, 9: 685.
New Voice from the South; a story. (M. L. Wells) Arena, 13: 503.
New West Education Commission. (C. R. Bliss) Educa. 13: 462.
New Woman in Old Rome; a story. (G. E. Wall) Chaut. 23: 343.
New Year's Day. (T. Hopkins) Eng. Illust. 12: no. 4, 14.
— in Malaya, A. (R. Wildman) Overland, n. s. 27: 76.
New Year's Day in Paris. (E. Crawford) Eng. Illust. 11: 347.
New Year's Days in Old New York. (E. Fawcett) Lippinc. 55: 136.
— Notable. All the Year, 74: 5.
New Year's Eve; a poem. (A. W. Brotherton) Cent. 21: 436.
New Year's Presents to Henry VIII. Reliquary, 32: 208.
New York City. American Museum of Natural History. (W. Taylor) Munsey, 6: 21.
— and State, Relations of. (A. C. Bernheim) Pol. Sci. Q. 9: 377.
— Apartment Houses in. (E. N. Blanke) Cosmopol. 15: 354.
— Arabs of. (N. Crynkle) Q. Illust. 2: 125.
— Architecture of. (A. G. Hyde) Gent. M. n. s. 48: 493.
— Art Schools of. (M. Field) Munsey, 8: 673.

New York City as a Literary Centre. Critic, **21**: 316. — (D. Sladen) Eng. Illust. **10**: 137.
— Baptist Church in. (R. H. Titherington) Munsey, **7**: 3.
— Boland Trade-school. Cath. World, **57**: 822.
— Botanic Garden. (G. L. Goodale) Science, n. s. **2**: 1.
— Bridging the Hudson at. (G. Lindenthal) Engin. M. **6**: 213.
— Burgher Guard of New Amsterdam. (L. D. Scisco) Am. Hist. Reg. **2**: 737.
— Cathedral of St. John the Divine. Archit. Rec. **2**: 45. — (A. Grant) M. Am. Hist. **29**: 172.
— Catholic Charities in. Cath. World, **59**: 702. **60**: 116.
— Central Park. (J. C. Hamilton) Munsey, **6**: 3. — (A. Wakeley) Munsey, **13**: 565.
— — Speed-road in. Garden & F. **5**: 109, 145.
— Chemical Bank. Bank. M. (N. Y.) **48**: 542.
— Chinese Quarter of. (W. Taylor) Munsey, **6**: 678.
— Citizenship of, Criminal Degradation of. (J. B. Leavitt) Forum, **17**: 659.
— City-hall Competition. Archit. Rec. **3**: 213.
— Commercial Blight of. (W. N. Black) Engin. M. **3**: 291, 463.
— Common Schools. (S. H. Olin) Harper, **90**: 584.
— Death-rate of, How it was reduced. (N. Straus) Forum, **18**: 361.
— Diet Kitchen Association. (Anna S. Hackett) Munsey, **8**: 276.
— Directory, 1665. Nat'l M. (N. Y. '91) **16**: 28.
— Early Schoolmasters of. (H. C. Kirk) Educa. **15**: 350.
— Edison Building. Archit. Rec. **1**: 133.
— Episcopal Church in. (R. H. Titherington) Munsey, **6**: 552.
— Evolution of. (J. J. O'Shea) Cath. World, **63**: 682. — (T. A. Janvier) Harper, **86**: 813. **87**: 15.
— Failure of Municipal Reform in 1895. (E. Porritt) National, **26**: 237.
— Fifth Avenue. (R. H. Titherington) Munsey, **6**: 123.
— First Book printed in. Bookworm, **3**: 89.
— First Impressions of Literary. (W. D. Howells) Harper, **91**: 62.
— Franchises of; a Chapter of Municipal Folly. (A. Bernheim) Cent. **28**: 149.
— Free Circulating Library, Financial Need of. Critic, **28**: 280.
— Freedom of Press in. (E. Lawrence) Nat'l M. (N. Y. '91) **18**: 113.
— Great Metropolitan Bridge. Soc. Econ. **9**: 329.
— Greater. (E. L. Godkin) Nation, **62**: 282. — Gunton's M. **10**: 341.
— — Government of. (F. V. Greene) Scrib. M. **20**: 418.
— — Politics in. Gunton's M. **10**: 166.
— — Symposium. Indep. April 16, '96.
— Greenwich Village. (T. A. Janvier) Harper, **87**: 339.
— — Government of, 1892, and how to reform it. (A. Shaw) R. of Rs. (N. Y.) **5**: 286.
— — Legacy of Blackmail from Colonial Days. (C. C. Buel) Cent. **27**: 769.
— Higher Life of. (A. Shaw) Outl. **53**: 132.
— Historic Homes in. (R. H. Titherington) Munsey, **7**: 571.
— in 1668–73. (A. G. Vermilye) Nat'l M. (N. Y. '91) **16**: 129.
— 1698–1743. Nat'l M. (N. Y. '91) **17**: 1–493. **18**: 1, 113.
New York City, 1743–53. (J. M. Gittermann) Nat'l M. (N. Y. '91) **18**: 209.
— 1761–68. Nat'l M. (N. Y. '91) **19**: 113, 229.
— in the Civil War. (T. F. Rodenbough) M. Am. Hist. **29**: 193.
— Jewish Charities of. (G. Gottheil) Munsey, **10**: 60.
— Landmarks of Manhattan. (R. Cortissoz) Scrib. M. **18**: 531.
— Letters of an Altrurian Traveller. (W. D. Howells) Cosmopol. **16**: 259, 415. **17**: 46–610.
— Libraries and the Library Problem in. (R. R. Bowker) Lib. J. **21**: 99.
— Library of University of. Critic, **27**: 252.
— Light in Dark Places; a Study of Better New York. (J. A. Riis) Cent. **31**: 246.
— Lispenard's Meadows. (T. A. Janvier) Harper, **87**: 746.
— Love Lane. (T. A. Janvier) Harper, **87**: 582.
— Manhattanville, Roman Catholic Convent-school at. (H. M. Sweeney) Cath. World, **57**: 462.
— Mercantile Library Building. Lib. J. **17**: 18.
— Metropolitan Museum of Art. (C. S. Johnson) Munsey, **6**: 145.
— Mt. St. Vincent, Roman Catholic Convent-school at. (M. J. Brunowe) Cath. World, **57**: 349.
— Movement for Housing Reform in. R. of Rs. (N. Y.) **14**: 693.
— Municipal Art. (C. S. Sargent) Garden & F. **9**: 21.
— Negro Plot in, 1741. Nat'l M. (N. Y. '91) **18**: 128.
— New Criminal Court Building. Archit. Rec. **3**: 429.
— A Night with the Roofers in. All the Year, **72**: 57.
— Old. (J. G. Wilson) Cosmopol. **12**: 313.
— Parks of, New. (E. S. Nadal) Scrib. M. **11**: 439.
— — Historical Reminiscences. (F. Morris) M. Am. Hist. **27**: 401.
— — Small. (W. Taylor) Munsey, **8**: 25.
— People in. (M. G. Van Rensselaer) Cent. **27**: 534.
— Picturesque. (M. G. Van Rensselaer) Cent. **23**: 164.
— Plan to improve and beautify. Soc. Econ. **2**: 65.
— Poets of. (B. Matthews) Cosmopol. **14**: 324.
— Police out of Politics. (Theodore Roosevelt) Cosmopol. **20**: 40.
— Police Scandals. Sat. R. **80**: 199.
— Poor in, Special Needs of. (J. A. Riis) Forum, **14**: 492.
— Presbyterian Church in. (A. C. Mackenzie) Munsey, **10**: 254.
— Public Baths of. (Amy L. Scudamore) Lend a H. **17**: 43.
— Public Library, Astor, Lenox, and Tilden Foundations. Lib. J. **20**: 84, 125.
— — Site of. Critic, **28**: 220. — (C. S. Sargent) Garden & F. **9**: 161.
— Public-school Situation in. (N. M. Butler) Educa. R. **12**: 196.
— Public-school System. (J. M. Rice) Forum, **14**: 616.
— Public Schools. Critic, **28**: 71.
— — Legislation for. Critic, **28**: 203.
— Reform in. (N. M. Butler) Educa. R. **11**: 300, 409, 512.
— Railroad Facilities of Suburban. (F. Crowell) Engin. M. **10**: 1029.
— Railroad Terminals and Harbor of. (W. N. Black) Engin. M. **5**: 631.
— Rapid Transit for. Am. Arch. **49**: 90.
— Records of the Ice Age about. (T. M. Prudden) Harper, **89**: 593.

New York City, Reformed Church in. (R. H. Titherington) Munsey, 6: 650.
— Riverside Park. (W. S. Bridgman) Munsey, 7: 131.
— St. Francis Xavier College Building. Archit. Rec. 4: 247.
— Salvation Army Building. Archit. Rec. 6: 77.
— Schools of. Am. J. Pol. 4: 616.
— Sea-robbers of. (T. A. Janvier) Harper, 89: 813.
— Slums of. Lond. Q. 78: 48.
— Society in. (M. W. Hazeltine) 19th Cent. 31: 762. Same art. Ecl. M. 118: 842.
— — in the Early Days of the Republic. (J. G. Wilson) M. Am. Hist. 29: 81.
— Spring in. (W. Frith) Temp. Bar, 105: 83. Same art. Ecl. M. 124: 843.
— Street Cleaning: Waring's "White Angels." (W. W. Ellsworth) Outl. 53: 1191.
— Sunday Closing in. (T. Roosevelt) Forum, 20: 1. — (T. Roosevelt) McClure, 5: 475. — (L. Windmüller) Forum, 20: 211.
— Sunday in New Netherland and Old New York. (A. M. Earle) Atlan. 78: 543.
— Superior Court of, in 1855. Green Bag, 4: 401.
— Unitarian Church in. (W. S. Bridgman) Munsey, 8: 131.
— Vigilance League of. (C. H. Parkhurst) No. Am. 156: 98.
— Wealth of. (T. F. Gilroy) No. Am. 157: 307, 403, 541.
— Were Dutch there in 1598? (D. Van Pelt) Nat'l M. (N. Y. '91) 15: 91, 279.
— West Side of, Charitable Work in. (A. B. Thaw) Lend a H. 10: 309.
— Wolfe Building. Archit. Rec. 5: 299.
New York State, Charities of. (J. P. Ritter) Soc. Econ. 7: 152.
— Constitution of, New. R. of Rs. (N. Y.) 9: 291.
— — and Catholic Schools and Charities. (J. T. McDonough) Cath. World, 62: 682.
— — in relation to Prison Labor. (W. P. Prentice) Lend a H. 15: 418.
— — Proposed Agnostic Amendment to. (T. McMillan) Cath. World, 60: 267.
— Constitutional Convention. Soc. Econ. 6: 211.
— Constitutional Revision in, Some Ideas on. (J. B. Uhle) Pol. Sci. Q. 9: 1.
— Court of Errors. (I. Browne) Am. Law R. 29: 321.
— Dutch Colonial Governors of. (J. G. Wilson) Nat'l M. (N. Y '91) 15: 337–571.
— Founder of. (J. W. De Forest) Am. Hist. Reg. 2: 881–1172.
— Is it more civilized than Kansas? (J. W. Gleed) Forum, 17: 217.
— National Guard. (E. E. Hardin) Outing, 25: 251, 427.
— — in Active Service in Brooklyn. (D. S. Mercein) Outing, 25: 517.
— Naval Militia. (R. S. Osborne) Munsey, 9: 3.
— Province of, Council of Appointment in. (J. M. Gitterman) Pol. Sci. Q. 7: 80.
— Rural Militia of the New Netherland. (L. D. Scisco) Am. Hist. Reg. 3: 335.
— University of. (W. C. Doane) No. Am. 158: 679.
— — Library Work of. (W. R. Eastman) Lib. J. 20: 267.
New York, Cruiser, Trial Trip of. (A. F. Matthews) Chaut. 17: 548.
New York Athletic Club on Travers Island. (O. Hackett) Munsey, 7: 389.
New York Bar Association. (A. O. Hall) Green Bag, 8: 450.
New York Canoe Club, Silver Wedding of. (R. B. Burchard) Outing, 28: 467.
New York Colleges. (J. N. Smith) Munsey, 6: 49.
New York Law School and the Harvard Law Review. (G. Chase) Am. Law R. 26: 155.
New York Magazine, First Illustrated Magazine published in N. Y. Bookman, 1: 234.
New York Sun, The. (E. J. Edwards) Munsey, 10: 20.
New York Tribune, The, in the Draft Riots. (J. R. Gilmore) McClure, 5: 445.
New York Yacht Club. (A. J. Kenealy) Outing, 24: 388.
New Zealand. (Sir R. Stout) Asia. R. 20: 86. — (E. Wakefield) Cosmopol. 13: 163.
— Alps of, In the. (E. A. Fitzgerald) Contemp. 68: 190. Same art. Ecl. M. 125: 480. Same art. Liv. Age, 206: 740.
— — Mannering's. Sat. R. 73: 72.
— Banking and Politics in. (S. J. Murray) Bank. M. (Lond.) 60: 593.
— Federation in. (R. Stout) 19th Cent. 33: 203.
— Glaciers, Exploration and Character of. (A. P. Harper) Geog. J. 1: 32.
— Harbors of. M. of Art, 11: 6.
— Homes in. All the Year, 72: 40.
— in 1892. (Countess of Galloway) 19th Cent. 32: 403.
— In the Wake of Captain Cook. Macmil. 71: 294.
— Land Laws of. (E. Reeves) Westm. 141: 297.
— Peculiarities of. Chamb. J. 70: 506.
— Playground of the Pacific. (W. C. Macgregor) Westm. 143: 319.
— Political and Social Reform in. (W. P. Reeves) National, 27: 834.
— Social Politics in. (Sir J. Vogel) Fortn. 59: 130.
— Southern Alps of, First Crossing of. (E. A. Fitz) Geog. J. 7: 483.
— State Experiments in. (Sir R. Stout) J. Statis. Soc. 55: 388.
— Travel and Discovery in, Fitzgerald's. Sat. R. 82: 221.
— under Female Franchise. (R. H. Bakewell) 19th Cent. 35: 268. — (M. G. Fawcett) Contemp. 65: 433.
— Westland Alps. Geog. J. 5: 61.
— Women of. Why they get the Franchise. (E. Reeves) Westm. 143: 35.
Newark, N. J. (F. W. Ricord) Nat'l M. (N. Y. '91) 17: 342, 464. 18: 265. 19: 98–299.
— Early Printers and Booksellers of. (J. P. Briscoe) Bookworm, 4: 145.
— Peddie Memorial Church Building. Archit. Rec. 2: 89.
Newberry, John S. Nature, 47: 276. — Nat. Sci. 2: 153.
Newberry Library, Chicago. How it was moved. (W. S. Merrill) Lib. J. 19: 11.
— Management of. Dial (Ch.) 17: 324.
— Musical Department of. (G. P. Upton) Music, 1: 97.
Newbery, John, the Publisher. Bookworm, 2: 121.
Newburgh, N. Y., Old Cantonment at. (R. Headley) New Eng. M. n. s. 13: 578.
Newbury, England. (E. Walford) Walford's Antiq. 8: 27.
Newbury, Mass., Soldiers of. (F. E. Blake) N. E. Reg. 50: 338.
Newcastle, Margaret, Duchess of. Temp. Bar, 99: 167. Same art. Liv. Age, 199: 596.
Newcastle-on-Tyne. (W. Reid) 19th Cent. 40: 461. Same art. Liv. Age, 211: 182.

Newcastle-on-Tyne, Museum of Natural History. (A. Meek) Nat. Sci. 7: 115.
— Natural Science in. (A. M. Norman) Nat. Sci. 7: 169.
Newell, Peter, with portrait. Bk. Buyer, 13: 348.
Newfoundland. (J. Murray) Canad. M. 7: 462. — (C. Fane) J. Soc. Arts, 41: 477.
— and French Fishery Rights. (J. P. Val d'Eremao) Asia. R. 20: 376. — (T. B. Browning) Law Q. 11: 248. — (J. W. Lowther) National, 25: 314.
— and the French Question. (P. A. Hurd) Westm. 139: 642.
— Commercial Collapse of. (A. R. Whiteway) National, 24: 822. — (P. T. McGrath) Nat'l M. (Bost.) 4: 563.
— Crisis in. (W. Greswell) Fortn. 63: 467. Same art. Liv. Age, 205: 98.
— Dialect. (George Patterson) J. Am. Folk-Lore, 8: 27. 9: 19.
— England and. (E. R. Spearman) Westm. 137: 403.
— First Plantation of. (J. F. M. Fawcett) Canad. M. 3: 41.
— Folk-lore of. (George Patterson) J. Am. Folk-Lore, 8: 285.
— Great Britain and France *vs.* (C. D. Collet) Asia. R. 13: 354.
— History of, Prowse's. Macmil. 74: 23. — Liv. Age, 209: 672. — (G. Smith) Am. Hist. R. 1: 185.
— in Revolt. Econ. R. 5: 236.
— Newspapers of. (I. F. M. Fawcett) Canad. M. 4: 422.
— Our Oldest Colony. Chamb. J. 72: 177.
— A Picture of. (J. Douglas) Nation, 63: 304.
— Politics in. (A. R. Whiteway) New R. 12: 295.
— a Review. Westm. 144: 127.
— Sentinel of the St. Lawrence. (P. C. Hurd) Eng. Illust. 13: 525.
— Treaty Obligations of, to France. (A. R. Whiteway) Month, 84: 204.
Newfoundland Regiments, The. (J. F. M. Fawcett) Gent. M. n. s. 56: 443.
Newhouse Tunnel at Idaho Springs. (A. Lakes) Engin. M. 10: 49.
Newland, Abraham, with portrait. Bank. M. (Lond.) 58: 635.
Newlyn and the Newlyn School of Painters. (W. C. Symons) M. of Art, 13: 199.
— A Painter's Snug Corner. Atlan. 71: 423.
Newman, F. W., and Protestant Prejudice. Eng. R. 17: 49.
— The Soul, her Sorrows and Aspirations. Eng. R. 16: 101.
Newman, John Henry. (T. V. Tymms) Chr. Lit. 10: 24 a. — (M. D. Conway) Open Court, 4: 2529, 2543. — (H. Goodwin) Contemp. 61: 49. — (R. M. Lovett) Harv. Mo. 15: 99. — (A. M. Fairbairn) Crit. R. 1: 119.
— Abbott on. Ath. '92, 1: 593. — Sat. R. 73: 519. — Spec. 68: 712.
— and Bishop Lightfoot. Ed. R. 178: 248.
— and Tennyson. Spec. 77: 74.
— Edinburgh Review on. Spec. 71: 172.
— Lead, Kindly Light. (T. V. Tymms) Good Words, 34: 665. Same art. Ecl. M. 121: 661.
— on Development of Christian Doctrine. Eng. R. 4: 386.
— Recollections of. (A. de Vere) 19th Cent. 40: 395. Same art. Liv. Age, 211: 148.
— Isaac Williams on. Spec. 68: 296.
Newnes, George; a Sketch of his Life. (R. Blathwayt) Idler, 3: 161.
Newport, R. I. (W. C. Brownell) Scrib. M. 16: 135.
Newport, R. I., in the Revolution. (C. R. Thurston) New Eng. M. n. s. 11: 3.
— Old. (O. Tiffany) Cosmopol. 15: 664.
Newport Symposium, A. (Mrs. Burton Harrison) No. Am. 163: 236.
News-getting for Country Papers. (A. Fosdick) Writer, 8: 145.
Newspaper, The, and the New Education. (F. E. Oliver) Educa. 13: 159.
— Daily. (J. T. Clark) Canad. M. 7: 101.
— — What it might be made. (W. M. Payne) Forum, 16: 355.
— Growth of a Great (London Times). Soc. Econ. 7: 345.
— Local, How to conduct. (J. A. Cockerill) Lippinc. 58: 395.
— of the Future. (J. A. Cockerill) Lippinc. 50: 220.
— Olden Time County. (H. E. Smith) Am. Hist. Reg. 1: 239.
— Significance of, in the U. S. (W. M. Fullerton) New R. 8: 655.
Newspaper Art and Artists. (A. Forman) Q. Illust. 1: 313.
Newspaper Cookery. (A. Barrows) Writer, 6: 67.
Newspaper Correspondent, The. (J. Ralph) Scrib. M. 14: 150.
Newspaper Correspondents, Some very Curious. (W. H. Bradley) Gent. M. n. s. 54: 17.
Newspaper Cuttings; a story. Belgra. 83: 159.
Newspaper Editing; Diversions of a Sub-editor. (J. Pendleton) Gent. M. n. s. 56: 120. Same art. Ecl. M. 126: 419.
— Editorial Copy Foundry. Lippinc. 57: 141.
Newspaper English. (F. Matthews) Chaut. 21: 302.
Newspaper Enterprise, Humours of. Chamb. J. 72: 423.
Newspaper Ethics. (M. Y. Beach) Writer, 8: 157.
Newspaper "Faking." (G. G. Bain) Lippinc. 54: 274.
— Humors of. (John Pendleton) Gent. M. n. s. 57: 39. Same art. Liv. Age, 210: 305.
Newspaper Illustrator's Story. (M. de Lipman) Lippinc. 50: 77.
Newspaper Illustrators in America, Early. (F. Beard) Our Day, 16: 85.
Newspaper Man as a Confidant. (A. E. Watrous) Lippinc. 49: 332.
Newspaper Office, Night in a Metropolitan. (F. Matthews) Chaut. 23: 332.
Newspaper Pictures. (E. L. Godkin) Nation, 56: 306.
Newspaper Press; a Paradox of Coöperation. (E. Ingle) Southern M. 4: 175.
— of Europe. (H. R. Chamberlain) Chaut. 20: 39.
— of the U. S. (F. Matthews) Chaut. 20: 162.
— Scotland, Beginnings of. (J. D. Cockburn) Scot. R. 21: 399.
Newspaper Reading. (W. A. Stille) Nation, 60: 218.
Newspaper Row and National Legislation. (A. Halstead) No. Am. 160: 249.
Newspaper Sensation. (L. N. Megargee) Lippinc. 52: 729.
Newspaper Women. (H. M. Winslow) Arena, 17: 127.
Newspaper Work for Women. (M. H. Welch) Am. J. Soc. Sci. 32: 110.
Newspapers, American. (H. King) Chaut. 22: 525.
— and Good English. (R. I. Attwill) Bost. 3: 543.
— Do they now give the News? (J. G. Speed) Forum, 15: 705.
— Endowment of. Dial (Ch.) 14: 35.

Newspapers, English, and Political Education. Atlan. 76: 571.
— — Literature in. (W. R. Nicoll) Bookman, 1: 32.
— Evening, English, Feature of. Spec. 71: 795.
— in Egypt. (W. F. Rae) 19th Cent. 32: 213.
— in France. (E. Delille) 19th Cent. 31: 474. Same art. Ecl. M. 118: 556.
— — Early Days of. (W. Burnet) Good Words, 33: 266. Same art. Liv. Age, 193: 572.
— in Germany. (C. Lowe) Ecl. M. 118: 209.
— in the U. S. (E. Delille) 19th Cent. 32: 13. Same art. Critic, 21: 98. Same art. Ecl. M. 119: 265.
— — Symposium on, in the "Forum" for August, 1893. Dial (Ch.) 15: 79.
— Index to. (R. R. Bowker) Lib. J. 18: 506.
— London Daily. (H. W. Massingham) Leis. Hour, 41: 231–740.
— of Europe. (T. C. Crawford) Munsey, 8: 376.
— Rights and Duties of. (S. Thompson) Open Court, 3: 2058.
— Sunday. *See* Sunday Newspapers.
— Women's. (E. March-Phillipps) Fortn. 62: 661.
— A Word to the Critics of. (C. R. Miller) Forum, 15: 712.
Newt, Vermilion Spotted, Life History of. (S. H. Gage) Am. Natural. 25: 1084.
Newton, Charles Thomas. (P. Gardner) Acad. 46: 476. — Ath. '94, 2: 797. — (S. L. Poole) National, 24: 616. — (R. C. Jebb) J. Hel. Stud. 14: xlix. — Nature, 51: 250.
— In Mitylene with. Blackw. 157: 596. Same art. Ecl. M. 124: 682.
Newton, Hubert A. Nature, 54: 394. — Pop. Astron. 4: 236.
Newton, Sir Isaac. (Robert Ball) Good Words, 36: 53.
— and Huygens. (A. Huet) Nature, 52: 270.
— Philosophical Method of. (L. R. Harley) Educa. 16: 596.
Newton Stone, The. (W. M. Ramsay) Acad. 42: 240. — (W. Stokes and others) Acad. 41: 542–614. 42: 14, 32. — (E. W. B. Nicholson) Acad. 44: 415.
Newton's Brain; a story. (J. Arbes) Poet-Lore, 4: 429–616.
Next House, The; a story. (J. C. Fletcher) New R. 12: 1.
Next Room, The; a story. (Octave Thanet) Harper, 93: 945.
Ney, Marshal M. Family Record of his Execution. (G. C. Genet) Cent. 30: 415.
— Mystery of. (C. H. Kidder) Munsey, 13: 277.
— Weston's Historic Doubts as to Execution of. (G. Hunt) Nation, 61: 119.
Nez Perces, Mythology and Religion of. (R. L. Packard) J. Am. Folk-Lore, 4: 327.
N'Gamiland, Sport and Natural History in. (H. A. Bryden) Longm. 21: 31.
Niagara, St. Andrew's Church. Canad. M. 5: 286.
Niagara Falls. Critic, 25: 181.
— and the Great Lakes. (F. B. Taylor) Am. J. Sci. 149: 249.
— — History of. (A. J. Herbertson) Knowl. 19: 223.
— as a Motor for the World's Fair. (J. Trowbridge) Chaut. 14: 441.
— as a Timepiece. (J. W. Spencer) Pop. Sci. Mo. 49: 1.
— Duration of. (J. W. Spencer) Am. Natural. 28: 859. Same art. Am. J. Sci. 148: 455.
— Electric Generation at. (L. B. Stillwell) Cassier, 8: 253.
— Electricity from. (J. Munro) Chamb. J. 70: 177. Same art. Liv. Age, 197: 567.
Niagara Falls, Industrial Village of Echota at. (J. Bogart) Cassier, 8: 307.
— Power from. (T. C. Martin) J. Frankl. Inst. 142: 287, 354. Same art. Am. Arch. 54: 89. — (A. Richardson) Good Words, 37: 183. — (E. A. Le Sueur) Pop. Sci. Mo. 45: 608. — (E. J. Edwards) McClure, 3: 423. — (C. Brown) Cosmopol. 17: 527. — Dub. R. 114: 421. — Nature, 50: 11. — (W. C. Johnson) Cassier, 5: 326.
— — Distribution of the Electric Power. (F. L. Pope) Engin. M. 10: 407. — (S. D. Greene) Cassier, 8: 333.
— — — Prof. Forbes on. (E. A. Le Sueur) Pop. Sci. Mo. 48: 198.
— — 3,000,000 Horse-power. (R. Grimshaw) Cassier, 3: 173.
— — Tunnel. (C. H. Werner) Cassier, 2: 73. — (A. H. Porter) Cassier, 8: 203.
— — Utilization of. (G. Forbes) Blackw. 158: 430. Same art. Ecl. M. 125: 507. — (A. V. Abbott) R. of Rs. (N. Y.) 12: 295. — (S. P. Thompson) Sat. R. 80: 134. — Dub. R. 112: 435. — (G. Forbes) J. Soc. Arts, 41: 90. — (Lyman Abbott) Outl. 52: 788. — (F. L. Stetson) Cassier, 8: 173.
— Power Plant. (H. H. Suplee) Cassier, 7: 85.
— Water-power of. Nature, 49: 482.
Niagara Literature. (J. Hayes) Bookworm, 4: 337.
Niagara Region in History. (P. A. Porter) Cassier, 8: 365.
Niagara Reservation. Critic, 28: 203. — (J. Chamberlin) Garden & F. 5: 575.
Niagara River since the Ice Age. (N. Upham) Nature, 50: 198.
Nibblings and Browsings. (F. D. Bergen) Atlan. 72: 373.
Nicaragua, Across, with Transit and Machéte. (R. E. Peary) Nat. Geog. M. 1: 315.
— and the Mosquito Coast. (R. N. Keeley, jr.) Pop. Sci. Mo. 45: 160.
— and its People. Sat. R. 79: 613.
— Games and Popular Superstitions of. (E. A. P. de Guerrero) J. Am. Folk-Lore, 4: 35.
— Northeastern, Recent Discoveries in. (J. Crawford) Science, 22: 269.
— Personal Impressions of. (G. Gaul) Cent. 24: 64.
— A Visit to. (M. R. Davies) Good Words, 37: 532.
— Walker's Expedition to, The Alamo Rangers in. (M. French) Overland, n. s. 21: 517.
Nicaragua Canal. (J. R. Proctor) Am. J. Pol. 2: 225. — (P. S. Cassidy) Cath. World, 62: 499. — (G. W. Davis) J. Frankl. Inst. 134: 1–109. — Pub. Opin. 14: 259, 298. — (H. Davis) Overland, n. s. 19: 247. — (G. W. Sherwood) J. Frankl. Inst. 139: 425. — Macmil. 72: 321. — Dub. R. 116: 411. — Pub. Opin. 16: 520. 17: 214, 463.
— Absence of Facts about. (C. B. Going) Engin. M. 11: 416.
— America's Need for. (W. Miller) Engin. M. 4: 799.
— and Commerce. (W. Miller) Forum, 12: 714.
— and the Economic Development of U. S. (E. R. Johnson) Ann. Am. Acad. Pol. Sci. 7: 38.
— and Great Britain. (A. S. White) Un. Serv. M. 9: 490.
— and Legislation in Connection with it. (G. P. Montague) Am. Law R. 27: 161.
— and the Monroe Doctrine. (L. M. Keasbey) Ann. Am. Acad. Pol. Sci. 7: 1.
— and the Surrounding Country. Dub. R. 118: 177.
— Colquhoun's. (G. S. Morison) Nation, 62: 125.
— Government Aid to. (J. T. Morgan) No. Am. 156: 195.

Nicaragua Canal, an Impracticable Scheme. (J. Nimmo, jr.) Forum, **21**: 21.
— Military Advantages to the U. S. (F. L. Winn) Overland, n. s. **23**: 489.
— Our Benefits from the. (A. S. White) No. Am. **161**: 720.
— Ours or England's? (C. De Kalb) Forum, **16**: 690.
— Outlook of. Sat. R. **79**: 341.
— Political Aspect. (W. L. Merry) Overland, n. s. **23**: 497. — (W. L. Merry) Forum, **12**: 721.
— Present State of. (A. W. Greely) Nat. Geog. M. **7**: 73.
— Route of, Advantages of. (J. W. Miller) Ann. Am. Acad. Pol. Sci. **7**: 32.
Nice, Capt. John, Diary of, 1775–78. Pennsyl. M. **16**: 399.
Nice, Drive from Paris to. (E. Johnson) Gent. M. n. s. **55**: 87.
— 2d Council of. Church Q. **42**: 448.
Nichol, John. (J. S. Cotton) Acad. **46**: 303. — (T. Watts) Ath. **'94, 2**: 530.
Nicholas, St., in England. Cornh. **71**: 482.
Nicholas, St., Pope, Who is? (W. J. D. Croke) Cath. World, **62**: 265.
Nicholas II. (W. T. Stead) R. of Rs. (N. Y.) **10**: 633. — With portrait. (M. Field) Munsey, **11**: 629. — R. of Rs. (N. Y.) **13**: 703. — (T. B. Preston) Chaut. **22**: 569. — Soc. Econ. **7**: 342. — Spec. **74**: 841.
— The Coronation at Moscow. (M. Creighton) Cornh. **74**: 305.
— Fêtes for. (J. B. Latham) Westm. **146**: 654.
— in Paris. (A. Laugel) Nation, **63**: 643.
Nichols, Francis Boude. (H. K. Nichols) Am. Hist. Reg. **2**: 788.
Nicholson, Brinsley. Acad. **42**: 312.
Nicholson, Sir Francis. (W. C. Ford) M. Am. Hist. **29**: 499.
Nicholson, W. N. P., and James Pryale, the Beggarstaff Bros. Idler, **8**: 519.
Nickel. (A. G. Charleton) J. Soc. Arts, **42**: 496.
— and its Uses. (J. T. Donald) Pop. Sci. Mo. **42**: 252.
— Treatment of Ores of. (A. G. Charleton) J. Soc. Arts, **43**: 609.
Nickel Region of Canada. (H. A. Hilyard) Canad. M. **1**: 305.
Nickeliferous Pyrite from Sudbury, Ont. (T. L. Walker) Am. J. Sci. **147**: 312.
Nicknames, Historical. (F. L. Oswald) No. Am. **161**: 254.
Nicky Binks; a story. (C. Nicholson) Eng. Illust. **12**: no. 5, 17.
Nicobar Islanders, Use of Narcotics by. (E. H. Maw) Anthrop. J. **23**: 232.
Nicol, Erskine. (W. W. Fenn) M. of Art, **2**: 180.
Nicolini, Adelina Maria Clorinda (Patti). *See* Patti, Madame.
Nicoll, W. Robertson, with portrait. Bookman, **1**: 15.
— Interview with. (H. Dixon) Sund. M. **25**: 303.
Nicolle, Leontine. (A. P. McIlvaine) Char. R. **2**: 116.
Nicolls, Richard. (E. Lawrence) Nat'l M. (N. Y. '91) **16**: 1.
Niehaus, Charles Henry. (R. R. Wilson) Mo. Illust. **12**: 391.
Niesz, Benjamin F., with portrait. (A. N. Towne) Nat'l M. (N. Y. '91) **16**: 732.
Nietzsche, Friedrich, with portrait. Bk. Buyer, **13**: 407. — (G. Schumm) Book R. **3**: 275. — Quar. **184**: 299. — (W. Wallace) Acad. **50**: 75. — Sat. R. **81**: 373.
— and Tolstoi, Moral Systems of. (Prof. Grote) Pub. Opin. **14**: 621.
Nietzsche, Friedrich, Philosophy of. (F. C. S. Schiller) Bk. Buyer, **13**: 407.
Nigel, Bishop of Ely. (J. H. Round) Eng. Hist. R. **8**: 515.
Niger, Christianizing the. (T. C. Collings) Sund. M. **24**: 307.
— England and France on the. (F. Lugard) 19th Cent. **37**: 889. Same art. Liv. Age, **206**: 87.
— Up the. All the Year, **71**: 414.
Niger Territories, The. (L. Darwin) National, **23**: 566.
Night of the Gods, O'Neill's. (W. W. Newell) J. Am. Folk-Lore, **7**: 328.
— on the River; a poem. (J. H. Keene) Outing, **26**: 151.
— When the, falls. Ecl. M. **122**: 268.
Night Hawks and Whip-poor-wills. (R. W. Shufeldt) Pop. Sci. Mo. **44**: 308.
Night Life. Cornh. **68**: 136.
Night Refuge for Workingmen at Turin. (W. E. Mantius) Am. Arch. **49**: 52.
Night Ride in Apache Land; a story. (W. R. Rowe) Overland, n. s. **19**: 142.
Night School. (J. G. Vibert) Cent. **29**: 554.
Night Thoughts. (G. F. Underhill) Time, **17**: 462.
Nightingale, Florence. (H. E. Banning) Chaut. **21**: 79.
Nightingale, Myth of the, in Greek Vase-paintings. (J. E. Harrison) M. of Art, **14**: 227.
— a poem. (F. Bierhoff) Outing, **26**: 395.
— Song of. (I. G. Tompkins) Music, **10**: 340, 451.
Nightingale's Nests. (C. J. Cornish) Sund. M. **25**: 607.
Nightingales and Cuckoos. Spec. **70**: 635.
Nightmare Page, The. (Octave Thanet) Scrib. M. **19**: 638.
Nihilism as it is, Stepniak's. Sat. R. **79**: 193.
— — Reply. (S. Stepniak) New R. **10**: 215.
— in Russia, and the Famine. (Countess Norraikow) Lippinc. **49**: 463.
Nihilist, The; a tale. (A. H. Seymour) Belgra. **84**: 279.
Nijhoff, Martinus. Acad. **46**: 232.
Nijni Novgorod Fair. Dub. R. **110**: 193.
Nikisch, Arthur, as Orchestra Leader. Sat. R. **79**: 827.
Nikko, Japan. (A. F. Mockler-Ferryman) Gent. M. n. s. **54**: 493.
— Temple of the Tokugawa. (C. T. Matthews) Archit. Rec. **4**: 191.
Nile, The. (J. N. Lockyer) Nature, **47**: 464. Same art. Liv. Age, **197**: 562. — (C. Scott-Moncrieff) Nature, **51**: 444. Same art. Liv. Age, **205**: 87.
— and Mountains of the Moon. Dub. R. **112**: 451.
— Battle of. (J. L. Laughton) Cornh. **74**: 147. — (Capt. Charrier) New R. **9**: 160.
— England and France on. (F. D. Lugard) National, **25**: 609. Same art. Liv. Age, **206**: 403.
— First Cataract. (G. Montbard) Art J. **48**: 6, 77.
— France and. (F. A. Maxse) National, **25**: 851.
— Notes on. Cornh. **68**: 25. — Ecl. M. **121**: 324.
— Sketches from. Outing, **23**: 284.
— Source of. Around World, **1**: 201.
Nile Campaign, Failure of. (Archibald Forbes) Un. Serv. (Phila.) **7**: 257.
Nile Corvée, The. (F. Cope Whitehouse) Nation, **55**: 373.
Nile Reservoir, Proposed. (J. P. Mahaffy) 19th Cent. **35**: 1013. Same art. Liv. Age, **202**: 38. — (F. Dillon) 19th Cent. **35**: 1019.
— and Philæ. (B. Baker) 19th Cent. **35**: 863. Same art. Liv. Age, **201**: 748. — (H. A. Harper) Leis. Hour, **44**: 300.

Nilsson, Christine, Glimpses of. (W. S. B. Mathews) Music, 10: 570.
Nilt, Cashmere, Battle of. Spec. 68: 600.
Nimbus and Aureole, in Art. (E. Schreiber) Am. Cath. Q. 17: 813.
Nîmes, Maison Carrée, Greek Horizontal Curves in. (W. H. Goodyear) Archit. Rec. 4: 446. — (W. M. Goodyear) Am. J. Archæol. 10: 1.
Nimrod in Assyrian Inscriptions. (A. H. Sayce) Acad. 42: 53.
1920. A Political Prophecy. Contemp. 68: 761. Same art. Liv. Age, 208: 3.
Nineteenth Century, Changes in the Intellectual Life at the Close of. (J. Wedgewood) Contemp. 70: 420. Same art. Ecl. M. 127: 721.
— Ends of. (Jane De F. Shelton) M. Am. Hist. 28: 98.
— Great Names of. Critic, 21: 240.
— Last Gift of. (N. S. Shaler) No. Am. 161: 674.
— Progress in. (E. A. Freeman) Chaut. 14: 433.
— Reformation of. (R. M. Meyer) Int. J. Ethics, 7: 63.
— This Enlightened Age. (J. R. Edwards) Westm. 137: 633.
Nineteenth Century Club and its Founder. (M. D. Conway) Open Court, 2: 1394.
Nineveh. Ashurbanipal, his Books and Buildings. (L. W. King) Illus. Archæol. 2: 65.
Ninia; a story. (L. Becke) Eng. Illust. 14: 283.
Niobrara, Fort, Nebraska. (P. Collier) New Eng. M. n. s. 8: 632.
Nippur, Arch at. (J. P. Peters) Am. J. Archæol. 10: 352.
— Court of Columns at. (J. P. Peters) Am. J. Archæol. 10: 439.
— Recent Results of the University of Pennsylvania Excavations at. (J. P. Peters) Am. J. Archæol. 10: 13.
Nirvana, Doctrine of. (Shaku Soyen) Open Court, 10: 5167.
— Karma and. (P. Carus) Monist, 4: 417.
Nitchevo: a Fragment of Russian Life. (G. B. Stuart) Blackw. 156: 430. Same art. Liv. Age, 203: 139. Same art. Ecl. M. 124: 93.
Nitragin; an Advance in Agriculture. (C. M. Aikman) Contemp. 70: 210.
Nitrate Fields, Chili. Blackw. 151: 437. Same art. Liv. Age, 193: 490.
Nitrates, Iodometric Determination of the. (H. Gruener) Am. J. Sci. 146: 42.
— — Method for. (F. A. Gooch and H. W. Gruener) Am. J. Sci. 144: 117.
Nitric Acid, Reduction of, by Ferrous Salts. (Charlotte F. Roberts) Am. J. Sci. 146: 126.
Nitrites and Nitrates, Estimation of, in One Operation. (Charlotte F. Roberts) Am. J. Sci. 146: 231.
Nitrogen, Fixation of, by Plants. (H. M. Ward) Nature, 49: 511.
— — in Algæ. (R. Beer) Nature, 51: 302.
— Free, How Plants utilize. (H. M. Ward) Sci. Prog. 3: 251.
— New Element in the Group of. (A. E. Tutton) Nature, 51: 258.
— of the Air as Food for Plants. (G. McGowan) Knowl. 18: 260.
Nitrogen Gas, Density of, Lord Rayleigh on. Nature, 50: 157.
Niuafou, Visit to. (B. T. Somerville) Geog. J. 7: 65.
Nive, Battles of the. Macmil. 73: 149.
Nivernais, Louis Jules Henri, Duke of, in England. (A. Dobson) Longm. 23: 297.
Nixie, The. (F. Van de G. Stevenson) Scrib. M. 3: 277.
Nixon, Robert. All the Year, 73: 210.
Nixy's Chord, The; a story. (H. H. Boyesen) Cosmopol. 19: 523, 635.
Nizam, City of the. All the Year, 75: 222.
No-account Creole, A. (K. Chopin) Cent. 25: 382.
No Resurrection! a poem. (M. A. M. H. Marks) Argosy, 59: 404.
No Sportsman; a story. (Fox Russell) Gent. M. n. s. 52: 63.
Noah Parker, Corporal; a story of the American Revolution. (W. Littlefield) Bost. 1: 422.
Nobility of Great Britain, Citizenship of the. Quar. 184: 270.
Noble, James Ashcroft. (J. S. Cotton) Acad. 49: 304.
— Essays. Ath. '93, 2: 906.
Nobody and Nothing. (G. L. Apperson) Gent. M. n. s. 57: 628.
Nocturnal Lights. All the Year, 75: 342.
Noel, Roden. Acad. 45: 456, 476. — Ath. '94, 1: 711.
— Poetry of. (N. Gale) Acad. 43: 280. — Reply. (R. Noel) Acad. 43: 306, 328. — (P. Addleshaw) Acad. 48: 105. — (J. A. Blaikie) Acad. 49: 216.
Noël-bird; a legend. (C. Vyvian) Belgra. 78: 59.
Noise, On the Gentility of. (H. P. Robinson) Chaut. 19: 726.
Noises, City, For the Suppression of. (P. G. Hubert, jr.) No. Am. 159: 633.
Nollekens, Joseph, and his Times, Smith's. Sat. R. 79: 375.
Nomadic Ideal in the Old Testament. (K. Budde) New World, 4: 726.
Nomadic Society. (C. D. Warner) Chr. Un. 45: 1087.
Nomenclature in Secondary Schools. (F. E. Partington) School R. 3: 219.
— Studies in, Kuntze's. (R. Pound) Am. Natural. 28: 1030.
— Zoölogical, Rules of, adopted by the Zoölogical Congress. (M. Fischer) Am. Natural. 26: 383. 28: 929.
Nomination Methods, A Suggested Reform in. (F. A. Cleveland) Pub. Opin. 20: 589.
Nominies. J. Am. Folk-Lore, 8: 81.
Nona Vincent; a story. (H. James) Eng. Illust. 9: 365, 491.
Nonconformist Forebodings. (I. G. Rogers) 19th Cent. 36: 790.
Nonconformists and the Church of England. (A. M. Mackay) Westm. 146: 388.
— and their Anxieties. Spec. 70: 414.
Nonconformity. (J. A. Picton) Time, 21: 206.
— in England, Decline in, Causes of. Spec. 70: 354.
— — Power of. (A. F. Marshall) Am. Cath. Q. 21: 583.
— Philosophy of. (W. Lloyd) Westm. 144: 552.
Nonjurors, History of. Eng. R. 3: 356.
Non-residents, Liability of, as Stockholders and Officers. (C. Reno) Am. Law R. 28: 518.
Nooning Tree, The. (K. D. Wiggin) Atlan. 73: 770.
Nordau, Max, with portrait. Bookman, 1: 157. — Critic, 26: 246. — With portrait. Bk. Buyer, 12: 224. — With portrait. Bk. News, 13: 381.
— Degeneration. (W. M. Ivins) Our Day, 15: 47. — (K. Cox; A. Seidl; M. W. Hazeltine) No. Am. 160: 735. — (G. Saintsbury) Bookman, 1: 178. — (E. Purcell) Acad. 47: 475. — Sat. R. 79: 323. — (A. L. Hodder) Nation, 60: 327. — (E. E. Hale, jr.) Dial (Ch.) 18: 236.
— — Prof. N. M. Butler on. (H. T. Peck) Bookman, 3: 403.
— — Deterioration of Soul. (Vernon Lee) Fortn. 65: 928.

Nordau, Max. Degeneration, its Value and its Errors. (C. Lombroso) Cent. **28**: 936.
— — a Reply to my Critics. (M. Nordau) No. Am. **161**: 80.
— — Reply of, to his Critics. Cent. **28**: 546.
— Entartung. Critic, **25**: 87.
— Inaccuracies of. (K. Cox) Nation, **61**: 45.
— Paradoxes. Sat. R. **82**: 89.
— Sketch of Life of. Idler, **9**: 14.
— The True Degenerate. (Charles Whibley) New R. **12**: 425.
Nore Light, Under the. (A. T. Pask) Time, **10**: 604.
Norfolk, Va., Inscriptions from Cemetery at. (E. W. James) N. E. Reg. **48**: 17, 336, 469.
Norfolk Broads, Birds on. (G. Stables) Leis. Hour, **42**: 672.
— Cruise on. (A. B. Dodd) Cent. **28**: 803.
— Physical Features of. (J. W. Gregory) Nat. Sci. **1**: 347.
Norfolk Flats, November on. Spec. **75**: 689. Same art. Liv. Age, **207**: 766.
Norfolk Island. Chamb. J. **72**: 252.
Norma, New Star in. (W. H. Pickering) Astron. **13**: 201.
Normal School, The, and the School of Pedagogy. (F. C. Foster) Educa. R. **7**: 383.
— at Paris. (R. A. Gregory) Nature, **52**: 570.
— Province of the. (J. W. Dickinson) Educa. **13**: 1.
Normal Schools in the U. S. (C. G. Ramsay) Educa. **17**: 232.
— Scope of. (M. V. O'Shea) Atlan. **73**: 811.
— State, Legitimate Work of. (A. W. Edson) Educa. **16**: 274.
Norman, Henry. (W. Roberts) Bookworm, **7**: 257.
— Appointment as Viceroy of India. Spec. **71**: 325.
Norman Tympana in Cornwall. (J. R. Allen) Illus. Archæol. **2**: 9.
Normandy and Brittany: Old Friends with New Faces. (K. S. and G. Macquoid) Good Words, **35**: 13, 117.
— Peasant Life in. (G. Käsebier) Mo. Illust. **3**: 269.
Norrköping, Sweden. (J. H. Vincent) Chaut. **18**: 131.
Norse and Irish Literature. (W. Larminie) Contemp. **68**: 575, 665.
Norse Remains in Neighborhood of Boston Bay. (G. Fowke) Am. Natural. **28**: 623.
Norsk Finmarken, Rambles in. (G. Lindesay) Fortn. **62**: 671.
North, Frederick, Lord. Temp. Bar, **98**: 53.
North, J. W. Painter and Poet. (H. Herkomer) M. of Art, **16**: 297, 342.
North, Marianne. (G. Murray) Acad. **41**: 272. — Book R. **1**: 59.
— Autobiography. Ath. '92, **1**: 269. — (A. B. McMahan) Dial (Ch.) **13**: 15. — Sat. R. **73**: 282. — Spec. **68**: 306. — Dial (Ch.) **15**: 64.
— Collection of Paintings at Kew. (H. V. Barnett) M. of Art, **5**: 430.
North and South, Growth of Wealth in. Soc. Econ. **8**: 65.
North and South from the Brooklyn Bridge; a poem. (M. Wilcox) Harper, **89**: 463.
North, Due. (Mrs. C. N. Jackson) Good Words, **34**: 396.
— Highest, Attainment of the. (D. L. Brainard) Scrib. M. **12**: 389.
North America, English Occupancy of. (A. Brown) Atlan. **70**: 465.
— Explorations of Coast of, Previous to Henry Hudson. (B. F. De Costa) Nat'l M. (N. Y. '91) **15**: 1.
North America, Fauna of, Effect of the Glacial Period on. (S. H. Scudder) Am. J. Sci. **148**: 179.
— Parkman's France and England in. (W. H. Withrow) Meth. R. **52**: 902. — Sat. R. **74**: 198.
— Parkman's Half Century of Conflict. Atlan. **70**: 414. — (W. Walker) Nation, **55**: 9. — (J. A. Doyle) Eng. Hist. R. **8**: 369. — (E. G. Mason) Dial (Ch.) **14**: 45.
— Pre-Columbian Literature of. (C. Thomas) M. Am. Hist. **28**: 27.
— Struggle of France and England for. (J. B. Ross) M. Am. Hist. **30**: 55.
— Who discovered it? (J. B. Shipley) Time, **23**: 1170.
North American Tales, Dissemination of. (F. Boas) J. Am. Folk-Lore, **4**: 13.
North Berwick, Scotland, and Vicinity. (F. Watt) Art J. **46**: 261.
North British Railway. (A. E. Lockyer) Eng. Illust. **10**: 939.
North Brother Island Hospital, N. Y. (J. A. Riis) Cosmopol. **13**: 291.
North Cape, Visit to. (E. M. Allaire) Outing, **29**: 242.
North Carolina; Charleston and the Carolinas. (J. Ralph) Harper, **90**: 204.
— Church and State in. (S. B. Weeks) J. H. Univ. Studies, **11**: nos. 5-6.
— Colonial, Landholding in. (J. S. Bassett) Law Q. **11**: 154.
— Constitutional Beginnings of. (J. S. Bassett) J. H. Univ. Studies, **12**: 105.
— Cross-section through. (A. B. Hart) Nation, **54**: 207.
— Eleventh Regiment. (W. J. Martin) So. Hist. Pap. **23**: 43.
— Fishing Tramp in. (B. Rush) Outing, **26**: 105.
— Folk-customs and Beliefs. (N. C. Hoke) J. Am. Folk-Lore, **5**: 113.
— Forty-ninth Regiment. (T. R. Roulhac) So. Hist. Pap. **23**: 58.
— Province of, Religious Development in. (S. B. Weeks) J. H. Univ. Studies, **10**: nos. 5-6.
— Regulators of. (W. H. Bailey) Am. Hist. Reg. **3**: 313-554.
— Road-building in. (D. A. Tompkins) Engin. M. **6**: 645.
— Slavery and Servitude in the Colony of. (J. S. Bassett) J. H. Univ. Studies, **14**: 179.
— Supreme Court of. (W. Clark) Green Bag, **4**: 457, 569.
— Town and County Resolutions of 1774 in. (G. Daves) M. Am. Hist. **30**: 88.
North Carolina Mountaineer Songs. (L. W. Edmands) J. Am. Folk-Lore, **6**: 131.
North Central Association of Colleges and Secondary Schools, Meeting of, University of Chicago, April 3 and 4, 1896. School R. **4**: 257.
North Coast and Eleanor; a story. (F. Wedmore) Art J. **44**: 85.
North Devonshire Ghost Story. (A. L. Paul) Eng. Illust. **11**: 1152.
North Pole, Artistic Expedition to. (J. v. Payer) Geog. J. **5**: 106.
— Nansen's Project for reaching. Spec. **69**: 731.
— Wanderings of the. (Sir R. Ball) Fortn. **60**: 171. Same art. Liv. Age, **198**: 625.
North Polar Basin. (H. Seebohm) Geog. J. **2**: 331.
North Polar Problem. (A. H. Markham) No. Am. **162**: 486.
— Regions. How can they be crossed? (F. Nansen) Geog. J. **1**: 1.

North Road, The Great, England. Chamb. J. 71: 689.
North Sea and Baltic Canal. (W. L. Clowes) 19th Cent. 38: 165.
— — Advantages of. Sat. R. 79: 437.
— Artist Life by. (H. W. Ranger) Cent. 23: 753.
— Geographical Evolution of. (A. J. Jukes-Browne) Contemp. 64: 704.
— Movements of Surface Waters of. (H. N. Dickson) Geog. J. 7: 255.
North Sea Fishermen, A Plea for. (G. Blake) National, 19: 719.
North Shore of Massachusetts. (R. Grant) Scrib. M. 16: 1. — (F. T. Robinson) New Eng. M. n. s. 10: 654.
North Star in Surveying. (W. A. McClean) Green Bag, 6: 288.
Northampton, Mass., Association of Education and Industry. (O. Rumsey) New Eng. M. n. s. 12: 22.
— Bank Robbery. (C. Moffett) McClure, 5: 257.
— Forbes Library. Lib. J. 19: 376.
Northampton, Eng., Borough Records. Ath. '95, 2: 494.
Northcote, Sir Henry, Note Books of. (Earl of Iddesleigh) Blackw. 155: 87.
Northcote, James, and William Hazlitt. (J. A. Noble) M. of Art, 7: 34.
— Hazlitt on. Sat. R. 77: 208. — Ath. '94, 1: 581.
Northern Winter's Welcome; a poem. (C. Turner) Outing, 27: 416.
Northmen, Discovery of America by. *See* America; Discovery.
Northrup, George W. The-man-that-draws-the-hand-cart. (E. Eggleston) Harper, 88: 466.
Northumberland, History of, Bateson's. Sat. R. 76: 600.
Northumbria, Pre-conquest Churches. Reliquary, 33: 1, 65, 140.
— Runic Crosses of. (J. M. Stone) Scot. R. 27: 292.
Northwest, Capitals of the. (J. Ralph) Harper, 84: 576.
— Conquest of, English's. (E. Coues) Nation, 62: 102.
— Educational Development in. (R. S. Robertson) M. Am. Hist. 27: 280.
— French Explorers in. (S. M. Davis) Nat'l M. (N. Y. '91) 15: 271.
— Inland Waterways for. (E. R. Johnson) R. of Rs. (N. Y.) 8: 536.
— Military Posts in, How England gained by holding. (C. Moore) M. Am. Hist. 28: 189.
— New Needs of. (W. R. Merriam) No. Am. 155: 37.
— Possibilities of. (S. A. Thompson) R. of Rs. (N. Y.) 8: 524.
Northwest Passage, Voyages in Search of, Christy's. Sat. R. 78: 49.
Northwest Passage; a poem. (R. L. Stevenson) M. of Art, 7: 198.
Northwestern University Library Building, Evanston, Ill. (L. Ambrose) Lib. J. 19: 338.
Northwestern Waters, Summer Outing on. (R. E. Strahorn) Cosmopol. 21: 473.
Norton, Eckstein. Nat'l M. (N. Y. '91) 16: 88.
Norway. All the Year, 76: 222.
— and Norwegians, Keary's. Sat. R. 73: 751.
— and Spitzbergen, A Short Cruise to. (Marquis of Ormonde) Good Words, 36: 737.
— and Sweden; the Case for Norwegian Liberalism. (J. E. Sars) Fortn. 64: 269. Same art. Liv. Age, 206: 643.
— — The Case for Sweden. New R. 12: 402.
Norway and Sweden, Political Crisis in. (M. S. Constable) Fortn. 63: 811.
— — Unification of. (C. Siewers) Fortn. 64: 282.
— Coast of, Up the. (G. C. Pease) Harper, 89: 375.
— Constitutional Struggle in. (W. H. Carpenter) Nation, 57: 153. — (H. H. Boyesen) No. Am. 157: 68. — (J. E. Olson) New Eng. M. n. s. 8: 429.
— Fjords of. (H. H. Boyesen) Cosmopol. 17: 151.
— Glimpses of. (F. Yeigh) Canad. M. 5: 79.
— Hospitality in. (H. H. Boyesen) Lippinc. 53: 267.
— in Winter. (A. A. Bulley) Temp. Bar, 94: 267. Same art. Liv. Age, 193: 88.
— Keary's. (W. H. Carpenter) Nation, 56: 165.
— Mockler-Ferryman on. Sat. R. 82: 194.
— Music in. (A. von Ende) Music, 6: 475.
— Out-door Life in. (H. H. Boyesen) Mo. Illust. 5: 7.
— Right Way to see. (H. L. Brackstad) Eng. Illust. 15: 464.
— Sledging in. (C. Edwardes) Outing, 25: 215.
— Sound and the Skager Rack. (M. Todhunter) Westm. 145: 404.
— Spirit of the Northland. (Coralie Glyn) Westm. 145: 410.
— The Tourist in. (W. H. Carpenter) Nation, 57: 325.
— Travelling in. (M. Howarth) Eng. Illust. 9: 750.
— Village Life in. (H. H. Boyesen) Chaut. 18: 1.
— Winter Day in. Chamb. J. 69: 836.
— Winter Journey up the Coast of. (R. B. Anderson) Scrib. M. 15: 489.
— Winter Sketches in. All the Year, 71: 587, 605.
Norwegian Club Exhibition. (H. W. Brewer) Argosy, 59: 365.
Norwegian Farmhouse, In a. (J. Bickerdyke) Chamb. J. 73: 282. Same art. Liv. Age, 209: 635. Same art. Ecl. M. 127: 119.
Norwegian House in England. (A. T. Sibbald) Am. Arch. 48: 121.
Norwegian Literature, 1891-92. (H. Jæger) Ath. '92, 2: 23.
— 1894-95. (C. Brinchmann) Ath. '95, 2: 21.
— 1895-96. (C. Brinchmann) Ath. '96, 2: 23.
Norwegian Literature, Modern. (B. Björnson) Forum, 21: 318, 398.
Norwegian Novel, The. (H. H. Boyesen) Bk. News, 8: 240.
Norwegians; an Idyllic People. (M. Beaumont) Sund. M. 25: 166.
Norwich, Connecticut. (L. W. Bacon) New Eng. M. n. s. 15: 161.
— Otis Library. (J. Trumbull) Lib. J. 18: 469.
Norwich, Eng., Castle of, as a Museum. (H. Woodward) Nat. Sci. 1: 691.
— Cathedral. (T. E. Champion) Canad. M. 3: 350.
— Leet Jurisdiction in, during 13th and 14th Centuries. Sat. R. 75: 43.
— Palace. (E. Venables) Sund. M. 24: 453, 560.
Nose, Human, Canals of, Ethnological Characteristics of. (W. C. Braislin) Science, 21: 169.
Noses. Sat. R. 75: 144.
— Character in. Spec. 70: 353.
— Types of. Sat. R. 76: 43.
Nostradamus, Michael. Walford's Antiq. 5: 165, 288. 6: 53, 207. 7: 30-284.
— Oracles of, Ward's. Spec. 68: 535.
Not above Diamonds; a story. All the Year, 71: 253.
Not Practical; a story. (A. Hope) Idler, 6: 659.
Not to be accounted for; a story. Argosy, 59: 500.
Notch in a Principality, A; a story. (F. B. Millard) New Eng. M. n. s. 7: 757.
Note of Enquiry, A; a story. (L. H. Armstrong) Belgra. 82: 270.

Notes, Payment of. Bank. M. (N. Y.) **48**: 578.
Notorycts Typhlops, Habits and Affinities of. (E. D. Cope) Am. Natural. **26**: 121.
Notovitch, Nicolas. (F. M. Müller) 19th Cent. **36**: 515.
— Unknown Life of Christ. (I. A. Douglas ; M. Mueller) 19th Cent. **39**: 667.
Notre Dame, Ind., St. Mary's Convent School. (E. A. Starr) Cath. World, **59**: 25.
Notre Dame Cathedral, Paris, and Mediæval Symbolism. (S. Beale) M. of Art, **16**: 422.
— — Stories in Stone from. (T. A. Cook) Scrib. M. **15**: 69.
Nottingham, Eng., Museum of Science and Art. (H. M. Cundall) Art J. **44**: 120.
— Trent Bridges at, 924–1871. (J. P. Briscoe) Walford's Antiq. **1**: 196.
See Midland Counties Art Museum.
Nourmandee ; a poem. (T. B. Aldrich) Harper, **86**: 71.
Nourse, Elizabeth C. (Clara McChesney) Mo. Illust. **13**: 3.
Nova Scotia. (F. Bolles) Atlan. **73**: 592, 781. — (A. W. Eaton) New Eng. M. n. s. **7**: 157. — (T. F. Anderson) New Eng. M. n. s. **8**: 730.
— about Cape Breton. (T. Mulvey) Canad. M. **7**: 264.
— as a Summer Resort. (T. F. Anderson) Outing, **20**: 231.
— Church founded by Connecticut Settlers. (A. W. H. Eaton) N. E. Reg. **46**: 219.
— Joseph Howe and his Times. (J. W. Longley) Canad. M. **2**: 207.
— A Yankee in Halifax. (Allan Eric) Canad. M. **4**: 401.
Novalis, *pseud.* *See* Hardenburgh, F. von.
Novel, The. (M. Field) Munsey, **12**: 371.
— America's First Homogeneous. (G. Willets) Writer, **8**: 78.
— and Drama, Moral Responsibility of. Critic, **25**: 325–356.
— and Novel-reading. Gent. M. n. s. **50**: 427.
— Hall Caine on. Critic, **27**: 355.
— Crawford on. (W. H. Hills) Writer, **7**: 136.
— Decadent. (E. Fuller) Lippinc. **57**: 427.
— Development of. (R. H. Titherington) Munsey, **8**: 281.
— English. (C. J. Billson) Westm. **138**: 602.
— Ethical Value of. (D. H. Hill, jr.) Southern M. **4**: 368.
— German, Beginnings of the. (J. G. Robertson) Westm. **142**: 183.
— Historical. (Geo. Saintsbury) Macmil. **70**: 256. Same art. Liv. Age, **202**: 681. **203**: 28, 495.
— — and American History. (L. Irving) M. Am. Hist. **29**: 338.
— How to write a. (S. Farina) Pub. Opin. **13**: 243.
— The Modern. (A. E. Barr) No. Am. **159**: 592. — Temp. Bar, **105**: 244. — Chamb. J. **72**: 262.
— — Emotional Tension and. (F. M. Crawford) Forum, **14**: 735.
— — The Picaresque. (James Fitzmaurice Kelly) New R. **13**: 59.
— Most Popular, in America. (H. W. Mabie) Forum, **16**: 508.
— of Incident. (Agnes Repplier) Chr. Un. **45**: 1243.
— Pedagogical Value of. (M. S. Merwin) Cosmopol. **15**: 36.
— Predominance of. (R. Burton) Dial (Ch.) **16**: 355.
— Prospective Transformation of. (D. F. Hannigan) Westm. **140**: 256.
— Purpose. (A. Lang) Critic, **25**: 30.
— — Plea for. (W. D. Moffatt) Critic, **22**: 230.
— The Romance and the. (M. Thompson) Chaut. **16**: 42.
Novel. Seventh Commandment. (M. C. Harris) Lippinc. **51**: 243.
— Study of the. (A. M. Logan) Nation, **63**: 264.
— The Three-volume. (W. Besant) Dial (Ch.) **17**: 185. — Macmil. **70**: 438.
— Tyranny of the. (E. Gosse) National, **19**: 163. Same art. Ecl. M. **118**: 704. — (D. F. Hannigan) Westm. **143**: 303. Same art. Ecl. M. **124**: 556.
— What is a? (F. M. Crawford) Forum, **14**: 591. — Same art. Critic, **22**: 12.
— with a Purpose, The. (Mrs. M. A. Ward) Lit. W. Bost. **23**: 260.
Novel Notes ; a story. (J. K. Jerome) Idler, **1**: 363, 488, 607. **2**: 44–651. **3**: 31–318.
Novel-reading. (L. de la Ramé) Fortn. **59**: 829. — (T. Martin) Lib. J. **17**: 241.
Novel-writers, Modern, Contentiousness of. (A. Repplier) No. Am. **163**: 395.
Novel-writing ; Cheating at Letters. (H. C. Bunner) Cent. **27**: 716.
Novel Collection of Curios ; a story. (K. May) Belgra. **82**: 41.
Noveiist, Art of the. (A. B. Edwards) Contemp. **66**: 225. Same art. Ecl. M. **123**: 515. Same art. Liv. Age, **202**: 771.
— as a Gentleman. (T. Maxwell) Book R. **2**: 115.
— The Irresponsible. Macmil. **72**: 73. Same art. Liv. Age, **205**: 744. Same art. Ecl. M. **125**: 68.
Novelists, Contemporary French. (A. Hornblow) Munsey, **12**: 483.
— English, of the Hour. (A. Leach) Munsey, **10**: 601.
— Female, Our Early. Cornh. **72**: 558. Same art. Liv. Age, **207**: 804.
— Great Realists and the Empty Story-tellers. (H. H. Boyesen) Forum, **18**: 724.
— New Scottish. Ed. R. **184**: 37.
— Some Contemporary. (J. L. Gilder) Chaut. **20**: 291.
— Some Forgotten. All the Year, **73**: 82.
Novels and Newspapers at the Church Congress, 1896. (R. Ogden) Nation, **63**: 324.
— and Novel-readers. (R. Burton) Dial (Ch.) **18**: 39.
— and Novelists, Modern. (D. E. Hervey) Book R. **3**: 245.
— as Sedatives. Spec. **73**: 108. Same art. Ecl. M. **123**: 555.
— Common, in Public Libraries. (C. H. Garland ; E. P. Thurston ; G. W. Cole ; A. W. Whelpley ; E. M. Coe) Lib. J. **19**: supp. 14–23.
— Danger-signals in. (R. Ogden) Nation, **62**: 71.
— Historical, and American History. (L. Irving) Nat'l M. (N. Y. '91) **18**: 258.
— Hundred Greatest. Lib. J. **17**: 55.
— Improper. (A. E. Barr) Bk. News, **7**: 359.
— Leading Boys from Reading. (T. C. Burgess) Lib. J. **21**: 144.
— Modern. (Lady Magnus) Good Words, **35**: 741.
— of Adventure and Manners. Quar. **179**: 530.
— Picturesque in. Chamb. J. **69**: 817.
— Plots in. (L. Stockton) Critic, **29**: 51.
— Reading of. (S. Axson) Citizen, **1**: 135.
— Recent, 1892. (F. Adams) Fortn. **58**: 13.
— Rise in the Price of. Gent. M. n. s. **54**: 215.
— Socialist. (M. Kaufmann) Lippinc. **55**: 138.
— Without a Purpose. (G. Allen) No. Am. **163**: 223.
November ; a poem. Cornh. **68**: 506.
— a poem. (A. C. Swinburne) M. of Art, **16**: 25.
— a poem. (F. Bierhoff) Outing, **21**: 136.
Noyes, James, Letter of, 1694. (S. B. Doggett) N. E. Reg. **49**: 285.

Noyes, Peter, of Sudbury, Mass., Descendants of. (F. H. Newell) N. E. Reg. 47: 71.
Noyes, William Curtis, with portrait. (A. O. Hall) Green Bag, 6: 545.
Noyes, William H., Documents in the Case of. And. R. 19: 601.
Noyes Inscription and Memoranda. (J. A. Noyes) N. E. Reg. 48: 18.
Noyon. (H. Zimmern) M. of Art, 6: 335.
Noyullo den, The; a story. (C. L. Hildreth) Munsey, 11: 543.
Nubecula, Great. (E. W. Maunder) Knowl. 18: 156.
Nubia, Devastation of. (J. P. Mahaffy) 19th Cent. 35: 1013.
— Notes from. (J. P. Mahaffy) Ath. '94, 1: 353, 451, 546.
Nucleolus, The. (R. Beer) Nat. Sci. 7: 185.
Nucleus of a Salon; a love story. (K. L. Johnson) Canad. M. 8: 30.
Nude, The, in Art. (W. H. Low and K. Cox) Scrib. M. 12: 741.
Number, Essence of. (G. B. Halsted) Science, n. s. 3: 470.
Number Forms. (G. T. W. Patrick) Pop. Sci. Mo. 42: 504.
— Pedagogical Value of. (A. R. Hornbrook) Educa. R. 5: 467.
Number Two in the Cloisters. Macmil. 68: 197.
No. 58; an Episode of the Columbian Exposition. (C. K. Rathbone) Outing, 26: 13.
No. 110; a story. (A. H. Sydenham) Un. Serv. (Phila.) 9: 113.
Numbers, Individuality of. (M. C. Whiting) Pedagog. Sem. 2: 107.
— Large. (H. Schubert) Open Court, 7: 3903, 3914.
— Mystic: Seven and Three. (A. Gaye) National, 21: 196. Same art. Ecl. M. 120: 766.
— Pictures and Hieroglyphs. Atlan. 77: 140.
Numerals, Indian. (E. F. Wilson) Science, 20: 9.
Numeration, Systems of. (T. J. A. Freeman) Am. Cath. Q. 18: 202, 412.
Numidian, The. (E. Eckstein) Liv. Age, 200: 77-586.
Nuñez, Alvar. (A. B. C. Grahame) 19th Cent. 40: 105.
Nuñez: a Spanish Apostle of Benthamism. (C. Kenny) Law Q. 11: 175.
Nunnery, Ups and Downs in an Old. (A. Jessopp) Good Words, 34: 205, 251, 422.
Nuremberg. M. of Art, 4: 488.
Nurse, District, Recollections of a. (E. R. Benedict) Eth. Rec. 3: 44.
— A Roman. (E. O. Kirk) Lippinc. 54: 107.
Nurse Edith; a story. (F. H. Holland) Canad. M. 2: 574.
Nurse Edith's Easter; a story. (E. S. Atkinson) Canad. M. 6: 552.
Nurse Elisia; a story. (G. M. Fenn) Good Words, 33: 433-837.
Nurse Miriam's Call; a story. (A. C. G. Sim) Theatre, 30: 27.
Nurseries: American Association of Nurserymen. Garden & F. 7: 249.
— at Bay Ridge, L. I. Garden & F. 9: 148.
— United States, at Short Hills, N. J. (W. N. Craig) Garden & F. 7: 378.
Nurseries, Day. (J. J. O'Shea) Cath. World, 61: 77. — (E. Carlyle) Char. R. 1: 365.
Nursery, Famous English. Garden & F. 6: 101.
Nursery Lands, Exhaustion of. (L. H. Bailey) Garden & F. 9: 259.
Nurserymen, Convention of, at Indianapolis. Garden & F. 8: 259.
Nursery Rhymes, Humor of. Spec. 72: 52.
Nursery Tales, Louisiana. (Alcée Fortier) J. Am. Folk-Lore, 1: 140. 2: 36.
Nurses, Amateur; an Accomplished Fact. (K. G. Wells) No. Am. 158: 255.
— and Nursing. (H. Jones) Good Words, 35: 554.
— Experiences of. (G. B. Burgin) Idler, 8: 423.
— in London Hospitals. (G. B. Burgin) Idler, 6: 282.
— Modern. (Emma L. Watson) National, 28: 567.
— of Great Men. (Mrs. E. M. Field) Sund. M. 24: 202. Same art. Liv. Age, 205: 251.
— Pupil, Working Hours of. (A. Nutting) Char. R. 5: 239.
— Royal British Association of. Sat. R. 73: 213.
— Training-schools for, of the Sisters of Charity. (T. Dwight) Cath. World, 61: 187.
Nursing. (Sir B. W. Richardson) Longm. 28: 30.
— District. (I. Hampton) Char. R. 1: 160.
— Improved Method of. (L. Darche) Lend a H. 15: 122.
— in London Hospitals. (G. B. Burgin) Idler, 8: 329.
— in Poor-Law Infirmaries. (J. L. de Pledge) Westm. 142: 173.
— Instructive District. (M. K. Sedgewick) Forum, 22: 297.
Nursing Habits, Some strange. (R. Lydekker) Knowl. 18: 97.
Nut Culture. (J. N. Rose) Garden & F. 8: 263.
— in the U. S. Garden & F. 9: 189.
Nutation, Diurnal, Determination of Constants of. (F. Folie) Science, n. s. 2: 613.
Nutlets, Dispersal of. (D. F. M. Pertz) Nat. Sci. 5: 284.
Nutrition. How Plants and Animals grow. (M. Miles) Pop. Sci. Mo. 43: 503.
Nuts and Nut-crackers. (P. Robinson) Contemp. 62: 555.
Nuttall, Thomas, with portrait. Pop. Sci. Mo. 46: 689.
Nyassa, Lake, Crater-lakes North of. (Dr. D. Kerr-Cross) Geog. J. 5: 112.
Nyassaland. England's Latest Conquest in Africa. (C. A. Orr) Cosmopol. 17: 35.
— Glave in. (E. J. Glave) Cent. 30: 589.
— Industrial Development of. (J. Buchanan) Geog. J. 1: 245.
— New Cypress of. Nature, 51: 85.
— Pacification of. (W. L. Clowes) New R. 10: 417.
— Southern, Routes and Districts in. (B. L. Sclater) Geog. J. 2: 403.
Nye, Edgar Wilson. Critic, 28: 150. — (M. S. Clarke) Writer, 9: 34.
— Portraits of. McClure, 1: 391.
Nymph of the Eddy, The; a story. (G. Parker) McClure, 1: 12.
Nymph-names, Alleged Confusion of. (J. P. Postgate) Am. J. Philol. 17: 30.

O Lark; a song. (A. Tennyson, music by Lady Tennyson) Argosy, 59: 320.
O Traveller by Unaccustomed Ways; a poem. (L. C. Moulton) Harper, 90: 675.
Oak, The. (N. M. Ward) Garden & F. 5: 287.
— The English. Garden & F. 8: 362.
Oak Chests. Cornh. 66: 73.
Oak-pruners. (J. B. Smith) Garden & F. 5: 557.
Oakham Pastures. Blackw. 151: 114. Same art. Liv. Age, 192: 590.
Oakland and Alameda County. (C. Hammerton) Overland, n. s. 27: 674.
Oaks at Paxtang, Pa. (M. L. Dock) Garden & F. 9: 293.
— Avenue of Live. Garden & F. 6: 2.
— Five Ornamental. Garden & F. 9: 432.

Oaks, Garry, in Oregon. (F. E. Lloyd) Garden & F. 7: 494.
— Golden-leaved, of California. Garden & F. 5: 121.
— How to identify certain Conifers and. Garden & F. 6: 397.
— in May. (E. J. Hill) Garden & F. 7: 192.
— Notes on North American. (C. S. Sargent) Garden & F. 8: 92.
— Quercus Texana. (C. S. Sargent) Garden & F. 7: 514.
— Royal and Notable. (G. Clinch) Eng. Illust. 15: 237.
— Tan-bark, of California. Garden & F. 5: 517.
Oarsmen, English. Are they Degenerate? (R. C. Lehmann) New R. 7: 619.
Oates Plot. Month, 81: 457.
Oath, A Remarkable. (W. W. Newell) J. Am. Folk-Lore, 7: 60.
Oath of Allegiance, The; a story. (E. S. Phelps) Atlan. 73: 465.
Oaths, Strange. (A. Hayden) Bookworm, 7: 77.
Oban Cave, The New. (W. J. L. Abbott) Nat. Sci. 6: 330.
Obeah Worship in East and West Indies. (M. Robinson and M. J. Walhouse) Folk-Lore, 4: 207.
Obeale: Witchcraft. Chamb. J. 72: 33.
Obediah Folger; a poem. (Gustave Kobbé) Cosmopol. 20: 424.
Obedience. (J. Worcester) N. Church R. 3: 344.
Obedient unto Death. (H. M. Butler) Sund. M. 21: 13.
Obelisk Dick's Fatal Blunder. (B. C. Truman) Overland, n. s. 28: 182.
Obelisks, Egyptian. Am. Arch. 45: 28.
Oberlin Campaign. (H. H. Russell) Our Day, 16: 497.
Oberlin Conservatory of Music. Music, 4: 268.
Obituaries, Newspaper. Chamb. J. 72: 353.
Object-glass Grating. (L. E. Jewell) Astron. 13: 44.
Object Glasses, Care of. (J. A. Brashear) Pop. Astron. 2: 9.
Obligation, Idea of, Analysis of. (F. C. Sharp) Int. J. Ethics, 2: 500.
O'Bryen, Richard, Letter of, 1790. (J. C. Clapp) N. E. Reg. 50: 51.
Observances, Value of. Spec. 71: 543.
Observation, Accuracy in. (H. Littlewood) Pop. Sci. Mo. 45: 533.
— and Recollection, Accuracy of. (F. E. Bolton) Psychol. R. 3: 286.
— by Pupils, Real and Sham. (H. L. Clapp) Educa. 12: 271.
— Errors of. (J. McK. Cattell) Am. J. Psychol. 5: 285.
Observatories, Mountain. (E. Whymper) Leis. Hour, 44: 699. — Chamb. J. 69: 246.
— of 100 Years Ago. (N. T. Lynn) Knowl. 18: 86.
Observatory on Top of Mt. Blanc. (I. M. Tarbell) McClure, 2: 289.
— Paris, Bureau of Measurements of. (Dorothea Khempke) Astron. 12: 783.
— U. S. National. (D. P. Todd) Nation, 54: 124.
Observing, Practice of. Spec. 69: 525.
Obstruction. *See* Filibustering.
Occult Manifestations. (W. C. Cooper) Arena, 14: 239.
Occult Science. The Tarot. Sat. R. 73: 249.
Occult Sciences, Waite's. Sat. R. 73: 156.
Occultations and Eclipses, Graphic Construction of. (W. F. Rigge) Pop. Astron. 4: 67.
Occultism, Practical, Mission of, To-day. (M. B. Peeke) Arena, 12: 198.
— True. (M. B. Peeke) Arena, 12: 73.
Occupation, — Author; a story. All the Year, 73: 586.
Occupations, Balance of. (R. C. Barnett) Am. M. Civics, 7: 205.
— Classification of, for Census Purposes. (H. Gannett) Am. Statis. Assoc. 4: 12.
— Hygiene of, Arlidge on. Spec. 69: 707.
— in the U. S., Classification of, in Census of 1890. (J. Bertillon) Am. Statis. Assoc. 3: 379.
— Injurious to Health. (C. Rolleston) Westm. 141: 417.
— Legal Regulation of, in N. Y. (L. D. Scisco) Am. M. Civics, 7: 649.
— Mortality and Morbidity according to. (J. Bertillon) J. Statis. Soc. 55: 559.
Ocean, Perils of. (F. L. Oswald) Chaut. 14: 688.
— Physical Condition of. (W. J. L. Wharton) Geog. J. 4: 252.
— Recent Contributions to Oceanography. Geog. J. 3: 302.
— Temperature of, at Various Depths. (W. J. L. Wharton) Nature, 51: 342.
— Troughs of. Around World, 1: 69.
— Wonders of. (F. M. Edselas) Cath. World, 62: 219.
Ocean Basins, Permanence of. (H. R. Mill) Geog. J. 1: 230. — (A. R. Wallace) Nat. Sci. 1: 418. — (A. J. Jukes-Browne) Nat. Sci. 1: 508, 737. — (E. Suess) Nat. Sci. 2: 180.
Ocean Currents. Chamb. J. 70: 422.
— Guinea and Equatorial. (J. Y. Buchanan) Geog. J. 7: 267.
Ocean Highways. (G. Hamilton; R. W. Rawson) J. Statis. Soc. 57: 1, 136.
— their Bearing on the Food and Wages of Great Britain. (G. Hamilton) National, 23: 482.
Ocean Meadows. Quar. 178: 363. Same art. Liv. Age, 202: 21.
Ocean Traffic by the Erie Canal. (Edward P. North) Forum, 13: 371.
Ocean Waves, Utilizing Power of. (A. W. Stahl) Cassier, 2: 39.
Oceanic Causeways, Recent. (E. Blanchard) Pop. Sci. Mo. 40: 540.
Oceanic Deposits, Ancient and Modern. (W. F. Hume) Nat. Sci. 7: 270, 385.
Oceanic Route, Short, to Europe and Canadian Ports. (O. P. Shannon) J. Pol. Econ. 4: 54.
Oceanography, Future of; Challenger Expedition. (A. Dohrn) Nature, 52: 121.
Oceans, Depth of, New Estimation of the Mean. Geog. J. 6: 267.
— Equilibrium of, Stability of. (T. J. J. See) Pop. Astron. 3: 178.
Ochtman, Leonard. (A. Trumble) Q. Illust. 2: 48.
O'Connell, Daniel, South Sea Discovery of. (S. P. Oliver) Ath. '94, 2: 253.
— Trial of. Ed. by Wallis. Sat. R. 78: 327.
O'Connell, Col. Daniel C. Ath. '92, 1: 464. — Spec. 69: 357.
O'Connor, William D. (M. Benton) Critic, 20: 184.
O'Conor, Charles, with portrait. (I. Browne) Green Bag, 7: 1, 83.
— Some Memories of a Great Lawyer. (W. Watson) No. Am. 161: 757.
October. Cornh. 74: 493.
— a poem. (M. Cawein) Cosmopol. 17: 669. Same art. All the Year, 75: 348.
— a poem. (A. C. Swinburne) M. of Art, 11: 403.
— a poem. (M. S. Anderson) Outing, 27: 15.
October Woods, In the. (J. K. Reeve) Lippinc. 54: 527.

Oculists of India, Native. Spec. 71: 627.
O'Daileagh, Muireagh; Adventures of a Poet-laureate. (M. F. Gibson) Gent. M. n. s. 54: 473.
Odd Neighbor. (C. C. Abbott) Lippinc. 54: 857.
Odd Volumes, The, Club of. (W. Roberts) Bookworm, 3: 305. — (E. D. North) Bibliographica, 2: 383.
Odds on the Gun. Lippinc. 55: 657.
Ode to Inspiration; a poem. (W. J. Dowler) Canad. M. 6: 575.
Ode to Silence; a poem. (W. W. Campbell) Canad. M. 6: 135.
Odell, W. H., Memoir of. (R. King) N. E. Reg. 46: 20.
Odense: The Capital of Fyen. Chamb. J. 71: 817.
Odors and the Sense of Smell. (C. Henry) Pop. Sci. Mo. 41: 682.
— Imitative. Chamb. J. 73: 389.
Odysseus and Kirke on a Bœotian Vase. (H. B. Walters) J. Hel. Stud. 13: 77.
Oettinger, Friedrich C. (C. Claus) Luth. Q. 23: 94.
Of the Blood Royal. (G. M. Cannon) New Eng. M. n. s. 14: 573.
Of the Blood Royal; a story. (W. M. Browne) Scrib. M. 11: 515.
Of Many Waters: a Dialogue. (J. A. Blaikie) New R. 13: 651.
Of a Meeting at Fulham; a story. (H. B. M. Watson) New R. 13: 564.
Of this Generation; a story. (H. S. Merriman) McClure, 8: 175.
Off Arran's Isle: a story. (K. Watson) Argosy, 58: 290.
Off Monomoy Point; a story. (W. E. Baldwin) New Eng. M. n. s. 6: 743.
Office Buildings, Design of. (George Hill) Archit. Rec. 2: 445. 3: 72, 169, 436.
Office-seekers, President Cleveland and. Pub. Opin. 15: 146, 215. — (L. Windmüller) Forum, 15: 478.
Office-seeking during Washington's Administration. (G. Hunt) Am. Hist. R. 1: 270.
— Quadrennial Raid. (C. Robinson) Soc. Econ. 5: 305.
Officers, Army, Education of. (J. P. Wisser) Un. Serv. (Phila.) 7: 109.
— — Rank of, Readjustment of. (C. J. Crane) Un. Serv. (Phila.) 13: 1.
Officialism. Spec. 70: 446.
Officials, Our Underpaid. (C. Robinson) Am. J. Pol. 3: 635.
Ogham of Castell Dwyran. (J. Rhys) Acad. 49: 35.
— the Oldest. (J. Rhys) Acad. 44: 153.
Ogham Inscription at Fordown. (A. Hutchinson) Illust. Archæol. 1: 124.
Ogham Inscribed Stone at Lewannick. (A. G. Langdon) Illus. Archæol. 2: 108.
Ogham Inscriptions in Ireland. (R. A. S. Macalister and others) Acad. 46: 118-558. 47: 13-239. 48: 32, 92.
— in Scotland. (C. H. Monro) Acad. 46: 330.
Oghams and Runes. (G. B. Rawlings) Knowl. 19: 232.
Ogilvie, G. Stuart. Sin of St. Hulda. Sat. R. 81: 396.
Ogilvy, Margaret. A Visit to J. M. Barrie's Mother. (Ellen T. Cunningham) Outl. 54: 562.
Oglethorpe, James, as a Landed Proprietor in Georgia. (C. C. Jones, jr.) M. Am. Hist. 28: 196.
Ogre of Alewife Cove. (E. M. Thomas) Atlan. 72: 231.
O'Hagan, T. Poems. (E. McManus) Canad. M. 1: 665.
Ohio. (C. F. Thwing) Harper, 93: 286.
— Boundary Disputes in, 1835. (C. E. Cheney) New Eng. M. n. s. 9: 180.
Ohio, Election of Governor of, in 1875. Am. J. Pol. 4: 433.
— Howells's Recollections of Life in. (W. H. Smith) Dial (Ch.) 18: 243.
— Legislative Crisis in, 1848-49. (A. E. Lee) Am. M. Civics, 6: 369.
— National Guard of. (W. H. C. Borden) Outing, 21: 406, 470.
— Supreme Court of, with portraits. (E. B. Kinkead) Green Bag, 7: 105, 168, 273.
— University of, Genesis of. (W. Boughton) M. Am. Hist. 30: 11.
Ohio Association in N. Y. (J. H. Kennedy) Nat'l M. (N. Y. '91) 15: 33.
Ohio Basin, Drainage Features of Upper. (T. C. Chamberlin and F. Leverett) Am. J. Sci. 147: 247.
Ohio Expedition of 1754. (A. Stephen) Pennsyl. M. 18: 43.
Ohio River, Ice Dam of. *See* Cincinnati Ice Dam.
— Upper, Inner Gorge Terraces of. (R. H. Hice) Am. J. Sci. 149: 112.
Ohrwalder, Joseph, Father. Blackw. 154: 341.
— Captivity in the Mahdi's Camp. Dub. R. 113: 814. — All the Year, 71: 582.
Oil. (T. J. A. Freeman) Am. Cath. Q. 19: 851.
— and Lamps, Safety Point in. Chamb. J. 73: 534.
— and Natural Gas Production. (S. D. Prentice) Cassier, 3: 405.
— Burning, by Compressed Air. (W. S. Collins) J. Frankl. Inst. 134: 266.
— Drilling for, near Philadelphia. (O. C. S. Carter) J. Frankl. Inst. 138: 230.
— Linseed, in Painting. (H. C. Standage) M. of Art, 14: 421.
— of Birch. (H. Trimble) Garden & F. 8: 303.
— on Rough Waters, Operation of. (G. W. Littlehales) Pop. Sci. Mo. 43: 494.
— upon Water. (A. Pockels) Nature, 50: 223.
Oil Lamp and its Contrivances. Reliquary, 36: 193.
Oil Painters, Institute of, Exhibition, 1893. Ath. '93, 2: 631.
Oil-river, Ten Days on an. (Z. Colville) Blackw. 153: 372. Same art. Liv. Age, 197: 370.
Oils, Drying, Boiling, and Bleaching. (N. N. Hartley) J. Soc. Arts, 41: 275.
— Essential. (T. J. A. Freeman) Am. Cath. Q. 20: 194.
— Fats, and Waxes, Analysis of, Benedikt on. (L. Archbutt) Nature, 52: 265.
— Mineral, Deblooming. (D. T. Marshall) Science, 19: 245.
Oka, Quebec, Silent Monks of. (T. P. Gorman) Cosmopol. 14: 143.
O'Keefe, Cornelius. (P. Hurley) Dub. R. 110: 351.
Okefinokee Swamp, An Archer's Sojourn in. (M. Thompson) Atlan. 77: 486.
Oklahoma. An Indian Commonwealth. (R. W. McAdam) Harper, 87: 884.
Olaf Jansen's Requital; a story. (F. Lynde) Munsey, 12: 427.
Old and Young, Gulf between. Spec. 69: 882.
— Plaint of the. (B. A. Crackanthorpe) Contemp. 65: 277. Same art. Liv. Age, 200: 605.
— The, *versus* the New; a story. (H. Mathers) Eng. Illust. 12: no. 3, 81.
— When are we? Chamb. J. 72: 305.
Old Age. Spec. 77: 513.
— and Death. (Colin A. Scott) Am. J. Psychol. 8: 67.
— and English Poor-law. (J. F. Wilkinson) Contemp. 64: 670.
— and Poets. (H. S. Pancoast) Poet-Lore, 3: 57.
— in English Villages. Spec. 70: 413.

Old Age: On growing Old. (H. C. Merwin) Atlan. 71: 349.
— Pauperism in. (C. Booth) J. Statis. Soc. 57: 235.
— Pensions for. Quar. 182: 254. — (J. W. Williams) Westm. 144: 193. — (J. F. Moulton) Fortn. 57: 465. — (J. Vogel) Fortn. 57: 753. — (J. Chamberlain) National, 18: 721. — (J. F. Wilkinson) National, 19: 285. — (L. Holland) National, 26: 849. — Quar. 174: 505. Same art. Liv. Age, 193: 771. — (J. F. Wilkinson) Contemp. 61: 554. — Bank. M. (Lond.) 54: 587. 56: 305, 477. — Lond. Q. 78: 241. — (W. M. Ede) Econ. R. 2: 179. — (L. R. Phelps) Econ. R. 3: 473.
— — and Friendly Societies. (J. Chamberlain) National, 24: 592. — Reply. (J. L. Stead) National, 25: 59.
— — and the State. (T. Mackay) J. Soc. Arts, 41: 343.
— — An Aspect of. (M. J. Farrelly) Int. J. Ethics, 4: 188.
— — Booth on. (J. Rae) Econ. J. 2: 379.
— — by Means of Municipal Dwellings. (E. Thomas) Econ. R. 5: 221.
— — Chamberlain's Scheme for. (W. L. Blackley) Contemp. 61: 382.
— — Economic Objections to. (T. Mackay) National, 19: 12.
— — Failure of, in Germany. (W. Bode) National, 19: 26.
— — in England. (R. Ogden) Nation, 54: 165. — (J. G. Brooks) Q. J. Econ. 6: 417. — (T. Scanlon) Westm. 137: 357.
— — in Practice. (H. W. Wolff) Contemp. 65: 887.
— — Problems of Pauperism and. (J. T. Baylee) Westm. 145: 67.
— — Some Economic Issues in regard to. (C. S. Loch) Econ. J. 5: 347.
— — A Successful Experiment. (G. Holloway) National, 19: 6.
— The Verdict of. (M. O. W. Oliphant) Blackw. 160: 555.
— Why grow Old? (N. E. Yorke-Davies) Gent. M. n. s. 50: 130. Same art. Ecl. M. 120: 497. Same art. Pop. Sci. Mo. 43: 226.
Old-age Homes in Austria. (E. Sellers) 19th Cent. 38: 338. Same art. Liv. Age, 206: 698.
Old and New Idyllists; a poem. (Lord Lytton) Nation, 21: 721. Same art. Ecl. M. 121: 458.
Old and New Time Book Prices. (W. Snyder) Bk. News, 11: 516.
Old Angeline, the Princess of Seattle; a story. (R. Simmons) Overland, n. s. 20: 506.
Old Bailey Prison, At the. (Edw. Aveling) Time, 23: 1098.
Old Barge, The. (T. St. E. Hake) Chamb. J. 69: 525–535.
Old Ben; a story. (V. C. McGie) Canad. M. 4: 514.
Old Ben's Bargain; a story. Chamb. J. 72: 173.
Old Bias's Vision. (V. F. Boyle) Cent. 26: 515.
Old Books Gossip. (F. Saunders) Bk. Buyer, 4: 7.
Old Boston Mary. (J. Flynt) Atlan. 74: 318.
Old Briar Pipe, The. Chamb. J. 71: 746.
Old Bundle, An; a story. (Marie Corelli) Idler, 7: 157.
Old Camp-fires rekindled. (W. S. Hutchinson) Overland, n. s. 21: 629.
Old Cripple-Dick. (A. Fleming) Good Words, 37: Xmas no., 45.
Old Days of New Burlington Street. (A. Bentley) Argosy, 60: 469.
Old-fashioned Folk in an East English Village. (A. Revett) Sund. M. 22: 310.
Old-fashioned Thanksgiving; a story. (H. Butterworth) Cent. 23: 30.
Old Flame; a tale. (C. G. Rogers) Canad. M. 1: 692.
Old Folks' Tales. (M. E. Francis) National, 26: 121.
Old Gallery, The. (S. Baring-Gould) Sund. M. 24: 23.
Old Garden Seat, The; a poem. (M. G. Watkins) Gent. M. n. s. 56: 264.
Old Gentleman of the Black Stock; a story. (T. N. Page) Harper, 89: 774.
Old Gervais; a story. (Mrs. Molesworth) Sund. M. 21: 398.
Old Grad's Story. (W. A. Wells) Bach. of Arts, 1: 356.
Old Jackson. (W. E. Norris) Good Words, 35: 176.
Old John's Easter Lilies; a story. (E. S. Atkinson) Canad. M. 5: 41.
Old Jones; a story. All the Year, 73: 417.
Old Jug Jurd'n. (H. C. Fairman) Southern M. 4: 312.
Old Kaskaskia; a story. (M. H. Catherwood) Atlan. 71: 1–433.
Old Lady in Black; a story. Argosy, 57: 83.
Old Lady Lazenbury. (R. M. Johnston) Cent. 30: 340.
Old Lady's Restoration, The. (G. King) Cent. 24: 724.
Old Letter, An. Idler, 1: 686.
Old Mademoiselle Varot; a character sketch. (M. C. Pratt) Chaut. 24: 83.
Old Maid's Counsel to the Young Man; a poem. (G. H. Best) Argosy, 57: 506.
Old Maid's Marriage, An. Chamb. J. 69: 552.
Old Maid's Mistake, An; a novel. (Mrs. Conney) Belgra. 86: 1–337. 87: 1–337. 88: 1–237.
Old Man Savarin; a story. (E. W. Thompson) McClure, 7: 267.
Old Man's Darling, An; a story. All the Year, 70: 108.
Old Man's Darling, An; a story. (C. J. Langston) Argosy, 54: 338.
Old Man's Garden, An; a story. (K. Watson) Belgra. 79: Christmas no., 62.
Old Men. Cornh. 65: 56. Same art. Ecl. M. 118: 306. Same art. Liv. Age, 192: 628.
Old Miss Pettifer; a story. All the Year, 72: 229.
Old Monmouth. (J. Ralph) Harper, 89: 327.
Old Mr. Tredgold. (M. O. W. Oliphant) Longm. 26: 111–551. 27: 1–553. 28: 1.
Old One-horned Stag, The. Macmil. 72: 241. Same art. Liv. Age, 207: 100.
Ol' Pap's Flaxen. (H. Garland) Cent. 21: 743, 912. 22: 39.
Old Place, The. Macmil. 66: 43.
Old Plute's Gobbler; a story. (C. E. Taylor, jr.) Outing, 27: 100.
Old Roses; a story. (G. Parker) Liv. Age, 194: 382.
Old Round Top, Montgomery Co., N. Y. (S. L. Frey) M. Am. Hist. 30: 23.
Old Salts; a poem. (P. Rivers) Outing, 23: 153.
Old School; a story. Cornh. 68: 637.
Old "Seventy-four" Frigate, An; a poem. (W. W. Story) Blackw. 156: 222.
Old Silver Trail. (M. E. Stickney) Lippinc. 56: 723.
Old Things, The. (H. James) Atlan. 77: 433–721. 78: 58–518.
Old Time Art and Artists: Early Newspaper Illustrators in America. (F. Beard) Our Day, 16: 85.
Old Trinity Chimes; a poem. (C. H. Crandall) M. Am. Hist. 27: 297.
Old Uncle Abe; a story. (A. M. Trotter) Argosy, 54: 525.
Old Uncle Vanderveer; a story. (E. Fawcett) Outing, 26: 108, 213.

Old Violin, An; a story. (R. Penn) Theatre, 30: 146.
Old Westminster, An. Argosy, 59: 481.
Old Wine and New in Literature. (A. Repplier) Atlan. 77: 688.
Old Woman's Romance. (E. M. Alford) Argosy, 57: 467.
Old-world Courtship, An. (C. Burke) Argosy, 60: 626.
Old-world Diary, An. (Sophia Beale) Univ. R. 6: 572.
Oldenburg, Henry. (H. Rix) Nature, 49: 9.
Ole Bull's Christmas; a poem. (Wallace Bruce) Chaut. 16: 338.
Ole Logan's Courtship. (W. A. Dromgoole) Arena, 10: 547.
Ole Miss's Last Tantrum. (M. M. Williams) Southern M. 4: 475.
Ole Rabbit an' de Dawg he stole; a story. (M. A. Owen) J. Am. Folk-Lore, 3: 135.
Olenellus, in the Green Pond Mountain Series, N. J. (C. D. Wolcott) Am. J. Sci. 147: 309.
Oleomargarine. (G. C. Caldwell) J. Frankl. Inst. 134: 190.
Oligochaeta, Recent Memoirs upon. (F. E. Bedard) Sci. Prog. 5: 190.
Oliphant, Laurence. (O. Smith) Time, 20: 373. — (E. Fairbairn) Westm. 137: 498.
— Boothism in the Life of. (J. K. Angus) Belgra. 80: 304.
Oliphant, Mrs. M. O. W., with portrait. Bk. Buyer, 10: 275.
— Cuckoo in the Nest. Spec. 69: 793.
— The Railway Man and his Children. Scot. R. 23: 42.
Olive-oil Making in Italy. (L. Dodge) Garden & F. 5: 485.
— near Florence. (I. M. Anderton) Good Words, 36: 384.
Olive Ranch, Californian. (E. Wallace) Overland, n. s. 21: 278.
Olives, Cultivation of, in Southern California. (W. M. Tisdale) Garden & F. 8: 168.
Olives, Mount of, A Night on. (D. Macleod) Good Words, 33: 27.
Oliver, Henry K. (J. W. Buckham) New Eng. M. n. s. 15: 387.
Olivia's Waiting-list. (C. Ticknor) New Eng. M. n. s. 15: 53.
Olmsted, Denison, with portrait. Pop. Sci. Mo. 46: 401.
Olmsted, Frederick Law. (M. G. Van Rensselaer) Cent. 24: 860.
Olney, Richard, Attorney-General, with portrait. Green Bag, 5: 257.
— and the Presidency. Atlan. 77: 676.
Ologies, Some. (Edgar Lee) Time, 16: 69.
Olympia, A Day at. (D. Osborne) Scrib. M. 19: 433.
— in its Ruins. (Commander Meryon) Good Words, 33: 592.
Olympiad, Anglo-Saxon, Proposed. (J. A. Cooper) 19th Cent. 32: 380.
Olympian Religion. (W. E. Gladstone) No. Am. 154: 487, 613.
Olympic Country, Washington. (S. C. Gilman) Nat. Geog. M. 7: 133.
Olympic Era of the Greeks. (J. Gennadius) Eng. Illust. 15: 217.
Olympic Games. (W. A. Robinson) Bach. of Arts, 2: 581. — (G. S. Robertson) Un. Serv. (Phila.) 16: 34.
— Can we revive the? (P. Shorey) Forum, 19: 313.
— Old. (A. Marquand) Cent. 29: 803.
Olympic Games, Revival of. (G. Horton) No. Am. 162: 266. — (John Patterson) Scot. R. 27: 276. — (J. G. Robertson) Fortn. 65: 944. Same art. Ecl. M. 127: 107. — (P. de Coubertin) Cent. 31: 39. — (R. B. Richardson) Scrib. M. 19: 453. 20: 267. — (W. S. Bensemer) New Eng. M. n. s. 14: 261. — (W. A. Elliott) Chaut. 23: 42. — Spec. 76: 511. — (A. Shaw) R. of Rs. (N. Y.) 10: 643. — (P. de Coubertin) Chaut. 19: 696. — (D. Kalopothakes) Nation, 61: 237. — (J. W. Laing) Bach. of Arts, 2: 372. — (G. Horton) Bost. 4: 315.
Omahas, The, Child-life among. (A. C. Fletcher) J. Am. Folk-Lore, 1: 115.
— Courtship and Marriage Customs of. (A. C. Fletcher) J. Am. Folk-Lore, 2: 219.
— Death and Funeral Customs of. (F. La Flesche) J. Am. Folk-Lore, 2: 3.
— Folk-lore of. (J. O. Dorsey) J. Am. Folk-Lore, 1: 213. 2: 190.
— Halthuska, Society of. (A. C. Fletcher) J. Am. Folk-Lore, 5: 135.
— Hunting Customs of. (A. C. Fletcher) Cent. 28: 691.
— Myths of. (J. O. Dorsey) J. Am. Folk-Lore, 1: 74, 204.
— Sacred Pole of the. (A. C. Fletcher) J. Am. Folk-Lore, 8: 249. — (A. C. Fletcher) Am. Antiq. 17: 257.
— Songs of. (J. O. Dorsey) J. Am. Folk-Lore, 1: 65, 209. 2: 271.
— Tribal Life among. (A. C. Fletcher) Cent. 29: 450.
Omaha Tale: Story of the Skull. (G. T. Kercheval) J. Am. Folk-Lore, 6: 199.
Oman, under British Protection. (J. T. Bent) Fortn. 60: 365.
Omar Khayyam. (J. A. Murray) Fortn. 66: 848. — Sat. R. 74: 223.
— Cult of, in England. (M. D. Conway) Nation, 57: 304.
Omega: the Last Days of the World; a story. (C. Flammarion) Cosmopol. 14: 744 — 15: 457.
Omens. Spec. 68: 739.
Omer Pasha. (A. Laugel) Nation, 61: 78.
Omnibus: Out and at Home. (A. R. Buckland) Good Words, 35: 397. Same art. Ecl. M. 123: 235.
Omnibus Story. All the Year, 73: 351.
Omnibuses; a Penny all the Way. All the Year, 70: 176.
On and Thebes, Astronomical History of. (J. N. Lockyer) Nature, 48: 318, 371.
On account of Emmanuel. (B. N. Taylor) Cent. 29: 51.
On a Barn Roof; a story. (J. A. Herne) Arena, 9: 131.
On Beethoven composing the Moonlight Sonata; a poem. (J. M. Templeton) M. of Art, 14: 188.
On the Betrothal of Brothers. (Evelyn Sharp) Idler, 6: 459.
On Black Butte; a story. (C. F. Brimblecom) Overland, n. s. 19: 387.
On Calais Sands. (A. Lang) M. of Art, 8: 409.
On a Christmas Altar; a story. (E. Marryat) Belgra. 77: 47.
On the Divide. (N. Cather) Overland, n. s. 27: 65.
On Frenchman's Bay; a story. (Mrs. Burton Harrison) Cosmopol. 18: 189.
On her Wedding Day. (G. G. Farquhar) Chamb. J. 71: 700.
On the Hill-side; a story. (N. Hopper) Eng. Illust. 15: 347.
On Kali's Shoulder; a story. All the Year, 73: 18–68.
On the Moor; a story. (J. Edgar) Gent. M. n. s. 56: 570.

On the Old Salt Road; a story. (F. A. Steel) Eng. Illust. **11**: 3.
On Pawnee Prairie; a story. (G. Smith) Cosmopol. **13**: 351.
On the River; a poem. (J. A. Blaikie) M. of Art, **9**: 521.
On Second Thoughts. (L. D. Morgan) Lippinc. **54**: 420.
On a Side-track. (M. H. Foote) Cent. **28**: 271.
On Sight; a story. (D. Gerard) Longm. **19**: 276.
On the Threshold. (Mrs. W. B. Carpenter) Sund. M. **25**: 29.
On the Way North; a story. (J. W. Tompkins) Munsey, **14**: 52.
Once Aboard the Lugger; a story. (A. Q. Couch) McClure, **1**: 515.
Once loved; a poem. (W. Graham) Belgra. **86**: 34.
"Once a Week;" a great Art Magazine. (Joseph Pennell) Bibliographica, **3**: 60.
One Afternoon. (L. Child) New Eng. M. n. s. **11**: 26.
One Brief Year; a poem. (M. Wilcox) Harper, **91**: 94.
One Day too Late; a story. (F. Beattie) Belgra. **83**: 365.
One-dimensional Manifold, Properties of a. (B. I. Gilman) Mind, **17**: 518.
One Good Guest, The; a story. (L. B. Walford) Good Words, **33**: 145-361.
One Hair White or Black; a story. (E. S. Moodie) Canad. M. **6**: 557.
One-horse Yarn, A. (E. Phillpotts) Idler, **2**: 21.
One Hour to live; a story. (J. N. Ervin) Our Day, **16**: 449-514.
One I knew the Best of All. (F. H. Burnett) Scrib. M. **13**: 60-798.
One in Charity. (S. K. Hocking) Sund. M. **22**: 1-793.
One Man who was Content. (Mrs. S. Van Rensselaer) Cent. **31**: 287
One More; a story. (W. Beatty) Idler, **7**: 497.
One of the Cloth. Macmil. **70**: 140. Same art. Ecl. M. **123**: 414. Same art. Liv. Age, **202**: 122.
One of the Few; a story. (K. Livingstone) Canad. M. **4**: 538.
One of the Forty. (A. Daudet) Univ. R. **1**: 140-567. **2**: 119-592.
One of Life's Ironies; a story. (M. Hill) Nat'l M. (Bost.) **4**: 434.
One of Our Criminals; a story. (R. C. Robbins) Harv. Mo. **17**: 89.
One of a Thousand; a story. (E. E. Rexford) New Eng. M. n. s. **6**: 783—**7**: 430.
One of us; balcony story. Cent. **24**: 544.
One Thing Lacking, The. (C. S. Coles) Outing, **26**: 427.
One Touch of Nature. (L. Child) New Eng. M. n. s. **13**: 399.
One Way to get a Rancho. (J. D. Mason) Overland, n. s. **23**: 250.
One Woman's Story; a study. (Margaret Deland) Cosmopol. **20**: 425.
One Woman's Way. (G. A. Hibbard) Cent. **27**: 275.
O'Neill, John. Acad. **47**: 61, 102.
O'Neill, Moira, *pseud.* *See* Higginson, Mrs.
O'Neill, Owen Roe. (E. D'Esterre Keeling) Acad. **50**: 26.
Onions, Cultivation of. (T. Greiner) Garden & F. **6**: 516.
— — in the South. (W. F. Massey) Garden & F. **6**: 6.
Only an Army Baby. (Mrs. K. T. Woods) Nat'l M. (Bost.) **5**: 151.
Only a Chinese Girl; a story. (G. De H. Browne) Munsey, **10**: 517.
Only a Fly; a story. (E. E. Hale) Chaut. **18**: 293.
Only Jack; a story. (E. St. Leger) Belgra. **81**: 83.
Only Jack; a story. All the Year, **73**: 496, 515.
Only Justice; a story. (W. B. Cameron) Canad. M. **6**: 434.
Only Kitty. (L. B. Walford) Longm. **25**: 414. Same art. Liv. Age, **204**: 526.
Only a Lassie; a story. (L. Hardy) Sund. M. **24**: 392.
Only a Pocket-handkerchief; a story. (L. B. Walford) Good Words, **35**: 417.
Only a Prescription; a story. (L. Creswicke) Belgra. **82**: 62.
Only Rose, The. (S. O. Jewett) Atlan. **73**: 37.
Only a Smudge; a story. (E. Yolland) Belgra. **81**: 414.
Only a Woman's Hand; a story. (W. Dixon) Belgra. **90**: 45.
Onondaga Indians, Customs of. (W. M. Beauchamp) J. Am. Folk-Lore, **1**: 195.
— Dances of. (W. M. Beauchamp) J. Am. Folk-Lore, **6**: 181.
— Folk-Lore of. (W. M. Beauchamp) J. Am. Folk-Lore, **1**: 44. **2**: 261. **6**: 173. **8**: 209.
— Superstitions of. (De Cost Smith) J. Am. Folk-Lore, **2**: 282.
— Witchcraft and Demonism of. (De Cost Smith) J. Am. Folk-Lore, **1**: 184.
Onslow, Arthur, and the Onslow Papers. Quar. **184**: 480.
Ontario and the West, Traders and Trade-routes in, 1760-83. (E. Cruikshank) Am. Antiq. **15**: 327.
— Early Artists of. (J. W. L. Forster) Canad. M. **5**: 17.
— Northern, Trip after Bark in. (T. C. Birnie) Canad. M. **1**: 206.
— Scottish Myths from. (C. A. Fraser) J. Am. Folk-Lore, **6**: 185.
Ontario, Lake, Aspects of. (J. Hague) Canad. M. **1**: 261.
— Birth of. (A. B. Willmot) Canad. M. **1**: 331.
Ontario Drain Tunnel and Electric Plant. (S. R. McKay) Engin. M. **9**: 1079.
Ontario Ladies' College, Whitby. (J. F. German) Canad. M. **5**: 72.
Ontario's Big Game. (J. Dickson) Canad. M. **4**: 3.
Ontology and Positivism. (P. Carus) Open Court, **4**: 2143.
— Epistemology and. (A. Seth) Philos. R. **3**: 568.
Onwhyn, Thomas, as a Graphic Humourist. (G. S. Layard) M. of Art, **19**: 393.
Oodeypore. (S. H. Dunn) Month, **88**: 536.
Oökinesis in Limax Maximus. (F. L. Washburn) Am. Natural. **28**: 528.
Opal of Carmalovitch. (M. Pemberton) Eng. Illust. **11**: 207.
— Superstitions of the. (Laura B. Starr) Westm. **141**: 685.
Open-air Evangelists. (G. H. Pike) Sund. M. **23**: 741.
Open-eyed Conspiracy. (W. D. Howells) Cent. **30**: 345, 607, 659, 836.
Open-field System in Northamptonshire. (G. L. Gomme) Ath. '95, **1**: 569.
Open Secret, An; a poem. (A. St. Johnston) M. of Art, **15**: 407.
Open Sesame. Argosy, **62**: 26.
Open Shutter; a story. (S. J. Weyman) Eng. Illust. **13**: 37.
Open Spaces in London, County Council and. (Earl of Meath) New R. **7**: 701.
Open Window and what came of it; a tale. (W. T. James) Canad. M. **1**: 68.
Opera, American, Plan and Plea for. (S. G. Pratt) Forum, **15**: 88.
— and Poor Acting. Sat. R. **79**: 724.

Opera before the Court of Reason. (W. F. Biddle) Atlan. **77**: 786.
— Comic, Decline of. (W. D. Adams) Theatre, **35**: 202.
— Endowed, Shall we have? (J. K. Paine) Forum, **13**: 507.
— English, How to obtain a School of. (J. F. Rowbotham) 19th Cent. **38**: 103.
— Grand. (N. Melba) Lippinc. **55**: 512.
— in England, Notes and Reminiscences of. (Sir A. Harris) New R. **9**: 257, 343.
— in Europe. (E. Morris) Music, **10**: 577.
— Italian, and German contrasted. Sat. R. **80**: 74.
— — Falstaff and the New. (J. A. F. Maitland) 19th Cent. **33**: 803.
— — in England. Sat. R. **79**: 649.
— Introduction to the English Stage. Theatre, **29**: 70.
— Lyric Drama and Libretti. (S. J. A. Fitzgerald) Theatre, **29**: 161.
— Old and New. (C. C. Billiani) Music, **4**: 616.
— Origin of the. (J. F. Rowbotham) Chamb. J. **69**: 705. Same art. Ecl. M. **120**: 159.
— Paris. Blackw. **158**: 157.
— — Gossip about. M. of Art, **7**: 436.
— Subsidized, in America. (K. Hackett) Music, **11**: 52.
Opera-house, A National. (A. W. Hutton) Contemp. **20**: 58.
Opera-houses, Famous, of Europe and America. (A. Hornblow) Munsey, **13**: 233.
Operatic Celebrities, English. All the Year, **71**: 233.
Operatic Singers, how trained in Italy. (E. P. L. MacDonald) Idler, **2**: 263.
Ophidia, Physiological Classification of. (A. Stradling) Science, **21**: 228.
Opie, Amelia. Temp. Bar, **98**: 485. Same art. Liv. Age, **198**: 707.
Opinions. (A. Repplier) Atlan. **73**: 545.
Opinions of a Philosopher. (R. Grant) Scrib. M. **13**: 777 — **14**: 357.
Ophir, Mount: King Solomon's Mines. (R. Wildman) Overland, n. s. **23**: 508.
Opisthoteuthidæ, The. (A. E. Verrill) Am. J. Sci. **152**: 74.
Opium and Hemp, Reports on. Spec. **74**: 570.
— Ennui and; a Chinese View. Temp. Bar, **102**: 506.
— in Ceylon. (Mary and Marg. Leitch) Lend a H. **12**: 49.
— Letter to the Opium Commission. (G. W. Des Vœux) 19th Cent. **35**: 323.
— Question of. (G. H. M. Batten and others) J. Soc. Arts, **40**: 444.
— — from Chinese Standpoint. Asia. R. **15**: 47.
Opium Commission, The. (L. Griffin) 19th Cent. **35**: 513.
Opium Dens, Chinese London and its. (J. Platt) Gent. M. n. s. **55**: 272.
Opium Eating, Lotus Eating and. (J. G. Alexander) Contemp. **66**: 337.
Opium Habit, Some Facts about the. Chamb. J. **73**: 294.
Opium Industry. (E. N. Baker) Econ. J. **6**: 114.
Opium Smoking. (E. H. Parker) Blackw. **159**: 570.
— in India. Sat. R. **77**: 10.
Opium-smuggling in India. Blackw. **151**: 669.
Opium Trade, British, Ravages of, in Asia. (A. P. Happer) Our Day, **10**: 545.
— in California. (F. J. Masters) Chaut. **24**: 54.
— Lambeth Conference and. (W. Butler; J. M. Foster) Our Day, **11**: 304.
Opium War, The Truth about the. (D. A. Wells) No. Am. **162**: 759. — (J. G. Alexander) No. Am. **163**: 381.
Opper, Henri Adolphe Stephan. *See* Blowitz, M. de.
Opportunity, Equality of, How to secure. (J. L. Cowles) Arena, **15**: 80.
— — Have we? (C. D. Wright) Forum, **19**: 301.
Optical Continuity. (F. Galton) Nature, **47**: 342.
Optical Illusion, Quantitative Determination of. (H. W. Knox) Am. J. Psychol. **6**: 413. — (R. Watanabe) Am. J. Psychol. **6**: 509.
Optical Phenomena, Some. All the Year, **76**: 34.
Optical Projection. (D. Salomons) Nature, **46**: 625.
Optical Time-content. (H. Münsterberg) Psychol. R. **1**: 51.
Optics, Modern, and the Microscope. (W. H. Dallinger) Nature, **47**: 409.
— Recent Progress in. (W. Le C. Stevens) Am. J. Sci. **150**: 277, 377. — (W. Le C. Stevens) Nature, **53**: 233.
— Wayside. (C. A. Wood) Pop. Sci. Mo. **40**: 616.
Optional Studies, Rigid Courses *versus*. (S. Thurber) School R. **3**: 206.
Optimism, American. Spec. **73**: 365.
— An Attempt at. (M. E. Ponsonby) 19th Cent. **40**: 474.
— E. Henri on. Spec. **72**: 221.
— Political. (I. W. Howerth) New Eng. M. n. s. **8**: 752.
Options and Futures. (W. D. Washburne) Am. J. Pol. **1**: 449.
— in Grain. (W. E. Bear) Contemp. **65**: 781.
Oracles, History of. (B. Williams) Gent. M. n. s. **48**: 21. Same art. Ecl. M. **118**: 270.
— Roman, Secret of. (R. Lanciani) Atlan. **75**: 310.
Orange Free State, Constitution of. (J. Bryce) Forum, **21**: 145.
Orange River, Africa. (H. A. Bryden) Chamb. J. **70**: 545.
Orange Society, The. (M. MacDonagh) Contemp. **70**: 215. — (Wm. Mackay) Time, **14**: 673.
Orangeism in Ireland. Eng. R. **5**: 192.
Orangemen in Ireland. Sat. R. **80**: 861.
Orange-tree, The. (T. H. B. Graham) Gent. M. n. s. **50**: 482.
Orange Crop in California. (W. M. Tisdale) Garden & F. **9**: 28.
Orange Culture in California and the Frost. (W. M. Tisdale) Garden & F. **9**: 56, 218.
Orange Industry, Rise and Fall of. (J. F. Richmond) Chaut. **22**: 451.
Oranges and Lemons, California. (C. H. Shinn) Garden & F. **5**: 561.
— Early California. (W. M. Tisdale) Garden & F. **9**: 508.
— Mandarin and Tangarine. Garden & F. **7**: 68.
— Satsuma, Hardiness of. (W. F. Massey) Garden & F. **5**: 103.
Orang-outang, The. (A. Keith) Nat. Sci. **9**: 316.
Oratorio, The First. (J. F. Rowbotham) Chamb. J. **70**: 689.
Oratory. Has it declined? (H. L. Dawes) Forum, **18**: 146.
— History of, Sears on. (E. H. Lewis) School R. **4**: 178.
— Is it a Lost Art? (E. J. Edwards) Chaut. **14**: 445.
— Political. (H. T. Peck) Bookman, **4**: 208, 324.
— Power of. (F. W. Gunsaulus) Our Day, **16**: 623.
— A School of. (J. H. Vincent) Chaut. **22**: 453.
Orcadia, In. Blackw. **154**: 224. Same art. Liv. Age, **199**: 109.
Orchard, First-born of the. (F. Wilson) Lippinc. **51**: 233.

Orchard, Looting of the [by Birds and Insects]. (P. Robinson) Contemp. 62: 709.
Orchard Trees, Early Bearing of. (T. H. Hoskins) Garden & F. 7: 496.
Orchard Street Disaster. (G. B. Waite) Am. Arch. 48: 18.
Orchards, Conservation of Water for. Garden & F. 7: 66.
Orchardson, William Quiller. (A. Meynell) M. of Art, 4: 276.
— The Art of. (Walter Armstrong) Portfo. no. 14.
— as a Dramatist. (W. Armstrong) Art J. 46: 33.
Orchestra, Evolution of the. (E. O. Heyler) Music, 7: 240, 349.
— The Modern. (A. Weld) Music, 3: 276, 438. 5: 497.
Orchestra Conducting and Conductors. (W. E. Apthorp) Scrib. M. 17: 384.
Orchid, Arachnanthe Cathcartii. (J. Weathers) Garden & F. 5: 153.
— Cypripedium Daisye Garden & F. 5: 460.
— Freak of a New England. Garden & F. 5: 142.
— Miltonopsis Bleni Splendens. (W. Robinson) Garden & F. 5: 197.
— Phajus Grandifolius. Garden & F. 5: 186.
— Swan's-neck. (R. A. Rolfe) Garden & F. 5: 88.
Orchid Notes. (M. Barker) Garden & F. 5: 572-596.
Orchids. (E. O. Orpet) Garden & F. 5: 559. — Garden & F. 6: 455. — (L. Irwell) Lippinc. 56: 827. — (L. Greenlee) Mo. Illust. 4: 186. — (W. A. Stiles) Scrib. M. 15: 190.
— Albinos Among. (A. M. Vail) Garden & F. 5: 395. — (J. F. Collins) Garden & F. 5: 299.
— as Window Plants. (J. N. Gerard) Garden & F. 6: 102.
— at Kew Gardens. (W. Watson) Garden & F. 9: 83.
— at Langwater Gardens. (T. D. Hatfield) Garden & F. 9: 147.
— at North Easton, Mass. (A. Dimmock) Garden & F. 5: 128. — (T. D. Hatfield) Garden & F. 7: 159.
— at Short Hills, N. J. (J. N. Gerard) Garden & F. 6: 69. — Garden & F. 7: 238. 8: 37.
— at Wellesley. (A. M. S. Rossiter) Garden & F. 7: 308.
— Beauty of. (M. G. Van Rensselaer) Garden & F. 7: 78.
— Cattleya Labiata. (E. O. Orpet) Garden & F. 8: 447.
— Joseph Chamberlain's, with portrait. (F. Dolman) Eng. Illust. 10: 879.
— Chinese. (A. B. Westland) Garden & F. 7: 76.
— Collecting, in Borneo, Destructive Effect of, on Forests. Sat. R. 76: 592.
— — Romance of. Chamb. J. 71: 257.
— Cultivation of. Garden & F. 7: 108, 247. — (E. O. Orpet) Garden & F. 7: 407.
— Cultivation of Mexican Lalias. (E. O. Orpet) Garden & F. 8: 17.
— Cultural Notes on. (E. O. Orpet) Garden & F. 9: 45, 247, 447. — (R. Cameron) Garden & F. 9: 54, 176. — (W. Watson) Garden & F. 9: 423. — (W. Magee, jr.) Garden & F. 9: 527.
— Cypripedium Arnoldiæ. (A. Dimmock) Garden & F. 7: 425.
— Cypripedium Insigne. (E. O. Orpet) Garden & F. 6: 506.
— Cypripediums. Garden & F. 6: 144.
— Cypripidum Bellatulum. (E. O. Orpet) Garden & F. 9: 528.
— Dendrobium Phalenopsis. (E. O. Orpet) Garden & F. 6: 467.
Orchids. Dendrobiums in Harvard Botanic Garden. (R. Cameron) Garden & F. 9: 137.
— Exhibition of, 1894. Sat. R. 77: 579.
— for Market Flowers. Garden & F. 6: 519.
— Hardy, for Out-door Cultivation. (E. H. Horsford) Garden & F. 6: 33.
— How they climbed the Trees. (J. Rodway) Longm. 22: 12.
— Hunting, in Demerara. Cornh. 70: 70. Same art. Ecl. M. 123: 364. Same art. Liv. Age, 202: 352.
— Hybridizing. Garden & F. 9: 446.
— in Flower. (E. O. Orpet) Garden & F. 9: 387.
— — in N. Y. City. Garden & F. 5: 129.
— in France. (M. L. de Vilmovin) Garden & F. 7: 84.
— Mitloina Vexillaria. (W. Robinson) Garden & F. 8: 194.
— New. (R. A. Rolfe) Garden & F. 5: 4-510. — (Wm. Robinson) Garden & F. 7: 65.
— New Cypripediums. Garden & F. 8: 63.
— Notes on. (E. O. Orpet) Garden & F. 6: 426. 8: 156. — (W. Watson) Garden & F. 7: 203. — (W. Watson) Garden & F. 8: 354. — (Emil Misch) Garden & F. 9: 106. — (H. G. Pratt) Garden & F. 9: 348.
— Noteworthy. (W. Watson) Garden & F. 8: 274.
— of Northeastern Mass. (T. D. Hatfield) Garden & F. 6: 378.
— A Season with the Native. (E. J. Hill) Garden & F. 8: 412, 422.
— Spot Disease of. (W. Watson) Garden & F. 8: 433.
— Thanksgiving for. (F. Boyle) 19th Cent. 32: 569.
Ordeal by Water, An. Liv. Age, 206: 57.
— History of an. (W. W. Newell) J. Am. Folk-Lore, 9: 147.
— Trial by, in Siam. (G. E. Gerini) Asia. R. 20: 156.
Ordelaffi, Barbara, Tomb of. (S. Thompson) M. of Art, 14: 373.
Orders, Foreign, and Decorations. (Edward Denloh) Cosmopol. 19: 294.
Ordinance of 1787, Part of Massachusetts Men in. (E. H. Tetlow) New Eng. M. n. s. 12: 55.
— Slavery and. (H. W. Quaintance) M. Am. Hist. 30: 75.
Ordination, Congregational, Validity of. (W. E. Griffis) Bib. Sac. 50: 588.
Ordnance, Heavy, in U. S., Present Development of. (W. H. Jaques) J. Frankl. Inst. 136: 19, 98.
— Testing Naval, in U. S. (P. Andrews) Nat'l M. (Bost.) 5: 137.
Ordre, L', de Bon-temps; a poem. (W. McLennan) Harper, 86: 393.
Ore-sampling Works, Public. (A. Williams, jr.) Engin. M. 3: 34.
Oregon, Discovery of. (E. G. Porter) New Eng. M. n. s. 6: 472.
— the Great Emerald Land. (C. H. Miller) Overland, n. s. 28: 641.
— History, Geography, and Resources of. (J. H. Mitchell) Nat. Geog. M. 3: 239.
— Missionary Work in, Early Methodist. (H. K. Hines) Meth. R. 53: 413.
— Sage Plains of. (F. V. Corille) Nat. Geog. M. 7: 395.
— Senatorships of, Memorable Contests for: Dolph's Defeat. (E. Hofer) Overland, n. s. 25: 460.
— Struggle for, N. J. Wyeth and. (J. A. Wyeth) Harper, 85: 835.
Oregon Campaign of '94. (E. Hofer) Overland, n. s. 24: 306.

Oregon Railway Decision. (E. Robertson) Jurid. R. 1: 130.
Oregon Trail, A Story of the. (J. B. Rhineheart) Overland, n. s. 23: 176.
Oregonian Characteristics. (A. Holman) Overland, n. s. 25: 202.
O'Reilly, John Boyle, Monument to. Critic, 28: 433.
Orendel, or the Legend of the Holy Coat of Trier. Scot. R. 20: 124.
Organ, The. (D. Spillane) Pop. Sci. Mo. 40: 623.
— Composers for, Early English. (B. Horner) J. Soc. Arts, 44: 505.
— History of. (W. F. Gates) Music, 2: 433.
— of St. Michan's Church, Dublin. (L. O. Cooper) Good Words, 37: 543.
— Possibilities of a Pure-toned. (J. C. Griggs) Music, 2: 483.
Organ Cases, Hill's Organs and. (B. Champneys) M. of Art, 6: 456.
Organ-grinding: Jersey and Mulberry. (H. C. Bunner) Scrib. M. 13: 641.
Organ Mountains, New Mexico. (C. H. T. Townsend) Science, 22: 313.
Organ-playing from Memory. (W. S. B. Mathews and others) Music, 4: 90.
Organisms, Conflict between, Geometrical Representation of the Relative Intensity of. (J. A. Ryder) Am. Natural. 26: 923.
— Problematic. (J. F. James) Am. Natural. 26: 5.
Organist at Glastonbury Abbey. Reliquary, 32: 176.
Organists, Leading, of France and Italy. (C. Eddy) Music, 11: 163.
Organs, Church. (A. G. Hill) Am. Arch. 44: 60, 85.
— and Organ Cases, Church. Am. Arch. 53: 35.
— of Middle Ages, Hill on. Sat. R. 73: 342.
Orgeas and Miradon. (F. Wedmore) 19th Cent. 38: 227. Same art. Liv. Age, 206: 761.
Oriel Bill. (J. D. Symon) Eng. Illust. 11: 455.
Orient, Spirit of. (J. H. Dubbs) Ref. Q. 41: 50.
Oriental Art and Archæology. (W. Simpson) Asia. R. 17: 349.
Oriental Congress, Stockholm, 1889. Asia. R. 9: 166.
— 1891, Place of Meeting. (G. W. Leitner) Asia. R. 10: 212.
— — Proceedings. Asia. R. 12: 157.
— 1894. Ath. '94, 2: 322, 350.
Oriental Languages, Transliteration of. (Monier Williams) Asia. R. 12: 397.
Oriental Social Life, Trumbull on. Sat. R. 79: 260.
Oriental Studies in Great Britain. (T. W. Davies) Asia. R. 13: 375.
— in Louvain, Beginnings of. (L. C. Casartelli) Dub. R. 119: 132.
Oriental Travel under Protest; a story. (J. K. Bangs) Mo. Illust. 3: 281.
Orientalism and Christianity. (J. K. Smyth) N. Church R. 1: 52.
Orientalists, Suggestion to. Spec. 69: 376.
Orientals, Official Relations with. (R. Meade) Asia. R. 12: 358.
Orientation of Greek Temples. (F. C. Penrose) Nature, 48: 42.
— — Influence of Egypt upon. (J. N. Lockyer) Nature, 48: 417.
— — Penrose on. Sat. R. 77: 368.
— Reverse Illusions of. (M. A. Binet) Psycholog. R. 1: 337.
Orienting Small Objects for Sectioning. (W. Patten) Am. Natural. 28: 360.
Origen and the Return to Greek Theology. (J. W. Falconer) Bib. Sac. 53: 466.
Origin of Thought; a story. (A. P. Valdés) Cosmopol. 16: 436, 542, 706. 17: 87, 185, 335, 485.
Original Retribution; a story. (C. N. Johnson) Canad. M. 4: 411.
Originality. Conventional and Original Minds. Spec. 69: 954.
— Decay of. (C. B. R. Kent) Ecl. M. 118: 161. Same art. Liv. Age, 192: 401.
— in Literature. (R. Burton) Dial (Ch.) 21: 212.
Oriole, Baltimore, Nest-building of. (S. Goodhue) New Eng. M. n. s. 9: 110.
Oriskany Fauna, Lower, in Columbia Co., N. Y. (C. E. Beecher) Am. J. Sci. 144: 410.
Orisons; a poem. (L. I. Guiney) Harper, 91: 75.
Orissa, the Holy Land of India. (J. M. Macdonald) M. of Art, 18: 150.
Orkhon Inscriptions. (E. H. Parker) Acad. 48: 547.
Orkney Isles. (T. P. White) Scot. R. 27: 195.
— Fauna of, Vertebrate, Buckley and Harvie-Brown on. Ath. '92, 1: 118.
Orizaba, Mount. (J. T. Scovell) Science, 21: 253.
— Ascent of. (A. Heilprin) Around World, 1: 21, 49.
Orleanism. New R. 13: 19.
— Non pas, mais royalisme. New R. 13: 290.
Orleans, Charlotte Elizabeth, Duchess of. Temp. Bar, 104: 494. Same art. Liv. Age, 205: 504.
Orleans, Henrietta, Duchess of. (F. Hawkins) Acad. 45: 241.
Orleans, House of. (T. C. Quinn) Munsey, 12: 235.
Orley, Bernard Van. *See* Van Orley.
Ormerod, Georgiana Elizabeth. Nat. Sci. 9: 276.
Ormsby, John. Acad. 48: 410. — Ath. '95, 2: 645.
Ormus, View of, in 1627. (W. Foster) Geog. J. 4: 160.
Ornament. (Sir H. Maxwell) Blackw. 153: 137.
— Classic, Evolution of. (W. H. Goodyear) Archit. Rec. 2: 165, 391. 3: 137, 263. 4: 88, 446.
— Evolution of. (C. H. Read) Portfo. 24: 112.
— Masters of. (L. F. Day) J. Soc. Arts, 41: 793–830.
— The Vine in. (L. F. Day) M. of Art, 13: 127, 151.
Ornamental Designs exhibited at South Kensington. (L. F. Day) Art J. 48: 315.
Ornithological Romance, An. (W. L. Alden) Idler, 1: 425.
Ornithology, American, Chamberlain on. (S. A. Hubbard) Dial (Ch.) 12: 385.
— — Progress in, 1886–95. (R. W. Shufeldt) Am. Natural. 30: 357.
— Economic and Scientific Questions in. (R. W. Shufeldt) Science, 22: 255.
— Recent Works on, 1893. (R. B. Sharpe) Nature, 49: 6.
Ornithophilous Pollination. (J. L. Hancock) Am. Natural. 28: 679.
Ornithopoda, Typical, of the American Jurassic. (O. C. Marsh) Am. J. Sci. 148: 85.
Oronhyatekha, the Mohawk Doctor. (M. T. Bayard) Canad. M. 7: 135.
Oropa, a Mountain Sanctuary in Piedmont. (E. C. Cook) Char. R. 4: 246.
Orphans, Treatment of. (S. Schindler) Arena, 8: 657.
Orpheus in Hades; a poem. (Lord de Tabley) 19th Cent. 34: 839.
Orrock, James, at 48 Bedford Square. (C. Monkhouse) Art J. 44: 12.
Ortegal to St. Vincent. (R. Benyon) Liv. Age, 197: 250.
Orthodoxy, The New. (P. Carus) Monist, 6: 91. — (E. H. Hall) New World, 1: 124.
— — and the Old. (G. A. Gordon) And. R. 19: 1.
— Progressive. (E. C. Smyth) New World, 1: 627. — Open Court, 1: 718.

Orthographic Union. Critic, **26**: 426.
Ortler Alp, A Slip on the. (C. S. Davison) Atlan. **72**: 319.
Ortolano, L., Altar-piece of. (G. Allen) Eng. Illust. **14**: 184.
Orvieto, Italy. (W. L. Alden) Idler, **2**: 35.
— Cathedral. (J. Cartwright) M. of Art, **5**: 514.
Osage River and Ozark Uplift. Science, **22**: 276.
— Meanders of. (A. Winslow) Science, **22**: 31.
Osama. Blackw. **159**: 438. Same art. Liv. Age, **209**: 259. Same art. Un. Serv. (Phila.) **15**: 394. — Sat. R. **77**: 452.
Osborn, Sir Danvers. (J. G. Wilson) Nat'l M. (N. Y. '91) **19**: 1.
Osborne, Francis: a 17th Century Chesterfield. (S. Peel) 19th Cent. **40**: 944.
Oscar II., King of Sweden. (H. Hjärne) Forum, **22**: 164.
Osgood, James Ripley. Critic, **20**: 305.
— Letters to. Critic, **26**: 484.
O'Shaughnessy, Mrs. Moulton's. Poet-Lore, **7**: 211.
O'Shea, John A. Roundabout Recollections. Spec. **69**: 471.
Oshkosh, Wisconsin. Chamb. J. **70**: 65.
Oskamull; a story. Chamb. J. **71**: 317–327.
Osman; an interlude. (C. W. Wood) Argosy, **55**: 211.
Osmium, Chemistry of. (A. E. Tutton) Nature, **47**: 400.
Osmotic Pressures, Applications of Theory of, to Physiological Problems. (E. Starling) Sci. Prog. **4**: 284. **5**: 151.
Osmund, Saint, Ancient Offices of. (F. E. Gilliat-Smith) Dub. R. **114**: 22.
Osmund, the Waterman; a story. (N. Hopper) Eng. Illust. **14**: 505.
Ospreys in Scotland, Last of the. Spec. **71**: 140.
Osric, King of Northumbria, How I found the Remains of. (H. D. M. Spence) Good Words, **33**: 388.
Ossets, The: a People Adrift. Liv. Age, **207**: 763.
Ossian, Author of. Spec. **73**: 50.
— Centenary of. Macmil. **74**: 62.
Ossipee Glens, N. H., and Whittier. (L. Larcom) New Eng. M. n. s. **7**: 192.
Ossoli, Margaret Fuller. (J. Lazarus) Cent. **23**: 923. — (E. L. Didier) Chaut. **23**: 387.
— in a New Aspect. Atlan. **78**: 550.
— Personality of. (Elsie Rhodes) Temp. Bar, **108**: 226. Same art. Liv. Age, **210**: 223.
Ostade, Adriaan van. (T. Cole) Cent. **26**: 215.
Ostriches at the London Zoo. (F. E. Beard) Chamb. J. **69**: 273.
Oswald, Jonathan. (W. S. Freas) Luth. Q. **22**: 341.
Oswego State Normal School. (W. M. Aber) Pop. Sci. Mo. **43**: 51.
Oswell, Wm. Cotton. (Thomas Hughes) Macmil. **70**: 307.
Other Half on Sunday: the Lone Bachelor. (H. V. Barnett) Eng. Illust. **12**: no. 3, 159.
Other Mother. (A. V. N. Dorr) New Eng. M. n. s. **7**: 649.
Other Side of the Wall; a story. (E. N. L. Fry) Belgra. **85**: 407.
Other-worldliness and Unworldliness. (J. M. Gibson) Sund. M. **22**: 748.
Otis Family of Montreal. (I. J. Greenwood) N. E. Reg. **46**: 211.
Otoe Tale: the Chief's Daughters. (G. T. Kercheval) J. Am. Folk-Lore, **6**: 199.
Ottawa Conference. (J. L. Payne) Canad. M. **3**: 186.
Ottawa River, On and in the. (W. Thomson) Outing, **26**: 431.
Otter, Silver. (H. Hutchinson) Longm. **24**: 68.
Otter Hunt, in Ireland. (T. S. Blackwell) Outing, **20**: 73.
Otter Hunting. (W. C. A. Blew) Eng. Illust. **10**: 92. — (G. Lascelles) Time, **3**: 295.
Otterburn, Battle of. Chamb. J. **70**: 465.
Ottolengui, Rodrigues. (S. L. Coles) Writer, **7**: 97.
Ottrelite-bearing Phase of a Metamorphic Conglomerate in the Green Mountains. (C. L. Whittle) Am. J. Sci. **144**: 270.
Otway, Thos. Citizen, **1**: 213.
Ouachita River, Up the, on a Cotton-boat. (S. Cooley) Cosmopol. **13**: 543.
Ouananiche, The, and its Canadian Environment. (E. T. D. Chambers) Harper, **93**: 107.
— Home of the. (E. T. D. Chambers) Canad. M. **5**: 33.
Oubliette, The. (M. H. Catherwood) Atlan. **77**: 781.
Oudeypore, the City of the Sunrise. (E. L. Weeks) Harper, **90**: 435. — (S. H. Dunn) Month, **88**: 536.
Oudh Police. (H. S. Clarke) Un. Serv. M. **7**: 1192.
Oudin, Eugene. Acad. **46**: 383.
Oudinot, Marshall. (A. Laugel) Nation, **58**: 344, 386.
Ought, Meaning of. (D. S. Miller) Int. J. Ethics, **4**: 499.
Ould Weatherglass. (M. Beaumont) Sund. M. **25**: 704.
Our Abbé; a story. (H. Duvar) Canad. M. **8**: 82.
Our Aromatic Uncle. (H. C. Bunner) Scrib. M. **18**: 169.
Our First Case; a story. All the Year, **76**: 255.
Our First Home Coverts. (H. Hutchinson) Longm. **27**: 606.
Our Glee Club; a story. (Penley Reyd) Gent. M. n. s. **57**: 316.
Our Ladies' Club. All the Year, **73**: 446.
Our Lady of the Angels. (D. E. Nelson) Lippinc. **57**: 137.
Our Lady of Ferrara in the National Gallery. (G. Allen) Eng. Illust. **15**: 149.
Our Mr. Jupp; a story. (G. Gissing) Eng. Illust. **11**: 631.
Our Ten-cent Boys. (E. Heaton) Good Words, **35**: 260.
Our Village; a story. (E. B. Harrison) Temp. Bar, **105**: 98. Same art. Ecl. M. **125**: 494. Same art. Liv. Age, **205**: 816.
Out of the Book of Humanity. (J. A. Riis) Atlan. **78**: 698.
Out of Bounds; a story. (B. Coll) Idler, **8**: 119.
Out-of-date Reformer; a story. Cornh. **72**: 151. Same art. Liv. Age, **206**: 788.
Out of her Class. (C. B. Davis) Cent. **25**: 357.
Out of the Night. (K. Tynan) Blackw. **160**: 550. Same art. Liv. Age, **211**: 656.
Out of Thun; a story. (R. Barr) McClure, **7**: 136.
Out of Town. All the Year, **71**: 173.
Out of the Workhouse; a story. Temp. Bar, **99**: 393. Same art. Liv. Age, **199**: 721.
Out Wand Way; a story. (A. J. Dawson) Idler, **10**: 498.
Outamaro. (T. Hopkins) Leis. Hour, **44**: 314.
Outdoor Life in England. Spec. **76**: 237.
Outdoor Relief. Is it so very Bad? (W. A. Hunter) Contemp. **65**: 305.
Outflanking Two Emperors. (M. Halstead) Cosmopol. **17**: 424.
Outlawed; a story. All the Year, **72**: 356–572.
Outlived Pain; a poem. (E. C. Cardozo) Cosmopol. **20**: 401.
Outpost Duty and Secret Service in War. Chamb. J. **70**: 650.

Outside the Chamber of Mirrors. (H. K. Horsfield) National, **19**: 431.
Outside the Dance Hall; a poem. (D. Fuguet) Cosmopol. **22**: 64.
Outward and Visible Signs; a story. (F. Norris) Overland, n. s. **23**: 241-502. **24**: 82, 375. **25**: 196.
O. V.; a Western Sketch. All the Year, **72**: 103.
Ovens and Stoves. Chamb. J. **70**: 86.
Over the Bars; a story. (E. Hilton) Our Day, **16**: 633.
Over the Devil's Back; a story. Argosy, **60**: 604.
Over the Edge of the World; a story. (F. A. Steel) Eng. Illust. **11**: 367.
Over Ifinger Joch; a story. (J. P. Rudd) Outing, **27**: 103.
Over Land and Sea; a story. (C. Stewart) Eng. Illust. **11**: 1250.
Over-mountain Men. (S. M. Burnett) Am. Hist. Reg. **1**: 313-421.
Over the Range; a sketch. All the Year, **71**: 229.
Overay, Thomas, Will of. Reliquary, **33**: 218.
Overbeck, Johannes. (W. Miller) Am. J. Archæol. **11**: 361.
Overberg, Bernhard. (J. Alexander) Cath. World, **56**: 659.
Overheard in a Paris Ball-room; a drama, adapted from Gyp. Eng. Illust. **12**: no. 5, 23.
Overland Monthly. (M. W. Shinn) Critic, **21**: 71.
Over-production. (U. H. Crocker) Q. J. Econ. **6**: 352.
— Reply. (T. V. Veblen) Q. J. Econ. **6**: 484.
Overture to Tannhäuser, The; a story. (E. F. Benson) Eng. Illust. **11**: 275.
Ovid and the Natural World. (E. M. Cesaresco) Contemp. **70**: 109. Same art. Liv. Age, **210**: 433.
Ovidiana. (R. Ellis) Am. J. Philol. **13**: 343.
Owd Lads; a story. (M. E. Francis) Blackw. **158**: 472. Same art. Liv. Age, **207**: 268.
Owen, David Dale, with portrait. Pop. Sci. Mo. **48**: 259.
Owen, John. (J. S. Cotton) Acad. **49**: 136.
Owen, Sir Philip Cunliff. Am. Arch. **44**: 41. — M. of Art, **17**: xxv.
Owen, Sir Richard. Ath. '92, **2**: 894. — Nature, **47**: 181. — Spec. **69**: 919. — Church Q. **40**: 345. — Dub. R. **112**: 437. — Liv. Age, **197**: 379. — (C. D. Sherborn) Nat. Sci. **2**: 16. — Leis. Hour. **42**: 319. **44**: 770. — Nature, **51**: 169.
— and the Evolution Movement. (H. F. Osborn) Nation, **61**: 66.
— and Old-world Memories. (L. A. Tollemache) National, **21**: 606.
— Hypotheses of. (St. G. Mivart) Nat. Sci. **2**: 18.
— Life of. (A. W. Benn) Acad. **47**: 73. — (S. A. Hubbard) Dial (Ch.) **18**: 17.
— Researches of, on the Invertebrata. (A. Crane) Nat. Sci. **2**: 23.
— — on the Vertebrata. (A. S. Woodward) Nat. Sci. **2**: 129.
Owen Glendower. *See* Glendower, Owen.
Owl, Ways of the. (F. Bolles) Pop. Sci. Mo. **41**: 313.
Owls. (E. K. Robinson) Time, **7**: 415.
Ownership, History of, Simcox's. Sat. R. **77**: 618.
Ownership Vote, The. (H. T. Wade) Westm. **143**: 316.
Oxalis, Cape. (W. E. Endicott) Garden & F. **5**: 392-524. **6**: 7.
"Oxbow" and "Bow." (Albert Matthews) Nation, **63**: 65.
Oxen, Ploughing. Chamb. J. **72**: 107.
Oxenstierna, Axel, Papers and Correspondence. (G. Edmundson) Eng. Hist. R. **7**: 777.
Oxford, England. Blackw. **158**: 420.
— Church of St. Mary Virgin. Church Q. 37: 101.
Oxford, High Street of, and Brasenose College. (T. G. Jackson) M. of Art, **12**: 332.
— How Built. (M. Hawke) M. of Art, **4**: 347, 401.
— New. (W. J. Gordon) Leis. Hour, **44**: 249-387.
— Old and New. (R. H. Titherington) Munsey, **7**: 57.
— Old Road to. All the Year, **75**: 31.
— Quiet Corners of. (E. E. Overton) Leis. Hour, **42**: 635.
Oxford Bible Helps, History of. Bookworm, **6**: 241.
Oxford Conference on Secondary Education in England. (A. T. Smith) Educa. **14**: 504.
Oxford Council of Dec., 1197. (J. H. Round) Eng. Hist. R. **7**: 501.
Oxford Idyll, An. Macmil. **69**: 298. Same art. Liv. Age, **200**: 748.
Oxford Movement. Eng. R. **1**: 145. **5**: 395.
— A forgotten. Liv. Age, **209**: 681.
— Rigg on. Church Q. **41**: 359.
— Significance of. (W. R. Thayer) Open Court, **3**: 2054, 2076.
Oxford University. (P. A. W. Henderson) Blackw. **155**: 342. — (A. M. Clarke) Cath. World, **61**: 491. — (A. Inkersley) Educa. **12**: 515.
— Advantages of. Harv. Mo. **14**: 1.
— American Collegian at. (J. Corbin) Bach. of Arts, **1**: 84-451.
— and Cambridge Universities as Publishers. Sat. R. **79**: 181.
— and Oxford Life. Church Q. **36**: 162.
— as seen by a Frenchman. Month, **75**: 161.
— B. A. Degree. (R. Jones) Our Day, **14**: 190.
— — What does it represent? (R. Jones) Educa. R. **4**: 447.
— before the Reformation. Quar. **174**: 1.
— Book-hunter at. Bookworm, **2**: 289.
— College Farms. Macmil. **75**: 22.
— Colleges of, and Agricultural Depression. (L. L. Price) J. Statis. Soc. **58**: 36.
— Colleges of, Clark on. (G. Smith) Nation, **54**: 113, 135.
— Corpus Christi College, History of, Fowler's. Sat. R. **75**: 353.
— Discipline at. (O. S. Jones) Idler, **10**: 464.
— Eights at. (M. N. Evans) New Eng. M. n. s. **8**: 441.
— English at. Sat. R. **78**: 525.
— Ethics at. (S. Alexander) Eth. Rec. **3**: 78.
— Forty Years Ago at. (A. F. Marshall) Bach. of Arts, **3**: 242.
— Heraldry of Colleges of. (A. Clark) Eng. Hist. R. **10**: 333.
— Hutton's Rixæ Oxonienses. Spec. **68**: 851.
— in the "Eights" Week. (E. Burnblum) Outing, **26**: 237.
— in Fact and Fiction. Blackw. **158**: 880. Same art. Ecl. M. **126**: 145.
— in the Long Vacation. Macmil. **74**: 274.
— in the Middle Ages. (F. C. Montague) Time, **17**: 53.
— in the '70s, Recollections of. Sund. M. **23**: 764.
— in the 13th Century. Macmil. **73**: 99.
— in Vacation. (E. L. Didier) Chaut. **16**: 177.
— Is it a University? (R. Jones) Educa. R. **9**: 485.
— Law Studies. (Sir F. Pollock) Law Q. **2**: 453.
— May Term at. (F. Adye) Good Words, **37**: 388. Same art. Ecl. M. **127**: 116.
— Memories of. (W. C. Lake) Good Words, **36**: 828.
— — in the Pre-æsthetic Age. (T. H. Escott) National, **24**: 232.
— Michaelmas Term at. (F. Adye) Bach. of Arts, **3**: 522. — (F. Adye) Good Words, **36**: 748. Same art. Ecl. M. **125**: 784.

Oxford, Modern Aspects of. (A. D. Godley) Portfo. **24**: 103–219.
— Museum of, Reforms in. (E. S. Goodrich) Nat. Sci. **5**: 128.
— My Days at. (E. H. Knatchbull-Hugessen) Time, **1**: 682.
— The New. (T. Arnold) Spec. **72**: 232, 267, 299.
— The New Degrees at. (W. C. Abbott) Nation, **62**: 321.
— Origin of. (A. F. Leach) National, **28**: 93. — (J. H. Round) Ath. '**96**, **1**: 810.
— Personal Recollections of. (Canon Oakeley) Time, **2**: 675.
— Poverty of. Chr. Lit. **12**: 43.
— Practical; a reply to Goldwin Smith. (L. A. Selby-Bigge) Contemp. **65**: 722.
— Press of. Book R. **3**: 155.
— — Editing of. Sat. R. **78**: 591, 602.
— Revisited. (G. Smith) Fortn. **61**: 149.
— St. Mary Hall. (W. K. Stride) Gent. M. n. s. **57**: 494.
— Science at. Nature, **54**: 225.
— Student-life at. (F. Grundy) Chaut. **22**: 312.
— Taylorian Galleries. M. of Art, **1**: 214.
— Three Centuries of. Macmil. **66**: 445.
— Undergraduate at, in the '40s. Sat. R. **74**: 590.
— Undergraduate Life at. (R. H. Davis) Harper, **87**: 779.
— Union, The. (E. H. Knatchbull-Hugessen) Time, **2**: 146.
— *versus* Cambridge. Temp. Bar, **101**: 371.
— *versus* Yale. (W. H. Grenfell) Fortn. **62**: 368.
— Wadham College. (P. A. Wright-Henderson) Blackw. **159**: 668.
— — Alumni of. (J. S. Cotton) Acad. **47**: 439.
— Zoölogy at. (S. J. Hickson) Nature, **52**: 549.
Oxfordshire, Palæolithic Remains in. (A. M. Ball) Antiq. n. s. **30**: 148, 192.
Oxus River, Source of. (G. N. Curzon) Geog. J. **8**: 15, 97, 239.
Oxygen and Hydrogen, Relative Densities of. (Lord Rayleigh) Nature, **46**: 101.
— Atmospheric, Origin of. (T. L. Phipson) J. Frankl. Inst. **142**: 436.
— in Air and in Aqueous Solution, Determination of. (D. A. Kreider) Am. J. Sci. **152**: 361.
— Liquid. (G. D. Liveing) Science, **20**: 169.
— — Magnetic Properties of. (J. Dewar) Nature, **48**: 89.
— Resuscitation by. Dub. R. **113**: 651.
— Spectrum of, in High Temperatures, Janssen on. Nature, **50**: 249.
— — Lime. (B. Hasselberg) Astron. **13**: 760.
Oyster Police, With the. (D. B. Fitzgerald) Lippinc. **56**: 699.
Oyster Supply of the U. S., Conservation of. (R. F. Walsh) Pop. Sci. Mo. **44**: 1.
Oysters, and Oyster Culture. (W. F. Nelson) Time, **18**: 327.
— Brightlingsea. (A. H. Japp) Argosy, **62**: 540.
— Culture of, and Disease. (T. E. Thorpe) Nature, **55**: 105.
— — in France. Chamb. J. **70**: 702. Same art. Liv. Age, **199**: 634.
— — on West Coast of France. Nature, **51**: 162.
— Pacific Coast. (J. G. Cooper) Overland, n. s. **23**: 648.
Ozark Mountains, Rambling Notes from. (L. S. La Mance) Garden & F. **5**: 526.
Ozark Series, Cambrian and. (G. C. Broadhead) Am. J. Sci. **146**: 57.
— Classification of. (A. Winslow) Am. J. Sci. **145**: 221.
Ozème's Holiday. (K. Chopin) Cent. **30**: 629.
Pablo's Fiesta. (H. E. Bandini) Overland, n. s. **24**: 70.
Pachanga, The Murder at. (M. W. Emerson) Lend a H. **15**: 279.
Pacific City, Mexico, and the Credit Foncier. (A. K. Owen) Lend a H. **9**: 344.
Pacific Encounter, A; a story. (M. E. Stickney) Lippinc. **51**: 3.
Pacific Ocean, Eastern, Dredging Operations in. (A. Agassiz) Nature, **45**: 281.
— Growing Greatness of. (L. A. Thurston) No. Am. **160**: 446.
— Influence of, on Political Relations. (Hyde Clarke) Asia. R. **10**: 273.
— Mystery of. (O. Smeaton) Westm. **144**: 29.
— Naval Control of. (M. Manson) Overland, n. s. **25**: 56.
— Northern, Seaside Resorts on. (F. F. Victor) Overland, n. s. **23**: 138.
— Western, Life in. (A. Inkersly) Chaut. **23**: 446.
Pacific Railroad, Indebtedness of, Funding the. (G. L. Johnson) Overland, n. s. **28**: 491.
Pacific Railroad Companies and the People of the Trans-Mississippi States. (G. H. Smith) Am. Law R. **29**: 189.
Pacific Railroad Debts. (R. T. Colburn) Ann. Am. Acad. Pol. Sci. **5**: 684. — (H. K. White) J. Pol. Econ. **2**: 424.
Packard, Silas S., with portrait. (J. H. Kennedy) Nat'l M. (N. Y. '91) **15**: 205.
Packet Lines, Boston and Liverpool. (H. A. Hill) New Eng. M. n. s. **9**: 545.
Packet-service, The Old. Macmil. **74**: 34. Same art. Liv. Age, **209**: 561.
Pacú Fishing on the Upper Paraguay. (H. H. Smith) Outing, **21**: 228.
Paddy Casey's Covey. (T. S. Blackwell) Outing, **24**: 424.
Paddy's Wife. (J. Mackie) Chamb. J. **73**: 269.
Paderewski. (W. Mason; F. M. Smith) Cent. **21**: 721. — (M. Bacheller) Munsey, **6**: 683. — Music, **1**: 83.
— and Liszt. (H. T. Finck) Nation, **56**: 308.
— in America. (H. T. Finck) Forum, **15**: 416.
— Playing of. Music, **1**: 587.
Padre's Earthly Hope; a story. (J. C. Bull) Munsey, **13**: 583.
Pæstum, A Day at. Argosy, **54**: Summer no., 28.
Pagan Review. (F. M. Bird) Lippinc. **51**: 249.
Paganiniana. Liv. Age, **192**: 760.
Paganism, Decay of. (E. Belfort Bax) Time, **22**: 52.
— Impending, in New England. (W. D. Hyde) Forum, **13**: 519.
— Influence of, upon Christianity. (F. W. Farrar) Sund. M. **21**: 730.
— Last Days of. Church Q. **34**: 162.
— New. Spec. **72**: 191.
— Roman, Christianity and. (St. G. Mivart) Chr. Lit. **10**: 56 a.
Pagans, Latter-day. Quar. **182**: 31. Same art. Liv. Age, **206**: 707.
Page, Richard Channing Moore, with portrait. Nat'l M. (N. Y. '91) **16**: 475.
Page, Thos. N., with portrait. Bk. Buyer, **4**: 284. — With portrait. Bk. News, **7**: 148.
Page from the Future, A; a story. (H. C. Davidson) Idler, **9**: 865.
Page from a Vicar's History. (F. Henniker) Eng. Illust. **13**: 379.
Page of Philosophy, A. Macmil. **72**: 389. Same art. Ecl. M. **125**: 667.
Pages from a Private Diary. Cornh. **74**: 93–817. Same art. Liv. Age, **210**: 688–731. **211**: 53.

Paget, Admiral Clarence E. Autobiography and Journals; ed. by Otway. Ed. R. **184**: 135. — Sat. R. **81**: 583, 654. — (W. Grey) Acad. **50**: 213. — (E. G. Johnson) Dial (Ch.) **21**: 34.
Pagliaccio's Courtship, The. (J. P. Rudd) Outing, **23**: 419.
Paheri, Tomb of, Tylor's. Sat. R. **80**: 602.
Pahlavi Texts translated by E. W. West. (J. G. R. Forlong) Asia. R. **16**: 410.
Pailleron, M. Cabotins. (A. Laugel) Nation, **58**: 211.
Pain, Barry. Critic, **21**: 73.
Pain and Pleasure. (B. I. Gilman) Am. J. Psychol. **6**: 3. — (A. Bain) Mind, **17**: 161. — (P. Carus) Open Court, **3**: 1987.
— — defined. (S. E. Mezes) Philos. R. **4**: 22.
— — in Education. (M. S. Gilliland) Int. J. Ethics, **2**: 289.
— — Origin of. (H. Nichols) Philos. R. **1**: 403, 518.
— Mystery of, in a New Light. (X. Clark) Open Court, **1**: 428.
— Physical. (H. R. Marshall) Psychol. R. **2**: 594.
— — and Pain Nerves. (C. A. Strong) Psychol. R. **3**: 64.
— Pleasure and Æsthetics, Marshall's. (W. James) Nation, **59**: 49.
— Psychology of. (C. A. Strong) Psychol. R. **2**: 329.
— Sensibility to. (H. Griffing) Psychol. R. **3**: 412.
Pain Nerves. (H. Nichols) Psychol. R. **2**: 487. **3**: 309.
Pains and Pleasures, Pathological. (T. Ribot) Monist, **6**: 176.
— Ribot on. (P. Carus) Monist, **6**: 432.
Paine, Henry W. (W. Matthews) New Eng. M. n. s. **10**: 189.
Paine, John Knowles. Music, **4**: 256.
Paine, Thomas. Acad. **50**: 519. — (E. P. Powell) Arena, **8**: 717. — (L. Stephen) Fortn. **60**: 267. — (R. G. Ingersoll) No. Am. **155**: 171. — (J. W. Chadwick) New World, **1**: 468. — (M. D. Conway) Open Court, **8**: 3951–4199.
— and Charles Bradlaugh. (M. D. Conway) Open Court, **5**: 2725.
— and Madame Bonneville. (M. D. Conway) Nation, **54**: 8.
— and the Republic of the World. (M. D. Conway) New Sci. R. **1**: 24.
— Conway's Life of. Ath. '92, **2**: 512. — (W. Lewin) Acad. **41**: 559. — Dial (Ch.) **13**: 132. — (J. W. Chadwick) Nation, **55**: 51. — Sat. R. **74**: 511. — Spec. **69**: 529. — Westm. **138**: 469.
— Escape of, from the Guillotine. (M. D. Conway) Ath. '94, **2**: 32, 97, 255, 288.
— Exhibition in London. (M. D. Conway) Nation, **62**: 10.
— the "Man without a Country" 100 Years Ago. (M. D. Conway) Nation, **59**: 477.
— A Minister *malgré lui*. (M. D. Conway) Nation, **60**: 87.
— Unpublished Letter of. (M. D. Conway) Nation, **62**: 118, 471. — Open Court, **5**: 3039.
Paine-Condorcet Declaration of Rights of 1793. (M. D. Conway) Open Court, **6**: 3159.
Painted Pavement at Tell-el-Amarna. (W. F. Petrie) Illus. Archæol. **1**: 204.
Painter, The; a poem. Canad. M. **5**: 469.
Painter I knew, A; a story. (W. W. Fenn) Art J. **44**: 275.
Painter's Art in England. (H. Townsend) Chaut. **20**: 259.
Painters. (H. Spencer) Contemp. **69**: 391. Same art. Pop. Sci. Mo. **4**: 697.
Painters and Critics: French and English. Ed. R. **183**: 143.
— Chats with. (W. Wood) Cent. **25**: 187.
— Dutch and French. (S. Beale) Am. Arch. **52**: 35.
— Early English. (E. Ollier) M. of Art, **7**: 515.
— French Gossip about some. (J. A. Blaikie) M. of Art, **6**: 234.
— Honors paid to. M. of Art, **5**: 85.
— Idealistic. (Margaret Field) Munsey, **9**: 587.
— Italian, Early, Art Studentship of. (J. P. Richter) 19th Cent. **32**: 271. Same art. Liv. Age, **194**: 799.
— — Morelli's. Ed. R. **176**: 329. — Sat. R. **74**: 172. — Spec. **69**: 534. — Liv. Age, **196**: 323.
— Karel van Mander's Book of the. M. of Art, **8**: 302.
— Multitude of, Whence comes? (M. B. Huish) 19th Cent. **32**: 720.
— Norwegian. (H. H. Boyesen) Scrib. M. **12**: 756.
— of Animals. (E. L. Grundy) M. of Art, **14**: 388.
— of Romanticism. (C. E. Meetkerke) Temp. Bar, **108**: 154.
— Portraits of. (J. P. Brodhurst) M. of Art, **10**: 300.
— Precocity of. (J. Oldcastle) M. of Art, **4**: 206.
— Relative Productiveness of. (J. A. Blaikie) M. of Art, **7**: 334.
— Women, Famous. (R. H. Titherington) Munsey, **12**: 261.
— — Some Noted. (H. L. Postlethwaite) M. of Art, **18**: 17.
— Venetian, of the Renaissance, Berenson on. (J. B. Fletcher) Dial (Ch.) **16**: 268.
Painting, British, in 1893. (W. Armstrong) Art J. **46**: 1.
— Classical, in France. (E. M. Ward) Mo. Illust. **12**: 239.
— Composition in. M. of Art, **7**: 434–489.
— Decorative, of the 19th Century, Havard's. (R. Sturgis) Archit. Rec. **5**: 94.
— Dutch, Contemporary. (L. G. Derby) So. M. **5**: 325.
— Effects of Light and Air in. (A. M. F. Robinson) M. of Art, **6**: 462.
— English. (W. H. Low) McClure, **6**: 256.
— — Pre-Raphaelite Brotherhood. (W. H. Low) McClure, **7**: 65.
— Fresco, Method of. (R. Rodd) Time, **8**: 642.
— Historical, in France. (F. Masson) Art J. **45**: 320. — (P. Gsell) Pub. Opin. **15**: 304.
— History of, by Woltmann & Woermann. M. of Art, **4**: 254.
— — Van Dyke's. Sat. R. **79**: 19.
— in America, Early Religious. (C. E. Clement) New Eng. M. n. s. **11**: 387.
— in England; Royal Academy. (D. S. McColl) Fortn. **59**: 881.
— in France. (W. H. Low) McClure, **6**: 145, 465. **7**: 293.
— — Realistic. (E. M. Ward) Mo. Illust. **12**: 443. — (W. C. Brownell) Scrib. M. **12**: 604.
— — Romantic. (E. M. Ward) Mo. Illust. **12**: 334. — (W. C. Brownell) Scrib. M. **12**: 431.
— — The Two Salons. (E. R. Pennell) Fortn. **59**: 774.
— in Germany. (W. H. Low) McClure, **7**: 161.
— in Italy. (W. H. Low) McClure, **7**: 225.
— in the 19th Century. Spec. **73**: 211. — (W. H. Low) McClure, **6**: 337.
— Italian, Kugler's Schools of. (J. Cartwright) M. of Art, **10**: 277.
— Modern. (W. H. Low) McClure, **7**: 415.
— — Muther's History of. (K. Cox) Nation, **63**: 368.
— Modern Religions. (P. R. Paulding) Munsey, **15**: 3.

Painting of Apelles. (W. von Schierbrand) Lippinc. **58**: 426.
— Painters, and Portraits. (H. S. Wilson) M. of Art, **1**: 230.
— Scottish School of. Blackw. **157**: 335.
— A Word about. (W. A. Coffin) Scrib. M. **15**: 499.
— Worship of the Ugly. (C. Monkhouse) National, **27**: 124.
Painting, House. Plea for Warm Tints. (M. C. Robbins) Garden & F. **5**: 189.
Paintings and Sculptures as Histrionic Studies. (W. Shaw-Sparrow) Art J. **47**: 27–85.
— Early Italian in the Jarves Collection at Yale College. (W. Rankin) Am. J. Archæol. **10**: 137.
— Famous, owned on the West Coast. Overland, n. s. **21**: 2. **22**: 634. **23**: 84–174.
— Famous Boston. (J. L. Wright) Bost. **3**: 413.
— Greek: Philostratus' Ancient Picture Gallery. (A. S. Murray) M. of Art, **5**: 371.
— of Old Masters, Recent Exhibitions of. (J. P. Richter) Art J. **47**: 88.
Paints and Painting, Chemistry of. (E. Bale) M. of Art, **14**: 50.
— — — Church on. (H. Müller) Nature, **45**: 241.
— Artist his own Color-maker. (A. P. Laurie) M. of Art, **15**: 115.
Pair of Glasses, A; a story. (G. L. Bent) Outing, **28**: 17.
Pair of Lovers, A. Cornh. **66**: 387. Same art. Liv. Age, **195**: 530.
Pair of Twins. (A. E. P. Searing) New Eng. M. n. s. **10**: 216.
Paisano, El, Enemy of the Rattlesnake. (T. N. Moyle) Overland, n. s. **23**: 462.
Pakua the Outlaw. (N. B. Emerson) Overland, n. s. **25**: 638.
Palace of Pan; a poem. (A. C. Swinburne) 19th Cent. **34**: 501. Same art. Ecl. M. **121**: 676.
Palæarctic and Nearctic Regions as to their Mammalia and Ibids. (A. R. Wallace; G. H. Carpenter) Nat. Sci. **4**: 433. **5**: 53.
Palæobotany and Evolution. (A. C. Seward) Sci. Prog. **1**: 108.
Palæolithic and Neolithic Period. (B. Dawkins) Anthrop. J. **23**: 242.
— — Continuity of. (J. A. Brown) Anthrop. J. **22**: 66.
Palæolithic Culture, Gravel Man and. (W. H. Holmes) Science, **21**: 29.
Palæolithic Floor near Dunstable, Eng. (W. G. Smith) Nat. Sci. **1**: 664.
Palæolithic Man in North America. (H. W. Haynes) Am. Antiq. **15**: 37.
Palæontology and the Biogenetic Law. (K. von Zittel) Nat. Sci. **6**: 305.
— Antarctic. (W. B. Scott) Science, n. s. **3**: 307.
— as a Morphological Discipline. (W. B. Scott) Science, n. s. **4**: 177.
— Avian, Recent Discoveries in. (C. W. Andrews) Sci. Prog. **5**: 398.
— Woods'. Sat. R. **79**: 287.
Palæopathology, Notes on. (R. W. Shufeldt) Pop. Sci. Mo. **42**: 679.
Palæospondylus, Devonian. (T. Gill) Science, n. s. **4**: 10.
Palæosyops, Parallelism in the Genus. (C. Earle) Am. Natural. **29**: 622.
Palæozoic Plants, A Type of. (A. C. Seward) Sci. Prog. **3**: 394.
Palæozoic Rocks, Lower, Life-zones in. (J. E. Marr) Nat. Sci. **1**: 134.
Palapye, South Africa, Visit to. (H. J. S. Mowell) Belgra. **91**: 294.
Palawan, Island of. Dub. R. **118**: 174.
Pale Girl's Face, A; the History of a Scoop. (E. Macpherson) Harper, **88**: 669.
Palemonium of the Lake Region. (E. J. Hill) Garden & F. **5**: 448.
Palenque Tablet, The. (C. Thomas) Science, **19**: 328.
Palermo, Italy. Around World, **1**: 58.
— Exhibition at, 1892. (J. W. Mario) Nation, **54**: 208.
— Principal Buildings of. (W. Wallis) Art J. **45**: 230.
— Quaint Customs of an Island Capital. (W. Cady-Scott) Cosmopol. **16**: 285.
Palestine and Egypt, 1400 B. C. (M. Jastrow, jr.) J. Bib. Lit. **11**: 95.
— — Prehistoric Times in. (J. W. Dawson) No. Am. **154**: 672. **155**: 68.
— Cities of, Early. (E. L. Curtis) Bib. World, **7**: 411.
— Cradle of Christianity. (J. Wells) Sund. M. **25**: 599.
— A Day in. (J. Wells) Sund. M. **25**: 261.
— Diary in. Spec. **69**: 286.
— Early. (W. H. Ward) Bib. World, **7**: 401.
— Excavations in. N. Church R. **1**: 461.
— The Favorite Walk in. (J. Wells) Sund. M. **24**: 751.
— From, to Attica. Spec. **69**: 319.
— Future of, Conder's. Spec. **69**: 962.
— Geography of. (J. S. Riggs) Bib. World, **4**: 1–421. **5**: 36.
— Historical Geography of. (C. Trotter) Geog. J. **4**: 450. — Sat. R. **78**: 50.
— — Smith's. Church Q. **40**: 371. — (C. R. Conder) Crit. R. **4**: 287.
— in 1400. (H. Zimmer) M. Chr. Lit. **5**: 357.
— Industries of. (W. M. Statham) Sund. M. **21**: 21, 185.
— Journey to, in 1480. Sat. R. **74**: 386.
— Patriarchal, Sayce's. Sat. R. **81**: 434.
— Pilgrims of. Ed. R. **177**: 63.
— Research in, Past and Future. (C. R. Conder) Contemp. **66**: 404.
Palgrave, Francis Turner, as a Poet. (E. K. Chambers) Acad. **43**: 29.
— Golden Treasury. Sat. R. **82**: 311. — (W. M. Dixon) Westm. **143**: 401.
— Vision of Life. Sat. R. **73**: 43. — Spec. **68**: 127.
Pâli and Prâkrit Words, Notes on. (R. Morris) Acad. **42**: 94–315.
Palisades of the Hudson, How to save. (C. S. Sargent) Garden & F. **7**: 391. **8**: 31.
Palissy, Bernard. (F. M. Robinson) M. of Art, **8**: 22.
— and his Work. (Mrs. C. R. Corson) Chaut. **15**: 330.
Pall Mall, My Campaign in. (A. Forbes) Univ. R. **3**: 373.
Palladia from Mycenæ. (E. A. Gardner) J. Hel. Stud. **13**: 21.
Palladio, Andrea. (A. Gilman) Am. Arch. **39**: 138.
Pallinsburn Gull Pond. (P. A. Graham) Longm. **27**: 75.
Pallium, The. (H. Thurston) Month, **75**: 305.
Palm, A British. (A. B. Rendle) Nat. Sci. **5**: 202.
Palm-oil at the Porte. Cornh. **70**: 598.
Palm Tree, California Fan. Garden & F. **8**: 472.
Palma, Caldera of. Cornh. **69**: 84. Same art. Liv. Age, **300**: 429.
Palmer, Sir Charles M., and Jarrow-on-Tyne. (F. Dolman) Eng. Illust. **12**: no. 5, 62.
Palmer, George, and the Town of Reading. (F. Dolman) Eng. Illust. **13**: 419.
Palmer, John M., Election to the U. S. Senate from Ill. in 1891. (W. H. Maguire) Nat'l M. (N. Y. '91) **15**: 97.
Palmer, Roundell. *See* **Selborne, Earl of.**

Palmer, Samuel. Ath. '92, 1: 441. — Sat. R. 73: 486. — (A. T. Story) Temp. Bar, 97: 79.
— Exhibition of Pictures by. M. of Art, 5: 122.
Palmerston, Lord. (J. A. Hamilton) Acad. 41: 559.
— Borough of. (T. J. M'Cormack) Open Court, 9: 4604, 4609.
— Marquis of Lorne's. Spec. 68: 371.
— The Queen and. (R. B. Brett) 19th Cent. 35: 912. Same art. Liv. Age, 202: 67.
Palmerston Ideal in Diplomacy. (E. M. Chapman) Cent. 29: 541.
Palmetto. (A. Kinney) Garden & F. 5: 215.
— Northern Limits of. (W. F. Massey) Garden & F. 5: 189.
Palmistry. Sat. R. 73: 146. 76: 238.
— as a Fine Art. (W. L. Courtney) Univ. R. 4: 401.
— Hands as Indicative of Character, etc. New Sci. R. 1: 442.
— in China and Japan. (S. Culin) Overland, n. s. 23: 476.
— Some Noteworthy Hands. (E. M. Forbes) New R. 10: 691.
Palms at Federal Point, Florida. (H. Wehrling) Garden & F. 6: 131.
— at Kew Gardens. Garden & F. 5: 398, 401.
— Bismarckia Nobilis. (W. Watson) Garden & F. 6: 244.
— Chemadarea Gladifolia. Garden & F. 8: 504.
— Cultivated in California. (J. C. Harvey) Garden & F. 6: 104.
— Notes on. (N. J. Rose) Garden & F. 8: 466.
— Tree, of the U. S. (C. S. Sargent) Garden & F. 9: 151.
— Washingtonia Filipera. Garden & F. 6: 535.
Paludina Vivipara, Development of. (M. M. Metcalf) Am. Natural. 26: 708.
Pamedomcook, Canoeing on the. (W. A. Brooks) Outing, 28: 361.
Pamela's Novel. (F. Madoc) Argosy, 57: 381.
Pamirs, The. Am. Natural. 27: 257. — (R. Michell) Asia. R. 14: 263. — (G. N. Curzon) Geog. J. 8: 15, 97, 239. — (F. E. Younghusband) J. Soc. Arts, 40: 292.
— and Adjacent Countries, Younghusband on. Nature, 45: 353. — Dub. R. 110: 450.
— and their Inhabitants. Dub. R. 114: 430.
— Dunmore on. Spec. 73: 752, supp. — Geog. J. 3: 115. — Nature, 49: vi.
— From Tian Shan to the. (H. Jones) J. Soc. Arts, 40: 202.
— Journeyings in. (Earl of Dunmore) Geog. J. 2: 385.
— Question of. Quar. 175: 507.
— Recent Events. Asia. R. 13: 17.
— Russia and. Spec. 69: 311. — Liv. Age, 192: 323. — (A. Vámbéry) New R. 7: 262.
— Travels through the Country of. Dub. R. 116: 409.
Pampas. (P. Kropotkin) Geog. J. 3: 318.
Pampas Grass and Pomegranate in California. (H. W. R. Strong) Overland, n. s. 25: 421.
Pampas Plumes. (S. E. A. Higgins) Overland, n. s. 21: 373.
Pamphlets. (H. M. Saunders) Temp. Bar, 108: 82.
— Ecclesiastical, Wars of. (G. L. Apperson) Gent. M. n. s. 53: 413.
— in Libraries. (W. Austin) Lib. J. 18: 143. — (W. S. Biscoe) Lib. J. 18: 236.
Pamunkey, Mystery of the Name. (W. W. Tooker) Am. Antiq. 17: 289.
Pan-making, Metal, in England. (A. W. C. Hallen) Walford's Antiq. 12: 150.
Panaceas, Moral. Spec. 71: 574.
Panaenus, Paintings by, on the Throne of the Olympian Zeus. (E. A. Gardner) J. Hel. Stud. 14: 233.
Panama. (M. E. Haines) New Eng. M. n. s. 14: 59.
— and Darien, A Trip to. (Richard U. Goode) Nat. Geog. M. 1: 301.
— Two Days on the Isthmus of. (W. S. Hale) So. M. 3: 343.
— Up the Coast from. (W. S. Hale) So. M. 4: 553.
Panama Canal, The. Macmil. 72: 321. — Pub. Opin. 14: 177.
— as it is. Chamb. J. 73: 558.
— President Carnot and. Spec. 69: 945.
— Condition of, 1892. (E. H. Seymour) 19th Cent. 31: 293.
— from a Car Window. (P. Stamford) Overland, n. s. 22: 104.
— New Company. Sat. R. 78: 482.
— Possibilities of a. (R. Ogden) Nation, 56: 229.
— Present Condition of. (O. A. F. Saabye) Engin. M. 7: 830.
— Route of. (R. T. Hill) Nat. Geog. M. 7: 59.
— Scandal of. (Maurice Barrès) Cosmopol. 17: 203. — (E. L. Godkin) Nation, 55: 426–490. — Pub. Opin. 14: 277, 563. 15: 286. — Sat. R. 74: 610. 75: 286, 313. — Spec. 69: 756–877. — (C. Schefer) Nation, 56: 7.
— — After the. (L. Andrieux) New R. 8: 374.
— — De Lesseps and. (G. W. Hinman) Chaut. 16: 587.
— — Mad. Cottu's Charge. Spec. 70: 344.
— State of the Works at. Dub. R. 118: 180.
— Story of a Colossal Bubble. (L. Lambert) Forum, 15: 12.
Panama Canal Congress, Recollections of the. (D. Ammen) No. Am. 156: 136.
Pan-Britannic Gathering, The. (J. A. Cooper) 19th Cent. 34: 81.
Pandean Pastimes. (F. D. Bergen) Atlan. 77: 625.
Pandora, Making of. (A. H. Smith) J. Hel. Stud. 11: 278.
Pandora; a story. (E. Y. Farmer) Canad. M. 3: 249.
Pandore; or, Les Deux Gensdarmes. Translated from the French of Nadaud. (Annie G. Wilson) Temp. Bar, 103: 219.
Pangeometry, Subconscious. Monist, 7: 100.
Panglima Muda, The. (R. Wildman) Overland, n. s. 24: 51–390.
Panic, Causes of. (H. C. Ager) Am. J. Pol. 4: 233.
— Facts touching a Revival of Business. Forum, 18: 379.
— of 1873. Bank. M. (N. Y.) 46: 392. — (H. White) Nation, 57: 76.
— of 1893. (W. Knapp) Am. J. Pol. 4: 656.
— — and the Banks. Bank. M. (N. Y.) 48: 721.
— — and the Credit Contraction in Europe. Bank. M. (Lond.) 57: 49.
— — and the Silver Movement. (A. B. and H. Farquhar) Am. J. Pol. 5: 84.
— — Bimetallist's View of. (A. F. Higgins) Outl. 48: 257.
— — Monometallist's View of. (L. Windmüller) Outl. 48: 257.
— — Phenomena of. (A. C. Stevens) Q. J. Econ. 8: 117.
— — Wage-earners' Loss during the Depression. (S. W. Dike) Forum, 18: 369.
Panics. (F. C. Howe) Am. J. Pol. 5: 449.
— and their Causes. (J. F. Bullitt) Southern M. 4: 394. — (J. W. Bennett) Arena, 9: 493.
— Periodicity of. (N. C. Frederiksen) Bank. M. (Lond.) 53: 189.
— — in the U. S. (E. V. Grabil) Am. M. Civics, 8: 366.
— Repression of. Spec. 71: 869.
See Financial.
Panlogism. (P. Carus) Monist, 7: 82.
Panmixia. (G. J. Romanes and others) Nature, 49: 599. 50: 5, 28, 196.
— Note on. (G. J. Romanes) Contemp. 64: 611.

Pannemaker, Stéphane; Wood Engraver. Scrib. M. 17: 601.
Panoply; a poem. (J. Cook) Our Day, 14: 120.
Pan-Slavism, Doctrine of. (S. Thomoff) Meth. R. 52: 259.
Pansychism and Panbiotism. (P. Carus) Monist, 3: 234.
Pantasote. J. Frankl. Inst. 142: 88.
Pantheism, Destruction of Boundaries by. (A. Kuyper) Meth. R. 53: 520, 762.
— Modern, and Gnosticism. (G. J. Stokes) Mind, 20: 320.
— Plea for. (H. Hensoldt) Arena, 12: 161.
Pantheon, New Facts concerning. (R. Lanciani) Atlan. 71: 721.
Panther-shooting in Central India. (C. J. Melliss) Scrib. M. 20: 529.
Pantomime, at Drury Lane Theatre, London. Idler, 9: 139.
— The "Book" of. (T. E. Pemberton) Theatre, 36: 25.
— Decadence of. (C. Dickens) Theatre, 36: 21.
— English, Genesis of. (W. J. Lawrence) Theatre, 34: 28.
— in the U. S. (W. J. Lawrence) Theatre, 36: 83.
— Origin of. Theatre, 29: 260.
— Revival of the. (T. C. Crawford) Cosmopol. 16: 278.
Paola in Italy; a story. (G. Hall) Harper, 90: 40.
Paolo Santi; a true tale. (A. Beresford) Argosy, 53: 329.
Paolo's Model; a story. (P. W. Roose) Argosy, 55: 285.
Papacy, The. (H. R. Haweis) Chr. Lit. 11: 230.
— and the Early Fathers. Church Q. 38: 27.
— and Italy. Spec. 75: 388.
— and the Primitive Church. Church Q. 39: 273. — (W. H. Kent) Dub. R. 115: 387.
— and the Primitive Saints. (L. Rivington) Dub. R. 113: 626.
— and the Revolution. Eng. R. 9: 255.
— and the U. S. (E. McGlynn) Forum, 16: 11.
— Church Unity and. (L. Johnston) Cath. World, 61: 433.
— Claims of, and the Primitive Church. Church Q. 39: 1.
— Creighton's History of. Church Q. 39: 357. — Dub. R. 116: 438.
— Early, Lightfoot on. Dub. R. 113: 836.
— France and. (C. B. R. Kent) Macmil. 67: 179.
— History of, during Reformation, Creighton's. Ath. '94, 2: 181.
— in Exile. Eng. R. 12: 344.
— Italy and. (R. Mariano) Int. J. Ethics, 4: 206, (F. Satoli) 347.
— Nationality and Residence of the next Pope. (B. O'Reilly) Am. Cath. Q. 17: 1.
— Origin and Authority of. (D. C. Butler) Dub. R. 113: 497.
— Pflugk-Harttung's Works on. (R. L. Poole) Eng. Hist. R. 7: 551.
— Policy of, towards America. Cath. World, 61: 528.
— Position and Aims of. (J. W. Gambier) Fortn. 64: 19. Same art. Chr. Lit. 13: 310.
— Temporal Power of, End of. Macmil. 72: 472.
— Territorial Sovereignty and. (B. O'Reilly) No. Am. 158: 211.
Papal Bull *In Cœna Domini*. Eng. R. 9: 96.
Papal Conclaves. Quar. 184: 505.
Papal Jurisdiction in Mediæval England. (J. Moyes) Dub. R. 115: 411.
Papal Supremacy. Eng. R. 8: 106.
Papaw Fruit. (L. C. Corbet) Garden & F. 8: 494.
Pape, Abraham de. Portfo. 24: 67.
Pape, W. A. C. (N. Crinkle) Mo. Illust. 3: 333.
Paper. All the Year, 75: 442.
— and Ink, Best. (R. T. Swan) Lib. J. 20: 163.
— Making of. (A. A. Black) Chaut. 17: 289.
— News, Making, from Wood. (G. B. Hanford) Engin. M. 3: 809.
— Recent Applications of. (E. Ratoin) Pop. Sci. Mo. 42: 207.
— Soluble. Chamb. J. 72: 22, 286.
— Water-marks on. (E. E. Thoyts) Antiq. n. s. 31: 326, 356.
Paper Currency, An International. (J. F. Hume) Am. M. Civics, 6: 48.
Paper Dollar, The. (M. M. Trumbull) Open Court, 3: 1609.
Paper-making Industry. (J. F. Hobart) Engin. M. 2: 488.
Paper Mill, A Natural. (V. G. Eaton) Pop. Sci. Mo. 48: 278.
— Rittenhouse, first erected in America. (H. G. Jones) Pennsyl. M. 20: 315.
Paper Money. (W. J. Gordon) Leis. Hour, 45: 21.
— Conditions for American Commercial and Financial Supremacy. (P. Leroy-Beaulieu) Forum, 20: 385.
— Government, An Appeal to retire. (M. Brühl) Forum, 15: 83.
— A New System of. (S. B. Gordon) Am. J. Pol. 4: 84.
— of Canada, 1685-1766. (R. M. Breckenridge) J. Pol. Econ. 1: 406.
Paper-staining, The Art and Craft of. (L. F. Day) Good Words, 36: 244.
Papias of Hieropolis, The Oracles ascribed to Matthew by. (A. Wright) Crit. R. 5: 11.
Papineau and his Home. (T. P. Gorman) Canad. M. 3: 237.
Papinian. (N. J. D. Kennedy) Jurid. R. 5: 297.
Papua, Picturesque. (O. M. Spencer) Cosmopol. 18: 653.
Papyri, Further Gleanings from. (J. P. Mahaffy) New R. 9: 526. Same art. Liv. Age, 199: 696. Same art. Ecl. M. 122: 24.
— Greek. (J. P. Mahaffy) Chaut. 16: 413.
— — in British Museum. Ath. '94, 1: 108.
— — Catalogue of. (B. P. Grenfell) Acad. 45: 60.
— Petrie Collection. Acad. 42: 267. — Ath. '92, 1: 111. — (J. P. Mahaffy) Ath. '92, 2: 160-818. — (J. P. Mahaffy) New R. 7: 549. Same art. Liv. Age, 196: 3.
— — Mahaffy on. (E. G. Mason) Dial (Ch.) 13: 49. — Ath. '94, 1: 472, 511.
— Recent Publications of. Church Q. 39: 88.
Papyrus Plant, The. (G. Ebers) Cosmopol. 15: 677.
Parable of the Sower. (R. W. Dale) Good Words, 35: 713.
Parables of Life. (Emilia F. S. Dilke) Univ. R. 5: 535.
Paracelsus, Theophrastus. (M. M. P. Muir) Nature, 50: 599.
Paradoxes, A Bundle of. Chamb. J. 72: 650.
Paragraph, Tyranny of the. (A. Waugh) National, 20: 743. Same art. Ecl. M. 120: 474.
— In Defence of the. (O. A. Fry) National, 21: 38.
Paraguay. (A. F. Baillie) J. Soc. Arts, 43: 353. — Lond. Q. 83: 74.
— Bibliography of. (R. Garnett) Bibliographica, 1: 262.
— A New Land of Promise. Chamb. J. 71: 97.
Paraguay River, Boggiani's Explorations among Tribes along. (H. H. Giglioli) Nature, 53: 545.
Parallax, A Lesson in. (O. E. Harmon) Pop. Astron. 1: 403.
Paramnesia, Prevalence of. (M. B. Simmons) Psychol. R. 2: 367.

Paraphernalia, Question as to. (T. F. Utley) Am. Law R. **30**: 556.
Paraphrases, Scripture, Scottish. (J. C. Hadden) Scot. R. **22**: 292.
Paraschos, Achilles. (E. M. Edmonds) Acad. **47**: 169.
Parasites. (A. E. Shipley) Sci. Prog. **1**: 78.
— Social. Spec. **71**: 108.
Parasitic Fungi of North American Forest-trees. (J. G. Jack) Garden & F. **5**: 37.
Parcel Post, A very Old. Walford's Antiq. **4**: 57.
Pardon of Gustave Majano; play in one act. (M. Pemberton) Eng. Illust. **16**: 270.
Pardoning Power. Lend a H. **14**: 141. — (M. M. Trumbull) Open Court, **7**: 3879.
Parenthesis, A; a story. (P. Trent) Argosy, **62**: 728.
Parents, Duty of, to Teachers. (A. H. Rich) Educa. **12**: 350.
— Education of, by their Children. (C. Sterne) Open Court, **1**: 642, 670.
— In Behalf of. (A. Repplier) No. Am. **157**: 225.
Paresis. (H. S. Williams) No. Am. **155**: 744.
Paretic Dementia. (S. V. Clevenger) Open Court, **5**: 3000.
Pariah, A; a story. (H. S. Merriman) Cornh. **74**: 52. Same art. Liv. Age, **210**: 446.
Pariah, The; a story. (A. Baird) Idler, **8**: 486.
Parini, Giuseppe. Macmil. **72**: 291.
Paris, L. P. A., Comte de. Temp. Bar, **99**: 83. Same art. Liv. Age, **199**: 415.
Paris and Helen. (A. Lang) Cosmopol. **18**: 173.
— Judgment of, in Greek Art. (J. E. Harrison) M. of Art, **5**: 502.
Paris, Academy of Fine Arts. (A. Laugel) Nation, **54**: 67, 106.
— Almshouses. (E. R. Spearman) Leis. Hour, **42**: 45-324.
— Along the Seine. (T. Child) Harper, **85**: 723.
— American Artists' Association of. (E. H. Wuerpel) Cosmopol. **20**: 402.
— American Society in. (M. B. Ford) Cosmopol. **15**: 72.
— Americans in. (R. H. Davis) Harper, **91**: 272.
— Antiquarian Ramble in. (F. Harrison) Fortn. **62**: 527. Same art. Ecl. M. **123**: 662. Same art. Liv. Age, **203**: 410.
— Architecture in, Domestic. (A. de Calonne) 19th Cent. **37**: 593.
— — since the Empire. (P. G. Hamerton) Portfo. **24**: 211, 238, 241.
— Art Club in, American Girls'. (E. M. Aylward) Scrib. M. **16**: 598.
— Art Schools of. (L. H. Hooper) Cosmopol. **14**: 59.
— Artistic Architecture of. Archit. Rec. **4**: 75.
— as a Book Centre. Bookworm, **6**: 349.
— Basilica of Montmartre. (J. M. Kiely) Cath. World, **63**: 398.
— Beggars of. (L. Paulian) Chaut. **19**: 55.
— Behind the Scenes in. All the Year, **72**: 546.
— Boulevards of. (T. Child) Harper, **85**: 855.
— — Life on the. (T. B. Preston) Chaut. **20**: 58.
— Burial Monopoly of. (E. R. Spearman) Forum, **13**: 265.
— Burials in. Leis. Hour, **42**: 397.
— Byvanck's Dutchman in. (S. Dewey) Westm. **140**: 446. — Spec. **69**: 530.
— Cabaret of the Chat Noir. (A. Galdemar) Eng. Illust. **11**: 185.
— Cafés of, Thirty Years Ago. All the Year, **71**: 568.
— The Capital of. Macmil. **75**: 97.
— Catacombs of. (N. W. Williams) Gent. M. n. s. **53**: 97.
Paris, Cheap Living in. (A. F. Sanborn) Lippinc. **55**: 496.
— Comédie-Française in 1893. (A. D. Vandam) New R. **8**: 319, 686.
— Commune of 1871, March on. (P. Shorey) Dial (Ch.) **20**: 167.
— Criminal Classes of. (B. Archdekan-Cody) Month, **74**: 212.
— Cyclone in. Nature, **54**: 481.
— Ecole des Beaux-Arts. (E. Flagg) Archit. Rec. **3**: 302, 419. **4**: 38.
— Education in, Free. (C. de Pratz) New R. **8**: 675.
— Englishman in. Ath. '92, **2**: 219. — Dial (Ch.) **13**: 178. — Sat. R. **74**: 79.
— — Authorship of. (F. Hawkins) Acad. **42**: 143.
— Excursion to, 1851. (T. Carlyle) Liv. Age, **192**: 77-230.
— Exhibitions in, 1892. (E. R. Pennell) Nation, **54**: 444.
— Experience in Cosmopolitan. Atlan. **72**: 139.
— Exposition, 1878. Buildings and Arrangement. M. of Art, **1**: 5, 29.
— — French Fine Art at. M. of Art, **2**: 15.
— — Industrial Art. M. of Art, **1**: 66-232.
— — Pictures of the British School. (H. Blackburn) M. of Art, **1**: 126.
— — Sculpture at the. M. of Art, **3**: 256.
— Exposition, 1890, Last Look at. (Sophia Beale) Univ. R. **6**: 113.
— Exposition, 1900. (Count Alphonse de Calonne) Archit. R. **5**: 217.
— — General Scheme. Am. Arch. **50**: 31.
— — Competitive Schemes for General Arrangement. Am. Arch. **47**: 62.
— — Congress and. (T. Stanton) No. Am. **161**: 753.
— Faculty of. (J. Leyland) Time, **10**: 356.
— Fairs in. (E. J. Hart) Idler, **6**: 419.
— Fortunes of, for the Last Fifty Years. Blackw. **160**: 336. Same art. Liv. Age, **211**: 195. Same art. Ecl. M. **127**: 598.
— German Entry into, March 1, 1871. Blackw. **154**: 609. Same art. Liv. Age, **199**: 676. Same art. Ecl. M. **121**: 794.
— The Gouvernante of. Liv. Age, **203**: 707.
— House Architecture of. (Fernand Mazade) Archit. R. **6**: 134.
— How the Poor live in. (T. B. Preston) Chaut. **21**: 313.
— in Mourning for President Carnot. (R. H. Davis) Harper, **90**: 700.
— in Spring. (W. Frith) Temp. Bar, **96**: 229. Same art. Liv. Age, **195**: 612.
— Indoor Life in. Blackw. **156**: 802. Same art. Liv. Age, **204**: 226.
— Literary. (T. Child) Harper, **85**: 489.
— Market of, Great. (A. F. Sanborn) Lippinc. **56**: 133.
— Municipal Laboratory. (I. M. Tarbell) McClure, **3**: 177.
— Musée Social in. (W. F. Willoughby) Ann. Am. Acad. Pol. Sci. **7**: 58.
— New Year's Day in. (E. Crawford) Eng. Illust. **11**: 347. — (Chas. Hervey) Time, **6**: 465.
— Next Siege of. (W. I. Clowes) National, **24**: 502.
— Note-book in. (A. D. Vandam) New R. **7**: 271, 481. Same art. Liv. Age, **195**: 427.
— Notre-Dame. *See* Notre-Dame.
— of the Revolution. (A. Laugel) Nation, **60**: 89.
— Old. (S. J. Cauffman) Lippinc. **50**: 528.
— Old Bastille. (H. S. Howell) Canad. M. **2**: 36.

Paris, Opera House, Museum and Library of. (B. Matthews) M. of Art, 9: 27.
— Palais Royal, a "Bijou" Parisian Theatre. All the Year, 70: 207.
— Pleasure Resorts of: the Marne. Art J. 44: 70, 107.
— Police of. (A. Shadwell) Eng. Illust. 9: 904.
— Poor in. Sat. R. 73: 267, 298, 324, 353.
— Present-day Aspect of. Time, 6: 553.
— Proletarian. (T. Child) Harper, 86: 185.
— Public Schools of. (L. Marillier) Educa. R. 12: 313.
— Quartier Latin. (J. H. Cameron) Canad. M. 1: 53.
— Quays of. (A. F. Sanborn) Lippinc. 58: 551.
— Recollections of, Clifton-Bingham's. Sat. R. 81: 459.
— Reminiscences of Old. Time, 7: 931.
— Riot in, June 11, 1870. (L. Halévy) Poet-Lore, 5: 603.
— Riots in, July, 1893. Am. Arch. 41: 132. — Spec. 71: 38.
— Salon, The. (Wm. Sharp) Time, 3: 702. 12: 670.
— — An Appreciation of Modern French Art. (M. H. Spielmann) M. of Art, 19: 369.
— — Art at. (C. Whibley) 19th Cent. 35: 905.
— — 1880. (J. Forbes-Robertson) M. of Art, 3: 423.
— — 1881. (J. Forbes-Robertson) M. of Art, 4: 379-453.
— — 1882. (J. Forbes-Robertson) M. of Art, 5: 413.
— — — Impressions of. Time, 7: 363.
— — 1883. American Pictures at. (W. C. Brownell) M. of Art, 6: 492.
— — 1884. American Artists at. (W. C. Brownell) M. of Art, 7: 492.
— — — French Art at. (W. C. Brownell) M. of Art, 7: 390.
— — 1887. M. of Art, 10: 311, 355.
— — 1888. (C. Phillips) M. of Art, 11: 338. — (H. Quilter) Univ. R. 1: 221, 325.
— — 1889. M. of Art, 12: 415.
— — History of. (R. Nobili) Cosmopol. 12: 268.
— — Origin of. (P. Villars) M. of Art, 4: 210.
— Salons, The Two. (Emily Crawford) Univ. R. 7: 206, 406. — (A. de Calonne) 19th Cent. 37: 1008. — (E. R. Pennell) Fortn. 61: 731.
— — 1891. (W. Armstrong) M. of Art, 14: 361.
— — 1892. Exhibitions, Summer. (C. Phillips) Art J. 44: 241, 272. — Sat. R. 73: 627. — (C. Nicholson) Acad. 41: 451-573. — (E. R. Pennell) Fortn. 57: 840.
— — 1893. Art J. 45: 216. — (C. Nicholson) Acad. 43: 400, 443. — (P. Phillips) M. of Art, 16: 325-397.
— — 1894. (André Michel) Ath. '94, 1: 653, 684, 747, 779, 811, 841. — (W. Sharp) Art J. 46: 185. — (C. Phillips) M. of Art, 17: 325, 379.
— — 1895. (C. Yriarte) Cosmopol. 19: 168. — (J. Bernac) Art J. 47: 182.
— — 1896. Art J. 48: 193.
— Salon of the Champs Elysées. (C. Phillips) M. of Art, 18: 361. — Am. Arch. 48: 119. — (C. Nicholson) Acad. 47: 408.
— Salon of the Champ de Mars. (C. Phillips) M. of Art, 18: 423. — Am. Arch. 48: 77. — Sat. R. 79: 647. — (C. Nicholson) Acad. 47: 385.
— Shall our Young Men study in? Arena, 13: 131.
— Show-places of, at Night. (R. H. Davis) Harper, 90: 125.
— Siege of, English Food Gifts after. Blackw. 157: 545. Same art. Liv. Age, 205: 543. Same art. Ecl. M. 124: 832. Same art. Un. Serv. (Phila.) 13: 523.
— Streets of. (R. H. Davis) Harper, 89: 701. — (I. M. Tarbell) New Eng. M. n. s. 9: 259.
Paris, Streets of, in 1850. Blackw. 156: 453. Same art. Ecl. M. 123: 747. Same art. Liv. Age, 203: 537.
— Study in, Cost of. (F. E. Thomas) Music, 8: 210.
— Suffering. (A. Laugel) Nation, 54: 28.
— Théatre Libre. (M. A. Belloc) New R. 10: 205.
— Theatres and Concerts in. (W. F. Apthorp) Scrib. M. 11: 3-628.
— Theatres in, from 1750 to 1790. Blackw. 153: 522.
— Under the Streets of. (J. J. Waller) Good Words, 35: 491, 548.
— Vignettes from. (Mary Negreponte) Westm. 139: 476. Same art. Ecl. M. 120: 225 — 121: 86.
— Women's Clubs. Leis. Hour, 45: 331.
— Workingmen's Cafés. (A. F. Sanborn) No. Am. 158: 251.
— Parish Councillor's Dilemma. (C. Hare) Longm. 29: 153.
Parish Councils. (T. W. Fowle; J. S. Montague) National, 22: 365.
— and Allotments. (B. King) New R. 9: 544.
— Bill for, in England, 1893. (W. B. Carpenter) Contemp. 64: 629. Same art. Spec. 71: 793. — Church Q. 37: 204.
— — Charities and the. (J. Darfield) Contemp. 64: 777. — Spec. 71: 830.
— — English Communes. Spec. 72: 290.
Parish Priest, The, before the Reformation. (A. Jessopp) 19th Cent. 36: 468. Same art. Liv. Age, 203: 346.
Parish Register, An Old. (W. J. Ferrar) Sund. M. 24: 410.
Parish Register Bill of 1882. (W. D. Macray) Walford's Antiq. 3: 109, 171.
Parish Registers; a story. (L. Kip) Overland, n. s. 22: 370.
Park, Edwards A. (A. H. Bradford) Chr. Un. 45: 540.
Park, Trenor William. (W. H. Maguire) Nat'l M. (N. Y. '91) 15: 655.
Park, National Military. (H. V. Boynton) Cent. 28: 703.
Park Lands and their Boundaries. (C. S. Sargent) Garden & F. 9: 421.
Parke, Walter, and Arthur Shirley. A Lost Sheep. Theatre, 29: 127.
Parker, Cortlandt. (F. W. Ricord) Nat'l M. (N. Y. '91) 19: 304.
Parker, Gilbert, with portrait. Bk. Buyer, 13: 333. — With portrait. Bk. News, 12: 193.
Parker, James H. Nat'l M. (N. Y. '91) 16: 478.
Parker. Dr. Joseph, Clergyman; a sketch. (R. Blathwayt) Idler, 4: 631.
Parker, Louis N. A Bohemian; a play. Theatre, 28: 199.
— Chris; a play. Theatre, 28: 253.
-- David. Gent. M. n. s. 49: 636. — Theatre, 29: 275.
Parker, Theodore, Grave of. (T. Stanton) Open Court, 5: 3063.
— Monument of, at Florence. M. Am. Hist. 27: 128.
— Optimism of. (M. D. Conway) Open Court, 3: 1655.
— Teachings of. (M. D. Conway) Open Court, 3: 1669.
— — Transient and Permanent in. (M. D. Conway) Open Court, 3: 1632.
Parkes, Sir Henry. (A. P. Martin) Cornh. 74: 220. Same art. Liv. Age, 210: 747. — Leis. Hour, 43: 722. — Quar. 178: 460. Same art. Liv. Age, 201: 771. — Spec. 73: 528. — (S. M. Hill) Acad. 46: 297. — Ath. '94, 1: 401. — Sat. R. 77: 367. — (E. W. Clement) Dial (Ch.) 17: 92. — (J. H. Wigmore) Nation, 58: 392, 407.

Parkhurst, Charles Henry. (E. J. Edwards) McClure, 2: 475. — With portraits. (H. Parker) Munsey, 12: 249. — (J. Cook) Our Day, 15: 233. — With portraits. (E. J. Edwards) McClure, 4: 149. — With portrait. Our Day, 16: 616.
— and the New York Police. And. R. 17: 515.
— and his Work. (A. C. Wheeler) Chaut. 20: 573.
— Character Sketch of, with portrait. (W. B. Murray) Our Day, 14: 287.
— Moral Reform by, in New York City. And. R. 19: 95.
Parkman, Francis. Ath. '93, 2: 698. — (J. B. Gilder) Critic, 23: 322. — (C. S. Sargent) Garden & F. 6: 471. — Lit. W. (Bost.) 24: 384. — (J. L. Walker) Nation, 57: 365. — Pub. Opin. 16: 153. — (J. Fiske) Atlan. 73: 664. — (J. Winsor) Atlan. 73: 660. — (J. Schouler) Harv. Grad. M. 2: 305. — (A. G. Bradley) Macmil. 69: 420. Same art. Liv. Age, 201: 259. Same art. Ecl. M. 122: 673. — With portraits. (H. Ward) McClure, 2: 185. — With portrait. Bk. News, 19: 5. — With portrait, Bk. Buyer, 7: 421. — (J. R. Lowell) Cent. 23: 44.
— and his Work. (J. H. Ward) Forum, 16: 419. — Spec. 71: 755.
— at Quebec. (J. M. Le Moine) Canad. M. 3: 493.
— Autobiography. Harv. Grad. M. 3: 453.
— Historical Works of. (E. J. Payne) Acad. 42: 164.
— In the White Mountains with. (D. D. Slade) New Eng. M. n. s. 11: 94.
— Reminiscences of, at Quebec. (J. M. Le Moine) Canad. M. 3: 493.
Parkman, George, Murder of. (G. C. Holt) Cosmopol. 91: 537.
Parks, American and English. Garden & F. 5: 458.
— and Boulevards; Work for the Municipal Art Society. (C. S. Sargent) Garden & F. 7: 11.
— and Park-planting. (C. S. Sargent) Garden & F. 8: 11.
— April Scene in Central Park, N. Y. Garden & F. 9: 332.
— Architectural Attack on Rural. (C. S. Sargent) Garden & F. 8: 351.
— Boards of, and their Professional Advisers. (C. S. Sargent) Garden & F. 7: 461.
— Boston. (S. Baxter) Garden & F. 7: 22.
— — and Vicinity. Garden & F. 6: 98.
— Boston Metropolitan, Movement for. (Sylvester Baxter) Garden & F. 5: 62. — Garden & F. 5: 421.
— Care of. Garden & F. 7: 127.
— Care of Urban. (C. S. Sargent) Garden & F. 8: 82.
— Central Park. Garden & F. 5: 350.
— City, Art Societies and. (C. S. Sargent) Garden & F. 6: 291.
— — Attacks on. (C. S. Sargent) Garden & F. 6: 22.
— — Elements of Beauty in. (C. S. Sargent) Garden & F. 7: 371.
— — Irrigation in. Garden & F. 7: 362.
— — "Keep off the Grass." (C. S. Sargent) Garden & F. 7: 291, 297.
— — Possibilities of. (Earl of Meath) New R. 11: 201.
— City Engineers and Public. (C. S. Sargent) Garden & F. 8: 91.
— County. (C. S. Sargent) Garden & F. 9: 221. — (T. H. Macbride) Pop. Sci. Mo. 49: 369.
— Defacement of. (C. S. Sargent) Garden & F. 8: 231.
— — in Buffalo. (C. S. Sargent) Garden & F. 8: 71.
— for Growing Cities. Garden & F. 5: 61.
— Forests and. Garden & F. 5: 542.
Parks. German Pleasure Ground. Garden & F. 5: 554.
— in New England. (M. C. Robbins) Garden & F. 5: 99.
— in New York City, Plan for. (M. G. Van Rensselaer) Garden & F. 9: 142, 158, 178.
— in Philadelphia, Small. Garden & F. 6: 248.
— Land for, Danger of Delay in acquiring. (H. W. S. Cleveland) Garden & F. 5: 131.
— Metropolitan, of Boston. (C. S. Sargent) Garden & F. 8: 171.
— Mission of. (H. L. Osborne) Am. M. Civics, 9: 171.
— Movement for, in U. S. (C. S. Sargent) Garden & F. 6: 221.
— National, in Canada. (C. S. Sargent) Garden & F. 6: 301.
— near Boston, Work on. (C. S. Sargent) Garden & F. 9: 171.
— Need of Efficient Park Service. (C. S. Sargent) Garden & F. 9: 181.
— Notable Project in New Jersey. (C. S. Sargent) Garden & F. 8: 141.
— Obliteration of. (C. S. Sargent) Garden & F. 9: 161.
— Parkways and Pleasure-grounds. (C. S. Sargent) Garden & F. 8: 192, 202. — (F. L. Olmsted) Engin. M. 9: 253.
— Playgrounds and. (C. S. Sargent) Garden & F. 7: 221. — (T. E. Will; H. L. White; W. Vrooman) Arena, 10: 274.
— Public, and Pleasure Grounds. (Lord H. G. Lennox) Time, 1: 275, 431.
— — Landscape Art in. (C. S. Sargent) Garden & F. 6: 191.
— — Tender Plants in. (W. McMillan) Garden & F. 6: 371.
— — U. S. Army as Guardian of. (J. D. W. French) Garden & F. 6: 95.
— — Water Front of. (C. S. Sargent) Garden & F. 6: 421.
— Public Reservations in the State of New York. (C. S. Sargent) Garden & F. 8: 151.
— Special Attraction in City. (C. S. Sargent) Garden & F. 8: 431.
— Standard of Taste for. Soc. Econ. 8: 321.
— Trees in. (C. S. Sargent) Garden & F. 9: 511.
— Use of Color in. (C. S. Sargent) Garden & F. 7: 281.
Parkway, River, at Boston. (C. S. Sargent) Garden & F. 9: 381.
Parley of the Kings; a poem. (H. H. Boyesen) Cosmopol. 15: 261.
Parliament, British. (J. W. Burgess) Chaut. 20: 17. — (J. M'Carthy) Contemp. 63: 108.
— and the Government of India. Macmil. 68: 449.
— Bargains in. (E. Porritt) No. Am. 158: 631.
— Conference of Colonial Members of. (J. F. Hogan) Contemp. 64: 713.
— Curious Acts of. (A. J. Gordon) Gent. M. n. s. 55: 187.
— Dissolutions of, Anecdotic Side of. (M. J. Griffin) Forum, 20: 91.
— — Memorable. (G. B. Smith) 19th Cent. 31: 713.
— Failure or Success in. (H. W. Lucy) New R. 7: 236.
— Future of, Burns on. Spec. 72: 424.
— Great Acts of. (T. Raleigh) Chaut. 21: 139.
— History of. Ed. R. 177: 389.
— — Smith's. Sat. R. 74: 772.
— in 1305, Maitland's. Ath. '94, 1: 273.
— in 1879. (T. H. Escott) Time, 1: 641.

Parliament. In Young Parliamentary Days. (H. W. Lucy) Fortn. **58**: 105. Same art. Liv. Age, **194**: 569.
— Intolerable Waste of. (J. Annand) New R. **15**: 215.
— Ireland blocks the Way in. (H. J. Gladstone) 19th Cent. **31**: 899.
— Long, and Dr. Gardiner. Blackw. **152**: 804.
— — Expulsion of, Cromwell and. (C. H. Firth) Eng. Hist. R. **8**: 526.
— Lords and Commons. Macmil. **69**: 241.
— Manners in. (J. M'Carthy) No. Am. **157**: 698. — Chamb. J. **70**: 10.
— Member of, Modern. Macmil. **67**: 304.
— — Tribulations and Advantages of Legislators. Chamb. J. **72**: 545.
— Members of. (G. O. Morgan) Time, **18**: 129.
— — Freedom of, from Arrest: Case of Sir Thomas Shirley. (G. W. Prothero) Eng. Hist. R. **8**: 733.
— — Payment of. (Sir C. G. Duffy; T. Mann; W. R. Elliston) Contemp. **63**: 480. — (Alex. B. Tulloch) 19th Cent. **38**: 27.
— The Old M. P. and the New. (G. A. B. Dewar) Westm. **146**: 628.
— The Prerogative of Dissolution. (L. G. Powers) Canad. M. **6**: 493.
— Press and. (H. W. Massingham) New R. **8**: 527.
— The Pulse of. (T. A. Spalding) Contemp. **67**: 695.
— A Queen's Minister's Business Day. Cosmopol. **22**: 87.
— Salisbury, Lucy's Diary of. Spec. **69**: 930.
— Sexcentenary of. (J. W. Root) Macmil. **71**: 252.
— Sittings of: stealing a Session. Blackw. **154**: 892.
— Torrens's Twenty Years in. Sat. R. **75**: 99.
Parliament of Religions. *See* Religions, Parliament of.
Parliament House of Scotland. (A. W. Renton) Green Bag, **4**: 62-543.
Parliamentary Fund. (Lord Wolmer) National, **25**: 158.
Parliamentary Government in England, Todd on. Spec. **71**: 119.
— The Outlook for. (H. Taylor) No. Am. **160**: 479.
Parliamentary Procedure. (J. Macy) Ann. Am. Acad. Pol. Sci. **3**: 306.
— *versus* Obstruction. Quar. **178**: 486.
Parliamentary Reform, Internal and External. (F. A. White) Westm. **146**: 517.
Parliamentary Reporting, Some Humors of. Macmil. **71**: 365. Same art. Liv. Age, **205**: 181. Same art. Ecl. M. **124**: 558.
Parliamentary Representation in England illustrated by the Elections of 1892 and 1895. (J. A. Baines) J. Statis. Soc. **59**: 38.
— is it compatible with Democracy? (M. Macfie) Westm. **142**: 323.
Parliaments and Ministries of the Century. (C. B. Roylance-Kent) Macmil. **70**: 19. Same art. Liv. Age, **201**: 732.
— Duration of. Spec. **68**: 521.
— of the World. (J. T. Kay) 19th Cent. **36**: 708.
— Sighele on. (H. Zimmern) Blackw. **158**: 227.
Parlor Conference Meeting. (A. G. Spencer) New Eng. M. n. s. **10**: 149.
Parlous Wholeness of Ephraim. (C. B. Fernald) Cent. **31**: 89.
Parnell, C. S., and Butt. (H. D. Traill) Fortn. **57**: 115.
— Was he badly treated? (W. O'Brien) Contemp. **70**: 678.
— *vs.* London Times. (G. W. Burnet) Jurid. R. **1**: 54, 226.
Parnell Commission, Story of. Green Bag, **6**: 362.
Parochial Schools in the United States. (A. Young) Cath. World, **59**: 444.
Parochial Self-government. (J. F. Wilkinson) New R. **10**: 95.
Parochial System. Eng. R. **2**: 329.
Parochial Visitation. Eng. R. **18**: 1.
Parodies. Spec. **70**: 670.
— and Parodists. (J. Buchan) Bookworm, **7**: 311.
Parody. Quar. **182**: 153.
Paronomasia in the Old Testament. (I. M. Casanowicz) J. Bib. Lit. **12**: 105.
Parr, Thomas. (E. A. King) Argosy, **55**: 430. — (C. Edwardes) Macmil. **70**: 372.
Parrett River, Eng., Valley of. (W. Greswell) Liv. Age, **192**: 106.
Parrots. Cornh. **65**: 167. Same art. Liv. Age, **193**: 43.
— I have known. Chamb. J. **72**: 796. Same art. Liv. Age, **208**: 243.
Parry, Charles C., with portrait. Nat'l M. (N. Y. '91) **19**: 85.
Parry, Dr. Charles Hubert H. National, **22**: 762.
— King Saul. Sat. R. **79**: 218.
— Music for The Frogs of Aristophanes. Theatre, **28**: 216.
Parsees, The. (C. Sorabji) 19th Cent. **34**: 605. Same art. Liv. Age, **199**: 762.
Parsi Calendar. When was it invented? (E. W. West) Acad. **49**: 348.
Parsi Religion. (D. Naoroji) Time, **20**: 526.
Parsimonious Liberality; a story. (E. J. Hardy) Argosy, **53**: 106.
Parsonage Building and Dilapidation. Eng. R. **7**: 253.
Parsons, Alfred, with portrait. Bk. Buyer, **9**: 5.
Parsons, Eben, and Fatherland Farm. (Mrs. S. E. P. Forbes) N. E. Reg. **50**: 59.
Parsons, Thomas W. (R. Hovey) Atlan. **71**: 264. — Critic, **21**: 139, 155. — Dial (Ch.) **13**: 173.
— A Portrait of. (T. B. Aldrich) Cent. **26**: 323.
Part of a Ghost: a Mystery. (W. H. Russell) 19th Cent. **36**: 222. Same art. Liv. Age, **202**: 741.
Parted Curtains, The; a story. (H. M. Hoke) Overland, n. s. **25**: 499.
Parthenon, Dimensions of. (A. Emerson) Am. J. Archæol. **11**: 335.
— Frieze of. (S. Reinach) Nation, **58**: 406. **59**: 121. — (A. W. Colgate) Am. Arch. **45**: 9. — (W. J. Stillman) Nation, **59**: 62. — (C. Waldstein) Nation, **58**: 329. **59**: 45.
— — Terracottas of. (A. H. Smith) J. Hel. Stud. **14**: 264.
— Inscription of. (B. I. Wheeler) Nation, **62**: 233.
— Sculptures of, Recent Additions to. (A. H. Smith) J. Hel. Stud. **13**: 88.
Partie Carrée, A; a story. (W. E. Norris) Harper, **88**: 539.
Parties and Sects. (C. R. Henderson) Pub. Opin. **20**: 173.
— Political, Evolution of. (S. M. Merrill) No. Am. **159**: 574.
— — Fusion of. (D. S. Remsen) Ann. Am. Acad. Pol. Sci. **8**: 32.
— — in England. (E. Porritt) Chaut. **21**: 264.
— — — Decay of Party Government. (F. Greenwood) Contemp. **70**: 352.
— — in the U. S., Beginnings of. (N. Brooks) Scrib. M. **17**: 48.
— — — Past, Present, and Future. (W. H. Brown) Am. M. Civics, **7**: 79.
— — — True Significance of Western Unrest. (C. S. Gleed) Forum, **16**: 251.
— — Inadequacy of Great. (W. B. Chisholm) Gunton's M. **10**: 293.
— — Limitations of. (W. B. Chisholm) Am. M. Civics, **8**: 624.

Parties, Limitations of Names of. (C. B. R. Kent) Macmil. 67: 420.
Parting and a Meeting, A; a story. (W. D. Howells) Cosmopol. 18: 183.
Partisanship, Blind, and Political Corruption. (J. S. Evans) Am. M. Civics, 7: 278.
Partly Celestial Tale, A. (E. L. Kellogg) Overland, n. s. 26: 315.
Partnership in Germany. (J. Hirschfeld) Law Q. 9: 62.
Parton, Arthur. (G. Cranmer) Mo. Illust. 12: 329.
Parton, Ernest. Art J. 44: 353.
Parton, James. (J. H. Ward) New Eng. M. n. s. 7: 627.
Partridge, The. (T. S. Kebbel) Macmil. 69: 312.
— The Irish. Macmil. 73: 43.
— Plea for. Spec. 71: 833.
Partridges, Barbary, A Day with. Outing, 19: 337.
Party, The Government. (F. V. Fisher) Westm. R. 140: 425.
— Government by. (G. E. Waring, jr.) No. Am. 163: 587. — (T. G. Kittrell) Am. J. Pol. 5: 295. — Quar. 179: 244. — (A. N. Laughton) Westm. 142: 361. — (C. Richardson) Ann. Am. Acad. Pol. Sci. 2: 518, 653.
— — Future of. (C. B. Roylance-Kent) Macmil. 68: 102.
— — on its Trial. (C. T. Catham) Gunton's M. 11: 257.
— Natural History of. (A. D. Morse) Yale R. 2: 74.
— What is a? (A. D. Morse) Pol. Sci. Q. 11: 68.
Party Journalism. Sat. R. 79: 612.
Party Loyalty, Ethics of. (G. W. Green) Forum, 20: 419.
Party Machinery in U. S. (J. W. Jenks) Chaut. 23: 23.
Party Obligation, Limits of. (H. Budd) Am. J. Pol. 5: 122.
Party Organization, the Curse of the Country. (W. E. Hodgson) Time, 13: 395.
— Principles of. (F. L. McVey) Gunton's M. 10: 144.
Party Rule in the U. S. (A. Stickney) Am. J. Pol. 1: 382.
Party System, English, Break-up of. (E. Porritt) Ann. Am. Acad. Pol. Sci. 5: 490.
Parvises and Porches. Chamb. J. 71: 534.
Pas de Quatre; a poem. (C. Monkhouse) M. of Art, 19: 13.
Pascal, Blaise. (W. Pater) Contemp. 67: 168. — Macmil. 68: 43. Same art. Liv. Age, 198: 169. — Spec. 70: 780.
Pascal, Gilberte; a Sister of Saints. (M. Libby) Cent. 24: 606.
Pascal, Jacquelin. (W. L. Courtney) Time, 17: 274.
Paschal Canon attributed to Anatolius of Laodicea. (A. Anscombe) Eng. Hist. R. 10: 515. — Reply. (C. H. Turner) Eng. Hist. R. 10: 699.
Paspati, A. G. (E. Freshfield) Ath. '92, 1: 92.
Pasquier, Etienne Denis, Duc de. Memoirs. Ed. R. 179: 1, 326. — Dial (Ch.) 16: 42, 264. — (A. Laugel) Nation, 58: 228, 250, 270. 59: 26. 60: 340.
Passage in a Tramp, A. (C. J. Cutliffe Hyne) Chamb. J. 72: 12.
Passage of the Statutes, The; a poem. (V. Hugo) Gent. M. n. s. 51: 416.
Passamaquoddy, Folk-Lore of. (J. W. Fewkes) J. Am. Folk-Lore, 3: 257.
Passamaquoddy Superstitions. J. Am. Folk-Lore, 2: 229.
Passed — with Honors. (C. Burke) Argosy, 59: 241.
Passing the Love of Women; a story. (E. Cummings) Southern M. 5: 78.
Passing of Jack Thompson. (W. C. Campbell) Overland, n. s. 24: 269.
Passing of Major Kilgore. (Y. E. Allison) Lippinc. 49: 3.
Passing of Sister Barsett. (S. O. Jewett) Cosmopol. 13: 59.
Passing of Spring; a story. (Gertrude Hall) Cosmopol. 16: 616.
Passing of Thomas. (T. A. Janvier) Harper, 85: 439.
Passini, Ludwig. (P. E. Pinkerton) M. of Art, 10: 127.
Passion Play at Höritz and Kindred Spectacles. R. of Rs. (N. Y.) 11: 671.
— at Selzach. (H. D. Rawnsley) Blackw. 160: 315. Same art. Liv. Age, 211: 299.
— at Vorder-Thiersee. (A. S. Peck) Cent. 29: 137, 163.
Passion Vine. Garden & F. 7: 264.
Passions and Manias. (F. L. Oswald) Open Court, 3: 1513, 1551.
— Sanctification of. (C. W. Rishell) Meth. R. 53: 380.
Pass'n's Grip, The. (R. Page) Lippinc. 52: 484.
Passover Hagadah, The. Temp. Bar, 98: 274.
— Samaritan. (A. R. Macewen) Good Words, 35: 50. — Liv. Age, 200: 505.
Past, The, and the Present. (E. P. Jackson) No. Am. 161: 380.
Past Gifts; a poem. Argosy, 59: 495.
Past Redemption; a story. (J. Maclaren Watson) McClure, 5: 333.
Paste for Labels. (H. Kephart) Lib. J. 18: 8.
Pastel, A. (C. K. Rathbone) Lippinc. 51: 617.
— The. (J. Benton) Critic, 22: 249.
Pastelle; a story. (C. S. Ross) Outing, 22: 244.
Pastels in Prose. (M. E. Wilkins) Harper, 86: 147.
Pasteur, Louis, with portrait. (J. A. Zahm) Cath. World, 56: 445. — (L. A. Stimson) Forum, 15: 93. — (P. C. Mitchell) New R. 13: 537. — (P. Geddes; J. A. Thomson) Contemp. 68: 632. Same art. Liv. Age, 207: 451. Same art. Ecl. M. 126: 11. — (G. S. Woodhead) Sci. Prog. 4: 229. — (H. W. Conn) Science, n. s. 2: 601. — (J. Marcou) Science, n. s. 2: 751. — (H. A. Miers and F. W. Andrewes) Nat. Sci. 7: 314. — (J. M. Charcot) Cosmopol. 18: 271. — Nature, 52: 550. — With portraits. (P. Frankland) R. of Rs. (N. Y.) 12: 541. — Sat. R. 80: 434. Same art. Ecl. M. 125: 800. — Spec. 75: 430. — Ath. '95, 2: 458. — (F. L. Oswald) Open Court, 9: 4663. — (G. M. Sternberg) Science, n. s. 3: 185. — (C. M. Aikman) Temp. Bar, 109: 375. Same art. Ecl. M. 127: 824.
— and his Life Work. (F. L. Oswald) Chaut. 22: 321.
— Final Entombment of. Nature, 55: 204.
— Funeral of. Nature, 52: 576.
— Method of Inoculation of. (G. W. Bulman) Nat. Sci. 2: 100.
— Scientist. (J. Tyndall) R. of Rs. (N. Y.) 12: 547.
— Scientific Work of. Dub. R. 118: 153.
— 70th Birthday. Nature, 47: 204.
Pasteur Institute. (F. Sarcey) Cosmopol. 18: 373. — (G. C. Frankland) Longm. 27: 363. — (I. M. Tarbell) McClure, 1: 327.
Pasteur-al Aid; a story. Belgra. 87: 71.
Pastime and Business. Chamb. J. 72: 801.
Pastimes, Pandean. (F. D. Bergen) Atlan. 77: 625.
Paston Letters. (W. Roberts) Ath. '96, 1: 447.
— New ed. by Gairdner, 1895. Sat. R. 80: 707.
Pastor among his People. (C. W. Heisler) Luth. Q. 24: 481.
— for the Times. (E. Miller) Luth. Q. 23: 173.
— Relation of Church Council to. (S. J. Taylor) Luth. Q. 24: 164.
Pastoral Office, Divine Estimate of. (M. MacGregor) Bapt. R. 14: 118.
Pastoral Work worth keeping. (J. A. Rondthaler) Our Day, 16: 464.

Pastorals. (E. H. Lacon Watson) Westm. 142: 440.
Pastoriza Pilgrimage. (L. M. R. Walker) Belgra. 84: 311. Same art. Liv. Age, 202: 637.
Patagonia. (J. R. Spears) Scrib. M. 17: 213.
— Memories of. (Florence Dixie) Westm. 139: 247.
— Plains of. (W. H. Hudson) Univ. R. 7: 549.
— Dr. Siemiradzki's Explorations in. Geog. J. 2: 158.
— Southern, New Discoveries of Fossil Mammalia of. (F. Ameghino) Am. Natural. 27: 439.
— Welsh in. Chamb. J. 71: 753.
Pataliputra, the Indian Troy. Am. Arch. 54: 83.
Patent Act, New German. (E. Schuster) Law Q. 8: 76.
Patent Law of Great Britain. Un. Serv. M. 11: 86.
Patent Law Practice, Engineering Knowledge in. (E. P. Thompson) Cassier, 6: 142.
Patent Laws. (E. P. Thompson) Cassier, 5: 267. — (W. C. Maude) Month, 86: 51.
— Are they Iniquitous? (H. Olerich) Am. J. Pol. 5: 543. — (W. E. Simonds) No. Am. 157: 679.
— Imperiled Dignity of Science and the Law. (J. Trowbridge) Atlan. 78: 491.
— Monopoly through. (Z. S. Holbrook) Bib. Sac. 53: 151.
Patent Office, U. S. (H. F. Shedd) Chaut. 15: 170, 281.
Patent Systems, American and Foreign. (C. L. Redfield) Engin. M. 6: 351.
— of England, History of. (E. W. Hulme) Law Q. 12: 141.
— of England and U. S. (A. W. Renton) Law Q. 7: 150. — (J. H. Bakewell) Law Q. 7: 364.
Patents and Monopolies. Cornh. 72: 256.
— Development of our Industries through. (H. F. Shedd) Chaut. 15: 37.
— English, How to take out. Chamb. J. 70: 406.
— for Methods. (W. F. Rogers) Am. Law R. 29: 559.
— Influence of, upon American Industries. (L. Mead) Cassier, 3: 113, 200.
— Infringement of, Liability of Public Corporations for. (V. H. Lockwood) Am. Law R. 26: 371.
— Meaning of the Recent U. S. Patent Decision. (P. Benjamin) Engin. M. 9: 189.
— Our Debt to Inventors. (R. H. Thurston) Forum, 19: 356.
Pater, Walter, with portrait. Bk. News, 13: 11. — (E. B. Titchener) Book R. 2: 201. — Quar. 182: 31. — Sat. R. 78: 118. — Critic, 25: 93. — (J. S. Cotton) Acad. 46: 102. — (T. H. Escott) National, 24: 232. — (L. Dyer) Nation, 59: 137.
— Blessedness of Egoism. (R. P. Jacobus) Fortn. 65: 384.
— Gaston de Latour. Sat. R. 82: 421.
— Imaginary Portraits. (A. Symons) Time, 17: 157.
— Miscellaneous Studies. (E. E. Hale, jr.) Dial (Ch.) 19: 279. — Sat. R. 82: 107.
— Personal Reminiscences of. (W. Sharp) Atlan. 74: 801.
— A Portrait. (E. Gosse) Contemp. 66: 795. Same art. Liv. Age, 204: 151. Same art. Ecl. M. 124: 103.
— Style of. (C. Dodgson) Acad. 49: 110.
— Work of. (E. E. Hale, jr.) Book R. 4: 69. — (L. Johnson) Fortn. 62: 352. Same art. Ecl. M. 123: 504.
Paternalism. (F. W. Howard) Cath. World, 59: 486.
— Dangers of. (G. F. Milton) Am. J. Pol. 5: 625.
— Foolish Fear of. (R. L. Bridgman) New Eng. M. n. s. 13: 244.
— Plutocracy and. (L. F. Ward) Forum, 20: 300.
Paternity; a poem. (V. Hugo) Gent. M. n. s. 50: 417.
Paterson, Gen. John. (B. Booth) New Eng. M. n. s. 11: 42.
— Egleston's Life of. (J. C. Welling) Nation, 59: 51.
Paterson, William. (W. A. Steel) Eng. Hist. R. 11: 260.
Patey, Janet Monarch. Acad. 45: 195. — Ath. '94, 1: 286.
Path of Murtoch, The; an Irish Story. (H. Frederic) Idler, 7: 457.
Pathology. (R. Virchow) Nature, 47: 487.
— and Transmission of Acquired Characters. (H. J. Tylden) Nature, 46: 302.
— Teaching of, Weichselbaum on. (A. A. Kanthack) Nature, 52: 241.
Pathos. Spec. 71: 710. — Spec. 72: 127, 162.
— of the Commonplace; a story. (B. Pain) Eng. Illust. 11: 19.
Patience. (J. G. Vibert) Cent. 29: 362.
Patience; a poem. All the Year, 72: 84.
Patmore, Coventry. Acad. 50: 496. — (R. Garnett) Bookman, 3: 325. — Ath. '96, 2: 797. — (J. H. Morse) Critic, 29: 365.
— Poems of Pathos and Delight. Sat. R. 80: 657.
— Poetry of. (Alice Meynell) Ath. '96, 2: 839.
— Recollections of. (R. Garnett) Sat. R. 82: 583.
— Rod, the Root, and the Flower. Sat. R. 79: 762.
Paton, Sir Joseph Noël. (G. R. Halkett) M. of Art, 3: 1.
— Life and Work of. (A. T. Story) Art J. 47: 97.
Patriarchal Remedies *vs.* Socialistic Remedies. (J. G. Brooks) Econ. J. 3: 226.
Patriarchs, Long-lived. (W. R. Harper) Bib. World, 3: 326.
— Narratives of, Historical Character of. (L. P. Paton) Bib. World, 2: 343, 420.
— Testaments of the Twelve, Jewish Authorship of. (F. C. Conybeare) Jew. Q. 5: 375.
Patrick, St., Birthplace of. (E. W. B. Nicholson) Acad. 47: 402, (A. L. Mayhew) 445, 466, 484, 507.
— Gradwell's. Sat. R. 73: 545.
Patriotic Societies, American. (M. Benjamin) Munsey, 14: 74. — Am. Hist. Reg. 3: 71–235.
— of the Civil War. (M. Benjamin) Munsey, 15: 322.
Patriotism. (W. H. Goodale) Am. M. Civics, 6: 353. — (E. L. Godkin) Nation, 54: 82.
— and Politics. (J. C. Gibbons) No. Am. 154: 385.
— Bryce on. Spec. 69: 816.
— Fountains of. (T. E. Davis) Am. M. Civics, 7: 408.
— from an Irish Standpoint. (W. Glenny-Crory) Time, 15: 449.
— Israelite View of. (J. Poucher) Bib. World, 4: 32.
— Local, Need of. (W. C. Lawton) Lippinc. 58: 548.
— Provincial. (J. P. Mahaffy) 19th Cent. 37: 1027.
— Reasonable. (Earl Meath) 19th Cent. 39: 295.
— True, in its Religious Aspects. (J. K. Smyth) N. Church R. 2: 354.
Patronage, Federal. Pub. Opin. 15: 98.
— — Distribution of. Pub. Opin. 14: 559, 589.
— — influencing Legislation. (C. J. Bonaparte) Good Govt. 12: 139.
Patronage Bill, English, 1895. (A. G. Edwards) National, 26: 409.
Patroons, The. (E. Anthony) Nat'l M. (N. Y. '91) 15: 194.
Patsy's Potlach; a story. (F. I. Vassault) Overland, n. s. 19: 461.
Patterns, The Lost Soul of. (A. E. Farman and G. C. Nuttall) Good Words, 37: 637.
Patti, Adelina, and the Old Songs. (G. F. Root) Music, 1: 428.
— at Craig-y-nos. (A. Warren) McClure, 1: 501.
Pattison, Dorothy Wyndlow, Sister Dora. (E. A. Gowing) Belgra. 89: 418.
Pattison, Mark, and Amiel. (R. M. Lovett) Harv. Mo. 13: 205.

Patty; a sketch. All the Year, **72**: 12.
Patty's Lovers; a story. (M. Mackintosh) Belgra. **88**: 380.
Paudheen Rhu; a sketch. All the Year, **72**: 518.
Paul, The Apostle. (G. Matheson) Chr. Lit. **14**: 535.
— and Ananias, before the Sanhedrin at Jerusalem. (S. L. Bowman) Meth. R. **56**: 570.
— and Barnabas, Call and Ordination of, to Missionary Work. (A. Sutherland) Meth. R. **53**: 562.
— and Inspiration. (G. T. Purves) Presb. & Ref. R. **4**: 1.
— and John, House of, at Rome. (Padre Germano) Am. J. Archæol. **7**: 25.
— and Seneca, Writings of, External Evidence as to. (C. M. Mead) Presb. & Ref. R. **4**: 289.
— before Agrippa. (W. H. P. Faunce) Bib. World, **7**: 86.
— before his Conversion. (F. Godet) Ref. Q. **41**: 250.
— Conversion of, as Evidence for Christianity. (A. B. Scherer) Luth. Q. **25**: 331.
— Experience on Way to Damascus. (E. D. Burton) Bib. World, **1**: 9.
— First Impressions of. (C. G. Montefiore) Jew. Q. **6**: 428.
— A Goaded Persecutor. (G. F. Genung) Bapt. R. **14**: 287.
— Gospel of. (F. H. Foster) Bib. Sac. **53**: 89.
— His Knowledge of Christ. (R. B. Drummond) Acad. **42**: 147.
— in Asia Minor. Church Q. **36**: 363.
— Mysticism of. (E. Y. Hincks) Bib. World, **2**: 326.
— on Mars Hill. (R. T. Stevenson) Meth. R. **54**: 353.
— — Did he preach there? (Richard Parsons) Meth. R. **56**: 546.
— Phraseology of, and Roman Law. (G. F. Magoun) Green Bag, **7**: 132. — (G. F. Magoun) Bib. Sac. **52**: 439.
— Psychology of. (A. J. Nelson) Meth. R. **56**: 722.
— Rabbinic Education of. (S. Weyler) And. R. **17**: 88.
— Theology of, and of John. (G. B. Stevens) Bib. World, **3**: 161.
— — Recent Studies in. (G. T. Purves) Presb. & Ref. R. **5**: 139.
— Visits of, to Jerusalem. (W. J. Beecher) Bib. World, **2**: 42.
— Voyage and Shipwreck. Eng. R. **13**: 257.
Paul I., Emperor of Russia. (F. Whishaw) Temp. Bar, **106**: 107.
Paul and Mignonette; the last of the Arcadians. (C. F. Howell) Overland, n. s. **25**: 297.
Paul Lorraine; a story. Belgra. **80**: 75.
Paula's Caprice; a story. (D. Gerard) Blackw. **155**: 94.
Paulie; a story. (Mary Deane) Temp. Bar, **98**: 585.
Paull, Richard James, with portrait. Bank. M. (Lond.) **53**: 667.
Paulsen, Friedrich. (A. W. Shaw) Educa. R. **8**: 363.
Paulton, Harvey and Edward. Niobe All Smiles; a Comedy. Theatre, **28**: 255.
Pauper Children, Boarding-out. (F. Davenport-Hill) Econ. J. **3**: 62.
Pauper Children of London. Sat. R. **81**: 365.
Pauper Lunacy and Pauperism. (T. W. L. Spence) Scot. R. **25**: 129.
Pauperism, Abolition of. (E. E. Hale) Am. J. Pol. **5**: 113. — (E. E. Hale) Lend a H. **13**: 21. — Lend a H. **14**: 83. **15**: 338. — (E. P. Powell) Lend a H. **17**: 329.
— and Charity. (J. C. Caldwell) Luth. Q. **24**: 39.
— and City Lot Farming. (C. S. Sargent) Garden & F. **9**: 91, 139.
— and Crime. (J. B. Weber) Char. R. **3**: 117.
— and Taxation. (B. Hall) Char. R. **1**: 115.
Pauperism, Booth on. Sat. R. **73**: 636. — Spec. **68**: 563.
— Chas. Booth and his Work. (M. McG. Dana) Gunton's M. **10**: 189.
— Correlation of, with Out-relief. (G. U. Yule) Econ. J. **5**: 603.
— in England and Wales, History of, from 1850, treated by Frequency-curves. (G. U. Yule) J. Statis. Soc. **59**: 318.
— in Great Cities. (R. T. Paine) Lend a H. **12**: 196.
— Manufacturing a New. (C. S. Loch) 19th Cent. **37**: 697.
— Old-age, Report of Commission on. (P. Green) Econ. J. **5**: 293.
— Prevention of. (E. E. Hale) Char. R. **1**: 39. — (O. Craig) Scrib. M. **14**: 121.
— Stigma of. (E. Cannan) Econ. R. **5**: 380.
— Would Personal Influence diminish? (Mrs. E. C. Bolles) Char. R. **2**: 410.
Paupers, Able-bodied, Places of Discipline and Training for. (A. N. Lincoln) Char. R. **4**: 87.
— Enumeration of. (C. Booth) J. Statis. Soc. **55**: 287.
— in England, Board of Guardians of. Macmil. **70**: 350.
— Sorting of. (E. Sellers) Eng. Illust. **9**: 332.
See Poor; Poverty.
Pavement Construction and City Growth. (S. Towle) Engin. M. **12**: 59.
Pavement Maintenance. (S. Whinery) Engin. M. **12**: 245.
Pavements, Carriage-way. Dub. R. **116**: 397.
— for Large Cities. (L. H. Isaacs) J. Soc. Arts, **42**: 61.
— Manufacture and Use of Brick for. (H. K. Landis) Eng. M. **11**: 1097.
— Municipal. (G. W. Elder) Overland, n. s. **28**: 274.
— Sidewalks, Roads, and Bridges. (W. Howard) Engin. M. **8**: 1014.
— Street. Am. Arch. **49**: 23.
Pavia, Certosa of. (J. Cartwright) M. of Art, **6**: 441. **7**: 45.
Paving in America. (W. Fortune) Cent. **24**: 894.
Paw Ducket's Coon-hunt. (Ed. W. Sandys) Outing, **26**: 434.
Pawnbrokers, Study of. (C. Bissell) Lippinc. **53**: 222.
Pawnbroking in Various Countries. (E. F. Baldwin) Outl. **52**: 173.
— "Ma Tante." (E. R. Spearman) Cosmopol. **16**: 747.
Pawned; a poem. All the Year, **54**: 12.
Pawnshops and Small Borrowers. (C. Barnard) Chaut. **19**: 69.
— Charity. (A. R. Kimball) Chr. Un. **45**: 791.
— French. (Rev. Wm. Burnet) Time, **20**: 437.
— How to municipalize the. (R. Donald) New R. **11**: 581.
— State, in Holland. (J. H. Gore) Forum, **21**: 228.
— Why not municipalize? (R. Donald) Contemp. **66**: 177.
Pawnee Hero Stories and Folk-Tales, Grinnell's. (F. Boas) J. Am. Folk-Lore, **3**: 80.
Pawnee Myth, Development of a. (G. B. Grinnell) J. Am. Folk-Lore, **5**: 127.
Pawnee Mythology. (G. B. Grinnell) J. Am. Folk-Lore, **6**: 113.
Pawnee Star Myth. (G. B. Grinnell) J. Am. Folk-Lore, **7**: 197.
Paxton, John R. (W. S. Bridgman) Munsey, **6**: 134.
Payer, Julius von. (B. Karageorgevitch) M. of Art, **19**: 399.
Paying in Person; a story. Cornh. **71**: 617. Same art. Ecl. M. **125**: 459.
Payment in Full. (E. E. Wood) New Eng. M. n. s. **13**: 210.
Payment in Promises to pay. Open Court, **3**: 1703.

Payments, Deferred, Standard of. (E. A. Ross) Ann. Am. Acad. Pol. Sci. 3: 293, (L. S. Merriam) 483. — (F. Fetter) Ann. Am. Acad. Pol. Sci. 5: 882.
— — Total Utility Standard of. (E. A. Ross) Ann. Am. Acad. Pol. Sci. 4: 425.
Payn, James. Backwater of Life. Spec. 74: 608.
— First Book of, with portrait. (J. Payn) Idler, 1: 649.
— Gleams of Memory. (J. Payn) Cornh. 70: 34, 138, 255. — Sat. R. 78: 511.
Payne, John Howard. (H. V. Clarke) Munsey, 7: 694.
Payne-Smith, Robert, Dean of Canterbury. Ath. '95, 1: 443.
Peabody, Andrew Preston, with portrait. (R. S. Rantoul) Harv. Grad. M. 1: 505. — (C. C. Everett) Harv. Mo. 16: 89. — (E. Lord) New Eng. M. n. s. 7: 639. — (P. S. Moxom) New World, 2: 329.
Peabody, Elizabeth Palmer. (W. Lewin) Acad. 45: 101. — (Jane M. Parker) Outl. 49: 214. — (M. S. Porter) Bost. 3: 340.
Peabody, George, Philanthropist. (W. E. Simonds) Char. R. 4: 242.
— Centenary of. Critic, 26: 145.
Peabody, Gen. Nathaniel, Sketch of. (W. C. Todd) N. E. Reg. 47: 297.
Peabody, Rev. Stephen, and wife. (W. C. Todd) N. E. Reg. 48: 171.
Peabody Museum, Harvard College. (S. R. Koehler) M. of Art, 12: 393, 404. 13: 47.
Peace, Agitation for, Present Position of the. (C. E. Maurice) Econ. R. 5: 252.
Peace, Armed. (S. Low) National, 26: 609.
— Conditions Essential to Universal. Am. J. Pol. 4: 104.
— Growth of Principles of, and the Methods of Propagating them. (B. A. Lockwood) Am. M. Civics, 6: 504.
— Permanent, Idea of. (O. Pfleiderer) Jurid. R. 8: 40.
— Plea for. (W. L. Stobart) Westm. 142: 135.
— Preservation of, Past and Present. (H. Hall) Time, 4: 672.
— Universal, Prospect of. R. of Rs. (N. Y.) 10: 635.
Peace Movement in Europe. (F. Passy) Am. J. Sociol. 2: 1.
— Modern. (A. H. Love) Am. J. Pol. 1: 607.
Peace Tribunal of the Nations. (E. E. Hale) Lend a H. 16: 176.
See Arbitration.
Peach, Chinese. Garden & F. 5: 438.
Peach-growing in Georgia. (L. J. Vance) Garden & F. 8: 248.
Peacock, Thomas Love. Sat. R. 73: 82.
Peak, The, Derbyshire, England. (E. Bradbury) M. of Art, 2: 173–277. — (E. Bradbury) Time, 7: 243.
Peakland, A Sunday in. All the Year, 76: 270.
Pear-borer. (J. B. Smith) Garden & F. 7: 373.
Pearce Amersom's Will; a story. (R. M. Johnston) Lippinc. 50: 683.
Pearceite, and the Crystallization of Polybasite. (S. L. Penfield) Am. J. Sci. 152: 17.
Pearl, Story of a. (E. W. Streeter) Good Words, 36: 340.
Pearl-diving and its Perils. (H. P. Whitmarsh) Cosmopol. 18: 564.
Pearl Fishing. (H. E. A. Coate) Time, 21: 646.
Pearl-shell Industry, New Phase of. Chamb. J. 70: 382.
Pearlin' Jean; a story. (J. M. Scott-Moncrieff) Liv. Age, 192: 209.
Pearls and Mother-of-pearl. (C. S. Pratt) Pop. Sci. Mo. 49: 390.
Pearls, Curiosities of. (H. J. Gibbins) Gent. M. n. s. 53: 306.
Pearls, Fishing, in Australia. (H. P. Whitmarsh) Cent. 21: 905.
— Scotch, and Pearl Hunting. (M. G. Watkins) Gent. M. n. s. 56: 626.
Pears, Cultivation of. (G. C. Butz) Garden & F. 5: 414.
— Late Keeping. (T. H. Hoskins) Garden & F. 6: 30.
— Pyrus Tschonoskii. (C. S. Sargent) Garden & F. 7: 54.
Pearson, Charles Henry. (J. S. Cotton) Acad. 45: 475, (H. A. Strong) 497. — Spec. 72: 786. 76: 594.
Pearson, Hugh. (A. K. H. Boyd) Longm. 24: 25.
Pearson, John, Bishop, Works of. Eng. R. 3: 441.
Pearson, Sir John. (M. Cookson) Law Q. 2: 373.
Pearson's Lane. (C. C. Abbott) Lippinc. 56: 251.
Peary, Josephine, with portrait. Around World, 1: 14.
— Among Eskimos. Spec. 73: 412.
Peary, Robert Edwin, Arctic Expedition of. (C. Moffett) McClure, 1: 156. — (C. C. Adams) Chaut. 18: 580.
— Arctic Work of. (C. C. Adams) Geog. J. 2: 303.
— Greenland Expedition, Second. (E. Astrup) Knowl. 18: 75.
— Portraits of. McClure, 1: 489.
Peasant, The; a sketch. Cornh. 71: 182. Same art. Ecl. M. 124: 412.
Peasant-farmer of Lancashire, The. Macmil. 72: 420.
Peasant Life in Normandy. (H. Glazebrook) M. of Art, 6: 468. 7: 215.
Pease, Joseph. Westm. 139: 414.
Peat Fuel. (L. Stern) Am. Arch. 45: 45.
— in Germany. (L. Stern) Cassier, 10: 111.
Peattie, Mrs. Elia W., with portrait. Bk. Buyer, 13: 607.
Peck, Commissioner Charles F., and Protection. Pub. Opin. 13: 513.
Peck, Jonas O. Meth. R. 54: 609.
Peck, Washington F., with portrait. Nat'l M. (N. Y. '91) 19: 73.
Peckham, Rufus W. (A. O. Hall) Green Bag, 8: 1.
Peckham, Wheeler H., Nomination of, for Supreme Court. Pub. Opin. 16: 427.
Peckinpaw's Pills; a story. (F. Crane) Cosmopol. 16: 340.
Pectoral Cross, The; a story. (J. Ingersoll) Outing, 29: 211.
Pedagogics in Germany. (C. Ufer) Monist, 1: 597.
— Psychology, Physiology and. (T. Hughes) Am. Cath. Q. 19: 790.
— Study of. (T. M. Balliet) Educa. 14: 65.
Pedagogy, Old and New, in Germany. (W. Rein) Educa. R. 11: 209.
— Psychology and. (W. L. Gooding) School R. 3: 556.
— Sociology and. (A. Tompkins) Am. J. Sociol. 1: 353.
— Study of, at Cornell University. (S. G. Williams) Educa. R. 3: 374.
Peddler's Peril; a story. (L. B. Miller) Harper, 90: 121.
Peddling; a Decayed Profession. Macmil. 72: 305.
Pedigree; Claims of Long Descent. (W. Clark) No. Am. 159: 756.
— Concerning our. (H. G. Wells) Gent. M. n. s. 50: 575.
— How to trace a. Walford's Antiq. 11: 238, 386.
Pedro, Dom. (J. Realf, jr.) Arena, 5: 366.
Peel, Arthur Wellesley, and his Predecessors. (H. D. Traill) Fortn. 63: 784. Same art. Liv. Age, 205: 621.
Peel, George Villiers, with portrait. Bank. M. (Lond.) 61: 387.

Peel, Sir Robert. (G. Peel) 19th Cent. 39: 596. Same art. Ecl. M. 126: 616. Same art. Liv. Age, 209: 500.
Peeping Tom and Lady Godiva. (E. S. Hartland) Folk-Lore, 1: 207.
Peerage, British. Quar. 177: 386.
— Sir B. Burke and the. Spec. 69: 922.
— Complete English, by F. Barlow. (C. M. Collins) Bookworm, 2: 115.
Peers, Representative, of Scotland. (W. C. Macpherson) Scot. R. 25: 344.
Peewit, Home of the. Spec. 68: 709.
Pei-Ho, In the River. (W. L. Clowes) Blackw. 155: 856. Same art. Liv. Age, 202: 46.
Peirce, Benj., Services to American Astronomy, with portrait. (T. J. J. See) Pop. Astron. 3: 49.
Peking. (M. R. Davies) Fortn. 62: 793. — (T. Child) J. Soc. Arts, 43: 207.
— Before and behind the Walls. Chamb. J. 72: 225.
— Recent Audience at, 1891. (R. S. Gundry) Ecl. M. 117: 479.
— a Threatened City. (M. R. Davies) Fortn. 62: 793. Same art. Liv. Age, 204: 54.
Peking Gazette and Chinese Posting. Longm. 29: 73. Same art. Liv. Age, 211: 642.
Peking University, Chinese Literati in. (M. L. Taft) Meth. R. 56: 921.
Pelagian Controversy and Augustine. (B. B. Warfield) Chr. Lit. 14: 465, 577. 15: 1-454. 16: 1-121.
Pelagic Crustacea, in Green Lake, Wisconsin. (C. D. Marsh) Am. Natural. 28: 807.
Pelargoniums. (W. Watson) Garden & F. 8: 294.
— Cultivation of. (W. N. Craig) Garden & F. 8: 226.
Pelasgi, Ancient, and their Descendants. (Pasco Wassa Pasha and P. Colquhoun) Asia. R. 11: 59.
Pelaya River, Sources of. (C. M. S. Pasley) Geog. J. 3: 105.
Pelecypoda, Proposed Classification of. (B. B. Woodward) Nat. Sci. 8: 239.
Pele's Last Appearance; a story. (M. H. Closson) Overland, n. s. 19: 318.
Pelham-Copley Letters, Some. (P. L. Ford) Atlan. 71: 499.
Pélléas and Mélisande; a prose play. (M. Maeterlinck) Poet-Lore, 6: 413.
Pelletan, Fanny. (F. M. Hoffman) Music, 9: 369.
Pellew, Edward. *See* Exmouth, Admiral Lord.
Pellew, George, with portrait. (W. D. Howells) Cosmopol. 13: 527. — Critic, 20: 133.
Peloponnese, Some Ancient Routes in. (W. Loring) J. Hel. Stud. 15: 25.
Pelton, Alonzo, with portrait. (H. L. Conard) Nat'l M. (N. Y. '91) 15: 191.
Pemberton Family. (W. K. Watkins) N. E. Reg. 46: 392.
Pembroke, George R. C. H., Earl of, Death of. (R. Talbot) Sat. R. 79: 687.
Pembroke, Mass., Baptisms in the Second Church at, 1748-1803. (Mrs. E. M. Avery) N. E. Reg. 49: 286, 426. 50: 177, 317.
Penal Colonies, Agricultural and Industrial. (A. Griffiths) No. Am. 163: 676.
Penal System, Our. (N. Nutt) Southern M. 4: 30.
Penances: Taxes of the Papal Penitentiary. (H. C. Lea) Eng. Hist. R. 8: 424.
Penck, Albrecht. Morphology of the Earth's Surface. (C. Lapworth) Geog. J. 5: 575.
Pender, Sir John, Art Collection of. (J. F. Boyes) Art J. 44: 161.
Pen-drawing, English, Harper on. Sat. R. 73: 424.
Pendulograph, The. (J. Andrew) New Sci. R. 1: 166.
Pendulum, The, and Geology. Liv. Age, 207: 50.
— Bifilar, for Measuring Earth-tilts. (C. Davison) Nature, 50: 246.
— Horizontal. (C. Davison) Nat. Sci. 8: 233.
— Movements of. (J. Milne) Nature, 53: 180.
— Use of a Free Pendulum as a Time Standard. (T. C. Mendenhall) Am. J. Sci. 143: 85.
Pendulum Escapement, New. (— Leman) Astron. 12: 882.
Pendulum Observations in Northern and Southern Hemispheres. (H. S. Schaw) Nature, 53: 222.
— Results of Recent. (G. R. Putnam) Am. J. Sci. 151: 186.
Penelope's English Experiences. (K. D. Wiggin) Atlan. 71: 79, 168.
Pengelly, William, Ath. '94, 1: 383. — Nat. Sci. 4: 389. — (W. B. Dawkins) Nature, 49: 536.
Penikese, Reminiscences of. (H. B. C. Beedy) Educa. 13: 339.
Peninsula Campaign, First Six Weeks of. (J. F. Rhodes) Am. Hist. R. 1: 464.
Peninsular War; Battles of the Nive. Macmil. 73: 149.
— Battle of St. Pierre. (W. H. James) Macmil. 70: 331.
— Unpublished Incident of. (Sir A. L. Freemantle) National, 23: 719.
Penitentiary at Kingston, Canada. (W. J. Macleod) Canad. M. 6: 3.
Penley, W. S., the Actor, at Home. (G. B. Burgin) Idler, 4: 171.
Penmænmawr, Braich y Ddinas on. (H. H. Lines) Antiq. n. s. 29: 11.
Penmanship, Microscopic. Bookworm, 6: 185.
— Writer's Cramp; its Recognition and Prevention. (K. West) Writer, 8: 13.
Penn, Granville, as a Scholar. (A. J. Edmunds) Pennsyl. M. 19: 119.
Penn, Wm., and Peter the Great. (H. Latchford) Arena, 11: 80.
— Essay towards the Present and Future Peace of Europe. New Eng. M. n. s. 15: 380.
— Family of. (H. M. Jenkins) Pennsyl. M. 20: 1, 158, 370.
— Genealogical Gleanings concerning. (J. H. Lea) Pennsyl. M. 17: 55.
Penn Family of Pennsylvania. Am. Hist. Reg. 1: 559.
Pennsylvania and her Public Men. (S. G. Fisher) Lippinc. 58: 114.
— Charter of, to Penn, Original of, Where is the? (W. B. Rawle) Pennsyl. M. 16: 86.
— Colonial, Corner of. (Bucks County.) (H. C. Michener) M. Am. Hist. 27: 225.
— Constitution of 1776, Adoption of. (P. L. Ford) Pol. Sci. Q. 10: 426.
— Eastern, Southern Ice Limit in. (E. H. Williams) Am. J. Sci. 149: 174.
— Election Laws of. (A. B. Bird) Citizen, 1: 14-160.
— First Regiment, Regimental Book of, 1782-83. Am. Hist. Reg. 2: 1449. 3: 44. — (L. B. Thomas; C. A. Hanna) Am. Hist. Reg. 3: 240-454.
— Flag of, Provincial. (F. O. Allen) Pennsyl. M. 18: 249.
— Folk-lore of. (D. G. Brinton) J. Am. Folk-Lore, 5: 176.
— — German. (W. J. Hoffman) J. Am. Folk-Lore, 1: 125. — (F. Starr) J. Am. Folk-Lore, 4: 321.
— Frontier Forts of. Pennsyl. M. 20: 257.
— Fundamentall Constitutions of, as drawn up by Wm. Penn. Pennsyl. M. 20: 283.
— German Churches of, Founding of. (J. H. Dubbs) Pennsyl. M. 17: 241.

Pennsylvania; Militia Regiments, Roster of Officers, 1802. (J. G. Leach) Pennsyl. M. 20: 122.
— National Guard of, and its Antecedents. (C. A. Booth) Outing, 23: 73-412.
— Northeastern, Gorges and Waterfalls of. Around World, 1: 123.
— Paper Currency. (C. W. Macfarlane) Ann. Am. Acad. Pol. Sci. 8: 50.
— Picturesque. (L. Knoche) Mo. Illust. 3: 41.
— Poets of, during the Provincial Period. (F. H. Williams) Pennsyl. M. 17: 1.
— Politics of, Early in 19th Century. Pennsyl. M. 17: 462.
— Rivers and Valleys of. (Wm. M. Davis) Nat. Geog. M. 1: 183.
— Slavery in. (A. R. M. Spaid) Am. Hist. Reg. 2: 1181.
— State College. (E. J. Haly) Cassier, 6: 119.
— University of. (F. N. Thorpe) Harper, 91: 285.
— — Ethics in. (G. S. Fullerton) Eth. Rec. 2: 220.
— — Liberal Tendencies in. (L. R. Harley) Educa. 17: 98.
— — School of Architecture. Am. Arch. 43: 152.
— — Science at. (L. R. Harley) Pop. Sci. Mo. 49: 440.
Pennsylvania Academy of Fine Arts. (C. McIlvaine) Q. Illust. 2: 10.
Pennethorne on Parnassus; a story. (F. Banfield) Gent. M. n. s. 52: 325.
Penny-in-the-slot Machines. Am. Arch. 38: 205.
Penobscot Bay. (E. A. Start) New Eng. M. n. s. 14: 579.
Penology in Europe and America. (S. J. Barrows) Arena, 11: 289.
— Modern. (G. R. Vicars) Gent. M. n. s. 53: 627.
— Modern Spirit of. (A. Winter) Pol. Sci. Q. 8: 445.
— Tendencies in. (S. J. Barrows) New World, 5: 67.
Pensée; a pansy story. (R. Metcalfe) Sund. M. 21: 550.
Pensioners in Essex Co., Mass. (G. A. Gordon) N. E. Reg. 49: 316.
Pensions, Civil, in Great Britain, Evils of. Sat. R. 80: 610.
— Old Age. *See* Old Age.
— State. (J. Rae) Econ. J. 2: 183. — (A. Marshall) Econ. J. 2: 186. — (H. C. Bourne) Macmil. 65: 312.
Pensions, U. S. Pub. Opin. 14: 4-273.
— Case of Justice Long. Pub. Opin. 15: 427.
— Federal and Confederate, contrasted. (M. B. Morton) Forum, 16: 68.
— Grand Army as a Pension Agency. (C. McK. Leoser) Forum, 15: 522.
— Half a Million Dollars a Day for. (J. D. Warner) Forum, 15: 439.
— in Legislation. (F. W. Blackmar) Chaut. 22: 284.
— Inside View of the Bureau. (A. B. Casselman) Cent. 24: 135.
— The Law and its Administration. (E. F. Waite) Harper, 86: 235.
— Patriotism, and Morality. (A. R. Foote) Am. J. Pol. 2: 638.
— Private, Anomalies of. (T. F. Dennis) Forum, 15: 377.
— Revision of the List. (R. P. C. Wilson; S. S. Burdett; W. C. Church) No. Am. 156: 416. — (W. G. Veazey; J. H. O'Neil; B. A. Enloe) No. Am. 156: 618. — Pub. Opin. 15: 377, 403, 451.
— Time to call a Halt. (H. W. Slocum) Forum, 12: 646.
— U. S. Bonds for. (H. White) Nation, 55: 466.
Pentecost, Dr. G. F., at Home. Sund. M. 24: 44.
Pentelikon. (Rennell Rodd) Univ. R. 5: 401.
Pentland Firth and Pentland Hills. (J. Rhys) Acad. 42: 132.
Pentlandite from Sudbury, Ont., etc. (S. L. Penfield) Am. J. Sci. 145: 493.
Peonage in Mexico. (W. L. Logan) Soc. Econ. 5: 98.
Peonies, Single-Flowered. Garden & F. 6: 304.
People, The, and Legislation. (L. V. Bennett) Am. J. Pol. 2: 610.
— of the Cities. (Alice French) Scrib. M. 16: 328.
— that we serve. (Alice French) Scrib. M. 16: 190.
— we pass; stories. (J. Ralph) Harper, 89: 695, 828. 90: 421, 781, 914. 91: 617.
"People the Best Governors," Book entitled. (H. A. Cushing) Am. Hist. R. 1: 284.
People who have failed, Why help? (W. F. Spaulding) Lend a H. 11: 175.
People's Kitchen, How to organize in London. (E. Sellers) 19th Cent. 37: 409.
People's Palace. (R. A. Gregory) Nature, 50: 114.
— Story of. (V. Sandars) Belgra. 71: 47.
See London, East.
People's Party, The. (C. W. Wiley) Am. J. Pol. 5: 651.
— Chasing a Political Phantom. (E. F. Howe) Am. J. Pol. 1: 603.
— Fallacies of. (E. Mead) Am. J. Pol. 1: 288.
— Strength and Weakness of. (E. McDonald-Valesh) Arena, 5: 726.
See Populists.
Peoples, Psychology of. (A. Fouillée) Chaut. 21: 452.
Pepins [Melon Pear]. Garden & F. 5: 95. — (W. M. Munson) Garden & F. 5: 173.
Pepper Tree. Garden & F. 8: 502.
Peppercorn, A. D. (J. S. Little) Art J. 48: 201.
Pepperell, Sir W., and the Capture of Louisburg. (V. Reed) New Eng. M. n. s. 12: 415.
Pepperellboro' (now Saco), Me., Marriages and Marriage Intentions in, 1768-75. (F. E. Blake) N. E. Reg. 50: 13.
Pepsine, Vegetable. Chamb. J. 69: 639.
Peptone. (W. D. Halliburton) Sci. Prog. 3: 35.
Pepys, Samuel. (C. Whibley) New R. 14: 367.
— and the Popish Plot of 1678. (J. R. Tanner) Eng. Hist. R. 7: 281.
— as a Bookman. (H. B. Wheatley) Bibliographica, 1: 155.
— Diary of. Quar. 183: 1.
— — Unpublished Pages of. (H. B. Wheatley) Liv. Age, 192: 172.
— — Wheatley's Bright's Edition. (G. Smith) Nation, 56: 457.
— Early Life of. (C. H. Firth) Macmil. 69: 32. Same art. Liv. Age, 200: 444. Same art. Ecl. M. 122: 112.
— Letter to. (A. Lang) Scrib. M. 14: 354.
— The Man. Macmil. 74: 345. Same art. Liv. Age, 211: 46.
— Notes on Little-known Painters. (A. Beaver) Art J. 45: 25.
Pequot Fight. (F. J. Kingsbury) Am. Hist. Reg. 1: 359.
Perak, Cave Dwellers of. (L. Wray) Anthrop. J. 26: 36.
Pérard, Victor, with portrait. Bk. Buyer, 13: 461. — (W. Carleton) Q. Illust. 2: 280.
Percentile Grades. (L. Gulick) Am. Statis. Assoc. 3: 321.
Perception of Rate of Movement in Direct and Indirect Field of Vision, Method of Comparing. (F. B. Dresslar) Am. J. Psychol. 6: 312.
— Recognition-theory of. (A. Allin) Am. J. Psychol. 7: 237.

Perception, Visual, and Attention, Development of. (H. Griffing) Am. J. Psychol. 7: 227.
Perchlorates, Quantitative Determination of. (D. A. Kreider) Am. J. Sci. 150: 287.
Perchloric Acid and its Application to the Determination of Potassium. (D. A. Kreider) Am. J. Sci. 149: 443.
Percussion Figures on Cleavage Plates of Mica. (T. L. Walker) Am. J. Sci. 152: 5.
Percy, Thomas, Bishop, Folio MS. of. (J. Pickford) Walford's Antiq. 1: 203.
Perdita's Candle. (M. Young) Cent. 29: 586.
Père Moineau; a story. Chamb. J. 71: 279–311.
Père Vulcan's Confession; a story. (F. Coppée) Cosmopol. 15: 368.
Pereda, José Maria de. (H. Lynch) Contemp. 69: 218. Same art. Liv. Age, 208: 692.
Perennials, Border of Hardy. (C. S. Sargent) Garden & F. 7: 331.
Perez, Antonio, More Light on. (M. A. S. Hume) 19th Cent. 36: 754.
Perfall, Baron Karl von. (J. G. Robertson) National, 25: 247.
Perfect; a story. (A. V. Chartres) Cosmopol. 22: 185.
Perfume Worship in all Ages. (E. Singleton) Cosmopol. 16: 476.
Perfumery, Manufacture of. Garden & F. 5: 340.
Perfumery Products. (J. N. Gerard) Garden & F. 9: 112.
Pergamon, Sculptures from. (T. Ely) Walford's Antiq. 2: 132.
Perigonimus Jonesii; a Hydroid supposed to be New, from Cold Spring Harbor, Long Island. (H. L. Osborn; C. W. Hargitt) Am. Natural. 28: 27.
Pericles and the Golden Age of Athens, Abbott on. (P. Giles) Eng. Hist. R. 7: 537.
— as an Art Patron. (F. M. Robinson) M. of Art, 11: 158.
Peridotite, Third Occurrence of, in Central New York. (C. H. Smyth, jr.) Am. J. Sci. 143: 322.
Perigord, Idle Hours in. (E. H. Barker) Temp. Bar, 98: 71. Same art. Liv. Age, 197: 811.
Périgueux, Churches of. (M. G. Van Rensselaer) Cent. 29: 918.
Perils, National. (J. F. Bartlett) Am. J. Pol. 2: 9.
Perimeter, A New. (J. E. Lough) Psychol. R. 3: 282.
Periodic Law, The. (J. M. Wainwright) New Sci. R. 2: 101.
— How far shall it be followed in teaching Chemistry? (F. P. Venable) Science, n. s. 2: 506.
— Some Difficulties in Presentation of. (F. P. Venable) Science, n. s. 4: 160.
Periodical, Cost of a French Illustrated. Gent. M. n. s. 55: 216.
Periodical Literature, Byways of. (A. E. Waite) Walford's Antiq. 11: 179. 12: 65.
— English. (W. R. Nicoll) Bookman, 1: 174.
Periodical Press, The, 1865–95. (T. H. S. Escott) Blackw. 156: 532.
Periodicals, American. Dial (Ch.) 13: 203.
— American Literary, General Catalogue of. (C. A. Nelson) Lib. J. 20: supp. 30.
— Bad Features of Good. (H. C. Bolton) Lib. J. 21: 317.
— Excursion among. (E. H. Blair) And. R. 18: 147.
— Use of. (W. H. Brett) Lib. J. 20: supp. 12.
Perjury, Petty. (M. D. Chalmers) Law Q. 11: 217.
Perkins, Abraham, Descendants of, in Plymouth County. (J. W. Porter) N. E. Reg. 50: 34.
Perles, Joseph. (W. Bacher) Jew. Q. 7: 1.
Perlycross. (R. D. Blackmore) Macmil. 68: 81–401. 69: 1–401. 70: 1–161.
Permian of Texas. (R. S. Tarr) Am. J. Sci. 143: 9.
Peroff, Basil. (N. Sobkô) M. of Art, 9: 315.
Perpetua, St., Passion of. (G. Canning) Month, 74: 340.
Perpetual Curate. Macmil. 68: 275. Same Art. Liv. Age, 199: 186.
Perpetual Motion Machine, The Redheffer. (C. Sellers) Cassier, 8: 523.—(H. Morton) J. Frankl. Inst. 139: 246.
Perplexing Manifestations; and that Last Sunday. (A. K. H. Boyd) Longm. 28: 172.
Perplexing Young Woman; a story. (Mrs. N. Fiennes) Belgra. 80: 95–442.
Perry, E. Wood. (M. T. Earle) Mo. Illust. 12: 531.
Perry, Nora. Critic, 28: 375.—Lit. W. (Bost.) 27: 168.
Perry, Commodore O. H. Victory on Lake Erie. (J. C. Ridpath) Chaut. 15: 135.
Perry, William Stevens, Bishop of Iowa. Nat'l M. (N. Y. '91) 19: 293.
Persecuting Spirit, Peril of encouraging the. (B. O. Flower) Arena, 16: 752.
Persecution and Tolerance, Creighton on. Sat. R. 79: 554.
— Religious. (A. F. Marshall) Am. Cath. Q. 19: 508. —Spec. 69: 283.
Persecution of the Curate, The. (R. Shindler) Idler, 5: 200.
Persecutions of Christians, Early. Church Q. 41: 26. Same art. Chr. Lit. 14: 587.
— Salvation *via* the Rack. (Julian Hawthorne) Cosmopol. 18: 482.
Perseid, Radiant. (W. H. S. Monck) Astron. 13: 344.
Perseids of 1895. (W. F. Denning) Nature, 52: 395.
Persepolis, Ruins of. (C. Smith) Macmil. 67: 256. Same art. Liv. Age, 196: 804.
Perseus and Andromeda in Greek Art. (J. E. Harrison) M. of Art, 8: 498.
— Legend of, Hartland's. (W. W. Newell) J. Am. Folk-Lore, 7: 329.
Perseverance: the Beginning and the Ending. (J. H. Vincent) Chaut. 20: 543.
Persia and Kurdistan, Travels in, Bishop's. Ath. '92, 1: 75.
— and the Persian Question, Curzon on. Ath. '92, 1: 719. — Atlan. 70: 550. — Blackw. 152: 615. — Ed. R. 176: 293. — Sat. R. 73: 717. — Nation, 57: 102. — Quar. 176: 166.
— Assassination of Shah of. (E. G. Browne) New R. 14: 651.
— Browne's Year among the Persians. Ath. '94, 1: 76. —Sat. R. 78: 271.
— By Caravan to. (E. H. Weeks) Harper, 87: 651, 813.
— Desert of, March through. (C. E. Biddulph) Asia. R. 12: 234.
— French Embassy to, under Richelieu. (M. G. De Rialle) Asia. R. 11: 163.
— From Ispahan to Kurrachee. (E. L. Weeks) Harper, 88: 231.
— From, towards the Caspian Sea. (H. L. Wells) Geog. J. 8: 501.
— Geography of. (F. J. Goldsmid) Geog. J. 6: 177.
— History of, Beginnings of. (H. H. Howorth) Acad. 41: 182–519.
— in Eastern Politics. Sat. R. 81: 466.
— in 1586, Italian Report on the Condition of. (H. F. Brown) Eng. Hist. R. 7: 314.
— Journey in, Collins's. Sat. R. 81: 582.

Persia, Journeys in, 1890-91. (H. B. Vaughan) Geog. J. 7: 24, 163.
— Lenz's World Tour awheel. Outing, 27: 382, 467. 28: 47-456. 29: 57.
— Military Strength of. (C. E. Biddulph) Un. Serv. M. 5: 582.
— On Things Persian. (J. C. Wills) Fortn. 65: 893. Same art. Liv. Age, 210: 21.
— Physical Geography. (C. E. Biddulph) Asia. R. 14: 43.
— Railways for. Asia. R. 11: 1. — Dub. R. 111: 189.
— Regeneration of. Asia. R. 10: 1.
— Reign of Terror in. (Sheikh Djemal ed Din) Contemp. 61: 238.
— Russia, England, and. (L. Griffin) 19th Cent. 40: 1.
— Shah of, in England. (A. Vámbéry) 19th Cent. 35: 451. Same art. Liv. Age, 201: 111.
— Stage in, The Modern. (J. Mew) Fortn. 65: 902. Same art. Ecl. M. 127: 230.
— Talks with a Persian Statesman. (H. R. Haweis) Contemp. 70: 73.
— Telegraph Department in. (A. Houtum-Schindler) Asia. R. 13: 321.
— Telegraphs and Trade Routes in. (H. L. Wells) J. Soc. Arts, 42: 534.
— under Nasr-ud-din Shah. Asia. R. 12: 1.
— Women in. (W. von Schierbrand) Lippinc. 55: 550. — (R. B. Karib) Cosmopol. 13: 668.
Persian-English Dictionary, Steingass's. Ath. '92, 2: 848. — Sat. R. 74: 399.
Persian Gulf, Ancient Trading Centres of. (A. W. Stiffe) Geog. J. 7: 644.
— under British Protection. (J. T. Bent) Fortn. 60: 365. Same art. Liv. Age, 199: 235.
Persian Lapidaries, Three. (A. Houtum-Schindler) Acad. 48: 526.
Persian Miracle Play, A. (M. Pechell) Belgra. 91: 209.
Persian Poetry. (Sir E. Strachey) Atlan. 71: 322. — (J. Buckham) Poet-Lore, 3: 1.
Persian Poets, Three. (J. H. Parsons) Gent. M. n. s. 55: 419.
Persigny, Duc de, Memoirs of. (Earl Cowper) 19th Cent. 39: 583. Same art. Liv. Age, 209: 545. — (A. Laugel) Nation, 62: 304.
Persimmon, The. Garden & F. 8: 262.
— American. (C. S. Plumb) Garden & F. 9: 442.
Persona. (F. M. Müller) Open Court, 1: 505, 543.
Personal Estate and Real Estate. (M. H. Box) Law Q. 3: 406.
Personal Liberty: Is it Desirable? (Joel Benton) Soc. Econ. 3: 210.
Personal Possessions. Spec. 71: 269. Same art. Ecl. M. 121: 513.
Personalities in Criticism of Officials. (E. L. Godkin) Nation, 55: 488.
Personality. (T. Ribot) Open Court, 3: 1586.
— Alterations of. (T. Ribot) Open Court, 3: 1695.
— — Binet on. (T. Courtier) Psychol. R. 1: 187.
— and Memory. (T. Ribot) Open Court, 4: 2709.
— as the Outcome of Evolution. (E. M. Caillard) Contemp. 65: 713. Same art. Ecl. M. 123: 15.
— Double. (W. R. Newbold) Pop. Sci. Mo. 50: 67.
— — and Double Brain. (T. Ribot) Open Court, 4: 2700.
— — and Double Soul. Open Court, 3: 1948.
— — and Submerged, and Phenomena of Modern Spiritualism. (A. N. Somers) Psych. R. 1: 314.
— — Problem of. (P. Carus) Open Court, 2: 1178.
— Experimental Method applied to. (T. Ribot) Open Court, 4: 2663, 2667.
Personality, Human and Divine; Illingworth's Bampton Lectures, 1894. Church Q. 40: 190.
— Nature of, as Illustrated by Twins. (T. Ribot) Open Court, 4: 2644.
— Physical Basis of. (T. Ribot) Open Court, 3: 1658.
— Rôle of Ideas in the Constitution of. (T. Ribot) Open Court, 5: 2742.
— Self and its Derangements. (W. R. Newbold) Pop. Sci. Mo. 49: 810.
Personality; a poem. (Archibald Lampman) Cosmopol. 18: 751.
Personality-suggestion. (J. M. Baldwin) Psychol. R. 1: 274.
Personifications, Veiled, in Literature. (E. H. Donkin) Gent. M. n. s. 54: 313.
Perspective, General Method of. (R. de Saussure) Am. Arch. 51: 40.
— Linear. (G. A. Middleton) Archit. Rec. 4: 464. 5: 378.
— — Some Constructions in. Am. Arch. 46: 48.
Perspective Illusions in Italian Churches. (W. H. Goodyear) Archit. R. 6: 163.
Perth, on the Swan River. Chamb. J. 71: 15.
Perth Museum of Natural History. (A. M. Rodger) Nat. Sci. 8: 41.
Perthshire. (J. H. Crawford) Scot. R. 23: 321.
— Idler in. (W. Canton) Good Words, 35: 570, 637, 712.
Peru, and the Head Waters of the Amazon. Dub. R. 116: 193.
— and its People. (A. F. Sears) Chaut. 17: 185.
— Business Opportunities in. (H. Guillaume) Engin. M. 7: 323.
— Central. Dub. R. 111: 190.
— Ceremony of the Quichuas of. (G. A. Dorsey) J. Am. Folk-Lore, 7: 307.
— Commerce and Resources of. (F. A. Pezet) J. Soc. Arts, 40: 411.
— Eastern, Social and Intellectual Condition of. (C. De Kalb) Harper, 85: 113.
— Incas of. Ecl. M. 127: 227.
— Rainy Period in, Indications of a. (A. E. Douglass) Science, 20: 231.
— Republic of. (A. F. Sears) New Eng. M. n. s. 7: 441.
— A Socialist State. (R. S. Long) Westm. 144: 605.
Perugia. (Mrs. F. W. W. Topham) M. of Art, 18: 105.
Perugini, Charles Edward. (S. F. Coles) Munsey, 9: 203.
Perugino, Pietro. (C. Phillips) Portfo. 24: 38, 59.
— An Altar-piece of. (G. Allen) Eng. Illust. 14: 535.
Perverse Cœlebs. (M. C. Smith) New Eng. M. n. s. 9: 117.
Pescadera, Chico; one Good Indian. (D. A. Goodsell) Chaut. 23: 179.
Pescadero Beach, California. (H. F. Lowe) Lippinc. 50: 372.
Pessimism. Church Q. 36: 116. — (A. Waters) Open Court, 8: 4073. — (A. Plummer) Thinker, 9: 526.
— and Poetry. (E. K. Chambers) Westm. 138: 366.
— and Progress. (S. A. Alexander) Contemp. 63: 75.
— Causes of. (C. H. Pearson) Fortn. 60: 441.
— in the Russian Novel. (E. G. Boner) Chaut. 22: 426.
— in the U. S. (G. Bradford, jr.) Atlan. 69: 363.
— Infection of. (G. Batchelor) New World, 5: 601.
— Natural Antidote to. (D. Pryde) Gent. M. n. s. 56: 162.
— Practical Suggestions of, to the Ministry. (G. H. Beard) And. R. 17: 272.

Pessimism, Significance of. (R. A. Holland, jr.) New World, 3: 295.
— Wenley's Aspects of. (J. F. Powicke) Crit. R. 4: 404.
Pessimist of Plato Road; a story. (G. Gissing) Eng. Illust. 12: no. 2, 51.
— Reply to a. (A. Austin) National, 19: 1. Same art. Ecl. M. 118: 614.
Pessimist Outlook, A. (C. Patmore) Fortn. 58: 88. Same art. Ecl. M. 119: 331. Same art. Liv. Age, 194: 697.
Pestalozzi, J. H. (C. J. Hamilton) Educa. R. 3: 173.
— and Herbart compared. (W. T. Harris) Educa. R. 5: 417. — (W. Rein) Forum, 21: 346.
— Leonard and Gertrude. (Nannie Brown) Educa. 15: 176.
Pestalozzian System, The. (G. S. Boutwell) Pop. Sci. Mo. 44: 55.
Pet of the Colony, The; a Story of Old Boston. (M. A. Denison) Bost. 2: 33.
Peter the Apostle; the Stone and the Rock. (T. C. Porter) Ref. Q. 39: 117-536. 40: 145, 292.
— England's Devotion to. (H. Vaughan) Dub. R. 110: 1.
— Gospel according to. (J. A. Robinson) New World, 3: 690. — (G. W. Cox) Acad. 45: 411. — (I. H. Hall) Bib. World, 1: 88. — (J. H. Bernard and others) Acad. 44: 275. — (A. J. Mass) Am. Cath. Q. 18: 313. — Church Q. 36: 385. — (J. Martineau) 19th Cent. 33: 905. 34: 633.
— — Additions to. (F. P. Badham) Ath. '93, 1: 605.
— — Did Polycarp have? (F. C. Conybeare) Acad. 44: 568.
— — Origin of. (F. P. Badham) Acad. 44: 91, 111.
— — Structure of. (J. R. Harris) Contemp. 64: 212.
— — True. (D. Kemble) Meth. R. 53: 357.
— Primitive Church, and See of. (S. F. Smith) Month, 81: 197.
Peter the Great, and William Penn. (H. Latchford) Arena, 11: 80.
Peter of Blois, Chronology of. Acad. 43: 59.
Peter Linnet's Interview; a story. (S. J. Duncan) Cosmopol. 15: 732.
Peter Teeter; a story. (C. N. Hood) Outing, 25: 244.
Peterborough, Saxon Monastery of. (J. J. S. Perowne) Good Words, 34: 810.
Peterborough Cathedral. Ath. '96, 2: 879. — Walford's Antiq. 3: 133.
— Recent Damage to. Sat. R. 79: 439.
Peterhof, Cronstadt and. (W. M. Inglis) Gent. M. n. s. 50: 619.
Peter's Wife; a novel. (Mrs. Hungerford) Belgra. 83: 1-337. 84: 1-337. 85: 1-337.
Peter's Wooing; a story. (P. Reyd) Gent. M. n. s. 56: 352. Same art. Liv. Age, 209: 509.
Peters, C. F. W. Nature, 51: 179.
Petey Burke and his Pupil; a story. (J. Ralph) Harper, 91: 617.
Peto, John. Acad. 42: 285.
Petöfi, Alexander. (Jessie D. Montgomery) Temp. Bar, 109: 405.
Petrarch and the Beginning of Modern Science. (G. B. Adams) Yale R. 1: 146.
— and the Carthusians. Am. Cath. Q. 19: 607.
— and Laura. (E. Gosse) Cosmopol. 17: 657.
— Correspondence of, Studies in. (H. W. Preston and L. Dodge) Atlan. 72: 89, 234, 395.
Petrel; Mutton Birds on Flinders Island. (H. H. Montgomery) New R. 7: 227.
Petrie, Flinders, Bronze Age Theory of. (H. W. Haynes) Am. J. Archæol. 9: 26.
Petrified Forest, The. (R. Wildman) Overland, n. s. 27: 9.
Petrographical Research, Methods of. (A. Harker) Sci. Prog. 3: 209.
Petrographs at Lake Pend d'Oreille, Idaho. (J. B. Leiberg) Science, 22: 156.
Petroleum, Deluge of, in 1886. (Chas. Marvin) Time, 14: 539.
— An Historical Sketch. (T. J. A. Freeman) Am. Cath. Q. 20: 404.
— Ontario, and its Products. (L. C. Campbell) Canad. M. 5: 321.
— Origin of. Chamb. J. 69: 593.
— Rise and Fall in. Chamb. J. 72: 678.
— Use of, in Prime Movers. (W. Robinson) J. Soc. Arts, 40: 960-1036.
Petroleum Engine, Brayton. Cassier, 2: 314.
Petroleum Fields of India. (R. D. Oldham) J. Soc. Arts, 42: 145.
Petroleum Industry. (P. MacQueen) Cosmopol. 12: 399.
Petroleum Motors for Carriages. Sat. R. 80: 8.
Petroleums, American Sulphur, Composition of. (C. F. Mabery) J. Frankl. Inst. 139: 401. 140: 1.
Petrology in America. (A. Harker) Sci. Prog. 5: 459.
Petronius. (C. Whibley) New R. 15: 451.
— Collignon's Study of. Spec. 70: 742.
— Friedländer's Cena of. (R. Ellis) Acad. 41: 256.
— Trimalchio's Feast. Macmil. 68: 203.
Petrossa, Treasures found at. M. of Art, 4: 148.
Pets and Sports of a Farmer Boy. (M. Halstead) Cosmopol. 12: 471.
— Garden. Spec. 70: 73.
— Possible. Spec. 68: 13.
— Royal. (G. B. Burgin) Idler, 3: 243. — (E. M. Jessop) Idler, 4: 3, 131.
Pettie, John. Ath. '93, 1: 255. — (W. M. Gilbert) Art J. 45: 206. — (R. Walker) Good Words, 34: 750. — (W. Meynell) M. of Art, 4: 11.
— House of. (H. Zimmern) M. of Art, 8: 89.
Pettitt, Henry. The Prodigal Daughter. Theatre, 29: 174.
Petty, Sir W. (Wm. L. Bevan) Am. Econ. Assoc. 9: 379. — Ed. R. 182: 45. — (C. H. Hull) Nation, 60: 288. — Liv. Age, 206: 323. — Lond. Q. 84: 263.
— Graunt or? Authorship of the "Observations upon the Bills of Mortality." (C. H. Hull) Pol. Sci. Q. 11: 105.
Pevtsof Expedition. (E. D. Morgan) Geog. J. 2: 55.
Pews, History of. (J. A. Sparvel-Bayly) Walford's Antiq. 12: 155, 231.
Pewter. (J. S. Gardner) J. Soc. Arts, 42: 627.
— Old English. Reliquary, 32: 148. 33: 202.
Pezant, Aymar. (H. Eckford) Q. Illust. 2: 163.
Pfefferkorn, John, and the Battle of the Books. (S. A. Hirsch) Jew. Q. 4: 256.
Pfeiffer, Ida. (A. King) Argosy, 56: 255.
Pfleiderer, Otto. Gifford Lectures at Edinburgh. Ath. '94, 2: 89. — Meth. R. 54: 794.
Phaleron, Bas-relief from. (N. E. Crosby) Am. J. Archæol. 9: 202.
Phantasms. (L. A. Weatherly) National, 19: 427. Same art. Ecl. M. 118: 780.
— In Defence of. (F. Podmore) National, 19: 234.
Phantom of the Brain; a poem. (A. G. Doughty) Canad. M. 7: 18.
Phantom of the High Sierras, A; a story. (M. Floyd) Overland, n. s. 21: 378.
Phantom of the Mines. (R. H. Syms) Cosmopol. 16: 739.

Phantom Death, The; a story. (W. C. Russell) Idler, 4: 221.
Phantom Fortune, A; a story. All the Year, 73: 562.
Phantom Governess, The. (T. R. Sullivan) Scrib. M. 20: 680.
Phantom Shepherd. (N. Guthrie-Smith) Good Words, 35: 630.
Phantom Ship, Legend of the. Chamb. J. 71: 381.
Phantom Trout of Sullivan County. (A. Livingstone) Outing, 26: 117.
Phantoms; a story. (C. Holland) Eng. Illust. 11: 577.
Phantoms of the Foot-bridge, The; a story. (C. E. Craddock) Harper, 88: 81.
Pharaoh of the Hard Heart. (W. M. F. Petrie) Cent. 30: 500.
Pharmacy, An Historic. (J. Hatton) Eng. Illust. 10: 166.
— Modern, Some Refinements of. Chamb. J. 71: 359.
Phasemeter, A. (J. Trowbridge) Am. J. Sci. 143: 232.
Pheasant, Macpherson on. Sat. R. 80: 272.
Pheasant-shooting in England. Sat. R. 82: 391.
Pheasants, At Home with the. (W. Bothams) Sund. M. 25: 679.
— Young, Observations on. (C. L. Morgan) Nature, 50: 575.
Phelps, Austin. (A. H. Bradford) Chr. Un. 45: 540.
Phelps, Edward J., with portrait. (A. S. Cameron) Nat'l M. (N. Y. '91) 19: 91.
Phelps, Elizabeth Stuart, Chapters from Life of. McClure, 6: 49-513. 7: 3-461. 8: 77.
— — Notice of. Critic, 29: 415.
Phelps, Wm. L., with portrait. Bk. Buyer, 13: 129.
Phenomenal and Noumenal, Oneness of. (P. Carus) Open Court, 3: 1541.
Phil; a story. (M. S. Hancock) Belgra. 78: 271. Same art. Liv. Age, 194: 737.
Philadelphia and the Bechstein Library. (M. D. Learned) Citizen, 2: 266.
— and the Keystone Bank. (B. Ferree) N. Eng. 56: 51.
— Architecture in. (W. P. Laird) Engin. M. 8: 75.
— as a Seaport. (F. A. Mahan) J. Frankl. Inst. 133: 186, 272. — (L. M. Haupt) J. Frankl. Inst. 133: 33.
— Business Directory of 1703. Am. Hist. Reg. 2: 725-1163.
— Charity Problem in. (S. McC. Lindsay) Citizen, 2: 263.
— Christ Church, Records. (C. R. Hildeburn) Pennsyl. M. 15: 486 — 17: 352.
— — Vestrymen of. (T. H. Montgomery) Pennsyl. M. 19: 518.
— City Councils of. (A. A. Bird) Citizen, 1: 186.
— Defences of, 1777. (W. C. Ford) Pennsyl. M. 18: 1-463. 19: 72-481. 20: 87, 213, 391.
— Description of, in 1754, Pownall's. Pennsyl. M. 18: 211.
— Fairmount Park. Garden & F. 5: 326.
— First Charter of City of, 1691. Pennsyl. M. 18: 504.
— Free Library of. Citizen, 1: 227.
— Hale Building. Archit. Rec. 3: 207.
— Health of. (J. S. Billings) Forum, 17: 595.
— Higher Life of. (Talcott Williams) Outl. 54: 144.
— Improvement of the Delaware River and the Harbor of. (J. Birkinbine) Engin. M. 9: 839.
— in 1698. Pennsyl. M. 18: 245.
— Mayor of. (A. A. Bird) Citizen, 1: 233.
— New. (C. Morris) Lippinc. 51: 221.
— Picturesque. (W. B. Banks) Munsey, 6: 251.
— Quakers in 1757-60, Directory of. Pennsyl. M. 16: 219.
— Record Building. Archit. Rec. 1: 261.
Philadelphia, Social Evil in. (F. M. Goodchild) Arena, 15: 574.
— Street Railway and the City. (A. A. Bird) Citizen, 1: 256, 286.
— Union for Practical Progress in. (D. Hirschler) Arena, 9: 548.
— Vernon Park. (T. Meehan) Garden & F. 5: 357.
— Water Supply. (A. A. Bird) Citizen, 2: 270, 299, 336.
Philadelphia and Reading R. R. Cases. (C. La R. Munson) Am. J. Pol. 2: 47. — Bank. M. (N. Y.) 46: 677.
Philae Island. (G. Montbard) Art J. 47: 289, 352.
— and the Nile Reservoirs. (H. A. Harper) Leis. Hour, 44: 300.
— Submergence of. (F. Dillon) 19th Cent. 35: 1019.
— Temple of. (A. S. Morison) Overland, n. s. 19: 208.
Philanthropists, Vagueness of. Spec. 70: 250.
Philanthropy and Atheism, Relations of. Spec. 69: 678. Same art. Ecl. M. 120: 54.
— and Morality. (J. O. S. Huntington) Int. J. Ethics, 3: 39.
— and Politics. (E. Kelly) Char. R. 2: 357.
— as Social Factor. (J. Visher) Lend a H. 15: 184.
— Failure of. Macmil. 73: 390. Same art. Liv. Age, 209: 230.
— from the Standpoint of Business. (J. H. Patterson) Pub. Opin. 20: 780.
— Hypocrisy of. Spec. 71: 743.
Philip II. of Spain. (A. Harcourt) Temp. Bar, 104: 251.
— his Visit to England in 1554. (M. A. S. Hume) Eng. Hist. R. 7: 253.
— in his Domestic Relations. (M. A. S. Hume) Fortn. 66: 536. Same art. Liv. Age, 211: 425.
— Passing of. (A. Harcourt) Temp. Bar, 105: 465.
Philip IV. (M. A. S. Hume) Gent. M. n. s. 49: 239.
Philip and his Wife. (M. Deland) Atlan. 73: 1-721. 74: 1-433.
Philips, Josiah, Case of. (W. P. Trent) Am. Hist. R. 1: 444.
Philippine Islands. (R. A. Lane) Cosmopol. 13: 409. — (H. A. MacPherson) J. Soc. Arts, 41: 577.
Philistia (in Piccadilly); a poem. (A. Lang) M. of Art, 7: 375.
Philistine, What is a? (G. Santayana) Harv. Mo. 14: 89.
Philistines, Country of the. (J. Wells) Sund. M. 25: 22.
Philistinism, Coming Triumph of. (Mrs. E. L. Linton) National, 26: 40.
Phillip, John. M. of Art, 1: 251.
— Exhibition of Pictures at Aberdeen. (G. R. Halkett) M. of Art, 4: 526.
Phillips, George. Acad. 41: 157.
Phillips, Stephen. Christ in Hades, and other poems. Sat. R. 81: 629.
Phillips, Watts. (F. Hawkins) Acad. 41: 343.
Phillips, Wendell. (R. J. Hinton) Arena, 13: 226. — (R. Wheatley) Meth. R. 52: 541.
— Letters to Lydia Maria Child. New Eng. M. n. s. 5: 730.
— A Poem. (I. McLellan) Lit. W. (Bost.) 23: 212.
Phillips Academy, Andover. (C. F. P. Bancroft) Educa. 14: 629.
Phillpotts, Eden. My Laughing Philosopher. Sat. R. 82: 68.
Philo of Alexandria. (C. G. Montefiore) Jew. Q. 7: 481. — (L. Cohn) Jew. Q. 5: 25.
— Contemplative Life. (F. C. Conybeare) Jew. Q. 7: 755.
— — Conybeare on. (S. M. Jackson) Presb. & Ref. R. 6: 769.

Philograph, Drawing with a. (J. F. Robertson) M. of Art, 16: 317.
Philological Congress at Philadelphia, Dec., 1894. Critic, 26: 22. — (L. W. Batten) Bib. World, 5: 124.
Philology, Literature and, Relations of. (O. F. Emerson) Educa. R. 5: 130.
Philoneism. (C. Lombroso) Monist, 1: 347.
Philornithus in the Park. Macmil. 70: 354. Same art. Liv. Age, 203: 371.
Philosopher in the Apple Orchard; a story. (A. Hope) Eng. Illust. 11: 413.
Philosopher with an Eye for Beauty. (R. B. Hale) Atlan. 76: 28.
Philosophers' Camp: Emerson, Agassiz, Lowell, and others in the Adirondacks. (W. J. Stillman) Cent. 24: 598.
Philosophical Congress, A. (L. J. Block) Educa. 13: 266.
Philosophical Terminology and its History. (R. Eucken) Monist, 6: 497.
Philosophy and Applied Ethics, A School of. (F. Adler) Eth. Rec. 2: 1.
— and Greek Social Life. (A. W. Benn) New World, 3: 418.
— and Industrial Life. (J. C. Murray) Monist, 4: 533.
— and the Natural Sciences. (S. T. Preston) Nat. Sci. 7: 253.
— and Political Economy, J. Bonair on. (D. G. Ritchie) Econ. R. 3: 541. — (W. Caldwell) J. Pol. Econ. 1: 607.
— Basil Concepts in, Ormond's. (A. Alexander) Philos. R. 3: 470. 4: 306.
— — Rejoinder. (A. T. Ormond) Philos. R. 4: 535.
— Bénard on. (P. Shorey) Philos. R. 3: 73.
— Cardinal Problems of. (B. C. Burt) Educa. 12: 389.
— Critical, and Idealism. (J. Watson) Philos. R. 1: 9.
— Erdmann's History of. Crit. R. 1: 83.
— Ejective. (T. P. Bailey, jr.) Am. J. Psychol. 5: 465.
— French. (L. Arreat) Open Court, 3: 1941.
— from Berkeley to Hegel. (E. D. Fawcett) Monist, 7: 41.
— German, of 19th Century. (F. Jodl) Monist, 1: 263.
— Greek, and German. (B. Winchester) Chr. Lit. 14: 225.
— — Early, Burnet's. Sat. R. 73: 695.
— Hill's Genetic. (G. A. Coe) Philos. R. 3: 81.
— History of, as applied to the Church. (C. M. O'Leary) Cath. World, 62: 36.
— — Fischer's. (F. Thilly) Philos. R. 2: 724.
— — Hegel on. Spec. 69: 929. — (A. W. Benn) Acad. 44: 559.
— in American Colleges. (G. A. Cox) Nation, 54: 282.
— in England; British Thought and Modern Speculation. (R. M. Wenley) Scot. R. 19: 141.
— in its National Developments. (W. Knight) Mind, 21: 60.
— in the U. S. (A. C. Armstrong, jr.) Educa. R. 10: 1.
— Indian and Greek, Connection between. (R. Garbe) Monist, 4: 176.
— — History of, Outlines of. (R. Garbe) Monist, 4: 580.
— — Vedânta and Sâmkhya Systems of. (R. Garbe) Monist, 4: 176.
— its Relation to Life and Education. (J. M. Baldwin) Presb. & Ref. R. 5: 36.
Philosophy, Method of, Old and New in. (H. Calderwood) Philos. R. 2: 641.
— Modern, History of, Falckenberg's. Sat. R. 80: 383.
— — Royce's. (G. S. Fullerton) Nation, 55: 53. — Sat. R. 73: 696.
— Nature and Aims of. (H. Jones) Mind, 18: 160.
— of Relative Existences. (F. R. Stockton) Cent. 22: 536.
— of Sosi. (Keijiro Nakamura) Monist, 4: 607.
— Our Need of. (P. Carus) Open Court, 7: 3783.
— Pillon's L'année philosophique. (F. Thilby) Philos. R. 4: 643.
— Practical Significance of. Time, 23: 1307.
— Practical Value of. (J. Royce) Eth. Rec. 2: 9.
— Province of. (W. R. Halstead) Meth. R. 52: 51.
— Recent German, Some Aspects of. (C. W. Hodge, jr.) Presb. & Ref. R. 7: 211.
— The Student of. (J. Royce) Harv. Mo. 18: 87.
— Study of. (J. E. Creighton) Book R. 3: 33.
— — When should it begin? (B. C. Burt) School & C. 1: 36.
— Summer School of. (J. C. Murray) Scot. R. 19: 98.
— Synthetic, and Theology. (H. C. Minton) Presb. & Ref. R. 7: 385.
— Terminology for. (W. Poland) Am. Cath. Q. 19: 629.
— Vaihinger on. (E. Adickes) Philos. R. 3: 201.
— What is? (J. G. Schurman) Chaut. 18: 26.
— Windelband's History of. (A. Fairbanks) Philos. R. 3: 480.
Philosophy of the Summer; a poem. (A. Cochrane) Temp. Bar, 99: 190. Same art. Ecl. M. 121: 633.
Phoebe; a story. (C. Young) Argosy, 62: 158.
Phœnician Colonization in Scandinavia. (C. W. Skarstedt) Asia. R. 20: 400.
Phœnician Inscriptions from Cyprus. (G. A. Cooke) Acad. 49: 59, 80.
Phœnix, The. Sat. R. 76: 38.
— Egyptian, Explanation of Mystery of. (T. J. J. See) Astron. 11: 457.
Phœnix, The; a story. (A. Strindberg) Poet-Lore, 6: 611.
Phœnix Park Tragedy. (Tighe Hopkins) Cosmopol. 21: 80.
Phonetic Alphabet, Winnebago. (A. C. Fletcher) J. Am. Folk-Lore, 3: 299.
Phonograph as Substitute for Books. (O. Uzanne) Scrib. M. 16: 221.
— in Music. (H. D. Goodwin) Music, 2: 144.
— Mechanical Memory of. (P. Carus) Open Court, 2: 1032.
Phonography, Sloan-Duployan and Pitman. (M. C. Johnstone) Westm. 145: 84.
Phonolitic Rocks from the Black Hills. (L. V. Pirsson) Am. J. Sci. 147: 341.
— from Montana. (L. V. Pirsson) Am. J. Sci. 150: 394.
Phosphate Industry of Florida. (F. B. Wilson) Engin. M. 4: 80. — (A. Allen) Engin. M. 6: 829.
— — Great Boom in. (A. Allen) Cosmopol. 14: 706.
Phosphate Nodules, Influence of Swamp Waters in Formation of. (C. L. Reese) Am. J. Sci. 143: 402.
Phosphate-rock Deposits of Tennessee. (L. B. Brown) Engin. M. 12: 86.
Phosphates, Land, of Ashley River District, S. C. (W. H. Dall) Am. J. Sci. 148: 296.
— of the World. (F. Wyatt) J. Frankl. Inst. 138: 330–412.
— Redonda. (F. W. Morse) Pop. Sci. Mo. 46: 78.

Phosphatic Chalk. (A. Strahan) Nat. Sci. 1: 284.
Phosphorescence. (S. P. Thompson) Sat. R. 82: 157.
— and Photographic Action at Low Temperatures. Dub. R. 116: 404.
— Bacteria of. Liv. Age, 204: 703.
Phosphoric Acid, Determination of. (H. Pemberton, jr.) J. Frankl. Inst. 136: 362. 137: 126.
— — Citrate Method. (F. Bergami) J. Frankl. Inst. 140: 139.
Phosphorus in Iron, Iodometric Method for Determination of. (Charlotte Fairbanks) Am. J. Sci. 152: 181.
Phosphorus Oxide. (A. E. Tutton) Nature, 45: 446.
Photographer and the Artist. (R. de la Sizeranne) Chaut. 17: 193.
Photographers, Amateur, Leading. (C. B. Moore) Cosmopol. 12: 421.
— American Women. (F. W. Crane) Munsey, 11: 398.
Photographic Perspective, Correction of. Dub. R. 114: 171.
Photographic Research, Laboratory for. (R. Hitchcock) Science, 20: 160.
Photographing Electrical Discharges. (W. E. Woodbury) Pop. Sci. Mo. 49: 305.
Photographing Game Animals; a New Sport in the Rocky Mountains. (A. G. Wallihan) Cosmopol. 19: 371.
Photographs, Composite. Are they Typical Pictures? (H. P. Bowditch) McClure, 3: 331.
— Copyright and. Art J. 48: 251.
Photography, Amateur, Experiences in. Outing, 20: 180.
— — of To-day. (W. S. Harwood) Cosmopol. 20: 249.
— and Criminal Inquiries. (Sir H. D. Littlejohn) Jurid. R. 8: 13.
— and Athletics. (W. I. L. Adams) Outing, 19: 404, 445.
— Anthropological Uses of. (E. F. im Thurn) Anthrop. J. 22: 184, 548.
— Art in, and Photographic Models. (A. Van B. Berg) Cosmopol. 21: 22.
— Artistic. (T. Runciman) Art J. 45: 113.
— Artistic Side of. (H. M. Steele) Q. Illust. 2: 321.
— as Evidence. (E. A. Jelf) Idler, 4: 517.
— as a Fine Art. (Kathryn Staley) Munsey, 14: 582.
— Astronomical. Liv. Age, 176: 387. — (H. C. Russell) Pop. Astron. 2: 310, 457. — (R. Hitchcock) Science, 19: 339. — (A. Morgan) Longm. 24: 183.
— — Astro-photographic Chart. (H. Jacoby) Astron. 12: 117.
— — at the Paris Observatory. (A. Fraissinet) Nature, 48: 617.
— — Micrometer for Measuring the Plates of the Astro-photographic Chart. (W. H. M. Christie) Astron. 12: 588.
— — Short Lenses in. (G. M. Searle) Astron. 12: 577.
— — Spectroheliograph. (G. E. Hale) Astron. 12: 241.
— — with Commercial Lenses. (W. Harkness) Astron. 11: 641.
— — with Small Cameras. (H. Wilson) Pop. Astron. 1: 26, 49.
— Boston Camera Club. (B. Kimball) New Eng. M. n. s. 8: 185.
— Camera and the Comedy, The. (Alex. Black) Scrib. M. 20: 605.
— Chemistry of, Advances in. (C. Jones) J. Soc. Arts, 42: 472.
Photography, Cloud. Nature, 53: 230.
— Detection of Crime by. (T. C. Hepworth) Chamb. J. 69: 326. Same art. Green Bag, 4: 516.
— Determination of Geographical Longitudes by. (H. G. Schlichter) Geog. J. 2: 423.
— Eclipse. (A. Taylor) Astron. 12: 267.
— Figure, Artistic Aspects of. (P. H. Emerson) M. of Art, 14: 310.
— Flash-light, by Electric Spark. (C. V. Boys) Nature, 47: 415, 421, 440.
— for Anthropologists. (M. V. Portman) Anthrop. J. 25: 75.
— Humors of Theatrical. Theatre, 29: 267.
— in Colors. (F. E. Ives) J. Soc. Arts, 41: 663.— (W. De W. Abney) J. Soc. Arts, 44: 587. — Nature, 53: 617. — Chamb. J. 73: 300. — Sat. R. 81: 546. — (Dr. Selle-Brandenberg) Chaut. 23: 718. — (J. Joly) Nature, 53: 91. — Pub. Opin. 15: 205. — (L. Weiller) Pop. Sci. Mo. 45: 539.
— — and the Photochromoscope. (F. E. Ives) J. Soc. Arts, 44: 517.
— — Lumière Lippmann. (F. E. Ives) J. Frankl. Inst. 137: 16.
— In Search of Paradise. (B. L. Harrison) Outing, 21: 310.
— in Technical Education. (E. Meldola) Nature, 45: 331.
— in Travel. Around World, 1: 7.
— Instantaneous. (H. B. Pritchard) M. of Art, 5: 70.
— Inventions in, Recent. (E. Wallace) No. Am. 162: 375.
— Is it an Art? (W. de W. Abney) M. of Art, 3: 302.
— Isochromatic. (B. Berenson) Nation, 57: 346.
— Landscape. (R. Derechef) Eng. Illust. 11: 1109.
— the New Eye of Science. (C. Flammarion) Cosmopol. 21: 484.
— Notes on. (W. A. Campbell) Un. Serv. (Phila.) 13: 64.
— of Invisible Objects. (J. J. Stewart) Knowl. 19: 61.
— of Rainbows. Dub. R. 118: 152.
— of Voice Production. (Rosa R. Holt) Music, 10: 333.
— Open Air. Art J. 44: 76.
— Optics of, Vogel on. (R. Meldola) Nature, 50: 589.
— Panoramic. Chamb. J. 70: 133.
— Perspective in. (H. Van der Weyde) J. Soc. Arts, 41: 591.
— Philadelphia's Contributions to. (J. F. Sachse) J. Frankl. Inst. 135: 271.
— Planetary, with Reflecting Telescope. (J. M. Schaeberle) Pop. Astron. 3: 280.
— Portrait, Development of. Bost. 1: 315.
— Relations of, to Art. (J. L. Breese) Cosmopol. 18: 137.
— Retinal. Dub. R. 118: 425.
— Roentgen Ray. (S. P. Thompson) Sat. R. 81: 35. — (J. W. Gifford) Knowl. 19: 73. — (H. J. W. Dam) McClure, 6: 403.— (T. J. McCormack) Open Court, 10: 4799.
See also Roentgen Rays.
— Sunshine through the Woods. (B. D. Halsted) Pop. Sci. Mo. 45: 313.
— up to Date. Chamb. J. 71: 389.
— Winter. (W. I. L. Adams) Outing, 19: 319.
— Woman Experts in. (C. B. Moore) Cosmopol. 14: 580.
Photogravure, Modern Methods in. (H. Wilmer) J. Soc. Arts, 43: 463.
Photo-intaglio Process, New. (L. E. Levy) J. Frankl. Inst. 134: 335.

Photometric Method Independent of Color. (O. N. Rood) Am. J. Sci. 146: 173.
Photometry. (W. De W. Abney) J. Soc. Arts, 42: 735, 747, 759.
— Improvements in. Nature, 51: 558.
Phototopography. (J. A. Flemer) Science, n. s. 2: 152.
— on the Alaskan Boundary. (O. J. Klotz) Canad. M. 3: 191.
Phrase that most influenced me; a sketch. (J. Alexander) Canad. M. 5: 511.
Phrases, Foreign, Prejudice against. (L. C. Bull) No. Am. 159: 509.
— Historical. Chamb. J. 72: 171.
Phrenology. (G. P. Serviss) Chaut. 15: 187.
— Old and New. Open Court, 1: 435.
Phroso; a romance. (A. Hope) Idler, 9: 98, 787. 10: 13-583. Same art. McClure, 6: 449-545. 7: 46-441.
Phrygia, Ancient Monuments of. (W. M. Ramsay) Contemp. 64: 563.
Phrygia Paroreus and Lycaonia, Notes in. (D. G. Hogarth) J. Hel. Stud. 11: 151.
Phyllida's Mourning. (G. W. Conant) Cent. 22: 786.
Phyllis Marsden's Love-poem; a story. (L. Hamilton) Chamb. J. 70: 652-679.
Phylogeny. (E. Haeckel) Open Court, 9: 4369-4458.
— and Ontogeny. (E. Haeckel) Open Court, 5: 2968.
— of an Acquired Characteristic. (A. Hyatt) Am. Natural. 27: 865.
Physical Catastrophe to America; a story. (A. Harvey) Canad. M. 2: 403.
Physical Condition of the American People. (E. Hitchcock, jr.) Chaut. 23: 151.
Physical Culture. (E. Sandow) Cosmopol. 17: 169.
— Extremes of Human Effort. (A. Macivor) Gent. M. n. s. 57: 259.
— Fad of. (M. L. Pratt) Educa. 15: 217.
Physical Education. (Earl of Meath) National, 20: 461. — (J. M. Buckley) Chaut. 14: 540, 613. 15: 33-277.
— at Wellesley College. (A. Shaw) R. of Rs. (N. Y.) 6: 545.
— Free Play in. (F. Lagrange) Pop. Sci. Mo. 42: 813.
— Past and Future of. (A. Mosso) Chaut. 23: 614.
— Physical Element in Education. (E. S. Richards) Pop. Sci. Mo. 47: 471.
— Problems of. (G. W. Fitz) Harv. Grad. M. 2: 26. *See* Physical Training.
Physical Exercise in Health and as Remedy. (J. M. Taylor) J. Frankl. Inst. 134: 223, 279.
Physical Geography. (A. R. Wallace) 19th Cent. 33: 391.
— Elementary, Tarr on. (A. D. Brigham) School R. 4: 176.
— in Elementary Teaching. (W. M. Davis) School & C. 1: 599.
— Teacher's Outfit in. (R. S. Tarr) School R. 4: 161, 193.
Physical Laboratory, National. (A. G. Webster) Pedagog. Sem. 2: 90.
Physical Life of Micro-organisms. (C. S. Wake) Open Court, 4: 2175.
Physical Phenomena, Implications of. (A. E. Dolbear) Psychic. R. 1: 7, 211. 2: 1.
— Psychical Implications of. (L. C. Howe) Psychic. R. 2: 203.
Physical Research, Economical Character of. (E. Mach) Open Court, 8: 4262, 4271.
Physical Training at Hemenway Gymnasium. (D. A. Sargent) Harv. Grad. M. 3: 169.
— at the Universities. (W. G. Anderson) Cosmopol. 21: 61.
Physical Training, Greatest Need of College Girls. (A. C. Pall) Atlan. 69: 102.
— in Childhood. (W. Channing) Educa. R. 10: 262.
— in the Public Schools. (M. V. O'Shea) Atlan. 75: 246.
— Indoor Apparatus for Outdoor Sports. Outing, 19: 275.
— Neglect of. (J. F. A. Adams) Educa. R. 11: 273.
— A Suggestion as to. (F. T. Fuller) Harv. Grad. M. 5: 200.
Physician, The, and the Social Question. (P. Gibier) No. Am. 160: 461.
— and Surgeon. (H. Spencer) Pop. Sci. Mo. 47: 164.
— College Education for, Best. (C. F. Thwing) Educa. 13: 195.
— Confessions of a. Arena, 6: 94.
— Effect of Occupation of, upon himself. (J. S. Billings) Int. J. Ethics, 4: 40.
Physician's Story, A. (T. Wilkins) Overland, n. s. 20: 544.
Physicians and Surgeons, Pay of. (G. F. Shrady) Forum, 18: 68. — (W. A. Hammond) No. Am. 158: 660.
— Lord Dunraven and the. National, 19: 280.
— of the Olden Days. (M. L. Sinclair) Gent. M. n. s. 55: 67.
Physics. (W. M. Hicks) Nature, 52: 472.
— and Sociology. (W. H. Mallock) Contemp. 68: 883. 69: 59, 233.
— Barker's. Sat. R. 78: 332.
— Comparison in. (E. Mach) Open Court, 8: 4283, 4288.
— Elementary, Teaching. (E. H. Hall) Educa. R. 4: 157. 5: 325.
— Grammar-school. (E. H. Hall) Educa. R. 6: 242.
— Lord Kelvin on. (O. J. Lodge) Nature, 50: 313.
— Laboratory Instruction in. (D. W. Hering) Science, 21: 211.
— Laboratory Work in, Chief End of. (A. E. Dolbear) Educa. R. 12: 348.
— Modern Views and Problems of. (D. W. Hering) Pop. Sci. Mo. 45: 511.
— Principles of, Gage on. (J. B. Ekeley) School R. 4: 235.
— Teaching of. (F. Guthrie) Pop. Sci. Mo. 43: 388.
— — Place of the Laboratory in. (A. D. Cole) Science, 21: 316.
— Theoretical, in Italy, Pozzo di Mombello on. Nature, 46: 439.
Physiognomy in Folk-Lore. (A. F. Chamberlain) J. Am. Folk-Lore, 6: 13.
— of Anarchists. (C. Lombroso) Monist, 1: 336.
Physiography as an Alternative Subject for Admission to College. (W. M. Davis) School R. 3: 632.
— Some Applications of, to History. (J. W. Redway) Educa. R. 8: 374.
— Teaching of. (P. Krapotkin) Geog. J. 2: 350.
— What is? (J. W. Redway) Educa. R. 10: 352.
Physiological Research, Present State of. Nature, 51: 58.
Physiologists, Modern: New Priesthood. (L. de la Ramé) New R. 8: 151.
Physiology and the Prevention of Disease. (J. M. Rice) Pop. Sci. Mo. 41: 308.
— and Psychology. (G. S. Fullerton) Psychol. R. 3: 1.
— — Verworn on. Nat. Sci. 8: 404.
— General, and its Relation to Morphology. (C. O. Whitman) Am. Natural. 27: 802.
— in 1894. Science, n. s. 2: 95.
— in the Schools. (S. H. Gage) Science, n. s. 4: 29.
— **Modern. (M. Verworn) Monist, 4:** 355.

Physiology, Modern, and Karl Ludwig. (J. B. Sanderson) Sci. Prog. 5: 1.
— — Scope of. (F. S. Lee) Am. Natural. 28: 380, 473.
— of the Excitable Tissues, Biederman on. (J. B. Sanderson) Nature, 51: 553.
— Science of, to-day. (A. Mosso) Chaut. 22: 305.
Physiology, Teaching of, in Schools. (M. Foster) Nature, 51: 487.
Physische Technische Reichsanstalt at Charlottenburg. Dub. R. 118: 148.
Pi Eta Society at Harvard. (E. A. Whitman) Harv. Grad. M. 3: 486.
Pianistic Retrospect. (E. Liebling) Music, 1: 509-583. 2: 68.
Pianists and Pianism. (A. Veit) Music, 5: 21.
— A Gossip about. (J. C. Hadden) Chamb. J. 72: 744.
— How they may differ, and yet each be Great. (F. M. Smith) Cent. 23: 628.
Pianner Mares, The; a story. (M. McC. Williams) Scrib. M. 12: 117.
Piano-forte, The. (D. Spillane) Pop. Sci. Mo. 40: 473.
— as a Factor in Musical Art. (J. S. Van Cleve) Music, 1: 336-496.
— Evolution of. (W. F. Gates) Music, 2: 205. — (J. Hoffmann) Nat'l M. (N. Y. '91) 16: 701.
— History of. (J. F. Runciman) Art J. 46: 142.
— Manufacture of. (J. Hatton) Eng. Illust. 9: 402.
— Religion of the. (G. B. Shaw) Fortn. 61: 255.
Piano Literature, Development and Character in. (A. Carpe) Music, 3: 256, 383, 510.
Piano Music, Philosophy of. (F. H. Clark) Music, 1: 613. 2: 98.
Piano-playing as a Revelation of Character. (J. C. Fillmore) Music, 1: 549.
— Beginner of the Future. (W. S. B. Mathews) Music, 5: 292.
— Cause and Effect in. (H. A. Kelso, jr.) Music, 6: 439.
— Controversy about Learning. (E. B. Perry) Music, 5: 207.
— Limits of Personal Rights in. (J. S. Van Cleve) Music, 7: 47.
— Philosophy in. (A. Carpe) Music, 2: 608. 3: 76-532.
— Touch in. Music, 6: 84, 317. 7: 179.
— — Graphics of. Nature, 52: 597.
— Radical Types of. Music, 1: 413.
Piano Practice, Wanted, the True Art of. (W. S. B. Mathews) Music, 1: 128.
Piano Teaching, Common Sense of. (E. Liebling) Music, 11: 22.
Piano Tuning. (E. E. Todd) Music, 5: 265.
Piatt, Donn, with portraits. (S. B. Hedges) Cath. World, 58: 99.
Piatt, John James, Poetry of. (E. D. Keeling) Acad. 44: 458. 48: 381.
Piatt, Sarah. Child-world Ballads. (E. D. Keeling) Acad. 48: 381.
Picaninny Peter. (M. Eyre) Longm. 20: 399.
Picardy, Ile de France and. (C. A. Cutter) Nation, 58: 343, 425. 59: 24.
Piccadilly. Chamb. J. 69: 417.
Pickerel, Jacking for. (E. W. Chubb) Outing, 26: 61.
Pickerel-fishing in South Jersey. (J. Gifford) Outing, 20: 303.
Picketts, The; a story. (R. W. Chambers) McClure, 7: 437.
Picnics, Rational, Plea for. Spec. 69: 13.
Pictish Inscriptions. (E. W. B. Nicholson and others) Acad. 45: 13-477. 48: 165, 186. 49: 427.
Pictish Tower in Shetland. (G. Goudie) Illus. Archæol. 1: 137.
Pictoglyphs, Indian, in California. (L. G. Yates) Overland, n. s. 28: 657.
Pictographs, Primitive, from Crete and the Peloponnese. (A. J. Evans) J. Hel. Stud. 14: 270.
Pictorial, Tyranny of the. (S. Fairfield) Lippinc. 55: 861.
Pict's House, Visit to a. (D. M. Ritchie) Science, 20: 43.
Picts, Sculptured Stones of. (G. F. Browne) M. of Art, 6: 15.
Picture, Evolution of a. (S. E. Waller) Art J. 45: 314.
— of Las Cruces. (C. Reid) Lippinc. 53: 147.
— of Saint Cloud, A; a story. (Gertrude Smith) Harper, 93: 540.
— on the Wall; a story. (K. Tynan) Eng. Illust. 14: 297.
Picture-cleaning. Chamb. J. 71: 609.
Picture Exhibition at the New Gallery. (F. Wedmore) M. of Art, 16: 289.
Picture Exhibitions, Hanging of Pictures at. (M. H. Spielmann) M. of Art, 10: 193.
— in Lower New York. (A. C. Bernheim) Forum, 19: 610.
Picture Galleries, Private: the Collection of John Forbes White. Good Words, 37: 813.
Picture Sales: Hamilton Palace. M. of Art, 5: 440.
— of 1894. Art J. 46: 310.
— of 1895. Art J. 47: 314. — (W. Roberts) 19th Cent. 38: 466.
— of 1896. (A. C. R. Carter) Art J. 48: 282.
Picture-writing of the American Indian, Mallery's. (L. Carr) Nation, 60: 34.
Pictures and Print. (J. Bell) Good Words, 33: 749.
— as Property. Spec. 69: 11.
— Conservation of. (J. C. Robinson) 19th Cent. 39: 608.
— How to hang. (L. F. Day) M. of Art, 5: 58.
— Lighting of. (N. Nisbet) Belgra. 77: 405.
— London, from the "Composition" Point of View. (S. Beale) Am. Arch. 53: 31.
— C. P. Matthews' Collection of. (A. Griffiths) M. of Art, 4: 265, 333.
— of the Year 1878. M. of Art, 1: 23.
— — 1879. M. of Art, 2: 125-280.
— — 1880. M. of Art, 3: 80-474.
— — 1881. M. of Art, 4: 302-397.
— — 1882. M. of Art, 5: 251.
— — 1895. (C. Phillips) Fortn. 63: 925. — (E. R. Pennell) Fortn. 64: 45.
— Prices of. (J. Oldcastle) M. of Art, 2: 197.
— Prize, American. M. of Art, 8: supp. 53.
— Remarkable Copies and Copyists of. (A. Beaver) M. of Art, 4: 450.
— Some, and their Prices. (W. Roberts) 19th Cent. 36: 286.
Pictures of a Curse, The; a story. (A. Upward) Idler, 9: 22.
Picturesque Place, Most, in the World. (J. and E. R. Pennell) Cent. 24: 345.
Piebald Rat, The. (E. Phillpotts) Idler, 10: 430.
Piece-rate System of Paying Labor. (F. W. Taylor) Econ. Stud. 1: 89. — (F. W. Taylor) Cassier, 8: 585.
Piece-work or Day-work. Cassier, 1: 55.
— Why Working-men dislike. (D. F. Schloss) Econ. R. 1: 311.
Pieces of Eight. Chamb. J. 71: 149.
Pied Piper of Hamelin, The. (E. Gutch) Folk-Lore, 3: 227.
Piedigrotta, Song of. Macmil. 73: 360.
Piedmont Plateau, Geographic History of. (W. J. McGee) Nat. Geog. M. 7: 261.

Piedmontite and Scheelite from the Ancient Rhyolite of South Mountain, Pa. (G. H. Williams) Am. J. Sci. 146: 50.
Pieper, Prof., and the Lutheran Manual. (J. B. Remensyder) Luth. Q. 24: 283.
Piers Plowman. Spec. 72: 756.
— Jusserand's. (G. L. Kittredge) Nation, 59: 86.
Pieta, Lakeport, and the Blue Lakes. (P. Weaver, jr.) Overland, n. s. 28: 303.
Pietism. (F. H. Williams) New World, 3: 218.
Piety, a Forgotten Virtue. Macmil. 72: 51.
Pig, The; Wild Traits in Tame Animals. (L. Robinson) No. Am. 161: 735.
Pigeon, Wild, of North America. (S. Pokagon) Chaut. 22: 202.
Pigeon Messenger Service, Naval. (H. A. Giddings) Outing, 25: 72.
Pigeons. Bost. 3: 351.
— Aerial. (G. Reynaud) Chaut. 23: 198.
— and Pigeon-netting. (W. L. Simpson) Outing, 25: 163.
— Homing, Method of. (C. F. Hodge) Pop. Sci. Mo. 44: 758.
— — Utilization of. (W. G. Tegetmeier) Nature, 45: 320.
Pigments, Ancient Egyptian. (W. J. Russell) Nature, 49: 374.
— and Vehicles of the Old Masters. (A. P. Laurie) J. Soc. Arts, 40: 125, 150, 171.
— Fading of, Mitigation of. Dub. R. 117: 444. — (W. De W. Abney) J. Soc. Arts, 43: 597.
— Modern, in Oil, Durability of. (A. P. Laurie) J. Soc. Arts, 40: 383. — Dub. R. 111: 181.
— Used by Children in Play. J. Am. Folk-Lore, 8: 151.
Pigmies. *See* Pygmies.
Pigott, E. S. Acad. 47: 199.
— and the Censorship of the Drama. Sat. R. 79: 280.
Pike, John Wm., Admiral. Geog. J. 4: 572.
Pike, Zebulon Montgomery. (E. Shippen) Un. Serv. (Phila.) 14: 55.
— Expeditions of, edited by E. Coues. (J. D. Butler) Am. Hist. R. 1: 362. — Nation, 61: 391. — (J. J. Halsey) Dial (Ch.) 19: 210.
Pike, About. (T. Southwell) Gent. M. n. s. 50: 463.
Pike's Peak and Colorado Springs. (M. L. Todd) Nation, 57: 245.
— and its Railroad. (M. L. Scudder) Nat'l M. (N. Y. '91) 17: 325. — (A. Spies) Cassier, 6: 99.
— Botanical Aspect of. (V. Havard) Garden & F. 6: 452.
— A Sunday on. (B. W. James) Around World, 1: 164.
Pilchard, Growth of. (J. T. Cunningham) Nature, 45: 255. — (M. Dunn) Nature, 45: 511.
Pilchards. (H. D. Lowry) Chamb. J. 70: 54.
Pilcomayo River, Journeys and Explorations on. (O. J. Storrr) Geog. J. 7: 82.
Pilgrim on the Gila, A: a story. (O. Wister) Harper, 91: 837.
Pilgrim Principle and the Pilgrim Heritage. (W. D. Hyde) Forum, 20: 480.
Pilgrim Sons, The; a story. (H. B. Fuller) Cosmopol. 19: 413.
Pilgrim Station. (M. H. Foote) Atlan. 77: 596.
Pilgrimage, Historical, Renaissance of. (L. P. Powell) R. of Rs. (N. Y.) 8: 411.
— — Revival of, in England. (W. T. Stead) R. of Rs. (N. Y.) 8: 420.
Pilgrimages to Mecca and the Propagation of Disease. (A. Proust) Chaut. 21: 574.
Pilgrim's Signs. (J. C. Wall) Illus. Archæol. 1: 237.
Pilgrims, The, not Puritans but Separatists. (T. W. Manchester) Nat'l M. (N. Y. '91) 15: 82.
— Women of. (Elizabeth C. Lovering) Bost. 1: 467.
Pilgrims of the Night; a story. (S. Doudney) Argosy, 61: 88-735. 62: 100-476.
Pilling, James C. (W. J. McGee) Science, n. s. 2: 150. — (R. V. Bain) Ath. '95, 2: 226.
Pillory, The, and the Whipping-post. (F. Watt) New R. 14: 687.
Pilot of Belle Amour, The; a story. (G. Parker) Cosmopol. 15: 334.
Pilotage, Compulsory. (R. G. Marsden) Law Q. 4: 51. — (C. E. Naylor) Overland, n. s. 28: 702.
Pilots. (W. J. Gordon) Leis. Hour, 42: 180.
Piloty, Carl von, and his Pupils. (E. M. Ward) Mo. Illust. 12: 152.
Pimento. Chamb. J. 70: 789.
Pin-money Workers. (S. M. Minturn) Lend a H. 14: 117.
Pin-wells and Rag-bushes. (E. S. Hartland) Folk-Lore, 4: 451.
Pinch and the Poorhouse; a story. (K. Tynan) Eng. Illust. 16: 265.
Pinch-me: the Story of a Little Servant-girl. Liv. Age, 203: 369.
Pinckney, Charles, Draft of a Federal Constitution by. (F. A. Myers) Nat'l M. (N. Y. '91) 15: 267.
Pindar. (E. Cumings) Music, 9: 613.
— Isthmian Odes, Bury's ed. Sat. R. 74: 28.
Pindemonte, Ippolito, Letters of. (J. W. Mario) Nation, 55: 103.
Pine, Robert Edge. Portrait of Rodney in Jamaica. (F. Cundall) Art J. 48: 333.
Pine, Distribution of Yellow, in Nebraska. (C. E. Bessey) Garden & F. 8: 102.
— Rate of Growth. (H. K. Mladziansky) Garden & F. 9: 72, 92.
— Royal, of New Hampshire. (W. H. Stone) New Eng. M. n. s. 15: 26.
— White. Garden & F. 5: 1.
— — Cultivation of. (J. D. Lyman) Garden & F. 5: 266.
— — Experimental Grove of. (J. D. Lyman) Garden & F. 9: 392.
— — for Timber. (Edmund Hersey and B. E. Fernow) Garden & F. 5: 609.
— — Forests of. (B. W. Davis) Cassier, 6: 408.
— — in the West. (C. A. Keffer) Garden & F. 8: 132.
— — Pinchot and Groves on. Garden & F. 9: 249.
— — Product per Acre. (B. E. Fernow) Garden & F. 9: 202. — (E. Hersey) Garden & F. 9: 402.
Pine Barrens of N. J. (B. E. Fernow) Garden & F. 8: 472.
— — Autumn Color in the Pines. (M. Treat) Garden & F. 8: 452.
— — Christmas in the Pines. (M. Treat) Garden & F. 8: 3.
— — Climbing Plants in. (M. Treat) Garden & F. 9: 492.
— — Heaths among the Pines in Early Winter. (M. Treat) Garden & F. 8: 492.
— — In the. (M. Treat) Garden & F. 8: 203, 262.
— — in August. (M. Treat) Garden & F. 9: 332.
— — in a Dry Summer. (M. Treat) Garden & F. 8: 362.
— — in Early Autumn. (M. Treat) Garden & F. 9: 412.
— — in Spring. (M. Treat) Garden & F. 9: 173.
— Winter Rambles in. (E. F. Hill) Garden & F. 5: 16-110.

Pine Boughs; a Salmon River Outing. (E. W. Wooster) Overland, n. s. 25: 173.
Pine Forests; Future of the Long-leaf Pine Belt. (L. J. Vance) Garden & F. 8: 278.
Pine Posts, Formula for. (J. H. Stanton) Am. Arch. 43: 112.
Pineapples Grown under Sheds in Florida. (P. H. Rolfs) Garden & F. 9: 274.
Pinehurst, South Carolina. (B. A. Goodridge) New Eng. M. n. s. 15: 321.
Pinelli, Bartolomeo. (E. Auber) Art J. 46: 284.
Pine Ridge, Indian Agency, Attack on. (T. H. Wilson) Un. Serv. (Phila.) 7: 562.
Pinero, Arthur Wing. (J. A. Hamilton) Munsey, 10: 247.
— Benefit of the Doubt. Sat. R. 80: 503.
— and Farce. (R. F. Sharp) Theatre, 29: 154.
— and the Literary Drama. Theatre, 31: 3.
— The Cabinet Minister. Gent. M. n. s. 48: 319.
— Notorious Mrs. Ebbsmith. Sat. R. 79: 346.
— Plays of, as Literature. (H. H. Fyfe) Theatre, 35: 324.
— Second Mrs. Tanqueray. Sat. R. 79: 249.
Pines. Bull Pine in the West. (C. A. Keffer) Garden & F. 8: 163.
— A Corner in. (M. C. Robbins) Garden & F. 5: 302.
— Florida. Garden & F. 5: 73.
— Pinetum at Wellesley, Mass. Garden & F. 5: 385. — (C. S. Sargent) Garden & F. 7: 451.
— Pinetum at West Chester, Pa. Garden & F. 6: 458.
— Pinus Ponderosa. (C. S. Sargent) Garden & F. 8: 392.
— Remarkable Group of. (M. C. Robbins) Garden & F. 8: 332.
— Scotch, in the West. (C. A. Keffer) Garden & F. 8: 142.
— Serotinous. (G. B. Sudworth) Garden & F. 5: 160.
— Table Mountain. (T. C. Porter) Garden & F. 6: 204.
— Western American Cone-bearers. (J. G. Lemmon) Garden & F. 5: 227.
Piney Branch Quarry Workshop. (T. Wilson) Am. Natural. 30: 873, 976.
Ping Yang, Battle of. How the News was told at Dragon Valley, October, 1894. (E. A. Irving) Blackw. 157: 138.
Pingree, Mayor, Potato-patch Plan of. (H. P. Pingree) Pub. Opin. 20: 109, 205. — Lend a H. 14: 404.
Pinochle Club, A Day of the. (J. Ralph) Harper, 89: 695.
Pinto, Ferd. Mendez. (S. Wheeler) Geog. J. 1: 139.
Piombo, Sebastiano del. *See* Luciani, S.
Piozzi, Mrs. H. L., in Italy. (M. S. Stillman) Nation, 54: 342.
Pipe, Primitive Smoking. (E. Lovett) Illus. Archæol. 2: 100.
Piper of Crag Ailsa; a story. (A. J. H. Antona) Outing, 26: 71.
Pipes. (H. V. Barnett) M. of Art, 6: 101.
— Chapter on. (J. Cassidy) Gent. M. n. s. 55: 17.
— Concerning. All the Year, 73: 245.
— Indian. The Calumet in the Champlain Valley. (G. H. Perkins) Pop. Sci. Mo. 44: 238.
Pipowder Courts. Green Bag, 5: 265.
Piracy in N. Y. (C. B. Todd) Nat'l M. (N. Y. '91) 16: 627.
— — Suppression of, 1698–1701. (W. L. Stone) Nat'l M. (N. Y. '91) 17: 1.
— in 13th and 14th centuries. Sat. R. 75: 262.
— of the Nimhok. (C. W. Mason) Eng. Illust. 12: no. 3, 125.
Pirarucú Fishing on the Amazon. (H. H. Smith) Outing, 28: 445.
Pirate in Petticoats, A; a story. (F. Dana) Harper, 87: 731.
Pirate Gold. (F. J. Stimson) Atlan. 77: 73, 222, 334.
Pirate's Paradise, A, in the West Indies. (G. H. Powell) Gent. M. n. s. 52: 21.
Pirates, Carolina, and Colonial Commeree, 1670–1740. (S. C. Hughson) J. H. Univ. Studies, 12: 241.
— Chinese, in the Fifties. (A. H. Markham) Idler, 10: 40.
Pirates, Illanum, A Fight with. (R. Wildman) Overland, n. s. 25: 514.
Pis-aller, A; a story. (A. Hope) Idler, 7: 435.
Pisano, Niccola, and the Renascence of Sculpture. (J. A. Crowe) 19th Cent. 39: 679. Same art. Ecl. M. 127: 153.
Pisano, Vittore. Sat. R. 82: 86.
Pisgah; a poem. (J. B. Tabb) Cosmopol. 18: 53.
Pisidia and Lycia, Inscriptions from. (G. F. Hill) J. Hel. Stud. 15: 116.
Pistol Exercise for Officers. Sat. R. 74: 99.
Piston Construction. (J. E. Sweet) Cassier, 9: 450.
Pit Dwellers of the Japanese Archipelago. Dub. R. 114: 430.
Pitch, Lake of, Trinidad. Chamb. J. 71: 810. — (S. F. Peckham) Am. J. Sci. 150: 33. — (S. F. Peckham and L. A. Linton) Am. J. Sci. 151: 193.
Pitch, Musical, Change of. (J. C. Hadden) 19th Cent. 38: 828.
— Educational Value of the International Pitch. (C. W. Grimm) Music, 3: 123.
— Standard for. (A. S. Hipkins) J. Soc. Arts, 44: 335.
Pitcher Plant. (W. H. Taplin) Garden & F. 5: 163.
Pitcher Plants, Cultivation of. Garden & F. 9: 176.
— Florida. (C. B. Palmer) Science, 20: 171.
— Home of. (M. Cristy) Good Words, 33: 758.
Pithecanthropus Erectus. (E. Dubois) Anthrop. J. 25: 240. — (O. C. Marsh) Science, n. s. 3: 789. — (O. C. Marsh) Am. J. Sci. 151: 475. — (A. Keith) Sci. Prog. 3: 348. — (W. J. Sollas) Nature, 53: 150.
— — Dubois, from Java. (O. C. Marsh) Am. J. Sci. 149: 144.
Pithecoid Man. (E. P. Evans) Pop. Sci. Mo. 46: 183.
Pitiful Surrender; a story. (J. P. Wisser) Un. Serv. (Phila.) 9: 560.
Pitman, John. (A. M. Earle) New Eng. M. n. s. 12: 407.
Pitsligo, Alexander, Lord. Temp. Bar, 103: 99. Same art. Liv. Age, 203: 67.
Pitt, Thomas, 2d Lord Camelford. Argosy, 60: 25. Same art. Liv. Age, 206: 503.
Pitt, William. (A. St. J. Clerke) Dub. R. 110: 25.
— Greatness of. (T. E. Kebbel) National, 18: 603. Same art. Liv. Age, 192: 707.
— Prophecy respecting Napoleon in Spain. (A. V. Dicey) Contemp. 70: 305, (Reply) 582.
— Rosebery's. (J. Skelton) Blackw. 151: 136. Same art. Liv. Age, 192: 680. — (S. Walpole) Eng. Hist. R. 7: 177. — (G. Smith) Nation, 54: 233. — (R. B. Brett) 19th Cent. 31: 7. — (R. S. Long) Westm. 137: 174.
— The Surrender at Saratoga. Macmil. 70: 193.
— War Policy of. Contemp. 61: 675. — Quar. 175: 70.
Pittsfield, Mass., Church and Meeting-houses of. (Mrs. H. M. Plunkett) New Eng. M. n. s. 9: 392.
— Literary Record of. Lit. W. (Bost.) 24: 92.
Pittsburg, Carnegie Library. Lib. J. 20: 382.
— Old Round Church. (O. O. Page) Pennsyl. M. 19: 351.
Pity, Progress of. Spec. 70: 320.

Pity of it, The; a story. (Z. D. Underhill) Harper, **93**: 739.
Piuro, Fate of. (G. S. Godkin) Argosy, **60**: 371.
Pius VI., Pope, and the French Directory. (F. S. Chatard) Cath. World, **64**: 1.
Pius IX. and the Revolution, 1846–48. (J. A. Mooney) Am. Cath. Q. **17**: 137, 463.
— Love Story of a Pope. (K. Roy) Canad. M. **5**: 555.
Piutes, In the Stronghold of the. (J. Adams) Overland, n. s. **22**: 583.
Pizzica, Pizzica; true story from Apulia. Temp. Bar, **96**: 377.
Place of Yellow Brick, The; a story. (S. H. Clarke) Temp. Bar, **109**: 552.
Place-names, Scottish. Ath. '92, **2**: 345. — (J. S. Blackie) Blackw. **156**: 38.
See Names.
Plagiarism. Lit. W. (Bost.) **27**: 216. — (C. Robinson) Writer, **8**: 109.
— and Coincidence. (J. C. Hadden) Scot. R. **27**: 336.
— Ethics of. (J. M. Driver) Meth. R. **52**: 405.
— Goethe on. (E. L. Hibberd) Writer, **8**: 147.
— Self-. Atlan. **72**: 429.
— Suspected. (F. Wicks) National, **19**: 423.
Plagiarists. Time, **23**: 929.
— Imitators and. (W. H. D. Adams) Gent. M. n. s. **48**: 502, 613.
Plague at Eyam in 1666. (C. Burke) Argosy, **54**: 463.
— on a Pleasure-boat. (J. S. Stevenson) Cent. **24**: 817.
Plain John Miller. (C. P. Burton) Outing, **28**: 329.
Plains, Across the. (J. W. Tate) Overland, n. s. **22**: 300.
— Treeless, of United States. (J. W. Redway) Geog. J. **3**: 209.
Planchette, Experience with. (E. T. Durgin) Psychic. R. **2**: 267.
Plane Spaces of *n* Manifoldness, Metrical Relations of. (E. Lasker) Nature, **52**: 340.
Plane Trees. (C. S. Sargent) Garden & F. **9**: 51.
Planetary Ephemeris. (J. Morrison) Pop. Astron. **4**: 32.
Planets. Are they inhabited? (G. M. Searle) Cath. World, **55**: 860. — (R. Ball) McClure, **5**: 147.
— Communication with. (A. Guillemin) Pop. Sci. Mo. **40**: 361.
— Configurations of. (E. E. Markwick) Knowl. **18**: 152.
— Habitability of. (R. S. Ball) Fortn. **62**: 718. Same art. Ecl. M. **123**: 818.
— Minor, Photographic Observation of. (Max Wolf) Astron. **12**: 779.
— Peep at. All the Year, **71**: 305.
— Picturing the. (J. E. Keeler) Cent. **28**: 455.
— What we know about. (G. P. Serviss) Chaut. **20**: 526.
Plant, A Cannibal. Liv. Age, **192**: 61.
Plant Anatomy, Elements of, Gregory on. (G. F. Atkinson) School R. **4**: 240.
Plant-breeding. (F. W. Card) Garden & F. **6**: 216. — (M. T. Masters) Nature, **54**: 138.
— at the Experiment Stations. (E. S. Goff) Garden & F. **8**: 292.
Plant Cells, Influence of Carbon Dioxide on Protoplasm of. (D. T. MacDougal) Science, n. s. **3**: 689.
Plant Doctor, The. (C. S. Sargent) Garden & F. **7**: 421.
Plant Doctors, Need of Competent. (J. W. Harshberger) Educa. **16**: 140.
Plant Forms in Decorative Art. (G. McKenzie) M. of Art, **1**: 74.
Plant Growth, Retarding by Low Temperature. (E. G. Lademan) Garden & F. **7**: 186.
Plant Individual, The, in Light of Evolution. (L. H Bailey) Science, n. s. **1**: 281.
Plant-lice. (M. V. Slingerland) Science, **21**: 48.
Plant Life of California, Picturesque. (C. H. Shinn) Cent. **22**: 834.
Plant-lore. (Mrs. F. D. Bergen) J. Am. Folk-Lore, **5**: 19.
Plant-names, Popular American. (S. Hayward) J. Am. Folk-Lore, **4**: 147. — (Mrs. F. D. Bergen) J. Am. Folk-Lore, **5**: 89, 179. **6**: 135. **7**: 89.
Plant Nomenclature, Ambiguity in. (B. L. Putnam) Educa. **15**: 550.
Plant-pests, Increasing Number of. (C. S. Sargent) Garden & F. **7**: 51.
Plant Structures, Origin of, Henslow's. Sat. R. **80**: 552.
Plantains and Bananas. Garden & F. **5**: 183.
Plantin-Moretus Museum, Antwerp. (W. A. Smith) Bookworm, **5**: 321. — (W. M. Conway) M. of Art, **6**: 360.
Plants, Arctic, during the Glacial Epoch. (A. G. Nathorst) Nature, **45**: 273.
— Bacterial Diseases in. (E. F. Smith) Am Natural. **30**: 626–912.
— Bedding-. (S. Parsons, jr.) Scrib. M. **17**: 329.
— Common Names of. Garden & F. **6**: 116.
— Diseases of, and Bacteria. (G. Murray) Nat. Sci. **4**: 129.
— — Legislation against. (C. S. Sargent) Garden & F. **6**: 401.
— Distinction between. (J. C. Arthur) Am. Natural. **29**: 961.
— Distribution of, Curious Facts on. (W. B. Hemsley) Knowl. **19**: 102–270.
— Dropsical Diseases of. (G. F. Atkinson) Science, **22**: 323.
— Fecundation of. (H. J. Webber) Science, **21**: 337.
— Folk-lore and Superstitions concerning. (B. D. Halsted) Chaut. **17**: 173.
— for Seashore. (J. W. Harshberger) Garden & F. **5**: 45.
— for Summer Decoration. (W. Tricker) Garden & F. **5**: 536.
— for Winter Decoration, Native. (Mary Treat) Garden & F. **6**: 141.
— Fossil, Lacoe Collection of. (G. B. Goode) Science, n. s. **4**: 8.
— Gases in Living. (J. C. Arthur) Am. Natural. **27**: 1, 98.
— Geographical Distribution as affected by Temperature. (C. H. Merriam) Nat. Geog. M. **3**: 228.
— House, Care of. Garden & F. **7**: 518.
— — for Shady Windows. (W. H. Taplin) Garden & F. **5**: 596.
— in Winter, Protection of. (J. G. Jack) Garden & F. **6**: 226.
— Insectivorous, of South Florida. (G. W. Webster) Science, **22**: 37.
— Irritability of. (F. Elfving) Nature, **49**: 466. — Nature, **49**: 586.
— — and Movement in. (D. T. Macdougal) Pop. Sci. Mo. **47**: 225.
— Life Action in. Sat. R. **82**: 131.
— Morphology of, Problems of. (C. MacMillan) Science, n. s. **3**: 346.
— Names of. Quar. **183**: 230.
— — Kew Index of. Nature. **49**: 241.
— Natural History of. (G. McCarthy) Chaut. **15**: 43–286.

Plants, New, of '92. (W. Watson) Garden & F. 6: 41–194.
— — in England. (W. Watson) Garden & F. 6: 183.
— Number of. (P. A. Saccardo) Am. Natural. 28: 173.
— of Indian Origin. (W. R. Gerard) Garden & F. 9: 252–302.
— Pestiferous. (B. D. Halsted) Pop. Sci. Mo. 41: 225.
— Protection and Dispersion in. (J. R. Jackson) Leis. Hour, 45: 26.
— Reserve Materials of. (J. R. Green) Sci. Prog. 3: 68, 476. 5: 60.
— Sexuality of, Discovery of. Pop. Sci. Mo. 42: 546.
— Sex-relation of, Terminology of. (L. H. Bailey) Science, n. s. 3: 825.
— Sleep of. Chamb. J. 71: 399.
— Stelar Theory. (A. G. Tansley) Sci. Prog. 5: 133, 215.
— Tender, in Public Parks. (W. McMillan) Garden & F. 6: 371.
— Useful, Experimental Work in the Improvement of. (C. S. Sargent) Garden & F. 6: 261.
— Wayside, in the Pines. (M. Treat) Garden & F. 7: 302.
— Winter, Decorative. (E. O. Orpet) Garden & F. 6: 18.
— Winter Flowering. (W. Tricker) Garden & F. 6: 18. — (R. Cameron) Garden & F. 6: 80.
Plasmogeny. (D. Bright) Open Court, 4: 2615.
Plaster for Walls and Ceilings. (J. B. King) Archit. Rec. 2: 515.
Plaster Work, Ornamental. (F. W. Pomeroy) Am. Arch. 48: 16.
Plastering, Staining of, Prevention of. (L. de C. Berg) Am. Arch. 50: 29.
Plataia, Excavations at, by American School, in 1891. (H. S. Washington) Am. J. Archæol. 7: 390.
— Votive Inscription from. (R. B. Richardson) Am. J. Archæol. 7: 406.
Plate, Corporation, and Insignia of Office of Towns of England and Wales, Jewitt and Hope's. (F. G. Stephens) M. of Art, 19: 324.
— Old Church, Ferguson's. M. of Art, 7: 418.
— Queen Anne. (W. Cripps) M. of Art, 5: 277.
— Sir Samuel Montagu's Collection. (F. S. Robinson) M. of Art, 19: 19.
Plate Matter for Newspapers. (H. Fielding) Bk. News, 7: 237.
Plateau Implements, Geology of, of Kent. (T. R. Jones) Nat. Sci. 5: 269.
Platform, The. (G. O. Morgan) Westm. 137: 289.
— Gladstone on. Spec. 68: 453.
— Jephson's Rise and Progress of. (A. Arnold) Acad. 41: 222. — Ed. R. 176: 275.
Platinochlorides, New Methods of obtaining. (M. C. Lea) Am. J. Sci. 148: 397.
Platinoid, Thermo-electric Properties of. (B. O. Peirce) Am. J. Sci. 148: 302.
Platinum, Consumption and Sources of. Dub. R. 113: 656.
Platinum Subchloride, Probable Existence of. (M. C. Lea) Am. J. Sci. 148: 397.
Plato. (W. Pater) Macmil. 66: 31. Same art. Ecl. M. 119: 65. Same art. Liv. Age, 193: 762.
— and Art, especially Music. (K. J. Belling) Music, 1: 197–317.
— and his Influence. Church Q. 35: 444.
— and Platonism, Pater's. (C. Dodgson) Acad. 43: 317. — (P. Shorey) Dial (Ch.) 14: 211. — (J. H. McDaniels) Nation, 57: 413. — (E. Gosse) New R. 8: 419. — Spec. 70: 422. — (W. Hammond) Philos. R. 3: 77.
Plato. Apology, Armenian Version of. (F. C. Conybeare) Am. J. Philol. 12: 399. 16: 300.
— Chronological Order of his Works. (W. S. Scarborough) Educa. 15: 213.
— Conception of the Good Life. (B. Bosanquet) New World, 2: 623.
— Dialogues, Jowett's Edition of 1892. (T. D. Seymour) Educa. R. 4: 270. — (P. Shorey) Am. J. Philol. 13: 349. — (W. S. Hough) Dial (Ch.) 13: 183. — Sat. R. 74: 82.
— Earlier Theory of Ideas. (R. P. Hardie) Mind, 21: 167.
— Educational Theories of. (H. G. Pearson) New Eng. M. n. s. 8: 758.
— Figures of Comparison in. (G. B. Hussey) Am. J. Philol. 17: 329.
— From the Reports of the Plato Club. (H. A. Aikins) Atlan. 74: 359, 470.
— Genius of. (W. Pater) Contemp. 61: 249. Same art. Ecl. M. 118: 454. Same art. Liv. Age, 193: 67.
— Half an Hour with. (H. M. King) Educa. 12: 481.
— Jowett's. Spec. 70: 47.
— Laws, Armenian Version, Book IV. (F. C. Conybeare) Am. J. Philol. 14: 335.
— — — Collation of. (F. C. Conybeare) Am. J. Philol. 15: 31.
— Lysis, Date of. (A. Wirth) Am. J. Philol. 16: 211.
— Parmenides; ed. by Waddell. Sat. R. 80: 529.
— — On the Interpretation of. (A. E. Taylor) Mind, 21: 297, 483.
— Republic, Ideas of Justice in. (P. Shorey) Eth. Rec. 2: 185.
— — Jowett and Campbell's. (P. Shorey) Nation, 61: 82.
— Where he taught. (J. Baker) Good Words, 33: 191.
Platonic Philosophy. Halévy, E. La Théorie platonicienne des Sciences. (P. Shorey) Philos. R. 5: 522.
Platt, Mrs. Mary J., Murder of, by Indians, at Pachango. (E. B. Howell) R. of Rs. (N. Y.) 10: 507.
Plattner Story, The. (H. G. Wells) New R. 14: 349.
Plattnerite. (W. S. Yeates) Am. J. Sci. 143: 407.
Platypus, Haunt of the. (S. Dickinson) Scrib. M. 13: 791.
Plausible Man, The. Ecl. M. 118: 129.
Plautus. Rudens, Sonnenschein's Edition. Ath. '92, 1: 190, 214.
Play, Educational Value of, and the Recent Play-movement in Germany. (J. L. Hughes) Educa. R. 8: 327. — (G. E. Johnson) Pedagog. Sem. 3: 97.
— of Young Animals, Groos on. Sat. R. 82: 415.
Play, The, Fifty Years at. (E. J. Goodman) Theatre, 33: 172.
— Modern Society. (C. Scott) Theatre, 34: 6.
— Single-act. (A. à Beckett) Theatre, 34: 204.
— A Study of the. (E. P. Powell) Open Court, 6: 3271. *See* Stage; Theatre.
Play Bills, Past and Present. (N. L. Parker) Theatre, 29: 8.
Play Writers and Censors. (A. Hornblow) Bookman, 3: 24.
Play-writing. Gent. M. n. s. 49: 423.
— Archer on. Sat. R. 73: 459.
— from the Actor's Point of View. (W. H. Crane) No. Am. 157: 325.
— Hints on. (E. K. Cowing) Writer, 7: 113.
— How successfully done. (J. Brooks) Cosmopol. 19: 212.
— Mistakes in. (G. B. Shaw) Sat. R. 82: 367.
Players, English, Loyalty of. (R. W. Lowe) Theatre, 37: 325.

Players, Strolling. Cornh. 72: 87.
Players' Club, New York City. (J. C. Harvey) Munsey, 12: 581.
Playfair, Sir Hugh Lyon, and St. Andrew's. Belgra. 83: 406.
Playgoers' Club. (R. J. Slade) Theatre, 31: 273.
Playgrounds for City Schools. (J. A. Riis) Cent. 26: 657.
— Municipal. (C. S. Sargent) Garden & F. 9: 501.
— Public, for Children. (Earl of Meath) 19th Cent. 34: 267.
Playhouse Sonnets. (H. W. Charlesworth) Canad. M. 1: 558.
Playing before Royalty. (A. à Beckett) Theatre, 33: 226.
— of The Bohemian Girl; a story. (E. Turner) Eng. Illust. 15: 514.
— Past and Present. (L. Wagner) Theatre, 37: 66.
Playing-cards, Origin of. (Stewart Culin) J. Am. Folk-Lore, 8: 250.
Playwright's Love Story. Argosy, 59: 236.
Playwright's Novitiate. (M. C. Harris) Atlan. 74: 515.
Playwrights and Players, Earnings of. (A. à Beckett) Theatre, 35: 209.
— Modern, and their Methods. Chamb. J. 69: 352.
— What they earn. Idler, 8: 285.
Plays, Accessorial Music in. (W. Beatty-Kingston) Theatre, 34: 143.
— Folk, in the Tyrol. (R. Barr) Idler, 4: 581.
— Pages on. (J. H. McCarthy) Gent. M. n. s. vols. 48-51.
— Why Theatrical Managers reject. (A. M. Palmer) Forum, 15: 614.
Plaza of Santa Marta. (H. Bindloss) Chamb. J. 73: 778.
Plea of Pan; a dialogue. (H. W. Nevinson) Contemp. 66: 390.
"Pleasant Sunday Afternoon" Movement in England. (R. Souttar) Our Day, 14: 222.
Pleasure. (Sir H. Maxwell) Blackw. 151: 22. Same art. Ecl. M. 118: 357. Same art. Liv. Age, 192: 643.
— and Pain. (A. Bain) Mind, 17: 161. — (A. Sidgwick) Mind, 18: 89. — (B. I. Gilman) Am. J. Psychol. 6: 3. — (H. R. Marshall) Mind, 19: 533. — (P. Carus) Open Court, 3: 1987.
— — defined. (S. E. Mezes) Philos. R. 4: 22.
— — in Education. (M. S. Gilliland) Int. J. Ethics, 2: 289.
— — Origin of. (H. Nichols) Philos. R. 1: 403, 518.
— — Pathological. (T. Ribot) Monist, 6: 176.
— — Ribot on. (P. Carus) Monist, 6: 432.
— Chemistry of. (J. C. F. Grumbine) Open Court, 4: 2692.
— Is it the *summum bonum*? (J. Seth) Int. J. Ethics, 6: 409.
Pleasure-pain and Emotion. (H. R. Marshall) Psychol. R. 2: 57.
— and Sensation. (H. R. Marshall) Philos. R. 1: 625.
— Emotions *versus*. (H. R. Marshall) Mind, 20: 180.
Plebiscite, The. (E. Meek) Canad. M. 2: 8.
Pleiades, The. (W. Schooling) Longm. 23: 626. (W. W. Payne) Pop. Astron. 1: 456. — Nature, 49: 366.
— Exterior Nebulosities of. (A. M. Clerke) Knowl. 18: 280.
— Nebulosities of. (E. E. Barnard) Astron. 13: 768.
— Occultation of, Dec. 10-11, 1894. (H. C. Wilson) Pop. Astron. 2: 176.
— Photograph of. (H. C. Wilson) Astron. 13: 192.
Pleistocene Fossils from Winthrop, Mass., Additional Species of. (R. E. Dodge) Am. J. Sci. 147: 100.
Pleistocene Marine Shore-lines on the South Side of the St. Lawrence Valley. (R. Chalmers) Am. J. Sci. 151: 302.
Plevna, Campaign of. Un. Serv. M. 11: 366, 464.
— Failure of Russian Artillery at. (E. S. May) Un. Serv. M. 11: 589.
Pleydell's Predicament. (C. E. C. Weigall) Argosy, 61: 287. Same art. Liv. Age, 209: 218.
Pliny and Magic. (E. Riess) Am. J. Philol. 17: 77.
Pliny, the Younger, Letters of. (S. B. Platner) N. Eng. 56: 63.
Plon, Eugene. Acad. 47: 337.
Plot and Counterplot; a story. (H. F. Lester) Argosy, 61: 216.
Plot-making. (E. E. Benton) Writer, 8: 96.
Ploug, Carl Parmo. Ath. '94, 2: 606.
Ploughin' o' th' Sunnyfields, Th'; a story. (M. E. Francis) Blackw. 160: 39. Same art. Liv. Age, 210: 529. Same art. Ecl. M. 127: 351.
Plover, Upland, With the. (J. R. Benton) Outing, 28: 433.
Plovers and their Peculiarities. (H. A. Bryden) Chamb. J. 70: 353.
Plucking of a Rosebud. (E. Esdaile) Longm. 20: 482.
Plum, Flowering and Fertilization of Native. (E. S. Goff) Garden & F. 7: 262.
— Prunus Watsoni. (C. S. Sargent) Garden & F. 7: 134.
— Prunus Orthosepala. (C. S. Sargent) Garden & F. 7: 184.
Plumbing. Archit. Rec. 1: 97.
— Recent Practice in, 1893. (G. Brown) Am. Arch. 41: 115.
— Trade Schools and their Influence. (E. N. G. Le Bois) Engin. M. 8: 646.
Plumblossom Beebe's Adventures; a story. (J. Ralph) Harper, 91: 943.
Plunket's Widow. Macmil. 71: 52. Same art. Liv. Age, 203: 733.
Plutarch, The New. (C. Whibley) New R. 12: 677.
Plutocracy and Paternalism. (L. F. Ward) Forum, 20: 300.
— Are we a? (W. D. Howells) No. Am. 158: 185.
— Menace of. (B. O. Flower) Arena, 6: 508.
Plymouth, Mass., Pilgrims' Church in. (A. Lord) New Eng. M. n. s. 7: 777.
Plymouth Idea. Lend a H. 15: 267.
Plymouth Schools, Old. (Mrs. A. M. Diaz) Bost. 1: 494.
Pneumatic Telegraphs in Paris. (S. E. Morss) Am. Arch. 47: 74.
Pneumatic Transmission, Progress in. (W. A. Smith) Engin. M. 4: 677.
Po River, Embankments of. (F. D. Adams) Science, n. s. 3: 759.
Poachers of Fish on Borderland of England and Scotland. (P. A. Graham) New R. 15: 585.
Poaching. (L'Aigle Cole) 19th Cent. 34: 470.
— and Poachers. Eng. Illust. 10: 811. Same art. Liv. Age, 199: 575.
Pobedonostseff, Constantine. (E. B. Lanin) Contemp. 63: 584.
Poblet, Ruins of. (C. W. Wood) Argosy, 62: 570.
Pocahontas. Our Lady of the James. (M. V. Terhune) Cosmopol. 16: 308.
Poe, E. A. (John Burroughs) Dial (Ch.) 15: 214. — (J. L. Onderdonk) Mid-Cont. 6: 166. — (C. Whibley) New R. 14: 612. — (B. M. Ranking) Time, 8: 352.
— and Charles Baudelaire. (E. Stuart) 19th Cent. 34: 65. Same art. Liv. Age, 198: 692.
— and the Brownings. (J. L. Onderdonk) Dial (Ch.) 14: 353.

Poe, E. A. Eureka, Addenda to, with Comments. Meth. R. 56: 9, 111.
— Friends of. (E. L. Didier) Chaut. 15: 723.
— Letters, in New York. Cent. 26: 854.
— — in the South. Cent. 26: 572.
— — in Philadelphia. Cent. 26: 725.
— Moral Nature of. (W. M. Griswold) Nation, 60: 381.
— Musical Possibilities of Poems of. (C. S. Skilton) Music, 7: 236.
— The New Poe. Atlan. 77: 551.
— Raven, Writing of. (F. A. Matthews) Bach. of Arts, 3: 328.
— Recollections of. (H. Paul) Munsey, 7: 554.
— Works. Ed. by Stedman and Woodberry. (D. L. Maulsby) Dial (Ch.) 18: 138.
— — Ed. by Stoddard. Sat. R. 81: 460.
Poems in Prose. (O. Wilde) Fortn. 62: 22.
Poems on Poems. Chamb. J. 70: 90. Same art. Liv. Age, 197: 187.
Poet, The, as Dreamer and Seer. Spec. 69: 14.
— Attitude of, towards his Critics. (F. B. Hornbrooke) Poet-Lore, 5: 135.
— Can he be Democratic? Poet-Lore, 7: 619.
— Democracy and the. (N. P. Gilman) New World, 3: 311.
— Function of the. (J. R. Lowell) Cent. 25: 432.
— — as Interpreter. Spec. 75: 516.
— in an Age of Science, The. (C. T. Goodwin) New World, 4: 121.
— in Carglen, A; a story. (A. Gordon) Gent. M. n. s. 48: 399.
— on the Wolds. (F. Wedmore) Fortn. 65: 751. Same art. Ecl. M. 126: 850.
Poetic Absurdities, Some. All the Year, 75: 354.
Poetic Criticism: Horace to Stedman. Poet-Lore, 5: 43.
Poetic Drama at Daly's Theatre. All the Year, 73: 420.
Poetic Expression, Nature of. (D. Dorchester, jr.) Poet-Lore, 5: 81.
Poetic License. (A. Quarry) Argosy, 58: 334.
Poetic Pride. (H. M. Sanders) Gent. M. n. s. 55: 203. Same art. Liv. Age, 206: 798.
Poetic Rhythms in Prose. (E. E. Hale, jr.) Atlan. 78: 227.
Poetical Literature, The Mother's Influence in Teaching. (M. J. Reid) Dial (Ch.) 20: 162.
Poetry. New R. 11: 475.
— and Eloquence. (J. Burroughs) Chaut. 15: 63.
— and Fine Art, Aristotle on. (E. E. Hale, jr.) Dial (Ch.) 18: 298.
— and Music. Macmil. 72: 102. — (W. M. Derthick) Music, 10: 24.
— and Pessimism. (E. K. Chambers) Westm. 138: 366.
— and Politics. (C. B. R. Kent) Gent. M. n. s. 50: 237. Same art. Ecl. M. 120: 562.
— and Science. (C. Thomas) Open Court, 3: 1727. — (H. Allen) Poet-Lore, 3: 232. — (W. H. Hudson) Pop. Sci. Mo. 45: 812.
— and Song in the U. S. in Colonial Days, Religious Thought as mirrored in. (B. O. Flower) Arena, 7: 64.
— Apologies for. (G. L. Apperson) Bookworm, 7: 111.
— Arabian, before the Days of Mohammed. (W. S. Blunt) New R. 14: 626.
— Aristotle's Theory of, Butcher on. (B. L. Gildersleeve) Nation, 60: 364.
— as a Profession. Critic, 21: 83.
— Bee-pastures of. (Arthur Grant) Time, 19: 60.
— Bohemian Popular. (J. J. Kral) Music, 3: 485.
— Consolations of. Macmil. 66: 387. Same art. Liv. Age, 195: 474.
— a Criticism of Literature. Dial (Ch.) 18: 133.
Poetry, English. Elizabethan Lyrics. Church Q. 34: 184.
— — since Pope. (M. Thompson) Chaut. 15: 320.
— Essence of. Atlan. 72: 137.
— European and Asiatic, Parallel Passages from. (W. A. Clouston) Asia. R. 10: 201.
— Feast of the Gods. (J. V. Cheney) Chaut. 19: 167.
— for Children, Some Notes on. (E. V. Lucas) Fortn. 66: 391. Same art. Liv. Age, 211: 131.
— Future of. (C. L. Moore) Forum, 14: 768. — (A. C. Benson) National, 25: 97.
— Gift for, Diffusion of. Spec. 71: 429.
— in England: Literary and Municipal Problems. (F. Harrison) Forum, 14: 644.
— in General and in Particular. Atlan. 73: 702.
— Inspirational. Psychic. R. 2: 308.
— Intimations of a New Dawn. (T. Bradfield) Westm. 143: 652.
— Life in. (W. J. Courthope) 19th Cent. 40: 260.
— Magic Verses. Temp. Bar, 104: 229.
— Mediocrity in. (A. Ainger) Macmil. 71: 92.
— Nature and Elements of. (E. C. Stedman) Cent. 21: 752 — 22: 859.
— New Form of, as shown in Browning. (D. G. Brinton) Poet-Lore, 2: 234.
— Obscurity in. Gent. M. n. s. 48: 430.
— of the Prison. (George Wyndham) New R. 12: 282.
— of To-day and To-morrow. Liv. Age, 196: 279.
— or Science? (W. K. Brooks) Science, n. s. 2: 437.
— The Permanent in. (W. Truitt) Overland, n. s. 24: 39.
— Plethora of. (W. E. Gladstone) Critic, 29: 45.
— Power and Place of. (J. V. Cheney) Chaut. 19: 37.
— Readers of. Spec. 68: 366.
— Recent. (W. M. Payne) Dial (Ch.) 14: 145. — Ed. R. 183: 488.
— — 1892. (T. W. Higginson) Nation, 55: 452.
— — Some Aspects of. (W. Wallace) Sat. R. 26: 114.
— Recent English. (W. M. Payne) Dial (Ch.) 18: 150.
— Sound in. (E. V. Eastman) Music, 10: 253.
— Stedman on. (A. G. Newcomer) Dial (Ch.) 14: 107.
— Use of, in School Study. (W. J. Rolfe) Poet-Lore, 6: 592.
— a World outside of Science. (T. W. Higginson) New World, 1: 689.
Poet's Christmas Eve; a poem. (C. G. Rogers) Canad. M. 6: 101.
Poet's Portmanteau; a story. (G. Gissing) Eng. Illust. 12: no. 5, 3.
Poets, American, and Music. (H. A. Clarke) Music, 6: 63–282.
— — of To-day. (D. H. Wheeler) Chaut. 22: 34.
— and Geographers. (W. Greswell) Blackw. 156: 515.
— and Poetry of the Century, Miles'. Ath. '92, 2: 545.
— and Versifiers, Contemporary. Ed. R. 178: 469.
— Children's. (A. Repplier) Atlan. 69: 328.
— Death of. Gent. M. n. s. 49: 537.
— Effects of Environment on: Lowlands *versus* Highlands. (E. Vicars) Poet-Lore, 6: 83.
— English, Living. (A. T. Q. Couch) Eng. Illust. 10: 900.
— English Minor. (H. D. Traill) 19th Cent. 31: 61. Same art. Ecl. M. 118: 298. Same art. Liv. Age, 192: 740.
— — — and others. (H. D. Traill) 19th Cent. 31: 410.
— Female, of the Century. Spec. 69: 258.
— Flowers and. (P. Robinson) Contemp. 63: 825. Same art. Liv. Age, 198: 419.
— Incomes of. Pub. Opin. 14: 214.
— the Interpreters of their Age, Swanwick's. Spec. 69: 100.
— Jacobean, Gosse on. Spec. 72: 506.

Poets Laureate, English. (R. H. Titherington) Munsey, 8: 525. — (R. H. Stoddard) Cosmopol. 14: 312. — (C. Newell) Poet-Lore, 4: 552, 599.
— — and the Laureateship, 1892. Spec. 69: 517.
— — Laureates and Poets. (R. Ogden) Nation, 62: 26.
— — Poet-laureateship, The. Temp. Bar, 106: 498. Same art. Liv. Age, 207: 787. Same art. Ecl. M. 126: 97. — Bookworm, 2: 297.
— — Question of. (H. T. Peck) Bookman, 2: 292.
— — Who shall follow Tennyson? Idler, 7: 400.
— Modern, and the Meaning of Life. (F. W. H. Myers) 19th Cent. 33: 93. Same art. Ecl. M. 120: 365.
— Music in. (H. A. Clarke) Music, 3: 239.
— of Provence. (C. Hartog) Contemp. 66: 496. Same art. Ecl. M. 123: 801.
— of the Pulpit. All the Year, 71: 341, 366.
— Older Living. Sat. R. 79: 648.
— Praise of, Adams'. Ath. '94, 1: 139.
— 17th-century, Reprints of. Gent. M. n. s. 48: 321.
— Some, and their Pastimes. Chamb. J. 72: 380.
— Swan-songs of. (A. Small) Gent. M. n. s. 49: 574. Same art. Ecl. M. 120: 241. Same art. Liv. Age, 196: 254.
— Two Modern. (H. D. Traill) Fortn. 63: 393. Same art. Liv. Age, 205: 161.
— The Younger. Liv. Age, 204: 470.
Poets' Corner, A. (V. Blackburn) New R. 12: 514.
Poetzsch, Paul. (C. Saunders) Mo. Illust. 11: 575.
Pogit Way; a story. (G. L. Furniss) Harper, 87: 110.
Poinsettias. (E. O. Orpet) Garden & F. 8: 486.
— Cultivation of. (W. N. Craig) Garden & F. 7: 76.
Point-aux-Pins; a story. (J. Blewitt) Canad. M. 5: 140.
Point of Contact. (A. Rothwell) New Eng. M. n. s. 11: 504.
Point of Knucklin' down, A; a story. (E. Higginson) McClure, 6: 71.
Point of Order. (E. S. Phelps Ward) Chaut. 18: 35.
Point of View, The; a Corsican story. (J. W. Dougherty) Overland, n. s. 23: 465.
Points of the Compass, Ceremonial Circuit of, among the Tusayan Indians. (J. W. Fewkes) Am. Natural. 26: 24.
Poison, Malayan Arrow. Anthrop. J. 21: 476.
Poison Ivy. (D. P. Penhallow) Garden & F. 8: 359. — (E. G. Lademan) Garden & F. 8: 399. — (T. J. Burrill) Garden & F. 8: 368.
Poisoned Tapestries, The; a story. (E. W. Champney) Munsey, 11: 576.
Poisoners, Can Chemical Analysis convict? (R. O. Doremus) Forum, 16: 229.
Poisoning of the Future. (S. S. Spriggs) New R. 9: 45.
Poisonous Plants. (Byron D. Halsted) Garden & F. 8: 172.
Poisons, Action of, Lew's System of. (J. C. Bay) Science, 22: 93.
— and their Antidotes. Chamb. J. 72: 155.
— Effects of, on Growing Plants. (F. W. Card) Garden & F. 9: 8.
— New Treatment for. (W. H. Wooster) Science, 20: 255.
Poitiers, Diane de. *See* Diane de Poitiers.
Poitiers. (J. Baker) Leis. Hour, 42: 666.
Pokagon, Simon; an Interesting Representative of a Vanishing Race. (B. O. Flower) Arena, 16: 240.
Poland, Future of. Sat. R. 79: 37.
— Partition of. (S. B. Perkins) Am. Hist. R. 2: 76.
Polar Expedition, Wellman's. Dub. R. 115: 177.
Polar Exploration, Continuous, Proposed System of. (R. Stein) Pop. Sci. Mo. 49: 321.
Polar Regions, Ancient. (W. Seton) Cath. World, 56: 485.
Polar Regions, Hunting in. (J. M. Mills) Outing, 23: 364.
Polar Research. Is it Remunerative? (E. W. Nye) Cosmopol. 19: 105.
Polar Sea, Treasure Islands in the. Ecl. M. 124: 472. *See* Arctic.
Polarization, Study in. (J. Daniel) Science, 21: 339.
Poldi-Pezzoli Collection. (C. L. Eastlake) 19th Cent. 33: 981.
Pole, Reginald. (H. W. Preston and L. Dodge) Atlan. 74: 641, 763.
Pole, Problem of the. (C. Morris) New Sci. R. 1: 59.
— The Race to. (H. Ward) New R. 11: 186. *See* Arctic; Antarctic; North Pole.
Police, County. (G. R. Vicars) Westm. 145: 280.
— French, Revelations of. (E. S. Delamere) Time, 6: 164.
— Metropolitan. Time, 15: 650.
— of London. Time, 20: 12.
Police Courts, London. (W. Holloway) Green Bag, 7: 405.
Police Force in Eleven Principal Cities of the United States. (R. Wheatley) Chaut. 7: 197.
Police Lodging Houses. (J. A. Riis) Chr. Un. 47: 84.
Police Matrons, Employment of, Progress in. (C. A. Kennard) Lend a H. 9: 180.
Police Reform. Lend a H. 8: 43.
Policeman, The. (W. Wemley) Eng. Illust. 12: no. 5, 83.
Policeman's story, The. Chamb. J. 70: 364.
Policies of the Nations of the World. (R. J. Hinton) Arena, 15: 815.
Polish Literature. (A. Belcikowski) Ath. '94, 2: 22.
— 1891–92. (A. Belcikowski) Ath. '92, 2: 24.
— 1892–93. (A. Belcikowski) Ath. '93, 2: 26.
— 1894–95. (A. Belcikowski) Ath. '95, 2: 23.
— 1895–96. (A. Belcikowski) Ath. '96, 2: 25.
Polish Summer Resort, A. (A. C. Coolidge) Nation, 63: 268.
Politeness, Chinese Face. Spec. 68: 264.
— Decline of. (A. E. Barr) Lippinc. 49: 84.
Political and Social Sciences, Study of. (E. J. James) Eth. Rec. 3: 8.
Political Assessments, Opinion of Attorney-Gen. Olney. Good Govt. 13: 139. — (D. B. Eaton) Good Govt. 14: 64.
Political Campaign Committees, A Plan for more Effective Management. (M. D. Harter) Forum, 14: 39.
Political Campaign Funds, Ethics of. (E. L. Godkin) Nation, 57: 262.
— Insufficient Restriction of. (J. B. Bishop) Forum, 15: 148.
Political Campaigning in Kentucky, Humors of. (E. J. McDermott) Cent. 28: 826.
Political Conventions in the U. S. (M. Halstead) Cosmopol. 13: 194.
Political Corruption, Blind Partisanship and. (J. S. Evans) Am. M. Civics, 7: 278.
— How best opposed. (T. E. Will) Arena, 10: 845.
Political Depravity of the Fathers. (J. B. McMaster) Atlan. 75: 626.
Political Differences and Moral Crimes. (E. A. Freeman) Univ. R. 4: 324.
Political Economy and Crime. (S. G. Smith) Lend a H. 17: 408.
— and Journalism. (J. S. Nicholson) Econ. J. 4: 393.
— and Morals, Relations between. (Lord Farrer) J. Statis. Soc. 57: 595.
— and Practical Life. (W. Cunningham) Int. J. Ethics, 3: 183.
— and Sociology. (R. Worms) Am. J. Sociol. 1: 146.

Political Economy, Christian. Eng. R. 7: 342.
— Church of England Economics. (C. S. Devas) Dub. R. 113: 661.
— Classical, Reaction in Favor of. (J. S. Nicholson) J. Statis. Soc. 56: 627.
— Cossa's. (O. L. Elliott) Dial (Ch.) 15: 336.
— Ely on. (S. Newcomb) J. Pol. Econ. 3: 106.
— Ethical, Need of. (C. H. Zimmermann) Meth. R. 52: 737.
— Four Schools of. (C. S. Devas) Dub. R. 110: 177.
— Hadley's. (W. G. L. Taylor) J. Pol. Econ. 4: 467. —(D. MacG. Means) Nation, 63: 68.
— History of. (G. Cohn) Ann. Am. Acad. Pol. Sci. 4: supp.
— in Elementary Schools. (S. N. Patten) Ann. Am. Acad. Pol. Sci. 5: 461.
— in Switzerland. (A. Oncken) Econ. J. 5: 133.
— Justice in. (G. Schmoller) Ann. Am. Acad. Pol. Sci. 4: 697.
— Last Word on. (E. Brentano) Univ. R. 2: 340.
— Literature of, Recent Tendencies in. (A. T. Hadley) Yale R. 3: 251.
— McCulloch's. Eng. R. 6: 96.
— Marshall's Principles of. (F. Y. Edgeworth) Econ. J. 5: 585.
— The New. (A. G. Fradenburgh) Meth. R. 55: 423.
— Nicholson's. (O. L. Elliott) Dial (Ch.) 17: 118.— (L. L. Price) Econ. J. 3: 658.—(S. Ball) Econ. R. 4: 526.
— Official, of Indiana. Soc. Econ. 8: 13.
— Philippovich on. (H. R. Seager) Ann. Am. Acad. Pol. Sci. 4: 168.
— Progress in. (C. F. Bastable) J. Statis. Soc. 57: 611.
— Relations of Economic Science to Practical Affairs. (L. L. Price) J. Statis. Soc. 58: 591.
— Saving *vs.* Spending. (L. Courtney) Contemp. 61: 642.
— Scope of. (S. N. Patten) Yale R. 2: 264.
— Sentimentalism and. (W. Kirkus) New World, 4: 225.
— Study of, in Japan. (Jinchi Soyeda) Econ. J. 3: 334.
— — in the U. S. (J. L. Laughlin) J. Pol. Econ. 1: 1.
— Tested by Prediction. (W. D. McDonnell) Econ. R. 4: 477.
Political Enthusiasm or Hysteria? (T. Mackay) National, 23: 468.
Political Ethics. (A. T. Hadley) Yale R. 1: 354.
Political Events, Record of. (W. A. Dunning) Pol. Sci. Q. vols. 7-11.
Political Evils, Remedies for. (H. Herzberg) Am. M. Civics, 7: 474.
Political Fatalism of To-day. Spec. 69: 589.
Political Grudges. Spec. 70: 766.
Political Independence, Growth of. (J. J. O'Neill) Am. J. Pol. 3: 557.
Political Inquiries, An Early Society for. (M. D. Conway) Open Court, 7: 3815.
Political Labor-parties. Soc. Econ. 1: 36.
Political Leaders of the Reconstruction Period. (E. G. Ross) Forum, 20: 218.
Political Lessons. (E. Meek) Canad. M. 1: 219.
Political Menace of the Discontented. Atlan. 78: 447.
Political Notions, Modern, Legal Aspect of Some. (R. L. Fowler) Am. Law R. 27: 369.
Political Obligation. (E. V. Raynolds) Yale R. 5: 31.
Political Organizations in the United States and England. (J. Bryce) No. Am. 156: 105.
Political Philosophy, American. (W. A. Dunning) Yale R. 4: 147.—(T. S. Blair) Gunton's M. 10: 270.
Political Platforms. Am. J. Pol. 1: 206.
Political Prophecy and Sociology. (H. Sidgwick) National, 24: 563.
Political Reform, A. (H. L. Sibley) Meth. R. 56: 610.
— True Basis of. (L. Satterthwait) Am. M. Civics, 7: 145.
Political Reputations, Thermometer of. (R. Stewart) Time, 18: 271.
Political Science and Constitutional Law, Burgess on. (T. Thornely) Eng. Hist. R. 7: 388.—Soc. Econ. 1: 225.
— Domain of. (Munroe Smith) Time, 15: 49.
— Introduction to, Seeley's. Sat. R. 81: 630.
— Relation of, to History. (J. W. Lowber) Am. M. Civics, 9: 64.
Political Science Quarterly, A Retrospect. Pol. Sci. Q. 10: 565.
Political Superstitions. Spec. 75: 263.
Political Verse, Saintsbury's. Spec. 68: 231.—Sat. R. 73: 516.
Politician, Character of the. New R. 12: 665.
— Making of a. All the Year, 72: 200.
Politician's Romance, A; a story. (R. C. Savage) Temp. Bar, 108: 420. Same art. Ecl. M. 127: 341.
Politics, American. (T. B. Preston) Monist, 2: 41.
— American Character in. (A. B. Hart) Chaut. 22: 142.
— American Nomination Law. (J. B. Smith) Soc. Econ. 3: 170.
— and Crime. (A. G. Warner) Am. J. Sociol. 1: 290.
— and Culture. (H. Seal) Westm. 144: 650.
— and Education. (C. H. Reeve) Am. J. Pol. 1: 250.
— Politics and Ethics. Quar. 175: 235.
— and Industry. (T. Whittaker) Macmil. 65: 221.
— and the Pulpit. (W. C. Doane) No. Am. 155: 41. —(C. D. Foss) No. Am. 155: 536.
— and the Saloon. (L. G. Janes) Soc. Econ. 6: 233.
— and Science. (K. Pearson) Fortn. 62: 334.
— as a Career. (G. F. Edmunds) Forum, 14: 445.
— — in England. (T. Raleigh) Chaut. 21: 27.
— as a Profession. (D. MacG. Means) Nation, 60: 85.
— Conscience in. (T. L. Cuyler) Chr. Lit. 15: 402.
— Disaster of Low. Soc. Econ. 6: 332.
— Economics and Party. Soc. Econ. 2: 257.
— Elements of, Sidgwick on. (J. H. Robinson) Ann. Am. Acad. Pol. Sci. 3: 211.—Ath. '92, 1: 143.— Ed. R. 175: 84.
— Empiricism in. (T. MacKay) National, 25: 790.
— Ethics and. (H. Macqueary) Am. M. Civics, 6: 86.
— in Boys' Schools. Spec. 69: 93.
— Liberty and Reaction in. Spec. 69: 844.
— Machinery in. Soc. Econ. 1: 329. 2: 1.
— Missing Link in Reform. (J. Benton) Soc. Econ. 5: 43.
— Money in. (J. W. Jenks) Cent. 22: 940.
— Non-partisan. (E. Lauterbach) Gunton's M. 10: 27.
— Non-partisanship a Municipal Necessity. (D. H. Bolles) Gunton's M. 10: 367.
— of the Future. (E. E. Hale) Lend a H. 17: 361.
— Practical. (F. T. Greenhalge) No. Am. 162: 154.
— — Authorities in. (E. L. Godkin) Nation, 54: 102.
— — The Manly Virtues and. (T. Roosevelt) Forum, 17: 551.
— Right and Wrong in. (Sir E. Strachey) Atlan. 72: 50.
— Science of. (A. J. G. Mackay) Jurid. R. 2: 1, 309.

Politics, Social Pressure in. (W. B. Chisholm) Am. M. Civics, 6: 449.
— Study of, in American Colleges. (J. A. Woodburn) Am. J. Pol. 4: 539.
— To a Friend in. (F. Eastman) Atlan. 76: 831.
— Why many Young Men are not in. (F. E. Clark) Pub. Opin. 19: 656.
Politics and the May-fly; a story. (J. Buchan) Chamb. J. 73: 301. Same art. Liv. Age, 209: 700.
Polity, Our Future. (T. B. Wakeman) Open Court, 5: 2790.
Polk, James K., Administration of. (J. Schouler) Atlan. 76: 371.
— Diary of. (J. Schouler) Atlan. 76: 235.
Polk, Leonidas. Sat. R. 77: 102. — Pub. Opin. 17: 106. — (A. H. Noll) Dial (Ch.) 16: 176. — (J. D. Cox) Nation, 58: 293. — So. Hist. Pap. 21: 321.
Polka, History of the. (J. J. Kral) Music, 9: 305.
Poll Book of an Election in New Jersey, 1739. (J. J. Thompson) Pennsyl. M. 18: 185.
Polledrara Ware. (C. Smith) J. Hel. Stud. 14: 206.
Pollen, Impotency of. (F. W. Card) Garden & F. 6: 153.
Pollice Verso. (E. Post) Am. J. Philol. 13: 213.
Pollination, Ornithophilous. (J. L. Hancock) Am. Natural. 28: 679.
— Yucca. (W. B. Marshall) Am. Natural. 26: 774.
Pollock, David George Hope, with portrait. Bank. M. (Lond.) 54: 527.
Pollock, Sir Frederick. Leading Cases. Spec. 69: 386.
Pollock Diamond Robbery. (C. Moffett) McClure, 4: 437.
Pollock's Surrender; a story. (B. Garland) Munsey, 13: 355.
Pollucite, Mangano-columbite and Microlite at Rumford, Me. (H. W. Foote) Am. J. Sci. 151: 457.
Polly; a story. (M. Watson) Eng. Illust. 11: 1189.
Polly Honeycombe. (A. Dobson) National, 25: 623.
Polo, Marco. (R. Parsons) Am. Cath. Q. 21: 43.
— Explorations of. (H. P. Margesson) New Eng. M. n. s. 6: 803.
Polo, Horsemanship and. (F. Keene) Lippinc. 49: 336.
— in the West. (J. B. Macmahan) Outing, 26: 385, 471.
— Modern, Millar's. Sat. R. 82: 140.
Poltalloch Drawings. Sat. R. 77: 227.
Poltergeist, Lang on. Spec. 71: 576.
Polyandry, Promiscuity and Survival. (S. Channing) Open Court, 5: 2896.
Polyas, Jacob. (E. M. Edmonds) Acad. 50: 130.
Polybasite and Tennantite, from Colorado. (S. L. Penfield and S. H. Pearce) Am. J. Sci. 144: 15.
Polycletan Head from the Metopes of Argive Heræum. (C. Waldstein) Am. J. Archæol. 9: 331.
Polygamists, Baptism of, in non-Christian Lands. (S. H. Kellogg) Presb. & Ref. R. 7: 285.
Polyglot, How to become a. (F. C. Higgins) Writer, 8: 112.
Polynesia. Eng. R. 9: 51.
— Asiatic Migrations. (R. A. Sterndale) Asia. R. 12: 324.
— Life in the Southern Seas. (J. E. Newell) Sund. M. 22: 22.
Polynesian Ornament, Symbolism of. (H. C. March) Anthrop. J. 22: 307.
Polynesian Races and Linguistics. (Emil Schneider) Asia. R. 13: 350.
Polytechnic Institutes of London. (R. A. Gregory) Nature, 50: 87, 114.
Pomaks of Rhodope. (J. D. Bourchier) Fortn. 60: 509.
Pomo Basket Makers. (J. W. Hudson) Overland, n. s. 21: 561.
Pomona; a story. (A. C. Maitland) Chamb. J. 70: 513–819.
Pompeii. Am. Arch. 46: 61.
— The New House in. (H. P. F. Marriott) Eng. Illust. 14: 449.
— Paintings at. (H. A. Kennedy) 19th Cent. 37: 86.
— — and their Relation to Hellenic Masterpieces. (T. Ely) J. Hel. Stud. 16: 143.
— — Origin and Styles of. (A. Melani) Am. Arch. 51: 21.
Pomponatius, P.; a Sceptic of the Renaissance. Quar. 177: 495.
Pompthero; a story. (L. A. North) Lippinc. 49: 348.
Ponca Myths. (J. O. Dorsey) J. Am. Folk-Lore, 1: 74, 204.
Ponca Songs. (J. O. Dorsey) J. Am. Folk-Lore, 2: 271.
Ponca Stories. (J. O. Dorsey) J. Am. Folk-Lore, 1: 73.
Poncha City, In. All the Year, 73: 395.
Pond, Nathan Gillette, Founder Society Colonial Wars. (L. Tracy) Am. Hist. Reg. 1: 213.
Pondland, South Africa, Annexation by England. Dub. R. 115: 174.
Ponds and Rock-pools, Scherren on. Sat. R. 78: 332.
Pong, Ancient Shan Kingdom of. (A. R. MacMahon) Asia. R. 10: 18.
Ponsonby, Miss Sarah. Gent. M. n. s. 55: 401.
Pont-Aven and Douarnenez. (H. Blackburn) M. of Art, 2: 6.
— Visit to. Belgra. 80: 283.
Pontefract Castle. (E. W. Kidd) Gent. M. n. s. 56: 389.
Pontiac's Lookout. (M. H. Catherwood) Atlan. 74: 35.
Pontine Marshes, Drainage of. Dub. R. 111: 192.
Ponting, Francis William, with portrait. Bank. M. (Lond.) 58: 357.
Pontius, W. H. (J. S. Van Cleve) Music, 4: 585.
Pontresina. (G. F. Browne) National, 25: 388.
Poole, Maria L. (A. M. Hale) Writer, 7: 180.
Pool Rooms and Pool Selling. (A. Comstock) No. Am. 157: 591.
— Gambling in, Suppression of, in Connecticut. And. R. 19: 358.
Poole, Reginald Stuart. Ath. '95, 1: 224. — (P. Gardner) Acad. 47: 154.
Poole, Wm. F. Ath. '94, 1: 347. — Dial (Ch.) 16: 165. — (W. I. Fletcher) Lib. J. 19: 81. — Music, 5: 739.
Poor, Mary, Diary of. (E. Mariotti) New Eng. M. n. s. 13: 316.
Poor, The Aged, Charles Booth on. (C. S. Loch) Econ. J. 4: 468.
— All Hands to the Pump. Sund. M. 23: 266.
— Amusements of. (M. Jeune) National, 21: 303.
— Care of, in Boston. (D. W. Waldron) Bost. 1: 481.
— Church *vs.* the State in the Concerns of. (M. O'Riordan) Cath. World, 60: 145.
— Commercial Relations of the. (J. B. Reynolds) Yale R. 5: 76.
— Dwellings for, The State and. (F. B. Vrooman) Arena, 12: 415.
— Education of; production of Learned Pigs. (Frances McNab) Temp. Bar, 109: 99.
— Employment for. (J. Mavor) 19th Cent. 34: 523.
— Hatred of, for the Rich. Spec. 76: 801.
— Housing of. (C. H. Blackall) Am. Arch. 52: 23, 63. — (J. W. Horsley) Econ. R. 3: 50.

Poor, How can a City best care for its? (H. S. Pingree) Our Day, 14: 254.
— How not to help. (J. H. Finley) Chaut. 18: 522, 650.
— in England. Quar. 179: 463.
— — and Wales, Booth's. Sat. R. 77: 671.
— — Relief of. (C. S. Loch) Econ. J. 3: 584.
— — What can the Government do for, at once? (J. T. Dodd) New R. 9: 191.
— in France, Public Assistance to. (E. G. Balch) Am. Econ. Assoc. 8: 265.
— in Great Cities. Scrib. M. 11: 399.
— — How should a City care for? (F. G. Peabody) Forum, 14: 474. — (C. G. Truesdell) Chaut. 15: 183.
— in Holland, How cared for. (J. H. Gore) Forum, 21: 228.
— in Naples. (J. W. V. Mario) Scrib. M. 13: 39.
— in New York, Special Needs of. (J. A. Riis) Forum, 14: 492.
— of London, Work of the Kyrle Society for the. M. of Art, 3: 210.
— of the World. (S. A. Barnett) Fortn. 60: 207.
— Oppression of, Banks on. (J. Lee) Char. R. 1: 179.
— Parasites of. Spec. 71: 136.
— Relief of, by means of Employment. (T. Mackay) Econ. R. 6: 183. — (C. Gardener) Open Court, 9: 4646.
— — How to administer, without creating Pauperism. (C. R. Henderson) Char. R. 5: 182.
— — in Boston. Lend a H. 12: 368.
— — — Emergency Work, 1893–94, Report. Lend a H. 13: 7.
— — in Italy. (F. S. Nitti) Econ. R. 2: 1.
— — in London. (C. S. Loch) Lend a H. 16: 436.
— — Indoor *vs.* Outdoor. Reply to Mr. Hunter. (W. Chance) National, 25: 667.
— — The Panic and. (R. Ogden) Nation, 58: 423.
— Riis on how the other Half lives. (Henry Powers) Soc. Econ. 1: 104.
— Thrift for. (C. Black; Lady F. Cavendish; Lady Montagu; Duchess of Rutland) New R. 7: 666.
— Trained Workers for. (O. Hill) 19th Cent. 33: 36. Same art. Liv. Age, 197: 156.
— True Pictures among the. Scrib. M. 16: 587.
Poor Clares, Order of, in the United States. (S. B. Hedges) Cath. World, 61: 380.
Poor Colonies of Holland. (J. H. Gore) Chaut. 22: 581.
Poorhouse, English, Month in. (M. B. Thacher) New Eng. M. n. s. 14: 452.
Poor Law and Old Age. Spec. 72: 461.
— Austrian System. (E. Sellers) Char. R. 3: 168.
— of Denmark, New, 1892. And. R. 17: 609.
— of England. (B. Bosanquet; A. Marshall) Econ. J. 2: 369.
— — Administration of. (J. F. Wilkinson) New R. 8: 59. — (C. S. Loch) Econ. J. 3: 425.
— — — An Experiment in. (Edith Sellers) Good Words, 36: 30.
— — — Recent Changes in. (E. Porritt) Yale R. 5: 88.
— — and Old Age. (J. F. Wilkinson) Contemp. 64: 670.
— — A Humane. Macmil. 67: 277.
— — Reform of. (S. A. Barnett) Contemp. 63: 322.
— — Sixty Years of. (E. Porritt) Soc. Econ. 4: 224.
— — Unpopularity of. (T. Mackay) National, 19: 762.
— — Women as Poor-law Guardians. (Matilda M. Blake) Westm. 139: 12.
— of Massachusetts and New York. (J. Cummings) Am. Econ. Assoc. 10: 481.
Poor Law, Politics and. (T. Mackay) Fortn. 63: 408.
— A Product of. Blackw. 160: 533.
Poor Law Clauses of the Local Government Bill. (T. Mackay) National, 22: 572.
Poor Law Statistics. (C. Booth) Econ. J. 6: 70.
Poor Laws, Early, in the West. (C. R. Henderson) Char. R. 3: 85.
Poor Millionaire. (M. L. Adams) New Eng. M. n. s. 6: 489.
Poor Mrs. Broom; a story. (E. R. Esler) Sund. M. 21: 470.
Poor Player; a story. (S. A Curzon) Canad. M. 4: 352.
Poor Yorick. (R. N. Stephens) Lippinc. 52: 455.
Poore Knights. Military Knights of Windsor. All the Year, 75: 484.
Pootoo, Our Lady of. (R. S. Gundry) National, 22: 491.
Pope, Albert Augustus, Portraits of. McClure, 1: 316.
Pope, Alexander. (W. S. Lilly) Dub. R. 114: 95. — (A. M. Williams) Gent. M. n. s. 55: 361. Same art. Ecl. M. 125: 620.
— Works, Denis' Edition. Spec. 68: 369.
Pope, Franklin Leonard; Obituary. Engin. M. 10: 295.
Pope at Home, The. (G. Amadi) No. Am. 155: 196.
— Election of: the next Conclave. (C. B. R. Kent) Macmil. 66: 23.
— Infallibility of. (J. Conway) Am. Cath. Q. 18: 677.
— — When is he Infallible? (J. Schroeder) M. Chr. Lit. 6: 51. — (S. M. Brandl) No. Am. 155: 652.
— Temporal Power of. (W. S. Lilly) New R. 6: 484. — Reply. (F. Crispi) New R. 6: 513. — Rejoinder. (W. S. Lilly) New R. 6: 732.
— — American Catholics and. (J. Schroeder) Am. Cath. Q. 17: 72.
— — Archbishop Vaughan on. Spec. 69: 489.
Pope Library. Critic, 27: 271.
Pope's Tasting-glass, The. (M. J. Plarr) Argosy, 60: 703.
Popes, as Promoters of University Education. (J. F. Hogan) Dub. R. 114: 278.
— Election of. (W. R. Thayer) Cent. 30: 138.
— — and Coronation of. (E. Beck) Dub. R. 119: 77.
— Gifts blessed by, Origin of. (A. E. P. R. Dowling) Dub. R. 114: 61.
— History of, Pastor's. (G. L. Burr) Am. Hist. R. 1: 526. — (T. B. Scannell) Dub. R. 111: 1. — Sat. R. 73: 80. — Spec. 69: 197. — Church Q. 35: 342. — Church Q. 41: 88. — Sat. R. 80: 50. — (T. B. Scannell) Dub. R. 117: 305.
— of the Renaissance, Personal Character of. (J. J. O'Shea) Cath. World, 61: 368.
Poplar Heterophylla for Lumber. Garden & F. 9: 13.
Poplars, American. Garden & F. 5: 277.
— Polygamous, and Willows. (J. G. Jack) Garden & F. 7: 163.
Popocatepetl and Volcanoes of Valley of Mexico. (O. H. Howarth) Geog. J. 8: 137.
Poppies, New. (Amy Whitman) Garden & F. 5: 163.
Poppies; a poem. All the Year, 75: 60.
Popular Literature, Religion and. (T. Hannan) Westm. 142: 608.
Popular Tales, Diffusion of. (T. F. Crane) J. Am. Folk-Lore, 1: 8.
Popularity, Sweets of. All the Year, 74: 222.
Population. Ed. R. 176: 431.
— and Area, Statistics of. (E. Levasseur) J. Statis. Soc. 55: 298.
— and Food Supply, Defoe and Malthus on. Soc. Econ. 7: 203.
— Are there too many of us? (E. B. Andrews) No. Am. 155: 596

Population, Doctrine of Malthus and Modern Society. (L. R. Harley) Am. M. Civics, 6: 13.
— in England and Wales, Probability of a Cessation of the Growth of. (E. Cannan) Econ. J. 5: 505.
— Law of, New Statement of. (S. N. Patten) Pol. Sci. Q. 10: 44.
— Malthus' Theory of. Soc. Econ. 2: 35.
— Neo-Malthusianism. (R. F. Clarke) No. Am. 163: 345.
— Notes on Methods of Estimating. (C. L. Wilbur) Am. Statis. Assoc. 5: 83.
— of the Earth. (J. S. Billings) Chaut. 16: 527. — Pop. Sci. Mo. 40: 400.
— of U. S. Was the Count in 1890 reasonably Correct? (H. Gannett) Am. Statis. Assoc. 4: 99.
— Question of. (A. Lyttleton) Econ. R. 1: 151. 2: 378.
— — New Lights on. Spec. 75: 361.
— Reversal of Malthus. (A. W. Tourgee) Am. J. Sociol. 2: 13.
— Urban. (C. D. Wright) Pop. Sci. Mo. 40: 459.
Populism, as an Honest Effort for the Securing of Better Conditions. (R. H. Williams) Am. M. Civics, 7: 195.
— Colorado's Experiment with. (J. F. Vaile) Forum, 18: 714.
— Deserts the Hotbed of. Soc. Econ. 8: 335.
— Trumbull as a Socialist. Soc. Econ. 7: 277.
Populist Movement. (F. L. McVey) Econ. Stud. 1: 135. — (F. E. Haynes) Q. J. Econ. 10: 269.
— National Convention, 1896. Pub. Opin. 21: 133. — (H. D. Lloyd) R. of Rs. (N. Y.) 14: 298.
Populist Party, The Mission of. (W. A. Peffer) No. Am. 157: 665.
— Rise and Doom of. (F. B. Tracy) Forum, 16: 240. *See* People's Party.
Populus Monticala. Garden & F. 7: 313.
Porcelain, Derby. (E. Bradbury) M. of Art, 7: 426.
— — Past and Present. (E. Bradbury) M. of Art, 6: 446.
— A Famous. Chamb. J. 72: 807.
— Old Blue and White Nankeen. (J. Grego) M. of Art, 10: 9. 13: 103.
— Oriental, Salting Collection of. (L. S. Myers) M. of Art, 14: 31.
Porcelains, Japanese and Chinese. (S. Arai) Lippinc. 54: 557.
Porches. (A. Saint-Paul; H. Nodet) Am. Arch. 41: 51.
Porcupines and other Spine-bearing Animals. (R. Lydekker) Knowl. 16: 101.
Porlock, England. M. of Art, 1: 169.
Pornic. (L. Lloyd) M. of Art, 4: 315.
Port Angeles, Washington. (W. R. McGarry) Nat'l M. (N. Y. '91) 16: 676.
Port Arthur, Battle of, Truth about. (F. Villiers) No. Am. 160: 325.
— Fall of. Spec. 73: 769.
— Massacre of. Spec. 74: 41.
Portal, Sir Gerald H. Geog. J. 3: 243. — Sat. R. 77: 119.
Portals. (A. Saint-Paul; H. Nodet) Am. Arch. 41: 63, 79.
Porteous Riot, The. (G. W. T. Omond) Scot. R. 20: 52. Same art. Liv. Age, 194: 793.
Porter, David, a Literary Chimney-sweep. Bookworm, 4: 367.
Porter, Col. Elisha, of Hadley, Mass., Diary of, 1776. (A. Morgan) M. Am. Hist. 30: 185.
Porter, Horace. (G. R. Miller) Munsey, 9: 200.
Porter, John, and Horse-training. Sat. R. 82: 423.
Porter, John K., with portrait. (G. P. Lowrey) Green Bag, 4: 353, 438.
Porter, Noah. And. R. 17: 407. — Spec. 72: 55.
— Merriam's. (J. W. Chadwick) Nation, 57: 435.
— Recollections of. (J. Cooper) Bib. Sac. 51: 493.
— Writings, List of. Lit. W. (Bost.) 23: 97.
Porter, William Henry. Bank. M. (N. Y.) 51: 161.
Portia; or, By Passions rocked. (Mrs. Hungerford) Time, 7: 1–988. 8: 60–271.
Portion of the Tempest, A. (Mary T. Wright) Scrib. M. 15: 712.
Portland, England, Prison Life at. (T. Hopkins) Leis. Hour, 45: 159, 256.
Portland, Maine, and its Environs. (R. E. Noble) Canad. M. 5: 189.
— Story of. (J. P. Baxter) New Eng. M. n. s. 13: 349.
Portland, Oregon, Library Association. (R. R. Bowker) Lib. J. 20: 77.
— River Improvement at. (G. W. Freeman) Engin. M. 3: 661.
Porto, Luigi da. An Immortal Story. (Eugene Benson) New R. 13: 94.
Portrait, A; a poem. (Edgar Fawcett) Cosmopol. 19: 412.
Portrait and the Man. (A. E. Brand) New Eng. M. n. s. 15: 156.
Portrait by Hunt, A; a story. (E. Robinson) Outing, 21: 128.
Portrait of a German Music-master; a story. Temp. Bar, 96: 244.
Portrait of Phillis Cromartie, The; a story. (F. Molloy) Temp. Bar, 98: 525.
Portrait of an Unknown Gentleman; a story. (S. Pickering) Eng. Illust. 10: 176.
Portrait Painter, The; a story. Argosy, 53: 505.
Portrait Painters, English. Sat. R. 79: 90.
— Society of. Ath. '94, 2: 535.
— — Exhibition, 1892. Ath. '92, 2: 72. — Spec. 69: 96.
— — — 1893. Ath. '93, 1: 676. — Sat. R. 75: 539.
Portrait Painters, The; a story. (B. Pain) Art J. 44: 201.
Portrait-painting in France, Pinset and Auriac's History of. (R. A. M. Stevenson) M. of Art, 8: 167.
— in its Historical Aspects. (J. Collier) 19th Cent. 39: 762. Same art. Liv. Age, 209: 771.
Portraits, Græco-Egyptian. (M. A. Peck) Mo. Illust. 13: 219.
— in Exhibitions, as an Index of Popularity. (J. A. Blaikie) M. of Art, 6: 418.
— in New Hampshire, of Public Men and others. (B. F. Prescott) N. E. Reg. 49: 177.
— of Artists. (J. Dow) M. of Art, 12: 206.
— of Women. (W. A. Coffin) Cosmopol. 18: 3.
— — at the Grafton Galleries. (F. G. Stephens) M. of Art, 17: 316.
Portraiture, Modern. (S. Beale) Am. Arch. 46: 71.
— of the American Revolutionary War. (W. L. Andrews) Bookman, 3: 211, 329.
Port-Reeve, Name and Office of. (J. H. Pring) Walford's Antiq. 6: 113–299.
— J. H. Pring on. (J. H. Round) Walford's Antiq. 5: 247, 282. 6: 23, 159.
Portsmouth, N. H. Old St. John's Parish. (F. W. Davis) New Eng. M. n. s. 11: 321.
— Profiles from, Old. (T. B. Aldrich) Cent. 24: 384.
Portsmouth Road, Old. All the Year, 73: 172.
Portugal, The Arts in. Eng. R. 6: 432.
— Finances of, in 1892; Portuguese Liquidation. Spec. 68: 190.
— Life in. Sat. R. 79: 473.
Portuguese Element in New England. (H. R. Lang) J. Am. Folk-Lore, 5: 9.
Portuguese Literature, English Neglect of. (E. Prestage) Acad. 43: 506.

Portuguese Sketches, Some. Cornh. 68: 196. Same art. Ecl. M. 121: 388. Same art. Liv. Age, 199: 52.
Portuguese Stories, translated. Folk-Lore Rec. 4: 141.
Poseidon, Trident of. (H. B. Walters) J. Hel. Stud. 13: 13. — (H. B. Walters) Acad. 41: 258.
Position, Judgments of, in the Retinal Field, Effect of Size Contrast upon. (J. M. Baldwin) Psychol. R. 2: 244.
Positivism and Ontology. (P. Carus) Open Court, 4: 2143.
— An Apologetic Irenicon. (T. H. Huxley) Fortn. 58: 557. — Reply. (F. Harrison) Fortn. 58: 713.
— The Reaction and its Lessons. (F. Harrison) Fortn. 64: 485.
Positivist Faith. (J. Sandison) Open Court, 6: 34, 66.
Possession in English Law. (C. Sweet) Jurid. R. 3: 121.
— in the Roman Law. (J. M. Lightwood) Law Q. 3: 32. — (H. Bond) Law Q. 6: 259.
Post, Albert Hermann. (P. Carus) Open Court, 9: 4650.
Post-eocene Formations of the Coastal Plain of Alabama. (E. A. Smith) Am. J. Sci. 147: 285.
Post-glacial Faults at St. John, N. B. (G. F. Matthew) Am. J. Sci. 148: 501.
Post-graduate Study. Ath. '94, 1: 313.
Post-obits and Equity. (J. M. M'Candlish) Jurid. R. 4: 25.
Post-office and Publicity. (F. E. Leupp) Nation, 56: 268.
— British, as a Newspaper Carrier. Sat. R. 82: 251.
— — Joyce's History of. Ath. '93, 2: 800. — Sat. R. 76: 711. — (W. P. Courtney) Acad. 44: 456. — (J. A. J. Housden) Gent. M. n. s. 52: 395. — Spec. 72: 89.
— — Modern. Time, 15: 708.
— — Plundering and Blundering. (J. H. Heaton) 19th Cent. 33: 994.
— — Rise of. (A. M. Ogilvie) Econ. J. 3: 443.
— in France. (C. J. Willdey) Un. Serv. M. 7: 732.
— in Germany. (C. J. Willdey) Un. Serv. M. 7: 934.
— in U. S. (C. J. Willdey) Un. Serv. M. 7: 1153.
— — Emancipation of. (J. R. Procter) Atlan. 77: 95.
Post-office Packet-service, Norway's History of, 1793–1815. Macmil. 74: 34.
Post-office Packets: a Forgotten Chapter in Naval History. Macmil. 70: 282. Same art. Liv. Age, 202: 694.
Post-office Scandals in the U. S. Pub. Opin. 15: 400.
Postage, British. Sat. R. 75: 202.
— Imperial Five-farthing. (J. H. Heaton) Fortn. 61: 338.
— Mulready's Envelope. Sat. R. 73: 487.
— Reform in. (C. W. Ernst) Critic, 28: 276.
Postage Stamps, United States. (J. T. Connor) New Eng. M. n. s. 13: 654.
Postal Progress in England, 1895. (J. Henniker Heaton) Contemp. 68: 1.
Postal Rates, Proposed Reduction in British Empire. Sat. R. 80: 404.
Postal Reformers, English. (T. L. James) Cosmopol. 15: 100.
Postal Savings Banks in Holland. (J. H. Gore) Forum, 21: 228.
Postal Service at New York. (C. W. Dayton) No. Am. 159: 24.
— English. National, 21: 647.
— Ocean. (T. L. James) Cent. 21: 944.
— Reforming the. (T. L. James) Chr. Un. 45: 100.
Postal Union, Universal. (C. J. Willdey) Un. Serv. M. 8: 118.
Poster, The Advertiser and the. (P. N. Boeringer) Overland, n. s. 28: 41.
Poster, Evolution of. (A. C. Sage) Lippinc. 58: 848.
— in Politics. R. of Rs. (N. Y.) 12: 285.
— Japanese War. (D. P. B. Conkling) Cent. 29: 936.
— Pictorial. (B. Matthews) Cent. 22: 748.
Posters, American, Past and Present. (H. C. Bunner) Scrib. M. 18: 429.
— and their Artistic Possibilities. (Gleeson White) J. Soc. Arts, 44: 168.
— and Book-covers, French. (A. Alexandre) Scrib. M. 17: 603.
— and Poster-designing in England. (M. H. Spielmann) Scrib. M. 18: 34.
— Art in. (F. Wedmore) Art J. 47: 43.
— Art of the Hoarding. New R. 11: 47. — Sat. R. 78: 657.
— Artistic, Moral Aspect of. (L. J. Rhead) Bookman, 1: 312.
— as a Means of Art Education. M. of Art, 4: 298.
Postes et Télégraphes; a story. (J. de Glouvet) Harper, 93: 362.
Posthumous Fame, Evolution of. (E. D. Warfield) M. Am. Hist. 30: 78.
Post-Laramie Deposits of Colorado. (W. Cross) Am. J. Sci. 144: 19.
Postman-poet of Bideford. (P. H. W. Almy) Sund. M. 25: 447.
Postmasters, Election of, by the People. (W. Clark) Arena, 10: 68.
— Fixed Terms for Fourth-class. (F. M. Loomis) Good Govt. 13: 78.
— Removal of. (E. L. Godkin) Nation, 56: 246.
Posture and its Indications. (T. Lander-Brunton) Pop. Sci. Mo. 42: 26.
Pot o' Beer. (Mrs. S. Batson) Longm. 21: 44.
Pot of Frightful Doom. (C. B. Fernald) Cent. 30: 369.
Potassium and Sodium, Separation and Identification of. (D. A. Kreider and J. E. Breckenridge) Am. J. Sci. 152: 263.
Potassium-lead Halides. (W. L. Wells) Am. J. Sci. 145: 121. 146: 190.
Potassium Permanganate and Sulphuric Acid, Certain Points in the Interaction of. (F. A. Gooch and E. W. Danner) Am. J. Sci. 144: 301.
Potato, the, History and Place in History of. (J. G. Speed) Chaut. 15: 554.
— in Shakespeare. (H. A. Evans) Acad. 41: 496. — (H. N. Ellacombe) Acad. 41: 542.
Potato Blight. (L. R. Jones) Garden & F. 9: 188.
Potatoes, Cultivation of. (C. S. Plumb) Garden & F. 6: 126. — (L. R. Jones) Garden & F. 6: 297.
Pot-boiler, A. (G. Allen) Longm. 20: 591. Same art. Liv. Age, 195: 561.
Potential a Bernoullian Term. (G. F. Becker) Am. J. Sci. 145: 97.
Potocka, Hélène Massalski, Countess. (S. C. Woolsey) Atlan. 76: 458.
Potomac River, Sediment of. (C. C. Babb) Science, 21: 342.
Potsdam and its Princes. (Jan Winn) Time, 19: 211.
Potter, Paul. (T. Cole) Cent. 26: 840.
Potteries of Aller Vale. (C. Monkhouse) M. of Art, 14: 349.
— Old London. (C. Cooper) Gent. M. n. s. 49: 120.
Potter's Art among Native Americans. (A. D. Le Plongeon) Pop. Sci. Mo. 49: 646.
Pottery, Ancient American, at the Peabody Museum. M. of Art, 12: 393, 404. — (S. R. Koehler) M. of Art, 13: 47.
— Ancient, Roseisle, Elgin. Reliquary, 36: 39.
— and China, Old English, in America. (A. M. Earle) Mo. Illust. 3: 116.

Pottery and Porcelain of the U. S., Barber's. (C. Cook) Nation, **58**: 295. — (A. M. Earle) Dial (Ch.) **16**: 212.
— Art, of Japan. (E. Hart) J. Soc. Arts, **40**: 315.
— — A Peep at an. (C. L. Hind) Good Words, **33**: 537.
— Artistic. (F. Miller) Art J. **47**: 311.
— Colors in. (W. Burton) J. Soc. Arts, **44**: 319.
— Dartmoor. Reliquary, **36**: 225.
— The "Della Robbia" Industry. M. of Art, **20**: 6.
— Early Italian Potters in France. (C. D. E. Fortnum) Acad. **43**: 88.
— English, Remarkable Kinds of. (R. H. Soden-Smith) M. of Art, **1**: 107.
— English-made American. (E. A. Barber) New Eng. M. n. s. **11**: 66.
— Glazes for. (W. P. Rix) J. Soc. Arts, **41**: 295.
— Inscribed, of the Pennsylvania Germans. (E. A. Barber) New Eng. M. n. s. **12**: 34.
— Japanese. (C. Holme) Art J. **44**: 154.
— — Bowes'. (E. Hart) M. of Art, **14**: 141.
— Kabyle. (M. A. W. Dunlop) M. of Art, **5**: 491.
— Korean. (M. A. W. Dunlop) M. of Art, **10**: 264.
— Martin-ware and Barum-ware. (C. Monkhouse) M. of Art, **5**: 443.
— Nicobar. (E. H. Man) Anthrop. J. **23**: 21.
— of American Indians. (W. J. Hoffman) Mo. Illust. **4**: 209, 377. **5**: 87, 216, 361.
— of Fiji. (A. St. Johnston) M. of Art, **7**: 336.
— of India. (E. F. Strange) Art J. **45**: 148.
— Old English. (A. H. Church) Portfo. **24**: 120, 143, 160.
— Pre-historic. (J. D. Butler) Am. Antiq. **16**: 44.
— Recent Artistic. (J. M. O'Fallon) Art J. **48**: 51.
— Solon's Art of the Old English Potter. (C. Monkhouse) M. of Art, **7**: 382.
— Stopping-point in Ornament of. M. of Art, **11**: 372.
— Worship of. (W. Roberts) Fortn. **61**: 817.
Pottery Industry, Recent Advances in. (E. A. Barber) Pop. Sci. Mo. **40**: 289.
Pouch-bearing Animals. (M. Bell) Month, **77**: 547.
Pouchet, Georges. Nat. Sci. **4**: 393.
Poultry Farming. Chamb. J. **72**: 241.
Poultry Keeping, Coöperative. Chr. Lit. **10**: 214.
Poultry-yard, Reminiscences of a. Blackw. **158**: 272. Same art. Liv. Age, **206**: 691.
Pound of Cure, A; a Story of Monte Carlo. (W. H. Bishop) Scrib. M. **15**: 285–768.
Pound Sterling; One-pound Notes, Guineas, etc. All the Year, **70**: 41.
Pour passer le Temps; a story. Argosy, **56**: 346.
Poussin, Nicolas. (R. Heath) M. of Art, **8**: 150. **10**: 368.
Pouvillon, Emile, Literary Work of. Sat. R. **79**: 408.
Poverty, Abolition of. (W. Graham) Am. M. Civics, **7**: 286. — Soc. Econ. **3**: 87.
— and Crime. (H. Thomas) Westm. **145**: 75.
— and Wealth. (E. W. Jackson) Am. J. Pol. **2**: 461, 589.
— Anti-poverty Movement. (V. B. Denslow) Open Court, **1**: 262.
— Art of making. (M. M. Trumbull) Open Court, **1**: 57: 97.
— Causes of. (J. H. Hyslop) Char. R. **3**: 383. — (A. G. Warner) Am. Statis. Assoc. **4**: 49. — Char. R. **4**: 142.
— — and Cure of. (J. Cook) Our Day, **13**: 28.
— How to abolish. (F. A. Burleigh) Am. J. Pol. **5**: 530. — (E. W. Dietrick) Am. J. Pol. **4**: 635.
Poverty in Cities, The Church and. (J. R. Commons) Char. R. **2**: 347.
— — Colonization as a Remedy for. (F. G. Peabody) Forum, **17**: 52.
— Is it diminishing? (J. A. Hobson) Contemp. **69**: 484. — Reply. (W. H. Mallock) 789.
— Modern, Significance of. (W. H. Mallock) No. Am. **159**: 288.
— or to Wealth, Is it more desirable to be born to? (F. R. Coudert and others) Munsey, **14**: 151.
— Problem of. (T. Cox) Am. J. Pol. **5**: 301. — (W. Gladden) Cent. **23**: 245. — (J. L. Davies) Univ. R. **1**: 373.
— Relief of, Principles and Methods of. (E. E. Hale) Lend a H. **13**: 120.
— Responsibility of. (E. M. Burchard) Am. J. Pol. **4**: 552. — (E. B. Dietrick) Am. J. Pol. **4**: 404. *See* Poor.
Powder, Smokeless. (C. A. Voigt) Un. Serv. M. **4**: 518. — (J. D. Dougall) Un. Serv. M. **7**: 1239.
— — and Future Wars. (W. W. Knollys) Un. Serv. M. **4**: 66.
— — and Tactics. Un. Serv. M. **11**: 229.
— — for Shotguns. (W. L. Colville) Overland, n. s. **26**: 442.
Powder and Paint; a story. (W. K. Clifford) Eng. Illust. **12**: no. 3, 165.
Powder Horns, Inscribed. (S. A. Green) N. E. Reg. **50**: 43.
— Rhymes from Old. (W. M. Beauchamp) J. Am. Folk-Lore, **2**: 117. **5**: 284.
Powder-making on the Pacific Coast. Overland, n. s. **26**: 423.
Powder-mills, Life and Work in. (C. Moffett) McClure, **5**: 3.
Powel-Roberts Correspondence, 1761–65. Pennsyl. M. **18**: 35.
Powell, Sir Francis, Sketch of. Art J. **45**: 272.
Powell, John Wesley, with portrait. Am. Antiq. **14**: 155.
Powellite from a New Locality. (G. A. Koenig and L. L. Hubbard) Am. J. Sci. **146**: 356.
Power, Acquisition of. (A. Reichenbach) Educa. **13**: 587.
Power, Coming Revolution in. (F. J. Patten) New Sci. R. **2**: 284.
— from Alternating Currents. (L. Duncan) Cassier, **11**: 104.
— Hydraulic, in London. (E. B. Ellington) Cassier, **11**: 95.
— Measurement of. (T. Gray) Cassier, **2**: 142.
— Sources of, in Nature. Chamb. J. **71**: 517.
— Storing. (G. Forbes) Cassier, **3**: 358.
— Transmission of. (C. Hering) Cassier, **1**: 449.
— — for Long Distances. (C. S. Bradley) Cassier, **3**: 337.
— — Rope-drive for. (R. Grimshaw) Cassier, **2**: 219. — (J. M. Dodge) Cassier, **5**: 64.
— without Cost: "Apergy." (C. Morris) New Sci. R. **2**: 174.
Power of Sympathy; the First American Novel. (W. H. Brown) Bost. **1**: 19–615. **2**: 39, 172, 270.
Powers, Daniel W., and the Powers Art Gallery. (W. A. Sherwood) Canad. M. **5**: 471.
Powers, Hiram, in Washington. Lippinc. **55**: 536.
Poynter, Edward J. (E. F. S. Pattison) M. of Art, **6**: 245.
Pozzo di Borgo, Count. Correspondence. Ed. R. **175**: 1. Same art. Liv. Age, **193**: 131.
Pozzuoli and the Tomb of Virgil; Littus Veneris. (A. Walters) Gent. M. n. s. **51**: 570.

Practical Reformation, A. (J. Barnes) Scrib. M. **20**: 708.
Practice Clavier, The, and the Mind in Playing. Music, **1**: 563.
— in Teaching Music. (H. G. Hanchett) Music, **6**: 520.
— Pedagogical Aspects of. (G. W. Kelsey) Music, **6**: 323.
Prado, Museum of the. (R. Cortissoz) Harper, **90**: 921.
Prague. (H. W. Sweny) M. of Art, **1**: 37.
Prairie Chicken in Manitoba. (R. S. Masson) Canad. M. **3**: 446.
Prairie Farms, Isolation of Life on. (E. V. Smalley) Atlan. **72**: 378.
Prairie-hen and its Enemies. (S. Goodhue) Cosmopol. **15**: 476.
Prâkrit Words, Notes on. (R. Morris) Acad. **43**: 245.
Prato, Memories of. (M. F. Robinson) Eng. Illust. **11**: 1238.
Pratt, Cornelia A., with portrait. Bk. Buyer, **13**: 603. — (J. B. Gilder) Critic, **29**: 213.
Pratt, Enoch. Critic, **29**: 189. — Lib. J. **21**: 450.
Pratt, Matthew, Autobiographical Notes of. (C. H. Hart) Pennsyl. M. **19**: 460.
Pratt, Samuel Jackson, Gleanings. (Earl of Iddesleigh) Blackw. **157**: 121.
Pratt Family and Trevice Family. (W. S. Appleton) N. E. Reg. **46**: 173.
Pratt Institute, Brooklyn, N. Y. (J. R. Campbell) Cent. **24**: 870. — (J. F. Hopkins) New Eng. M. n. s. **13**: 99.
— Free Library Building. Lib. J. **21**: 270. — Critic, **28**: 400.
Praxiteles, Art of, in the British Museum. (E. Sellers) 19th Cent. **37**: 682.
Prayer. (W. E. Fischer) Luth. Q. **26**: 411. — (J. Mudge) Meth. R. **53**: 707. — (B. Waugh) Sund. M. **24**: 422.
— An Ancient Posture in. (W. Stokes) Acad. **45**: 125, 150.
— and Science. (W. W. Kinsley) Bib. Sac. **49**: 89, 199.
— Book of Common, in Manx Gaelic; ed. by Moore. Sat. R. **80**: 116.
— A Defence of. (W. Barry) 19th Cent. **38**: 348. Same art. Ecl. M. **125**: 433.
— Did Christ unite with his Disciples in? (D. W. Forrest) Thinker, **9**: 330.
— for the Dead: Requiescat in Pace. Spec. **71**: 658.
— in Christ's Name. (H. Allon) Sund. M. **21**: 171.
— Life of. (W. M. Macgregor) Good Words, **33**: 427.
— Philosophy of. (William Jones) Meth. R. **56**: 77.
— to One Lord. (T. F. Wright) N. Church R. **1**: 264.
— True and False Notions of. (N. Pearson) 19th Cent. **37**: 813. Same art. Ecl. M. **125**: 45.
Prayer-book of Edward VI., First, Preparations for. Church Q. **35**: 33.
— Second, Preparations for. Church Q. **37**: 137.
Preacher, The, and his Province. (J. Gibbons) No. Am. **160**: 513.
— Functions of. What are they? (L. Abbott) Forum, **15**: 541.
— Modern, Double Advantage of. And. R. **19**: 349.
— Perils of. (W. E. Parsons) Luth. Q. **22**: 1.
— Personality of, in proclaiming the Truth. (W. E. Hull) Luth. Q. **22**: 198.
Preachers, American Pulpit. (C. J. Little) Chaut. **22**: 649.
Preachers, College-trained, Proportion of. (F. G. Peabody) Forum, **18**: 30.
— Famous English. (S. P. Cadman) Chaut. **19**: 184.
— Travelling, Inefficient, Compulsory Location of. (J. M. Buckley) Meth. R. **52**: 195.
Preaching. (M. Joseph) Jew. Q. **3**: 120.
— and Preachers. All the Year, **74**: 148. — Temp. Bar, **98**: 574. Same art. Ecl. M. **121**: 346. Same art. Liv. Age, **198**: 752.
— Apologetics in the Pulpit. (F. H. Foster) N. Eng. **56**: 125.
— The Christian Pulpit. (W. M. Baum) Luth. Q. **26**: 1.
— Doctrinal. (E. V. Gerhart) Ref. Q. **42**: 261.
— Effective. (H. C. Holloway) Luth. Q. **23**: 69
— for Applause. Spec. **68**: 82.
— in Italy, Mediæval. Church Q. **38**: 424.
— Lectures on, Carpenter's. Sat. R. **80**: 245.
— Modern, and Spurgeon. (F. W. Farrar) Sund. M. **21**: 239.
— of To-day. Chr. Lit. **16**: 87.
— Purpose of. (S. S. Seward) N. Church R. **3**: 419.
— Reality in. (C. H. Cutler) And. R. **17**: 580.
— Relation to Social Subjects. (J. W. Day) New World, **5**: 296.
— Subjective Conditions Essential to Highest Power in. (W. Swindells) Meth. R. **54**: 421.
— The Theme and the Times. (M. L. Young) Ref. Q. **43**: 266.
— Thoughts on. (A. R. Kremer) Ref. Q. **40**: 243.
Pre-Cambrian Geology, North American, Principles of. (C. R. Van Hise) Am. J. Sci. **152**: 205.
Precedent *versus* Justice. (L. Trumbull) Am. Law R. **27**: 321.
Precedent, A; a story. (A. M. Whitlock) Lippinc. **55**: 267.
Precedents, Value of. (J. W. McLoud) Am. Law R. **28**: 218.
Precious Stones. (H. A. Miers) J. Soc. Arts, **44**: 757, 769. — Nature, **49**: 319.
— Gems and Jewels. (T. J. A. Freeman) Am. Cath. Q. **20**: 641, 868.
— How to distinguish them. (H. A. Miers) Nature, **51**: 545.
— Colors of. (A. H. Church) M. of Art, **1**: 33.
— Stones of Fire. (E. B.) Argosy, **60**: 358.
— Setting of. (C. R. Ashbee) Art J. **46**: 182.
Predestination, Sovereignty of God in. (G. W. Northrup) M. Chr. Lit. **5**: 404 — **6**: 271.
— — Northrup on. (R. Watts) M. Chr. Lit. **7**: 52–240.
Prediction, Minute, and Modern Doubt. (A. W. Archibald) Bib. Sac. **49**: 546.
Predisposition, Reason and. (J. Burroughs) Open Court, **1**: 115.
Preface, A Curious. (F. Cherry) Bookworm, **2**: 245.
Prefaces. All the Year, **73**: 132.
Prehistoric Anthropology, Importance of. (T. Wilson) Am. Natural. **26**: 681, 809.
Prehistoric Craft Symbols and Religious Emblems. (S. D. Peet) Am. Antiq. **16**: 83.
Prehistoric Enclosures in Wisconsin. (T. H. Lewis) Am. Antiq. **16**: 357.
Prehistoric Man: First Artists of Europe. (S. Baring-Gould) Good Words, **34**: 600.
— in Jersey. (E. Lovett) Illus. Archæol. **1**: 209.
Prehistoric Peoples, Nadaillac on. (H. W. Haynes) Nation, **55**: 500.
Prehistoric Quadrupeds of the Rockies. (H. F. Osborn) Cent. **30**: 705.
Prehistoric Remains at St. Paul, Minn. (T. H. Lewis) Am. Antiq. **18**: 207.

Prehistoric Stone Implements, Manufacture of. (W. H. Holmes) Am. Antiq. 18: 309.
Prehistoric Trepanning and Cranial Amulets. (R. Munro) Fortn. 59: 208. Same art. Ecl. M. 120: 448.
Preisinger, Heinrich. Acad. 49: 220.
Prejudices, National. (J. C. Bayly) Int. J. Ethics, 6: 221.
Prelooker, Jaakoff. (J. G. C. Minchin) Acad. 49: 31.
Preludes; a poem. (C. Burke) Argosy, 61: 726.
Premium Butter. (A. E. Lawrence) New Eng. M. n. s. 13: 465.
Premium Plan for paying for Labor. (F. A. Halsey) Econ. Stud. 1: 75.
Premonitions. (R. Hodgson) Arena, 5: 175.
Prenatal Influence. (S. B. Elliott) Arena, 9: 417. 10: 307, 668.
— Effect of, on a Child. (B. O. Flower) Arena, 13: 243.
Prentice, George D. (J. R. Young) Lippinc. 51: 185.
Prentiss, Albert Nelson. (G. F. Atkinson) Science, n. s. 4: 523.
Prentiss, Sergeant Smith. (A. O. Hall) Green Bag, 8: 353.
Preparatory Schools. Blackw. 156: 45.
— Responsibilities of. (H. E. Starrett) Educa. 15: 74.
Pre-Raphaelite Brotherhood. (W. M. Rossetti) M. of Art, 4: 434. — (K. Cox) Nation, 56: 145.
Pre-Raphaelites, Collection of Pictures by. (C. Monkhouse) M. of Art, 6: 62. — Sat. R. 82: 59.
Pre-Raphaelitism. (C. Gurlitt) Pub. Opin. 13: 95.
— and Impressionism. (W. P. Frith) M. of Art, 11: 187.
Presbyterian, What makes a? (B. L. Agnew) Chaut. 17: 697.
Presbyterian Church, Heresy in. Pub. Opin. 17: 227.
— in America, Assemblies of. (N. M. Steffens) Presb. & Ref. R. 7: 665.
— — Beginning of. (J. A. Davis) Presb. & Ref. R. 7: 66.
— — General Assembly of. (W. G. Craig) Presb. & Ref. R. 6: 722.
— — Thompson's History of. (A. C. Zenos) Presb. & Ref. R. 7: 153.
— in Bermuda in 1620. (W. R. Notman) Presb. & Ref. R. 7: 630.
— in Canada, General Assembly of. (W. Caven) Presb. & Ref. R. 6: 735. 7: 676.
— in N. Y. City. (A. C. Mackenzie) Munsey, 10: 254.
— in Scotland, Assemblies of. (N. S. Walker) Presb. & Ref. R. 6: 717. 7: 660.
— — Walker on. (J. Laing) Presb. & Ref. R. 7: 551.
Presbyterian Reunion and a National Church in Scotland. Scot. R. 19: 177.
Presbyterian Union, The Kirk and. National, 22: 504.
Presbyterianism and Dr. Briggs. And. R. 18: 90.
— and Education. (D. S. Schaff) Ref. Q. 41: 65.
— Future of, in the United States. (C. A. Briggs) No. Am. 157: 1.
— Influence of, on the Individual. (A. R. MacEwen) Chr. Lit. 15: 321.
— Law of. (A. T. Innes) Jurid. R. 8: 159.
— Present Tendencies of. Church Q. 42: 303.
Prescience of Future Contingencies, Impossibility of. (L. D. McCabe) Meth. R. 52: 760.
Prescott, Wm. H. (S. Eliot) New Eng. M. n. s. 9: 515.
— A Centenary Sketch. (Kenyon West) Outl. 53: 745.
Present from Margate, A. Cornh. 69: 56.
Present-day Saga, A; a sea story. (H. Drachmann) Poet-Lore, 6: 394.
Presentations at Court; a farce. (W. Pett Ridge) Idler, 9: 442.
Presentiment; a story. Argosy, 55: 171.
Presents, Giving of. Spec. 69: 951.
Presidency of the U. S. (C. F. Adams) Soc. Econ. 4: 148.
President of the U. S. at Home. (H. L. Nelson) Harper, 89: 196.
— Election of. (J. B. McMaster) Atlan. 78: 328. — (F. H. Hardy) Fortn. 66: 309. Same art. Ecl. M. 127: 440.
— — by People, and Veto Power. (W. Clark) Arena, 10: 453.
— — The Campaign, how managed. (G. F. Parker) Contemp. 70: 636.
— — The Conventions, Humor and Pathos of. (J. B. Bishop) Cent. 30: 305.
— — The Electoral College. (L. C. Branch) Overland, n. s. 28: 551.
— — Electoral System, Our. (S. M. Merrill) No. Am. 163: 402. — Reply. (N. Ewing) No. Am. 163: 637.
— — — Danger ahead. (R. S. Taylor) Arena, 5: 286.
— — — Grave Danger in. (J. Schouler) Forum, 18: 532.
— — — Is it Republican? (J. A. Roebling) Am. J. Pol. 1: 480.
— — How shall we elect? (S. M. Davis) Am. M. Civics, 9: 337.
— — Methods of. (E. P. Clark) Nation, 55: 314.
— Third-term Idea. Pub. Opin. 19: 694. — (J. B. McMaster) Forum, 20: 257. — Sat. R. 80: 230.
Presidential Election, 1876: the Electoral Commission. (J. Honore) Atlan. 72: 521.
— — Vote in South Carolina. (R. M. Davis) Nation, 56: 139.
— 1892. (C. Logsdael and others) Am. J. Pol. 2: 30.
Presidential Election Years, Business in. (F. B. Thurber) No. Am. 155: 210. — (C. S. Smith) No. Am. 155: 426. — Bank. M. (N. Y.) 47: 401.
Presidential Electors, The Choice of. (E. J. Phelps) Forum, 12: 702.
President's Substitute, The; a story. (S. R. Bogue) Overland, n. s. 20: 134.
Presidents from Virginia, Long's Portraits of. (J. C. McCorvey) Nation, 57: 307.
— of Republics, with portraits. (H. Parker) Munsey, 12: 503.
— Other, that might have been. (J. Benton) No. Am. 162: 758.
— Reëlection of, Perils of. (B. D. Eaton) No. Am. 154: 691.
Press, The, and Law of Libel. (H. Fraser) Law Q. 7: 158.
— and the Party. (E. F. Howe) Am. J. Pol. 2: 432.
— and the Pulpit. (J. Leatham) Westm. 137: 601.
— Church and. (J. T. Bunce) National, 22: 387.
— — Relations of. (A. R. Buckland; P. W. Clayden; W. T. Stead) Chr. Lit. 11: 298.
— an Established. (W. E. Hodgson) Time, 10: 400.
— Fourth Estate. Gent. M. n. s. 53: 40. Same art. Ecl. M. 123: 336.
— International Congress of, Antwerp. Ath. '94, 2: 96.
— the Masses, and the Aristocracy. (W. E. Hodgson) Time, 10: 654.
— Mystery of. Spec. 70: 123.
— Pulpit, and Pew. (J. R. Creighton) Meth. R. 55: 68.
Press-day, and Critics at Picture Exhibitions. (M. H. Spielmann) M. of Art, 15: 186, 222.
Pressgang, The, and its History. Chamb. J. 71: 793. Same art. Liv. Age, 204: 126.
— in Orkney. Chamb. J. 72: 347.

Pressure, Death by, as a Penalty. (J. L. André) Antiq. n. s. **30**: 243.
Preston, Richard, sr. (S. Troth) Pennsyl. M. **16**: 207.
Prestwich, Sir Joseph. Ath. '96, **1**: 847. — Acad. **49**: 531. — (H. B. Woodward) Nat. Sci. **9**: 89.
Presumptive Proof, Problems of. (J. W. Clarke) Atlan. **72**: 100.
Pretender, The First, at Bar-le-Duc. (H. W. Wolff) Blackw. **156**: 226.
Pretenders, Character of. Spec. **73**: 334.
Pretty Miss Barneveld. (W. B. Allen) New Eng. M. n. s. **7**: 531.
Pretty Pierre; a story. (G. Parker) Eng. Illust. **9**: 583.
Previous Engagement, A; a comedy. (W. D. Howells) Harper, **92**: 28.
Prévost, Abbé Marcel. (A. Laugel) Nation, **63**: 174, 193. — (A. Hornblow) Bookman, **2**: 474.
— as a Story Writer. (F. Wedmore) Acad. **46**: 227.
— Manon Lescaut. (A. H. Millar) Gent. M. n. s. **57**: 402.
— Notre Compagne. Sat. R. **79**: 764.
Prévost-Paradol, L. A. (A. Laugel) Nation, **59**: 214.
Priam, Death of, Lecytas with. (E. A. Gardner) J. Hel. Stud. **14**: 170.
Price, J. Edward. Ath. '92, **1**: 188.
Price of a Cow. (E. W. Bellamy) Atlan. **77**: 763.
Price of the Lad, The. (A. Spode) Good Words, **37**: Xmas no., 20.
Price of a Man; a story. (F. Crane) Munsey, **14**: 147.
Price of God's Good Things, The. (F. Langbridge) Good Words, **36**: 326.
Price of a Proselyte, The. (H. Hill) Idler, **9**: 459.
Price of Romance, The. (R. W. Herrick) Scrib. M. **18**: 60.
Prices and Money. (S. McL. Hardy) Bank. M. (N. Y.) **50**: 790.
— Declining, Secret of. (T. L. Greene) Nation, **60**: 337.
— Delusion about. Soc. Econ. **6**: 65.
— Determination of, Geometrical Theory of. (L. Walras) Ann. Am. Acad. Pol. Sci. **3**: 45.
— Fall of, Battle of Standards and. (E. Atkinson) Forum, **19**: 143.
— — Effect of, in Canada. (J. B. Peat) Canad. M. **6**: 210.
— Falling, Some Effects of. (H. W. Farnam) Yale R. **4**: 183.
— High, An Era of. (D. MacG. Means) Nation, **63**: 116.
— in England, 1886–92. (A. Sauerbeck) J. Statis. Soc. **56**: 215.
— in U. S., Recent Investigations on. (F. W. Taussig) Yale R. **2**: 231. — (F. W. Taussig) Am. Statis. Assoc. **3**: 487.
— — under the McKinley Act. Q. J. Econ. **7**: 103.
— Index Numbers of. (A. Sauerbeck) Econ. J. **5**: 161.
— — Defence of. (F. Y. Edgeworth) Econ. J. **6**: 132.
— — Fallacy of. (C. W. Oker) J. Pol. Econ. **4**: 515.
— — Further Considerations on. (N. G. Pierson) Econ. J. **6**: 127.
— Money and, Price on. Sat. R. **82**: 69.
— The New Gold and the Fall of. (W. C. Mitchell) J. Pol. Econ. **5**: 84.
— of Wheat and Bread, Relative. (J. Kirkland) Econ. J. **6**: 475.
— Prosperity and. (C. B. Phipson) Westm. **141**: 652.
— Quantity of Money and, 1860–91. (S. M. Hardy) J. Pol. Econ. **3**: 145.
— Reasons why they are Low. (A. Williams) Engin. M. **8**: 781.
— Regulation of, Legal Theories of. (A. T. Hadley) Yale R. **1**: 56.
Prices, Statistics of, Theory and Practice of. (R. P. Falkener) Am. Statis. Assoc. **3**: 119.
Prickly Plants of California. (Emma S. Marshall) Overland, n. s. **24**: 604.
Pride. Spec. **69**: 157.
— English. Spec. **74**: 746.
Pride of Anne Havens. (D. E. Nelson) New Eng. M. n. s. **12**: 629.
Priest in Politics, The. (M. Davitt) 19th Cent. **33**: 139.
Priesthood of Israel and Egypt, Development of. (J. H. Breasted) Bib. World, **2**: 19.
Priestley, Joseph, in Domestic Life. (B. R. Belloc) Contemp. **66**: 567. Same art. Ecl. M. **123**: 775. Same art. Liv. Age, **203**: 478.
— Scientific Correspondence of, Bolton's. (J. T. Stoddard) Nation, **56**: 318.
Priestly Dues, Harmony of Pentateuch Respecting. (H. Hayman) Bib. Sac. **52**: 18.
Priggishness, What is? Spec. **68**: 807.
Prigs, Concerning. (M. Gray) New R. **14**: 303.
Prima Donna, The. Cornh. **71**: 73.
Prima Donnas, American. (O. Hackett) Munsey, **8**: 500.
Primary, The, the Pivot of Reform. (D. D. Field) Forum, **14**: 189.
See Caucus.
Primary Education and the State. (J. Clifford) Contemp. **69**: 441.
— Comparative Statistics of. (E. Levasseur) Am. Statis. Assoc. **3**: 481.
Primary Schools, Religious Problem in. (W. Sinclair) Westm. **145**: 56.
Primaticcio, Francesco. (A. M. F. Robinson) M. of Art, **8**: 254.
Primavera de Capri. (W. Sharp) Good Words, **33**: 396.
Prime, W. C. Along New England Roads. Garden & F. **6**: 23.
Prime Ministers, English. (S. Walpole) Fortn. **64**: 380. Same art. Liv. Age, **207**: 237.
Primer, The, and Literature. (H. E. Scudder) Atlan. **70**: 382.
Primer of Imaginary Geography. (B. Matthews) Scrib. M. **16**: 729.
Primitive Church and the Papal Claims. Church Q. **39**: 273.
Primitive Culture, Tylor on. (A. Macalister) Crit. R. **2**: 227.
Primitive Man in Modern Beliefs; poem. (H. Phillips, jr.) J. Am. Folk-Lore, **3**: 60.
Primogeniture. (W. S. Lilly) 19th Cent. **40**: 765.
Primrose, Two Forms of. (A. S. Wilson) Knowl. **18**: 102.
Primrose, The; a poem. (A. H. Japp) Argosy, **61**: 626.
Primrose League, The. (W. T. Marriott) National, **24**: 771. Same art. Ecl. M. **124**: 459. — Spec. **72**: 528.
Primrose League Party; a story. (S. C. Budd) Belgra. **81**: 282.
Primrose Path of Dalliance, The. (L. Lemmon) Southern M. **4**: 482.
Primroses, Chinese. (E. O. Orpet) Garden & F. **8**: 57.
— — at the Columbian Fair. (E. J. Hill) Garden & F. **6**: 94.
— — Cultivation of. (E. O. Orpet) Garden & F. **7**: 47.
Primulas in England. (W. Watson) Garden & F. **8**: 204.
Primum Tempus; a poem. (R. Kipling) Idler, **2**: 475.
Prince, Hezekiah, Diary of, 1793. New Eng. M. n. s. **9**: 723.
Prince Edward Island. (H. C. E. Childers) Good Words, **36**: 840. — (N. McLeod) New Eng. M. n. s. **10**: 749.

Prince Edward Island, Land Question in. (J. H. Hastam) Arena, **16**: 743.
— Prehistoric Shell Heap on. (J. W. Fewkes) Am. Antiq. **18**: 30.
Prince Pillowcase; a story. Temp. Bar, **108**: 373.
Prince Rupert's Emerald Ring; a story. Chamb. J. **72**: 300.
Prince Society's Publications. (E. D. North) Bibliographica, **2**: 371.
Prince's Love-story, A. (J. M. Cobban) Chamb. J. **71**: 216–264.
Princess Aline. (R. H. Davis) Harper, **90**: 240–595.
Princess and a Woman; a story. (R. McDonald) Munsey, **13**: 518, 631. **14**: 85.
Princess Désirée. (C. Black) Longm. **28**: 505, 609. **29**: 82, 111.
Princess Leiladin; a story. (M. von Ebner-Eschenbach) Chaut. **19**: 623.
Princess of Rattlesnakes; a story. (H. Miller) Lippinc. **50**: 399.
Princess Ratazanoff; a story. (C. M. Podgorski) Cosmopol. **12**: 733.
Princess Sonia. (J. Magruder) Cent. **28**: 3–774.
Princesses, Rejected. (E. Lewis) Cosmopol. **15**: 643.
"Princeton," U. S. Steamer, Explosion on, 1844. (W. W. Taylor) M. Am. Hist. **30**: 63.
Princeton College and Patriotism. (J. G. Hibben) Forum, **22**: 217.
— Glimpses of. (T. W. Hotchkiss, jr.) M. Am. Hist. **28**: 450.
— in the Nation's Service. (W. Wilson) Forum, **22**: 447. — (W. Wilson) Science, n. s. **4**: 908.
— 150th Anniversary of. Critic, **29**: 239, 265. — (W. M. Daniels) R. of Rs. (N. Y.) **14**: 446. — (E. Dowden) Sat. R. **82**: 668. — (H. van Dyke) Outl. **54**: 766. — Bach. of Arts, **3**: 439.
— Secret Societies of. (T. W. Hotchkiss, jr.) M. Am. Hist. **27**: 17.
— Spirit and Ideals of. (A. F. West) Educa. R. **8**: 313.
— Substitutes for Fraternities at. (J. L. Williams) Bach. of Arts, **2**: 189.
Principal, Public; Recovery from Third Person. (G. Urquhart) Am. Law R. **28**: 37.
Principals, Academy, Associated, of the State of New York. (F. H. Howard) School R. **4**: 99.
— School, Supervisory Work of. (J. G. Allen) School R. **1**: 291.
Principles of Miss Mehitabel; a story. Cornh. **73**: 379. Same art. Ecl. M. **126**: 630. Same art. Liv. Age, **209**: 277.
Pringsheim, Nathaniel. (D. H. Scott) Nature, **51**: 399.
Prinsep, Valentine. (W. Meynell) M. of Art, **6**: 405.
Printer's Marks. Bk. Buyer, **11**: 9.
Printers in N. Y., Colonial. Bk. Buyer, **13**: 8.
Printing. Bookworm, **7**: 173.
— and Printers, English, traced in the State Papers. (H. R. Plomer) Bibliographica, **2**: 204.
— Early, in Holland. (W. M. Conway) M. of Art, **4**: 190, 505.
— English Provincial Presses, 1478–1750. (W. H. Allnutt) Bibliographica, **2**: 23, 150, 276.
— Evolution of. (F. Allaben) Nat'l M. (N. Y. '91) **18**: 172.
— in America, the First. (C. R. Brainard) Nat'l M. (N. Y. '91) **15**: 136.
— — Colonial, in the 17th Cent. (C. R. Hildeburn) Nat'l M. (N. Y. '91) **17**: 49.
— in England; the First Book printed. (S. Urban) Gent. M. n. s. **54**: 537.
— Introduction into England, by Caxton. (R. B. Whittemore) Educa. **12**: 546, 616.
Printing, Invention of, Blades on. Ath. '92, **1**: 209. — (T. L. De Vinne) Nation, **54**: 15. — Sat. R. **74**: 311.
— Old-world, and Wood-cutting. (W. M. Conway) M. of Art, **7**: 68.
— Private, in France in 15th Century. (A. Claudin) Bibliographica, **3**: 344.
Printing-press, Early Labors of. (C. W. Currier) Cath. World, **63**: 59.
— Early Representations of. (F. Madan) Bibliographica, **1**: 223, 499.
Prints, Japanese Colored. (T. Duret) Art J. **46**: 342.
Printz, John, Governor of New Sweden. (Mrs. J. Mifflin) Am. Hist. Reg. **2**: 760.
Prior, Matthew. (E. Manson) Temp. Bar, **108**: 530. Same art. Ecl. M. **127**: 563. Same art. Liv. Age, **210**: 803.
Prior, Melton. (R. Compton) Idler, **8**: 337.
Prior Gilbert's Sister; a story. Temp. Bar, **104**: 71.
Prior's Cell; a ghost story. (D. Hale) Belgra. **77**: 296.
Pris; a story. Liv. Age, **192**: 272.
Priscilla, St., Cemetery of, Discoveries in. (W. R. Brownlow) Dub. R. **111**: 96.
Priscilla: a Tale of the Revolution. (C. F. Little) Un. Serv. (Phila.) **7**: 338.
Prism, Objective. Astron. **11**: 199.
Prisms, Longitudinal Aberration of. (C. G. Abbot and F. E. Fowle, jr.) Am. J. Sci. **152**: 255.
Prison, A Convent used as a. Cornh. **72**: 481.
— English County, In an. (G. R. Vicars) Eng. Illust. **10**: 712.
Prison Bars; a story. (M. L. Woods) Eng. Illust. **12**: no. 3, 151.
Prison Committee Report. (E. F. Du Cane) 19th Cent. **38**: 278.
Prison Industries and Discipline. (B. F. Sheets and others) Am. J. Pol. **3**: 490.
Prison Labor. (E. Smith) Lend a H. **15**: 408. — (C. E. Felton) Lend a H. **17**: 440.
— New Constitution of New York in relation to. (W. P. Prentice) Lend a H. **15**: 418.
— Uselessness of. (E. F. Du Cane) 19th Cent. **40**: 632.
Prison Life in England. (T. Hopkins) Leis. Hour, **45**: 159, 256.
Prison Malingering. Chamb. J. **73**: 244.
Prison Poetry. All the Year, **72**: 89.
Prison Problems. (F. L. Oswald) Open Court, **6**: 3402.
Prison Question. (C. J. Bartlett) Am. J. Pol. **2**: 86.
Prison Reform, Hopeful Side of. (W. F. Spalding) Lend a H. **9**: 198.
— in Japan. (W. N. Curtis) Lend a H. **14**: 341.
— What is? (W. C. Selleck) Am. M. Civics, **6**: 136.
Prison-ship Martyrs, Monument to. (A. M. Earle) Am. Hist. Reg. **2**: 1423.
Prison Statistics, International. (F. J. Mouat) J. Statis. Soc. **55**: 658.
Prison System, Massachusetts. (S. J. Barrows) New Eng. M. n. s. **8**: 31.
— of Ontario. Sat. R. **74**: 109.
Prison Treatment in England. Sat. R. **81**: 367.
Prisoner, Reflections of a. And. R. **17**: 265.
Prisoners, Shall they be reformed? An Important Step in Pennsylvania. (A. L. Bates) Am. M. Civics, **8**: 192.
Prisoners of Conscience; a story. (A. E. Barr) Cent. **30**: 672, 854.
Prisoners of Silence; a novel. (M. A. Dickens) All the Year, **75**: 97–601. **76**: 1–241.
Prisoners of War in England. Chamb. J. **71**: 13. Same art. Liv. Age, **200**: 317.
Prisoners on the Move. (E. R. Spearman) Fortn. **64**: 717.

Prisons and Prisoners. (G. R. Vicars) Gent. M. n. s. **50**: 53.
— Are they a Failure? (W. D. Morrison) Fortn. **61**: 459.
— British *vs.* Russian. (A. Webb) Nation, **54**: 109.
— Criminals and. (T. E. Will) Arena, **10**: 409.
— English. (A. West) 19th Cent. **39**: 150.
— English Gaols a Century Ago. (H. L. Carson) Green Bag, **6**: 313.
— Griffiths' Secrets of the Prison House. (W. S. Lilly) 19th Cent. **35**: 234. — Ath. '94, **1**: 41. — Sat. R. **77**: 23.
— in France, and their Inmates. (E. R. Spearman) Contemp. **66**: 550.
— in the Old World and the New. (A. Griffiths) No. Am. **158**: 332.
— London. Argosy, **55**: 156.
— Modern Penology. (G. R. Vicars) Gent. M. n. s. **53**: 627.
— Reformation of. (A. G. Warner) Char. R. **5**: 11.
— Reformatory, and Lombroso's Theories. (H. Zimmern) Pop. Sci. Mo. **43**: 598.
— — Do they lessen Crime? (A. J. Palm) Am. J. Pol. **1**: 109.
— Southern Soldiers in Northern. So. Hist. Pap. **23**: 158.
Pritchard, Charles. Acad. **43**: 480. — Ath. '93, **1**: 703. — (W. E. Plummer) Astron. **12**: 592. — Nature, **48**: 130.
Privacy, Privilege of. Spec. **69**: 733.
— Right to. Green Bag, **6**: 498. — (J. G. Speed) No. Am. **163**: 64.
Private Chivalry, A; a story. (F. Lynde) Munsey, **14**: 298.
Private the Honourable Fitz. (R. Penny) Temp. Bar, **109**: 562.
Private Interpretation (2 Pet. i. 20). (T. W. Chambers) Ref. Q. **42**: 242.
Private Jams; a story. (R. Penny) Temp. Bar, **106**: 186. Same art. Liv. Age, **207**: 724.
Private Jones of the Eighth; a story. (R. Monckton-Dene) Un. Serv. (Phila.) **9**: 155, 241.
Private Life, The; a story. (H. James) Atlan. **69**: 463.
Private Life of an Eminent Politician; a story. (E. Rod) National, **20**: 509 — **21**: 80.
Privateer "Dash." (E. C. Plummer) New Eng. M. n. s. **10**: 568.
Privateers, New York Colonial. (T. A. Janvier) Harper, **90**: 333.
Privy Council, with portraits. Green Bag, **7**: 65.
— Acts of. Ed. R. **175**: 145.
— under the Tudors. Quar. **177**: 131.
Prize Fighting and Boxing. Time, **22**: 258.
Prize-fights, Newspaper Reports of. (E. L. Godkin) Nation, **56**: 209.
Prizes, Naval, in War. (C. Johnstone) Un. Serv. M. **4**: 23.
Pro Patria Mea; a story. (C. F. Little) Un. Serv. (Phila.) **8**: 346.
Probability and Faith. (J. Morris) Dub. R. **111**: 365.
Probate Courts of Massachusetts. (G. White) N. E. Reg. **49**: 69.
Probation after Death. (J. W. Wellman) Our Day, **12**: 110. — Pub. Opin. **15**: 11.
Probation Work for Women. (H. M. Todd) Lend a H. **11**: 466.
Problems of the Age, Some. (F. W. Farrar) No. Am. **161**: 412.
— of the Day, Study of. (H. M. Bartlett) Am. J. Pol. **5**: 306.
Problems of the World, The Seven Intellectual. (A. Bierbower) Ref. Q. **42**: 443.
Process Pictures, Drawing for. (G. White) J. Soc. Arts, **43**: 277.
Procter, Adelaide Anne. (A. C. Kellogg) Cath. World, **63**: 521.
Proctor, Richard A. (H. MacQueary) Arena, **8**: 562. — With portrait. (C. R. Willard) Pop. Astron. **1**: 319. — (J. R. Sutton) Time, **21**: 316.
— Autobiographical Notes. New Sci. R. **1**: 393.
Procyon, Satellite of. (I. W. Ward) Nature, **55**: 153.
— Variable Proper Motion of. (S. W. Burnham) Astron. **13**: 434.
Prodigal Friend, A; a story. (S. E. Benet) Lippinc. **55**: 122.
Prodigal's Return; a story. (H. S. Merriman) Cornh. **74**: 361. Same art. Liv. Age, **211**: 206.
Prodigal's Return, The; a story. (F. Mathew) Idler, **2**: 424.
Production, About. (E. P. Powell) Am. M. Civics, **7**: 294.
— Cheap, and Low Wages. (H. Kingerly) Am. J. Pol. **2**: 308.
— English Theories of, Cannan on. (F. W. Taussig) Nation, **57**: 490.
— Uncertainty as a Factor in. (E. A. Ross) Ann. Am. Acad. Pol. Sci. **8**: 304.
— up to the Power Limit. (H. L. Arnold) Engin. M. **9**: 908.
Profession, In Search of a. (C. Carlyon-Jenkins) Sund. M. **23**: 162.
Professional Classes in England, Incomes of. (P. Collier) Forum, **16**: 774.
Professional Institutions. (H. Spencer) Contemp. **67**: 721, 898. **68**: 114–853. **69**: 100–547. Same art. Pop. Sci. Mo. **47**: 34–739. **48**: 49–841. Same art. Ecl. M. **126**: 645.
Professional Lover. (A. C. Grissom) New Eng. M. n. s. **8**: 377.
Professional Secrecy. Spec. **75**: 364.
Professional Training, Ideal in. (Mrs. D. Fulcomer) Educa. **16**: 473.
— Problem of. (J. J. Findlay) School R. **1**: 281.
Professions, Regulation of. (N. S. Shaler) Engin. M. **4**: 9.
— The Upward Pressure. (W. Besant) Scrib. M. **13**: 585.
— *vs.* Trade. Spec. **75**: 720.
Professor Fleg as a Fisherman. (H. Hutchinson) Longm. **21**: 419.
Professor of Theology, The; an Idyll. (E. F. Byrne) Temp. Bar, **96**: 533. Same art. Liv. Age, **196**: 336.
Prof. Van Wagener's Eye; a story. (W. L. Alden) Idler, **8**: 304.
Professor Weisheit's Experiment. (J. Hawthorne) Time, **14**: 513.
Professor's Aberration, The. (F. W. Snedeker) Cent. **23**: 600.
Professor's Butterfly, The. (H. A. Bryden) Chamb. J. **71**: 491.
Professor's Entertainment, The. Macmil. **68**: 38. Same art. Ecl. M. **121**: 565.
Professor's Holiday, The. (Pauline B. Mackie) Bach. of Arts, **2**: 160.
Professor's Jump, The; a story. (W. L. Alden) Idler, **8**: 18.
Professor's Letter, The; a story. (M. Hargrave) Gent. M. n. s. **55**: 325.
Professor's Skeleton, The; a story. Chamb. J. **69**: 45.
Professors, Age for Retirement of. Nature, **52**: 538.

Professors, Training of, Scholarships, Fellowships, and. (G. S. Hall) Forum, 17: 443.
— Universities and the Training of. (G. S. Hall) Forum, 17: 297.
Profit, Risk Theory of. (F. B. Hawley) Q. J. Econ. 7: 459.
Profit and Loss. (F. Harris) Fortn. 58: 374. Same art. Liv. Age, 195: 146, 205.
— Loria's Theory of. (C. A. Coriegliani) Q. J. Econ. 6: 344.
Profit-sharing. Cassier, 1: 50.—(W. Gladden) Lend a H. 16: 407.—(N. P. Gilman) Pub. Opin. 18: 472.
— and Coöperation. (B. Jones) Econ. J. 2: 616.— Lend a H. 9: 415.—(L. L. Price) Econ. J. 2: 442.
— and Gain-sharing. (H. R. Towne) Econ. Stud. 1: 51.
— at Ivorydale. (I. W. Howerth) Am. J. Sociol. 2: 43.
— Both Sides of. (F. G. Mather) Pop. Sci. Mo. 48: 401.
— Coöperators and. (W. E. Snell) Econ. R. 3: 201.
— Does it pay? (W. C. Proctor) Our Day, 14: 317.
— Economic Distribution *vs.* (Alfred Dolge) Soc. Econ. 2: 129.
— Experience with. Am. Arch. 51: 28.
— The Familistère at Guise. (O. Hancock) Fortn. 59: 418.
— in the U. S. (P. Monroe) Am. J. Sociol. 1: 685.—(N. P. Gilman) New Eng. M. n. s. 7: 120.
— Railroad. (J. W. Jenks) Char. R. 1: 299.
— Theory and Practice of. Cath. World, 58: 111.
— Two Examples of Successful. (F. W. Blackmar) Forum, 19: 57.
Profit-sharing Labor Unions of Antwerp. (J. H. Gore) Forum, 18: 117.
Profits and Interest. (A. T. Hadley) Ann. Am. Acad. Pol. Sci. 4: 337.
— Business and Insurance. (J. B. Clark) Q. J. Econ. 7: 40.
— — Are they too Large? (J. B. Mann) Pop. Sci. Mo. 42: 100.
— — not too Large. (P. F. Hallock) Pop. Sci. Mo. 42: 392.
— under the Law of Labor-value. (I. A. Hourwich) J. Pol. Econ. 2: 235.
Prognostications. (H. R. Plomer) Walford's Antiq. 8: 163.
Progress. (J. J. Valentine) Overland, n. s. 28: 428.
— American. (V. de Cleyre) Open Court, 5: 3040.
— Are we Old Fogies? (J. C. Ayres) Cosmopol. 19: 685.
— Christianity and the Ethical Spirit in relation to. (C. Ford) Westm. 146: 404.
— Limbo of. (F. Greenwood) Macmil. 67: 391.
— of the Century. (E. E. Hale) Lend a H. 15: 243.
— of Humanity. Meth. R. 54: 109.
— of Mankind. (E. Reclus) Contemp. 70: 761.
— Practical, Union for. (B. O. Flower) Arena, 8: 78.
— The Process of. (R. Weyler) Open Court, 1: 683.
— The Test of. Open Court, 5: 2916.
— Tides of. (F. L. Oswald) Open Court, 6: 3175.
— Why it is by Leaps. (G. Iles) Pop. Sci. Mo. 49: 216.
Progress Club-house, N. Y. Am. Arch. 47: 34.
Progression, Toryism and. (F. R. Y. Radcliffe) National, 20: 651.
Prohibition and the Drinking Habit. (D. B. Lady) Ref. Q. 43: 468.
Prohibition, M. F. Brown on. (G. B. Winslow) Am. J. Pol. 2: 259.
— by the State. Why it is not a Success. (A. M. Potter) Am. J. Pol. 3: 72.
— How Rum was reinstated in Iowa. (J. G. Woolley) Our Day, 16: 196.
— in England. (W. Lawson) No. Am. 157: 151.
— in Kansas. (D. C. Milner) Our Day, 16: 145.
— in Maine. (A. P. Rose) Nation, 55: 65.—(W. MacDonald) Nation, 62: 50.
— Is it practicable? (M. F. Brown) Am. J. Pol. 1: 570.
— Neal Dow's Watchwords for the 20th Century. (J. Cook) Our Day, 14: 12.
— Object Lesson in. (T. C. Down) 19th Cent. 37: 709.
— The Power of the Pulpit. (J. G. Woolley) Our Day, 16: 506.
— Voice of. (J. G. Woolley) Our Day, 16: 348.
Prohibition Party, Distinctive Features of. (B. W. Williams) Am. J. Pol. 3: 64.
— Plea for. (E. E. Bartlett) Arena, 6: 599.
Prohibitive Latin. (H. C. Elmer) Am. J. Philol. 15: 133, 299.
Prohibitory Liquor Laws, Abolish All. (A. Morgan) Pop. Sci. Mo. 44: 577.
— in Iowa. Soc. Econ. 8: 156.
— Should they be abolished? (T. D. Crothers) Pop. Sci. Mo. 45: 225.
Projectiles, Electrically Welded. (H. P. Maxim) Cassier, 2: 418.
— Small, Destructive Effects of. (V. Horsley) Nature, 50: 104.
Proletariat, Our American. Gunton's M. 10: 356.
Prometheus and the Caucasus. (F. D. Allen) Am. J. Philol. 13: 51.
— and the Fate of Zeus. (P. Carus) Open Court, 5: 2970.
— Unbound. (F. M. Holland) Open Court, 1: 483.
Prometheus Myth in Poetry. (H. A. Clarke) Poet-Lore, 4: 135.
Promise, A; a poem. (Maude Lyons) Cosmopol. 18: 529.
Promised Land, The; a story. (O. Wister) Harper, 88: 781.
Promises, Sacred Nature of. (K. T. Woods) Chaut. 17: 461.
Promising; a story. (A. Hope) Idler, 6: 13.
Promotion of Cadet Norcross. (N. Hapgood) New Eng. M. n. s. 15: 502.
Promotion of Pupils. (N. H. Whittemore) Educa. 12: 360.
Pronunciation; an Epidemic of Slovenliness. (G. W. Dancy) Theatre, 29: 97.
— of English, Common Sense in. Chaut. 22: 595.
Proof in Civil Cases in Scotland. (H. Begg) Jurid. R. 7: 1.
Proof of the Pudding; a story. Temp. Bar. 105: 55. Same art. Liv. Age, 205: 787.
Proof Positive. (D. C. Murray) Chamb. J. 72: 716-742.
Proof-reader, Equipment of. (D. Dane) Writer, 6: 121.
Proof-readers and Copy-holders. (J. A. Copeland) Writer, 6: 83.
Proof-reading: Fiend of Proof-sheets. Sat. R. 76: 698.
Propertius, Love Story of. (A. W. Verrall) Univ. R. 2: 197.
Property and Christian Beneficence. (D. R. Breed) Presb. & Ref. R. 5: 287.
— Christianity and. (C. Gore) Econ. R. 6: 391.

Property, Devolution of, on Death of Owner. (W. C. Maude) Month, 88: 546.
— Distribution of. (H. B. Brown) Am. Law R. 27: 656. — (C. B. Spahr) Outl. 49: 262.
— Division into Real and Personal Estate. (M. H. Box) Law Q. 3: 406.
— The Fathers on. (W. F. Cobb) Econ. R. 5: 191.
— Locke's Theory of. (D. G. Ritchie) Econ. R. 1: 29.
— Private, What justifies? (W. L. Sheldon) Int. J. Ethics, 4: 17.
— Redistribution of, Utmost Results possible from. (W. H. Mallock) National, 21: 26.
— Rights and Duties of, in our Legal and Social Systems. (J. F. Dillon) Am. Law R. 29: 161.
Prophecies, Fulfilled Cases of. (M. R. Libby) Psych. R. 1: 203.
Prophecy, The Israelitish. (C. H. Cornill) Open Court, 9: 4417.
— — Essential Elements of. (W. R. Harper) Bib. World, 5: 321.
— — Outline Topics in the History of. (W. R. Harper) Bib. World, 7: 39-352. 8: 37-375.
Prophecy of Columbus; a poem. (W. O. Croffut) Our Day, 11: 436.
Prophet, Function of the. (T. W. Chambers) Presb. & Ref. R. 5: 49.
— What is a? (L. Abbott) Chr. Lit. 14: 296.
Prophet, A; a story. (R. Marsh) New Eng. M. n. s. 7: 235, 322.
Prophetic Urn; a story. (W. Hinckley) Outing, 24: 407.
Prophets, Doctrine of, Kirkpatrick's. Church Q. 36: 424.
Propitiation, New Testament Idea of. (A. G. Voigt) Luth. Q. 25: 547.
Proportional Representation. *See* Representation.
Propositions, Distinction between Real and Verbal. (E. T. Dixon) Mind, 18: 339.
— Intensive Statement of Particular and Negative. (M. Washburn) Philos. R. 5: 403.
Prosaic Idyll, A; a story. Belgra. 88: 390.
Prose, Freedom of, Plea for. (R. P. Jacobus) Writer, 6: 30.
Prosencephalon of Telosts, Anatomy and Histology of. (C. L. Herrick) Am. Natural. 26: 112.
Prospect Park, Brooklyn, N. Y., Battle-ground in. (J. De Wolf) Garden & F. 6: 26.
Prospectograph. (A. Melani) Am. Arch. 48: 57.
Prosperity. Is it in Sight? (W. E. Connor and others) Am. M. Civics, 7: 324.
Prostitution and its Remedy. (E. O. Buxton) Am. J. Pol. 3: 39.
— A Study of. (J. W. Walton) Am. J. Pol. 3: 605.
— within the Marriage Bond. (B. O. Flower) Arena, 13: 59.
Prostration, Origin of. (E. P. Powell) Open Court, 8: 3978.
Protection. (G. Gunton) Pub. Opin. 20: 523.
— and Bimetallism. Soc. Econ. 9: 26.
— and Cost of Production. (R. Donald) Econ. J. 3: 145.
— and Democratic Party. (T. Cox) Am. J. Pol. 2: 24.
— and the Empire. (W. F. Lord) 19th Cent. 33: 1062. — Soc. Econ. 5: 47.
— and Farmers. Soc. Econ. 9: 10.
— and Free Trade. (J. Jarrett) Am. J. Pol. 1: 529.
— — Viewed Morally. (A. Walkley) Am. J. Pol. 3: 512.
— and Natural Monopolies. (J. R. Commons) Q. J. Econ. 6: 479.
— and Paternalism. Soc. Econ. 1: 257.
— and the Proletariat. (J. S. Morton) No. Am. 158: 641.
— and Prosperity, Curtiss on. Gunton's M. 10: 469.
Protection as a Campaign Issue in the U. S., 1892. Pub. Opin. 13: 466, 492. 14: 1.
— as Labor wants it. (H. H. Champion) 19th Cent. 31: 1027.
— Australia under. (M. Macfie) Econ. J. 3: 297.
— by Bounty. (A. R. Smith) Soc. Econ. 9: 196.
— Commissioner Peck and. Pub. Opin. 13: 513.
— Effect of, on Distribution of Wealth. (G. F. Milton) Am. J. Pol. 4: 515.
— England's Return to. (G. Gunton) Gunton's M. 10: 317.
— English Reasoning on. Gunton's M. 11: 92.
— Europe's Customs Union. (G. W. Hinman) Soc. Econ. 2: 233.
— Few Plain Words on. (A. L. Perry) New Eng. M. n. s. 8: 222.
— Free Trade, and Fair Trade. (Earl Grey) 19th Cent. 31: 38.
— French, and Swiss Retaliation. (E. Castelot) Econ. J. 3: 540.
— Future of English Labor. Gunton's M. 11: 325.
— a Help to a Few, a Hindrance to Many. (C. F. Crisp) Am. J. Pol. 1: 160.
— in Canada. (D. MacG. Means) Nation, 55: 215.
— — Results of. (D. MacG. Means) Nation, 61: 144.
— in England and the Labor Vote. Spec. 69: 439.
— in France. (Robert Donald) Univ. R. 4: 473.
— Is it gaining Ground? (D. MacG. Means) Nation, 54: 481.
— Is it Immoral? (D. Strange) Am. J. Pol. 4: 532. — (M. B. C. True) Am. J. Pol. 4: 214.
— Lancashire and the Cotton Duties. (W. Tattersall) Fortn. 65: 291.
— Modern System of. (F. W. Haine) Westm. 138: 138.
— Monometallism and. (C. S. Thomas) Arena, 10: 169.
— or Free Trade. (T. G. Shearman; G. Gunton; W. D. Lewis) Chr. Un. 46: 628, 629, 676, 677.
— Our National Ideal. Soc. Econ. 2: 141.
— Patriotism and. (G. Fiamingo) Econ. R. 6: 510.
— Rational. (W. F. Draper) Soc. Econ. 1: 365. 2: 18. 2: 225.
— Recent Literature on, 1893. (F. W. Taussig) Q. J. Econ. 7: 162.
— Ruin of American Farmer. (W. Maitland) 19th Cent. 32: 733.
— Scientific Validity of. (T. Cox) Am. J. Pol. 3: 359.
— Silver Senators and. Gunton's M. 10: 161.
— Socialism and. (E. L. Godkin) Nation, 58: 189.
— The South for, in 1896. (G. C. Sibley) Am. J. Pol. 3: 579.
— Tariff of 1789, Protective Purpose of. (W. Hill) J. Pol. Econ. 2: 54.
— to Home Industries, an Economical Mistake. Macmil. 71: 145.
— What Congress should do. Soc. Econ. 5: 65.
— Who pays the Tariff? Soc. Econ. 3: 297.
— Will Great Britain return to? (L. Irwell) Westm. 138: 349.
See also Tariff.
Protectionist Idea of Industry. (D. A. Wells) Am. J. Pol. 1: 225.
— Non-protectionist Idea. (W. T. Galbraith) Am. J. Pol. 1: 419.
Protectionist Reaction in France. (H. A. L. Fisher) Econ. J. 6: 341.
Protectionist Revival. (J. H. Round) National, 25: 497.
Proteids, Decomposition Products of. (T. G. Brodie) Sci. Prog. 4: 62.
— Synthesis of. (W. D. Halliburton) Sci. Prog. 4: 149.
Protest of the Wing Dormitory, The. (E. Phillpotts) Idler, 10: 184.

Protestant Controversy, Popular. (C. C. Starbuck) New World, 4: 696.
Protestant Episcopal Church, Broad and Narrow in. (S. D. McConnell) New World, 4: 201.
— Congress at Minneapolis. (H. B. Hudson) R. of Rs. (N. Y.) 12: 566.
— Contribution of, to Modern Religious Life. (F. Palmer) And. R. 17: 376.
— The First Colonial Bishopric, 1786. (H. Hall) Am. Hist. R. 1: 209.
— General Convention. (J. A. Locke) Cath. World, 62: 588.
— in America. Eng. R. 3: 101.
— in New York. (R. H. Titherington) Munsey, 6: 552.
— Journalism in. (G. A. Carstensen) Chaut. 21: 199.
— Pastoral Letter of the Bishops. (A. R. Kremer) Ref. Q. 42: 418. — (E. Gold) Forum, 19: 618.
— Restoration to Catholic Fellowship. (L. W. Bacon) Chr. Lit. 13: 297.
Protestantism and the New Ethics. (W. Clarke) Open Court, 1: 233.
— and the Reformation. (J. Reed) N. Church R. 3: 227.
— Aristocratic. (C. K. Whipple) Open Court, 1: 373.
— Catholicism, and Progress. (F. W. Howard) Cath. World, 62: 145.
— French, Social Movement in. (E. Bost) New World, 2: 256.
— in England. (A. F. Marshall) Am. Cath. Q. 17: 139. — (E. Peacock) Dub. R. 110: 325.
Protoceras, the New Artiodactyle. (H. F. Osborn) Nature, 47: 321.
Protoplasm. (H. W. Conn) Meth. R. 54: 27.
— Artificial, Bütschli on. (P. C. Mitchell) Nat. Sci. 2: 31.
Protoplastid Body and Metaplastid Cell. (J. E. S. Moore) Sci. Prog. 3: 323.
Protozoan, Daily Life of a. (C. F. Hodge and H. A. Aikins) Am. J. Psychol. 6: 524.
Proud Miss Fuller. (A. M. Peck) New Eng. M. n. s. 13: 117.
Proud Pynsents, The. (A. French) Scrib. M. 14: 549.
Prout, Ebenezer. Acad. 46: 454.
Prove it. (B. Coll) Idler, 2: 510.
Provence, Churches of. (M. G. Van Rensselaer) Cent. 27: 117.
— Embassy to. (T. A. Janvier) Cent. 23: 483-847. 24: 38.
— Impressions of. (A. M. F. Robinson) Contemp. 62: 647. Same art. Liv. Age, 195: 813. Same art. Ecl. M. 120: 56.
— Play in; Feast of the Marys. (J. Pennell) Cent. 21: 884.
— Poet's Wedding in. (C. A. Janvier) Critic, 26: 231.
— Poets of. (C. Hartog) Contemp. 66: 496. Same art. Liv. Age, 203: 562. Same art. Ecl. M. 123: 801.
— Some Legends of. (A. J. Dunn) Month, 83: 534.
Proverbs. Sat. R. 73: 739.
— and Phrases. (W. W. Newell) J. Am. Folk-Lore, 2: 153.
— — of Massachusetts. J. Am. Folk-Lore, 5: 60.
— English and Keltic. (J. Long) Folk-Lore Rec. 3: 56.
— Family Rhymes and. All the Year, 75: 498.
— in Chaucer. Chamb. J. 69: 574.
— Japanized Chinese. (Michitaro Hisa) J. Am. Folk-Lore, 9: 132.
Proverbs, Portuguese. (J. C. Branner) Overland, n. s. 21: 501.
— What are they? (C. A. Ward) Time, 8: 112.
Providence, R. I. (R. Grieve) New Eng. M. n. s. 13: 769.
— Merchants' Bank of. Bank. M. (N. Y.) 46: 644.
— Parks. (M. C. Robbins) Garden & F. 5: 590.
— Public Library Building. (W. E. Foster) Lib. J. 21: 364.
Providence Cottage; an Episode. (G. R. Burgin) Chamb. J. 70: 380.
Providences, Perplexing. (J. Watson) Sund. M. 25: 683.
Provident Loan Society of N. Y. Char. R. 3: 211.
Providential Leading; a story. (M. C. Parsons) New Eng. M. n. s. 6: 26.
Provincialism and London Culture. Spec. 75: 237.
— in America. (Caroline M. Beaumont) Bookman, 4: 232.
Provincialisms in England. Spec. 77: 640.
Provincials; Sketches of American Types. (Alice French) Scrib. M. 15: 565.
Prowl for the Picturesque, A. (C. S. Greene) Overland, n. s. 26: 205.
Prudhomme, Sully. Works. Spec. 69: 16.
Pruning of Fruit-trees, Some Points in. (T. H. Hoskins) Garden & F. 7: 144.
— of Trees. Garden & F. 5: 589.
— Unskilled. (C. S. Sargent) Garden & F. 7: 491.
Prussia, Archives of. (H. L. Osgood) Pol. Sci. Q. 8: 495.
— Gymnasia in, New Course of Study in. Acad. (Syr.) 7: 78.
— Kingdom of, Constitution of. (J. H. Robinson) Ann. Am. Acad. Pol. Sci. 5: supp.
— Liberty of Conscience in. (P. Carus) Open Court, 10: 4837.
— Schools in, Some Characteristics of. (E. J. Goodwin) Educa. R. 12: 453.
— under Frederick the Great, Tuttle's. (U. G. Weatherly) Am. Hist. R. 2: 145.
Prussing, Ernest. (W. M. Salter) Open Court, 3: 2023.
Pryde, James, and W. N. P. Nicholson. The Beggarstaff Brothers. Idler, 8: 519.
Prymers. (H. Littlehales) Antiq. n. s. 25: 99.
Psalmody, Rustic, Humors of. Cornh. 67: 56. Same art. Liv. Age, 196: 436.
Psalter, Greek, Early Papyrus Fragment of. Ath. '94, 2: 319.
— Mainz, of 1457. (Russell Martineau) Bibliographica, 1: 308.
— Translation of the Hebrew. Eng. R. 7: 71.
— Versification of, by Sternhold and Hopkins and their Followers. (J. C. Hadden) Gent. M. n. s. 56: 77.
Pseudonyms, American. Time, 17: 209.
— Value of a Pen Name. (M. E. J. Kelley) Writer, 6: 171.
Psiax, A Kylix by the Artist. (J. C. Hoppin) Am. J. Archæol. 10: 485.
Psyche and Eros, Some Ancient Representations of. (E. Lecky) M. of Art, 13: 386.
Psyche's Wanderings. (F. W. Cotton) Overland, n. s. 22: 481, 617.
Psychiatry and Criminal Anthropology. (C. Lombroso) Monist, 1: 186.
— or Psychological Medicine. (S. V. Clevenger) Open Court, 1: 207, 241.
Psychic, The, and the Spiritual. (M. B. Peeke) Arena, 13: 43.

Psychic, Autobiography of a. (E. Miner) Psychic. R. 1: 215.
— Experiences with a Private. (H. M. Poole) Psychic. R. 2: 256.
— Principles Governing. (J. E. Allen) Psychic. R. 2: 178.
— Sounds, Voices, and Physical Disturbances in the Presence of. (H. Garland) Psychic. R. 1: 226.
Psychic Dark Seances for Voices, etc. (B. O. Flower; H. Garland; T. E. Allen) Psychic. R. 2: 152.
Psychic Phenomena, Hudson on. (J. Jastrow) Dial (Ch.) 14: 359.
Psychic Realm, In the. (B. O. Flower) Arena, 10: 684.
Psychical Communication, A Story of. (L. Whiting) Arena, 13: 263.
Psychical Diagnosis of Disease. Psychic. R. 2: 118. — (L. B. Chandler) Psychic. R. 2: 214.
— Cases of. (L. A. Phillips) Psychic. R. 1: 106.
Psychical Experiences of a Clergyman. Psychic. R. 2: 200.
— Three. (M. E. Holden) Psychic. R. 2: 189.
Psychical Experiments at Milan. (A. M. Comey) Psychic. R. 2: 124.
Psychical Life, Central and Peripheral. (P. Carus) Open Court, 3: 1938.
— Nature of. (P. Carus) Open Court, 3: 1926.
— of Animals and Plants. (P. Carus) Open Court, 3: 1914.
— of Micro-organisms. (A. Binet) Open Court, 3: 1931. — (G. J. Romanes) Open Court, 3: 2063.
Psychical Phenomena, and Physical, Relations of. (A. E. Dolbear) Psychic. R. 2: 111.
— Implications of. (A. E. Dolbear) Psychic. R. 1: 7.
Psychical Research. (M. J. Savage) Arena, 5: 405 — 6: 677. — (O. J. Lodge) Psychic. R. 1: 60. — Ed. R. 181: 82. — (W. R. Newbold) Am. Natural. 29: 503. — (J. Cook) Our Day, 15: 233. — (W. James) Science, n. s. 3: 881. — (F. Podmore) Time, 23: 1251.
— and "Circles." (G. B. Stebbins) Psychic. R. 2: 42.
— and Science. (T. E. Allen) Psychic. R. 1: 52.
— Comedy of. (C. S. Minot) No. Am. 160: 217.
— Comparative. (A. Lang) Contemp. 64: 372 Same art. Ecl. M. 121: 548.
— Drift of. (F. W. H. Myers) National, 24: 190. Same art. Ecl. M. 123: 730. Same art. Our Day, 14: 91.
— Memory as a Factor in. (T. E. Allen) Psychic. R. 1: 366.
— Plea for. (M. M. Dawson) Psychic. R. 1: 335.
— Prejudice and. (T. E. Allen) Psychic. R. 1: 115.
— Society for. Time, 12: 410. — (F. Podmore) Time, 14: 192.
— Stead on. Sat. R. 76: 91.
— Ten Years in. (J. R. Cocke) Psychic. R. 2: 97.
— What it has accomplished. (W. James) Forum, 13: 727. — (F. Podmore) No. Am. 160: 331.
Psychical Science and Education. (A. F. Ewell) Psychic. R. 1: 293.
— Assured Results in. (M. J. Savage) Psychic. R. 1: 1.
Psychical States. In what Sense are they extended? (F. H. Bradley) Mind, 20: 225.
— What do we mean by the Intensity of? (F. H. Bradley) Mind, 20: 1.
Psychics and Physics. (C. W. Parsons) Psychic. R. 2: 144.
Psycho-folk-lorist, Protest of a. (A. Lang) Folk-Lore, 6: 236. — Reply. (E. Clodd) Folk-Lore, 6: 248.
Psychogenesis, Law of. (C. L. Morgan) Mind, 17: 72. — (D. J. Hill) Philos. R. 1: 481.
Psychography, Experiences in. (E. W. Gantt) Psychic. R. 2: 300.
— Experiment in. (S. Schindler; H. Garland) Psychic. R. 1: 131.
— in the Presence of Mr. Keeler. (A. R. Wallace) Psychic. R. 1: 16.
— Remarkable Cases. (B. O. Flower) Psychic. R. 1: 28.
Psychological Apparatus, New. (E. C. Sanford) Am. J. Psychol. 6: 575.
Psychological Laboratory, at Harvard. (H. Nichols) McClure, 1: 399.
— Equipment of. (E. C. Sanford) Am. J. Psychol. 5: 427.
Psychological Measurements. (E. W. Scripture) Philos. R. 2: 677.
Psychological Studies in Wellesley College. (M. W. Calkins) Pedagog. Sem. 3: 319.
Psychological Terms. (P. Carus) Open Court, 7: 3712.
Psychological Training, Need of. (E. W. Scripture) Science, 19: 127.
Psychologists, Congress of, in 1896. (J. M. Baldwin) Am. Natural. 30: 849.
Psychology. (E. B. Titchener) Science, n. s. 1: 426.
— Accurate Work in. (E. W. Scripture) Am. J. Psychol. 6: 427.
— Analytical, Stout's. Sat. R. 82: 195. — (H. M. Stanley) Dial (Ch.) 21: 254.
— and Education. (H. Nichols) Citizen, 1: 229.
— and Ethics in the High School. (C. S. Buell) Educa. 14: 36, 92.
— and Logic. (G. M. Stratton) Psychol. R. 3: 313. — (G. H. Howison) Psychol. R. 3: 652.
— and Metaphysics. (J. Watson) Philos. R. 2: 513.
— and Musical Composition. (F. Paulham) Music, 5: 28.
— and Pedagogy. (W. L. Gooding) School R. 3: 556.
— and Physiology. (G. S. Fullerton) Psychol. R. 3: 1.
— and Sociology. (L. F. Ward) Am. J. Sociol. 1: 618. — (S. N. Patten) Ann. Am. Acad. Pol. Sci. 8: 433.
— Applied, A Bit of. (H. W. Compton) Educa. R. 7: 343.
— Bibliography of Literature of, for 1895. (L. Farrand and H. C. Warren) Psychol. R. 3: supp.
— Biology, and Sociology, Relations of. (H. Spencer) Pop. Sci. Mo. 50: 163.
— Comparative, Morgan on. (W. R. Newbold) Am. Natural. 29: 388.
— — Problems of. (J. Jastrow) Pop. Sci. Mo. 42: 35.
— Desiderata in. (J. H. Hyslop) Philos. R. 4: 531.
— Doctrine of Conscious Elements. (E. B. Talbot) Philos. R. 4: 154.
— Epistemology, and Metaphysics. (A. Seth) Philos. R. 1: 129.
— — and Ontology, compared and distinguished. (S. H. Mellone) Mind, 19: 474.
— Experimental. (W. A. Stille) Nation, 54: 211. — (E. B. Titchener) Nat. Sci. 4: 446.
— — at the German Universities. (W. O. Krohn) Am. J. Psychol. 4: 585.
— — at Wellesley College. (M. W. Calkins) Am. J. Psychol. 5: 260.
— — International Congress of. (J. M. Baldwin) Nation, 55: 182.
— — Leipsic School of. (E. B. Titchener) Mind, 17: 206.
— for Normal Schools. (M. V. O'Shea) Educa. 16: 193.
— French and Italian. (J. Jastrow) Open Court, 3: 1956.
— Genetic, How to collect Data for Studies in. (Lillie A. Williams) Pedagog. Sem. 3: 419.
— German. (J. Jastrow) Open Court, 3: 1935.

Psychology in Great Britain and U. S. (J. Jastrow) Open Court, **3**: 2006.
— Individual. (C. Miles) Am. J. Psychol. **6**: 534.
— Infant. (Jas. Sully) Time, **13**: 447.
— Introspection and Experiment in. (A. Bain) Mind, **18**: 42.
— Ireland on. (J. Jastrow) Dial (Ch.) **16**: 46.
— Is it a Science? (G. T. Ladd) Psychol. R. **1**: 392.
— James on. Ath. '92, **2**: 246. — (J. Ward) Mind, **17**: 531. — (G. T. Ladd) Philos. R. **1**: 24. — Mind, **18**: 363, 509. — Reply, (F. H. Bradley) 366. — (W. L. Worcester) Monist, **2**: 417. **3**: 285. **4**: 129. — Reply. (W. James) Philos. R. **1**: 146.
— Külpe on. (M. Washburn) Philos. R. **3**: 345. — (E. B. Titchener) Dial (Ch.) **16**: 304. — (C. S. Peirce) Nation, **63**: 71.
— Ladd on. (J. P. Gordy) Philos. R. **1**: 299. — (J. G. Schurman) Philos. R. **13**: 13. — (E. B. Titchener) Philos. R. **3**: 723. — Psychol. R. **1**: 286.
— Marshall on. (B. I. Gilman) Philos. R. **3**: 342.
— Modern. (J. Ward) Mind, **18**: 54.
— — and Theories of Knowledge. (J. E. Creighton) Philos. R. **3**: 196.
— — Aspects of. (J. Jastrow) Open Court, **3**: 1907.
— — Growth and Spirit of. (E. A. Pace) Am. Cath. Q. **19**: 522.
— — Ward on. (C. A. Strong) Psychol. R. **1**: 73.
— Morgan's Introduction to. (W. R. Newbold) Am. Natural. **29**: 388.
— The New. (John Bigham) Meth. R. **56**: 345.
— — and Automatism. (A. Seth) Contemp. **63**: 555. Same art. Ecl. M. **120**: 740.
— — as a Basis of Education. (G. S. Hall) Forum, **17**: 710.
— — at Harvard University. (H. Münsterberg) Harv. Grad. M. **1**: 201.
— — Development of. (A. S. Weber) Ref. Q. **43**: 454.
— — H. von Helmholtz and. (C. Stumpf) Psychol. R. **2**: 1.
— — in Normal Schools. (L. A. Williams) Pedagog. Sem. **2**: 451.
— — in Undergraduate Work. (H. K. Wolfe) Psychol. R. **2**: 382.
— of Touch. (F. B. Dresslar) Am. J. Psychol. **6**: 313.
— Old and New. (P. Carus) Open Court, **4**: 2412.
— Past and Present. (J. M. Baldwin) Psychol. R. **1**: 363.
— Physiological, Laboratory Course in. (E. C. Sanford) Am. J. Psychol. **4**: 474. **7**: 412.
— Physiology, and Pedagogics. (T. Hughes) Am. Cath. Q. **19**: 790.
— Present State of. (W. R. Newbold) Am. Natural. **29**: 292.
— President's Address before American Psychological Association. (G. T. Ladd) Psychol. R. **1**: 1.
— Priority of Inner Experience. (W. Fite) Philos. R. **4**: 129.
— Progress of. (J. McK. Cattell) Pop. Sci. Mo. **43**: 779.
— Recent Books on. (E. B. Titchener) Dial (Ch.) **18**: 324.
— Relation of Logic to. (D. G. Ritchie) Philos. R. **5**: 585.
— Relations of Experimental. (E. A. Pace) Am. Cath. Q. **20**: 131.
— — to Other Sciences. (H. Griffing) Philos. R. **5**: 489.
— Scripture on. (W. M. Payne) Dial (Ch.) **19**: 287.
— Service of, to Education. (J. Sully) Educa. R. **4**: 313.
Psychology, Some Curiosities of Thinking. (M. A. Starr) Pop. Sci. Mo. **46**: 721.
— Standpoint of. (G. S. Fullerton) Psychol. R. **1**: 113.
— Sully on. (J. Brough) Acad. **42**: 113.
— Teaching of, to Teachers. (L. Witmer) Citizen, **2**: 158.
— 3d International Congress of. (J. M. Baldwin) Nation, **63**: 192.
— *vs.* Metaphysics. (I. Crook) Meth. R. **55**: 223.
— Vocabulary of. (E. B. Titchener) Am. J. Psychol. **7**: 78.
Psychometry, Science of. (J. R. Buchanan) Psychic. R. **1**: 101. **2**: 23.
— the Divinity in Man. (J. R. Buchanan) Psychic. R. **2**: 137.
— Experiments in. (M. M. Dawson) Psychic. R. **2**: 294.
— Illustrations of. (O. K. Crosby) Psychic. R. **2**: 193.
— The Sixth Sense. (P. Tyner) Arena, **10**: 37.
Psycho-physic Law, Psychometric Investigation of. (H. Münsterberg) Psychol. R. **1**: 45.
Psycho-physiology, Scope of. (C. L. Morgan) Nature, **49**: 504.
Ptah-hotep, the Radical of Ancient Egypt. (H. H. Bice) Open Court, **6**: 3303.
Pteridophyte Phylogeny. (C. MacMillan) Science, n. s. **2**: 183.
P'ti' Barouette; a story. (W. McLennan) Harper, **85**: 71.
Ptilolite and Mordenite, Note on Constitution of. (F. W. Clarke) Am. J. Sci. **144**: 101.
— New Occurrence of. (W. Cross and L. G. Eakins) Am. J. Sci. **144**: 96.
P'tit Matinic Monotone. (G. W. Edwards) Cent. **25**: 498, 857. **26**: 506.
Ptolemies, Laws of Succession among. (J. P. Mahaffy) Ath. '96, **2**: 164.
— Mahaffy on. (J. H. Breasted) Dial (Ch.) **20**: 359.
Ptolemy, Claudius, and his Works. (W. T. Lynn) Nature, **53**: 489.
Public, The, as Fetish. (A. B. Walkley) Theatre, **33**: 283.
— An Unregenerate. (E. Kuhe) Theatre, **34**: 208.
Public Art League of the U. S. Am. Arch. **51**: 86.
Public Building, Secretary of the Treasury on. Am. Arch. **51**: 34.
Public Buildings and Legislators. Am. Arch. **51**: 61.
— and Senators. Am. Arch. **44**: 28.
— U. S. Government Bureau of, Proposed. (F. Sewall) Am. Arch. **40**: 86.
Public Confession, A. (E. Mackubin) Atlan. **77**: 367.
Public Documents, U. S., Distribution of. (E. S. Morse) Pop. Sci. Mo. **45**: 459. Same art. Lib. J. **19**: 263.
— Printing and Distribution of. Lib. J. **20**: 13.
Public House, English. (A. Shadwell) National, **25**: 374.
— A Model, and its Lessons. (A. Shadwell) National, **25**: 632.
Public House Question. (F. J. Cestr) Jurid. R. **6**: 101.
Public Improvement, The Art of. (M. C. Robbins) Atlan. **78**: 742.
Public Institutions, Private Visitation of. (L. Twining) Char. R. **3**: 183.
Public Lands in Massachusetts. (C. S. Sargent) Garden & F. **7**: 351.
— in the U. S., Vacant, in 1893. (F. H. Newell) Science, **21**: 198.
Public Land Sales. Bank. M. (N. Y.) **50**: 189.
Public Library Limitations. Lit. W. (Bost.) **27**: 8.
See Libraries.

Public Officials, Payment of. (H. E. Foster) Am. J. Pol. 4: 611.
Public Opinion and the Law as Factors in Social Control. (E. A. Ross) Am. J. Sociol. 1: 753.
— Guidance of. (J. W. Jenks) Am. J. Sociol. 1: 158.
— Increasing Power of. (J. Quincy) Pub. Opin. 15: 478.
Public School Education in England, Products of. (A. W. Ready) New R. 15: 422.
— Scope of. (J. L. Spalding) Cath. World, 60: 758.
Public School Pioneering in New York and Massachusetts. (A. S. Draper) Educa. R. 3: 313. — Reply. (G. H. Martin) Educa. R. 4: 34. — Rejoinder. (A. S. Draper) Educa. R. 4: 241. — (G. H. Martin) Educa. R. 5: 232. — (A. S. Draper) Educa. R. 5: 345.
Public School Question. Pub. Opin. 16: 382, 431, 496.
Public School Reform in New York City. (S. H. Olin) Educa. R. 8: 1.
Public School System, Education of. (G. Buck) Am. J. Pol. 4: 294.
— Moral Problem in. (H. B. Ryley) School R. 3: 281.
Public Schools and Army Competitive Examinations. (H. Knollys) Un. Serv. (Phila.) 14: 160.
— and Good Citizenship. (C. R. Skinner) Am. M. Civics, 7: 87.
— and the Politician. (L. H. Jones) Atlan. 77: 810.
— and the Teachers. (Harriet H. Heller) Educa. 17: 165.
— Boston. Lend a H. 14: 126.
— Case of the. 1. The Witness of the Teacher. (G. S. Hall) Atlan. 77: 402.
— — 2. Teacher's Social and Intellectual Position. (F. W. Atkinson) Atlan. 77: 534.
— Civics and. (C. Greeley) Lend a H. 13: 189.
— Criminal Crowding of. (J. H. Penniman) Forum, 19: 289. 20: 547.
— Ethical Problem of. (W. F. Slocum, jr.) Atlan. 73: 674.
— Ethics of. (P. W. Search) Educa. R. 11: 134.
— for the Privileged Few. (C. S. Smart) Arena, 10: 462.
— Godless, Defence of. (W. W. Quatermass) Am. J. Pol. 4: 574.
— in England. Harper, 84: 722. — Sat. R. 76: 674.
— — Condition of, in 1892. Ath. '92, 2: 131.
— — in 1893. Ath. '93, 2: 129.
— — Methods and Morals of. New R. 9: 34.
— — — Defence of. (J. E. C. Welldon) New R. 9: 248.
— in Minnesota, Roman Catholic Church and. (L. B. Speare) Our Day, 9: 86.
— in the U. S., Encyclical Letter on. Am. Cath. Q. 18: 642. — Pub. Opin. 15: 301.
— — Fads in. (H. E. Starrett) Arena, 7: 603.
— — to free them from Politics. (J. M. Rice) Forum, 16: 500.
— — New Education and. (B. O. Flower) Arena, 8: 511.
— — Origin of. (A. D. Mayo) Educa. 12: 552.
— — Pope and. (W. J. Stillman) Nation, 57: 133.
— — Question of. Pub. Opin. 16: 257, 282.
— — Religious Instruction in. (J. H. Crooker) Westm. 144: 203.
— — Roman Catholics and. (J. Conway) Educa. R. 4: 236. — Reply. (C. B. Pallen) Educa. R. 4: 456.
— — Satolli and. (J. Cook) Our Day, 12: 228.
— — a Summary. (J. M. Rice) Forum, 15: 504.
— — System of. (J. M. Rice) Forum, 14: 145–429.
— — — Flaw in. (S. Schindler) Arena, 6: 59.
— Management of. (L. J. Block) Educa. 15: 199.
— Music in. (A. T. Cringan) Music, 2: 28.
— — Is it a Fad? Music, 3: 693.
Public Schools, Music in, A Teacher of. (G. A. Veazie, jr.) Music, 3: 175.
— Nation's Safeguard. (M. C. Jones) Am. J. Pol. 3: 643.
— of Boston. (J. M. Rice) Forum, 14: 753.
— of Chicago and St. Paul. (J. M. Rice) Forum, 15: 200.
— of Minneapolis, and others. (J. M. Rice) Forum, 15: 362.
— of New York City. (J. M. Rice) Forum, 14: 616.
— of Philadelphia. (J. M. Rice) Forum, 15: 31.
— Patriotism in. (C. P. Colegrove) Am. M. Civics, 9: 120.
— The Politician and. (L. H. Jones) Atlan. 77: 810.
— Pope's Pontifical Letter on. (G. Koerner) Open Court, 7: 3728.
— Popular Science in. (E. V. Brown) Educa. 16: 421.
— Recent Progress in. (W. J. Harris) Harper, 90: 789.
— Religious Teaching in. (L. Abbott) Cent. 27: 943.
— J. M. Rice on. Educa. 14: 530, 593. 15: 37–206.
— Roman Catholic, Failure of. (W. Hoyt) Our Day, 10: 721.
— Social Mission of. (W. D. Hyde) Educa. R. 12: 221.
— *vs.* Religious Education. (E. D. Daniels) N. Church R. 2: 12.
Public Speaking and Rhetoric in the American College. (H. A. Frink) Educa. 13: 129.
Public Ways, Use of, by Private Corporations. (S. L. Powers) Arena, 5: 681.
Public Works, Economics of Engineering. (H. N. Ogden) Science, n. s. 2: 539.
Publicans and Sinners; a chapter in the life of Mrs. Susan Piper; a story. Temp. Bar, 107: 525.
Publication, Date of, What is? (H. H. Field) Science, n. s. 2: 303.
Publicity, The Fetich of. (J. Macdonnell) 19th Cent. 17: 647.
Publishers and Authors; a Persistent Literary Superstition. (R. Ogden) Nation, 54: 297.
— — Relations between. (J. N. Porter) Time, 16: 399.
— and the Public. (H. M. Hoke) Writer, 9: 78.
— of 18th Century, Tricks of. Bookworm, 6: 305.
Publishing a Book. (G. H. Putnam) Writer, 9: 21.
— Hardships of. (W. Heinemann) Ath. '92, 2: 779, 888. — (W. Besant; A. M. Burges) Ath. '92, 2: 819. — (A. D. Innes) Ath. '92, 2: 855. — (W. Besant) Ath. '92, 2: 888.
— Random, and Rules of Priority. (T. R. R. Stebbing) Nat. Sci. 5: 337.
— The Revolution in Grub Street. (H. D. Traill) Fortn. 64: 78. Same art. Ecl. M. 125: 330.
Puckle's Club. (Austin Dobson) Bibliographica, 2: 407.
Pudd'nhead Wilson. (S. L. Clemens) Cent. 25: 233–817. 26: 17–232.
— Dramatized. Bost. 3: 382.
Pueblo Indians. (C. F. Lummis) Scrib. M. 12: 361.
— Discovery of. (S. D. Peet) Am. Antiq. 17: 339.
— Explorations among. (S. D. Peet) Am. Antiq. 18: 228.
— on the Northwest Coast. (J. Wickersham) Am. Antiq. 18: 21.
Pueblo Lands of San Francisco. (E. R. Taylor) Overland, n. s. 27: 22.
Pueblo Plan of Individual Teaching. (P. W. Search) Educa. R. 7: 154 — 8: 84.
Pueblos, Ancient and Modern, compared. (S. D. Peet) Am. Antiq. 18: 333.
Pueraria Thunbergiana. Garden & F. 6: 504.
Puerco Ungulates, Structure and Affinity of. (C. Earle) Science, 22: 49.

Puffery, Golden Age of. (Jas. L. Ford) Bach. of Arts, **1**: 502.
Pugilism, Lessons in Health from. (C. Barnard) Chaut. **15**: 667.
— Newspaper Apologies for. (W. Hoyt) Our Day, **11**: 432.
— *vs.* Progress. (C. Greeley) Lend a H. **15**: 437.
See Prize-fighting.
Pul, Jareb, Tiglath-Pileser. (J. Horner) Meth. R. **54**: 928.
Pullen, Eugene H. Bank. M. (N. Y.) **51**: 509.
Pullen, Robert. (J. H. Round) Ath. '**96**, **2**: 601.
Pullman, George M., with portrait. (R. H. Titherington) Munsey, **11**: 253.
— and Paternalism. (C. H. Eaton) Am. J. Pol. **5**: 571.
Pullman, Ill. How it was built. Soc. Econ. **7**: 85.
Pullman Car, In the. (E. W. Sanborn) New Eng. M. n. s. **12**: 467.
Pullman Strike. *See* Strike.
Pulpit, American, Decline of. (G. M. Royce) Forum, **16**: 568.
— and Ethics. (J. H. Clifford) Eth. Rec. **1**: 48.
— and the Press. (J. Leatham) Westm. **137**: 601.
— and Social Reform. (W. Gladden) Chr. Lit. **14**: 164.
— Elocution of. (J. V. O'Connor) Cath. World, **56**: 175.
— The Need of the. (Mary H. Norris) Meth. R. **55**: 430.
— The New. (H. R. Haweis) No. Am. **160**: 172.
— — A Word about. (C. E. Smith) No. Am. **160**: 508.
— The Old, and the New. (C. D. Foss) No. Am. **160**: 293.
— A Patriotic. (F. W. Hamilton) Am. J. Pol. **5**: 14.
— Poets of. All the Year, **71**: 341, 366.
— Power of. (J. G. Woolley) Our Day, **16**: 506.
— — Elements of. (B. D. Thomas) Bapt. R. **14**: 27.
— Press, and Pew. (J. R. Creighton) Meth. R. **55**: 68.
— Topics of To-day. (W. C. Preston) Sund. M. **25**: 289.
— Transformation of. (R. Ogden) Nation, **58**: 62.
Pulpit-censorship in New Amsterdam. (A. M. Dyer) Am. Hist. Reg. **1**: 507.
Pulpit Interchange, Question of. Chr. Lit. **11**: 16.
Pulpit-notices, Tyranny of. (M. G. Hansen) Ref. Q. **42**: 122.
Pulpits. (S. Baring-Gould) Sund. M. **24**: 93.
— Old. Am. Arch. **50**: 137.
Pulque, National Drink of Mexico. (A. Inkersley) Overland, n. s. **24**: 255.
Puma, The. (F. W. True) Science, **19**: 169.
Pump, Air-lift, Theory of. (E. G. Harris) J. Frankl. Inst. **140**: 32.
— Automatic Mercury Vacuum. (M. I. Pupin) Am. J. Sci. **149**: 19.
— Centrifugal, at Mare Island Navy Yard, Cal. (J. H. Cooper) J. Frankl. Inst. **138**: 251.
— A New Mine-. Cassier, **2**: 151.
Pumping Engine, of G. F. Blake Mfg. Co., Duty Trials of. (C. H. Peabody) J. Frankl. Inst. **135**: 167, 327.
— Steam, Modern. (W. M. Barr) Engin. M. **5**: 451, 593.
Pumping Machinery. (G. L. Clark) Cassier, **6**: 34.
— Electric. (C. A. Hague) Cassier, **9**: 257.
Pumpkin. Is it an American Plant? (J. W. Harshberger) Science, n. s. **3**: 889.
Pumps, Electric. (F. M. Wheeler) Cassier, **1**: 74.
— Some New. (G. L. Clark) Cassier, **3**: 298.
"Punch," The Life of, Spielmann's. Blackw. **158**: 866. Same art. Liv. Age, **208**: 82. — (R. Sturgis) Nation, **62**: 237. — Sat. R. **81**: 306.
— Prototypes of. Cornh. **71**: 305. Same art. Ecl. M. **124**: 536.
— Rivals of. (M. H. Spielmann) National, **25**: 654. Same art. Liv. Age, **206**: 563.
"Punch" Dinner, The. (M. H. Spielmann) M. of Art, **17**: 397. **18**: 89.
Punishment as seen by Children. (E. Barnes) Pedagog. Sem. **3**: 235.
— Darwinism and. (F. H. Bradley) Int. J. Ethics, **4**: 269.
— Evolution of. (E. B. Tylor) Acad. **49**: 49.
— Failure of. (Lady Cook) Green Bag, **7**: 454.
— of Criminals, Improvements in. (W. W. McLane) And. R. **17**: 393.
— Rationale of. (C. P. Woolley) Open Court, **1**: 134.
— Retributive. Spec. **73**: 173.
— Theory of. (J. Seth) Int. J. Ethics, **2**: 232.
Punishments, Ancient, in Massachusetts. Nat'l M. (N. Y. '91) **15**: 67.
— Military. (J. Mew) Un. Serv. M. **6**: 196.
Punjaub, In the. (J. H. Wick) Sund. M. **24**: 687.
— A Khud in. (E. Carrington) Leis. Hour, **45**: 49.
— Lahore and the. (E. L. Weeks) Harper, **89**: 651.
Punnett, John Trefusis. Acad. **43**: 417.
Punta Arenas: the Southernmost City in South America. Liv. Age, **202**: 380.
Pupasse. (G. King) Cent. **24**: 889.
Pupilla Oculi. (C. F. S. Warren) Bookworm, **4**: 117.
Puppett Show, Greek. All the Year, **74**: 206.
Purcell, Henry. (J. J. Shedlock) Acad. **48**: 443. — (C. H. H. Perry) National, **26**: 339. — (F. J. Crowest) Blackw. **158**: 819. Same art. Liv. Age, **208**: 149. — Temp. Bar, **107**: 593.
— and his Times. Sat. R. **80**: 758.
— Centenary of. Am. Arch. **51**: 39.
— Our Last Great Musician. (J. F. Runciman) New R. **13**: 599.
Purdue University. (W. F. M. Goss) Cassier, **2**: 249.
Pureney, Thomas; Prisoner Ordinary. (C. Whibley) New R. **12**: 570.
Purism and Impurism. (F. Morgan) Writer, **8**: 177.
Puritan Maiden's Diary. (A. E. H. Slicer) New Eng. M. n. s. **11**: 20.
Puritanism, Influence on National Character. (A. M. Earle) 19th Cent. **38**: 312.
— with the Chill on, and with the Chill off. (W. G. Blaikie) Good Words, **35**: 610.
Puritans and Jews. (J. G. Dow) Jew. Q. **3**: 52.
— and Play-actors. (W. Wheater) Gent. M. n. s. **50**: 178.
— as Christmas-haters. (S. Foxe) Nat'l M. (N. Y. '91) **17**: 150.
— Characteristics of. (B. Wendell) Harv. Mo. **14**: 45.
— in Holland, England, and America, Campbell's. (W. Walker) Nation, **55**: 147. — (J. A. Doyle) Pol. Sci. Q. **8**: 336.
— in New England. Lond. Q. **87**: 328.
Purity, Knowledge the Preserver of. (L. E. Scammon) Arena, **8**: 702.
— Moral, in Children. (A. H. Heinemann) Open Court, **3**: 1607.
— The Problem of. (W. S. Lilly) New R. **12**: 78.
Purloined Will, The. (H. Kern) Chamb. J. **73**: 541. Same art. Liv. Age, **210**: 817.
Purple Rhododendron, A. (J. Fox) Southern M. **3**: 584.

Purses, Pockets, and Personal Receptacles. (S. W. Beck) Cosmopol. **14**: 656.
Purveyance, English Custom of. Chamb. J. **70**: 508.
Pusey, Edward Bouverie. (G. A. Simcox) Acad. **44**: 359. — Church Q. **37**: 393. — Lond. Q. **81**: 205. — (C. K. Paul) Month, **79**: 528.
— and Mrs. Besant. (C. Chapman) M. Chr. Lit. **5**: 385.
— and Bishop Wilberforce. (R. G. Wilberforce) 19th Cent. **38**: 57.
— Liddon's Life of. Ath. '93, **2**: 481. — Sat. R. **76**: 414. — Spec. **71**: 548, 582. — (J. Gibb) Crit. R. **4**: 3. — Ed. R. **180**: 1. — Quar. **179**: 83. — (G. A. Simcox) Acad. **46**: 439. — Sat. R. **78**: 409. — (J. W. Chadwick) Nation, **58**: 51. — Ath. '94, **2**: 485. — (C. A. L. Richards) Dial (Ch.) **16**: 14. — Cath. World, **58**: 569. — (J. P. Sheraton) Presb. & Ref. R. **6**: 161. — Church Q. **39**: 336. — (B. B. Warfield) Presb. & Ref. R. **7**: 347.
Putnam, Mrs. George Haven. Acad. **48**: 110.
Putnam, Herbert. Critic, **26**: 187.
Putnam, Gen. Israel, Wolf-den of, Park at. (M. C. Robbins) Garden & F. **6**: 212.
Puvis de Chavannes, Pierre C. (K. Cox) Cent. **29**: 558. — (J. Cartwright) Art J. **48**: 190. — (C. Phillips) M. of Art, **8**: 60. — (B. Karageorgevitch) M. of Art, **17**: 73.
— Recent Work of. (J. Bernac) Art J. **47**: 47.
Puzzle, The. Cornh. **66**: 493.
Pygidium of Triarthrus, Appendages of. (C. E. Beecher) Am. J. Sci. **147**: 298.
Pygmies, Existence of. (D. MacRitchie) Acad. **47**: 37.
— — South of Mt. Atlas. (R. G. Haliburton) Asia. R. **14**: 79.
— in Europe. (J. Kollmann) Anthrop. J. **25**: 117.
— of Africa. (J. D. Caton) Atlan. **71**: 736.
— of Andaman Islands. (W. C. Preston) Sund. M. **23**: 600.
— of the Congo. Around World, **2**: 3.
— Quatrefages on. (W. H. Flower) Nature, **52**: 25.
Pygmies' Isle in the Hebrides. (D. MacRitchie) Antiq. n. s. **31**: 22.
See Dwarfs.
Pygmy, The, in the United States. (J. Weir, jr.) Pop. Sci. Mo. **49**: 47.
Pygmy Races of Men. (F. Starr) No. Am. **162**: 414.
Pyle, H., with portrait. Bk. Buyer, **5**: 335.
Pylos and Sphakteria, Topography of Region of. (R. M. Burrows) J. Hel. Stud. **16**: 1.
Pyramids, The. (C. W. Wood) Argosy, **56**: 129, 298.
— and their Builders. Eng. R. **5**: 87.
— Brick, of Dahchour, Egypt. Illus. Archæol. **2**: 111.
— of Gizeh, Road to. (C. H. Dana) Garden & F. **7**: 232.
Pyramid Builders and Temple Builders, Early. (J. N. Lockyer) Nature, **48**: 55.
Pyrenees, French. Church Q. **42**: 51. Same art. Liv. Age, **209**: 515.
— A Protestant Church in the. (W. Webster) Acad. **42**: 189.
— Through the, in December. (S. J. Weyman) Eng. Illust. **10**: 256.
Pyrethrums. (E. O. Orpet) Garden & F. **5**: 103.
Pyrochroa, Larva and Pupa of. (H. F. Wickham) Am. Natural. **28**: 816.
Pyrogravure. (P. G. Hamerton) Portfo. **23**: 165.
Pyroxenic Rock (azure-blue), from the Middle Gila, N. M. (G. P. Merrill and R. L. Packard) Am. J. Sci. **143**: 279.
Pyrus Betulifolia. (C. S. Sargent) Garden & F. **7**: 224.
Pythagorean Fancies. (H. Arthur) Canad. M. **5**: 184.
Pythagorics. (C. S. Peirce) Open Court, **6**: 3375.
Pytheas, the Discoverer of Britain. (C. R. Markham) Geog. J. **1**: 504.
Python, Power of. Spec. **73**: 556.
Pyx, Trial of the. Chamb. J. **69**: 454.

"Q." *See* Couch, Quiller.
Qirqisani, the Karaite, and Jewish Sects. (W. Bacher) Jew. Q. **7**: 687.
Quacks and the Reason of them. (A. Cartaz) Pop. Sci. Mo. **48**: 821.
— Medical Etiquette, and Secret Remedies. (E. Hart) Forum, **16**: 195.
Quadrilles at the Court of Napoleon I. (F. Masson) Cosmopol. **16**: 529.
Quadruple Alliance and Peace. Contemp. **66**: 761.
Quail and Quail Shooting. (J. A. A. Robinson) Overland, n. s. **20**: 285. — (E. W. Sandys) Outing, **21**: 25.
Quail, Blue, of the Cactus. (F. Remington) Harper, **93**: 651.
— Day with. (E. W. Sandys) Outing, **21**: 112.
— — in North Carolina. (C. Prescott) Outing, **21**: 373.
— Our National Game-bird. (C. D. Lanier) Harper, **87**: 672.
— Pennsylvania. Outing, **25**: 205.
— Valley, of California. (T. S. Van Dyke) Outing, **19**: 485.
Quail-shooting. (C. D. Wilson) Lippinc. **54**: 806.
"Quaker City," Cruise of. (M. M. Fairbanks) Chaut. **14**: 429.
Quaker Meeting, A, in England. (E. Pyne) Liv. Age, **192**: 36.
Quakers, Early Welsh, and their Emigration to Pennsylvania. (J. J. Levick) Pennsyl. M. **17**: 385.
— in Pennsylvania, 1682–1776. (A. C. Applegarth) J. H. Univ. Studies, **10**: nos. 8–9. — (A. C. Applegarth) M. Am. Hist. **28**: 353.
— Nantucket, in France. Atlan. **72**: 431.
— Persecution of, by the Pilgrims. (G. F. Tucker) Nat'l M. (N. Y. '91) **15**: 371.
— Southern, and Slavery, Weeks on. (W. P. Trent) Am. Hist. R. **2**: 178. — (G. W. Julian) Dial (Ch.) **21**: 38.
— What makes a Friend? (J. J. Cornell) Chaut. **19**: 45.
"Quamvis," Historical Syntax of. (H. D. Wild) Am. J. Philol. **17**: 347.
Quandary of the Bishop; a story. (H. B. M. Watson) New R. **12**: 113.
Quantock Hills, Witchery of the. (W. Greswell) Temp. Bar, **104**: 523.
Quarantine at New York. (W. T. Jenkins) No. Am. **155**: 585.
— — A Month of. (E. L. Godkin) No. Am. **155**: 737.
— National. Pub. Opin. **14**: 295, 323, 393.
— — Constitutionality of. (E. L. Godkin) Nation, **56**: 78.
— — Necessity for. (E. O. Shakespeare) Forum, **14**: 579.
Quaritch, Bernard. Bookworm, **2**: 33. — Walford's Antiq. **2**: 238.
Quarry at Piney Branch, D. C., and its Implements. (T. Wilson) Am. Natural. **30**: 873.
Quarrying by Fire of Granite in India. (H. Warth) Nature, **51**: 272.
— Methods of the Ancients. (W. F. Durfee) Engin. M. **7**: 474.
— Modern Methods of. (W. L. Saunders) Cassier, **2**: 338.
Quarterlies, Future of the. Spec. **75**: 551.
Quartz from North Carolina. (H. A. Miers) Am. J. Sci. **146**: 420.

Quartz Bowlder in the Sharon (O.) Coal. (E. Orton) Am. J. Sci. 144: 62.
Quashie. (F. Banfield) Gent. M. n. s. 50: 73.
Quaternary Depòsits of Russia, etc., Nikitin on. (A. A. Wright) Am. J. Sci. 145: 459.
Quaternary Time divisible in Three Periods. (W. Upham) Am. Natural. 28: 980.
Quatrefages, Jean L. A. de. Ath. '92, 1: 91.
Quebec. (B. J. Reilly) Cath. World, 63: 157.
— and the Early American Revolution, Coffin's. (W. L. M. King) J. Pol. Econ. 5: 105.
— Castle of St. Louis. (J. M. Le Moine) Canad. M. 6: 106.
— — under the Roses. (J. M. Le Moine) Canad. M. 6: 275.
— — Historic. (E. S. Tupper) Chaut. 15: 422.
— a Literary Rendezvous. (J. A. Cooper) Canad. M. 7: 511.
— Virginia and the Quebec Bill. (J. Winsor) Am. Hist. R. 1: 436.
— Winter Carnival at. (F. Fenton) Canad. M. 2: 487.
Quebec: a Discontented Province. (H. L. Nelson) Harper, 86: 873.
— Education in. (F. W. Grey) Month, 84: 75, 165.
— Election in, 1892. And. R. 17: 207, 405.
Quebec Act and the American Revolution. (V. Coffin) Yale R. 4: 171.
Queen Isabella; a poem. (M. B. Smith) Canad. M. 1: 701.
Queen Mary at Fotheringay; a poem. (H. E. Boulton) M. of Art, 10: 308.
Queen Mary's Holdfast; a story. Ecl. M. 120: 477.
Queen Mary's Jewels. (Andrew Lang) Good Words, 36: 372.
Queen of Clubs. (E. O. White) Atlan. 73: 653.
Queen of Holland and her Dolls. (W. Wright) Sund. M. 23: 327.
Queen of the May; a tale. (M. P. Williams) Belgra. 90: 154.
Queen of Portugal's Lover; a story. (P. Andreae) Eng. Illust. 15: 194.
Queen Till; a story. (Mary Pearle) Bost. 3: 71.
Queen's Marie, Mystery of. (A. Lang) Blackw. 158: 381.
Queen's Messenger, English. Quar. 174: 372. Same art. Liv. Age, 194: 26.
Queen's Reporter, The. (M. MacDonagh) Good Words, 36: 315.
Queen's Servant in Carglen, A; a story. (A. Gordon) Gent. M. n. s. 48: 61. Same art. Liv. Age, 192: 715.
Queen's Triplets, The; a story. (I. Zangwill) Idler, 2: 583.
Queen's University and its Founders. (J. J. Bell) Canad. M. 7: 19.
Queens of Europe, with portraits. (Marg. Field) Munsey, 11: 256.
— Some Unhappy. (G. Holme) Munsey, 14: 164.
Queensbury, 4th Duke of, Memoir of, by Robinson. Sat. R. 80: 15.
Queensland, Facts about. (R. Newton) Westm. 145: 568.
— Floods in, 1893. (H. O. Forbes) Geog. J. 1: 239. — Dub. R. 112: 458.
— Labor Party in. (A. Bertram) Contemp. 69: 399.
— Secret of her Downfall. (H. W. B. MacKay) Westm. 144: 152.
— To, in Search of Ceratodus. (W. B. Spencer) Nature, 46: 305.
— Wage-earners in. (G. M. L. Lester) Econ. R. 4: 345.
Queer Case, A. (E. S. Bates) Overland, n. s. 21: 613.
Quélern. The Gibraltar of France. (E. H. Barker) Temp. Bar, 106: 176.
Quenston Heights; a poem. (J. L. Kenway) Canad. M. 3: 540.
Quesnay, François. (S. Bauer) Econ. J. 5: 660.
— Tableau économique. (S. Bauer) Econ. J. 5: 1.
Question, A. (J. Vernon) Overland, n. s. 25: 207.
Question in Art, A; a story. (R. W. Herrick) Scrib. M. 17: 514.
Question of Courage. (F. Lynde) Lippinc. 54: 435.
Question of Penmanship. (L. B. Walford) Longm. 20: 159.
Question of Responsibility; a story. (I. Clark) Lippinc. 55: 110.
Questioning, Children's; Educative Value of. (H. L. Clapp) Pop. Sci. Mo. 49: 799.
Questions of the Day. (S. Low) Harper, 91: 142.
Quête de L'Enfant Jésus; a story. (H. Beaugrand) Canad. M. 2: 117.
Quibbling, Notes on. (G. H. Westley) Green Bag, 8: 106.
Quiberon, The Battle of, and its Influence on British Naval History. Macmil. 73: 420.
Quickhatch or Wolverine. *See* Wolverine.
Quicksands of Morecambe Bay. Sat. R. 77: 492.
Quicksands of Pactolus, The. (H. A. Vachell) Overland, n. s. 26: 182-641. 27: 42-619. 28: 17-262.
Quid mihi et tibi, Mulier? (A. E. Breen) Am. Cath. Q. 20: 399.
Quilter, H. Preferences. Spec. 69: 852.
Quimby, James M., with portrait. Nat'l M. (N. Y. '91) 19: 200.
Quimperlé, Finistère. (M. Creach) Belgra. 79: 269.
Quincy, Dorothy, Three Letters to. (H. C. Walsh) New Eng. M. n. s. 6: 531.
Quincy, Mass., Adams's Study of. (W. Walker) Yale R. 1: 368.
— Municipal Government in. (C. F. Adams) Forum, 14: 282. — (W. P. Garrison) Nation, 55: 197.
Quinn, Hannah. (K. T. Hinkson) New R. 14: 531.
Quintelle; a story. Belgra. 82: 90.
Quintilian, Peterson's. Spec. 68: 124.
Quintus Knox. (E. H. L. Watson) Gent. M. n. s. 55: 348.
Quiquern; a story. (R. Kipling) McClure, 5: 552.
Quirigua, Ruins of. (J. R. Chandler) Science, n. s. 3: 832.
Quite Inexplicable; a story. All the Year, 73: 33.
Quito. Sat. R. 77: 41-65.
Quivíra Myth, The. (C. F. Lummis) Scrib. M. 13: 466.
Quixotry. Spec. 76: 336.
Quong Lee; a story. (F. Lynde) Lippinc. 55: 246.
Quong Tin; a story of New York's Chinese Quarter. Idler, 2: 617.
Quotation. Temp. Bar, 102: 43. Same art. Ecl. M. 122: 781.
Quotations, Conversational. (C. Hussey) Chamb. J. 72: 591.
— Familiar, Traced Homewards. Macmil. 71: 47. — Same art. Ecl. M. 124: 89.
— Hackneyed. Spec. 69: 254.
— Happy, in Parliament. Liv. Age, 205: 317.
— Wood's and Bartlett's Dictionaries of. (W. H. Hills) Writer, 7: 90.

R, Sounds of. (A. M. Bell) Science, 20: 217.
Rabbeno, Ugo, on American Commercial Policy. (F. W. Taussig) Q. J. Econ. 10: 102.
Rabbis, Jewish, Great. (C. H. H. Wright) 19th Cent. 31: 905. Same art. Liv. Age, 194: 225.
Rabbit of the World, A; Moorland Idyll. (G. Allen) Eng. Illust. 12: no. 4, 94.

Rabbit Driving in the San Joaquin Valley. (C. S. Greene) Overland, n. s. 20: 49.
Rabbit Farming. Spec. 70: 700.
Rabbit Hunt, Pueblo. J. Am. Folk-Lore, 8: 324.
Rabbit Shooting. (T. E. Kebbel) Time, 20: 263.
Rabbit Woman, The; a story. (E. D'E. Keeling) Ecl. M. 126: 845.
Rabbiting with Ferrets and Greyhounds. (H. Rave) Outing, 27: 410.
Rabbits, Australian. Chamb. J. 71: 443.—(J. N. Ingram) Lippinc. 52: 751.
— for Food. Sat. R. 75: 410.
— in New Zealand. All the Year, 70: 340.—(J. N. Ingram) Lippinc. 54: 696.
Rabelais, François. Spec. 70: 290.
— at Home. Blackw. 155: 504.
— New Illustrated Edition. (F. Watt) Art J. 44: 379. —M. of Art, 9: 334.
Rabies, Skunk as a Source of. (V. L. Kellogg) Am. Natural. 29: 242.
Race by Rail. (F. M. Bird) Lippinc. 50: 242.
Race for Life, A. Macmil. 75: 133.
Race with the River; a story. (L. C. Shirley) Outing, 24: 47.
Race-prejudice. (M. Bloomfield) New World, 4: 23.
Racehorse, Decadence of English. (S. W. Reeves) Time, 1: 728.
— Warburton on the. Sat. R. 73: 752.
Racemosa; Snow-creeper of India. (A. B. Westland) Garden & F. 7: 56.
Races, Mixture of. (R. Mayo-Smith) Yale R. 3: 166.
— — Ancestry of Genius. (H. Ellis) Atlan. 71: 382.
— — and National Character. (L. R. Harley) Pop. Sci. Mo. 47: 86.
— Three Ruling, of Future. (H. Elsdale) Un. Serv. M. 4: 333-473.
Races. *See* Peoples.
Rachel and Leah. Macmil. 72: 362. Same art. Liv. Age, 207: 201. Same art. Ecl. M. 126: 354.
Rachel; a story. (E. E. Wilson) McClure, 6: 483.
Racine, Jean. Time, 13: 311.
— Shakespeare and. (P. Verlaine) Fortn. 62: 440.
— Some Thoughts on. Macmil. 74: 227.
Racing and Racing Men. (C. F. Gates) Overland, n. s. 28: 539.
— Our Turf's Transition. (F. Trevelyan) Outing, 28: 221.
— Team. (S. Scoville, jr.) Outing, 23: 151.
Racing Recollections, Custance's. Sat. R. 77: 95.
Racing Sandbaggers. (C. H. Chapman) Outing, 28: 114.
Radàmar I., King of Madagascar. (A. Zimmern) Temp. Bar, 104: 262.
Radcliffe, Ann. *See* Mowlson, Ann, Lady.
Radcliffe College. (J. B. Warner) Harv. Grad. M. 2: 329.—(H. L. Reed) New Eng. M. n. s. 11: 609.
— Fay House of. (A. Gilman) Harv. Grad. M. 4: 555.
Radcliffe Pedigree. (H. H. Edes) N. E. Reg. 50: 30.
Radegonda, Queen, Idyl of. (S. C. Upton) Cosmopol. 15: 363.
Radetzky, J. J. V. A. F. C. Sat. R. 73: 448.
Radiant Energy as a Probable Cause of the Solar Corona, the Comæ and Tails of Comets, and the Aurora Borealis. (S. J. Corrigan) Astron. 11: 362.
— Kirchhoff's Law of, Pringsheim on. (H. Crew) Astron. 11: 581.
— Transmission of, through Gaseous Media. (S. J. Corrigan) Astron. 11: 1, 108.
Radiator, Steam, Graduating. (J. T. Hawkins) Cassier, 3: 465.
Radical, New Type of. Spec. 73: 362.
Radical Unionism, Raison d'Etre of. Time, 16: 641.
Radicalism and Conservatism in Theology. (C. Clever) Ref. Q. 40: 228.
— in Scotland, Decay of. National, 20: 93.
Radicals, Old and New, in England. Macmil. 74: 153.
Radisson, Pierre-Esprit, and Groseilliers. (H. C. Campbell) Am. Hist. R. 1: 226.
Rae, John. Leis. Hour, 43: 126.—Nature, 48: 321. —Spec. 71: 206.
Raffles, Sir Thomas Stamford. (H. Allen) Pop. Sci. Mo. 50: 80.
Rag-busher and Pin-wells. (E. S. Hartland) Folk-Lore, 4: 451.
Rag Offerings and Primitive Pilgrimages in Ireland. (W. C. Borlase) Ath. '93, 1: 415.
Ragged and Torne and True; Ballad of the 17th Century. Eng. Illust. 15: 116.
Ragged School Union, The. (W. Besant) Contemp. 65: 688.
Rags; a story. (W. A. Dromgoole) Arena, 13: 492.
Rahel; a story. (E. Rhodes) Belgra. 82: 258.
Raigecourt, Marquis and Marquise de. Correspondence. Ath. '93, 2: 278.
Rail and Reed-bird. (E. W. Sandys) Outing, 28: 462.
Railroad, Building a, in the Southwest. (J. S. Coleman) Engin. M. 3: 81.
— from Jaffa to Jerusalem. Chamb. J. 71: 17.
— Gravity, American. (C. W. Whiting) Cassier, 8: 83.
— The Highest in the World. Chamb. J. 69: 129.
— in Asia, The. (C. Morris) New Sci. R. 1: 284.
— Industrial Services of. (E. R. Johnson) Ann. Am. Acad. Pol. Sci. 5: 897.
— Intercontinental, Problem of. (C. De Kalb) Forum, 13: 85.
— of the Future. (O. Smith) Engin. M. 3: 673.—(T. Voorhees) Engin. M. 8: 789.
— Relation of, to its Employees. (W. H. Canniff) Eng. M. 8: 977.
— Relations of Employee to. (C. Warman) Engin. M. 8: 985.
— to India, Proposed. (A. T. Frazer) J. Soc. Arts, 44: 793.
Railroad Accident and Emergency Service. (W. L. Derr) Engin. M. 10: 861.
Railroad Accidents. Bank. M. (Lond.) 53: 827.
— Causes of. (J. A. Hall) Engin. M. 9: 720.
— in the United States and England. (H. G. Prout) No. Am. 157: 707.
— Recent. (L. C. Loomis) Pop. Sci. Mo. 44: 314.
Railroad Accounting. (T. L. Greene) Pol. Sci. Q. 7: 598.
Railroad Affairs, Truth and Falsehood in. Meth. R. 53: 954.
Railroad Batteries and Armored Trains. (C. G. Boxall) Un. Serv. (Phila.) 14: 426.
Railroad Bonds, The Security of. (T. L. Greene) Nation, 54: 144.
Railroad Building and Manganese Mining in Colombia. (E. J. Chibas) Engin. M. 12: 426.
— Decline in. (T. L. Greene) Engin. M. 2: 575.
Railroad Classification, Uniform. (T. L. Greene) Nation, 54: 26.
Railroad Collision, A Pre-arranged. (A. C. Rogers) Cosmopol. 22: 125.
Railroad Collisions to Order. (C. Metters) Nat'l M. (Bost.) 5: 171.
Railroad Commission of Great Britain. Sat. R. 80: 537.
Railroad Competition. (H. T. Newcomb) Am. Statis. Assoc. 5: 65.
— Necessity of Limiting. (H. T. Newcomb) No. Am. 163: 121.

Railroad Consolidation in New England. (G. F. Seymour) New Eng. M. n. s. 14: 251.
Railroad Construction, Cost of Modern. (J. F. Wallace) Engin. M. 10: 472.
Railroad Corporations and Practical Politics. (C. Warman) Engin. M. 11: 8.
Railroad Couplings, Safety. (W. M. Mitchell) Engin. M. 5: 519.
Railroad Court of Last Resort wanted. (A. Morgan) Pop. Sci. Mo. 41: 212.
Railroad Economics. (W. M. Acworth) Econ. J. 2: 392.
Railroad Employees, Slaughter of. (H. C. Adams) Forum, 13: 500.
Railroad Exhibits at Chicago. (J. C. Trautwine) Cassier, 5: 178, 289.
Railroad Facts and Figures. (M. Philips) New Sci. R. 1: 448.
Railroad Failures and their Lessons, Recent. (S. Sterne) Forum, 17: 19.
Railroad Fares in Hungary; "Zone-Tariff" System of Minister Baross. (Dr. Körösi) R. of Rs. (N. Y.) 5: 562.
Railroad Finance, New Features in. (T. L. Greene) Nation, 55: 407.
Railroad Foreclosure, Rights of Material and Supply Men in. (C. A. Dickson) Am. Law. R. 30: 520.
Railroad Invasion of Asia. (C. Morris) Lippinc. 56: 83.
Railroad Invention, Review of. (C. P. Mackie) Engin. M. 9: 712.
Railroad Journey in Russia. Cornh. 65: 67.
Railroad Labor in America. (W. E. Hart) Soc. Econ. 1: 99.
— Problem of. (H. T. Newcomb) Pub. Opin. 21: 14.
Railroad Law, Preston on. Sat. R. 75: 102.
Railroad Legislation, The Farmer and. (H. C. Adams) Cent. 21: 780.
Railroad Machine Shop. (H. D. Gordon) Engin. M. 9: 705.
Railroad Management, First Principles in. (B. Reece) Engin. M. 9: 617.
— Fruits of Fraudulent. (J. S. Tait) Engin. M. 11: 407.
— German and American, compared. Am. Arch. 38: 206.
— Higher Education in. (G. B. Leighton) Harv. Grad. M. 3: 481.
— Reforms in. (H. Clews) Engin. M. 9: 635.
Railroad Mania, Credulous Side of. (John Pendleton) Gent. M. n. s. 57: 133.
Railroad Methods, English. (H. G. Prout) Scrib. M. 71: 545.
Railroad Monopolies. Sat. R. 75: 29.
Railroad Mortgages in the U. S. (A. Gallup) Law Q. 4: 300.
Railroad Operation, Economy in. (L. F. Lorec) Engin. M. 9: 271.
Railroad Party in Politics, A. (H. P. Robinson) No. Am. 156: 552.
Railroad Passengers, Grievances of. (L. A. Atherley-Jones) New R. 11: 135.
Railroad Pooling. (M. A. Knapp) Ann. Am. Acad. Pol. Sci. 8: 127. — (T. L. Greene) Nation, 55: 445.
— and the Reduction of Freight Rates. (H. T. Newcomb) Engin. M. 11: 1055.
Railroad Properties, Legalized Plunder of; the Remedy. (I. L. Rice) Forum, 17: 676.
Railroad Prosperity, The Importance of. (T. L. Greene) Nation, 59: 474.
Railroad Receiverships in Federal Courts. (H. C. Caldwell) Am. Law R. 30: 161.
Railroad Reform. (J. M. Lely) Time, 16: 525.
— Turning Point in. (M. E. Ingalls) Engin. M. 11: 621.
Railroad Reorganization in America. Bank. M. (Lond.) 57: 692.
Railroad Ride, Thousand-mile, on a Locomotive. (C. Warman) McClure, 2: 164.
Railroad Robberies. (W. A. Pinkerton) No. Am. 157: 530.
Railroad Securities, Advance in. (T. L. Greene) Engin. M. 9: 673.
— American, English Investment in. Univ. R. 1: 41.
Railroad Signal, A; a story. (J. Mackenzie) Gent. M. n. s. 55: 1.
Railroad Signaling. (G. H. Paine) Engin. M. 11: 814. — (R. Gordon) Science, 22: 118.
Railroad Stations, Architecture of. (B. L. Gilbert) Engin. M. 9: 649.
— Crowds and Panics at. Spec. 68: 558.
— European. (L. Benouville) Am. Arch. 40: 79, 95.
Railroad Station Gardens in California. (C. W. Shinn) Garden & F. 6: 413.
Railroad Stocks, British. Are they Good Investments? (T. F. Woodlock) Engin. M. 11: 238.
Railroad Systems of the U. S. (H. B. Plant) Cosmopol. 13: 677.
Railroad Tickets, Making. Chamb. J. 73: 118.
Railroad Traffic, Cost of, Distance not a Factor in. (J. L. Cowles) Engin. M. 5: 793.
Railroad Train, Pictures seen from a. (E. Bradbury) M. of Art, 3: 107.
Railroad Travel in England and America. (H. G. Prout) Scrib. M. 16: 399.
— Luxury as a Stimulus to. (H. G. Prout) Engin. M. 12: 213.
Railroad Traveling, Early. Cornh. 65: 413. Same art. Liv. Age, 193: 627.
Railroad Traveling Companions. Chamb. J. 70: 385.
Railroad Troubles, Remedy for. (G. Gary) Am. J. Pol. 5: 641.
Railroad Values, Decline in. Soc. Enon. 6: 85.
Railroad War. (H. J. Fletcher) Atlan. 74: 534.
Railroading as a Career. (B. Mansfield) Chaut. 19: 140.
— Legal Aspects of. (W. A. McClean) Cassier, 5: 39.
Railroading over an Earthquake. (C. Warman) McClure, 5: 415.
Railroads, American, and American Cities. (H. J. Fletcher) Atlan. 73: 803.
— — Van Oss on. Sat. R. 74: 720.
— and the Government. (J. S. Fisher) Am. J. Pol. 3: 82.
— and Municipalities. (D. A. Jones) Engin. M. 8: 813.
— and Ocean Steamers. Soc. Econ. 6: 283.
— and the State. (S. Sterne) Citizen, 2: 237. — (H. H. L. Bellot) Westm. 142: 1.
— and Waterways. (L. M. Haupt) Engin. M. 3: 9.
— and the World's Fair. (H. G. Prout) Engin. M. 6: 499.
— Bond Subsidies to, in Nebraska. (C. E. Tingley) Q. J. Econ. 6: 346.
— Brigandage on. (W. Hampton) No. Am. 159: 665.
— Broad Gauge, First and Last Days of. Temp. Bar, 95: 338. Same art. Liv. Age, 194: 672.
— City; Public Control of Urban Transit. (S. Baxter) Cosmopol. 18: 54.
— Court Management of. (S. D. Thompson) Am. Law R. 27: 481.

Railroads, Defaulting. Pub. Opin. 15: 490.
— Development of, at Home and Abroad. (J. S. Jeans) Fortn. 61: 365. Same art. Ecl. M. 122: 621.
— Early, in Boston. (L. P. Loring) Bost. 1: 299.
— Economy in Operating. (L. F. Lorec) Engin. M. 9: 7.
— Employees' Relief Departments of. (E. R. Johnson) Ann. Am. Acad. Pol. Sci. 6: 424.
— Fast Trains as related to Business Policy. (H. G. Prout) Engin. M. 12: 6.
— Federal Regulation of, Progress of. (H. T. Newcomb) Pol. Sci. Q. 11: 201.
— Freight Traffic Statistics. (C. P. Leland) Am. Statis. Assoc. 3: 611.
— The General Situation. (O. D. Ashley) Forum, 20: 266.
— Government, in a Democratic State. (W. M. Acworth) Econ. J. 2: 629.
— Government Control of, Steps toward. (C. D. Wright) Forum, 18: 704.
— Government Ownership of. (J. W. Mason) Am. J. Pol. 2: 355. — (T. V. Powderly) Arena, 7: 58.
— Great Systems of U. S. (J. B. Walker) Cosmopol. 19: 17.
— A Highway Robber. (L. de La Ramé) Fortn. 66: 83.
— Hours and Service on. (T. L. Greene) Nation, 54: 352.
— in Canada, Development of. (A. R. Davis) Chaut. 16: 435.
— in England. (J. Mavor) Q. J. Econ. 8: 280, 403.
— — and America. (W. M. Acworth) Engin. M. 5: 23, 197, 315.
— — Birth and Growth of the Broad Gauge. Gent. M. n. s. 55: 489.
— — British Railway Stocks as Desirable Investments. (W. J. Stevens) Engin. M. 11: 915.
— — One-class Question. Spec. 75: 923.
— — Problem of. (T. L. Greene) Nation, 56: 468.
— in India, in Native States. (E. Dicey) 19th Cent. 32: 752.
— in New York, State Aid to. (F. L. McVey) Soc. Econ. 7: 101.
— in Prussia, Government Policy of. (G. Cohn) J. Pol. Econ. 1. 179.
— — Recent Discussion on the Management of. (F. W. Taussig) Q. J. Econ. 9: 77.
— in the U. S. and Wall Street. (T. L. Greene) Engin. M. 3: 372.
— — Development of. (B. Mansfield) Chaut. 20: 1.
— — Problem of. (L. A. Sheldon) Arena, 5: 297.
— — Progress of, in 1892. (T. L. Greene) Engin. M. 4: 867.
— Irish. Fortn. 61: 138.
— Legislative Regulation of. (A. Fink) Engin. M. 9: 623.
— Light. (W. M. Acworth) Econ. J. 5: 86. — (W. M. Acworth) J. Soc. Arts, 43: 291.
— — for Farming Districts. Sat. R. 80: 793.
— — Mackay on. Sat. R. 82: 115.
— Mismanagement of. (W. M. Acworth) 19th Cent. 32: 938. — (C. B. Spahr) Chr. Un. 47: 506.
— Mountain. (J. H. Means and J. C. Branner) Chaut. 21: 426. — (G. E. Latham) Munsey, 8: 386.
— — of the Mining Regions. (J. R. Maxwell) Engin. M. 10: 61.
— A National Transportation Department. (H. J. Fletcher) Atlan. 76: 119.
— Nationalization of. (S. Schindler) Arena, 7: 209. 9: 460.
— — by Inches; the British Railway System. (E. E. Williams) New R. 13: 81.
— New, for England. Sat. R. 73: 714.
— Passengers on, Law and. Spec. 70: 189.
Railroads, Past, Present and Future. (Sir E. Watkin) Time, 1: 257.
— Problem of, Management of. (H. Clews) Gunton's M. 11: 337.
— — Partial Solution. (C. J. Buell) Arena, 12: 321.
— Question of, Economics of the. Soc. Econ. 6: 14.
— Rail for; the Reed System. Bost. 4: 407.
— The Railway Situation. (H. C. Adams) R. of Rs. (N. Y.) 10: 185.
— Rates on. (J. L. Cowles) Arena, 7: 702.
— — American. (H. T. Newcomb) Engin. M. 10: 624.
— — and Terminal Charges. (R. P. Williams) J. Statis. Soc. 59: 485.
— — Can they be cheapened? (H. T. Newcomb) Forum, 18: 250.
— — Decline in. (H. T. Newcomb) Pop. Sci. Mo. 47: 186.
— — in England, and the Common Weal. (W. A. Hunter) New R. 8: 332.
— — — and Trade. (W. M. Acworth) New R. 8: 165.
— — — New. (W. M. Acworth) Econ. J. 3: 134. — (J. S. Jeans) Fortn. 59: 223.
— — Passenger Fares, Freight Charges, and Free Passes. (W. Clark) Arena, 16: 937.
— — Question of, in Recent Railroad Literature. (S. Sherwood) Ann. Am. Acad. Pol. Sci. 3: 102.
— — Reasonable. (H. T. Newcomb) Ann. Am. Acad. Pol. Sci. 5: 335.
— — Wars in. Their Cause and Cure. (J. W. Midgley) Forum, 20: 519.
— Receivers for, Federal, South Carolina Memorial to Congress on. Am. Law R. 28: 161.
— South American, Development of. (C. De Kalb) Engin. M. 7: 7.
— Speed on; American Run that breaks the World's Record. (H. P. Robinson) Eng. Illust. 14: 653. Same art. McClure, 6: 247. — (H. G. Prout) No. Am. 157: 75.
— — Fast Trains of England and America. (G. Lodian) Cassier, 4: 3, 131.
— — in England, Possibilities of. Spec. 71: 332.
— — Increase of. (W. B. Le Vara) Engin. M. 4: 845.
— — Standards of Men, Machinery, and Track for. (H. G. Prout) Engin. M. 12: 413.
— State, in Australia. (W. Hill) J. Pol. Econ. 3: 1.
— The State and. (H. H. L. Bellot) Westm. 142: 1.
— State Aid to, in Missouri. (J. W. Million) J. Pol. Econ. 3: 73.
— State-owned, in Australia. (R. Speight) Engin. M. 4: 661.
— State Ownership of. (F. L. McVey) Gunton's M. 11: 54.
— Statistics of. (T. L. Greene) Nation, 59: 170.
— — Earnings of Passenger Trains. (M. Riebenack) Am. Statis. Assoc. 3: 519.
— — in the U. S., Recent Results in. (H. C. Adams) Am. Statis. Assoc. 3: 501.
— Symposiums. Indep. Oct. 6, '92; June 1, '93; June 7, '94; June 6, '95.
— Taxation of Gross Receipts. (F. J. Goodnow) Pol. Sci. Q. 9: 233.
Raimondi, Marc Antonio, the Savant of Peru. (M. H. Spielmann) M. of Art, 11: 355. — (C. De Kalb) Nation, 61: 42, 62.
Rain. (J. G. McPherson) Good Words, 34: 522.
— How Nature regulates. (R. L. Fulton) Science, n. s. 3: 546.
— in August. Nature, 52: 519.
— in Guiana, Coming of. (J. Rodway) Pop. Sci. Mo. 48: 652.
Rain and Ray; a poem. (J. Cook) Our Day, 13: 27.

Rain-baths, Modern. (W. P. Gerhard) Am. Arch. 43: 67.
Rainbow Camelia; a story. (F. Hume) Eng. Illust. 11: 819.
Rain Clouds; a honeymoon episode. (W. R. Walkes) Temp. Bar, 97: 373. Same art. Ecl. M. 120: 524. Same art. Liv. Age, 197: 354.
Rainfall of the Mississippi Valley, Origin of. (J. H. Patton) Pop. Sci. Mo. 44: 102.
— Records of, in British Isles. (G. J. Symons) J. Soc. Arts, 42: 298.
Rainfall Types of U. S. (A. W. Greely) Nat. Geog. M. 5: 45.
Rainfalls. (W. W. Wagstaffe) Gent. M. n. s. 54: 284.
— Great. (A. MacIvor) Gent. M. n. s. 54: 630.
Rain-gambling in Calcutta. Chamb. J. 72: 350.
Rain-god, Worship of. (S. D. Peet) Am. Antiq. 16: 341.
Rain-makers, Natural. (A. McAdie) Pop. Sci. Mo. 47: 642.
Rain-making. (F. Sanford) Pop. Sci. Mo. 45: 478.
— Artificial. Dub. R. 110: 445.
— Experiments by the U. S. Government. (G. E. Curtis) Engin. M. 3: 540.
— in Texas. Dub. R. 110: 192.
Raines Liquor-tax Law. Pub. Opin. 20: 453.
Rainy Afternoon, A. (G. A. Hibbard) Scrib. M. 15: 83.
Raisin Industry in California. Garden & F. 5: 268. — (J. Y. Goodman) Overland, n. s. 19: 493.
Rajahs of Sarawak. (H. Le Roux) Fortn. 62: 410.
Rajputana, Impressions of. (Alice Cameron) Temp. Bar, 101: 248. 102: 243. 103: 243. Same art. Ecl. M. 123: 197, 687.
— Painter's Impressions of. (E. L. Weeks) Harper, 89: 835.
— The Land of the King's Children. All the Year, 74: 521.
Rajputs, Red, Ethnology of. (C. Johnston) Asia. R. 16: 382.
Raking Straws; a story. (Mrs. Van R. Cruger) Cosmopol. 17: 305.
Raleigh, Sir Walter. Quar. 175: 287.
— and America, 1585. (E. G. Daves) Nat'l M. (N. Y. '91) 18: 147.
— New Fort in Virginia, 1585. (E. G. Daves) M. Am. Hist. 29: 459.
— Stebbing's. Spec. 68: 173.
Ralph, Julian, with portrait. Bk. Buyer, 12: 265.
Ralph Inglefield's Revenge; a story. (W. K. Tarpey) Temp. Bar, 102: 91.
Ralph Renton, Bachelor; a story. Temp. Bar, 106: 99.
Ralph Thornleigh's Picture. (F. D. Cuming) Chamb. J. 69: 711-758.
Ram Krishna Paramahamsa. (C. H. Tawney) Asia. R. 21: 111.
Ramabai Association. Lend a H. 10: 256.
— Report for 1893. Lend a H. 12: 261.
— Report for 1894. Lend a H. 14: 274, (J. W. Andrews) 329.
Râmarkrishna; a Real Mahatman. (F. M. Mueller) 19th Cent. 40: 306.
Ramazan. Sat. R. 77: 223.
Rambouillet, Julie, and La Guirlande de Julie. (T. W. Bradley) Bibliographica, 1: 291.
Râmchunderji; a story. (F. A. Steel) Macmil. 69: 234. Same art. Ecl. M. 122: 340.
Rameses II. as an Art Patron. (F. M. Robinson) M. of Art, 10: 305.
Rameses IV., What became of? (A. L. Harris) Gent. M. n. s. 51: 325.
Râmeswaram, Visit to a. (E. O. Walker) Gent. M. n. s. 51: 609.
Ramona, Tragic Sequel to. (E. B. Howell) R. of Rs. (N. Y.) 10: 507.
Ramsay, Allan, Junior, the Painter. (A. Dobson) M. of Art, 18: 309.
Ramsay, Andrew Crombie, Geikie's Life of. (F. W. Rudler) Acad. 47: 467. — Sat. R. 79: 485.
Ramsay, Sir Henry. (Dr. Geo. Smith) Good Words, 35: 345.
Ramsay, Prof. Wm. and Argon. (St. G. Odlum) Idler, 7: 443.
Ranch-Life: In the Sierra Madre with the Punchers. (F. Remington) Harper, 88: 350.
Ranches and Racing beyond the Rockies. (A. Bennett) Southern M. 3: 570.
Ranchman, English. Why he is a Failure. Longm. 26: 59.
Ranchwoman, The English. Longm. 28: 485. Same art. Ecl. M. 127: 549.
Rancho Chico, Some Trees at. (C. H. Shinn) Garden & F. 7: 332.
Rancho of Heavenly Rest; a story. (F. Heermans) Cosmopol. 12: 690.
Randolph, A. D. F. (W. M. Paxton) Presb. & Ref. R. 7: 687. Same art. Critic, 29: 33.
Randolph, John, of Roanoke. (P. Bouldin) Cent. 29: 712.
— and Henry Clay. Lippinc. 52: 443.
Randolph, Thomas, Poems of. Bookworm, 2: 225.
Ranelagh Gardens. (A. Dobson) Eng. Illust. 11: 33.
Range-Finders. Un. Serv. M. 10: 174.
Ranjit Singh. Sat. R. 74: 335.
— Griffin's. (G. Smith) Nation, 56: 107.
Ranke, Leopold von. Bk. Buyer, 3: 238.
— and the Beginning of the Seminary Method in Teaching History. (E. G. Bourne) Educa. R. 12: 359.
Rann, Jack. (C. Whibley) New R. 14: 220.
Ransoms, Some. Sat. R. 77: 175.
Raynard, A. C. Nature, 51: 179. — Ath. '94, 2: 865.
— and his Work. (W. H. Wesley) Knowl. 18: 25.
Rapallo, Italy, Historical Notes on. (P. H. Ditchfield) Antiq. n. s. 31: 78.
Raphael. (W. Pater) Fortn. 58: 458. Same art. Liv. Age, 195: 643.
— and the Fornarina. (J. Cartwright) M. of Art, 7: 323.
— at Urbino. (M. Robinson) M. of Art, 6: 434.
— Cartoons of, Criticised. (J. Brett) M. of Art, 17: 295.
— Crucifixion. (C. Phillips) Art J. 44: 335.
— Early Work of. (Julia Cartwright-Ady) Portfo. no. 1.
— How he quarrelled with the Marchesa Isabella. (L. E. Baxter) M. of Art, 12: 151.
— In Rome. (Julia Cartwright-Ady) Portfo. no. 20.
— Life of, Muntz's. (S. Colvin) M. of Art, 5: 213.
— Madonna Ansidei. (C. Phillips) M. of Art, 8: 136.
— Madonnas by, Different Types of. (G. Allen) Acad. 46: 428.
— Plagiarisms of. (C. Phillips) M. of Art, 9: 371.
— St. Cecilia of. (C. Duncan) M. of Art, 4: 6.
Rapid Transit. (C. D. Wright) Pop. Sci. Mo. 40: 785.
— Gravity System of. (B. S. Henning) Engin. M. 5: 167.
— in Cities. (T. C. Clarke) Scrib. M. 11: 567, 743.
— in London. Quar. 175: 476.
— Lessons in. (L. Heilprin) Engin. M. 3: 447.
— Some Speculations Regarding. (J. B. Walker) Cosmopol. 20: 26.
Rapisardi, Mario. (M. Hargrave) Gent. M. n. s. 50: 168.

Rare Editions, Slater on. (C. E. S. Chambers; H. Slater and others) Ath. '94, 1: 346–511.
Rare Specimen, A; a Canadian Sketch. (J. H. Stevenson) Canad. M. 1: 301.
Rarity's Jean. (A. Gordon) Good Words, 35: 96.
Raschen, Henry, Artist, with Sketches. (P. N. Boeringer) Overland, n. s. 27: 361.
Raspberries, Cultivation of. (E. Williams) Garden & F. 6: 176.
Rastell, John, and his Contemporaries. (H. R. Plomer) Bibliographica, 2: 437.
Rates. *See* Taxation.
Rather too much Energy. (J. W. Roosevelt) Scrib. M. 19: 611.
Rat-Catcher of Hamelin; a poem. (G. Hartwig) Blackw. 152: 491. Same art. Ecl. M. 119: 759. Same art. Liv. Age, 195: 639.
Rat-Lore, Recent. Spec. 75: 637.
Rat-Trap, A Night in a. Chamb. J. 72: 62.
Rats, Conjuring of. (W. W. Newell) J. Am. Folk-Lore, 5: 23.
— Land and Water. (Thos. Leyland) Time, 19: 327.
— on Shipboard. Chamb. J. 69: 523.
Rattlesnake, Bite of, Cure of, 1741. N. E. Reg. 46: 215.
Rationalism, Christian. Meth. R. 56: 445.
— Is it Rational? (R. T. Stevenson) Meth. R. 52: 586.
Rationality, Persistence of. (R. M. Wenley) Scot. R. 25: 226.
Raub Gravity Locomotive. (W. R. Covert) Am. J. Pol. 3: 207.
Ravachol, Trial of. Spec. 68: 596.
Ravenal, Daniel, of South Carolina. N. E. Reg. 49: 297.
Raven-Hill, L., the Illustrator. (G. White) Idler, 8: 125.
Ravenna and her Ghosts. (V. Paget) Macmil. 70: 380. Same art. Ecl. M. 123: 809. Same art. Liv. Age, 203: 272.
— Art of. (E. H. and E. W. Blashfield) Scrib. M. 12: 37.
Ravens in Somersetshire. (W. H. Hudson) Longm. 28: 150.
Ravenscroft, Francis, with portrait. Bank. M. (Lond.) 54: 827.
Rawlinson, Henry C. Ath. '95, 1: 313. — (J. S. Cotton) Acad. 47: 219. — Critic, 26: 189. — Nature, 51: 536. — With portrait. (F. J. Goldsmid) Geog. J. 5: 490.
Ray from a Jack-Lantern, A; a story. (L. M. Smith) Outing, 26: 287.
Raymond, Henry J. (J. R. Young) Lippinc. 51: 185.
Raymond Lee; a story. (H. W. Desmond) Architec. Rec. 1: 115–500. 2: 108–503. 3: 109–444. 4: 117.
Reaction, Type-Theory of. (J. M. Baldwin) Mind, 21: 81. — (E. B. Titchener) Mind, 20: 506. 21: 236.
— Types of. (J. M. Baldwin) Psychol. R. 2: 259.
Reaction Time with Reference to Race. (R. M. Bache) Psychol. R. 2: 475.
Reaction Times. (C. S. Dolley; J. M. Cattell) Psychol. R. 1: 159.
— Experimentation in. (R. Watanabe) Am. J. Psychol. 6: 408.
Reactions, Simple. (E. B. Titchener) Mind, 20: 74.
Read, Col. Charles. (J. G. Leach) Pennsyl. M. 17: 190.
Read, Mary; West Indian Amazon. All the Year, 76: 59.
Read, Nathan. (N. Read) N. E. Reg. 50: 434.
Read, Thomas Buchanan, with portrait. Bk. News, 4: 230.
Read Families. (J. Williamson) N. E. Reg. 50: 354.
Reade, Charles. (Catherine M. Reignolds-Winslow) Citizen, 1: 183.
— Novels. Gent. M. n. s. 48: 431.
Readers, Responsibility of. (R. Ogden) Nation, 59: 420.
Readers *vs.* Writers. Sat. R. 79: 410.
Readers, School, Contents of. (A. E. Kellogg) Educa. R. 8: 337.
Reading. Chamb. J. 70: 225. — Gent. M. n. s. 49: 431. — Meth. R. 55: 794.
— and Education. Dial (Ch.) 18: 101.
— and Readers. Sund. M. 22: 189.
— Education from. (J. B. Rieffer) Ref. Q. 40: 519.
— Educational Law of, and Writing. (H. E. Scudder) Atlan. 73: 252.
— Fatigue in. (H. Griffing and S. I. Franz) Psychol. R. 3: 513.
— for Boys. (E. M. Coe) Lib. J. 20: 118.
— for Children, Guiding of, by Teachers. (M. E. Merington) Lib. J. 20: 119.
— for the Young in Public Libraries. (L. E. Stearns) Lib. J. 19: supp. 81.
— Great Writers and their Favorite. All the Year, 73: 102.
— History of Literature of. (P. H. Ditchfield) Walford's Antiq. 11: 233.
— How and what Art Students should read. (J. E. Hodgson) M. of Art, 17: 342, 372.
— How to read. (A. Haultain) Blackw. 159: 249. Same art. Liv. Age, 208: 515. Same art. Ecl. M. 126: 577.
— in Farmers' Families. (E. E. Hale) Bk. News, 7: 147.
— in Public. (T. O'Hagan) Canad. M. 4: 248.
— in School, Object of. (W. M. Thayer) Educa. 15: 214.
— Libraries and Books. (C. A. Ward) Bookworm, 3: 17.
— makes a Dull Man. Bookworm, 4: 269.
— Notes on. Temp. Bar, 107: 560.
— of Adults and Children. (A. E. Bostwick) Lib. J. 21: 444.
— of the American People. (C. Snyder) Am. J. Pol. 4: 359.
— of Books, The Art of. (J. E. C. Welldon) National, 23: 213. Same art. Ecl. M. 122: 696.
— of Poor Children. (A. F. Sanborn) No. Am. 159: 377.
— of the Working Classes. (G. R. Humphrey) 19th Cent. 33: 690.
— Re- Spec. 77: 547.
— Summer. Dial (Ch.) 19: 7.
— Teaching of, Experiments in. (M. E. Burt) Dial (Ch.) 14: 172.
— What is? (O. T. Snow) Educa. 12: 422.
— What my Pupils read. (M. B. C. True) Educa. 14: 99.
— Youthful, of Literary Men. (E. Dickinson) Lippinc. 57: 841.
Reading Habits of Englishmen and Americans. (P. Collier) Forum, 18: 439.
Reading Public, Andrew Lang on the. Gent. M. n. s. 48: 321.
Reading Railroad, Affairs of. (T. L. Greene) Nation, 56: 155.
— and the Coal Supply. (A. A. McLeod) Forum, 13: 554.
Reading Railroad Combination, The. (D. MacG. Means) Nation, 55: 158.

Reading Railroad Receivership. (S. F. Van Oss) Bank. M. (Lond.) **55**: 556.
Real and the Ideal. (J. Burroughs) Dial (Ch.) **19**: 237.
— Heresy of the. (J. G. Dow) Dial (Ch.) **14**: 203.
Real Estate and Marriage. (H. Nelson) Law Q. **6**: 307.
— and Personal Estate. (M. H. Box) Law Q. **3**: 406. —(T. C. Williams) Law Q. **4**: 394.
— Gambling in. (T. C. Hall) Outl. **49**: 15.
Real Presence, Lutheranism and. (J. W. Santee) Ref. Q. **42**: 195.
Real Queen, A. (R. E. Francillon) Time, **8**: 1–605. **9**: 15–611. **10**: 1.
Realism, Allotropy of. (G. M. Hyde) Dial (Ch.) **18**: 231.
— and Art. (C. S. Darrow) Arena, **9**: 99.
— Aspects of. (E. E. Hale, jr.) Dial (Ch.) **14**: 169.
— Fallacies of. (W. R. Thayer) Open Court, **4**: 2361.
— in English Fiction. Liv. Age, **192**: 131.
— in Fiction, Limits of. (P. Bourget) New R. **8**: 201. Same art. Liv. Age, **196**: 737.
— Natural, Psychological Foundation of. (A. Fraser) Am. J. Psychol. **4**: 429.
— of To-day. (K. Cowper) 19th Cent. **35**: 618. Same art. Liv. Age, **201**: 293. Same art. Ecl. M. **122**: 648.
— on the Stage: is it overdone? (A. W. a Beckett) Theatre, **37**: 132.
— Passion for. (Hiram M. Stanley) Dial (Ch.) **14**: 238.
— Truer and Higher. Pub. Opin. **18**: 705.
— *versus* other Isms. (J. Kirkland) Dial (Ch.) **14**: 99.
Realists, Great, and Empty Story-tellers. (H. H. Boyesen) Forum, **18**: 724.
Reality and Causation. (W. W. Carlile) Mind, **20**: 82, 213.
Reality and Idealism, Ritchie on. (F. C. S. Schiller) Philos. R. **1**: 535.
— Bradley on. (A. Seth) Contemp. **66**: 694, 862.— Ath. '94, **1**: 403.—(J. Ward) Mind, **19**: 109, (F. H. Bradley) 232, (J. S. Mackenzie; A. Sidgwick; J. Ward) 205, 236, 378.—(J. S. Mackenzie) Int. J. Ethics, **4**: 246.
— Elements of, and Sensations. (E. Mach) Monist, **5**: 393.
— Well-springs of. (E. D. Fawcett) Monist, **5**: 363.
— What is? (D. G. Ritchie) Philos. R. **1**: 265.
Reason. Open Court, **7**: 3688.
— and Intuition. (C. L. Franklin) Monist, **3**: 211.
— and Predisposition. (J. Burroughs) Open Court, **1**: 115.
— and Will. (B. Bosanquet) Monist, **2**: 18.
— Function of, in Christianity. (W. B. Greene, jr.) Presb. & Ref. R. **6**: 481.
— Origin of. (L. Noiré) Open Court, **2**: 880.—(T. B. Saunders) Open Court, **4**: 2405–2534.
— Place of, in Theology. (H. C. Minton) Presb. & Ref. R. **7**: 84.
Reasoner, Is Man the only? (J. Sully) Pop. Sci. Mo. **40**: 506.
Reasoning, Teaching, as a Fine Art. (F. C. Sharp) Educa. R. **6**: 493.
Rebellious Heroine, A; a story. (J. K. Bangs) Harper, **93**: 15, 253.
Rebeur-Paschwitz, E. von. (C. Davison) Nature, **52**: 599.
Recall of Flathers. (C. D. Rhodes) Lippinc. **56**: 137.
Receivers and Judicial Assignees, Foreign. (S. T. Thompson) Green Bag, **6**: 118, 170.
Receiverships, Friendly, The Bane of. (H. Wollman) No. Am. **158**: 250.
Recidivist, The. (J. Weir, jr.) Am. Natural. **28**: 537.
Reciprocating Machinery, Automatic Balance of. (W. W. Beaumont) J. Soc. Arts, **42**: 205.
Reciprocity. (F. W. Taussig) Q. J. Econ. **7**: 26.
— American. (S. M. Davis) Am. J. Pol. **2**: 113.
— and the Farmer. (H. A. Herbert) No. Am. **154**: 414.
— and South America. (M. M. Trumbull) Open Court, **7**: 3543.
— Earl Grey on. (M. M. Trumbull) Open Court, **6**: 3503.
— Republican Policy of. (W. L. Wilson) Forum, **14**: 255.
— with Canada. (E. Wiman) Engin. M. **4**: 109, 337.
— with Cuba and South American Countries. Pub. Opin. **15**: 97, 121.
Recitation, Art of. Spec. **77**: 45.
— Unprepared, in Secondary Schools. (I. B. Burgess) School R. **4**: 13.
Recklessness, Growth of. Spec. **71**: 867.
Reclamation of Joe Hollends; a story. (R. Barr) Idler, **3**: 267.
Réclus, Elisée, and his Opinions, with portrait. (H. Zimmern) Pop. Sci. Mo. **44**: 402.
Recognition. (A. Allin) Am. J. Psychol. **7**: 249.
Recollection, Accuracy of, Measurements of. (J. McK. Cattell) Science, n. s. **2**: 761.
— and Observation, Accuracy of. (F. E. Bolton) Psychol. R. **3**: 286.
— Involuntary. (J. W. Donaldson) Science, **21**: 147.
— A Little Girl's. (Henriette Corkran) Temp. Bar, **103**: 551.
Recollections of Captain Wilkie, The. (A. Conan Doyle) Chamb. J. **72**: 40–57. Same art. McClure, **4**: 401.
— of our Old Country Home. (Canon Scott) Good Words, **36**: 157.
— of Yesterday, Some. Temp. Bar, **102**: 315. Same art. Ecl. M. **123**: 242.
Reconciliation; a poem. (J. A. Blaikie) M. of Art, **8**: 453.
Records, Historical Method of. (J. F. Hewitt) Westm. **143**: 5.
Recreation as a Fine Art. Sat. R. **76**: 210.
— Distraction *vs.* Spec. **72**: 368.
— Experiment in. Spec. **73**: 335.
— Physiology of. (C. Roberts) Contemp. **68**: 103.
— Science of. (W. Besant) Time, **14**: 11.
Recreations. (S. Cox) Sunday M. **21**: 258, 345.
— of Eminent Men. Chamb. J. **69**: 715.—(G. A. Townsend) Chaut. **15**: 582.
Recruits, Age and Physique of. (F. P. Staples) Un. Serv. M. **6**: 251.
Rector Warne's Heresy. (G. W. Ford) Lippinc. **54**: 675.
Rector's Gamecock. (G. W. Ford) Lippinc. **58**: 127.
Rector's Hat, The. (Noah Brooks) Scrib. M. **18**: 202.
Rectory Pew, The; a story. (N. Hopper) Eng. Illust. **15**: 143.
Recueil des Histoires de Troye, Authorship of. (H. O. Somers) Bibliographica, **1**: 31, 502.
Recusants in Derbyshire. Reliquary, **33**: 116.
— in Warwickshire and Worcestershire. Reliquary, **33**: 230.
Red Aleck; a sketch. (R. C. Macdonald) Canad. M. **2**: 589.
Red Beads, The; a poem. All the Year, **71**: 275.
Red Bodice and the Black Fly; a story. (A. Crawshay) Blackw. **156**: 66. Same art. Liv. Age, **202**: 463.

Red Bridal, The. (L. Hearn) Atlan. 74: 74.
Red-bud Tree. Garden & F. 8: 184.
Red Coats, A Chapter on. (J. W. Fortescue) Macmil. 68: 385.
Red Cross Hall, Southwark, Eng. (Mrs. R. Barrington) Eng. Illust. 10: 611.
Red Cross Knight, A; a poem. (A. L. Salmon) Gent. M. n. s. 55: 213.
Red Cross Society in Chino-Japanese War. (A. B. de Guerville) Munsey, 14: 47.
Red-drum Fishing at Oregon Inlet. (F. H. Newcomb) Outing, 22: 93.
Red Fan, The; a story. (F. Madoc) Argosy, 61: 542.
Red-hot Needle, The; a story. (H. F. Abell) Chamb. J. 77: 280-328.
Red Parasol; a story. (D. Blomfield) Outing, 26: 247.
Red Patrol, The; a story. (G. Parker) Eng. Illust. 12: no. 4, 33.
Red Room, The; a story. All the Year, 72: 37, 61.
Red Sea, Italian Colony on. (A. di San Giuliano) 19th Cent. 32: 436.
Red Sea Scenery, Buxton Letters on. Sat. R. 80: 599.
Red Stockade, The; a story. (Bram Stoker) Cosmopol. 17: 619.
Red Wolf, The; a poem. (B. Carman) Cosmopol. 15: 436.
Redemption by Love. (T. F. Wright) N. Church R. 3: 97.
— Haering on. (N. M. Steffens) Presb. & Ref. R. 7: 741.
Redemption of Bill Sheriffs. Chamb. J. 71: 760-790.
Redemptioner; a story in three scenes. (E. Eggleston) Cent. 24: 625.
Redemptioners, Pennsylvania. (L. R. Harley) New Eng. M. n. s. 15: 145.
Redfield, William C., with portrait. Pop. Sci. Mo. 50: 114.
Redgrave, Richard, Redgrave's Memoir of. (F. G. Stephens) M. of Art, 15: 26.
Redhouse, Sir James. Ath. '92, 1: 52.
Redlands. Garden & F. 7: 213.
Redonda and its Phosphates. (F. W. Morse) Pop. Sci. Mo. 46: 78.
Red-tape; the Seat of Justice. Macmil. 73: 198.
Redwood Forest, Cal. (C. H. Shinn) Garden & F. 5: 502.
— — Staging in. (N. Eames) Overland, n. s. 20: 113, 265.
Redwoods, Among the. (R. Wildman) Overland, n. s. 26: 494.
— of California. (W. G. Bonner) Cassier, 6: 195.
Reed, Edward T., Artist. Idler, 9: 499.
Reed, Ethel, Chat with. Bookman, 2: 277.
Reed, Thomas Brackett. (F. A. Munsey) Munsey, 9: 85. — With portraits. (R. P. Porter) McClure, 1: 375.
— and the Presidency. Atlan. 77: 250.
— and the 51st Congress. (T. Roosevelt) Forum, 20: 410.
Reeds, Dwellers in the. Chamb. J. 71: 454.
Reeve, Henry. Ath. '95, 2: 569. — (J. S. Cotton) Acad. 48: 338. — Ed. R. 183: 267.
Reeves, Lieut. Enos, Extracts from Letter-books of. (J. B. Reeves) Pennsyl. M. 20: 302.
Reeves, John Sims. (J. C. Hadden) Gent. M. n. s. 56: 274.
Reeves, William. (N. Moore) Acad. 45: 6.
Referendum, The. (C. B. Roylance-Kent) Macmil. 69: 15. — (D. MacG. Means) Nation, 58: 206. — (St. Loe Strachey) National, 22: 738. 23: 196. — (A. V. Dicey; G. N. Curzon; F. A. Maxse; Earl Grey; Lord Farrer) National, 23: 65. — (Edward A. Freeman) Univ. R. 7: 331.
Referendum, The, and other Forms of Direct Democracy in Switzerland. (E. V. Raynolds) Yale R. 4: 289.
— and Plebiscite. (G. W. Ross) Canad. M. 1: 445.
— and the Senate. (W. D. McCrackan) Lippinc. 55: 855.
— Balfour on. Spec. 72: 188.
— in America. Spec. 73: 494.
— in Switzerland. (N. Droz) Contemp. 67: 328. Same art. Liv. Age, 205: 3. Same art. Ecl. M. 124: 625. — (E. V. Raynolds) Am. J. Soc. Sci. 33: 213. — (W. D. McCrackan) Cosmopol. 15: 329. — (A. B. Hart) Nation, 59: 193. — Spec. 73: 234.
— — and in America. (A. L. Lowell) Atlan. 73: 517.
— in the U. S. Spec. 71: 904.
— The Initiative and. (C. W. Bowne) Arena, 16: 553.
— — How to introduce. (W. D. McCrackan) Arena, 7: 696.
— — in Switzerland. (J. M. Gregory) Pub. Opin. 18: 440.
— — Relation of, to Labor. (A. L. Lowell) Int. J. Ethics, 6: 51.
— Letters on. (C. B. Spahr) Outl. 50: 423.
— Movement for, and its Leaders. (E. Pomeroy) Arena, 16: 29.
Reffey; a story. (W. Balestier) Cent. 21: 561.
Reflections of a Bath Mirror. (C. J. Langston) Argosy, 60: 748.
Reflections of a Married Man. (R. Grant) Scrib. M. 11: 365-722.
Reflectors, Telescope. (D. W. Edgecomb) Pop. Astron. 2: 366.
Reflex Action, Instinct and Reason. (G. A. Reid) Fortn. 65: 269. Same art. Liv. Age, 208: 797.
Reflex Arc Concept in Psychology. (J. Dewey) Psychol. R. 3: 357.
Reflex-motions, Three Phases of. (P. Carus) Open Court, 3: 2084.
Reform and Reforms. (D. Mowry) Am. M. Civics, 7: 462.
— and Ultraism. N. Eng. 56: 1.
— Educational. (F. L. Oswald) Open Court, 5: 2875.
— Individual and Social. (B. Bosanquet) Time, 19: 312.
— A Notable Address. (J. G. Woolley) Our Day, 16: 625.
— Political Mission of. (L. P. Gratacap) Am. M. Civics, 7: 303, 368.
— Religion and. (W. Walsh) Westm. 142: 121. Same art. Ecl. M. 123: 433.
— within the Limits of Existing Law. (W. M. Salter) Int. J. Ethics, 3: 351.
Reform Forces, Union of. (W. Vrooman), Arena, 9: 540.
Reform Problems. (F. L. Oswald) Open Court, 1: 122.
Reform School, Educational Features of. (E. J. Wendell) Char. R. 3: 111.
— In a. Chamb. J. 69: 637.
Reform School Training, Aims, Methods, and Results of. (J. T. Mallalieu) Lend a H. 9: 99.
Reformation, The, and Civil Liberty. (D. H. Gaudin) Luth. Q. 22: 547.
— and Protestantism. (J. Reed) N. Church R. 3: 227.
— and Reunion. (G. W. E. Russell) 19th Cent. 40: 34.
— and Some of its Leading Spirits. (B. O. Flower) Arena, 11: 266.
— Extension of the. (R. F. Conder) Dub. R. 119: 378.
— in England. Eng. R. 12: 65.
— — Influence of Machiavelli on. (W. A. Phillips) 19th Cent. 40: 907.
— Making of the. (F. Manhart) Luth. Q. 22: 26.

Reformation, Undoing the Work of the. (F. W. Farrar) Contemp. 64: 60. Same art. Ecl. M. 121: 260.
— What did happen at. (A. Birrell) 19th Cent. 39: 655.
Reformation of James Reddy. (Bret Harte) Scrib. M. 13: 562.
Reformation or Retribution? (E. Smith; J. McKeen) Am. J. Soc. Sci. 31: 71.
Reformatories for Girls. (H. S. Everett) Lend a H. 10: 157.
— in California. (A. Drahms) Overland, n. s. 22: 424.
Reformatory and Industrial Schools. (J. Watson) J. Statis. Soc. 59: 255.
Reformatory Prisons as Schools of Crime. (W. P. Andrews) Forum, 13: 232.
Reformatory Work. (Mrs. I. C. Barrows) Char. R. 5: 192.
Reformed Church and Her Creed. (W. Rupp) Ref. Q. 42: 5.
— and Presbyterian Church, Alliance of. (W. H. Roberts) Presb. & Ref. R. 7: 679.
— Doctrines of. (S. Z. Beam) Ref. Q. 43: 44.
— in America, General Synod of. (T. W. Chambers) Presb. & Ref. R. 6: 731. — (D. S. Burrell) Presb. & Ref. R. 7: 672.
— — Pittsburg Synod, 25th Anniversary of. (A. E. Truxal) Ref. Q. 42: 203.
— — Progress of a Century in, 1793–1893. (J. H. Dubbs) Ref. Q. 42: 28.
— — Progress of Theology in. (T. G. Apple) Ref. Q. 42: 19.
— in New York. (R. H. Titherington) Munsey, 6: 650.
— in the U. S., 1793–1893. (A. E. Truxal) Ref. Q. 40: 366.
— — and Young People's Religious Organizations. (S. Z. Beam) Ref. Q. 41: 196.
— — Benevolent Work of the 19th Century. (C. Clever) Ref. Q. 41: 89.
— — Educational System of. (S. Z. Beam) Ref. Q. 41: 81.
— — Influence on Civil Government. (G. F. Baer) Ref. Q. 41: 291.
— — Religious Organizations in, and the Ordinances of the Church. (S. Z. Beam) Ref. Q. 41: 196.
— — Theological Progress of. (S. N. Callender) Ref. Q. 41: 133.
— — Theological Seminary at Lancaster, Dedicatory Sermon. (J. H. Dubbs) Ref. Q. 41: 275.
— of Germany and Rationalism. (J. I. Good) Presb. & Ref. R. 5: 227.
— Pastors of, Present Modes of Placing. (A. E. Truxal) Ref. Q. 39: 204.
Reformed Churches, Plan of Federation of. (S. J. Niccolls; N. N. Steffens; C. Clever; E. Daniel) Presb. & Ref. R. 5: 661.
Reformed Quarterly Review. Ref. Q. 43: 534.
Reformer, The Scholar as. (M. I. Swift) Open Court, 2: 868.
Reformer's Wife, A. (F. A. Steel) Macmil. 70: 452. Same art. Liv. Age, 203: 570.
Reformers, The Masses as. (M. I. Swift) Open Court, 2: 1055.
Reforms, Economic, The Church and. (C. H. Zimmerman) Arena, 10: 694.
— Progress of, during 1895. (W. F. Crafts) Our Day, 16: 5.
Refraction, Atmospheric, at Madison, Wis. (G. C. Comstock) Astron. 12: 769.
— Double, MacCullagh's Theory of. (A. B. Basset) Nature, 52: 595.
Refraction of Light upon the Snow. (A. W. Whitney) Am. J. Sci. 145: 389.
Refrigerating Apparatus. (C. Linde) J. Soc. Arts, 42: 322.
Refrigerating Machine, Large. Cassier, 1: 480.
Refrigerating Machines. (E. Penney) Cassier, 1: 153.
Refrigeration, Artificial. (D. Branson) Am. Arch. 43: 114.
— — through Lines from Central Stations. (D. Branson) J. Frankl. Inst. 137: 81. — (N. W. Smith) Cassier, 6: 315. — (J. E. Start) Engin. M. 5: 73.
Refugee Churches in England. (H. M. Baird) Meth. R. 54: 758.
Refugees, Protestant, Government of England and. (W. A. Shaw) Eng. Hist. R. 9: 662.
Refugees, The; a Tale of Two Continents. (A. C Doyle) Harper, 86: 244–913. 87: 78.
Refuse for Steam Raising. (T. W. Baker) Cassier, 7: 383.
— Power from. (F. W. Brookman) Cassier, 9: 569.
Refuse Furnaces. (W. P. Abell) Cassier, 10: 192.
Regal, Edward von. Nature, 46: 60.
Régamey, Félix. Okoma. M. of Art, 6: 256.
Regatta in Aztec Land, Winter. (A. Inkersley) Outing, 23: 302.
Regattas, Some. All the Year, 75: 183.
Regeneration and Faith. (H. Ziegler) Luth. Q. 23: 372.
— as a Force in Reform Movements. (C. M. Morse) Meth. R. 52: 876.
— Study of. (A. H. Daniels) Am. J. Psychol. 6: 61.
— through an Army. (A. M. Stoddart) Good Words, 37: 516.
— under the Old Covenant. (G. W. McSherry) Luth. Q. 26: 523.
— Washing of. (G. U. Wenner) Luth. Q. 26: 55.
Regenerators; a sketch. Canad. M. 1: 64.
Regensburg. (S. Beale) Am. Arch. 42: 133, 156.
— Musical Festival at. Sat. R. 78: 181.
Regicides in New England. (F. H. Cogswell) New Eng. M. n. s. 9: 188.
Regimental Mystery, A; a story. Chamb. J. 69: 268.
Regiments, British, and their Insignia. Chamb. J. 69: 609.
— Exchange of Stations. (H. R. Brinkerhoff) Un. Serv. (Phila.) 12: 29.
Regina, die Wälsche. (J. P. Rudd) Outing, 25: 3.
Regina looks in the Mirror. (L. C. Moulton) Cosmopol. 15: 411.
Reginald Blake, Financier and Cad; a story. (J. K. Jerome) Idler, 9: 637.
Registration Bill, Absurdities of the. (F. E. Eddis) National, 21: 557.
Regnal Years, Old Testament Reckoning of. (E. L. Curtis) J. Bib. Lit. 14: 125.
Regnault, Henri. (A. Meynell) M. of Art, 4: 69. — (W. G. Page) New Eng. M. n. s. 11: 704.
Regnier, Monsieur, Mystery of. (A. Forbes) 19th Cent. 35: 459.
Regret. (K. Chopin) Cent. 28: 147.
Regret of Spring; a story. (P. H. Burt) Cosmopol. 13: 63.
Rehatsek, Edward. (F. F. Arbuthnot) Bookworm, 6: 153.
Rehoboth, Mass. (G. Randall) New Eng. M. n. s. 11: 225.
Reid, Sir George. (B. Brown) M. of Art, 15: 196.
Reid, James, Picture Collection of. (R. Walker) M. of Art, 17: 153.
Reid, Whitelaw, Portraits of. McClure, 2: 20.
Reiff, Case of. (J. H. Dubbs) Ref. Q. 40: 55.

Reign of Terror, Women in. (J. G. Alger) National, 18: 639. Same art. Ecl. M. 118: 333. Same art. Liv. Age, 192: 606.
Reincarnation: is it a Natural Law? (T. Williams) Open Court, 7: 3898.
— Is it True? (J. R. Bridge) Open Court, 3: 1889.
Reindeer in Alaska. Lend a H. 10: 172. — (J. C. Cantwell) Chaut. 16: 562.
Reinecke, Carl. Music, 1: 174–212.
Reinhart, C. S., with portrait. Bk. Buyer, 11: 12. — (F. H. Smith) Q. Illust. 1: 147.
Réjane, Madame. (J. H. M'Carthy) Cent. 27: 839.
— and Sarcey. Critic, 26: 205.
— as Madame Sans-Gêne. Critic, 26: 169–189.
Rejected Manuscript, A; a story. (A. S. Hardy) Cosmopol. 16: 387.
Rejected Manuscript, The; a story. (E. S. Phelps Ward) Harper, 86: 282.
Rejection of MSS., Forms used for. (H. C. Cox) Writer, 7: 71.
— Reasons for. Writer, 7: 17, (M. A. Denison) 55.
Rejuvenation and Heredity. (C. S. Minot) Am. Natural. 30: 1, 89.
Relapses of Pap, The. (L. B. Bridgman) Overland, n. s. 25: 77.
Relation, Psychology of. (E. B. Titchener) Philos. R. 3: 193.
Relationship, Classificatory System of Australia. (L. Fison) Anthrop. J. 24: 360.
Relativity. (B. F. Underwood) Open Court, 1: 564.
Relic, Travels of a. (Le Cocq de Lautreppe) Cosmopol. 17: 478.
Relics of St. Eanswith. Illus. Archæol. 2: 47.
— Preservation of. Spec. 69: 382.
Relief by Work, Experiment in. (C. Gardener) Char. R. 4: 225.
Relief Work, Principles and Methods of. (W. Gladden) R. of Rs. (N. Y.) 9: 38, 179.
See Poor.
Reliefs, Archaic, at Dhimitzana. (G. C. Richards) J. Hel. Stud. 12: 41.
Religion, Æsthetic in. (J. W. Wright) Meth. R. 53: 90.
— and Density of Population. (E. Wiman) Pub. Opin. 15: 416.
— and Ethics, New Views of. (F. M. Holland) Open Court, 1: 519, 581.
— and Morality. (L. Tolstoi) Contemp. 65: 326. Same art. Liv. Age, 200: 798. Same art. Ecl. M. 122: 748.
— and Modern Science. (F. Jodl) Monist, 3: 329.
— and Philosophy, The Unification of. (M. C. O'Byrne) Open Court, 2: 1419.
— and Poetry. (S. Thurber) Educa. 16: 602.
— and Popular Literature. (T. Hannan) Westm. 143: 608. Same art. Ecl. M. 124: 181. — (J. S. Stahr) Ref. Q. 42: 272.
— and Reform. (W. Walsh) Westm. 142: 121. Same art. Ecl. M. 123: 433.
— and Science. (A. J. Du Bois) Cent. 27: 227. — (P. Carus) Open Court, 1: 405.
— — Marriage of. (C. S. Peirce) Open Court, 7: 3559.
— and the State. (J. Clifford) Contemp. 67: 433. — Reply. (W. H. Fremantle) Contemp. 67: 714.
— and Wealth. (W. Gladden) Bib. Sac. 52: 153.
— and the Working Classes. Eng. R. 15: 149.
— The Approaching New. (J. C. F. Grumbine) Open Court, 3: 1799.
— Art and, Reciprocity of. (F. M. Bristol) Meth. R. 54: 697.
— as Esprit de Corps. (J. Trevor) Time, 19: 429.
— Authority in. And. R. 17: 298.
Religion, Authority in, Fountains of. (F. R. Shipman) And. R. 17: 361.
— — Martineau on. (R. Rainy) Crit. R. 1: 5.
— — Place of. Church Q. 34: 265.
— — Seat of. (M. Dods) M. Chr. Lit. 5: 393. Same art. Chr. Un. 45: 12, 62.
— The Coming. (B. O. Flower) Arena, 8: 647. — (C. K. Whipple) Open Court, 3: 1623.
— Comparative. (J. F. Chaffee) Meth. R. 56: 409.
— — Nature and Scope of the Science of. (M. M. Snell) Bib. World, 8: 203.
— — Research in. (J. Jacobs) Folk-Lore, 1: 384.
— — Value and Danger of Study of. (F. N. Riale) Bib. World, 4: 14.
— Cosmopolitan. (C. A. Bartol) New World, 2: 51.
— Dawn of a New Era. (P. Carus) Forum, 16: 388.
— Definitions of, and Study of Non-Christian Religions. Bib. World, 6: 321.
— Divine and Human in. (F. M. Müller) Open Court, 5: 2819.
— Doctrine on. (E. V. Gerhart) M. Chr. Lit. 6: 321.
— Elizabethan. (F. G. Lee) Univ. R. 8: 238.
— End and Office of. (W. Elliott) Cath. World, 58: 57.
— Eternal. (G. M. McCrie) Open Court, 9: 4626.
— Ethics the only Basis of. (R. B. Marsh) Arena, 16: 448.
— Ethnic, and Christianity. (E. V. Gerhart) And. R. 17: 113.
— Everlasting Reality of. (J. Fiske) Chr. Lit. 14: 303, 419.
— Evolution of. (B. Bosanquet) Int. J. Ethics, 5: 432.
— — Caird on. Ath. '93, 2: 91. — (A. W. Benn) Acad. 43: 286. — (A. M. Fairbairn) Crit. R. 3: 198. — (W. B. Greene, jr.) Presb. & Ref. R. 6: 125. — (R. M. Wenley) Scot. R. 23: 143. — (J. Seth) Philos. R. 3: 69.
— for all Time. (L. R. Ehrich) Arena, 7: 385.
— — Ehrich on. (T. H. Pearne) Meth. R. 53: 747.
— From Despotism to Republicanism in. (J. Burroughs) Open Court, 1: 541.
— Future of. (A. Momerie) Fortn. 58: 834. — (J. H. Brown) Open Court, 4: 2127, 2157. — (M. M. Snell) Open Court, 7: 3823.
— History of, Teaching of. (J. Réville) Eth. Rec. 2: 223.
— Imagination in. (F. Tiffany) New World, 1: 264.
— in Business. (G. Hodges) Chaut. 15: 192.
— in Human Evolution. (F. Galton; B. Kidd) National, 23: 755, 763.
— in the U. S., Future of. (C. A. Briggs; A. H. Bradford) M. Chr. Lit. 6: 425.
— Is it Dead? (C. P. Geoffrey) Open Court, 3: 1943.
— Kernel of. (E. C. Hegeler) Open Court, 3: 2066.
— Liberal, Ground of all. (F. E. Abbot) Open Court, 3: 2012.
— — in America, Future of. (J. G. Schurman) New World, 1: 29.
— A Modern Conversation. (W. E. Hodgson) National, 21: 594.
— Modern Explanations of. (H. Schultz) New World, 2: 201.
— Monistic. What it is to me. (E. C. Hegeler) Open Court, 1: 725.
— My Grandmother's. (S. H. Morse) Eth. Rec. 3: 39.
— Natural. Church Q. 33: 323. — (F. M. Müller) Open Court, 4: 2350.
— — Seeley on. (E. Thurtell) Open Court, 6: 3255.
— New, Founding of a. (B. Carneri) Int. J. Ethics, 2: 492.

Religion. The New Eirenikon. (W. R. Sullivan) Westm. 142: 249. Same art. Ecl. M. 122: 629.
— of the Future. (A. Mathews) Bach. of Arts, 1: 775.
— of Letters, 1750–1850. Blackw. 154: 1. Same art. Ecl. M. 121: 334. Same art. Liv. Age, 198: 579.
— of a Literary Man, Le Gallienne's. (L. Johnson) Acad. 44: 477.
— of Savages, Lubbock on. (J. Carmichael) Pop. Sci. Mo. 48: 220.
— of Science. (P. Carus) Monist, 3: 352.
— of Soldiers and Sailors. (E. J. Hardy) Good Words, 33: 731.
— Old and New. (W. D. Gunning) Open Court, 3: 1883.
— on the Stage. Theatre, 35: 313.
— Pfleiderer on Morality and. (E. Ritchie) Philos. R. 5: 619.
— Philosophy and Development of, Pfleiderer on. (S. M. Jackson) Presb. & Ref. R. 6: 134.
— — Principal Fairbairn on. Bib. World, 6: 213.
— — Notion and Problem of. (O. Pfleiderer) Philos. R. 2: 1.
— Physical. (F. M. Müller) Open Court, 4: 2200–2249.
— — Müller's Gifford Lectures. Crit. R. 1: 381.
— Primitive. (C. B. Pallen) Am. Cath. Q. 18: 588.
— Reason, and Agnosticism. (A. Bodington) Westm. 139: 369. Same art. Ecl. M. 120: 752.
— Reason in, Supremacy of. (T. E. Allen) Arena, 7: 337.
— Romanes' Thoughts on. (A. F. Hewit) Cath. World, 62: 2. — (P. Carus) Monist, 5: 385.
— Savage, Limits of. (E. B. Tylor) Anthrop. J. 21: 283.
— Schleiermacher on. Spec. 70: 644.
— Scientific Treatment of. (D. J. H. Wood) Eth. Rec. 2: 23.
— Secularization of. (M. C. O'Byrne) Open Court, 1: 582.
— Separateness in. (G. J. Holyoake) Open Court, 1: 510.
— Services of Worship and Thought. (C. F. Dole) New World, 3: 488.
— Study of, Need of Systematic. (E. Buckley) Bib. World, 3: 119.
— Theoretical and Practical in. (G. A. Coe) Meth. R. 56: 394.
— True Necessity of. (A. W. Smith) Am. Cath. Q. 18: 345.
— Universal. (J. W. Chadwick) New World, 3: 401.
— — Possibility of. (I. N. Taylor) Arena, 16: 558.
— What can we give in Place of the Old Faith? (N. M. Salter) Eth. Rec. 1: 35.
Religions, Alleged Sympathy of. (J. H. Allen) New World, 4: 310.
— Ethnographic, and Ancestor Worship. (S. D. Peet) Am. Antiq. 15: 230.
— Foreign. (St. George Mivart) Cosmopol. 16: 609.
— Historical Study of, in America. (M. Jastrow, jr.) Bib. World, 1: 24.
— History of, in Modern Religious Education. (J. Réville) New World, 1: 503.
— Parliament of, 1893. Church Q. 41: 176. — (M. M. Trumbull) Monist, 4: 333. — (J. Cook) Our Day, 13: 37, (G. D. Boardman) 59. — (S. Gilbert and M. Müller) Chr. Lit. 10: 22, 291. — (A. F. Hewit) Cath. World, 59: 152. — (F. H. Stead) R. of Rs. (N. Y.) 9: 299. — (C. J. Little) Meth. R. 54: 208. — (C. C. Bonney) Monist, 5: 321. — (W. Pipe) Outl. 48: 385. — Open Court, 7: 3855, 3863. — (C. C. Bonney) N. Church R. 1: 73. — (C. H. Toy) New World, 2: 728. — (J. H. Barrows) R. of Rs. (N. Y.) 7: 303.
Religions, Parliament of, 1893, and the Barrows Lectureship. (G. S. Goodspeed) Bib. World, 5: 129.
— — and Breadth. Spec. 72: 81, 131.
— — as seen on Foreign Mission Fields. Meth. R. 56: 648.
— — Boardman on. Our Day, 13: 59.
— — Echoes of. (S. Wolkonsky) Cent. 26: 901. — (J. H. Barrows) Our Day, 13: 508.
— — Extension of. Monist, 5: 345.
— — A Peerless Bible in the. (J. Cook) Our Day, 13: 541.
— — Real Significance of. (F. M. Müller) Arena, 11: 1.
— — Reason at. (T. E. Allen) Arena, 8: 161.
— — Results of. (J. H. Barrows) Forum, 18: 54.
— — Results and Mission of. (G. T. Candlin) Bib. World, 5: 371.
— Statistics of Development of. (Fournier de Flaix) Am. Statis. Assoc. 3: 18.
— The Three. (J. S. Mackenzie) Int. J. Ethics, 2: 162, 327.
Religious, Why be? (M. Dods) Chr. Lit. 14: 146.
Religious Analysis of a New England Town. (W. B. Hale) Forum, 17: 71.
Religious Belief as a Basis of Moral Obligation. (E. P. Evans) Pop. Sci. Mo. 45: 83.
— Bases of, Upton's Hibbert Lecture on. Church Q. 39: 322.
— Fancies of a Believer. Blackw. 157: 237.
Religious Beliefs, Effect of Scientific Study upon. (H. S. Williams) Cent. 23: 273.
Religious Capacity. Spec. 69: 89.
Religious Conformity, Ethics of. (H. Sidgwick) Int. J. Ethics, 6: 273.
Religious Discussion, Limits of. (L. Coleman) No. Am. 156: 9.
Religious Doubt, Idealistic Remedy for. (D. W. Simon) Contemp. 62: 855.
Religious Education. (R. Gregory) Good Words, 33: 323. — (J. H. Jackson) Law Q. 12: 379.
— in Board Schools. (H. Adkins) Time, 8: 631.
— in England, Martineau on. Spec. 70: 599.
— in the Public Schools of the United States. (J. H. Crooker) Ecl. M. 126: 76.
Religious Equality and the Dissenters. Church Q. 34: 348.
Religious Evolution. (M. J. Savage) New World, 1: 216.
— Pure. Meth. R. 56: 629.
Religious Feeling and Literature. (A. A. Berle) Bib. Sac. 50: 261.
Religious Freedom and the Modern Pulpit. Time, 13: 430.
— Founding of Our. (M. D. Conway) Open Court, 2: 1163, 1175.
Religious Ideas, Good and Evil as. (P. Carus) Open Court, 9: 4642.
Religious Insanity. Eng. R. 6: 332.
Religious Instruction in England. Dub. R. 113: 886.
— in Public Schools. (N. S. Burton) And. R. 19: 33.
— in State Schools. (G. M. Grant) Educa. R. 3: 40. — (L. G. Janes) Educa. R. 4: 117.
Religious Intolerance in Tennessee. (B. O. Flower) Arena, 7: 120.
Religious Journalism and Journalists. (G. P. Morris) R. of Rs. (N. Y.) 12: 413.
— in Catholic Church. (J. J. Dunn) Chaut. 20: 712.
— in Congregational and Presbyterian Churches. (A. P. Foster) Chaut. 20: 585.
— in Protestant Episcopal Church. (G. A. Carstensen) Chaut. 21: 199.

Religious Liberty. (J. G. Hertwig) Am. J. Pol. 3: 430.
— and Popular Education. (Cardinal Vaughan) New R. 15: 97.
Religious People, Offence of. (J. Watson) Chr. Lit. 15: 48.
Religious Phenomena, Psychology of. (J. H. Leuba) Am. J. Psychol. 7: 309.
Religious Revolution, The Present. (J. C. F. Grumbine) Open Court, 5: 2975, 3001.
Religious Sentiment, The, and the Origin of Man. (A. Fogazzaro) Contemp. 68: 65. Same art. Chr. Lit. 13: 198.
— of Russia. (A. L. Beaulieu) Soc. Econ. 4: 13.
Religious Tableaux in Italian Churches. (W. H. D. Rouse) Folk-Lore, 5: 4.
Religious Teaching in the Elementary Schools. (T. J. Macnamara) Contemp. 69: 51.
— in London Board Schools. Ed. R. 180: 473. — (B. Herford) Contemp. 65: 271. — (A. Riley) National, 23: 514.
— in the Public Schools. (L. Abbott) Cent. 27: 943.
— Jowett on. (O. J. Simon) Jew. Q. 8: 245.
Religious Test Acts. (T. E. Bridgett) Month, 84: 58, 190.
Religious Thought in Ancient Greece and India. (H. Oldenberg) Open Court, 10: 5003.
— Modern. (T. B. Stork) Luth. Q. 23: 282.
— — Critical Review of Certain Phases of; a Reply. (S. Schwarm) Luth. Q. 22: 368.
— — Greek Elements in. (E. S. Carr) Bib. Sac. 53: 117.
— Philosophic Rise of. (H. Oldenberg) Open Court, 10: 4937.
— Progress of. (J. H. Fairchild) Bib. Sac. 49: 412.
Reluctant Evangelist, A; a story. National, 24: 415. Same art. Ecl. M. 123: 826. Same art. Liv. Age, 203: 776.
Remainders after Conditional Fees. (F. W. Maitland) Law Q. 6: 22.
Rembrandt. (H. Ward) Art J. 46: 23. — (M. G. Van Rensselaer) Cent. 25: 163. — (J. C. Robinson) 19th Cent. 37: 462. — (W. Armstrong) Portf. 23: 111.
— and his Art. Quar. 179: 365.
— and "The Night-watch." (T. Cole) Cent. 25: 170.
— and his Work. (J. M. Gray) Good Words, 35: 383.
— as an Educator. (H. C. Bierwirth) And. R. 17: 167.
— Ashburnham Picture by. (C. H. Middleton-Wake) Acad. 46: 452.
— Drawings of. (F. Wedmore) Acad. 41: 596.
— Dutuit's. (W. E. H.) M. of Art, 8: 418.
— Etchings of. (P. G. Hamerton) Portfo. 1894: no. 1.
— Individuality of. (M. G. Valbert) Pub. Opin. 15: 257.
— Life and Works of. (W. Armstrong) Fortn. 61: 234. Same art. Liv. Age, 200: 755. Same art. Ecl. M. 122: 413.
— Life of, Michel's. Sat. R. 77: 152. — (J. C. Van Dyke) Dial (Ch.) 16: 139. — (K. Cox) Nation, 58: 13. — Blackw. 154: 675. Same art. Liv. Age, 199: 707.
— Michel's and Simmonds's Lives of. Ath. '94, 2: 102.
— Paintings by; the Holford Collection. (F. Wedmore) Acad. 44: 78.
Remedies, Country. (S. Baring-Gould) Sund. M. 24: 240.
— Some Popular. Chamb. J. 72: 42.
— used in Former Times. (F. S. Potter) Time, 10: 530.
Remick Family Genealogy. (O. P. Remick) N. E. Reg. 47: 473.
Remington, Frederic, with portrait. Bk. Buyer, 11: 437.
Reminiscence of Old Bon Air; a story. (W. T. Hale) Southern M. 4: 184.
Reminiscence, A. (L. B. Bates) Overland, n. s. 23: 86.
Reminiscences and Anecdotes. (Gen. J. Cochran) Am. Hist. Reg. 1: 432.
Renaissance, The. (I. Zangwill) Critic, 28: 345.
— and the School, 1440–1580. (S. S. Laurie) School R. 4: 140, 202.
— Aspects of. (J. M. Stone) Month, 86: 473. 88: 98–502.
— Early, and Sculpture. (B. Fletcher, jr.) Archit. Rec. 2: 418.
— English. (E. Rivoalen) Am. Arch. 43: 15.
— French. (A. Saint-Paul) Am. Arch. 43: 51 — 44: 15.
— Homes of. (W. Wood) Cosmopol. 12: 671.
— in its Broader Aspects. (J. A. Symonds) New R. 7: 293. Same art. Liv. Age, 195: 451.
— in France. (G. A. T. Middleton) Archit. Rec. 6: 126.
— in Italy of To-day. (G. R. W. Scott) Our Day, 12: 121.
— Influence of, on Painting. (B. F. Fletcher) Archit. Rec. 4: 157.
— Italian. (A. D. F. Hamlin) Am. Arch. 44: 40 — 45: 85.
— Muntz's Precursors of the. (C. Monkhouse) M. of Art, 5: 495.
— The New Spirit. (J. A. Symonds) Fortn. 59: 4. Same art. Ecl. M. 120: 577.
Renaissance Art at Bardini's, Florence. (H. Ward) Art J. 45: 10.
Renan, Ernest. (J. Jacobs) Acad. 42: 311. — Ath. '92, 2: 484. — (G. Monod) Contemp. 62: 632. Same art. Ecl. M. 119: 844. — Critic, 21: 195. — Dial (Ch.) 13: 234. — (E. Crawford) Fortn. 58: 667. — (J. Taylor) M. Chr. Lit. 7: 249. — (P. Waddington) M. Chr. Lit. 7: 251. — (R. G. Ingersoll) No. Am. 155: 608. — Pub. Opin. 14: 21. — Sat. R. 74: 408. — Spec. 69: 491. — (A. W. Benn) Acad. 43: 497. — (M. D. Conway) Monist, 3: 201. — (A. W. Benn) New World, 2: 60. — (J. Darmesteter) New World, 2: 401. — With portrait. (G. Monod) Pop. Sci. Mo. 42: 831. — (A. Neubauer) Jew. Q. 5: 200. — (J. G. Colclough) Month, 76: 305, 472. — (J. S. Smith) So. M. 1: 431.
— after Thirty Years. (E. H. Hall) New World, 5: 493.
— and Christianity. (R. H. Hutton) National, 20: 301. Same art. Ecl. M. 120: 66.
— and Henriette; a memoir. (E. G. Johnson) Dial (Ch.) 20: 230.
— Another View of. Atlan. 71: 431.
— Berthelot and. (A. D. Vandam) Contemp. 68: 862.
— A Chat about. (A. D. Vandam) Fortn. 58: 678.
— Correspondence with his Sister. (A. Laugel) Nation, 61: 185.
— Detached Leaves. (A. Laugel) Nation, 54: 187, 226. — (S. J. Low) National, 19: 338.
— D'Hulst's Life of. Spec. 71: 176.
— Funeral of. (A. Laugel) Nation, 55: 316.
— Gaiety of. Spec. 68: 297.
— Glimpses of. Critic, 20: 119.
— Grant-Duff on. Spec. 70: 567.
— His Loss of Faith in Science. (J. Dewey) Open Court, 7: 3512.
— Philosophy of. (F. L. Oswald) Open Court, 6: 3447.
— Portraits of. McClure, 2: 345.
— Recollections of. (F. Pollock) 19th Cent. 32: 711.
— Table-talk of. (H. Le Roux) Fortn. 38: 685.

Renan, Ernest, Two Phases of Life of. (J. Dewey) Open Court, 6: 3505.
Renan, Henriette. Temp. Bar, 108: 362. Same art. Ecl. M. 127: 215. Same art. Liv. Age, 210: 439.—(E. F. S. Dilke) Ath. '94, 1: 709.
— by her Brother. Sat. R. 80: 86.
Renaudot, Théophraste, a 17th Century Reformer. (Edith Sellers) Temp. Bar, 101: 209. Same art. Liv. Age, 201: 20. Same art. Lend a H. 12: 211, 251.
— Old Journalism and New. (J. Macintyre) 19th Cent. 34: 596.
Réné; a story. (M. E. Wotton) Argosy, 61: 241.
Renée de France. (A. Laugel) Nation, 63: 287, 307.
Renewal, The; a story. (E. F. Benson) Cosmopol. 18: 44.
Reno Gang, Destruction of. (C. Moffett) McClure, 4: 549.
Rent. (A. Marshall) Econ. J. 3: 74.
— and Profit. (C. W. Macfarlane) Ann. Am. Acad. Pol. Sci. 5: 90.
— Curiosities of. Chamb. J. 73: 827.
— Essence of, and Place of, in the Distribution of Wealth. (T. L. Brown) Arena, 9: 81.
— Marginal, Concept of. (J. H. Hollander) Q. J. Econ. 9: 175.
Rent Day; a story. (Rhoda Broughton) Temp. Bar, 98: 228. Same art. Liv. Age, 198: 330.
Répin, Ílya; a Russian National Artist. (I. F. Hapgood) Cent. 23: 3.
Report of Chance, The; a story. (C. Burton) Temp. Bar, 95: 58.
Reporter, Metropolitan Newspaper. (A. F. Matthews) Chaut. 18: 164.
Reporter of the Evening Despatch; a story. All the Year, 72: 301.
Reporters, Parliamentary. (Wm. Maxwell) Time, 20: 469.
Reporting, Parliamentary, Some Humours of. Macmil. 71: 365.
Repplier, Agnes, with portrait. Bk. Buyer, 10: 633. (L. H. Bugg) Cath. World, 64: 74.
Representation and Independence, Balfour on. Spec. 73: 39.
— in New England Legislatures. (G. H. Haynes) Ann. Am. Acad. Pol. Sci. 6: 254.
— in Virginia. (J. A. C. Chandler) J. H. Univ. Studies, 14: 263.
— Modern Theory of. (L. R. Harley) Am. M. Civics, 6: 337.
— Proportional. (W. D. Foulke) Am. M. Civics, 7: 400.—(W. D. Foulke) Pub. Opin. 18: 634.—(J. R. Commons) Ann. Am. Acad. Pol. Sci. 2: 700.—(W. D. McCrackan) Arena, 7: 290.—(S. Cooley) New Eng. M. n. s. 8: 116.—(W. D. McCrackan) New Eng. M. n. s. 9: 698.—(F. M. Holland) Open Court, 8: 4191.
— — for Representatives in Congress. (J. M. Ashley) Arena, 14: 221.
— — The Fundamental Reform. (W. H. T. Wakefield) Am. M. Civics, 9: 365.
— — in 1844. (T. Gilpin) Ann. Am. Acad. Pol. Sci. 7: 233.
— — Miner's View of. (S. Neil) Time, 12: 257.
— — Municipal Reform by. (M. N. Forney) Citizen, 1: 278.
— — the Only Effective Moralizer of Politics. (C. H. Spence) Arena, 10: 767.
— — a Remedy for Misrule. (J. E. Whitney) Am. M. Civics, 8: 127.
— — Social Basis of. (J. W. Jenks) Ann. Am. Acad. Pol. Sci. 6: 381.
Representative in Congress, Position of, with respect to the People. (C. H. Lincoln) Ann. Am. Acad. Pol. Sci. 6: 117.
Representative Assemblies, The World's, of To-day; a study in comparative legislation. (E. K. Alden) J. H. Univ. Studies, 11: no. 2.
Representative Government and Federalism. (E. Meek) Canad. M. 6: 561.
Reprieve of Capitalist Clyve. (O. Wister) Lippinc. 52: 95.
Reproduction, Problems of. (M. Hartog) Contemp. 62: 92.
Reptiles, Man-eating. (A. Stradling) Chamb. J. 62: 475.
Reptilia, Distribution of, in North America. (E. D. Cope) Am. Natural. 30: 886, 1003.
— of the Baptamodon Beds. (O. C. Marsh) Am. J. Sci. 150: 405.
Reptilian Remains, from the Triassic of Northern California. (J. C. Merriam) Am. J. Sci. 150: 55.
Republic, Ideal, Brief History of an. (Robert Harton) Cosmopol. 20: 437.
— Is our, a Failure? (H. P. Judson) Soc. Econ. 9: 95.
— Race between the Empire and. Soc. Econ. 8: 24.
— A World-wide. (E. P. Powell) Arena, 5: 212.
Republican Clubs, National League of, Convention, 1894. Pub. Opin. 17: 308.
Republican Convention, 1896. Gunton's M. 11: 1.—Pub. Opin. 20: 805.
Republican League of the U. S. (L. A. Bond) Nat'l M. (N. Y. '91) 16: 110.
Republican Party, The, and the Farmer. (J. A. Waymire) Overland, n. s. 28: 592.
— Defeat of, 1892. (E. G. Salisbury) Am. J. Pol. 2: 388.—(C. H. Reeve) Am. J. Pol. 2: 603.
— Does it need Reorganization? (S. N. Dolph) No. Am. 156: 54.
— A Future for. (E. D. M'Creary) Am. J. Pol. 2: 644.
— Origin and Task of. (A. D. Morse) Pol. Sci. Q. 7: 522.
— Outlook for, 1894. (T. H. Carter) No. Am. 158: 423.
— — 1895. (C. T. Saxton) No. Am. 161: 536.
— Outlook and Duty of, 1893. (H. C. Lodge) Forum, 15: 250.
— What it stands for. (Horace Porter) Forum, 21: 722.
Republicanism in France. (F. V. Fisher) Westm. 139: 229.
— What is? (C. Thomas) Open Court, 10: 4863, 4897.
Republicans, European, Linton's. (W. R. Thayer) Nation, 56: 279.
Republics, Thoughts on. (G. Saintsbury) Citizen, 2: 84.
Repudiation. (E. M. Burchard) Am. J. Pol. 4: 330.
Reputation, Desire for, as affecting Authors. Spec. 72: 43.
Requiem; a story. (Pont da Lenha) Gent. M. n. s. 56: 1. Same art. Ecl. M. 126: 269. Same art. Liv. Age, 208: 335.
Resaca. (M. Thompson) Lippinc. 57: 667.
Rescue Mission Work. (A. F. Schauffler) M. Chr. Lit. 5: 437.
Research in Education. (H. E. Armstrong) Nature, 51: 463.
— the Vital Spirit of Teaching. (G. S. Hall) Forum, 17: 558.
Resemblance, Immediate. (W. James) Mind, 18: 208.
— Simple. (F. H. Bradley) Mind, 18: 83.
Reservations, Public, in Mass., Trustees of. (C. S. Sargent) Garden & F. 9: 331.
Residuary Legatee, The. (W. Pigott) Chamb. J. 73: 316.
Resistance Standards, New Apparatus for Exact Adjustment of. (E. G. Willyoung) J. Frankl. Inst. 135: 140.

Resolutions by Public Meetings: Verbal Poultices. Spec. 71: 545.
Respectability, A Word for. Spec. 68: 83.
Respectable, Meanings of the Word. (F. Hall) Nation, 61: 9.
Respiration, Comparative Physiology of. (S. H. Gage) Am. Natural. 26: 817. Same art. Nature, 46: 598.
— A Quarter of a Century of Work on. (C. F. Townsend) Knowl. 19: 200.
Responsibility, Free-will and. (D. G. Ritchie) Int. J. Ethics, 5: 409.
— Legal, and Arrested Brain Development. (T. S. Clouston) Jurid. R. 7: 38.
— Ritchie on. (J. H. Hyslop) Int. J. Ethics, 6: 101.
Rest: Greatest Need of College Girls. (A. P. Call) Atlan. 69: 102.
Rest; a poem. (A. L. Salmon) Gent. M. n. s. 53: 635.
Restaurants, Dockers'. (E. Sellers) Good Words, 35: 327.
— for the Laboring Classes. (M. M. Mallock) National, 21: 62.
— Old New York. (A. Fawcett) Lippinc. 54: 709.
Restless Dead, The; a story. Blackw. 152: 789. Same art. Ecl. M. 120: 99. Same art. Liv. Age, 196: 208.
Restlessness. Spec. 69: 10.
Restoration, Novelists of the. (W. H. Hudson) Time, 19: 566.
— Town Life under the. (W. C. Sydney) Gent. M. n. s. 49: 73.
Restoration, Universal. (A. F. Hewit) Cath. World, 59: 338.
Restoration House, The. (S. T. Aveling) Scrib. M. 13: 453.
Resurrection and Final Judgment. (E. B. Fairfield) Bib. Sac. 49: 62. 50: 487.
— as the Cardinal Feature of Apostolic Teaching. (P. Whitefoord) Chr. Lit. 15: 389.
— Immortality and. (G. Allen) Fortn. 60: 317.
— Dr. Heber Newton on. (G. M. Searle) Cath. World, 61: 387.
— of the Body. (C. L. Barringer) Luth. Q. 24: 499.
— What is the? (L. R. Fiske) Meth. R. 52: 177.
Resurrection, The; a sonnet. (E. Lee-Hamilton) M. of Art, 6: 374.
Rethel, Alfred. (J. M. Gray) Good Words, 34: 344.
Reticence in Literature. Spec. 75: 45.
Retina, Shadows of Blood-vessels upon. (C. L. Franklin) Psychol. R. 2: 392.
Retribution, Divine, and Providence, Greek and Hebrew Ideas of. (C. G. Montefiore) Jew. Q. 5: 517.
— Doctrine of, in Old Testament. (C. G. Montefiore) Jew. Q. 3: 1.
— — in New Testament. (J. F. Odgers) Jew. Q. 3: 13.
— — in Rabbinical Literature. (S. Schechter) Jew. Q. 3: 34.
Retribution; a story of the 17th Century. (H. Pyle) Harper, 86: 683.
Retrievers. (G. Lascelles) Time, 2: 415.
Retrospection; a poem. (C. A. Price) Belgra. 77: 315.
Rettig, John. (A. Ramsay) Mo. Illust. 4: 329.
Return of the Probationer. (E. F. Benson) Eng. Illust. 11: 999.
Return, The; a poem. (F. D. Sherman) Cosmopol. 20: 501.
Returned with Thanks. (G. B. Burgin) Good Words, 33: 804.
Returning a Verdict; a story. Cornh. 73: 57. Same art. Ecl. M. 126: 259. Same art. Liv. Age, 208: 210.
Retz, Gilles de Laval, Marechal de: Bluebeard. Belgra. 80: 58.
Retz, Paul, Cardinal de. Macmil. 70: 130. Same art. Liv. Age, 202: 101.
Reuchlin, Johann. (S. A. Hirsch) Jew. Q. 8: 445.
Reuleaux, Franz. (H. Zopke) Cassier, 11: 133.
Reunion of Christendom. (Earl Halifax) 19th Cent. 39: 850.
Reuter, Fritz. (Helen Zimmern) Time, 7: 734.
Réveillon, Le; a Christmas tale. (F. Fabre) Harper, 86: 85.
Revelation, Christian. Its Relation to Experience. (E. M. Caillard) Contemp. 69: 119.
Revelation, Divine. (J. F. Chaffee) Meth. R. 55: 99.
— Given as Man can receive it. (S. Domer) Luth. Q. 22: 161.
— Infallible. Can we have and do we need it? (T. E. Allen) Arena, 16: 986.
Revenge of Lucas Helm; a story. (F. M. F. Skene) Argosy, 61: 712.
Revenue, Sources of. (D. MacG. Means) Nation, 57: 185.
Revenue Customs; Adequacy of the System. (R. F. Hoxie) J. Pol. Econ. 3: 39.
Revenue-cutter Service, The U. S. (P. W. Thompson) Scrib. M. 11: 207.
Revenues, Public, Classification of. (E. R. A. Seligman) Q. J. Econ. 7: 286. 9: 279.
Revere, Paul, Ride of. (H. A. Giddings) M. Am. Hist. 29: 360. — (H. A. Giddings) Nat'l M. (N. Y. '91) 18: 37.
Reverend Peter Flannery; a story. (F. Mathew) Idler, 2: 170.
Reversible Love-affair, A; a story. (T. A. Janvier) Cosmopol. 15: 423.
Reviewers, Authors, and Publishers. (F. Wicks) National, 20: 640. Same art. Ecl. M. 120: 342.
— A Word for. (S. J. Low) National, 18: 799.
Reviews, English Weekly. (W. E. Hodgson) Fortn. 58: 508. Same art. Liv. Age, 195: 726.
Reviews, Should they be signed? (C. Thomas) Open Court, 7: 3788.
Revival of Religion, A; a symposium. (J. O. Peck and others) Meth. R. 53: 240.
Revivalists. *See* Evangelists.
Revolt, A; a short story. (R. Mace) Munsey, 11: 442.
Revolt of the ——, The; a story. (R. Barr) Idler, 5: 357. Same art. McClure, 3: 169.
Revolution, American, French Aid in. (M. G. Edmands) Nat'l M. (N. Y. '91) 17: 120.
— Massachusetts Daughters of the. (M. C. Pelletier) Bost. 2: 109.
— of '76. (F. A. Roe) Am. Hist. Reg. 2: 1401.
— Right of, and Authority of the State. (P. Carus) Open Court, 8: 3961, 3970.
Revolutions, Modern, and their Results. (K. Blind) No. Am. 154: 655.
— Renan on. Spec. 69: 521.
Revue des Deux Mondes. (L. Pollens) Critic, 29: 277.
Reward of Bravery, The; a story. (A. W. Tarbell) Bost. 4: 392.
Reward of the Unrighteous. (G. G. Bain) Cent. 23: 347.
Rewards, Theory of. (H. Rashdall) Econ. R. 2: 496.
Rey, Jean, Essays of. (L. A. Hallopeau and A. Poisson) Pop. Sci. Mo. 44: 247.
Rey, Jean F., Abduction of. (W. C. Dufour) Green Bag, 5: 261.
Reybaud, Madame Charles. Temp. Bar, 103: 63. Same art. Liv. Age, 203: 235.

Reymond, Madame, Acquittal of. Spec. **69**: 88.
Reynard the Fox, translated by Ellis. Sat. R. **77**: 696.
Reynell, Charles W. Ath. '92, **1**: 149, 245.
Reynolds, Edwin. Cassier, **1**: 346. — With portrait. (H. L. Conard) Nat'l M. (N. Y. '91) **18**: 64.
Reynolds, Sir Joshua. (J. C. Robinson) 19th Cent. **37**: 462. — M. of Art, **15**: 138. — (Fred Keppel) Scrib. M. **15**: 93.
— and his Models. (F. A. Gerard) Art J. **44**: 18.
— Lady Betty Delené and her Children. Sat. R. **79**: 39.
— Lady Cockburn and her Children. Portfo. **24**: 1.
— Painting of Samuel Johnson. Walford's Antiq. **4**: 1.
Rhabdomancy. (L. T. Vance) J. Am. Folk-Lore, **4**: 241.
Rhetoric and Public Speaking in the American College. (H. A. Frink) Educa. **13**: 129.
— Decay of. Spec. **68**: 672.
— for Science. (S. W. Balch) Educa. **16**: 223.
— Illogical. (F. A. Teall) Writer, **9**: 98.
— Scottish School of. (A. M. Williams) Educa. **13**: 142–488.
— Teacher's Outfit in. (J. F. Genung) School R. **3**: 405.
— Teaching of, Value of the Office-hour in. (C. S. Baldwin) Educa. R. **8**: 290.
Rhind, J. Massey. (N. MacDonald) Munsey, **14**: 671.
Rhine, Falls of the, in Winter. All the Year, **74**: 274.
— Scenery along. (F. Williamson) Art J. **46**: 294.
— The Upper. (F. L. Ford) Munsey, **7**: 546.
Rhizopods, Acid in the Digestion of Certain. (J. C. Hemmeter) Am. Natural. **30**: 619.
— Rocky Mountain. (E. Penard) Am. Natural. **25**: 1070.
Rhoads, Samuel, Mayor of Philadelphia, 1774. (H. D. Biddle) Pennsyl. M. **19**: 64.
Rhode Island. (E. B. Andrews) New Eng. M. n. s. **7**: 63.
— and Maryland; which established Religious Liberty first? (R. H. Clarke) Am. Cath. Q. **20**: 289.
— at the World's Fair. (J. C. Wyman) New Eng. M. n. s. **10**: 427.
— Glimpses of Old. (W. R. McGarry) Nat'l M. (N. Y. '91) **16**: 188.
— Population Tendencies in. (H. R. Palmer) New Eng. M. n. s. **14**: 159.
Rhodes, Cecil. (W. T. Stead) R. of Rs. (N. Y.) **13**: 317. — Westm. **145**: 660. — With portrait. (W. F. Day) Munsey, **11**: 462.
— and the Cape Parliament. New R. **14**: 587.
— and Jameson. (J. Verschoyle) Fortn. **65**: 483.
— and the Jameson Raid. Sat. R. **81**: 479.
— and South Africa. (J. C. Hopkins) Canad. M. **3**: 436. — (H. A. Bryden) Sat. R. **80**: 435.
— and the Transvaal. Fortn. **65**: 839.
— as a Monopolist. Sat. R. **80**: 400.
— Colonist and Imperialist. Contemp. **69**: 374.
— Influence in South Africa. Sat. R. **80**: 536.
— A Power for Peace in South Africa. Sat. R. **82**: 209.
Rhodes, James F., with portrait. Bk. Buyer, **9**: 667.
Rhodes, City of, Capitulation of, 1522. (R. Parsons) Cath. World, **59**: 502.
Rhodesia, Early Days in. (Lady H. Paulet) New R. **14**: 696.
— Gold Mining in. (W. F. Wilkinson) J. Soc. Arts, **44**: 687.
— of To-day, Knight's. Sat. R. **79**: 226.
— Two Years in. (L. Dècle) National, **27**: 531.
Rhododendron Land; a poem. (E. E. Hale) Cosmopol. **15**: 685.
Rhododendrons and Azaleas. (W. Goldring) Garden & F. **9**: 253.
— at the Columbian Exposition. (L. H. Bailey) Garden & F. **6**: 259.
— at Wellesley, Mass. (T. D. Hatfield) Garden & F. **9**: 267.
— Country Roads and. (C. S. Sargent) Garden & F. **8**: 271.
— Hardy. (J. McPherson) Garden & F. **6**: 178. — Garden & F. **7**: 268.
— in a Hard Winter. (H. H. Hunnewell) Garden & F. **8**: 209.
— in a Natural Wood. Garden & F. **8**: 252.
— Notes on. Garden & F. **8**: 214.
Rhone, a Feast-day on the. (T. A. Janvier) Cent. **29**: 409.
— Sketches on. (J. Pennell) M. of Art, **13**: 236.
Rhoscomyl, Owen. Jewel of Ynys Galon. Sat. R. **79**: 869.
Rhubarb. Chamb. J. **72**: 375.
Rhyme, Philosophy of. (E. Noble) Poet-Lore, **7**: 585.
Rhymes for a Little Girl. (T. B. Macaulay) Eng. Illust. **10**: 545, 629.
Rhyming Words. All the Year, **75**: 156.
Rhys, Ernest, Poetry of. (L. Johnson) Acad. **46**: 248.
Rhythm. (T. L. Bolton) Am. J. Psychol. **6**: 145.
— Music, and Muscle. (T. Allbutt) Nature, **49**: 340.
Ribot, Thos., and Modern Psychology. (E. Sokal) Open Court, **7**: 3655.
— on Diseases of Memory. (P. Carus) Open Court, **1**: 344.
— on Memory. (P. Carus) Open Court, **1**: 264.
— on Will. (P. Carus) Open Court, **1**: 455, 487.
Ricardo, David, Letters to J. R. McCulloch. (J. H. Hollander, editor) Am. Econ. Assoc. **10**: 611.
— in Parliament. (E. Cannan) Econ. J. **4**: 249, 409.
— Interpretation of. (S. N. Patten) Q. J. Econ. **7**: 322.
— on Currency. (J. Bonar) Econ. J. **6**: 64.
— Some Unpublished Letters of. (J. H. Hollander) Q. J. Econ. **10**: 209.
Ricasoli, Baron, Last Letters of. (J. W. Mario) Nation, **59**: 459.
Rice, Alexander H., Recollections of. (A. L. Stimson) Bost. **3**: 153, 260.
Rice, Culture of, in Japan, Mexico, and the U. S., Hygienic Aspect of. (A. S. Ashmead) Science, **20**: 57.
Rich Fool, The, and the Clever Pauper. (H. A. Vachell) Overland, n. s. **23**: 49.
Rich Men, Expenditure of. (E. L. Godkin) Scrib. M. **20**: 495.
— in a Republic, Uses of. (F. Harrison) Forum, **16**: 478.
— Legislation against. (D. MacG. Means) Nation, **57**: 40.
Rich Miss Girard, The. (H. Robertson) Scrib. M. **14**: 390.
Rich Miss Riddell; a story. Blackw. **155**: 167–645.
Richard of Glastonbury. (D. B. Camm) Month, **84**: 347.
Richard Maitland, Consul. (L. T. Meade and R. K. Douglas) Chamb. J. **71**: 631–679. **72**: 278–327.
Richard Peake, Ballad of. (R. Rodd) Eng. Illust. **11**: 555.
Richard and Robin; a story. (R. Grant) Harper, **90**: 139.
Richards, E. Windsor. Cassier, **7**: 176.
Richardson, Sir Benjamin Ward. Nature, **55**: 80.

Richardson, Henry Hobson. (H. Townsend) M. of Art, **17**: 133.
— and his Work. (E. Hale) New Eng. M. n. s. **11**: 513.
Richardson, John, Lieut., Letters of, 1776. Pennsyl. M. **16**: 202.
Richardson, Samuel, at Home. (A. Dobson) Scrib. M. **14**: 375.
Richardt, Christian. Ath. '93, **1**: 19.
Richborough. (A. Hall) Antiq. n. s. **27**: 207.
Richelieu, Cardinal. (J. B. Perkins) Chaut. **24**: 22.
— and Father Joseph. Quar. **183**: 339.
Richenda: a novel. (M. Moule) All the Year, **76**: 20–289.
Richmond, George. Ath. '96, **1**: 419.
Richmond, Eng., Lock and Tidal-Weir at. (J. B. Hilditch) J. Soc. Arts, **41**: 634.
Richmond, Va., Electric Railway in. (F. J. Sprague) Engin. M. **7**: 787.
— Soldiers' Home. So. Hist. Pap. **20**: 315.
Richter, Gustav. (M. Thompson) Chaut. **14**: 453.
Richter, Jean Paul. (L. E. Tiddeman) Belgra. **81**: 299. — (J. F. Wallace) Poet-Lore, **5**: 551. — (J. Forster) Chaut. **23**: 610. — Eng. R. **7**: 276.
Rickmansworth, England. (F. G. Kitton) Art J. **46**: 329.
Rico, Martin. (A. F. Jaccaci) Cosmopol. **13**: 272.
Riddles, Russian. Chamb. J. **70**: 479.
Ride for Dear Life. (C. Montague) Longm. **23**: 420.
Ride with "Starlight;" a story. (A. Barczinsky) Temp. Bar, **107**: 138.
Riders, Australian Rough-. (R. Boldrewood) Macmil. **69**: 430. Same art. Liv. Age, **201**: 429.
Rides, Long-distance. Chamb. J. **69**: 756. — Spec. **69**: 493. — (C. King) Cosmopol. **16**: 295. — (H. Romeyn) Outing, **22**: 45.
— — German View of. Sat. R. **74**: 531.
Ridgefield, Connecticut. (H. E. Miller) New Eng. M. n. s. **13**: 227.
Riding and Polo, Weir and Brown on. Ed. R. **175**: 34.
— Anderson on. Sat. R. **78**: 512.
— at Fences. Sat. R. **75**: 400.
Riding Recollections, Some. Macmil. **73**: 192.
Ridpath, John Clark. R. of Rs. (N. Y.) **11**: 294.
Rieger, Franz. (Edith Sellers) Temp. Bar. **107**: 335.
Riel Rebellion: Canadian Militia in Action. (H. J. Woodside) Outing, **22**: 227, 288.
Rienzi of Romance and History. (G. Todd) Leis. Hour, **45**: 770.
Rienzo, Cola di. (H. W. Preston and L. Dodge) Atlan. **71**: 62.
Rifle, Magazine: Development and Use. (W. A. Campbell) Un. Serv. (Phila.) **12**: 403.
— Repeating, in Hunting and Warfare. (J. A. A. Robinson) Overland, n. s. **20**: 141.
— Woodgate's Automatic. Sat. R. **76**: 11.
Rifle-fire, Modern. (J. M. Macartney) Un. Serv. M. **10**: 31.
Rifle-shooting in America, Military. (A. S. Jones) Outing, **28**: 470.
Rifles: Enfield Small-arms Factory. Chamb. J. **69**: 550.
— Making of. Nature, **47**: 163.
— Military. (W. L. Clowes) Un. Serv. M. **10**: 450.
Rigging and Sails. (A. J. Kenealy) Outing, **26**: 44.
Riggs, Mary. (A. R. Buckland) Sund. M. **24**: 674.
Righi, Sunrise on the. (F. B. Sauvel) Educa. **14**: 614.
Right-handedness. (F. E. Kavanagh) Citizen, **2**: 44.
— Origin of. (J. M. Baldwin) Pop. Sci. Mo. **44**: 606.
Righteous Woman, A; a story. (M. Watson) Eng. Illust. **13**: 531.
Rights and Duties. (J. S. Mackenzie) Int. J. Ethics, **6**: 425.
— Natural, Pedigree of. (W. Wallace) Time, **18**: 167.
Riis, Jacob A., with portrait. Bk. Buyer, **7**: 658.
Riker, Richard. (I. Browne) Green Bag, **8**: 141.
Riley, Charles Valentine. (E. P. Powell) Educa. **16**: 349. — (G. B. Goode) Science, n. s. **3**: 217. — (A. S. Packard) Science, n. s. **2**: 745. — Nature, **52**: 600.
Riley, Jas. Whitcomb, with portrait. Bk. Buyer, **5**: 96. — With portrait. Bk. News, **10**: 278. — (H. Garland) McClure, **2**: 219. — (R. R. Wilson) Munsey, **13**: 380.
Rimini, Francesca da. (J. Cartwright) M. of Art, **7**: 137.
Rimini. (H. Zimmern) Eng. Illust. **9**: 775.
— Historical. (E. M. Cesaresco) National, **19**: 612. Same art. Liv. Age, **194**: 600.
— To-Day. (E. M. Cesaresco) Portfo. **23**: 148, 158.
Ring out the Old, — Ring in the New; a poem. (H. M. Burnside) Argosy, **58**: 537.
Ringel d'Illzach, Medals by. M. of Art, **9**: 524.
Rings. (F. Peacock) Dub. R. **115**: 54.
— Famous. (M. J. Onahan) Cath. World, **63**: 254.
— Posy. Gent. M. n. s. **48**: 637. — (J. Evans) Longm. **20**: 26.
— — and Marriage. Chamb. J. **72**: 527.
Rings, Planetary, Formation of, as a Process of Disintegration. (W. Meyer) Astron. **12**: 407.
Rink, Hendrik. (R. Brown) Geog. J. **3**: 65.
Rio de Janeiro. (A. Montefiore) Time, **22**: 639.
— after the War of 1894. (C. A. Voigt) Un. Serv. M. **10**: 404.
Rio Grande: the American Congo. (J. G. Bourke) Scrib. M. **15**: 590.
— Popular Superstitions of the. (J. G. Bourke) J. Am. Folk-Lore, **7**: 119.
Rio Grande Valley, Language and Folk-Usage of. (J. G. Bourke) J. Am. Folk-Lore, **9**: 81.
Riot, Fireman's, at New Haven, 1858. (E. Smith) Bach. of Arts, **1**: 167.
— Law of. (J. B. L. Birnie) Jurid. R. **3**: 138.
Riots and Means of Suppression. (H. Romeyn) Un. Serv. (Phila.) **7**: 357.
— Featherstone and Other. (H. L. Stephen) National, **22**: 673.
— Law of. Spec. **71**: 421.
— Students', in Paris, in 1893. Am. Arch. **41**: 132.
Ripple's Relish; a story. All the Year, **75**: 468.
Rise and Fall of Religion at Duxbury Swamp. (W. Atkinson) Chamb. J. **72**: 553.
Rise of the Bottom Rail; a story. (J. A. Williams, jr.) Outing, **23**: 436.
Risk, an Economic Factor. (J. Haynes) Q. J. Econ. **9**: 409.
Ritchie, Mrs. Anne: Chapters from Some Unwritten Memoirs. Macmil. **66**: 17, 344. **69**: 443. **70**: 429. Same art. Liv. Age, **193**: 819. **195**: 108, 247. **201**: 226. **203**: 548.
— Unwritten Memoirs. (E. G. Johnson) Dial (Ch.) **18**: 8.
— Visit to, with portrait. (Mrs. B. Harrison) Bookman, **1**: 164.
Ritschl, Albrecht. (J. Orr) Chr. Lit. **11**: 135 a.
— Theology of. Lond. Q. **86**: 268. — (J. Orr) M. Chr. Lit. **6**: 417.
Ritschlianism. (C. Jensen) Luth. Q. **25**: 556.
Rittenhouse, David. (H. S. Davis) Pop. Astron. **4**: 1.
Rittenhouse Paper-mill, History of. (H. G. Jones) Pennsyl. M. **20**: 315.
Ritter vom Geiste, The. (E. Liebling) Music, **1**: 76–280.

Ritualism: the Bennett Case. Eng. R. 15: 111.
— Errors of. (F. W. Farrar) Contemp. 64: 60. Same art. Ecl. M. 121: 260. — Reply. (W. J. Knox-Little) Contemp. 64: 182. — Rejoinder. (F. W. Farrar) Contemp. 64: 351.
— in the Church of England, The Newest. (A. W. Grange) Am. Cath. Q. 18: 779.
Rival, The; a poem. (G. Hall) Harper, 90: 780.
Rival Swains; a story. (S. F. Bullock) Eng. Illust. 14: 588.
Rivalries of Long and Short Codiac. (G. W. Edwards) Cent. 28: 569, 869.
Rivals, The. (R. Wildman) Overland, n. s. 24: 613.
Rivals, The; a story. (F. Coppée) Harper, 85: 884.
Rivarol, Antoine. (G. E. Campbell) National, 19: 747.
River and Harbor Bills. (E. R. Johnson) Ann. Am. Acad. Pol. Sci. 2: 782.
River and Harbor Improvement. (N. C. Blanchard) No. Am. 158: 343.
— in United States, Rise and Progress of. (I. Y. Schermerhorn) J. Frankl. Inst. 139: 252.
River between, A; a story. (F. Guertin) Outing, 27: 180.
River Bank Protection by Fascines. Nature, 55: 156.
River Improvement Works. (C. D. Marx) Chaut. 21: 282.
River Song; a poem. (E. Nesbit) Argosy, 62: 252.
River Syndicate, The. (C. E. Carryl) Scrib. M. 18: 762.
Rivers, Banks of. (M. G. Watkins) Longm. 21: 531.
— Classification of. (W. M. Davis) Nat. Geog. M. 2: 81.
— Pollution of, How to stop. (F. Spence) Contemp. 64: 427.
— Temperatures of European. (H. N. Dixon) Geog. J. 6: 264.
— Tidal, Wheeler on. Ath. '94, 1: 648.
Rives, Amélie, with portrait. Bk. News, 7: 35.
— Novels. Spec. 69: 777.
Riviera, Bird's-eye View of. Blackw. 152: 769. Same art. Liv. Age, 196: 226. Same art. Ecl. M. 120: 145.
— de Ponente. (J. G. Dow) Good Words, 35: 827.
— Notes from. (Mrs. H. Chetwynd) Belgra. 86: 24.
— Run through the. Time, 6: 409.
— Wintering on. Around World, 2: 1.
Rivière, Briton. (W. W. Fenn) M. of Art, 2: 252. — (F. G. Stephens) Portfo. 23: 61, 77. — With portrait. R. of Rs. (N. Y) 9: 697.
Rivuli Montani. (J. Buchan) Gent. M. n. s. 53: 368.
Rix, Julian. (A. Black) Q. Illust. 1: 181.
Roach, Major Isaac, Journal of, with portrait. Pennsyl. M. 17: 129, 281.
Road, Common, as a Social Factor. (J. G. Speed) Chaut. 16: 547.
Road to Ruin, The; a poem. (Baroness de Bertouch) Belgra. 90: 64.
Road-building in a Southern State. (D. A. Tompkins) Engin. M. 6: 645.
Road Reform. (S. R. Downing) Am. J. Pol. 2: 438.
Roads. (M. M. Pope) Lippinc. 56: 570.
— and Boundaries, Ancient, of England. (J. R. Boyle) Antiq. n. s. 29: 57, 197.
— and Road Rollers. Cassier, 2: 302.
— Better, Need of. (M. Dodge) No. Am. 161: 125.
— Betterment of our Highways. (N. S. Shaler) Atlan. 70: 505.
— Common, Improvement of. (J. G. Speed) Lippinc. 55: 836.
— Country. (F. French) Scrib. M. 20: 375.
— — Preservation of. Garden & F. 5: 361.
Roads, French. (M. H. Catherwood) Atlan. 77: 355.
— (T. Stanton) Lippinc. 56: 538.
— Good. Bach. of Arts, 3: 384. — (Gen. R. Stone) Overland, n. s. 25: 234. — (C. F. Johnson) Overland, n. s. 28: 247, 443.
— — Economy of. (J. H. Wisby) Am. J. Pol. 3: 305.
— — An Industrial Revolution by. (A. A. Pope) Forum, 13: 115.
— — Symposium on. Indep. Feb. 6, '96.
— — Why we have so Few. (J. A. Beaver) Forum, 13: 771.
— How to improve. (R. P. Flower) No. Am. 157: 622.
— Improvement of. (E. P. Powell) New Eng. M. n. s. 7: 47.
— — Movement for. (L. M. Haupt) J. Frankl. Inst. 135: 1.
— in the U. S., Common. (I. B. Potter) Cent. 21: 803.
— Pavements, Sidewalks, and Bridges. (W. Howard) Engin. M. 8: 1014.
— Roman, in Yorkshire. (E. M. Cole) Antiq. n. s. 26: 206.
— — of Hampshire. (T. W. Shore) Antiq. n. s. 26: 263.
— State, in Massachusetts. (A. A. Pope) Lend a H. 14: 420.
— Village Streets and Country. (W. J. Beal) Garden & F. 9: 2.
Roadside Improvement. (L. F. Horner) Garden & F. 9: 427.
Roadsides in Autumn. (D. H. R. Goodale) Garden & F. 9: 402.
— Protection of. (M. G. Van Rensselaer) Garden & F. 6: 115.
Roan Mountain, V. Garden & F. 5: 325, 333.
— Frost Forms on. (H. R. Edson) Pop. Sci. Mo. 45: 30.
Roanoke, Lost Colony of. (E. Y. Wilson) Canad. M. 4: 500.
— Raleigh's Colony at. (J. P. Baxter) New Eng. M. n. s. 11: 565.
Roasting *vs.* Baking. Chamb. J. 70: 39.
Roba Nuova d' Italia; stories. (Clare Strong) Gent. M. n. s. 57: 276.
Robben Island, Lepers on. (F. MacNab) Temp. Bar, 106: 60.
Robbery on the French Coast, A. (A. Castaigne) Cent. 26: 926.
Robbia, Andrea della. Assumption of the Virgin, in Metropolitan Museum. (A. Marquand) Am. J. Archæol. 7: 422.
— and Luca della, Monuments of, in Italy. (A. Marquand) Scrib. M. 14: 681.
Robbia, Luca della, Madonna of. (A. Marquand) Am. J. Archæol. 9: 1.
— Monuments by, Unpublished. (A. Marquand) Am. J. Archæol. 8: 153.
Robbins, Ellen, Artist, Reminiscences of. New Eng. M. n. s. 14: 440, 532.
Robecchi, Luigi Bricchetti, Journeys of, in the Somali Country. Geog. J. 2: 359.
Robert Atterbury; a story. (T. H. Brainerd) Munsey, 14: 18-329.
Robert Elsmere, from an Ethical Point of View. (S. Coit) Eth. Rec. 1: 139.
Robert-Fleury, Tony, Paintings of. (J. Bernac) Art J. 46: 321.
Roberts, Charles G. D. (T. C. Marquis) Canad. M. 1: 572.
— Earth's Enigmas. (F. Sherman) Canad. M. 7: 179.
— Poetry of. (W. Sharp) Acad. 44: 334.

Roberts, Hugh, of Merion, Journal and Letter of. Pennsyl. M. 18: 199.
Roberts, Humphrey, Picture Collection of. (F. G. Stephens) M. of Art, 19: 41–170.
Roberts, John, of Merion. Pennsyl. M. 19: 262.
Roberts, Lord, of Kandahar. (A. Forbes) Eng. Illust. 9: 507. — Sat. R. 75: 396.
Roberts, Morley. My First Book, "The Western Avernus." Idler, 4: 91.
Robertson, Forbes, as Romeo, with portrait. Theatre, 36: 5.
Robertson, Frederick William. (R. E. Bisbee) Arena, 15: 187.
Robertson, George Croom. Ath. '92, 2: 419. — Acad. 42: 285. — Spec. 69: 446. — (A. Bain) Mind, 18: 1.
Robertson, James P. B. (A. W. Renton) Green Bag, 4: 158.
Robertson, John, with portrait. Bank. M. (N. Y.) 52: 176.
Robertson, Robert Henderson, Works of. (Montgomery Schuyler) Archit. R. 6: 184.
Robertson, Thos. Wm. (F. Hawkins) Acad. 43: 488.
— Life of, by T. E. Pemberton. Theatre, 30: 123. — Spec. 70: 192.
Robin Goodfellow; a Modern Fairy Tale. Good Words, 35: Christmas no., 61.
Robin Hood. (F. M. Wilson) Temp. Bar, 95: 401.
— Maid Marion on the Stage. (A. B. Walkley) Theatre, 28: 227.
Robin Hood; a story. (L. Jackson) Belgra. 81: 311.
Robinson, Alfred. Acad. 47: 192.
Robinson, A. M. F. Marguerites du Temps Passe. Spec. 69: 649.
Robinson, Dr. Anthony. (T. D. A. Cockerell) Am. Natural. 28: 775.
Robinson, C. D., Painter and Man. (C. S. Greene) Overland, n. s. 27: 34.
Robinson, Doane. (H. Austin) Bookman, 2: 477.
Robinson, F. Cayley. (A. L. Baldry) M. of Art, 19: 465.
Robinson, F. W. My First Book. Idler, 3: 205.
Robinson, Hugh. (F. Cundall) M. of Art, 5: 156.
Robinson, Rev. John, of Leyden, Some Descendants of. (A. S. Thurston) N. E. Reg. 48: 204.
Robinson, Jonah Leroy, a Poet of the Northwest. (J. Realf, jr.) Arena, 12: 308.
Robinson, Theodore. Critic, 28: 261.
Robsart, Amy, Fate of. Gent. M. n. s. 51: 429.
Rocamadour, France; an Albert Dürer Town. (E. R. Pennell) Harper, 87: 537.
Rocco and Sidora; a story. (E. Cavazza) Atlan. 70: 476.
Rochambeau, Gen. Comte de. (J. G. Rosengarten) Am. Hist. Reg. 3: 195.
Rochechouart, Gen. L. V. L. Memoirs. Ed. R. 178: 375.
Rochefort, Henri, and Art. Sat. R. 79: 722.
— at Home. (M. A. Belloc) Idler, 5: 260.
— Memoirs of. (A. Hornblow) Bookman, 3: 232. — (R. B. C. Graham) Sat. R. 82: 619. — Critic, 28: 373.
Rochelle Expedition, 1627. (J. S. Rothwell) Un. Serv. M. 6: 525, 624.
Rock Basins, Erosion of. (T. D. La Touche) Nature, 49: 39.
Rock Cutter and Trimmer, Improved. (E. Kidwell) Am. J. Sci. 149: 417.
Rock Fissure, A. (G. K. Gilbert) Science, n. s. 2: 117.
Rock Fusion, Fisher on. (C. Barus) Am. J. Sci. 146: 140.
Rock Garden. (T. D. Hatfield) Garden & F. 6: 395. 7: 285.
Rock Garden at Kew. (W. Watson) Garden & F. 5: 428.
— in June. (T. D. Hatfield) Garden & F. 7: 236.
Rock Island Express Robbery, The. (C. Moffett) McClure, 4: 245.
Rock Paintings and Pictographs of the Southwest. (L. W. Gunckel) Am. Antiq. 15: 223.
Rock-Pipits; a Seafarer's Home. (F. A. Fulcher) Argosy, 56: 114.
Rock-Pool, In a. (T. Wood) Sund. M. 23: 612.
Rockall Island, Visit to. Chamb. J. 69: 161.
Rockbridge Artillery, C. S. A. So. Hist. Pap. 23: 98.
Rockets. All the Year, 73: 11.
— in Warfare. Sat. R. 74: 412.
Rockport, Mass., Breakwater at. (H. Babson) New Eng. M. n. s. 11: 163.
Rocks and Minerals, Sections of, New Machine for Cutting. (G. H. Williams) Am. J. Sci. 145: 102.
— Flow and Fracture of. (L. M. Hoskins) Am. J. Sci. 152: 205.
— Foldings of. (J. L. Lobley) Knowl. 19: 162.
— Igneous, Causes of Variation in Composition of. (H. J. Johnston-Lavis) Nat. Sci. 4: 134.
— — Classification of. (A. Harker) Sci. Prog. 4: 469.
— — Natural History of. (A. Harker) Sci. Prog. 1: 12.
— — of the Yellowstone National Park, Age of. (A. Hague) Am. J. Sci. 151: 445.
— Plutonic Sequence of. (J. J. H. Teall) Nat. Sci. 1: 288.
Rocky Mts., Elevation along, in British America, since Cretaceous Period. (G. M. Dawson) Am. J. Sci. 149: 463.
— Family Camp in. (C. R. Conover) Outing, 22: 358, 420.
— Hunting in. (R. S. Hill) Outing, 26: 452.
— Lost in. (W. H. Grenfell) 19th Cent. 31: 839.
— Photographing Game in. (A. G. Wallihan) Cosmopol. 19: 371.
— Rifle and Rod in. (C. L. Marsh) Outing, 24: 303.
— A Summer Outing on Northwestern Waters. (R. E. Strahorn) Cosmopol. 21: 473.
— Wild Flowers of. (A. C. Carson) Mo. Illust. 13: 81.
— A Winter's Sport in. (W. A. Baillie-Grohman) Eng. Illust. 12: no. 3, 89.
Rockwood, Charles Greene, with portrait. (F. W. Ricord) Nat'l M. (N. Y. '91) 19: 301.
Rodbertus, K., Socialism of. (E. B. Andrews) J. Pol. Econ. 1: 50.
Rodents, Four New, from California. (S. N. Rhoads) Am. Natural. 27: 831.
— Home of. (R. Lydekker) Knowl. 17: 241.
— New, from California and Oregon. (S. N. Rhoads) Am. Natural. 28: 67.
Rodeo [Round-up] at Los Ojos, A. (F. Remington) Harper, 88: 515.
Rodin, Auguste. (C. Phillips) M. of Art, 11: 138.
— Rejection of, by the Royal Academy. (P. Leroi) M. of Art, 9: 394.
Rodney, Admiral George Brydges. Temp. Bar, 106: 318.
— and the British Navy of the 18th Century. Ed. R. 175: 166.
Rodway, James. The West Indies and the Spanish Main. Macmil. 74: 70.
Roe, E. P., with portrait. Bk. Buyer, 5: 304. — With portrait. Bk. News, 7: 1.
Roentgen, W. C., with portrait. Bk. News, 14: 601.
— Discoveries of. Critic, 28: 139.

Roentgen Rays. (A. A. Woodbridge) Bost. **3**: 570. — (H. S. Ward) Eng. Illust. **14**: 594. — Spec. **76**: 80. — (W. C. Röntgen) Nature, **53**: 274. — (H. Münsterberg) Science, n. s. **3**: 161. — (W. C. Röntgen) Science, n. s. **3**: 227. — Nature, **53**: 377. — (J. J. Thomson) Nature, **53**: 391. — (F. T. Thomason) Canad. M. **6**: 441. — (W. C. Röntgen) J. Frankl. Inst. **141**: 183. — R. of Rs. (N. Y.) **13**: 303. — (A. W. Goodspeed) Science, n. s. **3**: 394. — Dub. R. **118**: 421. — (E. J. Houston and A. E. Kennelly) J. Frankl. Inst. **141**: 241. — (P. H. Wynne) New Eng. M. n. s. **14**: 214. — (J. Trowbridge) Pop. Sci. Mo. **48**: 771. — Quar. **183**: 496. — Nature, **53**: 522, 613. — (J. J. Thomson) Nature, **53**: 581. **54**: 302. — (J. J. Stewart) Knowl. **19**: 121. — Nature, **54**: 109.

— and the Invisible World around us. (J. T. Bixby) Arena, **15**: 871.

— and the Soft Tissues of the Body. (J. Macintyre) Nature, **54**: 451.

— and their Uses. (O. Lodge) Sat. R. **81**: 422.

— Character and Effects. (A. W. Wright) Forum, **21**: 165.

— Diffuse Reflection of. (M. I. Pupin) Science, n. s. **3**: 538.

— Discovery of. (H. J. W. Dam) McClure, **6**: 403.

— Discovery of a New Radiance. (M. I. Pupin) Engin. M. **10**: 1021.

— Discovery of Our Day. (R. C. Auld) Our Day, **16**: 219.

— Electric Photography. (A. E. Dolbear) Cosmopol. **20**: 675.

— Electrification of Air by. (Lord Kelvin and others) Nature, **55**: 199.

— Experiments upon, and their Effects. (A. W. Wright) Am. J. Sci. **151**: 235.

— in America. (C. Moffet) McClure, **6**: 415.

— in Photography. (T. J. McCormack) Open Court, **10**: 4799.

— in Surgery. (W. W. Keen) McClure, **6**: 579.

— Nature of. (H. Schubert) Monist, **6**: 324.

— a New Form of Radiation. (W. C. Röntgen) Science, n. s. **3**: 726.

— The New Photography. (C. Barnard) Chaut. **23**: 75. — (S. E. Tilman) Cosmopol. **20**: 676.

— not Present in Sunlight. (M. C. Lea) Am. J. Sci. **151**: 363.

— Observations on. (H. A. Rowland; N. R. Carmichael; L. J. Briggs) Am. J. Sci. **151**: 247.

— Photographing the Unseen. (A. A. C. Swinton) Cornh. **73**: 290.

— Photography by. (A. A. C. Swinton) J. Soc. Arts, **44**: 357. — (J. Trowbridge) Scrib. M. **19**: 501. — (J. W. Gifford) Knowl. **19**: 61, 73.

— Recent Experiments with. Dub. R. **119**: 153.

— Recent Work on. Pop. Sci. Mo. **49**: 103.

— Reflection of, from Platinum. (O. N. Rood) Science, n. s. **3**: 463.

— Regular or Specular Reflection of, from Polished Metallic Surfaces. (O. N. Rood) Am. J. Sci. **152**: 173.

— Researches on. (A. M. Mayer) Am. J. Sci. **151**: 467.

— Search for Solar, on Pike's Peak. (F. Cajori) Am. J. Sci. **152**: 289.

— Source of. (A. A. Michelson) Science, n. s. **3**: 694.

— Stereoscopic Application of. (E. Mach) Monist, **6**: 321.

— A Symposium on. Cent. **30**: 120.

— Theory of. (A. A. Michelson) Am. J. Sci. **151**: 312. — (A. A. Michelson) Nature, **54**: 66.

— Triangulation by means of. (J. Trowbridge) Am. J. Sci. **151**: 245.

Roentgen's Curse; a story. (C. H. T. Crosthwaite) Longm. **28**: 469.

Roger, William. Spec. **76**: 130.

Rogers, Ezekiel. Roger Williams and Jane Whalley. N. E. Reg. **50**: 65.

Rogers, Henry. Eclipse of Faith. Eng. R. **17**: 273.

Rogers, Henry Darwin, with portrait. Pop. Sci. Mo. **50**: 258.

Rogers, Henry Wade. (H. L. Conard) Nat'l M. (N. Y. '91) **17**: 179.

Rogers, James Blythe, with portrait. Pop. Sci. Mo. **49**: 261.

Rogers, James Edwin Thorold. (H. de B. Gibbins) Econ. R. **1**: 86.

Rogers, John, Sculptor. (W. O. Partridge) New Eng. M. n. s. **13**: 705.

Rogers, Major, The Fate of; a Mystery of Ceylon. (H. Hensoldt) Arena, **11**: 71.

Rogers, Randolph. Pub. Opin. **12**: 465.

Rogers, Robert Cameron, with portrait. Bookman, **1**: 307.

Rogers, Robert Empie, with portrait. Pop. Sci. Mo. **49**: 837.

Rohlfs, Gerhard. (E. G. Ravenstein) Geog. J. **8**: 184.

Roi est mort, Le; a poem. (A. B. Paine) Outing, **23**: 331.

Roi est mort, Le; a poem. (A. Cochrane) Temp. Bar, **105**: 463.

Rokitansky, Victor. Ath. '96, **2**: 203.

Roland, Madame. (J. F. Spalding) Am. Cath. Q. **21**: 558. — (M. Dale) Belgra. **86**: 305. Same art. Liv. Age, **205**: 118. — (I. M. Tarbell) Scrib. M. **14**: 561.

— Daughter of. (A. E. Buchanan) Cath. World, **63**: 435.

Roland, Song of, and the Iliad. (A. Lang) National, **20**: 195.

Roll-call of the Reef, The; a story. (A. F. Q. Couch) McClure, **5**: 163. Same art. Idler, **7**: 581.

Rollright Stones and their Folk-Lore. (A. J. Evans) Folk-Lore, **6**: 6.

Rolls House. (W. J. Hardy) Leis. Hour, **42**: 53.

Rolph, John. (J. S. Cotton) Acad. **41**: 37.

Roman Altar at Lancaster. (R. E. Hoppell) Illus. Archæol. **1**: 124.

— at South Shields. Reliquary, **35**: 167.

Roman Amusements. Cornh. **69**: 418.

Roman Catholic, What makes a? (J. Conway) Chaut. **18**: 560.

— Why I became a. (F. Johnston) Cath. World, **55**: 375.

Roman Catholic Church, Aggression of. Eng. R. **14**: 416. **15**: 163.

— American Policy of. And. R. **19**: 230.

— Americanizing the. (B. B. Cahoon) Am. J. Pol. **2**: 376.

— — B. B. Cahoon on. (T. M. Crowley) Am. J. Pol. **2**: 534.

— and the coming Social Struggle. (C. Robinson) Am. M. Civics, **6**: 144.

— and the Higher Criticism. (M. M. Snell) Arena, **9**: 619.

— and Public Schools in Minnesota. (L. B. Speare) Our Day, **9**: 86.

— and the Salvability of Heretics. (C. C. Starbuck) Meth. R. **55**: 720.

— and the School Fund. (W. C. Doane) No. Am. **158**: 30.

— and Social Reform. (F. Howard) Cath. World, **63**: 286.

— and Social Struggle. (C. Robinson) Am. M. Civics, **6**: 144.

Roman Catholic Church as a Factor in Politics. (E. D. M'Creary) Am. J. Pol. 4: 119.
— Assurance of Salvation and Certainty of Belief in. (L. W. Bacon) Chr. Lit. 12: 193, 257.
— Attitude towards the Anglicans. (A. Jessopp) 19th Cent. 37: 961.
— Can it be Nationalized? (W. R. Claxton) Am. J. Pol. 3: 29.
— The Celestial Empire of the West. (A. Jessopp) Chr. Lit. 13: 147.
— The Coming Kingdom of Christ. (A. F. Hewit) Am. Cath. Q. 19: 225.
— Discussion over the Authority of, by a Catholic and an Anglican Bishop. (A. F. Marshall) Am. Cath. Q. 20: 557.
— Dispensing Power in. Dub. R. 116: 149.
— Dogma and Opinion within. (C. C. Starbuck) Meth. R. 54: 681.
— in Alabama. (M. E. Henry-Ruffin) Cath. World, 58: 233.
— in Bordeaux, 1350–1450. (E. Allain) Dub. R. 117: 373.
— in Corea. (E. M. Clerke) Dub. R. 116: 290.
— in England; the Pope and the Anglicans. (T. A. Lacey; Catholicus) Contemp. 70: 793.
— — Promised Support from Irish Revenue. National, 25: 453.
— — Restoration of the Hierarchy. (J. B. Milburn) Dub. R. 117: 347.
— in French Fiction. Macmil. 75: 140.
— in her History. (S. R. Seton) Am. Cath. Q. 18: 734.
— in Holland, Persecution of, under William III. (W. C. Robinson) Dub. R. 114: 381.
— in Russian Poland: Difficulties of the Episcopate. (M. E. Herbert) Dub. R. 117: 265.
— in the Sandwich Islands. (L. W. Mulhane) Cath. World, 68: 641.
— in the United States. (H. A. Brann) Cath. World, 54: 568.
— — O'Gorman's. (J. W. Chadwick) Nation, 61: 209. —(M. F. Egan) Cath. World, 62: 487.
— Journalism in. (J. J. Dunn) Chaut. 20: 712.
— Liberalism and. (B. Herford) Chr. Lit. 14: 49.
— Limitations of Private Judgment in. Am. Cath. Q. 17: 32.
— Magnetism of. Spec. 76: 370.
— Missions of, in Japan. (L. C. Casartelli) Dub. R. 116: 257.
— the Parent of Republics. (J. T. Scharf) Cath. World, 61: 290.
— Rigidity of. (W. Ward) 19th Cent. 38: 786. Same art. Chr. Lit. 14: 180, 256.
— Spiritual Treasures of. (W. Barry) Am. Cath. Q. 20: 176.
— Supremacy of, Testimony of Greek Church to. (A. E. Hewit) Am. Cath. Q. 19: 691.
— A True Ally of the Republic. (J. F. Loughlin) Forum, 15: 275.
— *vs.* the Doctrinaires in Social Economy. (M. O'Riordan) Cath. World, 59: 1.
— *vs.* Science. (H. G. Chapman) Bach. of Arts, 3: 338.
Roman Catholic Controversy. (R. Ogden) Nation, 56: 44.
Roman Catholic Education, State Support of. Eng. R. 11: 323.
— Subsidised. Eng. R. 7: 378.
Roman Catholic Educational Exhibit at the Columbian Exposition. (J. L. Spalding) Cath. World, 55: 580.
Roman Catholic Faith, Necessity for accepting. (A. W. Smith) Am. Cath. Q. 18: 345.
Roman Catholic Idea in the New Testament. (A. F. Hewit) Am. Cath. Q. 17: 673.
— in Prophecy, The. (A. F. Hewit) Am. Cath. Q. 17: 225.
Roman Catholic Missions, Outlook for, in the United States. (W. Elliott) Cath. World, 57: 757.
Roman Catholic Mystics of the Middle Ages. Ed. R. 184: 298.
Roman Catholic People's University in Germany. (J. H. McMahon) Cath. World, 57: 863.
Roman Catholic Policy concerning Popular Education. And. R. 17: 606.
— Present Position of. (G. Santayana) New World, 1: 658.
Roman Catholic Protectories and Reformatories. (R. H. Clarke) Am. Cath. Q. 20: 607.
Roman Catholic Reaction of Our Times. Ed. R. 184: 1.
Roman Catholic School System, in Rome. (F. Satolli) No. Am. 159: 641.
— of Great Britain. (T. McMillan) Cath. World, 55: 794.
Roman Catholic Schools and their Teaching. Dub. R. 110: 160.
— in New York and the Regents of the University. (J. F. Mullaney) Am. Cath. Q. 17: 634.
— in the United States. (G. D. Wolff) Am. Cath. Q. 17: 866.
Roman Catholic Summer School at New London, Conn., 1892. (J. A. Mooney) Cath. World, 55: 532. —(M. M. Sheedy) Cath. World, 56: 165.
— on Lake Champlain. Cath. World, 57: 67, 853.
Roman Catholic Superstition. Eng. R. 10: 324.
Roman Catholic Theory of Unity. Eng. R. 8: 354.
Roman Catholic Young Men's Societies. (M. J. Lavelle) Am. Cath. Q. 17: 98.
Roman Catholicism, Abjuration of. (D. H. MacVicar) Presb. & Ref. R. 5: 303.
— among Protestants, Growth of. (J. W. Ball) Luth. Q. 25: 409.
— and Apaism. (J. L. Spalding) No. Am. 159: 278.
— and Liberalism. (B. Herford) Chr. Lit. 14: 157.
— and Protestantism, Antagonism between. Eng. R. 2: 1.
— — the Coming Contest. (A. Young) Cath. World, 58: 457, 694.
— Attitude of the Protestant Mind towards. (W. C. Robinson) Cath. World, 54: 644.
— A Century of. (B. Morgan) Cath. World, 62: 433.
— Converts to. (R. H. Clarke) Am. Cath. Q. 19: 112. —Eng. R. 9: 96.
— — in U. S. (R. H. Clarke) Am. Cath. Q. 18: 539.
— France and. (G. Bonet-Maury) New World, 4: 516.
— in America. Chr. Lit. 16: 74.
— — Future of. (A. P. Doyle) Cath. World, 64: 206.
— in England, Asserted Growth of. (F. W. Farrar) Fortn. 64: 557.
— — Anglo-Catholic Movement. (J. A. Faulkner) Ref. Q. 39: 223.
— — 1860–1892. (St. G. Mivart) Am. Cath. Q. 18: 54.
— — Fifty Years Ago. (St. G. Mivart) Am. Cath. Q. 17: 161, 753.
— — Re-consecration of England to the Virgin Mary and St. Peter. Spec. 70: 729.
— — Will England become Roman Catholic? New R. 9: 182.
— in France. French Cardinals and the Republic. Spec. 68: 159.
— — French Royalists and the Catholics. Sat. R. 73: 707. —Spec. 69: 247.
— — Hildebrand in 1892. Spec. 68: 670.

Roman Catholicism in France. Pope and the French Bishops. Spec. **68**: 599.
— — Pope and the French Government. Nation, **55**: 47.
— in India. Month, **79**: 231.
— in Ireland, T. W. Russell and. (W. J. Walsh) Fortn. **57**: 415.
— in Madagascar. (T. Gilleran) Cath. World, **62**: 533.
— in Scandinavia. (F. Janssens) Cath. World, **60**: 586.
— in the U. S. "Cahenslyism" *versus* Americanism. (J. Conway) R. of Rs. (N. Y.) **6**: 43.
— — Encyclical "Longinqua" (Leo XIII.). Am. Cath. Q. **20**: 347. — Translation. Am. Cath. Q. **20**: 357. — Commentary. (J. Schroeder) Am. Cath. Q. **20**: 369.
— Is it Christianity? (L. T. Townsend) Our Day, **9**: 414.
— Liberal, The Holy Office and. (W. R. Sullivan) Westm. **140**: 489.
— — A Victory for. (R. Ogden) Nation, **54**: 374.
— Menace of. (W. J. H. Traynor) No. Am. **161**: 129.
— Modern. Eng. R. **16**: 16.
— A New-Church View. (J. Reed) N. Church R. **3**: 36.
— Needs of Humanity supplied by. (J. Gibbons) Cath. World, **58**: 1.
— or Naturalism. (A. F. Hewit) Am. Cath. Q. **21**: 477.
— Protestantism, and Progress. (F. W. Howard) Cath. World, **62**: 145.
— Pure *vs.* Diluted. (A. F. Hewit) Am. Cath. Q. **20**: 460.
— The Secret of. (W. Barry) National, **28**: 816.
— The Threatening Conflict with. (E. M. Winston) Forum, **17**: 425.
— Wordsworth on. Eng. R. **7**: 134.
Roman Catholics, American, and the Roman Question. (A. F. Hewit) Cath. World, **55**: 425.
— and Biblical Criticism. Contemp. **66**: 351.
— and the Public Schools. (J. Conway) Educa. R. **4**: 236. — Reply. (C. B. Pallen) Educa. R. **4**: 456.
— — Faribault Plan. Pub. Opin. **15**: 593, 619.
— — Symposium. Indep. Jan. 11, '94.
— Anti-Catholic Crusade. Pub. Opin. **16**: 573.
— French. (C. Jannet) Q. J. Econ. **7**: 137.
— Hostility to. (G. P. Lathrop; W. C. Doane) No. Am. **158**: 563.
— in Poland, Persecution of. Month, **80**: 166.
— in Rhode Island, Disfranchisement of. (J. R. Meade) Am. Cath. Q. **19**: 169.
— in the U. S., Bishop Doane and. (M. F. Egan) No. Am. **158**: 745.
— Loyalty of. (G. P. Lathrop) No. Am. **159**: 218.
— of England in Modern Times. (J. Morris) Month, **74**: 41, 356, 515. **75**: 27.
— of Russia. (B. J. Clinch) Cath. World, **59**: 757.
— Our Attitude towards. (H. K. Carroll) Meth. R. **55**: 231.
— Truthfulness of, in writing History. (D. J. Chapman) Dub. R. **119**: 1.
Roman Drama; Dramatic Satura and Old Comedy. (G. L. Hendrickson) Am. J. Philol. **15**: 1.
Roman Earthworks in Germany. (F. Haverfield) Acad. **46**: 285.
Roman Empire, Fall of, Cause of. (J. S. Hittell) Overland, n. s. **20**: 248.
— in 600 A. D. (J. B. Bury) Eng. Hist. R. **9**: 315.
Roman Law and Contemporary Revelation. (G. F. Magoun) Green Bag, **7**: 132.
Roman Law in the Middle Ages. (J. S. Taylor-Cameron) Jurid. R. **7**: 241. **8**: 118.
Roman Life and Story, Church's. Spec. **69**: 353.
Roman Literature, Ancient, Environment of. (W. C. Lawton) Poet-Lore, **7**: 113.
— History of, Teuffel's. Sat. R. **73**: 362.
Roman Paganism and Christianity. (St. George Mivart) 19th Cent. **34**: 822. — Ecl. M. **122**: 1.
Roman Poets, Nature in the Earlier. (E. M. Cesaresco) Contemp. **69**: 576. Same art. Ecl. M. **126**: 766.
— of Augustan Age, Sellar's. Sat. R. **73**: 222. — Spec. **68**: 608.
Roman Remains in England, Recent Discovery of. Acad. **44**: 157.
Roman See in the Early Church, Bright on. (L. Rivington) Dub. R. **119**: 11. — Sat. R. **82**: 375.
— Lightfoot on. Dub. R. **113**: 836.
Roman Society and Christianity. (St. G. Mivart) Cosmopol. **17**: 102.
Roman Therma, Fiesola. Reliquary, **35**: 129.
Roman Tile marked with Cross. Reliquary, **36**: 111.
Roman Villa at Brading. (F. P. Cobbe) M. of Art, **4**: 154.
— at Dareuth, Kent. Reliquary, **35**: 44.
Roman Wall, Hadrian's. (H. F. Abell) National, **19**: 812.
— in Scotland, Antonine. (W. M. Ramsay) Ath. '93, **2**: 105, 167.
Roman Women; a poem. (T. E. Brown) New R. **13**: 137.
Roman World in the Time of Christ. (J. Zimmerman) Luth. Q. **26**: 269.
Romance and Youth. Macmil. **65**: 285.
— Decadence of. (F. Harrison) Forum, **15**: 216. Same art. Critic, **22**: 244.
— Decline of. (D. F. Hannigan) Westm. **141**: 33.
— Writers of, German. (Levy-Bruhl) Pub. Opin. **13**: 21.
Romance, The, and the Novel. Chaut. **16**: 42.
— Persistence of. (R. Burton) Dial (Ch.) **15**: 380.
Romance; a poem. (O. C. Stevens) Harper, **90**: 679.
Romance, A: a story. All the Year, **71**: 373.
Romance in Late Fall. (M. Richardson) Lippinc. **56**: 693.
Romance, The, in the Life of Hefty Burke. (R. H. Davis) Harper, **86**: 225.
Romance of Ambrotype: a story. (H. Pyle) Harper, **94**: 11.
Romance of Belgravia, A. (C. F. French) Belgra. **82**: 409.
Romance of a Brown-paper Parcel. (T. W. Higginson) Cent. **30**: 572.
Romance of a Bullock Cart. (R. Bethune) Chamb. J. **71**: 696–742.
Romance of Casco Bay. (H. M. Sylvester) New Eng. M. n. s. **7**: 728.
Romance of Clovelly, A; a story. (K. D. Wiggin) Cosmopol. **19**: 277.
Romance of a Deck Chair. Chamb. J. **71**: 332.
Romance of Dull Town; a story. (J. W. Temple) McClure, **4**: 236.
Romance of the Faith. (H. D. Ward) Cent. **25**: 528.
Romance of Gray's Inn, A; a story. (A. Fleming) Gent. M. n. s. **54**: 217. Same art. Liv. Age, **205**: 401.
Romance of the Irish House of Lords; a story. All the Year, **72**: 370.
Romance of the Molehill Country. (U. L. Silberrad) Ecl. M. **127**: 693.
Romance of an Ox-team. (C. G. D. Roberts) Lippinc. **56**: 230.

Romance of Sergeant Clancy. (E. W. Hornung) Idler, 1: 334.
Romance of Spain. (C. W. Wood) Argosy, 59: 698. 60: 65–445.
Romance of a Stall, The. Macmil. 74: 118. Same art. Liv. Age, 210: 85.
Romance of the Stars; a story. (M. Proctor) Chaut. 22: 676. 23: 33–572.
Romance of a Store. Belgra. 89: 273.
Romance of Two Jubilees; a story. (G. F. Sams) Eng. Illust. 14: 119.
Romance of a Wooden Leg. (F. A. Schneider) Bach. of Arts, 2: 344.
Romanes, George John. Critic, 24: 379. — Monist, 4: 482. — With portrait. Nat. Sci. 5: 72. — (E. R. Lankester) Nature, 50: 108. — Ath. '94, 1: 713. — (L. Dyer) Nation, 58: 424. — Open Court, 8: 4111. — Quar. 183: 285.
— From Unbelief to Faith. (W. G. Horder) Sund. M. 25: 194.
— Life and Letters of. Critic, 28: 403.
Romanesque Revival. (M. Schuyler) Architec. Rec. 1: 7, 151.
Romano-British Articles, Wiltshire. Reliquary, 35: 91.
Romano-British Land Surface. Flint Flakes replaced. (W. G. Smith) Nature, 52: 222.
Roman's Villeggiatura, The. (E. M. Cesaresco) Contemp. 68: 509. Same art. Liv. Age, 207: 417.
Romans. Did they degenerate? (M. E. Case) Int. J. Ethics, 3: 165.
— Table Customs of. All the Year, 74: 76.
Romanticism, The New. (S. Axson) Citizen, 1: 69.
Rome. (S. B. Holabird) Un. Serv. (Phila.) 8: 571. 9: 27.
— after Thirty Years. Chamb. J. 73: 153. Same art. Ecl. M. 126: 686.
— American School at. (H. C. Butler) Critic, 26: 422.
— Ancient, and Modern London. (E. J. Gibbs) National, 19: 516. Same art. Ecl. M. 119: 179. Same art. Liv. Age, 194: 451.
— — — Gambling and Cheating in. (R. Lanciani) No. Am. 155: 97.
— — Archæological Notes from. (R. Lanciani) Ath. '92, 1: 313–799.
— — Commercial Law in. (F. P. Walton) Jurid. R. 5: 332.
— — Grandeur of. (R. Seton) Am. Cath. Q. 20: 55.
— — Middleton's. Sat. R. 73: 393. — Ath. '92, 2: 925.
— — Notes of. (R. Lanciani) Cosmopol. 15: 702.
— — Pageant at, 17 B. C. (R. Lanciani) Atlan. 69: 145.
— — Private Life in. (H. W. Preston and L. Dodge) Atlan. 69: 597, 819.
— and Italy. (R. de Cesare) Chaut. 22: 686.
— and its Churches. (O. Shipley) Cath. World, 61: 614.
— and its Recent Ruins. (T. Hughes) Am. Cath. Q. 20: 698.
— Architecture, Early Christian. (W. P. P. Longfellow) Arch. Rec. 4: 395.
— — the Sky-scrapers of Rome. (R. Lanciani) No. Am. 162: 705.
— Basilicas of. Temp. Bar, 109: 471.
— Canadian Bicycle in. (C. R. Boulton) Canad. M. 7: 333.
— Church of St. Clement. (P. J. Gloag) Good Words, 34: 594.
— Classical, Women of. (O. Walden) Time, 17: 318.
— Colosseum and its Builder. (E. S. Purcell) Time, 10: 56.
— Decline of. Soc. Econ. 2: 385. 3: 46.
— Ecole des Beaux-Arts, Prize Winners. Art J. 45: 333.
Rome, Faliscan Museum at. (W. J. Stillman) Nation, 58: 465, 483.
— History of, Shuckburgh's. Sat. R. 78: 269.
— How she governed her Provinces. (W. C. Morey) Bib. World, 2: 29.
— in the Middle Ages, Gregorovius on. Sat. R. 80: 350.
— in Paul's Day. (H. F. Burton) Bib. World, 3: 87.
— A Kaleidoscope of. (F. M. Crawford) Cent. 29: 323.
— Leo XIII. and the King of Italy. (W. L. Alden) 19th Cent. 39: 689.
— Modern: the Capital of a New Republic. (F. M. Crawford) Cosmopol. 15: 726.
— Modernized. Am. Arch. 45: 86.
— New, Impressions of. (L. Villari) Liv. Age, 192: 451.
— New Museum at. (F. Gautier) Antiq. n. s. 30: 59.
— Pagan and Christian, Lanciani's. (M. H. Morgan) Nation, 56: 53. — Atlan. 71: 401.
— The Pantheon. (L. Villari) M. of Art, 8: 142.
— a Pilgrimage to. Eng. R. 12: 322.
— Porta Magica at. (H. C. Bolton) J. Am. Folk-Lore, 8: 73.
— Prehistoric. (I. Taylor) Antiq. n. s. 25: 119, 144.
— Religious Organization in. (O. Shipley) Cath. World, 62: 50.
— Revisited. (C. R. W. Biggar) Canad. M. 4: 572. 5: 122, 201. — (F. Harrison) Fortn. 59: 702. Same art. Ecl. M. 121: 19.
— Riot in, February, 1889. (W. H. McCrackan) Arena, 5: 743.
— The Road to. Macmil. 72: 260, 366. Same art. Liv. Age, 206: 803. 207: 228.
— a Roman Reverie. (A. Austin) Fortn. 64: 593. Same art. Liv. Age, 207: 490.
— Saint Peter's. (F. M. Crawford) Cent. 30: 323.
— — and its Builders. Am. Arch. 36: 176. 37: 106.
— — Old. (H. W. Brewer) Month, 84: 319.
— Santa Maria Maggiore, Basilica of. (W. P. P. Longfellow) Archit. Rec. 2: 65.
— Society in, a Century ago. (C. Edwardes) National, 22: 796. Same art. Ecl. M. 122: 396. Same art. Liv. Age, 200: 593.
— Spring in. (L. Gittings) Outing, 26: 41.
Romeo and Juliet; an Immortal Story. (Eugene Benson) New R. 13: 94.
— Story of. (F. O'Keene) Theatre, 35: 149.
Romney, George. M. of Art, 2: 70.
— as an Investment. (W. Roberts) Temp. Bar, 109: 56.
Rônins, Forty-seven, Dickins' and Grausseron's Translations. (R. L. Stevenson) M. of Art, 6: 8.
Ronner, Henriette. (M. H. Spielmann) M. of Art, 14: 21.
— Cats of. (T. A. Janvier) Cent. 24: 852.
Ronzano, Italy. (B. O'Reilly) Harper, 91: 722.
Roof, Balance, for Telescope Buildings. (A. E. Douglass) Astron. 12: 207. — (C. A. Post) Astron. 12: 400.
Roof, the Ring, and the Robber. (W. P. Hooper) Idler, 8: 213.
Roof Garden. (E. P. Powell) Garden & F. 5: 125.
Roofing. (R. Rospide) Am. Arch. 36: 159–191.
Roofing-tiles, Terra-cotta, Older Forms of. Am. Arch. 35: 197. 36: 5–52.
Rookery, Annals of a. Liv. Age, 207: 637.
— First Nest of a. (P. Robinson) Contemp. 70: 46. Same art. Liv. Age, 210: 492. Same art. Ecl. M. 127: 516.
Rooks, Dispersal of Acorns by. (C. Reid) Nature, 53: 6.
Rooms 23 and 24; a story. (H. W. Lucy) Eng. Illust. 14: 19.
Roon, Albert von, Count. (A. Tanzer) Nation, 55: 497.

Roosevelt, Theodore. (J. A. Riis) Outl. 51: 1089. — (F. Morris) Chaut. 22: 586.
— as a Historian. (W. P. Trent) Forum, 21: 566.
— a Character Sketch. (J. Ralph) R. of Rs. (N. Y.) 12: 159.
— The Wilderness Hunter. Atlan. 75: 826.
Root, George Frederick. Ath. '95, 2: 234. — (W. S. B. Mathews) Music, 8: 502.
— and his Songs. (L. A. Coonley) New Eng. M. n. s. 13: 555.
Root to Stem, Transition from. (A. Maslen) Knowl. 19: 224.
Roots, Hairs of. (T. Jamieson) Science, 22: 354.
— of Peas, Beans, and Vetches. (J. P. Smith) Knowl. 17: 68, 91.
— Penetration of into Living Tissues. (R. Beer) Nature, 52: 630.
Rope Power-transmission. (J. M. Dodge) J. Frankl. Inst. 135: 437.
Ropes Pass, Texas. (W. Kent) Engin. M. 3: 340.
Rops, Felicien. (E. Verhaeren) M. of Art, 19: 164.
Rorby, Yorkshire, Reliquary, 33: 97.
Rorer, S. T., with portrait. Bk. News, 12: 279.
Rorke, Kate. (A. Croxton) Theatre, 30: 303.
Ros, Lady de, Swinton's Life of. (J. E. Roundell) Nation, 57: 124.
Rosa. (G. Pitrè) Atlan. 74: 624.
Rosa. (E. S. Morgan) Time, 20: 390-652.
Rosamond's Romance; a story. (G. A. Hibbard) Harper, 91: 219.
Rosamund, Fair. (W. W. Hunt) Gent. M. n. s. 54: 458.
Rosary, Ancient Poem on. (J. Moyes) Dub. R. 115: 444.
Roscher, William, Influence of, in England. (W. Cunningham) Ann. Am. Acad. Pol. Sci. 5: 317.
— Programme of, in 1843. (W. J. Ashley) Q. J. Econ. 9: 99.
Roscoe, William C. Poems. (R. Le Gallienne) Acad. 41: 367.
Rose, Edward. The Plowdens. Gent. M. n. s. 48: 423.
Rose in Poetry, Pathos of the. (J. A. Symonds) Time, 14: 397.
Rose of the Mire. (K. Jordan) Lippinc. 51: 365.
Rose of Yesterday, A. (F. M. Crawford) Cent. 31: 135, 182.
Rose on the Ghebir's Shrine. (J. G. Whittier) Cosmopol. 16: 258.
Rose Armistead; a story. (W. R. Hamilton) Un. Serv. (Phila.) 11: 261.
Rose Aylmer's Grave; a poem. Temp. Bar, 105: 534.
Rose Castle. (Canon Venables) Good Words, 35: 818.
Rose Garden in Jackson Park, Chicago. (F. C. Seavey) Garden & F. 8: 328.
Rosebery, Earl of. (H. W. Lucy) Eng. Illust. 9: 651. (J. M'Carthy) Forum, 19: 224. — Leis. Hour, 43: 428. — (St. L. Strachey) 19th Cent. 36: 489. — With portrait. (J. Chartres) Munsey, 11: 188. — With portrait. (W. T. Stead) R. of Rs. (N. Y.) 9: 422.
— Administration of. (C. W. Dilke) No. Am. 158: 534.
— — Record of. R. of Rs. (N. Y.) 12: 191.
— and Mr. Gladstone. (H. W. Massingham) Contemp. 65: 457.
— and the Liberal Crisis in England. (J. C. Hopkins) Forum, 17: 139.
— and the Liberal Party. (W. L. Stobart) Fortn. 64: 234.
Rosebery, Earl of, as Secretary for Foreign Affairs. Spec. 70: 182.
— as a Writer. Sat. R. 82: 78.
— Dalmeny and Devonshire. (T. H. S. Escott) New R. 11: 256.
— Failure of. Spec. 74: 888.
— Plan of. Liv. Age, 204: 47.
— Portraits of. McClure, 3: 34.
— Resignation of. (E. L. Godkin) Nation, 63: 283. — (E. Dicey) Fortn. 66: 746. — National, 28: 288.
— Scottish Home of; Dalmeny House and Park. (A. Lamont) Eng. Illust. 13: 236.
— Second Thoughts of. Fortn. 66: 615.
— View of, from a German Standpoint. (H. Delbrück) Fortn. 62: 770.
— — from a French Standpoint. (A. Filon) Fortn. 62: 761.
Roseland, Harry. (J. G. Speed) Mo. Illust. 3: 234.
Rosemary; a story. (F. Greenwood) National, 24: 123. Same art. Liv. Age, 203: 13.
Rosemary for Remembrance; a story. Temp. Bar, 94: 519. 95: 85. Same art. Liv. Age, 193: 786. 194: 118.
Rosen, Julius. Mrs. M. P.; an Adaptation by H. Vezin. Theatre, 28: 52.
Rosenthal, Toby Edward. (S. F. Coles) Munsey, 8: 614.
Roses. (W. H. Taplin) Garden & F. 6: 104. 7: 37. — (B. G. Johns) Sund. M. 21: 455.
— and Ancient Rose-growers. Quar. 182: 110.
— at Columbian Exposition. (L. H. Bailey) Garden & F. 6: 299.
— at Tarrytown, N. Y. Garden & F. 7: 168.
— at the Waban Conservatories. (T. D. Hatfield) Garden & F. 7: 8.
— Boston Rose Show. Garden & F. 6: 278.
— California. (H. G. Pratt) Garden & F. 5: 454, 598.
— Cherokee Rose. Garden & F. 8: 114.
— Christmas. (D. Dewar) Garden & F. 5: 42.
— Cultivation of. (W. H. Taplin) Garden & F. 5: 126-500. 6: 219, 327, 437. 7: 227. — (J. N. Gerard) Garden & F. 9: 326.
— Cultural Notes on. (T. D. Hatfield) Garden & F. 9: 487.
— Forcing Hybrid. (W. Scott) Garden & F. 9: 55.
— Garden of Single. Garden & F. 9: 257.
— Hybrid Brier. Garden & F. 6: 100.
— Hybrid Perpetual. (E. O. Orpet) Garden & F. 8: 516.
— — for Forcing. Garden & F. 7: 86.
— in Washington, D. C. Garden & F. 6: 538.
— New Hybrid. Garden & F. 5: 460.
— Notes on New. (W. N. Craig) Garden & F. 7: 487. 9: 415.
— Park of, at Nice. Garden & F. 5: 314.
— Seasonable Notes on. (W. H. Taplin) Garden & F. 8: 476.
— Single, Cultivation of. (J. G. Jack) Garden & F. 6: 286.
— Valley of, in Turkey. Blackw. 152: 647. Same art. Liv. Age, 196: 107.
— Wild, about Chicago. (E. J. Hill) Garden & F. 7: 322.
Roses, The. (F. E. Newberry) Lippinc. 54: 712.
Roses, Wars of the, Characters of. (H. H. Moore) Walford's Antiq. 5: 277. 6: 8.
Rosicrucians, Modern. Sat. R. 75: 425.
Rosita. (E. Mackubin) Atlan. 75: 769.
Roslin in its Catholic Days. Month, 85: 82.
Rosmini-Serbati, Antonio. (E. Thurtell) Open Court, 10: 4912.
— Philosophy of. (P. Carus) Open Court, 7: 3585.

Rosny, J. H. L'Imperieuse Bonté. (L. de la Ramé) Fortn. 61: 652.
Ross, Alexander; Pedant Schoolmaster of the Age of Cromwell. (F. Watson) Gent. M. n. s. 55: 459.
Ross, Clinton, with portrait. Bk. Buyer, 13: 230.
Ross, Janet. Four Clever Englishwomen. Critic, 22: 165.
Ross, Justin Charles. Acad. 50: 134.
Ross, Fort, and the Russians. (C. S. Greene) Overland, n. s. 22: 1.
Rosse, Earl of. (R. Ball) Good Words, 36: 541.
Rosseter, Philip. (G. Goodwin) Acad. 43: 199.
Rossetti, Christina G., with portrait. Bk. Buyer, 12: 21. — (E. Gosse) Cent. 24: 211. — (Lily Watson) Leis. Hour, 44: 244. — (J. B. Kenyon) Meth. R. 56: 743. — (G. Gilchrist) Good Words, 37: 822. — (Alice Meynell) New R. 12: 201. Same art. Liv. Age, 204: 569. — (A. C. Benson) National, 24: 753. Same art. Liv. Age, 204: 620. Same art. Ecl. M. 124: 490. — (D. Sutherland) Lit. W. (Bost.) 26: 40. — (W. Sharp) Atlan. 75: 736. — Sat. R. 79: 5. — (T. Watts) Ath. '95, 1: 16. — Pub. Opin. 18: 43. — Dial (Ch.) 18: 37. — Critic, 26: 16. — Acad. 47: 12.
— Memorial to. Critic, 28: 357.
— New Year's Eve. (A. C. Swinburne) 19th Cent. 37: 367.
— Passing of; a poem. (K. L. Bates) Dial (Ch.) 18: 135.
— Poetry of. (E. K. Chambers) Acad. 45: 162. — Critic, 26: 21. — (Alice Law) Westm. 143: 444.
— Reminiscences of. (K. T. Hinkson) Bookman, 1: 28. — (T. Watts) 19th Cent. 37: 355.
— Sacred Poetry of. (L. Johnson) Acad. 50: 59.
Rossetti, Dante Gabriel. (Val. Prinsep) Art J. 44: 129. — (F. G. Stephens) Portfo. 1894: no. 5. — (W. Sharp) Acad. 46: 72. — Quar. 184: 185. — (Janet Harper) Westm. 146: 312. — (G. Barnett Smith) Time, 7: 163.
— and his Family Letters. (F. M. Hueffer) Longm. 27: 465. Same art. Liv. Age, 209: 53.
— and his Sister Christina. (J. B. Kenyon) Meth. R. 56: 743.
— and the Pre-Raphaelite Movement, Wood on. Ath. '94, 2: 359.
— and W. B. Scott. (J. Skelton) Blackw. 153: 229.
— as a Painter. (S. Colvin) M. of Art, 6: 177.
— A Child's Recollection of. (L. H. Caine) New R. 11: 246. Same art. Liv. Age, 203: 102.
At the Grave of. (J. A. Noble) Bookman, 1: 170.
— Family Letters of. Sat. R. 80: 838.
— Jenny; a poem. (W. G. Kingsland) Poet-Lore, 7: 1.
— Letters. Art J. 44: 249. — (E. G. Johnson) Dial (Ch.) 20: 164.
— Letters and Memoir of. Critic, 28: 463.
— Letters of. (Ed. by G. B. Hill) Atlan. 77: 577–744. 78: 45–242.
— Poetry of. Lond. Q. 82: 104. — (W. B. Worsfold) 19th Cent. 34: 284. Same art. Ecl. M. 121: 851.
— Portraits of. (W. M. Rossetti) M. of Art, 12: 21–138.
— Reminiscence of. (Wm. M. Hardinge) Univ. R. 6: 398.
— Rosa Triplex. (F. G. Stephens) Portfo. 23: 197.
— Rossetti's Life of. (W. Sharp) Acad. 49: 213.
— A Study of. Time, 16: 469.
— Wood's. Sat. R. 77: 557.
Rossetti, Mrs. Lucy Madox, A Reminiscence of. (W. M. Hardinge) M. of Art, 18: 341.
Rossettis, The. Lond. Q. 87: 1. Same art. Liv. Age, 211: 500.
Rossi, Ernesto. (W. Beatty-Kingston) Theatre, 37: 11.
Rossi, Giovanni Battista de. (H. Meren) Am. Arch. 46: 43. — (T. J. Shahan) Am. Cath. Q. 20: 1.
— and his Work. Month, 76: 553.
Rossi, Luigi. Munsey, 12: 474.
Rossignol, Jean Pierre. Acad. 44: 31.
Rossignoli, Father, Escape of. Spec. 73: 775.
Rossini, Gioachino Antonio, Composer and Gourmet. Atlan. 75: 286. — Sat. R. 73: 450.
Rossiniana. (R. Pagliari) Ath. '92, 1: 284, 444.
Rosso, Il. (A. M. F. Robinson) M. of Art, 8: 206.
Rost, Reinhold. (C. Bendall) Ath, '96, 1: 218. — (J. S. Cotton) Acad. 49: 140.
Rostand, Edmond. (Princesse Lointaine) Sat. R. 79: 828.
Rostock, Germany. (E. P. Oberholtzer) Am. Arch. 48: 15.
Rotation, Motions of, Absoluteness of. (A. E. H. Love) Nature, 51: 198.
— Sensations of. (H. C. Warren) Psychol. R. 2: 273.
Rotch, William, Letters of, 1792. N. E. Reg. 46: 174.
Roth, Rudolf von. (A. A. MacDonell) Acad. 48: 55. — Ath. '95, 2: 130.
Rothenburg, Germany. Sat. R. 78: 350.
— Story of. (C. F. Dewey) Cosmopol. 21: 339.
Rothenstein, Will. Oxford Characters. Sat. R. 82: 504.
Rother, King, Romance of. (A. Menzies) Scot. R. 22: 33.
Rothesay, David, Duke of (1378–1402.) (Marquis of Bute) Scot. R. 19: 297.
Rothschild, Walter. Eng. Illust. 15: 210.
Rothschilds, The. (J. Benton) Munsey, 7: 37.
Roubillac, Louis Francis. (A. Dobson) M. of Art, 17: 202, 231.
Rouen, Pilgrimage to. (A. G. Hill) Walford's Antiq. 1: 65.
Rouergue, Wayfaring in the. (E. H. Barker) Temp. Bar, 95: 479. Same art. Liv. Age, 194: 759.
Roumania, Situation in, 1888. (H. Geffcken) Univ. R. 2: 184.
— Nationality of. (A. J. Patterson) Acad. 48: 177.
Roumanille, Josef. (M. L. Elmendorf) Poet-Lore, 2: 401, 449.
Roumelia, Revolution of. Time, 13: 620.
Round Pegs in Square Holes. (M. B. Godsall) 19th Cent. 39: 964.
Round Towers and Irish Art. (J. T. Hodgson) Canad. M. 4: 38.
— St. Fechlin, the Builder of. (E. Lawless) 19th Cent. 37: 421. Same art. Liv. Age, 205: 104.
Roundabout to Boston. (W. D. Howells) Harper, 91: 427.
Roundhead Order, Gen. Wilkinson's, 1801, Col. Butler and. Pennsyl. M. 17: 501.
Round-up, A. Chamb. J. 71: 671.
— Rodeo at Los Ojos, A. (F. Remington) Harper, 88: 515.
Rousing of Mrs. Potter. (Gertrude Smith) Cent. 23: 718.
Rousseau, J. J. (J. Sanderson) Open Court, 7: 3527. — (J. Forster) Time, 16: 159.
— Chuquet's. (A. Laugel) Nation, 59: 139.
— Some Thoughts on. Ecl. M. 122: 205.
Rousseau, Pierre-Etienne-Thédore. (D. C. Thomson) M. of Art, 11: 385.
Rousseauism Revived. Quar. 179: 414.
Roussel, Theodore, as an Artist. Acad. 46: 54.
Routing of a Ghost; a story. (J. J. à Becket) Cosmopol. 21: 521.
Roux, Maitre. *See* Rosso, Il.

Rowan-tree Inn. (Sir H. Maxwell) Good Words, 35: 814.
Rowdy, The: a story. (A. French) Cent. 23: 67.
Rowfant Club's Publications. (E. D. North) Bibliographica, 2: 383.
Rowing. (C. Mellen) Outing, 19: 463.
— at Yale and Harvard. (J. R. Finlay) Outing, 23: 457.
— College. Outing, 19: 389.
— in the Northwest. (A. W. Wack) Outing, 20: 307.
— The Essential in. (R. H. Dana) Harv. Grad. M. 4: 551.
— The Proposed Pan-Anglican Festival. (R. P. P. Rowe) Fortn. 58: 38.
— Six Months with a University Crew. (R. D. Paine) Outing, 24: 67.
See Boat-racing.
Rowing Indicator, A. (E. C. Atkinson) Nat. Sc. 8: 178.
Rowland, Henry Augustus, with portrait. (C. E. Lloyd) Pop. Sci. Mo. 49: 110.
Rowlandite, Description of. (W. E. Hidden and W. F. Hillebrand) Am. J. Sci. 146: 208.
Rowlands, Effie A., with portrait. Bk. News, 13: 10.
Rowlandson, Thomas, the Caricaturist. Bookworm, 2: 49.
Row'tilly Girl, The; a story. (D. S. Meldrum) National, 19: 824. Same art. Liv. Age, 194: 817.
Roxbury Latin School. (J. De Normandie) New Eng. M. n. s. 12: 388.
Roy, Captain J. J., Adventure of. (A. Harcourt) Temp. Bar, 107: 398.
Roy the Royalist. (W. Westhall) Lippinc. 49: 131.
Royal Academy, The. (C. Phillips) Acad. 49: 389-533. — (J. E. Hodgson and F. A. Eaton) Art J. 47: 143. — (S. Haras) Am. Arch. 48: 122. — (D. S. MacColl) Fortn. 59: 881. 61: 721.
— Admission of Pictures to. (W. Bayliss) M. of Art. 2: 62.
— and the New Gallery. (H. Statham) Fortn. 65: 958.
— and the Select Committee on Arts. (J. Penderel-Brodhurst) M. of Art, 9: 326.
— Architectural Drawings at. (E. J. Bell) M. of Art, 1: 249.
— Banquet. (M. H. Spielmann) M. of Art, 10: 228.
— Beginnings of. (H. V. Barnett) M. of Art, 9: 34.
— Dinners. (Dutton Cook) Time, 3: 117.
— Eight Presidents of. (F. Wedmore) Eng. Illust. 15: 3.
— Election Methods of. Art J. 45: 361.
— Elections, 1894. M. of Art, 17: xvii.
— Exhibition, 1878. M. of Art, 1: 40-135.
— — 1888. (H. Quilter) Univ. R. 1: 57.
— — 1889. M. of Art, 12: 224, 269.
— — 1891. (M. H. Spielmann) M. of Art, 14: 217, 253.
— — Winter, 1891-92. Ath. '92, 1: 58-219. — (C. Phillips) Art J. 44: 90.
— — 1892. (M. H. Spielmann) M. of Art, 15: 217, 253. — (C. Phillips) Art J. 44: 187-241. (C. Phillips) Acad. 41: 450-548. — Ath. '92, 1: 569-767. — (G. Moore) Fortn. 57: 828. — Sat. R. 73: 535, 568, 596. — Spec. 68: 642, 676.
— — Winter, 1892-93. Ath. '93, 1: 28-285. — (C. Phillips) Acad. 43: 17, 64, 111.
— — 1893. (M. H. Spielmann) M. of Art, 16: 217-294. — (C. Phillips) Acad. 43: 398, 420, 465, 487. — (R. A. M. Stevenson) Art J. 45: 241. — Ath. '93, 1: 542-770. — Sat. R. 75: 487-629. — Spec. 70: 573.
Royal Academy; Exhibition, 1894. (R. A. M. Stevenson) Art J. 46: 210. — (C. Phillips) Acad. 45: 399-481. — Ath. '94, 1: 583-842. — Sat. R. 77: 493-663. — (M. H. Spielmann) M. of Art, 17: 217-289.
— — 1895. (C. Phillips) Acad. 47: 407-548. — (R. J. Slade) Art J. 47: 161. — Sat. R. 79: 617. — Ath. '95, 1: 54-288. — (S. Beale) Am. Arch. 47: 53. — (M. H. Spielmann) M. of Art, 18: 241-321.
— — 1896. Art J. 48: 161. — Sat. R. 81: 470, 498. — M. of Art, 19: 257-355.
— Exhibitions, Making and Makers of. (H. Quilter) Eng. Illust. 10: 523.
— Hanging of Pictures. (W. Bayliss) M. of Art, 2: 133.
— in 19th Century. (J. E. Hodgson and F. A. Eaton) Art J. 47: 243. — (G. D. Leslie) Art J. 48: 183.
— Inquests and Commissions. (J. Penderel-Brodhurst) M. of Art, 9: 382.
— The "Instrument" of. (H. V. Barnett) M. of Art, 9: 57.
— New Associates of. Art J. 44: 94.
— Old Masters at. (C. Phillips) Acad. 41: 68-136. — (F. T. Palgrave) Acad. 41: 94. — (C. Phillips) Acad. 45: 17, 64, 107. 47: 40, 86, 109. 49: 41, 81, 140. — Ath. '94, 1: 21-318. — Sat. R. 77: 11-663. — (E. R. Pennell) Nation 60: 88. — M. of Art, 3: 198. 4: 201. 13: 145. 15: 145. 17: 109. 18: 161. 19: 161.
— Our Academicians and their Associates. (G. Moore) New R. 8: 665.
— Pictures at, 1890. (M. H. Spielmann) M. of Art, 13: 217, 253.
— Present Aspects of Art. (Wm. Sharp) Time, 5: 93.
— Receipts and Expenditure. (J. Penderel-Brodhurst) M. of Art, 9: 433.
— Scandals at. (J. Penderel-Brodhurst) M. of Art, 9: 453, 514.
— Schools of. M. of Art, 2: 59. — (M. H. Spielmann) M. of Art, 11: 55.
— — Winners of Prizes, 1893. (R. J. Slade) M. of Art, 17: 127.
— Student's Competition. M. of Art, 15: 174.
— Treatment of Living Artists by. Art J. 47: 158.
Royal Academy; a story. Temp. Bar, 95: 222.
Royal Archæological Institute, 1894 Meeting. Ath. '94, 2: 135, 201.
Royal Authors, Modern. (E. Davis) Canad. M. 4: 350.
Royal Canadian Society of Arts. (H. Ford) Canad. M. 3: 45.
Royal Colonial Institute. Catalogue of the Library. (H. L. Roth) Westm. 145: 140.
Royal Commissions as they are and as they should be. Spec. 74: 457.
Royal Courts of Justice, London. Description of the Buildings. (W. Armstrong) M. of Art, 5: 37.
Royal Families, Insanity in. (A. Bodington) Am. Natural. 29: 118.
— of England and Denmark, Marriages between. (J. D. Symon) Eng. Illust. 15: 303.
Royal Geographical Society, Address to. (C. R. Markham) Geog. J. 6: 1.
Royal Hospital at Kilmainham, near Dublin. Old Soldiers. (K. T. Hinkson) Good Words, 37: 454.
Royal Institute, Exhibition of Pictures, 1885. M. of Art, 8: 133.
Royal Jiltings, Certain. (E. F. Corby) Argosy, 60: 116.
Royal Marine; an idyl of Narragansett Pier. (B. Matthews) Harper, 89: 577, 651.
Royal Marriage, A; a story. (G. Bonner) Harper, 88: 267.
Royal Patriotic Fund. (H. E. Kearley) Fortn. 61: 634.
Royal Photographic Society. Nature, 50: 577.

Royal Reception, A; a story. Eng. Illust. 9: 810, 869.
Royal School of Art-needlework. M. of Art, 5: 219.
Royal Scottish Academy and Sir T. Dick-Lauder. Art J. 46: 271.
— and Glasgow Institute Exhibitions, 1879. (G. R. Halkett) M. of Art, 2: 184–265.
— Exhibition of Pictures, 1880. (G. R. Halkett) M. of Art, 3: 432.
— — 1881. (G. R. Halkett) M. of Art, 4: 260.
— 1893. (W. M. Gilbert) Art J. 45: 151. — Acad. 43: 136.
— — 1894. Acad. 45: 233.
— — 1896. Art J. 48: 154.
Royal Society of London. (M. D. Steele) Pop. Sci. Mo. 41: 531.
— Annual Soirée, 1894. Dub. R. 115: 159.
— 1894 Meeting. Nature, 51: 132.
— Library of. (E. W. Crofts) Bookworm, 5: 65.
— Rise of. (H. Rix) Leis. Hour, 45: 489–657.
Royal Society Conversazione. Nature, 52: 37.
Royal Society of Painters in Water-colors, Roget's History of. (F. G. Stephens) M. of Art, 15: 155.
"Royal William," First Steamer to cross the Atlantic. Chamb. J. 70: 369.
Royalty, Military Courage of. (A. Forbes) Contemp. 63: 189. Same art. Liv. Age, 197: 112. Same art. Un. Serv. (Phila.) 9: 348.
— A Study of. (L. de La Ramée) Forum, 21: 471.
— Summer Homes of. (H. W. Fischer) Munsey, 13: 406.
Rubber, India-. Spec. 77: 673. — (G. Allen) Longm. 24: 492.
Rubber-plants, Propagating. (W. Scott) Garden & F. 8: 7.
Rubber or Two, A; a story. All the Year, 73: 277.
Rube the Rat-catcher. Chamb. J. 69: 732.
Rubens, Peter Paul. (T. Cole) Cent. 28: 483.
Rubidium and Potassium Trihalides. (H. L. Wells and H. L. Wheeler) Am. J. Sci. 143: 475.
— Quantitative Determination of, by the Spectroscope. (F. A. Gooch and J. I. Phinney) Am. J. Sci. 144: 392.
Rubinstein, Anton. Ath. '94, 2: 723. — Pub. Opin. 17: 845. — Acad. 46: 431. — With portrait. Bk. News, 9: 71. — With portrait. (H. G. Ganss) Cath. World, 64: 193. — (H. R. Haweis) Fortn. 63: 27. Same art. Ecl. M. 124: 229. Same art. Liv. Age, 204: 451. — R. of Rs. (N. Y.) 11: 177. — Music, 7: 384.
— "Christus" at Bremen. (J. S. Shedlock) Acad. 47: 510.
— A Last Look. Atlan. 76: 287.
— the Man and the Musician. (A. McArthur) Cent. 28: 28.
— on other Composers. (H. T. Finck) Nation, 54: 36.
— Recollections of. (C. Saint-Saens) Music, 8: 423. — (J. Rodenberg) Music, 8: 437.
Rublee, Horace; a Fine Type of Journalist. (E. P. Clark) Nation, 63: 342.
Ruby Humming-bird, The; a story. (E. Phillpotts) Eng. Illust. 11: 377.
Ruchonnet, Louis, with portrait. (S. J. Capper) R. of Rs. (N. Y.) 8: 677.
Rude Awakening, A; a story. (Mrs. F. Copleston) Belgra. 79: 257.
Rudgis and Grim; a story. (M. Thompson) Cent. 22: 460.
Ruding, Walt. Evil Motherhood. Sat. R. 82: 230.
Rudini, Marquis, and Italian Politics. (L. de La Ramé) Fortn. 66: 350. Same art. Liv. Age, 211: 67.
Rudolf and Stefanie, Lakes. Nature, 49: 457. — Sat. R. 77: 232. — (A. M. Earle) Dial (Ch.) 16: 269.
Rue; "There 's Rue for you." All the Year, 73: 273.
Ruetimeyer, Ludwig. Nature, 53: 158.
Rugby and Oxford. (W. C. Lake) Good Words, 36: 666.
— Old School-list of. (J. W. Sherer) Time, 1: 176.
Rugs, Oriental. (S. G. W. Benjamin) Cosmopol. 14: 407.
Ruined Bookman; a story. (Chas. T. Lusted) Gent. M. n. s. 57: 486.
Ruined Faith-doctor, A. (C. R. Van Blarcom) Scrib. M. 18: 234.
Ruisdael, Jacob van. (T. Cole) Cent. 26: 363.
"Rule Britannia," Authorship of. (J. C. Hadden) 19th Cent. 40: 932.
Rum Punch at Podbury's; a story. (E. Phillpotts) Idler, 3: 336.
Rumford, Benjamin Thompson, Count. (F. M. Abbott) New Eng. M. n. s. 9: 463. — (G. E. Ellis) Atlan. 71: 213.
— Tyndall on. Sat. R. 73: 245.
Rumford, Me., Occurrence of Rollucite, etc., at. (H. W. Foote) Am. J. Sci. 151: 457.
Rumford Kitchen, The. Lend a H. 12: 14.
Ruminants, Distribution of. (R. Lydekker) Knowl. 15: 152.
Rumpety Case. (A. Fuller) Lippinc. 53: 790.
Rumsey, James, Steamboat Inventor. (J. Weir) Engin. M. 9: 878. — (G. W. Archer) Nat'l M. (N. Y. '91) 18: 132.
Runaways; a story. (F. W. Broughton) Theatre, 30: 45.
Runeberg, Johan L. (C. Fell-Smith) Time, 23: 714.
Runes and Oghams. (G. B. Rawlings) Knowl. 19: 232.
Runga's Revenge. (Mrs. Frank Penny) Chamb. J. 72: 685.
Runic Crosses of Northumbria. (J. M. Stone) Scot. R. 27: 292.
Running, Cross-country, History of, in America. (E. H. Baynes) Outing, 23: 484.
— International Athletic Match, 1895. (W. E. Curtis) Outing, 27: 157.
Runyon, Theodore, with portrait. Nat'l M. (N. Y. '91) 18: 295.
Rupee, Circulation of. (F. C. Harrison) Econ. J. 2: 256.
Rural Festivals, American. (C. C. Harrison) Cent. 28: 323.
Rural Life, Poetry of. Ed. R. 179: 61.
Rural Population, Decrease of the. (J. C. Rose) Pop. Sci. Mo. 42: 621.
— — in England. (G. B. Longstaff) J. Statis. Soc. 56: 380.
Rural Simplicity; a story. (B. Paine) Eng. Illust. 9: 307.
Rural Traditions. (B. Landreth) Un. Serv. (Phila) 12: 513.
Rurvenzori, Mount, Scott Elliot's Expedition to. Geog. J. 4: 349.
Rus in Urbe. (E. M. Thomas) Atlan. 74: 308.
Rush, Dr. Benjamin, and Gen. Washington. (P. L. Ford) Atlan. 75: 633.
— Letter of, in 1795. M. Am. Hist. 27: 68.
Rush, John, Descendants of. Pennsyl. M. 17: 325.
Rush, William. (E. L. Gilliams) Lippinc. 52: 249.
Rushton, Richard H., with portrait. Bank. M. (N. Y.) 52: 436.
Ruskin, John, with portrait. Bk. Buyer, 10: 191. — Church Q. 36: 439. Same art. Liv. Age, 199: 131. — (Henriette Corkran) Temp. Bar, 105: 515. — (F. Harrison) 19th Cent. 38: 958.
— and Mr. Stillman. (W. J. Stillman) Nation, 57: 447.

Ruskin, John, Art Teaching of, Collingwood on. (W. J. Stillman) Nation, 54: 16.
— as Art Teacher. (W. G. Kingsland) Poet-Lore, 5: 405.
— as a Letter-writer. (W. G. Kingsland) Poet-Lore, 5: 1, 67, 123.
— as a Master of Prose. (Frederic Harrison) 19th Cent. 38: 561.
— as a Political Economist. (W. J. Lhamon) Canad. M. 8: 45.
— as a Practical Teacher. (M. Kaufman) Scot. R. 24: 21. Same art. Liv. Age, 203: 155.
— at Home. (M. H. Spielmann) McClure, 2: 315.
— Collingwood's Life of. Art J. 45: 336. — Critic, 22: 401. — (W. M. Payne) Dial (Ch.) 15: 189. — Ath. '93, 2: 70. — (W. J. Stillman) Nation, 57: 159. — Spec. 70: 859.
— First Published Writings of. (W. R. Nicoll) Bookman, 1: 321.
— for Poet Laureate. Critic, 22: 311.
— in relation to Modern Problems. (E. T. Cook) National, 22: 823. Same art. Ecl. M. 122: 486.
— Influence of, on English Social Thought. New Eng. M. n. s. 9: 473.
— Letters by. (W. G. Kingsland) Poet-Lore, 8: 420.
— — 1840-45. Sat. R. 78: 274. — Spec. 73: 272.
— Letters of, with portrait. (G. Stronach) Eng. Illust. 10: 779. Same art. Liv. Age, 198: 813.
— — to Ernest Chesneau. (W. G. Kingsland) Poet-Lore, 7: 123, 255, 349.
— — to his Secretary. New R. 6: 273. Same art. Liv. Age, 193: 304.
— Life and Work of, Collingwood's. (M. H. Spielmann) M. of Art, 11: 417.
— Mania for. (Mrs. E. T. Cook) Good Words, 35: 538.
— on Gold. (W. G. Kingsland) Poet-Lore, 4: 113.
— Portraits of. (M. H. Spielmann) M. of Art, 14: 73, 121.
— Seven Lamps of Architecture. Eng. R. 15: 55.
— A Study in Development. Lond. Q. 81: 265.
— A Study in Love and Religion. (J. Telford) Meth. R. 55: 25.
— Titles of his Books. (Mrs. E. T. Cook) Good Words, 34: 477.
— Visit to the Museum of, at Sheffield. (E. Bradbury) M. of Art, 3: 57.
— Waldstein on. (W. Lewin) Acad. 46: 506.
— Writings of. (G. Saintsbury) Critic, 25: 115.
Russell, Charles, Lord Chief Justice. (G. H. Knott) Am. Law R. 28: 860. — Cath. World, 64: 243. — With portrait. Green Bag, 4: 97.
— at Home. (K. Tynan) Eng. Illust. 12: no. 2, 16.
Russell, John, Lord, Reid's. Sat. R. 80: 17. — (G. C. Williamson) M. of Art, 15: 73.
— Williamson's Life of. (C. Monkhouse) Acad. 46: 541.
Russell, John L., with portrait. Nat'l M. (N. Y. '91) 16: 730.
Russell, Rachel, Lady. (E. A. Gowing) Belgra. 78: 247.
Russell, T. W., and the Roman Catholic Hierarchy of Ireland. (W. J. Walsh) Fortn. 57: 415.
Russell, William, Lord, Widow of, Portraits of. (G. Scharf) Ath. '93, 1: 612.
Russell, W. Clark, with portrait. Bk. Buyer, 7: 95.
— How he writes his Sea-novels. (R. Blathwayt) Eng. Illust. 10: 863.
— Wreck of the Grosvenor. Idler, 2: 11.
Russell, Wm. E. (J. T. Wheelwright) Bach. of Arts, 3: 295.
— Memorial Address at Sanders Theatre, Cambridge. (C. E. Norton) Harv. Grad. M. 5: 177.
Russia. (E. Dicey) Fortn. 62: 817.
Russia. (S. Stepniak) Time, 23: 1145.
— Aim of, in Asia. (K. Blind) Un. Serv. M. 6: 400.
— and Northern Asia. (A. Vámbéry) Asia. R. 11: 13.
— and Bulgaria. (E. Dicey) Fortn. R. 65: 663.
— and China. (E. H. Parker) Asia. R. 22: 12. — (R. S. Gundry) Fortn. 58: 493.
— and the Czar's Death. Sat. R. 78: 475.
— and England. (A. J. French) Fortn. 63: 883. — (A. Vámbéry) No. Am. 160: 561. — (M. MacColl) Contemp. 67: 1.
— — in the Far East. Fortn. 65: 865.
— — and France. (T. H. S. Escott) Fortn. 66: 648. — Same art. Ecl. M. 127: 731.
— — A Meeting with Mr. Disraeli. (K. Blind) Time, 513.
— — Russo-English Alliance. (J. St. L. Strachey) National, 26: 741.
— — Why Russia distrusts England. (W. Reid) 19th Cent. 40: 509.
— and Europe. (E. J. Dillon) Contemp. 70: 609.
— and France, Alliance of. (P. de Coubertin) R. of Rs. (N. Y.) 13: 700.
— and Germany, in 1892. Spec. 68: 486.
— and her Rulers. (H. R. McElligott) Munsey, 10: 162.
— and India. Sat. R. 77: 315.
— and Peace. (K. Blind) Un. Serv. M. 7: 1291.
— and Russians, Notice of, in Oriental Literature. (F. H. Tyrrell) Asia. R. 17: 154.
— Apotheosis of. Blackw. 160: 135.
— Army of, Conspiracies in. (R. de Lipmann) Time, 16: 662.
— — In the Barracks of the Czar. (P. Bigelow) Harper, 86: 771.
— as a Field for Tourists. (E. Braddon) J. Soc. of Arts, 41: 396.
— Attitude of, during the Civil War in the U. S. (H. F. Cutter) Overland, n. s. 20: 311.
— Bargaining in. (I. F. Hapgood) Lippinc. 54: 680.
— Bed and Board in. (I. F. Hapgood) Lippinc. 57: 678.
— Beggars in, The Ways of. (Edith Sellers) Good Words, 37: 195.
— Censorship of the Press in. (R. G. Burton) Westm. 144: 135.
— a Change of Czars. Blackw. 157: 306. Same art, Liv. Age, 204: 579.
— Cholera and Cleanliness in. (E. B. Lanin) Fortn. 58: 304.
— Church of, State. (B. J. Clinch) Am. Cath. Q. 20: 449.
— — its Spiritual State and Possibilities. (Isabel F. Hapgood) Chr. Lit. 15: 239, 302.
— The Coronation at Moscow. (M. Creighton) Cornh. 74: 305.
See Nicholas II.
— Crisis in, 1892. Contemp. 62: 34. Same art. Ecl. M. 119: 367.
— Dissenters in, and the Russian Government. Sund. M. 22: 485, 547.
— Drama in. (H. S. Edwards) Theatre, 35: 213.
— Economic Condition of, in 1892. (T. Lloyd) Econ. J. 2: 398.
— Education in. (I. F. Hapgood) Lippinc. 58: 519.
— Empire of the Tsars, Leroy-Beaulieu's. Sat. R. 82: 139. — (I. F. Hapgood) Nation, 57: 216. — (R. B. Anderson) Dial (Ch.) 15: 222.
— English Influence in. (P. Bororykine) Contemp. 68: 50.
— Extradition Treaty with. (G. Kennan) Forum, 15: 283. — (J. B. Moore) Forum, 15: 629. — (E. L. Godkin) Nation, 56: 450. — Pub. Opin. 15: 93, 263. — (I. A. Hourwich) Yale R. 3: 68.

Russia, Famine in. (E. B. Lanin) Ecl. M. **118**: 93. — (E. Levasseur) J. Statis. Soc. **55**: 80. — (C. E. Smith) No. Am. **154**: 541. — (W. C. Edgar) R. of Rs. (N. Y.) **5**: 691.
— — and the Revolution. (S. Stepniak) Fortn. **57**: 358.
— — Nihilism and. (Countess Norriakow) Lippinc. **49**: 472.
— — Relief of. R. of Rs. (N. Y.) **5**: 37.
— — Relief Work for. R. of Rs. (N. Y.) **5**: 564.
— — — by the Younger Tolstoy. (J. Stadling) Cent. **24**: 560.
— — With Leo Tolstoy in the. (J. Stadling) Cent. **46**: 249.
— First English Ambassadors to. (J. Corbett) Macmil. **68**: 58. Same art. Liv. Age, **198**: 67.
— Foreign Policy of. (F. Engels) Time, **22**: 353, 525.
— Foreign Relations of. (S. M. Miller) Cath. World, **60**: 535.
— Free Labor in. (P. Bigelow) Contemp. **63**: 248.
— Georgian Treaties with. (V. E. Cherzekov) 19th Cent. **37**: 832.
— Germany's Secret Treaty with. National, **28**: 446.
— Imperial Guards, under Catherine the Great. (F. Whishaw) Un. Serv. M. **6**: 375.
— in Asia, as a Civilizing Force. (J. M. Hubbard) Atlan. **75**: 197.
See Pamirs.
— in 1892, Caprivi on. Spec. **69**: 758.
— in Europe. (G. G. Hubbard) Nat. Geog. M. **7**: 3.
— in the Mediterranean. Spec. **71**: 389.
— in the 19th Century, Mrs. Latimer's. Nation, **58**: 333.
— Industrial art in. (E. D. Morgan) J. Soc. Arts, **41**: 653.
— Judiciary of. (I. A. Hourich) Pol. Sci. Q. **7**: 673.
— Justice in, by Administrative Order. (A. Smith) Univ. R. **6**: 467.
— Life in a Russian Village. (J. D. Rees) 19th Cent. **35**: 813. Same art. Ecl. M. **123**: 40. Same art. Liv. Age, **201**: 560.
— Misinformation about. (I. F. Hapgood) Nation, **61**: 167.
— Mongolia and China. (E. Reclus) Contemp. **67**: 617. Same art. Liv. Age, **205**: 555.
— Music of. (E. B. Lewis) Music, **2**: 280, 371. — (C. Lichtenberger) Music, **6**: 506.
— Name of, Meaning of. (K. Blind) Scot. R. **22**: 325.
— Navy in Black Sea. (M. Rymaelje-Suwarof) Un. Serv. M. **4**: 395.
— — Under the Cross of St. Andrew. (V. Gribayédoff) Cosmopol. **16**: 673.
— — Volunteer Fleet. (J. D. Ross) Chamb. J. **72**: 341.
— New Era in. Cath. World, **63**: 525.
— The New Reign in. (V. Yarros) Chaut. **20**: 698. — (F. Volkhovzky) Canad. M. **4**: 357.
— Newton's Run through. Nation, **59**: 145.
— Nihilism in, Revival of. Sat. R. **80**: 338.
— Nihilists of. (Stepniak) Time, **13**: 253, 637.
— of To-day, and the Czar. (W. T. Stead) R. of Rs. (N. Y.) **4**: 667.
— — Stead on; Logic of a Despot's Advocate. (D. G. Ritchie) Westm. **137**: 268.
— On a Moor in. (F. Whishaw) Longm. **26**: 406.
— on the Pacific. Ed. R. **178**: 122.
— or England? (D. Mills) Canad. M. **4**: 518.
— Outskirts of Europe. (J. D. Rees) National, **23**: 766.
— Passports, Police and Post-Office in. (I. F. Hapgood) Atlan. **72**: 42.
Russia, Peasant Life in. (L. B. C. Wyman) Chaut. **15**: 57.
— Penury of. E. D. R. **177**: 1.
— People of. Leis. Hour, **43**: 627–795.
— Periodical Press in. (V. Yarros) Chaut. **18**: 545.
— Persecutions of Christians in. (L. Tolstoi) Contemp. **68**: 644.
— A Plea for. Contemp. **69**: 670. Same art. Liv. Age, **209**: 584.
— Politics in. After the Coronation at Moscow. (K. Blind) No. Am. **163**: 17.
— Present Condition. (P. Kropotkin) 19th Cent. **38**: 519. Same art. Ecl. M. **125**: 518. Same art. Liv. Age, **207**: 215.
— Railways and Exports of. (A. Laugel) Nation, **54**: 144.
— Rambles in, Hapgood's. Sat. R. **79**: 868.
— Regeneration of. (A. W. Sherman) No. Am. **162**: 507.
— Religious Problems of. (E. B. Lanin) Contemp. **63**: 584.
— Religious Sentiment of. (A. L. Beaulieu) Soc. Econ. **4**: 13.
— Rome, and the Old Catholics. (O. Novikoff) New R. **8**: 439.
— Six Weeks in. (M. E. Herbert) Dub. R. **116**: 89.
— South, Peasant-life of. Blackw. **158**: 805. Same art. Liv. Age, **208**: 35.
— Statesman of. Liv. Age, **193**: 98, 377.
— Strength of. Liv. Age, **211**: 331.
— A Study of. Atlan. **73**: 269.
— Stundists in, Persecution of. (E. B. Lanin) Contemp. **61**: 1.
— Superstitions of. Illus. Archæol. **2**: 54.
— Travels among the Peasants, Stevens'. Dub. R. **110**: 452.
— under Alexander III. Sat. R. **78**: 592.
— Village and Villagers in. (F. Whishaw) Temp. Bar, **99**: 193. Same art. Liv. Age, **199**: 689. Same art. Ecl. M. **121**: 740.
— Village Life in. (V. Yarros) Chaut. **19**: 131.
— A Voice for. (P. Botkine) Cent. **23**: 611.
— A Voice for the People of. (G. Kennan) Cent. **24**: 461.
— Western Frontier of. (P. Bigelow) Harper, **85**: 255.
— Why we left. (P. Bigelow) Harper, **86**: 294.
See Kirghese.
Russian Alliance, Alsace and the. (C. Schefer) Nation, **55**: 66.
Russian Ascendency in Europe. Fortn. **66**: 461.
Russian Bookseller and Publisher. (E. C. Grenville-Murray) Bookworm, **2**: 329.
Russian Church. (M. E. Herbert) Dub. R. **112**: 1. — (Isabel F. Hapgood) Outl. **53**: 1142.
Russian Costumes. (C. H. A. Bjerregaard) Mo. Illust. **13**: 161.
Russian Drama. (N. H. Dole) Poet-Lore, **1**: 487. **2**: 113, 566.
Russian Family, Life in a. Blackw. **160**: 692. Same art. Ecl. M. **127**: 749.
Russian Fiction, Early. (H. Wilson) Dub. R. **110**: 123.
Russian Fictional Literature. (R. G. Burton) Westm. **144**: 539.
Russian Folk-songs. (J. C. Fillmore) Music, **4**: 123.
Russian Intrigues in South Eastern Europe. (C. B. Roylance-Kent) Fortn. **60**: 105.
Russian Language, Professorship of, in U. S. (I. F. Hapgood) Nation, **55**: 29.
— Study of, Plea for. (N. H. Dole) Harv. Grad. M. **3**: 180.

Russian Literature. (P. Milyoukov) Ath. '94, 2: 22.
— 1891–92. (P. Milyoukov) Ath. '92, 2: 25.
— 1892–93. (P. Milyoukov) Ath. '93, 2: 27.
— 1893–94. (P. Milyoukov) Ath. '94, 2: 22.
— 1894–95. (P. Milyoukov) Ath. '95, 2: 24.
— 1895–96. (P. Milyoukov) Ath. '96, 2: 25.
— Decadence of. Lippinc. 58: 102.
— Stagnation in. (V. Yarros) Dial (Ch.) 20: 39.
Russian "New Woman," A; a story. Temp. Bar, 108: 518.
Russian Novels, Pessimism in. (E. G. Boner) Chaut. 22: 426.
Russian Propaganda. (A. Vámbéry) National, 21: 44.
Russian Summer Resort, Tzárskoe Seló. (I. F. Hapgood) Atlan. 72: 343.
Russian Spy, The; a story. (D'A. Hildyard) Belgra. 90: 75.
Russians at Home, The. Cornh. 66: 174. Same art. Liv. Age, 194: 808.
— in Boston. (G. Bamber) Lend a H. 8: 168.
Russia's Strength. (S. Wilkinson) National, 28: 220.
Russud, Custom of exacting, in India. (O. P. Sing) 19th Cent. 34: 802.
Rustication of Loll Toplis, The; a story. (T. Keyworth) Gent. M. n. s. 56: 109.
Rustlers, The. (A. McGowan) Lippinc. 52: 614.
Ruston, Joseph, Collection of Pictures. (C. Phillips) M. of Art, 17: 19–97.
Ruth Herrick's Assignment; a story. (E. G. Jordan) Cosmopol. 17: 365.
Rutherford, Mark. (W. R. Nicoll) Bookman, 3: 438.
Rutherford the Twice-born; a story. (E. L. Arnold) Idler, 1: 387.
Rutherfurd, Lewis M., with portrait. (J. K. Rees) Astron. 11: 689. — With portrait. Pop. Sci. Mo. 42: 404.
Rutherfurd Photographic Measures, Permanence of. (H. Jacoby) Science, n. s. 3: 505.
Rutland, Mass. (E. E. Barry) New Eng. M. n. s. 8: 762.
Rutland Papers. Ath. '92, 1: 18.
Rutty, Herbert Waring, with portrait. Theatre, 28: 297.
— Four Leading Men, a Comparative Estimate. (W. A. L. Bettany) Theatre, 29: 109.
Ruxton, G. A. F. (J. Munro) Good Words, 34: 547.
Ryder, Dick. Of the Man from Cornwall. (H. B. M. Watson) New R. 12: 345.
Ryder, John Adam. Nat. Sci. 6: 349. — (H. Allen) Science, n. s. 2: 334.
Rye and Winchelsea, England. Art J. 47: 257.
Ryland, William Wynne, Notes on. (E. Radford) Art J. 48: 237.
Rymer, Thomas. Bookworm, 2: 145.
Rype-shooting in Norway without Dogs. (G. A. Scott) Fortn. 61: 749.

Saadia. (M. Friedländer) Jew. Q. 5: 177.
Saas, Valley of, Art in the. (S. Butler) Univ. R. 8: 411.
Sabatier, P., with portrait. Bk. Buyer, 11: 373.
Sabbath, The American. (C. H. Hull) Nation, 56: 64.
— Anglo-Saxon. (F. Tupper, jr.) Nation, 56: 234.
— as a Civil Institution. (B. W. Williams) Am. M. Civics, 6: 432.
— Civilizing the. (M. D. Conway) Open Court, 6: 3495.
— English and American. Nation, 56: 122.
— in Puritan New England, Earle's. (W. W. Newell) J. Am. Folk-Lore, 4: 356.
— Observance of. (J. W. Love) Ref. Q. 43: 490.
Sabbath or Sunday, which? (M. G. Boyer) Luth. Q. 26: 122.
— Sabbatarianism: an Expensive Delusion. (F. L. Oswald) No. Am. 162: 125.
— Sunday, Authority of. (W. P. Schwarts) Luth. Q. 24: 100.
— Teaching of the Augsburg Confession on. (T. F. Reeser) Luth. Q. 26: 476.
Sabbath Breaker, The; a story. (I. Zangwill) McClure, 2: 159.
Sabbath-keepers, A Suggestion to. (A. R. Wallace) 19th Cent. 36: 604.
Sabbath Observance Bill, Lines on. (Marquis Wellesley) 19th Cent. 37: 1059.
Sabbath Reform, Practicable. (W. F. Crafts) Our Day, 13: 520.
Sabbaths and Weeks, Origin of. (A. B. Ellis) Pop. Sci. Mo. 46: 329.
Sabianism, or Sky Worship in America. (S. D. Peet) Am. Antiq. 16: 217.
Sabin, Joseph, with portrait. (W. L. Andrews) Bookman, 1: 381.
Sable Island. Chamb. J. 69: 314.
Sable Nimrod's Error, A. (D. Dodge) Outing, 23: 191.
Sabre, Revolver or? (W. P. Hall) No. Am. 161: 249.
Saccharine. (G. E. R. Ellis) Time, 18: 72.
Sacerdotalism. (F. W. Farrar) Contemp. 62: 48.
— Anglican. (G. M. Searle) Cath. World, 59: 273.
— Canon Knox Little on. (F. Peek) Contemp. 68: 826.
Sacher-Masoch, Leopold von. Bookman, 2: 401.
Sachs, Hans, Poet of the Reformation. (N. W. Clark) Meth. R. 55: 698. — With portrait. (M. A. Taggart) Cath. World, 59: 372.
— 400th Birthday Anniversary of. Critic, 25: 334.
— — Celebration in Germany. (K. Blind) National, 24: 392. Same art. Ecl. M. 124: 63.
Sachs, Julius, Physiological Papers of. Nature, 48: 513.
Sacking of Doe Castle; an Irish Story. (W. Packard) Nat'l M. (Bost.) 5: 253.
Sacking of Grubbville, The; a story. (A. F. Batell) Overland, n. s. 20: 573.
Sacramento Valley, Heart of the. (S. G. Wilson) Overland, n. s. 27: 185.
Sacraments and Forms in Christianity, Importance of. (J. M. Love) Ref. Q. 39: 473.
— and the Word, Objective Efficacy of. (J. A. Earnest) Luth. Q. 25: 289.
— as Means of Grace in the Lutheran System. (J. W. Richard) Luth. Q. 24: 348.
— Word of God in. (J. Tomlinson) Luth. Q. 23: 420.
Sacred Beetle, The; a story. (L. Græme) Chamb. J. 70: 343–393.
Sacrifice, Formula of. (H. J. Davenport) J. Pol. Econ. 2: 561.
— Human. (W. H. Gardner) Open Court, 8: 3991, 4000.
— Self-, Limits of Individual and National. (F. H. Bradley) Int. J. Ethics, 5: 17.
Sacrifices, Idea of, Origin and Development of. (D. B. Lady) Ref. Q. 39: 487.
Sad Fate of a New Woman; a story. (Julian Ralph) Cosmopol. 20: 548.
Saddle and Sentiment. (W. Gilman) Outing, 19: 309 — 21: 44.
Saddleton's Illusion; a story. (President Bates) Outing, 20: 397.
Sadi. Gulistan, translated by Sir E. Arnold. Longm. 23: 366. 24: 588.

Sadler, Walter Dendy. (F. G. Stephens) Art J. **47**: 193. — (W. L. Woodroffe) M. of Art, **19**: 265.
— The Gamesters; a painting. Art J. **47**: 253.
Sadness of Summer; a poem. (A. I. Muntz) Temp. Bar, **95**: 493.
Sadowa, Battle of. (S. B. Arnold) Un. Serv. (Phila.) **15**: 427.
Sadthu the Dacoit; a story. (F. Dixon) Eng. Illust. **13**: 473.
Safe No. 27; a story. (C. King) Chamb. J. **69**: 188.
Safed, Palestine. Chamb. J. **70**: 220. Same art. Liv. Age. **197**: 701.
Safely Deposited; a story. Chamb. J. **72**: 412.
Safes and Burglars. Chamb. J. **71**: 101.
Safety Devices for Machines. (J. H. Cooper) J. Frankl. Inst. **137**: 32.
Safford, Nathaniel Foster, Memoir of. (G. M. Bodge) N. E. Reg. **47**: 9.
Saga of Eric the Red. (H. H. Boyesen) Cosmopol. **16**: 467.
— of King Olaf Tryggwason, Stephton's. (W. H. Carpenter) Nation, **60**: 287.
Saga-growth. (F. Y. Powell) Folk-Lore, **5**: 97.
Saga Literature. (J. H. Wisby) Poet-Lore, **6**: 281.
Sagas of the Norse Kings. (H. H. Boyesen) Bk. News, **8**: 31.
Sage, Russell. (H. Parker) Munsey, **12**: 634.
Sage Plains of Oregon. (F. V. Corille) Nat. Geog. M. **7**: 395.
Saghalien, Island of. Dub. R. **113**: 668.
Saguenay Region. (E. J. Hill) Garden & F. **8**: 182, 193, 213.
— and Lake St. John. (E. T. D. Chambers) Canad. M. **3**: 361.
Sahara, Bird's-eye View of. (H. Michel) New Eng. M. n. s. **7**: 465.
— Caravan in. (A. F. Jaccaci) Scrib. M. **13**: 315.
— Geology of. (P. Lake) Sci. Prog. **3**: 370.
— Projected Railroad across. (E. S. Balch) Around World, **1**: 76.
— A Ride in. (J. H. Forbes) Good Words, **33**: 382, 453. Same art. Liv. Age, **194**: 505, 565.
— Tribes of. (Napoleon Ney) Cosmopol. **18**: 145.
Sailing. (A. J. Kenealy) Outing, **26**: 229.
— Fitting out for a Cruise. (A. J. Kenealy) Outing, **26**: 133.
Sailor, Merchant, Life of. (W. C. Russell) Scrib. M. **14**: 1.
Sails and Sailor-craft. (C. L. Norton) Outing, **22**: 256.
St. Agnes Macree. (A. W. Colton) New Eng. M. n. s. **15**: 443.
St. Alban, Legend of. (W. Proudfoot) Canad. M. **6**: 17.
St. Alban's Abbey. (F. G. Kitton) Antiq. n. s. **31**: 43. — (E. Liddell) Sund. M. **23**: 304. — (W. C. Sidney) Gent. M. n. s. **52**: 553.
— Restoration of. Am. Arch. **40**: 183.
St. Andrew's, Scotland. (A. Macdonald) Argosy, **56**: 53. — Chamb. J. **71**: 49. — (R. Williamson) Scot. R. **27**: 82.
— Cathedral of, Suspected Secret Passages under. Sat. R. **76**: 563.
St. Andrew's University and the Duke of Chandos. (J. M. Anderson) Scot. R. **25**: 41.
— Boyd's Twenty-five Years of. Ath. '92, **1**: 171. **2**: 475. — Blackw. **151**: 370. — Macmil. **65**: 391. — Sat. R. **73**: 192. — Spec. **68**: 204. — Church Q. **35**: 399.
— Excavations at. Sat. R. **77**: 92.
— Lang on. Spec. **72**: 555. — (W. J. Ashley) Nation, **59**: 290.
St. Angelo, Sea-cliffs of. (J. H. Adams) Mo. Illust. **4**: 139.
St. Anthony's Bread. (C. Robinson) No. Am. **161**: 379.
St. Augustine, Fla. (A. M. Fuller) Chaut. **15**: 203.
— Inscriptions at. (B. F. Leeds) N. E. Reg. **47**: 300, 433. **48**: 53, 461. **50**: 334.
St. Augustine Road, On the. (B. Torrey) Atlan. **72**: 365.
St. Augustine's Church, Hedon. Reliquary, **32**: 129.
St. Bartholomew's Day, 1572. (W. Loughnan) Month, **77**: 175.
— Eve of. (A. Laugel) Nation, **55**: 371.
— An Incident of. Gent. M. n. s. **48**: 539.
St. Bartholomew's Day, a poem. Argosy, **62**: 465.
Saint Bede went a Haymaking; a story. (C. Cotterell) Argosy, **60**: 245.
St. Benet, Abbey of, 1381. (W. Hudson) Antiq. n. s. **29**: 215, 256.
St. Bernard, Pious Monks of. (L. Hind) Eng. Illust. **14**: 334.
St. Botolph's Church, Aldgate, during the Reformation. (A. G. B. Atkinson) Eng. Hist. R. **11**: 522.
— Parish of, Troubles in, under the Protectorate. (J. A. Dodd) Eng. Hist. R. **10**: 41.
Saint Cashir, a Gentleman Adventurer of the Old Régime. (J. G. Bourinot) Canad. M. **6**: 152.
St. Catherine's Well, Newark-on-Trent. Reliquary, **36**: 52.
St. Clair, Maj.-Gen. Arthur. (K. V. Greenleaf) Am. Hist. Reg. **3**: 367.
St. Clair Lake. (C. M. Sinclair) Canad. M. **3**: 155.
St. Clair Tunnel. (J. J. Bell) Pop. Sci. Mo. **45**: 463.
St. Clair's Defeat. (T. Roosevelt) Harper, **92**: 387.
St. Cloud, Palace of, Ruins of. (G. I. Bigelow) Cosmopol. **14**: 553.
St. David's Church. (Miss M. A. R. Tucker) Walford's Antiq. **10**: 8, 58.
St. Dié, France, Baptismal Font of America. (F. H. Mason) Harper, **85**: 651.
St. Edmund's College, Ware, Eng., Ward's History of. Spec. **70**: 808.
St. Elias, Mt., Expedition to, 1890. Nat. Geog. M. **2**: 302.
— Exploration of. (I. C. Russel) Nat. Geog. M. **2**: 58.
— Glacial Fields of. (G. F. Wright) Nation, **54**: 48.
— Height of, Note on. (I. C. Russell) Nat. Geog. M. **3**: 215.
— — and Position of. (I. C. Russell) Nat. Geog. M. **2**: 231. — (T. C. Mendenhall) Nat. Geog. M. **5**: 63.
— Revisited. (I. C. Russell) Cent. **22**: 190.
St. Fin Barre's Cathedral, Cork. *See* Cork.
St. George and the Dragon. (C. A. Price) Belgra. **79**: 23.
St. George's Museum, Sheffield. (E. Bradbury) M. of Art, **3**: 57.
St. George's River, Medumcook, and Broadway, Me., List of Settlers in. N. E. Reg. **46**: 119.
St. Georges, Arreton. (A. B. Bibb) Am. Arch. **48**: 35.
St. Georges de Didonne, Haunt of Michelet. (Miss Betham-Edwards) Time, **19**: 155.
Saint-Germains, James II. at. (Herbert Vivian) New R. **13**: 525.
St. Gervais, Disaster at. (E. Fry) Knowl. **15**: 201. **16**: 1.
Saint Giles Mission. (F. W. Farrar) Chr. Lit. **10**: 148.
St. Helen's Mount, Ascent of. (F. G. Plummer) Am. Natural. **28**: 46.
St. Hilaire, J. B. *See* **Barthélemy St. Hilaire.**

St. James' Palace. (W. J. Loftie) M. of Art, **9**: 496.
— Memorials of, Sheppard's. Sat. R. **78**: 574.
St. James's Parish, Perkiomen, Montgomery County, Pennsylvania. (A. J. Barrow) Pennsyl. M. **19**: 87.
St. John, N. B., Post-glacial Faults at. (G. F. Matthew) Am. J. Sci. **148**: 501.
St. John, Lake, and the Saguenay. (E. T. D. Chambers) Canad. M. **3**: 361.
St. John River. (H. L. Spencer) M. of Art, **9**: 321.
— Canoeing on. (W. C. Gaynor) Outing, **28**: 109.
— Indian Legends of. (Edward Jock) J. Am. Folk-Lore, **8**: 193.
— On the Upper. (B. Torrey) Atlan. **73**: 324.
Saint Kevin and the Goose. Macmil. **72**: 188. Same art. Liv. Age, **206**: 397.
St. Kilda. (J. Sands) M. of Art, **19**: 242.
St. Lawrence Canal Route. (A. R. Davis) Canad. M. **3**: 148.
St. Lawrence County, N. Y., Metamorphism of a Gabbro occurring in. (C. H. Smyth, jr.) Am. J. Sci. **151**: 271.
St. Lawrence, Glacial Lake, of Professor Warren Upham. (R. Chalmers) Am. J. Sci. **149**: 273.
St. Lawrence River and Thousand Isles. (F. W. Falls) Canad. M. **4**: 148.
— Basin of, Late Glacial Subsidence and Reëlevation of. (W. Upham) Am. J. Sci. **149**: 1.
St. Lawrence Valley, Pleistocene Marine Shore-lines on the South Side of. (R. Chalmers) Am. J. Sci. **151**: 302.
St. Louis. (C. M. Woodward) New Eng. M. n. s. **5**: 589. — (J. Cox) New Eng. M. n. s. **9**: 98.
— Association of Painters and Sculptors, Exhibit of. Am. Arch. **48**: 108.
— the Convention City of 1896. R. of Rs. (N. Y.) **13**: 672.
— Examples of Architecture in. Arch. Rec. **5**: 393.
— Exposition, 1892. (J. Cox) Lippinc. **50**: 510.
— Fagin Building. Arch. Rec. **2**: 470.
— Higher Life of. (J. Snyder) Outl. **54**: 372.
— Libraries of, Private. Lib. J. **17**: 454.
— New. (J. Cox) Lippinc. **51**: 627.
— New Growth of. (J. Ralph) Harper, **85**: 917.
— Notes on City Government in. (A. Shaw) Cent. **30**: 253.
— Public Schools of. (J. M. Rice) Forum, **14**: 429.
— School and Museum of Fine Arts. (W. R. Hodges) M. of Art, **8**: supp. 85.
— Street Railways of. (W. H. Boyan) Engin. M. **8**: 449.
— Tornado at, 1896. (H. H. C. Dunwoody) Cosmopol. **21**: 440. — (N. O. Nelson) Lend a H. **17**: 103. — (H. W. Kirchner) Am. Arch. **52**: 102. — Nature, **54**: 104.
St. Luke's House, London. (Mrs. J. Stuart) Sund. M. **24**: 677.
St. Luke's Summer. All the Year, **73**: 302.
St. Malo, France. (K. W. Yeigh) Canad. M. **7**: 105.
— Legends of Old. Macmil. **73**: 182.
— Life of the Fisher People. Macmil. **73**: 336.
St. Martin-le-Grand, William the Conqueror's Charter, A. D. 1068. (W. H. Stevenson) Eng. Hist. R. **11**: 731.
St. Mary's, Carisbrook. (A. B. Bibb) Am. Arch. **48**: 35.
St. Mary's Loch. (W. L. P. Cox) Temp. Bar, **108**: 270.
St. Olaf's Day in the Faroes. Chamb. J. **69**: 378.
St. Osyth. All the Year, **71**: 522.
St. Paul, Minn. (J. Ralph) Harper, **84**: 576.
— and its New State House. Am. Arch. **50**: 81.
— Roman Catholic Visitation Convent at. (E. G. Martin) Cath. World, **57**: 745.
St. Paul's Cathedral and Library. Bookworm, **3**: 9.
— Decoration of. (W. B. Richmond) Am. Arch. **49**: 25. — (W. B. Richmond) J. Soc. Arts, **43**: 715. — M. of Arts, **17**: 177.
— Glass Mosaics of. (H. J. Powell) Contemp. **69**: 418.
— Interior of. (B. Champneys) M. of Art, **6**: 154.
— Jones's Portico of. Am. Arch. **54**: 6.
— Library. (A. C. Bickley) Bookworm, **1**: 233.
— Literary Associations of. Bookworm, **5**: 19.
— The New Mosaics at. Macmil. **74**: 16.
— Old Memories of. (W. C. Sydney) Gent. M. n. s. **50**: 447. Same art. Ecl. M. **120**: 849.
— Wren and. (B. Champneys) M. of Art, **5**: 321.
St. Paul's Churchyard, Round. All the Year, **76**: 17.
St. Paul's Cross, London. (F. Hawkins) Acad. **41**: 489.
Saint Paul du Var Re-discovered. (H. R. Haweis) Gent. M. n. s. **51**: 86. Same art. Ecl. M. **121**: 256.
St. Paul's School, London. (W. E. Milliken) Walford's Antiq. **8**: 264.
— Charity Commission and. Spec. **70**: 634.
St. Paul's-within-the-Walls, Rome, Mosaics by Burne-Jones, in. M. of Art, **18**: 256.
St. Peter's. *See* Rome.
St. Peter's Collegiate School, Adelaide, So. Australia. (A. Inkersley) Educa. **15**: 263.
St. Peter's School, York, Eng. (A. F. Leach) Fortn. **58**: 638.
St. Petersburg, Imperial Library at. Bookworm, **3**: 297.
— In the Streets of. Liv. Age, **196**: 375. Same art. Temp. Bar, **96**: 521.
— Névsky Prospékt, The. (I. F. Hapgood) Scrib. M. **12**: 301.
— Reminiscences of Society in. Longm. **20**: 145. Same art. Liv. Age, **194**: 308.
St. Pierre, Battle of. (W. H. James) Macmil. **70**: 331.
Saint-Saëns, Camille. (H. E. Krehbiel) Cent. **23**: 735.
— and Wagnerism. Music, **4**: 445. **5**: 249.
— Samson et Delila. Sat. R. **76**: 381.
— — Production of, in London, 1893. Ath. '**93**, **2**: 460.
Saint-Simon, Duc de, Boussier's. (A. Laugel) Nation, **54**: 428.
St. Skea; a story. (K. Bradshaw) Canad. M. **5**: 459.
St. Sophia. *See* Sancta Sophia.
St. Swithin's Monastery, The Last Years of. Macmil. **72**: 284. Same art. Liv. Age, **206**: 755.
St. Vincent, John Jervis, Earl of, Admiral. (A. T. Mahan) Atlan. **71**: 303.
St. Vincent, Island of. (J. R. Mozley) Blackw. **153**: 542. Same art. Liv. Age, **197**: 538.
Ste. Anne de Beaupré; a Famous Canadian Shrine. (J. J. Bell) Canad. M. **1**: 137.
Sainte-Beuve, Charles A., as Critic. Sat. R. **79**: 754.
Sainte Croix, Charles d'Escorches de. Temp. Bar, **94**: 191.
Saints, Epistemology of the. Meth. R. **56**: 120.
— Love of the. (V. Paget) Contemp. **67**: 499.
Saintsbury, George. Miscellaneous Essays. Sat. R. **74**: 313. — Ath. '**92**, **2**: 277. — Spec. **69**: 98.
— as a Critic. (E. K. Chambers) Acad. **47**: 459. — Sat. R. **79**: 257.
Saintsbury, William Noel. Ath. '**95**, **1**: 345.
Sal; a story. Temp. Bar, **99**: 575.
Sala, Geo. Augustus, with portrait. Bk. News, **14**: 339. — Critic, **27**: 409. — Ath. '**95**, **2**: 834. — (J. Macaulay) Leis. Hour, **44**: 512.
— Autobiography of. Sat. R. **79**: 223. — (E. G. Johnson) Dial (Ch.) **18**: 106.
— Home of. (B. Caralampi) M. of Art, **10**: 325, 427.
— London Pen and Gown in the Sixties and Since. (T. H. S. Escott) Fortn. **63**: 238.

Sala, Mrs. G. A. Famous People I have met. Spec. 68: 682.
Salacin as a Cure for Influenza. (T. J. Maclagan) 19th Cent. 31: 329.
— — Reply. (Earl of Dunraven) National, 19: 32.
Saladin, Age of. Quar. 183: 163.
Salagrama. (C. G. Leland) Asia. R. 15: 119.
Salamanders, Heart of some Lungless. (G. S. Hopkins) Am. Natural. 30: 829.
Salamis, Looking toward. (W. C. Lawton) Atlan. 70: 70.
Salamon, Louis S. J. F. de. Memoirs. Ed. R. 180: 61.
Sale of Uncle 'Rastus. (W. N. Harben) Lippinc. 54: 403.
Salem, Mass., Six Hours in. (C. F. Bragdon) Am. Arch. 39: 41.
Salem Kittredge, Theologue; a story. (B. Penny) Scrib. M. 12: 419, 591.
Salem Witch; a story. (E. M. Norris) New Eng. M. n. s. 5: 638.
Salemlek, The. Chamb. J. 71: 458.
Salerno to Sorrento, Highroad from. (J. H. Adams) Cent. 26: 337.
Sales, Humors of. All the Year, 76: 176.
Saline County, Mo., Old Fort of. (T. H. Lewis) Am. Antiq. 14: 159.
Salisbury, Lord. (H. D. Traill) National, 27: 401. — (W. F. Day) Munsey, 8: 55. — New R. 7: 55.
— Address at the Meeting of the British Association at Oxford, 1894. Dub. R. 115: 437.
— as Premier of England. (J. C. Hopkins) Chaut. 22: 703.
— Development of. (T. H. S. Escott) Fortn. 66: 91. Same art. Liv. Age, 210: 486.
— A Family of Statesmen. (J. M. Bulloch) Eng. Illust. 14: 429.
— from a French Point of View. (A. Filon) Fortn. 64: 803. Same art. Liv. Age, 208: 28.
— Second Ministry of. (G. Venables) Time, 15: 257.
Salisbury Cabinet, The Third. (W. T. Stead) R. of Rs. (N. Y.) 12: 177.
Salisbury, England. Green Rings of Old Sarum. (W. Canton) Sund. M. 23: 671.
Salisbury Cathedral. (G. D. Boyle) Sund. M. 24: 246, 344.
— Close of. (A. B. Bibb) Am. Arch. 53: 12.
— — and of Wells. (A. Ansted) M. of Art, 18: 263.
Salisbury Hall, Hertfordshire. (M. C. Gillington) M. of Art, 12: 45.
Salisbury Palace. (E. Venables) Sund. M. 24: 119, 188.
Saliva Charms. (Mrs. F. D. Bergen) J. Am. Folk-Lore, 3: 51.
Sally. (L. T. Meade) Chamb. J. 72: 652.
Sally Dows; a story. (Bret Harte) Eng. Illust. 10: 18–276.
Sallo, Denis de, Founder of the First Scientific Journal. (J. Boyer) Pop. Sci. Mo. 44: 690.
Salman and Morolf, ed. F. Vogt. (A. Menzies) Scot. R. 23: 296.
Salmon, The, and its Kin. Cornh. 72: 614.
— at London Bridge. Spec. 71: 237.
— Canned, The Story of. (C. Phillips-Wolley) Temp. Bar, 107: 410.
— Canning, in British Columbia. (C. K. Peacock) Good Words, 35: 605.
— Growth of. Spec. 70: 770.
— The Story of the. (A. Wilson) Chamb. J. 73: 355.
— Two Homes of the. Cornh. 70: 621.
Salmon Fisheries of Norway, The. Blackw. 157: 393.
Salmon Fishing. (H. A. Herbert) Cosmopol. 15: 487. — Outing, 26: 269.
Salmon Fishing and Canning on the Fraser. (H. H. Gowen) Canad. M. 2: 159.
— Heresies in. (W. E. Hodgson) National, 23: 57, (H. Maxwell) 340.
— on the Newfoundland Coast. (E. J. Myers) Outing, 22: 293.
— on Snake River. (F. C. Read) Outing, 27: 222.
— Ouananiche Fishing. (E. McCarthy) Outing, 23: 37.
Salmon-flies. (H. Maxwell) Blackw. 155: 223.
Salmond, S. D. F., with portrait. (A. B. Bruce) Bib. World, 8: 347.
Salmoné, Anthony Habib. Acad. 46: 556.
Salome, Wilde's. (E. E. Hale, jr.) Dial (Ch.) 17: 11.
Salomon, Otto. (J. S. Thornton) Educa. R. 5: 370.
Salon. No Parallel in England. Sat. R. 81: 497.
— Paris. *See* Paris.
Salons, The. (C. Phillips) Fortn. 66: 123.
— French, of the Ancien Régime. (A. Collyer) 19th Cent. 32: 553. Same art. Ecl. M. 119: 788.
— — Principles and Pastimes of. (I. M. Tarbell) Chaut. 18: 573, 699.
— — Women of, Mason's. Spec. 68: 533.
Saloon and Church as Political Antagonists. (J. G. Woolley) Our Day, 11: 12.
— and the Sabbath. (F. C. Iglehart) No. Am. 161: 467.
— Catholic Church and. (J. Ireland) No. Am. 159: 498.
— Christian Control of, Rainsford on. (E. E. Hale and others) Lend a H. 9: 1.
— Coffee-house as Counteraction to. (R. Graham) Char. R. 1: 215.
— Politics and. (L. G. Janes) Soc. Econ. 6: 233.
Saloons. American Anti-saloon League. (H. H. Russell) Our Day, 16: 551.
— Grog Shop *vs.* Civilization. (H. Price) Our Day, 16: 53.
— The Oberlin Campaign. (H. H. Russell) Our Day, 16: 497.
— Substitutes for. (F. P. Peabody) Forum, 21: 595.
Salpa, Genus. Nat. Sci. 5: 456.
Salt. Leis. Hour, 43: 801.
— Action of, upon Water. (R. B. Warder) Science, 19: 71.
— and its Manufacture. (T. J. A. Freeman) Am. Cath. Q. 19: 434.
— Manufacture of. (T. Ward) J. Soc. Arts, 43: 78.
— in the Weaver Valley, Eng. Chamb. J. 69: 774.
— Why Salt? (H. B. Tuttle) Cosmopol. 20: 94.
Salt and Gas Wells of China, The. (E. H. Parker) Chamb. J. 73: 545.
Salt Formation in Cheshire, Eng. Cornh. 66: 256. Same art. Liv. Age, 195: 421.
Salt Hill, Old Inns of. (J. W. Sherer) Gent. M. n. s. 49: 169.
Salt Monopoly in India, Evils of. (J. B. Pennington) Asia. R. 16: 313.
Salt Region, Cheshire. (S. Baring-Gould) Good Words, 34: 59.
Salt Water Day. (H. Garland) Cosmopol. 13: 387.
Salta and Jujuy-Jabez Land. Chamb. J. 72: 671.
Salutation, Etiquette of. Spec. 69: 158.
Salvage. Chamb. J. 71: 725.
Salvagia, Scotland. (R. B. C. Graham) Sat. R. 82: 279.
Salvation of a Missionary. (E. C. Martin) New Eng. M. n. s. 8: 78.
— Struggle for. (P. Michaelis) Open Court, 3: 1731.
Salvation Army. Lend a H. 14: 163. — (C. A. Briggs) No. Am. 159: 697. — (Mrs. Drummond) Time, 18: 641. — (J. Mavor) Univ. R. 8: 524.
— among the Slums. (Maud B. Booth) Scrib. M. 17: 102.

Salvation Army, and the Churches. (R. Ogden) Nation, **55**: 4.
— Annual Expenses. Lend a H. **14**: 208.
— as a Social Reformer. (G. E. Walsh) Chaut. **17**: 328.
— Blood and Fire Movement. (L. Katscher) Time, **12**: 531.
— Dissension in. Our Day, **16**: 197.
— General Booth and. (J. Cook) Our Day, **15**: 119.
— General Booth's Visit to U. S. Lend a H. **14**: 163.
— in India. (H. deh Booth-Tucker) Chr. Lit. **10**: 173 a.
— Inner History of the Origin of. (W. Booth) Our Day, **14**: 207.
— Night Shelters of. (W. C. Preston) Sund. M. **21**: 311.
— Organization of. (F. P. Noble) Pub. Opin. **12**: 533.
— Shelter in London. (H. Vivian) Sat. R. **80**: 862.
— — on Christmas Eve. (H. Vivian) Sat. R. **81**: 10.
— Social Scheme of. (G. E. Vincent) Am. J. Pol. **2**: 453.
— Socialistic Anarchists and. (J. Cook) Our Day, **13**: 532.
— Troubles of. Chr. Lit. **14**: 646.
— Truth about. (A. White) Fortn. **58**: 111.
Salvation Gap. (O. Wister) Harper, **89**: 673.
Salvation Lass, A; a story. (E. Earle) Belgra. **83**: 274.
Salvini, Alexander, with portraits. (M. Aldrich) Arena, **7**: 129.
Salvini, Tommaso, as King Lear. Theatre, **29**: 281.
— Autobiography. (T. Salvini) Cent. **23**: 230, 588. **24**: 90-927. — (J. B. Runnion) Dial (Ch.) **15**: 298.
— on Acting. Spec. **72**: 201.
— Reminiscences of. (E. Brain) Theatre, **35**: 16.
Salvo, Marquise de. Month, **78**: 228.
Sam Pendarn's Lady Daughter; a story. All the Year, **76**: 302.
Samaria. (J. S. Riggs) Bib. World, **4**: 279.
Samaritan Literature and Religion. (A. Cowley) Jew. Q. **8**: 562.
Samaritan Liturgy. (A. Cowley) Jew. Q. **7**: 121.
Samaritans, Nature's Good. (P. W. Roose) Argosy, **57**: 464.
Samarkand, From Baku to. (Frank Vincent) Cosmopol. **18**: 394.
— and Bokhara. (Frank Vincent) Cosmopol. **19**: 3.
— Through, to Ferghana. (M. Arnot) Good Words, **35**: 614.
Sambourne, Linley. (M. H. Spielmann) M. of Art, **11**: 329.
Sâmkhya Philosophy, The. Monist, **5**: 126.
Samoa. (F. M. Turner) Outing, **24**: 266, 354, 477.
— Disaster at, Story of the. (J. L. Woodruff) Cosmopol. **20**: 5.
— Fraser's. Sat. R. **79**: 382.
— German and English Interests in. (J. F. Rose-Soley) Westm. **146**: 277.
— Glimpses of. (H. H. Lusk) Mo. Illust. **13**: 107.
— Importance of Hawaii and. (W. F. Draper) Soc. Econ. **6**: 352.
— Our Troubles in. (E. L. Godkin) Nation, **58**: 358, 480.
— Question of, from an Ethical Standpoint. (M. M. Trumbull) Open Court, **3**: 1511.
— Scuttling out of. (E. L. Godkin) Nation, **58**: 380.
— Short Visit to. Time, **5**: 28.
— Sport in Samoan Craft. (F. M. Turner) Outing, **25**: 17.
— Stevenson on. Ath. '92, **2**: 343. — Sat. R. **74**: 251.
— Three Weeks in. (Countess of Jersey) 19th Cent. **33**: 52, 249. Same art. Liv. Age, **197**: 178, 215.
— A Visit to, and the Home of R. L. Stevenson. Westm. **143**: 551. Same art. Ecl. M. **125**: 61.
Samoan Elopement, A. (A. Mahaffy) Blackw. **160**: 508.
Samoan Stories. (J. Abercromby) Folk-Lore, **2**: 455. **3**: 158.
Samoan Waters, Boating Trip in. (F. M. Turner) Outing, **25**: 199.
Samoyads of the Great Tundra, Notes on. (A. Montefiore) Anthrop. J. **24**: 388.
— Sojourn among, Jackson's. Sat. R. **80**: 16.
Sampson, Deborah. (K. G. Wells) New Eng. M. n. s. **13**: 156.
Sampson, William. (I. Browne) Green Bag, **8**: 313.
San Antonio, Texas: Missions, Battle of Flowers. (J. D. Whelpley) Bost. **4**: 288.
San Domingo. *See* Santo Domingo.
San Donato, Shrine of, at Arezzo. (S. Thompson) M. of Art, **11**: 249.
San Fernando, Mission of, in California. (D. Lummis) Cath. World, **60**: 175.
San Francisco, Cal. (G. H. Fitch) Chaut. **23**: 659. — (R. L. Stevenson) M. of Art, **6**: 272.
— Architecture in. (E. C. Peixotto) Overland, n. s. **21**: 449.
— Chinatown, Night Scenes in. (W. H. Gleadell) Gent. M. n. s. **54**: 576. Same art. Ecl. M. **125**: 378.
— Chinese Quarter of. (J. H. Marr) So. M. **3**: 537.
— Civic Awakening in. (A. Knapp) Arena, **12**: 241.
— Election Machinery in. (W. A. Beatty) Overland, n. s. **21**: 27
— Emporium Building. Overland, n. s. **26**: 461.
— Guild of Arts and Crafts. (A. Lewis) Overland, n. s. **27**: 292.
— Midwinter Fair, 1894. Critic, **24**: 57.
— — Agriculture and Horticulture at. (C. H. Shinn) Overland, n. s. **23**: 393.
— — Architectural Effects. (E. Roberts) Overland, n. s. **23**: 341.
— — Art Display. (J. A. Stanton) Overland, n. s. **23**: 401.
— — Canadian Exhibit at. (F. W. Parks) Overland, n. s. **23**: 625.
— — Children's Day. (Phil. Weaver, jr.) Overland, n. s. **23**: 414.
— — Congresses at. (B. Moses) Overland, n. s. **23**: 371.
— — Is it a Benefit? (J. D. Phelan) Overland, n. s. **23**: 390.
— — Lighting of. (W. F. C. Hasson) Overland, n. s. **23**: 385.
— — Mineral Exhibit. (E. H. Benjamin) Overland, n. s. **23**: 409.
— — More Rambles on the Midway. (C. Hammerton) Overland, n. s. **23**: 527.
— — Nevada at. (F. W. Parks) Overland, n. s. **23**: 617.
— — Russia at. (N. M. Babad) Overland, n. s. **23**: 421.
— — Some Bread-winners of. (E. S. Bates) Overland, n. s. **23**: 374.
— — The Wild and Woolly at. (Ninetta Eames) Overland, n. s. **23**: 356.
— Municipal Conditions and the New Charter. (J. D. Phelan) Overland, n. s. **28**: 104.
— Pioneer Days in. (J. W. Palmer) Cent. **21**: 541.
— Restaurants of. (C. S. Greene) Overland, n. s. **20**: 561.
— Street Characters of. (F. E. Sheldon) Overland, n. s. **19**: 449.
— Water Front of. (C. S. Greene) Overland, n. s. **19**: 337.
— Water-supply of. (R. Wildman) Overland, n. s. **28**: 289.

San Francisco. Why the City of St. Francis? (A. Wey) Overland, n. s. **26**: 597.
San Francisco, Bay and Peninsula of, Vancouver's Visit to, in 1792. (W. H. McDougal) Overland, n. s. **20**: 602.
San Francisco Bay, A Triangular Trip around. (P. N. Boeringer) Overland, n. s. **28**: 533.
— Yachting in. (A. Inkersley) Outing, **28**: 70, 151, 313.
San Francisco College; a Pioneer School. (A. Inkersley) Overland, n. s. **28**: 544.
San Gimigniano, Italy. Spec. **70**: 732.
San José Scale in N. J. (C. S. Sargent) Garden & F. **9**: 41.
San Juan Region, Railroads and Mining in. (T. A. Rickard) Engin. M. **9**: 689.
San Marino, Ancient Commonwealth of. (A. B. Hart) Nation, **58**: 81.
— Carducci at. (J. W. Mario) Nation, **59**: 303.
— Smallest Republic in the World. (J. L. Hurst) Chaut. **21**: 73.
— Visit to. (W. Miller) Westm. **144**: 284.
San Pablo Rancho, Story of. (J. F. Sheehan, jr.) Overland, n. s. **24**: 517.
San Remo. (M. O. W. Oliphant) Good Words, **34**: 124.
San Salvador Refugees, Care of. (J. B. Moore) Am. Law R. **29**: 1.
San Serverino, Lorenzo da; a Third-rate Painter. (G. Allen) Eng. Illust. **14**: 407.
San Sisto Madonna, The; a poem. (E. P. Gould) Educa. **16**: 111.
Sanborn, Kate, with portrait. Bk. News, **12**: 463.
Sanchi Tope. (J. B. Braddon) Am. Arch. **49**: 92.
Sancta Sophia, Constantinople. (R. W. Schultz) Scot. R. **26**: 138. Same art. Liv. Age, **207**: 1. — (R. Davey) Art J. **47**: 33–75.
— and Byzantine Building. Ed. R. **181**: 460.
— Lethaby and Swainson's. Sat. R. **79**: 47.
Sanctification, Doctrine of. (J. Tomlinson) Luth. Q. **26**: 424.
— — Psychologically Developed. (C. W. Rishell) Meth. R. **52**: 513.
Sanctuary and Sacrifice. Baxter's Reply to Wellhausen. Church Q. **43**: 186.
— Right of. (G. H. Westley) Green Bag, **8**: 422.
Sanctuary; a poem. (L. I. Guiney) Harper, **90**: 751.
Sand, George. *See* Dudevant, Mme.
Sand, Musical. (F. A. Fulcher) Sund. M. **21**: 828.
— Rope of, To tie a. (A. L. Carter) Pop. Sci. Mo. **42**: 248.
Sand-blast Apparatus. (F. C. Brooksbank) Cassier, **10**: 277.
Sand-blast Processes. (J. J. Holtzapfel) J. Soc. Arts. **43**: 473.
Sand-eeling. (H. Heron) Chamb. J. **73**: 539.
Sand-mountain Aggression, A. (F. Lynde) Southern M. **4**: 567.
Sand Walker of Abblesey, The. Macmil. **67**: 223. Same art. Liv. Age, **196**: 403.
Sandal-wood. Darbya Umbellata. (C. S. Sargent) Garden & F. **7**: 74.
Sandals, Aboriginal, of North America. (O. T. Mason) Science, n. s. **2**: 134.
Sandars, Collett. Ath. '94, **2**: 224.
Sanday, William. (W. H. Day) Bib. World, **6**, 330. — (J. V. Bartlet) Chr. Lit. **15**: 41, 122.
Sandby, Thomas and Paul. (C. Monkhouse) Portfo. **23**: 194.
Sandeman, Albert George, with portrait. Bank. M. (Lond.) **59**: 713.
Sandeman, Sir Robert. (J. Macaulay) Leis. Hour, **45**: 791.
Sandeman, Sir Robert, and the Indian Frontier Policy. Asia. R. **20**: 131.
— Life and Work in India, Thornton's. Sat. R. **79**: 822.
Sandemanians. (G. W. Hallock) New Eng. M. n. s. **14**: 239.
Sanders, Basevi. Ath. '92, **1**: 153.
Sandford, Francis Richard. Blackw. **157**: 468.
Sandgate Landslip, The. (W. Topley) Geog. J. **1**: 339.
Sandham, Henry. (T. H. Allen) Q. Illust. **2**: 285.
Sandhurst Military College. (C. C. King) Un. Serv. M. **4**: 176–345.
Sandringham, A Peep at. (C. Beerbohm) Eng. Illust. **15**: 63.
Sands and Gravels, Shelly, on High Levels. (T. M. Reade) Nat. Sci. **3**: 423.
Sands, Musical. (A. MacIvor) Temp. Bar, **106**: 79.
Sandusky, Expedition to, 1782, Journal of. (G. Pilar von Pilchau) Pennsyl. M. **18**: 129, 293.
Sandwich Islands. *See* Hawaiian Islands.
Sandwich Man. (F. A. McKenzie) Eng. Illust. **13**: 73.
Sangir, Eruption at, June 7, 1892. Nature, **46**: 457.
— Island of, Disappearance of. Spec. **69**: 122.
Sangster, Charles; Canadian Poet. (E. H. Dewart) Canad. M. **7**: 28.
Sangster, Margaret E., with portrait. Bk. News, **13**: 337.
Sanitary Agents, Natural. Chamb. J. **70**: 534.
Sanitary Conferences, International. (S. Smith) Am. J. Soc. Sci. **32**: 92.
Sanitary Delusions. (F. L. Oswald) New Sci. R. **1**: 160.
Sanitary Dwelling, A. Am. Arch. **54**: 54.
Sanitary Engineering. (W. P. Gerhard) J. Frankl. Inst. **139**: 457. **140**: 56, 90.
Sanitary Experiments in Massachusetts, Notable. (W. T. Sedgwick) Forum, **20**: 747.
Sanitary Insurance. Bank. M. (Lond.) **57**: 936.
Sanitary Oversight of Dwellings. (M. I. Moore) Char. R. **4**: 434.
Sanitary Pilgrimage. (B. W. Richardson) Longm. **21**: 182.
Sanitary Progress in New York City. (C. F. Wingate) Engin. M. **3**: 316.
Sanitary Science, Growth of. Temp. Bar, **94**: 365.
— Hamburg's New Sanitary Impulse. (A. Shaw) Atlan. **73**: 787.
— in Massachusetts, Progress in. (G. W. Fuller) Science, **22**: 73.
— World's Debt to. (J. S. Billings) Chaut. **21**: 18.
Sanitation. (G. W. Steeves) Westm. **143**: 667.
— and Sociology. (M. Talbot) Am. J. Sociol. **2**: 74.
— in relation to the Poor. (W. H. Welch) Char. R. **2**: 203.
— Municipal Defects in American Cities. (J. S. Billings) Forum, **15**: 304.
— — in N. Y. and Brooklyn. (J. S. Billings) Forum, **16**: 346.
— — in Washington and Baltimore. (J. S. Billings) Forum, **15**: 727.
— Past and Ideal. (Sir B. W. Richardson) Longm. **26**: 274.
— Penalties of Ignorance. (Lady Priestley) 19th Cent. **38**: 579. Same art. Ecl. M. **124**: 726.
Sanskrit, A Study of. (H. Oldenberg) Open Court, **3**: 1487–1561.
— Study of. (F. M. Müller) Open Court, **4**: 2153.
Sanskrit Literature in India. (G. A. Jacob) Acad. **41**: 377. — Acad. **45**: 397.
Sant, James. (W. W. Fenn) M. of Art, **3**: 128.

Santa Barbara, Battle of Flowers at. (R. Wildman) Overland, n. s. 26: 50. — (S. A. Higgins) Chaut. 21: 531.
Santa Barbara Channel Islands. (L. G. Yates) Overland, n. s. 27: 538.
Santa Barbara Day in Winter, A; a poem. (H. W. Waring) Overland, n. s. 21: 172.
Santa Clara, Mission of, Vancouver's Visit to. (W. H. McDougal) Overland, n. s. 21: 45.
Santa Claus of Long Ago; a poem. (C. Cushnie) Eng. Illust. 11: 274.
Santa Cruz, Cal. (G. S. Mead) Nat'l M. (Bost.) 4: 573.
— Inscriptions at. (R. F. Leeds) N. E. Reg. 50: 49, 183, 303.
Santo Domingo, Gold and Silver in. (J. L. Laughlin) J. Pol. Econ. 2: 536.
— Monetary Reform in. (J. L. Laughlin) Atlan. 74: 107.
Santa Lucia Mountains, Over the. (M. L. White) Overland, n. s. 20: 449.
Santander, Dynamite Explosion at. Spec. 71: 656.
Santa Teresa. (B. Woodbridge) Overland, n. s. 28: 422.
Santhal Rebellion, 1855. (F. Middleton) Un. Serv. M. 7: 1063.
Santiago, Ancient Capital of Cuba. (J. T. Hyatt) Cosmopol. 19: 493.
Santiago, Chili. (M. Crommelin) Leis. Hour, 44: 725.
Santley, Charles. Reminiscences. Spec. 69: 735.
Saône River, Hamerton's. (C. N. Williamson) M. of Art, 11: 133.
Sap of Trees and its Movement. (C. R. Barnes) Science, 21: 239.
Saphir, Adolph, with portrait. (D. Macleod) Good Words, 34: 767.
Saporta, Gaston, Marquis de. Nat. Sci. 6: 278. — (A. C. Seward) Nature, 52: 57. — (L. F. Ward) Science, n. s. 2: 141.
Sappho. (E. Saltus) Lippinc. 51: 503.
— Secret of. (M. Thompson) Atlan. 73: 365.
Sapte, W., Jr. A Lucky Dog. Theatre, 29: 80.
Saracenic Metal-work. (S. Lane-Poole) Eng. Illust. 11: 905.
Saragossa, Spain. (C. W. Wood) Argosy, 62: 310, 434.
Sarah; a poem. (K. Carter) M. of Art, 10: 67.
Sarah Tingle's Young Man; a story. All the Year, 72: 108.
Saranac, Legend of. (H. Walworth) Am. Hist. Reg. 1: 159.
Saratoga, Battles of. (J. G. Nicolay) Chaut. 14: 387.
— Old and New. (L. A. Bond) Nat'l M. (N. Y. '91) 16: 313.
— With Burgoyne at. Macmil. 75: 71.
Sarawak. (J. Lawson) Gent. M. n. s. 54: 244.
— Rajahs of. (H. LeRoux) Fortn. 62: 410. Same art. Liv. Age, 203: 3.
Sarcey, Francisque, with portrait. Bk. Buyer, 10: 113.
— as Lecturer. Critic, 22: 166.
— Recollections of Middle Life. Dial (Ch.) 14: 241.
Sarcophagi, Sidon, New Museum and. (F. M. Müller) New R. 10: 17.
Sardinia, Problem of. (J. S. Fiske) Nation, 60: 161.
Sardou, Victorien. (A. Galdemar) McClure, 5: 71. — (A. W. Howard) Munsey, 12: 137.
— Fedora. Sat. R. 79: 725.
— Madame Sans-Gêne. (A. Laugel) Nation, 57: 445.
— Portraits of. McClure, 3: 343.
— Roosevelt's. Sat. R. 74: 204.
— Thermidor. (A. Galdemar) Fortn. 57: 770. — Sat. R. 73: 626.
Sargasso Sea, The. Chamb. J. 71: 309.
Sargent, Jo S., with portrait. R. of Rs. (N. Y.) 9: 685.
— and his Painting. (W. A. Coffin) Cent. 30: 163.
Sargon, Hezekiah, and Sennacherib. (J. Horner) Meth. R. 53: 74.
Sark, Scenery of. M. of Art, 1: 120.
Sarony, Napoleon. (L. Carr) Q. Illust. 2: 372.
Sarpi, Paolo. Quar. 176: 373.
— Robertson's. Sat. R. 78: 218.
Sarto, Andrea del. (W. J. Stillman) Cent. 21: 352. — (J. Cartwright) M. of Art, 6: 203.
Sartorio, G. Aristide. (H. Zimmern) Art J. 48: 105.
Sarum. *See* Salisbury.
Sassafras Tree. (C. S. Sargent) Garden & F. 7: 211.
Satan as represented in Art. (J. Leyland) M. of Art, 19: 261, 305.
Satellites, Evolution of. (A. M. Clerke) Knowl. 18: 205.
Satire, Humor, Wit, and Fun. (J. R. Lowell) Cent. 25: 124.
— Latin. Quar. 177: 152.
Satires and Satirists. (H. M. Sanders) Temp. Bar, 109: 76.
Satisfaction; a story. (A. E. Abbott) Idler, 7: 739.
Satolli, Francis, Archbishop. (T. S. Duhigg) Cath. World, 58: 305. — With portrait. (J. T. Smith) Munsey, 12: 291.
— An American Viceroy from the Vatican. (L. W. Bacon) Forum, 15: 268.
— and the Public Schools. (J. Cook) Our Day, 12: 228.
— Mission to America. (J. H. Vincent; L. W. Bacon; J. F. Loughlin) Forum, 15: 261.
Satsuma Hokusaï's Long Distance Ride; a story. (H. V. Barnett) Eng. Illust. 13: 135.
Satsuma Ware and its Imitations. (M. Kataoka) M. of Art, 13: 222.
Saturday Review, The. Time, 21: 30.
Saturn, The Feast of. (A. W. Verrall) Univ. R. 3: 84.
Saturn, Planet. (W. J. Lockyer) Nature, 50: 32.
— Rings of. (M. W. Meyer) Open Court, 4: 2595.
— — Meteoric Constitution of, Spectroscopic Proof of. (J. E. Keeler) Nature, 52: 164.
— Spectroscopic Observations of, at Allegheny Observatory. (J. E. Keeler) Pop. Astron. 2: 443.
Saturnian Metre. (W. M. Lindsay) Am. J. Philol. 14: 140, 305.
Sauces in Cookery. Sat. R. 77: 228.
Saul and David of the Steppe, A; a story. (M. A. Morrison) Good Words, 33: 163.
Saul of Tarsus. *See* Paul, St.
Saul, Son of Kish. (R. K. Eccles) Bib. World, 4: 432.
Saulsbury, Willard, with portrait. Green Bag, 4: 275.
Sault Ste. Marie Ship Canal. (J. J. Kehof) Canad. M. 1: 589.
Saumarez, James, Admiral. (A. T. Mahan) Atlan. 71: 605.
Saunders, John. Acad. 47: 297. — Ath. '95, 1: 443.
Saunders, Laurence, Citizen of Coventry. (M. D. Harris) Eng. Hist. R. 9: 633.
Saunders, William L. (A. M. Waddell) So. Hist. Pap. 20: 212.
Saunders's Social Yank. (D. Morley) Overland, n. s. 24: 177.
Sauppe, H. Ath. '93, 2: 456.
Savage, John, of Middletown, Conn., Family of. (J. F. Savage) N. E. Reg. 48: 311.

Savage, Richard. (T. Russell) Gent. M. n. s. **56**: 146.
Savage, Richard H., with portrait. Bk. News, **12**: 123.
Savage-Armstrong, George F. (E. Cavazza) New World, **1**: 519.
Savage Adornment. (A. T. Sibbald) Time, **8**: 504.
Savage Life, Habits and Customs of. (Lady Cook *née* Tennessee Claflin) Westm. **140**: 514.
Savagery and Survivals. (J. W. Black) Pop. Sci. Mo. **45**: 388.
Savages, Skill of. Chamb. J. **71**: 86.
Saved by a Ghost. (F. E. Myers) Overland, n. s. **27**: 535.
Saved by a Lie; a story. Temp. Bar, **95**: 351.
Saved by the Strike; a story. (M. Dyan) Belgra. **77**: 378.
Savidge, E. C., with portrait. Bk. News, **14**: 283.
Saville, George; Works. (H. C. Foxcroft) Eng. Hist. R. **11**: 703.
Savings of Workingmen, Management of. Bank. M. (N. Y.) **47**: 241.
— Small, and how to collect them. (E. Tapley) Char. R. **5**: 99.
Savings-bank Law, The. (H. White) Nation, **54**: 223.
Savings Banks. Bank. M. (N. Y.) **42**: 872. — Chamb. J. **70**: 394.
— Building Associations and. Gunton's M. **10**: 241.
— Duties of. Bank. M. (N. Y.) **48**: 756.
— Free Silver and the. (J. P. Townsend; C. H. Smith) No. Am. **162**: 347.
— in Great Britain. (H. W. Wolff) Contemp. **70**: 861.
— of Rhode Island. Bank. M. (N. Y.) **48**: 683.
— Postal. (E. T. Heyn) Ann. Am. Acad. Pol. Sci. **8**: 461. — (J. Wanamaker) Char. R. **1**: 342.
— — in England. Ed. R. **176**: 485. — Bank. M. (N. Y.) **47**: 452.
— School. (S. L. Oberholtzer) Ann. Am. Acad. Pol. Sci. **3**: 14.
— — as Educative and Reform Factor. (S. L. Oberholtzer) Lend a H. **15**: 202.
— — in England. Educa. R. **3**: 72.
Savonarola, Girolamo. (F. G. Stephens) M. of Art, **12**: 285.
— a 15th Century Revival. (J. H. Hobart) Harper, **91**: 555.
— his Friends and Enemies. (J. M. Stone) Month, **87**: 207.
— in History and Fiction. (J. J. Teague) Westm. **137**: 123.
Savoy, Palace of the. Walford's Antiq. **8**: 119.
Savoy Theatre, London, Rehearsing at the. (G. B. Burgin) Idler, **2**: 355.
Saw, Band-, American. (H. H. Suplee) Cassier, **1**: 319.
Saw Mill, The Modern. (W. H. Trout) Cassier, **11**: 83.
Sawdust Heroine, A; a story. (A. G. Sim) Theatre, **28**: 17.
Sawney's Deer-lick. (C. D. Lanier) Scrib. M. **17**: 93.
Saxe, Marshall, and the Marquis d'Argenson. Ed. R. **176**: 521.
Saxifrage, Cultivation of. (J. N. Gerard) Garden & F. **7**: 17.
Saxon Chronicles, Plummer's Edition. Sat. R. **74**: 204.
Saxon Doorway at Somerford-Keynes. Illust. Archæol. **1**: 46.
Saxons, South of England, and other Races of South Britain. (R. J. Horton-Smith) Anthrop. J. **26**: 82.
Say, Léon. (C. Gide) Econ. J. **6**: 318.
Sayce, A. H. (T. K. Cheyne) 19th Cent. **35**: 660.
— and the Critics. (S. R. Driver) Chr. Lit. **14**: 270.
— *vs.* the Archæologists. (A. A. Bevan) Contemp. **68**: 805.
Sayings and Doings of the Todds. (V. Roseboro') Cent. **30**: 298.
Scab, The. (A. French) Scrib. M. **18**: 223.
Scaffold, Travelling. Am. Arch. **47**: 92.
Scale Insects liable to be introduced into U. S. (T. D. A. Cockerell) Garden & F. **8**: 513.
Scales as Architectural Ornaments. (L. Passepont) Am. Arch. **36**: 65-193.
Scallop. (F. Maher) Pop. Sci. Mo. **49**: 534.
Scalping, History and Significance of. (A. A. Lambing) Nat'l M. (N. Y. '94) **19**: 251.
Scandal, The Love of. (O. S. Jones) No. Am. **160**: 124.
Scandinavia, Phœnician Colonization in. (C. W. Skarstedt) Asia. R. **20**: 400.
Scandinavian in the United States, The. (H. H. Boyesen) No. Am. **155**: 526.
Scandinavian Contingent in America. (K. C. Babcock) Atlan. **77**: 660.
Scandinavian Customs and Character. (H. H. Boyesen) Mo. Illust. **12**: 298.
Scandinavian Myths, Old. All the Year, **76**: 130.
Scandinavian Shipping, Development of. (A. N. Klær) J. Pol. Econ. **1**: 329.
Scandinavians in the Northwest. (K. C. Babcock) Forum, **14**: 103.
Scarabs, Myer on. Sat. R. **78**: 333.
Scarborough, Trip to. (F. G. Green) Bookworm, **4**: 21.
Scarborough Castle. (J. Leyland) Portfo. **23**: 173.
Scarlet Hunter, The; a story. (G. Parker) Macmil. **65**: 376. Same art. Liv. Age, **193**: 465.
Scarlet Letter, The; a poem. (W. M. Payne) Dial (Ch.) **13**: 263.
Scarron, P. Tales. Ath. '92, **1**: 496.
Scene-painters, Some famous. (W. J. Lawrence) M. of Art, **12**: 41.
Scene-painting. (W. Telbin) M. of Art, **12**: 92, 195.
Scenery. Cornh. **70**: 179. Same art. Liv. Age, **203**: 361.
— and the Imagination. (Sir A. Geikie) Fortn. **59**: 547. Same art. Liv. Age, **197**: 707. Same art. Ecl. M. **120**: 775.
— Defacement of. (C. S. Sargent) Garden & F. **8**: 81.
— English and American, Contrasts of. (E. S. Nadal) Cent. **26**: 28.
— Natural, Preservation of. Spec. **71**: 331.
— Origin of. Spec. **69**: 188.
— Restoration of. Spec. **73**: 237.
— Scenes in a Barrack School. (H. W. Nevinson) 19th Cent. **39**: 481.
— Note on. (C. Scott) 19th Cent. **39**: 871.
Scenes in the Voshti Hills; stories. (G. Parker) Eng. Illust. **12**: no. 6, 19. **13**: 23, 179, 276.
Schaff, Philip. Critic, **23**: 275. — (F. Bowen) Critic, **23**: 281.
Schamyl, A Forgotten Hero. Macmil. **72**: 213. Same art. Liv. Age, **206**: 373.
Scharf, Sir George. Acad. **47**: 363. — Ath. '95, **1**: 543.
Schedule-making, Experiment in. (W. H. Butts) School R. **2**: 412.
Scheele, Carl W. (T. E. Thorpe) Fortn. **60**: 665. — (T. E. Thorpe) Nature, **47**: 152.
— Monument to, at Stockholm. (F. Hoffmann) Pop. Sci. Mo. **42**: 685.
Scheffel, Victor. (T. W. Rolleston) Contemp. **68**: 716.
Schemata, Kant's Doctrine of. (H. H. Williams) Monist, **4**: 375.

Schenk, Martin; a Ballad of the Dutch and Spanish Wars. (W. Cairns) Temp. Bar, **107**: 392.
Schepen, Title and Office of. (J. W. De Peyster) Nat'l M. (N. Y. '91) **19**: 49.
Scherer, Jacob. (J. A. Brown) Luth. Q. **25**: 371.
Scheria, Localization of. (S. Butler) Ath. '**92**, **1**: 149.
Schiermonnikoog, Island of. (E. Lecky) Longm. **23**: 589. Same art. Liv. Age, **201**: 364. — (S. C. C. Glyn) Spec. **71**: 300.
Schiller, Johann F. von, and his Actors. (Chas. Hervey) Time, **4**: 544.
— Boyhood of. (Otto Brahm) Univ. R. **5**: 123.
— Maid of Orleans. Points of Contact with Shakespeare. (J. N. Willian) Poet-Lore, **7**: 169.
Schism, Heresy and. (W. E. Gladstone) Chr. Lit. **11**: 105 a, 129 a.
See Heresy.
Schlatter, Francis, the Healer. Chr. Lit. **14**: 196. — (A. B. Hyde) Chaut. **22**: 431.
Schleiermacher, F. E. D., and Christian Consciousness. (E. S. Carr) Bib. Sac. **53**: 668.
Schley, James Montfort, with portrait. (T. Johnson) Nat'l M. (N. Y. '91) **16**: 223.
Schliemann, Heinrich. (Karl Blind) Asia. R. **13**: 391. — With portrait. Bk. Buyer, **3**: 239.
— Excavations, Last. Ed. R. **175**: 399.
— — Schuckhardt on. Ath. '**92**, **1**: 120. — Spec. **68**: 22.
— Recollections of. (T. Stanton) Open Court, **5**: 2748.
— Reminiscences of. (J. I. Manatt) Atlan. **71**: 803.
Schmidel, Hulderico. (R. B. C. Grahame) 19th Cent. **38**: 805. Same art. Liv. Age, **207**: 798.
Schmidt, Allan. Acad. **43**: 271.
Schnadhorst, Mr., Case of. Spec. **73**: 687.
Schnapper-fishing off Sydney Heads. (F. G. Aflalo) Outing, **29**: 25.
Schneebergite, So-called. (A. S. Eakle and W. Muthman) Am. J. Sci. **150**: 244.
Schneider, George, with portrait. Nat'l M. (N. Y. '91) **16**: 604.
Schoelcher, Victor. (T. Stanton) Open Court, **8**: 4151.
Schoenefeld, Henry. Music, **5**: 81.
Scholar, The; a story. Cornh. **67**: 505.
— and his Function in Society. Dial (Ch.) **20**: 37.
— Mission of. (W. Rupp) Ref. Q. **41**: 421.
Scholarship, Preparatory. (A. Crosby) Overland, n. s. **27**: 322.
Scholarships, Fellowships, and the Training of Professors. (G. S. Hall) Forum, **17**: 443.
— in English Public Schools. Sat. R. **76**: 268.
Scholtz, Hermann. (M. Y. Mann) Music, **7**: 557.
School and College Conference at the University of Chicago. School R. **4**: 23.
School and Home, How they help or hinder each other. (W. M. Thayer) Educa. **14**: 68, 142.
— Board, Destruction of the. (J. Clifford) Contemp. **66**: 626.
— City, Administration. (A. P. Marble) Educa. R. **8**: 154.
— College, and Library. (T. W. Higginson) Cosmopol. **13**: 48.
— Conveyance of Children to, in Massachusetts. (G. H. Martin) Educa. R. **7**: 147.
— English Village. Macmil. **71**: 455.
— Hour in, Fatigue of. (M. E. Holmes) Pedagog. Sem. **3**: 213.
— Humor in the School-room. (T. L. Hughes) Canad. M. **1**: 367.
— in France [Institution Notre Dame des Victoires, Paris]. Liv. Age, **196**: 624.
— The Modern. (G. H. Martin) Educa. **13**: 519.
— A Parental. Lend a H. **8**: 90.
— 16th Century. (P. S. Allen) Eng. Hist. R. **10**: 738.
School, Voluntary, The Archbishops and. Spec. **74**: 813.
School Board Scandals. (Annie Besant) Time, **22**: 130.
School Boards, Large or Small? (C. B. Gilbert) Educa. R. **4**: 179. — (J. M. Greenwood) Educa. R. **4**: 386.
Schoolboys as they were; a Day's Bird's-nesting. Blackw. **159**: 606.
— English and American. (W. W. Goodwin) School & C. **1**: 99. — Pub. Opin. **12**: 631.
Schoolboys' Feast. (A. F. Leach) Fortn. **65**: 128.
School Children, Growth of, at St. Louis, W. T. Porter on. (F. Boas) Science, n. s. **1**: 225.
— Habitual Postures of. (E. M. Mosher) Educa. R. **4**: 339.
— in England, Physical and Mental Condition of. (F. Warner) J. Statis. Soc. **56**: 71.
— Tests of Senses and Faculties of. (E. W. Scripture) Educa. R. **5**: 52. — (J. McK. Cottell) Educa. R. **5**: 257.
— Uniforming of. (F. W. Ryder) Educa. R. **15**: 157.
School Customs, Some Curious. (John De Morgan) Bach. of Arts, **1**: 646.
School Discipline. (L. Dunton) Educa. **12**: 323, 399. — (A. Lewis) School R. **3**: 495.
— Dogma of Formal. (B. A. Hinsdale) Educa. R. **8**: 128.
School Ethics. (H. C. B. Cowell) Pop. Sci. Mo. **46**: 363.
School Excursion from Indiana to Virginia. (J. M. Rice) Forum, **18**: 20.
School Excursions in Germany. (J. M. Rice) Cent. **26**: 643.
School-girl, The; Character Note. Cornh. **70**: 486. — Same art. Ecl. M. **124**: 277.
School-girl's Romance. (N. Stuart) Eng. Illust. **13**: 163.
School Government: Fraternalism and Paternalism. (E. P. Powell) Educa. **13**: 468.
School-grounds. (C. S. Sargent) Garden & F. **8**: 491.
Schoolhouse as a Centre. (H. E. Scudder) Atlan. **77**: 103.
Schoolhouses, Architecture of. (C. H. Walker) Atlan. **74**: 825.
— Old. (F. B. Dreslar) Pedagog. Sem. **2**: 115.
School Hygiene. (W. H. Burnham) Pedagog. Sem. **2**: 9.
School Influences, Indirect. (Rev. Harry Jones) Time, **13**: 663.
School Journey, A. (C. C. Van Liew) Educa. R. **8**: 7.
School Law in Manitoba. (D'Alton McCarthy) Canad. M. **1**: 1.
School Legislation, Early, in Massachusetts. (G. H. Martin) New Eng. M. n. s. **8**: 526.
— in the U. S., Recent, 1893. (W. B. Shaw) Educa. R. **6**: 249. **8**: 258.
School Management, Philosophy of, Tompkins on. (C. H. Thurber) School R. **4**: 112.
School-master, The. (James Baldwin) Scrib. M. **15**: 171.
— at Home, A. Macmil. **74**: 444.
— in Old New York, The. (A. M. Earle) Bk. Buyer, **13**: 531.
— Reflections of a. Liv. Age, **210**: 425. **211**: 98.
Schoolmasters, Parish. Eng. R. **12**: 51.
— Standing of. Spec. **73**: 487.
School Orchestras of Boston. (E. B. Terhune) Bost. **3**: 559.
School Patriotism. (E. Peabody) School R. **3**: 498.
School Question, How to solve the. (M. B. O'Reilly) No. Am. **155**: 569.
— New Phase of. Bapt. R. **14**: 102.
School-ship "Saratoga." (E. E. Hale) Lend a H. **9**: 419.

School Superintendent, The American. (B. A. Hinsdale) Educa. R. 7: 42.—Reply. (W. H. Maxwell) Educa. R. 7: 186.
School Superintendents, Powers and Duties of. (W. A. Mowry) Educa. R. 9: 38.
— Tenure of Office of, Permanent. (W. A. Mowry) Educa. 15: 274.
School Supervision. (L. J. Block) Educa. 12: 558.—(A. W. Edson) Educa. 13: 391.
— City. (H. S. Tarbell) Educa. R. 3: 65.—(W. T. Harris) Educa. R. 3: 167.
— in Pennsylvania. (R. K. Buehrle) Educa. R. 8: 461.
— Rational, our Educational Problem. (W. Sinclair) Westm. 137: 672.
School Supply in the Middle Ages. (A. F. Leach) Contemp. 66: 674.
School System, American State, Inception of an. (A. S. Draper) Educa. R. 8: 105.
— — Pres. Draper on. (R. K. Buehrle) Educa. R. 8: 389.
— Free. (C. D. Cowell) Am. J. Pol. 3: 399.
School Systems, City. Dial (Ch.) 16: 290.
— — Organization of. (A. S. Draper and others) Educa. R. 9: 304.
School Ventilation as an Investment. (G. H. Knight) Pop. Sci. Mo. 46: 393.
Schools and the Doctors. (H. Sabin) Educa. 17: 129.
— and School-books. (A. A. Reade) Time, 7: 873.
— and School-house Architecture. (E. C. Gardner) Engin. M. 10: 478.
— Art for. (B. Ferree) Educa. 17: 1.
— Bible in the. (A. G. Herzfeld) Westm. 145: 197.
— — in Elementary. (J. G. Fitch) 19th Cent. 36: 817.
— Board, and Voluntary. (Bp. of Salford) National, 26: 448.
— — The Doomed. (R. F. Horton) Fortn. 66: 110.
— — Scientific Method in. (H. E. Armstrong) Pop. Sci. Mo. 46: 614.
— Church, in England, Archbishop Benson on. Spec. 71: 9.
— Common, in the Southern States. (A. D. Mayo) Chaut. 17: 71.
— — Proposed Changes in Course of Study in. And. R. 17: 197.
— — Taxation for Support of. (J. W. Mason) Am. J. Pol. 3: 590.
— Crowded, as Promoters of Disease. (H. D. Chapin) Forum, 19: 296.
— Denominational, in Canada. (T. W. Anglin) Cath. World, 58: 609.
— District, and Academies in Massachusetts. (G. H. Martin) New Eng. M. n. s. 9: 450.
— Elementary, and the Kindergarten. (C. C. Van Liew) Educa. R. 9: 172.
— Educational Values in. (M. V. O'Shea) Pop. Sci. Mo. 48: 675.
— Endowed. (A. C. Hill) School R. 1: 422.
— English Public. (A. G. Bradley) Bach. of Arts, 2: 657.
— Evening Free, in N. Y. Soc. Econ. 1: 218.
— Healthy, Struggle for. (J. J. Davies) Westm. 143: 47.
— in Large Cities, Organization of. (A. S. Draper) Educa. R. 6: 1.
— London, Religious Issue in. (J. G. Fitch) Educa. R. 9: 159.
— Massachusetts, before the Revolution. (G. H. Martin) New Eng. M. n. s. 9: 356.
— Millionaires' Gifts to. (S. P. Cadman) Chaut. 18: 695.
— Pauper, Child-life in. (S. A. Barnett) Time, 18: 188.
— Preparatory. Blackw. 155: 380.
Schools, Private, for Boys, in the U. S. (P. Collier) Cosmopol. 15: 655.
— — State Supervision of. (J. C. Mackenzie) School R. 1: 391.—(D. W. Abercrombie and others) School R. 1: 557.
— Public. *See* Public Schools.
— Religion in. (C. L. Slattery) New Eng. M. n. s. 7: 471.
— — A Bootless Wrangle about. (J. H. Hyslop) Forum, 16: 747.
— — in Elementary. (G. A. Spottiswoode) 19th Cent. 38: 135.
— — in Primary. (J. G. Fitch) 19th Cent. 36: 55.
— Religious Teaching in Board. (A. Riley) Chr. Lit. 10: 78.
— Rural, Possible Improvement of. (J. H. Blodgett) Educa. R. 12: 34.
— — Problem of. (H. Sabin) Educa. R. 10: 172.
— Secondary. *See* Secondary Schools.
— Sectarian, The Government and. (R. Ogden) Nation, 56: 22.
— — Problem of. (R. Ogden) Nation, 55: 386.
— Sixty Years Ago. (W. T. Adams) Bost. 3: 166.
— State Control of, Real Ground for. (G. H. Howison) Educa. R. 5: 424.
— Unsanitary, and Public Indifference. (D. H. Stewart) Forum, 20: 103.
— Voluntary, in England. (J. M. Wilson) Contemp. 67: 288.
— — Archbishop Benson and. Spec. 71: 906.
— — Claims of. (E. R. Wodehouse) National, 26: 628.
— — Crisis in. (H. Hayman) National, 22: 478.
— — Problem of. (R. Waddington) Westm. 146: 88.
— — *vs.* Board. National, 27: 315.
Schooners, Racing. (R. B. Burchard) Outing, 29: 48, 168, 252.
Schopenhauer, Arthur. (G. Koerner) Open Court, 8: 3983.—(M. Todhunter) Westm. 143: 364.
— and Music. (K. J. Belling) Music, 2: 8.
— Letters, Schemann's. (H. T. Finck) Nation, 57: 290.
— Life of, Wallace's. (F. J. Rae) Crit. R. 1: 315.
Schorlemmer, Carl. (H. E. Roscoe) Nature, 46: 394.
Schreiner, Olive, with portrait. Bk. Buyer, 6: 17.
— Story of an African Farm; a Reflection. (T. F. Husband) Westm. 141: 631.
Schreyer, Adolphe. (B. Karageorgevitch) M. of Art, 18: 133.
— and his Horses. (C. S. Johnson) Munsey, 11: 264.
Schroeder-Le Chatelier Law of Solubility applied to Solution of Salts. (C. E. Linebarger) Am. J. Sci. 149: 48.
Schrumpf, Gustave Adolphe. Acad. 43: 16.
Schubert, Franz. (A. Dvôrák) Cent. 26: 341.
— Schubertiana. (Mary Hargrave) Gent. M. n. s. 57: 620.
Schubin, Ossip, *pseudonym*. *See* Kürschner, Lola.
Schuetz, Dr. C. Acad. 42: 391.
Schultze's System of Descriptive Terms, Remarks upon. (A. Hyatt) Am. Natural. 28: 369.
Schumann, Clara. (J. S. Shedlock) Acad. 49: 453.
Schumann, Robert. (E. Grieg) Cent. 25: 440.
— Correspondence of. (E. W. Hubbard) Music, 4: 173.
— A Lyrical Poet. (J. Sohn) Forum, 22: 235.
— Piano Works of. (E. Liebling) Music, 5: 189-398.
— — Wanted: a Revised Edition of. (C. Sternberg) Music, 2: 23.
— Poet of the Pianoforte. (W. S. B. Mathews) Music, 5: 698.
Schurman, J. G., with portrait. Bk. Buyer, 10: 55.
Schwatka, Frederic. Critic, 21: 267.
Schweinitz, Lewis David von, with portrait. Pop. Sci. Mo. 44: 833.

Science. (P. Carus) Open Court, 7: 3520.
— Abstract, and Engineering, Interdependence of. (W. Anderson) Nature, 48: 65.
— Amateur in. (Grant Allen) New Sci. R. 1: 301.
— and Biblical Criticism. (C. de Harlez) M. Chr. Lit. 6: 465.
— and Biblical Facts. (V. M. Olyphant) Bib. World, 2: 92.
— and the Colleges. (D. S. Jordan) Pop. Sci. Mo. 42: 721.
— and Culture. (C. E. Bessey) Science, n. s. 4: 121.
— and Faith. (P. Topinard) Monist, 6: 28, 534.
— — Relations of. (G. Macloskie) Presb. & Ref. R. 6: 98.
— and Fine Art. (E. Du Bois-Reymond) Pop. Sci. Mo. 40: 751. 41: 16.
— and a Future Life, Myers on. (Wm. Payne) Dial (Ch.) 15: 141.
— and Mystery. Spec. 76: 162.
— and Poetry. (H. Allen) Poet-Lore, 3: 232. — (W. H. Hudson) Pop. Sci. Mo. 45: 812.
— and Religion. (A. J. DuBois) Cent. 27: 227.
— — The Harmony of. (P. Carus) Open Court, 7: 3553.
— — Natural Allies. (E. B. Andrews) New World, 3: 658.
— — Relation between. (S. H. Mellone) New World, 5: 506.
— and Theology, Warfare of, White on. (C. K. Adams) Forum, 22: 65. — (D. S. Jordan) Dial (Ch.) 21: 146. — Am. Hist. R. 2: 107.
— Appreciation of, by German Manufacturers. (H. E. Armstrong) Nature, 48: 29.
— as a Means of Human Culture. (F. Davis) Pop. Sci. Mo. 45: 668.
— at the Beginning of the 19th Century. (P. Carus) Chaut. 20: 33.
— Battles of. (C. Barnard) New Sci. R. 1: 216.
— by Coöperation. (T. Lindsay) Pop. Astron. 4: 84.
— A Century of. Quar. 180: 381. Same art. Liv. Age, 205: 771.
— A Century's Progress in. (J. Fiske) Atlan. 78: 13.
— The Creed of. Am. Cath. Q. 21: 518.
— Denominational. (St. G. Mivart) Fortn. 64: 423.
— Dogmatism of. (Mrs. B. Moore) New Sci. R. 2: 75.
— Educational and Industrial Value of. (H. S. Carhart) Science, n. s. 1: 393.
— Elementary, in the Public Schools. (A. C. Boyden) Educa. 12: 478.
— — in School Courses. (L. P. Hopkins) Educa. R. 3: 156.
— Elements of, Mivart's. Sat. R. 78: 214.
— Facts and Problems of. (W. Preyer) Open Court, 2: 1076–1407.
— Humanistic Element in. (H. S. Carhart) Science, n. s. 4: 124.
— Immaterial. (E. S. Moser) Pop. Sci. Mo. 44: 84.
— in Fetters. (St. G. Mivart) Dub. R. 116: 158. 117: 1.
— in a Literary Education. (A. H. Tolman) Pop. Sci. Mo. 49: 98.
— in Poetry. (T. E. Mayne) Westm. 141: 669. Same art. Ecl. M. 123: 343.
— in Secondary Schools. Dial (Ch.) 21: 7. — (C. M. Stuart) Nature, 53: 346. — Nature, 54: 308.
— in Universities. (T. E. Thorpe) Sat. R. 82: 254.
— Methods of, Educational Value of. (W. T. Sedgwick) Educa. R. 5: 243.
— Next Great Problems of. (R. H. Thurston) Forum, 14: 42.
— Notes on, Fichte's. (M. W. Calkins) Philos. R. 3: 459.
Science, Notes on the Progress of. (A. Heilprin) New Sci. R. 1: 370.
— or Poetry? (W. K. Brooks) Science, n. s. 2: 437.
— Pearson's Grammar of. (C. L. Morgan) Nat. Sci. 1: 300. — (St. G. Mivart) Nat Sci. 1: 497. — Ath. '92, 2: 356. — Nature, 46: 97.
— Physical, and the Truth of Scripture. (W. Caven) Pub. Opin. 15: 183.
— Politics and. (K. Pearson) Fortn. 62: 334.
— Popularising. (H. G. Wells) Nature, 50: 300.
— Progress of, Marmery's. Sat. R. 79: 586.
— Protestant, Christianity and. (W. J. Knox-Little) 19th Cent. 34: 353.
— Relation of, to Industry. (N. S. Shaler) Chaut. 22: 24.
— — to Morals. Open Court, 1: 154.
— Religion and: Symposium. Indep. Feb. 2, '93.
— Religion of. (P. Carus) Monist, 2: 600. — (P. Carus) Open Court, 7: 3511. — (M. M. Snell) Open Court, 7: 3799.
— — a Catechism. Open Court, 7: 3634–3672.
— — A. Harnack on. (P. Carus) Monist, 4: 494.
— a Religious Revelation. Open Court, 7: 3809.
— Salisbury on. Sat. R. 78: 150.
— Some Beginnings in. (C. Cobb) Pop. Sci. Mo. 49: 763.
— Some Relations of, to Morality and Progress. (G. Gore) Open Court, 1: 421, 458.
— Study of, Ethical Tendencies of. (J. A. Shott) Educa. 16: 161.
— Superstitions of. Spec. 77: 138.
— Teaching. (J. L. Howe) Science, 19: 233. — (F. Guthrie) Pop. Sci. Mo. 42: 520.
— — Disappointing Results of. (A. E. Dolbear) Educa. R. 8: 485.
— — in Public Schools of the U. S. (A. Nelson) School R. 1: 471.
— — in Schools. (W. B. Crump; G. Heath) Nature, 51: 56. — (H. E. Armstrong) Nature, 50: 631.
— — — and after School. (H. G. Wells) Nature, 50: 525.
— — in Secondary Schools. (C. F. Mabery) Science, 21: 197.
— The Tyranny of. (Catherine Walter) New Sci. R. 2: 341.
— Use of, to Christians. (E. M. Caillard) Good Words, 37: 52–604.
— *vs.* Theology. Open Court, 1: 43.
— Warfare of, New Chapters in. (A. D. White) Pop. Sci. Mo. Vols. 40–47.
— What is? (T. C. Chamberlin) Chaut. 18: 155. — (Mrs. H. O. Ward) New Sci. R. 1: 173.
Science Studies, Correlation of, in Secondary Schools. (J. M. Coulter) School R. 4: 65. — Reply. (W. M. Davis) School R. 4: 173.
Science Text-books. (E. P. Powell) Open Court, 5: 2855.
Sciences, Classification of the. (Wm. Knight) Univ. R. 5: 348.
— Natural, in Elementary Education. (S. G. Williams) School R. 1: 163.
— — in the College Curriculum. (W. L. Poteat) Science, 21: 170.
— Natural Philosophy and. (S. T. Preston) Nat. Sci. 7: 253.
— Relation of Abstract to Concrete. (S. N. Patten) Ann. Am. Acad. Pol. Sci. 5: 942.
Scienter, The. (W. A. McClean) Green Bag, 7: 76.
Scientific Books in Evidence. (J. H. Wigmore) Am. Law R. 26: 390.
Scientific Congresses. (J. M. Baldwin) Pop. Sci. Mo. 50: 196.

Scientific Education and Research. (H. E. Armstrong) Nature, 50: 211. Same art. Pop. Sci. Mo. 45: 630.
— Exact and Inexact. (T. Hughes) Am. Cath. Q. 19: 297.
— Public Schools and. (F. W. Caulfeild) New R. 13: 199.
Scientific Freedom, Christian Faith and. (J. A. Zahm) No. Am. 157: 315.
Scientific Literature, Card Catalogue of. (H. P. Bowditch) Science, n. s. 1: 182. — (F. B. Weeks) Science, n. s. 2: 75.
— Cataloguing of. Lib. J. 20: 81.
— — Coöperative. Lib. J. 20: 308.
— The Ideal Index to. (G. B. Goode) Science, n. s. 1: 433.
— International Bibliography of. (C. W. Andrews) Lib. J. 20: supp. 25.
— Proposed Catalogue of. Acad. 50: 84.
— — Dewey Decimal Classification. (W. E. Hoyle) Nat. Sci. 9: 43.
— Publication of. (H. E. Armstrong) Nature, 50: 159.
— Subject-index to. (J. C. Rowell) Lib. J. 20: supp. 27. — Nature, 52: 270. — Science, n. s. 2: 154.
Scientific and other Meetings, Success with. (G. Iles) Pop. Sci. Mo. 43: 463.
Scientific Method. (C. W. R. Crum) Ref. Q. 41: 344.
Scientific Problems of the Future. (H. Elsdale) Contemp. 65: 362. Same art. Ecl. M. 122: 612. Same art. Liv. Age, 201: 195.
Scientific Progress, 1866–91. (W. N. Rice) Bib. Sac. 50: 1.
— of the 19th Century. (P. Carus) Chaut. 21: 278.
Scientific Research, Endowment of. (Addison Brown) Nature, 51: 164, 186.
— Motive for. (H. H. Clark) Pop. Sci. Mo. 47: 501.
Scientific Schools. Requirements for Admission to. (T. C. Mendenhall) School R. 4: 713.
Scientific Situation, The London "Times" on. (W. B. Benham) Nature, 53: 73.
Scientific Societies of Italy. (W. C. Cahall) Pop. Sci. Mo. 42: 107.
Scientific Spirit, How to cultivate. Acad. (Syr.) 17: 167.
— Literature and. (O. L. Triggs) Poet-Lore, 6: 113. — (L. A. Sherman) Poet-Lore, 6: 323.
Scientific Studies, Religious Value of. (L. G. Janes) Open Court, 1: 571.
Scientific Thought, Transformation and Adaptation in. (E. Mach) Open Court, 2: 1087, 1115.
Scientist, Use of the Word. (F. Hall) Acad. 47: 169.
Scientists and Social Purity. (W. J. Corbet) Westm. 144: 574.
Scilly Isles, The. Chamb. J. 69: 401. — (H. Johnston) Good Words, 34: 311.
— and the Scillonians. Cornh. 67: 482. Same art. Liv. Age, 198: 100.
— A Summer in. (J. W. White) Atlan. 73: 738.
Scipio's Dream; a study. (A. Harvey) Canad. M. 5: 318.
Sclater, Philip Lutley. (G. B. Goode) Science, n. s. 4: 293.
Scolari, Filippo. (W. Mercer) Acad. 42: 464.
Scollard, Clinton, with portrait. Bk. Buyer, 13: 145.
Scorpion, Modest. Cornh. 68: 643. Same art. Liv. Age, 200: 175.
Scorpions and their Antiquity. (R. Lydekker) Knowl. 18: 150.
— and their Geographical Distribution. (R. I. Pocock) Nat. Sci. 4: 353.
— Habits of. (R. I. Pocock) Nature, 48: 104.
Scorpions, How and why they hiss. (R. I. Pocock) Nat. Sci. 9: 17.
— Sting of. (C. A. Mitchell) Knowl. 18: 20.
— Whip-, and their Ways. (R. I. Pocock) Knowl. 18: 272.
Scotch in America. (R. S. Robertson) M. Am. Hist. 27: 42.
Scotch and English Fairy Tales. (A. Lang) Folk-Lore, 1: 289.
Scotch Element in the American People. (N. S. Shaler) Atlan. 77: 508.
Scotch Fisher Child, The. (W. Gregor) Folk-Lore, 2: 73.
Scotch Highlanders and American Indians. (M. E. Strieby) Lend a H. 15: 376.
Scotch Highlands, Formation of. (H. P. Malet) Time, 22: 267.
Scotch-Irish in America. Pub. Opin. 17: 222.
Scotch Moor, A Day on a. (H. F. Witherby) Knowl. 18: 185.
Scotch People, Religiosity of. (J. Leatham) Westm. 144: 88.
Scotchman as a Householder, The. (G. Farquhar) Westm. 140: 635.
— Old-type. (R. B. C. Graham) Sat. R. 81: 542.
Scotchman's Adventures Abroad. (D. Macleod) Good Words, 34: 482. Same art. Liv. Age, 198: 567.
Scotchmen, Modern. (T. P. White) Scot. R. 24: 44. Same art. Liv. Age, 202: 795.
Scotland and English Courts. (T. Raleigh) Jurid. R. 2: 335.
— and the Unionist Cause. Scot. R. 23: 365.
— Battles of Preston and Falkirk. (J. Veitch) Blackw. 156: 98.
— Blackhal's Travels in, 1831–49. Eng. R. 4: 1.
— Castles of. (C. Turner) Mo. Illust. 4: 277.
— Celtic, Skene on. (T. Raleigh) Crit. R. 2: 25.
— Church and State in. Ed. R. 178: 223.
— Church of. *See* Church of Scotland.
— Coast of, Scenery of. (W. S. Dalgleish) Good Words, 33: 310.
— Coat-of-arms in, Right to use. (G. W. Campbell) Jurid. R. 4: 223.
— Conservatism in. (W. M. Ramsay) Westm. 196: 304.
— County Councils in. (W. C. Smith) Jurid. R. 1: 141.
— Court of Criminal Appeal for. (A. D. Blacklock) Jurid. R. 4: 150, 209.
— Disestablishment in. (D. Macleod) Contemp. 64: 259.
— Ecclesiastical History of. Eng. R. 7: 384. 8: 50.
— Ecclesiastical Parish in. (W. G. Black) Jurid. R. 6: 136.
— Ecclesiastical Situation in. (N. L. Walker) Presb. & Ref. R. 5: 216.
— Exchequer Rolls, edited by G. Burnett and J. G. Mackay. (J. Gairdner) English Hist. R. 7: 155.
— Free Church in, Walker on. (J. Laing) Presb. & Ref. R. 7: 551.
— Geology of. (A. H. Green) Nature, 47: 49.
— High Court of Justiciary, Archives of. (C. Scott) Jurid. R. 3: 197. 4: 32–293.
— Highlands of. *See* Highlands.
— in 1677, by Kirk and Thoresby. Sat. R. 74: 85.
— in 1892. Blackw. 155: 252.
— Journey to, in 1435. (J. J. Jusserand) 19th Cent. 37: 1036. Same art. Liv. Age, 206: 31.
— Land of the Raiders. (C. Blatherwick) Good Words, 36: Xmas no. 23.
— Land Law Reform in. (R. B. Haldane) Jurid. R. 2: 37.

Scotland, Law of, Sources of. (J. D. Wilson) Jurid. R. 4: 1.
— Letters relating to, January, 1650. (F. B. Bickley) Eng. Hist. R. 11: 112.
— Library of James VI. (G. F. Warner) Bookworm, 6: 201.
— Lowland, in the 18th Century. (J. Colville) Blackw. 152: 471. Same art. Liv. Age, 195: 515.
— Mar and Aberdeen. Quar. 184: 365.
— Marriage and Divorce in. (A. Scott) Westm. 146: 213.
— Mediæval, Cochran-Patrick on. Spec. 69: 292.
— Municipal Socialism. (A. Shaw) Jurid. R. 1: 33.
— New. (Francis Watt) New R. 13: 640.
— Off the Track in. (S. Hodges) M. of Art, 1: 209.
— Old Drove-roads of. Macmil. 72: 449.
— Parliament of, Ancient. (J. A. Lovat-Fraser) National, 21: 281.
— Parochialisation of. Time, 13: 529.
— Peasantry of. (W. G. Blaikie) No. Am. 159: 327.
— Picturesque. The Braes o' Mar. (P. MacQueen) Mo. Illust. 13: 137.
— Place-names of. (J. S. Blackie) Blackw. 156: 38.
— Popular Rhymes of, Chambers'. Sat. R. 73: 665.
— Reforms in Conveyancing in. (J. Burns) Jurid. R. 5: 38.
— Religious Progress in. (R. B. Drummond) Open Court, 1: 257.
— Reminiscences of. (R. Blackwell) Time, 10: 513.
— Rural, in the First Half of 18th Century. (H. G. Graham) Scot. R. 25: 104. Same art. Liv. Age, 204: 725.
— Rural Toilers of the North. (W. Diack) Westm. 145: 446.
— Sculptured Stones of, Bibliography of. (J. P. Edmond) Walford's Antiq. 3: 185.
— Social Life in, in the Olden Time. All the Year, 74: 249.
— Strickland's Lives of Queens of. Eng. R. 14: 245.
— Tartan Plaid. (B. M. Ranking) Time, 10: 50.
— Theological Drifts in, Present. (N. L. Walker) Presb. & Ref. R. 4: 25.
— Under the Roundheads. (J. Coville) Scot. R. 28: 103.
— Union of, with England. Ed. R. 176: 506.
— — How it was effected. (J. Downie) Scot. R. 20: 163.
— — How it has worked. (J. Downie) Scot. R. 20: 397.
— Universities of, Theological Tests in. (A. T. Innes) Jurid. R. 4: 301.
— Wild Fauna of. (J. H. Crawford) Gent. M. n. s. 52: 581.
— Wild Flora of. (J. H. Crawford) Gent. M. n. s. 54: 397.
— Wild Life of, Crawford's. Sat. R. 82: 170.
Scotland Yard, New. (R. Blomfield) M. of Art, 17: 330.
Scots Brigade, The First. Macmil. 74: 104.
Scots Law, Development of. (J. D. Wilson) Jurid. R. 8: 217.
Scott, Clement, as a Critic. Theatre, 37: 237. — Sat. R. 81: 548.
— as a Poet. Sat. R. 82: 282.
— Poet, Playwright, Critic. (M. A. Belloc) Idler, 8: 311.
Scott, Frederick George. (J. E. Wetherell) Canad. M. 4: 287.
Scott, James H., with portrait. Bank. M. (Lond.) 59: 917.
Scott, John, Chief Justice, Confessions of. Green Bag, 6: 59.
Scott, Matthew Thompson, with portrait. (J. P. Bishop) Nat'l M. (N. Y. '91) 16: 91.
Scott, Thomas, Grave of. (J. G. Wilson) Am. Hist. Reg. 1: 142.
Scott, Sir Walter, with portrait. Acad. 50: 596. — (E. K. Pearce) Gent. M. n. s. 48: 167. — (A. H. Millar) Scot. R. 23: 225
— and Mrs. Veal's Ghost. (W. Scott) 19th Cent. 37: 271.
— Constable and. Temp. Bar, 96: 473.
— Dickens, and Thackeray: are they Obsolete? (W. H. Mallock) Forum, 14: 503.
— First Love of. (G. Newcomen) Acad. 50: 236. Same art. Liv. Age, 211: 569.
— Heroes of. Gent. M. n. s. 51: 427.
— Heroines of, Age of. Atlan. 69: 139.
— The Historical Novel. (G. Saintsbury) Macmil. 70: 321.
— A House-party at Abbotsford. (N. L. Smith) Cosmopol. 19: 513.
— Journal and Letters, ed. by David Douglass. (A. H. Millar) Scot. R. 23: 225.
— Legal Lore of. (N. Newmark) Green Bag, 4: 541.
— Letters of. Blackw. 155: 15. Same art. Liv. Age, 200: 515. — Atlan. 73: 405. — Chamb. J. 71: 7. — (C. S. Peirce) Nation, 58: 105. — Spec. 72: 167. — (T. Hutchinson) Acad. 44: 539. — Dial (Ch.) 15: 384. — Ath. '93, 2: 725. — Sat. R. 76: 598.
— Life Scenes and Life Work of. (G. Holme) Munsey, 11: 622.
— Memorial and Relics of. Chamb. J. 73: 73.
— Monastery. (R. G. Moulton) Chaut. 20: 424.
— Novels ed. by Lang. Art J. 45: 234.
— — New Editions of. (G. C. Smith) Nation, 56: 370.
— Personal Recollections of. Argosy, 57: 26.
— Poems. Sat. R. 73: 368.
— — Dennis' ed. Spec. 68: 746.
— Quentin Durward. Gent. M. n. s. 48: 323.
— Some Portraits of. (F. G. Kilton) M. of Art, 19: 1.
— Voyage of, in the Lighthouse Yacht. (R. Stevenson) Scrib. M. 14: 492.
— Waverley Novels. Quar. 180: 431. Same art. Liv. Age, 205: 515.
— — after Sixty Years. (D. F. Hannigan) Westm. 144: 17.
— — Editions of. Book R. 1: 195.
— Woodstock. (R. G. Moulton) Chaut. 20: 673.
— — Dramatized by J. R. Sims and R. Buchanan. Theatre, 28: 307.
Scott, Wm. Bell, and D. G. Rossetti. (J. Skelton) Blackw. 153: 229.
— Autobiography. (W. Sharp) Acad. 41: 499. — (A. C. Swinburne) Acad. 41: 590. — (W. M. Rossetti) Acad. 41: 591. — (W. Minto) Acad. 42: 608. — Dial (Ch.) 13: 382. — Sat. R. 74: 692. — Ath. '93, 1: 113. — Spec. 70: 161.
— — The New Terror. (A. C. Swinburne) Fortn. 58: 830.
— — Sharp on. (W. Minto) Acad. 41: 541.
Scott, Winfield: Friendship with R. E. Lee. (J. W. Jones) Southern M. 4: 514.
Scotti, Giulio Cesare. (J. W. Sherer) Gent. M. n. s. 56: 459.
Scottish Artists, Society of. Acad. 44: 419.
Scottish Ballad Poetry, ed. by Todd. Sat. R. 75: 543.
Scottish Border, History and Poetry of, Veitch's. Blackw. 153: 865.
Scottish Elections of 1895. Scot. R. 26: 359.
Scottish Guard of France, The. Macmil. 73: 381. Same art. Liv. Age, 209: 94.
Scottish History and Poetry. (A. H. Japp) Scot. R. 23: 108.

Scottish Literature, Some Curiosities of. (W.W. Smith) Chaut. 21: 190.
— Walker's. (A. B. McMahan) Dial (Ch.) 14: 361.
Scottish Merchant of the 16th Century. (A. H. Millar) Scot. R. 22: 341.
Scottish Myths from Ontario. (C. A. Fraser) J. Am. Folk-Lore, 6: 185.
Scottish National Humor. (S. R. Crockett) Contemp. 67: 515. Same art. Liv. Age, 205: 259.
Scottish National Memorials. (J. M. Gray) M. of Art, 13: 383.
Scottish Novelists, New. Ed. R. 184: 37. Same art. Liv. Age, 211: 3.
Scottish Poetry before Burns. (J. C. Hadden) Scot. R. 25: 203.
— of the 16th Century. Sat. R. 74: 309.
Scottish Poets. (W. W. Smith) Chaut. 23: 421.
Scottish Vendetta, A. (H. Maxwell) 19th Cent. 36: 583.
Scout, The U. S. Government. (J. Crawford) Outing, 23: 148.
Scranton, Pa., Albright Memorial Library Building. Lib. J. 17: 236.
Scrap of College Lore; a story. (W. A. Dromgoole) Arena, 6: 750.
Scrap-book, My. Chamb. J. 73: 717.
— of Canon Alberic; a story. (M. R. James) National, 25: 132. Same art. Liv. Age, 205: 141.
Scrap-iron. Chamb. J. 73: 229.
Scratch, A, in Play. Chamb. J. 68: 822.
Screen in the Lumber Room; a poem. (A. Dobson) M. of Art, 9: 63.
Screw-propeller Boats, First. (F. B. Stevens) Cassier, 6: 323.
Screw Threads, An International Standard of. (T. Mudd) Cassier, 9: 563.
Scribner's Publishing House, History of. Scrib. M. 16: 793.
Scripture, Doctrine of. (T. M. Lindsay) Chr. Lit. 13: 29.
— Unshaken Truths in. (J. Cook) Our Day, 9: 285. *See* Bible.
Scrope, W. Sat. R. 76: 155, 298.
Scudamore, Frank I. (Sigma Smith) Time, 14: 278.
Scull, W. D., as a Novelist. (G. Allen) Acad. 50: 8.
Sculptor, A; how he works. (E. R. Mullins) Good Words, 35: 42.
Sculptor's Mistake, The; a story. (J. Lemaitre) Art J. 44: 5.
Sculptors. (H. Spencer) Contemp. 69: 285.
— Some Modern. (S. F. Coles) Munsey, 9: 507.
Sculpture, American School of. (W. O. Partridge) Arena, 7: 641.
— and Sculptors, American. (L. Taft) Chaut. 22: 387.
— Architectural. (E. I. Bell) M. of Art, 4: 245.
— at the Paris Universal Exhibition. M. of Art, 3: 256.
— at the Royal Academy, 1888. (C. Phillips) M. of Art, 11: 366.
— — in 1894. Sat R. 7: 125.
— Baffier's Gardener in Paris. (C. S. Sargent) Garden & F. 6: 152.
— Color in. (M. P. Souriau) Pub. Opin. 14: 261.
— Couleur in. Univ. R. 1: 524.
— Decorative, at the World's Columbian Exposition. M. of Art, 11: 383.
— — Use of. (E. R. Mullins) J. Soc. Arts, 40: 511.
— Early Chinese. (E. H. Parker) Acad. 50: 36.
— Exhibition of Old Masters at the Royal Academy. (A. Higgins) M. of Art, 11: 204.
Sculpture, French, Recent. (R. R. Wilson) Mo. Illust. 13: 195.
— Greek, at Cambridge. (J. E. Harrison) M. of Art, 7: 510.
— — Collignon on. Ath. '92, 2: 292.
— — Furtwängler's Masterpieces of. (R. Sturgis) Nation, 60: 148, 168. — (J. C. Van Dyke) Dial (Ch.) 19: 70. — Sat. R. 79: 812.
— — Lost Masterpieces of. Quar. 180: 61.
— — Overbeck on. Sat. R. 74: 748.
— — Pergamene Style, Various Works in. (L. R. Farnell) J. Hel. Stud. 11: 181.
— — Processes of. (E. A. Gardner) J. Hel. Stud. 11: 129.
— — Two 4th Century Children's Heads. (E. A. Gardner) J. Hel. Stud. 11: 100.
— in America, Development of. (W. O. Partridge) Forum, 20: 554.
— in Belgium, Renaissance of. (O. G. Destree) Portf. no. 23.
— in London, The Future of. (E. W. Gosse) M. of Art, 4: 281.
— in Sicilian Museums. (L. R. Farnell) J. Hel. Stud. 12: 46.
— Influence of Early Renaissance on. (B. Fletcher, jr.) Archit. Rec. 2: 418.
— of the Picts. (G. F. Browne) M. of Art, 6: 15.
— of the Year, 1889. M. of Art, 12: 369.
— — 1890. M. of Art, 13: 361.
— — 1891. (C. Phillips) M. of Art, 14: 402.
— — 1892. (C. Phillips) M. of Art, 15: 378.
— — 1893. (C. Phillips) M. of Art, 16: 56. — Sat. R. 76: 12.
— — 1894. (C. Phillips) M. of Art, 18: 67.
— — 1895. (C. Phillips) M. of Art, 18: 441.
— Outlook for, in America. (W. O. Partridge) New Eng. M. n. s. 7: 514.
— Place of, in Daily Life. (E. Gosse) M. of Art, 18: 326–407. 19: 9.
— Professional Institutions; Sculptor. (H. Spencer) Pop. Sci. Mo. 48: 557.
— Recent. (E. Gosse) Art J. 46: 138–306.
— Recent Architectural, and the Institute of Chartered Accountants. (R. Blomfield) M. of Art, 18: 185.
— Roman Copies and Greek Originals. (G. F. Hill) Illus. Archæol. 2: 81.
— Tuscan, of the Renaissance. (V. Paget) 19th Cent. 31: 938. Same art. Liv. Age, 194: 407.
Sculpture Society (of America). M. of Art, 16: xxix.
Sculptured Stones in Boroughbridge Church. Reliquary, 33: 168.
— in England. (G. F. Browne) M. of Art, 8: 78, 154.
— Stowford, Devon. Reliquary, 35: 228.
— Vortipore, Carmarthenshire. Reliquary, 35: 231.
Sculptures, French Exhibit of Historic. (C. M. Kurtz) Chaut. 16: 451.
— Greek: Did the Greeks paint them? (E. Robinson) Cent. 21: 869.
— Modern French, in the Luxembourg. (F. G. Stephens) Art J. 48: 206.
Scylla or Charybdis? (Rhoda Broughton) Temp. Bar, 105: 145, 291, 433. 106: 1–572.
Sea and Land. (N. S. Shaler) Scrib. M. 11: 611.
Sea, The, and its Spiritual Teachings. (J. R. Macduff) Sund. M. 22: 596.
— Apprentice Life at. (J. G. Rowe) Westm. 141: 675.
— At; a sketch. (M. Morris) 19th Cent. 40: 412. Same art. Liv. Age, 211: 292.

Sea, The, Chemical Changes between Water and Deposits. Nature, 51: 304.
— Color of. All the Year, 75: 40.
— Colors of. Chamb. J. 69: 534.
— Command of. Lond. Q. 85: 315. — Quar. 177: 329. — (J. F. Daniell) Un. Serv. M. 6: 170.
— Deep, Deposits in: Work of the "Challenger." (J. J. H. Teall) Nat. Sci. 1: 17.
— — Explorations of. (J. C. Beard) Cosmopol. 14: 532. — Spec. 72: 470.
— — Fauna of, Hickson's. Sat. R. 77: 156. — Around World, 1: 184.
— — Growth of Our Knowledge of. (G. W. Littlehales) Pop. Sci. Mo. 43: 39.
— — Physical Conditions of. (S. J. Hickson) Pop. Sci. Mo. 44: 461.
— — Salvage from, The Record in. Chamb. J. 73: 791.
— — Soundings in. (A. P. Crouch) 19th Cent. 40: 881.
— Depths of. (N. S. Shaler) Scrib. M. 12: 77.
— Disasters at, Lessening of. Sat. R. 73: 479.
— Freedom of. (J. G. Whiteley) New Eng. M. n. s. 9: 233.
— Impressions of a Blind Man. All the Year, 70: 162.
— Life in, Study of. (F. Houssay) Chaut. 18: 564.
— Literature of. Macmil. 68: 279.
— Microscopic Organisms of. (P. T. Cleve) Nature, 55: 89.
— Nature at. (F. H. Herrick) Pop. Sci. Mo. 44: 69.
— Old Man of the. (W. D. Gunning) Open Court, 1: 507.
— Rule of the Road at. (P. H. Colomb) J. Soc. Arts, 43: 326.
— Size of. (W. Schooling) Longm. 22: 255.
— Superstitions of. (J. D. J. Kelley) Cent. 26: 418.
— Weather Folk-Lore of. (W. Gregor) Folk-Lore, 2: 468.
— Why it is Salt. (G. W. Littlehales) Pop. Sci. Mo. 48: 273.
Sea Ballads: My Sailor, Galway Bay. (A. P. Graves) Harper, 89: 349.
Sea Change. (E. C. Stedman) Cent. 22: 503.
Sea Change, A; a story. (M. Robertson) McClure, 7: 362.
Seacoast-planting. (L. Ross) Garden & F. 8: 412.
Sea Cucumber. *See* Trepang.
Sea Deposits, Deep. (H. N. Hutchinson) Knowl. 16: 43–94.
Sea-dogs of England. (C. G. Lang) Good Words, 36: 808.
Sea Episode. (C. H. Rockwell) Lippinc. 52: 378.
Sea Fight, Our First Great. (P. Kent) Gent. M. n. s. 48: 54. Same art. Ecl. M. 118: 383.
Sea-fishing. (J. Bickerdyke) Blackw. 156: 418.
Sea-fowl and Samphire. Spec. 69: 316.
Sea-gull, The; a poem. All the Year, 76: 62.
Sea Islands, S. C., Hurricanes at. (J. C. Harris) Scrib. M. 15: 229–267.
— in War Time. (D. E. W. Spratt) Lippinc. 53: 780.
— Relief Work in, Report. (C. Barton) Lend a H. 12: 116.
Sea Kings, Elizabethan. (J. Fiske) Atlan. 76: 91.
Sea Life, Microscopic. Leis. Hour, 42: 558–845.
— in the 16th Century. (F. S. Bassett) Un Serv. (Phila.) 10: 33.
Seamen, English, in the 16th Century. (J. A. Froude) Longm. 22: 218–514. 25: 142–580.
— — Froude on. (W. H. Carruth) Dial (Ch.) 18: 341.
— Poor Jack. (C. Russell) Eng. Hist. 16: 3.
— Supply of. Chamb. J. 72: 275.
Sea Power. Fortn. 60: 849. Same art. Liv. Age, 200: 451.
— in History, Mahan on. Ed. R. 177: 484. — (C. H. Stockton) Nation, 56: 108, 126. — Atlan. 71: 556. — (F. N. Maude) National, 23: 110. — Liv. Age, 200: 451.
Sea Queen, The. (James Workman) Chamb. J. 73: 76.
Sea-robbers of New York. (T. A. Janvier) Harper, 89: 813.
Sea Sculpture. (H. W. Warren) Chaut. 24: 186.
Sea-serpent, the Great Unknown. (J. B. Holder) Cent. 22: 247.
Sea-service in England: Is it still Popular? Spec. 69: 490.
Seashore Resorts, Bathing at Continental. (J. H. Adams) Cosmopol. 19: 131.
Seaside Existence. All the Year, 73: 38.
Seaside Life in America. (F. H. Hardy) Cornh. 74: 605.
Sea Song; a poem. (G. A. Burdett) Outing, 26: 447.
Sea Songs, American. (A. M. Williams) Atlan. 69: 489.
Seaweeds, Artistic Value of. (H. L. Jelliffe) Mo. Illust. 5: 74.
— Olive-brown, Reproductive Organs of. (G. Murray) Sci. Prog. 3: 242.
— — Recent Researches on. (E. S. Barton) Nat. Sci. 4: 50.
— Recent Work on. (A. L. Smith) Nat. Sci. 8: 34.
— Study of, Murray's. Sat. R. 81: 380.
Seawomen. (M. B. Wright) Chaut. 14: 602.
Seaford, England. (G. C. Haité) Art J. 47: 331.
Seal, The: its Origin, Evolution, and Abolition. (H. C. McDougal) Am. Law R. 28: 37.
— Great, of England. (J. E. R. Stephens) Am. Law R. 30: 404.
— — of the United States. (E. T. Laader) M. Am. Hist. 29: 471.
Seals. All the Year, 70: 391.
— Antarctic. (W. S. Bruce) Knowl. 16: 221.
— Eared. Sat. R. 74: 329.
— Fur-. (R. Lydekker) Knowl. 19: 186.
— — Future of. Spec. 70: 569.
— — Passing of. (H. L. Nelson) Harper, 92: 462.
— — Rookeries of, in the U. S., Care and Conservation of. (H. W. Elliott) Cosmopol. 13: 245.
Seal-hunting; a Cruise to the Dutchman's Cap. (C. Stein) Blackw. 154: 439.
— 15th of June off Jan Mayen. All the Year, 74: 565.
— in the Antarctic. Pop. Sci. Mo. 43: 539.
— in the North Pacific. (M. Rees Davies) Macmil. 71: 214.
— on the Pacific Coast. Chamb. J. 70: 638.
Seal Fisheries, Aleutian Isles. (W. R. Shoemaker) Un. Serv. (Phila.) 11: 221.
— Decline of Fur Sealing. (M. Rees Davies) Gent. M. n. s. 57: 411. Same art. Ecl. M. 127: 661.
Seal Fisheries Dispute, Correspondence on. (H. White) Nation, 54: 204. — Spec. 68: 457.
Seal Fishing in Behring Sea. (C. H. Tupper) National, 28: 87.
Sealskin Purse, The; a story. (M. L. Molesworth) Longm. 19: 389.
Seamanship, Plea for. (C. H. Rockwell) Un. Serv. (Phila.) 8: 513.
Seamy Side, The. (W. Besant and J. Rice) Time, 1: 65–721. 2: 65–726.
Search after Culture; a true story. Blackw. 153: 441. Same art. Liv. Age, 197: 308. Same art. Ecl. M. 120: 649.
Search for an Ancestor. (S. A. Pryor) Cent. 27: 855.

Search for Mrs. Denbeigh; a story. (A. L. Provost) Outing, 28: 83.
Search-lights, Electrical. (H. Hutchins) Cassier, 1: 429. 3: 83.
— Large. (H. M. Norris, jr.) Cassier, 5: 398.
Seasons. As the Seasons Change. Ecl. M. 126: 802.
Seats of the Mighty. (G. Parker) Atlan. 75: 289-796. 76: 1-721. 77: 36, 187.
Seattle, Wash. (J. W. Pratt) New Eng. M. n. s. 8: 292.
— 1855-56. (T. S. Phelps) Un. Serv. (Phila.) 15: 40.
Seawell, Molly E., with portrait. Bk. Buyer, 13: 283.
— With portrait. (W. S. Walsh) Writer, 6: 41.
Sebastopol, Fall of. (W. H. Russell) Scrib. M. 13: 120.
— in the Trenches before. (W. Simpson) Eng. Illust. 14: 229.
— The Old Trenches at, Revisited. (G. Wolseley) Un. Serv. M. 10: 103.
—Winter and Summer in the Trenches of. (W. Simpson) Eng. Illust. 15: 33.
Sébillot, Paul, Scheme of, for Collection and Classification of Folk-Lore. (A. Nutt) Folk-Lore Rec. 3: 195.
Secession of Munich. (A. B. Bibb) Am. Arch. 51: 62.
Second Adventists: Waiting for the Millennium. Spec. 70: 322.
Second Edition, The; a story. (A. Crany) Overland, n. s. 20: 184.
Second Lieutenant Mackenzie; a story. (J. Lloyd) Munsey, 13: 493.
Second Mate's Yarn, The. Overland, n. s. 22: 123.
Second Missouri Compromise; a story. (O. Wister) Harper, 90: 534.
Second Mrs. Tanqueray, The. (J. H. McCarthy) Gent. M. n. s. 52: 98. — Theatre, 31: 139. — (A. Brereton) Theatre, 34: 152.
Second Spring, A; a story. (S. O. Jewett) Harper, 88: 114.
Second Thoughts. (E. S. Grew) Idler, 7: 97.
Secondary Education. Dial (Ch.) 16: 35. — (D. W. Abercrombie and others) Harv. Grad. M. 1: 376. — Month, 85: 305. — (W. H. Smiley) School R. 4: 523.
— and Higher, Support of, by the State. (A. D. Mayo) Educa. 12: 262, 335.
— and the London Board. Fortn. 65: 830.
— Buffalo Meeting of the N. E. A. Department of. (C. H. Thurber) School R. 4: 539.
— — — Programme of. School R. 4: 461.
— Important Reports for. School R. 4: 541.
— in England. (A. T. Smith) Educa. 14: 504.
— — Movement for Organizing. (A. N. Disney) School R. 2: 141.
— — Royal Commission on. (J. G. Fitch) Educa. R. 11: 1. — (H. Macan) J. Soc. Arts, 44: 305.
— — — Report of. (T. J. Macnamara) Fortn. 64: 893. — (H. E. Armstrong) Nature, 53: 79.
— in New York State. Critic, 24: 332.
— in the U. S., in Census Years. (J. H. Blodgett) School & C. 1: 14.
— — Programs of Committee of Ten. (M. A. Willcox) Educa. 15: 257.
— — Report of the Committee of Ten. (W. T. Harris) Educa. R. 7: 1. — (C. W. Eliot) Educa. R. 7: 105. — (C. De Garmo) Educa. R. 7: 275. — (C. F. P. Bancroft) Educa. R. 7: 280. — (J. E. Bradley) Educa. R. 7: 370. — (J. S. Clark) Educa. R. 7: 374. — (F. W. Parker) Educa. R. 7: 479. — (J. Sachs) Educa. R. 8: 75. — (J. G. Schurman; R. G. Huling) School R. 2: 83, 268. — (J. C. Mackenzie) School R. 2: 146, (J. M. Taylor) 193. — (O. D. Robinson) School R. 2: 366.
Secondary Education in the U. S., Reform of. (N. M. Butler) Atlan. 73: 372.
— — Regulation of. (N. M. Butler) Nation, 58: 44.
— National Uniformity in. (W. H. Butts) School R. 3: 65.
— Smith's. Sat. R. 74: 138.
— Tendency to Multiply Courses in. (P. H. Hanus) School R. 3: 193.
— Values in. (W. B. Jacobs) Educa. R. 9: 135.
Secondary School, What constitutes a. (J. E. Russell; J. G. Schurman; J. C. Mackenzie) School R. 4: 529.
— What constitutes a College, and what a. (R. H. Jesse) School R. 4: 274.
Secondary-school Programmes, Suggestions for making. (W. L. Hervey) Educa. R. 12: 84.
Secondary Schools. (J. L. Pickard) Educa. 15: 21.
— American and European compared. (B. A. Hinsdale) Dial (Ch.) 20: 195.
— and the Co-ordination of Studies. (L. E. Rector) Educa. 15: 283.
— and Higher Institutions, Closer Articulation between. (R. G. Huling and others) School R. 2: 594.
— College Preparatory Work in Relation to other Work in. (E. S. Hawes) Acad. (Syr.) 7: 153.
— Correlation of Science Studies in. (J. M. Coulter) School R. 4: 65. — Reply. (W. M. Davis) School R. 4: 173.
— Curriculum for. (W. T. Harris) Educa. 14: 579.
— German Methods in. (E. P. Drew) Educa. 15: 385.
— Home Readings for. (G. P. Du Bois) School R. 3: 485.
— How Colleges may help. (I. Thomas) Acad. (Syr.) 7: 140.
— of East London. (R. Mitcheson) Time, 21: 237.
— Preparation of Teachers for. (A. F. Nightingale) School R. 4: 129.
— Should Time be diminished in? (C. F. P. Bancroft) School R. 2: 156.
— University Inspection of. (P. H. Hanus) School R. 2: 257.
Secret, A. (A. Hope) Idler, 7: 3.
— of the Ball Cartridge, The; a story. (H. Hill) Chamb. J. 71: 46-62.
— of the Dead. (E. Yolland) Belgra. 87: 389.
— of the Hidden Room. (S. Jerome) Idler, 1: 292.
— of the Pines; a story. (H. M. Hoke) Outing, 28: 403.
— of Saint Florel, The. Macmil. 74: 1-465. 75: 1, 81.
— of Verloren Vlei. (H. A. Bryden) Chamb. J. 71: 807-823.
— of Wardale Court; a story. (A. Hope) Temp. Bar, 94: 219-559.
— of a Weed's Plain Heart. (H. Macmillan) Good Words, 36: 302.
Secret Northern Despatches. (W. H. Needham) Chamb. J. 71: 589-605.
Secret Service, Le Caron's. (F. A. Hamilton) Acad. 41: 557. — Ed. R. 177: 247.
Societies, Secret. (J. V. Collins) Lend a H. 16: 89.
— and Secret Tribunals. Chamb. J. 71: 502.
— C. A. Blanchard on. (F. T. Olsaver) Am. J. Pol. 1: 642.
— Folly, Expense and Dangers of. (C. A. Blanchard) Am. J. Pol. 1: 48.
— in China. Blackw. 160: 793. Same art. Liv. Age, 211: 852.

Secret Societies, Mussulman. (Napoleon Ney) Cosmopol. 17: 556. — Liv. Age, 202: 765.
Secretary of the Donga-Pa Mission; a sketch. (E. T. Kingsmill) Canad. M. 7: 50.
Secretary, The Private. Time, 18: 385.
Secretion, Physiology of, Pawlow's Researches on. (E. Starling) Sci. Prog. 4: 491.
Secrets, Keeping of. Spec. 71: 870.
— the Story of a Daisy Chain. Argosy, 53: 257.
Sectarian Schools, Public Appropriations for. (W. S. Linton) Our Day, 16: 235.
Sectarianism. (A. Mason) N. Church R. 1: 366.
— among Mohammedans. (D. A. Walker) Bib. World, 2: 15.
— Denominationalism and. (P. Schaff) Chr. Lit. 10: 144.
— Non-, Reign of. (T. McMillan) Cath. World, 59: 390.
Sects and Parties. (C. R. Henderson) Pub. Opin. 20: 173.
Secularism, How diffused. (G. J. Holyoake) Open Court, 10: 4959.
— Mission of. (F. L. Oswald) Open Court, 1: 29.
— The New. (W. Walsh) Contemp. 67: 117. Same art. Ecl. M. 124: 211.
Secularist Ceremonies. (G. J. Holyoake) Open Court, 10: 5088.
Secularists, Civil Rights of. (E. G. Taylor) Westm. 143: 117.
Sedan, After the Battle of. (A. Forbes) McClure, 5: 80.
— in '70. (B. v. Tauber-Harper) Southern M. 4: 115.
— Napoleon III. at. (A. Forbes) 19th Cent. 31: 419.
Sedan Chair of Queen Henrietta Maria. Reliquary, 33: 238.
Sedan-chairs. Chamb. J. 72: 91.
Sedding, John D. Sat. R. 73: 47.
Sediments, Ancient, Progress in the Study of. (J. E. Marr) Sci. Prog. 4: 1.
— — Study of. (J. E. Marr) Sci. Prog. 4: 313.
Seeboeck, W. C. E. Music, 3: 332.
Seebohm, Frederic, on the Tribal System in Wales. (W. J. Ashley) Pol. Sci. Q. 11: 310.
Seebohm, Henry. (H. Saunders) Geog. J. 7: 103. — Nature, 53: 105. — Ath. '95, 2: 794. — Spec. 75: 817.
Seed Exhibits at Columbian Exhibition. (L. H. Bailey) Garden & F. 6: 319.
Seed-raising in Germany. Garden & F. 5: 111.
Seedlings, Advance in Knowledge of. (A. B. Rendle) Nat. Sci. 1: 751.
Seeds, Adaptation of, to Facilitate Germination. (M. Rowlee) Science, 20: 189.
— and Fruits, Adaptations of. (J. W. Folsom) Pop. Sci. Mo. 43: 218.
— Dispersal of, by Birds. (H. N. Ridley) Nat. Sci. 8: 186.
— Distribution of, by the Department of Agriculture. (C. S. Sargent) Garden & F. 7: 381.
— Hygroscopic. (A. S. Wilson) Knowl. 19: 169.
— Latent Vitality of. (I. Giglioli) Nature, 52: 544.
— Unripe, Deviation in Development due to. (J. C. Arthur) Am. Natural. 29: 806, 904.
— Vegetable, Raising of. (G. C. Butz) Garden & F. 5: 139.
— Vitality of. (W. B. Hemsley) Nature, 52: 5.
Seegà, an Egyptian Game. (H. C. Bolton) J. Am. Folk-Lore, 3: 132.
Seeking Evidence; a story. (Elizabeth W. Durbin) Bost. 4: 330.
Seeley, John Robert. Acad. 47: 57. — (J. Jacobs) Ath. '95, 1: 86. — Quar. 182: 281. — (J. R. Tanner) Eng. Hist. R. 10: 507. — Sat. R. 79: 89. — (M. Todhunter) Westm. 145: 503. — (H. A. L. Fisher) Fortn. 66: 183.
— an English Monist. (X. Clark) Open Court, 2: 899, 948.
— Natural Religion. (E. Thurtell) Open Court, 6: 3255.
Seeley, Leonard Benton. Acad. 44: 390.
Seelye, Julius H. Critic, 26: 371.
— Administration of, at Amherst College. (J. Bigham) Educa. 13: 597.
Seen and Unseen, New Story of. Spec. 70: 446.
Seen by the Coppice; a story. Argosy, 61: 331.
See-saw; a story. (J. F. Foster) Eng. Illust. 16: 193.
Segantini, Giovanni. (H. Zimmern) M. of Art, 20: 25.
— Works of. (J. Carotti) Art J. 47: 69.
Seghers, Archbishop, True Account of the Murder of. (F. Barnum) Am. Cath. Q. 19: 154.
Segovia, Pablo de. Sat. R. 74: 742.
Segur, Count de. Napoleonic Memoirs. (A. Laugel) Nation, 58: 445.
Seidl, Anton. (O. Hackett) Munsey, 7: 308.
Seigneur's Shooting-party; a story. (M. G. Cundil) Outing, 26: 413.
Sein, Ile de. (E. H. Barker) Temp. Bar, 105: 378.
Seine, The, the Meuse, and the Moselle. (W. M. Davis) Nation, 59: 172, 194. — (W. M. Davis) Nat. Geog. M. 7: 189, 228.
— Parisian Fishing Ground. (R. F. Hemenway) Outing, 24: 109.
Seisin. (C. Sweet) Law Q. 12: 239.
— Beatitude of. (F. W. Maitland) Law Q. 4: 24, 286.
— Mystery of. (F. W. Maitland) Law Q. 2: 481.
Sekiya Seikei. Nature, 53: 443.
Selaginellas, Cultural Notes on. (W. Scott) Garden & F. 9: 516.
Selamlik, The. Liv. Age, 208: 572.
Selborne, Roundell Palmer, Earl of. Memorials. Sat. R. 82: 192. — (C. W. Colby) Nation, 63: 313, 322. — (G. H. Knoté) Am. Law R. 29: 695. — Lond. Q. 87: 355. — Spec. 74: 639.
Selborne, Eng. Chamb. J. 70: 321. — (W. H. Hudson) Contemp. 69: 277. Same art. Ecl. M. 126: 365. Same art. Liv. Age, 208: 752.
— and Gilbert White. (H. P. Palmer) Temp. Bar, 109: 113. Same art. Liv. Age, 211: 248.
— White's Natural History of. (C. S. Sargent) Garden & F. 9: 1.
— Wild Flowers of. (J. Vaughan) Longm. 19: 53. Same art. Liv. Age, 193: 637.
Selborne Priory, Story of. Macmil. 75: 49.
Selden, John. Table-Talk. Spec. 71: 489.
— — Reynold's Edition. Sat. R. 74: 689.
Selection and Education. (A. Fouillée) Pop. Sci. Mo. 43: 349.
— Artificial, and the Marriage Problem. (Hiram M. Stanley) Monist, 2: 51.
— Germinal. (A. Weismann) Monist, 6: 250.
— — Weismann on. (E. G. Conklin) Science, n. s. 3: 853.
— in Man. (J. Beddoe) Sci. Prog. 5: 384.
— Natural, All-sufficiency of. (A. Weismann) Contemp. 64: 309, 596.
— — and Lamarckism. (W. P. Ball) Nat. Sci. 2: 337.
— — and Use-inheritance. (V. Yanos) Science, 21: 156.
— — Henslow on. (A. R. Wallace) Nat. Sci. 5: 177.

Selection, Natural, Inadequacy of. (H. Spencer) Contemp. 63: 153-743. Same art. Ecl. M. 120: 382, 538. Same art. Liv. Age, 197: 67, 341. Same art. Our Day, 12: 131. Same art. Pop. Sci. Mo. 42: 799 — 43: 473.
— — Spencer on. (G. J. Romanes) Contemp. 63: 499.
— — Spencer *vs.* Weismann. (G. J. Romanes; M. Hartog) Contemp. 64: 50.
— Physiological, A. R. Wallace on. (G. J. Romanes) Monist, 1: 1.
— Reproductive. (K. Pearson) Nat. Sci. 8: 321.
— Sexual, Darwinian Hypothesis of. (G. N. Douglass) Nat. Sci. 7: 326, 398.
— Social Phases (or Processes) of. (C. C. Closson) Q. J. Econ. 11: 92.
Selections. Gent. M. n. s. 49: 321.
Selenic Acid, Determination of, by Potassium Permanganate. (F. A. Gooch; C. F. Clemons) Am. J. Sci. 150: 51.
— Iodometric Determination of Selenious and Selenic Acids. (F. A. Gooch and A. W. Peirce) Am. J. Sci. 151: 31.
— Reduction of, by Hydrochloric Acid. (F. A. Gooch and P. S. Evans, Jr.) Am. J. Sci. 150: 400.
— — by Hydriodic Acid. (F. A. Gooch and W. G. Reynolds) Am. J. Sci. 150: 254.
— — by Potassium Bromide in Acid Solution. (F. A. Gooch and W. S. Scoville) Am. J. Sci. 150: 402.
Selenite, Remarkable Occurrence of. (J. E. Talmage) Science, 21: 85.
Selenium, Gravimetric Determination of. (A. W. Peirce) Am. J. Sci. 151: 416.
— Method for the Separation of, from Tellurium. (F. A. Gooch and A. W. Peirce) Am. J. Sci. 151: 181.
Selenium Monoxide, Existence of. (A. W. Peirce) Am. J. Sci. 152: 163.
Self and its Derangements. (W. R. Newbold) Pop. Sci. Mo. 49: 810.
— — Bradley's View of. (J. S. Mackenzie) Mind, 19: 304.
— The Ego as Identity of. (P. Carus) Open Court, 7: 3900.
— The Hidden. (A. Bodington) Open Court, 4: 2604, 2621.
Self-assertion and Self-denial. (J. S. Mackenzie) Int. J. Ethics, 5: 273.
Self-consciousness, Implications of. (J. Royce) New World, 1: 289.
— Social Consciousness and Nature. (J. Royce) Philos. R. 4: 465, 577.
— — Two Critical Points in Royce's Paper. (J. E. Russell) Philos. R. 5: 395.
— Some Observations on the Anomalies of. (J. Royce) Psychol. R. 2: 433, 574.
Self-control, Social Law of. (F. H. Wines) Char. R. 5: 57.
Self-Culture Clubs of St. Louis. (E. N. Plank) Lend a H. 12: 27.
Self-defence, Art of. Chamb. J. 70: 241.
Self-denial and Self-assertion. (J. S. Mackenzie) Int. J. Ethics, 5: 273.
Self-development and Self-surrender. (S. Bryant) Int. J. Ethics, 3: 308.
Self-evident, The. (D. Newport) Open Court, 2: 1416.
Self-government. (W. S. Lilly) Fortn. 60: 787.
— in the Colonies. (D. Mills) Canad. M. 2: 533.
— A Return to the Basic Principles of. (L. Elseffer) Am. M. Civics, 7: 488.
Self-help, Teacher's Aid to. (W. M. Thayer) Educa. 12: 597.
Self-knowledge and Socrates. (J. I. Beare) Mind, 21: 227.
Self-knowledge, Modern. Spec. 70: 447.
Self-made Martyr; a story. All the Year, 73: 372.
Self-multiplication, Myers on. Spec. 68: 330.
Self-realization. (A. E. Taylor) Int. J. Ethics, 6: 356.
— as the Moral Ideal. (J. Dewey) Philos. R. 2: 652.
— Intuitionism and. (H. Calderwood) Philos. R. 5: 337.
Self-respecting Servant, A; a story. (G. Allen) Eng. Illust. 11: 471.
Selfish Man. (Marguerite Merington) Cosmopol. 22: 99.
Selfishness. (W. M. Salter) Open Court, 5: 2827.
— as an Ethical Theory. (W. M. Salter) Open Court, 5: 2867.
— Modern. Spec. 69: 380.
— Philosophy of. (V. de Cleyre) Open Court, 5: 2871.
— a Psychological Argument. (A. H. Heinemann) Open Court, 5: 2869.
— Pure: Is it Natural? Spec. 73: 77.
Selkirk, Alexander, Will of, 1720. (H. F. Waters) N. E. Reg. 50: 539.
Selkirk Mountains. Around World, 1: 10.
— Stalking the Haplocerus in the. (W. A. Baillie-Grohman) Eng. Illust. 13: 127.
Sellers, Nathan, Diary of, 1776-78. (H. W. Sellers) Pennsyl. M. 16: 191.
Selmeston Church, Sussex. Antiq. n. s. 31: 298.
Selous, Frederick C., with portrait. (W. T. Stead) R. of Rs. (N. Y.) 7: 425.
Selsey, Isle of. (C. R. L. Fletcher) Time, 19: 589. — (J. S. Little) Art J. 46: 171.
Semaphore, The. (H. D. Ward) Scrib. M. 14: 760.
Sembratowicz, Cardinal, with portrait. (B. J. Clinch) Cath. World, 63: 141.
Semi-Azimuths, Navigation by, Buller on. Nature, 49: 223.
Semi-Final, The; a story. (E. S. Grew) Idler, 9: 525.
Semites, Early, and Accad. Open Court, 9: 4651.
Semitic Literature, Drama in. (D. B. Macdonald) Bib. World, 5: 16.
Semitic Religions. Ed. R. 175: 325.
Semper, Carl. (J. Beard) Nature, 48: 271.
Senate, U. S., and the House of Lords. (J. C. Hopkins) Am. J. Pol. 5: 461. — (R. Ogden) Nation, 57: 184.
— and the Silver Question. Spec. 71: 506.
— The Attack on the. (C. D. Warner) Cent. 26: 374.
— Character Sketches of. (E. J. Edwards) Chaut. 19: 706.
— Decline of the. (M. M. Trumbull) Open Court, 7: 3895.
— Dignity of. (E. L. Godkin) Nation, 62: 230.
— Dilatory, and Trade Depression. (L. Windmüller) Forum, 17: 326.
— Freedom of Debate in. (E. N. Dingley) Am. J. Pol. 4: 49.
— Has it decayed? (Goldwin Smith) Sat. R. 81: 467.
— in the Light of History. Forum, 16: 272.
— Is it unfairly constituted? (S. E. Moffett) Pol. Sci. Q. 10: 448.
— Ought it to be abolished? (H. von Holst) Monist, 5: 1.
— Ought it to be reformed? (M. D. Conway) Monist, 5: 223.
— Our House of Lords. (J. F. Hume) Am. J. Pol. 4: 348.
— Reform of. (M. D. Conway) Open Court, 8: 4009.
— Rights of. Soc. Econ. 5: 271.
— Shall it rule the Republic? (H. von Holst) Forum, 16: 263.
— Situation in, in Oct., 1893. Pub. Opin. 16: 68.

Senate, U. S., Struggle in, 1893. (W. M. Stewart; H. C. Lodge) No. Am. **157**: 513. — (E. L. Godkin) Nation, **57**: 262.
— The West in the. (W. H. Bryant) Nation, **57**: 268.
Senates, New England, Colonial Origins of. (F. L. Riley) J. H. Univ. Stud. **14**: 101.
Senator Stanley's Story. (T. C. Crawford) Cosmopol. **15**: 686.
Senator's Daughters; a novel. (A. C. Wheeler) Chaut. **21**: 538, 665. **22**: 45–417.
Senators, United States, Choice of. (J. H. Flagg) New Eng. M. n. s. **14**: 190.
— Election of, by People. (W. Clark) Arena, **10**: 453. — (G. F. Edmunds) Forum, **18**: 270. — (J. Haynes) J. H. Univ. Studies, **11**: 547. — (W. P. Garrison) Nation, **54**: 44. — (J. H. Mitchell) Forum, **21**: 385.
— — Mode of. Pub. Opin. **14**: 391.
Sendschirli, Excavations at. (M. Jastrow, Jr.) Bib. World, **3**: 406. — (D. H. Müller) Contemp. **65**: 563.
Seneca and the Discovery of America. (E. G. Bourne) Acad. **43**: 130, 154.
— and St. Paul, External Evidence as to Writings of. (C. M. Mead) Presb. & Ref. R. **4**: 289.
Senior, N. W., Reminiscences of. (M. C. M. Simpson) New R. **8**: 214.
Sennacherib, Hezekiah and Sargon. (J. Horner) Meth. R. **53**: 74.
Señorita's Ghost, The; a story. Argosy, **54**: 473.
Senoussi; the Sheikh of Jerboub. Blackw. **156**: 27. Same art. Liv. Age, **202**: 274.
Sensation and Memory. (P. Carus) Open Court, **2**: 1431.
— and the Outer World. (A. Binet) Open Court, **3**: 1535.
Sensational Literature. All the Year, **71**: 224.
Sensations, Analysis of. (E. Mach) Monist, **1**: 48.
— and Elements of Reality. (E. Mach) Monist, **1**: 393.
Sense and Sentiment. (W. D. Howells) Outl. **51**: 304.
— Meaning, and Interpretation. (V. Welby) Mind, **21**: 24, 186.
Sense-impressions, Simple, Affective Tone of. (B. R. Major) Am. J. Psychol. **7**: 57.
Sense Stimulations, Simultaneous. (A. Tanner and K. Anderson) Psychol. R. **3**: 378.
Senses, the, "Mutual Aid Society" of. (S. M. Miller) Pop. Sci. Mo. **46**: 640.
— of the Lower Animals. (J. Weir, jr.) No. Am. **158**: 245.
— Origin of. Sat. R. **81**: 471.
— Physical, Education of. (J. S. Black) Educa. **16**: 68.
Sensible Woman, A; a story. (Mrs. A. Dean) Eng. Illust. **13**: 67.
Sensitive Plant, A; a story. All the Year, **75**: 400.
Sensitiveness, Transfer of, from Men to Inert Substances. (H. Gaullieur) Arena, **15**: 33.
Sensorial and Muscular Reaction. (A. R. Hill and R. Watanabe) Am. J. Psychol. **6**: 242.
Sensory Stimulation by Attention. (J. G. Hibben) Psychol. R. **2**: 369.
Sentence of Ostracism; a story. (F. Lynde) Munsey, **11**: 585.
Sentences, Indeterminate. (G. M. Buck) Am. M. Civics, **6**. 624.
— — for Penitentiaries. (W. F. Spalding) Lend a H. **16**: 23.
— Penal. (G. R. Vicars) Gent. M. n. s. **51**: 294.
Sententiousness. Spec. **70**: 602.
Sentiment, Aspects of. (J. B. Firth) Westm. **138**: 125.
— Value of. (Henry Lee) Am. Arch. **47**: 105.
Sentimental Tommy. (J. M. Barrie) Scrib. M. **19**: 13 — **20**: 561.
Sentimental Travelling. Macmil. **70**: 445.
Separated; a poem. (I. F. Mayo) Argosy, **61**: 597.
Separation, and its Bearing on Geology and Zoögeography. (A. E. Ortmann) Am. J. Sci. **152**: 63.
September; a poem. (A. C. Swinburne) M. of Art, **11**: 367.
September 13, 1894, on the N. P. R.; a story. (J. Heard) Scrib. M. **19**: 115.
Septuagint, Origin and History of. (C. van den Biesen) Dub. R. **117**: 41.
— Philonean Text of. (F. C. Conybeare) Jew. Q. **5**: 246. **8**: 88.
— *vs.* Hebrew Text. (H. H. Howorth) Acad. **45**: 149.
Sepulchral Art, Early Irish. Chamb. J. **71**: 555.
Sepulchral Cross-slabs, Some Ancient. (K. E. Stigan) Sund. M. **22**: 703.
Sepulchre, Holy, Site of. (M. MacColl) Contemp. **63**: 167.
Sequel, A; a story. Temp. Bar, **99**: 549.
Sequelæ, A Discourse on. Macmil. **70**: 28. Same art. Ecl. M. **123**: 104. Same art. Liv. Age, **201**: 549.
Sequoia Gigantea. Garden & F. **5**: 541.
Serao, M. Il Paese die Cuccagna. Atlan. **70**: 276.
Serapeum at Alexandria, Discovery of. Acad. **48**: 230.
Serapis. (F. Legge) Scot. R. **28**: 33.
Serenade, A; a poem. (W. Toynbee) Argosy, **58**: 304.
Serenade at Siskiyou; a story. (O. Wister) Harper, **89**: 383.
Serene's Religious Experience; an Inland Story. (C. A. Pratt) Cent. **23**: 285.
Serfdom, English, History of, Prof. Vinogradoff on. (W. J. Ashley) Econ. R. **3**: 153.
Sergeant Crœsus. (C. King) Lippinc. **52**: 643.
Sergeant O'Brien, of Siskiyou. (S. C. Garrison) Overland, n. s. **22**: 264.
Seriland. (W. J. McGee; W. D. Johnson) Nat. Geog. M. **7**: 125.
— Expedition to. (W. J. McGee) Science, n. s. **3**: 493.
Serious Dilemma of the Bishop of Oklaho; a story. (O. F. Adams) Munsey, **11**: 278.
Seriousness, Plea for. Atlan. **69**: 625.
Sergeant-at-Arms, The. (M. MacDonagh) Good Words, **37**: 699.
Sermione, A Morning at. (E. O. Kirk) Atlan. **70**: 776.
Sermon on the Mount. (W. B. Carpenter) Sund. M. **24**: 18–810.
— Free Translation of. (E. P. Burtt) Bib. World, **3**: 336.
— Lessons from. (W. M. Sinclair) Good Words, **35**: 571.
— Social Doctrine of. (C. Gore) Econ. R. **2**: 145.
— Spiritual Meaning of. (W. H. Mayhew) N. Church R. **3**: 192.
— What it Has to Do with the Gospel. (W. F. Cooley) Chr. Lit. **11**: 169 a.
Sermons, Some Modern. Church Q. **34**: 470.
— Traffic in. (B. G. Johns) 19th Cent. **31**: 197.
Serpent, The, and the Stage. (Dr. A. Stradling) Chamb. J. **72**: 237.
— as a Symbol of the Rain Cloud. (S. D. Peet) Am. Antiq. **16**: 367.
Serpent of the Nile, A; a story. (J. Graham) Good Words, **34**: 486.
Serpent Worship in Egypt. (A. H. Sayce) Contemp. **64**: 523. Same art. Ecl. M. **121**: 832.
Serpent's Tongue, The. (W. H. Hudson) Fortn. **60**: 198.
Serpents. Adders swallowing their Young. Sat. R. **79**: 279.
— Cobra and other. (G. R. O'Reilly) Pop. Sci. Mo. **46**: 67.
— Feeding of. (A. Stradling) Knowl. **18**: 1.

Sertularian Polypidoms. (P. L. Addison) Knowl. **19**: 141.
Serum Therapeutics. (F. W. Andrewes) Nat. Sci. **8**: 105.
— First Steps in. Nature, **53**: 138.
Servant of Jahveh. (W. H. Cobb) J. Bib. Lit. **14**: 95.
Servant Question, The. (M. Jeune) Fortn. **58**: 65.
Servants. (M. C. Hungerford) Lippinc. **56**: 566.
— Domestic. *See* Domestic Servants.
— Faithful. Gent. M. n. s. **47**: 106.
— in India. Chamb. J. **69**: 717.
— Ladies as. (E. M. Phillips) Fortn. **58**: 193.
— London, High and Low. (G. F. Millin) Eng. Illust. **11**: 939.
— Men, A Butler's View of. (J. Robinson) 19th Cent. **31**: 925.
— — in England. (V. Greville) National, **18**: 812. Same art. Liv. Age, **193**: 50.
— — in India. (C. T. Buckland) National, **18**: 663. Same art. Liv. Age, **192**: 667.
— Mistresses and. (C. G. J. Reeve) Longm. **21**: 497. Same art. Liv. Age, **196**: 659.
— Our Young. Longm. **25**: 631.
— Tyrannies of Private Life. (E. L. Linton) National, **26**: 170. Same art. Ecl. M. **125**: 707.
Servetus, Michael. (C. McRae) Gent. M. n. s. **48**: 120. Same art. Pop. Sci. Mo. **41**: 519. — (J. H. Allen) New World, **1**: 639.
— and Calvin. (P. Schaff) Ref. Q. **40**: 5.
— Trial of. (C. W. Shields) Presb. & Ref. R. **4**: 353.
Servia. Eng. R. **8**: 74. — (H. Vivian) New R. **15**: 656.
— Coup d'état in. (A. C. Coolidge) Nation, **56**: 330.
— Politics of, 1896. Sat. R. **82**: 31.
— Superstitions of. (G. Maxwell) Chamb. J. **70**: 537.
Service, Law of. (W. E. Brokaw) Am. J. Pol. **5**: 370.
— Types of. (J. Iverach) Thinker, **8**: 130.
Service of a Village Knight, The; a story. (Marian Bowen) National, **22**: 850. Same art. Liv. Age, **200**: 712.
Service Book of the 7th Century. Church Q. **37**: 337.
— of Aquitaine, Mediæval. (R. Twigge) Dub. R. **115**: 279. **117**: 57. **119**: 283.
Setting the Clock back. (C. J. Langston) Argosy, **60**: 409.
Settlements, University, in London. (T. C. Collings) Leis. Hour, **44**: 600–796.
Seume, Gottfried; a Poet among the Hessians. (C. Bierwith) Harv. Mo. **16**: 1.
Seva, Etymology of the Term. (C. Levias) Am. J. Philol. **16**: 28.
Seven and Three; Mystic Numbers. (A. Gaye) National, **21**: 196. Same art. Liv. Age, **197**: 666.
Seven Princesses; Drama. (M. Maeterlinck) Poet-Lore, **6**: 29, 87, 150.
Sevenoaks, Remarkable Barrow at. (W. J. L. Abbott) Anthrop. J. **25**: 130.
"Seven-up" Blaine's Conversion. Chamb. J. **72**: 804–820.
Several: Peculiar Uses of the Word. (F. Hall) Nation, **61**: 363.
Severn, Joseph. (R. B. Johnson) Acad. **41**: 318.
— Keats and. (William Graham) New R. **10**: 593.
— Life of, Sharp's. Ath. '92, **1**: 429. — Sat. R. **73**: 457.
— Roman Journals. (W. Sharp) Atlan. **69**: 631.
Severn River, from Source to Shrewsbury. (E. R. Dibdin) M. of Art, **19**: 482.
Sévigné, Madame de, with portrait. (A. S. Bailey) Cath. World, **59**: 608. — (E. L. Didier) Chaut. **24**: 4.
Seville. (D. Hannay) M. of Art, **7**: 327, 359. — (H. C. Chatfield-Taylor) Cosmopol. **21**: 3.
Seville, Corpus Christi in. (C. E. White) Lippinc. **55**: 273.
— Lay Brotherhoods of. (B. Evetts) Month, **77**: 491.
— Sevillana. (Mabel Thayer) Scrib. M. **19**: 169.
Sevillian Vignettes. (M. Wilcox) Cosmopol. **13**: 4.
Sewage, Disposal of, at Wayne, Pa. (G. E. Waring, jr.) Am. Arch. **37**: 5.
— — in the U. S. (G. W. Rafter) Engin. M. **2**: 496.
— — — Rafter on. (G. E. Waring, jr.) Nation, **58**: 239.
— — Methods of. (G. E. Waring, jr.) Cent. **25**: 939.
— — Waring on. (A. A. Woodhull) Nation, **59**: 221.
— Purification of, Future Methods of. (W. L. Hedenberg) Engin. M. **10**: 76.
— Treatment of, by the Aluminoferric Process. Chamb. J. **69**: 746.
Sewall, Arthur. (T. Roosevelt) R. of Rs. (N. Y.) **14**: 289.
Sewall, David, Library of. (F. Sewall) New Eng. M. n. s. **13**: 406.
Sewall, Rev. Joseph, Memoir of. (H. A. Hill) N. E. Reg. **46**: 3.
Seward, W. H. Attitude toward Compromise and Secession, 1860–1861. (F. Bancroft) Atlan. **74**: 597.
— Lothrop's Life of. Nation, **63**: 347.
— Recollections of. (J. M. Scovel) Lippinc. **51**: 237.
Sewer Gas and Disease. (A. C. Ranyard) Knowl. **17**: 57.
Sewer Rat in London. (W. Wemley) Eng. Illust. **14**: 369.
Sewerage of Charlottetown, P. E. I. (G. E. Waring, jr.) Am. Arch. **40**: 113.
— Shore Hydro-pneumatic System of. (U. H. Broughton) Am. Arch. **40**: 4.
Sewers and Sewage Disposal. (R. Hering) Engin. M. **8**: 1007.
— *vs.* Rivers. (S. Charlesworth) Gent. M. n. s. **56**: 630.
Sewing-machine, Story of the. Chamb. J. **72**: 597.
Sex and Art. (C. Scott) Am. J. Psychol. **7**: 153.
— Each, its own Moralist. (Emma Brooke) New R. **13**: 628.
— Feeling and Ideas of, in Children. (E. Barnes) Pedagog. Sem. **2**: 199.
— in Education. (Sir J. C. Browne) Educa. R. **4**: 164.
— in Mathematics. (D. E. Smith) Educa. R. **10**: 84.
— Material Relations of, in Human Society. (E. D. Cope) Monist, **1**: 38.
— Rôle of. (J. B. Haycraft) Nat. Sci. **7**: 193, 245, 342.
Sex Question in U. S. (E. D. Cope) Open Court, **3**: 2070.
Sexes, The, in the U. S., Distribution of, in 1890. (W. F. Willcox) Am. J. Sociol. **1**: 725.
— Relation of the. (A. Gilbertson) Westm. **144**: 571.
— — Knowledge a Young Woman's Right. (Mrs. W. M. A. Hawksley) Westm. **142**: 315.
— — A Study in. (A. E. Crawley) Anthrop. J. **24**: 430.
Sexual Characteristics. (F. L. Oswald) Open Court, **3**: 1812, 1922.
Sexual Ethics. (P. Carus) Open Court, **4**: 2675.
Sexual Problem, The. (Beswicke Ancrum) Westm. **141**: 512. **142**: 681.
— Rejoinder. (B. Ancrum) Westm. **143**: 171.
Sexual Purity. (J. Bellangee) Arena, **11**: 370.
Sexual Selection, On the Darwinian Hypothesis of. (G. N. Douglass) Nat. Sci. **7**: 326, 398.
Sexual Taboo. (A. E. Crawley) Anthrop. J. **24**: 116.
Sexuality, Fiction of. (J. A. Noble) Contemp. **67**: 490. Same art. Ecl. M. **124**: 745.
Seychelles, The. (A. Brauer) Geog. J. **8**: 372.
Sfax and Mahdia. (T. A. Archer) New R. **15**: 724.

Sforza, Caterina. (P. M. Watkins) Acad. 44: 411. — (J. Cartwright) Art J. 46: 115. — (H. Zimmern) Blackw. 159: 509. Same art. Liv. Age, 209: 451. Same art. Ecl. M. 127: 400.
Sforza Book of Hours. (J. C. Robinson) Bibliographica, 1: 428. — Blackw. 154: 128.
— Miniatures and Borders from, with Introd. by Warner. Sat. R. 78: 638.
Sgeul of Black Murdo, The; a story. (N. Munro) Blackw. 159: 266.
Shabby, Shy Man, A; a story. (G. B. O'Halloran) Gent. M. n. s. 52: 433.
Shad, The: Its Annual Pilgrimage. (A. H. Gouraud) Pop. Sci. Mo. 46: 818.
Shad-bush, Western. Garden & F. 5: 409.
Shad-float, On a. (D. B. Fitzgerald) Lippinc. 55: 692.
Shadow from the Moors; a story. Belgra. 83: 191.
Shadow of Death; a Tale of the Ashanti War. (C. Stein) Blackw. 155: 543. Same art. Ecl. M. 122: 812.
Shadow of Revenge, The; a story. (L. D. Mitchell) Outing, 20: 373.
Shadow on the Blind, The. Cornh. 70: 281.
Shadow on the Red House. (F. H. Cogswell) New Eng. M. n. s. 13: 452.
Shadow Boatswain, The; a poem. (B. Carman) McClure, 1: 205.
Shadowed; a story. All the Year, 72: 271.
Shadows from an Old Sun-dial. (Fred. Gale) Time, 8: 72-577.
— The Painter of. (M. A. M. Marks) Argosy, 61: 668.
Shaft Friction, Effect of Compression upon. (G. I. Alden) Cassier, 1: 8.
Shaftesbury, 3d Earl of, Relation to Utilitarianism. (E. Albee) Philos. R. 5: 24.
Shah Jehan, Story of. (Annie Besant) Univ. R. 3: 200.
Shaker Community, Union Village, Ohio. (J. K. Reeve) New Eng. M. n. s. 6: 349.
Shaker Romance, A; a story. (C. S. Haight) Munsey, 12: 625.
Shakers and Shakerism. (H. M. Poole) Open Court, 1: 449.
Shakspere, William. (J. Hamer) Belgra, 78: 398.
— Absence of Religion in. (G. Santayana) New World, 5: 681.
— The Advertiser's. (E. B. V. Christian) Gent. M. n. s. 50: 305.
— All 's Well that ends Well. (E. A. Abbey and A. Lang) Harper, 85: 213.
— — Performed by Irving Dramatic Club. Sat. R. 79: 150.
— Ancestry of. (J. P. Yeatman; H. P. Stokes) Acad. 48: 365, 388.
— and the Art of Painting. (W. W. Fenn) M. of Art, 12: 202.
— and his Contemporaries. (H. P. Stokes) Ath. '95, 2: 690.
— and the Copyright. (H. Davis) Atlan. 71: 256.
— and the Greek Tragedians. Hamlet and Orestes. (P. Stapfer) Poet-Lore, 6: 187.
— and the Jews. (J. W. Hales) Eng. Hist. R. 9: 652.
— and Lyly. (H. Davis) Poet-Lore, 5: 177.
— and a Municipal Theatre. (A. Dillon) Westm. 143: 418.
— and the Public. (Wm. Archer) Time, 12: 64.
— and Puritanism. (J. W. Hales) Contemp. 67: 54.
— and Racine. (P. Verlaine) Fortn. 62: 440.
— and Rhythm. (E. P. Mott) Poet-Lore, 4: 212.
— Antony and Cleopatra. (O. F. Emerson) Poet-Lore, 2: 71-188.
— — Comradeship of. (S. E. Peart) Poet-Lore, 4: 217.
Shakspere, William. Antony and Cleopatra, Moral Proportion and Fatalism in. (E. A. Moore) Poet-Lore, 7: 613.
— as a Citizen. (J. S. S. Glennie) Poet-Lore, 2: 1.
— as a French Hero. Liv. Age, 208: 446.
— as a Historian. Spec. 68: 265.
— As You Like it, Character in. (C. A. Wurtzburg) Poet-Lore, 4: 31, 81.
— — in 1896. (G. B. Shaw) Sat. R. 82: 585.
— at Elsinore. (J. Stefansson) Contemp. 69: 20.
— Authorship of, Baconian. (E. Reed) Arena, 6: 188-692. — (A. Nicholson) Arena, 7: 12. — (W. J. Rolfe) Arena, 7: 173, 279. — (F. J. Furnivall) Arena, 7: 441. — (I. Donnelly) Arena, 7: 733. — (A. R. Wallace and others) Arena, 8: 222. — (E. C. Stedman and others) Arena, 8: 366. — (M. J. Savage and others) Arena, 8: 492. — (R. A. Proctor) Arena, 8: 672. — (W. E. Russell and others) Arena, 8: 733.
— — Bacon "Farce" a tragedy. (E. G. Clark) Cosmopol. 5: 225.
— — Controversy on. (B. W. Ball) Open Court, 1: 585.
— — Literature on Baconian. Poet-Lore, 1: 69.
— Bartlett's Concordance to. (W. P. Garrison) Nation, 59: 218. — Critic, 25: 182. — (H. Corson) Dial (Ch.) 17: 193. — Sat. R. 78: 577.
— Beer-jug of. Spec. 70: 847.
— Birds and Beasts in. Quar. 178: 340. Same art. Liv. Age, 202: 155.
— Boydell's Gallery. (A. Beaver) M. of Art, 9: 218.
— Catholic View of. (J. Malone) Cath. World, 55: 716.
— Chronology, Study of. (A. Morgan) Cath. World, 62: 449.
— Commemorations of. (G. Morley) Belgra. 82: 72.
— Commemorative Festival. (Charlotte C. Stopes) Poet-Lore, 8: 342.
— Compliment of, to Brantôme. (C. H. Hunton) Poet-Lore, 4: 449.
— Coriolanus, Moral Proportion and Fatalism in. (E. A. Moore) Poet-Lore, 8: 86.
— Country of, Pilgrimage to. (C. C. Stopes) Poet-Lore, 4: 371.
— Critics of, Where they disagree. (L. Howard) Poet-Lore, 5: 143.
— Cymbeline at the Lyceum. (R. W. Bond) Fortn. 66: 635. — Sat. R. 82: 339.
— — Stage History of. Theatre, 37: 121.
— Did he write his Plays? (A. B. Farquhar) Am. J. Pol. 2: 245.
— Emendators of. (J. T. Kay) Time, 17: 308.
— English of, among Southern Negroes. (W. C. Elam) Lippinc. 55: 824.
— Fact and Fiction about. (H. Lacey) Theatre, 34: 88.
— Falstaff and Queen Elizabeth. (H. A. Kennedy) 19th Cent. 39: 316.
— — Dying Words of. (L. Richardson) Critic, 29: 333.
— First Editions of. Bookworm, 2: 314.
— First Folio. (T. F. Ordish) Bookworm, 1: 161-255.
— A French View of. (E. Brain) Theatre, 36: 208.
— Friendship of, with Mr. "W. H." and the Dark Lady. (L. W. Spring) Educa. 14: 599.
— Furness's Edition. Atlan. 76: 270.
— Genealogy of. (J. P. Yeatman; H. P. Stokes) Acad. 48: 272, 298, 342.
— Gloves of. (S. W. Beck) Walford's Antiq. 6: 103.
— Guesses at. (H. S. Wilson) Gent. M. n. s. 57: 423.
— Hamlet. Sat. R. 73: 126.
— — Oxford Edition, 1890. Sat. R. 78: 602.

Shakspere, William. Hamlet and Don Quixote. (I. Turgenief) Poet-Lore, **4**: 169.
— — and the Modern Stage. (M. Morris) Macmil. **65**: 357.
— — from an Actor's Prompt-book. (H. Beerbohm Tree) Fortn. **64**: 863.
— — from the Standpoint of Theology. (A. H. Ames) Meth. R. **53**: 369.
— — Guess at the Origin of. (A. T. Lyttelton) National, **28**: 532.
— — Moral Proportion and Fatalism in. (E. A. Moore) Poet-Lore, **7**: 191.
— Henry IV. and Falstaff on the Stage. (F. Hawkins) Theatre, **36**: 211.
— — in 1896. Sat. R. **81**: 500.
— Henry V., Ideal King of Shakspere. (L. W. Spring) Educa. **16**: 577.
— Henry VIII. Gent. M. n. s. **48**: 214, 427. — (W. Andrews) Theatre, **29**: 59. — Sat. R. **73**: 37.
— — at the Lyceum Theatre. (F. Wedmore) Acad. **41**: 70.
— — Authorship of. (E. Rose) Acad. **41**: 163–402.
— — on the Stage. (F. Hawkins) Eng. Illust. **9**: 291. — (R. W. Lowe and W. Archer) Longm. **19**: 249.
— Home and Haunts of. R. of Rs. (N. Y.) **5**: 567.
— How he illustrates Bacon. (H. M. Huguinn) Poet-Lore, **4**: 200.
— How to Study. (A. Morgan) Cath. World, **57**: 777.
— Ignorance concerning Coast of Bohemia. (C. Porter) Poet-Lore, **6**: 196.
— in Lexicography. (F. H. Teall) Dial (Ch.) **20**: 295.
— in Southwark. (L. Alldridge) Bookworm, **3**: 113.
— International, Illustrations to. (M. H. Spielmann) M. of Art, **14**: 231.
— Isabel, and Sophocles' Antigone. (W. L. Sheldon) Poet-Lore, **4**: 609.
— Italian Influence on. (C. F. Walters) Gent. M. n. s. **55**: 571.
— Juliet's "Runawayes Eyes." (J. W. Hales) Longm. **19**: 407. — (E. C. Stedman) Poet-Lore, **4**: 14.
— Julius Cæsar. (J. Wedgwood) Contemp. **63**: 356. — (W. J. Rolfe) Poet-Lore, **5**: 169, 424. **6**: 7.
— — and Browning's Strafford. Poet-Lore, **4**: 148.
— — Character of, Is it Ignoble? (A. R. Wall) Poet-Lore, **4**: 191.
— Kate "the Curst" as an Elizabethan "New Woman." (A. S. Way) Poet-Lore, **8**: 169.
— Katharine, and Ibsen's Nora. (E. Crowell) Poet-Lore, **8**: 192.
— King John, Moral Proportion and Fatalism in. (E. A. Moore) Poet-Lore, **8**: 139.
— King Lear at the Lyceum. (H. J. Jennings) Gent. M. n. s. **49**: 624, 634.
— — Famous Actors in. (H. J. Jennings) Gent. M. n. s. **49**: 509.
— — History of the Play. (G. W. Dancy) Theatre, **29**: 209.
— — Layamon's King Leir and Cordoille. Poet-Lore, **4**: 19.
— — on the Stage. (F. Hawkins) Eng. Illust. **10**: 157.
— Law in, Audacious. (Van Buren Denslow) Soc. Econ. **9**: 190.
— Love's Labor's Lost. (Sir E. Strachey) Atlan. **71**: 106. — (A. Lang and E. A. Abbey) Harper, **86**: 900. — (W. J. Rolfe) Poet-Lore, **1**: 84.
— Lovers in Plays of. (D. H. Wheeler) Chaut. **15**: 558.
— Macbeth. (J. F. Kirk) Atlan. **75**: 507.
Shakspere, William. Macbeth, at the Lyceum. (H. A. Kennedy) Univ. R. **3**: 135.
— — Lady, Stage Types of. (M. Ross) Poet-Lore, **5**: 90.
— — Materials for. (C. C. Stopes) Ath. '96, **2**: 138.
— — Studies in. (A. H. Tolman) Atlan. **69**: 241.
— — A Study of. (S. E. Hawley) Educa. **16**: 537.
— — Supernatural in. (W. Townsend) Canad. M. **3**: 199.
— Macbeth Revival, Stage Setting of. (M. H. Spielmann) M. of Art, **12**: 98.
— MacMonnies's Statue of. Critic, **28**: 312.
— Madness as portrayed by. (F. Winslow) Arena, **15**: 414.
— Master Reader of Humanity. (G. Holmes) Munsey, **10**: 117.
— Midsummer Night's Dream. (W. J. Rolfe) Poet-Lore, **1**: 184, 232, 280.
— — Edited by Daly. Sat. R. **80**: 43. — (E. E. Hale, jr.) Dial (Ch.) **19**: 176.
— — Furness's Edition. (G. L. Kittredge) Nation, **61**: 84. — Sat. R. **79**: 794.
— — Illustrated by Abbey. (A. Lang) Harper, **91**: 328.
— — Study of. (A. M. Lathe) Educa. **12**: 406.
— Miranda, and Tennyson's Elaine. (S. D. Davies) Poet-Lore, **5**: 15.
— Much Ado about Nothing. (W. J. Rolfe) Poet-Lore, **4**: 184. — (C. A. Wurtzburg) Poet-Lore, **6**: 491, 616.
— — Character in. (C. A. Wurtzburg) Poet-Lore, **6**: 126.
— — Dramatic Passion in. (C. A. Wurtzburg) Poet-Lore, **6**: 550.
— — Introduction to. (C. A. Wurtzburg) Poet-Lore, **6**: 70.
— Music in. (H. A. Clarke) Music, **1**: 519.
— Mutilated by A. Daly. Theatre, **35**: 63.
— Mutilators of, Early. (W. H. Hudson) Poet-Lore, **4**: 360.
— Natural History of, and Titus Andronicus. (P. Robinson) Contemp. **65**: 392. Same art. Ecl. M. **122**: 547. Same art. Liv. Age, **201**: 233.
— The Novelist in. (Hall Caine) New R. **11**: 120. Same art. Liv. Age, **203**: 259. Same art. Ecl. M. **123**: 388.
— Obscure Words in. (C. Mackay) Walford's Antiq. **1**: 190. **2**: 5.
— — A Reply. (B. Nicholson) Walford's Antiq. **3**: 177, 226.
— Old Saws of. (W. C. Elam) Lippinc. **58**: 567.
— on the French Stage. (F. C. de Sumichrast) Harv. Mo. **18**: 43.
— on the Labor Question; a Study from "The Tempest." (W. Schuyler) Open Court, **5**: 2931.
— Open-air Amateur Performances of. (M. A. Winston) New Eng. M. n. s. **10**: 167.
— Opening Scenes of his Plays. (C. W. Hodell) Poet-Lore, **6**: 169, 337, 452.
— Original Portrait of. (T. E. Pemberton) Theatre, **27**: 137.
— Physiognomy of. (T. F. Ordish) Bookworm, **1**: 121.
— Piscine Lore of. (C. Cordley) Gent. M. n. s. **54**: 30.
— Plays of, Should they be Acted? (W. H. Pollock) National, **19**: 231.
— Poems, Use of Alliteration in. (S. E. Bengough) Poet-Lore, **5**: 190.
— Portrait of, Supposed New. Acad. **48**: 552.
— Pseudo-Shakespearean Plays. (A. Morgan) Cath. World, **55**: 203, 397.

Shakspere, William, Recent German Works on. (C. H. Herford) Acad. 46: 44.
— Repetitions of. (W. T. W. Ball) New Eng. M. n. s. 13: 657.
— Richard III. performed in 1896. (G. B. Shaw) Sat. R. 82: 671.
— Romeo and Juliet, at the Lyceum Theatre, 1895. Sat. R. 80: 409.
— Romeo and Rosaline. (L. M. Griffiths) Poet-Lore, 1: 205.
— Some Characteristics of. (E. Caird) Contemp. 70: 818.
— Songs of. (S. L. Gwynn) Acad. 48: 369.
— Sonnets of. (I. Goodlet) Poet-Lore, 3: 505.
— — New Word on. (I. Goodlet) Poet-Lore, 4: 505.
— — The Stolen Key. (R. Shindler) Gent. M. n. s. 48: 70.
— Stage-life of; Gentle Will, our Fellow. (F. G. Fleay) Poet-Lore, 5: 7-612.
— Stratford Festival. (R. W. Bond) Macmil. 69: 451.
— Study of. (H. H. Furness) Poet-Lore, 1: 109.
— Supernatural in. (A. R. Wall) Poet-Lore, 5: 490, 557, 620.
— Taming of the Shrew. (A. Lang and E. A. Abbey) Harper, 90: 89. — (W. J. Rolfe) Poet-Lore, 8: 182.
— Teaching. (C. L. Maxcy) School R. 1: 105.
— Tempest, The. (A. Lang and E. A. Abbey) Harper, 84: 653.
— — Date and Occasion of. (R. Garnett) Univ. R. 3: 556.
— — Furness's Edition. Atlan. 70: 272. — (F. A. March) Nation, 55: 112.
— — Study Programme. (Charlotte Porter and Helen A. Clarke) Poet-Lore, 8: 347.
— Text of. (H. H. Furness) Poet-Lore, 3: 335.
— Tragedies. Moral Proportion and Fatalism of Passion in. (E. A. Moore) Poet-Lore, 7: 75-551.
— Twelfth Night. (A. Lang) Harper, 86: 327.
— — Acted in 16th Century Manner. Sat. R. 80: 75.
— — Clown in. (W. Townsend) Canad. M. 4: 59.
— Two Gentlemen of Verona. (A. M. Lathe) Acad. (Syr.) 7: 24. — (E. A. Abbey and A. Lang) Harper, 88: 134. — (W. J. Rolfe) Poet-Lore, 1: 130.
— — arranged by Daly. Sat. R. 80: 10.
— Variorum, Furness's. Spec. 69: 324.
— Venus and Adonis, Music of, Language as Illustrated in. (S. E. Bengough) Poet-Lore, 4: 562.
— Venus and Adonis, Who Wrote? (W. Truitt) Poet-Lore, 7: 28.
— Wendell on. (E. E. Hale, Jr.) Dial (Ch.) 18: 13.
— Winter's Tale. Acad. 41: 18. — (E. A. Abbey and A. Lang) Harper. 88: 710.
— Women of. (J. Hamer) Belgra. 77: 304. — (I. G. Tompkins) Chaut. 16: 74.
— The Young; a Study of Romeo. (J. J. Chapman) Atlan. 78: 707.
Shakspere Commemorations. (G. Morley) Poet-Lore, 2: 252, 306. 3: 204.
Shakspere Family Annals. Poet-Lore, 2: 258, 315.
Shakspere Year, 1891-92. Bookworm, 5: 249.
Shaksperean Courtship; a Tale. (F. L. Pollock) Canad. M. 7: 372.
Shaksperean Drama, Acted. (J. Murray) Overland, n. s. 22: 355.
Shall and Will. (R. Barr) Bookman, 2: 287. — (W. S. Liscomb) Educa. 12: 413.
Shamanism. (W. R. Morfill) Acad. 43: 350.
— in Siberia and European Russia. (M. Mikhailovskii) Anthrop. J. 24: 62, 126.
Shamrock, A Hunt for. (F. B. Sawvel) Educa. 15: 140.
Shan Hills, Peoples and Products of. (R. G. Woodthorpe) J. Soc. Arts, 44: 197.
Shane Desmond; a story. (F. Matthew) Idler, 2: 1.
"Shanghaed;" a Yarn in the Dog Watch. (E. Bevis) Canad. M. 4: 189.
Shanghai, Pilgrimage to. (A. L. Craig) Chaut. 17: 58.
— Republic of. (M. B. Dunnell) Overland, n. s. 24: 473.
Shannon, J. J. (A. L. Baldry) M. of Art, 20: 1. — (J. Creelman) Munsey, 14: 129.
Shans, Country of the. (R. G. Woodthorpe) Geog. J. 7: 577.
Shapleigh, Major John, Letter of, 1781. (J. S. H. Fogg) N. E. Reg. 50: 14.
Shareholders, Responsibilities of. Econ. R. 5: 127.
Shark Tales, Australian. Chamb. J. 69: 571.
Sharks, About. Chamb. J. 71: 551.
— as Ancestral Fishes. (B. Dean) Nat. Sci. 8: 245.
— Primeval, Problem of. (A. S. Woodward) Nat. Sci. 6: 38.
Sharp, Wm., with portrait. Bk. News, 11: 13.
— Vistas. (G. Cotterell) Acad. 45: 182.
Sharpness of Death, The. (E. K. Tompkins) Scrib. M. 14: 383.
Sharpshooter, The; a story. (J. A. Altsheler) Cosmopol. 21: 166.
Shasta, Mt., and the Crags. (R. Wildman) Overland, n. s. 28: 7.
— On the Crater of. (A. S. Packard) Pop. Sci. Mo. 50: 28.
— Path-finding up. (Geo. S. Meredith) Overland, n. s. 25: 45.
Shattuck, George Cheyne, Memoir of. (C. D. Bradlee) N. E. Reg. 48: 277.
Shaving. (H. Maxwell) Good Words, 36: 45.
Shaw, Albert, with portrait. (W. B. Murray) Our Day, 15: 225.
Shaw, G. B.: A Socialist in a Corner. (W. H. Mallock) Fortn. 61: 693.
Shawangunk Mountain. (N. H. Darton) Nat. Geog. M. 3: 23. — Garden & F. 5: 460-483.
— A Day on. (M. S. Holmes) Around World, 1: 171.
Shawe Genealogy. (M. F. King) N. E. Reg. 49: 64.
Shawmut Trestle, The; a story. (W. Atkinson) Chamb. J. 70: 28, 45.
Shays' Rebellion. (J. Canning) Am. Hist. Reg. 2: 1265.
She and Journalism; a story. (H. Robertson) Scrib. M. 16: 250.
She had a Familiar Spirit. (J. Bonner) Overland, n. s. 24: 467.
Shea, John Gilmary. (M. F. Vallette) Cath. World, 55: 55.
Shearing Stress, Transformation of Energy by. (M. C. Lea) Am. J. Sci. 146: 413.
Shearwater, The Manx. (T. D. Pigott) Blackw. 158: 257.
Shear-zone in Adirondacks. (J. F. Kemp) Am. J. Sci. 144: 109.
Shechem and Bethel. (H. Vogelstein) Jew. Q. 4: 513.
Shedd, Wm. G. T., with portrait. (J. De Witt) Presb. & Ref. R. 6: 295.
Sheep, The, and the Goat: Wild Traits in Tame Animals. (S. Robinson) No. Am. 161: 43.
— Cry of, Kratinos and Aristophanes on. (A. N. Jannaris) Am. J. Philol. 16: 46.
— Mountain, Hunting. (J. M. Oxley) Outing, 21: 317.
Sheep-shearing on Santa Rosa Island. Overland, n. s. 21: 492.
Sheffield, England. Sat. R. 80: 571.
— Museum and Art Gallery. (H. M. Cundall) Art J. 44: 279.

Sheffield Scientific School, Yale University, and the Farmers' Movement. Yale R. **2**: 4.
Sheik's Revenge, The. (S. J. Shields) Southern M. **3**: 591.
Sheldon, Mrs. M. French. A "White Queen" in Africa. (F. C. Williams) Chaut. **18**: 342.
Shell-fish Culture. (J. H. Fullarton) Scot. R. **22**: 162.
Shell Heaps of the St. John's River, Fla. (C. B. Moore) Am. Natural. **26**: 912. **27**: 8-708. **28**: 15.
Shelley, Harriet, In Defence of. (S. L. Clemens) No. Am. **159**: 108-333.
Shelley, Mary Wollstonecraft. Temp. Bar, **95**: 457. Same art. Ecl. M. **119**: 401. — (A. Armit) Scot. R. **20**: 254.
Shelley, Percy Bysshe. (K. West) And. R. **18**: 573. — (F. Adams) Fortn. **58**: 217. Same art. Ecl. M. **119**: 500. — Gent. M. n. s. **49**: 323. — (K. West) Lit. W. (Bost.) **23**: 276. — (C. A. Price) Belgra. **88**: 399. — (K. West) Chaut. **16**: 422.
— Adonais. (C. Fisher) Temp. Bar, **108**: 388.
— and Trelawney, Graves of. (J. L. Hurst) Critic, **27**: 285.
— and Vegetarianism. (K. West) Writer, **7**: 34.
— and Paul Verlaine. (Alice L. Wilson) Poet-Lore, **8**: 406.
— and Whitman. (I. H. Platt) Poet-Lore, **8**: 332.
— Ariel; a Poem in Memory of. (E. C. Stedman) Atlan. **70**: 145.
— as Prophet. Spec. **70**: 846.
— at Tremadoc. Macmil. **75**: 126.
— Centenary of. Critic, **21**: 72-111. — Dial (Ch.) **13**: 129. — (G. W. Alger) Poet-Lore, **4**: 315.
— — a poem. (W. Watson) Spec. **69**: 162. Same art. Ecl. M. **119**: 388.
— Chats with Jane Clermont concerning. (W. Graham) 19th Cent. **34**: 753.
— Grandfather of. (J. Malone) Cent. **22**: 634.
— Haunt of. Atlan. **71**: 855.
— His Life in his "Epipsychidion." (F. G. Fleay) Poet-Lore, **2**: 225.
— in Italy. (R. Garnett) Eng. Illust. **12**: no. 3, 143.
— Influence on Browning. (F. Converse) Poet-Lore, **7**: 18.
— Last Days of. (G. Biagi) Harper, **84**: 782.
— Letters to Elizabeth Hitchener. (W. G. Kingsland) Poet-Lore, **4**: 304.
— Memorial of, at Oxford. Ath. '92, **1**: 314. — Critic, **21**: 157.
— — at Viarreggio. Critic, **25**: 379.
— Monument to. Critic, **20**: 246.
— Place of, in Eng. Poetry. (D. H. Wheeler) Meth. R. **54**: 574.
— Poetical Works, edited by Forman. Ath. '93, **2**: 55, 90.
— Prometheus Unbound. (V. D. Scudder) Atlan. **70**: 106-391.
— Religious Faith of. (K. Parkes) Poet-Lore, **4**: 289, 397.
— Revolutionary Ideal of. (W. E. Smyser) Meth. R. **53**: 538.
— Triumph of Life. (S. Axson) Citizen, **1**: 209.
— Woodberry's Edition. (J. A. McDaniels) Nation, **56**: 68, 86. — (M. B. Anderson) Dial (Ch.) **14**: 244.
— Work of. (G. E. Woodberry) Cent. **22**: 622.
Shelley Concordance, Ellis'. Sat. R. **73**: 580.
Shelley Society, The. (A. Symons) Time, **14**: 182.
Shells. (M. W. Leighton) Pop. Sci. Mo. **50**: 46. — (D. Dale) Sund. M. **22**: 254.
— and Molluscs. Ed. R. **182**: 351.
— Dispersal of, Kew on. (C. Reid) Nature, **49**: 361.
Shells, Fossil, Fragments of, in Drumlins near Boston. (W. Upham) Am. J. Sci. **147**: 238. — (W. O. Crosby and H. O. Ballard) Am. J. Sci. **148**: 486.
Shelton, William Henry. Writer, **8**: 117.
Shelton Church. (S. Barber) Antiq. n. s. **26**: 14.
"Shenandoah," Cruise of the. So. Hist. Pap. **21**: 165.
Shepard, Charles Upham, Sketch of. Pop. Sci. Mo. **47**: 548.
Shepherd, Richard Herne. Ath. '95, **2**: 131. — Acad. **48**: 90.
Shepherd, Samuel. Walford's Antiq. **11**: 255.
Shepherd's Care on Salisbury Plain, The. (G. Fidler) Good Words, **36**: 741.
Shepherds' Midnight Mass in Alassio. (J. Leete) Argosy, **61**: 28. Same art. Liv. Age, **208**: 185.
Sheppard, Jack. (C. Whibley) New R. **12**: 318.
Sherbrooke, Robert Lowe, Lord. (J. Bryce) Nation, **55**: 141. — Sat. R. **74**: 125. — Spec. **69**: 149. — Lond. Q. **81**: 65. — Quar. **177**: 42. — (Goldwin Smith) Nation, **57**: 13.
— and Sir Alfred Stephen. (A. P. Martin) National, **23**: 682.
Sherburne, Eng. Ramblings in. (S. Beale) Am. Arch. **47**: 134.
Sheridan, Gen., Personality of. (T. R. Davis) Cosmopol. **13**: 209.
Sheridan, Richard B. Ed. R. **184**: 57. — (W. E. Gladstone) 19th Cent. **39**: 1037. Same art. Liv. Age, **210**: 225. — (H. A. Milton) Theatre, **27**: 332.
— Rae's Life of. (T. Hutchinson) Acad. **49**: 461. — (E. G. Johnson) Dial (Ch.) **21**: 11.
— School for Scandal, Morality of. Sat. R. **81**: 648.
Sheridan Family, The. Ed. R. **180**: 433. Same art. Liv. Age, **205**: 420.
Sheridan, Fort. (H. R. Brinkerhoff) Un. Serv. (Phila.) **8**: 271.
Sheriff of Siskyou, The; a story. (Bret Harte) McClure, **2**: 578.
Sherman, John. (F. A. Munsey) Munsey, **10**: 16.
— and W. T., Correspondence of. Cent. **23**: 88-892. — (J. D. Cox) Nation, **59**: 271. — (L. J. Block) Dial (Ch.) **17**: 228.
— as a Financier. (J. Prince) Am. J. Pol. **3**: 113.
— Open Letter to. (G. W. Pepperell) Arena, **11**: 345.
— Recollections. (G. W. Julian) Dial (Ch.) **19**: 325. — (A. G. Sedgwick) Nation, **62**: 80. — (E. L. Pierce) Am. Hist. R. **1**: 553.
— Story of His Own Career. (E. B. Andrews) R. of Rs. (N. Y.) **12**: 678.
Sherman, W. T., Models for Statue of. (Glenn Brown) Am. Arch. **51**: 53.
— Personal Recollections of. (S. H. M. Byers) McClure, **3**: 212.
— Raid into Mississippi. (A. G. Brackett) Un. Serv. (Phila.) **8**: 519.
— Recollections of. (H. C. King) Mo. Illust. **12**: 266, 376.
Sherwood, Mary Martha. Temp. Bar, **104**: 391. **105**: 228.
— History of the Fairchild Family. (F. A. Guthrie) Ecl. M. **126**: 698. — Longm. **21**: 579. Same art. Liv. Age, **197**: 548.
Sherwood, M. E. W., Recollections of. Lippinc. **49**: 244.
Shetland, Folk-lore of. (K. Blind) New R. **11**: 612.
— Pictish Tower in. (G. Goudie) Illust. Archæol. **1**: 137.
Shetland Islands, Folk-lore of. (J. J. H. Burgess) Scot. R. **25**: 91.
Shi King; Chinese Epic. Sat. R. **78**: 177.
— Jennings's Translation. Sat. R. **73**: 219.

Shibboleths, Lilly on. Spec. 68: 336.
Shikar, Thirty Years of. (E. Braddon) Blackw. 155: 276. 156: 387.
Shikaris, Two Great. Blackw. 137: 949. Same art. Liv. Age, 206: 150.
Shillaber, B. P. Autobiography. New Eng. M. n. s. 8: 511. 9: 88, 153, 625. 10: 29–286.
Shiloh, Battle of. So. Hist. Pap. 21: 215.
Shimonoseki, Straits of, The "Wyoming" in. (W. E. Griffis) Cent. 21: 844.
Shinkle, Amos. (H. Baker) Meth. R. 53: 177.
Shinto, the Old Religion of Japan. (N. Kishimoto) Pop. Sci. Mo. 46: 206.
Shinto Funeral, A. (A. Y. Sannomiya) 19th Cent. 40: 974.
Shinto Pantheon, The. (E. Buckley) New World, 5: 719.
Ship, War, Recent Construction. (H. L. Swinburne) Un. Serv. (Phila.) 8: 13.
Ship of State, Longfellow's. (W. Everett) Atlan. 76: 18.
Ship that found herself, The. (Rudyard Kipling) Idler, 8: 406. Same art. McClure, 6: 328.
Ship-building. Cyclops in London. Cornh. 67: 170.
— English and American. (J. S. Jeans) Cassier, 7: 72.
— in America. (W. H. Wiley) Cassier, 2: 157.
— in Quebec. (H. Fry) Canad. M. 5: 1.
— in the U. S. and Abroad. (P. Hitchborn) No. Am. 156: 398.
— on the Great Lakes. (H. H. Griffin) Engin. M. 4: 815.
Shipbuilding Tools, Modern. (J. A. Gray) Cassier, 9: 323, 455.
Ship Canals. (E. W. Hubbard) Un. Serv. (Phila.) 9: 199.
Shipka Pass, Crisis of the. (A. Forbes) Scrib. M. 13: 519.
Shipowners, Liability of, at Common Law. (E. L. de Hart) Law Q. 5: 15.
Shipping, American, Restoring. Gunton's M. 10: 256.
— and National Progress. (W. W. Bates) Soc. Econ. 1: 355.
— and Ship-building in California, Evolution of. (I. M. Scott and others) Overland, n. s. 25: 5, 122, 285.
— Economics of, American. (W. W. Bates) Soc. Econ. 1: 141.
— Ethics and Economics of. Soc. Econ. 6: 361.
— Our Neglected. (A. R. Smith) No. Am. 163: 470.
— Progress of, 1880–90. (J. Clover) J. Statis. Soc. 55: 205.
— Protection and Ocean Navigation. (W. W. Bates) Soc. Econ. 8: 353.
— Railways and Ocean Steamers. Soc. Econ. 6: 283.
— Scandinavian, Development of. (A. N. Klaer) J. Pol. Econ. 1: 329.
— Silver, Gold, and. (W. W. Bates) Soc. Econ. 7: 107.
— Some Facts about. (W. C. Ford) Nation, 63: 135.
— Subsidies and Bi-metallism. Soc. Econ. 8: 343.
— Unwise Taxation on. (C. E. Naylor) Overland, n. s. 28: 567.
Shipping Laws, Stringent, Our Need of. (F. Rotherham) No. Am. 161: 505.
Shipping Trade between the U. S. and the United Kingdom. (A. N. Klaer) J. Pol. Econ. 5: 1.
Ships, Abandoned. Sat. R. 75: 376.
— American. (S. A. Wood) Chaut. 17: 558.
— Ancient. (G. H. Preble) Un. Serv. (Phila.) 16: 297.
— — Torr's. Sat. R. 77: 365.
— Battle, Limit in. (J. M. Ellicott) Atlan. 69: 501.
Ships, Battle, of the Future. (P. H. Colomb) No. Am. 157: 412.
— — British, Construction of, Evolution of. (S. Eardley-Wilmot) Cosmopol. 14: 440.
— — — Past and Present. (A. H. Markham) Good Words, 34: 405.
See War Ships.
— before the Application of Steam. (D. Hannay) M. of Art, 7: 404.
— Capital invested on the Seas. (W. W. Carruth) Chaut. 15: 46.
— China Sea-clippers. Chamb. J. 69: 646.
— Derelict, Recent. Chamb. J. 71: 38.
— Free, shall we have? (E. Kemble) No. Am. 160: 85.
— Missing. Chamb. J. 69: 134.
— Modern. Chamb. J. 70: 710.
— Motion of, Resistance to. (T. M. T. Cazin) J. Frankl. Inst. 135: 209, 299, 364.
— Novel. Chamb. J. 72: 459.
— Protection of, System of. (W. W. Bates) Soc. Econ. 9: 112.
— Resistance of. (R. L. Newman) J. Frankl. Inst. 137: 218–308.
— Rigging and Sails. (A. J. Kenealy) Outing, 26: 44.
— Rolling of. Nature, 45: 559. Same art. Science, 19: 247.
— Scuttled. Chamb. J. 71: 166.
— Steel, Care of. (P. Hichborn) Cassier, 8: 109.
Ships' Lights, Visibility of. Nature, 52: 232.
Shipwreck. Time, 8: 144.
— My First. (R. C. Dowie) Chamb. J. 72: 366.
Shipwrecks, Some Memorable. (W. G. Smythies) Eng. Illust. 14: 389.
Shiras, George, jr., with portrait. Green Bag, 4: 553.
Shiré Highlands, The. (A. Werner) Gent. M. n. s. 56: 131. Same art. Liv. Age, 208: 788.
Shirley, Arthur, and Maurice Galley. The Cross of Honor. Theatre, 29: 124.
Shirley, E. P. (J. H. Round) 19th Cent. 35: 796.
Shirley, Sir Thomas, Case of. (G. W. Prothero) Eng. Hist. R. 8: 733.
Shoals, Isolated, not readily found. (G. W. Littlehales) Am. J. Sci. 151: 106.
Shoe and Leather Trade, Development of, in Massachusetts. (A. W. Brayley) Bost. 1: 38–651.
— in Massachusetts, Prominent Men in. Bost. 1: 173, 552.
Shoeblacks. (T. Mackay) Time, 21: 131.
— Among the. (C. Middleton) Sund. M. 24: 815.
— of Parnassus. (H. Lascaris) Chamb. J. 72: 772.
Shoeburyness. Chamb. J. 73: 235.
Shoemaker of Fougères; a story. (K. Macquoid) Harper, 92: 150.
Shoes and Shoemakers. Chamb. J. 69: 811.
— Fashions for the Feet. (R. Heath) M. of Art, 6: 504. 7: 115.
— Old, Romance of. (E. A. De Wolfe) Cosmopol. 12: 653.
— Unscientific, Foot Deformity as the Result of. (W. M. L. Coplin; D. Bevan) Science, 20: 99.
— Where the Shoe pinches. (A. J. Moore) Cosmopol. 13: 619.
Shoes, The; a story. Belgra. 86: 190.
Shooting at Swatow, China. (A. B. Hoff) Outing, 27: 357.
— Guns and. (E. W. Sandys) Outing, 27: 63.
— in Japan. (C. S. Hartman) Outing, 21: 427.
— Rough. (T. E. Kebbel) Time, 20: 153.
— Texas, Reminiscence of. (M. H. D.) Outing, 25: 457.

Shooting Woodcock. Sat. R. 78: 504, 532.
Shooting Season at Sandringham. Eng. Illust. 11: 128.
Shooting Stars. (W. F. Denning) Pop. Astron. 1: 208, 296, 345, 438.
— Cometary. (H. A. Newton) Astron. 13: 196.
Shop Assistants, Case of. (E. G. Salmon) Time, 13: 272.
Shop-girls, English. (M. A. Belloc) Idler, 8: 12.
Shop Management, Examples of Successful. (H. Roland) Engin. M. 12: 69, 270, 395.
Shopping, Ethics of. (M. Lady Jeune) Fortn. 63: 121.
Shore, The, and the Moorland. Chamb. J. 73: 577.
Short Story, Art of the. Dial (Ch.) 17: 183. — (W. H. Hills) Writer, 8: 48.
Shorthand for Schools. (H. M. Dean) Educa. 14: 227.
— Partial. (H. B. Lancaster) Writer, 9: 1.
— Pitman's: a Reply. (I. Pitman) Westm. 146: 338.
Shorthand Writing in Foreign Lands. (G. M. Fraser) Westm. 141: 189.
Shortley Wood, Eng., Sundown in. Spec. 71: 909.
Shot-putting. (M. W. Ford) Outing, 20: 280.
Shovel, The Steam. (A. W. Robinson) Cassier, 7: 187.
Show-child; a Protest. (I. A. Taylor) Longm. 27: 193. Same art. Liv. Age, 208: 112.
Shower, The; a poem. (F. D. Sherman) Cosmopol. 15: 737.
Shrike; "Beautiful and Brave was he." (O. T. Miller) Atlan. 76: 59.
Shrine, The Making of a. (Lily Wolffsohn) 19th Cent. 37: 313. Same art. Liv. Age, 204: 686. Same art. Ecl. M. 124: 482.
Shrine of St. Anthony; a story. (A. Macarthur) Eng. Illust. 14: 401.
Shrines, English. (V. Blackburn) Art J. 44: 177.
Shropshire, Ramble through. (R. O. Allsop) Eng. Illust. 11: 150.
Shrubberies, Roadside. Garden & F. 5: 613.
Shrubbery in Winter. (C. S. Sargent) Garden & F. 9: 41.
Shrubs, Earliest Flowering. (J. G. Jack) Garden & F. 7: 112.
— Late Flowering. (J. G. Jack) Garden & F. 6: 436.
— Native and Foreign. Garden & F. 9: 202, 212.
— Pruning. (C. S. Sargent) Garden & F. 9: 481.
Shudder, The, in Literature. (J. Clarétie) No. Am. 155: 136.
Shudderman, Soldier; a story. (N. Munro) Blackw. 154: 560. Same art. Ecl. M. 122: 129.
Shuffle-Shoon and Amber Locks; a poem. (E. Field) Pub. Opin. 18: 682.
Shuttleworth, Prof. Henry. (J. Milne) Sund. M. 24: 474.
Shylock and Harpagon, Specialists in Avarice. (I. A. Herrick) Educa. 14: 633.
— and Nathan the Wise. (R. Grossman) Lend a H. 12: 177.
Si, si, Señor; a story. (C. Grissen) Overland, n. s. 22: 314.
Siam and the Siamese. (H. H. Barroll) Cosmopol. 17: 3.
— Anglo-French Convention in. (F. Verney) 19th Cent. 39: 331. — (A. R. Colquhoun) Sat. R. 81: 93.
— Blue Book on. Asia R. 18: 294.
— Boundary Question. (G. N. Curzon) 19th Cent. 34: 34. *See also* Indo-China.
— Child's. Ath. '93, 2: 445.
— Commerce of. (C. S. Leckie) J. Soc. Arts, 42: 649.
— Crown Prince of. Open Court, 9: 4615.
— — in his English Home. (D. Trelawney) Eng. Illust. 13: 515.
Siam, France and. Spec. 70: 727. — Spec. 71: 453. — Pub. Opin. 15: 398. — Sat. R. 76: 88, 117. — (H. N. D. Prendergast) Asia. R. 21: 225. — (Muang-Thai) Asia. R. 16: 65. — (A. R. MacMahon) Un. Serv. M. 8: 164.
— — and England. (R. S. Gundry) National, 21: 577. — (G. N. Curzon; Mme. J. Adam) No. Am. 157: 268.
— — Blockade of Bangkok. Spec. 71: 132.
— — How the French first came into. (E. P. Thompson) Gent. M. n. s. 51: 493.
— — Relations with Great Britain. Asia R. 16: 60.
— French Movements in Eastern. (Sir R. Temple) Fortn. 60: 142.
— Future of. (H. Norman) Contemp. 64: 1.
— — from a Siamese Standpoint. (Muang-Thai) Asia. R. 21: 248.
— Journey Around. (J. S. Black) Geog. J. 8: 429.
— the Laos States. (E. Satow) J. Soc. Arts, 40: 182.
— Mekong-Menam Arrangement. (A. R. MacMahon) Asia R. 21: 232. — (Baron Textor de Ravisi) Asia. R. 21: 255.
— A Pageant in. (David Ker) Chamb. J. 70: 577. Same art. Liv. Age, 199: 440.
— Politics and Progress in. (G. Curzon) Fortn. 59: 454. Same art. Liv. Age, 197: 643.
— Question of. Blackw. 159: 461. — Un. Serv. M. 7: 1219.
— Railroad needed in. (A. R. Colquhoun) Sat. R. 82: 30.
— Railroads in. Dub. R. 110: 186. — Sat. R. 73: 475.
— Recent Progress in, 1893. (J. B. Breuer) Engin. M. 6: 32.
— Southwestern Provinces of. (H. W. Smyth) Geog. J. 6: 401, 522.
— Urgency in. (H. Norman) Contemp. 64: 737.
— Visit to Ruins in. (E. Satow) J. Soc. Arts. 40: 849.
Siao-ontai-shan, Journey to the Sacred Mountain of, in China. (A. H. S. Landor) Fortn. 62: 393. Same art. Ecl. M. 123: 596. Same art. Liv. Age, 203: 143.
Siberia, Across. (A. C. Coolidge) Nation, 61: 165, 203, 238.
— and its Exiles. All the Year, 70: 60.
— Arctic, Baron Toll's Expedition to. Geog. J. 3: 409. 5: 373.
— Kennan on. (I. F. Hapgood) Nation, 54: 35, 55.
— — Reply. (G. Kennan) Nation, 54: 108.
— Price's. Spec. 68: 714.
— Prison Life in. Belgra. 78: 76.
— Railroad across. (V. Gribayedoff) Cosmopol. 14: 559. — (F. Hobart) Engin. M. 5: 307. — Chamb. J. 70: 437. — Dub. R. 116: 193. — (P. Kropotkin) Geog. J. 5: 146.
— — Corea and the. Fortn. 64: 879.
— — Importance of. (H. Schönfeld) Engin. M. 7: 467.
— The Real, and Mr. de Windt. (F. Volkhovsky) Contemp. 61: 533.
— Recent Voyages in. (Capt. Wiggins) J. Soc. Arts, 43: 499.
— Russia and. (A. Vámbéry) Asia R. 11: 13.
— Sojourn among the Samoyads, Jackson's. Sat. R. 80: 16.
— Southern, Future of. Spec. 75: 515.
— The Truth about. (A. H. Keane) Acad. 41: 221.
— Tundra and Forest in. (H. Seebohm) Around World, 1: 73.
— Windt's. Spec. 69: 233.
Siberian Savages, Howard on. (F. Starr) Dial (Ch.) 15: 338.
Siberian Sea, State of. (J. Wiggins) Geog. J. 3: 121.

Sibley, Joseph C., as Presidential Candidate, with portrait. (H. M. Irwin) Am. M. Civics, 6: 616.
Sibyllenort Castle, Germany. (S. M. S. Pereira) Sund. M. 21: 527.
Sichel, Nathaniel. (E. W. Champney) Mo. Illust. 3: 199.
— Ideal Portraits of Classic Beauties. (C. M. Fairbanks) Chaut. 14: 705.
Sicilian Vespers, History of the War of. Eng. R. 15: 25.
Sicily, Ancient. Quar. 175: 319.
— and the United States, Trade between. (J. W. Mario) Nation, 58: 209.
— Archæological Notes from. (F. Halbherr) Ath. '92, 1: 830.
— Byeways in. (Susan Keppel) National, 20: 661. Same art. Liv. Age, 196: 506.
— Distress in. Sat. R. 77: 7.
— English Occupation of. Temp. Bar, 109: 332.
— The Fasci dei Lavatori and the Situation in. (E. Cavalieri) Chaut. 19: 13.
— First Act of Social Justice to. (J. W. Mario) Nation, 63: 102.
— Prof. Freeman and Prehistoric. (W. J. Stillman) Nation, 56: 328.
— Freeman's History of. (I. Taylor) Acad. 41: 461. — Ath. '92, 1: 597. — (F. W. Kelsey) Dial (Ch.) 12: 319. 13: 214. — (A. H. Cooke) Eng. Hist. R. 7: 117. — (G. W. Cox) Eng. Hist. R. 7: 539. — (W. R. Thayer) Nation, 55: 169. — Sat. R. 73: 543. 74: 400. — (J. B. Bury) Scot. R. 19: 26. 20: 300. — Spec. 68: 643. — (I. Taylor) Acad. 46: 295. — Sat. R. 78: 411,
— Martial Law in. (J. W. Mario) Nation, 58: 63.
— Outbreak in. Spec. 72: 5.
— Peasant Life in. (V. Mario) Chaut. 15: 316.
— Prisoners of. (C. S. Strong) Gent. M. n. s. 56: 412.
— Rambles in. (H. Mann) Good Words, 36: 173.
— Social Unrest in. (J. W. Mario) Nation, 57: 344.
— State of, Colajanni on. Spec. 72: 430. Same art. Liv. Age, 201: 246.
— Sulphur Mines of. (J. W. Mario) Nation, 54: 29.
Sick, Music for the. (A. E. Gether) Music, 7: 254.
— Treating the, New Methods of. (W. C. Krouss) Science, 22: 58.
"Sick Men," The Four, of the World. Liv. Age, 211: 830.
Sickness, National System of Notification and Registration. (A. Newsholme) J. Statis. Soc. 59: 1.
Siddons, Sarah. (E. Gosse) Cent. 24: 380. — (H. H. Fyfe) Theatre, 34: 212.
— Some Portraits of. (E. B. Nash) M. of Art, 10: 55.
Sidereal Ephemeris. (J. Morrison) Pop. Astron. 4: 90.
Sidewalks, Roads, Pavements, and Bridges. (W. Howard) Engin. M. 8: 1014.
Sidney, Margaret, with portrait. Bk. News, 11: 38.
Sidney, Sir Philip. (T. E. Brown) New R. 12: 415.
— Arcadia. Bookworm, 1: 145.
— Fox-Bourne's. Spec. 68: 206. — (G. Smith) Nation, 55: 247. — Sat. R. 73: 189. — Spec. 69: 198.
Siemens, Ernst W. von. Ath. '92, 2: 858. — Nature, 47: 153. — With portrait. Pop. Sci. Mo. 43: 831. — Sat. R. 76: 574. — Nature, 49: 25.
— Scientific and Technical Papers. (W. Watson) Nature, 52: 73. — Sat. R. 80: 512.
Siena, the City of the Virgin. (E. H. and E. W. Blashfield) Scrib. M. 29: 397.
— Cathedral, Pavement of. (L. F. Day) M. of Art, 17: 368, 410.
Sierra Leone, Wanderings in Hinterland of. (T. J. Alldridge) Geog. J. 4: 123.
Sierra Madre, In the, with the Punchers. (F. Remington) Harper, 88: 350.
— Indian Story of. (Dan De Quille) Cosmopol. 19: 180.
— Western, of Mexico. (O. H. Howarth) Geog. J. 6: 422.
Sierra Mts., a Tramp in. (H. P. Dyer) Outing, 26: 301.
Sierra Nevada, Wild Gardens of. (C. H. Shinn) Garden & F. 9: 343.
— Unexplored Regions of the High. (T. S. Solomons) Overland, n. s. 27: 477, 636. 28: 115, 509.
Sifre Zuta, Fragments of. (S. Schechter) Jew. Q. 6: 656.
Sight, Sense of, in Animals. Chamb. J. 70: 373.
Sightless, The [Les Aveugles]; a drama. (M. Maeterlinck) Poet-Lore, 5: 159–442.
Sign Language of Indians. (W. H. Wassell) Chaut. 23: 581.
Sign-painter, To a. Cornh. 67: 291.
Signal Service; a poem. (E. and A. Gleason) New Eng. M. n. s. 7: 101.
Signaling, Army. (H. A. Giddings) Outing, 26: 396. — (J. P. Finley) Un. Serv. (Phila.) 9: 540.
— in French Army. (W. C. P. Lethbridge) Un. Serv. M. 8: 574.
Sign-boards, London. (J. J. Doherty) Month, 88: 166.
— Notes on. M. of Art, 4: 474.
Signerolles Library, The. (A. Laugel) Nation, 58: 173.
Signorini, Telemaco. (H. Zimmern) Art J. 47: 265.
Signs and Omens from Nova Scotia. (Mrs. C. V. Jamison) J. Am. Folk-Lore, 6: 38.
— and Symbols. (E. Schroeder) Open Court, 6: 3431–3463.
Signs and Wonders; a story. Argosy, 61: 380.
Signs of the Times. (E. Atkinson) Engin. M. 9: 811. — (H. Thomas) Westm. 146: 84.
Sikhs, Political History of. (W. Irvine) Asia. R. 17: 420.
Sikyon, Theatre of, Excavations at, in 1891. (M. L. Earle) Am. J. Archæol. 7: 281.
Silchester, England: City of the White Walls. (H. D. M. Spence) Good Words, 35: 248, 318.
— Roman City of. (H. W. Young) Illust. Archæol. 1: 99. — Sat. R. 73: 71.
— — Discovery of Roman Remains at. Acad. 47: 549.
— — The Eagle and the Cross. All the Year, 72: 303.
— — Excavations at. (F. Haverfield) Ath. '94, 2: 836. — Illus. Archæol. 2: 22. — (W. H. St. J. Hope) New R. 9: 285. Same art. Liv. Age, 199: 349. — (W. H. St. J. Hope) Antiq. n. s. 27: 9. — (R. Le Schonix) Antiq. n. s. 29: 259.
Silence. All the Year, 72: 279.
Silence; a story. (E. M. Henry) Belgra. 79: 77.
Silence; a story. (M. E. Wilkins) Harper, 87: 213.
Silence Owen; a poem. Temp. Bar, 107: 591.
Silent Partners; a story. (C. A. Stearns) Overland, n. s. 21: 132.
Silent Pools, The; a story. Cornh. 70: 383, 490. Same art. Liv. Age, 203: 597, 654.
Silent Singer, The. (H. T. Griswold) Dial (Ch.) 13: 230.
Silent Voice, The; a play. (L. Alma Tadema) Harper, 93: 400.
Silent Witness, The; a story. (H. D. Ward) McClure, 6: 175.
Siletz Indians, Gentile System of. (J. O. Dorsey) J. Am. Folk-Lore, 3: 227.
Silk Culture in California. (E. R. Endres) Overland, n. s. 21: 508.
— in the United States. (A. Ferris) Chaut. 17: 342.

Silk Industry in England. (K. Parkes) National, 26: 212.
— — Plea for. (E. L. Linton) New R. 7: 335.
Silk Production in England, Decline of. Sat. R. 82: 306.
Silk-Spinner's Romance. (H. Hooton) Eng. Illust. 14: 475.
Silk-spinning Fly-larvæ. (H. Garman) Science, 22: 215.
Silks, British, Improvements in, since 1890. (T. Wardle) J. Soc. Arts, 43: 666.
Silladar Cavalry. (E. A. W. Stotherd) Un. Serv. M. 6: 484.
Siller Wedding; a story. Canad. M. 3: 190.
Silurian Strata near Penobscot Bay. (W. W. Dodge and C. E. Beecher) Am. J. Sci. 143: 412.
Silva of North America. (C. S. Sargent) Garden & F. 5: 83.
Silver a Money Metal. (J. T. Morgan) Arena, 16: 705.
— and the Alkali Metals, Some Double Halides of. (H. L. Wells and H. L. Wheeler) Am. J. Sci. 144: 155.
— and Gold, Production of. Bank. M. (Lond.) 60: 581.
— — — World's, 1871–94. Bank. M. (N. Y.) 50: 503.
— Collodial, Remarks on. (C. Barus) Am. J. Sci. 148: 451.
— The Cost of, and the Profits of Mining. (J. D. Hague) Forum, 15: 60.
— Discovery of. (E. Lord) New Eng. M. n. s. 12: 697.
— Facts about. Soc. Econ. 5: 290.
— from Mine to Mint. (M. C. Ihlseng) Cassier, 6: 3.
— Metallic, Solutions of. (M. C. Lea) Am. J. Sci. 148: 343.
— Method of Determining Small Percentages in Base Metals. (C. Whitehead) J. Frankl. Inst. 133: 470.
— Nevada. (C. H. Shinn) Pop. Sci. Mo. 49: 734.
— Production at Broken Hill, New South Wales. Dub. R. 117: 456.
— Production of, Future of. (E. B. Andrews) R. of Rs. (N. Y.) 8: 544.
— separated from Gold by Volatilisation. (J. W. Richards) J. Frankl. Inst. 141: 447.
— Soluble. Chamb. J. 73: 367. Same art. Liv. Age, 210: 319.
Silver [Money]. (W. E. C. Wright) Bib. Sac. 53: 708. — (F. G. Newlands) Pub. Opin. 12: 487.
— and Currency, Problems of. (H. H. Gibbs and H. Bacon) Forum, 14: 553.
— and Gold Fallacies. Soc. Econ. 5: 273.
— and the "Gresham Law." Soc. Econ. 7: 17. 9: 168.
— as it was, is, and should be. (A. J. Warner) Am. J. Pol. 1: 16.
— Boons and Banes of. (R. P. Bland; J. H. Rhoades) No. Am. 156: 171.
— Brussels Monetary Conference. (A. C. Tupp) Asia. R. 15: 132.
— A Century's Struggle for. (J. B. McMaster) Forum, 16: 1.
— Claims of Bi-metallists. Soc. Econ. 8: 257.
— Colorado's Mistake about. Soc. Econ. 6: 88.
— Correspondence on. Soc. Econ. 4: 297.
— Cost Theory of Value. Soc. Econ. 9: 27.
— Crisis in. (H. H. Gibbs) Forum, 14: 553.
— — in 1893. Spec. 71: 198.
— Debased, and British Trade. (E. E. Isemonger) National, 23: 788.
— Debts that Indicate Prosperity. Soc. Econ. 9: 47.
— Decline of, as Compared with Gold. (W. A. Campbell) Un. Serv. (Phila.) 13: 225.
— Depreciation of, with reference to Indian Currency. (J. S. Nicholson) Econ. J. 4: 59.
Silver, Doom of. (E. O. Leech) Forum, 15: 657.
— Downfall of Certain Financial Fallacies. (D. A. Wells) Forum, 16: 131.
— Experiment of U. S. with. (E. Mead) Am. J. Pol. 5: 398.
— Fall of, and its Causes. (E. O. Leech) Forum, 13: 439.
— — Is it a Benefit to India? (A. C. Tupp) Asia. R. 14: 11.
— A Farmer's Thoughts on. Am. M. Civics, 9: 166.
— Free Coinage of. (H. W. Seymour) Am. J. Pol. 3: 50. — (F. A. Walker) J. Pol. Econ. 1: 163. — (J. P. Dunn) J. Pol. Econ. 1: 436. — (E. P. Powers) J. Pol. Econ. 1: 597. — (A. C. Fisk) Arena, 8: 57. — (J. C. Henderson) Overland, n. s. 21: 305. — Pub. Opin. 15: 496. — (J. W. Jenks and others) Am. J. Soc. Sci. 33: 49. — (E. W. Bemis) Bib. Sac. 53: 728. — (J. B. Weaver) Chaut. 24: 67. — Soc. Econ. 8: 133.
— — After Effects of. (J. B. Clark) Pol. Sci. Q. 11: 493.
— — Agitation for. (H. White) Nation, 54: 103. — (M. D. Harter, Wm. F. Vilas, and J. C. Hemphill) Forum, 13: 281. — Pub. Opin. 12: 370.
— — American: Would it double Price of Silver in Markets of the World? (C. H. Spahr and J. L. Laughlin) R. of Rs. (N. Y.) 14: 306.
— — American Currency Cranks. (W. R. Lawson) Contemp. 70: 320. Same art. Ecl. M. 127: 583.
— — and Bank Circulation. (J. J. Knox) Forum, 12: 772.
— — and an Elastic Currency. (R. P. Bland) Forum, 13: 45.
— — and the Farmers. (J. M. Stahl) Forum, 22: 146.
— — and Life-insurance Companies. (J. A. McCall) Forum, 22: 136.
— — and the Loss of Southern Statesmanship. (J. C. Hemphill) Forum, 13: 295.
— — and National Prosperity. (W. P. St. John) Arena, 16: 581.
— — and the Savings Banks. (J. P. Townsend; C. H. Smith) No. Am. 162: 347.
— — and Trust Companies. (E. King) Forum, 22: 142.
— — and Wage-Earners. (C. R. Spahr and R. Mayo-Smith) R. of Rs. (N. Y.) 14: 560.
— — and Wages. (George Gunton) Gunton's M. 11: 157. — (R. Mayo-Smith) Pol. Sci. Q. 11: 464.
— — Argument for. (W. H. Harvey) Forum, 19: 401.
— — — Grotesque Fallacies of. (J. D. Warner) Forum, 19: 410.
— — Battle for. Pub. Opin. 18: 432.
— — the Blight of our Commerce. (M. D. Harter) Forum, 13: 281.
— — Compulsory Dishonesty. (B. Harrison) Forum, 22: 129.
— — Controversy on. Pub. Opin. 18: 496.
— — Cry for. (J. A. Cooper) Canad. M. 7: 378.
— — Cry for Fraudulent Money in America. (G. F. Parker) 19th Cent. 40: 516.
— — Debate on, in the Senate, May, 1892. (H. White) Nation, 54: 408.
— — Effect of an Appreciating Money. Gunton's M. 11: 233.
— — End of. (H. White) Nation, 54: 242.
— — Epidemic of. (J. S. Morrill) Forum, 21: 705.
— — Explained. (E. L. Godkin) Nation, 63: 206.
— — Folly of. (L. Windmüller) Forum, 13: 718.
— — A Foretaste of Socialism. (D. MacG. Means) Nation, 57: 206.
— — Hopes of. (R. P. Bland) No. Am. 158: 554.

Silver, Free Coinage of. Has the Election settled the Money Question? (W. J. Bryan) No. Am. 163: 703.
— — How it would affect us. (E. O. Leech) No. Am. 161: 34.
— — The Issue of 1896. (F. Parsons) Arena, 16: 881.
— — Monetary Crisis in America. (F. A. Walker) National, 27: 783. — (T. Lloyd) National, 28: 59. (G. Peel) 64; (J. H. Tilton) 70; (T. E. Powell; A. Hepburn; H. Schmidt) 269.
— — The New Superstition. (J. W. Mason) Am. M. Civics, 8: 581.
— — Some Outspoken Champions of, among Conservative Authorities of the East. (B. O. Flower) Arena, 16: 208.
— — Stewart Bill for, 1892. Pub. Opin. 13: 323.
— — Senator Stewart on. (M. Halstead) No. Am. 154: 666.
— — Thou shalt not steal. (I. L. Rice) Forum, 22: 1.
— — *vs.* Gold. (F. Parsons) Arena, 16: 770.
— — What shall the Ratio be? (W. M. Stewart; W. M. Springer; H. C. Hansbrough; R. P. Bland; J. Dalzell) No. Am. 155: 1.
— — Why does the South want? (J. T. Morgan) Arena, 14: 369.
— — Why the South wants it. (M. Butler) Arena, 15: 625.
— — Why the West needs it. (C. S. Thomas) Arena, 15: 897.
— — Would it bring European Silver here? (E. O. Leech) Forum, 13: 34.
— Free Coinage Catechism. (A. D. Noyes) Nation, 63: 23, 44, 82, 117.
— Free-silver Poison the Cause of Industrial Paralysis. (J. S. Tait) Engin. M. 11: 1001.
— Full-weight Dollar. Gunton's M. 10: 251.
— Future of. (R. P. Bland) No. Am. 160: 345.
— German Commission on. (J. Landesberger) Econ. J. 5: 95.
— Gold, and Shipping. (W. W. Bates) Soc. Econ. 7: 107.
— Greenbacks and. Pub. Opin. 15: 513.
— Has Congress Constitutional Power to demonetize? (J. S. Fisher) Am. J. Pol. 3: 313.
— Hoarding, in India. Bank. M. (N. Y.) 48: 210.
— in China, Effect of Fall of, on Prices. (G. Jamieson) J. Statis. Soc. 56: 646.
— in Commerce. (W. C. Ford) Pol. Sci. Q. 11: 478.
— in England, Legislative Bewilderment about. Spec. 71: 903.
— in India. (F. C. Harrison) Econ. J. 2: 653. — (S. Montagu) Fortn. 58: 545.
— — Crisis in, 1893. (Sir R. Temple) New R. 9: 148. — Sat. R. 76: 249. — (Sir G. Chesney) 19th Cent. 33: 116. — (E. Hubbard) National, 22: 68. — Spec. 71: 4.
— — — Effect of Fall in Value of Rupee. (Ameer Ali) 19th Cent. 33: 515.
— — — Indian Currency Experiment. (J. S. Nicholson) Contemp. 64: 339.
See also India, Currency of.
— in the U. S.: Can the U. S. restore the Bimetallic Standard? (G. C. Douglas) Arena, 9: 61.
— — The Currency Crisis in the United States. (M. Frewen) Fortn. 59: 762.
— — Exit Silver. (H. White) Nation, 57: 322.
— — Future of. (F. W. Taussig) Nation, 55: 196.
— — in the 53d Congress. (M. Frewen) National, 22: 542.
— — Law of 1890; Debate in Congress in 1890. (R. F. Hoxie) J. Pol. Econ. 1: 535.
— — — Imminent Danger from. (G. F. Williams) Forum, 14: 789.
Silver in the U. S. Law of 1890, India's Action and. (H. White) Forum, 15: 649.
— — — Repeal of. Pub. Opin. 15: 288–333, 379, 401, 424, 498, 517, 523, 570, 590, 614. — (J. L. Laughlin) R. of Rs. (N. Y.) 8: 282. — Sat. R. 76: 511. — Spec. 71: 294. — (H. White) Nation, 55: 404.
— — — — and the Financial Crisis. (F. W. Taussig) Econ. J. 3: 733.
— — — — Debate in the Senate. (H. White) Nation, 57: 166.
— — — — Vote on. Spec. 71: 623.
— — — Threat of. (W. F. Vilas) Forum, 13: 285.
— — — Why it should be repealed. (G. S. Coe) Forum, 12: 611.
— — — Working of. (F. Taussig) Econ. J. 2: 362.
— — Legislation on. (H. White) Nation, 55: 367.
— — — and its Results. (E. O. Leech) No. Am. 157: 42.
— — Money Famine in the U. S. (G. C. Douglass) Arena, 8: 401.
— — Politics of. (H. White) Nation, 54: 183.
— — Realism Regarding. (F. I. Vassault) Overland, n. s. 21: 544.
— — Rule of the Gold Kings. (W. M. Stewart) No. Am. 154: 552.
— — Situation in 1892. (F. W. Taussig) Am. Econ. Asso. 7: 7.
— — Situation in Colorado, 1893. (E. W. Bemis) R. of Rs. (N. Y.) 8: 277.
— — Use of, as Money. (A. B. Woodford) Ann. Am Acad. Pol. Sci. 4: 91.
— The International Situation. (F. W. Taussig) Q. J. Econ. 11: 1.
— — Is it Hopeless? (W. R. Lawson) Bank. M. (Lond.) 54: 795.
— Learning the Silver Lesson. (E. P. Clark) Nation, 59: 438.
— Lodge's Plan for coercing England. (E. L. Godkin) Nation, 58: 422.
— Malignant Effects of the Free-silver Delusion. (E. Atkinson) Engin. M. 9: 405.
— Marine Solution of the Money Question. (W. W. Bates) Soc. Econ. 4: 205.
— Monetary Question. (A. Del Mar) Soc. Econ. 9: 34.
— Money, Silver, Coinage. Soc. Econ. 2: 328.
— Notes on. (M. C. Lea) Am. J. Sci. 144: 444.
— Outlawry of. Bank. M. (N. Y.) 50: 170.
— The Outlook for. (O. Arendt) No. Am. 162: 674.
— Popular Superstitions on Money and Prices. Gunton's M. 11: 307.
— Present Status of. (C. B. Spahr) Am. J. Soc. Sci. 31: 27.
— Prices and Volume of Money. Soc. Econ. 8: 278.
— Question of. Bank. M. (Lond.) 53: 881. — (A. Carnegie; J. Lubbock) No. Am. 157: 354. — (J. F. Clark) Arena, 7: 471. — (C. J. Buell) Arena, 8: 191. — (W. W. Standish) Arena, 8: 314. — (D. Horton) Fortn. 60: 558. — (H. von Holst) R. of Rs. (N. Y.) 8: 280. — Chamb. J. 70: 614. — (P. Leroy-Beaulieu) Pub. Opin. 15: 447. — (Jay Cooke) Am. M. Civics, 8: 147. — (J. W. Longley) Canad. M. 7: 406. — (J. C. Levy) Overland, n. s. 28: 314. — Pub. Opin. 13: 4. — Spec. 69: 554. — (A. B. Woodford) Soc. Econ. 1: 23, 84.
— — and India. Bank. M. (Lond.) 56: 141.
— — Another View of. (J. S. Hopkins) Am. J. Pol. 3: 270.
— — Application of the Solution. Soc. Econ. 4: 321.
— — Bimetallic Parity. (C. Vincent) Arena, 8: 151.

Silver, Question of: Facts and Principles. (J. P. Irish) Overland, n. s. 27: 558.
— — from the International Standpoint. (H. S. Brooks) Overland, n. s. 21: 69.
— — The Gold Miner and the. (C. D. Lane) Overland, n. s. 28: 585.
— — in Congress. And. R. 19: 582.
— — in the Far East. (G. Peel) National, 27: 546.
— — The Law on. (W. J. McConnell) Overland, n. s. 27: 704.
— — Lloyd on. Sat. R. 74: 440.
— — Monometallism. (W. M. Stewart) Arena, 8: 277.
— — The Morning of a New Day. (G. C. Hill) Arena, 16: 455.
— — Neglected Elements in. Soc. Econ. 7: 148.
— — Public Sentiment in America on. (F. H. Hardy) Fortn. 66: 100. Same art. Ecl. M. 127: 310.
— — Present Aspect of. (J. W. Jenks) Am. J. Soc. Sci. 32: xxiii.
— — Recent Books relating to. (A. B. Woodford) Ann. Am. Acad. Pol. Sci. 3: 84.
— — Rehabilitation of Silver. (A. G. Schiff) Fortn. 60: 566.
— — Reply to "A Financial Seer." (C. S. Thomas) Arena, 16: 367.
— — Seven Facts about Silver. (W. W. Standish) Arena, 8: 418.
— — Silver or Fiat Money. (A. J. Warner) Arena, 8: 567.
— — The Silver Side. (C. S. Thomas) Cent. 25: 473.
— — Solution of. Soc. Econ. 4: 129.
— — up to Date. (M. Frewen) Fortn. 59: 101.
— — Western Warning to the East. (L. M. Keasbey) Forum, 16: 578.
— Redemption of. (J. G. Carlisle) J. Pol. Econ. 5: 82.
— Remedy for Monetary Sectionalism. Gunton's M. 10: 433.
— Remonetization of. (J. P. Jones) Arena, 16: 736.
— Secrecy of Legislation against. Soc. Econ. 8: 292.
— Seigniorage Bill. Pub. Opin. 16: 547. 17: 18, 42.
— Suggestion for Use of. (C. W. Wiley) Am. J. Pol. 3: 527.
— Symposium on. (R. P. Bland; T. F. Bayard; J. G. Blaine; John Sherman; M. D. Harter) Soc. Econ. 2: 321.
— Value of. (P. H. Leonard) Soc. Econ. 3: 43.
— Way to equalize Gold and. (J. H. Brown) Soc. Econ. 2: 271.
— Why it ceases to be Money. Pop. Sci. Mo. 43: 577.
Silver Chlorides, Notes on. (M. C. Lea) Am. J. Sci. 144: 446.
Silver Coin and Bullion in Commerce. (W. C. Ford) Nation, 63: 263.
Silver Coinage and Foreign Investors. Soc. Econ. 6: 91.
— historically considered. (H. D. McLeod) Engin. M. 8: 579.
— Need of an International Agreement. (F. H. Head) Forum, 17: 455.
— — Folly of Further Agitation. (J. C. Hendrix) Forum, 17: 467.
— Path to Safe Currency. Soc. Econ. 5: 193.
Silver Conference, Democratic, at Washington. Pub. Opin. 19: 233.
Silver Craze in the U. S. (J. F. Johnson) Econ. J. 5: 650.
— subsiding. (H. White) Nation, 61: 40.
— I. Germany's Attitude as to a Bi-metallic Union. (Count von Mirbach) II. The Silver Standard in Mexico. (M. Romero) No. Am. 160: 699.
in Ancient Times. No. Am. 160: 759.
Silver Craze, Present Aspect of the. (C. S. Fairchild) Forum, 20: 129.
— What is the? (L. Irwell) Westm. 143: 639.
"Silver Dollar, The Old." (J. O. Herdman) Contemp. 70: 504.
Silver Fields of Tasmania. (E. Braddon) Blackw. 152: 494.
Silver Haloid Molecule, Disruption of, by Mechanical Force. (M. C. Lea) Am. J. Sci. 143: 527.
Silver Hemisulphate. (M. C. Lea) Am. J. Sci. 144: 322.
Silver Industry in the U. S. (A. Williams, jr.) Engin. M. 5: 699.
Silver-Lead Smelting, American Practice. (W. R. Ingalls) Engin. M. 6: 859.
"Silver Lining" Claim; a story. Cornh. 65: 267.
Silver Miners, Debtors, and Money. (G. C. Hill) Am. J. Pol. 3: 543.
— Ancient, of Zacatecas. (C. S. Gleed) Cosmopol. 22: 130.
Silver-mining, Future of. (T. L. Greene) Nation, 57: 340.
— in South America. (O. F. Pfordte) Cassier, 6: 435.
— Outlook for. (A. Williams) Engin. M. 8: 443.
Silver Oxide, Estimation and Dehydration of. (M. C. Lea) Am. J. Sci. 114: 249.
Silver Party's Platform, The. (H. White) Nation, 62: 92.
Silver Plate by Gilbert Marks. (F. S. Robinson) M. of Art, 19: 437.
Silver Policy of the Administration, 1894: Opponents' View (C. B. Spahr); Supporters' View (R. Mayo-Smith) Outl. 49: 660.
Silver Senators and Protection. Gunton's M. 10: 161.
Silversmiths, Birmingham, and their Work. (J. M. O'Fallon) Art J. 46: 217.
Silver Standard Countries, Competition from. (W. C. Ford) Bank. M. (N. Y.) 51: 26.
— Dishonesty of. (J. F. Hume) Am. M. Civics, 8: 225.
Silver States: are they ruined? (D. H. Waite) No. Am. 158: 24.
Silver Thimbles. (G. Fosbery) Argosy, 56: 259.
Silver Thread, The. (J. Lloyd) Munsey, 11: 242–636. 12: 52–176.
Silverware, American. (A. St. Johnston) M. of Art, 9: 13.
— Old. (T. S. Woolsey) Harper, 93: 577.
— Old English. (S. L. Johnson) Cosmopol. 20: 509.
Silverwork, American. (H. Townsend) Am. Arch. 41: 26. — (H. Townsend) J. Soc. Arts, 41: 734.
Silveria Formation. (O. H. Hershey) Am. J. Sci. 152: 324.
Silverites and Jingoes. (E. Atkinson) No. Am. 161: 554.
Silvermead. (Jean Middlemass) Time, 8: 485, 649. 9: 46–633. 10: 27–389.
Silvester II., Pope. (R. Allen) Eng. Hist. R. 7: 625.
Sime, James. Ath. '95, 1: 379.
Sime, William. Acad. 47: 57.
Simeon, St., Shrine of, at Zara. (H. M. Cundall) M. of Art, 17: 392.
Simeon, Charles, Moule's. Spec. 69: 623.
Simian, Anthropoid. (A. F. Hewit) Cath. World, 62: 526.
Similkameen Indians of Brit. Columbia. (Mrs. S. S. Allison) Anthrop. J. 21: 305.
Simmons, Ichabod. (H. L. Conard) Nat'l M. (N. Y. '91) 17: 483.
Simms, William Gilmore. (W. Ervin) So. M. 1: 53.
Simocephalus, Notes on a Species of. (F. L. Harvey) Am. Natural. 28: 395.
Simon, Jules. Ath. '96, 1: 779. — Critic, 28: 432. — (P. de Coubertin) R. of Rs. (N. Y.) 14: 450.
— A Chat about. (A. D. Vandam) Fortn. 66: 148.
— Memories of. (A. D. Vandam) Sat. R. 81: 618.

Simon Ryan the Peterite; a story. (A. Jessopp) 19th Cent. 35: 588, 746. Same art. Liv. Age, 201: 434-613.
Simon Smith. (W. R. Mackay) Lippinc. 58: 696.
Simony, Friedrich. Geog. J. 8: 644.
Simony. (L. T. Dibdin) Contemp. 63: 213. Eng. R. 3: 179.
Simpatica; a story. (F. Schmalz) Belgra. 91: 313.
Simple Annal. (R. Pardepp) Longm. 27: 598.
Simple Case, A. (W. Payne) Cent. 22: 263.
Simple Simon; a story. (George Gissing) Idler, 9: 509.
Simple Solution, A; a story. All the Year, 74: 492.
Simple Story of a Tailor-made Overcoat. (R. Wildman) Overland, n. s. 27: 529.
"Simpleton, The;" a story. Chamb. J. 69: 829.
Simpletons; a novel. (T. Hardy) Harper, 90: 65.
Simplon Hospice, the, Winter at. Cornh. 71: 29.
Simplon Pass, Crossing the. (A. J. Halliday) Outing, 23: 309.
Simpson, Sir James. Introduction of Chloroform. (E. B. Simpson) Cent. 25: 412.
Simpson, Mrs. M. C. M. Reminiscences: In the Early Forties. (M. C. M. Simpson) New R. 8: 214. Same art. Liv. Age, 197: 90.
— — People I have Known. (M. C. M. Simpson) New R. 8: 475. Same art. Liv. Age, 197: 750.
Simpson Willoughby's Groom; a story. (A. Laith) Temp. Bar, 95: 393. Same art. Liv. Age, 194: 691.
Sims, Clifford Stanley. (W. Nelson) N. E. Reg. 50: 425.
Sims, George Robert, and C. Raleigh. The Grey Mare; farcical comedy. Theatre, 28: 150.
— and R. Buchanan. The White Rose; a drama. Theatre, 28: 307.
— My First Book. Idler, 2: 385.
Simulacra; a poem. (Will Hill) Cosmopol. 20: 441.
Sin in this and other Worlds. (A. E. Thomson) Bib. Sac. 51: 429.
— Origin of. (W. E. Fischer) Luth. Q. 25: 70.
— Philosophical. (H. C. Lea) Int. J. Ethics, 5: 324.
Sinai, Mt., Pattern in. (W. Milligan) Thinker, 9: 320, 512.
— Stony. (E. N. Buxton) 19th Cent. 37: 138. Same art. Ecl. M. 124: 320. Same art. Liv. Age, 204: 349.
— Where Was? (A. H. Sayce) Asia R. 16: 149.
Sinaitic Inscriptions, The. (C. J. Lyall) Acad. 41: 426.
Sinaola, Rock Inscriptions of. (O. H. Howarth) Anthrop. J. 23: 225.
Sincerity. (W. Goddard) N. Church R. 2: 67.
Sinclair, W. M., Archdeacon, at Home. Sund. M. 22: 615.
Sindbád, Namah. (A. Rogers) Asia. R. 13: 160.
Sin-eater, The. (E. S. Hartland) Folk-Lore, 3: 145.
— in Wales. (E. S. Hartland) Acad. 48: 387-545. — (J. P. Owen and others) Acad. 49: 14-428.
Sinecures. Spec. 75: 480.
Singapore; an Indian Station. (E. O. Walker) Gent. M. n. s. 55: 335. — (R. Wildman) Overland, n. s. 25: 45.
Singer awaiting an Answer; a poem. (M. Merington) Harper, 90: 582.
Singers, American. Music, 6: 141.
— — Opera for. (K. Hackett) Music, 10: 545.
— — and their Salaries. (E. Kuhe) Theatre, 35: 76.
— Fortunes in Voices. Chamb. J. 70: 665.
— of the Century, The. (H. W. Wack) Overland, n. s. 25: 339.
— of the Day. (J. Bennett) Eng. Illust. 9: 533.
— To. (K. Hackett) Music, 8: 135.
Singing: Ancient and Modern. (P. D. Aldrich) Music, 3: 150.
— and Elocution. (H. G. Hawn) Music, 7: 34.
— and the Wagner Opera. (J. S. Van Cleve) Music, 8: 144.
— Art of. (J. Howard) Music, 2: 188.
— Breath in. (K. Hackett) Music, 9: 11.
— Correct Breathing in. (J. Howard) Music, 7: 146.
— English Language in. (K. Hackett) Music, 7: 271.
— Enunciation in. (K. Hackett) Music, 9: 404.
— German. Sat. R. 81: 620.
— Is a Knowledge of Singing of Vital Importance? (J. W. Suffern) Music, 3: 70.
— Maurel on. Sat. R. 73: 679. 74: 71.
— Modern, Transition to. (F. H. Tubbs) Music, 9: 242.
— of the Bees and the White Omen; a story. (G. Parker) Eng. Illust. 12: no. 7, 23.
— off the Key. (K. Hackett) Music, 9: 123.
— Vowels in. (K. Hackett) Music, 9: 297.
— Words as Expression in. (H. Moore) Music, 5: 309.
Singing-games of Children. (G. W. Wood) Sund. M. 24: 56.
Singing Schools, Ulster. All the Year, 75: 233.
Singing-student in London, A. (J. Forsyth) Harper, 88: 385.
Singing Teacher of the 20th Century. (H. W. Greene) Music, 9: 33.
Single Tax a Delusion, not a Doctrine. Soc. Econ. 8: 51.
— Enough to solve the Labor Problem. (S. M. Gay) Arena, 15: 956.
— Superstition of. Soc. Econ. 8: 139.
Singleton, Eng. (B. Herford) Atlan. 69: 289.
Singular Abduction, A; a story. (R. Ottolengui) Idler, 7: 175.
Singular Cleverness of Toby Van Loo. [Kitwyk stories.] (A. E. King) Cent. 25: 226.
Singular Life, A. (E. S. Phelps) Atlan. 75: 1-721. 76: 77-433.
Singularly Deluded; a story. Blackw. 152: 155-821.
Sinibaldi, Paul Jean Raphael. M. of Art, 17: 420.
Sinjirli, German Discoveries at. (A. H. Sayce) Acad. 44: 322.
Sinking Funds. (E. A. Ross) Am. Econ. Assoc. 7: 313.
Sins, Minister's Power of Forgiving and Retaining. (W. Rupp) Ref. Q. 43: 65.
Sins of the Father. (J. B. H. Burland) Argosy, 58: 240.
Sintamaskin, a Midwinter Fairyland. (C. G. La Farge) Atlan. 78: 180.
Sion College Library. (A. C. Bickley) Bookworm, 1: 265.
Sioux, Mythology of. (C. A. Eastman) Pop. Sci. Mo. 46: 88.
— — Nanibozhu in. (J. O. Dorsey) J. Am. Folk-Lore, 5: 293.
— Religion of. (W. H. Wassell) Harper, 89: 945.
— Sketching among the. ("Man-afraid-of-his-name" Outing, 23: 3.
— Social Organization of. (J. O. Dorsey) J. Am. Folk-Lore, 4: 257, 331.
Sioux Massacre, 1862. (S. M. Davis) Nat'l M. (N. Y. '91) 16: 660.
Sioux War, Nebraska's National Guard in. (W. R. Hamilton) Outing, 28: 317.
Sir George Tressady. (Mrs. H. Ward) Cent. 29: 177-817. 30: 28-934.
Sir Harry Gray; a story. (C. A. Price) Belgra. 82: 312, 421.
"Sir John." (J. Kent) Gent. M. n. s. 51: 217. Same art. Liv. Age. 199: 401.

Sir Lancelot; a poem. (W. W. Campbell) Canad. M. **1**: 49.
Sir Michael. (F. Pollock) Macmil. **65**: 302. Same art. Liv. Age, **192**: 788.
Sir Reginald's Romance; a Corsican Love Story. Temp. Bar, **97**: 290, 438, 559.
Sir Simon's Courtship. (G. W. Hartley) Macmil. **70**: 241. Same art. Liv. Age, **202**: 531.
Sir William's Wife; a story. (W. E. Norris) Eng. Illust. **14**: 189.
Siráf, Ancient Trading Centre on the Persian Gulf. (A. W. Stiffe) Geog. J. **6**: 166.
Sirani, Elisabetta. (A. Isaacson) Belgra. **86**: 202.
Siren of Three-mile Bend; a story. (R. M. Dene) Un. Serv. (Phila.) **10**: 309.
Sirens, in Art. (J. E. Harrison) M. of Art, **10**: 133.
Sirius and its Companion. (D. Kirkwood) Pop. Astron. **1**: 205.
— and its System. (J. E. Gore) Gent. M. n. s. **50**: 14. Same art. Liv Age, **196**: 495.
— Color of, History of. (T. J. J. See) Astron. **11**: 269, 372, 550.
— in Ancient Times. (T. J. J. See) Pop. Astron. **2**: 193.
Sisal industry in the Bahamas. J. Soc. Arts, **44**: 407.
Sister. (H. S. Merriam) Blackw. **151**: 888. Same art. Ecl. M. **119**: 99. Same art. Liv. Age, **194**: 371.
Sister of the Annunciation; a story. (M. Merington) Harper, **89**: 857.
Sister Clare; a story. (G. Fosbery) Argosy, **58**: 550.
Sister Cordelia. Macmil. **70**: 468. Same art. Liv. Age, **203**: 466.
Sister Kathleen; a story. Belgra. **85**: 390.
Sister Refugia. (L. Craighan) Overland, n. s. **22**: 35.
Sisterhood of Cameron; a story. Belgra. **89**: 310.
Sisters, The; a story. (H. D. Loury) Eng. Illust. **12**: no. 4, 23.
Sita, The Rape of. (A. H. Gunlogsen) Open Court, **3**: 1622–1743.
Sitting, The Habit of. (F. Boyle) New R. **15**: 649.
Sitting Bull, True Story of the Death of. (E. G. Fechét) Cosmopol. **20**: 493.
Siwash Indians, of Puget Sound. (E. Meliss) Overland, n. s. **20**: 501.
Six Bulls to Die. (Mrs. N. Cutter) Cent. **24**: 659.
Six Jolly Serving-men. (J. A. Owen) Argosy, **60**: 631.
Six Merrie Wiyes of the West. (J. A. Owen) Argosy, **60**: 150.
Six Thousand Tons of Gold; a story. (K. E. Kirkwood) Chaut. **19**: 395–659. **20**: 48, 175.
Sixth Bench, The. (R. Barr) Idler, **2**: 78.
Sixth Sense, The. (P. Tyner) Arena, **10**: 37.
Sixth Sense; or, Another World; a story. (J. H. Rosny) Chaut. **23**: 589.
Size of Objects, Apparent. (W. H. R. Rivers) Mind, **21**: 71.
Size-Contrast, Effect of, upon Judgments of Position in Retinal Field. (J. M. Baldwin) Psychol. R. **2**: 244.
Skager Rack, The. (M. Todhunter) Westm. **145**: 404.
Skalds, Poetry of the. (W. A. Craigie) Scot. R. **28**: 331. Same art. Liv. Age, **211**: 685.
Skating. Ath. '**92**, **1**: 271. — Sat. R. **73**: 102. — Spec. **68**: 90. — (M. G. Watkins) Acad. **41**: 82. — (E. W. Sandys) Outing, **27**: 200.
— Fancy and Figure. (A. Grosvenor) New R. **14**: 152.
— in Fenland. (C. Silcock) Eng. Illust. **10**: 303.
— in Flanders. (C. J. K. Fenton) Argosy, **59**: 278.
— King Skate; a poem. (C. Turner) Outing, **25**: 267.
Skating, Speed in, Anatomy of. (R. T. McKenzie) Pop. Sci. Mo. **48**: 180.
— Stories of. Idler, **6**: 776.
Skeletal Variation, Individual. (F. A. Lucas) Science, **22**: 52.
Skeleton Construction and the Fire Department. (T. M. Clark) Am. Arch. **46**: 23.
Skeleton Hand, The. (A. MacLeod) Blackw. **156**: 527.
Skeletons, Primigenial. (H. P. F. Marriott) Pop. Sci. Mo. **48**: 14.
Skelt, Juvenile Dramas of. (R. L. Stevenson) M. of Art, **7**: 227.
Skelton, John. Table-Talk of Shirley. (G. Newcomen) Acad. **48**: 356. — Sat. R. **80**: 527.
ΣΚΗΝΑΩ, ΣΚΗΝΕΩ, ΣΚΗΝΟΩ. (M. H. Morgan) Am. J. Philol. **13**: 71.
Skene, F. M. F. Recollections. Blackw. **159**: 828.
Skene, William Forbes. Acad. **42**: 213. — Ath. '**92**, **2**: 323.
Skeptic, The Modern. (J. Burroughs) Open Court, **1**: 239, 322.
Skepticism, Agnosticism, Free Thought. (S. Dewey) Westm. **143**: 178.
— Modern, and Ethical Culture. (F. Adler) Forum, **16**: 379.
— Popular, and the Church. (S. A. Ort) Luth. Q. **26**: 555.
— a Self-evident Error. (C. Collins) Open Court, **1**: 723.
— True, Benefits of. (C. A. Little) Ref. Q. **40**: 414.
— Varieties of. Meth. R. **54**: 454.
— Wanted, a New. (S. Dewey) Westm. **143**: 31.
Skeptics of the Old Testament, Dillon on. (S. R. Driver) Contemp. **69**: 257.
Sketches and Studies by Old and Modern Masters. (J. Oldcastle) M. of Art, **4**: 84.
Sketches, A Set of. (H. Pyle) Cent. **25**: 210.
Sketching, Art of. (R. A. M. Stevenson) M. of Art, **9**: 124.
— An Artist's Idea of. (B. Day) M. of Art, **5**: 26.
— from Nature. (J. E. Hodgson) M. of Art, **16**: 302.
Sketching Club, Hints for Organizing a. (R. St. J. Tyrwhitt) M. of Art, **4**: 325.
Skies and Water-Carts. (A. R. Buckland) Sund. M. **23**: 768.
— Changeful. (C. C. Abbott) Lippinc. **57**: 846.
Skiff-racing, St. Lawrence. (C. B. Vaux) Outing, **20**: 324.
Skin, Sensibility of. (W. B. Pillsbury) Am. J. Psychol. **7**: 42.
— Sensations in, Experiments on. (H. Griffing) Psychol. R. **2**: 125.
Skinner, Otis, Actor. (A. Brownell) Bost. **3**: 190.
Skipper's Bible, The; a story. (E. Phillpotts) Good Words, **35**: 242.
Skipper's Treasure; a story. Argosy, **57**: 155.
Skipsey, Joseph. Songs and Lyrics. (W. Lewin) Acad. **42**: 147.
Skirt-Dancing. Sat. R. **73**: 741.
Ski-Running. (W. S. Harwood) Outing, **21**: 339.
Skis, Crossing an Alpine Pass on. (A. C. Doyle) McClure, **4**: 348.
Skopas, Art of, in the British Museum. (E. Sellers) 19th Cent. **37**: 682.
Skrine, John H. Joan the Maid. Sat. R. **81**: 402.
Skulls Discovered at Brandon, Suffolk. (C. S. Myers) Anthrop. J. **26**: 113.
— Two, from Nagyr. (W. L. H. Duckworth) Anthrop. J. **23**: 121.
Skunk, The, as a Source of Rabies. (W. Wade) Am. Natural. **29**: 242.

Sky-pilot; a Sketch of Western Life. (A. F. Chamberlain) Canad. M. 1: 582.
Sky-pilot; a story. (Mary S. Hancock) Gent. M. n. s. 57: 109. Same art. Liv. Age, 211: 168.
Sky Sign, A; a drama. (Mrs. A. Dean) Eng. Illust. 14: 311.
Sky Worship in America. (S. D. Peet) Am. Antiq. 16: 217.
Skye, A Legend of. (G. E. Wyatt) Good Words, 35: 342.
— Mountains of. All the Year, 74: 511.
Slade School of Art, London. Spec. 69: 595.
Slander; a poem. (E. Fawcett) Cosmopol. 14: 531.
Slang. All the Year, 73: 510. — Atlan. 71: 425. — (F. Hall) Nation, 57: 155.
— and Metaphor. (E. F. Andrew) Chaut. 23: 462.
— Dictionary of, Maitland's. (T. R. Lounsbury) Nation, 54: 469.
— Function of. (B. Matthews) Harper, 87: 304. — Pub. Opin. 15: 327.
— Rogue. (W. C. Wilde) J. Am. Folk-Lore, 2: 301. 3: 303.
— Thieves'. (C. H. Vellacott) Gent. M. n. s. 57: 346.
— Transplantation of. (T. W. Higginson) Pub. Opin. 15: 419.
Slapping Sal, The; a story. (A. Conan Doyle) McClure, 1: 206.
Slate, Temperature Variation of the Thermal Conductivity of. (B. O. Peirce and R. W. Wilson) Am. J. Sci. 150: 435.
Slates, Stratigraphic Position of Thomson. (J. E. Spurr) Am. J. Sci. 148: 159.
Slatin Pasha, Rudolph C. (E. A. Gowing) Belgra. 91: 125.
— Fire and Sword in the Sudan, trans. by Wingate. (F. D. Lugard) National, 27: 178.
— Ten Years' Captivity of. (S. E. Tillman) Cosmopol. 22: 139.
Slaughter-Houses, Public. (B. W. Richardson) New R. 8: 631.
Slava. (G. Maxwell) Folk-Lore, 2: 65.
Slave, The Value of a. Chamb. J. 73: 191.
Slave of the Lamp; a story. (H. S. Merriman) Cornh. 65: 1-590.
Slave of the Ring, A; a story. (A. Berlyn) Idler, 3: 661.
Slave of Summer, The. Macmil. 74: 199.
Slave-ships. Chamb. J. 70: 558.
Slave Trade, Present Causes of. Sat. R. 73: 66.
— to the United States, DuBois's Suppression of. Nation, 63: 498.
Slave Traders of New York. (T. A. Janvier) Harper, 90: 293.
Slavery, Abolition of, in the U. S. (J. B. McMaster) Chaut. 15: 24.
— and the Ordinance of 1787. (H. W. Quaintance) M. Am. Hist, 30: 75.
— and the Slave Trade in Africa. (H. M. Stanley) Harper, 86: 613. — (H. T. Cousins) Sund. M. 22: 166.
— How England forced the Slave upon America. (W. L. Scruggs) M. Am. Hist. 28: 32.
— in the Colony of North Carolina. (J. S. Bassett) J. H. Univ. Stud. 14: 179.
— in Connecticut. (B. C. Steiner) J. H. Univ. Studies, 11: nos. 9-10.
— in Old Deerfield. (G. Sheldon) New Eng. M. n. s. 8: 49.
— in East Africa. Dub. R. 114: 184.
— in Egypt; The Nile *corvée*. (F. Cope Whitehouse) Nation, 55: 373.
— in New Jersey, Early. Gunton's M. 11: 359.
Slavery in New Jersey, A Study of. (H. S. Cooley) J. H. Univ. Stud. 14: 419.
— in the Territories. (J. C. Welling) M. Am. Hist. 27: 132, 196.
— Letters of Colonel William Byrd on Slavery and Indented Servants, 1736, 1739. Am. Hist. R. 1: 88.
— Light on Underground Railroads. (W. H. Siebert) Am. Hist. R. 1: 455.
— Slave Power and the Money Power. (C. W. Cram) Arena, 8: 690.
— Southern Quakers and, Weeks on. (G. W. Julian) Dial (Ch.) 21: 38.
— under the British Flag. (F. D. Lugard) 19th Cent. 39: 335.
— when it went out of Politics. (N. Brooks) Scrib. M. 17: 338.
— White, in the Colony of Virginia. (J. C. Ballagh) J. H. Univ. Stud. 13: 269.
Slaves in New York, Price of, 1659-1818. (E. V. Morgan) M. Am. Hist. 29: 523.
— White, and Bond Servants, in the American Colonies. (A. B. Ellis) Pop. Sci. Mo. 42: 612.
Slavonic Folk-Lore. (W. S. Lach-Szyrma) Folk-Lore Rec. 4: 52.
Slavs, Early, Marriage among. (P. Kowalewsky) Folk-Lore, 1: 463.
Sledge Journey. (J. Diebitsch-Peary) Around World, 1: 1.
Sledging in Norway. (C. Edwardes) Outing, 25: 215.
Slender Romance. (R. M. Stuart) Cent. 29: 462.
Sleep, Chemistry of. (H. Wurtz) Pop. Sci. Mo. 46: 230.
— Loss of, Effects of. (G. T. W. Patrick and J. A. Gilbert) Psychol. R. 3: 469.
— — Patrick and Gilbert on. (H. C. Warren) Am. Natural. 30: 1061.
— Mental Action during. (A. Badington) Am. Natural. 30: 849.
— Reading before. Temp. Bar, 107: 560.
— Some Aspects of. Chamb. J. 72: 167.
Sleep; a poem. (A. Brown) Harper, 87: 250.
Sleepiness and Sleeplessness. (A. Schofield) Ecl. M. 123: 707.
Sleeping-car Company, Liability of, for Loss of Baggage. (S. Maxwell) Am. Law R. 27: 24.
Sleeping-car Tragedy; A. (W. L. Alden) Idler, 9: 41.
Sleeplessness. (A. S. Eccles) National, 23: 797. Same art. Ecl. M. 123: 406.
Sleepy Hollow as it is To-day. (J. N. Smith) Munsey, 7: 284.
Sleight-of-hand. (A. Herrmann) Lippinc. 52: 475.
Sleight-of-hand Experts, Psychological Notes upon. (J. Jastrow) Science, n. s. 3: 685.
Slieve League, Ireland. All the Year, 75: 413.
Sligachan and the Coolins. Cornh. 71: 375.
Sligo, Ireland, History of, Woodmartin's. Sat. R. 73: 423.
Slivinski, Joseph. Critic, 24: 112.
Slyfield House, Surrey. (B. Champneys) M. of Art, 9: 177.
Sloane, Wm. M., with portrait. Bk. Buyer, 13: 437. — Critic, 26: 294.
Slocombe, Fred. The Mill-stream: an Etching. Art J. 47: 285.
Sloths, Ground. (R. Lydekker) Knowl. 17: 73.
Sloyd, Distinguishing Characteristics of. (L. J. Woodward) Educa. 13: 296.
Sloyd System. (C. T. Work) Lend a H. 14: 356.
Slugs, Climate and. (T. D. A. Cockerell) Science, 21: 338.

Slum Work. (Mrs. L. O. Chant) Our Day, **16**: 433.
Slumming: Is it played out? (J. Adderley) Eng. Illust. **10**: 834.
Slums of London, Stamping out. (E. Marshall) Cent. **29**: 700.
— Only Cure for. (E. R. L. Gould) Forum, **19**: 495.
— Redemption of. (H. G. Mitchell) Meth. R. **55**: 262.
— Uninhabitable Houses in City. (W. Stevenson) Engin. M. **9**: 832.
Slye, Capt. Robert, Will of. (C. Johnston) N. E. Reg. **50**: 354.
Smailholm Tower, Scotland. Chamb. J. **70**: 337.
Small-pox, Investigations concerning the Etiology of. (J. C. Bay) Am. Natural. **29**: 699.
Small Talk. All the Year, **70**: 17.
— Perils of. (A. M. Hamilton) Cent. **29**: 739.
Smart, Christopher. (C. A. Ward) Walford's Antiq. **8**: 217, 260.
— Song to David. Sat. R. **81**: 606.
Smartness, Mallock on. Spec. **69**: 91.
— Society. Spec. **69**: 125.
Smedley, W. T., with portrait. Bk. Buyer, **11**: 77.
Smeed, E. C., and his Work. (H. Haupt) Engin. M. **4**: 115.
Smell; a Neglected Sense. (E. Dillon) 19th Cent. **35**: 574. Same art. Liv. Age, **201**: 502.
— Sense of, and Odors. (C. Henry) Pop. Sci. Mo. **41**: 682.
— — in Animals. Chamb. J. **69**: 741
— — in Maoris. Liv. Age, **196**: 448.
Smelt Fishing, Winter. (C. J. Kinsley) Outing, **19**: 394.
Smelting Process, The Pyritic. (P. Argall) Engin. M. **7**: 78.
Smetana, Bedrich. (J. J. Kral) Music, **9**: 145. **10**: 11, 155.
Smetham, James. (J. M. Gray) Acad. **41**: 189. — Lond. Q. **78**: 67.
— Letters. (W. J. Stillman) Nation, **54**: 116.
Smilax Glauca. Garden & F. **5**: 424.
— Pseudo-china. Garden & F. **5**: 52.
Smiley, James H. (H. L. Conard) Nat'l M. (N. Y. '91) **17**: 571.
Smith, Adam. Lond. Q. **85**: 96.
— and Alexander Hamilton. (E. G. Bourne) Q. J. Econ. **8**: 328.
— and his Friends. Ed. R. **182**: 221. Same art. Liv. Age, **206**: 771.
— Rae's Life of. Church Q. **42**: 104. Sat. R. **80**: 316.
— Relations of, to Recent Economics. (L. L. Price) Econ. J. **3**: 239.
Smith, Arthur H., with portrait. Bk. News, **13**: 51.
Smith, Charles E., with portrait. (L. A. Bond) Nat'l M. (N. Y. '91) **17**: 567.
Smith, Elizabeth Oakes. (W. M. Griswold) Critic, **23**: 361.
Smith, F. Hopkinson, with portrait. Bk. Buyer, **8**: 629. — With portrait. Bk. News, **10**: 99. — With portraits. (G. Willets) Munsey, **11**: 141.
— Portraits of. McClure, **1**: 492.
Smith, Geo. Adam, with portrait. (A. B. Bruce) Bib. World, **8**: 1.
Smith, Goldwin. Canad. M. **7**: 540.
— his "Views" on the Political History of the U. S. (W. Wilson) Forum, **16**: 489.
— in Literature and Politics. (J. C. Hopkins) Westm. **141**: 539.
— on Morality and Religion. (P. Carus) Open Court, **5**: 2765.
— Political Essays. Nation, **58**: 215.
Smith, Henry; an Old-world Parson. Macmil. **71**: 39.
Smith, Henry J. S., Works of. (P. A. MacMahon) Nature, **50**: 517.
Smith, Henry P. (P. King) Mo. Illust. **4**: 364.
Smith, Henry Preserved, Case of. And. R. **19**: 221.
Smith, John, Capt. Generall Historie. N. E. Reg. **47**: 205.
— in Virginia. (J. Fiske) Atlan. **76**: 350.
Smith, Dr. John, at Home. (A. W. Stewart) Sund. M. **24**: 661.
Smith, John Chaloner. Ath. '95, **1**: 384.
Smith, John Russell. Ath. '94, **2**: 644.
Smith, Joseph, the Bibliographer of the Friends. (A. C. Bickley) Bookworm, **1**: 30, 73.
Smith, Madeleine H., Trial of. (J. B. Atlay) Cornh. **74**: 639.
Smith, Mary. Two Types of Piety. Atlan. **73**: 834.
Smith, Richard, Diary of, in the Continental Congress, 1775–76. Am. Hist. R. **1**: 288, 493.
Smith, Robert Payne. Acad. **47**: 296.
Smith, Roswell. (W. Gladden) Cent. **22**: 310.
Smith, Samuel Francis, Author of "America." Bost. **3**: 224. — (C. E. L. Wingate) Critic, **27**: 349.
Smith, Samuel W.; an Oregonian Poet Hermit. (W. F. D. Jones) Overland, n. s. **25**: 375.
Smith, Sydney, and Social Reform. (A. W. W. Dale) Sund. M. **24**: 252. Same art. Liv. Age, **205**: 314.
Smith, Thomas Stuart, and his Institute at Sterling. (H. W. Bromhead) Art J. **48**: 307.
Smith, William. Acad. **44**: 319. — Ath. '93, **2**: 522.
Smith, William Henry. Lond. Q. **82**: 52. — Quar. **178**: 308.
— & Son. (W. M. Acworth) Eng. Illust. **9**: 795.
— — Bookstalls and Library of. (Wm. C. Preston) Good Words, **36**: 474.
— as a Colleague. (Lord Ashbourne) National, **22**: 592.
— Character of. (J. Hamilton) Acad. **45**: 164.
— Life of. (J. McCarthy) Good Words, **35**: 102.
Smith, Wm. Robertson. (J. G. Frazer) Fortn. **61**: 800. — (J. S. Cotton) Acad. **45**: 289. — Sat. R. **77**: 359. — Lit. W. (Bost.) **25**: 119. — (T. M. Lindsay) Sund. M. **23**: 410. — (J. Bryce) Nation, **58**: 308. — (F. C. Burkitt) Eng. Hist. R. **9**: 684. — Critic, **24**: 241. — Nature, **49**: 557. — Ath. '94, **1**: 445. — (T. M. Lindsay) Chr. Lit. **11**: 37.
— Doctrine of Scripture. (T. M. Lindsay) Chr. Lit. **12**: 23.
Smith College, Festivals in. (H. C. Seelye) Cent. **27**: 432.
Smithers; a story. (M. Thompson) Lippinc. **49**: 722.
Smith's Strike, The; a story. (F. Coppée) Temp. Bar, **95**: 117.
Smithsonian Institution. (G. B. Goode) Nature, **53**: 257, 281.
— its Origin, Growth, etc. (H. C. Bolton) Pop. Sci. Mo. **48**: 289, 449.
Smoke in London: How to make London Smokeless. (L. C. D'Oyle) Gent. M. n. s. **49**: 21.
— Problem of. Chamb. J. **71**: 177.
Smoke-preventing Appliances. (W. F. Sicard) J. Frankl. Inst. **138**: 58.
Smokeless Combustion. Dub. R. **114**: 425.
Smoking. Chamb. J. **72**: 143.
— Plea for Tobacco. (Lady C. Campbell) Eng. Illust. **11**: 81. — A Counter Blast; a Reply. (E. L. Linton) Eng. Illust. **11**: 85.
— Theory of. (H. Boult) Gent. M. n. s. **50**: 413.
Smoking-room, Travellers'. All the Year, **71**: 517.
Smollett, Tobias, Humphry Clinker. (A. Dobson) Longm. **22**: 370.

Smollett, Tobias. Roderick Random. (J. A. Nicklin) Gent. M. n. s. **56**: 453.
— His Translation of Gil Blas. (A. L. Mayhew) Acad. **42**: 313.
— in the South of Europe. Liv. Age, **192**: 507.
Smugglers, Highland. Good Words, **33**: 31.
Smugglers of the Clone, The; a story. (S. R. Crockett) Idler, **8**: 104.
Smuggling, Shore on. Ath. '**92**, **1**: 691.
Smyth, Egbert C. (A. H. Bradford) Chr. Un. **45**: 540.
Smyth, Frederick. (R. Morgan) Munsey, **9**: 372.
Smyth, John, Will of. Reliquary, **33**: 109.
Smyth Family of Maryland. (E. C. Neff) Am. Hist. Reg. **1**: 233.
Smyth's Channel and Magellan Straits. (A. P. Crouch) Un. Serv. M. **5**: 568.
Snail, The, Obnoxious to the Poets. Good Words, **34**: 685.
Snails, Land, Protective Devices and Coloration of. (H. A. Pilsbry) Pop. Sci. Mo. **42**: 187.
Snake, Garter, Habits of. (A. G. Mayer) Pop. Sci. Mo. **42**: 485.
— Milk, Color Variations in. (E. D. Cope) Am. Natural. **27**: 1066.
— Watching a, for an Hour. (W. Dennis) Science, **20**: 338.
Snake-bite, Cure for. (J. G. McPherson) Knowl. **18**: 164.
— Death from, in India. Chamb. J. **72**: 390.
— Inoculation against. (H. J. W. Dam) McClure, **3**: 460.
— New Treatment for. (W. H. Wooster) Science, **20**: 255.
— — Rational. Nature, **52**: 620.
— Treatment of, with Antivenine. (T. R. Frazer) Nature, **53**: 569, 592. **55**: 139. — (J. G. McPherson) Knowl. **18**: 175.
Snake Ceremonials at Walpi, Fewkes' (J. G. Bourke) J. Am. Folk-Lore, **7**: 324.
Snake Dance, Moki, Meaning of. (J. W. Fewkes) J. Am. Folk-Lore, **4**: 129.
Snake-eating Snakes. (H. Stewart) Good Words, **36**: 190.
Snake River Valley, in the. (J. R. Spears) Chaut. **15**: 298, 416.
Snake Story, The Best, in the World. Macmil. **74**: 373. Same art. Liv. Age, **211**: 251.
Snake-training. (A. Stradling) Chamb. J. **72**: 203.
Snake-venom and Anti-venomous Serum. (A. Calmette) Nature, **54**: 380.
Snake Yarns, Australian. Chamb. J. **69**: 640.
Snakes. (R. Lydekker) Knowl. **17**: 138. — (W. H. Hudson) Macmil. **67**: 451. — Quar. **174**: 423.
— and Hospitality; a Story of the Lesser Antilles. (E. Philpotts) Idler, **2**: 683.
— Brazilian. Chamb. J. **71**: 123.
— British Snake-Lore. All the Year, **74**: 569.
— Classification of. (E. D. Cope) Am. Natural. **28**: 831.
— Florida. (R. G. Robinson) Lippinc. **58**: 710.
— How they are fed. (F. A. Guthrie) Time, **3**: 610.
— Marine. (G. A. Boulenger) Nat. Sci. **1**: 44.
— of Nebraska, Catalogue of. (W. E. Taylor) Am. Natural. **26**: 742.
— Poisonous, in India. (E. C. Cotes) McClure, **2**: 466.
— Ring-, Our British. Chamb. J. **71**: 508.
— The Serpent's Strangeness. (W. H. Hudson) Fortn. **61**: 528.
— Some New North American. (E. D. Cope) Am. Natural. **29**: 676.
— Superstitions about. (A. Stradling) Chamb. J. **70**: 325.
Snakes, Venom of. (C. A. Mitchell) Knowl. **17**: 161.
— Venomous. (W. Seton) Cath. World, **55**: 695.
Snipe and Tiger Hunting in India. Blackw. **152**: 528.
Snipe, Modern. (T. S. Van Dyke) Outing, **27**: 353.
Snipe-hunt, A; a Story of Jim-Ned Creek. (M. E. M. Davis) Harper, **92**: 352.
Snipe-shooting. Sat. R. **78**: 656.
— Spring. (E. W. Sandys) Outing, **24**: 121.
Snow Genealogy, The. (Mrs. M. L. T. Alden) N. E. Reg. **47**: 81, 186, 341. **48**: 71, 188. **49**: 71, 202, 451.
Snow, Colored, Fall of, in Indiana, Jan. 8, 1892. (A. N. Somers) Science, **21**: 303.
Snow-Blanche; a Russian tale. Temp. Bar, **102**: 547.
Snow Crystals, Inner Structure of. (G. Nordenskiold) Nature, **48**: 592.
Snowdrops, Cultivation of. (S. Arnoth) Garden & F. **6**: 90. — (J. N. Gerard) Garden & F. **7**: 118. **8**: 137.
Snow-rollers. (E. W. Claypole) Science, **21**: 64.
Snow-shoeing in the White Mountains. (G. H. Taylor) Outing, **21**: 293.
Snow-shoer's Song; a Poem. (J. N. Doyle) Outing, **23**: 358.
Snow-storm in Humboldt Co., California, Jan., 1890. Overland, n. s. **20**: 539.
Snub, The. (K. M. Rabb) Lippinc. **54**: 565.
Snyders, Frans. M. of Art, **3**: 23.
So runs the World; a story. (F. Chaffee) Munsey, **12**: 389.
So Well Matched! a story. All the Year, **75**: 500, 525.
Soane, Sir John. (J. E. Hodgson and F. A. Eaton) Art J. **47**: 143.
Sobieski, Princess Clementina. (E. Lecky) Longm. **25**: 515.
Socager, the, in Domesday. (G. Law) Jurid. R. **8**: 279.
Social *vs.* Societary. (A. W. Small) Ann. Am. Acad. Pol. Sci. **5**: 948.
Social Agitation and Scholarship. (A. W. Small) Am. J. Sociol. **1**: 564.
Social Amelioration, Possibilities of. (J. J. McCook) Am. J. Soc. Sci. **32**: 160.
Social and Economic Legislation in the U. S. in 1891. (W. B. Shaw) Q. J. Econ. **6**: 227.
— — in 1892. (W. B. Shaw) Q. J. Econ. **7**: 187.
— — in 1893. (W. B. Shaw) Q. J. Econ. **8**: 230.
— — in 1894. (W. B. Shaw) Q. J. Econ. **9**: 195.
— — in 1895. (W. B. Shaw) Q. J. Econ. **10**: 218.
Social and Economic Science. (R. T. Colburn) Science, n. s. **4**: 558.
Social and Industrial Situation. (W. Gladden) Bib. Sac. **49**: 383.
Social and Political Sciences, Study of. (E. J. James) Eth. Rec. **3**: 8.
Social Apathy, Causes of. (T. C. Fry) Econ. R. **2**: 318.
Social Betterment. (N. P. Gilman) New World, **1**: 485.
Social Changes in Fifty Years. (Countess of Cork) 19th Cent. **31**: 465. Same art. Liv. Age, **193**: 346.
Social Classes in the Republic. (E. L. Godkin) Atlan. **78**: 721.
Social Compact Theory, Jefferson and. (G. P. Fisher) Yale R. **2**: 403.
Social Conditions; a Dialogue. (V. Lee) Contemp. **63**: 650. **64**: 90.
— Study of, by the Young, Value of. (J. W. Buckham) Lend a H. **15**: 24.
Social Constitution; Loria's *Bases économiques de.* Econ. J. **4**: 76.
Social Control. (E. A. Ross) Am. J. Sociol. **1**: 513, 753. **2**: 96–433.
Social Crimes. (Mrs. Lynn Linton) Chamb. J. **73**: 49.

Social Degeneracy, Symptoms of. (M. D. Conway) Open Court, **2**: 1429.
Social Democracy and Liberty. (F. V. Fisher) Westm. **141**: 643. Same art. Ecl. M. **123**: 289.
Social Discontent — I. Its Causes. (H. Holt) Forum, **18**: 664. II. Remedies. (H. Holt) Forum, **19**: 68, 169.
Social Doctrine of Sermon on the Mount. (C. Gore) Econ. R. **2**: 145.
Social Duty and Christianity. (V. H. Stanton) Econ. R. **3**: 87. — (W. H. Sanday) Econ. R. **3**: 348.
Social Economic Problems. (C. de Grafenried) Am. J. Sociol. **2**: 190.
Social Economics, Psychologic Basis of. (L. F. Ward) Ann. Am. Acad. Pol. Sci. **3**: 464.
Social Economy, Phases of. (F. B. Sanborn) Am. J. Soc. Sci. **31**: 44.
— State Intervention in. (A. L. Beaulieu) Pop. Sci. Mo. **41**: 463.
Social Evil: its Cause and Remedies. Eng. R. **11**: 1.
Social Evolution. (D. G. Ritchie) Int. J. Ethics, **6**: 165. — (E. M. Hardinge) Our Day, **15**: 255.
— and Historical Science. Westm. **146**: 619.
— Hub of. Soc. Econ. **3**: 200.
— Kidd's. Ed. R. **179**: 479. — (N. M. Butler) Educa. R. **7**: 385. — (G. B. Adams) Yale R. **3**: 99. — (A. W. Benn) Acad. **45**: 261. — Church Q. **38**: 311. — Sat. R. **77**: 420. — Spec. **72**: 292. **73**: 109. — (Lord Farrer) Contemp. **65**: 769. — (D. G. Ritchie) Int. J. Ethics, **5**: 107. — (A. R. Wallace) Nature, **49**: 549. — Ath. '94, **1**: 795. — (T. Roosevelt) No. Am. **161**: 94. — (H. C. Minton) Presb. & Ref. R. **6**: 136. — (W. D. Le Sueur) Pop. Sci. Mo. **47**: 38. — (J. A. Hobson) Am. J. Sociol. **1**: 299. — (J. G. Taylor) Educa. **15**: 457, 529. — (B. Kidd) 19th Cent. **37**: 226.
— — and his Parley with Religion. Canad. M. **6**: 52.
— Note on the Term. (G. McDermott) Am. J. Sociol. **1**: 596.
Social Forces. (L. F. Ward) Am. J. Sociol. **2**: 82.
— Theory of. (S. N. Patten) Ann. Am. Acad. Pol. Sci. **7**: suppl. 1.
Social Highwayman. (E. P. Train) Lippinc. **56**: 3.
Social Ideas and Social Realities in America. (W. B. Hale) Citizen, **1**: 103.
Social Intercourse, Gladstone on. Spec. **70**: 699.
Social Legislation in U. S., 1889-90. (L. S. Merriam) Econ. R. **1**: 234.
Social Liabilities. Spec. **69**: 765.
Social Morality. (J. H. Hyslop) Pub. Opin. **20**: 13.
Social Movement in French Protestantism. (E. Bost.) New World, **2**: 256.
Social Movements, Some Recent. (W. Taurnier) Soc. Econ. **4**: 348.
Social Organism, Some Material Forces of the. (J. W. Langley) Pop. Sci. Mo. **46**: 502.
Social Peace, Schulze-Gaevernitz on. Spec. **72**: 440.
Social Phenomena, Classification of. (A. Fairbanks) Bib. Sac. **53**: 133.
— Statistical Correlation between. (F. Y. Edgeworth) J. Statis. Soc. **56**: 670.
Social Philosophy, Fundamental Beliefs in my. (R. T. Ely) Forum, **18**: 173.
— Mackenzie's. Ath. '92, **1**: 528.
— Place of. (G. G. Wilson) Am. J. Soc. Sci. **32**: 139.
Social Philosophy for Churchmen. (T. C. Fry) Econ. R. **2**: 50.
Social Plaint, The. (E. B. Andrews) New World, **1**: 201.
Social Problem, The. (D. H. Wheeler) Meth. R. **53**: 554.
— The Contented Masses. (A. French) Forum, **18**: 204.
Social Problem in the U. S.: Social Quagmire and the Way out. (A. R. Wallace) Arena, **7**: 395, 525.
— Our. (R. H. Law) Westm. **145**: 674.
Social Problems and the Church. (M. E. Gates) Chaut. **18**: 136. — Dub. R. **113**: 801.
— and their Solution. (E. V. Neale) Econ. R. **2**: 518.
— at the Antipodes. (W. Booth) Contemp. **61**: 422. Same art. Ecl. M. **118**: 646.
— Ethical Solution of. (P. Ford) Westm. **144**: 298. Same art. Ecl. M. **125**: 731.
Social Progress, Ethics of. (F. H. Giddings) Int. J. Ethics, **3**: 137.
— Present Conflict for a Larger Life. (M. J. Savage) Arena, **10**: 297.
— Reason and Sentiment as Factors in. (C. W. Super) Meth. R. **56**: 94.
Social Purity. (C. Greeley) Lend a H. **13**: 343.
— Scientists and. (W. J. Corbet) Westm. **144**: 574.
Social Question, French Roman Catholics and. (C. Jannet) Q. J. Econ. **7**: 137.
— in Catholic Congresses. (J. G. Brooks) Int. J. Ethics, **6**: 204.
— Possible Solution of the. (C. G. Gümpel) Westm. **138**: 270.
— Cardinal Vaughan and the. (W. R. Sullivan) Westm. **141**: 126.
Social Questions, Church and. (W. G. Blaikie) Thinker, **8**: 8.
— Lilly on. (C. S. Devas) Dub. R. **111**: 426.
Social Reform. (A. Mason) N. Church R. **3**: 355.
— and the Pulpit. (W. Gladden) Chr. Lit. **14**: 164.
— The Church and. (W. Gladden) Chr. Lit. **14**: 68.
— Coming Social Condition. Soc. Econ. **4**: 354.
— Conservative Programme. (J. E. Gorst) 19th Cent. **38**: 3. Same art. Ecl. M. **125**: 337.
— Personal Element in. (Wm. MacDonald) Meth. R. **56**: 403.
— Relation of the Doctrine of Population to. (H. C. Adams) Open Court, **1**: 228.
— *vs.* War. (R. T. Ely) Our Day, **16**: 313.
— Where it should begin. (W. Gladden) Chr. Lit. **14**: 290.
— Woman's Part in. (C. Maynard) Arena, **7**: 476.
Social Reformer of the 15th Century, A. (Frank Goodrich) Yale R. **5**: 168.
Social Reformers, Ideals of. (W. Rauschenbusch) Am. J. Sociol. **2**: 202.
— Practical Hint to. (M. Jackson) Soc. Econ. **4**: 168.
Social Reforms, Relation of. (D. R. Dewey) Open Court, **6**: 3294.
Social Regeneration. (G. D. Herron) Char. R. **4**: 291.
Social Science and Individual Determinism. (G. Fiamingo) Ann. Am. Acad. Pol. Sci. **7**: 270.
— at Columbia College. Char. R. **3**: 288.
— Ethical Aspects of. (L. F. Ward) Int. J. Ethics, **6**: 441.
— French School of. (P. de Rousiers) Ann. Am. Acad. Pol. Sci. **4**: 128.
— in Business Life. (J. Habberton) Chaut. **15**: 682.
— in 19th Century. (F. B. Sanborn) Am. J. Soc. Sci. **30**: 1.
— in Theological Seminaries. (J. Tunis) Lend a H. **16**: 3.
Social Selection, Lapouge's. (C. C. Closson) J. Pol. Econ. **4**: 449.
— Phases of. (C. C. Closson) Q. J. Econ. **10**: 156. **11**: 92.
Social Settlements. (J. Addams) Forum, **14**: 345.
Social Spirit in America. (J. H. Crooker) Dial (Ch.) **15**: 17.
Social Statistics of Cities. (C. D. Wright) Pop. Sci. Mo. **40**: 607.

Social Struggles; a story. (H. H. Boyesen) Cosmopol. **13**: 592, 733. **14**: 97.
Social Subjects, Relation of the Preacher to. (J. W. Day) New World, **5**: 296.
Social Theorists and Business Men. (C. R. Henderson) Am. J. Sociol. **1**: 385.
Social Union. (W. Besant) Contemp. **64**: 272.
Social Unions of Edinburgh and Glasgow. (W. H. Tolman) Char. R. **2**: 332.
Social Webs, Moral Threads in. (E. S. Talbot) Econ. R. **4**: 153.
Socialism. (A. W. Benn) Acad. **47**: 161. — (J. W. Smith) Am. J. Pol. **2**: 67. — (M. Dods) Chr. Lit. **10**: 116 a.
Socialism according to Bebel. (S. Ball) Econ. R. **4**: 229.
— American. (F. L. Greene) Am. J. Pol. **4**: 414.
— Anarchism and. (P. Carus) Open Court, **1**: 754. **5**: 2856.
— and Canadian Democracy. (J. A. Cooper) Canad. M. **3**: 332.
— and Capital, Labor, Poverty. (J. Macgreggor) Bib. Sac. **49**: 30.
— and the "Christian Social Union." Church Q. **40**: 321.
— and Darwinism. (T. Kirkup) Econ. R. **1**: 531.
— and Democracy. Bach. of Arts, **3**: 454.
— and the Industrial Conquest. (W. N. Black) Engin. M. **3**: 787.
— and Marriage, Holland on. Spec. **72**: 365.
— and Militarism. (R. S. Long) Westm. **146**: 681.
— and a Municipal Commonwealth. (L. C. Barnes) Am. M. Civics, **6**: 260.
— and Natural Selection. (K. Pearson) Fortn. **62**: 1.
— and the New Testament. (D. H. Wheeler) Meth. R. **56**: 865.
— and the Rentier. National, **23**: 687.
— and the Republic. (J. La R. Burnett) Am. J. Pol. **2**: 63.
— and Selfishness. (R. L. Simpson) Canad. M. **5**: 285.
— and the Single Tax. (C. E. Benton) Am. J. Pol. **3**: 417.
— and Social Organization. (R. Flint) Good Words, **33**: 618.
— and Social Reform, Ely's. (A. T. Hadley) Forum, **18**: 184.
— and Society. (F. B. Sanborn) Am. J. Soc. Sci. **33**: 20.
— and Transcendentalism. (F. M. Holland) Open Court, **5**: 2812.
— Anti-Socialist Law, Twelve Years under. (Eduard Bernstein) Univ. R. **7**: 14.
— Are we becoming Socialists? (H. Weinstock) Our Day, **15**: 89.
— at Home and Abroad. (H. G. Keene) Fortn. **65**: 142.
— Belgian. (H. G. Keene) Fortn. **63**: 250.
— Benefactions of Capital. Soc. Econ. **8**: 357.
— R. Blatchford's. (T. Scanlon) Westm. **145**: 286.
— Catholic, Nitti's. (C. S. Devas) Dub. R. **118**: 117. — (F. P. Manhart) Luth. Q. **26**: 204. — (H. B. Learned) J. Pol. Econ. **4**: 391. — Sat. R. **80**: 352. — (F. C. Montague) Econ. J. **5**: 567. — Cath. World, **62**: 85.
— Christian. Church Q. **41**: 471. — (P. S. Moxom) New Eng. M. n. s. **10**: 20. — (Argyll) 19th Cent. **36**: 690. Same art. Ecl. M. **124**: 16. — (P. Monroe) Am. J. Sociol. **1**: 50. — (D. MacG. Means) Nation, **56**: 381.
— — Duke of Argyll's Views on. N. Church R. **2**: 117.
— — in France. Spec. **70**: 564.
— — Leavitt's Christian Democracy. Meth. R. **56**: 998.
— — The New. (H. Rashdall) Econ. R. **5**: 82. — (T. C. Fry) Econ. **5**: 95. — (J. Carter) Econ. R. **5**: 104, Quar. **179**: 1.
Socialism, Christian, What is? (J. Carter) Econ. R. **6**: 229.
— Christianity, and Communism. (W. S. Lilly) New R. **11**: 340.
— Clergy and. (R. Ogden) Nation, **58**: 323.
— Collapse of. (W. Lloyd) Westm. **143**: 597. Same art. Ecl. M. **125**: 158.
— Demand and Supply under. (W. H. Mallock) Forum, **20**: 193.
— Development of. (W. H. Mallock) Sat. R. **80**: 137.
— The Drift to. (A. Dunn-Gardner) Contemp. **65**: 110.
— Economic Lessons of. (H. Sidgwick) Econ. J. **5**: 336.
— Ely on. (E. W. Bemis) Dial (Ch.) **17**: 91.
— Ethical. (A. Fabian) Time, **13**: 47, 679.
— Ethics of. (E. L. Hicks) Econ. R. **6**: 467.
— Experiments by Colonisation. (E. Salmon) Fortn. **63**: 260.
— Fabian Economics. (W. H. Mallock) Fortn. **61**: 159, 393. Same art. Ecl. M. **122**: 433.
See Fabian Society.
— Familistère at Guise. (C. Hancock) Fortn. **59**: 418.
— Ferri's. (T. B. Veblen) J. Pol. Econ. **5**: 97.
— Flint's. (T. B. Veblen) J. Pol. Econ. **3**: 247. — Sat. R. **79**: 130. — (S. D. F. Salmond) Crit. R. **5**: 190. — (D. MacG. Means) Nation, **60**: 365.
— for Millionaires. (G. B. Shaw) Contemp. **69**: 204.
— French View of. Soc. Econ. **8**: 75.
— Future of, Richter on. Spec. **71**: 394.
— German, of To-day. Gunton's M. **10**: 279.
— — Origin of. (Levy-Bruhl) Pub. Opin. **13**: 155.
— — Program of. (W. Liebknecht) Forum, **18**: 652.
— Gilman on. (J. H. Crooker) Dial (Ch.) **15**: 17.
— Gladden on. (J. H. Crooker) Dial (Ch.) **15**: 17.
— Jay Gould and. (A. T. Hadley) Forum, **14**: 686.
— Growth of. (Bolton Hall) Chr. Un. **47**: 1067.
— Harm and Apology of. (A. F. Marshall) Am. Cath. Q. **18**: 151.
— Imperial, in Germany, Weakness in. (J. G. Brooks) Econ. J. **2**: 302.
— in England, The Present Outlook. (W. Morris) Forum, **21**: 193.
— in Europe. (C. Bradlaugh) Univ. R. **7**: 93.
— in France. (T. Marburg) Econ. R. **6**: 38.
— — its Present and Future. (Yves Guyot) 19th Cent. **34**: 860. Same art. Ecl. M. **122**: 70. Same art. Liv. Age, **200**: 114.
— in Germany. (E. Bernstein) Time, **22**: 276.
— — and Literary Sterility. (F. H. Geffcken) Forum, **14**: 660.
— in its Different Forms. (H. C. Ager) Am. J. Pol. **4**: 438.
— in Practice. (J. G. Brooks) Nation, **56**: 102.
— — in Roubaix, France. (R. Ogden) Nation, **58**: 79.
— in the U. S. (T. B. Preston) Arena, **7**: 90.
— — Progress of. (M. Kaufmann) Econ. R. **1**: 57.
— The Indictment of Dives. (W. S. Lilly) New R. **9**: 599. Same art. Ecl. M. **122**: 145.
— Is it advancing in England? (W. G. Blaikie) No. Am. **161**: 493.
— Is it a Remedy for Present Social Ills? (J. R. Endean) Westm. **139**: 508. Same art. Ecl. M. **121**: 1.
— its Growth and Outcome, Morris and Bax on. Gunton's M. **10**: 388.
— its Truths and Errors. (J. W. Longley) Canad. M. **6**: 297.
— Mallock's Forgotten Artist. Soc. Econ. **8**: 346.
— Menacing, in the Western States. (F. B. Tracy) Forum, **15**: 332.
— Modern, Fallacies of. (G. C. Brodrick) National, **19**: 300.

Socialism, Moral Aspects of. (S. Ball) Int. J. Ethics, 6: 290.
— The New, and Economics. (W. B. Weeden) New World, 2: 635.
— — and its Literature. (E. W. Gladden) Bk. News, 8: 413.
— a New Capitalist. (F. Adams) Contemp. 61: 87.
— Nicholson's Historical Progress and Ideal. (S. Ball) Econ. R. 5: 242.
— Norton on. Sat. R. 79: 352.
— Novels of. (M. Kaufmann) Lippinc. 55: 138.
— of Moses. (T. S. Potwin) Yale R. 3: 425.
— or Monopoly, Which? (R. E. O'Callaghan) Soc. Econ. 2: 287.
— Philosophic. (H. Genone) Open Court, 10: 4767.
— Present Position of. (R. D. Melville) Westm. 146: 543.
— Real Quintessence of. (W. H. Mallock) Forum, 19: 129.
— Republicanism *versus*. (W. Lloyd) Westm. 141: 258.
— Scientific, Rodbertus-Jagetzow on. (E. de Laveleye) Econ. R. 1: 172.
— Socialist Ideal. Soc. Econ. 1: 44.
— State, and Child Distress. (J. R. Diggle) National, 26: 519.
— — Should Capitalists advocate? (W. R. Cole) Westm. 143: 282.
— Trade Unions *vs*. Soc. Econ. 9: 373.
— Trumbull as a Socialist. Soc. Econ. 7: 277.
— Two Dialogues on. (J. M. Ludlow) Econ. R. 4: 328.
— Tyranny of, Yves Guyot on. Westm. 140: 404.
— *vs*. Protection. (W. F. Draper) Soc. Econ. 7: 22.
— Who will pay the Bills of? (E. L. Godkin) Forum, 17: 394. — (S. Baxter) Forum, 17: 699.
— Why it appeals to Artists. (W. Crane) Atlan. 69: 110.
— Woman and. (K. Knödel) Fortn. 63: 267.
Socialist and Lover; a story. (G. H. Hepworth) Chaut. 17: 397, 559.
Socialist Colony in Mexico. Dub. R. 114: 180.
Socialist Congress, International, 1896. (C. Edwards) Econ. J. 6: 460.
Socialist Controversy. (T. Mackay) Econ. R. 1: 194.
Socialist Millennium, How it would work. (E. Richter) R. of Rs. (N. Y.) 7: 438.
Socialist Propaganda, The. (Miss H. Dendy) National, 26: 108.
Socialist State, A. (R. S. Long) Westm. 144: 605. Same art. Ecl. M. 126: 176.
— Individual in a. (Lily W. Montagu) Westm. 146: 439.
Socialistic Remedies *vs*. Patriarchial Remedies. (J. G. Brooks) Econ. J. 3: 226.
Socialist's Dream. Soc. Econ. 2: 346.
Socialists and Communities. (E. L. Godkin) Nation, 58: 97.
— and Individualists, An Eirenikon to. (J. E. Symes) Westm. 142: 644.
— Catholic. (H. Zimmern) Leis. Hour, 41: 22.
— Congress of. (D. MacG. Means) Nation, 57: 149.
— English, in 1895, The Vicissitudes of. (E. Porritt) Yale R. 4: 365.
— "Opportunity" claimed by. (E. L. Godkin) Nation, 58: 43.
Societary *vs*. Social. (A. W. Small) Ann. Am. Acad. Pol. Sci. 5: 948.
Société d'Aquarellistes Français, Exhibition of Pictures. M. of Art. 3: 230.
Société de Dépòts et Comptes Courants, Fall of. Bank. M. (N. Y.) 46: 112.
Societies; the Great American Safety-valve. (W. B. Hill) Cent. 22: 383.
Societism and Individualism. (Z. S. Holbrook) Bib. Sac. 53: 540.
Society, Adaptation of, to its Environment. (W. D. Lewis) Ann. Am. Acad. Pol. Sci. 4: 37.
— and the Individual. (C. M. Moss) And. R. 18: 43.
— Characteristics of. (A. Haultain) Blackw. 155: 814.
— Fragments of, not to be neglected. (W. E. C. Wright) Char. R. 4: 113.
— Future of. (N. Arling) Westm. 140: 229.
— Inertness of. (M. H. Richards) Luth. Q. 25: 50.
— Man in. Poet-Lore, 6: 40.
— Mechanism of. (L. F. Ward) Am. J. Sociol. 2: 234.
— Methods of Studying. (A. W. Small) Chaut. 21: 52.
— Modern, Evolution of. (R. D. Melville) Westm. 143: 237. Same art. Ecl. M. 124: 577.
— Not in. (A. E. Barr) No. Am. 155: 302.
— Plans for Reforming: the Absurd Effort to make the World over. (W. G. Sumner) Forum, 17: 92.
— Relation of Classes in. (J. W. Love) Ref. Q. 43: 358.
— Sins of. (L. de La Ramé) Fortn. 58: 780. Same art. Ecl. M. 120: 121.
— Small's Study of. (G. McDermot) Cath. World, 61: 762.
— What is it? Time, 1: 235.
Society; a poem. (W. D. Howells) Harper, 90: 630.
Society of Antiquaries, Library of. (E. W. Crofts) Bookworm, 5: 257.
Society of Authors, Appeal of. Critic, 28: 100.
Society of British Artists, Exhibition, 1879. M. of Art, 2: 155.
— Exhibition, 1880. M. of Art, 3: 292.
— — 1886. M. of Art, 9: 161.
Society Islands, Cycling in the. (C. E. Trevathan) Outing, 19: 347.
Society Journalism explained. (E. Legge) Time, 12: 551.
Sociological Retrospect. (F. J. Kingsbury) Am. J. Soc. Sci. no. 34: 1.
Sociological Study, A Scheme of. (G. E. Vincent) Educa. R. 8: 452.
Sociology. (C. D. Hartranft) Cosmopol. 18: 127. — (T. F. Wright) N. Church R. 2: 107.
— and Anthropology. (L. F. Ward) Am. J. Sociol. 1: 426.
— — and Biology, Relations of. (H. Spencer) Pop. Sci. Mo. 50: 163.
— and Cosmology. (L. F. Ward) Am. J. Sociol. 1: 132.
— and Criminology. (Clark Bell) Am. M. Civics, 8: 93. — (C. Bell) Pub. Opin. 19: 587.
— and Pedagogy. (A. Tompkins) Am. J. Sociol. 1: 353.
— and Political Economy. (R. Worms) Am. J. Sociol. 1: 146. — (A. W. Small) J. Pol. Econ. 3: 169.
— and Psychology. (L. F. Ward) Am. J. Sociol. 1: 618. — (S. N. Patten) Ann. Am. Acad. Pol. Sci. 8: 433.
— and Sanitation. (M. Talbot) Am. J. Sociol. 2: 74.
— and Theology. (C. R. Henderson) Am. J. Sociol. 1: 381.
— Argyll's Unseen Foundations of Society. (D. MacG. Means) Nation, 56: 315. — (E. A. Ross) Pol. Sci. Q. 8: 722. — Quar. 176: 404. — Ath. '93, 1: 337. — Sat. R. 75: 128. — Spec. 70: 393.
— Biologic, Failure of. (S. N. Patten) Ann. Am. Acad. Pol. Sci. 4: 919.

Sociology, Christian. (S. Mathews) Am. J. Sociol. 1: 69–771. 2: 108–416. — (Z. S. Holbrook) Bib. Sac. 51: 537. — (H. S. McCowan) Our Day, 15: 62.
— — Strategic Points in. (W. F. Crafts) Our Day, 13: 189.
— Data of. (L. F. Ward) Am. J. Sociol. 1: 738.
— Early Social Self-government. (J. Simon) 19th Cent. 35: 628. Same art. Ecl. M. 122: 760.
— Giddings's Principles of. (D. MacG. Means) Nation, 63: 92. — (W. F. Blackman) Yale R. 5: 218. — (H. Sidgwick) Econ. J. 6: 426. — (C. R. Henderson) Dial (Ch.) 20: 330.
— in Ethical Education. (B. C. Mathews) Pop. Sci. Mo. 49: 373.
— in Germany, The Church and. (J. G. Brooks) New World, 1: 673.
— in Italy. (G. Fiamingo) Am. J. Sociol. 1: 335.
— in our Larger Universities. (I. W. Howerth) Char. R. 4: 198.
— in U. S., Present Condition of. (I. W. Howerth) Ann. Am. Acad. Pol. Sci. 5: 260.
— Music as a Factor in. (H. A. Moore) Music, 5: 525.
— Nature of. (B. Moses) J. Pol. Econ. 3: 24.
— The New. (G. Tyrrell) Month, 84: 502.
— — Church and. (G. McDermot) Cath. World, 62: 290.
— New Revival of. (L. G. Janes) Soc. Econ. 7: 294.
— Our Social Instincts. (E. P. Powell) Soc. Econ. 5: 220.
— Physics and. (W. H. Mallock) Contemp. 68: 883. 69: 59, 283.
— Place of, among the Sciences. (L. F. Ward) Am. J. Sociol. 1: 16.
— Political Prophecy and. (H. Sidgwick) National, 24: 563.
— Practical, Class in, Cincinnati, 1894. (C. M. Hubbard) Char. R. 4: 93. — (P. Tyner) Lend a H. 14: 424.
— Practical Christian. Soc. Econ. 9: 348.
— Practical Development of. (J. B. Reynolds) Pub. Opin. 20: 333.
— Principles of. (L. F. Ward) Ann. Am. Acad. Pol. Sci. 8: 1.
— Problem of. (G. Simmel) Ann. Am. Acad. Pol. Sci. 6: 412.
— Province of. (G. E. Vincent) Am. J. Sociol. 1: 473.
— Purpose of. (L. F. Ward) Am. J. Sociol. 2: 446.
— Recent Books on. (C. R. Henderson) Dial (Ch.) 19: 331.
— Relation of, to Scientific Studies. (F. H. Giddings) Am. J. Soc. Sci. 32: 144.
— Rests indirectly upon Biology. (L. F. Ward) Am. J. Sociol. 1: 313.
— Smith's Statistics and. (L. L. Price) Econ. J. 6: 85.
— Social Question. Soc. Econ. 1: 29, 91.
— Spencer's Principles of. Acad. 50: 481.
— Static and Dynamic. (A. W. Small) Am. J. Sociol. 1: 195. — (L. F. Ward) Pol. Sci. Q. 10: 203.
— Status of. Soc. Econ. 9: 360.
— Study in. (G. M. W. Bills) Am. J. Pol. 4: 113.
— A Study in. (E. D. McCreary) Meth. R. 55: 861.
— Study of, by Ministers. (M. L. Young) Luth. Q. 26: 365.
— Superiority and Subordination as Subject-matter of. (G. Simmel) Am. J. Sociol. 2: 167, 392.
— Terminology and. (H. H. Powers) Ann. Am. Acad. Pol. Sci. 5: 705.
Sociology, Theory of. (F. H. Giddings) Ann. Am. Acad. Pol. Sci. 5: supp.
— Traveller from Altruria. (W. D. Howells) Cosmopol. 14: 52, 251. 15: 341–738.
— What is? (Z. S. Holbrook) Bib. Sac. 52: 458.
Socrates as a Cross-examiner. (O. F. Hershey) Green Bag, 7: 138.
— once more. (H. M. Tyler) And. R. 19: 409.
Soda Deposits of United States. (T. M. Chatard) J. Frankl. Inst. 139: 271, 341.
Sodalite from Three New Localities. (L. M. Luquer and G. J. Volckening) Am. J. Sci. 149: 465.
Sodalite-syenite and other Rocks from Montana. (W. Lindgren) Am. J. Sci. 145: 286.
Sodium, Separation and Identification of Potassium and. (D. A. Kreider and J. E. Breckenridge) Am. J. Sci. 152: 263.
Sodom, Origin and Meaning of the Story of. (T. K. Cheyne) New World, 1: 236.
Soetbeer, Adolf. Bank. M. (Lond.) 54: 881.
Sofa Expedition and the West Indian Soldier. Blackw. 155: 699.
Sofas, Concerning. All the Year, 72: 582.
Sohni; a Story from Indus; a poem. Sir E. Arnold, Cosmopol. 14: 643.
Soil; Stones as a Source of Fertility. (T. H. Hoskins) Garden & F. 8: 288.
Soil-analysis, New Method of. (F. H. P. Coste) Nat. Sci. 8: 312.
Soil-moisture, Preservation of. (C. S. Sargent) Garden & F. 6: 411.
Soils, Chemistry of. (E. E. Call) Science, 20: 29.
— Hawaiian, Chemical Composition of. (A. B. Lyons) Am. J. Sci. 152: 721.
Sojourn in a Convent, A; a story. Temp. Bar, 108: 340.
Sojourner Truth. (H. Hendricks) Nat'l M. (N. Y. '91) 16: 665.
Sokoto Empire in 1894. (W. Wallace) Geog. J. 8: 211.
Solar System, Magnitude of. (W. Harkness) Astron. 13: 605. Same art. Am. J. Sci. 148: 230. — (J. E. Gore) Knowl. 18: 231. — (W. Harkness) Science, n. s. 1: 29.
Soldier, The American Private. (A. H. Sydenham) Overland, n. s. 21: 590.
Soldier, A, and a Gentleman. (J. McL. Cobban) Chamb. J. 68: 771–819.
— British, Life of a. (Seyley) Chaut. 20: 515.
— Courage of. (S. R. Elliott) Atlan. 71: 236.
— The English — as he was, and as he is. (H. Knollys) Blackw. 158: 850. Same art. Ecl. M. 126: 164.
— of the 16th Century, The. Macmil. 72: 171.
— of Fortune, A; a true story. (H. Pyle) Harper, 88: 103.
— of Seven, A; a story. (E. H. Fowler) Sund. M. 23: 543. Same art. Nature, 50: 532.
Soldier Caste, The. (W. Everett) Nation, 60: 251, 323.
Soldier-servant, The; a story. Cornh. 68: 146.
Soldier's Faith, The. (O. W. Holmes, jr.) Harv. Grad. M. 4: 179.
Soldier's Secret; a story. (C. King) Lippinc. 49: 259.
Soldier's Stratagem, The; a story. (E. E. Green) Ecl. M. 126: 126.
Soldiers, About. Blackw. 151: 873.
— and the People, Collisions between. Spec. 71: 357.
— Old, Mendacity of. (M. M. Trumbull) Open Court, 3: 1494.
— Physical Training of. (J. E. Pilcher) Un. Serv. (Phil.) 7: 321.

Soldiers, Recreation Workshops for. (E. J. Hardy) Un. Serv. M. 4: 368.
Soldiers' Aid Society; a story. (C. F. Little) Un. Serv. (Phila.) 11: 40.
Soldiers' Institutes. (M. Moore) Un. Serv. M. 4: 165, 222.
Soldiers' Pets. (Sir F. Middleton) Un. Serv. M. 5: 307.
Solenoids, Two-coil, Variable Action of. (W. S. Aldrich) J. Frankl. Inst. 133: 317.
Solèsmes, Restoration of the Benedictine Monastery of. (R. F. O'Connor) Am. Cath. Q. 20: 592.
Solférino, A Story of. Liv. Age, 208: 716.
Solitary Girl, The; a story. (A. Fairbairn) Eng. Illust. 10: 10.
Solitude — and a Crowd. All the Year, 74: 63.
Solly, Henry. Reminiscences. Spec. 72: 375.
Solomon, King, as an Art Patron. (F. M. Robinson) M. of Art, 10: 373.
— Riddles of, in Rabbinic Literature. (S. Schechter) Folk-Lore, 1: 348.
Solomon, Edward. Acad. 47: 87.
Solomon, Solomon J., Artist, a Chat with. (R. Compton) Idler, 10: 232.
Solomon Islands. (F. N. Wyley) Un. Serv. M. 7: 1255.
— Benjamin Boyd and. (J. F. Hogan) Chamb. J. 70: 593.
Solon, L., and his Work. (W. C. Monkhouse) M. of Art, 13: 173.
Solpugids, Structure of, Bernard on. (J. S. Kingsley) Am. Natural. 30: 653.
Solutions, Nature of. (E. P. Lewis) New Sci. R. 2: 188.
— New Means of Investigating. (M. C. Lea) Am. J. Sci. 145: 478.
— The New Theory of. (J. W. Rodger) Sci. Prog. 4: 377.
— Osmotic Pressure of. (J. W. Rodger) Nature, 47: 103. Same art. Liv. Age, 195: 718.
— Solid. (J. Walker) Sci. Prog. 5: 121.
Solway, Natural History of the. (G. S. Brady) Nature, 51: 322.
Somali Land, or, the Eastern Horn of Africa. (J. S. Leigh) Overland, n. s. 19: 642.
— British. Dub. R. 117: 168.
— Evidences of the Palæolithic Stone Age in. (H. W. Seton-Karr) Anthrop. J. 25: 271.
— Expedition through. (A. D. Smith) Geog. J. 8: 120, 221. — (F. G. Dundas) Geog. J. 1: 209.
— Dr. Donaldson Smith's Expedition in. Geog. J. 4: 528.
Sombre Wooing, A; a story. All the Year, 74: 136.
Somnambulism. (P. Carus) Open Court, 3: 1972.
"Some Mischief still." (A. C. Deane) Longm. 25: 622.
Some of my Country Kin; a poem. (Mrs. E. J. Nicholson) Outing, 28: 34.
Some Passages in the History of Letitia Roy. (M. E. Angus) Cent. 21: 933.
Somerled and the Sea-bird. (M. O'Neill) Blackw. 152: 228. Same art. Ecl. M. 119: 479.
Somerset, Lady Henry. (F. E. Willard) Chaut. 15: 76. — With portraits. (W. T. Stead) R. of Rs. (N. Y.) 8: 285.
— Interview with. (J. T. Stoddart) Sunday M. 25: 797.
Somerset House, Literary Research Room at. Chamb. J. 72: 587.
Somersetshire. Ed. R. 181: 346.
— Ancient Lake-Village in. (R. Munro) Antiq. n. s. 26: 247.
Somersetshire Valley, A. (W. Greswell) Liv. Age, 192: 106.
Sometimes; a poem. (G. P. Stuart) Argosy, 59: 149.
Somma, Monte, Ejected Blocks of. (H. J. Johnston-Lavis) Am. J. Sci. 147: 321.
Son of the Revolution. (A. French) Atlan. 77: 471.
Son of the Soil, A. (M. Branston) Macmil. 69: 59.
Sonderbund, War of the. (W. B. Duffield) Eng. Hist. R. 10: 675.
Song and Speech. (C. H. Brittan) Music, 3: 165.
— Modern, Some of the Difficulties of. Music, 8: 10.
Song; a poem. (E. Nesbit) Argosy, 58: 153.
Song before Sailing; a poem. (Bliss Carman) Cosmopol. 18: 330.
Song of Aegir. (Karl Blind) Scot. R. 27: 95.
Song of the Autumn Sea; a poem. (E. M. Richmond) Outing, 27: 156.
Song of the Balboa Sea; poem. (Joaquin Miller) Overland, n. s. 24: 353-576. 25: 25.
Song of the Banjo; a poem. (R. Kipling) New R. 12: 602.
Song of a Boat, A; a poem. (W. A. Wilber) Outing, 23: 128.
Song of the Camp; a poem. (F. C. Riehl) Outing, 28: 445.
Song of Dermot and the Earl, edited by Orpen. (F. Liebermann) Eng. Hist. R. 8: 129.
Song of the English, A; a poem. (R. Kipling) Eng. Illus. 10: 533.
Song of the Golden City; a poem. (C. Burke) Argosy, 59: 415. 62: 512.
Song of Psyche; a poem. (M. A. Curtois) Gent. M. n. s. 55: 535.
Song of the Road; a poem. (R. L. Stevenson) M. of Art, 9: 94.
Song-games, Diffusion of. J. Am. Folk-Lore, 6: 96.
— of Negro Children in Virginia. (M. O. Clarke) J. Am. Folk-Lore, 3: 288.
Songs and Ballads, English. (R. Noel) New R. 8: 47.
— and Singing. Music, 7: 482.
— Burlesque. (B. Boyle) Idler, 5: 294.
— Colonial patriotic. (J. L. Onderdonk) Am. Hist. Reg. 3: 472.
— English County, Broadwood and Fuller-Maitland's. Spec. 71: 202.
— for Soldiers. Sat. R. 75: 318.
— Gondoliers'. (L. A. Smith) Gent. M. n. s. 48: 486.
— of the Battle-field. (L. A. Smith) Lippinc. 54: 374.
— of England, Baring-Gould's. Sat. R. 80: 236.
— of the People. Spec. 68: 604.
— of the West, Gould and Sheppard's. Spec. 68: 122.
— of Yesterday. Liv. Age, 211: 108.
— Old, and New Laws. (E. L. Linton) Chamb. J. 70: 625.
— Old English, in American Versions. (W. W. Newell) J. Am. Folk-Lore, 5: 325.
— Popular. Cornh. 73: 405.
— — Makers of our. (E. Jarrold) Munsey, 13: 289.
— — Migration of. (H. T. Peck) Bookman, 2: 97.
— — of France. (E. C. Price) Contemp. 62: 105. Same art. Liv. Age, 194: 643.
— Some half-forgotten New England. (M. Barrows) New Eng. M. n. s. 12: 472.
— Students'. (L. A. Smith) Gent. M. n. s. 48: 174.
Sonnblick Mountain Observatory. Nature, 49: 204.
Sonis, General de. (T. L. L. Teeling) Am. Cath. Q. 19: 827.
Sonnenschein's Reader's Guide to Contemporary Literature. (W. E. Foster) Nation, 61: 331.
Sonnet, The English, and its History. (A. H. Japp) Gent. M. n. s. 51: 259.
— Tailed. (E. B. Brownlow) Poet-Lore, 4: 454.
Sonnet on the Sonnet; a poem. (Inigo Deane) Cosmopol. 20: 373.

Sonnet-literature, Curiosities in. (E. B. Brownlow) Poet-Lore, 3: 545.
Sonnets. (T. H. Rand) Canad. M. 6: 33.—(F. D. Stickney) Writer, 6: 76.
— Five. (W. Watson) Spec. 71: 944.
Sonny Keepin' Company. (R. M. Stuart) Cent. 30: 874.
Sonny's Diploma. (R. M. Stuart) Cent. 30: 781.
Sonny's Schoolin'; a monologue. (R. M. Stuart) Cent. 28: 931.
Sons of the American Revolution; California Society. (F. E. Myers) Overland, n. s. 26: 382.
Sons of God and Daughters of Men. (W. R. Harper) Bib. World, 3: 440.
Sons of Liberty, Gov. Morton and. (W. D. Foulke) Atlan. 72: 73.
Sonship, Our Divine. (W. Schaeffer) Ref. Q. 43: 207.
Soofeeism, Islam and. (Mohammed Barakatullah) Westm. 144: 674.
Sophia Dorothea, Queen of George I. Belgra. 77: 56.
—(M. E. Wemyss) 19th Cent. 31: 1008. Same art. Liv. Age, 194: 465.
Sophie. (Mrs. M. Singleton) Time, vols. 3-5.
Sophocles. Agamemnon, performed at Bradfield. Sat. R. 74: 15.
— Antigone, and Shakespere's Isabel. (W. L. Sheldon) Poet-Lore, 4: 609.
— — at Toronto University. Spec. 72: 369.
— Electra, at Iowa College. R. of Rs. (N. Y.) 6: 174.
— Jebb's Translation. Ath. '92, 2: 234.—Sat. R. 78: 17.
— Oedipus Coloneus. (A. E. Housman) Am. J. Philol. 13: 139.
— Oedipus Tyrannus at the Comédie Française. (W. A. Fox) Gent. M. n. s. 57: 186.
— — Doyle's Translation. Eng. R. 13: 151.
— Verbals in τος in. (C. E. Bishop) Am. J. Philol. 13: 171, 329.
Sorcery, Negro, in the U. S. J. Am. Folk-Lore, 3: 281.
Sorel, Agnes. (H. Bouchot) Cosmopol. 18: 35.
Sorel, Albert, Reception at the French Academy. (C. Nicholson) Acad. 47: 148.
Sorosis. (M. M. Merrill) Cosmopol. 15: 153.
— An Old-time. (H. Baldwin) Atlan. 74: 748.
Sorrento and Amalfi, Coasting by. (F. M. Crawford) Cent. 26: 325.
— Highroad from Salerno to. (J. H. Adams) Cent. 26: 337.
— The Plain of. (C. Q. Wright) So. M. 2: 100.
Sorrow of Rohab. (A. Bates) Harper, 84: 189.
Sot back; a story. (L. C. D'Oyle) Gent. M. n. s. 48: 1.
Sotheby's Principia Typographica, Two Plates in. (R. Proctor) Bibliographica, 3: 192.
Sothern, E. H., with portrait. (M. Aldrich) Arena, 6: 517.
Soudan, The. (J. Geddie) Chamb. J. 73: 614.
— The Advance into: What next? Blackw. 160: 297.
— Campaigning in. (H. C. S. Wright) Eng. Illust. 16: 413.
— Captivity of Slatin Pasha in. (S. E. Tillman) Cosmopol. 22: 139.
— Central, Slave Trade and Leprosy in. Dub. R. 119: 164.
— Conquest of. (A. Griffiths) Fortn. 66: 680.
— Devastation of. (W. T. Marriott) National, 20: 482.
— Fate of. Ed. R. 175: 232.
— Father Ohrwalder's Captivity in, Wingate's. Sat. R. 74: 508.
— Fighting in, Slatin Pasha's. Sat. R. 81: 352.
— First Invasion of. Un. Serv. M. 13: 359.
— The French. Quar. 179: 264.
Soudan, French Progress in Western, 1894-95. (S. P. Oliver) Asia. R. 20: 347.
— Mahdiism and, Wingate's. (J. M. Hubbard) Nation, 54: 470.—Spec. 69: 602.
— Northern. (J. T. Bent) Geog. J. 8: 335.
— Present State of. Dub. R. 112: 175.
— Recovery of. Blackw. 152: 875.
— Ruin of, Russell and Gattie's. Spec. 69: 103.
— Slatin Pasha and the. (F. D. Lugard) National, 27: 178. Same art. Liv. Age, 209: 323.
— A Talk with Father Ohrwalder. Blackw. 154: 341.
— Truth of the Dongola Adventure. (W. S. Blunt) 19th Cent. 39: 739.
Soudanese Soldier, Memoirs of a. (Ali Effendi Gifoon) Cornh. 74: 30-484.
Souffrière, Mt. St. Vincent, Crater of. Chamb. J. 70: 449.
Soul, The. (E. C. Hegeler) Open Court, 1: 393.
— and Spirit. (W. Wundt) Open Court, 4: 2587.
— The Animal Soul and the Human. (C. Sterne) Open Court, 2: 945, 1007, 1039.
— Breath and the Name of. (Lady Welby) Open Court, 5: 2893.
— The Discovery of. (F. M. Müller) Open Court, 5: 2835.
— Du Prel on. (F. C. S. Schiller) Philos. R. 3: 485.
— The, an Energy. (C. H. Reeve) Open Court, 9: 4359.
— Evolution of. (J. F. Clark) Arena, 16: 820.
— in Nature, Clifford on. (F. C. Conybeare) Monist, 2: 209.
— Iroquoian Concept of. (J. N. B. Hewill) J. Am. Folk-Lore, 8: 107.
— Monistic Theory of. (J. T. Bixby) New World, 1: 724.
— Nature of. (T. B. Wakeman) Open Court, 5: 3057.
— of Man, Carus on. Sat. R. 74: 452.
— Preëxistence of. (C. L. Barringer) Luth. Q. 23: 393.
— Supposed Uselessness of. (F. H. Bradley) Mind, 20: 176.
— Unity of the. Open Court, 5: 2883.
Soul, The; a Poem. (J. W. Powell) Monist, 5: app.
Soul at Fault; a story. (J. C. Bell) Canad. M. 5: 504.
Soul of Kainlain, The. (M. H. Closson) Overland, n. s. 22: 573.
Soul of Rose Dédé, The; a story. (M. E. M. Davis) Harper, 85: 250.
Soul-snake; a story. (F. G. Scott) Canad. M. 2: 350.
Soul's Awakening; a poem. Cornh. 67: 67.
Soul's Debt. (A. Brown) New Eng. M. n. s. 10: 121.
Sound, In the Realm of. Macmil. 67: 438.
— Localization of. (H. Münsterberg) Psycholog. R. 1: 461.
— Mystery of. (W. M. Clemens) Lippinc. 56: 283.
— Teaching of English Words by. (E. P. Moses) Educa. 15: 10.
Sound Effects, Peculiar. (A. A. Knudson) Pop. Sci. Mo. 45: 75.
Sound Intensities, Apparatus for Study of. (J. Jastrow) Science, n. s. 3: 544.
Sound of a Voice; a story. (B. Vye) Belgra. 87: 295.
Sound Smugglers Again; a story. (K. Cranford) Outing. 24: 373.
Sounding the Sea. (G. W. Littlehales) Pop. Sci. Mo 44: 334.
— Shortening Time for. (F. M. F. Cazin) J. Frankl. Inst. 138: 70.
Source, The. (H. Van Dyke) Scrib. M. 14: 705.
Source of the Stream, The. (Mrs. J. E. H. Gordon) Sund. M. 25: 368.
Sousa, John Philip. Music, 5: 254.

South, The, Agriculture in; Peons of the South. (G. K. Holmes) Ann. Am. Acad. Pol. Sci. **4**: 265.
— and the Black Man. (W. P. Garrison) Nation, **60**: 86.
— and its Problems. (L. B. Evans) Educa. R. **7**: 333.
— and its Resources: Symposium. Indep. March 7, '95.
— Art in. (W. Sartain) Southern M. **5**: 115.
— Before, During, and After the War. (E. P. Scammon) Cath. World, **54**: 875.
— The Common School in. (A. D. Mayo) Chaut. **17**: 71.
— Cotton Mills in. (E. Porritt) New Eng. M. n. s. **12**: 575.
— Economics and the Southern Problem. Soc. Econ. **2**: 352.
— Education in. (J. A. Dreher) Am. J. Soc. Sci. **33**: 185. — (A. D. Mayo) Educa. **16**: 257.
— — Higher. (E. A. Alderman) Educa. R. **11**: 29.
— Farmer in. (Alice French) Scrib. M. **15**: 399. — (F. W. Moore) Yale R. **3**: 56.
— Farms in, since the Civil War. (C. Meriwether) Nation, **57**: 264.
— in Amer. Literature. (J. R. Meader) So. M. **3**: 477.
— in Intellectual Development of U. S. Southern M. **3**: 602.
— Industrial Condition of, before 1860. (R. H. Edmonds) Chaut. **22**: 538.
— — after 1860. (R. H. Edmonds) Chaut. **22**: 669.
— Industrial Development of. (R. H. Edmonds) Engin. M. **4**: 1-513. — (W. C. Oates) No. Am. **161**: 566.
— Industrial Future of. (F. G. Mather) No. Am. **161**: 121.
— Industrial Progress of. (E. P. Alexander) Forum, **13**: 66. — (R. H. Edmonds) Forum, **13**: 673.
— Industrial Region of Northern Alabama, Tennessee, and Georgia. (J. Ralph) Harper, **90**: 607.
— Invention and Industry in. (B. H. Wise) Pop. Sci. Mo. **44**: 379.
— It is American. (J. W. Caldwell) Arena, **6**: 607.
— Land-holding in. Lend a H. **14**: 323.
— Lawlessness in, Suppression of. (J. M. Stone) No. Am. **158**: 500.
— Literary Workers of. (A. Leach) Munsey, **13**: 57.
— Literature in, Pioneers of. (S. A. Link) New Eng. M. n. s. **10**: 14.
— — since the War. (J. A. B. Scherer) Luth. Q. **26**: 493.
— New. (F. L. Oswald) Chaut. **15**: 541.
— — Is there a? (A. D. Mayo) Soc. Econ. **5**: 200, 358.
— — New Labor Forces at the. (T. T. Fortune) Open Court, **5**: 3007.
— — New Woman of. (J. K. Henry) Arena, **11**: 353.
— Old, Creed of. (B. L. Gildersleeve) Atlan. **69**: 75.
— Old Way to Dixie. (J. Ralph) Harper, **86**: 165.
— Permanence of Prosperity. Soc. Econ. **7**: 348.
— Political Revolution of. (J. Dowd) Gunton's M. **10**: 360.
— Problem of, Two Studies of. (B. Matthews) Cosmopol. **14**: 124.
— — and its Solution. (L. H. Blair) Our Day, **12**: 361.
— Resources and Development of. (H. Smith) No. Am. **159**: 129.
— Social Conditions of the. (G. F. Milton) Soc. Econ. **8**: 101, 163.
— Solid, Dissolving. (E. P. Clark) Forum, **22**: 263.
— Sound-money Sentiments in. (E. P. Clark) Nation, **58**: 341.
South, The; Southerner's Plea for Peace. (T. J. Middleton) Arena, **12**: 205.
— White Supremacy in. (J. H. Pitman) Am. J. Pol. **2**: 561.
— Women of, White. (E. B. Dodd) Southern M. **4**: 164.
— Women of, at Work. (O. R. Jefferson) Chaut. **17**: 348.
South Africa Co., British. Dub. R. **116**: 412.
South America. (G. G. Hubbard) Nat. Geog. M. **2**: 1.
— Civil Wars in. (E. S. Zeballos) No. Am. **159**: 150.
— Early Printed Books on. Bookworm, **3**: 143.
— Emancipation of, Pilling's. Ath. '93, **2**: 483.
— Nature's Triumph in. (J. Rodway) Pop. Sci. Mo. **46**: 456.
— Railroad to. (W. D. Kelley) Cosmopol. **15**: 389.
— — Surveys for. (J. D. Garrison) Engin. M. **4**: 577.
— — Would it Pay? (C. P. Yeatman) Engin. M. **5**: 51.
— Republics of. (F. L. Oswald) Open Court, **4**: 2587.
— Revolutions in, Mitre's. Sat. R. **75**: 496.
— Trade and Industry of. (E. M. Amores) Engin. M. **10**: 811.
— Trade of. (F. R. Clow) Q. J. Econ. **7**: 193.
South Atlantic Mystery, A; a story. Chamb. J. **70**: 749.
South Carolina, Charleston and. (J. Ralph) Harper, **90**: 204.
— Government of the Colony of. (E. L. Whitney) J. H. Univ. Stud. **13**: 1.
— New Constitution of. (A. Shaw) R. of Rs. (N. Y.) **13**: 66.
— State Dispensary. (R. I. Hemphill) Arena, **12**: 411.
— — Problem of. (E. P. Clark) Nation, **61**: 199.
— War in, 1894. (E. P. Clark) Nation, **58**: 246, 288. *See* Liquor Traffic.
South Dakota, National Guard of. (P. Leary, jr.) Outing, **22**: 77, 156.
South End House, Boston. Lend a H. **16**: 142.
South Kensington Museum, Art Instruction at. Art J. **46**: 196.
— Dyce and Forster Collection. (F. G. Green) Bookworm, **3**: 273.
— Entrance to. (F. Ford) M. of Art, **10**: 7.
— Exposure of Management. (M. H. Spielmann) M. of Art, **19**: 446.
— Frescoes by Lord Leighton. M. of Art, **19**: 373.
— Natural History at. Spec. **75**: 139. — (E. I. Bell) M. of Art, **4**: 358, 463.
— New Tapestry Court. M. of Art, **17**: 357.
— Reform for. (M. H. Spielmann) Contemp. **70**: 8.
South Kensington Schools, Distribution of Prizes. (L. F. Day) M. of Art, **19**: 472.
South Kerry and its Hotels, A Viceroy's Visit to. (M. O'C. Morris) Spec. **74**: 850.
South Mountain, Pa., Volcanic Rocks of. (G. H. Williams) Am. J. Sci. **144**: 482.
South Place Chapel; an Old London Society. (M. D. Conway) Open Court, **7**: 3751-3795.
— Conway's Centenary History of. (J. W. Chadwick) Nation, **59**: 203.
South Sea Bubble: the Financial Boom of the Last Century. Cornh. **73**: 482. Same art. Ecl. M. **126**: 776.
South Sea Trader, A. Macmil. **75**: 66.
Southampton, Old Road to. All the Year, **74**: 200.
Southern California Teachers' Association: Meeting at Los Angeles, March, 1896. (May L. Cheney) Overland, n. s. **27**: 545.
Southern Confederacy and the Pope. (J. Bigelow) No. Am. **157**: 462.

Southern Empire, Morton on. (W. D. Foulke) Dial (Ch.) 14: 214.
Southern Pacific Railroad. (F. Stratton) Cosmopol. 15: 280.
— Overland by. (F. C. W. Barbour) Chaut. 15: 391.
Southern Magazine, Making a. Southern M. 5: 50.
Southard, Milton I., with portrait. Nat'l M. (N. Y. '91) 17: 279.
Southey, Robert. (Geo. Saintsbury) Macmil. 71: 346. Same art. Ecl. M. 124: 779. Same art. Liv. Age, 205: 67. — (Mary C. Agnew) Temp. Bar, 107: 114.
— Letter by. National, 19: 704.
— Letters. Sat. R. 79: 486.
— Life and Correspondence. Eng. R. 15: 77.
— Ten Letters to. (S. T. Coleridge) Atlan. 73: 57.
"Southward Ho!" a story. Temp. Bar, 102: 229.
Southwark. Walford's Antiq. 1: 132.
Southwell, Father, the Euphuist. (H. Thurston) Month, 83: 231, 383.
Southwell Minster. Walford's Antiq. 6: 49.
Southwest, Flora of; a Characteristic Plant Group. (H. L. Clarke) Pop. Sci. Mo. 43: 786.
Southwold, Eng. (E. B. Brown) Eng. Illust. 10: 405.
Southworth, Mrs. E. D. E. N., with portrait. Bk. News, 9: 66.
Sovereign, State, Government: a Triad of Political Conceptions. (C. M. Platt) Pol. Sci. Q. 10: 292.
Sovereignty, Austin's Theory of. (J. Dewey) Pol. Sci. Q. 9: 31.
— Jean Bodin and Hobbes on. (W. A. Dunning) Pol. Sci. Q. 11: 82.
Sowers, The; a story. (H. S. Merriman) Cornh. 71: 1-561. 72: 53-641.
Sown on Sand; a story. (C. E. Morland) Belgra. 78: 94, holiday no.
Space, and Time as Mere Ideas. (P. Carus) Open Court, 3: 1600.
— Curvature of. (J. Dolman, jr.) New Sci. R. 2: 31.
— Four-fold, Realization of. (T. P. Hall) Science, 19: 272.
— Geometric and Actual. (J. Delbœuf) Monist, 4: 248.
— Homogeneous Division of. Nature, 49: 445, 469.
— Infinity of. Chamb. J. 71: 647.
— Interstitial. (T. D. Paret) J. Frankl. Inst. 140: 117.
— Perceptions of, Experiments in. (J. H. Hyslop) Psycholog. R. 1: 257, 581.
— Problem of the Three Dimensions of. (P. Carus) Open Court, 7: 3720.
— Tactual Estimation of. (G. S. Parrish) Am. J. Psychol. 6: 514.
— Visual Perception of. (E. C. Sanford) Am. J. Psychol. 6: 593.
Space-Sense. (A. E. Segsworth) Am. J. Psychol. 6: 369.
Space-threshold, Perception of Two Points not the. (G. Tawney) Psychol. R. 2: 585.
Spain. Along the Spanish Highways. (H. Lynch) Good Words, 35: 661.
— and the Jacobites. (Benjamin Taylor) Scot. R. 27: 253.
— and the Spaniards. Eng. R. 7: 1.
— The Artist in. (A. Griffiths) M. of Art, 4: 26.
— Artistic, as Shown by Kerr Lawson. (G. White) Idler, 8: 39.
— Church in, Meyrick on. (W. Webster) Acad. 41: 534.
— Church of. Eng. R. 18: 55.
— Colonies of. Spec. 74: 453.
Spain, Diercks's Geschichte Spaniens. (B. Moses) Am. Hist. R. 1: 523.
— Economic Condition of, in the 16th Century. (B. Moses) J. Pol. Econ. 1: 513.
— History of, Burke's. Ed. R. 182: 271. — (R. Lodge) Eng. Hist. R. 11: 537.
— Holy Week in. Cath. World, 58: 840.
— Iberian Peninsula. Chamb. J. 70: 609.
— In Distressful. Chamb. J. 73: 513.
— in the 15th Century. (B. O. Flower) Arena, 13: 192.
— Jews in, MS. Sources of History of. (J. Jacobs) Jew. Q. 6: 597.
— Memorial of Lord Burghley on Peace with Spain. 1588. (W. F. Tilton) Am. Hist. R. 1: 490.
— Memories of. (G. E. Vincent) Chaut. 15: 529.
— Midsummer in Southern. (E. R. Pennell) Cent. 30: 643.
— A Night and a Day in. (M. C. Harris) Atlan. 78: 647.
— Northern, Fueros of. (W. T. Strong) Pol. Sci. Q. 8: 317.
— On the Trail of Don Quixote. (A. F. Jaccaci) Scrib. M. 20: 135, 481.
— People of. Leis. Hour, 43: 457, 600.
— Protestants in, Proposed Episcopate for. Church Q. 38: 283.
— Relation of, to her Government. (L. Williams) No. Am. 163: 634.
— Romance of. (C. W. Wood) Argosy, 59: 78-698. 60: 65-706.
— Secrets from the Court of. New R. 10: 529, 662. 11: 35-594.
— Statesmen of. Liv. Age, 194: 294.
— Summer Resorts in, Lesser. (W. H. Bishop) Nation, 61: 254.
— Theatres and Actors in. (D. del Toboso) No. Am. 158: 628.
— Tour in. (L. M. R. Walker) Belgra. 77: 28.
— Twenty Years of Modern Monarchy in. (C. Benoist) Chaut. 20: 330.
— Up Gibraltar; to Tangier; into Spain. (L. R. Gracey) Chaut. 17: 515.
— Vignettes in. (H. R. Haweis) Contemp. 61: 732. Same art. Ecl. M. 118: 852.
— Village Communities in. Quar. 182: 483.
— West Coast of, and Wrecks. (R. Beynon) Leis. Hour, 42: 335.
— Wild, Chapman's. Nature, 47: 583.
Spalato, Diocletian's Palace at. (P. Fitzgerald) Gent. M. n. s. 53: 266.
Spangolite. (A. H. Miers) Nature, 48: 426.
Spaniard, Evolution of the. (H. C. Chatfield-Taylor) Cosmopol. 21: 238.
Spanish America, Descriptive Topographical Terms of. (R. T. Hill) Nat. Geog. M. 7: 291.
Spanish-American Families, Our. (H. E. Bandini) Overland, n. s. 26: 9.
Spanish-American Literature: Antòlogia de Poetas Hispano-Americanos. (A. R. Marsh) Nation, 60: 16, 33.
Spanish-Arabian Dames. (A. Grant) Time, 19: 295.
Spanish Armada. Quar. 182: 1. — Ed. R. 181: 59.
— and Turkey. (E. Pears) Eng. Hist. R. 8: 439.
— Defeat of. (W. F. Tilton) Atlan. 76: 773.
— Froude on. Ath. '92, 1: 625. — (M. A. S. Hume) Eng. Hist. R. 7: 567.
— Spanish Story of, Froude's. Sat. R. 73: 573.
— State Papers relating to, ed. by Laughton. Sat. R. 78: 434. 79: 387.
Spanish Art at the New Gallery. Am. Arch. 51: 88, 115, 131. — (E. R. Pennell) Nation, 62: 51.
Spanish Ballad-poetry. Spec. 72: 169, 233.

Spanish Blanks. (T. G. Law) Scot. R. 22: 1.
Spanish Calendar, 1538-42. Church Q. 33: 415.
Spanish Discussion, Current. Liv. Age, 211: 396.
Spanish Experience, A. (A. H. Studd) National, 22: 718.
Spanish Historiography. (J. G. Purón) Critic, 27: 187, 329.
Spanish Institutions of the Southwest, Blackmar on. (A. H. Noll) Dial (Ch.) 12: 349.
Spanish Invasion of England, 1588, Lord Burghley's Paper on. Am. Hist. R. 2: 93.
Spanish Language, Ramsey's Text-book of Modern. (A. R. Marsh) Nation, 60: 75.
Spanish Literature. (J. F. Riaño) Ath. '94, 2: 25.
— Birth of. (M. E. Blake) Cath. World, 56: 518.
— in 1891-92. (J. F. Riaño) Ath. '92, 2: 27.
— in 1892-93. (J. F. Riaño) Ath. '93, 2: 30.
— in 1893-94. (J. F. Riaño) Ath. '94, 2: 25.
— in 1894-95. (J. F. Riaño) Ath. '95, 2: 26.
— in 1895-96. (J. F. Riaño) Ath. '96, 2: 27.
Spanish Main, The. Macmil. 74: 70.
Spanish Military Life. Time, 1: 675.
Spanish Monarchy. (W. Fitzpatrick) Dub. R. 111: 297.
Spanish Music-hall. (A. Symons) Fortn. 57: 716.
Spanish Pioneers in America, Lummis's. (L. Carr) Nation, 58: 453.
Spanish Proverb, A; a poem. (T. A. Janvier) Cosmopol. 17: 202.
Spanish Society in Modern Fiction. (E. M. Clerke) Dub. R. 110: 102.
Spanning Spaces. Am. Arch. 49: 100.
Sparks, Jared, Adams's Life of. Nation, 57: 378.
— Pioneer in Historical Literature. Atlan. 73: 559.
Sparks, John, of Pike's Expedition. (E. Coues) Nation, 63: 9.
Sparrow, English. (J. Watson and others) Liv. Age, 192: 158.
— European House, in America. (H. C. Oberholser) Garden & F. 8: 112.
— A Good Word for the. (J. C. Atkinson) Macmil. 65: 457. Same art. Liv. Age, 193: 756.
— in the Zoo. (P. Robinson) Eng. Illust. 15: 163.
— The London. Spec. 76: 838.
Speaker of the House of Commons, Powers of. Spec. 68: 389.
Speaker of the House of Representatives, Follett's. (T. Roosevelt) Am. Hist. R. 2: 176. — (C. C. Nott) Nation, 63: 198. — (H. H. Smith) Chaut. 24: 191.
— of Legislative Bodies in England and America. (H. George, jr.) Arena, 5: 567.
Speakers of the House of Commons: Mr. Peel and his Predecessors. (H. D. Traill) Fortn. 63: 784.
Speaking, Extemporaneous, Preparation for. (J. Robinson) Writer, 8: 142.
Special Providence, A. (L. S. Furman) Cent. 31: 114.
Specialist, The. (E. H. L. Watson) Gent. M. n. s. 53: 467.
Specialization in Schools. (V. Wilker) Meth. R. 54: 442.
Special Correspondents. Spec. 68: 460.
Specialist, The. (Mrs. W. A. Kellerman) Science, 19: 161.
Specie Payment, Resumption of. (J. K. Upton) Scrib. M. 12: 124.
— — in Austria-Hungary. (F. Wieser) J. Pol. Econ. 1: 380.
— Origin of, without Aid of Natural Selection. (G. Henslow) Nat. Sci. 5: 257.
— Variation of, Bateson on. Sat. R. 78: 190.
Specimen Jones. (O. Wister) Harper, 89: 204.
Specs; a story. (W. LeC. Beard) Scrib. M. 20: 586.
Spectacled Schoolboys. (E. Hart) Atlan. 72: 681.
Spectacles. Chamb. J. 73: 525.
Spectra, Comparative, of High and Low Sun. Nature, 46: 211.
— of Flames, Influence of Pressure on. (G. D. Liveing; J. Dewar) Astron. 11: 215.
— of Metals, Infra-red. (E. P. Lewis; E. S. Perry) Astron. 13: 747.
— — New Method of Mapping. (H. Crew; R. Tatnall) Astron. 13: 741.
— of the Elements, Line. (C. Runge) Nature, 52: 106.
— Spark, of the Elements, Physical Characteristics of. (N. W. Hartley) Astron. 11: 223.
— Stellar, Distribution of Energy in. (E. C. Pickering) Astron. 11: 22.
— — Draper Catalogue of. (A. Fowler) Nature, 45: 427.
Spectral Publisher, The. (J. Albee) Dial (Ch.) 18: 261.
Spectral Well of Virginia. (A. E. Dolbear; T. E. Allen) Psych. R. 1: 197.
Spectre's Dilemma, A. (E. Phillpotts) Idler, 1: 194.
Spectres, Celebrated British. (E. Singleton) Cosmopol. 13: 566.
Spectro-Heliograph, The. (G. E. Hale) Astron. 12: 241.
Spectrograph, Potsdam. (E. B. Frost) Astron. 12: 150.
Spectroscope and its Applications. (J. E. Keeler) Pop. Astron. 1: 9, 102, 200. 2: 20.
— Grating, for Small Telescope. (D. E. Hadden) Pop. Astron. 3: 84.
— in Astronomy. (T. Reed) Pop. Astron. 2: 266, 301, 402. 3: 141.
— in Recent Chemistry. (R. A. Gregory) Fortn. 64: 298. Same art. Liv. Age, 206: 672.
— in Study of Variable Stars. (T. Reed) Pop. Astron. 3: 333.
— its Achievements. Chamb. J. 73: 506.
— Measuring Distances, Dimensions, and Masses of Binary Systems by. (F. R. Moulton) Pop. Astron. 3: 337.
— Modern. (J. S. Ames) Astron. 11: 28. — (F. L. O. Wadsworth) Astron. 13: 835.
— New, of Halsted Observatory. (C. A. Young) Astron. 11: 292.
— of Allegheny Observatory. (J. E. Keeler) Astron. 12: 40.
— of Royal Observatory, Edinburgh. (L. Becker) Astron. 12: 542.
— Star, of the Lick Observatory. (J. S. Keeler) Astron. 11: 140.
— Tulse Hill. (W. Huggins) Astron. 12: 615.
— Use of, for Sketching Solar Phenomena. (W. Sidgreaves) Astron. 11: 136.
Spectroscope Slits, Large, New Design for. (F. L. O. Wadsworth) Am. J. Sci. 148: 19.
Spectroscopic Investigations in the Swedish Royal Academy. (B. Hasselberg) Astron. 11: 793.
Spectroscopic Measurements, Application of Interference Methods to. (A. A. Michelson) Astron. 11: 884.
Spectroscopic Observations of Motion, Reduction of. (W. W. Campbell) Astron. 11: 319.
Spectroscopy, Astronomical, Scheiner on. (J. L. E. Dreyer) Nature, 50: 565. — (J. E. Keeler) Astron. 13: 688.
Spectrum, Infra-red. (S. P. Langley) Nature, 51: 12.
— Iron, as a Comparison Spectrum in Spectroscopic Determinations of Stellar Motion. (H. C. Vogel) Astron. 11: 151.
— — and the Periodic Law. (J. Parry) Nature, 45: 253.
— of β Lyræ. (J. E. Keeler) Astron. 12: 350.
— of Liquid Oxygen. (G. D. Liveing; J. Dewar) Astron. 11: 705.

Spectrum, Photographic, of Planetary Nebulæ and of the New Star in Auriga. (E. von Gothard) Astron. 12: 51.
— Rays of, Limit of Visibility of. (W. de W. Abney) Astron. 11: 296.
— Shifting of Lines in. (J. N. Lockyer) Nature, 53: 415.
— Stars of the First and Second Types of. (M. Maunder) Astron. 11: 145.
— Ultra-violet, of the Solar Prominences. (G. E. Hale) Astron. 11: 50, 821.
Spectrum Analysis. (J. J. Stewart) Knowl. 18: 149, 249, 282. — (A. A. C. Swinton) Time, 10: 625.
— its Spiritual Significance. (L. G. Hoeck) N. Church R. 3: 175.
Speculation, Utility of, in Modern Commerce. (A. C. Stevens) Pol. Sci. Q. 7: 419.
Speech. (Sir H. Maxwell) Blackw. 151: 828. Same art. Ecl. M. 119: 205.
— and Song. (C. H. Brittan) Music, 3: 165.
— Animal, Studies of. (E. P. Evans) Pop. Sci. Mo. 43: 433.
— Beginnings of. (G. Allen) Longm. 24: 58.
— Expressiveness of. (A. R. Wallace) Fortn. 64: 528. Same art. Liv. Age, 207: 369. Same art. Ecl. M. 125: 649.
— Natural Basis of. (C. R. Conder) Scot. R. 20: 338.
— of Children. (A. Stevenson) Science, 21: 118.
— Phonographic Studies of. (R. L. Garner) Forum, 13: 778.
— Psychology of. (J. M. Baldwin) Philos. R. 2: 385.
Speech to the Brutes, Man's. (A. H. Peters) Chaut. 21: 67.
Speech-reading, Subtle Art of. (Mrs. A. G. Bell) Atlan. 75: 164.
Speeches and Speakers of To-day. New R. 7: 422, 694.
— Great. (E. J. Edwards) Chaut. 14: 682.
Speed, Rotative, Limitation of. (C. T. Porter) Cassier, 4: 435.
— Variable, in Power Transmission. (H. C. Spaulding) Cassier, 3: 311.
Speed-regulating Mechanisms for Dynamo-engines. (W. S. Aldrich) Cassier, 2: 3.
Speedway. *See* Boulevard.
Spellers, Bad, Constitutional. (A. E. Wyckoff) Pedagog. Sem. 2: 448.
Spelling, American. (A. Lang) Critic, 21: 141. — (B. Matthews) Harper, 85: 277.
— Faculty of. Spec. 71: 363.
— A Fidgetty Question in: the Doubling of Letters. Liv. Age, 211: 358.
— Reformed, for U. S. Documents. (W. P. Garrison) Nation, 58: 360.
Spelling Reform, Future of. (B. E. Smith) Forum, 22: 367.
— in French. (F. Max Müller) Contemp. 63: 550. — Sat. R. 76: 258.
Spelman, Sir Henry. (C. F. S. Warren) Bookworm, 4: 17.
Spence, William. (Mrs. A. Crosse) Temp. Bar, 98: 356.
Spencer, Herbert, with portrait. (W. H. Hudson) Arena, 5: 273. — R. of Rs. (N. Y.) 12: 699.
— and the Synthetic Philosophy. (W. H. Hudson) Pop. Sci. Mo. 41: 1.
— as a Phrenologist. (B. Hollander) Westm. 139: 142.
— as a Thinker. (R. A. Proctor) Open Court, 1: 145.
— A Bible Lesson for. (M. A. Dodge) No. Am. 156: 87.
Spencer, Herbert, Ethical System of. (Van Buren Denslow) Soc. Econ. 8: 96.
— Guiding Principles. (G. H. Hudson) Educa. 16: 78, 144.
— Metaphysics. (T. C. Laws) Open Court, 8: 4039.
— on the Ethics of Kant. Open Court, 2: 1155, 1165.
— on Justice. (J. Iverach) Crit. R. 2: 75.
— on Militarism. (E. M. Lloyd) Un. Serv. M. 13: 157.
— Philosophy of. (H. C. Minton) Presb. & Ref. R. 7: 385. — (L. G. Janes) Open Court, 5: 2991.
— — Latest Phase of. (T. B. Wakeman) Open Court, 5: 2907.
— Political Ethics of. (L. F. Ward) Ann. Am. Acad. Pol. Sci. 4: 90.
— Political Philosophy of. (D. G. Ritchie) Time, 13: 643.
— Portrait of. McClure, 2: 315.
— Principles of Ethics. Church Q. 37: 84. — (J. Iverach) Crit. R. 2: 361.
— State *versus*. (D. G. Ritchie) Time, 14: 141.
— *vs.* Balfour. (St. Geo. Mivart) 19th Cent. 38: 261.
Spender, Mrs. Lilian (Headland). Acad. 47: 401.
Spendthrifts. (H. C. Black) Am. Law R. 28: 230.
Spenser, E., and England as he viewed it. (G. Serrell) Temp. Bar, 107: 423. Same art. Liv. Age, 209: 154.
— at Pendle Forest. Walford's Antiq. 5: 229.
Sperrylite, Notes on. (T. L. Walker) Am. J. Sci. 151: 110.
Spey River. (F. Walt) M. of Art, 9: 359, 416. — (A. Forbes) 19th Cent. 38: 68. Same art. Liv. Age, 206: 553.
Speyside. (D. Macleod) Good Words, 37: 193.
Sphakteria and Pylos, Topography of Region of. (R. M. Burrows) J. Hel. Stud. 16: 1.
Sphenophyllum. (A. C. Seward) Sci. Prog. 5: 427. — (W. C. Williamson) Nature, 46: 11.
Spice Factory, A Day in a. (J. Hatton) Eng. Illust. 9: 604.
Spicheren, Battlefield of. (F. Maurice) Un. Serv. M. 9: 413.
Spider, Harvest, Ash-gray. (C. M. Weed) Am. Natural. 26: 32.
— — Cinnamon, and its Variations. (C. M. Weed) Am. Natural. 27: 534.
— Striped; a Study in Variation. (C. M. Weed) Am. Natural. 26: 999.
Spiders and their Habits. Chamb. J. 71: 319.
— English. (R. I. Pocock) Nature, 49: 60.
— Habits of. (G. Allen) Longm. 20: 365.
— a Hunter of the Grass-tops. Atlan. 76: 139.
— Lungs of, Development of the. (O. L. Simmons) Am. J. Sci. 148: 119.
— Musical Boxes in. (R. I. Pocock) Nat. Sci. 6: 44.
— Suggestions on Origin and Evolution of Web-spinning in. (R. I. Pocock) Nature, 51: 417.
Spielhagen, F. Atlan. 70: 402.
Spies, Political. Quar. 177: 235.
Spies, the, Story of: Study in Biblical Criticism. (P. A. Nordell) Bib. World, 1: 168.
— — Nordell on. (W. H. Green) Bib. World, 1: 328.
Spifame, Raoul, the King's Double. All the Year, 73: 293.
Spiller, Jenny; Hogarth's Player-Friend. (W. J. Lawrence) Gent. M. n. s. 57: 224.
Spina Bifida and the Blastopore. (O. Hertwig) Am. Natural, 26: 782.
Spinner, Alice. (J. Knowles) 19th Cent. 35: 959.

Spinning Song. (M. C. Gillington) Overland, n. s. 21: 59.
Spinoza, Benedict. (W. L. Sheldon) Open Court, 6: 3127, 3135. — (J. Strauss) Gent. M. n. s. 50: 379.
— and Friedlander's Edition. (W. Knight) Crit. R. 2: 296.
— and the Old Testament. (B. Pick) Bib. World, 2: 112, 194.
— as a Moral Teacher. (F. Pollock) Time, 18: 416.
— Demonstration of Necessity, Critique of. (E. D. Roe, jr.) Bib. Sac. 51: 641.
— Ethic. (C. S. Peirce) Nation, 59: 344.
— — Conception of Immortality in. (A. E. Taylor) Mind, 21: 145.
— Idealism of. (J. C. Murray) Philos. R. 5: 473.
— Morals of, Worms on. (W. Knight) Crit. R. 3: 59.
Spinozism, History of. (J. Freudenthal) Jew. Q. 8: 17.
"Spinster," Use of the Word. Nation, 60: 11.
Spinster, The; a story. Cornh. 68: 79.
Spinsters and the Law. (R. V. Rogers) Green Bag, 5: 108.
Spir, African. (F. M. Müller) 19th Cent. 35: 942.
Spiral Weld Tube Machinery, Development of. (G. R. Green) J. Frankl. Inst. 133: 176.
Spire of St. Stephen's, The; a story. (E. W. Demeritt) McClure, 1: 410.
Spirea Bracteata. (C. S. Sargent) Garden & F. 7: 304.
— Longigemma. (C. S. Sargent) Garden & F. 7: 344.
Spirit and Matter. (E. M. Caillard) Contemp. 66: 422. Same art. Ecl. M. 123: 587.
— and Soul. (W. Wundt) Open Court, 4: 2587.
— Conservation of, and Origin of Consciousness. (F. C. Russell) Monist, 2: 357.
— Life of the. (L. Whiting) Arena, 17: 53.
— of the Times, The New. (D. Cortesi) Chaut. 23: 739.
— Science of. (H. Genone) Open Court, 9: 4410.
Spirit of the White Moth, The. Argosy, 61: 117.
Spirit-photographs. (H. R. Haweis) Fortn. 59: 116.
Spirit-writing. (B. F. Underwood) Arena, 7: 568.
— and "Speaking with Tongues." (W. R. Newbold) Pop. Sci. Mo. 49: 508.
Spiritual, The Psychic and the. (M. B. Peeke) Arena, 13: 43.
Spiritual Evolution. (E. A. Gowing) Belgra. 80: 251.
Spiritual Life, The. (V. Paget) Contemp. 62: 663. Same art. Ecl. M. 120: 86.
Spiritism and Immortality. (P. Carus) Open Court, 2: 1360.
Spiritualism. Month, 76: 1, 200. — (M. D. Conway) Open Court, 2: 1295. — (M. Dessoir) Open Court, 7: 3711.
— The Higher: Space and Matter. (J. E. Purdon) Open Court, 7: 3770.
— Materialism *vs.* (F. S. Billings) Psychic. R. 2: 317.
— Modern. (L. A. Fox) Luth. Q. 24: 1.
— Phenomena of. (Mrs. E. B. Duffey) Psych. R. 2: 8.
— — from a Theosophic View. (E. W. Wilcox) Arena, 8: 472.
— Possession and Mediumship. (W. R. Newbold) Pop. Sci. Mo. 50: 220.
— Savage. Longm. 23: 482.
— Two Views of. (H. A. Hartt) Arena, 10: 815.
Spiritualistic Hypothesis, Religious and Ethical Implications of. (M. M. Dawson) Psychic. R. 2: 241, (J. E. Allen) 271.
Spirituality, Knowledge and Feeling in. (F. W. Crowder) Meth. R. 56: 552.
Spitalfields. (Mrs. Brewer) Sund. M. 22: 172, 386.
Spitzbergen and Franz Josef Land. Dub. R. 119: 436.
— Visit of Training Squadron to, 1895. Geog. J. 6: 547.
Splash of a Drop, Photography of. (R. S. Cole) Nature, 50: 222.
Splendid Shilling, The; a story. (S. F. Bullock) Eng. Illust. 15: 86.
Splendid Time — ahead; a story. (W. Besant) McClure, 1: 440.
Splendide Mendax; a story. (S. Gwynn) Cornh. 74: 233. Same art. Liv. Age, 210: 574.
Spoerer, Friedrich W. G. Nature, 52: 417.
Spofford, Ainsworth R., with portrait. Bk. News, 12: 420.
— and the Library of Congress. (J. Hawthorne) Lippinc. 53: 517.
Spofford, Harriet Prescott, with portrait. Bk. Buyer, 6: 235.
Spoil of Office, A; a story. (H. Garland) Arena, 5: 253–749. 6: 104.
Spoil of the Puma, The; a story. (G. Parker) Cosmopol. 15: 80.
Spoils System and the Indian Service. (F. E. Leupp) Pub. Opin. 18: 570.
— Congress and. (C. Schurz) Good Govt. 14: 250.
— Consular Service and. (J. B. Angell and others) Cent. 26: 306.
— Demoralizing Influence of. (C. C. Andrews) Am. J. Pol. 4: 271.
— Do the Victors own the Spoils? (E. B. Reeves) Am. M. Civics, 6: 267.
Sponge and Sponges of the Florida Reef. (Kirk Monroe) Scrib. M. 12: 639.
Sponges, a Chat about. (T. Bird) Good Words, 37: 46.
— Development of. (H. V. Wilson) Am. Natural. 28: 439.
— Embryology of. (H. V. Wilson) Am. Natural. 28: 73.
— Recent and Fossil. (J. F. James) Am. Natural. 29: 536.
Spontaneity and Automatism. (E. Montgomery) Monist, 4: 44.
Spontaneous Combustion. (V. B. Lewes) Nature, 48: 626.
Spoon-fork. Reliquary, 33: 45.
Spoon Rack, Wooden. Reliquary, 36: 233.
Spoons, Antique. (T. W. Greene) M. of Art, 5: 160.
Sporophyte, Influence of Disturbed Nutrition on the Evolution of the Vegetable Phase of. (G. F. Atkinson) Am. Natural. 30: 349.
Sporozoa. (E. R. Lankester) Nat. Sci. 9: 111.
Sport and Literature. (C. Cordley) Gent. M. n. s. 49: 303.
— and Natural History, ed. by Crawfurd. Sat. R. 79: 353.
— and Soldiers. Sat. R. 78: 182.
— and Sportsmen. (E. Gambier Parry) New R. 11: 309.
— A Day with Canoe and Gun. (Nomad) Outing, 20: 114.
— Diguet on. (G. Greenwood) Westm. 139: 121.
— Horrors of. (Florence Dixie) Westm. 137: 49.
— in Art. Art J. 48: 230, 257.
— in Cheshire, History of. Walford's Antiq. 12: 193, 261.
— in the New Forest, Eng. (G. Lascelles) New R. 6: 353.
— in Norway. Blackw. 153: 584.
— in an Untouched American Wilderness. (F. Irland) Scrib. M. 20: 350.

Sport, International, In the Field of. (H. W. Lanier) R. of Rs. (N. Y.) **12**: 575.
— Ouida on. Gent. M. n. s. **48**: 640.
— Romance of. (C. Cordley) Gent. M. n. s. **55**: 475.
— Wild, in Costa Rica. (J. J. Peatfield) Outing, **23**: 96.
— Winter. (G. Lascelles) New R. **9**: 655. — (E. W. Sandys) Outing, **19**: 497.
Sporting Adventures in India. (E. Braddon) Blackw. **154**: 498, 618.
Sporting Ancestors, Our. Quar. **180**: 88.
Sporting Literature, Gems of. Gent. M. n. s. **49**: 107.
Sports and Sporting Grounds of the Northeast. Nat'l M. (Bost.) **5**: 71.
— Cruel. (H. S. Salt) Westm. **140**: 545.
— for Women. Sat. R. **73**: 369.
— Outdoor. (J. H. Mandigo) Chaut. **19**: 387.
— — in and around New York. (J. H. Mandigo) Chaut. **21**: 706.
— Rod and Gun in Canada. Outing, **20**: 241.
Sportsman's Journal, Notes from a. Macmil. **74**: 384.
Sportsmen, Yeomen and. (T. E. Kebbel) National, **19**: 548.
Sportswoman in Squirrel Land, A. (J. T. Wandle) Outing, **21**: 216.
Spots and Stripes in Mammals. (R. Lydekker) Knowl. **18**: 3.
Spotsylvania, Battle of. Soc. Hist. Pap. **21**: 228.
Spottswood's Expedition of 1716. (W. M. Thornton) Nat. Geog. M. **7**: 265.
Spraying Fruit Trees for Fungoid Diseases. Garden & F. **7**: 36.
Sprengel, Christian K. (J. C. Willis) Nat. Sci. **2**: 269.
Sprig of Heather; a story. (E. P. Oppenheim) Eng. Illust. **15**: 167.
Spring. (H. E. Ward) M. of Art, **5**: 231. — (R. Jefferies) Longm. **24**: 143.
— "Before the Swallow Dares." (P. Robinson) Contemp. **65**: 505. Same art. Ecl. M. **122**: 682.
— Coming of; a poem. (A. Austin) Blackw. **157**: 517. Same art. Ecl. M. **124**: 776.
— Glamour of. All the Year, **74**: 396.
— in Rome. (L. Gittings) Outing, **26**: 41.
Spring; a poem. (N. M'Cormick) Argosy, **58**: 81.
Spring in a Side Street; a story. (B. Matthews) Harper, **88**: 678.
Spring Cleaning. Spec. **76**: 665.
Spring Drive, A; a poem. (C. C. Rogers) Outing, **21**: 464.
Spring Flood in Broadway; a story. (B. Matthews) Harper, **92**: 696.
Spring Garden. (C. S. Sargent) Garden & F. **7**: 141.
Spring Song. (E. Nesbit) Argosy, **59**: 671.
Spring Song, A; a poem. (Elizabeth M. Johnstone) Temp. Bar, **98**: 126.
Springs, Hot. (J. L. Lobley) Knowl. **15**: 95.
Springboks, a Morning with. Sat. R. **78**: 555.
Springfield, Massachusetts. (C. E. Blake) New Eng. M. n. s. **9**: 574.
— Early History of. (F. Allaben) Nat'l M. (N. Y. '91) **16**: 561.
— Petition to Congress, 1819, for printing the United States Laws at. N. E. Reg. **47**: 461.
Springfield, Missouri, Succession of Fossil Faunas at. (S. Weller) Am. J. Sci. **149**: 185.
Sprinklers, Automatic. (C. J. H. Woodbury) Cassier, **1**: 261, 369.
Spruce, Richard. (A. R. Wallace) Nature, **49**: 317. — (C. R. Markham) Geog. J. **3**: 245. — Nat. Sci. **4**: 154.
Spruce, Muskeag. (H. B. Ayres) Garden & F. **7**: 504.
Spruce, Weeping. (T. H. Douglas) Garden & F. **5**: 591.
Spruce Forests, Wood Pulp Supply and. Garden & F. **9**: 363.
Spruce Trees of Eastern No. America. (C. S. Sargent) Garden & F. **9**: 351.
Spur of Circumstance. (G. Blanchard) New Eng. M. n. s. **7**: 494.
Spurgeon, Charles Haddon. (E. A. Gowing) Belgra. **86**: 244. — (H. C. Vedder) Bapt. R. **14**: 129. — Church Q. **34**: 198. — (W. B. Carpenter) Contemp. **61**: 305. Same art. Liv. Age, **193**: 311. — (H. R. Haweis) Eng. Illust. **9**: 503. — Ecl. M. **118**: 535. — (Newman Hall) Good Words, **33**: 233. — M. Chr. Lit. **5**: 489. — With portrait. (R. C. Houghton) Meth. R. **52**: 862. — (J. Cook) Our Day, **9**: 193. — With portraits. (W. T. Stead) R. of Rs. (N. Y.) **5**: 169. — Sat. R. **73**: 140. — Spec. **68**: 188. — (Wayland Hoyt) Chr. Un. **45**: 255.
— and Modern Preaching. (F. W. Farrar) Sund. M. **21**: 239.
Spy of France; a story. (J. A. Altsheler) Cosmopol. **21**: 279.
Square Diamond, The. (C. Ross) Scrib. M. **20**: 753.
Squares, Public. (T. M. Newton) Am. Arch. **43**: 52–135.
Squatter Life. All the Year, **72**: 136.
Squire, Passing of the. (E. Porritt) New Eng. M. n. s. **11**: 597.
Squire Jack. Temp. Bar, **97**: 55, 240. Same art. Liv. Age, **196**: 790. **197**: 8.
Squire Thorpe's Botany. Chamb. J. **73**: 765.
Squire's Dilemma, The; a story. Chamb. J. **70**: 201–263.
Squire's Niece Maria. (M. F. Haynes) New Eng. M. n. s. **6**: 461.
Squirrel, Flying, The Smallest. (R. Lydekker) Knowl. **18**: 27.
Squirrels. Spec. **77**: 761.
— at the Zoo. Spec. **73**: 267.
— Gray, of the U. S. (E. Ingersoll) Harper, **84**: 544.
— in Brown October, With the. (J. R. Benton) Outing, **25**: 21.
— Indian Legends of. (A. F. Chamberlain) J. Am. Folk-Lore, **9**: 48.
— Sociability of. (R. M. Kettle) Argosy, **54**: 431.
Srinagar; Venice of the East. (E. C. Tait) Sund. M. **21**: 735.
Stability, Specific, Variation and. (W. T. Thiselton-Dyer) Nature, **51**: 459.
Stables, Architecture of. (C. H. Blackall) Am. Arch. **54**: 11, 51, 67.
— Horse, in London. Am. Arch. **45**: 117.
Staël, Madame de. (E. L. Didier) Chaut. **24**: 6.
Staël, Chateau de. (J. Scott) So. M. **5**: 408.
Staël-Holstein, Auguste Louis de; A French Critic on England. Macmil. **69**: 435.
Stag-hunting in Devon and Somerset. (S. Malmesbury) No. Am. **156**: 186.
Stage: the Actress as Usurper of Man's Prerogative. (W. J. Lawrence) Gent. M. n. s. **56**: 551.
— American. (Fred. Daly) Time, **13**: 29, 169.
— Anglicisation of. (A. Brereton) Theatre, **37**: 314.
— — Beauties of. (J. P. Reed; W. S. Walsh) Cosmopol. **14**: 294.
— — Endowed Theatres and. (H. Modjeska) Forum, **14**: 337.
— — of To-day, 1888. (W. G. Elliot) Time, **19**: 534.
— and the Beauty Problem. (J. S. Metcalfe) Cosmopol. **22**: 13.

Stage and Literature. (W. Archer) Fortn. 57: 219.
— Art of Dressing an Historical Play. (S. Lucas) M. of Art, 17: 276.
— as a Career: An Actor's Experience. (R. de Cordova) Forum, 17: 622.
— as an Educator. (J. P. Walton) Westm. 142: 567.
— as a Profession, The. (F. C. Burnand) Time, 3: 88, 176.
— as a School of Art and Archæology. (H. Herman) M. of Art, 11: 332.
— as a Trade. Sat. R. 76: 678.
— Australian, Impressions of the. (E. Ballantyne) Theatre, 28: 186.
— Bible and the. Spec. 70: 155.
— Costume-designing for the. (L. Wingfield) M. of Art, 11: 403. — (P. Anderson) M. of Art, 17: 7.
— Decline of Scenic Art in America. (R. Marston) M. of Art, 17: 163.
— English, French Views of. (E. Brain) Theatre, 35: 195.
— — To-day. Theatre, 33: 89.
— — under Victoria. (H. Elliott) Theatre, 37: 242.
— from a Clergyman's Standpoint. (T. P. Hughes) Forum, 20: 695.
— in Fiction. (A. C. Deane) Theatre, 29: 104.
— in Relation to Paintings and Sculptures. (W. Shaw-Sparrow) Art J. 47: 27–85.
— The Juvenile Lead. (H. S. Wilson) Gent. M. n. s. 56: 72.
— Literature on. Dial (Ch.) 13: 336.
— Merits and Demerits of. Time, 12: 445.
— Misconceptions about. (H. Irving) 19th Cent. 32: 670.
— Nastiness on. Theatre, 37: 299.
— Paris, Favorites of. (A. Hornblow) Munsey, 11: 479, 591.
— Religion on the. Theatre, 35: 313.
— Revolving, in Munich Theatre. Am. Arch. 53: 83.
— Scenic Art on. (H. Herkomer) M. of Art, 15: 259, 316.
— Scottish, The Early. (N. R. Lawson) Time, 14: 584.
— — in the Last Century. Gent. M. n. s. 54: 332.
— Some Modernisms on. (H. W. Charlesworth) Canad. M. 1: 43.
— Talent and Genius on. (G. Barlow) Contemp. 62: 385.
— Toilers of. (A. Daudet) Theatre, 33: 1.
— Turkish. (R. Davey) Theatre, 37: 257.
Stage on the Road, A; a story. (A. Hope) Eng. Illust. 11: 253.
Stage Art To-day. Theatre, 33: 152.
Stage Costume. (A. Chasemore) Theatre, 37: 184.
Stage Costumes, Some Eccentric. (A. J. Daniels) Theatre, 29: 251.
Stage Curtains. (W. Telbin) M. of Art, 18: 335.
Stage-door Lover, A. Theatre, 28: 245.
Stage Dresser of 18th Century. Chamb. J. 69: 789.
Stage Effects, Some Realistic. Chamb. J. 73: 776.
Stage Production. (J. Hollingshead) Theatre, 37: 318.
Stage Scenery in the 18th Century. (W. J. Lawrence) M. of Art, 18: 385.
— Limitations of. (W. Archer) M. of Art, 19: 432.
— on Tour. (W. J. Lawrence) M. of Art, 19: 476.
— Reform in. (W. Telbin) M. of Art, 17: 44.
Stage-setting. (W. Archer) M. of Art, 6: 314.
Stage Spectacle, Development of, as exemplified in the Ballet of "Faust." (M. H. Spielmann) M. of Art, 19: 25.
Stage Spectacles. (A. Harris) M. of Art, 12: 109.
Stage-struck. (H. D. Trail) National, 19: 457. — Macmil. 73: 122.
Stage-coach. Development of the Overland Mail Service. (T. L. James) Cosmopol. 20: 603.
Stage-driver's Story. (S. Robie) Outing, 25: 81.
Stained-glass Windows of Church at Stamford Hill. (L. F. Day) Art J. 48: 197.
Stairs Expedition to Katangaland. (J. A. Moloney) Geog. J. 2: 238.
Stalagmites. Recent Analysis of Pele's Hair and a Stalagmite from the Lava Caves of Kilauea. (A. H. Phillips) Am. J. Sci. 147: 473.
Stalker, J. B., at Home. Sund. M. 22: 541.
Stamboloff, Stefan Nikoloff. (S. K. Vatralsky) Forum, 20: 317. — (J. G. C. Minchin) Acad. 48: 197. — (Henry Cust) New R. 13: 343. Same art. Ecl. M. 125: 563.
— Adverse View of. Sat. R. 80: 415.
— Assassination of. Sat. R. 80: 69.
— Beaman's Life of. (C. H. Cooper) Dial (Ch.) 19: 212. — Sat. R. 80: 381.
— Fall of. (E. Dicey) Fortn. 64: 391. Same art. Liv. Age, 207: 91. Same art. Ecl. M. 125: 747.
— Two Views of. (Lapcho and Mahaffy) Sat. R. 80: 103.
Stamboul, Old and New. (R. Davey) J. Soc. Arts, 44: 351.
— Revisited. All the Year, 74: 246.
Stamford Bridge, Battle of. (D. Lever) Gent. M. n. s. 55: 80.
Stamp-collecting Craze. (W. Roberts) Fortn. 61: 661. Same art. Ecl. M. 123: 128.
Stamp Mill, Evolution of the. (A. B. Paul) Overland, n. s. 25: 522.
Stampede on the Turkey Track Range. (W. C. Barnes) Cosmopol. 19: 437.
Stamps, Postage. (A. G. Bowie) Time, 16: 183.
Stamps Enclosed for Reply; a story. (H. Fielding) Eng. Illust. 14: 73.
Standard Oil Company. (C. Waggoner) Am. J. Pol. 3: 471.
— The Gospel of Greed. (R. Sherman) Forum, 13: 602.
— Lloyd on. (W. H. Smith) Dial (Ch.) 17: 230.
— Ten Years of. (S. C. T. Dodd) Forum, 13: 300.
Standards, Legislation relating to. (T. C. Mendenhall) Science, n. s. 4: 1.
Standing Committee System in American Legislative Bodies, Origin of. (J. F. Jameson) Pol. Sci. Q. 9: 246.
Stand-pipes for Fire Protection and Street Flushing. (L. L. Tribus) Engin. M. 10: 1040.
Stanfield Hall Murder. Green Bag, 6: 409.
Stanford, Leland. (C. H. Hepburn) Munsey, 9: 176. — With portraits. (A. Shaw) R. of Rs. (N. Y.) 8: 155. — Public Opin. 15: 308. — (J. S. Hittell) Overland, n. s. 22: 118.
— Educational Ideas of. (D. S. Jordan) Educa. R. 6: 136.
Stanford University. Chr. Un. 46: 26.
— Grounds of. (C. H. Shinn) Garden & F. 9: 227.
Stanhope, Edward. (St. J. Broderick) National, 22: 842. Blackw. 155: 299.
Stanhope, Lady Frederica Louisa, Tomb of, at Chevening. M. of Art, 3: 155.
Stanhope, Lady Hester Lucy. Temple Bar, 106: 368. 107: 480. Same art. Liv. Age, 209: 342. Same art. Un. Serv. (Phila.) 16: 126.
Stanislaus Augustus, King, Abduction of. All the Year, 74: 43. Same art. Liv. Age, 201: 62.
— Voltaire and. (H. W. Wolff) National, 19: 381.

Stanley, Arthur Penrhyn. Leis. Hour, 43: 285. — (M. E. Grant Duff) National, 22: 742. Same art. Ecl. M. 122: 456. — (A. K. H. Boyd) Longm. 23: 404. Same art. Liv. Age, 200: 643. — Quar. 178: 235. — Ed. R. 180: 1. — (G. Smith) 19th Cent. 35: 220. — Atlan. 74: 125. — Blackw. 155: 190. — (A. W. Benn) Acad. 45: 117. — Critic, 24: 59. — Spec. 72: 132, 164. — Church Q. 38: 1. — (D. Macleod) Good Words, 35: 274. — (C. A. L. Richards) Dial (Ch.) 16: 134. — Nation, 61: 226. — Crit. R. 4: 141.
— and Phillips Brooks at Plymouth. (G. E. Ellis) New Eng. M. n. s. 8: 3.
— and the Tractarian Movement. (A. V. G. Allen) New World, 3: 132.
— Imagination of. Spec. 71: 907.
— Letters and Verses, edited by Prothero. (W. H. Carruth) Dial (Ch.) 20: 271.
— Life and Correspondence of. (C. K. Paul) Month, 80: 305.
— Life and Influence of. Lond. Q. 82: 1.
— Recollections and Impressions of. (F. Arnold) Time, 10: 601.
Stanley, Henry Morton, with portrait. Bk. News, 5: 364. — (F. G. Carpenter) Chaut. 23: 444.
— as Leader and Comrade. (H. Quilter) Univ. R. 8: 313.
— Early Travels. Sat. R. 80: 446.
— Emin Pasha Expedition. (H. Quilter) Univ. R. 8: 469.
— In Camp with. (A. I. M. Jephson) Cosmopol. 12: 287.
Stanlowe Cell, Inventory of Goods. Reliquary, 33: 39.
Stannard, Mrs. H. E. V.: "My First Book." Idler, 4: 367.
Stannite and Some of the Alteration Products from the Black Hills, S. D. (W. P. Headden) Am. J. Sci. 145: 105.
Stanton, Clark. Acad. 45: 41.
Stanton, Dorothy. (E. D. Harris) N. E. Reg. 48: 421.
Stanton, Edwin M. (H. L. Dawes) Atlan. 73: 162.
— Recollections of, under Johnson. (H. L. Dawes) Atlan. 74: 494.
Stanwood Family of Brunswick, Me. (E. D. Hopkins) N. E. Reg. 50: 540.
Stapelia Gigantea. (W. Watson) Garden & F. 8: 514.
Star, Binary, Another Spectroscopic. (A. M. Clerke) Knowl. 18: 110.
— — Determination of Orbit of Companion of. (J. H. Boyd) Pop. Astron. 3: 19.
— Double, Orbit of, finding by Graphical Method. (S. W. Burnham) Pop. Astron. 1: 349.
— of Bethlehem. Nature, 47: 177.
— of the Sea, The. Liv. Age, 209: 172.
— Quadruple, Zeta Cancri. (Prof. Seeliger) Astron. 13: 802.
Stars and Molecules. (E. Ledger) 19th Cent. 38: 295. Same art Liv. Age, 206: 731.
— Binary, Method for determining Apparent Orbits of. (C. P. Howard) Astron. 13: 425.
— — Origin of. Dub. R. 111: 438. — (T. J. J. See) Knowl. 15: 81.
— Binary Systems of. (S. W. Burnham) Pop. Astron. 4: 169.
— Colors of. Liv. Age, 192: 186.
— Constitution of. (E. C. Pickering) Astron. 12: 718.
— Darkness behind the. (J. E. Gore) Gent. M. n. s. 53: 407. Same art. Liv. Age, 203: 625.
— Distances of. (W. W. Payne) Pop. Astron. 1: 129. —Pub. Opin. 13: 381.
Stars, Distances of, by Doppler's Principle. (G. W. Colles) Am. J. Sci. 145: 259.
— Distribution of. (A. M. Clerke) Astron. 21: 515. — (A. M. Clerke) Knowl. 16: 66.
— Double, Evolution of, See on. (G. H. Darwin) Nature, 47: 459. Same art. Astron. 12: 413.
— — Orbits of, Method of determining. (T. J. J. See) Astron. 12: 865.
— — Proper Motions of. (S. W. Burnham) Astron. 13: 14.
— — Systems of. (T. J. J. See) Astron. 12: 289.
— Fixed. (W. H. S. Monck) Pop. Astron. 1: 195, 300, 385. 2: 60, 108. 3: 62. 4: 259.
— Intelligible Signals between Neighboring. (F. Galton) Fortn. 66: 657.
— Modern Astronomy of. (F. R. Wegg-Prosser) Dub. R. 111: 268.
— Motion of, Photographic Determination of. (E. C. Pickering) Astron. 13: 521.
— Names of, from the Arabic, Pronunciation of. (R. H. West) Pop. Astron. 2: 209.
— New. (J. N. Lockyer) 19th Cent. 31: 341. Same art. Ecl. M. 118: 608. Same art. Liv. Age, 193: 323. — (A. Brester, jr.) Knowl. 18: 278.
— — and Variable. (J. E. Gore) Gent. M. n. s. 48: 392. Same art. Pop. Sci. Mo. 41: 396.
— Parallax of, Some Values of, by Method of Meridian Transits. (A. S. Flint) Science, n. s. 3: 617.
— — Pritchard on. Nature, 46: 612.
— Photographs of, Roberts on. (A. A. Common) Nature, 50: 447.
— Photometry of. (H. M. Parkhurst) Astron. 13: 652.
— Photographic Map of. Nature, 46: 274.
— Proper Motion of. (W. H. S. Monck) Astron. 11: 874.
— — Spectra and. (W. H. S. Monck) Astron. 11: 389. 12: 8.
— Scintillation of. (Lord Rayleigh) Astron. 12: 834, 921.
— Systems of, Life History of. (H. L. Clarke) Pop. Astron. 3: 489.
— Transits of, Photographic Method of determining. (F. H. Bigelow) Astron. 11: 42.
— The Universe of. Pop. Sci. Mo. 40: 545.
— Variable. (A. Brester) Knowl. 19: 107. — (P. S. Yendell) Pop. Astron. 4: 13. — (E. E. Markwick) Knowl. 19: 183. — (J. A. Parkhurst) Pop. Astron. 1: 125-460. 2: 18.
— — Long-period. (J. A. Parkhurst) Pop. Astron. 2: 215, 316.
— — Short Period. (P. S. Yendell) Pop. Astron. 2: 160, 202, 269, 362.
— — Red. (A. Brester, jr.) Knowl. 18: 251.
— — Study of. (P. S. Yendell) Pop. Astron. 3: 446.
— Velocity of, Spectroscopic Method of determining. (H. C. Vogel) Astron. 11: 203.
— What they are made of. (G. P. Serviss) Chaut. 21: 9.
— Wolf-Rayet. (W. W. Campbell) Astron. 13: 448.
Stars that never shone; a story. (W. Browne) Canad. M. 7: 171.
Star Chamber, Court of. (J. D. Lindsay) Green Bag, 6: 114-575. 7: 28.
— Modern. Time, 1: 633.
Star-showers of November. (W. F. Denning) Nature, 53: 7.
"Star-spangled Banner." (J. C. Carpenter) Cent. 26: 358.
— Origin of. Music, 1: 469.
"Star" System in Periodicals. (H. F. Bates) Dial (Ch.) 16: 38.

Stare Decisis, Doctrine of. (B. Winchester) Green Bag, 8: 257.
Starey, Alfred Butler. Critic, 23: 115.
Starfish, Psychological Life of. (C. Sterne) Monist, 1: 245.
Stark Munro Letters, The. (A. Conan Doyle) Idler, vols. 6-8.
Starkey Family of New England. (Emily W. Leavitt) N. E. Reg. 46: 144.
Starlight, Electrical Measurement of. (G. M. Minchin) Nature, 52: 246.
— Electromotive Force of. Dub. R. 117: 447.
"Starved Rock" in Illinois. (F. J. O'Reilly) Cath. World, 58: 473.
"Starving at Taskoma." (J. Heard, jr.) Cent. 21: 927.
Stas, Jean Servais. (V. Cornish) Knowl. 15: 74.— Nature, 46: 81.
State, Aid from the, Dangerous Absurdity of. (D. McG. Means) Forum, 17: 287.
— and Dwellings for the Poor. (F. B. Vrooman) Arena, 12: 415.
— as a Patient. (E. Fry) Contemp. 66: 849.
— Authority of the, Limits of. (J. M. Smith) Am. M. Civics, 9: 288.
— Does it Exist? (P. Carus) Open Court, 6: 3449.
— Federal, Nature of. (E. V. Robinson) Ann. Am. Acad. Pol. Sci. 3: 785.
— Has it Abdicated? (H. L. Wayland) Am. J. Pol. 2: 164. Same art. Am. J. Soc. Sci. 30: v.
— Hegel on. (L. F. Ward) Soc. Econ. 7: 32.
— Michel's *Idée de*. (R. Hudson) Am. Hist. R. 2: 148.
— a Product of Natural Growth. (P. Carus) Open Court, 8: 3944-3952.
— Rights of. (H. Rashdall) Econ. R. 6: 59.
— Sovereign, Government: a Triad of Political Conceptions. (C. M. Platt) Pol. Sci. Q. 10: 292.
State Bank Notes. Bank. M. (N. Y.) 49: 207.
— Tax on. Bank. M. (N. Y.) 48: 605.
State Bank Systems. Bank. M. (N. Y.) 47: 741-905. 48: 21, 96.
State Bank Tax, Repeal of the. (D. M. Stone) Forum, 13: 725.
— Shall it be repealed? (H. Bacon) Forum, 14: 571.
State Banking Systems. Bank. M. (N. Y.) 52: 50.
State Banks and Currency. (A. L. Ripley) Bank. M. (N. Y.) 50: 44.—(A. L. Ripley) Yale R. 3: 311.
— Revival of Circulation of. Bank. M. (N. Y.) 47: 321
— *versus* National Banks. Bank. M. (N. Y.) 47: 588.
State Charities of New York, 1894. (J. Tunis) Lend a H. 15: 49.
State Constitutions in the U. S., First. (W. C. Morey) Ann. Am. Acad. Pol. Sci. 4: 201.
State Government, Reform of. (G. Bradford) Ann. Am. Acad. Pol. Sci. 4: 883.
State Interference in Social Affairs. (J. S. Nicholson) Pop. Sci. Mo. 44: 196.
— Nature of. Westm. 137: 53.
— Principles of. (D. G. Ritchie) Time, 14: 29.
State Laws, Uniformity of. (J. L. Scott) Am. M. Civics, 8: 303.
State Legislation, Uniform. (F. J. Stimson) Ann. Am. Acad. Pol. Sci. 5: 829.
State Regulation of Prices and Rates. (W. H. Dunbar) Q. J. Econ. 9: 305.
State Rights and Federal Encroachments. (J. S. Fisher) Am. M. Civics, 6: 533.
State Secrets, Sanctity of. (A. D. Vandam) Sat. R. 82: 515.
State Sovereignty before 1789. (D. H. Chamberlain) Yale R. 2: 248.
State Surgery. (H. L. Wayland) Am. J. Soc. Sci. 32: 82.
State Trials, English, Wallis's. Sat. R. 75: 73.
State University Library Work. (C. Bennett) Educa. 14: 152.
Statecraft, Ethics of. (H. Seal) Westm. 146: 272.
Statehood, Candidates for, 1892. Pub. Opin. 14: 222.
States, Public Money of, Custody of. (E. R. Buckley) Ann. Am. Acad. Pol. Sci. 6: 397.
Statesmanship, An American Institute of. (W. T. Tredway) Am. M. Civics, 8: 628.
Statesmen, English, as Humorists. Spec. 74: 603.
— of Europe. Leis. Hour, 41: 238-809.
Stationers at the Sign of the Trinity. (E. G. Duff) Bibliographica, 1: 93, 175, 499.
Statistical Legislation in the U. S., Proposed. (R. P. Falkener) Am. Statis. Assoc. 3: 69.
Statistical Science, New Step in. (F. Galton) Nature, 51: 319.
Statistics, The A, B, C of. (T. A. Welton) Univ. R. 1: 419.
— Abuse of. Quar. 179: 463.
— and Morals, Relation between. (Lord Farrer) J. Statis. Soc. 57: 595.
— Dictionary of, Mulhall's. Sat. R. 73: 397.
— Frequency-curves applied to the History of Pauperism in England and Wales. (G. U. Yule) J. Statis. Soc. 59: 318.
— Industrial, Fallacies of. (S. N. D. North) Am. J. Soc. Sci. no. 34: 140.
— International Comparisons of. (R. Giffen) Am. Statis. Assoc. 3: 199.—Econ. J. 2: 209.
— Limitations and Difficulties of. (C. D. Wright) Yale R. 3: 121.
— Social and Industrial. (C. D. Wright) Gunton's M. 10: 219, 289.
— Study of. (R. Mayo-Smith) Pol. Sci. Q. 10: 475.
— Theory of, Westergaard on. (F. Y. Edgeworth) Nature, 46: 437.
— Uses of. (E. R. L. Gould) Pub. Opin. 20: 300.
Statue, Evolution of a. (F. Weitenkampf) Chaut. 19: 50.
Statues and Monuments, Surroundings of. (C. S. Sargent) Garden & F. 9: 71.
— at Large. (Bernard H. Becker) Time, 2: 91.
— Famous Equestrian. (R. Ker) M. of Art, 4: 339.
— New, in New York. (C. S. Sargent) Garden and F. 7: 321.
— of London. (E. I. Bell) M. of Art, 3: 7-133.
Statuettes. (R. J. Slade) M. of Art, 17: 385.
Staurolite, its Carbonaceous Inclusions. (S. L. Penfield and J. H. Pratt) Am. J. Sci. 147: 81.
Staveley Iron-works, Eng. Chamb. J. 70: 570.
Stavenhagen, Bernhard. (H. T. Finck) Cent. 27: 935.
Staves of Office. Antiq. n. s. 30: 246.
Staying Power of Sir Rohan, The. (F. R. Stockton) Scrib. M. 18: 745.
Stead, W. T. If Christ came to Chicago. (Goldwin Smith) Contemp. 66: 380.
— Portraits of. McClure, 2: 18.
— "Steadism" in Politics. (C. Waters) Westm. 137: 618.
Stealin' a Meetin' house. (A. M. Tirrell) New Eng. M. n. s. 8: 657.
Stealing a March on the Colonel; a story. (R. C. Drummond) Argosy, 59: 222.
Steam, Amount of Water suspended in. (W. R. Cummins) Cassier, 4: 49.
— and Electricity; a Study in Sociology. (A. A. Johnson) Am. M. Civics, 7: 343.

Steam and Hot Air for Power. Cassier, 1: 81.
— Cloudy Condensation of. (S. Bidwell) Nature, 49: 212.
— Dry, Methods for Securing. (R. C. Carpenter) Cassier, 2: 278.
— Future of. (F. H. Colvin) Cassier, 1: 334.
— High-pressure, Generating. (G. H. Babcock) Cassier, 2: 95.
— Manufacture of. Engin. M. 10: 500.
— New Method of using. Cassier, 3: 94.
— Power, Light, and Heat in City Blocks. (J. E. Talbot) Engin. M. 9: 457.
— Preventable Wastes of Heat in Generation and Use of. (W. Kent) J. Frankl. Inst. 140: 406.
— Superheated. (W. C. Unwin) Cassier, 7: 45.
— — in Steam Engines. (R. H. Thurston) Science, n. s. 4: 778.
— Superheating. (W. H. Patchell) Cassier, 10: 115.
Steamboat, James Rumsey the Inventor of the. (G. W. Archer) Nat'l M. (N. Y. '91) 18: 132.
— Where it was born. (Maggie Symington) New Sci. R. 1: 409.
Steamboating in the West and South. (W. Kennedy) Engin. M. 5: 731.
Steamboats, Early, on the Lakes. (J. F. Holloway) Engin. M. 7: 556.
— of the Hudson River. (S. W. Stanton) Engin. M. 8: 849.
Steam Boiler Efficiencies, Graphics of. (R. H. Thurston) J. Frankl. Inst. 138: 81–161.
Steam Engine, The. (W. H. Laurie) Cassier, 2: 359.
— Barring. (W. H. Booth) Cassier, 8: 528.
— Early History of. Cassier, 1: 14.
— Evolution of. (J. E. Sweet) Cassier, 6: 454.
— Foundation for, Replacing a. (C. A. Hague) Cassier, 6: 422.
— Heat Movement in Cylinders of. Cassier, 3: 308.
— in Modern Civilization. (C. H. Loring) Cassier, 3: 206.
— Marine, New. Cassier, 1: 225.
— Multiple-cylinder, Philosophy of. (R. H. Thurston) Cassier, 1: 3.
— Present and Prospective Economy of. (J. H. Barr) Cassier, 5: 387.
— Recent Designs. (G. L. Clark) Cassier, 5: 314.
— Remarkable Performance of. (C. T. Porter) Cassier, 7: 375.
Steam-engineering, Progress in. (R. H. Thurston) Engin. M. 5: 176, 349.
Steam-engineers: Why Some Men fail. (W. H. Wakeman) Engin. M. 8: 228.
Steam Engines and Boilers, Proper Connection of. (T. F. Scheffler) Cassier, 6: 447.
— — Significance and Value of Duty Tests for. (E. J. Armstrong) Engin. M. 12: 443.
— at World's Fair. (G. L. Clark) Cassier, 4: 32–333.
— Automatic, Economy of. (R. H. Thurston) Cassier, 3: 53.
— Breakdowns of. (J. E. Sweet) Cassier, 1: 24.
— Compound. Cassier, 1: 65.
— — and Triple-expansion, Power Distribution in Cylinders of. (W. M. Henderson) Cassier, 10: 23.
— — Non-condensing, Economy of. (R. C. Carpenter) Cassier, 3: 263.
— — Steam Distribution in. (F. M. Rites) Cassier, 2: 58.
— Contrasts in. (G. L. Clark) Cassier, 10: 457.
— Cylinders of, Heat-wastes in. (R. H. Thurston) J. Frankl. Inst. 142: 241.
— Direct-connected. Cassier, 2: 119–365.
— — and Dynamos. (T. G. Smith, jr.) Cassier, 7: 285.
Steam Engines, Efficiency in, Standard of. (R. H. Thurston) J. Frankl. Inst. 142: 442.
— First Stationary in America. (F. R. Hutton) Cassier, 6: 308.
— Governing of. (W. S. Aldrich) Cassier, 2: 374.—(F. M. Rites) Cassier, 3: 180.
— Governor for. (H. J. Conant) Engin. M. 8: 39.
— Insurance of. (H. B. Spence) Cassier, 8: 554.
— Marine, Triple-expansion. Cassier, 1: 166. 3: 149.
— Maximum Contemporary Economy. (R. H. Thurston) J. Frankl. Inst. 137: 247.
— Multi-cylinder, Test of. (S. M. Green and G. I. Rockwood) Cassier, 2: 9.
— of To-day. (G. L. Clark) Cassier, 8: 511.
— Oil Steam. (A. Spies) Cassier, 5: 95.
— Rotary, Old and New. Cassier, 1: 306.
— Points in the Selection of. (W. H. Wakeman) Engin. M. 11: 255.
— Semi-portable, in England. (W. Fletcher) Cassier, 4: 286.
— Tandem Compound. Cassier, 1: 486.
— — Thermal Analysis of. (R. H. Thurston) J. Frankl. Inst. 136: 241.
— Testing. (M. C. Ihlseng) Cassier, 1: 439.
— Triple-expansion, Experimental. (C. H. Peabody) Cassier, 1: 411.
— — Economy of. Cassier, 3: 64.
— Turbine. (J. H. Barr) Cassier, 10: 372.
— Use of Compound Stationary. (R. H. Thurston) Engin. M. 7: 837.
— Vertical, for Stationary Purposes. (C. H. Manning) Cassier, 10: 403.
Steam Gauges, High-pressure. (F. Budenberg) Cassier, 3: 189.
— and Pressure Gauges. (A. B. Calkins) Cassier, 1: 469.
— Pressure. (C. R. L. Lemkes) Cassier, 7: 496.
Steam Jackets, Influence of. (W. Kent) Cassier, 1: 116.
— Notes on. (W. Fletcher) Cassier, 3: 382.
Steam Locomotion on Common Roads. (W. Fletcher) Engin. M. 5: 493.
Steam Navigation, Origin and Developments. (G. H. Preble) Un. Serv. (Phila.) vols. 11–13.
— Progress in. (Mrs. M. J. Lamb) M. Am. Hist. 28: 161.
Steam Pipes, Water Rams in. (C. E. Emery) Cassier, 1: 135.
Steam Piping for Steam Plants. (W. A. Pike) Cassier, 5: 345.
Steam Power and Coal Bill. (T. Pray, jr.) Cassier, 1: 42, 162.
— Cost of. (W. C. Unwin) Cassier, 5: 352.—(C. E. Emery) Cassier, 8: 409.
Steamers, American Lake, for Ocean Traffic. (J. R. Oldham) Cassier, 8: 468.
— of Long Island Sound. (W. A. Fairburn) Engin. M. 9: 232.
Steamship, Auxiliary Machinery of. (H. L. Ebsen) Cassier, 6: 369.
— Genesis of the. (F. M. Holmes) Gent. M. n. s. 52: 500.
— Philosophy of. (W. F. Durand) Cassier, 3: 35.
Steamship Routes, Transatlantic. Chamb. J. 69: 262.
Steamship Service, Fast Atlantic. (E. Tupper) Canad. M. 7: 493.
Steamships. (C. H. New) Lippinc. 57: 660.
— "American Line" of. Pub. Opin. 14: 513.
— Atlantic. (H. Dyer) Scot. R. 19: 1.
— — Maginnis on. Sat. R. 74: 367.
— — Crew of. (W. H. Rideing) Cosmopol. 12: 679.

Steamships, Development of, in the 19th Century. (W. Sebree) Chaut. 20: 131.
— Early. Chamb. J. 70: 155.
— Fast. (F. Elgar) Cassier, 5: 83.
— Freight. (H. Russell) Eng. Illust. 10: 395.
— Great Atlantic Liners. (G. Holme) Munsey, 13: 118. — (S. W. Stanton) Engin. M. 10: 447.
— — Building of. (R. McIntyre) Good Words, 36: 134.
— — Latest and Greatest Cunarder. Engin. M. 5: 283.
— — Manœuvring Powers of. (P. H. Colomb) Nature, 49: 174.
— The New Cunarders. Chamb. J. 70: 293.
— Ocean. (J. N. Porter) Time, 17: 439, 532.
— — "Fürst Bismarck." (C. Warman) Idler, 7: 213.
— An Ocean Flyer. McClure, 4: 295.
— Speed of, Limits of. Spec. 70: 480.
— — Thirty Knots an Hour to Europe. (J. H. Biles) No. Am. 156: 717.
— Subdivision of, for Safety. (A. Ham) J. Frankl. Inst. 137: 71, 149.
— Transatlantic, 1819–55. (S. W. Stanton) Engin. M. 9: 1051.
— — 1856–80. (S. W. Stanton) Engin. M. 10: 245.
Stearns, Lewis French. And. R. 17: 307. — (F. B. Denio) And. R. 18: 1.
Stedman, Edmund Clarence. (H. W. Mabie) Bookman, 3: 421. — With portrait. Bk. Buyer, 12: 209. — With portrait. Bk. News, 7: 332. — (R. Cortissoz) Cent. 26: 899.
— and some of his Contemporaries. (Mary J. Reid) Overland, n. s. 25: 17.
Steel, Flora A. Miss Stuart's Legacy. Spec. 71: 690.
— On the Face of the Waters. Acad. 50: 488.
Steel, Conquest, over Cast Iron. (H. L. Arnold) Engin. M. 8: 1055.
— for Electric Machines. (H. F. Parshall) J. Frankl. Inst. 137: 93.
— Fusion of. (F. J. R. Carulla) Cassier, 1: 315.
— in Canada, Let us smelt our Own. (W. H. Merritt) Canad. M. 1: 181.
— Low in Carbon, Conditions causing it to be Crystalline. (W. F. Durfee) J. Frankl. Inst. 142: 110.
— Making, Revolution in. (W. Metcalf) Engin. M. 9: 1072.
— Manganese. (H. M. Howe) J. Frankl. Inst. 135: 114, 191.
— Production of, in Germany. New R. 14: 113.
— Structural. (J. Christie) J. Frankl. Inst. 141: 33.
Steel Castings. (H. L. Gantt) Cassier, 5: 355.
Steel Construction, Specifications for. (C. H. Blackall) Am. Arch. 46: 128.
Steel Forgings, Making of, in America. (H. F. J. Porter) Cassier, 10: 83.
Steel Ingots, Consolidating. (J. L. Sebenius) Cassier, 6: 31.
Steel Tool, A. (R. R. Bowker) Harper, 88: 587.
Steele, Gen. John. (S. C. Frazer) Am. Hist. Reg. 3: 644.
Steele, Richard, and "The Ladies' Library." Bookworm, 1: 49.
Steele, Thomas Sedgwick: With Brush and Rod. (C. S. Johnson) Munsey, 12: 577.
Steell, Gourlay. Acad. 45: 133.
Steen, Jan. (T. Cole) Cent. 25: 175.
Steenkirke, Battle of, and Waterloo. Sat. R. 76: 328.
Steeple-chasers and Chasing in Ireland. (T. S. Blackwell) Outing, 21: 419.
Steeple-Jacks. Chamb. J. 73: 365. Spec. 73: 488.
Steerage Passage from London to New York. (F. A. McKenzie) Eng. Illust. 12: no. 3, 43.
Stefen the Great, The Mother of. (Carmen Sylva) Sund M. 25: 73.
Stein, Lorenz von. (L. R. Phelps) Econ. R. 1: 89.
Steiner, Lewis H., Memorial of. (W. H. Ward) Lib. J. 17: supp. 10.
Steinway, William. (J. Hoffman) Nat'l M. (N. Y. '91) 16: 707.
Stelar Theory. (A. G. Tansley) Sci. Prog. 5: 133.
Stele, A, Commemorating a Victory in a Boat-race. (P. Gardner) J. Hel. Stud. 11: 146.
Stella. (Nellie Keith) Time, 8: 25, 175.
Stellar Space, Atmosphere of. (G. D. Liveing) Science, 22: 87.
Stellar System, New, Discovery of. (A. Searle) Atlan. 69: 814.
Stem to Root, Transition from. (A. Maslen) Knowl. 19: 224.
Stemmatoiulus as an Ordinal Type. (O. F. Cook) Am. Natural. 29: 1111.
Stencilled Stuffs. (L. F. Day) M. of Art, 20: 40.
Stendhal. (F. T. Cooper) Bookman, 3: 337.
Stenness, Standing Stones of. (M. Spence) Scot. R. 22: 401.
Step-brothers to Dives; a Moral without a Story. (L. B. Edwards) Harper, 89: 436.
Stephanie de Liancourt. Macmil. 73: 401.
Stephen, King, and Earl of Chester. (J. H. Round) Eng. Hist. R. 10: 87.
Stephen, Sir Alfred, Lord Sherbrooke and. (A. P. Martin) National, 23: 682.
Stephen, Sir James Fitzjames. (G. H. Knoté) Am. Law R. 26: 489. — Ed. R. 182: 418. — (J. Wedgwood) Contemp. 68: 520. — (F. Pollock) National, 25: 817. Same art. Liv. Age, 207: 45. — With portrait. Green Bag, 6: 161. — Spec. 72: 366. — Sat. R. 77: 273. — (C. K. Paul) Month, 84: 457.
— as a Legislator. (C. P. Ilbert) Law Q. 10: 222.
— Attitude towards Roman Catholicism. (B. Holland) National, 26: 29.
— Historical Work of. (F. Morgan) Green Bag, 6: 334.
— Leslie Stephen on. (J. G. Rosengarten) Am. Hist. R. 1: 351. — (J. B. Thayer) Nation, 61: 259. — Ath. '95, 1: 829. — Sat. R. 79: 865. — (A. W. Benn) Acad. 48: 23.
— an Unteachable Teacher. Spec. 74: 815.
Stephen, Leslie. (J. A. Noble) Bookman, 2: 399. — (W. E. Gladstone) 19th Cent. 38: 733.
Stephens, Alice Barber, with portrait. Bk. Buyer, 12: 392. — (F. W. Webber) Q. Illust. 1: 174.
Stephens, Charles Edward. Acad. 42: 78.
Stephens, George. Acad. 48: 130. — (R. N. Bain) Ath. '95, 2: 224.
Stephens, James Brunton. (O. Smeaton) Westm. 144: 491.
Stephens, Mrs., Actress. Acad. 49: 83.
Stephenson, Dr. Bowman, at Home. Sund. M. 22: 178.
Stephenson, George; the Father of Railways. (J. Hatton) Idler, 7: 647.
Stephenson, T. B., Homes for Children. (F. W. Farrar) Chr. Lit. 10: 276.
Stepniak. King Stork and King Log. (I. F. Hapgood) Nation, 62: 104.
Steppes, Deserts, and Alkali Lands. (E. W. Hilgard) Pop. Sci. Mo. 48: 602.
Stereochemistry. Nature, 49: 409.
— Progress in. (A. Eiloart) Nature, 54: 321.
— Review of. (S. W. Young) J. Frankl. Inst. 139: 56.

Stereoscope without Mirrors or Prisms. (H. Munsterberg) Psychol. R. 1: 56.
Sterna Wilsonii, Development of Wing of. (V. L. Leighton) Am. Natural. 28: 761.
Sterne, Laurence. Cornh. 66: 482. — (H. Paul) 19th Cent. 40: 995.
— at Home. Liv. Age, 196: 172.
— Life, by Fitzgerald. Sat. R. 81: 531.
— Philosophy of. (H. C. Merwin) Atlan. 74: 521.
— Tristram Shandy, Whibley's. Sat. R. 78: 510.
Sterner, Albert E., with portrait. Bk. Buyer, 11: 245.
Sternhold and Hopkins and their Followers. (J. C. Hadden) [Gent. M.] Liv. Age, 208: 365.
Stevens, Alfred. (W. Armstrong) M. of Art, 4: 215.
— and the Wellington Memorial. (W. Armstrong) 19th Cent. 31: 864.
— Stannus' Life of. (C. Monkhouse) M. of Art, 15: 303. — Ath. '92, 2: 326.
Stevens, Isaac N., with portrait. (A. N. Towne) Nat'l M. (N. Y. '91) 16: 366.
Stevens, William, Letter of, 1795. N. E. Reg. 48: 456.
Stevenson, Joseph. (J. H. Pollen) Month, 83: 331.
Stevenson, R. A. M., a Sane Critic. New R. 14: 87.
Stevenson, Robert Louis. (J. S. Cotton) Acad. 46: 533. — Critic, 25: 430–453. — Spec. 73: 813. — Pub. Opin. 17: 951. — Spec. 73: 881. — Sat. R. 78: 675. — (J. Jacobs) Ath. '94, 2: 863. — Lit. W. (Bost.) 25: 473. — Eng. Illust. 11: 768. — With portrait. Bk. Buyer, 3: 75. — Bk. Buyer, 5: 59. — With portrait. Bk. Buyer, 10: 641. — With portraits. Bk. Buyer, 11: 739. — With portrait. Bk. Buyer, 12: 12. — With portrait. Bk. News, 6: 489. — Bk. News, 13: 210. — (H. Charlesworth) Canad. M. 5: 27. — (C. D. Lanier) R. of Rs. (N. Y.) 11: 181. — (C. T. Copeland) Atlan. 75: 537. — Dial (Ch.) 18: 3. — With portraits. (W. Churchill and others) McClure, 4: 278. — (A. H. Japp) Argosy, 59: 226. — (Marcel Schwob) New R. 12: 153. — Ed. R. 182: 106. — Quar. 180: 324. — Lond. Q. 85: 1. — (G. L. Kittredge) Nation, 62: 37. — With portrait. Acad. 50: 562. — (Y. E. Allison) So. M. 5: 598.
— Across the Plains. Gent. M. n. s. 48: 638. — Sat. R. 73: 630. — Spec. 69: 99.
— and the Drama. (M. Watson) Theatre, 37: 311.
— and Edinburgh. (F. Watt) Art J. 48: 46.
— and his Writing. (M. G. Van Rensselaer) Cent. 29: 123.
— as a Dramatist. (L. Johnson) Acad. 43: 277.
— Autograph Letter. Cosmopol. 19: 259.
— Catriona [David Balfour]. Ath. '93, 2: 375. — Sat. R. 76: 333. — Scot. R. 23: 42.
— Collecting of Stevensons. (W. D. Ellwanger) Bach. of Arts, 1: 344.
— Critical Study of. (S. Gwynn) Fortn. 62: 776. Same art. Liv. Age, 204: 67. Same art. Ecl. M. 124: 154.
— Early Home of. (J. A. Ross) Good Words, 36: 181.
— Essays of. (R. Le Gallienne) Acad. 41: 462.
— Fables by. Spec. 75: 299.
— First Book, Treasure Island. (R. L. Stevenson) McClure, 3: 283. Same art. Idler, 6: 3.
— First Landing in N. Y. (L. E. Shipman) Bk. Buyer, 13: 13.
— Hero in Works of, Special Type of. Spec. 73: 171.
— Home of. Westm. 143: 551. Same art. Ecl. M. 125: 61.
— Home Life at Vailima. (L. Osbourne) Scrib. M. 18: 458.
— in his Home Life. (Isobel Strong) Scrib. M. 19: 531, 737.
Stevenson, Robert Louis. In Memoriam. (William Archer) New R. 12: 89.
— in Samoa, Short Visit with. Sat. R. 79: 38.
— Island Nights' Entertainments. (L. Johnson) Acad. 43: 473.
— Last Address and Will of. McClure, 5: 173.
— Library of, at Vailima, Samoa. (A. W. Mahaffy) Spec. 75: 762.
— Literary Work of, in College. (C. M. Robinson) Bookman, 1: 316.
— Personal Memories of. (E. Gosse) Cent. 28: 447.
— Plays of. Gent. M. n. s. 49: 529.
— Portraits of. (J. B. Paul) Ath. '95, 2: 328. — McClure, 2: 230.
— Rarer Writings of. Bk. Buyer, 12: 493.
— Recollections of. (A. Lang) No. Am. 160: 185.
— Religion of. (W. J. Dawson) Bookman, 4: 35.
— St. Ives. Acad. 50: 391.
— Some Aspects of the Work of. (Janetta Newton Robinson) Westm. 139: 601.
— Some Recollections of. (H. C. Baildon) Temp. Bar, 104: 325. Same art. Liv. Age, 205: 219.
— Songs of Travel. (E. Purcell) Acad. 50: 253.
— Stevensoniana. Critic, 26: 160. 27: 331.
— Style and Thought of. (Wm. Archer) Time, 13: 581.
— Tributes to. Critic, 26: 16–50.
— Vailima Letters. Idler, 9: 117. — Sat. R. 80: 689. — McClure, 5: 522. — (C. H. Genung) Nation, 63: 50.
— Weir of Hermiston. Sat. R. 81: 603. — (E. Purcell) Acad. 49: 521.
— With, in Samoa. Cornh. 70: 27. Same art. Ecl. M. 123: 257. Same art. Liv. Age, 202: 252.
— The Wrecker. Sat. R. 74: 77. — Spec. 69: 132. — (L. Johnson) Acad. 42: 103.
Stevenson, Mrs. Robert Louis, Portrait of. McClure, 3: 282.
Stewart, Mrs. Duncan. (A. J. C. Hare) Good Words 33: 661, 764. Same art. Liv. Age, 195: 753.
Stewart, Mrs. E. D. Mother Stewart, a Character Sketch, with portrait. (C. M. Nichols) Our Day, 15: 295.
Stewart, General Sir Herbert. (R. Mongan) Time, 12: 457.
Stewart, Sir Robert Prescott. (J. P. Mahaffy) Ath. '94, 1: 452. — (O. J. Vignoles) Acad. 45: 295.
Stewart, Royal House of. (James Hutton) Gent. M. n. s. 50: 281, 345.
Stickney, Edward S., with portrait. Nat'l M. (N. Y. '91) 16: 481.
Stiepevich, Vincent G. (A. Trumble) Mo. Illust. 5: 259.
Stiles, Ezra, Journal of. 1776. New Eng. M. n. s. 14: 317.
— Library of. (K. G. Wells) New Eng. M. n. s. 14: 181.
Stilicho, Flavius. (H. Maxwell) 19th Cent. 32: 389. Same art. Ecl. M. 119: 604. Same art. Un. Serv. (Phila.) 8: 450.
Stillman, William James. (W. P. Garrison) Cent. 24: 656.
Stilts and Stilt-walking. (M. Guyot-Daubes) Pop. Sci. Mo. 40: 467.
Stimuli, Agreeable and Disagreeable, Organic Effects of. (J. R. Angell and S. F. McLennan) Psychol. R. 3: 371.
Stirling, Mrs., afterwards Lady Gregory. (C. H. Dene) Eng. Illust. 14: 487. — (A. Escott) Theatre, 36: 86. — Acad. 49: 18.
Stirpiculture, Human. (W. J. Lhamon) Canad. M. 6: 403.
Stock, Collard J. Acad. 43: 80, 105.

Stock, New Issues of, at less than Par. (E. W. Huffcut) Am. Law R. 26: 861.
Stock Companies, Report of Departmental Committee. (H. Withers) National, 26: 129.
Stock Exchange, The, and the Public. (H. J. Jennings) Gent. M. n. s. 51: 420.
Stock Exchange Clearing Houses. (A. D. Noyes) Pol. Sci. Q. 8: 252.
Stock Exchange Gambling. Chamb. J. 73: 609.
Stock Exchange Investments. (Sir J. Vogel) Bank. M. (Lond.) 54: 10.
Stockholders, Duties of. Bank. M. (N. Y.) 46: 249.
Stock-sharing as a Preventive of Labor Troubles. (L. R. Ehrich) Forum, 18: 433.
Stock Speculation: the Gold Mining Madness in the City. (S. F. Van Oss) 19th Cent. 38: 537.
Stock-watering, Corporation. (T. L. Greene) Nation, 56: 307.
— Ethics of. (T. C. Frenyear) Ann. Am. Acad. Pol. Sci. 8: 509.
— Myth of. Gunton's M. 10: 274.
Stock-breeding, Science and, Mutual Relations of. (W. H. Brewer) Science, 22: 169.
Stockholm. All the Year, 73: 298, 318. Same art. Liv. Age, 199: 504.
— In a Stockholm Pension. Cornh. 68: 362.
— Winter in. Belgra. 86: 72.
Stocking, George, Family of. (E. E. Cornwall) N. E. Reg. 50: 171.
Stockton, Frank R., with portrait. Bk. Buyer, 2: 290. — With portrait. Bk. News, 7: 209. — With portrait. (E. M. Thomas) McClure, 1: 467.
Stockton, Cal., the Coming Chicago of the West Coast. (W. C. Ramsey) Overland, n. s. 26: 297.
Stoddard, Charles Warren. (C. H. Miller) Overland, n. s. 26: 376.
Stoddard, Mrs. Elizabeth, Poetry of. (W. Sharp) Acad. 50: 302.
Stoddard, Richard H., with portrait. Bk. Buyer, 2: 247. — With portrait. Bk. News, 5: 328.
— First Literary Acquaintances of. Lippinc. 53: 842.
— Seventieth Birthday of. Critic, 27: 11, 62.
Stoddart, James Henry. (M. White, jr.) Munsey, 13: 173.
Stoffels, Hendrickie. (J. F. White) M. of Art, 16: 308.
Stoke Pogis. (T. H. Bindley) Univ. R. 4: 114.
— Scene of Gray's Elegy. Chamb. J. 71: 395.
Stokers, Marine. Chamb. J. 70: 101.
Stokes Murder in Africa, The. (Lionel Decle) New R. 13: 585.
Stomach, Influence of, upon Mind. (W. Nathan) Westm. 146: 185.
Stomach Dwellers. (S. Baring-Gould) Good Words, 36: Xmas. no. 40.
Stomata, Respiratory Function of. (F. F. Blackman) Sci. Prog. 4: 13.
Stone, Horatio O., with portrait. (H. L. Conard) Nat'l M. (N. Y. '91) 16: 716.
Stone, James Madison. (H. L. Jillison) Mo. Illust. 13: 131.
Stone, Lucy. (Maria S. Porter) Bost. 3: 42. — (W. P. Garrison) Nation, 57: 302.
Stone, Marcus. (W. Meynell) M. of Art, 3: 83.
— and his Work. (C. S. Johnson) Munsey, 6: 421.
— at Home. (G. B. Burgin) Idler, 5: 173.
— Life and Work. (A. L. Baldry) Art J. 48: art annual.
Stone, Ormond, with portrait. (F. P. Matz) Pop. Astron. 3: 452.
Stone, Gov. William, of Maryland, Ancestry of. (E. Stone) N. E. Reg. 49: 314.
Stone, Art of Working in, Evolution of. (C. H. Read) Am. Natural. 28: 997. — (J. D. McGuire) Am. Natural. 29: 26.
"Stone of Destiny." (F. Barr) Good Words, 35: 848.
Stone Age of Connecticut. (J. Shepard) New Eng. M. n. s. 9: 327.
Stone Circles, British. (A. L. Lewis) Science, 21: 161, 274. 22: 17.
Stone Crosses of Somersetshire. Reliquary, 35: 216. 36: 139.
Stone Facing for Buildings, Adjustable. (J. L. Pelton) Am. Arch. 54: 74.
Stone Implements in Eastern U. S. (D. G. Brenton) Anthrop. J. 26: 59.
— of the Australian Type from Tasmania. (E. B. Tylor) Anthrop. J. 24: 335.
Stone Maiden, The; a Legend of Ancient Mani. (Mrs. M. C. Closson) Overland, n. s. 19: 130.
Stone Tools, Folk-Lore of. (F. Starr) J. Am. Folk-Lore, 4: 27.
Stoneware of Flanders. (C. Monkhouse) Portfo. 23: 248.
Stonehenge. (E. Barclay) Illus. Archæol. 1: 83.
Stonewall Brigade, History. (D. B. Conrad) Un. Serv. (Phila.) 7: 466.
Stonington, Conn., Aged Residents of, in 1893. (Mrs. H. A. Stanton) N. E. Reg. 48: 322.
— Contributions to the History of. (G. A. Gordon) N. E. Reg. 47: 459.
Stony Creek, Battle of. (E. B. Biggar) Canad. M. 1: 378.
Stony-Lonesome. (C. G. D. Roberts) Atlan. 78: 665.
Stony Point, N. Y., Capture of, in 1779. (W. Hull) M. Am. Hist. 28: 182.
— Operations at, 1779-80. (Original Letters) M. Am. Hist. 27: 465.
Stonyhurst. (P. Fitzgerald) M. of Art, 13: 354.
Stonyhurst College, by Gerard. Sat. R. 78: 274.
Stops of Several Quills: eleven Poems. (W. D. Howells) Harper, 90: 34.
Storage Batteries for Electric Traction. (P. G. Salom) Cassier, 7: 42.
Storage Battery, Evolution of. (M. Barnett) J. Frankl. Inst. 141: 296.
— Possibilities of. (P. G. Salom) Cassier, 7: 117.
Stores, Hours of, Regulation of, in England. Spec. 70: 381.
Storey, George Adolphus. (W. W. Fenn) M. of Art, 6: 353.
Storiation in Art. (H. Stannus) J. Soc. Arts, 41: 262.
Stories, Children's, Failure in. (R. E. Gregg) Writer, 8: 81.
— for Boys, How to Write. (W. O. Stoddard and others) Writer, 8: 127, 143. — (H. Castlemon) Writer, 9: 4. — (H. Alger, jr.) Writer, 9: 36.
— of Animals. (L. Meadows) Argosy, 61: 490, 598, 727.
— of British Battles. (J. D. Symon) Eng. Illust. 16: 77, 213, 335.
— of a Western Town. (Alice French) Scrib. M. 12: 135-684. 13: 208.
— Short, and Long. All the Year, 72: 79.
— — Writing of. (M. E. Child) Writer, 7: 129.
— Some Strange. (A. Quarry) Argosy, 57: 543.
Storm, Theodor. (J. G. Robertson) Gent. M. n. s. 55: 619.
Storm of March 11-14, 1888. (A. W. Greeley) Nat. Geog. M. 1: 37.
Storm Statistics at Bidston. (W. E. Plummer) Nature, 51: 272.
Storm Tracks. (F. L. Oswald) No. Am. 163: 115.

Storms, Dust and Sand, in the West. (J. A. Unden) Pop. Sci. Mo. **49**: 655.
— Equinoctial and Other. All the Year, **73**: 270.
— Law of, referring to North Atlantic. (E. Hayden) Nat. Geog. M. **2**: 199.
— of August, 1893. (W. C. Kerr) Science, **22**: 155.
— Winter, of Northern India. (H. F. Blanford) Nature, **45**: 490.
See Tempests.
Stormy Petrel; a poem. (T. H. Rand) Canad. M. **6**: 411.
Story, William Wetmore. (Mrs. Lew Wallace) Cosmopol. **21**: 404. — Critic, **27**: 234. — M. of Art, **2**: 272.
Story, The Short, in America. Critic, **23**: 608. — Atlan. **69**: 261.
Story I heard on the Cars, The. (E. V. Wilson) McClure, **1**: 224.
Story in Embroidery, A. (H. M. Gilchrist) Chamb. J. **72**: 826.
Story of Alcatraz. (A. H. Sydenham) Un. Serv. (Phila.) **13**: 219.
Story of an Artist. (E. Cumings) Music, **1**: 17–596. **2**: 93–620. **3**: 96, 194.
Story of a Beautiful Thing. (F. H. Burnett) Scrib. M. **15**: 722.
Story of Bessie Costrell. (Mrs. H. Ward) Cornh. **71**: 449, 562. **72**: 100. Same art. Scrib. M. **17**: 548, 680. **18**: 25.
Story of a Broken Life. Belgra. **89**: 192.
Story of a Child. (M. Deland) Atlan. **70**: 289, 446, 577.
Story of a Clock. (A. B. Edwards) New Eng. M. n. s. **7**: 564.
Story of a Club, The; a story. (A. Moffat) Cosmopol. **17**: 435.
Story of Conn-Eda; translated from the Irish. Folk-Lore Rec. **2**: 180.
Story of a Day. (G. King) Cent. **24**: 230.
Story of a Deccan Filly. (H. Nisbet) Idler, **4**: 511.
Story of Eleven Days. Liv. Age, **196**: 344.
Story of Engagements, A. (Q. Gordon) Belgra. **79**: Christmas no. 103.
Story of a Face, The. (Agnes J. Carr) Bost. **1**: 131.
Story of Fidelity. (E. Lambec) Chaut. **21**: 178.
Story of Hannah. (W. J. Dawson) Sund. M. **25**: 8–486.
Story of the Hinterland, A. Chamb. J. **73**: 823.
Story of his Life, The. Macmil. **74**: 300. Same art. Ecl. M. **127**: 679.
Story of an Hour, The. (H. Newman) Idler, **3**: 330.
Story of a Household Word. (L. Kip) Overland, n. s. **22**: 91.
Story of Kahuya Himé. (Trans. T. B. Harris) Chaut. **15**: 438.
Story of the Lagos Bar, A. Chamb. J. **73**: 461.
Story of the Late Mr. Elvesham. (H. G. Wells) Idler, **9**: 487.
Story of Lee Ping and "The Stork that lives a Thousand Years." (Guy Boothby) Chamb. J. **72**: 426.
Story of Léonie. (E. H. Miller) Chaut. **23**: 745.
Story of a Little Child. All the Year, **75**: 179.
Story of 'Liza Begg. Cornh. **70**: 61.
Story of Love and Faith. (Caspar Schenk) Un. Serv. (Phila.) **7**: 550.
Story of Margrédel. Blackw. **154**: 765. **155**: 27, 236, 395. Same art. Liv. Age, **200**: 164.
Story of a Mazurka, The. (E. F. Benson) Eng. Illust. **11**: 111.
Story of Meg. (M. Kendall) Longm. **21**: 505.
Story of the Metropolis. (H. C. N. Wilson) Canad. M. **3**: 216.
Story of the Miller. (N. W. Williams) Gent. M. n. s. **56**: 55.
Story of Miss Pi. (J. Ralph) Harper, **92**: 189.
Story of the Niger, A. (H. Bindloss) Temp. Bar, **109**: 104.
Story of the Northwest, A. (L. A. M. Bosworth) Overland, n. s. **21**: 98.
Story of O'Doud's Diggins. (R. M. Daggett) Overland, n. s. **24**: 491.
Story of the Other Wise Man. (H. Van Dyke) Harper, **86**: 277.
Story of a Path, The. (H. C. Bunner) Scrib. M. **16**: 754.
Story of a Penny Pencil. (S. A. Wedderburn) Outing, **29**: 119.
Story of a Portrait in Bruges; a story. (Georges Rodenbach) Cosmopol. **18**: 620.
Story of a Postcard. All the Year, **75**: 36, 69, 92.
Story of a Private Box. (F. Allston) Theatre, **28**: 85.
Story of the Sorcerer. (C. G. Leland) Idler, **7**: 257.
Story of a Story. (Caroline Ticknor) Cosmopol. **22**: 80.
Story of the Strange Chance Mine. Blackw. **159**: 219.
Story of Two Salons. Temp. Bar, **108**: 408.
Story of an Ugly Girl. (E. F. Andrews) Chaut. **20**: 462.
Story of Ung, The; a poem. (R. Kipling) Idler, **6**: 515.
Story without a Moral. (M. H. Fraser-Lovett) Lippinc. **50**: 661.
Story-teller, After-thoughts of a. (G. W. Cable) No. Am. **158**: 16.
— Speculations of a. (G. W. Cable) Atlan. **78**: 88.
Story-tellers, New, and the Doom of Realism. (W. R. Thayer) Forum, **18**: 470.
Story-telling. (A. Lang) Idler, **4**: 81.
— Gift of. (B. Matthews) Harper, **91**: 717.
Stothard, Thomas. (A. T. Story) Art J. **46**: 86.
Stoughton, Lieut.-Gov. William, Sketch of. (J. W. Dean) N. E. Reg. **50**: 9.
Stoughton, Mass., Records of Episcopal Church at, 1791–96. N. E. Reg. **46**: 14, 133, 351.
Stout, Francis A. (J. M. Read) M. Am. Hist. **28**: 432.
Stoves, American. (S. R. Koehler) M. of Art, **8**: 37, suppl.
— and Ovens. Chamb. J. **70**: 86.
Stowaways. Chamb. J. **72**: 489.
Stowe, Harriet Beecher, with portrait. Bk. News, **3**: 288. — (J. H. Morse) Critic, **29**: 1. — Ath. '96, **2**: 36. — (E. L. Didier) Chaut. **23**: 387. — Critic, **29**: 27. — (T. W. Higginson) Nation, **63**: 24. — (J. H. Ward) Forum, **21**: 727. — R. of Rs. (N. Y.) **14**: 177. — (R. Burton) Cent. **30**: 699. — (G. W. Cooke) New Eng. M. n. s. **15**: 3. — (J. R. Howard and others) Outl. **54**: 138, 143.
— at Cincinnati. (G. S. McDowell) New Eng. M. n. s. **12**: 65.
— Days with. (A. Fields) Atlan. **78**: 145.
— Reminiscences of. (E. S. Phelps) McClure, **7**: 3.
— Uncle Tom's Cabin. Eng. R. **18**: 80. — Spec. **68**: 434.
— — Story of. (C. D. Warner) Atlan. **78**: 311.
Strachey Family: The Old Hall and the Portraits. (Sir E. Strachey) Atlan. **71**: 626.
Stradanus, Johannes; the Landseer of the 16th Century. (W. A. Baillie-Grohman) Eng. Illust. **16**: 33.
Stradanus' Printing-office. (F. Maclan) Bibliographica, **1**: 223.
Straeten, Georges Van der. *See* Van der Straeten.
Strafford, Life of; Forster's or Browning's? (W. G. Kingsland) Poet-Lore, **6**: 555.

Strahan, William. Bookworm, **2**: 333.
Straight Edges, very accurate, Manufacture of. (F. L. O. Wadsworth) J. Frankl. Inst. **138**: 1.
Straight Flush, A. (F. Harris) Fortn. **58**: 265.
Straight Line and the Circle, Inductive Manual of, Myers's. (W. H. Butts) School R. **4**: 696.
Strains: Finite Elastic Stress-strain Function. (G. F. Becker) Am. J. Sci. **146**: 337.
— in Compound Framed Structures. (F. Schumann) Am. Arch. **46**: 87. **47**: 17, 30.
Strange Adventure, A. (W. W. Fenn) Argosy, **62**: 329.
Strange Adventure of Parson Trussbit. (R. Pardepp) Longm. **25**: 597. Same art. Liv. Age, **205**: 500.
Strange Adventures of John Percival. (Mrs. Oliphant) Chamb. J. **73**: 273–343.
Strange but True. (Donald MacLeod) Good Words, **36**: 404.
Strange Case of Thomas Blakewitch. (W. E. Lanham) Belgra. **89**: 178.
Strange Days that came to Jimmie Friday. (F. Remington) Harper, **93**: 410.
Strange Elopement, A. (W. C. Russell) Eng. Illust. **9**: 350.
Strange Experience of Mr. Tillotson; a story. Gent. M. n. s. **57**: 541.
Strange Expiation, A. (G. Winterwood) Good Words, **35**: Xmas no. 47.
Strange Fantasy, A. (C. B. Brown) Overland, n. s. **22**: 69.
Strange Office of a Pin; a story. (E. S. Drewry) Belgra. **81**: Holiday no. 55.
Strange People, A. Argosy, **59**: 249.
Strange Preacher, The; a story. Temp. Bar, **107**: 511. Same art. Liv. Age, **209**: 396.
Strange Premonition, A. (I. Garvey) Argosy, **61**: 588.
Strange Results of a Strange Wager. All the Year, **76**: 158.
Strange Story of Beethoven Koffsky. Temp. Bar, **94**: 425. Same art. Ecl. M. **118**: 629. Same art. Liv. Age, **193**: 392.
Strange Story of Mr. Robert Dalyell. (Mrs. Oliphant) Cornh. **65**: 85–312.
Strange Story of our Villa. (M. E. Penn) Argosy, **55**: 18.
Strange Touch of Nature, A. (M. A. M. Marks) Argosy, **61**: 540.
Strange Wound; a story. (W. R. Hamilton) Un. Serv. (Phila.) **13**: 128.
Stranger at "The Anchor;" a story. (M. F. S. Williams) Outing, **27**: 292.
Stranger at Boat O'Bruar, The; a story. (A. Gordon) Gent. M. n. s. **56**: 325.
Stranger in the Dress Circle, The. (Marion Robinson) Univ. R. **4**: 138.
Stranger in Elysia; a story. (C. D. Dick) Gent. M. n. s. **56**: 187.
Strangers, and taken in; a story. Cornh. **68**: 178.
Strasburg Commemoration of 19—, The. Contemp. **64**: 839.
Strategic Movement, A; a story. (E. O. Kirk) Atlan. **72**: 190.
Strategy, Modern. (W. H. James) Un. Serv. M. **9**: 263, 343.
Stratford de Redcliffe, Lord, The Attack on. (S. Lane-Poole) National, **24**: 316.
Stratford-on-Avon; by the Avon in April. All the Year, **72**: 367.
Stratham, N. H., Deaths in. (C. C. Hardy) N. E. Reg. **47**: 19, 477. **48**: 27, 337.
Strathnairn, Hugh Rose, Baron. (Lord De Mauley) Asia. R. **18**: 117.
Stratton Churchwardens' Accounts, 1512–1577. (F. Peacock) Dub. R. **119**: 121.
Strauss, Johann. (R. Aronson) Munsey, **14**: 12. — (E. Cuthwill) Music, **8**: 290.
Straw, Folk-Lore of. (C. G. Leland) J. Am. Folk-Lore, **5**: 186. — (John O'Neill) J. Am. Folk-Lore, **8**: 291.
Strawberries, Best Garden. (O. W. Blacknall) Garden & F. **5**: 186.
— Cultivation of. (E. S. Goff) Garden & F. **5**: 246. — (W. F. Bassett) Garden & F. **5**: 235. — Garden & F. **7**: 497. — (W. N. Craig) Garden & F. **9**: 257. — (E. O. Orpet) Garden & F. **8**: 257. **9**: 277. — Chamb. J. **72**: 216.
— — in New England. (G. E. Stone) Garden & F. **9**: 82.
— Early Growing. (O. W. Blacknall) Garden & F. **5**: 68.
— Selection of. (E. P. Powell) Garden & F. **5**: 210.
Strawberry, Whence came the Cultivated? (L. H. Bailey) Am. Natural. **28**: 293.
Strawberry-beds, Wintering. (O. W. Blacknall) Garden & F. **5**: 537.
Strawberry Hill. (E. L. Didier) Chaut. **14**: 577.
— and the Countess Waldegrave. (A. Badeau) Cosmopol. **12**: 535.
Strawberry Hill Press. (H. B. Wheatley) Bibliographica, **3**: 83.
Stream's Secret, The; a sketch. (M. Gray) New R. **15**: 18. Same art. Ecl. M. **127**: 248.
Street, Rev. Nicholas, Parentage of. (J. H. Lea) N. E. Reg. **46**: 257. **47**: 348.
Street Arabs, A School for. (E. R. Spearman) Scrib. M. **12**: 475.
— Teaching of. (A. R. Buckland) Sund. M. **21**: 607.
Street Boys, Paris. (M. Negroponte) Westm. **138**, 493.
Street Car Heating. (G. F. Greenwood) Cassier, **5**: 466.
Street Cleaning in N. Y. City. (C. S. Sargent) Garden & F. **9**: 251.
— New York and London. Soc. Econ. **7**: 193.
Street Music in London. Sat. R. **76**: 485.
Street Railway Building, Cost of. (T. W. Harris) Engin. M. **5**: 206.
Street Railways, Automatic Traction for. Blackw. **159**: 276.
— Electric, of Budapest: an Object Lesson for American Cities. R. of Rs. (N. Y.) **11**: 287.
— Gas Motor. (F. H. Mason) Cassier, **8**: 134.
— Great City. (R. I. Sloan) Chaut. **20**: 429.
— of St. Louis. (W. H. Bryan) Engin. M. **8**: 449.
— Power for. Chamb. J. **73**: 821. — (A. F. Sears) Cassier, **2**: 425.
— Traction on, Past and Future of. (F. J. Patten) New Sci. R. **2**: 193.
Streets, Clean, and their Benefits. (L. A. Maynard) Am. M. Civics, **9**: 298.
— Legislature and the. (F. J. Goodnow) Am. Law R. **26**: 520.
— Village, and Country Roads. (W. J. Beal) Garden & F. **9**: 2.
Strega's Curse, The; a story. (Lady M. Majendie) Argosy, **55**: 542. **56**: 58–405.
Strength of Timber: Is Young Weaker than Old? (B. E. Fernow) Garden & F. **8**: 467.
Stretton, Hesba, at Home. Sund. M. **22**: 398.
Strictly Vegetarian; a story. (K. Strange) Canad. M. **4**: 344.
Strike at Ann Arbor, Mich., 1893. (F. P. Sargent) No. Am. **156**: 561.
— — and the Law of Hiring. (G. McDermot) Cath. World, **58**: 670.

Strike, at Belfast, 1895. Sat. R. **80**: 681.
— at Brooklyn, Jan., 1895. Meth. R. **55**: 283.
— — Lesson of. (G. E. Richter) Arena, **13**: 98.
— at Buffalo. (T. Voorhees) No. Am. **155**: 407.— Pub. Opin. **13**: 490.
— at Carmaux, France, 1892. (C. Gide) Econ. J. **2**: 713.—(C. Schefer) Nation, **55**: 315.
— — Loubet and. Spec. **69**: 588.
— at Chicago, 1894. Yale R. **3**: 113.—(J. S. Jeans) 19th Cent. **36**: 259. Same art. Ecl. M. **123**: 442. —(H. von Holst) J. Pol. Econ. **2**: 485.—(C. B. Davis) Cent. **25**: 652.—(W. T. Stead) Contemp. **66**: 65. Same art. Ecl. M. **123**: 228.—(C. M. Depew) Our Day, **13**: 356.—(G. M. Pullman) Our Day, **13**: 364.—(T. B. Grant) Am. J. Pol. **5**: 190.—(J. W. Mason) Am. J. Pol. **5**: 392.—(H. White) Nation, **59**: 5.—Pub. Opin. **17**: 305, 514, 542.
— — and the Army. (J. J. O'Connell) Un. Serv. (Phila.) **15**: 299.
— — Pullman Strike Commission. (G. McDermot) Cath. World, **60**: 627.
— — — Report of. (D. F. Schloss) Econ. J. **5**: 83.— Pub. Opin. **17**: 809.—(R. Ogden) Nation, **59**: 376. (H. P. Robinson) Forum, **18**: 523.
— — Legal Aspects of. (Austin Abbott) Outl. **50**: 544.
— — Principles involved in. (D. McG. Means) Forum, **17**: 633.
— — Review of. (W. B. Harte) Arena, **10**: 497.
— Boot-makers', 1895. (W. B. Hoffman) Econ. J. **5**: 264.
— Cabmen's, in London, 1892. Sat. R. **73**: 297.
— Coal-miners, in England, 1892–93. Pub. Opin. **12**: 597.—Spec. **68**: 327.—(E. Bainbridge) Contemp. **65**: 1.—(C. M. Percy) Econ. J. **3**: 644.—(C. Edwards) Econ. J. **3**: 650.—(V. Nash) Fortn. **60**: 604.—(J. S. Jeans) 19th Cent. **34**: 791.—Sat. R. **76**: 322.—(S. A. Brooke) New Eng. M. n. s. **9**: 494. —(S. Woods) New R. **9**: 225.—Spec. **71**: 362, 454, 509, 736.—Soc. Econ. **5**: 350.
— — and after. (S. Olivier) Contemp. **64**: 749. Same art. Ecl. M. **121**: 730.
— — and a Minimum Wage. (F. D. Longe) Econ. J. **4**: 25.
— — at Broken Hill, Wales, 1892. (A. Duckworth) Econ. J. **3**: 148.
— — Christian Church and. (W. W. How; F. Williams; R. M. Grier) Chr. Lit. **10**: 153.
— — Economic Aspects of. (J. E. C. Munroe) Econ. J. **4**: 14.
— — Gladstone and. Spec. **71**: 705.
— Coal Miners', in the U. S., 1894. (Josephine S. Lowell) Char. R. **4**: 41.—(T. L. Greene) Nation, **58**: 381.
— Dock-laborers', 1889. (H. H. Champion) Univ. R. **5**: 157.
— — Some Results of. (J. G. Adderley) Econ. R. **2**: 202.
— Dock-laborers', at Hull, Eng., 1893. (C. Edwards) Econ. J. **3**: 351.—Spec. **70**: 512.—Sat. R. **75**: 479, 535.
— Durham, Among Miners on. Time, **1**: 353.
— Gas. (M. Hutchins) Time, **22**: 47.
— Homestead. (J. D. Weeks) Chr. Un. **46**: 113.—(E. W. Bemis) J. Pol. Econ. **2**: 369.—Soc. Econ. **3**: 108, 163.
— in Australia, 1890. (A. Duckworth) Econ. J. **2**: 425.
— in California, Railroad, 1893. (T. R. Bacon) Yale R. **3**: 241.
— in Post Office. (A. K. Donald) Time, **23**: 861.
Strike, Lancashire Cotton-spinners', 1893. Spec. **70**: 153.—Sat. R. **75**: 291.—(T. L. Greene) Nation, **56**: 287.—(E. Helm) Econ. J. **3**: 342.
— Lehigh Valley Railroad, 1893. Pub. Opin. **16**: 212.
— Miners'. (E. W. Bemis) Outl. **49**: 822.
— Shearers', in Western Queensland, 1894. (G. M. L. Lester) Econ. R. **5**: 392.
Strike at Colchester, The; a story. (T. B. Exeter) Lippinc. **56**: 679.
Strike at Mr. Mobley's, The. (M. Crim) Cent. **28**: 378.
Strike in Piñon Gulch. (F. Lynde) Lippinc. **56**: 93.
Strikes. Meth. R. **54**: 788.
— and Boycotts, Economics of. Soc. Econ. **4**: 257.
— and how to prevent them. Pub. Opin. **18**: 151.
— and Injunctions. (W. H. Upson) Bib. Sac. **52**: 549.
— and Lockouts, Ethics of. (C. H. Reeve) Am. J. Pol. **2**: 75.
— — in England, in 1890. (J. Burnett) J. Statis. Soc. **55**: 127.
— and their Remedies. R. of Rs. (N. Y.) **6**: 168.
— and Riots in Belgium, 1893. Pub. Opin. **15**: 66.
— and Strikers. (C. K. Davis; P. S. Grosscup) Engin. M. **7**: 864.
— and Trusts. (U. M. Rose) Am. Law R. **27**: 708.
— Causes and Losses of. (F. D. Huntington) Our Day, **14**: 130.
— Danger lurking behind. (W. N. Black) Engin. M. **7**: 459.
— from an Economic Standpoint. (E. D. M'Creary) Am. J. Pol. **5**: 241.
— Justice Harlan on. Pub. Opin. **17**: 663.
— How to avoid. (F. M. Holland) Open Court, **9**: 4535.
— How to prevent. (S. Bates) No. Am. **160**: 371.
— in America, History of. (A. A. Freeman) Engin. M. **6**: 176, 304.
— in Italy. (F. S. Nitti) Econ. J. **3**: 719.
— in Russia. Gunton's M. **11**: 253.
— in U. S., 1892. Sat. R. **74**: 215.
— — Lessons of. (H. C. Vedder) Bapt. R. **14**: 497.
— Investigation as to, in Foreign Countries. Pub. Opin. **21**: 557.
— Law of. (T. L. Greene) Nation, **59**: 281.
— Lessons of Recent Civil Disorders. (T. M. Cooley) Forum, **18**: 1.—(N. A. Miles; W. Hampton; H. P. Robinson; S. Gompers) No. Am. **159**: 180.
— Local and Sympathetic. (G. Koerner) Open Court, **8**: 4303.
— Modern Industrial Warfare. (J. W. Cunliffe) Westm. **140**: 109.
— Railroad, Congressional Remedy for. (E. L. Godkin) Nation, **60**: 120.
— Railroad Strikers' Case in California. (M. B. Woodworth) Am. Law R. **29**: 512.
— Recent Decisions on, 1893. Pub. Opin. **15**: 28.
— Society and. Soc. Econ. **8**: 129.
— Society and Sympathetic. Soc. Econ. **7**: 257.
— State and Social Law of. Soc. Econ. **7**: 75.
Strindberg, August. (J. H. M'Carthy) Fortn. **58**: 326. — Gent. M. n. s. **49**: 205.
— Plays and Novels of. Belgra. **86**: 137.
Stringer, Arthur J. Poems. (H. W. Brown) Canad. M. **6**: 88.
Stringer, Tommy. Lend a H. **16**: 243.
Stroke of Luck, A; a story. (Mrs. E. T. Cook) Gent. M. n. s. **56**: 541. Same art. Ecl. M. **127**: 160.
Stromboli, Mt., in 1891. (A. Ricco; E. Mercalli) Nature, **47**: 89.
Stromer, Ulmer; the First German Paper-maker. (E. Grosse) Pop. Sci. Mo. **42**: 94.

Strong, Dr. James, with portrait. Bk. News, 11: 517. — Meth. R. 54: 783.
Strong, Joseph D., jr. (C. S. Greene) Overland, n. s. 27: 501.
Strong, William Emerson, with portrait. (H. L. Conard) Nat'l M. (N. Y. '91) 15: 76.
Strong, William L. (T. C. Quinn) Munsey, 12: 361. — With portrait. (J. H. Kennedy) Nat'l M. (N. Y. '91) 15: 49.
Strontium, Quantitative Separation of, from Calcium. (P. E. Browning) Am. J. Sci. 143: 50, 386.
Structure and Style, Studies in, Brewster on. (E. H. Lewis) School R. 4: 470.
Structures, Status of. (O. F. Semsch) Am. Arch. 54: 79, 95.
Struggle for Existence, The, and Ethics. (L. Stephen) Pop. Sci. Mo. 44: 224.
Struwwelpeter. Spec. 73: 398.
Stuart, Lady Arabella and the Venetian Archives. Ed. R. 184: 483.
Stuart, Elizabeth, and her Family in Holland. (S. I. de Zuylen de Nyevelt) National, 18: 52. Same art. Liv. Age, 193: 297.
Stuart, Gilbert. (F. H. Sweet) Cath. World, 62: 114.
Stuart, H. Windsor Villiers. Ath. '95, 2: 535.
Stuart, Henry Benedict, Duke and Cardinal of York. (A. Shield) Dub. R. 119: 97.
Stuart, J. E. B. So. Hist. Pap. 23: 202.
Stuart, Margaret. Macmil. 66: 271. Same art. Liv. Age, 195: 162.
Stuart, Rose McE., with portrait. Bk. News, 13: 9.
Stuart, Royal House of, Banquo and Fleance Progenitors of. (J. A. Smith) Walford's Antiq. 7: 213. 8: 12.
Stuarts, Real or Bogus? (A. Forbes) New R. 8: 73.
Stubbs, C. W., Dean of Ely, at Home. Sund. M. 23: 664.
Student as Child, The. (H. Hapgood) Harv. Mo. 15: 11.
Student Associations, International. (W. H. Tolman) Educa. R. 5: 363.
Student life in Berlin. (A. F. M. Lange) Archit. Rec. 5: 65.
— in Mass. (Marion A. McBride) Bost. 3: 539.
— Scottish. Chamb. J. 71: 593.
Student Mobs, Medieval. (L. H. Weeks) Bach. of Arts, 2: 629.
Students, Theological; Qualities Requisite. (T. F. Wright) N. Church R. 1: 570.
Studies, Coördination of, German Contributions to. (C. DeGarmo) Educa. R. 4: 422.
— Correlation of. (H. T. Lukens) Educa. R. 10: 364.
— — in Elementary Education. (W. T. Harris and others) Educa. R. 9: 230.
— — Mr. Lukens on. (W. S. Jackman) Educa. R. 11: 72.
— — Necessity for Five Coördinate Groups. (W. T. Harris) Educa. R. 11: 323.
— — Practicable. (C. B. Gilbert) Educa. R. 11: 313.
— — Rational. (J. M. Rice) Forum, 19: 419.
— — Working Basis for. (C. De Garmo) Educa. R. 5: 451.
— Sequence of. (H. G. Wells) Nature, 51: 195.
Studio in a Boat, Henry's. (M. W. Freeman) Art J. 45: 201.
Studio-Decoration. (C. Cook) Mo. Illust. 4: 232.
Studio Flat, A; a story. (G. B. Stuart) Argosy, 53: 430.
Studio Receptions; the "Smoke." (M. H. Spielmann) M. of Art, 10: 80.
Study and Instruction, Methods of. (H. O. Kirk) Educa. 16: 230.
Study, Comparative Method of. (G. H. Johnson) Science, 21: 155.
— Course of, Attempted Improvements in the. (P. H. Hanus) Educa. R. 12: 435.
Study in Character; a story. All the Year, 73: 468.
Study in Contrasts; a poem. (W. Watson) Spec. 72: 13.
Study in Love; a story. (L. D. Mitchell) Outing, 25: 444.
Study Number Three; a story. (H. L. Bradley) Harper, 19: 752.
Study in Ochre, A. (E. V. Atkinson) Overland, n. s. 24: 45.
Stuff we are made of, The. (J. M. Hobson) Sund. M. 23: 331, 490.
Stukeley, William. Temp. Bar, 101: 394. Same art. Liv. Age, 201: 94.
Stump Orator, The; a poem. (L. D. Powles) Idler, 1: 398.
Stundism in Russia. (E. B. Lanin) Contemp. 61: 1.
Stundist's Papers, A. Good Words, 35: 488.
Stundists, Types of. Sund. M. 22: 690, 754, 830. *See also* Neo-Stundism.
Stupid, the, Sorrows of. Spec. 74: 897. Same art. Liv. Age, 206: 445.
Stupid Woman, A. (I. C. Vaughan) Good Words, 37: Xmas. no. 47.
Sturgeon-Fishing in the James River. (C. W. Coleman) Cosmopol. 13: 366.
— in Russia. (R. F. Walsh) Outing, 21: 157.
Stuyvesant, Peter. (B. Fernow) Nat'l M. (N. Y., '91) 15: 571.
Stygian Comedy; a sketch. (K. F. M. Sullivan) Canad. M. 8: 134.
Style c'est l'homme. (W. H. Mallock) New R. 6: 441. Same art. Ecl. M. 118: 793. Same art. Liv. Age, 193: 643.
Style, Literary. (R. L. Stevenson) [Contemp.] Writer, 9: 159. Gent. M. n. s. 48: 429. — Spec. 69: 445. — (J. Dennis) Time, 13: 71.
— — Conditions of. (D. H. Wheeler) Meth. R. 53: 910.
— — Paralyzers of. (F. M. Bird) Lippinc. 57: 280.
— — Realism. (R. L. Stevenson) M. of Art, 7: 24.
Subjective and Objective Relation. (G. M. McCrie) Monist, 4: 211.
Subjective Knowledge. (S. H. Mellone) Mind, 21: 388.
Sublime and the Beautiful, Theories of. (J. L. Powell) Dub. R. 119: 302.
Submarine Boats. (W. A. Dobson) Cosmopol. 20: 280. — (C. Sleeman) Un. Serv. M. 10: 578. 11: 24.
Submarine Mines, Torpedoes and. (F. L. Winn) Un. Serv. (Phila.) 8: 464.
Submarine Peaks, Form of Isolated. (G. W. Littlehales) Am. J. Sci. 151: 15.
Submerged Tenth. (E. E. Hale) Lend a H. 15: 83.
Submergence of Western Europe, Prior to Neolithic Period. (A. Crane) Science, n. s. 2: 2.
Subscription Books. Chamb. J. 72: 193.
Subsidies, British Shipping, Effects of. (T. Rhodes) Engin. M. 6: 54.
Substance, Category of. (W. Smith) Philos. R. 5: 246.
Sub-Treasury Plan. (C. C. Post) Arena, 5: 342.
Subterranean Adventure, A. Macmil. 73: 352. Same art. Liv. Age, 209: 248.
Subterranean Fauna of N. America, Origin of. (A. S. Packard) Am. Natural. 28: 727.
Subterranean Faunas. Nature, 52: 225.
Subterranean Mystery, A. (H. P. Bowden) Belgra. 87: 31.
Suburban "At Home," A; a farce. (W. Pett Ridge) Idler, 9: 49.

Suburban Homes. (R. C. Sturgis) Cosmopol. **21**: 180. — Garden & F. **9**: 271, 309, 312. — Garden & F. **5**: 445. — (Sylvester Baxter) Garden & F. **5**: 134. — Garden & F. **5**: 158.
Suburban Purse, Races for. (F. Trevelyan) Outing, **22**: 372.
Suburban Romance. (L. Street) Argosy, **59**: 124.
Suburbs: Outside the Walls. (B. Cane) Gent. M. n. s. **56**: 489.
Subways. (F. Foxcroft) New Eng. M. n. s. **13**: 193.
Success. All the Year, **74**: 463.
— Bitterness of. Sat. R. **79**: 474.
— Story of a. (L. Elsner) Eng. Illust. **11**: 889.
Suckling, Sir John, with portrait. Acad. **50**: 460. — Time, **11**: 352.
Sudan. *See* Soudan.
Sudermann, Hermann. Atlan. **77**: 697. — (J. D. Barry) Lit. W. (Bost.) **27**: 120. — Lit. W. (Bost.) **26**: 120. — (M. E. Braddon) National, **21**: 751.
— Novels of. (J. E. Hogarth) Fortn. **65**: 651.
Suez Canal, Difficulty about. (A. Milner) Time, **13**: 134.
— England's Right to the Suez Shares. (C. Whitehouse) Fortn. **60**: 405, 869.
— Romance of. (G. T. Ferris) Cosmopol. **16**: 663.
Suffering, Jesus Christ and the Problem of. (R. B. McGlashen) Thinker, **8**: 419.
— Problem of. (T. C. Chamberlin) Bib. World, **8**: 182.
— To Peace through. (Canon Scott) Sund. M. **24**: 533.
Suffering Saint, A. (H. P. Spofford) Eng. Illust. **16**: 167.
Suffolk, Eastern, Memories of. (S. Colvin) M. of Art, **8**: 221, 265.
— — A Study of. (G. M. McCrie) Gent. M. n. s. **55**: 10. Same art. Ecl. M. **125**: 395.
— Geology of. (W. Whitaker) Nature, **52**: 490.
— Moated Halls in. (J. E. Taylor) Good Words, **34**: 455.
Suffolk Leechcraft. (W. W. Groome) Folk-Lore, **6**: 117.
Suffrage. (E. E. Hale) Cosmopol. **14**: 476.
— Complete. (W. F. Collier) Westm. **137**: 680.
— Equal, Struggle for, in North Carolina. (J. S. Bassett) Am. M. Civics, **8**: 484.
— Exercise of. (A. B. Hart) Pol. Sci. Q. **7**: 307.
— History of, in the Legislation of the U. S. (F. W. Blackmar) Chaut. **22**: 28.
— a Natural Right. (E. C. Stanton) Open Court, **8**: 3959. — (E. P. Powell) Soc. Econ. **4**: 334.
— Next Extension of. (Emilia F. S. Dilke) Univ. R. **4**: 371.
— Relation of Voters to the State. (Joel Benton) Soc. Econ. **2**: 239.
— Should Voting be Compulsory? (M. S. Wise) Soc. Econ. **3**: 143.
Suffrage Campaign in California. (Adeline Knapp) Am. M. Civics, **9**: 46.
Sugar. Cornh. **69**: 369. Same art. Ecl. M. **122**: 827.
— as a Food. Dub. R. **114**: 424.
— Beet. (H. S. Adams) Cosmopol. **14**: 399.
— Cane. (R. Dykers) Southern M. **5**: 182. — (C. A. Barber) Knowl. **18**: 145.
— from Indian Corn. (F. L. Stewart) Science, **22**: 143–171.
— in Politics. (H. White) Nation, **58**: 462.
— in the U. S. (H. W. Wiley) Chaut. **15**: 290. **16**: 36.
— Industrial Opportunity for America. (E. Sowers) No. Am. **163**: 316.
— Manufacture of, in Egypt. Chamb. J. **70**: 137.
Sugar Bounties, The. (W. P. B. Shepheard) Time, **18**: 216.
Sugar Bounty Case. (H. C. Beach) Am. Law R. **29**: 801.
Sugar Industry of Peru. J. Soc. Arts, **44**: 751.
Sugar Machinery in Cuba. (A. W. Colwell) Cassier, **9**: 507.
Sugar Plantation. (Grace King) Chr. Un. **45**: 445.
Sugar Schedule, The. (H. White) Nation, **58**: 440.
Sugar Trust, Investigation of. Pub. Opin. **17**: 437.
Sugar-loaf Mountain, Mozambique. (W. A. Churchill) Geog. J. **4**: 352.
Suggestibility, Automatism, and Kindred Phenomena. (W. R. Newbold) Pop. Sci. Mo. **48**: 193, 375, 520, 641.
— of Children. (M. H. Small) Pedagog. Sem. **4**: 176.
Suggestion and Suggestibility. (P. Carus) Open Court, **3**: 2032. — (W. R. Newbold) Pop. Sci. Mo. **48**: 641.
— Cure by. Spec. **77**: 107.
— in Therapeutics. (W. R. Newbold) Pop. Sci. Mo. **49**: 342.
— Posthypnotic and Criminal. (W. R. Newbold) Pop. Sci. Mo. **49**: 230.
— Social Control by. (E. A. Ross) Am. J. Sociol. **2**: 255.
— Treatment of Disease by. (A. McL. Hamilton) Cent. **24**: 430.
Suggestions, Subconscious. (J. M. Baldwin) Book R. **2**: 177.
Suicide, among Women. (W. Ferraro) New R. **11**: 637.
— An Anatomy of. (A. M. Courtenay) Chaut. **23**: 273.
— and Genius. (C. W. Pilgrim) Pop. Sci. Mo. **42**: 361.
— and Insanity, Strahan's. (A. A. Woodhull) Nation, **59**: 35.
— and Modern Civilization. (F. L. Hoffman) Arena, **7**: 680.
— Can it be justified? Open Court, **5**: 2911.
— in Curb Street; a story. (N. Vynne) Theatre, **30**: 211.
— in New England, Statistics of. (D. R. Dewey) Am. Statis. Assoc. **3**: 158.
— Increase of. Spec. **72**: 678.
— Sentimental. Spec. **70**: 798.
— Sex Relation in. (F. L. Hoffman) Am. Statis. Assoc. **4**: 20.
— Sin of. (C. Cort) Ref. Q. **42**: 73.
— Sympathy in. Spec. **74**: 847.
— Toying with. Spec. **71**: 266.
Suicide, A; a story. (M. E. Wotton) Idler, **1**: 436.
Sullivan, Algernon Sydney. (L. A. Bond) Nat'l M. (N. Y. '91) **15**: 535.
Sullivan, Sir Arthur. Golden Legend. Sat. R. **79**: 124.
Sullivan, James F. The Flame Flower. (H. G. Wells) Acad. **50**: 459.
Sullivan, J. W., with portrait. Bk. Buyer, **12**: 334.
Sullivan, T. R., with portrait. Bk. Buyer, **10**: 141.
Sullivant, William Starling, with portrait. Pop. Sci. Mo. **48**: 690.
Sulphide of Carbon, A New. (A. E. Tutton) Nature, **49**: 275.
Sulphur in Roasted Sulphide Ores, Method for Determining. (H. F. Keller; P. Maas) J. Frankl. Inst. **139**: 286.
— Native, in Michigan. (W. H. Sherzer) Am. J. Sci. **150**: 246.
— A New Source of. (S. E. Tillman) Cosmopol. **22**: 224.
— Recovery of, from Alkali Waste. Chamb. **70**: 209.
Sultan, The, and his Harem. (R. Davey) Fortn. **64**: 790. Same art. Liv. Age, **207**: 553.
— and his Priests. (R. Davey) Fortn. **65**: 1. Same art. Ecl. M. **126**: 236. Same art. Liv. Age, **208**: 323.

Sultan, Fate of the. (E. L. Godkin) Nation, 61: 341.
— going to Pray. (J. F. Foster) Eng. Illust. 15: 459.
— A Negro. Spec. 74: 744.
Sultan's Egg, The. (J. A. Barry) Chamb. J. 71: 392-408.
Sultan's Fate, The; a story. (H. N. Crellin) Idler, 5: 251.
Sumac, Poison. (C. S. Sargent) Garden & F. 8: 404.
"Sumajh." Chamb. J. 70: 78. Same art. Ecl. M. 120: 517.
Sumatra. (C. Ericsson) Contemp. 70: 558. Same art. Liv. Age, 211: 508.
— Central, and Engano, Modigliani's Explorations in. (H. H. Giglioli) Nature, 46: 565.
— Deli in. (R. W. Egerton Eastwick) Fortn. 60: 634.
— Oeloes of. (M. J. Claine) Asia. R. 12: 227.
— Tobacco Plantation in. (J. Kechil) Good Words, 35: 808.
Sumiro-Accadians of Chaldea, Legends of. (A. Bodington) Am. Natural. 27: 14, 105.
Summer. (H. E. Ward) M. of Art, 5: 316.
— at Ashfurlong; a story. (R. M. Kettle) Argosy, 60: 36.
— Coming of. (R. Jefferies) Liv. Age, 192: 313.
— in the Heart of. (E. M. Thomas) Atlan. 72: 19.
Summer Campaign in Virginia. (G. G. Bain) New Eng. M. n. s. 11: 177.
Summer Evening at the Village Post-office; a story. Canad. M. 4: 557.
Summer-houses, Colonial. (J. De Wolf) Garden & F. 5: 63.
Summer Intimacy, The. (G. A. Hibbard) Scrib. M. 15: 363.
Summer Pleasures, Free, for the People in Boston. (K. G. Wells) New Eng. M. n. s. 6: 789.
Summer Resorts: where shall we go? Spec. 69: 221.
Summer Ride, A. (H. Rave) Outing, 28: 441.
Summer School, The. Dial (Ch.) 18: 312.
— and the Teacher. (H. G. Schneider) Educa. 17: 227.
Summer Schools. (Anna McC. Sholl) Bach. of Arts, 1: 465.
— Teachers' Scholarships in. (W. N. Davis) Educa. R. 12: 388.
Summer Suburban Communities. (C. F. Wingate) Engin. M. 3: 839.
Summer Visitors. (C. B. Selden) No. Am. 159: 235.
Summer Wooing, A. (G. E. Walsh) New Eng. M. n. s. 6: 181.
Summers and Winters at Balmawhapple; a story. Blackw. 153: 40-814.
Sumner, Charles. (G. F. Hoar) Forum, 16: 549.
— Dawes' Life of. (J. W. Chadwick) Nation, 54: 435.
— Grimke's Life of. (J. W. Chadwick) Nation, 54: 435.
— Personal Recollections of. (Marquis de Chambrun) Scrib. M. 13: 153.
— Pierce's Life of. (J. W. Chadwick) Nation, 57: 15, 29. — (G. P. Fisher) Yale R. 2: 120. — (W. H. Smith) Dial (Ch.) 15: 33. — Ath. '93, 1: 693. — Spec. 70: 775.
Sumter, Fort, Occupation of, April, 1865. (F. Jordan) Un. Serv. (Phila.) 14: 406.
Sun, The. (D. P. Todd) Science, n. s. 2: 29.
— among his Peers, The. (J. E. Gore) Gent. M. n. s. 49: 331. Same art. Ecl. M. 119: 692.
— and Sky, Photometric Observations of. Nature, 46: 284.
— Atmosphere of, Absorption of Heat in. (W. E. Wilson) Astron. 11: 46.
Sun, Atmosphere of, New Researches on. (M. H. Deslandres) Astron. 11: 60, 314.
— — Thermal Absorption in. (E. B. Frost) Astron. 11: 720.
— — Tranquillity of. (A. Brester, jr.) Astron. 13: 849.
— Automatic Check preventing Considerable Motion in Interior of. (A. Brester, jr.) Astron. 13: 218.
— Ball's Story of. (A. Fowler) Nature, 49: 382. — Sat. R. 77: 262.
— Carbon and Oxygen in the. (J. Trowbridge) Am. J. Sci. 151: 329.
— Contraction of, Helmholtz's Theory of. Pop. Astron. 3: 21.
— Corona of, Electro-magnetic Theory of. (H. Ebert) Astron. 12: 804.
— — Photographing, without Eclipse. (G. E. Hale) Astron. 13: 662.
— Diameter of, Variation of. (O. T. Sherman) Astron. 11: 513.
— Distribution of Heat on. (W. H. S. Monck) Astron. 13: 823.
— Disturbances on, 1891-92. (W. Sidgreaves; H. Turner) Astron. 11: 66.
— — July, 1892. (J. S. Townsend; W. Sidgreaves) Astron. 11: 815.
— Ephemeris of. (J. Morrison) Pop. Astron. 3: 24, 86.
— Faculæ of. (G. E. Hale) Astron. 13: 113.
— — and Prominences on, Photography of. (J. Evershed, jr.) Astron. 12: 628.
— Fuel of. (J. E. Gore) Gent. M. n. s. 48: 85. Same art. Ecl. M. 118: 312.
— Heat of. (R. Ball) McClure, 6: 75.
— Light of. (R. Ball) McClure, 6: 187.
— Magnetic Problem of, Status of. (F. H. Bigelow) Science, n. s. 2: 509.
— New Solar Records. (E. W. Maunder) Knowl. 18: 10.
— Notes on a Photograph of. (E. W. Maunder) Knowl. 18: 107.
— Observations of, First. (M. E. Byrd) Pop. Astron. 1: 216.
— Photographic Study of. (G. E. Hale) Astron. 11: 811.
— Photographing, Attempts at. (W. W. Payne) Pop. Astron. 2: 116.
— — at the Kenwood Observatory. (G. E. Hale) Astron. 11: 407.
— Physical Constitution of. (W. Sidgreaves) Astron. 12: 826.
— Physics of. (E. R. von Oppolzer) Astron. 12: 736.
— Place of, in Nature. (J. N. Lockyer) Nature, 51: 374-590. 52: 12-446.
— Polar Radiation from, and Atmospheric Pressures of U. S. (F. H. Bigelow) Astron. 13: 25.
— Prominence on, Enormous Velocity of a. (J. Fenyi) Astron. 11: 63.
— Prominences on, in 1891. (J. Evershed, jr.) Astron. 11: 426.
— — Photography of. (G. E. Hale) Astron. 11: 70.
— Protuberances on, Sept., 1893. (J. Fenyi) Astron. 13: 122.
— Radiation of Heat by. (W. Goff) National, 21: 143.
— Spectrum of, Recent Studies on. (A. L. Cortie) Astron. 11: 393.
— Spots on. (T. Perkins) Time, 11: 134.
— — and Air-temperature. Nature, 45: 271.
— — Distribution of. (E. W. Maunder) Knowl. 15: 128.
— — Group of, Feb., 1892, Phenomena observed on. (J. Fenyi) Astron. 11: 430.

Sun, Spots on, Group of, Spectrum of. (H. Crew; G. E. Hale) Astron. 11: 308.
— — June and July, 1892, and Terrestrial Magnetism. (G. E. Hale) Astron. 11: 917.
— — Large Group of, Aug. 28–Oct. 4, 1891. (A. L. Cortie) Astron. 11: 130.
— — Observations of, at Goodsell Observatory. (H. C. Wilson) Astron. 13: 293.
— — of August, 1894. (H. C. Wilson) Pop. Astron. 2: 49.
— — Radiation from. (W. E. Wilson) Astron. 13: 378.
— — Origin of. (E. von Oppolzer) Astron. 12: 419.
— — Solar Chromosphere in 1891 and 1892. (W. Sidgreaves) Astron. 12: 539.
— — Spectra of. (A. L. Cortie) Astron. 11: 587.
— — — Observations of. (J. N. Lockyer) Nature, 51: 448.
— Stellar Magnitude of. (J. E. Gore) Knowl. 18: 130.
— Symbols of, in Ancient Egypt. (F. W. Read) Knowl. 19: 127.
— Theory of. (A. Brester, jr.) Astron. 12: 914.
— Two Magnetic Fields surrounding. (F. H. Bigelow) Astron. 12: 706.
Sun and Moon Myth, Blackfoot. (G. B. Grinnell) J. Am. Folk-Lore, 6: 44.
Sun and Savior, The World's. (R. A. Proctor) Open Court, 1: 312.
Sun Dance Among the Sarcee Indians. (A. C. Shaw) Canad. M. 3: 10.
Sunbeam, Yacht, Voyage of the, Brassey's. (R. C. Burt) Eng. Illust. 14: 637.
Sunday at Sea. (R. MacIntyre) Sund. M. 25: 439.
— Continental, Shall we import? (J. Cook) Our Day, 12: 153.
— Country. Cornh. 70: 408. Same art. Ecl. M. 123: 632. Same art. Liv. Age, 203: 437.
— Dance Music on. Sat. R. 74: 246.
— in the U. S. Spec. 69: 411.
— — What it should be. (D. Swing) Forum, 13: 120.
— German-Americans and. (W. C. Doane) Forum, 20: 733.
— Observance of. (W. E. Gladstone) McClure, 4: 370. — (F. K. Levan) Ref. Q. 39: 106.
— — Huxley on. (Jane A. H. Simpson) Westm. 144: 266.
— — Is the Fourth Commandment binding upon Christians? (J. Cook) Our Day, 11: 439.
— — Laws concerning, in New England. (W. F. Crafts) Our Day, 11: 325.
— "Pleasant Sunday Afternoon" Movement. (G. Paton) Sund. M. 25: 375.
— Question of, Chief Justice of Nebraska upon. (W. C. Carter) Am. Law R. 27: 224.
— — Study of. (P. F. McSweeney) Cath. World, 62: 250.
— Rest on, a Civil Right. (J. Charlton) Canad. M. 8: 165.
— Value of, to Labor. (J. Cook) Our Day, 12: 324.
— — to Liberty. (J. Cook) Our Day, 12: 402.
— — to Religion. (J. Cook) Our Day, 12: 510.
— Who are the Chief Assailants of? (J. Cook) Our Day, 11: 274.
Sunday on Mount Royal; a poem. (C. A. Fraser) Canad. M. 1: 688.
Sunday Afternoon; a poem. (S. Swithin) Gent. M. n. s. 53: 200.
Sunday Afternoon, A; a story. (J. H. Shorthouse) Eng. Illust. 13: 257.
Sunday Closing in Operation. (H. L. Stephen) Fortn. 66: 285.
Sunday Closing of Public Houses, etc. (E. G. Salmon) Time, 12: 421.
— of Saloons in New York. Pub. Opin. 19: 38, 134, 167. — (F. C. Iglehart) No. Am. 161: 467.
Sunday Law of the Cherokees. (C. C. Nott) Nation, 57: 10.
Sunday Laws in Germany. (G. M. Whicher) And. R. 19: 565.
Sunday Newspapers. (J. Cook) Our Day, 11: 47. — (D. J. Burrell) Our Day, 12: 255.
— in the U. S. (Rob't Donald) Univ. R. 8: 78.
— Ought they to be abolished? (C. M. Nichols) Our Day, 14: 43.
Sunday Opening of Public Galleries. Spec. 76: 369.
— Present Situation of. (R. Winton; S. A. Barnett; Lord Hobhouse; G. J. Holyoake; M. H. Judge) Westm. 145: 485. — (J. Percival; Y. Guyot; A. Webster; J. Bright; B. J. Snell; J. A. Picton; F. Moscheles; M. D. Conway; H. Pratt; H. Rutherfurd; F. Long; W. H. Corfield) Westm. 145: 597. — (P. Blouët; H. V. Le Bas; W. Binns; G. Alexander; T. C. Horsfall; W. L. Thomas; Anna F. Parsons; Sophia Beale; Emily S. Judge) Westm. 146: 6. — (F. Peake) Westm. 146: 255. — (M. H. Judge) Westm. 146: 357.
— Triumph of. (S. Dewey) Westm. 145: 477.
Sunday Sam's Statute of Limitations; a story. (H. G. Paine) Harper, 94: 135.
Sunday-school, The, and Modern Biblical Criticism. (C. A. Briggs) No. Am. 158: 64.
— as a Factor in Public Education. (W. F. Crafts) Our Day, 10: 586.
— How the Bible should be studied in. (P. S. Moxom) Bib. World, 8: 229.
Sunday-school Lessons, Adaptation *vs.* Uniformity in. (E. Blakeslee) And. R. 18: 368.
— International System of. (M. S. Cressman) Luth. Q. 23: 274.
Sunday-school Movement of To-day. (E. T. Bromfield) Presb. & Ref. R. 5: 194.
Sunday-school Work and Bible Study in Light of Modern Pedagogy. (A. C. Ellis) Pedagog. Sem. 3: 363.
— Improvement of. (F. N. Peloubet) Bib. World, 4: 134.
Sunday Schools, Shortcomings and Opportunity of. (W. L. Hervey) R. of Rs. (N. Y.) 14: 702.
Sunday Societies, National Federation of. (R. S. Watson) Westm. 146: 498.
Sunday Society, Testimonial to M. H. Judge. (S. A. Barnett) Westm. 146: 19.
Sunday Worship. (C. K. Whipple) Open Court, 1: 95.
Sunderland, Dorothy Sidney, Countess of. Church Q. 36: 337. Same art. Liv. Age, 199: 101. — Spec. 69: 853. — Sat. R. 74: 544.
Sunderland Library. Walford's Antiq. 1: 35, 78, 255. 2: 145. 3: 35.
Sun-dials. (W. Hogg) Am. Arch. 37: 41. — (E. S. Bates) Overland, n. s. 22: 498.
— Primitive, in Upper Egypt. (E. A. Floyer) Ath. '95, 2: 458.
Sunflower-farming in Russia. Chamb. J. 69: 390.
Sun-myth, A; a poem. (W. E. Windus) Gent. M. n. s. 54: 534.
Sun-pillar, The. (S. Barber) Knowl. 18: 132.
Sunrise and Sunset. Foreglows and Afterglows. (J. G. McPherson) Gent. M. n. s. 52: 269. Same art. Ecl. M. 122: 700.
Sunrise in the Catskills; a poem. (J. L. R. Burnett) Outing, 24: 151.
Sunset; a poem. (M. Kendall) M. of Art, 8: 272.
Sunset till Dawn, From. All the Year, 71: 29.

Sunset Club in "Darkest England." (M. M. Trumbull) Open Court, 5: 2768.
— on the Jury System. (M. M. Trumbull) Open Court, 5: 2832.
Sunshine and Life. (G. C. Frankland) Longm. 26: 532. Same art. Ecl. M. 125: 555.
— and Rain. (P. Robinson) Contemp. 64: 415. Same art. Liv. Age, 199: 311. Same art. Ecl. M. 121: 484.
Sunshine Johnson, Murderer. (Luke Sharp) Good Words, 33: 22.
Sunstruck; a story. (G. M. Fenn) Chamb. J. 69: 7-73.
Sun-worship, Survivals of. (F. D. Bergen) Pop. Sci. Mo. 47: 249.
Sunyarsees and Trappists, Kipling on. Spec. 73: 555.
"Super Hanc Petram;" a tale of Leo XIII. (H. A. Kennedy) Contemp. 70: 340.
Superannuated, Bitter Cry of the. (W. Routh) National, 21: 430.
Superior, Lake. (J. Ralph) Harper, 84: 685.
— With a Fishing Tug on. (H. J. Woodside) Canad. M. 1: 673.
Supernatural, The. (C. B. Brewster) And. R. 19: 513. — (I. Zangwill) Critic, 26: 41.
— and the Higher Criticism. (A. W. Benn) New World, 4: 429.
— and its Imitations. (A. F. Marshall) Am. Cath. Q. 19: 813.
— and Natural. (B. P. Bowne) Meth. R. 55: 9.
— in Crime. Green Bag, 5: 191.
— Intellectual Basis of the. (A. F. Hewit) Am. Cath. Q. 18: 628.
— King on the. Sat. R. 74: 513.
— Natural Origin of. (F. M. Müller) Open Court, 4: 2278.
— Philosophical Basis of. (J. Bascom) New World, 4: 279.
Supernaturalism, Origin, Perpetuation and Decadence of. (R. G. M. Browne) Westm. 140: 115. Same art. Ecl. M. 121: 410.
Superstition and Fact. (A. Lang) Contemp. 64: 882. Same art. Ecl. M. 122: 104.
— Contemporary, Mallock's. Sat. R. 79: 835. — Ath. '95, 1: 665.
— Curiosities of. Chamb. J. 69: 684.
— in Religion and Science. Open Court, 2: 837.
— Recent Recrudescence of. (E. P. Evans) Pop. Sci. Mo. 48: 73.
— Survival of. (E. F. Seat) Lippinc. 56: 428.
Superstitions, Celestial, Survival of. (G. A. Peck) Chaut. 19: 751.
— Chinese. (E. T. C. Werner) Time, 23: 955.
— Connecticut. (E. M. Backus) J. Am. Folk-Lore, 8: 192.
— Current. (Mrs. F. D. Bergen and W. W. Newell) J. Am. Folk-Lore, 2: 12, 105.
— — Bergen on. (F. Starr) Dial (Ch.) 21: 36. — (W. W. Newell) J. Am. Folk-Lore, 9: 55.
— Elworthy on. Sat. R. 79: 482.
— in American Life. (L. J. Vance) Open Court, 3: 1823, 1951, 1961.
— of Childhood on the Hudson River. (M. H. Skeel) J. Am. Folk-Lore, 2: 148.
— of Cornwall. Macmil. 73: 36.
— of Georgia. (R. A. Moore) J. Am. Folk-Lore, 7: 305. 9: 226.
— of Newfoundland. J. Am. Folk-Lore, 9: 222.
— of North Germany. All the Year, 75: 419.
— of the Rio Grande. (J. G. Bourke) J. Am. Folk-Lore, 7: 119.
— of the Sea. (J. D. J. Kelley) Cent. 26: 418.
— of West Sussex. (C. Latham) Folk-Lore Rec. 1: 7.
Superstitions; Old Scottish Cures. (A. W. Stewart) Gent. M. n. s. 53: 419.
— Other People's. (L. M. J. Garnett) Ath. '95, 1: 443.
— Popular. (T. E. Champion) Canad. M. 3: 25. (W. J. Hoffman) Pop. Sci. Mo. 50: 92.
— Survivals of. Spec. 71: 403.
— West Country. (C. Leigh) Belgra. 81: 407.
Supper in a Sheep Rancher's Jacal; a sketch. (L. B. Colson) Canad. M. 1: 586.
Supply and Demand, Law (?) of. (A. B. Woodford) Soc. Econ. 3: 350.
— — Law of, Modern Version of. (R. H. Thurston) Science, n. s. 4: 817.
Supply at Saint Agatha's. (E. S. Phelps) Cent. 25: 868.
Suppose; a poem. (M. A. M. Marks) Argosy, 60: 702.
Supreme Court, U. S. (G. A. Benham) No. Am. 163: 505.
— as Expounder of the Constitution. (J. C. Rosenberger) Am. Law R. 30: 55.
— Carson's. Nation, 54: 251, 268.
— Chief Justice of the United States, or of the Supreme Court? (W. A. Richardson) N. E. Reg. 49: 275.
— Constitutional Duty and Power of. (J. Parke) Am. Law R. 30: 357.
— Judges of. (D. H. Wheeler) Chaut. 23: 531.
— Should it be reorganized? (J. M. Ashley) Arena, 14: 221.
— Vacancy in. (E. P. Clark) Nation, 61: 129.
Suretyship. Bank. M. (N. Y.) 48: 901. 49: 21, 104.
Surgeon's Guest; a story. Cornh. 68: 431, 544.
Surgeon's Miracle, The; a story. (J. Kirkland) McClure, 1: 555.
Surgeon's Wife, A; a story. (A. Buckler) Belgra. 89: 64.
Surgery, American Achievements in. (G. F. Shrady) Forum, 17: 167.
— and Superstition. (F. R. Fowke) Nature, 48: 87.
— Modern. (H. P. Dunn) 19th Cent. 35: 775. Same art. Ecl. M. 122: 798. — (P. F. Chambers) Munsey, 8: 407.
— — Symposium. Indep. Sept. 12, '95.
Surnames, English. Quar. 180: 207.
— — and Hereditary Genius. (E. O. Addy) Gent. M. n. s. 54: 86.
— Manufacture of. (F. Chance) Acad. 45: 329.
— Middle-class. (G. Walford) Gent. M. n. s. 56: 63.
— Protection for. (Lord Dundonald) 19th Cent. 35: 132.
Surratt, Mrs., Trial of. (A. O. Hall) Green Bag, 8: 195.
Surrey, Earl of. (W. G. Howard) Harv. Mo. 14: 54.
Surrey, England, Commons of. M. of Art, 3: 52.
— its Geological Structure. (J. L. Lobley) Knowl. 18: 6.
— Highlands of. Time, 7: 832.
— Out of Doors in. (H. E. Ward) M. of Art, 6: 287.
— Walks in. (H. E. Ward) M. of Art, 7: 375.
Surrey Hills in March. Blackw. 153: 387.
Surrey Ponds. Spec. 71: 744.
Surtees, Robert, as a Poet. (F. Peacock) Dub. R. 112: 130.
Surveying and Mapping a City. (C. H. Rice) Engin. M. 9: 1066.
— Marine. Chamb. J. 70: 342.
"Surveyor," Ship, Capture of. (H. D. Smith) Un. Serv. (Phila.) 7: 363.
Survival. (A. K. H. Boyd) Longm. 28: 598.
Survival of the Fittest, The; a story. McClure, 7: 469.

Survival of the Unfit. (A. Bodington) Open Court, 6: 3327, 3337.—(H. D. Chapin) Pop. Sci. Mo. 41: 182.
Survivals and Folk-rhymes. (E. B. Taylor) Acad. 43: 73.
Susa, Acropolis of. (F. Goldsmid) Geog. J. 1: 437.
Susanna. (N. A. Cox) Cent. 26: 354.
Suspense. Spec. 73: 238.
Suspension Cable and Tow-line, Primitive Types of. (W. F. Durfee) Cassier, 7: 35.
Suspiciousness. Spec. 71: 75.
Susquehanna: Origin and Signification of the Name. (W. W. Tooker) Am. Antiq. 15: 286.
Susquehanna Express Robbery. (C. Moffett) McClure, 5: 366.
Susquehanna Valley, Lower, Notes on Glacial Gravels in. (H. B. Bashore) Am. J. Sci. 151: 281.
Sussex, Geological Structure of. (J. L. Lobley) Knowl. 18: 90.
— Great Forest of. (T. H. B. Graham) Gent. M. n. s. 50: 260.
— Hare on. Ath. '94, 1: 635.
— In the Down Country. (G. R. Tomson) M. of Art, 17: 206.
— The South Downs as a Sketching Ground. (W. W. Fenn) M. of Art, 6: 207.
Sutherland, Duchess of, Imprisonment of. Spec. 70: 512.
Sutherland Book, Fraser's. Blackw. 157: 702.—Ed. R. 181: 404.
Sutherland Folk-lore. (Frank Rinder) Scot. R. 28: 246.
Sutherlandshire Lochs, Among the. Temp. Bar. 97: 424. Same art. Liv. Age, 197: 234.
Suttner, Bertha von. Die Waffen Nieder! (F. Hertz) Int. J. Ethics, 2: 201.
Suzerain, Rights of a. (M. McIlwraith) Law Q. 12: 113.
Suzerainty, Feudal and Modern. (W. H. H. Kelke) Law Q. 12: 215.—Reply. (M. McIlwraith) Law Q. 12: 228.
Svastika, The, as both Sun and Fire Symbol. (H. G. M. Murray-Ayneley) Nature, 35: 559.
Svendsen, Charles C. (C. J. O'Malley) Mo. Illust. 12: 437.
Swagger, Decline of. Spec. 68: 197.
Swallows, Starved, in England, 1886. Chamb. J. 70: 158.
See Chimney-swallows.
Swan, Annie S., at Home. Sund. M. 23: 38.
— Works. Scot. R. 23: 32.
Swan, John Macallan. (R. A. M. Stevenson) Art J. 46: 17.—(C. Monkhouse) M. of Art, 17: 171.
Swan-shooting. (J. C. Bliss) Outing, 19: 328.
Swans and Swan Songs. (J. E. Field) Gent. M. 53: 250.
— Resort of, at Abbotsbury, Eng. Spec. 68: 603.
Swansea, Lord. The Man and the Town. (F. Dolman) Eng. Illust. 12: no. 2, 60.
Swanton Mill. (A. Jessopp) 19th Cent. 32: 416.
Swarm of Bees; a story. (N. M'Cormick) Argosy, 57: 431.
Swayne, Wager, with portrait. (J. H. Kennedy) Nat'l M. (N. Y. '91) 15: 201.
Swearing, Art of. (E. Valdes) Belgra. 88: 366.
Sweating, Government, in the Clothing Contracts. (J. Macdonald) New R. 11: 471.
Sweating System. (J. Lee) Am. J. Soc. Sci. 30: 105.—(J. Lee) Char. R. 2: 100.—(H. White) Lend a H. 17: 115.
— A Defence against. (H. W. Wolff) Econ. R. 4: 166.
Sweating System, Immigration and. (G. E. Walsh) Chaut. 18: 174.
— in 1893. Am. J. Soc. Sci. 31: 63.
— in Germany. (J. C. Brooks) Am. J. Soc. Sci. 30: 59.
— in Massachusetts. (H. G. Wadlin) Am. J. Soc. Sci. 30: 86.
— in New York City. (J. M. Mayers) Gunton's M. 11: 98, 277.
— in Philadelphia. (F. M. Goodchild) Arena, 11: 261.
— in United Kingdom. (D. F. Schloss) Am. J. Soc. Sci. 30: 65.
— Legislation on. (J. Lee) Am. J. Soc. Sci. 30: 138.
— Question of. (D. F. Schloss) Econ. R. 2: 452.
— Where they make Clothing. Gunton's M. 11: 26.
Sweden. (Marie A. Brown) Time, 16: 585.
— and Norway, Political Crisis in. (M. S. Constable) Fortn. 63: 811. Same art. Liv. Age, 205: 634.
— — Political Quarrels of. Sat. R. 79: 501.
— Case for, against Norway. New R. 12: 402. Same art. Liv. Age, 205: 279.
— in 17th Century. Oxenstierna's Papers and Correspondence. (G. Edmundson) Eng. Hist. R. 7: 784.
— Royal Family of. (H. W. Fischer) Munsey, 14: 202.
Swedenborg, Emanuel, Allegations against. (L. F. Hite) N. Church R. 1: 500.
— and the Occult. (J. Goddard) N. Church R. 3: 379.
— and Modern Philosophy. (C. S. Boswell) National, 18: 93.
— as a Scientist. (S. Beswick) N. Church R. 1: 413.
— compared with Aristotle. (F. Sewall) N. Church R. 2: 161.
— Patmore influenced by. (P. Sewall) N. Church R. 2: 592.
— Precision in Use of Terms. (S. M. Warren) N. Church R. 1: 129.
— Unfavorable Estimates. (T. F. Wright) N. Church R. 2: 85.
Swedenborgian Belief and the Church Universal. (W. Denovan) N. Church R. 1: 237.
— concerning Truth and Good. (J. Whitehead) N. Church R. 3: 553.
— New-Jerusalem Age. (T. A. King) N. Church R. 1: 349.
Swedenborgian Church and the Christian World. N. Church R. 1: 118.
— and the Lord's Coming. (T. A. King) N. Church R. 1: 349.
— compared with Old Jerusalem. N. Church R. 1: 623.
— Its Believers' Position in the World. (H. C. Hay) N. Church R. 3: 214.
— Its Growth. (T. F. Wright) N. Church R. 2: 275.
— Its Intellectual Mission. (F. Sewall) N. Church R. 1: 393.
— Preaching Different from Other Denominations. (F. Sewall) N. Church R. 3: 389.
— Science in. (E. Cranch) Open Court, 1: 374.
— What it stands for. (J. Reed) N. Church R. 1: 161.
Swedenborgian School, Aim of a. (A. E. Goddard) N. Church R. 1: 383.
Swedish Cathedral Churches. Reliquary, 33: 208.
Swedish Literature, 1891–92. (H. Tigerschiöld) Ath. '92, 2: 30.
— 1892–93. (H. Tigerschiöld) Ath. '93, 2: 32.
— 1894–95. (H. Tigerschiöld) Ath. 95, 2: 28.
Sweet, John E. (F. A. Halsey) Cassier, 1: 474.
Sweet Bells out of Tune; a story. (Mrs. B. Harrison) Cent. 23: 13–858. 24: 23.
Sweet Experience, A; a story. (Marta Freddi) Idler, 2: 483.
Sweet Girl Graduate, A. (B. A. Barnett) Argosy, 62: 243.

Sweet 'Laases; a story. (W. A. Drumgoole) Arena, 17: 151.
Sweet Marjory; a story. (S. B. Kennedy) Outing, 27: 259, 344.
Sweet Pea; a story. (P. Crawford) Belgra. 79: 165.
Sweet Punch; a monologue. (J. L. Steffens) Harper, 88: 126.
Sweet Singer; a story. All the Year, 70: 517.
Sweetheart Manette. (M. Thompson) Lippinc. 54: 147.
Sweethearts; a story. (A. C. Doyle) Idler, 5: 451. Same art. McClure, 3: 400.
Swift, Benj., with portrait. Bk. Buyer, 13: 601.
Swift, Jonathan, Dean. Church Q. 33: 440. — (M. O. W. Oliphant) Cent. 24: 401. — (W. Barry) Contemp. 69: 644.
— as an Advertiser. (J. Manning) Bookworm, 7: 107.
— "Cadenus and Vanessa." (E. Solly) Walford's Antiq. 7: 4.
— Collins's Life of. Ath. '93, 2: 87.
— "Conduct of the Allies." (E. Solly) Walford's Antiq. 7: 103.
— Journal to Stella. (A. Dobson) Longm. 22: 30. Same art. Liv. Age, 198: 42.
— Three Books on. (W. E. Grey) Acad. 44: 143.
— Was He ever in Love? (Thos. Tyler) Time, 3: 532.
— Will of. (R. Anslow) Bookworm, 1: 375.
Swiftiana in "The Gentleman's Magazine." Bookworm, 2: 39.
Swimmers, The. Macmil. 73: 30.
Swimming. (H. Oelrichs) Lippinc. 49: 230. — (E. W. Sandys) Outing, 28: 285.
— and Darwinism. (L. Robinson) 19th Cent. 34: 721.
— Practical Lessons in. (W. A. Varian) Outing, 22: 279.
Swinburne, A. C., and the Meaning of Life. (F. W. H. Myers) 19th Cent. 33: 93.
— as a Critic. (S. J. E. C. Hankin) Acad. 46: 547. — (D. F. Hannigan) Westm. 142: 142.
— Astrophel and other Poems. (E. D. A. Morshead) Acad. 45: 429. — Spec. 72: 828. — Ath. '94, 1: 701. Sat. R. 77: 472.
— Ethics of his Poetry. Sat. R. 81: 95.
— Lamb, and Webster. (W. Archer) New R. 8: 96.
— Poems, Theology of. (R. Shindler) Ecl. M. 118: 109.
— Religion of his Poetry. Sat. R. 81: 296.
— The Sisters. Ath. '92, 2: 31. — Gent. M. n. s. 49: 212. — Sat. R. 73: 602. — Spec. 69: 19. — (G. Cottrell) Acad. 42: 5.
— Studies in Prose and Poetry. (C. Coupe) Dub. R. 116: 338.
— Tale of Balen. Sat. R. 82: 166. — (E. D'Esterre-Keeling) Acad. 49: 481.
Swindles, London. Argosy, 59: 496.
— Paris. (C. Moffett) Lippinc. 57: 565.
Swinfen *vs.* Swinfen, Case of. Green Bag, 7: 581.
Swing Song; a poem. (W. Allingham) M. of Art, 8: 301.
Swipes; a tale. (L. H. Foote) Overland, n. s. 25: 227.
Swiss Idyls. (W. D. McCrackan) New Eng. M. n. s. 12: 713.
Swithin, St.: a Home-made Saint. (E. MacMahon) Belgra. 81: 251.
Switzerland. (J. M. Vincent) Nation, 54: 383.
— Alcohol Monopoly in. (J. King) Econ. R. 3: 212.
— Alpine Tit-bits. (F. T. Wethered) Gent. M. n. s. 49: 390.
— as a Nursery of Politics. (J. King) And. R. 19: 269.
Switzerland as a School of Politics. (A. W. Hutton) Time, 23: 1271.
— Constitution-making in. (S. M. Lindsay) Nation, 57: 425.
— Democracy in Miniature. (M. O'Brien) Nation, 57: 152.
— Democracy of, Model. (S. H. M. Byers) M. Am. Hist. 28: 42.
— Economics in. (A. Oncken) Econ. J. 6: 308.
— Federal Court of. (W. A. B. Coolidge) Law Q. 4: 409. 5: 149.
— Government of; a President of no Importance. (W. D. McCrackan) No. Am. 163: 118.
— House Industries in. (W. H. Dawson) Econ. J. 6: 295.
— In "Chalet" Land. Cornh. 72: 143. Same art. Liv. Age, 206: 633.
— Infantry of. Macmil. 73: 106. Same art. Liv. Age, 208: 101.
— McCrackan's History of. (J. O. Pierce) Dial (Ch.) 14: 85.
— the Model Republic, Baker's. Sat. R. 81: 79.
— Mountaineering in, Marsh's. Sat. R. 80: 511.
— Naturalist in a Swiss Forest. (C. Parkinson) Eng. Illust. 11: 67.
— the Oeschinen See, and the Gemmi Pass. (S. Hodges) M. of Art, 3: 9.
— Political Experiments in. (L. Wuarin) Ann. Am. Acad. Pol. Sci. 6: 361.
— Politics in. (J. Macy) Am. J. Sociol. 2: 25.
— Referendum in. (N. N. Withington) New Eng. M. n. s. 9: 563. *See also* Referendum.
— a Republic. (Karl Blind) Time, 19: 268.
— Solutions of American Problems in. (W. D. McCrackan) New Eng. M. n. s. 11: 448.
— State and Federal Government in, Vincent on. Spec. 69: 262.
— Theological Instruction in. (P. W. Snyder) Bib. World, 1: 109, 184, 278, 445.
— Village Life in. (E. Macpherson) Chaut. 18: 515.
— Vox Populi. (A. B. Hart) Nation, 59: 193.
Sword, Burton's Book of the. (D. Hannay) M. of Art, 7: 259.
— A Highly Ornate, from North Australia. (R. Etheridge, jr.) Anthrop. J. 24: 427.
Sword-actors, Yorkshire. (T. M. Fallow) Antiq. n. s. 31: 138.
Sword Exercise, The New. Un. Serv. M. 13: 98.
Sword-lore of Japan. (L. H. Weeks) Lippinc. 56: 833.
Sword-play. Sat. R. 77: 442.
— in Japan. (K. Hirai) Outing, 25: 466.
— Old, Hutton on. Sat. R. 73: 637.
Swords, Japanese. (B. S. Lyman) J. Frankl. Inst. 141: 13.
— of Washington. (T. A. Washington) N. E. Reg. 48: 21.
— Testing. Sat. R. 76: 514.
Swordsmanship, Army. Sat. R. 75: 264.
— on the Stage. (W. H. Pollock) Theatre, 36: 321.
Sword-fish of the Indian Ocean. (N. Pike) Outing, 21: 306.
Sybel, Heinrich von. Acad. 48: 110. — Ath. '95, 2: 193. — (Munroe Smith) Bookman, 2: 205.
Sydney, New South Wales, Making of. (W. B. Worsfold) Un. Serv. M. 8 : 336.
Syenite (Saganaga), Geological Age of. (A. R. C. Selwyn) Am. J. Sci. 143: 319.
— Nepheline, in the Township of Dungannon, Ontario. (F. D. Adams) Am. J. Sci. 148: 10.
Symbiosis of Stock and Graft. (E. F. Smith) Am. Natural. 29: 615.

Symbol, Migration of, Alviella's. Sat. R. **78**: 479.
Symbolism, Christian. (E. Sedding) Antiq. n. s. **29**: 159.
— Early Christian. (R. Seton) Am. Cath. Q. **17**: 491.
— in Art. (A. Beaver) M. of Art, **4**: 234.
— in French Literature. Spec. **68**: 579.
— on the Stage. (R. F. Sharp) Theatre, **30**: 203.
Symbolists, French. Bookman, **1**: 89, 161.—Scrib. M. **13**: 337.
Symbols. (H. Zimmern) Pop. Sci. Mo. **46**: 539.
— and Signs. (E. Schroeder) Open Court, **6**: 3431–3463.
— Migration of. (H. W. Haynes) Nation, **60**: 386, 404.
— used by Uncultivated Races. Sat. R. **77**: 525.
Symington, James. (H. M. Steele) Q. Illust. **2**: 18.
Symington, William, Life and Works of. (W. Fletcher) Cassier, **6**: 67.
Symmetry. (E. Mach) Open Court, **8**: 4015.—(H. Munsterberg) Psychol. R. **1**: 483.
— and Incident. (A. Meynell) Fortn. **62**: 705.
Symon, Arthur. London Nights. Sat. R. **80**: 176.
Symonds, John Addington, with portrait. Bk. Buyer, **10**: 197.—With portrait. Bk. News, **11**: 429.—(A. R. Cluer) Fortn. **59**: 874. Same art. Liv. Age, **198**: 362. Same art. Ecl. M. **121**: 91.—(R. Noel) Gent. M. n. s. **51**: 304.—Ath. '93, **1**: 506.—Sat. R. **75**: 456.—Critic, **22**: 277.—(J. S. Cotton) Acad. **43**: 371.—Dial (Ch.) **14**: 264.—(F. Sewall) New World, **3**: 704.—(F. Harrison) 19th Cent. **39**: 979. Same art. Liv. Age, **210**: 166. Same art. Ecl. M. **127**: 525.—Quar. **182**: 31. (E. G. Johnson) Dial (Ch.) **18**: 205.—(F. P. Nash) Nation, **60**: 281.—(W. Sharp) Acad. **47**: 95.
— Art Essays. (K. Cox) Nation, **58**: 87.
— as an Essayist. (R. Le Gallienne) Acad. **43**: 213. —(W. I. Way) Dial (Ch.) **14**: 180.
— Brown on. Sat. R. **78**: 709.
— Life of. (H. F. Brown) 19th Cent. **37**: 342.
Sympathies, Human, and Religious Capacity. Spec. **69**: 123.
Sympathy and Antipathy; drama. (D. Leighton) Eng. Illust. **12**: no. 1, 53.
— Antipathy and. (S. Bryant) Mind, **20**: 365.
— Merit and Vice of. (C. P. Woolley) Open Court, **1**: 550.
Symphony illustrated by Beethoven's Fifth in C Minor. (P. H. Goepp) Atlan. **75**: 39.
Symphony Rehearsal, A Boston. (W. E. Walker) Bost. **1**: 248.
Sympsychograph, The; a Study in Impressionist Physics. (D. S. Jordan) Pop. Sci. Mo. **49**: 597.
Synaesthesia. (M. W. Calkins) Am. J. Psychol. **7**: 90.
Synagogue Service, Ancient. (E. D. Burton) Bib. World, **8**: 143.
"Synechism," Issues of. (G. M. McCrie) Monist, **3**: 380.
Synesius, a Pupil of Hypatia. (H. W. Preston and L. Dodge) Atlan. **75**: 371.
Synods of the Church. Eng. R. **16**: 126.
Synthesis, Nature of Intellectual. (J. E. Creighton) Philos. R. **5**: 135.
Synthetic Method. (A. B. Forman) Lend a H. **8**: 340.
Syon House. (E. Balfour) M. of Art, **7**: 221, 300.
Syria and Asia Minor, Early History of. (J. E. Gilmore) Eng. Hist. R. **10**: 1.
— Coast of. (W. Wright) Sund. M. **22**: 663, 743.
— In. (F. Carrel) Fortn. **62**: 562.
— Jottings in. (G. Thomas) Eng. Illust. **9**: 898.
Syria, Languages of, Early. (R. C. Conder) Scot. R. **21**: 279.
— Railway in. All the Year, **74**: 8.
— Six Months in, Parry's. Sat. R. **79**: 700.
Syriac Gospels and Text Tamperings. (W. F. Steele) Meth. R. **55**: 398.
— The New. (A. J. Maas) Am. Cath. Q. **20**: 543.—(F. A. Gast) Ref. Q. **42**: 141.—(F. W. Farrar) Chr. Lit. **12**: 224.—(A. S. Lewis) Acad. **47**: 315. —(J. R. Harris) Contemp. **66**: 654.—(W. C. Allen; F. C. Badham) Acad. **46**: 512.
Syriac Language—the Language of Christ. (Agnes S. Lewis) Cent. **31**: 307.
Syrian Desert. (A. Klein) Blackw. **151**: 722.
— Wright's Trips in. Dub. R. **118**: 433.
Syringia Pekinensis. Garden & F. **7**: 384.
Szarvas, Gabriel. Acad. **48**: 339.
Székely Tales. (P. Gave) Folk-Lore, **4**: 328.

Τὰ στοιχεῖα τοῦ κόσμου in Gal. iv. 3, and Col. ii. 8. (E. Y. Hincks) J. Bib. Lit. **15**: 183.
Taaffe, Edward, Count. (E. B. Lanin) Contemp. **63**: 279.—Temp. Bar, **99**: 497. Same art. Liv. Age, **199**: 809.
Taaffe Family of Austria. Spec. **71**: 872.
Tabasheer. (G. F. Kunz) J. Am. Folk-Lore, **5**: 64.
Tabb, Rev. John B. (M. Gordon Hale) Bach. of Arts, **2**: 791.—With portrait. Bk. Buyer, **13**: 227.
Tabernacle, The. (J. Strong) Bib. World, **1**: 270.—(W. H. Green) Presb. & Ref. R. **5**: 69.
Tablecloth designed by Crane. (L. F. Day) Art J. **47**: 286.
Table Customs. Chamb. J. **70**: 161.
Table Manners, Evolution of. (L. J. Vance) Lippinc. **55**: 531.
Table Talk. Good Words, **35**: 185–843.
Tables and Table Customs. (J. H. Pollen) M. of Art, **9**: 105.
Tabley, Lord de. *See* De Tabley.
Taboos of Commensality. (A. E. Crawley) Folk-Lore, **6**: 130.
Tabreez to Khoi. (F. G. Lenz) Outing, **28**: 386.
Tachygraphy, 14th Century. (T. W. Allen) J. Hel. Stud. **11**: 286.
Tacitus, Annals, ed. by Furneaux. Sat. R. **73**: 421.—Ath. '92, **1**: 238.
— Dialogues, Notes on. (A. Gudeman) Am. J. Philol. **12**: 444.
— Dialogus de Oratoribus, Authorship of. (R. B. Steele) Am. J. Philol. **17**: 289.
— — Notes to Gudeman's Edition of. (R. B. Steele) Am. J. Philol. **17**: 45.
— — Peterson's. Ath. '94, **1**: 140.
— Quill's Translation. Spec. **69**: 648.
— Recent Editions of. Ed. R. **179**: 76.
Tacoma, Washington. (H. M. Howard) New Eng. M. n. s. **7**: 793.
— City Library. (R. R. Bowker) Lib. J. **20**: 78.
Tacoma, Mt., *vs.* Mt. Rainier. Nation, **56**: 329.
Tact of Miss Aspinwall-Jones. (W. E. Baldwin) Outing, **25**: 349.
Tactics and Strategy, Coming Revolution in. (H. Elsdale) Contemp. **62**: 245. Same art. Un. Serv. (Phila.) **8**: 355.
—1859–1890. (Von Boguslawski) Un. Serv. M. **4**: 109, 249.
— Modern. Un. Serv. M. **4**: 51.
— Recent European Improvements. (A. S. Frost) Un. Serv. (Phila.) **7**: 215.
Tadema, Laurens Alma. *See* Alma Tadema, L.
Tadousac, Quebec. (A. T. Sadlier) Cath. World, **57**: 307.

Tadpoles, My. Chamb. J. 73: 189.
Tadpoles; a story. (F. Wyatt) Theatre, 28: 32.
Taeping Rebellion, Hake on. Spec. 68: 583.
— Personal Recollections of. (E. Forester) Cosmopol. 21: 625. 22: 34, 209.
Tafilet, Oasis of, Harris's. Dub. R. 118: 435.
— a Journey to. (W. B. Harris) Geog. J. 5: 319.
— the Land of Dates. Chamb. J. 73: 321.
Tags and Clichés. Cornh. 70: 301.
Tahiti: a South Sea Island. Liv. Age, 200: 29.
Tahoe, the Gem of Californian Lakes. Chamb. J. 73: 472.
Tail-like Formations in Men. Pop. Sci. Mo. 40: 347.
Tailoring by Steam. (D. Paton) Good Words, 34: 527.
Tails attributed to Englishmen in Mediæval Times. (P. Toynbee and others) Acad. 43: 83, 107, 154.
Tain, Scotland, Antiquities of. Sat. R. 73: 443.
Taine, Hippolyte A., with portrait. Bk. Buyer, 10: 97.—(G. Monod) Contemp. 63: 518. Same art. Liv. Age, 197: 579. Same art. Ecl. M. 120: 661. — Critic, 22: 150, 183.—Dial (Ch.) 14: 165, 223. — Ath. '93, 1: 311.—Spec. 70: 317.
— and the Science of Criticism. (L. E. Gates) Nation, 56: 193.
— Dislike of Publicity. (R. Ogden) Nation, 56: 249.
— Le Régime Moderne. (B. Holland) National, 28: 36.
— Personal Reminiscence of. (J. E. C. Bodley) Blackw. 153: 609.
— Posthumous Work of. (A. Laugel) Nation, 57: 463.
Tait, Archibald Campbell. Leis. Hour, 42: 412.
Taj Mahal, The. (G. F. Pentecost) Sund. M. 23: 592. — Chamb. J. 71: 261.
Takin' in of Old Mis' Lane, The; a story. (E. Higginson) McClure, 4: 83.
Taking Sides on Questions of the Day, Difficulty of. (W. L. Sheldon) Int. J. Ethics, 6: 77.
Taku Glacier. (E. R. Scidmore) Around World, 1: 177.
Talbots of Malahide. Walford's Antiq. 4: 251.
Talc, Rose-colored Lime-and-alumina-bearing Variety of. (W. H. Hobbs) Am. J. Sci. 145: 404.
Tale of Accrá, A. Chamb. J. 72: 254.
Tale of a Christmas Day. (J. Barnes) Bach. of Arts, 2: 43.
Tale of a Dartmoor Fog. Chamb. J. 70: 251.
Tale of the Fens, A. (N. W. Williams) Belgra. 88: 431.
Tale of Germany; a story. (H. C. N. Wilson) Canad. M. 2: 485.
Tale of a Goblin Horse. (C. C. Nott) Scrib. M. 13: 373.
Tale of the Karroo, A. Chamb. J. 70: 636.
Tale of the Mercantile Marine; a story. (H. Bindloss) Temp. Bar, 108: 397.
Tale of Mere Chance. (S. Crane) Eng. Illust. 14: 570.
Tale of Narragansett. (C. Hazard) N. Eng. M. 5: 805.
Tale of Old Edinburgh, A. (J. M. Cobban) Chamb. J. 71: 552-600.
Tale of the Sea. (G. J. Romanes) Longm. 26: 51.
Tale of a Tail-Girl, The. (H. Bell) Idler, 10: 451.
Tale of Ter-rew Love Triumphant; an Extravaganza. (K. Strange) Canad. M. 5: 525.
Tale of To-day. (B. L. Clay) New Eng. M. n. s. 14: 660.
Tale of Twin Souls, A. (F. Wishaw) Idler, 9: 131.
Tale of Two Studios; a story. Blackw. 154: 30.
Tale of a Wedding-cake. Argosy, 54: 419.
Talent and Genius on the Stage. (G. Barlow) Contemp. 62: 385.
Tales of a Smuggler. (S. S. Boynton) Overland, n. s. 22: 511.
"Tales of Terror," Authorship of. Acad. 45: 35.
Tales of the Thames. (M. Pemberton) Eng. Illust. 13: 396, 489.
Tales of Wayside Inns. (H. Lye) Canad. M. 1: 131, 224, 297.
Taliesin; a masque. (R. Hovey) Poet-Lore, 8: 1, 63.
Talismans. Reliquary, 33: 162, 193. Spec. 71: 396.
Talk at a Country House. (Sir E. Strachey) Atlan. 42: 607. 73: 46-625.
Talking and Writing. (J. Monteith) Educa. 16: 268.
Tall Master; a story. (G. Parker) National, 20: 108. Same art. Liv. Age, 195: 664.
Talleyrand. Atlan. 70: 115.
— and Randolph. (M. D. Conway) Nation, 57: 211.
— Lady Blennerhassett's. (F. Clarke) Fortn. 63: 60.
— Memoirs of. (H. M. Stephens) Acad. 42: 43.—(A. Laugel) Nation, 54: 337.
Tallien, Jean L. (B. S. Knolly's) Belgra. 78: 23.
Talma: French Histrionic Story. (A. H. Wall) Time, 9: 734.
Talmud, Study of, in 13th Century. (J. H. Weiss) Jew. Q. 1: 289.
Tam Miller; a poem. (M. McKenzie) Canad. M. 8: 34.
Tame Surrender, A; a story. (C. King) Lippinc. 55: 291.
Tamenend (Tammany), Grave of. (H. C. Mercer) M. Am. Hist. 29: 255.
Tamerlane the Great. (E. S. Holden) Overland, n. s. 22: 380.
Tamils. Around World, 1: 78.
Tammany Hall. (H. C. Merwin) Atlan. 73: 240.—(W. Taylor) Munsey, 9: 131.—(E. J. Edwards) McClure, 4: 445, 569.
— Future of. (E. L. Godkin) Nation, 59: 356.
— points the Way. (H. C. Merwin) Atlan. 74: 680.
— under John Kelly. (E. J. Edwards) McClure, 5: 325.
Tana River, R. M. Ormerod's Journeys on. Geog. J. 8: 283.
Taney, Roger B., with portrait. (E. S. Taney) Green Bag, 7: 361.
Tanganyika, Lake; the Heart of Africa. All the Year, 71: 77.
Tanghim, or the Poison Ordeal of Madagasca. Chamb. J. 71: 714.
Tangier. (J. Reid) Good Words, 36: 535.
— and Algiers. Around World, 1: 113.
— British Occupation of. (W. F. Lord) 19th Cent. 34: 1009.
— Problem of. Spec. 68: 110.
— Two Days at. (F. W. Cornish) Time, 21: 259.
Tanjore. All the Year, 75: 390.
Tanks and Fountains, Literary. Time, 7: 280.
Tanna, Mission Work in, Dr. Paton's. Sund. M. 23: 806.
Tannhäuser, New Ballad of. (J. Davidson) Sat. R. 81: 642.
Tannin Value of Some North American Trees. (H. Trimble) Garden & F. 9: 162.
Tanning Properties of Three North American Trees. (H. Trimble) Garden & F. 8: 293.
Tanoux, Adrien Henri. (P. G. Hamerton) Scrib. M. 16: 435.
Tantalus; a poem. (W. J. Henderson) M. of Art, 10: 14.
Tante Cat'rinette. (K. Chopin) Atlan. 74: 368.
Tao. (W. Davies) Atlan. 73: 182.
Taoism. Open Court, 10: 5155.
Taormina Note-book. (G. E. Woodberry) Cent. 24: 677.
Tapestries, American. (S. R. Koehler) M. of Art, 9: 209.
— and Costume. Spec. 72: 647.

Tapestry. (A. Cole) Eng. Illust. 11: 1041.
— The Great, by Burne-Jones and W. Morris, in Exeter College Chapel, Oxford. (H. D. Rawnsley) M. of Art, 17: 284.
— of the New World. (F. D. Bergen) Scrib. M. 16: 360.
— of St. John's Church. Walford's Antiq. 3: 138.
— Tynecastle, Making of. Art J. 48: 81.
Tapestry Painting. M. of Art, 3: 458.
Tapir, Hunting a. (A. Chamberlain) Outing, 22: 21.
Tapirs. (C. Earle) Science, n. s. 4: 934.
— Recent and Fossil. (J. B. Hatcher) Am. J. Sci. 151: 161.
Tarahumaris; American Cave-dwellers. (C. Lumholtz) Scrib. M. 16: 31.
— Dances and Plant Worship of. (C. Lumholtz) Scrib. M. 16: 438.
— Life and Customs of. (C. Lumholtz) Scrib. M. 16: 296.
Tarakanoff, Elizabeth, Princess. (S. Marchant) Belgra. 89: 203.
Tarantula-killer, The. Chamb. J. 72: 15. Same art. Liv. Age, 204: 511.
Tardy Compensation, A. (M. L. Adams) New Eng. M. n. s. 10: 63.
Target-shooting, Inanimate. (M. C. Allen) Overland, n. s. 26: 438.
Tariff, American, — its Past and its Future. (J. S. Jeans) Ecl. M. 120: 215.
— and Business. (T. B. Reed) No. Am. 158: 110.
— and the Constitution. (A. P. Winston) J. Pol. Econ. 5: 40.
— and the Constructive Arts. (R. H. Thurston) Cassier, 1: 183.
— and the Consuls. (E. L. Godkin) Nation, 57: 340.
— and Trade. (S. G. Horwitz) Am. J. Pol. 1: 364.
— and Wool. (T. Cox) Am. J. Pol. 1: 231.
— at the Chicago Convention, 1892. (W. L. Wilson) No. Am. 155: 280.
— Carey and Greeley on. Soc. Econ. 7: 134.
— Customs Administrative Act, The. (C. S. Hamlin) No. Am. 158: 222.
— Customs Union for British Empire. Soc. Econ. 7: 291.
— Danger in Hasty. (R. H. Wolff) Forum, 15: 666.
— Economists and the Public. (S. M. Macvane) Q. J. Econ. 9: 132.
— English View of American. Soc. Econ. 4: 100.
— Ethics of the Controversy. (O. L. Elliott) Overland, n. s. 23: 281.
— for Revenue; what it really means. (D. A. Wells) Forum, 14: 51.
— Gorman Law. Soc. Econ. 7: 129, 198.
— Hill on. Pub. Opin. 17: 66.
— How to do it. (W. M. Springer) No. Am. 156: 129.
— in France. Sat. R. 73: 143.
— in Germany, Policy of, Past and Present. (H. Villard; H. W. Farnam) Yale R. 1: 10.
— in Great Britain: Common Sense at last. (C. E. H. Vincent) National, 19: 667.
— in Legislation. (J. A. Woodburn) Chaut. 23: 9.
— in New York State, Statistics of, Peck's Report on. (H. White) Nation, 55: 158.
— Incidence of Tariff Taxation. Soc. Econ. 5: 343.
— Injustice of Our System. (E. Mead) Am. J. Pol. 2: 189.
— Is the Duty added to the Price? Gunton's M. 10: 103.
— Labor Troubles and. (C. J. Harrah) Engin. M. 4: 411.
— Legislation on. (H. White) Nation, 62: 91.
Tariff, McKinley and Wilson. Pub. Opin. 19: 326.
— McKinley Bill and the Cost of Living. (N. W. Aldrich) Forum, 14: 242.
— — English Views of the. (T. H. Farrer) Forum, 14: 310.
— — Prices under. Q. J. Econ. 7: 103.
— Mandate of the Election, 1894. Soc. Econ. 9: 321.
— Moderate, Proposed for England. (Lord Masham) Sat. R. 82: 311.
— Necessity for Immediate Reduction. (A. A. Healy) Forum, 16: 405.
— New, 1894. (F. W. Taussig) Pol. Sci. Q. 9: 585. — (F. W. Taussig) Econ. J. 4: 573. — Blackw. 156: 573. — Soc. Econ. 6: 1.
— — and of 1890. Pub. Opin. 17: 541, 615.
— — Compromise Amendments. Pub. Opin. 17: 157.
— — Passage of, by Senate. Pub. Opin. 17: 329.
— — Principle and Method of. (W. L. Wilson) Forum, 16: 544.
— Not a Local Question. (H. Kingerly) Am. J. Pol. 1: 496.
— of 1789, Protective Purpose of. (W. Hill) J. Pol. Econ. 2: 54.
— of 1828, Minimum Principle in, and its Recent Revival. (S. B. Harding) Ann. Am. Acad. Pol. Sci. 6: 100.
— One Phase of. (H. White) Nation, 58: 78.
— Our National Object Lesson. Soc. Econ. 5: 1.
— Past and Future of. (J. S. Jeans) Fortn. 58: 746.
— Plan for an Automatic Business-like. (W. J. Coombs) Forum, 16: 413.
— The Practical Issue. (D. MacG. Means) Nation, 55: 178.
— Probable Effects of Free Wool. Soc. Econ. 7: 145.
— Protective, Constitutionality of a. (C. Reno) Am. Law R. 27: 519.
— Question of. (H. White) Nation, 63: 379.
— — British View of. (L. Irwell) Am. J. Pol. 1: 395.
— The Real Issue. (G. G. Vest) No. Am. 155: 401.
— Reductions of, and Fiat Money. (Raymond E. Dodge) Gunton's M. 10: 126.
— Reed-Dingley Revenue Bill. Gunton's M. 10: 36.
— Reform of, and Monetary Reform. (E. B. Andrews) No. Am. 158: 464.
— — Blunders in. (W. T. Galbraith) Am. J. Pol. 4: 79, Reply, 190. — (R. Baker) Am. J. Pol. 4: 155.
— — Canadian. (J. W. Russell) Am. M. Civics, 8: 244.
— Retrospective and Prospective. (D. A. Wells) Forum, 14: 697.
— "Revenue Only" Tariff Unconstitutional. Soc. Econ. 6: 75.
— Revision of, 1893. Pub. Opin. 15: 568.
— — Question of. (L. M. Neiffer) Am. J. Pol. 4: 392.
— Should the Administration, 1893–7, change it? (E. Mead) Am. J. Pol. 2: 98.
— Shouting Prosperity in. Soc. Econ. 7: 210.
— Silver and. Pub. Opin. 17: 412.
— Situation of. (E. E. Russell) Am. J. Pol. 5: 526.
— Socialism *vs.* Protection. (W. F. Draper) Soc. Econ. 7: 22.
— Sound Economics in Congress. Soc. Econ. 6: 129.
— What shall be done with the? Soc. Econ. 9: 345.
— What will the Democrats do? (J. DeW. Warner) Engin. M. 5: 267. — (B. M'Millin; J. Dalzell; W. J. Bryan) No. Am. 157: 493.
— What would I do with it if I were Czar? (A. Carnegie) Forum, 19: 18.
— Who pays the Tariff? Soc. Econ. 3: 297.
— Wilson Bill. (H. White) Nation, 57: 404, 480. — Pub. Opin. 16: 186–310. — (R. Q. Mills) No. Am. 158: 235.

Tariff, Wilson Bill, Canada and. (E. Wiman) Engin. M. 6: 125.
— — Effect of, on Gold Standard. (H. B. Russell) Am. J. Pol. 4: 167.
— — for a Deficit only. (A. Clarke) Forum, 16: 696.
— — Home Industries and. (C. S. Smith; E. Kemble; A. K. Miller; W. H. Dimond) No. Am. 158: 312.
— Wool and Woolens in the. Soc. Econ. 6: 22.
Tariff Policy, Our. (J. Dalzell) Am. J. Pol. 1: 172.
— First Stages of. (W. Hill) Am. Econ. Assoc. 8: 461.
Tariff Retaliation, Salisbury on. Spec. 68: 735.
Tariffs of the American Colonies. (W. Hill) Q. J. Econ. 7: 78.
— Preferential. (C. Tupper) Fortn. 58: 137.
Tarpon, Adventure with a. (F. J. Wells) Outing, 25: 389.
— Graining the. (W. B. Hobbs) Outing, 23: 491.
— The Silver King at Home. (J. L. Wood) Cosmopol. 17: 30.
Tarpon-fishing in Texas. (E. A. Bailey) Blackw. 158: 281.
Tarragona, Spain. (C. W. Wood) Argosy, 62: 442.
Tartans. (J. M. Gray) Scot. R. 23: 269.
Tartar Emetic, Standard Solutions of, Stability of. (H. Gruener) Am. J. Sci. 146: 206.
Tartars, Parker's Thousand Years of the. (E. Simcox) Acad. 48: 239.
Tartary and Thibet, Huc on. Eng. R. 16: 398.
Tartini. (J. F. Rowbotham) Good Words, 34: 18.
Tartuffe, What was? (H. M. Trollope) Blackw. 154: 641.
Tarlton, Richard. (C. T. J. Hiatt) Theatre, 29: 65.
Tarn River. (E. H. Barker) Temp. Bar, 94: 251.
Tarumensian Woods, In the. 19th Cent. 36: 244. Same art. Liv. Age, 202: 756.
Tashkent, A Winter in. (T. G. Allen, jr.) Bach. of Arts, 1: 297.
Tasmania. (A. Webb) Nation, 62: 95.
— and her Prospects. (E. Braddon) Asia R. 12: 91.
— Crocoite from. (C. Palache) Am. J. Sci. 151: 389.
— History of. (E. Braddon) Asia. R. 12: 335.
— Internat. Exhib. at Hobart, 1894. (G. C. Levey) J. Soc. Arts, 42: 481.
— Something about. Time, 8: 317.
Tasmanians as Representatives of Palæolithic Man. (E. B. Tylor) Anthrop. J. 23: 141.
Tasset, Marianne. (J. G. Alger) Scot. R. 22: 363.
Tassie, James, and the Foulis Academy. (J. M. Gray) M. of Art, 17: 150.
— and William. (F. Wedmore) Acad. 45: 172.
Tasso, Torquato. Quar. 182: 508.
— his Centenary and his Legend. (M. V. Cherbuliez) Chaut. 22: 171.
— Milman's Life of. Eng. R. 13: 125.
Taste, Good. (A. Birrell) Scrib. M. 17: 115.
— A Question of. (E. F. Benson) 19th Cent. 34: 458. Same art. Ecl. M. 121: 604.
Tate, A. Norman. Nature, 46: 298.
Tate, Henry. Collection of Paintings. (W. Armstrong) Art J. 45: 65–297. 46: 177–193.
— — and the National Gallery of British Art. (M. H. Spielmann) M. of Art, 16: 145–263.
Tatian, and the Date of the Fourth Gospel. (J. R. Harris) Contemp. 64: 800.
— Diatessaron. (W. R. Cassels) 19th Cent. 37: 665.
— — Reply. (J. Rendel Harris) Contemp. 68: 271. Same art. Chr. Lit. 13: 268.
Tatra Group, Geography of the. Geog. J. 2: 255.
Tattooed Face of King Tawhaio. Reliquary, 35: 155.
Tattooing. (C. M. Salwey) Asia. R. 22: 141.
Tattooing, Art of. (T. Hopkins) Leis. Hour, 44: 694, 774.
— Savage Origin of. (C. Lombroso) Pop. Sci. Mo. 48: 793.
Tauchnitz, Baron C. B., with portrait. Bookman, 2. 156. — (J. Stanton) Critic, 27: 281. — Acad. 48: 130.
— Recollections of. Critic, 27: 281.
Taufers, in the Tyrol. (C. Weeks) M. of Art, 3: 463.
Taunton, Mass. (S. V. Cole) New Eng. M. n. s. 14: 65.
Tautphœus, Jemima, Baroness. (M. L. Thompson) Atlan. 74: 114. — Critic, 24: 12.
— Works. Belgra. 85: 67.
Tax, Business, in Prussia. (J. A. Hill) Q. J. Econ. 8: 77.
— Income. *See* Income Tax.
— on Ground Rents: Who would pay it? (R. Balmforth) Westm. 143: 297.
— Single. (C. E. Benton) Am. J. Pol. 2: 347. — (I. Feinberg) Am. M. Civics, 6: 1. — (R. W. Joslyn) Am. M. Civics, 6: 310. — (S. M. Gay and F. E. Russell) Arena, 13: 284, 411. 14: 1–401. — (C. B. Whitehead; E. B. Brokaw; F. E. Russell) Arena, 15: 196.
— — and Socialism. (C. E. Benton) Am. J. Pol. 3: 417.
— — and Transportation. (W. E. Brokaw) Am. J. Pol. 4: 369.
— — Ethics of. (J. Lee) Q. J. Econ. 7: 433. — (G. Bernard) Am. M. Civics, 8: 518.
— — in Actual Operation. (H. Garland) Arena, 10: 52.
— — in Delaware. (Priscilla Leonard) Outl. 52: 303. 53: 666.
— — Land Question and. (S. B. Riggen) Arena, 10: 332.
— — the Middle Ground of Social Philosophies. (G. S. Robbins) Arena, 13: 472.
— — Reply to A. Kitson. (G. Bernard) Am. M. Civics, 7: 425.
— — Simplicity of. (S. H. Leech) Arena, 16: 892.
— — Theory of, Critique of. (H. W. B. Mackay) Am. J. Pol. 4: 302.
Taxes, Evading Some. Sat. R. 78: 122.
— New and Old. (M. Q. Holyoake) Chamb. J. 73: 313.
— Shifting of. (T. N. Carver) Yale R. 5: 258.
Taxation, American and English Conditions of. Soc. Econ. 6: 269.
— American, and Politics. (E. J. Shriver) Westm, 141: 60.
— and the Farmers. (J. Middleton) Am. M. Civics, 6: 523.
— and Finance. (S. Laing) Univ. R. 3: 149.
— and Pauperism. (B. Hall) Char. R. 1: 115.
— Curiosities of. (M. Q. Holyoake) Temp. Bar, 99: 345.
— Direct, Madison on. (W. C. Ford) Nation, 60: 322.
— — Problem of. (G. F. Milton) Pub. Opin. 16: 98.
— Economics of Rating. (G. Crosoer) Westm. 146: 322.
— Equitable Distribution of. (W. E. Weyl) Pub. Opin. 13: 49. — (R. Luce) Pub. Opin. 13: 51. — (B. Hall) Pub. Opin. 13: 52.
— Ethical Basis of. (W. W. McLane) And. R. 18: 549.
— Graduated. Blackw. 155: 729. — (J. G. Godard) Econ. R. 5: 39.
— — in the Canton de Vaud. (W. B. Duffield) Westm. 144: 401.
— Hadley on. (G. Turrell) J. Pol. Econ. 4: 508.
— Illinois Labor Report on. Gunton's M. 10: 197.
— in Chicago and Philadelphia. (J. R. Commons) J. Pol. Econ. 3: 434.

Taxation in Connecticut, History of, 1636–1776. (F. R. Jones) J. H. Univ. Stud. 14: 345.
— in England, Inequality of Local Rates. (E. Cannan) Econ. J. 5: 22.
— — A New Departure in. (Sir L. Playfair) No. Am. 160: 285.
— — Proposed Revolution in. Spec. 72: 73, 131.
— in Japan. (G. Dropero) Q. J. Econ. 6: 492.
— — Origin and Growth of. (T. Okada) Ann. Am. Acad. Pol. Sci. 3: 82.
— in the United States. (E. Atkinson) Engin. M. 10: 194.
— Incidence of. (H. L. Davies) Westm. 144: 370.
— Inheritance Tax, Theory of. (M. West) Pol. Sci. Q. 8: 426.
— Just. (J. Whidden Graham) New Eng. M. n. s. 6: 706.
— Land, in Japan. (S. Sugiyama) Gunton's M. 11: 6.
— Local and Central, Relation between. (W. H. Smith) Econ. J. 5: 175.
— Local, "Betterment" and. Quar. 178: 185.
— — in England, Growth and Incidence of. (G. H. Murray) Econ. J. 3: 698.
— — in Scotland. (B. Taylor) Scot. R. 25: 360.
— — Injustice of. (J. St. L. Strachey) National, 27: 710.
— — its Amount and Burden. (W. M. J. Williams) Fortn. 61: 758.
— National. Open Court, 2: 778, 800.
— Natural [*i. e.* Land], Shearman's. Sat. R. 82: 143.
— New Canon of. (E. A. Ross) Pol. Sci. Q. 7: 585.
— of Church Property. (F. D. Bovard) Overland, n. s. 27: 167. — (S. Mosby) No. Am. 163: 254. — (M. C. Peters) No. Am. 163: 633. — (J. E. Larmer) Am. J. Pol. 1: 502. — N. Eng. 56: 177.
— — Should it be taxed? (W. H. Laird) Am. M. Civics, 6: 543.
— — Why it should be taxed. (M. C. Peters) Forum, 18: 372.
— — Why it should not be taxed. (J. M. Farley) Forum, 17: 434.
— of Land Values. (A. Withy) Westm. 143: 626.
— of Large Estates. (R. T. Colburn) Ann. Am. Acad. Pol. Sci. 4: 82.
— A Plea for Variety in. (H. Withers) National, 26: 641.
— Poor Man's Budget. (W. M. J. Williams) Fortn. 61: 306.
— Popular Mistakes about. Soc. Econ. 6: 199.
— Principles of. (D. A. Wells) Pop. Sci. Mo. 48: 1–721. 49: 29–577. 50: 145.
— Progressive, in Theory and Practice. (E. R. A. Seligman) Am. Econ. Assoc. 9: 1.
— — Theory of. (E. R. A. Seligman) Pol. Sci. Q. 8: 220.
— Recent Literature on. (E. A. Ross) Dial (Ch.) 14: 17.
— Recent Reforms in. (E. R. A. Seligman) Yale R. 3: 352. 4: 40.
— Reform in Prussia, Plan of. J. Pol. Econ. 1: 315.
— Relation of, to Monopolies. (E. R. Johnson) Ann. Am. Acad. Pol. Sci. 4: 764.
— St. Paul Method of Assessing Real Estate. (F. R. Clow) J. Pol. Econ. 5: 71.
— Seligman's Essays in. (L. L. Price) Econ. J. 6: 81. — (C. H. Hull) Am. Hist. R. 1: 565. — Sat. R. 81: 607.
— Seligman on. (C. H. J. Douglass) Yale R. 1: 323.
— Shifting and Incidence of. (E. R. A. Seligman) Am. Econ. Assoc. 7: 123.
Taxation, Shifting and Incidence of, Seligman on. (E. A. Ross) Ann. Am. Acad. Pol. Sci. 3: 444. — (A. C. Miller) J. Pol. Econ. 1: 285, 450. — (E. R. A. Seligman) J. Pol. Econ. 1: 444.
— State and Federal. (R. Ogden) Nation, 55: 444.
Taxidermist, The. (G. W. Cable) Scrib. M. 13: 679.
— A Country. (A. J. Goodson) Eng. Illust. 15: 77.
Taxidermy. (J. C. Beard) Scrib. M. 20: 66.
— as a Fine Art. Nat. Sci. 5: supp.
— The Preservation of Wild Animals. (R. W. Shufeldt) Cosmopol. 21: 297.
— Sportsman's. (L. H. Smith) Outing, 23: 405.
Taxpayer under Home Rule. Blackw. 154: 587.
Tay River, Scotland. (D. S. Graham) Art J. 46: 233.
Taylor, Bayard. M. Am. Hist. 29: 136.
— Memorial Library. Critic, 29: 189.
Taylor, Charles H. (E. J. Edwards) McClure, 7: 144. — (F. A. Munsey) Munsey, 14: 276.
Taylor, Edmund Dick. (H. L. Conard) Nat'l M. (N. Y. '91) 16: 209.
Taylor, Edward T. [Father Taylor.] (C. A. Bartol) New World, 2: 479.
Taylor, Hobart C. Chatfield-. (M. Abbott) Writer, 8: 150.
Taylor, Gen. James, of Kentucky. (Mrs. J. Van Voast) Am. Hist. Reg. 1: 57.
Taylor, Jeremy, Life of. Eng. R. 9: 315.
Taylor, John, the Water Poet. Bookworm, 3: 369.
Taylor, John, Librarian at Bristol. (J. Baker) Ath. '93, 1: 473.
Taylor, Thomas. (A. Waters) Open Court, 10: 4908.
Taylor, Tom. (J. Oldcastle) M. of Art, 4: 66.
Taylor, Wm. M., with portrait. Book News, 11: 431. — Chr. Lit. 12: 289.
Taylor, Gen. Zachary. (R. D. St. John) Chaut. 21: 205. — (A. R. Watson) Lippinc. 52: 220.
Taylor Collection of Pictures at Aston Rowant. (C. J. Weeks) M. of Art, 5: 309.
Taylor Family. The Old Morton and Taylor Estates, Dorchester, Mass. (D. Clapp) N. E. Reg. 46: 78.
— of Virginia and Kentucky. Am. Hist. Reg. 2: 1001.
Taylor of Baronsgate; a story. Macmil. 67: 321. Same art. Liv. Age, 197: 224.
T' Bonnie Lass o' t' Fells. (C. A. B. Massicks) Belgra. 84: 374.
Tchampa, History of. (E. Aymonier) Asia. R. 16: 140, 365.
Tchebicheff, P. L. Nature, 52: 345.
Tea. (A. G. Stanton) J. Soc. Arts, 43: 189.
— and other Staple Drinks, Consumption of, in Great Britain. (C. H. Denyer) Econ. J. 3: 33.
— Brick. Liv. Age, 192: 318.
— A Cup of. (Mrs. A. H. Green) Good Words, 35: 748.
— Landing of, in Philadelphia, 1773, Opposition to. (F. D. Stone) Pennsyl. M. 15: 385.
Tea at the Mains; a story. Blackw. 151: 257. Same art. Liv. Age, 193: 74.
"Tea will be provided;" a story. (E. S. Grew) Idler, 6: 727.
Tea Ceremony of Japan. (J. K. Matumoto) Lippinc. 56: 115.
Tea Culture in Darjeeling. (G. W. Christison) J. Soc. Arts, 44: 624.
Tea-gardens and Masquerades 100 Years Ago. All the Year, 74: 277.
Tea Party of Edenton, N. C., in 1774. (R. Dillard) M. Am. Hist. 28: 81.
Tea Supply of the U. S., The. (E. H. Miller) Nat'l M. (Bost.) 4: 553.
Tea-time in the Village. (M. E. Francis) Blackw. 160: 520. Same art. Liv. Age, 211: 417.

Teacher, The, as an Individual. Dial (Ch.) 19: 275.
— as a Professional Expert. (A. B. Hart) School R. 1: 4.
— Certificated, in England, Position of. (J. H. Yoxall) New R. 8: 536.
— Dignity of. (G. M. Hyde) Critic, 27: 111.
— Influence of, in Politics. (G. J. Luckey) Am. J. Pol. 1: 200.
— Self-training of. (J. E. C. Welldon) Contemp. 63: 369.
— Substitution of, for Text-book. (J. M. Rice) Forum, 19: 681.
— What he owes to Himself. (M. A. Jordan) Acad. (Syr.) 7: 275.
Teachers, Address to. (C. L. Morgan) Monist, 5: 354.
— Characteristics of Best, as recognized by Children. (H. E. Kratz) Pedagog. Sem. 3: 413.
— Confessions of Public School. Atlan. 78: 97.
— Duty of, to Pupils. (J. Gibbons) No. Am. 163: 56.
— Duties of Parents to. (A. H. Rich) Educa. 12: 350.
— for Secondary Schools, Training of. (W. B. Jacobs) Educa. R. 11: 245.
— Higher Pay and a Better Training for. (J. G. Speed) Forum, 20: 247.
— Letters to. (W. S. B. Mathews) Music, 5: 213.
— Manners of, Influence of. (A. F. Palmer) Acad. (Syr.) 6: 571.
— Modern, Influence of. Time, 5: 233.
— Parochial School, Institutes for. (B. E. Burke) Cath. World, 64: 249.
— Pay of, in England, in Girls' Schools. (S. Bryant) Econ. J. 4: 94.
— Pensions for. (E. Gray) Contemp. 65: 453.
— Preparation of, for Secondary Schools. (A. F. Nightingale) School R. 4: 129.
— Primary, in England, Security of Tenure for. Westm. 139: 554.
— Professional Training of. (M. V. O'Shea) Pop. Sci. Mo. 45: 796.
— — and American Universities. (G. S. Hall) Forum, 17: 148.
— Public School, Appointment of. (J. C. Hendrix) Educa. R. 3: 260.
— Ratio of Men to Women in the High Schools of the United States. School R. 4: 86.
— Salaries of. (J. P. Garber) Educa. 15: 583.
— Salaries of Women. School R. 4: 687.
— Secondary, Professional Preparation of, in the U. S., Atkinson on. (M. K. Smith) School R. 1: 688.
— Superannuation of. (A. Reichenbach) Educa. 16: 385. — (T. J. Macnamara) Westm. 139: 623. — (Sir R. Temple) Fortn. 59: 477.
— — of Elementary. (W. A. Hunter) Contemp. 65: 84. — (F. H. Wiltshire) Westm. 145: 539.
— Training of. (H. S. Tarbell and others) Educa. R. 9: 209.
— — in the Province of Ontario, Canada. (G. W. Ross) School R. 1: 400.
— — New York College for. (W. L. Hervey) R. of Rs. (N. Y.) 5: 424.
— Water Travel for. Educa. 15: 554.
Teacher's College, The. (R. B. Holt) Cosmopol. 16: 579.
Teachers' Meetings, Should Papers dealing with Matters of Scholarship, or Papers on Method, be the Chief Feature of? (F. W. Kelsey) School R. 4: 594.
Teaching. (H. Spencer) Pop. Sci. Mo. 48: 265.
— Freedom of. Dial (Ch.) 17: 103.
Teaching, Gregory's Seven Laws of. (J. M. Richardson) Educa. 15: 413.
— Individual, Pueblo Plan of. (P. W. Search) Educa. 7: 154. 8: 84.
— Laboratory, of Large Classes. (A. Hyatt) Science, n. s. 1: 197.
— — — in Botany. (W. F. Ganong) Science, n. s. 1: 230.
— — — in Zoölogy. (H. C. Bumpas) Science, n. s. 1: 260.
— Motor Activities in. (E. R. Shaw) Pop. Sci. Mo. 50: 56.
— Music. (F. W. Wodell) Music, 11: 159.
— Objective Method, Bitter End of the. (I. F. Foster) Educa. R. 7: 290.
— of Beginning Chemistry. (P. C. Freer) Science, n. s. 4: 130.
— Our Improved Methods in. (A. D. Hodges) Nation, 63: 401.
— Personal Factor in. (F. A. Comstock) Educa. 15: 527.
— Practice, in Normal Schools. (J. W. Cook) Educa. R. 3: 267.
— — Value of. (W. J. Milne) Educa. R. 3: 69.
— Research the Vital Spirit of. (G. S. Hall) Forum, 17: 558.
— Tendency of, Responsibility of Teacher for. (B. A. Greene) And. R. 19: 51.
— A Trade or a Profession? (J. G. Schurman) Forum, 21: 171.
— Training of College Graduates for Work of. (S. T. Dutton) Educa. 16: 523.
— University, Original Research and Creative Authorship the Essence of. (G. B. Halsted) Science, n. s. 1: 203.
Teaching Force, The; Normal Schools as a Source of Supply. (E. T. Pierce) Overland, n. s. 28: 219.
Teak Forests of Burmah. (C. S. Sargent) Garden & F. 9: 311. — (D. Brandis) Garden & F. 9: 318-428.
Teak-wood, Where it grows. (M. M. Pope) Cent. 26: 890.
Teay Valley, West Virginia. (W. M. Davis) Science, n. s. 2: 40.
Teche, Bayou, Down the, in a Cat-rig. (A. B. Paine) Outing, 23: 106.
Technic, Psychological. (H. A. Kelso, jr.) Music, 2: 346.
Technical Education, Advance of. (R. A. Gregory) Nature, 51: 379.
— and Commercial Competition. (B. Samuelson) Sat. R. 82: 390.
— Economic Element of. (L. S. Randolph) Cassier, 5: 194.
— Progress and Prospects of. (P. Magnus) J. Soc. Arts, 41: 426.
— Progress of. (R. A. Gregory) Nature, 49: 185.
— Relations of Academic and. (N. S. Shaler) Atlan. 72: 559.
— Schools of Practical Arts. Soc. Econ. 9: 18.
Technical Instruction in London. (H. L. Smith) Contemp. 61: 741.
Technical Journals in America. (C. H. Werner) Cassier, 2: 226.
Technical School and the University. (F. A. Walker) Atlan. 72: 390.
Technical Schools for Girls on the Continent. (M. Mulhall) Contemp. 70: 136.
Technical Training, Need of. (Lord Brabazon) Time, 14: 546.
Technique in Art. Spec. 74: 719.

Technological Schools. (R. H. Thurston) School R. 1: 523.
Teck and its Duchy. Chamb. J. 69: 65.
— Dukes of. Liv. Age, 192: 764.
Tee-To-Tum Club, New York City. (W. H. Tolman) Char. R. 2: 371.
Tee-to-tum Movement. (H. O. Thomas) And. R. 17: 415. — (H. O. Thomas) Econ. R. 2: 351.
Teese, Frederick H., with portrait. Nat'l M. (N. Y. '91) 18: 303.
Teeth, Civilization and. Nature, 50: 53, 148, 199.
— Human, Degeneration of. (J. L. Williams) New R. 7: 466.
— in Mammals, Succession of. (H. F. Osborn) Am. Natural. 27: 493.
— — Ameghino on the Evolution of. (E. D. Cope) Am. Natural. 30: 937.
— of Sioux Indians. (Wi berforce Smith) Anthrop. J. 24: 109, 446.
Teetotalism in London, Origin of. (H. A. Glass) Sund. M. 24: 492.
— Moral Basis of. Spec. 70: 799.
Teheran to Tabreez. (F. G. Lenz) Outing, 28: 295.
Tehuantepec Interoceanic Route. (E. L. Corthell) Engin. M. 8: 259.
Tehuantepec Railway. (M. Romero) Engin. M. 6: 872.
Tehuantepec Ship-railway. (E. L. Corthell) Nat. Geog. M. 7: 64.
Teichmüller, Robert. (H. F. Young) Music, 7: 511.
Telautograph, The. All the Year, 73: 177.
— Gray's. Dub. R. 114: 173. — (W. Maver, jr.) Engin. M. 5: 217. — (E. Gray) Cosmopol. 15: 123.
Telegony. (F. Finn) Nat. Sci. 3: 436.
Telegraph and Telephone, Legal Aspects of; Essential Parts of an Efficient Postal Service. (W. Clark) Am. Law R. 29: 675.
— — Properly Parts of the Post-office System. (W. Clark) Arena, 5: 464.
— — Romance of the. Chamb. J. 69: 21.
— Between England and India. (E. O. Walker) J. Soc. Arts, 42: 217.
— Central Station, St. Martin's-Le-Grand. (J. Munroe) Time, 1: 485.
— The First News Message by. (J. W. Kirk) Scrib. M. 11: 652.
— Future of. J. Frankl. Inst. 140: 472.
— Government Control of. (R. T. Ely and W. Clark) Arena, 15: 49. — (L. Abbott; W. L. Wilson; F. Parsons) Arena, 15: 242–947. 16: 70–629. 17: 9.
— — Semi-jubilee of, in England. Gent. M. n. s. 54: 522.
— in the British Empire, An Imperial System for. (J. H. Heaton) Contemp. 63: 537.
— in England. (W. Clark) Arena, 13: 372.
— in France, A Century of. (W. Lodian) Pop. Sci. Mo. 44: 791.
— in War. (Carl Reichmann) Un. Serv. (Phila.) 10: 103.
— Operation of. Chamb. J. 70: 199.
— Possibilities of Mechanical Transmission. (P. B. Delany) Engin. M. 10: 39.
— Russo-American: Project of 1864–67. (W. H. Dall) Nat. Geog. M. 7: 110.
— The State and the. Chamb. J. 72: 161. Same art. Liv. Age, 205: 187.
Telegraph Cables, Atlantic, Two New. Chamb. J. 71: 303.
— Submarine. (J. Munroe) Leis. Hour, 44: 18–183.
Telegraph Company, Liability of, for Mental Suffering. (W. C. Rogers) Am. Law R. 29: 209.
Telegraph Department in Persia. (C. E. Biddulph) Asia. R. 13: 99.
Telegraph Establishment, Inclusion of, in Civil Service. (W. H. Preece) Good Govt. 13: 108.
Telegraph Systems of the World. (H. Muir) McClure, 5: 99.
Telegraphic Codes and Cipher Messages. Chamb. J. 71: 379.
Telegraphic Mistake, A. (H. F. Lester) Argosy, 57: 558.
Telegraphing without Wires. (J. Trowbridge) Chaut. 15: 54.
Telegraphs, The, of the Bond-aided Pacific Railroads. (L. S. Merriam) Pol. Sci. Q. 9: 185.
— Pacific, Proposed. (H. L. Webb) Engin. M. 6: 845.
Telegraphy as it used to be. (G. Lodian) Cassier, 8: 34.
— Delany System. J. Frankl. Inst. 142: 91.
— Machine, New System. (P. B. Delany) J. Frankl. Inst. 141: 1.
— Submarine, Smith's. Sat. R. 73: 253.
— up to Date. (G. J. Varney) Lippinc. 54: 571.
Tel-el-Amarna Tablets. Ed. R. 178: 1. — (J. H. Mitchiner) Knowl. 16: 25. — (H. Hayman) Thinker, 9: 408. — (Mrs. W. Hope) Sund. M. 23: 274. — Acad. 46: 15.
— in the British Museum. Nature, 46: 49.
— "Men of Judah" in. (M. Jastrow, jr.) J. Bib. Lit. 12: 61.
— Testimony of. (H. Hayman) Bib. Sac. 50: 696.
Tel-el-Hesy Excavated, Bliss's. Sat. R. 78: 298. — (J. P. Peters) Nation, 59: 13.
Tele-photography. (T. R. Dallmeyer) J. Soc. Arts, 41: 379.
Telepathy. (C. B. Newcomb) Arena, 15: 822. (R. Hodgson) Chaut. 16: 409.
— and W. T. Stead. (A. Bryne) Canad. M. 2: 131.
— Experience in. (E. T. Durgin) Psychic. R. 2: 267.
— Experimental. (T. E. Allen) Arena, 11: 227.
— Theory of. (T. E. Allen) Arena, 12: 116.
Telephone, The. (M. Brooks) Cassier, 8: 3.
— and the Post-office. (Duke of Marlborough) New R. 6: 320.
— City Control over. (H. C. McDougall) Am. Law R. 30: 381.
— History of. (W. C. Jones) Cassier, 8: 71.
— 950 Miles by. (A. Dickson) Cassier, 3: 71.
— of To-day. (H. L. Webb) New Eng. M. n. s. 10: 461.
Telephone, The; a Domestic Tragedy. Temp. Bar, 107: 106.
Telephone Industry, Future of. (H. L. Webb) Engin. M. 2: 753.
Telephones: Past, Present, and Future. (J. H. Heaton) New R. 10: 540.
Telephoning without Wire, Preece's Experiments In. Spec. 69: 764.
Telephony, Long-distance, Practical Value of. (H. L. Webb) Engin. M. 4: 876.
Telescope, Field of View of, Diameter of. (T. H. Blakesley) Knowl. 18: 154.
— How it aids Ordinary Vision. (W. W. Payne) Pop. Astron. 3: 81.
— Pleasures of. (G. P. Serviss) Pop. Sci. Mo. 45: 213. 46: 289, 466, 738. 47: 508.
— Possibilities of. (A. G. Clark) No. Am. 156: 8.
Telescopes, Common: What they will show. (G. E. Lumsden) Canad. M. 2: 217.
— Giant. (J. E. Gore) Gent. M. n. s. 54: 342.
— Great, of the Future. (A. Clark) Astron. 12: 673. — (E. E. Barnard) Pop. Astron. 2: 245.

Telescopes, Great, Simple Mounting for, in the Field. (F. H. Bigelow) Astron. 11: 257.
— Large and Small, as showing Planetary Detail. (W. F. Denning) Nature, 52: 232.
— Large Reflecting, Mounting of. (H. Grubb) Knowl. 17: 98.
— Large Refracting, Engineering Problems in Construction of. (W. R. Warner) Astron. 12: 695.
— Mountings and Domes of. (W. H. Pickering) Astron. 13: 1.
— Objectives of, Glass for. (J. A. Brashear) Pop. Astron. 1: 221, 291.
— Reflecting and Refracting. Dub. R. 117: 158.
— Refracting, Adjusting Object Glasses of. (J. A. Brashear) Pop. Astron. 2: 57.
— 20-inch Equatorial of Chamberlain Observatory. (H. A. Howe) Astron. 13: 709.
Tell, William, and Rudolf von Warta. (K. A. A. Biggs) Gent. M. n. s. 52: 156.
— Gisler on. (W. A. B. Coolidge) Eng. Hist. R. 11: 360.
Tellurium by Precipitation as the Iodide, Determination of. (F. A. Gooch and W. C. Morgan) Am. J. Sci. 152: 271.
— with Potassium, Rubidium and Cæsium, Double Halides of. (H. L. Wheeler) Am. J. Sci. 145: 267.
Telubin River. (H. Louis) Geog. J. 4: 219.
Temblor, A, in the Mad Mule Mine. (F. M. Stocking) Overland, n. s. 22: 81.
Temecula Cañon. (T. S. Van Dyke) Outing, 22: 432.
Temperaments. (A. E. J. Legge) National, 18: 713.
Temperance, Agencies of. (A. Shadwell) National, 27: 262.
— and the Social Question. Dub. R. 113: 801.
— The Old Fight and the New. (P. S. Henson) Our Day, 16: 453.
— Physical Foundations of. (Sir B. W. Richardson) Longm. 27: 141.
— Quality of Liquors as related to. (T. B. Griffith) Dub. R. 110: 363.
— Scientific. (D. S. Jordan) Pop. Sci. Mo. 48: 343.
— — Instruction in Public Schools. (A. F. Newton) Am. M. Civics, 8: 30. — (E. S. Martin) Bach. of Arts, 2: 774. — (F. E. Willard) Arena, 12: 10.
Temperance Crusade, Miss Willard's. Chr. Lit. 10: 348. 11: 30.
Temperance Education, Scientific, of the Masses. (M. H. Hunt) Our Day, 11: 89.
Temperance Movement, Duty of Church Members in. (J. Cook) Our Day, 11: 407.
— in England, Advanced Party in. (W. S. Caine) Contemp. 63: 47.
— — Deadlock in. (G. Wyndham) Contemp. 63: 61.
— in the U. S., Outlook for, in 1892. (F. E. Willard) Our Day, 10: 866.
— — State of, in 1893. Pub. Opin. 16: 194.
Temperance Needs in Foreign Lands; a symposium. Our Day, 9: 391.
Temperance Organizations in England. (F. W. Farrar) M. Chr. Lit. 7: 199.
Temperance Problem, The, Past and Future. (E. R. L. Gould) Forum, 18: 339.
Temperance Question, Scientific Aspect of the. (A. E. T. Longhurst) Westm. 140: 8.
Temperance Saloons. (G. T. Ferris) Soc. Econ. 3: 218.
Temperance Scheme, Jayne's. Sat. R. 74: 160.
Temperance Societies, Old-Time. (P. F. McSweeny) Cath. World, 62: 482.
Temperance Work, Prospects of, in Mission Fields. (Mrs. J. Cook) Our Day, 13: 371.
Temperature in Buildings, Influence of. Am. Arch. 53: 68.
— in the 26.68 Day Solar Magnetic Period, Inversion of. (F. H. Bigelow) Am. J. Sci. 148: 435.
— Present Status of High Temperature Research. (C. Barus) Am. J. Sci. 148: 332.
Temperature Coefficients, Determination of. (E. G. Willyoung) J. Frankl. Inst. 135: 140.
Tempest, Adolphus Vane, with portrait. Theatre, 29: 23.
Tempest, Marie, Experiences of. (M. Tempest) Munsey, 10: 480.
Tempest Island. (N. H. Dole) New Eng. M. n. s. 9: 51.
Tempests, Laws of. (A. Angot) Chaut. 20: 707.
Templars, Crime of the. (J. E. Crombie) Gent. M. n. s. 51: 337.
— Michelet on. Eng. R. 1: 1.
Temple, Frederick, as Archbishop of Canterbury. (R. Ogden) Nation, 63: 323.
Temple, Second, Builders of. (W. Betteridge) Bib. Sac. 53: 231.
Temple Builders and Pyramid Builders, Early. (J. N. Lockyer) Nature, 48: 55.
Temple Newsam and its Art Collection. (S. A. Byles) M. of Art, 16: 208.
Temple-sculptures, Greek, Subjects of. (F. B. Tarbell; W. N. Bates) Am. J. Archæol. 8: 18.
Temple Students and Temple Studies. (D. W. Douthwaite) Green Bag, 6: 411, 456.
Temples and Temple Cities. (B. W. Ball) Open Court, 1: 351.
— Greek, Dates of. (F. C. Penrose) Nature, 45: 395.
— — Lighting of. (M. M. Lathbury) Acad. 41: 70.
Tempted by the Devil; a story. (A. C. Doyle) Cosmopol. 19: 561.
Ten Brink, Bernhard. (T. G. Foster and H. F. Heath) Acad. 41: 133. — (Geo. Hempl) Dial (Ch.) 12: 434.
Ten Dollars a Day — no Canvassing. (P. G. Hubert, jr.) Lippinc. 54: 657.
Ten-shilling Cigar; a story. (W. E. G. Fisher) Eng. Illust. 15: 233.
Ten-shilling Tragedy, A. (J. Reid) Good Words, 37: Xmas no. 5.
Ten-Times-One Corporation: Report, 1892–93. Lend a H. 12: 60.
— — 1893–94. (E. E. Hale) Lend a H. 13: 56.
Ten Tribes: Where are They? (A. Neubauer) Jew. Q. 1: 14–408.
Tenacity *vs.* Strength. (H. B. M. Buchanan) Argosy, 60: 487.
Tenancy in the U. S. (G. K. Holmes) Q. J. Econ. 10: 34.
Tenant of the Shag Rock. (W. E. Norris) Longm. 26: 155.
Tenants' Ball. Cornh. 65: 156.
Tendencies of Othello Perkins. (H. Campbell) New Eng. M. n. s. 7: 113.
Tendency, What is a? (A. W. Bennett) Sci. Prog. 3: 143.
Tender Mercies of the Good, The. (C. R. Coleridge) Sund. M. 24: 1–793.
Tenderfoot Ink-slinger, The. (W. C. Platts) Chamb. J. 71: 345–376.
Tenement House, Home in. (L. T. Ames) New Eng. M. n. s. 7: 594.
— Homes of the Poor. (A. T. White) Chaut. 16: 442.
— Problem of, in New York. (E. M. Valesh) Arena, 7: 580.
— Question of. (M. Bradshaw) Lend a H. 15: 261.
— the Real Problem of Civilization. (J. A. Riis) Forum, 19: 83.

Tenement-house Work. (H. Fox) Lend a H. **10**: 41.
Tenement-house Workers in Boston. (W. L. Hicks) Am. J. Soc. Sci. **30**: 103.
Tenement Houses and Tenants. (K. Bocock) Soc. Econ. **6**: 111.
— an Attempt to give Justice. (A. Eilvart) Char. R. **3**: 343.
— Berlin. (C. de Kay) Am. Arch. **49**: 49.
— Census of, in Boston. (J. Tunis) Lend a H. **12**: 56.
— Curse of. (W. H. Talman) Arena, **9**: 659.
— Evil of, in New York, and its Cure. (E. Flagg) Scrib. M. **16**: 108.
— in New York city, Evictions from. (W. P. McLoughlin) Arena, **7**: 48.
— — Life in. (W. T. Elsing) Scrib. M. **11**: 697.
— — Problems of. (E. T. Potter) Char. R. **1**: 129.
— Life in, Relation to the Family. Lend a H. **12**: 323.
Tenement Street, Anatomy of a. (A. F. Sanborn) Forum, **18**: 554.
Tenements, Improved. (G. W. Da Cunha) Am. Arch. **52**: 123.
— Model. (W. H. Tolman) Arena, **16**: 595.
— Working-Class in London. (E. Porritt) No. Am. **160**: 120.
See Homes; Housing.
Teneriffe. Liv. Age, **211**: 663.—(C. E. Jefferey) Month, **85**: 255. **86**: 96.
— Winter in. Month, **75**: 333.
Tengger, or the Great Sand Sea of Java. Chamb. J. **71**: 732.
Teniers, David the Younger. (T. Cole) Cent. **28**: 772.
Tennessee, East, Over-mountain Men of. (S. M. Burnett) Am. Hist. Reg. **1**: 313-421.
— Industrial Conditions of. (T. Ralph) Harper, **90**: 607.
— Middle, Mountaineers of. (A. Moffat) J. Am. Folk-Lore, **4**: 314.
— Supreme Court of. (A. D. Marks) Green Bag, **5**: 120-275.
Tenniel, Sir John. (M. H. Spielmann) M. of Art, **18**: 201.
— Political Cartoons of. (E. C. Reynolds) Cosmopol. **12**: 588.
Tennis in England, in 1892. Sat. R. **74**: 645.
— in California. (J. F. J. Archibald) Overland, n. s. **20**: 363.
— Some Developments of. (J. M. Heathcote) National, **23**: 500.
Tennis Balls; from the Memoirs of a Minister of France. (S. J. Weyman) Eng. Illust. **12**: no. 2, 35.
Tennis Court Oath, The. (J. H. Robinson) Pol. Sci. Q. **10**: 460.
Tennyson, Alfred. (J. Jacobs) Acad. **42**: 335.—(S. H. Thayer) And. R. **18**: 460. (T. Watts) Ath. '**92**, **2**: 482, 555.—Blackw. **152**: 748.—With portrait. (M. F. Egan) Cath. World, **56**: 149.—(S. A. Brooke) Contemp. **62**: 761.—Critic, **21**: 254-285.—(G. Stewart) Cosmopol. **14**: 169.—Dial (Ch.) **13**: 231.—Gent. M. n. s. **49**: 535.—Liv. Age, **195**: 446.—Lit. W. (Bost.) **23**: 372.—(A. Ainger) Macmil. **67**: 76.—(H. Van Dyke *et al.*) Critic, **21**: 203-237.—(J. W. Chadwick) Nation, **55**: 276.—(E. Gosse; H. Paul) New R. **7**: 513. Same art. Liv. Age, **195**: 707.—Pub. Opin. **14**: 43.—With portraits. (W. T. Stead) R. of Rs. (N. Y.) **6**: 557. Sat. R. **74**: 405.—Spec. **69**: 484.—Westm. **138**: 589.—With portrait. Bk. News, **11**: 68.—(W. Ward) Critic, **29**: 46.—(A. Fields) Harper, **86**: 309.—Ecl. M. **120**: 31.—Church Q. **35**: 485.—With portrait. (W. T. Stead) Our Day, **11**: 19.—(H. V. Clarke) Munsey, **7**: 189.—(J. S. Smith) So. M. **2**: 145.
Tennyson, A., and Browning as Spiritual Forces. (C. C. Everett) New World, **2**: 240.
— — Love and Duty in. (E. F. R. Stitt) Poet-Lore, **4**: 271.
— and O. W. Holmes; a Parallel, with portraits. Cath. World, **60**: 521.
— and the Meaning of Life. (F. W. H. Myers) 19th Cent. **33**: 93.
— and Whitman, Relations of, to Science. (J. Burroughs) Dial (Ch.) **14**: 168.
— and Whittier, with portraits. (T. V. Powderly) Arena, **7**: 1.
— the Artist. (H. W. Mabie) Chr. Un. **46**: 786.
— as a Humorist. (H. D. Traill) 19th Cent. **35**: 761.
— as a Nature Poet. (T. Watts) 19th Cent. **33**: 836. Same art. Ecl. M. **120**: 837. Same art. Liv. Age, **198**: 28.
— as Poet of the English People. (G. W. Alger) Poet-Lore, **8**: 325.
— as the Poet of Evolution. (T. Watts) 19th Cent. **34**: 657. Same art. Liv. Age, **199**: 611.
— as the Religious Exponent of his Age. (J. Wedgwood) Sund. M. **22**: 34.
— as a Thinker. (H. S. Salt) Time, **23**: 1055.
— Aspects of. (H. D. Traill) 19th Cent. **32**: 952. Same art. Liv. Age, **196**: 415.—(J. Knowles) 19th Cent. **33**: 164. Same art. Liv. Age, **196**: 515.
— at Aldsworth. (F. G. Kitton) Gent. M. n. s. **54**: 53. Same art. Liv. Age, **204**: 434.
— At the Laureate's Funeral. In Memoriam, Oct. 12, 1892; a poem. (Argyll) National, **20**: 581.
— Becket. Sat. R. **75**: 146.
— — at the Lyceum Theatre. Spec. **70**: 253.—(F. Wedmore) Acad. **43**: 158.—(J. Hatton) Art J. **45**: 105.
— Bibliography. Critic, **21**: 211.
— S. A. Brooke on. Ed. R. **181**: 485.—(A. Waugh) Acad. **46**: 24.—Spec. **73**: 18.—(F. Adams) New R. **10**: 311.
— Browning, and Taylor. Eng. R. **14**: 65.
— Characteristics of. (J. Knowles) Same art. Critic, **22**: 67.
— Classical Poems. (H. Paul) 19th Cent. **33**: 436. Same art. Liv. Age, **197**: 407.
— Dante and. (F. T. St. Thackeray) Temp. Bar, **102**: 387. Same art. Ecl. M. **123**: 352.
— Death of Œnone and other Poems. (L. Johnson) Acad. **42**: 403.—Poet-Lore, **4**: 640.—Ath. '**92**, **2**: 695.—Sat. R. **74**: 536.
— Dissenters about, A Word with. (P. Shorley) Dial (Ch.) **14**: 102.
— Earliest Manuscript of. Critic, **28**: 81.
— Earliest Poems of. Critic, **22**: 333.
— Early French Estimate of. Ath. '**92**, **2**: 554.
— Early Recollections of. Temp. Bar, **101**: 203. Same art. Liv. Age, **200**: 618.
— Elaine, and Shakspere's Miranda. (S. D. Davies) Poet-Lore, **5**: 15.
— Fancy of. Spec. **68**: 458.
— The Foresters. (W. Watson) Acad. **41**: 341.—Sat. R. **73**: 391.—Ath. '**92**, **1**: 491.—(J. H. McCarthy) Gent. M. n. s. **48**: 528.
— — Maid Marian on the Stage. (A. B. Walkley) Theatre, **28**: 227.
— Friendships of. (E. C. Martin) McClure, **2**: 54.
— Funeral of. (T. R. Macquoid) Lit. W. (Bost.) **23**: 388.—Liv. Age, **195**: 510.—Spec. **69**: 516.
— Gallic Study of. Univ. R. **4**: 529.
— Genius of. Spec. **69**: 528. Same art. Ecl. M. **119**: 808. Same art. Liv. Age, **195**: 505.
— Homes of, at Aldworth and Faringford. (G. Allen) Eng. Illust. **10**: 145.

Tennyson, A. Idyll of Guinevere. (P. Cameron) Cath. World, 63: 328.
— Idylls of the King. (W. Walsh) Gent. M. n. s. 50: 500.
— — Littleday's Essays on. Sat. R. 75: 248.
— In the Laureate's Footsteps. (G. Winterwood) Good Words, 33: 670.
— In Memoriam. (W. J. Rolfe) Poet-Lore, 7: 428.
— — How to Study. (H. A. Clarke) Poet-Lore, 5: 574.
— Influence of, in the U. S., Sources and Extent of. (H. W. Mabie) R. of Rs. (N. Y.) 6: 553.
— King Arthur at the Lyceum Theatre. (H. J. Jennings) Gent. M. n. s. 54: 202.
— Lady of Shalott, Celtic Element in. (A. R. Brown) Poet-Lore, 4: 408.
— Latest Verses. Gent. M. n. s. 49: 641.
— Life of, Bellezza's. Ath. '94, 2: 486.
— Literary Sensitiveness of. (A. Austin) National, 20: 454. Same art. Ecl. M. 120: 230.
— Locksley Hall, and Locksley Hall Sixty Years After. Poet-Lore, 5: 34.
— Louth Grammar School. (J. W. Hales) Gent. M. n. s. 49: 562.
— the Man and the Poet. (D. Dorchester, jr.) Meth. R. 55: 409.
— Maud, Fauvel's French Translation of. Spec. 69: 325.
— Monument to, Proposed. Critic, 26: 303–471. 27: 31–447.
— New Lights on. (W. V. Taylor) Sund. M. 23: 344.
— on the Future Life. Spec. 70: 283.
— Philosophy of. Time, 8: 53.
— Place of, in Poetry. (E. E. Hale, jr.) Dial (Ch.) 14: 101.
— Plays of, and Dramatic Sentiment. (L. J. Block) Poet-Lore, 8: 512.
— a Poem. (A. C. Swinburne) 19th Cent. 33: 1. Same art. Ecl. M. 120: 249.
— a Poem. (D. Beale) Spec. 69: 595.
— Poems, Art and Architecture in. Am. Arch. 38: 87.
— Poetical Tributes to. (T. H. Huxley; F. W. H. Myers and others) 19th Cent. 32: 831.
— Poetry of. Quar. 176: 1.
— — Romantic Elements in. (L. E. Gates) Harv. Mo. 15: 45.
— Portraits of. (T. Watts) M. of Art, 16: 37, 96.
— The Princess. Eng. R. 9: 286.
— Recollections of. (J. A. Symonds) Cent. 24: 32.
— Religion of. (W. H. Savage) Arena, 9: 582.
— Ruskin, and Browning, Ritchie on. Dial (Ch.) 13: 339.
— Sale of Birthplace of. Critic, 29: 149.
— Songs by. (L. J. Block) Poet-Lore, 7: 127.
— Study of, in Class. (H. M. Reynolds) Educa. 13: 359.
— Talks with. (A. G. Weld, jr.) Contemp. 63: 394. — (W. Ward) New R. 15: 76. Same art. Liv. Age, 210: 323. Same art. Ecl. M. 127: 317.
— Tennysoniana. Acad. 45: 57, 81. — Ath. '92, 2: 517, 741. — Critic, 21: 315. — Sund. M. 22: 50, 122, 201.
— Theology of. (E. Parsons) Meth. R. 54: 917. — Spec. 69: 642. Same art. Ecl. M. 119: 853.
— Trees and Flowers of. Temp. Bar, 103: 358. Same art. Ecl. M. 123: 783. Same art. Liv. Age, 23: 807.
— Tributes to. Dial (Ch.) 13: 265.
— Turncoat. (J. J. Davies) Westm. 142: 558.
— Ulysses, Literary Genealogy of. (A. S. Cook) Poet-Lore, 4: 499.
— Visit to. (W. J. Rolfe) Critic, 21: 285.
— The Voice of. (H. Van Dyke) Cent. 23: 539.
— Was he Consistent? (G. P. Lathrop) Am. Cath. Q. 18: 101.
Tennyson, A. Was he either Gnostic or Agnostic? Spec. 70: 10. Same art. Liv. Age, 196: 561.
— Waugh's Life of. (R. Le Gallienne) Acad. 42: 427. — Sat. R. 74: 473.
— Waugh's Study of. Spec. 70: 82. — Dial (Ch.) 14: 53. Same art. Liv. Age, 197: 18.
— Women of. (E. Parsons) Chaut. 23: 621.
— Works. Spec. 68: 201.
Tennyson's Pilgrimage. (M. D. Conway) Open Court, 6: 3455.
Tennyson, Emily, Lady. (T. Watts-Dunton) Ath. '96, 2: 227. (E. Parsons) Critic, 29: 149. (E. Parsons) Writer, 9: 125.
Tennysons, The, A Visit to, in 1839. (B. Teeling) Blackw. 155: 605. Same art. Ecl. M. 123: 79. — Liv. Age, 201: 536.
Tenth Wave, The; a drama. (V. Hunt) Eng. Illust. 11: 1175.
Tenures, Singular Ancient. (T. B. Trowsdale) Walford's Antiq. 3: 77, 240.
Terburg, Gerard. (T. Cole) Cent. 28: 377.
— Michel's. (P. Macnab) M. of Art, 11: 91.
Terence. Phormio, at Harvard. (F. G. Ireland) Educa. R. 8: 54.
Teresa, Santa. Lond. Q. 82: 288. Same art. Liv. Age, 203: 195.
— Graham's Life of. (W. Webster) Acad. 45: 491. — Church Q. 39: 30. — Sat. R. 78: 103. — Spec. 72: 792, 826. — Liv. Age, 203: 195. — (M. Chanler) Book R. 2: 153.
Terns of Little Green Island, Maine. (A. H. Norton) Science, 22: 91.
Terra Cotta, Characteristics of. (James Taylor) Archit. Rec. 1: 63.
— in Modern Buildings. (G. M. R. Twose) Engin. M. 8: 203.
— in New York City. (James Taylor) Archit. Rec. 2: 137.
Terra Incognita. (Agnes Repplier) Cosmopol. 20: 661.
Terrapin, Diamond-back. (D. B. Fitzgerald) Lippinc. 55: 241.
Terrible Devotion, The; a story. (P. Vernon) Argosy, 62: 466.
Terrible Experience of Plodkins. (R. Barr) Idler, 1: 159.
Terrible Piece of Nonsense, A; a story. (F. Lindsay) Belgra. 77: 150.
Terrier, Boston. (C. F. Leland) Outing, 23: 464.
Terriss, Ellaline, with portrait. Theatre, 37: 332.
Terriss, William. (H. Aspden) Theatre, 30: 243.
Terror, the, End of. (R. Wilson) Atlan. 76: 762.
Terry, Edward, with portrait. Theatre, 28: 47.
Terry, Ellen, with portraits. (E. M. McKenna) McClure, 2: 457. — Theatre, 34: 160.
— as Anne Oldfield. (A. Brereton) Theatre, 35: 21.
— as Queen Katharine. Theatre, 28: 101.
— — a sonnet. (T. Watts) M. of Art, 15: 309.
Terry, Fred. Four "Leading Men," a Comparative Estimate. (W. A. L. Bettany) Theatre, 29: 109.
Terry, Marion, as Mrs. Erlynne. Theatre, 28: 201.
Tertiary Floras of the Yellowstone National Park (F. H. Knowlton) Am. J. Sci. 152: 51.
Tertiary Geology of Calvert Cliffs, Md. (G. D. Harris) Am. J. Sci. 145: 21.
Tesla, Nikola, with portrait. Bk. News, 12: 311. — (W. T. Stephenson) Outl. 51: 384. — (N. W. Perry) Engin. M. 7: 779. — (T. C. Martin) Cent. 25: 582.
— and the Electrical Outlook. R. of Rs. (N. Y.) 12: 293.
— and his Works. (F. J. Patten) New Sci. R. 1: 81.
— Laboratory of, Burning of. (T. C. Martin) Engin. M. 9: 101.

Tesla Oscillator, The. (F. J. Patten) New Sci. R. **2**: 113.
— and other Inventions. (T. C. Martin) Cent. **27**: 916.
Test Case. (W. Laidlaw Peel) Longm. **21**: 165.
Testator, In Presence of a. (J. Schouler) Am. Law R. **26**: 857.
Testimony, Human, Value of, Fitzarthur on. Spec. **68**: 401.
Testing, Methods of. (G. C. Henning) Cassier, **6**: 497.
Testing Apparatus, New. (T. Gray) Cassier, **2**: 439.
Teton Dakota Ghost Story. (J. O. Dorsey) J. Am. Folk-Lore, **1**: 68.
Teton Folk-Lore. (J. O. Dorsey) J. Am. Folk-Lore, **2**: 133.
Teutonic Mythology. (F. Y. Powell) Folk-Lore, **1**: 118.
— Rydberg's. (W. W. Newell) J. Am. Folk-Lore, **2**: 244.
Tewfik Pacha, Recollections of. (E. Dicey) 19th Cent. **31**: 233. Same art. Ecl. M. **118**: 388. Same art. Liv. Age, **193**: 167.
Tewkesbury, England. (J. P. Brodhurst) M. of Art, **10**: 348.
Tewkesbury Abbey. (H. D. M. Spence) Good Words, **33**: 15, 111.
Texas. (S. B. Maxey) Harper, **87**: 561.
— Botanical Journey in. (E. N. Plank) Garden & F. **9**: 62–232.
— Botanical Notes from. (E. N. Plank) Garden & F. **6**: 15–313. **7**: 23–342. **8**: 72, 193.
— Clays of, and their Origin. (W. Kennedy) Science, **22**: 297.
— Native Sulphur in. (E. A. Smith) Science, n. s. **3**: 657.
— Plants of, Some. (J. Reverchon) Garden & F. **6**: 63.
— Ranch Life in, Jaques on. Sat. R. **78**: 162.
— Struggle of, for Independence. (W. H. Mayes) M. Am. Hist. **29**: 235. — (W. H. Mayes) Nat'l M. (N. Y. '91) **17**: 448.
"Texas." (N. Mackubin) Cent. **25**: 294.
Texas Legend; a story. (S. Crane) Eng. Illust. **15**: 271.
Text-book, Substitution of Teacher for. (J. M. Rice) Forum, **19**: 681.
Text-books, Why Teachers should go beyond. (S. T. Frost) Educa. **12**: 278.
Textile Fabrics, Egyptian, at South Kensington. (F. Fond) M. of Art, **12**: 132.
— Pattern Designing in, History of. (P. Schulze) J. Soc. Arts, **41**: 534.
— Tricks with. Econ. R. **4**: 318.
Textile Schools. Soc. Econ. **9**: 18.
Texts and Mottoes. Cornh. **68**: 52.
Texture, Functions of, in the Arts. (J. Brett) Art J. **45**: 117.
Thackeray, W. M. (H. Corkran) Temp. Bar, **103**: 551.
— Barry Lyndon, The Real. (W. E. G. Fisher) Eng. Illust. **14**: 625.
— Chapters from some Unwritten Memoirs. (Mrs. Ritchie) Macmil. **66**: 17.
— Dramatic Adaptations of Works of. (C. P. Johnson) Ath. '96, **2**: 107. — Ath. '92, **2**: 171.
— Genealogies of. (E. C. K. Gonner) Time, **20**: 501, 603.
— Illustrations of the Ballad of Lord Bateman. Harper, **86**: 124.
— Legal Career of. Green Bag, **7**: 372.
— Letter of, to Macready. Critic, **28**: 430.
— Letters of. (W. Sichel) Time, **18**: 19.
— Little Girl's Recollections of. (H. Corkran) Ecl. M. **124**: 345. Same art. Liv. Age, **204**: 311.
— London of. *See* London, Thackeray's.
— Morality of his Art. (C. W. Hutson) Educa. **12**: 531.
— Place of, in Literature. (F. Harrison) Forum, **18**: 326. — Sat. R. **78**: 553.
— Portraits of. (F. G. Kilton) M. of Art, **14**: 289.
Thackeray, W. M., Portraits of, by himself. (G. S. Layard) Liv. Age, **192**: 125.
— Reminiscences of. (F. St. J. Thackeray) Temp. Bar, **98**: 373. Same art. Ecl. M. **121**: 237. Same art. Liv. Age, **198**: 504.
— Scott, and Dickens: are they Obsolete? (W. H. Mallock) Forum, **14**: 503.
— Some Notes upon. (G. Fiennes) New R. **10**: 337, 499.
— A Study for Colonel Newcome. (J. W. Irvine) 19th Cent. **34**: 584. Same art. Liv. Age, **199**: 563. Same art. Ecl. M. **121**: 645.
— Thackerayana. (C. C. Harrison) Critic, **26**: 447. **27**: 80.
— Uncompleted Works of. (C. P. Johnson) Walford's Antiq. **8**: 81.
— Was he a Cynic? Time, **17**: 188.
Thackeray MS. in Harvard College Library. (T. R. Sullivan) Scrib. M. **14**: 281.
Thames Bridge. Am. Arch. **48**: 110.
Thames River. (A. Watson) M. of Art, **6**: 485. **7**: 107, 251. — (W. Taylor) Munsey, **7**: 444. — Time, **7**: 219.
— and its Poetry. (A. Lang) M. of Art, **5**: 377.
— Down, from Oxford to Moulsford. (A. Inkersley) Bach. of Arts, **3**: 195.
— Evenings on the. Time, **5**: 705.
— Father Thames; a story. (R. Penn) Theatre, **28**: 7.
— Fishing on. All the Year, **70**: 344.
— Henley Regatta Reach. (R. Mackenzie) Eng. Illust. **9**: 725.
— in Winter. Spec. **70**: 14. Same art. Liv. Age, **196**: 575.
— New River. Cornh. **68**: 249.
— On the. (R. Radclyffe) Time, **15**: 277.
— Revolution of. (J. W. Gregory) Nat. Sci. **5**: 97.
— Scenes along. (E. R. Pennell) Art J. **46**: 97.
— Shores of. (J. Penderel-Brodhurst) M. of Art, **7**: 452.
— Upper. (E. Boyer-Brown) Leis. Hour, **42**: 691.
— Watermen of. Chamb. J. **73**: 129.
Thamugas, the Numidian Pompeii. (N. G. Batt) Spec. **68**: 638.
Thanet, Octave (pseud.). *See* French, Alice.
Thankfulness. (E. J. Hardy) Good Words, **34**: 241.
Thanks of the Municipality, The; a story. (J. Barnes) Harper, **93**: 146.
Thanks to the Snake. (B. Patterson) Chamb. J. **71**: 525.
Thanksgiving at the Farm; a story. Cornh. **72**: 172.
Thanksgiving Breakfast, A; a story. (H. P. Spofford) Harper, **91**: 923.
Thanksgiving Day in the U. S., Beginnings of. (L. L. Gracey) Chaut. **16**: 174.
Thanksgiving Day's Bear Hunt. (H. S. Habersham) Outing, **21**: 116.
Thanksgiving Dinner, A. (B. Matthews) Harper, **88**: 28.
Thanksgiving Morn; a poem. (D. McCaig) Canad. M. **4**: 116.
Thanksgiving-time Fancies. Scrib. M. **18**: 557.
Tharmapala, the Buddhist. (Anna Ballard) Open Court, **10**: 5173.
That Beast "Beauty;" a cat story. (K. Hare) Idler, **3**: 96.
That Dog uv Seke Simmons. (J. A. Williams, jr.) Outing, **21**: 286.
That Fine Carriage; a story. (E. Whelpton) Sund. M. **22**: 464.
That Good may come. (E. Wharton) Scrib. M. **15**: 629.
That Heliograph! a story. (S. de Havilland) Belgra. **78**: Holiday no. 67.

That Insidious Game. Chamb. J. 71: 283.
That Night at Pukkapore. (G. B. Stuart) Argosy, 58: 427.
That Snipe. (T. C. James) Idler, 7: 72.
That There Mason; a story. (C. Russell) Idler, 8: 4.
That Wife of Mine; a story. (John Strange Winter) Idler, 8: 204.
Thaumasite, Occurrence of, at West Paterson, N. J. (S. L. Penfield and J. H. Pratt) Am. J. Sci. 151: 229.
Thaxter, Celia. (A. Fields) Atlan. 75: 254. — With portrait. Bk. News, 12: 343. — Critic, 25: 147. — Lit. W. (Bost.) 25: 280. — (G. S. Lee) Critic, 28: 209.
Theatre: Actor, the Manager, and the Public. (J. Malone) Forum, 20: 235.
— Amongst the "Gods." (M. Pemberton) Theatre, 29: 74.
— and Music-hall in England, Distinction between. Spec. 68: 673.
— at Bath, History of, Penley's. Sat. R. 74: 459.
— by Daylight. (H. S. Wilson) Gent. M. n. s. 54: 445. Same art. Ecl. M. 125: 37.
— The Church and. Sat. R. 81: 98.
— Duty of Church as to. (N. Hall and H. C. Shuttleworth) Chr. Lit. 11: 302.
— English, Five Years of Progress in. (W. A. L. Bettany) Theatre, 32: 239.
— French, Peculiarities of. (W. Thorpe) Theatre, 33: 51.
— How to enjoy the. (J. J. Wood) Theatre, 29: 15.
— in London. (G. S. Street) New R. 12: 547.
— — Outlook of, 1892. Sat. R. 74: 220.
— in Poland. Sat. R. 73: 385, 507, 737.
— Independent, in New York. (J. L. Ford) Lippinc. 49: 371.
— Municipal. (Sir H. Irving) Theatre, 33: 216.
— National, Functions of. (W. Poel) Theatre, 31: 162.
— of To-day. (C. Maynard) Cosmopol. 12: 725.
— Panic in, Gateshead, Eng., 1892. Spec. 68: 12.
— Parson, the Play, and the Ballet. (H. R. Haweis) Univ. R. 1: 248.
— Royalty, Reminiscences of. (F. C. Burnand) Univ. R. 2: 577.
— 16th Century Playhouse. (W. Archer) Univ. R. 1: 281.
— A Standard. (T. R. Sullivan) Atlan. 75: 686.
Theatre Libre of Paris. Sat. R. 79: 213.
Theatre-building for American Cities. (D. Adler) Engin. M. 7: 717–814.
Theatres. (E. A. E. Woodrow) Am. Arch. 50: 7, 51, 85.
— American. (H. Townsend) Am. Arch. 35: 28.
— and Opera Houses, The Grand. (P. Fitzgerald) Theatre, 33: 111.
— Architecture of. (E. A. E. Woodrow) Am. Arch. 44: 18, 59, 119. 45: 35, 71. 46: 24–124. 47: 15–132. 48: 36, 55. 49: 35, 118. — (G. Redon) M. of Art, 18: 129.
— Bad Air in. (C. S. Montgomery) Engin. M. 3: 190.
— Building, Regulations for. Am. Arch. 36: 38–103. 37: 22–118.
— Construction and Interior Arrangement of. (C. J. Hexamer) J. Frankl. Inst. 134: 43.
— Endowed, and the American Stage. (H. Modjeska) Forum, 14: 337.
— Fire in, Prevention of. (E. A. E. Woodrow) J. Soc. Arts, 40: 785.
— Laws affecting. (R. V. Rogers) Green Bag, 6: 259, 321, 376.
— London. Antiq. n. s. 30: 254.
Theatres, Early London, Ordish on. (G. M. Hyde) Dial (Ch.) 18: 47. — (E. K. Chambers) Acad. 48: 139. — Sat. R. 78: 462.
— — 1550–1650. (H. F. Randolph) New Eng. M. n. s. 10: 318.
— Literature on. (W. P. Gerhard) Am. Arch. 52: 124.
— Municipal. (W. H. Pollock) Theatre, 34: 15. — Sat. R. 81: 300.
— New York. (W. J. Henderson) M. of Art, 9: 401.
— — Week in. (J. G. Speed) Forum, 19: 118.
— On the Licensing of. (C. Dickens) Theatre, 34: 10.
— Safety in. (W. P. Gerhard) Am. Arch. 44: 133. 45: 4–25.
— Stages in. (E. O. Sachs) Am. Arch. 54: 97.
Theatrical Criticism, The Public and. (C. Dickens) Theatre, 33: 220.
Theatrical Illusion. (C. Dickens) Theatre, 35: 192.
Theatrical Managers, Policy of Leading. (W. A. L. Bettany) Theatre, 32: 182.
Theatrical Portraits in the Deanery of Hereford. (T. E. Pemberton) Theatre, 33: 235.
Theatrical Revolution; a story. Theatre, vols. 31–33.
Theatrical Season in New York. (J. S. Metcalfe) Cosmopol. 18: 279.
Theatrical World of 1894, Archer's. Sat. R. 79: 476.
Theatrical Year, 1891–92; a résumé. (W. D. Adams) Theatre, 29: 49.
Theatricals: Jullien's "La Comédie à la Court." M. of Art, 6: 524.
Thebes, Explorations at. (P. E. Newberry) Acad. 49: 513.
Their Christmas Meeting; a story. (F. W. Snedeker) Cent. 23: 305.
Their Cousin Lethy. (R. M. Johnston) Cent. 27: 467.
Their Exits and their Entrances. (G. A. Hibbard) Cent. 26: 75.
Their Journey's End. Cornh. 72: 288.
Their Last Race; a story. (F. Mathew) Idler, 2: 576.
Their Passport into Paradise; a story. (I. J. Armstrong) Eng. Illust. 14: 525.
Their Reason; a story. (N. Verne) Theatre, 30: 3.
Their Story. (G. A. Hibbard) Harper, 88: 756.
Their Wedding-day; a story. Chamb. J. 70: 190.
Theism. (J. M. Williams) Meth. R. 52: 89.
— and after. (E. D. Fawcett) Westm. 142: 446.
— as a Scientific Hypothesis. (J. S. Vaughan) Dub. R. 110: 52.
— Christian, Peerlessness of. (J. Cook) Our Day, 13: 133.
— Foundations of. (E. D. Cope) Monist, 3: 623.
— Philosophy of, Fraser on. (J. Seth) Philos. R. 5: 406.
— Recent Arguments for. (A. W. Benn) Acad. 45: 181.
— Theistic Argument of St. Thomas. (Brother Chrysostom) Philos. R. 3: 148.
Them Old Cheery Words; a poem. (J. W. Riley) Cent. 31: 294.
Theobald, Lewis, the Poison of Shaksperian Criticism. Quar. 175: 102.
Theocracy. Eng. R. 14: 150.
Theocritus. (J. Kendall) Poet-Lore, 7: 307.
Théodulfe, Bishop of Orleans. Church Q. 37: 377.
Theologian, Confessions of a. Arena, 6: 219.
Theological Education and its Needs. (C. A. Briggs) Forum, 12: 634.
— in England, Inadequacy of. (D. W. Simon) Our Day, 9: 15.
Theological Faculties, German, Signs of the Times in. (G. R. W. Scott) Our Day, 9: 155.
Theological Schools, Methodist. Meth. R. 56: 618.

Theological Seminaries, Improvement of. (C. F. Thwing; B. B. Warfield) Chr. Lit. 13: 135.
— Presbyterian, Methods of Control of. (W. H. Roberts) Presb. & Ref. R. 4: 94.
Theological Seminary, Relation of, to Previous Bible Study. (O. H. Gates) Bib. World, 8: 265.
Theological Teaching, Freedom of. (J. H. Ecob) New World, 4: 495.
Theology, Aims and Progress of. (J. S. Banks) Chr. Lit. 12: 94.
— Biblical: its History and its Mission. (G. H. Gilbert) Bib. World, 6: 358.
— — What it is, and its Method. (G. B. Stevens) Bib. World, 1: 5.
— Burlesque in. (R. Ogden) Nation, 54: 7.
— Christian, Gordon's. (A. H. Plumb) Bib. Sac. 53: 325.
— Christocentric Idea in. (J. W. Etter) Pub. Opin. 12: 408.
— Claims of, as a Study. (F. H. Foster) Overland, n. s. 22: 506.
— Current, and Reformed compared. (J. A. De Baun) Presb. & Ref. R. 7: 459.
— Decadence of. (J. Burroughs) No. Am. 156: 576.
— Dogmatic, Bavinck on. (G. Vos) Presb. & Ref. R. 7: 356.
— — Tanquerey's. (A. F. Hewit) Cath. World, 60: 611.
— German, Liberal and Ritschlian. And. R. 19: 44.
— — Our Relation to. (W. Rupp) Ref. Q. 40: 473.
— in Germany since Kant, Pfleiderer on. (C. C. Everett) Philos. R. 1: 88.
— in the University and the Seminary. (A. M. Fairbairn) Chr. Lit. 14: 169.
— Old, and the New Philosophy. (G. J. Low) Open Court, 9: 4734.
— Old Testament, Schultz on. Spec. 71: 371.
— Persistence of Dogmatic. (G. G. Greenwood) Westm. 144: 528.
— Planetary Limitations in. (F. Sewall) N. Church R. 1: 101.
— Present-day, Stearns on. (T. Nichols) Presb. & Ref. R. 5: 730.
— Progress in. (R. G. Hobbs) Meth. R. 55: 913.
— Rabbinic. (S. Schechter) Jew. Q. 8: 363.
— — Some Aspects of. (S. Schechter) Jew. Q. 6: 405, 633. 7: 195. 8: 1.
— Reason in, Place of. (H. C. Minton) Presb. & Ref. R. 7: 84.
— Recent Scientific. (H. G. Chapman) Bach. of Arts, 3: 55.
— Scholastic and Mystic, in the Middle Ages. (P. Schaff) Ref. Q. 40: 336.
— Scientific, and the Church of To-day. (O. Pfleiderer) And. R. 17: 133.
— Scientific Study of, Cox on. Spec. 71: 336.
— Sociology and. (C. R. Henderson) Am. J. Sociol. 1: 381.
— Strong's Manual of. Church Q. 35: 281.
— Studies in, Denny's. Church Q. 40: 479. — (J. Laidlaw) Crit. R. 5: 150.
— Systematic. (B. B. Warfield) Presb. & Ref. R. 7: 242.
— — Miley's. (J. L. Girardeaux) Presb. and Ref. R. 6: 172.
— — Nature and Scope of. (D. W. Simon) Bib. Sac. 51: 587.
— — Right of. (B. B. Warfield) Presb. & Ref. R. 7: 412.
— Thoroughness in. (R. A. Armstrong) New World, 2: 709.
Theories, Architecture of. (C. S. Peirce) Monist, 1: 161.
Theories carried into Practice. Econ. R. 3: 23.
Theory and Practice. (H. Sidgwick) Mind, 20: 370.
— Logical, Present Position of. (J. Dewey) Monist, 2: 1.
— Pure, A Plea for. (W. Cunningham) Econ. R. 2: 25.
Theosophical Society, The. (W. F. Kirby) Time, 12: 47.
— True Story of, Olcott's. Sat. R. 81: 378.
Theosophy. (J. M. Thoburn) Meth. R. 52: 530. — Month, 74: 1.
— and its Evidences. (W. D. Strappini) Dub. R. 110: 337.
— and Protestantism. (F. B. Doherty) Cath. World, 61: 182.
— Marvels of. Month, 74: 173.
— Modern, in its Relation to Hinduism and Buddhism. (M. M. Snell) Bib. World, 5: 200, 258.
— Mueller's Gifford Lectures. (A. Macalister) Crit. R. 3: 255. — Sat. R. 75: 467.
— New Religion. (E. D. Walker) Arena, 7: 213.
— Progress of, in the United States. (E. T. Hargrove) No. Am. 162: 698.
— Recent, in its Antagonism to Christianity. (W. J. Lhamon) And. R. 19: 570.
— Scientific. (J. R. Buchanan) Arena, 15: 59, 425.
— True Character of. Month, 74: 321.
— What it is. (Annie Besant) Outl. 48: 665.
Thera, Vases from. (C. Torr) Acad. 42: 177.
Theralite in Costa Rica, Central America, Occurrence of. (J. E. Wolff) Am. J. Sci. 151: 271.
Therapeutics. Limitations of the Healing Art. (H. Nothnagel) Pop. Sci. Mo. 41: 77.
— Suggestion in. (W. R. Newbold) Pop. Sci. Mo. 49: 342.
There is Sorrow on the Sea; a Lincolnshire story. (G. Parker) Idler, 7: 297.
There was a Little City; a story. (G. Parker) New R. 12: 589.
Thermal Expansion, Effect of Residual Viscosity on. (H. D. Day) Am. J. Sci. 152: 342.
Thermodynamic Law, Graphics of. (R. H. Thurston) J. Frankl. Inst. 141: 27.
Thermodynamics, Graphical. (R. de Saussure) Am. J. Sci. 149: 21.
Thermo-electrics, Elementary Expression in. (C. Barus) Am. J. Sci. 147: 366.
Thermo-metamorphism in Scotland. (G. Barrow) Nat. Sci. 4: 198.
Thermometer, Evolution of. (G. T. Holloway) Sci. Prog. 4: 413.
— Volume Measurement of an Air Thermometer Bulb. (W. G. Cady) Am. J. Sci. 152: 341.
Thermophone, The. (G. C. Whipple) Science, n. s. 2: 639.
These Streams of Life; a poem. (J. H. Bryant) Cosmopol. 19: 660.
Thessalonica. (E. D. Burton) Bib. World, 8: 10.
Thessaly, Mid-winter in. (Sir H. Maxwell) Blackw. 153: 412. Same art. Liv. Age, 197: 422.
Thetford Abbey, Escutcheons in. Walford's Antiq. 1: 252.
Thetis, U. S. S., Arctic Cruise, 1889. (Chas. S. Stockton) Nat. Geog. M. 2: 171.
Thiarthrus, Thoracic Legs of. (C. E. Beecher) Am. J. Sci. 146: 467.
Thibet. *See* Tibet.
Thiébault, Paul, Général. Ed. R. 181: 429.
— Memoirs. (A. Laugel) Nation, 57: 368. 59: 321, 339. 61: 425, 445. — Sat. R. 82: 424. — Acad. 50: 418.

Thief, Repentant, on the Cross. (W. E. Barton) Bib. Sac. 53: 100.
Thiers, L. A. Spec. 69: 290.
— redivivus. (H. von Holst) Nation, 60: 108, 127.
— Rémusat's. (F. T. Marzials) Acad. 41: 535.
Thieves, Making of, in New York. (J. A. Riis) Cent. 27: 109.
Thing, Origin of a, and its Nature. (J. M. Baldwin) Psychol. R. 2: 551.
Things in Themselves, Are there? (P. Carus) Monist, 2: 225.
Things Together, Knowing of. (W. James) Psychol. R. 2: 105.
Thinking all over. (Paul Tyner) New Sci. R. 2: 203.
— Some Curiosities of. (M. A. Starr) Pop. Sci. Mo. 46: 721.
Third Finger of the Right Hand; a story. Argosy, 53: 151.
Third Relief, The. (G. I. Putnam) Scrib. M. 16: 629.
Third Time of Asking. (M. E. Francis) Longm. 26: 389. Same art. Liv. Age, 206: 657.
Third Traveller, The; a story. Argosy, 62: 682.
Thirlmere Scheme, The. Chamb. J 71: 705.
Thirlwall, Bishop, and the Irish Church Bill of 1869. (W. Alexander) National, 25: 81.
Thirsk, Railroad Accident at. Sat. R. 74: 561.
Thirteen Club. Spec. 72: 82.
Thirteenth Brydain, The; a story. (M. Moule) All the Year, 70: 210—71: 42.
Thirteenth Guest, The; a story. (A. H. Drury) Argosy, 60: 609, 680.
Thirteenth of February, The; a story. (E. Allbutt) Belgra. 90: 180.
Thirty-nine Articles, Gibson's. Church Q. 42: 391.
Thirty-shilling Pieces, Plea for. (J. Evans) Longm. 21: 47.
Thistle, Russian, So-called. (C. E. Bessey) Am. Natural. 28: 427.
Thlinkets of Alaska. (A. M. Bugbee) Overland, n. s. 22: 185.
Thom, Rev. John Hamilton. (M. Cholmondeley) Temp. Bar, 103: 479.
Thomas Aquinas, St., Political Theories of. (A. J. Carlyle) Scot. R. 27: 126.
— Theistic Argument of. Philos. R. 3: 148.
— Theories of, on Church and State. (R. W. Carlyle) Econ. R. 6: 76.
Thomas à'Becket. Eng. R. 6: 37, 370.
— Ancient Offices of. (F. E. Gilliat-Smith) Dub. R. 114: 22.
— An Episode in the Life of. (E. Venables) Macmil. 69: 49.
— The Real. (A. Lambert) 19th Cent. 33: 273.
— Sermons for the Festivals of. (W. D. Macray) Eng. Hist. R. 8: 85.
Thomas, Arthur Goring. Ath. '92, 1: 413.—Sat. R. 73: 358.
Thomas, Charles Louis Ambroise. Critic, 28: 130.—(J. A. F. Maitland) Theatre, 36: 140.
Thomas, Edith, Blind-mute, Anagnos on. Lend a H. 14: 372.
Thomas, Edith M. Bk. Buyer, 2: 129.—With portrait. (R. H. Stoddard) Bk. Buyer, 5: 56.
Thomas, Ernest Chester. (J. S. Cotton) Acad. 41: 206.
Thomas, Frederick, Medallion Portraits by, on the National Portrait Gallery. M. of Art, 18: 429.
Thomas, Gen. G. H., Coppée's Life of. (J. D. Cox) Nation, 58: 125.
— Piatt and Boynton's. (J. D. Cox) Nation, 57: 332, 351.
— Piatt's Life of. (A. C. McClurg) Dial (Ch.) 17: 36.
Thomas, Capt. John, of Braintree. (J. W. Porter) N. E. Reg. 49: 172.
Thomas, Sidney Gilchrist. (A. G. Bartley) Acad. 41: 160.
Thomas, Theodore, in Chicago. Music, 1: 81.
Thomas and the Elf Queen; a poem. Folk-Lore Rec. 2: 165.
Thomas Cathro's Clock. Macmil. 73: 321. Same art. Liv. Age, 209: 12.
Thomas of Parkworth's. (C. H. Chase) New Eng. M. n. s. 11: 628.
Thomas the Rhymer. Chamb. J. 69: 481.
Thomason, James. (J. W. Sherer) Macmil. 68: 269.
Thompson, Basil, as Prime Minister of the Friendly Islands. Sat. R. 79: 101.
Thompson, Benjamin. *See* Rumford, Count.
Thompson, Mrs. Bowen. (A. R. Buckland) Sund. M. 24: 462.
Thompson, David. (C. H. McIntosh) Canad. M. 8: 150.
Thompson, Elizabeth. *See* Butler, Elizabeth.
Thompson, Francis. (A. McC. Sholl) Bach. of Arts, 2: 625.—With portrait. Bk. Buyer, 11: 298.—Church Q. 39: 457.
— a New Poet. (C. Patmore) Fortn. 61: 19.
— Poems. (H. D. Traill) 19th Cent. 35: 229.—Ath. '94, 1: 143.—(G. R. Tomson) Acad. 45: 302.—Liv. Age, 203: 403.
— Sister-songs. Sat. R. 80: 16.
— a Study in Temperament. Lond. Q. 83: 25. Same art. Liv. Age, 203: 403.
Thompson, Sir Henry, and the Vegetarians. (H. S. Salt) Time, 14: 61.
Thompson, Jacob. (L. Jewitt) M. of Art, 4: 32.
Thompson, Sir John. (O. A. Howland) Canad. M. 5: 420.—With portrait. (J. A. J. McKenna) Cath. World, 60: 816.
— and his Critics. (T. L. P. O'Hanly) Canad. M. 1: 413.
— a Poem. (A. M. Belding) Canad. M. 4: 536.
Thompson, Dr. Mary. (J. Visher) Lend a H. 16: 45.
Thompson, Maurice, with portrait. Bk. News, 10: 349.
Thompson, William Hale, with portrait. Nat'l M. (N. Y. '91) 16: 345.
Thompson, Rev. William Hepworth. (P. Fitzgerald) Gent. M. n. s. 48: 600.
Thompson, William P., with portrait. (L. A. Bond) Nat'l M. (N. Y. '91) 18: 72.
Thompson, Wordsworth. (E. King) Mo. Illust. 4: 131.
Thompson, Zadoc, with portrait. Pop. Sci. Mo. 46: 262.
Thompson Family of Connecticut. (Mrs. M. Richardson) Am. Hist. Reg. 3: 481.
Thomson, David, Widow of. (F. W. Hackett) N. E. Reg. 47: 76.
Thomson, Hugh, with portrait. Bk. Buyer, 13: 148.
Thomson, Humphry. Passages from an Autobiography. (E. Dowden) Fortn. 60: 425.
Thomson, James; a Poet of the Woods. (H. Haliburton) Good Words, 34: 467.
— Seasons, Interleaved Copy of. (D. C. Tovey) Ath. '94, 2: 131.
Thomson, James ("B. V."), Poetry of. Sat. R. 79: 215.
Thomson, James, Prof. Nature, 46: 129.
Thomson, Joseph. Acad. 48: 110.—Ath. '95, 2: 195.—(J. W. Gregory) Nature, 52: 440.—With portrait. (E. G. Ravenstein) Geog. J. 6: 289.
Thomson, William, Archbishop, Bullock's. Quar. 174: 287.

Thoreau, Henry David. (B. Torrey) Atlan. 78: 822. — Belgra. 81: 375. — (G. Stewart) Canad. M. 4: 101. — (C. C. Abbott) Lippinc. 55: 852.
— and Thomas Cholmondeley. (F. B. Sanborn) Atlan. 72: 741.
— as a Prose Writer. (H. M. Stanley) Dial (Ch.) 21: 179.
– Correspondence with Emerson. (F. B. Sanborn) Atlan. 69: 577, 736.
— Familiar Letters; ed. by Sanborn. (L. J. Block) Dial (Ch.) 17: 228.
— Poems of Nature. Sat. R. 81: 55. — (F. B. Sanborn) Scrib. M. 17: 352.
Thorgils, Voyage of, along Coast of Greenland, 1000 A. D. (B. F. DeCosta) Nat'l M. (N. Y. '91) 16: 38.
Thorium, a Rare Metal. (T. L. Phipson) Knowl. 19: 140.
Thorn in the Flesh; a story. Cornh. 68: 623.
Thorns, North American. (T. Meehan) Garden & F. 7: 292, 312.
— of Plants. (H. Coupin) Pop. Sci. Mo. 46: 433.
Thornton, James Howard. Memories of Seven Campaigns. Sat. R. 80: 661.
Thornton, William. (Glenn Brown) Archit. Rec. 6: 53.
Thornton Abbey, Lincolnshire. Reliquary, 36: 1.
Thornycroft, Hamo. (E. W. Gosse) M. of Art, 4: 328.
Thornycroft, John I. (C. J. Cornish) Cassier, 9: 398.
Thornycroft, Mrs. Mary. (F. G. Stephens) M. of Art, 18: 305.
Thornycroft, Thomas, House of. (H. Zimmern) M. of Art, 6: 512.
Thorold, Anthony W., Bishop of Winchester. (A. C. E. Thorold) Sund. M. 24: 620.
— at Farnham Castle. Sund. M. 22: 247.
— Day with, at Selsdon Park. (E. A. Parry) Good Words, 37: 467.
— Simpkinson's. Church Q. 43: 51.
Thorwaldsen, Albert Bertel. (C. S. Johnson) Munsey, 9: 293.
Those Souvenir Spoons; a story. (M. Sidney) Harper, 85: 568.
"Though One rose from the Dead;" a story. ("Rita") Belgra. 79: Christmas no. 85.
Thought and Action, Unity of. Westm. 140: 407. Same art. Ecl. M. 121: 685.
— and Language. (F. M. Müller) Monist, 1: 572.
— — F. M. Müller on. (G. J. Romanes) Monist, 2: 56.
— and Thing, Unity of. (R. Lewins) Monist, 4: 208.
— before Language: Deaf-mute's Recollections. (W. James) Philos. R. 1: 613.
— Conflict between the Old and New in. (H. Höffding) Int. J. Ethics, 6: 322.
— Dread of. Spec. 69: 442. Same art. Ecl. M. 119: 711.
— Free, Stages of. (G. J. Holyoake) Open Court, 10: 4880, 4888.
— in America, Future of. (E. D. Cope) Monist, 3: 23.
— Mechanism of. (A. Binet) Fortn. 61: 785. Same art. Ecl. M. 123: 174.
— Nature of. (P. Carus) Open Court, 3: 2009. — (T. Whittaker) Monist, 5: 104.
— the Parent of Originality. (M. E. Cole) Open Court, 1: 743.
— The Simplicity of. (F. M. Müller) Open Court, 1: 337, 365.
— Thicker than Blood. (F. M. Müller) Open Court, 3: 2043.
— Transference of, Experiments in. (E. M. Sedgwick) New R. 7: 306.
— Transitional Eras in. (A. C. Armstrong, jr.) New World, 4: 484.
Thought-Conception. (C. S. Wake) Open Court, 7: 3682.
Thought-Transference, Podmore on. Sat. R. 78: 435.
Thoughts, Free. (F. L. Oswald) Open Court, 1: 433.
Thousand Isles. (F. W. Falls) Canad. M. 4: 148.
— Trolling among. (A. R. Carrman) Outing, 24: 366.
Thread, Spool of. (H. Hendry) Good Words, 34: 757.
Thread of Mystery, A; a story. (L. D. Mitchell) Outing, 27: 372.
Three and Seven: Mystic Numbers. (A. Gaye) National, 21: 196. Same art. Liv. Age, 197: 666.
Three to One; a story. Idler, 1: 275.
Three-bottle Comedy. (W. E. Norris) Longm. 22: 532. Same art. Liv. Age, 199: 584.
Three Cameos. (G. W. Steevens) New R. 14: 76. Same art. Ecl. M. 126: 304.
Three Chancellors, The. (T. Barth) New R. 11: 557.
Three Chapters; a story. (G. B. Stanton) Cosmopol. 18: 739.
Three Cigarettes; a story. (G. Fosbery) Argosy, 56: 435.
Three Commandments in the Vulgar Tongue. (G. Parker) Atlan. 73: 615.
Three Fates. (V. Woods) Lippinc. 56: 818.
Three Fates. (F. M. Crawford) Longm. 19: 225–577.
Three Fives; a Texan Romance. (C. Logsdail) Canad. M. 1: 147.
Three Gentlewomen and a Lady; a story. (M. J. Judah) Arena, 8: 756.
Three Hours Late; a story. (A. E. Ferris) Overland, n. s. 19: 602.
Three in Green; a story. (Gertrude Hall) Cosmopol. 21: 528.
Three in Paradise; a story. (I. Gilchrist) Gent. M. n. s. 57: 217.
Three Men and Two Bears; a story. (C. Warman) McClure, 4: 193.
Three-mile Run, A; a story. (W. Hendrick) Outing, 20: 403.
Three Miraculous Soldiers; a story. (S. Crane) Eng. Illust. 15: 104.
Three Moods of Midnight; poem. (G. Pellew) Cosmopol. 13: 528.
Three Old Sisters, The, and the Old Beau; a story. (M. E. Wilkins) Harper, 92: 854.
Three Shots at a Sunbeam; a poem. (G. M. Whicher) Educa. 16: 169.
Three-stranded Yarn, A; a story. (W. C. Russell) Cosmopol. 18: 356. 19: 57–547.
Three Travellers. (W. W. Fries) Arena, 16: 796.
Three Travellers; a poem. (J. V. Cheney) Cosmopol. 17: 160.
Three-Volume Novel, A. (A. Hope) Eng. Illust. 12: no. 1, 65.
Three-Volume Novel, The. (R. Ogden) Nation, 59: 115.
Thrift, Economic Direction of. (W. Aldrich) Soc. Econ. 5: 36.
— in Great Britain. (R. Hamilton) Econ. J. 2: 290.
"Thrift;" a story. All the Year, 75: 610.
Thrift; a story. (L. Dougall) Atlan. 76: 217.
Thring, Edward. (G. W. Brooks) Educa. 14: 6.
Thring Museum. Sat. R. 77: 550.
Through the Gate of Tears; a story. Cornh. 73: 284.
Through the Ranks; a story. (Mrs. Leith-Adams) All the Year, 73: 217–625. 74: 19, 45.
Through the Windows: Two Glimpses of a Man's Life. (F. E. Lester) Atlan. 75: 785.
Throwing the Fifty-six Pound Weight. (M. W. Ford) Outing, 21: 29.
Thucydides. Spec. 72: 54.
— Book III.; ed. by Spratt. Sat. R. 81: 486.
— Grote's Interpretation of ἀνέλπιστοι. (W. S. Scarborough) Educa. 12: 286.

Thuenen, H. J. von. On Theory of Natural Wages. (H. L. Moore) Q. J. Econ. **9**: 291, 388.
Thule and the Tin Islands. (T. H. B. Graham) Gent. M. n. s. **51**: 176.
Thulstrup, Thure de, with portrait. Bk. Buyer, **12**: 439. — (P. Maxwell) Q. Illust. **1**: 48.
Thumann, Paul. (G. L. Carey) Chaut. **16**: 65.
Thumb — the Sign of Contempt. All the Year, **76**: 42.
Thumb-books. Sat. R. **77**: 361.
Thumb-nail Sketches. (G. W. Edwards) Cent. **22**: 457, 756.
Thumb Notes. Chamb. J. **68**: 797.
Thunder. (A. L. Alger) Pop. Sci. Mo. **43**: 651.
Thunder Storm, The; a poem. (H. M. Chadwick) Educa. **16**: 49.
Thunderbolt of the Assyrians, The. (E. Bonavia) Acad. **47**: 405.
Thunderbolt's Mate; a story. (E. W. Hornung) Chamb. J. **69**: 154–200.
Thurloe, John, Secretary. Macmil. **70**: 291. Same art. Liv. Age, **202**: 707.
Thurlow, Edward, Lord. (W. P. Courtney) Temp. Bar, **107**: 25. Same art. Liv. Age, **208**: 195.
Thurneysen and Havet, Law of, Establishment and Extension of. (L. Horton-Smith) Am. J. Philol. **17**: 172.
Thurston, Robert H. Cassier, **1**: 36.
Thynne, William. (J. Maskell) Walford's Antiq. **8**: 1–295.
Thyroid Gland, Diseases of, New Departure in Treatment of. Chamb. J. **70**: 273.
Tiahanuaco, Ruined Cities of. (A. H. Keane) Acad. **44**: 36.
Tiara in the Louvre, The Disputed. (S. Reinach) Nation, **63**: 157.
Tiber River, The. (W. Davies) M. of Art, **9**: 133, 196.
Tibet. All the Year, **70**: 300.
— Among People of. (I. I. Bishop) Leis. Hour, **42**: 238–450.
— and Central Asia, Travels in. Church Q. **39**: 55.
— Attack on. (D. G. Whitley) Gent. M. n. s. **54**: 618. Same art. Liv. Age, **206**: 218.
— Bishop's Among the Tibetans. Around World, **2**: 4.
— Bonvalot's. Sat. R. **73**: 338. — Ath. '92, **1**: 144.
— Bower's Diary of a Journey across. (A. C. Coolidge) Nation, **59**: 88. — Sat. R. **78**: 23.
— Driven out of. (W. W. Rockhill) Cent. **25**: 877.
— An Englishwoman in. (A. R. Taylor) National, **22**: 25. Same art. Liv. Age, **199**: 422. Same art. Ecl. M. **121**: 598.
— Folk Songs of Ladak and Baltistan. Dub. R. **114**: 433.
— Flora of Central. Garden & F. **7**: 263.
— A Hermit Nation. Chamb. J. **70**: 677.
— Journey across. (H. Bower) Geog. J. **1**: 385. — (St. G. R. Littledale) Geog. J. **7**: 453.
— Knight on. Dial (Ch.) **15**: 9.
— Lansdell's Ride to Little. Geog. J. **3**: 119. — Chamb. J. **71**: 81. — All the Year, **74**: 29.
— Literature of. (A. W. Croft) Acad. **42**: 174.
— Macaulay Mission. (J. H. Ryley) Time, **19**: 75.
— Map of. (J. T. Walker) Geog. J. **4**: 52.
— New British Markets in. (C. E. D. Black) 19th Cent. **38**: 247.
— Occult Science in. (H. Hensoldt) Arena, **10**: 181, 366, 648.
— Pratt's. Spec. **68**: 885.
— Some Notes on. (Annie R. Taylor) National, **23**: 81. Same art. Liv. Age, **201**: 41.
— South-eastern, Habits of Natives of. Dub. R. **112**: 449.
Tibet, Travels in. Ed. R. **175**: 540.
Tibetan Books. (A. Croft) Acad. **48**: 75.
Tibetan House-demon. (L. A. Waddell) Anthrop. J. **24**: 39.
Tibullus at his Farm. (E. M. Cesaresco) Contemp. **69**: 106. Same art. Liv. Age, **208**: 430.
Tichborne Case, A French. Chamb. J. **71**: 93.
Tick Island, Supplementary Investigation at. (C. B. Moore) Am. Natural. **26**: 568.
Ticking of the Clock. (Mrs. A. Baldwin) Longm. **24**: 275. Same art. Liv. Age, **202**: 310.
Ticknor, Anna, and her Study at Home. Lit. W. (Bost.) **27**: 346.
Ticks. (A. D. Michael) Nat. Sci. **1**: 200.
Tick Pest in the Tropics. (C. A. Barber) Nature, **52**: 197.
Ticonderoga. Un. Serv. (Phila.) **15**: 340.
— Battle of. (J. G. Nicolay) Chaut. **15**: 143. — Macmil. **73**: 281. Same art. Liv. Age, **208**: 611.
Tidal Wave in Japan, 1896. *See* Japan.
Tides, Fisher's New Hypothesis of. (G. F. Becker) Am. J. Sci. **146**: 137.
— Power from the. (G. E. Walsh) No. Am. **161**: 509.
— Rigidity and the Earth's Age. (O. Fisher) Am. J. Sci. **145**: 464.
Tidiness. Liv. Age, **204**: 61. — Spec. **73**: 807.
Tie that binds; a Christmas Play. Bost. **3**: 276.
Tiemann's to Tubby Hook. (H. C. Bunner) Scrib. M. **14**: 177.
Tientsin, English at, 1860–62. (W. H. James) Un. Serv. M. **11**: 175.
Tiepolo, Giambattista. (L. Villari) M. of Art, **19**: 452.
Tierra del Fuego. (D. R. O'Sullivan) Fortn. **59**: 36. Same art. Liv. Age, **196**: 472.
Tierreich, Das. Nat. Sci. **8**: 305.
Tietjen, Friedrich. Nature, **52**: 320.
Tiffin, Edward. (I. Smucker) Nat'l M. (N. Y. '91) **16**: 672.
Tiflis. (W. B. Harris) National, **26**: 827. Same art. Liv. Age, **208**: 549.
Tiger trapped. (R. Baum) Lippinc. **52**: 503.
Tiger-hunt. (J. H. Porter) Outing, **26**: 3.
— in Borneo. (J. T. Van Gestel) Lippinc. **58**: 382.
— in Nepaul. (E. N. Braddon) Sat. R. **80**: 373–403.
— Malay. (J. H. Porter) Outing, **28**: 368.
Tiger Hunting and Snipe Hunting in India. Blackw. **152**: 528.
— in India. (J. H. Porter) Outing, **28**: 140.
— in Mysore. (R. C. Woodville) Harper, **85**: 706.
Tiger-lion and Lion-tiger Hybrids. (V. Ball) Nature, **47**: 390.
Tiger Skin, The. (E. L. Hall) Bach. of Arts, **3**: 755.
Tigers: how they are hunted and killed. Chamb. J. **71**: 781.
Tiglath-Pileser, Jareb, and Pul. (J. Horner) Meth. R. **54**: 928.
Tilden, Lieutenant John Bell, Extracts from Journal of, 1781–2. (J. B. T. Phelps) Pennsyl. M. **19**: 51–208.
Tilden, Samuel J. (J. C. Carter) Atlan. **70**: 433.
— as a Lawyer, with portrait. (A. O. Hall) Green Bag, **7**: 49.
— Bigelow's Life of. (E. G. Johnson) Dial (Ch.) **18**: 291. — (J. D. Cox) Nation, **60**: 385. — (E. M. Shepard) Am. Hist. R. **1**: 174.
Tilden Trust and why it failed. (J. L. High) Atlan. **72**: 481.
Tilden Trust Library. Critic, **21**: 125. — Gent. M. n. s. **49**: 640. — (J. Bigelow) Lib. J. **17**: 378. — Lib. J. **17**: 484.
— and the New York City Hall. Lib. J. **18**: 77.

Tilden Trust Library, Proposed Location of. Garden & F. **5**: 421.
— What shall it be? (John Bigelow) Scrib. M. **12**: 287.
Tiles, Artistic. (L. F. Day) Art J. **47**: 343.
Tiles, Stamped, from Argive Heræum. (R. B. Richardson) Am. J. Archæol. **9**: 340.
Tilford, Frank, with portrait. (T. Johnson) Nat'l M. (N. Y. '91) **16**: 359.
Till Death — and After; a tale. (W. Richards) Belgra. **91**: 258.
Tillage, Ethics of. (P. H. Bryce) Canad. M. **1**: 460.
Tim Slather's Ride. (G. P. Hurst) Overland, n. s. **25**: 37.
Timber, Culture of, Notes on. (F. A. Waugh) Garden & F. **8**: 502.
— Hard-wood, in the South. (C. Mohr) Garden & F. **6**: 21.
— Problem of, in the South. (C. Mohr) Engin. M. **4**: 685.
— Strength of, Coefficients for Transverse. (F. E. Kidder) Am. Arch. **44**: 121.
— Tests of, Government. Am. Arch. **50**: 101.
Timber-cruiser, The. (J. Chambers) Cent. **25**: 671.
Timber-supply of the U. S. (C. S. Sargent) Garden & F. **6**: 181.
Timbuctoo. Chamb. J. **73**: 797.
— the Mysterious. Spec. **77**: 934.
Time and Common Sense; a Dialogue. (H. Sidgwick) Mind, **19**: 441.
— and Consciousness. (C. A. Strong) Psychol. R. **3**: 149.
— and the Hegelian Dialectic. (J. E. McTaggart) Mind, **18**: 490. **19**: 190.
— and Space as Mere Ideas. (P. Carus) Open Court, **3**: 1600.
— and the Succession of Events. (J. L. McIntyre) Mind, **20**: 334.
— Divining the. Spec. **69**: 315.
— Infinite Divisibility of. (J. Shaw) Good Words, **36**: 235.
— Infinitesimal, Phenomena of. (E. L. Nichols) Nature, **49**: 113.
— Measurement of; a Historical Study. (J. F. Hewitt) Westm. **146**: 23, 117.
Time Machine, The; a story. (H. G. Wells) New R. **12**: 98-577.
Time Observations with Transit Instrument. (C. B. Hill) Astron. **12**: 212.
Time-process, Metaphysics of the. (F. C. S. Schiller) Mind, **20**: 36.
Time-service of Harvard College Observatory. (E. C. Pickering) Science, **19**: 87.
Time Standard, Use of a Free Pendulum as. (T. C. Mendenhall) Am. J. Sci. **143**: 85.
Time Standards of Europe. (H. R. Mill) Nature, **46**: 174.
Time-stars, Groups of, for Amateur Astronomers. (E. Iliff and L. Waterbury) Pop. Astron. **2**: 74.
Timely. (H. C. Stickney) Lippinc. **57**: 859.
Time's Prisoner; a poem. (L. C. Moulton) Cosmopol. **15**: 749.
Times, The. *See* London Times.
Timon to the Athenians; a poem. (E. M. Thomas) Cosmopol. **18**: 14.
Tin, Mine of, in California. (E. Knight) Overland, n. s. **19**: 169.
— World's Store of. (E. W. Claypole) Engin. M. **2**: 435.
Tin Mine, Story of a. Macmil. **73**: 435.
Tin-mines, Cornish. Chamb. J. **70**: 470.
Tin-plate Industry in England, Decline of. Sat. R. **82**: 435.
Tin-plates, American. Am. Arch. **37**: 190.
Tinaja Bonita, La; a story. (O. Wister) Harper, **90**: 859.
Tinatotherium Beds, The. (J. B. Hutcher) Am. Natural. **27**: 204.
Tinctumutation. *See* Color, Change of.
Tinnie, a Study in Philanthrophy. (A. B. Paine) Overland, n. s. **26**: 275.
Tintagel; a poem. (H. F. Wilson) M. of Art, **15**: 272.
Tintern Abbey; a poem. (H. J. Green) Belgra. **87**: 429.
Tintometer, The. Chamb. J. **73**: 85.
— Lovibond's, Scientific Value of. (F. W. Edridge-Green) J. Soc. Arts, **40**: 213.
Tintoretto. (W. J. Stillman) Cent. **22**: 742.
Tinworth, George. (C. Monkhouse) M. of Art, **6**: 340.
Tio Juan; a story. (M. Kingsley) Harper, **86**: 386.
Tipping. Idler, **3**: 674.
— Economic Effects of. Gunton's M. **11**: 13.
Tipú Sultan, Bowring's. Sat. R. **77**: 202.
Tiryns, Schliemann's Discoveries at. (K. Blind) Time, **12**: 143.
'T is he that striveth not, is dead; a poem. (C. H. Page) Cosmopol. **21**: 543.
"'T is Love that makes the World go round;" a story. (E. Davies) Argosy, **59**: 375.
Tissandier, Gaston. (R. H. Sherard) McClure, **4**: 493.
Tisserand, François Felix. Nature, **54**: 628.
Tissington MSS. and Rebellion of 1745. (R. M. Grier) Antiq. n. s. **30**: 22, 62.
Tissot, James, and his Life of Christ. (R. H. Sherard) M. of Art, **18**: 1.
— Illustrations of the Gospels. (T. Stanton) Cent. **26**: 244.
— Paintings of Christ. (S. Beale) Am. Arch. **52**: 102.
Tit for Tat; a story. All the Year, **74**: 330.
Tithe Acts, The Church and the. (H. R. Farquharson) National, **26**: 379.
Tithe Redemption: a Solution. (C. Reade) National, **28**: 139.
Tithes in England and Wales. (R. Brown, Jr.) Pol. Sci. Q. **7**: 244.
— Question of, in Wales. (A. Griffith-Boscawen) National, **22**: 97.
Titian. (W. J. Stillman) Cent. **21**: 576. — (W. Bayliss) M. of Arts, **5**: 550.
— Lafenestre's. (J. Cartwright) M. of Art, **10**: 242.
— Madonna in the Hermitage: is it by Giorgione or Titian? (C. Phillips) M. of Art, **18**: 347.
— Summer Pilgrimage of. (L. E. Baxter) M. of Art, **16**: 29.
Title-page, The. Gent. M. n. s. **48**: 107.
— History of. (Alfred W. Pollard) Univ. R. **4**: 205, 357.
— Wanted, a Book for a. (G. S. Layard) Good Words, **37**: 32.
Title-pages, Spurious. Bookworm, **2**: 24.
Titles of Honor. (W. Everett) New Eng. M. n. s. **13**: 60. — Spec. **72**: 647.
Titmice. Spec. **72**: 230, 300, 371.
Tivoli, A Villa at. (A. W. Verrall) Univ. R. **7**: 253.
Tlemçen, Africa, and its Vicinage. (W. Sharp) Art J. **46**: 46.
— and its Mosques. (E. Barclay) Eng. Illust. **9**: 412.
To a Baby Kinswoman. (A. C. Swinburne) 19th Cent. **36**: 1008.
To Barbara; a poem. (D. S. Jordan) Pop. Sci. Mo. **47**: 538.
To a Child: in Fancy; a poem. (G. E. Montgomery) Cosmopol. **20**: 288.
To a Child of Fifteen; a poem. (E. Gosse) M. of Art, **17**: 169.
To a Coquette; a poem. (H. DeB. Porter) Belgra. **90**: 179.

To Dame Nature; a poem. (J. F. Sullivan) M. of Art, **13**: 137.
To Dianeme; a poem. (R. Herrick) M. of Art, **18**: 255.
To a Friend; a poem. (D. Fuguet) Cosmopol. **21**: 527.
To a Gardener; a poem. (R. L. Stevenson) M. of Art, **9**: 320.
To the Gates of Hell; a story. (C. E. Morland) Belgra. **79**: 56.
To Her; a story. (T. R. Sullivan) Scrib. M. **13**: 185.
To his own Hindrance; a story. Argosy, **53**: 414.
To History unknown; a tale. (S. E. Asling) Canad. M. **1**: 239.
To a Hyacinth Bulb; a poem. (A. A. Mosher) Cosmopol. **21**: 668.
To Know; a poem. (B. Pares) Gent. M. n. s. **55**: 102.
To love or to be loved; a poem. (W. J. Lampton) Cosmopol. **21**: 361.
To May. (E. G. Booth) Longm. **26**: 380.
To an Old Sun-dial; a poem. (Will Hill) Cosmopol. **21**: 60.
To right the Wrong. (A. E. Bayly) Good Words, **34**: 1-793.
To a Skylark; a poem. (Will Hill) Cosmopol. **19**: 536.
To Sleep; a poem. (L. C. Moulton) Cosmopol. **20**: 388.
To the Soil of the Earth; a story. (H. Pyle) Cosmopol. **13**: 217.
To those coming; a poem. (E. Thomas) Cosmopol. **14**: 360.
To the Unknown God; a story. Belgra. **81**: Holiday no. 7.
To the Uttermost Farthing; a story. (F. Bell) Theatre, **30**: 190.
Toad, The Midwife. (C. Hartmann) Nat. Sci. **8**: 392.
Toad Lore. Chamb. J. **73**: 158.
Toad-stools, Rights and Wrongs of. (C. McIlvaine) New Sci. R. **1**: 106.
Toad's Treasure, The; a story. (E. L. Linton) Eng. Illust. **10**: 561.
Toads: Bufo of the Jewelled Head. (G. Winterwood) Good Words, **35**: 684.
Toast. Cornh. **74**: 354.
— and Sentiments. Time, **7**: 922.
Tobacco, Abuse of. (G. J. Cowley-Brown) National, **21**: 571.
— and the Tobacco Habit. (J. Rochard) Pop. Sci. Mo. **41**: 670.
— Ceremonial Use of. (J. Hawkins) Pop. Sci. Mo. **43**: 173.
— Enemies of. All the Year, **72**: 55.
— Home of. (E. V. Howard) Gent. M. n. s. **57**: 352.
— Nicotiana. Ecl. M. **125**: 420.
— A Pipe of. (L. H. Weeks) Bach. of Arts, **1**: 364.
— Stray Leaves from the Indian Weed. (E. V. Howard) Gent. M. n. s. **56**: 245.
Tobacco Books. Bookworm, **3**: 193.
Tobacco Factory, A. (J. Hatton) Eng. Illust. **9**: 299.
Tobacco Industry. (J. B. Carrington) So. M. **5**: 581.
— of India and the Far East. (C. Tripp) J. Soc. Arts, **44**: 367.
Tobacco Money; a story. (J. A. Tyson) Idler, **8**: 170.
Tobacco-pipes, Old English. Chamb. J. **73**: 495.
Tobacco Plantation, A Sumatran. Liv. Age, **204**: 445.
Tobacco-smoking, Antiquity of. Macmil. **74**: 289.
Tobogganing in Middle Georgia. (Caroline Le Conte) Overland, n. s. **22**: 475.
— in Switzerland: a New Sport. Scrib. M. **19**: 45.
Tocqueville, Alexis de. (A. V. Dicey) National, **21**: 771.
— Souvenirs. (Lord Acton) 19th Cent. **33**: 883. — (A. Laugel) Nation, **56**: 270, 310. — Atlan. **72**: 120.
Todas of the Nilgherries. Dub. R. **111**: 449.
Todd Memorial Lectures. (W. Stokes) Acad. **44**: 31, 52, 73.
Toft and Croft. Cornh. **69**: 521.
Toilers of the City. (B. A. Clarke) Idler, **5**: 193.
Toilet, History of the. (L. Bourdeau) Chaut. **22**: 717.
Tokens, Traders'. Chamb. J. **71**: 662.
Toki Murata; a story. (S. Reed) Cosmopol. **14**: 418.
Tokyo, Artificial Caves at. (Shogoro Tsuboi Rigakushi) Asia R. **13**: 279.
Told, Silas; Mariner and Methodist. (A. Dobson) Temp. Bar, **97**: 363. Same art. Liv. Age, **197**: 300.
Told by the Colonel. (W. L. Alden) Idler, vols. **1-3**.
Told by Oyhee Joe. (R. Wildman) Overland, n. s. **25**: 253.
Told in Confidence; a story. (C. E. Shute) Eng. Illust. **11**: 1211. Same art. McClure, **3**: 116.
Told in the Dog Watch. Overland, n. s. **25**: 310.
Told over a Stile; a story. (L. Wyndham) Canad. M. **6**: 23.
Tolerance in Taste. Spec. **75**: 687.
Toll, Baron von, Expedition to New Siberian Islands. (C. Siewers) Knowl. **18**: 105.
Tollemache, W. F., Lord, and his Anecdotes. (L. A. Tollemache) Fortn. **58**: 74. Same art. Liv. Age, **194**: 652.
— "the Laborer's Lord." (F. Impey) New R. **9**: 299.
Tolstoi, Lyof, with portrait. Bk. Buyer, **3**: 296. — (M. Thompson) Bk. News, **6**: 9. — With portrait, Bk. News, **7**: 268. — (Mad. Dovidoff) Cosmopol. **12**: 719. — (R. H. Reade) Good Words, **33**: 448. — (E. M. L. M'Dougall) Sund. M. **21**: 706. — With portrait. (F. Handley) Our Day, **15**: 71.
— and the Gospels. Pub. Opin. **19**: 51.
— and Nietzsche, Moral Systems of. (Prof. Grote) Pub. Opin. **14**: 621.
— and Non-resistance. (E. H. Crosby) Outl. **54**: 52.
— and Primitive Christianity. (W. D. Gunning) Open Court, **1**: 398.
— as he is. (I. F. Hapgood) Munsey, **15**: 555.
— Decline of his Philosophy. (V. Yaros) Chaut. **18**: 703.
— Famine Relief Work of. (J. Stadling) Cent. **24**: 249, 560.
— from an Ethical Standpoint. (W. L. Sheldon) Eth. Rec. **2**: 65.
— Kreutzer Sonata. (P. K. Rosegger) Open Court, **5**: 2795. — (C. K. Whipple) Open Court, **5**: 2796. — (E. J. Dillon) Univ. R. **6**: 293.
— on Patriotism. (A. Laugel) Nation, **59**: 171.
— Philosophy of Life. (E. H. Crosby) Arena, **15**: 279.
— Visit to. Cornh. **65**: 597. Same art. Liv. Age, **194**: 210.
— What to do. (H. Wood) New Sci. R. **1**: 184.
— Work of, in the Famine Districts. (E. J. Dillon) R. of Rs. (N. Y.) **5**: 39.
Tolstoi Club, Our. (D. Prescott) Cent. **21**: 761.
Toltec Idol, The; a story. (T. P. Terry) Outing, **22**: 106.
Toluca, Mexico. (C. E. Hodson) Cath. World, **55**: 845.
"Tom — 'e Know'd;" a story. Temp. Bar, **104**: 509. Same art. Liv. Age, **205**: 271.
Tom o' the Blueb'ry Plains. (K. D. Wiggin) Atlan. **72**: 773.
Tom's Liza. (E. Elmer) New Eng. M. n. s. **6**: 668.
Tom's Second Missus. (M. E. Francis) Longm. **27**: 63. Same art. Liv. Age, **207**: 525.
Tom Grogan. (F. H. Smith) Cent. **29**: 238-761.
Tom Puckle; a story. (L. Street) Argosy, **57**: 435.
Tom Sawyer, Detective; a story. (S. L. Clemens) Harper, **93**: 344, 519.
Tomatoes and their Preservation in Italy. Chamb. J. **73**: 799.

Tomatoes, Cultivation of. (W. W. Tracy) Garden & F. 9: 37.
— under Glass. (W. E. Britton) Garden & F. 9: 526.
— Yellow-fruited. (F. A. Waugh) Garden & F. 8: 138.
Tomb of Burns, The; a poem. (W. Watson) Spec. 75: 14.
Tomb of a Prophet; a story. Argosy, 57: 122.
Tombs of the Caliphs. (C. W. Wood) Argosy, 55: 29.
Tombs of the Kings of England, Wall's. Sat. R. 74: 373.
— of the Popes at Viterbo. (A. L. Frothingham, jr.) Am. J. Archæol. 7: 38.
— Sculptured, in Italy. (S. Thompson) M. of Art, 3: 95.
Tombstones, Sculptured, of Argyllshire. (R. C. Graham) Illus. Archæol. 1: 90.
Tomes, Sir John. Nature, 52: 396.
Tomkinson, W., Cavalry Officer under Wellington. (J. E. Roundell) Nation, 59: 14. — Macmil. 71: 393.
Tomlins, Wm. L. Story of a Child Trainer. (M. B. Powell) Cosmopol. 21: 582. Music, 2: 62.
"Tommyrotics." (H. E. M. Stutfield) Blackw. 157: 833.
To-morrow's Wait; a poem. (T. F. Mayo) Argosy, 59: 768.
Tomson, Mrs. Graham R., Poetry of. (W. Watson) Acad. 41: 30.
Tomtit. (O. O. Howard) Overland, n. s. 28: 403.
Tomtom; a poem. (Mary Brotherton) Temp. Bar, 98: 69.
Tonbridge School Laboratories. (A. Earl) Nature, 52: 88.
Tone, Theobald Wolfe. (R. Dunlop) Acad. 44: 431. — Sat. R. 76: 517. — (A. Birrell) Contemp. 65: 46. Same art. Liv. Age, 200: 477. — Ath. '94, 1: 797.
Tone-space, an Unknown Quantity. (J. P. White) Music, 4: 160.
Tonga, Parliament of, Opening of. Blackw. 153: 512. Same art. Liv. Age, 197: 603.
Tongue, Use of, Legal Enactments on. (R. V. Rogers) Green Bag, 4: 376.
Tonia; a Story of Crime from Poverty. (L. de La Ramée) Cosmopol. 20: 190.
Tony. (M. A. P. Stansbury) New Eng. M. n. s. 8: 454.
Too Constant; a poem. Argosy, 61: 595.
Too Late; a story. (W. C. Platts) Belgra. 81: 396.
Too True; a poem. (W. C. Monkhouse) M. of Art, 12: 241.
Tool, Philosophy of the. Open Court, 7: 3735.
Toole, J. L., the Actor. (R. Blathwayt) Idler, 3: 301.
— Luncheon with. (J. Hatton) Idler, 7: 315.
— Reminiscences. Spec. 68: 782.
Toombs, Robert. (A. E. Allaben) Nat'l M. (N. Y. '91) 16: 299.
— Stovall's. (J. W. Chadwick) Nation, 54: 363.
Toovey, James. Ath. '93, 2: 388.
Top, A Curve-tracing. (C. Barus) Science, n. s. 4: 444.
Topaz; a story. (M. A. M. Marks) Argosy, 61: 421.
— Water in. (P. Jannasch; J. Locke) Am. J. Sci. 147: 386.
Topley, William. Acad. 46: 259. — Nature, 50: 579. — Nat. Sci. 5: 389.
Topographic Methods. (J. A. Flemer) Science, n. s. 2: 15.
— American. (A. Fowler) Nature, 51: 274.
Topographic Models. (Cosmos Mindeleff) Nat. Geog. M. 1: 254.
Topographical Changes, Causes which influence. (L. G. Yates) Am. Natural. 26: 1.
Topsel, Edward. Cornh. 69: 304.
Torcello, Italy: an Afternoon Tea. (H. L. Bradley) Atlan. 70: 388.
Torlonia, Prince Alessandro. (E. S. Morgan) Time, 15: 39.
Tormenting, Pleasure of. Spec. 71: 109.
Torn Cloak, The. (Maxime Du Camp) Good Words, 36: Xmas no. 62. Same art. Ecl. M. 126: 120.
Tornado, St. Louis. (H. H. C. Dunwoody) Cosmopol. 21: 440.
Toronto as a Municipal Object-Lesson. (A. Shaw) R. of Rs. (N. Y.) 10: 165.
— Castle Frank, History of. (H. Scadding) Canad. M. 5: 155.
— Parliament Buildings. (F. Yeigh) Canad. M. 1: 101.
— University of, and its Presidents. (W. H. Fraser) Canad. M. 6: 541.
Toronto Art Students' League. (R. Holmes) Canad. M. 4: 171.
Torosaurus, Skull of. (O. C. Marsh) Am. J. Sci. 143: 81.
Torpedo, Bushnell's Submarine, Sergeant Lee's Experience with, 1776. (H. P. Johnston) M. Am. Hist. 29: 262.
— Future of the, in War. (P. H. Colomb) No. Am. 160: 396.
— Whitehead, in the U. S. Navy. (Robert Hanna) Cosmopol. 19: 405.
Torpedo Boat, From Queenstown to Sheerness in a. (F. T. Jane) Eng. Illus. 10: 552.
— in the Year 1900, A Cruise in a. (F. T. Jane) Good Words, 37: 597.
Torpedo Boats. All the Year, 71: 101. — Chamb. J. 69: 374. 72: 198.
— in British Navy. (H. O. Arnold-Forster) Sat. R. 80: 339.
— Weakness of. Sat. R. 80: 339.
Torpedo-catcher, Life on Board a. (F. T. Jane) Eng. Illust. 11: 1097.
Torpedoes and Submarine Mines. (F. L. Winn) Un. Serv. (Phila.) 8: 464.
— Evolution of. (Eugene Robinson) Un. Serv. (Phila.) 11: 1.
— Forerunners of. (A. A. C. Galloway) Un. Serv. M. 9: 196.
— in Action. Chamb. J. 73: 781.
— in Coast Defence. (A. M. D'Armit) Cosmopol. 12: 659.
Torr, A. C., and Vincent, William Thomas. Cinder-Ellen, up too late; a Burlesque. Theatre, 28: 96.
Torres Straits, Legends from. (A. C. Haddon) Folk-Lore, 1: 47, 172.
Torrey, Henry Warren. (S. M. McVane) Harv. Mo. 17: 131.
Torrigiano, Pietro. (E. S. Roscoe) M. of Art, 3: 226. — (F. M. Robinson) M. of Art, 9: 18.
Torrington, Earl of, and the Battle of Beachy Head. Macmil. 72: 222.
Torso from Daphne. (R. B. Richardson) Am. J. Archæol. 9: 53.
Torts, Malice in Law of. (W. E. Ormsby) Law Q. 8: 140.
Torture by Hope. (V. de l'I. Adam) Poet-Lore, 6: 303.
— European Law of. (A. W. Barber) Pop. Sci. Mo. 44: 648.
— Forms of. All the Year, 70: 136.
— Horror of. Spec. 71: 908.
Toryism and Progression. (F. R. G. Radcliffe) National, 20: 651.
— Death of. Spec. 75: 4.

Total Abstinence. (H. Jones) 19th Cent. **40**: 875.
Totem Posts at the World's Fair. (J. Deans) Am. Antiq. **15**: 281.
Totemism in the Evolution of Theology. (C. K. Barnum) Pop. Sci. Mo. **42**: 395.
Totnes. (S. Baring Gould) Good Words, **35**: 470.
Totokomila and Lisayae; a poem. (J. V. Cheney) Cosmopol. **13**: 666.
Tottel, Richard. (H. R. Plomer) Bibliographica, **3**: 378.
Totteridge; a Hertfordshire Village. (J. Telford) Good Words, **34**: 744.
Tottie; a New Zealand Episode. (H. G. Smith) Good Words, **33**: 598. Same art. Liv. Age, **195**: 438.
Touch. (John Heitz) New Sci. R. **2**: 237.
— and Taste in Animals. Chamb. J. **69**: 583.
— Psychology of. (F. B. Dresslar) Am. J. Psychol. **6**: 313.
Touch and Go; a story. (M. G. McClelland) Lippinc. **49**: 366.
Touch of Spring, The; a story. (D. S. Meldrum) Blackw. **157**: 442. Same art. Ecl. M. **124**: 527. Same art. Liv. Age, **205**: 78.
Touchstone, The; a fable. (R. L. Stevenson) McClure, **6**: 300.
Toulon and the French Navy. (W. L. Clowes) 19th Cent. **34**: 1023.
Toulouse. Academie des Jeux Floraux. (C. A. Janvier) Critic, **21**: 110.
— in Summer. (E. R. Pennell) Harper, **87**: 707.
Touraine, At a Country House in. (Chas. Hervey) Time, **5**: 639.
— Chateaux of. Sat. R. **73**: 334.
— in Autumn. All the Year, **76**: 247.
— Through, on Wheels. (H. Maxwell) Blackw. **160**: 251. Same art. Liv. Age, **210**: 625. Same art. Ecl. M. **127**: 486.
Tourist Ticket, A. Macmil. **73**: 299.
Tourist's Problem, The. National, **26**: 279.
Tournaments and Matches. Cornh. **68**: 84.
Tourney, The; a poem. (H. P. Spofford) Cosmopol. **20**: 3.
Tout, Development of the French Word. (R. de Poyen-Bellisle) Am. J. Philol. **16**: 66.
Tower, Charlemagne, with portrait. Bk. News, **13**: 311.
Tower by the Sea; a story. (A. Beresford) Argosy, **54**: 390.
Tower of St. Sepelain; a story. (R. R. Ottley) Argosy, **59**: 252.
Towers and Turrets. (A. Saint-Paul) Am. Arch. **45**: 15, 23.
— Famous. (G. Holme) Munsey, **12**: 518.
— Old, at Liège. (A. Elliot) Illus. Archæol. **1**: 150.
— of Silence in India. (W. Bourchier) Eng. Illust. **10**: 582.
Town or Country? (E. L. Linton) New R. **9**: 375. — Same art. Ecl. M. **121**: 690.
— the Small, Doom of. (H. J. Fletcher) Forum, **19**: 214.
Town and Gown Rows at Yale. (H. E. Howland) Bach. of Arts, **1**: 1, 160.
Town Government in Maine. (W. MacDonald) Nation, **60**: 197.
— in New England, Adams's Study of. (W. Walker) Yale R. **1**: 368.
— on Cape Cod. (A. B. Hart) Nation, **56**: 343.
Town Halls. (E. Rümbler) Am. Arch. **42**: 55-83.
Town History, The. (A. Titus) N. E. Reg. **49**: 191.
— Study of, in Schools. (C. K. Bolton) New Eng. M. n. s. **14**: 94.
Town Holdings. Quar. **176**: 222.
Town Life. Ecl. M. **119**: 320. Same art. Liv. Age, **194**: 683.
— in the 15th Century, Mrs. J. R. Green's. (E. P. Cheyney) Ann. Am. Acad. Pol. Sci. **6**: 137. — (A. Law) Econ. R. **4**: 375. — Ed. R. **180**: 289. Same art. Liv. Age, **203**: 579. — Sat. R. **77**: 423.
— in the Middle Ages, Beginnings of. (W. J. Ashley) Q. J. Econ. **10**: 359.
— Three Centuries ago. (Rhys Jenkins) Gent. M. n. s. **57**: 531.
Town Lot No. 1303; a story. (A. French) McClure, **2**: 330.
Town Meeting, The. (E. E. Hale) Cosmopol. **13**: 241.
— the Aryan Mark. (A. C. Brackett) Harper, **85**: 577.
Towns, Names of, American. (R. C. Faris) Chaut. **19**: 723.
— Rise of. Cornh. **66**: 624.
Township, Anglo-Saxon. (W. J. Ashley) Q. J. Econ. **8**: 345.
Toynbee, Arnold. (H. B. Adams) Char. R. **1**: 12.
— and his Work. (M. McG. Dana) Gunton's M. **10**: 40.
Toynbee Hall. (C. Bailey) Econ. R. **6**: 88. — (F. S. Boas) Time, **23**: 749. — Students' Residences at. (H. S. Lunn) Chr. Lit. **10**: 95.
Trachytes, Ischian. (H. S. Washington) Am. J. Sci. **151**: 375.
Trace. (J. M. Soames) Contemp. **61**: 809. Same art. Ecl. M. **119**: 112.
Tract 90. Eng. R. **3**: 157.
Tractarian Movement, Dean Stanley and the. (A. V. G. Allen) New World, **3**: 132.
— Poetry of. N. Eng. **56**: 239.
Tracy, John M. (M. Tracy) Mo. Illust. **3**: 109.
Trade and Capital, Ethics of, as Related to Popular Government. (D. A. Gorton) Am. M. Civics, **8**: 153, 255.
— and the Tariff. (S. G. Horwitz) Am. J. Pol. **1**: 364.
— Depression of. (W. H. Houldsworth) National, **25**: 213. — Ed. R. **182**: 1.
— — What Causes? (L. Irwell) Chaut. **18**: 307.
See Financial Crisis.
— Foreign, Our. (F. T. Newbery) Cent. **29**: 786.
— — Unbalanced. (R. Ogden) Nation, **54**: 104.
— How Distrust stops. (E. Atkinson) No. Am. **157**: 25.
— How to revive. (A. Withy) Westm. **143**: 626.
— in Ancient Times. (C. R. Conder) Scot. R. **19**: 74. Same art. Liv. Age, **193**: 22.
— International. (Earl Gray) Am. J. Pol. **2**: 449.
— — Balance of. (D. Strange) Am. J. Pol. **4**: 1. — (E. L. Rector) Am. J. Pol. **4**: 326.
— Philosophy of. Eng. R. **8**: 35.
— Recent Legislation in restraint of. (C. F. Beach, jr.) Am. J. Sociol. **1**: 657.
— Revival of. Spec. **75**: 327.
— — in U. S. Bank. M. (Lond.) **59**: 688.
— Tendency of, to forsake Large Centres. Bank. M. (Lond.) **54**: 18.
Trade Disputes. Westm. **138**: 303.
Trade-marks in 15th Century. Reliquary, **33**: 86.
Trade-Organizations, Changes in. (H. J. Falk) Econ. J. **6**: 542.
Trade Schools. (J. Lee) Am. J. Soc. Sci. **33**: 208. — Lend a H. **12**: 33. — Argument for. (J. Lee) Char. R. **5**: 113.
— for the Many. (S. F. Hubbard) Lend a H. **14**: 415.
— New York City. (L. Mead) Engin. M. **3**: 55.
Trade Statistics, Classification of. (F. C. Hicks) Am. J. Statis. Assoc. **3**: 65.
— of Various Countries, Comparability of. (A. E. Bateman) Am. Statis. Assoc. **3**: 533. — Same art. J. Statis. Soc. **57**: 394.

Trade-teaching in Germany. All the Year, 75: 521.
Trade Unionism, British, Representative Institutions in. (S. Webb and B. Webb) Pol. Sci. Q. 11: 640.
— Broader. Soc. Econ. 9: 207.
— History of. (Lyman Abbott) Outl. 51: 264.
— in England. Soc. Econ. 7: 332.
— Brentano on. (H. Dendy) Econ. J. 5: 488.
— Method of Collective Bargaining. (S. and B. Webb) Econ. J. 6: 1.
— Methods of the New. Quar. 180: 138.
— Origin of. (W. A. S. Hewins) Econ. R. 5: 200.
— Primitive Democracy in British. (S. and B. Webb) Pol. Sci. Q. 11: 397.
— To your tents, oh Israel! (Fabian Society) Fortn. 60: 569.
— The Trend of. (H. W. Massingham) Fortn. 58: 450.
— Wanted, a Newer. (M. Stobart) Westm. 143: 23. Same art. Ecl. M. 124: 289.
— Weak Points in. (L. Irwell) Engin. M. 5: 460.
— Webb's History of. (J. A. Hamilton) Acad. 46: 95. — Sat. R. 77: 555.
Trades Union, First Incorporated. (C. Cowley) Soc. Econ. 9: 44.
Trades Union Congress, Liverpool. (Clementina Black) Univ. R. 8: 182.
Trades Unions. Soc. Econ. 1: 55.
— American Federation of Labor. Gunton's M. 10: 134.
— and Civilization. Soc. Econ. 3: 275.
— Are they Benefit Societies? (S. and B. Webb) Econ. R. 6: 441.
— Coercion by. (C. Black) Contemp. 62: 547.
— English, Congress of, 1892. (J. Rae) Econ. J. 2: 727. — (T. R. Threlfall) 19th Cent. 32: 614. — Spec. 69: 341. — Open Court, 5: 2987.
— — — 1893. (C. Edwards) Econ. J. 3: 694. — Spec. 71: 361.
— — — 1895. (C. Edwards) Econ. J. 5: 636. — Spec. 75: 295. — Am. Arch. 49: 136. — Sat. R. 80: 337.
— in the United Kingdom. (J. M. Ludlow) Atlan. 78: 687.
— Insignificance of Vote of. (F. Wicks) 19th Cent. 35: 602.
— Legal Disabilities of. (B. Holland) 19th Cent. 37: 393.
— New Serfage in England. Spec. 70: 475.
— Popular Mistakes about. (W. P. D. Bliss) Pub. Opin. 20: 620.
— Recent Decisions concerning. Yale R. 2: 8.
— Should they be incorporated? (K. Bocock) Soc. Econ. 3: 269.
— Tailoring Trade. Sat. R. 82: 346.
— Tendencies of. Soc. Econ. 7: 215.
— *vs.* Socialism. Soc. Econ. 9: 373.
— Women's, Progress of. (E. March-Phillipps) Fortn. 60: 92. Same art. Ecl. M. 121: 226.
— A Word to. (J. W. Jenks) Char. R. 1: 55.
Trades and Faces. (L. Robinson) Pop. Sci. Mo. 47: 627.
— Queer. (R. Edgarton) Lippinc. 51: 355.
— *vs.* Professions. Spec. 75: 720.
Trading Companies. (J. H. Finley) Chaut. 14: 403, 529.
Tradition, Law of. (J. C. F. Rupp) Luth. Q. 22: 252.
— Testimony of, MacRitchie's. (C. G. Leland) J. Am. Folk-Lore, 3: 319.
Traditions, Final Batch of. All the Year, 76: 203.
— of the Elders, Some. All the Year, 75: 209, 369, 582.
— Problematic. (F. L. Oswald) Open Court, 3: 2028.
Trafalgar, Battle of. (B. Clement) Cornh. 71: 478.
Trafalgar, Battle of, and To-day. (H. W. Wilson) National, 28: 354. Same art. Ecl. M. 127: 758.
— from the Spanish Side. (W. L. Clowes) Cornh. 74: 435. Same art. Ecl. M. 127: 669.
Trafalgar Captains, The. (W. L. Clowes) 19th Cent. 38: 576. Same art. Un. Serv. (Phila.) 14: 512.
Trafalgar Day; a poem. (A. C. Swinburne) 19th Cent. 38: 713.
Tragedy and the Problem of Life. (P. Carus) Open Court, 2: 1120.
Tragedy at Millager, Me.; a story. (E. Myers) Canad. M. 4: 365.
Tragedy of the Comedy, The. (C. B. Fernald) Cent. 29: 98.
Tragedy of Elmtop; a story. (M. White, jr.) Munsey, 11: 583.
Tragedy of the Great North Road; a story. (R. L. Stevenson) Cosmopol. 20: 147, 289.
Tragedy of Khartoum; a story. (C. E. Barns) Munsey, 13: 273.
Tragedy of Mr. Thomas Doughty; a story. (J. Corbett) Macmil. 68: 258. Same art. Liv. Age, 199: 146.
Tragedy of South Carolina; a story. (F. W. Dawson) Cosmopol. 20: 53.
Tragedy of Trade. (M. Langdon) Lippinc. 54: 560.
Tragedy of Two Ambitions, A. (Thos. Hardy) Univ. R. 2: 537.
Tragedy Writers and Tragedy Writing. Theatre, 29: 118.
Tragic Muse, The; a story. Argosy, 62: 502.
Trailing Arbutus, Transplanting. (R. Ridgway) Garden & F. 5: 202.
Trailing Yew; a story. (P. Stapleton) Cosmopol. 12: 480, 563.
Traill, H. D. Fables and Fantasies. Spec. 69: 294.
— To; a poem. (W. Watson) Spec. 73: 340.
Traill, Mrs. (H. Burnham) Canad. M. 4: 390.
Train for Tarrow's. (V. W. Cloud) Lippinc. 59: 542.
Train Robbers, How to repel. (J. T. Knight) No. Am. 160: 254.
Tramp, American, considered geographically. (J. Flynt) Cent. 25: 99.
— at Home. (J. Flynt) Cent. 25: 517.
— Autobiography of a. (F. M. F. Skene) Belgra. 81: 167.
— The City. (J. Flynt) Cent. 25: 706.
Trampdom, Border Land of. (C. W. Noble) Pop. Sci. Mo. 50: 252.
Tramping Trip, Outfit for. (W. H. Hobbs) Outing, 26: 207.
Tramp's Diary, A. Spec. 75: 518.
Tramps. (J. J. McCook) Char. R. 3: 57. — Spec. 71: 509. 74: 781.
— Caring for. Pub. Opin. 15: 407.
— Census of, and its Revelations. (J. J. McCook) Forum, 15: 753.
— Children of the Road. (J. Flynt) Atlan. 77: 58.
— German, Life among. (J. Flynt) Cent. 24: 803.
— German Labor Colonies for. (F. G. Peabody) Forum, 12: 751.
— How Baltimore banished. (E. R. L. Gould) Forum, 17: 497.
— How Men become. (J. Flynt) Cent. 28: 941.
— My Friend the Tramp. (D. C. Macnicol) Good Words, 34: 275.
— Problem of. (E. Hofer) Overland, n. s. 23: 628. — (J. J. McCook) Lend a H. 15: 167.
— — in Baltimore. (M. S. Briscoe) M. Chr. Lit. 6: 458.
— — New Phases of. (J. J. McCook) Char. R. 1: 355.

Tramps, Rights of. (E. Hubbard) Arena, 9: 593.
— Trades-union. Chamb. J. 70: 661.
— Treatment of, in Small Cities. (J. W. Bradshaw) Char. R. 5: 335. — Lend a H. 17: 266.
Transatlantic Mails. (J. H. Heaton) No. Am. 159: 424.
Transatlantic Transit, Quick. (A. Corbin) No. Am. 161: 513.
Transcendentalism and Materialism. (E. M. Caillard) Contemp. 70: 78.
— of Emerson. (F. C. Lockwood) Meth. R. 56: 702.
Transit, Ideal. Atlan. 72: 809.
Translation, Art of. Quar. 182: 324. Same art. Liv. Age, 207: 387.
— at Sight. (C. T. Williams) Educa. 13: 88.
— Ethics of. Macmil. 72: 401.
Translations, Tudor. (W. A. Raleigh) Fortn. 64: 415. Same art. Liv. Age, 207: 171.
Transmigration, Forms of Belief in. (J. Wier) Meth. R. 54: 565.
Transplanted Boy, A; a story. (C. F. Woolson) Harper, 88: 425.
Transportation. Spec. 71: 425.
— Ethics and Economics of. Soc. Econ. 6: 361.
— A National Department of. (H. J. Fletcher) Atlan. 76: 119.
— Single Tax and. (W. E. Brokaw) Am. J. Pol. 4: 369.
— Taxes on. (W. M. Acworth) 19th Cent. 31: 134.
— Theory of. (C. H. Cooley) Amer. Econ. Assoc. 9: 235.
Transvaal and the Hollanders. Sat. R. 81: 505.
— and the Matabele Rising. (R. N. Cust) Asia. R. 22: 330.
— Armenia and the. (M. MacColl) Fortn. 65: 313.
— Boer, Briton, and Africander in the. (F. I. Ricarde-Seaver) Fortn. 65: 111.
— Boers and Uitlanders. Quar. 184: 532.
— British in. (E. L. Godkin) Nation, 62: 192.
— Chartered Company. National, 27: 454. — (H. O. Arnold-Forster) National, 27: 516.
— — French View of the. (L. Dècle) National, 27: 531.
— Constitution of. (J. Bryce) Forum, 21: 145.
— Crisis in. National, 26: 717. 27: 6.
— Eastern, Game Fields of. Nature, 53: 467.
— England in. (A. A. Baumann) Sat. R. 81: 94.
— The English Government and the Boers. (W. B. Worsfold) Contemp. 69: 473.
— German Intrigues in. (W. R. Lawson) Contemp. 69: 292.
— Gold Production in. Dub. R. 112: 457.
— Impressions of. (M. Prior) Eng. Illust. 16: 21.
— In Praise of the Boers. (H. A. Bryden) 19th Cent. 39: 381.
— Invaders of. (C. C. Adams) Chaut. 22: 713.
— Mineral Resources of. (J. L. Lobley) Knowl. 19: 49.
— Naturalist in, Distant's. Spec. 68: 882.
— Pretoria Prisoners, Case of. (G. G. Ramsay) New R. 15: 479, 524.
— Prisons of, from the Inside. Chamb. J. 73: 134.
— Problems of. (K. Blind) No. Am. 162: 457.
— Mr. Rhodes and. (An Imperialist) Fortn. 65: 839.
— Story of an Amateur Revolution. (Johannesburg Resident) Fortn. 65: 605. Same art. Ecl. M. 126: 650.
— The Trouble in. New R. 14: 128.
— — Mr. Chamberlain's Inheritance. (E. B. Iwan-Müller) New R. 14: 572.
— True Motive and Reason of Dr. Jameson's Raid. (G. S. Fort) 19th Cent. 39: 873.
— The Water-gate of the. Chamb. J. 72: 824.
Transylvania, Month's Trip in. (A. T. Sibbald) Time, 14: 452.
Trap Sheets of Holyoke and Deerfield, Massachusetts. Proofs of their Contemporaneousness with the Sandstones. (B. K. Emerson) Am. J. Sci. 143: 146.
Trapping and Home-made Traps. (E. W. Sandys) Outing, 23: 136.
Trappists, Monastery of, Gethsemane, Ky. (A. Hendricks) Lippinc. 57: 712.
— A Night with the. (E. H. Barker) Temp. Bar, 99: 47. Same art. Liv. Age, 199: 353.
Travancore, Trip to. (E. W. Quin) 19th Cent. 31: 255.
Travel, Art of. (Viscount Lymington) Time, 19: 143.
— European, Early Days of. Cornh. 73: 504.
— Foreign, Hints to Art Students on. (J. W. Case) Am. Arch. 47: 71, 83, 93, 100.
— Teaching by; a School Excursion from Indiana to Virginia. (J. M. Rice) Forum, 18: 20.
— Where to spend a Holiday. (M. Jeune; A. Symons; J. Verschoyle) Fortn. 62: 293.
Traveler from Altruria; a story. (W. D. Howells) Cosmopol. 14: 52 — 15: 738.
Travellers, Lady. Blackw. 160: 49. Same art. Liv. Age, 210: 279.
Travelling. (H. Quilter) Univ. R. 8: 147.
— Holiday, Coöperative; Touring Clubs of London and Manchester. R. of Rs. (N. Y.) 6: 54.
— in Europe, Practical. (A. T. Bolton) Am. Arch. 44: 146.
— On Modern. (V. Paget) Macmil. 69: 306. Same art. Ecl. M. 122: 380. Same art. Liv. Age, 200: 634.
— Sentimental. Macmil. 70: 445. Same art. Ecl. M. 123: 837. Same art. Liv. Age, 203: 694.
Travelling with Half a Million; a story. Argosy, 55: 113.
Travelling with a Reformer. (S. L. Clemens) Cosmopol. 16: 207.
Travelling Companions, Involuntary. Spec. 71: 268.
Travelling Men, Convention of, at Terre Haute, Ind. Bost. 4: 375.
Travels, Imaginary. All the Year, 72: 569.
Travis Hallett's Half-back. (Frank Norris) Overland, n. s. 23: 20.
Trawler, The, and the Line Fishermen, The Case of. (W. A. Smith) Chamb. J. 73: 423.
Trawling, Beam. (J. M. Laing) Blackw. 151: 712.
— with Gloucester Fishermen. (J. Z. Rogers) Outing, 23: 401.
Treason in Roman Law. (A. H. J. Greenidge) Jurid. R. 7: 228.
Treasure, Hidden. All the Year, 71: 369. — Chamb. J. 73: 186.
— — in India. Chamb. J. 72: 479.
— of Sacramento Nick. (G. Boothby) Macmil. 70: 339.
— of Shagul, The. (S. L. Yeats) Macmil. 72: 231.
— Seeking Buried. Chamb. J. 71: 541.
Treasure Cave on Oahu, The; a story. (M. H. Closson) Overland, n. s. 19: 577.
Treasure Islands in the Polar Sea. Chamb. J. 72: 9. Same art. Liv. Age, 204: 315.
Treasury, Independent, Influence of, on Business. (D. Kinley) Ann. Am. Acad. Pol. Sci. 3: 180.
Treaty-making in Africa. (F. D. Lugard) Geog. J. 1: 53.
Tree, Herbert Beerbohm. (G. Parker) Lippinc. 55: 117. — Critic, 26: 91. — (W. A. L. Bettany) Theatre, 28: 69.
— and Mrs. Tree. Critic, 26: 110. — (W. A. L. Bettany) Theatre, 32: 75.
— — in Sloane Street. Eng. Illust. 14: 498.

Tree, Herbert Beerbohm, as Falstaff. Critic, 26: 150.
— as Hamlet. Ath. '92, 1: 159. — Gent. M. n. s. 48: 316. — Spec. 68: 398. — (H. D. Traill) National, 19: 225. — Theatre, 28: 148. — Critic, 26: 168.
— — More about. (Oliver Bluff) Theatre, 28: 175.
Tree, The, as a Schoolmaster. Garden & F. 5: 85.
Tree Butchers. Garden & F. 5: 589.
Tree Culture, Interesting Experiment in. (C. A. Dana) Garden & F. 8: 442.
Tree-felling, Sentimentalism and. (C. S. Sargent) Garden & F. 6: 311.
Tree Flora of the Chiricahua Mountains, Arizona. (J. W. Toumey) Garden & F. 8: 12, 22.
Tree-hoppers on the Bittersweet. (W. H. Gibson) Harper, 87: 432.
Tree-life, Meaning of. (H. L. Clarke) Am. Natural. 28: 465, 572.
Tree-planting at Childbirth. (E. S. Hartland) J. Am. Folk-Lore, 8: 323.
— by Village Improvement Societies. Garden & F. 6: 189.
— in Cities. (C. S. Sargent) Garden & F. 7: 21.
— in Towns. Garden & F. 5: 2.
— on Mt. Hamilton. (C. H. Shinn) Garden & F. 6: 45.
Tree Worship and Ghost Worship. (G. Allen) Pop. Sci. Mo. 42: 489, 648.
Trees. (G. Cadell) Gent. M. n. s. 49: 251. — (M. G. Watkins) Longm. 22: 453.
— Among the. (A. C. Brackett) Harper, 93: 601.
— and Shrubs, Native, about Montreal. (J. G. Jack) Garden & F. 7: 383, 393, 403, 413, 423.
— — Notes on. (J. G. Jack) Garden & F. 7: 195–326.
— Beauty of, in Spring. Garden & F. 5: 265.
— Dangerous Enemies of Street. (C. S. Sargent) Garden & F. 9: 141.
— Deciduous, in Winter. (C. S. Sargent) Garden & F. 7: 501.
— Diseases of, Hartig's. Sat. R. 79: 102.
— Exhaustion of Soil by. (B. E. Fernow) Garden & F. 8: 142.
— Field Mice and Bark Destruction. (J. G. Jack) Garden & F. 7: 6.
— Flowers of the Forest. (E. Step) Good Words, 37: 424.
— Forest, Distribution of Some, in the Southern States. (C. Mohr) Garden & F. 6: 372.
— — Internal Decay of. (F. J. Hill) Garden & F. 5: 207.
— — of the Sierra Nevada. (C. Palache Overland, n. s. 21: 337.
— — Parasitic Fungi of. (J. G. Jack) Garden & F. 5: 37.
— Forms of. (Gustave Eisen) Garden & F. 5: 322. 5: 334.
— — as determined by Water Supply. (W. P. Wilson) Around World, 1: 158.
— Fruit, Late Ornamental. (J. G. Jack) Garden & F. 6: 507.
— Glory of. Spec. 73: 519.
— in October. Garden & F. 5: 505.
— in Parks. Sat. R. 81: 322. — (C. S. Sargent) Garden & F. 9: 511.
— in Winter, Aspect of. Garden & F. 5: 50.
— Japanese, in Rhode Island. (E. W. Davis) Garden & F. 6: 468.
— London. (H. Maxwell) New R. 10: 580.
— Memorial. Garden & F. 5: 530.
— Mexican, New Species of. (C. G. Pringle) Garden & F. 6: 303.
Trees, Newly Planted, Care of. (C. S. Sargent) Garden & F. 6: 211.
— North American, Notes on. (C. S. Sargent) Garden & F. 6: 130.
— of Minor Importance for Western Planting. (C. A. Keffer) Garden & F. 8: 122.
— of Nebraska, Report on the Native. (C. E. Bessey) Garden & F. 5: 46.
— of Northern U. S. (A. C. Apgar) Garden & F. 5: 431.
— Pruning of Street. Garden & F. 8: 514.
— Street. (C. S. Sargent) Garden & F. 8: 221.
— Texas, Notes on Some. (J. Reverchon) Garden & F. 6: 503, 524.
— Transplanting. (C. S. Sargent) Garden & F. 7: 431.
— Under the Apple Tree. (B. D. Halsted) Chaut. 23: 415.
— Why Lightning prefers to strike Certain. Nature, 53: 393.
— Winter Aspect of. (C. S. Sargent) Garden & F. 8: 121.
See also Forestry.
Tregarthon of the Red Hand; a story. (Mrs. A. Fraser) Belgra. 79: 150.
Tregellas, Walter Hawken. (W. P. Courtney) Acad. 45: 475. — Ath. '94, 1: 741.
Treitschke, Heinrich von, Memories of. (W. H. Dawson) Sat. R. 81: 449.
Trek, The Longest on Record. (H. A. Bryden) Chamb. J. 72: 395.
Tremain, Madam. Macmil. 71: 142.
Tremayne's Madness; a story. All the Year, 74: 589.
Trent, Council of, Froude on. Sat. R. 81: 457. — (F. H. Foster) Am. Hist. R. 2: 135. — (W. H. Kent) Dub. R. 119: 324.
Trentham Hall. (J. F.-Robertson) M. of Art, 4: 89, 204.
Trenton Falls, N. Y., Original Rocks of. (T. G. White) Am. J. Sci. 152: 430.
Trepang. (W. Marshall) Pop. Sci. Mo. 42: 515.
Trepanning, Prehistoric. Cornh. 66: 512. — Pop. Sci. Mo. 42: 535. — Illus. Archæol. 1: 52.
— — and Cranial Amulets. (R. Munro) Fortn. 59: 208.
Trésor du Lac, Le. (André Theuriet) Univ. R. 3: 21.
Trespass, Early Case of, in Maine. Green Bag, 7: 15.
Trespasser, The. (G. Parker) Lippinc. 53: 98–807.
Trespassing on the Tsar; a story. (Y. Yegorevitsch) Cornh. 74: 202. Same art. Ecl. M. 127: 387. Same art. Liv. Age, 210: 799.
Treves, Holy Coat of. (R. F. Clarke) Antiq. n. s. 25: 8.
Trevice Family and Pratt Family. (W. S. Appleton) N. E. Reg. 46: 173.
Treviso, the Last Home of Mrs. Billington. (W. B. Squire) National, 26: 512.
Trevor Perkins; a Platonic Episode. (H. Crackanthorpe) Eng. Illust. 15: 473.
Trial by Newspaper. (A. O. Hall) Green Bag, 6: 308.
Trial Trip of a Cruiser. (W. F. Sicard) Harper, 90: 524.
Trials among the Jews, Procedure in. Green Bag, 6: 336.
— Achilli *versus* Newman. Green Bag, 6: 11.
— Ardlamont Case. Green Bag, 6: 69.
— Case against C. Kent. Green Bag, 6: 526.
— Case of W. Dove. Green Bag, 6: 371.
— Case of Mrs. Lyon and Mr. Home. Green Bag, 6: 222.

Trials, Criminal, in England: an Autumn Circuit. Cornh. **65**: 295. Same art. Liv. Age, **193**: 351.
— Frederic Manning *versus* Maria. Green Bag, **7**: 15.
— Regina *versus* Bellingham. Green Bag, **7**: 130.
— Stanfield Hall Murder. Green Bag, **6**: 409.
Trials of Faith. (J. Watson) Sund. M. **25**: 259.
Trianon, Marie Antoinette in Petit. (G. Bapst) Cosmopol. **17**: 387.
Triarthrus Beckii, Antennæ and other Appendages of. (W. D. Matthew) Am. J. Sci. **146**: 121.
— Larval Form of. (C. E. Beecher) Am. J. Sci. **146**: 378.
— Morphology of. (C. E. Beecher) Am. J. Sci. **151**: 251.
Triassic Dinosauria, Notes on. (O. C. Marsh) Am. J. Sci. **143**: 543.
Tribal Law in the Panjâb. (B. H. Baden-Powell) Asia. R. **22**: 46.
Tribal Life among the Omahas. (A. C. Fletcher) Cent. **29**: 450.
Tribal Society, Ethics of. (E. P. Evans) Pop. Sci. Mo. **44**: 289.
Tribal System in Wales, Seebohm's. (F. W. Maitland) Econ. J. **5**: 589.
Tricoupis, Charilaos, a Greek Prime Minister. (J. W. Jenks) Atlan. **73**: 365. — (J. D. Bourchier) Fortn. **66**: 36. Same art. Liv. Age, **210**: 670.
Tricoupis, Spiridion, Notes on. Sat. R. **81**: 391.
Trident of Poseidon. (H. B. Walters) J. Hel. Stud. **13**: 13.
Trieste. (J. W. Mario) Nation, **55**: 162.
Trilby. (G. Du Maurier) Harper, **88**: 168 — **89**: 351.
Trilbyana. Critic, **25**: 381-454.
Trilobites from the Lower Helderberg Group, Larval Forms of. (C. E. Beecher) Am. J. Sci. **146**: 142.
— Limbs of. (P. Lake) Knowl. **19**: 68.
— Zoölogical Position of. (H. M. Bernard) Sci. Prog. **4**: 33.
Trim Exploit, A; a story. (M. Hunt) Liv. Age, **192**: 393.
Trimen, Henry. (W. B. Hemsley) Nature, **54**: 628.
Trincomali as an English Naval Base in East Indies. Un. Serv. M. **13**: 461.
Tring, England, Rothschild Museum at. (A. S. Woodward; C. D. Sherborn) Nat. Sci. **2**: 57.
Trinidad, Cycling Trip in. (H. Macbeth) Outing, **27**: 433.
— with Harden Hickey as King. (H. Frederic) Sat. R. **80**: 137.
Trinidad Treasure, The. (C. J. Cutliffe Hyne) Chamb. J. **72**: 108.
Trinitarian Controversy, A Way out of the. (J. M. Whiton) New World, **2**: 434.
Trinitarianism, New England. (L. L. Paine) New World, **5**: 272.
Trinity as seen in the Material Creation. (J. S. Vaughan) Dub. R. **112**: 16.
— Doctrine of the. (L. L. Paine) New World, **4**: 664.
— — (G. J. Low) Open Court, **10**: 4791.
— — Dawn of. (C. Waterer) Westm. **144**: 441.
— Mystery of. (E. Sherwood) Meth. R. **54**: 584.
— Pesello's Painting of, 1422. (R. S. Perrin) Open Court, **1**: 288.
— Place of, in Dante's Divina Commedia. (D. M. O'Connor) Dub. R. **118**: 370.
— really Unity. N. Church R. **3**: 258.
See also Athanasianism.
Trinity College, Cambridge, Library of, Sinker on. Sat. R. **73**: 215. — Ath. '**92**, **1**: 493.
Trinity College, Dublin. (J. Cooke) Acad. **42**: 23. — Ath. '**92**, **2**: 53. — (W. R. Scott) Eng. Illust. **9**: 743. — (J. P. Mahaffy) 19th Cent. **32**: 77. — Quar. **175**: 162.
Trinity College, Dublin, Tercentenary of. Sat. R. **74**: 344.
Trinity University, Toronto. (A. H. Young) Canad. M. **7**: 395.
Trinucleus, Structure and Appendages of. (C. E. Beecher) Am. J. Sci. **149**: 307.
Triple Alliance and Peace. Sat. R. **78**: 315.
— England and the. (F. Greenwood) National, **27**: 555.
— in Danger. (E. B. Lanin) Fortn. **61**: 119.
Tripoli, Early Remains in. (H. S. Cowper) Ath. '**95**, **1**: 649.
— Journey in Tarhuna and Gharian of. (H. S. Cowper) Geog. J. **7**: 150.
Trissino, Leonardo, An Italian Adventurer. Macmil. **74**: 211. Same art. Liv. Age, **210**: 468.
Trist, Mr., Pre-Raphaelite Pictures of. (C. Monkhouse) M. of Art, **6**: 62.
Tritton, Charles Ernest, with portrait. Bank. M. (Lond.) **61**: 705.
Tritubercular Theory, H. F. Osborn on. (E. S. Goodrich; C. I. F. Major) Nature, **50**: 6, 101.
Triumph of the Cross. (Emilia F. S. Dilke) Univ. R. **5**: 253.
Triumph of Faith. (J. P. Ritter) New Eng. M. n. s. **12**: 113.
Triumph of Hector. Macmil. **71**: 267.
Triumph of Marie Laviolette; a story. (D. C. Scott) Scrib. M. **12**: 232.
Triumph of Mind. (M. G. L. Underwood) New Eng. M. n. s. **8**: 627.
Triumph of Mogley. (R. N. Stephens) Lippinc. **49**: 89.
Trobriand Islands, Ethnographical Collections. Reliquary, **36**: 49.
— Wood-carving in. (A. C. Haddon) Illus. Archæol. **1**: 107.
Trochosphaera Solstitialis, Occurrence of, in Illinois River. (C. A. Kofoid) Science, n. s. **4**: 935.
Trochu, Gen., Memoirs. (A. Laugel) Nation, **63**: 382, 419.
Troitsa, Monastery of, Russia. Time, **8**: 515.
Trojan War, The. (G. W. Cox) Acad. **41**: 495.
Trollhattan, Falls of. All the Year, **71**: 445. Same art. Liv. Age, **196**: 185.
Trollope, Anthony. (W. P. Trent) Citizen, **2**: 297. — (T. H. S. Escott) Time **1**: 626.
— Place of, in Literature. (F. Harrison) Forum, **19**: 324.
Trollope, Edward, Bishop of Nottingham. Ath. '**93**, **2**: 855.
Trollope, Frances. (G. Newcomen) Acad. **49**: 171.
— Domestic Manners of the Americans. Critic, **25**: 422. — (W. P. Garrison) Nation, **59**: 345.
— Life and Literary Work of. Sat. R. **80**: 841.
Trollope, Thomas A. Ath. '**92**, **2**: 704. — (W. Mercer) Acad. **42**: 483.
Troop-leading, Studies in. (G. F. R. Henderson) Un. Serv. M. **6**: 306, 433.
Troops, Civil Employment of. (J. C. Gresham) Un. Serv. (Phila.) **7**: 476.
— Conveyance of, by Railway. (J. S. Rothwell) Un. Serv. M. **4**: 215, 310. — (G. Findlay) Un. Serv. M. **5**: 37[illegible]
— — by Sea. (J. S. Rothwell) Un. Serv. M. **4**: 125.
— Transportation of, by Wagon and Rail. (H. R. Brinkerhoff) Un. Serv. (Phila.) **7**: 429.
Troost, Gerard, with portrait. Pop. Sci. Mo. **45**: 258.
Tropical Colony, Wanted a. (Frederick Boyle) New R. **13**: 272.
Tropical Cultivation, Delusions about. 19th Cent. **36**: 38. Same art. Liv. Age, **202**: 417.
Tropical Forests, Animals of. Spec. **70**: 321.

Tropical Fruit Trees. (B. F. Herrick) Pop. Sci. Mo. 48: 751.
Tropics, A Sleepless Night in the. Chamb. J. 68: 769.
Trotting Road-teams and their Drivers. (E. B. Abercrombie) Outing, 29: 8.
Troubadour Land, Sport in. (R. T. Mullin) Canad. M. 4: 110.
Troubadours, Modern. (J. F. Rowbotham) Westm. 144: 562.
— Rowbotham's. Sat. R. 79: 418.
Trouble, Hall's Does God send? (S. T. Lowrie) Presb. & Ref. R. 6: 187.
Trouble in the Bric-a-brac Mission. (W. H. Bishop) Scrib. M. 13: 751.
Troubled Spirit, A; a story. (A. Armstrong) Eng. Illust. 10: 313.
Troubles of a Hostess; a story. Argosy, 61: 162. Same art. Liv. Age, 208: 594.
Troublesome Lady. (P. Stapleton) Lippinc. 52: 3.
Trout and Trout Lake. Outing, 26: 236.
— English. (H. Maxwell) Blackw. 158: 493.
Trout of the Chalk Stream. (B. G. Johns) Good Words, 33: 166.
Trout-fishing. (H. P. Beach) Outing, 22: 121.—(J. Newman) Outing, 22: 331.—(A. M. R. Gordon) Outing, 24: 340.—(E. W. Sandys) Outing, 28: 144.
— at the Head Waters of the Navarro. (L. Johnson) Overland, n. s. 24: 380.
— begins. (W. E. Hodgson) National, 19: 44.
— Episode of. (J. K. Mumford) Outing, 28: 381.
— in Devonshire. (H. Hill) Outing, 22: 231.
— in England, Future of. (J. Bickerdyke) Sat. R. 82: 437.
— in Ireland. Outing, 26: 99.
— in Lake Superior. (W. O. Henderson) Outing, 28: 180.
— in New England. (C. F. Danforth) New Eng. M. n. s. 8: 497.
— in New Zealand. Macmil. 70: 122.
— in Norway. Sat. R. 79: 691.
— in the Traun. (H. Van Dyke) Scrib. M. 14: 91.
— May Day's. (H. P. Beach) Outing, 24: 137.
— Mountain, Memory of. (R. L. Warner) Outing, 24: 150.
— with a Camera. Outing, 20: 272.
— Yuba Dam. (A. M. R. Gordon) Canad. M. 5: 145.
Trout Lake, Washington. (H. T. Finck) Nation, 57: 342.
Trouting Tattle. (Sir H. Maxwell) Blackw. 155: 555.
Trowbridge, John Townsend, Portraits of. McClure, 2: 343.
— Some Confessions of a Novel-writer. Atlan. 75: 316.
Troy-myth, Accretions to, after Homer. (W. C. Lawton) Poet-Lore, 8: 14.
Troy, N. Y., Beginnings of. (Mrs. M. J. Lamb) M. Am. Hist. 28: 1.
Troy Town, England, Revisited. (A. T. Q. Couch) Eng. Illust. 12: no. 1, 88.
Troyon, Constant. Art J. 45: 22.
Truants and Incorrigibles, Care of. (E. P. Seaver) Educa. R. 7: 423.
Truax, Chauncey S., with portrait. Nat'l M. (N. Y. '91) 19: 210.
Truck Legislation and the Home Secretary's Bill. (S. N. Fox) Fortn. 63: 593.
True Avouch of mine own Eyes. (E. Crowe) Belgra. 91: 190.
True History of Our Cooks; a story. (F. C. Baylor) Cosmopol. 21: 649.
True Story of an Irish Courtship. All the Year, 73: 325.
True Tales of the Old West. (R. M. Daggett) Overland, n. s. 25: 62, (C. L. Canfield) 142, (S. S. Boynton) 258, (C. D. Robinson) 261, (S. S. Boynton) 354, 491. 26: 172. (G. A. Hamilton) 27: 211, (Emma A. Thurston) 276, (J. H. Lawrence) 369, (J. C. Brown 510, (E. K. Rountree) 617.
Truffles. Chamb. J. 69: 182.
— Hunting for. (G. Fidler) Eng. Illust. 11: 158.
— — in Wiltshire. (P. A. Graham) Longm. 25: 531.
Trumbull, John, Artist. (E. S. Bartlett) New Eng. M. n. s. 13: 607.
— an Historian in Color. (C. H. Hyde) M. Am. Hist. 28: 296.
Trumbull, Lyman, with portrait. (R. Linthicum) Arena, 12: 33.
Trumbull, Matthew Mark. Open Court, 8: 4079.
Trumbull Genealogy, Contributions to. (J. H. Lea) N. E. Reg. 49: 148, 322, 417.
Trumpet of Fame, The. (H. D. Traill) Univ. R. 7: 114, 189.
Trumpeter, The. (M. H. Foote) Atlan. 74: 577, 721.
Trumpeter and the Child; a story. (J. C. Bell) Canad. M. 5: 59.
Trumpeter of the Troop. (T. H. Wilson) Cent. 29: 428.
Trumpets, Concerning. All the Year, 72: 567.
Trust, Breach of, Indemnity against. (W. C. Smith) Jurid. R. 8: 105.
Trust Companies. Bank. M. (Lond.) 56: 165.
Trustee Act, 1888, England. (L. L. Shadwell) Law Q. 6: 50.
Trustees and Mortgagees. (A. J. P. Menzies) Jurid. R. 5: 241.
— Defaulting, Remedy for. Sat. R. 77: 123.
Trusteeship and Agency. (C. Sweet) Law Q. 8: 220.
Trusteeships, Administration of, by Joint-stock Companies. (T. C. Poole) Law Q. 5: 395.
Trusting in the Dark. (H. C. G. Moule) Philos. R. 2: 71.
Trusts, Administration of. (J. H. Tait) Jurid. R. 8: 386.
— and Trustees. Chamb. J. 71: 71.
— and Corporations. (L. G. McPherson) Pop. Sci. Mo. 45: 289.
— and Monopolies as Modern Highwaymen. (W. O. McDowell) Our Day, 11: 424.
— and Unions. (L. J. Gage) Open Court, 2: 959.
— and Wages. (F. H. Cooke) Soc. Econ. 9: 107.
— Anti-trust Campaign. (A. W. Tourgée) No. Am. 157: 30.
— and a Substitute for Strikes. Spec. 71: 422.
— Common Sense on. Gunton's M. 11: 402.
— Economic Errors of. Soc. Econ. 4: 65.
— in the U. S. (J. Jenks) Econ. J. 2: 70.
— — Von Halle on. Sat. R. 80: 351.
— Modern, Tyrrel's Case and. (J. B. Ames) Green Bag, 4: 81.
— Some Legal Decisions with regard to. (G. Bryan) Am. M. Civics, 9: 352.
— Their Own Corrective. (G. A. Rich) Pop. Sci. Mo. 44: 740.
Truth. (P. Carus) Open Court, 7: 3596.
— and Error, Meaning of. (D. S. Miller) Philos. R. 2: 408.
— and Fiction. (M. W. Meyer) Open Court, 2: 1451.
— and Tests of Truth. (A. Hodder) Philos. R. 5: 1.
— and the White Lie. (E. M. Thomas) Atlan. 76: 836.
— as apprehended and expressed in Art. (G. F. Genung) New World, 3: 527.
— Criterion of. (P. Carus) Monist, 1: 229.

Truth, Human, The Personal Equation in. (R. P. Halleck) Pop. Sci. Mo. 46: 792.
— Inspiration and. (W. Lloyd) Westm. 137: 16.
— Loyalty to, Two Forms of. (W. R. Harper) Bib. World, 7: 241.
— Religious. (J. Burroughs) Open Court, 6: 3319.
Truth, Sojourner. *See* Sojourner Truth.
Truth-hunting. Time, 23: 1289.
Truth about Stoutenbrough; a story. (J. Lloyd) Munsey, 13: 651.
Truth Toy-show, The. (W. C. Preston) Sund. M. 23: 120.
Truthfulness. *See* Veracity.
Truths, Shady. (L. H. Courtney) Contemp. 61: 642. Same art. Ecl. M. 119: 16.
"Try for Her in Fifty;" a sea story. (W. C. Russell) Good Words, 35: 55.
Tryer's Bell; a story. Temp. Bar. 94: 376.
Trying Our Wings; a story. All the Year, 73: 138.
Tryon, Admiral Sir George. Spec. 71: 10.
— and the Victoria Disaster, with portrait. (W. T. Stead) R. of Rs. (N. Y.) 8: 169.
Tryon, Dwight Wm., with portrait. (R. Cortissoz) Harper, 91: 171.
Tsavo and the Taita Highlands, Visit to. (C. W. Hobley) Geog. J. 5: 545.
Tschaikowsky, Peter Iltitsch. (J. S. Shedlock) Acad. 44: 422. — Ath. '93, 2: 670. — (J. de Zielinski) Music, 5: 271. — (F. W. Root) Music, 5: 306.
Ts'ets'ā'ut, Traditions of the. (F. Boas) J. Am. Folk-Lore, 9: 257.
Tsetse Fly Disease. (W. F. H. Blandford) Nature, 53: 566.
Tsimsian Language, Von der Schulenburg on. (A. S. Gatschet) Nation, 59: 180.
Tsimsian Proverbs. (Miss O. Morrison) J. Am. Folk-Lore, 2: 285.
Tuam Cathedral. Reliquary, 32: 95.
Tuan Roseden's Story, The. Temp. Bar, 96: 505. Same art. Ecl. M. 120: 206. Same art. Liv. Age, 196: 142.
Tuatara, The, a Remarkable Lizard. (J. Buckland) Eng. Illust. 16: 381.
Tube-making, Wrought-iron. (R. T. Crane) Cassier, 6: 64.
Tuberculosis and its Prevention. (T. M. Prudden) Harper, 88: 630.
— Royal Commission on, Pathological Results of. (S. Martin) Sci. Prog. 3: 335.
Tubing, Flexible. (G. R. Redgrave) J. Soc. Arts, 40: 429.
Tübingen, Germany, and its Catholic Scholars. (G. F. X. Griffith) Cath. World, 60: 23.
Tubman, Harriet. (L. B. C. Wyman) New Eng. M. n. s. 14: 110. — (R. B. Holt) Chaut. 23: 459.
Tucker, Charlotte. (A. R. Buckland) Sund. M. 24: 611.
Tudor, Margaret. Intrigues in Scotland. Scot. R. 24: 225.
Tuer le Mandarin. All the Year, 75: 377.
Tufts, Col. Gardiner. And. R. 17: 80.
Tug of War; a story. (W. E. Norris) Harper, 89: 565.
Tugboats. (E. Beynon) Leis. Hour, 42: 251.
— and Their Work. Chamb. J. 71: 343.
Tuileries, Life in the, under the Second Empire. (A. L. Bicknell) Cent. 25: 643. 28: 709.
Tuke, Daniel Hack, with portrait. Pop. Sci. Mo. 47: 625.
Tuke, James Hack, and his Work. (S. Buxton; H. Hodgkin) Contemp. 69: 860. Same art. Liv. Age, 210: 144.
Tulips, About. (J. N. Gerard) Garden & F. 8: 207.
— Cultivation of. (E. O. Orpet) Garden & F. 7: 176.
— Cultural Notes on. (W. Watson) Garden & F. 9: 223.
— Notes on. (Max Leichtlin) Garden & F. 5: 224.
Tulle and its Government Factories of Arms. Chamb J. 69: 693.
"Tully's Head," At. (A. Dobson) Scrib. M. 15: 516.
Tumors, Extirpation of, Early. (J. W. S. Gouley) Pop. Sci. Mo. 42: 337.
Tunbridge Wave. Chamb. J. 71: 762.
Tunbridge Wells, Old Road to. All the Year, 73: 367.
Tundale, Vision of. (W. A. Craigie) Scot. R. 26: 92.
Tungsten, Atomic Weight of. (E. F. Smith and E. D. Desi) J. Frankl. Inst. 139: 290.
Tungstous Oxide, etc., associated with Columbous Oxide. (W. P. Headden) Am. J. Sci. 145: 280.
Tunicata, Budding among the. (W. Garstang) Sci. Prog. 3: 43, 250.
Tunis. (S. J. Weyman) Leis. Hour, 41: 14. — (E. S. Purcell) Time, 7: 696.
—French in. (Count Gleichen) Fortn. 61: 538. Same art. Liv. Age, 201: 470. — (J. St. Loe Strachey) National, 25: 21.
— Italian Power in. (T. A. Archer) New R. 15: 724.
— Tints and Tones of. (H. Haynie) Cosmopol. 17: 670.
Tunisia, Through Northern. (Wm. Sharp) Good Words, 36: 16.
Tunnel-building, Difficulties of. (E. Low) Engin. M. 3: 199.
Tunnelling by Compressed Air. (E. W. Moir) J. Soc. Arts, 44: 567.
Tunnels, Great. (R. Jamison) Chaut. 21: 32.
— Iron-lined. Chamb. J. 71: 495.
Tupelo-trees; Nyssa Sylvatica. Garden & F. 7: 273.
Turacin, the Animal Pigment. (A. H. Church) Nature, 48: 209. — Dub. R. 115: 156.
Turanian Blood in the Anglo-Saxon Race. (M. V. B. Knox) Meth. R. 53: 697.
Turbines, How to Test. (S. Webber) Cassier, 8: 605.
— Niagara. (C. Herschel) Cassier, 3: 387.
— Steam. Cassier, 3: 94. — (J. H. Barr) Cassier, 10: 372.
Turenne, Life of, Hozier's. Liv. Age, 192: 152.
Turf, American, Status of the. (F. Trevelyan) Outing, 19: 468. 20: 33, 129.
— in Lord George Bentinck's Day. Belgra. 80: 27.
Turgenev, Ivan. (M. Todhunter) Westm. 146: 141.
— Episode in Life of. (N. H. Dole) Arena, 10: 401.
— Howells on. Critic, 26: 295.
— Letters of. (L. Katscher) Univ. R. 8: 577.
— Mother of. (H. H. Boyesen) Cent. 26: 249. — (I. F. Hapgood) Nation, 58: 447.
— On the Eve. Tr. by C. Garnett. Sat. R. 79: 675.
Turgot, A. R. J. Life and Writings. (D. L. Shorey) Dial (Ch.) 19: 138. — Sat. R. 80: 413. — (W. B. Duffield) Acad. 47: 458.
Turkey, Administration of Justice in. (D. Démétriadés) Jurid. R. 3: 145, 245.
— American Treaty Rights in. Our Day, 14: 168.
— Americans in, Troubles of. (R. Ogden) Nation, 54: 443.
— America's Duty to Americans in. An Open Letter to the Hon. John Sherman. (C. Hamlin) No. Am. 163: 276.
— Army of. (C. B. Norman) Un. Serv. M. 11: 611.
— — in Olden Time. (F. H. Tyrell) Asia. R. 8: 398. 9: 30.
— Art Impetus in. (J. P. Peters) Cent. 23: 546.
— The Caliph and his Duties. (Ahmed Riza) Contemp. 70: 206.
— The Crisis in the East. (K. Blind) No. Am. 162: 84.

Turkey, Education of Women in. (M. M. Patrick) Forum, 21: 440.
— England's Policy in. Fortn. 65: 286.
— English Policy toward. Sat. R. 80: 466.
— English Trade with, The Dawn of. (W. J. Hardy) Good Words, 37: 590.
— Inhabitants and Customs of. (G. B. Burgin) Idler, 7: 515.
— Is it Progressing? (Ibrahim Hakki) Asia. R. 13: 265.
— Is the Sultan the True Khaliph of Islâm? (H. A. Salmoné) 19th Cent. 39: 173. — (G. W. Leitner) Asia. R. 21: 65.
— Lenz's World Tour Awheel. Outing, 29: 150, 267.
— Letters on. (G. M. Müller) Longm. 28: 135, 239. Same art. Ecl. M. 127: 85, 190. Same art. Liv. Age, 210: 99–254.
— Misgovernment in. (W. S. Blunt; E. F. DuCane) 19th Cent. 40: 838.
— Naval Position of. (S. Eardley-Wilmot) Un. Serv. M. 6: 382.
— or Russia? (M. MacColl) Fortn. 64: 943.
— Present Condition of Mohammedan Women in. (R. Darcy) Fortn. 64: 53.
— Press in. (H. A. Salmoné) 19th Cent. 36: 716.
— Question of, in its Religious Aspect. (J. W. Gambier) Fortn. 66: 521.
— Question of, Turkish Note on. National, 26: 569.
— — Symposium. Indep. March 5, '96.
— The Real. (C. Kitchin) Time, 19: 413.
— Real Rulers of. (H. A. Salmoné) 19th Cent. 37: 719.
— Remarks on Ibrahim Hakki Bey's Article. (Hyde Clarke) Asia. R. 14: 129.
— The Selamlik. (M. A. M. Marks) Argosy, 61: 84.
— The Stage in. (R. Davey) Theatre, 37: 257.
— A World Crisis. (H. H. Van Meter) Our Day, 16: 35.
— Young. (K. Blind) Fortn. 66: 830.
Turkeys, Tracking, Trial of. (E. W. Sandys) Outing, 29: 153.
— Wild, Gunning for. (W. C. Elam) Lippinc. 56: 811.
— — On the Trail of. (C. D. Lanier) Harper, 89: 881.
— — Two Tries for. (E. W. Sandys) Outing, 25: 292.
— — Virginia. (A. Mulville) Outing, 25: 391.
Turkish Embassy in London. Eng. Illust. 16: 131.
Turkish Flagship, Seizure of. (Demetrios Bikelas) Scot. R. 27: 117. Same art. Liv. Age, 208: 506.
Turkish Guilds. (C. Sutcliffe) Fortn. 66: 820.
Turkestan, Afghan, Excursion to. Dub. R. 116: 189.
— Chinese, Takia-Makan Desert of. (S. Hedin) Geog. J. 8: 264, 356.
— Russian. (Paul Gault) Asia. R. 16: 50.
— Trip to. (H. Bower) Geog. J. 5: 240.
Turks and Mongols, Cahun's. (A. C. Coolidge) Nation, 62: 495.
— Origin of the. (E. H. Parker) Eng. Hist. R. 11: 431.
Turn of the Wheel, The. Chamb. J. 69: 620.
Turned around: Mental Somersault. Atlan. 71: 566.
Turner, John Bice, with portrait. Nat'l M. (N. Y. '91) 16: 711.
Turner, Joseph M. W. (J. Penderel-Brodhurst) M. of Art, 8: 510. — (J. E. Hodgson; F. A. Eaton) Art J. 45: 162–324.
— at Farnley Hall. (S. A. Byles) M. of Art, 10: 295.
— Harbours of England, Ruskin on. Sat. R. 80: 180.
— Portraits of. (L. Cust) M. of Art, 18: 245. — (C. Monkhouse) Scrib. M. 20: 89.
— Water-Color Art of. (T. Sulman) Good Words, 37: 688–758.
Turner, J. M. W. Yorkshire Drawings, Early History of. Ath. '94, 2: 326.
Turner, Robert Samuel. Bookworm, 2: 177.
Turner, Valentine C., with portrait. (H. L. Conard) Nat'l M. (N. Y. '91) 16: 714.
Turner on the Loire. Music, 3: 113.
Turning again of Lady Drummond; a story. (E. Chilton) Temp. Bar, 101: 62.
Turnpike, On an Old American. (A. G. Bradley) Fortn. 66: 291. Same art. Liv. Age, 210: 617.
Turpentine. Gathering Naval Stores. (L. J. Vance) Pop. Sci. Mo. 48: 469.
Turpentine Farm, A, in Georgia. Chamb. J. 73: 14. Same art. Liv. Age, 208: 254.
Turpin's Ride to York. Ecl. M. 124: 696.
Turquoise, New Localities for. (W. E. Hidden) Am. J. Sci. 146: 400.
Turtle, Land of the. All the Year, 71: 227.
Turtle Chase, in the Indian Ocean. (G. H. Westley) Outing, 25: 249.
Tusayan, The Kivas and Kisis of. (E. Ingersoll) Mo. Illust. 3: 341.
— Ceremonials of. (J. W. Fewkes) J. Am. Folk-Lore, 8: 265.
— — the Pá-lü-lü-koñ-ti. (J. W. Fewkes and A. M. Stephens) J. Am. Folk-Lore, 6: 269.
— Ceremonial Circuit of the Cardinal Points among. (J. W. Fewkes) Am. Natural. 26: 24.
— History and Architecture of. (S. D. Peet) Am. Antiq. 18: 1.
— Initiation Ceremony. (J. W. Fewkes and A. M. Stephens) J. Am. Folk-Lore, 5: 189.
Tusayan Monsters, Destruction of. (J. W. Fewkes) J. Am. Folk-Lore, 8: 132.
Tuscan Farmhouse, A. (I. M. Anderton) Good Words, 36: 702.
Tuscan Folk-story, A. (I. M. Anderton) Good Words, 35: 301.
Tuscan Highlanders at Home. (E. S. Morgan) Time, 17: 716.
Tuscan May-day; a poem. (A. M. F. Robinson) M. of Art, 8: 141.
Tuscan Mezzadria. (E. S. Morgan) Time, 14: 153.
Tuscan Shrine, A. (Edith Wharton) Scrib. M. 17: 23.
Tuscany, Love-songs of the Peasantry of. (H. C. Dana) Cath. World, 58: 685.
— Nationality in. (Grant Allen) National, 22: 83. Same art. Ecl. M. 121: 837. Same art. Liv. Age, 199: 195.
— North, Notes on. (V. Paget) M. of Art, 7: 1.
Tuscarora Conspiracy in Carolina. (H. M. Thompson) Nat'l M. (N. Y. '91) 19: 138.
Tusitala in Vailima; a poem. (E. Gosse) McClure, 5: 170.
Tuskegee Negro Conference; 4th Annual Session. (R. C. Bedford) Lend a H. 14: 247.
Tuskegee Normal and Industrial Institute. (B. T. Washington) Chaut. 18: 197. — (A. Shaw) R. of Rs. (N. Y.) 9: 436. — (E. E. Lane) Lend a H. 13: 17.
— Industrial Education at. (B. T. Washington) Our Day, 16: 79, 343.
— One Woman's Influence in Alabama's Black Belt. Our Day, 16: 339.
Tusks and their Uses. (R. Lydekker) Knowl. 16: 121.
Tussock Moth. (Dr. E. B. Southwick) Garden & F. 8: 308. — (V. H. Lowe) Garden & F. 8: 314.
— White-marked, in Chicago. (J. L. Hancock) Am. Natural. 28: 326.
Tussore Silk. (G. Wallis) M. of Art, 2: 47.
Tutor's Wife, The; a play. (A. Hennequin) Bost. 3: 442.
Tuttiet, Miss Mary G., with portrait. Bk. News, 12: 43.

Tuxedo Club, The. (J. N. Smith) Munsey, 6: 161.
Tuxedo Park, N. Y., Art and Engineering at. (J. S. Haring) Engin. M. 2: 459.
Twain, Mark. *See* Clemens, S. L.
Tweddell, Ralph Hart. Cassier, 7: 260.
Tweed Ring, Rise and Overthrow of. (E. J. Edwards) McClure, 5: 132.
Tweedside; The Men of the Hills. Macmil. 72: 298.
— A Night on the Heather in the Glens. Macmil. 72: 356.
'Tween Man and Man. (A. E. Abbott) Idler, 5: 626.
Twelve Numbers, Carol of the. (W. W. Newell) J. Am. Folk-Lore, 4: 215.
Twentieth Century. (H. B. Brown) Forum, 19: 641. — (T. H. Pearne) Meth. R. 55: 608. — (C. Morris) Lippinc. 53: 138.
Twenty-dollar Bill. (A. Tassin) Lippinc. 58: 108.
Twenty-first of October; a story. (Kenneth Grahame) New R. 13: 359.
Twenty-four — Four: a story. (E. S. Phelps) Harper, 92: 264.
'20 Port. Temp. Bar, 101: 454.
Twenty Years; a poem. (W. Whitman) M. of Art, 11: 348.
Twice in Jeopardy. (F. B. Livingstone) Green Bag, 6: 373.
Twice Told; a story. (G. F. White) Eng. Illust. 13: 309.
Twickenham; Literary Suburb of the 18th Century. (W. C. Sydney) Gent. M. n. s. 49: 589.
Twilight, The Astronomy of. (O. E. Harmon) Pop. Astron. 4: 148, 252.
Twilight; a poem. Cornh. 68: 622.
Twilight of a Life, The; a story. All the Year, 70: 492.
Twilight Night; a poem. (M. A. M. Marks) Argosy, 62: 214.
Twin Bank Holidays; a story. (C. Scott) Idler, 6: 53.
Twining, Louisa. Autobiography. Sat. R. 77: 48.
Twins; a story. (R. Marsh) Idler, 8: 504.
Two by Four; a story. (R. S. Jones) Munsey, 12: 596.
Two in the Bush; a story. (F. F. Moore) Idler, 6: 575.
Two in a Gondola; an Olympian Idyl. (A. Fairbairn) Idler, 1: 639.
Two in the "Other Half." (E. O. Hays) Lippinc. 53: 830.
Two of a Kind; a story. (R. Barr) Idler, 5: 147.
Two of a Trade. (F. W. Robinson) Idler, 1: 181.
Two of a Trade; a story. (W. W. Jacobs) Idler, 10: 649.
Two Beasts; a story. (G. S. Duff) Arena, 13: 135.
Two Beauties of the Backwoods; a story. (C. C. Farr) Canad. M. 6: 221, 322.
Two Black Bags; a story. All the Year, 74: 611.
Two Brothers; a Russian Story. (J. Prelooker) Sund. M. 24: 37.
Two Brothers; a tale. (R. Lucas) Belgra. 78: 45.
Two City Girls' Experiences in holding down a Claim. (L. E. M. Smith) Overland, n. s. 24: 145.
Two Days; a poem. New R. 13: 536.
Two Eistedfodds, The; a story. (E. M. T. Fitzjohn) Belgra. 78: holiday no. 43.
Two Episodes in a Coward's Life. Liv. Age, 200: 232.
Two Fetches; a story. (J. Bond) Theatre, 30: 39.
Two Glacier Accidents; a story. (F. Gribble) Idler, 2: 192.
Two Gourmets of Bloomfield; a story. (Alice S. Wolf) Overland, n. s. 20: 299.
Two Handicaps; a story. (C. Shelley) Outing, 28: 268. 370.
Two Holiday-meets; a story. Belgra. 80: 294.
Two Ideals Realized; a story. (Alice Powell) Belgra. 83: 52.
Two Idlers in Camp. (H. Church) Outing, 26: 392.
Two Lepers. (M. Eyre) Longm. 20: 264.
Two Letters; a story. All the Year, 73: 305, 333.
Two Market Days at Cummerthwaite. (Sarah S. Homer) Chamb. J. 72: 760.
Two Mates, The; a story. (Edward Heins) Gent. M. n. s. 53: 541.
Two Mayors of Bottitort; from the Memoirs of a Minister of France. (S. J. Weyman) Eng. Illust. 12: no. 3, 133.
Two Men and a River; a story. (M. Roberts) Eng. Illust. 15: 449.
Two Miracles; a story. (W. L Alden) Cornh. 74: 654.
Two Modern Prodigals; a story. (J. F. McKay) McClure, 8: 69.
Two Mormons from Muddlety; a story. (L. E. Mitchell) Harper, 93: 191, 436, 587.
Two Mrs. Elder Greens; a story. (P. McClure) Munsey, 11: 77.
Two-Ocean Pass. (B. W. Evermann) Pop. Sci. Mo. 47: 175.
Two Old Boys. (P. S. Colyar) Lippinc. 58: 815.
Two Painters, The; a poem. (A. Dobson) M. of Art, 5: 340.
Two Points of View; a story. (J. T. K. Tarpey) Temp. Bar, 107: 76.
Two Proper Prides; a story. (H. D. Traill) National, 21: 386. Same art. Liv. Age, 197: 790. Same art. Ecl. M. 121: 111.
Two Republics or One? (H. L. West) No. Am. 162: 509.
Two Roses, The; a poem. (J. Turner) Gent. M. n. s. 48: 420.
Two Sacrifices; a poem. (E. Arnold) Cosmopol. 20: 502.
Two Shadowy Rivals. (R. M. Johnston) Cent. 28: 144.
Two Sides to a Saint. (L. W. Bacon) Chr. Lit. 12: 129.
Two Silver Bullets; a story. (W. B. Foster) Munsey, 11: 475.
Two Strings to his Bow. (W. Mitchell) Atlan. 73: 169, 339.
Two Studies of Old Men; Stories. (M. Negreponte) Westm. 138: 631.
Two Women. (Sir H. Cunningham) Macmil. 67: 285. Same art. Liv. Age, 196: 759.
Two Writers. (J. L. Ford) Cosmopol. 22: 103.
Two-Year-Old Heroine, A. (F. Trevelyan) Outing, 21: 17.
Tyburn Tree. (F. Watt) New R. 15: 692.
Tycho Brahe. (C. E. Furness) Pop. Astron. 3: 221.
Tyler, Cyril. Music, 3: 271.
Tyler, James G. (J. G. Speed) Q. Illust. 2: 24.
Tynan, Katherine. *See* Hinkson, Katharine T.
Tynan, Patrick J. P., and his Disclosures. Sat. R. 82: 345.
— Kearny, and Haines, Extradition of. National, 28: 293.
Tyndall, John. Ath. '93, 2: 811. — (H. Hale) Critic, 23: 389. — Dial (Ch.) 15: 377. — Pub. Opin. 16: 249. — Sat. R. 76: 641. — (T. H. Huxley) 19th Cent. 35: 1. Same art. Liv. Age, 200: 259. Same art. Ecl. M. 122: 220. Same art. Pop. Sci. Mo. 44: 637. — (H. Spencer) Fortn. 61: 141. Same art. Pop. Sci. Mo. 44: 819. — (P. C. Mitchell) New R. 10: 77. — (F. L. Oswald; M. D. Conway) Open Court, 8: 3927, 3943. — (G. Allen) R. of Rs. (N. Y.) 9: 172. — With portraits. (H. Spencer) McClure, 2: 401. — Dub. R. 114: 174. — (J. W. Gregory) Nat. Sci. 4: 10. — Around World, 1: 60.

Tyndall, John, and his American Visit. (E. A. Youmans) Pop. Sci. 44: 502.
— as a Materialist. (J. G. Hibben) No. Am. 158: 122.
— Death of. Critic, 23: 382.
— New Fragments. Ath. '92, 1: 347. — (A. W. Benn) Acad. 41: 293.
— Scientific Work of. (Lord Rayleigh) Pop. Sci. Mo. 46: 658.
Tyne River, The. (A. Watson) M. of Art, 6: 114.
Tynedale, England, Castles, Churches, and Tributaries of. (E. Browne) Art J. 45: 38, 73.
Tyneside, Reminiscences of. Chamb. J. 73: 218.
Tyng, Rev. S. H., with portrait. Bk. News, 9: 258.
Type, Century's Printer on the Century's. (T. L. De Vinne) Cent. 29: 794.
Type-setting by Machinery. (W. E. Crane) Engin. M. 2: 513. — (J. Southward) J. Soc. Arts, 44: 74.
Type-writing Machines. (H. C. Jenkins) J. Soc. Arts, 42: 839, 855.
Typewriter, Bar-lock, of Chas. Spiro. J. Frankl. Inst. 137: 321.
— a Coming Necessity in Schools. (F. H. Kasson) Educa. 15: 615.
Typewriter, Being a. (L. C. Bull) Atlan. 76: 822.
Type-writers and Writers. (Edw. Aveling) Time, 23: 1322.
Type-writing, Present Educational Aspects of. (F. H. Palmer) Educa. 12: 622.
— Rules for copying MSS. in. (W. H. Hills) Writer, 7: 82.
Type-written Letter, The; a story. (R. Barr) Idler, 2: 597. Same art. (R. Barr) McClure, 2: 445.
Types, Current, Written Portraits of. (Edith Sichel) Time, 20: 509, 645. 21: 42.
Typhoid Fever and Rainfall. (W. P. Mason) J. Frankl. Inst. 140: 212.
— Oysters and. Nature, 51: 391, (G. C. Frankland) 415.
— Treatment of. (C. E. Page) Arena, 6: 450.
Typography, History of. (W. Blades) Bookworm, 1: 84-212.
Typological Museums. (Lt.-Gen. Pitt-Rivers) J. Soc. Arts, 40: 115.
Tyrant's Apology, The; a story. (G. Gissing) Eng. Illust. 13: 297.
Tyrol, Among the Snow Mountains of. (A. E. W. Mason) Temp. Bar, 104: 411. Same art. Ecl. M. 124: 611. Same art. Liv. Age, 205: 113.
— at the World's Fair. (Charlotte H. Coursen) Munsey, 9: 231.
— Austrian, Holiday in the. (A. McLean) Belgra. 80: 408.
— Bicycle Trip in the. (S. Greer) Outing, 28: 254.
— Charterhouse of. Good Words, 33: 180. Same art. Liv. Age, 193: 418.
— Folks-play in the. (R. Barr) Idler, 4: 581.
Tyrrell, Robert Yelverton. (H. A. Hinkson) Critic, 22: 149.
Tzarskoe Selo; an Imperial Pleasure Place. (I. F. Hapgood) Cosmopol. 20: 641.

Uffizi Gallery, Florence, Misnamed Pictures in. (C. A. J. Ffoulkes) M. of Art, 13: 189.
Uganda. (R. W. Felkin) Asia. R. 14: 93. — Asia. R. 15: 55. — (G. S. Mackenzie) Fortn. 62: 882.
— Ashe on. (C. H. Cooper) Dial (Ch.) 20: 136.
— Best Route to. (G. F. S. Elliot) Contemp. 68: 15.
— British Mission to, 1893. Spec. 73: 51.
— Catholic Prospects in. (R. L. Keegan) Month, 78: 475.
— Chronicles of, Ashe's. Sat. R. 79: 97.
— Commercial Future of. Dub. R. 113: 670.
Uganda, Compromise on. Spec. 72: 780.
— Controversy about, End of. Spec. 69: 345.
— Evacuation of. Spec. 69: 485.
— France and. Spec. 68: 773.
— Land of the Nile Springs, Colvile's. Sat. R. 80: 551.
— Past and Present. (R. P. Ashe) Sund. M. 23: 397, 478.
— Sir G. Portal on. Spec. 72: 495. — Dub. R. 115: 455. — Sat. R. 77: 666.
— Problem of. (J. Thomson) Contemp. 62: 786. — (Sir C. W. Dilke) Fortn. 59: 145.
— Shall it be retained? (J. G. Rogers) 19th Cent. 33: 219.
— Side-lights on. (H. Waller) Blackw. 152: 127. Same art. Ecl. M. 119: 304.
— Situation in. Dub. R. 112: 451.
— The Troubles in. (G. S. Mackenzie) Fortn. 58: 23. Same art. M. Chr. Lit. 6: 363. — (F. D. Lugard) Fortn. 58: 689. — (W. J. Smith) New R. 7: 92.
— Truth About. (K. Vaughan) Month, 76: 153.
Uganda Railway, Proposed. (H. M. Stanley) Sat. R. 79: 719.
Ugliness of Modern Life, The. (L. de la Ramé) 19th Cent. 39: 28.
Ugly, the, Worship of. (C. Monkhouse) National, 27: 124. Same art. Ecl. M. 126: 665.
Ugly Little Woman, An; a story. (N. Vynne) Gent. M. n. s. 49: 325.
Ugly Man, The. (L. Street) Argosy, 56: 516.
Uhland, Poems of, Hewett's. (C. von Klenze) School R. 4: 628.
Uist, North, Glance at. All the Year, 74: 104.
Uitlanders, The Case for. (C. Leonard) New R. 14: 454.
Ullathorne, Wm., Archbishop. (A. F. Marshall) Am. Cath. Q. 18: 329.
— Autobiography. Spec. 70: 294.
Ulphilas, and the Conversion of the Goths. (A. G. Hopkins) And. R. 18: 162.
Ulrich of Lichtenstein. Cornh. 67: 69.
Ulster. National, 19: 449.
— and the Confederate States. (C. de Polignac) 19th Cent. 33: 927.
— and Home Rule. Contemp. 62: 16. — (St. L. Strachey) 19th Cent. 31: 877. Same art. Ecl. M. 119: 166. Same art. Liv. Age, 194: 195. — (J. G. Colclough) Contemp. 63: 761.
— Annals of. (W. Stokes) Acad. 50: 182, 223.
— Facts and Figures. (T. Sinclair) Contemp. 64: 29.
— Home Rule for. Spec. 68: 487, 835.
— — and the Protestants. (W. E. Ball; H. P. Hughes) New R. 7: 1.
— Taxation of, under a Home Rule Parliament. (G. McDermot) Cath. World, 56: 393.
Ulster Singing Schools. All the Year, 75: 233.
Ulstermen in America. Spec. 68: 869.
Ultra vires Doctrine: should it be applied to Business? (F. H. Cooke) Am. Law R. 28: 222.
Ultramontanism *vs.* Americanism. (L. Johnston) Cath. World, 59: 731.
Umbeyla Campaign, 1863. Un. Serv. M. 6: 457.
— Reminiscences of. (W. F. Mitchell) Chamb. J. 72: 812.
Umbria, Valleys of. (S. Thompson) M. of Art, 2: 236.
Una at Desford; a story. (B. Pain) Idler, 2: 518.
Unacted Crime. (G. H. Burrow) Eng. Illust. 11: 746.
Unanswered Prayers; a poem. (E. W. Wilcox) Cosmopol. 19: 217.
Unattractive Girl. (M. G. L. Underwood) New Eng. M. n. s. 9: 659.

Unauthorized Intervention, An; a story. (D. L. Johnstone) Chamb. J. **72**: 337-406.
Unbalanced People. (F. H. Wines) Lend a H. **16**: 166.
Unbelief, Grief at. (P. Carus) Open Court, **7**: 3579.
Unbidden Guest; a story. Argosy, **57**: 332.
Unbidden Guest; a story. All the Year, **71**: 132, 151.
Unbidden Guest; a story. (E. W. Hornung) Longm. **24**: 76-628.
Unc' Ananias; a story. (M. E. Seawell) Lippinc. **50**: 97.
Unc' Israel's Eli; a story. (F. Lynde) Munsey, **12**: 540.
Unchurched Classes; symposium. Indep. Jan. 5, '93.
Uncanny Bairn, The. Cornh. **66**: 274. Same art. Ecl. M. **119**: 515. Same art. Liv. Age, **195**: 459.
Unclaimed, The Great. Blackw. **157**: 591. Same art. Liv. Age, **205**: 438.
Unclaimed Estates. (H. S. Everett) Atlan. **77**: 240.
Unclaimed Money in Chancery. Time, **15**: 79.
Uncle Duke's "B'ar" story. (L. Gilfillan) Outing, **19**: 409.
Uncle Lock's Legacy. (J. Payn) Idler, **1**: 405.
"Uncle Nat;" a story. (W. Cary) Cosmopol. **13**: 378.
Uncle Obadiah's Uncle Billy. (W. H. Shelton) Cent. **24**: 307.
Uncle Onesimus; a story. Cornh. **69**: 612.
Uncle Remus traced to the Old World. (A. Gerber) J. Am. Folk-Lore, **6**: 245.
Uncle Richard; a story. (A. M. Meadows) Belgra. **80**: 394.
Uncle Seth. (H. M. North) New Eng. M. n. s. **14**: 476.
Unconditional Surrender, An; a drama. (D. Leighton) Eng. Illust. **13**: 267.
Uncrowned King, An; a Romance of High Politics. Blackw. **158**: 769. **159**: 38-851. **160**: 67-206.
Undaunted Spirit. (L. Baldwin) Longm. **27**: 476.
Undecyphered Significance; a poem. (G. Wyndham) New R. **13**: 484.
Undefinable, The; a story. (Sarah Grand) New R. **11**: 320, 433. Same art. Cosmopol. **17**: 745.
Under a Bush of Lilacs. (J. Arbes) Poet-Lore, **4**: 318.
Under the Cherry-tree; a story. (D. Gerard) Chamb. J. **70**: 430-444.
Under Cover of the Darkness. (T. R. Sullivan) Scrib. M. **13**: 716.
Under Dog, The; a story. (L. T. Meade) Sund. M. **21**: 195, 274.
Under the Fair Divinities. Overland, n. s. **22**: 437.
Under False Pretenses; a story. (L. D. Mitchell) Outing, **22**: 319.
Under a Grass Roof; a story. (Dailey Dale) Sund. M. **21**: 624-837.
Under a Grey Vail; a story. (M. Pireau) Belgra. **89**: 211-433. **90**: 96-433. **91**: 102, 225.
Under the Headin' of Thruth. (B. Lindsay) Overland, n. s. **28**: 281-638.
Under the Knife. (H. G. Wells) New R. **14**: 1. Same art. Ecl. M. **126**: 605.
Under the Pines. (M. W. Glascock) Overland, n. s. **22**: 148.
Under Police Protection; a story. (S. Radford de Meissner) Scrib. M. **12**: 772.
Under Seal of Confession. Macmil. **68**: 357.
Under Sentence of the Law; a story of a Dog. (F. V. Stevenson) McClure, **1**: 34.
Under the Shadow of Tyburn-tree; a story. (Caroline Brown) Cosmopol. **21**: 417.
Under the Shadows of the Church; a story. (Mrs. F. W. W. Topsham) Sund. M. **24**: 458, 554.
Under a Spell. (M. E. S. Penn) Argosy, **59**: 161.
Under a Strange Seal; a story. (P. Andreae) Eng. Illust. **14**: 615.
Under the Tricolour. (P. de Nanteuil) Good Words, **37**: 55-846.
Under a Village Spire. (W. J. Ferrar) Sund. M. **24**: 835.
Under the Willow; a story. (Mrs. A. Fraser) Belgra. **78**: 148.
Under the Yellow Flag; a story. All the Year, **75**: 517.
Under the Yoke of the Butterflies. (Hon. A. Herbert) Fortn. **57**: 44.
Underclothing Question, The Great. (S. W. Beck) New R. **11**: 534, 606. **12**: 222.
Underflow as related to Irrigation. (H. V. Hinckley) Engin. M. **10**: 84.
Undergraduates, Religion of. (A. C. Deane) 19th Cent. **38**: 673. — (H. Legge) 19th Cent. **38**: 856. — (A. C. Deane) 19th Cent. **38**: 987.
Underground City in Turkestan. Dub. R. **110**: 194.
"Underground Railroad" and one of its Operators. (J. E. Champion) Canad. M. **5**: 9.
— Light on. (W. H. Siebert) Am. Hist. R. **1**: 455.
Underground Railways of London. Am. Arch. **50**: 135.
Understanding, Human; Relation of Hume's Treatise to the Inquiry. (W. B. Elkin) Philos. R. **3**: 672.
— Locke's Essay concerning Human. (J. E. Creighton) Philos. R. **3**: 601.
Understudy, The; a story. (R. Barr) McClure, **6**: 58.
Underthrust Folds and Faults. (E. A. Smith) Am. J. Sci. **145**: 305.
Underwood, B. F., Resignation as Editor of "The Open Court." Open Court, **1**: 622.
Underwood, Francis Henry. (J. T. Trowbridge) Atlan. **75**: 108. — (J. MacArthur) Critic, **25**: 192.
Underwriter, Capture and Burning of the. (D. B. Conrad) Un. Serv. (Phila.) **7**: 598.
Undine, The White Lady and. Eng. R. **3**: 69.
Undiscovered Murder, An. (T. R. Sullivan) Scrib. M. **16**: 176.
Undivined Tragedy, An; a story. (L. A. Tadema) Harper, **88**: 615.
Undoing of David Lemwell, The; a story. (L. B. Bridgman) Overland, n. s. **20**: 206.
Undying Fire; a story. (Mrs. St. L. Strachey) Belgra. **86**: 153.
Unemployed, The. (W. R. Bousfield) Contemp. **70**: 835. — (A. White) Fortn. **60**: 454. — (S. A. Barnett) Fortn. **60**: 741. — Lend a H. **12**: 126. — (T. E. Will) Arena, **10**: 701. — (C. D. Wright) Soc. Econ. **2**: 71.
— and Relief Measures in the U. S., Notes on the History of. (C. C. Closson) J. Pol. Econ. **3**: 461.
— Colonies for. (H. E. Moore) Contemp. **63**: 423.
— A Colony of the. (J. Flynt) Atlan. **78**: 793.
— Demands of, Senator Hoar on. Our Day, **13**: 257.
— Duty of the State toward. (H. C. B. Cowell) Pub. Opin. **16**: 121.
— Early Experiments with, in England. (A. R. Brewster) Q. J. Econ. **9**: 88.
— Eight-hours Day and. (J. Rae) Contemp. **63**: 790.
— Emergency Work for, in Providence. (E. W. Blake) Lend a H. **14**: 13.
— English Cities and. (E. Porritt) Char. R. **3**: 373.
— Experiment in Behalf of. (F. W. Speirs) Char. R. **1**: 304.
— Government Work for. (B. O. Flower) Arena, **9**: 822.

Unemployed, House of Commons Committee on the. (G. H. Duckworth) Econ. J. 6: 143.
— How Baltimore helped. (E. R. L. Gould) Forum, 17: 497.
— How to help the. (H. George) No. Am. 158: 175.
— in American Cities. (C. C. Closson, jr.) Q. J. Econ. 8: 168, 453, 499.
— — Relief for. (A. Shaw) R. of Rs. (N. Y.) 9: 29.
— in England, Children of. (J. Law) New R. 8: 228.
— in German Cities. (J. G. Brooks) Q. J. Econ. 7: 353.
— in London. A Winter's Experiment. (H. V. Toynbee) Macmil. 69: 54.
— in Massachusetts. (J. G. Brooks) Econ. J. 4: 361.
— in New York City, Five Months' Work for. (Mrs. C. R. Lowell) Char. R. 3: 323.
— Insurance of. (J. G. Brooks) Q. J. Econ. 10: 341.
— Labor Colonies and. (J. Mavor) J. Pol. Econ. 2: 26.
— Lack of Employment—its Cause and Cure. (E. Withy) Westm. 145: 123.
— Massachusetts Investigation of. (C. C. Closson) J. Pol. Econ. 3: 488, 492. —(J. G. Brooks) Econ. J. 5: 477.
— Methods of Dealing with. (A. Streeter) Month, 80: 153.
— Methods of Relief for. (J. S. Lowell) Forum, 16: 655.
— Movement of, in the U. S. Pub. Opin. 15: 499.
— Necessity of State Aid to. (S. Coit) Forum, 17: 275.
— Problem of. (J. A. M. Macdonald) New R. 9: 561. — Soc. Econ. 6: 11.
— — Future. (J. G. Brooks) Ann. Am. Acad. Pol. Sci. 5: 1.
— — Real. (R. Ogden) Nation, 59: 6.
— Public Work for, in Hartford, Objections to. (J. J. McCook) Char. R. 3: 236.
— Relief of, by Extra Public Service. Char. R. 3: 132.
— — Reports. Am. J. Soc. Sci. 32: 1.
— Remedies for Organized Vagrancy. Pub. Opin. 17: 69.
— Shall the State furnish Labor for? (H. C. B. Cowell) Am. J. Pol. 3: 456.
— Treatment of. (S. O. Preston) Char. R. 3: 218.
— What shall we do with? Soc. Econ. 6: 81. — (E. L. Godkin) Nation, 57: 481.
— Work for the Workless. (A. Withy) Westm. 141: 233.
Unemployment. (G. W. Lee) Lend a H. 14: 185.
— Economic Cause of. (J. A. Hobson) Contemp. 67: 744.
— Meaning and Measure of. (J. A. Hobson) Contemp. 67: 415.
Unexpected Guests, The; a Farce. (W. D. Howells) Harper, 86: 211.
Unexpected Legacy, An. (A. Turner) Cent. 26: 413.
Unfinished History, An. (E. Lynn Linton) Univ. R. 3: 187, 335.
Unfinished Rubber, An. Macmil. 70: 115. Same art. Liv. Age, 202: 174. Same art. Ecl. M. 123: 206.
Unfinished Story. (R. E. Burton) New Eng. M. n. s. 9: 242.
Unfinished Task. (W. J. Lacey) Longm. 23: 163. Same art. Liv. Age, 199: 785.
Unforgotten; a poem. (H. M. Burnside) Argosy, 59: 345.
Unfortunate Expedition, An; a story. Chamb. J. 73: 173.
Unfortunate Jest; a story. (Mrs. E. M. Davy) Belgra. 77: 394.
Unillumined Verge, The; a poem. (R. Bridges) Cosmopol. 14: 458.
Union for Practical Progress. (T. E. Will) Arena, 10: 263.
Union for Practical Progress, How to organize, in the Villages and Country Districts. (T. E. Will) Arena, 12: 59.
Union; a poem. (A. C. Swinburne) 19th Cent. 33: 725.
Union with Imogene. (H. S. Wilson) Gent. M. n. s. 57: 615.
Union Jack, British, as a National Emblem. Spec. 70: 769.
Union Pacific Railway. (J. P. Davis) Ann. Am. Acad. Pol. Sci. 8: 259.
— Driving the Last Spike of. (S. Dillon) Scrib. M. 12: 253.
— Reorganization of. (H. White) Nation, 61: 286.
Union Theological Seminary. (W. E. Griffis) Chr. Un. 47: 311.
Unionidæ, N. American, Relationship and Distribution of. (C. T. Simpson) Am. Natural. 27: 353.
— of the Mississippi Valley found in the St. Lawrence and Atlantic Draining Areas. (C. T. Simpson) Am. Natural. 30: 379.
— of Spoon River, Fulton Co., Ill. (W. S. Strode) Am. Natural. 26: 495.
Unionist Party; Alliance or Fusion? (E. Dicey) 19th Cent. 37: 904.
Unique Instance, A; a story. (A. Elliot) Belgra. 82: 392.
Unique Ordeal, A; a story. (I. Lamaison) Overland, n. s. 19: 348.
Unitarian, What makes a? (G. L. Cary) Chaut. 18: 686.
Unitarian Church in N. Y. City. (W. S. Bridgman) Munsey, 8: 131.
Unitarian Movement, Allen's. (J. W. Chadwick) Nation, 59: 106.
Unitarian's Gospel, A. (C. E. St. John) New World, 3: 623.
Unitarianism and its Future, Mrs. Humphry Ward on. Spec. 73: 170.
— and its Grand-children. (M. D. Conway) Open Court, 1: 46.
— and Judaism. (M. H. Harris) No. Am. 160: 632.
— and Philanthropy. (F. G. Peabody) Char. R. 5: 25.
— The New. (E. H. Hall) New World, 2: 536.
United Presbyterians of Scotland and their New Service Book. (W. F. Faber) Ref. Q. 39: 193.
United States, Ability of, to carry on an Offensive War. (W. R. Hamilton) Un. Serv. (Phila.) 14: 395.
— Advance in, during One Hundred Years. (S. G. Brock) Fortn. 60: 116.
— America as a Power. (A. Maclure) 19th Cent. 39: 906. Same art. Ecl. M. 127: 54.
— American Life through English Spectacles. (A. S. Northcote) 19th Cent. 34: 476. Same art. Ecl. M. 121: 471. Same art. Liv. Age, 199: 226.
— American Situation. (J. C. Hopkins) Econ. R. 5: 62.
— and the Anglo-Saxon Future. (G. B. Adams) Atlan. 78: 35.
— and Chili, 1892. Pub. Opin. 12: 419, 448. — Spec. 68: 156.
— and Great Britain; an Anglo-American Alliance. (A. S. White) No. Am. 158: 484.
— — Future Trade Relations. (R. S. McCormick) J. Soc. Arts, 40: 524.
— — Naval Union of; Reply to A. Carnegie. (G. S. Clark) No. Am. 158: 353.
— — Relations between. (J. B. Moore) National, 27: 470. Same art. Ecl. M. 127: 145.
— — — True. (D. A. Wells) No. Am. 162: 385. — Reply. (M. W. Hazeltine) No. Am. 162: 594.

United States and the Pan-Britannic Movement. (J. A. Cooper) 19th Cent. 38: 462.
— and Japan, Treaty Relations of. (J. L. Atkinson) Our Day, 9: 273.
— Annexation to: "Manifest Destiny." (C. Schurz) Harper, 87: 737.
— — Policy of Annexation. (S. E. Baldwin) Yale R. 2: 131.
— Army, and other Land Forces. (M. R. Davies) Un. Serv. M. 13: 173.
— — as a Military Training School. (E. Hudson) Forum, 15: 604.
— — Clothing and Equipage. (H. Romeyn) Un. Serv. (Phila.) 9: 447.
— — Company Discipline. (A. K. Taylor) Un. Serv. (Phila.) 7: 372.
— — Detached Service. Un. Serv. (Phila.) 13: 402.
— — Engineer Battalion. (H. Warner) Un. Serv. (Phila.) 15: 420.
— — Engineer Corps, Worthless Work by. (G. Y. Wisner) Engin. M. 2: 427.—Reply. (W. R. King) Engin. M. 2: 664.—Rejoinder. (G. Y. Wisner) Engin. M. 2: 743.
— — Increase of. (H. C. Egbert) Un. Serv. (Phila.) 16: 377.
— — Mrs. Lane's Old Days in. (C. King) Dial (Ch. 14: 80.
— — Needed Reforms in. (J. Gibbon) No. Am. 156: 212.
— — New Jersey Cavalry in, 1794. (E. J. Cleveland) N. E. Reg. 47: 27.
— — New Weapons of. (V. L. Mason) Cent. 27: 570.
— — Ninety-day Men of '63. (B. Landreth) Un. Serv. (Phila.) 12: 111.
— — Non-commissioned Officer, Status of. Un. Serv. (Phila.) 9: 340.
— — Organization of the Line. (A. D. Schenck) Un. Serv. (Phila.) 13: 107.
— — Plea for Increase of. (H. R. Brinkerhoff) Un. Serv. (Phila.) 14: 489.
— — Promotion in. (E. A. Root) Un. Serv. (Phila.) 7: 139.
— — Proposed Increase of. (G. D. Ruggles) No. Am. 159: 728.
— — Reform of. (G. Y. Wisner) Engin. M. 3: 66.
— — Reforms needed in Paper Work. (A. M. Palmer) Un. Serv. (Phila.) 9: 322.
— — Reorganization of. (W. A. Campbell) Un. Serv. (Phila.) 11: 305.
— — Reorganization of Artillery. (A. H. Sydenham) Un. Serv. (Phila.) 10: 451.
— — Standing. (G. Howard) Chaut. 17: 156.
— — Uniform of. (C. D. Hine) Un. Serv. (Phila.) 13: 406.
— Blackwood's History of. (Fred. S. Dickson) Bach. of Arts, 3: 1.
— Bonds: are they voidable? (A. C. Houston) Am. J. Pol. 4: 644.
— A Britisher's Impressions of. (Earl of Meath) 19th Cent. 33: 493.
— Bryce's American Commonwealth. (A. C. McLaughlin) Dial (Ch.) 14: 310.
— Bureau of Animal Industry. (G. W. Hill) Chaut. 14: 549.
— Campaign of 1896, Issues of: symposium. Indep. Oct. 8, '96.
— Cavalry in Mexican War. (W. B. Lane) Un. Serv. (Phila.) 15: 482. 16: 14, 110.
— Census, Eleventh. (R. P. Porter) J. Statis. Soc. 57: 643.
— Circuit Courts of Appeals. (H. Budd) Law Q. 9: 51.
United States, Civilization, Social Order, and Morality in. Blackw. 151: 617. Same art. Ecl. M. 119: 1.
— Claims against, Notable and Curious. (K. Field) Green Bag, 7: 12.
— Coast Defence. (W. T. Denniston) Un. Serv. (Phila.) 15: 381.
— Commerce, Needs of. (W. F. Prosser) Un. Serv. (Phila.) 15: 291.
— — Our Foreign Trade and our Consular Service. (C. D. Warner) No. Am. 162: 274.
— Commercial Era for, New. (G. W. Medley) Forum, 15: 24.
— Congress. A Congress out of Date. Atlan. 77: 98.
— — Legislation and Events, 1774-1895, Moore's. Sat. R. 80: 479.
— — Reminiscences of, 36th and 37th. (J. Hutchins) M. West. Hist. 12: 616. 13: 75, 208, 359.
See Congress.
— Constitution. (J. W. Burgess) Chaut. 22: 11, 139, 267, 395.
— — Amendment to, proposed by Pennsylvania, 1809. Pennsyl. M. 18: 194.
— — Amendment of Preamble of. Pub. Opin. 17: 46.
— — Foster's Commentaries on. (H. P. Judson) Am. Hist. R. 1: 562.
— — 14th Amendment, Citizenship under. (M. B. Woodworth) Am. Law R. 30: 535.
— — God in. (W. C. Wood) Our Day, 12: 473.—(A. E. Truxal) Ref. Q. 43: 254.
— — Greek History and. (J. F. Jameson) Chaut. 17: 285.
— — Massachusetts Report on Amendments, 1790. Am. Hist. R. 2: 99.
— — Origin of the Supreme Judicial Power. (R. L. Fowler) Am. Law R. 29: 711.
— — Stevens's Sources of. (C. C. Nott) Nation, 59: 30.—(S. E. Baldwin) Yale R. 3: 97.—Sat. R. 78: 294.
— — Unwritten, Tiedeman on. (G. H. Smith) Am. Law R. 27: 52.—(J. O. Pierce) Dial (Ch.) 13: 18.
— — Von Holst's History of. Atlan. 70: 838.—(J. D. Cox) Nation, 55: 32.
— Court of Appeals. (L. Trumbull) Am. Law R. 26: 204.
— — Jurisdiction and Practice of. (W. L. Murfree) Am. Law R. 26: 544.
— Courts of. Green Bag, 8: 381.
— — Federal Jurisdiction in Case of Corporations. (S. D. Thompson) Am. Law R. 29: 864.
— Credit of the Government, Wall Street and. R. of Rs. (N. Y.) 12: 31.
— Currency. Bank. M. (N. Y.) 48: 401.—Chamb. J. 73: 113.
— — and Finance. Bank. M. (Lond.) 61: 32-236.
— — and State Banks. (A. L. Ripley) Bank. M. (N. Y.) 50: 44.
— — Volume and Character of. Bank. M. (N. Y.) 48: 39.
See Currency.
— Defenceless Condition. (C. H. Rockwell) Un. Serv. (Phila.) 8: 144.
— — Our Defenceless Coasts. (G. N. Southwick) No. Am. 162: 317.
— Democracy in, Checks on. (G. W. Smalley) 19th Cent. 35: 873.
— — Peril of. (A. Matthews) Bach. of Arts, 3: 44.
— Department of Agriculture, Year-book of. (C. S. Sargent) Garden & F. 8: 421.
— Diplomacy, Democratic, Two Years of. (C. K. Davis) No. Am. 160: 270.
— Diplomatic Service. Official Residences for American Diplomats. (T. Stanton) Lippinc. 57: 698.

United States, Eastern, as a Field for Enterprise. (J. G. Cannon) Engin. M. 3: 802.
— Economic and Social Condition of, in 1893: Letters of an Altrurian Traveller. (W. D. Howells) Cosmopol. 16: 110, 218.
— Economic Development of, and Nicaragua Canal. (E. R. Johnson) Ann. Am. Acad. Pol. Sci. 7: 38.
— Education in, System of. (E. J. James) Citizen, 1: 157.
— Electoral System; Should it be abolished? (N. T. Mason) Am. J. Pol. 2: 423.
See President, Election of.
— Expansion of. (E. D. Warfield) M. Am. Hist. 27: 272.
— Expenditures of, Control of. (N. H. Thompson) Pol. Sci. Q. 7: 468.
— Federal Intervention. (W. W. Quartermass) Am. J. Pol. 5: 266.
— Finances: The Bond and the Dollar. (J. C. Ridpath) Arena, 15: 266, 439, 555.
— — The Coming System of National Credit. (A. C. Houston) Am. M. Civics, 6: 172.
— — Congress and Financial Control. Nation, 63: 451.
— — Deficiency of Revenue the Cause of our Financial Ills. (J. Sherman) Forum, 21: 129.
— — Government and the Bond Syndicate. (B. Ives) Yale R. 4: 10.
— — in 1893. Bank. M. (N. Y.) 47: 641.
— — — Annual Treasury Report. Pub. Opin. 16: 308.
— — in 1894. (H. White) Nation, 58: 24.
— — — Financial Year and the Outlook. Forum, 18: 636.
— — — Our Family Skeleton. (J. F. Hume) No. Am. 158: 728. — (C. Howell) No. Am. 159: 88.
— — in 1895. Pub. Opin. 18: 141.
— — Muddle of. (J. S. Morton; W. M. Springer; H. W. Cannon) No. Am. 160: 129.
— — Our Reviving Business. (J. H. Eckels) No. Am. 161: 340.
— — Our "Uncle Samuel" and his I. O. U.'s. (P. T. Sexton) No. Am. 162: 249.
— — The Peril of the Treasury. (G. S. Boutwell) No. Am. 159: 416.
— — Secretary Carlisle's Report. (H. White) Nation, 57: 486.
— — The Ship of State adrift. (A. Carnegie) No. Am. 162: 641.
— — Should the Government retire from Banking? (W. C. Cornwell) Forum, 18: 641.
— — The Treasury Reserve and the Bond Syndicate. (A. D. Noyes) Pol. Sci. Q. 10: 573.
— — The Turning of the Tide. (W. C. Ford) No. Am. 161: 187.
— — Twenty-five Years of Political Finance. (E. Cary) Pol. Sci. Q. 11: 222.
— — Under Republican Management. (R. Ogden) Nation, 54: 350. 55: 25.
— Financial Experiments of. (J. H. Eckels) Bank. M. (N. Y.) 50: 36.
— Financial Legislation, Our Experiments in. (J. H. Eckels) No. Am. 159: 689.
— Financial Policy. (H. F. Bartine) Arena, 16: 251.
— Financial Predicament of. (H. B. Russell) Am. M. Civics, 7: 415.
— Fish Commission. (C. B. Hudson) Cosmopol. 18: 460.
— Foreign Policy of. (W. D. McCrackan) Arena, 8: 145.
— — An Alliance with England the Basis of a Rational. (S. Sherwood) Forum, 21: 89.
— — Our Blundering. (H. C. Lodge) Forum, 19: 8.
United States, Foreign Policy of, under President Harrison. (R. Ogden) Nation, 55: 140.
— — — The Bering Sea, Barrundia, and Itata Cases. (T. S. Woolsey) Yale R. 1: 162.
— Foreign Relations. (T. S. Woolsey) Am. J. Pol. 1: 351.
— Foreign Service, Educated Men in. Dial (Ch.) 16: 230.
— Foreign Trade of, A Hindrance to. (T. R. Jernigan) No. Am. 163: 438.
— — Our Trade with South America. (T. C. Search) No. Am. 163: 716.
— Foreigners on. (A. A. Hayes) Westm. 137: 422.
— Foremost Nation of the World. (Col. Snowden) Am. Hist. Reg. 3: 65.
— Franco-American's Notes on. (T. Stanton) Westm. 141: 195.
— Future of the Republic. (G. W. Thompson) Am. M. Civics, 9: 149.
— Geologic Atlas of. Science, n. s. 3: 647.
— Geological Survey. (J. W. Powell) Chaut. 14: 669. — (C. D. Walcott) Pop. Sci. Mo. 46: 479. — (M. Baker) Geog. J. 6: 252. — Science, n. s. 2: 58.
— — Cost of. (E. O. Wolcott) Engin. M. 4: 221.
— — Prof. Wright and. (T. C. Chamberlin) Dial (Ch.) 14: 7.
— — Reasons for Supporting. (N. S. Shaler) Engin. M. 4: 225.
— — Recent Geographical Work by. Geog. J. 4: 147. — Nature, 53: 462.
— — Tribute of the French Academy to American Geological Exploration. Pop. Sci. Mo. 43: 95.
— German Appraisal of. Atlan. 75: 124.
— Government, Contributions of, to Social Science. (C. D. Wright) Am. J. Sociol. 1: 241.
— — Departments of, Reports of. Sat. R. 76: 191.
— — A Dual Organization. (H. H. Perry) Am. M. Civics, 8: 9.
— — Hart's Essays on. (C. C. Nott) Nation, 58: 70.
— — Law of the Administration in America. (E. Freund) Pol. Sci. Q. 9: 403.
— — My Business Partner. (U. D. Eddy) Forum, 13: 379.
— — Theory and Practice of American Popular Government. (F. W. Grey) Westm. 140: 175. Same art. Ecl. M. 121: 433.
— Government Buildings, Failure of. (M. Schuyler) Forum, 17: 609.
— Government Printing Office. (B. L. Putnam) Educa. 15: 118.
— Government Publications. (W. F. Willoughby) Yale R. 5: 143. *See* Public Documents.
— History, Adams's. Spec. 68: 126.
— — Andrews's. (A. C. McLaughlin) Dial (Ch.) 18: 111. — Nation, 60: 77.
— — Channing's. (C. W. French) School R. 4: 694. — (A. C. McLaughlin) Am. Hist. R. 2: 161.
— — Civil War. (A. Alison) Blackw. 157: 740.
— — — Anecdotes of. (M. E. W. Sherwood) Lippinc. 51: 89.
— — — Attitude of Russia during. (H. F. Cutter) Overland, n. s. 20: 311.
— — — Army of Northern Virginia, Allan's. (J. D. Cox) Nation, 56: 85.
— — — Battles and Casualties of Massachusetts Regiments. (T. W. Higginson; Mrs. F. W. Jaques) N. E. Reg. 46: 31.
— — — Border Statesmen of. (N. S. Shaler) Atlan. 69: 245.
— — — Borderboy's Recollections of. (G. A. Cook) New Eng. M. n. s. 10: 164.

United States; History: Civil War, Bravest Deed of. (T. J. Mackey) McClure, 3: 272.
— — — California Defenders of the Union. (F. E. Myers) Overland, n. s. 28: 53.
— — — Causes of. (J. Wheeler) So. Hist. Pap. 22: 24.
— — — Country Boy's Recollections of. (A. D. Smith) New Eng. M. n. s. 5: 812.
— — — Division and Reunion, Wilson's. (J. C. Welling) Nation, 56: 278.
— — — Federal and Confederate Armies in. (J. S. Ward) So. Hist. Pap. 20: 238.
— — — Great Cities in. (T. F. Rodenbough) M. Am. Hist. 29: 193.
— — — Health of the Survivors of. (Dr. J. S. Billings) Forum, 12: 652.
— — — London Times on. (C. K. Tuckerman) M. Am. Hist. 27: 290.
— — — Memories of a Confederate Boy. (R. Y. Toombs) New Eng. M. n. s. 9: 46.
— — — The North in. (J. B. McMaster) Chaut. 15: 152.
— — — Reconstruction in, Scott on. (G. W. Julian) Dial (Ch.) 20: 11.
— — — Responsibility for. (S. Webster) Pol. Sci. Q. 8: 268.
— — — Riddle's Recollections of. (G. W. Julian) Dial (Ch.) 19: 12.
— — — Ropes on. (C. H. Cooper) Dial (Ch.) 18: 48. — Nation, 59: 384.
— — — Running the Blockade. (E. H. Ferguson) Lippinc. 52: 493.
— — — Songs of. (A. M. Williams) J. Am. Folk-Lore, 5: 265.
— — — Story of a Regiment in. (A. W. Tourgee) Cosmopol. 18: 69.
— — — Three Critical Periods in the Diplomatic Relations of the U. S. with England. (T. H. Dudley) Pennsyl. M. 17: 34.
— — — A War-time Aurora Borealis. (E. W. Mayo) Cosmopol. 21: 134.
— — — What it has not done. (H. Olerich) Am. J. Pol. 3: 628.
— — — Why the Confederacy failed. (D. Rose) Cent. 31: 33.
— — — Why the Men of '61 fought for the Union. (J. D. Cox) Atlan. 69: 382.
— — Colonial; Domestic and Social Life. (E. E. Hale) Chaut. 14: 397, 525.
— — — Fisher's. (W. Walker) Nation, 54: 471.
— — — Old-time Gleanings, Curious. Chamb. J. 69: 362.
— — — Thwaites's. (J. A. Doyle) Eng. Hist. R. 7: 379.
— — Colonial Memories and their Lesson. (Mrs. C. V. R. Erving) M. Am. Hist. 27: 325.
— — Dramatic Scenes in. (R. H. Titherington) Munsey, 8: 10, 381. 9: 345.
— — Fiske's. (W. H. Mace) School R. 4: 108.
— — Four Epochs in. (B. O. Flower) Arena, 16: 928.
— — French and Indian War, 1754–1760. (J. G. Nicolay) Chaut. 15: 10.
— — How to study. (H. E. Chambers) M. Am. Hist. 29: 37.
— — Leading Families in. (H. King) Chaut. 21: 387.
— — McMaster's. (A. B. Hart) Forum, 19: 375. — (F. W. Shepardson) Dial (Ch.) 18: 319.
— — — Vol. 3. (C. H. Haskins) Dial (Ch.) 13: 13.
— — of Last Quarter-century. (E. B. Andrews) Scrib. M. 17: 269–720. 18: 71–593. 19: 60–469.
— — — Andrews on. Nation, 63: 458.
— — Political, Goldwin Smith's "Views" on. (W. Wilson) Forum, 16: 489. — Dial (Ch.) 15: 181. — Ath. '93, 2: 517. — (W. P. Garrison) Nation, 57: 293. — Spec. 71: 518.
United States; History: Providence in. (T. F. Dornblaser) Luth. Q. 24: 386.
— — Reconstruction Period, Political Leaders of the. (E. G. Ross) Forum, 20: 218.
— — Rhodes's. Gunton's M. 10: 310. — (J. D. Cox) Nation, 55: 498. — (J. D. Cox) Nation, 61: 117. — (G. W. Julian) Dial (Ch.) 19: 68.
— — Schouler's. (J. C. Welling) Nation, 54: 75.
— — War of 1812. (H. Frederic) Eng. Illust. 14: 573.
— — Working Manual of, Mace on. (W. J. Chase) School R. 4: 113.
— Ideal of the American Commonwealth. (J. W. Burgess) Pol. Sci. Q. 10: 404.
— in 1892, Four Centuries of Progress. Pub. Opin. 14: 84.
— in 1893. (Lady H. Grey-Egerton; Lady J. Sykes) No. Am. 156: 449.
— in International Law. Blackw. 154: 479.
— Independence and Union. (L. R. Harley) Am. M. Civics, 7: 187.
— Industries of, Development of. Pop. Sci. Mo. 40: 289 — 41: 496.
— Intellectual Progress. (G. F. Parker) 19th Cent. 35: 729.
— Is our Republic a Failure? (H. P. Judson) Soc. Econ. 9: 95.
— Judiciary, Criticism of. (W. H. Taft) Am. Law R. 29: 641.
— — Danger of the. (H. Wollman) No. Am. 160: 377.
— Jurassic Formation of Atlantic Coast of. (O. C. Marsh) Science, n. s. 4: 805.
— Land of Social Contrasts. (J. F. Muirhead) Arena, 6: 180.
— Legislation, Political and Municipal, in the Various States, 1895. (E. D. Durand) Ann. Am. Acad. Pol. Sci. 7: 411.
— Life in, Rousiers on. Sat. R. 74: 517.
— Life-saving Service. Uncle Sam's Life-savers. (F. G. Carpenter) Pop. Sci. Mo. 44: 346.
— Literature in, in 1891. (H. W. Mabie) Forum, 12: 797. *See* American Literature.
— Loans of. Bank. M. (N. Y.) 51: 20, 151. 52: 152–581.
— A Look Ahead. (A. Carnegie) No. Am. 156: 685.
— Maps of, Earliest. (H. Gannett) Nat. Geog. M. 4: 101.
— Military Academy. (A. T. Sibbald) Un. Serv. M. 9: 366.
See West Point.
— Military Policy: Wanted — a Definite Policy. (C. H. Rockwell) Un. Serv. (Phila.) 8: 413.
— Militia: Our Sailor Soldiers. (E. B. Mero) Outing, 25: 63.
— Monetary Condition of. (J. A. Quarles) Am. M. Civics, 8: 181.
— Monetary Situation in. (W. Lewis) Econ. Stud. 1: 215.
— National Debt of. (A. B. Nettleton) Chaut. 16: 271.
— National Enterprises of. (E. E. Hale) Lend a H. 11: 243.
— Naval Academy. (T. R. Lounsbury) Harper, 92: 201.
— — Life and Study at. (W. G. Richardson) New Eng. M. n. s. 8: 305.
— Naval Observatory, New, Latitude and Longitude of. (J. R. Eastman) Astron. 12: 699.
— — Reorganization of. Nation, 59: 228.
— Naval Weakness of. (W. L. Cathcart) Cassier, 10: 409.
— Navy. (L. Nixon) Cassier, 7: 99.
— — Administration of. Nation, 56: 154.
— — American Men for. (F. M. Bennett) Un. Serv. (Phila.) 11: 101.

United States; Navy: American Naval Power in the Future. (A. T. Mahan) Harper, 91: 767.
— — American Sailor-soldiers. (E. B. Mero) Outing, 26: 309.
— — Apprentice System in. (A. V. Wadhams) And. R. 17: 35.
— — Difficulties in Construction of New Ships. (R. Ogden) Nation, 57: 341.
— — during the Civil War. (R. S. Collum) Am. Hist. Reg. 1: 113-325. — Un. Serv. M. 10: 124-337.
— — Engineer Corps. (F. M. Bennett) Un. Serv. (Phila.) 11: 507. 12: 1, 129.
— — Fleet, Constitution and Organization. (C. C. Todd) Un. Serv. (Phila.) 9: 505.
— — Growth of. Un. Serv. M. 7: 1308. 8: 185, 390.
— — Hawaii and our Future Sea-power. (A. T. Mahan) Forum, 15: 1.
— — History of, Maclay's. Sat. R. 79: 54. — (C. H. Stockton) Nation, 60: 35.
— — in 1844. (D. G. Adee) Un. Serv. (Phil.) 14: 262.
— — Is the Value of our Fast Cruisers overestimated? (D. Ammen) No. Am. 158: 77.
— — Lesson from the "Chicago." Fortn. 62: 30.
— — Maclay's History of. Dial (Ch.) 16: 300.— (C. H. Stockton) Nation, 58: 455.
— — Memorable Exploits of. (R. H. Titherington) Munsey, 8: 10.
— — Modern War Vessels of. (W. A. Dobson) Pop. Sci. Mo. 44: 164.
— — New, Development of. Pub. Opin. 15: 76.
— — Politics in. (E. L. Godkin) Nation, 56: 173.
— — Rebuilding. (H. P. Mawson) Lippinc. 49: 357.
— — Reorganization of the Personnel of the Navy. (Wm. McAdoo) No. Am. 159: 457.
— — Sea Power of the U. S. (C. H. Cramp) No. Am. 159: 137.
— — Spirit of. (R. Ogden) Nation, 58: 284.
— Navy Department and Naval Officers. (E. L. Godkin) Nation, 56: 399.
— Notes and Currency Situation. (M. L. Muhleman) Bank. M. (N. Y.) 50: 486.
— Overland through. Cornh. 65: 637.
— Pensioners, Essex Co., Mass. (G. A. Gordon) N. E. Reg. 49: 316.
— People of: Are they prosperous? (B. O. Flower) Arena, 7: 197.
— Perils, National. (J. F. Bartlett) Am. J. Pol. 2: 9.
— Political Campaign of 1892; symposium. Indep. Sept. 29, '92.
— Political Parties in. (F. W. Hewes) Chaut. 14: 407.
— Political System, A New. (A. Schaumberg) Am. J. Pol. 3: 168.
— Political Upheavals in, Historic. (T. B. Reed) No. Am. 160: 109.
— Politics: Constitutional Union Party of 1892. (C. F. Richardson) Yale R. 3: 144.
— — Corruption in. (A. S. Northcote) 19th Cent. 35: 692.
— — The Hayes Administration. (J. D. Cox) Atlan. 71: 818.
— — in 1892, and in England; Impending Elections. (A. Carnegie) 19th Cent. 32: 141.
— — — Dissolving Political Régime. (W. N. Black) Engin. M. 3: 181.
— — — How the New York Senate was captured. (M. Hale) Forum, 13: 179.
— — — Party Government on its Trial. (G. Smith) No. Am. 154: 583.
— — — Platforms and Principles. (W. P. Garrison) Nation, 55: 404.
— — — A Political Parallel: 1844, 1892. Atlan. 69: 395.
United States; Politics: Presidential Contest, 1892. (C. Logsdael and others) Am. J. Pol. 2: 30. — (W. H. Smith) Am. J. Pol. 2: 619. — Atlan. 69: 116. — (T. F. Bayard; G. F. Hoar) Forum, 13: 409. — (A. B. Hart) New R. 7: 579. — (G. Smith) 19th Cent. 32: 345. Same art. Ecl. M. 119: 565. — (J. G. Blaine) No. Am. 155: 513. — Spec. 68: 805. 69: 550. — (P. Ross) Westm. 138: 229, 597.
— — — — Cleveland and Tammany. (E. L. Godkin) Nation, 55: 384.
— — — — Declination of Blaine. Pub. Opin. 12: 471. — Spec. 68: 226.
— — — — Democratic Outlook. (W. F. Harrity) No. Am. 155: 551.
— — — — Democratic Revolt in New York. (F. R. Coudert) Forum, 13: 169.
— — — — Election Week. Blackw. 152: 892.
— — — — For whom shall I vote, and why? (J. Schouler and others) Forum, 14: 390.
— — — — Economic Significance of. Soc. Econ. 3: 321.
— — — — Fraud Issue a Failure. (L. Satterthwait) Am. J. Pol. 2: 412.
— — — — Hill's "Plan of Campaign." Pub. Opin. 12: 311.
— — — — Hill's Record revised. (J. B. Bishop) Nation, 54: 182.
— — — — McKinleyism and. (R. Donald) Contemp. 66: 489.
— — — — The Man or the Platform. (M. S. Quay and others) No. Am. 154: 513.
— — — — Michigan, Presidential Electors of. (E. B. Winans) No. Am. 154: 439.
— — — — Nomination of Bidwell. Pub. Opin. 13: 321.
— — — — Nomination of Cleveland. (M. Halstead) Cosmopol. 13: 585. — Pub. Opin. 13: 295. — Letter of Acceptance. Pub. Opin. 13: 613.
— — — — Nomination of Harrison. Pub. Opin. 13: 247. — (M. Halstead) Cosmopol. 13: 507. — Letter of Acceptance. Pub. Opin. 13: 537.
— — — — Nomination of Weaver. Pub. Opin. 13: 319.
— — — — Paramount Questions of. (S. Pennoyer) No. Am. 155: 477.
— — — — The Party Platforms. Soc. Econ. 3: 65. — Atlan. 70: 688.
— — — — Republican Defeat, Foreign Joy at. (R. Ogden) Nation, 55: 467.
— — — — Results of. Pub. Opin. 14: 147. — Spec. 69: 674.
— — — — A Symposium. (W. M. Springer; T. E. Watson; J. C. Burrows) Arena, 6: 198. — (M. A. Dodge and others) Arena, 6: 300.
— — in 1893; President Cleveland and the New York Senatorship. Pub. Opin. 14: 319.
— — — The Situation. (T. B. Reed) No. Am. 157: 257. — (G. Smith) 19th Cent. 34: 131. Same art. Ecl. M. 121: 269.
— — — State Elections. Pub. Opin. 15: 520. 16: 165.
— — — — Meaning of the Election. Soc. Econ. 5: 321.
— — — Will the Democracy divide? Pub. Opin. 15: 495.
— — in 1894: Elections, Meaning of. (J. W. Babcock; C. J. Faulkner) No. Am. 159: 742. — Soc. Econ. 7: 321.
— — — Issues of. (W. L. Wilson; T. B. Reed) No. Am. 159: 385.
— — — The Present Administration. (T. B. Reed) No. Am. 159: 1.
— — — Results of Democratic Victory. (H. C. Lodge) No. Am. 159: 268.

United States; Politics in 1894: Silver and the Tariff at Washington. Fortn. 61: 837.—(Lord Farrer; M. Frewen; J. S. Nicholson; F. J. Faraday) Fortn. 62: 116.
— — in 1895. (M. Frewen) National, 26: 595.
— — — Election, Benefits and Dangers of. (J. Wanamaker and others) Am. M. Civics, 6: 81.
— — — Is an Extra Session needed? (C. Tracey; B. Storer; J. Patterson; R. G. Cousins) No. Am. 160: 257.
— — — A Last Tribute. (T. B. Reed) No. Am. 160: 385.
— — — Political Parties and the Public Peril. Soc. Econ. 9: 161.
— — in 1896. (E. L. Godkin) Forum, 21: 257.
— — — American Silver Rebellion. (T. E. Powell) National, 27: 686.
— — — An Analysis of Agricultural Discontent in the United States. (C. F. Emerick) Pol. Sci. Q. 11: 433.
— — — Are the Farmers Populists? (J. M. Stahl) No. Am. 163: 266.
— — — Democratic View. (W. E. Russell) Cent. 29: 73. — Republican View. (T. Roosevelt) Cent. 29: 68.
— — — The Duty of the Hour. (W. Miller; R. P. Bland) No. Am. 163: 362.
— — — Duty of the Republican Administration. (J. H. Eckels) No. Am. 163: 696.
— — — Free Silver Craze. (G. Smith) Sat. R. 82: 103–538. — (A. R. Colquhoun) Sat. R. 82: 129.
— — — The Lamp of Experience. (T. L. Ford) Overland, n. s. 28: 470.
— — — Money and the Masses in America. Quar. 184: 564.
— — — New Political Deals. (W. B. Chisholm) Gunton's M. 11: 442.
— — — Political Outlook. (B. R. Tillman) National, 28: 189.
— — — Presidential Election. (G. W. Steevens) Blackw. 160: 859. — Yale R. 5: 113, 233. — (F. H. Hardy) Fortn. 66: 568. — National, 28: 12, 153. — National, 28: 271. — National, 28: 429. — (F. F. Browne) National, 28: 452.
— — — — Chicago Convention. (I. L. Rice; A. D. White) Forum, 22: 1.
— — — — Effect of Republican Victory. (T. C. Platt) No. Am. 163: 513.
— — — — The Final Word. (A. J. Pillsbury) Overland, n. s. 28: 594.
— — — — If Silver wins: 1. The Shrinkage of Wages (L. Windmüller). 2. Inevitable Constitutional Changes. (W. Clark) No. Am. 163: 456.
— — — — Issues and Prospects of the Campaign. (W. E. Chandler; J. Quincy) No. Am. 163: 175.
— — — — Its Lessons and Warnings. (A. D. White; D. MacG. Means; G. Smith) Forum, 22: 414.
— — — — Lessons from. (F. H. Hardy) Fortn. 66: 894.
— — — — Outlook as Europeans view it. (P. Leroy-Beaulieu) Forum, 21: 525.
— — — — Premonitions of. Sat. R. 81: 364.
— — — — A Visitor's Glimpse of the Contest. (A. S. Eccles) National, 28: 199.
— — — — The Vital Issues. (L. Abbott) R. of Rs. (N. Y.) 14: 544.
— — — The Safe Pathway of Experience. (T. B. Reed) No. Am. 163: 385.
— — — The Ship of State adrift. (A. Carnegie) No. Am. 163: 496.
— — — Silver Politics across Seas. (E. J. Shriver) Westm. 146: 487.
United States; Politics: The League as a Political Instrument. Atlan. 69: 258.
— — The New. (R. J. Hinton) Arena, 11: 216.
— — Our Situation viewed from without. (G. Smith) No. Am. 160: 547.
— — Perils of Our National Elections. (G. F. Edmunds) Forum, 12: 691.
— — Political Organizations in the U. S. and England. (J. Bryce) No. Am. 156: 105.
— — Some Ante-bellum Politics. (G. W. Julian) No. Am. 163: 195.
— — Wanted, a New Party. (T. V. Powderly) No. Am. 155: 592.
— Population of, and its Distribution. (C. D. Wright) Pop. Sci. Mo. 40: 368.
— — Assimilation of Nationalities. (R. Mayo-Smith) Pol. Sci. Q. 9: 426, 649.
— — Geographical Distribution of. (H. Gannett) Am. Statis. Assoc. 3: 551.
— — Growth and Distribution of. (F. A. Walker) Chaut. 14: 655.
— — Movements of. (H. Gannett) Nat. Geog. M. 4: 21.
— — Native and Foreign-born. (C. D. Wright) Pop. Sci. M. 41: 756.
— Power and Wealth of. (M. G. Mulhall) No. Am. 160: 641.
— Presidency of. (C. F. Adams) Soc. Econ. 4: 148.
— — An American Birthright. (J. G. Hertwig) Am. J. Pol. 2: 43. — (W. W. Phelps) Am. J. Pol. 2: 300. — (D. Mowry) Am. J. Pol. 2: 616. *See* President.
— Printing-office: Government as a Great Publisher. (A. R. Spofford) Forum, 19: 338.
— Progress of, 1880–90. (R. H. Edmonds) Engin. M. 5: 14.
— — Trend of. (R. H. Thurston) No. Am. 161: 297.
— Public Documents, Catalogue of, Ames's. (W. P. Garrison) Nation, 60: 103.
— Public Lands. The Stepchild of the Republic. (W. E. Smythe) No. Am. 163: 37.
— Races and Nationalities in, Statistical Data on. (R. M. Smith) Am. Statis. Assoc. 3: 429.
— Recent Books on. (E. Reclus) Geog. J. 6: 448.
— Recognition of, by the Dutch Republic. (W. E. Griffis) Chaut. 17: 715.
— Reconstruction in, Recollections of. (J. Chester) Un. Serv. (Phila.) 14: 122.
— Religious Forces of, Carroll on. (A. H. Noll) Dial (Ch.) 16: 141.
— Republic, The; Endurance by Means of Revolution. (W. Macomber) Am. M. Civics, 6: 190.
— — in the Court of Reason. (T. B. Grant) Am. J. Pol. 5: 580.
— — is it a Failure? (H. P. Judson) Am. J. Sociol. 1: 28.
— — Some Reasons why it may endure. (C. W. Eliot) Forum, 18: 129. — Pub. Opin. 17: 691.
— — — President Eliot on. (T. B. Grant) Am. J. Pol. 5: 580.
— Senate. *See* Senate.
— Senators, Reminiscences of. (W. K. Benedict) Chaut. 17: 454, 598, 649.
— Shaler on. (J. D. Cox) Nation, 59: 466.
— Social and Economic Legislation in, Recent. (F. J. Stimson) Yale R. 5: 251.
— Social Crisis in, Origin of the. (Viscount de Frousac) Canad. M. 1: 660.
— Social Legislation, 1889–90. (L. S. Merriam) Econ. R. 1: 234.
— Society in. (A. W. Small) Chaut. 22: 15.

United States; Southern Peninsula of, Geography of. (J. N. MacGonigle) Nat. Geog. M. 7: 381.
— States made from Territories. (J. A. Woodburn) Chaut. 4: 411, 533.
— Statesmen of, Hilliard on. Sat. R. 73: 633.
— Supreme Court. (E. J. Phelps) Jurid. R. 2: 122.
— — Athenian Parallel to. (T. D. Goodell) Yale R. 2: 64.
— — Carson's History of. (H. L. Boutell) Dial (Ch.) 12: 326.
— — Politics and. (W. D. Coles) Am. Law R. 27: 182.
— Statute Law in. (S. E. Baldwin) Law Q. 3: 158.
— Territorial Extension of, Fallacy of. (W. G. Sumner) Forum, 21: 414.
— Territory of, Acquisition of. (N. A. Miles) No. Am. 161: 561.
— Treasury Department, Old Employees in. (E. I. Renick) Good Govt. 13: 79.
— Village Life in, Kipling on. Spec. 68: 522.
— Weather Bureau River and Flood System. (W. L. Moore) Nat. Geog. M. 7: 302.
— Welfare of; what it demands. (J. P. Altgeld) Am. M. Civics, 8: 207.
U. S. Military Academy. *See* West Point.
U. S. Sanitary Commission. (J. H. Benton, jr.) Lend a H. 13: 209.
Universe, Construction of. (J. E. Gore) Knowl. 18: 8.
— Dimensions of. (G. P. Serviss) Chaut. 21: 143.
— The Far Distances in our. (Agnes Giberne) Chamb. J. 73: 212.
— An Ideal. Ecl. M. 118: 471.
— Is it Infinite? (Sir R. Ball) Fortn. 59: 620. Same art. Ecl. M. 121: 32. Same art. Liv. Age, 198: 90.
— The Unseen. (R. S. Ball) Monist, 5: 553.
— *versus* World. Sat. R. 78: 594.
— The Visible. (A. D. White) Pop. Sci. Mo. 44: 433.
— — Gore's. (A. Taylor) Nature, 47: 193.
Universalism, The Bible and. (W. W. Gleason) Chr. Lit. 13: 102.
— a Progressive Faith. (A. N. Alcott) New World, 3: 38.
Universalist, What makes a? (C. H. Eaton) Chaut. 19: 443.
Universalist Thought, Progressive Changes in. (M. D. Shutter) Arena, 14: 144.
Universities, American, Great. (C. W. Super) School & C. 1: 513.
— — Some Thoughts on. (A. M. Fairbairn) Our Day, 15: 187.
— in Canada, Parliamentary Representation of. (T. Hodgins) Canad. M. 5: 115.
— — Victoria. (H. Hough) Canad. M. 7: 205.
— English, and the Reformation. (L. C. Casartelli) Dub. R. 117: 416.
— Need of, in the U. S. (H. E. von Holst) Educa. R. 5: 105.
— of England, Need of more Scientific Research. (W. Ramsay) Sat. R. 82: 308.
— — Thoughts on. (E. A. Freeman) No. Am. 157: 722.
— European, Women in. (A. Zimmer) Forum, 19: 187.
— French, and Spanish. (L. H. Weeks) Bach. of Arts, 2: 467.
— — Instruction in. (L. S. Rowe) Ann. Am. Acad. Pol. Sci. 2: 494.
— — Question of. (C. V. Langlois) Pol. Sci. Q. 9: 510.
— — Reconstruction of. (G. Compayré) Educa. R. 4: 475.
— German. (A. R. Crook) Chaut. 23: 560.
— — Crisis in. (James E. Russell) Educa. R. 9: 391.
Universities, German, Paulsen on. (B. A. Hinsdale) Dial (Ch.) 18: 294. — Sat. R. 80: 271.
— of Italy. (F. Martini) Chaut. 19: 452.
— of the Middle Ages, The Poor Scholar and the. Macmil. 74: 222.
— — Rashdall's. (N. M. Butler) Nation, 62: 309, 327. — Ed. R. 184: 82. — (G. B. Adams) Am. Hist. R. 1: 520. — (J. Wells) Scot. R. 28: 56. — Quar. 183: 445. — Church Q. 43: 80. — (B. A. Hinsdale) Dial (Ch.) 20: 67.
— of Russia. (C. T. H. Wright) Scot. R. 20: 105. — Pub. Opin. 13: 480.
— Origin of, Compayré on. Sat. R. 79: 259.
— Sociological Function of. (M. I. Swift) Open Court, 3: 2021.
— State. (R. T. Ely) Cosmopol. 19: 648.
— — Religious Instruction in. (H. S. Piatt) Educa. 16: 395.
— Transmission of Learning through. (N. S. Shaler) Atlan. 73: 115.
University, The American. (E. G. Hirsch) Am. J. Sociol. 1: 113.
— and the Workingman. (Seth Low) Soc. Econ. 1: 7.
— as a Scientific Workshop. (F. Paulsen) Pop. Sci. Mo. 46: 170.
— for London, The Proposed. (K. Pearson) Acad. 31: 273. 39: 417.
— — Report on a. Nature, 40: 121, 149.
— Function of a. (G. W. Prothero) Scot. R. 28: 346.
— National, Do we need a? (E. P. Powell) Educa. 16: 513.
— A New State, for England. (S. H. Boult) Westm. 137: 298.
— The Next American. (W. MacDonald) Forum, 21: 671.
— of Illinois, Architecture at. Am. Arch. 46: 82.
— of London. Spec. 61: 164.
— — Future of. Sat. R. 79: 149.
— of Vermont. (R. E. Lewis) New Eng. M. n. s. 15: 64.
— of Wisconsin. (D. B. Frankenburger) New Eng. M. n. s. 8: 10.
University Colleges: Their Origin and Methods. (Brother Azarias) Am. Cath. Q. 18: 830. 19: 25.
University Education in the U. S. (C. J. Bonaparte) Harv. Mo. 14: 133.
— President Low on. Nation, 56: 6.
— Worth of. (A. P. Peabody) Harv. Grad. M. 1: 1.
University Extension. (R. G. Moulton and others) Bk. News, 9: 339. — (W. Boughton and others) Bk. News, 10: 21–78. — (L. L. Gardner) Acad. (Syr.) 7: 14. — Atlan. 69: 713. — (C. W. Super) Educa. 12: 330. — (J. B. Thompson) Lib. J. 17: supp. 6. — (C. M. Moore) Cath. World, 57: 27. — (M. G. Brumbaugh) Educa. 13: 482, 552, 611.
— and Public Libraries. (T. L. Montgomery) Lib. J. 19: supp. 64.
— Defence of. (W. C. Lawton) Citizen, 1: 85.
— Doubts about. (G. H. Palmer) Atlan. 69: 367.
— Facts about. (M. E. Sadler; L. E. Stuart) 19th Cent. 36: 371.
— Farce of. (C. Whibley) 19th Cent. 36: 203, 598.
— Future of. (I. M. Gardner) School & C. 1: 348.
— History of the English Movement. (M. G. Brumbaugh) Educa. 13: 421.
— in Canterbury; a sketch. (R. H. Davis) Harper, 86: 789.
— in Great Britain, Coöperation in relation to. (J. T. Taylor) Citizen, 1: 137.
— in Music. (W. S. B. Mathews) Music, 1: 309.
— in Oxford. Church Q. 38: 409.

University Extension in the U. S. (W. T. Harris and others) Bk. News, 9: 362. — (A. M. Earle) 19th Cent. 38: 308. — (E. J. James) Our Day, 9: 79. — R. of Rs. (N. Y.) 6: 701. — (M. G. Brumbaugh) Educa. 13: 482.
— Nationalization of. (C. H. Henderson) Pop. Sci. Mo. 40: 500.
— New Career for College Men. (E. J. James) R. of Rs. (N. Y.) 7: 578.
— New Phase of. (M. B. Snyder) Science, 19: 1.
— of Catholic Summer School. (J. F. Mullaney) Am. Cath. Q. 18: 166.
— Problems of. Dial (Ch.) 13: 297.
— Two Experiments in. (G. M. Grant) School & C. 1: 129.
— University Participation, a Substitute for. (A. B. Hart) Educa. R. 6: 42.
University Extension Congress, London, 1894. (J. Davidson) Educa. R. 8: 350.
University Extension Movement. (F. C. Williams) Open Court, 5: 3016.
University Extension System. (F. S. Boas) Time, 21: 436.
University Idea. (R. A. Woods) And. R. 17: 98.
University Library: its Larger Recognition in Higher Education. (C. E. Lowrey) Educa. 14: 520.
University Life, Mediæval. (Brother Azarias) Am. Cath. Q. 18: 122.
University Press. Dial (Ch.) 13: 295.
University Question in France. (C. Schefer) Nation, 56: 451.
University Reform, The Schoolmaster and. (E. D. Warfield) Educa. 12: 455.
University Settlement; Andover House, Boston. Lend a H. 11: 183. — (R. A. Woods) Char. R. 2: 160.
— in Philadelphia. (H. Fox) Lend a H. 11: 43.
— in Whitechapel. (S. A. Barnett) Time, 1.
— Scientific Aspect of. (F. A. C. Perrine) Science, 21: 91.
University Settlement Movement. Gunton's M. 10: 429.
University Settlements. (S. A. Barnett) Chaut. 18: 393. — Lend a H. 12: 204. — (S. A. Barnett) 19th Cent. 38: 1015. Same art. Ecl. M. 126: 183. — (Percy Alden) Outl. 50: 906, 1090. — (E. Cummings) Q. J. Econ. 6: 257.
— Idea of. (R. A. Woods) And. R. 18: 317.
— Place of. (V. D. Scudder) And. R. 18: 339.
— Women's. (M. Talbot) Econ. R. 5: 489.
University Spirit, The. (J. M. Coulter) Educa. R. 4: 366. — (J. Pierce) Educa. 12: 354.
University Symposium. Dial (Ch.) 20: 95.
University Systems. (P. Geddes) Fortn. 60: 509.
University Teaching, East and West. (S. A. Barnett) New R. 8: 700.
University Training and Citizenship. (W. Wilson) Forum, 18: 107.
Unknowable, The. Open Court, 1: 667.
Unknown Glen, An. (A. T. Story) Art J. 44: 149.
Unknown Parts of the World. (H. R. Mills) McClure, 3: 540.
Unlived Life of Little Mary Ellen; a story. (R. McEnery Stuart) Harper, 93: 697.
Unlooked-for Turn, An; a story. Chamb. J. 69: 110–126.
Unpaid Governess, An; a story. Temp. Bar, 106: 116. Same art. Liv. Age, 207: 146.
Unpardonable Liar, An; a story. (G. Parker) Eng. Illust. 11: 51, 162.
Unprincipled Woman, An; a story. All the Year, 76: 282.
Unqualified Assistance; a story. (G. H. Page) Argosy, 54: Summer no. 76.
Unregarded Singer, An; a story. (K. Watson) Theatre, 32: 313.
Unresolved Discord, An; a story. (W. E. Norris) Longm. 24: 592. Same art. Liv. Age, 203: 425.
Unromantic Affair, An; a story. Overland, n. s. 21: 19.
Unsatisfactory Lover. (Mrs. M. H. Hungerford) Lippinc. 52: 515.
Unseen Land, The; a poem. (J. Runciman) M. of Art, 16: 51.
Unsigned Portrait, An; a story. (R. H. Russell) Scrib. M. 15: 250.
Unsolved. (H. O'S. Dixon) Cosmopol. 22: 28.
Unsolved Mystery, An; a story. All the Year, 71: 638. 74: 355.
Unspoken Water. (M. Hunt) Longm. 26: 633.
Untaught by Experience. (R. B. Hale) New Eng. M. n. s. 11: 484.
Unto the Third and Fourth Generation; a story. (H. Caine) Munsey, 13: 241–455.
Untrammelled Art; a poem. (J. F. Sullivan) M. of Art, 14: 168.
Unwin, William Cawthorne. Cassier, 7: 76.
Up and down Old Brandywine; a poem. (J. W. Riley) Cosmopol. 17: 15.
Up Horse Mountain. (D. R. Goodale) New Eng. M. n. s. 13: 220.
Up in the Morning Early. Macmil. 71: 138.
Up the Yangtsze; a story. (L. Boehm) Belgra. 86: 272. Same art. Liv. Age, 205: 171.
Upanishads and the Brahmans. (C. Johnston) Open Court, 10: 5079.
— Teaching of the. (W. Davies) Atlan. 72: 178.
Upper Canada College. (W. A. Neilson) Canad. M. 1: 451.
Upsala. (C. Edwardes) Chamb. J. 72: 473.
Upson, William Ford, with portrait. (J. H. Kennedy) Nat'l M. (N. Y. '91) 15: 426.
Ural Mountains, Southern: Results of Recent Journeys. Geog. J. 6: 181.
Urania Institute, Berlin. (E. S. Holden) Engin. M. 2: 782.
Urban VI., Pope, Election of, More Light on. (C. G. Hebermann) Am. Cath. Q. 18: 407.
Urdu Translation of National Anthem. (G. W. Leitner) Asia. R. 15: 374.
Uredineæ, Homologies of. (C. E. Bessey) Am. Natural. 28: 989.
— Occurrence and Distribution of. (M. A. Carleton) Science, 22: 62.
Urgent Private Affairs; a story. (R. Dowling) Chamb. J. 69: 89–137.
Uriel Acosta; a story. (I. Zangwill) Cosmopol. 21: 257.
— dramatized. (K. Gützkow) Poet-Lore, 7: 6–333.
Urmi; a Poisoned Queen. (C. Sorabji) 19th Cent, 33: 112.
Urrabieta, Daniel Vierge, Portraits of. McClure, 1: 123.
Uruguay, Christmas Deer-hunt in. (G. A. Stockwell) Canad. M. 6: 114.
— Debt of, Scaling of. (R. Ogden) Nation, 54: 47.
Use of Friends; a novel. (C. C. Jenkins) Belgra. 87: 156.
Useful People. Cornh. 67: 277.
Ushant, With the Islanders of. (E. H. Barker) Temp. Bar, 103: 221.
Using what we have. (A. H. Japp) Argosy, 55: 488.
"Usque ad mortem;" a story of China. (R. Allen) Temp. Bar, 108: 204.

Ussher, James, Carr's Life of. (R. C. Browne) Acad. 49: 5.
Usury, Ecclesiastical Treatment of. (H. C. Lea) Yale R. 2: 356.
— Extortionate, Evils growing out of. (A. B. Mason) Char. R. 4: 446.
— in Law, in Practice, and in Psychology. (G. K. Holmes) Pol. Sci. Q. 7: 431.
— Money and. (H. Clews) No. Am. 154: 480.
Utah, Admission of. (J. Cook) Our Day, 11: 364.— Pub. Opin. 16: 309.—Our Day, 13: 231.
— and Statehood; symposium. Indep. Feb. 9, 16, '93.
— as an Industrial Object-lesson. (W. E. Smythe) Atlan. 78: 610.
— Ruins of Southern. (W. K. Moorehead) Am. Antiq. 14: 324.
— Will Polygamists control the New State of? (G. Miller) Forum, 18: 462.
— Brigham Young and Modern. (J. A. Cockerill) Cosmopol. 19: 501.
Ute Indians, Exodus of. (H. F. Bond) Lend a H. 8: 230.
Ute Children, Games of. J. Am. Folk-Lore, 4: 231.
Utilitarian Philosophy, Some Aspects of. (T. E. Mayne) Westm. 141: 429.
Utilitarianism. (A. L. Hodder) Int. J. Ethics, 3: 90.
— Human Cost and. (J. A. Hobson) Econ. R. 6: 10.
— Relation of Shaftesbury and Hutcheson to. (E. Albee) Philos. R. 5: 24.
— Theory of, and the Formulation of Normal Laws. (S. N. Patten) Ann. Am. Acad. Pol. Sci. 7: 426.
Uxmal. (W. D. Foulke) Mo. Illust. 12: 256.
Uzanne, Octave, with portrait. Bk. Buyer, 11: 201.

Vacant House, A; a story. (G. G. Kitton) Argosy, 60: 635.
Vacaresco Incident in Roumania. (H. W. Fischer) Munsey, 14: 32.
Vacarius, Magister. (F. Liebermann) Eng. Hist. R. 11: 305.—(A. Jessopp) Eng. Hist. R. 11: 746.
Vacation Camps and Boys' Republics. (A. Shaw) R. of Rs. (N. Y.) 13: 572.
Vacation Notes of a Canoeist. (C. B. Vaux) Outing, 20: 429.
Vacations and Physical Culture. (J. M. Buckley) Chaut. 15: 445.
— How Long should they be? N. Church R. 3: 597.
Vaccination, Commission on. (M. Morris) 19th Cent. 40: 658.—(J. A. Picton) Contemp. 70: 484.
— — Report of. Nature, 55: 15.
— Dangers of. (W. B. Hidden) No. Am. 159: 124.
— an Error. (A. Milnes) Arena, 14: 244, 392.
— Experiment in, in Milton, Mass., 1809. (S. W. Abbott) New Eng. M. n. s. 15: 346.
— Lady M. W. Montagu and Modern Bacteriology. (Mrs. H. M. Plunkett) Pop. Sci. Mo. 45: 359.
— Our Duty in regard to. (T. G. Stewart) Blackw. 160: 703.
— Protective Inoculation for Cholera. (S. T. Armstrong) Pop. Sci. Mo. 42: 223.
Vacuum Discharge Streamers, Interaction of. (M. I. Pupin) Am. J. Sci. 143: 263.
Vagabond's Christmas in Tahiti, A. (J. C. Werner) Overland, n. s. 26: 590.
Vagabonds, Married. (M. E. Richmond) Lend a H. 16: 103.
— — Proper Treatment of. (M. E. Richmond) Char. R. 4: 401.
Vailima Letters. (R. L. Stevenson) McClure, 5: 522.
Vaillant, Auguste: Evolution of a Dynamiter. (R. Ogden) Nation, 58: 5.
Val d'Arno. (C. J. Bayne) Atlan. 77: 625.
Val-des-Bois. An Object-lesson in Christian Democracy. (V. M. Crawford) Fortn. 65: 58.
Valediction, A; a poem. (W. Toynbee) Gent. M. n. s. 56: 530.
Valencia, Spain. (C. W. Wood) Argosy, 62: 694.
Valentine Forsyth's Harvest; a story. All the Year, 71: 396.
Valera, J. Pepita Ximénes. (C. Patmore) Fortn. 58: 91. Same art. Ecl. M. 119: 333. Same art. Liv. Age, 194: 699.
Valeria; a story. (H. B. Stimson) Belgra. 91: 198.
Valiant Ignorance, A; a novel. (M. A. Dickens) All the Year, 72: 1-553. 73: 1-193.
Valkyrie III. (E. L. Snell) McClure, 5: 381.
Vallauris Pottery. (C. Monkhouse) M. of Art, 6: 30.
Valle di Pompei, Rosary of. (Lily Wolffsohn) 19th Cent. 37: 313.
Vallée d'Aspe: a Paradise of Peasant Lords. (J. C. Graham) Good Words, 37: 785.
Vallejo, Don Jaime. (C. H. Shinn) Lippinc. 54: 834.
Vallejo, General M. G., Reminiscences of; a Modern Knight. (E. B. Powell) Harper, 86: 786.
Valley of Childish Things, and other Emblems. (E. Wharton) Cent. 30: 467.
Valley of Sheitan; a story. (H. Hill) Chamb. J. 69: 825, 838.
Valley Forge. (H. M. Jenkins) Pennsyl. M. 17: 431.
Valley Path; a story. (W. A. Dromgoole) Arena, 15: 139-1017. 16: 138-656.
Valleys, Inaccessible. (A. R. Wallace) 19th Cent. 33: 391. Same art. Liv. Age, 197: 498.
Valmy, Battle of, 1792. (S. Wilkinson) Un. Serv. M. 6: 46.
Valois, Spring in Woods of. (M. Darmesteter) Contemp. 64: 198. Same art. Ecl. M. 121: 417.
Valparaiso. Leis. Hour, 44: 585.
— Capture of. Un. Serv. M. 4: 506. 5: 185.
Value, Austrian Theory of. (S. M. MacVane) Ann. Am. Acad. Pol. Sci. 4: 348.
— Economic, What is? (A. Kitson) Am. M. Civics, 6: 348.
— Evolution of the Idea of. (W. G. L. Taylor) J. Pol. Econ. 3: 414.
— Hedonistic Interpretation of Subjective. (H. W. Stuart) J. Pol. Econ. 4: 64.
— Idea of. (S. Alexander) Mind, 17: 31.
— International Theory of. (F. Y. Edgeworth) Econ. J. 4: 35, 424, 606.
— Measure of: is its Appreciation in the Interest of the Creditor? (G. A. Story) Overland, n. s. 28: 112.
— Natural, Tendencies of. (E. A. Ross) Yale R. 2: 173.
— — Wieser on. (W. K. Firminger) Econ. R. 5: 423. —(D. I. Green) Ann. Am. Acad. Pol. Sci. 6: 512.
— Notes on the Theory of. (J. S. Mackenzie) Mind, 68: 425.
— Shrinkage of. (M. M. Trumbull) Open Court, 2: 1325.
— Standard of. (E. B. Dietrick) Am. M. Civics, 7: 243.—(J. Bascom) Q. J. Econ. 10: 54.
— — New. (W. Bagehot) Econ. J. 2: 472.
— Subjective, and Exchange. (H. W. Stuart) J. Pol. Econ. 4: 208, 352.
— Theories of, and Standard of Deferred Payments. (F. Fetter) Ann. Am. Acad. Pol. Sci. 5: 882.
— Theory of. (F. von Wieser) Ann. Am. Acad. Pol. Sci. 2: 600.
— Ultimate Standard of. (E. v. Böhm-Bawerk) Ann. Am. Acad. Pol. Sci. 5: 149.— (E. v. Böhm-Bawerk and F. G. Edgeworth) Econ. J. 4: 719.— (J. B. Clark) Yale R. 1: 258.

Value, Unit of, in all Trade. (E. Atkinson) Engin. M. 5: 555.
Valves of a Corliss Engine, How to adjust. (T. Pray, jr.) Cassier, 1: 270.
Valves, Water, Improvements in. (J. Richards) Cassier, 4: 378.
Vampire Lore. (L. J. Vance) Open Court, 7: 3607.
Vampires, Concerning. Chamb. J. 73: 730.
Van Alen, J. J., Nomination of. Pub. Opin. 16: 20, 67. — (E. L. Godkin) Nation, 57: 240. — H. M. Janeway) Am. J. Pol. 4: 186. — (C. Robinson) Am. J. Pol. 4: 57.
Vanadic Acid, Reduction of. (P. E. Browning) Am. J. Sci. 152: 185.
Vanadium, Application of Organic Acids to Estimation of. (P. E. Browning and R. J. Goodman) Am. J. Sci. 152: 355.
Van Beers, Jan. (M. H. Spielmann) M. of Art, 15: 397.
— at Home. (M. A. Belloc) Idler, 5: 27.
Vanbrugh, John. Ath. '94, 2: 234. — (C. Dalton) Ath. '94, 2: 299.
— Works, Ward's. Sat. R. 75: 268.
Van Buren, John, with portrait. (A. O. Hall) Green Bag, 7: 209.
Vancouver, Across, from Alert Bay to Tahsis Canal. (W. W. Bolton and J. W. Laing) Overland, n. s. 28: 621.
— and Hawaii. (H. H. Gowen) Canad. M. 2: 451.
"Vandalia" Wreck at Samoa. (H. Webster) Un. Serv. (Phila.) 12: 303.
Van den Broeck, Clémence. (P. McArthur) Mo. Illust. 5: 58.
Vanderbilt, Cornelius. (W. S. Bridgman) Munsey, 6: 34.
Vanderbilt, Geo. W. Forest in North Carolina. (C. S. Sargent) Garden & F. 8: 481.
Vanderbilt, William H., House of, New York. (S. G. W. Benjamin) M. of Art, 6: 137.
Vanderbilt University, Student Life at. (W. B. Nance) So. M. 5: 468.
Vanderbilts, The. (R. H. Titherington) Munsey) 12: 71.
Vanderdecken; poem. (B. S. Parker) Cent. 29: 758.
Vanderfelt, E. H., as Judah. Theatre, 28: 152.
Vander's Marget. Good Words, 37: Xmas no. 29.
Van der Straeten, Georges. (M. H. Spielmann) M. of Art, 15: 310.
Van Dyck, Anthony. (T. Cole) Cent. 27: 210. — M. of Art, 5: 422. — (F. M. Robinson) M. of Art, 9: 522. (J. A. Blaikie) M. of Art, 10: 198.
— at the Court of Charles I. (F. M. Robinson) M. of Art, 10: 65.
Van Dyke, Henry, with portrait. Bk. Buyer, 11: 285.
— (Katherine H. Parker) Bost. 1: 386.
Van Elten, Kruseman. (A. Black) Mo. Illust. 3: 214.
Van Haanen, Cecil. (P. E. Pinkerton) M. of Art, 10: 1.
Vanini, Giulio Cesare, in England. (R. C. Christie) Eng. Hist. R. 10: 238.
Vanished; a story. (J. S. Fletcher) Chamb. J. 73: 137.
Vanished Bride, The; a story. Argosy, 62: 122.
Vanishing Illusions. (J. Watson) Sund. M. 25: 468.
Vanitas Vanitatis; a story. (E. Penrose) Argosy, 60: 98.
Vanity and Humility. Spec. 70: 218.
— Crawford on. Spec. 68: 523.
— Destructive. Spec. 73: 106.
— Food of. Liv. Age, 192: 191.
Van Lennep's Cowardice. (J. E. McMahon) Overland, n. s. 27: 17.
Van Loeninga, A. *See* Loeninga, A. van.
Van Muyden, Evart. Critic, 22: 130.
Vannes, College of, Sixty Years ago. (Jules Simon) Forum, 21: 659.
Van Norden, Warner, with portrait. Nat'l M. (N. Y. '91) 17: 93.
Van Orley, Bernard. (W. S. Sparrow) M. of Art, 11: 391.
Vanuxem, Lardner, with portrait. Pop. Sci. Mo. 46: 833.
Van Wagener's Flying Cat; a story. (W. L. Alden) Idler, 10: 698.
Van Zile, E. S., with portrait. Bk. News, 14: 327.
Vapor Bath of Ghantur. (A. Walker) Bib. World, 3: 53.
Vaporization, Relations between Temperature, Pressure, and Latent Heat of. (C. E. Linebarger) Am. J. Sci. 149: 380.
Vaqueros, Last of the. (Alan Owen) Overland, n. s. 27: 249.
Varallo, Italy, Sacro Monte at. (E. M. Lynch) Cath. World, 59: 174.
Vardhamâna Jnâtriputra. (J. T. Bixby) New World, 5: 541.
Variation after Birth. (L. H. Bailey) Am. Natural. 30: 17.
— and Evolution. (W. A. Gain) Science, 22: 7.
— and Specific Stability. (W. T. Thiselton-Dyer) Nature, 51: 459.
— Animal, Bateson on. Ed. R. 182: 78. — (W. F. R. Weldon) Nature, 50: 25. — (P. C. Mitchell) Nat. Sci. 5: 371.
— in Animals and Plants. (W. F. R. Weldon) Nature, 51: 449.
— in Animal Life, Discoveries in. Sat. R. 79: 312.
— Influence of Islands on. Sat. R. 80: 204.
— Inherent Error in Views of Galton and Weismann on. (W. K. Brooks) Science, n. s. 1: 121.
— Ontogenic and Phylogenic. (H. F. Osborn) Science, n. s. 4: 786.
— Organic. (C. Morris) Am. Natural. 29: 888.
— A Study of Leuciscus Balteatus (Richardson). (C. H. Eigenmann) Am. Natural. 29: 10.
Variations and Mutations. (W. B. Scott) Am. J. Sci. 148: 355.
— Individual. (G. Henslow) Nat. Sci. 6: 385.
Variety Entertainment, Triumph of. (A. B. Walkley) New R. 7: 505.
Variscite from Utah. (R. L. Packard) Am. J. Sci. 147: 297.
Varnish on Paintings, Robinson on. Art J. 46: 326.
Vasari, Giorgio. (F. M. Robinson) M. of Art, 8: 250.
— in the Light of Recent Publications. (B. Berenson) Nation, 56: 271.
Vase, Alkmene, formerly in Castle Howard. (A. S. Murray) J. Hel. Stud. 11: 225.
Vase-fragments from Acropolis of Athens. (G. C. Richards) J. Hel. Stud. 14: 186.
Vase-painting, Archaic Pediment Reliefs and. (C. L. Brownson) Am. J. Archæol. 8: 28.
Vase-paintings, Greek. Spec. 72: 468.
Vases, Attic, Orphic Myths on. (C. H. Smith) J. Hel. Stud. 11: 343.
— by Phintias, Two. (H. S. Jones) J. Hel. Stud. 12: 366.
— Fragments of, from the Acropolis of Athens. (G. C. Richards) J. Hel. Stud. 14: 381.
— Greek. (H. B. Walters) Knowl. 19: 36, 91, 151, 267.
Vasey, George. Science, 21: 145.
Vassar College, Festivals in. (E. E. Boyd) Cent. 27: 437.
— a Generation of College Women. (F. M. Abbott) Forum, 20: 377.

Vassili. (S. Pickering) Macmil. 66: 277. Same art. Ecl. M. 119: 465.
Vatican, The. (F. M. Crawford) Cent. 30: 577.
— Archives of. (C. H. Haskins) Am. Hist. R. 2: 40.
— Library of, Origin and Development of. (N. Hone) Month, 84: 404.
— — Recent Work in. (E. Soutif) Am. Cath. Q. 20: 750.
— Observatory of. (J. A. Zahn) Cosmopol. 18: 599. — (R. A. Gregory) Nature, 49: 341.
Vatican Council, Personal Reminiscences of the. (J. C. Gibbons) No. Am. 158: 385.
Vaughan, Henry, the Silurist. (L. I. Guiney) Atlan. 73: 681.
— Grave of. (L. I. Guiney) Critic, 27: 446. — (L. I. Guiney) Ath. '95, 2: 492.
— Silex Scintillans of. Bookworm, 1: 408.
Vaughan, Herbert A., Archbishop. (H. T. Smart) M. Chr. Lit. 6: 196. — (H. C. Kent) Cath. World, 55: 385. — With portrait. (W. Ward) Eng. Illust. 10: 219.
— and the Social Question. (W. R. Sullivan) Westm. 141: 126.
— Poisoning the Wells of Catholic Criticism. (E. S. Purcell) 19th Cent. 39: 514.
Vaughan, Father Jerome. Blackw. 160: 668.
Vaughan, Kate. (J. Hollingshead) Theatre, 36: 257.
Vaulting, Pole. (M. W. Ford) Outing, 20: 42.
Vautier, Benjamin. (H. M. Zimmern) M. of Art, 8: 8.
Vauvenargues, Marquis de. (W. F. Rae) Temp. Bar, 102: 23. Same art. Liv. Age, 201: 687.
Vaux, Wm. S. W. (Fred. Gale) Time, 158.
Vaux, Château de. (A. Laugel) Nation, 59: 246.
Veda, Discoveries of, by Chinese, Persians, Missionaries and Scholars. (F. M. Müller) Open Court, 4: 2307. — (H. Oldenberg) Open Court, 3: 1547.
— Gods of. (H. Oldenberg) Open Court, 10: 4919.
— Interpretation of. (M. Bloomfield) Am. J. Philol. 12: 414. — (F. M. Müller) Acad. 42: 134, 364.
— — and the Hindu Epic. (H. Oldenberg) Open Court, 3: 1561.
— Religion of. (H. Oldenberg) Open Court, 10: 4872.
— Study of, and Ethnology. (H. Oldenberg) Open Court, 10: 4889.
Vedânta Philosophy, The. (G. A. Jacob) Acad. 46: 155. — (A. Gumlogsen) Open Court, 4: 2131.
Vedder, Elihu, with portrait. Bk. Buyer, 12: 321. — (A. M. F. Robinson) M. of Art, 8: 120.
— Recent Work of. (W. C. Brownell) Scrib. M. 17: 157.
Vedic Epoch, History of. (H. Oldenberg) Open Court, 3: 1573.
Vedic Language, Reduplication of Nouns and Adjectives in. (E. W. Hopkins) Am. J. Philol. 14: 1.
Vedic Religion, What is? (H. Oldenberg) Open Court, 10: 4895.
Vedic Syntax, Delbrück on. (W. D. Whitney) Am. J. Philol. 13: 271.
Vega, Lope de. Columbus. Sat. R. 75: 150.
Vegetable Diet. (W. Paget) 19th Cent. 31: 577. Same art. Pop. Sci. Mo. 44: 94.
Vegetable Malformations. (B. D. Halsted) Pop. Sci. Mo. 42: 318.
Vegetable Monsters. (E. Step) Good Words, 35: 107.
Vegetable Physiology, Development of. (J. C. Arthur) Science, n. s. 2: 360.
— Two Schools of, in Germany and England. (E. L. Gregory) Am. Natural. 26: 211, 279.
Vegetable Sculpture in China. (A. B. Westland) Garden & F. 7: 92.
Vegetables, Azotic Nutrition of. (R. G. Abbott) New Sci. R. 2: 268.
— for Private Gardens. Garden & F. 8: 126.
— Our Imported. (R. H. Wallace) Chamb. J. 73: 519.
Vegetarianism. (T. P. Smith) Fortn. 64: 753. Same art. Ecl. M. 126: 68. — (A. de Neuville) Pub. Opin. 15: 181. — Spec. 70: 767. — Time, 8: 698.
— Against. Sat. R. 73: 92.
— Plea for. Time, 8: 144.
— — Answer to Plea for. (J. W. Power) Time, 8: 390.
— Practicability of. (O. A. Shrubsole) Westm. 145: 312.
— Shelley and. (K. West) Writer, 7: 34.
Vehmgerichte, The. Chamb. J. 69: 833.
Vehmic Courts of Westphalia. (G. H. Westley) Green Bag, 8: 440.
Veii, a Dead City of Etruria. All the Year, 70: 33.
Veil of Moses. (P. J. Gloag) Thinker, 8: 308.
Veiling of the Soul. (J. Watson) Sund. M. 25: 590.
Veitch, John. Acad. 46: 172. — Ath. '94, 2: 322.
— History and Poetry of the Scottish Border. (A. H. Japp) Scot. R. 23: 108.
Veitch, Sophie F. F. Margaret Drummond, Millionaire. Scot. R. 23: 32.
Velasquez, Diego Rodriguez de Silva y. (C. C. Cooper) Lippinc. 51: 75. — M. of Art, 6: 82.
— Art of, Stevenson's. Sat. R. 81: 78.
— in Madrid. (E. R. Pennell) Nation, 59: 323, 339.
Velocimeter, The Newest. (S. E. Tillman) Cosmopol. 20: 336.
Venetian Art at the New Gallery. (C. Phillips) Fortn. 63: 423. — Am. Arch. 47: 73, 122. — (E. R. Pennell) Nation, 60: 69.
Venetian Melancholy. (J. A. Symonds) Fortn. 59: 256. Same art. Ecl. M. 120: 513.
Venetian Painters of the Renaissance, Berenson on. (J. B. Fletcher) Dial (Ch.) 16: 268.
Venezuela, Republic of. (N. Bolet-Paraza) New Eng. M. n. s. 7: 220.
— and Guiana, Glimpses of. (W. N. King) Cent. 30: 358.
— as a Sister Republic. (R. Ogden) Nation, 62: 4.
— before Europe and America. (G. H. D. Gossip) Fortn. 65: 397.
— Belles of Caracas. (W. N. King) Cosmopol. 22: 29.
— Boundary Question. (J. C. Ropes) Bach. of Arts, 2: 725. — (H. Thurston) Month, 87: 153. — (H. R. Mill) Nature, 53: 200. Same art. Liv. Age, 208: 294. — National, 26: 573, 737. — (B. H. Thwaite) Fortn. 65: 231. — (T. S. Woolsey; O. S. Straus; I. L. Rice) Forum, 20: 705. — (Sir D. P. Chalmers) Jurid. R. 8: 1. — (A. Carnegie) No. Am. 162: 129. Pub. Opin. 20: 6. — Pub. Opin. 19: 584. — (W. L. Scruggs) R. of Rs. (N. Y.) 12: 695. — (H. S. Somerset) 19th Cent. 38: 758. Same art. Liv. Age, 207: 545. — Pub. Opin. 19: 838. — (R. Ogden) Nation, 61: 286.
— — American View of. (E. J. Shriver) Westm. 145: 117.
— — and Arbitration. (H. O. Arnold-Forster) Sat. R. 82: 180. — (J. Morley) 19th Cent. 40: 320.
— — — The Lawlessness of Arbitration. (E. Reich) New R. 15: 62.
— — and the Monroe Doctrine. (H. C. Lodge) No. Am. 160: 651.
— — British Case. (L. J. Maxse) National, 27: 277.
— — British Feeling on. (J. Bryce) No. Am. 162: 145.
— — A British Guiana Colonist on. (N. D. Davis) Nation, 62: 72.

Venezuela; Boundary Question, President Cleveland on. (E. L. Godkin) Nation, 61: 420. — Pub. Opin. 19: 766.
— — The Commission on. (E. L. Godkin; S. M. Macvane) Nation, 62: 7, 24.
— — Common Sense and Venezuela. (E. Dicey) 19th Cent. 39: 7. Same art. Ecl. M. 126: 207.
— — The Correspondence concerning. (E. L. Godkin) Nation, 61: 458.
— — Duty of Congress. (I. L. Rice) Forum, 20: 721.
— — Evidence of Maps. (C. R. Markham) Geog. J. 7: 277, 309.
— — Facts about the Boundary. (J. Bolton) 19th Cent. 39: 185.
— — French View. Sat. R. 81: 32.
— — Issue between Great Britain and America. (H. M. Stanley) 19th Cent. 39: 1.
— — Jingoism or War upon Domestic Industry. (E. Atkinson) Engin. M. 10: 801.
— — The Law in the Case. (V. Denslow) Nation, 61: 358.
— — Legal Merits of the Case. Soc. Econ. 9: 339.
— — Olney Doctrine and America's New Foreign Policy. (S. Low) 19th Cent. 40: 849.
— — Our Duty in the Crisis. (J. Wheeler; C. H. Grosvenor) No. Am. 161: 628.
— — Plea for Peace in. Critic, 28: 25.
— — The Seamy Side of British Guiana. (F. Comyn) 19th Cent. 39: 390.
— — Settlement of. (E. L. Godkin) Nation, 63: 360.
— — — and Canada. (G. T. Blackstock) Canad. M. 8: 170.
— — W. E. Curtis on; Perversion of History. Macmil. 74: 237.
— Eastern Boundary of. (J. S. Cotton) Acad. 48: 567. — (H. C. Lea) Nation, 61: 345.
— Government, People, and Boundary. (W. E. Curtis) Nat. Geog. M. 7: 49.
— Natural Features of. (F. A. Fernald) Pop. Sci. Mo. 48: 510.
— A Peep at. All the Year, 71: 57.
— Some Notes about. (T. R. Dawley, jr.) Cosmopol. 20: 410.
Vengeance of the Dead. (R. Barr) Eng. Illust. 11: 835.
Vengeance of Pendleton, The. (A. McEwen) Overland, n. s. 26: 283.
Venice. (H. Mereu) Am. Arch. 41: 158, 197. — Cath. World, 63: 478. — (E. O. Kirk) Lippinc. 50: 642. — (S. B. Holabird) Un. Serv. (Phila.) 8: 425.
— Academy, Rearrangement of the. (A. French) Nation, 61: 61.
— Ancient, Society in. (C. Edwardes) National, 20: 160. Same art. Ecl. M. 119: 761. Same art. Liv. Age, 195: 579.
— Arts and Industries of. (P. Molmenti) Chaut. 21: 686.
— Brown's History of. (W. R. Thayer) Nation, 57: 175. — Spec. 70: 827.
— Church of Santa Maria dei Miracoli. Reliquary, 35: 193.
— Fashions of the 18th Century in. (V. Malamani) Chaut. 22: 564.
— Fêtes in, Past and Present. (F. Cooley) Chaut. 19: 651.
— From, to the Gross-Venediger. (H. Van Dyke) Scrib. M. 13: 135.
— Gondola Days in. (F. H. Smith) So. M. 3: 228.
— Gondoliers of. (L. A. Smith) Gent. M. n. s. 48: 486.
Venice, The Grand Canal. (Henry James) Scrib. M. 12: 531.
— Impression of. (H. W. Massingham) Eng. Illust. 11: 243.
— in Easter, Impressions and Sensations. (A. Symons) Harper, 90: 738.
— in Lent. All the Year, 70: 321.
— Interior Decorations in. (G. E. Campbell) Art J. 45: 253.
— Literary Landmarks of. (L. Hutton) Harper, 93: 205.
— of Titian. (W. Bayliss) M. of Art, 5: 50.
— Outdoor. (G. E. Campbell) Art J. 44: 38.
— Pictures in, Re-viewed. (Kenyon Cox) Nation, 57: 188.
— a Poem. (E. Fellner) Outing, 25: 443.
— Restorations at. (W. J. Stillman) Nation, 55: 256.
— St. Mark's, Preservation of. M. of Art, 3: 115.
— To-day. Am. Arch. 51: 130.
— The Venetian Day. (R. S. Peabody) Atlan. 76: 477.
— Venetian Ducali. (J. W. Bradley) Bibliographica, 2: 257.
— Wells of. (W. Scott) Univ. R. 8: 393.
Venner, Thomas, the Boston Wine-cooper and Fifth-Monarchy Man. (C. E. Banks) N. E. Reg. 47: 437.
Ventilation and Warming of Dwellings. Pop. Sci. Mo. 41: 831.
— — Blower System of. (W. B. Snow) Cassier, 4: 97.
— — of Tall Buildings. (L. Allen) Engin. M. 9: 476.
— Expired Air and Problems of. Pop. Sci. Mo. 48: 583.
— Insensible. (J. M. White) Am. Arch. 45: 107.
— Making the House Healthful. Pop. Sci. Mo. 47: 573.
— of Large Buildings. (A. R. Wolff) J. Frankl. Inst. 138: 45, 116.
— Practical Suggestions respecting. (J. H. Kellogg) Am. Arch. 47: 136.
— An Unsettled Question in. (L. Allen) Engin. M. 7: 207.
Ventimiglia, Antiquarian Exploration at. (W. Jackson) Walford's Antiq. 4: 298. 5: 58.
Ventriloquism, Ganthony on. Sat. R. 77: 291.
Venus Accroupie, in the Louvre. (R. Jefferies) M. of Art, 10: 331.
— of Milo, Attempt towards the Restoration of. (J. Bell) M. of Art, 17: 16.
Venus, Planet. (W. J. Lockyer) Nature, 46: 468. 49: 413. — Nature, 53: 367. — (P. Lowell) Pop. Astron. 4: 281.
Venus-slippers. (L. Greenlee) Mo. Illust. 4: 283.
Véra Blavatsky; a story. (E. Staniforth) Eng. Illust. 10: 411. Same art. Liv. Age, 197: 653.
Veracity. (H. Spencer) Pop. Sci. Mo. 41: 482.
Vera Cruz. Around World, 1: 43.
— Landing of Gen. Scott at. (W. B. Lane) Un. Serv. (Phila.) 11: 553.
Verbs, Weak, Third Class of, in Primitive Teutonic and Anglo-Saxon. (M. Sweet) Am. J. Philol. 14: 409.
Verdi, G. (F. J. Crowest) Blackw. 158: 566. Same art. Ecl. M. 125: 786. — (E. Swayne) Music, 5: 111.
— Falstaff; an opera. (J. S. Shedlock) Acad. 45: 442. — (V. Stanford) Fortn. 59: 445. — Sat. R. 75: 200. — Ath. '93, 1: 227.
— — Mackenzie on. Sat. R. 75: 655.
— Old Age of. (E. Panzacchi) Chaut. 18: 654.
— Operas of. Sat. R. 81: 596.
— Otello; an Opera. Sat. R. 78: 430.
Verestchagin, Basil. (N. Sobkô) M. of Art, 7: 184.

Verga, Giovanni. (H. Zimmern) Critic, 20: 217.
— a True Realist. (J. W. Mario) Nation, 57: 305.
Verhaeren, Emile. (V. M. Crawford) Fortn. 66: 715. Same art. Liv. Age, 211: 835.
Verlaine, Paul. (Jos. T. Stickney) Bach. of Arts, 3: 18. — With portrait. Bk. Buyer, 10: 643. — With portrait. Bk. Buyer, 13: 353. — With portraits. Bookman, 1: 89. — (A. Symons) National, 19: 501. — (A. Symons) New R. 9: 609. — Critic, 23: 397. — (A. Symons) Sat. R. 81: 34. — (A. Symons) Ath. '96, 1: 54. — Critic, 28: 47, 80, 134. — (A. Manston) Temp. Bar, 108: 329. Same art. Liv. Age, 210: 508. — (E. Dujardin) Univ. R. 6: 412.
— and Shelley. (Alice L. Wilson) Poet-Lore, 8: 406.
— Confessions. Sat. R. 79: 731.
— Invectives. Sat. R. 82: 338.
Vermin, What are? Sat. R. 74: 274.
— What constitutes? Sat. R. 76: 156.
Vermont at the World's Fair. (H. H. McIntyre) New Eng. M. n. s. 10: 3.
— An Early Combat in, 1709. (B. C. Steiner) M. Am. Hist. 28: 215.
— Election in 1892. (E. P. Clark) Nation, 55: 196.
— Supreme Court of. (R. S. Taft) Green Bag, 5: 547. 6: 16, 72, 122, 176.
Verne, Jules, with portrait. Bk. Buyer, 7: 281. — With portrait. Bk. News, 8: 380. — (R. H. Sherard) McClure, 2: 115.
— Portraits of. McClure, 1: 218.
Verney, Harry. Geog. J. 3: 340.
Verney Family during the Commonwealth. Sat. R. 79: 866.
— Home Life of. (L. B. Lang) Longm. 26: 143. Same art. Liv. Age, 206: 43.
— Memoirs. (A. Galton) Acad. 41: 501. — Ath. '92, 1: 751. — Gent. M. n. s. 49: 105. — Sat. R. 73: 689. — Ed. R. 176: 411. — Spec. 69: 135. — Liv. Age, 195: 680. — Lond. Q. 79: 1. — Church Q. 36: 136. — (J. F. Kirk) Atlan. 71: 371.
Vernon's Aunt; an Oriental Story. (S. J. Duncan) Idler, 5: 3-617.
Verona. (S. Thompson) M. of Art, 10: 253.
Veronese, Paul. (W. J. Stillman) Cent. 22: 581.
Verrazzano and Gomez in N. Y. Bay, 1524. (D. Van Pelt) Nat'l M. (N. Y. '91) 15: 488.
Verse, Blank. Has it Laws? (J. B. Perry) Poet-Lore, 8: 528.
— Political. (C. B. R. Kent) Gent. M. n. s. 50: 237.
— A Practical Use of. (R. Stevens) No. Am. 161: 634.
— Practical Uses of. (R. F. Horton) Sund. M. 24: 827.
Verse-making and Man-making. (W. E. Gladstone) New R. 15: 116.
Versification, Brewer on. Spec. 70: 574.
Verses, Magic. Liv. Age, 204: 549.
Vert and Gules; a story. (G. Hall) Cosmopol. 17: 686.
Vertebrate Paleontology in the American Museum. (H. F. Osborn) Science, n. s. 2: 178.
Vertebrate Skeleton, Origin of. (J. S. Kingsley) Am. Natural. 28: 635.
Vertebrates, Lowest of, and Origin. (T. Gill) Science, n. s. 1: 645.
— Nervous Systems of. (P. Carus) Open Court, 4: 2228.
Very Light Railway, A; a story. (Jane Barlow) National, 24: 278. Same art. Liv. Age, 203: 396.
Very Modern Historian; a story. All the Year, 75: 589.
Very Strange Case, A; a story. (W. Hinckley) Outing, 21: 221.
Vesalius, the Anatomist. (G. M. Cullen) Month, 80: 30.
Vespucci, Amerigo. (E. Lawrence) Harper, 84: 909.
— Autograph Manuscript of. M. Am. Hist. 29: 169.
— Book by, Fraudulent. (J. Winsor) Nation, 56: 234.
Vespucci, Amerigo, in India. Ath. '94, 1: 86.
— Markham's Letters of. Critic, 26: 59. — (J. Winsor) Nation, 59: 220.
Vespucci, Simonetta de'. (J. Cartwright) M. of Art, 9: 466.
Vessels, Cellulose Protection for. (B. P. Wiltberger) J. Frankl. Inst. 140: 53.
Vesuvius, Eruption of, July 3, 1895. (H. J. Johnson-Lavis) Nature, 52: 343.
— Under Shadow of. (E. Fawcett) Cosmopol. 22: 3.
Veteran, The; a story. (S. Crane) McClure, 7: 222.
Veterinary Physiology, Smith's. Sat. R. 74: 518.
Veterinary Science, The Importance of. (C. F. Adams) Harv. Grad. M. 3: 188.
Vetulonia, Primitive Dome with Pendentives at. (A. L. Frothingham, jr.) Am. J. Archæol. 9: 213.
Vézalay Abbey. (W. Pater) 19th Cent. 35: 963.
Vézère, In the Valley of the. (E. H. Barker) Temp. Bar, 98: 399. Same art. Liv. Age, 199: 33.
Vianden Castle. (S. Beale) Am. Arch. 38: 145.
Viaud, Julien [Pierre Loti, *pseud.*]. Quar. 176: 433. — With portrait. Bk. Buyer, 9: 203. — (M. J. Onahan) Cath. World, 60: 191. — (E. Delille) Fortn. 57: 233. — (M. Adam) McClure, 4: 476.
— and Feuillet. Sat. R. 73: 411.
— and the Sea. Scot. R. 26: 343.
— Death and Pity. (L. de La Ramé) Fortn. 57: 548.
— Modern Paganism and. Spec. 68: 493.
— Some Aspects of the Work of. (J. Fitzgerald) Westm. 140: 31.
Vibert, Jehan Georges; an autobiographical sketch. Cent. 29: 78.
— Pictures by. Cent. 29: 551, 719, 941.
Vibration, Sympathetic; an Old Miracle, New Science. (Mary Parmele) New Sci. R. 2: 344.
Vibrations of Buildings. (J. R. Milne) Am. Arch. 53: 38.
Vibratory Circuit, Operation of the. (J. E. W. Keely) New Sci. R. 1: 457.
Viburnums as Garden Plants. Garden & F. 9: 304.
Vicar-general, Office of. (G. Peries) Am. Cath. Q. 20: 313.
Vicar of Wrocksley, The. (J. Stafford) Chamb. J. 72: 747.
Vicar's Secret; a story. Cornh. 65: 41. Same art. Liv. Age, 192: 523.
Vice-Presidency. How to make it Attractive. (Linton Satterthwait) Am. M. Civics, 9: 53.
Vice-President, Whom shall we elect for, in 1896? (D. Mowry) Am. M. Civics, 9: 295.
Vice-Presidential Candidates, The three, 1896. (T. Roosevelt) R. of Rs. (N. Y.) 14: 289.
Victim of Circumstances, A; a story. (K. F. Hills) Belgra. 88: 303.
Victim of Circumstances, A. Blackw. 153: 69. Same art. Ecl. M. 120: 329.
Victim to Art, A. All the Year, 71: 13.
Victor Emmanuel II. Argosy, 60: 242.
Victor, Prince, of Hohenlohe. Fortn. 58: 366. Same art. Liv. Age, 195: 311.
Victoria, Queen and Empress. (E. Arnold) Forum, 20: 667.
— and Art. (J. Oldcastle) M. of Art, 3: 283.
— and her Children. (S. P. Cadman) Chaut. 20: 643. 21: 1.
— and Lord Melbourne. (R. B. Brett) 19th Cent. 34: 967.
— and her Prime Ministers. (R. B. Brett) 19th Cent. 35: 248, 639, 912. Same art. Liv. Age, 200: 2, 579. 201: 451.
— as a Ruler. Liv. Age, 211: 343.

Victoria, Queen, Early Ancestors of. (H. W. Wolff) National, 18: 740. Same art. Ecl. M. 118: 479. Same art. Liv. Age, 193: 78.
— in Politics. (F. H. Hill) National, 19: 153. Same art. Liv. Age, 193: 579.
— The Longest Reign in English History. (J. Ashton) Eng. Illust. 16: 103.
— Reign of. Ed. R. 183: 1. Same art. Liv. Age, 208: 450.
— Sixty Years Sovereignty. (T. E. Champion) Canad. M. 7: 565.
Victoria, Empress of Germany, as an Artist. (A. St. Johnston) M. of Art, 9: 300.
Victoria Mary of Teck, Princess. New R. 9: 1.
Victoria, Australia, Government of, Jenks on. (D. G. Ritchie) Eng. Hist. R. 7: 803. — Sat. R. 74: 339.
— Land Boom and Banking in. (M. Macfie) Bank. M. (Lond.) 53: 65.
— Village Settlements in. (H. F. Tucker) Econ. R. 3: 514.
Victoria, B. C., Bridge Disaster, May, 1896. (C. H. Gibbons) Bost. 4: 388.
"Victoria," Loss of the. (Sir G. P. Hornby) Fortn. 60: 290. — (F. Elgar) Nature, 49: 102, 124, 151. — Pub. Opin. 15: 310. — Sat. R. 76: 34. — Spec. 68: 192. 71: 7, 103. — (G. P. Hornby) Un. Serv. M. 7: 1109. 8: 50. — (G. P. Hornby) Un. Serv. (Phila.) 10: 334.
— — Lesson of. (W. McAdoo) No. Am. 157: 145.
— — Manœuvring Powers of Steamships. (P. H. Colomb) Nature, 49: 174.
— — Responsibility for. Sat. R. 76: 513.
— — — Admiral Tryon and. (W. T. Stead) R. of Rs. (N. Y.) 8: 169.
— — Verdict of the Court Martial. (V. Lushington) National, 22: 141.
Victoria Hall, Geneva, Switzerland. Am. Arch. 47: 21.
Victoria Nyanza, Exploration of. Dub. R. 110: 189.
— Railway to, A Parliamentary View of. (R. Temple) Fortn. 57: 704.
— — Plea for. (T. H. Parke) Un. Serv. M. 6: 203.
— — with the Railway Survey. (J. W. Pringle) Geog. J. 2: 112.
Victorian Anthology, Stedman's. Dial (Ch.) 19: 237.
"Victory," H. M. S. (F. A. Walker) Southern M. 4: 59.
Victory of the Grand Duke of Mittenheim; a story. (A. Hope Hawkins) McClure, 6: 280.
Victory through Self-surrender. (J. Cook) Our Day, 14: 311.
Vienna, Musical Celebrities of. (W. von Sachs) Harper, 93: 622.
— People's Kitchens in. (E. Sellers) 19th Cent. 36: 744.
— Popular Life in. (W. Singer) Harper, 84: 215.
— Recent Events in Municipal History of. (L. S. Rowe) Citizen, 1: 282.
— Visit to, in 1856. Belgra. 87: 363.
See Austrian Museum of Art and Industry.
Vierge, Daniel, with portrait. Bk. Buyer, 13: 505.
— Drawings by. Spec. 69: 822.
— the Father of Modern Illustration. (A. F. Jaccaci) Cent. 24: 186.
— Illustrations to Pablo de Segovia. (M. H. Spielmann) M. of Art, 16: 52. — (P. G. Hamerton) Portfo. 23: 227.
Viewy Folk. (Mrs. L. Linton) Fortn. 65: 595.
Vigil of McDowell Sutro; a story. (B. Matthews) Harper, 93: 758.
Vigilance Committee of '56. (A. B. Paul) Overland, n. s. 24: 433–622.
Vignettes from Nature. (R. Jefferies) Longm. 26: 253.
Vignettes of Manhattan. (B. Matthews) Harper, 88: 28–678. 89: 222, 457.
Vignoles, Chas. B. (Fred. Gale) Time, 20: 611.
Vigny, Alfred de. Spec. 69: 473.
Vijayanaga, Deserted City of. (C. Rolleston) J. Soc. Arts, 44: 529.
"Viking," Voyage of. (H. H. Boyesen) Chaut. 18: 420.
Viking's Tomb at Taplow. Walford's Antiq. 5: 14.
Viking Expeditions, Swedish Part in. (W. Roos) Eng. Hist. R. 7: 209.
Vikings, The, and what we owe to them. (S. Kneeland) Open Court, 1: 259.
— Norway and the. (Capt. M. Anderson) Nat. Geog. M. 5: 132.
Village, Mediæval, Study of Typical. (W. W. Fowler) Q. J. Econ. 9: 151.
Village of Old Age. (W. Ramal) Cornh. 74: 381. Same art. Liv. Age, 211: 310.
Village Alien; a story. (V. Roseboro') Cent. 22: 908.
Village Communities in Spain. Quar. 182: 483.
— Japanese. (B. H. Baden-Powell) Asia. R. 21: 366.
Village Community, Destruction of. (W. J. Ashley) Econ. R. 1: 358.
Village Craft; a story. (Mary Hartier) Gent. M. n. s. 55: 433. Same art. Liv. Age, 207: 655.
Village Fragment, A. (Mary Hartier) Gent. M. n. s. 51: 378. Same art. Ecl. M. 121: 705.
Village Homes, Picturesque. (Mary Campbell Smith) Westm. 141: 243.
Village Improvement as a National Issue. (B. G. Northrop) Our Day, 10: 574.
Village Improvement Societies, Work of. (B. G. Northrop) Forum, 19: 95.
— Work of Women in. (C. S. Sargent) Garden & F. 8: 121.
Village Legacy, The. Macmil. 65: 279. Same art. Liv. Age, 193: 17.
Village Life in England. (T. L. Papillon) Macmil. 65: 418. Same art. Ecl. M. 118: 767.
— — Another View of. (H. S. Blatch) Westm. 140: 318.
— — in Olden Time. (F. Gale) Eng. Illust. 9: 320.
— in France. Contemp. 65: 376. Same art. Liv. Age, 201: 29.
— Twenty-five Years of. (J. Vaughan) Longm. 21: 304. Same art. Liv. Age, 196: 628.
Village Maid, A; a poem. (A. Salmon) M. of Art, 14: 115.
Village Mystery, A; a story. (F. G. W.) Argosy, 61: 627.
Village Romance, The. (V. Roseboro') Cent. 21: 774.
Village Shop, The. Chamb. J. 73: 12.
Village Stradivarius, A. (K. D. Wiggin) Atlan. 75: 61, 205.
Village Watch-tower; a story. (K. D. Wiggin) Atlan. 69: 375.
Villages, English Midland, Statistics of. (J. Ashby; B. King) Econ. J. 3: 1, 193.
Villainage in England. Church Q. 38: 169. — (C. Elton) Law Q. 8: 117. — (I. S. Leadam) Pol. Sci. Q. 8: 653.
— — Andrews and Seebohm on. Sat. R. 74: 288.
— Vinogradoff on. (F. Seebohm) Eng. Hist. R. 7: 444. — Sat. R. 73: 74, 160.
Villaines, France, Coöperative Society at. (L. F. Scott) Econ. J. 3: 529.
Villains of Fiction. Chamb. J. 70: 517.
Villars, Claude L. H., Duc de. (W. O'C. Morris) Eng. Hist. R. 8: 61.

Villas, Old Lombard and Venetian. (Vernon Lee) Am. Arch. **53**: 6, 78, 86.
Villiers de l'Isle Adam, Philippe A. M. de. (W. Sharp) Acad. **45**: 388. — Sat. R. **77**: 208.
Vincennes, Dungeons of. (T. Hopkins) Leis. Hour, **45**: 697, 786.
Vincent, Frank, with portrait. Bk. News, **14**: 34.
Vincent, Henry Hyam. *See* Barnett, Henry Hyam Vincent.
Vincent, John Heyl, with portraits. (I. M. Tarbell) McClure, **5**: 240.
Vinci, Leonardo da. (E. Müntz) Portfo. **24**: 153.
— at the National Gallery. (J. P. Richter) Art J. **46**: 166.
— a Cartoon by. (J. Cartwright) M. of Art, **7**: 448.
— Genius of. (J. J. O'Shea) Cath. World, **61**: 235. — Chamb. J. **70**: 443.
— New Reading of. Atlan. **73**: 414.
— Our Lady of the Rocks. (E. J. Poynter) Art J. **46**: 229.
— Pioneer in Science. (W. R. Thayer) Monist, **4**: 507.
— The Romance of. (A. de Calonne) 19th Cent. **38**: 411.
— St. Anne. (A. Marks) Ath. '92, **1**: 540, 798. — (E. Müntz) Ath. '92, **1**: 673. — (A. Marks) M. of Art, **16**: 186.
Vine, The, in Ornament. (L. F. Day) M. of Art, **13**: 127, 151.
Vineland, Whereabouts of. (L. G. Power) New Eng. M. n. s. **8**: 174. — (D. Boyle) Canad. M. **4**: 19.
Vines, Architecture and. (C. S. Sargent) Garden & F. **7**: 241.
— Climbing Plants on Boston Buildings. (S. Baxter) Garden & F. **7**: 433.
Vinet, A. (J. V. Bartlett) Chr. Lit. **10**: 17 a.
Vineyards, English. Spec. **73**: 369.
— French. (M. Betham-Edwards) Sund. M. **24**: 592.
Vining, Miss Mary, Revolutionary Belle. (Mrs. H. G. Banning) Am. Hist. Reg. **2**: 1190.
Vintage Time, In. Cornh. **71**: 633. Same art. Liv. Age, **206**: 226. Same art. Ecl. M. **125**: 414.
— South Australian Sketch. Chamb. J. **69**: 465.
Violante. (W. Armstrong) Portfo. **23**: 23.
Violet; a Story of To-day. (C. E. Arbuthnot) Belgra. **84**: 195.
Violets, Birdsfoot, in Cultivation. (C. A. Farley) Garden & F. **5**: 226.
— Cultivation of. (T. D. Hatfield) Garden & F. **5**: 176. — (G. F. Atkinson) Garden & F. **6**: 536. — (E. O. Orpet) Garden & F. **7**: 428. **9**: 366. — (W. N. Craig) Garden & F. **7**: 105, 497. — (T. D. Hatfield) Garden & F. **8**: 66.
— Disease in. (E. O. Orpet) Garden & F. **5**: 381. — (C. S. Plumb) Garden & F. **5**: 417.
— Notes on. (E. O. Orpet) Garden & F. **8**: 87, 107, 506.
Violets; a poem. (A. H. Japp) Argosy, **61**: 489.
Violin and its Ancestry. (W. F. Gates) Music, **3**: 680. **4**: 78.
— for Ladies. (J. Y. Taylor) Lippinc. **49**: 629.
— Origin of. (B. Brandt) Music, **8**: 584.
Violin Music. Sat. R. **79**: 282.
Violin Playing in the Past. (E. Drake) Music, **9**: 176.
Violin Strings, Silkworm-gut, How made. Music, **10**: 1.
Violinist's Adventure; a story. (M. E. S. Penn) Argosy, **59**: 474.
Violinists, American. Music, **2**: 39.
Violins, Collecting, Romance of. Cornh. **72**: 34. Same art. Liv. Age, **206**: 481. Same art. Ecl. M. **125**: 267.
— New, for Old. (E. Heron-Allen) New Sci. R. **1**: 87.
Viollet-le-Duc, Eugène E., Side-lights on. (M. Rouvet) Am. Arch. **40**: 65–118.
Violoncello of Jufrow Rozenboom. (A. E. King) Cent. **23**: 643.
Vionville, Battle of. (A. E. Turner) Un. Serv. M. **9**: 496. **10**: 43.
Viperiana. (A. Stradling) Chamb. J. **71**: 348.
Virgil. Æneid: the Epic of Piety. Macmil. **72**: 51.
— Archaisms in, Noted by Servius. (R. B. Steele) Am. J. Philol. **15**: 164.
— as a Magician. (K. V. Coote) Good Words, **37**: 662. Same art. Liv. Age, **211**: 437. Same art. Ecl. M. **127**: 737.
— in the Country. (F. M. Cesaresco) Contemp. **67**: 644. Same art. Liv. Age, **205**: 697.
— in the Middle Ages, Comparetti on. (W. H. Johnson) Dial (Ch.) **19**: 381. — Sat. R. **80**: 599.
— Tomb of: Littus Veneris. (A. Walters) Gent. M. n. s. **51**: 570.
— Tunison on. (W. H. Johnson) Dial (Ch.) **19**: 381. — J. Am. Folk-Lore, **2**: 83.
Virgilium Vidi; a poem. (T. H. Warren) Macmil. **67**: 478.
Virgin, The Yoke of the. (A. M. Logan) Nation, **58**: 369.
"Virgin of the Rocks" in the National Gallery. (J. P. Richter) Art J. **46**: 300. — (F. W. Burton) 19th Cent. **36**: 79.
Virgin-birth. (F. P. Badham) Acad. **47**: 485, (F. C. Conybeare) 508.
Virginia and Maryland, Early Relations between. (J. H. Latané) J. H. Univ. Stud. **13**: 129.
— and the Quebec Bill. (J. Winsor) Am. Hist. R. **1**: 436.
— Bruce's Economic History of. (J. J. Halsey) Dial (Ch.) **20**: 267. — (W. C. Ford) Nation, **62**: 399, 419. — (S. B. Weeks) Yale R. **5**: 94. — (W. B. Weeden) J. Pol. Econ. **4**: 537. — (A. Brown) Am. Hist. R. **1**: 538.
— Church of, Disestablishment of. (W. F. Carne) Cath. World, **60**: 108.
— Cycling through. (J. B. Carrington) Outing, **28**: 204.
— Educational and Literary Efforts in, History of. (J. B. Henneman) Nat'l M. (N. Y. '91) **15**: 377.
— From England to, and back. (Spencer Ryder) Time, **4**: 1.
— Homes of, Old. (V. Cousins) Munsey, **14**: 711.
— in the Revolutionary Period. (W. W. Henry) M. Am. Hist. **27**: 114.
— Journey in, in 1891. (E. S. Nadal) 19th Cent. **32**: 319.
— Last Colony of Roanoke. (E. Y. Wilson) Canad. M. **4**: 500.
— The London Company; a Seminary of Sedition. Atlan. **77**: 313.
— The Old Dominion. (T. N. Page) Harper, **88**: 4.
— On an Old American Turnpike. (A. G. Bradley) Fortn. **66**: 291. Same art. Ecl. M. **127**: 817.
— Quaint Records of. (T. T. Upshur) Pennsyl. M. **16**: 64.
— Religious Toleration in, Struggle for. (H. R. McIlwaine) J. H. Univ. Stud. **12**: 7.
— Representation in. (J. A. C. Chandler) J. H. Univ. Stud. **14**: 263.
— Sport in. (H. Hutchinson) Longm. **20**: 510.
— Starving Time in Old. (J. Fiske) Atlan. **76**: 748.
— Supreme Court of Appeals of. (S. S. P. Patteson) Green Bag, **5**: 310, 361, 407.
— Tertiary Changes in the Drainage of S. W. (M. R. Campbell) Am. J. Sci. **148**: 21.
— Through Virginia awheel. Outing, **28**: 323.

Virginia, University of. (W. Baird) Educa. R. 12: 417.
— Voting in, 1896. Nation, 63: 384.
— White Servitude in the Colony of. (J. C. Ballagh) J. H. Univ. Stud. 13: 263.
Virginia Antiquities, Association for Preservation of. (M. M. P. Newton) Am. Hist. Reg. 1: 9.
Virginia Company of London. (A. Brown) N. E. Reg. 47: 205.
— Manuscript Records of, 1619–24. (A. Brown) M. Am. Hist. 29: 371.
Virginia Sportsman, A. Macmil. 73: 223. Same art. Liv. Age, 208: 398.
"Virginius," Surrender of, 1873. (M. P. Handy) Lippinc. 50: 757.
Virial Theorem of Clausius. (C. E. Baskevi) Nature, 52: 413, (R. E. Baynes) 568.
Virieu, Henri de. (A. Laugel) Nation, 55: 387, 429.
Virtue, John Sprent. Acad. 41: 350.
Virtue, Teleology of. (W. Smith) Int. J. Ethics, 5: 181.
Virtues, Commonplace. Do they pay? Spec. 68: 263. Same art. Ecl. M. 118: 500.
— Philo on. (W. A. Hammond) Philos. R. 5: 193.
— The Positive. (T. Davidson) Open Court, 1: 426, 490, 517.
Viscosity, Isothermals, Isopiestics and Isometrics relative to. (C. Barus) Am. J. Sci. 145: 87.
— of Mixtures of Liquids. (C. E. Linebarger) Am. J. Sci. 152: 331.
Vision, Acute, Point of, in Vertebrates. (J. R. Slonaker) Am. Natural. 30: 24.
— Animal. Spec. 74: 784.
— Defective, in School Children. (S. D. Risley) Educa. R. 3: 348.
— Direct Control of the Retinal Field. (G. T. Ladd) Psychol. R. 1: 351.
— Displacement of Crosslines in. (F. B. Dresslar) Am. J. Psychol. 6: 275.
— Light Intensity and Depth Intensity. (T. R. Robinson) Am. J. Psychol. 7: 518.
— Normal Defect of, in the Fovea. (C. L. Franklin) Psychol. R. 2: 137.
— Persistence of. (E. S. Ferry) Am. J. Sci. 144: 192.
— Recurrent. Dub. R. 116: 183.
— without Inversion of Retinal Image. (G. Stratton) Psychol. R. 3: 611.
Vision not dreamt of in the Philosophies; a story. (B. M. Dawson) Arena, 15: 136.
Vision of Augustin Nypho, The; a story. Temp. Bar, 99: 94.
Vision of Fulfilled Desire. (E. E. Hale, jr.) New Eng. M. n. s. 9: 307.
Vision of the Great Spoon-bill. (W. H. Hudson) Sund. M. 25: 198.
Vision of Lost Atlantis; a poem. (J. G. Clark) Arena, 16: 332.
Visit from the Sea; a poem. (R. L. Stevenson) M. of Art, 8: 21.
Visiting, Friendly, On Personal Service and. (L. D. Wald) Char. R. 4: 229.
Visiting Cards, Venetian. (H. F. Brown) M. of Art, 7: 275.
Visitor and his Opinions; a Story of the Unseen. (M. O. W. Oliphant) Blackw. 153: 481. Same art. Liv. Age, 197: 473. Same art. McClure, 2: 27.
Visitor's Books. (Mrs. E. T. Cook) Good Words, 36: 334.
Vista in Central Park. (B. Matthews) Harper, 89: 457.
Visual Sensations, Subjective. (W. R. Gowers) Nature, 52: 234.
Visyenos, George. (E. M. Edmonds) Acad. 49: 405.
Vital Question, A. (G. A. Hibbard) Cent. 27: 763.
Vital Statistics and the Race Problem. Pub. Opin. 13: 32.
— Ethnic Influences of. (W. Z. Ripley) Am. Statis. Assoc. 5: 18.
— of Baltimore and District of Columbia compared. (A. A. Woodhull) Nation, 58: 190.
— Recent Contributions to Literature of. (G. N. Calkins) Am. Statis. Assoc. 4: 103, 340.
Vitaline. Spec. 68: 706.
Vitalism, Neo-. (F. A. Welby) Nature, 51: 43.
Vitality, Comparative. Ecl. M. 118: 239.
— Suspended, in Plants and Animals. Chamb. J. 72: 38.
Vitascope, Stage Scenery and the. (G. P. Lathrop) No. Am. 163: 377.
Viterbo, Tombs of Popes at. (A. L. Frothingham, jr.) Am. J. Archæol. 7: 38.
Vitté, Sergé J., with portrait. R. of Rs. (N.Y.) 8: 655.
Viviparidæ, North American, Geographic Distribution of. (R. E. Call) Am. J. Sci. 148: 132.
Vivisection. (F. P. Cobbe) National, 19: 144. — (L. J. Wallace) Westm. 137: 245. Same art. Ecl. M. 118: 617. — (J. E. McLean) New Sci. R. 2: 220. — Science, n. s. 3: 421.
— at the Church Congress, 1892. Nature, 46: 557.
— Benefits of. (A. C. Jones) Fortn. 59: 112.
— and Brain-surgery. (W. W. Keen) Harper, 87: 128.
— Controversy on. (R. F. Clarke) Dub. R. 115: 96.
— Ethics of. Pub. Opin. 20: 110.
— in Naval Study. (R. Ogden) Nation, 59: 336.
— Morality of. (E. Bell) Contemp. 62: 849. — (V. Horsley; M. A. Ruffer) 19th Cent. 32: 804. — Reply. (J. Moorhouse) 19th Cent. 32: 980.
— New Priesthood. (L. de La Ramé) New R. 8: 151.
— Question of. (C. F. Hodge) Pop. Sci. Mo. 49: 614, 771.
— Richardson on. Sat. R. 82: 114.
— Women, Clergymen, and Doctors. (E. Hart) New R. 7: 708. — Reply. (B. Wilberforce) New R. 8: 85.
Vivisectionist. (C. Wells) Lippinc. 57: 546.
Vizetelly, Henry. Reminiscences. Spec. 72: 16.
Vizier's Doom, The; a story. (H. N. Crellin) Idler, 5: 593.
Vladivostock, Visit to. Dub. R. 117: 162.
Vlest, Russia: a Concord of the Steppe. (F. Prevost) Temp. Bar, 95: 175. Same art. Liv. Age, 194: 300.
Vocabulary, Ethics of a. (F. B. Sawvel) Educa. 15: 489.
— Psychological. (E. B. Titchener) Am. J. Psychol. 7: 78.
Vocal Culture in its Relation to Literary Culture. (H. Corson) Atlan. 75: 810.
Vocal Method at the Italian Opera. (F. W. Root) Music, 1: 142.
Vocations, Study of Four. (C. Barnard) Chaut. 17: 169. — (W. W. Carruth) Chaut. 17: 299.
Vogler, George Joseph, Abbé. New Eng. M. n. s. 9: 506.
Vogt, Karl. Nature, 52: 108.
— Huxley and. (E. Haeckel) Fortn. 64: 464.
Vogüé, Melchior de. Spec. 71: 372.
— The Academician of Life. Atlan. 72: 424.
Voice, The American. Atlan. 78: 852.
— American Conversational. Why it is Bad. (F. Osgood) Forum, 19: 501.
— and Spiritual Education, Corson on. (E. Mims) Dial (Ch.) 20: 235.
— in a Million, A. (C. Black) Eng. Illust. 14: 165.

Voice of Authority, The; a story. (E. A. Alexander) Harper, 92: 674.
— of the Future. (A. F. Sheardown) Music, 5: 160.
— of the Mountains, The; a poem. (J. G. Clark) Arena, 7: 629.
— Relation of, to Ministerial Success. (G. K. Morris) Meth. R. 52: 914.
— Speech-tone. (Frank Austin) Univ. R. 8: 299.
— Wagner and. (C. Tetedoux) Music, 3: 1.
Voice Culture. (K. Hackett) Music, 8: 281, 571.
— Aria-giving Method of. (K. Hackett) Music, 7: 360.
— in Schools. (Z. Richards) Educa. 14: 608.
— Italian Method of. (F. W. Root) Music, 7: 118.
Voice Figures. (M. W. Hughes) Good Words, 37: 104.
Voice Production in Song and Speech. (T. Kelly) Month, 77: 346.
— Photographed. (Rosa B. Holt) Music, 10: 333.
Voice Teacher, Evolution of. (H. W. Greene) Music, 1: 557.
Voice Training. (E. E. Evans) Music, 6: 620.
Voices from Afar. (E. M. Thomas) Atlan. 74: 252.
Voices of the Empty House, The. (G. Villari) Argosy, 61: 187.
Voiture, Vincent. Liv. Age, 200: 366.
Vokins, William. Acad. 48: 370.
Volapük. (A. A. Post) Arena, 5: 556.
— Scientific. Nat. Sci. 5: 55.
Volcanic Dykes, Influence of, upon Littoral Life and Scenery. (J. Hornell) Nat. Sci. 4: 112.
Volcanic Eruptions in California, Recent. (G. W. Wright) Am. Natural. 27: 813.
Volcanic Rocks from Gough's Island, South Atlantic, Note on. (L. V. Pirsson) Am. J. Sci. 145: 380.
— of South Mountain. (G. H. Williams) Am. J. Sci. 144: 482.
Volcano, Interior of. Around World, 1: 63.
— Sicilian, Birth of. (A. S. Packard) Pop. Sci. Mo. 46: 577.
— Youngest, in the U. S. (J. S. Diller) Nat. Geog. M. 5: 93.
Volcanoes and Igneous Intrusions. (I. C. Russell) Pop. Sci. Mo. 50: 240.
— Hull on. Spec. 69: 796.
— Science of, Johnston-Lavis on. Nature, 50: 66.
Voldomir, The Princess of. (M. Costello) Gent. M. n. s. 48: 152. Same art. Ecl. M. 119: 390.
Volga River, Harvest-tide on. (I. F. Hapgood) Atlan. 69: 314.
— A Journey on. (I. F. Hapgood) Atlan. 69: 231.
Volkmar, Gustav. Ath. '93, 1: 86.
Volney, Count: his Prophecy. (C. L. Daniels) Open Court, 7: 3707.
Volta, Alessandro, with portrait. Pop. Sci. Mo. 41: 117.
Voltaire. (H. S. Ashbee) Bookworm, 3: 73.
— and Mlle. Dunoyer. (F. Hawkins) Theatre, 33: 126.
— and England. (N. H. Kennard) National, 19: 783.
— and King Stanislas. (H. W. Wolff) National, 19: 381.
— as King. (F. M. Holland) Open Court, 1: 6.
— Espinasse's. (F. Hawkins) Acad. 42: 600.
— in England. (A. F. Sieveking) Ath. '92, 2: 194.
— François Tronchin and. (A. Laugel) Nation, 61: 308.
Voluntary Action. (G. F. Stout) Mind, 21: 354.
Volunteers of '85; a poem. (S. Livingston) Canad. M. 2: 421.
Voodoo Tales, Owen's. (F. S. Bassett) Dial (Ch.) 14: 338.
Voodoo Worship in Hayti and Louisiana. (W. W. Newell) J. Am. Folk-Lore, 2: 41.
— — Myth of. (W. W. Newell) J. Am. Folk-Lore, 1: 16.
Voodooism. (S. Culin) J. Am. Folk-Lore, 2: 232.
Voorhees, Daniel W., with portrait. (H. Parker) Munsey, 10: 495.
Vorbei; a story. (A. N. Meyer) Harper, 87: 927.
Vortex Motion; Action of Force is Spiro-vortex. (Mrs. Bloomfield Moore) New Sci. R. 2: 217.
Voshli Hills, Scenes in the; a story. (G. Parker) Eng. Illust. 12: no. 6, 19.
Voter, The Rural. (H. Maxwell) National, 18: 578.
Voting in Virginia in the Colonial Period. (J. F. Jameson) Nation, 56: 309.
— Secret. (J. B. Bishop) Nation, 55: 368.
— Venal, Alarming Proportion of. (J. J. McCook) Forum, 14: 1.
— — Methods and Remedies. (J. J. McCook) Forum, 14: 159.
Voyage across the World, A; a story. (E. C. Kitton) Argosy, 54: 171.
Voyage in the Dark. (R. E. Robinson) Atlan. 75: 172.
Voyage in Spain; a poem. (W. Brunton) Outing, 26: 44.
Voyage of Bran: Irish Saga, edited by Meyer. (W. W. Newell) J. Am. Folk-Lore, 8: 334.
Voyagers; a poem. (E. M. Thomas) Cosmopol. 17: 422.
Vries, Matthias de. Acad. 42: 193.
V'ronica Mary; a story. (I. L. Cassilis) Belgra. 91: 35.
Vuequellin, Madame. Am. Hist. Reg. 2: 1447.
Vulgarism in English Speech. (E. F. Andrews) Chaut. 22: 721.
Vulgarity, A Dialogue on. (T. Chapman) 19th Cent. 39: 624.
Vultur of Apulia. (Rennell Rodd) Time, 23: 740.

Wa, The Wild; a Head-hunting Race. (J. G. Scott) Liv. Age, 208: 478.
Wabanaki Legends. (Mrs. W. W. Brown) J. Am. Folk-Lore, 3: 213.
Waddington, Wm. H. (J. B. Latham) Time, 14: 438.
Wade, Sir Thomas. Acad. 48: 110.
Wadham College, Oxford. (H. M. Minchin) Acad. 43: 528.
— Alumni of. (J. S. Cotton) Acad. 47: 439.
Wadhams, Edgar P., Bishop, with portrait. (C. A. Walworth) Cath. World, 55: 317-826. 56: 104-407.
Wadsworth Athenæum, Hartford, Conn. Critic, 22: 115.
Wage-contract, The, and Personal Liberty. (C. Reno) Pop. Sci. Mo. 41: 644.
Wage-earners, Pending Problems for. (A. E. Outerbridge, jr.) J. Frankl. Inst. 141: 337. Same art. Pop. Sci. Mo. 49: 57.
— Protection of. (W. F. Draper) Soc. Econ. 1: 365.
Wager of the Marquis de Merosailles, The; a story. (A. Hope Hawkins) McClure, 6: 198.
Wages. (M. M. Trumbull) Open Court, 3: 1539, 1559, 1572, 1595.
— and Capital, Taussig's. (E. Cannan) Econ. J. 6: 441. — (W. Hill) J. Pol. Econ. 4: 523.
— and Cost of Living in the Garment Trades. (I. Eaton) Am. Statis. Assoc. 4: 135.
— and Currency Depreciation. Gunton's M. 11: 332.
— as a Criterion of Civilization. (W. E. Hart) Soc. Econ. 1: 173.

Wages, Average, Changes in the Uuited Kingdom, 1860-91. (A. L. Bowley) J. Statis. Soc. 58: 223.
— Basis of. (J. D. Sands) Am. J. Pol. 1: 337.
— "Boke Longyng to a Justice of the Peace" and. (E. A. McArthur) Eng. Hist. R. 9: 305.
— Cheaper Living and the Rise of. (C. D. Wright) Forum, 16: 221.
— Course of, in the U. S., since 1840. (C. D. Wright) Am. Statis. Assoc. 3: 496.
— Economic Effects of Low and High. (J. A. Hobson) Contemp. 64: 811.
— Economy of High. Soc. Econ. 6: 193.
— English Gang System. Soc. Econ. 2: 163.
— Free Silver and. (R. Mayo-Smith) Pol. Sci. Q. 11: 464.
— Giffen on. Spec. 70: 120.
— High, Economy of. Ed. R. 179. 33. Same art. Ecl. M. 122: 289.
— — in the U. S. (E. Waxweiler) Soc. Econ. 8: 204.
— Importance of a New Point of View. Soc. Econ. 1: 113.
— in Ancient Greece. (F. B. Jevons) Econ. J. 6: 470.
— in England: Equity of the Rural Wage-rate. (C. Reade) Westm. 138: 57.
— — Fluctuation of Purchasing Power of. (G. F. Steffen) 19th Cent. 33: 932.
— in Foreign Countries. Am. J. Soc. Sci. 33: 127.
— in London, County Council and. Spec. 69: 880, 917.
— in the U. S. (E. Levasseur) J. Pol. Econ. 4: 166.
— — and in Great Britain, 1860–1891. (A. L. Bowley) Econ. J. 5: 369.
— Industrial Remuneration, Basis of. (D. F. Schloss) Econ. J. 2: 608.
— Iron Law of. (C. Drake) Am. M. Civics, 8: 285.
— A Living Wage. (W. Cunningham) Contemp. 65: 16. — (H. Bell) National, 22: 783. — (H. Thomas) Westm. 145: 297.
— — Plea for. (L. R. Phelps) Econ. R. 4: 519. — (R. Halstead) Econ. R. 5: 350.
— Low, and Cheap Production. (H. Kingerly) Am. J. Pol. 2: 308.
— Municipal Progress and the Living Wage. (D. M. Means) Forum, 20: 11.
— Natural Law in the Economic World. (J. C. Kimball) Soc. Econ. 2: 193.
— New Theories of. (D. MacG. Means) Nation, 59: 59.
— Piece-rate System and Shop Management. (F. W. Taylor) Engin. M. 10: 690.
— Problem of, in England. Spec. 71: 105.
— Ratio of, to Product. (Van Buren Denslow) Soc. Econ. 9: 268.
— — in Manufactures. (W. F. Draper) Soc. Econ. 4: 84.
— Sliding-scale of South Wales. (H. Read) Econ. J. 4: 332.
— Source of, and Boehm-Bawerk's Definition of Capital. (J. B. Veblen) Q. J. Econ. 6: 247.
— Standard Rate of. (S. and B. Webb) Econ. J. 6: 356.
— — Evolution of a. (R. L. Bridgman) Am. M. Civics, 7: 633.
— Statistics of, Evolution of. (C. D. Wright) Q. J. Econ. 6: 151.
— Theory of, and of Profits. Soc. Econ. 7: 269, 284.
— — and Recent Theories of Value. (T. N. Carver) Q. J. Econ. 8: 377.
— — Savans to the Rear! (W. J. Armstrong) Arena, 12: 97.
— Trusts and. (F. H. Cooke) Soc. Econ. 9: 107.
Wages, Von Thünen's Theory of Natural. (H. L. Moore) Q. J. Econ. 9: 291, 388.
— What is a Fair Wage? (C. Black) New R. 8: 587.
Wages-fund Doctrine at the Hands of the German Economists. (F. W. Taussig) Q. J. Econ. 9: 1.
Wages of Self-denial; a story. All the Year, 75: 563.
Wages of Sin, The. (L. Malet) Univ. R. vols. 5–8.
Wagner, Richard. (Mrs. E. W. Hubbard) Chaut. 21: 305. — (P. Carus) Open Court, 3: 1850.
— and his Work. (H. Badger) Music, 3: 654.
— and his Works, Finck's. (W. P. Garrison) Nation, 57: 122. — (W. M. Payne) Dial (Ch.) 14: 306.
— and the Music of the Future. (W. S. B. Mathews) Music, 9: 341.
— and the Voice. (C. Tetedoux) Music, 3: 1.
— and Weber. Sat. R. 80: 106.
— at Munich. (V. Blackburn) New R. 13: 545.
— The Case of. (F. Nietzsche) Fortn. 64: 367.
— Flying Dutchman. Sat. R. 80: 574.
— in Chicago. Dial (Ch.) 19: 321.
— Influence of. Sat. R. 79: 251.
— — on Present-day Composers. (A. Seidl) No. Am. 158: 86.
— — on Vocal Art. (J. S. Van Cleve) Music, 2: 167, 380.
— Krehbiel on. Sat. R. 74: 80.
— Nibelungen, Women of. (H. Moore) Music, 2: 573.
— Opera at Bayreuth. (L. A. Bourgault-Ducoudray) Chaut. 17: 63.
— Operas, Legends of. (G. Holme) Munsey, 10: 593.
— Parsifal. (L. S. Russell) Music, 3: 49.
— — Gatty's. Sat. R. 78: 275.
— Prose Works, tr. by Ellis. Sat. 77: 235. 80: 437.
— Realism of. (E. S. Kelley) Music, 10: 37.
— Siegfried, 1892. Sat. R. 73: 743.
— — Début in London. Sat. R. 78: 506.
— — in England. Sat. R. 79: 827.
— Tristan and Isolda. Sat. R. 82: 10. — (A. B. Mitchell) Music, 7: 549.
Wagner Revulsion of 1892. (E. W. Naylor) Music, 4: 241.
Wagneriana. (H. T. Finck) Nation, 54: 400.
Wagner, Battery, Defence of. (H. D. D. Twiggs) So. Hist. Pap. 20: 166.
Wahl, Louis, with portrait. (H. L. Conard) Nat'l M. (N. Y. '91) 16: 609.
Waifs; a story. (H. T. Johnson) Idler, 8: 133.
Waifs of Fighting Rocks; a story. (C. McIlvaine) Lippinc. 55: 3.
Wain, Louis. (R. Compton) Idler, 8: 550.
Waite, R. Thorne. (R. J. Slade) Art J. 44: 182.
Waiting for the Train; a story. (W. L. Alden) Idler, 4: 643.
Waiting Rain, The; a poem. (E. M. Ladd) Overland, n. s. 21: 77.
Wakefield, Mass., Lakeside Park. (S. Baxter) Garden & F. 5: 411.
Walberswick, Eng. (E. B. Brown) Eng. Illust. 10: 405.
Waldegrave, Frances, Countess, and Strawberry Hill. (A. Badeau) Cosmopol. 12: 535.
Waldenses at Valdese, N. C. (C. J. Ryder) Lend a H. 13: 333.
Wales, The Prince of. (M. D. Conway) Open Court, 5: 3026.
Wales. (D. C. Macdonald) Lippinc. 58: 820. — Belgra. 79: 203. Same art. Liv. Age, 195: 702.
— and her Language, Southall's. Sat. R. 74: 420.
— Atlas of, in the 18th Century. (F. O. Whitaker) Gent. M. n. s. 57: 138.
— Church in. (A. Griffith-Boscawen) National, 20: 668. — (A. G. Asaph) 19th Cent. 38: 111. — Blackw. 157: 141.

Wales, Church in, Debate on. (R. Wallace) Sat. R. 79: 438.
— — Disestablishment of. (R. Ogden) Nation, 60: 273. — (L. T. Dibdin) 19th Cent. 36: 100. — Quar. 179: 145. — Spec. 72: 574, 606. — (R. E. Webster; A. Griffith-Boscawen) National, 23: 449.
— Church History of, Hughes's. (J. H. Matthews) Dub. R. 116: 363.
— Future of. (H. Davies) Westm. 140: 369.
— Gallant Little. (A. Webb) Nation, 54: 393.
— Intermediate Education Act of. (H. Holman) School R. 2: 286.
— Land in, Royal Commission on. (Lord Stanley of Alderley) National, 23: 89.
— North, A Nook of. Blackw. 156: 681.
— Parish in, in the Interregnum. (N. Jones) Eng. Hist. R. 9: 339.
— Politics in; a Warning. (A. Griffith-Boscawen) National, 22: 97.
— Sacred Wells in. (J. Rhys) Folk-Lore, 4: 55.
— Seebohm's Tribal System in. (C. M. Andrews) Am. Hist. R. 1: 120. — Sat. R. 80: 318. — (J. W. Thompson) J. Pol. Econ. 4: 400. — (J. W. Thompson) Dial (Ch.) 20: 273.
— Settlement of. (W. B. Dawkins) Fortn. 58: 517.
— A Summer Month in a Village of. (S. N. Carter) Cent. 25: 859.
— Under Cader Idris. (Mrs. H. E. V. Stannard) Belgra. 85: 404.
— University for. (J. E. McTaggart) National, 22: 835.
— The Wallace of. (A. H. Wall) Time, 7: 21, 174.
— Wild. (C. Stuart) M. of Art, 13: 19, 62.
Walewein, Romance of. (W. P. Ker) Folk-Lore, 5: 121.
Walford, Thomas. (B. F. DeCosta) New Eng. M. n. s. 12: 305.
Walker, Charles Pyndar Beauchamp. (W. H. Goodenough) Geog. J. 3: 241.
Walker, Frederick. Acad. 50: 535.
— and his Work. (C. Phillips) Portfo. 1894: no. 6.
— Harbour of Refuge; painting. Art J. 45: 277. — (J. W. North) M. of Art, 17: 12.
Walker, Gen. James T. Nature, 53: 469. — (C. R. Markham) Geog. J. 7: 320.
Walker, John. (S. Groves) Cassier, 2: 452.
Walker, Joseph H., with portrait. Bank. M. (N. Y.) 52: 313.
Walker, Sears Cook, with portrait. Pop. Sci. Mo. 46: 116.
Walking. (J. Hawthorne) Lippinc. 49: 481. — (M. W. Ford) Outing, 22: 64.
— as a Pastime. (E. L. Richards) Cent. 26: 539.
— Literary Tramps. (M. B. Wright) Macmil. 66: 439.
Walking Delegate, A. (R. Kipling) Cent. 27: 289.
Walking Skirt, A; a poem. (George Wyndham) New R. 12: 77.
Walking-sticks. [Insects.] Chamb. J. 70: 330. — (L. N. Badenoch) Good Words, 36: 270. — (S. H. Scudder) Harper, 88: 454.
Walkley, Arthur Bingham, with portrait. Theatre, 28: 247.
Wall Paintings, Ashampstead Church. Reliquary, 36: 53.
— at Kirkby Hall. Reliquary, 35: 15.
Wall-paper Decoration. (L. F. Day) M. of Art, 15: 189.
Wall-papers and Stencilling. (T. R. Spence) J. Soc. Arts, 41: 362.
— Choice of. (L. F. Day) M. of Art, 15: 165.
Wall Street. (E. G. Riggs; C. J. Rosebault; C. J. Fitzgerald) Munsey, 10: 351.
— The Railroads and. (T. L. Greene) Engin. M. 3: 372.
Wall Street Wooing, A; a story. (B. Matthews) Harper, 93: 99.
Wallace, Gen. Lew, with portrait. Bk. Buyer, 10: 357. — With portrait. Bk. News, 6: 301. — (H. V. Clarke) Munsey, 8: 62.
— Portraits of. McClure, 1: 19.
— Prince of India. (C. W. Currier) Cath. World, 60: 306.
Wallace, Prof. A. R., on Darwinism. (J. C. F. Grumbine) Open Court, 5: 2813.
Wallachs of Macedonia. (W. R. Morfill) Acad. 44: 15.
Wallala Beds, So-called, as a Division of the California Cretaceous. (H. W. Fairbanks) Am. J. Sci. 145: 473.
Waller, Edmund. Poems, Drury's Edition. Sat. R. 75: 212. — Spec. 70: 133.
Waller, John Francis. Ath. '94, 1: 149.
Waller, Lewis. Four "Leading Men," a Comparative Estimate. (W. A. L. Bettany) Theatre, 29: 109.
Waller, S. E. Experiences in finding Art Subjects. Art J. 48: 289.
Wallenstein's Camp. (F. Schiller) Blackw. 151: 231.
Wallis, Dorothy. Sat. R. 74: 55.
Wallis, Sir Provo, Brighton's. Spec. 69: 167.
Walloomsac, Battle of. (S. D. Locke) Nat'l M. (N. Y. '91) 15: 629.
Walls, Castle. (W. Jackson) Walford's Antiq. 2: 186.
— Our Old Town. Cornh. 73: 179. Same art. Liv. Age, 209: 42.
Walnut-tree, Hybrid. (C. S. Sargent) Garden & F. 7: 434.
Walpi Flute Observance. (J. W. Fewkes) J. Am. Folk-Lore, 7: 265.
Walpole, Horace. Temp. Bar, 102: 79. Same art. Liv. Age, 201: 740. Same art. Ecl. M. 123: 114.
— and his Editors. (H. Toynbee) Acad. 50: 99.
— Letters of. (V. D. Rossman) Cath. World, 60: 806.
Walpole, Sir Robert, as a Collector of Pamphlets. (J. Hayes) Bookworm, 4: 81-217.
Walrus Hunting in the Arctic Regions. (L. L. Dyche) Cosmopol. 20: 347.
Walter, John, Editor London Times. Soc. Econ. 7: 345. — Ath. '94, 2: 642.
Walters Art Gallery, Baltimore. (M. Reizenstein) New Eng. M. n. s. 12: 545. — (Mrs. M. J. Lamb) M. Am. Hist. 27: 241.
Waltham (England) Cross. (W. Dampier) Walford's Antiq. 8: 205.
Walther von der Vogelweide. (W. A. Phillips) 19th Cent. 40: 67.
Walton, Elijah. (T. G. Bonney) M. of Art, 4: 107.
Walton, Izaak, 1593-1683. (W. F. Stockley) Chaut. 16: 193. — (R. Le Gallienne) New R. 9: 141. Same art. Ecl. M. 121: 558. — (A. Cargill) Scrib. M. 14: 267.
— Complete Angler. Critic, 23: 127.
— — and its Bibliography. (J. L. High) Dial (Ch.) 14: 237.
Waltz, The. (J. F. Rowbotham) Argosy, 57: 291.
Walworth, Clarence A., Poetry of. (S. W. Holcomb) Cath. World, 57: 770.
Walworth, Reuben Hyde, with portrait. (I. Browne) Green Bag, 7: 256.
Wanderer's Song; a poem. (R. Rodd) M. of Art, 10: 212.
Wandering Jew, The, at the Salpêtrière. (H. Coupin) Pop. Sci. Mo. 44: 525.
— In the Track of. Cornh. 71: 164. Same art. Liv. Age, 204: 739.
Wanderings in Bookland. (R. Le Gallienne) Idler, 9: 113, 446, 719, 886. 10: 112, 254, 406, 535.

Wandesford, William, Letters of, to Sir Rowland. Eng. Hist. R. 9: 548.
Wanita: a Legend of Kentucky. (E. Wildman) Overland, n. s. 28: 212.
Wanque River, Nicaragua. (J. Crawford) Science, 21: 174.
Wanted, Four Good Rock-drillers. Chamb. J. 73: 715.
Wanted: a Situation. (H. Allen) Cent. 27: 349.
Wapiti Hunting in Manitoba. Outing, 19: 419.
Wapping. An Old Wapping Picture. Chamb. J. 71: 33.
War. (N. A. Miles) Cosmopol. 21: 142.
— Abolition of. (H. C. Vrooman; T. E. Will) Arena, 11: 118.
— against War. (J. H. Wisby) Soc. Econ. 4: 139.
— Amenities of. (A. Griffiths) Un. Serv. M. 6: 272.
— amongst Various Human Races. (C. Letourneau) Westm. 144: 504.
— Anglo-American, The Cost of an. (E. Atkinson) Forum, 21: 74.
— and Civilization. (W. D. Le Sueur) Pop. Sci. Mo. 48: 758.
— and Evolution. (C. Thomas) Open Court, 2: 1355.
— and Progress. (L. G. Janes) Soc. Econ. 3: 331.
— Art of, Dragomiroff's Views on. Un. Serv. (Phila.) 12: 201.
— — Evolution of. (H. Elsdale) Un. Serv. M. 11: 569.
— as a Remedy. (E. L. Godkin) Nation, 54: 64.
— Benefits of. (A. J. Palm) Am. J. Pol. 1: 327.
— The Coming. Un. Serv. M. 6: 226, 337.
— Cost of. (G. H. Hubbard) N. Eng. 56: 222.
— The Distress of Nations. (J. M. Beck) Am. M. Civics, 7: 1.
— End of. (W. H. Jeffrey) Soc. Econ. 5: 32.
— Ethics of. (B. Nicholson) Canad. M. 6: 333.
— European. Is it inevitable? (H. Elsdale) Un. Serv. M. 5: 337, 449.
— Financial Incidents of. (A. C. Galt) Canad. M. 5: 453.
— Follies and Horrors of. (W. C. Doane) No. Am. 162: 190.
— Future of. (F. Lee) Cent. 28: 422.
— How it begins. (G. P. Lathrop) No. Am. 162: 195.
— How to abolish. (W. H. Jeffrey) Am. J. Pol. 1: 492.
— How to avoid. No. Am. 162: 119.
— Human Animal in. (H. W. Wilson) Un. Serv. (Phila.) 16: 234.
— a Hundred Years hence. (E. Gautier) Engin. M. 3: 223.
— in Legislation. (H. E. Bourne) Chaut. 22: 151.
— International Agreements and the Sufferers in. (J. King) Westm. 143: 492.
— Lines of Communication in. (H. G. Sharpe) Un. Serv. (Phila.) 13: 27.
— Modern Blockade, Mahan on. (H. O. Arnold-Foster) Sat. R. 80: 755.
— Natural History of Warfare. (N. S. Shaler) No. Am. 162: 328.
— Next Great: a Forecast by Colomb *et al.* Sat. R. 81: 230.
— of 1812. (J. A. Stevens) M. Am. Hist. 29: 419. — (A. C. Sharpe) Un. Serv. (Phila.) 7: 275. — (C. Warwick) Am. Hist. Reg. 2: 1469.
— — a Neglected Chapter. (A. F. Hunter) Canad. M. 4: 302.
— a Poem. (Archibald Lampman) Cosmopol. 20: 481.
— Renaissance of. (E. Field) Un. Serv. (Phila.) 9: 100.
— Right to wage. (F. J. Lippitt) Nation, 54: 86.
— Rumors of, and Resultant Duties. (J. W. Miller) Forum, 21: 237.
— Should it be abolished? (W. H. Jeffrey) Am. J. Pol. 3: 436. — (E. P. Powell) Arena, 12: 353.
War, The Solution of. (H. P. Mendes) No. Am. 161: 161.
— Study of. (H. C. Taylor) No. Am. 162: 181.
— Use of Text Books in. (R. Harrison) Un. Serv. M. 9: 111.
War among the Fairies; a story. All the Year, 75: 372.
War of the Roses; a story. (W. A. Dromgoole) Arena, 5: 481.
War Artist, Experiences of a. (I. Montagu) New R. 11: 624.
War Artists and War Pictures. (H. Skinner) M. of Art, 15: 62.
War Chief of the Tontos, A. (C. P. Johnson) Overland, n. s. 28: 528.
War Correspondence as a Fine Art. (A. Forbes) Cent. 23: 290.
War Correspondent, Modern. (V. Gribayêdoff) Munsey, 13: 34.
War Correspondents. Ed. R. 183: 129.
War Debt; a story. (S. O. Jewett) Harper, 90: 227.
War-ship, Construction of a. (H. L. Swinburne) Un. Serv. M. 5: 164.
— Designing and Building of. (W. A. Dobson) Cosmopol. 16: 395.
— Forty-eight Hours in. (C. Eaglestone) Un. Serv. M. 4: 138.
— Nerves of. (P. Benjamin) Harper, 92: 631.
War-ships, American, Speed in. (W. S. Aldrich) No. Am. 162: 48.
— Modern. (A. H. Battey) Munsey, 16: 57.
— — Electricity on. (H. Hutchins) Cassier, 1: 429. 2: 207.
— — of the U. S. Navy. (W. A. Dobson) Pop. Sci. Mo. 44: 164. — (W. H. Jaques) Engin. M. 6: 187.
— Test and Value of Speed in. (P. H. Colomb) No. Am. 162: 59.
See also Ships.
War Tax of Europe, The. (W. J. Gordon) Liv. Age, 202: 125.
Warbeck, Perkin. (J. Stevenson) Month, 75: 508.
Warble Fly. (W. F. Kirby) Nature, 51: 154.
Warburton, Eliot, Works of. Eng. R. 17: 198.
Ward, Gen. Artemas, Letter of, 1775. (J. S. H. Fogg) N. E. Reg. 50: 20.
Ward, Charles E. D. Leader of Men; a comedy. Sat. R. 79: 216.
Ward, Edward Matthew. (H. W. Sweny) M. of Art, 1: 14.
Ward, Mrs. Humphry. (J. S. Steele) Critic, 24: 265. — (H. James) Eng. Illust. 9: 399. — Bk. Buyer, 5: 381. 6: 270. 12: 282. — With portrait. Bk. News, 10: 311.
— at Home. Critic, 27: 188.
— David Grieve. Sat. R. 73: 133. — (J. A. Noble) Acad. 41: 149. — Ath. '92, 1: 141. — (J. Wedgwood) Contemp, 62: 217. — Ed. R. 175: 518. — Spec. 68: 268.
— Marcella. (F. M. Crawford; H. W. Mabie) Book R. 1: 273. — Ed. R. 180: 108. — (L. Johnson) Acad. 45: 363. — Lond. Q. 82: 205.
— — and other Novels. Church Q. 38: 455.
— — and Pembroke. Atlan. 74: 272.
— — a Notable New Book. (H. W. Mabie) Forum, 17: 249.
— Robert Elsmere. Time, 18: 723.
— — The Attack on. (W. W. Salter) Open Court, 2: 1372.
— — The Real. (F. R. Statham) National, 28: 252.
— Sir George Tressady. Nat'l M. (Bost.) 5: 298. — Sat. R. 82: 397. — Acad. 50: 423. — Atlan. 78: 841. — (J. A. Cooper) Canad. M. 8: 179.

Ward, Mrs. Humphry. Sir George Tressady, and the Political Novel. (H. D. Traill) Fortn. 66: 703. Same art. Liv. Age, 211: 647.
— Story of Bessie Costrell. Sat. R. 80: 436.
Ward, Wilfrid. (W. S. Lilly) 19th Cent. 35: 948.
— Essays. Crit. R. 4: 134. — Spec. 71: 875.
Ward, Wm. George. Book R. 1: 56. — (P. Bayne) Crit. R. 3: 341. — (W. Wilberforce) Dub. R. 115: 1.
— and the Catholic Revival. Ed. R. 178: 331. — Spec. 70: 738, 774. — (J. W. Chadwick) Nation, 57: 140. — (R. H. Hutton) 19th Cent. 35: 226.
— in the Roman Catholic Church. Church Q. 37: 67.
— Witnesses to the Unseen. (J. Owen) Acad. 46: 127, 168.
Warder, Ann, Diary of, Extracts from. (S. Cudbury) Pennsyl. M. 17: 445. 18: 51.
Wardite. (J. M. Davison) Am. J. Sci. 152: 154.
Wareham, England. (J. S. Little) Art J. 48: 143.
Warfare, Modern, Evolution and Revolution in. (S. Wilkinson) Contemp. 62: 412.
— Science of, Improvements in. (C. E. Munroe) Chaut. 16: 27.
Warham, Archbishop, Threatened Prosecution of, in 1532. (J. Moyes) Dub. R. 114: 390.
Waring, Herbert. *See* Rutty, Herbert Waring.
Waring, John Edward. (F. Mary Wilson Parsons) Temp. Bar, 107: 253. Same art. Liv. Age, 208: 723.
Waring's Peril. (C. King) Lippinc. 51: 259.
Wark, Old Castle of. (C. H. Dick) Gent. M. n. s. 54: 156.
Warming and Ventilating of Dwellings. Pop. Sci. Mo. 41: 831.
Warner, Charles and Grace, with portraits. Theatre, 36: 343.
Warner, Charles Dudley, with portrait. Bk. Buyer, 6: 55. — With portrait, Bk. News, 8: 2.
Warner, Olin, Sculpture of. (F. C. Brownell) Scrib. M. 20: 429.
Warner, Susan. Wide, Wide World. Critic, 21: 236.
Warrants, State, A New System of. (H. L. Weed) Arena, 15: 465.
Warren, John Byrne Leicester. *See* De Tabley, Lord.
Warren, William, Pioneer Underwriter, with portrait. Nat'l M. (N. Y. '91) 16: 349.
Warren and Barrington, R. I., Burials at. N. E. Reg. 48: 442.
Warren, Fort, How we escaped from. (J. W. Alexander) New Eng. M. n. s. 7: 208.
Warriorism, The Secret of. (E. L. Godkin) Nation, 54: 222.
Wars, Three. (E. Zola) New R. 6: 210–455.
Wart and Wen Cures. (J. Hardy) Folk-Lore Rec. 1: 216.
Warta, Rudolf von, and William Tell. (K. A. A. Biggs) Gent. M. n. s. 52: 156.
Warton, Thomas, and Machyn's Diary. (H. E. D. Blakiston) Eng. Hist. R. 11: 282.
Warwick the Kingmaker, Oman's Life of. (J. Tait) Eng. Hist. R. 7: 761.
Warwick Castle and its Art Treasures. (J. M. Gray) M. of Art, 14: 1.
Warwick St. John; a story. Belgra. 91: 275.
Was he a Coward? a story. (V. Garskine) Gent. M. n. s. 52: 109. Same art. Ecl. M. 123: 92.
Was he Human? (W. B. Foster) Bost. 3: 19.
Was I a Coward? Chamb. J. 73: 809.
Was it a Dream? a story. Argosy, 56: 42.
Was it the Good Bear? a story. (A. French) McClure, 2: 61.
Was it Right? Was it Wrong? (O. Schreiner) New R. 7: 397.
Was she justified? a story. (E. M. Halliday) Munsey, 12: 289.
Washbourn, J. R. (S. Lee) Ath. '93, 2: 591.
Washing-day on a Western Ranch. All the Year, 73: 13.
Washington, Booker T., Life Work of. Our Day, 16: 79.
Washington, Mrs. Booker T. One Woman's Influence in Alabama's Black Belt. Our Day, 16: 339.
Washington, George. (Woodrow Wilson) Harper, 92: 169–930. 93: 169–843. — (R. H. Clarke) Am. Cath. Q. 21: 250.
— Account Books of. (J. M. Toner) Pennsyl. M. 16: 75.
— after the Revolution, 1784–99. (W. S. Baker) Pennsyl. M. 18: 389. 19: 22–428. 20: 41, 176, 334.
— and his Mother. (J. M. Toner) M. Am. Hist. 28: 368.
— and Robert Morris, Correspondence of. (E. L. Gilliams) Nat'l M. (N. Y. '91) 15: 390.
— Birthday of, How made a Holiday. (W. G. Chase) Bost. 1: 513.
— — Proper Time for Celebration of. (J. Meyer) Am. Hist. Reg. 1: 547.
— Birthplace of, Preservation of. (C. S. Sargent) Garden & F. 7: 1.
— Books about, New. (W. C. Ford) Nation, 56: 297.
— Christianity the Moulding Power of his Character. (F. W. Conrad) Luth. Q. 26: 89.
— Description of Person and Height of. M. Am. Hist. 29: 66.
— Do we know? (L. Irving) M. Am. Hist. 29: 222. — (L. Irving) Nat'l M. (N. Y. '91) 17: 437.
— Early Military Order of, 1775. N. E. Reg. 46: 30.
— English Ancestry of. (J. M. Read) Ath. '94, 1: 377.
— Family of, in Virginia Life. (A. H. Wharton) Lippinc. 57: 577.
— — in Official Life. (A. H. Wharton) Lippinc. 57: 865.
— Farewell Address. (W. W. Phelps) Am. M. Civics, 7: 466. — Am. M. Civics, 8: 434.
— First Portrait of. M. Am. Hist. 29: 275.
— Footprints of. (H. H. Ragan) Chaut. 22: 515, 643. 23: 1, 131.
— Genealogy of. (W. C. Ford) Nation, 55: 373.
— Houdon's Statue of. (N. B. Winston) M. Am. Hist. 30: 3.
— in Boston. (I. Allen) New Eng. M. n. s. 9: 688.
— in his Relations with Catholics. (R. H. Clarke) Am. Cath. Q. 21: 636.
— Itinerary of, 1775–83. (W. S. Baker) Pennsyl. M. 15: 394.
— Last Letters of. Ath. '95, 1: 504.
— Letter of, in 1785, Fragment of. M. Am. Hist. 28: 60.
— Letter to Joseph Reed, 1779. (W. H. Egle) Pennsyl. M. 16: 83.
— Love Affairs of. (W. E. Curtis) Chaut. 20: 599.
— Manuscript Prayer-book. (E. C. Lee) Am. Hist. Reg. 1: 535–767.
— Mother of. (M. D. Conway) Open Court, 6: 3385.
— — and Birthplace of. (E. B. Washington) Cent. 21: 830.
— Office-seeking during his Administration. (G. Hunt) Am. Hist. Reg. 1: 270.
— Original Portraits of. (C. H. Hart) Cent. 21: 593.
— Portrait of, Stuart's Lansdowne. (C. H. Hart) Harper, 93: 378.

Washington, Portraits of, G. W. P. Custis's Opinion of. Pennsyl. M. 18: 81.
— — Savage's. (J. Winsor) Harv. Grad. M. 3: 502.
— — Stuart's. (W. H. Downes) New Eng. M. n. s. 9: 767.
— — Two Unpublished. (H. S. Stabler; E. B. Washington) Cent. 25: 544.
— — Unpublished Life. (C. H. Hart) McClure, 8: 112.
— Purchase of Braddock's Field by. (M. D. Conway) Nation, 60: 122, 145.
— Relics of, in England. (M. D. Conway) Nation, 55: 491.
— Religion of. (M. D. Conway) Open Court, 3: 1895.
— Religious Character of. (W. S. Perry) Chr. Lit. 10: 53 a.
— Dr. Rush and. (P. L. Ford) Atlan. 75: 633.
— Siemering's. Nation, 57: 83.
— Some of his Kin. (Mrs. M. S. Payne) M. Am. Hist. 30: 181.
— Swords of. (T. A. Washington) N. E. Reg. 48: 21.
— Visit to, at Mt. Vernon, in 1785. (J. Hunter) Pennsyl. M. 17: 76.
— Writings of, Ford's Edition. Ath. '94, 1: 437.
— Youth of. (J. M. Toner) M. Am. Hist. 27: 378.
Washington, John, of Virginia, New Facts about. (A. C. Quisenberry) M. Am. Hist. 30: 68.
Washington, John, 2d, The Will of. (W. C. Ford) Nation, 57: 44.
Washington, Mary. (H. E. Hayden) M. Am. Hist. 30: 47.
Washington, Robert, Letter of, 1775. N. E. Reg. 47: 324.
Washington Family of Garsden. (J. E. Nightingale) Ath. '92, 1: 180.
— of Maidstone. (M. D. Conway) Ath. '92, 1: 88.
— Home of, in England. (A. Branscombe) Munsey, 14: 553.
— of Virginia. (Mary L. and Louise A. Mayo) Munsey, 16: 313.
— Will of Mrs. Margaret Washington, Hawtayne, 1616. (G. H. Hawtayne) N. E. Reg. 47: 303.
Washington, D. C. (J. Ralph) Harper, 90: 657. — Leisure Hour, 44: 354. — (J. Hawthorne) Lippinc. 52: 70.
— Afternoon Receptions in. (Mrs. S. F. Parsons) Chaut. 20: 213.
— as a Spectacle. (F. M. Crawford) Cent. 26: 483.
— Asiatic and South American Legations at. (C. M. Conger) Munsey, 7: 411.
— Before the War. (M. E. W. Sherwood) Lippinc. 54: 259.
— British Attack on, 1814. (R. S. Rogers) Nat'l M. (N. Y. '91) 18: 231.
— Burning of, 1814. (Original Letter) M. Am. Hist. 27: 467.
— Cairo Apartment House. Archit. Rec. 4: 473.
— Capitol, History of. (Glenn Brown) Am. Arch. 52: 51-99. 53: 3-75. 54: 3-81.
— City Government of. (M. N. Lee) Chaut. 22: 39, 164.
— European Legations at. (C. M. Conger) Munsey, 7: 259.
— Ford's Theatre, Fall of, June 9, 1893. Pub. Opin. 15: 267.
— Historic Houses of. (T. S. Hamlin) Scrib. M. 14: 475.
— in Lincoln's Time. (N. Brooks) Cent. 27: 140.
— Local Names near. (W. H. Babcock) J. Am. Folk-Lore, 1: 146.
— Parks of. Am. Arch. 47: 72.
— Plan of. (C. B. Todd) Am. Arch. 53: 53.
Washington, Roman Catholic University at. (H. M. Sweeney) Cath. World, 57: 95.
— Society in. (H. L. Nelson) Harper, 86: 586, 674.
— Special Correspondents at. (T. C. Crawford) Cosmopol. 12: 351.
— the Winter before the War. (H. L. Dawes) Atlan. 72: 160.
Washington, the Evergreen State. (J. Ralph) Harper, 85: 594.
— Forests of. (L. H. Wall) Garden & F. 5: 57.
Washington, Mount. (J. H. Ward) New Eng. M. n. s. 8: 547.
Washington Correspondent. (E. J. Gibson) Lippinc. 54: 715.
Washington Memorial Arch. Critic, 26: 329.
Washington National Park. (C. Snyder) R. of Rs. (N. Y.) 9: 163.
Wasp, Study of a. (J. McN. Wright) Science, 20: 220.
Wasps. (G. Allen) Longm. 23: 521.
— at Home. Spec. 71: 267.
— Plague of. Dub. R. 114: 170.
— Statistics of Observations upon. (F. Y. Edgeworth) J. Statis. Soc. 59: 358.
Wassilieff, Sophie, The Female Nihilist. Idler, 3: 431-648. 4: 43-306.
Waste. Chamb. J. 73: 337.
— City's, Disposal of. (G. E. Waring) No. Am. 161: 49.
Waste in Building. (W. A. Rodman) Am. Arch. 45: 100.
Waste-paper, Government. Chamb. J. 73: 747.
Waste Products, Cotton-seed Oil. (F. G. Mather) Pop. Sci. Mo. 45: 104.
— made useful. (L. Playfair) No. Am. 155: 560. — Chamb. J. 71: 591.
Wasted; a poem. (W. Meynell) M. of Art, 9: 502.
Watch, Mechanism of. (H. E. Duncan) J. Frankl. Inst. 139: 81.
Watch in the Night, A. (H. P. Spofford) Harper, 88: 147.
Watch Schools, Swiss. (T. B. Willson) Pop. Sci. Mo. 46: 62.
Watcher, The; a poem. (C. Turner) Outing, 23: 144.
Watches, Early Artistic. (G. F. Kunz) Mo. Illust. 3: 313.
Watchmaker's Wife, The; a story. (F. R. Stockton) National, 21: 240.
Watchman, The. (M. H. Foote) Cent. 25: 30.
Watchmen's Songs. (L. A. Smith) Good Words, 37: 671. Same art. Liv. Age, 211: 345.
Water, Analysis of, Value of. (W. P. Mason) Science, 21: 258.
— Analyses of, Interpretation of. (J. C. Thresh) Am. Arch. 47: 65.
— and Air, Relation of, to Temperature and Life. (G. G. Hubbard) Nat. Geog. M. 5: 112.
— and Well-worship. (A. W. Moore) Folk-Lore, 5: 212.
— as Food and Drink. (T. G. Allen) Chaut. 23: 324.
— Color of. (D. Fitz Gerald and W. E. Foss) J. Frankl. Inst. 138: 401. — (C. Vogt) Pop. Sci. Mo. 41: 246.
— Condensing, Worthington Cooling Tower for Continuous Use of. (J. H. Cooper) J. Frankl. Inst. 141: 417.
— Data relating to. Am. Arch. 47: 126.
— Density of, at Different Temperatures. (A. F. Nagle) Cassier, 2: 378.
— Drinking, Sand Filtration of. (G. W. Fuller) Engin. M. 6: 663. — (A. Hazen) J. Frankl. Inst. 142: 366.
— Flow of, through Pipes. Cassier, 1: 79.

Water, Methods for the Determination of. (S. L. Penfield) Am. J. Sci. **148**: 30.
— Poison in the Cup. (N. E. Yorke-Davies) Gent. M. n. s. **51**: 517.
— Pure, as a Hygienic Factor in Prisons. (D. N. Rankin) Lend a H. **15**: 327.
— — for Drinking and Cooking. (S. P. Axtell) Engin. M. **11**: 67.
— Purification of. (F. Davis) Engin. M. **2**: 819. — (R. Hering) J. Frankl. Inst. **139**: 135, 215.
— — by Chemical Treatment. (W. G. Tucker) Science, **20**: 34.
— — by Iron. (F. A. Anderson) J. Soc. Arts, **44**: 267.
— Surface-film of. (L. C. Miall) Nature, **46**: 7.
— Transporting Power of. (W. H. Wheeler) Longm. **26**: 422.
Water Bacteriology and Cholera. (G. C. Frankland) Longm. **23**: 171.
Water Bugs, Giant; a Family of Water Kings. (C. M. Weed) Pop. Sci. Mo. **45**: 443.
Water-closets: Latrines of the East. (E. S. Morse) Am. Arch. **39**: 171.
Water-color Painters, Royal Society of; Exhibition of 1892. Ath. '**92**, **1**: 379, 442. — Ath. '**92**, **2**: 823.
— — of 1893. (C. Monkhouse) Acad. **43**: 400. — Ath. '**93**, **1**: 351, 511. — Ath. '**93**, **2**: 813.
— — 1894–95. (W. Sharp) Art J. **47**: 60.
— Royal Scottish Society of. Acad. **43**: 459.
Water-color Painting in America. (C. S. Johnson) Munsey, **8**: 637.
— in England. (J. D. Linton) M. of Art, **11**: 150.
— — Poor. Sat. R. **81**: 344.
— — Redgrave's. (M. S. Stillman) Nation, **55**: 73.
Water-color Sketching from Nature. (E. M. Wimperis) Leis. Hour, **44**: 624.
Water-colors, Action of Light on. (A. H. Church) M. of Art, **11**: 233.
— Institute of Painters in. Ath. '**94**, **1**: 352, 545.
Water-courses, in Relation to the Public. (C. S. Sargent) Garden & F. **7**: 231.
Water-garden. (J. N. Gerard) Garden & F. **6**: 296, 349.
— at Clifton, N. J. (J. N. Gerard) Garden & F. **6**: 434.
Water-hens. (H. F. Witherby) Knowl. **17**: 212.
Water-horse, A; a story. (M. Crommelin) Argosy, **59**: 215.
Waterhouse, John William. (J. A. Blaikie) M. of Art, **9**: 1.
Water-lilies. (J. N. Gerard) Garden & F. **5**: 477. — (J. N. Gerard) Garden & F. **7**: 354.
— and Extreme Heat. (W. Tricker) Garden & F. **9**: 356.
— at Yarmouthport. Garden & F. **5**: 441.
— Cultivation of. (J. N. Gerard) Garden & F. **5**: 439. — (W. Tricker) Garden & F. **6**: 406. — Garden & F. **7**: 24.
— from Seed. (W. Tricker) Garden & F. **6**: 79. **9**: 334.
— Hardy. (J. N. Gerard) Garden & F. **8**: 267.
— Hybridizing. (G. W. Oliver) Garden & F. **9**: 53.
— Notes on. (W. Watson) Garden & F. **6**: 364.
— Nympea Gigantea. Garden & F. **6**: 40.
— A Winter Water-garden. Garden & F. **8**: 18.
Water-lily, Blue, from Mexico. (J. W. Rose) Garden & F. **8**: 205.
Water Pipe, Cast-iron. (F. H. Lewis) Cassier, **8**: 17.
Water-plants. Nelumb lutea. (J. W. Manning) Garden & F. **9**: 373.
Water-power. (W. C. Unwin) Am. Arch. **42**: 8. — (J. Richards) Cassier, **2**: 22. — (S. Webber) Cassier, **9**: 375.
— and Electric Transmission. (C. E. Emery) Cassier, **9**: 219.
— Cost of. (S. Webber) Cassier, **8**: 415.
— in Switzerland. (H. H. Suplee) Cassier, **11**: 3.
— Use of, in Europe. (T. Turrettini) Cassier, **8**: 322.
— Value of. (C. T. Main) Cassier, **2**: 26.
Water-powers, Development of Unused. (S. Webber) Cassier, **5**: 213.
— of the Western States. (A. G. Allan) Engin. M. **9**: 17.
Water Spirits, The Toll of the. (C. Battersby) Sund. M. **25**: 666.
Water Supplies for Cities. (F. Davis) Engin. M. **3**: 227. — (R. Hering) Engin. M. **9**: 450.
— — Contamination of. (F. J. Thornbury) Chaut. **24**: 197.
— — Filtration of. (E. F. Smith and others) J. Frankl. Inst. **141**: 321. — (R. Hering) Engin. M. **11**: 627.
— — Prospective Use of Salt Water. (S. McElroy) Engin. M. **6**: 821.
— Public, Investigation of. (F. Davis) Engin. M. **10**: 439.
— Purification of. (G. H. Rohe) Lend a H. **17**: 166.
Water Supply. Am. Arch. **44**: 137.
— Gravity Systems of. (G. W. Rafter) Engin. M. **2**: 633.
— Locating a Public. (D. W. Mead) Engin. M. **10**: 876.
— of London. Sat. R. **73**: 356.
— — History of. Sat. R. **73**: 384.
— — Public *vs.* Private Ownership of. (J. Lubbock) Sat. R. **82**: 617.
Water-towers in Massachusetts. Garden & F. **5**: 410.
Water-wheel, Pelton. J. Frankl. Inst. **140**: 161.
Water Wheels, Tangential. (J. Richards) Cassier, **5**: 117.
Water Works. Distribution Mains and Fire Service. (J. T. Fanning) Cassier, **2**: 180–291.
— Naples. Am. Arch. **46**: 49.
Water Works Machinery. (C. L. Newcomb) Cassier, **10**: 168.
Water Works Standpipes. (W. Kiersted) Cassier, **8**: 41.
Watercress and Flower-girl Mission. (F. W. Farrer) Chr. Lit. **11**: 25.
Waterford, Louisa Stuart de Rothsay, Marchioness, Art of. (H. W. Brewer) Argosy, **59**: 534. — (W. M. Hardinge) Temp. Bar, **103**: 49. Same art. Liv. Age, **203**: 175. — Ed. R. **179**: 382. — Sat. R. **77**: 151. — Dial (Ch.) **16**: 204.
Waterford Cathedral. Reliquary, **32**: 33.
Waterloo, Battle of, Cavalry in, Wood on. Sat. R. **80**: 784.
— — Did Grouchy cause Defeat of Napoleon? (F. L. Huidekoper) Un. Serv. (Phila.) **15**: 197.
— — Literature of. (H. M. Stephens) Acad. **41**: 174.
— Campaign of. Gent. M. n. s. **52**: 251. — (W. O'Connor Morris) Temp. Bar, **97**: 257. Same art. Liv. Age, **196**: 707.
— — Contemporary Letter on. (F. G. Leeds) 19th Cent. **33**: 430. Same art. Liv. Age, **197**: 292.
— — Disputed Passages of. (W. O'Connor Morris) Eng. Hist. R. **10**: 55.
— — Inner History of. (A. Forbes) 19th Cent. **33**: 416. Same art. Liv. Age, **197**: 283.
— — Ropes on. Harv. Grad. M. **2**: 31. — (J. D. Cox) Nation, **56**: 183. — (W. O. Morris) Acad. **44**: 103, 125. — (J. Kirkland) Dial (Ch.) **14**: 275. — Sat. R. **75**: 350.

Waterloo Banquet, At the. Cornh. **72**: 48.
Waterman, Mark. (W. H. Downes) M. of Art, **18**: 269.
Watertown, Mass. (W. H. Savage) New Eng. M. n. s. **6**: 237.
Waterways, Deep, Commerce and. (L. M. Haupt) J. Frankl. Inst. **141**: 81, 171.
— — Problem of. (E. V. Smalley) Forum, **19**: 746.
— Do they benefit Railroads? (L. M. Haupt) Engin. M. **3**: 9.
— from the Ocean to the Lakes. (T. C. Clarke) Scrib. M. **19**: 103.
— Interior, from N. Y. to the Gulf Coast. (S. M. Miller) Un. Serv. (Phila.) **12**: 503.
Watson, John. [Ian Maclaren.] (W. R. Nicoll) Bookman, **2**: 311. — With portrait. (J. A. Noble) Bookman, **1**: 93. — (D. M. Ross) McClure, **7**: 387. — With portrait. Bk. News, **14**: 584.
— Afterwards. (E. S. Phelps) McClure, **5**: 329.
— as Lecturer. (G. S. Lee) Critic, **29**: 218.
— at Home. (D. Paton) Sund. M. **25**: 37.
— Doctor of the Old School. Sat. R. **81**: 557.
— Kate Carnegie. Acad. **50**: 425.
— Revival of Sentiment, "Days of Auld Lang Syne." Our Day, **15**: 317.
Watson, Sereno. Garden & F. **5**: 121. — Nature, **45**: 494.
Watson, Thomas, Sermon before the Synod of Durham in 1556. Dub. R. **119**: 412.
Watson, Thomas E. (T. Roosevelt) R. of Rs. (N. Y.) **14**: 289.
Watson, William. (H. D. Traill) Fortn. **63**: 393. Same art. Ecl. M. **124**: 616. — (C. J. Goodwin) New World, **4**: 121. — (Q. McC. Sholl) Bach of Arts, **2**: 612. — With portrait. Bk. Buyer, **10**: 7. — Book R. **1**: 26. — (James MacArthur) Chr. Un. **47**: 114. — (J. A. Noble) Critic, **22**: 154.
— and the Laureateship. Critic, **21**: 332.
— as an Essayist. (F. Wedmore) Acad. **43**: 430.
— as a Poet, with portraits. Bookman, **2**: 182. — Sat. R. **80**: 71.
— Excursions in Criticism. Spec. **70**: 488.
— Father of the Forest and other Poems. Sat. R. **80**: 615. — (G. Cotterell) Acad. **48**: 479.
— Insanity of. Critic, **21**: 365.
— Lachrymæ Musarum. (G. R. Tomson) Acad. **42**: 476.
— Odes and other Poems. Spec. **73**: 810.
— Poems. Spec. **69**: 819. — (E. K. Chambers) Acad. **41**: 246. — Church Q. **39**: 457. — (E. Purcell) Acad. **47**: 28.
— Poet of Poetry. Atlan. **71**: 694.
— Poetry. (D. F. Hannigan) Westm. **139**: 265. Same art. Ecl. M. **120**: 647. — Ath. '93, **2**: 121.
— Serious Verse of. (L. Magnus) Blackw. **158**: 121. Same art. Ecl. M. **125**: 347. Same art. Liv. Age, **206**: 425.
Watt, James, and Ocean Navigation. (F. Elgar) Nature, **51**: 475.
Watteau, Antoine. (C. Phillips) Portf. no. **18**.
Watterson, Henry. (M. M. Casseday) Mid-Cont. **6**: 3.
Watts, Geo. Frederick, with portrait. (G. Campbell) Cosmopol. **14**: 273. — (W. Meynell) M. of Art, **1**: 241. — (E. Monkhouse) Scrib. M. **16**: 693.
— Description of his Equestrian Statue of Hugh Lupus. M. of Art, **3**: 150.
— Painter of the Eternal Truths. (L. T. Meade) Sund. M. **23**: 15, 96.
— Pictures of. (C. Monkhouse) M. of Art, **5**: 177.
Watts, Theodore, the Literary Critic. Idler, **5**: 500.
Watty Whyte; a story. (A. Stuart) Idler, **6**: 735.
Watusi, The. (L. Decle) Anthrop. J. **23**: 423.
Waugh, Benjamin, and British Children, with portrait. R. of Rs. (N. Y.) **4**: 693.
Wauna, the Witch-maiden; a story. (A. H. Sydenham) Un. Serv. (Phila.) **10**: 546.
Wauters, Emile. (M. H. Spielmann) M. of Art, **10**: 397. — (A. J. Wauters) M. of Art, **17**: 181.
— and his Portraits. (F. T. Buck) Munsey, **15**: 608.
Waverley Oaks. (J. Kendall) New Eng. M. n. s. **14**: 227.
Waves. (E. M. Caillard) Good Words, **34**: 763. Same art. Ecl. M. **121**: 801. — (V. Cornish) Knowl. **19**: 6–281.
— and Rays. (P. Spies) Open Court, **6**: 3239, 3247.
Wax-myrtles of Seacoast of North America. (C. S. Sargent) Garden & F. **7**: 474.
Way it always ends; a duologue. (W. Thorold) Canad. M. **6**: 34.
Way of Fate; a poem. (G. de C. Curtis) Cosmopol. **21**: 151.
Way of a Will. (W. T. Nichols) Lippinc. **57**: 104.
Way of the World, The; a story. All the Year, **70**: 12.
Way of the World; a poem. (C. G. Rossetti) M. of Art, **17**: 304.
Way to my Heart; a poem. (D. H. Cornish) Argosy, **59**: 221.
Way, the Truth, the Life, Hort's. Church Q. **38**: 379.
Way we flirt now; a story. (H. Rawdon) Cornh. **74**: 620.
Wayfaring God, The. (W. J. Dawson) Good Words, **37**: 586.
Wayland, Francis. Lend a H. **14**: 173.
Wayne, Anthony, Campaign against North West Indians. (J. Brooke) Pennsyl. M. **19**: 387.
— Letters relating to Death of. (I. Craig) Pennsyl. M. **19**: 112.
— Stillé's. (J. C. Welling) Nation, **57**: 68, 86.
— Victory at Stony Point. (T. Roosevelt) Harper, **92**: 702.
Wayside Calvary, A; a poem. (A. Lamont) Argosy, **58**: 495.
Wayside Harvest, A. (L. B. Bridgman) Overland, n. s. **27**: 402.
Wayside Shrine; a poem. (I. Deane) Cosmopol. **13**: 174.
Wazan. (W. B. Harris) Blackw. **152**: 419. Same art. Ecl. M. **119**: 584. Same art. Liv. Age, **195**: 289.
"We," The Editorial. (A. W. Dennis) Writer, **7**: 88.
We, of the Stylus; a story. (T. G. Taaffe) Cosmopol. **18**: 550.
Weak Imitation, A; a story. (L. Merrick) Eng. Illust. **11**: 932.
Weald, In the. Blackw. **152**: 273.
Wealden, The, Age of. (O. C. Marsh) Am. J. Sci. **151**: 234.
Wealden Ironworks. All the Year, **73**: 184.
Wealer, The; a Story of the Times. (A. Knapp) Arena, **12**: 323.
Wealth and Christian Sociology. (S. Mathews) Am. J. Sociol. **1**: 771.
— and its Distribution. (E. N. Dingley) Am. J. Pol. **3**: 274.
— and Education. (H. G. Ager) Am. J. Pol. **3**: 483.
— and Morality. (W. E. Hart) Soc. Econ. **3**: 96.
— and Poverty. (E. W. Jackson) Am. J. Pol. **2**: 461, 589.
— Apology of Dives. (W. Barry) National, **28**: 228.
— Aristocracy of, in the U. S. (R. M. Reeves) Am. M. Civics, **8**: 23.
— Census on Distribution of. Soc. Econ. **6**: 137.

Wealth, Concentration of. (E. Pomeroy) Arena, **17**: 82. — (G. K. Holmes) Pol. Sci. Q. **8**: 589.
— Distribution of, Commons on. (O. L. Elliot) Dial (Ch.) **17**: 119.
— Divisibility of. (W. H. Mallock) New R. **8**: 463.
— Duty of. (A. Carnegie) Char. R. **5**: 33.
— English, Christianity and. (D. H. Wheeler) Chaut. **20**: 650.
— Ethics of. (W. H. Quaintance) Am. J. Pol. **3**: 1.
— The Gospel of. (John O'C. Power) Univ. R. **6**: 347.
— Gratuitous Benefactions of. (T. B. Stork) Soc. Econ. **8**: 357.
— How it is distributing itself. Soc. Econ. **5**: 257.
— in Existence, Computation of Value of. (G. K. Holmes) Am. Statis. Assoc. **4**: 75.
— in France and England. (W. J. Harris) J. Statis. Soc. **57**: 452.
— in the U. S. Spec. **68**: 364, 367.
— Initial Anarchist. (G. H. Sandison) Soc. Econ. **3**: 289.
— Its Proper Earning and Use. (W. H. Alden) N. Church R. **2**: 396.
— Labor, and Ability. (W. H. Mallock) National, **21**: 474.
— Limitation of, by Taxation. (C. W. Buck) Southern M. **5**: 167.
— New; a Study of the Source of Income. (W. Smart) Pol. Sci. Q. **9**: 445.
— Northern. Why it grows faster than Southern. Soc. Econ. **8**: 65.
— Obligations of: Indictment of Dives. (W. S. Lilly) New R. **9**: 599.
— of France and of other Countries. (A. de Foville) J. Statis. Soc. **56**: 597.
— or Poverty, Is it more desirable to be born to? (F. R. Coudert and others) Munsey, **14**: 151.
— Possession of. All the Year, **70**: 529.
— Prevailing Jealousy of. (W. N. Black) Engin. M. **7**: 646.
— Producers of, Who are the Chief? (W. H. Mallock) No. Am. **156**: 648.
— Production and Consumption of, by the Nation. (G. B. Waldron) Arena, **15**: 654.
— Productivity of the Individual. (W. H. Mallock) No. Am. **157**: 580.
— Public Effect of Great Fortunes. Soc. Econ. **8**: 272.
— Race for, in the U. S. (E. Fawcett) Eng. Illust. **11**: 43.
— Relations and Responsibilities of. (A. P. Peabody) And. R. **19**: 321.
— Right Use of. (J. M. Buckley; R. S. MacArthur) M. Chr. Lit. **5**: 399.
— — Symposium. Indep. Jan. 7, '92.
— Social and Ethical View of. (G. M. Steele) Meth. R. **55**: 751.
— Social Function of. (P. Leroy Beaulieu) Pop. Sci. Mo. **48**: 829.
— Social Ministry of. (H. C. Adams) Int. J. Ethics, **4**: 173. — Soc. Econ. **6**: 150.
— Spontaneous Diffusion of. (W. H. Mallock) National, **21**: 792.
— Three Factors of. (F. J. Kingsbury) Am. J. Soc. Sci. **31**: 1.
— Two Kinds of. (L. G. Bostedo) Am. M. Civics, **9**: 130.
— Unequal Distribution of, the Impediment to Production. (F. Minton) Econ. R. **1**: 517.
— Use and Abuse of, in Industry and Commerce. Ed. R. **178**: 139.
— Use of. Sat. R. **79**: 750.
— What is? Chamb. J. **70**: 737.
Weapons, Aboriginal, of California. (L. G. Yates) Overland, n. s. **27**: 337.
— Ancient Scottish. (J. M. Gray) Scot. R. **23**: 269.
— Curious. Chamb. J. **69**: 61.
— Military Operations as affected by the New. (F. Lee) Cent. **28**: 422.
— New, of the U. S. Army. (V. L. Mason) Cent. **27**: 570.
— Secret. Sat. R. **77**: 250.
Weariness. (M. Foster) 19th Cent. **34**: 337. Same art. Ecl. M. **121**: 577.
Weather and Climate, Study of. (R. H. Scott) Longm. **22**: 62.
— and Mental Action. Pop. Sci. Mo. **47**: 568.
— and Weather Wisdom. (E. O. Kirk) Atlan. **76**: 481.
— in England. Spec. **69**: 285.
— Influence of, on Diseases. (O. Gotthilf) Chaut. **21**: 85.
— — on Mind. Pub. Opin. **12**: 378.
— Psychic Effects of the. (J. S. Lemon) Am. J. Psychol. **6**: 277.
— Seven-day Period. (H. H. Clayton) Am. J. Sci. **152**: 7.
— A Short Cycle in. (J. P. Hall) Am. J. Sci. **145**: 227.
— Six-and-seven-day Weather Periods. (H. H. Clayton) Am. J. Sci. **147**: 223.
Weather Bureau in relation to Science and Industries of the Country. (E. L. Moore) Science, n. s. **2**: 576. Same art. Nature, **53**: 187.
Weather Fallacies. (R. Inwards) Nature, **52**: 377.
Weather Forecasting, Scientific. (G. J. Symons) Sci. Prog. **1**: 1. — (R. H. Scott) New R. **9**: 416.
— Commercial Value of. (E. B. Dunn) Engin. M. **9**: 1.
— for Long Periods in India. (D. Archibald) Nature, **55**: 85. — (D. Archibald) Sat. R. **82**: 646.
— Possibilities of Long-range. Nature, **51**: 212.
— Value of, to Agriculture and Inland Commerce. (M. W. Harrington) R. of Rs. (N. Y.) **12**: 303.
Weather-lore. (F. D. Bergen and W. W. Newell) J. Am. Folk-Lore, **2**: 203.
— Popular. Spec. **71**: 796.
Weather-making, Ancient and Modern. (M. W. Harrington) Nat. Geog. M. **3**: 35.
Weather Preferences of Authors. (Pauline W. Roose) Temp. Bar, **105**: 186.
Weather Prevision. Ed. R. **181**: 514.
Weather Prophets, Modern. Spec. **71**: 12.
Weather Record of 14th Century. Reliquary, **33**: 100.
Weather Service, A Colonial. (A. McAdie) Pop. Sci. Mo. **45**: 331.
Weather Studies at Blue Hill. (R. L. Bridgman) New Eng. M. n. s. **12**: 40.
Weather Wisdom. (P. H. W. Almy) Gent. M. n. s. **53**: 548.
Weaver Family of New York City. (I. J. Greenwood) N. E. Reg. **47**: 48.
Weavers of Bradford, Eng., Work and Wages of. (J. B. Firth) Econ. J. **2**: 543. — (H. L. Holder) Econ. J. **3**: 715.
Weaving, A Revolution in. (S. G. Wilson) Overland, n. s. **28**: 279.
Web-spinning in Spiders, Suggestions on the Origin and Evolution of. (R. I. Pocock) Nature, **51**: 417.
Webb, Sidney and Beatrice. (F. Harrison) 19th Cent. **35**: 956.
Webb, Thomas Stallad. Temp. Bar, **97**: 405.
Webbe, William. (A. C. Benson) Gent. M. n. s. **56**: 99.
Weber, Carl M. von, and Wagner, Richard. Sat. R. **80**: 106.
Weber, William Edward, with portrait. Pop. Sci. Mo. **40**: 548.

Weber's Law, New Instrument for. (J. H. Leuba) Am. J. Psychol. 5: 370.
Webster, Mrs. Augusta. (T. Watts) Ath. '94, 2: 355.
Webster, Ben, with portrait. Theatre, 29: 23.
Webster, Daniel. (W. C. Todd) Green Bag, 8: 229.
— and Monistic Religion. (T. B. Wakeman) Open Court, 3: 2093.
— and the War Spirit. (R. Ogden) Nation, 60: 141.
— Debt to Mason in Dartmouth College Case. (W. S. G. Noyes) Am. Law R. 28: 356.
— A Glance at. (M. Chamberlain) Cent. 24: 709.
— An Hour with. (H. King) M. Am. Hist. 27: 455.
— Incident in the Life of. (W. I. Crandall) M. Am. Hist. 29: 252.
— Reply to Hayne. (C. J. Little) Chaut. 22: 290. — (R. C. Winthrop) Scrib. M. 15: 118.
Webster, John. (W. Poel) Acad. 42: 339.
— Duchess of Malfi. Gent. M. n. s. 49: 633.
— — and Amalfi. Theatre, 29: 148.
— Lamb, and Swinburne. (W. Archer) New R. 8: 96.
Webster, Joseph D. Nat'l M. (N. Y. '91) 16: 338.
Webster, J. W. Murder of Geo. Parkman. (G. C. Holt) Cosmopol. 19: 537.
Wedderburn, Alexander. *See* Loughborough, Lord.
Wedding at Capri; a story. (P. Heyse) Cosmopol. 16: 318.
— in Greece. Gent. M. n. s. 49: 338. Same art. Liv. Age, 195: 553.
— in the Pistoiese. (I. M. Anderton) Good Words, 35: 546. Same art. Liv. Age, 202: 634.
— in Telos, Protracted. (J. T. Bent) Eng. Illust. 8: 672.
Wedding, A; a story. (J. Gordon) Lippinc. 49: 496.
Wedding-cake, Evolution of. (A. C. Sage) Lippinc. 57: 409.
Wedding Dance Mask, County Mayo. (Earl of Southesk) Illust. Archæol. 1: 205.
Wedding Journey of Mrs. Zaintree, born Greenleaf. (W. H. Shelton) Scrib. M. 14: 247.
Weddings, New England. (P. M. Cole) J. Am. Folk-Lore, 6: 103.
— Shoe-throwing at. (J. E. Crombie) Folk-Lore, 6: 258.
Wedgwood, Josiah. (A. H. Church) Portfo. 1894: no. 3.
— and his Latest Biographer. Chamb. J. 72: 65.
— Old London Potteries. (C. Cooper) Gent. M. n. s. 49: 120.
Wedgwood Pottery. (A. H. Church) Portfo. 1894: no. 3.
Wedmore, Frederick, Collection of Prints. (F. Wedmore) Art J. 46: 6-70.
— English Episodes. (G. Cottrell) Acad. 46: 440. — Sat. R. 79: 162.
— Renunciations. (G. Cotterell) Acad. 42: 601.
Weeds, Destroying, by Act of Congress. (C. S. Sargent) Garden & F. 7: 511.
Weeds; a story. (R. McE. Stuart) Harper, 94: 105.
Weeks and Sabbaths, Origin of. (A. B. Ellis) Pop. Sci. Mo. 46: 329.
Weight. (A. G. Greenhill) Nature, 46: 247.
Weights and Measures, Confusion in. (T. C. Mendenhall) Science, 21: 79.
— Determination of the Division Errors of a Straight Scale. (H. Jacoby) Am. J. Sci. 151: 333.
Weil, Gottlieb. Acad. 47: 237.
Weimar, Two Days in. (E. Sigrid) Canad. M. 5: 250.
Weir, John Alden. (E. King) Mo. Illust. 5: 29.
Weir, John Jenner. Nat. Sci. 4: 392.
Weir to Mill, From. Blackw. 156: 510. Same art. Ecl. M. 123: 701.
Weird Story of Adela Grove. (E. F. Byrrne) Argosy, 54: Summer no. 61.
Weird Violin, The; a story. Argosy, 56: 522.
Weird Warning, A; a story. (R. J. McNeil) Argosy, 60: 507.
Weiser, Conrad. (P. C. Croll) Am. Hist. Reg. 1: 221.
Weiser Family of Pennsylvania. (H. M. M. Richards) Am. Hist. Reg. 4: 176.
Weismann, August, Concessions of. (L. F. Ward) Pop. Sci. Mo. 45: 175.
— Romanes on. Nature, 49: 49.
Weismannism, Critical Remarks on. (G. J. Romanes) Open Court, 7: 3775.
— Once More. (H. Spencer) Contemp. 66: 592.
Weiss, Bernhard, with portrait. (J. H. Ropes) Bib. World, 8: 177.
Weissenburg, Battlefield of. (F. Maurice) Un. Serv. M. 9: 77.
Weist-Hill, —, Musician. Acad. 41: 22.
Weitling, William, a Neglected Socialist. (F. C. Clark) Ann. Am. Acad. Pol. Sci. 5: 718.
Weld, Habijah. (M. L. Starr) Am. Hist. Reg. 3: 360.
Welfare, Principle of. (H. Höffding) Monist, 1: 525.
Well, Breathing, in Kansas. (J. T. Willard) Science, 20: 337.
— Deep, at Wheeling, W. Va. (W. Hallock) Am. J Sci. 143: 234.
Well-being and Suffering, Problem of, in the Old Testament. (H. Creelman) Bib. World, 7: 255, 325.
Welland Canal. (C. N. Dutton) Canad. M. 1: 255.
Welldon, J. E. C. Gerald Eversley's Friendship. Sat. R. 80: 82.
Wellesley, R. C., Marquis, Governor-Generalship of. Spec. 72: 110. — Sat. R. 76: 416.
Wellesley College. (L. M. Hodgkins) New Eng. M. n. s. 7: 361.
— Festivals in. (K. L. Bates) Cent. 27: 441.
Wellesley, Mass., Gardens at. (H. H. Hunnewell) Garden & F. 6: 229.
Wellington, Lord, Assye and. (F. Maurice) Cornh. 74: 291. Same art. Liv. Age, 211: 284.
— Maxims and Opinions of. Eng. R. 4: 280.
Wells, David A., on the Downfall of Financial Fallacies. (G. Wilson) Arena, 11: 27.
Wells, H. G. Island of Dr. Moreau. (P. C. Mitchell) Sat. R. 81: 368.
— Time Machine. Sat. R. 80: 86.
Wells and its Cathedral. (E. R. Pennell) M. of Art, 12: 9.
— and Salisbury, Closes of. (A. Ansted) M. of Art, 18: 263.
— Church on. Sat. R. 78: 488.
Wells Cathedral, Vicar's Close at. (A. B. Bibb) Am. Arch. 46: 79.
Wells College, Festivals in. (A. A. Wood) Cent. 27: 442.
Wells Memorial Institute, Relief Work of. (H. S. Dudley) Ann. Am. Acad. Pol. Sci. 5: 377.
Wells Palace. (Canon Church) Good Words, 36: 389.
Wells and Lochs, Guardian Spirits of. (W. Gregor) Folk-Lore, 3: 67.
— Artesian, Power from. (A. L. Baumgartner) Cassier, 8: 548.
— Bore Hole, for Town Water-supply. (H. Davey) Cassier, 7: 244.
— Holy. (R. C. Hope) Antiq. n. s. 25: 156. 26: 63-213.
— — of Scotland. (R. C. Hope) Antiq. n. s. 27: 102, 216. 28: 62, 262. 29: 29. 30: 25. — Antiq. n. s. 31: 26.
Well-worship. (A. W. Moore) Folk-Lore, 5: 212.
Welser, Philippina. (J. Cartwright) M. of Art, 7: 305.

Welsh Bards and Eisteddfodds. Walford's Antiq. **4**: 71.
Welsh Eisteddfod. Music, **4**: 541.
Welsh Romance and Superstitions. (T. E. Kebbel) Time, **21**: 138.
Wendish Meres, Among the. (B. Marshall) Sund. M. **24**: 699.
Wends, The: Remnant of a Great Race. (H. W. Wolff) Westm. **137**: 538. Same art. Ecl. M. **119**: 636.
Wenlock, Old, and its Folk-Lore. (C. M. Gaskell) 19th Cent. **35**: 259. Same art. Ecl. M. **122**: 407. Same art. Liv. Age, **200**: 721.
Wenlock Abbey. (C. McGaskell) Good Words, **35**: 392.
Wentworth, Isabella, Lady. (W. T. Hardy) Liv. Age, **192**: 180.
Wenzell, Albert B. (P. Maxwell) Q. Illust. **1**: 97. — With portrait. Bk. Buyer, **13**: 636.
Were-wolf. Sat. R. **78**: 288.
Wesley, J., as a Scientist. (W. C. Cahall) Meth. R. **52**: 77.
— English Dictionary by. (H. B. Wheatley) Bookworm, **1**: 15.
— Methodism of. Eng. R. **8**: 314.
— a Methodist Evolutionist. (J. W. Lee) Southern M. **4**: 348.
Wesley Ghost, The. (A. Lang) Contemp. **68**: 288.
Wessex, England, Conversion of. (F. S. Holmes) Eng. Hist. R. **7**: 437.
— Country of Thomas Hardy. Temp. Bar, **108**: 150.
Wessex Philosophy. (E. B. V. Christian) Gent. M. n. s. **51**: 239. Same art. Ecl. M. **121**: 479. Same art. Liv. Age, **199**: 377.
West, Benjamin. M. of Art, **2**: 43.
— Career of. (Mrs. M. J. Lamb) M. Am. Hist. **27**: 217.
— Letters. (T. Stewardson) Pennsyl. M. **18**: 219.
West, the, Are the People of, Fanatics? (J. K. Miller) Arena, **13**: 92.
— Business in, 1893. (T. L. Greene) Nation, **57**: 131. — (A. Williams, jr.) Chaut. **18**: 184.
— California to Texas, from a Car Window. (D. A. Goodsell) Chaut. **18**: 552.
— Discontent of. Is a Revolution at hand? (J. E. Bennett) Arena, **16**: 393.
— Feeling towards the East. (W. V. Allen) No. Am. **162**: 588.
— in Literature. (H. Garland) Arena, **6**: 669.
— Is it discontented? (J. E. Bennett) Overland, n. s. **28**: 456.
— — a Local Study of Facts. (J. H. Canfield) Forum, **18**: 449.
— Letter to a Friend from the Far. (F. Eastman) Atlan. **73**: 711.
— Literary. Dial (Ch.) **15**: 173.
— Literary Emancipation of. (H. Garland) Forum, **16**: 156.
— The Loyal. (H. M. Teller) No. Am. **162**: 757.
— Mr. Godkin on; a Protest. (C. S. Gleed) Forum, **21**: 641.
— Problem of the. (F. J. Turner) Atlan. **78**: 289.
— Roosevelt's Winning of the. (F. J. Turner) Nation, **60**: 240. — (F. J. Turner) Am. Hist. R. **2**: 171.
— Settlements in, Prior to 1776. (G. C. Broadhead) M. Am. Hist. **29**: 332. — (G. C. Broadhead) Nat'l M. (N. Y. '91) **18**: 17.
— Struggle for. (J. B. McMaster) Lippinc. **49**: 758.
— Wealth and Business Relations of. (C. S. Gleed) Forum, **14**: 631.
West African Story, A. Chamb. J. **73**: 125.
West Drayton, England. (J. P. Brodhurst) M. of Art, **10**: 73.
West Florida; a Short-lived American State. (H. E. Chambers) M. Am. Hist. 27: 24.
West Indian Commissioners, Work of. (A. W. Renton) Jurid. R. **2**: 155–357.
West Indian Slave Insurrection; a story. (G. W. Cable) Scrib. M. **12**: 709.
West Indian Soldier and the Sofa Expedition. Blackw. **155**: 699.
West Indies, The, and the Spanish Main, Rodway's. Macmil. **74**: 70. — Sat. R. **81**: 558.
— as a Winter Resort. (H. F. Abell) Westm. **137**: 277.
— Aspects of Nature in. (W. K. Brooks) Scrib. M. **14**: 101.
— British Troops from. (C. Pearson) Un. Serv. M. **9**: 150.
— Dissatisfaction in. (C. B. Heygate) National, **19**: 141.
— Expedition to, 1655. (J. W. Fortescue) Macmil. **69**: 184. Same art. Ecl. M. **122**: 252. Same art. Liv. Age, **200**: 539.
— Fauna of, in South Florida. (T. D. A. Cockerell) Nature, **46**: 458.
— in 1892. (Lord Brassey) Fortn. **59**: 633.
— Merchant's Voyages to, in 1805. (P. A. Grotjan) Scrib. M. **15**: 205–505.
— Patchwork in Black and White. (G. Blake) National, **19**: 73. Same art. Liv. Age, **193**: 422.
— Rebellion in, 1795–96. (J. W. Fortescue) Macmil. **70**: 456.
— Reminiscences of. (J. M. Moody) Canad. M. **1**: 560.
West Jersey, Colony of, State of, 1681. Pennsyl. M. **18**: 158.
West Paterson, N. J., Occurrence of Thaumasite at. (S. L. Penfield and J. H. Pratt) Am. J. Sci. **151**: 229.
West Point. (A. T. Sibbald) Un. Serv. M. **9**: 366.
— Can it be made more useful? (J. Gibbon) No. Am. **160**: 668.
— Educational Methods at. (P. S. Michie) Educa. R. **4**: 350.
— How to make it more useful. (F. A. Mitchell) No. Am. **159**: 61.
West-Saxons, Northern Settlements of. (J. Beddoe) Anthrop. J. **25**: 16.
West Springfield, Mass., Parish Records of. (E. N. Bagg) New Eng. M. n. s. **11**: 441.
West Sussex Superstitions. (C. Latham) Folk-Lore Rec. **1**: 7.
West Virginia and the Civil War. (E. Parker-Scammon) Cath. World, **57**: 505.
Westbrook, Col. T., and others, Letters of, 1724. N. E. Reg. vols. **46–49**.
Westbury, Lord, Wit and Wisdom of. (W. B. Duffield) Cornh. **74**: 517.
Westcar Papyrus, The. (J. H. Cooke) Bib. World, **4**: 49.
Westchester Creek, Chronicles of. (John Baynes) Univ. R. **8**: 90, 271.
Westcott, B. F. Gospel of Life. Church Q. **36**: 310.
Westerly, R. I. Religious Study of a Baptist Town. (W. B. Hale) Forum, **18**: 694.
Western Brook, A. (C. B. Going) Outing, **28**: 390.
Western Daisy Miller. (C. M. Girardeau) Lippinc. **54**: 814.
Western Dinner Party. All the Year, **72**: 319.
Western Landscapes. (H. Garland) Atlan. **72**: 805.
Western Life, Provincial Peculiarities of. (E. W. Howe) Forum, **14**: 91.
Western Mystery, A; a story. Belgra. **78**: 158.
Western Nations and Eastern Markets. (H. S. Hallett) 19th Cent. **35**: 379.

Western Posts and the British Debts. (A. C. McLaughlin) Yale R. **4**: 58.
Western Reserve. (R. Shackleton) New Eng. M. n. s. **14**: 323.
Western Reserve University. (E. O. Stevens) New Eng. M. n. s. **14**: 163. — (E. O. Stevens) Educa. **14**: 282.
Western State-making in the Revolutionary Era. (F. J. Turner) Am. Hist. R. **1**: 70, 251.
Western Traffic Association, The. (F. A. Walker) Forum, **13**: 743.
Westminster and its Abbey. Lond. Q. **86**: 18.
— and St. James's. Ed. R. **183**: 449.
— Besant's. Sat. R. **80**: 583.
— Old. (M. L. Sinclair) Gent. M. n. s. **52**: 343.
— St. Margaret's Church; The Parish Church of the House of Commons. (M. L. Sinclair) Gent. M. n. s. **51**: 386.
— Some Curiosities of. (M. L. Sinclair) Gent. M. n. s. **52**: 608.
Westminster Abbey. (H. B. Fuller) Cent. **23**: 700. — (John Telford) Meth. R. **56**: 758.
— About. (F. W. Farrar) Univ. R. **8**: 33.
— Actors and Actresses in. Cornh. **67**: 373. Same art. Liv. Age, **197**: 756.
— and its Last Abbot. (F. G. Lee) Univ. R. **7**: 350.
— and its Monuments. (H. P. B. Downing) M. of Art, **17**: 300.
— Bradley's. (W. J. Loftie) M. of Art, **19**: 247.
— Chapter House at. Walford's Antiq. **1**: 17.
— Epitaphs in. (F. W. Farrar) M. Chr. Lit. **5**: 306.
— From the Organ Loft in. (J. F. Bridge) Good Words, **37**: 22.
— Future of. (F. W. Farrar) No. Am. **154**: 705.
— Jerusalem Chamber. (E. D. Morris) Presb. & Ref. R. **7**: 595.
— Library of. (A. C. Bickley) Bookworm, **1**: 305.
— Rambles in the Precincts. Good Words, **34**: 535.
— The Statuary in. (F. W. Farrar) Good Words, **34**: 104. Same art. Ecl. M. **120**: 640.
— Sunday Morning in. (K. M. Warren) Sund. M. **25**: 793.
Westminster Abbey, the Valhalla of England's Poets. (J. Conway) Cath. World, **59**: 835.
— Wax Effigies in. (A. G. Bradley) Eng. Illust. **11**: 61.
Westminster Confession, Proposed Revision of. (C. A. Briggs) And. R. **18**: 124.
Westminster Palace. (R. G. Kingsley) Art J. **45**: 33.
Westminster Play, At the. (G. H. Dixon) Theatre, **35**: 337.
Westminster Review, John Stuart Mill and. (C. M. D. Towers) Atlan. **69**: 57.
Westmoreland, Priscilla, Countess of. Ed. R. **179**: 382.
Westmoreland, Mountaineering in. (J. F. Fraser) Eng. Illust. **13**: 107.
Weston, Thomas, and his Family. (C. Johnston) N. E. Reg. **50**: 201.
Westward; a poem. (J. Kavanagh) Argosy, **57**: 414.
Westwood, John O. (G. H. Carpenter) Nat. Sci. **2**: 150. — (J. S. Cotton) Acad. **43**: 15.
Wet Day; a poem. (Isa J. Postgate) Gent. M. n. s. **57**: 96.
Wey Hill Fair. Spec. **77**: 548.
Weyman, Stanley J., with portrait. Bk. Buyer, **11**: 109. — With portrait. Bk. News, **12**: 459. — (R. H. Sherard) Idler, **7**: 671. — (R. E. Prothero) 19th Cent. **35**: 244. — Lit. W. (Bost.) **25**: 254. — Critic, **24**: 360.
Weyman, Stanley J. From the Memoirs of a Minister of France. Sat. R. **80**: 501.
— Novels of. (G. Richards) Acad. **46**: 371.
Weymouth, Mass. Corrections and Additions in Savage's Genealogical Dictionary. (J. W. Porter) N. E. Reg. **46**: 185.
Whale, Sperm, and its Food. (J. Y. Buchanan) Nature, **53**: 223. — (F. T. Bullon) Nature, **54**: 102.
Whale Fishery in Arctic Ocean. (A. Conan Doyle) Idler, **1**: 625. Same art. McClure, **2**: 391.
Whaleman's Log, Stray Leaves from a. (J. T. Brown) Cent. **23**: 507.
Whaler Pluck; a poem. (S. L. Johnson) Cosmopol. **20**: 508.
Whales. Chamb. J. **70**: 542.
— and Whaling. Sat. R. **80**: 865.
— Toothed, and their Ancestry. (R. Lydekker) Knowl. **16**: 161.
Whaling in the Antarctic. All the Year, **75**: 296.
Whaling-ground, A Day on the Solander. Chamb. J. **71**: 186.
Whaling Industry. (H. L. Aldrich) Engin. M. **8**: 234.
Whalley, Jane. Ezekiel Rogers, Roger Williams and. N. E. Reg. **50**: 65.
Whalley Abbey, Inventory of Goods. Reliquary, **33**: 34.
Wharfedale, Sketches in; a story. Temp. Bar, **95**: 517.
Wharton, Anne Hollingsworth, with portrait. Bk. News, **14**: 414. — (H. S. Morris) Writer, **9**: 40.
Wharton, Edward Ross. (J. S. Cotton) Acad. **49**: 488.
Wharton, Henry Thornton. (J. S. Cotton) Acad. **48**: 185.
Wharton, Philip, Duke, Robinson's. Sat. R. **82**: 569.
What awoke Hans Zeibenstroother. (C. B. Todd) New Eng. M. n. s. **13**: 92.
What the Angels think; a poem. (W. J. Lampton) Cosmopol. **20**: 664.
What became of Dennis Martin? (J. A. Riis) Cent. **30**: 913.
What befell the Slave-seekers; a story. (James Deans) J. Am. Folk-Lore, **1**: 123.
What the Flood brought down. (P. E. Quinn) Idler, **5**: 302.
What followed a Knock. (H. C. Davidson) Idler, **1**: 447.
What it feels like to fight a Duel. (C. J. Cutliffe Hyne) Chamb. J. **73**: 221.
What the Madre would not have; a story. (R. C. V. Meyers) Harper, **91**: 18.
What a Naughty Boy did; a story. (M. Douglas) Argosy, **54**: 258.
What Necessity knows; a story. (L. Dougall) Leis. Hour, **42**: 1–795.
What she could; a story. (J. M. Watson) McClure, **4**: 537.
What will Mrs. Grundy say? All the Year, **74**: 209.
Wheat: British Production under Free Trade. Social Econ. **8**: 201.
— Culture of, in Ohio, Forty Years of. (C. E. Thorne) Science, **19**: 48.
— Price of. (A. D. Noyes) Nation, **63**: 378.
— — and Food Supply. (T. B. Veblen) J. Pol. Econ. **1**: 365.
— — since 1867. (T. B. Veblen) J. Pol. Econ. **1**: 68.
— Prices and Supply of. (R. F. Crawford) J. Statis. Soc. **58**: 75.
— Production and Consumption of, in England. (R. H. Wallace) Chamb. J. **72**: 419.

Wheat, Production of, in Canada. (S. C. D. Roper) Canad. M. 3: 468.
— Situation in, 1894. (W. M. Grosvenor) Bank. M. (N. Y.) 50: 26.
Wheat Crops of the World. (A. C. Stevens) Bank. M. (N. Y.) 50: 782.
Wheat Farming, Future. (W. Aldrich) Soc. Econ. 6: 224.
— No-profit Line in. Soc. Econ. 8: 222.
Wheat-growing, Science in. (P. P. Dehérain) Pop. Sci. Mo. 50: 101.
Wheatley, Leonard Abercrombie. Acad. 47: 544. — Ath. '95, 1: 838.
Wheatley, Phillis. (P. M. Cole) Chaut. 18: 599.
Wheel of the Lough Run; a story. Cornh. 68: 483.
Wheel of Love, The. (A. Hope) Scrib. M. 18: 149, 374.
Wheel of Time; a story. (H. James) Cosmopol. 14: 215, 348.
Wheel of Time; a story. (F. Guertin) Outing, 26: 347.
Wheels within Wheels; a story. All the Year, 76: 181.
When Angry, count a Hundred. (E. Cavazza) Cent. 22: 597.
When the Century came in; a story. (Mrs. B. Harrison) Scrib. M. 12: 170.
When the Century was Young; a story. Argosy, 54: 155. Same art. Liv. Age, 195: 181.
When the Gorse is in Flower; a story. (A. E. Holdsworth) Eng. Illust. 16: 219.
When Hester came. (B. N. Taylor) Lippinc. 52: 739.
When the Kitchen is Dark. (H. Stewart) Good Words, 36: 93.
When Leaves were Green; a novel. (S. Hodges) Argosy, 59: 1-513. 60: 1-641.
When Memory is no more; a poem. (W. Toynbee) Gent. M. n. s. 54: 102.
When she was Thirty; a story. (L. C. Moulton) McClure, 2: 141.
When Time has slumbered, (J. Ralph) Harper, 89: 613.
When we two parted. (M. Bradford-Whiting) Gent. M. n. s. 51: 277. Same art. Ecl. M. 123: 705.
When the World was Young; a poem. (E. J. Poynter) M. of Art, 16: 84.
When the Worst comes to the Worst. (W. R. Nicoll) Sund. M. 25: 505, 627.
Where the Clues met. (H. S. Edwards) Lippinc. 56: 802.
Where Fancy was bred; a story. (O. Wister) Harper, 92: 574.
Where had John been? a story. (H. H. Gardener) Harper, 93: 575.
Where he belongs. (E. E. Hale) Lend a H. 15: 113.
Where Ignorance is Bliss; a story. (R. Barr) McClure, 4: 455.
Where the Plane-trees grow; a story. (K. Watson) Argosy, 56: 205.
Where Thame windeth; a poem. (K. Strange) Canad. M. 4: 245.
Where the Treasure is; a story. Chamb. J. 73: 61.
Where were the Boys? a story. (J. Habberton) Outing, 19: 339.
Which is it? a tale. (E. J. Toker) Canad. M. 1: 73.
Which Miss Charteris? a story. (C. G. Rogers) Outing, 21: 347.
Which was the Murderer? a story. (R. Barr) Eng. Illust. 11: 269.
Which was the Princess? (M. Moffat) Nat'l M. (Bost.) 5: 145.
Which was the Thief? a story. (E. L. Keyes) Un. Serv. (Phila.) 13: 440.
Whiff of Hades; a story. (L. Creswicke) Belgra. 80: 176.
Whigs, End of the. (B. C. F. Costelloe) Time, 14: 257.
— Future of the. (W. E. Hicks) Time, 14: 385.
— of Colonial New York. (C. H. Levermore) Am. Hist. R. 1: 238.
— Passing of the. (N. Brooks) Scrib. M. 17: 199.
While Joanna was away; a story. (H. Erroll) Temp. Bar, 102: 341. Same art. Liv. Age, 202: 233.
Whim and a Chance. (W. T. Nichols) Lippinc. 57: 291.
Whipping of Uncle Henry. (W. N. Harben) Lippinc. 58: 828.
Whipping-post, The, and the Pillory. (F. Watt) New R. 14: 687.
— in Delaware. (Priscilla Leonard) Outl. 53: 55.
Whipple, Edwin P., as Essayist. (T. W. Hunt) Bib. Sac. 50: 30.
Whip-poor-will as named in American Languages. (A. S. Gatschet) Am. Antiq. 18: 39.
Whip-poor-wills and Night Hawks. (R. W. Shufeldt) Pop. Sci. Mo. 44: 308.
Whirligig of Fortune. (T. R. Sullivan) Atlan. 77: 797.
Whirligig of Time, The. (G. A. Hibbard) Cent. 26: 737.
Whirligig of Time. (L. F. Austin and A. R. Ropes) Eng. Illust. 11: 499-979.
Whirlpool, Naruba, Through the. Chamb. J. 70: 49.
Whiskey, Kentucky. (W. E. Bradley) Southern M. 4: 615.
Whiskey Insurrection: New Jersey Cavalry in the United States Army, 1794. (E. J. Cleveland) N. E. Reg. 47: 27.
Whist. Blackw. 157: 64.
— and its Masters. (R. F. Foster) Mo. Illust. 13: 15-295.
— Duplicate. (G. Fletcher) New R. 11: 490.
— English, and English Whist Players. Temp. Bar, 97: 527. 98: 103. Same art. Liv. Age, 197: 515. 198: 217.
— How to play. (E. C. Howell) Bost. 3: 374, 455, 591.
— in America. (F. W. Crane) Cosmopol. 19: 196.
— What America has done for. (H. Jones) Scrib. M. 20: 540.
Whist-table, The. (Fred. H. Lewis) Time, 2: 55.
Whistler, James Abbott McNeil. McClure, 7: 374. — (C. W. Dempsey) M. of Art, 5: 358.
— Paintings of. (D. S. MacColl) Art J. 45: 88-134. — Sat. R. 73: 357.
— To-day. (W. Sickert) Fortn. 57: 543.
— Triumph of. (E. R. Pennell) Nation, 54: 280.
Whitaker, Joseph. Ath. '95, 1: 643.
Whitaker, J. Vernon. Ath. '95, 1: 87.
Whitby. (Hal Souther) Time, 8: 460.
White, Andrew Dickson, with portrait. (G. L. Burr) Pop. Sci. Mo. 48: 546.
White, Edward D., Appointment of, to Supreme Court. Pub. Opin. 16: 521.
White, Major-Gen. Sir G. (E. C. H. Price) Eng. Illust. 10: 251.
White, Gilbert, and Selborne. (H. P. Palmer) Temp. Bar, 109: 113. — (W. W. Fowler) Macmil. 68: 182. Same art. Liv. Age, 198: 674. — Spec. 70: 849.
White, Henry Kirke. (Alice Law) Westm. 142: 276.
White, Joshua. (H. L. Conard) Nat'l M. (N. Y. '91) 17: 560.

White, Stephen V. (F. A. Munsey) Munsey, **7**: 15.
White, William H. Acad. **50**: 315.
White Blot, A; the story of a picture. (H. Van Dyke) Scrib. M. **18**: 693.
White Company, The, and Sir John Hawkwood. Macmil. **73**: 232.
White Edith; a poem. (T. B. Aldrich) Scrib. M. **12**: 33.
White Foxglove; a poem. (T. E. Brown) New R. **13**: 454.
White Heron; a story. (M. G. McClelland) Lippinc. **50**: 3.
White Horse Hill. Spec. **76**: 629.
White House, In the. (Alice E. Lewis) Munsey, **15**: 643.
White Islander. (M. H. Catherwood) Cent. **24**: 222–729.
White Lady, The, of German Legend. (Emma H. Nason) Munsey, **9**: 178.
White Lilac; a story. All the Year, **73**: 212, 235.
White Mountains: Alone on Osceola. (W. M. Cole) New Eng. M. n. s. **12**: 758.
— Cycling in. (P. C. Stuart) Outing, **26**: 372.
— Forests of. Garden & F. **5**: 517.
— Map of. Around World, **1**: 151.
White Owl's Cry, The; a poem. (W. Packard) Outing, **27**: 219.
White Pawn, The; a story. (E. Hughes) Eng. Illust. **13**: 227.
White Plains, N. Y., in the Revolution. (Mrs. M. J. Lamb) M. Am. Hist. **28**: 241.
White Redoubt; a story. (E. Nesbit) Argosy, **60**: 92.
White Road, The. Macmil. **74**: 145. Same art. Liv. Age, **210**: 245.
White Sea Letters, 1893. (A. Trevor-Battye) Longm. **24**: 403, 469.
White Seal, The; a story. (R. Kipling) National, **21**: 845.
White Sister, A; a story. (M. S. Hancock) Belgra. **85**: 288.
White Spider, The. (H. S. Edwards) Cent. **31**: 130.
White Weaver, The. (G. Parker) Macmil. **66**: 462.
Whitefield, in the Middle Town of. (H. M. North) New Eng. M. n. s. **12**: 286–719. **13**: 95.
Whitehall. (W. J. Loftie) Portfo. no. 16.
— Palace. Chamb. J. **70**: 698.
Whither and why; a poem. (M. A. M. Marks) Argosy, **61**: 116.
Whither? a Study of Tendency. (D. A. Goodsell) Meth. R. **53**: 9.
Whiting, Rev. Samuel, Chaplain of Sir Nathaniel Bacon and Others. (C. H. Townshend) N. E. Reg. **50**: 465.
Whitlocke's Swedish Embassy. (E. Edwardes) Gent. M. n. s. **51**: 127. Same art. Liv. Age, **198**: 805.
Whitman, Walt. Acad. **41**: 325. Same art. Ecl. M. **118**: 690. — (W. Boughton) Arena, **6**: 471. — With portrait. (D. G. Watts) Arena, **5**: 228. — (T. Watts) Ath. '92, **1**: 436. Same art. Ecl. M. **118**: 690. — Atlan. **69**: 831, 851. — (C. D. Lanier) Chaut. **15**: 309. — (J. Burroughs) Critic, **20**: 198. — Critic, **20**: 215. — (H. Munroe) Critic, **20**: 231. — (C. Aldrich) Critic, **20**: 245. — Critic, **20**: 268. — (J. J. Halsey) Dial (Ch.) **12**: 317. — (P. W. Roose) Gent. M. n. s. **48**: 464. — (W. H. Garrison) Lippinc. **49**: 621. — Lit. W. (Bost.) **23**: 126. — (T. W. Higginson) Nation, **54**: 262. — (G. D. Black) New Eng. M. n. s. **6**: 710. — Sat. R. **73**: 378. — (W. Lewin) Acad. **44**: 185. — Temp. Bar, **99**: 252. — (J. Burroughs) Lippinc. **51**: 753. — (O. L. Triggs) Poet-Lore, **5**: 289. — (J. Burroughs) Chr. Un. **45**: 636. — (R. H. Titherington) Munsey, **14**: 138. — (N. P. Gilman) New World, **3**: 311. — (M. D. Conway) Open Court, **6**: 3199. — (G. Sarrazin) Univ. R. **6**: 247.
Whitman, Walt, and R. W. Emerson, Friendship of. (W. S. Kennedy) Poet-Lore, **7**: 71.
— and his Art. (J. Burroughs) Poet-Lore, **6**: 63.
— and Murger. (H. L. Traubel) Poet-Lore, **6**: 484.
— and Shelley. (I. H. Platt) Poet-Lore, **8**: 332.
— and Tennyson, Relations of, to Science. (J. Burroughs) Dial (Ch.) **14**: 168.
— Artistic Atheism of. (H. L. Traubel) Poet-Lore, **5**: 498.
— Aspects of. (H. McCulloch, jr.) Harv. Mo. **14**: 122.
— Boston Criticism of. (J. Burroughs) Poet-Lore, **4**: 392.
— Burroughs and others on. Poet-Lore, **6**: 95.
— Conversations with. (H. L. Traubel) Arena, **15**: 175.
— Democracy of. (W. B. Harte) New Eng. M. n. s. **6**: 721.
— Estimate of. Overland, n. s. **19**: 55.
— Greek Traits in. (E. C. Monck) Poet-Lore, **7**: 327.
— in Boston. (S. Baxter) New Eng. M. n. s. **6**: 714.
— in Europe. (R. I. Zubof) Writer, **6**: 65.
— in relation to Christianity. (E. C. Monck) Poet-Lore, **7**: 607.
— in War-time: Familiar Letters. Cent. **24**: 840.
— A Note on. (E. Gosse) New R. **10**: 447. Same art. Liv. Age, **201**: 495.
— The Poet of Democracy. (J. Burroughs) No. Am. **154**: 532.
— Religion of Poems of. (M. J. Savage) Arena, **10**: 433.
— Short Reading Course in. Poet-Lore, **6**: 644.
— Swinburne on. (R. Noel) Time, **17**: 653.
— Whitmaniana. (W. M. Payne) Dial (Ch.) **15**: 390.
Whitman College, Early Years of. (A. J. Anderson) Educa. **12**: 364.
Whitmore's Brook. (A. F. Rice) Outing, **26**: 128.
Whitney, William Collins. (R. R. Wilson) Mo. Illust. **11**: 612.
Whitney, William Dwight. (C. R. Lanman) Atlan. **75**: 398. — (T. D. Seymour) Am. J. Philol. **15**: 271. — (J. T. Hatfield) Dial (Ch.) **16**: 353. — Ath. '94, **1**: 805. — (C. R. Lanman) Nation, **58**: 442. — Pub. Opin. **17**: 252. — Critic, **24**: 410. — (A. H. Sayce) Acad. **45**: 499.
Whitsunday Fight; a story. (H. Drachmann) Poet-Lore, **7**: 405.
Whit-Tuesday at Old Eton. (J. W. Sherer) Gent. M. n. s. **50**: 476.
Whittier, John Greenleaf. (W. Lewin) Acad. **42**: 237. — Ath. '92, **2**: 354. — (G. E. Woodberry) Atlan. **70**: 642. — (J. V. Cheney) Chaut. **16**: 299. — Critic, **21**: 151–168, 182. — (O. W. Holmes) Critic, **21**: 221. — (T. C. Hadden) Gent. M. n. s. **49**: 408. Same art. Liv. Age, **195**: 469. — Lit. W. (Bost.) **23**: 332. — (T. W. Higginson) Nation, **55**: 199. — (F. C. Sparhawk) New Eng. M. n. s. **7**: 293. — Pub. Opin. **13**: 584. — (M. Harrison) Sund. M. **21**: 766. — (B. O. Flower) Arena, **15**: 965. — With portrait. Bk. News, **5**: 8. — (A. Fields) Harper, **86**: 338. — Same art. Critic, **22**: 47. — (E. S. Phelps) Cent. **23**: 363. — (F. C. Iglehart) Meth. R. **53**: 43. — (J. O. Murray) Presb. & Ref. R. **4**: 450. — (Mary Negreponte) Westm. **139**: 7. Same art. Ecl. M. **120**: 377. — (I. F. Mayo) Leis. Hour, **42**: 164. — Lond. Q. **79**: 224. — (H. V. Clarke) Munsey, **7**: 279. — Pub. Opin. **18**: 114.
— and Curtis. R. of Rs. (N. Y.) **6**: 280.
— and Slavery. (S. Willard) Dial (Ch.) **13**: 175.
— and Tennyson, with portraits. (W. J. Fowler) Arena, **7**: 1.
— as I knew him. (M. B. Claflin) Arena, **15**: 26.
— **Autobiographical Sketch.** Our Day, **10**: 724.

Whittier, J. G. Ballad of the Countess. New Eng. M. n. s. 7: 809.
— Bibliography of Original Editions of. Bk. Buyer, 12: 216–499.
— Birthplace of, Haverhill, Mass. (Miss J. G. Tyler) M. Am. Hist. 29: 50.
— Desultoria on. (C. F. Bates) Cosmopol. 16: 303.
— Education of. (E. D. Mead) Bk. News, 2: 99.
— First Printed Poems of. New Eng. M. n. s. 7: 506.
— Funeral of. (C. H. Dall) New Eng. M. n. s. 7: 652.
— His Faith and Character. (C. F. Bates) McClure, 2: 125.
— Homes of. (W. S. Kennedy) New Eng. M. n. s. 7: 275.
— Hussey Ancestry of. (A. H. Quint) N. E. Reg. 50: 295.
— Life and Poetry. Atlan. 74: 693.
— The Man. (B. O. Flower) Arena, 16: 406.
— A Modern Apostle of Lofty Spirituality. (B. O. Flower) Arena, 16: 543.
— Personal Recollections of. (C. F. Grimke) New Eng. M. n. s. 8: 468.
— Pickard's Life of. (J. W. Chadwick) Nation, 59: 410.
— Poem on: Poet's Tributes to a Poet. Dial (Ch.) 13: 176.
— Portraits of. McClure, 5: 513.
— Prophet of Freedom. (B. O. Flower) Arena, 16: 106.
— Religion of. (W. H. Savage) Arena, 10: 153.
— Religious Beliefs of. (C. M. Cobern) Meth. R. 55: 245.
— Reminiscences of. Bookman, 1: 230, 309. — (E. S. Phelps) McClure, 7: 114.
— Snow-Bound. Poet-Lore, 6: 102.
— Some Personal Reminiscences of. (C. C. Hussey) Arena, 15: 376.
— Spiritual Career of. (J. D. Chadwick) New World, 2: 88.
Whittier Reform School. Pub. Opin. 17: 338.
Whittington, Richard, Glimpses of. Time, 15: 665.
Who broke up de Meet'n'? a story. (W. A. Dromgoole) Arena, 8: 255.
Who did sin, this Man or his Parents? a tale. Canad. M. 7: 571.
Who is my Mother? Matthew xii. 46–50. (J. V. Tracy) Am. Cath. Q. 19: 712.
Who rang the Bell? a story. Argosy, 53: 169. Same art. Liv. Age, 193: 183.
Who was he? a story. (C. A. Fraser) Canad. M. 3: 480.
Who was Lost and is Found. (M. O. W. Oliphant) Blackw. 155: 745 — 156: 1–624.
Whortleberry Gathering in West England. Sat. R. 80: 139.
Why I enlisted; a reminiscence. (W. F. Mitchell) Chamb. J. 73: 205.
Why should we care? a poem. (J. V. Cheney) Harper, 91: 95.
Whymper, E., with portrait. Bk. Buyer, 9: 97.
Wickford, R. I., St. Paul's Episcopal Church. (A. M. Earle) New Eng. M. n. s. 7: 577.
Wiclif, John. Beginnings of his Activity in Ecclesiastical Politics. (J. Loserth) Eng. Hist. R. 11: 319.
— Birth and Parentage of. (L. Sergeant) Ath. '92, 1: 344, 405. — (B. Peacock) Ath. '92, 1: 436. — (F. D. Matthew) Ath. '92, 1: 469. — Ath. '92, 1: 503.
— on English and Roman Law. (F. W. Maitland) Law Q. 12: 76.
— Portraits of. (L. Sergeant) Ath. '92, 2: 393.
— Sergeant's Life of. Spec. 70: 390.
Wiclif Society, History and Work of. (R. Buddensieg) Crit. R. 3: 280. 4: 71.
Wicliffites, English and Bohemian, Intercourse between, in early 15th Century. (R. L. Poole) Eng. Hist. R. 7: 306.
Widdin Fortress, Bulgaria, Herbert on. Sat. R. 82: 449.
Widgery, Wm. Henry. Ath. '94, 2: 122.
Widow, "Bewitched" and "Grass." (F. Hall) Nation, 56: 215. — (G. Hempl) Nation, 56: 292.
Widow's Tale; a story. (Mrs. Oliphant) Cornh. 68: 92–318.
Widows. (F. C. Baylor) Lippinc. 57: 412.
— in India, Home for. Lend a H. 9: 269.
Wiener, Jacques, Léopold, and Charles. (F. Alvin) M. of Art, 15: 55.
Wiertz, Antoine Joseph. (E. B. Bax) M. of Art, 3: 99.
Wiertz Museum, Brussels. (E. B. Bax) M. of Art, 3: 142.
Wife, Contribution of, to Family Income. (A. H. Bigg) Econ. J. 4: 51.
Wife, The; a poem. (T. Woolner) M. of Art, 13: 302.
Wife manufactured to Order; a story. (A. W. Fuller) Arena, 13: 305.
Wig-wearing. (C. E. Gildersome-Dickenson) Good Words, 35: 621.
Wiggin, Kate Douglas, with portrait. Bk. Buyer, 8: 285.
Wiggins, Carleton. (G. P. Lathrop) Mo. Illust. 4: 305.
Wigglesworth, Michael. (M. W. Leighton) Am. Hist. Reg. 3: 545.
Wight, Isle of. Ed. R. 176: 234. — (C. J. Cornish) Portfo. 19: no. 7.
— Rambles in. (M. B. Huish) Art J. 44: 225–312.
Wigmore, Herefordshire, Eng.; an old village. Gent. M. n. s. 57: 334.
Wigwam, The. (H. T. Stanton) So. M. 2: 18.
Wilberforce, Bp. Samuel. (Lord Cowper) 19th Cent. 35: 938. — Sat. R. 73: 308.
Wilburton, Manor of, History of. (F. W. Maitland) Eng. Hist. R. 9: 417.
Wilcox, Ella Wheeler, with portrait. Bk. News, 10: 392.
Wild, Edward Augustus, Sketch of. (Bradford Kingman) N. E. Reg. 49: 405.
Wild, James William. (R. S. Poole) Acad. 42: 489. — Art J. 45: 120.
Wild Animals, Capture and Training of. (R. Blathwayt) McClure, 1: 26–219.
— in Captivity. (C. Moffett) McClure, 2: 544. 3: 71.
Wild Beasts as they live. (C. J. Mellis) Scrib. M. 18: 705.
Wild Boy of Pindus. Spec. 68: 50.
Wild Cat, Hunting the, in Southern California. (H. E. Bandini) Overland, n. s. 19: 281.
— in Scotland, Anecdotes of. (N. Lochaber) Good Words, 33: 237
Wild-cats at the London Zoo. Spec. 72: 465.
Wild Drive in Ireland; a story. Temp. Bar, 103: 535. Same art. Liv. Age, 204: 79.
Wild-fowl in Sanctuary. Spec. 68: 397.
— on Holkham Lake. Liv. Age, 208: 381.
Wild-fowling, Art of, Chapman's. Sat. R. 81: 355.
Wild Gilroys, The; a story. (R. M. Kettle) Argosy, 54: 199.
Wild Irish Girl, A; a story. All the Year, 70: 6, 37.
Wild Life, Glimpses of. (J. Burroughs) Cent. 22: 560.
Wild, Unutterable Desire; a poem. (W. T. James) Canad. M. 8: 78.
Wilde, Lady. Ath. '96, 1: 220.
Wilde, Oscar, The Disgraee of. Pub. Opin. 18: 374.
— Ideal Husband. Sat. R. 79: 44.

Wilde, Oscar. Importance of Being in Earnest. Sat. R. 79: 249.
— Lady Windermere's Fan. Gent. M. n. s. 48: 426. — Spec. 69: 767. — Theatre, 28: 200.
— New Views of. (P. H. W. Almy) Theatre, 32: 119.
— Salomé. Sat. R. 74: 18.
Wildebeest Hunt in Africa. Sat. R. 80: 865.
Wildenbruch, Ernst von. Poet-Lore, 3: 481.
Wilderness, Battle of. (J. R. Turner) So. Hist. Pap. 20: 68.
— Cavalry Surgeon's Experiences. (A. P. Clarke) Un. Serv. (Phila.) 11: 138.
Wilderness Vengeance; a story. All the Year, 70: 588.
Wiles, Irving R., with portrait. Bk. Buyer, 11: 387.
Wilkes, John. Westm. 140: 291.
Wilkie, Sir David. (A. Quarry) Argosy, 58: 112. — (G. D. Leslie) Art J. 48: 183.
Wilkins, Mary E., with portrait. Bk. Buyer, 8: 53. — With portrait. Bk. News, 11: 227. — Critic, 20: 13.
— as Prize Winner. Critic, 26: 484.
— Giles Corey, Yeoman. Critic, 22: 256.
— Madelon. Sat. R. 82: 16.
Wilkinson, Jemima. Lend a H. 10: 126.
Wilks, Mark. Acad. 45: 476.
Will, The. (C. K. Heath) New Sci. R. 2: 263.
— and Education. (G. M. Steele) Educa. 16: 353.
— and its Training. (M. B. Peeke) Arena, 14: 487
— and Reason. (B. Bosanquet) Monist, 2: 18.
— Attention and. (A. F. Shand) Mind, 68: 450.
— Baldwin on. (R. B. Johnson) Science, 19: 62.
— Diseases of. (T. Ribot) Open Court, 8: 4031–4055.
— Dynamic Theory of. (C. De Garmo) Educa. 16: 337.
— Free, Methodist Doctrine of. (T. M. Griffith) Meth. R. 54: 556.
— Freedom of. (E. D. Roe, jr.) Bib. Sac. 51: 641. — (F. Thilly) Philos. R. 3: 385.
— — and Inhibition. (J. H. Hyslop) Philos. R. 1: 369.
— General, Reality of. (B. Bosanquet) Int. J. Ethics, 4: 308.
— Ossification of. Spec. 68: 11. Same art. Liv. Age, 192: 567.
— Pathology of. (W. Seton) Cath. World, 59: 60.
— Psychology of, Fouillée on. (W. James) Philos. R. 2: 716.
Will to believe, The. (W. James) New World, 5: 327.
Will, Shall and. (W. S. Liscomb) Educa. 12: 413.
Will you walk out with me, Miss? All the Year, 75: 158.
Willard, Archibald M. (J. F. Ryder) New Eng. M. n. s. 13: 483.
Willard, Edward S. (A. Stoddart) Lippinc. 51: 768. — Idler, 9: 335.
— A Day with. (L. A. Lathrop) Theatre, 32: 59.
Willard, Emma. (Elizabeth Cady Stanton) Westm. 140: 538.
Willard, Frances E., with portrait. (W. T. Stead) R. of Rs. (N. Y.) 6: 427. — (Lady H. Somerset) Outl. 53: 1184.
— Great Britain's Welcome to. (Lady H. Somerset) Our Day, 11: 249.
— an Interview and Life Sketch, with portrait. (G. T. B. Davis) Our Day, 16: 247.
— Meeting in Honor of, in London, Jan. 1893: Noise and Nonsense. Spec. 70: 76.
— Portraits of. McClure, 1: 390.
Willemite, Contributions to the Crystallization of. (S. L. Penfield) Am. J. Sci. 147: 305.
Willette, Adolphe. (B. Karageorgevitch) M. of Art, 19: 109.
William, St., of Norwich. (A. Jessopp) 19th Cent. 33: 749. Same art. Liv. Age, 198: 195.
William the Conqueror, Are we all Descendants of? (G. Clarke) No. Am. 160: 117.
— Flight from Valognes. Macmil. 71: 439.
— Home of. Art J. 47: supp. 17.
William III., of England. Westm. 141: 601.
William II., Emperor of Germany. Contemp. 61: 457. Same art. Ecl. M. 118: 673. Same art. Liv. Age, 193: 515.
— and Bismarck. Contemp. 62: 153. Same art. Ecl. M. 119: 420. — Spec. 69: 7.
— and Constitutional Liberty. (P. Bigelow) Cosmopol. 20: 17.
— and German Politics. (F. C. Howe) Am. J. Pol. 2: 1.
— and his Family. (H. W. Fischer) Munsey, 12: 45.
— and Religious Education. Spec. 68: 423.
— as a Sportsman. (H. W. Fischer) Munsey, 13: 637.
— Free-trade Tendency of. (P. Bigelow) Forum, 13: 212.
— Lowe's. Sat. R. 82: 92.
— on Dancing. Spec. 68: 51.
— on Providence. Spec. 68: 288.
— Portraits of. McClure, 1: 310.
— Stud-farm and Hunting Forest of. (P. Bigelow) Harper, 88: 742.
— War of, with Disbelief. Liv. Age, 193: 60.
William the Marshal, History of. (P. Toynbee) Acad. 47: 289.
William the Silent and his Times. (A. A. Pfanstiehl) Ref. Q. 42: 102, 365.
— Putnam's Life of. (C. H. Cooper) Dial (Ch.) 19: 330. — (R. S. Long) Acad. 48: 287.
William and Margaret, Ballad of. (W. L. Phelps) Harv. Mo. 13: 191.
Williams, Daniel, Library of. (A. C. Bickley) Bookworm, 1: 141.
Williams, Eleazar. (J. D. Butler) Nation, 58: 417, (E. H. Williams, jr.) 446.
See Louis XVII.
Williams, Ephraim, Some Old Letters of. Scrib. M. 17: 247.
Williams, Sir George, Founder of Y. M. C. A. (Lord Kinnaird) Outl. 54: 774.
Williams, George Fred. (B. O. Flower) Arena, 16: 872.
Williams, George Huntington. Nat. Sci. 5: 234.
Williams, Haynes. (W. W. Fenn) M. of Art, 4: 485.
Williams, Isaac, and the Oxford Movement. Church Q. 34: 332.
Williams, J. T., Collection of Pictures. (C. de Kay) M. of Art, 9: 386.
Williams, Jesse Lynch, with portrait. Bk. Buyer, 12: 437.
Williams, Prof. M. Monier. (E. A. Reed) Book R. 1: 77.
Williams, Roger. (A. H. Newman) M. Chr. Lit. 5: 271.
— Early Statements relative to the Early Life of. (J. W. Dean) N. E. Reg. 50: 169.
— Ezekiel Rogers, Jane Whalley and. N. E. Reg. 50: 65.
— Strauss's. (W. Walker) Nation, 59: 35.
Williams, Rev. Samuel. (M. A. Green) New Eng. M. n. s. 12: 495.
Williams, Samuel Wells. Bk. Buyer, 1: 29.
Williams, Wm. Mattieu. Knowl. 16: 12. — With portrait. Pop. Sci. Mo. 45: 548.
Williams College. (L. W. Spring) New Eng. M. n. s. 9: 161. — (Clifton Johnson) Outl. 48: 715.

Williams Family Record. (H. W. Lloyd) Pennsyl. M. 18: 239.
Williamsburg, Va., Battle of. (R. L. Maury) So. Hist. Pap. 22: 106.
Williamson, W. C. (L. F. Ward) Science, n. s. 2: 145. — Pop. Sci. Mo. 47: 576. — Nat. Sci. 7: 141. — (H. Solms-Laubach) Nature, 52: 441.
Willie; a story. (W. L. Alden) Idler, 5: 89.
Willix, Balthazar. (F. W. Hackett) N. E. Reg. 50: 46.
Willoughby Wedding, The; a story, (C. M. Priest) Belgra. 91: 75.
Willow at Grand Pré; a poem. (T. H. Rand) Canad. M. 2: 197.
Willow, Diamond, in South Dakota. (T. H. Williams) Garden & F. 8: 493.
Willow-farming. Chamb. J. 71: 277.
Willows. (G. Allen) Longm. 29: 33.
— Notes on some Arborescent, of North America. (M. S. Bebb) Garden & F. 8: 363-482.
— Polygamous Poplars and. (J. G. Jack) Garden & F. 7: 163.
Will's Coffee-house. Ecl. M. 120: 83.
Wills, C. J. Behind an Eastern Veil. Sat. R. 79: 50.
Wills, Mrs. Janet. Ath. '92, 2: 590.
Wills, William G. (Henriette Corkran) Temp. Bar, 108: 281.
Wills. Temp. Bar, 105: 410. Same art. Liv. Age, 206: 365.
— and Inheritance, Laws regarding. (Lady Cook) Westm. 143: 187.
— Curious. Green Bag, 7: 119.
— Eccentric. Green Bag, 5: 188.
— Ethics of. (T. C. Fry) Econ. R. 3: 190.
— Jewish Ethical. (I. Abrahams) Jew. Q. 3: 436.
— Last, and Testaments. Cornh. 67: 505. Same art. Ecl. M. 120: 811.
— Litigation arising from. (J. F. Hume) Am. J. Pol. 4: 278.
— Litigation over, How to check. (R. S. Ransom) No. Am. 156: 661.
— Making of, Madness and. Spec. 69: 879.
— of some Rich and Famous People. (H. L. Biddle) Chaut. 18: 456.
— Oral. (J. Schouler) Law Q. 2: 444.
— Probate Forms of Massachusetts. N. E. Reg. 48: 296.
— Right of Disposal by Will. (J. Cooper) Ref. Q. 41: 16.
— Suffolk County, Mass. (W. K. Watkins) N. E. Reg. 48: 323, 457.
Wilmington and the Long Man. (G. Clinch) Eng. Illust. 15: 510.
Wilson, Alexander, the Great Naturalist. (H. Coyle) Chaut. 18: 180.
Wilson, Charles H.; the Man and the Town. (F. Dolman) Eng. Illust. 13: 351.
Wilson, Sir Daniel. (Mrs. C. H. Dall) Am. J. Soc. Sci. 30: xxiii. — (H. Hale) Critic, 21: 94. — Acad. 42: 130, 151. — With portrait. (H. Hale) Pop. Sci. Mo. 44: 256.
Wilson, Francis, A Talk with. Music, 8: 178.
Wilson, James. Works. (J. O. Pierce) Dial (Ch.) 20: 236.
Wilson, John; "Crusty Christopher." (H. A. Beers) Cent. 23: 361.
— Sporting Articles by. Sat. R. 75: 511.
Wilson, John, Scotch Vocalist, Grave of. (J. G. Wilson) Am. Hist. Reg. 1: 143.
Wilson, Richard. (E. Ollier) M. of Art, 5: 353.
Wilson, T. W., the artist. (W. Lawler) Idler, 9: 123.
Wilson, William L., as a Tariff-reform Leader. (H. L. Nelson) Forum, 18: 352.
Wilson Bill, Passage of. Pub. Opin. 16: 451, 616.
Wiltshire Evening; a poem. (W. S. Senior) New R. 12: 576.
Wilton House. (G. Winterwood) Good Words, 35: 448. — (M. P. Jackson) M. of Art, 3: 323, 369.
Wimbledon Camp, 20th Middlesex Rifle Volunteers at. (H. V. Barnett) M. of Art, 6: 389.
Wimborne Minster, The Library at. Bookworm, 2: 153.
Winchell, Alexander, with portrait. Pop. Sci. Mo. 41: 837.
Winchelsea and Rye, England. Art J. 47: 257.
Winchester Cathedral. (T. E. Champion) Canad. M. 6: 199. — (Canon Benham) Good Words, 34: 695.
Winchester College. (J. S. Cotton) Acad. 41: 317. — (L. Johnson) Acad. 45: 73.
— 1793 and 1893. (A. F. Leach) Contemp. 64: 74. — Quar. 177: 358.
— Kirby's Annals of. Spec. 68: 783.
Wind as a Factor in Geology. (G. P. Merrill) Engin. M. 2: 596.
— as a Motive Power in the United States. (F. Waldo) R. of Rs. (N. Y.) 12: 299.
— Internal Work of the. (S. P. Langley) Am. J. Sci. 147: 41.
— Relations of the Diurnal Rise and Fall of the Wind in the United States. (F. Waldo) Am. J. Sci. 150: 235.
— Velocities of, in the United States, Daily March of. (F. Waldo) Am. J. Sci. 149: 431.
Wind, The; a poem. (R. L. Stevenson) M. of Art, 7: 367.
Windigo, The. (M. H. Catherwood) Atlan. 73: 526.
Windmill, Modern Uses of. (R. H. Thurston) Eng. M. 4: 719.
Windmills and Meteorology. (P. J. de Ridder) Pop. Sci. Mo. 46: 522.
Window Gardening. (J. N. Gerard) Garden & F. 6: 157.
— Rose's Window and Parlor Gardening. Garden & F. 9: 9.
Window Lights and their Value. (J. L. Greenleaf) Pop. Sci. Mo. 44: 354.
Winds, Hot, of the Prairies. (C. S. Sargent) Garden & F. 8: 331.
Windscheid, Bernhard Josef Hubert, German Jurist. (M. Smith) Pol. Sci. Q. 10: 664. — (A. Rivier) Jurid. R. 5: 8.
Windsor Castle, Queen's Private Apartments at. Time, 1: 145.
— Royal Library. Bookworm, 7: 329.
— Treasures at. (E. M. Jessop) Idler, 7: 631, 755.
"Windsor Castle" The, a Famous Packet-ship. Chamb. J. 71: 522.
Windsor Forest, Hughes' History of. Spec. 68: 242.
Wine Cellars of Warsaw. Sat. R. 80: 341.
Wine-growing in California. (W. Roberts) Fortn. 59: 394.
Wines, California. (C. F. Oldham) J. Soc. Arts, 42: 195.
— at Chicago Exposition, 1893. (C. F. Oldham) J. Soc. Arts, 42: 112.
— — German Wine Building. (L. H. Bailey) Garden & F. 6: 329.
Wingate, J. Lawton. (J. L. Caw) Art J. 48: 73.
Wings of a Dove, The. Macmil. 73: 462.
Winifred Power's Candlestick. (L. Hardy) Sund. M. 24: 614.
Winnebago Customs and Beliefs. (Mrs. F. D. Bergen) J. Am. Folk-Lore, 9: 51.

Winnebago Folk-Lore. (J. O. Dorsey) J. Am. Folk-Lore, 2: 140.
Winnebago Phonetic Alphabet. (A. C. Fletcher) J. Am. Folk-Lore, 3: 299.
Winning of the Biscuit-shooter, The; a story. (O. Wister) Harper, 88: 52.
Winning a Christmas Bride. (A. C. Vance) Outing, 25: 269.
Winning of Paddon Manor; a story. Chamb. J. 70: 796, 813.
Winslow, Anna Green: a Boston Schoolgirl in 1771. (A. M. Earle) Atlan. 72: 218.
— Diary, ed. by A. M. Earle. Sat. R. 79: 15.
Winslow, William Copley, with portrait. (S. D. Peet) Am. Antiq. 15: 181.
Winslow Family, Letters of, 1783–97. (E. J. Carpenter) New Eng. M. n. s. 15: 150.
Winter, John Strange. *See* Stannard, Mrs. H. E. V.
Winter, Wm., with portrait. Bk. Buyer, 13: 389. — (F. E. Partington) Book R. 1: 176. 2: 266. — (P. Robinson) M. of Art, 5: 125.
Winter in the Country. (E. F. Brewtnall) M. of Art, 13: 163.
— in New England. (Clifton Johnson) Chr. Un. 47: 171.
— in the West of England. Sat. R. 79: 278–311.
— in a Wintry Wilderness. (F. Bolles) Atlan. 71: 92.
— a Poem. Argosy, 59: 160.
— Picturesque. (M. G. Watkins) Gent. M. n. s. 48: 481.
— A Walk in. (C. C. Abbott) Lippinc. 55: 255.
Winter's Tale, The; Performance by Saturday Morning Club, Boston. Bost. 2: 1.
Winter Assizes. Cornh. 69: 145.
Winter Climbers. (M. Barker) Garden & F. 5: 162.
Winter House-party. (C. C. Harrison) Cent. 29: 734.
Winter Pastimes, Canadian. (E. W. Sandys) Outing, 21: 183.
Winter Picnic, A. (Van Eps) Outing, 23: 273.
Winter-resorts, American. (A. M. Hamilton) Forum, 15: 52.
Winter Shifts of Animals. Blackw. 151: 446. Same art. Liv. Age, 193: 427.
Winter Shore, The. Chamb. J. 72: 641. Same art. Liv. Age, 200: 315.
Winter Sketches in Norway. All the Year, 71: 587, 605.
Winter Sunshine. (G. Boscawen) Blackw. 153: 219.
Winter Twilight in Provence; poem. (R. W. Gilder) Cent. 30: 136.
Winter Wind; a poem. (N. Boyce) Outing, 27: 312.
Winter's Day in Mid-forest. (F. Whishaw) Longm. 27: 586. Same art. Liv. Age, 209: 554. Same art. Ecl. M. 126: 671.
Winter's Tale, A. Chamb. J. 69: 494. Same art. Liv. Age, 195: 60.
Winter's Walk, A. Macmil. 75: 120.
Winters, Old-fashioned. (A. W. Jarvis) Good Words, 36: Xmas no. 6.
Winthrop, John, Farm of, Bedford, Mass. New Eng. M. n. s. 6: 325.
— his Defense of his Administration. (F. Allaben) Nat'l M. (N. Y. '91) 17: 251.
— Homestead of. (H. A. Hill) New Eng. M. n. s. 13: 727.
— An Injustice done to. M. Am. Hist. 29: 275.
Winthrop, Robert C. (W. Everett) Harv. Grad. M. 3: 293.
— Reminiscences of. Atlan. 75: 116.
Winthrop, Mass. (W. H. Gardner) Bost. 2: 571. — (A. W. Cobb) New Eng. M. n. s. 6: 645.
Wiradthuri Tribes, The Burbung of. (R. H. Mathews) Anthrop. J. 25: 295.
Wire-netting in Glass, Shuman's Process for Embedding. Am. Arch. 43: 127.
Wire-rod Rolling. (R. W. Hunt) Cassier, 6: 249.
Wire-rope Transportation. (W. Hewitt) Engin. M. 7: 18.
Wires, Electrical, Formulæ for. (E. R. Keller) J. Frankl. Inst. 140: 455.
Wirral, Submerged Forests of the, in Cheshire. (H. O. Forbes) Knowl. 19: 145.
Wisby, Sweden; the Eye of the Baltic. (Augusta Nash) Temp. Bar, 98: 215. Same art. Liv. Age, 198: 431.
Wisconsin, Library Association of. (L. E. Stearns) Lib. J. 21: 189.
— Library Legislation in. Lib. J. 21: 187.
— Library Movement in. Lib. J. 21: 183.
— State Historical Society of. Lib. J. 20: 204.
— — Collections of. M. Am. Hist. 28: 228.
— — Library of. (R. G. Thwaites) Lib. J. 21: 175.
— State Library. (J. R. Berryman) Lib. J. 21: 177.
— Summer School of Library Science. (K. L. Sharp) Lib. J. 21: 192.
— Township School Libraries in. (F. A. Hutchins) Lib. J. 21: 185.
Wisconsin Base-level, A. (C. R. Van Hise) Science, n. s. 4: 57.
Wisdom. (W. B. Yeats) New R. 13: 285.
Wisdom Tooth, The. (D. Christie Murray and H. Herman) Liv. Age, 188: 163.
Wise, Thomas J. Bookworm, 7: 193.
Wise Woman, The. Chamb. J. 71: 221.
Wisest Aunt telling the Saddest Tale; a story. (A. Lang) Eng. Illust. 16: 11.
Wish Fulfilled, A. (L. Hearn) Atlan. 75: 90.
Wissant: "Guizzante" of Dante. (H. A. Redpath) Acad. 41: 543.
Wistar Museum of Anatomy. Pennsyl. M. 18: 90.
Wistaria, Chinese. Garden & F. 6: 252.
Wister, Owen, with portrait. (N. H. Banks) Bookman, 2: 275. — (S. G. Fisher) Writer, 7: 130.
Wit and Humor. (D. Hack Tuke) Univ. R. 5: 282. — (A. Repplier) Atlan. 70: 801.
— — Irish. (R. A. King) Belgra. 77: 186. — (J. O'C. Power) Time, 22: 474.
— of Man, The. Macmil. 70: 204. Same art. Liv. Age, 202: 497.
— Old-fashioned. All the Year, 75: 463.
— A Professor of the Dry. (P. Fitzgerald) Gent. M. n. s. 48: 600.
Witch, Black, in Devonshire. Spec. 68: 526.
Witch of Dulditch; a story. (Mary E. Mann) Temp. Bar, 104: 543.
Witch of Endor and Prof. Huxley. (A. Lang) Contemp. 66: 165.
Witch of Shawshine. (A. E. Brown) New Eng. M n. s. 5: 764.
Witch of Yell, The. Macmil. 70: 304.
Witch-burning at Clonmel. Folk-Lore, 6: 373. — (E. F. Benson) 19th Cent. 37: 1053.
Witch Kate; a yarn. (R. G. Denig) Outing, 25: 433.
Witch Maid, The; a story. (M. P. Smith) Argosy, 62: 633.
Witch Prosecution. Open Court, 10: 4892.
Witchcraft. (J. M. Buckley) Cent. 21: 408.
— Belief in. (P. Carus) Open Court, 10: 4883.
— — in Russia. (F. Whishaw) Longm. 27: 42.
— Evil Spirits. (J. H. Long) Pop. Sci. Mo. 43: 357.
— in Connecticut. (C. Levermore) New Eng. M. n. s. 6: 636.
— in New England. (Gertrude Savage) Bost. 1: 197.
— in New Mexico. J. Am. Folk-Lore, 1: 167.
— in 19th Century. Green Bag, 3: 94.

Witchcraft in Norfolk, Eng. (C. Roper) Harper, 87: 792.
— in Salem and in Europe. (S. G. W. Benjamin) New Eng. M. n. s. 9: 412.
— in Somersetshire. Spec. 72: 231. Same art. Liv. Age, 200: 766.
— Iroquois. (DeCost Smith) J. Am. Folk-Lore, 1: 184.
— Onondaga. (DeCost Smith) J. Am. Folk-Lore, 2: 277.
— Origin of Mediæval Belief in. (F. Legge) Scot. R. 21: 115.
— Salem, Stories of. (W. S. Nevins) New Eng. M. n. s. 5: 664, 717. 6: 36, 217.
Witchcraft; a story. (L. Dougall) Atlan. 76: 740.
Witches and Witchcraft. (A. M. Judd) Belgra. 81: 24.
— Weird Sisters. (Esther Singleton) Cosmopol. 20: 301.
Witch's Castle; a story. (Carman Sylva) Eng. Illust. 11: 353.
Witch's Spell, The; a story. (E. E. Fowler) Argosy, 56: 170.
With Cobb & Co. in Far Inland Australia. (J. A. Barry) Chamb. J. 71: 188.
With Compliments and Thanks; a story. (A. C. Deane) Temp. Bar, 104: 123. Same art. Liv. Age, 204: 146.
With Costs. (Mrs. Newman) Time, vols. 3-5.
With a Drawing by Boucher; a poem. (C. Monkhouse) M. of Art, 9: 193.
With Edged Tools; a story. (H. S. Merriman) Cornh. 68: 1, 561. 69: 93-659.
With Faithful Heart; a poem. Argosy, 62: 81.
With his Life; a story. (P. Gordon) Belgra. 84: 174.
With Iron Will; a story. (T. St. E. Hake) Chamb. J. 69: 397-409.
With Madness in his Method; a story. (F. I. Guertin) Eng. Illust. 13: 437. Same art. McClure, 3: 313.
With Pick and Shovel. (H. R. Eliot) Overland, n. s. 22: 597.
With the Quarrymen; a story. All the Year, 71: 426.
With the Smugglers; a story. All the Year, 72: 374, 397.
Witherle's Freedom. (C. A. Pratt) Cent. 26: 98.
Witherspoon, John, in the American Revolution. (M. C. Tyler) Am. Hist. R. 1: 671.
Within Sound of the Saws. (C. G. D. Roberts) Longm. 22: 171.
Withrow, Eva, California Painter, with sketches. (P. N. Boeringer) Overland, n. s. 27: 161.
Withrow Water Right; a story. (M. C. Graham) Atlan. 70: 623, 785.
Wittgenstein, Princess, Funeral of, at Rome. Atlan. 71: 570.
Witty Encounters in the Courts. Green Bag, 7: 449.
Wives, English. Spec. 69: 284.
— for Sale. All the Year, 71: 324.
— Maltreatment of. (M. S. Crawford) Westm. 139: 292.
— Representative. Sat. R. 80: 540.
— A Study in: French. (M. O'Rell). English. (G. Allen). German. (K. Blind). Scandinavian. (H. H. Boyesen) No. Am. 161: 427.
Wizard of the Cascade; a story. (S. C. Kendall) Outing, 27: 362.
Wizardry, Problem in. Spec. 72: 531.
Wizard's Cross; a story. All the Year, 75: 348.
Woad Mill, English. (F. Darwin) Nature, 55: 36.
Woadwax; Nourishing Poor Soil. Garden & F. 7: 318.
Wobbegong of Botany Bay, The. Liv. Age, 210: 823.
Woburn, Eng. Experimental Fruit Farm. Nature, 52: 508.
Woburn, Mass., Public Library, Local Collection of. (W. R. Cutter) Lib. J. 17: 420.
Woe to the Vanquished; a story. (G. E. Mitton) Argosy, 62: 609.
Woerth, Battle of. (L. Hale) Contemp. 61: 821. — (Lonsdale Hale) Un. Serv. (Phila.) 8: 164.
— Battlefield of. (F. Maurice) Un. Serv. M. 9: 280. 13: 547.
Woerishofen, Visit to. (A. Quarry) Argosy, 59: 745.
Woffington, Margaret ["Peg"]. (A. Dobson) M. of Art, 8: 256. — (C. J. Hamilton) Time, 8: 430.
Woking, Oriental University Institute. Asia. R. 20: 180.
Wolcott, Dr. John. (P. MacNab) M. of Art, 11: 242.
Wolf, Henry. Scrib. M. 17: 20.
Wolf, Joseph, Life of, Palmer's. Sat. R. 80: 806.
Wolf, Rudolf. Astron. 13: 112. — Nature, 49: 266.
Wolf Battue. (F. Whishaw) Longm. 21: 203. Same art. Liv. Age, 196: 247.
— in Podolia. (G. E. Stanley) Blackw. 159: 212. Same art. Liv. Age, 208: 620.
Wolf-hound, Irish. Good Words, 37: 827.
Wolf-hunt, A; a story. (P. M. F. Selmes) Outing, 22: 469.
Wolf-hunting in Russia. (E. J. Dillon) Eng. Illust. 9: 313.
Wolfe, Catherine, Collection of Paintings. Nat'l M. (N. Y. '91) 18: 180.
Wolfe's Cove; a story. (M. H. Catherwood) Atlan. 73: 79.
Wolff, Albert. Critic, 20: 28.
Wolfram von Eschenbach, French Words in. (L. Wiener) Am. J. Philol. 16: 326.
— Titurel. (J. Goddard) Walford's Antiq. 1: 138. 2: 10, 244.
Wolf's Life, The; a story. (J. H. Millar) New R. 13: 215.
Wolf's Point Episode; a story. (E. Traughber) Munsey, 12: 472.
Wollaston, Francis, Amateur Astronomer. (W.T. Lynn) Knowl. 19: 202.
Wolseley, Lord. (W. F. Day) Munsey, 8: 261.
— and Sir E. Hamley. (F. Maurice) Un. Serv. M. 11: 414, 439.
— the New Commander in Chief. (G. T. Denison) Canad. M. 5: 495.
— Reminiscences of. Sat. R. 80: 611.
Wolstenholme, Elizabeth Clarke. (E. Ethelmer) Westm. 145: 424.
Wolverhampton, Eng., Museum and Art Gallery. (H. M. Cundall) Art J. 44: 282.
— Municipal Art Gallery. (C. Whibley) M. of Art, 11: 65.
Wolverine; the Beaver Eater. (H. T. Martin) Pop. Sci. Mo. 44: 811.
Wolverine, The; a story. (S. Marchant) Belgra. 80: 194.
Wolves, A Night among. (F. Whishaw) Outing, 27: 307.
Woman. (H. E. Harvey) Westm. 145: 193.
— Advance of, during last Fifty Years. (Mary A. Livermore) Bost. 1: 81.
— The American. (C. de Varigny) Pop. Sci. Mo. 43: 383.
— — in Politics. (E. Kinnicutt) Cent. 27: 302.
— and her Work: aut Cæsar aut nihil. (A. Repplier) Scrib. M. 16: 118.
— and Labor. (K. Pearson) Fortn. 61: 561.
— and Primitive Culture, Mason's. Sat. R. 79: 815.

Woman and Socialism. (K. Knödel) Fortn. 63: 267.
— as Embodied Obstruction. (H. Campbell) Arena, 15: 371.
— as an Inventor and Manufacturer. Pop. Sci. Mo. 47: 92.
— Ascent of, Devereux's. Sat. R. 82: 43.
— The Average, in Politics. Spec. 72: 819.
— Battle of, in Great Britain. (W. G. Blaikie) No. Am. 163: 282.
— Cause of, is Man's Cause. (F. E. Willard) Arena, 5: 712.
— 14th-Century Ideals of. (E. B. Stone) Lippinc. 56: 100.
— from the Standpoint of a Naturalist. (W. K. Brooks) Forum, 22: 286.
— A Half Century of Progress. (M. L. Dickinson) Arena, 15: 361.
— An Ideal, of Olden Days. (B. J. Snell) Sund. M. 22: 674.
— in Antiquity. Meth. R. 56: 314.
— in India, Billington's. Sat. R. 79: 262.
— in Marriage. Argosy, 59: 405.
— in the Socialistic State. (E. L. Godkin) Nation, 58: 359.
— in Society To-day. (A. E. U. Hilles) Arena, 16: 263.
— in the World's Parliament. (J. Cook) Our Day, 13: 335.
— Lacour on. Sat. R. 80: 205.
— The Making of. (L. V. de Fabeck) Westm. 145: 544.
— The Malcontent. (T. P. White) Scot. R. 25: 270.
— The Modern, and Marriage. (E. Bisland) No. Am. 160: 753.
— — Out-of-doors. (A. W. Sears) Cosmopol. 21: 630.
— A National Waste. (Ellen S. H. Ritchie) Westm. 144: 545.
— The New. (L. de la Ramé) No. Am. 158: 610. — Cornh. 70: 365. — Sat. R. 79: 646, 687.
— — and her Debts. (C. de Graffenried) Pop. Sci. Mo. 49: 664.
— — and Shakespeare. Cath. World, 64: 158.
— — Foibles of. (E. W. Winston) Forum, 21: 186.
— — How to court. Idler, 6: 192.
— Non-political. Spec. 68: 605.
— On Being a. Liv. Age, 211: 62.
— Physical Insensibility of. (C. Lombroso) Fortn. 57: 354.
— Place of, in Art. Gent. M. n. s. 51: 639.
— — in Modern Life. (J. Adam) Fortn. 57: 522. Same art. Ecl. M. 118: 668.
— — in Pagan Times. (H. H. Boyesen) Forum, 20: 311.
— Progress of. (Mary Scharlieb) Univ. R. 2: 289.
— — in 1894. (F. E. Willard) Our Day, 13: 571.
— Psychology of. (G. T. W. Patrick) Pop. Sci. Mo. 47: 209.
— Retrogressive Pathways. (M. J. Eastman) Am. M. Civics, 7: 31.
— Rights of, Wollstonecraft's Vindication of. (C. L. Franklin) Nation, 52: 163.
— The Rule of the Lay-woman. (H. M. Batson) 19th Cent. 39: 98.
— Sisterhood of, Lacking. Sat. R. 79: 785.
— the Soft Sex. (Mrs. Haweis) Good Words, 37: 36.
— Tyranny of. (Ellen Gosse) New R. 10: 615.
— under the English Law. Ed. R. 184: 322.
— under Monasticism, Eckenstein's. (W. Webster) Acad. 49: 277. — (C. L. Franklin) Nation, 63: 90. — (J. M. Vincent) Am. Hist. R. 2: 120.
— Women's Excitement over. (H. Watterson) Forum, 16: 75.
Woman in the Camp; a Christmas Sketch. (H. Garland) Arena, 11: 90.
Woman intervenes, A; a story. (R. Barr) Idler, 7: 601, 767. 8: 51–563.
Woman of Asbestos. (E. Pullen) Lippinc. 57: 77.
Woman of the Plains; a story. (P. Stapleton) Lippinc. 49: 750.
Woman of the Saeter, The; a story. (J. K. Jerome) Idler, 3: 579.
Woman of Sicyon, A; a story. All the Year, 74: 469.
Woman of Stone, The; a story. (R. Barr) Idler, 5: 459.
Woman of Thirty, A; a story. All the Year, 70: 542, 565.
Woman who did the Right; a story. (S. C. Budd) Belgra. 91: 337.
Woman Journalist, Experiences of a. Blackw. 153: 830.
Woman Movement in Germany. (A. Russell) 19th Cent. 40: 97.
Woman Physician abroad, Letters from an American. (S. Solomons) Chaut. 23: 756.
Woman Question. (J. P. MacCorrie) Cath. World, 63: 605.
— among Catholics. Cath. World, 57: 669.
— Danger of the. (A. G. P. Sykes) Westm. 143: 396.
— a Decade of Fads. (R. Gourlay) Canad. M. 6: 67.
— from a Bio-sociological Point of View. (G. Ferrero) Monist, 4: 261.
— New Aspect of. (S. Grand) No. Am. 158: 270.
— Some Thoughts on. (G. Travers) Blackw. 156: 689.
— the Wail of the Male. Gent. M. n. s. 53: 360.
Womanhood, By Right of. Temp. Bar, 102: 109. Same art. Liv. Age, 201: 699.
— Christian. (F. W. Farrar) Chr. Lit. 14: 74.
— in the Iliad. (W. C. Lawton) Atlan. 71: 784.
— in Modern Poetry. (V. D. Scudder) Poet-Lore, 1: 449.
— New. (H. H. Boyesen) Lippinc. 56: 126.
— Old and New Ideals of. (C. Porter) Poet-Lore, 3: 269.
Womanliness and Womanishness. Spec. 71: 742. Same art. Ecl. M. 122: 68.
— as a Profession. (A. Gorren) Scrib. M. 15: 610.
Woman's Art Exhibition in Paris. Fortn. 58: 628.
Woman's Board of Missions. (E. P. Gould) Educa. 13: 536.
Woman's Case; a story. (S. A. Underwood) Arena, 6: 344.
Woman's Commonwealth. (C. M. Huntington) Soc. Econ. 3: 285.
Woman's Education Association of Boston. (A. E. Chandler) Lib. J. 20: 305.
Woman's Exchange; The. (L. M. Salmon) Forum, 13: 394.
Woman's Exchange of Simpkinsville; a story. (R. McE. Stuart) Harper, 86: 454.
Woman's Judgment, A; a sketch. Argosy, 56: 422.
Woman's Loyalty, A; a novel. (I. D. Hardy) Belgra. vols. 77–79.
Woman's Luncheon, A. Atlan. 76: 194.
Woman's National Council. (F. E. Willard) Am. J. Pol. 1: 139. — Pub. Opin. 18: 243.
Woman's Share in Primitive Culture, Mason on. (M. L. Miller) Dial (Ch.) 18: 323.
Women, Almshouse; a study. (Mary R. Smith) Am. Statis. Assoc. 4: 289.
— American, Marriage of, to German Noblemen. (E. von Wedel) Cosmopol. 12: 754.

Women, American, married abroad, Legal Status of. (R. Sewell) Am. Law R. 26: 358.
— American Life and Physical Deterioration of. (C. Edson) No. Am. 157: 423.
— among the Early Germans. (L. P. Bates) Chaut. 20: 724. 21: 90, 219, 343.
— and Civic Education. (W. B. Scaife) Pub. Opin. 20: 429.
— and the Law. (Matilda M. Blake) Westm. 137: 364.
— and Men, Mutual Relations of. (A. Clerk) New R. 13: 375.
— and Money. (E. S. Atkinson) Canad. M. 1: 277.
— and their Money. Spec. 69: 413. Same art. Ecl. M. 119: 667.
— and Nature of Music. (H. A. Clarke) Music, 7: 453.
— and Science. (M. N. Maugras) Pub. Opin. 14: 305.
— and the Universities. (J. B. Bury) Sat. R. 81: 269.
— and the World. (B. M. Rickoff) No. Am. 157: 423.
— and Worship in Burmah. (V. Greville) 19th Cent. 31: 1001. Same art. Ecl. M. 119: 132.
— Are Clever or Stupid, more attractive to Men? Idler, 8: 87.
— Are they protected? (M. M. Blake) Westm. 137: 43.
— Arts relating to, and their Exhibition in Paris. (O. Uzanne) Scrib. M. 13: 503.
— as Dramatists. All the Year, 75: 296.
— as Editors. (M. E. Sangster) Forum, 20: 445.
— as Inventors. (L. Mead) Chaut. 18: 464.
— as Journalists. Spec. 70: 800.
— as Landscape Gardeners. Garden & F. 5: 482.
— as Librarians. (M. S. R. James) Lib. J. 18: 146.
— as Official Inspectors. (L. Twining) 19th Cent. 35: 489.
— as Physicians. The History of a Movement. (E. G. Anderson) Fortn. 59: 404.
— as Shopkeepers. Idler, 8: 478.
— as Students in Design. (A. M. Gordon) Fortn. 61: 521.
— as Travellers. Blackw. 160: 49.
— Associations for the Advancement of. Open Court, 1: 561.
— Bookbinding as an Occupation for. (E. H. Nordhoff) Lend a H. 15: 429.
— Brain of. (L. Büchner) New R. 9: 116. Same art. Ecl. M. 121: 404.
— Brotherless. Spec. 74: 644.
— Canadian. (S. Blackburn) Canad. M. 5: 574.
— Capacity of, for Industrial Union. (E. A. Holyoake) Westm. 139: 164.
— A Certain Deficiency in. (J. C. Fletcher) Univ. R. 1: 398.
— Characteristics of. (F. L. Oswald) Open Court, 3: 1812.
— Citizenship for, Full. (P. L. Edwards) Green Bag, 7: 217.
— Claims of. Spec. 72: 463.
— College, After Careers of. (A. M. Gordon) 19th Cent. 37: 955. Same art. Ecl. M. 125: 559. Same art. Liv. Age, 206: 110.
— — and Matrimony, again. (F. M. Abbott) Cent. 29: 796.
— — in Literature. (F. A. Doughty) Critic, 27: 210. — (M. M. Miller; A. Estrem) Critic, 27: 282.
— — Pay of. (F. M. Abbott) No. Am. 163: 337.
— — Self Help among American. (E. L. Banks) 19th Cent. 39: 502.
Women, College, What becomes of. (C. F. Thwing) No. Am. 161: 546.
— The Conceited Sex. (W. S. Walsh) No. Am. 159: 369.
— Congress of, 1891. (I. Howland) Chaut. 14: 589.
— Congresses of, at Chicago, 1893. Pub. Opin. 15: 225.
— Courage in. (H. Quilter) Fortn. 63: 979.
— Creative Faculty in. Critic, 20: 42. — 21: 112. — (M. E. Seawell) Critic, 21: 35.
— Criminal. (L. Puibaraud) Char. R. 5: 364. — (H. Zimmern) Pop. Sci. Mo. 44: 218.
— — Lombroso on. Sat. R. 79: 603.
— Criticism of. (C. D. Wilson) Southern M. 4: 194.
— Cruelty and Pity in. (G. Ferrero) Monist, 3: 220.
— The Cry of. (E. Bisland) No. Am. 158: 757.
— Degrees for. Ath. '96, 1: 118.
— — at Oxford. (M. G. Fawcett) Contemp. 69: 347. — Spec. 76: 334. — (F. C. Conybeare) Acad. 49: 157. — (T. Case) Fortn. 64: 89.
— Discontented. (A. E. Barr) No. Am. 162: 201.
— Dress of, Economic Theory of. (T. Veblen) Pop. Sci. Mo. 46: 198.
— Early American, Earle on. Sat. R. 81: 357.
— Economic Function of. (E. T. Divine) Ann. Am. Acad. Pol. Sci. 5: 361.
— Economic Progress of. Soc. Econ. 2: 337.
— Educated, New Employments for. (Lady Knightley) New R. 9: 577.
— Education of. Macmil. 68: 33. — (A. Witte) Educa. 15: 229. — (H. Quilter) 19th Cent. 37: 940.
— — at the German Universities. Ath. '95, 1: 643. — (J. B. Steffens and others) Nation, 58: 116–271. 59: 232.
— — at Leipzig. (A. Luxenberg) Nation, 59: 247, (J. B. S.) 268.
— — At the Parting of the Ways. Atlan. 76: 691.
— — at the University of London. (E. C. Barney) Nation, 58: 286.
— — at the University of Paris. (J. B. Steffens) Nation, 58: 151.
— — Colleges for. (Anne McC. Sholl) Bach. of Arts, 1: 752. — (C. F. Thwing) Outl. 49: 747, 828, 871, 918.
— — — and Physical Training. (R. G. Huling) Educa. R. 7: 78.
— — College Life for Women. (E. Aitken) Sund. M. 25: 99.
— — An Educational Interlude. (F. Harrison) Fortn. 65: 355.
— — Female Brains and Girls' Schools. (G. Miller) Gent. M. n. s. 50: 31. Same art. Ecl. M. 120: 355.
— — Girls' Schools in France. (Mrs. Sandford) Macmil. 66: 116. Same art. Ecl. M. 119: 217. Same art. Liv. Age, 194: 217.
— — Higher. (R. T. Ely) Chr. Un. 45: 1025. — (J. Tetlow) Educa. R. 11: 105.
— — — as Graduate Students at Yale. (A. T. Hadley) Educa. R. 3: 486. — (T. Dwight) Forum, 13: 451.
— — — as Students at Oxford. (M. A. H. Rogers; A. Sidgwick) Educa. R. 3: 497. — Spec. 68: 232.
— — — College for. (M. A. Jordan) Atlan. 70: 540.
— — — College Education of Young Women. (C. F. Thwing) Pub. Opin. 16: 9.
— — — Colleges for, Normal Training in. (F. A. Walker) Educa. R. 4: 328.
— — — College Girls, A Word to. (L. Whiting) Chaut. 16: 336.
— — — Imperial University for. (G. F. Browne) 19th Cent. 33: 857.

Women, Education of, Higher, in European Universities. (M. F. Crow) Nation, **54**: 247.
— — — Sociology in. (S. W. Dike) Atlan. **70**: 668.
— — — University. R. of Rs. (N. Y.) **6**: 48.
— — — Women and the Universities. (M. S. Aldis) Contemp. **63**: 387.
— — in England. (W. C. Abbott) Nation, **63**: 26.
— — in France. (K. de Forest) Scrib. M. **14**: 632.
— — — Secondary. (M. Dugard) Educa. R. **14**: 257.
— — — What French Girls study. (H. C. Dana) Atlan. **69**: 204.
— — in Italy. Educa. R. **7**: 177.
— — in the South. (M. V. M. Woodward) Educa. R. **7**: 466.
— — — Higher. (C. F. Smith) Educa. R. **8**: 287.
— — Movement for, in Germany. (A. Witte) Educa. **13**: 37.
— — Private Schools for Girls. (A. C. Brackett) Harper, **84**: 943.
— — Recent Tendencies in. (M. R. Smith) Pop. Sci. Mo. **48**: 27.
— — Technical Schools for. (H. C. Parker) Canad. M. **1**: 634.
— — University. (Goldwin Smith) Sat. R. **81**: 392.
— — — in Europe. (A. Zimmern) Forum, **19**: 187.
— — — University Degrees for Women. Fortn. **63**: 895.
— — — University Opportunities for. (L. Frank) Educa. R. **8**: 471.
— — Where shall Polly go to School? (E. E. Hale) Cosmopol. **13**: 111.
See also Co-education.
— Emancipation of, Morals, Manners, and. Blackw. **152**: 463. Same art. Ecl. M. **119**: 777.
— Emancipation of Women from. (W. Schuyler) Open Court, **8**: 4186.
— Employment of. (A. A. Bulley) Fortn. **61**: 39.
— Employments of: Counting-room and Cradle. (M. Harland) No. Am. **157**: 334.
— The Encroachment of. (C. Whibley) 19th Cent. **39**: 495.
— English. Are they Legally Inferior to Mohammedan Women? (Rafi-un-din-Ahmad) Asia. R. **11**: 410.
— Evolution of, Gamble's. (C. L. Franklin) Nation, **58**: 452.
— Exemption of, from Labor. (L. F. Ward) Monist, **4**: 385.
— Extravagance of, in New York. Spec. **75**: 852.
— Factory Legislation for. (E. March-Phillipps) Fortn. **63**: 733.
— Financial Dependence of. (C. S. Bremner) No. Am. **158**: 382.
— French, Group of Eminent. (E. L. Didier) Chaut. **24**: 3.
— Friendly Societies for. (Elizabeth S. Haldane) National, **28**: 559.
— Fruit Farmers in California. (A. V. Wakeman) Chaut. **20**: 596.
— Great, of the Old Regime. Cath. World, **63**: 656.
— Gymnastic Training of, Anthropometrical Study of Effects. (C. J. Enebuske) Am. Statis. Assoc. **3**: 600.
— Hebrew Life of. (Dr. Cholzner) Asia. R. **17**: 438.
— Helpless *vs.* Self-reliant. (L. S. La Mange) Lend a H. **11**: 296.
— Honor among, Code of. Spec. **72**: 45.
— Impasse of. (A. L. Lee) Westm. **141**: 566.
— in Art. (S. Beale) Am. Arch. **45**: 85. — (E. W. Champney) Q. Illust. **2**: 111.
— in the Art Crafts. (F. Miller) Art J. **48**: 116.
— in Assemblies. (C. S. Oakley) 19th Cent. **40**: 559. — Reply. (H. McIlquham) 19th Cent. **40**: 777. Same art. Liv. Age, **211**: 572.
Women in Banks. Bank. M. (N. Y.) **48**: 833.
— in Business. (M. E. J. Kelly) Lippinc. **57**: 850.
— — How Many are going? Chaut. **21**: 337.
— in Church Work, Place of. (Mrs. J. Butler; Mrs. S. Amos; Mrs. B. Booth) M. Chr. Lit. **6**: 30.
— in Civic Reform. (M. R. Smith) Pub. Opin. **20**: 141.
— in the Colonies. (Gilbert Parker) New R. **11**: 409.
— in the Columbian Exposition. (Mrs. P. Palmer) Am. J. Pol. **1**: 124.
— in the Community and in the Family. (M. S. Gilliland) Int. J. Ethics, **5**: 38.
— in the Elections of England. Spec. **75**: 109. — (M. Jeune) No. Am. **161**: 451.
— in England, and Local Government. (Earl of Meath) No. Am. **157**: 423.
— — in the Time of Charles II., Johnstone on. Sat. R. **74**: 197.
— — Our Grandmothers and Their Grandmothers. (Matilda M. Blake) Westm. **137**: 608.
— in English Life, Hill on. (A. B. McMahan) Dial (Ch.) **21**: 117.
— in English Politics. (M. G. Fawcett) Forum, **14**: 453. — (E. Porritt) New Eng. M. n. s. **10**: 222.
— in 14th Century, Advice to. (E. B. Stone) Lippinc. **56**: 100.
— in French Prisons. (E. R. Spearman) 19th Cent. **37**: 798.
— in Greek History. (E. F. Wheeler) Chaut. **16**: 401.
— in Greek Literature. (E. F. Wheeler) Chaut. **16**: 531.
— in Industrial Pursuits. (W. Aldrich) Soc. Econ. **5**: 227.
— in Journalism. (E. Crawford) Contemp. **64**: 362. Same art. Ecl. M. **121**: 811. — (E. G. Jordan) Lippinc. **51**: 340.
— in the Learned Professions. Pub. Opin. **14**: 401.
— in Literature at the World's Fair. (E. E. Clarke) Lib. J. **19**: 47.
— in the Middle Ages. (E. B. Stone) Lippinc. **58**: 281.
— in the Mission Field. (A. R. Buckland) Sund. M. **24**: 194.
— in Painting and Poetry. (William Sharp) Portfo. **1894**: no. 7.
— in Politics. (B. A. Lockwood) Am. J. Pol. **2**: 385. — (W. W. Phelps) Am. J. Pol. **2**: 578.
— in Recent Fiction. (W. M. Salter) Open Court, **9**: 4383.
— in the Public Worship of the Churches of Paul. (G. H. Gilbert) Bib. World, **2**: 38.
— in the Pulpit. (F. M. Holland) Open Court, **6**: 3121.
— Industrial Position of. (E. F. S. Lady Dilke) Fortn. **60**: 499.
— Insurrection of. (J. B. Bury) Fortn. **58**: 651.
— Intellectual Force of, Waste of. (M. G. Van Rensselaer) Forum, **13**: 616.
— International Council of. (M. D. Conway) Open Court, **2**: 930.
— Labor of, and Child Labor in Germany. Soc. Econ. **5**: 287.
— — in England. Soc. Econ. **9**: 363.
— — in N. Y. (A. S. Daniel) Am. J. Soc. Sci. **30**: 73.
— Literary, Womanliness of. (J. W. Abernethy) Lippinc. **55**: 570.
— Literary Ladies. Temp. Bar, **108**: 576. Same art. Ecl. M. **127**: 466.
— Married, Debts of. (E. C. C. Firth) Law Q. **8**: 62.
— — Property of, in Anglo-Saxon and Anglo-Norman Law. (F. G. Buckstaff) Ann. Am. Acad. Pol. Sci. **4**: 233.
— Medical, in Fiction. (S. Jex-Blake) 19th Cent. **33**: 261.

Women, Medical Employment for. (A. T. Vanderbilt) Time, 18: 43.
— Men, and Home. Spec. 75: 78.
— Men's Missionary Work among. (B. Morgan) Harper, 90: 880.
— Mohammedan, in Turkey, Present Condition. (R. Davey) Fortn. 64: 53. Same art. Ecl. M. 125: 305.
— — their Social Status and Legal Rights. (L. M. J. Garnett) 19th Cent. 37: 57. Same art. Ecl. M. 124: 220.
— Money-making. Spec. 77: 852.
— Mothers and Daughters. (G. B. Harrison) 19th Cent. 35: 313.
— Nagging. (C. Edson) No. Am. 160: 29. — Reply to Dr. Edson. (I. Somerset; H. P. Spofford; M. Harland) No. Am. 160: 311. — Reply. (C. Edson) No. Am. 160: 440. — Last Word on. No. Am. 160: 634.
— National Council of. (Countess of Aberdeen) Arena, 11: 338.
— Natural Debarments of, from Political Service. (F. P. Matheson) Am. M. Civics, 7: 591. — (F. O. Immler; A. L. Cornwall) Am. M. Civics, 8: 271. 9: 78.
— Need of Legislative Protection for. Soc. Econ. 7: 88.
— A New Union for. (H. Morgan-Browne) Westm. 138: 528.
— Newspaper Work for. (M. H. Welch) Am. J. Soc. Sci. 32: 110.
— Next Step forward for. (B. O. Flower) Arena, 6: 635.
— of Fiction. (H. S. Wilson) Gent. M. n. s. 53: 34.
— of the French Salons, Mason's. Spec. 68: 533.
— of Imperial Rome, and English Women of To-day. (M. Dale) Westm. 141: 490.
— of Lyrical Love. (M. Gray) New R. 15: 708.
— of the North and South U. S. compared. (Mrs. H. B. Boulden) Nat'l M. (Bost.) 5: 262.
— of Paris. (L. de San Carlos) No. Am. 157: 560.
— of the Restoration. Gent. M. n. s. 49: 211.
— of To-day as Wives and Mothers. (M. C. Jones) Am. J. Pol. 2: 583.
— of the United States. (C. Logsdail) Canad. M. 1: 264.
— on Horseback. (L. Beck) Munsey, 15: 23.
— Oppression of. (E. D. Cope) Open Court, 8: 4103.
— Organization of. (E. A. Holyoake) Lend a H. 10: 430.
— Part of, in Political Sins. (E. W. Winston) Am. M. Civics, 6: 573. — Reply. (E. R. Meredith) Am. M. Civics, 7: 172. — (F. A. Burleigh) Am. M. Civics, 9: 429.
— Persian. (W. v. Schierbrand) Lippinc. 55: 550.
— Philanthropic Work of. Spec. 71: 490.
— Physical Education of. (A. Mosso) Pedagog. Sem. 2: 226.
— Physical Training for. (Hope W. Narey) Bost. 1: 98.
— Plea for, by a Woman. Westm. R. 139: 282.
— Poetry of, Non-creative Faculty in. (E. Gosse) Critic, 22: 37.
— Political Rights and Duties of. (G. F. Talbot) Pop. Sci. Mo. 49: 80.
— Political Status of. (J. Howard) Chaut. 18: 477.
— Portraits of. (W. A. Coffin) Cosmopol. 18: 3.
— Position of, in the Church. Pseudo-judicial Declaration of 1888. (W. F. Warren) Meth. R. 56: 81.
— — — Real Judicial Declaration of 1888. (G. G. Reynolds) Meth. R. 56: 87.
Women, Position of, in Industry. (H. Dendy) National, 23: 806.
— Professions accessible to. Westm. 139: 381.
— Progress of. (C. A. Channer) Good Words, 34: 830.
— Proposals of Marriage by. Spec. 68: 492.
— Renaissance of. (I. Somerset) No. Am. 159: 490.
— Revolt of the Daughters. (M. Jeune) Fortn. 61: 267. — (M. E. Haweis) 19th Cent. 35: 430. — (B. A. Crackanthorpe) 19th Cent. 35: 23, 424.
— — Reply from the Daughters. (K. Cuffe) 19th Cent. 35: 437. — (A. W. P. Smith) 19th Cent. 35: 443.
— Right of, to Work. Spec. 71: 330.
— Rights of. All the Year, 75: 150.
— — Nearing the Rapids. (E. L. Linton) New R. 10: 302.
— — Public. Cath. World, 59: 299.
— — The Strike of a Sex. Quar. 179: 289.
— Rivalries of, Famous. (G. Atherton) Lippinc. 54: 514.
— Roman; Claudia and Cornelia. (F. Tonge) Gent. M. n. s. 56: 305.
— Sexual Taboo. (A. E. Crawley) Anthrop. J. 24: 219.
— Smoking for. (E. B. Harrison) 19th Cent. 36: 389.
— Some Colonial. (A. H. Wharton) Cosmopol. 16: 651.
— Some Notable, of the Past. (E. Stuart) Lippinc. 54: 846.
— Southern and Northern. (E. Eliot) Southern M. 5: 199.
— Spanish. (E. Carrel) No. Am. 157: 560.
— Specialization of Function in. (H. S. Blatch) Gunton's M. 10: 349.
— Sphere of, Who shall prescribe? (E. B. Deitrick) Am. J. Pol. 3: 155.
— Suffrage for. (C. W. Wiley) Am. M. Civics, 8: 376. — (A. B. Tweedy) Pop. Sci. Mo. 49: 241. — Critic, 25: 151. Same art. Liv. Age, 203: 742. — (A. Schaumburg) Am. J. Pol. 5: 412. — Critic, 25: 63. — Open Court, 1: 411. — (P. Carus) Open Court, 5: 2747. — (Marion F. Pease) Time, 14: 325. — (W. Snoad) Westm. 138: 52. — (C. H. Matters) Westm. 143: 534. — (H. H. Gardener) Arena, 15: 67. — (M. E. Brooks) Am. M. Civics, 6: 158.
— — and the Teaching of St. Paul. (E. Lyttelton) Contemp. 69: 680. Same art. Chr. Lit. 15: 220, 284.
— — Arguments against. (J. M. Williams) Bib. Sac. 50: 331.
— — as a Weapon in Vital Reforms. (J. W. Howe) Our Day, 9: 23.
— — Attitude of Southern Women on. (A. R. Watson) Arena, 11: 363.
— — Benefit of. (H. A. Marsh; M. A. Hamm; D. T. S. Dennison; L. Wheelock; B. A. Lockwood; M. F. Ormsby) Am. M. Civics, 8: 605.
— — Constitutional. (W. S. Harwood) No. Am. 162: 632.
— — Bishop Doane and. (M. N. Lee) Arena, 15: 642.
— — Does Maternity preclude Politics? (F. F. Victor) Am. M. Civics, 8: 457.
— — Dual Suffrage. (E. Q. Norton) Arena, 16: 748.
— — Effect of, on Posterity. (J. Weir, jr.) Am. Natural. 29: 815.
— — Fallacy of the W. C. T. U. (E. W. Winston) Am. J. Pol. 5: 479.
— — Feminine Politics. (T. E. Kebbel) Time, 20: 491.
— — Gladstone on. Spec. 68: 550.

Women, Suffrage for, in Canada. (E. M. Luke) Canad. M. 5: 328.
— — in England. (M. G. Fawcett; L. H. Courtney; S. M. S. Amos) Contemp. 61: 761.
— — — Bill for, 1892. Spec. 68: 598.
— — in France. (T. Stanton) Open Court, 8: 4127.
— — in New Zealand. (M. G. Fawcett) Contemp. 65: 433. — (N. Young) Westm. 142: 666. — 19th Cent. 35: 268.
— — in Practice. (D. H. Waite; L. Crounse) No. Am. 158: 737.
— — Last Protest against. (J. L. Hughes) Arena, 10: 201.
— — Movement for, Results of. (M. A. Greene) Forum, 17: 413.
— — — Status and Future of. (M. P. Jacobi) Forum, 18: 406.
— — Petticoat Government. (M. O'Rell; H. P. Spofford; M. Bottome) No. Am. 163: 101.
— — Pro and Con. Pub. Opin. 17: 491.
— — Right of. (Anna Shaw) Am. J. Pol. 1: 309. — (C. H. Chapman) Arena, 16: 570.
— — — and Expediency of. (G. F. Hoar) Cent. 26: 605.
— — The Rock ahead in. Open Court, 1: 326.
— — Some Later Aspects of. (W. C. Doane) No. Am. 163: 537.
— — South Australia's Victory for. (C. H. Spence) Canad. M. 5: 276.
— — Useless Risk of. (M. Hale) Forum, 17: 406.
— — Why New Zealand Women get the Franchise. (E. Reeves) Westm. 143: 35.
— — Why they do not want it. (W. C. Doane) No. Am. 161: 257.
— — Why Women should have the Ballot. (J. Gibbon) No. Am. 163: 91.
— — Wrongs and Perils of. (J. M. Buckley) Cent. 26: 613.
— Surplus of, New View of. (A. Kenealy) Ecl. M. 118: 84.
— Trades-Unions for. (C. de Graffenreid) Lend a H. 10: 103.
— — Progress in. (E. March-Phillipps) Fortn. 60: 92.
— Two Interesting: Mrs. Anne C. L. Edgren and Prof. S. V. Kovalevsky. Chamb. J. 71: 154.
— Tyranny of the Kitchen. (C. Selden) No. Am. 157: 423.
— Unappreciated. (M. N. Wishard) Chaut. 16: 340.
— under the Jewish and Christian Religions. (Mrs. R. Charles) Sund. M. 23: 340, 388.
— under Monasticism. Lond. Q. 87: 113.
— Wage-earning, The Condition of. (C. de Graffenreid) Forum, 15: 68.
— — of America and Europe. (H. Campbell) Arena, 7: 153. — 8: 172.
— Wages of. (S. M. Davis) Am. J. Pol. 4: 63. — (K. Stephens) No. Am. 162: 377.
— — Deductions from. Sat. R. 78: 530.
— — Webb on. (M. G. Fawcett) Econ. J. 2: 173.
— — Why they are paid less than Men. (C. D. Wright) Forum, 13: 629.
— Wages of Needlewomen. (W. H. Wilkins) 19th Cent. 34: 329.
— Wild, Defence of. (M. Caird) 19th Cent [illegible]: 811. Same art. Ecl. M. 118: 540.
— — Partisans of. (E. L. Linton) 19th Cent. 31: 455.
— Work of. (C. G. Robertson) Econ. R. 5: [illegible]7.
— — and Wages of. (E. M. Abdy-Williams) Time, 13: 539.
— — in the Church. (G. U. Wenner) Luth. Q. 26: 471.
— Working. Spec. 70: 426.
Women, Working, Paris Municipal Refuge for. (H. Zimmern) Char. R. 2: 226.
— — Society and. (C. S. Davidge) Cosmopol. 15: 223.
— Young, Symmetrical Development of. (C. E. Brewster) Pop. Sci. Mo. 42: 217.
— Young Woman's Right to Knowledge. (Mrs. W. M. A. Hawksley) Westm. 142: 315.
Women Bachelors in London. (M. G. Humphreys) Scrib. M. 19: 600.
— in New York. (M. G. Humphreys) Scrib. M. 20: 626.
Women Compositors. (Amy Linnett) Econ. R. 2: 42.
Women Convicts, Women Keepers for. (M. W. Noble) Chaut. 18: 467.
Women Laborers in Factories and Shops. (Alice L. Woodridge) Soc. Econ. 5: 154.
— in Trades and Commerce. (Chas. Barnard) Soc. Econ. 5: 146.
Women Novelists in Italy at the Present Day. (M. Hargrave) Gent. M. n. s. 53: 145.
Women Poets of the Day. (R. Le Gallienne) Eng. Illust. 11: 649.
Women-workers. Spec. 74: 713. Same art. Ecl. M. 125: 132.
— English Conference of, 1895. (M. P. Marshall) Econ. J. 6: 107.
— in Mission Fields. (A. R. Buckland) Sund. M. 23: 458.
Women Writers, Canadian, with portraits. (T. O'Hagan) Cath. World, 63: 779.
— Four, of the West. (M. J. Reid) Overland, n. s. 24: 138.
Women's Christian Association Libraries. (S. W. Cattell) Lib. J. 19: 121.
W. C. T. U., Fallacy of. (C. E. Cawthorne) Am. M. Civics, 6: 298.
Women's Clubs. (Mrs. A. M. Diaz) Bost. 2: 383.
— The Castilian Club. (Mrs. A. M. Diaz) Bost. 3: 175.
— Federations of. (E. M. Henrotin) Arena, 17: 120.
— in Mass. (Mrs. A. M. Diaz) Bost. 2: 179, 288, 516.
— N. E. Woman's Club. (Mrs. A. M. Diaz) Bost. 3: 483.
— N. E. Woman's Press Club. (Mrs. A. M. Diaz) Bost. 3: 367.
— Political. (Kate M. Bostwick) Mo. Illust. 13: 304.
— their True Character. (Mrs. A. M. Diaz) Bost. 3: 59.
Women's Colleges, American, Festivals in. Cent. 27: 429.
Women's Rights Movement in France, Progress of. (J. E. Schmahl) Forum, 22: 79.
Women's Rights Question in Rome, B. C. 195. (A. Harvey) Canad. M. 4: 395.
Women's Settlements in Bethnal Green. (Mrs. Mace) Good Words, 36: 613.
Wonder-witch. (M. G. McClelland) Lippinc. 53: 715
Wonderful City, The; a poem. (E. G. Curtis) Arena, 15: 1030.
Wonderful Experience Meeting, A. (W. A. Dromgoole) Arena, 9: 534.
Wonderful Visit, The. (R. F. Horton) Good Words, 37: 91.
Wood, Lieut.-Gen. Sir H. E., with portrait. (E. C. H. Price Eng. Illust. 10: 251.
Wood, Sir H. E. Life by Williams. Sat. R. 73: 721.
Wood, Mrs. Henry. (A. H. Japp) Leis. Hour, 44: 392.
— and Worcestershire. Argosy, 56: 463.
— Memorials of. (J. M'Cormick) Argosy, 59: 22.
Wood, John Warrington. (T. Wilmot) M. of Art, 14: 136.
Wood and Wave Notes. (Edith M. Thomas) Overland, n. s. 24: 461.
Wood, Construction in, Better. Am. Arch. 35: 106–172. 36: 27.

Wood, Hard, Kiln-drying of. (O. S. Whitmore) Pop. Sci. Mo. 45: 375.
— — Remaining Resources of the U. S. in. (C. Mohr) Engin. M. 4: 378.
— Preservation of. (O. Chanute) Cassier, 7: 301.
Wood-carving. (G. A. Rogers) M. of Art, 4: 120, 226.
— and Iron Work, Peyre's Collection. (L. F. Day) Art J. 47: 279.
— and Wood Carvers. (J. E. Knox) Am. Arch. 51: 142.
— in 1896. (F. Miller) Art J. 48: 311.
— in the Trobriands. (A. C. Haddon) Illust. Archæol. 1: 107.
— Some East Indian. (L. F. Day) M. of Art, 9: 328.
Wood-carvings, Peyre Collection at South Kensington. M. of Art, 19: 316.
Woodcuts as Bindings. (Paul Kristeller) Bibliographica, 1: 249.
— in Early Printed Works. Bookworm, 4: 237.
— Mitchell Collection of. (C. Dodgson) Acad. 47: 282.
— of Gothic Books. (W. Morris) J. Soc. Arts, 40: 247.
— of Old and Modern Books. (W. Morris) Bookworm, 5: 193.
— Transference of, in 15th and 16th Centuries. (A. W. Pollard) Bibliographica, 2: 343.
Wood-engravers. Scrib. M. 17: 20–689. 18: 167–718.
— Old German. (R. Walker) Good Words, 33: 808.
Wood-engraving. (H. Holiday) M. of Art, 2: 26–284. 3: 93, 123. — (W. Dampier) Walford's Antiq. 1: 306
— as a Fine Art, Future of. (W. B. Gardner) J. Soc. Arts, 44: 611.
— Books with Woodcuts printed at Pavia. (Paul Kristeller) Bibliographica, 1: 347.
— Chatto's Treatise on. (H. V. Barnett) M. of Art, 5: 237.
— — Jackson's Share in. (M. Jackson) M. of Art, 5: 314.
— Early, in Holland. (W. M. Conway) M. of Art, 4: 190, 505.
— Early Venetian. (A. W. Pollard) Bibliographica, 3: 122.
— Florentine Book-illustration. (Paul Kristeller) Bibliographica, 2: 81, 227.
— in America, Linton's History of. (H. V. Barnett) M. of Art, 8: 127.
— — Timothy Cole and. (E. Bale) M. of Art. 16: 138.
— in England and America, Present Condition of. (M. H. Spielmann) National, 25: 48. Same art. Ecl. M. 124: 549.
— — True Condition of. (J. Pennell) National, 25: 343.
— in Lyons in the 15th Century. (N. Rondot) Bibliographica, 3: 46.
— Japanese. (W. Anderson) Portfo. no. 17.
— Linton on. Art J. 45: 293.
— Old World Printing and. (W. M. Conway) M. of Art, 7: 68.
— Present and Future of. (W. B. Gardner) M. of Art, 19: 57.
— Reproduction of Dream of Poliphilus. Sat. R. 77: 47.
— Wood-cut Books of Ulm and Augsburg. (W. Morris) Bibliographica, 1: 437.
Wood-pigeons, London. Spec. 74: 748.
Wood-pulp Floor Mosaics. (Louis Stern) Am. Arch. 47: 106.
Wood-pulp Supply and our Spruce Forests. Garden & F. 9: 363.
Wood Sections, Solar Prints of. (B. D. Halsted) Pop. Sci. Mo. 45: 313.
Wood-stave Pipe for Conveying Water. (A. Lakes) Engin. M. 9: 462.
Woodberry, Geo. E., with portrait. Bk. Buyer, 8: 7.
Woodbury, Levi, Memoir of. (C. L. Woodbury) N. E. Reg. 48: 9.
Woodcock in England. Sat. R. 82: 669.
Woodcock Shooting in Illinois. Outing, 22: 427.
— on the Upper Mississippi. (T. S. Van Dyke) Outing, 20: 293.
Wooden Dish from the Hebrides. Reliquary, 36: 241.
Wooden Legs. All the Year, 71: 279.
Wooden Peg. (W. Grant) New Eng. M. n. s. 8: 609.
Woodlands, English, in May. Spec. 70: 601.
— of New England. (T. H. Hoskins) Garden & F. 7: 279.
— Prairie. (E. J. Hill) Garden & F. 7: 412.
Woodman, The; a poem. (R. L. Stevenson) New R. 12: 17.
Woodman, The; a story. (Mrs. F. Harrison) Temp. Bar, 109: 91. Same art. Liv. Age, 211: 84.
Woodpecker. Is it Useful? (J. B. Smith) Garden & F. 6: 483.
— Ivory-billed. (Inez de Campo) Overland, n. s. 26: 211.
Woodpeckers. (H. F. Witherby) Knowl. 16: 64.
Woods, American, Hough's Specimens, part III. Garden & F. 6: 529.
Woods in Winter. (B. G. Johns) Good Words, 34: 31.
— Leafless, and Gray Moorlands. National, 24: 366.
— Natural Beauty of the. (G. F. Schwarz) Garden & F. 9: 357.
— Path through. (J. Buckham) Outing, 23: 395.
Woodward, Geo. Austin, with portrait. Bk. News, 14: 592.
Woodward, R. Henry, Works of. Eng. R. 9: 85.
Woodward Family; MS. Genealogy by Rev. S. Woodward. (Mary F. Peirce) N. E. Reg. 50: 301.
Wood-work in Huntington Church, Yorkshire. Reliquary, 32: 235.
— Interior. (A. C. Nye) Am. Arch. 35: 56. 38: 54.
— Limerick Cathedral. Reliquary, 33: 129.
— Trinity Church, Hull. Reliquary, 32: 166.
Wood-working, Art of, Progress in. (C. E. Tompkins) Engin. M. 4: 194.
Woodworth, Samuel, and the "Old Oaken Bucket." (G. M. Young) New Eng. M. n. s. 5: 661.
Wooing of Teige, The. Liv. Age, 211: 398.
Wooing of William. (M. E. Francis) Longm. 28: 253. Same art. Liv. Age, 210: 269.
Wool and the Tariff. (T. Cox) Am. J. Pol. 1: 231.
— and Woolens. (H. White) Nation, 54: 5.
— — Duties on, in the U. S. (F. W. Taussig) Q. J. Econ. 8: 1.
— Consumption of. (J. T. Busiel) Am. J. Pol. 4: 490.
Wool Situation in the World. (S. N. D. North) Bank. M. (N. Y.) 50: 328.
Woolens and Worsted of Yorkshire. (R. C. Gill) Art J. 47: 22.
Woolhouse, W. S. B., with portrait. Bank. M. (Lond.) 53: 349.
Woollett, Sidney. (J. Hawthorne) Lippinc. 49: 107.
Woolley, John G. Character Sketch: with portrait. Our Day, 16: 125.
Woolman, John, and Stephen Girard. (G. M. Hammell) Meth. R. 55: 741.
Woolmer Forest, Rambles of a Naturalist in. Macmil. 73: 365. Same art. Liv. Age, 209: 308.
Woolner, Thomas. Acad. 42: 341. — Ath. '92, 2: 522. — Sat. R. 74: 442. — (F. G. Stephens) Art. J. 46: 80. — M. of Art, 16: viii, 71.
Woolsey, Rev. Benjamin. (G. M. Clapham) New Eng. M. n. s. 9: 201.
Woolson, Constance Fenimore, with portrait. Bk. Buyer, 6: 309. — With portrait, Bk. News, 11: 263. — Critic, 24: 73.

Worcester, Eng., Hastings Museum at. (J. Ward) Antiq. n. s. 27: 14.
— Musical Festival at, 1893. Sat. R. 76: 353.
Worcester Cathedral. (C. Parkinson) Gent. M. n. s. 49: 294. — (T. T. Shore) Sund. M. 23: 86.
— Book of Ecclesiastical Collections made about 1000 A. D. (M. Bateson) Eng. Hist. R. 10: 712.
Worcester Consistory Court. Reliquary, 32: 230.
Worcester, Mass., Churches of. (C. M. Lamson) New Eng. M. n. s. 5: 768.
Worcestershire and Mrs. Henry Wood. Argosy, 56: 463.
Word of God, The. (T. F. Day) Bib. World, 2: 189.
Word-painting. (A. D. B. Atkinson) Portfo. 23: 206.
Words. (A. Repplier) Atlan. 71: 364.
— and Phrases, Anglicised, Stanford Dictionary of. Spec. 69: 531.
— and Tones; poem. Argosy, 59: 542.
— Common Mistakes about. Chamb. J. 69: 151.
— The Craft of. (V. Paget) New R. 11: 571.
— Division of, at end of Lines. (W. R. Thayer) Nation, 57: 270.
— English, 150 New. (H. A. Schuler) Writer, 7: 21.
— — Teaching by Sound. (E. P. Moses) Educa. 15: 10.
— "Index Expurgatorius" of, W. C. Bryant's. Writer, 7: 154.
— Linguistic Parvenus. (E. F. Andrews) Chaut. 23: 216.
— Magic of. Spec. 73: 518.
— Rise and Fall of. (D. Lever) National, 20: 188. — (W. H. Johnstone) National, 20: 430.
— Study of. (W. F. Parsons) Educa. 15: 536.
Wordsworth, Charles. Autobiography. Ath. '93, 2: 57. — Sat. R. 75: 545. — Church Q. 33: 372. — Spec. 69: 845.
Wordsworth, William. (T. W. Hunt) Bib. Sac. 53: 28. — (J. V. Cheney) Chaut. 15: 588. — (A. Copeland) Meth. R. 52: 249.
— and Allston. Ath. '94, 2: 233.
— and Sir George Beaumont. (J. A. Noble) M. of Art, 7: 206.
— and Carlyle — a Literary Parallel. Temp. Bar, 106: 261. Same art. Liv. Age, 207: 356.
— and Nature. (A. F. Sanborn) Open Court, 4: 2447.
— Ballads, Philadelphia Reprint of. Ath. '94, 1: 213.
— Castle of Indolence Stanzas. (T. Hutchinson) Fortn. 62: 685.
— his Home and Works. (P. Oléron) Cath. World, 61: 349.
— Knight's Edition of. (T. Hutchinson) Acad. 50: 5, 233. — Sat. R. 81: 559.
— Literary Democracy of. (J. W. Bray) Poet-Lore, 8: 306.
— Notes on Two Recent Editions. (T. Hutchinson) Acad. 44: 170-486.
— Parson Sympson. Temp. Bar, 107: 63. Same art. Liv. Age, 208: 357.
— Poems, Chronology of, and Collation of Text. (T. Hutchinson) Acad. 44: 170, 211.
— Poetical Works, edited by Dowden. Ath. '93, 2: 218, 259.
— Quantock Poems. (W. Greswell) Temp. Bar, 107: 530.
— Some Unpublished Letters of. Cornh. 67: 257. Same art. Liv. Age, 197: 323.
Wordsworth Country on Two Shillings a Day. (A. F. Sanborn) Atlan. 76: 514.
Work and Morality. (W. Ferrero) Forum, 22: 358.
— and Wages in Hotels and Restaurants. (C. H. d'E. Leppington) Good Words, 33: 754.
— and Workers, How to bring together. (J. A. Riis) Forum, 18: 122.
Work, Furnished by Government, in France, 1848. (R. Ogden) Nation, 58: 324.
— Joy of. All the Year, 72: 418.
— Law of Demand in. (W. B. Chisholm) Am. M. Civics, 8: 34.
— Relief in the form of, Uses of. (G. B. Buzelle) Char. R. 1: 257.
Workhouse Administration. (L. R. Phelps) Econ. R. 5: 261.
Workhouse Girls and Women, How to help. (E. M. L. McDougall) Sund. M. 22: 347.
Workhouse Visiting, Amateur. All the Year, 73: 635.
Working in the Dark. Chamb. J. 73: 771.
Working-class Homes, Improvement of. (H. M. Bompas) Fortn. 64: 738.
Working-class Settlements in Mulhouse and Milan. (C. Hancock) Fortn. 62: 94.
Working-classes, English, Mental Deterioration in. (G. R. Stetson) Pub. Opin. 18: 666.
— Housing of, in London. (E. Porritt) Pol. Sci. Q. 10: 22.
— Present Condition of. (Dr. A. Crespi) Time, 21: 483.
— Progress of. (D. McG. Means) Nation, 55: 467.
Working-girl, The New York. (Mary G. Humphreys) Scrib. M. 20: 502.
Working Girls' Clubs. (H. Campbell) Pub. Opin. 18: 600. — (G. H. Dodge) Pub. Opin. 18: 762. — (M. W. Coleman) Char. R. 4: 307. — (C. S. Davidge) Scrib. M. 15: 619.
Working Lads' Club, A. (P. Emerson) Sund. M. 24: 111.
Workingman, The American. (E. Levasseur) Yale R. 5: 122. — (Alice French) Scrib. M. 16: 100.
— and Immigration. (J. W. Knight) Char. R. 4: 363.
— as his Own Capitalist. (W. O. McDowell) Our Day, 10: 625.
Workingmen, Budgets of. (H. Higgs) J. Statis. Soc. 56: 255.
— Club Homes for Unmarried. (W. Moffatt) Blackw. 156: 701.
— Clubs for. (J. Wells) Econ. R. 4: 59.
— — in the East End. (F. Eardley) Good Words, 36: 227.
— Diet and Wages of. (T. Oliver) Fortn. 62: 513.
— English and Foreign. Spec. 70: 696.
— Governmental Care for. (C. C. Johnston and M. C. Lea) Cent. 23: 954.
— Homes for. Lend a H. 12: 99.
— — in New York City. R. of Rs. (N. Y.) 14: 693. *See* Homes.
— of America. (J. Conway) Cath. World, 56: 490.
— Plain Words to. (F. Woodrow) Cent. 23: 134.
— Plea for. (W. I. Simmons) Cath. World, 58: 424.
— Social Condition of. (R. D. St. John) Chaut. 18: 329.
Working-men Directors. (G. Livesey) National, 27: 103.
Workingmen's Boys, Professions or Trades for. (F. Morgan) New Eng. M. n. s. 6: 752.
Workingmen's Colonies of Germany. (E. M. Burbank) Chaut. 18: 680.
Workmanship, Deterioration of Modern. Am. Arch. 48: 88.
Workmen, Trade Life of, Duration of. (R. Donald) Econ. J. 2: 176.
Works and Faith. (E. V. Gerhart) Ref. Q. 40: 460.
Workshop, Education for. (F. A. C. Perrine) Engin. M. 3: 209.
— Evolution of. (C. J. Hexamer) J. Frankl. Inst. 138: 175.

Workshop, Three Months in, P. Göhre on. (C. R. Henderson) Char. R. 4: 256.
World, Age of. (H. N. Hutchinson) Knowl. 15: 161.
— Below, The. (E. M. Abdy-Williams) Time, 14: 78–734. 15: 84–607.
— External, and the Social Consciousness. (J. Royce) Philos. R. 3: 513.
— Is it Better or Worse than it was? (H. Jones) Time, 20: 587.
— Is it growing Better? Symposium. Indep. Oct. 5, '93.
— Map of, on Scale of 1:1,000,000. (A. Penck) Geog. J. 1: 253.
— Mechanical Conception of. (W. Harrison) Meth. R. 55: 932.
— One, but that Infinite! (T. B. Wakeman) Open Court, 3: 1925.
— One Government for. (G. C. Sibley) Am. J. Pol. 3: 197.
World of Chance; a novel. (W. D. Howells) Harper, 84: 694 — 85: 927.
World-sorrow, The. (J. Watson) Sund. M. 25: 729.
Worldliness, What is? Meth. R. 55: 121.
Worldly Young Woman, A. Idler, 6: 88.
World's Fair, 1893. *See* Chicago.
Worlds, Life in Other, Possibility of. (Sir R. S. Ball) Fortn. 62: 718. Same art. Ecl. M. 123: 818.
Wormeley, Katharine P. Bk. Buyer, 6: 61.
Wormwood Scrubs Prison. (G. R. Vicars) Sund. M. 25: 399.
Worries of Life, The. (B. J. Snell) Sund. M. 21: 444.
— Small. Spec. 68: 85.
Worry, The Policy of. Liv. Age, 209: 443.
Worship, Christian. (G. U. Wenner) Luth. Q. 22: 451.
— — and Edification. (F. P. Manhart) Luth. Q. 24: 516.
— — Early History of Divine Service. Church Q. 41: 395.
— — Fundamental Principles of. (C. S. Albert) Luth. Q. 23: 449.
— — Hymnology and Music in. (J. M. Schick) Ref. Q. 39: 504.
— — its Spirit and its Forms. (J. C. Koller) Luth. Q. 25: 427.
— in Ancient Egypt, Astronomy and. (J. N. Lockyer) 19th Cent. 32: 29.
— in Spirit and in Truth. (G. Rietschel) Luth. Q. 25: 105.
— Public, Voluntary System in Maintenance of. Lend a H. 13: 83.
— Services of, and Thought. (C. F. Dole) New World, 3: 488.
— Theory of Cultus. (W. Rupp) Ref. Q. 43: 277.
— What constitutes True? (E. S. Johnston) Luth. Q. 24: 216.
Worth, the Paris Dressmaker. Blackw. 157: 790.
Worth of a Lass, The; a story. Temp. Bar, 102: 517.
Worth Keeping. (J. A. Rondthaler) Our Day, 16: 464.
Worthington Cooling Tower for Continuous Use of Condensing Water. (J. H. Cooper) J. Frankl. Inst. 141: 417.
Wotton, Sir Henry. (F. Watson) Gent. M. n. s. 48: 273. Same art. Liv. Age, 193: 432.
Wotton, Reinfred; a story. (T. Carlyle) New R. 6: 1–285.
Wotton House. (G. Allen) M. of Art, 10: 145.
Wound, Mortal, What is a? (J. N. Hall) Overland, n. s. 20: 530.
Wounded in War, Future of the. (A. Forbes) Scrib. M. 15: 781.
Wounded Knee, The Fight at. (W. E. Dougherty) Overland, n. s. 19: 357.
Wounded Soldiers, First Actions of. (G. L. Kilmer) Pop. Sci. Mo. 41: 155.
Wourali: a Tale of British Guiana. Chamb. J. 73: 46.
Wraith of the Shark God; a story. (N. Douglas) Overland, n. s. 19: 548.
Wrangel, Field-Marshal Count. (A. Bothmer) Un. Serv. M. 6: 543.
Wranglers, Senior. (C. G. Nuttall) Gent. M. n. s. 57: 116.
Wreck of the "Columbia;" a story. (S. Newcomb) Harper, 93: 466.
Wreck of the "Petrel;" a story. (N. Eames) Overland, n. s. 21: 358.
Wrecked Vessel, Saving a. (G. Kobbé) Engin. M. 7: 509.
Wrecker, The; a story. (R. L. Stevenson and L. Osbourne) Scrib. M. 11: 85 — 12: 57.
Wrecks and Salvage. (D. Owen) Westm. 140: 483.
— Raising of. Chamb. J. 69: 438.
Wreford, H. G. Liv. Age, 199: 511.
Wren, Sir Christopher, and St. Paul's. (B. Champneys) M. of Art, 5: 321.
— Towers of. (B. Champneys) M. of Art, 5: 206.
Wren, Wood. (W. H. Hudson) Longm. 28: 590.
Wrens. (O. T. Miller) Atlan. 69: 791.
— of Travis County, Texas. (C. D. Oldright) Science, 22: 15.
Wrestling. (H. F. Wolff) Lippinc. 51: 206.
Wright, Frances. (Eliz. Lee) Gent. M. n. s. 52: 518. — (F. M. Holland) Open Court, 9: 4623.
Wright, George Frederick, with portrait. Pop. Sci. Mo. 42: 258.
— and the Geological Survey. (T. C. Chamberlain) Dial (Ch.) 14: 7.
— and his Critics. (E. W. Claypole) Pop. Sci. Mo. 42: 764.
Wright, John; in Memoriam. (C. W. Wood) Argosy, 57: 196.
Wright, Joseph, of Derby. (C. Monkhouse) M. of Art, 6: 383. — (E. Bradbury) Time, 8: 590.
Wright, Mabel Osgood. Critic, 29: 319.
Writer, The, and his Hire. Dial (Ch.) 15: 211.
Writer's Cramp. (J. Wolff) Writer, 7: 65.
Writers, Advice to. Lippinc. 58: 140.
— and Speakers. (H. N. Crellin) Gent. M. n. s. 55: 484.
— Combination of. Writer, 6: 67.
— Mistakes of. (G. T. Bicknell) Writer, 8: 61.
— Mistakes of Tried. (L. B. Edwards) Writer, 8: 64.
Writing and Talking. (J. Monteith) Educa. 16: 268.
— and Writing-masters. All the Year, 70: 394.
— Automatic. (B. F. Underwood) Arena, 6: 74.
— Composing before or at Time of. (E. E. Benton) Writer, 9: 145.
— Craft of. (V. Paget) New R. 11: 571.
— Indian, Origin of. (A. A. Macdonell) Acad. 50: 330.
— Inspiration in. (E. E. Benton) Writer, 9: 109.
— Living by. (A. Fosdick) Writer, 8: 93.
— Man before. Liv. Age, 211: 410.
— Mirror-, and Left-handedness. (M. Strach) Pedagog. Sem. 2: 236.
— Shortened. (H. M. Dean) Educa. 14: 294.
See Handwriting.
Writing on the Wall, The; a story. (R. H. Davis) Harper, 88: 773.
Writing to Rosina. (W. H. Bishop) Cent. 24: 141, 264.

Writing Masters, Early English. (E. F. Strange) Bibliographica, **3**: 156.
Writing Material of Antiquity. (G. Ebers) Cosmopol. **16**: 102.
Writing Materials, Early. (T. Hopkins) Leis. Hour, **44**: 162.
Written in Golden Sand; a story. (Mrs. J. S. Lloyd) Belgra. **78**: 17, Holiday no.
Wrong Black Bag, The; a story. (A. Lewis) Chamb. J. **70**: 125. Same art. Liv. Age, **197**: 172.
Wrong Jimmie; a story. (W. S. Arnold) Canad. M. **7**: 250.
Wrong Prescription, The; a story. (M. E. Hawker) Good Words, **34**: 49.
Wrong Road, The; a story. (Sarah Grand) Eng. Illust. **14**: 221.
Wrong Trump, The; a story. (Emma A. Thurston) Overland, n. s. **20**: 314.
Wrought-iron Work in Charleston, S. C. Am. Arch. **47**: 104.
Wroxeter: the English Pompeii. (C. Edwardes) Chamb. J. **71**: 657.
Wu t'ai Shan, the Great Buddhist Sanctuary of North China. (W. W. Rockhill) Atlan. **75**: 758.
Wyatt, Henry Lawson. (S. B. Weeks) Nat'l M. (N. Y. '91) **17**: 56.
Wyatt, Sir Thomas, Sonnets of, and their Sources. (E. B. Brownlow) Poet-Lore, **3**: 127.
Wye-land, June-days in. (C. Parkinson) Gent. M. n. s. **48**: 592.
Wye River, England. (S. Hodges) M. of Art, **1**: 85.
Wycherley, William. Citizen, **1**: 237.
Wycliffe. *See* Wiclif.
Wyeth, Nathaniel J., and the Struggle for Oregon. (J. A. Wyeth) Harper, **85**: 835.
Wyllie, William Lionel. (H. V. Barnett) M. of Art, **7**: 309.
Wyman, Michigan, Archæological Remains at. (F. W. Kelsey; M. Jastrow) Nation, **54**: 71.
Wyman Genealogy, Contributions to. (M. Wyman) N. E. Reg. **50**: 43.
Wyndham, Charles, with portrait. Theatre, **36**: 194.
— as Bob Sacket. Theatre, **28**: 50.
— as Peregrine Porter. Theatre, **28**: 153.
Wynne, Frances. (K. Hinkson) Longm. **23**: 66.
Wyoming, State of. (J. Ralph) Harper, **87**: 63.
— Journey to the Devil's Tower in. (T. Moran) Cent. **25**: 450.
"Wyoming," The, in the Straits of Shimonoséki. (W. E. Griffis) Cent. **21**: 844.
Wyzewa, Téodor de, as a Critic. Sat. R. **79**: 796.
— as Essayist. Sat. R. **82**: 106.

X-rays. *See* Roentgen Rays.
Xanthia; a legend. (F. M. F. Skene) Argosy, **55**: 380.
Xanthoceras Sarbijolia. Garden & F. **6**: 284.
Xavier, Jerome, Gospel according to. Asia. R. **10**: 184.
Xenophon's Harriers, A Day with. Macmil. **71**: 182. Same art. Ecl. M. **124**: 376.

Yacht, The, as a Naval Auxiliary. (W. McAdoo) No. Am. **161**: 170.
— Decoration of a. (A. Brassey) M. of Art, **5**: 103.
— Racing, Problem of. (G. A. Stewart) No. Am. **158**: 749.
— Sailing, of To-day. (C. L. Norton) Outing, **22**: 184.
Yacht "Chispa," Cruise of the. Overland, n. s. **21**: 617.
Yacht "Minnie's Mark," The; a story. (J. C. Tucker) Overland, n. s. **19**: 53.
Yacht Modeling, Miniature. (F. Bassford) Outing, **25**: 400, 503.
Yacht Race, How to report. (W. E. Robinson) Writer, **8**: 129.
— My First International. (W. Henn) Outing, **24**: 33.
Yacht Races for the America's Cup, 1895. Pub. Opin. **19**: 358. — (D. Rolleston) Eng. Illust. **14**: 177. — (W. J. Henderson) McClure, **5**: 373.
— Cup Champions and their Crews. (R. B. Burchard) Outing, **26**: 481.
— Cup Champions of 1895. (R. B. Burchard) Outing, **26**: 377.
— International. (Earl of Dunraven) No. Am. **155**: 706.
— — The America's Cup Defenders, Old and New. (W. P. Stephens) Cent. **24**: 520.
— International Racing and National Supremacy on the Sea. (W. P. Stephens) Engin. M. **10**: 1.
— — in 1893. (G. A. Stewart) No. Am. **157**: 88. — (A. J. Kenealy) Outing, **22**: 381. **23**: 161.
— — Story of the America's Cup. (R. Jope-Slade) Blackw. **154**: 189.
— on the Solent. (A. E. Payne) Eng. Illust. **10**: 818.
Yachting around San Francisco Bay. (C. H. Shinn) Outing, **21**: 465.
— Coast and Island. (F. W. Pangborn) Cent. **22**: 14.
— Continental. Blackw. **160**: 402.
— Evolution of the Forty-six-footer. (G. A. Stewart) Outing, **20**: 55, 124, 189.
— From the German Ocean to the Black Sea. (T. Stevens) Outing, **20**: 3–464.
— From Sloop to Cutter in America. (A. J. Kenealy) Outing, **23**: 225.
— in England, History of. (W. J. Gordon) Leis. Hour, **43**: 622.
— in San Francisco Bay. (A. Inkersley) Outing, **28**: 70–313.
— Lake Yacht Racing Association. (P. S. Peer) Outing, **26**: 315.
— Leaves from a Sketcher's Note-book. M. of Art, **3**: 243, 408.
— Model, Science and Sport in. (F. R. Burton) Engin. M. **6**: 63.
— New York Yacht Club. (A. J. Kenealy) Outing, **24**: 388.
— on the Great Lakes. (E. S. Hoch) Nat'l M. (Bost.) **4**: 411, 537.
— Outlook for 1893. (C. L. Norton) Outing, **22**: 47.
— Seawanhaka Yacht Club Race. (R. B. Burchard) Outing, **26**: 488.
— Sullivan on. Sat. R. **77**: 620.
— Through an Autumn Gale. Outing, **27**: 124.
Yachts; Cradle of the English Cutter. (A. J. Kenealy) Outing, **23**: 132.
— English Racing. (D. Kemp) Eng. Illust. **9**: 827.
— Getting into Commission. (R. B. Burchard) Outing, **28**: 230.
— Half-raters. (R. B. Burchard) Outing, **28**: 350.
— Model, their Building and Fittings. (F. Bassford) Outing, **27**: 484. **28**: 60.
— of New York Harbor. (W. J. Henderson) Engin. M. **2**: 802.
— Rating of. Sat. R. **74**: 618.
— Steam, Fast. (C. H. Werner) Cassier, **2**: 323.
— 30-foot Class. (R. B. Burchard) Outing, **28**: 412.
— 20-raters. (R. B. Burchard) Outing, **28**: 301.
Yachtsman's Song; a poem. (J. W. Merrill) Outing, **24**: 128.
Yahgan Indians, How Christians destroyed a Tribe of. (J. R. Spears) Chaut. **21**: 58.
Yahgan Language, Structure of. (T. Bridges) Anthrop. J. **23**: 53.

Yale University. (A. T. Hadley) Harper, 88: 764.
— Alumni Wit at. Bach. of Arts, 3: 633.
— and Harvard in the West. (C. F. Thwing) Harv. Grad. M. 1: 194.
— and Harvard Boat-race. (W. A. Brooks) Harper, 89: 181.
— at Henley. (W. B. Curtis) Outing, 28: 199.
— Athletic. (J. W. Allen) Munsey, 12: 125.
— Cost of Education at. Yale R. 3: 117.
— Pres. Dwight's Decennial at. (B. J. Hendrick) Bach. of Arts, 3: 173.
— Ethics in. (G. T. Ladd) Eth. Rec. 2: 217.
— Glimpse of. (G. Santayana) Harv. Mo. 15: 89.
— Oxford *vs.* (W. H. Grenfell) Fortn. 62: 368.
— 100 Years Ago. (R. S. Baldwin) M. Am. Hist. 28: 280.
— The Prom. from Girls' Point of View. (Florence Guertin) Bach. of Arts, 2: 364.
— Secret Societies at. (R. Hughes) Munsey, 11: 286.
— Senior Society Elections at. (W. Camp) Bach. of Arts, 3: 74.
— Town and Gown Rows at. (H. E. Howland) Bach. of Arts, 1: 1, 160.
Yalu, Battle of the. (P. N. McGiffin) Cent. 28: 585. — (G. P. Horney) Un. Serv. M. 10: 137.
— — Lessons from the. (A. T. Mahan) Cent. 28: 629.
Yam Custom, The. Macmil. 73: 115.
Yancey, William Lowndes. (A. W. Dillard) So. Hist. Pap. 2: 151.
Yandell, Enid. So. M. 5: 504.
Yangtze-Kiang River. (W. B. Harris) Liv. Age, 192: 406.
— and its Gorges. Dub. R. 110: 187.
"Yankee," Private Armed Brig. (G. C. Mason) Am. Hist. Reg. 4: 161.
Yankee Twang. Spec. 75: 269.
Yaqui Indians, The. Chamb. J. 73: 750.
Yarmouth, Eng. All the Year, 71: 378.
Yarmouth Bloaters and Red Herrings. Chamb. J. 70: 811.
Yarrow and its Inscribed Stone. (J. Veitch) Blackw. 154: 648.
— in Song and Story. (F. Watt) Art J. 45: 180.
— of Wordsworth and Scott. (J. Veitch) Blackw. 151: 638. Same art. Liv. Age, 194: 156.
Yat; a Digger Indian story. (E. I. Hoffman) Overland, n. s. 26: 489.
Yates, Edmund. (T. H. S. Escott) New R. 11: 87. — Acad. 45: 437. — Ath. '94, 1: 679.
— Last Days of. (Marie Corelli) Temp. Bar, 102: 378.
Yeames, William Frederick. (W. W. Fenn) M. of Art, 4: 196.
Year, Origin of. (J. N. Lockyer) Nature, 45: 487. 46: 104. 47: 32, 228.
Year Ago, A; a poem. (H. M. Burnside) Argosy, 59: 685.
Year Books, 11-12 Edward III. Walford's Antiq. 4: 181.
Yeast, Taka Koji, a New Substitute for. Chamb. J. 72: 454.
Yeates, Jasper, with portrait. (B. C. Atlee) Green Bag, 5: 393.
Yeates, W. B., Poetry of. (L. Johnson) Acad. 42: 278. — (E. Rhys) Acad. 49: 151.
Yedaya Bedaresi. (J. Chotzner) Jew. Q. 8: 414.
Yellow book, The. Critic, 24: 360.
Yellow-book Style. Sat. R. 79: 730.
Yellow Dog, A; a story. (B. Harte) McClure, 5: 235.
Yellow Fever in Demerara. Cornh. 66: 266.
Yellow Globe; a Midnight story. (A. W. Drake) Cent. 25: 18.
Yellow Gown, The; a poem. (K. Carter) M. of Art, 11: 377.
Yellow Men of India. (C. Johnston) Asia. R. 15: 102.
Yellow Wall-paper. (C. P. Stetson) New Eng. M. n. s. 5: 647.
Yellowstone Lake, Overhead Sounds in the Vicinity of. (E. Linton) Science, 22: 244.
Yellowstone National Park. (C. S. Sargent) Garden & F. 7: 131. — (D. S. Jordan) Around World, 1: 148. — (D. S. Jordan) Pop. Sci. Mo. 40: 447. — Garden & F. 5: 181.
— Age of Igneous Rocks of. (A. Hague) Am. J. Sci. 151: 445.
— Boundaries of. Garden & F. 5: 241.
— Chittenden on. (E. Coues) Nation, 62: 219.
— Fossil Forests of. (S. E. Tillman) Pop. Sci. Mo. 43: 301.
— Tertiary Floras of. (F. H. Knowlton) Am. J. Sci. 152: 51.
Yemen, Journey Through, Harris'. Ath. '94, 1: 767.
— Literature of Jews in. (A. Neubauer) Jew. Q. 3: 604.
— Rebellion in. (W. B. Harris) Blackw. 153: 301.
— Travels in, and History of. Dub. R. 115: 172.
Yeoman and Sportsmen. (T. E. Kebbel) National, 19: 548.
Yeomanry, English. Macmil. 74: 401. — (L. Parsey) Un. Serv. M. 6: 58. — (E. Frewen) Un. Serv. M. 7: 830.
— — 1794-1894. (C. W. Thompson) Un. Serv. M. 9: 165.
Yeomen of the Guard. Liv. Age, 192: 381.
Yerdon, Switzerland; Day in Pestalozzi-Town. (K. D. Wiggin) Overland, n. s. 19: 33.
Yerex, Albert E.; with portrait. (W. R. McGarry) Nat'l M. (N. Y. '91) 16: 497.
Yerkes, C. F., Picture Collection of. (F. G. Stevens) M. of Art, 18: 96-165.
Yew, The World-old. Chamb. J. 69: 449.
Yew-trees. (C. S. Sargent) Garden & F. 9: 261.
Yoe, Peter L., with portrait. (H. L. Conard) Nat'l M. (N. Y. '91) 15: 318.
Yonge, Charlotte M., with portrait. Bk. News, 9: 5.
York, Prince George of Wales, Duke of. New R. 8: 609. Same art. Liv. Age, 198: 307.
York, Edward A., Last Duke of. Liv. Age, 194: 252.
York, Dukes of, Some. All the Year, 71: 34.
York, Eng. Liv. Age, 199: 387. — Lond. Q. 80: 307.
— in 16th Century. (M. Sellers) Eng. Hist. R. 9: 275.
— Minster of. (A. P. Purey-Cust) Good Words, 35: 552, 597.
— and its Associations. (J. A. Floyd) Cath. World, 63: 725.
— Priory Church of Holy Trinity. Reliquary, 35: 26.
— A Ride to. Cornh. 71: 246.
— St. Peter's School. (A. F. Leach) Fortn. 58: 638.
York, Pa., Incidents in History of. (G. Neisser) Pennsyl. M. 16: 433.
York County, Old, Me., Records of. (G. A. Gordon) N. E. Reg. 49: 46.
Yorkshire and Lancashire, Nomenclature in. Walford's Antiq. 4: 69.
— British and Roman Roads in. (E. M. Cole) Antiq. n. s. 26: 206.
— Coast Scenery. (J. Leyland) Portfo. 23: 16, 39.
— Haunts of J. R. Lowell in. (E. Skelding) Atlan. 76: 181.
— Local Rhymes and Sayings. Folk-Lore Rec. 1: 160.
Yorkshire Good Cheer, Some. (E. Skelding) Atlan. 78: 419.
Yorkshire Parish Tea, A. (B. Atkinson) Sund. M. 23: 176.
Yorktown, Siege of. (E. C. Haynes) Chaut. 15: 1.

Yorktown Campaign, 1781. (J. W. de Peyster) Un. Serv. (Phila.) 16: 305.
Yoruba-speaking Peoples, Ellis's. Sat. R. 77: 256.
Yosemite, The. (R. W. W. Cryan) Westm. 143: 78.
— and the Big Trees. (R. Wildman) Overland, n. s. 28: 199.
— Camping Trip to. (Mrs. W. C. Sawyer) Chaut. 17: 612.
— Memories of. (W. H. Gleadell) Gent. M. n. s. 57: 245. Same art. Ecl. M. 127: 837.
— Panorama of, Painting a. (C. D. Robinson) Overland, n. s. 22: 243.
— a Poem. (J. L. Spalding) Cosmopol. 18: 727.
Yosemite National Park. (C. H. Shinn) Garden & F. 5: 74. — Garden & F. 5: 193.
Youghal. (G. M. Synge) Leis. Hour, 42: 157.
Youmans, E. L., Fiske's Life of. (F. Starr) Dial (Ch.) 16: 330.
Young, Arthur. (F. S. Stevenson) Westm. 39: 109. — (L. Stephen) National, 27: 489. Same art. Liv. Age, 210: 108.
Young, Brigham, and Modern Utah. (J. A. Cockerill) Cosmopol. 19: 501.
— How he was arrested for Polygamy. (E. Steptoe) Overland, n. s. 28: 677.
Young, Edward D. Geog. J. 8: 644.
Young, George, Lord. (A. W. Renton) Green Bag, 4: 414.
Young, The, Moral Instruction of. (F. Adler) Eth. Rec. 2: 83.
Young Barneby; a story. (A. H. Marshall) Eng. Illust. 13: 521.
Young Dr. Jarvis; a story. Munsey, 13: 147.
Young Dog's Dance. (G. B. Grinnell) J. Am. Folk-Lore, 4: 307.
Young Love; a story. (L. Dougall) Temp. Bar, 105: 1. Same art. Liv. Age, 205: 534.
Young Man, Modern, as Critic. (Robt. Buchanan) Univ. R. 3: 353.
— The Employer and the. (E. W. Bok) Cosmopol. 16: 727.
— in Business. (E. W. Bok) Cosmopol. 16: 332.
Young Men and the Church. (F. C. Iglehart) Meth. R. 55: 386. — (E. W. Bok) Cosmopol. 18: 317.
— Displacement of. (J. L. Payne) Canad. M. 1: 467.
— in the Colleges. (H. T. Fowler) Harper, 92: 688.
— in Literature. Contemp. 65: 177.
— in Politics. Pub. Opin. 12: 404.
— — A Republican's View. (Thos. L. James) Chr. Un. 46: 280.
— — A Democrat's View. (J. C. Hendricks) Chr. Un. 46: 581.
Y. M. C. A. among the Indians. (Antonio Apache) Lend a Hand, 17: 337.
Young Men's Institute, Catholic. (F. J. Murasky) Overland, n. s. 28: 407.
Young Mr. Ainslie's Courtship. (F. C. Philips) Time, 20: 1-561. 21: 1-337.
Young People's Movement in the Church; Symposium. Indep. July 7, '92.
Young People's Society of Christian Endeavor. (F. E. Clark) And. R. 17: 573. — (F. E. Clark) Our Day, 9: 317.
Young People's Writing. (E. E. Hale) Bk. News, 8: 1.
Young Person, The. Dial (Ch.) 20: 61.
— The Modern. Belgra. 86: 61.
Young Robin Gray. (F. Bret Harte) Good Words, 35: 130. Same art. McClure, 3: 448.
Youth and Old Age. (F. L. Oswald) Open Court, 3: 1683, 1741.
— its Proper Ideal. (J. Worcester) N. Church R. 3: 1.
— Wagner on. Spec. 71: 369.
Youth: a poem. (F. N. Thorpe) Harper, 90: 711.
Youthful Reminiscence, A. (H. H. Boyesen) Lippinc. 55: 417.
Ypres. (J. Maskell) Walford's Antiq. 10: 195.
Ysaye, Eugène. (H. E. Krehbiel) Cent. 27: 670.
Yuba Dam Trout; a sketch. (A. M. R. Gordon) Canad. M. 5: 145.
Yucatan, Hill Caves of, Mercer on. (F. Starr) Dial (Ch.) 20: 71.
— Notes on. (H. C. Mercer) Am. Natural. 29: 507.
— since the Conquest. (Alice D. Le Plongeon) M. Am. Hist. 30: 158.
Yucca Moth and Yucca Pollination. (C. V. Riley) Pop. Sci. Mo. 41: 171.
Yuccas, Notes on the Names of. (C. S. Sargent) Garden & F. 9: 104.
— Tree, in the U. S. (C. S. Sargent) Garden & F. 8: 301.
Yukon, Fort, Boundary North of. (H. Turner) Nat. Geog. M. 4: 188.
Yukon River, Down the. (W. Ogilvie) Canad. M. 1: 531, 642. 2: 45.
— Expedition to. (C. W. Hayes) Nat. Geog. M. 4: 119.
Yule Guest, The; a poem. (B. Carman) Cosmopol. 14: 163.
Yule Log, The. (G. Winterwood) Ecl. M. 118: 132.
Yumi, the Japanese Long Bow. (R. C. Denig) Outing, 21: 83.
Yun-Nan, From, to British India. (Prince Henry of Orleans) Geog. J. 7: 300.
Yuruks, The, Ethnologic Study of. (A. T. M. d'Andria) Pop. Sci. Mo. 43: 184.
Yves, Saint, Legend of. (Tr. F. L. Snow) Green Bag, 6: 142.

Zabara, Joseph, and his "Book of Delight." (I. Abrahams) Jew. Q. 6: 502.
Zacatecas, Mexico. (C. Reid) Cath. World, 56: 297.
— Ancient Silver Mines of. (C. S. Gleed) Cosmopol. 22: 130.
Zambesi River, Chinde Entrance to, Discovery of. (D. J. Rankin) Fortn. 58: 824.
— Travels in the Basin of. (E. Foa) J. Soc. Arts, 42: 338.
Zambesia, England's Interest in. Sat. R. 73: 319.
— Twenty Years in. (F. C. Selous) Geog. J. 1: 289.
Zamindari Estates in Bengal, Origin of. (B. H. Baden-Powell) Q. J. Econ. 11: 36.
Zamora, Alfonso de. (A. Neubauer) Jew. Q. 7: 398.
Zangwill, Isaac, with portraits. Bk. Buyer, 11: 744. — With portrait. Bk. News, 13: 417.
— The Master. Sat. R. 79: 656.
— My First Book. Idler, 3: 629.
Zangwill, Louis. World and a Man. Sat. R. 82: 65.
Zante. (J. P. Mahaffy) Sund. M. 23: 272.
— Earthquakes in. Dub. R. 112: 453.
Zanzibar. (J. E. C. Bodley) Univ. R. 3: 405.
— Seyid Burgash, Sultan of. (A. L. Royce) Un. Serv. (Phila.) 7: 127.
Zanzibari, Rehabilitation of. Dub. R. 119: 429.
Zaragoza. *See* Saragossa.
Zealous Moslem, The; a poem. (E. G. Curtis) Arena, 15: 474.
Zeballos, Estanislao. Critic, 23: 90.
Zebehr Pasha. (Sir W. T. Marriott) Fortn. 64: 101.
Zebra, Domestication of. Around World, 2: 7.
Zebras. Sat. R. 76: 413.
Zee-Wee. (H. H. Boyesen) Overland, n. s. 24: 229.
Zeke Cleghorn's Wife. (E. M. Leyden) Southern M. 4: 271.
Zeitun. (A. Nazarbek) Contemp. 69: 513.

Zendavesta and First 11 Chapters of Genesis. (A. Kohut) Jew. Q. 2: 223.
— Date of the. (F. Max Müller) Contemp. 64: 869.
Zenger, John Peter, and Andrew Hamilton. (B. C. Steiner) Pennsyl. M. 20: 405.
Zenobia, a Commonplace Girl; a story. All the Year, 73: 355-477.
Zenon, Emperor, and the Isaurians. (E. W. Brooks) Eng. Hist. R. 8: 209.
Zeolites, The, Constitution of. (F. W. Clarke) Am. J. Sci. 148: 187.
Zermatt Valley in Winter. All the Year, 54: 325.
— A Wet Day in. Belgra. 91: 35.
Zero, Search for the Absolute. (H. J. W. Dam) McClure, 3: 557.
Zeyneb, Princess, Chennels's. Liv. Age, 198: 515.
Zi-ka-wei Observatory, near Shanghai, China. (S. Chevalier) Science, n. s. 2: 17.
Zimbabwe; Latest Marvel of South Africa. All the Year, 70: 366. — Dub. R. 110: 459.
— Excavations at. (J. T. Bent) Anthrop. J. 22: 124.
— Ruins of. Dub. R. 112: 447.
— — Historical Evidence as to. (H. Schlichter) Geog. J. 2: 44.
Zinc and Copper, Alloys of. (T. K. Rose) Nature, 55: 130.
Zinc-bearing Spring Waters from Missouri. (W. F. Hillebrand) Am. J. Sci. 143: 418.
Zinc-mining, Joplin District. (H. S. Wicks) Engin. M. 6: 699.
Zincke, Foster Barham. Acad. 44: 192.
Zinto; an Episode. (H. T. Munn) Outing, 29: 256.
Zirconium, Double Fluorides of. (H. L. Wells and H. W. Foote) Am. J. Sci. 151: 18.
Zittel, Alfred von. Nat. Sci. 4: 163.
Zizka, John, and the Reformation in Bohemia, 1415-24. Macmil. 72: 346. Same art. Liv. Age, 207: 297.
Zo they Zay; a story. (O. Hartier) Gent. M. 53: 217. Same art. Liv. Age, 203: 340.
Zodiacal Light. Dub. R. 110: 174. — (E. E. Barnard) Pop. Astron. 1: 337. 2: 29.
Zoellner's Figures and Other Related Illusions. (J. Jastrow) Am. J. Psychol. 4: 381.
Zogbaum, R. F., with portrait. Bk. Buyer, 12: 135.
Zohar and Bahir. (A. Neubauer) Jew. Q. 4: 357.
Zola, Emile, with portrait. Bk. News, 10: 504. — (E. A. Vizetelly) Book R. 4: 31.
— and his Work. (W. H. Gleadell) Westm. 140: 614.
— as an Evolutionist. (Y. Blaze de Bury) New R. 7: 188.
— at Home. (R. H. Sherard) McClure, 2: 411.
— The *Idée Mère* of. (E. L. Linton) Univ. R. 1: 27.
— in England. Spec. 71: 427.
— Interview with. Critic, 21: 83.
— La Débâcle. Ath. '92, 2: 278. — (G. Moore) Fortn. 58: 204. — Spec. 69: 228.
— Literary Creed of. Time, 18: 563.
— Moral Teaching of. (V. Paget) Contemp. 63: 196. Same art. Ecl. M. 120: 437.
— My Impressions. (G. Moore) Eng. Illust. 11: 477.
— Philosophy of Life. (R. E. S. Hart) Fortn. 66: 257.
— Rome. (A. Hornblow) Bookman, 2: 120. — (W. Barry) National, 27: 816. — (E. C. Townshend) Westm. 146: 532.
— Sketch of his Life. (V. R. Mooney) Idler, 3: 498.
— Towards the Appreciation of. (E. C. Townshend) Westm. 143: 57.
Zolaism, Downfall of. (W. Lecky) Cath. World, 61: 357.
Zoo, Byways at the. (H. Scherren) Eng. Illust. 15: 268.
— How to see the. Liv. Age, 211: 241.
— Life at the, Cornish's. Nature, 51: 276.
Zoö-geography, Marine. (A. E. Ortmann) Science, n. s. 3: 739.
Zoölogical Explorations in the Far North. (C. C. Nutting) Am. Natural. 29: 45.
Zoölogical Nomenclature, Change in. (J. T. Cunningham) Nat. Sci. 8: 309.
Zoölogical Record, International. (H. H. Field) Nature, 47: 607.
— Bibliographical Reform and. (H. H. Field) Nat. Sci. 6: 333.
Zoölogical Regions. (A. R. Wallace) Nature, 49: 610.
Zoölogical Station at Naples, Publications of. (A. Dohrn) Nature, 48: 440.
— Portable, in Bohemia. Nat. Sci. 5: 370.
Zoölogists, International Congress of. (S. J. Hickson) Nat. Sci. 7: 333.
Zoölogy as a Factor in Mental Culture. (S. H. Gage) Science, n. s. 4: 207.
— Bibliography of. (H. H. Field) Lib. J. 20: supp. 29.
— in the High School. (C. M. Weed) Am. Natural. 28: 1003.
— in Wood and Stone. (S. Beale) Sund. M. 25: 584.
— New International Bibliographical Bureau for. (H. H. Field) Science, n. s. 2: 234.
— Nomenclature in. Acad. 49: 179. — (T. R. R. Stebbing) Nat. Sci. 8: 254. — (T. Gill) Science, n. s. 4: 581.
— — of the Magazines. (W. M. Webb) Univ. R. 8: 288.
— since Darwin. (L. von Graff) Nat. Sci. 9: 193, 312, 364.
Zoöphily, Ethics of. (F. P. Cobbe) Contemp. 68: 497.
— Jesuit: a Reply. (G. Tyrrell) Contemp. 68: 708.
Zorilla, José. Ath. '93, 1: 121.
Zorn, Anders; a Swedish Etcher. (M. G. Van Rensselaer) Cent. 24: 582.
Zoroaster and the Bible. (L. H. Mills) 19th Cent. 35: 44.
— and Persian Dualism. (J. T. Bixby) Arena, 5: 694.
— The God of. (L. H. Mills) New World, 4: 47.
— Yasna XLVI, a Hymn of. (L. H. Mills) Am. J. Philol. 17: 71.
— Zoroastrian Religion, Ancient, Moral and Ethical Teachings of. (A. V. W. Jackson) Int. J. Ethics, 7: 55.
Zoutpansberg Gold-fields. (F. Jeppe) Geog. J. 2: 213.
Zulu War, Battle of the Eclipse. (E. B. Biggar) Canad. M. 2: 26.
Zululand, Two Lost Kingdoms. (E. B. Biggar) Canad. M. 2: 256.
Zumalacarregui, Tomas. Sat. R. 73: 330.
Zuñi, Chimney Corners in. (E. Ingersoll) Mo. Illust. 3: 251.
— Folk-tale of the Underworld. (F. H. Cushing) J. Am. Folk-Lore, 5: 49.
— Music of. (J. C. Fillmore) Music, 5: 39.
Zunz, Leopold. (L. I. H. Weiss) Jew. Q. 7: 365.
Zupitza, Julius. (K. Bruel) Ath. '95, 2: 101.
Zurich, Church in. (J. I. Good) Presb. & Ref. R. 6: 593. — (A. S. Napier) Acad. 48: 51.
Zuider Zee, Draining of. Liv. Age, 194: 823. — Dub. R. 116: 191. — Am. Arch. 47: 102. — (P. H. Schoute) Geog. J. 1: 234.
— Reclaiming the. Chamb. J. 70: 245.
— Round about the. (Mrs. G. C. Davies) Outing, 22: 126.